PREFACE

Although this volume of *Obituaries from The Times* is chronologically the first, it is in fact the third to appear. Obituaries from 1961-70 and from 1971-75 have already been published and these two volumes have established themselves as valuable works of reference. *The Times* obituaries have of course been a natural source for scholars for many years but it has proved very useful to have the main obituaries in volume form.

In this volume there are 1,450 entries. There is of course some overlap with the relevant volume of the *Dictionary of National Biography* which appeared some years ago, but twenty-eight per cent of the notices refer to British subjects who do not appear in the *Dictionary of National Biography* and twenty-nine per cent are foreign subjects. These of course were not eligible for the *Dictionary of National Biography* and in many cases adequate alternative biographies are hard to find.

There can unfortunately be no doubt which is the most celebrated figure to have died in the period we cover. It is Joseph Stalin. Inevitably his biography reflects the limitations of contemporary opinion and information which has been overtaken by subsequent discoveries and research. Nevertheless his obituary is itself of historical interest. Judgments tend to require less change when they are made of figures who have played a less central part in the historical process. Lord Halifax, John Foster Dulles or Senator Joseph McCarthy provide good examples of the interesting figures who played their part in history without exercising a dominant role.

The great commanders of the second world war tended to survive into the 1960s, though with Guderian, Gamelin and Graziani the "Gs" provide an intriguing group. Marshal Pétain qualifies both as a soldier and as a political figure.

All of these obituaries are *The Times* obituaries. We receive and publish many appreciations contributed from outside. We have not republished these appreciations, interesting though many of them are.

It will be noticed that there are a number of obituaries which have not been republished, of figures who might be expected to appear, where we considered that the original obituary notice, written with knowledge available at the time, might be misleading.

Obituaries are a very important part of the coverage of *The Times* as a journal of record and they go back, though not with their present regularity, to the very early days of *The Times,* when we published obituary notices of some of those who suffered in the French Revolution. We attach great importance to ensuring the quality of these obituaries and believe that this volume is not unworthy as a representation of them.

WILLIAM REES-MOGG
Editor of *The Times*

March 1979

COMPILER'S NOTE

Among the obituaries from the decade of the Nineteen Fifties, those of Stalin and Einstein relate to world figures who this year (posthumously) become "centenarians". More than 40 others who were born in 1879 are also represented here. Both 1878 and 1880 may well have been better producers of men and women, but in this volume some remarkable women appear who were born in 1879 and may help serve to indicate the variety of lives which such volumes cover—women like Frieda Lawrence (widow of D. H.), Lady Londonderry (the hostess), Annie Kenney (the suffragette), Lady Dudley (Gertie Millar) from the English stage, Ethel Barrymore and Ella Shields from the American, and Janet Trevelyan.

The 1,450 entries can be divided as follows: U.K. 64 per cent, Rest of Europe 18 per cent, the Americas 11 per cent, the Antipodes 3 per cent, Asia 3 per cent and Africa 1 per cent—proportions not significantly different from those in the previous volumes, except that it was too early for Africa to throw up significant victims of conflict, as happened in the Sixties and Seventies.

Many entries include references to persons whose obituaries were reprinted in the volumes covering 1961-70 and 1971-75. Such references are marked with asterisks, and in pages 779-780 the relevant volume and page number of each is indicated. Where two related obituaries appear in this volume, the indication "q.v." is given.

On pages 783-790 appears a breakdown of the fields of activity of the persons obituarized in this volume, with page numbers—a system which one reviewer finds unnecessary in a book alphabetically arranged, but one which can make an entry easier to find for the many readers not handy with alphabetical order. The reviewer tends also to forget that many readers need to discover for the first time that interesting or important people in their own fields have died: with the grouping of obituary subjects in pages 783-790 the young history teacher who has not read *The Times* daily will quickly learn which historians, studied at university, have since ended their careers.

Some inconsistencies in the treatment of titles are due to changes in *The Times* style over the ten year period.

The criteria for selection remain as before. In the words of Mr. William Rees-Mogg, Editor of *The Times*, in his preface to the first volume: "The selection has been made with regard to the public importance of the subject of the obituary, the intrinsic interest of what was written about him, and the need to reflect a wide range of nationalities and walks of life which *The Times* obituary columns encompass."

All the reprinted obituaries have stood the test of a critical public. Where factual errors were noted, they have been corrected. But judgments stand as they were delivered in the 1950s, and the student has the opportunity to compare them with any reappraisal by later generations.

F.C.R.

OBITUARIES FROM THE TIMES 1951-1960

including an Index to all Obituaries and Tributes
appearing in The Times during the years 1951-1960

Compiler: **Frank C. Roberts** (Home News Editor, *The Times* 1965-1968)

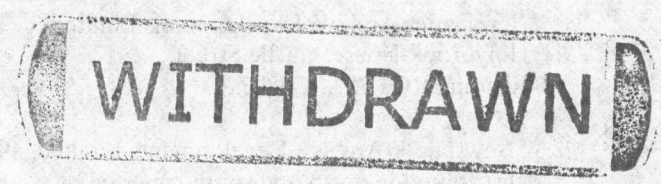

NEWSPAPER ARCHIVE DEVELOPMENTS LIMITED
MECKLER BOOKS

Newspaper Archive Developments Limited,
Holybrook House, Castle Street,
Reading RG1 7SN, England.

Distributed in north and south America by
Meckler Books,
520 Riverside Avenue,
Westport, Conn. 06880, U.S.A.

ISBN 0 903713 96 9
ISBN 0 930466 16 0

In preparing this and previous volumes valued advice and assistance were received from Colin Watson, Obituaries Editor of *The Times.*

Photoset and made-up by The Creative Press (Reading) Ltd.,
42-44 Portman Road, Reading.
Printed by Unwin Brothers Limited, Old Woking, Surrey.
Bound by G. & J. Kitcat Ltd., Shand Street, London SE1.

* NOTE ON USE OF ASTERISKS IN THESE PAGES *

An asterisk after the name of a person referred to in one of these obituaries indicates that a biography of the named person appears in a volume of this work that has been published previously:—*Obituaries from The Times 1961-1970* or *Obituaries from The Times 1971-1975.* These volumes are obtainable from Newspaper Archive Developments Limited. A consolidated list of these biographies included in former volumes appears on pages 779-780 of this book, and gives the required volume and page references.

The indication [q.v.] is used only where a person referred to is himself the subject of an obituary in this present volume.

A

Prince Abdul Illah, Crown Prince and formerly Regent of Iraq, who was killed in the rising in Iraq with King Faisal [q.v.] and General Nuri es Said [q.v.] on July 14, 1958, aged 45, combined the qualities of a prince and of a statesman.

A much travelled man, he was at home in east and west alike. He had no personal ambitions; his loyalty was given first to the training and later to the advising of the young King Faisal, his nephew.

But Prince Abdul Illah was a far-sighted politician, a man with the knack, disconcerting at times, of seeing the truth of a subject even when it was being deliberately hidden from him and accepting it with a philosophical smile.

He never wavered in his support of Iraq's ties with the west.

Abdul Illah was born in 1913, the only son of the late King Ali of Hejaz, and so had a *de jure* claim to the Kingdom of Mecca. He became Regent of Iraq in 1939 on the sudden death of King Ghazi. Later that year he proclaimed Iraq's support for the Allied cause, but in 1941 he was deposed in Rashid Ali's *coup* and narrowly escaped with his life on that occasion.

After the suppression of the revolt he returned to Baghdad and again issued an appeal for Iraqi support of the Allies. In 1943 he visited London for the first time and was a guest at Buckingham Palace. It was in this year that he was made Crown Prince as heir to the throne in the event of King Faisal dying without issue.

After the war he visited Washington, Ottawa, and London. In 1951, after the death of King Abdullah, he was recognized as Head of the Hashemite Royal Family. In 1952 he accompanied the young King Faisal, who had just left Harrow, on a state visit to the United States, and on their return they were invited by the Queen for a short stay at Balmoral. His 14 years of regency came to an end with King Faisal's accession in May 1953. Since then he had remained a constant traveller and a close adviser of the King.

He was three times married, but had no children.

July 23, 1958.

King Abdullah—See **Jordan.**

The Duke of Abercorn, who was the first Governor of Northern Ireland, died at his London home on September 12, 1953. He was 83.

He was admirably qualified, both by the traditions of his family, which has played a notable part in the history of England and Scotland as well as Ireland, and by his own character and record, for the difficult post he was called upon to assume in December 1922. He came new to the office; the office was also new. He had to make his own precedents as the constitutional head and King's deputy in the infant Ulster state, in circumstances of great delicacy and even danger. He had the advantage, especially valuable in Ireland, of splendid physique and a commanding presence, and it soon became evident that he possessed courage and resolution, as well as dignity, tact and an attractive geniality, together with a working knowledge of the business and industrial activities of the Six Counties north of the border.

The most noble Sir James Albert Edward Hamilton, third Duke of Abercorn, K.G., P.C., K.P., a godson of King Edward VII, was born on November 30, 1869, the eldest son of the second duke, who was a member of the household of the Prince of Wales (King Edward VII) for more than 40 years, and was also a founder of the Irish Loyal and Patriotic Union, afterwards the Irish Unionist Alliance, and an active supporter of Sir Edward Carson's leadership in Ulster. Though the dukedom is a modern creation, he inherited on the death of his father the barony of Paisley in the peerage of Scotland, created in 1587, and other ancient titles. Thus he was also Earl of Abercorn and Baron of Aberbrothick, Abercorn, Hamilton, Mountcastle and Kilpatrick, in the peerage of Scotland; Duke of Abercorn, Marquess of Hamilton, Viscount Strabane, Lord Hamilton, and Baron of Strabane and Mountcastell, in the peerage of Ireland; and Marquess of Abercorn and Viscount Hamilton in the peerage of Great Britain. Only two other noblemen, the Marquess of Lansdowne and the Earl of Verulam, hold distinct peerages in all three kingdoms. The respective claims of the Dukes of Abercorn and the Dukes of Hamilton to the French dukedom of Châtellerault are explained in an appendix to Volume I of *The Complete Peerage (Second Edition, p.465).*

The late Duke went to Eton in 1883 as Lord Paisley and was in Walter Durnford's house; he became Marquess of Hamilton in 1885 and left the next year. He served first with the Royal Inniskilling Fusiliers and in 1892 he joined the 1st Life Guards and served with the regiment until 1903. Afterwards he became a major in the North Irish Horse.

Meanwhile a long and happy partnership was inaugurated by his marriage in 1894 to Lady Rosalind Cecilia Caroline Bingham, D.B.E., only daughter of the fourth Earl of Lucan. As Marquess of Hamilton he captured Londonderry City from the Nationalists in 1900, and kept the seat till he succeeded to the dukedom in 1913. When Victor Cavendish succeeded to the dukedom of Devonshire in 1903, he succeeded him as Treasurer of the Household, and held the post till the fall of the Unionist Government, becoming one of the Opposition whips when the Liberals took office. Like his father, who was one of the promoters of the charter of the British South Africa Company, he took an active part in the administration of Rhodesia, and his eldest daughter, Lady Mary Kenyon-Slaney, has Rhodesia as one of her names.

As Governor of Northern Ireland the Duke, almost from the beginning, was spared much of the criticism which was freely lavished on the new Ministers. His straightforwardness and sincerity, as well as his fidelity to his constitutional position and his devotion to the welfare of Ulster, seemed to be recognized even by the strongest opponents of partition. The community soon began to realize how greatly indebted it was to the Governor's unobtrusive work, much of which was done behind the scenes. He was reappointed in 1928 for a further term of six years. It was a striking tribute to him when in 1931 the King, on the recommendation of the Prime Minister of Canada, offered him the Governor-Generalship of the Dominion, but the Duke, convinced that he could render better service in Ulster, asked leave to decline. His decision gave great satisfaction in Ulster, which was increased when he accepted a further extension of his term for six years from December 1934.

The Duke, who was created a K.P. in 1922, received the Knighthood of the Garter in 1928; his three immediate predecessors in the dukedom had been Knights of the Garter.

Hillsborough Castle, co. Down, the seat of Lord Downshire, was bought by the Office of Works to be the official residence of the Governor. When in 1934 a fire did serious damage to the building the residents of Hillsborough vied with one another in helping the police and fire brigade to save valuable pictures and furniture, an indication of the popularity already won by the Duke and Duchess.

It was the outbreak of the war in 1939, however, and the Duke's continuation in office for nearly six years during its progress, which perhaps revealed most clearly the immense value of his services to the Province, to the United Kingdom and to the united cause. Again, in 1940, he made it known that he would have been happy to retire after nearly 20 years in this onerous office, but he intimated his readiness to continue as Governor until the end of the war in Europe, and it was in fact only when this had been achieved that in July of 1945 he resigned his office. Ably supported by the Duchess, he threw himself completely into the manifold duties of state and of benevolence which greatly increased as the years passed. Both were assiduous in the round of war work, and it is common knowledge that their staff used to wonder how they contrived to interest themselves in all the many war movements and charitable organizations to which they gave their patronage with almost ceaseless visits to camps, hospitals, training schools, work depots and the centres of the great industries, while maintaining all the normal functions of their office.

When, in 1944, the Duke and Duchess celebrated their golden wedding, it was the occasion for a demonstration of affection and regard, probably unexampled in the public life of Ulster. A heavy fall in the grounds of Baronscourt just before his retirement in 1945 incapacitated the Duke for some time, but his ultimate recovery was complete.

After the Duke's retirement the Duchess and he spent practically all their time in London, where both occupied themselves with their customary zeal and enthusiasm in assisting good causes, especially those associated with Ulster. The Duke was president of the London Ulster Association and Club, and constant in his attendance at their functions. He was also a leading freemason, an inheritance from his distinguished father, who was for a generation one of the most notable personalities in the order. After an early initiation from his distinguished father, he rose to high rank.

The Duke is succeeded by his elder son, the Marquess of Hamilton, who was born in 1904, and was formerly in the Grenadier Guards. He married in 1928 Lady Mary Kathleen Crichton, sister of the Earl of Erne, and has two sons and a daughter.

September 14, 1953.

Sir Patrick Abercrombie, F.R.I.B.A., F.S.A., who died at his home in Berkshire on March 23, 1957 at the age of 77, had been for many years the leading figure among British town planners and one of the few town planners to achieve world-wide renown.

The progressive nature of British town planning legislation is largely due to his pioneer work and the ideas he propagated as a teacher and a practitioner during a long and active career. He held successively the chairs of Civic Design at Liverpool University and of Town Planning at University College London, and his development and reconstruction schemes for cities and regions in many parts of the world reached their climax in the County of London Plan which he produced in 1943 in conjunction with J. H. Forshaw. His activities and his influence for good covered an immensely wide field. He was, for example, one of the founders of the Council for the Preservation of Rural England and was the first president of the International Union of Architects.

Leslie Patrick Abercrombie was born in 1879 at the Manor House, Ashton-upon-Mersey, one of a family of nine, among his juniors being Lascelles Abercrombie, the poet. His father, William Abercrombie, a Fifeshire man, practised as a stockbroker in Manchester, but his private interests were literary and artistic. Patrick's mother, Sarah Ann Heron, was of Yorkshire stock. He had his schooling at Locker's Park preparatory school, Hemel Hempstead, and at Uppingham.

From early years he had wanted to be an architect, and at about the age of 20 he was apprenticed to a Manchester architect, moving on some three years later to the office of Sir Arthur Thornely, in Liverpool, where he spent a further three years. Wider fields opened out for him then with his appointment as junior lecturer and studio instructor in the Liverpool University School of Architecture, where he was infected with the enthusiasms of that great architectural teacher, Professor C. H. Reilly.

When the first Lord Leverhulme founded the Liverpool Chair of Civic Design in 1910, Abercrombie (by this time Reilly's chief assistant) became lecturer and research fellow under the new professor, Stanley D. Adshead. At the same time there was founded the *Town Planning Review,* the first journal to be devoted to this subject in Great Britain, and Abercrombie's literary bent and growing knowledge made him the obvious choice as editor. With Adshead he was the chief contributor to the first few volumes, making many bold and fruitful suggestions for the right development of Merseyside. Abercrombie's fellowship took him abroad every year, and he visited Paris, Vienna, Brussels and Berlin, specializing in the study of capital cities and garden cities. In 1913 came his first notable success when, in collaboration with Sydney A. Kelly, he won first premium in an international competition for the replanning of Dublin. The book on this subject did not appear until 1923, by which time several of the centrally situated buildings had been destroyed in civil warfare. It was some 25 years after the acceptance of the plan that its implementation began.

In 1915 Adshead was translated to University College London and Abercrombie succeeded him in the Liverpool Chair, which he occupied for 20 years. He was a good and fluent lecturer, well liked by his students, and though he founded no special school of thought in town planning he did great work in the all-round, balanced study of his subject, and he was frequently called into consultation by local authorities wishing to embark on large-scale replanning.

He produced schemes for Sheffield (1924), East Kent (with John Archibald, 1925), Doncaster, Bristol and Bath (1930), Sheffield again (1931), and Cumberland (with Sydney Kelly, 1932). Of all these plans he took pride in that relating to Doncaster, which was worked out on the satellite principle and was the first regional report to be published in Britain. In 1923 Abercrombie and his brother Lascelles were asked to report on the preservation of Stratford-on-Avon, and he also collaborated in the Thames Valley preservation scheme. He worked out a plan for a new civic centre at Plymouth. He paid five or six visits to Palestine, doing much work there, and with A. C. Holliday planned a new site and buildings for the University of Ceylon.

When Adshead retired in 1935 Abercrombie again took his place, this time as Professor of Town Planning at University College London. From 1936 he was also consultant architect to the Department of Health for Scotland. He was co-founder of the Council for the Preservation of Rural England and later chairman of its executive, and produced enlightened and practical works in this field entitled *The Preservation of Rural England* (1926) and *Town and Country Planning* (1933).

By far the most important of Abercrombie's planning projects was the great County of London Plan, which he produced in collaboration with J. H. Forshaw (a former student of his at Liverpool and later architect to the London County Council). This ambitious scheme was published in 1943 and was the product of a considerable number of experts working under the direction of Forshaw and Abercrombie. Among its main principles were the zoning of population densities, the creation of a coherent road system for fast traffic, and the isolation from the main flow of London traffic of a number of "precincts", such as the university area in Bloomsbury, the area round St. Paul's, the Temple and so on. It also dealt exhaustively with the questions of open spaces, the siting of industry, transport, the reconstruction of bomb-damaged areas, the preservation of a green belt, and many other problems, and it strongly emphasized the need to preserve, and indeed to cultivate, the character traditional to each locality. Abercrombie's constant preoccupation with the human side of his profession—his conception of a town as primarily the setting for human life, rather than a mere pattern of roads—was in fact what made his work so beneficial an influence on town planning generally.

Although his road plan was drastically revised and his plans for moving the central markets and some of the railway termini have been indefinitely postponed, Abercrombie's scheme for London is still the basis of official plans for controlling and directing its growth. The new towns now growing up round London are also the direct outcome of reports prepared by him on the future development of the region, and the New Towns Act was formulated largely according to his advice.

After the war Abercrombie, with various collaborators, drew up plans for the development of Plymouth, Edinburgh, Hull, Warwick and Bournemouth, and of the Clyde and West Midlands regions. His services were sought by the Colonial Office on more than one occasion and he wrote reports on the planning of Hongkong and Cyprus. He also advised the Emperor of Ethiopia* on the replanning of Addis Ababa.

In 1946 he retired from his chair at London

University. He had been knighted the year before, and among the other honours he received were the Royal Gold Medal for Architecture in 1946 and the Gold Medal of the American Institute of Architects in 1949. He had formerly been president of the Town Planning Institute and a member of the Royal Fine Art Commission and of the Royal Commission on the Location of Industry.

Abercrombie had an excellent prose style and was a conversationalist of considerable endowment, able and ready to discourse with ease and brilliance on subjects far removed from his speciality. He had a close-clipped manner of speech and a ready wit. A great believer in co-operation, he had numerous partners and collaborators, with whom he worked loyally and well. He inspired his subordinates with enthusiasm and confidence, and was often known to do quiet and secret kindnesses to those about him.

Up to the end of his life he pursued his many interests with sparkle and energy, travelling much on their behalf. As late as 1956 he spent six weeks in Addis Ababa, putting the last touches to his plan for that city, and he gave much time to the International Union of Architects, whose conferences in various capitals he attended, contributing much to their success.

He married Emilia Maud, daughter of Robert Gordon, and had a son and a daughter. His wife died in 1942.

March 25, 1957.

Lord Aberdare, who was killed in a car crash in Yugoslavia on October 4, 1957 at the age of 72, was a brilliant player of ball games and one of the best known sportsmen of his time. Whether it was cricket, rackets, tennis, golf, shooting or lawn tennis, he showed a natural aptitude. His physical fitness and powers of endurance were remarkable. He was the open rackets champion of the British Isles at the age of 46, and amateur tennis champion of the British Isles at 53.

In later years he devoted himself more closely to the work of the Order of St. John of Jerusalem, and to the service of youth and education. He was Prior for Wales of the Venerable Order of the Hospital of St. John of Jerusalem and was especially active in encouraging the work in the industrial areas of its offshoot, the St. John Ambulance Association. He was also a member of the Joint Committee of the Order of St. John and the British Red Cross Society, and in association with these various duties and interests was his presidency of the Welsh National School of Medicine of the University of Wales.

Lord Aberdare also sat on the Research Board for the Correlation of Medical Science and Physical Education. He was a member of the executive of the National Playing Fields Association, and of the National Trust, as well as the Standing Committee of National Parks. He took much of the advice that he prescribed for others, especially during his chairmanship of the National Fitness Council, and as chairman of the International Congress for Physical Education, Recreation and Rehabilitation.

He took a keen interest in the National Association of Boys' Clubs, of which he was chairman, and the Queen's Institute of District Nursing. He was also a member of the Miners' Welfare Committee and of the executive of the International Olympic Committee, serving on the organizing committee for the Olympic Games in London in 1948. A member of the national youth committee of the Board of Education from 1939 to 1942, he was honorary adviser to the J. Arthur [Lord] Rank* Organization on Children's Cinema Clubs.

The Right Hon. Clarence Napier Bruce, third Baron Aberdare, of Duffryn, in the County of Glamorgan, in the Peerage of the United Kingdom, was born on August 2, 1885, the second son of the second baron, and was educated at Winchester and New College, Oxford. He was in the XI at Winchester and got his Blue at Oxford, playing for the university against Cambridge in 1907 and 1908. Later he was to play for Middlesex and the Gentlemen. He represented Oxford at golf from 1905 to 1908, at tennis from 1906 to 1908, and at rackets from 1905 to 1908. In 1907 he won the Oxford University Silver Racket.

In 1911 Bruce was called to the Bar by the Inner Temple. He was a captain in the 2/1 Glamorgan Yeomanry, a temporary lieutenant in the 2nd Life Guards, and later with the 2nd Battalion of the Guards Machine Gun Regiment, and was also attached to Headquarters, 61st Division. He was demobilized with the rank of captain in 1919. He was honorary colonel of 282 (Welsh) Field Brigade, R.A. (T.A.). From 1940 to 1945 he served as a major with the 11th Battalion of the Surrey Home Guard.

Bruce won the rackets amateur championship in 1922 and 1931, was 10 times doubles champion, and was champion of the United States doubles in 1928 and 1930. He was singles champion of Canada in 1928 and 1930 and doubles champion there in the latter year. In 1931 he became open champion of the British Isles.

At tennis Bruce was amateur champion of the United States in 1930, and of the British Isles two years later and again in 1938. He represented Great Britain in the Bathurst Cup no fewer than 18 times and was six times winner of the Coupe de Paris. He was five times winner of the M.C.C. Gold Prize and nine times winner of the Silver Prize. A fine match player, his good style and amazing endurance made him outstanding.

He succeeded his father in the title in 1929, his elder brother, Captain the Hon. Henry Lyndhurst Bruce (3rd Battalion, The Royal Scots) having been killed in action on December 14, 1914. He married, first, in 1912 Margaret Bethune (Betty), the only daughter of Mr. Adam Black, of Danescross, Hook Heath, Woking, who died in 1950, and by whom he had two sons and two daughters. His second marriage, to Miss Grizelda Hervey, took place in the month before he died.

He is succeeded in the family honours by the Hon. Morys George Lyndhurst Bruce, who was born on June 16, 1919, and who married in 1946 Maud Helen Sarah, only daughter of Sir John Dashwood, Bt., by whom he had two sons.

October 5, 1957.

William Abingdon, M.B.E., the stage director, died on December 13, 1959 in London at the age of 71. He will be remembered for a long series of successful productions at Drury Lane Theatre, first for Basil Dean [d. 1978] and later for Ivor Novello [q.v.].

"Bill" Abingdon, as he was generally known, was born at Highgate on July 1, 1888, the son of W. L. Abingdon, a well-known actor, and was educated at Thanet College and St. Francis Xavier, Bruges. He made his first stage appearance at His Majesty's Theatre in February 1910 as a member of Sir Herbert Tree's company in *The O'Flynn* and he remained with Tree for two years. But even at this early stage of his career his thoughts were turning to stage management rather than to acting. In 1912 he was stage manager for a play *Very Much Married* at the Little Theatre. It achieved little success and after acting in *Within the Law* at the Haymarket he returned to His Majesty's. When he was demobilized from his war service in the Royal Field Artillery he abandoned acting altogether and took up stage management as a career.

At that period he owed much to Basil Dean, who had great faith in his abilities. For him Abingdon stage managed a number of successful productions, including *The Blue Lagoon* in 1920, *Will Shakespeare* in 1921, *East of Suez* in 1922, a revival of *The Gay Lord Quex* and *Hassan* in 1923. In February 1924 Dean was appointed joint managing director of Drury Lane and he took Abingdon with him to stage manage *London Life* and the notable production of *A Midsummer Night's Dream.* Dean resigned his Drury Lane appointment in January 1925 but this time Abingdon did not follow him and he was associated with Drury Lane for the rest of his stage career. He contributed largely to the success of a long series of productions including *Rose Marie, The Desert Song, Showboat, The New Moon, The Three Musketeers, The Land of Smiles* and *Cavalcade* and then, when Ivor Novello took over at Drury Lane, Abingdon's successes continued with *Careless Rapture, Crest of the Wave, Henry V* and *The Dancing Years.*

When E.N.S.A. took over in 1939 Abingdon remained as staff controller in charge of equipment and he held the position throughout the war. Probably nothing in his whole career gave him greater pleasure than his appointment as secretary of the Drury Lane Fund, which was founded by David Garrick, and which has continued since his day as an independent benevolent institution, of which only Drury Lane actors, actresses and stage officials can be members. His services to the theatre were recognized when he was made M.B.E.

December 15, 1959.

"Abu Saud"—See **Dickson.**

Marcus Adams, the outstanding child photographer of his day and photographer to the Royal Family for more than 30 years, died on April 9, 1959 while staying with relatives at North Stoke, Oxfordshire. He was 83.

He first photographed the Queen in 1926, when she was only eight months old, and continued his studies of her until she was 15. The Prince of Wales and Princess Anne sat for him; his last royal portrait was of Princess Anne in 1955. He retired in 1957.

Adams in his later years would rarely photograph adults. His methods were unorthodox, and he handled children marvellously well; he once said that his work was nine-tenths psychology and one-tenth mechanics. He made his studio more like a living room, and camouflaged the camera. Children took to him readily, he played with them and won their confidence, and the camera caught their characters unawares. His backgrounds were a specialty in which his considerable competence as a painter in water colours and oils assisted him. Frequently, where he thought it appropriate, he painted in a suitable background in the process of developing his negatives; his colleagues recall, for example, his coverage of a fancy ball when he conceived different backgrounds to suit the dress each child was wearing.

During his long career he photographed tens of thousands of children, and examples of his work have gone all over the world. One of his favourite portraits was of the Queen, when she was learning to walk at the age of 15 months, stepping hesitantly away from her nurse with a rattle in her hand. A little book which he had published in 1935, a collection of amiable reflections and skilful illustrations, entitled *The Rhythm of Children's Features,* began with a picture of "the beautiful hands of H.R.H. Princess Elizabeth of York," and to her it was by permission dedicated.

Marcus Algernon Adams was born in Southampton on May 16, 1875, the second of three generations of Court photographers, for his father, Arthur Walton Adams, was one of the first and his son and partner, Gilbert Adams, has had the royal warrant extended to him. Educated at York House School, University College, Reading, and in Paris, Adams took up photography in 1889 and formed his own company in 1919. He opened his famous children's studio in London in 1926. He was an honorary Fellow of the Royal Photographic Society, having served for many years on the council, and of the Institute of British Photographers, and a member or honorary member of various photographic and art societies in Britain and America, where his reputation was as high as in Britain. Travelling was among his favourite recreations, and he lectured and exhibited in many countries.

He had a striking presence, being of medium height and wiry, with a great shock of black hair which faded towards the end. Carpentry and ancient history were among unexpected occupations of his leisure; he had a passion for gardening and flowers, and claimed to be most at home in the country.

He married in 1904 Lillie Maud Farr; Gilbert Adams is their only child.

April 11, 1959.

Lord Addison, who had a long and distinguished career in both Houses of Parliament culminating in the leadership of the Labour Party in the House of Lords, died at his home near High Wycombe, Buckinghamshire, on December 11, 1951 at the age of 82.

His political career falls into two parts. In the first, when he was a member of the Liberal Party, he held important Ministerial offices in the Lloyd George Coalition Government during and after the 1914-18 war. In the second phase, after he had left the Liberal and joined the Labour Party, he held successive Ministerial posts in three Labour Governments. He was an able administrator, forceful in character, sincere in his ideals, and forthright in Parliamentary debate. His occasional asperities were fully redeemed by his kindly human feeling and generosity. It was typical of the man who had denounced the Opposition in the House of Lords for, as he alleged, obstructing the will of the people on the Iron and Steel Bill, that he should also pay warm tribute to the absence of a sense of class distinction which he found among the peers. "I don't know anywhere," he said in an address to the Oxford University Labour Club in 1949 "where there is a more complete absence of snobbery than the House of Lords . . . there is no distinction of class or type, and Labour peers who have come new to the place have been received with the same openness and friendliness as anybody else."

The Right Hon. Sir Christopher Addison, first Viscount Addison and Baron Addison, of Stallingborough, in the County of Lincoln in the Peerage of the United Kingdom, K.G., P.C., was born on June 19, 1869, on a farm at Hogsthorpe, in Lincolnshire, and his early contact with farming life and its difficulties and hardships made an impression upon him that remained throughout life. This early experience peculiarly fitted him to fill the post of Minister of Agriculture in the second Labour Government. He never lost interest in the practical problems of agriculture and he acquired more than an amateur's knowledge of the art of apple culture. Educated at Trinity College, Harrogate, and at St. Bartholomew's Hospital, he became after the conclusion of his medical course a lecturer and demonstrator in anatomy and later he was Professor of Anatomy in University College, Sheffield. A Fellow of the Royal College of Surgeons (where he was Hunterian Professor in 1901), a member of several boards of medical studies, and at one time secretary of the Anatomical Society of Great Britain and Ireland, Addison was editor for some years of the *Quarterly Medical Journal* and prepared the twelfth edition of Ellis's *Demonstrations of Anatomy.*

He first entered the House of Commons in 1910 as Liberal member for the Hoxton division of Shoreditch and he continued to represent that constituency until 1922. Deeply interested in social problems, he was brought close to Lloyd George when the latter was carrying his Insurance Bill through Parliament, and in debate he showed a complete mastery of the scheme. He had been appointed Parliamentary Secretary to the Board of Education in 1914, and after war broke out and Lloyd George became Minister of Munitions, Addison became Under-Secretary to that Ministry. In this office he was of great assistance to the Minister and was praised by Lloyd George for having saved the country large sums of money by the system of costing which he introduced. Later, when Lloyd George became Prime Minister in the Coalition Government, Addison succeeded him as Minister of Munitions, and he was sworn of the Privy Council. During the closing phases of the war he was given the post of Minister in charge of post-war reconstruction.

After the General Election of 1918 and the Lloyd George Government had been returned with an overwhelming majority, Addison was appointed President of the Local Government Board; when that department was shortly afterwards reorganized as the Ministry of Health, and he became its first political head, his career moved into a stormy phase. There was a clamant need for houses after the interruption of building during the war and Addison promoted an ambitious programme of State-assisted housing, which involved the payment of large subsidies. There was an outcry against the heavy cost to the taxpayer which the scheme involved and on this issue relations between Lloyd George and his energetic colleague became strained. In 1921 Addison left the Ministry of Health to become Minister without Portfolio, but the campaign against him did not abate but rather increased, and Addison resigned from the Government.

This break with the Lloyd George Government was followed shortly afterwards by Addison's transfer of allegiance from the Liberal to the Labour Party. His conversion to Labour was marked by the publication in 1922 of his book, *The Betrayal of the Slums,* in which he defended his housing policy and sharply attacked those who had rejected it. Two volumes on *Practical Socialism* followed. In the General Election of 1929, which brought the Labour Party to power, he was elected Labour member for Swindon. Ramsay MacDonald, the new Prime Minister, appointed him Parliamentary Secretary to the Ministry of Agriculture, and a year later Minister of Agriculture. Addison showed a remarkable grasp of the duties of that office and was acutely alive to the difficulties and needs of agriculture. He sponsored the first of the Agricultural Marketing Acts.

From this time onward Addison's membership of the House of Commons was somewhat intermittent. He lost his seat at the 1931 General Election and he was an outspoken critic of the National Government. Although he was elected again for Swindon at a by-election in 1934 he held the seat only until the next General Election in 1935. He occupied part of the time he was out of Parliament in writing the two volumes of his personal diary,

Four and a Half Years, covering the period from June 1914 to January 1919, which were specially interesting because they contained the recommendations which he had made as Minister of Reconstruction.

Yet another phase of Addison's political career began when he was raised to the peerage in 1937. When the Labour Party came to office in 1945 he was appointed Dominions Secretary (he was given a step in the peerage in the same year) and he was head of that department when it became the Ministry of Commonwealth Relations in 1947. At his own request he was relieved of the heavy duties of the office in view of the demands made upon him as Leader of the House of Lords, and he was appointed Lord Privy Seal and later Paymaster-General. Before he left the office of Commonwealth Relations, however, Lord Addison, in his seventy-ninth year, went to Australia by air as leader of the British delegation at the Canberra talks on the Japanese treaty. He became Lord President of the Council when Morrison* vacated that office on becoming Foreign Secretary. Throughout all the controversies in which he took part when the Government's nationalization measures came before the House Lord Addison held the affectionate regard of the peers, a feeling which found cordial expression when his illness compelled him to be absent from his post of duty.

He was twice married, first to Isobel, daughter of the late Archibald Gray, by whom he had two sons and two daughters, and who died in 1934; secondly, in 1937, to Dorothy, daughter of Mr. J. P. Low. He is succeeded by his son, Major the Hon. Christopher Addison, who was born in 1904.

December 12, 1951.

Julius Ochs Adler, who achieved distinction both as a newspaper man and as a soldier, died in New York on October 3, 1955 at the age of 62.

Born on December 3, 1892, at Chattanooga, Tennessee, he was educated at Lawrenceville School and Princeton. His mother was a sister of Adolph S. Ochs, who from 1896 until his death in 1935 was publisher of the *New York Times.* Even before he left Princeton it was taken for granted that Adler would join his uncle's organization, but soon after he had joined it the United States entered the war against Germany in the spring of 1917 and Adler was granted a commission in the cavalry. He went to France with the 7th Division in command of an infantry company and took part in the fighting in Lorraine to such effect that he was awarded the Distinguished Service Cross by General John J. Pershing.

After demobilization he became vice-president and treasurer of the *New York Times,* and was gradually allotted increasingly important duties in the management of the paper. His interest in military matters still remained strong, however, and he remained on the reserve. For the whole period between the wars he strongly supported the Citizens' Military Training Camps and he also played a large part in supporting many charitable organizations in New York.

As time passed, his interest in the *New York Times* was increasingly absorbed by supervision of the work of the business and mechanical departments, but he also had a share in shaping general policy. After the death of Adolph Ochs in 1935 Adler became general manager, while still retaining the posts of vice-president and treasurer.

He was quick to see the danger of the Nazi domination of Germany and he redoubled his efforts to get adequate training camps organized in 1940, and in October of that year he resumed full military duty. After intensive training he took his unit to the Pacific theatre and for three years took part in the fighting in Hawaii and New Guinea, until a breakdown in health brought his repatriation in 1944. A serious operation had to be performed, but he recovered sufficiently to resume his duties with the *New York Times.*

After the collapse of the German armies he flew to Germany and visited a number of concentration camps. His experiences he used for a series of revealing articles. He was able to send a series of eye-witness dispatches on the arrival of the United States Third Fleet in Tokyo Bay after the surrender of Japan. Though he had been chiefly concerned with the business side of the paper, these articles and dispatches showed that he was an all-round newspaper man.

He married in 1922 Miss Barbara Stettheimer and there were a son and two daughters of the marriage.

October 4, 1955.

King Amanullah, former King of Afghanistan, died in a nursing home at Zurich on April 25, 1960. He was 68.

When Amanullah, third son of Habib Ullah, was born on June 1, 1892, the throne of Afghanistan had been held for 11 years by its strong and ruthless conqueror, the Amir Abdur Rahman. He died in 1901, after craftily and successfully playing Russia against Britain, and was succeeded by his son, the no less crafty Habib Ullah, whose outstanding performance was to keep strictly neutral during World War One, irrespective of Berlin's rather primitive efforts at winning his support.

A favourable treaty with Moscow, concluded on February 28, 1921, which was undoubtedly a factor in securing British confirmation of his independence in the following November, was a first fruit of this inheritance for Amanullah, for he had, unexpectedly, succeeded to the throne in 1919.

Habib Ullah was murdered on February 21, 1919, a sequel to a typically Asiatic palace intrigue in which his eldest son had been involved, and when Amanullah was made Amir he was expected to follow in the steps of his predecessors as a stern, tradition-bound ruler bent upon preserving the medieval seclusion of his country.

He soon began to shock his grandees, who had hitherto held nearly unlimited delegated power within their provinces. He changed his title to that of king, opened negotiations with countries of unbelievers, and sent Afghan students to learn their ways and languages. Then, finding that the advantages he had won from Britain after some skirmishing were not to outlive the duration of his three years' treaty, he decided to get in touch personally with other western nations.

Amanullah encouraged German trading and engineering enterprise in Kabul, started the building of a huge modern palace, and brought about innovations which—while meant to improve the living and hygiene of his people—clashed with many old-established prejudices, and the material interests of a nation still entirely dependent upon primitive handicrafts.

In the autumn of 1927 Amanullah started on a European tour with a huge suite and bodyguard, all arrayed in sumptuous and colourful uniforms. His main target besides other capitals was Berlin, where he was to be the first foreign ruler to pay an official visit since Germany's defeat in 1918. The German Republic duly acknowledged this honour, though not without some sarcastic comment. Amanullah had a triumphant reception in a richly decorated capital, which had put one of the former palaces at his disposal, and started buying whatever took his fancy—from machinery to knick-knacks, from cheap, modern carpets to an enormous stain-glass decoration for his new palace, with some modern weapons thrown in. When he finally left, with some trainloads of goods, he expressed his gratitude by granting pompous decorations, and titles as Afghan dukes and counts, to some of the higher republican officials, who, however, were forbidden by the Weimar Constitution to take any of them.

The results of his prolonged absence and his indiscriminate pandering to Western modernism were to prove the last straw to his apparently neglected subjects. Shortly after his return revolts broke out, during which parts of the regular army—nominally 40,000 men—went over to the traditionalists, rising against Amanullah, and there were bloody battles for Kabul.

He was forced to abdicate, and with his family and sufficient funds he left the country in January 1929 to settle where, next to Germany, he had found the warmest reception—in Italy.

As a reformer, Amanullah failed, not for lack of good intentions, but for lack of wisdom in the timing of the changes he wanted to bring about.

April 26, 1960.

The Aga Khan, who died on July 11, 1957, aged 79, had more varied claims to fame than any contemporary Indian, and for many years exercised a marked influence on imperial and international affairs. That influence was invariably used for the maintenance and advancement of good relations between the British Commonwealth and the countries of the Near and Middle East.

He exemplified the culture of the east and west in happy combination. A large part of the public thought of him only as a great and pleasure-loving figure on the Turf, the owner of five Derby winners, though this was no more than one facet of his versatile personality. A Persian by descent and an Indian by adoption, he spoke the principal languages of Europe with great fluency, and knew the leading figures in every western country as well as those of Asia. A keen and rapid thinker, he was invariably interesting in philosophical, political or religious argument. He was especially fond of Persian poetry. His wide reading of English, French and German books of the day, and of both occidental and oriental classics, though never paraded, enriched his conversation. In fact he gained an extraordinary versatility from the good use he made of his exceptional opportunities.

The Right Hon. the Aga Sultan Sir Mohamed Shah, G.C.S.I., G.C.I.E., G.C.V.O., G.C.M.G., the third holder of the title "Aga Khan" bestowed by the British Government, was born at Karachi on November 2, 1877. He was descended in the direct line from Fatima, the daughter of the prophet Mohamed, of the Beni-Fatimite Caliphs who ruled in Egypt in the time of the Crusades, and of the Kwaja dynasty in Persia. He was thus the spiritual head of an Islamic sect, the Ismailis, scattered over Asia and Africa, and variously estimated to number from 10 to 12 million.

The first holder of the title of Aga Khan, Hasan Ali Shah, was born in Persia in 1800, and his royal kinsman, Fateh Ali Shah, made him Governor-General of Kerman. Incurring the displeasure of his master, he fled with his followers southwards and gave great assistance to British arms both in the First Afghan War and in Napier's campaign for the conquest of Sind. Hasan Ali Shah settled in Bombay with several thousand followers. He died there in 1881. His eldest son and successor lived to enjoy the title for only four years, being succeeded in 1885 by the subject of this memoir, his only son, then a lad of eight, so that the tenure of the Imamate of his son extended over nearly 70 years, and he was the forty-ninth Head of the Ismaili community.

He never forgot the care, skill and judgment with which his mother guided his upbringing, and except when he was in Bombay wrote to her almost daily. Aga Khan III was still in his middle teens when, in the Hindu-Muslim riots in Bombay in 1893, he gave peremptory orders to his Ismaili followers to keep out of the sanguinary quarrel. Lord Curzon nominated him to the Viceroy's Legislative Council, where he assisted Lord Kitchener in his efforts to obtain increases of imperial service troops from the Indian states. His first visit to Britain was made before the end of the nineteenth century and all through life he cherished the memory of the kindness of Queen Victoria. She invited him to dine and spend a night at Windsor Castle. This was the beginning of his long close personal association with successive British sovereigns, and particularly with Edward VII.

The influence of his Highness on the Islamic world in general and the Indian Muslims in particular was beneficial to British relations with the East. A turning-point was reached in Indian constitutional history when in 1906 the Aga Khan headed a Muslim deputation to the Viceroy, Lord Minto, and stated the case for encouraging the community to abandon its obscurantist aloofness from political life. Of the All-India Muslim League, which he thereupon formed, he was president in the first constructive years.

During the Turco-Italian and two Balkan Wars, as on many other occasions, the Aga Khan took the risk of incurring personal unpopularity by his efforts to soothe the fears of Indian Muslims and to induce in them a sense of proportion. His doctrine on the value to both sides of friendship between Great Britain and the Islamic world was of crucial importance when war broke out in 1914. He was in East Africa at the time, and cabled immediately to the *jamats* (councils) of his Ismaili followers stressing the obligation to remain loyal to the British Crown. When Turkey threw in her lot with Germany he issued a manifesto to the Muslim world on the same lines. Secret missions of diplomatic importance to Egypt, Switzerland and elsewhere were entrusted to his Highness, and some of them yielded important results.

His remarkable study of Indian and Middle East affairs in *India in Transition* (1918) was not only consistent with his post-war criticisms of the severity of the peace terms but had its effect on the final shaping of Indian political reforms. It was in the same spirit that he laboured unceasingly to secure the mitigation, ultimately obtained, of the allied terms to Turkey.

The Aga Khan was a delegate to the three sessions of the Round-Table Conference in London in 1930-32. Not only did the Muslims appoint him their leader but he was chosen to be the chairman of the entire British-Indian delegation. His rooms at the Ritz Hotel were the venue of many anxious and secret negotiations, some of them lasting to the small hours of the morning. In 1933 he was chairman of the British-Indian delegation to the resulting Joint Select Committee of both Houses of Parliament presided over by the late Lord Linlithgow, which was a prelude to the passing of the India Act of 1935. The remarkable achievement of securing a unanimous report from the delegation was due in no small measure to his efforts to adapt communal claims to the interests of India as a whole.

When the Second World War broke out he was on the Riviera, and on the downfall of France he went to Switzerland for medical treatment, remaining there throughout the war period. Apart from the immediate issue of a manifesto to his followers enjoining loyal support of Britain, he was unable to play any notable share in promoting Allied aims, as he had done in the 1914-18 War. He was not seen in England until the summer of 1947. There were critics who felt that he should have managed somehow to leave France for some part of the Empire he had so long served. He had, however, a succession of illnesses, and these stood in the way of his acceptance of offers from Delhi of high diplomatic office abroad when a fixed date had been given for the attainment of Indian independence. He took up Persian citizenship in 1949 while remaining a British subject. A feature of the Aga Khan's guidance of his followers in his later years was that of instructing them to be loyal to the countries they dwelt in. While adhering to their Islamic faith they should adopt the dress and customs of the inhabitants.

The Aga Khan's relative immobility due to illness led him to respond to many suggestions that he should write an autobiography. This was dictated at his villa above Cannes and published in 1954. It was a most readable and informing narrative, marked by the mellow wisdom and engaging frankness of his later years.

His Highness married in youth a cousin in her teens. There was no issue and the union was dissolved. In 1908 he married an Italian lady, Teresa Magliano, who was a sculptor of merit. There was born to them a child who died in infancy and in 1911 Aly Khan [q.v.], who shared his father's love of the Turf, was born. The Begum died in 1926 and in December 1929 his Highness married Mlle. Andrée Carron, a lady of much charm and ability. A son, Sadruddin, who has been educated mainly in the United States, was born to them. The union was dissolved in the Geneva courts in 1942. He married in 1944 at Vevy Mlle. Yvette Larbousse, who has participated fully in his interests and pursuits. She nursed him with assiduous care in the recurring illnesses of his advanced age.

His Highness was made a K.C.I.E. in 1898, and promoted G.C.I.E. in 1902. He was made a G.C.S.I. in 1911 and a G.C.V.O. in 1923. In 1955 he was appointed G.C.M.G. As the Indian Orders ceased to be given when power was transferred in 1947 he probably stood alone outside the Royal Family in the possession of these four Grand Crosses. In 1934 he was sworn of the Privy Council, being the first Indian other than members of the Judicial Committee to be given this honour. He was also Hon.LL.D. of Cambridge University.

The Aga Khan derived from his father a love of horseflesh, and when he was still quite young his colours were seen on the Indian racecourses. Next he raced in France, and he was still only a visitor to the English turf when the 1914-18 War led to a suspension of racing. But he had already given close study to bloodstock rearing; the Hon. George Lambton bought for him, and after the war he visited the English turf not merely to win races but to breed the winners of big races and to show what could be done by close study after the foundations had been securely laid.

His first notable victory in England was winning the Queen Mary Stakes at Ascot in 1922 with Cos. Two years later he won the 2,000 Guineas with Diophon, and the St. Leger with Salmon Trout. Although Mumtaz Mahal, a public heroine in her day, cost him 9,100 guineas and won him £14,733 in stakes, he had paid 14,000 guineas for the beaten Aftab and £17,000 for the unsuccessful Feridoon. In 1930 he realized a cherished ambition by winning the Derby with Blenheim, and in the same season the Eclipse Stakes with Rustom Pasha and the Cesarewitch with Ut Majeur. He headed the list of winning owners with remarkable frequency, and in 1935 his triumphs reached their climax when Bahram won the three classic races of the year open to colts. In the history of the turf only 13 other horses had gained this triple crown, and of these only one, Ormonde, had never, like Bahram, been beaten.

In 1936 the grey Mahmoud won the Derby in the fastest time for the Epsom course ever recorded, and Taj Akbar, which was second, also belonged to the Aga Khan. Both Bahram and Mahmoud were sold to the United States as stallions, Bahram for £40,000 and Mahmoud for £20,000. The Aga Khan's mark has been left on the General Stud Book and the influence will be felt for generations. It was unfortunate that he saw fit to export his successful sires, thus losing that valuable result of endeavour and clever thinking to British bloodstock breeding.

In 1940 he again won the St. Leger, this time with Turkhan, and also provided the runner-up in Stardust. Tehran repeated this success in 1944, was third in the 2,000 Guineas, and had a long-remembered struggle with Ocean Swell in the Derby before succumbing by a neck. The good judgment of the Aga Khan and his eldest son caused them to buy a half share in My Love before the 1948 Derby. He duly won, and at the same meeting Masaka won the Oaks for them. Palestine added the 2,000 Guineas to this great list of triumphs in 1950. Finally Tulyar appeared, bred from a mare bought from P. Beatty, and won the Derby, Eclipse, King George and Queen Elizabeth, and St. Leger before being sold to the Irish Government for £250,000. The Aga Khan disposed of his studs in Britain in 1954, and his interest in racing there tended to decline thereafter.

July 12, 1957.

Vice-Admiral Sir William Agnew, K.C.V.O., C.B., D.S.O., who fought several brilliant actions in the Mediterranean in the last war and who was captain of H.M.S. Vanguard during the royal tour of South Africa in 1947, died suddenly at his home at Alverstoke, Hampshire, on July 12, 1960. He was 61.

William Gladstone Agnew was born on December 2, 1898, the fifth son of Charles Morland Agnew, O.B.E., second son of Sir William Agnew, first baronet. He went to sea from Dartmouth when the First World War began and was a midshipman in the battleships Glory and Royal Oak and sub-lieutenant of the destroyer Skilful during hostilities. In 1923 he was selected to specialize in gunnery and became gunnery officer of the cruiser Durban in China and of the Queen Elizabeth, Mediterranean flagship, from which he was promoted to commander in 1932. He returned to the Queen Elizabeth in 1936 as executive officer and in 1938 was appointed to command the seaplane carrier Pegasus.

In 1940 he took command of the light cruiser H.M.S. Aurora, a name that was soon to inspire a very healthy respect in the Italian Navy. In October 1941 Agnew sailed from Scapa in Aurora with H.M.S. Penelope (Captain A. D. Nicholl). His small squadron was called Force K and at Gibraltar he was joined by two destroyers; all then sailed for Malta.

On November 8 an R.A.F. aircraft reported a convoy 40 miles east of Cape Spartivento. "It is now known," wrote Captain S. W. Roskill, in *The War at Sea, Vol. 1,* "that it consisted of seven merchant ships with a close escort of six destroyers and a support force of two heavy cruisers and four more destroyers, in all greatly superior to Force K. Agnew left harbour before dark, gained contact in the very early hours of the next morning and in a brief, crushing night action sank all the merchant ships (some 39,000 tons) and one destroyer of the escort . . . By 1 p.m. on the ninth Force K was back in Malta harbour completely unscathed. Its action, in the C.-in-C.'s words, had been a brilliant example of leadership and forethought and the Italian Navy was, we now know, badly shaken . . .". The effect on Rommel's reinforcements was immediately marked. Agnew was made C.B. for this splendid action.

Soon afterwards Force K sailed again, co-operating with a cruiser force from Alexandria in a search for two ships carrying fuel from Greece to Benghazi. Agnew in Aurora, in company with Penelope and the destroyers Lance and Lively, found the enemy convoy 100 miles west of Crete and completely destroyed it. The German staff reported that the sinking of these ships made the fuel supply of the Luftwaffe in Africa critical.

In December 1942 the Aurora formed part of a light force of three cruisers and two destroyers which sank four supply ships and two destroyers of an enemy convoy bound for Tunisia. Of this action another officer of the force said: "Aurora hit everything she fired at and left us flames to shoot. All we had to do was engage flame after flame." Agnew was awarded a D.S.O. in 1943 and a Bar to it in 1944 for outstanding courage, resolution, leadership and devotion to duty in H.M.S. Aurora during operations in support of the successful landings on the Italian mainland. In January 1944 he was appointed in command of the Navy's Gunnery School at Whale Island, holding that position until selected to command the Vanguard in 1946.

He was Director of Personal Services and Deputy Chief of Naval Personnel, Admiralty, from 1947 to 1950 and in July that year he retired at his own request.

July 13, 1960.

Mabell Lady Airlie, G.C.V.O., G.B.E., close friend of Queen Mary [q.v.] for over 50 years, died on April 7, 1956 at her home in London at the age of 90.

She was Lady Mabell Frances Elizabeth Gore, Countess of Airlie, the eldest daughter of the fifth Earl of Arran, and she married the eighth Earl of Airlie in 1886. Her husband was killed during the South African War in 1900 at Diamond Hill, near Pretoria, after gallantly leading his regiment, the 12th Lancers, in a successful charge which saved the guns. Two years later Queen Mary, then Princess of Wales, invited Lady Airlie to join her household as Lady of the Bedchamber. The years drew the bonds of friendship ever closer. Queen Mary's death just over three years ago was a great blow to Lady Airlie and she had been in failing health for some time.

In spite of her duties at Court Lady Airlie found time to examine with critical insight many of the letters and papers that had been preserved by her own family and those connected with it. The first fruits of these researches appeared in 1921 and comprised a volume of letters by the first Lady Melbourne and her daughter, Emily, entitled *In Whig Society, 1775-1818.* There emerges a vivid picture of the last ripe autumn days of the great Whig ascendancy, which the passing of the Reform Act of 1832 brought to an end. Lady Melbourne, as brilliant as a diamond and almost as hard, is scarcely less typical of the period than Lady Holland herself. The next year there appeared more of Emily's letters, under the title, *Lady Palmerston and Her Times,* which evokes a far more sympathetic personality and one to whom it is clear her second husband, Lord Palmerston, owed a great deal.

Eleven years were to pass before another volume appeared. The material belonged to a later period and the social climate had begun to change, though even the Reform Bill, Chartism, and, finally, the Crimean War had evidently less effect on those within the charmed circle than is often now supposed. Lady Airlie's great-uncle, Colonel Strange Jocelyn, went through the Crimean War as an officer of the (then called) Scots Fusilier Guards. He was not a very brilliant letter-writer, but Lady Airlie put historians in her debt by publishing his letters from the Crimea, under the title *With the Guards We Shall Go,* in 1933.

About Lady Airlie there seemed still to cling something of the spirit of her Whig ancestors. In their strength of mind and steadfast refusal to follow fashion unless it definitely commended itself to their own exacting standards, she certainly resembled them. With her striking appearance, with masses of white hair piled up, usually beneath a large picture hat, she could easily have been the subject of a portrait by Gainsborough, and she rarely deserted that old and elaborate fashion. She was active in numerous charitable causes and was for many years a member of the council and of the executive committee of the Red Cross.

April 9, 1956.

Alain—See **Chartier.**

The Duke of Alba died on September 24, 1953 at the age of 74.

Don Jacobo Fitzjames Stuart y Falcó, 17th Duke of Alba, was born in Madrid on October 17, 1878. His father was the sixteenth Duke of

Alba, and he descended on his mother's side from the ducal house of Fernán Núñez. He was educated at Beaumont College and at Madrid University, where he took a degree in law. From an early age he travelled widely in four continents and went on expeditions to hunt big game.

At the same time he developed strong literary leanings, and it is true to say that intellectual interests occupied the greater part of his life, for the Duke was no dilettante or dabbler in the arts but an accomplished author, a keen student of political questions and international affairs, and a most careful historian whose published works include biographical studies of his famous ancestors, the third Duke of Alva (as he was known to his contemporaries in Tudor England) and James FitzJames, Marshal of France, on whom James II conferred the dukedom of Berwick.

The bearer of numerous hereditary titles dating from the fifteenth to the eighteenth centuries, a close friend of Don Alfonso XIII, and a convinced liberal monarchist who served his royal master as Minister of State and of Education, "Jimmy" Alba, as he was called by his intimates, represented to rare perfection, in his person, demeanour, and temperament, the Spanish nobility at its best. Lean and lined, frail in looks but abounding in energy, alert of mind and caustic of wit, he was always and above all the aristocrat—not by mere accident of illustrious birth, like some of his rank in Spain, but positively, actively, ineluctably: the cultivated prototype of dynastic pride, dignity, and intelligence.

The seventeenth Duke of Alba was fourteen times a grandee of Spain, a descendant of the Conde-Duque de Olivares and, by baton sinister, the inheritor from James II of the royal name with which the abolished duchy of Berwick is associated in the history of three kingdoms.

The list of his titles is long and fine-sounding, for it includes the dukedoms of Arjona, Huéscar, Montoro, and Liria-Jérica, the county-duchy of Olivares, the counties of Lerín, Lemus, Miranda, Castañar, Monterrey, Osorno, Siruela, Ayala, Andrade, Casarrubios, Fuente de Valdepera, San Esteban de Gormas, and Fuentidueña, and the marquisates of Algaba, Carpio, Barcorrota, Coria, La Mota, San Leonardo, Villanueva del Río, and Villanueva del Fresno.

To meet him in London or in Madrid, wintering in Switzerland or in Scotland for the shooting, to visit the Palacio de Liria before it was damaged during the civil war, or to be shown his sumptuous library and the splendid pictures of his collection round the corner, to dine in his company at the Nuevo Club, to play chess or discuss politics with him was to encounter a cultured and attractive personality, at once friendly and imposing, for the Duke was as punctilious and punctual in private life as he was affable and courteous in an official capacity, as Minister of the Crown or as General Franco's* Agent—and later his Ambassador—in London.

The inventory of his numerous public posts and academic distinctions was hardly less impressive than that of his titles of nobility. He was a Senator of the Realm in his own right, a member of the permanent Council of Grandees, as also of the National Assembly, and President both of the Royal Academy of History and of the custodianship of the Prado Museum. He belonged to over a score of cultural societies and associations, including the Fine Arts and Spanish academies, the British Academy, the Rockefeller Foundation, the National Geographic Society of New York, the Friends of Toledo, and the committee in charge of the Caves of Altamira.

The Duke, who had represented the Nationalist cause in London during the civil war, was appointed Ambassador to the Court of St. James's in 1939; he resigned from the post six years later in protest against General Franco's steadfast refusal to heed Don Juan's claims as Pretender to the Spanish throne.

In 1920 he married Maria del Rosario de Silva, daughter of the Duke and Duchess of Híjar y Aliaga. She died in 1934, leaving one child of the marriage, Cayetana.

September 25, 1953.

The death occurred on February 24, 1957 of the Russian novelist **Mark Aldanov,** one of the principal surviving literary figures of the Russian "emigration."

Like the majority, perhaps, of the Russian writers of his generation, Aldanov was antipathetic from the start to the Soviet régime. By temperament and upbringing, however, he was marked out for a more bitter and more stubborn hostility to the Bolshevist scheme of things than most of his fellow exiles. Born Mark Alexandrovich Landau in Kiev, on November 7, 1889, he completed his education in Paris and had travelled widely in Europe before the Revolution. A student of history, a writer of an ironical turn of mind, politically a socialist of moderate stamp, he discovered in the Bolshevist Revolution those excesses of the Russian spirit against which as a writer he had from the very first set himself. His antagonism to the new dispensation in Russia was to grow more virulent as his period of exile, which was passed mainly in France, lengthened.

It is chiefly as an historical novelist that, under the pseudonym of Aldanov (he was also known for a time as Landau-Aldanov), he achieved genuine and individual distinction. In evoking the Napoleonic period of history, however, the period above all others to which he was attracted , he almost always had in mind parallels with the present and seldom failed to provide his own ironical slant on contemporary affairs. On essentially historical and political subjects he could indeed be an uncommonly acute and pungent writer. Apart from a biographical study of Lenin (1921) and an essay in the same year on "Clemenceau and Ludendorff," he wrote a comparative study of the French and Russian Revolutions that is still of considerable interest and whose conclusions bear closely upon the temper of his fiction of the French revolutionary era.

His first novel, *Saint Helena,* in which a reasonable enough fancy pervades his reading of the authentic historical evidence, achieves a humorous and sometimes witty good sense and is probably the most artistically accomplished of his books in that kind. It was this, at any rate, which led one critic to discover in Aldanov's Latin spirit a degree of likeness with Lytton Strachey. Each of the volumes of the trilogy begun with *The Ninth Thermidor,* though vividly conceived, is a less happily composed, less harmonious affair. The cool astringent irony is there, and the anti-heroic sentiment embodied in the young Russian hero has an almost Stendhalian quality, but each volume carries too heavy and confusing a load of historical allusion. The middle volume, *The Devil's Bridge,* is perhaps the best balanced.

A novel of Aldanov's that created some stir when it appeared in translation in America and, later (1945), in Britain is *The Fifth Seal.* Written, it would seem, or partly written, at the time of the Moscow trials and the great purge in Russia, this novel describing the ways of a small group of Soviet diplomatic representatives in western Europe is marked by anti-Soviet feeling of a withering satirical fury. It is, artistically speaking, disproportionate feeling, yet Aldanov's is a remarkable and at times powerful performance. Two years later came a translation of *For Thee the Best,* a novel about Byron, somewhat disjointed in construction and sourly pessimistic in tone. *Before the Deluge,* which gave a kaleidoscopic picture, in the Tolstoy tradition, of Europe—and primarily Russia—in the 1870s came out in 1948, *Tenth Symphony,* a book of five stories in 1950, and *The Escape,* a novel set in Russia at the time of the Revolution, in 1952. He wrote also *Live as You Wish* and *Night in Ulm,* which was being translated at the time of his death.

Aldanov was, without question, a writer of exceptional talent, although—as with almost all the other Russian writers in exile—it was talent which reflected the progressive inner weakness of the deracinated.

February 26, 1957.

Queen Alexandrine—See **Denmark.**

Liaquat Ali Khan—See **Liaquat.**

The Very Rev. Cyril A. Alington, D.D., successively Headmaster of Shrewsbury and of Eton, and then Dean of Durham, died at his home in Herefordshire on May 16, 1955 at the age of 82.

Cyril Argentine Alington was born in 1872, the son of the Rev. H. G. Alington, of Candlesby, in Lincolnshire. He was educated at Marlborough, where he was in the cricket XI, and gained a scholarship at Trinity College, Oxford: he was in the First Class in Classical Moderations, also in Greats, and was elected to a Fellowship at All Souls. He was Sixth Form Master at Marlborough for a short time, and then went to Eton, where he became Master in College in 1904 till he was appointed Headmaster of Shrewsbury in 1908. On the retirement of Dr. Lyttleton he was made Headmaster of Eton, where he was from 1917-33, when he accepted the Deanery of Durham.

Such is the bare outline of his career, and though he made his mark at school, at Oxford, at Shrewsbury, and at Durham, it is probable that he will be most generally remembered as the Headmaster of Eton. He married in 1904 Hester, daughter of the fourth Lord Lyttelton, and had four daughters and two sons, of whom a son [Giles Alington, q.v.] and three daughters survive him. He was a remarkably gifted man, with a very quick brain, a great capacity for work, many interests, wide sympathies, and a keen sense of humour. He was also fond of games, being a most useful cricketer and very difficult to beat at fives or rackets. He enjoyed riding, and at one time was often seen on horseback at Eton. Extremely good looking, especially in his robes, he was a most inspiring preacher to boys, and there are surely very many old Etonians and Salopians who remember how much they looked forward to and enjoyed hearing his sermons, addresses, and fables, which were delivered so naturally and impressively in their school chapels.Especially remarkable at Eton were the voluntary evening services in Holy Week, when Chapel was completely full.

He was not a very profound scholar nor a great divine, in the sense that he produced work that was redolent of research; but he was so thoroughly human and sensible and so sincere in his beliefs that the many and various books which he found time to write on religious subjects have probably achieved more towards the purpose for which they were intended than many more ponderous and erudite volumes.

As a schoolmaster, besides being so effective in the pulpit, he was a lively imaginative teacher, sometimes perhaps mystifying as well as stimulating—the rapidity with which his brain worked and the mass of quotations with which his remarkable memory was stored being sometimes none too easy to follow. He certainly worked for Shrewsbury and for Eton with all his heart, and it is possible that his time at the former school was the happiest of his life; there he had his own way entirely for the first time, when he was young and enthusiastic; there, besides the memory of the man there are many abiding memorials to his energy and good sense that keep his name alive. At Eton he was not so powerful, and he was not an Etonian—some rather narrow-minded people resented that—but he did much for the work, discipline, and general life of the school, and the Drawing Schools were due to him as was the King of Siam's garden, the most generally popular of improvements made in recent years at Eton.

As a writer, besides the religious works already mentioned, he tried his hand at novel writing, light verse, hymns, songs, opera, and once at a short historical study. Probably he was most successful at light verse; at times in his shorter poems, especially in his lines to retiring masters, he was exceptionally happy, and he was at his best here because he wrote so fast, and it was this speed which makes his novels and more serious works sometimes seem to lack in lasting power—whereas the shorter poems were thrown off as they should be, the genuine product of a quick and ready wit and a truer insight than many would have given him credit for. For Alington was in reality a most genuine man; in spite of his mannerisms, and a certain self-consciousness which to some may have seemed the real man, he was the kindest and most charitably minded of men.

He was a staunch believer in the public schools and certainly he did much for the two of which he was headmaster. Though no great reform in education is associated with his name at Eton during his time there was maintained a high standard of efficiency, with the school full to overflowing, and he was the inspiring spirit. Cheerfulness, industry, and humour are three great assets; when associated with a keen brain, a strong will, and sincere religion, as they were in Alington, and adorned by an athletic frame, a splendid presence and fine face, it is not surprising that he became the headmaster of two great schools, or that his memory is clearly imprinted in the minds of hundreds of boys, not even the most critical of whom could deny his greatness as a preacher.

After 26 years of headmastership, Alington accepted the Deanery of Durham, and at once was thrilled with the beauty of his new home and the interest of his work. Unfortunately he became a martyr to arthritis and in his later years was very lame, and so unable to be as active as he wished, but his courage and spirit never failed, and he and his wife will be remembered there with great affection, for he did much for the services and the building and made a habit of showing all and sundry round his beloved cathedral, to the very great delight of many, to whom his impressive appearance and ready tongue added enormously to their enjoyment, while Mrs. Alington was always actively employed in giving help and sympathy to every philanthropic undertaking in the district.

There was a very general and genuine regret when in 1951 he retired. Retirement for him did not mean any slackening in intellectual work, though arthritis gradually confined physical movement. In his beautiful home in Herefordshire, tended lovingly by his wife, he continued almost to the end of his life to publish volumes of scholarship, reminiscence and fiction; in November 1954 his tribute in verse to Sir Winston Churchill* on his eightieth birthday appeared in *The Times.*

May 17, 1955.

Giles Alington, Dean and Senior Tutor of University College, Oxford, died on February 24, 1956 at Oxford at the age of 41.

He was the elder son of the late Dr. Cyril Alington [q.v.], Headmaster of Eton and Dean of Durham, and was born on May 29, 1914. He entered Crace's House at Eton while his father was still Headmaster, and in time became Captain of the Oppidans. From Eton he went as an exhibitioner to Trinity College, Oxford, his father's old college. After taking his degree in *Literae Humaniores* he went to the United States, where he taught for a short period at St. Paul's School, Concord, New Hampshire.

On his return to England he became assistant secretary to the National Association of Probation Officers, but in 1939 he underwent a serious operation and he was unfit for military service. He later became secretary of the Evian Refugee Committee, in which capacity he returned in 1940 to the United States to attend a conference. On the advice of the Embassy he remained in America and again did some teaching at St. Paul's. In 1941 he returned to England to take up an appointment on the War Office Army Education staff. A year later he was back at Oxford as secretary of the Oxford University Courses for the American, Canadian, and British Forces, which were attended during the war by more than 7,000 officers and other ranks. In this post he revealed his unusual gift for organization, and a capacity for informal friendship, whether with Generals or G.I.s.

In June 1944 he was elected Fellow and Praelector in Modern History at University College, Oxford, and at once he assumed a leading part in the life of the college. His rooms were open to any member of the college, senior or junior, whether they wanted his advice or simply the pleasure and surprises of his conversation. In 1940 he had published a book, *The Growth of America,* and in his teaching he remained especially interested in the history of the United States. His most congenial period in English history was the eighteenth century, and at the time of his death he was working on the manuscript of a book dealing with politics and persons in the reign of George III. In 1946-47 he was Junior Proctor. He had been Dean of his college since 1945, and in 1948 the governing body invited him to become Senior Tutor also, the first time in the history of the college that these two posts had been combined.

In spite of the very full part he played in the life and government of the college, Alington also engaged in many outside activities. He was appointed a magistrate in 1950 and he was specially valued by his colleagues for his work in the Juvenile Court and in probation. He became a visiting justice both at Oxford Prison and at the Campsfield Detention Centre at Kidlington. He was Chairman of the City of Oxford Youth Employment Committee. In the summer of 1953 and again in 1955 he was secretary of the Fulbright Conference on American Studies.

It is doubtful whether any other Oxford don of this generation has been more devoted to his undergraduates or has done more to shape their lives. Those who came to him in trouble could count upon his utter discretion and practical sympathy; if more was possible, his help was never limited merely to advice. Few of his closest friends were aware that he was often himself in physical pain. Those who saw him in his last illness will not forget his exemplary courage and courtesy. What chiefly remains in the memory is his largeness of personality, the grasp and trenchant wit of a penetrating mind, his quite unusual executive ability, and his humanity. He moved easily in many kinds of company and in any company his presence was impressive.

He was unmarried and is survived by his mother and his three sisters—the Countess of Home, Mrs. R. A. B. Mynors, and Mrs. J. C. V. Wilkes.

February 25, 1956.

To the present generation **Maud Allan,** who died on October 7, 1956, is merely a name remembered vaguely. But 40 years ago she created a considerable sensation in London by her dancing of *The Vision of Salome,* provoking much criticism, both favourable and otherwise. She was a classical dancer of exquisite grace and almost perfect technique, and critics were unanimous in acclaiming her as the greatest living exponent of the poetry of motion. Her performances were rather more than dancing; they were, indeed, a remarkable series of realistic and finely acted episodes, and for 20 years she created a furore wherever she appeared.

She was born in Toronto, Ontario, the daughter of Dr. William Allan and his wife (also a doctor), Isabel Maud Hutchinson. On her father's side she was of English stock, on her mother's partly Irish, partly Scottish. She was educated at San Francisco, where her parents had settled, and she studied at the School of Music there under E. S. Bonelli, with a view to becoming a professional pianist. Later she went to the Royal High School for Music in Berlin, where she gained the friendship of several famous musicians, especially of Joachim. It was not until 1903 that she made her *début* as a professional dancer, appearing at the Royal Conservatoire, Vienna, in a programme of classical dances. Afterwards she danced in Brussels and Paris, and then toured the leading cities of Germany, Switzerland, Austria, and Hungary.

At Maríenbad in September 1907 she was commanded to appear before King Edward VII, and in the following March she made her first appearance in London at the Palace Theatre. It is no exaggeration to state that she took London by storm, and she remained at the Palace without a break for eight months. She made many return visits to London besides touring the world.

She also appeared as an actress in London, at the Court Theatre in April 1918, as Salome in Oscar Wilde's play of that name, and at the Lyceum, in April 1932, as the Abbess in a revival of *The Miracle.* She was the author of a small book, *My Life and Dancing,* published in 1908, and of various essays and articles on the art of the dance.

October 8, 1956.

George Allison, manager of Arsenal Football Club from 1934 to 1947 and the first F.A. Cup Final commentator for the B.B.C., died on March 13, 1957 at his home at Golders Green, London. He was 73.

George Frederick Allison was born in Hurworth-on-Tees, co. Durham, and began his career as a judge's secretary. He then turned to journalism, and after experience in Tees-side, Newcastle upon Tyne, and Plymouth, went to London to work on a sporting paper. In 1912, having secured an exclusive interview with Lord Kitchener, he was given a job with an American newspaper. His position as European correspondent of the Hearst [q.v.] group Sunday magazine *The American Weekly,* which he joined a year later, lasted for over 30 years.

Broadcasting next claimed his attention as a sideline. In 1927 the B.B.C. asked him to make the second soccer commentary ever broadcast—on a match between the Corinthians and Newcastle United at Crystal Palace on January 29 of that year. That rich, deep voice was soon known to millions. His commentaries of football matches were always full of colour. Somehow he caught the atmosphere of an occasion in a magical way and when the Cup Final of 1928 was granted a running commentary—the first Cup Final broadcast—his was the voice that told the story.

In due course Allison became a director of Arsenal Football Club. By then Arsenal, managed by the famous Herbert Chapman, had won a place of world fame in sport. When Chapman died in 1934 the one man big enough to step into his shoes was Allison. To become manager he resigned his directorship of the club. To follow the tradition and the golden success established by Chapman was a huge task. But Allison, by his acute sense of showmanship, business acumen, and knowledge of players, kept Arsenal's name in the forefront.

He was a born impresario and put that talent to full use in the game of football which he loved. He brought Drake, Crayston and others to Highbury and under his direction Arsenal proceeded to gain the League Championship in 1934, 1935, and 1938, as well as winning the F.A. Cup in 1936. To reach the top is difficult enough: to stay there is infinitely more difficult. Allison maintained Arsenal at the peak and that was the measure of his many qualities. In 1947, after the difficult years of war, he finally retired, a man of wide horizons, who had made his mark.

March 14, 1957.

Sir Richard Allison, C.V.O., C.B.E., F.R.I.B.A., chief architect, H.M. Office of Works from 1920 to 1934, died at his home on September 29, 1958 at the age of 89.

Allison is said to have owed his first big job to exceeding his instructions. Shortly after the death of Queen Victoria, the late Lord Esher, permanent head of the Office of Works, which was then housed in two converted dwellings on the site of the present War Office, asked Allison, who was a draughtsman, to look at some rough sketches of a scheme for extending the space in front of Buckingham Palace. Guessing that the question of a memorial to the Queen was in the air, Allison drafted a new scheme, providing not only for a memorial but also for the treatment of The Mall as an approach to it. Lord Esher took the sketch to a secret conference then considering the question of a memorial, and within an hour young Allison was told that his plan had been unanimously accepted by the committee.

The story well suggests Allison's broad vision and habit of looking ahead. He was closely associated with Sir Aston Webb in carrying out the work, and the suggestion for a triumphal arch at the Charing Cross end of The Mall, which materialized as Admiralty Arch, was his. Later he was put in charge of the scheme, which included the Office of Works and other buildings in Whitehall.

For three years Allison served as "diplomatic architect" and travelled about Europe designing legations and embassies, as at Stockholm and Cetinje, in Montenegro. When the Serajevo assassination took place he was making his final inspection of the British Legation at Cetinje. At the outbreak of war his clerk of works was arrested and only just managed to escape internment by the Germans. The legation was never used, and after 1918 when Montenegro ceased to be a separate country, it was sold. Allison also rebuilt the Tokyo Embassy after the earthquake.

During the First World War Allison was chiefly engaged on hospitals. What he always regarded as his finest work of the kind was the hospital built in Richmond Park by the British Red Cross for wounded Americans. It was begun when the United States entered the war, and was within a few weeks of completion when the Armistice came and it was demolished.

The completed buildings on a large scale that best represent Allison's powers are the New Science Museum, South Kensington, the King Edward Building of the General Post Office, and Cornwall House, Waterloo Road. He was also responsible for the stone restoration of the Houses of Parliament.

Allison's larger buildings in stone are distinguished by a simplicity in the handling of what has been called "Whitehall Classic," and by courage and enterprise in comparatively new methods of construction. Shortly before his retirement in 1933 after 45 years of service he said in an interview that as he had grown older he had realized more and more the need for simplicity. On the same occasion he put in a plea for brick as a building material. It was in fact in brick that Allison's more personal taste as an architect was expressed. He designed many post offices, telephone exchanges and employment exchanges up and down the country.

Allison, who was the second son of Joseph Charles Allison, was born in 1869. He was educated at a choir school and studied art at the Lambeth School of Art. Entering the Office of Works at the age of 20, he was for 12 years employed on the temporary staff, being appointed Assistant Architect in 1901, Architect in 1911, Principal Architect on the retirement of Sir Henry Tanner in 1914, and Chief Architect in 1920.

September 30, 1958.

Lord Altrincham, who was Joint Parliamentary Under-Secretary of State for War in the crucial years 1940-42, and Minister Resident in the Middle East in 1944-45, died at his home at Badminton, Gloucestershire, on December 1, 1955 at the age of 76, after a long illness.

A journalist for the sake of supporting the ideals of Joseph Chamberlain; a soldier in the 1914-18 War who gained rapid promotion; a traveller who ranged the Dominions and colonies again and again both as a student and on the staff of the Prince of Wales [later Duke of Windsor*]; a member of Parliament; Governor of Kenya; a Minister of the Crown, and latterly a member of the House of Lords, the true key to his life was his almost fanatical devotion to the Empire.

The Right Hon. Sir Edward William Macleay Grigg, K.C.M.G., K.C.V.O., D.S.O., M.C., first Baron Altrincham, of Tormarton, Gloucestershire, in the peerage of the United Kingdom, was born on September 8, 1879, the only son of Henry Bidewell Grigg, C.I.E., I.C.S., and Elizabeth, eldest daughter of Sir Edward Deas-Thomson, Colonial Secretary of New South Wales. He had, therefore, imperial service in his blood and knew India from his cradle. From Winchester, where he was a scholar, he passed on, again as a scholar, to New College, Oxford, and in 1900 obtained a second class in Classical Moderations and in 1902 a third class in *Lit. Hum.* In the latter year he also won the Gaisford Greek Verse Prize. He moved to London in 1903 with the intention of becoming a journalist and was appointed to the editorial staff of *The Times* as secretary to the editor, the late G. E. Buckle.

Grigg's next move was to the *Outlook,* of which he was assistant editor under the late J. L. Garvin in 1905-06. Then, after an interval of two years spent in travel in the United States, Canada, Australia, New Zealand, and India, he returned to control the colonial department of *The Times.* This post, for which the experience and knowledge he had gained in his two years' journeying particularly suited him, he held from 1908 until his resignation in 1913. Thereafter he was for a short time joint editor of the *Round Table,* the last position which he was to hold in journalism.

On the outbreak of war in 1914 Grigg, who was then 35, joined the Army, was granted a commission in the Grenadier Guards and joined the second battalion. His advance in his new profession was exceptionally rapid. Having served for about a year with his battalion at the front he was transferred to the staff as G.S.O.3 of the Guards Division. During the Battle of the Somme he acted as brigade-major, and finally, some two years later, was promoted G.S.O.1 of the Guards Division in March 1918 at the moment when the enemy's almost overpowering attack had provoked one of the supreme crises of the war.

After the cessation of hostilities Grigg served for a time as secretary of the Army Reorganization Committee, and in 1921, two years after his appointment as military secretary to the Prince of Wales, he resigned his commission with the rank of lieutenant-colonel. For his services during that war and after it he was awarded the M.C. and D.S.O. and was created a C.M.G. and C.V.O. in 1919. In 1920 he was advanced to K.C.V.O. He was also a Chevalier of the Order of Leopold II and an Officer of the Legion of Honour.

Either directly or indirectly, as military secretary to the Prince of Wales during his tours of Canada, Australia, and the West Indies; as private secretary to Lloyd George at the time of the Imperial Conference of 1921 and in the next year; as secretary to the Rhodes Trustees from 1923 to 1925; and lastly as Governor of Kenya, Grigg was to be closely connected with the Dominions and colonies. His wide knowledge of them was indeed to be his principal asset, and when he entered the House of Commons in 1922 as National Liberal member for Oldham it was to prove of the greatest value to him.

Eminently fitted by his training for a post of the kind, Grigg was appointed in 1925 to be Governor and Commander-in-Chief and High Commissioner of Transport of Kenya Colony, an important but contentious position which he was to fill with much distinction until 1931. He went there with his wife whom, as the Hon. Joan Dickson-Poynder, only child of the first Lord Islington, he had married two years before. During his Governorship she was to take a deep interest in the many problems he was called upon to face and was to prove a great assistance to him.

In September 1930, his term as Governor having drawn almost to its close, Grigg returned to England, expressing, as he left, high confidence in the future of the colony he had served so well. Early in the new year his voice was heard on the political emergencies of the time and in March he accepted the invitation of the Central Leeds Conservatives to contest that constituency at the next election. Shortly afterwards he published a pamphlet, *Three Parties or Two?* an appeal to Conservatives and Liberals to co-operate in the restoration of national welfare and imperial security. When, however, in the autumn the election came he withdrew a Parliamentary candidature which had every prospect of success in favour of the former Labour member who proposed to stand as a National candidate. It was a patriotic and characteristically unselfish action.

During 1932 Grigg made some interesting and valuable speeches on public occasions, and also served as chairman of the Milk Reorganization Commission. In May of the next year he was selected to contest the Altrincham Division as the Conservative candidate at a by-election. Attempts were made to rouse the Conservative votes against him in view of the attitude he had adopted towards the Indian problem; but he was eventually elected by a majority over both his opponents' polls combined. He therefore returned to the House of Commons, where his knowledge and experience of imperial affairs made him a prominent figure. In the years that followed he continued to speak frequently upon domestic and imperial affairs; and as the European situation grew more ominous his speeches reflected a growing anxiety. In 1936 he published *The Faith of an Englishman* and two years later *Britain Looks at Germany,* in which he urged the peril to Britain of her insufficient protection against air attack.

Grigg became Parliamentary Secretary of the Ministry of Information in September 1939. It was a post for which he had obvious qualifications, but in early 1940 he went as Financial Secretary to the War Office, and a little later was appointed joint Parliamentary Under-Secretary of State for War. This position he held until 1942. A little later he became, at the request of the Foreign Secretary, chairman of a small committee to advise upon hospitality in regard to the Americans in Great Britain. Then in 1943 he published *The British Commonwealth,* in which he argued that nothing less than the whole Empire could speak on equal terms with the United States, the U.S.S.R., and China, considered the problem of co-ordinating a greater unity, and fell back eventually upon a regional organization in virtue of which each Dominion would be charged with special responsibilities for safeguarding imperial interests in its own sphere. The next year his *British Foreign Policy* discussed the future of Great Britain's international relationships. On November 21, 1944, his appointment was announced as Minister Resident in the Middle East, in succession to Lord Moyne after the latter's assassination by members of the Stern gang in October of that year, and he was sworn a member of the Privy Council.

In 1945 he was raised to the peerage. The same year the post lapsed, shortly after he had announced that he would not stand for re-election as an M.P. In 1948 when Lady Milner's [q.v.] editorship of the *National Review* came to an end, Lord Altrincham took over, and continued as editor when that publication merged with the *English Review* and became the *National and English Review.*

There were two sons and a daughter of the marriage. The elder son, the Hon. John Edward Poynder Grigg, who was born in 1924, served in the Grenadier Guards during the last war, and has been associated with his father in the editorship of the *National and English Review,* succeeds to the title.

December 2, 1955.

Shah Aly Khan, the elder surviving son of the late Aga Khan [q.v.], died on May 12, 1960, at the age of 48. He was known throughout the world as a keen sportsman, inheriting his father's love of the Turf and skill in the breeding of famous racehorses, as a man of attractive personality, and as having once served the allied cause as a soldier in the 1939-45 War. He was a volatile man of immense energy and lived a strenuous life of travel, sport and pleasure.

The late Aga Khan married Theresa Magliano, an accomplished Italian artist and sculptor in 1908. Their first son died in infancy and Aly Khan was born to them on June 13, 1911. The child was delicate and was not sent to any preparatory or public school and as his parents were frequently away from their French home he had a somewhat lonely childhood. He was placed under the tutorship of the late C. M. Waddington, a Carthusian member of the Indian Educational Service, who was for some years Principal of the Rajkumar College, Rajkot, for the training of the sons of ruling Princes. Subsequently Aly Khan studied for the Bar at Lincoln's Inn, but was never called.

As a boy of 12, Aly Khan went to India with his mother to join the Aga Khan, and thus for the first time saw for himself something of the religious responsibilities devolving on his father and the profound reverence in which he was held by his Ismaili followers. His mother died when he was 15. The Aga Khan married Mlle. Carron in December 1929.

Aly Khan fully inherited his father's keen interest in racing but, unlike him, was a gentleman jockey, and rode more than 100 winners. In later life he joined the Aga Khan in the management of his large racing stud and in the rearing of famous winners. He was also keen in the athletic field, and from time to time sustained broken bones and other injuries.

In 1931 Aly Khan registered his own racing colours with the Jockey Club. Credited with an amazing flair for picking promising horses, he built up a chain of stud farms in Ireland and in France which he directed himself. In 1946 he became a full co-proprietor with his father when he bought a half-share in all his brood mares, yearlings and foals.

When war broke out in 1939 the Aga Khan was under medical treatment in Switzerland. He heartily encouraged his son's desire to be of the utmost service to the allied cause. After a visit to London to discuss matters with friends of his father, Aly Khan joined the French Foreign Legion and was sent to the Middle East to serve under General Weygand* in Beirut, as a cavalry officer. After the short campaign in Syria he crossed the frontier to Palestine, and joined the British forces in Jerusalem. He was allotted intelligence work and made frequent broadcasts to the Muslim peoples of the Middle East, urging them to give their utmost support to the allied cause.

He was gazetted to the Wiltshire Regiment and rose to the rank of lieutenant-colonel. He was transferred to Cairo and continued to serve in the Intelligence branch. He was decorated with the Croix de Guerre with palms, and the Bronze Star Medal (United States).

He married first, in 1936, the Hon. Joan Barbara, eldest daughter of the third Baron Churston, by whom he had two sons. This marriage was dissolved and he married secondly, Rita Hayworth, the film actress, by whom he had a daughter. This marriage also ended in divorce.

One of his sons, Karim, is now the Aga Khan.

Aly Khan was named head of the Pakistan delegation to the United Nations early in 1958 and devoted considerable time to his duties there. He was elected a vice-president of the General Assembly within a few months and in 1959 he became vice-chairman of the Peace Observation Commission.

He was to have gone from France to Argentina to present his credentials as Pakistan Minister in Buenos Aires, in addition to his United Nations post, and to have attended the 150th anniversary celebrations of the Argentine Republic.

May 13, 1960.

King Amanullah—See **Afghanistan.**

Queen Amelie—See **Portugal.**

Dr. B. R. Ambedkar, the champion of the outcastes of India and their outstanding figure, died at his home in New Delhi on December 6, 1956. He was 63. His name will figure prominently in any history of the socio-political evolution of India in the closing years of British Rule. On the attainment of independence in 1947 Nehru* elected him as Law Minister, and this post he retained until he resigned in 1951.

Bhimrao Ramji Ambedkar, Ph.D., D.Sc., M.A., barrister-at-law, was born on April 11, 1893 in a small Ratnagiri village on the Konkan coast of Bombay. His father was an Army pensioner "passing rich" on Rs.50 (£3 15s.) a month, and thus better off than many of the caste Hindus by whom, following the custom of centuries, he was spurned as an outcast. The boy was made to feel the bitterness of "birth's invidious bar" by being relegated with the children of sweepers outside the village school house, on the chance of hearing the tuition given within to caste children, and this experience was repeated when his father moved to Satara.

In spite of these and many later handicaps and humiliations arising from the Hindu caste system, Bhimrao carved his way to distinction and leadership, and was big both physically and mentally. The determination and courage of this thick-set, spectacled man were writ large upon his features; but he gave little evidence in manner and address of the wide scholarship gained by assiduous study in three continents, for he failed to acquire polish. From the Elphinstone College, Poona, he went to Baroda and attracted the attention of the farsighted and liberal Maharaja Sayaji Rao III, who granted a scholarship enabling Bhimrao in 1917 to enter Columbia University, New York, to read economics and sociology. He also studied at Bonn University, and in London took courses at the School of Economics, did research work in the India Office Library, and kept terms at Gray's Inn, being called to the Bar in 1923. A teetotaller and non-smoker, he lived with a frugality that a promising poor Scots student could not surpass. When with his doctorates and his M.A. he returned to India he could do so only by part-working his passage and a loan from a British friend, repaid in later years.

The Maharaja Gaekwar gave orders for his entry into the Finance Department of the State but he was completely ostracized by caste colleagues and was refused living accommodation suitable to his status, so he had to resort to the insanitary and poverty-stricken quarters of the sweepers and other menial workers. He then took up law practice in Bombay, was appointed to the Chair of Economics at the Sydenham College of Commerce there, was made a fellow of the university, and an examiner in Economics and Law.

All this time he was preparing to be a Moses to lead his people, variously known as the Untouchables, the Depressed Classes, the Scheduled Castes, and (Gandhi's selection) the Harijans (sons of God) from the degradation of their centuries of abasement under Brahmanical teaching and example. He established a weekly paper in their interests, and rejecting Congress claims to promote the needed reforms and "change of heart" he organized an Independent Labour Party composed largely of this unfortunate section of the people. He was nominated to the Bombay Legislative Assembly in their interests.

It was inevitable that he should represent these 50 million or 60 million at the three sessions of the Indian Round Table Conference in London in the early thirties and should serve with the Joint Parliamentary Committee which was the prelude to the 1935 India Act. His insistence on the needs for separate electorates for these people was strenuously opposed by Gandhi, but figured in the Communal Award made "in the absence of agreement of the parties" by the Prime Minister, Ramsay MacDonald. On his return to India Gandhi led a civil disobedience campaign and was interned. His essayal to "fast unto death" unless the Depressed Classes were brought into the general (Hindu) electorates aroused intense excitement in Indian political circles and tremendous pressure was brought to bear upon Ambedkar to give way, since the award could not be modified save at the instance of the parties directly concerned.

So there came into existence the Poona Pact, whereby candidates chosen by the Scheduled Classes at a primary election later ran the gauntlet of the general constituencies for the seats specifically reserved for this section of the public. Though a compensatory provision was for a substantial increase in the number of seats allotted to his people—148 instead of 78—Ambedkar never ceased to regret the terms of settlement.

The whole story is told in much detail in Ambedkar's largely autobiographical *What Congress and Gandhi have done to the Untouchables* (1940). Among other products of his busy hand and brain was a favourable exposition of the Pakistan plan in an India not suited for democracy on the strictly western model; and works on economic subjects so varied as small holdings, the problem of the rupee, and the evolution of finance in British India.

When Lord Linlithgow [q.v.] further Indianized his executive council in July 1942, Ambedkar was appointed and given the portfolio of Labour. He condemned in no uncertain language the resort soon after of the Congress Party to what Gandhi himself described as "open rebellion" when the Japanese enemy was at the gates of India. Ambedkar was an efficient and purposeful departmental head.

The setting up of an interim National Government at New Delhi in September 1946 left him free to pay a visit to Britain to press his views with intensity of conviction on leading public men.

He was appointed Law Minister in 1947, and in that capacity had a leading part to play in the framing of the voluminous constitution. Though given to outbursts of ill-humour, he piloted the measure through with great skill.

He resigned in October 1951. He had for some time been unhappy about recent developments in Indian affairs and, in particular, took strong exception to the Hindu code measure promoted by the Cabinet, because he felt that it did not sufficiently safeguard the full rights of citizenship of the Depressed Classes.

He maintained his activity until his death, one of his last gestures having been to attend the world Buddhist conference at Katmandu in November 1956 a few weeks after publicly embracing that religion together with some thousands of his followers.

Dr. Ambedkar married in 1948 as his second wife Laxmi Kabir, a Brahmin, of Bombay.

December 7, 1956.

L. S. Amery, C.H., died in his sleep on September 16, 1955 at his home in London, at the age of 81, after long and devoted service to the public.

He was above all else an imperialist. In the 1920s he held the offices of First Lord of the Admiralty and Secretary of State for the Colonies. Then, in the critical days of the spring of 1940, after 10 years of private membership, he was made Secretary of State for India and for Burma. Here for five years he played a foremost part in the political reorientation under which his successors planned a two-Dominions settlement of the Hindu-Muslim controversy.

One of the most consistent supporters of the fiscal policy of Joseph Chamberlain, he devoted himself to empire development and solidarity. His wholehearted devotion to imperial preference and unity gave to his political actions an uncompromising vigour and sometimes an appearance of impatience with anything short of the most drastic measures. There was, however, no doubt of his complete sincerity or of his great abilities. He had travelled widely and his knowledge of the British Commonwealth and Empire was probably unrivalled. Before he entered Parliament he had been for a number of years on the editorial staff of *The Times.* After his defeat in the general election of 1945, his vigour unabated, he embarked on the major task of writing his memoirs, of which three volumes have been published, the last only in August 1955. These, written in fine, nervous language, constitute a major contribution to the political history of this century, and will be indispensable to future historians.

Leopold Charles Maurice Stennett Amery was the eldest son of Charles F. Amery, of Lustleigh, South Devon, and of the Indian Forest Department. He was born at Gorakpur, in the United Provinces of India, on November 22, 1873, and was educated at Harrow and Balliol College, Oxford. His career at the university was distinguished. He took a first class in Classical Moderations in 1894, a first in *Lit. Hum.* in 1896, and was elected a fellow of All Souls a year later. Having already represented Harrow as a gymnast, he received his half-Blue as a cross-country runner, and added to his activities as athlete and scholar a catholic and, at that time, not very clearly defined interest in politics which permitted him to call himself a Liberal Imperialist and to be a member simultaneously of a Tory club and of the Fabian Society. But two things at least were already clear in his mind—a sense of imperial unity which never deserted him, and a hearty detestation of orthodox Free Trade.

When he came down from Oxford he prepared for a call to the Bar and acted for about a year as private secretary to Leonard Courtney, afterwards Lord Courtney of Penwith. Meanwhile, he pursued what were always his strongest personal interests, the study of modern languages, for which he had a brilliant gift, and the study of foreign politics on the spot. When travelling through Turkey and the Balkans he attracted the attention of *The Times* and this led to a long connexion with Printing House Square. After a temporary appointment to Berlin, he went to London as an assistant to Sir Valentine Chirol, and remained a member of the editorial staff until 1909. During this period he acted as manager and organizer of the group of correspondents who had represented the paper in South Africa and was primarily responsible for *The Times History of the South African War.*

Meanwhile Amery had been called to the Bar by the Inner Temple in 1902 and had begun his political career in 1906 by unsuccessfully contesting East Wolverhampton as a Unionist and Tariff Reformer. In this constituency, which he fought three times, he had unbroken misfortune. Defeat in 1908 by only three votes was acclaimed in Unionist circles as a moral victory. The party was in the trough of a wave and Amery, an uncompromising supporter of the most bitterly controversial sections of its programme, had nearly succeeded in carrying off a Liberal prize. There were naturally strong hopes for the future. But in January 1910 the majority against him was increased by over 800 and at the end of the same year, when he shifted his attack to Bow and Bromley, he was beaten again, this time by George Lansbury. Five months later, in May 1911, he was returned unopposed for South Birmingham, subsequently the Sparkbrook Division, a constituency which he represented unbrokenly for the 34 years of his Parliamentary life.

During the 1914-18 War he saw service in Flanders and the Balkans, and had his share of adventure before returning to the House of Commons at the end of 1916. He was in the Caledonia when she was torpedoed by a submarine in the Mediterranean and escaped capture only by concealing himself—he was small in stature and easy of concealment—in the stern sheets of a small open boat which was afterwards picked up by a hospital ship.

When the War Cabinet was formed, Amery, who had long ago been one of the group of young men who were associated with Lord Milner in South Africa, became its assistant-secretary, and he afterwards served on the staff of the War Council at Versailles and on the personal staff of the Secretary of State for War. When Lord Milner went to the Colonial Office in 1919 he chose Amery to be his Parliamentary Under-Secretary and Amery remained there until 1921, when he became Parliamentary and Financial Secretary to the Admiralty. On the fall of the coalition he became First Lord and the Admiralty circular criticizing the economies recommended by the Geddes Committee brought him for the first time prominently to the notice of the public.

He remained at the Admiralty until the general election of 1923, continuing, though doubtless against the grain, the policy of naval reduction which had resulted from the Washington conference. Meanwhile his mind was working once more upon his lifelong problem of Imperial unity. It was not surprising that, when Stanley Baldwin went to the country on the fiscal question, Amery should be in the forefront of the battle, and when the experiment had failed and his party had modified its policy for the future, his opinion remained firm. While agreeing that modification was necessary in order to secure party unity and being prepared to take his place on the Front opposition Bench, he insisted in a letter to Baldwin, designed "to make his position clear at the first possible moment", that the "permanent facts of the situation" were unaffected.

When in 1924 the Conservative Government was returned to power, Amery became Secretary of State for the Colonies, an office to which he was suited by inclination, study and experience. Baldwin had pledged himself against preference duties on staple articles of food, and Amery was, in view of his lifelong beliefs, galled by the restriction; but there were other possibilities and he set himself to explore and exploit them. Meanwhile, he made the development of Empire trade the text of many of his speeches. In 1925 it was decided to create a new Secretaryship of State for Dominion Affairs, though at first the new department was vested in the Colonial Secretary. This arrangement was calculated to facilitate visits by the holder of the office to various parts of the Empire. In the same year he went to Iraq, which had presented him with one of his earliest problems. He was also the first Conservative Minister to visit the newly-constituted Irish Free State. In 1926 came the Imperial Conference, and Amery expressed himself particularly pleased at the agreement reached in regard to the future relations of the Mother Country with the Dominions, by virtue of which the equality of the partners was recognized.

In March 1927 he announced his intention of making a six months' tour of the Dominions. In May he realized a long-cherished idea of bringing the Governments of the Colonial Empire together in a colonial conference. The results were excellent and he and a number of delegates went on to Paris, where they were entertained by the French *Union Coloniale.* In July he sailed for Southern Africa and went on to Southern and Northern Rhodesia, whence he returned by Bechuanaland. He then proceeded in s.s. Ulysses to Australia. He landed in Western Australia and toured the Commonwealth. Then, in late November, he arrived in New Zealand. On December 3, a remarkable article under the dateline "s.s. Ulysses (at sea)" appeared in *The Times.*

After New Zealand where in some spare hours he indulged his love of mountain climbing, Amery left for Canada, arriving at Victoria, B.C., early in January. He held conferences with Ministers at Ottawa and negotiated in regard to Empire settlement. At last, on February 3, he sailed for home, his visit commemorated by the naming after him of a mountain in Alberta. He had travelled 55,000 miles and delivered some 300 speeches, some of which he published in *The Empire in the New Era* (1928). He was already the author of several political works which had appeared before the 1914-18 War.

Greatly invigorated by his tour, Amery settled down to the application of the lesson. He was even more strongly convinced of the possibilities of Imperial Preference than before. The general election was, however, approaching. It went against his party and in the early summer of 1929 the second Labour Government took office. In August he was back in Canada and with a guide made the first ascent of Mount Amery, which is more than 10,000ft. in height. It took him 13 hours.

While in opposition Baldwin defined his policy in regard to safeguarding, but he was too cautious for Amery, who publicly expressed his disappointment. Subsequent developments of Conservative policy in this respect went far, however, to remove his difficulties. In October 1930 Amery published *Empire and Prosperity,* in which he presented his arguments against Free Trade, and his preference proposals.

When in 1931 Ramsay MacDonald's Coalition Government was formed Amery, the champion of protection, had no place in it, and it was to be nearly 10 years before he sat in a Cabinet again. The authority with which he spoke on Empire matters, and the forcefulness of his personality insured, however, a hearing for his criticisms of the Government's fiscal policy and the other political pronouncements which he made from time to time. He was all for a firmer foreign policy and for greater vigour in rearmament. He was also a critic of the Munich settlement. As chairman of the Empire Economic Union Amery had published, with an introduction by himself, a series of reports under the title *A Plan of Action.* It appeared almost on the eve of the important Economic Conference of 1932. Three years later, in *A Vision of Empire,* he registered a confession of his political faith, and in 1939 he produced *The German Colonial Claim,* followed in the same year by *Days of Fresh Air,* an account of his many travels. This was supplemented in 1946 by *In the Rain and the Sun,* which gave his walking and mountaineering experiences.

When after Munich the war clouds were gathering Amery's record gained him the ear of the House as perhaps never before. After Neville Chamberlain had in September 1939 told the House that a state of war existed between Great Britain and Germany, and Arthur Greenwood [q.v.] rose to speak for the Opposition, there were cries of "What about Britain?" and "Speak for the working classes", but from Amery came the cry: "Speak for England".

The long months of the "phoney war" dragged on until in May 1940 came Amery's own turn to speak for England in his most celebrated speech. In the peroration, delivered in a tense and silent House, pointing directly at Chamberlain, he quoted Cromwell's famous words when turning out the Long Parliament: "You have sat here too long for any good you have been doing. Depart, I say, and let us have done with you. In the name of God, go!"

In the new Administration he became Secretary of State for India and Burma. Amery's record as a staunch upholder of Empire disposed Indian Nationalists to view the choice with some misgiving which was, however, tempered by the reflection that in the controversies on Indian Reform which had divided the Conservative Party a few years earlier he had stood sturdily for the advances authorized by the India Act of 1935.

He took charge in Whitehall when most of the Indian provinces were being administered by their Governors without Ministers or Legislatures, as the Congress Cabinets had resigned by way of protest against India coming automatically into the war without prior consultation by the Central legislature. Under the influence of Gandhi's pacifism the Congress Party was showing increasing hostility to the war effort, and the Muslim League, without actively hindering, stood aloof. Amery gave whole-hearted support to the Viceroy, Lord Linlithgow [q.v.] in the building up of India's ever-growing and magnificent contribution to the defeat of the Axis Powers.

These achievements were the more impressive since in the late summer of 1942, when Japan was overrunning Burma and battering at the gates of India, the Congress Party resorted to a campaign of what Gandhi himself described as "open rebellion", especially serious in areas of eastern India forming the springboard of the eventual reoccupation of Burma. This subversive "Quit India" movement had to be put down with a firm hand. Next came the grave anxiety of the Bengal famine of 1943-44, which was unfairly exploited by a Communist opponent in the 1945 General Election.

Through all these troubles the Secretary of State never wavered in the pursuit of his ideal of bringing India into free and equal partnership within the British Commonwealth, and of preparing Burma for a corresponding advance. He was the inspirer of successive efforts to prepare the way to complete autonomy for India by agreement between the various parties. His consistency is shown in *India and Freedom,* a reprint of his speeches on the subject published in 1942. The August offer of 1940 accepting the principle that India should work out her own future constitution; the increasing and ultimately almost complete "Indianization" of the Viceroy's Executive Council; the wide offer taken to Delhi by Sir Stafford Cripps [q.v.] in the spring of 1942—these and other steps were inspired by the Secretary of State with a steadfastness of purpose made the more significant by the well-known reluctance of his chief, Winston Churchill*, to promote any fundamental disturbance of the British role in India. As the buffer between the Prime Minister and the Viceroy, both men of determined views, he had no easy task. He might have secured more active support from colleagues in the Coalition Cabinet had not his restless energy and amazing industry made him prone to write letters and memoranda to them on any matters, whether directly affecting his own office or not. He also found time to show Indian and Burmese visitors great hospitality in his book-filled house in Eaton Square.

In the great Labour victory of 1945 Amery lost the seat for Sparkbrook Division of Birmingham he had held for 34 years. Yet at a time of grave family anxiety he continued many of his activities, and though a septuagenarian he did not dismiss from his mind the hope of one day returning to the House of Commons. He was one of the first of experienced public men to urge the importance of a speedy withdrawal of control of India from Whitehall as a necessary step for effective settlement between the two main parties—the Congress and the Muslim League—whose antagonisms had so stood in the way of the success of his own official efforts. He supported both the original announcement in February 1947 of a time limit for the transfer of power to Indian hands, and the later decision to antedate the British withdrawal by more than 10 months, on the basis of the setting up of the two dominions of India and Pakistan. On the day of the latter announcement, in one of his many letters to *The Times* he described the policy as constituting "a wise decision." In various other fields he still made his influence felt. He was strongly opposed to the American loan on the ground that the conditions imposed by Washington were inimical to the full and free maintenance of Imperial Preference.

Besides his memoirs, published under the general title of *My Political Life,* he wrote a number of other books after his retirement from Parliament. All manifest an unabated intellectual vigour and enjoyment of the adventure of thinking, coupled with felicity of expression. He also returned to journalism and, among other pieces, contributed some striking articles to *The Times,* notably a retrospect of the South African War and a commemorative piece on the centenary of Lord Milner's birth.

In all his activities Amery had the constant and understanding support of his wife, Florence*, daughter of the late John Hamer Greenwood, and sister of the first Viscount Greenwood. Mrs. Amery gave devoted service in the war as chairman of the Indian Comforts Fund, which looked after the needs of Indian prisoners of war on the Continent, and of Indian naval men and seamen in the British ports. Sewing parties were organized all over the British Isles, and Mrs. Amery was in daily attendance at the headquarters at India House. For this important work she received in 1945 the rare decoration of the Crown of India.

The tragedy of the younger of the two sons of the marriage need not be enlarged on here; the elder son carries on his father's work in the House of Commons.

September 17, 1955.

Sir Alan Anderson, G.B.E., who, during the last four years of the 1939-45 war, filled the posts of Controller of Railways at the Ministry of War Transport and Chairman of the Railway Executive, died on May 4, 1952 in London, aged 75.

He brought to his work wide business experience, from the shipping world as a director of various important lines and as a former director of the L.M.S. Railway. He devoted many years to the organization of trade and represented the City of London in Parliament from 1935 until 1940, when he retired because of the demands of his work as chairman of the Wheat Commission.

Alan Garrett Anderson was born in 1877, the son of James George Skelton Anderson and Dr. Elizabeth Garrett Anderson. His father was a man of conspicuous character and ability and his mother was a brilliant woman who performed outstanding work for women in the field of medicine.

He was educated at Elstree School, where he won an Eton scholarship. From Eton he went to Trinity College, Oxford, and started at once to read Greats, taking a pass in Mods. at the end of his second term. A keen oarsman, he rowed in the Trinity Eight in 1895, was given his Leander, and won the Ladies' Plate at Henley. He stroked Fours for Trinity at Henley in 1896-97, winning the Visitors and the Wyfold Cups respectively. Gifted with superb health and physique, he might have excelled at all ball games, but with him sport of all kinds always took second place to work.

In 1897 he entered his father's firm, Anderson, Anderson, and Company, joint managers at the time with Frederick Green and Company of the Orient Steam Navigation Company, and he became a partner in 1900. In 1911 he was elected a director of the Midland Railway, and when this later became the London, Midland and Scottish Railway he was appointed to the new board. When war broke out in 1914 he volunteered for active service. The part to be played by shipping, however, was soon realized, and he was placed in a reserve category, but every week-end he was engaged on heavy manual labour in connexion with the production of munitions. During 1915-16 Runciman, who was then President of the Board of Trade, employed him at various operations of blockade, chiefly in connexion with nickel. In October 1916, Anderson was appointed vice-chairman of the Royal Commission on Wheat Supplies. A month later he formed the Wheat Executive and became its first chairman. This organization was adopted as a model for a number of other Allied partnerships, and he was largely responsible for the excellent work done.

In April 1917, when the United States joined the allies, he was a member of Balfour's mission to Washington, and assisted to set up the control of wheat in America and Canada. Shortly after his return from the United States he was appointed Controller at the Admiralty and filled a difficult position in an able and efficient manner. In 1918 he became a director of the Bank of England and held the position of Deputy Governor during 1925-26. In 1924-25 he was president of the Chamber of Shipping. Among other important offices he held are those of vice-president and president of the International Chamber of Commerce, president of the Institute of Marine Engineers, and president of the Association of Chambers of Commerce.

He was a Deputy-Lieutenant of the City of London and High Sheriff of the County of London in 1922. In addition to being a director of Anderson, Green and Company, Limited, managers of the Orient Line, he was a director of the P. & O. and British India companies, and of the Suez Canal Company. His appointment as chairman of the Railway Executive in August 1941 arose from the need to co-ordinate more efficiently transport for war purposes. That body functioned as the Minister of War Transport's agent.

His mother's work for hospitals touched a responsive chord in him, and he rendered valuable help to the Elizabeth Garrett Anderson Hospital. He was closely connected with the work of King Edward's Hospital Fund and played an important part in founding in 1921 the British Provident Association for Hospital and Additional Services. Any practical means of alleviating suffering found in him a generous supporter.

Anderson possessed a magnetic personality, a keen sense of humour, and had a great capacity for absorbing details, but he always thought on a big scale and was a strong individualist. A willingness to delegate work and readiness to back up his staff enabled him to tackle successfully large and varied problems and were not the least potent factors in his success.

His interests were varied. He was for some years a Governor of Eton College, a member of the Royal Commission on the National Debt, a member of the Fishmongers' Company, honorary treasurer of the London School of Medicine for Women and of the Royal Free Hospital, and a trustee of the Seamen's Pension Fund. He was particularly fond of yachting and frequently travelled to Continental conferences in his own yacht. He was made a K.B.E. in 1917 and promoted G.B.E. in 1934.

He married, in 1903, Muriel Ivy, the daughter of G. W. Duncan, of Richmond, and had two daughters and two sons, who have both risen to positions of importance in the shipping world. The elder, Colin, who was knighted in 1950, was president of the Chamber of Shipping in 1949, and was first chairman of the Ministry of Labour's London Seamen's Port Welfare Committee. The younger son, Donald Anderson*, is chairman and managing director of the P. & O. and the British India lines.

May 5, 1952.

Sir David Anderson, president of the Institution of Civil Engineers in 1943-44, died at Dura, Cupar, Fife on March 27, 1953 at the age of 72.

Born on July 6, 1880, he was educated at Dundee High School and St. Andrews University and began his career as assistant to the late Sir Benjamin Baker, K.C.B. Later he joined the late Sir Basil Mott, Bt., as chief assistant and was subsequently taken into partnership, the style of the firm being Mott, Hay and Anderson.

The most important work of the firm was the design and construction of the Mersey Tunnel, but much bridge building also stands to the credit of the firm, including Southwark Bridge, Tyne Bridge, Wearmouth Bridge and Tees Bridge. With his partners Anderson was consulting engineer to the Central London and the City and South London tube railways. He was responsible, as joint consulting engineer for the London Passenger Transport Board (later the London Transport Executive), for the realignment of the Central line to Newbury Park, Ilford.

As consulting engineer to the Corporation of London he was concerned with the maintenance of the four Corporation bridges over the Thames. He was employed by the Ministry of Transport as joint engineer for the projected tunnel under the Thames at Dartford and he was also engineer for the Tyne tunnels. In 1949 he was appointed by the Minister of Works to be chairman of a committee to secure the maximum efficiency and economy in the use of steel. Sir David Anderson, who was knighted in 1951, served in the Royal Engineers during the 1914-18 war and was demobilized with the rank of captain.

He married first in 1907 Isabella Corbet, daughter of Mr. Robert Anderson, of Dundee. She died in 1929; in 1935 he married his first wife's sister, Agnes Gilchrist, who survives him.

March 28, 1953.

Sir John Anderson—See **Waverley.**

General Sir Kenneth Anderson, K.C.B., M.C., died in Gibraltar on April 29, 1959 at the age of 67.

Anderson was in command of the First Army from the time of the North African landings in 1942 until the victorious end of the Tunisian campaign in May 1943. Lacking in the characteristics which catch the public eye, he could hardly have been described as an inspiring figure. But he was a sound, energetic, tenacious, and skilful commander who had difficulties of supply, politics, and terrain to combat as well as a determined enemy. The successful plan of attack by the First Army in the final stages of the campaign was very much his own. Later, from 1947 to 1952, he was Governor of Gibraltar. His rise in the Army was both regular and rapid—he mounted by the regimental rather than the staff ladder—and he was given command of an army corps before he was 50. He followed the world of politics closely and spent most of his leisure in foreign travel.

Kenneth Arthur Noel Anderson was born on Christmas Day, 1891, educated at Charterhouse and Sandhurst, and gazetted to the Seaforth Highlanders in 1911. The 1st Battalion of the regiment was then serving in India, and Anderson arrived just in time to see the famous Delhi Durbar of King George V. In 1914 he went with his battalion, which formed part of the 7th (Meerut) Indian Division, to France and took part in the hard fighting of that winter. He was promoted captain in 1915, and at the end of the year was appointed adjutant of the 23rd Northumberland Fusiliers (Tyneside Scottish). On July 1, 1916, the opening day of the Battle of the Somme, he was gravely wounded and won the Military Cross for gallantry in action. He lay for many months in hospital, and it was nearly a year and a half before he was fit enough to rejoin his regiment, then in Palestine. He was in time to take part in Allenby's final victorious offensive.

He was adjutant to the Scottish Horse from 1920 to 1924. He then returned to India and to regimental duty, this time with the 2nd Seaforths. After passing through the Quetta Staff College and serving for a short time at home as G.S.O. 2 of the 50th (Northumbrian) Division in 1930 he was back again in India in command of the 2nd Seaforths. In that year he reached successively the brevet and substantive rank of lieutenant colonel at the age of 38. With his regiment he took part in operations on the North-West Frontier, for which he was mentioned in dispatches.

After service in Palestine Anderson was promoted colonel and in 1934 took over command of the 152nd Brigade of the 51st Highland Division at Inverness. Even now his regimental connexion was maintained; for this was the Seaforth and Cameron Brigade. He then made yet another visit to India, acting for a year as G.S.O. 1 of the 4th Indian Division, which was to produce so splendid a record under the test of war. Then, at the end of 1937, he was appointed to command the 11th Brigade at Colchester. He trained it strenuously with inadequate equipment and took it out to France in 1939. During the later stages of the Dunkirk evacuation he was placed in command of the 3rd Division and promoted major-general. For his services on this occasion he was awarded the C.B.

During the period between Dunkirk and the expedition to French North Africa Anderson commanded successively the 1st Division, VIII Corps, II Corps, and Eastern Command, becoming acting lieutenant-general in May 1941 and temporary lieutenant-general in May 1942.

In the autumn of 1942 first General Alexander* and then General Montgomery was nominated to the command of the British First Army in the landings in French North Africa which were being prepared for under the supreme command of General Eisenhower.* But changes in the Middle East commands took them to other appointments and Anderson was chosen to fill the post. His name was entirely unknown to the public, though well and honourably established in the Army, and even in the Army he aroused respect rather than enthusiasm. The task which he undertook was one of immense difficulty and complexity. In the belief that more French support might be expected for an American than for a British operation, the main part in the landings was given to American forces. Thereafter the heaviest weight was transferred to British shoulders and Anderson first co-ordinated and then commanded II United States Corps and XIX French Corps in addition to his own First Army, until in February 1943 18th Army Group headquarters was set up under General Alexander. The enemy, though inferior in numbers in the whole theatre of war, was able to concentrate superior strength in vital sectors. Anderson found his tanks ineffective in battle with the Germans, his air support weak, and his French allies unwilling at first to enter under his command. In the early stages it certainly appeared from time to time that there was too much dispersion in the British dispositions, but it is by no means certain that the responsibility was Anderson's. In May 1943 his patience and inflexibility of purpose were rewarded by one of the most complete victories in the annals of warfare. He was later advanced to K.C.B.

On his return home from Tunis Anderson was given command of the Second Army in the United Kingdom, and was transferred in January 1944 to Eastern Command. His last purely military appointment was as G.O.C.-in-C. East Africa Command in 1945. Two years later he was appointed Governor of Gibraltar.

In his first broadcast to the people of Gibraltar Anderson said that he and his wife were appalled at the conditions of some houses in the colony. With the return of the part of the population which had been taken off during the war, housing conditions were deplorable; and their amelioration was one of the most notable achievements of his governorship. But it was not achieved without a good deal of local resentment at the new taxes which were imposed to raise a contribution towards the cost of house building. Anderson's term of office is also memorable for the constitutional reforms in 1950 which established a Legislative Council, and for the warmth and interest which the Governor and Lady Anderson showed to all classes of the community. His term of office, originally three years, was twice extended and he retired in 1952.

He married in 1918 Kathleen Lorna Mary, daughter of Sir Reginald Gamble, Comptroller and Auditor-General in India. They had a son, who was killed in action in Malaya in 1949, and a daughter.

April 30, 1959.

Maxwell Anderson, the distinguished American playwright and Pulitzer prizewinner, who was admitted to hospital in Stamford, Connecticut, after suffering a stroke, died there on February 28, 1959, in his seventy-first year.

He had been engaged in arranging for the production of a new play, his thirty-third, called *Madonna and Child.* He was also in the early stages of writing the libretto for a musical comedy called *The Art of Love,* which was to be based on Ovid's poems but in a modern New York setting.

Probably he deserves to be chiefly remembered for his part in re-establishing a rhythmical form of language as a normal mode of speech in plays of contemporary life. In this respect Anderson was a pioneer in the theatre of the 1930s in his own country, and the style of his more serious work such as *Winterset* has had significance for playwrights in England too, though he never achieved on the stage in Britain the success which frequently came to him on the boards at home.

Anderson was born on December 15, 1888, in the small town of Atlantic, Pennsylvania. He was the son of a Baptist Minister, and got his schooling in various places where his father held a pastorate, before going west to the University of North Dakota, where he graduated in 1911. Later, while teaching English in a high school, he took the degree of master at Stanford University, California, and in more recent years endowed a scholarship there to be held by authors of new plays in verse.

Though Anderson wrote a play and acted in it as an undergraduate, poetry rather than drama seems to have been the main interest of his youth. Journalism, first in North Dakota, then in San Francisco, later in New York, where he became dramatic critic of *The New Republic* and contributed to the *Evening Globe* and the *Morning World,* was his means of livelihood. He helped to found a poetry magazine entitled *The Measure.* In 1923, however, his play *The White Desert,* a tragedy in blank verse, was produced in Stamford, Connecticut, and though it failed immediately, he decided to go on with playwriting. The very next year his *What Price Glory?*—a tale of two marines in wartime and their women—written in collaboration with Lawrence Stallings, was a sensational success on Broadway. He gave up journalism at once, finished (again in collaboration with Stallings) two new plays which were then produced, and published a collection of his poems *You Who Have Dreams*—all in 1924, his *annus mirabilis.*

Anderson maintained his position for the next 30 years with a succession of plays, some in verse, others in prose, some contemporary, others historical, in their setting. The first of these, *Saturday's Children*—with youth and marriage for its theme—appeared in 1927; in 1933 *Both Your Houses*—an attack on political corruption—was awarded a Pulitzer prize; in 1938 he became together with Elmer Rice* and Robert Sherwood [q.v.] a founding member of the Playwrights Company which sponsored the production of all his subsequent plays; and in 1956 the last of them, *The Golden Six,* was presented off Broadway without much success. In between these dates came other milestones of his career: *Elizabeth The Queen, Mary of Scotland, Valley Forge, Winterset, The Masque of Kings, High Tor, Key Largo, Storm Operation, Joan of Lorraine, Anne of the Thousand Days,* and—two dramatizations of novels by other writers—*Lost in the Stars* (from *Cry, the Beloved Country*), and *The Bad Seed.* At least three of these were made the subjects of effective films.

Anderson gained importance as a dramatist by the experimental dialogue that he wrote in his most forceful plays, and this in turn owed its distinction to the incentive behind what was best in his work generally. He wished to establish the dignity of the individual, of each individual in the sight of the community, more especially to re-establish it when it had been lost sight of or traduced, as Mio in *Winterset* wishes to re-establish the good name of his father, executed for a crime of which he was not guilty. This wish is the mainspring of the action in *Winterset,* but it also determined the style of speech characteristic of the people in Anderson's other verse-plays. What they say is always, in a sense, an attempt to justify themselves, not by argument, but by an avowal of their feelings, such as the use of poetry in drama encourages while that of prose normally discounts. Dialogue as Anderson hammered it out was a sort of anti-prose, a redressing of the balance in favour of what people would like and ought to say, but normally dare not and cannot. An oppressive stone is, as it were, rolled back, and from below the place where it was voices are heard speaking with some difficulty, as in a key passage in *Winterset*:

The Judge: You
will not repeat this? It will go no further?
Mio: No.
No further than the moon takes the tides—no
further
than the news went when he [my father] died
when you found him guilty
and they flashed that round the earth.
Wherever men
still breathe and think, and know what's
done to them
by the powers above, they'll know. That's all
I ask.
That'll be enough.

March 2, 1959.

John Miller Andrews, C.H., M.P., Prime Minister of Northern Ireland from 1940 to 1943, died on August 5, 1956 at the age of 85.

He had been, as Minister of Labour and later as Minister of Finance, a member of the Northern Irish Government since its creation. A quiet though thoroughly competent man, he was little known outside his own province until he was called to succeed the late Lord Craigavon in its highest political office. His predecessor had possessed a strong and rugged character and had commanded an immense respect. He had also had a long experience in the House of Commons and was a popular figure in London political life.

Andrews had a more limited experience of affairs and far fewer political connexions. He was, moreover, at the time of his succession advanced in age. Even in Ulster there were some doubts as to how far his authority would extend over a party which, having been in power for many years, had begun even in Lord Craigavon's days to show occasional signs of restiveness. At the beginning of his term of office as Prime Minister he might have done wisely to broaden the basis of his Government by the introduction of fresh or younger blood. He possessed, however, the characteristic Ulster qualities of steadfastness and single-mindedness. There was no question where he stood, and the fact that it was as a rule in the footprints of his predecessor was accounted to him as a merit.

John Miller Andrews was born in 1871, the eldest son of the late Rt. Hon. Thomas Andrews, D.I., of Ardara, Comber, co. Down. His mother was Eliza, daughter of the late James Alexander Pirrie, of Belfast. He was educated at the Royal Academical Institution in that city. He then served his apprenticeship in his father's flax spinning firm at Comber, of which he was later to become managing director, and spent some time with the firm of James Taylor and Sons at Carrickfergus. He was at one time a director of the Belfast and co. Down Railway, but on becoming a Minister he resigned from the board.

Andrews was chairman for a number of years, and later president, of the Ulster Labour Unionist Association, and became a member of the executive committee of the Ulster Unionist Council. Afterwards, as Prime Minister, he became its president. He had therefore played a considerable part in Ulster politics when, on the establishment of the Parliament of Northern Ireland in 1921, he was returned as a member for co. Down. He continued to represent this constituency until 1929, after which date he represented Mid-Down until his retirement in 1953.

On the formation of the first Northern Irish Cabinet Andrews was appointed Minister for Labour, a position which he occupied until 1937. He was well qualified for it both by temperament and by his knowledge of labour conditions. His honesty of purpose and his skill in handling the problems of his department were recognized even by those who politically were strongly opposed to him. When, therefore, on the death of the Rt. Hon. E. M. Pollock in 1937 a vacancy arose in the Ministry of Finance his appointment to it was received with considerable satisfaction. He was a sound and experienced man of business and negotiated a "financial unity" scheme with the British Treasury which worked to the advantage of both countries.

In 1940 Lord Craigavon, who for nearly 20 years had been Prime Minister of Northern Ireland, died. Andrews was next to him in rank and, pending the election of a party leader by the Ulster Unionist Council, accepted the Premiership. Shortly afterwards he made it clear that in so far as he was concerned there would be no change in Ulster policy. He said that while the Ulster people were all anxious to live on friendly terms with the people of the South it must be as neighbours and not as partners in an all-Ireland republic. "We stand," he declared, "with Britain both in peace and war."

In January 1941 the Ulster Unionist Council elected him to the leadership and he was there confirmed in office. In announcing his policy he expressed his strong desire for improvements in social conditions, and particularly in an extension of medical services, but expressed a fear that it would be necessary to wait until after the war for many of the reforms he would have liked to achieve.

Although he had had 22 years of continuous office in Ulster when, in 1943, he handed over the reins of the premiership to Sir Basil Brooke, later Viscount Brookeborough*, he was by no means in the mood for retirement from public service. He retained his seat in the Parliament of Northern Ireland, and applied himself with energy to his family interests in the great flax enterprise bearing his name, his duties as landowner and cultivator, and especially to his work for the Grand Orange Council. In 1949 he was appointed Imperial Grand Master of The Grand Orange Council of the World, a selection which took place at the twenty-third triennial conference of the council held in Belfast a year after he had become Grand Master of the Institution of All Ireland.

In 1902 he married Jessie, daughter of the late Joseph Ormrod, of Morelands, Heaton, Bolton. She died in 1950, and a son and two daughters survive him.

August 6, 1956.

Roy Chapman Andrews, the American explorer and leader of many expeditions into Central Asia, and for many years Director of the American Museum of Natural History in New York, died at the age of 76 on March 11, 1960.

He was best known, perhaps, as the man who discovered fossilized dinosaur eggs in the Gobi desert of Mongolia, where he also mapped out large areas previously unknown to science.

He was born on January 26, 1884, at Beloit, Wisconsin, and after studying at the college there and at Columbia he started on his first work of exploration in Alaska in 1908. In the two following years he was naturalist on board the United States ship Albatross, which made an extended voyage round the Dutch East Indies and Borneo. In 1911-12 he was in North Korea and in 1913 with the Borden expedition in Alaska once more. In 1917 he was leader of the first Asiatic expedition of the American Museum of Natural History in south-west China but its work was interrupted by the entry of the United States into the war and he returned to serve for two years with the United States Intelligence Service, for which work his extensive travels and knowledge of foreign lands eminently fitted him.

After the war he led the third expedition of the museum to Central Asia and Mongolia, where he found great fossil fields and the eggs which first revealed to scientists that the dinosaur did not bear its young alive. During that expedition he did much work of great value to botany, zoology, geology, geography, and archaeology.

He recounted many of his observations and experiences in a long series of books, which were widely read. His first was on whale hunting. Then came a group of five on his work in China, *Camps and Trails in China, Across Mongolian Plains, On the Trail in Ancient Asia, The Ends of the Earth* and *The New*

Conquest of Central Asia. He then wrote two books on the general work of exploring, and lastly *This Amazing Planet,* in which he set forth many of the strange facts he had found out in various parts of the world.

He received many honours for his work. Among them were the gold medals of the Philadelphia Geographical Society, of New York Explorers' Club, of the American Geographical Society, and of the Swedish and Hungarian Geographical Societies.

Andrews did much to popularize science and scientific subjects, for he had a flair for simplifying these subjects for the layman and giving them the excitement of a tale of adventure. He also lent an air of romance to the search for the fossils of prehistoric animals. His headquarters for his many expeditions into Central Asia was the palace of a Manchu prince in Peking and it was in the courtyards of this beautiful building that representatives of the world's Press were first shown such finds as *Baluchitherium,* the largest known land mammal, fossils of the shovel-toothed mastodon, fossilized dinosaur eggs and other remarkable scientific discoveries.

The real object of the Central Asian expeditions was to find remains of ancient man. His chief at the American Museum of Natural History, Dr. Henry Fairfield Osborne, had developed the theory that Central Asia was the place of origin and centre of distribution for much of the mammalian life of the world, including very early man. The Andrews expeditions made important scientific discoveries bearing on the Osborne theories, but never had the luck to uncover remains of early man. Ironically the various remains of *Sinanthropus Pekinensis* were found at Chowkowtien, only 35 miles west of Peking, the first by a Swedish scientist.

After his retirement from the Directorship of the American Museum of Natural History Andrews lived in Connecticut, and from his home there came a stream of articles and books on the many and varied subjects that interested him. He also interested himself in the Boy Scout movement, and in 1952 was given the Silver Buffalo award of the National Council of Boy Scouts in America. In the last years of his life he made his home in the beautiful Carmel Valley of California.

He had a wide circle of friends in all parts of the world. In the twenties he was a popular figure in Peking and his house there the mecca of hundreds of travellers. At home he found recreation in polo, steeplechasing, and hunting.

March 14, 1960.

Sir William Angliss, the pioneer of Australia's meat export trade, died in Melbourne on June 15, 1957. He was 92.

William Charles Angliss was the son of a tailor and was born at Dudley, Worcestershire, in 1865. He left his first employment as a butcher's boy in London and emigrated to the United States and thence to Australia, where he arrived at the age of 19 with only a few shillings in his pocket. He borrowed money to open a butcher's shop; it prospered and he bought another and branched out into land and cattle stations. From those small beginnings he built up a large organization of sheep and cattle stations throughout Australia, freezing and processing works in Melbourne and elsewhere, a chain of retail butchers, and other interests including drapery and insurance.

He started the frozen meat trade in the 1890s, shipping meat to the goldfields of Western Australia during the gold rush. The South African War gave him an opportunity to extend the trade to the United Kingdom. He represented Australian meat exporters at the Ottawa conference in 1932. Just before the Second World War he sold most of his meat interests to the Vestey organization, of which he became chairman in an advisory capacity.

His charitable gifts were on a most generous scale. They included a large station property to the "Big Brother" movement to encourage the immigration of boys from England, and property at Bacchus Marsh to the Northcote Children's Immigration Trust. From 1912 until 1952 he was a member of the Legislative Council of Victoria, and he was knighted in 1939.

He married Jacobina Victoria, daughter of Francis Grutzner, of Melbourne. She was appointed C.B.E. in 1949. There was a daughter of the marriage who has died.

June 17, 1957.

Joyce Anstruther—See **Placzek.**

"Archimedes"—See **Edmonds.**

Former Bishop of the Arctic—See **Fleming.**

Colonel Sir Charles Arden-Close, K.B.E., C.B., C.M.G., F.R.S., who died at Winchester on December 19, 1952 at the age of 87, was Director-General of the Ordnance Survey during the 1914-18 war, President of the Royal Geographical Society at the time of its centenary, and a scientific geographer of the first rank. He combined with great technical knowledge a cultivated mind with manifold interests, and possessed practical ability much above the average. Keen, alert, energetic, he infused new life into all that he undertook or directed.

A son of Major-General Frederick Close of Shanklin, Isle of Wight, Charles Frederick Close (he changed his name to Arden-Close in 1938) was born on August 10, 1865, and after attending the Royal Military Academy, Woolwich, was gazetted to the Royal Engineers at the age of 19. Sent to India, he was attached to the Survey of India, and his training in that distinguished school was an advantage he was never slow to acknowledge. When over 40 years later he received the Victoria Medal of the Royal Geographical Society—an award given only for exceptional services in pure science—he declared that he believed he owed the distinction chiefly to having served on the Survey of India, and that he had never ceased to thank his lucky stars that he had had that experience in India. He returned home with a remarkable reputation for a young man, and in 1895 was placed in charge of the British commission which in conjunction with a German commission surveyed the Nigerian-Cameroon frontier: a difficult piece of work in partly unknown country inhabited by warlike and suspicious pagan tribes.

Returning once more from Africa, he became chief instructor at the School of Military Engineering and in 1905 chief of the geographical section of the General Staff. While so employed he was called upon in 1910 to take part in settling a curious frontier tangle in Central Africa. When, in the days of the partition of Africa, the diplomats in Europe were carving up the continent, certain frontiers in the Great Lake region were made to depend on the thirtieth meridian. Twenty years later it was found that the meridian was not where it had been thought to have been, and for a time the "wandering meridian" became notorious and troublesome. German, British, and Belgian interests were all involved. It took three months of hard work—Arden-Close being the British representative—to straighten out the tangle. This was not done on the spot, but in Brussels with the aid of trustworthy maps.

In 1911 Arden-Close was appointed Director-General of the Ordnance Survey. Here he soon made his mark; the maps were produced more artistically and great pains were taken over place names—a matter, even in England, of much complexity. Another of Arden-Close's interests was seen in the appointment of an archaeological surveyor to the Ordnance staff. To Arden-Close also was due the rehabilitation of the primary triangulation; he encouraged the production of the "Million Map"—to cover the whole world; and he had much to do with the establishment of the Colonial Survey Committee. Also to him fell, as Boundary Commissioner, the readjustment of the Parliamentary constituencies under the Representation of the People Act of 1917. The normal work of the Ordnance Survey was inevitably much interrupted by the 1914-18 war, when the demands of the Army for technical help were insistent. Throughout the war Arden-Close gave unstinted support to his brother Sapper, Colonel E. M. Jack, the officer in charge of the topographical section in France and Flanders. When in 1922 Arden-Close went on retired pay, it was Jack who succeeded him as Director-General of the Ordnance Survey.

Freed from War Office duties, Arden-Close devoted himself to historical, archaeological, and chiefly geographical interests—he regarded them as inseparably linked. He had long been a Fellow of the Royal Geographical Society, had been honorary treasurer, a councillor, and now became a vice-president and the chief adviser of the society on geodesy and kindred subjects. It was in June 1927 that he received from the hands of David Hogarth, the president, the Victoria Medal; in the following November Hogarth died suddenly, and the council of the society at once appointed Arden-Close to the vacant office. No man was better equipped for the task, and under his three years' rule the society greatly increased in usefulness and popularity. His business ability was of much value in all the arrangements for the erection of the new buildings of the society in Kensington Gore. The buildings were completed in time for the centenary celebrations, which happily fell in the last month of Arden-Close's presidency—in October 1930.

He remained an alert observer until an advanced age, his 12 essays on some of the byways of geographical studies being some of the best things of the kind that have appeared in recent years. They were published in one volume in 1947. He had meanwhile led a busy life as president of the International Population Union from 1931 to 1937, as president of the Hampshire Field Club for two terms (1929-32 and 1935-36), and as president of the International Geographical Union from 1934 to 1938. He also did a great deal of useful and important work as chairman of the Palestine Exploration Fund from 1930 to 1945. His volume *The Map of England* was published in 1932. He also wrote, besides various technical papers, a *Text Book of Topographical Surveying,* and in 1926 published a valuable record, *The Early Years of the Ordnance Survey.*

Arden-Close, who was appointed C.M.G. in 1899, C.B. in 1916, and K.B.E. in 1918, was elected F.R.S. in 1919. He married in 1913 Gladys Violet, daughter of Theodore Percival, who survives him, together with a son and a daughter of the marriage.

December 22, 1952.

Reginald Arkell, whose whimsical and various talent as librettist, versifier, story-teller, and editor had a popular following for nearly 40 years, died on May 1, 1959 at his home in Wiltshire at the age of 76. Of the dozen revues and musical comedies in which he had a hand the best known was *1066 and All That,* first produced in 1935 and revived after the war. His most notable novel, *Old Herbaceous,* was a best-seller in Britain and America and translated into several languages.

He was born at Lechlade, Gloucestershire, on October 14, 1882, and trained as a journalist. One of his plays, *Columbine,* was produced in London and New York before war broke out in 1914, and on his return to civil life in 1919 after service with The King's Own Yorkshire Light Infantry and The Norfolk Regiment he turned his attention to the writing of librettos and lyrics. His name was associated with many of the most successful light entertainments produced in London between the wars, from *Jumble Sale* in 1920 to *Moonshine* in 1940.

He was the editor of the magazine *Men Only,* which, he said, women insisted on reading because of its title. He retired from Newnes [q.v.], the publishers, in 1954. His own output was considerable; he was a frequent broadcaster, and among a number of volumes of light verse he will be remembered for the series *Green Fingers, More Green Fingers,* and *Green Fingers Again,* rounded off in 1950 after 16 years with *And a Green Thumb. Old Herbaceous* came out in 1950 and *Charley Moon,* a rather less restrained fancy which was made into a film, in 1953.

Bridge without Sighs in 1934 enabled him to poke fun at his favourite game. His attitude towards bridge is well summed up by his own description in *Who's Who* of his chief recreation:—

"I always like to call a slam;
That is the sort of fool I am."

He used to describe his hobbies as walking and talking. Much of his walking was done in the Cotswolds and most of his talking in the Savage Club, where he was a well loved figure. He had a bubbling wit and was rich in repartee and it was always certain that even a lethargic club circle would spring into life and laughter the moment he joined it.

He married Elizabeth Evans, in her younger days a talented actress. They had one son.

May 2, 1959.

Dr. William Joscelyn Arkell, F.R.S., a Fellow of Trinity College, died at Cambridge on April 18, 1958. He was 53.

At an early age Arkell reached a unique position in the realm of geological research as a foremost authority on the Jurassic rocks and on the classification of the Jurassic ammonites, fossils which provide the means of identifying and correlating these strata throughout the world.

He was elected a Fellow of the Royal Society in 1947. He was an honorary member or correspondent of several foreign geological societies, including those of the United States of America, France, and Germany; and of the Paleontological Society of America. He was Lyell Medallist of the Geological Society of London (1949), Thompson Gold Medallist of the National Academy of Sciences, Washington (1944), von Buch Medallist German Geological Society (1953).

Arkell was born on June 9, 1904, son of James Arkell, of Highworth, Wiltshire, and he went up to New College, Oxford, from Wellington College. He took first class honours in geology in 1925 and began his researches on the Corallian rocks which stretch in an unbroken ridge from his family home at Highworth as far as Cumnor, where he later made his Oxford home. He extended his work to other areas of Jurassic rocks and to the fossil fauna contained in them. In 1933, before he had reached the age of 30, he published *The Jurassic System in Great Britain,* a monumental work published by the Clarendon Press containing mature consideration of structural geology, sedimentation processes, palaeography and faunal classification in addition to stratigraphical correlation of the Jurassic throughout Britain. A continuous series of research papers followed and about 100 geological publications stand under his name. In addition to memoirs on stratigraphy, he published three monographs for the Palaeontographical Society.

He was lecturer in geology at New College from 1929 to 1933 and research fellow there from 1933 to 1940. Work with the Ministry of War Transport from 1941 to 1943 was ended owing to a sudden attack of ill-health. In 1947 he was elected to a Research Fellowship at Trinity College, Cambridge, but before he left Oxford he published *The Geology of Oxford* (1947). His *Oxford Stone* (1947) is both a history of the various building stones used in Oxford since Norman times and a critique of their geological origins and weathering properties. He had already in 1937 written a private report (with L. H. Dudley Buxton) for the university on sources of building stones for university and college building repairs and extensions.

In the congenial atmosphere of Trinity College and the Sedgwick Museum, Arkell continued and extended his work. In the following years he made expeditions to Arabia, Egypt, Algeria and many countries of Europe. Geological workers in his own and allied fields of research consulted him freely and visited him from all over the world. His *Jurassic Geology of the World* (1956) brought together his world-wide researches into a comprehensive whole. His section of the *International Treatise on Invertebrate Paleontology,* a collaborative work, was published in 1957.

He was generous in his encouragement of young workers in Jurassic stratigraphy and palaeontology, and especially so to the amateurs who came under his influence, many of whom he stimulated to progress from collecting to serious research.

He is survived by his widow and three sons.

April 22, 1958.

Michael Arlen, a novelist and short-story writer who enjoyed a great vogue in the 1920s, died on June 23, 1956 in New York at the age of 60, after a long illness.

Those who were young when Michael Arlen was young will remember *The Green Hat,* that airy compound of romantic fancy and epigrammatic facility which "shocked" a seemingly all too shockable reading public and which brought the author his greatest success. Published in 1924, the novel reflected an unexacting fashion of the "post-war" period for verbal smartness, youthful cynicism, and a display of equally immature romantic temperament. To do him justice, Arlen—in whom there was always a hint, doubtless derived from his foreign parentage, of the onlooker—was not taken in by his own pose of pert and wearied sophistication. He was a clever young man, and knew it, and he exploited his vein of cynical if shallow wit and sentimental artifice with much shrewdness. He even tried, in later books, to get away from it and to contrive something of more genuine imaginative substance, but was by then too firmly rooted in the Mayfair-ish style that had brought him popular favour.

He had few illusions, as a matter of fact, on the subject of his literary ability and indeed once said that he had become very popular on the strength of a very slender talent and that the Mayfair background was merely a gaudy trapping for a kind of New Arabian Nights fantasy. He rightly made hay while the sun shone and his slight, elegant figure, immaculately attired by the best hatters, tailors, outfitters, and shoemakers in London, was to be seen at every resort of fashion, getting either into or out of his enormous yellow Rolls-Royce.

This phase ceased soon after his marriage and he retired to the south of France, where he lived until the outbreak of war in 1939. He managed to return to England and was for a short time a public relations officer in the Midland Region. He then settled in the United States and seldom visited the country he was brought to as a boy.

Of Armenian parentage, born Dikran Kouyoumdjian at Rustchuk, Bulgaria, on November 16, 1895, he changed his name by deed poll to Michael Arlen, and became a naturalized British subject in 1922. He had been educated at Malvern and, after some hesitation, plumped for authorship as a career. His two earliest books, *The London Venture* and *The Romantic Lady,* seem to have met with little attention, but *Piracy,* published in 1922, a novel about smart and fashionable people, or about people who were represented as smart and fashionable, made up for any neglect he had suffered until then.

The story had for a hero a precociously tired young man and reeled off a string of witticisms and aphorisms, of which a few were urbane and happy and many more were inclined to be cheap. Next year came a volume of nicely calculated short stories, *These Charming People,* most of which were amusing enough in their cynical-romantic idiom, and a year later Arlen brought out *The Green Hat,* a schoolboyishly alluring portrait of a *femme fatale.* It sold prodigiously and was adapted for the stage, though with less success than had been hoped.

In two novels that followed, *Young Men in Love* (1927) and *Lily Christine* (1929), he was plainly intent on showing he could do better, in a strictly literary sense, than *The Green Hat. Lily Christine* is, indeed, probably his best and most serious performance as a novelist. *Men Dislike Women* (1931) and *Hell! said the Duchess* (1934) are characteristic alike in title and manner: while among the books that came afterward the latest of all, *Flying Dutchman,* issued in 1939, is an exercise in topical fantasy with a keener edge of cynical wit than usual. Arlen lived in virtual retirement in later years.

He married, in 1928, Atalanta, daughter of Count Mercati. There were a son and a daughter of the marriage.

June 25, 1956.

William Armstrong, C.B.E., director of the Liverpool Repertory Theatre for more than 20 years, died on October 5, 1952 at his home near Birmingham.

He was born in Edinburgh on November 30, 1882, the son of John and Annie Armstrong, and educated at Edinburgh University. He studied music and was for some years a school master before he decided to train for the stage under F. R. Benson. His first London appearance was at His Majesty's Theatre in June, 1909, as Cinna in *Julius Caesar,* and he subsequently played many parts under the managements of Tree, Bourchier, J. B. Fagan, and Matheson Lang. He went to the Glasgow Repertory Theatre, where he met Madge McIntosh, the producer, who shortly afterwards recommended him to Liverpool. In September 1914 he joined the Liverpool repertory company. He moved on to Birmingham in 1916, and from 1917 to 1919 toured camp theatres. In September 1920 he was with the Everyman Theatre repertory company; and in 1922 he toured with Mrs. Patrick Campbell as Lövborg in *Hedda Gabler.*

Armstrong's acting and general ability had made a great impression in Liverpool, and when, in 1922, it was decided to find a young producer who might save the Playhouse from bankruptcy, Armstrong accepted the post. Mrs. Patrick Campbell was a prophet of doom, and said: "I could have made a great actor of you, and now you're throwing away your chance. You're going to be a little man who sits in an office and makes *lists."* But he soon proved that he was much more than that. He embarked on a programme that, while it preserved the true spirit of repertory, removed serious anxieties of the financial sort by 1925. He was made a director of the company in 1923, and his skill in play selection and production, his eye for good acting, and his happy combination of enterprise and prudence in business management commended him more and more to the supporters of repertory. He put on a very varied list of significant pieces by modern British dramatists—some of them (like St. John Ervine's* *The Ship*) for the first time on any stage—as well as modern drama from America, like Susan Glaspell's *Inheritors* and Elmer Rice's* *The Adding Machine.* He also established a tradition that there should be a really first-rate play for children every Christmas. The Playhouse under his management enlisted and trained actors and actresses with extraordinary success, so that in time the West End stage was full of its graduates—of whom Diana Wynyard*, Richard Bird, and Robert Donat [q.v.] are typical names. Scenic designers like Aubrey Hammond, Doris Zinkeisen, and Mary Adshead were also used.

Armstrong continued to direct the theatre and resigned only in 1944. He took enormous pains with detail, and held his company not by hard discipline but by the affection they all bore him. He was a generous, sensitive figure, endowed with a lively sense of humour and not free from a little pardonable vanity. Between 1941 and 1945 he produced several plays in London, and in 1945 he was appointed assistant director to Sir Barry Jackson* at the Birmingham Repertory Theatre. He resigned in 1947 on account of ill-health and spent the winter of that year in South Africa. But he returned to London in 1948, and directed the production at the St. James's of *Don't Listen, Ladies,* adapted from Sacha Guitry [q.v.].

October 6, 1952.

Yvonne Arnaud, the actress, died in hospital in London on September 20, 1958 at the age of 67. She was taken to hospital seven weeks earlier, when she suffered a cerebral haemorrhage.

Her death removes from the stage an actress of abundant charm; it was impossible to resist her. Yet she was much more than a delightful creature with whom every playgoer instantly fell in love; she was the wittiest of actresses, too, witty in the essentially theatrical way in which a gesture has all the effect of an epigram.

There was a moment, for instance, in a comedy of the 1930s, when she played the wife of a vain man who felt it his duty to leave her and so prepared himself for a big emotional parting. To his astonishment, and to ours, she promptly agreed, held out her hand and wished him goodbye as coolly as though he had merely been paying a call. Twenty-five years later one can still see the gesture and still hear the whole house breaking spontaneously into applause. And who that saw her Lady Kitty in a revival of *The Circle* towards the end of the war will forget a very different impression of her, when the preposterously kittenish old woman silently began to weep as she turned the pages of the photograph album and saw herself as she used to be?

Had she not achieved fame as one of the most polished comedy actresses of her time, she could in all probability have done so as a pianist—in fact her first appearances in entertainment were on the concert platform.

Born at Bordeaux on December 20, 1890, she won a first prize for piano playing at the Paris Conservatoire at the age of 12 and thereafter toured as a child prodigy both in Europe and in the United States. Her first stage appearance was something of an accident. In 1911 there was a lull in her concert engagements in Britain and she decided to see what the theatre had to offer. She had had no special stage training but she managed to obtain a small part in *The Quaker Girl* at the Adelphi and from that time she never looked back. A pretty, dark-eyed girl, she used to describe her voice as something of a croak. But it had individuality and with her broken English and her infectious, gurgling laugh she was soon popular with audiences and with her fellow players. When *The Girl in the Taxi* was produced in 1912 she scored an immense success which she repeated when the musical comedy was revived on later occasions.

In 1915 she appeared in the French mime play *L'Enfant Prodigue,* to which she contributed a clever picture of the mercenary and heartless Phrynette. The play depended for its success largely on a charming musical score, and several times she played the piano accompaniment. She had parts in musical comedies including *Kissing Time* and *The Naughty Princess,* but she felt that her future lay in straight acting and she was ready to turn her hand to anything from Shakespeare to roaring farce.

She played in two of the most successful productions of the Tom Walls and Ralph Lynn* series: *Tons of Money,* which ran for nearly two years, and *A Cuckoo in the Nest,* in which, at the height of farcical catastrophes, she always remained a monument of imperturbability. The production of J. B. Fagan's play *And so to Bed* is still remembered with gratitude by many playgoers for the delightful performances of Edmund Gwenn [q.v.] and Miss Arnaud as Mr. and Mrs. Samuel Pepys.

At least four of her performances in the middle period of her career call for special mention. In 1941 there was the production of Miss Margery Sharp's play *The Nutmeg Tree* in which Miss Arnaud sketched with amused and tender lines the character of a woman whose response to a gaily offered embrace was instinctive, and whose warm-hearted and generous nature could not be repressed by the false dignity imposed upon her by the need not to shock a priggish daughter. In Congreve's *Love for Love* at the Phoenix in 1943 her performance as Mrs. Frail was outstanding among a brilliant cast.

Perhaps the greatest success of her career was in Arthur Macrae's farcical comedy *Traveller's Joy* which was produced at the Criterion in 1948 and ran for over 900 performances. Her part was that of a rich woman who, having exhausted her legal travelling allowance in Sweden, was forced to rely on her wits. She was as bewitchingly mischievous as ever; yet, as a critic said, hers was a humour with persistently romantic overtones.

She scored a great success again in the production of Alan Melville's comedy *Dear Charles,* in which she was as charming, as serenely resourceful and as suprisingly august as she had ever been, and once again she proved that, if she had three admirers in the comedy, she had a cohort of admirers among playgoers. Her last engagement in the theatre was in *The Big Tickle* which opened in May 1958.

She appeared in many British films, and first broadcast in the early days of radio. She was afterwards heard in classical and straight plays as well as musical comedy and became a popular member of radio and television panel games where she was able to give free play to her charming personality.

She married in 1920 Mr. Hugh McLellan.

September 22, 1958.

Princess Arthur of Connaught—See **Fife.**

Inejiro Asanuma, chairman of the Japan Socialist Party, who was murdered on October 12, 1960 at the age of 63, was born on a remote island in Tokyo Bay.

In 1922 he graduated from the political department of Waseda University, like many politicians before him. He was politically conscious as a student and a year after his graduation joined the mineworkers' union. He soon made his mark as a trade union official and held the post of secretary-general of the Labour Farmer Party until that organization was disbanded by a Government order which aimed at suppressing all left-wing political activity.

He was elected member for Tokyo in the Lower House elections of 1936 and for most of the rest of his life remained a member of Parliament. Soon after the war he became a member of the central executive committee of the Japan Socialist Party and later was appointed its secretary-general. When, in 1950, the Socialists split into right and left wing factions Asanuma followed Nishio, later chairman of the rival Democratic Socialist Party, and Katayama, the ill-starred Socialist Prime Minister, into the right wing group with which he had always been identified. When the two Socialist wings were reunited in 1955 his experience and ability to compromise assured his re-election as secretary-general and in the autumn of 1959 he was appointed the party chairman. As chairman he inclined towards the left, especially after the birth of the more moderate Democratic Socialists. Nominally, however, he belonged to the right wing faction, who were not too happy about Asanuma's drift leftwards.

Nevertheless, he was a popular figure even with those who did not agree with his views. He was a critic of the foreign policy of the United States and had made several visits in recent years to Communist China. His last visit was in March, when he went to Peking as the leader of a socialist mission. During that visit he said that the United States was the common enemy of Japan and Communist China. He lived to see trade unionism in Japan grow to tremendous proportions after the end of the last war. His own untiring efforts in this cause, which earned him an assortment of nicknames, including "Bulldog" and "Human Locomotive", did much to bring this about. He was well known to radio and television audiences and his powerful frame, crowned by a large head and a shock of black hair, helped to make him a familiar figure.

His audiences appreciated his showmanship and his eloquence, while his activity was astounding for a man of his years. He was, in fact, a man of action rather than a political theorist, and it was reputed that his grasp of Marxist dialectics was none too sure. In spite of his popularity and influence it is doubtful whether he would ever have become Prime Minister. The task of keeping the Opposition in place and his own "troops" in order at the same time might well have proved too much for him. Asanuma was not the tough, determined leader, but a rather mild man who had built up his reputation and popularity on his gifts as a peacemaker and on his ability to ride out factional storms. Although at the time of his death he tended to identify himself with an extreme brand of socialism, this had come about more by force of circumstance than by choice.

October 13, 1960.

Alberto Ascari, who was killed at Monza autodrome on May 26, 1955 at the age of 36 trying a Ferrari car belonging to his friend Eugenio Castellotti, was the leading racing driver in Italy.

He was only six years old when his father, Antonio Ascari, himself one of Italy's greatest drivers, was killed when his Alfa-Romeo overturned in the French Grand Prix of 1925 at Montlhéry. Like many other Italians, the young Ascari started his racing career on motor cycles, beginning in 1935 at the age of 17 and competing in many races with Sertum, Gilera, and Bianchi motor cycles. His first car race was in 1940, when he drove a Ferrari in the Mille Miglia, which was run that year on a closed circuit. After the war he drove a Maserati, winning the San Remo Grand Prix and finishing third in the 1948 championship of Italy. After driving a Maserati in South America (where he won the Buenos Aires Grand Prix) in the early part of 1949, Ascari joined the Scuderia Ferrari with his friend and mentor L. Villoresi, gaining the title of European champion after winning the European (Monza), Swiss, and Monaco Grands Prix, the *Daily Express* International Trophy at Silverstone, and the Coupe des Petits Cylindrées.

In 1950 he won the German Grand Prix, the production car race at Silverstone, and the Peña Rhin race at Barcelona, and in the following year he became runner-up to Farina* in the world championship by winning for Ferrari the San Remo, Monza, German, and Italian Grands Prix, and the Ulster Trophy. Ascari reached the height of his fame in 1952 and 1953, when he won the world championship two years running. In both years he was virtually invincible, his successes including the European, British, German, and Italian Grands Prix in 1952, and the Argentine, Dutch, Belgian, British, and Swiss Grands Prix in 1953. At many circuits he set up new record lap speeds.

All these victories were gained on Ferrari cars, but in 1954 he left Ferrari to join the Lancia firm, which had announced its intention of building a team of Grand Prix cars. With a sports car of this make he achieved one of the great ambitions of every Italian driver in winning the Mille Miglia—his only success, indeed one of his few races, that year. It was as the first driver in the Lancia team that he competed in the European Grand Prix at Monte Carlo in the weekend before his death and had a narrow escape when his car plunged into the harbour. Ascari himself suffered only a ducking and slight facial injuries. At Monaco he showed that in spite of a year's absence from the Grand Prix racing circuits he had lost none of his virtuosity, because with an evidently slower car he succeeded in practice in equalling the fastest time for the Monaco circuit achieved the day before by Fangio, the 1954 world champion and member of the Mercedes-Benz team.

Ascari was universally liked and respected in British motor racing circles, one of his most admirable traits being his generous praise of other drivers' ability. Another endearing characteristic was his devotion to his family. When in 1953 he was world champion for the second time he said to reporters: "The credit is not all mine and Ferrari's. A lot belongs to him." As he spoke he pointed to the portrait of a greying man with smiling eyes and reckless mouth, Antonio Ascari, his father, who was also 36 when he died. Alberto Ascari was also deeply attached to his wife and his two children, all of whom survive him.

May 27, 1955.

Professor A. W. Ashby, C.B.E., who died at Oxford on September 9, 1953, had retired only in December 1952 from the directorship of the Oxford Institute for Research in Agricultural Economics. He had been active to the end, having lectured during August in Denmark and, even later, to dockers at the annual conference held at Oxford.

He was born at Tysoe, in Warwickshire, in August 1886, the eldest son of the late Joseph Ashby, J.P., a farm worker and Methodist lay preacher, who played a prominent part in the radical agitation for allotments and smallholdings. From 1899 to 1909, after attending the village school, Ashby worked on his father's smallholding. He then went to Ruskin College and took the diploma (with honours) in economics and political science in 1911. From 1912 to 1915 he was the first holder of the Board of Agriculture research scholarship in agricultural economics. With the help of this scholarship he continued his studies at the University of Wisconsin, where he was honorary fellow in political science in 1915. On his return he served on the staff of the wartime food production department from 1917 to 1918.

From 1920 to 1924 Ashby was senior research assistant at the Oxford Institute under its first director, Dr. C. S. Orwin [q.v.]. In 1924 he was appointed advisory lecturer and head of the department of agricultural economics at the University College of Wales, Aberystwyth. His work at Aberystwyth was recognized in 1929 by his elevation to the first professorship in agricultural economics in Britain. It was entirely fitting that in 1946 Ashby should return to Oxford to succeed Dr. Orwin as director of the Agricultural Economic Research Institute. He was made a fellow of Lincoln College in 1947.

Ashby was one of the most prominent and influential members of the small group who pioneered the study of agricultural economics in Britain. In the academic field his influence was exercised, first, in the building up of the new department at Aberystwyth, through which several generations of students passed, many of whom now hold responsible positions in agrarian affairs and, secondly, by his guidance of the Oxford Institute after 1946, notably in the expansion of teaching facilities in addition to the pursuit of research.

His background and his somewhat unorthodox training ensured, however, that to him agricultural economics could never be a mere academic subject. He conceived its development as an essential factor in the amelioration of farm pupils' and rural life. Hence the prominent part which he played in the formation of the Agricultural Economics Society, of which he was a president, and in the activities of the International Conference of Agricultural Economists, of which he was one of the vice-presidents from 1949-1952. His interest in international affairs and in the encouragement of overseas students was unflagging, and it gave him great pleasure to accept an invitation to visit India in 1949 to advise on the development of teaching and research in agricultural economics in that country.

Ashby served on numerous official and unofficial committees since he first served on the Royal Commission on Agriculture in 1919. Some of his most influential work was done in this capacity and particularly in the field of cooperation and agricultural marketing. It was largely his enthusiasm and guidance which determined the continuance of the Welsh Agricultural Organizations Society when the sister English societies ceased to exist in 1920.

He was a member of the (Linlithgow) departmental committee on prices of farm produce in 1922-23. His knowledge of the problems of milk marketing was probably unrivalled, and behind the scenes he played a prominent part in the planning of the Milk Marketing Board. He had been one of the impartial members of the Agricultural Wages Board since 1924. He had also served on, and passed through the chair of, both the Council of Agriculture for England and the Council of Agriculture for Wales.

Ashby was a prolific writer on all the economic and essential aspects of the agrarian problem, but his writings are mostly scattered in various journals, notably the journal of the proceedings of the Agricultural Economics Society and the Proceedings of the International Conference of Agricultural Economists. The variety of his interests probably accounts for the fact that he never found time to write the standard work on agricultural economics which so many had hoped his leisure would permit him to do.

He leaves a widow and one son.

September 11, 1953.

Hitoshi Ashida, a former Prime Minister of Japan, died in Tokyo on June 21, 1959 after a long illness. He was 71.

He was regarded as an idealist rather than a practical politician, standing above the factional struggles and personal rivalries of Japanese political life. His early years in the Japanese Foreign Service laid the basis of his profound grasp of international problems and his ability to judge his country's position with rare detachment. He was for many years the liberal Democratic Party's leading foreign affairs adviser. He was a man of great intellectual integrity and sound judgment, and his approach to politics was moderate and liberal.

Ashida entered the Foreign Service after graduating at Tokyo University in 1912, and served in Russia, France, and Turkey. He resigned through disagreement with the Government's Manchurian policy, and became president of the *Japan Times.* His political career began in 1943 when he was elected to the Lower House. After the war he became chairman of the Diet committee which drafted the new constitution, and as such was largely responsible for the wording of Article Nine which, he held, denied war potential to Japan while recognizing her right to self-defence. He was, with Ichiro Hatoyama, [q.v.], one of the Democratic Party's founders and became its president in 1947.

Ashida was the last Foreign Minister in the coalition Government headed by Mr. Katayama, and he became Prime Minister in 1948 with Socialist support. Unfortunately, charges of bribery against his Finance Minister forced Ashida to resign and cast a shadow over his last years. Though finally cleared of all suspicion in 1958, he never again played a leading political role.

June 22, 1959.

Lena Ashwell (Lady Simson, O.B.E.) who died in London on March 13, 1957, was an actress whose emotional force and sincerity were perhaps unique in the English theatre during the comparatively short time during which she played leading parts.

Her successes were made in modern plays; but she had a quality which might have made her a fine Shakespearian actress, for everything that she did rang true. There was nothing meretricious or artificial about her work. Moreover, she had that indefinable power of being able, in big moments, to hold an audience.

She was born on September 28, 1872, on board the training ship Wellesley, moored in the Tyne, being the third daughter of Commander Charles Ashwell Boteler Pocock, R.N., captain of the ship. She had several brothers, one of whom, Roger Pocock, founded the Legion of Frontiersmen and became known as a traveller and author. Both parents were profoundly religious, and looked to Lena's early education on Christian principles. In 1880, when she was eight years old, Commander Pocock resigned from his ship and went to Canada, where he made a home at Brockwell, overlooking the St. Lawrence, and became a minister.

The family soon followed, and after two years moved to Toronto, where the girls were educated at Bishop Strachan's School for Young Ladies, becoming boarders there after their mother's death in a carriage accident. Lena matriculated early, and in 1888 was sent to Lausanne for finishing in French and grounding in music, attending the ordinary Swiss state school and the Conservatoire. Her voice promised a singer's career, so after some months she went to London to study at the Royal Academy of Music.

Early in 1891 she abandoned music for the stage on the advice of Ellen Terry. Her first two years were hard and unremunerative. She owed her first part (that of Martin in *The Pharisee*) to Malcolm Watson, dramatic critic to the *St. James's Gazette.* This was on March 30, 1891. In 1892 she toured with Sir George Alexander in *Lady Windermere's Fan,* but had only a very small part. Her first important parts in London were at the Comedy Theatre, under the management of J. Comyns Carr; and it was in his *King Arthur* at the Lyceum under Henry Irving that she took the part of Elaine in 1895; but she still had her craft to learn and was handicapped by a strong Canadian accent of which it took her some time to rid herself. A worse handicap was an unsuccessful first marriage which she was unable to dissolve until 1908, when (in October) she married the surgeon Henry Simson, F.R.C.S.(Edin) and later K.C.V.O., with whom she lived in great happiness until his death in 1932.

Meanwhile Lena Ashwell's stage career made steady advance. Her first real "hit" was in the part of Blanche Ferreby in *Her Advocate* in September 1895; yet even this did not put her into the front rank, and it was her rendering of Mrs. Dane in Henry Arthur Jones's play *Mrs. Dane's Defence,* with Charles Wyndham, in the autumn of 1900 which established her position as one of the three or four leading actresses in London. In 1906 she started in management on her own account, opening with *The Bond of Ninon* (she herself taking the name part) and following this with *The Shulamite,* in which she played Deborah. Both productions were artistically triumphant but financially disastrous.

In the autumn of the same year Lena Ashwell went to America, repeating her London successes in the latter-named play and in *Mrs. Dane's Defence.* On her return to London in 1907 she secured the lease of the Great Queen Street Theatre, which she opened in October as the Kingsway Theatre, with Anthony Wharton's excellent play *Irene Wycherley.* Cicely Hamilton's *Diana of Dobson's* was put on in February 1908 and attained great popularity. She retained the Kingsway until the end of 1915, but in the meanwhile she had taken the chief part in the first production of Barrie's *Twelve Pound Look* at the Duke of York's in 1910. Early in 1911 she was in America once more; in May of that year she played Rosalind in *As You Like It* at Stratford-on-Avon; while in February 1915 she was in *Fanny's First Play* at the Kingsway.

After giving up management Miss Ashwell devoted all her energies to the entertainment of the troops, first in France and later in Malta, Palestine, Egypt and the Rhineland. By 1919 she had no fewer than 25 companies at work. She raised £100,000 in funds, and was awarded the O.B.E. for her distinguished services.

In 1920 she started her "Once-a-Week Players", working with Clement Attlee (Lord Attlee*) to provide good and inexpensive drama for the people in various London town halls.

Then followed the Lena Ashwell Players, who in 1924 acquired the old Bijou Theatre in Bayswater, renamed the Century Theatre, and went on producing there until 1929. The companies were not very highly trained but part of their purpose was the discovery of new talent, and the derisory prices charged for the seats in a very little theatre made any substantial profits impossible. Many playgoers will nevertheless remember thankfully their opportunities of seeing at the Century Ibsen and other good drama not easily or frequently available elsewhere.

Lena Ashwell was a woman of personal beauty and charm, whose influence in the theatre of her generation was always salutary. In the period of agitation for woman suffrage she did some work for the Actresses' Franchise League, serving on several deputations. Another notable service to women engaged in acting, painting, and literature, was the foundation of the Three Arts Club, in which she played a considerable part.

In 1936 she brought out a well-written book of memoirs called *Myself a Player,* which showed her wide charity and reflected a serious moral tone that never degenerated into priggishness.

March 15, 1957.

Charles Herbert Aslin, C.B.E., who died on April 18, 1959, at the age of 65, was formerly county architect of Hertfordshire, and was president of the Royal Institute of British Architects in 1954-55. He was an honorary fellow of the American Institute of Architects.

His principal contribution to architecture was his development of prefabricated building. In 1946 he realized that the Butler Education Act would demand in his county an abnormal volume of new school building. Rather than compete for scarce building labour and materials, he decided on the then novel course of developing a form of prefabricated unit construction. This employed lightweight welded steel framing which was clad with various materials in slab or sheet form. It involved the careful detail design and dimensioning of hundreds of components and the making of arrangements with manufacturers for their production. The system had to be adaptable to all sizes and plan arrangements of schools and, indeed, no two of his schools are identical, though all have a strong family resemblance. Because this was then quite foreign to normal building procedure, it at first involved difficulties with the Ministry of Education and the Treasury.

The system proved remarkably successful, being both inexpensive and quick to erect, though the buildings were in no sense temporary. In 1955 his hundredth new school was opened by the Minister of Education. By then the fame of Hertfordshire schools had spread widely. Foreign architects came in large numbers to study them and the system of construction was extensively used all over the country. In various forms the ideas incorporated in it have now become absorbed into building vernacular.

The schools are also aesthetically pleasing. Aslin pioneered in the use of colour in schools. Revolting against the traditional cream and green paintwork and brown woodwork, he boldly went in for delicate pastel shades, emphasized by small areas of strong colour. In spite of much head shaking by those who feared damage by rough small boys, the new colour schemes were a triumphant success. Today they are almost universal in new British schools.

Aslin was essentially a team leader. He operated through a staff of young architects whom he encouraged and inspired. He freely acknowledged that many of the detail ideas came from members of his staff and were worked out to reality by groups of them. In this he was of his time. The traditional conception of the great architect, surrounded by assistants, has given place today to that of the team, or group of teams, consisting of qualified men under a leader—an idea perhaps borrowed from war experience. Aslin was one of the first to adopt it and his friendly and wise personality made it a success. Always there was great competition among newly graduated architects for places in his office.

He became president of the R.I.B.A. just after building licensing had been abolished and there was long-absent feeling of architectural freedom in the air. In his inaugural address he said that this was the right time to study the structure of the profession and the training of architects. He said he wanted to see a highly skilled and united profession giving service to a country in which building would be sponsored about equally by the State and private enterprise. The lead he then gave has since been followed actively by the R.I.B.A.

Aslin studied at the Sheffield University Department of Architecture and in 1926 became architect to the county borough of Rotherham. From 1926 to 1929 he was deputy county architect of Hampshire and he then became borough architect of Derby, where he carried out the central improvement scheme, building new municipal offices, police courts, bus station, open markets, and riverside gardens. In 1925 he became a member of the Institution of Structural Engineers. From 1945 he served on the R.I.B.A. council, acting as chairman of numerous committees. He was president of the Nottingham, Derby, and Lincoln Architectural Society from 1941 to 1943.

Aslin was one of those who make friends easily, but who is respected by them. Always charming and apparently easy going, he had an inner firmness, hence, perhaps, his success as the president of a vigorous society of professional men and as the leader of a team of architectural individualists. Behind both charm and firmness he retained his native Yorkshire shrewdness, pretension or pomposity in others being seen through and met with a quizzical smile.

In his last presidential speech he paid a warm tribute to the help he had received from his wife, who, with a daughter, survives him.

April 20, 1959.

Lord Asquith of Bishopstone, who died suddenly on August 24, 1954 at his home in London, had been a Lord of Appeal in Ordinary since April 1951. Previously he had been a Judge of the King's Bench Division from March 1938 until 1946, and a Lord Justice of Appeal from 1946 to 1951.

The Right Hon. Cyril Asquith, Lord Asquith of Bishopstone, was the fourth son of Lord Oxford and Asquith and was born in 1890. His mother (who died in 1891) was a daughter of Dr. Frederick Melland, of Rusholme, Manchester. He went to Winchester and thence to Balliol College, Oxford, winning an open scholarship, as his father and elder brother, Raymond, had done before him. Like them, he also obtained firsts in the two classical schools and the Craven scholarship, also the Hertford, and, like Raymond, he won the Ireland and Eldon scholarships. In 1913 he was elected a Fellow of Magdalen. The following year, on the outbreak of war, he joined as a second lieutenant the Queen's Westminster Rifles, and in due course was promoted captain. He was called to the Bar by the Inner Temple in 1920, and he soon obtained a good junior practice, but not too large to prevent him in 1925 accepting the post of Assistant Reader in Common Law to the Inns of Court. He took silk in 1936 and was appointed Recorder of Salisbury in the ensuing year. As a leader Asquith's practice was high class, but never a large one, and Lord Maugham's [q.v.] choice of him, at the age of 48, in 1938, came as a surprise to the Bar.

Nevertheless, it was recognized that he had the qualities out of which the best type of Judge is evolved. From the first Asquith created a good impression, and with increasing experience he soon added distinct strength to a team of King's Bench Judges, at the time a strong one. He was learned, careful, and courteous, and with much of his father's dignity, never descended to facetiousness or irrelevance. Before his appointment to the Court of Appeal he several times sat there as an additional Lord Justice.

He was sometimes considered unduly lenient in the sentences he imposed. He was, in 1939, appointed the High Court Judge attached to the General Claims Tribunal. In 1943 he presided over the Commission of Higher Education in the Colonies, and in 1944 he was made chairman of the very important Royal Commission on Equal Pay for Equal Work as between men and women.

This question at the time was the subject of bitter controversy and much evidence from opposite points of view was taken at length. It was not until November 1946 that the report was published. For the present purpose it is sufficient to say that the majority report, in which the chairman concurred, pointed out that the Commission were not asked to submit recommendations but only to provide an analysis from which those responsible would draw their own conclusions, and the analysis that was the result of their labours will be of the highest value to those charged with framing policy in the future. In February 1946 he was appointed a Lord Justice of Appeal in the place of Lord Justice MacKinnon, who had died suddenly in the previous month, and remained in the post until he became a Lord of Appeal in Ordinary, when a life peerage was conferred upon him.

The late Judge was a man of wide general culture, as will have been gathered from his academic career. He was the author of *Versions from a Shropshire Lad* and *Trade Union Law for Laymen;* but he will be chiefly remembered as the joint author, with J. A. Spender, of the excellent life of his father, the Prime Minister.

He married in 1918, Anne Stephanie, daughter of the late Sir Adrian Pollock, K.C.M.G., who survives him together with two sons and two daughters.

August 25, 1954.

Lord Astor, the second Viscount, who died on September 30, 1952 at the age of 73, was a man of wide interests and much practical capacity, who combined unflagging industry and considerable administrative gifts with a whole-hearted devotion to the public weal.

The Right Hon. Waldorf Astor, second Viscount Astor, of Hever Castle, in the county of Kent in the peerage of the United Kingdom, was born on May 19, 1879. He was the eldest son of the first Viscount Astor and of Mary Dahlgren, of Philadelphia. His father, who was born an American citizen, settled in England in 1889 and became a British subject 10 years later. Waldorf's entire upbringing was therefore English. He went to A. C. Ainger's house at Eton in 1893, and was Captain of the Boats in 1898. Then he went to New College, Oxford, where he represented Oxford at polo, steeplechasing, and sabres, and took his degree in history. In 1910 he was returned to Parliament as (joint) Unionist member for Plymouth and there commenced a long career of public service in the course of which he first held office in 1917 as Parliamentary Private Secretary to Lloyd George, then Prime Minister. A few months later he moved to the new Ministry of Food as Parliamentary Secretary, and thence served from 1919 to 1921 as Parliamentary Secretary to the new Ministry of Health. These offices indicated the main bent of his interests. He was devoted to the welfare of agriculture, and deeply concerned in measures of many kinds for improving the health of the people and raising the general standard of life.

His contribution to the study of agriculture included three books, the first of which, *Land and Life,* was produced in 1932 with the collaboration of Dr. Keith A. H. Murray. This was followed in 1933 by *The Planning of Agriculture* and in 1938 by a broader study entitled *British Agriculture,* to which B. Seebohm Rowntree [q.v.] and others contributed. His views on agriculture were distinguished by two very strong convictions. In the first place, he stood in the forefront of those who, at a time when the broader interests of the industry were much misunderstood and gravely neglected, urged upon their countrymen the danger and folly of that shortsighted attitude. History has endorsed their argument and placed it beyond further controversy. His other main conviction was the unwisdom of preferring arable cultivation to livestock.

Later, in 1936, he became chairman of the joint committee of agricultural, economic, and health experts appointed by the League of Nations to study the problem of nutrition in relation to public health and the effect of improved nutrition on the consumption of agricultural products. The report of that body, issued in August 1937, received world-wide attention and has profoundly influenced the action of the United Nations, which is now equipped with a permanent food organization. After the war, with Rowntree, he returned to the question of the evolution of agriculture in *Mixed Farming and Muddled Thinking.*

From his first connexion with Plymouth in 1910 he became a devoted servant of that great city and found in it a field for beneficent social activities of the practical type which most strongly appealed to him. Various undertakings, all of which Lord Astor endowed, came into being year by year and gradually extended their activities. Of these Virginia House, commemorating Lady Astor's* Virginian origin, was perhaps the most remarkable. Founded as an institution for girls in the 1914-18 war, it was steadily enlarged by the acquisition of neighbouring property till it embraced a large hall and cinema, three clubs, a library, a billiard-room, a welfare centre for mothers, and a beautiful nursery. Lord Astor was made a freeman of the city 26 years after his first arrival in it, and later served as Lord Mayor for five consecutive terms, resigning finally in 1944 because control of the reconstruction plans had passed into party hands.

Many of his gifts to the city, which included, besides Virginia House, the Astor Playing Field, the Mount Gold Institute, the University Hall of Residence, and the Astor Housing Estate, had been obliterated by air attacks in common with a very large surrounding area. He played an active part in securing plans for its rebuilding and in pressing for an extension of the borough which would enable these plans, which were drawn in the main by Professor Abercrombie [q.v.], to be carried into effect. The curtailment of them, imposed partly by local feeling and partly by the city's failure to obtain the extensions of area which they required, was a source of deep disappointment to him.

It was a pity that his succession to the family honours in 1919 put an end to his career in the House of Commons. Lord Astor held very strongly that a peer should not be disqualified from Parliamentary service in the popular House, and endeavoured, by way of test, to decline the title and keep his seat as a member for Plymouth. The legal authorities, however, found that a member of the Commons who inherited a peerage must automatically and compulsorily resign his seat, and he had no choice but to comply. He served thereafter as Parliamentary Secretary to the new Ministry of Health, but was compelled for reasons of health to resign that very congenial post in 1921. The Lloyd George Coalition Government fell in the following year, and office never came his way in subsequent Governments. One reason for this is probably to be found in the fact that from 1919 onwards he set aside his own political ambitions in order to further the political career of his wife.

He had married in 1906, as her second husband, Nancy Witcher, daughter of the late C. D. Langhorne, one of the Virginian sisters made famous by Charles Dana Gibson, the pen-and-ink artist, who was himself married to the eldest one. In addition to very attractive looks, Lady Astor had a personality of great vitality and charm which took the political world by storm when she was elected member for the Sutton division of Plymouth in her husband's place. As the first woman to enter the Mother of Parliaments she naturally became at once a figure of nation-wide interest, and she rapidly justified her place by the courage with which she championed women's interests in Westminster and Whitehall. Thereafter the limelight fell almost exclusively on her, but her husband's judgment and public spirit were always of much influence behind the political scene and they radiated through the wide range of acquaintance, great and small, which the Astors gathered round them at Cliveden, the Hoe, and St. James's Square. There were four sons and a daughter of the marriage.

At one time the so-called "Cliveden set" became indeed a legend industriously diffused by credulous or imaginative writers throughout the world, and Lord Astor found it necessary in 1938 to prick the bubble by writing to *The Times.* While, however, it was always absurd to associate Cliveden with conspiracies for any particular set of views, it was throughout the period between wars a political country house in which the leaders of many utterly dissimilar causes and parties met and exchanged a comprehensive variety of views. Lord Astor liked to listen, whether or not he agreed, and Lady Astor could be counted upon to provoke a controversy or initiate a game at any moment when her guests seemed to want that kind of entertainment. For distraction from politics there was always good golf or tennis to be played—in the company, often, of such experts as Helen Wills; there was a lovely garden to be explored, with a historic cemetery commemorating Canadian and other Empire soldiers who had died at the Cliveden Hospital in the 1914-18 war, very near at all times to Lord Astor's heart. There were the brood mares to be visited and admired. For in this latter field, from boyhood onwards, Lord Astor's interest never flagged. Breeding is planning and in all his activities he had a careful planning mind.

The stud was begun by the acquisition of that great mare Conjure. Lord Astor bought her for £100 while he was still at Oxford and she became the first mare of the Cliveden thoroughbred stud. Among the good horses who were her descendants were Winkipop (1,000 Guineas), Short Story (Oaks), Pennycomequick (Oaks), Mannamead (unbeaten), and Instantaneous (dam of Court Martial and Way In). In 1907 Popinjay was brought into the stud. From her line came Book Law (St. Leger), Saucy Sue (Oaks), Pogram (Oaks), Pay Up (2,000 Guineas), Rhodes Scholar (Eclipse Stakes), and Early School (unbeaten).

A further brood mare, Maid of the Mist, was bought at auction from Sir William Bass for 4,500 guineas in 1911. Her family included Buchan (Eclipse Stakes twice and champion sire 1927), Craig an Eran (2,000 Guineas and Eclipse), Sunny Jane (Oaks), Saltash (Eclipse), Tamar (second in the Derby), St. Germans (second in the Derby), and Mitrailleuse. Altogether Lord Astor won 11 classic races and innumerable other prizes. The Derby always eluded him, but the stud's success must be considered unusually swift and splendid and its contribution to English thoroughbred bloodstock great.

Lord Astor was given control of the *Observer* by his father during the 1914-18 war. The newspaper was edited by J. L. Garvin, who collaborated happily with the proprietor for a quarter of a century and made the central columns of the paper a resounding pulpit which no public man could ignore. But difficulties arose between them towards the end of that period, and in 1942 the partnership ended for reasons which (in spite of rumour to the contrary) had nothing to do with the leadership of the nation in war or with the freedom proper to editors in the great English tradition. The *Observer* is now safeguarded by a trust which guarantees its independence. One of his sons, David Astor, has been its editor since 1948. Cliveden House, built in 1850-51 by Sir Charles Barry, the architect of the Houses of Parliament, with its gardens and lovely woods, was handed over to the National Trust in 1942 with an endowment providing for upkeep on the understanding that Lord Astor and his family might continue to reside there so long as they wished to do so.

Lord Astor leaves behind him a record of high service to a very wide community. He was the least assuming of human beings, but to all his activities as landowner, sportsman, and public man he brought a solid competence and a quiet, endearing enthusiasm which won the affection of all who knew him. His character was profoundly Christian; his religious faith was strong; and his life was a constant proof that wealth and goodness are not incompatible companions. No man who was born, as he, to great possessions, has ever worked harder for the happiness of his fellow-men.

He is succeeded in the family honours by his eldest son, the Hon. William Waldorf Astor,* who was born in 1907 and married in 1945 the Hon. Sarah Katharine Elinor Norton, daughter of the sixth Lord Grantley. They have one son, who was born in December 1951.

October 1, 1952.

Lord Athlone, the first and last Earl, who died at Kensington Palace on January 16, 1957, in the course of his long life occupied positions of high distinction in many branches of the public service. He was 82.

The Right. Hon. the Earl of Athlone, K.G., P.C., G.C.B., G.C.M.G., G.C.V.O., D.S.O., F.R.S., was born at Kensington Palace on April 14, 1874, being the youngest son of the first Duke of Teck and Princess Mary. He was thus the great grandson of King George III, who was born more than 200 years before his great-grandson's death—an unusually long gap for four generations. As the brother of Queen Mary [q.v.] he was great-uncle to Queen Elizabeth II.

He was christened Alexander Augustus Frederick William Alfred George and until 1917 he was known as His Serene Highness Prince Alexander. He went to Eton, where he achieved some distinction as a cricketer and added to his popularity with his fellows by his power of mimicking his tutor, Austen Leigh. From Eton he went straight to Sandhurst and in 1894 he was gazetted a second lieutenant in the 7th Hussars. He saw active service in the Matabele Campaign and was mentioned in dispatches. He also fought throughout the South African War and took part in the relief of Mafeking. For his services in this campaign he was awarded the D.S.O.

In 1904 Prince Alexander married Princess Alice, the only daughter of the Duke of Albany (Queen Victoria's youngest son). During the next few years he began to take an increasingly big part in charitable and public work. His marriage, coupled with his sister's position as Princess of Wales, meant that he was more in demand for functions of this kind than would normally have been the lot of a collateral member of the Royal Family. In those years he was especially closely connected with the Middlesex Hospital, of which he was chairman, and it was in part due to his work and encouragement that a special cancer ward and laboratory were established there before the 1914-18 War.

At this period of his life the Prince's capacity for hard and efficient work, his conscientiousness and his reliability were appreciated by all who were brought into contact with him; but they were not, perhaps, generally recognized. It was therefore something of a surprise when it was announced in the summer of 1914 that the Prince was to succeed the Duke of Connaught as Governor-General of Canada. The Duke was the first member of the Royal House to hold the governorship-general, although Lord Lorne, who was connected with the Royal Family by marriage, had been Governor-General in the 1880s. For the most part governors-general had been members of the English nobility of some prominence in politics, and the implication that it was now to become the preserve of the Royal Family was not welcomed by the whole of Canada. No doubt this outcry, which was based on an imperfect appreciation of the facts, would have quickly died away when the Prince had arrived in Canada; in fact it was never put to this test, since the war intervened, and the Prince was soon in France on active service.

At the outbreak of the war in 1914 Prince Alexander was a major in the 2nd Life Guards, to which he had been transferred from the 7th Hussars.

He then served throughout the war and was twice mentioned in dispatches. During the closing months of the war he was the head of the British Mission with the Belgian Army.

In 1917 the Prince relinquished the title of Serene Highness and all styles of his German nobility, assumed the surname Cambridge, and was created Earl of Athlone and Viscount Trematon in the County of Cambridge.

When the war ended it was clear that an important future lay before Lord Athlone. It was therefore no surprise when it was announced in 1923 that he had been appointed Governor-General of South Africa in succession to Prince Arthur of Connaught. His term of office coincided with a difficult spell of South African internal politics, feeling being sharply divided by reason of the nationalist policy pursued by General Hertzog and his Cabinet. These divisions came to a head over what was known as "The Flag Controversy", which centred on the General's proposal that South Africa should have its own flag in addition to the Union Jack. It needed someone outside and above the dispute to give the necessary impetus to agreement—a delicate task which was undertaken and fulfilled by Lord Athlone. In 1927 the British Government received a request from General Hertzog that Lord Athlone should extend his governorship-general by a further term of four years. At the same time the King created him K.G. When the close of his eight years as Governor-General came, in 1931, it was clear that he had won unqualified approval from all sections of South African opinion.

On his return to England Lord Athlone was appointed Governor and Constable of Windsor Castle in succession to Lord Esher. In the same year he was elected Chancellor of London University—thereby perpetuating a connexion which had begun when his great uncle, the Duke of Sussex, had been one of the original sponsors of a university in the metropolis. He was chancellor of the university for 23 years.

In March 1938, with Princess Alice he paid an official visit to Arabia, which included the first English royal visit to Saudi Arabia. The visit was extremely successful.

After his return from South Africa Lord Athlone was no doubt looking forward to a period of leisure and retirement, but this was not to be, and in 1940 he was appointed Governor-General of Canada—undertaking when he was 68 an appointment which, but for the 1914-18 War, he would have taken up 26 years before. His term of office in Canada, which expired soon after the end of the war, was constitutionally uneventful. The Governor-General's relations with Mackenzie King and his Ministers were of the happiest, and he remained aloof from all questions of party politics. Having a thorough understanding of the representative character of his position, he executed his constitutional duties with tact and discretion and maintained the reputation of the Crown.

In March 1946 Lord Athlone, who had earlier requested that his period of office should not be extended, left Canada, and returned to England after a short holiday in the West Indies. Four years later he paid a longer visit to that part of the Empire when Princess Alice was installed as first Chancellor at the inauguration of the University College of the West Indies in Jamaica. He never ceased to take a special interest in Canada, and one of his last acts as Chancellor of London University was to confer an honorary degree on L. S. St. Laurent.*

He is survived by Princess Alice and by their daughter May Helen Emma, who married in 1931 Colonel Sir Henry Abel Smith. The peerage becomes extinct.

January 17, 1957.

Katharine Duchess of Atholl, D.B.E, HON. D.C.L., HON. LL.D., F.R.C.M., former Hon. Colonel of the Scottish Horse, and one of the first women to hold ministerial office in Britain, died on October 21, 1960 in Edinburgh. She was born in 1874.

Her busy life covered a remarkable span of public duty, from the time of her marriage in the reign of Queen Victoria until 60 years later. An author and scholar as well as a politician and a great aristocrat, she held honorary doctorates of the universities of Oxford, Glasgow, Manchester, Durham, Columbia, Leeds, and McGill. Completely sincere, grave and alert, her tiny, upright, hawk-like figure was poised with an innate dignity that was reinforced by the greatness of her moral stature. Always in earnest, she found it impossible to compromise in matters of principle, and was sometimes carried into extreme positions by the logic of her views. As a result she was often misunderstood, and her steadfast opposition to all forms of totalitarianism led her into paradoxical situations. Utterly unselfish, kind and good, she was the soul of honour and incapable of meanness. Politically a Tory, she was bred in the Whig tradition, and was a hard-working, tireless and thorough liberal humanist, whose life was devoted to the public interest. She leaves no children.

She was the widow of Brigadier-General the 8th Duke of Atholl, K.T., P.C., G.C.V.O., D.S.O., Lord Lieutenant of Perthshire, a former Lord Chamberlain, Lord High Commissioner to the General Assembly of the Church of Scotland, and a Grand Master Mason of Scotland, one of the greatest Highland figures of his time. Her own aristocratic roots in Perthshire also went very deep. Her father, Sir James Ramsay of Banff, 10th Bart., LL.D., Litt.D., 25th Laird since 1232 in the unbroken male line, was a well-known historian, gained a double first at Oxford and was a continental mountaineer who celebrated his eightieth birthday by walking 25 miles across the Atholl hills.

Kitty Ramsay married the future Duke of Atholl in 1899. When her husband succeeded to the dukedom in 1917, she turned Blair Castle into an auxiliary hospital and served as its commandant. At its inception she had become president of the Perthshire Branch of the Red Cross. Before that war she served on the committee that investigated the medical and nursing services in the Highlands and Isles. After the war she was elected chairman of the Scottish Board of Health's Consultative Council for the Highlands and Islands.

She entertained many distinguished visitors at Blair Castle, among them, in 1921, Lloyd George, then Prime Minister, who wanted talented women of all parties in the Commons and pressed the Duchess to stand for Parliament. Two years later Lord Haldane hinted at Liberal and Labour support should she stand as a Unionist. Accordingly in 1923 she was elected Unionist M.P. for Kinross and West Perthshire. But she immediately wrote an article in the *Spectator* firmly opposing Mrs. Pankhurst's [q.v.] scheme for a "Women's Party" in Parliament. In 1924 she was appointed Parliamentary Secretary to the Board of Education; she and Margaret Bondfield [q.v.] being the first two women ever to become Ministers in a British Government.

During the financial cuts of 1927 her personal intervention with Stanley Baldwin saved the educational grants to local authorities from being merged in the general block-grant system. She took an active part in the Imperial Education Conference that year, and next year was responsible for the Atholl Report on examinations for part-time students. Although she ceased to be a Minister when the Conservative Government fell in 1929, she held her seat in the Commons.

In Opposition the Duchess joined an all-party committee to prevent enforced circumcision of Kikuyu girls, and represented them at an international conference on African children in Geneva. She was hotly opposed by native reactionaries, especially by Jomo Kenyatta, who strongly upheld this cruel custom.

The Duchess commented that "there was something very unsympathetic about him". From this time onwards her life was devoted to combating totalitarianism in all its forms.

When the war that she had foreseen broke out, the Duke and Duchess had already prepared hostels at Blair Castle and four Atholl shooting lodges to receive refugee children from Glasgow, while her brother-in-law, Lord James Murray, arranged for 400 more children to be sheltered in Mid-Atholl. After Dunkirk she became secretary of the local invasion committee to organize civil co-operation with the military. The remaining years of her life were tirelessly devoted to exposing and combating the Soviet menace, to supporting the cause of the unhappy Poles, Czechs, and Hungarians, also the Baltic and Balkan peoples abandoned to the Russian yoke, and to organizing practical assistance for refugees from communist tyranny. She who had made her curtsy to Queen Victoria, had known Kitchener and Baldwin and Madariaga, now befriended Kravchenko*. It seems fitting that the last decoration she received was the Order of Polonia Restituta, conferred on the Duchess by the exiled President of Poland. In 1958 she published her autobiography, including the life of her husband and appropriately called *Working Partnership.*

October 22, 1960.

Henry Ernest Atkins, formerly Principal of Huddersfield College and an outstanding chess player—he won the British Chess Championship nine times—died in hospital at Leicester on January 31, 1955 at the age of 82.

The son of Edward Atkins, of Leicester, he was born on August 20, 1872, and was educated at Wyggeston Grammar School. He went up to Cambridge with a scholarship at Peterhouse in 1890 and was bracketed Ninth Wrangler in 1893.

In 1894 he took a First in Part II of the Mathematical Tripos, and four years later he was appointed an assistant master at Northampton and County School. From 1902 to 1908 he was assistant master at Wyggeston Grammar School, and in 1909 he was appointed Principal of Huddersfield College. He retired in 1938.

He showed his promise at chess as an undergraduate at Cambridge, where he played in the University team; but he first came into prominence at the Hastings Minor Tournament of 1895, where he was equal second, Maroczy taking the first prize. Thereafter until 1911 he had a period of almost unbroken success in English tournaments. He won the S.C.C.U. tournaments in 1896 and 1897 and the Amateur Championship Trophy at Bath in 1900.

From 1904 to 1911 he played regularly in the British championship, winning it every year except the first, when he tied with Napier and lost the play-off. He tied with J. H. Blake in 1909 and with the late F. D. Yates in 1911, but was successful both times in the play-off. During this period he represented Great Britain regularly in the cable matches against the United States, curiously enough with rather limited success. He also played for England in the pre-1914 international matches against Holland.

After the 1914-18 War, although he took relatively little part in competitive chess, he did take part in the London International Tournament of 1922, and won some fine games, notably against Rubinstein and Tartakower [q.v.]; his form was, however, uneven. In 1924 and 1925 he again appeared in the British championship and won it on both occasions. He twice represented England in the International Team Tournament for the Hamilton Russell Cup, at London in 1925 (the first of the series) and again at Warsaw in 1935.

In 1937 he again represented England against Holland, himself and R. P. Michell on the English side being the only players who had taken part in the pre-1914 series. He played on the fifth board against L. Prins, winning one and losing one—the latter an exceptionally fine game by the young Dutch player which virtually decided the match. In the same year, having now retired from his professional work, Atkins again took part in the British championship, and came fourth. It was noticeable that his ignorance of modern opening theory handicapped him; if he succeeded in extricating himself from his opening difficulties he was more than a match for his younger rivals.

He is survived by his widow.

February 1, 1955.

Sir Ivor Atkins, who died on November 26, 1953 at his home at Worcester three days before his eighty-fourth birthday, was formerly organist of Worcester Cathedral, and was known to the wider musical public chiefly through the Three Choirs Festivals, which he directed triennially at Worcester from 1899 to 1948. These festivals ceased during both wars and it was primarily due to Atkins's initiative that they were revived in 1920 and placed on a firmer financial basis, which has enabled them to be carried on with unflagging success ever since. It was for this service particularly that Atkins was knighted in 1921.

Born at Llandaff on November 29, 1869, Ivor Algernon Atkins began his career as an organist there; later he was assistant to G. R. Sinclair at Truro and at Hereford, and so entered the Three Choirs orbit. He became organist of Worcester Cathedral in 1897 after four years as organist at Ludlow, and completed a half-century of service to the music of the city and the cathedral. His first festival in 1899 produced a good deal of adverse criticism of himself as a conductor, a fact hardly to be wondered at, considering that the system of these festivals requires the cathedral organist suddenly to assume control of soloists, choir, and orchestra, without special training in the delicate art of conducting. Atkins was an excellent organist, a fine church choir trainer, and what is called a good all-round musician. He was not a born conductor, but he gave great attention to matters of organization and he greatly widened the repertory of these festivals.

His 1902 festival introduced *The Dream of Gerontius,* which was the beginning of the close association of Elgar with the Three Choirs. He brought the American Horatio Parker to England for a performance of one of his works and gave a first festival commission to Walford Davies. Szymanowski's *Stabat Mater* and Kodaly's* *Missa Brevis* were similar testimonies to his enterprise and catholicity of taste which were produced by him at the last festival for which he was responsible. He was the conductor to make Bach's *St. Matthew Passion* a more or less regular feature at Three Choirs Festivals, and in conjunction with Elgar prepared the edition for use thereat which has now become the most used English edition of the work. He also edited the *St. John Passion* and Brahms's *Requiem.* He had, though essentially an executant musician, something of the scholar's mind, which he employed during his leisure both before and after his retirement in the cathedral library on subjects ranging beyond music. Atkins had a fine and impressive presence; his tall figure in morning coat at all Three Choirs Festivals was a familiar and friendly feature of those gatherings, even after his retirement in 1950.

He married in 1899 Katherine, daughter of the Rev. E. Butler, of Llangoed Castle, who survives him together with a son of the marriage.

November 28, 1953.

Sir Edward Tindal Atkinson, K.C.B., C.B.E., Director of Public Prosecutions from 1930 until 1944, died in a nursing home on December 26, 1957. He was 79.

Edward Hale Tindal Atkinson was the only son of the late Henry Tindal Atkinson, county court judge, and his uncle was the late Sir Edward Tindal Atkinson, K.C., a Railway and Canal Commissioner. His grandfather, too, was one of the last of the Serjeants-at-Law and county court judge at Wimborne. He was born in 1878, and went to Harrow in May 1892 to Marshall's house, and to Trinity College, Oxford, where he graduated in 1899. He was called to the Bar by the Middle Temple in 1902, and joined the South-Eastern Circuit and the Herts and Essex Sessions, where he enjoyed a large, chiefly criminal, practice.

He was recognized as an able counsel, and in 1929, as a junior, received the unusual honour of being elected a Bencher of his Inn; he was also a member of the Bar Council. In 1929 also he was appointed the first Recorder of Southend-on-Sea.

Before assuming office as Director of Public Prosecutions, he had had some varied administrative experience as a Referee under the National Health Insurance Act for the Ministry of Health, and Chairman of Inquiry Committees for the Ministry under that Act. During the war of 1914-18 he was a lieutenant in the R.N.V.R. and a major in the Royal Air Force. At the Peace Conference he was a member of the Air Section of the British Delegation, and British Secretary of the International Air Commission in Paris in 1919.

In March 1930 Sir Archibald Bodkin [q.v.], who had held the office of Director of Public Prosecutions for 10 years, retired, and the Home Secretary, J. R. Clynes, nominated Tindal Atkinson to the post. The appointment came as a surprise to the public, for, unlike Sir Archibald Bodkin or his predecessor Sir Charles Mathews, Tindal Atkinson's name—at any rate in London—had not been prominently associated with the criminal law.

But Clynes had been well advised by those who knew the qualifications of the new director, and the appointment was soon seen to have been a wise one. Tindal Atkinson had had more experience of practical affairs than the ordinary practitioner in the criminal courts and some practical acquaintance with administration. To the always responsible, and often delicate duties of his office he brought a shrewd and cautious mentality that was seldom at fault, and his judgment as to what cases his department should take up and how they should be conducted was usually sound. His outlook on life was kindly and essentially human, and with the frailties of mankind he was tolerant, so long indeed as they were not too much in conflict with his own high moral standards. With the Bar and with his official colleagues Tindal Atkinson was extremely popular, and to the latter he was always accessible and helpful. On his retirement after attaining the usual age limit in September 1944, a tribute was paid him at the Central Criminal Court, where the presiding High Court Judge, the leaders of the Bar present, and the officials of the Court all testified to the respect and affection in which the director was held. He was shortly after appointed chairman of the Central Price Regulation Committee and presided over it until 1953.

He was appointed C.B.E. in 1919 for his post-war service, and made K.C.B. in 1932. He was also a Chevalier of the Legion of Honour. He was a bachelor, and was often to be found at the Athenaeum, where his interesting and gaily humorous personality will be especially missed. Mention should also be made of his intimate knowledge of his native county of Dorset in all its aspects: fauna, flora, and geological, and remains, primeval, Roman and medieval.

December 27, 1957.

Mary Ann Bravery Attlee, a sister of Lord Attlee* and for nearly 40 years a missionary in South Africa, died in a nursing home at Salisbury on September 6, 1956 at the age of 81.

Her father was a solicitor in London, and Mary was born at Putney in 1875. As a girl she wanted to go to India as a missionary, but her father liked to have his family about him; therefore she waited until after his death before beginning her life work. Her health was not considered good enough for India, so she went to South Africa in 1910 to work for the South African Church Railway Mission. She was licensed as a lay worker by the Archbishop of Cape Town, and did much Sunday school work. For a time she acted as Diocesan Inspector of Sunday Schools at Johannesburg.

When the general secretary of the Railway Mission died she took his place for four and a half years at headquarters in Westminster. She resigned because she was anxious to go back to South Africa to work for the coloured people, for she had realized how much they were in need of friends. She became house-mother for a year at a school for half-caste girls taken out of native kraals in Swaziland who were nobody's children. They were trained for domestic service at the school and put into employment at the Cape, where they found friends in the old-established community of coloured people.

Miss Attlee's work was interrupted when she returned to look after an old aunt in England for nearly three years until she died. Then she went back to work for the Cape Town Diocesan Mission to the Moslems. This brought her into close contact with the coloured people, especially the girls, and led her to start social and Christian work among them. She began with a club room in a cottage, and as the work developed she collected money for an institute in which the coloured people could have a concert hall of their own, a club, and classrooms. She received very little encouragement but with characteristic quiet determination she persevered, and eventually a very fine institute was built at a cost of £13,000 in Claremont, a suburb of Cape Town.

She called it the "Janet Bourhill Institute" after her friend and fellow-worker. Lord Clarendon [q.v.], who was then Governor-General of South Africa, gave his name to the concert hall. Miss Attlee was the first superintendent of the institute and working early and late she made it a very active centre of social welfare among the coloured people. During a cold and wet winter many of the coloured people living in wretched little hovels scattered about the Cape Flats were flooded out of their so-called homes. Miss Attlee at once formed the "Cape Flats Distress Association," now well known as "Cafda," which organized relief.

When Miss Attlee reached the age of 70 she decided to return home to her family, leaving her work in good hands. After some years, however, she returned to the Cape and again interested herself actively in the community centres she had formed. When she finally left South Africa, at the age of 75, the quayside at Cape Town was thronged with weeping coloured people as well as with Europeans whom she had made her friends.

September 7, 1956.

John August—See **De Voto.**

Frederic Austin, who died on April 10, 1952 in hospital in London, little more than a week after his eightieth birthday, was a versatile musician who made a mark in several fields, as singer, composer, teacher, and, most conspicuously, as the editor of the Playfair production of *The Beggar's Opera* at the Lyric Theatre, Hammersmith.

It was the combination of operatic experience, a singer's sense of style, and a composer's sound musicianship that made the success of Austin's version of *The Beggar's Opera.* He realized the figured basses and composed interludes in a manner suggestive, but not slavishly imitative, of the eighteenth century, and scored the whole most delicately for an orchestra in which, again, by the use of harpsichord and viols, the atmosphere of the period of the original production of 1728 was created. He appeared himself on the stage as Peachum in the earlier days of the opera's astonishing run, and a little later he edited *Polly* in the same manner.

This editorial work, his other labours in the cause of English opera as artistic director of the short-lived British National Opera Company, and his previous success as a baritone singer of distinction somewhat obscured his work as a serious composer, and only a few songs, of which his setting of "The Twelve Days of Christmas" is certainly one, keep his name before the public in this capacity. An orchestral rhapsody "Spring" was performed at a Promenade concert in 1907, a symphonic poem, "Isabella," was produced two years later in his native Liverpool, and a Symphony in E flat was given at one of Balfour Gardiner's concerts in 1913. A cantata, *Pervigilium Veneris,* produced at the Leeds Festival of 1931, showed him working on a large scale and experimenting not quite successfully with the modern idioms that had come into vogue since his youth. Since then only incidental music to plays and an overture, "The Sea Venturers," written for his own and the Bournemouth Orchestra, then under the direction of his son, Richard Austin, had come from his pen. Yet, though he had latterly composed little, his wide musical culture and great experience made his advice of great value to younger colleagues and he continued to teach to a ripe old age.

Frederic Austin was born at Liverpool of a musical family in 1872. He began his career as an organist and taught harmony at the Liverpool College of Music. He made his debut as a singer in London in 1902 and quickly established himself as an interpreter not only of standard works like *Elijah,* but of the newer music like Delius's "Sea Drift," in which he sang the baritone solo at its first performances. He launched out into opera in 1908 in Richter's performances of *The Ring* in English at Covent Garden and he took important parts in such dissimilar works as *Elektra, Tales of Hoffmann,* and *Tiefland,* in Sir Thomas Beecham's* famous seasons of 1910 and 1915. He was an acceptable recitalist of songs, since his acute sense of style enabled him to treat all these different kinds of singing in their proper and different manners. This sense of style he no doubt owed to his wide general training and musicianship. In him a diversity of gifts were happily combined so that each branch of the art he practised was enriched by the others, with the further advantage that his career never ended but continued to serve the art of music in Britain in many capacities.

April 12, 1952.

Professor John Langshaw Austin, O.B.E., since 1952 White's Professor of Moral Philosophy in the University of Oxford and thus a Fellow of Corpus Christi College, died at the age of 48 on February 8, 1960.

Born on March 26, 1911, the son of Geoffrey Langshaw Austin, he was educated at Shrewsbury, where he won a classical scholarship to Balliol College, Oxford. After a distinguished record as an undergraduate he won a Fellowship at All Souls College in 1933 and in 1935 was elected to be Fellow and Tutor in Philosophy at Magdalen College.

During the 1939-45 War he worked for some time in a branch of Military Intelligence. Legends tell how generals and brigadiers paced the corridors, trying to summon up courage to consult the captain whose knowledge of their business so greatly and so candidly exceeded their own. He retired with the rank of lieutenant-colonel. He served as Junior Proctor in the university in 1949-50. Two years later he succeeded Professor H. J. Paton in White's Chair of Moral Philosophy.

Inside the university community Austin was greatly respected, and timidly liked. Though his pungent dicta achieved wide currency, in ordinary conversations he did not try to electrify or scarify. Frivolity was not in his nature but earnestness did not monopolize it. The university lecture list sometimes contained the entry *"Sense and Sensibilia:* by J. Austin."

For individuals who needed or might need his help he was unfailingly and unflaggingly considerate. He was a man to have on one's side in trouble. Intellectually exacting, he treated his pupils as persons for whom, as well as from whom, he wanted the best. A scrupulous and judicious examiner, he alarmed by his rigorous standards not the candidates, but his fellow-examiners. During his year as Proctor, the undergraduates were emancipated from a number of archaic prohibitions; it was the dignitaries of the university who learned to quail before him. Already in his early days in All Souls he began to have a powerful influence upon philosophical thinking in Oxford. Latterly this influence was making itself felt throughout the philosophers of the English-speaking world. In 1955 he spent several months in the United States, where, based on Harvard as William James Lecturer, he visited the philosophy departments of a score of universities. It is pleasant to recall how, for once, he broke into hyperbole and said that his time in America had been a marvellously good time.

He published little. His translation of Frege's *Foundation of Arithmetic* is his only production of book length. The student of Austin's own thoughts has access only to a few papers in the Proceedings of the Aristotelian Society and a British Academy lecture. His great impact derives almost entirely from his utterances in discussions, seminars, and lectures. In theoretical disputes, as in disputes about college or university policy, he knew what he was for and what he was against: it was in such matters that the flint in him showed itself in his face, his voice, and his bearing.

His vocation was not to provide philosophical messages, whether comforting or disquieting but to give philosophy a discipline. Where the ambitious and precipitate philosopher treats as superficial blemishes the cracks and unevennesses in his conceptual pathway, to Austin these seemed to be the likely symptoms of beginnings of subterranean crevasses. The philosopher needs to train himself to scrutinize the concrete details of the workings of the language in which we think, negotiate, and converse. Unalarmed by the repeated reproach that he was reducing philosophy to philology, he drilled himself and others in the guess-free techniques of determining the specific forces of expressions and the interplays of these forces.

To have learnt from Austin just how, for example, *negligence* differs from *inadvertence* is to have learnt much more than this; it is to have learnt in part how, in the formulations of very abstract doctrines and questions, to sort out what is girder and what is façade, and, more than that, which girders support which parts of the load. When colleagues fretted at his unreadiness to neglect the negligible, his attitude was that of the expert rock-climber when adjured to shut his eyes and jump for it. Undoubtedly his passion for the minutiae was only in part the desire that philosophy should, at last, begin to have its own discipline. He was also a collector of specimens.

The magnitude of his philosophical influence will not become assessable in the near future. It has provoked hostilities which do not matter, and healthy philosophical reactions, which do matter. The course of philosophical thought will be greatly different from what it would have been without him. If it is different from what he would have wished, even this may be what he would have wished.

He married in 1941 Jean, daughter of the late C. R. V. Coutts, and they had two sons and two daughters.

February 10, 1960.

Joseph Avenol, the second—and last—Secretary-General of the League of Nations, died at Nyon on the Lake of Geneva on September 2, 1952 at the age of 73.

His predecessor, Sir Eric Drummond, as the late Lord Perth [q.v.] was in 1933, when Avenol took over from him at Geneva, had received his training in diplomacy; Avenol's preparation was in the financial service, which in France, at any rate during the years of the stability of the franc before 1914, had habitually attracted high intelligence and talent. Although concerned almost exclusively with matters of finance until 1933, much of his work during the previous 10 years, as deputy secretary-general of the League, had necessarily been on the highest international level. It was in large measure under his practical direction, indeed, that the policy of extending loans under League auspices to countries threatened by financial collapse was inaugurated. A man of patent integrity of mind, widely travelled, a good European, frank and deliberate in speech, simple and unaffected in his manner of life, he gave himself sincerely and in the most conscientious fashion to the practical ideals of an international order.

Joseph Louis Anne Avenol, who was born on June 9, 1879, at Melle, Deux-Sèvres, joined the Inspection Générale des Finances in 1905. Within five years he had risen to be Inspecteur-Général. Soon after the outbreak of war in 1914 he gained further promotion and in 1916 became a member of the French financial mission in London. He continued to serve the mission until 1923, simultaneously holding a place on the Supreme Economic Council in 1919, on a variety of inter-Allied commissions, and on the finance committee of the League of Nations. In these multiple capacities he took part in all the international conferences of the period concerned with the related problems of reparations and inter-Allied debts, and was made an honorary K.B.E. in 1921.

In January 1923 the deputy secretary-general of the League, Jean Monnet, resigned and Avenol was appointed his successor. Even then he continued to occupy himself in the first place with matters within his special competence, in the work of the financial and economic section, co-operating with Sir Arthur Salter, its chief [later Lord Salter*].

In 1923 he went to Hungary and some two years later to Estonia to arrange for financial assistance to those countries. The World Economic Conference convened at Geneva in 1927 came under his care, and he took an active part in the preparatory work for the scheme of economic union in Europe projected by Briand in 1930-31. He was chosen to succeed Sir Eric Drummond in December 1932 and entered upon his duties in the ensuing summer.

He served the League as secretary-general with conspicuous ability and dignity, but the foundations laid at Geneva in 1919 were shifting rapidly in 1933. Avenol himself perceived very clearly the fatal drift of events and lent himself with admirable discretion to the discussion of suggestions for the reform of the League.

In 1936, the year after Germany had left the League, he paid a visit to Britain and lectured at Oxford (where an honorary degree was conferred upon him) and at Cambridge. The outbreak of war in 1939 marked the virtual end of his direction of the League secretariat, but he did not actually resign until August 31, 1940. Four years later, after he had been living in the Haute Savoie, he took refuge in Geneva.

September 3, 1952.

Allan Aynesworth (Edward Abbot-Anderson), the actor, died on August 22, 1959 at Camberley at the age of 95. On his retirement in 1938 the English stage lost a player who, whether as a young man or a man of riper years, had been almost without a rival in certain lines of part in high comedy.

Born at the R.M.C., Sandhurst, on April 14, 1864, the third son of General E. Abbot-Anderson, he came from a family of conservative traditions. His eldest brother rose to the rank of brigadier-general; the other, Maurice, made his name as a physician. To break away from such traditions in the 1880s required courage, but Aynesworth, fortunately for him, was sent to complete his education in France, where a *Sociétaire* of the Comédie Française provided an opportunity for him to study the technique of French acting. His determination to be first rate, his respect of acting as an art, his insistence on clarity of diction and intimate timing, his reluctance to undertake parts to which he felt he could not do justice, not least his *panâche*—all this may be traced to the influence of the French theatre upon him in his formative years.

He obtained a small part in London in Tree's production of *The Red Lamp* in 1887, then went as a student to Sarah Thorne's Company at Margate in order to learn his business more thoroughly. In 1888 he was at the St. James's Theatre under John Hare and W. H. Kendal, when as General de Pontac in *The Ironmaster* he took the first of many subsequent parts in Pinero's plays. Other parts in Pinero followed from 1889 to 1891 at the Court, where Aynesworth appeared under the management of Arthur Chudleigh, in 1912 at the Duke of York's, and in 1915—his last Pinero play—at the St. James's.

It was, however, in 1895 at the St. James's that he caught the public eye as a star by creating the part of Algernon Moncrieff in *The Importance of Being Earnest.* In *The Times* he was praised for having caught "the right vein of grave extravagance."

In 1912 he joined the select group of London's actor-managers, making a successful start at the New Theatre with 200 performances of *Ready Money:* In 1913 he took the Garrick Theatre and later shared with Bronson Albery* the management of the Criterion.

During the war theatres were asked to keep open so as to provide entertainment for troops on leave. Aynesworth was in demand both as actor and producer, and he also contributed to the success of charity performances. Those who saw *The Circle,* by Somerset Maugham* in 1921 will not forget the rotund perfection of his performance as Lord Porteous, especially in those scenes which he and Lottie Venne played together. He appeared in a revival of *The Circle* 10 years later, and in 1938 said goodbye to the theatre at the end of the long run of Laurence Housman's [q.v.] *Victoria Regina.*

He acted in 25 London theatres, most frequently at the Haymarket and the St. James's; and he took part in plays written by over 50 contemporary dramatists. He never appeared in anything by Shaw (though for a while he rehearsed a part in *You Never Can Tell*) or Granville Barker, for his interest was centred in the comedy of character and he was not sympathetic to the drama of ideas. His favourite part was Charles Surface, which gives a nice indication of his general outlook. He had worked with almost every eminent actor and actress of his day; and appeared before Queen Victoria, King Edward VII and Queen Alexandra, King George V and Queen Mary [q.v.], and King George VI* and Queen Elizabeth.

"Tony" Aynesworth was a delightful companion, with a fund of humorous anecdotes, devoid of ill humour, about the men and women he had acted with or known. He was happy in the country where he could fish, shoot and enjoy his garden. He was a lifelong member of the Beefsteak Club and of the Garrick Club, where his portrait hangs.

August 25, 1959.

Ruby M. Ayres, the romantic novelist, died on November 14, 1955 in a nursing home at Weybridge after a long illness. She was 72.

Ruby Mildred Ayres was born at Watford on January 28, 1883, the daughter of an architect. Her talent for writing romantic fiction became apparent at an early age, for while at school she discovered, from the appreciation of her schoolmates, that she could write to satisfy the feminine taste for romance. She saw no reason why she should not exploit this talent and her output soon became prodigious. Indeed, of her day and age, she became synonymous with romantic fiction.

At the age of 25 she published her first novel, *Richard Chatterton, V.C.,* and it sold in large numbers. Serial stories from her pen appeared, too, in the daily Press and were immensely popular. Thus she embarked on the long list of novels which, in a writing life of over half a century, were to reach 150. Her attitude to writing was purely professional and she is recorded as saying: "First I fix the price. Then I fix the title. Then I write the book." At times she produced 15,000 to 20,000 words a day. She was, in fact, never afraid of hard work and was a forthright, yet kindly person, who knew just what was expected of her and who did not hesitate to supply the "mixture as before."

In 1909 she married Reginald William Pocock, a London insurance broker, who died some six years ago. There were no children of the marriage.

November 15, 1955.

B

Admiral Oscar Charles Badger, a distinguished American commander in the Pacific during the Second World War, died of a heart attack on November 30, 1958 at his home at Long Island. He was 68 and is remembered at large for the "No hits, no runs, no errors" signal he sent to Admiral Halsey [q.v.]—borrowing a superlative from baseball—on the surrender of the Yokosuka naval base.

Badger came of a long naval line (his father was commander-in-chief of the Atlantic Fleet at the outbreak of the First World War) and was serving until he retired in 1952 as commander of the eastern sea frontier and the Atlantic reserve fleet. Since then he had been associated with the Sperry Corporation (which produces gyroscopes and bomb sights) and the Prudential Insurance Company; he was also active in planning for civil defence. As an expert on supply problems he had assisted the combined Chiefs of Staff at the war conferences at Quebec and Cairo, and not long before retiring had taken strong issue before a Senate investigating committee with General MacArthur's* recommendations for extending the Korean War.

It was Badger who led the flotilla parade into Tokyo Bay at the end of the war after his Task Force 31 had cleared the minefields for the landing of allied occupation forces; and subsequently he directed "Operation Magic Carpet", which brought home four million service men from the Pacific theatre. He had seen action as a squadron commander off the Solomon Islands and the Bismarck archipelago and directed attacks on Iwo for the American landings there.

Before assuming command of the entire naval area east of the Rockies he was responsible in 1947 for the disposal of radioactive vessels used in the atomic tests at Bikini; he was naval adviser to the American delegation at the 1951 Assembly of the United Nations, and a year later commanded the western Atlantic submarine area under N.A.T.O.

Badger took his commission as a member of the 1911 class of the Naval Academy, and in 1914 he took part in the Mexican campaign while serving in the battleship Utah; he won the Medal of Honour as leader of the first American landing party at Vera Cruz; and during the First World War commanded the destroyer Worden in the Atlantic.

Between the wars he served alternately at sea and in the Pentagon, and before receiving command of the North Carolina in 1941 he was chief of staff and assistant chief of naval operations (logistics) to the Third Fleet's battleship division under Admiral King [q.v.]. He was decorated with the Navy Cross and four Legions of Merit, besides the Medal of Honour.

He leaves a widow, two daughters and eight grandchildren.

December 3, 1958.

Marshal Pietro Badoglio, Duke of Addis Ababa, Marquis of Sabotino, Marshal of Italy, Cavalier of the Santissima Annunziata, and for nearly a year Prime Minister of Italy after the fall of Mussolini, died on October 31, 1956 at Grozzano, in north-west Italy, at the age of 85.

Born of yeoman stock in 1871 in the Piedmontese village of Grazzano, Monferrato, he first saw active service in 1896, in the disastrous war against the Abyssinians, and he served in the Tripoli war. At the outbreak of war in 1914 he was a lieutenant-colonel, and in 1916 he was promoted colonel. His share in the capture of Monte Sabotino, one of the keys to Gorizia, established his military reputation, won him promotion to the rank of general, and many years later brought him his marquisate. In the final battles on the Piave and at Vittorio Veneto, Badoglio was at the side of General Diaz, Cadorna's successor, as his Chief of Staff, and to Badoglio fell the honour of heading the commission which on November 4, 1919, concluded the armistice with the Austrians at Villa Giusti.

After the 1914-18 War Badoglio was created a senator, and he went as special envoy to Romania and later to the United States. At the time of the march on Rome (October 28, 1922) Badoglio was said to have told the King of Italy that with a handful of troops and a whiff of grapeshot he would sweep the fascists away. Anyhow Badoglio was known not to favour fascism and, since he was far too popular in the Army and the country to be dismissed, he was temporarily side-tracked by being appointed Ambassador to Brazil in 1924-25.

In June 1925, he was made Marshal of Italy, and later in the same year he resumed the post of Chief of the General Staff of the Army which he had already held soon after the conclusion of the 1914-18 War but had given up in 1921. He also took up in 1925 the appointment of Chief of the General Staff, a post quite distinct from that of Chief of the General Staff of the Army. Between 1928 and 1933 Badoglio held the post of Governor of Libya and carried on campaigns to pacify the rebellious tribes of Tripoli and Cyrenaica. Two years later Badoglio was back in Africa. In November 1935, shortly after he had returned from an inspection of the Tigre front and made a report to Mussolini, he was sent out to take the place of the fascist De Bono as commander-in-chief against the Abyssinians, whom Mussolini had attacked in the face of the League of Nations.

Badoglio was criticized for devoting many weeks to reorganization, but when once he had launched his offensive he carried it to a swift conclusion and entered Addis Ababa in the early summer of 1936. He conducted his campaign with ruthlessness, seeking the "complete annihilation of the enemy" in battle, according to a book he wrote, and he is generally credited with having used poison gas in some form, though the circumstances have remained somewhat obscure. For a short time he acted as Viceroy of Abyssinia, and then returned to Rome, where he was given a triumphal welcome. The King created him a Duke and the Fascist Party insisted upon making him an honorary member.

From that time until the outbreak of the 1939-45 War little was heard of Badoglio. He was thought to have disapproved of the signature of the alliance with Germany in 1939, but nevertheless he was reconfirmed in his post as Chief of the General Staff in the following November, although he had reached the age limit of 68. At the close of the following year, however, he resigned soon after the opening of Mussolini's attack upon Greece, which he was believed to have opposed.

This episode marked Badoglio's final rupture with fascism, and made him the man increasingly mentioned as a successor to Mussolini. When, therefore, after a stormy meeting of the Fascist Grand Council, Mussolini was driven to resign on July 25, 1943, Badoglio's appointment was widely expected. His task, especially for one who had held aloof from politics, was extremely difficult. He had to manoeuvre on three fronts. Having declared in his first proclamation that "the war continues", he had to face the victorious allied forces, though convinced that Italy was irreparably beaten. He had to face his German allies, who doubted his intention to carry on the fighting. He had to face the Italian nation, very many of whom were clamouring for peace. The people were soon dissatisfied with the extent of his anti-fascist measures, sweeping as they were, and with the composition of his Cabinet. In the September, simultaneously with the allied invasion of the Italian mainland, it was announced that an armistice had been signed five days before. This helped to clear the air so far as the allies were concerned, but the Germans reacted swiftly and easily disarmed many of the Italian troops. The King and Badoglio had to leave Rome for allied-occupied Italy.

The allies did their best to facilitate Badoglio's task, especially after the declaration of war on Germany on October 13, by accepting Italy as co-belligerent. But Badoglio's call to the people to unite in ejecting the Germans, in spite of his pledge to widen his Government as soon as possible by the inclusion of representatives of every political party and his promise that the people should be free after the war to choose their own form of democratic government, continued to find a serious stumbling-block in the King, Badoglio's devotion to whom was deep and unswerving. While some of the parties were prepared to cooperate on this basis, anti-fascist leaders such as Count Sforza [q.v.] and Benedetto Croce [q.v.] refused to join his Cabinet unless the King abdicated.

Throughout the winter of 1943-44, in spite of another reconstruction of the Cabinet, the bickerings went on. But on February 22, 1944, Churchill* made it clear that, at least till Rome was reached, the Allies would support Badoglio. On April 12 the King finally consented to announce his "definite and irrevocable" decision to withdraw from public life and to appoint Prince Umberto Lieutenant of the Realm on the day the Allies reached Rome.

All these developments greatly strengthened Badoglio's arm, as it appeared, and after he had formally resigned he formed a new Cabinet on April 21 which contained representatives of the six leading parties, and included as Ministers without portfolios such men as Croce, Sforza, Togliatti*, and Rodino. But on the occupation of Rome by the allies the opposition to the Marshal, so clearly manifested in Naples, was reinforced by the uncompromising attitude of the Rome politicians. A resolution was passed on June 8, 1944 by the united representatives of the parties against acceptance of office under him in his endeavour to form the wider Cabinet to which he was pledged. He immediately tendered his resignation to the Crown Prince, who sent for the former Prime Minister, Bonomi.

In 1946 Badoglio published his history of Italy during the 1939-45 War, in which he set out to answer some of the attacks of his many critics. Then, nearly 75 years of age, he slipped quietly and uncomplainingly into retirement.

November 1, 1956.

Dr. Leo Baeck, an outstanding leader of modern Judaism, died in hospital in London on November 2, 1956 at the age of 83.

Born at Lisa, then in the Province of Posen, on May 23, 1873, he studied at Breslau and Berlin and served as rabbi in Oppeln (1897-1907) and Düsseldorf (1907-12). In 1912 he was appointed one of the rabbis of the Berlin Jewish Community and lecturer in Homiletics and Midrash at his *alma mater,* the Hochschule für die Wissenschaft des Judentums. Save for a period on active service as a German Army chaplain during the 1914-18 War, he remained in these positions until the institutions concerned ceased to function. Baeck's powers as a preacher, teacher, writer, and thinker were in themselves sufficient to give him a commanding position among the rabbis of Germany, but that position was enhanced by administrative abilities of no mean order. In 1922 he became President of the Union of German Rabbis and a few years later Grand President for Germany of the powerful Jewish fraternal and philanthropic organization, the Order of B'nai Brith. Though not a Zionist he was one of the founders of the Jewish Agency for Palestine. Religiously Baeck belonged to the moderate liberal wing of Judaism; in 1939 he became President of the World Union for Progressive Judaism in succession to his English collaborator, Dr. Claude G. Montefiore.

His outstanding service was rendered from 1933 onwards, when, overtaken by the crisis created by the Nazi victory, the Jews of Germany established a representative organization, the Reichsvertretung der Juden in Deutschland. Of this organization Baeck was elected president and to him fell the task of negotiating with the Nazis in a constant endeavour to mitigate the severity of their oppression, of keeping high the morale of German Jewry, and, at the same time, of preparing its dissolution. He received many invitations to take up positions outside Germany, but preferred to remain with his people until the end.

He continued his work after the outbreak of the war until, in January 1943, he was arrested and dispatched to the Terezin concentration camp, in which he passed his seventieth birthday. There he found many of his relatives and close friends, whose number gradually diminished as they were removed to the death camps. Even there Baeck did not forget his vocation as a teacher, organizing classes in philosophy and religion in spite of the German ban. He seems to have inspired a certain amount of respect even among his captors. As he said of his experiences under the Nazis at the time of his liberation: "Although I never bent, sometimes even taking risks and being threatened with arrest, those in power, strangely enough, always treated me with a certain respect and even acquiesced to my refusing to yield to their demands."

Baeck's experiences in a concentration camp did not impair his vitality. He settled in London, where, besides many friends, he had a married daughter, and at the first opportunity he became a British subject. When the Society for Jewish Study was organized he became its president and principal, and he was elected President of the Association of Synagogues in Great Britain, a small group of reform congregations. But his activities were not confined to this country. He took up the position of visiting professor at Hebrew Union College, Cincinnati, Ohio, spending his winters there. He also lectured at the Hebrew University of Jerusalem and, in spite of his advanced age, frequently travelled on the continent of Europe in the course of his public work.

The afternoon of Baeck's life was convulsed by a tornado: the evening was one of serene glory. As one of the few leaders of European Jewry to emerge from the holocaust he evoked a lonely reverence; his steadfast course under the Nazi régime made him a hero, and his resilience enabled him to continue his work from his new home.

Baeck's philosophy of Judaism is unfolded in his *Das Wesen des Judentums* (1905), which passed into eight editions in German and of which an English edition was published, under the title of *The Essence of Judaism*, in 1936. His collected essays and addresses were published under the title *Wege im Judentum* in 1933. He also published a volume on the Pharisees in 1937, *Die Romantische Religion* (1922), *Das Evangelium* (1938), and *Aus drei Jahrtausenden* (Essays in the History of Judaism) in 1938. In England he delivered, and later published, the Arthur Davis Memorial Lecture *Changes in Jewish Outlook* (1947).

November 3· 1956.

Max Baer, whose death occurred in Hollywood on November 21, 1959 at the age of 50, was heavyweight boxing champion of the world from June 14, 1934, until June 13, 1935.

He won the championship by knocking out the Italian Primo Carnera* in 11 rounds, and lost it when he was surprisingly outpointed by

James Braddock* over 15 rounds. Baer began his professional boxing career in 1929 and had his last contest in 1941. The following year he entered the United States Army. After the war he made something of a reputation as a cabaret comedian with another former world champion, the light-heavyweight Maxie Rosenbloom.

If professional boxing is, as was recently said, "show business with blood", then Max Baer was one of its outstanding exponents. He was a natural comic and had one of the hardest right-hand punches of any of the great heavyweights. Early in his career one of his opponents failed to recover consciousness after being knocked out. Many believe that Baer was so haunted by this that he never afterwards punched his full weight.

Baer showed little of the dedication that has led other men to world boxing titles. He loved the bright lights, was not fond of training, and would often play to the gallery in most important bouts. On the occasion when he beat Carnera for the title both men at one stage slipped to the floor and Baer took the opportunity to remark, "Last one up's a cissy!" Yet he took the contest seriously enough to put Carnera down 11 times before the referee stopped the exchanges.

Maximilian Adelbert Baer was born on February 11, 1909, in Omaha, Nebraska, but his family soon moved to California, and here it was that he entered boxing after an inspiring victory in a spontaneous fist fight. By the time of his retirement he had had 54 bouts, of which he had won 43 inside the distance. His most memorable victory was over Max Schmeling, whom he stopped in 10 rounds in 1933, three years before Schmeling beat Joe Louis. Baer met Louis in his first contest after he had lost the title to Braddock, but the young, smooth-moving negro was far too good for him and won by a knock-out in the fourth round.

After this setback Baer announced his retirement but then made a successful comeback. In 1936 he took part in 18 bouts in three months and the next year he visited England for bouts with Tommy Farr and Ben Foord. Farr outpointed Baer over 12 rounds but Foord was stopped in the ninth round after a courageous display. Baer beat Farr in a return bout in New York in 1938, but Lou Nova temporarily stopped any further progress when he defeated Baer in 11 rounds. Baer had one more happy period, in 1940, when he beat both Tony Galento and Pat Comiskey inside the distance, but then another defeat at the hand of Nova finished his career for good.

November 23, 1959.

Lady Bailey, D.B.E., a former champion airwoman and the first woman to fly across the Irish Sea, died on August 29, 1960 at her home at Kenilworth, near Cape Town. She was 69 and the widow of the South African millionaire Sir Abe Bailey.

In 1928 the International Aviation League awarded her a trophy as champion airwoman of the world, and in 1930 she was made a Dame of the British Empire for her services to aviation. What she did as a pioneer of aviation for women was for her own satisfaction, and it was only when it had been done that she discovered the needs and opportunities which her exploits had revealed. As the wife of Sir Abe Bailey and the mother of a family, she already filled an important place in English and South African society. Flying was to carry her to still greater prominence, not so much because of her exceptional skill as because of the courage with which she turned it to practical use. After a long solo flight to the Cape in 1928 her husband expressed the hope that she would not attempt to fly back. She did fly back, and after many difficulties returned to her starting point without injury.

Her flight to Cape Town between March 9 and April 30, 1928, was one of the finest feats that a woman has accomplished. Within a fortnight of her arrival she was continuing her tour, and for the next 14 months she was flying in most of the countries on the West Coast and making her way gradually homewards.

Before she started for the Cape she had climbed in a Gypsy Moth, with Mrs. Geoffrey de Havilland as passenger, to a height of 18,000ft., and so had made a height record at that time (July 1927) for light aircraft. In 1927, 1929, and 1930 she took part in the King's Cup race, and in the latter two years she flew in the International Challenge Competition round Europe. In January 1930 the Royal Aero Club awarded her the Britannia Trophy in acknowledgment of her African flight.

She flew frequently in later years, and took a course of instruction in instrument or blind flying. She was the first woman in the country to obtain a certificate of proficiency.

She joined the London Aeroplane Club, and took her pilot's licence at Stage Lane, Hendon. She may be regarded as the pioneer of air touring for women with standard aeroplanes and engines.

A daughter of the late Lord Rossmore of Monaghan, she married Sir Abe Bailey in 1911 and had two sons and three daughters.

August 30, 1960.

Dr. Cyril Bailey, C.B.E., who died at his home at East Hanney, near Wantage, on December 5, 1957 at the age of 86, was for many years a notable and friendly figure both in his own college of Balliol and in Oxford generally. He did an astonishing amount of varied work.

Within what are commonly supposed to be the narrow limits of an academic career he lived a full, rich, and useful life, distinguished by its large contributions to scholarship and by its even larger contributions to the lives of all who came into close contact with him.

Born on April 13, 1871, Cyril Bailey was the eldest son of Alfred Bailey, barrister-at-law and at one time Fellow of University College, Oxford. He gained a scholarship at St. Paul's School, and in a few years took his place in the long succession of finely trained classical scholars who were sent up to Oxford (and particularly to Balliol during Jowett's mastership) by F. W. Walker, the high master, whom Jowett described as the greatest idealist in education in his day. He entered Balliol as a scholar of the college in 1890, won the Hertford and Craven Scholarships in the next year, and took a first-class in Classical Moderations in 1892 and in Literae Humaniores in 1894. He had a love of great music, and his skill as an actor and a producer of plays enlarged the range of his activities. He was a singing member of the Oxford Bach Choir to the end of his Oxford life; he produced with great success more than one play of Aristophanes, and his influence upon the affairs of the O.U.D.S. for many years was most valuable. In his younger days he was also a keen cricketer and a hockey player, and became a good mountaineer, spending many holidays in the Alps, and he was an early member of the Alpine Club.

In 1894 he was elected a Fellow of Exeter College, and worked there for eight years, first as classical lecturer and afterwards also as Tutor. In 1902 he returned to Balliol as a Fellow of the College, in succession to Evelyn Abbott. In 1916 he was appointed to one of the Jowett Fellowships founded by Lord Newlands, and in 1931 to the Craig-Sellar Fellowship. He held various college offices, but his main work was that of a tutor and lecturer in classics.

His lectures were exhaustively prepared and admirably delivered, and he was second to none as a teacher of Latin and Greek composition. At the same time he was preparing and publishing works connected with the subjects of his special studies—Lucretius, Epicurus, and the Religion of the Romans. His text of Lucretius appeared in 1898, and a second edition in 1922, his translation in 1910. In 1907 he published a small but excellent handbook on the Religion of Ancient Rome; in 1921 an edition of Ovid's *Fasti, Book III*; in 1926 a text of Epicurus, with a translation and an extensive commentary; in 1928 a history of the Greek Atomists and Epicurus; and in 1932 a volume entitled *Phases in the Religion of Ancient Rome,* based on the Salter Lectures delivered in 1929 in the University of California, where he spent a fruitful six months as Visiting Professor. In 1947 appeared his critical, interpretative edition of Lucretius in three volumes.

All his writings show lucidity and orderliness, his scholarship was marked by learning and sound judgment, with none of the venturesomeness which is indifferent to evidence, but with plenty of good suggestions based upon careful study.

Readers of *The Times* have reason to be grateful to him for his work as Oxford University correspondent from August 1919 to August 1932. He was always energetic in promoting the education of women at Oxford, and from 1921 onwards was chairman of the council of Lady Margaret Hall, which is greatly indebted to his wise guidance; his interest in the Balliol Boys' Club (in St. Ebbe's parish) was unceasing, and he was for some time chairman of the Oxford Juvenile Organizations' Committee.

Profoundly religious, and a Churchman of broad and charitable views, he was called upon for advice and help by those in authority in the Church. He was a governor of St. Paul's School from 1901, and of Worcester Cathedral King's School from 1919, and was a member of the Council of Marlborough College from 1932. He took his full share of service on university boards and committees, and of examinerships of all kinds. He was a Delegate of the Clarendon Press—an office which is no sinecure—and after some years' service was appointed a Perpetual Delegate.

In all university affairs he maintained a sane balance between conservatism and progressiveness, and of no one was it more certain than that any issue which arose would be dispassionately judged. In 1932 he was elected Public Orator *omnium consensu,* his gift for ceremonial Latin (not unmixed with humour) having already been well proved. Two years later the university conferred on him the honorary degree of D.Litt.

Yet, with all this accumulation of duties, he performed each one of them as if it were his only care; and no outside interest interfered with his devotion to the college of which he was for more than 30 years one of the main pillars. Here he was trusted by all. How much he did for the well-being of his pupils and friends will never be told. But it is certain that he never dropped a friend or pupil, or refused his help even to the most uncompromising. Always bearing others' burdens as if it were just the natural thing to do, he never looked for recognition; and public recognition came to him comparatively late. He was elected a Fellow of the British Academy in 1933, and he had previously been made an Hon.D.Litt. of Durham and the University of Wales, an Hon. LL.D. of Glasgow, and an Hon. D.L. of California. During the war of 1914-18 he worked at the Ministry of Munitions and was made M.B.E. Subsequently, he was promoted C.B.E. In 1934 he was president of the Classical Association.

In 1912 he married Gemma, daughter of Dr. Mandell Creighton, Bishop of London, a marriage which brought great happiness and increased his usefulness. Their Oxford home at the King's Mound, with the family of a son and three daughters, will be a delightful memory to many. Some part of the vacations was spent almost every year in reading-parties, in many of which Mrs. Bailey joined, and the party included both men and women students. Cyril Bailey was an ideal member of a reading-party, and not least in its lighter moments.

December 6, 1957.

The Rev. A. V. Baillie, K.C.V.O., Dean of Windsor and Registrar of the Order of the Garter for 27 years, died on November 3, 1955 at his home at Baldock, Hertfordshire, at the age of 91. He will be remembered chiefly for his achievement in carrying out the restoration of St. George's Chapel.

At the time of his appointment to the Deanery in 1917, and for many years afterwards, his position was one of great difficulty, though he showed admirable tact and patience in dealing with it. His predecessor, and a succession of canons, had been completely dominated by that remarkable man, John Dalton, who had been installed canon so far back as 1885. Dalton's energy, his impatience of opposition and his stentorian vocal powers were undiminished up to his death, in 1931, at the age of 92.

It had been known for some time that, owing to settlements and decay, the fabric of St. George's was in a dangerous condition and, soon after the end of the 1914-18 War had made work possible, the urgent reports of the architects insisted that it must be begun immediately. With great energy the new Dean faced the task of raising the large sums needed—sums which, as usually happens, proved to be much larger than originally were expected. The keen personal interest of King George V was a powerful factor in encouraging contributions. Yet there were times when it seemed that the work must come to a standstill through lack of funds, and once almost all the workmen had to be withdrawn. Yet the Dean never allowed himself to be discouraged, and redoubled his efforts until at last, in the autumn of 1930, 10 years after its beginning, the great work of restoration was triumphantly completed. It had cost rather more than £180,000.

After its restoration St. George's Chapel became a far more active religious force than before. The congregations increased greatly. The nave was now often used for great special and central services, and Baillie himself was more interested in such special functions than in the normal Sunday and weekday services. In 1934 the Chapter had to undertake another large enterprise, when the lease of the buildings serving as the choir school expired. It was resolved to purchase the freehold and to re-equip the buildings as a first-rate preparatory school. In the long-drawn out and often difficult negotiations that were necessary the Dean had little part, but once more he used his personal influence most successfully with wealthy and generous friends.

Albert Victor Baillie was the third son of Evan Montagu Baillie, and the grandson of Evan Baillie, of Dochfour. His mother was a sister of Lady Augusta Stanley, wife of Dean Stanley. He was born on August 9, 1864, and owed his Christian names to the fact that he was a godson of Queen Victoria, his mother's intimate friend. From Marlborough he went to Trinity College, Cambridge, where he took his degree in 1886. In the following year he joined Bishop Lightfoot's "Brotherhood" at Auckland Castle—a group of young men reading for holy orders, to whom Lightfoot stood in much the same relationship as did Dr. Vaughan to his "Doves" at the Temple.

Baillie was ordained by Bishop Lightfoot in 1888. After three years at South Shields he went to London as curate of St. Paul's, Walworth, and soon afterwards was appointed domestic chaplain to Randall Davidson, who had lately left the Deanery of Windsor to become Bishop of Rochester. When, long afterwards, Baillie himself became Dean of Windsor, he used to speak with unbounded admiration of Davidson's tact and sagacity. His next posts were a curacy and an incumbency in Plumstead, and in 1898 he was appointed Rector and Rural Dean of Rugby. In the same year he married the Hon. Constance Elizabeth Hamilton-Russell, fifth daughter of the eighth Viscount Boyne. This was in every way an ideal marriage. No one ever met Mrs. Baillie without realizing her charm, her sympathy, her goodness. As a correspondent wrote in *The Times* after her death in 1924, "men and women of all classes found in her friendship the greatest strength they knew."

The 14 years at Rugby were probably the most successful of Albert Baillie's ministerial life. Rugby was a large and important parish with a very varied population. Under the control of the rector were a number of district churches, and he had a staff of seven or eight curates to assist him. He was always excellent with young men, and the relationship between him and his curates was a pattern of its kind. The personal attractiveness and kindness of the rector and his wife made them extremely popular, and this in turn enabled them to secure all the lay helpers they needed to carry on the numerous parochial organizations.

From 1905 to 1908 Baillie was an honorary Canon of Worcester; when Rugby passed into the newly created diocese of Coventry he became an honorary Canon of St. Michael's, Coventry, and in 1912 left Rugby to be vicar and Sub-Dean of St. Michael's. For various reasons the Coventry setting was less congenial to him than Rugby had been, and his friends rejoiced at the promotion which gave him the distinguished post of Dean of Windsor. He loved young men, and was never happier than when he had a group of them in his library. He had also a passion for the stage, and among his most frequent visitors at the Deanery were members, both eminent and obscure, of the theatrical profession.

The coming of war in 1939 necessarily reduced Baillie's outside interests and occupations, compelling him to spend far more time at Windsor. His stall in St. George's was still rarely occupied except on special occasions, but he found a congenial task in looking after the Guardsmen stationed in the Castle. Almost daily he entertained some of them, drawn from all ranks, in his house, and he conducted a special service for them in the Castle on Sunday mornings.

To the end of his life Baillie retained a youthful enthusiasm, especially over any new possession. It might be a new friend, or a picture he had just bought—of pictures he had a really expert knowledge—or a book which its author had sent him: whatever it was, for the time being he could hardly talk of anything else. He himself edited the letters of Lady Augusta Stanley, and, with Hector Bolitho*, wrote a memoir of Dean Stanley. In 1934 he published a small book entitled *The Making of a Man,* which attempted to reproduce in print some of his conversations with young men on life and religion. His autobiography, *My First Eighty Years,* was published in 1951. It gives a true and vivid picture of the life of a truly good man. But his talk was incomparably better than his writing. He knew a vast number of people, many of whom used him unsparingly. It is not as an ecclesiastic that Albert Baillie will be remembered. But his memory will be widely cherished as that of a magnificent friend with a childlike heart—assuredly the tribute which he himself would have counted best of all.

November 4, 1955.

The Very Rev. Dr. John Baillie, C.H., a distinguished and influential figure in Scottish church life and in the ecumenical councils of the churches, who was Moderator of the General Assembly of the Church of Scotland in 1943-44, and one of the Presidents of the World Council of Churches from 1954, died in Edinburgh on September 29, 1960. He was 74. From 1934 to 1956 he was Professor of Divinity in the University of Edinburgh, and from 1950 to 1956 he was Principal of New College, Edinburgh, and Dean of the Faculty of Divinity.

John Baillie was a son of the manse, and was born at Gairloch on March 20, 1886, the eldest son of the Rev. John Baillie. In a brilliant and amply fulfilled scholastic career from the Inverness Royal Academy to Edinburgh University and the Universities of Jena and Marburg, Baillie gathered all the philosophical honours of his day. His clear and lucid mind was matched with an ease in public speaking for which he had plenty of exercise in his four years in the First World War in France under the Y.M.C.A. There his wide range of lectures were popular and memorable among the troops. This experience laid the beginnings of his dominant concern for the expression of religious truth in terms which the ordinary man can understand and which made his own books a delight to read.

After his wartime experiences Ballie went to North America as professor at the Auburn Seminary, later to Emmanuel College, Toronto, and then to Union Theological Seminary, New York, as Roosevelt Professor of Systematic Theology. He was always at home in the American scene, and when the call came to serve his own church again in Edinburgh in 1934 he saw to it that the annual flow of American students to the Scottish capital was always warmly welcomed and furnished with a due supply of subjects for doctoral theses. The generations of "Baillie men" in the Scottish ministry owed to him that excellent mixture of philosophy and theology which characterises the finest traditions of Scottish academic discipline. He was always a students' man, rebuking shoddy work and demanding the best for the high calling of the ministry.

In 1943-44 he was Moderator of the General Assembly of the Church of Scotland, and a year before that had presided over one of the most significant commissions ever formed by the Scottish Church, which resulted in the famous report, *God's Will in Our Time,* which had a worldwide circulation. It bears the stamp of Baillie's thought all the way through.

This experience led on naturally to Baillie's formative part in the shaping of the modern phase of the ecumenical movement and the creation of the World Council of Churches. He always liked his Presbyterianism to be thought of as part of the great reformed tradition which had so mightily influenced Europe and America, but he understood and had a great respect for other traditions. In all the preparations for the Amsterdam and the Evanston Assemblies of the World Council Baillie was a leader, and at the Evanston Assembly he was elected as one of the council's six presidents. His handling of press conferences at Evanston was a masterly performance. He could interpret to the popular press the most intricate theological discussion with an astonishing clarity even for those newsmen who wanted it all in words of two syllables and not too many of them.

While there was no brilliant flash in his lecturing and debating he could always be depended on to straighten out a tangle with direct and pawky humour. When in 1956 the World Council of Churches Central Committee at Davos wished to send a message to the Patriach of Moscow, Baillie pleaded for point and brevity. When the inordinately lengthy telegram was approved he slipped down to the post office at Davos and discovered it would cost 150 dollars to send. Armed with this compelling news he soon got his more pithy message agreed to.

But there was something more about John Baillie than was revealed in his work as scholar and church statesman. It is best seen in his *Diary of Private Prayer* and in the most gracious of his many books, *And the Life Everlasting,* where his inner resources of faith and belief are intimately revealed. He was Chaplain to the Queen in Scotland and a D.Litt. and Hon. D.D. of Edinburgh University. Both Princeton and Yale honoured him with degrees, as did other Canadian and American universities. He was made a Companion of Honour in 1917. He was Chaplain to King George VI [q.v.] in Scotland and to Queen Elizabeth, and since 1956 had been an extra chaplain.

In 1919 he married Florence Jewel, of Caterham, and they had one son.

September 30, 1960.

Captain Bruce Bairnsfather, who died on September 29, 1959 aged 71, was fortunate in possessing a talent, limited but very real, which suited almost to the point of genius one particular moment and one particular set of circumstances; and he was unfortunate in that he was never able to adapt, at all happily, his talent to new times and new circumstances.

During the First World War, however, his drawings of the ordinary soldier's life in Flanders in the trenches, and the ruins of villages just behind the trenches, achieved an immense popularity. They did indeed, primitive in artistic technique though they were, succeed in making something genuinely, if grimly, funny out of a situation which was far from comic.

Bruce Bairnsfather was born in India, in July 1888, the son of Major T. H. Bairnsfather. He was educated at Westward Ho!, joined the Warwickshire Militia in 1911, and became a civil engineer.

On the outbreak of war he joined The Royal Warwickshire Regiment, with whose first battalion he served after going to France in November 1914. He became a captain in July 1915, and continued to serve in France until 1916, and his first "Fragments From France" (as the famous series of drawings was headed) were sent to *The Bystander* from the western front.

It was this fact, and their absolute authenticity as by-products of a fighting soldier's life, that made their broad jesting at danger and discomfort bearable. Bairnsfather created broadly caricatured, but still recognizable types of soldier in his heavily moustached, tomato-nosed, Old Bill; the young chinless boy with a cigarette eternally hanging from his lip (was his name Bert?); and all the rest. The legends under his drawings, too, were often brilliant in their unfeeling sardonic wit. "Well, if yer knows of a better 'ole, go to it" (under a picture of two wretched lonely soldiers in a shell hole, while all hell breaks loose above them); and (for a drawing of two soldiers, one old, one young, sheltering in a barn with a vast gap in the wall) "Who made that 'ole?" "Mice." These attained a currency that was nation-wide—and probably far more than that.

Six collections of "Fragments from France" were published. *The Better 'Ole* was the title of a successful play, written by Bairnsfather in collaboration. And Old Bill had a variety of theatrical and film incarnations, continuing, in fact, down to the Second World War, in which from 1942 to 1944 Bairnsfather was an official cartoonist attached to the United States Army.

Bruce Bairnsfather did an immense number of things—stage appearances, lecture tours, drawings in periodicals, several books (among them an autobiography *Wide Canvas* published in 1939), journalism and illustrations, but he never repeated the success of that one outstanding comic "moment of truth" in World War I.

In 1921 he married the Hon. Mrs. M. Scott, and they had one daughter.

September 30, 1959.

C. H. Collins Baker, C.V.O., the art historian, who was keeper and secretary of the National Gallery from 1914 to 1932, and was afterwards in charge of research in the history of art at the Huntington Library, California, died on July 3, 1959 at the age of 79.

Charles Henry Collins Baker, the son of John Collins Baker, a solicitor of Ilminster, Somerset, was born on January 24, 1880, and was educated at Berkhamsted and at the Royal Academy Schools. He had talent as a landscape painter, being capable of a fine design, if sometimes uncertain as a colourist. He exhibited at the New English Art Club in one of its best periods, and was secretary of the club from 1921 to 1925; his work is represented in the Manchester, Leeds, and Huddersfield galleries. He did not, however, find sufficient encouragement to justify him in devoting himself primarily to painting, and gave an increasing share of his time to art history and criticism. He contributed art criticism to the *Outlook* before succeeding D. S. MacColl as art critic of the *Saturday Review.*

In 1911 Collins Baker was appointed private assistant and secretary to the director of the National Gallery, Sir Charles Holroyd, and in 1914 he was promoted to the position of keeper and secretary. On the director's retirement in 1916 Sir Charles Holmes was appointed to succeed him, and Holmes and Collins Baker then settled down to a long and successful partnership in control of the gallery. One of their earliest tasks, during the 1914-18 War, was the housing of 900 of the gallery's best pictures in the unused Tube station in the Strand, where they were safe from air raids. Collins Baker made a brave attempt to get to the front as a motor driver, but he was rejected on medical grounds.

As an art historian Collins Baker made his reputation with his masterly book on *Lely and the Stuart Portrait Painters* (1912), which has done much to remedy the absence of reliable literature on the painting of the period. Studies of Crome and of P. de Hooch were published in 1921 and 1925. His book on *Dutch Painting of the Seventeenth Century* (1926) is notable for an invaluable account of the genre painters. In 1934 appeared his *British Painting.*

After many fruitful years—during which his pioneer efforts in publishing postcards and photographs at the gallery deserve to be mentioned—Collins Baker felt that persistent differences of opinion with a prominent member of the board made it impossible for him to remain at the National Gallery. His great friend Sir Charles Holmes had retired in 1928, and in 1932 Collins Baker submitted his resignation and accepted an appointment at the Huntington Library, California. It was regretted in London art circles that his experience and knowledge would no longer be available, and the post of director of another London gallery was, in fact, offered to him, but proved unacceptable.

Collins Baker had been appointed Surveyor of the King's Pictures in 1928 in succession to Sir Lionel Cust, and he retained this office until 1934, when he was made C.V.O. His catalogue of the principal pictures at Windsor Castle appeared in 1937. He later published a catalogue of the Huntington Art Gallery, and, with his wife, *The Life and Circumstances of James Brydges* from papers among the Stowe manuscripts purchased by Henry E. Huntington in 1925. He retired from his post in California in 1949, but continued to advise the Huntington Library on their purchases in England.

He married in 1903 Muriel Isabella, daughter of H. R. T. Alexander, Taxing Master of the Supreme Court, and they had one daughter.

July 6, 1959.

Lord Baldwin of Bewdley, the second earl, died in a London hospital on August 10, 1958. He was 59.

Oliver Baldwin was everything by turns—soldier, in the Irish Guards and later in Armenia and Georgia, politician, author, playwright, and journalist, soldier again, politician again and lastly Colonial Governor—but nothing long. But the tag does not apply. Most of these activities were permanent expressions of one side or another of his character, and his character remained unaltered.

Kindly, generous, loyal, always ready to help the poor or disregarded, he was also a man who stuck firmly to convictions formed early in life. He showed physical courage on the battlefields of northern France as early as 1918; his moral courage was exhibited many times in his political career, not least when he joined the Social Democratic Federation, when his father, Stanley Baldwin, was already Prime Minister and leader of the Conservative Party.

The contrast between the Conservative father and the Socialist son was the cause of much—mostly ill-informed and often ill-natured—speculation in the twenties and thirties. But few of the speculators knew that Oliver Baldwin explicitly refused to take any financial help from his father after that time and insisted on earning his own living, or that their political differences never lessened the natural sympathy and affection between father and son.

The Rt. Hon. Oliver Ridsdale Baldwin, second Earl Baldwin of Bewdley and Viscount Corvedale of Corvedale, in the county of Salop, in the Peerage of the United Kingdom, was born on March 1, 1899, the elder son of Stanley and Lucy Baldwin, of Astley Hall, Worcestershire.

His early upbringing was appropriate to the time and his father's position as owner of a great iron and steel business and a Conservative member of Parliament (Stanley Baldwin entered Parliament in 1908). Private school at St. Aubyn's, Rottingdean, was followed by four years at Eton. Baldwin never thought highly of the education he received at Eton—like his near contemporary, Sir Osbert Sitwell*—and in his autobiography, *The Questing Beast,* which he published at the age of 33, he described his time there as "the most useless and unhappy years of my life up till then".

The strains of nonconformity which he inherited from both sides of his family provide another, more personal, explanation both of Baldwin's feelings about school and of much of his later activity in politics and writing. On his father's side this strain—nonconformity allied with Highland blood—came from Louisa Baldwin, Stanley Baldwin's mother and one of the five daughters of the Rev. George Macdonald, a Wesleyan minister in Wolverhampton. Three of his sisters married, respectively, John Lockwood Kipling, Edward Poynter, and Edward Burne-Jones.

Baldwin left school in July 1915, but had to wait until May 1916 before he could begin serving with the Cadet Battalion into which the Cambridge O.T.C. had been transformed.

In June 1917 he was commissioned in the Irish Guards and went to France in May 1918, where he took part in much frontline fighting. Demobilized in June 1919, he spent a month as acting-Vice-Consul at Boulogne and the early months of 1920 in Algeria and Morocco. A meeting at Alexandria in August 1920 with the President of the Armenian Republic resulted in his departure for Erivan with the rank of colonel in the Armenian Army and the task of training Armenian troops to take part in the war with Turkey.

His experiences between then and the summer of 1921 when he returned to England are summed up in the title of the book he wrote about them—*Six Prisons and Two Revolutions.*

Soldiering was one of Baldwin's first and enduring loves. He wrote in his autobiography about his enjoyment of the training at Cambridge and later. When war began again in 1939 he went back to the Army as soon as he could. After some time he was re-employed, not as a regimental officer, but in several interesting jobs in intelligence.

After joining the S.D.F. in 1922, Baldwin naturally took to Labour politics. He fought Dudley in 1924 and again in 1929, when he won the seat. Defeated at Chatham in 1931, he did not return to Parliament until July 1945, when, as Viscount Corvedale, he was elected as Labour member for Paisley, which he had fought unsuccessfully in 1935.

His short career in the Commons ended finally when he succeeded his father as second Earl in 1947. Soon afterwards he was appointed Governor and Commander in Chief of the Leeward Islands.

Baldwin's behaviour at Government House was on occasions eccentric and he openly criticized the action of the British Government in sending out missions of inquiry and inspection, and expressed the view that the money thus spent would have been far more usefully employed in the improvement of living and working conditions in the Leeward Islands. Eventually he was recalled by Arthur Creech Jones,* the Colonial Secretary, ostensibly for consultation on policy. When he arrived in England he talked to the Press about his expectations of a "carpeting" by the Cabinet and expressed doubts as to whether he would be allowed to return.

His utterances were as outspoken as his speeches as Governor had been, and it was expected that he would be asked to resign. However, V. C. Bird, one of the principal Labour leaders of the island, followed Baldwin to England to plead his cause. Baldwin, after apologizing for some of his statements, returned to the island and resumed office. He was afforded an ecstatic welcome by the people of St. John's, the capital of the Leeward Islands.

The truth of the matter is that Baldwin was quite genuinely appalled at the conditions which he found in the Leeward Islands, some of the poorest in the West Indies. Owing to his lack of experience of colonial administration he did not know how to set about the task of reform. His generous instincts, combined with his lack of practical knowledge, resulted in his giving vent to his feelings in a way which delighted the islanders but, not unnaturally, exasperated the authorities at home.

In retrospect, the Leeward Islands can be said to have profited from his Governorship. The publicity attracted to them by Baldwin's behaviour stimulated the Government into sending out a number of able administrators, who subsequently carried out many of the reforms which Baldwin would no doubt have instituted had he known how to set about them.

August 12, 1958.

Solomon Bandaranaike, who died on September 26, 1959, from wounds inflicted earlier by a Buddhist monk, had been Prime Minister of Ceylon since 1956. He was 60.

He will be of significance in his country's history as the leader of the first organized movement to identify the public life of Ceylon with Asian, rather than with Western, outlooks upon international affairs.

Solomon West Ridgeway Dias Bandaranaike was born in January 1899 of a wealthy Sinhalese noble family. His father, Sir Solomon Diaz Bandaranaike, was a great landowner, a personal friend of the English Royal Family, and a devoted partisan of British rule in Ceylon. The young Solomon had an English governess before he went to St. Thomas's College in Colombo; and the Christian pro-British atmosphere of his upbringing was further continued when he came to complete his education at Christ Church, Oxford. He soon showed himself a brilliant speaker, and was elected secretary of the Oxford Union in his last year.

At Oxford he developed an enthusiastic attachment to Sinhalese nationalism and became an impassioned advocate of self-government for Ceylon. After being called to the Bar he returned to Ceylon and lived the life of a wealthy young barrister. But before long he resigned his practice, gave up his former "English" hobbies of tennis and riding, learned the Sinhalese language thoroughly, and identified himself with Sinhalese, as opposed to British culture. The ideals of Gandhi made a powerful appeal to him; he learned to use the spinning wheel and customarily wore home-spun clothes. He renounced Christianity and became a Buddhist.

Entering political life as an exponent of Sinhalese language and customs, he became secretary to the Ceylon National Congress, but soon broke away to form his own organization, the Sinhala Maha Sabha. In the first real parliamentary election held in Ceylon his party won a number of seats, but joined with the United National Party to form the Government. Bandaranaike became Minister of Health and Local Government—a position which he had held in the now superseded Council of Ministers.

Before long he broke with his colleagues, and just before the 1952 elections he formed a new group, the Sri Lanka Freedom Party. Although he did not win against the United National Party he secured growing support from persons who looked on communism as an acute danger; and who realized that public opinion was tiring so rapidly of the continued rule of the United National Party, with its conservative outlook and open opposition in international affairs to the alignment of small Asian countries under Nehru's* leadership, that Sir John Kotalawala and the U.N.P. would not be able to retain power for long.

It was probably this growing feeling that Bandaranaike's moderate Socialism and strong Sinhalese nationalism were stabilizing factors of great value in Ceylonese politics which swept him into power in the elections of 1956. He had formed a moderate left-wing coalition to fight the U.N.P.; he won an absolute majority and found himself with a free hand to form his cabinet as he wished. He soon showed his intention of breaking completely with Sir John Kotelawala's right-wing foreign policy by negotiating with Britain for the withdrawal of British naval and air forces from Ceylon; by cultivating close relations with Nehru; and by adopting for Ceylon the outlook of neutralism in the cold war, of which India was the leading exponent.

The British Government accommodated him in arranging for the gradual rendition of the British bases to Ceylon sovereignty; and although he continued to identify himself with a specifically Asian view of international politics, Ceylon's relations with Britain remained cordial. In domestic affairs he had rather a rougher passage. Friction with the Tamil minority over the use of the Tamil language was averted only at the last moment under a threat of passive resistance. It was this delicate situation which prevented him from carrying out his intention of attending the Prime Ministers' Conference in London in July 1957.

Bandaranaike promised the Tamil leaders in 1957 to grant recognition to Tamil as the language of the rational minority. But the agreement was never implemented and in April 1958 he said that it would have to be reconsidered because of continued unrest over the language issue.

A month later, during an outbreak of rioting, 158 people lost their lives in five days and a state of emergency was declared. Public confidence in Bandaranaike was not to be regained. It was not only the confidence between Sinhalese and Tamils that had been lost, it was the confidence in the workings of government and the forces of public order.

In recent months Bandaranaike's Government had not had an easy passage. The defection of the Marxist Party from the Government coalition in May left Bandaranaike controlling only 50 seats in the 101-member house.

September 28, 1959.

Leslie Banks, C.B.E., who died at his home in London on April 21, 1952 at the age of 61, was one of the most distinguished and versatile actors on the London stage, and his achievements as a producer of plays and a director of films in the last 20 years were also notable.

His versatility enabled him to play a diversity of parts, ranging from Shakespearian characters to roles in modern comedies, and the list of the plays in which he took leading parts would run to considerable length. Disinclined by nature to be flamboyant, he could nevertheless impart a flourish to his acting on occasion, and the humorous characters he portrayed were interpreted with a subtle understanding and restrained relish which found much favour with theatregoers.

Born at West Derby, Liverpool, on June 9, 1890, Leslie James Banks was the son of George and Emily Banks. He obtained a classical scholarship at Trinity College, Glenalmond, and afterwards became a classical scholar at Keble College, Oxford.

His first stage appearance was at the town hall, Brechin, in 1911, as Old Gobbo in *The Merchant of Venice* in Sir Frank Benson's company. He acquitted himself so well in the part that he was engaged to tour during the next 12 months with another of the Benson companies visiting theatres in the south of England. In the ensuing year he joined a touring company sponsored by George Dance, but a year later he threw in his lot with a band of players, selected by H. V. Esmond and Eva Moore [q.v.], to tour the United States and Canada. His first part in New York, at the famous Garrick Theatre, in 1914, was as the porter in *Eliza Comes to Stay*. Until then he had not been seen on the London stage, but after returning to England he accepted an engagement at the Vaudeville to play the part of Lord Murdon in *The Dangerous Age*, in May 1914.

War in Europe interrupted his stage career, and he spent the next four years in The Essex Regiment.

Banks returned to the stage as a member of Lena Ashwell's [q.v.] Repertory Company in 1919, with which he played important parts until a year later, when he signed on for a season at the Everyman Theatre, Hampstead. His capabilities were quickly recognized by London managements, and he soon became an actor of established reputation. In 1924 he again visited New York, where he appeared as Captain Hook in *Peter Pan*.

In the years that followed he fulfilled many important engagements at London theatres, among his outstanding successes being leading parts in such plays as *Service, Clive of India, Man of Yesterday,* and *The Taming of the Shrew*.

He made several more visits to America between his appearances in the West End. During the 1939-45 war there was little diminution in his stage activity, and he toured the country, as well as performing in London, in several productions for which he, himself, was responsible. In April 1943 he played Mr. Tattle in *Love for Love,* which ran at the Phoenix Theatre for over a year, and afterwards was with John Gielgud in a distinguished season of repertory at the Haymarket, which kept him fully occupied from October 1944 to June 1945. He then toured among the troops in Germany.

By no means the least important part of

Banks's work was as a producer of plays and films, and among his many productions were *Crime and Punishment, Asleep, The Eldest Son, The Flying Squad, The Lady with A Lamp, The Infinite Shoeblack, Too True to be Good* (in New York), and *Emma Hamilton.* From 1932 he was also in constant demand as a film actor and appeared in many notable pictures.

He married in 1915 Miss Gwendoline Haldane Unwin, and there were three daughters of the marriage.

April 23, 1952.

Warren Bardsley, the Australian cricketer, died at his home at Collaroy, near Sydney, on January 20, 1954 at the age of 69, after a long illness. He was one of the great figures of cricket, a man almost universally accepted as the true yardstick by which an outstanding left-hand bat might be measured. For many years he was considered, along with Clem Hill, the best left-hander Australia ever produced.

Warren Bardsley was born at Warren, New South Wales, whence he derived his Christian name.

His first appearance in big cricket was for New South Wales against Queensland in the 1903-4 season, but it was in February 1908 that he really made his mark by scoring a century against the M.C.C. touring team. Bardsley first went to England in 1909, and though his earlier scores were disappointing the Australian selectors retained their faith in him and were rewarded when he made 136 and 130 in the fifth Test match at Kennington Oval against an England attack which included such bowlers as S. F. Barnes* and W. Rhodes.* This was the first occasion on which a century was scored in each innings of a Test match. This achievement has since been repeated several times, but Bardsley's partnership of 180 with S. E. Gregory in the second innings remains as the best opening stand for Australia against England. He made only one other century off England's bowlers, 193 not out at Lord's in 1926, carrying his bat throughout the innings.

Besides his four tours to England in 1909, 1912, 1921, and 1926, Bardsley visited South Africa and New Zealand, and helped to spread the gospel of cricket to Fiji, the United States, Canada, and Bermuda. Altogether Bardsley appeared in 41 Test matches (30 against England and 11 against South Africa) and scored 2,469 runs for an average of 40.47. Among Australians only Sir Donald Bradman and A. L. Hassett have exceeded his 53 centuries in first-class cricket.

By modern standards, influenced by the remarkable scores of Bradman, his record is not exceptional, but, as a famous contemporary, C. G. Macartney [q.v.], said of him in 1936: "It was not the number of runs he made but his presence in the side that inspired the confidence of his colleagues and doubt in the opposition." His opponents' view was expressed by Sir Jack Hobbs*, who said: "I cannot imagine a more pleasant type of fellow, but he was always a thorn in our side on the cricket field. He was one of the best left-handers of the upright, classical school I have ever seen."

January 21, 1954.

Marie (Mrs. Edward) Baring—See **Hall.**

Rowland Thomas Baring—See **Cromer.**

Sir Ernest Barker, described in *The Times* as "a rare humanist", died on February 17, 1960 at the age of 85.

Ernest Barker was born on September 23, 1874. His father was a small farmer in the parish of Bredbury, in north-east Cheshire, where the boy grew up on the lower slopes of Werneth Low, a hill which has a wide prospect of the Lancashire plain. He went from the village school to Manchester Grammar School. He was a tall, lanky boy, with a long, dreamy face which was melancholy in repose but which lit up into a bright and friendly smile. He was sensitive to the beauty of words and was a great reader.

In 1893 he won a classical scholarship at Balliol and began an academic career of unusual distinction. He was Craven Scholar, took firsts in Classical Moderations and Greats, and, after another year's work, a brilliant first in Modern History (1898). In the same year he was elected to a prize fellowship at Merton, and in 1899 he accepted a lectureship in modern history at Wadham. In 1900 he married, and, having no private means, he was for some years obliged to take a large number of pupils, a circumstance which, if it checked his impulse to historical investigation, led to a memorable association with several of the men's and women's societies. Recognition came in 1909. As fellow and tutor, first of St. John's (1909-13) and then of New College (1913-20), he took a leading part in the work of the School of Modern History. His lectures on English constitutional history were crowded and he was a really great tutor. Indeed, throughout his busy and versatile life he was always at his best as a lecturer and as the intimate friend and adviser of the young.

A fine classical scholar and a devoted reader of English literature, blessed with an apt memory, and ready speech, with a touch of pungent quaintness in it, he won instant recognition. He never suffered from reticence and was, by turns, unaffectedly critical and sentimental. Social and political problems were for him human realities, not matters of academic interest. The influence of T. H. Green, still strong at Balliol in his time, was at work in him. He liked to talk about his early days and to revisit the haunts of his boyhood, and he was helped rather than hindered by a persistent northern accent which, it is said, he firmly believed that he had long outgrown. Many stories, some of which are true, are told about him, and nearly always with affectionate appreciation. His ready mind in a simple nature would have delighted Jane Austen. Her delicate pen would have traced in his portrait sense and sensibility alike.

In the business of the university and especially during the year when he was one of two very popular proctors (1909-10) he lost the diffidence which had clung to him, and during the 1914-18 War, when he was a member of the Oxford Hebdomadal Council, his natural independence found free play. He acquired a taste for administration and, to say nothing of abortive schemes, was largely responsible for the highly successful short courses for men who had had military service, and for the system of rotating groups for the scholarship examinations in classics and modern history. As Dean of New College he was, as one would expect, very happy in dealing with the large crowd of undergraduates who, though inured to military discipline, might have been expected to chafe at the restrictions of college life.

In 1920 Barker succeeded Dr. Ronald Burrows as principal of King's College, London. In Oxford he had taken a full share of academic business, but the problems of administering a large London college were new to him. He did a difficult task with courage, and his usual frankness, and he delighted in the social occasions with which it was accompanied. Yet, though not unsuccessful, he did not feel so much at home as he had felt at Oxford. He missed the easy intimacies and the indulgence in caprice which are hardly compatible with the steady drive and the ability to "lie low" expected of the head of a college in a rapidly growing university.

In 1928, on the foundation of a new chair of Political Science in Cambridge, Barker was appointed Professor and was elected to a Fellowship at Peterhouse. He arrived exuberant and full of reforming schemes, and a university that steels itself somewhat against an enthusiast allowed him to revise the syllabus of his own subject. He established a scheme to allow students of political science to visit foreign countries. He sought to promote a wider study of sociology. Engagingly frank, ever ready to wonder, loving a story against himself, and preserving some attractive childlike qualities, he won affection more often than he won agreement, and became a pleasing legend in Cambridge while still alive. With students he was happiest of all perhaps on intimate occasions—when, after dinner, for example, he would declare to them that "history must be written with a full mind" (and the word "full" as he pronounced it conveyed all its amplitude of meaning); or he would tell stories of old Oxford days for an entire evening, or he would be amusing in what he would concede (and in what he would refuse to concede) to undergraduates who pressed upon him radical views on the subject of sex.

His extra-university activities were numerous; his interest in schools and in adult education never declined; he was chairman of the Community Centres and Associations Committee. With a certain sense of duty he went to Nazi Germany to talk about Oliver Cromwell. For three years before he reached the age of 65—an age which he was totally unable to consider suitable for retirement—he was an indefatigable chairman of the Faculty

Board of History; and when war broke out in September 1939, in spite of his retirement from his professorship, he consented to serve a further period to carry the board through the initial crisis.

He could not fail to make his presence felt wherever he was, but in Cambridge he was more than a local figure. He was now free to make and keep in touch with a wider world. He became a publicist, expressing himself in papers, addresses and letters to *The Times.* As Lowell Lecturer at Harvard he strengthened his American connexions. He had always possessed a power of intense concentration and an enviable gift of easy expression. These qualities are revealed in two early books which are still widely read, his treatise on Greek political thought and his masterly little book on the Crusades. His work at Cambridge was informed by a wider experience, as an administrator, a member of the Advisory Committee of the Board of Education, and a political thinker who never lost touch with events and every day life. One might or might not agree with him, but one could never deny that his intelligence was very much alive.

All this was a good preparation for his most ambitious work, the introduction to his translation of the section of Gierke's famous treatise, which he published in 1939 under the title *Natural Law and the Theory of Society.* He had already published his works on Greek political theory, on *Political Thought in England from Herbert Spencer to Today* and on *National Character.* If these manifested the "full mind" he demanded from the historian how much more was this demonstrated by his *Ideas and Ideals of the British Empire* and *Reflections on Government.* In 1948 his charming memories of his boyhood and early manhood were issued by the National Council of Social Service and were re-published as Part II of his more extended autobiography, *Age and Youth* (1953). He had acted as chairman of the Books Commission appointed by the conference of eight Allied Ministers of Education during the Second World War; and when this commission appointed a History Committee he presided also over this. At the suggestion of the History Committee the Allied Ministers of Education approved the plan of a large-scale history of European civilization which should be produced by absolutely independent scholars, and of which Barker was appointed one of the editors in 1944. This work appeared in three volumes in 1954 under the title *The European Inheritance.* In 1955 Barker produced *From Alexander to Constantine,* and in 1957 *Political Thought in Byzantium.*

Yet, admirable though his books are, the fact remains that the man was bigger than his books. To think of Ernest Barker is to think, first and foremost, of one who, once met, can never be forgotten, a man of surprising candour, naive curiosity and effortless vitality. He repelled a few, attracted many, aroused the interest of all. In many ways he was an extraordinarily intelligent child, and he influenced others with the unconscious fearlessness of a child. In all that he did he was always the same, a critical yet sensitive Liberal, not particularly careful of others, yet tender-hearted, easily stirred by the plight of those in adversity, happy in phrase as in disposition, often uncannily acute, and sometimes unexpectedly perverse.

He was twice and very happily married. His first wife, by whom he had a son and two daughters, was Emily Isabel, daughter of the Rev. R. Salkeld, of Dukinfield; she died in 1924. He married secondly in 1927 Olivia Stuart, only daughter of J. S. Horner, of Mells. There were a son and a daughter of this marriage.

Merton College made him an honorary fellow in 1931, Peterhouse in 1939, and he received the honorary degree of Doctor of Laws from various universities, including Edinburgh and Harvard. He was knighted in 1944.

February 19, 1960.

Dame Lilian Barker, D.B.E., who will long be remembered for her beneficent work as Governor of the Borstal Institution for Girls at Aylesbury, died on May 21, 1955 while on holiday at Hallsands, a fishing village in Devon. She was 81.

Lilian Charlotte Barker was born in London in 1874, daughter of the late James Barker, of Swefling, Suffolk. She was educated at Whitelands College, Chelsea, and began her career as a teacher in elementary schools conducted by the L.C.C. and soon showed an unusual ability. She was asked to take over a class of boys—an unheard of thing in those days—and, distracted by her mother's recent death, she was glad of the challenge. She was so successful that she was asked to take on a class of inexplicably aggressive girls. Within a year every girl in the school was trying to get into the "awful" class and the class were behaving like angels.

Clearly, even then she had proved she was no ordinary woman, but those were the days of the women's suffrage agitation and she might well have ended her career as principal of the L.C.C. Women's Institute in Cosway Street, Marylebone, to which post she had been promoted, but for the outbreak of war in 1914. Then the call for women of administrative ability and courage was clamant and she began her war service while still at her old post by organizing classes for training in Red Cross work, invalid cookery, and so forth. In the summer of 1915 she was appointed first Commandant of the Women's Legion Cookery Section, and the pioneer work she did in training cooks for the Army laid the foundations on which the women's services were subsequently built.

Her next post was one of very much greater responsibility and scope, for as Lady Superintendent of Woolwich Arsenal she had control in the end of some 30,000 women and girls employed there, where women had never before been employed. Canteens, cloakrooms, ambulance rooms, rest rooms had to be provided and to this already heavy task she added the self-imposed duties of organizing recreation outside the Arsenal walls, visiting the sick, providing homes for holidays and convalescence, and for the care of unmarried mothers and their babies, raising funds herself for these unofficial services.

After the end of hostilities she joined the staff of the Ministry of Labour and became Executive Officer of the Central Committee on Women's Training and Employment, in which capacity she was responsible for the administration of £600,000 granted for the purpose of providing training and maintenance of women "who could prove economic detriment due to the War".

In 1922 the post of Governor of the Borstal Institution for Girls at Aylesbury fell vacant and someone at the Home Office, showing unusual imagination for those days, suggested Dame Lilian's name. She was not particularly keen to begin on what, in fact, became her greatest work, first because appointment meant a considerable loss of salary, and she only consented to take on the work on condition that she had a completely free hand. She took up her duties in May 1923, and the impact of her personality was at once felt. It must be remembered that a Borstal Institution is a state training school for persistent law-breakers between the ages of 16 and 21, for whom other forms of treatment, such as probation and reformatory schools, have been tried without success. Out of such material decent citizens have to be made and it requires unfailing courage and a faith proof against the bitterest discouragement. These qualities Dame Lilian possessed in the highest degree. To them she added an abundant humanity and complete integrity. Some critics viewed her approach as too sentimental.

The introduction of pleasantly furnished rooms, comfortable beds, appetizing food, organized games, a swimming-pool, and all the other less tangible things—the "little unremembered acts of kindness and of love"—were looked on askance, but they paid dividends. The girls responded and many became her lifelong friends. She could be brusque, she could be formidable, but, with wry humour, she preferred to punish by making the punishment, if possible, fit the crime. For instance, one girl, who smashed up her bedroom furniture, was given a heap of bones to pound. Her square-cut figure, usually severely dressed in tweeds and with her hair in the close Eton crop of 30 and more years ago, became a welcome and heartening sight to her charges, who soon came to realize that here they had someone—perhaps the first in all their lives—in whom they could confide, and they knew that their confidences would be received with sympathy tempered by common sense.

When she retired from her post in 1935, she was appointed an Assistant Commissioner of Prisons, the first women ever to be appointed, and she finally retired in 1943.

Her epitaph comes from her own lips: "I have laughed more people into being good than if I had preached for hours."

May 23, 1955.

Senator Alben Barkley collapsed and died on April 30, 1956 while making a speech at a mock Democratic Convention at Washington and Lee University, Lexington, Virginia, at the age of 78.

He had just told the meeting he would "rather be a servant in the house of the Lord than sit in the seat of the mighty." Then he faltered and fell. Doctors administered oxygen and students, who had been wildly cheering his address, sat silently as he lay on the platform. He had laughingly told the meeting that he would not himself be a candidate for President this year.

The "Convention" continued after Senator Barkley's body was removed on a stretcher because Paul Holstein, the Mayor of Lexington, who was on the speakers' platform, told students that he believed it would have been Barkley's wish not to have the gathering cut short.

Alben William Barkley was born on November 24, 1877, in Graves County, Kentucky, where his father had a tobacco farm. As a boy he had to work his way through school at Clinton. Then he took to the road, selling kitchen utensils to make enough to take him to Emory College and the University of Virginia.

He first held public office as a prosecuting attorney in his home state of Kentucky. Later he became a County Court Judge. He was elected to the House of Representatives in 1913 and from then on was continuously in Congress, from 1927 as a Senator, and for the 1949-52 period as Vice-President.

Senator Barkley was for 10 years the Senate majority leader during the Roosevelt era. Many Americans had seen him on television on the day he died, when he spoke at the tenth anniversary dinner of the popular interview programme "Meet the Press."

At an age when most men are content to sit in a rocking chair on the front porch, he was still campaigning vigorously for the Democratic Party. A lifelong servant of the party, his political career started when he campaigned on mule-back through the Kentucky mountains for the post of prosecuting attorney of McCracken County. In 1909 he was elected a County Court Judge. He started his Congressional career as a member of the House of Representatives in 1913 in President Wilson's term. There, his southern drawl and ready smile, mixed with salty, old-style oratory, soon made him a popular figure. In 1926 he was elected to the Senate and served there in important positions until his seniority, his capacity for hard work and tremendous popularity with his Democratic Party colleagues won him the role of President Truman's* running mate in the 1948 Presidential elections.

Only once did he spurn party lines. In 1944 President Roosevelt vetoed the Tax Reduction Bill as "relief for the greedy and not the needy." Senator Barkley had agreed, against his conviction, to support the veto, but when he had read the veto speech he regarded the language used as a reflection on Congress. He made an impassioned speech breaking with Roosevelt and resigning the leadership of his party in the Senate. President Roosevelt apologized, and expressed the hope that Senator Barkley would be re-elected leader, which he was.

In all Senator Barkley was majority leader for 10 years—six years longer than anyone else in Democratic history, and a record cut short only by the Republican victory of 1946. Throughout his career he was known as a staunch friend of Great Britain and he was a sterling champion of loans it received since the war.

May 1, 1956.

The Right Rev. Ernest William Barnes, D.D., F.R.S., formerly Bishop of Birmingham, died on November 29, 1953 at his home in Sussex at the age of 79.

He was born in Birmingham on April 1, 1874. His father was John Starkie Barnes. He received his early education locally before entering King Edward's School, from which he won a mathematical scholarship, in 1893, to Trinity College, Cambridge. In the Mathematical Tripos, part I, 1896, he was bracketed second Wrangler with two other Trinity men, and he was placed in the first division of part II in 1897. He won the first Smith's Prize in 1898, and his election to a fellowship of Trinity followed, naturally, in the same year, and the college was to be his home until 1915. In 1906 he gained his doctorate of science and in 1909 was made a Fellow of the Royal Society.

His first office in college was that of mathematical lecturer (1902), and in the same year he was ordained deacon by the Bishop of London. He succeeded to a tutorship in 1908, and to his pupils was a wise and careful guide.

He was steadily making a name for himself as an outspoken preacher, courageous in tackling controversial subjects, and in 1915 Asquith, having a strong liking for academic attainments, even when they were mathematical, nominated him to the Mastership of the Temple. Barnes was not happy about the war, which had broken out in the previous year, and, being a man quite devoid of fear, would sometimes express sentiments which made the more patriotic Benchers furious. It said much for the new Master that he retained his personal popularity, but in 1918 there were Templars who chuckled when their pacifist Master was chosen—by Lloyd George, of all men—for the canonry of Westminster.

There Barnes put in some very useful work, helping Bishop Ryle with the finances of the Abbey and with the useful work of the Westminster Spiritual Aid Society. His sermons remained as challenging as ever.

This outstanding pulpit influence, coupled with utterances of a more elaborate and technical kind at conferences of "Modern Churchmen" at Oxford or Cambridge, soon gave Barnes an assured position among the men who counted in the world of religious intellect. Then in the summer of 1924, Ramsay MacDonald was faced with his first (and only) episcopal vacancy, caused by the breakdown in health of Dr. Russell Wakefield, Bishop of Birmingham. MacDonald naturally desired that his first nomination should be of a specifically "Labour" character, and his friends were ready with the choice which he should obviously make.

The announcement was made on August 1, 1924, and the new Bishop was soon in deep difficulties. Throughout the whole of his episcopate he gave himself unreservedly to controversy on behalf of truth as he saw it, and believing as he did that the cause was of much more importance than the individual, he often showed a lack of consideration for his opponents.

Inheriting a diocese which had got out of hand on ritual matters (Barnes described it as a "bear garden") he proceeded to root out the custom of perpetual reservation, which was plainly illegal. The score or so of clergy who refused to obey his rulings became known as rebels and the controversy continued during the whole of his episcopate, only diminishing by the death or removal from the diocese of the recalcitrants. But the letter of the law which in this instance he so strongly upheld was treated by him with scant respect on other occasions. For example, on one occasion he refused to institute an incumbent, even when ordered to do so by Mr. Justice Bennett in the Chancery Division.

A happier and more fruitful side of his episcopate was shown in the close relations which he established with the Free Churches, and he stretched institutional religion to its utmost limits in his search for the underlying unity of the Spirit. In the same way, believing that in Christ Jesus there is neither male nor female, he encouraged the ministry of women beyond the limits allowed elsewhere in the Church of England.

He had no particular gift for the preaching of pastoral sermons and his confirmation addresses were often occupied with subjects which seemed extraneous. But he proved himself an able and conscientious administrator of diocesan affairs—the appeal for "one hundred thousand guineas" in 1935 was carried through with complete success, leading to the building of 13 new churches and six church halls—and had he possessed a larger understanding of the psychology of the clergy, and allowed his natural goodness of heart to modify the severity of his logical judgments, he could have achieved even more.

His extreme pacifism during the 1939-45 War, which prevented him from attending a National Day of Prayer or associating himself with any kind of club for "war workers," reduced his civic contacts very considerably, and the sombre addresses which he delivered during that period gave little encouragement to clergy or laity. He was concerned only to witness to his pacifism, with which his whole spiritual experience was bound up.

It will always remain a matter of controversy whether his extremely able and independent mind should ever have been harnessed to episcopal tasks. On the one hand it gave the modernist movement which he represented a chance to justify itself within the institutional life of the Church of England; on the other hand it brought a mind scientifically trained but alien to many types of spiritual experience into control of a mechanism requiring delicate and sympathetic treatment. It cannot be said that the experiment was wholly successful.

Much that he wrote became automatically sensational and controversial because of the fact that it was written by a bishop. This does not apply to his Gifford Lectures on "Scientific Theory and Religion," delivered in 1933, which were a notable contribution to the subject, but it applies very definitely to his book *The Rise of Christianity,* published in 1947. This book, as coming from a bishop, raised serious questions for the Church, though it provided little that was new for the attention of the scholar. In the autumn of the same year the book was publicly condemned by the Archbishops of Canterbury and York, speaking in their respective Convocations, as seriously minimizing the essential doctrines of the Church of England.

Barnes, however, was not by his previous history or temperament the man to submit meekly his own judgment to that of anyone else, or to care much about the embarrassment he might cause anyone by his actions. He was convinced that he had a mission to free Christianity from its accretions, and to present it in such a way that it might be acceptable to young people trained in a scientific age. He returned from Convocation with no thought of resignation in his head. He resigned the bishopric in May 1952 because of ill health.

No memoir of this remarkable man would be complete without some reference to his charm and courtesy as a host in his own house. Many who had formed quite a different idea of the bishop from his public utterances were completely disarmed on closer acquaintance by the gracious atmosphere of Bishop's Croft, to which the presence of his wife—Adelaide, daughter of the historian, Adolphus Ward—contributed an equal share.

November 30, 1953.

Sir George Barnes, who died on September 22, 1960 at the age of 56, combined to a remarkable degree an instinct for cultural activities with a highly developed administrative talent. During his long years in charge of B.B.C. Talks, then as the first Head of the Third Programme, later as Director of Television, and finally as Principal of the University College of North Staffordshire, he put these gifts to significant use.

A man of great charm of manner, he had a wide circle of friends in many fields. But his easiness of approach and his seeming ability to get on terms with almost anyone did not weaken his force of character or his determination, once his mind was made up, to see a thing through. "There is a thin strip of well-tempered steel running through that willowy young man," one of his closest colleagues once said. It was a good description.

George Reginald Barnes was born on September 13, 1904. His father was Sir Hugh Shakespear Barnes, K.C.S.I., K.C.V.O. Barnes was educated at the Royal Naval Colleges at Osborne and Dartmouth and it was his ambition to go into the Navy. He was ultimately rejected because of his sight. This fact remained a regret to him all his life. His interest in naval affairs, although it had to become a hobby, remained undiminished.

When he had to leave Dartmouth he proceeded to King's College, Cambridge. The idea then was that he might try for the Foreign Office, but, when the moment came, he felt the call of the Navy too strong and he returned to the Royal Naval College, Dartmouth, as an assistant master. He stayed there from 1927 to 1930, then joined the Cambridge University Press as assistant secretary.

Those who remember him there would agree that he had not been born with those administrative gifts which he showed in later life. He was in fact a rather untidy worker in those days. But, even then, his will was apparent. And five years later—in 1935—he began the first major part of his career, joining the B.B.C. Talks Department. He stayed with the corporation for 21 years. From the very beginning his work, first as a talks producer and later as Director of Talks, brought him into touch with a wide circle of people. This was further enlarged when he paid his first visit to the United States in 1945.

The American visit was in fact the turning point in his life. He returned with his horizons widened, with a final access of assurance which never deserted him, and with an urge to widen his experience. When the Third Programme was established Barnes was the obvious choice to give the idea practical form. The impact Barnes made on the listening public was immediate. When the programme had been running six months there was a small spate of articles marking its significance. Such a major series of broadcasts as "The Ideas and Beliefs of the Victorians", with its elaborate preliminary research and planning, brought something quite new to broadcasting. (The series was later published as a book). His lifelong devotion to music was given expression in a number of equally ambitious and unconventional music programmes. From the beginning he was determined that the Third Programme should have a character all its own. This he achieved. He had a strong social conscience, which was reflected in his work.

In 1948 Barnes joined the B.B.C. Board of Management as Spoken Word Director; and was put in charge of television in 1950. An aspect of this that pleased him was that it brought him into closer touch with the theatre. Irene and Violet Vanbrugh were his aunts, and Sir Kenneth Barnes [q.v.] his uncle. He was always proud of his stage connexions. In 1953 he had the distinction of being the only man ever to be knighted during a royal visit to the television studios, the Queen conferring the honour on him at Lime Grove in October of that year.

Barnes had never made any secret of the fact that he regarded his work in television as only an interlude. There was never any question of its filling the rest of his life. Nonetheless, it came as a surprise to his friends—and it was a great loss to the B.B.C.—when he resigned from the corporation in 1956 to become Principal of the University College of North Staffordshire at Keele.

The move was, however, part of a pattern that can be traced through Barnes's career. He had started out as a schoolmaster; in B.B.C. talks he had shown a strong educational impulse; one of his main concerns in television had been its proper use in schools. By this time too the administrator in him had become uppermost. He regarded the Keele experiment as a challenge, both in conception and organization. Undoubtedly he missed many of the attractions and amenities of London. But his university career brought him new interests at a vital stage of his life.

Among the bodies on which he served at one time or another were the Council of the Royal College of Art, the British Film Institute, the Standing Commission on Museums and Galleries, the Council of Industrial Design, the Wedgwood Society, and the British Pottery Manufacturers' Federation. Durham conferred a D.C.L. on him in 1956.

In early life Barnes published, with Commander J. H. Owen, four volumes of the *Private Papers of the Fourth Earl of Sandwich.* His friends always urged him to write more. But with his keen interest in music, his passion for sailing, his determination to do a motor tour of France every year, his collecting interests which ranged from Trollope first editions to Wedgwood cream ware, he never had time to write that study of the British Navy in the early nineteenth century which was always a kind of Shangri-la to him.

Barnes married Anne, the daughter of Dr. Henry Bond, who survives him with their only child, a son.

September 23, 1960.

Sir Kenneth Barnes, Principal of the Royal Academy of Dramatic Art, died at Kingston Gorse, Sussex, on October 16, 1957 at the age of 79.

It is doubtful whether in the whole history of the theatre any one man did more to secure sound training for the young actor and actress, and he lived long enough to see a dream of Sir Herbert Tree's brought to full fruition, and to receive the plaudits of everybody who loves the theatre when the academy celebrated its golden jubilee in the summer of 1954.

Kenneth Barnes was born at Exeter on September 11, 1878, the son of Prebendary Reginald Barnes and the brother of two great actresses, Irene and Violet Vanbrugh, who were, in later life, to have much to do with the fortunes of the R.A.D.A. Educated at Westminster School and Christ Church, Oxford, he was for a time in the Civil Service. Later he was engaged in journalism and it was not until 1909 that his association with the academy began. "Mr. Tree's Academy of Dramatic Art" began its work in April 1904 in the dome above His Majesty's Theatre.

Tree admitted that acting could not be taught but he contended that those endowed with the power to act could be taught and his faith was justified. In a few months it became necessary to find separate premises. The venture moved to Gower Street, to a house which Bernard Shaw described as the "Theatre Royal Back Drawing Room." In 1909 Kenneth Barnes was offered at a salary of £250 the task of looking after the academy. He was on a year's probation but he remained there for the rest of his life with the exception of the interruption of the 1914-18 War, when he served with The Hampshire Regiment in India, Mesopotamia and Siberia.

Under Barnes's direction the academy made great strides and the accommodation in Gower Street had to be continually expanded. It was a severe blow when in 1941 its theatre was destroyed by an enemy bomb. Barnes, however, regarded the incident as a great opportunity for further development and plans were soon under consideration for the construction of a larger and better equipped theatre. In November 1952 Queen Elizabeth the Queen Mother laid the foundation-stone of the new building which, by a happy decision, was called the Vanburgh Theatre as a tribute to Barnes's two sisters, who had done so much during their careers both for the stage in general and the R.A.D.A. in particular.

The Queen Mother showed her continued interest in the academy when in May 1954 she attended a special performance at Her Majesty's Theatre to celebrate three occasions: the jubilee of the academy and of Dame Sybil Thorndike's [d. 1976] first stage appearance; and the centenary of the birth of Tree. A prologue by Sir Alan Herbert* was spoken by Dame Edith Evans [d. 1976] and Kenneth Barnes was commemorated in the following lines:—

"But keep a cheer or two for Kenneth
Barnes,
Who should be honoured by a song of
Arne's,
For he insists, in spite of Danny Kaye,
On English spoken in the local way."

Many of the players who took part in the performance had received their stage training at the academy, and the imposing list of those who have passed through its portals showed that the belief both of Tree and of Barnes that such an institution was a vital necessity for the continued welfare of the theatre was fully justified.

In his busy life Barnes found time to write a number of plays, two of which were presented during his military service at Simla. When the Ex-students of the Academy Club was formed in 1921 its first production was his play *Undercurrents,* which dealt with psychoanalysis. When the Partnership Players staged *The Letter of the Law* in 1924 there was quite a family flavour about it, for the author was Barnes and two of the leading players were his sister Violet and his niece Prudence.

Barnes was knighted in 1938. During the 1939-45 War he acted as general secretary of E.N.S.A.

He married in 1925 Daphne, daughter of Sir Richard Graham, Bt. There was a son of the marriage.

October 18, 1957.

Dr. L. D. Barnett, C.B., the eminent oriental scholar and Indian linguist, died on January 28, 1960 at the age of 88.

On August 30, 1959 he celebrated the sixtieth anniversary of his entry into the service of the British Museum and, though he had retired from the Keepership of the Department of Oriental Printed Books and Manuscripts in 1936, he was still active, for he had returned to the museum in 1947 to take charge of its Indian books and manuscripts. He was indeed steadily at work, as an assistant keeper in his old department, until the onset of his last illness in November, and had almost finished a catalogue of Punjabi books.

Lionel David Barnett was born in Liverpool, the son of B. Barnett of that city, on October 21, 1871. He was educated at the High School, Liverpool Institute, Liverpool University and Trinity College, Cambridge. At Cambridge he took both parts of the Classical Tripos in Class I.

Barnett entered the Department of Oriental Printed Books and Manuscripts of the British Museum in 1899 and became Keeper of the Department in 1908. On his retirement he was made C.B. He had a very wide knowledge of oriental languages, especially those of India, and was in fact one of the principal authorities in England on Indian literature. He was Professor of Sanscrit at University College, London, and Lecturer in Indian History at the London School of Oriental Studies, where he was also Librarian from his retirement from the British Museum until 1947.

He translated many oriental texts and published in addition *Hinduism* (1906), *Brahma Knowledge* (1907), and other volumes in "The Wisdom of the East Series" and *Antiquities of India* (1913). He catalogued Sanscrit, Pali, Prakiit, Tamil, Kannada, and other oriental books in the British Museum. Barnett also translated a number of works on Greek and Latin literature and wrote *The Greek Drama* (1900).

With Dr. H. A. Strong he published in 1901 *A Historical Reader of Early French.*

In his own community Barnett was specially interested in Jews' College (the Jewish theological seminary) and the Congregation of Spanish and Portuguese Jews, or Sephardim, of which he was a member by adoption. Of the council and education committee of the former he was for many years an active member. In his synagogue he held at one time or another most of the honorary offices, retiring as Elder and Chairman of the Archives Committee. In the latter capacity he edited two interesting and valuable volumes of selections from the archives.

He was a firm and consistent opponent of Zionism and of everything else that savoured of political Judaism, and as an oriental scholar looked askance at many of the developments of modern or colloquial Hebrew. He was made a Fellow of the British Academy in 1936.

He married Blanche, daughter of the late Rev. B. Berliner, minister of the St. John's Wood Synagogue, and is survived by a son, Dr. Richard Barnett, also a distinguished member of the staff of the British Museum and since 1955 Keeper of the Department of Western Asiatic Antiquities, who has followed him in honorary office in the Spanish and Portuguese Jewish community, and by a daughter.

January 29, 1960.

Don Pío Baroja, one of the great figures of modern Spanish letters, died on October 31, 1956 in Madrid at the age of 83, after a long illness.

It is many years since any moderately well read Spaniard would have thought of disputing Don Pío Baroja's right to be considered the "grand old man" of Spanish letters. He belonged to "the generation of '98," that group of young writers who sought by a kind of patriotic introversion to soothe and restore Spain's national *amour propre* after her bitter defeat by the United States. Baroja's reputation dates therefore from the first quarter of the century. He wrote close on 100 books, but they have long been neglected by the modern reader, and he cannot be said to have found a wide foreign public at any stage of his quietly yet deservedly successful career as a literary artist.

His novels were translated into many languages, but their titles are as unfamiliar to the present generation outside Spain as the author's name itself, which is as famous on the other hand, among his fellow countrymen as those of Palacio Valdés, Benavente [q.v.], Blasco Ibáñez or Azorín. In the company of his contemporaries Baroja's eminence was taken for granted, and he ranks to this day above all other Spanish prose-writers since Galdós (1843-1920), for he survived or must be held to have surpassed in stature such rivals as Pardo Bazán, Pérez Lugín, Valle-Inclán, León, Espina, Ayala, and Fernández Flórez.

Critics have sometimes reproved him for the ruggedness of his style, but none would deny him humour, humanity, observation and narrative skill. Nor is it possible to overlook the rebellious temperament disclosed, with lively imagination, in his earlier books.

"I have battled with the language as best I might," he confessed on the threshold of his eightieth year, "always trying to avoid the stock phrase and the ready-made idea. The first essential of style is efficiency; you go in for elegance afterwards, if you can manage it." A voracious reader, he modelled himself, by his own admission, on Dickens, Poe, Balzac, Stendhal, Turgenev, and Dostoevsky. In his youth he travelled widely in Spain and visited France, England, and Italy, in order to absorb impressions that are reflected in some of his novels.

Pío Baroja Nessi was born on December 28, 1872, at San Sebastian. His father was the author of the first Basque opera and of popular songs in the Basque language. The young Baroja studied medicine at Valencia and took a medical degree in Madrid at the age of 21. Returning to his native province, he set up a practice at Cestona, but tired of it very soon and moved back to the capital, where he earned his living for a while as a painter and engraver, when he was not engaged in business or managing a bakery in partnership with his brother Ricardo, who died in 1953 and was well known as a painter and etcher. He also began contributing assiduously to various newspapers, and in 1900, at the age of 28, having abandoned the medical profession, he published his first collection of short stories, which he entitled *Vidas sombrias (Dark Lives).* Among his best-known novels are *Zalacaín el aventurero, Idilios vascos, La cuidad de la niebla, Las inquietudes de Shanti Andia, La dama errante, Mala hierba, Paradox Rey, El árbol de la ciencia,* and the historical series entitled *Memorias de un hombre de acción,* in 17 volumes. His own memoirs, also published by instalments, bear the title, *From the Last Bend in the Road (Desda la última vuelta del camino).*

The outbreak of the civil war surprised Don Pío in Navarre. In the previous year, 1935, he had been elected a member of the Spanish Royal Academy. He spent some months in Paris, returning to Spain in 1937, and again in 1940, after another sojourn in France. He was regarded with uneasiness bordering on suspicion by the hotheads of the new régime; but lask of appreciation never disturbed the old man's peace of mind. He was a stubborn, uncompromising Basque, who had seen many changes in his day. But that was long ago, and it would come again, for his work was behind him and with Basque pride he believed, with more than a little justification, that his name would live on while the Spanish language is spoken and read.

November 1, 1956.

Sir Lancelot Barrington-Ward, K.C.V.O., F.R.C.S., Surgeon to King George VI for the whole of his reign, and since then Surgeon to the Queen, died on November 17, 1953 at his home near Bury St. Edmunds, Suffolk, at the age of 69.

He earned an international reputation by his attainments in the profession of surgery and particularly by his work for children. Appointed as a young man to be a house surgeon at the Hospital for Sick Children, Great Ormond Street, his work came at a time when the special surgery of childhood was attracting some of the giants of surgery and, as a distinguished pupil of some of these pioneers, he himself eventually became a distinguished teacher. His success as a children's specialist was due not only to the ability, knowledge, and skill he concentrated upon his patients but also to the possession of that "way with children" which is an essential for the children's specialist. Gentle and infinitely patient in his dealings with little sufferers, meticulous in diagnosis, and masterly in treatment, he was rewarded by an unusual measure of trust and affection. In regard to his adult patients he exhibited a similar sensitiveness and understanding, with the result that those who had once turned to him in illness or anxiety continued to entertain the warmest feelings towards him. He was indeed a remarkable and many-sided man, who in his young days had been an outstanding player of Rugby football.

Lancelot Edward Barrington-Ward was born at Worcester on July 4, 1884, second son of the late Canon M. J. Barrington-Ward, D.D., and one of a family of five sons, all of whom were to make their mark in their respective callings. He was educated at Westminster and at Bromsgrove, at both of which he was a classical scholar, and later was a classical exhibitioner at Worcester College, Oxford. Having decided upon a medical career he went to Edinburgh University, where in 1908 he received the degrees of M.B. and Ch.B. with honours. At the University he attained distinction also as a first-class Rugby footballer, played for it in six seasons, and was captain of the XV in 1908. He also represented England in four Rugby Internationals.

In 1910 he became a F.R.C.S., Edinburgh, and in 1912 a F.R.C.S., England. He secured his Ch.M. at Edinburgh, again with honours, in 1913, and in the same year was awarded the Chiene Medal in Surgery. He also studied at the Middlesex Hospital.

In 1910 Barrington-Ward's appointment as house surgeon at the Hospital for Sick Children inaugurated a connexion with Great Ormond Street, which was to last the whole of his career and eventually to be crowned by his appointment as its senior surgeon. In December 1914 he became a member of its surgical staff, but interrupted his duties in order to act as surgeon-in-chief of Lady Wimborne's Hospital at Uskub in Serbia. For his services at this period he was awarded the Grand Cross of St. Olav and the Order of St. Sava. After his return to his own country he found himself in a rapidly growing practice which was not confined to the treatment of children, for an appointment to the staff of the Royal Northern Hospital enabled him to do important and brilliant work among adult patients as well.

He was interested especially in abdominal surgery and his *Abdominal Surgery of Children* became a standard book. He also edited and wrote much of *Royal Northern Operative Surgery* and made a number of contributions to various surgical journals. In 1935 he was created a K.C.V.O., and in the following year was appointed Surgeon to King George VI [q.v.], on whom he had performed an operation for appendicitis as far back as 1918. He performed similar operations on Princess Margaret and Princess Alexandra of Kent. He became senior surgeon to the Royal Northern Hospital, consulting surgeon at Wood Green Hospital and Sutton Hospital, and was a Fellow of the Royal Society of Medicine, and an ex-president of its section on the diseases of children. In 1952 he became Hunterian Professor at the Royal College of Surgeons of England.

In 1917 he married Dorothy Anne, second daughter of the late T. W. Miles. A vital and attractive woman, she did valuable work for Great Ormond Street Hospital and the Peter Pan League. She died in 1935, leaving him with three daughters. In 1941 he married as his second wife Catherine, only daughter of the late E. G. Reuter, of Harrogate, who survives him together with a son of the marriage.

November 18, 1953.

Ethel Barrymore, the stage and film actress, died in Hollywood, at the age of 79, on June 18, 1959. Her long triumphant career on the American stage was preceded by a brief but romantic descent upon London.

She was born at Philadelphia on August 15, 1879. With her elder brother, Lionel [q.v.], and her younger brother, John, she came on the mother's side of two very old theatrical families, the Lanes and the Drews. Her mother, Georgie Drew, sister of the eminent actor, John Drew, the younger, married an Irishman named Blythe, who acted with Modjeska and others under the name of Maurice Barrymore.

Born on the stage, as the players say, Ethel Barrymore made her first public appearance at the age of 14, playing Julia in *The Rivals* at the Empire Theatre, New York. Then her uncle, John Drew, took her up and by 1897 she was actress enough to be brought to London by William Gillette in *Secret Service.*

With her full share of the Barrymore-Drew good looks, and a full share also of their adventurous high spirits, she was soon the talk of the town. Sir Henry Irving, entreated by his son Laurence, who had fallen in love with her, took her on tour in *The Bells* and also engaged her for the Lyceum production early in 1898 of Laurence's play *Peter the Great.* Rehearsing and wooing at the same time Laurence became engaged to her, but neither the play nor the engagement lasted long.

Also in that memorable season Ethel Barrymore became engaged to Gerald du Maurier. She accompanied him on a fishing holiday he was taking with two friends at Waterville in Kerry, and there that engagement too was broken off. She returned to America towards the end of 1898, preceded by news of her betrothal to a duke, an earl, an Indian prince. Though her social life in London had not been quite as eventful as that, her success had been as brilliant in the salons as on the stage, as she recalled with vivacious enjoyment in her *Memories,* published in 1956.

After her return to New York, she was chosen by Charles Frohman in 1901 for his leading lady, and thus began a long career of success and popularity, during which she appeared in many of the great parts in the repertory of English and American old and modern comedy, and acted also Juliet, Ophelia (to the Hamlet of Walter Hampden) and Marguerite Gautier.

London, which hugged its memories, saw all too little of her. In 1904 she was over to act in Hubert Henry Davies's play *Cynthia* (her cousin Kate in Davies's play of that name was one of her most charming impersonations); and in 1934 at the Palladium she acted in Barrie's *The Twelve-Pound Look.* But New York, where she opened her own Ethel Barrymore Theatre in 1928, may well be excused for being reluctant to spare so much beauty, charm and talent.

Her work in films began in 1914, and when she had overcome her initial dislike of the medium she was much admired in many successful films. She played with her two brothers in *Rasputin and the Empress,* and she won an Academy award in 1944 for her supporting role in *None But the Lonely Heart.*

Her marriage to Russell Griswold Colt, of

which there were three children, was dissolved in 1923.

June 19, 1959.

Lionel Barrymore, the veteran actor, died in hospital at Hollywood, California, on November 15, 1954, at the age of 76.

To the present generation he was known simply as a film star, not only in Britain but also in his native America. He had been, however, an actor of more than average ability in the legitimate theatre with many striking successes to his credit before his last stage appearance in 1925. He was a powerful actor in many parts and his performance of Macbeth gained him considerable kudos.

He was born at Philadelphia on April 28, 1878, the eldest child of the British-born actor Maurice Barrymore, who was well known on the London stage for several years. His mother was Georgie Drew, daughter of the Irish-born actor-manager John Drew the elder, by his wife Louisa Lane, for many years the "grand old lady" of the American stage. He received his early education in London and made his first appearance at the old Fourteenth Street Theatre, New York, in December 1893 in a small part in *The Road to Ruin,* in his grandmother's company.

For some years he appeared in a series of melodramas which were popular at the period, such as Augustus Thomas's *Arizona,* J. A. Herne's *Sag Harbor,* &c., and in 1901-02 he was a member of Charles Frohman's company in *The Second in Command* and *The Mummy and the Humming Bird.* In 1905 he played Pantaloon in Barrie's play of that name, after which he was absent from the stage for some years owing to ill-health. In 1917 he made a notable impression as Colonel Ibbetson in a dramatization by John N. Raphael of George du Maurier's novel *Peter Ibbetson,* in which his famous younger brother, John Barrymore (who died in 1942), played the title-role.

In 1918 he had further success when he played the leading part in Augustus Thomas's drama *The Copperhead,* followed, a year later, by a striking performance in *The Jest,* in which he shared the honours with his brother John. It was in 1921, at the Apollo, New York, that he played Macbeth. Other successful parts he undertook were in *The Claw* (1921) and *Laugh, Clown, Laugh* (1923). His last performance on the New York stage was in the part of Nicholas Snyders in *Man or Devil* at the Broadhurst Theatre in 1925.

Barrymore began his career in films as far back as 1909, in the "silent" days, when he acted in innumerable pictures for the old Biograph company. His first screen appearance was in *Friends,* a D. W. Griffith production. He appeared, intermittently, in films from 1915 to 1925, and since that date had devoted himself exclusively to that medium. His great experience on the stage stood him in good stead when "talking" pictures came in, and he produced the first outstanding "sound" film—*Madame X.* Later he directed *The Rogue Song* in which Lawrence Tibbett achieved instant fame, and, although he was to have directed Norma Shearer in *A Free Soul,* he became so interested in the dramatic part of the father that he played it himself. As a result he was awarded the "Oscar", the Academy award for the best screen performance of 1931. Seven years later he was awarded the Speech Arts Medal.

Notable films in which he acted were *Grand Hotel, Rasputin and the Empress* (with John and Ethel Barrymore [q.v.], his sister, who survives him), *Christopher Bean, Treasure Island, Guilty Hands, David Copperfield, Captains Courageous, Test Pilot, A Yank at Oxford, You Can't Take it With You, A Guy Named Joe,* and, more recently, *Duel in the Sun* and *Down to the Sea in Ships.* One of his greatest successes was the part of Dr. Gillespie in the *Dr. Kildare* series of films.

He was the author of two books, a novel and a history of the Barrymore family, and in later years, when crippled by arthritis, he devoted much of his time to etching—he had studied art in Paris while young—and composing. Some of his music, including a symphony, was performed by British and American orchestras.

He was twice married. His first marriage, to Miss Doris Rankin, a well-known actress, the daughter of Mr. McKee Rankin, was dissolved, and he later married Miss Irene Fenwick, also an accomplished actress. She died in 1936.

November 17, 1954.

Sir Charles Bartlett, managing director of Vauxhall Motors for 23 years and chairman from 1953 until December 1954, died at his home near Harpenden, Hertfordshire on August 10, 1955 at the age of 65.

A Gloucestershire man, Charles John Bartlett was born on December 12, 1889, and left the village school at the age of 12 to work in a bicycle shop. He did not enjoy his work there and decided to take up gardening, studying books on the subject, bought with his hard-earned pennies, and visiting the gardens in the neighbourhood to get practical experience. Then came the outbreak of war in 1914, and the wound he received at Loos compelled him to abandon his early ambition to lead an outdoor life.

After his discharge from the Army he joined the London office of General Motors Ltd., the English subsidiary of the General Motors Corporation of America, as a clerk, and in six years he had risen to be managing director of that company. He was appointed managing director of Vauxhall Motors in 1930, when the company's 2,000 employees were producing 1,400 vehicles a year in a factory with a floor space of 11 acres. When he retired there were 14,500 employees producing 130,000 vehicles a year in a factory covering 85 acres.

A career of such distinguished service, of such success from small beginnings, and with the handicap of the prolonged after-effects of a severe wound is notable. It might augur a ruthless determination merely to get to the top. In Bartlett's case there certainly was determination and an immense capacity for hard work over long hours. He expected others to work, too. Nevertheless, the excellent labour relations in the factory at Luton bear witness to his enlightened approach to the human problems arising in all factories in which most of the work must be dully repetitive. He was untiring in his efforts to create a better understanding of these problems, and his concern for the well-being of his company's workpeople was deep and strong.

Though his main interest was necessarily in the manufacture of motor vehicles, his early love of horticulture persisted throughout his life, as did his interest in many country sports. He was a Fellow of the Royal Society of Arts, a Deputy Lieutenant for Bedfordshire, and a past-President of the Royal Society for the Prevention of Accidents. In 1944 he was knighted in recognition of his own and his company's contribution to the war effort.

He married in 1925 Emily May, daughter of Henry Pincombe, of Arlington, Devon, who survives him.

August 11, 1955.

W. J. Bassett-Lowke, the founder of the famous firm of model makers, of Northampton and High Holborn, died on October 21, 1953 at the age of 76.

Wenman Joseph Bassett-Lowke was born in 1877 at Northampton. Engineering was in his blood. His grandfather established the engineering and boiler-making business of Bassett and Sons in Northampton in 1859. His father was also an engineer and it was while he was apprenticed to his father's works of J. T. Lowke and Sons that the firm of Bassett-Lowke took shape. Frustrated by the difficulties of getting well-designed components to meet his model-making needs, he decided to produce them for himself and for others faced with the same problem.

In this he was helped by his father and by his friend, H. F. R. Franklin. They advertised in the *Model Engineer,* then just established. A mail order business sprang up and the firm of Bassett-Lowke was born. The first of the famous catalogues was issued in 1899. Since then his models of railways, ships, and engineering equipment, many of them exquisite replicas of their prototypes, have become world famous.

Bassett-Lowke was a director and one of the founders of the Northampton Repertory Theatre, and since his election as a member of the Northampton Town Council in 1930 he played a prominent part in municipal activities. He retired from the council in 1952, after having been an alderman for seven years.

October 23, 1953.

Daisy Bates, C.B.E., famous for her life-long work among the Australian aborigines, died in Adelaide on April 19, 1951 at the age of 90.

Born in 1861 of Irish parentage, she was engaged in journalism in London before going out to Western Australia in 1899, partly in connexion with a pastoral lease in which she was interested and partly to investigate charges of white cruelty towards the natives, which were eventually found to have been made through a misunderstanding of native needs. Having reached her destination, she remained to become the devoted friend of the aborigines and lived among them as a solitary European for 35 years. In the days of early railway construction she made her own way along the shores of the Great Australian Bight and then settled at Ooldea, where she pitched her tent and spent a number of years.

The labours which Daisy Bates thus undertook were sustained by no faith in the future of the race she sought to serve. She realized that what she called "this last remnant of palaeolithic man" was doomed, but she determined that as far as she could she would make its passing easier. Her sustained efforts were not, however, without reward. The aborigines realized she was their friend. They talked to her as they would to no other, and even admitted her to their tribal rites from some of which their own women were excluded on pain of death. Thus she became known among them as their *Kabbarli* or grandmother.

In time she accumulated a unique store of knowledge and collected a mass of material which she presented to the archives at Canberra. Her efforts to help the aborigines absorbed her intensely until 1935 when, refusing all invitations to live with admiring friends, she left Ooldea for a camp on the Murray River in order, while still doing what she could for her former charges, to sort and prepare her great collection of notes.

In 1939 her book *The Passing of the Aborigines* was published and received favourable mention in *The Times.* Its final verdict was that "among these decadents to-day no anthropological study of social laws is necessary; only the administration of British rule founded on our highest and best traditions." Above all else she believed in the British character.

In 1945 she collapsed and was taken to hospital and as a result she had to retire from the active life among the aborigines to which she had dedicated herself. She was said to have had an unequalled knowledge of native dialects and was an expert on every branch of bush lore. In 1933 she was made a C.B.E.

April 20, 1951.

Charles Bathurst—See **Bledisloe.**

Harry Batsford, chairman and managing director of Messrs. B. T. Batsford, the well-known publishers, died suddenly in London at the age of 71 on December 20, 1951.

He was the only son of Henry George Batsford and grandson of the founder of the business, Bradley Thomas Batsford, and was born on April 18, 1880. He entered the family business just before the turn of the century and in 1917 succeeded his uncle, Herbert Batsford, as chairman and managing director.

The firm had earlier established a considerable reputation for beauty of printing and illustration and under Harry Batsford this was greatly enhanced. The reproductions of architectural compositions have always been of a particularly high standard and they have in most cases been accompanied by well-written and informative texts. Batsford's work in this field was recognized in 1926 by his election as honorary A.R.I.B.A.

He was himself the author of many of the books published by the firm, among them *How to See the Country; London: Work and Play; London: Historic Buildings;* and he also collaborated with Charles Fry in *The Cathedrals of England, The Greater English Church, The Parish Churches of England, The English Cottage, The Face of Scotland,* and *The Face of Ireland.*

His knowledge of English architecture and the English countryside was extensive. This knowledge has been recognized almost without exception by all the authors whose books were published by the firm, who frequently mentioned their indebtedness to him in their prefaces. He had travelled extensively by foot, bicycle, and car all over the British Isles. His knowledge of English villages, parish churches, and country houses was unsurpassed and surprised all the experts with whom he came into contact.

Largely under his guidance and direction the term "a Batsford book" became a household word in the book trade, and during his period of office the policy of the firm changed from that of a specialized architectural publisher to one of a more general and popular list, without, with the exception of the war years, any deterioration in the standard of production.

December 21, 1951.

Gaston Baty, whose ingenious and imaginative stage settings of the French classics and of his own adaptations of foreign and indigenous works will be remembered, died at Pélussin, near Saint-Etienne, on October 13, 1952.

He was born in 1885, near Saint-Etienne, and was educated at the Dominican College at Oullins, near Lyons, and afterwards at Munich, where he intended to study the history of art, but turned to the theatre and worked under Fritz Erler* and Max Reinhardt.

On his return to France shortly before the war of 1914-18 he made the acquaintance of Firmin Gémier, with whom, in 1919, he produced *La Grande Pastorale* at the Cirque d'Hiver and, in 1920, Saint-Georges de Bouhélier's *Les Esclaves* at the Théâtre des Arts and Shaw's *Arms and the Man,* Shakespeare's *Taming of the Shrew,* and Lenormand's *Le Simoun* at the Comédie des Champs-Elysées. When Gémier was appointed director at the Odéon in 1921 Baty founded his own company, "Les Compagnons de la Chimère," which for three years published its own magazine.

In 1924 he became director of the tiny Studio des Champs-Elysées and there, with the production of Jean-Victor Pellerin's *Têtes de Rechange* and the great success of Simon Gantillon's *Maya,* he established his reputation as a producer of unusual plays. He continued his success at the Théâtre de l'Avenue with Gantillon's *Départs* (1929); and, from 1931 onwards, at the Théâtre Montparnasse, with his own adaptations from Flaubert (*Madame Bovary,* 1936), Dostoevsky (*Crime et Châtiment,* 1933), and Cervantes (*Dulcinée,* 1938).

In 1921 Baty founded and edited a little theatrical review called *Masques,* which ran for several years, and in 1922 he expounded his ideas on the theatre in a book called *Le Masque et l'Encensoir.* In 1928 he brought out another book, called *Visage de Shakespeare.*

His interpretations of French classics were often severely criticized. He presented *Le Malade Imaginaire* (1929) as a farce which ended in tragedy—the death of Molière. He transposed the *Caprices de Marianne* (1936) into a nineteenth-century setting, with interludes of eighteenth-century carnival. His production of Labiche's *Un Chapeau de Paille d'Italie* at the Comédie Française (1938) was attacked as a betrayal of the spirit of French farce. Yet his stage pictures linger in one's mind—the fearful shadows of the doctors on the walls of the Imaginary Invalid's room, the cemetery in *Les Caprices de Marianne,* the magnificent *salon* in Labiche's farce. There are others, too—the Rembrandtesque interiors of *Le Dibbouk,* the dazzling African whiteness of the Casbah scenes in *Prosper* (1934), the theatre-box in *Madame Bovary,* the opening scene of the towering Atlantic liner at the quayside in *Départs,* the sinister staircase in *Crime et Châtiment.*

October 15, 1952.

Vicki Baum, the novelist, and author of the best-seller *Grand Hotel,* died in Hollywood on August 29, 1960. She was 64.

As a writer Vicki Baum was never pretentious, but was thorough, workmanlike and, above all, a superb story-teller. She was widely travelled, completely cosmopolitan in outlook, and could transmute what she saw, heard and suspected into novels of strong plot, meticulous and accurate detail and dramatic content.

She was born in Vienna on January 24, 1896, the daughter of Herman and Matilda Baum. She was educated at the High School of Music in her native city and married Richard Lert, the conductor. In 1930 *Grand Hotel,* excellently translated from its original German by Basil Creighton—she was always fortunate in this respect—reached the English reader. It was a remarkable book, the study of a number of human beings who at the same moment were guests in a large and luxurious hotel in Berlin. The authoress, handling a complex plot, showed that she possessed skill of a high order. She also exercised a remarkable power of description. A year later the story, adapted for the English stage by Edward Knoblock, was lavishly and efficiently produced at the Adelphi Theatre.

The overall success of the book—a best-seller of the century in every sense—was enormous; it was a Book Society choice on both sides of the Atlantic, produced by Max Reinhardt and the New York Theatre Guild and made into a film by M.G.M., who fielded for the occasion two Barrymores [q.v.], Greta Garbo, Joan Crawford [d. 1977], and Wallace Beery.

Vicki Baum went to the United States in 1931 to see the dramatized version of *Grand Hotel*, intending to stay two weeks, but she fell in love with the country, took her family over from Europe, and settled in California to become an American citizen.

She continued to write a novel almost every year up to the Second World War; *Results of an Accident; Martin's Summer; Secret Sentence; A Tale from Bali;* none was less than competent; none attained the success of *Grand Hotel.* But *Nanking Road* drew out the best that was in her. A story of modern China, it was shrewd, exciting, ironically humane, and a delicate commentary on the values of western civilization from a standpoint as near to the Confucian as the author could attain.

In *Marion Alive* in 1943 she essayed another long novel which proved as absorbing as any of its predecessors. It traced the story of a woman from her childhood in Vienna, through London, New York, Nazi Germany and Vienna, and ended in Switzerland. Long, like *Nanking Road,* but extremely accomplished; larger than life perhaps, but how many stories worth reading are not?

Of her later novels perhaps the best were *The Weeping Wood* and *Ballerina*—which came out in 1958 and gave Vicki Baum an excellent opportunity to describe the birth of a ballet.

Though she loved America she told a recent visitor from England: "The longer I am away from Europe the more European I feel". Probably, as a true writer, who was modest about her talent, she felt both at ease everywhere, and so never thoroughly at home in any place.

August 31, 1960.

Sir Arnold Bax, K.C.V.O., the Master of the Queen's Musick, who died on October 3, 1953, was not only a prolific composer in all forms of music except opera, but a good writer who, while associated with the literary group of Irish writers, including his brother, Clifford Bax*, in Dublin at the turn of the century, wrote short stories and novels, as he relates in his autobiography, *Farewell my Youth.* He would have been 70 in another month.

Arnold Edward Trevor Bax was born in London on November 8, 1883 and the Celtic streak in his artistic personality was a matter of environment rather than heredity, but the romanticism which informed all his music and made him something of a Bohemian in character was congenital. Indeed, it was a matter of some surprise that he accepted official honours and appointments for which he was not temperamentally fitted. He contrived to avoid the university and spent instead five years at the Royal Academy of Music, where he studied composition with Frederick Corder.

The refusal of discipline and the hostility which he showed to his pastors and masters—we have his own words for it—ultimately damaged his art, since the luxuriance of his imagination was never wholly controlled to the point of its most effective expression. His seven symphonies, which are a testimony to the fertility of his talent and the power of his imagination, fail to clinch their own argument because they protest too much and too long and to the casual ear they are too rhapsodic, but closer study reveals that they are concerned with issues proper to symphonic treatment. The first, in E flat (1922), sets out its problems starkly enough and the two following symphonies seem to be devoted to their resolution. The fourth is more cheerful and owes its inspiration to the sea, the fifth deals with legend and is his best symphony, approached most nearly by No. 7 (1938), in which also there is much sheer romantic beauty inspired by nature.

The symphonies were heralded by a series of orchestral tone-poems in which Bax first found his freedom from the influences of Wagner and Strauss which had weighed upon his earlier work, subsequently destroyed. In "In the Faery Hills" (1909), the first of many works inspired by legend, he achieved his mature style and followed it up with "Tintagel," his best known work, "The Garden of Fand," "November Woods," and "Mediterranean," all of which reflect his personal vein of romanticism in rich and fully saturated orchestral tone.

His liking for richness of colour and texture did not however ward him off from chamber music—on the contrary he was attracted to it precisely by the problems of colour and texture which it presents. He tackled these problems by employing novel combinations of instruments, as for example in the sonata for harp and viola, the nonet for strings, wood-wind and harp, and the quintet for oboe and strings. He also used the more conventional forms, including the string quartet and the piano sonata. He was a prolific writer of songs, but his tendency to elaboration impedes their lyrical impulse. For a short time he wrote choral music, where the two tendencies that are at war in the songs come together with the happiest results in the motet "Mater ora filium," a splendid piece of modern polyphony. Two choral works with orchestra, both short, are "St. Patrick's Breastplate" (1924) and "The Morning Watch" written for the Three Choirs Festival of 1935.

Bax received the Beethoven Gold Medal of the Royal Philharmonic Society in 1931 and was made an honorary Doctor of Music at Oxford in 1934 and at Durham in 1935; he was knighted in 1937. In 1942 he succeeded Sir Walford Davies as Master of the King's Musick, and of the Queen's Musick in 1952. It was not a good appointment, since although it has unprescribed duties the office ought not to be regarded as a sinecure or an honour but rather as an official position. Bax was not cut out for official duties and found their performance irksome. Yet during his time in office he composed the march for Malta, G.C., which was played at the funeral of King George VI [q.v.], trumpet fanfares for the wedding ceremony of the Queen and the Duke of Edinburgh, and a special march for the Coronation, which was played immediately after the National Anthem had been sung.

October 5, 1953.

Walter Bayes, R.W.S., the painter and writer on artistic subjects, who was a founder member of the Camden Town group, died on January 21, 1956 at his home at Hampstead. He was 88.

It might be an overstatement to say that Bayes was too intellectual for a painter, but it is certainly true to say that he excelled in what has been called the science of picture making, including perspective and the proportioning and balancing of colour. He was an academic artist in the sense in which the French rather than the English would understand the description, and his artistic ancestor was Poussin. This character, while it left Bayes's own work rather cold and dry in feeling, made him an admirable teacher and critic of art. His influence, in matters of construction rather than of execution, can be traced in the work of several contemporary artists who were trained under him at the Westminster School of Art; and his writings in the old *Athenaeum,* of which he was art critic from 1906 to 1916, afterwards holding the same position on the *Saturday Review,* were among the most fundamental of his time.

Bayes was a son of A. W. Bayes, painter and etcher, and brother of Gilbert Bayes, the sculptor, and Jessie Bayes, the illuminator and decorative designer. Educated at University College School, he studied art at evening classes only, except for three months at the Westminster School of Art. In one book of reference Bayes was described as "painter and decorator of buildings and theatrical scenery," and the description covers his more characteristic activities. Interesting examples of his decorative work are to be found in the Regent Cinema Theatre, Brighton, where, about 1919, he collaborated with the architect. His "The Underworld," a large painting of East Londoners, sheltering from an air-raid in a Tube station, exhibited in the Academy of 1918, was bought for the Imperial War Museum, where he is also represented by a design for tapestry of "Survivors from a Torpedoed Ship." His work is also represented in the Tate Gallery and in public galleries at Liverpool, Manchester, Dublin, and Johannesburg.

He was a fairly regular exhibitor at the Royal Academy of both figure subjects and landscapes, mostly painted in the South of France. Among the more important were "The Ford," 1917, purchased out of the Chantrey Bequest Fund for the Tate Gallery; "Pulvis et Umbra," 1919; "Oratio Obliqua," 1920; "Les Jeux sont faits," 1925; "Evening with Canaletto," the central group of a large composition executed for the Oxford Cinema, 1936; and "Martigues," 1938. The title of "Lilac and Gold," exhibited in 1940, gives a hint of Bayes's taste in colour, the general tonality of his pictures recalling Poussin, whom he resembled in other respects. His figure subjects often had a characteristically sardonic flavour.

Slightly grim and cynical at first acquaintance, Bayes quickly became friendly and communicative to anybody he found to be seriously interested in art. It pleased him to pose as a disappointed man, and in the preface to the catalogue of an exhibition of his works at the Leger Galleries in 1934 he described himself as an "amateur"—which was true only in so far as easel pictures might be regarded as leisure products of one of the most professional of artists in his own field of mural decoration. He had highly developed ideas about the relationship between painting and architecture, and for a time he taught mural decoration at the school of the Architectural Association. He also lectured on perspective for a period of years at the Royal Academy of Arts and the Slade School. His period as head of the Westminster Art School was from 1918 to 1934; and later, from 1944 to 1949, he was director of the painting school of the Lancaster School of Arts and Crafts. He was also for some years principal examiner in drawing and painting to the Board of Education.

As a writer on art Bayes was both sound and witty. Besides his contributions to periodicals, including the *Architectural Review*, he published at least three books: *The Art of Decorative Painting*, in 1927; *A Painter's Baggage*, illustrated with brilliant pen drawings, in 1932; and *Turner, a Speculative Portrait*, in 1931. The last, which is preoccupied with Turner's love affairs, real or supposed, and periodical disappearances from respectable society, is thoroughly characteristic of Bayes's ironical attitude to life.

He married in 1904 Miss Katherine Teller, and had two sons.

January 23, 1956.

Sir William Beach Thomas—See **Thomas.**

Michael Beary, who died in hospital in London on October 8, 1956 at the age of 60, was one of the most stylish riders of the century and had great success between the two wars.

It was his misfortune that his Irish temperament did not adjust itself to caution in financial matters in the years when he was at the top. In the saddle it was a different matter, for there he had rare judgment and the coolest head. His riding was not all professional, and he was often seen going with the best out hunting on winter days when his brother jockeys were holidaymaking in sunnier countries. The disappearance of his lean, trim figure from the racecourse means that another remarkable character has gone.

Born in co. Tipperary in December 1895, he rode his first winner, Hainesby, at Bath in May 1913, but he was still riding in 1955; and in December 1954, he had a mount over hurdles for the first time since before the war.

In 1954 he rode his last winners on the flat. After an interval of training, in which he prepared the winner of the 2,000 Guineas in 1951, Ki Ming, he had returned to the saddle to take the ride on Victory Roll in the Derby of 1953, but finished unplaced. He gained his only Derby success in 1937, on Mrs. G. B. Miller's Mid-Day Sun, the first Epsom Derby to go to a woman owner.

He won three other English "classic" races: on Udaipur in the Oaks of 1932; on Trigo in the St. Leger of 1929; and on Ridge Wood in the same race 20 years later. In the 1956 season he had been training a few horses at Stockbridge, Hampshire, and won two races with Boerchalke.

Apart from his "classic" wins he will always be remembered for the great race he rode on Lord Coventry's filly Verdict to snatch the Cambridgeshire of 1923 by a neck from the French champion, Epinard. He gained a Cesarewitch success in 1930 on the Aga Khan's [q.v.] good stayer, Udaipur, and on an even better stayer, Brown Jack, he won the Chester Cup in 1931. He had many other handicap successes and rode several Irish "classic" winners. He could have ridden Trigo and Blenheim, both Derby winners, but chose the wrong mounts in these races.

He was injured several times, twice had his licence withdrawn for a short period, and was bankrupt three times, but he always came back smiling.

Like Steve Donoghue, he modelled his style on the great Danny Maher, and he had a most persuasive way with two-year-olds.

It was Donoghue who really gave him his start, for when Beary was apprenticed to "Atty" Persse [q.v.] he wanted to ride Hainesby at Bath, but was refused permission to leave the Stockbridge stables by the head lad. Donoghue smuggled him away in his car, took him to the course, and Beary rode his first winner, in such dashing style that other mounts soon followed.

October 10, 1956.

Sidney Bechet, the jazz musician, died in Paris on May 14, 1959, his sixty-second birthday.

Sidney Bechet was one of the most notable survivors from the almost legendary golden age of New Orleans jazz. He was born in New Orleans on May 14, 1897, the seventh child of a negro shoemaker, and was very early attracted to music-making, practising secretly on a clarinet borrowed from his brother. His mother encouraged his interest and bought him his own clarinet, on which he proceeded to teach himself to such effect that he was playing in public by the time he was 10, and the next year deputized for George Baquet in the celebrated Olympia Band. His (self-taught) fingering was, and remained, eccentric, but his technique on the clarinet was already formidable, and soon he had formed the tiny Silver Bell band which also included two of his brothers, before he was persuaded to join the Eagle Band, one of the great bands of New Orleans between 1911 and 1914.

He did a variety of jobs during his early years, including a vaudeville act in which he took his clarinet to pieces while playing it, and periods in New Orleans with King Oliver and in Chicago with Eddy Venson; and in 1919 he visited Europe for the first time, touring with Will Marion Cook—at which period he first took up the soprano saxophone, subsequently his favoured instrument, though he continued all through his career to play the clarinet as well.

Though he returned to America in 1923, Europe, and especially France, held ever afterwards a great attraction for him; he was in Paris with Noble Sissle's band from 1925 to 1930, when he returned with the band to America and stayed with it until 1938; some of his best recordings date from this period, especially those made in 1932 with a recording group, of which he was the guiding light, called the New Orleans Footwarmers.

During the late 1930s and the war years his fame, along with the popularity of the "classical" jazz style he represented, suffered something of an eclipse, but with the great revival of New Orleans jazz after the war he at once regained his pre-eminent position, settling in Paris in 1949 and thereafter visiting the United States only fairly infrequently. His last appearance in Britain was at a triumphant concert at the Albert Hall in 1956.

Sidney Bechet was often called "the poet of jazz," and this is a fair description of much of his work, especially on the clarinet, but it does not perhaps suggest the tremendous energy and attack which characterized most of his best work, or his endless fund of melodic invention.

His rich and subtle *vibrato* playing can be well appreciated in some of his recorded clarinet numbers, notably *Blues in Thirds* and *Kansas City Man Blues,* but one must turn to his classic saxophone work to enjoy fully his vigorous drive and the nervous energy of his playing, with its clear outlines and incisive attack. Happily, there exist some superlative recordings of his artistry on both instruments, and his influence is noticeable in the work of some prominent jazz-men of the younger generation, but his highly personal gifts will be sadly missed from the contemporary jazz scene.

May 15, 1959.

In the early and sudden death of **Diana Beck** on March 3, 1956 after an operation, medicine lost a distinguished brain surgeon. A wide circle of friends, colleagues, and patients were deprived of one whose generosity, skill, and devotion will ever be remembered.

Of Scottish descent, Diana Jean Kinloch Beck was born at Chester on June 29, 1902, and received her schooling at the Queen's School there. She then proceeded to the London School of Medicine for Women (the Royal Free Hospital) where after graduation she soon displayed a flair for surgery and undergraduate teaching. Her election as F.R.C.S., Edinburgh, in 1930 and F.R.C.S., England, in

1931 confirms her status as a surgeon. Though an accomplished general surgeon she decided shortly before the last war to specialize in neuro-surgery and was trained for this at Oxford by the late Sir Hugh Cairns [q.v.].

The outbreak of war prolonged her stay there, and some years were spent in general surgery and the care of military cases, with the addition of research and the teaching of undergraduate students in the newly established school at the Radcliffe Infirmary. In 1943 she was appointed consultant neuro-surgeon to the Royal Free Hospital, but the emergencies of war took her in 1944 first to Chase Farm, Enfield, and later to Bristol in charge of an E.M.S. neuro-surgical unit. Her appointment to the Middlesex Hospital in 1947 was the crown of her career and provided the happiest years of her professional life. This appointment was remarkable; it was the first time that a woman was given the charge of men in a consultant capacity in a major London teaching hospital. She entered fully into the life of the place, in teaching, committees, and social activities, and soon gained the affection of colleagues and students. One of her early patients at the Middlesex was the late A. A. Milne [q.v.]. A tribute was paid in the recent obituary notice in *The Times* to the "remarkable feat of surgery" which preserved Milne's life at that time.

Diana Beck's fastidious femininity and small stature belied the innate strength derived from power of will, self control and immense enthusiasm which carried her through the exacting trials of endurance intrinsic to her speciality. Though her frail constitution was often sorely taxed she was never happier than when working at full stretch. Overwhelmingly interested in people, she was gifted in the handling of patients, quickly gaining their confidence and often their personal devotion. Her keen powers of observation and insight contributed to her fine diagnostic skill and doubtless guided her in her choice of what to do and when.

Her many friends will cherish the memory of her open-hearted generosity and the help she was ever ready to give to those in trouble. Wherever she lived, her surroundings were as elegant and tasteful as her own personal attire. She had a collector's eye for everything choice. Her home was a focal point of warm hospitality. Her last illness and operation were faced with characteristic courage, although the hazards were formidable. She was optimistically planning her convalescence and ultimate return to work when the end came without warning.

March 6, 1956.

May Lamberton Becker, long one of the foremost among American literary critics and journalists, whose death occurred at Epsom on April 27, 1958 at the age of 84, was best known to booklovers on the European side of the Atlantic as an adviser on reading for young people, as the author of inviting popular biographies, and, to the friends of Anglo-American understanding, as the co-founder of the transatlantic "Books Across the Sea" exchange, which in its seventeenth year flourishes as a committee activity of the English-Speaking Union of London and New York.

In New York, where she was born on August 26, 1873, and in literary circles throughout the United States, she will be remembered as the sole conductor for over 40 years of the weekly "Reader's Guide" feature of questions and answers on the choice of books and reading. She had originated this feature for the New York *Evening Post* and transferred it to the *Saturday Review of Literature* at the invitation of Henry Seidel Canby. Later she continued it in the New York *Herald Tribune* Weekly Book Section under the editorship of Irita van Doren. The "Reader's Guide" feature ended with her retirement at an advanced age, and to the end showed no abatement of the enthusiasm and insight which had made its conductor the trusted friend of two generations of librarians, publishers, and booksellers in every state of the Union.

Before entering into journalism at the age of 16 she had given evidence of genuine vocation to a career which would illustrate a kind of relation to books and readers which is becoming rarer: that in which the massive figures which spell success to a publisher count for little beside the triumph of having introduced the right books or authors to their predestined individual readers. In middle life her lectures on current literature and the drama brought her a reputation among publishers as a trustworthy discoverer and interpreter of important new writers. She married, in 1893, the pianist and composer Gustave L. Becker.

When her only daughter, Beatrice Warde*, went to work in London in 1927, England became Mrs. Becker's summer home. Her lifelong affection for Britain then found expression in a series of "Letters from London." At the outbreak of the Second World War, at the age of 66, she was persuaded to return to New York (much against her inclination), and her forthright voice was one of the first to break the conscientious silence of neutrality that had descended upon American writers at that time.

Her *Introducing Charles Dickens,* written during the first year of the war, gave her favourite author something beyond a perceptive literary tribute: for the American royalties purchased and equipped the Charles Dickens Ambulance which arrived in Ealing on the eve of its worst night of bombing; those of the English edition were turned over to such causes as would comfort "families like the Cratchits," whose small homes had been shattered by enemy action.

On a cabled hint that Americans in London needed, to offset Nazi propaganda among them, new books about their country which wartime import difficulties had made unobtainable in England, Mrs. Becker presented over 70 new publications to the American Outpost in Great Britain. A return present of new British books, not then known in America, led to the formation of the "Books Across the Sea" societies to foster such practical uses of "books as ambassadors." Her *Presenting Miss Jane Austen,* published in London a few years ago, and her introductions to the Rainbow Classics for young people, endeared her name to a new generation of readers on both sides of the Atlantic. In recent years Mrs. Becker contributed to the columns of *The Times Literary Supplement.*

April 29, 1958.

The twelfth **Duke of Bedford** was found dead from an accidental gunshot wound on October 11, 1953, at the age of 64. His death deprived the British peerage of one of its least conventional members—a man who had quite literally "no time" for the obvious and usual pursuits favoured by the majority of those occupying a comparable status.

From his middle twenties onwards he was dominated by two powerful forces which interacted on his nature—an austere and pious evangelical Christianity and a keen social sense which impelled him to try to discover some way out of the current economic ills.

The courses into which he was led by this dual impulse were never such as to commend themselves to the majority in Britain. In other words, he was an obstinate heretic both in theology and politics, and was looked upon by the conventional-minded as a crank. No political party could hold him and no label describe him. He often acted in a manner that lacked discretion, and he was accused quite unfairly by detractors of being in turn a communist and a fascist. In fact, he wandered about from cause to cause, always favouring those least popular. He had abundant energy and high moral earnestness, but a lack of logic in his make-up often caused him to take geese for swans; and he was inclined to underrate the material difficulties which stood in the way of policies he advocated from time to time.

The Most Noble Hastings William Sackville Russell, twelfth Duke of Bedford, Marquess of Tavistock, Earl of Bedford, Baron Russell of Chenies, Baron Russell of Thornhaugh, in the county of Northampton, Baron Howland of Streatham, in the county of Surrey, all in the Peerage of England, was born on December 21, 1888, the only child of the eleventh duke. His father was a noted landowner and generous patron of Woburn Abbey Hospital, and his mother became an air pilot, and died while on a solo flight in 1937.

The Marquess of Tavistock (to give the Duke of Bedford the name under which he became known as a social campaigner) succeeded to the family honours on August 27, 1940; and it was a matter of much grief to him that his succession to vast estates and responsibilities should have occurred during a great war which he deemed unnecessary and which robbed him of immediate opportunities for service to his tenants. He formally withdrew from the Church of England and refused to continue the financial support his father had always given to the local churches in Bedfordshire.

He was educated at Eton and Balliol, and

was for some time in the 10th Battalion, The Middlesex Regiment; but the military life was desperately uncongenial to him; and when war broke out in 1914 he, having pacifist convictions, was by no means sorry to be classified C3 on grounds of bad eyesight. He felt very strongly, however, the urge to render some form of non-combatant service, and early in the course of the war was put into touch with the Oxford branch of the Y.M.C.A., which was running a camp centre at Purbrook Hill, near Portsmouth. He chose to be just an ordinary helper, and for five years carried out duties ranging from washing-up to the taking of New Testament study circles.

From 1919 onwards he was busily and happily occupied in Christian and social work of various kinds, his aim being to integrate the Christian ethic with a scheme of public order which should abolish poverty and provide a wide measure of social justice. The preservation of peace bulked large in his mind, and to forward it he joined the Fellowship of Reconciliation. Another organization which drew him into its fold was the Conference on Christian Politics, Economics, and Citizenship ("Copec"). But his most fruitful work, in his own view, was done for the Discharged Prisoners' Aid Society.

About 1928 he was presented with a copy of Marshall Hattersley's *This Age of Plenty*. He did not then pretend to be a social theorist, and found the economic arguments of Social Credit heavy going (as many have done before and since); but he gave close study to the book and began to think it likely that Major Douglas's [q.v.] theory offered a solution to the problem of poverty existing in a world of plenty, without the disadvantages either of Socialism or of the current monetary and economic system. He brought prominent Social Crediters and orthodox economists together in debate; and, being convinced that the former had in nine cases out of 10 the better of the argument, embraced Social Credit with enthusiasm. He became one of the most ardent exponents of the theory, and wrote *The Road to Real Success, Poverty and Over-Taxation,* and a flood of pamphlets (which he would forward to a very large number of people, both prominent and obscure).

As a liberal evangelical Christian he had always felt that the participation of Christian people in war was immoral. His pacifism strengthened as the years went on, but it changed somewhat in character and texture, and he came to believe that war could be avoided by closer contact between legislatures and people and by the readjustment of economic stresses. The 1939-45 war seemed to him to have been avoidable, and he found himself unable to see eye to eye with press and politicians on this big issue. In April 1940 he approached the German Legation in Dublin and secured from a personage there a statement of the terms on which it was alleged that Germany would be prepared to cease fighting. This was, of course, irregular and unofficial, and nothing resulted from it save a pamphlet called *The Fate of a Peace Effort* and a good many hard words in Parliament and elsewhere, spoken and written by those with a more urgent sense of the necessity to stamp out the evil of Nazism.

The Duke of Bedford never belonged to a political party except John Beckett's "British People's Party," of which he became chairman on its formation in April 1939. Its paper programme included monetary reform; the protection of the small shopkeeper against trusts; security of employment; and electoral reform. It failed to secure any public support, and Beckett was imprisoned under the Defence Regulations shortly after the war had begun. An attempt to revive the organization after the end of the war was a dismal failure.

The Duke inherited from his father a keen interest in natural history, particularly in the keeping of animals both in his own park and in the collections of the Zoological Society of London. He was attracted especially to the study of parrots, pheasants, fish, deer, and bison (both American and European), all of which he kept at Woburn. To the Zoological Society he rendered most generous service, especially perhaps by enabling a herd of the very rare Père David's deer to be started at Whipsnade as an offshoot of his own large herd at Woburn. As a member of the council of the society, and for a time chairman of its gardens committee, his knowledge and advice were of very great value. He wrote a book on *Parrots and Parrot-like Birds in Aviculture,* and published a pamphlet on developing a homing strain of budgerigars.

In November 1914 he married Louisa Crommelin Roberta Jowitt, daughter of the late Mr. R. J. Whitwell, of Thornbury Lodge, Oxford. They had two sons (of whom the elder, the Marquess of Tavistock, inherits the family honours) and a daughter.

October 12, 1953.

Sir Max Beerbohm died on May 20, 1956 in a nursing home at Rapallo, after an illness of several weeks. He was 83 and had been in a coma for more than 24 hours. His last words before he became unconscious were: "Grazie per tutto" (thank you for everything). They were addressed to his doctor and Elisabeth Jungmann, who had looked after him for the last few years and whom he had married secretly on April 20.

There have not, for many years now, been more than a handful of living British writers whose reputation is universally acknowledged, and of these none has shown himself so fastidious, within the strict limits of a varied output, as Max. His death removes, therefore, a writer and draughtsman who is likely to prove irreplaceable and who, moreover, has suffered no setback in a fame which has grown steadily during the last 60 years. Furthermore, it removes a human personality who endeared himself to successive generations of readers and friends without ever making a demand upon the admiration or the loyalty which was freely accorded him.

On August 24, 1872, when Henry Maximilian Beerbohm was born in a quiet Kensington backwater, it cannot have seemed likely that a family which had already given proof of unusual vitality had only now reached its apogee. Of Baltic descent, Sir Max's father had settled in London, where he carried on the family business of corn merchant and for many years ran two commercial papers, *Beerbohm's Evening Corn Trade List* and *Beerbohm's Morning Shipping List.*

He married in 1849 Constantia Draper, who bore him four children, of whom the most distinguished later became known as Sir Herbert Tree; and after her early death he married her sister, Eliza, by whom he had four daughters and one son, Max. Of Max's school education we know, by his own confession, that "my delight in having been at Charterhouse was far greater than had been my delight in being there." But he was not actively unhappy. His gift for caricature had early asserted itself, and by the time he reached Merton College, Oxford, in 1890, the pattern of his future life was already definable.

His first published drawings appeared in the *Strand Magazine,* and his first prose in such undergraduate journals as the *Isis;* before long, however, he attained a wider circle through his friendship with William Rothenstein, who in turn introduced him to Wilde and to Beardsley, his exact contemporary. When, therefore, *The Yellow Book* appeared, in 1894, Max was at once put to contribution, and wrote a set of essays which reached their final form in a volume demurely entitled *The Works of Max Beerbohm,* introduced to the world by the exceptionally perceiving publisher, John Lane, when their author was no more than 23. In the same year his first collection of caricatures was published, and a connexion formed with the *Saturday Review,* of which, when Bernard Shaw resigned the post, he became dramatic critic during the 12 years which ended with his marriage in 1910 to the oustanding American actress, Florence Kahn.

They lived at Rapallo, except during the two war periods. With the years honours gathered fast about him. In 1935 he founded a fresh reputation as an outstanding broadcaster, and in 1939 he was knighted. Academic recognition was bestowed on him, first by Edinburgh and then by Oxford; and during the last decades of his life it is safe to assert that he was universally accorded a position in the world of English art and letters which left all competition out of court. Before the turn of the century Shaw had attached to his name the tag "incomparable"; and, indeed, there is no English contemporary to whom he can strictly be compared. The good fortune which always accompanied him was clouded only by the death of his first wife in 1951; from that time onward, however, he was fortunate enough to be able to resign the conduct of a small household to Fräulein Jungmann, who towards the end of his life had similarly cared for the Beerbohms' old friend and sometime neighbour in Italy, Gerhart Hauptmann. As already recorded, Sir Max married her a month before he died.

The peculiar gift upon which Max's reputation reposes may be defined as the gift of intimacy. Both as a writer and as a draughtsman he excelled at gaining the confidence of his public—to an extent, indeed, which makes the very word "public" wholly inapposite. He drew each reader aside, he murmured his neat, his apparently casual reflections into every private ear. Rising to fame at a period when both writers and artists of distinction had adopted, almost as a matter of course, a large prophetic utterance, Max suddenly brought the pitch of his art down to a conversational level. Once, it is true, in *Zuleika Dobson,* he wrote to the full scale of a novel; yet, for all its felicity, *Zuleika Dobson* is hardly likely to be accounted his most successful work.

He was essentially a miniaturist, excelling in such evocations, half-story and half-essay, as "William and Mary," which appeared in the collection, *And Even Now.* In these few pages he showed, what no one who knew him in private life ever doubted, that in addition to rare qualities of wit, detachment, and observation, he had a heart—a heart perhaps too tender to be readily exposed to the perils of print. For in general his range was limited not only in scale but in feeling. It was in delicate withdrawals that he showed his paces, in refusals of commitment.

The extreme refinement of this approach to literature was not without its perils. It led, for instance, to a care for language which sometimes fell into preciosity. Words like "disbuskined" and "irrepleviable" may add a glow-worm light to his pages, but they exasperate as well; his syntax was often wilful; and his treatment of the reader at times was no better than arch. Yet there can be few writers in modern times who, under a surface appearance of casual ease, hid a more impressive arsenal of resources. He was at home in several languages, and his reading was firmly based on classical models. He always knew, therefore, exactly what he was doing.

Not suprisingly, he became a parodist—a parodist, moreover, whose special skill reflects an exceptionally keen critical gift. "The Mote in the Middle Distance," his parody of Henry James in *A Christmas Garland,* is in its way as pointed a comment as any in his considerable body of overt criticism. For in both fields he made it his business to show that he was not easily to be taken in. Where other minds asserted their acceptance, Max preferred to turn aside with a shrug. Whether his subject were Shakespeare or Shaw, he was equally unimpressed by the opinions of others. And in his dramatic criticism, especially, although he was keenly alive to the interests of the contemporary theatre, it was literature rather than pure criticism which engaged his weekly interest. He took out of his themes exactly what he needed but nothing else, and what he needed was always a fresh light thrown on some aspect of his own nature.

To read Max is thus to be lost in the delightful mazes of an endless autobiography. Even when, as in *Seven Men,* he is composing, a set of imaginary portraits, it is the portraitist, no less than the sitter, who remains in the memory. Not T. Fenning Dodworth but the tone in which Dodworth's appalling triumphs are recounted gives his story an undying resonance. Indeed, it was seldom necessary for Max to compose a story. He merely set his automata in motion, content to describe his own airy circles about them as they move to their appointed anti-climax. And when he withdrew himself a little, in order to allow his story a more conventional play, as in *The Happy Hypocrite,* there is an immediate sense of absence. We do not really want to know more about Lord George Hell; we want Max.

Hence it is to the essays and broadcasts that a contemporary reader is most likely to turn. In these, without much heed to the subject in hand, Max can play the part of the entrancer. On music-halls, on Bloomsbury, on Swinburne, and Watts-Dunton in the most famous essay of all, "No. 2 The Pines," he turns the sharp and affectionate eye which has revealed for us a fresh dimension of wit-writing. Just as Congreve or Berkeley or (in a mood more nearly akin to Max) Wilde used dazzling gifts of precision in order to tantalize the reader with glimpses of a vista which he will never be allowed fully to explore, so Max in his essays extrudes deceitful promises of intimacy. Here I am, he says: you have only to look and listen; in a moment you shall seize me and I shall be wholly yours. Yet in that moment he has vanished again, nimble as a squirrel.

All that he leaves behind is as imponderable as a scent, elusive even, the smiling farewell of the Cheshire cat. He will have been writing, it may be, on "The Top Hat"—that is to say, on himself. A recollection or two, an evocative glimpse of the past, a general opinion here and there turn about the "black but shining old monument" which, however impersonal he may pretend it, is so clearly perched on a particular head: the essay contains no more than these. Yet it leaves an aura behind—an emanation which cannot easily be accounted for by purely literary analysis. Once again, by something like a trick of intonation, Max has given his legion of unknown readers the illusion, not that he is taking them into his confidence, but—still more flatteringly—that they could perfectly well take him into theirs.

This personal gift stood him in excellent stead as a draughtsman. For one thing, he had known most of the eminent men and women of his time—or at least he had known the Londoners, for it is among the many curious aspects of his art that in spite of close family connexions with the Continent and long residence abroad he always remained a Londoner, and an old-fashioned Londoner at that. Then, his sympathetic intuition was so acute that he grasped the essence of a personality even when his subject was known to him only by hearsay or observation. It was appropriate that Max's complexion of mind should lead him to caricature, for he had no pretensions whatever to be a pure artist; colour and line interested him chiefly in so far as they enabled him to make immediate comments on life, and not, as with caricaturists such as Sem or Caran d'Ache, for their own sake as well. Because it was more often Max's intention, in any medium, to catch a mood than to develop a theme, his caricatures serve his purpose almost better than his prose.

It is not necessary to recapitulate his successes in the field nor to speculate on his powers of suggestion. No doubt he subtly and permanently coloured the reaction of his public to such figures as Edward VII or the Rossetti circle, and to a handful of notabilities, like Mrs. Humphry Ward, who remain in our affection largely because for a moment they caught Max's amused eye. In 10 volumes, the best of which appeared immediately after the 1914-18 War, a panorama of English social life has been displayed with all the resources of irony and of a general good humour which is all the more compelling for an occasional hint of savagery; and the retrospective exhibition at the Leicester Galleries which marked his eightieth birthday in 1952 showed that there are still unpublished riches waiting for posterity.

Behind a lifetime of work in different spheres an enigma remains, however. Max's life was devoted to the construction of a *persona.* In a few fastidious volumes he gave the best of that *persona* a permanent outline, and in addition he has left a large body of miscellaneous work, all of which is informed by the same consistency of intention. Yet at the back of it all stands someone who remains mysterious: behind Max there is a Henry Maximilian who preferred the modest solitude of Rapallo to any fame or familiarity not of his own choosing. He was far from a recluse. Visitors, if he liked them, he enjoyed. On his rare visits to England he was by no means averse to the ritual gestures of an eminent man, such as lunching with Lady Colefax; and if he hated letter-writing he shared a fault not uncommon among men of talent. Yet he was not to be snared. And of all his large circle of friends and acquaintances there must be few indeed who would venture to say that they really knew him as he was. Like Lord George Hell, he has chosen his mask, and it fitted to perfection: exactly what lay beneath that smiling urbanity we may never know.

May 21, 1956.

Sir George Beharrell, D.S.O., who died on February 20, 1959 at his home in Hertfordshire at the age of 85, had been prominent in both the transport and the rubber industries, and held high positions in government service in time of war.

He was an acknowledged authority on transport; he knew more than most about railways and railway law; he became one of the best known figures in the rubber industry; and mastered the art and technique of civil aviation when, both as a science and as a method of getting about the world, flying was emerging from its infancy. He was as capable under an emergency in the nation's service as he was in the direction of industry, a man of prodigious knowledge, and insatiable capacity for work, and yet a man who was never too busy to accept new responsibilities, to probe new ideas, to indulge his recreations, and to cultivate his friends.

John George Beharrell was born at Almondsbury, near Huddersfield, on March 11, 1873, the son of George Beharrell, a schoolmaster, who died when his son was still a boy. His legacies to his son were a fine character, a mathematical mind, and a head for figures.

Young Beharrell first went to King James's School, Almondsbury, had private tuition, and eventually found his way to Leeds University, although in the meantime he had started the career, to which he was to return, in the offices of the North-Eastern Railway at York. His first job was in the clerical department, which was given to him at the age of 15, and for which he was paid £15 a year.

After the interruption of completing his education, his progress at York was rapid and spectacular. Because of his flair for statistics, he was given a succession of quick promotions so that at 41, when the 1914-18 War broke out, he was assistant goods manager and commercial agent.

His brilliant work in the swift mobilization and dispatch of the men of Northern Command, and his part in producing a complicated railway service for purely military needs, such as the nation had not before known, brought him to the attention of the Government, and particularly of Lloyd George, who in 1915 got him into the Ministry of Munitions as Director of Statistics and Requirements. When he had set the department going, he was sent to France with the rank of lieutenant-colonel as Assistant Director-General of Transportation, working with Sir Eric Geddes and Sir Philip Nash. Not long afterwards he became Assistant Inspector-General of Transportation in all the theatres of war, and in May 1917 he was transferred to the Admiralty with the rank of Director of Statistics. The title, however, was ambiguous. In fact, he was appointed mainly to deal with the anti-submarine campaign when the German menace to shipping was at its height, to analyse the copious and intricate data at the Admiralty.

After the war Beharrell joined the Ministry of Transport upon its formation in 1919 as Director-General of Finance and Statistics, and in 1921 he was attached as financial adviser to the Geddes Committee on National Expenditure. He was with the famous "axe" committee for something more than a year, until he left the Civil Service to go into business.

In October 1922 he joined the Dunlop Rubber Company and became joint-managing director in November 1923. Already he knew something about rubber production and manufacture, and within a short time he mastered its intricacies and became one of the acknowledged leaders of the industry. In 1926 he became president of the India Rubber Manufacturers' Association, an office he held for two years, and from 1927-29 he was president of the Society of Motor Manufacturers and Traders. For the year 1932-33 he was president of the Federation of British Industries, from 1933 to 1936 president of the Institute of the Rubber Industry, and in 1935 chairman of the Sixth International Congress for Scientific Management.

Three years later he was appointed to the Prime Minister's Panel of Industrialists, and for nine years until 1943 he was on the Advisory Panel of the International Rubber Relations Committee. In April 1942 he was made Director-General of Raw Material Controls at the Ministry of Supply, but he resigned on account of ill-health two months later.

Although in later years Beharrell was always thought of primarily as the acknowledged spokesman of the rubber industry—he was from 1937 to 1949 chairman of the Dunlop Company, and president until 1957—he derived much satisfaction from his position as chairman of Imperial Airways, a post in which he succeeded his old friend Geddes.

Although he ostensibly retired in 1949, he kept up many of his activities. He was fond of his gardens at Harpenden, was an *habitué* of the Reform Club, and would from time to time call in at the Dunlop headquarters in St. James's Street, where his son, George Beharrell, succeeded him as deputy chairman and managing director.

Many distinctions were conferred upon him. He received the D.S.O. in 1917 and was knighted in 1919. He had the Order of the Crown of Belgium, was a Commander of the Orders of St. Maurice and St. Lazarus of Italy, and of Orange-Nassau of the Netherlands.

He married in 1898 Kate, daughter of Joseph Ripley, by whom he had three sons and a daughter.

February 21, 1959.

Dr. Eduard van Beinum, principal conductor of the Amsterdam Concertgebouw Orchestra, jointly with Willem Mengelberg from 1937 to 1943 and since 1943 alone, died on April 13, 1959 at rehearsal. Since the war his powerful features and dark hair had become familiar to audiences in a dozen countries. He was notable for the modesty and clarity of his conducting, habitually without a baton; he was able to bring the best out of his players as a unit while eschewing demonstrative impositions of his will, and to inspire the most conventional programmes with rare life and spirit.

He had been in ill-health for some time, and was said to have been kept alive in recent months by the use of drugs. After rehearsing the first two movements of a symphony by Brahms—a composer whose work he excelled in interpreting—he was taken ill and died at once. The news was followed by the cancellation of concerts throughout Holland. He was to have taken the orchestra on a tour of Britain in May. Dr. van Beinum was 58.

When he took the Concertgebouw to London in 1946 for the first time after the war he demonstrated that the tradition of brilliant playing had survived, without the excesses which sometimes marred Mengelberg's interpretations. In 1949 and 1950, as principal conductor of the London Philharmonic Orchestra, he did much to repair its deficiencies and strengthen its qualities; his last appearance in London was in October 1958, when his conducting of the Philharmonia Orchestra during part of the Beethoven series recalled just such a service in his first year with the Philharmonic. He first took the Concertgebouw to America in 1954; in 1956 he was invited to be guest conductor with the Los Angeles Philharmonic and a year later was appointed music director. He had played in most of the principal centres of Europe, including the Edinburgh Festival.

Van Beinum was born into a family of musicians at Arnhem on September 3, 1901, and by the age of 16 was a member of the town's symphony orchestra. He studied as a pianist and in harmony and composition at the Amsterdam Conservatoire, and after service with several orchestras and choirs in small provincial towns was appointed conductor of the Haarlem Orchestra in 1927. He had already made his name as a brilliant pianist and a competent performer on violin and viola. In 1931 he was appointed second conductor at the Concertgebouw at a time when its great reputation was being established.

The value set upon him became notably apparent six years later, when he was invited to become conductor of the Residentie Orchestra at The Hague, and the committee of the Concertgebouw, to keep his services, appointed him "first conductor" and joint conductor with Mengelberg. In 1943, when Mengelberg was dismissed for alleged collaboration with the Germans, van Beinum had the task of re-establishing the orchestra's great prestige alone.

His success was demonstrated by the international acclaim accorded him in his jubilee year with the Concertgebouw in 1956. In addition to the many speeches which marked his investiture as a Grand Officer of the Order of Orange Nassau, the audience heard the recorded voices of musicians from abroad, including Sir Adrian Boult and Dame Myra Hess*. In the same year he was awarded a doctorate by Amsterdam University. He held decorations from six other countries.

He married in 1927 Sepha Jansen, the violinist, by whom he had two sons.

April 14, 1959.

Major-General John Hay Beith, C.B.E., M.C., **(Ian Hay)** died on September 22, 1952 in a nursing home near Petersfield, Hampshire, at the age of 76. Under the name of "Ian Hay" he was widely known as novelist and playwright.

For some years before the outbreak of war in 1914 "Ian Hay" was coming to be known as an author of gay, apparently inconsequent, yet carefully wrought stories. The appearance in 1915 of *The First Hundred Thousand,* which impressed upon a notoriously unmilitarist public the lighter aspect of Kitchener's Army, set the seal on a reputation already high. The qualities he displayed in that celebrated book were abundantly manifested through many years thereafter in a large number of novels and plays.

"Ian Hay" wrote to please, and to this end he drew unselfconsciously upon a boisterous sense of fun which held the residual virtue of his schooldays, and upon two strains in him that seemed to bear the mark of his Scottish ancestry—a strain of humour that is commonly described as pawky, and a strain of lively and ceremonious sentiment, which sometimes trembled on the verge of sentimentality. He was remarkably successful from the start of his literary career and had never any need to court popularity. Indeed, it would have been quite foreign to his delightfully simple and modest nature to do so. He would have been the last to claim that his work was in any way profound, but within the limits set by his particular talents he was a careful and conscientious craftsman who would have scorned to give to a loyal public less than the best of which he was capable.

Born on April 17, 1876 at Manchester, the son of Scottish parents (his father, John A. Beith, came from Altnacraig, Oban), John Hay Beith descended from a family that had given to the Church some of its best known and most loyal ministers at the time of the Disruption in 1843. All through his life he retained an ardent affection for Scotland and Scottish things; the Royal Company of Archers (whose history he wrote) had no more loyal member than he. With his brothers he went to school at Fettes, where one of his contemporaries was Lord Simon [q.v.]. Even as a schoolboy he had a marked bent for the amateur theatre. From school he went on to St. John's College, Cambridge, where he took a second class in the Classical Tripos. He then returned to Fettes as master of one of the lower forms and remained there until he had established himself as a writer. Much of his early work is coloured by his experience at Fettes, the fruits of which are most directly apparent in *The Lighter Side of School Life* (1914) and in his play *Housemaster* (1938).

His first novel, *Pip,* appeared in 1907 and was an immediate success. It was followed by *The Right Stuff* (1908), *A Man's Man* (1909), *A Safety Match* (1911), *Happy-Go-Lucky* (1913), *A Knight on Wheels* (1914), all of them cheerful and optimistic in temper, all of the right stuff and happy-go-lucky, their good feeling saved from insipidity by its seasoning of piquant humour.

Beith volunteered for service in 1914, served as a captain with the Argyll and Sutherland Highlanders in France, and was mentioned in dispatches and awarded the M.C. *The First Hundred Thousand,* consisting of sketches describing life in his own battalion from September 1914, when it began squad drill, until a twelvemonth later at Loos, appeared serially in *Blackwood's Magazine,* and in volume form was one of the most popular books of the period. Presented as the story of a typical unit of Kitchener's Army, these gay and extraordinarily lighthearted sketches were of more than ordinary practical value in the circumstances, though they resolutely, perhaps too resolutely, turned away from the brutal face of war. A second volume, *Carrying On,* appeared in 1917, and *The Last Million,* in 1919, written chiefly for Americans, described—less spontaneously—the arrival in France of the American citizens' army in 1918. Beith was a member of the British War Mission to the United States during the last two years of the fighting and lectured to American audiences with very considerable effect.

None of his novels written after the war of 1914-18 enjoyed the great popularity of the early ones, but, as playwright, "Ian Hay", from 1919, when *Tilly of Bloomsbury* was produced, until almost the close of his career, was a name to conjure with. His instinct for the theatre, his natural high spirits, and his shrewd craftsmanship apart, he had two unusual endowments in writing for the stage. One which he shared with a near-contemporary, H. A. Vachell [q.v.], was the knack, a seemingly instinctive skill, of translating any of his novels into a play—or of translating any of his own plays, for that matter, into a novel. The other was a very real gift for collaborating with somebody else. "Ian Hay" wrote plays—light comedies verging on farce—in collaboration with Sir Seymour Hicks, P. G. Wodehouse (Sir Pelham Wodehouse*), Stephen King-Hall (Commander Lord King-Hall*), Guy Bolton, Anthony Armstrong [d. 1976] and A. E. W. Mason, and almost all of them enjoyed good fortune.

Tilly of Bloomsbury (which owes a great deal to Arthur Bourchier) and *A Safety Match* were both romps, perhaps—entertaining romps—rather than drama; *The Happy Ending* (1922) had somewhat more substance and more sentiment; *Baa, Baa, Black Sheep* (written with P. G. Wodehouse), *The Middle Watch* (written with Stephen King-Hall), and *The Sport of Kings,* all produced in the same year, 1929, were uproarious and attractive nonsense. His last play, produced in 1951 and written in collaboration with L. du Garde Peach, was *The White Sheep of the Family.* Slight in theme though it was, and based on a well-worn trick of paradox, it yet manifested the deftness of touch the public had so long enjoyed.

Besides the novels he continued to write, "Ian Hay" published several volumes of short stories, some of them collections of early work which had fugitively appeared in magazines. In 1938 came *The King's Service,* an attempt to give an informal history of the British infantry soldier in peace and war, which is said to have so impressed [Lord] Hore-Belisha*, then Secretary of State for War, that he appointed the author Director of Public Relations.

After he had resigned his appointment at the War Office in 1941, the sternness of the struggle with the Axis Powers seemed to have caused "Ian Hay" to engage in tasks at variance with his gifts. His tribute to Malta, G.C., in *The Unconquered Isle, America Comes Across, Arms and the Men,* and other works of like nature, though lit as usual with humour and sentiment, were serious in intention and failed in effect because the lightness and deftness which had served their author so well in his novels and plays were inappropriate to the theme. If, however, the serious side of his nature did not find expression in his writing it often did in his life, as his membership for nearly a quarter of a century of the governing body of Guy's Hospital amply proves.

He married in 1915 Helen Margaret, the only daughter of the late P. A. Speirs, who survives him.

September 23, 1952.

Lord Hore-Belisha—See **Hore-.**

The Rt. Rev. G. K. A. Bell, D.D., Bishop of Chichester from 1929 until early 1958 and previously Dean of Canterbury, died on October 3, 1958 at his home at Canterbury. He was 75.

The Anglican Bench has rarely lacked men of outstanding eminence and, among such, none in recent years has rivalled the distinction, particularly in international affairs, of George Kennedy Allen Bell. He was never able to be contentedly diocesan or even insular; "his mind ranged as widely as the Anglican Communion"; and though the most loyal of Anglicans he became something of a world churchman.

He himself in some sort summed up his attitude a few months before he resigned his bishopric. "Not for me", he said, "a fugitive and cloistered Church, which refuses to face the problems and crises of the modern world—clearly though I recognize and value room for special vocations to contemplation and prayer, and missionary and nursing work".

Bell was born in Hayling Island on February 4, 1883. He was the eldest son of Canon J. A. Bell, Vice-Dean of Norwich Cathedral and a former popular Vicar of Wimbledon, who died in 1934. He was educated at Westminster and Christ Church Oxford, where he took a First Class in Classical Moderations and a Second in Literae Humaniores, graduating in 1905. In 1904 he had won the Newdigate Prize and he continued to write poetry from time to time all his life. Some of it attained the level of "Departure", which was published in *The Times* of January 3, 1916. In August 1932 he wrote a "Song of the Sussex Church Builders" which was set to music by Dr. Martin Shaw, and published in support of the bishop's appeal for 100,000 contributors to a scheme for building new churches.

He received his theological training at Wells and was ordained in 1907 to a curacy at Leeds, leaving in 1910 to become lecturer (in Classics and English) and Tutor at his old college, Christ Church, where he was student from 1911.

In 1914 began a long and happy association with Canterbury, first as Resident Chaplain to the Archbishop and from 1924 to 1929 as Dean. His tenure of office as Dean was marked by an immense number of improvements. These included the abolition of visitors' fees; the broadcasting of services on notable occasions; the restoration of Lanfranc's People's Altar in the nave; the daily offering of organized intercession by the use of a rota diocesan, inter-diocesan and Provincial; the reorganization of the Chapter Office, and the scheme of "Friends of Canterbury Cathedral". His active interest embraced town-planning at Canterbury and the special problems of the Aylesham mining area.

An invitation to some Nonconformist divines to preach (though within the limits of the 1920 Lambeth Conference conditions) attracted considerable attention, as did also the performance in the nave of the Cathedral of John Masefield's* *Coming of Christ* with music by Gustav Holst and settings by Charles Ricketts. Later, as a diocesan bishop, he issued in 1943 a carefully framed statement in Synod of regulations for occasional interchange of preachers with other denominations, based on the recommendations of the Lambeth Conference of 1920 and 1930.

His positions, first as Archbishop's Chaplain and then as Dean, were far from exhausting his energies. In Leeds, he had done notable pastoral work among men through the Church of England Men's Society, and he continued his association with the society, helping it to push forward various schemes. He took a lively interest in the trade union movement, and in 1952 he accepted an invitation to become a member of the National Union of Public Employees.

He was Assistant Secretary of the Lambeth Conference of 1920 and Episcopal Secretary of the 1930 Conference. He was a member of the Archbishops' Commission on Social and Industrial Problems in 1917; member of the Joint Committee of the Convocations of Canterbury and York on the Church and Marriage appointed in 1931; member of the Church Assembly Commission on Church and State appointed in 1930; president of the Religious Drama Society of Great Britain since its formation.

From 1925 to 1929 he was Pro-Prolocutor (3rd) of the Lower House of the Convocation of Canterbury. He was also chairman of the Joint Committee of the Convocations of Canterbury and York on Relations between the Church of England and the Church of South India in 1950 and 1955, and chairman of the Conference between representatives of the Church of England and the Methodist Church in 1956.

The first of the series of important official visits made by him to other countries in furtherance of the ecumenical movement was that of 1925, when he was appointed lecturer on the Olaus Petri Foundation at Upsala in Sweden; in 1938 he assisted at the consecration of three bishops there. In 1946 he was able to fulfil a longstanding engagement to give a series of lectures in the same university centre on "The Anglican Church and Christian Unity"; the latter occasion was combined with a visit to Norway, whose Primate was shortly afterwards his guest at Chichester.

Perhaps his most memorable visit to Sweden was that of 1942. Years later he described how he had been approached independently by two German pastors, Dr. Hans Schönfeld and Dr. Dietrich Bonhöffer, pre-war friends of his, who had travelled from Berlin to Stockholm at great risk to themselves. They spoke of a growing movement of revolt against Nazism in which both the Evangelical and Roman Catholic churches were playing a leading part. Would the British encourage the leaders of such a revolution to hope for negotiations if the "arch-gangsters" were removed? Bell informed Sir Anthony Eden [Lord Avon, d. 1977] and Winant, the American Ambassador, of the approaches, but subsequently the Foreign Secretary told Bell that in the national interest no reply should be given. This Bell deemed negative and wrong and he did not hesitate to say so.

In 1948 he attended the First Assembly of World Council of Churches, at Amsterdam, and was appointed chairman of its Central Committee. In the following year he was invited by the Bishops of Australia to spend two months there. He then went for a short time to New Zealand at the invitation of the National Council of Churches, before paying a short visit to South India on his way home. He returned to India for the World Council of Churches Central Committee early in 1953. In 1954 he went to Minneapolis for an Anglican Congress before attending the Second Assembly of World Council of Churches, at Evanston, at which he relinquished his chairmanship of the Central Committee and became honorary president of the W.C.C.

Bell had been so obviously marked out by intellectual and organizing ability for promotion that his nomination to the See of Chichester in 1929 caused only mild surprise that the promotion should have come quite so soon and he long remained one of the youngest members of the episcopal bench. This was the more noted because he retained then, and indeed in some degree throughout his life, a curiously youthful appearance, which was the outward expression of a mind that kept to an astonishing degree the zest and vigour and freshness of youth. As a bishop he was as active in extra-diocesan enterprises as he had previously been in extra-decanal ones, to the immense benefit of the Church at large but not always to the entire satisfaction of his diocese; some of his best friends felt that too much of his energy was consumed in the service of causes and interests remote from diocesan needs and problems, yet he strongly maintained the traditional view that English bishops were bishops of England with wider responsibilities than to their dioceses alone, and as time went on it came to be increasingly seen that his external activities involved no neglect of his more immediate responsibilities.

His knowledge of the parishes and of his clergy and indeed of the laity as well was intimate and detailed, and it may be doubted whether any of his contemporary bishops knew their dioceses better. He had great administrative gifts and was ever fresh and fertile in resource.

The affection felt for Bell by clergy and laity was shown in 1954, when he celebrated his silver jubilee as Bishop. To mark the occasion Professor William Coldstream was commissioned to paint the Bishop's portrait. The result was not uniformly admired by the subscribers, the artist suggested that another should be found, and A. R. Middleton Todd was chosen. The original portrait was subsequently given by Bell to the Tate Gallery.

No one ever called Bell's moral courage in question. In character he was a combination of gentleness and modesty, even to diffidence, with outspokenness in the expression of opinion unpopular at the moment, and a remarkable determination in carrying out his plans. He was sharply criticized in many quarters for his exposure of the anti-Christian trend of Hitlerism at its beginnings, and even more sharply, 10 years later, for deprecating the allied policy of bombing cities and civilian homes in Germany.

Bell will be permanently remembered for his *Life of Randall Davidson* published in 1935. This monumental work in two volumes, totalling over 1,300 pages, is far more than a mere personal biography and has already run into three editions. Its subject was intimately associated for something like half a century—save for a few years during his successor's Primacy—with almost all the great movements in the life of the Church and with not a few of those in the life of the State; and Bell's pages present a series of deft summaries of the basic issues in each crisis, with graphic pictures of the protagonists.

He married in 1918 Henrietta Millicent Grace, eldest daughter of the late Canon R. J. Livingstone and the Hon. Mrs. Livingstone. There were no children, Mrs. Bell took a full share of her husband's labours in many fields.

October 4, 1958.

Sir Hesketh Bell, G.C.M.G., who died in a nursing home in London on August 1, 1952 at the age of 87, had had a long and distinguished career in the public service.

Henry Hesketh Joudou Bell was born in the West Indies in December 1864, the eldest son of the late H. A. J. Bell. He was educated in Brussels and Paris, and entered the Civil Service of Barbados in 1882. He held various junior appointments in the West Indies until 1889, when he was transferred to the Gold Coast as a supervisor of Customs. In 1891 he was promoted to be chief assistant treasurer, and was further promoted to the receiver-generalship of Bahamas in 1894. He was appointed a member of the Executive Council of the colony and represented Harbour Island in the House of Assembly in 1895-96.

About this time he had the good fortune to attract the attention of Joseph Chamberlain, and his progress in the Colonial Service was rapid. He became Administrator of Dominica in 1899 and, with characteristic energy, set to work to develop his small domain. In this he was greatly helped by a grant of £15,000 which had been made by the Imperial Government in 1898 for the construction of roads in the island. Owing to the mountainous nature of the country, the lack of roads had been one of the most serious obstacles in the way of its development.

The Protectorate of Uganda was transferred from the care of the Foreign Office to that of the Colonial Office in 1905 and, in the same year, Bell was appointed Commissioner. The title of "Commissioner" was changed to "Governor" in 1907; and he thus became the first Governor of the protectorate. Among the problems which confronted him on assuming the administration by far the most formidable was that of the sleeping-sickness epidemic. To cope with this outbreak it became necessary to remove large parts of the native population from the tsetse infested shores and islands of Lake Victoria and to enforce extensive measures of segregation and control. By his vigorous action Bell succeeded in bringing the epidemic under control, but not before it had more than decimated the population and dealt the Protectorate a staggering blow from which it only recovered after the lapse of many years. Realizing how large a part questions of transport played in the development of the tropical colonies and protectorates, he introduced motor-transport into the country. Empire cotton-growing was also one of his enthusiasms, and in Uganda he was able to give it full scope. For his special services in Uganda Bell, who had been made a C.M.G. in 1903, was promoted K.C.M.G. in 1908.

In 1909 he was appointed Governor of Northern Nigeria and his tenure of office was marked by a steady development of the protectorate. The establishment of the Civil Service was considerably increased, and good progress was made with various public works. Perhaps the most important of the latter was the construction of the main trunk line from the navigable Niger at Baro to Kano (356 miles), the great market of the Hausa states. This had been begun in 1907 and was completed in 1912, while a start was made with its extension towards the Banchi tin-fields. The Durbar which was held at Kano in January 1913, a few months after the close of Sir Hesketh Bell's terms of office, may be quoted as an instance of the progress achieved by the country during his administration. On that occasion practically all the chiefs of the protectorate with their retinues attended, to the number of some 20,000 horsemen and 40,000 foot. In 1912 Sir Hesketh made way for Sir Frederick (later Lord) Lugard (to whom the Home Government had entrusted the task of amalgamating Northern and Southern Nigeria and then undertaking the government of the combined protectorates) and was appointed Governor of the Leeward Islands. Here he remained until 1915, when he was appointed Governor of Mauritius.

Of French extraction and with a perfect command of the French language, he found himself in a congenial atmosphere in a colony in which the French tradition is very strong. During the 1914-18 war Mauritius suffered in no way by direct action on the part of the enemy; and, after the war, the enormous rise in the price of sugar brought great prosperity to the colony; the gross value of the crop of 1920-21 was estimated at £20m. By imposing a duty of 5 per cent on the sugar exported during that period the local Government was able to establish a development fund of about £1m. to be employed in promoting the progress of the sugar industry and carrying out works of public utility. This was not a popular measure among the planters at the time, but the Governor's foresight was justified when, with a steady decrease in the price of sugar, the colony fell on evil days. He was regarded by the poorer classes of the community as their friend, and he gave practical proof of his sympathy with them when he arranged for the building by Government of a model village of small houses in the suburbs of Port Louis capable of housing from 800 to 900 persons.

Sir Hesketh Bell had a singular gift of clear and interesting exposition, without prolixity. Some of his dispatches on sleeping-sickness and cotton-growing were models of their kind. In his retirement his interest in African affairs continued active and manifested itself in many letters to *The Times*. One letter of his, on the introduction of an Indian elephant into Uganda in the hope of teaching the African elephant how to work, was an example of his power of combining information and humour. He was much exercised as to the effect of the cinema on the African native, and was an earnest advocate of some form of censorship which would prevent the display of films likely to undermine native respect for European morality and ways of life.

After his retirement from the governorship of Mauritius in 1924 (when he was promoted G.C.M.G.), he paid a visit to Java and French Indo-China in 1926, the outcome of which was a book entitled *Foreign Colonial Administration in the Far East*. The value of this work was recognized by the Royal Empire Society in 1929, when it presented him with the gold medal granted annually to the writer of the best book of the year dealing with Empire questions. Latterly he was greatly impressed by the desirability of a comparative study of British and French systems of governing tropical dependencies, with a view to bringing into more general use the best features of both the "indirect" and the "direct" methods of administration.

Sir Hesketh was a man of many interests. He painted well in water colour; he helped to design the Mauritius War Memorial which was a great success and attracted attention outside the colony; and he had a sound knowledge of architecture. A hobby, inspired no doubt by his early years in the West Indies, was the study of witchcraft. As long ago as 1889 he published his first book on the subject and his interest in it remained with him all his life, his last book, published in 1948, being entitled *Witches and Fishes*. He was unmarried.

August 5, 1952.

Sir Thomas Bell, K.B.E., who as marine engineer, shipbuilder, and administrator was identified with the Clydebank shipyard for 60 years, died at Helensburgh, Dumbartonshire on January 9, 1952 at the age of 86.

Born in 1865 at Sirsawa, British India, the son of the late Imrie Bell, M.Inst.C.E., he was educated at King's College School and the Royal Naval Engineering College, Devonport, and went to Clydebank, which was then owned by James and George Thomson, as a draughtsman in 1886. He rapidly rose to a managerial position, being finally appointed resident director in 1909. In announcing his retirement from that post in 1935, the chairman of Messrs. John Brown and Co., who acquired the yard in 1899, said that "for the last 25 years he has been Clydebank—the equipment, the organization, the choice of personnel, and above all the success of Clydebank have been his". Though he retired from the post of resident director he remained on the board until 1946 when he finally retired on account of advancing age.

Almost from the start of his career he was recognized as an engineer and designer of outstanding ability and he constantly acted on the principle of making each ship an advance over its predecessor. Thus the destroyers designed under his direction attained greater and greater speeds from the earlier vessels of 21 knots to the 36 knots and over of the later models. It was his enterprise, too, which brought about the change from reciprocating engines to turbines in the big transatlantic vessels.

Among famous ships with the construction of which he was associated were the Carmania, Lusitania, Aquitania, Empress of Britain, and Queen Mary, and among naval vessels the Tiger, Repulse, and Hood. During the 1914-18 war, from May 1917 to December 1918, he was Deputy Controller of Dockyards and Shipbuilding at the Admiralty, and he was created K.B.E. in 1917.

He married in 1900 Helen, daughter of the late Malcolm Macdonald. She died in 1926 and he is survived by a daughter.

January 10, 1952.

Commander Carlyon Wilfroy Bellairs, a naval writer and critic, and formerly member of Parliament for Maidstone, died at his home at Barbados on August 22, 1955 at the age of 84.

For 25 years up to his retirement from Parliament in 1931 Commander Bellairs was a prominent speaker whenever naval debates took place in the House, and was always heard with attention. He excelled, however, more when in opposition to the Government of the day on defence problems than when supporting them. At one time he was a prolific writer on naval topics in the daily and weekly Press.

Carlyon Wilfroy Bellairs was the son of Lieutenant-General Sir William Bellairs, and a grandson of the Sir William Bellairs who served with the 15th Hussars in the Peninsular and Waterloo campaigns. Born on March 15, 1871, he entered the Royal Navy in 1884. He was specially promoted lieutenant in 1891, taking "firsts" in all examinations for that rank. He served as lieutenant for 11 years, the latter part of the time as a torpedo officer, in which capacity he invented a number of ingenious devices which were adopted in the Navy, and also a graphical system of plotting light and darkness for each day of the year, on which he read a paper, by invitation, before the Royal Geographical Society. Unfortunately, his eyesight prevented him pursuing a career in the service which appeared so full of promise, and he retired on that account in 1902.

He had been permitted by the Admiralty, whilst on half pay, to act as Special Correspondent for *The Times* in the naval manoeuvres of 1900 and 1901, and it was as publicist that he was mainly occupied for the next few years. It was said that his dispatches from the manoeuvres were more in the nature of leading articles than accounts of the operations, and certainly his bent was more towards polemics or, as he himself called them, Navy politics. The moment was an opportune one for an officer of his abilities, for the German Navy Law had just been passed, and the movement for the expansion of the British

Fleet to meet this new menace was beginning. Lieutenant Bellairs, as he then was, soon became familiar to the public by his initials, "C.B.", in the *Daily Graphic* and other journals, attached to contributions which did much to re-awaken the national interest in the vital importance of an adequate Navy.

He entered Parliament in 1906 as Liberal member for King's Lynn. But his opposition to the Government on defence measures, and particularly on the economies effected in the administration of the Navy and the curtailment of the shipbuilding programme, led to differences with his party, and he eventually crossed the floor of the House in 1909. He was also at issue with the Liberal Government over Home Rule and all legislation which he regarded as of a Socialistic tendency.

When he came to contest Salford West in the January 1910 election, Admiral Lord Charles Beresford commended him to the electors for the "yeoman service" he had done as an M.P., "pluckily fighting single-handed (he was the only naval officer in the House) the cause of the defence of an Empire. Defeated at Salford and Walthamstow in 1910 elections, it was not until 1915 that he re-entered the House as Conservative member for Maidstone. He was promoted commander, retired, in 1911, and in 1913 was elected at Lewisham to the London County Council, on which he served until 1915.

After the 1914-18 War, Commander Bellairs came specially into prominence as a critic of the conduct of the Battle of Jutland on the British side. Purporting to represent the views of younger naval men, he vigorously attacked the "Material school", as he termed it, which he alleged to have been in control at the Admiralty, and eulogised instead what he called the "Historical school". Jutland he held to be the outcome of wrong teaching and a false doctrine of war, and he embodied these views in a book, written in 1919, entitled *The Battle of Jutland: The Sowing and The Reaping.* He was also the author of two volumes of poems and was a former president of the Poetry Society. After retirement from Parliament he settled in Barbados. In 1954 he made some of his property there available for a research centre for the study of plant and animal life, for which McGill University had plans.

He married in 1911 Charlotte, daughter of Colonel H. L. Pierson, of Laurence, Long Island, United States. She died in 1939.

August 24, 1955.

Hilaire Belloc, a great master of the English language, died in ripe old age on July 16, 1953, from illness after accidental burns in his study. Through half a century of continuous and enormous creative energy, in poems, essays, biographies, histories, novels, satires, and light verses, Hilaire Belloc added, year by year, and often several times in one year, to the riches of English prose and verse.

The versatility that made him tackle and triumph in so many forms of writing sprang from a magnificent delight in the things of this world and of the next. Faith, humanist no less than Catholic, was his inspiration as an artist. It gave wings to his imagination and to his sense of comedy. He could laugh louder in print than any man of his day, and he could be tender without lapsing into sentimentality. His relish for controversy, which was a by-product of his riotous pleasure in the causes and the sights and scenes he loved, misled many readers into regarding him as, primarily, a special pleader for his Church and for his highly idiosyncratic opinions on political history. It is as a pure artist, a man of honourable achievement as an author, that his name will live. The style of the poet and of the prose writer expressed a many-sided man in the round. It was forthright, vivid, sure in instinct for the right word, scornful of cant and *cliché,* civilized in the eighteenth-century manner without being ponderous.

Blood told in his genius. On his father's side he was the direct descendant of a distinguished officer in Napoleon's armies. Through his mother he could claim Joseph Priestley as an ancestor. He was born at La Celle, St. Cloud, a village between Versailles and St. Germain, on July 27, 1870. Louis Belloc, his father, was a barrister whose family, of Basque origin, had settled at Nantes some 200 years ago, and owned large sugar plantations in the French Indies. Early in the nineteenth century they were ruined by the British blockade. Belloc's grandfather became a noted painter, and a portrait of his beautiful wife, painted in 1830, hangs in the Louvre.

Left fatherless at the age of two, Belloc, and his sister (who became Mrs. Belloc Lowndes), were brought up chiefly in England, but they were often in France, knew the language, and were shaped by French modes of thought. He was educated at the Oratory School under Newman. Her served in the French artillery, but as the only son of a widow his period with the Colours was limited to one year. His regiment was stationed at Toul, near the German frontier, and that brief spell left a deep mark on him. In 1892 he went up to Balliol, was elected to a Brackenbury history scholarship, and took a first. President of the Union and prominent at college debating societies, he stood out among his contemporaries as an eloquent—and a violent—orator.

Some of his finest poetry came out in 1895 in his first book, *Verses and Sonnets.* This caused no more stir than do most first volumes of poetry. *The Bad Child's Book of Beasts,* which came out in the next year with Lord Basil Blackwood's pictures, at once reached a wide public. *Danton* in 1899 was the forerunner of a long series of historical studies. They were accompanied, over the years, by essays and reflective travel books, of which *The Path to Rome* in 1902, enlivened by the author's own drawings and sketches, is the most famous. But others in this *genre,* notably *Hills and the Sea* and *Esto Perpetua* (both 1906), *The Four Men* (1912), and *The Cruise of the Nona* (his favourite yacht), 1925, were as perfect.

When he was about 30 Belloc became naturalized and, in 1904, he was adopted as prospective Liberal candidate for South Salford. He was elected in the landslide of 1906, but he was never at home in the House of Commons. His fervent individualism, which led him to see Socialism as the begetter of a servile state. made him critical of the Liberal alliance with Labour. The Party Whips found him an awkward back-bencher, and after being elected again at the first General Election of 1910 he did not stand at the second. Instead, he joined Cecil Chesterton in writing *The Party System* and followed up this broadside with satirical novels, popularly known as "Chesterbellocs" because they were enlivened by the pencil drawings of G.K.C. The 1914-18 war brought him fame as a military commentator that did some harm to his reputation. His simplifications were too drastic and his prophecies by no means always correct.

As a historian, his great strength was a warm and unacademic sense of the past that made him write as though he had been alive at the times he was describing. A master of narrative and of portraiture, he marred some of his work—and played into the hands of his numerous learned enemies—by inaccuracies of detail and dogmatic over-confident excursions into the polemical and ideological fields he loved—not always wisely. But, even at his most controversial, he stimulated readers, inspiring them with his consciousness that the past is never dead and challenging them to examine the accepted—and transitory—orthodoxies of the universities. Men and battles, clashes of faith and of policy, the small change of vanished ages come alive in his historical studies.

His poetry, light verse and essays will be longer remembered. By his friends—down to generations born after he had achieved fame—he will be cherished in recollection as an inspiring talker, letter-writer and travel companion by land and water. He could—and would—sing French and English songs on the least encouragement and he was at ease in and added richness to any company of any age or rank. His conversation was, sometimes, Rabelaisian, and, often, in its combination of piety and good sense, Johnsonian.

Belloc married, in 1896, Elodie Agnes, daughter of John Hogan, of Napa, California. He was never the same after her death in 1914. He leaves one son and two daughters. His eldest son, Louis, was killed flying over the German lines in August 1918. His youngest son, Peter, died in April 1941, when serving as a captain of Royal Marines. He has a surviving son, Hilary, in Canada. His elder daughter, Eleanor, married Mr. Reginald Jebb, M.C., and she and her husband have for many years tended her ageing father. The younger daughter, Elizabeth, is unmarried and has published several volumes of lyric poetry.

July 17, 1953.

The death of **Jacinto Benavente,** the most distinguished and influential of Spanish dramatists and the founder of a modernist drama of ideas, occurred in Madrid at the age of 87 on July 14, 1954.

Jacinto Benavente was born in August 1866 in Madrid. As a good Madrileño, he was early attracted by the theatre. He was essentially cosmopolitan, a citizen of every country, and indeed of every class, eager to associate with the humble or humiliated underworld of cities, and, like Pio Baroja [q.v.], to study the "vidas sombrias". Later he travelled widely and acquainted himself with many European literatures. In 1896 the aged critic Valera wrote of Benavente, then author of *El Nido Ajeno* (1894) and *Gente Conocida* (1896), that "he will soon be, if he is not already, one of the most celebrated and discreet of our dramatic authors". "Discreet" may not convey the full meaning of the Spanish "discreto", but it well describes Benavente's genius. As to his fame, it grew steadily year by year and extended to other countries of Europe and to America; in 1922 it was crowned by the award of the Nobel Prize for literature.

Enthusiastic Spanish admirers began to bracket his name with that of Shakespeare, but the comparison was unwise. Himself a devoted admirer of Shakespeare, Benavente founded in Spain a modernist drama of ideas; his art works by allusion, ingenious irony, and suggestion rather than by the presentation and contrast of great human passions. His satire, always oblique and effective, based on keen observation of the life and habits of the middle classes, was levelled against empty show, shams, and false generalities. It is possible to trace a growing idealism in his work, the poet gaining on the satirist and cynic.

Benavente himself claimed that he created a public for his plays, not his plays for the public. He wrote at a time of strong reaction against the powerful effects, purely external and sometimes melodramatic, and declamatory emphasis of the drama of Echegaray and the Romantics. Benavente's dramatic effects are all internal. He cured the Romantic drama of its fever; and, thought some critics, nearly killed the drama as well. But with a people so alive to the dramatic as are the Spanish, the process was no doubt salutary.

Besides realistic plays of contemporary life, he delighted in humorous and philosophic fantasies such as *The Prince Who Learned Everything Out of Books* (1909) and *The Butterfly That Flew Out to Sea* (1926). Butterfly, rainbow, spider's web are words that occur readily to any critic of Benavente's drama; but the airy lightness of his plays is apt to be insidiously deceptive; there is more than meets the eye, there is solid structure beneath the frivolous surface, gravity of matter under the gaiety of manner, nor are they often out of touch with reality. Their contemporary, almost topical, character may cause some of his plays to age, but most of them will scarcely lose their place, a high place in Spanish literature.

In 30 years Benavente wrote 50 plays and still went on writing; his complete works fill over 30 volumes. Admirable English translations of 16 of the plays were published by Underhill in four volumes in 1923 and 1924. The high-water mark of Benavente's achievement is generally considered the play produced in 1907, *Los Intereses Creados,* a brief play with more imaginative power than was usual in his work. This was first produced in London as *The Bias of the World* by the Stage Society in 1912, and in 1920 as *The Bonds of Interest,* the first production of the Everyman Theatre. *The Passion Flower* in an English version by Underhill was produced at the Everyman in 1926; *The Princess* in 1929 by the Stage Society; and *Constanza,* renamed from *The School of Princesses,* by the Festival Theatre, Cambridge, in 1930. Under the Primo de Rivera* régime Benavente's play, *For Heaven and the Altars,* was vetoed in 1928, at a time when his *Pepa Doncel* was arousing the ire of the Clericals. In 1934 he scored successes with *The Fabricated Truth* and *Bread Eaten out of the Hand,* and *Ni Al Amor Ni Al Mar,* a much stronger play, quickly followed.

None of his plays is a masterpiece, but many of them are masterly in their deftness of touch, psychological insight, skill in dialogue, quick play of ideas, ironical humour, and sensitive reaction to the requirements of the stage: Benavente was himself an actor. This thin little man, playing dominoes and munching chocolates, might seem an insignificant figure; but one soon noticed that his expressive face, with its broad forehead, long delicate nose, small pointed beard, and arrogantly curled moustache, had strength and fineness as well as supple penetration and mobile wit. He had a serious purpose and even something of the Stoics' creed.

He continued writing to the end and in 1950 at the age of 84 he was still the most active author in Spain. He had been invested with the Grand Cross of Alfonso the Wise in 1944 and in 1950 the Medal of Labour was conferred upon him to commemorate the seven plays he wrote during the summer of 1950. Only in April 1954 his new play, *El Marido de Bronze,* was presented in Madrid and he was known to be working on two further plays when struck down by his last illness.

July 15, 1954.

Julien Benda, famous as the author of *La Trahison des Clercs,* died on June 7, 1956 at his home near Paris at the age of 90.

His thesis, from which he never deviated—at the cost of a certain increasing austerity and bitterness, but not without revealing nobility as well as pride—is that the function of the *Clerc* (scholar, man of letters or scientist) is to uphold and where necessary to proclaim the ideals of perfect disinterestedness and of attachment to absolute truth. *La Trahison des Clercs* is its manifesto; a negative one as the title suggests. It attacks Sorel, Maurras [q.v.], Barrès, Bergson and many other French contemporaries, and also the Germanic influences Benda detected behind their thought. All his life and work led up to this book and developed again from it. Even his novels are concerned with this theme.

Since the study of mathematics early set his standard of intellectual integrity, and he not only despised all experimentalism—including the kind which is necessary for the sciences—but actually prided himself on his lack of visual interest and of emotional perception, it is not surprising that the novels are not his most inspiring works. The inevitable clash of the spiritual and the practical, which provides the theme for his novel *L'Ordination,* was to him the supreme problem. There could be no compromise: for him, indeed, "Mary hath the better part".

Born in 1866 in Paris, Julien Benda first studied at the École Centrale des Arts et Métiers, but soon found that he had a call for the humane professions and turned over to the Sorbonne, where he took a degree in literature. Affected first by Spinoza and then by Bergson, who, though his senior by only two years, had already made a name for himself, Benda started to write essays; his first published book, *Dialogue à Byzance* (1900) dealt with the main subject of France's public life at the period, the Dreyfus affair. He attracted wider attention, however, only when he started to publish the *Cahiers de la Quinzaine,* which he edited from 1910 to 1914, and in which he laid the foundations of his school of thought. A philosophical novel, *L'Ordination* (translated into English under the title *The Yoke of Pity*) and three books against Bergson's teachings followed each other rapidly.

Another novel *La Croix des Roses* (1923), followed by *Lettres à Mélisande* (1925) preceded his main work *La Trahison des Clercs* (translated into English under the title *The Great Betrayal*) that was to win an international reputation for Benda. It soon became one of the most quoted—and misquoted!—books of the period, for it contained a deadly chastisement of the trend to subordinate and to exploit spiritual values for political ends. Benda followed it up with *La fin de l'éternel* (1929), *Esquisse d'une histoire des Français à la récherche d'une nation* (1932) and, when the Nazi danger began to assume menacing proportions in 1933, *Discours à la Nation Européenne,* all books of an anti-Romantic Frenchman, who fights for his spiritual inheritance against what he considers dangerous, or frivolous, innovators.

In *La jeunesse d'un Clerc* (1936) and *Un Régulier dans le siècle* (1938) he takes up again the subject of his "Trahison" . . . this time himself the cleric, the monk in the service of intellectual faith, of a cultural nationalism *à l'outrance.* His next book, *La grande épreuve de la démocratie,* was written when the Nazi forces had invaded Paris. Its manuscript was smuggled out of the city, and it appeared in New York in 1942, where it made a deservedly great impression; for the vigour of its septuagenarian author had apparently increased rather than decreased. A deep, lucid self-analysis, a reasoned rejection of all conventions leading to the restriction of freedom, and a coldly surgical dissection of all customary or traditional snares diverting pure intelligence are the characteristics of this, perhaps unlovable, but certainly admirable, thinker and writer whose work had long given him a claim to a seat among the French "Immortals".

June 8, 1956.

Sir Ernest Benn, the second baronet, publisher, and an unrepentant individualist in an age when all parties accept the fundamental tenets of collectivism, died in hospital at Oxted, Surrey, at the age of 78, on January 17, 1954.

Sir Ernest John Pickstone Benn, of Old Knoll, second baronet, C.B.E., was born on June 28, 1875, the eldest son of Sir John Williams Benn, the first baronet. Sir John Benn was mainly known for his long service to the Progressive cause on the London County Council. When he died in 1922 he was the only member of the L.C.C. who had been one of the original members when the Council was created in 1889. Ernest Benn's mother was Elizabeth, daughter of the late John Pickstone, of Hyde. She had married John Benn in 1874 and she died in 1928.

Benn was educated at the City Central Foundation Schools in Cowper Street, City Road, which he left, having failed to pass the London Matriculation examination, at the age of 16, and entered his father's office as a junior office boy. His father was a furniture designer and had started a journal called the *Cabinet Maker.* After three years as office boy Benn went on the road as a traveller for the journal. Then, in 1900, with the help of his father, he acquired the *Hardware Trade Journal,* and this—run side by side with the successful *Cabinet Maker*—marked the beginning of the publishing house of Benn.

The pains and gains of the early days of struggle—when he had very little money but a rich store of energy and dauntless courage—he graphically and with a striking frankness described in his *Confessions of a Capitalist,* which he published in 1925, and in a more recent volume of recollections and reflections, *Happier Days.* By hard effort the firm branched out—publishing a number of trade journals and journals specifically designed for the export field. Ernest Benn was the inspiration and the energy behind this growth, for his father was deeply engrossed in public life. Sir John Benn more than once acknowledged that "the bricks for the House that Benn built were well and truly laid by my eldest son".

It was Ernest Benn, too, who conceived the project, in the early twenties, of establishing the book publishing company of Ernest Benn Ltd., and he gathered together a fine string of distinguished authors. Not all his publishing enterprises met with success, but he never regretted the experiments, and some of them he regarded as among what he called "my glorious failures". In 1926 he realized a long cherished ambition when he built his new offices, Bouverie House, lifting, as he was wont to say, the trade and technical press to where it belonged, right into the heart of Fleet Street. Although his appointment, in 1934, to succeed Lord Revelstoke as chairman of the United Kingdom Provident Institution meant a severance of his close application to the day-by-day work of the great publishing house he built up, he remained a director of Benn Brothers Ltd.

Benn was known to a wider public as a champion of the rights of the individual against the increasing encroachment by the State. In the early twenties he was writing and speaking of the growing activities of the State in the same terms that others began to use 20 or more years later. (His *Letters of an Individualist to The Times* gathered together the most important of a long series published between 1921 and 1926). He looked forward gloomily to the day when a party would come to power with the slogan: "You have the baby; we do the rest". In 1930, in *Account Rendered: 1900-1930,* he was already complaining that the social services were placing too heavy a burden upon prosperity.

During the twenties and thirties and even since then—his last broadside against the collectivist State, *The State the Enemy,* was published only a year before he died—Benn contributed a steady stream of books, pamphlets, and letters condemning modern government "as a busybody in other men's matters". In *Modern Government,* published in 1936, he held that the best government is that of which there is least. He saw evil in government interference in the money market, in a monopoly broadcasting service, in extended social services—the Beveridge* Report seemed to him "a cruel red herring drawn across the path of sanity"—and, indeed, in every form of government activity to improve the condition of the people.

It was easy to mock his views—for he knew no middle way and was often exaggerated in the emphasis of his warnings. He was a Palmerstonian Liberal born out of his time. But there was a value, during the years of his active career, in having the views of such a Liberal consistently and robustly expressed. He was the spokesman of no interest but of an idea—of one aspect of liberalism which not even a collective society, if it wishes to remain free, dare ignore. His protests—deliberately addressed to the leaders of industry, of the Churches, and in politics, and not to the mass of men—helped to prevent the assumptions of collectivism from being accepted too easily, though he himself would have said that he had failed in this. At a time when capitalism was intellectually on the retreat he could speak forthrightly of the "immorality of collectivism".

He ignored much that did not fit into his theory. In his most recent book he spoke of the decline in Britain's economic strength as though it were directly due to the increasing functions of bureaucracy and not to the changed economic position of the country in the contemporary world. He overlooked—or explained away inadequately—the real improvements in human welfare caused by increasing government activity. But there were truths to be found in his one-sided gospel—of the virtues of hard work and of competition, and of the dangers of too readily allowing the State a free hand. He himself was a latterday representative of the successful Victorian business man and he carried the creed of his type bravely and with no apology until his death.

In 1903 he married Gwendoline Dorothy, daughter of Mr. Frederick Andrews, of Edgbaston. They had three sons and two daughters and he is succeeded in the baronetcy by his eldest son, Mr. John Andrews Benn, a director of Benn Brothers Ltd. and a director of Ernest Benn Ltd. He married, in 1929, the Honourable Ursula Helen Alers Hankey, only daughter of the first Baron Hankey*. They have two sons and three daughters.

January 18, 1954.

William Wedgwood Benn—See **Stansgate.**

F. S. Bennett, one of Britain's most famous pioneer motorists, was found dead in his bed at the Royal Automobile Club, London on December 22, 1958 at the age of 84. He had become a resident of the club.

Frederic Stanley Bennett was born on April 21, 1874, at Warrington. He was educated at Frodsham and Manchester University, afterwards serving an apprenticeship in the railway locomotive works at Crewe. For a time he worked in an electrical firm, but his main career started when he joined the Anglo-American Motor Company, where he was responsible for introducing the Oldsmobile and Cadillac cars to Britain.

In 1908 he conceived the idea of staging a test at Brooklands to demonstrate the interchangeability of the parts used in Cadillac cars. Three cars were stripped down completely and the parts intermingled before reassembly. For this test, and the introduction of the electric starter to Europe, Bennett was twice awarded the Dewar Trophy.

He took part in most of the motor trials in the early years of the century. During the 1914-18 War he went to the United States on a Government mission in connexion with food production problems. He became a councillor and trustee of the Society of Motor Manufacturers and Traders in 1906, and was vice-president in 1928-29 and 1933-34. He was a member of the Ministry of Transport Technical Advisory Committee on road research, vice-chairman of the R.A.C. in 1947-49, and Master of the Worshipful Company of Coach Makers and Coach Harness Makers in 1950-51.

Among his many services to the motor industry was the introduction of the general trade licence plate. Bennett was an inveterate motorist to the end of his life, competing in the annual London to Brighton run on many occasions. In 1953, when he was vice-president of the Veteran Car Club, he re-enacted the 1,000-mile reliability test of 1903, driving the same 6½ horse-power Cadillac with which he competed in the trial 50 years earlier. On successive days he travelled from the Crystal Palace to Margate, Eastbourne, Worthing, Folkestone, Southsea, Bexhill, Winchester, and Brighton, and back again each day.

He became president of the Veteran Car Club of Great Britain in the following year, and in 1955 he led a processional column of old cars to Hastings carrying a detachment of guardsmen to mark the golden jubilee of the Automobile Association. He was married, and leaves a son and a daughter.

December 23, 1958.

E. C. Bentley, the author of *Trent's Last Case,* one of the few authentic classics of detective fiction, and of comic verses which have added a new word to the English language, died on March 30, 1956 after a short illness at the age of 80.

Bentley held, as a result of this dual distinction, what might fairly be regarded as a unique position among English writers. It is more than 50 years since the first clerihew appeared in print and only a little less since *Trent's Last Case* dazzled and delighted a public that had begun to weary of the infallible sleuth of convention; and the younger generation today may not realize how fresh and individual was Bentley's performance in either case. Trent, after all, returning to life after a lapse of years, found himself encompassed by a rival host of brilliant and all too human amateurs fired by his example; while in his later phase the creator and master of the clerihew was obliged to match his skill with a horde of clever disciples and imitators. Today some of the newcomers may seem to shine more brightly. But of Bentley's originating genius in either capacity there can be no question.

He blazed these trails in the midst of an active and successful career in journalism. Born on July 10, 1875, the son of J. E. Bentley and his Scottish wife, M. R. Clerihew, Edmund Clerihew Bentley was educated at St. Paul's School and at Merton College, Oxford. A school fellow at St. Paul's was G. K. Chesterton, who remained a friend for life; at Oxford, where he was president of the Union, his contemporaries and friends included F. E. Smith, John Simon [Viscount Simon, q.v.], John Buchan, and Hilaire Belloc [q.v.].

Bentley was called to the Bar in 1901, but did not practise. In the following year he joined the staff of the *Daily News,* taking his place, under A. G. Gardiner, among the brilliant group of Radical journalists, who included C. F. Masterman, Herbert Paul, H. W. Nevinson, H. N. Brailsford [q.v.], and R. C. K. Ensor [q.v.]. At times he was acting editor of the newspaper. Then, in 1912, with an open-mindedness in matters of party politics that was permissible and perhaps indeed natural in those years, he transferred as leader-writer to the Conservative *Daily Telegraph,* where he remained until 1934.

It was while still a schoolboy that he had turned his hand, with some assistance, it seems, in the early stages, from G. K. Chesterton, to the composition of that brief and emphatic form of verse which served the uses of quintessential biography. The earliest and not the least celebrated of clerihews runs:—

Sir Humphry Davy
Detested gravy.
He lived in the odium
Of having discovered sodium.

Biography for Beginners appeared in 1905, and the relish for its comic salt and savour was to grow in succeeding years. Not all the specimens were equally happy and pertinent—sometimes the nonsense lacked authentic biographical content—but few were wholly without the felicity of the unexpected.

Then, in 1912, came *Trent's Last Case,* which was largely written in the small hours of the morning, after the newspaper job for the day was done. If this was not the detective novel to end all detective novels, it was at least the story of a successful amateur which cast the gravest suspicion upon the perfection of the Holmesian method. Artist, journalist, amateur of genius, Trent reasoned his way towards a complete and brilliant solution of the murder mystery, only to discover almost by chance that the real truth had evaded him and that he had in fact failed miserably. Here, in brief, almost for the first time, was the sleuth as human being.

More Biography, in 1929, stimulated the taste for a variety of English nonsense verse which drew so innocently upon the resources of the instructed mind. In 1936, after long years of persuasion and entreaty, Bentley produced, in collaboration with a friend, H. Warner Allen, another of Trent's cases—*Trent's Own Case.* Ingenious, resourceful, pleasantly if somewhat haphazardly decorated, this is good detection, though hardly a fellow to the earlier masterpiece; few of the complications are inherent in the intellectual essentials of the case. *Trent Intervenes* (1938) earns a similar criticism; and *Elephant's Work* (1950), a detective story of the highest improbability, fell far below his own standard. In 1939 *Baseless Biography* provided 50 new specimens together with pictures by the author's younger son, Nicolas Bentley.

In 1951 *Clerihews Complete* came out, a "definitive" edition with some suppressions and some textual changes. A few months after the outbreak of war in 1939 Bentley rejoined the staff of the *Daily Telegraph* and proved of inestimable value. An informal volume of autobiography, *Those Days,* in which he evoked the social and intellectual atmosphere of his early boyhood and drew a shrewd and telling comparison with the present, appeared in 1940.

Bentley, who was quiet and reserved in manner, was a man much liked and admired by those who knew him. He married in 1902 Violet, daughter of General N. E. Boileau, and there were two sons of the marriage.

March 31, 1956.

Bernard Berenson died in Florence on October 6, 1959 at the age of 94. His death has taken from the scene one who achieved in his lifetime the status of a legend.

To the villa near Florence in which he spent so many and such fruitful years came men and women from all parts of the world to visit one whose claim to fame was not only founded on a sureness of judgment unique in all that touched the classical schools of Italian painting, but also enlarged by a devoted application to the art of life. For although it may be true to say that especially in the field of artistic attributions Berenson's judgment was more generally respected than that of any other critic of his time, the attraction he exercised upon others was pre-eminently that of a sage, a humanist, and a stimulator.

The eldest son of Albert Berenson, of Boston, Massachusetts (who himself died a centenarian), Bernard Berenson was born in Lithuania on June 26, 1865, of Jewish stock. He was taken in boyhood by his parents to America, where, after a year at the Boston Latin School and at Boston University, he went to Harvard. After two years of further study in Oxford, Berlin and Paris, he abandoned his first interest, literature, in order to study pictorial art. His reputation as an expert grew rapidly, partly from the advice he gave such private collectors as Mrs. Jack Gardner, of Boston, partly from a long collaboration with the late Lord Duveen, and partly from his own activities as scholar and collector.

In 1900 he married Mary, widow of B. F. C. Costelloe, daughter of Robert Pearsall Smith, Philadelphia, thus becoming brother-in-law to Logan Pearsall Smith and to the late Mrs. Bertrand Russell. Left a widower in 1945, and childless, he owed much to the kindness of Signorina Mariano, the friend and collaborator who long supervised the conduct of his household, and his peculiar gift of gaining the devotion of friends and students made of his villa, I Tatti, Settignano, a unique centre of activity and—what satisfied his sense of fitness no less—sensible pleasure.

The sagacious calm of his life was rudely interrupted by the events of the 1939-45 War. In 1943 Berenson was forced to hide under diplomatic protection in the Tuscan countryside, and there he occupied his time in writing a volume of reflections, *Aesthetics, Ethics, and History,* the publication of which in 1948 greatly reinforced his international reputation. Other books followed; few writers, indeed, have produced so substantial an *oeuvre* between the age of 80 and 90. And with his *Sketch for a Self-Portrait*—a book best read, incidentally, in the admirable French translation of Mme. Charles Du Bos—the world came to know something of that intimate charm which made of B.B., as he was almost universally known, so loved a friend. His cosmopolitanism, his astonishing range of interests, his quick intuition, backed by inflexible scholarship, his knowledge of people and places, were brushed lightly on to a small canvas; and for the first time the humanist concealed behind the expert became something of a public figure.

Berenson's chief task had been set in train, however, many years before. It was to publish what may be called standard lists of the Italian painters, revised and corrected in the attribution of their works by the light of the latest research, including his own. For this purpose he took the different schools of Italy in turn, and published four volumes between 1894 and 1907. In 1932 these four volumes were combined in one, under the title of *The Italian Painters of the Renaissance,* and a further edition was brought up to date in 1952.

In this combined volume a good many doubtful works, formerly omitted from the lists, are readmitted, the object being to include "every work that shows the distinct trace of the artist's creative purpose, whether largely or only in small part by his own hand, whether done in his studio or on his initiative, or whether mere copies of lost works". Many of Berenson's attributions have been questioned by other experts, but the exacting scholarship and power of concentration involved in the preparation of the lists is universally recognized, and they remain a standard of reference which cannot be neglected. In his own field of scholarship, indeed, his influence may be compared with that of another son of eastern Europe, Sir Lewis Namier [q.v.], in the sphere of historical method.

It was characteristic of Berenson that, with succeeding editions, the imponderables played a greater part in his judgments—not, as might be supposed, from the leniency of age so much as from a growing sense of the limitations of science in the sphere of art. Asked to define his own skill, he once, in conversation, called himself "the lawyer of painting"—and it was his habit scrupulously to submit every problem to an extremely systematic method of examination. Yet this scientific approach was balanced by imagination and an ardent aesthetic sense. He never lost a keen sense of the relationship between art and life: indeed, the catch phrase "life-enhancement" remains as his criterion of all good art.

Over the years, while he was becoming a rich man and a distinguished collector through his own expertise, he was also amassing an exhaustive library of humanism ultimately designed for his old university of Harvard: a library among the most splendid of any which have been formed in our time. Among his books he nourished a personal quality which became ever more important in his own life—a sense of proportion. Early in life he had become a Roman Catholic, if of an individual complexion. And in whatever he touched, however widely his fancy roved, his humanist temper remained one which Erasmus himself would not have disowned.

To meet B.B. could be an unforgettable pleasure—though he was fully capable of making it an unforgettable pain. For he did not suffer fools gladly, and pretensions he bore with not at all. The small figure, the glancing eyes, the sensitive lips behind a neat beard, the hands which stayed so beautifully young, even at the age of 90, will long remain in the memory of those who saw them; just as the swallow-like darts of his talk, the salt of his wit, and his laughing command of the unexpected will persist, for many, as the ideal of good conversation. That academic honours came to him, that he was an honorary citizen of Florence, a member of the American Academy of Arts and Letters, and a recipient of many international honours as well, need not be said. He would himself prefer to be remembered as the *genius loci* whose refreshing presence will long be felt among the noble rooms of his library.

October 8, 1959.

Dr. Eivind Berggrav, Bishop of Oslo and Primate of Norway from 1937 to 1950, died at the age of 74 in January 1959. His death reawakens many memories of the heroic stand he made for the Christian faith during the war years in Norway when faced with the combined authority of the puppet Quisling and the occupying forces of Nazi Germany. He was a revered figure in the ecumenical movement and was vice-president of the World Council of Churches.

Eivind Josef Berggrav, born in Stavanger in 1884, was not a natural churchman although his father was a Lutheran bishop. He had no intention of entering the ministry as a young man and university student, but turned to high school teaching for 10 years. After a visit to Germany, during the First World War, and also to Britain, his mind turned to Christian theology, and he was ordained a pastor at Hurdal in 1919.

He was at once drawn into the developing ecumenical movement through the Stockholm Conference of 1925, and after his consecration as Bishop of Hallogoland in 1929 he shared the hardships of the fur trappers, the seamen, and fishermen of the far north, where he was greatly beloved. His preaching and teaching were based on the central truths of the Christian faith, its links with the common life, and its unique place in the universal life of man.

When war was imminent in 1939 he worked hard (as Bishop of Oslo) by way of the World Alliance for Friendship through the Churches to avert the catastrophe by visiting Britain, France, and Germany, but when the Nazis overran Norway in 1940 he girded himself and his clergy for resistance. The fight was opened by the pastoral letter of the Norwegian Church bishops of February 1941 with its key sentence: "When the authorities allow violence and injustice in society and when they oppress souls, then it is that the Church is the guardian of conscience". When Quisling was installed as puppet Prime Minister the Dean of Trondheim Cathedral was ordered to arrange a ceremony of glorification, and in protest Berggrav and over 800 of his clergy resigned. Summoned to Quisling's presence, Berggrav was accused of being a "triple traitor" and worthy of execution, to which the Bishop replied, "Well, here I am".

This brought Berggrav to the centre of Norwegian national life and its resistance movement, which the Nazis realized would only be sharpened if they made him a martyr. Himmler himself took the trouble to interview the Bishop, who commented afterwards: "He appeared sympathetic and intelligent during the conversation and I felt that at heart he respected my views entirely. He explained that it would be stupid to make a martyr of me. He said: 'There is another way to break your power and influence and that is to let you be forgotten.'"

In April 1942, he was arrested with three other prominent clergymen, taken to the Bredtvedt concentration camp, and charged with high treason, but, as the Bishop later told a British newspaper correspondent, his quisling advocate was "converted" and at great personal risk spoke up so strongly for him that he was himself in danger and fled to Sweden.

Quisling's position *vis-à-vis* the Church, so valiantly led by Berggrav, was not as strong as it would have appeared to be and the Primate was soon "released" and for three years confined under house arrest at Asker, his country cottage, where he was proud of having chopped 14 cords of firewood, and where the secret liaison with the resistance movement throughout Norway was carried out.

It was during this period that he learnt through the coded radio that his friend Archbishop Temple had publicly prayed for him in Canterbury. Many visitors came secretly to the cottage, and on several occasions the Bishop himself was smuggled into conferences in the Norwegian towns. His guards politely forgot to electrify the fence, two metres high, round the cottage.

With Norway liberated Berggrav's wartime renown brought him into leadership of the ecumenical movement and he addressed crowded meetings in Europe and America. He was a close friend of the late Bishop Bell [q.v.], who had visited him on more than one occasion and who had entertained him at Chichester. His rugged, upright frame, simplicity and directness of speech, and excellent English (which he perfected in captivity) won him not only admiration for his wartime courage but affection and respect for his post-war vision of churchmen of all traditions united to meet the threats of omnicompetent states, and to witness to the eternal truths of the Christian faith.

In November 1945 he went to London to receive, at the hands of Dr. Fisher [Lord Fisher of Lambeth*] the Lambeth Cross instituted by Archbishop Lord Lang in 1940 for award to leaders of other Churches in Europe who had rendered exceptional service to the cause of Christian unity. For England he had a warm regard and it was he who suggested that the most fitting place for the headquarters of the United Bible Societies to be situated was London. He was a former president of the united body and attended the third jubilee of the British and Foreign Bible Society in London in 1954.

For nearly 50 years he was editor of the periodical *Church and Culture.* He published also *The Prisoner's Soul and Our Own;* and *Land of Suspense.* In 1943 *With God in Darkness* and other papers illustrating the Norwegian Church conflict, edited by Dr. Bell and Canon H. M. Waddams*, was published in Britain.

January 16, 1959.

Lavrenti Pavlovich Beria, who held almost supreme power while Stalin [q.v.] was alive—as head of the Soviet police force and Minister of the Interior—was shot on December 23, 1953 by a firing squad after a secret trial. The Moscow official newspaper *Izvestia* carried the curt announcement on December 24.

So ended the first round in the struggle for power that broke out almost immediately after Stalin's death early in March. The outside world can have no certain means of knowing how far the charges against Beria were proved; neither can it know how far Beria made confessions of plotting against the Soviet Government. Two plain facts are, however, ominous. Beria was held in prison for six months, and then the trial was in secret. The combination of these two facts strongly suggests that Beria, in spite of all rigorous questioning, did not confess enough to allow the present Soviet leaders to parade him before the public as a broken and confessed plotter. They had to fall back upon a law of 1934 which allows a trial to be held in secret without any defending counsel.

When Stalin died, Beria naturally stepped into place as one of the triumvirs with Malenkov and Molotov. It seemed that Malenkov would lead the Communist Party and be directly responsible for internal affairs, Molotov would have foreign affairs under his control, and Beria would have all the security forces. Everything, it was said, would be done through committee work; no one man would have absolute power. Yet July 9 brought the news that Beria was arrested, dismissed from the Communist Party, and accused as a traitor.

No fall was ever more sudden or more complete. Malenkov, for one reason or another, found that he could not leave Beria with the degree of power which he exercised when they were equals under Stalin. Stalin had been the top of the pyramid; all the strings of power led up to him. When the top of the pyramid was removed the links of power were broken, and the other leaders came to distrust the amount of power that remained—outside their direct command—with Beria. They felt that they had to gain direct command themselves, and they could do it only by removing Beria.

Beria was accused of seeking supreme power for himself and, especially, of seeking to gain power by appointing his own men in some of the outlying Republics like Georgia and the Ukraine. Georgia and the Ukraine are notoriously proud and restless areas of the Soviet Union, and it would be natural for Beria, with his special responsibilities, to appoint men whom he could trust to key positions in their administration. That would be no less than his duty. He was himself a Georgian and took a special interest in the Republics. Beyond that point, surmise has to begin. It cannot be known whether he was deliberately bolstering his own power in the outlying areas because he felt his power slipping from him in the centre.

The plain truth is that he lost in the inevitable struggle for power—and he lost, in spite of his great power, because the other leaders made sure that they had the Army behind them. The record of his own career earns him no pity. He became head of the secret police after the great purges of the middle thirties, and he was ruthless in consolidating the régime and running the great prison camps in all parts of the Soviet Union. The outside world hardly knew him at all. In appearance he was deceptively mild, with his clerkly face, his pince-nez and his quiet manner.

He was born in 1899 into a poor peasant family in the Sukhum region of Georgia, in the village of Mercheuli, and received his early education in an elementary school at Sukhum. In 1915 he left for Baku, where he entered a technical college. In this same year Beria had already come into contact with Marxist ideas and he began to organize an illegal Marxist study group. Two years later, in March 1917, he joined the Bolshevik faction of the Russian Social Democratic Revolutionary Party, and became the organizer of a Bolshevist group in his college. In 1917 he was conscribed into the Tsarist army.

At the time of the revolution he left the army and returned to Baku, where he tried to complete his studies in technology although most of his time was taken up by active participation in the work of Bolshevist organizations in Baku. Thenceforward until the final setting up of Soviet power in Azerbaijan in April 1920, Beria was the organizer and director of an illegal group of Bolshevik technicians.

By this time Beria had developed considerable talent for underground organization, and in 1921 the Bolshevik party decided to direct him to work in the Caucasian Cheka, and thenceforward until about 1931 Beria worked almost exclusively in the organs of the Secret Police. He became a vice-president of the Cheka in Azerbaijan and Georgia, president of the Georgian G.P.U., then president of the Caucasian State Police, and finally a member of the O.G.P.U., and the chief representative of that body in Transcaucasia.

Beria's task while serving in the Transcaucasian Secret Police was the unearthing and elimination of all anti-Bolshevist groups in the area, and he was subsequently decorated with the Order of the Red Banner of the Republics of Georgia, Armenia, and Azerbaijan for his "successful struggle against counter-revolutionaries". In 1931 the central committee of the Communist Party of the U.S.S.R. discovered some "deviations" inside the leadership of the Bolshevist Party organization in Transcaucasia, and the central committee in Moscow charged the central committees of the Caucasian Republics with the task of correction. Beria was transferred from his post in the Caucasian State Police in October of that year and appointed second secretary of the central committee of the Georgian Communist Party. In the ensuing year he was appointed to the post of first secretary of the same body.

At the seventeenth party congress in 1934 Beria's record secured his election to the central committee of the Communist Party of the U.S.S.R., but except for a short period in 1936, when he served as a member of the editorial commission for the presentation of the Stalin Constitution, he remained in the south until 1938. After the conclusion of a succession of widespread purges in that year, Beria was brought back to Moscow to succeed Yezhov—the former Chief of the State Police, who had been executed. Beria was appointed Commissar for Internal Affairs, a post which he held throughout the whole period of the war.

During the 1939-45 War he held a number of other responsible posts in addition to his ministerial duties. In February 1941 he was appointed a vice-president of the Council of People's Commissars of the U.S.S.R.; he became responsible for the Public Security Department, and in June 1941, together with Stalin, Molotov, Voroshilov*, and Malenkov, he was appointed to a vice-presidency of the State Committee for Defence, on which body he was responsible for domestic policy. In 1943 he was given additional tasks in connexion with the speeding up of the production of arms and war supplies, for the successful fulfilment of which in the difficult conditions of war he was awarded the title of Hero of Socialist Labour. Not only was he engaged with problems of arms production and public security in war, but from time to time he gave his attention to problems of food production and organization at the front. He was a member of the Committee for Economic Rehabilitation of Liberated Areas in the same year, and in the ensuing year he was finally elected to full membership of the Politburo, having been a "candidate" member since 1940. He was accorded the title of Marshal of the Soviet Union in July 1945. By the end of the 1939-45 War, Beria had risen high in the ranks of the Soviet Communist Party, and his many other duties forced him, in January 1946, to ask for release from his post as Commissar for Internal Affairs. He was generally believed to be in charge of Soviet atomic developments. In 1951 he again appeared to be in charge of internal affairs.

After his downfall in July there was much speculation outside Russia whether he had been a "liberalizer" or a "Stalinist" in his views on the future organization of Soviet society. In fact, the chief struggle that led to his downfall and death seems to have been a tense conflict of personalities and power.

December 24, 1953.

Henry Bernstein, who over a very long period had been one of the most prolific and most consistently successful French playwrights in the Paris theatre, died in hospital there on November 27, 1953 after an operation. He was 77.

Bernstein's was a genuine gift for the theatre, at least for the more conventional aspects of the commercial theatre. His special talent was for the strong situation, the tense scene, the display of emotional violence—in a word, for melodrama and its more obviously theatrical devices. At his normal level of "powerful" drama he gave no more thought to character than was strictly necessary for his immediate purpose and even seemed deliberately to favour a certain crudeness of language. Yet this fabricator of conventional strong drama could also display, when he chose to do so, no little psychological penetration and delicacy and could even bring off a touch of genuinely poetic sentiment. Success in the theatre, however, seems always to have been Bernstein's principal concern (the commercial theatre in London and New York was no less obediently his than that of Paris), and partly as a result he was continuously involved in the peculiar warfare of French theatrical politics. Never lacking in personal courage, he had fought no fewer than eight duels before 1914, and at the age of 62 engaged in a duel with Edouard Bourdet, the administrator-general of the Comédie Française and himself a dramatist of distinction.

Henry Bernstein, who was of Jewish parentage, was born in 1876 in Paris. Information concerning his early years is hard to come by, but he spent two years as an undergraduate at Cambridge, rowed with some distinction, developed pronounced Anglophile sympathies, and maintained, even at that age, that wealth and luxury were indispensable to art, which could not flourish without them. Success in the theatre came to him at the start with *Le Marché* (1900), followed by *Joujou* and *Le Détour* (both 1902), the latter a facile piece extolling the charm of easy morals as compared with respectability. *Le Bercail,* produced in 1904 at the Gymnase, which was the scene of most of his triumphs during the next 30 years, exhibits Bernstein in his fresher and more attractive vein, but on the other hand the still more successful *La Rafale,* a year later, is one of his most brazenly machine-made efforts. An English adaptation appeared in London in 1906 as *The Whirlwind.*

Le Bargy appeared in the earlier of these two plays, Réjane in the other. Bernstein was handsomely served by his actors all through the earlier part of his career; among others who assisted his reputation were Lucien Guitry and the elder Coquelin. Abroad he made a particular hit at the St. James's in London in 1909 with a version of the stagey *Le Voleur,* with George Alexander and Irene Vanbrugh in the leading parts. This play had been produced in Paris in 1906, as was *La Griffe;* and they were followed in 1907 by *Samson,* which completed the series of Bernstein's earlier and most violent plays, in which he exploited moral turpitude with a brutality which seemed to aim at playing on the nerves rather than the emotions of the spectators. With *Israel* (1908) his manner began to evolve not towards less theatricalism, for he remained theatrical to the last, but towards less melodrama and towards a greater elaboration in presenting a picture of social life and to some extent of character; although his penetration into character was never profound, any more than was his power of discussing a serious theme.

The production at the Comédie Française in 1911 of *Après Moi,* a melodrama on his favourite themes of love and money, was attended by a remarkable series of events. Nightly disturbances of a general anti-Semitic character, though directed against Bernstein personally on the ground that this playwright specially favoured by the Comédie Française had in youth fled to Brussels before completing the full period of his military service, were organized inside and outside the theatre by a group associated with the *Action Française.* There were arrests—Léon Daudet was among those arrested—the performances were suspended, the play was eventually withdrawn, and Bernstein fought three duels in succession, the second and third (each with pistols and swords) with Daudet, both of them being wounded, without being reconciled. Next year, however, *L'Assaut,* put on at the Gymnase, a drama of political intrigue, brought Bernstein his greatest triumph to date.

After the 1914-18 War Bernstein appears to have decided no longer to write for managers and for actors already famous, but to become his own manager and to form his own actors, which he was fully capable of doing, as he was a marvellously able stage director. He first became manager of the Gymnase, where so many of his early successes had appeared; and there he produced not only *Judith* but *La Galerie des Glaces* (1924), *Félix* (1936), *Le Venin* (1927), *Mélo* (1929), and *Le Jour* (1930). Then, in 1933, he produced *Le Bonheur,* which he had written for Yvonne Printemps [d. 1977].

Bernstein lived in New York from 1940 to 1946, having reached America at the time of the downfall of France. Vichy deprived him of French citizenship in 1941. On his return to Paris after the war Bernstein opened the Ambassadeurs theatre in the Champs-Elysées, converted from the former café-concert of the same name into the most luxurious playhouse in Paris. Here he produced two plays, *Après, Après* in 1946 and *La Soif* in 1950. For the chief part in the latter play he took Jean Gabin [d. 1976], a star of the films, who had never before appeared in the theatre.

November 28, 1953.

W. H. Berry, whose reign as a comedian in the West End will be long remembered, died at his home at Herne Bay, Kent, on May 2, 1951 at the age of 81.

William Henry Berry was a Londoner and was born on March 23, 1870. As a very small boy he was entranced by the bright lights of Lord George Sanger's circus at Astley's Amphitheatre. His first introduction to the theatre came when, at the age of 14, he was apprenticed to Keith, Prowse and Co. The firm's name was an open sesame which gave the stage-struck lad the *entrée* to every theatre and he was not shy in asking for complimentary seats. So it was that from an early age he saw all the great ones of the past and this yearning for the footlights, kindled at Astley's, was fanned into flame.

His first step was to become assistant business manager to Wilson Barrett at the old Globe Theatre. Barrett's departure for Australia threw Berry out of work until he found himself in the Ediswan electric lamp factory at Tottenham. Then it was that he first discovered his talent as an entertainer, and after office hours he was kept busy at local dinners and concerts, until he was able to give up working in the factory. Some 12 years as a concert artist in the winter and a seaside pierrot in the summer followed.

It was a hard but invaluable training, first on the old Wellington pier at Yarmouth, and later with the Bohemians at Broadstairs. One night the audience included George Grossmith, Jnr., and Ivan Caryll, and the former asked Berry if he and his wife would care to appear in one of George Edwardes's musical comedies. Such were the foundations of a life devoted to the making of good honest fun.

With Lily Elsie* he appeared in *The Merry Widow;* then followed *The Dollar Princess, A Waltz Dream, The Count of Luxembourg. Tina* was followed by *High Jinks* and then his greatest success, *The Boy,* in which he played Mr. Meebles, the magistrate who found himself in the farcical position of having to pronounce judgment on those who had been with him the previous night in a raided night club.

Berry was one of the earliest broadcasters and was on the air in 1922 in pre-Savoy Hill days, and in 1938 took the part of Mr. Micawber in a series of Dickens broadcasts.

He was married twice, first to Miss Kitty Hanson, whom he met when she was a typist in his Ediswan lamp days. They were devoted partners in the home and in their work until her death in 1947. At the age of 77 he married Mrs. Agnes Lydon, who had nursed him through a severe illness.

May 4, 1951.

Lord Bessborough, the ninth earl, who died on March 10, 1956 at his home, Stansted Park, Hampshire, was Governor-General of Canada from 1931 to 1935. He was 75.

Although he will not rank in Canadian history among the greater holders of that office, he discharged its duties with energy and conscientiousness. Before his succession to his father's peerage he had been, as Lord Duncannon, for some years Member of Parliament for Dover.

The Right Hon. Vere Brabazon Ponsonby, G.C.M.G., ninth Earl of Bessborough in the Peerage both of Ireland and of the United Kingdom, Viscount Duncannon of the Fort of Duncannon, co. Wexford, and Baron Bessborough of Bessborough, co. Kilkenny in the Peerage of Ireland, and Baron Ponsonby of Sysonby and Baron Duncannon of Bessborough in the Peerage of the United Kingdom, was born on October 27, 1880. The eldest son of the eighth Earl by his marriage with Blanche Vere, C.B.E., daughter of Sir John Guest, Bt., M.P., he came of an old Cumberland family, one of whom, his ancestor Sir John Ponsonby, had commanded a regiment of cavalry under Oliver Cromwell and had settled in co. Kilkenny.

Educated at Harrow under Dr. Welldon and at Trinity College, Cambridge, he took his degree and was called to the Bar by the Inner Temple in 1903. He also served as a lieutenant in the Bucks Yeomanry and later became a captain in the Territorial Force Reserve. In 1906, the year that his father succeeded to the Earldom of Bessborough, he unsuccessfully contested Carmarthen as a Unionist. In 1907 he entered the London County Council as a Municipal Reformer and representative for East Marylebone and remained a member of it for three years.

In January 1910 (he was then Lord Duncannon), he was returned to Parliament for Cheltenham, but was defeated in the general election of the following December. In 1913 he re-entered Parliament as member for Dover, which he continued to represent until his father's death in 1920. During the war, with the exception of a period of service as G.S.O.3 in

Gallipoli, he was on the Staff in France under his close friend Sir Henry Wilson. After the war he entered the City and became chairman of the San Paulo Railway and deputy chairman of De Beers Consolidated Mines, and sat on other boards.

In 1931 Lord Bessborough was appointed Governor-General of Canada, created a G.C.M.G., and sworn of the Privy Council. The appointment caused some surprise as, although he had visited the Dominion once or twice, he was almost unknown there. The facts, however, that Lady Bessborough was, albeit a Protestant, French, the first of her race to be Vicereine at Rideau Hall, and that he also had a good command of the French language, commended his régime to the French-Canadian people. His parliamentary experience, moreover, helped him in the performance of his duties, though during his time no serious constitutional problem such as Lord Byng had had to face arose.

During his earlier Canadian career Lord Bessborough did not enjoy a widespread popularity. A certain stiffness of demeanour, largely the result of shyness, and a quick temper handicapped him in his intercourse with Canadians; and his insistence upon the full rigours of ceremonial etiquette contrasted unfavourably with the friendly democratic ways to which Lord Byng and Lord Willingdon had accustomed them. In 1934 there was a particularly unfortunate incident. On the occasion of a visit to a public function at Toronto he found that there was nobody to receive him. The neglect was due to error; but when eventually the Mayor appeared, Lord Bessborough rebuked him in the presence of others for discourtesy to the King's representative. It led to his being made the target of more outspoken press criticism than any of his recent predecessors had incurred, and, since he had a high sense of his duty, he was deeply distressed by it. Forced, however, to realize that he had few friends in Canada who would come at need to his defence, he changed his ways, and for the remainder of his time there did his utmost to make himself agreeable. Consequently he succeeded in retaining a considerable measure of good will.

During his Governor-Generalship he made a valuable contribution to the cultural life of the Dominion. An ardent patron of the drama—he had a private theatre at his seat at Stansted Park where he regularly produced plays, though it was destroyed by fire in 1942—he was distressed by the lack of Canadian support for it, and therefore, with much enthusiasm and success, he promoted a revival of the National Drama Festival which had been inaugurated by Lord Grey. It became, as a result of his efforts, a flourishing annual institution. In all his activities—he was very hospitable and travelled widely—he was ably assisted by Lady Bessborough, who, throughout his term, was extremely popular with all classes. In September 1935, he left the Dominion to be succeeded by Lord Tweedsmuir, and two years later he was created an earl of the United Kingdom in recognition of his services. (The earldom had previously been only in the peerage of Ireland).

In 1936 he had become president of the Council of Foreign Bondholders and in 1937 succeeded Sir Austen Chamberlain as chairman of the League Loans Committee. In September 1940 he was invited by the War Cabinet to set up a department attached to the Foreign Office to co-ordinate the activities of all the Government departments and voluntary organizations, British and French, concerned with the welfare of the French in Great Britain.

In recognition of his work at the head of that department he was created a Knight of the Grand Cross of the Legion of Honour. In his later life Lord Bessborough published three books. He was co-editor of *Lady Bessborough and her Family Circle* (1940), and he edited *The Diaries of Lady Charlotte Guest* (1950) and *The Diaries of Lady Charlotte Schreiber* (1952).

Lord Bessborough married, in 1912, Roberte, the only daughter of Baron de Neuflize, C.V.O., of Paris, who survives him. There were three sons and a daughter of the marriage. The second son died in 1925 when he was ten years old, and the youngest son died in 1951 as a result of a traffic accident when he was on military duty in Germany. The eldest son, Viscount Duncannon, succeeds to the family honours. He was born in 1913 and married, in 1948, Mary, daughter of Charles A. Munn, of New York, by whom he has a daughter.

March 12, 1956.

Antonin Besse, HON. K.B.E., HON. D.C.L., OXFORD, who died at Gordonstoun School, Elgin, on July 2, 1951 at the age of 74, accumulated great wealth as a general merchant and shipowner in the Middle East, particularly in the Red Sea and Gulf of Aden areas. It is, however, by his magnificent gesture in endowing a college, St. Antony's, in the University of Oxford that he will be chiefly remembered in Britain.

With the death of Antonin Besse, Oxford mourns one of her most munificent and also one of her most modest benefactors. For some time, at his urgent request, his identity was kept secret. Even when he allowed his name to be mentioned he at first declined, with genuine modesty, to accept the degree of Doctor of Civil Law. When he was at last prevailed to accept it he requested that it should not be at the *Encaenia* but on a separate and more private occasion. It was actually conferred on him on June 18, 1951, before a well-attended meeting of Congregation which paid him the warmest tribute, for his gift to Oxford is very great. New colleges are seldom founded in modern times. Pembroke in the seventeenth, Worcester in the eighteenth, Hertford and Keble in the nineteenth centuries are the only examples at Oxford. It is gratifying that M. Besse, with Mme. Besse and his family, were able in June to visit Oxford and see the college established and working. M. and Mme. Besse gave a garden party in the college grounds to a large number of members of the university.

It was in May 1948 that Besse through his solicitor first approached the university. His idea then was to found and endow a college in some English country house which was to be affiliated to the university and to receive a number of French students. Besse was moved to this by his admiration for English university trained men, especially Oxford men, whom he had frequently employed. The university view was that the college had better be in Oxford and since Besse was anxious for haste it was suggested that his aim would be more speedily and effectively fulfilled if he could arrange for existing colleges to accept French students. This led to the allocation of part of the funds which he had offered to eight colleges and halls who were thus enabled to extend their buildings and to accept students from France. As reported in *The Times* in June, the colleges have begun to accept French students, some have completed the additional building, others are setting it in hand.

In September 1948 Besse visited Oxford in strict anonymity and it was suggested that Ripon Hall, the theological college with fine buildings and grounds on Boars Hill, might be acquired and transport provided to make it easily accessible from Oxford. Negotiations for this scheme fell through and it was not till the summer of 1950 that the building called Halifax House in Woodstock Road was allocated by the university for the foundation of St. Antony's.

On May 1, 1950, the university appointed Mr. Deakin, Fellow of Wadham College, to be the first Warden, and he began with the utmost speed and efficiency to bring the college to life. It came to being in October 1950, and has now completed its first academic year. It has now four Fellows and expected to have in 1952 from 25 to 30 students, of whom at least six would be French. The college was originally limited to graduate students and is mainly devoted to such students, but there is no statutory limitation. It is already becoming a centre of graduate study and the Warden gives his assistance to the other colleges which have shared Besse's benefaction in arranging for the admission of French graduates to Oxford.

When one reflects on the influence over 50 years of the Rhodes benefaction on Oxford and the ties which it has made between Oxford and the English-speaking world oversea, it is clear that in the course of time Besse's foundation, conceived by him with such liberality and enthusiasm, should have the same beneficent effect on the relations between Oxford and the academic world of France from which since medieval times many malign incidents of history have severed us.

July 5, 1951.

Aneurin Bevan, Deputy Leader of the Opposition and M.P. for Ebbw Vale since 1929, who died at his home at Chesham, Buckinghamshire at the age of 62, on July 6, 1960 was one of the most prominent, vivid and controversial personalities in the Labour movement. He was a politician of brilliant if uneven talent, often at odds with the party leadership, a parliamentary performer whose wit, pugnacity and scintillating verbal imagery could dazzle and delight the House.

His unpredictability baffled and fascinated friend and foe; he could inspire the deepest affection and the liveliest enmity. The complexity of his character matched—and largely explained—the diversity of his political career. Within a few years of having launched, as Minister of Health, his National Health Service he had resigned from the office of Minister of Labour over differences with his Government on defence and social service expenditure. His leadership of the dissident group which became known as the Bevanites made him a storm centre of controversy within the Labour movement, and for a time in 1955 the party whip was denied him. Few could have predicted then that about four years later he would become Deputy Leader of the Opposition.

The transformation from the fiery rebel to the more mellow statesmanlike figure he became may be said to date from his selection as party spokesman on foreign affairs. But it was not an easy process, and it involved him in one of the most testing encounters of his career with those who had once been his most ardent followers. He risked forfeiting the esteem of many of them when at the party conference of 1957 he argued powerfully against a motion for the unilateral renunciation of nuclear weapons. It was not the only time he puzzled and disappointed his supporters.

Bevan was in fact a much misunderstood figure. It was customary to compare him with David Lloyd George, but apart from their Celtic fervour the two had little in common. Bevan, surprisingly enough, was not a natural orator, and some would argue that there was ground for saying he was not an orator at all. Certainly he professed a contempt for oratory. He was a thinker, capable, while on his feet, of clothing in shimmering phrases the thoughts which darted through his lively mind. Although he was one of the most effective platform speakers of his day, he had a genuine distaste for large public meetings and, unlike Lloyd George, he was often at his worst in face of interruptions.

He was not a real demagogue because he continually asserted the necessity for basic principle. It was a favourite contention that while the expediencies of political life might enforce the modification of principle, it was impossible to construct a principle upon a series of modifications. His political outlook was undoubtedly influenced by bitter experiences in South Wales and in his work underground in the coal mines at the age of 13. Basically he was an anti-Conservative, believing profoundly in the class struggle, but he realized that a healthy democracy could function only if the citizens were educated to an adequate social conception. He foresaw a future in which the working classes would want to acquire a first-class copy of a Renoir as much as a Cup Final ticket.

Bevan was a dilettante in the best sense of the word. He had much in common with Charles James Fox, and in this respect one recalls Pitt's own appreciation of his lifelong adversary. When a distinguished Frenchman expressed surprise at Fox's dominance of Whig politics Pitt replied, "Ah, but you have never been under the wand of a magician".

Aneurin Bevan was born at Tredegar, Monmouthshire, in November 1897, the son of a coal miner. He was educated at Sirhowy Elementary School, and after leaving it in 1910 went into the mines. After some years of employment there—it was eventually terminated by nystagmus—he went to the Central Labour College. Later he became increasingly prominent in the councils of the South Wales Miners' Federation and was particularly active in connexion with the great strike of 1926. In 1929 he was returned as Labour member for the Ebbw Vale division of Monmouthshire, a constituency which was to remain loyal to him throughout his political career.

In his early days in the House Bevan confined himself to speaking on mining matters. He had, however, a faculty for debate and a power for concentration in argument which were soon to impress his fellow members and to win him a reputation for forceful vitality. In 1934 he married Miss Jennie Lee, who until 1931 had been Labour member for North Lanark and was one of the Left wing of the Labour Movement. She was returned for Cannock in 1945.

In March 1939 Bevan, who had joined the "United Front" movement, of which Sir Stafford Cripps [q.v.] was the most prominent member, received a letter from the secretary of the Labour Party threatening his expulsion unless he dissociated himself from it. The expulsion was confirmed at the annual party conference at Whitsuntide, and it was not until December that Bevan was received back into the Labour Party.

In the war years Bevan was as frank a critic of Churchill's* as he had been of Chamberlain's administrations. He was, moreover, prepared on occasion to indulge in what appeared to be a personal dislike for Churchill, who once described him as a "merchant of discourtesy".

In May 1944 Bevan led a challenge to the Government and to his own party, which very nearly resulted in a second expulsion, over Defence Regulation 1AA which prescribed heavy penalties for the instigation of strikes in essential industries. The outcome was that the party organization decided that he should be expelled unless he would give written assurances of loyalty. This he promptly gave and later in the year he was elected to the National Executive of the Labour Party.

With characteristic self-confidence Bevan accepted the post of Minister of Health in the Labour Government of 1945. He carried through Parliament the Local Government Act of 1948, and with the Minister of National Insurance he was joint sponsor of the National Assistance Act of the same year, which wound up the Poor Law. Under his regime Britain, and principally British local authorities, produced far more new dwellings, temporary or permanent, than any comparable country in Europe, but at a cost which was almost certainly excessive.

Bevan's health scheme was one which he honestly believed, in spite of the opposition of the leaders of the British Medical Association, would be welcomed by the doctors themselves. He produced a Bill based on the Coalition scheme with certain daring changes, never before contemplated even by the Labour Party, such as the nationalization of hospitals, their management by "mixed" regional boards, and the stopping of the sale of publicly-remunerated general practices. The Health Act was a masterly attempt to cut the Gordian knot of contending interests by a bold compromise not wholly to the liking either of the Labour Party or of the doctors, but sufficiently imaginative to earn for Bevan the respect of all parties in Parliament and at least the respectful neutrality of the consultants and specialists.

These early hopes were soon dashed, partly by psychological blunders on the part of Bevan and some of his less responsible political supporters, no less by the attitude of the B.M.A. leaders. When Bevan became Minister they gave him neither quarter nor credit for the many unpalatable changes he forced his own party to accept. In spite of his noticeably cynical realism and flexibility, Bevan was not free of doctrinaire ideas, which he betrayed in emotional remarks about the sale of practices and in his long insistence on a "basic salary" for every general practitioner. The B.M.A. made effective use of all this in its campaign. Even his self-imposed silence during most of 1947, when negotiations with the medical representatives were resumed after the passing of the Act, was turned against him.

The revulsion of feeling became general at the end of 1947, when the doctors' negotiating committee came back crestfallen from their talks with Bevan without a single one of the major concessions which the B.M.A. was demanding. The doctors prepared themselves without enthusiasm for a boycott of the service due to start in July. Bevan was at first tempted to be equally stubborn. But by early April he was persuaded to make a final effort at reconciliation. He was wise enough and big enough to swallow his pride. The basic salary was made optional, he promised an amending Bill to make the introduction of a full-time medical service impossible without fresh legislation, and met the doctors' leaders once again to agree on a final settlement. This quarrel, so belatedly settled, hampered the smooth launching of the new health service, but the blame for it does not rest wholly on Bevan.

From the completion of the administrative and legislative measures necessary to implement the National Health Service, Bevan's Ministerial career reached its zenith. But he felt himself in a situation of increased isolation in the Cabinet. Many of his colleagues resented the constant advice and criticism they received from the *Tribune* newspaper which, if Bevan had no direct association with it, was edited by close and intimate associates and frequently gave expression to views identical with his. In particular Bevan was known to distrust a good deal of the foreign policy of the Labour Government.

In fact the Labour Cabinet had at times been an uneasy coalition and disputes in the Cabinet over nationalization of steel and over foreign policy had aggravated this division. In 1947 Sir Stafford Cripps attempted a palace revolution for the removal of Attlee* which Bevan emphatically refused to support. But though he worked on terms of apparent amity with Attlee, the two men never established a mutual understanding.

In 1947 and again in 1950 a group of Labour backbenchers, many close associates of Bevan, published pamphlets under the titles of *Keep Left* and of *Keeping Left,* highly critical of Labour Government policy, and the second of these pamphlets appeared on the very eve of the election of 1950 and aroused considerable controversy. Bevan was already under attack. In 1948 in a speech on the inauguration of the National Health Service he was reported as describing Conservatives as "lower than vermin", and though he declared that in the context it applied to the South Wales coalowners of the last century the observation was criticized by a number of his parliamentary colleagues.

Immediately after the election of 1950 which returned the Labour Government with a bare majority to half a dozen, the presentation of supplementary estimates for the Health Service amounting to nearly £100m. resulted in a motion of censure in which Bevan came under heavy attack. He was compelled to agree to a declaration by Sir Stafford Cripps imposing a ceiling upon National Health expenditure.

In October 1950 Sir Stafford Cripps resigned the Chancellorship owing to ill health and was succeeded by Hugh Gaitskell*. During the Christmas recess of 1950 it became known that following discussions in Washington the Cabinet had agreed to a very large increase in defence expenditure which would inevitably involve anxiety among Labour members. There was considerable talk about ministerial resignations.

In January Bevan became Minister of Labour. He was aware that a resignation by him at such a moment would involve him in old and buried hostilities, and cause deep cleavage in the movement, and he was known to be genuinely reluctant to take this course. The proposals in the Budget involving charges amounting to some £12m. in respect of certain National Health Services, and the reduction by £100m. of the surplus standing to the credit of the National Insurance fund were the ultimate reasons which brought about in April the resignation from the Government of Bevan and of the President of the Board of Trade, Harold Wilson, and of John Freeman.

The resignations led to widespread controversy in the country and in the Labour Party. On the whole the trade unions, through their leaders and the official central organizations of the Labour Party, condemned Bevan, while he received increasing support from the constituency parties. He naturally became the leader of those Labour members who had been principally critical of Cabinet policy and the group of members who had been responsible for the publication of the *Keep Left* pamphlet was rapidly enlarged until it numbered about 50 Labour members, and was responsible for the publication of two more pamphlets, the latter of which, *Going Our Way,* published under the auspices of *Tribune* and critical of Government financial policy, appeared on the eve of the parliamentary election of 1951 which resulted in the return of a Conservative Government.

At the annual conference of the Labour Party preceding the election an effort had been made to close the ranks, but some bitterness was caused by the result of the election for constituency party representatives on the Labour Party National Executive in which the Minister of Defence, Shinwell, lost his seat after a very long membership while Bevan headed the poll and three of his supporters obtained seats. From this period the word Bevanite was constantly used to denote those Labour members whose votes would usually be cast in support of the policies advocated by Bevan. But a number of well-known Labour members included among this number were never members of the Bevanite organization.

After the defeat of the Labour Government it was soon made clear that the Parliamentary Labour Party was not prepared to tolerate what was referred to as a "party within a party" and there were early demands for the reimposition and enforcement of standing orders to be followed by strong disciplinary action. In March 1952 on the defence debates a three-line whip was issued which took the unprecedented course of instructing Labour members to vote not only for the Opposition amendment but also in support of the Government White Paper. There was in fact a large abstention on the vote on the amendment and 57 members, including Bevan, voted against the Government on the main question. There was an immediate demand for an expulsion of these 57 members from the party and at the meeting of the Parliamentary Party Attlee moved a resolution calling for the reimposition of standing orders and for written undertakings to be called for from the members concerned.

Ultimately a more moderate amendment moved by George Strauss calling for party unity and the reimposition of standing orders was carried by a substantial majority.

When the results of the constituency party elections were announced it was found that both Herbert Morrison* and Hugh Dalton* had been defeated. Two more Bevanites had been added to the executive, James Griffiths* being the only supporter of official policy to retain his seat. The deep cleavage in the Parliamentary Labour Party continued and the pattern remained the same. Bevan could count on overwhelming support from the constituencies and gained no additional support in the Parliamentary Labour Party. Bevan was faced with the dilemma of either refusing to submit himself for election to the Shadow Cabinet or of offering himself for election and remaining there in a permanent minority and bound by minority decisions.

In 1952 he offered himself for election and secured the last of the 12 seats. His position was a singularly uneasy one and in 1954 a scene in the House of Commons, in which in a supplementary question on the South East Asia Treaty Organization Bevan was regarded as having strongly dissociated himself from the view just expressed by Attlee, resulted in a formal rebuke of Bevan and his resignation from the committee. The vacancy thus created was, under the rules, filled by the runner-up at the preceding election, who was Harold Wilson, Bevan's principal lieutenant, and it was believed that his acceptance of office resulted in a weakening of the understanding between them.

In March 1955 the continued controversy within the Parliamentary Labour Party which had ranged over German rearmament, the use of the hydrogen bomb, and the necessity for discussions with the U.S.S.R. seemed to have been brought to a head when, at a meeting of the Parliamentary Labour Party, Attlee moved a resolution for withdrawal of the whip from Bevan. This was finally carried, after the narrow rejection of a compromise resolution, by a majority of 141 to 112.

The National Executive of the Labour Party then discussed the expulsion of Bevan from the Labour Party. Attlee, who had undoubtedly been surprised by the narrow majority in the Parliamentary Party, moved a resolution for postponement and for discussion with Bevan which was carried by one vote only; and after Bevan had given assurances of his desire to conform to the constitution of the party, the Executive, again by one vote only, decided not to expel him though Gaitskell and Morrison were among those voting for expulsion. A week or two later, in face of a general election, the parliamentary whip was restored.

Bevan gave up his seat on the National Executive of the Labour Party to enter into a contest for the office of treasurer of the party left vacant by the death of Arthur Greenwood [q.v.]. This brought him into direct conflict with Gaitskell, who had been nominated by the principal trade unions. Bevan had declared that while he knew immediate defeat was inevitable he would continue the contest for some years.

In December of 1955 Attlee resigned his leadership of the party and a ballot resulted in 157 votes being cast for Gaitskell, 70 for Bevan, and 40 for Morrison, Bevan in fact retaining almost exactly the support he had had throughout the controversy.

Bevan made clear his intention to accept this decision and he did not contest the position in 1956. Gaitskell and Bevan both made efforts to arrive at an understanding and in the course of the violently controversial debates on the Suez question they achieved a close association, co-operative if not cordial. Gaitskell in assigning roles in the Shadow Cabinet first entrusted Bevan with colonial affairs in which he at once proceeded to take a very keen and active interest. In a later re-allocation of duties Bevan was entrusted with the shadow role of foreign affairs, a position which he had always particularly desired.

During this period Bevan's parliamentary style noticeably mellowed and his speeches became less aggressive. He adopted a parliamentary technique of offering thoughtful and constructive suggestions, but presented with the old artistry and inflection and in a manner which began to command increasing respect on both sides of the House.

But the new statesmanlike Bevan found himself in a sharp dilemma at the 1957 Party

Conference when he had to oppose a composite motion demanding unilateral renunciation by Britain of nuclear weapons. One of the arguments he used in encompassing its defeat—with trade union help—was that its passage would mean sending a British Foreign Secretary naked into the conference room.

Some months later he angered some of his hearers when in a Commons debate he appeared to put a gloss on those words, and there were murmurs of "over-diluted Bevanism". Some of his former adherents gathered themselves into a "ginger group" under the resuscitated title of "Victory for Socialism", and their activities prompted a move to unite Labour forces behind an agreed policy on disarmament and nuclear tests. His championship at public meetings of the official line brought him under noisy protests from those who spurned it. In April 1959 he startled the Commons by flinging into a Foreign Affairs debate a blunt declaration that a Labour Government would stop all hydrogen bomb and atomic tests at once. At this time he was much preoccupied with the dangers of rearming Germany, and in general his responsibilities as "shadow" to the Foreign Secretary imbued his speeches at times with a certain melancholy foreboding about international events as evolving "with all the inevitability of an ancient Greek drama". Some of his speeches seemed to lack his former buoyancy and ebullience, though one he made in the early days of the new 1959 Parliament, advocating the televising of the House, recaptured the old brilliance in full.

Bevan had gone with Gaitskell to Moscow in the summer recess of 1959 but they came home immediately the date of the general election was announced. Bevan was returned by Ebbw Vale with a majority increased by more than 1,000, and soon after the new Parliament met he was elected Deputy Leader of the Opposition on the resignation of James Griffiths. In all the heart-searching in which the Labour Party engaged after their decisive defeat, many of the rank and file who feared a retreat from essential Labour policies, particularly on public ownership, looked hopefully to Bevan. Whether, at the party's grand inquest at Blackpool, they got the reassurance they desired seemed to be left in some doubt. But they revelled in the sparkle of his wit and basked in the mellowness of his mood.

The bitterness which sometimes entered into Bevan's political utterances was completely absent from his private life. His marriage to Miss Lee was singularly happy and the visitor to his house in London or later to his farm in Buckinghamshire had the rare privilege of being entertained by two outstanding parliamentary personalities of exceptional charm.

Bevan loved the good things of life and there were few subjects on which he could not talk with considerable knowledge and none on which he could not talk attractively. He delighted in conversation for its own sake. A genuine appreciation of art and literature was reinforced by a remarkable memory. His philosophical outlook had moved from a Marxist foundation to an appreciation of the theories of Jose Rodo on the Protean nature and perfectibility of man. He might be found cheerfully, brilliantly, but without ostentation, discussing in painting the modernism of Braque* or approving the exquisite drawing of Fragonard, quoting from such widely varied poetry as Chesterton and Crabbe or illustrating a musical disquisition with records of Stravinsky* or of Negro spirituals. He was generous to a fault and kindly and considerate in adversity.

July 7, 1960.

Ernest Bevin, Lord Privy Seal and formerly Foreign Secretary, who died at his London home after a heart attack on April 14, 1951, at the age of 70, was for the greater part of his life an outstanding figure in the British trade union movement. After sterling service as Minister of Labour and National Service in Churchill's* war-time Coalition Government and as Foreign Secretary in the years immediately after the war, he had gained a place in men's hearts few could equal, and his death is deeply mourned not only by his own countrymen but by all the free nations of the world.

He went to the Foreign Office at a critical juncture in the history of British foreign policy. The balance of world power had been entirely upset by a great war and no one could predict what the role of Britain would be in the future international order. She had emerged from the war militarily weaker than either her Russian or American allies; her economic assets, on which her influence had largely been founded in the past, had been ruthlessly cast away in support of the war effort; her people were tired, and the election campaign had revealed a strong demand for speedy demobilization and a quick return to the routine of peace. Unless these disadvantages were overcome Britain's influence on the peace settlement would be small and she might quickly sink to the status of a second-rate Power.

Bevin faced his task with little of the traditional equipment. His experience of negotiation was confined almost entirely to trade disputes, and his information about foreign countries was derived, apart from his numerous journeys abroad in international trade union business, largely from a diligent study of Foreign Office telegrams during his membership of the War Cabinet. His parliamentary experience consisted of five years on the Government Front Bench. Nevertheless he showed himself capable of taking firm and clear decisions, and he applied to the conduct of foreign policy the same large views and infinite capacity for detailed work as he had shown in organizing the country's man-power while Minister of Labour in the war-time coalition.

The keynotes of Bevin's foreign policy were honesty and frankness. He believed that Britain stood for certain simple and clear-cut principles which could be universally applied, and that British influence depended on championing them wherever they were challenged. These principles were fidelity to the pledged word, the right of nations to determine by free elections their own forms of government, and respect within the nation for the rights of individuals and groups. Liberal idealist as he was, however, Bevin was a shrewd judge of the politically possible. No peace settlement could last unless it had the support of the great Powers, and Bevin was ready to compromise in order to get that support. He believed that compromise should never involve moral confusion or hypocrisy and should never be purchased at the cost of certain essential and enduring interests of Britain and Europe. He believed that the common task of administering Germany could be a bond of union between east and west; he was convinced that a rigid division of control in Germany was incompatible with a stable Europe. It was not until repeated attempts to agree with Russia had failed that he bent himself with zeal to creating a close partnership in western Europe and to the independent organization and unification of the western zones in Germany.

Whatever the final judgment on Bevin's foreign policy, it displayed some characteristically British qualities—courage, frankness, shrewdness, and practicality. A powerful speaker, he usually carried away his audience but was sometimes carried away himself, indulging in large and generous conceptions which bore little relation to reality. His language was seldom precise and he relied mainly on the impression produced by his strong personality. When at the conference table he came rapidly to earth, concentrated rigorously on practical essentials—the result apparently rather of instinct than of any process of logical thought—and had a healthy contempt for legal formulas. His chief defects as a parliamentarian were undue sensitiveness to criticism and a tendency to attribute malice to all who attacked him. As the Prime Minister mentioned in his broadcast last night [April 15, 1951], Bevin came to Parliament too late in life to become a real House of Commons man. He was often too proud to disarm criticism by explanation. His robust and generous nature, on the other hand, won the hearts of all who knew him intimately, and it was no secret that he was Churchill's favourite Labour colleague in the coalition.

Apart from his work as Foreign Secretary since the war, Bevin played an important part in shaping the economic policy of the Labour Government and he worked closely with Sir Stafford Cripps [q.v.] in aiming at the goal of solving the balance of payments problem and making Britain independent of external aid. Before he died he had seen both these objectives achieved.

In addition to his great practical commonsense Bevin had a fertile mind and constantly produced new ideas. Had he been able to devote himself to politics as a younger man his thinking might have modified some of the more rigid doctrines of Socialism. As it was he had never the leisure, or perhaps the vital urge, to dissect the *clichés* learned in an earlier generation, and the burdens of responsibility and ill-health which at last weighed him down left him clinging to well-worn beliefs which some of his own thought had sometimes appeared to challenge.

Ernest Bevin was humbly born in a labourer's home in the Somerset village of Winsford in 1881. His parents died while he was still a child. After living for a few years with a married sister he became a farmer's boy for his keep and sixpence a week.

When but 13 and with no more than a few shillings of worldly wealth, he abandoned the country for the town. Making his way to Bristol he first became kitchen boy in a restaurant, where he had his meals and was paid a shilling a day. Presently he became a van boy, then a tram conductor, and later a van driver. Town life brought him into contact with trade unionism and the Social Democratic Federation. Attendance at a Sunday afternoon meeting gave him an opportunity for public speaking and argument and he steered his course for full-time trade union employment. At a time when there were no State unemployment benefit, no State sickness or medical benefit, and when the mass of labouring men, notwithstanding what friendly societies were able to do, was helplessly driven to Poor Law relief in days of adversity, Bevin became the champion of Bristol's unemployed. On a memorable occasion, while the Dean was preaching, he led a company of the workless into the cathedral, where they stood in well-behaved files, mute witnesses of want and social neglect.

His trade union career began with his appointment as secretary to a carmen's branch of the Dockers' Union. He was appointed assistant national organizer in 1913 and assistant general secretary to Ben Tillett in 1920. The first time he attended a Trades Union Congress was in 1915. He was not yet a national figure even in trade unionism, though his progress was to be rapid. His industrial horizons were broadened that year by a visit to the United States as a fraternal delegate to the American Federation of Labour, and at home he had a foretaste of large-scale administration as a member of the Government's Port and Transit Committee which regulated the supply of dock labour during the years of submarine warfare.

He leapt suddenly into fame when he conducted the case for the dockers before a wage tribunal set up by the Government in 1920. Against him was an eminent King's Counsel. Bevin himself marshalled the evidence and stated the arguments of the men. His opening speech, well documented and fortified with figures, occupied more than two days, and he immediately won the honorary title of the "dockers' K.C." The court conceded nearly all that he claimed. To him the result was more than an industrial victory; it was a vindication of his belief that, given a competent and independent tribunal, the workers could obtain justice by reason and conciliation more successfully than by striking and without the loss and suffering that a stoppage of work must inflict on the men themselves, on industry, and on the country.

For all that, Bevin was unable to rely always on argument and reasonableness. The temper in his own union was not favourable to conciliation a few years later when the dockers struck work, against his advice, in resistance to a reduction of wages during a trade depression; nor again when he thought circumstances favourable for a renewed claim, and was met with resistance and a challenge. So, soon afterwards, came a London transport workers' strike and Bevin, the conciliator, appeared in the public eye as a centre of industrial storm. This was undeniably a period of militancy for Bevin and it was to rise to a higher pitch still in 1926 when the organized workers rallied to the support of the miners.

Perhaps the General Strike was, as he later saw it, the culminating point in the conflict of two philosophies. Its failure and its cost and the long-continuing industrial ill-will brought him again to explore the ways of industrial understanding. In the autumn of 1926 he was one of a delegation of employers and trade union leaders which undertook a Government mission to investigate industrial methods in the United States. A year later he warmly approved the discussions between a group of industrialists led by Sir Alfred Mond (the first Lord Melchett) and members of the General Council, and he deeply resented the Trades Disputes Act of that year as a vindictive reprisal for the General Strike. After serving on the Macmillan Committee on Finance, Bevin took a still more prominent part in shaping industrial labour's economic policy. He had an increasing part, too, in the study of international relations, both economic and political, and in the work of the International Labour Organization. He was president of the T.U.C. in 1937. In the following year he attended the Commonwealth Relations Conference in Sydney and, partly for reasons of health, he extended his tour.

Bevin was one of the architects of the modern trade union structure which attached the unions more closely to each other and called for higher qualities of leadership in the T.U.C. General Council. He clung to the democratic principle in trade union control, he accepted decisions taken against his advice, but he never shirked the duties of leadership or wanted the courage to incur unpopularity in advancing his opinions. The original basis of his strength in trade unionism was among the unskilled workers. Beginning with the dockers and the road transport workers, and bringing in the unskilled men of many industries who were weak through isolation, he constructed the great Transport and General Workers' Union on a wholly new pattern.

It was not until he was 59 and approaching retirement that Churchill summoned him in 1940 to join the Coalition Government as a member of the War Cabinet to undertake the immense and delicate task of organizing the nation's man-power. At the Ministry of Labour he was an immediate success. He knew his own mind. He went prepared with ideas and with ways of carrying them out, and he took control of his department and set it to work out his plans. The department responded with something more than the traditional loyalty of the Civil Service, for it felt with him the compulsion of the national emergency and recognized in him a man of leadership and initiative. His reputation in the trade unions, combined with his immense energy, made it possible for him to obtain from his fellow trade unionists a voluntary abrogation of many of the traditional safeguards of labour in order fully to mobilize the national effort.

He could thus justly claim in 1943 that Britain was the most highly organized of the belligerent countries. At the same time he made a full contribution to the deliberations of the War Cabinet. Apart from the part which he played in the direction of the war Bevin was mainly responsible for devising the demobilization scheme, which returned millions from the forces to civil life with smooth efficiency and a fairness of treatment acknowledged by all. During this period he made an intensive study of foreign affairs, and when Attlee's* Government was returned those who knew Bevin regarded his qualifications for the post of Foreign Secretary as far superior to those of any of his colleagues.

He was appointed to that office in the middle of the Potsdam Conference in July 1945. Attlee recalled last night [April 15, 1951] his vivid recollection that when Bevin went to Potsdam at short notice he showed an immediate grasp of the problems there. Almost at once he had to embark on the task, destined to prove more difficult than even pessimists had supposed, of maintaining agreement between the great Powers in shaping the peace settlement. Two practical objectives were before him, the making of peace with the satellite countries and the achievement of a more permanent and stable settlement in Germany than was provided for by the Potsdam agreement.

Nine months of arduous negotiation failed to yield agreement with Russia on some of the most important aspects of the peace treaties with Italy and the other German satellites. Finally Bevin, with full American support, proposed to submit the uncompleted drafts to a general peace conference. This meant that the disputed points would be debated in public. After months of exhausting vituperation the Paris Peace Conference ended with the agreed drafts approved without any material change and the blank spaces left by the great Powers unfilled. At the end of 1946 the Council of Foreign Ministers, meeting in New York, at length approved the terms of the peace treaties with Italy, Bulgaria, Romania, Hungary, and Finland. This success was little more than formal, as later events painfully showed, but it was a triumph for Bevin's personal method of diplomacy.

A more serious test of inter-allied cooperation was Germany—whether the four Powers could agree on an economic and political programme by which a reunited Germany would become self-supporting and self-governing. But the Russians refused to contemplate economic and political unity except on the basis of a highly centralized Germany closely tied to the Soviet Union by an obligation to pay reparations out of current production (in practice the burden would have fallen on the western occupying Powers). At the end of 1947, having just sat through the third of a series of abortive Councils of Foreign Ministers, Bevin reconciled himself to the fact that the western Powers must go their own ways in their own zones, even if the consequence was to confirm the partition of the Reich.

Having changed his course, Bevin, with his American and French colleagues, pursued the new one with great courage and determination. Both were needed. On June 20, 1948, soon after the three western Powers, with the support of the Benelux countries, had decided to bring into being a federal government in western Germany, the Soviet Government severed their land and water communications with Berlin. This faced the western Powers, as the Soviet Government thought, with the choice of abandoning their programme for western Germany or quitting the German capital. Bevin had never any doubt that the western Powers must resist this kind of pressure, and few doubts that, barring physical interference by the Russians, the airlift organized by the British and American air forces would succeed. In the event, the Russians, as Bevin had expected, decided not to play the game too dangerously. They were beaten by a combination of air lift and counter-blockade imposed by the western Powers on the communications of their eastern zone; and at Lake Success on May 4, 1949, they signed an agreement by which both sides restored normal facilities.

Meanwhile the Soviet Government had shown itself ready to exploit and perpetuate post-war poverty and misery everywhere for the purpose of enthroning its power throughout all Europe. In spite of what he called the "ambulance" work of Unrra, Bevin in the middle of 1947 felt depressed about the outlook for European democracy and civilization. Britain, as he said in a later speech in Washington, could see what needed to be done, but no longer had the means. Then he heard on his radio on the morning of June 7, 1947, [General] George Marshall [q.v.], the United States Secretary of State, make a speech at Harvard in which he hinted at substantial economic help for Europe if the European Powers would organize themselves for mutual help. That, said Bevin, was "like a lifeline to sinking men". He promptly took the initiative, which led to the formation of the 16-nation O.E.E.C. as the instrument of European recovery.

He had always wanted, Bevin told the House of Commons in January 1948, the widest European co-operation, including that of Russia. But Russian aims and standards had defeated him, and in the same speech he ventilated for the first time the idea of Western Union. It involved the effective co-ordination of the free nations of Europe for political, defence, and economic purposes. Already in March 1947 he had signed the Treaty of Dunkirk with France. On March 17, 1948, conversations initiated by him reached their conclusion in the signature of a treaty of mutual assistance between Britain, France, Belgium, Holland and Luxembourg. In the interval the whole western world had been shocked by the Communist *coup* which destroyed the independence and free institutions of Czechoslovakia, and in June the Senate of the United States passed the Vandenberg [q.v.] resolution welcoming the association of the United States with regional agreements. On April 4, 1949, Bevin signed in Washington the North Atlantic Treaty, which united for defence purposes Canada and the United States with eight countries of Europe, and in the negotiation of which he had played a most important part.

Bevin was an architect of Western Union in its broadest sense. He saw his country in a position to act as pivot of an association of sovereign States covering North America, Western Europe, and the British Commonwealth. He was reluctant to compromise it by letting the United Kingdom become integrated in a West European State. It was only under strong pressure from France, which is preoccupied with the German danger, that he committed Britain to a tentative step in that direction by agreeing to the Council of Europe.

The conduct of British policy in the other parts of the world faced Bevin with many anxious decisions. Those on Palestine were the most controversial. He was convinced that the policy which in the long run would best serve the interests of the western Powers in the Middle East must be based on the fact that the great majority of the inhabitants of the Middle East are Arab. He would not impose a Jewish State on them, and he could not, without gravely compromising Anglo-American relations, impose a settlement unacceptable to the Jews. So when his efforts to bring Jews and Arabs to a bargain failed, he placed the problem in the lap of the United Nations, with the warning that Great Britain would take no hand in implementing any recommendations which were not accepted by both Arabs and Jews. With great pertinacity, and in face of much criticism, he stuck to his course, to the point of pulling out the British administration and troops, and leaving the Jews and Arabs to fight it out. His own solution was overborne by the facts, and he would neither seek nor support any other.

Bevin was able in 1946 to negotiate a new treaty and protocols with the Egyptian Foreign Minister, Sidky Pasha. They provided for the withdrawal of British troops from Egypt, and, as Bevin understood it, for the full right of self-determination of the Sudan. But the Sudan protocol was interpreted differently by Egypt and became a dead letter. On his way home from the Commonwealth Foreign Ministers' conference at Colombo in January 1950 he stopped at Cairo, where he had an encouraging exchange of views with the Egyptian Prime Minister and Foreign Minister on the possibilities of reopening negotiations.

The Communist revolution in China created new problems for the British Government in the Far East and south-east Asia. His action in recognizing the new Government on January 6, 1950, was regarded by many as precipitate. The Communist Government was undoubtedly in control of the whole of the mainland of China, but the United States, France, and several of the British Dominions were for one reason or another not in a position to extend recognition.

With the Communist victory in China, south-east Asia had become an emergency area. On Bevin's initiative the Commonwealth Foreign Ministers met at Colombo early in 1950 to discuss how the Commonwealth could help countries in the region to achieve firmer economic foundation for a democratic and independent political life. Before he died he had the satisfaction of seeing large concrete programmes worked out for the development of agriculture and industry in the Commonwealth countries of south-east Asia, to be supported by technical assistance and funds from outside the region.

In his last year of office Bevin's activity was reduced by indifferent health. His devotion to duty was undiminished, but he appeared to have no longer the vigour of mind and body, which had helped to make him so influential in international negotiation, or to be capable of the effort required to make British foreign policy fully known and understood by the people of his own country. He went to New York in the autumn for the international gatherings that produced the plan for the North Atlantic Defence Force, including Germany, and in general worked hard to make the Atlantic Treaty a going concern.

On March 10 he laid down the heavy burden he had borne at the Foreign Office since the summer of 1945 and was succeeded by Herbert Morrison [later Lord Morrison of Lambeth*]. His services in the Cabinet were, however, far too valuable for Attlee to dispense with them and the position as an elder statesman he had achieved by his services in war and in the peculiarly delicate international situation that succeeded it made his presence in the Government indispensable. He was therefore appointed Lord Privy Seal in the place of Lord Addison [q.v.] who took over Mr. Morrison's office of Lord President of the Council. There was naturally some redistribution of functions between the offices, but the paramount consideration was that discussions in the Cabinet and its committees should continue to have the benefit of a voice which from its first great triumph as that of "the dockers' K.C." to its forceful and inspiring reiteration of democratic principles at conference after conference on international affairs was recognized throughout the world as the authentic utterance of Britain's faith.

April 16, 1951.

Lord Baldwin of Bewdley [Oliver Baldwin] —See **Baldwin**.

The death of **Gilbert Beyfus,** Q.C., at his home at Haslemere on October 30, 1960, robbed the Bar and the general public of a direct descendant of the great jury leaders of the last century.

Gilbert Hugh Beyfus was born on July 19, 1885, the son of Alfred Beyfus, a solicitor, and Emma, the daughter of Robert Plumstead. He was educated at Harrow and at Trinity College, Oxford, and was called to the Bar by the Inner Temple in 1908. In the days when young members of the Bar devilled without payment, hoping only for the experience it brought them, the outbreak of the First World War must have appeared as a throwing aside of years of painstaking and laborious effort. Beyfus interrupted his career and was commissioned into the 3rd Battalion, The Duke of Wellington's Regiment in August 1914 as a second lieutenant. He served with the 2nd Battalion in Flanders in 1915 and in April that year was wounded at Ypres. A month later he was taken captive and remained a prisoner of war until December 1918. In 1919 he retired as a captain, having been mentioned in dispatches.

On leaving the Army he returned to the Bar and began to rebuild his practice. Within three years he made his second and final bid to enter Parliament; in 1910 he had unsuccessfully fought the Cirencester division of Gloucestershire as a Liberal. In 1922 he contested the Kingswinford division of Staffordshire as a Coalition candidate but again he was unsuccessful. Many great advocates have been singular failures in the House of Commons but it was to be expected of Beyfus that, had he been returned as a member, he would not have been one of their number.

Beyfus now turned his attention from politics and gave himself solely to the Bar. The golden rewards were there for the taking and he steadily acquired a varied and lucrative practice. In 1933 he took silk, and in 1940 he was made a Bencher of his Inn. As a leader he naturally found himself concerned more and more in the field of libel and slander; for it is largely in such cases that a barrister with a civil practice encounters a jury and Beyfus was an advocate who was completely at home with them.

Advocacy, it has been said, means essentially the exerting of the whole of one's charm and ability to make a doubtful case look unanswerable. Today's style of advocate is conversational, quiet, almost mundane. The floridity and emotion of other ages is now out of place; its effect on the present-day jurymen would probably be disastrous, and its exponent ridiculous. The hush which descended on Westminster Hall when Erskine was on his feet will not be witnessed again; his oratory, and that of Marshall Hall, has gone, but in Beyfus the Law Courts found a worthy successor. For he was able to combine to an extraordinary degree their eloquence with the modern style. In large measure it fell to him to show the Bar that a simple lucid use of today's words goes hand in hand with eloquence; and that great advocacy is the lively fashioning of commonplace and everyday speech, stamped with the character of the person who utters it. Sometimes Beyfus spoke for 10 minutes; once he made a speech, from the briefest of notes, which lasted six days.

Great as he was as an advocate, it was as the exponent of cross-examination that Beyfus excelled. Simple and direct, but wily as Serjeant Ballantyne, he would relentlessly harry a witness until the truth was out; if there was anything to be concealed, better not to go into the witness box to face him. Better to hear him ask the jury why X had not been willing to answer a few questions. As with his speeches, so with his cross-examination Beyfus relied on simplicity and a mastery of detail to give the lie to what had been said with every appearance of honesty and truth.

With his large and fashionable practice, principally concerned with defamation and divorce, he appeared in *causes célèbres.* The more recent cases which spring to mind are the Marchioness of Winchester's action against Mrs. Fleming, the Ortiz-Patino libel action, Aneurin Bevan's [q.v.] action against the *Spectator,* the Brighton conspiracy, and the Liberace case; more recently still, Mrs. MacPherson's action against the Duchess of Argyll, which was the last case he took before he retired. He was constantly before the public eye and his health inevitably suffered from the burden of a heavy practice. Yet in spite of two serious operations, one at the age of 73, he returned and continued apparently undiminished in vigour. The difficulties which beset him at this stage of his career, when he was often engaged in more than one Court at the same time, would have been no light thing for a more youthful man and Beyfus must often have been thankful, as have many, for a clerk who arranged these matters so smoothly.

Apart from his mastery of the arts of advocacy, Beyfus took a special interest in the law of gaming and wagering and he was briefed to appear in the famous Aspinall gaming case. He used to maintain that all games were a mixture of chance and skill except one, Snap, which was a game of pure skill.

Perhaps it was from his background that Beyfus derived a measure of his success; in common with the late Mr. Justice [Sir Travers] Humphreys [q.v.], his father was a solicitor and so the law must have played a part in his upbringing as a child and a young man. As well, his father was keenly interested in the stage and had collaborated with D'Oyly Carte. The characteristics of the actor are to some extent found in the successful advocate, although, as Beyfus himself pointed out, an advocate writes his own lines. Beyfus inherited and retained his father's interest in the theatre and to the end of his life was a member of the Savage Club.

Beyfus married, in 1929, Margaret Malone, by whom he had one son; his second marriage, in 1949, to Joan Grant was dissolved, and he married for the third time, in 1953, Eileen Louisa Hill, who survives him. He retired from practice in May 1960, having some two years before received the congratulations of the Bench and Bar on the fiftieth anniversary of his call. When he retired it was greatly feared that with him went a tradition which could never be replaced; it is difficult to see who his successor will be.

October 31, 1960.

The Nawab of Bhopal, who died on February 4, 1960 at the age of 65, was an important figure in the prolonged discussions which preceded the transfer of power in India in August 1947, for in the last four of the 26 years of the existence of the Chamber of Princes he was its Chancellor. He combined marked gifts of statesmanship with great distinction in the athletic field.

Air Vice-Marshal His Highness Sir Hamidullah Khan Sikandar Saulat, Nawab Ruler of Bhopal, G.C.S.I., G.C.I.E., C.V.O., was born on September 8, 1894, being the youngest of the three sons of that accomplished lady, Sultan Jehan Begum, who skilfully ruled the state from the death of her regnant mother in 1901 to 1926. Her gifts of insight led her to eschew for her youngest and favourite son residence at the Chiefs' College at Indore; she sent him to the Mahomedan Anglo-Oriental College at Aligarh (subsequently created a university, of which he later became Chancellor).

He captained the cricket XI and won his hockey cap. He became one of India's most famous polo players and had the exceptional handicap of nine goals. In 1937 he brought his unbeaten polo team to Britain, comprising 45 ponies, their attendants and five players. He introduced cycle-polo in India and organized its growth. He was also a keen yachtsman, fisherman, and lawn tennis player. His love of big game shooting could be amply gratified in the game reserves of his personal estates in Bhopal.

The Begum took care to interest him in administrative work as soon as he came down from college. He gained experience both in the law and justice and the finance departments of the state, and for six years from 1916 he was Chief Secretary. Through life he worked hard as well as played hard, his custom being to spend six hours daily at his desk or in other administrative labours.

His two elder brothers died in 1924, both leaving two sons. The Begum claimed that under Islamic law and in accordance with local family custom her surviving son instead of the eldest grandson should succeed to the Rulership, and she bent her energies to securing his recognition by the Viceroy. The first decision at Delhi was adverse; but the Begum went to England with Hamidullah, and privately intimated that she would not leave until she had gained her way. Prolonged and exhaustive researches into history and precedent brought further considerations under review, and the Begum was informed in March 1926 by the Viceroy, through the Secretary of State (Lord Birkenhead), that the Government was prepared to recognize Hamidullah as heir apparent.

Within a few weeks of her return to Bhopal the Begum abdicated in his favour. She lived for another four years to be his shrewd counsellor. Thus, contrary to all reasonable expectation in youth, he became ruler of a Muslim state second in importance only to Hyderabad, with an area of close on 7,000 square miles and a population of more than 800,000. In pursuit of his progressive policy he established a legislature, and gathered round him able and experienced administrators, as, for instance, Sir Joseph Bhore. As a sportsman he was a man after Lord Willingdon's own heart and that Viceroy, visiting the state in 1933, spoke of his "amazing sense of anticipation".

By this time the Nawab had become an outstanding figure among the hereditary rulers. He had long been a member of the small standing committee of the Chamber of Princes, and in March 1931 was elected Chancellor in a close contest with the late Maharaja of Patiala but resigned in the following year. He took an active part in the three sessions of the Indian Round Table Conference in London. He was re-elected to the Chancellorship in 1944. He gave most generous help to the war effort of the allies and maintained the strong loyalty of his House to the King Emperor. But in the negotiations for the transfer of power he was not one of the Princes who hankered after some measure of British protection, for he was keen that Indian autonomy should be complete. He was called upon to represent his Order in discussions with the Cabinet Mission in 1946, and he counselled his brother Princes to seek an evolutionary solution. He hoped for and worked for a settlement under which the Princes would be able to take a full and combined share in the development of an independent India. He aimed at their forming a third neutral and balancing dominion within the sub-continent. In the absence of an effective press and opposed by the full force of the leaders of the National Congress and the Muslim League, the plan was stillborn.

With a view to gaining a neutral position for his state on certain understandings, he signed in 1947 the instrument of accession to the Union. His plan to bring into being a constituent assembly was not favourably regarded by the States Ministry in Delhi, nor were his ambitions—notably to be Governor-General of Pakistan—gratified. But this Muslim-ruled state among the many Hindu principalities in Central India secured a special position. Instead of being merged into a geographical group like the great majority of the states, it was centrally administered and his rule was no more than titular. He was promised that for a period of five years there would be no change in this status without his consent. It was stated in Parliament in March 1951 that the Nawab had given an assurance that if, after investigation, changes were planned to merge Bhopal with any neighbouring principalities, he would extend his co-operation in the best interests of the people.

The Nawab left no sons and the succession devolves on his eldest daughter, the Begum Abiba, a noted sportswoman and an air pilot of distinction, yet full of feminine charm. So the headship of the state (now merely nominal) reverts to the female line in which it was held for 100 years before Hamidullah succeeded in 1926. Another daughter of the Nawab is the wife of the Nawab of Pataudi [q.v.], "Pat", captain of the Indian cricket Test team in 1947.

February 5, 1960.

Prince Antoine Bibesco died in Paris on September 2, 1951 at the age of 73.

Born in Paris in 1878, he was a member of a family of the old nobility and a descendant of George Demetrius Bibesco, Sovereign Prince of Wallachia. In 1920, after being attached for some years to the Romanian legations in Petrograd and London, he was appointed Romanian Minister in Washington. It was a period during which relations between America and Romania were difficult, and exchanges between the two countries sometimes reached the point almost of acerbity.

In January 1926 Prince Bibesco was recalled to the Foreign Office in Bucharest. It was understood at the time that a conflict had arisen between him and Titulesco, the Romanian Minister in London, who was head of the Romanian Debt Commission and was sent to the United States to negotiate a settlement of Romania's debt to America.

Whatever the truth about that conflict, there was no truth in one suggestion which was then sometimes made—that Romania might have secured a more favourable debt settlement if it had not been for Prince Bibesco's mishandling of the situation. Those who were in a position to know were not hesistant in their tribute to the skill and courage with which he supported his country's interests. In February of the following year he was appointed Romanian Minister to Madrid. He remained there until 1931. In 1937 he became Romanian delegate on the International Commission for the Danube in Geneva.

Prince Bibesco, who in 1919 married Lady Elisabeth Asquith, daughter of the first Earl of Oxford and Asquith by his marriage to Margot Tennant, was himself a playwright of light comedies. These, such as *Laquelle?* which was produced at the Théâtre des Mathurins in 1927 and at the Gate Theatre in 1932, and *Mon Héritier,* also produced at the same two theatres, had a particular reputation for being comedies of the "risky" sort. They had also wit and a style of their own and, slight though they might be, were lively entertainments.

Princess Bibesco, remembered by the general public for her original talents as a writer and by her friends for her charm and wit, died in 1945. There was one daughter of the marriage.

September 4, 1951.

Lord Bicester, a leading figure in the City for well over 50 years, died on February 17, 1956 at his home at Bicester, Oxfordshire, at the age of 88.

The Right Hon. Vivian Hugh Smith, first Baron Bicester, of Tusmore, in the county of Oxford, in the peerage of the United Kingdom, was born on December 9, 1867. He was educated at Eton, where he boarded at Dalton's and his tutor was E. L. Vaughan, and at Trinity Hall, Cambridge. He came of a family which had already distinguished itself in finance and commerce. His father, Hugh Colin Smith, was for a long time the head of Hay's Wharf, the fortunes of which he did much to build, and he made his mark in the City from an early age. He was elected a director of the Bank of England in 1876 and was Governor of the Bank in 1897 and 1898. Vivian Hugh Smith, his eldest son, followed his father into the City, and on coming down from Cambridge went into the Hay's Wharf business, where he carried on his father's work. His brother, Owen Hugh Smith, is now the head of the business, which, next to the Port of London Authority, is probably the largest wharfage enterprise in London.

When still in his thirties, however, he became a partner in J. S. Morgan and Co., the merchant banking firm, which had been founded as George Peabody and Co. by that famous merchant banker George Peabody, and has since changed its name to that of the subsequent senior partner, who was the father of John Pierpont Morgan I. From then onwards Vivian Smith made J. S. Morgan and Co.—which later changed its name to its present title of Morgan, Grenfell and Co.—the mainspring of his career. He was a partner—and after the firm became a private company a director—for over 40 years; for most of that period in association with his cousin Edward Grenfell. Under the guidance of these two the importance and status of the firm, already great, increased progressively. It handled countless important financial transactions on behalf of Governments, home industries, and oversea trade.

Two special developments helped to spread the firm's influence and interests into diverse parts of the world. The previous head of the firm, Junius Spencer Morgan, though he made his career in this country, was born an American and came originally from Boston. His son, John Pierpont, decided to return to America, where he founded the firm of J. P. Morgan and Co., which was later to become the largest and most powerful banking firm of its kind in the world. Close relations between Morgan, Grenfell and Co. in London and J. P. Morgan and Co. in New York naturally existed from the first. At a later stage Vivian Hugh Smith, through his friendship with the late Sir David Yule, took an important interest in Andrew Yule and Co., the well known Eastern merchants, and in the associated London firm of George Yule and Co. (later Yule, Catto and Co.), of which he had been chairman for many years.

Vivian Smith's career was for long intimately bound up with that of Morgan, Grenfell and Co., of which he was one of the two principal partners, and of which later, when the firm was incorporated, he eventually became chairman. Outside Morgan Grenfell, though he was a director of several large companies, his main business interest was in the Yule firm and in the Royal Exchange Assurance, where he had the remarkable record of being a director for well over 50 years and Governor since 1914. He gave much of his time and energy to the affairs of the Royal Exchange Assurance, and the huge growth of this institution over that period was mainly due to his work and his vision. Part of that expansion was due to the acquisition of other assurance businesses, and these acquisitions which took place largely on his initiative proved uniformly well chosen. In his special bias towards enterprises which were developing the new line of motor insurance, he showed a foresight which, however obvious it may seem in retrospect, was very far from general at that time.

In his business and public life the City, with its work and traditions, and his own special cares of Morgan Grenfell and the Royal

Exchange Assurance, always came first. He was indeed one of the outstanding men in the City for over half a century and few people in the whole of the City's history can have achieved a comparable record of eminence over so long a period. He was bound to the City alike by his own interests and by family ties. He was the eldest of six brothers, all of whom showed the ability which had established the family's fortunes in earlier generations. Four of the six made their careers in the City and between them they provided the managing directors of two of the City's leading merchant banks, a senior partner of one of its leading Stock Exchange firms, and a head of the original family firm of Hay's Wharf. The other two entered the Navy, in which both had distinguished careers and retired as admirals. The Hugh Smiths indeed acquired an almost unique position as a well known City family dispersed among different firms and different activities. Vivian was perhaps, as was appropriate to the eldest son, *primus inter pares.*

Though he was never very actively engaged in politics and never entered Parliament, he played a prominent part in the political life of the City of London. He was chairman of the Conservative and Unionist Association of the City for many years. But even so, he was probably less interested in party politics than in maintaining contacts between the City of London and the Governments of the day. And although he was not much in the public eye he was active in maintaining such contacts for many years. Neville Chamberlain paid a public tribute to his work in that sphere. He was raised to the peerage in 1938.

He was indeed a notable representative of the City. He had in full measure the best and most typical of its talents and abilities. Anybody thinking of Lord Bicester would think first of the reasonable and fair-minded attitude with which he approached every problem, his anxiety that in any transaction all concerned should not only get, but should feel that they were getting, a fair deal. This more than anything was the clue to his fame and success as a negotiator. People never felt that he had taken any advantage of them or concealed anything. Moreover, he had infinite patience and hated to abandon any negotiation once he had begun it.

In addition to intellectual and administrative ability of a high order he had a quick, clear, and farseeing eye both for people and for economic and commercial developments. There were many ventures to which he committed himself or his business that appeared problematical or worse to many of his contemporaries, but these duly justified his confidence. His ready appreciation of human talents led to numerous business associations and personal friendships with men who were later to win fame in financial and other spheres; and it is of interest to record that it was at his instigation that the present Lord Catto [q.v.], later to be appointed Governor of the Bank of England, but at that time a young and comparatively unknown man, joined the firm of Andrew Yule and eventually became Lord Bicester's partner in Morgan Grenfell.

Lord Bicester had the advantage of a charming and dignified presence and a natural gift for friendship; perhaps one of his most noticeable and valuable personal traits was the calm, reassuring, and unruffled manner which was the outward sign of an inner steadiness of mind and judgment. Indeed, in his work, his character, and his person alike, he was the very embodiment of the City at its best. Though the City and family life left him with only limited time for public work, he took an active part in the civic and other activities in his home county of Oxfordshire. He had been Lord Lieutenant of the county since 1924. These duties he discharged as quietly and unostentatiously but with the same assiduous determination as he devoted to his duties in the City.

In the realm of sport his great interest lay in hunting and horses. For many years he was chairman of the Bicester Hunt Committee, though in his later years he gave up hunting himself. He was keenly interested in steeplechasing and always had a few horses in training (they were always 'chasers—he never took much interest in the "flat"). For a number of years he usually had a horse in the Grand National, though he never succeeded in owning a winner. But his interest never flagged and he was still in the habit well beyond his eightieth year of travelling to Ireland by air for a short weekend in search of likely horses.

He married in 1897 Lady Sybil Mary McDonnell, daughter of the eleventh Earl of Antrim. There were three sons and four daughters of the marriage. His heir is the Hon. Randal Hugh Vivian Smith, who joined his father in Morgan, Grenfell and Co. when in his early twenties and is now one of the managing directors of the firm. He married in 1922 the Hon. Dorothea Gwenllian James, the eldest daughter of the third Lord Northbourne, and there are two daughters of the marriage.

February 18, 1956.

S. J. Lamorna Birch, or "Lamorna Birch", as he was generally called, who died on January 7, 1955 at his home in Cornwall at the age of 85, was exclusively a landscape painter in oil and watercolours. Much of his work was done in Cornwall, in and about the beautiful Lamorna valley, near Penzance, where he settled in 1902 and from which he took his name in order to distinguish himself from another artist named Birch who was a member of the neighbouring Newlyn colony.

Cornish by adoption, Birch was in effect a Lancashire man, though he was actually born on June 7, 1869, at Egremont in Cheshire. The eldest of a family of 10, he left school at the age of 12 to become an office boy at Manchester, devoting his leisure to his two passions of painting and fishing. Indifferent health sent him at the age of 16 into some mills in the country near Lancaster, where he did a certain amount of industrial designing. He was already making a local reputation when, at the age of 20, he paid his first visit to Cornwall, putting up at the farm of Bolleit at the head of the Lamorna valley and becoming extremely popular in the Newlyn colony. Advised to go to Paris he studied for 11 months at Colarossi's, but Cornwall had his heart, and until his marriage in 1902 he divided his time between Bolleit and Lancashire, finding opportunities to combine art with trout fishing in both places. He was elected A.R.A. in 1926, becoming full R.A. in 1934. He is represented in practically all the provincial public art galleries in England, and also in the United States, Canada, New Zealand, South Africa and Australia. Most of his one-man shows in London were held at the galleries of the Fine Art Society, New Bond Street, but the artistic fruits of a combined painting and trout fishing tour in New Zealand in 1937 were shown at the Greatorex Galleries, Grafton Street. Birch was a very regular exhibitor at the Royal Academy, seldom failing to send the full number of works allowed to members.

Largely a self-taught artist, Birch had a distinct talent and definite limitations. He was both a good descriptive draughtsman, of rock and tree forms in particular, and a delicate colourist, but in the combination of drawing and colour, particularly in oil painting, he was apt to over-do the colour—possibly in response to the robust taste of his North Country patrons, who remained faithful to him—so that the sensitiveness of his delineation of natural features was obscured. Probably his best work was in watercolours—he was a member of the Royal Society of Painters in Water Colours—of the tinted drawing type. In them his charm of line found unhindered expression.

Birch, who was an athletic, bearded man, looking very much younger than his years, with the bright eyes and eager manner of a terrier, was the best of companions in any grade of society. Though he could hardly be described as a marine painter Birch naturally made many studies of the rainbow-tinted sea off the Cornish coast, and he took an active part in the business of the sea, associating on equal terms with the few crabbers and longliners at Lamorna, who were devoted to him, and sharing the dangers of their lonely trade. As a fly-fisherman for trout and salmon Birch was in the first rank. He tied his own flies to perfection, and to see him cast into the wind through a small opening in the bushes that fringed the Lamorna stream, in which a half-pounder was a monster, was to witness a truly artistic performance.

Birch married Miss Emily Houghton Vivian, a Cornish lady who had been his pupil. She died in 1944 and he is survived by two daughters of the marriage.

January 8, 1955.

Field-Marshal Lord Birdwood, sometime Commander-in-Chief in India and later Master of Peterhouse, Cambridge, who died on May 17, 1951 at the age of 85, will be best remembered for his leadership of the Australian and New Zealand Forces in the 1914-18 war. He inspired their confidence and admiration, and they gave him loyal and whole-hearted support through many difficult days in the forlorn

Gallipoli enterprise and in France.

The Right Hon. Sir William Riddell Birdwood, first Baron Birdwood, of Anzac, and of Totnes, first baronet, G.C.B., G.C.S.I., G.C.M.G., G.C.V.O., C.I.E., D.S.O., was born on September 13, 1865 and was educated at Clifton and Sandhurst. He was gazetted to the 12th Lancers in 1885, but in 1886 exchanged into the 11th Bengal Lancers. In 1899, in his thirty-fourth year, ambitious and enthusiastic, he went on special service with the Indian contingent to South Africa. In 1901 Lord Kitchener called Birdwood to his staff, and in the following year gave him the post of Military Secretary.

Late in 1902 Birdwood returned to India to be Assistant Military Secretary to the Commander-in-Chief. Then he was appointed A.A.G. at Simla. In 1905 he was given the brevet of colonel. Lord Kitchener, on arrival in India at the end of that year as Commander-in-Chief, appointed him Military Secretary, but, in characteristic fashion, permitted him to leave Simla in order to serve as Chief Staff Officer to the Mohmand expedition in 1908. For the action at Khargha Birdwood received the D.S.O., and was soon afterwards made a C.I.E. Birdwood next took command of the Kohat Brigade, and held it for two years, when he became Quartermaster-General in India. In 1912 he was made Secretary to the Army Department.

On the outbreak of war in 1914 Kitchener, then at the War Office, chose Birdwood to lead the Australian and New Zealand contingents then assembling in Egypt, and he commanded them in their historic landing on the Gallipoli peninsula. Then the hard struggle began. He knew how to adapt his manner to the temperament of the Australians, while his courage placed him high in their esteem. When Sir Ian Hamilton was recalled he handed over command on the peninsula to Birdwood until his successor, Sir Charles Monro, arrived. Monro promptly recommended evacuation, whereat Kitchener telegraphed to ask if the corps commanders were agreed upon this step. Birdwood gave weighty reasons for opposing withdrawal. On receiving this report, forwarded by Monro, Kitchener decided to go out himself, and meantime telegraphed privately to Birdwood, telling him to reconnoitre for a fresh landing at Bulair and that he would be given command in place of Monro. Birdwood wired back that such a landing could end only in disaster, and added: "I sincerely trust that Monro will remain in command here". When evacuation was decided upon Monro was placed in command of the Mediterranean Expeditionary Force while Birdwood was given command on Gallipoli.

Early in 1916, after reorganization in Egypt, I Anzac Corps arrived on the Western Front and took over a part of the line near Armentières. Here the Australians were not long in confirming their reputation for courage and hard fighting. In July the corps was brought down to the Somme, where the great offensive had just been launched with disappointing results. Birdwood was given general command of the Australian Imperial Forces in September. The next heavy fighting falling to the Australians was in the Third Battle of Ypres. During the ensuing winter I and II Anzac Corps were reorganized. The five Australian divisions were placed all together in one corps, named the Australian Corps. Finally, after it had been decided to reorganize the Fifth Army, its command was entrusted to Birdwood in May 1918.

He received the thanks of Parliament, with a grant of £10,000 in October 1919 and was then created a baronet. In the summer of 1920 he returned to India, this time to command the Northern Army. In March 1925 he was promoted Field-Marshal and selected to succeed Lord Rawlinson in the following November.

Birdwood never had the opportunity of shining as a strategist or as an independent commander; none the less, to his talent for handling certain types of men in the field his whole career bears eloquent witness. He remained a "character", a virile personality rather than a master of war. He had a remarkable memory for the names and faces of old comrades, and loved riding to some village within reach of Delhi or Kohat and talking in the vernacular with the veterans of former campaigns. He was A.D.C. to King Edward VII from 1908 to 1910 and to King George V from 1910 to 1911; he was A.D.C. General to the King from 1917 to 1922, and later Gold Stick in Waiting. He was appointed Honorary General in the Australian Military Forces in 1920, and Colonel of the 12th Lancers in the same year.

In 1935 he was elected president of his old school, Clifton, and in the same year was appointed Captain of Deal Castle. He had been elected an honorary fellow of Peterhouse, Cambridge, in 1920, and in 1930 he was invited to be Master. It was this novel and happy choice which lead him to entitle his reminiscences, published at the end of 1941, *Khaki and Gown.* All through life he kept a diary and on this he drew freely for an autobiography which throws much light on the many operations in the field in which he had taken part. It also bears testimony to the wide range of his friendships and his love of good stories. In 1945 he wrote a pendant entitled *In My Time: Recollections and Anecdotes.* Birdwood's seven years at Cambridge were among the happiest in his life. It was with the keenest regret both of the college and himself that he "went down" in June 1938.

Birdwood was disappointed when war broke out in 1939 that he could no longer take an active part, but a good deal of work of a ceremonial and philanthropic kind fell to him. As Deal Castle was no longer tenable he lived in his beloved West Country, at Batcombe, in Somerset, but afterwards at Hampton Court Palace in a house the gift of the King. He took a keen interest in service and Indian questions, and his lament at the passing of the old order in the Indian Army found expression in the House of Lords after his elevation to the peerage in 1938. It gave him great pleasure to receive in August 1950 a letter from General Cariappa, the C.-in-C. of the Indian Union Army, a warm tribute to British officers and men of the former Army in India and an assurance of the desire and intention to maintain the best traditions inherited from them. He also contributed letters to *The Times* on occasion. In his last years defective sight hampered his activities.

Lord Birdwood had a domestic life of great happiness. He married in 1894 Janette, eldest daughter of Colonel Sir Benjamin P. Bromhead, Bt., C.B. For her services in India she received the rare decoration of the Crown of India. She died in 1947. They had one son and two daughters. The son Lieutenant-Colonel the Hon. Christopher Bromhead Birdwood, late Indian Cavalry, who now succeeds, was A.D.C. to his father in France during 1918-19. In 1931 he married Elizabeth Vere, daughter of Lieutenant-Colonel Sir George Ogilvie, and they have a son and a daughter.

May 18, 1951.

Lord Lindsay of Birker—See **Lindsay.**

Sir Oswald Birley, one of the most successful portrait painters of his time, who counted among his sitters several members of the Royal Family, died at his home in London on May 6, 1952, aged 72.

Oswald Hornby Joseph Birley, M.C., son of Hugh Francis Birley, was born at Auckland, New Zealand, in 1880. Taken to England at an early age, he was educated at Harrow and Trinity College, Cambridge, and studied painting in Dresden, Florence, and under Marcel Baschet at the Julian Academy in Paris. Sargent was an early influence upon his style. In 1914 he enlisted in the 10th Battalion of the Royal Fusiliers and served with the battalion for a year. From 1916 to 1919 he was with the Intelligence Corps in France with the rank of captain, and won the Military Cross.

Birley was a member of the Royal Society of Portrait Painters, later becoming vice-president, the International Society and the Royal Institute of Oil Painters, and showed at their exhibitions as well as at the Royal Academy. His Academy pictures were portraits in oil, mostly of men, soldiers in particular, and a large proportion of them were presentation portraits commissioned by public bodies. Among the important people painted by him were the Queen when she was Princess Elizabeth; King George V and Queen Mary [q.v.], for Windsor Castle; King George V, for the National Museum of Wales, Cardiff, as one of a series of presidents of the museum painted by Birley; King George VI [q.v.], for the Royal Naval College Greenwich, Lincoln's Inn, and the Royal Agricultural Hall; the King and Queen of Siam; Field-Marshal Sir Henry Wilson; Lord Irwin and Lord Willingdon, for the Viceroy's House, New Delhi; Lord Baldwin; Mr. and Mrs. Neville Chamberlain; Lord Swinton*; Lord Rutherford, for the Royal Institution; Lord Craigmyle, for the board room of the P. & O. offices; Mr. Gandhi; Sir Abe Bailey; Sir Robert Witt [q.v.] and Madame Karsavina. At the Academy of 1941 Birley was represented by "At Printing House Square", showing the chairman, editor, and manager of

The Times in 1937. In 1946 he painted Churchill*, and in the following year Attlee*. He had recently completed a portrait of General Eisenhower*. He was knighted in 1949.

He is represented at the National Portrait Gallery by a portrait of the first Lord Birkenhead, and at the Luxembourg Museum, Paris, by "Mirror Portrait" (bought for the Edmund Davis Collection in 1915), and a later portrait of Mamie Cartier. There are works by him in the National Art Gallery, New Zealand, and at Birmingham and Liverpool. Birley painted several portrait groups. At the 1939 exhibition of the Royal Society of Portrait Painters he showed a huge stagebox group, dated 1910, of Haddon Chambers, the dramatist, Colonel William Egerton, and two Edwardian ladies. An eminently "safe" rather than an inspiring portrait painter, he was occasionally a little clumsy and was too much inclined to dwell on superficial glitter; but he had good ideas of arrangement and a masculine bluntness of statement that won respect. Very little of Sargent's influence survived in his later work, which seemed to be modelled rather on the great Spaniards of the seventeenth century.

With his neat moustache, well-tailored clothes, and genial manners, Birley looked more like a soldier than an artist. During the war of 1939-45, in which he served as a major in the Home Guard, he lost the use of his right eye when it was injured by a splinter in an accident at a gun demonstration in Sussex. He travelled extensively in the United States, Mexico, Siam and India. He was interested in music and the ballet, and he had some ability as an architect and helped to design his own house in St. John's Wood.

In 1921 he married Rhoda Vava Mary, daughter of Robert Lecky Pike, D.L., of Kilnock, Tullow, co. Carlow, Ireland, with whom he shared an interest in Indian philosophies and religions. They had a son and a daughter.

May 7, 1952.

Former Bishop of Birmingham—See **Barnes.**

Air Marshal W. A. Bishop, V.C., C.B., D.S.O. & BAR, M.C., D.F.C., to mention only his British decorations, who won the Victoria Cross for most conspicuous bravery, determination, and skill when, flying independently, he destroyed four enemy aircraft near Cambrai in 1917, died at Palm Beach, Florida on September 11, 1956 at the age of 62.

Born at Owen Sound, Ontario, on February 8, 1894, William Avery Bishop was the son of William Avery Bishop, Registrar of Grey County, Ontario. After receiving his education at the Royal Military College, Canada, he joined the Canadian Militia in 1911. After war broke out in 1914 he was granted a commission in the Canadian Cavalry and was drafted to France with a cavalry unit. When he was sent to Netheravon to be trained as an observer towards the end of 1915 he was refused permission to qualify as a pilot on the ground that his nerves were not good enough, and that he had not enough "go".

He was highly indignant. Nevertheless, though the courses on wireless and photography interested him but little, he paid the greatest attention to everything connected with gunnery so that by the end of his training he was by far the best aerial shot on the station. At length he was allowed to qualify as a pilot, and between April and August 1917 he won the M.C., the D.S.O. twice, and the V.C.

The exploit for which he was decorated with the Victoria Cross was an almost unbelievable feat of arms. Bishop had been flying solo behind the German lines in search of a German airfield. Spotting one, he found it deserted so he flew on until at last he came upon a new airfield about 12 miles inside the territory held by the enemy. There he saw seven new Albatros machines in a neat row, waiting to move off, some with their engines running. From a height of about 50ft. he fired at them with his Lewis gun, and a mechanic who was starting one of the engines was seen to drop. Bishop rose in a spiral and, seeing that one machine had begun to climb, he swooped down and when about 60ft. from the ground fired 15 rounds into its tail. The machine was sent crashing.

Turning, he saw that a second machine had risen from the ground, and at once he let it have 30 rounds at a range of about 150 yards. That aeroplane went sideslipping into a tree. By this time he was the focal point of an intense concentration of fire of all kinds. Nevertheless, when he saw two more machines had risen, he chased one of them, and, catching it with the full blast of his machine-gun, had the satisfaction of seeing it crash about 300 yards from the airfield. Then he emptied a whole drum of ammunition into a fourth Albatros, and, having no more ammunition, waved a farewell and flew back to his station.

He then went home to Canada on leave and was married in October, 1917, to Miss Margaret Eaton Burden, daughter of Mr. C. E. Burden and niece of Sir John Eaton. They had a son and a daughter. After his return to England he was awarded the D.F.C. in June 1918.

After the war he settled down in England and became concerned with various business interests, not unnaturally chiefly connected with flying. In 1929 he became chairman of British Air Lines, and a night and day air taxi service was established. Later he returned to Canada, and became vice-president of the McColl Frontenac Oil Company and a director of a number of other enterprises. A signal honour was conferred upon him in January 1936, when he was appointed the first Canadian Air Vice-Marshal. Promoted Air Marshal in 1939, he served during the last war as Director of the Royal Canadian Air Force and had much to do with the Empire training scheme, in which Canada played such an important part.

September 12, 1956.

Lord Asquith of Bishopstone—See **Asquith.**

Jussi Björling, who died on September 9, 1960 after a heart attack at his summer home near Stockholm, at the age of 49, was one of the finest lyric tenors of our age. Naturally endowed with a voice of wide compass and considerable dynamic range, he employed it with unusual artistry and a fine sense of style.

Johan Jonathan (Jussi) Björling was born on February 2, 1911, and began his career at the age of six as treble in a vocal quartet, the other members of which were his father and his brothers Karl Johan Olof and Karl Gustav (Gösta), who was himself a member of the Stockholm Royal Opera Company from 1941 until his death in 1957. The family quartet was trained by the father, and their public appearances took them as far afield as the United States, where they toured in 1919 and 1921.

After two years at the Stockholm Conservatory, where the English tenor John Hislop was one of his teachers, Björling entered the Royal Opera School in 1930, the year in which he first appeared at the Royal Theatre as Don Ottavio in *Don Giovanni,* Arnoldo in *William Tell,* and Jonathan in Nielsen's *Saul and David.* Between 1931 and 1939, as a member of the Stockholm Royal Opera, he sang some 50 roles; not only those in the popular Italian operas in which, as his international reputation grew, he came increasingly to specialize, but also such parts as Florestan in *Fidelio,* and Lensky in Tchaikovsky's *Eugene Onegin.* In spite of his activities in international opera, he continued to sing in Sweden, and in 1944 was appointed Court Singer.

Guest appearances at Vienna, Prague, and Dresden in 1935 laid the foundations of his international reputation; America first heard him, both as a concert singer and in opera, with the Chicago Opera Company in 1937.

From 1938 onwards he appeared frequently with the New York Metropolitan Opera. London, however, saw him comparatively rarely; he sang at Covent Garden in 1939, and did not return until March 1960, when he suffered a heart attack in the wings of the theatre as he was about to make his entry as Rodolfo in one of several performances of *La Bohème.* He insisted on continuing with the performance, and though his singing, on that occasion as always, pleased by its artistry and restraint, his ill health was probably responsible for a certain stiffness in his acting. Between these two appearances on the opera stage he gave recitals in London and elsewhere on several occasions. His recital of operatic arias in the Festival Hall in 1952 was one of the most conclusive triumphs that concert hall has known.

Though the almost traditional itinerary of the opera star prevented English audiences from knowing him in the flesh so well as they would have wished (London, it is to be feared, seems no longer to be an essential port of call in an opera singer's triumphal progress), his rare visits—and his many gramophone recordings—endeared him to British operagoers.

His treatment of the stock Italian operatic repertory is in itself a sufficient demonstration of an unusually mature artistry. If in his early days he was sometimes inclined to prove that he could play Hercules rarely, he came to develop a musicality and sense of style that, in such operas as *Pagliacci*, was no less than a vindication of the composer's original intentions. Such arias as "Vesti la giubba", sung straight, with meticulous phrasing and dependence upon the melodic line so complete that it eschewed any addition to the composer's text, are typical of the integrity of style he brought to even the most hackneyed roles, and it is fortunate that his gramophone records remain to provide a model for his successors.

In greater works his performances were always marked by his complete absorption in the composer's text and his refusal to cheapen it with conventional but unmusical tricks. His occasional excursions into the realms of non-operatic song, though carried out with sincerity and musicianship, never achieved the sense of complete authority that marked his performances in opera; it was the stage and the task of embodying a character in music that brought out the best in his art.

September 10, 1960.

Robert Blackburn, one of the pioneers of the aircraft industry in Britain and the founder of the Blackburn and General Aircraft Company, died at his home at Exeter on September 10, 1955 at the age of 70. He had attended the Farnborough Air Display twice in the previous four days.

Robert Blackburn flew an aeroplane in 1909. He had designed and built it himself. He wrecked it on its first flight on Marske sands, between Saltburn and Redcar, and, learning by his experience, abandoned it for a new design, which duly flew from the sands at Filey in the following year. He had been intended for his father's heavy engineering company in Leeds and had taken the engineering course at Leeds University, but he saw the Wright brothers fly in France and thereafter nothing but aircraft engineering would content him.

When flying changed the direction of his career, Robert Blackburn had been sent for further training and practical experience into the office of a consulting civil engineer in Rouen. While he was there in 1908 the Wrights gave their first demonstration in Paris and he saw it. He returned time after time to watch the flying at Issy and soon abandoned his position at Rouen and established himself in a Paris *pension* where, in his top-floor room, he completed the detailed design of his first aircraft in a few months—a monoplane.

Returning to Leeds and his father's works, he soon had several departments of Thomas Green and Sons unofficially making parts of the projected aircraft. This met with firm disapproval when it was discovered, and the "jobs" were pitched out of the works, but "Master Robert" was by now deemed incurable and his father helped him to set up a small workshop of his own in Leeds. There his first aircraft, including an all-steel military monoplane of 1911, were built and from there they were sent to the sands at Filey to fly. B. C. Hucks, who afterwards became a famous pilot, joined Blackburn in 1910 and for several years he did most of Blackburn's flying while the proprietor concentrated on design and construction. He turned also to the flying side of the new art and for 18 months ran a flying school at Hendon. Orders for aircraft were few until war broke out in 1914.

In the following year his private venture was turned into a public company as the Blackburn Aeroplane and Motor Company and a big factory in Leeds was acquired. Design now began to turn specially towards seaplanes and several floatplanes were produced. After that war, the works were moved to Brough, near Hull, and the company found itself specializing in naval types of aircraft. A new company, North Sea Aerial and General Transport Ltd. was also formed to enter the operational and instructional field.

Blackburn's early enthusiasm never deserted him. His company built nearly every kind of aircraft at various times, from small two-seaters for the amateur pilot to the biggest kind of military flying-boats. It produced one of the first dive-bombers for the Navy, the Skua, and a torpedo bomber, the Barracuda, which saw a fair amount of service. Early in the 1939-45 War it built a two-engined flying-boat with a retractable bottom. This was designed to give ample clearance above the water for the airscrews during take-off without adding to hull drag. This piece of work had been done at the Clydeside works, which were organized at Dumbarton in 1936 under an arrangement with the shipbuilding company of William Denny and Brothers. At about the same time, the Cirrus Hermes Engineering Company, makers of light aero-engines, was merged with the company, which became known as Blackburn Aircraft Ltd. This was to be changed a few years after the war, following another merger, to Blackburn and General Aircraft Ltd.

The company then became responsible for the development of a big, four-engined freighter, the Beverley, which was adopted as a troop and Army equipment transport. In its post-war form the company also kept its interest in small engines up to date by acquiring the British rights in the French Turboméca range of gas turbines. In all these expansions and developments Robert Blackburn was the prime mover as chairman and joint managing director. He also took a leading part between the wars in helping Greece to establish a naval aircraft factory near Athens and was decorated with the Golden Cross of the Order of the Redeemer for his services in that undertaking. As a good businessman, he generally succeeded in keeping his works busy on the production of various types besides those designed by the company.

He was successful, too, in building into his own company a corporate spirit which led many workers to spend their whole working lives in it and to give it a high personal loyalty. So he carried on into a new industry the old touch of the family firm which his father had exercised in his Leeds works.

Robert Blackburn may never have had an outstanding success among his aircraft but they were always sound, efficient, workmanlike jobs, and those which went into production were interspersed with others that gave designers and workmen all the satisfaction and excitement of breaking new ground or attempting something on an unusual scale. Mixed with the shrewdness of the Yorkshireman in Blackburn was a love of enterprise for the fun of it and of adventure for the variety it brought.

He was born in 1885. He was twice married and is survived by his second wife and by two sons and four daughters.

September 12, 1955.

Betty-Ann (Mrs. Alexander) Blackford—See **Davies.**

Algernon Blackwood, who as novelist and short-story writer inhabited that world of fantasy which is pervaded by the supernatural, died in London on December 10, 1951.

Although its simpler thrills and crude horrors may present a fluent pen with no great difficulty, the fiction of the weird and the uncanny has always been an exacting form of literature. Algernon Blackwood brought to it uncommon gifts. He had a genuinely poetic vein of language and an individual inventive fancy; he could also be engagingly light and airy and could enter with delicate insight into the mind of childhood. Yet the perils of the supernatural in literature remain. The numbers of effective ghost stories, for instance, is notoriously small, and, in spite of all his qualities, it was only now and then that Blackwood slipped past the guard of incredulity which ensures a good night's rest even to the habitual reader of ghost stories. True, he had his authentic triumphs when he did so—more, perhaps, than almost any of his contemporaries.

Born in 1869, Algernon Henry Blackwood was the son of Sir Arthur Blackwood, K.C.B., at one time financial secretary to the Post Office, and Sydney, Duchess of Manchester, widow of the sixth Duke. His father became a conspicuous figure in the evangelical movement, and the boy was sent to school with a Moravian Brotherhood in the Black Forest. Later he went to Wellington and proceeded to Edinburgh University. At 20 he was packed off to Canada to fend for himself. He fell into the hands of swindlers and, at the end of a year, had parted with his slender resources. All but penniless he made for New York. After an assortment of odd experiences, which are described with telling detachment in a volume of autobiography, *Episodes before Thirty* (1923), he joined the staff of the New York *Sun* and later of the *New York Times*. For a time he was in the dried milk business. Then in 1906 appeared his first book, *The Empty House*.

In his earlier work Blackwood seemed to put his trust above all else in his powers of bizarre fancy and in a fertility of language which tempted him to try to create illimitable vistas by verbal associations alone. He was inclined, in fact, to write prose poems, and, in the way of writers of prose poems, he frequently carried a suggestion of hollowness. His feeling for the macabre in time grew more assured, and in some of his stories of hauntings, spiritual influences and the like he came very near to achieving the creepiness or the effect of physical horror at which he aimed. In this first phase of his work he was in the tradition of Poe rather than in that newer and more difficult tradition, which is specially associated with *The Turn of the Screw.*

He uncovered a child's mind in a fantasy entitled *Jimbo* (1909), the story of a small boy who, having been tossed by a cow, flew in his dreams. In *The Human Chord* (1910) he exhibited a remarkable sympathy with the half-morbid fancifulness of a child's mind. An imaginative effort of a different kind was *The Centaur* (1911), in which an Irishman afflicted by *Wanderlust* communicates from the Caucasus a latter-day vision of the morning of the world. There was at least one genuine curdling of the blood to be had from the stories in *Pan's Garden. A Prisoner in Fairyland* was, in its own way, a *tour de force* of poetic fantastication; there were stories for other than the credulous—stories which were told, indeed, with almost too studied a persuasiveness—in *Incredible Adventures.*

In 1915 Blackwood, in collaboration with Violet Pearn, adapted *A Prisoner in Fairyland* for the theatre. Produced as *The Starlight Express,* with music composed by Sir Edward Elgar, the play charmed by its fairy philosophy but lacked something of dramatic power. In 1920 *The Crossing,* which he had written in collaboration with Bertram Forsyth, was put on at the Comedy Theatre. The play had, it seems, few of the qualities considered necessary for stage performance, but there was a section of the public which was more interested in the subject of life after death than in the niceties of dramatic art, and by this section of the public the play was well received. In the following year, *Through the Crack,* again written with Violet Pearn, made children's entertainment of a nicely imaginative kind.

Blackwood's pace slackened during the 1920s. There was a collection of stories, *Wolves of God,* two or three of them very good indeed, in 1921; and in the same year came a novel, *The Bright Messenger,* which was in some sort a sequel to the earlier *Julius Le Vallon* and of a similarly mystical temper. After that, however, maturity of imagination in his chosen field seemed to arrest his powers of expression. But his virtuosity as a storyteller in a vein of the supernatural is handsomely displayed in two collections, *The Dance of Death* (1927) and *Shocks* (1935). Between these two volumes came *Dudley and Gilderoy* (1929), the story of the adventures of a parrot and a somewhat over-philosophical cat. A large selection of his stories, *The Tales of Algernon Blackwood,* was published in 1938 and another, *Tales of the Uncanny and Supernatural,* in 1949. Late in life he achieved an immense reputation as a story-teller on television, a rôle in which he was terrifyingly effective.

December 11, 1951.

Field-Marshal Sir Thomas Blamey, G.B.E., K.C.B., C.M.G., D.S.O., Deputy Commander-in-Chief in the Middle East under Lord Wavell, and later Commander-in-Chief of Allied land forces in Australia, died at Melbourne on May 27, 1951 after a long illness, at the age of 67.

One of the oustanding soldiers of Australia, he first made an enviable reputation as a staff officer and was selected by Sir John Monash as his Chief of Staff during the closing stages of the 1914-18 war. In the earlier stages of that war he had shown his mettle as a staff officer in the Gallipoli operations and later in France as a battalion and a brigade commander, and when war again broke out in 1939 he had already achieved high rank. As Deputy to Lord Wavell in the Middle East he shared the glory of those brilliant victories which gleamed so brightly in the early, dark days of the war. No commander could have wished for a more loyal subordinate.

When, after Pearl Harbour, Australia was threatened with invasion Blamey was placed in charge of all Allied forces in Australia. There again he exhibited that quickness of perception, grasp of detail, and appreciation of difficulties and the means of surmounting them that he had shown in the famous order to the Australian Army Corps in France which began the great Allied offensive leading to victory in 1918. That order was used, as Sir John Monash predicted that it would be, in staff colleges and schools of military instruction for many years all over the world.

Thomas Albert Blamey was born at Wagga, New South Wales, on January 24, 1884. He was educated for the teaching profession, but at the age of 22 joined the Australian Permanent Force. Some five years later he was sent to the Staff College, Quetta, where most Australian staff officers were trained before the establishment of Duntroon Military College in 1913. On qualifying he was sent to the North-West Frontier, where he first saw active service, and was then transferred to the staff of a Territorial division in England.

He was thus in Europe when war broke out in 1914 and was posted to the Australian force in Egypt as a divisional intelligence officer. He was present at the landing at Gallipoli in the spring of 1915 and played a large part in organizing the evacuation in the autumn. His capacity was then shown to effect for, contrary to the almost universal view that evacuation must cost enormous losses, the Anzacs were withdrawn without the loss of a single man.

After a period as a battalion and then a brigade commander had shown that he could be as effective in the field as on the staff, he was selected by Sir John Monash as his Chief of Staff when the latter was in command of the Australian Army Corps. Monash has left his opinion of him on record: "He possessed a mind cultured far above the average, widely informed, alert, prehensile. A Staff College graduate, but not, on that account, a pedant, he was thoroughly versed in the technique of staff work and in the *minutiae* of all procedure. Some day the order which he drafted will become a model for staff colleges and schools for military instruction". The order to which Sir John Monash referred was the operational order for the Australian attack in France in 1918, which initiated the final Allied offensive. It was for long used as a model at Camberley and elsewhere.

Blamey's services during the war were mentioned seven times in dispatches; he was awarded the D.S.O. in 1917, was made a C.M.G. in 1918, and in the course of the next year he was made a C.B., while serving as Deputy Chief of Staff of the Australian Imperial Forces. In 1922 he was appointed Australian defence representative at the War Office and he was Second Chief of the General Staff in Australia from 1923 until 1925, when he was appointed Chief Commissioner of Police in Victoria. His resignation from that post in 1936 was due to an ill-advised attempt to protect the reputation of a subordinate. He was not unemployed for long, however, for in 1938 he became Controller-General of the Australian recruiting secretariat and, from the outbreak of war in 1939 until his appointment to the command of the special Australian force organized to take part in the defence of the Middle East in 1940, he was chairman of the Australian Man-Power Committee.

The Australian forces in the Middle East were a major part of Lord Wavell's heroic band, and Blamey, who had been promoted lieutenant-general towards the end of 1939, became in the spring of 1941 Deputy Commander-in-Chief, Middle East. As such he was in charge of the ill-fated expedition to Greece and recalled in his order of the day at the outset of the operation that Australians had been called on just 26 years before to fight on the northern shores of the Mediterranean. The history of the withdrawal is too well known to need more than passing reference, and later in the year Blamey, who was promoted general in September, was called home to report. Japan's sudden entry into the war had altered the strategic position of Australia and during the winter of 1941-42 all Australian forces were withdrawn from the Middle East to strengthen the defence in the south-west Pacific.

To meet the threat of invasion Blamey was put in charge of all Allied forces in Australia with the widest powers to make adjustments in organization. He had no doubt of the magnitude of the task nor of the magnificent troops he had led in the Middle East, which were now again under his command in very different circumstances. A long and hard struggle in the jungles of Papua ensued, which eventually led to the Japanese surrender there. Thus was the immediate threat to Australia diminished, though by no means eliminated. General MacArthur's* invasion of the Philippines had cut off large numbers of Japanese troops in the more southerly islands, and it fell to the forces under the Australian commander to deal with these. The difficulty of the country and problems of supply prolonged these operations and they were still going on in the numerous islands off the northern and eastern coasts of Australia when Japan surrended in the autumn of 1945.

A short time after the surrender, Sir Thomas Blamey, who had been knighted in 1935, promoted K.C.B. in 1942, and created G.B.E.

in the course of the next year, resigned his command, having made specific recommendations about the future defence organization of Australia, including the numerical strength of her peace-time army and general defence policy. He was promoted to the rank of Field-Marshal in the Australian Military Forces in 1950.

He was twice married, first, in 1908, to Minnie, daughter of the late Edwin Millard, by whom he had one son. His first wife died in 1935 and in 1939 he married Olga, daughter of the late Henry Farnsworth.

May 28, 1951.

Leo Blech, the German conductor and composer, died at his home in west Berlin on August 24, 1958. He was 87.

Born at Aachen on April 22, 1871, Blech studied music under Bargiel and Rudorff in Berlin and later under Humperdinck at the Royal Academy of Music at Munich. In 1893 he was appointed conductor at the opera of his home town Aachen. From there, in 1899, he went as first conductor to the German Theatre at Prague. Finally, in 1906, he was chosen to be chief conductor and General Musical Director of the then Royal State Opera of Berlin, with a number of sonorous titles to his name: "Staatskapellmeister", "Königlicher Musikdirektor", and the like. Personally modest, though an exacting conductor, he was soon as well known abroad as in Germany and frequently visited Stockholm and Riga.

In 1923 he became artistic director of the Deutsches Opernhaus, in 1924 of the Berlin Volksoper, in 1925 of the Vienna Volksoper, and in 1926 he returned to Berlin as conductor of his first theatre.

The exacting obligations of his work as the musical director of one of the greatest opera houses somewhat affected his creative work as a composer. Even so, he produced four operas and two operettas, several of them with great and widespread success; the operas: *Das war ich* (1902), *Alpenkönig und Menschenfeind* (1903), *Aschenbrödel* (1905), and *Versiegelt* (1908); and the operettas: *Die Strohwitwe* (1920) and *Rappelkopf* (1924). He furthermore wrote a number of symphonies, choral music, orchestral works, piano music, and many songs.

In 1937, while fulfilling an engagement at Riga, he was advised that the political situation was such that it would be inadvisable for him to return to Germany. In Riga, therefore, he remained until the progress of the war and the extension of German influence meant that Riga was no longer a certain place of refuge. He moved on to Sweden and there secured the appointment of conductor at the Stockholm Royal Opera. He also occasionally made appearances on the concert platform. In September 1949 he returned to Berlin and took up the musical activities he had been obliged to abandon 12 years earlier. He was conductor of the West Berlin Civic Opera Orchestra until he retired in 1954.

If less brilliant perhaps than some of the many famous musicians among his contemporaries, experts as well as the discriminating public, who listened to his performances in the course of the long years during which he wielded the baton, appreciate Blech as one of the most conscientious, knowledgeable, and tasteful masters of his art.

August 26, 1958.

Lord Bledisloe, formerly Governor-General of New Zealand and one of the foremost experts on agriculture in this country, died at his home at Lydney, Gloucestershire, on July 3, 1958. He was 90.

His long and devoted services to the cause of agriculture will ensure that his memory will remain green for many years. Even before the 1914-18 war he was urging that Britain should grow more food, and as M.P. for South Wiltshire he attempted to form an agricultural party embracing members of all other parties. A survivor of a class of men who over the centuries have proved to be the backbone of England, the efficient country gentleman, he conducted his own estate with respect for tradition coupled with eager experiment in newly proved methods and, moreover, played his full part in local and national government. As Governor-General of New Zealand he proved to be perhaps the most popular representative of the Crown who has ever been appointed to that Dominion, and his good will tour of New Zealand and Australia in 1947 on behalf of the Royal Agricultural Society of England forged new and firm links between the peoples of those distant Dominions and their relatives at home.

The Right Hon. Sir Charles Bathurst, first Viscount Bledisloe, of Lydney, in the county of Gloucester, in the peerage of the United Kingdom, P.C., G.C.M.G., K.B.E., was descended from Benjamin Bathurst, M.P., a younger brother of the first Earl Bathurst. His father was Charles Bathurst, of Lydney Park, his mother Mary Elizabeth, only daughter of Colonel Thomas Pasley Hay. He was born on September 21, 1867, and was educated at Sherborne, Eton, and University College, Oxford. He showed an early interest in agriculture by taking a course of study at the Royal Agricultural College, Cirencester, where he was a gold medallist and later chairman of the governors; he also held the gold and silver medals of the Royal Agricultural Society of England, of which he was a life member and president in 1946. In 1892 he was called to the Bar by the Inner Temple and practised in the Chancery Division and as a conveyancer. He had served as a captain in the Royal Monmouthshire Engineers and during the 1914-18 war was Assistant Military Secretary at the Salisbury Training Centre.

In 1897 he became a Verderer of the Forest of Dean; but it was not until January 1910, when as a Unionist candidate he was elected for the Wilton Division, that he became known as a champion of agriculture. He was not long in the House before he established a reputation for knowledge of his subject, for he could speak with authority and lucidity on both the scientific and practical aspects of farming. At first he was less appreciated than he might have been, for, although strenuous in his advocacy, his length and breadth of vision were apt to carry him away from the case in hand, and the weight and impressiveness of his arguments were therefore impaired. He suffered indeed from the defects of his qualities both in regard to the multiplicity of his interests and in his scrupulous wish to be fair.

In 1916 he was appointed to represent the Food Controller (Lord Devonport) in the Commons, and succeeded him as chairman of the Royal Commission on the Sugar Supply and Director of Sugar Distribution. He was created a K.B.E. in 1917 and in the ensuing year was created Baron Bledisloe, of Lydney—Bledisloe being the name of the ancient hundred which included the Lydney Park estate, at that time still in his father's ownership. In the first Baldwin administration he was a member of the Agricultural Advisory Commitee and its Imperial Economic Conference sub-committee, but he resigned in August 1923, in consequence of the preparations for the admission of Canadian pedigree breeding cattle to Britain. In the second Baldwin administration he was Parliamentary Secretary to the Ministry of Agriculture and was sworn of the Privy Council in 1926.

Lord Bledisloe was appointed chairman of the Royal Commission on Land Drainage in 1927. In the next year he went to Argentina to study questions in relation to the export of meat to Great Britain, and in 1928 resigned his office in the Government in order to take up the appointment of chairman of the Imperial Grassland Association.

He was appointed Governor-General of New Zealand in 1929. In view of his expert agricultural knowledge there could not have been a more appropriate selection, and it was warmly welcomed in the Dominion. He was created a G.C.M.G., and took over his duties in March 1930. The next year there was a severe earthquake, which caused heavy loss of life and property at Napier and Hastings. He was on the scenes of devastation as soon as possible and furnished a full report. This and the fact that he offered to share up to 45 per cent of his salary in the deductions which the depression imposed on public officials deepened the excellent impression he had made. In 1933 he made a Pacific cruise, and in 1934 went to Australia. When he left the next year he and Lady Bledisloe—she was an immense help to him—received many tokens of the sincere affection with which they had come to be regarded by the people of New Zealand. He was created a viscount in recognition of his services and received an Hon. D.C.L. from Oxford.

In 1938 he went to South Africa as chairman of a Royal Commission to investigate the possibility of closer union of Southern Rhodesia, Northern Rhodesia, and Nyasaland.

In his private capacity Lord Bledisloe occupied many offices of importance in the great agricultural societies. He was at different and sometimes the same time president of the Central Chamber of Agriculture, of the Central Landowners' Association, of the British Dairy

Farmers' Association, and of the Bath and West Agricultural Society; chairman of the committee of the Lawes Agricultural Trust (Rothamsted) and of the agricultural research committee of Bristol University; chairman of the Farmers' Club, and successively vice-president and president of the Royal Agricultural Society of England. He was also a Fellow of the Chemical Society, a vice-president of the British Science Guild, and an Hon. D.Sc. of Bristol University. From 1935 to 1938 he was president of the National Council of Social Service, and in 1939 president of the Museums Association. He was, too, president of the Empire Day Movement.

In addition to the services which he rendered to agriculture as head of active organizations, his example as a practical farmer was hardly less important. The home farm at Lydney bore testimony to his enterprise and ability to harmonize science and practice. While respectful towards established methods he was not deterred from putting possible alternatives to the test. Naturally he had his disappointments, but his farming showed how much can be accomplished by a practical mind endowed with vision, imagination, and patience.

Lord Bledisloe was a Knight of Grace of the Order of St. John of Jerusalem, an Hon. LL.D. of Edinburgh, an Hon. Fellow of University College, Oxford, and a Fellow of the Society of Antiquaries.

In 1898 he married the Hon. Bertha Lopes, daughter of the first Lord Ludlow, by whom he had two sons and a daughter. She died in 1926, and he married secondly, in 1928, the Hon. Alina Kate Elaine, second daughter of the late Lord Glantawe, and widow of Mr. T. Cooper-Smith. She died in 1956, and the family honours pass to his elder son, the Hon. Benjamin Ludlow Bathurst, Q.C., who was born in 1899, and married in 1933 Joan, the only daughter of the late Otto Krishaber. There are two sons of the marriage.

July 4, 1958.

Ernest Bloch, composer, died in Portland, Oregon on July 15, 1959. He was 78.

He was born at Geneva in 1880, of Jewish parents. His decision to devote his life to music was made at the age of 11, and during his early years both violin and composition occupied his attention. As a student in Brussels he studied the former with Ysaye and the latter with Rasse, and from Brussels he went to Frankfurt-on-Main for further composition lessons with Knorr. The most ambitious of his several early works was a symphony in C sharp minor written at the age of 20, a work which later attracted the favourable attention of Romain Rolland; but, owing to difficulties of obtaining performances of his music, Bloch was obliged to return to Geneva where for a while he took over his father's business.

An invitation in 1916 from Maud Allan [q.v.], the dancer, to accompany her in the capacity of conductor to America led to a happy change of fortune. In 1917 Dr. Karl Muck, director of the Boston Symphony Orchestra, invited him to conduct a performance of his *Three Jewish Poems,* and this not only resulted in further concerts of his music but also in several important teaching appointments.

For five years Bloch was director of the Cleveland Institute of Music, and from there he moved to California to take over the same position at the San Francisco Conservatoire, where he remained till 1930. It was during this American visit that much of Bloch's chamber music—possibly his most significant music—was written, also the lesser known *America* Rhapsody for orchestra (which gained the prize offered by the *Musical Quarterly)* and the *Helvetia* Symphony, the last two works as tributes to the land of his adoption and the land of his birth.

It was in 1930 that the kindness of a friend relieved him of the financial necessity of earning a living, and he was able to return to Switzerland and live a life of isolation in mountain hamlets. *The Sacred Service* for choir and orchestra and the *Violin Concerto* were the most important compositions of this period. In 1934 he paid a brief visit to Britain, playing, conducting and talking about his music, and as an outcome of this visit the Ernest Bloch Society was founded in London for the purpose of introducing his music to a wider public. But war clouds were gathering fast in Europe, and realizing the embarrassments of his presence there he decided to return to America.

In latter life he continued to be creative: a piano concerto, written in 1946-48, was first performed at the Edinburgh Festival in 1951, and in that year also, as a kind of codicil, a Scherzo Fantasque was first heard in England at a Promenade Concert. He wrote a third string quartet in 1945, a fourth in 1951-52, and in the latter year a Sinfonia breve.

Though it is as a Jewish composer that Bloch will first and foremost be remembered in future years—the first Jewish composer ever to give a distinctive voice in music to the spirit of his race—the appeal of his music is not limited by its nationalist or racial tendencies. It is possible to discern other influences at work in it—notably that of the Orient. Just as Gauguin turned from European culture to the primitive Tahitians for inspiration, so Bloch frequently travelled in imagination to Bali and its neighbouring islands in the eastern seas. He had no sympathy with the cold-blooded musical experiments carried out around him in his youth, and felt always that art should be created "rather by instinct than by intelligence, rather by intuition than by will", to use his own words.

July 16, 1959.

Henry Blogg, G.C., B.E.M., the famous coxswain of the Cromer lifeboats, in which he served for 53 years with skill and devotion, died in hospital at Cromer on June 13, 1954 at the age of 78.

Henry George Blogg was born on February 6, 1876, and became a member of the Cromer crew at 18 and second coxswain in 1902. He had a record in life-saving, unequalled in the lifeboat service, which became a legend in his lifetime. During his career he was responsible for saving 873 lives and displayed not only the highest heroism but skill, character, and above all leadership. Holder of the George Cross and the British Empire Medal, he was awarded the Silver Medal of the R.N.L.I. four times and the Gold Medal three times. Only one other man has ever held three Gold Medals—Sir William Hillary, the founder of the Royal National Life-boat Institution in 1824. In spite of the honours and fame which came to him, Blogg remained a modest man, who hated to appear on public platforms.

He won his first Gold Medal in 1917 when the Swedish steamer Fernebo ran aground after an explosion. The second was in 1927 when the crew were taken off the sinking Dutch tanker Georgia. The third was in 1941 when the first Cromer lifeboat saved 88 men from four ships in convoy which had gone aground on Happisburgh Sands. He was awarded the British Empire Medal for the same deed and the George Cross in the same year.

After his retirement in 1947 he was awarded an annuity by the Royal National Life-boat Institution and his portrait was painted by Mr. T. C. Dugdale [q.v.].

At a ceremony in 1948 No. 1 lifeboat at Cromer was named after Mr. Blogg by Admiral of the Fleet Sir John Cunningham.* In the last few years of his life he had heart trouble and in June 1953 he collapsed when attempting to help three other fisherman, two of them his nephews, whose boat sank in sight of the promenade.

June 15, 1954.

In **Dr. Eric Blom,** who died after a period of poor health on April 11, 1959, good journalism and sound scholarship were compounded in equal measure and were devotedly placed at the service of the art of music. His last article, on Handel, appeared in *The Observer* on April 12. Although frail in physique—he was deformed in his shoulders—he attained his seventieth birthday on August 20, 1958, and was always a prodigious worker. For the last year or two he had been seen less at concerts, but with the exception of the years he spent as music critic of the *Birmingham Post* (1931 to 1946) he had been a familiar figure in London music for 40 years.

Eric Walter Blom was born in German-speaking Switzerland of partly Danish descent—he had an expert knowledge of German—but was of British nationality and spent all his working life here. He was educated privately and he largely taught himself music while he worked for a firm of music publishers. He came before the public first as a writer of programme-notes for Henry Wood's concerts along with Rosa Newmarch. His first critical post was with the *Manchester Guardian,* for which he wrote notices of London events from 1923 to 1931. Like Ernest Newman [q.v.]

before him, he moved from that journal to the *Birmingham Post,* and remained with it for 15 years till 1946, when he returned to London chiefly in order to edit the fifth edition of Grove's *Dictionary of Music and Musicians.*

He resumed newspaper work for *The Observer* in 1949 and though he relinquished the reporting of musical events a couple of years ago he continued to write for it regularly. Another piece of journalism in which his scholar's mind was particularly valuable was his editorship of the quarterly periodical *Music and Letters.* He undertook this voluntary labour when its founder, Arthur Fox-Strangways, relinquished control in 1937. In 1950 its proprietor, the late Richard Capell, edited it while Blom was busy on *Grove,* but Blom resumed his direction of it in 1954 and made it over on Capell's death to a company in which the Royal Musical Association, of which Blom was a council member, and the Oxford University Press are represented.

As an author Blom had a dozen books, an encyclopaedia, and several translations from the German to his credit. His interests ranged widely and he was fond of some of the secondary composers, so that he called his first book *The Stepchildren of Music* (1923). He followed this with a serious study in aesthetics, *The Limitations of Music* (1928). But his chief love was given to Mozart, and his short biography in the *Master Musicians* series, which he edited for Dent, is about as good as a book of that size could be. He followed it many years later with a selection of Mozart's letters for Pelican. If he never wrote a big book it was because he devoted his vast learning to dictionaries, Dent's *Everyman* that will go into a coat pocket and *Grove* which runs to nine stout volumes. He was the first of the editors who succeeded Sir George Grove to make that monument of humane learning a systematic work of reference. He was himself systematic, and the mark of his green ink on a proof was familiar to every one of his fellow writers and to the young contributors he gathered around him for the *Master Musicians* series.

He was shy but not unsociable and he had an almost feline wit. He was public-spirited in his voluntary work for the art, which included the chairmanship of the Central Music Library and membership of several advisory panels. For these distinguished services to music he was made C.B.E. in 1955 and awarded a D.Litt. by Birmingham University in the same year.

His wife, whom he married in 1923, died before him, but he leaves a son and a daughter, who is the wife of his *Observer* colleague, Paul Jennings.

April 13, 1959.

The Right Rev. A. W. F. Blunt, D.D., Bishop of Bradford from 1931 until 1955, died on June 2, 1957 at his home in Yorkshire at the age of 77.

He was a scholar who preferred pastoral work to an academic career, and it may be doubted whether his outstanding intellectual gifts and a remarkable power of expression gave as much to the Church as they might have done if he had not been called to the Bench. Although he had little interest in diocesan administration, his industry and high ideals won him great respect in the Northern Province. His influence during his later years lessened by reason of a want of balance in his public utterances.

Alfred Walter Frank Blunt was born on September 24, 1879. He obtained scholarships both at Marlborough and Exeter College, Oxford. He had a distinguished university record, obtaining first classes in Classical Moderations and Literae Humaniores, and after a year's school-mastering at Wellington College he was elected fellow and classical lecturer of Exeter College in 1902. Two years later he was ordained, and in 1907, feeling the strong call of parochial work, quitted Oxford for a curacy in Nottingham. When his vicar left in 1909 the Bishop of Southwell recognized Blunt's marked abilities by appointing him to the living, after no more than two years' tenure of the assistant-curacy.

Ten years later he was moved to the important parish of St. Werburgh, Derby, with a large industrial population. Here he worked with much success from 1917 until 1931, becoming also an honorary Canon and Rural Dean of Derby. In 1931 the see of Bradford fell vacant by the translation of Dr. Perowne, its first bishop, to Worcester, and the nomination of Blunt to succeed him seemed eminently suitable. In one respect he differed from his predecessor and from the prevailing churchmanship of the Bradford diocese; both were definitely Evangelical, while Blunt's sympathies were no less definitely Anglo-Catholic. But at this stage of his career Dr. Blunt (Oxford gave him a D.D. in the year after his consecration) was wisely restrained in putting forward from pulpit and platform his ecclesiastical and political views, which indeed seem to have been less extreme at this period than they were afterwards to become. He gained widespread approval by his personal kindliness.

In fact, he overworked badly, with lamentable consequences. At no long intervals he had four nervous breakdowns, and when he was physically well enough to carry on his duties the strain still showed itself by turning the tolerant and judicious prelate into an ardent controversialist. That he should himself adopt socialism of an extreme type as his political creed was felt to be a matter for his private judgment, but when he began to regard almost every important sermon and address to his diocese as an opportunity for stating that creed in provocative language, the regret caused, and the harm his influence suffered, were great. In later years he became more sympathetic with the Evangelical school of thought and more critical of socialism.

On one occasion, however, the notoriety he gained by one of his public utterances was purely fortuitous. Towards the end of 1936 King Edward VIII's matrimonial project was no secret to those with inner knowledge. But it was still unsuspected by a large proportion of the public, and for some time the British press with self-imposed restraint made no allusion to it. The Bishop of Bradford was not among those with knowledge of what was imminent, but a chance phrase of his in an address to his diocesan conference sounded by accident like a direct allusion to this topic. It was so interpreted by many newspapers, which argued that it set them free from the need of any further reticence. The Bishop had said that the King would abundantly need God's Grace if he were to do his duty faithfully. "We hope that he is aware of his need. Some of us wish that he gave more positive signs of such awareness". When he wrote the speech some two months before it was delivered he had not heard the rumours surrounding the King [later the Duke of Windsor*]. He was later shown some American newspaper cuttings; but, as he recalled many years later, he decided not to delete the passage as "it had nothing to do with Mrs. Simpson".

It is not by this unlucky incident that he should be remembered, but as a most unselfish and devoted bishop, whose ardour caused him to become, in both physical and other ways, a martyr to overwork. He had always been a voracious reader of books of all kinds, and once confessed to having read all the novels of Jane Austen 30 times. Some of his numerous books, too, will remain as scholarly and able statements of the Anglo-Catholic position. He resigned his bishopric in August 1955, and had been in failing health for some time before he died.

He married Margaret Catherine, daughter of Lieutenant-Colonel J. Duke, and there was a son and two daughters of the marriage.

June 4, 1957.

The death on December 31, 1957 at his home near Petersfield of **Sir Archibald Bodkin,** K.C.B., removed a prominent public figure who for half a century had been closely connected with the administration of criminal justice. He was 95. From 1920 until 1930 he had been the Director of Public Prosecutions, and for many years previously he had been one of the leaders of the criminal bar, and a prosecuting Counsel for the Crown. After his retirement he was for many years chairman of the Devon Quarter Sessions.

Archibald Henry Bodkin might be said to have been born into the traditions of the criminal law; for his grandfather, Sir William Bodkin, the legal writer and authority on the Poor Law, was appointed chairman of the old Middlesex Sessions in 1859, and held the office until 1874, being later succeeded in the post by his son, W. P. Bodkin, Archibald's father. W. P. Bodkin, who died at an advanced age in 1900, was a well known Highgate resident, and when other arrangements were made for the old Middlesex Sessions, he became chairman of the Highgate Bench, an office he held for many years. Archibald was also a nephew of Sir Harry Poland, the greatest criminal lawyer of his day.

Born on April 1, 1862, the fifth son of his father, he was educated at Cholmeley School, Highgate, and he was called to the Bar in 1885 by the Inner Temple, of which Inn he was made a Bencher in 1915, and naturally adopted the criminal branch of the law for a career. At that time Poland had for long been the outstanding figure at the Old Bailey Bar, and no doubt his nephew made his start there under the most favourable auspices. He soon acquired an extensive practice in the criminal courts of the metropolis and on the South-Eastern Circuit, which he joined, and in 1892 he was appointed Junior Treasury Counsel at the Central Criminal Court and Senior Counsel in 1908, retaining the latter post until his appointment in 1920 as Director of Public Prosecutions in which office he succeeded the late Sir Charles Mathews.

It will thus be observed that of Bodkin's 35 years of active practice at the Bar, 28 were spent as prosecuting Counsel for the Crown, a post which his particular cast of mind enabled him to fill with eminent success. His industry was unsparing and his accuracy in detail never at fault, while his knowledge of criminal law and practice was second to none. His work filled his life; Sundays were often spent in drawing indictments; and the legend in the Temple that a Christmas evening had once seen him leaving his chambers with a bundle of papers was probably true. As a prosecuting counsel his mastery of his cases and his earnest and deliberate manner made him a dangerous opponent; but it should be added that he always maintained the best traditions of the Bar of fairness to the prisoner. He was constantly also retained for the defence, and he had a large licensing business; but otherwise his practice was limited to the criminal Courts.

There were few important criminal trials at the Old Bailey between 1892 and 1920 in which his name does not appear, and during the war of 1914-18 he was responsible for the prosecution of every spy tried. He had succeeded, in 1901, his uncle, Sir Harry Poland, as Recorder of Dover, and after his retirement in 1930 he was reappointed to that office. In July 1920, on the death of Sir Charles Mathews—the first holder of the post of Director of Public Prosecutions after its separation from the office of the Solicitor to the Treasury—it was no surprise that Sir Archibald Bodkin (he had been knighted in 1917) was appointed to succeed him.

To his new office Bodkin brought the qualities of thoroughness and conscientiousness for which he had been distinguished at the Bar, and over a difficult period he filled the post with success. Perhaps he was never quite at home as the head of a department, and he used regretfully to say that having all his life done his own work, he found delegation difficult and feared that he would never learn its art, which is the first that a successful administrator must acquire. During his tenure of office his department did not escape public criticism on several occasions, notably in connexion with the Savidge case in 1928, though the commission which examined the whole circumstances exonerated the Public Prosecutor from blame, and it was shown that his action had been strictly in accordance with the established practice of his office.

A case that arose the following year, in which he induced the Attorney-General to give his fiat for preferring a voluntary bill of indictment before the Grand Jury after the discharge of a prisoner by the Chief Magistrate (the late Sir Chartres Biron), which resulted in the acquittal of the accused, raised more justifiable criticism, and was the subject of an article in *The Times*.

It was sometimes suggested that his department showed rather too decided a tendency to interfere in cases that might better have been let alone, notably where questions of morals (in the narrower sense) and books were concerned. There was perhaps some force in these criticisms. But, on the whole, Bodkin's conduct of his office was neither in advance of nor behind the average public opinion of the time in such matters, and certainly his actions were always dictated by the high standards of rectitude which distinguished his career. Such defects as he had, perhaps a rather more liberal education and rather wider intellectual interests outside his profession would have corrected.

After his retirement, which at the request of the authorities was delayed for some three years, he was chairman of the Committee on Firearms in 1934, and of one on "share-pushing" in 1936. He was also for 15 years chairman of the Devon Quarter Sessions, to commemorate which a Sir Archibald Bodkin Prize for criminal law was established in 1948 at the University College of the South West at Exeter.

With the profession Bodkin was deservedly popular, and anyone meeting him for the first time would have had difficulty in believing that his genial, bustling personality had been officially responsible across long years for putting many thousands of his fellows under lock and key and bringing not a few to suffer the supreme penalty of the law. His death removes an upright and able public servant and the news of it will be received with grief in many quarters.

He was created K.C.B. in 1924.

Sir Archibald Bodkin married, in 1891, Maud Beatrice, daughter of the late Rev. R. Wheler Bush.

January 3, 1958.

Humphrey Bogart, the American actor, died on January 14, 1957 in Hollywood. He was 57.

For over 20 years—since his playing of the Dillinger-like part of Duke Mantee in *The Petrified Forest,* which won him much praise—his seamed, sardonic cast of countenance and mordant tongue had been familiar to cinema audiences all over the world.

Bogart was born in New York on June 23, 1899, the son of Dr. Belmont Bogart, a physician, and his wife, who as Maud Humphrey had made a name for herself as a watercolour artist and commercial illustrator. He was educated at Trinity School, New York, and at Phillips Academy, Andover, Massachusetts, whence he was expected to go to Yale, but this intention was not fulfilled. The United States had entered the First World War and Bogart joined the Navy. He had always been attracted to the theatre and as soon as the war ended he joined the staff of a promoter of theatrical ventures as manager of a travelling company.

However, he determined to act and made his way to New York, where he made his first appearance in 1922 in *Drifting.*

Thereafter he appeared regularly in plays and it was not until 1930 that he went to Hollywood. Of his first efforts he himself later said they were "a flop". He returned to the stage and it was only after the success of the play *The Petrified Forest* that he again turned to the screen, to make an immediate impact with the film of the play with Leslie Howard and Bette Davis.

There followed many other films, and notable among his earlier successes was *Dead End,* in which Bogart played the part of a gangster; and a gangster on the screen he often was, but a gangster with a difference. If Clark Gable [q.v.] may be said to stand, in the parts he plays, for the uninhibited American male, the happy extrovert whom every college boy would wish to be, the lad for the girls and the lad for the liquor, Bogart represented a contrasting, yet allied, type of American hero.

He dwelt in the shadows and was on the other side, so far as the police and the law were concerned, but that was because the police and the law were themselves often shown as corrupt. He was the masculine counterpart of the girl of easy virtue who has a heart of gold. Typical was the role he played in *The Big Shot.* Here he was, of course, the "big shot", the head of a gang which took beatings-up and murder in its stride, and yet at the end he gave himself up rather than see an innocent man, a man he did not even know, electrocuted. It is, of course, wildly improbable that the "big shot" would do any such thing and, to make the climax convincing, some powerful acting would seem necessary. But that was not Bogart's way. "He has charm and he doesn't waste energy pretending to act", wrote James Agate. "He has a sinister-rueful countenance which acts for him. He has an exciting personality and lets it do the work".

Certainly Bogart seemed to do little more than project his film personality on to the screen and leave it at that, but it was astonishing how much he could convey with a suggestion of pathos in that husky voice of his, with a shadow of a smile wryly turned against himself, and, in films which gave him a chance, a film, for instance, such as John Huston's *The Treasure of the Sierre Madre,* he showed that his acting could be positive, even though it never moved far away from the essential Bogart.

Bogart appeared in a great number of films, among then *High Sierra, The Maltese Falcon, Across the Pacific, The African Queen, To have and Have Not, Casablanca,* and *The Caine Mutiny,* and, while other reputations waxed and waned, he went on unchanged and unchangeable in calm, complete command of himself, the situation and the screen. He had what Kent found in Lear—authority.

January 15, 1957.

Sir Harold Boldero, the well-known physician and medical administrator, died at his home in London on November 30, 1960. He was Registrar of the Royal College of Physicians from 1942 until his death, and a former Dean of Middlesex Hospital Medical School.

Harold Esmond Arnison Boldero was born in August, 1889, the elder son of John Boldero, J.P., of Mark Cross, Sussex. Educated at Charterhouse and Trinity College, Oxford, where he represented the university at athletics in 1911 and hockey in 1912, he did his clinical studies at Middlesex Hospital, qualifying with the Conjoint Board Diploma in 1915.

Serving in the B.E.F. from 1915 to 1919, Boldero rose to the rank of major in the R.A.M.C., being mentioned twice in dispatches. He already showed his talent for administration by becoming D.A.D.M.S. Returning to civil life he had junior appointments at the Middlesex Hospital, eventually being elected to the staff there as assistant physician. He obtained his B.M. Oxford in 1920 and D.M. in 1925. His M.R.C.P. was obtained in 1922 and he was elected F.R.C.P. in 1933. He showed an early interest in diseases of children and worked as a clinical assistant at the Hospital for Sick Children, Great Ormond Street, in 1921. This interest he continued in his early years on the staff at the Middlesex Hospital, where the junior physician in those days looked after the children. He also was on the staff of the Evelina Hospital for Children and St. Saviour's Hospital.

It was, however, as a medical administrator that Boldero became best known. The posts of Dean of the Medical School of the Middlesex Hospital and sector officer in the Emergency Medical Service during the First World War brought him great opportunity for his talents. The University of London recognized this, and he became a member of the Senate and served for many years as chairman of the Board of Advanced Medical Studies. He was an original member of the North West Metropolitan Regional Hospital Board and an experienced negotiator on various committees that represented the medical profession in discussions with the Ministry of Health.

The Royal College of Physicians also recognized his ability and he served first as treasurer and then as registrar for many years, especially during the period of Lord Moran's [d. 1977] presidency. They made a perfect pair in promoting the college's influence during the events leading up to the creation of the National Health Service.

Boldero's own life was clouded by tragedy. His wife, Margery, daughter of Arthur Dunn, whom he married in 1917, was an invalid for some years before her death in 1950 and the elder of his two sons died in a shooting accident. He himself had a severe illness about this time but he recovered to throw himself once more into the work he so much enjoyed. Boldero was knighted in 1950.

Whether on the hockey field, as in his younger days, or in the committee room, he conducted his "game" with skill and shrewdness, with a courtesy to his opponents and a frequent light remark when tension needed to be eased. Middlesex Hospital and the college were his whole life for a long period, and he will be greatly missed by all his colleagues.

December 2, 1960.

David Bomberg, the painter, died on August 19, 1957 in hospital in London, at the age of 67.

He had been painting in the Andalusian Sierras when he became ill. Accompanied by his wife he rode down from the mountains on horseback on the way to Gibraltar, where he was nursed for several weeks before travelling back to London to enter hospital.

He was more of a painter and less of a theorist than were most of the young Jewish artists who "took the town" during the first decade of the present century. His early efforts were encouraged by Sargent, and there was evidently some resemblance between the two painters in both visual alertness and the capacity for direct and forcible representation with the brush. But what was forcible in Sargent tended to become violent in Bomberg, and the violence would have been excessive if it had not been contained by an architectural or structural emphasis that was hardly thought of in Sargent's day. There was indeed in the work of Bomberg a good deal that tempted a play upon the first half of his name; an effect of high tension, as if between the explosive impulse of the painter and the ordering capacity of the architect; and this was enough to mark the difference between the two generations.

Bomberg was born at Birmingham in 1890. He studied at the Slade School and was an original member of the London Group when it was founded in 1914. During the First World War he served in France, and later did work for the Canadian War Memorial. Afterwards, under the auspices of the Zionist organization, he was sent to Palestine, and in 1924 he extended his travels to Petra.

The results of these excursions were shown at the Leicester Galleries in 1928, and they excited great interest by their purely pictorial character and complete freedom from literary, sentimental, or archaeological bias. There was nothing in them to suggest that Bomberg was familiar with the Bible narrative, much less that he had ever heard of the "rose-red city" of the hackneyed quotation. Such complete independence of vision in the presence of historically important subjects is rare, and creates its own effect of veracity. Having asserted his own vision of "Mount of Olives" and "The Holy City" Bomberg spared no pains to make it intelligible to others, and the paintings were full of technical expedients to assist those who came to the subjects through their reading, such as the suggestion of topographical detail by variations in the thickness of pigment.

Bomberg's exclusively painter-like attitude to things in general made him look rather a rebel even at the London Group, which, at any rate under the Roger Fry régime, had its academism of design. But there was no suggestion that Bomberg wanted to startle; it was just that he wanted to paint.

It is an open question whether Bomberg was drawn to savage mountain country by spiritual impulse or simply because it suited his style of painting. Certainly nobody has conveyed more forcibly the tragic quality of the landscape of Spain, where Bomberg was caught by the civil war and with his wife and two young children had to join the stream of refugees. Shown at the London Group, his paintings made at this time were justly described as interesting documents, but their documentary character was, so to speak, a by-product of the intensity with which the subjects were realized.

August 20, 1957.

By the death of **Margaret Bondfield,** C.H., which occurred on June 16, 1953 in a nursing home at Sanderstead, Surrey, at the age of 80, the British Labour movement lost one of its most notable women, a trade union organizer of idealistic and practical temper during almost half a century.

The loss is not the Labour movement's only, for "Maggie" Bondfield was a woman of lovable temperament and unusually wide human sympathies. Though she was the first of her sex to attain Ministerial rank, her parliamentary career covered only six years in all. She was, first and foremost, a trade unionist rather than a politician, and the essential part of her work for what a generation ago was called social betterment was carried out elsewhere than at Westminster. The tribute to her energy and devotion was fully deserved when in 1923 she became the first woman chairman of the General Council of the T.U.C.

Margaret Grace Bondfield was born in humble circumstances at Chard, Somerset, on March 17, 1873, one of 11 children of a lace-maker. At the age of 13 she became a supply teacher to infants in a local board school. Two years later she left teaching and went to Brighton to serve in a colonial outfitter's shop, and for the next 11 years she worked in various London and provincial shops. Conditions under which the majority of shop assistants worked in those days were hard. Hours—a 70-hour week was not uncommon—and pay apart, the living-in system was the cause of many evils and abuses. "Maggie" Bondfield (the diminutive clung to her all through her career) soon reached the conclusion that the only hope of putting matters right lay in trade unionism. In 1894, four years before the formation of the National Union of Distributive and Allied Workers, she joined the Shop Assistants' Union; two years later, on its amalgamation with another union, she became its assistant secretary, remaining in that post until 1908, when she resigned to take up wider activities.

Sir Charles Dilke's Shop Bill had been introduced in 1896. Miss Bondfield made contact with him and Lady Dilke, and this association, together with her friendship with Mary Macarthur, led to vigorous propaganda on behalf of women in industry. In those days of trade union organization women who entered industry were regarded by many of the men with whom they worked as interlopers. Much of Bondfield's prentice work as a union organizer was concerned with breaking down this prejudice. One instrument to her hand was the Women's Trade Union League. Another was the National Federation of Women Workers, founded in 1906.

On launching out into political activities she threw in her lot with the Independent Labour Party, serving after a time on its executive. After the death of Mrs. Ramsay MacDonald she became organizing secretary of the Women's Labour League, and in 1914 she occupied a similar post with the National Federation of Women Workers. During the war of 1914-18 she was a member of the Central Committee on Women's Employment, of the Trades Union Advisory Committee to the Ministry of Munitions, and of the War Emergency Workers National Committee. Like other prominent members of the I.L.P., she maintained an essentially pacifist attitude during the course of the war.

After the women's vote had been won Margaret Bondfield pressed forward tirelessly with her work of labour organization. In 1920, as T.U.C. delegate, she attended the convention of the American Federation of Labour and also visited Russia. The International Labour Office of the League of Nations had from the first awakened the liveliest hopes in her—with Mary Macarthur she went to its first conference, at Washington, in 1919—and she attended further conferences at various times during 1921-27. In 1924 she was the official representative of Great Britain on the governing body. Mary Macarthur had died in 1921 and Miss Bondfield took over from her, among other responsibilities, the chairmanship of the Standing Joint Committee of Industrial Women's Organizations. She also became vice-president of the International Federation of Working Women. With the merging in 1920 of the National Federation of Women Workers in the General Workers' Union she also became the latter's chief woman officer and remained in the post until March 1938.

She had received in 1923 the highest honour the British trade union movement could confer—the chairmanship of the General Council of the T.U.C. She was the first woman to occupy this office, just as 24 years earlier she had been the first woman to attend the annual union conference as delegate.

In 1923 also she entered Parliament as the Labour member for Northampton. Her quality was recognized by her appointment, early in 1924, as Parliamentary Secretary to the Ministry of Labour in the first Socialist administration. The same year she headed a delegation sent to Canada by the Overseas Settlement Committee, and continued to serve on that body till 1929.

Bondfield lost her seat at the General Election of 1924 and remained outside Parliament until 1926, when she was returned for Wallsend at a by-election with a majority of over 9,000. In the formation of the second Socialist administration she was an obvious choice as Minister of Labour. She held that office until 1931, having meanwhile been sworn of the Privy Council; she was one of the many conspicuous Labour casualties in the General Election of 1931. After a further defeat by the same candidate, Irene Ward, she decided in 1936 not to stand again for Wallsend, but her interest in politics and industrial organization remained unabated. In 1938, at the age of 65, she undertook the journey to the United States and Mexico in order to study labour conditions there. More recently, however, she had withdrawn noticeably from public affairs, but some three years ago came again before the public as the authoress of her admirably written reminiscences, *A Life's Work*.

Her pioneering spirit and selfless devotion to the practical causes she made her own were widely recognized. Hers was not a sentimental humanitarianism. She appealed always to reason and presented a documented case innocent of rhetoric. As a speaker she was perhaps more successful on the public platform than in the House, though she had a good voice and a command of English which bore testimony to wide reading. Her generous nature and real sense of humour looked out from a pleasant, alert, bright-eyed countenance surmounted by a broad and thoughtful brow.

She received the freedom of her native Chard in 1930 and was made an honorary LL.D. of Bristol in the same year. She was appointed a Companion of Honour in 1948.

June 18, 1953.

Sir David Bone, C.B.E., who died on May 17, 1959, at his home in Surrey, was formerly Commodore of the Anchor Line and the author of many books and articles on life at sea.

As a master-mariner David Bone was unlike any of Conrad's men, even McWhirr. He had an easy sense of fun, though it was masked by the rigid countenance which watchful restraint puts on the face of a dutiful man. His ship was more important than her master. But his ready understanding of his fellows—he knew hard times himself; he knew the worst at sea—made him a commander to find devotion, he did not know why. He was a modest man. His figure was stocky and stiff, his toes inturned a little for stubbornness, and his eyes heavy-lidded through lonely consideration of circumstance, which could be inimical. The vagaries of the weather and the cunning of his fellows rarely had him off guard.

David William Bone was born in 1874 in Glasgow, and the ships and shipyards of the Clyde took his early wonder; when he sought entertainment, it was to watch, sitting on a bollard, the business of one of the famous Loch Line of clippers. His father was a journalist with a special knowledge of ships and the shipyards, and what naval architects and engineers were aiming at on the Clyde. He had other sons named James*, who became London editor of the *Manchester Guardian,* and Muirhead [q.v.], the artist. But David was cast for a sailor; he thought all the best things were beyond the horizon.

It was lucky for readers that he had also respect for the dignity of English prose. He read the classics, and perhaps he was helped, in his use of words, by the need for them to be laconic and peremptory when shouted at sea into the wind; ambiguity there can be disastrous. His first voyage was made in 1891 in the Scottish ship City of Florence, Antwerp to San Francisco. He took his first trick at the wheel off Cape Horn; the wheel had just before "kicked" a helmsman over it, and injured him. They were 183 days out to the Golden Gates. There he learnt much, at the worst coast in the world for sailors. Seafaring had its grim side. Desired landfalls came only after seas that could mean overwhelming in a latitude far south, besides drifting without water afterwards in the doldrums of the Pacific.

Naturally, after survival, he loved it. He kept a diary from the beginning and, on his first voyage, he had lived as a man in danger. Before he sat for his certificate as master mariner he had been round the world in the barque Loch Ness, under a driver and a severe master, known as "Bully" Martin; and went on in Anchor Line steamers to the Far East and to New York. It was when he was third mate of that company's Australia (3,600 tons) that he went from Bombay to Cape Town. The South African war had begun.

Thereafter he was to have his fill of war; he was Commander—at last—of that company's flagship Cameronia in 1916, with 2,700 troops on board. It was a calm and brilliant day in the Mediterranean, and he was on the bridge, thinking no evil, when suddenly "broken hatch-covers, coal, shattered débris, a huge column of sea-water soared skywards in a hurling mass to fall in torrents on the bridge, to bear us down". The troops swarmed up in a near panic, most of them at sea for the first time, making for the boats. Then a small boy, the bridge-deck messenger, picked up his master's megaphone, and in a shrill treble cried: "Steady, you men down there. Steady up. Ye'll no do any good for yersels crowdin' up the ledders!" They steadied, and 2,571 of them got away. The Commander grabbed a stay of a destroyer alongside as his ship went from under him, and thus he left the bridge that had given him higher standing in his profession.

In 1939 he was on the point of retiring, when the Germans broke loose once more. There was another Cameronia for him and this time she was to transport not troops but children, a thousand of them, with cots and perambulators; and fellowship and pity had left the sea. He was not to be convoyed. He was to speed to America independently, remembering for his guidance the fate of the Athenia a little before. Though this had sufficient of the navigation called "by luck and by God", something still depended on the knowledge and skill of the liner's anxious master. He got them over.

He related much of his wartime service in *Merchantmen-at-Arms,* 1919, and *Merchant Rearmed,* 1949. Other of his books are *Broken Stowage,* 1925, *Capstan Bars,* 1931, and a novel of the sea, *The Queerfella,* 1952. An anthology of sea-pieces is sadly imperfect if it does not include a chapter from his first book, *The Brassbounder* (1910), describing the way a dangerous cape was weathered in a gale; or else some other passage from that veracious and vivacious book. His last book was his life-story, *Landfall at Sunset,* a story altogether as felicitous as its title.

Bone was knighted in 1946 and was an LL.D. of Glasgow University. He married in 1922 Mary Helen Bell, daughter of Mr. Archibald Cameron. She died in 1952. They had a son and a daughter.

May 18, 1959.

The death of **Sir Muirhead Bone,** on October 21, 1953 at Oxford at the age of 77, deprived the world of art of one of the greatest draughtsmen our age has produced. His special province was the rendering of great masses of buildings under construction or demolition, with all the attendant paraphernalia, in such a manner that out of superficial chaos there emerged a beautiful and ordered design. He also did portraiture, and notable work during the 1914-18 War as an official artist at the front. In the war of 1939 to 1945 he again made many drawings, both at sea and on land in the factories and among the ruins of bombed London.

Born at Partick, Glasgow, on March 23, 1876, he was the fourth of eight children of David Drummond Bone, a newspaper reporter. He attended a local school, where he made friends with Francis Dodd (later to win fame as a portrait etcher), whose sister he was in due course to marry. Leaving school at 14 he worked at art in the evenings under Archibald Kay, R.S.A., and then presently under Francis Newbery at the Glasgow School of Art. Architecture was his day-time occupation, and he served three years' articles at it, but he was more interested in drawing buildings in his spare time, and at 18 gave up all idea of being an architect. For a short period he worked in a "home crafts" shop which used to close in the summer months, enabling Bone to go on painting expeditions with Dodd. Very soon he decided it must be art or nothing, and after a few months on the *Scots Pictorial* he worked independently. Paintings and some unimportant lithographs were his initial productions, but early in 1898 he made his first etchings and drypoints. During the next winter he attended a life class, and in 1899, bearing six Glasgow etchings and introductions to D. S. MacColl and Lord Carlisle, he went to London.

Bone's introductions led to his meeting Legros, Tonks, and J. P. Heseltine, not to mention the dealer, Dunthorpe, who gratified him by buying a print. Gradually he made a few sales and some of his pieces were hung at the New English Art Club and the Royal Academy, but there was no question yet of firing the Thames. Indeed, in 1900 he decided to settle at Ayr as an art master, hoping to earn enough to allow of marriage; but no pupils enrolled, and the wedding had to be deferred for three years. Nevertheless, he arranged, through a friend, a small exhibition at Emmanuel College, Cambridge, illustrated and partly wrote *Glasgow in 1901,* with the collaboration of his brother James* and A. H. Charteris, showed at the Glasgow international exhibition of that year, arousing favourable comment from Charles Aitken and Campbell Dodgson, and in the winter took up residence in London again.

During 1902 and 1903 some splendid London drawings appeared in the *Architectural Review.* Bone made various interesting friends of like tastes, such as William Rothenstein, David Muirhead, and Wilson Steer, had a first public exhibition at the Carfax Gallery, and found most congenial subjects in the demolition of Wych Street, which ran over part of the site of Aldwych, and Newgate Prison. It was the firm of print publishers, Obach, with which G. Mayer, later of Colnaghi's, was then connected, which set him on his feet by making him an advance on an edition of the etching *Southampton.*

He had used various papers for his early prints, but in 1903 he found at a printing works a large stock of old, creamy-tinted, soft-textured Japanese paper which greatly enhanced the effects he desired. It lasted him for four whole years. Soon after Bone's marriage Obach published a set of *Ten Drypoints,* which included Bone's first London subjects. In 1905 a visit to Scotland produced one of his finest prints, *Ayr Prison*; from the same year dates the fine drawing *The Demolition of St. James's Hall;* 1906 saw several noteworthy British Museum subjects, the illustration of Gertrude Bone's novel *Children's Children,* and the appearance of a full-dress article on his work by Campbell Dodgson in the Viennese magazine *Die Graphischen Künste.*

Bone was then only 30, yet his course was set fair. He had a good showing at the Franco-British Exhibition of 1908, and as early as 1910 he was adjudged worthy of more than a page in Thieme and Becker's *Allgemeines Lexikon der bildenden Künstler.* Etching and drypoint remained his preferred media, though he also carried out many works of superlative quality in sepia or pencil. In 1916 William Rothenstein mooted the scheme of sending one or more official artists to the front. Colonel Repington and Lady Cunard forwarded the idea, which was taken up by the Government, and Bone was sent to France with a lieutenant's commission. Later on he served with the Fleet, and his great mass of war drawings forms one of the most important sections of the Imperial War Museum. After the Armistice he lectured on the war art of his contemporaries and was instrumental in inspiring many sales. In 1925 he did the pictures for a delightful book by his journalist brother, James, entitled *The London Perambulator.*

Like Sir William Nicholson and many others, Bone found a world of joy and inspiration in the landscape and old towns of Spain. He penetrated into every corner of the Peninsula, held exhibitions of Spanish drawings at Colnaghi's in 1930 and 1931, and in 1936 produced a huge, sumptuous collector's book called *Old Spain,* priced at 100 guineas a copy. His knighthood in 1937 was welcomed by all interested in art.

Bone's painting period (in which Claude Monet was his chief enthusiasm) was soon over, and from his early twenties he is to be considered chiefly as a black-and-white man. He continued, however, to produce occasional coloured drawings and his oil painting "Mine-laying off Iceland", done during the 1939-45 War, is in the Imperial War Museum. He came to etching under the spell of Whistler and Méryon, but neither the atmospheric subtlety of the one nor the drama of the other seems to have aroused him to emulation.

In his love of complicated detail it may not be far-fetched to detect the Scottish racial strain that has produced a nation of Bible commentators, metaphysicians, and engineers. Nothing pleased him more than a building in course of construction, with all its scaffolding and planks, or some bewildering harbour scene, containing forests of masts and jungles of chains and derricks. A remarkable *tour de force* of his later years was the huge drawing of the view over the ruins from St. Bride's Church to St. Paul's Cathedral. Another was his interior of the Painted Hall at Greenwich.

Bone married the writer, Gertrude Helena, daughter of the Rev. Benjamin Dodd, by whom he had two sons, the elder, Stephen [q.v.], being himself a well-known artist and critic. The younger, Gavin, Fellow and Tutor of St. John's College, Oxford, died in 1942, and an exhibition of drawings by him was held at the Ashmolean in 1944.

October 23, 1953.

Stephen Bone, who died in London on September 15, 1958, at the age of 53, was a painter of authentic gifts and a perceptive art critic who followed his own star and never mingled in artistic politics.

Undoubtedly environmental conditions were propitious for him; and he developed his powers by hard work and extensive travel in Great Britain and abroad. In landscapes in oils he perhaps found his best medium, specializing in out-of-the-way or apparently ordinary scenes which most artists would have passed by, and making out of them pictures in which strong composition and fine paint quality were marked. He was also a portraitist of more than average ability, and several of his works in this kind found their way into public collections.

Stephen Bone was born at Chiswick on November 13, 1904, the son of that great graphic artist, Sir Muirhead Bone [q.v.], and his wife, Gertrude, the writer, whose maiden name was Dodd. Francis Dodd, R.A., the eminent etcher-portraitist, was his uncle, and on the paternal side he was also the nephew of James Bone* of the *Manchester Guardian.* When a child of seven Stephen was taken to Italy, living there for two years and acquiring the language (which he later forgot). He began to draw in infancy, and always intended to be an artist. He was sent to Bedales, and while there (at the age of fifteen) he had a water-colour accepted by the New English Art Club.

Leaving school in 1920, he went with his father on a European journey which covered France, Spain, Italy, Turkey, and Norway; and then for two years lived at the Hampshire village of Steep, continually painting and going abroad each summer. In the autumn of 1922 he went to the Slade, where he made his first figure drawings and drew much of value from the teaching of Henry Tonks. In the summer of 1924 he made the first of many visits to Sweden, and now left the Slade.

Bone's professional career began in adolescence with wood-engraved book illustrations for W. H. Davies's *Selected Poems* and George Bourne's *The Farmer's Life,* which were soon followed by two of his mother's books, *The Furrowed Earth* and *Mr. Paul.* At the Paris International Exhibition, 1925, he won a gold medal for wood-engraving. He decorated several more books by Gertrude Bone; and then, after a long interval, collaborated with Mary Adshead in a delightful children's book, *The Little Boy and his House* (1936), in which the medium was colour lithography.

Bone worked at first a good deal in water-colour, but did not neglect oils and wood-engraving. In 1926 he held a show at the old Goupil Gallery in conjunction with Robin Guthrie and Rodney Burn. The following summer was spent at the delightful estate of the Swedish sculptor Carl Milles [q.v.] at Lidingö; and Bone took a glance at Finland on the way home. In 1928 he carried out a big and very excellent mural scheme for the escalator arch at Piccadilly Circus station. This painting was unfortunately removed in favour of advertisements some years later.

In 1929 Bone married Mary, daughter of Professor S. D. Adshead, the architect and town planner. They went off to Bologna, Athens, and Rhodes, then settled for a time in Galway, and in the autumn returned to London, in time for the opening of another show of Bone's work at the Fine Art Society's galleries. Bone settled in Hampstead (if he could ever be said to "settle" anywhere), but remained an inveterate traveller, seeing nearly every country in Europe and nearly every part of the British Isles.

To Stockholm he went again and again, finding the Swedish civilization and landscape highly congenial; and from there he brought some of his best work. One of his biggest exhibitions was held at the Galerie Moderne there in 1937. Others took place at the Lefèvre Galleries, in galleries at Glasgow and Dundee, and at Ryman's, Oxford, where in 1936 he showed "Landscapes of Forty-one Counties", the catalogue including a map of the British Isles with reference numbers instead of picture titles. A little later he wrote a guide-book to the Scottish Highlands.

All these topographical preoccupations did not mean that Bone was a topographical painter in the literal and restricted sense. His work was naturalistic, but was very carefully composed and learnedly integrated as to pattern. The most unpromising corners held out attraction to him, and he dignified them by his broad fresh treatment and fine feeling for colour. He was no abstract theorist, but followed where his taste and feelings led.

Bone was a member of the New English Art Club, and frequently showed at the Royal Academy. His portraits were well-wrought, and made the fullest use of appropriate background and accessories to comment on the character of the sitter. His "Charles Aitken" was acquired by the Tate, and others went to Dundee and Manchester. In general he favoured wood panels rather than canvas.

In recent years he had become widely known for his art criticism in the *Manchester Guardian,* and as a broadcaster reached a large public through his appearances on the television programme "Animal, Vegetable and Mineral" and as one of "The Critics" on Sunday mornings. His comments on the air were always marked by common sense that was not incompatible with a sensitive response.

He was an admirable reporter of current exhibitions, level-headed and objective, and always made plain to his readers what sort of pictures he was discussing. To his fellow journalists he was a kindly and helpful colleague.

In the Second World War he was an official naval war artist.

Bone was a tall, thin man, precise of speech, sparing of commentary, and happily free from jealousy of the work of others.

He is survived by his widow, two sons and a daughter.

September 16, 1958.

Sir Edgar Bonham-Carter, K.C.M.G., C.I.E., who died suddenly on April 24, 1956 at his home near Alton, Hampshire, less than a month after his eighty-sixth birthday, had spent a long career in the service of the Crown, in the Sudan, where the establishment of the present legal and judicial system was largely due to his initiative, and later in Mesopotamia, where as Senior Judicial Officer and Judicial Adviser he was instrumental in adapting the Turkish legal system to present day needs. The London County Council, housing and town-planning were among the activities of his later years.

The fifth son of the late Henry Bonham-Carter, he was born on April 2, 1870. He was educated at Clifton, under Dr. Wilson, and New College, Oxford, where he was in the University Rugby Football XV in 1891, and an English international. He took honours in jurisprudence in 1892. In Lincoln's Inn he read in the chambers of Edward Beaumont, in whose pupil room so many distinguished lawyers, including a future Lord Chancellor (Lord Buckmaster) and several Judges, learned their law, and he was called to the Bar by that Inn in 1895. Four years later he entered the service of the Sudan Government as Legal Secretary, and later he was Official Member of the Council of the Governor-General of the Sudan.

Bonham-Carter's appointment entailed devising and initiating an entirely new system of law, both civil and criminal. The latter was based largely on the Indian Penal Code; the former—in the compilation of which he had the assistance of the late Sir William Brunyate, another of Edward Beaumont's pupils, then Judicial Adviser in Egypt—was primarily based on the English rules of justice, equity and good conscience, until in time precedents and case law evolved. In the eyes of the natives Bonham-Carter's work was recognized as the ideal embodiment of justice; the new epoch was for long spoken of as "the epoch of justice", in contradistinction to the days of Dervish oppression and Egyptian rule. No tribute can be too great for the man who inaugurated it.

When, in 1919, he was asked to undertake similar service in Mesopotamia, just free from Turkish rule, his good judgment was shown by his making no attempt to lay down new foundations, but by building up and modernizing the system he found there. As a result, on the termination of the British Mandate, Iraq was not left with a superimposed system of English law which had no roots in the country.

While he was in Iraq he had greatly interested himself in the rich archaeological heritage of the country. With a legacy of £5,000 from Gertrude Bell and at the request of the Bell family, who were wondering whom they could get to raise the necessary funds, he became the honorary secretary of the British School of Archaeology in Iraq and succeeded in establishing the school on a firm basis. He was its first chairman and continued in office until 1950. He made many friends in Iraq, particularly Nuri Pasha [q.v.], who was always a welcome visitor to Bonham-Carter's home in London.

When he returned to England in 1921 he entered on a period of busy retirement. For three years from 1922 he represented North-East Bethnal Green as a Progressive on the London County Council and from 1929 to 1939 he was chairman of the First Garden City Ltd., Letchworth. He was also chairman of the National Housing and Town Planning Council from 1940 to 1942. Much of his time was taken up by his work for the National Trust as a member of the council, and of the executive and finance committees of that body, and he was also president of the Commons Preservation Society.

Since 1953 he had been president of the North-East Hampshire Agricultural Association; though increasing lameness had in later years tended to keep him increasingly at his wife's beautiful estate at Binsted Wyck, he nevertheless took a lively interest in the conduct of the farms there.

Sir Edgar Bonham-Carter, besides the English honours specified, held the First Class Order of the Nile. He married in 1926 Charlotte Helen, daughter of the late Colonel William Lewis Kinloch Ogilvy, C.B., and leaves no issue. Lady Bonham-Carter did much good work on the Borough Council of Paddington, where she and her husband lived, and elsewhere, during the last war. She trained as a pilot and worked in Transport Command in the earlier part of the war, and later worked in the German section of the Foreign Office.

April 25, 1956.

Captain Charles George Bonner, V.C., D.S.C., R.N.R., late of the Merchant Navy, who was awarded the Victoria Cross for his gallantry in a "Q" ship against German submarines in 1917, died on February 8, 1951 at his home in Edinburgh at the age of 67.

Born at Shuttington, Warwickshire, in 1884, he was the youngest son of Samuel Bonner, J.P., of Aldridge, near Walsall, and was educated at Sutton Coldfield Grammar School, Coleshill Grammar School, and in H.M.S. Conway. At the age of 21 he had passed all the necessary examinations for the master mariner's certificate, which he was duly awarded.

On the outbreak of the 1914-18 war he joined the Royal Naval Division as an able-bodied seaman, but was transferred to the Royal Naval Reserve with the rank of sub-lieutenant. Later he served under Commander (now Vice-Admiral) Gordon Campbell, V.C. [q.v.], the organizer of the "mystery", or "Q", ships to combat the growing menace of submarines. Bonner won great distinction in the various actions with submarines in which he took part, and his services were recognized by the award to him of the D.S.C. in 1917.

Later that year, when serving with Campbell in the Dunraven, Bonner won the Victoria Cross in an action which has been described as the greatest of its kind between a "Q" boat and a submarine.

After the war Bonner rejoined the Mercantile Marine, and his name again came prominently before the public in 1925 when, as captain of the salvage tug Bullger, of Leith, he succeeded, in spite of adverse conditions, in refloating the Copenhagen steamer Elizabeth from a reef at Johnstone's Point, Campbeltown.

In 1917 he married Alice Mabel, daughter of the late Thomas Partridge, of Walsall.

February 9, 1951.

Rosie Boote—See **Headfort.**

Florence (Mrs. Bramwell) Booth, who died on June 10, 1957 at her home in Berkshire, was the widow of the second General of the Salvation Army and herself the leader for many years of its work among women. She was 95.

Florence Eleanor Soper was born at Blaina, South Wales, in 1861, the daughter of Dr. Soper. Her career was determined in 1880. She was 18 and like other girls of her age and class enjoying the London season, when she went, out of curiosity, to hear Mrs. Catherine Booth, wife of the founder of the Salvation Army, speaking at Steinway Hall. That experience determined her to join the movement. Her family strongly opposed her resolution; and their opposition was renewed when 18 months later she announced her intention of accepting the proposal of marriage which was made to her by Bramwell Booth, the General's son.

Her first task was as one of a party sent to Paris to start the Salvation Army in France. They paraded the streets with placards, distributed tracts and held meetings, and Florence Soper (she was not yet married) had a first taste of the hostility and ridicule which she was often to meet with in her life's work.

Back in London, she was put in charge of rescue work in the East End of London, where child prostitution was rife. She was appalled and dispirited by the conditions she found there. On her first visit a barrow boy, jeering at her uniform, flung a potato which hit her on the side of the head. "That potato cheered me up; it roused me", she characteristically recalled afterwards. It roused her to bring the energies of the Salvation Army to bear against the vice and squalor she witnessed; and working with Josephine Butler, W. T. Stead and others they secured the passage of the Criminal Law Amendment Act and the raising of the "age of consent". She continued for 30 years to guide the women's social work of the Salvation Army and she was frequently consulted as an expert by royal commissions and other bodies. Later she was a justice of the peace for the London district and a visiting magistrate at Holloway prison.

General Booth appointed his son's wife a commissioner in 1888, and as such she led the Salvation Army field officers, both men and women, throughout the country. She introduced a number of reforms, one of which gave more pay to officers with children. Motherhood and family life were among her chief concerns. She was a member of the Birthrate Commission 1915-18. The Home League, which is conducted by every Salvation Army Corps throughout the world, was her idea.

She lacked the natural eloquence of her husband's family, but she possessed an unusually penetrating voice which served her well at public meetings. These she conducted in many parts of the United Kingdom, on the Continent and in North America. For six years she was in charge of the evangelistic work of the Salvation Army in the United Kingdom, and she was later responsible for the training of Salvation Army officers.

Her husband succeeded his father as General in 1912 and, although Mrs. Booth's prominence in the affairs of the Salvation Army by no means depended on her husband's position alone, that increased her importance as in later years his deafness caused him to rely on her more and more.

Firm in her opinions, she was also receptive to new ideas. She worked enthusiastically for women's emancipation, though she was not altogether complacent afterwards about its fruits. Handsome, and vigorous in mind and body, she educated her elder girls herself. Her two sons and five daughters all grew up to service in the Salvation Army. They were strictly brought up in the family tradition of leadership in the Salvation Army, and it was a personal disappointment to Mrs. Booth that the control passed out of her family after the removal from office of her husband in 1929. Bramwell Booth died later in the same year.

June 11, 1957.

Hubert Cecil Booth, who died at a nursing home in Croydon on January 14, 1955 at the age of 83, was the inventor of the vacuum cleaner and, until 1952, chairman and joint managing director of the British Vacuum Cleaner and Engineering Company, Ltd., which he founded after his invention.

Born in Glasgow in 1871, the son of a Glasgow merchant, Booth received his engineering training at the Central Technical College. For many years he was in practice as a consulting engineer and he was responsible for the design and construction of many important bridges, both in Britain and oversea. He also played a leading part in the design of the big wheels in Paris, Vienna, Earls Court, and Blackpool in the early years of the century.

His invention of the vacuum cleaner was in 1901, the idea coming to him, it is said, while he watched a demonstration of a machine for blowing dust from carpets invented by an American engineer. His first vacuum cleaner was on wheels and operated in the street, tubes being taken into the house. His machine made its reputation when it was used to clean the royal carpet in Westminster Abbey before the coronation of King Edward VII. The King, who was impressed by news of its performance, commanded a demonstration at Buckingham Palace. A vacuum cleaner was thereafter installed at the palace and at Windsor Castle.

It was not until some years later that his right to the title of inventor was established beyond any doubt in the High Court. Booth applied the principle not only to household uses but also to a wide field of industrial purposes of value in reducing the hazards of industrial disease.

He was a fellow of the City and Guilds of London Institute and a member of the Institution of Civil Engineers.

January 15, 1955.

Air Chief Marshal Sir John N. Boothman, K.C.B., K.B.E., D.F.C., A.F.C., died on December 29, 1957 at the age of 56.

Boothman, as a senior officer of the Royal Air Force, was armed at all points. He was one of the finest pilots his service has produced—he piloted the aircraft which won the Schneider Trophy outright for his country—he flew with great gallantry in the earlier part of the Second World War, he had wide technical knowledge of aircraft and their engines, and he brought to the Air Staff and Ministry of Supply and to his commands at home and abroad a combination of innate leadership and a lively and penetrating mind, allied to a most likeable personality.

The fact that Sir John was at the right moment no respecter of persons or, for that matter, of empty tradition, enhanced his reputation among those who knew the quality of his great contribution to the many important appointments he was called upon to fill.

He developed his love of flying as a schoolboy, and his determined pursuit of aviation brought him a remarkable early achievement in that field—a flight with the pioneer aviator, Colonel Cody. The latter entered for a race in 1911 that required a passenger, took with him the young Boothman, then aged 10, as the lightest passenger he could find willing and anxious to venture into the air in a "flying machine". If Boothman had not had this determined interest in becoming a pilot he might well have become discouraged in his early attempts to join the Royal Air Force, which were frustrated because of his youth. Although only 17, the young Boothman got himself accepted instead as a voluntary motor driver to the French Red Cross and went out to Salonica with an ambulance unit. He served from January to September 1918 in this capacity and was awarded the Croix de Guerre (Bronze Star).

Born on February 19, 1901, the son of the late T. J. Boothman, of Wembley, John Nelson Boothman was educated at Harrow County School, which he left in 1917, seeking some form of war service. After the war he took up private flying at Hendon nearby and continued his efforts to make service flying his career. His efforts eventually met with success in March 1921, when he was accepted for a short service commission in the General Duties Branch. After service in Constantinople in the early 1920s he returned home to take the flying instructor's course at the Central Flying School and stayed on as an instructor there. He spent three happy years at C.F.S. before going out to the Middle East, where he flew with Nos. 55 and 30 Squadrons in Iraq, which he was to command 18 years later.

In February 1930 he was selected for training in high speed research flying, which led on inevitably to membership of the High Speed Flight, which was set up in 1931 to compete for the Schneider Trophy and the world's speed record in the fine aircraft that were then giving Britain an undisputed lead in Service aviation.

On September 13, 1931, Boothman flew a Supermarine S 6 B round the course over the Solent at an average speed of 342 m.p.h. to win the Schneider Trophy outright for Britain. Later the same day it fell to another member of the High Speed Flight, Flight Lieutenant George Stainforth, to break the world's air speed record in the same type of aircraft.

From Calshot it was a natural step for him to be posted to the Aircraft and Armament Experimental Establishment to continue his work in the same field. He was for more than four years engaged in this type of flying before taking the 1935 Staff College course.

Before war came he had rounded off his experience with three years of air staff duties but was commanding his first squadron, No. 44, in September 1939. His experience with operational units and in experimental flying led to his being sent to the Air Ministry at the end of 1939 for duty in an air staff branch dealing with fighter operations. In July of the following year he went to Bomber Command headquarters for operational staff duties from where he was posted to command Waddington in March 1941.

With his oustanding qualities and experience, however, his was not a settled procession of appointments, and in October 1941 he was sent out to Washington on temporary duty as adviser to the American Army Air Force on the operational lessons that the Royal Air Force had so hardly won in the hostilities up to that time. It was not inapt that at the end of the war he should become the recipient of the American D.F.C. and Commander, Legion of Merit.

Boothman returned to take up command of another base, at Finningley, towards the end of 1941, where he remained until the summer of 1942, when he was back in the Air Ministry for duty in the Directorate of Operational Requirements. A year later he went as Air Officer Commanding No. 106 Wing at Benson—later, as its functions and scope increased, No. 106 Group. In this command he was concerned with much of the vital reconnaissance that had to be done to ensure the success of D-Day. In this appointment, as in all others, he flew whenever his duties permitted.

It gave Boothman pleasure and satisfaction to return to the Aeroplane and Armament Experimental Establishment at Boscombe Down as its commander in July 1944. A year later he was promoted to Air Vice-Marshal and went to the Air Ministry as Assistant Chief of Air Staff (Technical Requirements), possibly as highly qualified for such a post as any officer could be. He spent more than three years in this exacting post, recommending the trends that R.A.F. equipment should take for the future. The fruits of his thinking can be seen in the Air Force operational squadrons of today.

In November 1948 he was appointed A.O.C. Iraq, and it was during his stay in that country that he was first troubled with illness which he made light of. He was nearly two years there before he went back to London to become Controller of Supplies (Air) in the Ministry of Supply in September 1950, with the acting rank of Air Marshal.

His vital task at the Ministry of Supply gave him outlet for the full employment of his talents and experience for the next three years, at the end of which his service career was crowned by his appointment as Air Officer Commanding-in-Chief, Coastal Command, which he became in November 1953. His health give him a certain amount of trouble during his days at Northwood but he served a full term before his retirement from the Service in April 1956.

His son, Flying Officer P. J. Boothman, followed his father into the Royal Air Force and they had perhaps the unique distinction of attending the same investiture in 1945 to receive the same decoration, the Distinguished Flying Cross. Flying Officer Boothman was killed in a flying accident the following year.

Boothman was awarded the Air Force Cross in 1931, made C.B. in 1944, K.B.E. in 1951, and K.C.B. in 1954.

December 31, 1957.

The belated report from Moscow of the death two years ago [1952] in a Siberian prison camp of **Michael Borodin** brings the story of one more Bolshevist old guard to what has now become the orthodox conclusion.

It is unlikely that Borodin will ever win a prominent place in the Communist pantheon of fame, because his principal work was to secure the early victories of the Kuomintang in China. As adviser to the Canton Government during its struggle for power after the 1914-18 War, Borodin taught Dr. Sun Yat-sen two indispensable lessons without which the Kuomintang could hardly have hoped to defeat the "warlords" and independent generals also competing for power. First, he emphasized the need for a disciplined party and, secondly, the need for a revolutionary movement of which the party would become the general staff. Both lessons were concerned with the technique of revolution rather than the mystique of Marx-Leninism.

Borodin was the Bolshevist organizer of a bourgeois revolution. His success was also his undoing, as, when the Chinese Communists were expelled from the Kuomintang and later fought their way to power, Borodin found himself on the wrong side of the ideological fence. His death in Siberia then became only a matter of time and even the reported appeal for clemency of Mao Tse-tung [d. 1976] was of no avail to save him.

Michael Borodin, who was born in about 1890, was of non-Russian (probably Lettish) origin. He emigrated to the United States as a young man and went to an Indiana university, where he acquired fluent English. (It was in English that he always communicated with the Chinese).

Returning to Russia with the revolution, he became a leading agent of the Communist International and before being sent to China took part in Communist agitation in many countries, including the United States, Mexico, Spain and Turkey. In 1922 he was sent by the Communist International to England to attend to the financial side of the propaganda conducted by the Communist Party of Great Britain. At that time Soviet money was being spent freely in Britain, and Borodin was able to persuade a number of the delegates to the Blackpool conference to start a minority movement in the Miners' Federation, with a view to affiliation with the Red International of Labour Unions. After six weeks of this work he went back to Russia. When he returned, this time to Glasgow, he was promptly arrested, sentenced to six months' imprisonment for contravention of the Aliens' Order, and recommended for deportation.

In 1923 Borodin began his life's main work in China. Soviet Russia, threatened on her western frontiers by Polish and potential British hostility, sought to ensure for herself at least security in the east and in particular to guard against Japan by befriending China. Secondly, Russia regarded the development of Chinese nationalism, with its likely effect on Asian nationalism generally, as likely in the long run to bring about divisions in the imperialist camp. Borodin was therefore dispatched to Canton to advise the Nationalists on how best to unite China, in the hope that Russian assistance would earn Chinese good will.

Since part of the Kuomintang programme was to free China from foreign domination, Borodin's activities were regarded in Britain with profound suspicion. He became a western bogy man of immense proportions in the 1920s. In fact, however, the evidence suggests that he was a moderating influence on the Kuomintang in this respect, pointing out to them that to take on Britain at the very outset of their march to power in China was a foolish and impracticable dissipation of strength and purpose.

Borodin retained a sure footing through all the maze of intrigue and counter-intrigue which accompanied the rise of the Kuomintang to power. When the National Government was established under a Kuomintang Executive Committee, Borodin, besides a prominent part in its organization, was invited by Hu Han-min, the Foreign Minister, to become High Adviser to the Foreign Ministry. In that capacity he revolutionized Chinese diplomacy. Under his influence the National Government not only assumed from the outset a position of equality with all foreign Powers—arrogating to itself the right, which it certainly did not possess, to speak for China as a whole—but also adopted an aggressive policy which, as military successes followed, led to the gradual abandonment in law of some foreign concessions in China, and of all but the most elementary of foreign rights.

It seemed as though Moscow's policy were about to come to full fruition, when Borodin made a false move. Under his influence the Central Executive Committee began to show its independence by contradicting Chiang Kai-shek's* orders to the Army; by abolishing at its third plenary session in Wuhan in March 1927 the Political and Military Councils; and by passing a resolution that Communist Party and Kuomintang must together rule China. Communist accession to power was contrary both to Sun Yat-sen's expressed wishes and to the repeated declarations of Moscow. Chiang bided his time, and when the favourable moment came formed a separate Government at Nanking.

Borodin's work for the Kuomintang was from the start strongly criticized inside Russia, where support of a bourgeois régime was regarded as unworthy of a Communist State. When, however, the Nationalist-Communist rift became open, and later when the Communists were clearly going to win, the Soviet Government took the obvious way of living down their earlier support of the Kuomintang. First they dismissed Borodin and later put him in a concentration camp.

October 14, 1954.

Dr. Mario Borsa, for many years Milan Correspondent of *The Times,* who died in Milan on October 6, 1952, was an Italian whose robust love for his own country, in whose cause he was called upon to suffer many things, only heightened his appreciation of another people. During all his adult life, England and her people, her institutions, both political and social, her country, her work and her pastimes, were in his heart second only to his own.

Mario Borsa was born in 1870 in the province of Milan. The country home of his childhood was to form the background of one of his most delightful books, as the countryman's sagacity was to prove one of his most powerful gifts during his career. Having studied at Milan University, seen the then Liberal Italy at its best and learned to love the ideal of freedom, political and personal, for which his country was striving, he went as a young man to London and began his active life as a journalist. He remained for many years as London Correspondent of the *Secolo,* at that time the greatest Italian Liberal newspaper, and in 1910-11 returned to Milan as editor.

During his life in England, Borsa identified himself to a remarkable extent with the Liberal party—understanding and in some respects idealizing the aims of English Liberalism as few men, either English or foreign, have done. More than that, his own ardent intellect, nourished in all that was great in the tradition of Cavour and the other leaders of Italian unity, penetrated beneath the seeming contradictions in much of our party politics and social life, and examined in writing and in speech those principles, striking deeper than parties and persons, from which our national character has grown.

Borsa's direct mind and impetuous will could ill tolerate half-speech or half-measures of any kind where he felt a principle to be in danger. It is not surprising that during his first years as editor of the *Secolo,* when the Tripoli war broke out, he earned bitter unpopularity for a time by his fearless opposition to it. His victory in a libel suit brought against his paper by certain Italian journalists in 1915 certainly added power to his paper, and possibly caution to his pen. The *Secolo* held during his editorship a unique position among Italian newspapers. With the coming of Fascism such an organ of free speech was at once suspect. Mario Borsa was forced to retire, and the character of the *Secolo* was changed.

From such a blow to the ideals of a strenuous lifetime only a brave man could recover. Borsa did recover; and during the long period of his enforced silence in his own country—he was debarred from all work on Italian newspapers—he held the post of the Milan Correspondent of *The Times.* In that capacity his dispatches and articles kept readers well informed on the latest developments of Italian life and politics. He wrote several books, most notable among them *La Cascina sul Po,* published in 1920 and translated some 10 years later into English as *The Farm on the River Po.* It is in part autobiographical, being the story of an Italian whose early life is passed in the patriarchal surroundings of a Lombard homestead, with the struggles of the "Risorgimento" still vivid in his mind, whose journalistic work brings him to England as a young man, and who returns to his own country as a mature thinker. Into this simple framework the author put the reflections of a lifetime; his own passion for nature, his friendships, his patriotism. Another volume, *La Caccia nel Milanese,* reflects in a more specialized way Borsa's love of and lively interest in national life and sport.

In person tall and fine looking, Borsa possessed an ardour which was always young, and a sincerity which illuminated all his work. His wit was keen, but its Italian edge had perhaps been softened by long contact with the more misty outlines of English humour; in talk he was vivacious and apposite; in friendship he was constant; in heart he was humble, and gave to his country a love which refused to be rebuffed by adversity.

In the early days of Fascist power his name stood high on the index of Italians hostile to the Blackshirt movement, and he spent some time in prison without any charge being brought against him. Persecution enhanced his ideals. When Mussolini joined Hitler in war, Borsa became a fugitive and spent long periods in remote hill caves. The collapse and withdrawal of the Germans brought him inevitably back to Milan, where he immediately set to work, at the age of 75, to build up the *Corriere della Sera* (now become the *Corriere d'Informazione*) to something resembling its old glory, in the forefront of the Italian Press. For two years he laboured incessantly at his editorial desk, and he was the recipient of many tributes, Italian and British, for the achievement of his old age.

After relinquishing the editorship of the *Corriere della Sera*—the highest post to which an Italian journalist can aspire—Borsa, in spite of his advanced age, did not retire from active journalism, but continued to contribute occasional articles, more especially on foreign policy, to *La Stampa* of Turin. His greater leisure enabled him, however, to enjoy more fully his favourite recreation of shooting, which he continued almost to the day of his death.

October 7, 1952.

Professor Percy Boswell, F.R.S., who was Professor of Geology at the Imperial College of Science and Technology and head of the Department of Geology, Oil Technology and Mining Geology from 1930 to 1938, died at Ruthin on December 22, 1960.

Percy George Hamnall Boswell was born at Woodbridge, Suffolk, in 1886, the eldest son of G. J. Boswell, of Ipswich, and educated at Ipswich, the Royal College of Science, and the Royal School of Mines. He was first appointed a demonstrator in geology at the Royal College in 1914, but in 1917 went to Liverpool University as Herdman Professor of Geology, where he was to remain until 1930, when he came to London University.

Boswell worked as a geologist over a very wide field, but perhaps his most important contributions concern the recent geology of East Anglia, where he was a pioneer in making sense of the stratigraphy of the area with its record of alternate advances and retreats of ice. He did notable work, too, on the prehistoric tools of the area.

During the First World War, when he served as scientific adviser in geological matters to the Ministry of Munitions, Boswell was called upon to investigate British supplies of moulding sands for use in metal foundries and, as a result, became a recognized authority as a sedimentary petrologist. He acted as adviser for the Metropolitan Water Board for some 20 years from 1934, being concerned with the falling water table under London, and his opinion was often sought as a consultant elsewhere.

Boswell was much interested in scientific education, serving the British Association as general secretary from 1931 to 1935 and as treasurer from that year till 1943. He was president of the Prehistoric Society in 1936 and of the Geological Society of London,

1940-41.

In 1939 he married Hope, the youngest daughter of William Blount Dobell.

December 23, 1960.

Rutland Boughton, composer of *The Immortal Hour,* the most successful English opera of its generation, died at the age of 82 on January 25, 1960.

Boughton had a number of other operas to his credit, all of them founded on the technique of the Wagnerian music-drama infused with a more specifically English element derived from our choral tradition. He stuck to his principles and was an unrepentant romantic at a time when taste had set in the other direction.

Boughton was born at Aylesbury on January 23, 1878. He was largely self-taught until he went to the Royal College of Music in 1900 to study under Stanford and Walford Davies. He stayed there only a year and earned a living afterwards in a theatre orchestra, until Sir Granville Bantock found him a teaching post at the Midland Institute at Birmingham, which he retained till 1911. Meantime his compositions, mostly symphonic poems and pieces for orchestra, were played by Henry Wood and other conductors, including a cantata, *Midnight,* to words from Edward Carpenter's *Towards Democracy,* at the Birmingham Festival of 1909. He also wrote a monograph on Bach, which was to be followed many years later by a larger, politically tinged interpretation of the same composer. At intervals through his career he wrote chamber music, a violin sonata, two string quartets, and an oboe sonata for his daughter Joy, a capable oboist, for whom also he wrote a concerto. But opera was his chief business.

Having discovered the Wagnerian aesthetic just when its sway was declining, he embraced it wholeheartedly and, with Reginald Buckley as librettist, embarked on a cycle of music dramas based on Arthurian legends. He settled at Glastonbury in 1914, where he began a series of festivals like a miniature English Bayreuth. *The Immortal Hour,* to words by Fiona Macleod, first saw the light there in the primitive conditions of a small stage in the local assembly rooms with only a piano for orchestra. Here, too, Boughton's other successful opera, *Bethlehem,* a happy setting of the Coventry mystery play in a frame of carols, a thoroughly English piece in comparison with the Celtic twilight of *The Immortal Hour,* was produced in 1916, along with an instalment of the Arthurian cycle, *The Round Table.*

There was an interruption in the later years of the first German war but the Glastonbury festivals were resumed from 1919 to 1924, during which time *The Birth of Arthur, Alkestis* (to Gilbert Murray's [q.v.] translation of Euripides), and *The Queen of Cornwall* (a setting of Hardy's play) were successively produced in the somewhat cramped conditions that no ingenuity or art or devotion (all of which were present in abundance) could wholly overcome. Boughton's own skill as an orchestrator probably suffered a little from lack of opportunity of hearing his scores as he conceived them.

The Glastonbury scheme after some hopes for its expansion ultimately failed, but meantime *The Immortal Hour* had achieved a great popular success and ran for a long time in Birmingham and London. *Bethlehem* also found popularity among amateurs. Both works in their different ways triumph by their tunefulness; *Alkestis* relies more on the chorus than on either melody or characterization; *The Queen of Cornwall* combines these merits but calls for more dramatic power than the composer can supply without overdriving his music into becoming forced and fussy.

The Lily Maid (which he gave at Stroud in 1937 and which Sir Steuart Wilson brought to London the following year), still moving in the land of Astolat, employs a chorus which takes no part in the action and shows the composer's old power of conveying sincere emotion in lyrical strains.

He subsequently wrote two more music dramas from the Arthurian legends, *Galahad* and *Avalon.*

January 26, 1960.

Tom Bourdillon, who died in a climbing accident in the Alps on July 29, 1956, at the early age of 32, was one of the oustanding mountaineers of his generation.

His exploits on the Chamonix Aiguilles led the way to that remarkable regeneration of British mountaineering in the Alps which, for the first time for many years, enabled British climbers to accept the challenge of new standards of performance set by Continental mountaineers.

His technical excellence was matched by his extraordinary determination and his refusal to accept failure, qualities which were so clearly displayed when he was a member of the team that conquered Everest. But for the unlucky breakdown of their oxygen apparatus, he and Evans might have reached the summit, in spite of the fact that they were attempting the prodigious climb all the way from the South Col.

Bourdillon was a man of great charm; as a companion he was delightful. Outstanding were his warmth and sincerity, his sympathy for suffering, his quick anger at injustice done to others, his humour, and perhaps above all his inflexible loyalty.

Thomas Duncan Bourdillon was born in 1924 and after attending a preparatory school at Newquay went to Gresham's School, Holt. During the latter part of the last war he served with the Army in the Middle East, and after demobilization went up to Oxford. After taking his degree he joined the staff of the Ministry of Supply as a physicist and worked on rocket research. His private researches in conjunction with his father, Dr. R. B. Bourdillon, and Dr. Griffith Pugh helped to evolve the oxygen apparatus which made the conquest of Everest possible. He was a member of Eric Shipton's [d. 1977] expedition in 1951 which discovered the southern route to the summit of the mountain.

He was an extremely shy man, very reserved, with a halting, rather precise manner. Yet he was a man who held extremely strong personal convictions, somewhat at variance with his large size and apparent diffidence. Soon after the war he was climbing in the Alps and began high grade climbs. He first became noticed after a climb which was the first British ascent of the north face of the Dru, then one of the most formidable climbs in the Alps. It was a very difficult rock climb; rock climbing was, in fact, his speciality and his passion.

He did a lot of other climbs, took part in the 1951 Everest expedition, and the Cho Oyu expedition in 1952, accompanied by his wife, who survives him together with two young children.

August 1, 1956.

Sir Harold Bowden, second baronet, G.B.E., president of Raleigh Industries, died at the age of 80 on August 24, 1960.

He was well known in the world of industry and in sport. As chairman for many years of the Raleigh Cycle Company, in which office he succeeded his father, Sir Frank Bowden, first baronet, founder of the concern, in 1921, he was one of the largest employers of labour in Nottingham, and the firm's product, the Raleigh Cycle, was known throughout the world.

He was chairman of the British Olympic Association from 1931 to 1935 and in that capacity he attended the Olympic Games at Los Angeles in 1932. He gave much of his time to raising funds for the support of British Olympic teams and in arousing interest and enthusiasm for all branches of athletics.

He was an excellent advertisement for his product. As a child he had been frail in health and, to recruit it, took up cycling; he gave it up when he was nearing 80.

Bowden was born on July 9, 1880, and educated at Clifton and at Clare College, Cambridge. In 1899 he entered the family business.

If he was a shrewd man of business he was also an enlightened employer of labour on several showings. Shortly after the international conference at Locarno he wrote a letter to *The Times* calling for a new spirit in industry and a conference at Christmas between picked leaders from employers and labour to draw up a charter of peace. Moreover, he was willing, as he said, to "back his optimism to the extent of defraying the expenses of such a conference". It was not his fault that nothing came of the plan.

He acted generously after the General Strike; the first year of the profit-sharing scheme he had introduced produced a shareout of over £15,000 among the Raleigh workers. Eight hundred of his men had earlier gone on sympathetic strike and it was a condition of the scheme that a man should be in continuous employment for the whole 12 months; but he chose to ignore the action of the 800, saying he assumed "they acted under the influence of bad leadership". During the trade depression he was actively occupied with new plans for fresh and more extensive credit to provide greater employment.

He was twice president of the British Cycle and Motor Cycle Manufacturers' Association, and was a vice-president of the Federation of British Industries. In 1933 he was High Sheriff of Nottinghamshire.

He was four times married. The baronetcy passes to his only son, Frank, who was born in 1909.

August 25, 1960.

Marjorie Bowen, one of the most fertile English writers of historical fiction, who wrote also under the names of George R. Preedy and Joseph Shearing (not to mention three or four other names which it is believed conceal her identity), and who in private life was Mrs. Arthur L. Long, died in hospital in London on December 23, 1952.

Marjorie Bowen, born Margaret Gabrielle Campbell, wrote with singular facility. She had imagination, a vividly picturesque historical sense, and an unhesitating feminine instinct for the elements of dramatic narrative; with these resources she had determined at the very outset to earn her living by writing fiction. This she did in time with little apparent difficulty. So vast, however, became the volume of her work that it threatened to overwhelm the reading public she had made her own, and it was perhaps this anxiety that led her to adopt the device of appearing to be several authors at the same time.

Born at Hayling in Hampshire in 1888, the daughter of Vere Campbell and Josephine Elizabeth Ellis, Margaret Gabrielle Campbell came of Moravian and clerical stock, but was brought up in penurious and eccentric circumstances which were to leave her with an ineradicable dislike of bohemianism. She was educated spasmodically in Paris, Rome, and London, but largely, in her own phrase, by life and by herself.

In 1912 she married Zefferino Emilio Costanza, a Sicilian, by whom she had two children, of whom the first died in infancy. She was living with her husband during the 1914-18 war in Italy when he fell ill; she nursed him in circumstances of hard and bitter privation, which she struggled to alleviate by her writing, until his death in 1916. In the ensuing year she married as her second husband Arthur L. Long, by whom she had two more sons.

She had made a precocious and brilliantly successful start as historical novelist in 1917, when she published *The Viper of Milan.* Greeted enthusiastically by a host of distinguished people, several famous writers among them, that opulent piece of story-telling gripped the public fancy and became a best-seller. For some years afterwards she wrote in the most difficult and adverse circumstances, and it was only by extreme persistence that the author of *Defender of the Faith, The Carnival of Florence, The Rake's Progress, Mr. Washington,* and the rest built up her reputation with a public made gratifying and all but painlessly aware of the pageant of history. Book succeeded book in astonishing profusion. Her normal purpose in selecting a historical period—Renaissance Italy, say, or Revolutionary France—or more often a historical character—Mary Stuart, Lady Hamilton, William Hogarth, John Wesley, or indeed any striking figure in history—was to exhibit in the personal passions and crises of the past an unfailing human resemblance to the present.

Throughout the 1920s and 1930s the flood of "Marjorie Bowens" continued. No year passed without one, few without several more than one. In 1928, for instance, there were no fewer than seven. It is difficult to pick and choose among all these volumes. In *The Netherlands Displayed* (1927), in which she returned to a setting she had employed before, she gave evidence of a genuinely inquiring interest in the intricacies of government in the later seventeenth century; *Brave Employments* found her once more in Jacobite Ireland; in *Dickon* (1929) she attempted a bold rehabilitation of Richard III. In the middle 1930s came a soundly informed trilogy on the spirit of the Renaissance *(The Golden Roof, The Triumphant Beast, Trumpets at Rome),* and another trilogy on the spiritual life of seventeenth-century England—*(God and the Wedding Dress, Mr. Tyler's Saints, The Circle in the Water).* And there were quite a number of biographies and historical studies proper, sandwiched between these works of fiction.

It was in 1928, Marjorie Bowen's most fecund year, that "George R. Preedy" published *General Crack,* which he regularly followed every year with another book. In adaptation it served also for the first of several stage plays for which he was responsible. He, too, was a historical novelist of bustling and romantic temper, who kept fairly close to recorded fact while imposing his own interpretation of motive upon his characters. Like Marjorie Bowen's, his work varies markedly in quality. *Violante,* which appeared in 1932, was, perhaps, his most successful, certainly his grimmest, book. In that same year "Joseph Shearing" joined "Marjorie Bowen" and "George R. Preedy" in production.

In 1939 Marjorie Bowen published a volume of autobiography, *The Debate Continues,* under her maiden name, Margaret Campbell.

December 27, 1952.

Air Chief Marshal Sir Frederick Bowhill, G.B.E., K.C.B., C.M.G., D.S.O. & BAR, who died at his home in London on March 12, 1960 at the age of 79, had a remarkable and distinguished career of some 50 years in the Merchant Navy, the Royal Naval Air Service, and the Royal Air Force.

He was undoubtedly one of the most colourful personalities of his day. Although he rose to the highest ranks of the R.A.F. the tang of the sea remained with him. With his stern, weather-beaten face, and with shaggy eyebrows of a vivid red hue which earned him the affectionate nickname of "Ginge", he made a striking figure. Meeting him for the first time, people were apt to regard him as cold and rather awe-inspiring, but behind this hard, bleak façade he hid a kindly nature and a keen sense of humour.

Bowhill had the capacity to command respect and obedience, but without apparent effort he inspired the confidence of his men and won their lasting affection and admiration. He was reticent about his own achievements but unstinting in giving credit to subordinates and in making known the successes of others. A bachelor until he was 52, Bowhill's work was his consuming interest, and he showed skill, ingenuity and foresight in every task with which he was entrusted. He will best be remembered for his work as Commander-in-Chief of Coastal Command during the early part of the 1939-45 War, for the big part he played in building up the Atlantic bomber ferry, by means of which American and Canadian aircraft were delivered to Britain, and as the first head of Transport Command.

At the age of 16 Bowhill's ambition to enter the Royal Navy was frustrated by his failure to pass the examination for a cadetship in H.M.S. Britannia. Where Bowhill failed, success was gained by his friend, a boy named Teddy Evans, who eventually gained fame as Evans of the Broke. Bowhill also went to sea, but as an apprentice in sail on a barque carrying coal to South Africa. In those days conditions were rough and hard and the food provided for seamen little better than in Nelson's day.

One voyage of 199 days from San Francisco to Antwerp is believed to have been a "slow record" even for a sailing ship. The vessel in which Bowhill was third mate took six weeks to round the Horn, and for weeks the crew had to subsist on the cargo of grain. On his travels under sail Bowhill read medical text books with the object of qualifying as a doctor in case he did not make progress at sea. It was 17 years before he achieved his long-cherished ambition of being admitted to the Royal Navy, though he had earlier seen service in the R.N.R. From sailing ships he went to the P. & O. Line, and it was while he was serving in steamships that the Wright Brothers made their first heavier-than-air flight and gave Bowhill his lasting interest in aviation. When he was 32 he heard that the Admiralty were contemplating experiments with aircraft, and read an announcement offering tuition in flying for £75. He took leave from the Merchant Service, qualified as a pilot, and was accepted by the Royal Navy. From that time onwards his love of the sea was shared with a passion for flying, and he regarded it as a fortunate chance that some of his commands enabled him to enjoy both.

Of a Scottish Border family deriving its name from Bowhill village, near Selkirk, Frederick William Bowhill was the son of Colonel J. Bowhill, The Wiltshire Regiment, and was born on September 1, 1880, at Morar, Gwalior, India. He was educated at Blackheath and in the Thames Nautical College (H.M.S. Worcester). His early career was spent in the Merchant Service, from 1896. He became a midshipman in the R.N.R. in 1898 and was promoted to sub-lieutenant in 1904 and lieutenant in 1911. He learnt to fly on a Bristol biplane on Salisbury Plain, his pilot's certificate being dated January 21, 1913. Three months later he transferred to the Royal Navy as a supplementary lieutenant, and was appointed to the naval flying school at Eastchurch as flying officer. When war began in August 1914 he was placed in command of the seaplane carrier Empress, which operated in the North Sea and off the Belgian coast. On September 26, 1914, he was promoted to flight commander, continuing in the Empress. Seaplanes at that time were decidedly experimental, and when loaded with bombs could not rise from any but the lightest of seas. Yet on Christmas Day 1914 those from the Empress were among the seven which raided Cuxhaven. In October 1915 Bowhill was recalled to the Admiralty to organize a seaplane unit for Mesopotamia, and from January 1916 with the rank of squadron commander he commanded it there. From August 1916 to March 1918 he commanded the R.N.A.S. unit working off the coast and inland in East Africa. While there he was promoted to wing commander in June 1917 and in February 1918 was awarded the D.S.O.

On the formation of the R.A.F. on April 1, 1918, he was graded as lieutenant-colonel, and during the concluding months of the war commanded a wing in the Aegean Group, where he gained a bar to the D.S.O. During 1919 he served in Russia, at Constantinople, and in the Mediterranean. He was appointed C.M.G. and awarded the Russian Order of St. Vladimir and the Greek Order of St. Saveur.

In the post-war establishment of the R.A.F. on August 1, 1919, he received a permanent commission as wing commander. From October 1919 to June 1920 he was chief of staff and second-in-command of the successful operations against the Mad Mullah in Somaliland, for which he was again mentioned in dispatches (the sixth time). Promoted to group captain in January 1921, he was shortly afterwards appointed chief staff officer in the Coastal Area (later Coastal Command). In February 1925 he again went east to command the aircraft depôt at Aboukir, Egypt, and in October 1926 was posted to Iraq as chief staff officer. While there he was promoted to air commodore in July 1928.

For two years from May 1929 he was Director of Organization and Staff Duties at the Air Ministry, and in May 1931 became Air Officer Commanding, Fighting Area (later Fighter Command), receiving promotion to air vice-marshal in July 1931. He returned to the Air Ministry in July 1933, as Air Member for Personnel on the Air Council, and held the post for four strenuous years, which saw the start of rearmament and a vast expansion of numbers and training facilities. He was made C.B. in June 1935 and promoted to K.C.B. in January 1936.

From August 1937, he was Air Officer Commanding-in-Chief, Coastal Command. This was the command he held during the first two years of the War of 1939-45, when Coastal Command aircraft co-operated with the Navy in vast areas between Norway and Gibraltar and far out into the Atlantic searching for and attacking U-boats and German warships, protecting our convoys and carrying out reconnaissance.

When war began the command had only 171 aircraft at its disposal, many of them of inferior performance, and to make the best use of his available strength Bowhill instituted what became known as "scarecrow" patrols. These were carried out by Tiger Moth training aircraft carrying neither bombs nor guns, which flew over the U-boat routes from Germany to the Atlantic, frequently forcing them to submerge by unfounded fear of an attack. It was a Coastal Command aircraft which spotted the notorious German "hell ship" Altmark, with British sailors aboard as prisoners, off the Norwegian coast in 1940.

When Bowhill left Coastal Command it had the remarkable record of having escorted more than 4,000 convoys, made about 500 attacks on U-boats, and destroyed many other German vessels.

In June 1941 he was selected to command the organization in Canada which became necessary to take delivery from the newly formed Flight Ferry Command of the United States Army Air Corps and fly to the United Kingdom the large numbers of aircraft produced in American factories. In March 1943 he took on a still larger task on being appointed Air Officer Commanding-in-Chief, Transport Command. In addition to controlling the operations of the R.A.F. transport squadrons at home, this new command became responsible for the organization and control of strategic air routes, for all oversea ferrying, and for the reinforcement moves of squadrons to and between oversea theatres. The Ferry Command at Montreal became a subordinate formation. Sir Frederick held the Transport Command until February 1945. On retiring, he was appointed to the United States Legion of Merit, Degree of Commander, the citation stating that he had "manifested an exceptional degree of interest in promoting the most effective and cordial relationships with the American Air Transport Command".

He was created G.B.E. in the 1941 birthday honours. From 1946 to 1957 he served as Chief Aeronautical Adviser to the Ministry of Civil Aviation (later the Ministry of Transport and Civil Aviation), for which he received the warm thanks of the Government. In 1945 he was elected Master of the Honourable Company of Master Mariners.

Bowhill was married in 1932 to Dorothy, widow of Wing Commander A. B. Gaskell, and daughter of R. H. Arlingham-Davies.

March 14, 1960.

Sir Arthur Lyon Bowley, C.B.E., one of the distinguished British statisticians who came to the fore in the first decade of this century, died on January 21, 1957 at Haslemere.

Bowley was born on November 6, 1869, the son of the Rev. J. W. L. Bowley, vicar of SS. Philip and Jacob, Bristol. He went to Christ's Hospital and to Trinity College, Cambridge, where he was bracketed Tenth Wrangler in 1891. Under the influence of Marshall, he applied his mathematical abilities to problems in economic statistics. He gained the Cobden Prize in 1892 with his *A Short Account of England's Foreign Trade in the Nineteenth Century* (published 1893, third edition 1922). He also obtained the Adam Smith Prize in 1894 and his Cambridge Sc.D. in 1913.

On leaving Cambridge he taught mathematics at St. John's School, Leatherhead, from 1893 to 1899 and his interest in statistics developed rapidly. By 1895, the critical date in his career, he had already published the first of what was to be a long series of articles in the *Journal of the Royal Statistical Society*. In that year Sidney Webb and others founded the London School of Economics with Hewins as first director. On Marshall's recommendation, Hewins invited Bowley to become one of the small staff of lecturers at the school; few of them were much older than Bowley himself and all had other main occupations. He worked in close association with such teachers as Cannan, Graham Wallas, Hobhouse, and Mackinder, men of wide and diverse interests. At that time statistics was not taught, at least as a separate discipline, at any British university and Webb wanted it treated as a practical subject—"not statistical theory, but statistics for junior Civil servants". So, as Bowley himself noted later, the school's time-table included from the outset in October 1895 "a statistical course which continued on Wednesday evening at 5.45 or 6 for perhaps 38 years with little intermission".

For 19 years, from 1900 to 1919, Bowley combined a lectureship at the London School of Economics with teaching in mathematics and economics at University College, Reading, where Mackinder was Principal for some years. Though the school had become part of the University of London, it did not proceed rapidly to appoint either professors or full-time teachers. It was not until the period 1907-1914 that chairs in the main subjects were established; Bowley was given the title of professor in 1915 and he was elected to a newly established chair in statistics in 1919, a post he held until his retirement in 1936. He was made Emeritus Professor in the same year.

He was a diligent teacher, but in his care as an expositor he made little or no concession to the student mind. In research work he was meticulous to a degree and demonstrated a wide range of interest in economic and social affairs. He wrote a great deal, much of lasting value, particularly in economic and social statistics. His influence as a teacher was great though perhaps more at the postgraduate than at the undergraduate level. The late Lord Stamp, in his work on British incomes and property, for example, freely acknowledged his indebtedness to Bowley, whose student he was. He cannot be regarded, however, as a pathbreaker either in the development of statistical methodology or in economics. Marshall referred to him in private as "plodding" and endeavoured to persuade him to seek the "many in one and one in many" in economics; but Bowley did not regard such a broad task as within his scope, preferring to confine himself to the immediate applications of his subject. His most original and fruitful contributions were in the application of sampling techniques to social surveys; his pioneer work here was subsequently developed in market research and in other fields.

He was at his best in the role of a wise and experienced counsellor and his reputation in this respect was very high, both in Britain and abroad. The International Statistical Institute owed much to him, as a member from 1903, treasurer from 1929 to 1936 and again from 1947 to 1949, and as the author of several reports sponsored by the institute. He was a member of the Council of the Royal Statistical Society as early as 1898, always active in its affairs, becoming president in 1938-40.

When the journal *Economica* was founded at the London School of Economics in 1921, Bowley was an early contributor and served with Cannan and Graham Wallas on the editorial board. Later, when the London and Cambridge Economic Service was started in 1923, he acted as editor and member of the Executive Committee from the outset; he remained editor until 1945 and his regular contributions to the bulletins of the service continued until the end of 1953. He was a founder member of the International Econometric Society, serving as a member of council from 1933 to 1947 and as president in 1938-39. He was acting Director of the Oxford University Institute of Statistics for a wartime period (1940-44).

He served on several official committees in Britain, particularly those on the cost of living, and he contributed to the series of publications of the League of Nations in the early 1920s. His authority on the measurement of subsistence levels and the cost of living was recognized in the invitation given him by Sir William Beveridge [Lord Beveridge*] to be one of a sub-committee of four to advise on subsistence level for the purpose of the Beveridge Report on Social Insurance and Allied Services.

He travelled extensively, influencing statisticians in many parts of the world. With Professor Sir Dennis Robertson* he went to India on the mission which resulted in the publication of *A Scheme for an Economic Census of India* (1934).

He was created C.B.E. in 1937 and Knight Bachelor in 1950.

Of a reserved and retiring disposition, but with a very dry sense of humour, Bowley made and retained many friends who share with a very large body of pupils the loss of an untiring worker in the field of economic and social statistics.

He married in 1904 Julia, daughter of Thomas Hilliam, of Spalding, Lincolnshire, who survives him together with the three daughters of the marriage.

January 23, 1957.

Sir Leslie Boyce, who died on May 30, 1955 in hospital at Gloucester at the age of 59, achieved many distinctions, the greatest of which was that of being the first citizen born in a British Dominion oversea, and remaining within the Empire, to be elected Lord Mayor of London.

The honour, though unique in the annals of the City, was more than a gesture of regard for him, or his native country, Australia; he had earned it by service in local government, not only in London but in Gloucester, as that city's representative in Parliament for many years, and by taking a leading part in its business and social affairs. He had hoped that during his term of office he could do something to strengthen the ties between London and the Commonwealth. It gave him great pleasure to welcome to London the Commonwealth representatives who attended the Finance Ministers' conference at the beginning of his year of office. He was also exploring the possibility of calling a meeting in London of the civic heads of all the more important towns and cities in the Commonwealth. As a result of the death of King George VI [q.v.] he postponed his social engagements for the first two months of the new reign. Those engagements which were postponed had then to be fitted into the already crowded programme.

Boyce was not an ostentatious figure, but his strength of character struck everyone who met him. He was an extraordinarily hard worker—just before his illness he was working an 18-hour day—and, whether pursuing his own business or attending to the Lord Mayor's business at the Mansion House, he was at his desk when most people were still thinking of getting up for breakfast.

Born at Taree, New South Wales, on July 9, 1895, the son of the late Charles Macleay Boyce, of Sydney, Harold Leslie Boyce was educated at Sydney Grammar School. He had no time to embark on a career before the outbreak of war in 1914, when he joined the Australian Imperial Forces and in the next three years saw service in Egypt, Gallipoli, and on the western front. Invalided to South Australia in 1917, he soon recovered and started a one-man recruiting campaign, raising an infantry unit in command of which, in the same year, he returned to France and active service.

At the end of the war he went to Balliol College, Oxford, on a Huth scholarship and two scholarships awarded by the Rhodes Trust. He read for the Bar and in 1922 was called by the Inner Temple. As a barrister he became interested in the League of Nations and for some time acted as technical adviser to the Australian representative before the Permanent Mandates Commission at Geneva, being appointed later a substitute delegate and legal adviser at the third Assembly of the League.

He lived on the outskirts of Cheltenham, where he was soon taking a prominent part in several of the leading local industries and political activities, and in 1929 he secured election as Conservative M.P. for the neighbouring city of Gloucester. He retained the seat until the general election in 1945, and during the time he was at Westminster displayed an unremitting zeal on behalf of his constituents and exerted considerable influence when wider questions affecting the Empire were under discussion. He was a member of the Empire Parliamentary delegation sent to Northern Rhodesia in 1930, and his knowledge of imperial matters contributed materially to the success of the mission. He was elected Sheriff of Gloucester in 1941.

His association with the Corporation of the City of London began after the 1939-45 War, when he was elected alderman for the Ward of Walbrook. A liveryman of the Worshipful Companies of Loriners and Carpenters, he was chosen as Senior Sheriff of the City in 1947, and his election as Lord Mayor came in 1951 as a signal honour not only to a distinguished Australian but to the Commonwealth.

Though some of the customary pageantry of the Lord Mayor's Day procession was dispensed with, the procession was halted outside Australia House, where the High Commissioner presented the new Lord Mayor with an illuminated address from the Prime Minister of Australia, congratulating him on his outstanding achievement.

He was created a K.B.E. in 1944 and was one of his Majesty's Lieutenants and a Justice of the Peace for the City of London. His commercial activities were varied and extensive, and in 1946 he led an important trade mission to China representing the whole of the industries in the United Kingdom.

He married in 1926 Maybery, daughter of the late Edward Philip Bevan, of Melbourne. There were three sons of the marriage, of whom the eldest, Mr. Richard Leslie Boyce, succeeds to the baronetcy conferred upon his father at the end of his term of office as Lord Mayor of London.

June 1, 1955.

Lord Bracken, the first viscount, died in London on August 8, 1958 after a long illness. He was 57.

An ebullient, full-blooded, energetic, and highly intelligent personality disappeared from British public life with his death. Success was, as the saying is, "written all over" Bracken from an early age; and one shrewd observer said of him that "he seemed to have conquered London, to have got to know everyone, and to have been able to make the most important do his bidding before he was 30".

The Right Hon. Brendan Bracken, P.C., first Viscount Bracken, of Christchurch, in the county of Southampton, in the peerage of the United Kingdom, was born in 1901, son of the late J. K. A. Bracken, of Ardvullen House, Kilmallock, co. Limerick. He was sent to Australia at an early age, and had most of his schooling in Sydney; but in 1920 (having, it is strongly believed, made his own choice among the public schools) he turned up at Sedbergh, a self-assured young man with his own cheque book, who entered himself and paid his own fees.

He remained at Sedbergh for less than a year, but even in that short time he impressed the staff by his adult mind, his interest in world affairs, and his skill as a debater. Going to no university, Bracken turned his attention to the newspaper world. Having both money and ability, this precocious young man was already, in 1922, running *English Life* with Robert Lutyens. One of the important elements in his early business career was his connexion with the Eyre family and the family publishing firm of Eyre and Spottiswoode. He formed this friendship with the Eyre family early in life and from a young age he was a director of Eyre and Spottiswoode and a trustee of the principal Eyre family trust. The Eyre family and publishing interests were in effect his partners in the formation of the publishing group which he constituted in the 1920s.

The group included *The Financial News, Investors' Chronicle, The Banker, The Practitioner,* a controlling interest in *The Liverpool Journal of Commerce,* and a half share of *The Economist.* These various interests were acquired during a short period and were organized under the general umbrella of a holding company called Financial Newspaper Proprietors of which he was managing director.

He was keenly interested in architecture, as an intelligent layman, and when the Liverpool Roman Catholic Cathedral was mooted he passed word to the Archbishop, Dr. Downey [q.v.], by Professor Reilly, that if Sir Edwin Lutyens was appointed architect he would subscribe munificently towards the funds. As the world knows, Lutyens was in fact called upon, but though *post hoc,* it may not have been *propter hoc.* Through the private mediation of Professor Reilly also, Bracken acquired a controlling interest in a Liverpool shipping daily.

Bracken proved to be a wise and far-seeing man of business. His relationships with his staff were pleasant, for he detested sycophancy, had the knack of bringing out the best qualities of those who served him, and appreciated enterprise and straight dealing.

In 1929 Bracken was elected to Parliament as a Conservative for the North Paddington division, and he continued to sit for that constituency after successive re-elections, having by 1935 increased his majority to 7,228. To the Press Gallery and the House in general he gave the impression of being a young man of great assurance, verging almost on truculence, showing special interest in colonial questions. He was firmly convinced of the necessity and urgency of Empire development, saying that if Britain did not act some other nation would certainly do so. He deprecated the Austrian loan in 1933, saying "Why lend money to rebuild the slums of Vienna when we have slums of our own?"

Initially he showed some energy as a backbencher, but his strong criticisms of a foreign policy based on appeasement were not calculated to bring him advancement. He foresaw the gradual drift into war; and his views in this matter were very similar to those of Sir Winston Churchill*. In spite of the quarter-century's difference in their ages the two men became fast friends. When Sir Winston Churchill went to the Admiralty at the outbreak of the last war he took Bracken with him as parliamentary private secretary. In 1940 Bracken was sworn of the Privy Council; and in the summer of 1941 he succeeded Mr. Duff Cooper [later Lord Norwich, q.v.], as Minister of Information.

When he took over the Ministry Bracken succeeded to a tangle of interests and circumstances which made his job most difficult; but he began to use methods which promised better things for this troubled and awkward department. In an early speech he said: "If, as Minister, I cannot get news into the papers, the sooner I depart from the premises the better for all concerned". One of his first acts was to arrange with Cable and Wireless, Ltd., for cheaper rates for Empire news cables. Another was to release to all the cinemas a captured German propaganda film, for he held (rightly, as it proved) that this brutal film, far from working to German advantage, would stiffen the resolution of Hitler's enemies.

With his great gift for personal relations, whether they were with American, Commonwealth, foreign, or British journalists, Bracken soon showed exactly what a Minister of Information's relations with the Press should be. He was also highly successful in the team he picked to work with him. It can be said that from the time Brendan Bracken and Cyril Radcliffe [Lord Radcliffe, d. 1977] came together in 1941 as Minister and Director-General the Ministry of Information justified itself. The Press and the broadcasting authorities both came to respect Bracken because they found by experience that he was no mere mouthpiece of other Ministers. On occasions he was prepared to fight them all, including the Prime Minister, if he thought they were on the wrong tack where the providing of information about the war was concerned.

In 1945 he achieved renewed political advancement and prominence—though this was to prove only the prelude to a gradual retreat from political life. He became First Lord of the Admiralty in Sir Winston Churchill's caretaker government of 1945 and was one of the party's active leaders during the 1945 general election campaign. He was selected to give one of the Conservatives' major party political broadcasts; on the radio, indeed, he was the principal second string to Sir Winston Churchill, whose close friend and disciple he was, in launching the main line of attack on Labour.

But after the Government's defeat in the 1945 election he returned immediately to a great expansion of his business interests and from that time onwards his business interests really came first, as he never returned to political office. His most notable appointment was to the chairmanship of the Union Corporation, one of the City's leading mining finance houses, with large interests in the South African gold mining industry. He had been a close friend and collaborator of Sir Henry Strakosch, who had been chairman of the Union Corporation for many years and had died in 1943. It was supposed that it had always been Sir Henry Strakosch's intention that Bracken should succeed him and he was appointed to the chairmanship in 1945 almost immediately after the Conservative Government had resigned. He gave most of his energies to his work as chairman of the Union Corporation and made many extensive visits to South Africa on the corporation's behalf.

Meanwhile, his large and long-standing interests in the world of financial and economic publishing underwent a fresh expansion. His group in 1945 acquired the *Financial Times,* which had previously been controlled by Lord Camrose [q.v.]; soon afterwards the two daily financial newspapers were amalgamated as *The Financial Times.* Bracken remained chairman of the group, though he no longer undertook the active executive control as he had before the war.

In the later 1940s he suffered somewhat seriously from intermittent ill-health and it came as no great surprise when he did not return to office with the Conservative Government in 1951. He had been defeated in 1945 in his old constituency of North Paddington but was later returned in a by-election at Bournemouth. But at the end of 1951 he had come to the conclusion that continued membership of the House of Commons would put too much strain on his health, and in January 1952 he announced his intention to resign his seat in the Commons.

Relief from the burden of Parliamentary duties left him more time for fulfilling his now very considerable business responsibilities. It also perhaps left him more time to pursue the literary and cultural interests which meant a great deal to him throughout his life. His business responsibilities, notably as chairman of the Union Corporation and of the publishing group which he had founded, were discharged with undiminished zest and skill in spite of occasional periods of illness, and he found more time to indulge his love of reading (his knowledge of English literature was exceptionally wide and detailed). He also liked to give any of his time that could usefully be given to the affairs of Sedbergh School, of whose governors he was chairman. His interest in and knowledge of the graphic arts were recognized in his appointment as a trustee of the National Gallery in 1955.

Bracken was a tall man with a great mass of ginger hair. He was well read, quick, and a remarkably fertile conversationalist, of whom it has been said that "conversation was his hobby". He shared Sir Winston Churchill's liking for a good cigar. He had a pretty wit, and many anecdotes collected about its exercise. One of these may bear relating. On his entry into Parliament he was asked what he thought of the new Prayer Book. "My dear sir", he answered, "we print it".

Lord Bracken was unmarried, and there is no heir to the peerage.

August 9, 1958.

Former Bishop of Bradford—See **Blunt.**

Amy M. Bradford, who died at Folkestone, Kent, on January 7, 1951 at the age of 91, was the mother of four sons, two of whom won the V.C., one the D.S.O., and one the M.C. A second M.C. was won by the youngest son, as well as his V.C. All four fought in the first world war, and only the eldest, now Sir Thomas Bradford, of Durham, survived, having been wounded and awarded the D.S.O. Three of the brothers served in The Durham Light Infantry and one in the Royal Navy. Their sister, Mrs. Bradford's only daughter, is the wife of Lieutenant-Colonel H. L. Cremer, of The Grange, Chartham, Kent. Their father was the late Mr. George Bradford, of Milbanke, Darlington.

The second son, Lieutenant-Commander George Nicholson Bradford, was killed at Zeebrugge on St. George's Day 1918, his thirty-first birthday, in one of the bravest exploits of that memorable action. He was in command of the naval storming parties in Iris II, which could not anchor to the parapet of the mole because of the motion. A lieutenant who tried to scale a ladder without the ship being secured was killed on the parapet, and Lieutenant-Commander Bradford went to certain death by climbing a derrick and jumping on to the mole with the parapet anchor. He secured the ship and was immediately killed by machine-gun fire. His body fell into the sea and was not recovered. The V.C. was awarded posthumously.

The third son, Lieutenant James Barker Bradford, of The Durham Light Infantry, won the Military Cross in France, and died of wounds on May 14, 1917, at the age of 27.

The youngest of the brothers, Brigadier-General Roland Boys Bradford, also joined The Durham Light Infantry, and was awarded the Military Cross. On October 1, 1916, when serving as lieutenant, he saved the right flank of his brigade and of the division by an act of conspicuous bravery and leadership in attack, for which he was awarded the Victoria Cross. His battalion was in support when the situation of a leading battalion became critical and its commander wounded. Lieutenant Bradford asked permission to command the exposed battalion as well as his own, and by fearless energy under fire he rallied the attack, captured and defended the objective, and so secured the flank. He was afterwards promoted captain, then made brevet major, and at 25 was the youngest brigadier-general in France. He was killed in action in France in November 1917.

The brothers were educated at the Royal Naval School, Eltham.

On more than one occasion Mrs. Bradford took her place at the Folkestone observance of Remembrance Day, wearing the two Victoria Crosses and a Military Cross.

January 9, 1951.

H. N. Brailsford, a leading English socialist intellectual and an author and political journalist of an uncommonly cultivated stamp, died on March 23, 1958 in London at the age of 84.

His socialism, which was always of an internationalist character and which might be described as extreme but not extremist, was the key to almost everything that he did or wrote. Few men held more firmly or more consistently than Brailsford to an ideal of political and social justice; and none showed greater alacrity, in seeking to further that ideal, in embracing difficult or unpopular causes.

In his championship of the weak or the oppressed, or merely of those who complained of oppression, Brailsford had something in common with the late H. W. Nevinson. But while there was something of romantic knight errantry in Nevinson's noble crusades, Brailsford's was essentially a reasoned and rationalist left-wing inspiration. Inevitably it led him at times, in spite of both a warm humanity and a clear brain, into certain doctrinaire extravagances. Internationalism, the right of national self-determination, and social and economic equality were all joined in his mind in a vision of ending man's exploitation of man. Hence his enlistment in the Greek forces in the war with Turkey in 1897, his relief work in Crete and Macedonia, his ardent support of women's suffrage, his sympathy with the wrongs of Ireland, with the Indian claim to independence, with the professed aims of Soviet Russia. Hence his constant prodding of the British Labour Party and his desire for "a European Revolution" at the close of the Second World War. Brailsford was in no sense "anti-British", of course; it was his case against "imperialism" which made him an unsparing critic of British policy.

Born at Mirfield, in Yorkshire, in 1873, the son of the Rev. E. J. Brailsford, Henry Noel Brailsford was educated at Glasgow University, where he took philosophical and classical honours and where, after further courses of study at Oxford and Berlin, he was for a time assistant to the professor of logic. He threw up his post to serve as a volunteer in the Greek Foreign Legion. His experiences in the war against Turkey he described afterwards in a novel, apparently his first book, entitled *The Broom of the War-God.* Brailsford took to political journalism with ease and conspicuous success, and was leader-writer to, successively, the *Manchester Guardian, Morning Leader, Tribune, Daily News, Daily Herald,* and *The Nation.* He was never a mere armchair journalist, but travelled in Europe, the near East, America, Russia, and India. Nor was he merely political-minded. His range of interest was wide, his cultivation of mind deep and scholarly and he wrote with imaginative power and often with striking felicity.

In 1907 he had joined the Independent Labour Party, which was then the popular intellectual driving force behind the Labour movement as a whole. His propaganda for international socialism attained its fullest measure in the book he published in 1914, *The War of Steel and Gold,* an anatomy of the imperialist phase of finance capitalism and in some respects the most notable of all his books. Of necessity his attitude at the outbreak of war was one of strong opposition to British participation. In an article on the origins of the war, which originally appeared in the *Contemporary Review* and was afterwards reprinted in pamphlet form, he spoke of this "utterly unnecessary war with Germany", for which he held Imperial Russia responsible in the first place. A subsequent pamphlet styled "Belgium and 'a Scrap of Paper' " was impounded by the British authorities and destroyed. Brailsford was one of several Englishmen who in 1917 outlined a plan for a "League of Nations". After the armistice he advocated direct action for the purpose of influencing the terms of peace. In the "khaki election" he contested, unsuccessfully, Montrose Burghs.

Possibly the most notable event in Brailsford's journalistic career was his editorship of the *New Leader,* the weekly organ of the I.L.P., from 1922 until 1926. With the assistance of a strong team of contributors, among them Shaw, Wells, E. M. Forster*, Bertrand Russell* and others, he maintained exceptionally high literary and artistic standards, and there can be little doubt that the cultural stimulus he thus gave to Labour politics and policy was sorely missed on his departure.

Brailsford did not spend all his energies in journalism. His *Shelley, Godwin, and Their Circle,* published in the Home University Library, is still a minor classic in its kind, and his little book on Voltaire, published in the same series in 1935, is no less remarkable. Among his polemical works and volumes of political interpretation are *Socialism for Today* (1925); *How The Soviets Work* (1927), which exhibits a high enthusiasm, in spite of certain critical reservations, for the "new civilization" of the Bolshevik experiment; *Rebel India* (1932), which was based on first-hand impressions; *Property or Peace?* (1934), in which he looked forward to a world federation of Socialist republics; *Subject India* (1943); and *Our Settlement with Germany* (1944).

For some years before his death, while in failing health, he had been engaged in a work on the extremer Puritan sects of the seventeenth century.

March 24, 1958.

Dennis Brain, the justly renowned hornist, was killed on the Barnet by-pass early on September 1, 1957 as he was returning from the Edinburgh Festival. He had appeared in two capacities—as the principal horn of the Philharmonia Orchestra and as the leader of the wind ensemble which bears his name—and it was his frequent practice to drive back to London in his fast car after concerts.

Dennis Brain, who was born on May 17, 1921, and educated at St. Paul's School and at the Royal Academy of Music, was the son of an equally famous father, the late Aubrey Brain, who was first horn in the B.B.C. Symphony Orchestra from its foundation until the war. His grandfather had also been a horn player. The son was a better player than the father, on the father's own testimony, which is saying a lot. At the academy he studied the horn under his father and the organ with G. D. Cunningham, making his *début* in 1938 in a Bach series with his father and the Busch Chamber Players.

Thereafter he steadily increased his virtuosity on the horn and his stature as a musician until his was an international name. Works were composed for him by Elizabeth Lutyens, Paul Hindemith*, and Gordon Jacob, and Benjamin Britten [Lord Britten, d. 1976] had him in mind when writing his "Serenade for tenor horn and string orchestra". The last work written to display Brain's talents was Malcolm Arnold's concerto performed in July 1957 at the Cheltenham Festival.

The traditional uncertainties of the instrument never seemed to have occasioned a fluffed note from him and no technical difficulties ever appeared to cause him the slightest apprehension. He professed to have no nerves, though his playing lacked nothing in musical sensitiveness, but insensitiveness to risk seems to have exacted a heavy price and English music will be poorer by the loss of so brilliant an executant at the early age of 36.

September 2, 1957.

Constantin Brancusi, who died in Paris on March 16, 1957 at the age of 81, was perhaps the most famous of all the sculptors of what is loosely called the "modern" school. He did for sculpture very much what Picasso* did for painting, and what men like Le Corbusier* and Walter Gropius* did for architecture; that is to say, he reduced its elements to their lowest terms in respect of both form and content.

Brancusi was a Romanian, born into a peasant family, but like other foreigners who found their inspiration in Paris, he is generally associated with the French school. He went to Paris in 1904 having previously studied at the Bucharest Academy. He first attracted attention by reason of a number of works which cast naturalism aside, and which, to some eyes at least, belonged rather to the field of solid geometry than to that of sculpture as formerly known. The process ran parallel to that of Cézanne in painting, and constituted a kind of artistic generalization. Spirals, circles, egg-shaped objects, formed part of his production; but there were also "portrait busts" which attempted to generalize facial characteristics in the same broad way that the other shapes related to other aspects of nature. He favoured hard materials, including onyx, marble, and bronze. His works were much shown and canvassed in France, and first appeared in London at the Allied Artists' exhibition of 1913.

Among British sculptors two at least, Henry Moore and Barbara Hepworth*, have been strongly influenced by Brancusi. The United States Customs Department at one stage was less perceptive. When in 1927 his bronze "Bird in Flight" was imported into that country the Customs declined to recognize it as a work of art and charged duty on it as a "bronze product".

Brancusi belongs to the early age of steel furniture, ferro-concrete architecture, and abstract painting; and his ultimate place will depend on what estimation is given to the school in general. Partisans find in him "a vision almost of a man who has reached after intense struggle a final stillness and certainty". There is no doubt but that his range is limited; but for the present, at any rate, Brancusi's work enjoys considerable renown, and is found in many important public and private collections.

March 18, 1957.

Sir Frank Brangwyn, R.A., who died on June 11, 1956 at his home at Ditchling, Sussex, at the age of 89, was an artist of wide range and great achievement.

It would be altogether too simple a statement to say that his work is more remarkable for quantity than quality, but the inclination is nevertheless to dwell on his range, variety, and fertility rather than on the artistic merits of any individual example of his work, or even of his work in any particular medium—and his output included architecture at one end of the scale and book illustration at the other. Some 35 years ago he was the one living English artist, just as Henry Moore is now, of whom any foreigner had heard and his prestige in this country was correspondingly great. He executed commissions from all over the world—his Japanese admirers were so numerous and influential that in 1920 a Brangwyn Museum was projected in Tokyo. His birthplace, Bruges, of course, has a Brangwyn Museum, so has Orange, in Vaucluse. The United States, Canada and Mexico boast some of his large murals, and the paintings he originally executed for the Royal Gallery of the House of Lords now decorate the Guildhall at Swansea.

He was the first living artist whose works were selected for a retrospective exhibition in the Diploma Gallery of the Royal Academy. That was in 1952. The great murals had, of course, to be represented by drawings and cartoons, but the effect of so wide a range of such a comprehensive artist's work showed, however much taste might have changed from that current in his heyday, his great achievement and widespread influence. Some, indeed, felt that, like Shakespeare, "he was too full of quotations", for his work offered a rich quarry for the practitioners of applied or commercial art, which has been exploited to the full and often vulgarized in the process. From being too much praised he was too much neglected until rediscovered some four years ago. What stands out now is his ability to produce designs that are really adapted to their large scale—an aptitude so rare among English artists that it may account more than anything else for his great reputation abroad.

Welsh by extraction and a Roman Catholic in religion, Frank William Brangwyn was born on May 13, 1867, at Bruges, where his father, William Curtis Brangwyn, an ecclesiastical architect and craftsman, who designed the church of St. André, in Bruges, was working at church embroideries, and was registered as "Guillaume François". When the family returned to England Brangwyn worked at the Victoria and Albert Museum, and, as a boy of 15, was brought to the notice of William Morris by an architect named Macmurdo. Morris employed the boy in making cartoons for textiles. His first painting, "A Bit of the Esk", was exhibited at the Royal Academy in 1885. The sale of this picture to a shipowner sent Brangwyn, who was getting tired of the more or less mechanical work he did for Morris, to sea as a cabin-boy. He visited Tunis, Tripoli, Smyrna, Trebizond, and Constantinople, and later made voyages to Spain, Russia, and South Africa.

These experiences, and to some extent the watercolours of Arthur Melville, profoundly influenced his style, and from being a painter in tone he became a composer in colour. But though for a good many years Brangwyn continued to paint easel pictures and exhibit them at the Academy and elsewhere—he is represented at the Tate Gallery by "The Poulterer's Shop", a Chantrey purchase of 1916, and in the Luxembourg Museum by "Market in Morocco", bought by the French Government in 1895—they are not the works by which he will be chiefly remembered.

Brangwyn was essentially a decorative painter of a romantic disposition, and he needed the wall for the full expression of his personality. An early and very successful example of his work in this kind, thoroughly in keeping with the spirit of the place and the rather robust ornament of the interior, was the decoration of Skinners' Hall, in the City of London, and other examples of his mural painting are at the Royal Exchange, Christ's Hospital, the central hall of Selfridge's, the church of St. Aidan, Leeds, the Canadian House of Parliament, Ottawa, and the Court House, Cleveland, Ohio, but it was in connexion with what came to be known as the House of Lords Panels that Brangwyn's name became familiar to thousands who had never heard of him before.

In 1925 it was announced that the late Lord Iveagh had offered to complete the decoration of the Royal Gallery at the House of Lords at a cost of £20,000, and the offer was accepted on the understanding that the scheme would harmonize with that for the Peers' War Memorial. Rather belatedly the Royal Fine Art Commission was asked to express an opinion on the evidence of five out of the 13 panels proposed. The verdict of the commission was unfavourable on the grounds that the panels were out of harmony with their surroundings. This judgment did not go unquestioned. Seven members of the Royal Academy sent a joint letter to the Press urging delay until more of the work was available for inspection, and there were letters to *The Times* in Brangwyn's favour from two artists of such different views as W. R. Sickert and Sir A. S. Cope, R.A., but the scheme was finally rejected.

After much discussion about what to do with the panels it was announced in 1933 that Lord Iveagh* (son of the original benefactor) and his co-trustees had offered them to the Corporation of Swansea to be placed in the assembly hall of the new Guildhall designed by Sir Percy Thomas, F.R.I.B.A. In the bright light of the Brangwyn Hall, as it is called, the panels make a rather less good impression than they did in the dim interior of the Royal Gallery, which suggests that Brangwyn knew what he was about in the first instance.

In 1932 Brangwyn, with José Maria Sert, the

Spaniard, and Diego Rivera, the Mexican, was commissioned to paint panels representing aspects of modern American civilization for "Radio City", the huge Rockefeller wireless centre in New York.

Brangwyn practised nearly all the visual arts and crafts, from architecture to book illustration. Examples of his work in architecture are the British Pavilion for use at the Biennial Exhibitions in the Public Gardens at Venice, and the façade, in an unusual variety of Portland stone, of the Rowley Gallery in Kensington Church Street. In 1930 there was a comprehensive exhibition of Brangwyn's furniture, pottery, carpets, and interior decorations at a large shop in Oxford Street.

His most important work in book illustration was *The Way of the Cross,* an interpretation in 12 drawings engraved by the Sun Engraving Company of the "Stations", with a commentary by G. K. Chesterton, published in 1935. It is only necessary to compare these drawings with representations of the same subjects by Eric Gill to see how definitely Brangwyn was an "expressionist".

He was a generous giver, and not only of his own works, such as the collections of his etchings and lithographs that he presented to various public galleries at home and abroad. In 1935 he gave to the Brussels Museum a painting "The Fortune Teller", by his friend Count Albert de Belleroche, which he described as "one of the finest examples of flesh painting I have seen". The following year, in association with Arthur H. Macmurdo, the architect who had introduced him as a boy to William Morris, he gave a collection of 148 works by contemporary and other artists to The Water House, Walthamstow, once the home of William Morris, on its conversion into a Morris Museum.

Though his reputation fluctuated and he himself lived a retired life Brangwyn did not lack honours in his own country. An LL.D. of the University of Wales, he was elected A.R.A. in 1904 and R.A. in 1919, and in 1941 he was knighted. In 1932 he was awarded the Albert Medal of the Royal Society of Arts for services to decorative and commercial art and he was the recipient of many foreign distinctions. As was natural, Belgium in particular delighted to do him honour. In 1936 a Brangwyn Museum containing works by him was inaugurated at Bruges and at the same time he was elected an honorary citizen of the city of Bruges, and a deputation from the municipal authorities came over to his home to make the presentation. In 1947 a house at Orange, in Vaucluse, France, to which works by both Brangwyn and Count Albert de Belleroche had been given by the son of the latter, Count William de Belleroche, as a mark of the friendship between France and Britain, was opened as a Brangwyn and Belleroche Museum by Edouard Daladier*, who was a native of Orange.

For a good many years Brangwyn lived at Temple Lodge, a secluded house in a walled garden not far from Hammersmith Broadway. Later he migrated to Ditchling, Sussex, where there is a settlement of Roman Catholic artists and craft workers. It was in connexion with Ditchling that Brangwyn made one of his rare excursions into print, in a letter to *The Times* of July 29, 1941, urging delay in granting permission for a residential estate in that neighbourhood until the regional plan had been decided.

To meet Brangwyn was to recognize the boy who had never grown up. With his round, bearded face and stocky figure, generally clad in blue serge, he looked more like a merchant skipper than a man who would like to be mistaken for one. In conversation he had the habit of expletives—the word being generally followed by, "if you'll excuse me"—a habit that accorded amusingly with his tendency to dramatic emphasis in painting. He mixed very little in society, but he was hospitable to casual visitors interested in art, and though he was inarticulate in public and would open an exhibition with a gesture when a speech was hoped for, he would talk interestingly in a *tête-à-tête.* What struck one most was his combination of imagination and severe technical practicality.

A good deal has been written about Brangwyn, the most substantial publications being *Brangwyn, A Study of Genius at Close Quarters,* by Philip Macer-Wright (1940); and *Brangwyn Talks* (1944) and *Brangwyn's Pilgrimage* (1949), both by Count William de Belleroche.

Brangwyn married Miss Lucy Ray, who predeceased him by many years. They had no children.

June 13, 1956.

L. C. Braund, the cricketer, who died at his home in London on December 22, 1955 at the age of 80, was one of the leading lights of the Somerset eleven in the opening years of the twentieth century and one of the most useful all-round players in England.

Leonard Braund was born on October 18, 1875, and under his birth qualification, when he was 20 years old, was tried for Surrey, but then proceeded to qualify for Somerset. His desertion of the county of his birth was little noted, but it soon became clear that Surrey had lost a good man. While qualifying he gained experience with the Crystal Palace eleven, then under the management of W. G. Grace, and in 1899 he made 125 against the Australians, his first 100 in a big match. In 1900 he played once for Somerset, but the M.C.C. decided that his claim to represent the Western county was not satisfactory, and another season passed before he was properly qualified. In 1901, the summer in which he became a regular member of the Somerset side, he was brilliantly successful as a batsman and as a slow bowler. For the county he scored nearly 1,000 runs, and took nearly 100 wickets, while all told his figures were 1,587 runs and 120 wickets.

It was in this his first season that he played a prominent part in what is usually pronounced by students of cricket history to be one of the most curious county matches ever played. Up to the middle of July that summer Yorkshire had an unbeaten record, while Somerset was one of the lowest competitors on the list, so that their visit to Leeds must have been regarded with some equanimity by the home players. Colour was lent to this attitude by the opening stages of the contest. On the first evening Somerset were all out for 87, and Yorkshire had replied with 325. It is said that the visitors that evening booked seats on the south train for the Tuesday afternoon, expecting that the match would be finished by lunch-time. However, in their second innings the Somerset men began by making 222 for the first wicket, that superb batsman, Lionel Palairet, scoring 173 and Braund supporting him well with 107. The side went on to make 630, and Yorkshire were rattled out for 113, Braund taking four for 41.

In the winter of 1901-02 Braund had his first experience of Test Match cricket. He made one of a side taken to Australia by A. C. Maclaren. The success of Braund as an all-rounder was one of the few bright spots of the tour. He realized to the full the hopes that were formed of him, coming out second in the batting averages, and taking more wickets than anyone else. He did well enough to ensure a further trial when the Australians visited England in the summer of 1902, and was chosen for all the Tests. But this time he did little; he scored 65 in the fourth match, but his bowling was ineffective. He never played in another Test in England, but he went twice more to Australia, once under Sir Pelham Warner* in 1903-04, and again under A. O. Jones. His batting more than once was useful, but as an all-rounder Braund seemed to be a spent force. Indeed it was a marked feature of this gifted player's career that, compared with that of some of his contemporaries, it was so short.

He gave up playing for his county after the 1914-18 War, and became a first-class umpire, retiring in 1938. Later he had the misfortune to have both legs amputated; but in spite of this he was often seen at cricket matches, and in 1949 he was made an honorary member of the M.C.C.

December 24, 1955.

Bertold Brecht (or, as he preferred for long to be called, Bert) died in east Berlin of a heart attack on August 14, 1956. He was 58.

For long one of the most controversial figures in the European theatre, he had an immense output, not only of original work but also of adaptations from the Chinese, the Russian, and the English theatre. The adaptations are, however, so free that they really have become fresh works, the most famous of which is *The Threepenny Opera,* lately seen in London. Founded on Gay's *Beggar's Opera,* it is, nevertheless, so far from the original that little but the names of the characters remains. Other adaptations are from Gorki's *Mother,* Farquhar's *The Recruiting Officer,* and Marlowe's *King Edward the Second.*

Of his original work it may be said that he substitutes a kind of picaresque theatre, reminiscent of the early picaresque novel, by not merely abandoning the dramatic unities but by deliberately forcing them from the stage. *Mother Courage and Her Children,* for instance, covers a period of decades in a series of small, vivid scenes, very like those sketched by Fielding and Smollett. But the scenes, as played by the Berliner Ensemble, have a stark reality, which permits no escape from the hard things in everyday life. This, though it has been attempted before, has never been achieved with such intensity and will, perhaps, be judged as his major contribution to the European theatrical tradition.

With his wife, Frau Weigel*, he founded his own theatrical company in east Berlin in 1949 which found a permanent home in the old Theater am Schiffbauerdamm. Since most of his outstanding works were written between 1922 and 1948, before he settled in east Berlin, his recent fame rested largely on his imaginative productions of the Berliner Ensemble and successful performances of his plays in the western capitals.

Bertold Brecht was born on February 10, 1898, at Augsburg, the son of a manufacturer. He studied natural sciences and philosophy at Munich and Berlin universities. His earliest associations at Munich after the 1914-18 War were with a group around Lion Feuchtwanger [q.v.], but he soon felt happier in the company of revolutionary communists. His first plays, *Drums in the Night* and *Baal,* won him the Kleist literary prize in 1922. International acclaim followed seven years later with the first performance in Berlin of *The Threepenny Opera,* for which he wrote the text and Kurt Weill the music. It ran for more than 250 performances in the German capital and swept over the country on an immense wave of popularity, helped largely by Weill's catchy tunes. Bert Brecht soon aroused the displeasure of the National Socialists. As early as 1930 they provoked rioting at Leipzig and Frankfurt-am-Main during performances of the opera *The Rise and Fall of the Town of Mahagonny,* another joint work of Brecht and Weill.

When Hitler came to power Brecht sought asylum successively in Denmark, Sweden, and Finland, until 1941, when he settled in the United States after an adventurous journey across the Soviet Union and Persia. He returned to Germany in 1948 on a visit and accepted an offer from the east German Government to conduct his own theatre in his own way in east Berlin. In spite of occasional ideological lapses, which earned him remonstrations from the Socialist Unity Party and in 1951 obliged him to withdraw *The Interrogation of Lucullus* from the State Opera in east Berlin, Brecht remained utterly loyal to the régime in power and used his international prestige constantly on behalf of the "World Peace Movement". His former friends could never believe that he did so from conviction. They thought rather that he had struck a deliberate bargain for the sake of his theatre in east Berlin and his truly brilliant ensemble, which alone interpreted his dramatic language in the way he demanded.

August 16, 1956.

Sir Charles Bressey, C.B., C.B.E., a road engineer well known for his study of the highway needs of Greater London, and author of the report that bears his name, died on April 14, 1951 at the age of 77.

Born on January 3, 1874, Charles Herbert Bressey was educated at the Forest School, Walthamstow, and abroad, and was articled to his father, John T. Bressey, F.R.I.B.A., of Wanstead, Essex. During the 1914-18 War he served with the Royal Engineers in France and Flanders, attaining the rank of lieutenant-colonel and becoming O.B.E. and Chevalier of the Legion of Honour.

On his return to England he was appointed Divisional Road Engineer for London under the Ministry of Transport in 1919, Chief Engineer in 1921, and Principal Technical Officer in 1928, vacating the last position in 1935. Thus for 15 years he was closely associated with the great arterial road works carried out in the London area during that period, and when in 1934 Leslie [Lord] Hore-Belisha [q.v.], then Minister of Transport, decided to have a comprehensive survey made of the traffic needs of Greater London and a long-term plan of highway development prepared he was appropriately selected, with Sir Edwin Lutyens as consultant, to undertake the task.

His survey occupied three years, and his report, a document notable alike for the boldness of some of its proposals and for its wealth of detail, appeared in 1938, a full summary of its contents being published by *The Times* as a special section on May 17, 1938.

No immediate action was taken to bring the proposals of his report into practical effect, and the outbreak of war in 1939 and the destruction subsequently wrought on London by enemy bombing materially affected the problem. The authority with which he could speak on the subject was, however, recognized by his appointment as vice-chairman (Sir Edwin Lutyens being chairman) of the Royal Academy Planning Committee, which was formed in 1940 and held an exhibition of plans in 1942; and again in 1943 by his selection by the British Council, at the invitation of the Spanish Government, to visit Madrid and lecture under the auspices of the town planning authorities. A past president of the Chartered Surveyors' Institution and of the Junior Institution of Engineers, he was a vice-president of the Institute of Transport, an honorary member of the Institution of Royal Engineers, the Town-planning Institute, and the Institution of Municipal and County Engineers, and a member of the Permanent International Commission of Road Congresses. He became C.B.E. in 1924 and C.B. in 1930, and received a knighthood in 1935.

In 1902, he married Margaret, daughter of Mr. Francis C. Hill, of Wanstead. There were two sons of the marriage.

April 16, 1951.

Dr. Francis Brett Young—See **Young.**

James Bridie—as Dr. O. H. Mavor, who died on January 29, 1951 at the age of 63, was most widely known—was a dramatist who from 1931 onwards contributed much stimulating and original work to the theatre.

His plays combined humour, fantasy, and shrewd characterization. To Glasgow he was also known as one of its prominent physicians, for some time a consultant and later visiting physician at the Victoria Infirmary, and as a citizen who took a lively interest in Scottish cultural organizations, especially the Scottish National Theatre Society. The division of his professional interests was never clear cut; and he continued to live in Glasgow and remained always the complete Lowland Scot self-depicted in *One Way of Living.*

Bridie was a dramatist of superb gifts, but either he was never able to keep them all working at full pressure throughout the writing of a single play or he lacked the formal sense without which the best of dramatic ideas cannot be brought to a satisfactory conclusion. His first acts were often brilliant; his last acts too often disconcertingly inconclusive, as though he had tired of his theme and, satisfied that the play in hand contained a sufficiency of entertaining matter, was thinking of his next. The play fully worthy of his gifts, though continually expected, did not come.

Yet for 20 years on end he enriched the theatre with a succession of comedies which delighted by their unconventional view of character, the effectiveness of the situations in which character was exhibited, the relation of ideas and people to the author's own sinewy sense of fact and the humour, which could be mischievous, tender, ironic, uproarious.

Perhaps the two plays in which Bridie's powers are shown must fully extended are *A Sleeping Clergyman* and *Mr. Bolfry.* In the first he argues that we had better not interfere with Nature's biology since she may, if left alone, redeem apparently irretrievable blunders, and, anyway, we are in no position to teach her how to work less wastefully; and in the second he makes it appear that a Calvinist minister and the Devil have more in common with each other than has an agnostic with either. But more successful as works of art than these plays are *Tobias and the Angel* and *Jonah and the Whale,* for here other storytellers have provided the beginning, the middle, and the end and his re-tellings are quick with invention and apt comment.

Bridie's first professional dramatic production took place at the Lyric Theatre, Glasgow. The play, *The Sunlight Sonata,* was signed with the pseudonym of "Mary Henderson". *The Switchback* was first produced by Sir Barry Jackson* at Birmingham in 1929, and was seen at the Malvern Festival later in the year. With *The Anatomist,* produced at the Westminster Theatre in 1931, Bridie made his first real success, the play, which dealt with Dr. Robert Knox and the body snatchers, Burke and Hare, running for 127 performances. *Tobias and the Angel* followed in 1932, and *A Sleeping Clergyman* was put on at the Malvern Festival in the following year. After appearances in Edinburgh, Birmingham, and Glasgow, it went to London and ran for nine months at the Piccadilly Theatre. Thenceforth Bridie was an established and a prolific playwright. *Mary Read,* which he wrote with Claud Gurney, ran for over 100 nights in 1934, and among the more durable of the great variety of plays which followed may be mentioned *Susannah and the Elders* (1937), *Mr. Bolfry* (1943), *Dr. Angelus* (1947), and *Daphne Laureola* (1949). For the Edinburgh Festival in 1950 he wrote *The Queen's Comedy.*

Osborne Henry Mavor was born at Pollokshields, Glasgow, on January 3, 1888, the son of Henry Mavor, an engineer, and his wife, Janet Osborne. (His pseudonym, Bridie, came from his maternal grandmother). His infancy was passed at East Kilbride, in the country. At six he was brought back to Glasgow, and went successively to a dame school, to the Glasgow High School for a year, and to the Glasgow Academy. His father was a friend of the artists of the Glasgow School, and Mavor himself showed some talent for art, but it was decided that he should take up medicine, and he was accordingly entered at Glasgow University. He was a not too assiduous student, who spent a great deal of his time in writing plays for undergraduate performance and in contributing caricatures and literary matter to the university magazine; but at length, in 1913, he graduated, and went to the Glasgow Royal Infirmary for a year as house physician and casualty house surgeon.

Immediately on the outbreak of war in 1914 Mavor put his name down for medical service, and by October he was in France with a field ambulance. He served in the Ypres salient, at Arras, and on the Somme, and was invalided home in February 1917. After a short period of light duty in Edinburgh he was sent out to Mesopotamia, and for the rest of the war he was there, in India, Persia, Transcaucasia, and Constantinople, finishing with nine months at Baku.

He went into general practice at Longside, Glasgow, assisted in the psycho-therapeutic clinic, and was appointed extra physician at the Sick Children's Hospital Dispensary. He set up as a consultant in 1923 and also held a chair at the Anderson College of Medicine for a time.

January 30, 1951.

Professor J. L. Brierly, C.B.E., Emeritus Professor of International Law in the University of Oxford, died at his home there on December 20, 1955 at the age of 74.

James Leslie Brierly was born on September 9, 1881, and was the son of the late Sydney Herbert Brierly, woollen manufacturer, of Huddersfield. Educated at Charterhouse and at Brasenose College, Oxford, where he was a classical scholar, he was elected to a prize Fellowship in Law at All Souls in 1906 and called to the Bar by Lincoln's Inn in 1907. He had the good fortune to work in the chambers of F. H. [later Lord] Maugham, [q.v.], and it was to Maugham's instruction in drafting as well as to his classical studies that he owed the lucidity and neatness of his prose style. Three years after being called to the Bar, Brierly returned to Oxford to succeed W. M. Geldart as law lecturer of Trinity College, where he became a Fellow and his All Souls Fellowship expired in 1913.

Although he occupied academic positions for the rest of his professional life, he always took an active part in practical affairs, and in his legal work he never lost contact with the realities of social and ethical problems. During his second Oxford period he was a member of the Board of Guardians. In 1914 he was granted a commission in The Wiltshire Regiment and later on in the war he served on the staff of the Adjutant-General in the War Office and was appointed O.B.E. After the armistice he served as D.A.A.G. in the Army of the Black Sea with the brevet of major. In the Near East he made the acquaintance of Miss Ada Foreman, whom he married in 1920, and by whom he had one son.

In the year of his marriage he became Professor of Law in the University of Manchester, and, though his stay there was short, he rendered notable service by thoroughly reorganizing the staff and curriculum of the faculty. In 1922 he succeeded Sir Henry Erle Richards in the Chichele Chair of International Law, which carried with it a Fellowship in his old college of All Souls. He had already contributed to the study of international law by his English translation of Richard Zouche's *Juris et Judicii Fecialis Explicatio* in Holland's edition of this work. His inaugural lecture as Chichele Professor was published in the *British Year Book of International Law* in 1924.

To the same journal, which he edited alone or jointly with Professor Pearce Higgins for seven years, and to other publications, British and foreign, he afterwards contributed a long series of articles and notes dealing with current questions of international law and relations. Most of these had particular reference to the work of the League of Nations and international instruments relating to the organization of peace or to the more political and philosophical aspects of international law. In 1928 he published the first edition of his short book, *The Law of Nations,* an introduction to the law of peace, including the settlement of disputes, a masterpiece of common sense and clarity of statement.

Brierly lectured at the Hague Academy of International Law on two occasions. On the first the subject was "Le Fondement du Caractère Obligatoire du Droit International"; on the second he gave one of the long courses delivered each year under the title of "Règles Générales du Droit de la Paix" (1937), a general statement in 235 pages covering most of the ground of the law of peace.

He lectured to less specialized audiences in America and in half a dozen European countries. Nor was his interest in international law confined to the study or the class room or to broadcasting, in which he was extremely effective. He was the British member of the committee of experts for the codification of international law which was appointed by the Council of the League of Nations in 1924 and held numerous meetings until 1927 in preparation for the Hague Codification Conference in 1930. He was from time to time appointed by one or other of the organs of the League to report upon the legal aspects of pending disputes, and he accompanied the Emperor of Ethiopia* to Geneva in 1938 in order to help him in the critical Assembly of that year.

He was without doubt one of the sanest and best-balanced international lawyers of his generation. His training in English law had made him a sound lawyer, but without cramping his outlook and making him too "positivist". He could not be regarded as a typical "positivist", for his philosophical training made him alive to the limitations of law between States and caused him to deplore the too early eclipse of natural law as a source of the development of new rules of law.

Outside the sphere of international law he was responsible, with Sir John Miles, for the seventeenth and eighteenth editions of Anson's *Law of Contract,* and for a book of *Cases Illustrating the Law of Contract.* In Oxford he took a full share in university administration and in the life of the city. He served for six years on the Hebdomadal Council, and for 13 as curator of the University Chest; he was a delegate of the University Press throughout the whole period of his professorship and until he reached the age of 70.

On the outbreak of war in 1939 he joined the staff of the organization set up for Government research by the Royal Institute of International Affairs, where his wide knowledge and unruffled judgment were of the greatest value. He also served on the Advisory Committee under Defence Regulation 18B, which reviewed the cases of British subjects who were interned. After retiring from his Oxford chair he was for two years Professor of International Relations in Edinburgh.

It was inevitable he should be much in request for public work, and not only because of his ability and his eminent fairness of mind. Few men of such acute intellect combined as he did unshakable principle with deep sympathy for all who suffer, whether from misfortune or from injustice. His practical kindness to refugees or to his poorer neighbours was inexhaustible.

His manner was quiet, and his friendly smile lighted up a face usually grave and a little austere. If he had been less unselfish in personal things, he might have written the great work of which his colleagues knew him to be capable; but countless men and women would have been the losers.

December 22, 1955.

Harold Brighouse, the playwright and author, well known in earlier years as a leading figure among the "Manchester school" of dramatists, collapsed and died in London on July 25, 1958 on the eve of his seventy-sixth birthday.

Together with Stanley Houghton, Allan Monkhouse and others, Harold Brighouse in the years before and immediately after the War of 1914-18 helped to put Manchester on the theatrical map, and in so doing contributed to the real (if minor) influence brought to bear on English drama of the period by the productions of Miss Horniman's repertory theatre in that city during 1907-21. It is more accurate, perhaps, to speak of the "Manchester drama" than of a Manchester school of dramatists; for what Brighouse and the others did was to apply their mind and imagination to the distinctive verities of life and character in Manchester in order to transfer them in appropriate terms to the stage. In the result, at any rate in the earlier phase, they achieved a type of realism, at once homely and luminous, that entered closely into the texture of the "new drama" of the period before 1914. Admittedly the realism hovered now and then on the edge of the bleakly insignificant, but for the most part it had a singular force of veracity and comic illumination.

Born at Eccles, Lancashire, on July 26, 1882, and educated at Manchester Grammar School, he began work with a cotton firm but gravitated towards Miss Horniman's theatre and was writing plays soon after it had been founded. They were generally produced for the first time in Manchester, at any rate until 1921, after which they were commonly first performed by the Liverpool repertory company. His earliest plays were *Dealing in Futures* (1909) and *Graft* (1911), after which came *The Odd Man Out,* a gay if slightly obvious comedy, which was produced at the Royalty Theatre in London in 1912. *The Game* (1913), which recalled Houghton's *Trust the People,* was followed, two years later, by *The Hillarys,* written in collaboration with Houghton; and then, in the next year, Brighouse scored an indubitable hit with *Hobson's Choice,* a richly funny and rumbustious Lancashire comedy of an amiable bully, drunkard, and skinflint and his managing daughter. No one who saw him in the play is likely to forget Norman McKinnel's performance as old Hobson. A film was made of it; it has remained a favourite of provincial repertory; and it was revived in the West End as recently as 1952.

Other plays that followed included *Other Times* (1920), a mid-Victorian period piece; *Mary's John* (1924), a witty comedy, though one which did not quite maintain its promise, of a young man from the provinces who planned to take London by storm; *What's Bred in the Bone* (1927), another comedy of Lancashire character; and a not too successful piece entitled *It's a Gamble* (1928).

Besides full-length plays Brighouse also wrote many one-act plays, several of which were outstandingly popular with amateur theatrical bodies. He was at the same time author of some half a dozen novels of which the earliest, *Fossie for Short,* appeared in 1917, and which included one he made in 1927 out of *Hindle Wakes.* A rather reticent autobiography, *What I Have Had,* appeared in 1952.

During the Second World War he was attached for a time to the intelligence staff at the Air Ministry. In later years he was a member of the literary staff of the *Manchester Guardian,* and he was chairman of the dramatic committee of the Authors' Society in 1930-31.

July 26, 1958.

Carl Brisson died in hospital in Copenhagen on September 26, 1958 at the age of 62.

He was born in Copenhagen on December 24, 1895, and in his early days was a well known figure in the sporting life of Denmark. At the age of 15, fighting under his real name of Carl Pedersen, he won the amateur lightweight boxing championship of Denmark, and later became the welterweight champion of Middle Europe and Scandinavia. He made his first stage appearance in Denmark in 1916, then went to Sweden to appear in films, and as a cabaret singer toured in South Africa with considerable success.

When he appeared in England for the first time in a sketch in the variety theatres it was realized that in him there was a potential musical comedy star, for he possessed many of the essential ingredients including a pleasant singing voice, a bubbling sense of humour, curly hair, and considerable dancing skill.

It can be truly said of him, however, that he established a world-wide reputation in a single night. This was at Daly's on May 19, 1923, when he took the part of Prince Danilo in an admirable revival of *The Merry Widow,* in which George Graves repeated his performance of Baron Popoff, which he had created 16 years before, and Evelyn Laye followed Lily Elsie* as the Widow.

The occasion must have been an ordeal for a stranger coming from a foreign country, for at that time the names of Joseph Coyne and Prince Danilo were synonymous. It was to Brisson's credit that he made no attempt to model himself on his predecessor. As a result he succeeded in presenting a very appealing figure to the audience and, with his broken English and consistent display of youthful petulance, soon made the onlookers cease to regret that Coyne, who was in the audience and who had received a tremendous ovation when he entered the theatre, was in the auditorium and not on the stage.

Brisson always declared that Danilo was his favourite part, and this is not surprising, for it was closely linked up with his fortunes at many stages of his career. In January 1932, he toured his own company in *The Merry Widow,* with his sister Tilly as a principal dancer, and when the production went to the Hippodrome later in the year the audiences found that Brisson still had exceptional dash and energy and that he still danced with sparkling humour and fiery grace.

As a critic of the time said, he played his part with all the joy of a man running a race that he knows he will win. It was during this period of his success that he founded a charity club among those who had written to him expressing their appreciation of his acting, singing, and dancing and one of its principal objects was to raise funds for the Cancer Hospital.

He was again seen as Danilo at Los Angeles in 1951, and those who saw the production could scarcely credit the reports that he had first played the part 28 years earlier. This may have been partly due to the fact that he was a man of abounding energy and vitality who always insisted on keeping himself physically fit.

Brisson had another great London success in December 1930 in *Wonder Bar* at the Savoy. It was an adaptation from a German musical comedy, the whole action of which took place in a night restaurant. By the device of not lowering the curtain before, during or after the performance the audience seemed to become a part of the company on the stage and to share in the excitement and the light relief. Brisson's work showed that he would make an ideal master of ceremonies, and in his later career he occupied that position in many cabaret entertainments in London and in the United States.

In 1949 he was back in his native Denmark, where he was knighted by King Frederik*, and in the summer of that year he appeared with great success at the London Palladium in a one-man entertainment. Six years later, in a West End cabaret, immaculate in white tie and tails with a gardenia in his buttonhole, he was singing Danny Kaye's song "I'm Hans Christian Andersen" and one could not help feeling that the number was appropriate for a poor Danish boy who had reached the heights.

In 1957 he was given a tremendous reception when he appeared at Berns, the Stockholm music hall where he had first sung 40 years before.

September 27, 1958.

Former Bishop of Bristol—See **Woodward.**

Harry Edgar Broadsmith, who died in the Isle of Wight on September 25, 1959, was associated with early aeronautical developments in both England and Australia. He was 69.

Educated at Manchester Grammar School, he received his engineering training at the Lancashire and Yorkshire Railway Locomotive Workshops at Horwich, Lancashire, and served for several voyages as a marine engineer with the Furness Withy Line. He joined the firm of A. V. Roe and Co. Ltd. in November 1912 and together with Roy Chadwick worked upon the design of the famous Type 504 Avro. Later, as the company's outside representative at Brooklands track, he was associated with the delivery and acceptance trials at Farnborough of the first of the 504s to be delivered to the Royal Flying Corps.

In August 1914 he returned to Manchester and was engaged in the building up of facilities for the large production then foreseen, and was later appointed works manager and chief engineer, becoming responsible for the large wartime output from several Manchester factories.

In September 1919 he left England to live in Sydney, New South Wales. Appointed Avro representative for Australasia, he took with him several 504K demonstration machines and a quantity of "knocked down" parts for local assembly.

With Australian associates he formed the Australian Aircraft and Engineering Company Ltd., leasing a large area at Manscot, near Sydney, to provide a base for the company's flying operations. This proved to be the first step towards development of what is now

Australia's international airport.

He established the first Australian aircraft factory and, being an expert on aeronautical timbers, he carried out the first systematic investigation of Australian timbers to determine their suitability for aircraft construction. Arising from this work his firm received a contract from the Commonwealth Government for the construction of a number of Avro training machines for the Royal Australian Air Force, using Australian timbers to his recommendations, and subsequently for a prototype six-seater civil type machine built to his designs.

Broadsmith was one of the original directors of Saunders-Roe Ltd. He joined forces with Sir Alliott Verdon-Roe [q.v.] and John Lord in December 1928, when they acquired a controlling interest in the firm of S.E. Saunders Ltd., and was appointed technical director and general manager, taking up his duties at Cowes during January 1929. A short time later the firm was renamed Saunders-Roe.

Under his direction a programme for the production of a series of monoplane amphibious flying boats was embarked upon, the first of which, named "Cutty Sark", was designed, built and test flown within a period of 13 weeks, and was exhibited at the Aero Show held at Olympia in June of that year.

The "Cutty Sark" served as a medium scale development for the Saro "Cloud", the prototype of which was produced in 1930 and subsequently adopted by Coastal Command, R.A.F. for navigational training, whereby the new Saro Company received their first "production" order from the Air Ministry.

During the Second World War Broadsmith was appointed by the Minister of Aircraft Production, Lord Beaverbrook*, to organise the facilities for the reception, design and manufacture of modifications, installations and testing to British operational standards, for Catalina flying boats—then arriving from America in quantity.

He resigned from Saunders-Roe after the war to take up practice as a consultant, and returned to Australia in 1948. At the time of his resignation he was joint managing director of the company, and director of Saro Laminated Wood Products and Saunders Shipyard Ltd.

September 30, 1959.

Sir Thomas Brocklebank, fourth baronet, the well known Liverpool ship owner, died suddenly at his home near Ruthin, North Wales, on September 15, 1953.

Thomas Aubrey Lawies Brocklebank was born on October 23, 1899, the son of Sir Aubrey Brocklebank, third baronet, and the Hon. Grace Mary Jackson, daughter of the first Baron Allerton. He represented the sixth generation of his family with Liverpool shipping interests. Thomas Fisher, of Whitehaven, who died in 1810, left a son, Wilson Fisher, of Kickle, Cumberland, who married, in 1812, Anne, daughter of Daniel Brocklebank, of Whitehaven, and sister of Thomas Brocklebank, of Stanfield, near Liverpool. Their only son, who was born in 1814, assumed by royal licence in 1845 the surname and arms of Brocklebank in lieu of Fisher, and he was created a baronet by letters patent in 1885.

Brocklebank—whose father was a director of the Great Western Railway, the Suez Canal Company, the Cunard Steamship Company, and other companies—was educated at Eton and Trinity College, Cambridge. He joined the family firm of ship owners, Thomas and John Brocklebank, Limited, of Liverpool, in 1922, becoming a director five years later. In 1927 he was made a director of Crosfields Oil and Cake Company, and two years later also joined the board of the Cunard Steamship Company, Limited.

In that year, when he succeeded his father in the baronetcy, he first became a member of the Mersey Docks and Harbour Board. In 1938 he was the first of its members to be elected to the newly created office of deputy chairman, and he succeeded Sir R. D. Holt as its chairman in 1941, holding the position until 1948.

In 1940 Brocklebank was elected chairman of the Thames and Mersey Marine Insurance Company and a director of the L.M.S. Railway Company, Limited, and in July 1943 became deputy chairman of Cunard White Star, Limited, of which company he was one of the original directors. He was also at one time a director of the Midland Bank, Limited and of the Royal Insurance Company, Limited. After the 1939-45 War, while he was deputy chairman of Cunard White Star, Limited, he played an important part, as deputy chairman of the company's shipbuilding committee, in setting out a considerable programme of new work as well as of reconversion from war to peace-time requirements. When the chairmanship of the company fell vacant in 1946, following the death of Sir Percy Bates, he asked that he should be left free to devote himself to this work.

Brocklebank, who had lived at the family home at Sandiway, Cheshire, until 1952, was a prominent member of the Sandiway Golf Club. He took a great interest in association football and became chairman of the Chester Football Club board in 1938. On relinquishing this post 12 years later, he became president of the club.

He was unmarried, and is succeeded in the baronetcy by his younger brother, Mr. [later Sir] John M. Brocklebank*, who was born in 1915 and is unmarried.

September 17, 1953.

Louis Bromfield, the American novelist who was for many years a leading "best-seller", died in hospital at Columbus, Ohio, on March 19, 1956 at the age of 59.

He was a prolific writer who, having achieved success and the good favour that goes with it, was apparently able to produce all that he wished by working a few hours a day only. His was a genuine enough talent, though after a serious beginning he made no bones about commercializing it. Fluent in style, with a shrewd eye for the dramatic theme and the colourful background, unfailingly expansive and large-hearted in sympathy, he could be relied upon for entertainment as an adroit and resourceful story-teller of the larger than life variety. He became, on the whole, increasingly opulent in story-telling manner, but never lost the practised and self-assured touch with which he concealed, or tried to conceal, a superficial quality of imagination. His occasional essays in political writing evinced a strong anti-British bias.

Louis Bromfield was born at Mansfield, Ohio, on December 27, 1896, the son of Charles and Annette Bromfield. He went to Cornell University, where he studied agriculture, and then to Columbia, where he switched over to a course in journalism. He had made some reputation for himself as a versatile journalist when, during the 1914-18 War, he volunteered as an ambulance driver in France and then served in a liaison capacity with a division in the Army of General Mangin. For his services he was awarded the Croix de Guerre and the Legion of Honour.

With the return of peace he made his home for many years just outside Paris, where a villa he owned became a recognized meeting place for writers, artists, and celebrities of various kinds, American and European. Here, with intervals during which he paid visits to New York and Hollywood and contributed critical articles to American newspapers, he settled down as a practising novelist.

His first novel, *The Green Bay Tree,* appeared in 1924. It tells a somewhat irresolute story about a heroine from the American Middle West who moves to and fro between America and Paris, and contrives to mingle a fresh, sincere quality with a curious note of arrogance. A year later came *Possession,* and a year later still Bromfield produced *Early Autumn,* a study of a decaying and over-proud New England family that was lively and persuasive and that was awarded a Pulitzer Prize. Comparatively speaking, however, these were still *succès d'estime,* and it was not until *The Strange Case of Miss Annie Spragg* appeared in 1928 that the author was firmly set on the road to recognition and popularity. In its mixture of deliberate, almost aggressive artifice and genuine narrative power this novel about an elderly spinster in Italy, who received the stigmata, is typical of at any rate the better works of fiction that Bromfield wrote in the years that followed.

They are of several different kinds. *Twenty Four Hours* (1930) and *A Modern Hero* (1932), for instance, are both of the clever and flagrantly artificial type. On the other hand, *The Rains Came,* published in 1937, with which Bromfield at last attained success on a really big scale, is an elaborate exercise in romantic persuasion, with an ornately coloured Indian setting thrown in for extra and spectacular effect. After that there evidently seemed to be a good reason for a degree of relaxation on his part. *Night in Bombay* (1939), *Wild is the Rose* (1941), and *Until the Day Break* (1942) were all done in a rather lush novelette idiom, but Bromfield then made a handsome recovery with *Mrs. Parkington* (1943), a shrewd and experienced piece of work about the raffish and golden age of New York society.

His novels, several volumes of short stories, and three or four plays apart, Bromfield published in 1946, under the title of *Pleasant Valley*, a book about his farming experience in southern Ohio which included an instructive account of various experiments of his own. It was marked by decided views on soil fertility and other matters. With part of the considerable sum of money which *The Rains Came* had earned for him he had purchased a farm near his birthplace—characteristically, perhaps, the farm was called Malabar, after the place where the novel had been written—and afterwards tended to regard himself as a farmer almost as much as a writer. It was a luxuriously equipped farm, and Bromfield, who was also very much a New York clubman, did a great deal of entertaining there.

He married, in 1921, Miss Mary A. Wood. She died in 1952 and there were three daughters of the marriage.

March 20, 1956.

Although he never became Chief of the Air Staff or a Marshal of the Royal Air Force, **Air Chief Marshal Sir Robert Brooke-Popham,** G.C.V.O., K.C.B., D.S.O., C.M.G., A.F.C., who died on October 20, 1953 at the age of 75 in hospital at Halton, influenced immensely the formative years of the Royal Air Force. It fell to him to put through many of the most significant developments in its earlier years.

Under his name and title, or as "Brookham", as he was more intimately known, he will be remembered as one of the great names in his service. As the holder of comparatively high rank at the end of the 1914-18 War it might have been expected that he would be inevitably cast for an important part, but he had exceptional qualities of mind and character that made their own distinctive contribution to the important posts he held in the difficult years between 1919 and 1937. He had a feeling for the air which had led him to this new calling when military aviation was in its infancy, and as it grew so did his clear appreciation of its potentialities and role.

This understanding was perhaps typified by a public speech made in the City of London during the height of the Battle of Britain. As a commander whose operational experience might have given him a bias towards the fighter, he pleaded with his audience to subscribe towards funds for bombers, for, as he said, to win a war it required an offensive which in the air only the bomber could give. As the first Commandant of the Royal Air Force Staff College, and later as Commandant of the Imperial Defence College, his sound strategic thinking had great influence. His highest appointment, to be Commander-in-Chief, Far East, ended in the disaster of the fall of Singapore and this demoralizing blow led to a great deal of criticism. A sober assessment of the situation when it could be made showed that the overriding factors were outside the power of any commander-in-chief to alter or control.

Henry Robert Moore Brooke-Popham was born on September 18, 1878, at Mendlesham, near Stowmarket, a son of the late Henry Brooke, of Wetheringsett Manor, Suffolk. He assumed the additional name of Popham by royal licence in 1904. Educated at Haileybury and Sandhurst, he received his first commission in The Oxford Light Infantry (later the Oxfordshire and Buckinghamshire Light Infantry) in 1898. In 1910-11 he passed through the Army Staff College at Camberley. Immediately after graduating he showed originality by learning to pilot an aircraft at Brooklands. He was awarded, in 1911, the 108th certificate issued by the Royal Aero Club.

Early in 1911 an Air Battalion of the Royal Engineers was formed, with one airship company and one aeroplane company. Brooke-Popham joined this battalion in 1912, and was posted to the aeroplane company. Captains who had passed the Staff College were rare in the little band of pioneer Army pilots, and before a month had passed Brooke-Popham found himself in command of the aeroplane company. A year later the Air Battalion of the Royal Engineers was transformed into the Royal Flying Corps, and the Aeroplane company became No. 2 Squadron, R.F.C. (Military Wing). On the formation of No. 3 Squadron Brooke-Popham was given command of it, and he threw all his energy into training that squadron in the functions which it was believed would fall to the lot of the aeroplane in war. In those days only one function was envisaged for aircraft, namely reconnaissance.

When war broke out in 1914, Brooke-Popham, by that time a temporary major, had given over the command of No. 3 Squadron to Major (later Marshal of the Royal Air Force Sir) John Salmond* and went to France on the staff of the R.F.C. In March 1915 he formed the 3rd Wing at St. Omer with Nos. 4 and 16 Squadrons as the operational units. He commanded this wing at the battles of Neuve Chapelle and Aubers Ridge. As chief staff officer at the headquarters of the R.F.C. he drew up in August 1915 a notable memorandum in which he pointed out that while the British Expeditionary Force had grown from four to 30 divisions, the Royal Flying Corps had only increased from four squadrons to 11 while its work had very greatly increased.

Later, when he was in charge of the equipment of the R.F.C., among the important steps which he took was the placing of an order with French firms for 50 Hispano-Suiza 150 h.p. aero engines. The supply of aero engines had always been the greatest difficulty of the R.F.C., which had to rely chiefly on France for motive power. The Hispano-Suiza engine had just come to the fore, and the promptness of Brooke-Popham in securing a supply for the British flying corps eased the situation to no small degree. For his war services he was awarded the D.S.O. and A.F.C., as well as being mentioned in dispatches four times. In 1918 he was appointed C.M.G., and the following year C.B.

He became Controller of the technical side of aircraft production at the Ministry of Munitions in 1918 and on transferring permanently to the Royal Air Force in the course of the next year he became an air commodore. For a time he was Director of Research at the Air Ministry, but in November 1921 a new and very important post was entrusted to him. The Air Force instituted a Staff College at Andover, on the lines of the Army Staff Colleges at Camberley and Quetta. The science of an air campaign, as apart from mere co-operation with the Army or the Navy, was a novel idea, and the study called for much original work. That this very important college made a good start in life was chiefly due to the qualities of its first commandant.

In 1926 the Air Defence of Great Britain Command was formed, with a fighting area and a bombing area. Brooke-Popham was the first officer appointed to command the fighting area. In the air exercises held in 1927 he had under his command the corps of coast watchers, the searchlights, and the anti-aircraft artillery as well as fighters. He was by that time an air vice-marshal, and in the Birthday Honours of 1927 he had been made K.C.B.

In the autumn of 1928 he was sent to Iraq as Air Officer Commanding, which entailed responsibility for the internal peace of the country as well as for the security of its frontiers. In 1929 the High Commissioner in Iraq, Sir Gilbert Clayton, died, and until his successor arrived Brooke-Popham acted as High Commissioner. Promoted to Air Marshal in 1931, he was appointed Commandant of the Imperial Defence College, the first R.A.F. officer to fill this key defence post. After two years at the I.D.C. he was appointed A.O.C.-in-C., Air Defence of Great Britain and for two years devoted an unrivalled experience to shaping and strengthening this important command.

At this point in his highly successful career many might well have expected one of the principal appointments in the Air Ministry would have come to him. But it was not to be. In August 1935 he was selected to fill the revived appointment of Inspector-General of the Royal Air Force, having been promoted Air Chief Marshal at the beginning of the year. His somewhat nebulous duties were suddenly replaced by work more to his liking by the development of the Abyssinian crisis. In a theatre where the air arm was of paramount importance it was essential to have adequate air defence against the Italian Regia Aeronautica if war came. "Brookham" was an inevitable choice, and he was sent out to act as A.O.C.-in-C., Middle East.

His special task ended, he returned to England and in March 1937 retired at his own request. This was followed by his appointment as Governor and Commander-in-Chief of Kenya. He held this post with great distinction and while he confirmed all the promise he had shown in Iraq of becoming a first-rate administrator and diplomat he did not neglect the military side and saw to it that an extensive scheme for the defence of the colony was built up, a logical sequence to the work he had already carried out as A.O.C.-in-C., Middle East. When war broke out in 1939, he relinquished the post of Governor of Kenya to rejoin the active list. As chief R.A.F.

representative of the United Kingdom Air Mission to Canada, he helped to initiate the great Commonwealth air training plan, and the following year headed another air mission to South Africa to explore the possibilities of extending this air training to the Union.

The announcements in November, 1940, that he was to become Commander-in-Chief, Far East, occasioned the greatest interest. The command was created to co-ordinate the control of the defences in that theatre, and for the first time an air officer was given a major post of this kind. Singapore, Malaya, Burma, and Hongkong were within his command, and his proved powers of co-ordination and tactful inspiration had the widest scope. There was much inertia to contend with, and in the short time the new Commander-in-Chief had to work in before Japan struck almost everything militated against him. The general strategy of the war dictated that forces in the deserts of the Middle East and on the hard-pressed Russian front, where desperate warfare was raging, must have absolute priority over a theatre only under threat of war. Inevitably, supplies and reinforcements could only be too small and too late. Having as an air officer carried through so many innovations with consummate skill, it was all the greater disappointment to Sir Robert that in this greater experiment he was to have neither the means nor the time to succeed.

On his return to England he reverted to the retired list in May 1942. During the latter years of the war he continued to serve his country in whatever way he could, as president of the Navy, Army, and Air Force Institute, as Inspector-General of the Air Training Corps, and as the author of excellent training pamphlets for service use. He was Principal Air A.D.C. to the King from 1933 to 1937, and was made a G.C.V.O. in 1935.

He married in 1926 Opal Mary, second daughter of Mr. Edgar Hugonin, who survives him together with a son and a daughter.

October 21, 1953.

Dr. Robert Broom, F.R.S., the distinguished South African palaeontologist whose researches between 1897 and 1910 proved the origin of mammals from reptiles, and from 1936 until his death threw new light on the origin of man, died at Pretoria, South Africa, on April 6, 1951 at the age of 84.

Born on November 30, 1866, at Paisley, Scotland, he was the second son of John Broom (shawl-designer and in later life art connoisseur). He was delicate in childhood, but at the age of six he acquired an interest in natural history, which was fostered by his father's circle of friends. He became assistant to the Professor of Chemistry at Glasgow University, and while there graduated in science and medicine, but his mind was soon bent on the problem of the origin of mammals—according to Huxley mammals had possibly evolved from amphibia, according to Owen from reptiles.

In 1892 he went to Australia to practise medicine and to get an opportunity of studying the egg-laying mammals and marsupials. After five years he moved to South Africa, where, maintaining himself by medical practice, he began his studies on the golden moles and on the fossil reptiles of the Karroo formation (Permian and Triassic ages). In 1903 he was made Honorary Keeper of Fossil Vertebrates in the Capetown Museum, and at the same time gave up his medical practice to become Professor of Geology and Zoology at Stellenbosch University. Within seven years he had published nearly 100 papers, mainly describing the reptiles, many of them proving to be mammal-like forms, whose remains he had collected from the Karroo beds.

After a visit to London in 1909 he went to the United States to examine the carnivorous reptiles from the Permian rocks of Texas, preserved in the American Natural History Museum, New York, and as a result he was able to establish their close relationship with some of the Karoo forms. He had resigned from the posts which he held at Stellenbosch and Capetown, but he continued his palaeontological work with great energy. After the outbreak of war in 1914 he worked as a surgeon in the London Ear, Nose, and Throat Hospital and then joined the R.A.M.C., but on being told that he was "too old for active service" he went back to South Africa and settled as a general practitioner in Griqualand West.

After partial retirement in 1929 he wrote three books, including his great work *The Mammal-like Reptiles of South Africa,* and at the same time he maintained an astonishing output of scientific papers; but at the end of three years he found it necessary to return to medical practice.

In 1934 General Smuts persuaded him to accept the post of Keeper of the Transvaal Museum, Pretoria. He continued to devote time to research on fossil reptiles and mammals, but his mind was now chiefly working on the problem of the origin of man. He had recognized the probable significance of Professor Raymond Dart's discovery in 1924 at Taungs, in Bechuanaland, of a young skull of a fossil man-like ape, *Australopithecus,* and in 1936 he resolved to try to find an adult skull of this creature in the bone caves of the Transvaal dolomites. Within six weeks of this resolve he had discovered the Sterkfontein skull, and two years later the Kromdrai skull. Other specimens came to light, and in 1946 he published jointly with G. W. H. Schepers a book entitled *The South African Fossil Ape-Men.*

From a study of this and much more material, dating, it would seem, from the end of the Pliocene or beginning of the Pleistocene period, it became evident that the creatures were remarkably human in many ways. They might well have been man's ancestors, or closely related to them, but it was generally objected that their brains were far too small to be admitted as human. Broom's eventual discoveries at Swartkrans, in the Transvaal (made with the assistance of I. T. Robinson), showed that the *Australopithecines* were very diverse or variable, and that some had heads possibly approaching the human size. Broom's efforts were unflagging, and only in 1950 he discovered two more skulls with brain cases of a size to bring them definitely into the human category.

The advances in knowledge due to his work received world-wide recognition. In 1928 he was awarded one of the two gold medals of the Royal Society of London. Among the numerous honours conferred on him, one which gave him peculiar pleasure was the award in 1949 of the Wollaston Medal of the Geological Society of London.

His scientific work was the outcome of an insatiable curiosity combined with abounding energy, and it owed much to his remarkable memory, his keen eye for minute differences, his capacity for rapid judgment, his flair for collecting, and—a small but important point—the facility with which he could make pencil sketches. Although the greater part of his research was on fossils, his outlook was essentially that of a biologist. As he looked at a fossil bone he was thinking in terms of the nerves and muscles which once gave it life.

Broom was married in 1893 to Miss Mary Baird Baillie.

April 9, 1951.

Douglas Clifton-Brown—See **Ruffside.**

Dame Edith Mary Brown, D.B.E., M.A., M.D., M.R.C.O.G., L.R.C.P., L.R.C.S., died at Srinagar, Kashmir, on December 6, 1956. She was 92. A pioneer in the training of Indian women doctors and midwives in modern western methods, she was the founder and for half a century the principal of the Ludhiana Christian Medical College for Women.

Edith Mary Brown was born in 1864 and received her early education at Croydon High School. At Girton College, Cambridge, she took honours in the Natural Science Tripos. After medical training at the Royal Free Hospital she was sent out by the Zenana branch of the Baptist Missionary Society and landed in Bombay on November 9, 1891.

At that time by age-long tradition the orthodox Hindu woman would on no account have the services of a medical man, whether trained in modern or in the ancient systems of medicine followed in India; she was dependent for help in her confinement on the services of the superstitious *dai* or nurse, who was always of low caste and, from a surgical point of view, unbelievably dirty. Trained Indian women doctors or nurses were almost unknown, and throughout the peninsula only one or two women's hospitals existed.

To the transformation since wrought Edith Brown made an outstanding contribution. She soon left the society to which she was accredited to launch out on her own distinctive career of service. In January 1894 a gift of £50 from a Bristol lady enabled her to rent an old schoolhouse at Ludhiana, in the Punjab, with six Indian women students, using a small hospital near by for clinical teaching. From this small beginning the first medical school for women in India developed into a great institution housed in fine buildings with classrooms, laboratories, and a hospital with 200 beds, and having an average of 300 students in the medical, nursing, and pharmacy schools. The work was inspired by a strongly evangelical outlook and attracted support, not only from an active London Auxiliary, with branches in Edinburgh and Glasgow, but also by auxiliaries in the United States, Canada, Australia, and New Zealand. Substantial grants were made by the Punjab Government. In 1932 the tireless and devoted founder was created a Dame Commander of the Order of the British Empire.

When the jubilee of her arrival in India was celebrated in November 1941 the college had sent forth for work in all parts of India 411 doctors, 143 nurses, 168 dispensers, and over 1,000 midwives, all fully trained. In the following year she handed over the principalship to Dr. Aileen Pollock, and became Emeritus Principal and honorary treasurer. At 83 she was still active and an inspiring force, when the work was jeopardized in the summer of 1947 by the outbreak of communal savagery in the Punjab preceding and accompanying the attainment of independence by India and Pakistan. The considerable staff of Muslim employees fled across the border and Sikh and Hindu refugees poured in. But such was the place of the college and hospital in the regard and confidence of the people that it was entirely immune from attack and became a haven of refuge.

The work of succouring the refugees was immediately taken in hand and the hospital was made a general one for the time being. Many of the women pupils of the school had fled, but as conditions improved the classes were fully resumed. The East Punjab Government continued the support which had been given by the authorities of the undivided province.

December 10, 1956.

Lieutenant-General Sir John Brown, K.C.B., C.B.E., D.S.O., F.R.I.B.A., who died on April 4, 1958 at his home at Northampton, was the most famous Territorial Army officer of his generation, and the first to reach the rank of lieutenant-general.

He also made a name for himself as an architect, combining with great success his civil career with his military duties.

Born on February 10, 1880, the elder son of Alderman John Brown, of Abington, Northampton, he was educated at Magdalen College School, Brackley. He qualified as an associate of the R.I.B.A. in 1921 and became a Fellow in 1930. For many years he was in practice at Northampton in partnership with A. E. Henson and was responsible for a great variety of buildings. He also practised in London. As an architect he combined professional competence with keen business qualities, but he was far more widely known for his unique parallel career as a soldier.

Joining the 1st Volunteer Battalion, The Northamptonshire Regiment, in 1901, he continued his service as a Territorial when it became the 4th (T.A.) Battalion, and accompanied it at the Suvla landing in August 1915 and in the Palestine campaign that followed. From 1924 to 1928 he commanded the 162nd (East Midland) Infantry Brigade. In 1937 he was appointed Deputy Director-General of the Territorial Army, being the first serving Territorial Officer to occupy that position, and he became Deputy Adjutant-General (T) at the War Office in 1939 and served in that capacity until his retirement under the age limit regulation in August 1941, when he received the thanks of the King for his long and valuable services. He was granted the honorary rank of lieutenant-general.

At the War Office he supervised the new welfare scheme for the Army which was established in November 1939 as a result of his initiative. In its initial stages the work was financed by money which he collected. He was responsible for the starting of the service libraries from which many millions of books and magazines were supplied to the troops, and he also held the office of chairman of the Council of Voluntary War Work which comprised the religious and philanthropic bodies and which controlled thousands of canteens and mobile canteens in Britain as well as in the Near East.

From the inception of the British Legion he had taken a close interest in all branches of its activities and from 1930 to 1934 was chairman. He was also for many years a member of the Society for Army Historical Research and in 1938 he was elected Vice-President. Many honours were bestowed upon him, and his services in the First World War gained for him the D.S.O. in 1918; in 1923 he was appointed C.B.E.; in 1926 C.B.; and in 1934 he was advanced to K.C.B. He was Master of the Worshipful Company of Pattenmakers from 1942 to 1944 and again in 1950-51.

In 1904 he married Annie Maria, third daughter of the late Alderman S. Tonsley, of Northampton, and had two sons.

April 7, 1958.

W. J. Brown, Independent member of Parliament for Rugby from 1942 to 1950, and general secretary of the Civil Service Clerical Association from 1919 to 1942, died on October 3, 1960.

Of lively resource and intelligence, equipped with notable powers of advocacy, as politician and journalist seldom averse from a momentary exhibition of showmanship, W. J. Brown made up by his own efforts for any initial sense of disadvantage with which he started his career. He made a precocious beginning when, as a boy clerk, aged 15, he gave evidence on behalf of himself and his fellows before the Royal Commission on the Civil Service in 1911, presenting a remarkably well-argued case for modifying the conditions of what was then a blind-alley occupation. He made a distinct impression upon the members of the commission and had the satisfaction of eliciting from them positive recommendations which were promptly acted upon.

This youthful feat established his reputation, which in later years preceded him through all the diverse negotiations he undertook as secretary of the Civil Service Clerical Association with the Treasury or with particular departments. His experience in this capacity served him to rather mixed advantage, perhaps, in the House of Commons. He spoke pointedly and to practical purpose on Civil Service affairs and on most aspects of public administration, but in other respects he was, on the whole, though agile and forceful in manner, inclined to be a shade too demonstrative and wanting in judgment. As an Independent member, however, who had left the fold of the Labour Party, he undoubtedly tried to live up to what he thought was expected of him, and indeed exhibited an aggressive mind of his own on such topics as Russia and the power of the trade unions.

Born in 1895, the son of Joseph Morris Brown, a sanitary inspector, and Rose Spicer, William John Brown was educated at an elementary school in Margate and a grammar school in Sandwich before going as a boy clerk to the Post Office Savings Bank in 1910. It was as the moving spirit of the Boy Clerks' Association that he determined the royal commission should become fully acquainted with the facts of their grievance. He became an assistant clerk at the Office of Works in 1912, and, in 1919, after the cessation of hostilities, general secretary of the newly formed Civil Service Clerical Association. This body Brown nursed through its early phases with conspicuous industry, persistence, and adroitness. Indeed, he made the whole cause of trade unionism in the Civil Service his own, and in 1923 virtually engineered the defeat of the Government on a Civil Service issue. The C.S.C.A. continued to expand and prosper, its membership owing a great deal to Brown's skill and resource in negotiating better conditions of service.

Elected Labour member for West Wolverhampton in the general election of 1929, Brown was one of the small body of Labour supporters in the House discontented with the Government's rate of progress who rallied to Sir Oswald Mosley's New Party. He lost his seat in the debacle of 1931, and did not return to Parliament until 1942, when he stood as an Independent for Rugby at a by-election against a Conservative opponent and won by a narrow majority. The National Council of Labour had pronounced against him during the campaign, for—the wartime electoral truce apart—Brown had for some time been opposed to various aspects of Labour policy, and had, indeed, left the party; but the local Labour Party gave him its support. He was again returned for the same constituency at the general election in 1945, on this occasion in a close triangular contest in which the official Labour candidate was at the bottom of the poll. By this time he was frequently at loggerheads with Labour policy as that was represented by "Transport House".

With his re-election he ceased to be general secretary of the C.S.C.A. and became parliamentary general secretary. Differences rapidly developed with the executive committee of the association, however, and, in connexion with proposed changes in the terms of his agreement with the association, in 1947 Brown preferred a charge in the House that pressure was being brought to bear on him by an outside body. The report of the Committee of Privileges, however, did not uphold his complaint, though a Government motion declared that it was inconsistent with the dignity of the House or a member's duty to his constituents to enter into any contractual agreement with an outside body controlling or limiting his freedom of action in Parliament.

He was bottom of the poll at Rugby in 1950 and the following year he opposed Dr. Edith Summerskill as an Independent at Fulham West. In a three-cornered fight he came second.

Brown was fluent and effective on the platform and as a sound and television broadcaster, and was a shrewd and able journalist; there was a thoughtful half-religious and almost humble side to his nature that was reflected in his journalism of the better sort. He wrote a history of the C.S.C.A., produced a *Civil Service Compendium,* a small volume on his travels in Russia, another volume on his travels in the United States, and was also the author of an interesting, self-assertive and at times exasperating volume of autobiography *So Far* (1944), and of an excellent little popular guide to Parliament.

He married in 1917 Mabel, daughter of H. Prickett, and there were two sons and a daughter of the marriage.

October 5, 1960.

Maurice Browne, who gave long and distinguished service to the theatre as producer, actor, and author, died in hospital at Torquay on January 21, 1955 at the age of 73.

The eldest son of the late Rev. F. H. Browne, sometime headmaster of Queen Elizabeth's School, Ipswich, he was born on February 12, 1881. From Temple Grove he obtained a scholarship to Winchester and thence went as a scholar to Peterhouse, Cambridge. He left in 1900 to serve for the remainder of the South African War in the 49th Imperial Yeomanry. A short period as a schoolmaster followed, which he did not find congenial and then, fired by the enthusiasm of a Cambridge friend, the late Harold Monro, who was some two years his senior, he embarked on the risky business of publishing verse.

He and Monro started the Samurai Press in 1906, and though the venture was anything but a financial success it was the germ from which the Poetry Bookshop and, in part, the Georgian Poets grew. Monro remained, a cheerful prisoner in the little corner of Bloomsbury he had made his own for the rest of his life, bringing together poets and lovers of poetry. Browne, while remaining on terms of close friendship with Monro, went off to conquer other worlds.

With Ellen Van Volkenburg he founded the Chicago Little Theatre in 1912; its fame soon led to a movement for the production of intimate drama throughout the United States. The movement was further accelerated by the organization of a repertory company by the partners in 1918. For the next few years he gained experience in production, presenting plays as far apart in period and character as the *Medea, The Trial of Joan of Arc, Candida,* and *Mr. Faust.* He returned to London in 1927 with little money but a much enhanced reputation.

His first appearance on the London stage was at the Arts Theatre as Adolf in *Creditors* towards the end of 1927. Before the year was out he had presented at the same theatre the much discussed *La Prisonnière.*

In the course of the next year he made a number of successful appearances and early in 1929 entered on the management of the Savoy Theatre. Meanwhile he had gathered up the threads of his old friendships. Among these pre-eminent was that with Harold Monro, who brought to him a play by a young insurance clerk who had served in The East Surrey Regiment in France during the 1914-18 War; the young man was R. C. Sherriff* and the play *Journey's End.* It had been produced by the Stage Society when Browne presented it at the Savoy with such immense success that it was subsequently seen all over the English-speaking world.

At last Browne had attained real financial success and he used it to finance such worthy ventures as *Hamlet,* with Mr. (now Sir) John Gielgud as the Prince, *Street Scene* and an international season with Alexander Moissi and the Pitoëffs [q.v.]. He collaborated with the late Robert Nicholls in writing the prophetic *Wings Over Europe,* which was presented with Ellen Van Volkenburg at the Globe in 1932. Losses on these and other ventures did not defeat him and he continued both to act and to produce in London until he was invited by the University of California to be the "artist in residence", in 1949, in recognition of his services to the theatre.

Latterly, he had been living quietly in Devon.

January 22, 1955.

Clarence Bruce—See **Aberdare.**

Sir Robert Bruce, editor of the *Glasgow Herald* from 1917 until 1936, died at his home at Glasgow on March 27, 1955 at the age of 83.

Under his editorship the *Glasgow Herald* continued to exert a profound influence on the commercial and industrial life of the west of Scotland and over its social and intellectual activities, and Sir Robert Bruce was at the same time one of the most notable and successful Scottish journalists of recent times. When he retired from active work on December 31, 1936, he had served for 50 years as a journalist and during that time worked for only three newspapers. For more than 20 years he was stationed in London as the chief representative of Scottish newspapers and during that time he was a familiar figure in the Press Gallery at the House of Commons and in the Lobbies, where he made many lifelong friends among members of his own craft and among politicians not only from Scotland but from all parts of the country.

He was born at Alloa, Clackmannan, on October 26, 1871. At the age of 15 he left school and secured his first employment on the staff of the local newspaper, the *Alloa Advertiser.* He then moved to Aberdeen, where he joined the staff of the *Aberdeen Journal,* and before he was 23 years old he was sent to London as its representative. Three years later he had done so well that he attracted the attention of the owners of the *Glasgow Herald* and was appointed their representative in London. At that time their office in Fleet Street was largely one man's job and from 1898 till 1913 he served the *Herald* in a whole host of capacities, as reporter, special correspondent, Parliamentary sketch writer, lobby correspondent, London correspondent, and head of the London office.

Only a man of robust health, strong will, and determination could have carried on successfully all the work he took upon himself during all these years. Yet he got through it all with much success and without any seeming overstrain, and at the same time was able to make and develop many associations and friendships with those whom he met in the course of his daily work. In 1914 he was summoned back to Glasgow to undertake the duties of assistant editor, and in 1917 he succeeded Harcourt Kitchin, formerly of *The Times,* as editor. During the 20 years that he held that office the *Glasgow Herald* maintained a high standard of news. In its presentation it adopted some more modern methods in the use of new type and headlines, but its aim was to give a sober, reliable, unbiased account of current events, while at the same time affording a reasonable commentary for the benefit of its readers.

Sir Robert Bruce found time for other work outside his regular duties as editor, and kept himself abreast of the times by constant travel and association with people of other lands. He was a Fellow of the Institute of Journalists and its president in 1926. He was a Fellow of the Royal Society of Edinburgh, a Deputy Lieutenant of the County of Glasgow, and a Justice of the Peace. He received the honorary degree of LL.D. from the universities of Glasgow, St. Andrews, and Toronto. He was knighted in 1918.

After he retired he became a member of the Scottish Committee of the London Midland and Scottish Railway and he was one of the trustees of the Scottish National Library in Edinburgh. In fact he continued to serve his native country, and particularly Glasgow, where he lived for the rest of his life. In 1941-42 he was Lord Dean of the Guild of Glasgow and from 1944 to 1947 president of the Royal Philosophical Society of Glasgow. He was a member of the Alness Committee which examined the question of grants to the Scottish universities and he was the acting chairman of the Ministry of Labour Committee on distressed areas.

April 22, 1955.
(News summary after period of non-publication).

The Rev. Francis Rosslyn Courtenay Bruce, D.D., F.L.S., rector of Herstmonceux, Sussex, until Christmas 1955, died on January 19, 1956 at the age of 84.

Born on August 14, 1871, he was the son of Canon Lloyd Stewart Bruce, whose father, Sir James Bruce, second baronet, fought at Waterloo. His mother having died during his early childhood, he was brought up with his three brothers and seven sisters by their uncle, Archbishop Thomson, of York. He was educated at St. Edward's School and Worcester College, Oxford, where he was secretary of the Union, having competed for the presidency with Hilaire Belloc [q.v.]. He rowed for his college and was an all-round athlete.

While a curate at St. Anne's, Soho, at the turn of the century, he started campaigns for more humane conditions for stage children and for the education of poor mothers in the care of their babies. During the 1914-18 War he accompanied Noel Buxton (later Lord Noel-Buxton) on his missions in the Balkans and America, and also served with the troops in France as a chaplain.

When the country living controlled by his family at Clifton, Nottinghamshire, fell vacant in 1904, he was presented to it. Eight years later he became vicar of St. Augustine's, Edgbaston, Birmingham: thence he went to Herstmonceux, where he stayed for his remaining 33 years. He did much to beautify the ancient church of Herstmonceux, and fancifully explained how supernatural agencies had introduced new embellishments, for which the necessary faculty had not first been obtained from higher ecclesiastical authority.

Such unorthodoxy of behaviour stood as a barrier to the preferment that his abilities and devotion undoubtedly deserved. But the truth of his life lay in the happiness he brought to countless thousands by the gaiety of his company and the healing of his consolation, which sprang from his deep love of all fellow creatures. He saw all as good. He condemned no one as bad.

Rosslyn Bruce's lifelong pastime was the care and breeding of animals. Horses, monkeys, birds, mice, rats, iguanas, snakes, dogs, ferrets, even bears and an elephant all passed through his cherishing hands. He was known as the greatest expert on smooth fox terriers, and bred several champions. He judged at dog shows far and wide. One of Queen Victoria's pets was a Skye terrier from his kennels.

He married in 1908 Rachel, the eldest daughter of Richard Hanbury Joseph Gurney, J.P., D.L., of Northrepps Hall, Norwich. She survives him with their two sons, three daughters, and 19 grandchildren.

January 21, 1956.

Colonel F. C. Bryant, C.M.G., D.S.O., C.B.E., Provost Marshal, Middle East during the 1939-45 War and conqueror of Togoland at the beginning of the 1914-18 War, died on March 27, 1956 at the age of 76.

Frederick Carkeet Bryant was born on December 10, 1879. He went to Harrow, where he played in the football XI of 1896-97, and then passed into the Royal Military Academy. He was gazetted to the Royal Artillery in 1898. In 1909-10 he was adjutant of the VI Brigade, R.H.A., at Trowbridge, and then secured employment with the West African Frontier Force.

At the beginning of August 1914 he was acting Commandant of the Gold Coast Regiment at Kumasi, and speedily completed the mobilization of the unit. He was fully aware of the importance of capturing the powerful wireless station at Kamina, and his plans to do so practically coincided with the scheme General Dobell, Inspector-General of the West African Frontier Force and then in London, was about to formulate. When notice of the declaration of war was received preparations were well advanced. Next day, on his own initiative, Bryant demanded the surrender of Togoland.

On August 7 the Colonial Office ordered that if Lome, on the coast, surrendered it was to be occupied, but that there should be no advance on Kamina, 100 miles inland, without further reference to London: Bryant (a captain of only seven years seniority) protested, through W. C. F. Robertson, the Acting Governor, claiming freedom of action, and that same evening the Germans surrendered Lome with practically the whole of the coastal territory.

The French had already moved from Dahomey to co-operate in the occupation of Togoland, and Bryant was then permitted to move against Kamina. As he was placed in command of the Allied forces he was given the necessary local rank. The advance on Kamina began on August 14 and, after a few sharp engagements, the Germans surrendered on August 26 after they had destroyed the wireless station.

Major Bryant—he was promoted to that rank in the Royal Artillery in October 1914—remained on the West Coast until March of the following year, being created C.M.G. for his services, while the French Government made him an Officer of the Legion of Honour. He then served on the Western Front, first as a battery commander and later in command of an artillery brigade, until 1918. In 1917 he was awarded the D.S.O., was given the brevet of lieutenant-colonel in January 1918, and received two "mentions". He retired in September 1920 but was re-employed during the 1939-45 War first as D.P.M., Northern Command, and from 1940 to 1945 as Provost Marshal, Middle East.

In 1915 he married Rosamund, second daughter of the late Philip Beresford Hope. She died in 1953.

March 29, 1956.

Charles Buchan, M.M., the former Sunderland and Arsenal footballer, and for many years a familiar broadcaster, died while on holiday with his wife near Monte Carlo on June 25, 1960. He was 68.

Born at Plumstead, S.E., he first attracted attention by his skilful play as an inside-right while he was a member of the Woolwich Polytechnic team in 1909. The following year he moved to Northfleet, and a season later signed as a professional for Leyton. His transfer to Sunderland a few months later was at a fee of £1,250, a record at that time.

He had not been long with Sunderland before he was picked out for representative honour, appearing for the Football League against the Scottish League in 1912, and in the following year he appeared in his first international match, England against Ireland. It was in this season that his club won the League championship, and he played for Sunderland against Aston Villa in the Cup Final, Sunderland losing 1-0.

During the First World War he served in the Grenadier Guards, won a Military Medal, and was later commissioned in the Sherwood Foresters.

He was transferred to Arsenal in 1925 with a transfer fee of £2,000 plus an arrangement for his new club to pay Sunderland £100 for each goal he scored that season. His total of 19 League goals and two Cup goals cost Arsenal a further £2,100. He was captain of Arsenal at the 1927 Cup Final, when they were beaten 1-0 by Cardiff.

In 1928 he turned to full-time journalism, becoming a sports writer for the *News Chronicle* (then the *Daily News*). He was a director of his own company, set up in 1951, Charles Buchan's Publications Ltd., to produce the magazine *Charles Buchan's Football Monthly* and other sporting publications.

The name of Charles Buchan is woven into the fabric of the game the world over and his place is assured. His passing is yet one more sad link broken with a past when the British were the acknowledged masters of football. And Buchan in his time was an accepted master among the masters.

Indeed, it used to be said that he was too clever for his own colleagues in attack, a dismal but probable reason why he was granted only six international caps. But trophies and accolades are not the only rewards in life. He had his in other ways; in his wide circle of admirers and friends in all walks of life, his infectious optimism, and in the undying gratitude of players who absorbed some of his patient exposition of his own skills.

Charles Buchan was a generous companion and a great character. He could argue black was white with the force and conviction of a Carson, and it was said that he was the only player who ever got his own point of view across famous Herbert Chapman, the architect of the great Arsenal. That in itself was worth a Cup Final medal.

A long-legged artistic attacker in any of the inside forward positions, he could beat his man by a slight turn of the body and a deceptive movement of the foot. In fact, he could sell as brilliant a "dummy" with the foot as any Rugby football man ever sold with his hands. But it was all his tactical appreciation and his sharp brain, thinking several moves ahead, that often left opponents and colleagues alike bemused.

Also a fine cricketer and golfer, Buchan's stories were legion, as are the tales about him.

Apocryphal or not, they were always worth an ear. One story concerned one of the two losing Cup finals in which he appeared—the first, for Sunderland as a lanky stripling in 1913, the other for Arsenal in 1927. It was at the old Crystal Palace in the year before the First World War, in the presence of a crowd of 120,000—a world record then—that Clem Stephenson, the Aston Villa inside-left, turned to Buchan on the field of play and said: "I dreamed last night that we should win 1-0 with a goal headed by Barber". Sure enough, Villa won the Cup by way of Barber's head.

Buchan could spin a yarn as easily as ever he sent opposing defences into a spin. And with it all, sucking his beloved pipe, he proved himself, when his playing days were over, to be both a *bona fide* journalist of integrity and a shrewd judge of the business of journalism.

June 27, 1960.

George Buchanan, P.C., who for 26 years was one of the group of Clydeside members of Parliament, before he attained Ministerial rank and membership of the Privy Council, died on June 28, 1955 at his home in Glasgow at the age of 64.

With his big, burly frame and shock of sandy hair he was a formidable figure throughout the period of over a quarter of a century in which he sat in the House of Commons, among the intransigent representatives of the Clydeside divisions. Often intemperate of language—he was suspended many times—he gave an impression of hardness and even harshness which constantly belied his true nature. He knew the Glasgow poor better than most of his colleagues, and during the time of the depression and the means test he both moved and troubled the House by his untutored eloquence on the theme of unemployment and corrupting idleness.

He had set his course early, and, with all the bitterness which sometimes seemed to be his whole nature, he was a man of integrity. His one interest was to raise the standard of life of the lowest paid workpeople, and to this end—as M.P., as Under-Secretary for Scotland, as Minister of Pensions, and as chairman of the National Assistance Board—he bent his whole effort.

He was born on November 30, 1890, in the Gorbals district of Glasgow, the son of George Buchanan, of Kilberry, Argyllshire. His early experience of poverty made him a champion of the underdog on every possible occasion, and to further his ends he grasped every opportunity to supplement the knowledge he had gained at the Camden Street School in his native city. He went to work in an iron foundry on leaving school and became a pattern maker. While still in his teens he joined his union and the then struggling Independent Labour Party, and his aggressive oratory enabled him to forge ahead in both organizations. After being for many years a member of the executive of the United Pattern Makers' Association he was appointed its chairman in 1932, by which time he had represented the constituency in which he was born for about 10 years. From 1918 to 1923 he was also a member of the Glasgow Corporation.

Though one of a small *coterie* of Labour extremists associated with the late James Maxton, he exhibited in his early days none of the qualities which endeared his leader even to avowed opponents. Indeed few who succeed in securing a seat in the House of Commons have been able to withstand its mellowing influence with such determination. He persisted in acting contrary to its rules of procedure and alternately entertained and outraged his fellow members. Outspoken to the point of rudeness, he seemed incapable of tolerance and was regarded even by his closest associates as a "Parliamentary problem". Yet eventually he became a reformed character, and that his conversion was genuine and lasting cannot be denied. His loyalty to his fellow men in the trade union and Labour movement had never been in doubt, for, as long ago as 1934, although a poor man, he had refused a Government offer of £2,000 a year, as a member of the Statutory Committee on Unemployment, rather than desert the cause to which he had devoted his life.

Just before the 1939-45 War he rejoined the Labour Party, from which he had resigned in 1932, and the seal of his defection from the extreme left was placed by his acceptance of the office of Joint Parliamentary Under-Secretary for Scotland with Tom Fraser in 1945. He had been offered the post of Minister of National Insurance but took the Scottish Under-Secretaryship principally because he hoped that he could in that office follow his lifelong ambition to improve housing conditions in Scotland. Two years later he became Minister of Pensions, in which capacity he soon acquired a reputation for the wisdom and kindliness with which he administered the department, one of the most exacting in the Government. He was constantly having to deal with problems for which there was no ready-made solution and his handling of cases of hardship involving ex-service men and women aroused widespread appreciation. There was less surprise than satisfaction when in 1948 he was sworn of the Privy Council, and a few months later appointed chairman of the newly created National Assistance Board. This necessitated his resignation from the House and he left with the most sincere expressions of good will and hopes for his future success from all sides.

The responsibility of the chairman of a new organization is a heavy one, for on him largely lies the responsibility for forming the traditions on which work will proceed. Buchanan, as Minister of Pensions, had already manifested his broad sympathies in filling a notoriously difficult office in which human problems constantly arise. As chairman of the National Assistance Board he was confronted with problems of a similar character. Applicants to the board were sure of sympathetic treatment, consonant with the necessity for care in the disbursement of public funds.

When his five-year period of office expired he continued to serve as a member of the board, and by then the tradition he set was firmly established. His successor as chairman, Sir Geoffrey Hutchinson, Q.C., speaking at East Ham, was able rightly to say: "He has left behind at the National Assistance Board an immense tribute to his public service, kindliness and generosity of temperament, which have made him loved by all".

He married in 1924 Miss Annie McNee.

June 29, 1955.

Jack Buchanan, who died in a London hospital on October 20, 1957, belonged to the gay tradition of dude comedians. He went on to the stage before the First World War and continued as actor, manager, and film producer almost up to the end. But he will be remembered most affectionately for the seemingly lazy but most accomplished grace with which he sang, danced, flirted, and joked his way through musical shows between the wars. The tall figure, the elegant gestures, the friendly drawling voice, the general air of having a good time, cheered up the most languid house from stalls to gallery.

He projected across the footlights a pleasant world (the latest kind of publicity spoils it with the label "glamorous") in which all the girls are pretty, well-dressed, and out for fun, cocktails are always to be had by ringing for Jeeves and overdrafts raise a hearty laugh. One of his shows was called *Top Hat and Tails* and that would have done for almost all the others. His singing may have been nothing in particular. As a dancer he never reached the acrobatic perfection of an Astaire. He did not let himself go in fooling in the manner of a Hulbert*. But his style of comedy was all his own; he took everything, from tunes to wisecracks, in an easy stride. He knew how to make the most of looks, charm, and manner. His secret was that he could take an audience into his confidence and persuade them, by exquisitely good manners in acting, that they too would have felt at home in the elegant Edwardian society, as depicted on the light-comedy stage in which he had his roots. Jack Buchanan was the last of the "knuts".

Born at Helensburgh, near Glasgow, he made his first appearance on the regular stage at the Apollo in 1912. Between 1914 and 1918 he began to show his individuality in pieces that old soldiers have not forgotten—*Tonight's the Night, Bubbly,* and *Tails Up!* After *A to Z* in 1921 he went into management with *Battling Butler* and then in 1924 he played at Times Square Theatre, New York, in André Charlot's [q.v.] Revue. Back in England he toured with *Boodle* and then, alternating between Britain and America, scored a series of successes. The Charlot connexion continued. As producer or actor and sometimes both he was always to be heard of. There were *Sunny, That's a Good Girl, Wake Up and Dream, Stand Up and Sing* (of which he was part author with Douglas Furber), *This'll Make You Whistle, The Last of Mrs. Cheyney, Canaries Sometimes Sing, Don't Listen Ladies, Castle in the Air,* and *As Long as They're Happy*—titles that prove at once his consistency and his versatility. They span the period between the late twenties and the early fifties and trace his development into a skilful actor in light comedy. In 1940 he made his first pantomime appearance and gave a new look, which went down very well, to Buttons.

Though never robust he threw himself into filming as actor—or director—wending his jaunty way through *Monte Carlo, Good Night Vienna* (how hauntingly he sang George Posford's songs), *Yes, Mr. Brown, Come Out of the Pantry, The Middle Watch, When Knights Were Bold, The Band Wagon* (with Fred Astaire), and the bilingual *Major Thompson.* He controlled the Garrick Theatre, directed the King's Theatre, Hammersmith, appeared on television both in Great Britain and in the United States, and in many broadcasts both before the Second World War and after.

He married in 1949 Susan Bassett, of New York.

October 21, 1957.

Zetton Buchanan (Mrs. E. L. Buchanan), who was taken prisoner by the Arabs after her husband had been murdered in the Mesopotamian rising of 1920, died on March 16, 1959 at her home in London at the age of 50. Her account of the experience, *Captured by the Arabs,* was later serialized in *The Times* before being published as a book.

Zetton Chesnay was born in London and spent her childhood in France. She was only 18 when she married Captain E. L. Buchanan and only 20 when she joined him at Shahraban, a little town some 60 miles north-east of Baghdad, where he was assistant irrigation officer. There was one other Englishman at the station, and shortly before it was attacked a British officer moved in with 50 Arab levies and two British sergeants. The British at the station ultimately numbered seven.

Under attack, on August 13, 1920, most of the levies deserted. Only Mrs. Buchanan and the assistant grass-farm manager, Mr. Baines, escaped of the British party, and were taken prisoners. Mrs. Buchanan threw herself on the mercy of the elderly Shaikh Majid, a cousin of the leader of the attacking tribesmen, and soon regretted it: "It was not a pleasing face which I saw. The eyes were small and watery, close together and very shifty, set in a rather long, sallow face with a white beard".

Majid was "disgusted" at her desire to see her husband's body, and consigned her to the harem where she spent several horrified days. "The women were here, but far from beautiful . . . but nothing else of the conventional picture (of a harem) and certainly the perfume was not that of incense. The courtyard was a square of uneven mud, with dirt and filth all over it. In the centre was a horse trough, also made of mud. Rooms, which might more properly be called hovels, led off all round the square . . . There was a mysterious room which was always kept locked . . . a veritable bluebeard's chamber".

In this distressing institution, described in Mrs. Buchanan's exact, unadorned prose, scores of women lived a monotonous life with nothing to do. Even tidying up was rare. Most of them, she wrote, "might fitly be described by the term 'cat' ". The shaikh's wife would have been "an elegant, handsome old lady if only she had washed. The common recreation was quarrelling, but a report the day after the murders that the British had been driven out of Baghdad drove the women wild with joy".

The captive was later moved to better quarters, those of the assistant political officer's clerks, which she shared with Baines, who had been badly wounded, two Indians and an Egyptian. They looked after her well and protected her from the guards, one of whom tried to shoot her. Relief came on September 6 when Majid, fearing for his safety, had her sign a chit clearing him of complicity in the rising. She was taken to his house and wrote a note to accompany the white flag which prevented the relieving column under Conyngham from shelling the town.

The lack of protection of Shahraban, and the failure of communications before it fell, created some scandal at the time. Mrs. Buchanan returned to England and, after writing her book, which received wide notice, returned also to private life and her long widowhood. She preserved a taste for travel, and in the course of indulging it went round the world three times.

March 17, 1959.

Sir Peter Buck, K.C.M.G., D.S.O., M.D., D.Sc., for many years Director of the famous Bishop Museum, Honolulu, died in hospital there on December 1, 1951.

A child of the union of an Irish father and a Maori mother, he will always be known among his mother's people, for whom he did so much, both directly and through the great distinction as a scientist to which he attained, by his Maori name, Te Rangi Hiroa.

He started life with few advantages. His mother died while he was an infant and he found himself treated at school as a Maori. "The only way I could hold my own", he once said, "was to keep a lap or so ahead and I had little difficulty in doing that". However, he succeeded in qualifying in medicine and, after serving the Maori people as a medical officer of health, he entered the New Zealand Parliament and joined the Cabinet as Maori representative. He had much to do with the regeneration of the Maoris and in interpreting their way of life to New Zealanders of European descent. Later he extended his studies and his influence to the whole of Polynesia, and as Director of the Bishop Museum in Honolulu, containing the most comprehensive ethnological collection in the Pacific, he became the indispensable guide and friend to students of the culture of the South Seas throughout the world.

Peter Henry Buck was the son of W. H. Buck and Ngarongo-ki-tua. He was educated at Aute College, Otago Medical School, and the University of New Zealand. After serving as a house surgeon at Dunedin hospital in 1904 he was appointed medical officer of health to the Maoris in 1905. In 1909 he became the representative in the New Zealand Cabinet of the Maori race and retained the post until 1914 when he went on active service with the New Zealand Expeditionary Force. He served in Egypt, Malta, and Gallipoli, and, after commanding a Maori pioneer battalion, joined No. 3 New Zealand General Hospital, where he remained until demobilization. He then became Director of Maori Hygiene.

Meanwhile, though he had already made a considerable reputation in the medical profession, he had turned more and more to the study of ethnology. He began a long list of publications on the subject with a treatise on the evolution of Maori clothing, and by 1932 his reputation stood so high that he was invited to become visiting professor at Yale. He served several terms there, the last in 1939. He was created K.C.M.G. in the Birthday Honours of 1946.

December 3, 1951.

Hermann Buhl, the Austrian climber who conquered Nanga Parbat in the summer of 1953 lost his life on June 27, 1957. He was a member of the Austrian Karakoram expedition which climbed the Broadpeak, and he fell while trying to scale the Chequlsia peak in the Baltoro region.

Buhl, who electrified the climbing world in July 1953 by going alone to the summit of Nanga Parbat—eighth highest mountain in the world—a few weeks after the successful British ascent of Everest, did not start his mountaineering with any particular advantages. His family was poor and he himself thin and frailly built. But what he lacked in physique he made up for by his great determination. He had a passion for mountains, and this, since he lived at Innsbruck, he was able to satisfy on the ridges and rockfaces of the Karwendel and the Wetterstein. He began climbing shortly before the last war and was out in the high places whenever he could manage it, his climbs becoming ever more difficult as his experience grew. Even during the war he found time to attack some grim face or other.

After the war he extended his range first to the Dolomites, then to the Western Alps, and made his *début* at Chamonix by ascending the north face of the Charmoz. He had always driven himself hard, and now turned the screw tighter on the great wall of the Marmolada in winter, on the man-killing Eigerwand, on the Péteret ridge of Mont Blanc, and on the Chamonix Aiguilles. This determination to see how far he could go lay behind his solo climbs, particularly the solitary ascent of the north-east wall of the Piz Badile, prefaced and rounded off by a hundred-mile cycle journey.

He was a climber to be reckoned with when he was invited to join the 1953 Nanga Parbat expedition. Although first attempted by the English climber Mummery with two British companions and a few Gurkhas in the 1890s, Nanga Parbat had become a peculiarly German preserve owing to the attempts—unsuccessful and twice attended by disaster—of three expeditions of Austrian and German mountaineers in the 1930s, expeditions from which the Nazi spirit of fanaticism was by no means absent.

Though not, perhaps, bedevilled politically, Buhl's splendid and courageous ascent of Nanga Parbat early in July 1953 was later to become the subject of acrimonious debate and a court action by the leader of the expedition, Dr. Herrligkoffer.

Shortly after the climb Peter Aschenbrenner, who was in charge of the climbing party, and Herrligkoffer appeared to give conflicting accounts of Buhl's achievement. One was reported to have said it had taken place on July 3, the other on July 4. But in any case there remained Buhl's great feat of endurance and resolution. Starting out alone from the highest camp he reached the summit at 7 o'clock in the evening, survived a night at 26,000ft. on a narrow ledge with no spare clothes, and in spite of appalling weakness and dehydration lived to tell the tale.

July 17, 1957.

Admiral Sir Henry Tritton Buller, G.C.V.O., C.B., died on August 29, 1960 at the age of 86.

His name is chiefly connected with the action with the Kaiser Wilhelm der Grosse, the first of the German raiders on the oversea trade routes to be destroyed on August 26, 1914. For nine years after the war, he was the Flag Officer Commanding the Royal Yacht.

Buller was the second but eldest surviving son of the late Admiral Sir Alexander Buller, G.C.B., of Erle Hall, Plympton, Devon. He was born on October 30, 1873, and entered the Britannia as a cadet in January 1887, in the same month that his father became a rear-admiral. In May 1889 young Buller was appointed midshipman to the battleship Benbow, in the Mediterranean, on which station his father was Superintendent of Malta Dockyard, exchanging later first into the Camperdown, flagship of Admiral Sir Anthony Hoskins, and afterwards into the Victoria, which succeeded the Camperdown as flagship, and was lost with many lives in collision with her in June 1893. By that date, Buller had moved into the Active, flagship of the Training Squadron. In 1897 he went to the North America and West Indies Station as Flag Lieutenant to Vice-Admiral Sir John (afterwards Lord) Fisher, Commander-in-Chief, on board the Renown. In 1899 Fisher became Commander-in-Chief in the Mediterranean, taking the same flagship with him, and Buller also went there as Flag Lieutenant. Three years later, he joined the Royal yacht Victoria and Albert, and in August 1904 was promoted to commander.

Buller was appointed commander of the R.N. College, Dartmouth, in 1908 and served there until his promotion to captain in 1911. He was made M.V.O. in April 1911, on the occasion of the Prince of Wales completing his term at the college. In November 1911 he became Flag-Captain in the Zealandia to Rear-Admiral A. Y. Moggridge, commanding the Home Fleet at Portsmouth, and in 1913 was appointed to command the cruiser Highflyer, seagoing training ship for the "special entry" cadets from public schools. The Highflyer had only been on this duty for 11 months when the war broke out. She landed her cadets at Devonport, and proceeded to join the Ninth Cruiser Squadron, on the Mid-Atlantic or Finisterre Station, under Rear-Admiral J. M. de Robeck. Her first war service was to take back to Plymouth the captured Tubantia, an afterwards famous Dutch liner, carrying German gold and reservists.

She was next heard of for a creditable exploit, the destruction of the Kaiser Wilhelm der Grosse, the first of the German armed merchant raiders to escape from the North Sea into the Atlantic, on August 26, 1914. The Highflyer found this vessel coaling off the Rio de Oro, West Africa, and after an action of an hour and a half she was sunk, with the loss of only one man killed and five slightly wounded in the British ship.

Buller was for a time Senior Naval Officer of a Squadron which included various armed merchantmen. He remained in the Highflyer until May 1916 and afterwards became Naval Assistant to the Second Sea Lord, Admiral Sir Cecil Burney.

On April 1, 1922, he hoisted his flag as Rear-Admiral Commanding H.M. Yachts, and he held this command for nine years, being promoted to vice-admiral and admiral while still in the Victoria and Albert. While in command of the yacht he was also Naval Aide-de-Camp to the King. He utilized much of his spare time in affairs connected with the welfare of naval officers and men, and was the first President of the Royal Naval Benevolent Trust, incorporated by Royal Charter in 1922, to take over the Grand Fleet and kindred Funds for the relief of cases of necessity or distress. He was promoted to Admiral in April 1931 and later in the month retired at his own request.

Buller married in 1919 Lady Hermione Stuart, only daughter of the seventeenth Earl of Moray. They had three sons and one daughter.

August 31, 1960.

Ivan Bunin, one of the last great names of the pre-revolutionary generation of Russian writers, who had lived in exile, mainly in France, since 1919, died on November 7, 1953 in hospital in Paris at the age of 83.

To English readers Bunin is probably still best known for his long short story, "The Gentleman from San Francisco", which, though by no means one of his most characteristic works, is a feat of austere and sombre imaginative power that merits a place among the best short stories of modern times. In its haunted sense of mortality it derives plainly from the spiritual teaching of Tolstoy, who had always a more potent influence on Bunin than foreign critics were for long disposed to recognize. Its curiously formal, coldly ironical style, pervaded by a kind of reserved lyrical emotion, is very much his own.

Bunin is generally described as a "classical" writer, whose masters in the Russian tradition—Tolstoy apart—were Turgenev and Goncharov. This is only to say that he had little in common with the prevailing school of social naturalism of his day in Russia. Having made his beginnings as a poet, it was as a prose writer of a fine drawn lyrical quality—lyrical in cast of imagination—who in much of his early work seemed indeed to follow directly in the wake of Chekhov—that he stamped himself most deeply upon the sensibilities of his contemporaries. A greater artist, in the technical sense, than Gorky, he seemed likely, in the years before 1917, to rise to the stature of the greatest of all Russian writers. But, although he produced fine work in the early years of exile, he eventually suffered the normal fate of the exile, and his later stories reflect only dimly his former powers.

Ivan Alexeyevich Bunin was born on October 22, 1870, at Voronezh, in the district of Elets, in the province of Orel, of an old and impoverished family of country gentry. The central Russian scenes of his boyhood provide a setting for much of his best action. He attended the *gymnasium* at Elets, but his later studies were haphazard and informal. At the age of 19 he left home to become a local government clerk at Kharkov and afterwards worked at Orel and Poltava. He had begun to write both verse and prose at an early age, and in 1891 he published his first volume of poetry. Two years later he was awarded the Pushkin prize for literature for a translation of Longfellow's *Hiawatha* (he also produced spirited translations of Byron's *Manfred* and *Cain*).

Although in the succeeding years his work was issued by the publishing firm Znanie, founded by Gorky, Bunin was in imaginative temper far removed from the realism of Gorky and his school. He was equally far removed from the aesthetic and mystical philosophy of the Symbolists. Aloof in manner, reserved and somewhat caustic of temperament, he followed a highly individual literary path. He was a great traveller—few Russian writers have travelled so constantly or so far afield. Apart from regular visits to France and Italy, between 1907 and 1914 he visited Turkey, Greece, Syria, Palestine, Egypt, North Africa and Ceylon; the last three winters before the outbreak of war in 1914 he spent in Capri in the company of Gorky.

In 1909 he was elected an honorary fellow of the Russian Academy. Next year he published his first full-length work of fiction, *The Village,* which draws a sombre and powerful picture of the darkness of Russian peasant life. It has something of the same effect as Chekhov's *Peasants,* though it is more formless, and it provoked heated controversy. Of the shorter works that followed, one of the most impressive is *Sukhodol* (1912), which describes, in similarly unsparing fashion, the decay of a family of country gentry. The collection of short stories Bunin published in 1917, which included "The Gentleman from San Francisco", contains examples of his best work.

Bitterly hostile to the Bolshevists from the very start, during the civil war he edited for a time a "White" newspaper in Odessa. He left Russia in 1919 and settled in France. He continued steadily to write. A volume of memoirs, *The Accursed Days,* is filled with implacable hate and contempt for the new rulers of Russia. The sense of exile is strong in a story like "Mitya's Love", stronger still in what is his most ambitious effort, the unfinished autobiographical novel *The Life of Arseniev,* beautifully written but altogether too shadowy of substance, of which the first part, written during 1927-29, was published in an English translation in 1933 under the title *The Well of Days.* In that year also Bunin was awarded the Nobel Prize.

He wrote relatively little afterwards, though a collection of his stories belonging for the most part to the year 1939 was published in an English translation, under the title of *Dark Avenues,* 10 years later, and a volume of criticism and reminiscences entitled *Memories and Portraits* appeared some two years before he died.

November 9, 1953.

Admiral Sir Robert Burnett, G.B.E., K.C.B., D.S.O., who died in London on July 2, 1959 at the age of 71, will be chiefly remembered for his share in the destruction of the German battle cruiser Scharnhorst on December 26, 1943. This was the third occasion on which he had served with distinction in action with enemy forces in northern waters in the defence of convoys to Russia.

The Soviet Government, in recognition of his great assistance to it, made him a member of the Order of Suvarov, and among other honours he received from the University of his native Aberdeen the honorary degree of Doctor of Laws. In his earlier career he was a great sportsman and athlete, and had done much for the advancement of physical and recreational training in the Navy.

Robert Lindsay Burnett was the fourth son of J. A. Burnett, of Kemnay, Aberdeenshire, and a younger brother of the late Air Chief Marshal Sir Charles Burnett. He was born on July 22, 1887. Educated at Bedford School, and at Eastmans, Southsea, he entered the Britannia as a naval cadet in January 1903, and went to sea in May 1904, as midshipman of the cruiser Amphitrite in China. In 1911 he was appointed physical training officer at Shotley training establishment and in 1913 to the staff of the physical training school at Portsmouth. In this branch of the service he may be said to have been the outstanding officer of his time. He became sabre champion of the Navy, and at one time was on the lists of qualified referees for boxing, rugby and association football, hockey, and water polo.

During the First World War he served as lieutenant in the destroyer Laertes, in the Harwich Force, commanded torpedo boat No. 26, and from July 1916 the destroyers Acheron and Nessus. From 1920 to 1922 he was fleet P. and R.T. officer in the Mediterranean, and in 1922-23 held a similar appointment in the Atlantic Fleet. In July 1923 he became Assistant Director of Physical Training and Sports at the Admiralty, and was reappointed on his promotion to commander at the end of 1923 until May 1925. For a few months in 1928 he returned to his former post as A.D.P.T.S. at the Admiralty, and in December of that year became executive officer of the battleship Rodney.

During the next two years he commanded the Eighth Destroyer Flotilla on the China Station in the Keppel, and from 1933 to 1935 was Director of Physical Training and Sports and in command of the P.R.T. School at Portsmouth. His next appointment was in command of the new cruiser Amphion, which he took to the Africa Station, where he became flag captain and chief of staff to the Commander-in-Chief from 1936 to 1938.

In March 1939 he took up the post of Commodore at the Royal Naval Barracks, Chatham, where he served during the first year of the Second World War. From the autumn of 1940 he commanded the minelaying squadron as acting rear-admiral until his substantive promotion in January 1941. In March 1942 he took over the command of the destroyer flotillas of the Home Fleet, and in the following December was made C.B. for his "daring, skill and resolution in taking a convoy to North Russia in the face of sustained and relentless attacks by enemy aircraft and submarines".

On December 31, 1942, he was in command of the covering force of another Russian convoy, the destroyer escort of which engaged a superior German force off the North Cape and prevented its interfering with the convoy. More powerful British forces arrived in support and engaged the enemy, who escaped in the low visibility with loss and damage. Burnett was awarded the D.S.O.

In January 1943 he was moved to another command in the Home Fleet, that of the Tenth Cruiser Squadron, and reappointed on his promotion to vice-admiral on December 9, 1943. Seventeen days later, on Boxing Day, with his flag in the Belfast, he played an outstanding part in the operations which resulted in the sinking of the German battle cruiser Scharnhorst, which had attempted to attack another Russian convoy. He was created a K.B.E. for his good services in the pursuit and destruction of the Scharnhorst, for great determination and skill throughout the action, and in twice driving off the enemy, thus saving the convoy. In May 1944 he was made Commander-in-Chief, South Atlantic Station, where he served for the customary two years, a period which saw the end of the war. He was promoted to K.C.B. in the birthday honours in 1945, and in September 1946 to admiral. From December 1947 until his retirement in 1950 he was Commander-in-Chief at Plymouth. He was advanced to G.B.E. in 1950.

For four years, from 1950 to 1954, he was chairman of the White Fish Authority.

He married, in 1915, Ethel Constance, daughter of R. H. Shaw.

July 3, 1959.

General Sir John Burnett-Stuart, G.C.B., K.B.E., C.M.G., D.S.O., died at his home at Avington Park, near Winchester on October 6, 1958. He was 83.

John Theodosius Burnett-Stuart was born on March 14, 1875, and educated at Repton and Sandhurst. He joined the Rifle Brigade in 1895 and served with the Tochi Field Force before going to South Africa. As a captain he was with the 4th Battalion of his regiment in Egypt and he graduated at the Staff College under Lord Rawlinson in 1904.

He went to the War Office during the Esher reforms, was in the Directorate of Operations, and in 1910 went to New Zealand as Director of Operations.

He was instructor G.S.O.2 at the Staff College, Camberley, from September, 1913, to August 4, 1914, which was the last course before war broke out. After holding several staff appointments in France during the first year and a half of the war he was promoted to brigadier general and made B.G.S. of VII Corps under General Snow in February, 1916. In the Cambrai battle of November 1917 VII Corps was on the flank of the main attack and played no part in the assault. But Burnett-Stuart gave repeated warnings that a German counter-offensive was being mounted—warnings which were unfortunately disregarded by the higher command. Thus the German counter-stroke attained a great initial surprise and success, penetrating deeply into the sector held by VII Corps, but was eventually brought to a halt by the well-directed defence.

In December 1917 Burnett-Stuart was promoted major-general and made Deputy Adjutant-General at G.H.Q.—a post which he held until the end of the war. In 1920 he was sent out to India as G.O.C. of the Madras District, and thus had to deal with the Malabar rising of 1921, but in 1922 he was brought back to fill the key post of Director of Military Operations and Intelligence in the War Office—a post which he held under two successive Chiefs of the Imperial General Staff, Lord Cavan and Sir George Milne.

After four years' tenure of this post he was given command in 1926 of the 3rd Division, in the Southern Command, and Colonel A. P. Wavell (later Field-Marshal Earl Wavell) was selected as his G.S.O.1.

In 1927 the first Experimental Mechanized Force was assembled on Salisbury Plain and placed under the higher direction of Burnett-Stuart. He criticized the motley components of the force and pointed out that the infantry would not be capable of keeping pace with the rest of the force in battle unless they were mounted in armoured cross-country vehicles. He also urged that the "enthusiastic experts and visionaries" should be brought in to aid in the new experiments, saying: "It doesn't matter how wild their views are if only they have a touch of the divine fire—I will supply the common sense of advanced middle age".

That conclusion showed profound insight and a clear perception of the basic requirement of the success of the new experiments. Unfortunately, he had an early disagreement with Colonel [later Major-General John*] Fuller, who had been chosen to command the new force. More unfortunately still, that led to the appointment of a new commander, who was much less progressive, and Burnett-Stuart himself came to be increasingly disappointed with the methods by which the force was trained.

When on the staff in France he had been very sceptical about the value of tanks, but in the post war years he changed his views, although still inclined to be excessively critical of their defects and variable in his views. On the other hand he also failed to see eye to eye with the G.O.C.-in-C., Southern Command, General Montgomery-Massingberd, who was much more conservative.

From 1931 to 1934 Burnett-Stuart was G.O.C. British Troops in Egypt, and there became a supporter and advocate of the possibilities of using mechanized forces in desert warfare.

In 1934 he returned home to become on promotion G.O.C.-in-C. of Southern Command, and held that post until April 1938, when he was succeeded by his former staff officer, General Wavell. That was Burnett-Stuart's last appointment before retirement.

But he had been very near to the highest appointment in the Army. When Montgomery-Massingberd retired from the post of C.I.G.S. in April 1936 Burnett-Stuart was a leading candidate for the succession and certainly the most fluent of all the candidates. But he had clashed too often with Montgomery-Massingberd to have a chance of being recommended as his successor by the outgoing C.I.G.S.

"Jock" Stuart, as he was generally known in the Army, was a man of sparkling mind, lively imagination, and long range if variable vision. He had an impish turn of humour, which handicapped his progress, but together with his informality of manner made him much beloved by his subordinates. Although he could be devastating in criticism and witticisms, he was remarkably free from malice.

He was A.D.C. General to the King from 1935 to 1938 and Colonel Commandant 1st Battalion, The Rifle Brigade, from 1936 to 1945. He was awarded the D.S.O. in 1900, made C.M.G. in 1916, C.B. in the following year, and created K.B.E. in 1923. In 1932 he was advanced to K.C.B. and in 1937 to G.C.B.

October 8, 1958.

Tommy Burns, who died on May 9, 1955 at Vancouver at the age of 74, was heavyweight boxing champion of the world for some two years before he was defeated by Jack Johnson at Rushcutter's Bay, Sydney, New South Wales, in 1908. He was the only Canadian to win the world title.

Tommy Burns, whose real name was Noah Brusso, was born at Hanover, in Canada, in 1881, and so was 27 years of age when he arrived with the title of boxing champion of the world and a personality and presence never before quite experienced in Britain, at any rate in boxing circles.

Known as "Tammy" to a growing number of friends, who in spite of everything could not help liking and admiring him, he was publicized, and publicized himself, as "Emperor Burns" or "The Little Corporal". Burns certainly was very like some of the pictures of Napoleon. He had the same clearly defined features and penetrating gaze—when he wished—and a tuft of hair over the forehead helped in the illusion. He had an acute mind to match. His physique, too, was compact and far from vast or hulking.

Burns was in fact the smallest man ever to win the world title under the Queensberry rules—no more than 5ft. 7in. in height and about 12½ stones in weight. He must have realized that he could never hope to become one of the real giants of the ring and, pursued by the black shadow and challenges of Jack Johnson, he travelled widely and held on to his title profitably and worthily enough for about two years.

He had been little known when he became the world champion through defeating Marvin Hart, the American light heavyweight, to whom the great James Jeffries had bequeathed his title on retirement. Jeffries could have overwhelmed Hart in double quick time but it took Burns 20 rounds in which to win on points in February 1906 at Los Angeles, California.

It was soon after that that Burns saw a future in Britain. When he arrived he was matched first of all with the reigning British champion, Gunner Moir, and the preliminary meeting between Burns and a committee of the National Sporting Club, composed of a number of famous sportsmen, probably had to be seen and heard to be fully appreciated, or even believed. Burns, adopting the attitude of a Napoleon and a business tycoon in one, laid down his own terms and got them. On the very night of the fight Burns demanded that the purse be handed over before he entered the ring. He ended a bitter argument by declaring: "That cuts no ice with me. I want the referee to hold the money". And so it had to be.

It says a lot for Burns that both he and the club became quite friendly when they came to know each other better. Incidentally, Gunner Moir, a robust but slow and extremely moderate boxer, was first out-classed and then knocked out scientifically in 10 rounds.

After his victory over Moir at the N.S.C. he startled a very different crowd of spectators by appearing at Wonderland in the East End in his tuxedo. Having arrived outside the ring he set about discussing with his friends a supper party arranged for only an hour or so ahead. His opponent, Jack Palmer, of Newcastle, meanwhile sat uneasily in his corner and had to wait some time before Burns stripped for action and disposed of his man inside four rounds. Palmer's form had not been improved by the conversation he had heard. A similar pantomime contributed to the even easier demolishment of Jem Roche in Ireland.

Decisive victories over the well-known Bill Squires and Bill Lang in Australia preceded Burns's Waterloo at Rushcutter's Bay, Sydney, Australia, in December 1908. This was inevitable in spite of a series of brilliant delaying actions and, when the time came, he went down defiantly and bravely as everyone who knew him well felt sure he would. It was not a pretty end, but it was a gallant one. Johnson was a master of the insolent jibe in the ring, when all was going well, but Burns at least held his own at Rushcutter's Bay in the face of certain defeat. Johnson, over two stones the heavier man and six inches the taller, immensely strong and perhaps the best counter-fighter of all the world champions, set out to massacre Burns and he would have spent more than 14 rounds enjoying it if the police had not intervened. Burns, however, had assured himself beforehand of what at the time was a unique financial recompense. He had insisted upon a purse of "£6,000 win, draw, or lose" and that figure proved to be the first of the big purses which subsequently had to be offered to any world champion before he could be prevailed upon to risk the loss of a title which now represented a small fortune.

Years later, after the 1914-18 War, Burns returned to Britain and lost to Joe Beckett* in London in 1920 in seven rounds. For some years afterwards he was the licensee of an hotel in Newcastle and then operated a "speakeasy" in New York during the prohibition period. He became an evangelist in 1935 and went to Vancouver a fortnight before he died to enter a religious order.

May 12, 1955.

Christine Burrows, sometime Principal of St. Hilda's Hall, Oxford, and of the Oxford Society of Home Students (later St. Anne's College) died at Oxford on September 10, 1959 at the age of 87.

Christine Mary Elizabeth Burrows was the only and posthumous child of Henry Parker Burrows, of Maidenhead, and Esther Elizabeth Bliss, who came of a family once well known in Oxford and Chipping Norton. She was educated at Cheltenham Ladies' College; in 1891 she went up to Lady Margaret Hall to read history; but at the end of her second year she was summoned to help her mother, whom Miss Beale had selected to be Principal of St. Hilda's, the new hall for women students which she had just founded in Oxford.

The self-sacrificing devotion which Miss Burrows brought to the task of acting as senior student and helping her mother, to whom she was warmly attached, to understand Oxford life led, in the opinion of many of her friends, to the loss of her chance of a first class. She gained a second class in modern history in 1894, and became tutor in history at St. Hilda's and later vice-principal. It was largely due to her that the hall took its place as quickly as it did among the other foundations for women in Oxford, since neither Miss Beale nor Mrs. Burrows was familiar with the problems of the enterprise. Miss Burrows's wisdom helped to keep her mother on the right track and eased her relations with the first students, who were at an age of which Mrs. Burrows had had little experience.

Miss Burrows succeeded her mother as Principal in 1910 and carried the hall through the earliest phase of expansion after the First World War. In 1919, however, she felt it right to retire, at the early age of 47, in order to live with Mrs. Burrows, whose health was failing. In 1921 she was appointed to the principalship of the Society of Oxford Home Students (now St. Anne's College), which did not entail residence. Here for nine years she did a great work in collecting a tutorial staff and laying the foundations of a corporate existence; but at the end of 1929 she again retired to look after her mother.

After the latter's death in 1935 Christine Burrows continued to live in Oxford and to occupy herself with many tasks there. One of her greatest pleasures was to show strangers round Oxford, to which she was an incomparable guide. The work which she did for the English Speaking Union and also as hospitality secretary of the Oxford branch of the British Federation of University Women brought her into touch with many visitors from oversea and she greatly enjoyed entertaining them.

Miss Burrows was a firm supporter of women's rights, though never a militant suffragist. In the thirties she was a member of the Archbishops' committee on the place of women in the Church and, although she signed its report, she did not alter her opinion that the ordination of women to the priesthood was right and would come in time. Many of her friends felt that she might have made her mark as an historian if she had not been over-conscientious in giving up so much to the necessities of others. She was the kindest and most generous of friends: no trouble or financial sacrifice was too much if it would help a former student or one of her beloved colleges. In many ways she had always seemed older than her age, for she had imbibed much of her mother's Victorian cast of manners; but this was united with an insistence that women should take their proper part in the world and an interest in contemporary developments which placed her in touch with modern opinion.

September 11, 1959.

Sir Montague Burton collapsed and died on September 21, 1952 at the age of 67. Starting his own business before he was 20 on borrowed capital of £100, he established in a few years a vast and prosperous organization.

Montague Maurice Burton was born on August 15, 1885. He started working in a Sheffield tailors' shop, and before he was 20 a relative lent him £100 with which to start a business of his own; he opened a shop in Chesterfield. He was soon struck by the exceptionally bad conditions which existed in the clothing industry at the beginning of the century. He became convinced that these conditions, far from cheapening garments, made them in fact more expensive to the consumer, because of low output of indifferent quality.

He believed it was possible to change this by using more modern methods, by creating efficient factories, pleasant to work in, by employing well-paid labour, and by engaging in mass-production. At Chesterfield he flourished, and within a few years other shops were opened in his native city of Sheffield, in Manchester, Leicester, and Mansfield, where he gradually began to put into practice the ideas which were to become the main interest of his life.

Burton was little more than 20 when his first factory, employing 56 workers, opened at Leeds, already the world's centre of the wholesale clothing industry. In less than 30 years the company of Montague Burton Limited, which he had formed in 1929 to take over his multiple tailoring enterprises, was employing directly more than 10,000 men and women in conditions which were widely praised, and more than 100,000 indirectly, in various subsidiary processes of clothing manufacture.

Since then it has expanded still further. He was able to claim, long before he died, that not only was his company paying the highest wages for clothing manufacture in Europe, but that it held the undisputed leadership of all similar firms in its welfare work. The great Hudson Road mills at Leeds work to a clock-like precision, with special lighting and air conditioning, an expert staff of doctors, dentists, nurses, and chiropodists in constant service at the clinics, and canteens which are prepared to serve meals to every worker, on the premises.

His benefactions, particularly to universities, were considerable. Altogether he made about a dozen gifts to universities and colleges, endowing chairs of industrial relations at Cambridge, Cardiff, and Leeds, of International Relations at Oxford, Dublin, and the London School of Economics, and a lectureship at Nottingham. He created also several prize funds in literature and art, and himself wrote two travel books, with some shrewd sidelights on many of the personalities he had met and, in many cases, entertained at the Burton works or at his home at Harrogate. He avoided party politics, but he was interested in the work of various industrial and commercial organizations, and some years ago represented Great Britain at the conference of the Federation of British Empire Chambers of Commerce in New Zealand.

He had a very special interest in and concern for the welfare of Jewish people, and had for many years generously supported educational and charitable institutions in Palestine, both before and since the establishment of the State of Israel. One other of his interests which should not be overlooked was his encouragement of the literature indigenous to the north country, especially Yorkshire, and he was one of the main sponsors of the week-end gathering of Yorkshire authors from all parts of the kingdom which assembled in Bradford in 1939. He was an honorary LL.D. of Leeds University, of which he had been such a constant benefactor.

He was knighted in 1931.

In 1909 he married Sophia Amelia, daughter of the late Maurice Marks, of Worksop, Nottinghamshire, and there were three sons and a daughter of the marriage, all of whom survive him.

September 23, 1952.

Dr. Fritz Busch, who died suddenly in London at the age of 61 on September 14, 1951, was a conductor of the front rank, and his loss to the art of music will be felt the world over.

Though a German, steeped in the great German tradition, he had a catholicity of taste which enabled him to serve first his native land and then Britain, after the tragic disruption of German music by Hitler, in the work he did to make Glyndebourne unique. He served also Latin America, in his tenure of office at the Buenos Aires Opera, and more recently Denmark, where he trained the Danish State Radio Orchestra, which he conducted at the Edinburgh Festival in 1950 and was to have conducted at the Festival Hall in the week he died.

Fritz Busch came of a musical family—his brother is Adolf Busch, the violinist and leader of the Busch String Quartet, in which their younger brother, Hermann, is the cellist. He was born at Siegen, Westphalia, on March 13, 1890. In 1905 he entered the Cologne school of music, and made such progress that, in1909, he was made conductor of the State Theatre at Riga, and three years later started on successful tours of the world's capitals. In 1914 he was called up, got a commission, distinctions, and was wounded. After the war he was appointed General Director of Music at the Stuttgart National Theatre; in 1922 he moved, in the same capacity, to the more ample opportunities of Dresden.

His reign at Dresden was brought to a sudden end by an uproar engineered by the Nazis after an incident in which he had shown impatience with a singer who had greeted him with the Nazi salute. He promptly left Dresden, realizing more quickly than most Germans the true nature of the new spirit abroad in the land. He promptly found an equivalent position at the Teatro Colon in Buenos Aires which, however, he soon exchanged for the musical direction of the Copenhagen State Radio.

John Christie* engaged him for his new venture at Glyndebourne in 1934 and Dr. Busch at once established his reputation in Britain as a virile, faithful and extremely skilful interpreter of Mozart.

When Copenhagen fell into Hitler's hands he migrated to America, where he wrote his memoirs, which were published in 1946. Although he was less well known on English concert platforms than his brother, his return to Glyndebourne in 1950 was warmly welcomed because his constant collaboration with Carl Ebert, as producer, made the Glyndebourne operas unique in their musico-dramatic unity.

In 1951 he conducted the whole of the Glyndebourne season in four Mozart operas and the whole of the Edinburgh Festival's operatic programme consisting of *Don Giovanni* and Verdi's *La Forza del Destino.* His beat, like his bearing, was one of quiet authority; his interpretations were fully alive without fuss or idiosyncrasy but devoted wholly to the projection of the music as he conceived the composer to have intended it.

September 17, 1951.

Dr. E. M. Butler, D.LITT., Professor Emeritus of Cambridge University, died in London on November 13, 1959 at the age of 73.

Eliza Marian Butler was one of the few women of her generation who made a great mark in academic life and won for herself a special position in the small and special world where learning and letters are united. She came of an Anglo-Irish family, but her father, Theobald Fitzwalter Butler, after failing to make a fortune in Australia, settled in Lancashire, where Eliza Butler, the third daughter, was born on December 29, 1885. He had strong, if eccentric, views on the education of his children, and Elsie, as everyone called her, was sent to school first in Germany and then in Paris, and finally in Cheltenham. More by accident than by predilection she found herself teaching German, though she had no great love for the Germans and thought most of them both absurd and dangerous—an impression formed by her youthful knowledge of the Kaiser's Germany and confirmed by later events. She was an excellent linguist, thoroughly at home not only in German and French but later in Russian and Italian, and she had a great love for the best literature of all countries. But in a specialized academic society she had to teach where teaching was needed, and German happened to provide her first opportunity for a post.

Miss Butler began her career as an assistant lecturer at Newnham College, Cambridge, where her deep admiration for Jane Harrison and Pernel Strachey blinded her to the narrowness which is liable to hamper learned ladies gathered in a single college. When the 1914-18 War came she saw many of her predictions fulfilled, but her professional interest in German made her suspect to the Cambridge police, who accused her of signalling to the enemy. She found a happy release from war conditions at home by serving with the Scottish Women's Hospitals in Russia and Macedonia. In later years she looked back on this time as the happiest in her life.

She returned to Newnham in 1920, but found it changed; and her ironical, playful spirit fretted in a society from which her old friends had departed. She comforted herself by hard work and in 1926 produced a solid and scholarly work, *The Saint-Simonian Religion.* She claimed that nobody read it, but it was in fact highly readable, as everything that she wrote always was, but the subject was perhaps too far from the main road to attract students or even dons. She followed it in 1929 with *The Tempestuous Prince,* about Bückler-Muskau, which shocked some of her colleagues by its levity but remains a charming, perceptive, and learned account of an extraordinary man. Forced as she was by circumstances to write about Germany, she tended to choose subjects off the beaten track which appealed to her taste for the unusual, but in *The Tyranny of Greece over Germany* she struck home in her distrust of "Germanentum" and exposed the fallacy that the German notion of Hellenism has been a liberating force for Germans.

In 1936 she was appointed professor of German at Manchester University; in 1945 she returned to Cambridge as Schröder Professor of German, and held the post till her retirement in 1951. She was an excellent lecturer, lively, stimulating, and learned. She carried bravely the burden of committees and examinations. She opened the eyes of her students not only to what was best in German literature but to much beyond it, and especially to a humane and tolerant vision of life. She continued to write with unbated zest—studies of Heine, Goethe, and the Faust legend—and in *Rainer Maria Rilke* (1940) produced a most perceptive and sympathetic study of genius at work.

Among her later works, *The Myth of the Magus* (1947) and *Ritual Magic* (1949) reflected another side of her character, but had the same distinction and originality. She also published two not very good novels, and, in 1959, a delightful volume of reminiscences, *Paper Boats.*

Dr. Butler's Irish origin gave her a degree of high spirits which made those duller than herself think that she was not always serious enough about her work. She was in fact extremely serious, worked very hard, and was most careful to get her facts right. Her originality and much of her appeal lay in her imaginative and literary power. She saw her subjects through her own unusual and often mocking vision, and she left the impression that even the most distinguished men could be absurdly silly at times. Yet just for this reason she brought life into themes which seemed to have been sunk for ever in a bog of excessive learning, and behind her gaiety there was indeed a most human and courageous personality. She believed in liberty and in the good things of life, and she made no compromise or concession in her long struggle for them. She was the most enchanting companion, provocative, encouraging, witty, and wise. Among the learned ladies produced by Cambridge she has a very high place.

Dr. Butler was an honorary D.Litt. of London and Oxford universities.

November 14, 1959.

Sir Harold Butler, K.C.M.G., C.B., one of the founders and later director of the International Labour Office at Geneva and the first Warden of Nuffield College, Oxford, died at Reading on March 26, 1951 at the age of 67.

Coming from an academic home, he would have been happy and useful in an academic career. He had a scholarly mind and the disposition which enables a man to plan out his work and then proceed to execute it without haste or worry. These qualities, coupled with a personality which made him always respected and effective in common-room, conference, and interview, were invaluable in the career of public administration which occupied so many of the most fruitful years of his life. Industrious and devoted and easy to get on with, he was courageous and insistent when some issue of principle arose. It is no secret that his resignation from the I.L.O. was largely due to increasing efforts to appoint men to the higher posts for political ends, which, in his view, would defeat the purposes of good administration, though a greater inducement for him to resign was the offer of the post of Warden of the new Nuffield College at Oxford. It was, perhaps, the greatest disappointment of his life that the exigencies of war took him away from a most congenial task.

Harold Beresford Butler was the eldest son of the late Dr. A. J. Butler, the noted classical scholar and sometime Bursar of Brasenose College, Oxford. He was born on October 6, 1883, and was educated at Eton and Balliol College, Oxford, where he was Brackenbury Scholar and Jenkyns Exhibitioner. After taking a first in *Literae Humaniores* in 1905 he was elected a Fellow of All Souls and in 1907 joined the old Local Government Board. In the next year he was transferred to the Home Office. Having in the meantime entered the Territorial Army, he applied for permission to join his unit on the outbreak of war in 1914, but, though he pursued his case to the extent of obtaining an interview with the Home Secretary, his services were considered too valuable for the Civil Service to lose. Though he was grievously disappointed at the time, there is no doubt that his continued contact with his chief, the late Sir Malcolm Delevingne, himself a pioneer in international labour relations, was of material benefit to the development of Butler's own ideas and achievements in that sphere.

He was largely responsible for the memorandum submitted by the British Government to the Peace Conference in 1919, which did much to pave the way for the drafting of Part XIII of the Treaty of Versailles. Butler was assistant general secretary to the Commission on International Labour Legislation, and, armed with the memorandum he had taken a large part in drafting, did his work so well that Part XIII (the "Labour Charter"), by which the International Labour Office was set up, agreed substantially with the British proposals. It was only by a narrow margin of votes and a manoeuvre which took many members of the governing body by surprise that the late M. Albert Thomas was preferred to Butler as the first director of the organization. The circumstances of his own election made Thomas at the outset suspicious of the man whom with some hesitation he made his deputy director; and Butler had this added difficulty that, though he had already won a reputation for imaginative and creative ability, he had now in some sort to become a restraining influence upon an explosive genius.

If Thomas deserves credit for the way he modified his original attitude, Butler deserves no less for his loyal acceptance of a difficult situation and his development of it into a close partnership unsuspected by the world at large. Each learned from the other and in the end became perfectly complementary. When the partnership was dissolved by Thomas's sudden death in 1932, Butler was the obvious successor and quickly showed that the qualities that had won him distinction a dozen years before had been laid aside, not lost. His quiet mastery of his subject contrasted with Thomas's oratorical brilliance but was no less effective, and the record of ratifications of conventions continued to show progress. Nobody, perhaps, could have kept Germany and Italy in the organization; Butler, however, met the challenge and called in the New World to redress the balance of the Old. His great achievement in bringing in the United States, which was not in the League of Nations, was amplified and extended by his practical appreciation of the importance of all the non-European countries.

He had been offered the task of organizing Nuffield College, and returned to Oxford to enter upon his new duties in 1939. He had time to do little more than collect a nucleus of Visiting Fellows, find and commission an architect, and begin to make plans for dovetailing the new society with Oxford when war broke out. Founding a college is not a thing to be hurried, but time to work out his plans thoroughly was not granted him and very soon he was taken away to serve as Regional Commissioner at Reading. He succeeded in securing his release from that post late in 1941 so that he could take part in the war-time activities of the nascent organization at Oxford, and for a time worked in close harmony with Professor G. D. H. Cole [q.v.], who was later appointed Sub-Warden. He was, however, again called away in 1942 to take charge of the British Information Service in the United States, and, realizing that he would have no chance of carrying out any plans he might make (since the retiring age would end his term of office in 1946), he insisted on resigning the Wardenship.

In Washington, where he held the rank of Minister, he was no stranger, and his record in international affairs was such as to earn him an enthusiastic welcome. By concentrating on unadorned information about what the British people were doing and enduring he succeeded in counteracting the results of enemy propaganda and of the inevitable indifference of the man in the street to events taking place so far away. On their side, the Americans soon learned that British information was to be trusted and used it more and more to build up the morale of their own people.

After the end of the war he took no new post but was very active in the movement for the Council of Europe and travelled extensively in Europe and America. Previously he had been too much immersed in administration to give rein to his bent for writing, though occasional articles in *The Times*, notably his character sketch of the late J. G. Winant (his successor as director of the I.L.O.), when the latter was appointed United States Ambassador to the Court of St. James's, and his book *The Lost Peace*, on the inter-war years, proved his ability. With the cares of office behind him, he hoped to be able to write more extensively, and the first fruits of this ambition, *Confident Morning*, a striking and original volume of reminiscences, was published a few months before he died.

He married in 1910 Olive, the youngest daughter of Mr. S. A. W. Waters. She proved a sterling and sympathetic helpmate throughout their long and happy partnership, and was a vivacious and indefatigable hostess. There were two sons and a daughter of the marriage.

March 28, 1951.

Sir Montagu Butler, K.C.S.I., C.B., C.I.E., C.V.O., C.B.E., formerly Master of Pembroke College, Cambridge, Mayor of Cambridge, Governor for two terms of the Central Provinces, India, and later Lieutenant-Governor of the Isle of Man, died at Cambridge on November 7, 1952 at the age of 79.

Montagu Sherard Dawes Butler was the third of the 10 sons of Spencer Percival Butler (1828-1915), Conveyancing Counsel to the Office of Works. Three of his brothers were also knighted for public services. At Haileybury, which he entered in 1886, he distinguished himself in fencing and rifle shooting, and was racquets and paperchase captain. At Pembroke College, Cambridge, where he was a scholar, he took a first-class in the Classical Tripos, Parts I and II, with special distinction in the latter, and he was University Bhaonagar Medallist. He was president of the Union, a distinction in which he was in due time followed by his elder and only surviving son, R. A. Butler, the Chancellor of the Exchequer [later Lord Butler of Saffron Walden].

He passed the Indian Civil Service examination of 1895, and went out to the Punjab at the close of the next year. He was settlement officer of the Kotah State in 1904, and later was on special duty, successively, under the Foreign and Financial Departments of the Government of India, and was then Deputy Home Secretary. In the autumn of 1912 he was made joint secretary of the Royal Commission on the Public Services in India, of which the late Lord Islington was chairman. As Deputy Commissioner of Attock in the 1914-18 war, he took an active part in the Punjab recruitment drive for the Indian Army. When the Montagu-Chelmsford Reforms came in, in 1921, he was made President of the enlarged Legislative Council of the province. Some 18 months later he was appointed Secretary to the Government of India in the Department of Education, Health, and Lands, and in the spring of 1924 he was selected to be President of the Council of State.

Early in 1925 Butler went to Nagpur as Governor of the Central Provinces, his elder brother, the late Sir Harcourt Butler, being then Governor of Burma. "Monty" had not Harcourt's social *flair* but had a like knack in the handling of men. The sterile nature of non-cooperation was now beginning to be appreciated, and in the 1926 elections the Swarajists, who had been in the majority, retained less than a quarter of the total seats. To the composing of wrangles and the greater efficiency of administration Butler brought tireless energy and high ambition. He made a gap in the ranks of non-cooperation by appointing S. B. Tambe, hitherto a leader of the Swarajists, the Home Member, and later Tambe acted for four months as Governor. Other ardent disciples of the Gandhian cult were turned into loyal cooperators through the tonic effect of responsibility for administration. Towards the close of his five years' tenure Butler was reappointed for another full term.

Confronted by the revival throughout British India of the civil disobedience campaign, he met the challenge with patience and restraint. So far as possible recourse was had to the ordinary law, and the special Ordinances issued by the Government of India were very little used. The Governor did his utmost to uphold the spirit of the Constitution and invited non-official opinion even on the "reserved" side of the dyarchial system. Further, he took prompt and energetic measures to meet the economic depression so general in the early thirties. He had the great advantage of the support of a gifted wife, whom he had married in 1901. She was Ann, youngest daughter of a well-known publicist of former days, Dr. George Smith, C.I.E. Their family comprised two sons and two daughters. Lady Butler was Chief Commissioner of Girl Guides in India, and hospital and health development in the Central Provinces were her constant preoccupation. In 1929 she was awarded the Kaisar-i-Hind medal, 1st class.

In the autumn of 1933 Butler resigned to become Lieutenant-Governor of the Isle of Man. To the problems and peculiarities of Manxland his energy and resource were zealously applied. Some labour trouble led up to a brief general strike, but very soon both employers and employed rallied to the Lieutenant-Governor. He left the island at the end of September 1937 on his election as Master of Pembroke College, Cambridge. He had been elected a Fellow before going out to India, and from 1925 had been an honorary Fellow. The choice was the more appropriate from the long connexion with Cambridge of a family which had provided four generations of double firsts.

Thus Butler had a congenial sphere; Pembroke had lately suffered a disastrous series of losses and he quickly applied himself to a reorganization of college finance. When war broke out in 1939 he tackled the many problems which arose with characteristic speed and thoroughness. The town, like the university, was not slow to recognize his powers, and he served on the borough council, being elected mayor in the autumn of 1941. He was also on the Council of the Senate and the Financial Board. Early in 1943 his younger son, Jock, who had entered upon a career of great promise at the Home Office, was killed almost immediately after being commissioned in the Royal Air Force. This was a heart-breaking blow; but Butler's indomitable sense of duty sustained him in carrying out his many war-time tasks with undiminished vigour and he naturally took a deep pride in the brilliant achievement of his elder son.

His term of office as master having been extended to the statutory limit, Butler retired in 1948, but he remained in Cambridge as Senior Fellow of Pembroke, and there was no decline in his interest in, and affection for, the college. Though he was a man of affairs rather than of learning, Butler had a profound respect for scholarship, and probably the achievement in which he took most pride was his distinction in the second part of the Classical Tripos. Still greater was his pride in his college, to which he rejoiced to devote the energies of his later years.

November 8, 1952.

Sydney Elizabeth Butler (Mrs. R. A. Butler), wife of the Right Hon. R. A. Butler [later Lord Butler of Saffron Walden], died on December 9, 1954 at her home, Stanstead Hall, in Essex, at the age of 52.

Sydney Elizabeth Butler was born on August 24, 1902, the only daughter of Samuel Courtauld, head of the great manufacturing house of Courtauld; and the strength and poise manifest in her bearing throughout all her days were drawn from a long line of forebears, masters in their own right.

She married, at 24, into another notable family, this time of scholars, the Butlers, of Cambridge. From that day the marriage became one of those entirely successful things about which, as Chesterton once said in another context, nothing whatever is chronicled. The two halves made a whole.

Her family came originally from a potent French stock, such as so often enriched the life of this island. Le Sieur Pierre Courtauld, merchant, Huguenot, is noted as residing in the Isle of Oleron, off La Rochelle, in the 1680s. His son, Augustine Courtauld, fled to England at the time of the Revocation of the Edict of Nantes. Augustine's son and grandson were goldsmiths and silversmiths in London. The grandson, Samuel Courtauld the First, still attended the French Church. His wife, too, was French, Louisa Ozier, born in Poitou. Her father was a silk weaver in London; and here in 1750, so long ago, began the Courtauld connexion with silk. George Courtauld, his son, entered the silk trade in earnest, as an apprentice throwster, in 1775; and the long story of Courtaulds thereafter belongs to the industrial history of England.

This family history is inseparable from any biography, however short, of Sydney Courtauld. For she incarnated, both in mind and body, this long tradition. She had the craftsman's delight in lovely work. The French pictures—Cézanne, Seurat, Renoir, Manet—which she inherited from her father, were to her an endless pleasure and inspiration. She was chairman of the Home House Trustees, under London University, and maintained her general interest in art, both there and in connexion with the National Art-Collections Fund. But she had also the craftsman's pleasure in the use of her hands.

She had a student's brain; she left Newnham in 1924 with a degree in history. Her interest in music, which was intense, was intellectual as well as emotional. But the strong blood of her ancestors precluded the possibility of her becoming any kind of blue-stocking. The very name, Sydney Butler, conceded to her by common consent, carried the stamp of energy, of individuality. Here was the mistress of the house, the manager of the farm. Here was the matriarch, mother of three sons and a daughter. Here was the rider to hounds, the country-woman; here, above all, was the clear, direct knowledge of her surroundings and her ideals, which was her hall-mark. This great managing power expressed itself notably in the organization of a wide home life, which she shared, in particular, with friends—to whom she was as staunch as steel—rather than with acquaintances.

She would not bow her head to circumstance, not an inch; not even at the end. During the war she maintained the household at Stanstead at full pitch. But there was, deep and pervading, a gentler strain. She not only ran a wartime house, with three young sons and a baby daughter. She added to their number a little Polish boy, a refugee; of whom one can only say that she had, thereafter, four sons, instead of three.

Needless to say, she was interested in politics; and, as in all her walks of life, interested in the techniques as well as the ideals. She was good on the doorstep, good on the platform. And both were needed, for agricultural Essex is no Tory preserve. Yet she enjoyed getting off that string; and nothing pleased her more than to meander off across the Continent by car, with such of the family as could be collected, and to cut herself adrift from mails and telegrams.

She was dark, slight, short, vital. Her eyes sparkled, lighting up her whole face. She had a certainty of movement which made her stand out in any company. But her essential quality was of that aim. She flew like an arrow. None of this has any meaning apart from her setting; which was that of her family; her husband, her sons, and her daughter, a unit complete in itself, interested in the outside world, but finding it in no way essential. It is a paradox, for one so deep in public life. But without that paradox, no public life can reach its highest point.

December 10, 1954.

Frank Butters, who died in December 1957, at the age of 78, was one of the great racehorse trainers. He won 15 English classic races and was on 35 occasions second or third.

With Bahram he won the triple crown, the 2,000 Guineas, the Derby, and the St. Leger, and in addition he trained classic winners in Ireland, Austria, Hungary, Germany and Italy. Bahram, who was never beaten, won nine races, worth £39,686.

Butters won the Derby two years in succession with Bahram and Mahmoud. His other classic winners in England were the 1,000 Guineas with Fair Isle; the 2,000 Guineas with Bahram; the Oaks with Beam, Toboggan, Udaipur, Light Brocade, Steady Aim, and Masaka; and the St. Leger with Fairway, Firdaussi, Bahram, Turkhan and Tehran. He was the leading trainer in England on seven occasions, and in these years alone he won stakes to the value of £419,716.

Born near Vienna, he was the eldest son of Joe Butters, who trained on the Continent. Young Butters was sent to England to be educated, and then returned to Austria and assisted his father for three years before becoming private trainer to Mautner de Markhom. He won the Austrian and Hungarian Derbies with San Geraro, and subsequently nearly every race of any importance on the Continent.

After the First World War he went to Italy and took charge of the Raza Bellatta stud. During his stay in that country he won nearly 1,500 races, including all the classics. In 1926 he became assistant to George Lambton at Newmarket and the following year was appointed trainer of Lord Derby's horses under Lambton's management. His success was immediate, but the arrangement lasted for only four years because of the owner's decision to cut his racing expenses. Butters then found himself unemployed at the age of 52. He set up as a public trainer, rented Fitzroy House at Newmarket from Sir Victor Sassoon* and quickly made his mark again. He was later able to purchase the property.

He began to train for the Aga Khan [q.v.] in 1931 and during that year, with only 17 horses, he won £17,545 in stakes.

In 1932 Butters had a remarkable training achievement. He ran four horses for the Aga Khan in the St. Leger and they finished first, second, fourth and fifth. Two years later he won nine of the 28 races run at Ascot. They were worth £19,350.

At that time he had one of the most brilliant collections of two-year-olds ever seen in one stable. They were all winners and included Bahram. They largely contributed to the £88,843 won by the trainer in stake money in 1934.

If asked to name the best horse he ever trained, Butters would plump for Fairway, which he insisted was superior even to Bahram. This horse was upset by the crowd at Epsom before competing in the Derby, but he won the St. Leger, Eclipse Stakes and the Champion Stakes (twice). At the stud Fairway has proved a great stallion. He was champion in 1936, 1939, 1943 and 1944. He sired the Derby winners Blue Peter and Watling Street.

Frank Butters was one of the very great trainers of this century. He did not spare his horses in the matter of work, and it was often hinted by critics that he overdid their training. The fact remains that the results he achieved were remarkable. He did not believe in waiting until the actual race to find out whether his representative was good enough. By means of stripped gallops and full dress trials he knew the capabilities of his horses with astonishing accuracy, and when he said that he thought he would win he was rarely wrong. His unlucky accident when returning from superintending work on the Heath caused his retirement at a much earlier date than expected, for he carried his years lightly then.

January 2, 1958.

Dr. P. A. Buxton, C.M.G., F.R.S., who died at his home at Gerrards Cross, Buckinghamshire, on December 13, 1955 at the age of 63, had been director of the Department of Entomology at the London School of Hygiene and Tropical Medicine since 1925 and Professor of Medical Entomology in the University of London since 1933. He was one of the world's leading authorities on the relation of insects to human and animal disease, and was especially noted for his work on the tsetse fly and trypanosomiasis.

Patrick Alfred Buxton was born on March 24, 1892, the eldest son of the late Alfred

Fowell Buxton, banker and sometime chairman of the London County Council, by his wife Violet, daughter of the Very Rev. T. W. Jex-Blake, D.D., headmaster of Rugby and afterwards Dean of Wells. He was educated at Rugby School and at Trinity College, Cambridge, where he read the Natural Sciences Tripos. He was a Fellow of his college from 1916 to 1921. Having completed his medical training at St. George's Hospital, he qualified as M.R.C.S., L.R.C.P. in 1917 and saw war service in Mesopotamia and N.W. Persia. He obtained the Cambridge Diploma in Tropical Medicine and Hygiene in 1921 and then accepted the appointment of entomologist to the Government of Palestine. He held this post for two years and was then selected to lead a medical and scientific expedition to Samoa.

The years 1924 and 1925 were spent in Samoa, Tonga, the Ellice Islands, and the New Hebrides in the investigation of hygienic conditions, prevailing diseases, and insects of medical importance. The knowledge gained on this expedition enabled Buxton to produce two volumes of *Researches in Polynesia and Melanesia* (1927-28), which were published under the auspices of the London School of Hygiene and Tropical Medicine, and a monograph on *Insects of Samoa and other Samoan Terrestrial Arthropoda* for the British Museum of Natural History in 1935. He later made several journeys to Africa to study the tsetse fly problem, to which he made great contributions, and his life-work culminated in his memoirs on *Trypanosomiasis in Eastern Africa* (1948) and *The Natural History of Tsetse Flies,* a volume of 800 pages which was published only in 1955.

Buxton was elected a Fellow of the Royal Society in 1943 and in 1947 he was made a C.M.G. He was a member of the Medical Research Council and of the Colonial Medical Research Committee, and a Fellow of the Royal Society of Tropical Medicine and Hygiene. In 1953 he was awarded the Linnean Gold Medal. He married Muryell Gladys, fourth daughter of the late Rev. Hon. Talbot Rice. Of this marriage there were two sons and four daughters; one of the sons predeceased his father.

December 15, 1955.

Rear-Admiral R. E. Byrd, the distinguished American explorer and airman, died on March 11, 1957 at his home in Boston, Massachusetts. He was 68.

Richard Evelyn Byrd, second son of Richard Evelyn Byrd and his wife Eleanor Bolling, *née* Flood, was born at Winchester, Virginia, on October 25, 1888, of an old Virginia family. At the age of 12, when he visited Manila, he insisted on returning home by India and Europe, thus travelling round the world.

Educated at the Virginia Military Academy, the University of Virginia, and the United States Naval Academy, where he was a noted footballer, Byrd was appointed an ensign in the United States Navy in 1912. After some three years' service, during which he twice saved the lives of drowning men and showed both ability and originality as an officer, he was retired, much to his chagrin, on account of a broken ankle incurred years before at football. Soon afterwards, when the United States entered the war in 1916, he was recalled for departmental work, but in autumn 1917 succeeded in being sent to learn flying at the U.S. Naval Air Station in Pensacola. There he revealed unusual talent, particularly on the technical side, and some of the scientific devices used in his later expeditions were first planned at this time. During the last five months of the war he was a commander in the United States Air Force, and was on duty at Halifax, Nova Scotia, but he retired after the war.

Thenceforward aviation and the improvement of the navigating instruments used in flying were his chief study. In 1921 he was in England, and just missed going up in the [airship] R38, which exploded over the Humber.

In 1925 he accompanied the Macmillan Expedition to Etah, in West Greenland, and with Floyd Bennett as a companion traversed in an aeroplane some 3,000 miles of the region north-west of Etah. This first experience of Polar flying proved invaluable to him later. In April 1926 50 volunteers led by Byrd and equipped by the United States Navy Department, the United States Shipping Board, the National Geographic Society and private patrons, sailed from Brooklyn for King's Bay, Spitsbergen. Thence Byrd and his pilot, Floyd Bennett, were to attempt a flight to the North Pole in a three-engined Fokker monoplane. May was chosen for the attempt since, though it is the coldest month in the Arctic, it is the time of least fog. On arrival at Spitsbergen the only available berth was found to be occupied by a Norwegian ship. The aeroplane had to be taken ashore over shifting ice by means of a raft of planks and boats, and for several days the crew worked 24 hours at a stretch to prepare a track from which the aeroplane could take off.

On May 9 the flight was begun in brilliant sunshine, which made steering and the estimation of drift comparatively easy. An hour from the Pole an oil leak started in the third motor, but when Byrd wrote a note to the pilot asking what could be done, there came the reply that they would get to the Pole first and then discuss the matter. Actually the motor did not stop, and the flight to the North Pole and back to King's Bay, 1,360 miles, was accomplished in 15½ hours. A great welcome awaited the expedition on its return to New York. The freedom of the city was conferred on both Byrd and Bennett, President Coolidge presented to Byrd the National Geographic Society's Hubbard gold medal (awarded only four times before) for "valour in exploration", and to Bennett the society's special gold medal, and Byrd was given the rank of commander (retired) in the United States Navy.

In June 1927, after many experiments with Fokker aeroplanes, during which he broke his arm and Floyd Bennett was seriously injured, Byrd, with three companions—Bert Acosta, Lieutenant Noville, and Bernt Balchen—decided to attempt a transatlantic flight from New York to Paris, following the steamship lines, a longer route than that taken by Lindbergh*, but one on which they were less likely to encounter high winds or fogs. The flight, begun on June 29, must have been a nightmare, for the Atlantic proved to be blanketed in fog. Although every air station in France was watching for the American aeroplane, it eventually came down in the sea 200 yards from the shore at Ver-sur-Mer, Calvados, after a flight of approximately 4,200 miles in 42 hours. The crew were exhausted, having flown for hours over Britanny and Normandy, uncertain of their direction by reason of a faulty compass, and having seen neither sky nor sea since leaving America. They presented to President Doumergue a casket containing part of the original star-spangled banner, and Poincaré, the Prime Minister, made Byrd a commander of the Legion of Honour. On their return the Mayor of New York presented the crew of the America with the Medal for Valour.

In 1928 Byrd determined to make an aerial survey of the unknown regions of the Antarctic and a flight to the South Pole. The estimated cost of £171,000 was largely contributed by the American public.

In October Byrd left California for New Zealand, where the Eleanor Bolling and other ships were to meet him at Dunedin. Dunedin was left on December 2, and by Christmas Day the expeditionary party, consisting of 43 men, with three aeroplanes, a Ford, a Fokker and a Fairchild, were safely landed at the chosen base on the western shore of the Bay of Whales, in about 78° 30″S. latitude. Amundsen had used the same base, but the Americans could not have landed their aeroplanes at any other spot.

An extensive and highly equipped camp, called "Little America", was soon built. During the next three months several aeroplane flights were made, and then and in the following November and December large tracts of land lying east, north-east and south-east of the Bay of Whales were mapped from the air. These included, east of 150° W. longitude, which was the eastern boundary of the area claimed by Great Britain, the district named Marie Byrd Land, the Edsel Ford Mountains, and the Rockefeller Range, which consists of some 40 peaks of granite and pre-Cambrian rock rising to over 2,000ft. West of the 150° line Byrd named a tract lying between 150° and 155° W. longitude Scott Land in memory of his heroic predecessor, and "the Matterhorn" an outlier of the Rockefeller Range. In these flights, which were always carried out in close touch, by wireless, with the base, the pilots where Byrd himself, Harold June and Bernt Balchen, while Captain Ashley McKinley took the photographs. The coastline N.E. of the Bay of Whales, extending up to King Edward VII Land, was also gradually mapped for some 400 miles.

From April to November the winter darkness kept the expedition inactive, but on November 25-29 Byrd, with Balchen as his pilot, June as wireless operator, and McKinley as photographer, made a flight in the Ford aeroplane to the South Pole and back, a distance of 1,600 miles. He dropped on the Pole the United States flag wrapped round a stone from the grave of his companion in the North Polar flight, Floyd Bennett. At 86° S. latitude the aeroplane had to rise to 11,000ft. to clear a great complex of mountains ("The Hump") which rises about Axel Heiberg and Liv Glaciers, and this was accomplished only by throwing out some hundreds of pounds of reserve provisions.

Meanwhile a geological party led by Professor Lawrence Gould had sledged southwards on November 19, and before their return in the following January the members had reached 86° 27′′ S. latitude, explored Mount Nansen, and examined several ranges east of it.

In February much anxiety was felt about the expedition, as its supplies were nearly exhausted and the Ross Sea was so packed with ice that it was dangerous for a ship to enter; but Captain Melville, of the City of New York, after a battle with ice and storms which lasted several days, succeeded in getting his ship into the Bay of Whales and in taking the whole party off, although the aeroplanes had to be left behind.

Honours were now heaped upon Byrd. President Hoover* had already conferred upon him the rank of rear-admiral (retired) in the United States Navy, and to the medals which he had previously received—the Congressional Medal of Honour, the Congressional Life Saving Medal, and the Medal of Honour—the Royal Geographical Society added the Patron's Medal. He published a full account of the work done by his expedition in *Little America* (1930), to which Professor Gould contributed a chapter on the geological survey.

A second Antarctic expedition followed in 1933, its objects being to map and claim land areas about the Pole, to determine what natural resources could be utilized by man, and to study weather and geological conditions. Seventy members, including the scientists and crew, took part. The start was again made from New Zealand, but the expedition's two ships, the Jacob Ruppert and the Bear of Oakland, encountered great difficulties in entering the Bay of Whales, and the party was not established at Little America until February 1934. An advanced camp was planned 400 miles south of Little America, where two or three scientists, isolated from the world except by wireless, would spend the Antarctic winter taking meteorological observations. Weather, however, made it impossible to proceed farther than 123 miles southward, and then there were supplies for only one man. Byrd therefore decided to remain completely alone there for seven months in order to obtain a continuous meteorological record. On March 28 he was left at his post, called Bolling Base. On June 20 the main party were alarmed by a wireless request from Byrd to send tractors to fetch him back as he had "a bad arm" and only his hand wireless set was working.

Winter darkness still reigned, there were frequent blizzards, and the temperature was about 71° below zero when the tractor expedition, commanded by Dr. Thomas Poulter, set off to the rescue on June 24. The attempt, and a second one on August 6, were unsuccessful. The third attempt was made on August 9, again under Poulter, and after the rescuers had fought their way for 66 hours through darkness and over most difficult ridges and crevasses they sighted the beacon burning over Byrd's hut. He had hot soup waiting for them, although himself almost too weak to stand as a result of fumes from his kerosene stove, which had made him ill in June. From that time he had been unable to use the stove or to cook proper food, though the temperature was at times 80° below zero. Nevertheless he had continued his meteorological observations. So near was he to death that he left notes (afterwards concealed) for the tractor party in case they should not arrive in time.

In November a flight by Byrd and June seemed to confirm the admiral's opinion that the Antarctic was not a single unbroken continent, but that a sea-level passage divided the land masses of the Pacific Quadrant and the Queen Maud Range in about 170° E. longitude. After a further survey eastward he reported seeing a vast plateau east and south of the Edsel Ford mountain range (75° to 78° S.) and adjoining Marie Byrd Land. This plateau, in his opinion, was the long-sought connexion between the mountains of western Antarctica and the Andes. In December the geological party, led by Quin Blackburn, reported the discovery of coal and fossils at the head of the Thorne Glacier in the Queen Maud Range, 182 nautical miles from the Pole.

His party had sighted many new mountains and glaciers, but their activities had been hindered by continuous violent winds. Nevertheless, they had established the fact that the plateau encircling the South Pole was connected with the recently discovered Marie Byrd Land, as Byrd had thought, and that the Leverett Glacier in the Queen Maud Range was really a sub-plateau, 2,500ft. above sea-level. From within 20 miles of the head of the Thorne Glacier no mountains were visible to the southward, and the mountains to the east bore north-eastward and seemed to diminish gradually in height.

In 1946, with 13 vessels, 4,000 men and 17 aircraft, Byrd went south once more and much useful exploration was carried out. On his return in March 1947 310,000 square miles of the Antarctic had been discovered and mapped by the airmen, and 535,000 square miles of little known areas, of which 15 per cent had probably never been seen before, had been mapped. A month earlier he had flown yet again over the South Pole, in company with another aircraft, dropping, *en passant,* a carton containing flags of all the 54 states belonging to the United Nations.

Byrd had been appointed head of the United States Navy's operation Deep Freeze in Antarctica some time before, but had been ill for several months, and so had been unable to take over direct supervision of the area.

His last visit to Antarctica was 14 months before he died, when he made his third flight over the Pole.

March 13, 1957.

C

James Branch Cabell, the American novelist, author of *Jurgen, Figures of Earth,* and other fantasies, died on May 5, 1958 at the age of 79.

Cabell's novels were, perhaps, very much a matter of taste. Those that were most highly esteemed by his admirers, the novels which had for setting the imaginary medieval realm of Poictesme, combined allegory with an elaborate and somewhat old-fashioned turn of rhetoric in a spirit of high romantic disillusionment.

Cabell brought invention and gusto, as well as a habit of irony that seemed to derive from Anatole France, to his variations on the themes of the old chap-books and books of *gestes*, and at his happiest provided gracefully light and amusing reading. But the total effect of his rather too fluent work, marked as it was by doubtful poetry, discreet impropriety, and easy pessimism, seemed to the more critical reader thin and unsatisfying.

However, until recent years he had a faithful public, who were not put off by either the monotony of the ancient trappings he affected or the vagueness of his symbolism. It was larger in the United States than in Britain, though after the publication of *Jurgen* most of the volumes he had produced during the preceding 15 years were duly brought out in England.

He was born in Richmond, Virginia, the old Confederate capital, on April 14, 1879, the son of Robert Gamble Cabell and Anne Branch, whose families were among the oldest of colonial days. His sentiment of pride where Richmond (the "Lichfield" of his earlier novels) and the South were concerned was always strong, and he achieved no little fame in his own state as a genealogist and local historian.

He graduated at the oldest college in the United States, William and Mary, in Williamsburg, and was for two years an instructor there in French and Greek. He then engaged in journalism in Richmond, to which he returned after an interval on the staff of the *New York Herald*; abandoned journalism for the more leisurely mode of writing of his early essays in fiction—mostly short stories; engaged for a time in coal-mining in West Virginia; and, finally, settled down to work as a novelist and as a genealogist and student of Virginia's history.

His earliest volume, *The Eagle's Shadow*, appeared in 1904 and seems to have made little stir. But the decoratively opulent way with history of the short stories in *Gallantry* (1907) and *Chivalry* (1909) already carried a plain hint of what was to come. In the two or three novels that followed Cabell hesitated between a contemporary setting for his play of fancy and a more remote background, but with *The Cream of the Jest* (1917) he arrived at his characteristic style of narrative. *Jurgen* (banned for a time in several states) appeared two years later, and the rich pictorial colour, the grotesque invention, and the air of melancholy wisdom of this fabulous tale of a little pawnbroker in medieval France proved irresistible to many readers.

Cabell repeated his success in *Figures of Earth* (1921), in which the figure of Manuel the Redeemer bore a close enough resemblance to that of Jurgen, and retained the same manner throughout almost the whole of his succeeding work. Apart from the novels, *The Silver Stallion, Something About Eve, The King was in His Counting House, Hamlet had an Uncle,* and *The First American Gentleman,* in 1926 he produced a kind of apologia, *Straws and Prayer Books,* which appeared to reflect the pessimism of the disappointed novelist and which for some readers was at once more enlightening and more genuinely entertaining than his fiction. The novels of his later period include *The Witch-Woman* (1948) and *The Devil's Own Dear Son* (1949).

He married, in 1913, Priscilla Bradley, by whom he had a son. She died in 1949, and in the following year he married Margaret Waller Freeman.

May 7, 1958.

Mildred Cable, who as a member of the China Inland Mission crossed the Gobi desert five times with her two friends and colleagues, died on April 30, 1952 in London.

Mildred Cable liked to speak of her life as beginning when she went as a missionary to China shortly after the Boxer rebellion. From the time she was a schoolgirl she felt that she had a definite vocation. She held it while she was studying science in London, and when it was said that China would be closed for a long time after the Boxer trouble, her strategic mind moved her to go then—while the door was still open. The young enthusiast was sent to Eva French as a junior worker at Hwochowrin, in Shansi. Educational work was being developed among Chinese women and girls and the two missionaries took a small school, where the girls had to have unbound feet. It quickly became a large and important boarding school. For seven years they worked together and after they had been home on furlough Eva's sister, Francesca [q.v.], returned to China with them. All became convinced that they had to respond to a need in central Asia.

They obtained a roving commission from the China Inland Mission in 1926 to adapt themselves to what they found. They hired a room, where they kept their boxes, and became nomad missionaries. For 15 years thereafter they were always on the move. They went to the edge of the Gobi desert, and whenever they heard of an oasis in country not charted they went there, taking the Gospel message and Bibles in Chinese with them. They crossed the whole length of the Gobi desert five times with numerous detours. They learned to sleep anywhere; they spoke Chinese and Turki, and they found it easier always to wear Chinese dress. The local people loved them and the Muslims respected them for what Mildred Cable called "the combination of our grey hairs, celibate state, and pilgrim life".

They were not only missionaries but explorers. Each time they returned to England scientific societies and universities asked them to lecture on their findings. Although they had but one aim on their journeys—to spread the message of Christianity—yet they gathered a great deal that was of unique interest to the geographer, the archaeologist, the philologist, and the student of human nature.

When missionary work in the Gobi desert was no longer possible the travellers turned to help the British and Foreign Bible Society, which had helped them in their pioneer work. As one country after another was closing to the Bible they felt it was time to get it in before too late. Mildred Cable threw herself into organizing the women's work of the society, serving on committees for India, Asia, Australia, and Africa, and eventually became a vice-president. She also spoke a great deal to big organizations of women's societies.

During their brief holidays the three friends wrote books about their travels and tried to interpret the Chinese people to Great Britain. Mildred Cable was awarded the Lawrence of Arabia medal for 1942 for her book *The Gobi Desert*, written with Francesca French, and she was also awarded the Livingstone medal. Other books in collaboration with one or other of her friends include: *A Desert Journal; Through Jade Gate and Central Asia; China: Her Life and Her People.*

May 2, 1952.

Sir Andrew Caird, K.B.E., who died at his home in London on December 15, 1956 at the age of 86, was one of Lord Northcliffe's picked men and a powerful Fleet Street figure in the first two decades of the century.

Northcliffe once described Caird as "the Scot I employ to see that no halfpennies are wasted in my business", and it is, perhaps, as the cautious guardian of newspaper finance that Caird will be best be remembered by past generations of Fleet Street.

He was born at Montrose in 1870 and was educated at Montrose Academy and University College, Dundee. He began in journalism in Scotland, then went south to Manchester, where he worked for six guineas a week as a sub-editor on Hulton's *Daily Dispatch.* At 31 he left for London to join Lord Northcliffe's *Daily Mail.* He worked at first in the Parliamentary Press Gallery, and then, as Night Editor, he vigorously upheld the Scots sub-editorial tradition of meticulous accuracy. Many of the "young lions" on the reporting staff those days had cause to wince at his cutting criticism of their "fancy writing" when all he wanted was "facts".

There was something of the forbidding touch of the schoolmaster as he prowled round Carmelite House—always in black morning coat and usually chewing at his pipe. His shrewd dark eyes, close-cropped hair and bull-like neck gave him a severity of appearance which softened on closer acquaintance. It was not long before Northcliffe decided that Caird's flair for finance and organization should be used on the commercial as well as the editorial side. He was made a director, with a special eye on expenses. Indeed, he admitted that he was the accepted brake on Northcliffe's weakness for generosity. In 1922 he became managing director and vice-chairman of Associated Newspapers. He was also a director of Anglo-Newfoundland Company.

In 1917 he accompanied Northcliffe to the United States with the British War Mission, and he acted as administrator of the headquarters of the mission in New York. For these services he was created K.B.E. in 1919. His long service and friendship for Northcliffe were marred in 1922 when in one of his famous *communiqués* Northcliffe made a statement about Caird and another director (Walter Fish) which they considered to be libellous and a writ was served on Northcliffe; but it was withdrawn because of Northcliffe's tragic illness.

He resigned his position with Associated Newspapers in 1926, and went to India in 1927-28 to reorganize the *Statesman,* of Calcutta, and was chairman and managing director of the newspaper while he was there. On his return he twice contested the St. Ives Division of Cornwall as Conservative candidate, but was both times defeated by his Liberal opponent. During his years of success and position in London he did not forget his native town of Montrose. He was a generous benefactor of the poor and destitute of the town, and this was recalled when the freedom of Montrose was conferred on him in 1935.

Caird was one of the early representative members of the Newspaper Proprietors' Association and he gave a lively speech in July 1956 at the fiftieth anniversary of its incorporation. Those who worked with him will remember him as a man without humbug.

He married in 1896 Anne, daughter of William Davidson, of Montrose, and there were two sons and two daughters of the marriage. Lady Caird died in 1933.

December 17, 1956.

Sir James Caird, BT., who was long an active and successful shipowner but was best known generally for the prominent part he took in the restoration of H.M.S. Victory and in the formation at Greenwich of the National Maritime Museum, died on September 27, 1954 at his home in London at the age of 90. He had been a complete invalid for the last five years.

He was born on January 2, 1864, and went to Glasgow Academy. He left there in 1878 and became a junior member of the staff in Glasgow of Graham and Co., East India merchants. On going to London he joined Turnbull, Martin and Co., managers of the Scottish Shire line of steamers, for which in 1884 the Elderslie was built. She was claimed to be the first steamer specially constructed for the carriage of refrigerated meat. In 1903 Caird became sole partner of Turnbull, Martin and Co., and owner of the Shire Line, which he sold later to the Clan Line. He continued, however, to be a director of shipping and other companies.

Until the beginning of 1948 he was chairman of the Smithfield and Argentine Meat Company; then, at the forty-fifth meeting, he announced his resignation and that of three other British directors on the completion of the disposal of control of the company to the Argentine Farmers' Union (known as C.A.P.) representing 300,000 Argentine farmers. Caird continued to maintain an office in the City and attended to business daily. He remained extremely alert, had an excellent memory and was distinguished by vigour such as might be expected of a man many years younger. In the 1914-18 War Caird became chairman of the Standard Shipbuilding Company, of Chepstow.

In association with the late Admiral Sir Doveton Sturdee, who was in command at the successful naval fight at the Falkland Islands, Caird issued an appeal for the preservation of H.M.S. Victory which, in the end, he restored at his own cost. All his life Caird devoted himself and his fortune with remarkable singleness of purpose to the preservation of maritime records and relics. Not only does the National Maritime Museum owe its existence to his interest and generosity but H.M.S. Victory would not today be the attraction it is if he had not provided an initial sum of £50,000 to enable the work of restoration to begin, and again at a later date a further £15,000 so that the work could continue.

When the buildings at Greenwich were vacated by the Royal Hospital School, he offered to defray the cost—eventually nearly £80,000—of converting the class rooms and dormitories into galleries. In addition to this sum, and during the same period, he was constantly providing new exhibits to place in the galleries. He had already placed the print room on a firm foundation by his purchase of the Macpherson collection of prints, engravings, and drawings, &c., which with insurance and incidentals cost him over £108,000; and he had greatly enhanced the ship model section by his purchase of the "Mercury" collection for £30,000.

He became a keen collector in all sections of the museum, and in order to secure for the navigation room the instruments necessary to show navigational aids from the earliest times he purchased large collections from abroad as well as in Britain. Every section of the museum owes its existence to his generosity, and especially is this so with the library and manuscripts department. In 1946 the manuscripts department received the magnificent gift of the Naval MSS. from the Phillips Collection, and a little later he saved for the nation the collection of relics from Trafalgar House. His benefactions to the oil paintings department were so numerous that, were they to be removed, it would be necessary to close half the galleries of the museum as the walls would be so bare.

The efforts to save the Implacable, made in February 1949, bring to mind similar efforts to save this ship more than 25 years ago, when under the auspices of Admiral of the Fleet Sir Doveton Sturdee a "Sea Fund" was launched to enable the ship to be dry-docked and examined. On this occasion Caird provided the sum of £15,000 to cover the expense of dry-docking and repairs, which were undertaken in Devonport Dockyard, and then guaranteed the sum of £1,000 per annum for a period of 10 years to provide for her upkeep.

In 1894 he married Henrietta, daughter of the late William Stephens. She died in 1953, and he was survived by a daughter of the marriage.

September 29, 1954.

Sir Hugh Cairns, K.B.E., D.M., F.R.C.S., Nuffield Professor of Surgery in the University of Oxford, died in hospital there on July 18, 1952 at the age of 56.

Hugh William Bell Cairns was born on June 26, 1896 in South Australia. From Adelaide High School he went to Adelaide University. He served in the 1914-18 War, first in the ranks and, after taking the M.B., B.S. degrees in 1917, as a captain in the Australian Army Medical Corps, and saw active service in the Middle East and France.

He was at Balliol as a Rhodes Scholar from January 1919 until the middle of 1920, and in the latter year rowed for Oxford against Cambridge. Between 1921 and 1925 he held house appointments at the Radcliffe Infirmary, Oxford, and the London Hospital. He was Hunterian Professor at the Royal College of Surgeons in 1925, and in 1926 and 1927 was in the United States as a Rockefeller Travelling Fellow. It was then that he became a pupil and ardent disciple of Harvey Cushing and acquired the interest in neurosurgery which was to win him an international reputation. From 1926 to 1937 he was at first assistant honorary surgeon—this was an appointment for a general surgeon—and later neurosurgeon to the London Hospital.

While he remained in private practice he eschewed all the usual habits of a fashionable surgeon. He had no consulting rooms in Harley Street and made all his patients consult him at the London Hospital. Nevertheless he quickly built up a valuable practice. Though he was a surgeon of remarkable skill and originality—he was for instance the first English surgeon to remove a pineal tumour, though the operation had, quite unknown to him, been already performed in Germany and the United States—his main interests were always in the advancement of medical knowledge.

He was an active advocate of the establishment of a clinical medical school in Oxford; and when Lord Nuffield* first intimated his intention to endow the Oxford Medical School Cairns, working always cordially with Sir Farquhar Buzzard, was, it might be said, the mainspring of the scheme. Many of his early papers on the subject remain on record, and they show his remarkable prescience as to the lines of development which the school must follow, and particularly of the important part which the non-medical scientist would play in it. It was no surprise to anyone that in 1937 Cairns at the age of 41 was elected the first Nuffield Professor of Surgery in the newly expanded medical school at Oxford.

There was at that time open to him a choice of careers, with their own attractions. He already had an international reputation as a brain surgeon and could have won fame and a big income in that capacity; or he could have devoted himself to pure research and the pursuit of academic fame, free from the distractions both of practice and of teaching. He chose, however, to combine teaching and research, sacrificing leisure, fame and income in the process. He thus built up a school in which the wise and inspired but self-effacing help he gave to this work won him the devotion of generations of students.

His approach to any problem may be illustrated by one example from his work as consultant neurosurgeon to the Army, in which he held the rank of brigadier during the 1939-45 War. He devised the form of crash helmet which saved innumerable dispatch riders from injury or death; and as a by-product of the research on that question he helped to devise a leg-shield for motor-cyclists which had a remarkable effect in preventing fractures. Another of his striking successes in his work for the Army was in working out with Sir Howard [later Lord] Florey* the clinical uses of penicillin in the treatment of war wounds.

After the war his energies were for the time distracted, like those of every one in the university, by the problem of meeting peace-time demands in overcrowded buildings. Nevertheless, he found time to visit Australia and New Zealand as the first Sims Commonwealth Professor appointed by the Royal College of Surgeons, and during his tour completed the negotiations between the Australian and the English Royal Colleges, by which each college recognized the primary examinations of the other.

A later visit to the United States brought him up to date with the advances made in neurosurgery during the war. More recently he was keenly interested in surgical procedures designed to alleviate mental disease. He developed an operation which bears promise of being more selective and less damaging in its effects than others in common use. In his own department the research on which he was mainly engaged personally was the treatment of tuberculous meningitis with streptomycin; in this he made notable advances on work begun in America.

He married in 1921 Barbara Forster, daughter of the late A. L. Smith, sometime Master of Balliol. Lady Cairns survives him together with two sons and two daughters of the marriage.

July 19, 1952.

General Avila Camacho, who died on October 13, 1955 at the age of 58, was President of Mexico from 1940 to 1946, and led his country to join the United Nations in 1942.

Manuel Avila Camacho was born at Teziutlán, in the State of Puebla, on April 24, 1897, the son of a small farmer, Manuel Avila Castilla, and his wife, Euprosia Camacho de Avila. He was intended for the profession of accountancy, but in 1914 broke his course in this subject to take part in the successful rising against Huerta. Thereafter he was an army man. In many conflicts which were so long the normal accompaniment of Mexican politics he found himself on the right side. In 1923 he was fighting with Cárdenas* and Calles to suppress rebellion; in the next year he obtained special mention in dispatches for his defence of Moralia; and in the Cristero rebellion of 1927 he astonishingly met a rebel leader at an inn, and within an hour had persuaded him to lay down his arms. Even more amazing as a diplomatic feat was his purely verbal conquest of no fewer than 12 rebel generals at Michoacan in 1929.

Under President Rodriguez, Camacho served as chief of staff at the Ministry of War, and he there acted with such success that in the Administration of President Cárdenas he was made Secretary for National Defence. He did a great deal towards the modernization of the Mexican Army's equipment by purchases from the United States; and he crowned his own military career by an action against the bandit Cedillo which earned him the highest army rank.

He remained a loyal supporter of Cárdenas, and when, early in 1939, he resigned from the Cabinet to start his campaign for the presidency, he was backed not only by the Party of the Mexican Revolution but by Lombardo Toledano, head of the radical C.T.M. (Confederation of Mexican Workers). By November he had behind him not only these influential bodies but the National Farm Confederation and the Government party. He was duly elected at the polling of July 7, 1940; and though Almazán complained that his adherents had been forcibly prevented from voting, the election was confirmed, and in November President Roosevelt accredited a representative to his Government. He served his full term and was succeeded in 1946 by President Valdes.

General Camacho had a very strong scholarly strain, and was a devoted student of history, biography, and sociology. One of his favourite diversions was polo, and he kept a string of ponies and put forth a winning team in the 1936 Olympic Games. In person he was big for a Mexican, with heavily moulded features, black hair and eyes, and bushy eyebrows.

October 14, 1955.

Professor Emile Cammaerts, C.B.E., the distinguished Belgian writer, who had long made his home in Britain, for many years Professor of Belgian Studies and Institutions in the University of London, died on November 2, 1953 at his home at Radlett, Hertfordshire.

Scholar, poet, Belgian patriot, interpreter of his own country—he remained always a Belgian citizen—and, in another sense, interpreter of England also, Emile Cammaerts filled a notable and distinctive place in English life and learning, and for 40 years and more contributed as much as any man to the cultural exchanges and the strengthening of cultural ties between Britain and Belgium. His burning patriotism stamped itself deeply upon English minds in 1914, and there must be many today who remember the powerful, indeed the electrifying, effect of his poem, "Carillon", to which Elgar wrote the music, when his wife, Tita Brand-Cammaerts, recited it at the Queen's Hall in December of that fateful year. His passion of patriotism, which did not diminish between the two world wars, broke into flame again when disaster came in 1940.

Born in Brussels, Emile Cammaerts had won a reputation as a poet of fine lyrical temper before he settled in England in 1908. His verse always retained a quality of heightened simplicity, an air of enchanted innocence; at its happiest it attained a directness of imaginative experience that for an English reader was reminiscent of Blake. Besides verse and verse plays he wrote art criticism and gave early evidence of his English tastes and sympathies by translating Ruskin and G. K. Chesterton. In 1910 a fairy-tale play of his, *The Two Hunchbacks*, was produced in London. During the War of 1914-18 his poems, many of them commemorating the fighting on Belgian soil, appeared in their original French with translations from his wife's hand.

With the return of peace Cammaerts settled down to the grateful task of interpreting the Belgian past and present for English readers. A deep knowledge of English literature and an impassioned love in particular of English poetry provided constant stimulus in his interpreter's part. His *History of Belgium*, which appeared in 1921, was not a work of original research, but it exhibited wide learning and an acute grasp of cultural values and was written with fine historical imagination. In *The Treasure House of Belgium* (1924) he dealt illuminatingly with Belgian art and literature, more especially of the modern period. The other side of this labour of love was evidenced in the engaging appreciation, on a faint note of Anglomania, of *The Poetry of Nonsense* (1927), by which he meant in the first place the distinctively English tradition of nonsense of Edward Lear and Lewis Carroll. Cammaerts lectured frequently both in England and in Belgium on English themes, and his *Discoveries in England* (1930) are in a familiar vein of candid and not unflattering friendship.

He wrote profusely in the years that followed and on a great variety of subjects. There were books on Rubens and on G. K. Chesterton; a volume on *Albert of Belgium, Defender of Right*, and an informed and balanced study, entitled *The Keystone of Europe* (1939), which set the history of the Belgian dynasty against the general background of European politics; and two or three novels of a thoughtful but somewhat formless stamp. Catastrophe in Belgium in 1940 drew from him, in the year following, *The Prisoner at Laeken*, a sober and persuasive vindication of King Leopold.

The death of his son Pieter, killed while serving in the R.A.F., was a blow which brought with it an inner crisis of belief. In successive volumes, *Upon This Rock* and *The Flower of Grass,* he set down his meditations upon death and the meaning of existence and recorded his conversion from the humanist agnosticism of earlier years to an acceptance or re-acceptance of the Christian faith and ethic. In *The Peace that was Left* (1945) he submitted the world emerging into peace to the test of his restored belief and thenceforward his published work took on the character of a Christian apologist.

The Devil Takes the Chair (1949) and *For Better, For Worse* (1950) both propound the view that moral principles devoid of divine authority are not enough.

November 3, 1953.

Charles Campbell, O.B.E., director of the British Information Services in Washington, died on December 17, 1956 at Knoxville, Tennessee.

He was born in Liverpool in 1904 but spent most of his life in the United States. His father, Henry James Campbell, was the New Orleans representative of the Liverpool shipping firm of Frederick Leyland and Company.

Charles Campbell grew up in New Orleans, was educated at Tulane University, and later worked on a newspaper, the *Item*, in that city from 1923 to 1942. When war broke out in 1939 he offered his services to the British Embassy and in 1942 he joined the staff of the British Information Services in Washington.

With the late Sir Wilmot Lewis, for so many years Washington Correspondent of *The Times*, Charles Campbell was something of an institution in the complex diplomatic and journalistic world of Washington. Ambassadors and Ministers might come and go, but he seemed always to be there—to be turned to for help and advice by American and Briton alike. Such a position can be achieved only by those with a profound knowledge of the country to which they are accredited, and with the perhaps more important virtue of sensing what the citizens of that country want to know.

In their time Wilmot Lewis and Charles Campbell were certainly the most unconventional and colourful representatives of British interests, and also the most accessible. It is doubly tragic that Campbell's death should have come at a time when Anglo-American understanding needs more than ever before the personal touch of a Lewis or a Campbell in Washington, particularly in the National Press Club where over the years so many difficulties and misunderstandings have been resolved by a talk with Campbell, so many breaches prevented by his ability to sustain in a city of ever-changing values his own reputation as one who never swerved in his devotion to both Britain and the United States.

In Washington he was one of the best known and most liked men in journalistic and diplomatic circles. He was held in fond esteem as Britain's "unofficial ambassador", a role for which he was fitted not only by his intimate knowledge of American life and politics but by the essential "Englishness" which never left him—although most of his life was spent in the United States—and which was of that rare kind which draws the affection and respect of Americans.

December 19, 1956.

Vice-Admiral Gordon Campbell, V.C., D.S.O., who died in hospital on October 3, 1953 at the age of 67, was the best known of the captains of the "Q"-boats, or mystery ships, fitted out as one of the special means of combating the enemy submarines during the 1914-18 War. In this work his coolness, patience, and persistence were shown to a degree amounting to genius. The V.C., D.S.O. and two bars, the Croix de Guerre, and the insignia of Officer of the Legion of Honour were among the honours earned by him, and he also won his promotion to captain at the early age of 31.

When war broke out in 1914 Campbell was a lieutenant in command of the destroyer Bittern at Devonport, and had given no evidence of that exceptional capacity which he afterwards displayed. The fitting out of ships for decoy purposes, however, gave him his chance. On October 21, 1915, he commissioned the tramp steamer Lodorer as a "Q"-ship, changing her name to Farnborough on passage to Queenstown. All that winter she cruised off the south-west coast of Ireland, and the patient training and well-laid schemes of her captain were rewarded on March 22, 1916, when she engaged and sank "U.68", one of the newest German submarines. The antics of the "panic party" in abandoning the Farnborough so completely deceived the "U"-boat that she came to the surface, and by holding on to the last minute Captain Campbell was able to use his 12-pounders and depth charges with the certainty of destroying the enemy. For this action he was promoted to commander and awarded the D.S.O.

Nearly a year passed before his next success, but on February 17, 1917 a torpedo was seen approaching and was allowed to strike, causing a big hole in the vessel's side. All men not needed took to the boats, with Campbell and his "action party" concealed on board the sinking ship waiting for a chance to fight. After 20 minutes, which seemed like days, the submarine, which proved to be "U.83", broke surface and came within range, when the "Q.5", as the Farnborough had been renamed, made short work of her. But the "Q"-boat was herself in a parlous condition, so much so that within an hour Captain Campbell reported to the vice-admiral at Queenstown, in a most pathetic message: "Q.5 slowly sinking respectfully wishes you goodbye". Fortunately, a destroyer and sloop arrived to begin attempts at towing, which eventually ended in the ship being brought into Berehaven. It was for this affair that Captain Campbell was awarded the V.C.

He was then appointed to the collier Vittoria, which was known under a number of other names, and on June 7, 1917 accounted for "UC.29" in the Atlantic. A bar was added to Captain Campbell's D.S.O. and he was promoted to post rank.

In the collier Dunraven he fought, on August 8, 1917 what is considered the epic fight of all the "Q"-boat duels, although the submarine escaped. It took place in the Bay of Biscay, 130 miles west of Ushant. Soon after the submarine began firing, a lucky shot exploded a depth charge in the Dunraven's poop and set fire to the ship, but patiently the captain waited for a chance to attack. Two hours after the submarine had been sighted, another explosion hurled the 4in. gun and its crew into the air, and thus revealed the nature of the ship to the enemy.

Still Captain Campbell held on, and actually signalled by wireless to all H.M. ships, "Keep away for the present", although he knew his ship was severely damaged and about to be attacked again. After a torpedo had struck the Dunraven abaft the engine-room, the captain sent away more of his crew in boats and on a raft, to convey the impression that she had been entirely abandoned. He afterwards got off two torpedoes, but unfortunately without success. As nothing more could be done, urgent assistance was called for, and two destroyers and a patrol boat came up in time to pick up the Dunraven's crew.

As Admiral W. S. Sims, in a letter to the captain, said, "The standard set by you and your crew is worth infinitely more than the destruction of a submarine. Long after we are both dust and ashes, the story of this last fight will be a valuable inspiration to British (and American) naval officers and men." Captain Campbell received a second bar to his D.S.O. and was personally thanked for his services by the War Cabinet. He did not return to the mystery ships, but took command of the light cruiser Active, and finished the war in command of a destroyer flotilla. He afterwards commanded the cadets' training cruiser Cumberland, and the boys' training ship Impregnable, while in November 1922 he was appointed Captain-in-Charge at Simonstown.

After his return from the Cape in the spring of 1925, he held one more command, that of the Tiger, gunnery firing ship at Portland, from November 1925 to July 1927. In April 1928 the working of the seniority rule brought him at the age of 42 to the head of the captain's list, with its inevitable result of promotion to rear-admiral. He was informed that he would be placed on the retired list in what he referred to in his autobiography (*Number Thirteen*, published in 1932) as a regular stereotyped letter "rather less gracious than one would send to a cook who had served you for two years." Because of his early promotion to captain, he had been unable to qualify for the maximum pension, which is determined partly by length of service. In the *London Gazette* of May 8, 1928, however, it was notified that the King, on the advice of the Privy Council, had approved an Admiralty memorial that an additional Greenwich Hospital Pension of £100 a year be awarded to him, "in recognition of his distinguished and exceptional services during the War." The grant was to be regarded as an exceptional and isolated case, and not to be drawn into a precedent for the future. After his retirement he published a volume on *Mystery Ships,* and also achieved some success as a lecturer.

His excursion into politics was in its way as dramatic as his "Q"-boat exploits. When the National Government decided to appeal to the country in 1931 he made a spontaneous offer to contest Burnley because the Socialist leader, Arthur Henderson, was there; his offer was accepted. "I would not have gone anywhere", he said, and he disavowed any party ties. He had never belonged to a political party or taken a hand in politics before. He stood as a Nationalist, claimed as his colours the White Ensign, and hung on the wall of his private office the torn flag he had had on active service. He polled 35,126 votes against the 26,917 cast for Henderson. In the House, from which he retired in 1935 on medical advice, he took little part in debate except when service matters were under discussion. The success of his earlier books gave him a taste for writing, which he was able to indulge because, owing to the condition of his heart, he was unable to take part in more active pursuits. The results, though not outstanding, were workmanlike and readable, particularly his studies of Captain Cook and other naval men.

The son of Colonel Frederick Campbell and grandson of Sir John Campbell, the seventh baronet, the late Vice-Admiral was born in 1886. His mother was Emilie, eldest daughter of Donald Maclaine, of Lochbuie, Argyllshire. He entered the Royal Navy from Dulwich College in January 1900 and two years later was appointed midshipman of the Prince George in the Channel. In October 1903 he joined the light cruiser Flora in the Pacific. His is another instance of a successful commander in battle not being specially good at examinations, for he did not take a single "first" in passing for lieutenant, but got through with four "seconds" and two "thirds". He joined the destroyer service as a sub-lieutenant in 1906, being appointed to the Arun, in the Channel Fleet, but it was not until April 1913 that he attained his first independent command, in the Bittern.

He married in 1911 Mary Jeanne, daughter of Mr. H. V. S. Davids, and there were two children of the marriage, a son and a daughter.

October 6, 1953.

James Campbell, general secretary of the National Union of Railwaymen, and a member of the T.U.C. General Council, who died on November 6, 1957 from injuries in a motor accident in Russia, was born in Glasgow on April 17, 1895.

He came of a railwayman's family; his father was a Glasgow guard and an active trade unionist, and young Campbell was introduced to the local branch at an early age. After leaving school, Campbell became a ticket collector at Glasgow; he joined the N.U.R. in 1911, a member of the same branch as J. B. Figgins, who was his predecessor as general secretary.

After the First World War Campbell worked as a shunter; he was also a branch secretary and in 1937 was elected to the union executive. He became a divisional organizer the following year. Before his election as assistant general secretary in 1948 he had worked in Doncaster and Ireland. In 1953 he took over the post of general secretary—one of the leading offices in the trade union movement—at the age of 57.

Although comparatively unknown to the general public until he became general secretary of his union less than five years before he died, "Big Jim" Campbell has since become a national figure. His period of office has been one of recurring wage crises. On more than one occasion he has had to threaten the possibility of a strike, the first time at Christmas in 1954. In spite of this he was generally respected and liked.

Nobody could possibly have described him as a "wild man". He was cautious, quiet, and patient, but determined. He had both the railways and trade unionism in his blood and might be said, perhaps, to belong to the old school of trade union leaders, just as he was a socialist of the old school. One of the last—and probably most lasting—impressions of him was as he stood on the rostrum at the Labour Party conference at Brighton, moving the reference back of the new fangled policy statement on public ownership.

He accepted his defeat there with his usual calm. However tense a situation, he never became flustered or ill-tempered. His personality did a great deal to increase public sympathy for the railway workers, whose case he put so often with a sincerity and honesty that were never questioned.

He rose to the leadership of his union rather because of his organizing ability than because of his eloquence as a speaker. He was not an outstanding figure on the T.U.C. General Council, though he was always heard with respect. His heart seemed to be in his work for his own union rather than in that of the wider movement. He came to the General Council too late to hope for the highest T.U.C. honours.

With his slight Scottish accent, he had a quiet humour and an unfailing sense of proportion. He did not always, it was said, agree with the decisions of his own union, but he always accepted them with unquestioning loyalty and carried them out to the best of his ability. He had presented a new wage claim only a few days before he left England, and had he lived would have had perhaps the most critical struggle of his career during the coming months. His leadership will be greatly missed during the difficult days ahead.

November 7, 1957.

Dame Janet M. Campbell, D.B.E., M.D., M.S., died on September 27, 1954 in London at the age of 77, after a long illness. She was senior medical officer for maternity and child welfare to the Ministry of Health and chief woman medical adviser to the Board of Education from 1919 to 1934.

Janet Mary Campbell was born in 1877, daughter of George Campbell of Barnham, Sussex, and received her medical training at the London School of Medicine for Women. She graduated M.B., B.S. in 1901, proceeding to M.D. in 1904, and to M.S. in the next year at London University. After acting as house surgeon and house physician at the Royal Free Hospital in 1902 and as senior resident medical officer at the Belgrave Hospital for Children in 1904, she was appointed an assistant school medical inspector under the London County Council in 1905. Three years later she became a medical officer to the Board of Education. When the Ministry of Health was formed in 1919 she received the additional appointment of medical officer for maternity and child welfare. She retired in 1934.

In the course of her long career she was a member of the Women's Committee of the Liquor Control Board, the Health of Munition Workers Committee and the War Cabinet Committee on Women in Industry, the Committee on the Training of Midwives, the Committee on Maternal Mortality, the Departmental Committee on Hospital Construction, and the Health Committee of the League of Nations, on which she did much valuable work from 1930 to 1936.

In 1917 she had prepared a report for the Carnegie United Kingdom Trust on the Physical Welfare of Mother and Children, and the most important of her reports to the Ministry of Health and the Board of Education were those on the teaching of obstetrics and gynaecology in 1923, the training of midwives in the same year, maternal mortality in the following year, the protection of motherhood in 1927, infant mortality two years later, high maternal mortality in certain areas in 1932, and maternity services in 1935. She attacked the most pressing problem which the maternity and child welfare movement had brought to light, the excessive mortality and morbidity attendant on childbirth, and firmly advocated greater coordination and improvement of all available services.

She was created a D.B.E. in 1924, and was an honorary Doctor of Hygiene of Durham University, and a justice of the peace for Surrey and for Gloucestershire.

In 1934 she married Mr. Michael Heseltine, C.B., registrar of the General Medical Council. He died in 1952. In 1940 she resumed the surname of Campbell.

September 29, 1954.

Margaret Campbell—See **Bowen**.

The Rev. Reginald J. Campbell, for many years one of the most prominent and popular preachers first in the Congregational ministry and then in the Church of England, died at his home near Uckfield, Sussex, on March 1, 1956 at the age of 89.

Reginald John Campbell was born in London on January 29, 1867, of Ulster stock which had come originally from Argyll. His father was a minister of the United Methodist Free Church, but the boy spent most of his earlier years in the North of Ireland among Presbyterian kinsmen. He was delicate from his childhood, fond of books, and conscious in a special degree of the mysterious beauty of Nature. He joined his parents in Nottingham in his youth, continued his studies at the University College, and for a time taught in various schools, but, discovering the need of a university degree in that profession, he went up to Oxford after his marriage to Mary Elizabeth, daughter of Mr. James Slack, of Nottingham.

Before that time he had been confirmed and was a communicant of the Church of England. At Christ Church he came under the influence of Dr. Francis Paget, the Dean, and thought of seeking holy orders, but before he left Oxford he came to the conclusion that the Anglican Church could not satisfy him, and in 1895 he left it to become the minister of Union Street Congregational chapel at Brighton.

His success was instantaneous, and soon a larger building was secured. To a striking personal appearance—his refined and delicate face was even then crowned by snow-white hair—he added no sensational attitudes or pulpit mannerisms. He preached the great themes of evangelical religion, and his hearers felt that his sympathy responded to their needs.

When Dr. Joseph Parker was no longer equal to the claims of the City Temple he asked Campbell to carry on his famous Thursday mid-day services, and on his death his associate was appointed his successor. The church was crowded by thousands who came to regard Campbell as the one man to be appealed to in every difficulty of faith or conduct. Early in 1900, during the South African War, he made a tour through Cape Colony, where he caught enteric fever, and this weakened him for many years. In 1903 he visited America, where he was welcomed enthusiastically.

When in 1906 Campbell launched his *New Theology* a hot agitation followed. Many believed that he had gone over to Unitarianism. But in truth there was little intellectual weight in Campbell's book, its rather loose statements were easily refuted by Bishop Gore and others, and Campbell himself soon came to regret that he had written it, and withdrew it from circulation.

He continued to attract large congregations to the City Temple. But the physical strain of his work there became increasingly severe. He was expected to preach twice each Sunday and also on Thursday mornings and to preach sermons which could at once be put into print. He asked the deacons of the City Temple to appoint an assistant minister in order to lighten this burden. This they were unwilling to do, knowing that the rather curious congregation which filled the pews came solely to hear the Rev. R. J. Campbell. As his intimate friends of this period knew, it was this friction with his office-bearers that took a large part in causing Campbell's return to the Church of England.

Accordingly, after 12 years at the City Temple, in 1915, Campbell was ordained by Bishop Russell Wakefield and joined the staff of Birmingham Cathedral. In 1917 Canon Carnegie, then Rector of St. Margaret's, nominated him to the living of Christ Church, Westminster. Carnegie's idea was that here Campbell would have a preaching centre of his own and would build up a large congregation while the parochial duties of the cure might be discharged by an assistant curate. But this scheme was not successful. It is true that a large congregation came to hear Campbell, but it was composed mainly of the same people who had helped to throng the City Temple in earlier years.

To minister to this special class was a feat of which few men were capable, and Dr. Campbell's (Oxford gave him an honorary D.D. in 1919) work in doing it was of undoubted value. Yet he was never so effective in the Anglican Church as he had been in his Nonconformist days. He would not stoop to the sensational methods that attract crowds of a certain type, while to thoughtful people many of his sermons seemed little but a succession of commonplaces, though charmingly delivered. He was not happy at Christ Church, and after four years there took charge of what had been F. W. Robertson's church at Brighton. There he remained from 1924 until 1930, when he was appointed by the Bishop of Chichester to a residential stall in his Cathedral.

In this post he began new work. Always a wide and rapid reader, of late years he had given himself to a systematic study of theological literature, and most of the new books of importance came to him for review in an ecclesiastical newspaper. He now set himself to make his knowledge serviceable to his brother clergy and the laity, and his main business in life became teaching instead of preaching. His Bishop gave him the formal title of Canon-Teacher. He lectured at Chichester Theological College, addressed study circles throughout the diocese, and attracted both clergy and laity to special courses of instruction at Elfinsward, the charming diocesan retreat house at Haywards Heath.

His first wife had died in 1924. Three years later he married Miss Ethel Gertrude Smith. Her constant help and support did much to ease the burden of his later years, but he had never been robust, and in 1936 failing health, with increasing deafness, caused him to resign his residentiary canonry. He preserved, however, as Chancellor and Prebendary his tie with Chichester Cathedral. When Campbell resigned his stall in the Cathedral in 1946 the Bishop conferred on him the title of canon emeritus. During the remainder of his life he lived near Uckfield, preaching occasionally, and continuing to give many lectures and devotional addresses. During the war, in spite of his age and infirmities and the death in 1943 of his second wife, he gallantly took charge of the parish in which he lived.

Personally he was a man of great charm. After being at a comparatively early age a world-celebrity, he seemed after his return to the English Church to slip swiftly and suddenly into the background, but he was not in the least soured by this experience. His natural goodness and the intensity of his personal religion made him immune against such dangers. If it be said that the Anglican Church failed to make full use of him two facts can be urged in reply. The first is that, remarkable in their own way as were Campbell's powers as a preacher, they seemed far more effective in a Nonconformist than in an Anglican setting. The other is that the spiritual counsel and religious instruction given by him in his later years may well have had more lasting value than anything he accomplished at the height of his fame as a popular preacher. Today a multitude of souls must still be grateful for the help given them by R. J. Campbell, and will cherish his memory with gratitude.

March 2, 1956.

Sir Ronald Hugh Campbell, G.C.M.G., British Ambassador to Portugal from 1940 to 1945, died at Lymington, Hampshire, on November 15, 1953 at the age of 70.

He was a diplomatist of great and deserved reputation who during a brief but most important period was British Ambassador in Paris. From the beginning of his career he had been marked for high appointment, and there was no surprise among those who knew him when in 1939 he moved in a single step from the Legation in Belgrade to the Embassy in Paris. Usually the Ambassador to France has graduated through one or two Legations and an Embassy before promotion to that senior post; but Campbell had long been recognized as one of the ablest and soundest men in the service and was recognized to possess special qualifications. There, and afterwards at Lisbon, he rendered invaluable services to his country.

Ronald Hugh Campbell was born on September 27, 1883, the eldest son of Sir F. A. Campbell, K.C.M.G., C.B., Assistant Under-Secretary of State for Foreign Affairs from 1906 to 1911. In 1907 he passed a competitive examination and was appointed a clerk in the Foreign Office. Three years later he became a third secretary and accompanied Lieutenant-General Sir A. Paget on his special embassy to the Courts of Munich, Stuttgart, and Sofia to announce the accession of King George V. The next year he was in attendance on the representative of Venezuela at the Coronation. Then from 1913 to 1919 he was private secretary to the Permanent Under-Secretary of State for Foreign Affairs and in this capacity served Sir Arthur Nicolson (later Lord Carnock) and Lord Hardinge of Penshurst. It was excellent training and he made the most of it. In 1917 he was created a C.M.G.

While in attendance at the Peace Conference of 1919 Campbell was promoted second secretary and in July 1919 became, until 1920, private secretary to Lord Curzon of Kedleston, then Acting Secretary of State for Foreign Affairs.

In the same year he was promoted to first secretary. An Acting Counsellor in 1928, he shortly became Counsellor in the Foreign Office, and in 1929 was appointed Envoy Extraordinary and Minister Plenipotentiary in Paris, where on many occasions he acted as Chargé d'Affaires. During the seven years he spent there he was extremely popular and made numbers of friends in every class of French society. In 1935 he was transferred to Belgrade and in 1936 promoted K.C.M.G. He did excellently at Belgrade. Many of his dispatches home were models of what diplomatic dispatches ought to be, clear, balanced, explanatory, and revealing.

In July 1939 Campbell's appointment to succeed Sir Eric Phipps as Ambassador in Paris was announced. When the appointment was first hinted in France it was immediately clear that no more popular selection could have been made, and one of the leading newspapers, *Excelsior*, expressed the general satisfaction in the headline *"L'Ecossais bien venu"*.

On his way through London he was sworn of the Privy Council and arrived in Paris early in November. He was soon to fulfil the expectations of the French. In January 1940 he delivered a spirited and wholly admirable speech to the American Club in Paris in which he claimed for the war that "to us it is a simple struggle between right and wrong". Seeing it as a fight for the same principles as those of the colonists of 1776 enlarged and projected upon the international plane, he held that Great Britain had gravitated to her natural plane with, instead of against, France and the United States, and expressed his sympathy with the idea that the close Anglo-French cooperation which then existed might be made the nucleus of a new world order of mutual help.

Campbell's mission was unfortunately to prove of brief duration. Returning to London after the fall of France, he was employed at the Foreign Office and promoted G.C.M.G. Then, in November 1940, he was transferred to Lisbon, where he succeeded Sir Walford Selby* in another post of first importance, and took up his duties in the course of the next month. Early in 1942, at a time when the Germans in an effort to make mischief were saying that Great Britain was severing relations with Portugal because of disagreement over the Allied landing in Timor, he returned to London to consult on this and other much wider matters. In Portugal he was once again to live up to his reputation as one of the ablest of his country's diplomatic representatives.

His dispatches, dry and sardonic, but remarkably informative, surpassed in quality even those he had sent from Paris in the early days of the war. Though much of his work has had necessarily to remain secret, he lifted a corner of the veil in a speech which he gave in July 1945, at the end of his term of office, when he entertained President Carmona [q.v.] at dinner at the British Embassy. Before D Day, he said, Portugal stopped all supplies of wolfram to Germany at the request of the British Government and by prompt action permitted the seizure of all German documents in Portugal. She also contributed to the successful outcome of the Battle of the Atlantic by allowing Great Britain to use the Azores as a base from August 1943 onwards. Only those who have taken part in such delicate negotiations in wartime can appreciate the close attention to detail necessary and the nerve required to take risks which must on occasion be taken. Sir Ronald Campbell, by his superb handling of affairs in what seemed to many a backwater during the war, deserved well of his country when he came to his well-earned retirement in 1945.

In 1908 he married Helen, daughter of the late Richard Graham. She died in 1949 and he is survived by his only son.

November 17, 1953.

Roy Campbell, poet and man of action, was killed in a motor accident on April 23, 1957, when a car driven by his wife crashed into a tree near Setubal in Southern Portugal. He was 56.

Sudden death by violence would have had no terrors for him. He had always lived adventurously, often dangerously; he delighted in taking risks and joining battle with the men and women and the causes that he hated. But pugnacity in him was no more than the reverse side of a passionate and a humble sincerity. No poet of the last thirty years has done more original work or compromised less with the current fashions of the literary world.

Campbell was an individualist, a traditionalist and a fiery scorner of much that was accepted by his articulate contemporaries as being commonplace truth. But to call him a poet of the right is merely to use a convenient label. It does not explain the beauty of his lyrics nor the marvellous sweep of his narrative descriptive power.

The restlessness that sent him roaming from place to place and sampling all manner of odd jobs, afloat and on land, was symptomatic not of inner uncertainty but of a magnificently virile consistency. He knew what he wanted from life and from art; there was no room for half-measures or pale shades in his philosophy.

I will go stark: and let my meanings show
Clear as a milk-white feather in a crow
Or a black stallion on a field of snow.

As an artist and as a man of action, he lived up to that ideal.

Ignatius Roy Dunnachie Campbell was born in Durban on October 2, 1901. His father, Dr. Samuel George Campbell, was of Northern Irish stock and the family was well known in Natal for breeding men and women of marked character.

Campbell's mother, Margaret Dunnachie, was half French and gave him a literary background uncommon in the colonial atmosphere of Edwardian South Africa. She came of a family that had known Browning, Tennyson, and the pre-Raphaelites. Campbell went to Durban High School and just missed the First World War, though not before he had tried to get into it under age. A year at Oxford found him sharing a tutor with William Walton, who, as Campbell has recorded, "introduced me to the people who have influenced and helped me most in my subsequent career".

In 1924 *The Flaming Terrapin* made his name. Here was a poet not afraid of polychromatic imagery and one able to handle it without lapsing into rhetoric, though not always escaping monotony. The South African origins of the writer were plain. He could not have written as he did had he not known the great seas that roar around the Cape. Colonial verse writers have sometimes been given the benefit of the doubt by polite critics at the centre of things.

Campbell needed no such concessions, and he was at once acclaimed in his own right as a young poet in the first rank.

At that time he had already been married for two years having, as he loved to describe, laid violent siege to the lady of his heart, Mary Margaret Garman, and married her in 1922. Matrimony, bringing with it two daughters, was no more a handicap than was literary fame or the open doors of Bloomsbury to the young poet's zest for roving. The Campbells were for a time in the wilds of Wales. They lived in the remote corners of Provence, in Spain, in Portugal and in Rome. He fought for Franco* in the Spanish War and he and his wife and daughters were received into the Roman Catholic Church.

The gamut of adventures he ran would have provided marvellous material for a picaresque novel had he not regarded that form of self-expression as beneath contempt. He saved the Carmelite Archives of Toledo during the siege. He was mentioned three times during the Spanish War by General Quiepo de Llano.

His miscellaneous peace-time activities were no less remarkable. He had been a sailor, he twice won the steer-throwing competition of Provence in the early 1930s, he gained the Silver Picador's Jacket in Madrid and never lost his enthusiasm for bull-fighting. He served in the last war in the ranks in East and North Africa until he was disabled and discharged with the rank of sergeant. A heavy limp and a host of memories were his legacy from those years.

On demobilization, he joined the Literary Advisory Board of the B.B.C. Some of those who thought they knew him best prophesied that his impatient individualism would prevent him from fitting in at Broadcasting House. But his four years there from 1945 to 1949 in fact gave him a chance which he took with enthusiasm of encouraging good work in poetry.

His own output had never flagged. *The Wayzgoose* (1928) gave proof of a rollicking pleasure in satire, slapdash, painfully wounding to individuals, epigrammatic in flashes, sprawling and careless in stretches. As his targets here were South African, most of his venom meant nothing in Britain. But in *The Georgiad* (1933), which he called a satirical fantasy in verse, he pitched into well known English literary figures. It would be a nice point to decide whether the brilliance of the wit or the gratuitous nature of the offensiveness most struck detached readers. Campbell in this vein—and he worked it out, also, in some pungent shorter verses— was nearer to Byron than to Pope. He could be very funny indeed, but he missed the polished felinity of the little crippled master.

As a lyricist he never flagged. *Adamastor* (1930), *Flowering Weeds* (1933), *Mithraic Emblems* (1936), *Talking Bronco* (1946), contain such unmatched perfection as "The Zulu Girl" and "Horses on the Camargue"—to name only the most familiar.

He wrote two autobiographical books, *Broken Record* and *Light on a Dark Horse.* As a translator he deserves to be spoken of among the top very few.

Roy Campbell's renderings of Baudelaire, St. John of the Cross, Lorca, and other Spanish and Portuguese writers are felicitous as only a poet who had caught the spirit as well as the music of the originals could make them. His other writings include *Flowering Rifle* and *Taurine Provence.* He contributed to *The Times Literary Supplement* on many occasions. In October 1956 a poem of his there included this quatrain:

At my approach all pedagogues grow
raucous.
Collective age-groups raise a cackling cry
Like the New Critics, or the crazy caucus,
Or poultry when a falcon cruises by.

The falcon has now come to an end of his cruising; but he will live on in his own books and in anthologies.

April 25, 1957.

Captain Victor Campbell, D.S.O., O.B.E., R.N. (RETD.), a member of Scott's expedition to the Antarctic in 1911-13, died on November 19, 1956 at Cornerbrook, Newfoundland. He was 81.

Victor Lindsey Arbuthnot Campbell was born on August 20, 1875, the son of Captain Hugh Campbell, R.N. He was First Officer of the Terra Nova, which took Scott's party to the Antarctic and, according to Apsley Cherry-Garrard [q.v.], in his hands "the routine and discipline of the ship was most efficiently maintained. I was very frightened of Campbell". That was on the voyage out, before the comradeship of the Antarctic had broken down reserve.

Campbell was placed in command of the Northern Party which carried out sledging and geological work from Cape Adare southwards. It was arranged that they should be taken off by ship and brought back to the main base before winter set in in 1912. But gales and pack ice prevented the ship from reaching them, and Campbell's party, who were enduring the gales in their camp, concluded that it had been wrecked. The journey down the coast at that season was out of the question, so Campbell with his five companions prepared to winter there. Food was short and three of the men were dispatched to kill all the seal and penguin they could find. The rest meanwhile excavated a dug-out in a large snowdrift, 6ft. down, 12ft. by 9ft. in area and 5ft. 6in. high. There from March to September they passed the winter with blubber to eat, and *David Copperfield,* the *Decameron* and the New Testament to read. On September 30 they set out on the 200-mile sledge journey to Hut Point, which they reached at the beginning of November.

For his part in the expedition Campbell was specially promoted to commander. During the 1914-18 War he took part in the Dardanelles Expedition and was awarded the D.S.O., to which he received a bar in 1917. He had lived in west Newfoundland since 1922.

He married, in 1902, Lilian Mary, daughter of Lieutenant-General Sir H. H. Settle.

November 21, 1956.

Lord Campion, who died onApril 6, 1958 at the age of 75, had spent the whole of his distinguished career of 42 years at the Palace of Westminster, and from 1937 until 1948 he had been Clerk of the House of Commons.

With discretion, intelligence, and a retentive memory stored with historical precedents he carried on the tradition of his post of accessibility and helpfulness on which front benchers and back benchers, and indeed the Chair, had come to rely, and especially during the difficult years of the 1945 Parliament, when party feeling had often lowered the dignity of the House and seriously impeded the conduct of public business.

He will also be remembered for (among other works) his admirable *Introduction to the Procedure of the House of Commons* and for his editorship of the fourteenth edition of the century-old classic, Erskine May's *Parliamentary Practice*. With him dies much learning of the laws and customs of the House of Commons.

Sir Gilbert Francis Montriou Campion, G.C.B., Baron Campion, of Bowes, in the county of Surrey in the Peerage of the United Kingdom, was the son of John Montriou Campion, of the Public Works Department in India, where Gilbert Campion was born on May 11, 1882. He was educated at Bedford School, under the successful headmastership of J. S. Phillpotts, and he went up to Hertford College, Oxford, with a classical scholarship, where he took a first in Mods, and graduated in 1905 with a first in Lit. Hum. In the competition for the Civil Service he seems to have been disappointed with his place, and in 1906 he accepted from Sir Courtenay Ilbert a nomination for a clerkship in the House of Commons. In 1913 Ilbert selected him to visit the Legislatures of several Continental countries and study their comparative methods. The results of this expedition, neatly tabulated, appeared soon afterwards as an appendix to Ilbert's evidence given before the Select Committee on Procedure over which Sir Thomas Whittaker presided.

He joined the Army early in the 1914-18 War and was a captain in the R.A.S.C. He was invalided home from France, and on his recovery he served as secretary to two important commissions of inquiry, the first being the Bryce Second Chamber Conference. As unanimity was lacking, Bryce made his report in the form of a letter, which bore witness in warm terms to Campion's abilities as well as to his wide and accurate knowledge of parliamentary institutions at home and abroad.

The second inquiry was Speaker Lowther's Conference on Devolution. The general scheme of the Lowther plan, with its Regional Grand Councils, was believed to have been substantially Campion's work. Official promotion followed steadily. In 1921 he was appointed to "The Table", becoming Second Clerk Assistant and Clerk Assistant in 1930. In 1937 he succeeded Sir Horace Dawkins as Clerk of the House at the end of the latter's 46 years of service. During Campion's term of office he was an indispensable witness before various select committees on questions of procedure and privilege and, in 1941, on the disqualification involved by acceptance of an office of profit under the Crown.

In August 1946 the new Labour Government, faced with a heavy programme, set up another Select Committee on Procedure, and Campion was invited to produce his own suggestions for reform, which, if they did not find acceptance as a whole, yet served as a useful framework for discussion. To the question of Parliament sitting for more days in the year than it normally does he was definitely opposed. "If", he said, "the House sits very much more than it does now, which is about 30 weeks in the year, the result will be to take the last stage in altering the types of membership, because it would be necessary to rely on whole-time service."

In July 1948 he decided to retire, and the general regret of all parties was eloquently expressed on a motion by the Leader of the House, Herbert Morrison [Lord Morrison of Lambeth*] conveying its appreciation of his services, which was supported by Winston Churchill*, Clement Davies*, and [Lord] Maclay [q.v.]. The following month he set out on an official tour of the Dominion Parliaments, lasting five months, in the course of which he visited Ceylon, New Zealand, Australia, South Africa, and Southern Rhodesia. The following year he was appointed Clerk of the Consultative Assembly of the Council of Europe, which began its first meeting at Strasbourg in August, 1949. On November 13, 1950, he contributed a special article to *The Times,* pointing out some of the defects of its organization and procedure.

Campion's *Introduction to the Procedure of the House of Commons,* already referred to, was first issued in 1929, and has been recast in a later edition. It was originally designed as a first-aid manual for new members, but it came to contain practically everything that an M.P. ought to know, and is now indispensable. Of greater importance was his new edition of Erskine May's *Parliamentary Practice,* to which he devoted some 12 years' preparation. Whole chapters were rewritten, fresh sections were inserted, the proper relation between footnotes and the text was re-established, and the excellent index made the book easier to consult than before. After much consideration it was found possible to contain the work in one volume, which was published in May 1946, and was the subject of a special article of commendation in *The Times.*

An article of interest that he contributed to the columns of *The Times* was one on the Commons Journals on November 8, 1947. In 1952 he edited a composite study of parliamentary government in Great Britain, contributed to by many of the leading English jurists and others, his own contributions being his original lecture on "Parliamentary Procedure Old and New" and a chapter on "Parliament and Democracy". In 1946 he was elected to an honorary fellowship of his old college, Hertford, and in 1950 Oxford made him a D.C.L.

He was made C.B. in 1932, K.C.B. in 1938, G.C.B. in 1948, and he was raised to the peerage in 1950. He married in 1920 Hilda Mary, daughter of the late W. A. Spafford. At their pleasant home at Abinger Hammer, near Dorking, he had constructed a golf green ingeniously testing the approach from a succession of tees, and he won the trophy in the Parliamentary Golf Handicap in 1948.

He sketched and painted, too, with an amateur's enjoyment and some modest success.

April 7, 1958.

With **Lord Camrose,** who died on June 15, 1954 in hospital at Southampton, little more than a week before his seventy-fifth birthday, there passes one of the most respected and successful figures in the British Press.

Lord Camrose entered the world of newspapers as a boy. Even at his zenith, working newspaper-man that he was, he exerted close personal control over his newspapers. From the beginning he was destined to be an editor as well as a proprietor. Punctilious and exact, he was genial and accessible; a man who, never forgetting the struggles of his own youth, took into account the needs, not only material, of those employed in his enterprises. Of his technical abilities as a journalist the newspapers which were his chief care stood witness. Thus, when it came under his control, that great newspaper the *Daily Telegraph,* while losing none of its traditional trustworthiness and stability, drew from him new life and vigour. Moderate in view, firm in principle, and faithful to the high traditions of the older generations that had reigned in Peterborough Court, he was destined from the moment he acquired the *Daily Telegraph* to become an influence of immense importance in British journalism.

The Right Hon. William Ewert Berry, first Viscount Camrose, of Hackwood Park, in the County of Southampton, Baron Camrose, of Long Cross, and a baronet, was born on June 23, 1879, the second son of the late Alderman John Mathias Berry, estate agent, of Gwaelodygarth, Merthyr Tydfil. All three sons of the alderman were to become peers. The eldest, the late Henry Seymour Berry, who had extensive interests in coal, iron, and steel, was created Lord Buckland.

The alderman's household was reasonably prosperous, but not affluent. William started his career at 14 on the *Merthyr Times.* Having remained in South Wales for five years, and worked on various papers, he made his way to London in 1898, where he became a reporter on the *Investor's Guardian* at 35s. a week. Losing his position there, he had a period of three months' unemployment, but was then taken on as reporter by the Commercial Press Association. One day he had to report a meeting of Harmsworth Brothers (as the Amalgamated Press was known), when his knowledge of company law enabled him to make a useful suggestion about procedure. After the meeting Alfred Harmsworth invited him to apply to him for a post. Nothing came of it. William Berry proceeded aided by his own resources.

By 1901 Berry, a young man of 22, although he possessed only a very small capital, ventured into ownership, and started the *Advertising World,* most of which he was, at first, to write himself, in addition to canvassing for and laying out the advertisements. The paper made a profit. As a result William brought up his brother Gomer, who was four years his junior, from Wales, and while the elder of the two concentrated on the editorial side the younger applied his energies to the business management. This apportionment of responsibilities was to continue for 35 years of the brothers' joint work in Fleet Street. In 1905 they sold the *Advertising World,* bought a publishing business, and founded *Boxing* and a number of other periodicals. When Franklin Thomasson's ill-fated *Tribune* was on its last legs (a tragedy portrayed in Sir Philip Gibbs's *The Street of Adventure*) the Berrys looked into its possibilities, but found no hope of resuscitation. Their active career at this period earned for them the sobriquet of "the Busy Bees".

The year 1915 brought to the Berry brothers their first really important enterprise, the acquisition of the *Sunday Times.* William Berry was lunching with the late James White, the financier, when White was approached by West de Wend Fenton, traveller and journalist, who had an option on the paper. Berry took up the option, and then found himself face to face with the principals, who included Dr. Jameson (of the Raid), Sir Basil Zaharoff, the armaments manufacturer, and Sir Arthur Steel-Maitland. All three were anxious about future policy and made many difficulties, but Berry at length brought them into line and completed the purchase without any hampering conditions. He remained editor-in-chief for 21 years, greatly improving this old-established paper and maintaining its position as one of the few British weekly newspapers which catered for all the needs of the cultivated reader.

Soon after taking over the *Sunday Times* the Berry brothers bought the St. Clement's Press, which printed the paper. With it went the control of the *Financial Times,* which in 1925 was amalgamated with the *Financier.* The operations of the partners now took on ever-increasing pace and momentum, and they acquired, often for enormous sums, large numbers of printing, publishing, and paper-making concerns. Among the more important were Weldons, publishers of magazines for women, with about 20 subsidiaries; the publishing business of Cassell and Co.; Kelly's Directories, and the *Graphic* publications. In 1924 they took over the Hulton group, of Manchester (including the *Daily Dispatch,* the *Manchester Evening Chronicle,* the *Sunday Chronicle,* and the *Athletic News*). In the following year they bought the Newcastle group (the *Chronicle* and others), the Glasgow group (*Daily Record, Evening News,* &c.), and sundry journals in Aberdeen, Sheffield, and South Wales. William Berry was now a baronet, the creation dating from 1921.

In 1926 the Berry brothers made their biggest deal, acquiring from the executors of Lord Northcliffe the vast business of the Amalgamated Press, comprising over 100 periodicals and a department which issued encyclopaedias and similar books of reference, the printing works at London and Gravesend, and the Imperial Paper Mills at Gravesend. Further big paper interests followed a year later, when the Berrys bought Edward Lloyd, Ltd., one of the largest paper mills in the world.

In December 1927 the late Lord Burnham, its proprietor, was in search of a likely purchaser of the *Daily Telegraph.* At a meeting between him, his nephew, then Colonel Fred Lawson, the Berry brothers and Sir Edward (now Lord) Iliffe [q.v.] it was arranged that the three last-named should take entire control as from January 9, 1928. The Lawson family yielded their financial interests in the concern, but Colonel Lawson (now Major-General Lord Burnham) remained manager. Changes were then made in make-up and policy; the plant was considerably modernized; great new offices sprang up in Fleet Street, and within five years the circulation had been trebled. Lord Burnham's confidence that under the new management the traditions of the paper would be maintained was justified, and the *Daily Telegraph* in the Berrys' hands continued to combine a high literary standard with moderation, conscientiousness, and stability in opinion. In 1929 Sir William Berry was raised to the peerage.

At the beginning of January 1937 the long-continued partnership between the Berrys was at last severed. It was felt by both, and by Lord Iliffe, that the great expansion of their newspaper interests demanded a reorganization. Lord Camrose therefore took over Lord Kemsley's* interest in the *Daily Telegraph* and part of Lord Iliffe's, resigned from Allied Newspapers and Kelly's Directories, and took up the Kemsley and Iliffe holdings in the Amalgamated Press, Ltd., and the Financial Times, Ltd. (He parted with his holding in the *Financial Times* in 1945.) In August 1937 Lord Camrose acquired the *Morning Post,* and two months later amalgamated it with the *Daily Telegraph.*

Shortly after the outbreak of war it was announced that Lord Camrose had joined the Ministry of Information as Chief Assistant to Lord Macmillan, the Minister and Controller of Press Relations. He remained there for a few weeks only, and then announced in the House of Lords that in the process of reconstructing the Ministry he had "organized himself out of a job", but stated that he would gladly give Lord Macmillan what assistance he could from outside. In the New Year Honours of 1941 he was raised to a viscounty. His admirable survey, *British Newspapers and their Controllers,* appeared in 1947.

In 1905 he married Mary Agnes, eldest daughter of the late Thomas Corns. There were four sons and four daughters of the marriage, and the heir to the title is the Hon. John Seymour Berry, who was born on July 12, 1909.

June 16, 1954.

Dr. Charles Camsell, C.M.G., the explorer, formerly deputy Canadian Minister of Mines and Resources, died on December 19, 1958 at his Ottawa home. He was 82.

Camsell's English father, Captain Julian Camsell, went to Canada with the Royal Canadian Rifles, sold his commission to join the Hudson's Bay Company, and later became the company's chief factor. It was said that not even Lord Strathcona himself was more intimately associated with the inner history of the Great West and the Far North. Charles, one of 11 children, was born on February 8, 1876, at Fort Liard near the British Columbia-Yukon border, where supplies came once a year.

He was educated at St. John's College and Manitoba University, Winnipeg, Queen's University, Kingston, and later took post graduate courses in geology at Harvard and the Institute of Technology, Boston, Massachusetts. Thereupon he folded up the documentary evidence of his academic achievements, packed his kitbag and for six years lost himself in the Canadian North, carrying out extensive exploration of the basin of the Mackenzie river and then of the regions to the west towards the Pacific.

Camsell's expeditions into a land at once beautiful and inhospitable were often attended by appalling hardships; in 1897 he nearly starved in an attempt to reach the Klondike gold field by an especially difficult route.

In 1900, with the geologist Mackintosh Bell, he was on the shore of Great Bear Lake when they noted mineral stain including cobalt bloom and reported it. Twenty-nine years later an investigation of this report by a prospector led to rich pitchblende discovery. Wherever he was, whether at Coppermine or the Great Slave Lake, he kept his eyes open and put his time and training to good use with scientific observations. He was geologist to the Algoma Central Railway in 1901, to the Canadian Northern Railway in 1902-03, and in 1904 joined the Geological Survey of Canada. In the following 16 years he was responsible for the original exploration and mapping of some of the larger rivers of north-western Canada. From 1918 until he was appointed Deputy Minister of Mines and Resources in 1920, he was in charge of the British Columbia and Yukon branch of the survey. When he retired from his post as Deputy Minister in 1946 he had held, among other offices, those of Commissioner of North-West Territories and chairman of the Dominion Fuel Board.

Camsell's achievements were widely honoured. He was awarded the Murchison grant of the Royal Geographical Society for exploration in Northern Canada in 1922 and the Founders Medal in 1945. In 1930 he was president of the Royal Society of Canada and two years later of the Engineering Institute of Canada. He was first president of the Canadian Geographical Society. He published numerous memoirs and papers on the geography and geology of British Columbia and Northern Canada. In 1935 he was made C.M.G.

He married in 1905 Isabel Doucie, daughter of W. Thomas, of Swansea, by whom he had a son and two daughters.

December 22, 1958.

Albert Camus, one of the best known and most influential French writers, and winner of the Nobel Prize for literature in 1957, was killed in a motor accident near Sens on January 4, 1960. He was 46.

Few French writers of this century have been more versatile or more influential than Camus. He first attracted wide public attention immediately after the war as a moving spirit, and later editor, of the Resistance paper *Combat.* His name was thereafter generally coupled with that of Sartre, although there was in fact very little to link them beyond the respect which they shared as two main architects of French intellectual life after the rigours of the Occupation. For the past 15 years, as playwright, novelist, philosopher, journalist, and publisher, Camus had steadily enlarged his reputation and clarified his ideas. His death at the age of 46 robs him of the logical fulfilment of an exceptional gift.

Albert Camus was born in Algeria in 1913. His parents were of mixed French and Spanish stock, and his mother was early left a widow. He was brought up, therefore, in great poverty; but he won a scholarship to the *lycée* in Algiers, and might have taken up a teaching career had he not fallen ill with tuberculosis at the age of 17. Up to that time his main interest had been football; but after a partial recovery he drifted through various jobs into writing. A practical interest in the theatre followed; he travelled widely in Europe; and only settled in France in 1940, where he worked for *Paris-Soir.*

North Africa, however, remained his spiritual home, and after the defeat he returned there for two further years. His clandestine work with the Resistance gave him further insights into the plight of man in our century—the main theme of all his work—and by the end of the war he had already a body of writing behind him which brought him at once into the forefront of his contemporaries. Much of what he had to say is implicit in the short book of essays, *Noces* (1938), which not only contains some of the most beautiful prose written in our time but also states the themes which never ceased to preoccupy him. The beauty of the world which surrounded his childhood, the elemental consolations of sun and sea, were all-important to him. At the same time he was keenly aware of the poverty and suffering which afflict even the most beautiful of worlds, and he was not prepared to accept any supernatural consolation for the plight of mankind. The experience of the Spanish Civil War touched him on the raw; it prepared his attitude to the still more obsessive conflict of 1939. Above all, his early work showed that Camus was interested in people, in people of every sort and condition. He never for long fell victim to the blandishments of abstract theorizing.

In the same year he wrote a play, *Caligula,* which embodies a persistent idea with which his name has been long associated, that of "the absurd". *Caligula* is a remarkable achievement for a man of 25; it has been called "a controlled inquiry into the chemistry of nihilism". Caligula condemns himself to the utter solitude of absolute and valueless power. His gesture is absurd; but then it was Camus's contention that only by realizing his own absurdity could man regain a lost dignity. The universe is indifferent to him; very well, he will show himself indifferent to the universe.

During the war he worked these ideas into the two books which brought him fame, *L'Etranger* and *Le Mythe de Sisyphe.* The former is a novel told in the first person singular, and the latter is a study of suicide. Meursault, the centre of the novel, is a murderer; the strong preoccupation with death which stamps both books can be put down in part to the period at which they were written, and in part to the precarious state of Camus's health. At the same time they are not in the least pessimistic. Camus recognizes that death is the central point of existence; he might have sympathized with Rilke's insistence that nothing in our life is more important than the achieving of our own death. But he is in no way a passive victim. And indeed, his ennobling appeal to mankind is to take for a model the resolution of Sisyphus. The task may be meaningless and absurd; its performance is none the less essential for that.

The circumstances of the Resistance led Camus to test his theories against hard experience. Without ever being a communist he began by giving at least his respect to communist fellow-fighters in the Resistance. He uttered a famous phrase: "Pessimiste quant à la destinée humaine, je suis optimiste quant à l'homme". And a volume of articles, later republished under the title *Actuelles,* shows how vividly his mind grappled with the problems which beset an alert humanist in the closing months of the war and the opening years of uneasy peace. His *Lettres à un ami allemand* (1945) provide one of the most generous comments on these problems; and it was followed two years later by his first major international success, *La Peste.* This novel remains the best introduction to Camus's work—a carefully wrought metaphysical novel the machinery of which can be compared to Sophoclean tragedy. The plague in question afflicted Oran in the 1940s; and on one plane the book is a straightforward narrative. Into it, however, can be read all Camus's native anxieties, centred on the idea of plague as a symbol.

Dissatisfied with the corresponding echoes which he perceived in France, Camus at the same time joined Sartre in founding a political movement which split in two when Sartre accused Camus of moving away from the Left, and a long public controversy ensued. It is clear, however, that Camus was primarily a writer and only intermittently a politician. He returned to the theatre with two further plays, of which *Les Justes* (1949) was the more successful; he wrote what may emerge as his most enduring book, *L'Homme Révolté* (1952), a synthesis of his attitudes to contemporary problems; he published a further novel *La Chute* (1956), which disappointed admirers, and a collection of short stories. Having already, in 1947, received the Prix des Critiques for *La Peste,* he was awarded the Nobel Prize for literature in 1957.

As a personality, Camus was a disarming and impressively modest man. He carried with him none of the bitter existentialist flavour with which his enemies credited him, but talked with a charming simplicity which concealed firm determination. So Mediterranean a writer could hardly hope to be appreciated at his full value in Northern countries, and the reception of his books in England—nearly all have been translated—shows that he has consistently puzzled those of his readers who did not share his own experience of life. Yet he impresses even those who do not admire his agnostic humanism with the brave and tolerant seriousness with which he allows cheerfulness to keep breaking through a deep natural pessimism. No one in his lifetime wrote better prose than he, no one better blended conviction and grace of style. As time went by he was less willing to involve himself in public affairs, and his public silence on Algerian affairs—however strongly he felt about them in his heart—caused some surprise among those who recalled his quick response to similar dangers in the 1930s and 1940s.

But he had come to grips, of recent years, with his true vocation, and planned a series of books which might have combined the two strands of his thought as novelist and thinker. Freedom he valued above everything. If he derived from any single master it was from Bakunin. But he had known so active a role in the life of his own dual country—Algeria and France—that he could never have been content with reducing his thought to a set of theoretical formulae. Hence a certain capacity recurs in those of his writings where he adopts a didactic tone, since the very root of his teaching was that people must be free to make their own mistakes. His early death has taken away not only one of the most vigorous but also one of the most intrepid and endearing of our masters.

He leaves a widow and two children.

January 5, 1960.

The Italian conductor **Guido Cantelli** was killed in an aircraft accident near Paris on November 24, 1956 at the age of 36. Since he had already by the time he was 30 given proof of ability so exceptional as to put him into the line of Toscanini [q.v.] and de Sabata, the loss to the musical world, which is always short of first-rate conductors, is severe both now and for the foreseeable future.

Guido Cantelli was born at Novara on April 27, 1920. He showed musical ability early—he was organist at the church of his home town when he was ten, and conducted the local choral society from the age of 14. He was sent to the Milan Conservatory, where his principal studies were composition and conducting. He returned as conductor of the local theatre in his native town in 1943 but the end of the war caught him in its toils, compelling him to join the Italian army to fight for principles which he rejected as Nazi impositions. His adventures led him to a labour camp in Germany, thence to hospital in Italy from which he escaped to Milan, only to be held as a hostage by fascist troops.

After the liberation of Italy he resumed conducting, beginning with orchestral concerts with the orchestra of La Scala. He quickly established a reputation in Italy and was already internationally known when he went with the Scala Orchestra to the Edinburgh Festival of 1950 along with Victor de Sabata. The next year he conducted the Philharmonia Orchestra in the newly opened Festival Hall. Thereafter he was a regular visitor. Curiously, for an Italian, he had only recently taken up operatic conducting, but he had just been appointed to La Scala. Now his death precludes us for ever from gauging our probable loss in this field.

As a conductor he had shown himself a stylist—his first London concert had a German programme, and at his second, when Vivaldi's *The Seasons* was played, he had observed the scholarly prescriptions for its period. His last appearance in Britain was in Verdi's *Requiem* in the summer, which showed the combination of Italian force with taste and appreciation of style. Force came not merely from temperament but from a careful stick technique, which too many conductors discard to the detriment of precision.

Toscanini had perceived his ability as long ago as 1948, when he invited him to conduct the N.B.C. Orchestra of New York at the age of 28. His association with de Sabata has been already mentioned, and his succession to the first place among Italian conductors was already assured at the early age of 36.

November 26, 1956.

Jonathan Cape, the publisher, died at his London home on February 10, 1960 at the age of 80.

Herbert Jonathan Cape was born in London on November 15, 1879, though his family came from Ireby in Cumberland. His education was brief and in his early teens he began his literary career as an errand-boy at Hatchard's bookshop in Piccadilly. In 1899 he switched to publishing at the London office of Harper and Brothers, where he worked in turn as clerk, general utility man, and traveller. From 1904 till 1920 (with an interval for military service in the first war) he was on the staff of Duckworth and Company, first as London representative and then as manager.

In 1920 he was appointed manager of the Medici Society, and there he met a young man called G. Wren Howard, who showed promise of business acumen and a gift for book-production. They decided to join forces, and the new publishing house of Jonathan Cape Ltd. opened its doors at 11 Gower Street on January 1, 1921.

Realizing his need of literary advice, Cape had engaged the services of Edward Garnett, the prince of publishers' readers, whom he had known at Duckworth's. The combination worked excellently: Garnett was freer than ever before to foster talent and shape a publisher's list, while Cape's experience and Howard's technical skill rapidly brought the new firm to the fore.

Their first book was a new nine-guinea, two volume edition of C. M. Doughty's *Travels in Arabia Deserta*, which had been out of print for 30 years. It is probably true to say that in 1921 no one but Garnett would have recommended such a risky undertaking, and no one but Cape would have had the courage to carry it out. The edition sold out, as did its several successors, and the book's publication brought the firm into contact with T. E. Lawrence, for whom they in due course published *Revolt in the Desert* (1927), *Seven Pillars of Wisdom* (1935), and *The Mint* (1955). Writing of the early years it would be impossible not to mention that best-seller of Percy Lubbock's*, *Earlham*, of which four impressions were called for in its year of publication, 1922.

Nowadays, the sidewalks of New York are thronged with London publishers in search of masterpieces or best-sellers, but in the early 1920s such enterprise was unknown, and Cape's first visit to America was such an unchallenged feat of pioneering that he immediately enriched his list with three future Nobel Prize-winners—Sinclair Lewis [q.v.], Eugene O'Neill [q.v.], and Ernest Hemingway* as well as Sherwood Anderson, H. L. Mencken [q.v.], Dorothy Canfield, and many others.

Meanwhile, the purchase of the one-man business of A. C. Fifield brought the works of Samuel Butler and W. H. Davies under the Cape imprint, and in 1925 the firm moved to its present home at 30 Bedford Square. Gradually and steadily throughout the 1920s and 1930s the name of Jonathan Cape came to represent books of high literary quality, elegantly produced, and efficiently marketed. The new names of H. E. Bates*, Eric Linklater*, Christopher Isherwood, and others combined with the fabulous success of Mary Webb to establish Cape as a fiction publisher. Arthur Ransome's* Swallows and Amazons series and the Dr. Dolittle books of Hugh Lofting created new fashions in children's books, while history was well served by the publication of the first works of J. E. Neale*, C. V. Wedgwood, Duff Cooper [Lord Norwich] and A. L. Rowse. Poetry was represented by Robert Frost*, William Plomer*, Cecil Day-Lewis*, and Andrew Young. Cape's various cheap series—in particular the Travellers Library—held the field until the arrival of Penguin Books, whose potentialities Cape was, incidentally, one of the first to foresee.

Inevitably the adventurous young firm grew in stature and solidity with the years, and when in November 1959 Cape was given a dinner in celebration of his eightieth birthday he was hailed on all sides as the grand old man of the publishing trade.

He had no outside interests; publishing was his life, and he may truly be said to have possessed all the qualities necessary for success in that exacting profession. Not least of these is that mysterious brand of intuition known as "flair", which is neither an intellectual nor a business attainment, but rather an instinct or hunch—and here Cape was remarkably gifted. Some of his shots in the dark misfired but many more scored bull's-eyes.

He was a tall man of distinguished presence, dignified upright carriage and military stride. He was always neatly dressed, and his spacious room in Bedford Square, lined with the books he had published, was meticulously ordered. He was intensely methodical.

Reputed a shrewd bargainer, he was capable of great generosity, and of inspiring affection and loyalty. A stroke some years ago impaired his speech, but he recovered with admirable determination and courage, and worked to the end, as he would have wished. He was three times a widower and is survived by two sons and three daughters.

February 11, 1960.

Archbishop of Cape Town—See **Clayton.**

Francis Carco, the French novelist, died on May 26, 1958 at the age of 71.

A writer of finished and captivating style, with perhaps as elegant and beautifully modulated a gift of language as any of his generation, Carco found his themes as a rule in the artistic Bohemia and the underworld of the Paris of yesterday. He had a place of his own at the *soirées* of Paul Fort [q.v.] at the Closerie des Lilas and knew and wrote of the company there; his volumes of reminiscences published in the 1930s provide some of the sharpest and most revealing impressions that we have of Fort, Apollinaire, Moréas, Modigliani, and the others. But in his most powerful fiction it is a more sordid, more corrupt world that he evokes with incomparable lightness and grace. Besides his novels, he wrote poetry and criticism and also collaborated with various hands at different times in the writing of plays.

Francis Carcopino-Tussoli (for this was the cumbersome real name he abbreviated) was born on July 3, 1886, in Nouméa, New Caledonia, the son of a civil servant. When he was 14 the family returned to France, settling at Villefranche-de-Rouergue. He became a teacher in the *lycée* of Agen, but neglected his work for poetry, some examples of which appeared in the Marseilles *Nain Jaune* and in the Paris review *La Phalange.* After a short time at Agen he went to Toulouse; thence to Rodez; and thence to Grenoble, where he did his military service. In 1907 he founded a journal called *Pan,* and in 1909 was appointed secretary of the magazine *Le Feu.*

In 1910 Carco arrived in Paris with no prospects. A friend secured him a small Government post, and he devoted his evenings to the frequenting of Montmartre cafés. These noisy evenings notwithstanding, he continued to write verse, published several volumes at his own expense, and was then advised by the novelist, Charles Henry Hirsch, to quit Paris and set to work in earnest in the country. He went to Nice, and in due course returned to Paris with several parcels of manuscript. A small post as art critic on *L'Homme Libre* just kept him from starvation; but at last, in 1914, he placed his first novel, *Jésus la Caille,* with no less distinguished a publishing house than the Mercure de France. The prestige thus won opened the way for him into a variety of journals.

But for the moment war intervened, and Carco went to it first as a corporal in a field bakery and from the end of 1916 as a pilot in the air force. Three more volumes of fiction, *Au Coin des Rues, Les Malheurs de Fernande,* and *Les Mystères de la Morgue* were published in 1918, all of them dealing with the Paris *demi-monde.* In 1922 Carco reached the highest point in his development as a novelist with *L'Homme traqué,* which was awarded the Prix du Roman by the French Academy. This short novel (translated into English as *The Noose of Sin*), set in the neighbourhood of Les Halles, is an analytical study of the mind of a murderer overtaken by fear, and is done with faultless objective clarity and strength.

His novels and poetry apart, Carco's familiarity with the *milieu* and the aspirations of the Paris school of painting gave a considerable authority to such works of mingled biography and criticism as his essay on Vlaminck [q.v.] and his *La Légende et la Vie de Maurice Utrillo* [q.v.], the latter a powerfully illuminated and revealing portrait. He wrote critical studies of Hirsch and Paul Bourget, a biography of Villon in novel form (an ideal subject, one would have thought, but rather disappointing in the event), and—among other telling novels of the kind—*Rue Pigalle,* which projected a little world of moral anarchy in as pure and light a style as Carco ever encompassed. His most important books in the thirties were volumes of memoirs.

He was very much in the centre of things in literary and artistic Paris, and was known, colloquially speaking, to everybody. Among his social accomplishments was the ability to sing all the popular Parisian songs with a verve and sympathy that would have ensured his success in any *café-chantant* if his ambitions had turned that way.

May 28, 1958.

Lord Carisbrooke died on February 23, 1960 at the age of 73.

The Most Hon. Sir Alexander Albert Mountbatten, G.C.B., G.C.V.O., first Marquess of Carisbrooke, Earl of Berkhampsted and Viscount Launceston, was born on November 23, 1886, the eldest son of the late Prince Henry of Battenberg by his marriage to Princess Beatrice, youngest daughter of Queen Victoria. He was educated at Wellington and in the Britannia, and served in the Royal Navy from 1902 to 1908. Later he received a commission in the Grenadier Guards and served in the War of 1914-18 with his regiment and afterwards on the Staff. His services were mentioned in dispatches.

After the war he took up a business career, for a time working as a clerk in the offices of Lazard Brothers, the bankers. Subsequently he joined the boards of several large firms.

His engagement to Lady Irene Denison, the only daughter of the second Earl of Londesborough, was announced in May 1917. He was still Captain His Highness Prince Alexander of Battenberg; he had been granted the title of "Highness" by Royal warrant in December 1886. In the interval before the marriage, at King George V's request, he discontinued by Royal warrant the style of "Highness" and assumed the surname of Mountbatten. Then on July 17, 1917, he was created Marquess of Carisbrooke, Earl of Berkhampsted and Viscount Launceston. Two days later the marriage was celebrated in the Chapel Royal and was attended by the King and Queen, Queen Alexandra, and the other members of the Royal Family.

In the War of 1939-45 Carisbrooke served in the R.A.F.V.R. and in 1953 was appointed an honorary Group Captain. In 1949 he became honorary Colonel of the 1st (C) Battalion, The London Rifle Brigade (The Rifle Brigade).

He was a senior steward of the National Greyhound Racing Club, president of the Bribery Prevention League, and London president of the Old Contemptibles.

He was created K.C.V.O. in 1910, G.C.V.O. in 1911, and G.C.B. in 1927. He also had Belgian, Russian, and Spanish Orders, the French Croix de Guerre with palms, and the Order of the Nile.

His wife died in 1956. They had one daughter, Lady Iris Victoria Beatrice Grace, who married in 1941 Captain H. O'Malley, Irish Guards. The marriage was dissolved in 1946 and she resumed the surname of Mountbatten in 1949.

February 24, 1960.

Sir Ernest Rock Carling, the distinguished surgeon, who died suddenly in London on July 15, 1960, was the third son of the late F. R. Carling, of Guildford.

He was born in 1877 and received his medical education at Westminster Hospital Medical School. In 1900 he served in South Africa with the Imperial Yeomanry Field Hospital. He qualified with the Conjoint Diploma in 1901 and in the following year obtained honours and a gold medal at the M.B. examination of London University. He became a Fellow of the Royal College of Surgeons in 1904 and was from the first obviously marked out for the surgical staff of the hospital at which he trained.

When in due course he was elected to the surgical staff of Westminster Hospital he fully justified the hopes which he had raised and for a long term of years he served his hospital with devotion and distinction. He was also appointed surgeon to the Seamen's Hospital, Greenwich, and acted as consulting surgeon to the Chislehurst, Watford, and Hornsey hospitals. In the 1914-18 War he served in Flanders and France with the rank of major, R.A.M.C. (T.F.).

Rock Carling's activities extended beyond the merely operative part of surgery. He was a pioneer in the use of radium and took a large part in establishing the radium centre at Westminster Hospital, and in 1929 (with Sir J. Paterson Ross) published a book of instruction in radium practice. His width of vision was recognized by his being chosen as a member of the Medical Research Council and of the Radium Trust.

He was a good lecturer and examiner; for 10 years he served as a member of the court of examiners of the Royal College of Surgeons. For some years he acted as Dean to Westminster Hospital Medical School. When the decision was taken to rebuild the hospital and medical school Rock Carling entered into the project with enthusiasm and his constructive ability was of the greatest assistance in determining the plans of the new buildings. To him largely belonged the original idea of having complete units comprising out-patients and in-patients on the one floor. He was ever ready to give his time and ability to unravel some knotty point of organization or administration.

At the outbreak of the Second World War he was appointed Consultant Adviser for Casualty Services to the Ministry of Home Security and Ministry of Health and in this capacity he did most valuable service at a critical period of the war. He also took part in the Ministry of Health Survey of the Hospital Services. He developed a keen interest in the social side of medicine and was a member of the executive council of the Institute of Almoners. He was also closely associated with the Nuffield Provincial Hospitals Trust.

At the time of his death Rock Carling was consultant adviser, Ministry of Health, Atomic Energy Authority, and Home Office (C.D.), chairman of the Advisory Committee on Medical Nomenclature, Somerset House, and a member of several important committees concerned with health in the atomic age.

Though a short man of spare build, Carling had kindly eyes which looked keenly from under dark eyebrows and indicated the clear-thinking mind behind them. His opinions were given deliberately and clearly and carried conviction. His personality was attractive and will be greatly missed in the surgical world.

He married Petra, daughter of the Rev. E. D. Rock, by whom he had two sons. His wife died in 1959.

July 16, 1960.

The Right Rev. Dom Aelred Carlyle, O.S.B., founder of the Anglican Benedictine community of Caldey Island, most of whose members were received into the Roman Catholic Church in 1913, died in hospital on October 14, 1955 at the age of 81.

Benjamin Fearnley Carlyle was born at Sheffield on February 7, 1874, and was educated at Blundell's School, Tiverton. In 1892 he began his medical training at St. Bartholomew's Hospital, London, but never qualified. In his twentieth year, after he had paid several visits to Buckfast Abbey, he became convinced that he was called to revive the Benedictine Order in the Church of England.

A start was made in 1896 when Carlyle, who now styled himself Brother Aelred, began to live a quasi-monastic life with a few like-minded young men on the Isle of Dogs, in the East End of London. After a long series of uprootings from one place to another during the next 10 years, the little community managed to secure possession of the Isle of Caldey, South Wales. It was not long before Anglo-Catholics were talking of this Benedictine community as "the greatest phenomenon in the Anglican Communion at the present day".

Within seven years, however, the bubble burst. It was Dr. Gore, Bishop of Oxford, who convinced the abbot and the majority of his monks that their devotional life and liturgical observances would only be justified on a strictly papal basis of authority. Feeling unable to fall into line with other Anglican religious communities, Abbot Aelred and 22 of his community made their corporate submission to the Holy See on March 5, 1913.

By October 1914 Aelred Carlyle had been professed as a Roman Catholic Benedictine monk, ordained priest, and blessed as abbot. His health broke down under the strain of his responsibilities, and in 1921 he resigned his office.

He found a new and very different sphere of work in British Columbia, where for the next 30 years he devoted himself to many kinds of missionary activity. He worked among the Indians in the Okanagan, was first resident priest at Princeton, then moved to Ocean Falls, where he ministered to a widely scattered flock on the Pacific Coast. In 1937 Archbishop Duke appointed him editor of the diocesan newspaper, port chaplain, and chaplain to a home for old men.

The ex-abbot by this time had become one of the clergy of the archdiocese of Vancouver, and had been dispensed from his monastic obligations. It was he who was mainly responsible for the erection of an "Apostleship of the Sea" club in Vancouver, but he will be remembered chiefly for his self-sacrificing work among prisoners. The men and boys in the gaols of Vancouver were his vast "family". They loved and trusted him. Father Carlyle had such exceptional gifts for dealing with outcasts that it is strange that he should ever have thought that his vocation was to be a strictly enclosed and purely contemplative monk. He was a born missionary.

By 1951 he felt that the time had come to retire from active work. Before leaving Vancouver he was presented with a golden key of the city as a token of respect and affection. He returned to England after an interval of more than 30 years, and found an eventide home at Prinknash Abbey—the community he had founded. With special permission from the Holy See he was allowed to renew his monastic vows. Until his health gave way, he lived as a simple monk at Prinknash Abbey, with nothing to distinguish him from the rest of the community.

October 15, 1955.

Marshal Antonio Carmona, President of Portugal, who died on April 18, 1951, had been Head of the State of Portugal for nearly a quarter of a century. The régime of which he was the symbol brought much needed stability to his country.

Dom Antonio Oscar de Fragosa Carmona sprang from a family with strong military traditions and was born in 1869. By the end of the war of 1914-18 he had won for himself in influential military and political circles a reputation for efficiency and perspicuity which in the then turbulent conditions of Portuguese public life was bound to bring him to the front sooner or later.

The occasion came in 1926. In May of that year a military *pronunciamiento,* the eighteenth since the establishment of the Republic in 1910, resulted in the fall of President Machados's Government. The revolt was provoked by the corruption and inefficiency of successive administrations, and was organized by Commander Mendez Cabeçadas and General Gomez da Costa in association with General Carmona. These three took charge of affairs on the resignation of President Machados. The triumvirate was, however, far from harmonious. First Cabeçadas was eliminated; and then Gomez da Costa, an honest soldier whose reforming zeal was untempered by patience or tact, was overthrown.

General Carmona became Prime Minister, Minister for Foreign Affairs, and Minister for War. In November 1926 he assumed by decree the position of Head of the State, pending the election of a constitutional President, and became virtual dictator. His reforms, excellent in themselves and long overdue, had the result of raising up against him a motley but formidable array of enemies. The opposition was well organized, and arms were smuggled over the Spanish frontier. In February 1927 troops garrisoned at Oporto mutinied, and the revolt rapidly spread to Lisbon. A railway strike hampered the movements of the troops on whom Carmona could rely and a serious armed struggle ensued. The revolt delayed the carrying out of his programme of reform. Yet it had cleared the situation, and Carmona was now able to act with a freer hand.

He himself was anxious to revert as soon as possible to a constitutional form of government. In April 1929 he was elected President of the Republic by a plebiscite of the nation, and thereupon proceeded to temper the military character.

In 1928 a new figure had entered the scene. This was Dr. Oliveira Salazar*. At the time of the revolution of 1926 Dr. Salazar was Professor of Economics in the University of Coimbra, where his reputation was so high that he was offered the task of straightening out the muddled and muddied finances of the nation. He seems to have held the post no more than a week and then to have returned to Coimbra. His reputation and the impression he made remained, however, and he was appointed Finance Minister. From then onward the direction of affairs passed more and more under his control. He became Prime Minister in July 1932 and introduced the *Estado Novo* which is the basis of the Portugal of today. It was the practice of critics to speak of him, not of Carmona, as the "dictator". The truth is that the President found in Dr. Salazar the perfect partner, whose judgment and sagacity he trusted and whose integrity was unimpeachable. General Carmona became more and more the conventional but never the merely ceremonial Head of the State.

The fundamental basis of President Carmona's foreign policy was the alliance with Great Britain, and with that went the development and preservation of the Portuguese empire, the fourth largest in the world. In 1938 he undertook an extensive tour of the Atlantic and West African possessions, being the first Head of the State to do so. The next year, at the age of 70, the President visited Portuguese East Africa, accompanied by Senhora Carmona, and, as was the case with the earlier tour, the occasion was taken to emphasize the closeness and warmth of Anglo-Portuguese relations.

The unleashing of Axis aggression on the world, and its European consequences, filled the later years of the President's long life with new anxieties. The crisis followed the civil war in Spain, with its complications for Portugal herself. In 1940, with the Germans at the Pyrenees and at one time threatening to thrust down into the Peninsula, Portugal had to take serious stock of her position. Her oversea possessions were a rich prize. The Azores would be an invaluable base for U-boats and *Luftwaffe.* Precautions were taken, and in particular strong garrisons and naval forces were sent to the Azores to serve, as the President himself said when he visited the islands in 1941, as "sentinels of our national honour".

Throughout those anxious years he made no secret of where his sympathies lay in the struggle, and was much moved when the ship bringing him back from the Azores crossed the track of a British naval squadron and the belligerent guns accorded him a sovereign's salute. Nevertheless he was determined, as he said, to keep Portugal a zone of peace in the midst of war.

Though past 70, he consented to stand again in 1942 for the Presidency, and the people's gratitude to the man who had given them first internal peace and who had maintained the neutrality of the country in the midst of a world-wide struggle was shown in an overwhelming vote of over 80 per cent. The strain, however, had begun to tell. Nevertheless, in spite of age and ill-health, he continued in office and, having been promoted to the rank of marshal in 1943, was re-elected President in 1949.

April 19, 1951.

Mary Endicott Carnegie, widow of Canon W. H. Carnegie, formerly rector of St. Margaret's Westminster, died on May 17, 1957 at the age of 93. Her first husband was Joseph Chamberlain—she was his third wife—who died in 1914. It was two years after his death that she married Carnegie as his second wife. He died in 1936.

She was born on March 16, 1864, the only daughter of W. C. Endicott, who, after studying law at Harvard, became Associate-Justice of the Supreme Court of Massachusetts, the state of which his ancestor, John Endicott, of Dorset, had been the first Governor. Through her mother she was related to another noted Massachusetts family, the Peabodys. At the time her first meeting with Joseph Chamberlain took place her father was Secretary for War in President Cleveland's first Administration.

Their first meeting was in the autumn of 1887, at Washington. At the time he was one of the British delegates on the Fisheries Commission. The engagement was kept secret, for public opinion in America was very sensitive while the Fisheries Treaty remained undecided, and his forthcoming marriage was not even announced to his English friends until just before he sailed, in the November of 1888, for New York. They were married on November 15, in the Church of St. John at Washington, in the presence of the President of the United States and Mrs. Grover Cleveland. After a honeymoon spent on the Riviera Chamberlain took his bride home to England early in 1889, and when they arrived at Birmingham they were received with a most unusual public demonstration of social esteem.

From the day of this remarkable reception she became closely associated with her husband's fellow townsmen and townswomen. She took a close personal interest in all philanthropic, social, and municipal enterprises connected with Birmingham life, and she much enjoyed entertaining Chamberlain's old friends and acquaintances during the many long sojourns made by her each year at Highbury.

The keenest curiosity was also felt in general and political London society concerning the personality of Mrs. Joseph Chamberlain. By her gentleness, her unaffected simplicity, and her eager interest in all that concerned her distinguished husband's life and career she may truly be said to have won all hearts. Those who were present remembered long afterwards the delightful impression she produced at the first drawing room held in 1889, when, rather to the surprise of the more old-fashioned ladies present, she wore blue instead of the traditional bridal white.

Keenly alive though she was to every side of political life, she was yet too fully absorbed in her husband's manifold interests to play any public, or even semi-public, role of the kind so often played by the wives of distinguished statesmen, and her low, clear voice was never heard on any platform. During the last year of his tragic illness she may be said to have never left her husband for more than an hour or two at a time. Her rare appearances were most eagerly welcomed by whatever circle of men and women had the good fortune of her temporary company. Her conversation was most agreeable, because always moderate in tone, and instinct with a real knowledge of life and sympathy with human nature. This was particularly shown at the gatherings, often attended by her during the early autumn months of each year, of a women's luncheon club which also had the privilege of possessing Lady Dorothy Nevill as a member. There, most happily at ease, and in an atmosphere free from controversial discussion, the quick, though always gentle, wit of Mrs. Chamberlain (as she then was), and her keenly expressed interest in all that was going on, had the freest play.

May 20, 1957.

Former King Carol II—See **Romania.**

Dr. Hans Carossa, the German poet and novelist, died in September 1956 at Rittsteig, near Passau, at the age of 77.

In the closing phase of the Second World War he brought all his influence to bear to ensure that the old and historic city of Passau should be preserved from senseless destruction and should be surrendered to the American troops who were then rapidly advancing on it. Hitler's hangmen had condemned him to the gallows for his bold endeavour, but fortunately the Americans saved him at the last minute.

Those who knew Carossa personally will never forget the benign face and meditative expression of this doctor and novelist. Influenced and encouraged by Hugo von Hofmannsthal, Carossa had his roots in the grand tradition of the western world. Although no denominationalist, he was a deeply religious man who, like Goethe, believed in the eternal order of life and made moderation, enlightenment, and purity the principles of his own practice. To understand others he searched the recesses of his own soul. Only thus, he believed, could the destiny and the way of thinking and feeling of others be grasped. In his many novels he spurned the gloss, but instead remorselessly uncovered the diseased and the bad, the disharmonies and the failings, as the way to healing and fulfilment.

The son of a physician in the small mountain spa of Tölz, in Upper Bavaria, Hans Carossa was born on December 15, 1878, and was educated at Landshut and Würzburg and Leipzig universities. After gaining his M.D. degree he established himself as a general practitioner at Passau in 1903. Soon after he set up at Munich in 1914, however, war broke out and he entered military service as a medical officer and was wounded in 1918.

Before the war he had already, in 1910, published a volume of verses, and in 1913 a novel, *Dr. Bürgers Ende*, creating but little impression. Yet this medical "Werther" novel in the form of a diary was to become famous, years later; its subject became a favourite one with Carossa, taken up again in *Die Schicksale Dr. Bürgers* and in *Der Arzt Gion* (1931). The autobiographical nature of his novels was emphasized even more in *Eine Kindheit* (1922) and in *Verwandlungen einer Jugend* (1928), which were translated into English in 1930 and established him with the Anglo-Saxon public, after fame had come to him in his own country with his *Romanian Diary* (1924), unanimously praised as the most beautiful and poetic book of the 1914-18 War.

Two semi-philosophical books followed: *Führung und Geleit* and *Lebensgedenkbuch* (both 1933). With another, *Geheimnisse des reifen Lebens* (Secrets of Mature Life), he got, in 1936, into the bad books of the Nazis, who boycotted him and his works. There is but one other book of his during the Hitler régime of 12 years, with the ambiguous title *Das Jahr der schönsten Täuschungen* (*The Year of Most Beautiful Deceptions*), which was published in 1941.

Apart from that, and ever since, Carossa had published mostly poems, his collected verses in 1938, and *Verse an das Abendland (Poems for the Occident)* in 1947. His total *oeuvre* is weighty, but small in size; apart from the books mentioned, nearly all by now published in foreign languages, there are two lesser novels, *Die Flucht* (1916) and *Ostern* (1920); yet, ever since the end of the 1939-45 War Hans Carossa's stature as author, poet, and thinker has grown in the esteem of the German-speaking world.

A modest, searching, and honest writer, a man of a clearer *Weltanschauung* than many of his fellow-countrymen, free, in his autobiographical works, from the negative, destructive, or morbid trend of so many of his contemporaries, he is distinguished by his deep humanity and his sensitive conscience. He had a warm heart, and an easy grace of style such as make for major poets.

He was honoured as one of them, by the Munich Prize for Poetry in 1928, by the Swiss Gottfried Keller Prize, and in 1938, though ostracized by the Nazis, by the Frankfurt Goethe Prize. In pre-Nazis days he was made a member of the Prussian Academy of Arts, but had lived retired from public life in a little mountain resort since 1933.

September 18, 1956.

Vice-Admiral Alfred Carpenter, V.C., who was awarded the Victoria Cross for the most conspicuous bravery he displayed as commander of the Vindictive in the historic St. George's Day raid on Zeebrugge on April 22-23, 1918, died at his home in Gloucestershire on December 27, 1955 at the age of 74.

Born on September 17, 1881, Alfred Francis Blakeney Carpenter was the son of the late Captain Alfred Carpenter, D.S.O., and grandson of Commander Charles Carpenter, R.N., who entered the Royal Navy in 1810 and assisted in the capture of the American privateer Rattlesnake in 1814. After receiving his education at a private school, Carpenter entered the Royal Navy in 1896, and before he had reached the rank of sub-lieutenant, which he did in 1901, he had seen a considerable amount of fighting. In 1898 he was on service in Crete during the massacres which took place there; two years later he was in China with the Naval Brigade which was landed in consequence of the Boxer Rebellion, and he gained the China medal. In 1903 he was promoted to lieutenant, and specialized in navigation. He received his next step in 1911 when he became lieutenant-commander. The year before the outbreak of the 1914-18 War he specialized in war staff duties, and he received the thanks of the Admiralty for a number of special inventions. In the same year he was presented with the silver medal of the Royal Humane Society for saving life at sea.

When war was declared he was in the Iron Duke on Admiral Sir John (afterwards Admiral of the Fleet Earl) Jellicoe's staff, to which he had been appointed in July 1914. He continued to serve on the staff until November 1915, when he was promoted to the rank of commander and appointed navigating commander of H.M.S. Emperor of India. After two years in that post he was called to the Admiralty to take up a position on the Admiralty War Staff in the

Plans Division, which he held until the next year. He was privy, of course, to the arrangements which were being made for the April raid on Zeebrugge, and the appointment which probably gave him the most pleasure in his long and distinguished naval career was his selection to command the Vindictive in the raid.

The story of the gallant men who went forth on the St. George's Day exploit has become one of the great stories of the British Navy which will be told and told again, and one of the greatest figures in it was Commander Alfred Carpenter, as he then was. As the officer in command of the Vindictive he set a magnificent example to all those under his command by his calm composure while navigating mined waters, and by his skilful seamanship in bringing his ship alongside the mole at Zeebrugge in darkness. His vessel was within a few yards of the mole when the enemy suddenly became aware of what was happening. At once a murderous fire rained down from the batteries, machine-guns, and rifles—and the fire was concentrated on the bridge on which Carpenter stood. The Vindictive succeeded in making fast alongside the mole, and then Carpenter personally supervised the landing of the men.

During the whole time he showed most conspicuous bravery and did much to induce similar behaviour on the part of the ship's company. He walked round the decks and standing in the most dangerous and exposed positions directed operations and encouraged the men. It was stated officially that "by his encouragement to those under him, his power of command and personal bearing, he undoubtedly contributed greatly to the success of the operation." Indeed, his conduct made such an impression on those with whom he was serving that he was selected by officers of the Vindictive, the Iris II, and the Daffodil, and of the naval assaulting force, to receive the Victoria Cross under Rule 13 of the Royal Warrant dated January 29, 1856. The notification of the award was published in the *London Gazette* of July 22, 1918.

For his services at Zeebrugge Carpenter was also specially promoted to captain, received the Croix de Guerre with Palm, and was made an officer of the Legion of Honour. Later in 1918 he was sent on a lecture tour of Canada and the United States, and when he returned to England was appointed to the Naval Intelligence Department, and to the command of a war course for naval officers at Cambridge. He remained in his appointment until 1920. His next move was to the command of the light cruiser Carysfort. When he relinquished that post he took charge in the autumn of 1923 of the Senior Officers' Technical Course at Portsmouth. Then he went in February 1924 to Chatham to take up the triple post of Captain of the Dockyard, Deputy-Superintendent, and King's Harbour Master. On leaving Chatham in 1926 he was given command of the Benbow, and the next year he transferred to the Marlborough, in which he stayed until 1928. In August 1929 he was promoted to flag rank and then went on to the retired list, further promotion to the rank of vice-admiral coming to him in 1934.

It is fortunate that Vice-Admiral Carpenter should have written the book *The Blocking of Zeebrugge*, which he published in 1921. This authentic account written by one who was better able than any other man to tell the story of the great adventure is half a study of naval tactics and half a pen portrait of a great adventure. The first part of the book dealt with the technical aspects of the operations, and the second part with the actual attack, beginning with the vice-admiral's signal "St. George for England", and the reply "May we give the Dragon's tail a damned good twist". The absorbing chapters that followed gave a vivid account of that fiery twisting.

In his younger days Vice-Admiral Carpenter was a good cricketer and lawn tennis player, and later in life he became as good a golfer. He had many other interests, among which were astronomy and psychology. He married in 1903 Maud, daughter of the Rev. Stafford Tordiffe. She died in 1923. There was one daughter of the marriage. Secondly, he married in 1927 Hilda Margaret Alison, daughter of the late Dr. W. Chearnley Smith.

December 28, 1955.

The Rev. Dr. S. C. Carpenter, D.D., Master of the Temple from 1930 to 1935 and Dean of Exeter from 1935 to 1950, died on August 19, 1959 at Exeter. He was 81.

He was a writer of distinction, one who could make a religious book not only interesting but entertaining without resorting to flippancy. His *Church and People 1789-1889*, which was published in 1933, has become a standard work. In this study of English religion in the nineteenth century no aspect, theological, ecclesiastical, social, or philosophical seemed to escape him. To each he brought the trained judgment of a sympathetic mind fortified by omnivorous reading.

He did not believe that the Church either could or should turn a blind eye to temporal problems. "It is the doctrine of the Incarnation which causes Christians to concern themselves with housing, leisure, unemployment", he wrote in 1934, adding, drily, that in his study of history he had observed that no one complained about the parson meddling with politics except when the message was unwelcome. Nevertheless it would be wrong to write him down as a "political" clergyman, for he had very definite views on what was fair for the pulpit and what was not. He was a gifted preacher, searching, scholarly, persuasive, with a high, chiselled voice which sounded "as though each word had been the subject of some discipline".

Spencer Cecil Carpenter, son of Robert Spencer Carpenter, was born on November 3, 1877, and educated at University College School, London, where his father taught for nearly 30 years, and Caius College, Cambridge. He took a second class in the Classical, a first in the Theological Tripos, and won the Carus Greek Testament Prize. He was ordained in 1902 to the curacy of St. Paul's, Newington, and was successively Sub-Warden of Queen's College, Birmingham, Vice-Principal of Westcott House, Cambridge, and Warden of his college mission in Battersea. From 1913 to 1922 he was fellow, tutor, and lecturer of Selwyn College, Cambridge, and was then appointed vicar of Bolton. From 1916 to 1922 he was examining chaplain to the Bishop of Southwark and from 1927 to 1931 to the Bishop of Manchester.

August 20, 1959.

Sir Edgar Bonham-Carter—See **Bonham.**

Joyce Cary, the novelist, died at his home at Oxford on March 29, 1957 after a long illness. He was 68.

Never among the more popular novelists in Britain, though always held in the highest respect by critical opinion, Joyce Cary gave himself seriously, perhaps too seriously, to the problems of the novelist's craft. In all that he wrote he demonstrated an unswerving artistic integrity. Drawing in the first place upon his experience as a political officer in Nigeria, he produced a series of novels with an African setting in which he brought a lively realistic humour to his observation of Negro psychology, and set down with unsentimental force and candour the effects of the white man's administration.

Then, with *Herself Surprised*, published in 1941, which was awarded the James Tait Black memorial prize, he started to explore a vein of serio-comic Anglo-Irish narrative which at its happiest provided a feast of character and sly fun. The exploration, though rewarded until the end by rich finds of idiosyncratic comedy, grew progressively more laboured. He seemed to develop a love of virtuosity for its own sake, and his later work, while often illuminating in its riotous and extravagant habit, is inclined to be over-elaborate in conception and rather too mannered in style. Yet as a novelist he never lost either the storyteller's instinct or an ironical, thoughtful, and sometimes poetic gift of insight.

Born on December 7, 1888, Arthur Joyce Lunel Cary was the eldest son of Arthur P. C. Cary, of Wadeford, Somerset, and Charlotte Joyce. Much of his boyhood was spent in Ireland, in Donegal, which provides the setting of what is perhaps the most delightful and most poetical of his novels, *The House of Children.* He was sent to Clifton and proceeded to Trinity College, Oxford, where much of his reading apparently consisted of works of philosophy. Undecided on the choice of a career, he studied art in Edinburgh, served with the British Red Cross and a Montenegrin battalion in the Balkan War of 1912-13, and for a time assisted Sir Horace Plunkett in the field of Irish co-operative organization. In 1913 he joined the Nigerian political service, where he remained, except for an interval with the Nigeria Regiment during the Cameroons campaign of 1915-16, until 1920, when he resigned for reasons of ill-health.

He was 43 when he wrote his first novel, *Aissa Saved*, in which he drew a remarkable objective picture of conditions in Nigeria, and leavened with nice irony his doubt of the white man's success in improving Negro morals. A year later, in 1933, came *An American Visitor*, again set in British Nigeria, in which his grasp of native psychology was perhaps obscured by the political parable he tacked on to the story.

The African Witch, published in 1936, had a more complex and less harmonious theme than either of the two earlier books, was not quite so readable and, as so often happens in these circumstances, proved much more successful. Three years later Cary produced *Mister Johnson*, the best of his African novels, a felicitous blend of analytical realism with vivid storytelling of an Africa that recalls *King Solomon's Mines*.

Two novels about children followed. *Charley is My Darling* (1940), a sympathetic and amusing study of a group of boys from a London slum evacuated to a West Country village, does not lack distinction but otherwise belongs to an all too common type of fiction of the period. *The House of Children* (1941), on the other hand, written round the experience of the author's early years in Donegal, is a jewel of a book, faultlessly clear and unsentimental in its evocation of the sensibilities of childhood. In the same year appeared *Herself Surprised*, which for many of Joyce Cary's admirers is likely to remain the most imaginatively satisfying and the most finished of his works. Closely modelled in style and spirit upon *Moll Flanders*, so that at times it leaves an impression of almost pure pastiche, the story of his Sara shines with an irresistibly sly and humane humour that is very much the author's own. Sara's story is resumed in two more first-person narratives and from two different angles, in *To Be a Pilgrim* (1942) and *The Horse's Mouth* (1944), but the effect is very different. Both books preserve something of the cunning humour of the earlier work, but Cary was now carried away by the spell of his own artifice and the experimentalist and conscious stylist in him ran riot.

The chief work of Cary's later years is another trilogy, *Prisoner of Grace* (1952), *Except the Lord* (1953), and *Not Honour More* (1955), in which he again casts an identical set of characters into differently angled first-person narratives. Once more the conception is somewhat top-heavy, the imaginative purpose too rigidly preconceived; the wife, the lover and the political bigwig of a husband are all enigmas of one sort or another and rarely come quite alive. But the humour is still there, filling the interstices of a strongly felt study of moral predicaments in politics and personal relationships. His fiction apart, Cary was the author of two small volumes, *Power in Man* (1939) and *The Process of Real Freedom* (1943), each designed as a philosophical statement of his liberal creed; of *The Case for African Freedom* (1941); and of a long allegorical poem, *The Drunken Sailor* (1947).

In his later years, partly because of ill health, Cary lived a relatively secluded life in Oxford. Tall, thin, loose-limbed, quiet and undemonstrative in manner, his speculative turn of mind was always apparent in conversation with him.

He married, in 1916, Gertrude Margaret Ogilvie. There were four sons of the marriage. His wife died in 1949.

March 30, 1957.

W. F. Casey, Editor of *The Times* from 1948 until 1952, died in London on April 20, 1957 at the age of 72.

His long and varied career as a journalist, beginning in 1913 and covering two world wars and two phases of uneasy peace, was all spent in the service of *The Times*. He was unique among editors of *The Times* in his first-hand knowledge of all branches of the paper's journalistic activities at home and abroad. He had learnt by this long experience, wedded to his own peculiar intuitive good sense and understanding of men and affairs, to pick out the relevant facts upon which sober news and sound views depend: his judgment, shrewd and swiftly formed, stood him in equally good stead as a leader writer and in the editorial chair.

This weight of professional competence was carried light-heartedly and, as a wide circle of men and women in all walks of life knew, he was a witty, unassuming, and friendly companion. No editor of *The Times* has been more well or more widely loved. His friendly approach, particularly to those who had earned his esteem, was a byword, but even they quickly discovered that to presume on this side of his character in order to persuade him into a betrayal of the principles by which he ruled his life was to court a sharp and telling rebuke. In a temperament so urbane there was little room for anger, but the rare occasions on which urbanity was ever seen to desert him were in response to shallow thought, because he considered it to be dishonest.

William Francis Casey was born in Cape Town on May 2, 1884, the son of Patrick Joseph Casey, of Glenageary, co. Dublin. He was educated in Ireland at Castlenock College and Trinity College, Dublin, where he spent two years at the medical school. But, abandoning medicine for the law, he was called to the Irish Bar in 1909. While he was reading for the law he acted briefly, in a part-time capacity, on the business side of the Abbey Theatre, of which Yeats and Lady Gregory were then directors. Casey used to dismiss this brief legal phase of his career characteristically—summing it up as: "One year, one brief, one guinea".

He decided to seek his fortune in London, having, before doing so, won the reputation of being a young dramatist of promise. Two of his plays, *The Suburban Groove* and *The Young Man from Rathmines*, were produced at the Abbey Theatre. An introduction to Sir Bruce Richmond* led to writing reviews for *The Times Literary Supplement*. Then, shortly before war broke out in 1914, the future editor was offered work during the holiday season as a sub-editor in the sporting room. Casey had found a profession in which he was to be happily and profitably employed until his retirement. After a spell as a foreign sub-editor he was posted as acting correspondent in Washington in 1919 and transferred to Paris in 1920, where he remained for the next two years.

From 1923 until 1928 he was chief foreign sub-editor and was then promoted to the foreign leader writing staff. He attended many sessions of the League of Nations at Geneva and followed events in Europe in a spirit of sympathy towards French rather than German aspirations. He became an assistant editor in 1935 and, on the retirement of Geoffrey Dawson in 1941, he was appointed by the new editor, R. M. Barrington-Ward, as his deputy. After the sudden death of Barrington-Ward in 1948 Casey succeeded him. Increasing ill-health handicapped him through his last years in Printing House Square. But he continued, until his retirement, to keep a close watch on affairs and to make the influence of his poise and fairmindedness felt in the policies of the paper.

Many qualities go to make a responsible journalist, and Casey possessed most of them, above all the most fundamental one of principle. Whatever his own views on any subject, he was inflexibly insistent that the facts, however disagreeable they might be to him, were fully and accurately reported. He could form a judgment on the spur of the moment, as is sometimes inevitable in such work as his, but he seldom had reason afterwards to regret what he had decided. Tactful in the handling of the work of other men, he would alter it, with speed and felicity, when he felt that lucidity, truth, or common sense required it. As a writer he had the gifts of clarity and of an easily read style, and in his time he handled with distinction a remarkably wide range of subjects.

Those who knew his early work in the theatre felt that he should not have allowed the pressure of other responsibilities to combine with an easy-going temperament to discourage him from tackling more ambitious plays. The keen watch he kept on the comedy of life, his warm heart, and his freedom from sentimentality might have stood him in good stead had he chosen to explore his own possibilities as a dramatist. He wrote two novels, *Haphazard* in 1917 and *The Private Life of a Successful Man* in 1935, but neither of these gave evidence of more than some talent for the writing of fiction.

The wit and the relish for political and social scenes which were so marked and so delightful a feature of Casey's personality found easy expression in conversation at the clubs where he delighted to relax. The Athenaeum, the Garrick, the Beefsteak, and the Savile have lost in him a member who kept up, almost until the last, the art of good talking which is so often said to be on the wane. Casey could "rattle"—his own word for himself off duty—with the best of civilized men. But he never ceased to be a serious student of home and foreign politics. Controversialists who mistook his bland, modest air for the marks of a lightweight frequently found themselves out of their depths and worsted in argument with him. Eminent public figures no less than the rank and file went through that experience.

He married, in 1914, Amy Gertrude Pearson-Gee, daughter of the late Henry Willmott. There were no children of the marriage. He was an honorary LL.D. of his own university, Dublin.

April 22, 1957.

The Right Rev. William Wilson Cash, D.S.O., O.B.E., D.D., Bishop of Worcester since 1941 and formerly general secretary of the Church Missionary Society, died in a nursing home in Worcester on July 18, 1955 at the age of 75. He had been ill for some time and his impending resignation was announced in June.

A great missionary in his younger days and an eloquent speaker in Arabic, his qualities of leadership, efficiency, and above all his spiritual force led to his appointment during the War of 1914-18 as assistant principal chaplain to the Egyptian Expeditionary Force in Palestine. The same qualities raised him to a position of powerful influence over the largest missionary society of the Church. He was a firm advocate of cooperation in missions, in the large aspects of policy and statesmanship no less than in such enterprises as an African literature bureau. Indeed, it was as a thinker and leader on the ultimate objectives of policy that he was able to enlist the support of evangelical missionary enterprise for large cooperative aims in building up the younger native and other churches overseas.

William Cash was a Cheshire man whose early home was at Sale. He was born on June 12, 1880, the son of James Cash, who worked for 25 years on the editorial staff of the *Manchester Guardian.* He was educated at the Cambridge School, Sale, and went out to the mission field as a layman under the Egypt General Mission in 1901. He joined the C.M.S. Egypt Mission in 1909 and was ordained the following year, working at Menouf.

As an Army chaplain he saw much service during the First World War. At the end of 1916 he joined the headquarters of the Army operating in Sinai, was with Allenby's Army on its move through Palestine, and after the capture of Jerusalem he preached at the thanksgiving service in St. George's Cathedral, Jerusalem. From 1918 to 1920 he was assistant principal chaplain. He was five times mentioned in dispatches and was awarded the D.S.O. and made an O.B.E. Demobilized in 1920, he was appointed secretary of the C.M.S. missions in Palestine, Egypt, and the northern Sudan. In 1924 he was appointed home secretary of the C.M.S., and on January 1, 1926 general secretary.

It was an extraordinarily fortunate choice for the C.M.S., for it gave to that society through difficult years (which included the heavy impact of the economic depression upon the primary producers of colonial lands, as well as the rather bewildered reactions abroad to the Prayer Book controversy at home) one of the great missionary leaders of modern times. The course which he steered was a kind of middle way between the instinctive evangelical tendency towards an exclusive alignment with Free Church or Continental Protestant missions, and the opposite policy of merging the evangelical tradition in a "common pool" wherein Anglican Catholic traditions would have predominated because of their organization. He believed in the preservation of the evangelical tradition as such, and in the maintenance of the distinctively C.M.S. influence in all the numerous oversea dioceses and institutions where it operated; but he believed also in active cooperation with other and more Catholic traditions. His was thus a unifying policy, and in the event it strengthened evangelical influence. Of his oversea tours special mention should be made of that in 1931, when he led a C.M.S. delegation to the churches of Australia and New Zealand.

Cash's indirect influence on the missionary world through other missionary leaders was enormous, and part of it was exercised through his books. He wrote innumerable articles in the missionary magazines, devotional booklets, and aids to Bible study. Among his more lasting works are *The Moslem World in Revolution* published in 1925 and still valuable on its subject; *The Expansion of Islam* (1928); *Christendom and Islam* (1937); and *The Missionary Church* (1939). The last is one of the best general books on modern missions and may be commended, for example, to sentimentalists who for the sake of picturesque savage survivals would oppose "the replacing of the fear-religions by the Christian liberty of the Children of God".

In 1933 Cash was made Prebendary of Weldland in St. Paul's Cathedral, and in 1939 Chaplain to the King. On November 1, 1941, he was consecrated Bishop of Worcester. He was an inspiring bishop. The keynotes of his episcopate were contained in two or three sentences in his earliest letters to the diocese: "Our patriotism will be all the stronger as we place God in the centre of our lives. To turn away from Him because of the war is to turn our backs on the one hope of our nation"; and again: "Prayer is the secret of power".

One of his earliest steps was the formation of a diocesan prayer fellowship. At the same time he was insistent that "the multiplication of church services does not necessarily mean increased spiritual power". Old methods, he told his diocesan conference in June 1942, might have to be scrapped and new ways tried. If the nation would not come to the church, then the church must go to the nation, that by every available channel the Gospel of Christ might be known. An example of his own new methods was the appointment each year of four of the younger clergy to be his private chaplains and so see something of other parishes than their own.

His comments on broad issues of politics were always cautious, but they were definite. He did not believe that peace could be realized "through leagues, pacts, and covenants, through organizations and councils", but only "through a changed human nature and a new way of life based on good will". Under him the primary emphasis was always upon the reality of faith and upon prayer.

In 1949 he was summoned to take his seat in the House of Lords. His health deteriorated in 1954 and his diocesan work became necessarily intermittent. He returned from a recuperative visit to Spain and shortly afterwards announced that he would retire at the end of September.

He married, in 1906, Alice Maude Ladkin, who had also worked in Egypt as a missionary before her marriage. She died in 1953. They are survived by a son and two daughters.

July 19, 1955.

General Sir Robert Archibald Cassels, G.C.B., G.C.S.I., D.S.O., C-in-C of the Army in India, 1935-41, died on December 23, 1959 at the age of 83.

Cassels was in the Indian cavalry and came to notice early in his career as an officer of outstanding capacity, although he saw no active service before the First World War. Then, in Mesopotamia against the Turks, he proved himself a skilful and energetic commander and his advancement was assured. He was born on March 15, 1876, and received his commission in January 1896, arriving in India in the following March. After being attached to the 1st and then to the 10th Bombay Infantry, and serving as A.D.C. to the Political Resident at Aden, he was transferred to the 5th Punjab Cavalry and, in 1901, to the 2nd Bombay Lancers, better known by its later title of 32nd Lancers. He had been promoted lieutenant in 1898.

He was appointed adjutant of his regiment in 1903, got his captaincy in 1905, and from February 1906 until he passed into the Staff College at Quetta in 1907 he was A.D.C. to the commander of the Quetta Division. After graduating he was appointed in 1909 brigade-major of the Meerut Cavalry Brigade, and in 1911 he went to the 7th (Meerut) Division as G.S.O.2. At the beginning of 1913 he returned to the 32nd Lancers for his last spell of regimental duty, being promoted major in 1914.

In September, soon after the outbreak of the war, he left his squadron on appointment as D.A.A.G. at the headquarters of the Army. When General Nixon assumed command in Mesopotamia in April 1915 Cassels was selected to be D.A.A.G. with the headquarters of the Expeditionary Force, and in December he went to the III (Indian) Corps as G.S.O.1. In this capacity he served throughout the four attempts made, under General Aylmer, to relieve Kut-al-Amara, and in May 1916 he became G.S.O.1 on the staff of the 14th (Indian) Division. With the division he took part in Maude's victorious advance to Baghdad. After the occupation of the city he was placed in command of a mixed force of cavalry—two squadrons of his old regiment—guns, and aircraft which operated with success in the Khalis canal area in April 1917, taking its share in the successful action of Istabulat and in the passage of the Adhaim river.

In 1917 he was transferred to the Cavalry Division as G.S.O.1 and in August he went to the headquarters of the Mesopotamian Expeditionary Force as Brigadier-General, General Staff; but he was glad to get command in

November of the 11th Cavalry Brigade, which he led until after the war. In March 1918 his brigade played a prominent part in the action of Khan Baghdadi on the Euphrates; and in the October advance up the Tigris it led the way, so that it reached Mosul on November 3 after the armistice with Turkey had been signed.

His services as staff officer and commander were rewarded with one brevet in 1916 and another in 1917; he was awarded the D.S.O. in 1918 and created a C.B.; and he received eight "mentions".

At the beginning of 1919, when not yet 43 years of age, he was promoted major-general, and in November he took command of the 5th Cavalry Brigade in Egypt, where he stayed three months; his next appointment was in December 1920 when he was selected to be Cavalry Adviser at Army headquarters in India; and three years later he was given command of the Peshawar District, which he held for four years. After promotion to lieutenant-general in April 1928 he was appointed Adjutant-General in May, and he attained the rank of general in 1929. In the following May he left Army headquarters to become G.O.C.-in-Chief Northern Command, and during his four years' tenure of this post the Frontier was comparatively quiet, no major operations being necessary. In November 1935 he succeeded Sir Philip Chetwode as Commander-in-Chief in India with a seat on the Governor General's Executive Council. He retired in 1941.

Cassels was created C.S.I. in 1920, and promoted K.C.B. in 1927 and G.C.B. in 1933. In 1940 he was advanced to G.C.S.I. From 1929 to 1933 he was an A.D.C. General to the King; and he was appointed Colonel of the 7th Light Cavalry in 1933 and Colonel Commandant of the Indian Signal Corps in 1936.

He married Florence Emily, daughter of Lieutenant-Colonel H. Jackson, in 1904, and leaves one son, General Sir James Cassels.

December 24, 1959.

Dr. George Clark Cathcart, who died in a nursing home in Edinburgh on January 4, 1951 at the age of 90, was the doyen of British ear, nose, and throat specialists, but it will be of interest to a wider public that he was the founder in 1894 of the Promenade Concerts, the influence of which upon musical appreciation in Britain has been incalculable.

Dr. Cathcart's father was the greatest friend of Robert Louis Stevenson's father, and young George was accustomed to walk with his elders (often including R. L. S.) after church to the Chain Pier at Granton and home to the Sunday midday dinner of those days. He went to school at Loretto and, after graduating at Edinburgh, voyaged to Australia and back in a sailing ship, was a pupil at Naples of Scafati, one of the last teachers of the old Italian *bel canto*, in order to cure a stammer, and then in 1891 qualified M.B., proceeding in 1908 to M.D. He left Edinburgh—mainly because he was known there as Charles Cathcart, the surgeon's young brother—for London as a resident at the Children's Hospital, Great Ormond Street, and subsequently became resident house surgeon to Edward Law and McNeill Whistler (elder brother of the painter) at the old London Throat Hospital (later amalgamated with Golden Square Hospital), to which in due course he was appointed honorary surgeon.

In his earlier days in practice he was greatly interested in problems of the voice, and the chief motive behind his founding of the Promenade Concerts was his enthusiasm to prevent vocal strain by insisting on the orchestral instruments being tuned to French pitch and not to the higher concert pitch, as was then usual. In order to do this he had to buy the necessary instruments in Brussels, though eventually the various members of the orchestra acquired them from him. He was also insistent that his young friend Henry Wood, in whose future he had great faith, should be the conductor of the series of concerts. Even the famous fountain in the middle of the parterre was one of his ideas. Then a young bachelor of independent means, Dr. Cathcart was content to lose several thousand pounds in launching the Promenade Concerts.

Dr. Cathcart was a sound oto-laryngologist, a safe and careful operator, who kept well within the limits of his knowledge and ambitions, and at the height of his career he had one of the best consulting practices in London. In 1926 he revised—indeed, he completely rewrote—his late friend Hunter Tod's textbook, *Diseases of the Ear*, published 20 years previously, and most otologists considered the revised edition even better than the original; in 1931 he published a small book, *The Treatment of Chronic Deafness*. Innumerable singers and students of singing—few if any of whom ever paid him a professional fee—found in him a true friend and adviser.

He never married. Freemasonry was to him almost a religion and he was a Past Master of the University of Edinburgh Lodge and a member of Grand Lodge. He still played a good game of golf—learned long ago at Musselburgh—when he was nearly 80. It was reminiscent of another era to see him, between the two great wars, in his black velvet dinner jacket presiding benevolently at the head of the table in his panelled dining room in Upper Wimpole Street, the cabinets at either end of it lit up to show his collection of eighteenth-century glass, pieces of massive Irish cut glass on the Sheraton sideboard, and the table illuminated by candles in old glass candlesticks, with some of the most interesting company in London round the table and some of the best claret in the world upon it.

January 6, 1951.

Lord Catto, who died on August 23, 1959 at the age of 80, was the first Governor of the nationalized Bank of England. He was appointed Governor by the King under the Bank of England Act, 1946, having previously been elected Governor of the Bank in April 1944, when it was still a private institution, and he was thus Governor during the whole delicate period of transition. He had previously served as Financial Adviser to the Chancellor of the Exchequer from 1940 to 1944. Before taking up these high public appointments he had a distinguished and successful business career as a merchant banker.

The Right Hon. Sir Thomas Sivewright Catto, Bt., P.C., C.B.E., first Baron Catto, of Cairncatto, Aberdeenshire, in the Peerage of the United Kingdom, was born on March 15, 1879. Several generations of Cattos had carried on business as merchants at Peterhead. His father, William Catto, moved from Peterhead with his wife and four young sons to Newcastle upon Tyne, where Thomas Catto was born. When Thomas was six months old his father died and the family returned to Peterhead, where, with his brothers, he attended the old Peterhead Academy. Later the family returned to Newcastle. Thomas won a scholarship at Heaton School (Rutherford College) at Newcastle and completed his education there.

Leaving school in 1895 at the age of 16, Catto entered the office of a Newcastle shipowning firm, the Gordon Steam Shipping Company Ltd., and there he had four years' thorough grounding in the elements of commerce in general and shipping in particular. But evidently he could not see the opening for which he was looking, and in 1898, at the age of 19, he answered an advertisement for an appointment. As a result he was engaged as private secretary to W. H. Stuart, an English shipper and merchant who had extensive business connexions in Russia and in the Near and Middle East. Within a few years Stuart made him his manager. After six years he joined MacAndrews and Forbes, a large and well known merchant house with a large trade in Russia and the Near and Middle East. His rise with his new employers was again rapid, and within two years he had been appointed deputy to David Forbes, the general manager for the whole of Europe and the East. In 1908, still only 28, he was transferred to New York as first vice-president of the MacAndrews and Forbes American house. He remained in the United States for 11 years.

The outbreak of the 1914-18 War found him still in the United States, and that war brought him his first acquaintance with public service and the world of politics and public administration. In the early months of the war the Admiralty was looking for somebody of proved business ability who was familiar with the American scene and at the same time had some knowledge of Russia. Thomas Catto's qualifications were apparent and he was duly appointed British Admiralty representative on the Russian Mission in New York. When the United States entered the war in 1917 he was transferred to the British Food Mission, and eventually in 1918 became chairman of the British and Allied Food Missions in the United States and Canada.

In 1919 he returned to business life, but in a still more important capacity. His abilities had for a long time won high esteem from Lord Bicester [q.v.], then Vivian Hugh Smith, head of the eminent London merchant banking firm of Morgan Grenfell and Co., which was closely associated with the New York house of J. P. Morgan and Co., and also with the great Indian merchant house of Andrew Yule and Co., of Calcutta. At that time Sir David Yule, head of Andrew Yule and Co., was looking for somebody to succeed him. Thomas Catto was introduced to Sir David Yule by Lord Bicester and was duly invited to join the firm and to succeed Sir David Yule as its head. He served as head of Andrew Yule and Co. for 12 years—from 1919 to 1931—and during this period not only was he a dominant figure in the commercial life of India and the Far East but also was called on to discharge various public duties. Among other public appointments he was a member of the Indian Government (Inchcape) Retrenchment Commission of 1922-23.

In 1928 he became a managing director of Morgan Grenfell and Co., with which firm he was already closely connected as head of Andrew Yule and Co. For the next few years he divided his time between India and London, and both then and later he interested himself deeply in Indian problems and general questions of post-war reconstruction and finance. He made London his headquarters more definitely from 1931 onwards. He became a director of the Bank of England in March 1940. In 1936 he was created a baron for his services to India.

The 1939-45 war once again interrupted his business life and drew him over to the sphere of public administration. In April 1940, he succeeded Lord Woolton* as Director-General of Equipment and Stores in the Ministry of Supply and became a member of the Supply Council. In July of that year he was appointed to the position—a post specially created for the war and unpaid—of Financial Adviser to the Chancellor of the Exchequer.

The last and most important phase of his career started on April 18, 1944, when he was elected Governor of the Bank of England in succession to Montagu Norman. Lord Catto had a difficult role to fulfil, since his predecessor had virtually built the Bank of England organization as it then existed and had established a personal ascendancy not only over the Bank but over the whole City. At the same time the idea of the Bank's role as an instrument of Government policy—an idea welcomed by Norman—had become more firmly entrenched. Lord Catto, with his many years of banking and commercial experience on the one hand, and his four years at the Treasury on the other, was an obvious choice for the dual responsibility to Government and City. But a still more delicate and invidious task was in store for him, as the Labour Government came into power 14 months after his election as Governor, and the nationalization of the Bank of England was one of the earliest and most urgent items on the Labour programme.

Any Governor who had to negotiate terms and conditions with the Government and had to act as the intermediary between the stockholders and the Treasury, and also between the clearing banks and the Government on matters of general banking regulation, was bound to lay himself open to suspicion and criticism. Lord Catto came in for his full share of this, though the criticism was seldom ventilated in public, and he showed plainly at the time that he was sensitive to this criticism and anxious to rebut any suggestion that he had been more sympathetic to the policy of the Government than to the views and interests of the City which he was expected in some ways to represent. His speech in the House of Lords defending the terms (though not the principle) of the Bank of England Bill and his evidence in Committee caused much comment, some of it critical, in banking circles. But in the end most people were willing to agree that he had done what should have been expected of the Governor in the circumstances—that he had succeeded in preserving the individuality, independence, and established organization of the Bank of England almost intact in form in spite of the change of ownership.

The building of the organization of the Bank of England in its modern form was not Lord Catto's work; it was essentially the child of Montagu Norman. Nor did Lord Catto remain long enough after nationalization—for he retired in 1949—to play a major part in shaping its development as a national institution. His Governorship was associated essentially with the transition to public ownership under the Labour Government.

Apart from his exceptional ability in the field of ordinary business and finance he had the breadth of outlook, the personality, and the diplomatic sense to find his way easily in the difficult public and political tasks which fell to his lot. He was a natural leader and seemed to find it as easy to gain ascendancy in negotiation as to impose his authority over the institutions which he controlled. This power of leadership rested entirely on quick wit, intelligence, humanity, and strength of will. For it was achieved in spite of unusually small stature and quietness of manner.

Lord Catto had many interests outside the world of banking, business, and public life, and there was nothing which was at all times dearer to his heart than his native heath in Aberdeenshire. Long ago he purchased the farm Cairncatto on which stands an ancient cairn, reputed to mark the site of a battle fought in the remote past, and from which he took his title. He made his own Scottish home in Aberdeenshire a few miles away from Cairncatto at the House of Schivas, which he had extensively restored between 1931 and 1937. Shortly after he retired he accepted the chairmanship of the committee on Scottish finance and trade statistics which reported in 1952.

In 1910 he married Gladys, daughter of Stephen Gordon, of Elgin, who survives him. There were four children of the marriage. His only son, the Hon. Stephen Gordon Catto, who was born in 1923, succeeds him as second baron.

August 24, 1959.

Hugh Gascoyne Cecil—See **Quickswood.**

Lord Cecil of Chelwood, who died on November 24, 1958 in a nursing home at Tunbridge Wells at the age of 94, was one of the remarkable sons of Lord Salisbury, the Prime Minister, who impressed themselves by their strongly individualistic idealism on public life in the earlier years of this century. His scholarly, distinguished figure, the eagle-like profile, and the high domed forehead were familiar to parliamentarians from Edwardian days onwards.

He held high offices of State. But he will be best remembered as an architect of the League of Nations; he began his advocacy of it as early as September 1916. On Lord Cecil's eightieth birthday, in 1944, Winston Churchill* in a letter to him, wrote "My dear Bob . . . this war could easily have been prevented if the League of Nations had been used with courage and loyalty by the associated nations. . . . You are entitled to mellow reflections even while the storm still rages." That tribute to Lord Cecil's main work in life will stand as the verdict of history.

The Right Hon. Edgar Algernon Robert Gascoyne Cecil, P.C., C.H., Q.C., Viscount Cecil of Chelwood, of Grinstead in the county of Sussex in the Peerage of the United Kingdom, was the third son of the third Marquess of Salisbury. His mother was the daughter of Baron Alderson. He was born on September 14, 1864, when Lord Salisbury was a member of the House of Commons as Lord Robert Cecil. Robert went like his brothers Hugh and William to Eton and to University College, Oxford, where he worked at law. He was called to the Bar by the Inner Temple in 1887. He was very successful at the Parliamentary Bar and was an active member of the Bar Council, to whom he presented in 1918 the bulk of his library of legal books, many of which had come to him from the library of Lord Chancellor Selborne, whose son was his brother-in-law. Lord Robert in 1889 married Lady Eleanor Lambton, and they had a small country home at Chelwood, near Uckfield.

In January 1906, Lord Robert was elected Unionist member for East Marylebone, in spite of the free-trade views which he was at no pains to conceal from the tariff reformers who opposed his selection. In January 1910 he and George Bowles together fought Blackburn unsuccessfully as Unionist free-traders, Philip Snowden being one of the successful candidates; and in December 1910 he fought North Cambridgeshire against Neil Primrose. But in November, 1911, when he became Chairman of the Hertfordshire Quarter Sessions, he was returned at a by-election for the Hitchin Division of Hertfordshire. In 1913 he published *Our National Church*, written in collaboration with the Rev. H. J. Clayton. Lord Robert was always a staunch and devoted churchman, like the rest of his family, and here his thesis was the existence through the centuries of a covenant between Church and State to help each other in uplifting national life.

A few months after the outbreak of the Great War he became Under-Secretary of State for Foreign Affairs. Sir Edward Grey was overworked and troubled by his eyesight. To Lord Robert therefore there fell more work and responsibility than usually falls to an Under-Secretary, as in the case of the Orders in Council of March 1915. With Balfour later on he was working with an intimate friend and cousin. He became a Privy Councillor in June 1915, and in February 1916 he became Minister of Blockade, with Cabinet rank, while remaining Under-Secretary of State. Early in 1918 he was appointed Assistant Secretary of State, and for frequent periods he acted as head of the Foreign Office. Of those relations with our allies which were not in charge of the Admiralty or the War Office many were connected with the blockade of the enemy or with the distribution of supplies to friends, and both of these activities were the work of his Contraband Department. Relations with neutrals turned upon the blockade almost entirely. Lord Roberts was responsible for most of the comprehensive series of agreements with the traders of the United States, Holland, Switzerland, and Scandinavia by which Britain obtained the virtual control of their external trade with a minimum of friction.

When the Cabinet decided that the truce which had endured for so long should be ended and that the Welsh Church Disestablishment Act should be put into operation as soon as the war was over Lord Robert resigned for conscience' sake. In his electoral campaign which followed the Armistice he declared in a characteristic manner that to him it seemed "doubly repulsive" to divert the funds of the Church to secular purposes "when we have been vouchsafed the great victory which has crowned our arms". On the day after the Armistice (November 12) he was installed as Chancellor of Birmingham University. Although his resignation had deprived him of the place that might have been his in the Peace Conference at Paris in 1919, he was made chairman of the Supreme Economic Council, whose purpose was to undo the effects of the blockade by restocking Europe and to set trade going again.

While he was still at the Foreign Office he had drawn up a memorandum outlining a future League of Nations, and in Paris at this time began the work which was to dominate the rest of his career. He had taken a deep interest in the early discussions of what President Wilson's idea of a League of Nations should mean and in the studies and suggestions of Lord Phillimore and others. Now he was appointed head of the British section of the Conference that was to deal with the League. The drafting of the Covenant brought him and Sir Cecil Hurst* into close touch with General Smuts, Colonel House, and M. Fromageot. Lord Robert saw that President Wilson had thought out none of the practical difficulties and details and had had no experience of European politics, and the burden of drafting fell largely to Lord Robert and to General Smuts. He did not consider the Covenant perfect, but had reason to be thankful that one so near his own ideal should be incorporated in the Treaty.

General Smuts, who was in South Africa in 1920, appointed him to represent the Union at the first Assembly of the League. Thus he began to take the place at Geneva which he held later on as the delegate of Great Britain, and for some years his position was second to none. In 1921 he went into opposition at home. He was impatient with the Government. He wanted them to adopt a more "European" attitude, of which a real keenness to get Germany into the League would have been the proof. In this and in the doctrine which he was preaching to deaf ears, that "the existence of a prosperous Germany is essential to the economic life of Europe", he knew that British policy was not the chief obstacle, but he demanded more positive effort than the Government would make. In the following March he went to Canada and addressed scores of meetings in the United States on the League.

In 1923 he entered the new Conservative Government as Lord Privy Seal, an office which left him free to devote himself to the League and to represent this country at Geneva.

Towards the end of the year his never very robust health being exhausted by the double strain of work in Parliament and for the League, he was created a peer as Viscount Cecil of Chelwood. A year later, when the Unionist Government returned to power, Lord Cecil was made Chancellor of the Duchy, and so again was a Cabinet Minister with freedom to work for the League. He was also elected Rector of Aberdeen University and delivered an address on the party system.

It was undoubtedly chiefly due to Lord Cecil that the draft Treaty of Mutual Assistance was produced by the League of Nations. He was greatly disappointed at the reception at home and by the League of the work that he and his colleagues had done. When the Protocol was produced next year (1924) he appreciated the merits of a proposal resting on the principles of arbitration, security, and disarmament, but he held that all the objections raised against his Treaty applied equally to the Protocol.

In 1927 he went to Geneva with the First Lord of the Admiralty and his experts in answer to the invitation of the United States to discuss the limitation of Naval Armaments. The Conference consisted only of the United States of America, Great Britain, and Japan, but it failed, and Lord Cecil addressed a letter to the Prime Minister, Stanley Baldwin, announcing his resignation from the Cabinet, and giving as his chief reason that "on the broad policy of disarmament the majority of the Cabinet and I are not really agreed". In this, as Baldwin wrote to him, he probably exaggerated the difference of opinion, because he was tired out and needed rest and freedom for a time. Lord Cecil was determined to work for disarmament outside the Government. It may be said that a man who twice resigned office and twice differed from his party when out of office was a difficult colleague, and there is some truth in the judgment. But no one could fail to respect Lord Cecil's obedience to conscience. In 1937 he was awarded the Nobel Peace Prize.

In 1941, a year and a half after the outbreak of the second German war, Lord Cecil published *A Great Experiment*, an "autobiography", which, in fact, consisted of an account of his conception and championship of the League of Nations. He attributed its failure mainly to the selfishness and timidity of the Governments of the greater Powers; and in a memorandum on "World Settlement after the Present War" showed that he still believed in the machinery set up in 1920. Agreed and universal reduction of armaments was still his fundamental remedy, and he hardly seemed to give sufficient importance to Article XIX of the original Covenant, which covered the revision of treaties. The book is valuable as an authoritative if personal account of the rise and decline of the League.

In the spring of 1946, when he was 81, he flew to Geneva to attend the winding-up of the League of Nations which he had done so much to create and shortly afterwards he was made honorary life president of the newly formed United Nations Association.

In 1949 appeared *All the Way*, a much fuller and more intimate autobiography than *A Great Experiment*, containing some vital and enchanting memories of Hatfield and its vigorous individualistic family. In 1956 he was made a Companion of Honour.

Cecil retained his interest in current affairs to the last and though hampered by deafness he continued to visit the House of Lords from time to time.

November 25, 1958.

Admiral Sir Dudley de Chair—See **de Chair.**

Mrs. Joseph Chamberlain—See **Carnegie.**

Sir Edmund Chambers, K.B.E., C.B., died at his home at Beer, Devon, on January 21, 1954. He was 87.

An educationist of wide learning, patient, persevering, and, above all, prodigiously industrious, he wrote much on the men of genius, and the history, events, and customs of the Elizabethan age. His work was no less penetrating and precise when it came to writing on such outstanding personalities as Samuel Taylor Coleridge and Matthew Arnold, or on the lyrics and poems of the spacious past.

Though several of his books were monumental in conception and size, they were also fascinating in content. His work *The Elizabethan Stage*, published in 1923, consisted of four substantial and strictly factual volumes, while another, *Sir Thomas Wyatt and Collected Studies*, represented painstaking labour over a period of 40 years. Most of his books brought to light new information on matters that had hitherto been overlooked or disregarded by other researchers. In delving into the origins of some of the quaint practices that had survived from bygone times he examined, as it were with a microscope, the evidence of a common source of inspiration. His books without exception were hailed by the critics as masterpieces of erudition and research.

Edmund Kerchever Chambers was born in Berkshire on March 16, 1866, the eldest son of the Rev. William Chambers, Fellow and Tutor of Worcester College, Oxford. He was educated at Marlborough and Corpus Christi College, Oxford, where he was Chancellor's English Essayist in 1891 and was later elected an honorary Fellow. In the following year he entered the Education Department, and from that time, although he eventually reached the office of Second Secretary to the Board of Education, he devoted all his energies to literary and cultural pursuits throughout his long and distinguished career.

He edited many poetical works, including *English Pastorals* (1895), *Donne's Poems* and *Vaughan's Poems* (1896), *Red Letter Shakespeare* (1904-8), *Early English Lyrics* (with F. Sidgwick, 1907), *Aurelian Townshend's Poems* (1911), and the *Oxford Book of Sixteenth Century Verse* (1932). His first more ambitious literary effort was a masterly study of the medieval stage, published in 1903, but it was not till about 20 years later that he began to put in book form the exhaustive researches that established his name as an author of exceptional merit in a field offering almost unlimited scope. Each volume that proceeded from his facile pen explored new avenues of inquiry, and from 1923, when his brilliant survey of the Elizabethan stage created a sensation in literary circles, his labours were unremitting.

His subsequent works included: *Shakespeare: A Survey* (1925), *Arthur of Britain* (1927), a penetrating study of the Arthurian legend, *William Shakespeare* (1930), *The English Folk-Play* (1933), *Sir Henry Lee: An Elizabethan Portrait* (1936), *Eynsham under the Monks* (1936), a study of English medieval village life, *Samuel Taylor Coleridge* (1938), *A Sheaf of Studies* (1942), *Shakespearean Gleanings* (1944), *English Literature at the Close of the Middle Ages* (1945), *Sources for a Biography of Shakespeare* (1946), and *Matthew Arnold: A Study* (1947). He was a Fellow of the British Academy, and was made a C.B. in 1912, and appointed K.B.E. in 1925.

He married, in 1893, Eleanor Christabel (Nora), daughter of John Davison Bowman, who survives him. There were no children of the marriage.

January 22, 1954.

Sir John Chancellor, G.C.M.G., G.C.V.O., G.B.E., D.S.O., who during his long life achieved a considerable reputation as an administrator, died at his home in Lanarkshire on July 31, 1952 at the age of 81.

John Robert Chancellor was born in Edinburgh on October 20, 1870, the second son of C. E. Chancellor, of Woodhall House, Juniper Green, Midlothian. From Woolwich he joined the Royal Engineers in 1890, and was with the Indian contingent in the Dongola expedition of 1896. In the Tirah Expedition of 1897-98 he was in charge of the Sirmur Imperial Service Sappers, and was present at the capture of the Dargai Heights, the capture of the Sampagha and Arhanga passes, and the operations in the Bara Valley. His services were mentioned in dispatches and he was awarded the D.S.O. Passing through the Staff College in 1902, he was appointed a staff captain in the intelligence department of the War Office in the following year. A year later he was appointed assistant secretary (military) to the Committee of Imperial Defence; and he was secretary to the Colonial Defence Committee in 1906. In 1911 he was appointed Governor of Mauritius, and in 1916 Governor of Trinidad and Tobago. He was appointed the first Governor of Southern Rhodesia in 1923.

In Rhodesia Chancellor fully justified the reputation of a capable and progressive administrator which he had already achieved. As a Royal Engineer his opinion, always shrewd and practical, was valued in regard to the various works which the young colony was then considering or commencing. In the interests of both races, the first Governor stood firmly for a segregation so far modified that it would not, by isolating the natives from the Europeans, condemn them to "moral, intellectual, and material stagnation". Accordingly, he expressed disapprobation of such ideas as that the "proper native policy was to drive all the native races north of the Zambesi", equally with the suggestion that a solution of the problem was to be found in the fusion of white and black. Justice, sympathy, and above all common sense, firmly and consistently applied, was the only means, he urged, by which a *modus vivendi* taking all the factors into consideration, could be established.

As High Commissioner of Palestine, to which post he was appointed in 1928, Chancellor found himself in a vastly different *milieu*—a mandated territory in which on religious and economic grounds the establishment of a "national home" by Jewish incomers had roused acute resentment among the indigenous Arab population. His period of office proved a difficult one, and though he was energetic and effective in restoring order after the numerous excesses perpetrated by fanatics in the name of religion, he ended his term in 1931 on a note of disappointment at a farewell reception given by the Mayor of Jerusalem.

In his later years his wide range of interests and deep knowledge of colonial problems found expression in manifold activities. His chairmanships included the Agricultural Marketing Facilities Committee, the International Conference on Locusts, the Trustee Savings Bank Association, and the British Livestock Commission. In 1940-41 he was vice-chairman of the British Council. He was also a member of the Colonial Empire Marketing Board, and of the Colonial Development Advisory Committee, and member of the Council and Foreign Secretary of the Royal Geographical Society. His colonial interests also found expression in the vice-presidency of the Royal Empire Society and membership of the council of the Royal African Society and of the International Colonial Institute, and he held a number of directorships of commercial enterprises with colonial interests.

In 1903 he married Elsie, third daughter of G. Rodie Thompson, J.P., D.L., of Lynwood, Ascot, who survives him.

August 2, 1952.

Raymond Chandler, the author, died at his home at La Jolla, California, on March 26, 1959. He was 70.

Raymond Thornton Chandler was an American citizen born in Chicago of Quaker parents on August 23, 1888. They sent him to school at Dulwich College and he completed his education in France and Germany. He then tried his hand at schoolmastering, soldiering in a Canadian infantry regiment, accountancy, and the oil business. Finally he settled in America and began writing fiction. He served his apprenticeship in the "pulp" magazines of the late 1920s and early 1930s. "When in doubt", he said, "have a man come through the door with a gun in his hand": and he retained considerable respect for the technical honesty of that kind of story.

His mature thrillers became something of a cult among intellectuals. They were praised by literary critics, who normally despise crime fiction. Their originality has been confirmed by a host of imitators; but it would be untrue to say he founded a school, rather he defined a school. Dashiell Hammett* was his master. He admired Hammett's effect of realism, his sharp, aggressive attitude to life, and a style of writing which, Chandler insisted, was not personal to Hammett but inherent in the American language for him that can get it.

Chandler held strong views of what he called "the simple art of murder". He spoke disrespectfully of *The Hound of the Baskervilles* and *The Purloined Letter*; he ridiculed *Trent's Last Case*; he had no patience with the classic detective story which depends on contriving a problem and deducing the answer. His dispute with John Dickson Carr [d. 1977] on this subject split the upper echelons of crime writers.

Chandler's own success depended not so much on his plots or the shock value of their toughness as on the faceted irony of his style and his acridly atmospheric picture of Californian civilization. Modern crime, he believed, and therefore modern crime stories, belong to "a world gone wrong"; but "down the mean streets a man must go who is not himself mean, who is neither tarnished nor afraid". Such a man was Chandler's hero, Philip Marlowe, the lonely, sardonic, inflexibly honest private detective who provides the highly moral heart of all his books.

"Everything a writer learns about the art or craft of fiction", said Chandler, "takes just a little away from his need of drive to write at all. In the end he knows all the tricks and has nothing to say."

Raymond Chandler's fame rests on seven novels and a few relatively undistinguished short stories. *The Big Sleep*, which established his reputation on both sides of the Atlantic, was first published in 1939. His last book, *Playback*, appeared in 1958 after a long interval during which he wrote nothing. Gleams of the old brilliance were still there to confound his imitators: Philip Marlowe was still there, unfrightened and unstained; but the book was only the shadow of a shade. Raymond Chandler, having mastered his art, had nothing more to say.

He had already said a great deal in a very

small compass. His name will certainly go down among the dozen or so mystery writers who were also innovators and stylists; who, working the common vein of crime fiction, mined the gold of literature.

March 28, 1959.

R. W. Chapman, C.B.E., the scholar and eminent authority on the works of Samuel Johnson and Jane Austen, died in Oxford on April 20, 1960. He was 78.

Robert William Chapman was born at Eskbank, near Dalkeith, on October 5, 1881, the youngest of the six children of Edward Chapman, an Anglican clergyman working in Scotland, and Hannah Cannon, a Yorkshire woman. His father died when he was three, and his mother settled near Dundee. From the High School there Chapman obtained the first bursary at St. Andrews, where he learnt Greek from John Burnet and whence he went up to Oriel, with the Adam de Brome Scholarship, in 1902. He took Firsts in Classical Moderations and Greats and won the Gaisford Greek Prose Prize. Shortly after taking his degree Chapman became assistant to the Secretary of the Clarendon Press, Charles Cannan, whom he succeeded in 1920. Apart from absence in 1914-18, when he served with the Artillery in the Salonika force, the rest of his life was spent in Oxford, of which it may truly be said that it became a part of him and he of it.

At the Press his main concern, apart from administrative duties, was with editions and lexicography, both English and Greek, but at that time the *Oxford English Dictionary* was under way, and in its examples Chapman's touch is discernible.

On the completion of the Oxford Dictionary Chapman was made an Honorary D.Litt. of the University (he was also Hon. LL.D. of St. Andrews) and from 1931 to 1947 he was a fellow of Magdalen. He became a fellow of the British Academy in 1947. He resigned his secretaryship of the Clarendon Press in 1942, and devoted his retirement to literary leisure and to the completion of his edition of Dr. Johnson's letters (in three volumes they came out in 1952). It is by this work, and by his editions of Jane Austen's novels and letters, that Chapman will be remembered; they will never be superseded, and they have set a standard for scholarship in such fields. The detailed (but never over-laboured) textual and explanatory annotations, the copious and cunningly devised indexes (in the planning of which he claimed with justice to be a pioneer) were the fruit not merely of a long-developed skill in the mechanics of bookmaking but of an encyclopaedic knowledge of the worlds his authors lived in and described. He was the leading "authority" on Jane Austen, and perhaps the leading Johnsonian of his day.

Textual criticism was his foible, and he indulged it widely: he published an emendation in the *Republic* which was approved by Housman, and he tried his skill with notable success on the text of Trollope, of whose works he had a remarkable knowledge. He explained and defended his sense of the importance of textual criticism in a number of papers, several of which were collected under the title *Portrait of a Scholar.* The "scholar" was Ingram Bywater, whose worthy disciple he was, and the essay is an acknowledged masterpiece of miniature portrait-painting. Chapman's critical gifts were not confined to textual questions or to "classical" writers; he was a devout admirer of Henry James; and he wrote English himself with ease, exactness and distinction.

Chapman was a very learned man who wore his learning very lightly. Few of his acquaintances can have suspected that among his "hobbies" were Greek particles, early English punctuation, and lexicography; but students will recognize, and experts have acknowledged, his contributions to learning in these fields. In his work for the Clarendon Press he displayed surprising administrative and financial gifts; and among the publishing enterprises with which he was particularly associated were the tracts of the Society for Pure English and the series of type-facsimiles of eighteenth-century poems produced by the Oxford Press in the 1920s. He was an expert bibliographer, a book-collector in his own special fields, and a valued "Friend" of the Bodleian.

Achievement apart, Chapman was a "character". Lanky in face and figure, aristocratic (or at least lofty) in bearing and manner, there was a natural distinction about all he said and wrote and did. He never allowed himself to be a martyr to convention in social intercourse, and he made few allowances for the fool or the Philistine, as some of his colleagues at Magdalen had cause to know. Nor was his knowledge of the world limited by academic boundaries; he had friends on both sides of the Atlantic, and was as much at home at a City dinner or a country-house party as in a common room. Rarely divorced from his bicycle, and never (it seemed) from his bicycle-clips, his figure was a familiar one in the streets and bookshops of Oxford; and perennial showers of letters, amusing, allusive, and all but indecipherable, kept him in constant touch with a wide range of acquaintances. He was a member of several societies, convivial and learned, and could be relied on for a review, a paper, or an after-dinner speech, enlivened with a wit which could be caustic and was never stereotyped. He was for many years a valued contributor to *The Times Literary Supplement.* He was made C.B.E. in 1955.

In 1913 Chapman married Katharine Metcalfe, then a tutor of Somerville, who shared his interest, and assisted in his studies, in Jane Austen, and by whom he had three sons and one daughter, all of whom (with her) survive him.

April 22, 1960.

André Charlot, who died at Hollywood on May 20, 1956 at the age of 73, was for many years one of the foremost personalities in the London theatre as the creator of the famous Charlot *revues.*

Above all a master in the art of spectacular and topical entertainment, he was for long a formidable and at some periods successful rival of such skilled contemporary showmen as Sir Charles Cochran [q.v.]. While he never claimed to have originated the *revue* type of entertainment, he certainly did as much to make it popular as any theatrical man of his time, and there were times when he had three or four *revues* at leading London theatres at the same time.

André Eugene Maurice Charlot was born in Paris on July 26, 1882, and educated at the Lycée Condorcet. He first became press manager, then business manager, and eventually manager of several of the most important Paris theatres, including the Châtelet, Palais-Royal, Fémina, Folies-Bergère, Ambassadeurs, and Alcazar. Then in July 1912 he was appointed joint manager of the Alhambra, London, of which he later became managing director for three years.

Specializing in the production of *revues*, a form of stage presentation then beginning to take definite shape in London, he produced a long series of successes which brought his name into prominence. Eventually the Charlot technique reached a point at which it was unmistakable, and although the French producer inspired many imitators they generally lacked the masterly touch that characterized his creations. Yet the ingredients of his shows seldom varied in essentials.

For one thing, the title hardly mattered provided it was short, catchy, and therefore easily remembered. Such titles as *Kill that Fly, Eightpence a Mile, Keep Smiling, Now's the Time, Cheep, Buzz-Buzz, Just Fancy, Puss-Puss, Now and Then, Rats,*and *Pot-Luck* were typical, and though virtually meaningless served their purpose. For the rest they were merely labels for bright, swift-moving, spectacular entertainments concentrating on the assembly on the stage of a beauty chorus in lavish dresses or dazzling costumes, and individual performers of exceptional merit. Many hardworking stage aspirants who have since become celebrities in the theatre, or on the films, were given their first opportunity of appearing in public by Charlot.

Among the spectacular productions for which he was responsible during the quarter of a century in which he largely set the pace and pattern of London entertainment there were many of outstanding merit. *Wonder Bar* at the Savoy in December 1930 established a new standard of excellence. *London Calling* and other musical pieces with which his name was identified had long and successful runs. Charlot was also a pioneer of the cabaret form of entertainment, and in addition to putting on *The Midnight Follies* at the Hotel Metropole in 1922 he produced similar attractions at the Hotel Splendide and Grosvenor House.

Yet such are the economics of spectacular entertainment that in 1931 Charlot felt compelled to file his petition in bankruptcy. He gained his discharge in the course of the next year and soon had a number of new shows running in London, including *Men About the House, Charlot's Char-a-Bang,* and *Dancing City,* but in 1937 his last *revue* ran for only six nights. He went to California, and in the following year was engaged by the Paramount Picture Corporation as technical adviser. Though he had never been himself a player, he took minor parts in a number of successful films, but it was not until 1941 that he appeared on the stage, and then only as a *compère.* His sympathy with the Allied cause in the war was shown by his production at Hollywood of an ambitiously staged *revue* in the best Charlot tradition, the profits from which he contributed to the British War Relief Fund.

For a long period before going to Hollywood he was associated with the B.B.C., for whom he produced about 50 complete shows for broadcasting. He was also founder of the Sunday Play Society, inaugurated as long ago as 1928. Though proud of his British nationality, he remained in California during the later years of his life.

May 22, 1956.

Emile Chartier, whose philosophical work published under the pseudonym "Alain" had for many years a great influence in France, died on June 2, 1951 at the age of 83.

By profession a teacher of philosophy first at Rouen and later at the Collège Henri IV, in Paris, he took the pen-name "Alain" in memory of the poet whom Margaret of Scotland stooped to kiss, and, though his formal teaching had no small influence on generations of students, it was by his published work that he wielded an influence second only to that of Bergson. Since Carlyle, perhaps, no philosopher more deeply honoured labour and the labourer, especially men whose work lies in the fields. Nevertheless man and man's work, though so important, are not all. Mind, for which all the rest exists, is limitless and imponderable and the different essential forms of man's spirit, although of varying values, are none of them negligible.

In the eyes of "Alain" the origin of all religions is extremely simple: is, in fact, neither more nor less than the dim unconscious memories of infancy. As a philosopher, therefore, one need not believe in order to admire the splendid flowering of these memories and since religion is an original, fundamental fact of our development, the philosopher must make his account with it, even extol it if, on the whole, its action prove beneficent. Such is his position in *Les Dieux*, published in 1935.

Had "Alain" kept to such fundamental questions his own influence might have been more beneficent than in fact it turned out to be when the *débâcle* of 1940 brought to many thinking Frenchmen re-examination of their, perhaps, too lightly accepted pacifism. "Alain's" famous *Éléments d'une doctrine radicale* must bear much of the blame for this and a perusal of the work makes it easy to see why he felt that collaboration with the conqueror was the best course. His systematic scepticism and resignation, however, which found expression time and again in the reconstructed *Nouvelle Revue Française,* which was to be the Trojan horse by which Goebbels hoped to take the citadel of French culture, was less deadly than the impression made by the passionate faith of the Nazis. The decline in "Alain's" influence must, therefore, be dated from those disastrous days, and though he continued to publish after the war the spirit of the time had passed him by.

June 5, 1951.

Edna Woolman Chase, until her recent retirement editor-in-chief of the three editions of *Vogue,* died in hospital in Sarasota, Florida, on March 19, 1957. She was 80.

She began her career with the magazine at the age of 18 when it was still a small weekly devoted to the interests of society in Newport and New York. From addressing envelopes she advanced quickly to the editorial staff and when the magazine was taken over in 1909 by the late Condé Nast he made her managing editor. Together they remodelled the magazine and created the character in which it is known today.

She helped to found the British edition in 1916 and the French edition in 1922, and by frequent European visits steered these two editions throughout their early years. Edna Chase pioneered much that is now taken for granted in fashion reporting and magazine editing.

Edna Chase had great influence, also, on the fashion trade, and the first American fashion show was arranged by her during the First World War. The Paris dress designers were then at a standstill, and Edna Chase persuaded American dress manufacturers to create fashions of their own and to employ as advertisers women with a special feeling for style and trends.

In support of her effort to make New York a style centre she organized fashion shows attended by women of social distinction. The proceeds of these went to French war relief.

In 1954 she published her autobiography *Always in Vogue*, which is a history of the magazine no less than the story of her life—for indeed the two were one and the same. She was a woman of courage, integrity, humour, and shining common sense. Though her whole career was spent in what, to some, has proved a rarefied and heady air, she kept her feet firmly on the ground of everyday life, and never lost touch with the ordinary reader. She had the great editor's instinctive sense of readers' needs, and in their interests perpetually questioned the clarity and meaning of photographs, layout, and copy. The leading photographers and illustrators of the day were happy to work with her. They, like her colleagues of three nationalities, respected her for her undaunted and single-minded devotion to the magazine, and loved her for her warmly human sympathy.

By her first marriage to Mr. Francis Dane Chase she had one daughter, Ilka, the writer and actress.

Her second marriage was to Mr. Richard Newton, who died in 1950.

March 22, 1957.

Sir Atul Chatterjee, G.C.I.E., K.C.S.I., who died at Bexhill on September 8, 1955 at the age of 80, was one of the most distinguished Indian members of the Indian Civil Service of his day, and rose to high responsibility and influence.

After membership of the Government of India he was for six and a half years High Commissioner in London, and it was due to his initiative and effort that India House in Aldwych was built. He took no small share in the work of the League of Nations, especially as president of the tenth session of the International Labour Conference, and as member for some years of the Governing Body of the I.L.O. For five years he served on the council of the Secretary of State for India, and was subsequently reappointed as Adviser at the India Office.

Atul Chandra Chatterjee was born on November 24, 1874, the son of Rai Saheb Hem Chandra Chatterjee. From the Presidency College, Calcutta, he obtained a Government of India scholarship, and entered King's College, Cambridge. He headed the list in the I.C.S. open competition of 1896, being the first Indian to do so, and won the Bhownugger medal in 1897. He was posted to the United Provinces, and his keen interest in economics led to his selection by Sir John Hewett in 1907 to make a special inquiry into the industries of the territory. His report provided a model which was followed in other provinces. For four years from 1912 he was Registrar of Co-operative Credit Societies.

Sir James (afterwards the first Lord) Meston, made him Revenue Secretary to the Government in 1917, and in 1919 he scored another record for an Indian member of the I.C.S. when Sir Harcourt Butler made him Chief Secretary. Later in the year he went to Washington to represent India at the first International Labour Conference. On returning to India, he was made a member of the Munitions Board; and when, phoenix-like, there emerged from its ashes the Department of Industries and Labour, he became its Secretary. Early in 1923 he was chosen by the first Lord Reading to become a Member of the Executive Council in charge of the Department. Under his influence India was the first country to ratify the Washington Convention on maximum hours of labour. He was the inspirer and guide of many important reforms in factory and mining legislation and administration, such as that providing for reasonable workmen's compensation.

Chatterjee was a member of the Government of India for a little less than two years, as he went to London at the beginning of 1925 to replace Sir Dadiba Dalal as High Commissioner for India. The administrative experience of Sir Atul, who was made a K.C.I.E. on appointment to London, was much needed, for office affairs were somewhat out of hand. At an early stage he appointed an unofficial committee to advise him on the methods by which the education department of his office could render more effective service to the 2,000 young people from India normally in the British Isles for purposes of study.

In administrating the stores department Chatterjee gave loyal support to the declared policy of purchasing Government supplies in India to the fullest possible extent, and also of buying in the cheapest market compatible with quality and punctuality of delivery. The trade department of his office under Sir Harry Lindsay was strengthened by the addition of a publicity section and by the appointment of commercial advisers who were experts on Indian timber and minerals.

An enduring monument to Chatterjee's tenure is India House, Aldwych. Soon after taking charge he impressed on Lord Reading the urgent need for providing the High Commissioner with headquarters not unworthy to compare in dignity and architecture with those of his contemporaries from the Dominions. Under plans prepared by Sir Herbert Baker, India House was erected in Aldwych at a cost to India revenues of some £324,000. India House was formally opened by King George V in the summer of 1930, when Sir Atul was made K.C.S.I. The existence of this remarkable building gave a fitting home for Chatterjee's successors on the coming of independence in 1947. In order that he might see India House brought to completion and the enlarged office in full working order, Chatterjee's quinquennial term was twice extended; so that he filled the High Commissionership for six and a half years. On retirement from that office in 1931 he was appointed a member of the Secretary of State's Council for the statutory period of five years.

In 1942 he returned to London as Adviser to the Secretary of State for India and served as such until February, 1947. Chatterjee reached a position of influence in peaceful international counsels such as was not attained by any other contemporary Indian official. He represented India at the International Labour Conference in 1921, and from 1924 for six consecutive annual sessions, and again in 1933. He was appointed a member of the governing body of the I.L.O. for five years in 1926, was vice-president in 1932, and president in the following year. In 1927 he had the great honour of being elected president of the tenth International Labour Conference.

Chatterjee, with his close knowledge of detail and his genial manner, was well equipped for this responsibility. He was a representative of India at the 1927 League of Nations Assembly; and he was leader of the I.L.O. delegation to the abortive World Economic Conference in 1932. He also served the League as vice-president of the Consultative Economic Committee; member of the Permanent Central Opium Board, and member of the Allocations Committee. He was Indian delegate to the London Naval Conference of 1930. In the inter-Imperial field his outstanding contribution was his leadership of the Indian delegation to the Ottawa Conference in 1932. The delegation secured the important preferential trade agreement which subsisted between Britain and India for five years, and for a couple of years thereafter during the negotiations conducted in London and Delhi for a new agreement. This service was followed by Chatterjee's promotion to G.C.I.E. He was from 1925 a member of the Imperial Economic Committee.

Chatterjee also left his mark in the field of thought and scholarship. In 1936 there was brought to completion a long and careful collaboration with his fellow United Provinces civilian, the late W. H. Moreland, by the publication of *A Short History of India*, which told the story in the light of the most recent research, and concentrated on the evolution of Indian culture and its response to successive foreign contacts. His collaborator had died when at the end of 1947 Chatterjee prepared a revised third edition bringing the story up to the attainment of Indian independence. He was also the author of *The New India* (1948). Chatterjee had been constitutionally correct as the agent in the United Kingdom of the Government of India in refusing to express opinions on the political problems of his native land; but his discriminating Nationalist sympathies were apparent in his public writings, as also in private conversation.

Chatterjee long served on the Council of the Royal Society of Arts and was chairman of that body in the first two years of the 1939-45 War. He was also for many years vice-chairman of the council of the East India Association, and was a member of the council of the Royal Asiatic Society. In his years of retirement he had frequent illnesses and at the time of his death had long been an invalid, though he was known to be preparing his autobiography.

Sir Atul's first wife, Nina Mukerjee, was a talented Bengali lady. She died in his relatively early Service days, leaving two daughters, one of whom married a son of the first Lord Sinha, and the other became the wife of Mr. S. N. Gupta, C.I.E., I.C.S., the first Indian Trade Commissioner at Hamburg. Sir Atul married secondly in 1924 Dr. Gladys Mary Broughton, O.B.E., D.Sc., barrister-at-law, formerly of the Indian Educational Service and afterwards Adviser to the Government of India in the Labour Department on questions affecting the welfare of women and children. As a charming hostess and a lady of wide and studious interests she contributed greatly to his success.

September 9, 1955.

Olga Chekhov—See **Knipper.**

Lord Cecil of Chelwood—See **Cecil.**

Apsley Cherry-Garrard, the Polar explorer, died on May 18, 1959 in London after many years of illness. He was 73.

Apsley George Benet Cherry-Garrard was born on January 2, 1886, the only son of Major-General Cherry-Garrard. He went to Winchester and then to Christ Church, Oxford, where he was a distinguished oar, rowing in the crew which won the Grand Challenge Cup in 1908. After a trip round the world he met Dr. E. A. Wilson at a shooting party in Scotland, and it was through Wilson that he was selected, though not a scientist, by Scott as a member of his last expedition.

He was one of the youngest and certainly the quietest of Scott's civilian officers but quickly gained the confidence of the leader. As a result he shared in all the major journeys of that long expedition, in particular in what turned out to be a desperate one with Wilson and Bowers to seek Emperor penguins' eggs in the darkness and cold of an Antarctic winter. He himself confessed later that it was unwise of Wilson to have taken him because of his bad eyesight and the necessity for glasses. Yet it was on this perilous journey that there was cemented a rare friendship between the three men which was to affect the younger man's whole outlook on life. There was a spiritual communion between those three fine characters which could endure anything—anything except its disruption by death which was to come eight months later. He parted from his friends at the top of the Beardmore Glacier, about 300 miles from the Pole, to see them again but once more, a year later, lying dead at their last camp.

When he got back to the base there began a series of misfortunes which upset the well laid plans. A very bad ice year prevented the ship from picking up the Northern Party of six men who had to winter in a cave in the ice. It delayed the ship for over a month in picking up the four fit men of the western geological party. On top of that Lieutenant Evans arrived back from the Pole journey stricken almost to death with scurvy and carried for the last 90 miles by his seaman companions, Lashly and Crean.

Everything seemed to have gone awry, and so it came about that Cherry-Garrard was the only officer on the spot to go towards Scott with a dog team, and he had only the Russian boy dog-driver as companion, to take some necessary food out to One-Ton depôt, 130 miles away, and perhaps meet Scott returning from the Pole.

Cherry-Garrard was the only officer who had never managed to master the art of navigation by theodolite observations, but at the time that did not seem to matter since the orders, from Scott himself, were that the dog party was not to go beyond the depôt, up to which there were snow cairns to mark the route.

They reached there before Scott's estimated time of arrival, with four days' spare food for the dogs. They might have gone farther south to endeavour to meet Scott on that trackless plain, but it would have been risky and it was settled out of hand by Dimitri's collapse. As was later known, the nearest the parties ever were to each other was 70 miles. No fault lay with Cherry-Garrard: it was the unfortunate circumstances above-mentioned which prevented a stronger party with more food being available to meet Scott, added to Scott's general instructions that there should be no risks taken.

These details seem necessary to explain why, in later years, Cherry-Garrard could never forget the expedition and subconsciously, against all reason, felt that he should have gone on alone to try to meet his friends, which would only have added two more deaths to the tragedy. The shock of losing his friends took effect slowly.

During the succeeding winter of waiting till the sun's return permitted a search party to travel, he was withdrawn and very quiet but as unselfish as ever and as mindful of everyone's welfare. He was of great assistance to the leader, Surgeon Atkinson, in planning the search journey. He was one of that party and he it was who suggested the epitaphs for Captain Oates—"Hereabouts died a very gallant gentleman"—and for the memorial cross to the Pole party—"To strive, to seek, to find, and not to yield".

Returned to England, he recovered his spirits for a while and when the First World War began he raised a squadron of armoured cars and took it to Flanders. He had never quite recovered from his strenuous journeys in the Antarctic and he had soon to return to England and was invalided out of the service. He spent the remaining years of the war in doctors' hands at his ancestral home of Lamer Park at Wheathampstead, and began to write the classic of polar narrative, *The Worst Journey in the World.* Having G. B. Shaw as a near neighbour, and being in a circle which included Arnold Bennett and H. G. Wells, besides other writers and artists, he no doubt received some inspiration, but the work was his own, and the telling quotations from his original diary prove that he was a writer of some brilliance even when he was writing for his own eyes alone.

He recovered some of his bodily strength in the early 1920s, but the shadow of the Scott tragedy still hung over his mind and altered his interests, almost reversing many of them. He gave up shooting, became almost hostile to fox hunting, and disappointed the churchmen who had been accustomed to his support in the parish. His relaxations were book-collecting (first editions if possible) and cruises in the Mediterranean, but he still lived with the polar expedition and would talk of little else.

In 1939 he married Angela, the daughter of Kenneth Turner, of Ipswich, and for a time he recovered some of his flair for conversation and some interests in a wider prospect than the past. The war years were hardly such as to help him to regain full mental balance and he became more withdrawn, more introspective than ever, and ceaselessly worried about his health. To his friends of earlier days this was a tragedy; they felt it was a case of a once noble mind now overthrown and disordered by dwelling on a far-off past of glorious friendship and perhaps a needlessly uneasy conscience about the part he played.

Whether he could ever have repeated the literary success that came to his *Worst Journey* is a moot point, but that book will remain for all time a triumph of the art of narrative and a memorial to the men whose death took most of the savour of life from their young colleague.

May 19, 1959.

Lord Cherwell, the distinguished scientist and formerly Professor of Experimental Philosophy at Oxford, died there on July 3, 1957. He was 71.

The Rt. Hon. Frederick Alexander Lindemann, P.C., C.H., F.R.S., Viscount Cherwell, of Oxford, Baron Cherwell, of Oxford, in the peerage of the United Kingdom, was the younger son of Adolph Frederick Lindemann and Olga Noble, and was born at Baden-Baden on April 5, 1886. The paternal grandfather was an Alsatian who decided to retain French citizenship after 1871 and make his home in Paris. The father was a wealthy engineer, with varied business interests, who had married an Englishwoman and settled as a naturalized Englishman at Sidmouth, in Devon.

Lindemann and his elder brother grew up there in a happy, wealthy and cultured home where family affection was strong. He was sent for a short time to Blairlodge School at Polmont and then to a gymnasium at Darmstadt where the curriculum was of the thorough, Continental type. The family were great travellers, with friends all over Europe. In consequence Lindemann early became a good linguist with a wide knowledge of the Continent. He was a devoted son, and it was largely his father's love of astronomy and skill as an instrument maker that inclined the son to mathematics and physics.

He entered the University of Berlin late, studied under Rubens, Planck and Nernst, and took his Ph.D. degree there in 1910. Atomic heats, low temperatures, the quantum theory and the special theory of relativity were then the great subjects of study. Lindemann's doctoral dissertation on the atomic heat of metals at low temperatures marked him out as a man with a future in a laboratory where many brilliant young men were working. After Berlin Lindemann continued his work, both experimental and theoretical, in Paris.

By 1914 he had published much in physics and his reputation there was so high that he was given the directorship of the R.F.C. experimental physics station at Farnborough. Both in the laboratory and as experimental pilot he showed his metal. His courage, his flair for the essential point of a problem, his quickness in argument, his wide knowledge, and his complete independence of opinion on everyone and everything, stood him in good stead. His best known exploit at Farnborough was his demonstration of the safest way of pulling an aircraft out of a spin. Lindemann first evolved a mathematical theory of how an aircraft got into a spin, deduced from theory the simplest way of getting it out of it, then learnt to fly; next, in due course, put his machine into a spin, applied his principles, found they did what he had predicted they would do, landed it and then quietly and modestly reported the incident. This demonstration was not a fluke. He showed courage in repeating it at other times, and he underwent similar trials in testing later theories. When flying ordinarily, it should be said, he was not a very good pilot.

In 1919 he was offered and accepted a chair of physics at Oxford. This was the professorship of Experimental Philosophy attached to the then moribund Clarendon Laboratory. It carried with it a fellowship of Wadham College, which became an honorary fellowship in 1956, and, after 1921, a Studentship of Christ Church, which he retained after retirement. Oxford was glad to welcome this tall, fine-looking, well-dressed, rich, athletic, Continentally educated stranger with a low voice and an informing and critical tongue, who in his fastidious way was a "card". At Wadham, where he lived for a few years before going to a stately set of rooms in Christ Church, he met Lord Birkenhead, and, through him, his friend Winston Churchill*. Through them Lindemann formed a wide acquaintanceship among those who lived in country houses and combined rank and wealth with interest in politics. He was himself a good host, putting his rooms and his cars at the disposal of his friends. In the midst of luxury he preserved an attractive simplicity. He was an abstainer, a non-smoker, and a life-long vegetarian.

In 1920 Lindemann was elected a Fellow of the Royal Society. His success in the following 20 years as a professor was partial only. A fair stream of published work came from his laboratory, after he had refurnished it and partly endowed it, but he never went hard and continuously at one important thing. He preferred to busy himself and his young men with a succession of smaller researches in various branches of physics.

He was temperamentally averse from the hard drudgery of experimental work and more content to be a director, adviser, and stimulator of young research men than their co-worker and leader. As a lecturer he was adequate. He lectured late in the forenoon in a low voice, with few of the arts of an expositor, but his matter was good and read well. Everything, indeed, that he published was a model of clear expression. He was devoted to Oxford and to the advancement of science as a subject of study and research there, and worked harder for this end in private than in committees or on boards of faculties. Largely through his influence and efforts the new Clarendon Laboratory in the Parks, then by far the best of its kind in the country, was built and equipped by the university in 1939. He resigned his chair on reaching the age of 70 in 1956 but retained his home in Christ Church. A measure of the change which had been effected during the years that he had been in charge of the Clarendon can be gained by the fact that when he took over there was no research of any kind going on in physics and fewer than 10 undergraduates were reading the subject. Today there are over 40 senior research workers, 120 advanced students reading for higher degrees, and some 250 undergraduates reading physics.

In 1937 Lindemann, who felt very strongly the necessity of an immediate large increase in British air power and the great need for state endowment of research for all scientific problems involved in the mastery of the air, stood for Parliament at a by-election as Independent Conservative candidate for Oxford University. He was unsuccessful but the defeat only made him more pertinacious in bringing before those in power the gravity of the situation as it seemed to him. Churchill, a friend of long standing, then out of office, held the same views, and it was not surprising, after the outbreak of war when Churchill took office, that Lindemann was given the post of his personal assistant, which he retained to the end of the war. His main task in that post was to advise the Prime Minister generally.

He was there not as a specialist primarily concerned with difficult scientific problems but as a man of completely independent judgment, with a wide experience of French and German mentality, whose views on problems involving numbers and quantities of any kind were found to be unbiased and useful. At first he was a target for criticism. Those who disliked him—and they were many—saw him largely as a thwarter of designs he personally did not care for. Some Ministers and Civil servants thought it irregular that one of no higher status than a private secretary should have the powers of a cabinet minister.

Criticism on this point was partly allayed when Lindemann was created Baron Cherwell in 1941. The position was further regularized in the following year by his being given ministerial rank and sworn of the Privy Council as Paymaster-General. This office he held from 1942 to 1945. Throughout the war he toiled hard at the many problems the Prime Minister referred to him. Highly confidential work of this kind cannot at this stage be easily assessed, but it is believed on good authority that at times it was of the highest value.

When Churchill formed his Government in 1951 he again called on Cherwell to assist him and once more appointed him Paymaster-General. Between 1951 and 1953 Cherwell was the Prime Minister's adviser on atomic energy research and development and on scientific and statistical matters generally. He resigned his Cabinet post in October 1953 to resume his academic duties but it was made clear that his personal advice would continue to be available to the Prime Minister and the Government on atomic energy questions and other scientific matters. He was made C.H. in the same year.

In 1954 he was appointed a member of the United Kingdom Atomic Energy Authority set up under the Atomic Energy Act and with his wide experience made a powerful contribution to the progress of atomic energy in Great Britain. He was advanced to a viscounty in 1956.

He had downright views on the testing of hydrogen bombs, and speaking in a defence debate in the House of Lords in May 1957 he said that he could not understand how anyone with a logical mind could argue that Britain ought to have thermonuclear weapons but ought not to test them. The argument that the tests constituted a danger to the health of humanity was "unmitigated nonsense".

He was unmarried and by his death the peerage becomes extinct.

July 4, 1957.

Zetton Chesney—See **Buchanan.**

Frank Chester, the cricket umpire, died at his home at Bushey, Hertfordshire, on April 8, 1957.

Chester might have won as much fame as an all-round cricketer had it not been for the loss of his right arm when serving with the R.F.A. in Salonika during the First World War.

Born in January 1896, he first played for Worcestershire in 1912, and in the following season, at the age of 17½, scored three centuries. In addition his high, easy action secured him 43 wickets. Already he seemed set for a great career. In *Wisden's Almanack* of 1914 it was remarked that few players in the history of cricket had shown such form at his age. It seemed "only reasonable to expect that when he has filled out and gained more strength he will be an England cricketer". Already he was the youngest century maker in English first-class cricket and in 1914, during an innings of 178 not out against Essex, he had the temerity to hit J. W. H. T. Douglas for four 6's.

Debarred by his injury from further active participation, he first stood as an umpire in county cricket in 1922 and in the 33 years until his retirement in 1955 he achieved a great name not only as a Test match umpire (he acted in 56 of these) but also as an authority on the game and its laws. On his retirement a special tribute was paid him by R. Aird, secretary of the M.C.C., who recalled the exceptional standard Chester had always set.

In some curious way his presence on the field could be sensed even by the uninformed. All umpires must err on occasion, but Chester made very few mistakes, gifted as he was with an unusual keenness of sight at the length of the wicket. Moreover, he gave some correct decisions that have passed into cricket history. Autocratic though he may have been in bearing and speech, his fearless impartiality and scrupulous approach to all problems justly earned him the reputation of perhaps the greatest of all umpires.

There was a time when Chester became recognized as well nigh infallible. It is told, for example, how once at Lord's he rejected, to everyone's astonishment, an appeal for a catch at the wicket. The batsman said later that he had not touched the ball and Chester, to put minds at rest, indicated that it had grazed the off stump without dislodging a bail. This is just one example of his extraordinary judgment which was joined, of course, to considerable powers of concentration. Sir Donald Bradman once wrote that with Chester umpiring he would have no hesitation whatever in trying to leg glance a ball which in his opinion was pitched on the leg stump but would have missed the leg stump had it been allowed to pass. With few other umpires, he said, would he have attempted the shot.

Chester used to exercise a measure of control over a match. He was not an insignificant figure in a white coat but a well-loved, respected personality who passed judgment with a wisdom of Solomon. Starting as an umpire when all his faculties were keen he set for himself, and achieved, new standards, and anyone whose umpiring experience does not extend beyond the fathers' match will understand that he must have been a man not only of deep knowledge and diligent application but also of the highest principles.

April 9, 1957.

Peter Cheyney, whose crime stories have achieved a wide circulation for many years past, died in London on June 26, 1951 at the age of 55.

Reginald Evelyn Peter Southouse-Cheyney was the son of A. W. T. Cheyney and Katharine Southouse and was born on February 22, 1896. He attended Hounslow College and the Mercers' School and began his career as a clerk in a solicitor's office. He soon tired of office routine, and at the age of 16 went on the stage and made a number of boyish essays at playwriting and verse. This phase was cut short by the outbreak of war in 1914 and he joined the Inns of Court O.T.C., being later gazetted to The Royal Warwickshire Regiment. At the second battle of the Somme he was severely wounded and on recovery was given a staff appointment.

After demobilization he gravitated to Fleet Street, and after supporting himself as a free-lance for some years formed an agency for supplying stories and feature articles to newspapers and magazines. In 1928 he was appointed editor of the *St. John Ambulance Gazette,* a position he was to hold until 1943, and in 1933-34 he spent some months as news editor of the *Sunday Graphic.*

He had for some years been interested in the methods of crime investigation and in 1936 published his first crime story, *This Man is Dangerous,* which was an immediate success. Other stories followed in quick succession, all with a background of crime and all aimed rather to pass an idle half-hour or so than to probe character. Tough, transatlantic figures—notably Caution and Callaghan—pass before the reader in urgent sequence and the technique of suspense is cleverly exploited.

If none of the numerous stories, which averaged about two a year since 1936, leaves very much impression on the mind, they have an efficiency and slickness which is *sui generis* of this type of fiction. He took the business of production seriously and as early as 1932 set up an organization the objects of which were not only to market his wares efficiently but also to keep abreast of the latest developments in the perpetual war between criminals and society.

He married in 1948 Loretta Theressa, daughter of Mr. W. F. Groves, of Westchester County, New York.

June 27, 1951.

Former Bishop of Chichester—See **Bell.**

Prince Chichibu, brother of the Emperor of Japan, died of jaundice on January 3, 1953 in Tokyo at the age of 50.

Prince Atsunomiya Yasuhito—the title of Chichibu was conferred on him at his majority—was the second son of the late Emperor Taisho, and was born on June 25, 1902, the year of the signing of the Anglo-Japanese Alliance. Until he was 15 years of age the prince attended the Peers' School in Tokyo; then, having decided on a military career, he was sent to the Military Preparatory Academy, and afterwards to the Military Academy. On leaving the Academy he decided to enter not the Guards but an ordinary line regiment; he took up residence in barracks in Tokyo and shared in every way the spartan life of a Japanese officer. An all-round sportsman, he rode, fenced, shot, swam, skied, played tennis, and occasionally golf, and there were few important athletic or sporting gatherings which he did not attend.

Prince Chichibu was also an enthusiastic mountaineer and made some difficult ascents of the Japanese Alps.

When he went to England in 1925 to study life there he had conscientiously devoted much time to studying those aspects of modern Japan which might usefully be compared with conditions in Britain. Thus he had visited many factories and public institutions and had gone down a coalmine. His visit was a remarkable innovation in the customs of the Japanese Imperial House, for no son of a living emperor had ever before made his home in England for so long a period, and it was a conspicuous expression of the new spirit prevailing in Japan.

After seeing at close quarters many aspects of British government and public life, the Prince took a holiday mountaineering in Switzerland. He climbed the Matterhorn on the day of his father's birthday, which is celebrated in Japan as a national festival, and also ascended the Jungfraujoch and Monte Rosa. After his return to England in September 1926 he went into residence at Magdalen College, Oxford, to lead the life of an ordinary undergraduate. He intended to stay there a year, but the illness and death of his father, the Emperor, obliged him to return to Tokyo in January, 1927. His premature departure was regretted not only by the Prince himself but by many friends he had made. In 1926 the King conferred on him the G.C.V.O.

On the succession of his brother as Emperor, Prince Chichibu devoted much time to social welfare and to the cause of science. He was president of the Japan Association for the Encouragement of Science, and Japan's progress in the scientific field owed much to him and to other members of the Imperial Family.

In 1937 he went to England with his wife, the daughter of Mr. Matsudaira, a former Ambassador in London and Washington, to represent Emperor Hirohito at the coronation of King George VI [q.v.]. Before returning to Japan he visited Germany and saw Hitler.

He maintained his interest in sport, and was president of the Japan Rugby Football Association. He welcomed the Oxford Rugby team which toured Japan in late 1952.

A man of simple tastes, Prince Chichibu was perhaps the most democratic of Japan's princes, and was opposed to the militarist party which came to power in his country. When war broke out in 1939 he did not conceal that his sympathies lay with the allies, and when Japan intervened in 1941 it was reported that he remained under surveillance in various parts of Japan, but never in Tokyo.

January 5, 1953.

J. B. Chifley, Leader of the Opposition in the Australian Parliament, died suddenly in hospital in Canberra on June 13, 1951. He had been Prime Minister of Australia from 1945 to 1949. He was 65.

A close friend and colleague of his predecessor, John Curtin, Chifley was a Labour leader of a similar quiet strength of character, who likewise exerted a firmly unifying influence within the Australian Labour Party. Although at the time of Curtin's death he had no ambition for the leadership of the party, he would undoubtedly have been Curtin's own choice, and this fact, together with his strong sense of duty and his conscientiousness as an administrator, marked him out for the succession.

Not an eloquent speaker, he had from the beginning exhibited uncommon Parliamentary skill and tact, had proved himself an able and resourceful Treasurer (his reluctance to engage in press conferences and public appearances did not tell against him), and was liked and respected on both sides of the House. When he became Prime Minister he promptly declared his intention of following in Curtin's footsteps and throughout his tenure of office did indeed display a similar moderation of mind and sense of responsibility. In the restless after-war years he constantly urged the need for trade union discipline; he did not hesitate to impress upon Parliament and people how vitally necessary it was for Australia to make a larger contribution to the defence of the British Empire; while to his own supporters he was always characteristically sparing of promises.

On his visits to Britain for the Commonwealth talks in 1946 and 1949 he impressed all whom he met by his shrewd good sense and painstaking clarity of purpose, while during his visit in 1948 for consultations on economic and immigration problems he made many friends. Tall, of spare build, not of very robust health—though he had been a keen Rugby footballer in his youth—Chifley was imperturbable of temperament and enjoyed the political advantage of a quiet sense of humour.

The Rt. Hon. Joseph Benedict Chifley, P.C., was born on September 22, 1885, at Bathurst, New South Wales, the son of Patrick and Mary Anne Chifley, both of Irish ancestry. His father was a blacksmith, and the boy left the Patrician Brothers' High School in Bathurst at the age of 15, took a job in a general store, and then joined the New South Wales railways department as a shop-boy, becoming successively cleaner, fireman, and engine-driver. He eventually became a prominent figure in the Railway Locomotive Engine-Drivers' Union—a body which has given the Australian Labour Party so many of its right-wing leaders—having appeared for his union, often with notable success, in both state and federal arbitration courts. He first stood for Macquarie, a constituency of which Bathurst was the centre, as a candidate for the Federal House of Representatives in 1925, but was not elected until three years later. Curtin entered Parliament at the same time, and the two sat together on the back benches and formed a close and lasting friendship.

Chifley's Parliamentary career was rather chequered. Appointed Minister for Defence in the Scullin [q.v.] Government in 1931, he lost his seat in the electoral *débâcle* of that year and did not return to Parliament until the General Election of 1940. But he served on the Royal Commission on monetary and banking systems during 1935-36, and the experience and knowledge he gained in the course of its protracted sittings, which led to his appointment as Commonwealth Treasurer in 1941, stood him in good stead in putting through the Curtin Government's radical banking legislation. In the following year he was given the additional portfolio of Minister for Post-War Reconstruction. But he surrendered this office in the subsequent reorganization of the Government, and as Treasurer was recognized as holding the third place in the Cabinet. His Budget statements were frank and clear, and, encouraged by the example of the Beveridge* Report, he worked to good purpose on a comprehensive scheme of social insurance in Australia.

During the illness of Curtin and in the absence of Mr. Forde (who had on several occasions served as deputy Prime Minister) in San Francisco, Chifley became acting Prime Minister in April, 1945. In July Curtin died, and Forde received an interim commission from the Duke of Gloucester* as Governor-General.

A week later, however, Chifley was chosen as leader of the Labour Party and became Prime Minister. He made few changes in the Cabinet and soberly and purposefully pursued the moderate policy that was expected of him. After his visit to Britain during April-May 1946 he went on to Washington to discuss Pacific problems with President Truman* and thence to Japan.

In the election campaign of that year he claimed that the country had been offered no real alternative to Labour policy, and in the result the Labour mandate was renewed, though with a slightly reduced majority. As Prime Minister and Treasurer Chifley himself submitted to Parliament the Government's proposals for nationalizing the private trading banks. This policy, however, created a storm which, coupled with increasing labour unrest in Australia, led to the defeat of the Labour Party in 1949 and Chifley's supersession by Menzies as Prime Minister.

He married, in 1914, Miss Elizabeth Mackenzie, who took no part in public life. There were no children of the marriage.

June 14, 1951.

Professor V. Gordon Childe, the eminent prehistorian, who died in Australia in a fall over a cliff in the Blue Mountains, was 65. His body was found on October 20, 1957.

Vere Gordon Childe was born at Sydney, New South Wales, on April 14, 1892, the son of the Rev. S. H. Childe. He received his early education locally, leaving Australia in 1914 with a Graduate Scholarship in Classics for the Queen's College, Oxford. He returned to Australia with a B.Litt. and a first in Greats, and for a couple of years was private secretary to the Premier of New South Wales—a period described by himself as "a sentimental excursion into Australian politics".

This over, his life's work really began in 1922 with a period of travelling and study in Central and Eastern Europe which culminated in the appearance of the first of his great works *The Dawn of European Civilization* (1925) and *The Aryans* (1926). In 1927 he was appointed Abercromby Professor of Prehistoric Archaeology in the University of Edinburgh, a post which he held until 1946. He then became University Professor of Prehistoric European Archaeology and Director of the Institute of Archaeology in the University of London, retiring in advance of his time in 1956, in order (characteristically) to simplify the lot of his successor, whose task it would otherwise have been to transfer the institute to its new building in Gordon Square within a few months of his taking office.

His name first came to the notice of the general public in the 1920s when he supervised the excavations of a curious prehistoric village at Skara Brae, on the west coast of the Orkney mainland.

Of Gordon Childe it can truly be said that he was a scholar of international repute; and of international repute in the widest sense. The products of his thought not merely inspired his colleagues of all nationalities working in the same or related fields; some of them were intended for, and reached, a wider public—and this without any watering-down of ideas and views to suit the supposed tastes of the bookstalls. *The Dawn,* as it has now come to be called, appeared in its fifth edition in 1950; it has been translated also into French and Russian. *What Happened in History,* first published in 1942, sold more than 300,000 copies and has appeared in Italian, German, Dutch, and Swedish editions. Curtains, of whatever material, did not impede him. *Man Makes Himself* has had American and Chinese editions; and the list of translations is not complete.

Childe's own view of his contribution to knowledge—and he was his own most severe critic—was that it lay in "interpretative concepts and methods of explanation" rather than in the assembly of fresh evidence about the past, whether from excavations or from the study of museum collections. As a classicist his original approach to prehistory was by way of comparative philology; his aim was to identify the primitive culture of the Indo-Europeans and with it their geographical source and connexions. From this "naturally fruitless" search he turned to the creation of a chronological framework for Central Europe which was set out first in *Dawn* and subsequently, in modified form, in *The Danube in Prehistory,* to bring out clearly the significance of the Danube as the great thoroughfare by means of which (though other routes played their part) "civilization" was spread through Europe.

In this and subsequent developments Childe's receptiveness of ideas and readiness to apply and extend them, his awareness and knowledge of what was happening on the Continent, were of the utmost value. To archaeologists who were wedded to "classical" ideas with their strong element of "art-history", or who, on the other hand, saw prehistory as a sequence of "types" of flints or other artifacts, the concept of a culture as representing a people and being composed of the sum total of what they used, made, and thought (so far as their thoughts could be determined) was something new. So, too, the part played in human settlement by factors which may broadly be called geographical—climatic changes, soil variations, and the like—was also not appreciated in Britain apart from one or two scholars, such as J. L. Myres [q.v.], and following him O. G. S. Crawford [q.v.], who had long been protagonists of the geographical approach in archaeology.

The *Dawn* showed cultures and migrations of cultures as events in history which in this particular context constituted the spread of the industrial revolution based on the introduction of farming and food production, which is now universally accepted as the criterion of the Neolithic Age during the third millennium B.C. From this much else flowed. Prehistorians in general no longer confuse "culture" with chronology. The old "periods" were regarded as being of universal application, fixed in time, with no sense of the variations and fluctuations, of the overlapping in space and time between different groups which become recognizable under the definition of culture which Gordon Childe more than any other scholar sought to disseminate. This must serve for the present occasion as but one example of the lasting contribution made by his thinking to the study of man's past.

Childe was not an easy man to know, but colleagues and students will remember him for a rare sweetness of nature and for his high sense of duty towards them and towards the subject to which he devoted his life. His too infrequent outspoken comments displayed an unexpected shrewdness; but he was never malicious and he was never guilty of unkindness or of lack of consideration for others.

October 21, 1957.

The death of **Audrey Christie (Mrs. John Christie)** on May 31, 1953 after a long illness is a very serious blow to the whole enterprise which has given first-rate opera at Glyndebourne, for her part in its creation and development amounted to very much more than the distinguished and charming impersonations she gave there in the *soubrette* parts of Mozart's operas, which were what the public knew of her at first hand.

Under her maiden name of Audrey Mildmay she sang with the Carl Rosa Opera Company before she married John Christie* in 1931. Together they evolved the Glyndebourne Opera and by her wish the festival in 1953 opened on June 7 in spite of her death.

Grace Audrey Louisa St. John Mildmay was the daughter of the Rev. Sir Aubrey Neville St. John Mildmay, tenth baronet, and was born in Sussex on December 19, 1900. She got her first musical instruction, however, at Vancouver, where her father was the first vicar of the parish of Penticton. She began to study singing in London with Johnstone Douglas and in Vienna with Theodore Lierhammer and Jani Strasser, whom she took to Glyndebourne as chief vocal coach when the opera was being planned in 1933. She toured Canada and the United States in *The Beggar's Opera* in 1927-28, and returned to the part of Polly in the wartime production of that opera by Glyndebourne in 1940. She joined the Carl Rosa Company in 1929 and sang Nedda and Zerlina for it.

Her stature as an artist was only fully revealed on the night when the Glyndebourne Opera House first opened its doors to the public in June 1934; she appeared as Susanna in *Figaro,* and with her rather light silvery voice and delicious characterization established her claim to be a Mozart singer in the best tradition. She added Norina in *Don Pasquale* to her roles in 1938. During the war she was in America, where she was forced to earn a living by accepting concert engagements. This was the end of her active career as a singer, but she continued the part she had played from the beginning as adviser to her husband and his associates in artistic and practical matters.

It is an open secret that it was she who determined the character which Glyndebourne opera was to take when John Christie first began seriously to think of providing for Britain something comparable to what he heard abroad. Mrs. Christie came down decisively on the side of professional opera of the highest standards instead of semi-amateur opera of the sort which has indeed proved its value over and over again but is a very different thing from international opera of the standard of a festival. It is less generally known that hers was one of the minds from which the spark was struck that ultimately fired the project for an international festival at Edinburgh. Illness prevented her participation as hostess at Glyndebourne in 1951 and 1952, but her ideas abour repertory and the singers to execute it were still a formative influence. She leaves a son and a daughter.

June 1, 1953.

I. I. Chundrigar, who was Prime Minister of Pakistan for a short period in the autumn of 1957, died on September 26, 1960 in a London hospital. He was for some years Leader of the Muslim League Party.

Ismail Ibrahim Chundrigar was born in 1897; he was educated at the university of Bombay, where he read law. His political career began on his election to the Ahmedabad Municipal Council in 1924 and continued during his service on the Bombay Legislative Assembly between 1937 and 1946. In October of the latter year he was appointed Minister of Commerce in the interim Government in Delhi and held the same portfolio in the first Government of Pakistan from August 1947.

Later he was Ambassador in Kabul, and Governor successively of the North-West Frontier Province and Punjab. In August 1955 he became Law Minister in the Government of Chaudhri Mohammad Ali, thus playing a leading part in piloting the Pakistan constitution through its final and tortuous stages; and on the formation of Hussain Suhrawardy's* Government in the autumn of 1956 Chundrigar succeeded him as Leader of the Opposition.

In less than a year he was to succeed him as Prime Minister, for on October 11, 1957, Suhrawardy resigned after a dispute between the partners in the coalition he led, the Republican Party and the Awami League. Six days later Chundrigar, by this time a most experienced politician, was commissioned by the President, Major-General Mirza*, to form a new Government. On October 18 the new Prime Minister was sworn in. His Government soon ran into trouble, for its proposal to replace the joint electorate system with two separate electorates did not please those who felt that they would be worse placed by a change of system, the Awami League, dissident members of the Krishak Sramik Party, the National Awami Party, and the East Pakistan Hindus. Early in December Chundrigar offered his resignation. At the President's request he attempted to form a new Ministry, but in this he was unsuccessful. Not long afterwards he was succeeded by Malik Firoz Khan.

At the time of his death Chundrigar was chairman of the Company Law Commission.

September 27, 1960.

Lord Ivor Churchill, who died in London on September 17, 1956 at the age of 57, was one of the several men of title who bettered the good example of eighteenth-century English noblemen by collecting contemporary instead of ancient works of art.

Many English and French artists will remember his name with gratitude. Not less so because his personal preferences were for modern French painting and sculpture; for patronage of contemporary art of any kind by a person of social consequence is almost bound to affect public opinion and so benefit British artists indirectly. Paintings and sculptures from his collection were often to be seen at loan exhibitions, and apart from this way of spreading the light he took an active, though unobtrusive, part in the work of the Contemporary Art Society.

The younger son of the ninth Duke of Marlborough, and Consuelo, daughter of the late William Kissam Vanderbilt, of New York, who after the dissolution of her marriage with the Duke in 1921 married Lieutenant-Colonel Jacques Balsan, Ivor Charles Spencer-Churchill (or Ivor Churchill as he preferred to be called), was born on October 14, 1898. He was educated at Eton and Magdalen College, Oxford, and during the 1914-18 War served in the R.A.S.C. He inherited artistic interests from his mother, who as Madame Balsan was well known in the artistic world of Paris and like Winston Churchill* himself was active in fostering Anglo-French relations, and from his father, whose efforts to preserve, rehabilitate, and beautify Blenheim were lifelong.

Except in connexion with art Lord Ivor's name was seldom mentioned. He took no part in public affairs and held no public appointments, and he was more often to be seen at art exhibitions or meetings or in artists' studios than at any other kind of social gathering. Pale and slight, he gave the impression of great physical delicacy. From his casual manner at exhibitions nobody would have supposed that he was keenly interested in and well informed about what he saw, but it was only necessary to exchange a few words with him in front of a picture to find that he missed nothing and had very definite tastes. He preferred, he said, painting of the more solid kind, and it was not surprising that his collection should contain a larger proportion of sculpture than is common.

A full description of Lord Ivor's collection in his home on Chelsea Embankment, where he was a neighbour of the late George Eumorfopoulos, was given in *The Times* of June 27, 1928, in an illustrated article forming one of a series on "Private Art Collections" published that year. It was said then that sooner or later anything that had given special pleasure in an exhibition of modern French paintings was likely to be found in the Churchill collection, so that to run through it was to experience a series of delighted recognitions. To recall some of the pictures—Cézanne, and Dunoyer de Segonzac*, the former with the self-portrait of "Cézanne au Chapeau", a "Montagne Sainte Victoire", and seven other works, all accepted by Venturi in his complete catalogue of the artist, and the latter with "Les Buveurs", were naturally prominent, but the collection was as catholic as was consistent with the avowed preferences of its owner.

Consistency, indeed, was the mark of the collection. Historically it began with Corot and Ingres, and the early "Cliffs" by the former and "Etude pour Ste. Germaine de Pibrac" by the latter might be called the "key" pictures to its formation. As links between Corot and Cézanne through the atmospheric preoccupations of Impressionism there were two splendid landscapes: "Ste. Adresse", by Monet, and "La Côte de l'Hermitage", by Camille Pissarro. Seurat was an obvious figure, but the range was wide enough to include "Les deux Raies", by Matisse, and two of Bonnard's most celebrated paintings, "La Fenêtre" and "Nude in Bath", which last is now in the modern foreign collection at the Tate Gallery, presented by Lord Ivor through the Contemporary Art Society in 1930. His independence of judgment was shown by several Brittanny landscapes by Jean Frélaut, an artist who has not yet found general acceptance by English collectors.

Though Lord Ivor's artistic interests were chiefly across the Channel he did not ignore contemporary British art and in the august company of the noble draped figure of "Pomona" and other works by Maillol and several pieces by Despiau there were two important things by Frank Dobson, R.A.*: "Cornucopia", of 1927, and "Torso", of the following year. But, as was said, Lord Ivor's value to British art was not to be measured by his personal acquisitions alone. By securing the works of his choice from the accidents of time he conferred benefits on art in general and contributed to raising the level of taste in the country. The collection was, of course, not static and over the years changed a good deal, with Lord Ivor's preference for the solidity of Segonzac gradually asserting itself.

When the war clouds began to gather he wisely moved his home and collection to the village of Steep, near Petersfield, and took up fruit farming with energy and enthusiasm, though he kept a *pied à terre* in London. His home was, of course, a centre for the many French friends he had made in the past and who had been uprooted from their homes by the war. Unobtrusive, as was his wont, he yet played a significant part in preserving the bonds of friendship between France and Great Britain during that testing time and the conferment of the Legion of Honour on him was a due recognition of his many services to a cause that was very near his heart.

He married in 1947 Elizabeth, daughter of J. C. Cunningham, who survives him together with a son of the marriage.

September 18, 1956.

Lord Cilcennin, P.C., First Lord of the Admiralty from 1951 to 1956, died in London on July 13, 1960. He was 56.

Better known as "J. P. L." or "Jim" Thomas, he sat in the House of Commons for 24 years as Conservative member of Parliament for Hereford. By his death his party lost a distinguished and sincere servant. He had, in fact, been in politics since his early twenties, and had held many ministerial posts before becoming First Lord of the Admiralty in the Conservative Government formed by Winston Churchill* in October 1951.

In his early days in the Commons he was Assistant Private Secretary to Stanley Baldwin, and later served as Parliamentary Private Secretary to the late J. H. Thomas, and then to Sir Anthony Eden [Lord Avon, d.1977]. It was a remarkable coincidence that both of "Jim" Thomas's chiefs should have had to resign high office and that their Parliamentary Private Secretary should have helped them to prepare, and heard them deliver, amid scenes of intense emotion, their resignation speeches in the Commons.

It was his loyalty to his chiefs that made J. P. L. Thomas such an outstanding Parliamentary Private Secretary. Stanley Baldwin would speak in the highest praise of his young lieutenant, and it was a great joy to him that "Jim" Thomas spared so much time to visit him in his lonely wartime retirement.

J. P. L. Thomas never married. He was, in fact, well known as one of the "most eligible bachelors" in the House of Commons. He was universally popular, and possessed much charm and tact.

James Purdon Lewes Thomas was born on October 13, 1903, son of the late J. Lewes Thomas, and was educated at Rugby (he was chairman of the governors at the time of his death) and Oriel College, Oxford, where he graduated with honours. Choosing a political career, almost immediately after leaving Oxford he went into the Conservative Central

Office, where he was afterwards to make such a deep impression upon the party machine and the organization generally. For two years he was engaged on the educational side of the work for the Central Office, and greatly extended its scope.

In 1929, when only 25, he was invited to fight the Llanelly Division of Carmarthenshire. He was defeated in this safe Labour division, and a few months afterwards he joined the secretariat of Stanley (afterwards the first Earl) Baldwin, where he greatly extended his political experience and knowledge. A year or so later, in the election of 1931, he contested the Hereford division and was returned with a majority of more than 7,000 votes. In that year he became Baldwin's assistant private secretary, and a few months later was to begin a long period of service and close personal friendship with J. H. Thomas, whose Parliamentary Private Secretary he was, as Secretary of State for the Dominions, and moved with him in the same capacity to the Colonial Office. In April 1937 he became Parliamentary Private Secretary to Anthony Eden, then Foreign Secretary, and again he moved with his chief when Eden went to the Dominions Office just before the war broke out in 1939.

When Churchill formed the wartime Coalition Government in May 1940 he chose Thomas to be one of the Government Whips, appointing him a Lord Commissioner of the Treasury. Thomas's personality was ideal for a job of this character, for he was liked by members of all parties, and was assiduous in his duties. In September 1943 he was appointed Financial Secretary to the Admiralty, with which Department of State he was destined to remain until the electoral landslide in 1945. This was a post which gave him his first intimate knowledge of the workings of a great Department of State, and he impressed the Commons, both by his speeches and by his complete mastery of his duties under A. V. (afterwards Viscount) Alexander*.

He survived the 1945 debacle and went back to the Conservative Central Office as vice-chairman of the Conservative and Unionist Party. For six years he assisted R. A. Butler to formulate the new Conservative policy, and to retrieve the electoral fortunes of his party. There is little doubt that in the part he played in the selection of new candidates, and in the development of his old enthusiasm—the party's youth organizations—he had a considerable hand in the Conservative victory of October 1951.

Churchill recognized this, and awarded Thomas the Ministerial "plum" he had always coveted—the First Lord of the Admiralty. He enjoyed his work, and did much for the Navy at a difficult period.

When Sir Anthony Eden became Prime Minister in 1955, Thomas continued at the Admiralty, but it soon became an open secret that he was anxious to retire. In the New Year Honours of January 1956 he was created Viscount Cilcennin, of Hereford, in the county of Hereford, but it was not until nine months later that Viscount Hailsham succeeded him at the Admiralty.

Still comparatively young, Lord Cilcennin found much interesting work to occupy him in his retirement. He became chairman of the new Welsh Independent Television Authority, and accompanied the Duke of Edinburgh on his world tour. He was appointed Lord Lieutenant of Herefordshire in 1957.

July 14, 1960.

The death of **Sister Margaret Clare,** O.B.E., at Tunbridge Wells, at the age of 80, in September 1956 brought to an end a long life devoted up to the day of her death, to vigorous and adventurous activities in social and educational welfare, particularly among British families in Egypt.

A daughter of the Rev. Wilson Brown, of Stoke by Nayland, Sister Margaret was frail in body, not five feet high, and suffered from the day of her birth from grievously defective eyesight and a defective heart. But these disabilities were counteracted by the clearest and calmest vision in social and political problems, an amazing capacity for drive, and inflexible determination to get things done when she felt that a wrong should be righted or help given.

She entered a religious order and in 1910 went to Cairo for her health, but, ignoring doctors' orders, she immediately plunged into social work. In Shoubra, a poor district of Cairo, she discovered a neglected community of poor British, whose male members mostly worked for the Egyptian Railways. At once she started a welfare centre to help them. At the same time she was equally shocked by the extent of the brothel area in Cairo, and became the principal founder of the International Bureau for the Suppression of Traffic in Women and Children. In this work she was strongly supported by Sir Thomas Russell [q.v.], then Chief of Police. She also had support from the Bishop of London, and from General Sir Archibald Murray, whose financial help enabled her to open a hostel for girls and women who wished to escape from a life of misery.

The 1914-18 War created a new British community in Egypt where many Service men were demobilized, marrying girls of other nationalities and creating new problems. Sister Margaret established the British Benevolent Fund, enrolling many willing workers and raising immense sums of money. The fund remains as one memorial to her, continuing to help many unfortunate British individuals and families. She also started girl guides in Egypt.

But the most spectacular of Sister Margaret's activities in Egypt was her creation of the English School in Cairo. In 1915, finding many British children unable to go home for schooling, she cajoled the authorities into lending her a closed German school in Boulac; and in her own way obtained furniture and teaching staff. As the years passed her vision extended and she visualized an English School where the poorest British child could obtain British education on public school lines. Later she extended the privilege to boys and girls of other nationalities, with the result that today her school, with magnificent buildings surrounded by trees at Heliopolis, has over 700 pupils, a large proportion of them boarders.

This continual work played havoc with her health, and Sister Margaret retired to France, more than usually ill. But in 1935 the late Lord Lloyd, then High Commissioner, invited her to revisit Egypt at his own expense to examine the condition of social and educational work in the British communities. After that visit she returned to England where she started the Anglo-Egyptian Aid Society to help in rehabilitating and establishing British families compelled through circumstances to go to England. For many years she was its honorary secretary and principal caseworker, but ill health again terminated this work. She died as its president. For her services to the British community in Egypt she was appointed O.B.E.

In her work with the Anglo-Egyptian Aid Society in London and the English School in Cairo, Sister Margaret was, year after year, supported by warm personal understanding and sympathy from Queen Mary [q.v.] and since her death by the Princess Royal*. But her death leaves a grievous gap in the lives of hundreds of men, women, and children who have reason for appreciating her unfailing activity in helping them, her broad-minded understanding and her saintliness.

October 4, 1956.

Lord Clarendon, Lord Chamberlain from 1938 until 1952, and a former Governor-General of the Union of South Africa, died at his home in London on December 13, 1955 at the age of 78.

Much of his life was spent in public service. He brought to it high ability, a vigorous sense of duty, and a most engaging charm. Added to these was a spontaneous tact more effective, perhaps, in practice than the most studied diplomacy. It went far to smooth his way through life. Gifted as well with the ability to form impartial judgments, he had all the qualities which under modern conditions make for the success of a representative of the Sovereign in a self-governing Dominion. In South Africa he did conspicuously well. In him there passed a great aristocrat, who was also a great and kindly gentleman.

The Rt. Hon. Sir George Herbert Hyde Villiers, sixth Earl of Clarendon, and Baron Hyde, of Hindon, Wiltshire, K.G., G.C.M.G., G.C.V.O., was born on June 7, 1877, the only son of the fifth Earl by his wife Lady Caroline, daughter of the third Earl of Normanton. He was, therefore, of the junior branch of the house of Villiers, the first Earl having been the second son of the second Earl of Jersey. His grandfather, the third Earl, had, in the reign of Queen Victoria, three times been Secretary of State for Foreign Affairs.

Lord Clarendon was educated at Eton, where he was in Walter Durnford's House. From 1902 to 1905 he was extra A.D.C. to the Lord Lieutenant of Ireland. In 1914 he succeeded his father.

A Conservative in politics, he was, from 1919 to 1921, Chancellor of the Primrose

League. From 1921 to 1922 he was a Lord in Waiting to the King, and from 1922 to 1925 Chief Conservative Whip in the House of Lords and Captain of the Honourable Corps of Gentlemen at Arms. From 1925 to 1927 he held office as Parliamentary Under-Secretary of State for Dominion Affairs and Chairman of the Overseas Settlement Committee.

In these capacities he made an extended tour of Canada to investigate the working of the group system of settlement. He returned to report that the experiment was the most successful in which any Government had hitherto engaged. From 1927 to 1930 he was chairman of the British Broadcasting Corporation, a position which he filled with tact and competence.

Early in 1930 it was announced that Lord Clarendon was to succeed Lord Athlone [q.v.] as Governor-General of South Africa. It presented a great though an exacting opportunity, for the régime of his predecessor, ably assisted as it was by Princess Alice, had been immensely popular. Before his departure he was created a G.C.M.G. In January 1931 he was sworn in at Cape Town, and started his career with, in the eyes of the Afrikaans speakers of the Union, the initial advantage that he had been appointed on the recommendation of General Hertzog.

He lived up to every expectation. All that the King's representative could do to serve the end of South African unity was done. Sedulous in avoiding any entrenchment on the constitutional prohibitions which attached to his office, he nevertheless exerted a wise and salutary influence. He made it his duty to know every part of the Union, and he and Lady Clarendon identified themselves with beneficent works and social service of every kind. In 1935 he suffered a grievous loss in the death, as the result of a shooting accident, of his eldest son, Lord Hyde. On the news of this tragedy, a wave of spontaneous sympathy swept over the Union. When in the same year his term of office was extended the announcement was received throughout South Africa with keen satisfaction.

During his term of office he had seen the Union pass through the lean and difficult period which followed the world depression. When in 1937 he left it, it was enjoying a great prosperity. Before he sailed the South African Prime Minister expressed the "appreciation of the Government and the gratitude of the people" for the manner in which he and Lady Clarendon had sought to advance the national harmony in a spirit of impartial devotion to duty. On his return to London he was created a Knight of the Garter.

During the period of his Governor-Generalship Lord Clarendon sold The Grove at Watford, an eighteenth century house, which, in his grandfather's day, had been a famous political centre, frequented by the Palmerstons, Lady Holland, Macaulay and other great figures.

In 1938 he was appointed Lord Chamberlain in succession to Lord Cromer [q.v.], and, in the same year, Chancellor of the Order of St. John of Jerusalem. In 1941 Kyre Park, which he and Lady Clarendon had lent to the British Red Cross Society and the South African Red Cross, was opened as a convalescent home for other ranks.

During much of Lord Clarendon's period of office as Lord Chamberlain the ceremonial side of his work was interrupted or greatly reduced by the Second World War and conditions of the years immediately after it. When the war ended he assisted King George VI [q.v.] in adapting state ceremonies to the changed circumstances of the time. He will perhaps be most vividly remembered, as Lord Chamberlain, for his courtesy, for his fine voice, which sounded particularly impressive at investitures, and for the dignity and fortitude with which he overcame the handicap of lameness. He resigned on medical advice in 1952.

He married in 1905 Adeline Verena Ishbel, D.G.St.J., only surviving daughter of Captain Herbert Haldane Somers Cocks, and sister of the sixth Baron Somers, by whom he had two sons, the elder of whom died in 1935, and a daughter. The heir is his grandson, George Frederick Laurence Hyde Villiers, Lord Hyde, who was born in 1933.

December 14, 1955.

Sir William Henry Clark G.C.M.G., K.C.S.I., who died on November 22, 1952 at the age of 76, had had a long, varied, and distinguished career in the public service both at home and overseas, in India, Canada, and South Africa.

His outstanding qualities were quickmindedness, courage, and a sense of humour which amounted at times almost to irreverence for the accepted opinion or personality. His mental agility was shown by the speed and thoroughness with which he adapted himself to special job after special job. His courage was no less evident. He faltered before none of the novel and difficult situations which he so often had to face. A year of ill-health which at one time threatened to end his official career was only surmounted by the almost gay gallantry with which he endured it. His sense of humour always became acute in proportion to the seriousness of the matter in hand.

Born on January 1, 1876, he was the elder son of the late J. W. Clark, well known for many years in Cambridge as a fellow and tutor of Trinity College and later as Registrar of the University. He went to Eton in 1889 as a colleger, and was in the "select" for the Newcastle in 1893 and 1894. Then he went up to Trinity College, Cambridge, where he was a scholar, and obtained a first class in the Classical Tripos.

In 1898 he passed high in the Civil Service examination and was appointed in the following year to the Board of Trade. Within a short time his capacity and energy attracted attention, and when a Royal Commission headed by Sir James Mackay (afterwards Lord Inchcape) was appointed in 1901 to negotiate a new commercial treaty with China as a result of the Boxer rebellion, he was selected for the post of secretary, and accompanied the Commissioners to Shanghai.

Another Royal Commission was appointed in 1903 to investigate certain irregularities in connexion with the supply of food to the South African Expeditionary Forces, and to inaugurate a system that would prevent their recurrence in the future, and Clark was given the post of secretary.

When the Conservative Government were defeated at the end of 1905 Lloyd George became President of the Board of Trade. He selected Clark as his chief private secretary, and on his transfer to the Exchequer induced his successor at the Board of Trade to allow him to take Clark with him.

Clark was appointed Member for Commerce and Industry in the Executive Council of the Viceroy of India in 1910 for the usual term of five years. The appointment was a bold one. Clark was young for so important a post; he had no Indian experience; and he had to make good among those who had the advantage over him in both respects, and who might naturally be expected to feel that there was no need to go outside the Indian service to find a fully qualified candidate for the appointment. It tells the story of Clark's career to record that he was equal to the test; that he soon became an efficient representative of the interests with which his duties were concerned.

After six years' tenure of the appointment he returned to England in 1916 and reverted to his old department, the Board of Trade, becoming Comptroller-General of its commercial intelligence department. Towards the close of the 1914-18 war it was deemed essential to devise some organization for fostering British trade abroad in the difficult and obscure conditions which were the inevitable sequel of the world-wide upheaval. With this object the commercial intelligence department was expanded into the Department of Overseas Trade. Clark naturally became the first Comptroller-General of the new department, and for 10 years he showed all his characteristic energy and resource in grappling with the problems which the business community and Governments alike piled upon the shoulders of the new organization.

It was during this period, and thanks to the vision and zeal of his department, that the British Industries Fair became an institution of national and permanent importance, and that a policy of British participation in international exhibitions was evolved and practised.

To give effect to the resolution adopted by the Imperial Conference of 1926 as to the further development of the existing system of communication between His Majesty's Governments, the Government in the United Kingdom took steps in 1928 to appoint a representative in Canada with the title of High Commissioner.

He was one of the official advisers to the British delegation to the Ottawa Conference of 1932. He discharged his duties as High Commissioner with marked ability and success, and his term of office, normally five years, was extended in 1933 for another year.

He left Canada in 1934 to fill the even more difficult post of his Majesty's High Commissioner for Basutoland, the Bechuanaland Protectorate, and Swaziland, and was the first holder of this reconstituted office, which until his appointment had been styled High

Commissioner for South Africa and High Commissioner in the Union of South Africa for his Majesty's Government in the United Kingdom. He displayed in the post his customary ability and tact, and resigned in the summer of 1939 to succeed Sir Halford Mackinder as chairman of the Imperial Shipping Committee, and retired from the Civil Service in the course of the next year.

During the years of his retirement he was a constant attendant at the meetings of the Royal Empire Society, of which he had been chairman of the council, and more than once entertained the members with his trenchant and witty reminiscences and comments on current problems. His last official work was to tour in 1946, on behalf of the Dominions Office, the oversea posts under the control of the department to report on staff and establishment questions.

He was made a C.S.I. in 1911, a K.C.S.I. in 1915, a K.C.M.G. in 1930, and G.C.M.G. in 1937. He married in 1909 Anne Elizabeth, daughter of Mr. W. J. Monsell and widow of Mr. W. Bennett Pike. She died in 1946, and he is survived by a son and two daughters.

November 24, 1952.

Professor Sir Fred Clarke, who died suddenly on January 7, 1952 at his home in London, was a well-known figure in educational circles in Britain and in the Dominions.

He was born in 1880. After taking a first in Modern History at Oxford he was appointed to the Chair of Education in University College, Southampton, then known as Hartley College. His long and dominant interest in the Dominions may have dated from 1911, when he was appointed as the first holder of the Chair of Education in South Africa College, now the University of Cape Town. In the 18 years in which he held this chair he took an active interest in public affairs. In addition to the normal work of a university professor he was acting as chairman of the national conferences which led to the passing of the Juveniles Act and legislation regulating apprenticeship.

He was an official delegate of the Union Government at the International Labour Conference at Geneva in 1925 and the Imperial Education Conference in London in 1927. From 1929 to 1934 he was Professor of Education at McGill University, Montreal.

It was at about this time that the University of London Institute of Education, under the directorship of Professor Sir Percy Nunn, was beginning to attract students in considerable numbers from oversea and especially from the British Colonies and Dominions. It was felt that if the institute could be strengthened as a common centre of advanced studies in education, and if there could be brought to it from the Dominions promising young men and women destined later to occupy positions of weight and influence, the whole cultural and educational development of the Commonwealth might benefit. The Carnegie Corporation of New York made generous provision for a number of fellowships to be awarded to selected teachers and educationists of experience from the Dominions, and for a man of high standing in the educational world of one of the Dominions to be chosen for the appointment as adviser to oversea students. Professor Clarke was invited to accept this post and went to the institute in 1935. A year later he was appointed university professor of education and director of the institute in succession to Professor Sir Percy Nunn.

Of the nine years in which he held this office all but the first three were overshadowed by war, yet they compassed a notable stage in the development of the institute. With his intimate knowledge of two of the Dominions and his administrative ability, Clarke was able to bring the scheme rapidly into action and, when the outbreak of war inevitably suspended the oversea work of the institute, 32 Carnegie Fellows had returned to Australia, Canada, South Africa, and New Zealand to spread the news of the work being done in London.

As soon as the war was over students from all parts of the Commonwealth and from countries abroad came to the institute, and now number more than 250 each year. It was Sir Fred Clarke who undoubtedly gave the institute its international character.

When war denied him a full opportunity to pursue his interest in Commonwealth affairs, his energies found other outlets nearer home. As an active member of the National Union of Teachers he worked to promote a sense of high responsibility within the teaching profession. He had a peculiarly happy way with an audience of teachers, and he never spared himself a long journey (though perhaps at times he should have done so) to meet a group of teachers. As a member of the McNair Committee he was a strong advocate of the participation of the universities in the training of teachers, and he took his part in framing the policy under which his own institute assumed wider responsibilities, and other institutes were created on a similar pattern throughout the country.

He was the first chairman of the Central Advisory Council for Education (England), and the report on "School and Life" bears many marks of his influence. He was a leading spirit in the promotion of the National Foundation for Educational Research in England and Wales, and the first chairman of its executive committee under the presidency of the Minister of Education. He was knighted in 1943, and retired from the directorship of the institute in 1945. The institute was, however, happy to retain his services as adviser to oversea students until his death.

January 8, 1952.

Dr. Louis Clarke, Director of the Fitzwilliam Museum, Cambridge, from 1937 to 1946, died on December 13, 1960. He was 79.

By his death the university, his college and his many friends lost one of the most striking and well-loved Cambridge figures of his generation.

The fourteenth child and tenth son of Stephenson Clarke, Louis Colville Grey Clarke was born on May 2, 1881. Educated at Trinity Hall, of which he was later elected a fellow, most of his working life was connected with the university. By training an archaeologist, he was interested in all forms of art, ancient and modern. He travelled extensively, in Central and South America, Abyssinia (which he visited twice) and other parts of Africa; and took part in excavations in New Mexico (1923) and on several occasions in Hungary. He was an Honorary Fellow of the Society of Archaeological and Historical Arts of Hungary, and was awarded the Hungarian Order of Merit.

His first appointment was as Curator of the Museum of Archaeology and Ethnology. He held the post from 1922 to 1937 and during this time did much for its collections and continued afterwards as a regular benefactor. As Director of the Fitzwilliam Museum he followed Sir Sydney Cockerell*, who in 30 years of office had attracted many benefactions, including substantial sums for extensions of the building. The outbreak of war soon after Clarke's appointment gave him fewer big opportunities of this kind, but he arranged more than 40 exhibitions during the war, in spite of lack of staff, and by 1944 the museum had more visitors than in 1937 or 1938.

His firm foundation in the past, historical knowledge and open mind enabled him to do much intensive work among the collections, throwing fresh light on the old and extending the range of the new. One of his first efforts was a special exhibition of the engravings of Robert Nanteuil, selected from the magnificent collections of prints presented to the museum by John Charrington. Moreover, he initiated an immense improvement in the arrangement and furnishing of the principal rooms. On his retirement he became Honorary Keeper of the Prints and himself continued to make many generous gifts to the collections. A bust of him by Epstein [q.v.] was presented to the museum by his friends on his retirement. Clarke published no books, but he contributed articles to various journals. In 1959 he received the honorary degree of LL.D., an honour rarely conferred by the university on one of its own resident members.

He was a Fellow of the Society of Antiquaries and was President of the Cambridge Antiquarian Society in 1927-29. Long a member of the council of the Royal Geographical Society, he was also deeply interested in the work of the Scott Polar Research Institute at Cambridge, and had many friends among explorers.

Clarke, who was elected a Fellow of Trinity Hall in 1929, was much beloved there. He took a particular interest in successive improvements in the appearance of the college, and his comments in college meetings had a special flavour of independence and originality. Living as a bachelor in his large house off the Grange Road, he introduced many people of all ages to a better appreciation of beautiful things. He was an extensive and discriminating collector, and had a notable collection of Augustus John's* paintings and drawings. His wide circle of friendship and his astonishing fund of historical knowledge and personal recollection about families and people belonging to a vanishing society brought a breath of fresh air into academic life. Finally, his anonymous acts of generosity probably exceeded those which are known.

December 15, 1960.

Tom Clarke, who died in a nursing home at Colchester on June 18, 1957 at the age of 73, belonged to the picked company of Northcliffe's young men who carried on, between the wars, the professional traditions of that great journalist.

His heart at the outset of his career was in writing, but he became an extremely successful news editor and afterwards, at the *News Chronicle,* an editor of high competence and considerable distinction. There were few, indeed, in London who understood the technique of newspaper production better.

Born at Bolton on June 6, 1884, he was the youngest son of the late Joseph Clarke, who was of Irish descent, and worked for an insurance company. His mother was a Baptist, and saw to his religious upbringing. In spite, however, of her efforts, he refused at the age of 16 to be baptized. His brother, Allan, took him into the office of the *Northern Weekly*; and he learnt German and a little French, and began to write. After a year or two of this employment his brother introduced him to Dennis Hird, Warden of Ruskin Hall, and he obtained a year's scholarship there. Hird exerted a considerable influence over him, but he decided when his scholarship ran out to leave Ruskin Hall and take to journalism. He eventually obtained work at £1 a week on the *Lewisham Journal.*

When he was 19 his employer, F. G. Kellaway, afterwards Postmaster-General, suggested that he should enlarge his experience. He therefore applied for a reportership on the *South China Morning Post* and, somewhat to his surprise, obtained it. Young though he was, he did extremely well. The Russo-Japanese War brought him opportunities of correspondents' work for important London and American journals, and he was a special correspondent of the *Daily Mail* and *Chicago Tribune* in French Indo-China during the cruise of the Baltic Fleet. When the war ended he returned to London and sought employment, but was unsuccessful and went back to Bolton. Eventually, however, he obtained work as a reporter on the *Manchester Evening Chronicle.* A good article on the flying meeting at Blackpool in 1909 drew attention to him and he went to the *Daily Sketch* as news editor. Thence in 1911 he moved to the foreign staff of the *Daily Mail,* and in 1913 became night news editor of that journal.

After the 1914-18 war, in which he served, Lord Northcliffe promoted him to be news editor, and in 1920 sent him to the United States and Canada to study newspaper methods. After Lord Northcliffe's death he went to Australia and became assistant editor of the *Herald,* Melbourne. In 1926 he returned to London to become, first, managing editor of the *Daily News* and then editor of the *News Chronicle,* a position which he held until 1933, when owing to divergence of his views from those of the board he resigned. In 1935 he became Director of Practical Journalism at London University. He was deputy director, news division, Ministry of Information, from 1939 to 1940 and then joined Edward Hulton (as he then was) and his colleagues in the development of the chain of specialized news agencies which had been set up under the title of Britanova as the parent company.

Clarke went out in 1940 to establish an organization in South America with headquarters at Buenos Aires, and in a few short months had achieved what London headquarters thought the impossible: a substantial branch serving a large number of the most influential newspapers south of Panama. Circumstances which neither the chiefs in London nor Tom Clarke himself could control, and which were certainly not to his discredit, compelled his recall, and he returned to London where at headquarters in Norfolk Street he assumed editorial direction.

Of his books the first had appeared in 1931. This was *My Northcliffe Diary.* It was a faithful presentation of his former chief in action; but it was less convincing as an exposition of a remarkable and elusive mentality. Certain obvious questions such as what were the mainsprings of Lord Northcliffe's actions were left without satisfying answer. *Marriage at 6 a.m.* (1934) contained his impressions of Australia; and *Round the World with Tom Clarke* (1937) was the story of a journey and suggested that the evolution of thought within the Empire was not sufficiently understood by British politicians, newspapermen or students. *My Lloyd George Diary* appeared in 1939, *The Word of an Englishman* in 1934, and *The Devonshire Club* in 1944. In the summer of 1950, when for a year or two Clarke had been little seen in London, and dark reports about his health were coming from his home in Surrey, his many friends and the reading public were delighted to have evidence of his recovery with the appearance of a new book from his pen, *Northcliffe in History.* This had a varied reception, not on account of its writing, for Clarke could not help writing well, but because many critics felt that he had failed to live up to his claim that his was "an intimate study of Press power". He was, however, an eager newspaper controversialist to the last.

He married first, in 1910, Elizabeth, only daughter of Richard Weddington. The marriage was dissolved and he married secondly Shiela, daughter of Harry Green.

June 19, 1957.

Paul Claudel, who as poet, dramatist and Roman Catholic apologist was one of the most original and significant literary figures in France, and who had also had a distinguished diplomatic career, having served as French Ambassador in Tokyo, Washington, and Brussels, died in the early hours of February 23, 1955 at the age of 86.

In France Claudel's poetry and plays, which have a common imaginative source, found from the start a rapt and profoundly attentive, though not very large, public. In proclaiming, in the poetic symbolism of a devout Roman Catholic mysticism, the supremacy of the absolute, he seemed to restore to power a tradition in French thought that had been all but fatally weakened by the relativist philosophy popularized by Bergson. To this imaginative assertion of Roman Catholic dogma Claudel added a striking originality. What in some degree gave him his hold upon the literary sensibilities of his French readers, even of those who stood at the opposite intellectual pole to him, was the force and suggestion of his metrical invention. As with Rimbaud, perhaps the formative influence, both aesthetic and metaphysical, upon Claudel as writer, his experiments with the long unrhymed periods of his verse reflected a continuous struggle of mind and spirit.

They were recognized as such in France. Abroad, however, and especially in Protestant countries, Claudel's work evoked in the first place only doubt and hesitation. In England he seemed all too often not merely obscure, as without doubt he frequently is, but wilfully and pointlessly obscure; his hieratic manner of utterance seemed to cloak only a habit of rhetoric. That view of him has necessarily changed. Claudel still means much more to a Frenchman than he can mean to anybody else. For all its Spanish setting, *Le Soulier de Satin,* not to speak of *L'Annonce Faite à Marie* or of *L'Otage,* is woven into the fabric, after all, of French historical sentiment.

Paul Louis Charles-Marie Claudel was born on August 6, 1868, in a village of the Champagne country, Villeneuve-sur-Fère-en-Tardenois. His family had its roots deep in the soil of France; his father, *conservateur des hypothèques,* came of sound Vosges stock, his mother was proud of her unmixed Champagne ancestry.

He attended the *lycée* at Bar-le-Duc at the same time as Raymond Poincaré, and then studied with a private tutor at Nogent-sur-Seine. In 1882 he was living with his mother and sister in Paris. At the Lycée Louis-le-Grand in the capital he was not a particularly promising pupil—he loathed both Latin and mathematics—and failed at his *baccalauréat.* But in the top form, where he studied philosophy under the celebrated Burdeau, to whose potent hortatory influence Maurice Barrès bore witness, his intellectual faculties were sharply stimulated. He knew nothing as yet of unquestioning belief; in adolescence Renan was the light to which he turned, and by a strange coincidence it was Renan who handed him his prize on the last day of school in 1883.

Two things at this early period made a deep impression upon him, quickening his discontent with the rationalist mode of philosophy in which he had seemed likely to acquiesce. One was the death of his grandfather, the other was his discovery of the poetry of Rimbaud.

In the year 1890 he had entered the Diplomatic Service and thus embarked upon a career which was to take him away from France during much of the greater part of the next 40 years. It is not an insignificant thing that most of Claudel's work, which brings an impassioned lyrical sentiment to its statement of French and French-Catholic tradition, was written while he was abroad. He was appointed Vice-Consul in New York in 1893, then proceeded to China, where he served successively in Shanghai, Peking, and Tientsin, and during the later part of the period before 1914 went, in turn, to Prague, Frankfurt, and Hamburg. In 1916 he became Minister in Rio de Janeiro, where, incidentally, he took the composer Darius Milhaud* as a member of his staff. He was Minister in Copenhagen three years later, and was Ambassador in Tokyo during 1921-26, Ambassador in Washington during 1927-33, and Ambassador in Brussels during 1933-35.

A member of Mallarmé's circle, and a close friend of André Gide [q.v.], which he remained in spite of their subsequent religious differences and his failure to convert Gide, Claudel took from the beginning a firm footing in the French literary world of his day. Yet the prose poems of *Connaissance de l'Est* (1900) left on many a slightly bewildered impression, as also did the poems of *Cinq Grands Odes* (1910)—and this in spite of the declaration of aesthetic philosophy which he had made three years earlier in his *Art Poétique.* The plays themselves—*Tête d'Or, La Ville, L'Echange, La Jeune Fille Violaine,* the strange *Partage de Midi* (which goes back to 1906 and waited for republication until a year or two ago only)—these carried a clear enough message as Christian mystery plays. But the range of their poetical—and theological—implications did not become fully apparent until the production of *L'Annonce Faite à Marie,* the haunting tale of two sisters in the France of Joan of Arc, of whom one became a leper and saint while the other knew earthly joys and sorrows.

For the rest, it is barely possible to do more than mention some of the more notable plays that preceded what is, by common consent, Claudel's masterpiece, *Le Soulier de Satin.* There is, first, the subtle trilogy of three French generations placed providentially in opposition to the Papacy—*L'Otage, Le Pain dur,* and *Le Père humilié.* Besides these, there is *L'Ours et la Lune,* described as a farce for a marionette theatre, a magnificent compound of poetry, humour, and humanity. But it is to *Le Soulier de Satin* that one must go for the highest expression of Claudel's originality and his most impassioned statement of belief in Divine Grace.

A version of the play which he prepared for theatrical performance during the German occupation was produced by the Comédie-Française in 1944. It had long been a reproach to the Académie-Française that he was not a member, but amends were made at last when he was triumphantly elected after the liberation. In those later years Claudel's literary work had consisted chiefly of commentaries on Holy Scripture.

Relatively few translations from the vast body of his work have appeared in English, and the number of full-length studies devoted to that work is smaller still. Only in autumn 1954, however, an illuminating commentary by Dr. Joseph Chiari appeared under the title *The Poetic Drama of Paul Claudel.* Some 12 months earlier Jean-Louis Barrault's company gave a new and striking production in Paris of *Le Livre de Christophe Colombe*; and in the last weeks of his life Claudel watched the rehearsals in preparation for a new production of *L'Annonce Faite à Marie* at the Comédie-Française, and attended the first night only in the week before he died.

February 24, 1955.

Brooke Claxton, D.C.M., a former Canadian Minister of Defence, died on June 13, 1960. He was 61 and had given notable service in several spheres of Canadian life.

The son of Albert George Brooke Claxton, K.C., he was born on August 23, 1898, and educated at Lower Canada College and McGill University (where he was later a part-time Professor of Commercial Law).

At the age of 19 he was a battery sergeant-major with the Canadian artillery in France and won a D.C.M. Subsequently he became a prominent lawyer in Montreal and in politics was soon recognized as one of the Liberal Party's ablest organizers, fluent in English and French, and with the ability to fire enthusiasm.

In 1944 he was taken into the Cabinet of Mackenzie King as Minister of National Health and Welfare, and many assumed he was being groomed as King's successor. In fact, Claxton suggested after the war was won that the Minister of Justice, Louis St. Laurent*, be asked to take the External Affairs portfolio as a means of keeping him in public life. St. Laurent accepted and later became Prime Minister, while Claxton took the thankless job of Defence Minister with the task of reorganizing the Canadian forces for peace—later made the more difficult by the demands of the Korean War.

He worked long hours and his interests ranged far beyond his department into the fields of social security and education and overall political strategy. Although the Liberals were re-elected in 1953 he retired a year later and became vice-president and manager for Canada of Metropolitan Life Insurance.

But his public service was yet not done. He was made chairman of the Canada Council on its formation in 1957, and entrusted with the task of distributing federal funds to assist universities and promote the study and enjoyment of works of art, the humanities and social sciences.

He is survived by his wife, the former Helen Galt Savage, one son and a daughter.

June 15, 1960.

Sir Henry Clay, formerly Warden of Nuffield College, and a lifelong student of economic and social questions, died on July 29, 1954 in hospital at Middelburg, in Holland, where he was on holiday, after a road accident. He was 71.

He was born at Bradford in 1883, and was educated at the local grammar school and at University College, Oxford. At the early age of 24 he became Warden of the Neighbour Guild Settlement, and two years later threw himself into the movement for extending university lectures to the Workers' Educational Tutorial Classes.

Clay lectured to these classes in Leeds, London, and Oxford for eight years, and was then attached to the Ministry of Labour as a wartime assistant from 1917-19. He was elected a Fellow of New College, Oxford, in 1919, but retained his Fellowship only two years, during which he was special correspondent on industrial questions to the New York *Evening Post.*

In 1922 he was appointed Jevons Professor of Political Economy at Manchester University, exchanging his Chair in 1927 for a specially created Chair of Social Economics. His reputation as an economist at that time rested chiefly upon his little book *Economics: An Introduction for the General Reader*, published in 1916, and his study of *The Problem of Industrial Relations*, published in 1929. His gifts of sobriety of statement, sanity of judgment, and lucidity in exposition combined with painstaking industry and shrewd common sense to cause him to become a popular speaker and writer.

Though he came under the influence of Marshall, who lectured for a time at Balliol before he became Professor at Cambridge, Clay was far removed from the Cambridge School.

In everything he wrote Clay was hard-headed, often penetrating, and always clear. In 1925 he accepted an invitation from the Union Government of South Africa to serve on the Economic and Wage Commission set up to inquire into the cost of living, wages, &c. In 1929 he presided over the Section of Economics and Statistics at the meeting of the British Association in Cape Town.

Clay left Manchester in 1930 to take up an appointment under the Securities Management Trust, formed under the auspices of the Bank of England. The task of economic research into British industry was congenial to a man of his type, and the removal to London enabled him to meet his fellow economists at the Political Economy Club, to which he had been recently elected. Soon the ominous signs of the depression which came to a head in August 1931 cast their shadows before and Clay was not slow to note their significance. His address to the Insurance Institute early in the year was a fitting warning to business circles in Britain, but by February 1932 in the fifth of the Halley Stewart lectures of that year he showed that his thought had already moved on to the consideration of the whole effect of the depression on world trade.

His position and influence were much enhanced in 1933 by his appointment to the post of Economic Adviser to the Governors of the Bank of England, and though his work was thenceforward done rather behind the scenes than in public his influence was known to be considerable. With the late Sir Hubert Henderson [q.v.] he assisted the late Lord Stamp to make a comprehensive survey of the war plans of all Government Departments, a task which occupied this powerful team for some two years, and Clay was then, in 1941, given leave of absence from the Bank to act as Economic Adviser to the Board of Trade, with a view to reconstructing the commercial and industrial life of the country after the end of hostilities.

In his post as Warden of Nuffield College, Oxford, which he held from 1944 to 1949, he manifested a charm and tolerance in the best academic tradition, without, however, giving way on any question of importance.

Frail in appearance and reserved in demeanour, he attracted and retained the affection of a wide circle of friends, by whom his loss will be deeply regretted. Almost his last published work appeared in *The Times* in 1951 when he contributed two articles analysing the not very sound assumptions underlying the Monopolies and Restrictive Practices Act of 1948.

He was twice married, first to Gladys, daughter of Arthur Priestman. She died in 1941, leaving three sons and a daughter.

Clay married secondly in 1951 Rosalind, daughter of the late A. L. Smith, sometime Master of Balliol, and widow of E. Murray Wrong.

August 2, 1954.

The Most Rev. Geoffrey Hare Clayton, D.D., Archbishop of Cape Town since 1948, died suddenly in Cape Town on March 7, 1957. He was 72.

A former Chaplain and Fellow of Peterhouse, Cambridge, he was a scholar and theologian, and at the same time a great diocesan administrator. As Bishop of Johannesburg he was undoubtedly one of the ablest bishops in the church of the Province and he had made outstanding contributions to the Native cause in South Africa.

The son of a former Bishop of Leicester, Clayton was born on December 12, 1884. He was educated at Rugby and at Pembroke College, Cambridge, where he was Bell scholar and graduated in 1906 with a first class in the Classical Tripos Part I. In 1907 he took a first class in the Theological Tripos Part II and won the George Williams Prize. In 1908 he was ordained to the Chaplaincy of Peterhouse, Cambridge, and was elected to a fellowship there, which he held until 1924. From 1914 to 1919 he was a temporary Chaplain to the Forces and was mentioned in dispatches. He was successively Vicar of St. Mary's the Less, Cambridge (1918-1924), and Vicar of Chesterfield (1924-1934). He was Rural Dean of Chesterfield from 1925 to 1928; Lecturer from 1925 to 1934; Examining Chaplain to the Bishop of Derby from 1927 to 1934; and Archdeacon of Chesterfield and Hon. Canon of Derby from 1928 to 1934, in which year, on May 1, in St. Paul's Cathedral, London, he was consecrated Bishop of Johannesburg. Fourteen years later he was made Archbishop of Cape Town.

A bachelor, and a man with no hobbies, he was an extraordinarily hard worker, rising at 7 a.m. and often not going to bed until 2 a.m. Much of his success as an administrator was undoubtedly due to this capacity for sustained hard work, but he had also the wise and genial judgment of men and things that so often goes with a sense of humour. One felt as though that great laugh of his echoed through South Africa, and that in face of it and of the deep spirituality as well as human sympathy that lay behind it, prejudices and every kind of meanness must vanish away. To a remarkable extent they very often did.

The force of his personality seemed to pervade the whole diocese, and even native priests and catechists in remote areas felt that his eye was upon them and the personal example of his own titanic labours ever before them. Kind and sympathetic to all his clergy as he was, he nevertheless expected to get, and as a rule did get, the last ounce of effort out of each of them. Part of his secret undoubtedly lay in his leadership on large questions. Though a latecomer to South Africa, and in spite of his academic background—or perhaps because of it—he showed a wonderful power of picking up the threads of South African problems quickly.

Clayton's thinking about them was often penetrating and original, and South Africans of all classes from General Smuts downwards listened to his opinions with respect. A minor illustration of this was provided at the opening of the Johannesburg Exhibition, when, instead of felicitations on the organization and output of the gold industry, he contributed the criticism that the exhibit relating to the pygmies was lamentably insignificant. That was typical of his attitude. For him the real problems of Africa were essentially human problems.

Clayton was strongly opposed to the policy of Apartheid. In a B.B.C. broadcast in 1954 he said that acts forbidding mixed marriages were wrong in principle and unnecessary in practice and that the existing form of Apartheid prevented Africans from making the contribution they could make to the welfare of the country. It was also hampering their economic and cultural development.

On another occasion he warned South Africans that they were laying up a "terrible heritage" for the future. There could be no real peace or mutual confidence when legislation was based on fear. This, he said, was the curse of South Africa.

Differences of opinion between the churches and the Nationalist Government—and also within the churches themselves—have often, in recent years, been acute and debated in anger.

Clayton, throughout his long sojourn, first in the Transvaal and then in the Cape Province, sought, consistently and without in the least yielding on matters of principle, to bring men together. He remained, in the heat of a contest in which few of the protagonists can be said wholly to have kept their dignity, always a Christian gentleman and a scholar. His wise and moderating influence will be sadly missed.

March 8, 1957.

Sir George Clerk, G.C.M.G., C.B., formerly British Ambassador in Paris, died on June 18, 1951 at the age of 76.

In appearance he was almost a stage ambassador—tall, erect, and faultlessly dressed. He had also those gifts of tact and sympathy which do so much to oil the machinery of international relations. For all his apparent dilettantism, however, he was a hard and effective worker and few diplomats have been possessors of memories more capacious and retentive. His forceful handling of a difficult situation saved the Hungarians in 1919 when they were in danger of complete ruin from defeat, foreign invasion, and internal strife. He did much to foster friendly relations with Turkey at a particularly difficult time and his outstanding service in strengthening the bonds of friendship between Britain and France in the threatening days before the outbreak of the 1939-45 war was recognized by the signal award of the Grand Cordon of the Legion of Honour.

George Russell Clerk was born on November 29, 1874, the only son of General Sir Godfrey Clerk, K.C.V.O. He went to Eton in 1888 and four years later he entered New College, Oxford (of which he was to become an Honorary Fellow), where he took classical honours. After studying abroad he passed the Foreign Office examination and was appointed a clerk in 1899. Normally his life should have been spent in London, but he volunteered for foreign service. One of his first appointments was in attendance on Prince Albert of Belgium at the Coronation of King Edward VII in 1902, and it was then that he first made the acquaintance of the heroic King whose death put Europe into mourning 32 years later during Clerk's short tenure of the office of British Ambassador in Brussels.

From 1903 to 1907 he was an assistant in the British Agency at Addis Ababa. There followed alternate appointments abroad and in the Foreign Office. When war broke out in 1914 he was at home and except for two special missions he stayed in the Foreign Office for the duration of the war.

He was already recognized as one of the most promising of the younger men in the service, and was made head of the newly constituted war department of the Foreign Office. It was in this capacity that in 1917 he attended the Rome Conference, where the four principal Allied Governments discussed the military situation at Salonika and in Macedonia, and made plans for the military and naval campaigns of 1917. A few weeks later he accompanied Lord Milner to Petrograd on a mission the object of which was to secure more efficient cooperation with the Russians. They arrived at a period more pregnant with tragedy than any other in Russian history. Rasputin had been murdered a month before; a month later, with the Tsar's abdication, came the beginning of Russia's collapse.

When the Peace Conference opened in Paris and Mr. (later Lord) Balfour accompanied the Prime Minister and the British delegation to France, Lord Curzon acted as Secretary of State at the Foreign Office and appointed Clerk his private secretary. As Lord Hardinge,

Sir E. Crowe, and Sir W. Tyrrell were all in Paris, Clerk was in practice also Under-Secretary of State. In the following September he was appointed Minister to the newly formed Czechoslovak Republic and was almost immediately sent on a special mission to the Romanian Government to bring about a settlement of the confused situation in Hungary. This task was achieved after several weeks of difficult and complicated negotiations.

In 1926 he succeeded Sir Ronald Lindsay as Ambassador to the Turkish Republic and was sworn of the Privy Council. Relations between Great Britain and Turkey were then far from cordial. Memories of Britain's moral support of the Greek invasion of Anatolia in 1919 were still vivid in the minds of the Nationalist Party. The new Ambassador immediately set out to dispel Turkish suspicions and gradually gained the confidence of the Republican Government. When in the autumn of 1933 Clerk was moved to Brussels sincere regret was felt by the Turkish official world as well as by the British colony in Istanbul.

Brussels was but a stepping stone to Paris, to which capital Clerk was appointed in March 1934, after less than three months in Belgium. In Paris he had the heavy task of maintaining the unusually high standard set by his predecessor, [by then] Lord Tyrrell, but his outstanding gifts enabled him to come finely through that severe test. During his term of office the Italo-Ethiopian war, the progressive violations of the Treaty of Versailles, and the Spanish conflict enabled him to show the measure of his ability and tact and to reveal not only the depth of his affection for France and all she stands for in Western civilization but also his conviction that the closest ties of friendship between Britain and France were as necessary then as they are now. When he retired in 1937 the keenest regret was expressed on all sides in Paris, a regret which he reciprocated.

Sir George Clerk, who had been made C.M.G. in 1908, a C.B. in 1914, and promoted K.C.M.G. in 1917, was promoted G.C.M.G. in 1929.

He married in 1908 Muriel, daughter of Mr. E. R. Whitwell. Lady Clerk is an artist with an extensive range both in medium and subject.

June 20, 1951.

Douglas Clifton Brown—See **Ruffside.**

Sir Charles Arden-Close—See **Arden-.**

Blanche Clough, Principal of Newnham College, Cambridge, from 1920 to 1923 and previously Vice-Principal, died on June 14, 1960 at the age of 98.

The death of Blanche Athena Clough breaks a link with the great pioneers of women's education, and removes a remarkable personality.

As the youngest daughter of the poet Arthur Hugh Clough, she was born in 1861 at Combe Hurst, Richmond, a few months before the death in Florence of her father, whom she never saw.

Much of her childhood was spent in the house of her grandparents, Mr. and Mrs. Samuel Smith, with whom Mrs. Clough and her young family partly made their home. With them at Combe Hurst (at that date a real country house), and later at Embley in Hampshire (previously the home of Miss Clough's cousin, Florence Nightingale, and her parents), "Thena" Clough imbibed that knowledge and love of the country which remained with her all her life. Birds and butterflies were her special delight, and she was deeply interested in the New Forest, where in later years she had her home. She was not, however, fated to pass her life in rural surroundings. She spent about four years at school, at the Miss Metcalfes' at Hendon, then recently established as one of the efforts of that time to improve girls' education. There she made some life-long friends, including Augusta and Eleanor Butcher, the two eldest daughters of Dr. Jex-Blake of Rugby, and others.

After a few years at home she entered Newnham College, following family traditions; for there were strong links with the women's movement on both sides, her mother being nearly related to Florence Nightingale and Barbara Bodichon, one of the founders of Girton, while her father's sister was Anne Jemima Clough, a founder and the first Principal of Newnham.

Miss Clough's work at Newnham filled nearly the whole of her life. She went up as a student in 1884, and stayed on first as secretary to her aunt, and after Miss Clough's death in 1892, as Assistant Secretary and Assistant Treasurer. In 1896 she was appointed Tutor in charge of Clough Hall, and in 1920 she succeeded Katharine Stephen as Principal of the college. She held this office till 1923, but continued as a member of the Council and of the Governing Body.

Outside the college, too, she was actively engaged in helping forward the interests of girls and women. She was a valued member of the Council of Roedean School, St. Felix School, and the Perse Girls' School, and of the Women's University Settlement, Southwark; she worked with the constitutional societies to obtain the suffrage for women; and was a faithful member of the London and National Society for Women's Service, and of the Women's Employment Federation. At the invitation of Herbert Fisher she represented the Cambridge Women's Colleges on the Royal Commission which investigated the Universities of Oxford and Cambridge after the 1914-18 War.

In these different directions, and especially at Newnham, Miss Clough found scope for her remarkable powers of mind and character. The college was for her a place in which women had an opportunity to liberate their minds, and to develop freely in a stimulating and friendly atmosphere, and she was active in initiating and pressing forward any changes of a progressive nature.

The endowment of research fellowships and studentships, the placing of the salaries of the college lecturers on a satisfactory basis, the constitutional change by which the college was granted a royal charter in 1917, the comprehensive scheme for enlarging and improving the college buildings—these were but a few among the many matters to which she contributed courageous thinking, clear and unhurried judgment, wise counsel, and a certain noble generosity which marked all she did.

No one worked harder for the admission of Cambridge women to membership of the university, but she showed no bitterness or discouragement in defeat. And amidst all the work which was involved in these larger issues, Miss Clough never lost sight of the individual students. The impression she made on them was a lifelong one, and the number of those who owe her a debt that can never be repaid must be countless. Her interest in human beings as such was indeed so spontaneous, so warm, so effortless, that throughout her life it brought her innumerable and devoted friends.

In her younger days she was one of a brilliant Cambridge group—Stephens, Custs, Butchers, Lloyds—and she was always intimate with the Darwins, the Maitlands, the Batesons, and the Protheros. Many were the delightful tales she could tell, in her deep voice, of the university figures who gave so special a flavour to the society of that simpler age.

In her later years she remained as keenly interested as ever in the world around her, and as ready to give her invaluable help in any direction: at the age of 80 she insisted on undertaking the collection of national savings from the cottages near her Hampshire home. Miss Clough's death brings to an end the age of the pioneers of women's emancipation, and with them she will always be remembered as an unconquerable lover of justice and freedom.

June 15, 1960.

Lord Clydesmuir, industrialist, parliamentarian, sometime Secretary of State for Scotland, and the last British Governor of Bombay, who acted four times as Viceroy and Governor-General of India, died on October 31, 1954 at his home at Carluke, Lanarkshire. He was 60.

The Right Hon. Sir David John Colville, first Baron Clydesmuir, of Braidwood, in the county of Lanark, in the peerage of the United Kingdom, P.C., G.C.I.E., T.D., J.P., and Lord Lieutenant of Lanarkshire, was born on February 13, 1894, being the only son of the late John Colville, sometime Liberal M.P. for North-East Lanarkshire. The late peer belonged to the third generation of the family which conducted the steelmaking firm of David Colville and Sons Ltd., which has contributed so largely to the industrial history of Scotland. In intervals from high public appointments he was an active member of the directorate of the firm and also of the Glasgow Chamber of Commerce. He was educated at Charterhouse and Trinity College, Cambridge, where he took his degree in 1914. During the 1914-18 War he was on active service with the 6th Battalion, The Cameronians, being twice wounded.

In 1922 Colville unsuccessfully contested in the Unionist interest the Motherwell and Wishaw division and similarly failed at a by-election in North Midlothian and Peebleshire in January 1929, but was returned there at the general election four months later. Debonair and genial, he was also a hard, efficient worker, and soon made his mark in the House both as a keen protectionist and as a strong upholder of Scottish interests. Within two years he was Parliamentary Secretary to the Department of Overseas Trade. He was made Under-Secretary for Scotland in 1935, and a year later was sworn of the Privy Council and selected for the key post of Financial Secretary to the Treasury. He entered the Cabinet as Secretary of State for Scotland in May 1938. On the fall of Chamberlain's Ministry in May 1940 he went on war service as a temporary colonel on the Staff, and he became honorary colonel of his old unit, the 6th Battalion, The Cameronians.

In the spring of 1943 he succeeded Sir Roger Lumley (now Lord Scarborough*) as Governor of Bombay. He went to the Town and Island in most anxious times, for there was great unrest in India owing to the Congress leaders' opposition to the war effort. Like other Governors in Congress-dominated provinces Colville ruled under Section 93 of the 1935 India Act without Cabinet or Legislature, local knowledge being provided by official "advisers". In these unfavourable conditions he quickly won widespread trust and regard, being greatly assisted therein by the wife he had married in 1915. She was Agnes Ann, elder daughter of Sir William Bilsland, Bt. She did much social service, was awarded the Kaisar-i-Hind gold medal, and became in 1946 one of the last ladies to be appointed to the Order of the Crown of India. There were two daughters and a son of the marriage.

Colville was the first (and last) former Secretary of State to hold a governorship in India since the assumption of direct rule by the Crown in 1858. In view of his wide experience this was a fortunate circumstance as it enabled a departure to be made from the long tradition that the senior in tenure of the three "Presidency" Governors should act when occasion called as Viceroy and Governor-General. So when Lord Wavell went home twice in 1945 to confer with the British Cabinet, Colville went to Delhi as temporary Viceroy. He acted again in December 1946, and also in May 1947, when Lord Mountbatten went to London on the direction of the Prime Minister (Clement Attlee*) to give the final form to the proposals for ante-dating by some 10 months the transfer of power on the basis of partition. He was admirably fitted by his courtesy and tact for holding the fort in these difficult circumstances, and his contributions to the private discussions of urgent questions were valued. There was no precedent for such frequent temporary tenures.

The confidence reposed in Colville, as also in General Sir Archibald Nye*, by the new independent Government at New Delhi was such that both were invited to continue in office for the time being, and Colville was Governor for some five months after the transfer of power. His advancement to a peerage in the New Year Honours of 1947 was welcomed in Bombay. On returning home Lord Clydesmuir re-entered the steel business of Colvilles, Ltd., and was an occasional participant in House of Lords debates. He was made a Governor of the B.B.C. at the beginning of 1950.

He is succeeded in the peerage by his only son, Major the Hon. Ronald John B. Colville, M.B.E., T.D., who was born on May 21, 1917, and married in 1946 Joan Marguerita, daughter of Lieutenant-Colonel E. B. Booth, D.S.O. They have two sons and a daughter.

November 2, 1954.

Albert Coates, who died on December 11, 1953 at the age of 71 in South Africa, where he had been living in retirement for several years, was a conductor of international experience and repute whose success was so great that it constantly raised the question why it was not greater. The answer is probably to be found in the mysterious fact that cosmopolitanism often cuts a man's roots and that in consequence his art somehow withers in the end.

Coates was the son of a Yorkshireman married to a Russian. He was born in St. Petersburg in 1882, educated in Liverpool, musically trained at Leipzig, and launched on his career at the Dresden Opera. Thence he went back to St. Petersburg, where he was principal conductor of the opera for five years. He left Russia soon after the Revolution, and in the years immediately after the 1914-18 War made a great reputation for himself in Britain, conducting the London Symphony Orchestra from 1919 onwards, Beecham* opera seasons, and the Leeds Festivals of 1922 and 1925. In 1923 he undertook concerts in America and in 1925 special performances at the Paris Opera. Since that time he had travelled incessantly, conducting everywhere in Europe (including Russia once more) and America.

He was, however, never long away from English musical life and every other year or so turned up at Covent Garden, at provincial festivals, and at principal London concerts. Yet when our need of experienced conductors was acute at the end of the 1939-45 War we had no permanent post to offer him or suitable mitre for him to wear. He went to South Africa in 1946 to direct the Johannesburg Symphony Orchestra.

His all-round experience was unequalled by any other British conductor (including Beecham). He first appeared in London with the London Symphony Orchestra in 1910, but made his name during the Covent Garden season of 1913, when he shared the Wagner performances with Nikisch, with whom he had studied at Leipzig. But when he returned in 1919 it was as a specialist in Russian music that he chiefly won his great repute. He knew the Russian operas, had studied composition under Rimsky-Korsakov, and had been friendly with Scriabin, of whose large-scale works he became the advocate and interpreter. But in spite of his training in Germany and his European experience his interpretations of the Viennese classics were less acceptable.

Even in much more recent times the structure of classical symphonies seemed to be an uncongenial way of thinking to a mind which worked on other lines. And since English musical life outside oratorio is founded for good or ill on the classical symphonies, Coates failed to win for himself the highest reputation among his own countrymen. He never ceased, however, to be to them a present help in times of dearth. His enormous experience, a comfortable sense of confidence which exuded from his large physical frame, and his catholicity of knowledge if not sympathy, made his performances of all kinds of works, including even such a one as Walton's *Belshazzar's Feast,* which he undertook for the Huddersfield Choral Society's centenary, secure and vivid.

His compositions in somewhat similar fashion fell between the two stools of national character and international sympathy, with a resulting ambiguity of achievement. The chief were operas on typically English themes, Samuel Pepys and Pickwick. *Samuel Pepys* was given in German at Munich in 1929, *Pickwick* in English at Covent Garden in 1936, but it seemed as though Wagner and the Russians stood between the composer and his subject, which really demanded, at any rate in the case of *Pickwick,* the traditional English style of the ballad opera. A symphonic poem "The Eagle", dedicated to the memory of Nikisch and produced at the Leeds Festival of 1925, is the chief of Coates's non-operatic compositions.

December 12, 1953.

Eric Coates, known as a composer of light music to an older generation who bought, sang, and listened to his song "Stonecracker John", and to a mid-wars generation as the composer of the *Three Elizabeths* and the *Knightsbridge March,* died on December 21, 1957 at the age of 71.

He was born at Hucknall, in Nottinghamshire, showed his talent early, learnt the violin as a boy, but entered the Royal Academy of Music in 1906 with a scholarship for viola. He was a pupil of Lionel Tertis* and for composition went to Frederick Corder. He started professional life in chamber music, being violist successively in the Hamburg, Cathie, and Walenn Quartets, but in 1912 he joined Henry Wood's Queen's Hall Orchestra as leader of the violas.

During the six years he remained an orchestral player, which may have done something to blunt his susceptibilities to great music, he began to turn out songs, of which the words by Fred Weatherley expressed the kind of sentiment that appealed to the audiences of the ballad concerts, of unlamented memory, and thence to amateur singers. Coates, who had an undoubted gift for orchestration, also began to write suites and marches suitable to the light orchestras also associated with the ballad concerts.

From 1918 onward he devoted himself to

this kind of music, which ultimately fell between the two stools of really popular jazz and serious music. But he was skilful, conscientious, and successful in works like "The Three Bears", "The Three Men", "Wood Nymphs", which were descriptive pieces, fundamentally commonplace no doubt, but well written, easy on the ear, and lightly sentimental.

In his autobiography, published in 1953, Coates, writing modestly to reveal a simple, friendly personality, said roundly: "I am a very ordinary man", and so he was, but with an extraordinary talent for music. If his compositions never rose above the unadventurous level of the popular and the obvious, they gained an enormous currency because he knew from his own nature what the ordinary man feels and thinks. Coates did not write with his tongue in his cheek. If his music is superficial, it is also sincere.

He married in 1913 Phyllis, daughter of Francis Black, who survives him with their son.

December 23, 1957.

Wells Wintemute Coates, O.B.E., the architect, died in Vancouver, British Columbia, in June 1958. He was 62.

Not many architects can have had a wider preliminary experience or a more cosmopolitan training than Wells Coates, who was one of those principally responsible for introducing modern architecture into Britain in the nineteen-thirties. He had a fine taste and a passion for research, and although he had several interesting buildings to his credit, he was unlucky in obtaining fewer opportunities to build than his talents deserved.

Coates, who was the son of the Rev. Harper Havelock Coates, D.D., Professor of Comparative Religion and Philosophy, his mother being of Canadian parentage, was born in Tokyo, Japan, on December 17, 1895. He was educated under private tutors and learnt the Japanese method of painting from a native artist. At the age of 18 he left Japan for a cruise round the world, visiting China, the Philippines, Java, Sumatra, Burma, India, Ceylon, and Europe, arriving in Canada in time to matriculate at McGill University, where two years later he graduated with degrees in both arts and science.

During the First World War Coates joined the Canadian forces and later served as a fighter pilot in the R.A.F. Afterwards he engaged in a variety of occupations, including lumbering and journalism, in Canada.

Coates went to London in 1929. His first works in architecture were shops and showrooms in various parts of London, which attracted a good deal of interest by their skilful planning for space-economy and lean elegance of design. At that time the severe reduction of a building to its essentials was something of a novelty. Without looking temporary these shops and showrooms had something of the lightness of the bazaar stall, and there is some reason to suppose that in designing them, as also in his domestic work, Coates remembered the light structures of the Far East, with their sliding panels instead of permanent walls to divide internal space, and their sparing decoration; yet there was never any obviously Oriental flavour in his designs.

Coates was one of the founders, in 1933, of the modern Architectural Research Group. Through it, as well as independently, he showed a life-long interest in the changing nature of architecture in relation to the modern world, and in the need for closer cooperation between architecture and engineering. In his own practice as a designer he was much more than an architect, creating at different times furniture, radio-sets (for many years the sets of his design were the best-looking on the market), original engineering structures and, in recent years, sailing boats on unorthodox principles. He had a sympathetic understanding of all branches of modern art and was one of the founders, also in 1933, with Paul Nash, of the group called Unit One.

His first substantial building was Lawn Road flats, Hampstead, a pioneer design, sociologically as well as architecturally, based on the idea of the minimum flat, completely equipped, for people who want to "live light" and have no desire to accumulate personal possessions. The flats became for many years afterwards, especially during the war, a centre of intellectual life unique of its kind, and the residence of well-known refugee architects.

They were followed by blocks of flats in Brighton and Kensington, the latter a most successful experiment in split-level planning. He was one of a group of architects who designed the studio and other interiors at Broadcasting House, London, when the building was first completed. He was elected F.R.I.B.A. in 1938 and R.D.I. in 1944. After the Second World War (during which he had a distinguished career as a staff officer in the R.A.F. and was appointed O.B.E.) he resumed practice in London and was responsible, among other things, for the National Film Theatre at the South Bank Exhibition, 1951.

In recent years he lived and worked mostly in Canada, where he undertook a number of large-scale planning projects, including the design of Iroquois, a new town to be built on the banks of the enlarged St. Lawrence seaway, and a study for the redevelopment of downtown Vancouver.

Wells Coates was an interesting talker on all subjects connected with art and science and a charming and friendly host. One of his talents as a host was that of being himself an excellent cook, especially of Japanese dishes. As a young man he was somewhat temperamental and moody, but he mellowed with the years and impressed everyone who worked with him by the serious belief in right principles that lay behind even his most fanciful designs. For him modern design was not a fashion but a cause demanding unquestioning devotion, and modern architecture in England owes a great deal to him.

In 1927 he married Marion Chamier, daughter of Frank Grove, consulting engineer, and leaves one daughter.

June 20, 1958.

John Cobb, who died while attempting to break the world's water speed record at Loch Ness on September 29, 1952, was one of the most successful drivers of track and record-breaking motor-cars in the history of motor racing. In both forms of motor racing he brought renown to Great Britain by his exploits at home, on the Continent, and in the United States. The boat Crusader in which he met his death was his first venture at speed on water.

John Rhodes Cobb was born on December 22, 1899, at Esher, Surrey, the son of Rhodes H. Cobb, and was educated at Eton and Trinity Hall, Cambridge. In business life he was a fur broker, and before the 1939-45 war he was commissioned by the Soviet Government to sell the annual Russian pelt stock. During the war he served first in the R.A.F. and from 1943 to 1945 as an Air Transport Auxiliary ferry pilot. He was one of the most modest and reticent of racing drivers. He never sought publicity and he raced and broke records for the sheer love of the sport. The outer circuit at Brooklands will always be remembered as his happy hunting ground, and no one surpassed him in knowledge of the track, courage, and driving skill at high speed.

He began his racing career at Brooklands in the early 1920s, driving a big 10-litre F.I.A.T. which had been made before the 1914-1918 war but was still capable of lapping the track at about 110 m.p.h. He then acquired a faster mount in one of the eight-cylinder Leyland-Thomas cars previously raced by J. G. Parry-Thomas. With this car Cobb scored several victories, following them up with many more when he bought the 10½-litre Delage driven with success some years before by the Frenchman René Thomas.

He became sufficiently accustomed to the 130-135 m.p.h. lap speeds possible with the Delage to want something even faster, and at his request Reid Railton [d. 1977] designed, and Thompson and Taylor made, the famous Napier-Railton car which was to prove the fastest machine ever raced on Brooklands track. Before the war caused the track to close Cobb had raised the Brooklands lap record to the formidable figure of 143.44 m.p.h. The Napier-Railton was extraordinarily successful in breaking long-distance records, both at Montlhéry and on the Bonneville salt flats, Utah, where Cobb drove the car for the first time in 1935. On that visit to the United States he set up a new world's record for one hour at 152.7 m.p.h. and raised the world's 24-hour record to 134.7 m.p.h. While doing so he broke all the records for intermediate times and distances from 100 miles to 3,000 miles at speeds of over 130 m.p.h. These records were subsequently beaten by Captain George Eyston and later by Jenkins, the American driver.

The culminating point in his career came when he broke the world's land speed record with an entirely new car designed by Railton. He took this car to Bonneville salt flats in 1938, Eyston, the holder of the existing record of 312 m.p.h., making the journey at the same time with his Thunderbolt car. Eyston was the first to beat the record with a speed of 345.49 m.p.h., but Cobb persevered and finally exceeded this figure with a speed of

350.20 m.p.h. He held the record for only one day, however, before Eyston went out once more and recorded a speed of 357.53 m.p.h. In the following year, 1939, Cobb tried again and this time beat the record by the handsome margin of 12 m.p.h., raising it to 369.7 m.p.h.

After the war Cobb returned to Utah with the Railton, and on September 16, 1947, increased the record to 394.2 m.p.h. In one direction he reached a speed of 403.135 m.p.h. and thus became the first man to exceed a speed of 400 m.p.h. on land. For this astonishing feat of courage he was awarded the Segrave Trophy for that year. This record speed, which is almost impossible to visualize, is likely to stand for many years.

September 30, 1952.

Sir Charles Cochran, who died on January 31, 1951 in hospital in London at the age of 78, was the great showman of his generation. He began, with a production of Ibsen, a career which included the promotion of boxing matches and the management of circuses.

The small boy whose zest never faded in him liked entertainment to be on the grandest possible scale, but the business sense which led him to see big and to seize opportunities in every kind of entertainment did not prevent him from bringing to the stage a natural good taste which asserted itself and became by assiduous cultivation in many countries a flair for the first rate in diverse kinds of theatrical art.

London was for a long stretch of years—during which he made and lost fortunes—as much indebted to his taste as to his indefatigable enterprise. With his name are associated Reinhardt's production of *The Miracle* at Olympia; the Diaglihev Ballet and La Chauve-Souris; seasons of Lucien Guitry, Duse, Brieux, and Pirandello; the London Pavilion as the home of the *dernier cri* in *revue*; Noël Coward's* early *revues* and his *Calvacade*, and such plays as Sean O'Casey's* *The Silver Tassie* and Barrie's *The Boy David*; the Holborn Stadium and the Wells*-Beckett* and the Beckett-Carpentier* fights; Olympia again, and the Hackenschmidt*-Madrali match; with roller skating and the rodeo and with the management of such different public entertainers as Lenglen, Mistinguett*, and Houdini. He was never to be found in slavish pursuit of what the public was supposed to want. He trusted his sense of the best.

Charles Blake Cochran, born on September 25, 1872, at Lindfield, Sussex, son of James Elphinstone and Matilda Cochran, was educated at Brighton, and in 1887 made his first appearance on the stage there as Henry VII; in the cast was Aubrey Beardsley, who, like himself, was already intensely interested in things theatrical.

At 16 Cochran was articled to a surveyor in Brighton. He was determined to go on the stage, however, and in August 1890 actually got an engagement at Dover—only to be incontinently "sacked" after his first performance.

By the end of the year he had bought a steerage passage to the United States, where for some two years he led a hard and precarious life in touring companies. He was not a success as an actor; yet the great American actor, Richard Mansfield, saw that if Cochran could not act he had managerial ability, and appointed him his private secretary. Cochran now began to make contact with authors and actors of note. In 1895 he quarrelled with Mansfield and set up in New York a school of acting, in partnership with E. J. Henley. That year also saw his first production, Ibsen's *John Gabriel Borkman.*

Late in 1897 Cochran returned to London. Mabel Beardsley introduced him to the *Yellow Book* circle. He met Max Beerbohm [q.v.], William Rothenstein, Ernest Dowson, Charles Conder, and other comparable figures. For some time he worked as a journalist, but the theatre was in his blood. Seeing *Cyrano de Bergerac* in Paris, he conceived the idea that Mansfield should put it on in New York, and, the old quarrel having been quickly composed, the thing was done, with Cochran as secretary.

Cochran's next step was to set up business in Chancery Lane as a theatrical agent. Gradually he won success in management, acting in turn for Mistinguett, Ethel Levey, Houdini, the "escapist", and the great wrestler, Georges Hackenschmidt, whom he matched at Olympia in 1904 against Madrali, the "Terrible Turk". His first London production, *Sporting Simpson*, put on at the Royalty in 1902, had not been a success. Until the outbreak of the 1914-18 war, however, he had arranged numerous grandiose spectacles and introduced "crazes" (like roller-skating, which flourished from 1909 up to 1914), which affected social habit. His greatest production of those years was *The Miracle*, which opened at Olympia on Christmas Eve, 1911.

The 1914-18 war differed very materially from that of 1939-45 in the conditions it dictated to the entertainment industry. There was, indeed, something like a theatrical "boom", and the prevailing mood, of troops and public alike, called for gaiety, lightness, and colour to offset the grim business in hand. In this need Cochran saw his opportunity to stage *revues.* He began at the Ambassadors with *Odds and Ends.* Then as general manager of the Empire he scored another resounding success with *Watch Your Step.* After several more *revues* and musical comedies, Cochran produced the two sociological plays by Brieux, *Damaged Goods* and *The Three Daughters of M. Dupont.* In 1917, at the Oxford Music Hall, he put on Bruce Bairnsfather's [q.v.] light show, *The Better 'Ole,* which, after starting quietly, attained a run of 817 performances. At the Pavilion in 1918 he produced *As You Were.* This ran for a year.

Cochran was now a power in the entertainment world. In 1919 he took control of the Garrick and Aldwych theatres and the Holborn Stadium, where he promoted many notable fights, including Bombadier Wells v. Joe Beckett and Beckett v. Carpentier. He was responsible for the production in 1920 of *London, Paris, and New York,* but the same year was thrown out of his stride by a long illness. Recuperating in Spain the next year, he met Diaghilev and Stravinsky*, and learnt of the remarkable Russian troupe called La Chauve-Souris. Brought over to England, this company gave brilliant and original light entertainment. Cochran's next ventures were a season for Lucien Guitry and a return of Eleonora Duse at the age of 63.

Ever on the look-out for something new, Cochran promoted the rodeo, a cowboy entertainment, at Wembley in 1924. Unfortunately on the first night a steer broke its leg; the word went round that the rodeo was cruel and brutal and the success he had hoped for did not materialize.

Noël Coward was by that time rapidly rising to fame as a playwright, actor, and composer. Cochran and he collaborated in many ventures, including *This Year of Grace* (1928) in which Coward also acted, but the biggest of them was *Cavalcade,* in 1931. Cochran ran a Pirandello season in 1925 and sponsored Chaliapine at the Albert Hall in 1927. Another serious play he brought to London was Sean O'Casey's *The Silver Tassie* (1929). Sir James Barrie's *The Boy David,* with Elisabeth Bergner in the title part, was one of his few failures.

In the thirties his best remembered pieces are *Ever Green, Helen* (an adaptation by Sir Alan Herbert* of Offenbach's *La Belle Hélène*), a revival of *The Miracle* at the Lyceum, and *Nymph Errant.* After the war Cochran and Sir Alan Herbert joined forces again in *Big Ben, Bless The Bride,* and *Tough At The Top. Bless The Bride* was Cochran's last big success. In January 1951 he had formed a new company and, when he met with his fatal accident, he was contemplating a number of further productions, including *The Lion and the Unicorn,* which has been indefinitely postponed.

Cochrane was at various times chairman and managing director of the Palace Theatre, manager of the Albert Hall, president of the Actors' Benevolent Fund, and a governor of the Shakespeare Memorial Theatre. He wrote four books of reminiscences, called *Secrets of a Showman* (1925), *I Had Almost Forgotten* (1932), *Cock-a-doodle-do* (1941), and *A Showman Looks On* (1945). He married Miss Evelyn Alice Dade, who survives him.

February 1, 1951.

Captain Sir Archibald Cochrane, G.C.M.G., K.C.S.I., D.S.O., who died at Gifford, East Lothian, on April 16, 1958, rendered outstanding naval service in the 1914-18 War and sat in the House of Commons for nine years. He was Governor of Burma during the anxious years from 1936 to 1941 when the country was separated from British India and was given a dyarchial constitution. He was 73.

Archibald Douglas Cochrane, second son of the first Baron Cochrane of Cults and Lady Gertrude Julia Georgina Boyle, first daughter of the sixth Earl of Glasgow, was born on January 8, 1885. He entered the Royal Navy in 1901 and served in various stations.

Early in the 1914-18 War he was in command of a submarine in the North Sea, being present at the battle of Heligoland Bight. In the spring of 1915 he took submarine E7 to the Dardanelles and operated for some months in the Sea of Marmora, doing great damage to enemy shipping, and, after blocking the railway line near Kava Burnu by bombarding it from the sea, shelled a troop train and blew up three ammunition cars attached to it. For these exploits Cochrane and two other officers were awarded the D.S.O. in September of that year. Later, seeking to re-enter the Sea of Marmora, the submarine met with a mishap and Cochrane was taken prisoner. In August 1918, with seven other officers, he escaped from the prison camp at Yozgad. After an adventurous journey of 450 miles across Asia Minor they managed to reach Cyprus and a bar was added to Cochrane's D.S.O. Retiring from the Navy with the rank of Commander, Cochrane took a fishing boat from the north-east of Scotland to the Mediterranean, where he engaged in commercial shipping for a year.

At the general election of 1924 he won East Fife in the Unionist interest, but lost the seat in the 1929 general election. At a by-election in Dunbartonshire in 1932 he was again returned to Parliament. His speeches were infrequent but were marked by championship of the small man.

At a time of much division of opinion among the Conservative majority in the House regarding the far-reaching proposals for Indian reforms leading to the 1935 Act, he gave his support to Government policy, and he did his full share of committee work in this connexion.

In February 1936 it was announced that Sir Hugh Stephenson* was retiring from the Governorship of Burma in order to give his successor the opportunity of some experience of conditions of the Province before its separation from British India on April 1, 1937. Cochrane was selected for the Governorship and had a year under the old conditions before being called upon to introduce the dyarchial system freed from the supervision of the Viceroy in New Delhi.

The choice was appropriate from the point of view of the marked individualism of the Burmese people, which appealed to his independent mind. There was about him, however, a quiet reserve and Scottish caution which prevented his real worth and strong human sympathies being fully understood, except by a small circle of intimate friends. In Rangoon high officials found him unduly reticent and quiet when administrative matters were under discussion. His tendency seemed to be to regard the dyarchial stage as already at an end. As in British India, where the reforms took effect on the same date, April 1, 1937, there was considerable hesitation on the part of leading politicians as to their acceptance of ministerial office, but in a short time this difficulty was overcome.

In 1938 political immaturity and racial antagonism, notably between the large Indian business element and the Buddhist majority, led to severe rioting starting in Rangoon. In September Cochrane found it necessary to exercise his reserve powers under the Rangoon (Emergency) Security Act, giving increased powers of arrest to responsible police officers, but a civil disobedience movement gained many adherents. During this period large supplies of food and material were passing through Burma into China to aid that country in resisting the Japanese invasion.

In the summer of 1939 Cochrane went home, but returned by air when the prospect of war became imminent. His sympathies with Burmese aspirations were an important factor in the support being given to the Allied cause at that critical juncture. Many political, religious, social, and industrial organizations passed resolutions expressing loyalty to the Crown and a desire to assist in the war effort. In October the Governor established a Burma Defence Council to facilitate resistance to Japanese threats, and nine subsidiary boards were set up, each under a part-time director. At the same time Cochrane gave public assurances of the intentions of the British Government to facilitate Burmese attainment of self-government within the Commonwealth. In September 1940 Hitler's Government signed a treaty with Japan recognizing her claim to hegemony in East Asia. In view of this threat to Burma her defence forces were largely increased and compulsory service was introduced for Europeans.

Voluntary contributions from the Burmese people poured into the war funds. Early in 1941, while the chief effort of the enemy was the conquest of Malaya, Japan took definite steps to bring to an end the flow of supplies to China by the Burmese road. The country was on the brink of invasion when in the spring Cochrane, on the completion of his five-year term, was succeeded by Sir Reginald Dorman-Smith [d. 1977].

This retirement gave Cochrane a welcome opportunity to render combatant service to the Allied cause. He rejoined the Royal Navy with the rank of acting captain, and until the end of the war was in command of a large armed merchant cruiser. Subsequently he became a director of the Standard Life Assurance Company. In 1955 he accepted the chairmanship of a working party appointed by the Scottish Council (Development and Industry) to investigate the economic conditions and prospects of Midlothian. He was created K.C.S.I. in 1936 and G.C.M.G. in the following year.

He married in 1936 Julia Dorothy, only daughter of the first Baron Cornwallis, and there were a son and a daughter of the marriage.

Lady Cochrane was particularly helpful to her husband during the anxious years of his Governorship, when she had to be separated from her young children. Their sacrifice was much appreciated in a country where women play so great a part in current affairs and the shaping of opinion. This impression was deepened by her ready understanding, keen sympathy, and great personal charm. From 1941 to 1951 she was Commissioner for England, Girl Guides Association, and then became its President. She was made C.B.E. in 1952.

April 18, 1958.

Maurice Codner, the portrait painter, died in London on March 10, 1958. He was 69.

He was an industrious and plodding kind of painter rather than a brilliant one, but he could be relied upon not to fall below a certain level, and he had both a feeling for character and a capacity for dealing effectively with elaborate costumes, such as uniforms and official robes.

Codner, who was a member of the Royal Society of Portrait Painters, was a regular exhibitor at the Royal Academy, making his first appearance there in 1928.

He was born in 1888, the son of William Squires Codner, and educated at the Stationers' Company School. In the First World War he was commissioned in The Royal North Devon Hussars and served in France.

Among those who had sat to him were King George VI [q.v.], Queen Elizabeth the Queen Mother, Field-Marshal Lord Alexander of Tunis*, Field-Marshal Lord Milne, and Sir Seymour Hicks, as "The Man in Dress Clothes". (Actors lent themselves particularly well to his eye for the dramatic in composition.)

Codner's portrait of King George drew many people to the annual exhibition of the Royal Society of Portrait Painters in 1951. It showed the King as Captain-General of the Honourable Artillery Company, in field-marshal's uniform with Garter robes. The canvas, eight feet high, hangs at Armoury House, headquarters of the Honourable Artillery Company. The portrait of the Queen Mother was awarded the Silver Medal of the Salon at Paris in 1954.

Another of Codner's portraits that attracted much favourable comment was that of Sir George Broadbridge, Lord Mayor of London, in Coronation robes, reproduced in *The Times* in November, 1937, and afterwards shown at Guildhall.

Evidently Codner took his idea of a portrait from the great men of the eighteenth century, from Reynolds in particular, and it was not without relevance that he should have been for some time curator of the collection at Kenwood.

March 11, 1958.

Sir Robert Waley Cohen, K.B.E., who was connected with the Shell group for over 50 years and was a prominent member of the Anglo-Jewish community, died on November 27, 1952 at his home in London at the age of 75.

He was born in London on September 8, 1877, the second son of Nathaniel Louis Cohen, a member of the leading Ashkenazi Jewish family into which even Nathan Mayer Rothschild, the first Rothschild to settle in England, was proud to marry. His mother was a daughter of Jacob Waley, Professor of Political Economy in University College, London, and a member of another of the leading Anglo-Jewish families. He was educated at Clifton and Emmanuel College, Cambridge, of which latter he was a scholar.

On leaving Cambridge in 1901 Waley Cohen entered the service of the Shell Transport and Trading Company in the expectation of being sent to one of its foreign stations in a subordinate capacity. Normally he should have spent a few months in preliminary training at headquarters, but in the course of these few months he proved himself so valuable to the company that he was never sent abroad. He remained in London and rose rapidly, becoming ultimately a managing director.

Although the Shell group was for the greater part of his active commercial life his principal business interest, Waley Cohen took also at times an active part in the management of other important trading companies, including the Eastern and African Corporation, Baldwins, Limited, and the United Africa Company. He was also chairman, and had served as treasurer, of the Ramsay Memorial Fellowship Trustees, and vice-chairman of the Council of University College, London.

Himself a university man, who had made a considerable success in business, he was always an advocate of the employment in the great commercial undertakings of men straight from one or other of the universities. This cause he was able to support not only by the introduction of recruits into the many companies with which he was connected but also by persuasion with the directors of other similar undertakings and also on the appointments board of his own university. During the 1914-18 war he held a commission in the Royal Navy, which, however, did not interfere over-much with the pursuit of his very valuable civil duties. He was as a rule in his office at Shell House during the day and slept there at night in charge of an anti-aircraft gun on its roof.

The calls of his business interests and his public work, together absorbing much of his time, yet left him leisure to carry on the tradition of his family in the service of the Jewish community. The Cohens had been among the leading members of the Central Synagogue in Great Portland Street from its opening as the first London synagogue of any size outside the City. In this synagogue, like other members of his family, he accepted office while still a young man, being successively treasurer, vice-president, and, on the death of Lionel de Rothschild, president. In the last-mentioned capacity he was the virtual if not the nominal lay head of Anglo-Jewry. He was also for a time an active vice-president of the Jewish Board of Deputies which is, according to its constitution, the representative body of Anglo-Jewry. Waley Cohen at one time or other held many other honorary offices in the Jewish community. He was chairman of the Jewish Memorial Council, president of the Education Aid Committee and for a long period an active member of the council of Jews' College and of the Anglo-Jewish Association.

Although never a formal Zionist or even officially connected with the Jewish Agency for Palestine, Waley Cohen always took a deep interest in the development of Palestine and the future of its Jewish inhabitants. He visited the country several times as chairman of the Palestine Corporation and of the Economic Board for Palestine, British companies, formed on the lines of public utility corporations, for the encouragement of industry and agriculture in that country.

It was on one of these visits, in 1935, that he and Lady Waley Cohen met with a motor accident to which she succumbed. Lady Waley Cohen was the only daughter of Henry Edward Beddington. He is survived by two sons and a daughter.

November 29, 1952.

Professor G. D. H. Cole, who died suddenly on January 14, 1959 at the age of 69, was one of the best-known and most distinguished of the "Labour intellectuals", and devoted remarkable gifts of intellect and character to the Labour cause.

Born on September 25, 1889, George Douglas Howard Cole was the only son of the late George Cole, of Ealing. From St. Paul's School Douglas Cole went up to Balliol in 1908 as a classical Exhibitioner, and, besides two first classes, he won the Jenkyns Exhibition, the principal college award at Balliol for those reading "Greats". In 1912 he was elected to a seven-years prize fellowship at Magdalen, where he had rooms overlooking the deer park.

In spite of these examination successes, his chief interests even as an undergraduate lay outside his work for the Schools. He made various literary experiments in prose and verse, but he was not long in finding his true bent. He went up to Oxford already a socialist; and in his first term started a socialist magazine, the forerunner of a number of other periodicals, none of them long-lived, which he afterwards edited. In the University Fabian Society he became a leading figure, and it was in its study groups of undergraduates that he did the preliminary work for his first public success, which he gained with *The World of Labour,* published in 1913.

This book, a survey of the labour movement all over the world, was a mature specimen of a kind of book of which he wrote many more in later years, a rapid and orderly collection of facts over a wide field, with confident judgments, sometimes provocative in manner, and comparatively little elaborate argument. For a short time Cole was in charge of the teaching of philosophy at the Armstrong College, Newcastle; but from the outbreak of war in 1914 he lived mainly in London and devoted himself to labour affairs.

Holding pacifist opinions, he gave energetic assistance in the preparation of the labour case in a number of disputes. He became an official of the Amalgamated Society of Engineers; and the Labour Research Bureau, of which he was acting secretary, served as a general staff for the labour side in industrial relations. During the war he also published several books, of which one, *The Payment of Wages,* was praised by Edgworth, no friend to Cole's principles, as a "little classic".

In the later part of the war Cole, seeking for a socialism more imaginative and more positive than the Fabianism of the time, was one of the leaders of Guild Socialism, which then had its spell of popularity. In 1918 he married Margaret, one of the daughters of Professor J. P. Postgate. She became his collaborator in innumerable writings and organizations, and built up a position of her own in literature and public life. They had three children.

When Cole, after the war, served as secretary to the labour side of the Joint Industrial Conference, it seemed as if he might become an active labour leader; but he had no inclination to follow up his successes in that direction. He had displayed an extraordinary capacity for hard work, a great power of leading and inspiring those who worked under him, with a readiness in speech and a power of commanding masses of intricate detail which made him a very skilful negotiator; but he did not find it easy to work patiently with or under other people, and he never repressed his distaste for the pretences and pomposities of ordinary public life.

For the first few years after the war the centre of his activity was in adult education, in which he had taken part from the beginning of his career, and he both taught with great success and took a prominent part in the work of administration.

He also wrote regularly in the *New Statesman* on labour matters. It was in this period that he began to write historical books; the two best known among these, the *Life of William Cobbett* and the *Short History of the Working Class Movement* started him on subjects to which he also made many minor contributions. For Cobbett, as for Defoe, Robert Owen, the Chartists and William Morris, he had an affectionate enthusiasm that made him almost an antiquarian. He was a great buyer of books, and he built up a very large collection of works of every kind on social history which now forms part of the library of Nuffield College, Oxford.

It was in 1923 also, during his convalescence after a serious illness, that he began, with his wife, to write detective novels. By a regular output of these they became popular with a new public not interested in social economics.

Cole's health suffered from the overwork and frequent journeys of his adult education period, and in 1925 he returned to Oxford as the first holder of the Mynors Fellowship at University College, and Reader in Economics in the University. His lectures, packed with matter, without artifice but delivered with intense conviction, were very successful.

After a year or two he began to divide his week between his college rooms and a large Victorian house at Hendon, which he made still larger by additions. There his wife and family lived. In Oxford his main enthusiasm was for the University Labour Club. It was largely through his efforts that this became a highly organized body with hundreds of undergraduate members, closely linked with the Labour Party. In later Oxford years Cole took a considerable share in the administration of the various bodies connected with social studies, and, on its foundation, he became a Fellow of Nuffield* College.

His position among the cross-currents of labour politics was never altogether simple; although instinctively favourable to extremists and "ginger-groups"; he frequently worked for practical compromise. About 1929 he turned more definitely than ever before towards parliamentary methods, and he was adopted as Labour candidate for the King's Norton division of Birmingham; but a breakdown in health, which was discovered to be due to diabetes, forced him to give up his candidature.

Although he became permanently dependent on insulin and on carefully observing a regimen, his power of work and his literary output were no less than they had been before. A member of some of the left-wing groups of the 1930s, he became also chairman of the executive committee of the Fabian Society in 1939-46 and 1948-50. Since 1952 he had been president. Ramsay MacDonald, as Prime Minister, made him a member of the Economic Advisory Council when it was formed, and this helped to broaden his interest from labour questions to national and international economics generally, on which, among other subjects, he wrote voluminously from about that time. Not long before the outbreak of the second German war, he was adopted as Parliamentary Labour candidate for Oxford University.

In the new war the enemy plainly meant to destroy everything Cole believed in, and it was impossible for him to be, as in 1914, indifferent to the national cause.

In 1940 he worked as a temporary civil servant for the Man-Power Survey of the Ministry of Labour. On the conclusion of this work he found in Oxford a task well suited to his powers and his previous experience in the Social Reconstruction Survey which Nuffield College was commissioned to carry out for the Government. Of this Cole became chairman, and he built it up at lightning speed into a productive, if unconventional, machine. In 1944 he became Professor of Social and Political Theory and, in virtue of this office, a Fellow of All Souls College. University College and Balliol subsequently elected him to honorary fellowships. During his tenure of the chair he wrote his longest work, which may prove to be his most important, the three volumes on the history of socialist thought. On retiring under the age limit in 1957 he became a Research Fellow of Nuffield College.

Strikingly handsome in person, he was essentially an indoor man, hospitable, and with a fine appreciation of poetry and the arts. He was popular in all the circles he moved in, even among those who differed most strongly from his opinions, and this he owed as much to his courage and straightforwardness as to a charm of manner which few could resist at close quarters. In business he had many controversies, some of which degenerated into quarrels; and in his writings he sacrificed style and depth of thought to a rapidity of composition which made him rather a great journalist than a profound thinker.

His most important and original contributions to thought belonged to the borderland between economic and political theory. Although he wrote so much, he never wrote ineffectively. The scores of volumes which he published did a remarkable work in disseminating knowledge and provoking thought, quite apart from their effect, which must have been great, though it cannot be measured, in making converts to his ways of thinking.

He never ceased to adapt his views to the needs, if not the moods, of changing times, so that he cannot be labelled as belonging to any particular species of socialism; but he never wavered in his belief that, as against its opponents, "labour is always right". To him "labour" meant the organized labour movement: those working men who knew him and those, many times more numerous, who read his books, had steady confidence in him as one of their friends.

January 15, 1959.

Colette, one of the most famous modern French novelists, died at her home in Paris on August 3, 1954 at the age of 81.

It is almost necessary to have lived in Paris and to have known something of that side of it which is sometimes called Bohemian but is really luxuriously immoral, if one is to appreciate the most vivid figure among Colette's literary creations—the portrait, several times repeated, with slight variations, of the superannuated *demi-mondaine.* One must know Paris if one is to understand how accurate it is in its frankness and its entire absence of compromise. But even without that experience it is easy to feel that the portrait must be accurate because it is so human. Everything that Colette touched became human; human, that is to say, within the animal limits of humanity, but truly human within those limits.

She felt deeply everything concerned with the senses—all the senses—and she had the literary instinct to be able to convey those feelings in her books. Everything that she did came from instinct rather than accomplishment, although she was a most conscientious artist, and re-wrote and altered her work many times before she let it go. She was all instinct, like the cats with which she loved to be surrounded, like the flowers that she loved to see and touch and smell. She was a complete sensualist; but she gave herself up to her senses with such delicacy of perception, with such exquisiteness of physical pain as well as physical ecstasy, that she ennobled sensualism almost into grandeur. The love affairs of her novels were her own love affairs. Everyone knew that she had suffered as she made her heroine in *Chéri* suffer. And yet the thing never offended, as that sort of autobiography usually offends. She had transmuted it into art.

She was always known as Colette and not as Madame Colette, although it was, in fact, the name of her family, and not her Christian name. She was born in 1873 in a village in Burgundy, daughter of a tax collector, who had been a captain in the Zouaves and had lost a leg in the Italian wars, and of a mother from whom she inherited a love of flowers and birds and trees, that love of nature, in fact, which never left her. She was christened Sidonie Gabrielle and was educated in the village, but on her own account devoured a wide range of literature, from Rabelais and Voltaire to Zola. It was, however, when her family left the village for the neighbouring town and she was 17 years old that her real education in the hard and bitter school of life began. For there she met her evil genius, the witty and cynical journalist and critic Henri Gauthier-Villars, who wrote under the pseudonym of "Willy".

He carried her off into the boulevard life of Paris and they were married when she was 20. For the next dozen years she worked as a sort of literary slave to her husband; and her first three books, *Claudine à l'école* (1900), *Claudine à Paris* (1901), and *Claudine s'en va* (1902) were actually published as his. They at once had a considerable success, partly of scandal, for "Willy" had deliberately encouraged her naturally outspoken nature, but also partly of literary appreciation, and when, in 1904, she brought out her first book under her own name, the charming *Dialogue des Bêtes* (between a cat and a bulldog) she began slowly to establish herself. She had then ended "Willy's" tyranny and left him. She divorced him two years later, but he lived for a quarter of a century more.

To earn her living after the divorce—she was then a woman of 33—she took to the stage, and appeared at several music-halls; but in spite of making the sort of attempt to shock the public which was perhaps to be expected from her background, she was not a success. Her experience of the theatre was, however, of use to her in writing her first really successful novel. This was *La Vagabonde* (1910), in which the central character is an actress. Her marriage to Henry de Jouvenel in the same year gave her an opening on *Le Matin* of which he was foreign editor, and she regularly wrote stories and articles for that paper.

Between 1913 and 1919 Colette was a very busy woman. She was in charge of the fiction department of *Le Matin*, acted as publisher's reader and dramatic critic, and ran columns of her own in *Le Figaro, Vogue,* and *Demain.* For a large part of the 1914-18 War she acted as nurse at a hospital on her husband's estate, near St. Malo. Her best known novels appeared respectively in 1920 and 1926 under the titles of *Chéri* and *La Fin de Chéri.* Colette was made a Chevalier of the Legion of Honour in 1920, and after her eightieth birthday promoted to Grand Officer. She also became a member of the Goncourt Academy.

Between the two wars her literary standing in France was very high, and she continued to write effectively almost to the end of her life. Foreign critics, like Arnold Bennett (who of course knew his Paris), have rated her among the masters. Her life has been written by Jean Larnac, and among appreciative essays there is one by Mary Duclaux. She never used dictation or a typewriter, and one of her foibles was to have a whole selection of fountain-pens at hand when writing, using one nib or another as the mood dictated.

In person she was dark, and beautiful after an exotic fashion. She wore "bobbed" hair long before this style became general among women. Her hobbies were gardening and interior decorating, and, of course, her cats.

Colette leaves no children. Her second marriage was dissolved in 1934, after which she married Maurice Goudeket, journalist and man of letters.

August 4, 1954.

Constance Collier, who died in hospital in New York on April 25, 1955 at the age of 77, was an actress whose range was limited by her imposing physique, deep voice and great but rather overwhelming beauty.

In an earlier theatrical age she might well have been a majestic tragedy queen. In our own she rather tended to dwarf the other members of the casts with whom she acted, and it was not by mere accident that her most outstanding successes were made with Beerbohm Tree, himself a tall man, who had some difficulty in finding actresses to match him. Of these successes, undoubtedly the greatest was her Nancy in J. Comyns Carr's stage version of *Oliver Twist,* in which Tree himself gave a notable performance as Fagin; but her Cleopatra in *Antony and Cleopatra*—also with Tree—was so fine as to have been described by a leading critic as "superb and terrible". In her later years she developed another side to her histrionic talent, and became a mistress of finished and biting comedy.

She was born at Windsor on January 22, 1878, and was the daughter of an actor, C. A. Hardie, and his wife, Lizzie Collier. She was only six years old when she made her first stage appearance, which was as a child in *The Silver King* with Wilson Barrett. In her teens she was in the chorus and playing small parts at the Gaiety under George Edwardes; but in 1896, when she was still only 18, she was once more with Wilson Barrett, playing the chief part in his religious melodrama *The Sign of the Cross.* In 1900 she was the Lady Sneerwell in a revival of the *School for Scandal* at the Haymarket, and later in the same year scored her first marked success at the same theatre as Lady Castlemaine in Fred Terry's production of *Sweet Nell of Old Drury.* She joined Tree at His Majesty's in 1901 and appeared in *Ulysses, Eternal City, Twelfth Night* (as Olivia), and *Julius Caesar.* In 1905 came her Nancy in *Oliver Twist,* in the following year Poppaea in *Nero,* and, in 1907, Cleopatra, which she afterwards played with Tree on a visit to Berlin.

In 1913 she joined the American actor William Faversham in the United States and played Portia in *Julius Caesar* and Emilia in *Othello* with him. From 1916 to 1919 she was again in America, but in 1920 she appeared once more in London as the Duchess of Towers in the play which J. N. Raphael had adapted from George du Maurier's novel *Peter Ibbetson.* In 1929 she appeared in New York as Countess Flordi Folio in *Serena Blandish,* but by the end of that year she was back again in London, and she alternated between New York and London for the next three years. In 1933 she settled in Hollywood, and appeared in many films. She collaborated in the authorship of two plays, *The Rat* and *Downhill,* with Ivor Novello [q.v.], who wrote them under the pseudonym of David L'Estrange. In 1929 she published her reminiscences, with the title of *Harlequinade: The Story of My Life.*

Her husband, the actor Julian L'Estrange, died in 1918. For many months towards the end of her life she was blind, but late in 1954 she left hospital in New York after a successful operation for cataract.

April 27, 1955.

José Collins, who died on December 6, 1958 in an Epping hospital, had not been seen on the professional stage for many years. But in the early part of the century she established a great reputation with her striking appearance, her beautiful voice, and her great dramatic ability. She was 71.

From 1917 to 1923, first at Daly's Theatre and afterwards at the Gaiety, she was certainly the uncrowned queen of the musical comedy kingdom. Her great success in *The Maid of the Mountains* has become almost a legend and those who, like the writer, were present at its first West End performance, enjoyed an unforgettable experience.

José Collins was born in London on May 23, 1887, her mother being Lottie Collins, one of the great music hall artists of her time. As a child José appeared with Sir Harry Lauder and when he sang "I Love a Lassie" she was the Little Bluebell that illustrated it. In 1904 at the age of 17 she was playing in a touring company of *A Chinese Honeymoon* and at Christmas 1905 she was again appearing with Lauder in a Glasgow pantomime *Aladdin.* Music hall engagements and touring companies followed and in 1911 she boldly went out to America without a contract and was so successful that she did not return to England until early in 1916.

In May of that year she appeared at Daly's in *The Happy Day* as a member of a star-studded company and in the second act she was given two elaborate song-scenes. It was a daring experiment but it is recorded that the enthusiasm aroused by her second contribution seemed to be as great as that occasioned by the first. She was obviously destined for a highly successful career but few could have anticipated that within a year she would be the leading lady of Daly's Theatre. The production of *The Maid of the Mountains,* first at Manchester in December 1916, and then at Daly's on February 10, 1917, came in the dark days of the First World War and brought into the theatre beautiful music, colourful acting, and glorious stage mounting to delight not only those who were forced to remain in London but the troops on leave from overseas.

Daly's became the Mecca of all who wanted to get away for a few brief hours from the grim realities of everyday life. José Collins's song "Love will find a way" was soon being whistled and sung in the streets and trenches. Harold Fraser-Simson wrote most of the music, but additional numbers were provided by J. W. Tate, whose first wife had been Lottie Collins.

José Collins's forceful personality was soon realized by all concerned with the theatre and it is said to have been on her insistence that *The Maid of the Mountains* ended on a happy note. In her book of reminiscences, published in 1932, she wrote that Frederick Lonsdale [q.v.], the author, had intended that Teresa and her brigand lover should part for ever but, she added, "with a little pressure from Mr. Oscar Asche (the producer) and much weeping from me, Mr. Lonsdale agreed to a happy ending".

The original production ran for 1,352 performances and José Collins missed very few of them. It was always understood that the run could have been still longer if Miss Collins had not insisted that the time had come to call a halt. Her dressing room at Daly's was described by a writer of the period as the loveliest he had ever seen—a large symmetrical compartment with a rose du Barri colour scheme of decoration, a small grand piano, an Adam bureau laden with books, among them a complete set of the novels of Alexandre Dumas, uniformly framed sketches of actors and actresses, and a floor strewn with toys for the children who loved to convert her boudoir into a teatime playground.

The Maid of the Mountains was followed by a series of notable successes including *The Southern Maid, Our Peg,* and *Sybil* and, in December 1921, a revival of *The Maid of the Mountains.* The greatness of Daly's had been built up by George Edwardes and continued after his death by Robert Evett but when the theatre was sold to James White a change came over the scene. Macqueen Pope [q.v.] recorded that one night White and a party of his friends walked unceremoniously into the dressing room of the leading lady. When he declared that he had bought the theatre and it was now his property, she ordered him out of the room. As a result of this and other incidents White lost the services of Evett and Miss Collins. Evett took with him to the Gaiety the leading lady and other members of the company and he also took with him the spirit and the atmosphere of Daly's.

José Collins scored considerable successes in *The Last Waltz, Catherine,* and *Our Nell* in which she played Nell Gwynne with a vivid red wig. At the end of the run of the last-named production Evett and Miss Collins left the Gaiety. In 1925 she was financially interested in the production of *Frasquita,* a gypsy play at the Prince's, and again she acted with the assurance of one who understood absolutely the part she was playing and sang delightfully numbers for which Franz Lehar had written the music. But it was not a financial success and when a receiving order was made against her in the following year she attributed her position to the losses incurred on *Frasquita* (which only ran for four weeks) and to the nervous breakdown which followed. Thereafter she played in variety but she never regained her commanding position in the theatre.

She was married three times. Her marriages with Mr. Leslie Chatfield and Lord Robert Innes-Ker were dissolved. Her third husband, Dr. G. B. Kirkland, whom she married in 1931, survives her. She gave up the stage to nurse for him during the Second World War when he was a major in the R.A.M.C. She trained as a nurse and worked voluntarily at hospitals where he was stationed. It was a great change from her stage career but Miss Collins had the happy knack of taking everything in her stride and she accepted both success and failure with equanimity. To the older generation of playgoers Teresa of *The Maid of the Mountains* will always remain a happy memory.

December 8, 1958.

Peter Collins, who died after an accident in the German Grand Prix on August 3, 1958, was one of the leading racing motorists in the world.

In 1956, his first season as a member of the Ferrari team, he won two of the *grandes épreuves*—the French and Belgian Grands Prix.

Peter John Collins was born in 1931 at Kidderminster, where his father is a well-known motor distributor. After serving his apprenticeship as a motor engineer, Collins took up motor racing with a 500 c.c. Cooper at the age of 17, and soon made his name as a fast and safe driver in spite of his extreme youth.

It was not until he had served another apprenticeship, this time in motor racing with a small car, that he was allowed to graduate to larger cars. In 1952 he had a full Grand Prix season with John Heath's H.W.M. team, which did so much to bring on promising drivers as well as uphold British prestige, and with the Aston Martin team in sports car events. His best performance was to win the Goodwood nine-hour race with Griffith in an Aston Martin, while for H.W.M. he took second place to Villoresi (Ferarri) at Sables d'Olonne. He also finished third in the Luxembourg 500 c.c. race in a J.B.S.

At the beginning of 1953 Collins went to Florida for the Sebring 12-hour race, in which he drove brilliantly to lead the field after three hours, when his co-driver, Duke, took over and unhappily went off the course a few laps later. Collins did well for David Brown's Aston Martins that year, however, for he won the Tourist Trophy and was second in the Goodwood nine-hour race, both with Griffith as his co-driver, and was third in the Silverstone sports car race in July. He continued to race for H.W.M. abroad, but without much success. As a member of the Aston Martin team Collins was third in the 1954 Argentine 1,000 kilometre race with Griffith as his co-driver, won the sports car race before the British Grand Prix, and was second at the same track in May and at the Aintree meeting in October.

Invited by G. A. [Tony] Vandervell* to join his stable for Grand Prix events, Collins finished second to Moss (Maserati) with a Vanwall at Goodwood and was seventh in the Italian Grand Prix. With the big Thinwall Ferrari Special, the fastest car he had yet driven, Collins made the fastest lap at the inaugural meeting at Aintree in May and won minor races at Goodwood in June and September.

In 1955 Collins moved over to the B.R.M. camp for formula races while continuing to drive for Aston Martin in sports events. It was with the Maserati used by the Owen* organization for trying out ideas for the new B.R.M. that Collins won the big race at Silverstone in May, setting up a new lap record. Driving the powerful 16-cylinder B.R.M., he won a race at Goodwood and the *formule libre* race at Aintree in September.

At that meeting Collins was entered to drive the new Formula I B.R.M. in its first race, but the car developed a fault in practice and crashed, fortunately without injury to the driver. A few weeks later Collins raced the car at Oulton Park and was lying third when he retired.

For Aston Martin he was second, with Frere, at Le Mans, third in the Goodwood nine-hour race with Brooks, second at Aintree, and third at Oulton Park. But his outstanding performance that year, and the one that probably decided Enzo Ferrari to invite him to join his team for the 1956 Grand Prix season, was to share with Moss the driving of the winning Mercedes-Benz in the Targa Florio in Sicily.

Few British drivers have had a more successful international season than Collins enjoyed as a member of the Ferrari team in 1956. Like his friend and rival, Stirling Moss (who won at Monaco and Monza), Collins won two of the *grandes épreuves*—the Grands Prix of France and Belgium—and he shared the wheel of the second car to finish in the British, Italian, and Monaco Grands Prix.

For several months he was actually leading in the contest for the world championship and eventually finished second. In sports car races he won the Tour of Sicily and the Monza 1,000 kilometre race (with J. M. Hawthorn [q.v.]), and was second in the Mille Miglia and in the Swedish Grand Prix (with Graham Hill*) for Ferrari. Partnered with Moss he again finished second at Le Mans in an Aston Martin.

He began the 1957 season well by winning the opening race at Syracuse and the Naples Grand Prix, but it was not until the current season, beginning in South America, that he secured another major success, winning the 1,000 kilometre race at Buenos Aires with P. Hill. He also won the 12-hour race at Sebring, Florida. He was second in the 1,000 kilometre race at the Nürburgring with J. M. Hawthorn and his third *grande épreuve* was the British Grand Prix in July 1958.

Collins married in 1957 Louise Cordier, daughter of Dr. Andrew Cordier*, deputy secretary-general of the United Nations.

August 4, 1958.

Ronald Colman, the film actor, died at Santa Barbara, California, on May 19, 1958. He was 67.

Although, as a young man, Ronald Colman had considerable experience of the stage, it was as a film actor, and above all a film actor of the talking era, that he established his reputation and made his name widely known. For throughout his film career he represented to filmgoers all over the world all that typified the English gentleman. Colman in his films revealed an unfailing graciousness and style. His voice was cultured and quiet: his manners were impeccable. And his performances gave the impression that there was still a place for dignity and restraint in the noisy world which Hollywood so often loved to picture on the screen.

He was born at Richmond, Surrey, on February 9, 1891, the son of Mr. Charles Colman. He was educated at Littlehampton, and from boyhood wanted to go on the stage. His first ventures in this direction, as a young man of 18, were as an amateur, but he soon became prominent for his work with the West Middlesex Dramatic Society, gaining rather more than a local reputation.

In 1914 came his first opportunity to act professionally, but he had barely embarked on his chosen career when war broke out. He went to France with the London Scottish, of whom he was already a member, and saw some severe fighting, culminating with the Battle of Mons. His was no easy war and by 1916, no longer fit, he was invalided out of the service. As soon as he regained sufficient strength, however, he resumed acting, and his first appearance was with Lena Ashwell [q.v.] at the London Coliseum in *The Maharani of Arakan* as Rahmat Sheikh. Thereafter he was several times seen on the London stage in such plays as *Partnership, The Misleading Lady* and *Damaged Goods.*

In 1920 he went to America, touring first with Robert Warwick in *The Dauntless Three,* and subsequently with Fay Bainter, later like himself to play in many films, in *East is West.* Early in the following year he played the temple priest in *The Green Goddess,* with George Arliss, at the Booth Theatre, New York, afterwards fulfilling two further engagements in that city at the Empire in *La Tendresse* and at the 39th Street Theatre in *The Nightcap.*

He first appeared in films in England in 1917 and began his film career in America in 1923, in *The White Sister,* with Lillian Gish, while in 1926 he appeared in one of the best silent pictures ever made—Herbert Brenon's *Beau Geste.*

But it was, of course, the coming of sound that gave Colman his great opportunity and it was Sam Goldwyn*, of United Artists, who really discovered him and set him on the road to fame.

Colman made a large number of films for United Artists, his earliest talking pictures including *Raffles, Arrowsmith,* and *Cynara.* Later films included *A Tale of Two Cities, Under Two Flags, Lost Horizon, The Prisoner of Zenda, The Light that Failed, Random Harvest, A Double Life,* for which he won an Academy Award in 1947, and, of course, a small part in Mike Todd's [q.v.] *Around the World in 80 Days.*

His acting range was perhaps not great, but he was capable of revealing a sincere and moving emotion, and his good looks and cultured manners made him an impressive hero of the classic English school. Of all his many parts, one must be remembered above all others—that of Sydney Carton, "the most complete Gentleman in Dickens". No film actor of his era, or indeed of any subsequent era, could have better delivered the most famous of all last words: "It is a far, far better thing. . . ."

To the modern generation of filmgoers Ronald Colman may not today be so very well known; but to those of the pre-war period he will always be thought of with affection as the most complete gentleman of the cinema.

May 20, 1958.

Sir David Colville—See **Clydesmuir.**

Sir Frank Colyer, K.B.E., LL.D., F.R.C.S., L.D.S., who died on March 30, 1954 at the age of 87, was regarded as the doyen of dental surgeons in Britain and enjoyed a world-wide reputation as an authority on the anatomy, human and comparative, and the diseases of the teeth.

He was also a leading authority on the history of dentistry, particularly on the evolution of dental instruments, and his researches in this direction were greatly facilitated by his position as a trustee of the Hunterian collection and as honorary curator of the Odontological Museum of the Royal College of Surgeons. He was consulting dental surgeon to Charing Cross Hospital and to the Royal Dental Hospital, and in the course of his long career had held many other official appointments.

James Frank Colyer was born on September 25, 1866, and was trained at Charing Cross Hospital and at the Royal Dental Hospital. He qualified first as a dental surgeon, taking the L.D.S. diploma of the Royal College of Surgeons in 1887, and two years later he obtained the full medical qualification of M.R.C.S., L.R.C.P. After acting as house surgeon and demonstrator of operative dentistry at the Royal Dental Hospital he was appointed full surgeon, and from 1904 to 1909 he held the office of dean. In 1893 he was elected dental surgeon to Charing Cross Hospital, and he subsequently became consulting dental surgeon to the Croydon War Hospital, the Queen's Hospital at Sidcup, and the Ministry of Pensions. The textbook *Dental Surgery and Pathology,* which he wrote with Evelyn Sprawson, reached an eighth edition in 1942, and his other writings included books on *Dental Disease and its Relation to General Medicine, Chronic Dental Periodontitis,* and *Variations and Diseases of the Teeth of Animals* (1936).

His historical interests were shown in his book *John Hunter and Odontology* and in his comprehensive *Old Instruments for Extracting Teeth,* which was published in 1952. In 1900 he undertook the honorary curatorship of the odontological museum at the Royal Dental Hospital, and he retained this office when the museum was moved first to Hanover Square and then to the Royal College of Surgeons. The serious damage suffered by the college collections in the air raids of May 1941 was a great blow to him, but he took his share in the task of salvage and repair and continued to work at his catalogue of old dental instruments. He was universally respected and loved in his profession, and he received many honours. He was president of the Odontological Section of the Royal Society of Medicine in 1919, having previously held the offices of honorary secretary and editor under its parent body, the Odontological Society of Great Britain. In 1932 he became the first president of the British Society of Dental Surgeons.

He married in 1895 Lucy Olivier, daughter of the late George Simpson. She died in 1950, and he is survived by a son and a daughter of the marriage.

April 1, 1954.

Sir Ninian Comper, who died on December 22, 1960 in London at the age of 96, was an architect and craftsman of more than passing distinction. In learning, and in the breadth of his grasp as a designer, he was much more than a medievalist. His extraordinary assimilation of the Gothic idiom placed him entirely apart from literary revivalists. It was as a craftsman that he regarded himself, eschewing professional recognition and public applause, although by any reckoning his output was phenomenal.

John Ninian Comper was born in Aberdeen on June 10, 1864. His father was a priest of the Scottish Episcopal Church and a leader of the Anglo-Catholic Revival in Scotland. His godfather was the hymnologist John Mason Neale. Anglo-Catholicism was, therefore, the earliest, as it was always the primary, influence in his life. He was educated at Glenalmond, and, after drawing for a term in Ruskin's School at Oxford and then spending a year between South Kensington and the office of C. E. Kempe, he was articled to Bodley and Garner. Like Bodley, he became a rigid opponent of architectural education and of any system of examination for artists. On the same grounds, he later opposed the influence of diocesan advisory boards, fearing mediocrity.

Comper was a traditionalist, but in no narrow sense. Without rejecting the technical inspiration of the Renaissance, he regarded its architecture as fundamentally secular, whereas his aim was to give form and expression to places of religious worship. To Comper, a religious building was something infinitely subtle in which the interior was always what counted most. Indeed, he designed from the altar outwards; and to the altar every proportion and detail, every refraction of light, every embellishment, were subordinated. To this end he bent the whole of his powers seeking in carving, glass, and plaster, to emulate the great period of Gothic art. He built and wrought under the compulsion of a deep spiritual insight. Yet he remained in a true sense an architect.

He proclaimed his testament when he wrote: "There will be no wholesomeness for architecture till, abandoning all this talk about self-expression and the expression of the age, we settle down again to real work and the concentration of all our time and energies on meeting our real needs by beauty of proportion and detail in whatever style we build. No one expresses the age better than the engineer who designs an aeroplane, and no one is further from any set intention of doing so. His sole preoccupation is to make it fly".

Apart from notable restorations at Southwark Cathedral; Lound, Suffolk; Wymondham Abbey, Norfolk; and St. Clement, Eastcheap; among Comper's best-known works are St. Mary, Wellingborough; the Crypt Chapel of St. Mary Magdalene, Paddington; the Warrior's Chapel in Westminster Abbey; the Chapel for All Saints Sisterhood, London Colney; and St. Philip, Cosham. His designs for a cathedral at Aberdeen, made in 1930, had later to be abandoned.

As a decorative artist Comper had few rivals, expressing himself with equal confidence in burnished gilding, in fabrics, and in glass. The stained glass in East Meon Church, Hampshire, is a beautiful continuation of an ancient art. He was also responsible for the Parliamentary war memorial window in Westminster Hall (1952); the Royal Window in Canterbury Cathedral (1954); and the east window in Holy Trinity Church, Coventry (1955). He was knighted in 1950.

In 1890 Comper married Grace Buckhall, who died some years ago and who is buried at St. Mary's, Wellingborough. There were two sons and one daughter of the marriage.

December 23, 1960.

Dr. Karl Taylor Compton, who died on June 22, 1954 in New York at the age of 66, was one of the greatest scientists of recent times in the United States, and was appointed president of the Massachusetts Institute of Technology in Boston in 1930. His retirement from the institute was celebrated in 1949 by a three-day Convocation, which was addressed by Sir Winston Churchill*, who made a memorable review of world affairs.

Although he was a national figure as a pure scientist and although he played an exceptionally active part in public affairs, his years at the Institute—America's, and perhaps the world's, most important school of applied science—were those of his highest achievement. His lifelong interest was the integration of science with public affairs, and at a time when science was playing an ever increasing part in industry Compton set himself to inspire his students with a sense of service to the community, and in the years which immediately followed his appointment, when many industries were at a standstill, he did much to help them on the way to recovery and to find work for men who had passed through his school.

Compton was born at Wooster, in Ohio, on September 14, 1887. He went to school and college there and graduated with distinction in science at Wooster College in 1909. He remained there for a year as instructor in chemistry and in 1910 was appointed instructor in physics at Reed College, Portland, Oregon. In 1915 he was appointed assistant professor of physics at Princeton, and in 1919 was promoted to be professor of physics and held that position until 1930, when he was appointed head of the Massachusetts Institute of Technology. In his last year at Princeton he was also chairman of the department of physics there.

He retired from the Massachusetts Institute in order to accept President Truman's* invitation to become head of the Research and Development Board of the United States National Military Establishment. This was only the last of a series of public appointments which were too numerous to mention here in full. From 1943 to 1945 he was chief of the Office of Scientific Research and Development; in 1943, chairman of the United States radar mission to Britain; in 1944, a member of the Committee of the Secretaries of Navy and War on Post-war Research. As far back as June 1941 he had urged all-out aid to Britain, and during the war was Stimson's adviser on testing and using atomic bombs.

In February 1946 Compton, who never allowed his convictions to be silenced, was one of the few leading scientists who did not support the McMahon [q.v.] Bill for atomic energy control. Although he supported civilian control, he argued that the leading scientists in the country should help to define policy but not be required to administer it. He supported the controversial appointment of David Lilienthal as head of the Atomic Energy Commission. The same strongly worded convictions were to be found in most of his public pronouncements on national policy.

It is almost impossible to pick out the actions of this remarkable man which most clearly characterized the width of his vision and the alertness of his mind. Two may be taken as examples. At the Massachusetts Institute of Technology he broadened the whole curriculum, introducing many courses in the humanities, so that the students might have some understanding of the social and humane implications of their studies.

Secondly, at the Institute as well as in the wide fields of science and public affairs, he constantly advocated the need for stimulating basic scientific research in America. He held that America's achievements in science had been in development rather than discovery and that this could only be remedied by encouraging pure scientific research. (At the M.I.T. he insisted that technology should be more closely related to pure science.) The loss of so liberal a scientist at this moment in America's history will be deeply felt.

He was twice married.

June 24, 1954.

Philip Connard, C.V.O., R.A., Keeper of the Royal Academy, 1945-49, died in a Twickenham hospital on December 8, 1958. He was 83.

His career illustrates the virtue of hard work, native talent, and single-hearted devotion to one's chosen task; for Connard was of humble origin and, without influence or more than the average amount of luck, won for himself a very real and sound position in the recent annals of British art.

Born at Southport on March 24, 1875, the son of David Connard, he had the minimum of state schooling and then went into the building trade as a house painter. But it was another kind of painting that interested him, so he attended evening classes and succeeded in carrying off a national school scholarship for textile designing which took him to South Kensington. Next he won a British Institute prize of £100, and at once set out for Paris, optimistically hoping to complete a two-year period of painting there.

Naturally enough this was not feasible without additional resources, so after a few months Connard returned to London, where he found some illustrative and kindred tasks which served to meet his immediate needs until he secured a staff post as master at the Lambeth School of Art.

Meanwhile he had begun to submit work to open exhibitions, notably that of the New English Art Club. Two excellent judges there, Professor Henry Tonks and P. Wilson Steer, were not long in recognizing his merit; and with their support he was elected to the club. He retained his post at Lambeth for some years, but an increasing practice (chiefly as a decorative painter) in due course enabled him to work independently. Portraiture occupied some of his time, and he became a member of the National Portrait Society, but up to the 1930s he was best known as a painter in oils of romantic decorative landscapes with figures or birds.

Water-colour he took up in middle life, but once started on this technique he very soon showed a subtle appreciation of its possibilities, and was made an associate of the Royal Society of Painters in Water-Colours, quickly rising to full membership. With the Royal Academy his dealings were unusual, for he did not submit work there until elected an Associate in 1918. Thereafter he was regularly seen at Burlington House, and became an Academician in 1925. His one-man exhibitions were usually held at Barbizon House, for that very able dealer, D. Croal Thompson, had been among the early admirers of his work.

Connard was entrusted with a number of important decorative commissions, including the admirable murals on the theme of "Royal Residences" in the Doll's House room at Windsor Castle and two panels for the main ballroom at Delhi. For the liner Queen Mary he executed a decorative panel 26ft. by 14ft. on the general subject of "England" in one of the principal dining saloons. Various works of his were bought by the Chantrey trustees, and he is represented in the Tate Gallery, the Luxembourg, the national galleries of Eire and Canada, and the municipal collections of Liverpool, Manchester, Aberdeen, Melbourne, Sydney, Cardiff, Bradford, Oldham, Blackburn, Huddersfield, and Southport. In his latter years he lived at Richmond, in a house overlooking the Thames, where he painted many riverside scenes.

Connard's work falls into some four divisions. First in time are his decorative compositions in oils, which consist of landscapes treated with considerable stylization, usually including figures of Harlequin, pierrettes and the like, or birds. Of bird-motifs he was very fond, and though they were properly conventionalized in accord with a more or less strict decorative scheme, all were based on painstaking studies from life made at the Zoo. These compositions were graceful, airy, and highly individual in conception.

Portraits and interiors form the next group, and here Connard was sound without being inspired. The later "realistic" landscapes in oils, many of them done at Richmond, were utterly unlike the decorations just named. Poetically conceived and very subtly executed, their main intention was to capture pearly grey misty atmospheric effects, delicately suffused with light.

Finally there are his watercolours, which are in the highest degree ethereal and which, again mostly concerned with delicate shades of atmosphere, reach a very high level of attainment. Connard was versatile, and never became set in any formula. He was unaffected by post-impressionist and kindred theories, and his work has a "handwriting" that is unmistakable. He was appointed C.V.O. in 1950.

Connard was twice married, first to Mary (who died in 1927), daughter of Archdeacon Collyer, by whom he had two daughters, and second, in 1933, to Georgina Yorke, of Twickenham, who figures in many of his later interior paintings.

December 9, 1958.

Princess Arthur of Connaught—See **Fife.**

Mabel Constanduros, a popular entertainer in her plays, novels, and above all in broadcasts, died on February 8, 1957 in hospital at Chichester at the age of 77. She had been carrying on with her work until three weeks before her death.

She was born in London, the daughter of R. S. Tilling and granddaughter of Thomas Tilling, a pioneer of horse-drawn omnibuses. She attended Sutton High School, Dulwich High School, Mary Datchelor School, and the Central School of Speech Training.

In an autobiography, *Shreds and Patches,* published in 1948, she recorded the trepidation with which she approached Savoy Hill to offer her services to the B.B.C. in 1925, having been prevailed upon by her friends to uncover her facility in recitation. Her anxiety was misplaced: her natural broadcasting talent was recognized by the producers and very quickly by the audience as her "Buggins Family" sketches became a regular feature. Four years later she made her *début* on the London stage in a sketch at the Coliseum. Later she appeared in *Derby Day,* as Ann of Cleves in *The Rose Without a Thorn,* and as Madam Wang in *Lady Precious Stream* in 1935. She continued to act in the West End until 1938 and made a further appearance in *Murder Duel* immediately after the war. By then, however, she was already better known as a playwright.

Three for Luck was her first play, a polite farce of mild matrimonial entanglements, and she took a part in it herself when it was put on at the Westminster Theatre in 1934. She later collaborated most fruitfully with her nephew, Denis Constanduros. Perhaps the most successful of their joint plays was *Acacia Avenue*, a comedy of suburbia, first produced in 1943. Together they wrote a large number of plays for broadcasting. She also turned her hand to novel writing, excelling again in *A Nice Fire in the Drawingroom* at drawing for an amusing story on the gentility of lower middle-class manners. Just before Christmas 1956 she made her only appearance on television.

Her kindness and charm in private life made her much loved by her family and many friends. She married Athanasius Constanduros, an insurance broker. He died in 1937, and there was a son of the marriage.

February 9, 1957.

Sir Gerald Lenox-Conyngham—See **Lenox-.**

Dr. Arthur Bernard Cook, F.B.A., Vice-President of Queens' College, Cambridge, and Emeritus Professor of Classical Archaeology in the university, died on April 26, 1952 at his home at Cambridge. He was 83.

Arthur Bernard Cook was born on October 22, 1868, the eldest son of William Henry Cook, M.D., of Hampstead, and of Harriet Bickersteth Cook. He went to St. Paul's School, where, as a foundation scholar and exhibitioner, he began an exceptionally brilliant academic career. He won a major scholarship at Trinity College, Cambridge, in 1887, and a Craven University Scholarship in 1889; in the same year he carried off the Chancellor's Gold Medal for English verse and two years later became Chancellor's Senior Medallist for Classical Learning; in 1892 he won the Members' Latin Prize. Meanwhile, Cook sat for the Classical Tripos, obtaining in 1889 and 1891 the highest classes in both parts. The rewards of this industry and brilliance were a Fellowship at Trinity College in 1893, which he held for six years, and the Professorship of Greek at Bedford College, London, to which he was appointed when only 24.

Cook's classical interest turned at first towards philosophy, and in 1895 he published a work on *The Metaphysical Basis of Plato's Ethics*, but he soon inclined more towards the religion and beliefs of the classical world, and especially towards archaeology as the primary source for the study of ancient religion. He was able to devote himself properly to this study only when he resigned the chair at Bedford College in 1907 to become Reader in Classical Archaeology in the University of Cambridge in the following year. Queens' College had elected him to a fellowship and classical lectureship in 1900. From this time on Cook began in earnest to build up his important collection of antiquities, his fine library, and the materials for his great life work, *Zeus, a Study in Ancient Religion.* The first part of this work appeared in 1914, the second in 1925, and the third and final portion in 1940. These five volumes of *Zeus* contain a wealth of learning and research which can be paralleled only in the late Sir James Frazer's *Golden Bough*; and, like Frazer, Cook wrote with exceptional charm and clarity. His text was lightened by confining the learning to long footnotes, and enlivened by thousands of illustrations. Besides *Zeus* he published many articles in the classical and anthropological journals and was editor from 1928 onward of a series of handbooks of archaeology.

When the Laurence Chair of Classical Archaeology in Cambridge was founded in 1931 Cook became the first professor. He gave up the chair on reaching the retiring age in 1934. Cook's somewhat frail appearance was in marked contrast to an untiring energy which sometimes betrayed him into overtaxing his strength. Saintly, learned, witty, a man full of sympathy, no Cambridge scholar within living memory has inspired more love and affection in his friends and pupils. Never did great scholarship sit more lightly upon any man's shoulders. He may best be described as a great humanist.

In 1894 he married Emily, daughter of George Thomas Maddox, of Hampstead. She died in 1943, leaving a daughter.

April 28, 1952.

Alfred Duff Cooper—See **Norwich.**

Sir Alfred William Cope, K.C.B., who, as Assistant Under-Secretary for Ireland in 1920-22, acted as an intermediary between Lloyd George's Government and the Sinn Fein leaders before and after the establishment of the Irish Free State, died at his home at Seaford, Sussex, on May 13, 1954. He was 77.

He began his career in the Customs and Excise Department and after some 25 years' service was in 1919 appointed second secretary at the Ministry of Pensions, going there for the purpose of reorganizing that Ministry, which was then in a rather disordered condition. In the summer of 1920 he was sent to Dublin as Assistant Under-Secretary for Ireland and Clerk of the Irish Privy Council. Cope himself stated later that he was not selected by Lloyd George for the post, but that he was sent to Ireland by the permanent head of the Civil Service, a statement which was elicited by a certain amount of public discussion in 1922.

When the Sinn Fein's activities were followed by the militarization of the Royal Irish Constabulary under General Tudor reprisals and counter-reprisals took place, and Cope, taking his career in his hands, abandoned the traditional methods of Dublin Castle's peace parleyings and got into direct personal contact with the Sinn Fein leaders. In his position it was not easy for him to do this, but he convinced the Sinn Fein leaders that he meant to play straight with them. The negotiations which he undertook at considerable danger to himself were approved by his superiors and he was eventually able to bring about a state of affairs whereby the treaty of 1921 could be signed.

After the signing of the treaty he remained in Ireland to direct the evacuation of Dublin Castle, and for the greater part of 1922 he was the principal civil official of the British Government there. His achievement was entirely a success of personality, backed by great courage and a remarkable capacity for hard work. At the end of 1922 he resigned his position and retired from the Civil Service to assist Lloyd George in the organization of his election campaign. He was general secretary of the National Liberal Party until 1925.

In that year he left politics and embarked upon a business career, becoming managing director of Amalgamated Anthracite Collieries, Ltd., a position which he held until 1935. In 1939 he took up a voluntary post in the Lord Privy Seal's department, under Sir John Anderson (Lord Waverley [q.v.]), with whom he had worked in Ireland. He was also elected chairman of Seaford Urban Council in 1939.

May 14, 1954.

Dr. Maurice Copisarow, whose sudden death from coronary thrombosis, in his seventieth year, occurred in Manchester on April 15, 1959, achieved a distinguished record of scientific research under conditions of great adversity.

Permanently blinded at the outset of his career in defence research, and often in acute pain, he went on to publish scientific works of importance.

Copisarow was educated at Owen's College, Manchester, where he graduated in chemistry in 1913. Dalton Research Scholar from 1914 to 1916 and Honorary Research Fellow between 1916 and 1919, he gained his D.Sc. in Manchester in 1925. His principal work was carried out much later, however, and in recognition of special services to Britain he was placed on H.M. Civil List.

At the outbreak of the First World War, before either specifications or experience were adequate for the production of T.N.T. safely, a succession of disastrous explosions occurred, killing two or three hundred in the T.N.T. plants of northern England and Scotland. Copisarow, then 25, submitted an idea, and was invited to build up a T.N.T. analytical laboratory at Gorton, responsible to the Ministry of Munitions. He quickly diagnosed the trouble, and his recommendation to use a water instead of the prevailing alkali washing system was successfully adopted.

By the end of the war large quantities of dangerous waste products had accumulated and he discovered a means of converting them into dyestuffs, gelatinous dynamite, and other industrial products. The danger of contact with phosgene and T.N.T. were partly unknown at the time. As a result of his work he gradually lost his eyesight.

He fitted up a small laboratory at home and continued experimental work, but the practical approach to problems after a few years slowly gave way to the theoretical in which he seemed to be gaining some new insight. It was during this period that he put forward his generalized theory of allotropy, his coordination of periodic structures, and established new relationships between inorganic and living forms.

When the Second World War came he was eager to help solve some of the nation's food problems. In this field he was able to produce timely results of his physiological work on grassland improvement, on the reclamation of brackenland, and in fruit and vegetable preservation.

His interests in physiology extended to the animal world in the post-war years, and led him to investigate enzyme and virus activity and, specifically, the biochemistry of influenza. There followed a number of important theoretical studies, which appeared in the *Edinburgh Medical Journal,* on the biochemistry of cancer, its influences and causes, the effect of carcinogenic agents, and its biochemical control. Upon reading Copisarow's review, in 1952, on the "History of Human Cancer", a surgeon, the late Lord Webb-Johnson [q.v.], wrote of him: "The production of such a comprehensive review and the sound judgment which pervades the whole presentation is really a most remarkable piece of work. I am astounded that an unsighted man has been able to accomplish it."

But Copisarow made light of his handicap, shunned publicity, and simply wished for his work to be judged according to its merits. No single judge, over such a wide range of scientific endeavour, is adequate to do this, but one who knew him well once wrote: "His work is characterized by high originality combined with accurate experimentation. It is impossible to fail to recognize in him an investigator whose brain teems with ideas which he somehow manages to put to the experimental test." This was the opinion of Sir Robert Robinson, O.M.*, his former teacher in Manchester in 1936.

Copisarow was a man of fine bearing, energetic, brave, and kind. Throughout his life he was supported by a devoted wife, who survives him, together with their son, who is Scientific Counsellor at the British Embassy, Paris, and their daughter.

April 24, 1959.

A. E. Coppard, who died in hospital in London on January 13, 1957 held almost as high a place as any among the English short-story writers of the past quarter of a century. A story-teller of strongly individual gifts, with a feeling at once robust and sensitive for the oddities, the humours, the mischances, and raw melodrama of country life, he achieved at his best a delightful blending of poetry and realism. He was not always at his best, it is true, and in his later work the extravagance which had always pursued his original fancy, and which had streaked even the happiest of his collections, degenerated into mere arbitrariness or caricature. But stories like *The Higgler* and *The Field of Mustard* are to be counted among the most attractive modern examples in the language.

Alfred Edgar Coppard was born at Folkestone, the child of humble parents, on January 4, 1878. Beyond a reference to his education at an elementary school in Brighton there is little to be gathered of his early life; Coppard was not a writer who lived in the public eye. He made a late beginning as an author, or at any rate as a published author: his first collection of short stories, *Adam and Eve and Pinch Me,* appeared in 1921, when he was 43. (It was the first book, incidentally, issued by the Golden Cockerel Press.) His unusual talent was apparent at the start, as also was his study of at any rate one of the masters of the form, Chekhov, then an all too evident model; but the realism of these early stories was apt to be smothered by fantasy or whimsy, often of a rhetorical colour. The same failing characterized many of the tales in *Clorinda Walks in Heaven,* published in the following year. A year later, however, in the collection entitled *The Black Dog,* Coppard's gifts came to maturity.

There are one or two failures among the stories in this volume and several which are imperfectly resolved. But the others exhibit a vitality, a fund of sensuous appreciation, and a warmth and delicacy of insight that are captivating. The mingling of poetry and realism, as in the title story, is effected with a remarkable air of spontaneity, while the lighter studies of rural types and manners draw a singular ease and fidelity from the author's feeling for English idiosyncracy. The succeeding volume, *Fishmonger's Fiddle* (1925), again includes several tales which are insubstantial in fancy or of a somewhat too rollicking humour, but it also contains *The Higgler,* a story quick with life and poetry and truly irresistible, and others only a degree inferior in liveliness and imaginative perception. The gem of the next collection, *The Field of Mustard* (1926), is the title story, in which the conversation of three village women going over their experience of life is once more lifted to a rare plane of poetic truth. Coppard reaches his highest general standard, perhaps, in this volume.

He had a great variety of story-telling moods and manners, although his distinctive cast of imagination was apparent in them all. It was in his rural comedies and dramas, however, that he achieved his happiest effects: his labourers, publicans, farming people, village craftsmen, poachers, and country "characters" generally were drawn with alert and unsentimental feeling, their talk reproduced with admirable justice and precision, from the inside. Yet it was not merely in turning away from the rural scene that Coppard faltered in artistic aim; a certain flamboyance and prankiness gained steadily upon him. There are good stories still in *Silver Circus* (1928), *Nixey's Harlequin* (1931), and *Dunky Fitlow* (1933), but side by side with an increasing virtuosity goes a mounting passion for the jocose and for the far-fetched farcical conceit. In his later volumes, indeed, the illuminated truth to nature has almost disappeared. *You Never Know, Do You?* (1939) and *Ugly Anna* (1944) are both disappointing volumes. His last two volumes of stories were *Dark-eyed Lady* (1947) and *Fearful Pleasures* (1952).

Coppard was a poet as well as a writer of short stories, and here, too, though his quality was undoubted, the varying levels of his power of communication accounted for a lack of adequate recognition. There was genuine poetry in the free verse of *Hips and Haws* (1922), still more in the volume he brought out in 1926, *Pelagea and other Poems*, the best of which was cast in traditional forms of verse. A volume of *Collected Poems* appeared in 1928 and a small volume, *Cherry Ripe*, in 1935. At the time of his death Coppard had just finished going through the page proofs of the first volume of his autobiography covering the period of his life up to the early twenties, under the title *It's Me, Oh Lord.*

Coppard, who for many years had been living near Dunmow, Essex, where he was active in the Home Guard during the Second World War, was a vivid personality, dark and gipsy-like in appearance—certain gipsy ways entered into his love of the open air—and, when the mood was upon him, a brilliant and arresting talker. He married Winifred May de Kok, of Bloemfontein, and had one son and one daughter.

January 14, 1957.

Frances Cornford, the poet, died on August 19, 1960 at Cambridge. She was 74.

Frances Cornford, daughter of Sir Francis Darwin and Ellen Darwin (*née* Crofts), half-sister of Bernard Darwin*, and a granddaughter of Charles Darwin, was born on March 30, 1886, at Cambridge, where her father was Reader in Botany. She was educated at home, and in 1908 married Francis Macdonald Cornford, Fellow of Trinity College, Cambridge, and later Lawrence Professor of Ancient Philosophy. She had five children, three sons and two daughters, of whom the second son, John, was killed in Spain in 1937, aged 21, when a member of the International Brigade.

Mrs. Cornford's first volume, *Poems,* published in 1910, brought her a somewhat embarrassing fame, for the triolet: *To a Fat Lady Seen from a Train*—

"O why do you walk through the field in gloves,
Missing so much and so much?"

became a stock anthology piece and provoked a loud burst of derision from G. K. Chesterton—

"Why do you flash through the flowery meads,
Fat-headed poet that nobody reads?"

And, indeed, for many years few of the general public read any of Mrs. Cornford's poetry, except for those notorious and quite unrepresentative lines. Gradually, however, with the publication of later volumes—*Different Days* (1928), *Mountains and Molehills* (1934), *Travelling Home* (1948)—the quiet but distinctive quality of her work began to be recognized. In 1954 her *Collected Poems* were the choice of the Poetry Book Society, and in 1959 she was awarded the Queen's Medal for Poetry.

Precision and unpretentiousness are perhaps the main characteristics of her verse. Her poems, often only a quatrain in length, never pretend to be more than they are. She was among those poets who ignored the revolution in diction led by T. S. Eliot* and Ezra Pound* yet, at the same time, she conducted a minor revolution of her own. So that while there was nothing in her language which was obviously new, neither was there anything archaic or out of date.

She began to write as a troubled agnostic with a certain resentment at man's predicament, but eventually the resentment disappeared and was replaced by an acceptance under protest but without rancour of the human lot.

Much of her life was spent in or round Cambridge, and some of her most pleasing lines describe that "sober, fruitful, unemphatic land". These words, moreover, apply equally well to her poetry. She had an ear that never failed her and an exquisite sense of what to leave unsaid:

"So let me in this Cambridge calm July
Fruitfully live and undistinguished die".

Fortunately for her readers, Mrs. Cornford was granted only the first half of her wish.

August 22, 1960.

Sir Kinahan Cornwallis, G.C.M.G., C.B.E., D.S.O., died on June 3, 1959 at his home at North Warnborough, Basingstoke. He was 76.

The name of Sir Kinahan Cornwallis ranks with those of a small number of outstanding Englishmen—and one outstanding Englishwoman—who helped to shape the fortunes of Iraq. First as Adviser to the Ministry of Interior, later as Ambassador, his influence was as deep as that of Sir Percy Cox, Sir Arnold Wilson and Gertrude Bell, Tall, rugged imperturbable, he seemed cast in the great proconsular mould, and on the rare occasions when it seemed necessary could assume the proconsular manner. But he was always easy of access, simple, humorous, and abounding in common sense.

Cornwallis was born on February 19, 1883, and educated at Haileybury and University College, Oxford. He was a remarkable athlete, representing Oxford against Cambridge for four years in the quarter mile and for three years in the half mile, including, among his successes, a new university record for the latter in 1904. He was President of the Oxford University Athletic Club from 1904 to 1906.

Cornwallis was one of the Blues who chose the Sudan Civil Service for a career. Here he remained for eight years, until the outbreak of war brought him, like other Arabic speakers, to wider military and political responsibilities. He became Director of the celebrated Arab Bureau in Cairo, of which T. E. Lawrence was a junior member, and subsequently a political officer with the Army in Syria, which brought him into contact with the Emir Faisal. This was the beginning of a long collaboration between the two men, and it was suitably to Colonel Cornwallis (as he had become) that the task of offering the throne of Iraq was deputed by Curzon in December 1920, after the Emir had been expelled from his Syrian kingdom by the French. He accompanied Faisal [q.v.] in the journey which took him from Jeddah to his new kingdom in June 1921.

In the years of the mandate, when Iraq was finding her feet as a state and a nation, Cornwallis's official position was that of Adviser to the Ministry of Interior. This was certainly the key post in the country, since the Ministry controlled all administration and the police.

The mandatory power was responsible for the ultimate security of the country, and for preparing and developing its institutions for the day of independence. Cornwallis was the clearing house of policy. On his strength, tact, and sympathy much depended. But, in addition to his official post, he also acted as personal adviser to King Faisal.

Cornwallis saw the mandate end and Iraq admitted to the League of Nations. He retired in 1935, and as a special mark of appreciation was invested with the First Class of the Order of Rafidain by King Ghazi. His association with Iraq seemed at an end.

But he was to be recalled at the most critical period of the war and on the eve of an open breach between Britain and Iraq. On April 1, 1941, the pro-Axis junta of officers known as "the Golden Square" carried out a *coup d'état.* The Regent took refuge in the American Embassy. It was at this moment that Cornwallis, who had been nominated to succeed Sir Basil Newton as Ambassador, arrived in Baghdad. Rashid Ali became Prime Minister, and Cornwallis's first task was to inform him that, in conformity with the Anglo-Iraq treaty, troops were being sent from India to Basra. Negotiations continued in a steadily deteriorating atmosphere. By the beginning of May Cornwallis and nearly 400 British subjects were besieged in the Embassy compound.

The rebellion lasted a month, and it fell to Cornwallis to arrange the formal terms by which the defeated units of the Iraq Army surrendered to the relief force which had carried out a brilliant campaign across the Syrian desert.

For the next four years he remained as Ambassador, guiding Anglo-Iraqi relations through the difficult problems of war. Large numbers of troops—Indians and Poles as well as British—were stationed in Iraq, which looked, until the end of 1942, as though it might well become a theatre of war. Even after this threat had been removed there were the shortages, high prices, and other complications to deal with. As long as Cornwallis was in the large white Embassy on the west bank of the Tigris there was general confidence that all complications could be overcome. Political problems were another matter. The most acute of these remained in comparatively cold storage until after the war.

After his retirement in 1945 Cornwallis was for a time chairman of the Middle East committee of the Foreign Office. He was a director of the British Bank of the Middle East. He was twice married.

June 5, 1959.

Lou Costello, the American film comedian, died at Beverly Hills, California, on March 3, 1959 at the age of 52.

His real name was Louis Francis Cristillo, and he was born on March 6, 1906, at Paterson, New Jersey. He began his career as a prize fighter, then became a shop assistant before buying a $100 car and making the trip to Hollywood. There his first job was a labourer at M.G.M. studios. Later he became a stunt man and was injured while jumping from a second storey window, doubling, it is said, for Dolores Del Rio.

Recovering. he went into burlesque and subsequently teamed with Mr. Bud Abbott. After several years of equivocal fortunes in the theatre, the team of Abbott and Costello suddenly achieved notice on radio, in the Kate Smith Show; moving on to Broadway, their success in *Streets of Paris* (a musical which also brought stardom to the late Carmen Miranda) led to a film contract with Universal. Their first film was *One Night in the Tropics* (1940); and between then and 1957, when the team finally split, Abbott and Costello made almost 40 films together. In Britain they appeared together on the stage, at the Palladium in 1953. Costello did little film work after the partnership broke, although in latter months he was seen in television shorts.

Abbott and Costello enjoyed great popularity throughout most of their career; and between 1941 and 1951 appeared frequently among Hollywood's "top ten money-making stars". Their success was not confined to America; and in Italy they were offered the unusual compliment of local names, being known there as Gianni e Pinotto. Their style of comedy was broad and hectic slapstick; and their films were mostly coarse parodies of popular Hollywood *genres.* In the early forties they hit at Westerns, detectives, and thrillers of the day; in later years following popular taste Abbott and Costello Went to Mars, Met Dr. Jekyll and Mr. Hyde.

Costello was of course the funny man of the team. His special species of clown was The Baby, though he had not the refinement of the great exponents of this type—Langdon and Laurel [q.v.]—nor the lost and winning quality of Jerry Lewis.

Short, flabby, and distinctly plain, he was always slapped and painfully ill-treated; and his shortcoming as a clown was that he had neither those moments of grandeur with which W. C. Fields used to dismiss the trials of existence, nor yet sufficient charm to make us feel really sympathetic towards him. His best moments were when, in a crisis, he alone saw the true perils of the situation, but since excitement almost reduced him to gibbering incoherence, his flashes of foresight were of no use to anyone.

Even at their best, however, Abbott and Costello fell far short of Laurel and Hardy [q.v.], upon whom much of their work was so closely based.

In private life Costello enjoyed a long and happy married life and leaves a widow and four daughters. He had earned very large sums from his films and was noted for his extravagance but also for his generosity. In 1945 he endowed the Lou Costello Jnr. Youth Centre in Los Angeles, in memory of his only son, who died in infancy.

March 5, 1959.

Lord Cottesloe, C.B., one of the outstanding authorities on the rifle and himself a first-class marksman, died on July 19, 1956 at his home in Buckinghamshire, of which county he was for many years Lord Lieutenant. He was 94. Up to his eighties, he still shot regularly at Bisley.

The Right Hon. Sir Thomas Francis Fremantle, third Baron Cottesloe, of Swanbourne and of Hardwicke, in the county of Buckingham, in the peerage of the United Kingdom, and a baronet, was born on February 5, 1862, the eldest son of the second Lord Cottesloe. He early evinced remarkable prowess with the rifle and was in the Eton Shooting VII in 1879 and 1880. In the latter year the team won the Ashburton Shield.

When he went up to Oxford, where he attended Balliol, he represented the university each year he was there in both the Chancellor's Plate and Humphry Cup teams—Oxford won seven out of the eight events. In 1884, his last year at Oxford, he was in the "Queen's Sixty" (2,200 competitors shot for the Queen's Prize that year). Other years in which he was in the final stage were 1893 and 1921.

He first shot for the Elcho Shield in 1885 and from 1920 to 1928 was captain of the English team competing for that trophy. He was also captain of the successful British team in the match for the Palma Trophy at Ottawa in 1902 and in the return match at Bisley in the next season. At Bisley in 1909 he was captain of the Olympic team and again in 1910 he was captain of the British team in the Empire match. For many years he shot for the House of Lords in the annual match against the Commons and held innumerable trophies of success in individual events.

He was hardly less distinguished in ballistic research, which he began as early as 1887 at first in collaboration with W. E. Metford and then with Sir H. Holford. He took over the latter's range at Wistow and shot there up to 2,000 yards to determine the trajectories described by various bullets fired from different makes of rifle; and with A. Mallock, F.R.S., he determined the extreme range of the S.M.L.E. with Mark VII ammunition by a new method in 1909 and 1911.

For many years he was chairman of the Small Arms Committee at the War Office and was also an associate member of the Ordnance Board. He was sent in 1900 on a special mission to report on the safety of ranges in various countries on the Continent and he held a commission for many years from 1881 in the Volunteers and then in the Territorial Army, gaining both the V.D. and the T.D.

His career as an administrator of rifle shooting began in 1889 when he was appointed assistant secretary of the National Rifle Association, and so had much to do with the removal from Wimbledon and the establishment of the headquarters of the association at Bisley. He was elected to the N.R.A. council in 1891 and was chairman from 1930 to 1939. For many years he was chairman of the Public Schools Rifle Matches Committee and contributed to the N.R.A. prize list, giving a challenge trophy in 1927. He also originated the collection of small arms at Bisley Camp. With A. P. Humphry, a former secretary, he wrote a history of the N.R.A. from its foundation in 1859 to 1909, which was published in 1914. Other books he produced are *Notes on the Rifle* (1896). *The Book of Rifle* (1901), and *The Englishman and the Rifle* (1946). He also contributed to several editions of the official *Text Book of Small Arms.* He was also for a number of years president of the Society for Army Historical Research.

Lord Cottesloe, who succeeded to the family honours in 1918, married in 1896 Florence, daughter of the late Thomas Tapling. She died in April 1956, having borne him four sons and four daughters. The eldest son died unmarried in 1915 of wounds received in Flanders and the third son died before he reached his teens. The family honours therefore devolve on the second son, the Hon. J. W. H. Fremantle, T.D., who was born in 1900 and married in 1926 Lady Elizabeth Harris, daughter of the fifth Earl of Malmesbury. There are two children—a son and a daughter—of the marriage, which was dissolved in 1944.

July 20, 1956.

By the untimely death of **Sir Reginald Coupland,** K.C.M.G., C.I.E., on November 6, 1952 at the age of 68, Oxford lost one of her foremost scholars and the Empire one of its most devoted servants.

Reginald Coupland, who was born in 1884, was a scholar of Winchester and New College. He obtained a first class in *Literae Humaniores,* his brilliant work in ancient history exciting the special attention of the examiners. In 1907 he was elected to a teaching fellowship at Trinity, where he made his mark as an enthusiastic and successful tutor in ancient history. Yet, as in the case of other Wykehamists of his generation, his interest early turned to the study of the problems of the modern world. In 1913 the Beit Lectureship in Colonial History became vacant after the tenure of Lionel Curtis [q.v.], and though as yet he had done no work in this field Coupland was selected as his successor. The choice was brilliantly vindicated and led in due course to his election, in 1920, to the Beit Chair in the same subject.

Soon after his accession to the chair the School of Philosophy, Politics, and Economics, known as "Modern Greats", was instituted, and Coupland had much to do with working out the details of the politics side of the course, in which the political structure of the British Empire figures as a special subject. But the activity which gave him the greatest pleasure and brought him into closest contact with young and old interested in his subject was the Ralegh Club, an undergraduate society for the discussion of imperial questions, of which he was the guiding spirit during the whole of the inter-war period until its activities were suspended in the Michaelmas term of 1939.

As a historian Coupland's name will certainly live in academic annals, for his tenure of the chair was marked by a substantial volume of first-class work in what had previously been a neglected field. Under Coupland, colonial history came of age and took its place beside the older historical studies in which he himself had learnt his craft. Considering that he was not a rapid worker and that his health was always delicate Coupland's output was remarkable; and it was all on the same high level.

His earliest volume dates from the war of 1914-18, when, being debarred by his health from war service, he edited the war speeches of Pitt, having the rare experience of being able to re-issue the volume, still as fresh as ever, with a preface by Winston Churchill*, in 1940. His book on the Quebec Act, issued in 1925, is still the best account for the general reader of that turning-point not only in Canadian but in imperial history.

He had the power of presenting large issues through the great figures who embodied them. Thus his books on *Wilberforce* (1923), *Raffles* (1926), and *Kirk on the Zambesi* (1928) were works of sound scholarship on their respective themes. Coupland had early become interested in the humanitarian aspects of imperial rule; indeed it was the moral appeal of the problem of the backward peoples of the Empire which had drawn him from classical studies. He followed up his study of Wilberforce, in the centenary year of abolition, by an account of the British anti-slavery movement. Two other books which belong to this period are *The American Revolution and the British Empire* (1930), which throws a floodlight on the period, so often neglected, between the end of the First Empire and the Durham Report, and *The Empire in These Days* (1935), a collection of essays which mingles vivid description with sound constitutional learning.

The work by which Coupland himself would have wished chiefly to be judged was that which he devoted, in the years before the war, to the history of East Africa. Here his gifts of accurate scholarship, lucid presentation, and felicitous style are seen to the best advantage. In *East Africa and her Invaders* (1938) he brought together for the first time from very scattered sources the history of the coast from Greek times to 1856, the vivid account of the Arab settlements showing traces of his early interest in Greek colonial activities; the central figure of the book is, however, that picturesque personality Seyyid Said, Sultan of Muscat. A later volume, *The Exploitation of East Africa,* is sufficiently described by its sub-title, "The slave-trade and the scramble". Here the centre of the stage is occupied by a Scot, Sir John Kirk, of whose papers Coupland made full use and to whom he was able to render tardy justice.

Coupland was no mere armchair student of the Empire. His African studies were vivified by several lengthy visits to that continent—to South Africa in 1913, when he threw himself into a plan for preserving the records of the up-country Boers, to East Africa in 1928, and to

West Africa in 1933. He visited the West Indies in 1936 and on his return drew attention to the conditions which later excited the criticism of the Royal Commission. These were all journeys undertaken in a private capacity, but two important public duties also fell to him, necessitating long stays overseas. In 1923 he went to India as a member of the Royal Commission, presided over by Lord Lee of Fareham, on the Superior Civil Services in India, and in 1936-37 he served in Palestine under Lord Peel as a member of the Royal Commission on the affairs of that country. It can now be revealed that in each case it was mainly due to his persuasive efforts that a minority report was averted. The report of the Palestine Commission, with its masterly and indeed almost classic account of the social and political conditions of that divided community, bears the characteristic traces of Coupland's hand, both in its analysis and in its presentation. It was a matter of unaffected disappointment to him that the policy put forward in the report, which seemed at first to find favour, was eventually set on one side.

He had, however, the satisfaction of being a member of the India Office Committee which drafted the constitution of Burma, serving also as an official adviser at the Burma Round Table Conference.

Coupland was unmarried, but he had a wide circle of friends, both in Oxford, where, from 1920 to 1948, he was a Fellow of All Souls, and among present and past members of the Indian and Colonial Services, many of whom he had met in the fields. It had been his intention to devote his later years to an intensive study of the methods of government in the Colonial Empire. He abandoned this project on the outbreak of war and took over the editorship of the *Round Table,* which he had already held in 1917-19. But soon after L. S. Amery's [q.v.] advent to the India Office he gave up his editorship and embarked on a study of the constitutional problem of India and it was in pursuance of this task, sponsored by Nuffield* College, that he travelled to the East and the results of his work were published under the auspices of Nuffield College.

He was thus in a position to render signal service to the mission which went to India under Sir Stafford Cripps [q.v.], and though the eventual solution of the Indian problem was at variance with his views, which tended towards federation, his studies had thrown a clear light on many hitherto obscure aspects of the matter.

Though he resigned his Chair at Oxford in 1948, he continued his studies of Imperial affairs to the end of his life and was, indeed, on the way to South Africa to make further investigations at the time of his sudden death.

November 7, 1952.

Augustine Courtauld, a brave and resourceful explorer, died on March 3, 1959 at the age of 54.

He will be especially remembered for his fortitude in 1930-31 when, a member of a British expedition which went to Greenland to study meteorological conditions relating to air operation, he volunteered to man alone the station on the central ice plateau. There he remained for five months until in May 1931 he was relieved by H. G. Watkins. His experiences he later recounted in a series of articles published in *The Times.*

Courtauld, who was a son of Samuel Courtauld, for many years a director of Courtaulds Ltd., was born in 1904 and educated at Charterhouse and Trinity College, Cambridge.

He began his "Greenland days" early, taking part in two expeditions in 1926 and 1929, the latter being led by the Polar explorer, Sir James Wordie. A main object of those two expeditions was to explore the mountainous region of north-east Greenland. Much good work was done and in 1929 Courtauld was one of the party which reached the top of Petermann Peak, some 11,000ft. above sea level.

In July 1930 Courtauld went with the British Arctic Air Route Expedition to Greenland, which had as its object the studying of meteorological conditions with a view to the establishment of an air route to Canada.

A station was established on the ice-cap some 150 miles from the base of the expedition, which itself was some 35 miles from the settlement of Angmagsalik. In October Lieutenant-Colonel F. Spencer Chapman* and others, including Courtauld, led an expedition to the ice-cap, but owing to bad weather—in 14 days fewer than 30 miles were covered—and other causes the ice-cap station was not reached until December 3. At the station there were then two men.

In view of the bad weather it was felt by Chapman and his comrades that the station should be evacuated. Courtauld, however, insisted that there was no need for so doing, that he was well fitted to stand a prolonged period alone, and that he stay on upon his own responsibility. In these circumstances the rest of the party left the ice-cap station for the base.

Courtauld was thus left behind, at his own wish. He had provisions to last up to the middle of May and fuel until the end of April. It was therefore arranged that he should be relieved by the beginning of May. A relief party of three left the base camp on March 9, reached the vicinity of the ice-cap station on March 26, but were unable to locate it on account of bad weather. A Moth aircraft sent out on March 26 also failed to find the station. The relief party returned to the base with the news of their failure, and on April 21 Watkins and two companions set out on another search, taking with them provisions for five weeks.

Courtauld's home was a circular dome-shaped tent 10ft. in diameter with double walls. It was covered by a snow house and through the top protruded a metal ventilator about 2in. across.

When Watkins and the relief party arrived in May they skied right over the roof; only the ventilator showed. Courtauld for two months had been snowed up and for the latter part of his time had been in darkness. In 1932 he was awarded a Polar Medal by King George V.

In 1935, in company with Professor L. R. Wager*, Mr. Jack Longland, and others, he was again in Greenland.

Courtauld, who served in the Royal Navy in the War of 1939-45, was a Deputy Lieutenant for Essex, a Justice of the Peace and a county councillor. In 1953 he was High Sheriff of the county. He had been a member of the Cruising Association since 1926 and was president from 1957 until his death.

He wrote an autobiography, *Man the Ropes,* and later compiled an admirable collection of Polar writings, *From the Ends of the Earth.* In 1956 he announced his intention of establishing a substantial fund to help various bodies which "had been hobbling along for years" such as charitable organizations associated with religious work and educational facilities among boy scouts.

Some years ago he gave a lifeboat—now stationed at Walton-on-Naze—in memory of his mother.

His marriage to Mollie, daughter of F. D. Montgomerie, took place in 1932. They had four sons and two daughters.

March 4, 1959.

Albert P. de Courville—See **de Courville.**

Bishop of Coventry—See **Gorton.**

Admiral Sir Walter Henry Cowan, BT., K.C.B., D.S.O., M.V.O., died on February 14, 1956 in hospital at Leamington at the age of 84.

He had a distinguished career, and was created a baronet for his services in command of the British naval forces operating in the Baltic immediately after the 1914-18 War. As a lieutenant, he had exceptional opportunities in land campaigns in Africa, culminating in duty as A.D.C. to Lord Kitchener and Lord Roberts in the South African War. Later he built up a high reputation as a destroyer commander, and became Assistant to the Admiral of Patrols in the North Sea.

In 1939, at the age of 68, he persuaded the Admiralty to re-engage him for the duration of the 1939-45 War, and in 1941 he served as liaison officer with the Commandos during their raids on the North African coast. Later he was attached to an Indian regiment, the 18th King Edward VII's Own Cavalry, and served with them in all the operations in the Western Desert in which they took part, including the famous "Balaclava" charge against the German guns at Mechili, until he was captured at Bir Hacheim in 1942. After repatriation in 1943 he was awarded a bar to the D.S.O. he had won in 1898 and he joined the 2nd Commando Brigade in Italy in January 1944.

When war broke out in 1914 he had command of H.M.S. Zealandia in the Grand Fleet. In February 1915 he joined the Battle Cruiser Force, under his former colleague Vice-Admiral Beatty, as Flag Captain in the Princess Royal to Rear-Admiral Osmond Brock. For his service in this vessel at the Battle of Jutland he was appointed C.B. In July 1917 he was made Commodore Commanding the First Light Cruiser Squadron of the Grand Fleet on board the Caledon, and it was while so employed that he was promoted to rear-admiral on September 2, 1918, and reappointed. When this squadron was selected for duty in the Baltic, which it performed throughout 1919, Cowan was faced with difficult and delicate tasks.

Ably led by Cowan, the work of the squadron was the more praiseworthy because it came after the long strain of war and when other forces were able to enjoy a relaxation of effort. Cowan commanded the squadron for three years, hauling down his flag in the Delhi on July 5, 1920. In the following March he took command of the Battle Cruiser Squadron.

After about two years on half pay, he hoisted his flag again on June 30, 1925 as Commanding Officer on the Coast of Scotland and Admiral-Superintendent of Rosyth Dockyard. This post he held for a year only, as he was selected for the more important duty of Commander-in-Chief on the North America and West Indies Station, with his flag in the Calcutta. It was during his two years there that this station was extended to include South America, its title being altered to the America and West Indies Station. He was promoted to Admiral from August 1, 1927, and hauled down his flag on the expiration of his term in command on July 22, 1928.

Walter Henry Cowan was the son of Walter Frederick James Cowan, of Alveston, Warwickshire, J.P., who died in 1914. He was born on June 11, 1871, and entered the Britannia as a naval cadet in 1884. Lord Beatty was among his term-mates there, and the two joined their first seagoing ship together in 1886. This was the Alexandra, flagship in the Mediterranean Station (then at the zenith of its importance) of Vice-Admiral H.R.H. the Duke of Edinburgh. In 1887 Cowan went to the Temeraire, in the Channel Squadron, and in 1889 to the Volage, in the Training Squadron.

His first 10 years' naval duty were comparatively uneventful. Nor did he shine at examinations, for he took only third-class certificates in all subjects except seamanship, in which he got a second. Consequently he served some time as a sub-lieutenant, and did not become a lieutenant until 1892. Part of his sub-lieutenant's time was passed in the Boadicea, flagship in the East Indies, under that popular admiral, Sir William Kennedy. In 1894 he was nominated for duty on the Africa Station in the light cruiser Barrosa, and this gave him his first chance of distinction. In the following December the Barrosa lent her assistance to the French gunboat Ardent when aground up the Niger, and Cowan was among those who received the thanks of the French Government. In 1895 he was landed for service with the punitive expedition under Rear-Admiral Bedford against King Koko, of Nimby, and for this he received the General Africa Medal, with clasp for Brass River.

Six months later a similar undertaking claimed his services, and he was landed for duty with the expedition under Rear-Admiral Rawson at Mombasa for the punishment of M'buruk, the rebellious Arab chief. The latter's stronghold at M'Weli was captured on August 17, 1895.

Cowan was concerned in the Benin expedition 18 months later. Commanded by Rear-Admiral Rawson, this was landed for the punishment of the King of Benin for the massacre of the political expedition. Cowan, who was in charge of carriers, was mentioned in dispatches, and was awarded the Benin clasp. It was also while in the Barrosa that he won the Bronze Medal of the Royal Humane Society, for rescuing from drowning, during operations against rebels in the Pongwe River, East Africa, a sepoy of the 24th Baluchistan Regiment.

Further and more serious land fighting claimed his attention in 1898. He had command of the gunboat flotilla on the Nile during the operations in the Sudan, and was present at the battles of Atbara and Khartoum. In addition to the medal for this duty, he was awarded the D.S.O. A year later he served as staff officer to the Sirdar (Sir Reginald Wingate [q.v.]) during operations against the Khalifa. In bringing his work to the notice of the authorities, Sir Reginald Wingate said: "He is a most zealous and energetic officer, and afforded me much assistance throughout the operations". He added the Sudan 1899 and Gedid clasps to his medal, and was appointed a member of the 4th Class of the Medjidieh. Towards the end of 1899 he was selected for duty as Aide-de-Camp to Lord Kitchener, and after 11 months in this capacity he became Naval Aide-de-Camp to Lord Roberts. For this war he was awarded the South African Medal, and in June 1901 was promoted to commander, at the comparatively early age of 30.

In this rank he served in the Resolution, flagship at Holyhead, and early in 1903 was given command of the Falcon and of a group of early destroyers at Devonport. In this branch his qualities of thoroughness and zeal proved very successful, and from July 1905 he was made Commander (D) in the scout Skirmisher to command torpedo craft in commission in reserve.

He had been appointed M.V.O. in 1904, in commemoration of escort duty. After his promotion to captain at the end of 1906, he was retained on destroyer work as Flag Captain in the Sapphire to Rear-Admiral R. A. J. Montgomerie, commanding torpedo craft of the Home Fleet; and in 1908, still in the Sapphire, he took command of the destroyer flotillas of the Channel Fleet under Lord Charles Beresford. He had an important share in the organization and training of a class of vessel which proved to be of the greatest importance in the war.

In October 1910 he commissioned the new cruiser Gloucester for the Home Fleet, but in May 1912 he was recalled as the first occupant of the post of Assistant to the Admiral of Patrols (Rear-Admiral de Robeck). He resumed sea command in February 1914 as Captain of the Zealandia, Third Battle Squadron.

He married in 1901 Catherine Eleanor Millicent, daughter of Digby Cayley. She died in 1934. There is no heir to the baronetcy.

February 15, 1956.

Dr. Alfred Cox, O.B.E., medical secretary of the British Medical Association from 1912 to 1932, died on August 31, 1954 in a nursing home at Brighton at the age of 88.

Alfred Cox was born in a working-class home in Middlesbrough in 1866. Later his parents moved to Darlington, where his early life was spent. He entered the medical profession, as he once said, by the back door as a dispenser's assistant.

On his twenty-first birthday he became a student in the Medical School at Newcastle upon Tyne in the University of Durham, and carried on his studies while still working as a dispenser under conditions of some penury and hardship. He qualified in 1891. Those were the days of club practice, and Cox learnt from bitter experience in his practice at Gateshead the conditions from which national health insurance delivered the general practitioner. In 1898 he was instrumental in forming the Gateshead Medical Association, of which he became honorary secretary.

In 1900 he became a member of the committee which hammered out what is still virtually the constitution of the association, with its representative body. He forsook the north of England and his practice in 1908, having been chosen from among many candidates as deputy medical secretary of the B.M.A. at a salary of £500 a year.

His first big job was to help in preparing the association's evidence to the Royal Commission on the Poor Law. His chief was Dr. (later Sir James) Smith Whitaker, and when Smith Whitaker accepted the office of deputy chairman of the National Health Insurance Commission—an action which was regarded by many in the association as going over to the enemy—Cox succeeded to the uneasy seat of medical secretary. With the outbreak of war in 1914 came the setting up of the Central Medical War Committee, of which Cox was joint secretary, and at the end of the war he was appointed O.B.E. in acknowledgment of his services. He was due for retirement under the age limit in 1931 but, 1932 being the centenary year of the association, his term of office was extended to cover that event, when he was presented with a testimonial and a great tribute was paid him both by the leaders and the rank and file of the association. He was also awarded the gold medal of the association.

Retirement from official duties meant no slackening in his activities. He had already helped to found the *Association Professionnelle des Médecins,* out of which the present World Medical Association has developed, and the international exchanges which his work brought about afforded him great satisfaction.

He also served as part-time secretary of the British Health Resorts Association, the object of which was to make British spas and other resorts better known, and another activity was the part-time medical secretaryship of the London Public Medical Service. In 1950 he wrote his autobiography, *Among the Doctors,* ending it with the words: "I have had a happy life, and, nearing the end of it, have much to be thankful for. I can say, as few men can, that I have done just the work I wanted to do, and through it have made a host of friends, amongst whom have been many of the salt of the earth."

He married Florence, the daughter of Thomas Cheesman. She died in 1927.

September 1, 1954.

André Coyne, the designer of the Kariba dam and the builder of the Malpasset dam, above Fréjus, which collapsed in December 1959, died in Paris at the age of 69 on July 21, 1960.

Although well-known to his fellow engineers not only in France but throughout the world, it would, perhaps, be true to say that few laymen would recognize his name—even those who have seen the remarkable dams (over 100) built to his design in France, Africa and elsewhere.

A big dam is a beautiful sight at any time, and the technical innovations which Coyne introduced in the past 30 years have made the dams of his design exceptionally satisfying to the eye.

He received his engineering training at the École Polytechnique and qualified as Ingénieur des Ponts et Chaussées. After an interval of service in the air force in the 1914-18 War—for which he received the Croix de Guerre and the Distinguished Flying Cross—Coyne entered the French Civil Service, in what is the equivalent in many countries of the public works department, the Service des Ponts et Chaussées. After some years of service in the 1920s at the port of Brest, he transferred to the Service d'Aménagement of the River Dordogne. His specialization on the technique of dam-building culminated in 1935 with the establishment of a new section of the department—the Service Technique de Grands Barrages—of which he was made head. In 1941 he became Inspector-General of his original department—the Ponts et Chaussées—and retired from the Civil Service after the 1939-45 War. Since retirement he had had a busy practice, both French and international, as a consulting engineer.

Kariba was begun in a series of strikingly beautiful constructions not only in France itself but in Portugal, Luxembourg, Belgium, and Poland, in Morocco, Tunisia, and the Union of South Africa, and in some Asian countries. Many of these earlier works themselves earned superlatives—the highest pure arch dam in Africa or the longest span in a multiple arch. The Kariba project, completed earlier in 1960, has earned others—the largest man-made lake in the world and the longest pure arch dam in the world, the highest Zambezi flood recorded during its building—and will doubtless qualify for more in the future.

The official report as to the causes of the Fréjus catastrophe of December 1959, in which nearly 400 people lost their lives, stated that the disaster was apparently due to a fault in the rock on which the dam was based. The report made it clear that no mistake was made in the construction of the dam itself. At the time of the disaster there was much speculation that the design of the dam—completed in 1957—was to blame for its collapse. One end of it was linked to the rock foundation by a concrete shoulder and there were allegations that either the engineers had made the dam too thin or that the concrete had given way.

The report, however, exonerated both designer and builder. The calculations on which the design was based, it said, were sound and both the dam and its concrete shoulder were correctly constructed.

July 22, 1960.

Commander Lionel Kenneth Philip Crabb, O.B.E., G.M., R.N.V.R., whose death was presumed by the Admiralty after trials with certain underwater apparatus near Portsmouth in the last week of April 1956, was one of the most daring and enterprising "frogmen" during and after the Second World War. He was 46.

While he was serving at Gibraltar in 1942 as a mine and bomb disposal officer, he and his unit had to dispose of bombs under water as well as on land, and he operated wearing a Davis emergency escape set. At the time of the Italian surrender in 1943 he was operating in north Italy and was commissioned to take charge of anti-frogmen activities, keeping the northern Italian ports clear for British warships and landing-craft. By purely peaceful persuasion he got the Italian frogmen to clear Leghorn harbour of German mines.

At the end of the war he was in Venice and did experimental work there. Later he undertook anti-frogmen activities at Haifa during the period immediately before the founding of the Jewish State in Palestine.

He was at the Admiralty research station at Teddington when the submarine Truculent went down in the mouth of the Thames in very tricky sea conditions and considered that he could reach the submarine more quickly than a conventional diver. He went down with another frogman, named James Hodges, and was the first man to reach the conning tower of the Truculent and report no sign of life.

He was a moving spirit in the development and use of the underwater television camera that located the submarine Affray in the English Channel. For some time up to 1954 he was working for the Duke of Argyll, investigating the galleon at Tobermory, but in April 1955 he was recalled for duty with the Royal Navy.

April 30, 1956.

Sir John Craig, C.B.E., an outstanding figure in the British iron and steel industry, died at his home in Wishaw, Lanarkshire, on February 1, 1957. He was 82. For nearly 70 years he had been associated with the great concern of Colvilles, of Glasgow, latterly as honorary president, having joined it as an office boy at the age of 13 in 1888.

Within 22 years he had become a director and under his guidance it grew to one of the greatest concerns of its kind, with extensive development plans in progress. He was a man of indomitable will, frank and rugged in speech, and a great champion of free enterprise in trade. He was also, throughout his career, deeply interested in youthful ambitions and in providing every facility to help those with initiative and promise.

John Craig was born on December 11, 1874, the son and grandson of skilled ironworkers. His father, Thomas Craig, a furnaceman, and strict Presbyterian, had followed his trade from his home at Clydeside to Motherwell and from the local day school his son went into the Colville offices at a wage of five shillings a week. He graduated from the counting house to the departments turning out steel, and within 10 years had a considerable knowledge of all branches of the business. At that time Colvilles was a family business and although its reputation stood high there was nothing in its history or its activities at the turn of the century to suggest that it would make such enormous developments within the next 50 years.

Great opportunities came with the insistent demand for steel on the outbreak of war in 1914, and two years later, on the death of the two remaining members of the Colville family, Craig was appointed chairman of the directors at the age of 42. He remained at the helm through the ensuing period of boom conditions and the long depression in the early 1920s, and there is no doubt that it was largely due to his skill and foresight, during the years which followed until the outbreak of war in 1939, that the company was able to maintain its position in national and world markets.

War again changed the position not only of the British steel industry but also of Colvilles' place within it. While still controlling the Clydeside works and holding important office within the various national metallurgical organizations, Craig saw the industry continue to grow under the pressure of national and world demands for steel. Ten years after the ending of hostilities British output had been increased by something like six million tons and total output was approaching 20 million tons in 1955. Early in 1955 he announced expansions to the company costing nearly £14m., with a replanning of its activities to deal almost entirely with pig iron, which it was both producing and importing in increasing quantities. To the last he had complete faith that the new era of prosperity which had overtaken the British steel industry had all the elements of permanence about it, and it was upon these grounds that he embarked upon, and justified, the immense expansions.

He was also on the boards of a number of other companies, some of them closely allied with the Colville parent business. He was also a director of the shipbuilding firm of Harland and Wolff, the Steel Company of Scotland Ltd., the Ardrossan Harbour Co. Ltd., the Scottish Mutual Assurance Society Ltd., and other companies, and he was a Deputy Governor of the Bank of Scotland. He had been president both of the National Federation of Iron and Steel Manufacturers and of the Iron and Steel Institute, and for some years was a member of the council of the Federation of British Industries.

He was made a C.B.E. in 1918 and knighted in 1943. In 1951 an Honorary Doctorate of Laws was conferred upon him by Glasgow University. He was a Deputy Lieutenant of the county of Lanarkshire and a Justice of the Peace.

He married in 1901 Jessie Sommerville, and they had two sons and three daughters.

February 2, 1957.

Sir Robert Craigie, P.C., G.C.M.G., C.B., British Ambassador in Tokyo from 1937 to 1941, died at Winchester on May 16, 1959 at the age of 75.

Robert Leslie Craigie was the only son of Admiral R. W. Craigie. He entered the Foreign Office in 1907 and held diplomatic appointments in Berne, Sofia, and Washington. But his main services during the early part of his career were in Whitehall and in connexion with international conferences. He was secretary of the conference relating to the New Hebrides in 1914, and during the 1914-18 War he was British representative on the Inter-Allied Blockade Committee. In 1930 he accompanied Ramsay MacDonald to Washington and he was afterwards placed in charge of naval negotiations at the Foreign Office, taking a prominent part in the negotiation of the Naval Treaties of 1930 and 1936.

His appointment as Ambassador in Tokyo in 1937 was unexpected. He arrived at a particularly unpromising moment when the Japanese were refusing to apologize for the wounding of the British Ambassador at Nanking. His strenuous efforts to improve matters were temporarily successful, and he was encouraged in his resolution to repair relations between the two countries by personal conversation with the Emperor and the considerate approaches of many Japanese persons of rank and talent. But he had to contend with a series of difficulties in an atmosphere heated by war and anti-British propaganda, and the emphasis he laid in public on the convergence of Japanese and British interests and the hopes he built on the presence of liberal elements in the Japanese Government gave rise to some criticism in London and Washington.

The final failure of his endeavours came with the resignation of Prince Konoye and the appearance of General Tojo as Prime Minister. Two months later Japan entered the war against the United States and Britain. Craigie and his staff were interned for six months until they were granted safe conduct and a ship to take them home.

In a book published in 1946, *Behind the Japanese Mask,* he set out his recommendations for the reconstruction of defeated Japan. The abolition of Imperial rule would, he thought, lead quickly to chaos: "With Army domination eliminated, with Shintoism shorn of its nationalistic trends, and with the spiritual side of the Imperial influence emphasized at the expense of the temporal, the Japanese teaching profession would be free to revert to its normally liberal and progressive practices in the education of the country's youth."

From 1945 to 1948 Craigie was United Kingdom representative to the United Nations War Crimes Commission, and he headed his country's delegation to the Geneva conference for protection of the victims of war in 1949. He was sworn of the Privy Council in 1937.

He married in 1918 Pleasant, daughter of P. A. Stovall, at that time United States Minister at Berne. She died in 1956, and they are survived by their son.

May 18, 1959.

Sir William Craigie, an outstanding authority on the Northern languages and joint editor of the *Oxford English Dictionary* from 1901 to 1933, died on September 2, 1957 at Watlington. He was 90.

The labours of the lexicographer and the philologist—Craigie was both—are sometimes believed to be unattractive, both to the labourer and to those who peruse his labours, but Craigie had joy in his researches and if there was drudgery in the compiling of his works it was skilfully disguised.

In a long life of scholarship he performed much, rendering outstanding service to Scandinavian, Icelandic, and Frisian studies as well as to English in several of its branches. He was a leading authority on Anglo-Norman.

William Craigie was born on August 13, 1867, at Dundee, the son of James Craigie. He began to study Scots literature with the aid of *Jameson's Dictionary* while still at school at Dundee, finding even at this stage of his career words of which Jameson appeared to have no cognizance. He took his M.A. degree at St. Andrews in 1889 with honours in classics and philosophy. Elected a Bible clerk at Oriel College, Oxford, in 1889, he took first classes both in Classical Moderations and in the final honour school of *Lit. Hum.*

Before he left St. Andrews he had begun the study of Danish and Icelandic, and in 1892 went to Copenhagen to spend a year in enlarging his knowledge of Scandinavian languages. On his return he took up an appointment at his old university as Assistant Lecturer in Humanity which he occupied until 1897, the year in which he joined the staff of the *O.E.D.* Here he joined forces with Sir James Murray, Henry Bradley, and Dr. C. T. Onions*. It was said that he used to spend 11 months of each year for 20 years, working more than seven hours a day, on this massive piece of erudition.

In 1928, in recognition of the valuable work of Craigie and Dr. Onions in bringing the *New English Dictionary* to a successful conclusion, the Royal Society of Literature conferred honorary Fellowships upon them.

For some years he was Professor of English at Chicago University and while in the United States edited the *Historical Dictionary of the American English.*

Craigie was Lecturer in Scandinavian Languages at the Taylor Institution, Oxford, 1905-16, Fellow of Oriel, 1917-25, and later an honorary Fellow of the college.

His scholarly output never flagged. On his ninetieth birthday in August 1957 he was said to be working "several hours each day" on an Icelandic-English dictionary. His published works included a *Primer of Burns; Religion of Ancient Scandinavia; Icelandic Sagas; Easy Readings in Old Icelandic; The Poetry of Iceland* (in the *Oxford Book of Scandinavian Verse*); *A Dictionary of the Older Scottish Tongue,* and many papers and articles on Scottish, Gaelic, and Scandinavian subjects.

He was knighted in 1928 and many academic distinctions were conferred upon him. He was a D.Litt. of Oxford, Cambridge, Calcutta, Michigan, and Wisconsin, and at a ceremony at Oriel College on his 85th birthday a group of friends and what were described as his "intellectual beneficiaries" presented him with his portrait and a bibliography of his works.

He married in 1897 Jessie Hutchen. She died in 1947.

September 3, 1957.

Sir Edmund Craster, Bodley's Librarian at Oxford from 1931 to 1945, died on March 21, 1959 at the age of 79.

One of the greatest in the line of Bodley's librarians, and deeply respected by all who worked with him or knew him or his work, he was not one of the "familiar figures" of Oxford. Few passers-by would recognize the excellent portrait of him carved on one of the stone corbels in the Old Bodleian quadrangle. He rarely spoke in public, for a strange impediment made unbroken speech impossible, though it could add point and even effectiveness in private conversation or during discussions in a meeting of the body which he liked to describe as "my curators".

As generations of Fellows of All Souls knew, he was an affable, kind, witty, and levelheaded man, anything but a recluse; but he was also a very busy and hard working man, guided by strong principles of conduct.

Herbert Henry Edmund Craster was born on November 5, 1879. He was a Northumbrian, a son of Edmund Craster, of Beadnell Hall. His family, long connected with the fishing village of Craster, near Alnwick, was one of country squires and soldiers, steeped in the tradition of dignified loyalty which has maintained such quality in the gentry of Northumberland, so that the county never ceases to provide its stream of statesmen, public servants, reformers, and scholars.

The historical work by which he made his name as a scholar was begun in 1904, a year after he had passed from Clifton and Balliol, where he gained his Firsts in Greats and History, to the dignified opportunities of All Souls. As editor of the great *History of Northumberland,* one of the noblest monuments which England has produced of local patriotism and intelligence, he was responsible for three of its massive volumes (1907-14); much of them he wrote himself.

Craster's labours gave him just the experience required in a custodian of manuscripts which are in frequent use. It made him a palaeographer, familiarized him with manuscript collections of various kinds, such as the muniments at Durham and the Dodsworth manuscripts in the Bodleian, taught him how to relate record and literary evidence and deepened his first-hand knowledge of English history. Hence, when he joined the staff of the Bodleian as a sub-librarian in 1912, he was well equipped for the task with which he was especially entrusted, the completion of the Summary Catalogue of Western Manuscripts begun by Dr. Falconer Madan.

Some important collections in the library had been catalogued and calendared in the nineteenth century, but a great deal of work remained to be done. Dr. Madan had himself dealt (1895 to 1906) with the uncatalogued manuscripts acquired in the eighteenth and nineteenth centuries. Craster was mainly responsible for a volume on the more recent acquisitions (1924) and the work on the manuscripts received in the seventeenth century, which as a whole had not been catalogued since 1697. His first volume on these appeared in 1922, the second, due to Madan, Craster, and Denholm-Young, in 1937, after Craster had become librarian.

Craster became Keeper of the Western Manuscripts in 1927 and succeeded Sir Arthur Cowley as Bodley's Librarian in 1931. Although some people wondered whether this deliberate and retiring scholar would be strong enough to carry through the great scheme of library extension upon which the University had at last reached a general, if hesitant, agreement, his claims were in fact irresistible, and those who knew him best had no fears.

As second in command he had never pressed his personal views, which were in favour of a new library, a counterpart to the new library at Cambridge, and he had found, as well as given, great satisfaction in his congenial labours among the manuscripts.

But he was much more than this. He was a man of strong clear views, and a master in systematic planning. Those who worked most closely with him were astonished by the ease with which he took control of the affairs of the library and elaborated in detail the programme of years required to give effect to the Report of the Bodleian Commission which the University had appointed. Obviously Craster, as a sub-librarian, had been giving his mind to the problems as well as to the history of the library.

His patient thoroughness never failed him. No obstacle, however unforeseen or intricate, made him lose heart or disturbed his equanimity. He was a sensitive man and at times he suffered extremely, but few suspected this and fewer still were aware of it. His task was peculiarly difficult, for the University scheme was one for extension of the existing accommodation, not for a new Bodleian. It was extraordinarily complicated and involved constant adjustment of the daily activities of the library to the requirements of the future. The congestion in the old library was so great that a few months' delay in the execution of the programme approved by the University and the Rockefeller trustees would have meant chaos.

For some years before the outbreak of war in 1939 the building committee and its planning sub-committee were concerned with the reorganization of the old library and the Radcliffe Camera and with the innumerable problems and incidental difficulties prescribed by the internal arrangement of Sir Giles Scott's [q.v.] new building.

At the same time, working through the standing committee of the curators, the librarian carried through a whole series of revisions, long overdue, affecting the status, stipends, and pensions of the staff, and the financial position of the Bodleian. Also, the compilation of the new catalogue went steadily forward.

One of Craster's greatest services to the library was his *History of the Bodleian Library, 1845-1945,* written after his retirement as librarian and published by the Clarendon Press in 1952. The book is written with learning and authority, and might well have been dull, but is in fact one of the best and most vivacious accounts ever written of a great library.

He was knighted in the year of his retirement from the library (1945). He had taken his doctorate at Oxford, and became an honorary doctor of letters in the Universities of Cambridge, Durham, and Leeds. His later years were passed happily in his Oxford home and in All Souls, where he was at ease. He could look back there on several academic generations and remember many interesting men.

In 1940 he had edited a collection of the political speeches of the statesman who had been elected a Fellow of the college on the same day as he had been, Lord Halifax [q.v.], Chancellor of the University.

Craster's own interests found a centre in the Codrington Library of the college, of which he became librarian in 1946.

March 23, 1959.

Dr. Osbert G. S. Crawford, the archaeologist, died suddenly during the night of November 28/29, 1957 at his home near Southampton. He was 71.

Osbert Guy Stanhope Crawford was born at Bombay on October 28, 1886, the son of C. E. G. Crawford, a Judge in the Indian High Court, and a member of an Ayrshire family with various links with the south. His mother dying shortly after he was born, Crawford spent his early years in the care of his father's sisters, first in London then at East Woodhay, near Newbury. From there he went to Marlborough, his father's old school, for what he later called his "internment": a period which he did not enjoy, though he acknowledged much benefit from contacts with one or two of his teachers, and through F. B. Malim in particular first developed the interest in field-archaeology and the reality of things in the countryside which was to run like a brightly-coloured thread through so much of his later thought and action.

At Oxford, where he found himself rather against his will at Keble, he set out to continue his education on classical lines, but with a growing lack of conviction. His interest in archaeological matters continued and developed as a parallel vocation activity; and it was in the course of this that he came into contact with H. J. E. Peake, who lived near his home at Boxford.

A lifelong friendship resulted; and Crawford never failed to acknowledge the benefits that he had derived from both Peake and his wife. Peake's views certainly helped to guide him in his crucial decision to drop Greats in favour of the Geography Diploma course and a pass B.A. obtained only after various academic vicissitudes. At this time he had begun to make his first contributions to archaeology; and they were on original lines. His diploma thesis was an archaeological field survey of the Andover district, and he also produced in 1911 a distributional study of Early Bronze Age antiquities which anticipated the application of these methods by other scholars in Britain as a means of assessing the strength and direction of early cultural and trading activity.

Archaeological careers outside the classical field were no easy matter in the years before 1914, and though Crawford finally established himself with the Wellcome Expedition to the Sudan under Reisner at Abu Geili, this opportunity was cut short by the outbreak of World War One.

Here, after a spell in the infantry, later developments were anticipated in several ways. Crawford was first of all attached to the survey division of the Third Army as a photographer; and later realized a long-standing ambition to join the R.F.C. when he became an observer, being finally shot down and taken prisoner early in 1918. (It is typical of the man that as occasion offered throughout this time he continued to pursue his archaeological field work, whether at home on leave, or behind the lines in France: during this time he produced the first draft of his important book *Man and His Past*). An attempt to escape preceded the Armistice. After it came another period of uncertainty and odd jobs, one of which took him on a surveying and excavating project into north Wales. Shorts as an article of male attire were not then what they have since become; and Crawford's shorts created a sensation among the lady members of a visiting learned society—as, on occasion, other items of unconventional clothing have tended to do since.

In 1920 appointment by Sir Charles [Arden-] Close [q.v.] as first Archaeology Officer of the Ordnance Survey finally set Crawford's feet on the road for which he was pre-eminently suited: it was as if his previous activities had been undertaken with the deliberate intention of fitting him for the Ordnance Survey's archaeological work. Here, side by side with routine revision aimed at correcting the inaccuracies on the published maps, with very limited help, he set out on the policy of producing "period maps"—maps which should aim at presenting a cartographical picture of Britain at various stages in her history. The best known of the series was the *Map of Roman Britain,* which his successors have recently reissued in a much elaborated and highly successful version. Crawford's work at the Ordnance Survey in this and in other fields was carried out in far from easy circumstances, with inadequate staff and limited facilities; he had to fight for his ideas against unsympathetic official outlook. His methods were not always those best calculated to win over the unconvinced, but the experience did not sour him and he remained usually on good personal terms with people whose official decisions were often against him. It was typical of him, also, that when a last minute evacuation of his Archaeological Branch became necessary under the threat of bombing during the Second World War he should have left until the last his personal library, on which the branch had relied for works of reference that were not at that time in the Survey's library. His books were destroyed; the valuable and irreplaceable records of the branch were saved.

Crawford's official work at the Ordnance Survey set a standard which has not been achieved by any similar organization in the world; and it is gratifying to know that it continues to-day on an enhanced scale. An important element in it was his application of air photography to archaeological work, now accepted and generally recognized as an outstanding contribution to research.

His other achievement was the foundation and maintenance through all the difficulties of war and post-war of his journal *Antiquity*, which now enjoys a universal reputation. *Antiquity* combines in a unique fashion at once the scholarly and the readable; not its least attractive feature has been the pungent direct style of its editor, who has not hesitated on occasion to express himself in forceful terms, whatever the effect on some of his more sensitive readers.

Throughout his working life the period maps and *Antiquity* absorbed most of his creative effort. A feature of his thought has at all times been an originality of approach which has more than once led him to anticipate developments which later have come to be generally accepted.

Crawford's outstanding characteristic was his independence of spirit: he maintained his attitudes regardless of their personal consequences. He did not suffer fools gladly; he abhorred humbug and showed his abhorrence at times with embarrassing clarity. But he was also fair minded, a good friend, and an inspiration to all who knew him.

He was made C.B.E. in 1950 and was an honorary Litt.D. of both Cambridge and Southampton Universities.

November 30, 1957.

Sir Stafford Cripps, Q.C., who died in Zürich on April 21, 1952, three days before his 63rd birthday, was for 20 years one of the most remarkable individual forces in British politics. He had been ill and in a clinic for several months.

He had all the virtues and all the weaknesses of a "man with a mission": utter integrity, an unsparing devotion to the cause he upheld, and great courage; but with these went a native impatience of the restrictions implicit in political action and a tendency to overlook the human factor in any given situation. Having formed his own ideas, it seemed to him a rather burdensome necessity that they should have then to be submitted to the test of facts—and await the decision of minds less competent, less far-seeing than his own.

His intellectual ability was apparent in everything he did. Before he was called to the Bar he established, while still a young man, a considerable reputation as a chemist; then, in his remarkably successful career at the Bar, he displayed a formidable gift for unravelling legal intricacies which brought him attention even when he was a junior; and finally when, from 1947 to 1949, he found himself in command of Britain's economic front, the country soon felt that, whatever his other failings, here was a man equal to his stupendous task.

Richard Stafford Cripps, was born on April 24, 1889, the fifth child and fourth son of Charles Alfred and Theresa Cripps. His father, later the first Lord Parmoor, was of an old, traditionally Conservative family, which had lived for generations at Cirencester; his mother was one of the Potters, a radical north country family of the manufacturing class: Beatrice Potter, afterwards Mrs. Sidney Webb, was her sister. The character of his parents ensured that Cripps was brought up to think and feel seriously on religious and social questions. His mother died when he was only four, but her influence lived after her. She left to her husband a revealing letter, outlining the way in which she would like her children to be brought up: "I should like their living to be of the simplest, without reference to show or other follies. I should like them trained to be undogmatic and unsectarian Christians . . . taking their religious inspiration directly from the New Testament". Again, this time addressing her eldest son, she wrote: "When you grow up you will find heaps and heaps of work of every sort and kind waiting to be done, and never imagine that God has not given you the power to take your share in helping the world to better and nobler things."

These quotations reveal the high seriousness which characterized the men and women of Theresa Cripps's class and generation, and go a long way to account for the unselfconscious dedication to the service of others which was to mark Cripps's actions throughout his life. His education was straightforward: at 12 he followed his father to Winchester, and from there won a chemistry scholarship to New College, Oxford. His papers were so impressive that they were sent to Sir William Ramsay at University College London, and Cripps accepted an invitation to go and work under him. Academic distinctions followed one after the other: at 22 he was part author of a paper on *The Critical Constants and Orthoberic Densities of Xenon,* read before the Royal Society. Cripps was, however, already reading for the Bar: his father was and his grandfather had been distinguished lawyers. In 1913 he was called to the Bar by the Middle Temple and a year later, being medically unfit for the Army, he went to France as a Red Cross lorry driver. He was recalled in the following year for work in the explosives department of the Ministry of Munitions and for a time was assistant superintendent of the Government factory at Queensferry. While there he suffered from the intestinal disease which, in various forms, was to recur throughout his life. Cripps never again enjoyed good health.

In 1919 Cripps returned to the Bar. While still a junior he distinguished himself by his remarkable capacity for hard work: he always knew the smallest details of any case with which he was concerned. In the early twenties he made his name in the Duff Development Company case—which raised complex questions of constitutional law—and so impressed the Colonial Office solicitor that he began at once to brief Cripps in the Privy Council. Similarly he was briefed by the London County Council in the inquiry into railway charges, and his success there led to his employment at the Parliamentary Bar. In 1926 he took silk, and was then the youngest K.C. From then on his reputation grew with each big case in which he appeared, notably patent and compensation cases. It is worthy of note that these were not jury cases, but cases in which his formidable knowledge of the law and extreme lucidity of exposition left him without a rival. He might have been less successful if he had practised in a branch of the law which required that he should appeal to and win over a jury.

While he was building up one of the most lucrative legal practices of the day, Cripps's mind was turning to the wider problems of the world. Again the influence of his father—now Lord Parmoor—was apparent. Not that he shared his father's pacifism during the 1914-18 war; but he was drawn into the "World Alliance to promote international friendship through the Churches", of which his father was a moving spirit. It was characteristic of Cripps that once he attached himself to this movement he became impatient because it did not achieve results overnight. Between 1923 and 1929 he was both the treasurer of the alliance and its most energetic advocate on scores of platforms throughout the country. But the need to see immediate results killed his enthusiasm, and by 1929 he was searching for a fresh instrument, a new outlet, for his missionary zeal.

The year, 1929, is itself significant. In the first Labour Government his father, who had long since abandoned the traditional Conservatism of his family, had accepted the post of Lord President of the Council, and his uncle, Sidney Webb, was appointed President of the Board of Trade. Now the second Labour Government was in office, and Lord Parmoor was again Lord President and Sidney Webb was Colonial Secretary. Moreover, apart from these personal influences, the disorders of the world were too apparent to be ignored. "And what has the organized body of Christians done?" asked Cripps. "Nothing—at least nothing that has had the slightest impact upon the forces of materialism that are responsible for these outrages on civilization". Shortly afterwards a direct approach from Herbert Morrison [later Lord Morrison of Lambeth*] brought him face to face with the choice which his father had already made, and in 1929 Stafford Cripps joined the Labour Party.

Cripps had been a member of the Labour

Party for little more than a year when he was appointed Solicitor-General. A seat was immediately found for him at West Bristol and in January 1931 he was returned to Parliament with a safe majority. He soon made his mark as a skilful advocate, but he had had little opportunity to prove himself before Ramsay MacDonald's decision to form a National Government split the Labour movement and undermined its position in the country. Cripps refused an invitation to serve in the new Government.

For the next four years the Labour Party lived in an atmosphere of crisis. The distrust of Parliamentary institutions which the 1931 crisis had provoked was accompanied, perhaps inevitably, by a revolt against "gradualism". Almost immediately Cripps became the spokesman of those who were prepared, in his own words, to "risk a breakdown while making a rapid change-over to Socialism". As ever, he was impatient for results and intolerant of anything which delayed action. In 1932 he helped to found the Socialist League, a body of Socialist intellectuals who stood clearly on the left of the party: he was its main financial support. Over the succeeding months he was again and again to be publicly associated with its more revolutionary proposals, which included an attack on Parliamentary institutions by "the immediate introduction of an Emergency Powers Act to forestall any sabotage by financial interests" and the abolition of the House of Lords. He sometimes went even farther and embarrassed his party by virulent attacks on the monarchy.

Yet in spite of these indiscretions Cripps's revolutionary fervour gave the Labour Party just the tonic it needed, and in 1934 his popularity among the rank and file was acknowledged by his election to the party's National Executive. This label of respectability was, however, not to stick for long. At the very moment when the Labour Party was breaking with its pacifist past and declaring its support for League of Nations sanctions against Italy, Cripps was arguing more vehemently than ever that "If war comes before the workers in Great Britain have won power, that war will be an imperialistic war". Here was a fundamental difference of opinion, and Cripps resigned from the Executive. At the 1935 annual conference of the party he and those who thought like him suffered a resounding defeat, and it was open to doubt whether Cripps could long remain inside it.

His dissatisfaction with the party ("the trouble is that it has no clear idea of its objectives or strategy") and its impotence in Parliament led him in 1936 to advocate a "British United Front of the Working Class" to defeat the National Government. His energies were now devoted to bringing together the Labour Party, the Communists, and the I.L.P. The Labour Executive did not hold its hand for long. In March 1937 it declared that membership of the Labour Party was incompatible with membership of the Socialist League. The Socialist League was dissolved. A few weeks later the Executive took its second step, announcing that any member of the Labour Party appearing on a public platform with any member of the I.L.P. or the Communist Party would be expelled automatically. Cripps challenged this decision at the 1937 annual conference, but was overwhelmingly defeated. Nevertheless at the same conference the constituency Labour parties returned him to the Executive.

It was in the autumn of 1938, in the Commons debate on the Munich agreement, that a new note began to creep into Cripps's pronouncements on foreign policy. The obvious threat from Nazi Germany was compelling him to a new view of world affairs. The immediate need, he now declared, was "the strength to maintain the rule of law internationally", and the first step to be taken was the removal of Neville Chamberlain's Government from office. He was no longer concerned that it should be replaced by a United Front of the Working Class, for he was now prepared to look for allies among the Liberals and even the dissident Conservatives. So started his advocacy of the Popular Front, inviting "the cooperation of every genuine anti-Government party, or group of individuals". When he publicly announced a programme for a Popular Front campaign, he was asked by the Executive to withdraw it; and on refusing to do so was expelled from the Labour Party.

War came quickly, and as Independent M.P. for West Bristol he used all his personal influence to forward the policies he thought desirable; and it is a tribute to his personal standing that during the summer and autumn of 1939 he was always able to get a hearing, and often a sympathetic hearing, from his political opponents. It was, in fact, with the help of Lord Halifax [q.v.], then Foreign Secretary, that towards the end of 1939 he set out on a world tour. He visited India, Burma, China, Russia, and the United States. It had a double importance, enabling him to explain British war aims to other nations, and giving him that wider view of world affairs which hitherto he had lacked.

Since before the Russo-German pact of August 1939 Cripps's first object had been to prevent Germany and the Soviet Union from becoming actual allies in the field. His visit to Moscow, early in 1940, had convinced him that this could be done, and he returned to England in the early summer of 1940 urging that every effort should be made to win Russia away from the German connexion. He even offered to go himself to Moscow to explore the possibilities of a trade agreement. A few days later, on May 20, 1940, the new British Government under Winston Churchill* invited him to go to Moscow as British Ambassador. He left by aircraft four days later. He was to remain in Moscow until January 1942. It was a vital period in the development of Anglo-Soviet relations, and during it the main obstacles to Anglo-Soviet cooperation were abruptly removed by the German invasion of Russia. Cripps's appointment was not, in fact, an entirely happy one. He had long been under the impression that a convinced socialist like himself would be able to speak to the Soviet leaders in terms they could understand, and so gain their confidence. In fact, he had no such success. Four months after his arrival he had to confess that "there is no development of any sort in our relations with the Soviet Government", and in the succeeding months Cripps found himself more and more isolated from the Russian leaders.

At the end of the year, at the time of Molotov's visit to Hitler in Berlin, Cripps was complaining that he had received only a "very ridiculous" reply to his inquiry about the purposes of the visit. In January the Russians seemed to him "more sphinx-like than ever"; and so the uncertainty continued until June 22, 1941, when overnight Russia and Britain found themselves allies. Cripps was at the time in London and during his visit was sworn a member of the Privy Council. He returned quickly to Moscow, but the second phase of his term as Ambassador did not result in any solid or significant achievements. The pact of mutual assistance, concluded on July 12, 1941, was more a formality than a diplomatic stroke. Late in 1941 Anthony Eden [Lord Avon, d. 1977] arrived in Moscow for his conference with Marshal Stalin [q.v.] and Molotov, which was to mark the beginning of a closer collaboration between the two allies. A few weeks later Cripps returned to England. Although his ambassadorship had not been strikingly successful, Cripps was now a national figure of rather less notoriety and greater reputation than before the war: this was emphasized by a remarkable broadcast which he made soon after his return from Moscow, which captured the popular imagination.

This unexpected success, coupled with the fact that he was a man whose outstanding ability should not be wasted, made it inevitable that he would be given a high post; and in February 1942 he was appointed Lord Privy Seal, Leader of the House of Commons, and a member of the War Cabinet. Again it was an unhappy appointment—for personal reasons. He had a habit of scolding the House and speaking to it rather as a school mistress might to a disobedient class, which caused considerable irritation.

While he was Leader of the House Cripps set off on a new mission—this time to India—which put to the test some of his fondest beliefs of pre-war years. In 1940 he was apt to attribute all the responsibility for India's difficulties to the "British Government's refusal to grant self-government to the Indian people". He now went out as the sincere and enthusiastic advocate of a plan for granting self-government to India "immediately on the cessation of hostilities". In spite of every personal effort he could not persuade the Indian leaders to accept it, but he had translated the Indian problem into terms which the outer world could understand, and the atmosphere in India itself had improved.

On his return from India—his replacement as Leader of the House of Commons being inevitable—Cripps was appointed Minister of Aircraft Production. It was a step down to a lower political rank, and Cripps hesitated before accepting the post. There had been personal differences between him and Churchill which explained his disappearance from the War Cabinet. The temptation to leave the government altogether and regain the careless freedom and irresponsibility of a back-bench critic must have been great. It was typical of Cripps that he chose otherwise. As it turned out, his years at the Ministry of Aircraft Production were outstandingly successful: the man with a mission became the man with an immediate task to be performed, and he performed it supremely well.

This experience fitted him well for the post of President of the Board of Trade, to which he was appointed by Clement [later Lord] Attlee* in July 1945. (Cripps had been readmitted to the Labour Party earlier in the same year). He immediately showed that he took a broad view of his tasks. In his election broadcast he had stressed the importance of efficiency in industry and it was to this that he turned his attention. One of his first actions was the appointment of a "working party" (representing workers and employers and including four independent members as well) to consider the measures needed for the reorganization of the cotton industry. The same pattern was followed for other key export industries. In the summer of 1946 he left his departmental responsibilities to join the mission of three Cabinet Ministers who visited India to seek a peaceful solution of Indian problems. The plan which the mission took with it did not, however, gain complete acceptance: the hostility between the Congress Party and the Muslim League proved insurmountable.

Meanwhile the economic situation at home was deteriorating. There was the fuel crisis in the early months of 1947 and, even more threatening, the ever-increasing dollar deficit. Cripps was still only President of the Board of Trade with a strictly departmental brief. Yet during the summer of 1947 it was he, with his emphasis on increased exports and reduced imports and his call for increased production, who seemed to appreciate the needs of the moment and have the political courage to face them. The legend of "austerity Cripps" began to grow, but however much the people might grumble there could be no doubt that they drew constant reassurance from his frank statement of the facts. It came as no surprise therefore, and as a great relief to the mass of the nation when on October 8, 1947, he was appointed to the new post of Minister for Economic Affairs. A few weeks later Hugh Dalton's* Budget disclosure led to his resignation and Cripps succeeded him as Chancellor of the Exchequer. He was now in a position of unprecedented power and influence.

The essentials of his economic policy, rigid concentration on exports, a carefully worked out system of priorities in the distribution of raw materials designed to bring this about, an austere fiscal policy aimed at checking inflation, and the reduction of Government expenditure, commanded general approval. Cripps, however, was convinced that disaster could be avoided only by the personal effort of every member of the community. He saw clearly that, economic doctrines apart, there was a strict limit to the material incentives which could be offered to managers and workers at a time of general shortage. The profits system could not in itself be a sufficient stimulus to production at a time when scarcely enough was being produced to satisfy the basic needs of the community. Workers must be persuaded to new efforts, in the full knowledge that for a long time to come there would be comparatively little for them to buy with their wages.

Equally, indirect taxation could not be an effective answer to inflation while labour shortages enabled the trade unions to exact higher wages to meet every increase in the cost of living. Even price control, stringent as under Cripps's direction it was, was inadequate to suppress inflation so long as the black market continued, and legislation against the black market could never wholly succeed without becoming totalitarian in character.

The same applied to the control of wages. A general, simultaneous, but discriminating control of wages over the whole of industry would involve a more comprehensive and detailed exercise of power than any Government could undertake without serious risk of becoming undemocratic. Cripps saw, with a clarity unequalled by any of his colleagues, the limitations of legislative and administrative action. He was soberly and rationally convinced that nothing but a process of fundamental moral regeneration would avert calamity.

What were mere pious platitudes in the mouths of others were Cripps's deepest convictions, based not only on his personal faith as a Christian and an Anglican but on a clear and remorseless analysis of social and economic facts. He was convinced that the Government must take the lead in austerity. The cheap money policy of his predecessor at the Treasury, Dalton, had the deliberate purpose of encouraging expenditure by local authorities at a time when every consideration of economic and fiscal expediency demanded economy. This policy he abandoned. In his capacity as coordinator of national economic policy Cripps maintained continuous contact with both sides in industry, fixing production targets and allocating raw materials accordingly. He won the confidence of the business world to a greater extent than any other socialist Minister and he inspired all who worked with him with his own high and exacting sense of duty. It was clear to all who knew him that he had not only an honest regard for the public interest but a clear grasp of what the public interest required, an assumption which could not be so easily made about all his colleagues.

On October 20, 1950, Cripps's resignation was announced. For some time he had clearly been unwell and had already been on leave for two and a half months. He said that he hoped to resume public work some 12 months later, but instead of recovering he grew steadily weaker. The strain of his long years in office—except for a few weeks in the summer of 1945 he had held a public post of one kind or another for more than 10 years—had told heavily on him. He was completely exhausted. It was the price he had to pay for his selfless devotion to public duty.

In 1911 he married Isobel, second daughter of the late Commander Harold Swithinbank. She was a tireless and enthusiastic partner throughout their married life, and Cripps owed much to her constant care and cooperation. She, a son, and three daughters survive him.

April 22, 1952.

Dr. Benedetto Croce, one of the most influential philosophers of the last 40 years, died at Naples on November 20, 1952 at the age of 86. He had suffered a stroke two years earlier but recovered, and his death was due to complications arising from an attack of influenza.

Few figures will loom so high as that of Benedetto Croce in Italy's history since the unification. His long life was a record of unparalleled activity in all the fields which can broadly be called the humanities. An immense erudition, a wide and almost unceasing production, the highest possible quality of scholarship and a peculiar felicity in bringing learning into contact with life: such merits alone would suffice to account for the impact of Croce upon his fellow-countrymen. His unflinching defence of the ideal of liberty during the darkest hours of reaction deserves the gratitude and admiration not only of the Italians but of the civilized world.

Benedetto Croce was born on February 25, 1866, at Pescasseroli, in the Abruzzi, of wealthy middle-class South Italian stock. He received his first education at Naples in strict Roman Catholic and conservative surroundings. In 1883 he lost both his parents in the earthquake of Casamicciola, when he himself was buried in the ruins for several hours and was severely injured. Silvio Spaventa, a relative of the family and an eminent liberal politician, offered the young orphan hospitality in Rome. The years spent in the Italian capital had a decisive influence on the formation of the future philosopher and statesman. At the university, where he read law, Croce was particularly inspired by the teaching of Antonio Labriola, who later became his friend. Thus through many channels did Croce absorb the elements which were to combine into his interpretation of life. Early in his youth he had experienced a religious crisis which led him to abandon the formal practices of the Church, though never to renounce the name of a Christian.

Marxism was revealed to him in the critical version elaborated by Labriola. Hegelism had long been flourishing in South Italy. These different influences were moulded by a strong individual personality as well as by a tradition which, as a South Italian, Croce had, so to speak, in his blood, and which hailed in Vico its master. Philosophy Croce conceived from the start as a means for a better understanding of history. Styling himself an idealist against the prevailing positivism of the late nineteenth century, he vindicated the creative power of man in thought as well as in action. He set himself the task of assessing the cultural heritage of his country and of his generation.

The year 1903 marked the beginning of the constructive period of Croce's activity. In that year the publication of the review *La Critica* was begun. It embodied for a period of nearly half a century the results of Croce's researches and meditations, of his reading of past records as well as of all that was published of any importance in Europe and oversea. Croce's close collaborator in the first years of *La Critica* was Giovanni Gentile; but the friendship between the two men turned to bitter enmity in later days with the political rift over fascism. Another valid collaborator of Croce was a young publisher of Bari, Laterza by name. Casa Editrice Laterza soon came to be respected as one of the most serious among Italian publishing firms. The years 1902-1917 also saw the completion of Croce's philosophical system. That system was set forth in the four volumes of the *Filosofia dello Spirito (Estetica—Logica—Filosofia della Pratica—Teoria e Storia della Storiografia)*. These works were translated into most languages. They established Croce's reputation all over the world. He was awarded an honorary D.Litt. by the University of Oxford in 1923.

Up to the outbreak of the 1914-18 war Croce had kept almost entirely aloof from practical politics. He had been made a Senator of the Kingdom of Italy in 1910 in recognition of his outstanding literary achievements. In 1915 he opposed the intervention of Italy in the war; but he loyally supported his Government in the war effort. As Minister of Public Instruction in Giolitti's Cabinet of 1920 he introduced a Bill for the reform of the education system which had been dominant in Italy since the formation of the Italian state. Paradoxically enough, the reform was carried through only by the fascists. It proved in the end to be one of the most successful obstacles to the thorough indoctrination of Italian youth with fascism.

On the advent of Mussolini in 1922 Croce at first took up a sympathetic attitude. He went into opposition only after the final installation of totalitarianism in 1925, but from that date onwards his rejection of fascism grew more and more uncompromising. He was, however, able to carry on the publication of *La Critica* and with his editorial work. In those years Croce's name and Croce's liberalism became the rallying point of all that was still healthy and enlightened in Italy. He himself, true to his well known dictum that "all history is contemporary history", turned more and more to the work of the historian. His writings on Italian and European history, and especially his *Storia d'Italia dal 1871 al 1915* (1928) and his *Storia d'Europa nel secolo XIX* (1932) partake of historical scholarship as well as of political pamphleteering. Two books on aesthetics and historiography (*La Poesia* (1936)—*La Storia come Pensiero e come Azione* (1938)) gave the final touches to his philosophical construction.

The Axis alliance and the intervention of Italy on the side of Nazi Germany could only appear to Croce, as indeed to the best among his fellow-countrymen, as the final undoing of all that Italy had been building for over a century. He never made any secret of his belief in the allied cause, though deeply partaking of the tragic fate of his people and warning them against the perils of the advancing communist tide. From the day when, in the autumn of 1943, almost at the same time as Mussolini was removed by the Germans, Croce was rescued from the mainland by a British detachment and brought safely to harbour in Capri, the old man was called upon to play a prominent part in the restoration of free institutions in liberated Italy. It is no doubt too soon to say whether that part was always timely and well advised. A Minister without Portfolio in Badoglio's [q.v.] and Bonomi's successive Cabinets, Croce was also the president of the reconstituted Italian Liberal Party. Himself a monarchist, he well saw the folly of King Victor Emmanuel III's refusal to abdicate, and the necessity of creating a moderate, intermediate party between the two extremes of resurgent nationalism and of revolutionary propaganda.

Yet Croce's influence undoubtedly contributed to give the Liberal Party a strongly conservative and anti-clerical bias. He shared the responsibility for the overthrow of Parri's Coalition Government which led to the disruption of the spirit that had animated the movement of Italian resistance in the north. As a member of the Constituent Assembly in 1946-47 Croce severely criticized and opposed the inclusion of the Lateran pacts in the new constitution, the setting up of regional autonomy, as well as the acceptance of the peace terms imposed upon Italy by the allies, which he denounced as unduly harsh and unjust.

Croce's resignation in November 1947 of the presidency of the Liberal Party marked his retirement from active politics. But the almost symbolical meaning of Croce's return to his real and lasting vocation had already been significantly underlined some months before in the foundation of the Istituto Italiano per gli Studi Storici at Naples. The institute was devised to provide and foster postgraduate research in the field of the humanities, of law, and economics. It has its seat in Croce's own palazzo at Naples. Croce retained the presidency of the institute during his last years. There, for the first time in his life, he devoted some of his time to direct teaching and lecturing. There, also, among the admirable collection of books which he assembled, young students, both Italian and foreign, will continue to work in that tradition of truly European civility which Croce himself did so much to enliven and to preserve.

He leaves a widow and four daughters, two of whom are well known in Italy as writers.

November 21, 1952.

Lord Cromer, who was Lord Chamberlain of his Majesty's Household from 1922 to 1938, died suddenly in a nursing home in London on May 13, 1953 at the age of 75.

Son of a greatly distinguished father and in his early days a diplomatist, he became in later life a courtier in the best sense of the word. The office of Lord Chamberlain is anything but a sinecure and he performed its many duties with the conscientiousness and efficiency which were characteristic of him. As censor of plays he was brought into a special relationship with the stage, and, since he exerted the charm of an obvious sincerity and good will, was on excellent terms with the theatrical profession. On his retirement the London managers expressed in an address which they presented to him their "abiding gratitude for the courtesy and patience in which you have never failed, and for the sagacity which you have so constantly exhibited".

In the 1939-45 war, as chairman of the executive committee of the Red Cross and St. John War Organization, he performed excellent work, particularly during the difficult days of its establishment.

The Right Hon. Sir Rowland Thomas Baring, P.C., G.C.B., G.C.I.E., G.C.V.O., second Earl of Cromer, Viscount Errington, of Hexham, Northumberland, Viscount Cromer and Baron Cromer, of Cromer, Norfolk, was born on November 29, 1877. His father, the first Earl, who died in 1917, attained fame as his Majesty's Agent and Consul-General in Egypt and a Minister Plenipotentiary in the Diplomatic Service. His mother was Ethel Stanley, daughter of the late Sir Rowland Stanley Errington, Bt. He was educated at Eton and entered the Diplomatic Service in 1900. In 1902 he was promoted third secretary. Having served at Cairo, Teheran, and St. Petersburg, he was transferred in 1906 to the Foreign Office where, having been promoted second secretary, he was private secretary to two successive Permanent Under-Secretaries of State, Lord Hardinge of Penshurst and Lord Carnock.

On the outbreak of war in 1914 Lord Errington joined the special reserve of the Grenadier Guards and from 1915 to 1916 was A.D.C. to the Viceroy of India, Lord Chelmsford. He was then appointed Equerry in Ordinary and assistant private secretary to King George V, and in 1920, on relinquishing this post, became an Extra Equerry in Ordinary and was created a C.V.O. Meanwhile in 1917 he had succeeded his father. From 1920 to 1921 he was Chief of Staff to H.R.H. the Duke of Connaught during his Indian Mission and, in the following year, to H.R.H. the Prince of Wales* on his visit to India and the East.

Lord Cromer was appointed Lord Chamberlain of his Majesty's Household and sworn of the Privy Council in 1922. It was a position for which he was admirably suited and he continued to discharge its many duties with distinction until 1938, when he was appointed Permanent Lord-in-Waiting to King George VI [q.v.]. He has been a Permanent Lord-in-Waiting to the Queen since August 1952. During his term of office the arrangements for the Silver Jubilee imposed especially heavy duties on him and in recognition of his services on that occasion he was awarded the Royal Victorian Chain.

In 1926 Lord Cromer was elected on the nomination of the First Lord of the Treasury to the Board of the Suez Canal. He also held other important directorships. In 1927 he was created a G.C.V.O. and in 1932 a G.C.B. From 1939 to 1940 he was chairman of the British Red Cross and St. John War Organization, and in the latter year became a private in the 1st Somerset Home Guard. Deeply interested in the work of hospitals, he was president of the

National Hospital for Diseases of the Heart, and chairman of the Cheyne Hospital for Children. A vice-president of the Gordon Memorial College at Khartoum, he was also chairman of King George's Pension Fund for Actors and Actresses, and of the Entertainments National Service Association International Advisory Council. In 1934 he was president of the M.C.C.

He married in 1908 Lady Ruby Elliot, Lady of Grace of St. John of Jerusalem, the second daughter of the fourth Earl of Minto, who is the authoress of *Lamuriac, Unfettered Ways,* and *Such Were These Years.* They had three children, a son and two daughters, and the family honours now devolve upon the son, Viscount Errington, who was born in 1918 and married in 1942 the Hon. Esmée Mary Gabrielle Harmsworth, younger daughter of the second Viscount Rothermere. They have a son and a daughter.

May 14, 1953.

Canon E. C. Crosse, D.S.O., M.C., who died on December 11, 1955 in London at the age of 68, was Headmaster of Ardingly College, Sussex, from 1933 to 1945.

He went there from Shrewsbury, where he had been chaplain for a short time, and before that he had been Headmaster of Christ's College, Christchurch, New Zealand, and assistant master at Marlborough under Sir Frank Fletcher [q.v.] and Sir Cyril Norwood [q.v.].

In the 1914-18 War he had a distinguished record as an Army chaplain at the front in France and Italy, and wrote some pamphlets and books on his work and his experiences there which attracted considerable attention. He had an innate gift for handling boys and young men, winning their confidence as their leader through the readiness with which he built up close and lasting friendships. His experiences in the war and in New Zealand had greatly broadened his outlook on life and through them he was enabled to bring his boys to a fuller and more sympathetic understanding of the modern world and of the part which they might and should play in it. He was an excellent teacher, patient and inspiring, and an even better headmaster, for he was full of confidence and was a wise and courageous leader.

Ernest Courtenay Crosse was born on March 18, 1887, and was educated first at Bedford Grammar School and then at Clifton, where his father had gone before him. From there he won a classical exhibition at Balliol College, Oxford. There he took a second class in Classical Moderations and a second in *Literae Humaniores* in 1910. He was appointed an assistant master at Marlborough in 1911 by the late Sir Frank Fletcher, another old Balliol man, and remained there until the outbreak of war in 1914. He had in the meantime taken orders and he resigned from Marlborough to go on active service. He was appointed a temporary chaplain to the forces early in 1915.

At first he was attached to 8 Division and was soon at the Western Front, where he won for his bravery in action the Military Cross and the Distinguished Service Order and was three times mentioned in dispatches. Soon after he received as well the Croix de Guerre. In 1917 he was promoted to be Senior Chaplain of 7 Division and went with that formation to Italy, where he served through the critical phases of the campaign and up to the final rout of the Austrian Army. He has left an account of this episode of the war in his volume *The Defeat of Austria as seen by the Seventh Division,* which was published in 1920. He also wrote two shorter works on his experiences at the front devoted more to the work he had in hand. Both appeared in 1917, one entitled *The Place and Worth of a Chaplain with the Fighting Troops* and the other *The God of Battles—A Soldier's Faith.* They won the attention not only of chaplains and churchmen but also of soldiers from all parts, for they were written from a chaplain's experiences and devotion to duty and the service of his fellow soldiers.

In 1919 he returned to Marlborough and taught there for two years. He was appointed in 1921 to Christ's College, Christchurch, and having seen much of New Zealand troops in Britain and France he was able to settle down at once to his work there. He made many friends during his nine years there and married Miss Joyce Williams, daughter of Canon A. T. Williams, of Napier Cathedral. They had three sons (of whom two survive) and a daughter.

He resigned his position in 1930 and returned to England, serving for a time as chaplain at Shrewsbury under H. H. Hardy [q.v.] before he was appointed to Ardingly in 1933. He remained there until 1946 when he became Rector of Henley-on-Thames. He held the prebend of Highleigh in Chichester Cathedral from 1944 to 1947.

December 14, 1955.

Sir Edward Crowe, K.C.M.G., who died on March 8, 1960 at the age of 82, had a long and fruitful career in the public service, much of which was spent in the Far East. He was on a visit to his son, Colin Crowe, British Chargé d'Affaires in Cairo, when he died.

Edward Thomas Frederick Crowe, son of A. L. Crowe, sometime British Vice-Consul at Zante, Ionian Isles, was born on August 20, 1877, and educated at Bedford School. He began his career in the Far East in 1897 as a student interpreter in Japan, held appointments at Yokohama, Kobe, and Tamsui, and in 1918 was appointed Commercial Counsellor at the Embassy in Tokyo. From 1924 to 1928 he was seconded for service as Director of the Foreign Division in the Department of Overseas Trade and when in April 1928 Sir William Clark [q.v.], Comptroller of the department, was appointed High Commissioner in Canada, Crowe was chosen to succeed him. During his term of office, which lasted until the autumn of 1937, he rendered important services to British trade and did much to foster commercial relations with the Far East.

Both before his retirement and after he served on many important committees. He was a member of Viscount Goschen's Committee on the Law relating to Trade Marks, Lord Gorell's* Committee on Art and Industry, and of Lord Fleming's Committee on Public Schools. From 1928 to 1937 he was vice-president of the board of governors of the Imperial Institute, and for the same period vice-president of the International Exhibitions Bureau at Paris.

He was president of the Royal Society of Arts from 1941 to 1943, of the Japan Association in 1951-52, of the Old Bedfordian Club from 1938 to 1946, and governor, the Harpur Trust, Bedford, from 1938 to 1945. He was chairman of Croda, Ltd., and a director of W. T. Henley's Telegraph Works Company Ltd., Marconi's Wireless Telegraph Company, and the English Electric Company, Ltd. Crowe was made C.M.G. in 1911, received a knighthood in 1922, and in 1930 was advanced to K.C.M.G.

He married in 1901 Eleanor, daughter of W. H. Lay, H.B.M. Consul at Chefoo, China, by whom he had two sons and a daughter. His wife died in 1947.

March 9, 1960.

Crown Princess of Norway—See **Norway.**

Former Bishop of Croydon—See **Woods.**

R. J. Cruikshank, C.M.G., who died on May 14, 1956 at his home in London at the age of 58, had been editor of the *News Chronicle* from 1948 to 1954 and was widely respected and liked as a journalist who distinguished himself in Fleet Street and as a foreign correspondent in America. Since his resignation he had borne with fortitude a long and distressing illness.

Robert James Cruikshank was born in London on April 19, 1898, of a Northern Ireland father and a Kentish mother. They were poor and "Robin" (as he was known to his many friends) Cruikshank did not have a formal education. He was a great reader from his youth onwards and he had a catholic range of interests. Shortly before the 1914-18 War he joined the *Bournemouth Guardian* as a reporter, and he returned to that paper after serving in the Army. The great promise of his work attracted the attention of a veteran south coast journalist, Borthwick, who recommended him to the then news editor of the Liberal *Daily News.* Having begun as a reporter and then taken charge of the features page, he was sent to the United States in 1928.

His seven years in America won him a reputation as a serious, perceptive observer of the complicated political and social scene, and a writer who did not allow speed to be an excuse for neglecting style. He returned as assistant editor of his paper, which by then had amalgamated with the *Daily Chronicle,* and in 1936 he was appointed editor of its evening partner, the *Star.* This post he held until 1941, when he was called away as Director of the American Division of the Ministry of Information, and then as Deputy Director-General of the British Information Services in the United States. Not all journalists found translation to the Civil Service agreeable, but Robin Cruikshank made the best of both worlds. He brought to his public duties the energy, the integrity, and the sense of humour that buoyed him up in his professional career. He was appointed C.M.G. in the Victory Honours and was released to resume his work in Fleet Street.

He became editor of the *News Chronicle* and a director of Daily News Ltd. in 1948, and he had already done good work as a governor of the Old Vic and a delegate to the Sub-commission on Freedom of Information of the Human Rights Commission of the United Nations.

These diverse activities did not prevent him from continuing to write books. *The Double Quest*, 1936, had shown that as an author no less than as a journalist he was worth reading on American affairs. This was followed by *Roaring Century* in 1946, *The Liberal Party* in 1949, *Charles Dickens and Early Victorian England* in the same year, and *The Moods of London* in 1951. Cruikshank would be absorbed in each theme as he took it up, and his enthusiasm for it came infectiously through to readers. A happy disposition and a complete absence of pomposity endeared him to colleagues in his own and other newspapers and to acquaintances in all walks of life.

He married, in 1939, Margaret Adele, daughter of Dr. J. A. MacKnight, of California, who survives him together with two daughters of the marriage.

May 15, 1956.

Though the name of **Ely Culbertson,** who died at Brattleboro, Vermont, at the age of 64 in December 1955 is best known not as an expert, but as *the* expert on contract bridge, he had other aspects of his character and other activities which he himself considered of greater moment.

Ely Culbertson was born on July 22, 1891, in Romania, the son of an American oil prospector and the daughter of a Russian general. He spent his early years mostly in Russian Caucasia, but studied literature and the social sciences at Geneva University and L'École des Sciences Économiques et Politiques in Paris. After getting into trouble with the Tsarist Government as a revolutionary, he left Russia and finally arrived in the United States in 1922, already well to do as his father had made money out of his oil prospecting. In the intervals of studying at American universities, he played agitator and hobo from the Rockies to Mexico, and in 1923 he married Josephine Murphy, a notable bridge player and author and lecturer on the game.

[Mrs. Culbertson died on March 23, 1956].

For years they made an almost unbeatable partnership and, having perfected the approach system of auction, extended it to contract bridge as the forcing system. The Culbertson articles, books, and lectures on bridge attained an unprecedented popularity, which extended far beyond the territories of the United States and, after the celebrated month of play in 1930-31 between the Culbertsons on the one side and Lenz and Jacoby (Jacoby was replaced by Winfield Liggett, jun., during play) on the other, which the Culbertsons won by 8,980 points, they were supreme in the bridge world.

The large fortune Culbertson made from his writing and lecturing on bridge he largely devoted to advocating schemes of social betterment, and before the end of the last war he evolved a plan for world federation. Towards the end of his life, indeed, he devoted more of his time, energy and money to these causes then he did to the pastime which had made his name famous throughout most of the western world. So was the circle of his life completed. He had begun as a social reformer, branded by the Tsarist Government as a revolutionary, and he ended as a social reformer, his youthful impetuosity mellowed by age and experience.

December 29, 1955.

Dr. Winifred Cullis, Professor Emeritus of Physiology in the University of London, and vice-president of the British Federation of University Women, of which she was president in 1925-29, died suddenly in London on November 13, 1956 at the age of 81.

Winifred Clara Cullis was born at Gloucester on June 2, 1875, the younger daughter of Frederick John Cullis. She was educated at King Edward VI's High School for Girls, Birmingham, and Newnham College, Cambridge, where she was Professor Sidgwick Scholar. She took the Natural Sciences Tripos, Cambridge, Part I in 1899 and Part II in 1900, and in the following year she was appointed demonstrator in physiology at the London (Royal Free Hospital) School of Medicine for Women. In 1903 she became lecturer, and in 1912 was appointed head of the Department of Physiology in place of Dr. T. Brodie. In 1919 the University of London conferred on her the title of Professor of Physiology.

The fullness of Winifred Cullis's life may be gauged by reviewing the numerous activities she took in her stride. Among these were lectures for the National Health Society, and the National Society for Combating Venereal Disease, broadcast lectures in the B.B.C. schools' programme, courses of lectures on physiology at the London School of Economics, and extension lectures for the University of London. Her wonderful personality and her brilliance as a teacher and lecturer were recognized internationally and she received a number of invitations to lecture abroad. Those which she was able to accept included an invitation from the University of Toronto to act as Professor of Physiology, for the winter session 1917-18, in place of the late Professor T. Brodie.

The following year she gave the Ellen Richards Memorial Lecture at Vassar College, United States, and this foundation later conferred on her an LL.D. *honoris causa.* Also in that same year (1919) she was sent by the Colonial Office to Gibraltar and Malta to lecture to the troops, and for her services in this connexion she was appointed O.B.E. In 1929 she was promoted C.B.E. in recognition of her continued public services. In 1936 the Government of South Australia invited her to attend the Centennial Conference at Adelaide, and in 1937 she was a member of the British delegation to the meeting of the Indian Association for the Advancement of Science.

During the last war she travelled extensively for the Ministry of Information. Before Japan came into the war, she crossed the United States to Japan and proceeded thence to China, the East Indies, Australia and New Zealand, following an extensive lecture programme *en route.* Later she visited Canada, and she also paid two visits, each of some months' duration, to the United States, where she was head of the women's section of the British Information Services. Shortly after the war the R.A.F. invited her to undertake a flying tour of their establishments in Cairo and East Africa, where she gave a series of stimulating and instructive lectures, and helped most successfully to relieve some of the monotony of post-war service life.

Professor Cullis enjoyed these lecture tours immensely, but it is certain that always in the front of her mind were her two abiding interests—physiology and her work to assist in securing for professional women an equal status with men. In furthering this latter aim (to secure for women equality of status) she felt it was of utmost importance that university women should cooperate, and thus she was one of the founders of the British Federation of University Women, as well as of the International Federation, and she played a constant and leading part in the work of these federations from their inception.

Winifred Cullis had great qualities of both mind and heart. She was a loyal, generous, and devoted friend; and though a shrewd judge of people was also very tolerant and kindly. She possessed sound common sense and a high moral courage, and would fight with pertinacity for what she felt was right.

Her beautiful speaking voice and charm of manner were great assets; and the speed with which she established a friendly atmosphere between herself as lecturer and the members of a large and heterogeneous audience was little short of miraculous. Moreover, she did far more than stir up a passing interest in a cause; she had the gift of inspiring in others an enthusiasm which declared itself in long and patient work.

Her name is perpetuated in the Winifred Cullis Lecture Fellowship of the British-American Association, and her memory will long be cherished.

November 15, 1956.

Arthur John Cummings, who died on July 4, 1957 in a London nursing home after a long illness, established a great reputation as political editor, leader writer, and columnist on the *News Chronicle* in the years between the two World Wars. He was an ardent Liberal and although many of his views found little favour with the leaders of the other political parties they were always accepted as a sincere expression of a faith which few journalists of his generation interpreted with greater clarity.

It was a great blow to him when the split between the followers of Asquith and Lloyd George shattered the fortunes of his party but he never swerved in his own beliefs. When he retired in 1955 his editor and great friend, R. J. Cruikshank [q.v.], wrote that he was essentially a patriot journalist of the Hazlitt and William Cobbett type who never minded what enemies he made if he knew his cause to be good.

Cummings was born at Barnstaple the son of a highly respected Devon journalist and had it not been for his father's breakdown in health he would probably have adopted the law as his career. Instead, he joined the staff of the *Devon and Exeter Daily Gazette* as a Jack-of-all-trades reporter. He undertook everything from leader writing to musical criticism and sometimes delivered pronouncements on the state of the stock markets. Later he left the West and went to Sheffield and then after four years on the Western Front joined the *Yorkshire Post* as an assistant editor.

His association with the *Daily News* and afterwards with the *News Chronicle* began in 1920 and lasted for more than 35 years. It was a difficult period for Liberal journalists but Cummings established an international reputation by the great vigour he showed in tackling the problems of the time. He was probably at the height of his powers in the early 1930s. In 1931 he toured the United States for his paper and a year later attended the Economic Conference at Ottawa, from which his dispatches were widely read. In 1933 he was at the Reichstag Fire Trial in Germany and at the trial of the British engineers at Moscow.

He was one of the two English journalists who were granted permission by the Russian Embassy in London to report the case, and the book which he afterwards wrote caused a lively controversy. The primary object of the book was to describe at first hand an extremely dramatic experience: and in this he succeeded admirably. But when he came to discuss the background of the case he was not so successful. As a Liberal he found the Soviet dictatorship extremely distasteful, disliking its harshness, its narrow-mindedness, and its ignorance of the outside world; but as an English Liberal he was also convinced that most of what he had read in the opposition newspapers at home was grossly exaggerated, if not actually invented. He was convinced that not only the British Press, but the British Ambassador, the Foreign Office, and the Government completely lost their heads and that the only sane and cool-headed people in Moscow were himself, a few American correspondents, and last, but not least, the Soviet Government. In the months preceding the outbreak of war in 1939 Cummings strove to warn the nation of the peril ahead, and when the war came his "Spotlight" column was read by politicians of every shade with tremendous interest, although many of them disagreed violently with the views he expressed.

In 1953 the Institute of Journalists chose Cummings as its president. When he delivered his presidential address in November the Press Council had just begun its work and he declared his support for it. In the same speech he deplored the increasing Parliamentary tendency to raise questions of privilege. Privilege, he declared, was a word which hung threateningly over the heads of the conductors of the press and there was something prophetic in his remark that there was a risk of making Parliamentary privilege a future excuse for pompous or frivolous claims which would make it exceedingly hard for the press and other commentators to indulge effectively, if at all, in many forms of necessary or legitimate criticism.

He married Nora, daughter of Arthur Suddards, by whom he had a son—now a successful political cartoonist—and a daughter. Cummings was the brother of Bruce Frederick Cummings (W. N. P. Barbellion), to whose remarkable book *The Journal of a Disappointed Man* he wrote an introduction.

July 6, 1957.

Homer S. Cummings, who died on September 10, 1956 in Washington at the age of 86, was Attorney General of the United States under President Franklin D. Roosevelt from 1933 to the end of 1938.

He was not originally designated for that post when President Roosevelt completed his selections for his first Cabinet and it was then intended that he should go to the Philippine Islands as Governor. But before the Cabinet took Office Senator Walsh, of Montana, who had been first choice for the post of Attorney General, died and Cummings was invited to take his place as a temporary appointment until a suitable successor could be found. He soon proved to be so successful in the administration of the Department of Justice at Washington that he remained there for over five years.

When he accepted office gangs of terrorists, which had thriven largely on their profits from the illicit liquor trade under prohibition, were at the height of their power and had spread a reign of terror all over the country by their internecine battles with one another and their unscrupulous methods of holding large sections of the community up to ransom. The Department of Justice, of which Cummings was the head, could deal with crime only in so far as it involved breaches of federal laws or movements from one state to another. So the detection and punishment of crime were left mainly to local authorities who were hampered by a diversity of laws and procedure and the difficulty of bringing wrongdoers back to face trial.

Cummings at once began to take a much wider view of his responsibilities and powers than any of his predecessors and stepped in boldly to arrest and prosecute criminals who had in the slightest way offended against the federal laws in such matters as taxes, use of the mails, robbery of banks or fleeing from one state to another. Before long some of the most notorious gangsters were imprisoned in federal penitentiaries for long terms for failure to pay income tax. Cummings also increased and strengthened the police force of his department, enrolling a large number of young men of university education and dauntless courage. They were specially trained for their work in every way, equipped with firearms and instructed to shoot to kill when dealing with the most desperate criminals. This force soon became popularly known through the films as the "G-Men", or Government men. They prepared lists of those who were particularly wanted for their criminal activities and before long most of these were either dead or in prison.

Though his successful campaign against crime was the most notable part of his work at the Department of Justice it was by no means all. Cummings was also the chief legal adviser to the Cabinet on all matters pertaining to the legislation required to put into effect the proposals of the New Deal. He had also, when that legislation was attacked in the courts, to prepare for its defence, and though he had an able staff of subordinates to help him in this work he often appeared in the Supreme Court in person to argue the Government's case.

Before he went to Washington to join the Cabinet Cummings was known as a successful lawyer in the town of Stamford, Connecticut, and as a Democratic politician who had more than once taken a leading part in the business of the national party conventions and their inner committees. He had been a candidate for election to the House of Representatives in 1902 and for the Senate in 1916, but was beaten each time, for Connecticut had been for many years a Republican stronghold. He was temporary chairman of the party convention in San Francisco in 1920 when Roosevelt was nominated for the vice-presidency. Four years later he was chairman of the committee on resolutions at the Democratic Convention held in New York, and at the Convention in Chicago in 1932 he led the delegates who were pledged to secure the nomination of Roosevelt, and quickly won the whole assembly of delegates to his side.

Homer Stillé Cummings was born in Chicago on April 30, 1870. After attending Yale, where he graduated in law in 1893, he settled at Stamford, Connecticut, remained in practice there until he became Attorney General, and returned after his resignation in 1939. He was mayor of the town for three terms, between 1900 and 1906, and for nine years Corporation Counsel, or legal adviser to the town council. Later he was for 10 years State Attorney for Fairfield County, Connecticut.

He took a lively interest in local affairs, particularly trade, prisons, and the enforcement of the law. He was the leading Democrat in the state and for many years its representative at the national conventions of the Democratic Party, but until the era of the Roosevelt administration his party was always in a minority in the state.

While he was in practice at Stamford, he acted as counsel in several legal cases which attracted wide interest.

In 1937 he published, in collaboration with Carl McFarland, *Federal Justice,* a history of the Department of Justice in Washington, of which he had then been head for more than four years. Later in that year appeared *We Can Prevent Crime* and in 1939 *The Tired Sea.*

In 1893 he married Miss Cecilia Waterbury. She died in 1939, and in 1942 he married secondly Miss Julia Alter.

September 13, 1956.

Frédéric Joliot-Curie and **Irène Joliot-Curie** —See **Joliot-**

J. M. Curley died on November 12, 1958 in Boston.

James Michael Curley, generally described as the last of the big "city bosses", died in the city which had been the scene of so many triumphs and disasters during a picturesque political career of half a century. He would have been 84 in a week, and had shown every sign of recovering from a recent abdominal operation, described in his fulsome language as "just another campaign"—and the Democratic landside in the previous week's election had acted as a spur to his fighting spirits.

Nearly two years before, he made an astonishing recovery from another operation and boasted that he would live to 125—as Mayor of Boston, his favourite office—but he had a relapse and a team of seven doctors could not save him. The last rites were administered by one of his sons, Father Francis Curley, of the Jesuit Order.

Politics and litigation were as meat and wine to the irrepressible Curley, the son of poor Irish immigrants whose descendants, largely under the impetus of his colourful personality, were to rise to the dominant position they now hold in local affairs. Only in the summer he was unsuccessfully seeking an injunction against the film version of the novel *The Last Hurrah* on the grounds that it was an invasion of his private life; its Boston author has denied that his book had anything to do with Curley—though it certainly seems difficult to portray a Boston politician and wholly avoid him. He served four times as mayor, three terms as a congressman in Washington, and once as Governor of Massachusetts; when he was not winning elections he was losing them and a Republican-minded legislature was accused many years ago of passing a single term law solely to prevent Curley from becoming the perennial Mayor of Boston.

Some say that he never had a machine but rose by sheer force of personality, a knowledge of other men and understanding of his Irish people, who had come to the promised land to be confronted with placards on the mill gates "No Irish need apply". In 1902, at any rate, he formed a "Tammany club" in Boston which became a power in local politics before its dissolution and saw him in 1910 returned to Congress from which he resigned four years later to serve his first term as mayor.

These were the days when the Irish had just begun to fight and they gloried in his verve and the simulated Oxford accent with which he gibed at the "royal purple" living in the big houses on Beacon Hill. Leaving school at the age of 16, he worked as a grocer's clerk to help support his widowed mother, but by dint of his own efforts he became known as one of the best read men in Massachusetts.

His speeches were peppered with quotations from the classics with which he was widely conversant; his resonant dramatic voice was cultivated as a youth from appearances in Dion Boucicault plays at the Dudley Street opera house in Boston. In later years he would often speak of his rise from the "shanty Irish" quarter in which he was born as an example of what could be done by hard work.

He was frequently in trouble with the law and was twice sent to prison—the first time as a young alderman of 20 for taking a postman's examination in someone else's name. Campaigning for re-election from prison he dwelt on the lengths to which he would go for a friend and was returned by a large majority.

In 1946 he was convicted in Washington on a charge of fraud arising from his connexion with a firm of so-called engineering consultants who undertook to secure Government contracts for their clients and collected fees of $60,000 (some £21,600) for unrendered services. Curley, then serving one of his terms as mayor, waged a long legal battle to escape an 18-month sentence; while on bail he returned to Boston to be greeted by a huge crowd of admirers and a brass band playing "Hail the Conquering Hero" on which he remarked: "These things exhilarate you, they cheer you up".

On losing a final appeal on grounds of ill-health he stated in court, "You are sentencing me to death"—and a few days before he had sought and received the last rites of the Roman Church. President Truman* commuted the sentence a few months later and Curley returned to resume office in Boston; the city clerk who had served as temporary mayor ran against his chief in a later campaign and beat him.

In his day, of course, Curley was a power in the Democratic Party and was one of the earliest supporters in Massachusetts of Franklin Roosevelt. He led a Roosevelt slate in the Democratic primary of 1932 against the more numerous supporters of Al Smith and having been beaten appeared at the party convention with a *lei* round his neck as an official delegate of Puerto Rico—a feat which he never explained.

He had looked as a reward for his services to a Cabinet post or the American Embassy in either Ireland or Italy, and rejected Roosevelt's offer of the ambassadorship to Poland. Through the years he was constantly involved in law suits, often for alleged libel, and was once directed by the Supreme Court of Massachusetts to pay $500 a week to the city treasury in respect of $42,000 judged to have been taken in graft.

By this time Curley was occupying a fashionable mansion in Jamaica Way, where in later life he browsed in his well-stocked library, advised political leaders, and schooled his sons in the arts of oratory and rhetoric. But when his political fortunes ebbed he was always ready to move back to the thickly populated west end from which he rose.

After serving a term as governor from 1924 he was beaten in three successive elections by members of patrician families which he had so often chided; an attempt to enter the United States Senate was defeated by the youthful Cabot Lodge, to whom he referred in his speeches as "little boy blue".

It was characteristic of him that on retiring from the governor's mansion he married for a second time on the morning of his successor's inauguration.

Curley came back strongly during the last war and was again elected to Congress; in 1945, at the age of 71, he was returned to a fourth term as mayor of Boston, an office that had seen the peak of his power.

November 13, 1958.

Lionel Curtis, C.H., Fellow of All Souls, Oxford, the most distinguished exponent in Britain of federalist ideas and of the concept of a world state, died at his home at Kidlington, near Oxford, on November 24, 1955 at the age of 83.

Of strong and all but wilful personality, heroically single-minded, he exercised a shaping influence upon some of the principal events in the evolution of the British Empire into the British Commonwealth. At no period of his career did Curtis occupy an outstanding public position; his activities were largely behind the scenes of public life. His power lay indeed in his personal enthusiasm and persuasiveness rather than in any gift of popular leadership. Possessed by an unbounded zeal for the causes which he made his own, most notably for the cause of Imperial federation (which in later years he preferred to call organic union), he threw himself into the task of prosecuting them with complete self-abandonment and with a commanding vigour which pressed the best energies of his friends, whether they would or no, into his service. In thus enlisting their aid he had no thought of recognition either for himself or for them. So long as the practical aim he had in mind was realized, it was a matter of complete indifference to him that his personal contribution, which was so often the decisive factor, remained unknown to the world at large. Grave in demeanour, relentless in enthusiasm, his appearance suggested the possession of prophetic powers. As a writer he will be best remembered for the three volumes of his *Civitas Dei.*

Lionel George Curtis was born on March 7, 1872, in a deeply religious home and was educated at Haileybury and at New College, Oxford. Though he graduated in the honours school of *Literae Humaniores,* his academic career was not specially distinguished, nor perhaps was he ever to be a true scholar. He formed close and enduring friendships, however, with such men as Lionel Hichens and Richard Feetham and remained throughout his life a devoted son of his college. His first contact with public affairs was as private secretary to the Rt. Hon. Leonard Courtney, M.P. (later Lord Welby), in the latter's capacity of chairman of the London County Council. Twice during this employment—partly under the guidance of Octavia Hill, to whom he often paid warm tribute in later years—Curtis set himself the task of gaining experience of the working of the Poor Law by assuming the guise of a tramp and begging on the highroads and sleeping in workhouses. The earnestness of the undertaking was characteristic of the times and of the man.

Studies of this type, however, were interrupted in 1899 by the South African War. He enlisted in the City Imperial Volunteers, saw some fighting, and served until the occupation of Pretoria in 1900. This was the period when Lord Milner* was gathering about him the band of young Oxford men who were to become known as the "Kindergarten". Curtis, as one of Milner's private secretaries, became an early member. His first administrative task was to organize the beginnings of municipal self-government, under a nominated council, in Johannesburg. In March 1901 he was appointed acting town clerk, an office in which, in spite of an amusing oversight now and then, he showed conspicuous ability.

His next appointment was as Assistant Colonial Secretary of the Transvaal in charge of Local Government. He held that position until 1907 (by which time he had been called to the Bar by the Inner Temple) and then resigned in order to devote himself, as a member of the nominated Upper House of the Transvaal Legislature, to the movement towards South African union. Curtis displayed the most astonishing energy and resource in furthering the plan of unification of the four separate colonies—a plan from which every principle of his subsequent faith in world peace through federal union is derived. He formed a number of "closer union" societies and, with Philip Kerr, afterwards Lord Lothian, founded *The State,* a monthly journal. And he himself drafted a document in which he presented the case for organic union in South Africa. This, after considerable modification, was adopted by Lord Selborne (who had succeeded Milner) and became known as the Selborne Memorandum. Curtis was content to have made the initial move and had no part in the subsequent Convention.

His work in South Africa accomplished, he was led to apply the experience he had gained there to the Empire as a whole. For the next 30 years, in season and out of season, Curtis preached the doctrine of imperial federation, urging the need for a constitution which would unite Britain and the self-governing Dominions in a new Commonwealth entity; and then, for the rest of his life, he advocated a still wider federal unity in the approach to a world State. Meanwhile, assisted by Philip Kerr, its first editor, and others, he founded the *Round Table* as a quarterly journal for the dissemination of Liberal-imperialist ideas. He remained to the last a member of the editorial committee of that publication.

In 1912 he was appointed Beit Lecturer in Colonial History at Oxford. The outbreak of war in 1914 gave fresh point and emphasis to his plea for an imperial Parliament, and in 1916 he published what was intended as the first part of an ambitious work, *The Commonwealth of Nations* (this marked the first recorded use of the term), in which he argued his federalist case to impressive purpose. The work was prepared in consultation with his friends of the "Kindergarten" and with the Round Table groups overseas; but they would not accept it as an expression of their collective opinion, and it appeared eventually under Curtis's name alone.

In the years after the Treaty of Versailles Curtis's studies and labours were unremitting. He was largely instrumental in promoting and raising funds for the Royal Institute of International Affairs, in which he retained until the end a close and active interest.

The fruits of his conscientious application to the problem of India appeared in the volume entitled *Dyarchy,* published in 1920; Curtis's contribution to the recommendations of the Montagu-Chelmsford report was, without doubt, considerable. Elected a research Fellow of All Souls College, Oxford, he established himself in his permanent home at Kidlington. But there was still work for him to do in varied fields abroad.

After India Curtis addressed himself to the Irish question and was summoned from Oxford to be secretary to the British delegation which negotiated the Irish Treaty, remaining as adviser on Irish affairs at the Colonial Office until 1924. Next he turned to China, paid a prolonged visit to the Far East, and in 1932 Curtis produced *The Capital Question of China.*

The phase of personal exploration ended, Curtis settled down to the writing of *Civitas Dei,* which he published in three volumes between 1934 and 1937. His object was to discover "a guiding principle in public affairs", and to this end he surveyed the main currents of human history. The course of history, he sought to show, was ultimately guided by human beliefs, and in a closely packed study he envisaged the growth of the commonwealth ideal into a society transcending the limits of nationality. The book was open to criticism by both historians and theologians, but there was no mistaking the author's fire and sincerity. From this point onwards Curtis returned with unabated vigour to his imperial and federalist doctrines.

Inevitably, after years of single-minded preaching and propaganda they had lost something of their freshness; nor did the arguments he employed in favour of creating without delay a supra-national state in the West always strengthen his otherwise cogent illustration of the anarchy which the continued existence of sovereign states threatened.

But the outbreak of war in 1939 served only to confirm and deepen his faith. During the war years he published several pamphlets, in which the ideal of a federal United States of the World beckoned ever more brightly to him, and followed them up in the years of peace with further essays on the same theme. Criticisms that, on the most obvious practical grounds, the time for a world State was not yet he met with insistent warnings of disaster. But the most notable production of his last years was a volume, *With Milner in South Africa* (1951), consisting largely of transcripts of the diary-letters he wrote from South Africa to his mother in England, which in its youthful zest and curiosity makes the happiest reading. Two years before, to the great pleasure of his friends and of all who knew of his real achievement, the award of the Companionship of Honour was conferred on him. Other distinctions would have meant little, but with this he was delighted because it had also been bestowed upon his great friend, Lord Lothian.

In 1920 he married Patricia, youngest daughter of the late Prebendary Scott, of Tiverton.

November 25, 1955.

Dr. Ernst Robert Curtius, one of the most learned literary historians in Europe, died in Rome on April 19, 1956, less than a week after his seventieth birthday.

Born on April 14, 1886, he received his early education at the Protestant gymnasium at Strasbourg and then studied at Berlin and Heidelberg. He held teaching posts successively at Marburg, Heidelberg, and Bonn in which the breadth and depth of his learning quickly became evident and attracted students. Though through these he has exercised wide influence, his written work has been and will continue to be of considerable significance. Quite early in life he realized that the main stream of European culture flowed from Rome, so it is all of a piece with the development of his thought that his earliest published works should be preponderantly concerned with French literature and thought.

There appeared in 1919 *Die Literarichen Wegberieter des Neuen Frankreich,* the chapters of which were lectures Dr. Curtius had delivered at Bonn before the 1914-18 War, brought up to date. It is significant in that few Germans at that period made any attempt to appraise, as Dr. Curtius appraised, French literature between 1871 and 1919, and it is a feat of great sympathetic understanding.

There followed volumes on Balzac and Maurice Barrès, and in 1925 another major study entitled *Französischer Geist im Neuen Europa,* in which Proust's work receives appreciative attention; and there is, in another of the essays comprising the book, a suggestively drawn comparison between Paul Valéry and Hölderlin. Another admirable study of French culture was published in 1930 stressing its Roman origin.

Many years of work went to the making of his great study, *Europäische Literatur und Lateinisches Mittelalter,* which appeared in 1948 and was translated into English in 1953. The range of reading displayed is formidable. From Homer to Valéry and Eliot*, Dr. Curtius seems to have read everything in six or seven languages with an appreciation of all their many echoes, not only of the classical authors but of those medieval Latinists whose names even are hardly a memory to-day. Thus when he reads John Donne he is reminded of Abelard and Sidonius Apollinaris.

A trick of versification in Calderon is shown to be common form with Walafrid Strabo and his Carolingian contemporaries and—striking detail—the Latin motto over the door of the Globe Theatre in Southwark in 1599 read: *"Totus mundus agit histrionem"*, and soon a play was shown there containing the phrase "All the world's a stage". Whence came the motto? From some Roman classic? No, Dr. Curtius tells us, it comes from a work of varied learning and philosophy composed by John of Salisbury in 1159. And so Dr. Curtius has driven home his lesson that to be a European one must have become *civis Romanus.*

April 21, 1956.

Lady Curzon of Kedleston, G.B.E., widow of the first and last Marquess Curzon of Kedleston, K.G., P.C., G.C.S.I., G.C.I.E., died on June 29, 1958.

She was Grace Elvina, daughter of J. Monroe Hinds, sometime United States Minister in Brazil, and she married first Alfred Duggan, a South American of considerable fortune. There were two sons and a daughter of the marriage.

Her marriage to Curzon (whose first wife had died in 1906) took place in 1917. "When you read before long in the papers", wrote Curzon to Lord Lamington in December 1916, "that I am going to marry Mrs. Duggan, pray believe that I am doing a wise thing which will make us both happy and brighten my often desolate life."

His hopes were abundantly fulfilled. His wife, a woman of elegance and great beauty—which shines forth from Sargent's portrait now in the Tate Gallery—came, saw, and conquered English high society, and Curzon's house became once more a centre of brilliant social life; it also became the scene of fateful and historic gatherings.

They were indeed a superb pair. If she was beautiful, she was also kindly and good natured and her graceful companionship meant much to her husband. It was his habit wherever he might be to unburden himself in letters which were a mixture of high politics, tender affection, and warm self-revelation. How well she understood him—and his was a complex character that long baffled his contemporaries—is made plain in her *Reminiscences* which appeared in 1955. Him they showed to be an extraordinary, a very human, and by no means a superior person in the sneering sense of the expression. Herself was revealed as a woman of charm and gentle wit.

July 1, 1958.

The Right Rev. Charles Edward Curzon, D.D., Bishop Suffragan of Stepney from 1928 to 1936, and Bishop of Exeter from 1936 to 1948, died on August 23, 1954 in hospital in London. He was 76.

He was born in 1878, the son of Edward Curzon, of Kensington, and was educated at Lancaster Grammar School and at Christ's College, Cambridge, where he won a Tancred Studentship in Divinity in 1897. He graduated in 1900 with a Second Class in the Classical Tripos. After further study at Sarum Theological College he was ordained in 1901 to the curacy of St. Andrew's, Fulham, and remained there some three years. He left it in 1904 to undertake secretarial and organizing work for the Additional Curates' Society. His first incumbency was at St. Oswald's, Millhouses, Sheffield, where he was vicar from 1908 to 1916. In 1917 he became Vicar of Goole, and in 1920 he returned to London to take up the important post of secretary of the London Diocesan Fund. His work there was marked by vigour and ability, and continued until 1926, when he was appointed Vicar of St. Barnabas, Kensington.

In October 1928 he was consecrated Bishop Suffragan of Stepney and presented to the rectory of St. Margaret's, Lothbury. At the time of consecration all six of his predecessors were still living—an unusual and probably unique state of affairs. His work in Stepney was hard, and his clergy had good cause to appreciate his full understanding of their special troubles and difficulties. In this his practical experience of parochial work was of much assistance to him. He was particularly earnest in his work among the large Jewish population of the East End, and his special duties demanded much tact and understanding, but his sympathies with Jewry both at home and abroad never failed him, and he was held in warm affection by many Jewish friends.

In 1936 he received the Lambeth doctorate and was appointed to the See of Exeter on the death of the Right Rev. Lord William Rupert Ernest Gascoyne-Cecil, D.D. He soon showed that he was not only an able administrator, of curiously all-round competence though with special gifts in financial matters, but a man who brought keen spiritual insight and shrewd constructive common sense to bear on a great variety of Church spheres and problems. Perhaps he was most deeply interested in youth work and moral welfare, for he was concerned with the social and recreational needs of youth and with the "right" of young people "to be protected from books which may poison the mind".

He was a quiet, simple, "matter of fact" speaker, with a gift of dry humour, but his sincerity and directness, even his understatements, could be at times profoundly moving. He was an inspiring leader in war-time, praising and strengthening the courage of the common man and woman; comforting the bereaved; himself quite undismayed by the great loss of churches and other property in Plymouth; inspiriting all with his own faith that God would defend the cause of human dignity and freedom.

For a number of years he was chairman of the Central Council for Women's Church Work, but this position he felt bound to relinquish when the grim reality of enemy action seemed to call for his almost constant presence in his diocese. He also did much to further plans for Church extension and inaugurated a diocesan campaign for the building of new churches.

In 1948 he resigned, and became chairman of the Grey Coat Hospital Foundation. He was keenly interested in educational matters and because of his past association with the London Diocesan Fund was exceptionally well versed in matters relating to education. It gave him much satisfaction that he was able to recover sufficiently from a severe operation to lay the foundation-stone of the new Grey Coat Hospital in Grey Coat Place, London, in July 1954.

He married, in 1903, May, daughter of the Rev. E. O. Vincent, of Worthing, who survives him together with a son and a daughter.

August 24, 1954.

Kate Cutler, a star of musical comedy and later a talented and accomplished actress, died on May 14, 1955 at her home in London.

A daughter of Henry Cutler, an artist and singer, she was born in London on August 14, 1870, and was early trained—partly at the Conservatoire in Watford—as a singer in opera. "An ideal Cherubino", said one of her instructors; and her first engagements were actually in Lecocq's *Pepita* (1888) and Planquette's *Paul Jones* (1889) at Toole's Theatre. But for the young breadwinner the lure of musical comedy, then in its lively youth, was irresistible.

Kate Cutler was engaged for *In Town* at the Gaiety in 1893, and for a decade or more she was one of the theatrical beauties whose photographs were gazed at in the Regent Street windows of the Stereoscopic Company. In *The French Maid, Little Miss Nobody, Flora-Dora, A Chinese Honeymoon, The Girl from Kay's,* and their like at the Gaiety, and other theatres, her fine voice and method, her adequate knack of dancing, and her talent in acting combined with her trim figure and pretty face to win high favour with her managers and the public.

After *The Spring Chicken* in 1905 she gave up the lyric stage and devoted herself to comedy. Her first engagement of any importance was with Tree in 1907 for his revival of *The Red Lamp.* Success awaited her in Roy Horniman's *Bellamy the Magnificent* in 1903 and in A. E. W. Mason's *The Witness for the Defence* when she took up the part just vacated by Ethel Irving.

Sir George Alexander was among those with whom she acted; but for the most part the busy years were filled with tours and revivals, or with new ventures in the smaller theatres, to which she brought a rich sense of comedy and an even finer accomplishment. One of her best remembered feats was to keep the audience helpless with laughter while, as a middle-aged lady, she became, slowly and abstractedly, less and less able to control the many sheets of a pre-war number of *The Times.*

May 18, 1955.

D

Sir Ratanji Dinshaw Dalal, C.I.E., M.R.C.S., M.R.C.P., D.P.H.(LOND.), late Indian Medical Service, died in Belgaum on April 6, 1957 at the age of 88. He was probably the last survivor of the large number of medical men hastily recruited in 1896-97 to cope with the outbreak of bubonic plague in Bombay city.

He was born to a Parsee family in the Broach district of the presidency on July 27, 1868. From the Grant Medical College, Bombay, he went to London for study at University College and St. Bartholomew's Hospital. He was R.M.O. at the Finsbury Dispensary when, early in 1897, he was called back to Bombay where bubonic plague, conveyed by rats in shipping from the Far East, was taking firm hold and many thousands of people were fleeing, on account of natural fear and of aversion from government measures of prevention, some of which went much against the ingrained ideas of the people. The migration spread the disease far and wide, and within two of three years scarcely any part of the country was wholly free from it. The riots against preventive measures in Bombay and elsewhere sowed some of the seeds of subsequent political unrest.

Dalal took an active part in laboratory research, following on Dr. Haffkine's discovery of anti-plague vaccine. His clinical studies also covered the widespread diseases of cholera, guinea worm, and smallpox. In 1903 he was admitted to the Indian Medical Service without undergoing the usual competitive tests. In 1913 he was appointed deputy sanitary commissioner for the southern division of the presidency, and ten years later became Assistant Director of Public Health. He exercised a marked influence on the work of local government authorities in this connexion.

For two years before his retirement from the public service he was director of the Vaccine Institute at Belgaum, and carried out experiments which greatly raised the potency of the vaccine there manufactured. Throughout his service, and thereafter, he was active in Red Cross work.

From 1930 to 1945, as a member of the Central Legislative Assembly he showed gifts of effective debating. He was made C.I.E. in 1936 and was knighted in 1942.

April 10, 1957.

Viola (Mrs. John) Dallyn—See **Meynell.**

Claude Dampier, the comedian, died on January 1, 1955 in hospital, aged 76.

Born in Clapham, London, he began work as apprentice to an architect, but before long he was appearing at Drury Lane in the chorus and earning thirty shillings a week.

Later he went to Australia and it was while he was there that he developed the distinctive stage character for which he later became famous in Britain. With mouth agape and his face frozen in an imbecile smile, he kept up a patter of benign, slow-witted inanity, of which "Mrs. Gibson" was the central theme.

This imaginary character had its origin in a performance in Australia when he "dried up" on stage and kept up a conversation with a non-existent member of the audience. He played also in South Africa and on his return to Britain he found a ready market for and audiences responsive to his particular brand of humour.

He was married to Miss Billie Carlyle.

January 3, 1955.

Sir William Cecil Dampier, F.R.S., SC.D., (known through the greater part of his life as Dampier-Whetham), died on December 11, 1952 at the age of 84. As secretary of the Agricultural Research Council from 1931 to 1935 he steered that body to success in its first very difficult years.

He was born on December 27, 1867, the son of Charles Langley Whetham and Mary Ann, youngest daughter of Thomas Dampier, of Yeovil, Somerset. He traced a family connexion with Dampier, the famous explorer and scientific observer of the period of William III, in whom he took a keen interest, as also in the history of another ancestor, the Roundhead Colonel Nathaniel Whetham, whose biography he wrote in 1907. In 1897 he married Catharine, daughter of Robert Durning Holt, of Liverpool, a lady of exceptional knowledge, talent and charm, who cooperated with her husband in the production of his *Life of Colonel Whetham* and his better known *History of Science.* She died in March 1952 and he is survived by five daughters. He was knighted in 1931.

Dampier, with an enormous capacity for work and for enjoying work and recreation, was never idle. His background for many years was his small country house of Hilfield Manor, Dorset, and the dairy farms belonging to it lying along the foot of the chalk downs. There, when not in London or Cambridge, he lived a country life in all its aspects of work and active leisure: he read widely in many forms of serious study including history; he shot and hunted; and above all experimented in agriculture. It was to his laboratory that Dr. Leonard Harding took his Royal Society research on new ways of extracting lactose from whey.

His devotion to Trinity, Cambridge, was lifelong. He became a Fellow in 1891, was college lecturer from 1895 to 1922, tutor from 1907 to 1917, and senior tutor (a post of great responsibility) from 1913 to 1917; and in later years, when his chief work lay in London and Dorset, he was a most wise and active member of the estates committee of his college and a well known and well loved figure in combination room. His sage counsel was also freely given to the Cambridge Preservation Society, of which body he was an ardent and active member.

His interests and his zeal for the public went far beyond Cambridge. Perhaps his greatest work in life was done as secretary of the Agricultural Research Council. He was also a member of the Central Agricultural Wages Board, and was one of the Development Commissioners. He was an ideal adviser to Government bodies, independent, yet absolutely devoted to the public interest. Many of his scientific and agricultural publications are to be found in the *Transactions* of the Royal Society, of which he became a Fellow in 1901; he also wrote numerous volumes of which the following are specimens: *Solution and Electrolysis* (1895); *Theory of Solution* (1902); *Theory of Experimental Electricity* (1905); *History of Science* (1929); various works on eugenics; *Studies in Nature and Country Life; Politics and the Land;* and *Dairy Research.*

His financial knowledge and economic insight rendered his advice on agricultural and other matters all the more valuable and safe. By temper, character, gifts, and training he was a perfect example of the academic and the man of science devoting himself to national affairs and public service. He was at once a man of the world and of the college study, trained in the laboratory and on the country estate, with an inexhaustible zeal to be active for the public welfare, which grave ill health and advancing years could not tame. His goodness of heart was salted by a shrewdness that was seldom deceived. His character, apparent in all that he said and did, was that of a humorous, quiet, steady wisdom at the service of "strong benevolence of soul."

December 12, 1952.

Fred Darling, who bred Pinza, winner of the Derby in 1953, died suddenly on June 9, 1953 at his home at Beckhampton on the Marlborough Downs, less than a month after his sixty-ninth birthday.

He was a man who lived for his horses. Nothing was allowed at Beckhampton which might tend to interfere with the strict routine which he mapped out for their good. Consequently he was a firm disciplinarian in the stables, but consequently, too, his charges throve and in time carried the hall mark of physical excellence which became associated with the inmates of his stable. Such singleness of purpose achieved its object and he became the greatest of the trainers.

From his stable came not only Pinza but six other Derby winners, four winners of the 2,000 Guineas, two of the 1,000 Guineas and the Oaks, and three of the St. Leger, and when he retired in 1947 he had won over £825,000 for his patrons in stake-money.

Descended from a great racing family, he was born on May 15, 1884, and served his apprenticeship at Newmarket. For a short time he rode as a jockey and in 1913 took over the Beckhampton establishment, which his father had already rendered famous with a glittering host of successes culminating with his greatest achievement, the training of Galtee More, winner of the "triple crown" in 1897. Fred Darling's first great success was in 1916 when he won the St. Leger with Hurry On, a colt he always regarded as the best he ever trained.

Sun Chariot who won three classics in the colours of King George VI [q.v.], was probably the best filly he had in his care. Darling was one of the few trainers who won a Derby with a horse of his own. This happened in 1940 when Pont L'Évêque beat a big field, including his better fancied stable companion, Tant Mieux.

Thinking of his horses constantly and studying their peculiarities, he came in time to possess an almost uncanny knowledge which enabled him to turn out runners for big races with their preparation timed to a minute. Callers who had the pleasure of going round evening stables with him, or of sitting over an after-dinner drink, were amazed by the fact that he could switch from the discussion of his leading classic hope to a detailed plan for the future of the least of his horses, showing that none escaped the hours of study and thought. It was a bitter blow for such a man to be forced to give up active participation in the work of the stables which had become so famous.

June 10, 1953.

Richard W. Darré, formerly Hitler's Minister of Agriculture, died in September 1953 in a private clinic at Munich. He was 58.

Darré was born in Argentina in 1895, of a family of French origin (he always denied this in Germany), and was educated at King's College, Wimbledon. He associated himself with the Nazis in 1930, and was the party's agricultural expert. He was appointed Reich Minister for Food and Agriculture when Hitler came to power, and set out to establish himself as the leader of the peasants—"the source of the country's strength," as he called them. It was in accordance with this aim that as early as May 1934 he chose Pomerania (the scene in the past of much dispossession of peasants by big landowners) to attack the great estate-owners.

This strain was maintained in another significant early speech, at Altenesch, in Oldenburg, in which Darré attributed all the peasants' revolts and wars of German history to the greed of territorial princes. Now, he added, the peasants had united in a single, firm block, behind their leader, Adolf Hitler, who "came of peasant stock." Darré was playing his part in building up a Nazi mythology.

His success in winning the support of the peasants pleased Hitler and Darré remained in office until the third year of the war. His description of Nazi war aims, given in December of 1940, together with the promise that "England will be destroyed as Carthage was destroyed", seemed to overlook the peasants, for the conquered territories of Europe, he said, were to be "distributed among worthy members of the Nazi Party and German soldiers".

He was removed from office in May 1942 "for reasons of ill-health". The news came at a time when the food supply in Germany was causing the military and civil authorities considerable anxiety, and there is little doubt that Darré was jettisoned as a scapegoat. Even the peasants—overworked and anxious over their harvests after a cruel winter—had little to feel thankful for at the time. Darré was captured in 1945 and indicted in the war trials at Nuremberg in November 1947. He was convicted by the United States military tribunal in 1949 and sentenced to seven years' imprisonment for his part in the confiscation of property from Polish and Jewish farmers. His release came in the following year and he had lived for the past two years in Bad Harzburg.

Darré, though not one of the most prominent of the Nazi leaders, will always be interesting because he was characteristic of the Nazi idealist. He was the prophet of Nazi "ideological agricultural policy", of the *Blut und Boden*—Blood and Soil—theory, which sought to identify Nordic blood and German soil. There was a wealth of ethnological, economic, and historical speculation in his theory, which was expounded in many works, including a strange treatise, *Der Schwein in der Volksgeschichte—The Pig in Folklore*—in which he proved this animal to be the symbolic beast of Nordic Europe. His racial theories—which had their ludicrous side in the classification of German women into four categories— led him during the war to be one of the most outspoken exponents of the German ambition to rule as a master race in a continent the rest of whose peoples would be slaves—"a modern form of medieval slavery".

September 7, 1953.

Gwendolen Darwin—See **Raverat.**

Jo Davidson, the most famous of American sculptors, died at Azay-le-Rideau in the Loire valley on January 2, 1952 at the age of 68 after a heart attack.

Though like all sculptors of his generation he was greatly indebted to Rodin, the latter's influence did not so much help Davidson to find Rodin as help Davidson to find himself. His work, particularly his portrait busts upon which his fame chiefly rests, has been called impressionistic; it is, however, not impressionistic in the sense used of the painters of the Barbizon School, but impressionistic in manifesting the artist's reaction to the interplay of appearance and personality in the sitter. This ability to make the dead clay seem to live was Davidson's supreme achievement and, though he developed his skill in obtaining his effects as he grew older, his ability is as clearly marked in his early portrait bust of William Morris's daughter, May Morris, as in such a recent work as the bust of Ernie Pyle, the American war correspondent.

He was born in New York City on March 30, 1883, of Russo-Jewish parentage, and joined the Art Students' League at the age of 15. Meanwhile he had begun to earn his living in a variety of odd jobs. His chance came when he was employed to clean out the studio of Hermon A. McNeill, then teacher of sculpture in Yale University. McNeill paid him $4 a week and this enabled Davidson to attend evening classes.

Davidson then began to execute portraits in burnt wood which became a vogue, and so was able to earn enough to attend day classes. He won a scholarship for a sculptured group which enabled him to go to Paris, where he enrolled himself as a student at the École des Beaux Arts. That institution, however, did not give him what he wanted and he shortly left it to work by himself. By 1911 his work had already attracted attention in the Salon d'Automne and the New Spring Salon and commissions for portrait busts began to flow in.

During the 1914-18 war Davidson had the idea of modelling "plastic history"; Masaryk, Pershing, Foch, and Clemenceau sat for him; then he went to Russia where he hoped to have Lenin as a sitter. He never achieved this ambition but a number of other members of the Soviet Government sat to him, including Chicherin.

Among his other sitters were Gandhi, President Franklin D. Roosevelt, John D. Rockefeller, Albert Einstein [q.v.], George Bernard Shaw, Marshal Tito, Charlie Chaplin [d. 1977], and Chaliapin. He had lately rêturned to France from Palestine, where he had been working on one of his biggest commissions—a series of busts of leading Israeli personalities. He had executed 12 of these busts, including President Weizman [q.v.] and David Ben-Gurion* and had planned to return to Palestine in February 1952 to complete his task. He had suffered from heart trouble for some years and was warned that he must not work so hard as he had been accustomed to do. His temperament, however, forbade him to take life easily and though he had recently had two heart attacks he continued his work and thus brought on his last attack, from which he succumbed.

He was twice married, first in 1909 to Mlle. Yvonne de Kerstrat. She died in 1934 and he married secondly in 1941 Miss Florence Gertrude Lucius, who survives him together with two sons of his first marriage.

Janaury 4, 1952.

Major-General Sir John Davidson, K.C.M.G., C.B., D.S.O., died on December 11, 1954 in a nursing home. He was 78.

He was Conservative member of Parliament for the Fareham division of Hampshire from 1918 to 1931 and Colonel-Commandant of The King's Royal Rifle Corps from 1937 to 1945, and had seen service in the South African War and in the 1914-18 War, in which he held many staff appointments and was one of the most trusted General Staff officers of Field-Marshal Earl Haig. His very efficiency as a staff officer stood in his way of attainment of command; for he was retained by Haig in the same General Staff appointment, as head of the Operations Branch, during the whole period in which Haig was Commander-in-Chief.

It so happened that this post was of more than usual importance, and Davidson, together with the late Brigadier-General John Charteris (also later an M.P.). head of the Intelligence Branch, became Haig's confidant in an unusual degree; Davidson was consulted by him as to operations, prepared and issued his orders, and was present at all the important conferences with the French and with the Army commanders. Only once did he disagree with his chief and that was in 1917 over the decision to carry out the Cambrai operation.

John Humphrey Davidson was born on July 24, 1876, the son of George Walter Davidson, of Queen's Gate, South Kensington, and was educated at Harrow and Sandhurst. He was gazetted to The King's Royal Rifle Corps in 1896, and joined the 1st Battalion in Mauritius, where it remained until 1899 when it embarked for the Cape. The battalion was at Pietermaritzburg in September 1899, whence it marched to join Sir William Penn Symons's brigade, and thus took part in the frontier fight at Talana, in which the general was mortally wounded, and the colonel and four officers of the 1st K.R.R.C. were killed.

After being besieged in Ladysmith the battalion fought its way, under Sir Redvers Buller's command, through the Eastern Transvaal to the Delagoa Bay railway line; subsequently it was engaged only in minor operations and in building blockhouse lines, and in July 1901 Davidson left it to become adjutant of Rimington's Guides and later of Damant's Horse, and took part in many "drives". He was mentioned in dispatches, received the D.S.O., and earned nine clasps to his two war medals. He was promoted captain and became adjutant of his battalion.

For a time after the war he was stationed in Malta, and in February 1905 he was one of a detachment sent to form part of the international force in Crete, then under a high commissioner; but at the end of the year he left to enter the Staff College at Camberley on nomination. He went straight from the college as G.S.O.3 to the Military Training Directorate of the General Staff, War Office, for two years, and thence to be Brigade-Major, 5 Infantry Brigade, at Aldershot. His efficiency and tact came to general notice when during the railway strike in 1911 he was brigade-major to the troops camped in Victoria Park, Hackney; soon after he was appointed an instructor at the Staff College in general staff duties, training and tactics; and in 1913 he received the brevet of major.

The outbreak of war in 1914 found him still at the college, and his mobilization appointment being G.S.O.3 (Intelligence), III Corps, he joined its headquarters in France during the retreat from Mons, and took part in the battles of the Marne and the Aisne, and the fighting round Armentières. When in December 1914 the First Army was formed, under Sir Douglas Haig, Davidson was lent to its headquarters for the special duty of extracting the Indian Corps from the waterlogged trenches in the Lys valley, where it had been thrust to fill a gap; the relief took 10 days, and he had to report progress personally to Haig each evening.

On the termination of this duty Haig asked for his permanent appointment to the General Staff of the First Army as operations officer, and he joined as a temporary colonel, subsequently receiving the brevets of lieutenant-colonel and colonel. When in December 1915 Haig became Commander-in-Chief he took Davidson with him as Director of Operations with the rank of brigadier-general. In 1917 he was promoted major-general. At the close of the war Davidson was created a K.C.M.G.; he had previously been appointed C.B. (in 1917) and had received a number of foreign decorations.

It was already well known that Haig's friends had little chance of advancement after the Armistice; so Davidson accepted an offer to stand for Parliament, and was elected, as already recorded. He remained in the House of Commons for 12 years, serving as chairman of the Select Committee on the Training and Employment of ex-Service men, and of the King's Roll National Council, and being for some years president of the Union Jack Club. After leaving Parliament he devoted himself to business activities, being among other things chairman of the Bank of Australia from 1937 to 1949 and chairman of Dalgety and Co. from 1939 to 1947. He was also deputy-chairman of Gresham Insurance Societies; a director of the National Bank of Egypt, of Vickers Ltd., and of other companies.

In his old age, in 1953, after the *Official History*, of which he approved, had appeared, Davidson wrote an account of the higher command in 1916 to 1918 in *Haig, Master of the Field*—a title bestowed on Haig by the principal German military society. The book was particularly designed to exhibit Haig's difficulties and the strength of character he displayed in overcoming them, without alluding to the very prominent position that the author occupied on the Headquarters Staff.

He married in 1905 Margaret, the youngest daughter of John Peter Grant, of Rothiemurchus, Inverness-shire, who survives him together with a daughter.

December 13, 1954.

Lieutenant-Colonel Wilfred Bennett Davidson-Houston, C.M.G., died on September 18, 1960 at Esher at the age of 90.

Born on January 3, 1870, he was the second son of the Rev. B. C. Davidson-Houston, Rector of St. John's, Sandymount, Dublin, and chaplain to the Lord Lieutenant of Ireland. He went first to Corrig School, Ireland, and then to St. Edward's, Oxford. In 1887 he was commissioned in the 5th Royal Dublin Fusiliers. He joined the British South Africa Company Police in 1890 and at the beginning of 1894 he was appointed an Assistant Inspector in the Gold Coast (Hausa) Constabulary.

In 1894 Prempeh, King of Kumasi, threatened to attack the Attabubus, a tribe in the northern part of Ashanti, but a detachment of the Gold Coast Constabulary, which included Davidson-Houston among its officers, was sent to the country under the command of Colonel Sir Francis Scott, Inspector-General of the Constabulary, and the attack was averted. At the same time it was suggested to Prempeh that he should agree to the establishment of a British Residency in his country. He was unwilling to grant this request and it was at length decided to send an expedition to Kumasi under the command of Sir Francis Scott. In January 1896 Kumasi was occupied, and Prempeh made his submission to the Governor. Davidson-Houston commanded the advance guard of the column, and was mentioned in dispatches.

The armed constabularies of the West African Colonies were transferred in 1898 into units of the West African Frontier Force, which had been originally enrolled for service in Northern Nigeria, and Davidson-Houston was granted the rank of captain in the new force. He had already been promoted captain in the home army in 1892. He acted as Resident in Ashanti from 1899 to 1900.

In March of the latter year the Governor visited Kumasi and attempted to gain possession of the "Golden Stool". Like most Europeans at that time he considered the stool to be the king's throne, and was not aware that the Ashantis regarded it as containing the soul of the nation, and believed that if it were captured or destroyed the Ashantis would perish. Attempts to find the stool failed, and rebellion began with an attack on Hausa soldiers who were searching for it. Kumasi was then closely invested by the Ashantis, provisions ran short, and a part of the garrison with the Governor cut their way out. The rest were relieved by Colonel (afterwards Sir James) Willcocks, commanding the Ashanti Field Force, on July 15 after some severe fighting. Subsequently the Ashantis were routed at Aburen.

In a dispatch contained in the paper on the expedition which was presented to Parliament, the Governor referred to the valuable assistance he had received from the Acting-Resident. In 1901 Davidson-Houston volunteered for service with the British Expeditionary Force in South Africa, and was appointed Staff Officer at Wanenton. He served until the end of the war, and was awarded the Queen's Medal and five clasps.

On his return to the Gold Coast he was appointed a commissioner in Ashanti, and between 1903 and 1905 he acted as Chief Commissioner. In 1906 he was appointed Commissioner of Montserrat. He represented the Leeward Islands at the Imperial Conference on Education which was held in London in 1911; and in a similar capacity he attended the Canada-West Indies Reciprocity Conference held in Ottawa in 1912.

On the outbreak of the First World War he volunteered for service in Europe, and was appointed D.A.Q.M.G., Central Force, in 1915. In 1916 he was attached to the Headquarters Staff of the Eastern Command, and in 1917 to the Headquarters Staff of the 1st Army of the British Expeditionary Force. In 1918 he was made Deputy-Controller of Labour, France.

Among the duties he was called upon to perform in the early stages of the war was that of visiting the small island of Herm, off the coast of Guernsey, to arrange for the removal of its occupants, Prince Blücher, his family, and household.

At the end of 1918 Davidson-Houston was promoted to be Administrator of St. Lucia. The principal event during his term of office was the change in the constitution of the island. He acted as Governor of the Windward Islands on various occasions between 1923 and 1926.

In 1927 he was appointed Chief Secretary to the Government of Nyasaland, and acted as Governor in 1929-30. He retired in the latter year. He was created C.M.G. in 1911.

He married in 1898 Annie Henrietta, only daughter of E. Langley Hunt, and by her he had two sons. His wife died in 1940.

September 20, 1960.

Dr. T. B. Davie, Principal and Vice-Chancellor of the University of Cape Town since 1948, died in hospital in London on December 14, 1955 at the age of 60.

Thomas Benjamin Davie was born in 1895, and educated at the University of Stellenbosch, South Africa, and at the University of Liverpool. He was commissioned in the Royal Air Force in 1918 and after the war returned to South Africa where he taught science in several high schools, the last being Parktown Boys' High School, Johannesburg. In 1924 he went to Liverpool where he studied medicine and took his F.R.C.P. He was junior lecturer in pathology in the university from 1929 to 1931 and was then for three years pathologist to the Corporation Hospital, Liverpool. He returned to the university as senior lecturer in pathology in 1933. In 1935 he was appointed to the chair of pathology at Bristol. He transferred three years later to the George Holt chair at Liverpool, remaining in that post until 1946, when he became dean of the faculty of medicine. His medical publications include a *Textbook of Pathology* in which he collaborated with Professor J. H. Dible, whom he succeeded as professor at Liverpool.

Davie's appointment as Principal and Vice-Chancellor of the University of Cape Town in 1948 came at a crucial time in the history of the universities of South Africa. The stiffening of the attitude of the National Government on the question of *Apartheid* did not, of course, affect the four Afrikaans-speaking universities (Orange Free State, Potchefstroom, Pretoria, and Stellenbosch), for they never have admitted native or coloured students; and the full impact of the Government's attack fell on the Universities of Cape Town and Witwatersrand. South African universities, like those elsewhere, found themselves compelled to rely more and more on financial support from the State and it therefore required great moral courage for Cape Town and Witwatersrand to continue to adhere to their traditional practice of admitting students capable of benefiting from a university education without regard to race or colour. In maintaining this position no man played a more vital part than Davie. Though he was both firm and uncompromising in his opposition to *Apartheid* in the universities, he maintained his attitude with a degree of statesmanship and moderation which earned the respect of his opponents.

At the vice-chancellor's residence overlooking Table Bay the Davies dispensed hospitality on a liberal scale. Their circle of friends in Cape Town and indeed South Africa included leading members of the commercial and industrial communities as well as the world of education and many a Commonwealth scholar travelling on a boat which made Cape Town a port of call has vivid memories of the warm welcome he received from the Davies.

His later years were marked by a series of long and painful illnesses but he refused to be daunted and his courage and equanimity remained with him to the end. When he died he had visited London with his wife to represent the University of Cape Town at the installation of Queen Elizabeth the Queen Mother as Chancellor of the University of London in November.

He married in 1921 Vera C. Roper, who survives him. There were no children.

December 15, 1955.

Betty-Ann Davies, the well-known actress, who was in private life Mrs. Alexander Blackford, died on May 14, 1955 in hospital at Manchester, six days after an operation for appendicitis. She was 44.

Born on December 24, 1910, she was educated at Goudhurst College, Kent, and made her first appearance on the stage at the London Palladium in 1926 in the chorus of the revue *Life.* In the course of the next year she was picked by C. B. Cochran [q.v.] as one of the original members of his troupe "Cochran's Young Ladies" in the revue at the London Pavilion *One Dam Thing After Another.* She appeared also in its successor, *This Year of Grace,* at the same theatre. It was a singularly fortunate chance that she had arrived right in the middle of the West End theatre business before she was 18 and had succeeded in holding her advantage. That she had both beauty and charm goes without saying, but only marked and genuine talent could have carried her through a career which exhibited no setbacks and many triumphs.

The long tale of her successes extends over more than a quarter of a century, and it would be tedious to reiterate all of them here. Nevertheless, mention should be made of her excellent interpretation of Susie Dean in *The Good Companions* before, in 1934, she took up cinema work to the exclusion for four years of work in the theatre. She reappeared in the West End at the Little Theatre in 1938 in *Nine Sharp,* and stayed on for its successor, *The Little Revue,* in which she shone in a company that included Cyril Ritchard, Joyce Grenfell, and Hermione Baddeley, Her first "straight" dramatic part was Wanda Baring in *Morning Star* in 1942 at the Globe, and she then toured in the same part with Emlyn Williams. As Elvira in *Blithe Spirit* at the Duchess in 1943 she exhibited just that odd fantasy which brought out the comedy of the situation. Her greatest triumph, however, was in taking over the part of Blanche du Bois, originally played by Vivien Leigh*, in *A Streetcar Named Desire.*

May 16, 1955.

David Igor Davies—See **Novello.**

Joseph Davies, who died on May 9, 1958 in Washington at the age of 81, was United States Ambassador in Moscow in 1937-38 and later undertook important diplomatic missions during the war for President Roosevelt and President Truman*.

As Ambassador in Moscow his judgment both of Russia's military potential and of the international diplomatic scene was shrewd and, as it afterwards turned out, remarkably accurate. But he was led to take too optimistic a view of Russia's post-war intentions. This, combined with advancing years and indifferent health, contributed to his retirement from public life after 1945.

Joseph Edward Davies was born at the small town of Watertown, Wisconsin, on November 29, 1876. His parents were both natives of Wales, his father having come from the southern part of that country, and his mother, who was well known in many parts of America as a singer of hymns and a revivalist preacher under her maiden name of Rachel Paynter, from Anglesey. Davies himself once showed what he could do in this line when he delivered an impassioned address on liberty and democracy before the National Eisteddfod at Cardiff in 1938.

Davies was brought up in humble surroundings. He earned the money to take him through college by working in his spare time as a physical training instructor, and graduated in 1898 at the University of Wisconsin. Called to the Bar of Wisconsin in 1901, he started in practice for himself in the following year and was then appointed state's attorney and held that office for a couple of years. Soon after Woodrow Wilson's inauguration as President in 1912 Davies was given the post in Washington of Commissioner of Corporations, and he became chairman of the Federal Trade Commission two years later.

He retired from his official post in 1918, and then built up for himself an extensive legal practice at Washington. His work was then concerned largely with foreign affairs. He acted as counsel for the Government of Mexico in an international inquiry in 1920, for the Government of Peru in the arbitration with Chile over the Tacna-Arica dispute, and also for the Republic of Santo Domingo, as well as in an arbitration case between the United States and Egypt.

In 1936 he was nominated by President Roosevelt Ambassador in Moscow. His firm faith in individualistic capitalism and his large personal fortune (two years earlier he had married, as his second wife, Mrs. Hutton, the only child and heir of Charles W. Post, the breakfast-food manufacturer) did not prevent him getting on good terms with the Soviet leaders and appreciating the strength of their country. In the earliest phase of his diplomatic mission he was convinced that the only hope of peace lay in the creation of a London-Paris-Moscow axis. Before he left Russia he had come to the conclusion that the European democracies were driving Stalin [q.v.] into

Hitler's arms. In 1942 he gave extracts from his official correspondence and private journals in a book called *Mission to Moscow.* He came out of its pages as a first-rate diplomatic observer and something of a prophet. A film was made of it, in which living statesmen were impersonated by actors, and there were not wanting critics both of the film and the book who complained that they gave too rosy a picture of the Soviet régime and too infallible a character to Davies's judgment.

In 1938 Davies was transferred to Brussels and at the beginning of the war he was recalled to Washington as a special adviser to the Secretary of State, Cordell Hull [q.v.]. In the war he was an eloquent advocate of close alliance with Russia, both militarily and in the ultimate peace settlement. In the summer of 1943 President Roosevelt selected him to be the bearer of a personal message to Stalin; and in June 1945 President Truman sent him, with the rank of ambassador, to confer with the British Government about the forthcoming Potsdam meeting. He brought, among other proposals, the suggestion that the President should have a preliminary meeting alone with Stalin. This idea Churchill* quickly and effectively squashed. Davies attended the Potsdam conference in the capacity of special adviser to the President.

May 10, 1958.

Peter Llewelyn Davies, founder of the firm of publishers that bears his name and its chairman at the time of his death, died on April 5, 1960 after falling in front of a train at Sloane Square Underground station, London. It had often been said that it was Davies, as a boy, who inspired J. M. Barrie to create the character of Peter Pan.

The association between the Davies family and Barrie was a long one. The boy Peter was one of the five sons of Arthur Llewelyn Davies, a barrister, and the beautiful Sylvia du Maurier, one of the five children of George du Maurier and thus a sister of Gerald du Maurier. Probably in 1898 Barrie noticed the three elder boys, George, Jack, and Peter (wearing, it is said, red berets made by their mother from her grandfather-in-law's judicial robes) during their daily walks in the neighbourhood of the Round Pond. Barrie had with him his large St. Bernard which did tricks; he had also his incomparable gift of telling tales and in other ways entertaining the young.

While the acquaintance was growing in Kensington Gardens a close friendship was developing between Barrie and his wife and the children's parents, who became, like Maurice Hewlett, A. E. W. Mason, and the Will Merediths, part of the Barrie circle. The association between Barrie and the children was to have a marked effect on J. M. B.'s writing, in particular in the creation of *Peter Pan.* As Denis Mackail* said in *The Story of J. M. B.*: "On and on they (the stories) went, this year, next year, and for long after that. Each little Davies in turn became a listener and a character in them at the same time. . . . Peter Pan wasn't always a protagonist . . . but he was there oftener than not, and all that was afterwards written of him was only a fraction of what the little Davieses were told."

In 1906 Arthur Davies underwent a serious operation for the removal of a sarcoma. The surgeons believed that they had conquered, but a few months later the disease returned and no further operation was possible. He died the following year at the age of 44. Barrie thereupon instantly assumed entire financial responsibility for the widowed mother and all five sons.

Peter went to Eton; like his brother George, he was a good cricketer but luck just kept him out of the XI. He served with distinction in the K.R.R.C. in France in the War of 1914-18 and won a Military Cross. In the 1920s he went up to Walter Blackie in Edinburgh to learn about typography and book production. Then, with Barrie's ever-present help, and the assistance of Hodder and Stoughton, he underwent a "trial trip" in London before setting up with an imprint of his own in 1926. Peter Davies became a limited company in 1932 and in 1937 became one of the Heinemann group. In June that year Barrie died at the age of 77. Peter Davies had been at the nursing home almost day and night throughout J.M.B.'s illness and was present when he died. King George V sent him a personal message of sympathy.

Davies married in 1932 the Hon. Margaret Leslie, twin daughter of the ninth Lord Ruthven. They had three sons.

April 7, 1960.

Sir William Llewelyn Davies, who died at his home at Aberystwyth on November 11, 1952 at the age of 65, was librarian of the National Library of Wales, in which, after five years of teaching and three of service in the 1914-18 war, he spent all his working life.

Born on October 11, 1887, at Plas Gwyn Schoolhouse, near Pwllheli, he was educated at Portmadoc County School and the University College of Wales, Aberystwyth, taking his degree in 1909 with honours in Welsh and proceeding to the degree of M.A. in 1912 with a dissertation on sixteenth and seventeenth century Welsh poets. Among the teaching posts he held was that of part-time lecturer in Celtic studies at Cardiff University College, and during the 1914-18 war he served first with the Royal Artillery and later with the Army Education Service, in which he held a commission. He was appointed to the staff of the National Library of Wales in 1919.

The library had been founded by Royal Charter in 1907 and opened in 1909. The first national librarian, the late Sir John Ballinger, had enthusiastically pursued the founders' ideal of providing a worthy home for the many priceless collections of Welsh literature and records then still remaining in private hands in old country houses, such as the Peniarth and Wynn of Gwydie MSS., both of which were deposited in the library in his time. By the Copyright Act of 1911 the library was added to those benefiting from free deposit of new books, and suffering from the duty of housing them and making them available. In all this, but especially by the creation of a department of duplicates for the lending of books from Aberystwyth to other libraries and to students in Wales, and most of all, naturally, in his own field of Welsh literature and history, Llewelyn Davies was Ballinger's lieutenant, having indeed the advantage over his chief of being really bilingual and a native Welsh scholar. In 1930, therefore, when Ballinger retired, the appointment of Davies to succeed him was received with general pleasure.

During the 1939-45 war he more than repeated the precedent of the war of 1914-18, when the National Library, on its remote western coast, had housed many valuable collections from more exposed libraries. In 1939-45 the danger was greater and so was the service which Davies carried out on his Governors' behalf and himself largely promoted. Aberystwyth was the temporary home of countless treasures—and of the officials sent there to watch over them.

To the collections of manuscripts Davies made vastly larger additions than even his predecessor; no doubt owners were more willing than they had been to give or deposit their collections. In 1941 he started publishing the useful series of *Handlists of Manuscripts,* as supplements to *The National Library of Wales Journal,* which he had founded two years earlier, to anticipate the necessarily slow appearance of full catalogues. He also for many years edited the journal of the Welsh Bibliographical Society, and the journals of Merioneth and Cardiganshire Historical and Antiquarian Societies. In 1937, when the completed library building was formally opened by King George VI and Queen Elizabeth, he published *The National Library of Wales, a survey of its history, its contents, and its activities.*

Davies was knighted in 1944. He was a vice-president of the British Records Association, a Fellow of the Society of Antiquaries and of the Library Association, a Historical MSS. Commissioner, and served on countless similar bodies, while in Wales itself he was one of the leading spirits in every organization promoting the intellectual life of the Principality; a list of the offices he served would be tedious. The University of Wales conferred the honorary degree of LL.D. upon him in 1951, and in March 1952 he was appointed High Sheriff of Merioneth.

He married, in 1914, Gwen, daughter of Mr. Dewi Llewelyn, of Pontypridd, who survives him together with a daughter of the marriage.

November 12, 1952.

Gordon Daviot—See **Elizabeth Mackintosh.**

John W. Davis, who died in hospital at Charleston, South Carolina, on March 24, 1955 at the age of 81, will be widely remembered in Britain as one of the most distinguished and popular ambassadors who have ever represented the United States at the Court of St. James's.

Appointed by President Wilson to succeed the late Walter Hines Page at the end of the 1914-18 War, his mission coincided with the difficult period of the drafting of the Peace Treaties, their rejection by the American Senate, and the mortal illness of his friend, the President. A man of aristocratic bearing, natural dignity, and transparent sincerity of character, he was also one of the best speakers of his day. A most distinguished lawyer who had also unusual diplomatic gifts, he was convinced of the importance of Anglo-American friendship to the future of the world, and did all within his power to further it.

John William Davis was born on April 13, 1873, at Clarksburg, West Virginia, and was educated at Washington and at Lee University, Lexington. There he studied Law and, having finished his course, stayed on for a year as assistant professor of that subject. Then, in 1897, he entered into practice with his father in his native town and continued to reside there until 1913. As a young man he was strongly attracted to politics and at the age of 26 was elected a member of the West Virginian House of Delegates and sat in it for a short period. A Democrat in allegiance, he accepted in 1910 nomination to Congress for the first district of West Virginia and won a seat which for 20 years had been Republican. At Washington he did some valuable work in forwarding the great missions of fiscal currency and banking reform with which Woodrow Wilson began his Presidency. Then, in 1913, he was appointed Solicitor-General of the United States.

In 1918 Davis, who had become a fast friend of President Wilson, went to Berne as a member of an American commission on the exchange of prisoners, and, while still in Europe, was chosen to succeed Page as United States Ambassador to the Court of St. James's. The wisdom of the President's selection was to be amply vindicated. London had only to see and hear him to realize the quality of his personality. His heart as well as his intelligence was in his task and he had lively faith in the possibilities of Anglo-American relationship. As he became better known he was increasingly in request as a speaker on public occasions and always acquitted himself to perfection. When, on a change of Administration, he left in 1921, he was regarded as a proved and trusted friend.

Davis returned to the United States a comparatively poor man, and resumed his legal practice in partnership with his friend, the late Frank L. Palk. In 1922 he was elected president of the American Bar Association, and was thereafter to become one of the greatest and most successful members of his profession. In 1924, however, he was drawn suddenly into the forefront of American politics as a compromise Democratic candidate for the presidency. There had been a fierce struggle for the nomination between McAdoo and Governor "Al" Smith, when an exhausted Convention turned to him and, on the hundred and third vote, he received the necessary majority. It soon appeared, however, that he was engaged in a hopeless conflict. At the election he carried no state outside the "solid South", and even there he suffered some losses. The result was an overwhelming defeat for the Democrats.

Thereafter he retired from active political contests, though his advice was sought from time to time on important public issues. The Democratic policy of Franklin D. Roosevelt, entailing as it did vast expenditure and what he regarded as interference with vital individual rights, proved after Roosevelt's first term to be too advanced for one of his cautious and conservative temperament. He remained, however, throughout his life a fast friend of Great Britain, who never lost an opportunity of giving evidence of his affection for her. For many years he was president of the American branch of the English-Speaking Union.

Davis was a striking figure, of good stature, dignified and intellectual in bearing. He had an easy manner, a friendly approach, and was a humorous and delightful talker. Modest though he was, he was far from timid, and if provoked was capable of a rapier-like reply. In his later years he lived in a quiet and sedate house on Long Island in the society of well-chosen friends of his own kind. He was, however, not forgotten on either side of the Atlantic. When he visited Britain to receive an honorary degree at Oxford in 1950 he was entertained by the Pilgrims and three years later, on his eightieth birthday, while still president of the Pilgrims of the United States, he was appointed an honorary G.B.E.

March 25, 1955.

Sir Ronald Davison, well known between the wars as an authority on unemployment and social insurance, died at his home at Shiplake-on-Thames on September 29, 1958 at the age of 74.

Ronald Conway Davison was the son of George Davison, who, in the early days of the box camera, gave up a career in the Inland Revenue to create and build up Eastman's vast Kodak organization in Europe. He was born in March 1884 and educated at Charterhouse and Oriel College, Oxford.

He was one of the group of socially minded Oxford men (Lord Beveridge* was another) who went on from university to Toynbee Hall to make the problems of unemployment and the unemployed their special study. After two years at Toynbee Hall (1908-10), he entered the Labour Department of the Board of Trade in 1912 to work under William Beveridge in the recently created labour exchange service and to help organize the newly formed social insurance schemes. He remained at the Ministry of Labour (as it later became) for the next 16 years, being concerned after 1917 chiefly with training schemes for disabled ex-Servicemen.

In 1928, at the age of 43, he left the Civil Service to devote himself to writing and lecturing in England and North America, a change made financially possible by his father's death. A year later he published his first and best book, *The Unemployed: Old Policies and New,* lucid, unbiased, informative, though confined to treatment of the unemployed rather than prevention of unemployment. There followed numerous well informed articles, several in *The Times,* discussing developments in insurance and assistance schemes for the unemployed, and drawing attention to the different methods adopted in contemporary American essays in social security. *British Unemployment Policy,* surveying the transformation effected since 1931, appeared in 1938.

During the decade before the Second World War Davison's advice on most aspects of social security policy was in frequent demand from many quarters. In the depths of the economic depression his closest associates, though he held aloof from politics, were in the short-lived National Labour Party. But his energy and enthusiasm went mainly into the building up of Political and Economic Planning, the independent research institute whose anonymous "broadsheets" did so much to break the intellectual deadlock among economists and politicians spellbound by the economic crisis.

He played a leading role in the discussions, part study groups and part indignation meetings, of Civil servants, businessmen, scientists, and others which took place at P.E.P., and from which emerged so many practical ideas for restoring social and economic health by expansionist policies.

During the war of 1939-45 Davison was one of the P.E.P. team which gave evidence to the Beveridge inquiry into social security. After the Beveridge report's publication he spent some years in publicizing and stimulating critical discussion of the report's ideas, both in writings and in lectures to the Forces oversea.

His many friends will recall with regretful pleasure the high-minded but ever stimulating hospitality always awaiting them at his house, first in Holland Park, later at Shiplake; and frequenters of the Tate Gallery restaurant will miss the quietly genial gentleman who for several decades was to be seen lunching on most Fridays with the late Sir Frank Tribe [q.v.] and other colleagues, all now distinguished, who had spent their formative years at the Ministry of Labour.

Davison's first wife, Sheila Grant, whom he married in 1911, died in 1923. He married again in 1926, and was knighted in 1938. He is survived by his second wife, Emily Whiteman, and by two sons and two daughters.

October 2, 1958.

Dr. Clinton Joseph Davisson, the American physicist, died on February 1, 1958. He was 76.

In 1937 he shared with G. P. (Sir George Paget) Thomson*, F.R.S., the Nobel Prize for Physics for their experimental discovery of interference phenomena in the irradiation of crystals by electrons.

A graduate of the University of Chicago, Davisson taught physics at the Carnegie Institute of Technology before joining the engineering department of the Western Electric Company, predecessor of the Bell Telephone Laboratories. His connexion with the Bell firm continued until 1949. From 1947 to 1949 he was Professor of Physics at the University of Virginia.

Some years before de Broglie had advanced his theory as to the wave structure of matter, some American scientists, working under Davisson, had already carried out experiments which could subsequently be interpreted in favour of de Broglie's basic assumption. These experiments involved a study of the scattering of a beam of electrons when reflected by the surface of a crystal, e.g., a nickel crystal.

The irregular distribution of the reflected electrons with maxima in certain definite directions was remarkable and difficult to explain. After de Broglie had published his theory, and further experiments had been carried out under more precise experimental conditions, Davisson was able to establish that his observations agreed well with the results which could be expected if the electrons were scattered in the same way as wave radiation incident on a crystal.

The phenomenon was thus of exactly the same nature as that observed earlier in the case of reflection of X-rays by a crystal.

The experiments of Davisson and his colleagues presented great technical difficulties and it was, therefore, of the greatest importance to receive confirmation of the new wave structure theory of matter from other quarters. G. P. Thomson, the son of J. J. Thomson, succeeded in demonstrating the reflection and diffraction of electrons in thin crystalline layers in a direct, simple and very obvious manner. While Davisson used electrons of relatively low velocities, Thomson carried out his experiments with very fast electrons capable of penetrating thin metal foils.

In 1935 the Royal Society awarded its Hughes Medal to Davisson. During the Second World War he worked on the application of electron devices to communications equipment used by the armed forces.

February 4, 1958.

Brigadier-General Charles Dawes, Vice-President of the United States from 1925 to 1929, and United States Ambassador to the Court of St. James's from 1929 to 1932, died suddenly at his home at Chicago on April 23, 1951 at the age of 85.

Charles Gates Dawes was born on August 27, 1865, at Marietta, Ohio, the son of General Rufus R. Dawes, who came of stock originally settled at Sudbury, in Suffolk. He was educated at Marietta College. After a brief period as a railway engineer, he went to the Cincinnati Law School where he took the degree of LL.B. in 1886 and, having been admitted to the Bar, started practice in Lincoln, Nebraska.

His natural financial talent, however, soon asserted itself. In 1894 he published a book on *The Banking System of the United States* and in the same year he gave up the practice of law to go into business. His life had already been varied enough, but in 1896 came the event which was destined finally to decide the course of his career. William J. Bryan that summer won his first nomination as Democratic candidate for the presidency. His Republican opponent was William McKinley. Dawes was treasurer of the Republican campaign committee which, under Mark Hanna, had its headquarters in Chicago.

On McKinley's election as President, Dawes, a very young man for the position, was appointed Comptroller of the Currency. During the five years for which he occupied that office he was in extremely close touch with the President and, more than any other person, acted as the confidential go-between of the White House and Senator Mark Hanna and other chiefs of the Republican organization. In his capacity of Comptroller of the Currency, Dawes had necessarily become familiar with the intricacies of finance. He retired from the office in 1901 and in the following year organized the Central Trust Company of Illinois which, under his presidency, quickly grew to be a very successful and powerful institution; and Dawes himself became recognized as one of the outstanding financial personalities in the country—a fact which was to be of great importance to the allies in the 1914-18 war.

When in 1915 the mission under the late Lord Reading visited the United States on behalf of the first Anglo-French loan, much pressure was brought to bear on American banks in opposition to the loan, by Germans and other friends of the Central Powers in the United States. Dawes, however, let it be known that he and the Central Trust Company proposed to back the loan with all their strength. Without his action it is very doubtful if the loan could have succeeded.

As soon as America entered the war, Dawes applied for a commission and it was as a lieutenant-colonel of engineers that he went to France. Soon, however, General Pershing took him on to his staff and shortly thereafter he was appointed chairman of the purchasing board of the American Expeditionary Force. In that capacity he was universally regarded by his own countrymen as having done very good work. What was also important was that his experience confirmed his natural sympathies with England. He found, as he often said himself, that he could both work with and trust Englishmen though he did not hesitate to make fun of British methods. When he was discharged in 1919 it was with the rank of brigadier-general and besides decorations from each of the allied countries (including a Companionship of the Bath) he was awarded the American Distinguished Service Medal.

When testifying before the Congressional commission appointed to inquire into war expenditure he proclaimed boldly his sympathy with England. German-Irish, "anti-British" influences strove in various ways (especially by inquiries as to the cost of transporting the American troops to Europe) to elicit evidence injurious to Great Britain: "I don't like this criticism of the British", he said. "I am not in sympathy with this Irish-American and hyphenated stuff. I am not a politician or looking for a job. . . . I am no more ashamed to stand up for England than I am for the United States; and I thank God that in a crisis like this there were no bickerings between the English-speaking peoples". It was true that he was not a politician nor looking for a job; but his courage and outspokenness then probably did more to pave the way to his subsequent election to the vice-presidency than any other individual act of his life.

In 1921 President Harding appointed Dawes the first Director of the Federal Budget. It was thus natural that he should be one of two Americans nominated in 1923 by the Reparations Commission to serve on what was known as the first committee of experts—later known as the Dawes Committee, of which he was chairman. The "Dawes Plan" made his name world-famous, and also earned for him the award of the Nobel Peace Prize. He himself, however, lost no opportunity of disclaiming all personal credit, declaring that whatever good had been achieved by the commission was due to the work of Owen Young and the British representatives, the late Lord Stamp and Sir Robert (later Lord) Kindersley [q.v.]. When the Dawes Plan came before the London Conference in August 1924 he had already been nominated as Republican candidate for the vice-presidency, with Coolidge as the presidential candidate. He worked very hard in the campaign that followed, and the size of the Republican majority in November was undoubtedly largely due to his personal popularity and the influence of his speeches.

In March 1925 he entered on his duties as Vice-President of the United States, chief among which is the task of acting as presiding officer of the Senate. His vigorous and outspoken methods produced at first some rather angry scenes, but as time passed the Senate came to learn that General Dawes was not a mere rough-and-tumble Westerner but that behind the ruthlessness of his rulings and the frankness of his language there lay, for use when required, an infinite fund of tact, of courtesy, and of patience; and that, besides being a soldier, a banker, and a politician, the Vice-President was also a cultured gentleman of wide reading and great knowledge of the world. Before the end of his term he was as respected in the Senate as he was popular in the country. For a time it looked as if he was likely to be the Republican presidential nominee in 1928. The Convention, however, preferred Herbert Hoover*.

Of the line of distinguished men who have filled the office of President of the United States, Hoover was the first who, at the time of his accession, had travelled much and had, especially, any first-hand knowledge of European conditions and public men. The relations between Great Britain and the United States were at the moment in a delicate condition, owing to the recent failure of the Conference on Naval Disarmament at Geneva; and these relations had been made none the easier by certain utterances of the retiring President, Coolidge. Happily the new President understood how essential not only to their own welfare but to the peace of the world it was that there should be cordiality and friendship between the English-speaking peoples.

Dawes, then, was indicated as the ideal man for the post of American Ambassador in

London, to fill the vacancy caused by the retirement of Houghton; and when, in June 1929, he arrived in England he was warmly welcomed. The impression which he made in the first weeks after his arrival only increased that feeling of cordiality. The Labour Government, under Ramsay MacDonald, had just come into office, though with a minority in the House of Commons. By the activity which he showed in getting immediately on intimate terms with the Prime Minister and by the tone of his speeches he gave evidence of his determination to work for a better understanding between the nations. The degree of D.C.L. which Oxford conferred upon him in June 1929 was a token of the universal friendliness with which he was regarded.

He left London for Geneva to sit as American observer on the committee of the Council of the League of Nations examining the Sino-Japanese conflict in Manchuria in 1931. Then he sailed for home, and in mid-Atlantic suddenly decided to resign his diplomatic post in London and telegraphed his decision to Washington.

Soon after his arrival in the United States he was appointed president of the Reconstruction Finance Corporation set up to mitigate the effects of the slump, and latterly he had been chairman of the board of the City National Bank and Trust Company of Chicago. He published a number of volumes of memoirs dealing with his work on the Reparations Commission and as Ambassador to Britain.

He married in 1889 Caro, daughter of William H. Blymer. There were three daughters and a son of the marriage.

April 25, 1951.

Professor R. M. Dawkins, for many years Bywater and Sotheby Professor of Byzantine and Modern Greek in the University of Oxford, and an Honorary Fellow of Exeter College, collapsed and died on May 4, 1955 in Parks Road, Oxford. He was 83.

Richard MacGillivray Dawkins was born in 1871. His father was Rear-Admiral Richard Dawkins, R.N., and his mother a cousin of John Doyle, Fellow of All Souls. After leaving Marlborough he spent a period as a lonely student in London lodgings, rather unhappily attending engineering courses at King's College. At this time he became momentarily interested in theosophy and it was characteristic that he determined as a consequence that he must at once teach himself Sanskrit. This achievement led to a scholarship at Emmanuel College, Cambridge, where, going up rather older than the average undergraduate, he was able to follow his natural bent for classical and philological studies. In 1904 he won a Fellowship at Emmanuel and in 1906 he was appointed Director of the British School at Athens, a post which he resigned in 1914 when an inheritance gave him financial freedom to pursue his first love, philology.

From 1916 to the end of the 1914-18 War he served with the Navy on counter-espionage in Crete, and there are few villages or monuments in that island of which he had not an intimate knowledge at first hand. From 1920 to 1939 he held the Bywater and Sotheby Chair of Byzantine and Modern Greek Language and Literature at Oxford, and after his retirement Exeter College most wisely elected him an Honorary Fellow and allowed him to retain his rooms in college. Some years before his death he had the misfortune to break his thigh, a disability which with unconquerable fortitude he refused to allow to impede his industry in scholarship. His industry, indeed, was continuous, and throughout his life articles and reviews in learned journals, both British and foreign, continued to pour out.

As Director of the British School at Athens he conducted excavations at the temple of Orthia at Sparta with a skill which may fairly be said to have revolutionized the technique of digging in Greece. There were other excavations at Phylakopi, on Melos, and on Cretan sites. When not so engaged he was travelling widely, and besides his numerous reports and papers in archaeological journals, his philological studies resulted in the publication of *Modern Greek in Asia Minor,* which is an account of the strange dialects spoken by the Greeks who then still lived in Cappadocia. The material which he subsequently collected in Pontus, where he was almost caught by the outbreak of war in 1914, was never published.

During his tenure of the Bywater Chair his most considerable publication was a translation with commentary of the Cypriot *Chronicle of Makhairas.* Much of the dialect material which he had recorded for philological purposes was in the form of folk-tales and this led him to an increasing interest in folk-tales themselves. The two major works of his retirement were the translation with commentary of *Forty-five Stories from the Dodekanese* and a comprehensive corpus of Greek folk-tales, in which for each story a large number of Greek variants are discussed, thus establishing the essential peculiarities of the Greek form of the story. He also published in 1952 a short and admirable memoir of Norman Douglas [q.v.].

All his scholarly work was distinguished by meticulous accuracy informed by an extraordinarily wide background of general knowledge. His interests in letters and in the arts, except music, for which he had no ear, were catholic and he was no mean botanist, an interest which he owed to one of his masters at Marlborough. He knew the principal European languages and was a fluent conversationist in most of them, while he had a reading knowledge of not a few unusual tongues. He was keenly observant and prepared to be interested in everything; he had a retentive memory and a wide general knowledge of European history. This made him a good and profitable traveller. There were few Mediterranean lands of which he did not know something, and of all parts of the Greek-speaking world from Calabria to Pontus he had a quite exceptional knowledge. He could be severe with humbug or pretension and in scholarship he was not fond of ingenious nonsense, but his critical attitude was positive. He was more delighted to discover the spark of interest in a human being or in a book than to elaborate the defects which might accompany their qualities. His friendships in consequence covered almost as wide a range as his reading.

To the end of his life he retained an inexhaustible liking for and patience with the young. There must be many an Exeter man who will remember going as an undergraduate for the first time into "the Professor's" room. "A funny old man", he may well have thought at first, with his high-pitched laugh and his nervous mannerisms. Perhaps the undergraduate hoped to show off as an expert on modern art or French literature or some other matter, which he knew was not the Professor's subject, though he believed it to be his. How soon he would find himself out of his depth on his chosen topic, though gratefully realizing that he was not being put in his place but being treated as a conversationist with something interesting to say! That kind of experience is real education.

May 6, 1955.

R. C. Dawson, who died on September 15, 1955 at his home at Newbury, at the age of 89, was one of the few men to have trained winners of both the Derby and the Grand National. It is now 57 years since Drogheda, in whom he also had a share, won the great race at Aintree, and Dawson will be better remembered by the racing public for his great success as a trainer under Jockey Club Rules at Whatcombe and, in particular, during the period when he trained there for the Aga Khan [q.v.].

Richard Cecil Dawson was born in Ireland on November 27, 1865, the son of Richard Cuming Dawson, who both trained and bred racehorses. After leaving Dublin University he began to own horses in 1886 and had his first winner at Waterford two years later. He had charge of a stud farm near Dublin for several years, but in 1897 he decided to go to England. He at once settled down as the presiding genius of Whatcombe, near Newbury, where McNaughton was nominally the trainer. Whatcombe came into the limelight in 1902 when The Solicitor won the Hunt Cup at Ascot and Mauvezin the Stewards' Cup at Goodwood. Both these horses were owned by Lord Carnarvon, for whom Dawson had most of his early successes as a trainer. In 1904 he sent out Robert le Diable to win the City and Suburban, the Doncaster Cup, and the Duke of York Stakes, and his victories were followed in the years that came after by the successes of such as Missavia Valens and Buckwheat and the misfortune of Mustapha, who had the bad luck to finish second in three successive Cambridgeshires, two of them being won by Christmas Daisy.

Dawson moved to Newmarket during the 1914-18 War, having trained Fifinella to win the war Derby and Oaks of 1916, but he was back at Whatcombe in 1919. Almost at once the old tale of victory in famous races was continued. Tangiers won the Summer Cup on Dawson's favourite course, the local Newbury, and also the Ascot Gold Cup after Buchan had been disqualified.

Soon afterwards came that long period

when Dawson was to win nearly every great race in the land as the Aga Khan's first trainer in England. Cos was the first of the Aga Khan's winners, but then came the immortal Mumtaz Mahal, Diophon, Salmon Trout, Teresina, Ziverist, and others who made Dawson the leading trainer in 1924. He headed the list again in 1929 with a winning total of £74,754, this being mainly due to the performances of the two colts he trained for Barnett, of Belfast, Trigo and Athford. Trigo won the Derby, the St. Leger, and the Irish St. Leger, and Athford the Newbury Spring Cup and the Jubilee Handicap at Kempton Park. Le Voleur and Parmiz did well for the Aga Khan, and Dawson's stallion Blandford had established himself as one of the great sires of all time. In the following year Dawson won his second Derby when another son of Blandford, Blenheim, gained the Aga Khan his first victory in the greatest of all races.

After 1931 the Aga Khan's horses were trained mainly at Newmarket; they left Whatcombe in that year. Dawson remained in his old stables, but although he always had one or two useful horses he did not from that time take the same part in English racing as formerly. He still took a great interest in Newbury, but he was getting old and his appearances on other racecourses were rare.

During the 1939-45 War, however, he went to Salisbury to see his useful stayer Mazarin win several races, and to Windsor and Ascot when he had a runner. At the end of 1944 he nearly brought off a remarkable owner's double when Giraud and Misty Morning finished second in the Cambridgeshire and Cesarewitch respectively, and he retired in the following year.

September 17, 1955.

Arthur Deakin, P.C., C.H., C.B.E., who died on May 1, 1955, had been general secretary of the biggest trade union in Britain—the Transport and General Workers' Union—for some 10 years.

Latterly he had dominated the General Council of the Trades Union Congress as no man had done before him, even Ernest Bevin [q.v.]. It was seldom indeed that any policy he supported failed to become the policy of the T.U.C. The secret of his influence lay partly in the huge block vote of the unions he led, but no less in the strength of his character. Without exceptional intellectual qualities or eloquence, he ruled by force of will combined with an integrity which was recognized by his most bitter opponents, of whom there were many, for his domination naturally provoked enmity. He loved a fight and his weapon was the bludgeon, not the rapier. Anyone who saw him at the Trades Union Congress, a solid figure with legs astride, face shining red, hurling himself at enraged Communists with all the delegates in uproar, could not but feel that those were among his happiest moments.

He never minced his words or hesitated to rebuke those who, he thought, deserved it, whether the victim were an incautious member of the general council, a pretentious Communist, a pin-pricking Bevanite or even the great Confederation of Shipbuilding and Engineering Unions, whose carefully worked out plan for the future of the engineering industries he publicly dismissed—to their intense indignation—as "a mumbo jumbo of meaningless words and phrases". Though lesser men in the movement criticized and abused him, at heart most of them liked him because he remained one of them, talking their language and fighting their battles. They liked him because of his determination not to accept a knighthood. They liked him for his contempt of politicians. More than once he said that nothing would induce him to go to "that place", by which he meant the House of Commons.

He was not a man who could understand other people's points of view. When outsiders criticized his union, the union founded by Ernest Bevin, whom he deeply admired, and which absorbed the whole of his energies, he attributed it either to ignorance or malice. He was always ready to forgive ignorance—and no man can have had to forgive it more often—but where he saw malice he did not easily forgive. His most serious weakness was his inability to understand the point of view of his own members when they rebelled against the authority of his union. Since the union could not be wrong, in his view, the Communists and trouble makers were to blame.

He once said privately that he dreaded his retirement, which was to have taken place in November 1955. It was his habit to go to Transport House early and work late, and his job absorbed his energies so that life would have been empty for him without it. Yet, with the generosity which was another of his characteristics, he decided not to stand for election for another year on the General Council as he might have done. It would not, he said, have been fair to his successor.

Though his health had been bad in his last year or two, he appeared in good form in the week before he died when encountered outside Transport House. He spoke with pride of the part he had played in settling the newspaper strike and of the efforts he was making to help to avert a railway strike. He was not a clever man but he was determined, obstinate, courageous, and intensely loyal to his union, to the Labour movement, and to the country. If John Bull could be a trade union leader—as he might be in these days—Arthur Deakin could well have been regarded as his incarnation.

Arthur Deakin was born in 1890 at Sutton Coldfield, in Warwickshire. His father, who was a cobbler, died when Arthur was a child, and on his mother's remarriage the family moved to Merthyr Tydfil. At the age of 13 he started a job for 4s. a week at Guest, Keen and Nettlefolds' plant at Dowlais, where he had to work incredibly long hours. Socialism was then sweeping through the Welsh valleys, and the young man was deeply stirred by Keir Hardie and others who used to address meetings outside the gates of the factory. This revelation that life had other things to offer besides hard work led him to read widely, and by the time he was 19 he was a regular attendant at night school.

During the years of the 1914-18 War he became increasingly concerned with the affairs of his trade union, in 1919 becoming a full-time official of the Dock, Wharf, Riverside and General Workers' Union and later, on its amalgamation, of the Transport and General Workers' Union. He was based on Shotton in Flintshire and got to know intimately the detailed workings of pretty well all the trades in the area, including passenger transport, and became known as an able and patient negotiator.

Deakin became also a Labour member of the Flintshire County Council, of which he later became an alderman and eventually chairman.

In 1932 he was called to London by the headquarters of his union and offered the post of national secretary of the General Workers' group. Here his great administrative abilities were noted by the general secretary, Ernest Bevin, who three years later made him his assistant. The relationship between the two men was remarkably close and in the years that led up to 1939 it was perhaps not always realized what an influential part Deakin played in the life of the country's largest trade union. It was in the Bevin tradition of being an efficient organizer and administrator rather than of being an agitator that Deakin followed, and more than anyone he was typical of the new type of trade union official, who is conscious of representing a body which is an integral part of modern society, and who is very much aware of the responsibilities which his power lays on him. Deakin himself put down the union official's chief needs as being the ability to examine every problem objectively and see both sides, skill in negotiation and advocacy, and power to stick to his case and know his facts.

In the innumerable conferences and long hours of negotiation which make up any trade union official's life Deakin showed that he possessed these abilities to the full, and when during the early years of the war Bevin joined the Cabinet there was little doubt that Deakin was the best person to act as the union's general secretary and to take Bevin's place on the General Council of the T.U.C. He at once became involved in the job of helping to increase war production and in the many adjustments attendant on the establishment of the country's wartime routine. Among a mass of activities there stand out his advocacy of more drastic measures to provide relief for the victims of air-raids and his investigation of the many delays in transport. He was a member of the Government's War Transport Council and of the committee set up to advise the Production Executive.

In addition to these invaluable if rather humdrum activities, on several occasions he demonstrated a staunch independence, as when on business in Sweden in 1943 he explored the possibilities of peace with M. Vuori, secretary of the Finnish trade union movement (for which he received both official and much public disapproval), and when together with the executive of his union, he opposed Sir Oswald Mosley's release from detention under Regulation 18B. In 1944 he visited the French battle fronts.

After Labour's victory at the polls in 1945 and the certainty that Bevin would remain in the Government, Deakin was confirmed by a clear majority over his five opponents in the general secretaryship. Nor long afterwards he had to deal with the sensational unofficial strike of the Smithfield market transport drivers. He came in for much criticism for not being in touch with the rank-and-file members of his union whose structure was thought by many to be too cumbersome, and for allowing the negotiations over the men's claims to drag on for nine months, but in the end he maintained his authority as the men's leader. At all times he showed his belief in the strictly regular forms of trade union procedure and carried on relentless war against the unofficial strike, maintaining that the only hope lay in what he called the education of the members of trade unions.

When the true facts of the country's economic plight were fully appreciated, Deakin reacted in a way which was typical of his independence of mind. Refusing to accept the position that preference was due to any section of the community, he had led the opposition to the suggestions of the miners' trade union leaders and others that special inducements should be offered to workers in the undermanned industries and at the same time he had as hotly opposed any suggestion of direction of labour. Less than two months later he decided that a choice could be made between the two evils and caused a mild sensation by advocating what he called a "limited amount of direction". He was also very conscious of the dangers of inflation and never tired of pointing out that to secure wage increases was pointless if price increases followed. Although not one of the Labour movement's most forceful Socialists, he saw an ultimate solution to the country's difficulties through the gradual restriction of the field of private enterprise and in the belief that use rather than profit should be the motive behind production.

It was the conviction that the trade unions were but a part of the community and must not seek to dominate it that led him to take so firm a line over the unofficial strikes at the docks and in transport, and he was never tired of pointing out that strike action must not be used as a political weapon. Communists and fellow travellers time after time denounced him for the very good reason that he meant trade unionism to work within the economic system and not to be an instrument to wreck it. That attitude on his part was well exemplified by his denunciation of the World Federation of Trade Unions at the meeting in Paris in 1948, while he was actually president of the body. Then he characterized the federation as nothing more than an instrument for the furtherance of Soviet policy and led the British delegates from the hall. The American and the Dutch delegations also left.

Even after the Conservative Party came back into power, Deakin continued to urge restraint in wage claims, holding rightly that wages must be linked with production. On the other hand, he could not approve of the early economies, nor was he happy over the policy of rearmament or the general monetary policy. Nevertheless, he understood truly the place of trade unionism in the body politic and he was always anxious to show how the place won by the pioneers could be more securely held and more truly enjoyed by tolerance and good manners.

His reward was the regard of a great company of his fellows and this received official recognition by the award of the C.H. in 1949 and the signal honour of inclusion in the Privy Council in 1954.

May 2, 1955.

Colonel W. de Basil, whose ballet company was for many many years well known in Europe and America, died on July 27, 1951 in Paris.

He was at one time an officer in the Russian Army, but after the revolution went to western Europe and entered the profession of theatrical management. He had already had some experience of management of ballet and opera when in 1925 he joined Prince Zeretelli in the direction of a Russian opera company which appeared at the Lyceum Theatre in a repertory including *Russlan and Ludmilla, Boris Godunov,* and *Prince Igor,* with Chaliapine in the principal parts. After Diaghilev's death René Blum formed the Ballets Russe de Monte Carlo, and in 1932 de Basil became a co-director of the company, which had the great advantage of the services of Serge Grigoriev* as *régisseur* and Balanchine and Massine as choreographers.

The directors, however, did not always agree and René Blum soon retired to form another company, leaving de Basil in charge. His policy was to bring out the younger generation of dancers and though in its early days the company suffered from the inevitable comparisons with that of Diaghilev, who had had the proved resources of the old Imperial Ballet to draw upon, as time went on the performances of de Basil's young dancers triumphantly justified his bold decision. The company toured with success in Europe and America and worthily presented such pieces as Massine's three "symphonic" ballets, *Les Présages, Choreatium,* and *Symphonie Fantastique,* and it was also responsible for the revival of Fokine's *Le Coq d'Or.*

Though de Basil had not the same extraordinary *flair* as Diaghilev in his best days for seeing the presentation of a ballet as a whole—dancing, music, and *décor*—and his productions therefore lacked the overwhelming impact of such masterpieces as *La Boutique Fantasque* and *The Three-Cornered Hat,* he maintained ballet as a living tradition at a time when, the genius of Diaghilev having gone, there was a real danger of decline and, by keeping up public interest, he undoubtedly did much to pave the way for the later triumphs of the Vic-Wells company.

July 30, 1951.

Admiral Sir Dudley R. S. de Chair, K.C.B., K.C.M.G., M.V.O., who died at his home at Rottingdean on August 17, 1958 at the age of 93, was responsible for the organization of the North Sea blockade in the 1914-18 War and was the senior admiral in the Royal Navy at the time of his death.

Dudley Rawson Stratford de Chair was the eldest son of Dudley Raikes de Chair, and was born on August 30, 1864. Entering the Royal Navy in January 1878, at which time King George V and his elder brother, the Duke of Clarence, were cadets in the training ship Britannia, he passed out as midshipman in 1880 and was appointed to the Alexandra, flagship in the Mediterranean, in which he served for nearly three years. He was thus in the vessel at the bombardment of Alexandria on July 11, 1882, after which he was landed in the town with the Naval Brigade. He was taken prisoner by Egyptian cavalry when on special service alone outside the British lines. After six weeks of captivity he was released to rejoin his ship. After the occupation of Cairo by the British troops he was selected by Lord Wolseley to carry dispatches to Alexandria. He received the Egyptian medal, Alexandria clasp, and Khedive's bronze star.

In 1886 he was selected to specialize in the torpedo branch, and joined the Vernon schoolship. At the end of his two-year course he remained in the establishment for another two years as a junior staff officer, and on July 1, 1890, became torpedo lieutenant of the battleship Inflexible in the Mediterranean. On leaving her in 1892 he returned to the Vernon for staff duties, and except for a year as torpedo lieutenant of the Channel flagship, the Royal Sovereign, in 1893-94, he remained in the torpedo school as a staff officer until his promotion to commander in June 1897. He was commander of the Doris, flagship of Admiral Sir Harry Rawson at the Cape, from July 1897 to July 1899, and for the next three years commander of the Majestic, flagship in the Channel, and he was promoted captain on June 26, 1902.

His first three years as a captain were spent in Washington, where he was Naval Attaché, and on returning to England he commanded successively the cruisers Bacchante and Cochrane. From January 1909 to July 1911 he was Naval Assistant to the Controller of the Navy (Lord Jellicoe), and for a year after that he was captain of the battleship Colossus in the Home Fleet, until his turn came on July 31, 1912, for promotion to rear-admiral.

Following a period of special Admiralty service, he succeeded Lord Beatty on March 1, 1913, as Naval Secretary to the First Lord (Winston Churchill*). In June 1914 he took up the post of Admiral of the Training Service, but when war broke out a few weeks later he hoisted his flag in the cruiser Crescent as Rear-Admiral Commanding the Tenth Cruiser Squadron, and proceeded to establish the Northern Patrol, in the latitude of the Shetlands, for the blockade of Germany.

De Chair commanded this force until March 6, 1916, and the importance of his services towards winning the war can scarcely be exaggerated. It may be recalled that no blockade of Germany in the strict sense was declared until the Order in Council of March 11, 1915, but from the very beginning the Navy took action to intercept the passage of contraband goods to the enemy. The North Sea blockade took the form of strategically placed units of patrolling squadrons, chiefly armed merchant cruisers, all out of sight of each other, but within easy steaming distance. Usually the vessels were about 20 miles apart, and as each was afforded a clear view of 15 miles to the horizon no blockade runner could pass between them without being seen by one or both. The number of ships which ran the blockade was negligible, and its operation became increasingly effective as the war progressed. On an average, some 80 ships of all kinds were intercepted and examined weekly on the high seas by Admiral de Chair's squadron. Several ships of the squadron fell victim to submarines or mines with heavy loss of life. As Lord Jellicoe said in his book on the Grand Fleet: "The decisive effect of the blockade did not become apparent until the end, when the final crash came, and it was seen how supreme an influence on the result of the war this powerful weapon had exercised".

De Chair relinquished his command to take up the special post of Naval Adviser to the Foreign Office, where the need was felt for a senior officer with first-hand experience of the conditions of a modern blockade. He remained there until September 23, 1917, when—having reached his turn for promotion to vice-admiral—he hoisted his flag in the Dreadnought in command of the Third Battle Squadron, stationed in the Channel. On July 23, 1918, he was appointed to the office of Admiral Commanding Coastguard and Reserves and on November 25, 1920, was advanced to full Admiral. He was president of the interallied commission on enemy warships in 1921-23 and was then placed on the retired list.

In the same year he was appointed Governor of New South Wales, where he remained until 1930. His term was notable for the trial of strength in 1926-27 between the Governor and the Labour Premier, Mr. Lang. In 1926 the Government introduced a Bill to abolish the Legislative Council or second chamber. The Governor had previously consented to appoint 25 members to the council, but Lang, fearing that that was still insufficient to carry the measure, requested the Governor to appoint 20 more members, including women. De Chair however refused to make any further appointments during the lifetime of that Parliament.

He married in 1903 Enid, younger daughter of H. W. Struben, of South Africa. They had two sons, one of whom is Somerset de Chair, the writer and former member of Parliament, and a daughter.

August 19, 1958.

Albert Pierre de Courville, who died on March 7, 1960, will be remembered as one of the earliest producers, at the Hippodrome and other London theatres, of spectacular revue in the years round about the First World War.

Born in London in 1887 and educated partly in Switzerland, he began his working life in an electrical engineer's office, but quickly left it for the Corn Exchange, where his knowledge of foreign languages proved useful. He became a reporter on the *Daily Mail* and the *Evening News,* and in this capacity covered the disaster at the Courrières mine in Northern France and the wreck of the Great Eastern Railway steamer Berlin.

But he found his true vocation in the course of a visit to America in 1909. The success of one of the first revues of the Ziegfeld Follies in New York suggested to him that this new form of entertainment would suit London and, on his return to England, he abandoned journalism for the theatre.

His earliest ventures, however, were not in the field of revue. He began by introducing the French diabolo champion to audiences at the Holborn Empire, but, after some weeks, the championship was challenged and lost, and de Courville then introduced the Sicilian Players, with Mimi Aguglia and Giovanni Grasso, to the Lyric. He later attached himself to Sir Edward Moss, founder of Moss' Empires and builder of the London Hippodrome, and was entrusted with the job of finding "attractions" on the Continent.

Among his first engagements was the Oriental dancer, Sahary Djeli. He persuaded Leoncavallo to conduct *Pagliacci* and Mascagni, at about £2,000 a week, *Cavalleria Rusticana.* Mascagni, as de Courville mentioned in a book of reminiscences published in 1928, was difficult to deal with, for he had a way of suddenly stopping the orchestra and demanding the removal of some player he disapproved of.

Thereafter, de Courville produced *The Eternal Waltz* and *Arms and the Girl,* but another visit to America revealed the possibilities of jazz to him and he brought over Shirley Kellogg, who became his first wife, for *The Blue House* and *Hullo, Ragtime. Hullo, Ragtime* was followed at the Hippodrome by *Hullo, Tango,* and de Courville was lucky enough to discover Violet Loraine [q.v.] in the provinces. With *Zig-Zag* he embarked on even more lavish spectacle, and he took this show over to the Folies Bergère in 1918. He launched two big productions in London during the first year of the post-war period: *Joy-Bells* with George Robey [q.v.] and Shirley Kellogg, at the Hippodrome—his ninth show at that theatre—and *The Whirligig,* with Maisie Gay and Morris Harvey, at the Palace.

But spectacular revue was not his sole interest. He produced an intimate revue, *Pins and Needles,* in 1921—to find de Courville at the Royalty, Edmund Gwenn [q.v.] in revue, and a Grand Guignol sketch in a song and dance show was a surprise to last playgoers over Whitsuntide, a critic said. In 1922 he staged an adaptation of a French fantasy *Arlequin,* with a big emotional scene for Godfrey Tearle [q.v.] in his motley at the bedside of a dying girl, and in 1924 he brought D. Hay Petrie, the most brilliant Shakespearian clown of the early days at the Old Vic, from the Waterloo Road to the Vaudeville, and presented him in *The Looking Glass.* Petrie's song, "Oh, Shakespeare, you're the best of all, but you can't fill the fourteen-shilling stall", highlights more than one difference between the theatre of his day and ours.

None of these three productions made money and he was obliged to wind up his management soon afterwards. Together with James White he founded the Embassy Club in Bond Street.

De Courville entered films during the 1930s and was responsible for making 10, including a vehicle for Jessie Matthews, *There Goes the Bride,* in studios in Britain and three in Hollywood. He put on no fewer than 12 plays of different kinds in New York between 1940 and 1946, and returned to London in 1948 to produce *Lute Song,* an American musical melodrama with a Chinese setting, at the Winter Garden. The cast was headed by Yul Brynner and Dolly Haas. It is not, however, stars of the present epoch, but Harry Tate, Ethel Levey, George Robey, Shirley Kellogg, that de Courville's name will now recall.

After the dissolution of his marriage with Miss Kellogg in 1925, de Courville married Mrs. Edith Kelly Gould.

March 16, 1960.

Brigadier-General Sir Wyndham Deedes, C.M.G., who died in hospital in London on September 2, 1956 at the age of 73, had an exceptionally active and strenuous career but one divided into two singularly divergent compartments. For many years he served with distinction in the Army and for a short time in administrative posts in Egypt and Palestine, and after his retirement from public service he devoted himself almost entirely to social service in the East End of London.

Born on March 10, 1883, the younger son of the late Colonel H. G. Deedes, of Saltwood Castle and Sandling Park, Kent, he was educated at Eton. After leaving school he joined The Rifle Brigade, just in time to see some active service in the South African War. Able, hardworking, a clever linguist, and at that period of his life a man of normal ambitions, he did not remain long at regimental soldiering but went to the Near East as an inspector in the Turkish Gendarmerie, when an international inspectorate was formed for Macedonia in consequence of the Mürzsteg programme.

In the course of his five years in Turkey he learned to speak and write Turkish better probably than any other Englishman of the century. On one occasion, indeed, when he was inspecting a lunatic asylum in the company of two Turkish officers of gendarmerie whom he had not met previously, an inmate addressed him as a British officer and tried to explain that he was not mad at all. Deedes's Turkish companions afterwards remarked to him that now indeed they had proof of the patient's lunacy, to which Deedes retorted that the madman had recognized his nationality while they had not.

His knowledge was to stand him in good stead later on. After the 1914-18 War came and the Dardanelles expedition was decided upon, his exceptional local knowledge, his type of mind, and his inclinations marked him out for intelligence work; and during 1915 and a part of 1916 he served in that capacity on General Sir Ian Hamilton's staff at Imbros. For his services at the Dardanelles he received the D.S.O. After the Armistice he was clearly marked out to go to Constantinople as military attaché. There, however, he only remained for a year, being sent to Egypt as Director-General of Public Security in 1919.

In the meantime a remarkable change of outlook had taken place in him. The 1914-18 War had given him an impulse towards the study of the Bible, particularly of the Prophetic Books, and the Balfour Declaration had awakened in him an interest in and sympathy with Zionism that grew ever deeper. Concurrently with the development of these interests there came a loss of interest in professional and more mundane things; and, from having been in social intercourse, outlook, and habits a normal man of the world, he became practically an ascetic.

On the appointment of Sir Herbert (later Lord) Samuel* to be first High Commissioner of Palestine, Deedes, who had now become known as a strong Zionist, was appointed to be the first Chief Secretary to the Palestine Government, and took up this appointment in 1920, retiring shortly afterwards from the Army with the rank of brigadier-general. In 1921 he was created a knight bachelor, but this was the last honour which he would accept.

For the next two and a half years he worked with complete devotion, and with an almost inhuman industry and expenditure of physical power, to help to create the new Administration, having constantly before him the inspiration, which he derived from the Prophetic Books, that it was the privilege of England to help the Jewish people to a new dispensation. If it cannot be said that he was the ideal administrator—there was perhaps too much of the visionary in him, and too great a dislike of the petty things inseparable from administration, for that—he was utterly unsparing of himself in carrying out his arduous duties. The Zionists of Palestine regarded him to all intents and purposes as one of their own leaders; the Arabs found his complete command of Turkish a great help to official intercourse.

At the end of 1922 he decided to retire from the public service in order to devote himself to work in the East End of London. He had not married, and, after a period of residence at the Oxford House, he and his mother set up house together in an East End slum, which he made his headquarters for the social service to which he thereafter devoted himself. At the same time he maintained his active interest in Zionism.

The outbreak of war in 1939 and the bombing of London gave him fresh opportunities for service and, in addition to his social work, he undertook the duties of information officer for the London region under the Ministry of Information. Then, in 1941, he was elected to the L.C.C. His long and selfless devotion to his fellow men was recognized by his election as chairman of the London Council of Social Service and, though 10 years ago he was seriously ill, he maintained to the end a lively interest in the things on which he had set his heart over 30 years ago.

September 4, 1956.

Lady de Frece—See **Tilley.**

By **Alcide De Gasperi's** death at the age of 73, on August 19, 1954, Europe and the world lost a Christian statesman of whom the reputation and the respect in which he was generally held were so great in his lifetime that they cannot easily be greater in history. An adequate account of the later years of his career must become in fact a history of post-war Italy. For eight years, from December 1945 until July 1953 this quiet, devout man controlled the destinies of Italy as Prime Minister and sometimes as Foreign Minister as well. The new Italy that had to learn again all the lessons which it forgot in 20 years of fascism owes De Gasperi a debt which is less only in degree than that which the first Italy owed to Cavour.

In spite of his long-lasting pre-eminence of position De Gasperi never knew, or at least never yielded to, the temptations of power. He was an idealist in that he believed passionately in the great truths and sought assiduously for their recognition. But he was also a politician of consummate skill, fully aware that politics is the art of the possible. Time and time again his opponents, in striving to upset him, succeeded only in upsetting themselves, while De Gasperi had not apparently moved a finger.

This almost uncanny touch sometimes evoked from those who observed it a comparison with Giolitti, who also kept Italian democracy going, after a fashion, by *transformismo*—the method of playing off one political force or personality against another. But there is, in fact, little valid comparison between the two men. De Gasperi, the idealist, the internationalist, who had patriotism without nationalism, political skill without demagogy, and, above all, a strong sense of public duty without a trace of personal ambition, occupies a place all to himself in the annals of modern Italian history.

Alcide De Gasperi was born in the then Austrian province of Trento on April 3, 1881, and by the time he had reached the University of Vienna, 22 years later, was a confirmed and active Italian irredentist. In 1904 he was arrested by the Austrian police for his part in the agitation for an Italian literary and cultural centre at Innsbrück. In the Austrian elections of 1911 he was chosen to sit in the Diet at Vienna as one of the deputies for the Trento, and there he continued to work for Italian rights and interests, finally resigning his seat in 1918.

With the passage, under the peace treaties, of this part of the Habsburg domains to Italy De Gasperi became an Italian citizen, and in 1921 was elected for the Trento district to Parliament, sitting as a leading member of the *Partito Popolare,* the progressive Catholic party (the forerunner of the Christian Democrat Party) which he and Don Sturzo had together formed. This Austrian background gave De Gasperi a breadth of experience and outlook which has often been denied to Italian leaders. Years later it was to place him, with his native command of the German language, in a very special position *vis-à-vis* Dr. Adenauer*, the Chancellor of western Germany, and Robert Schuman*.

From the very first De Gasperi was resolutely anti-fascist, and together with others of the same outlook he helped to form, after Matteotti's murder in 1924, the *Aventine*—a group of deputies who abandoned Parliament in protest at fascist methods and ideas. In 1926 the fascists dissolved the *Partito Popolare,* suppressed the newspaper—*Il Nuovo Trentino*—that De Gasperi had edited for 20 years, and finally arrested and condemned De Gasperi to four years' imprisonment. He was rescued from this by the intervention of the Vatican, and in 1928 he was given a post as an assistant in the Vatican library. Here he remained, poor but at least unmolested, until Mussolini's fall in 1943. With the German occupation of Rome De Gasperi became prominent in clandestine activities, working for, among other things, the restoration of the old *Partito Popolare* on a new basis and with the new name of Christian Democracy.

In June 1944 he became a Minister in the first Government to be constituted after the allied entry into Rome. Six months later he became Minister of Foreign Affairs, a post he retained in the Parri Government in the following summer. In that capacity it was his sad duty to go to London, where the Foreign Ministers of the Great Powers were beginning to discuss the peace treaty of Italy, to defend as best he could the interests of his defeated and stricken country. On December 10, 1945, he succeeded Signor Parri as Prime Minister, after a crisis in which he himself, as head of the powerful Christian Democrat Party, played an outstanding role. His task was unenviable, as the economy of Italy had become chaotic and the bright hopes of national unity and political cohesion which had immediately succeeded the liberation had already begun to fade.

The facts proved to be no better than the prospects. The treaty, against which De Gasperi had pleaded with such eloquence at the Paris peace conference, was a bitter pill for Italy to swallow, while at home it was becoming increasingly clear that the Communists, and the Socialists led by Nenni (with whom De Gasperi had been hidden during the war and for whom he always retained a certain feeling), were spoiling for a fight. The crisis came in the middle of May 1947. Though both Communists and Socialists were members of the coalition, Togliatti Palmiro and Nenni, their respective leaders, now freely attacked the Government. With a courageous and decisive gesture designed to bring everybody face to face with their responsibilities, De Gasperi resigned. A few days later, after the failure of two elder statesmen to form an administration, he was back again, this time with a minority Government of Christian Democrats and ready for an emergency programme to save the country from the economic ruin threatening it.

Anxious months of agitation followed, during which Communists and Socialists made resolute attempts to overthrow the Government and De Gasperi by any means. The Prime Minister's firmness in face of this threat contributed in large part to the triumph which the Christian Democrat Party and its allies enjoyed at the polls in April 1948, in the first general election held under the new Constitution. This defeat in free elections of the Communists was a turning-point for Italy, and perhaps for western Europe, and De Gasperi was fully entitled to be considered the chief architect of victory.

He formed his fifth Ministry in May 1948 consisting of the four-party coalition which had won the day on April 18. Although there were in the coming years to be changes in this team, brought about by the withdrawal of one or other of the smaller parties, De Gasperi never relinquished the idea that as broadly based a government as possible was best in the interests of national unity. He disliked always the notion of a one-party Christian Democrat Government, just as he rejected the efforts of those who tried to link the Christian Democrats more closely with the Church. His conception of the great, sprawling, often unruly party of which he was the leader was that of a central grouping serving as the keystone of a parliamentary coalition. As for the Church, De Gasperi was a devout Catholic but almost an "anti-clerical" in the historical and political sense of the term.

The years that followed made him more and more of an international figure. Together with Count Sforza [q.v.], his Foreign Minister, he set to work patiently to reinstate the new democratic Italy in the framework of international relations. Against the fiercest opposition from the Communists and in face of doubts even from some of his own party, De Gasperi skilfully helped to pilot Italy into the North Atlantic Treaty Organization. From the very first he was an ardent supporter of the idea of a united Europe. He had his own special difficulties here, for the disgruntlement which Italy had felt at the peace treaty was renewed at regular intervals by outbursts of agitation over Trieste, in which neo-fascists and communists alike joined in accusing De Gasperi and Sforza of betraying Italy's interests.

To an unhappily large degree De Gasperi was for these years the prisoner of the Trieste question. If he erred in his approach it was because, as a political leader, he failed to get the Italians to realize that they could never receive full satisfaction in this matter. The three-Power declaration of 1948 (in which the United States, the United Kingdom and France supported the return of the whole of the Free Territory of Trieste to Italy) inevitably changed its import after the break between Tito and the Cominform. He must have seen this as clearly as anyone outside Italy, but caught in the crossfire of national and nationalistic feeling, he tended to keep his views to himself, with the result that time made a solution harder, instead of easier.

In the course of 1951 De Gasperi, accompanied by Sforza, met the French Prime Minister and Foreign Minister at Santa Margherita; went to London for talks with Attlee* and Morrison*—talks which had, at least at the time, the happy appearance of "burying the past"—and was received by King George VI [q.v.] and addressed members of both Houses of Parliament; received Dr. Adenauer in Rome, and went to the United States, where, among other successes, he made a striking address to Congress. At the same time he was deeply involved in the preparations for the forming of a coal and steel pool, as envisaged in the Schuman Plan, and for the setting up of a European army, in which German contingents should play their part. By the end of 1951 he had the satisfaction of seeing the N.A.T.O. Powers meet in Rome and the *de facto* revision of the Italian peace treaty, for which he and Sforza had worked from the day of its signature, agreed to by the non-Russian signatories.

Meanwhile, at home the programme of social reform was slowly taking shape. Land reform, fiscal reform, investment plans for absorbing unemployed—all began to bear some sort of fruit. De Gasperi paid several visits between 1950 and 1952 to the "forgotten south" of Italy to see for himself the appalling conditions of these regions. As he once remarked privately, "It would all be so much easier to get the things done that needed doing if they could be done autocratically". It was very far from his mind that this in fact was the best way, and so month after month he sat patiently upon the ministerial bench in the Senate or the Chamber listening to the debates or defending and explaining the measures on which his Government needed action or approval. He was no orator, but possessed a nimbleness in debate which generally assured him the victory in any brush with his critics. It seemed during these years that this modest, quiet, unexciting man had become almost a one-man administration and any prospect of a possible successor was looked for in vain.

Although by this time over 70, he campaigned with more than the vigour of a young man for the local elections in northern Italy in 1951, and in the south in 1952. (His campaign tour before the 1953 general election was perhaps an even more astonishing feat of endurance). The neo-fascists had by now become a force to be reckoned with, and many thought that in order to defeat the communists, the Christian Democrats should ally themselves with these unrepentants of the Right on the principle that ends justify the means. De Gasperi rejected this idea altogether and fought the battle with equal energy against Right and Left. His appeal now, as always, was for national unity in face of threats to freedom from wherever they came. His faith in the commonsense of his countrymen never wavered and, supported by this confidence, he continued to bear the great burden of duty.

By the autumn of 1952 preparations were being made to hold a general election in 1953 for a new Chamber of Deputies, and De Gasperi, now at the head of his seventh consecutive Government, decided, together with his ministerial collaborators, to introduce an Electoral Reform Bill which would ensure an ample working majority for the party or group of parties obtaining a bare majority at the elections. The Bill was ferociously attacked inside and outside Parliament by the Socialists and Communists. In the end it passed, but failed in its object. By the narrow margin of 57,000 votes the Christian Democrats and their allies failed to gain an absolute majority. This result was a severe personal blow to De Gasperi, made heavier when on July 28, 1953 his eighth Ministry was rejected by the Chamber of Deputies and the veteran Italian statesman, for the first time after the war, returned to his place on the party benches as a simple deputy.

For some time past he had occasionally indicated that he would welcome a respite from ministerial responsibilities, and he now left the field open to younger men and began to devote himself to the organization of his Christian Democrat Party as its political secretary. This did not prevent him from continuing his efforts on behalf of European unity, and early in 1954 he was elected president of the six-Power coal and steel pool, which he had always hoped would form the basis for the creation of a European Defence Community and ultimately of a European political community. One of his last important activities was to preside over the annual congress of his party in Naples in June 1954. The congress showed that new and younger Christian Democrat leaders were coming to the fore, and De Gasperi again felt the time had come to make way for new blood. He therefore relinquished his post as political secretary to Fanfani. He was then elected president of the party and continued to be guide, counsellor, and friend to his successor in party and ministerial posts.

De Gasperi's literary output was considerable, most of his published work being concerned with politics and social studies. In June 1953 he visited Britain to receive the Honorary degree of Doctor of Civil Law which was conferred upon him by Oxford University. He was entertained during his stay by Sir Winston Churchill* with whom he discussed Anglo-Italian relations and European problems.

He married in 1921 Signora Francesca Romani, who survives him together with four daughters.

August 20, 1954.

Walter de la Mare, O.M., C.H., died on June 22, 1956 at his home at Twickenham at the age of 83.

His was a poetic spirit of rare imaginative delicacy, and he brought to his verse and his prose an apprehension of seen and unseen mystery that words other than his own can but dimly convey. In the opinion of many he has a claim to be considered the most magically evocative of English poets since Tennyson.

This most modest of men, Walter John de la Mare, was born at Charlton, Kent, on April 25, 1873. His father, of Huguenot descent, was James Edward Delamare, churchwarden and brother of Abraham Delamare, Rector of St. Thomas's, Woolwich, and his mother was Lucy Sophia, daughter of Dr. Colin Arrot Browning, naval surgeon at Woolwich Dockyard, and a distant kinsman of Robert Browning. He was educated at the choir school of St. Paul's Cathedral, where he started the school paper, *The Choristers' Journal.* At Easter 1890 he entered the city office of the Anglo-American Oil Company, where he worked until, in 1908, the grant of a civil list pension enabled him to give all his time to literature.

In 1895 a short story called "Kismet" appeared in the *Sketch* above the name of Walter Ramal. Soon afterwards Roger Ingpen persuaded St. Loe Strachey, then editor of the *Cornhill,* to read another tale by this same Ramal; and in 1896 "The Mote" was published in the magazine, to be followed by other stories no less eagerly accepted. In 1902 came the first book, *Songs of Childhood,* still by Walter Ramal. In 1904 a first novel followed, *Henry Brocken,* then the *Poems* of 1906. In 1908, when he left the City, de la Mare, now Ramal no longer, did some reviewing for, among other journals, *The Times Literary Supplement.*

There is some pleasantly illuminating bibliographical detail concerning these early years of writing in the critical study of him by his friend, Forrest Reid, which appeared in 1929. In later years de la Mare lectured a good deal, both in England and in the United States. There was no mistaking his hand in a review; and his lectures were as enlivening as his talk. But English literature will know him as poet, a story-teller, and an anthologist.

The first thing that all would say of Walter de la Mare is that he made the best poetry for children that ever was written. His delight in the fact and the appearance, his love of strange and resounding names, his clean freedom from affectation and from moralizing showed not that he understood what children like, be it nonsensical or mournful or what not, but that the child in himself was living still. Stevenson is didactic and sentimental by the side of him; and only Blake carried so much of the child into maturity. The peculiar quality of Walter de la Mare lay in his combination of the child and the man. He began and he ended, it has been said, in wonder. The delighted or terrified wonder of the child led straight into the wonder of the man, the thinker, so intensely aware of the fact and the appearance, and he could not stop at them, but must go through them to a reality of another kind which he apprehended no less keenly. In "The Memoirs of a Midget" and other stories he chose an odd point of view because everything was odd to him. In "The Return" and other stories he chose subjects of fear and horror because, of all things, fear most quickens the sense of the wonder of life. The world of dream and vision was as real to him as the world of sense; and from Bayswater (as in his only play, *Crossings*) one may step at once into enchanted woods. And with the intense labour of the artist (labour of which the effort stands out in some of his earlier work not in his true vein) he made for himself the perfect expression, especially in the rhythm of his verse, for this joy and wonder and fear. Thus from "fragile, flower-like loveliness" to romping nonsense, from a child's happy chant to reverent probings into mystery, he made the English verse and prose that he needed.

His later work attests a continuous deepening of his sensibilities and visionary questionings. He could never spend the riches of his imagination, and it is scarcely possible to do more than catalogue some of the volumes which appeared under his name during the last 20 years or so. There was a further collection of poetry, *Poems, 1919 to 1934,* and in 1942 all his poetry for adults was collected into one edition.

Among his individual volumes of stories there were *On the Edge* (1930), *The Lord Fish* (1933) and *The Wind Blows Over* (1936), in all of which he conjures a landscape just this side of the frontier of dream or across it. There were three enchanting anthologies: *Early One Morning* (1935), which holds his reflections on childhood; *Behold, This Dreamer* (1939), an anthology in verse and prose of the musings of the dreaming mind; and the anthology, a rich and golden harvest, entitled *Love* (1943).

In 1945 came a volume, *The Burning-Glass, and other Poems,* in which the fusion of the homely and the ethereal had all his wonted magic, and two years later, in his seventy-fourth year, *The Traveller*—a parable that lies at the heart of perhaps every poem that Walter de la Mare wrote—bore witness to his sense of the transitoriness of natural things and of the ultimate reality. It is a poem that sums up the poet's inward grace of vision.

His latest work, *Winged Chariot* (1951), *Private View* (1953), and *O Lovely England* (1954), deepens and strengthens the impression of his earlier poems. And in 1955, when he was 82, appeared another collection of stories, *A Beginning,* which contained passages as good as he had ever written and even included a new and successful experiment.

He was made a Companion of Honour in 1948 and to this was added the Order of Merit in the Coronation Honours, and he had honorary degrees conferred by Cambridge, St. Andrews, Bristol, and London. In 1944 he was elected an honorary Fellow of Keble College, Oxford, and in 1955 he was made an honorary member of the American Academy of Arts and Letters.

He married Constance Elfrida, a sister of Roger Ingpen. His family life was of intense interest, significance, and value to Walter de la Mare. To think of him, indeed, is not to think first of his writings. It is to enjoy once more in retrospect his scarcely less than enchanting personality. It was well said of him by a friend that he combined the best qualities of a man, of a woman, of a child, and of a dog. He had the appeal which can only vaguely be described as "dearness". And to talk with him was to be so lit by his keenness, his power, and his charm that every talk was too short.

His wife died in 1943, and he is survived by two sons and two daughters. The elder son, Richard de la Mare, is a director of the publishing firm of Faber and Faber.

June 23, 1956.

Marshal de Lattre de Tassigny—See **Lattre.**

Jack de Leon, who died on September 21, 1956 at Richmond, Surrey, after a heart attack at the age of 55, was a forceful and beneficent influence on the London stage for far longer than would seem possible for his age.

Born on August 12, 1901, he was educated at University College School, Hampstead, and made so early a start in the theatre that he felt it necessary to put up his age by four years for fear that managers would not take him seriously. He was only in his early twenties when, with his sister, Delia Dellvina, he broke new ground in theatrical management by going out to the suburbs to found a theatre with the avowed object of trying out new plays. Such was the origin of the "Q" Theatre, which opened in the last month of 1924 not with a new play but with a revival of Gertrude Jennings's successful comedy, *The Young Person in Pink.*

Those early days meant hard and unremitting work in selecting and mounting play after play. That, together with a genuine flair, was the secret of his success in management which lasted for upwards of 25 years. Far enough from the West End to make it a real centre for local playgoers, drawn from the affluent surrounding districts, the little theatre proved not only a monetary success but a cultural force and a boon to new and young playwrights, actors, and actresses.

Of the hundreds of new plays and important revivals presented there, more than 60 were transferred to the West End and among the many subsequently successful playwrights given their first chance at the "Q" is [Sir] Terence Rattigan [d. 1977], whose first comedy, *First Episode,* was produced there in 1934. There was a brief episode, between 1938 and 1940, when he conducted the Embassy, another suburban theatre, in conjunction with the "Q", but this came to an end in 1940 when the Embassy was bombed. In 1949 he gave up active direction of the "Q" Theatre for some time, but resumed it in the course of the next year and produced his own version of Part 1 of Goethe's *Faust.*

He had had by that time a whole string of successful productions at West End theatres to his credit, including Aldous Huxley's* *The Giaconda Smile* at the New Theatre and some of the plays he himself wrote in collaboration with Jack Celestin, of which *The Man at Six* is the best known. Most of these are little more than good theatre of the "whodunit" variety, but one play, a fantasy based on an episode vaguely alluded to in Everard Meynell's life of Francis Thompson, manifests a sensibility and delicacy of touch which proved most moving when it was produced at the "Q" in 1933.

De Leon's last production in London was *The Count of Clerambard,* at the Garrick Theatre. He was taken ill a few weeks before the play was due to come on and for the first time in his life he missed one of his own first nights. During his last, inactive months he tried his hand at writing radio plays, and one of these was given by I.T.V. on September 20.

He leaves a widow and a daughter.

September 22, 1956.

General Sir Beauvoir de Lisle, K.C.B., K.C.M.G., D.S.O., who died at his home in London on July 16, 1955 at the age of 90, may be regarded as a striking type of the British "fighting" general produced by the First World War. A stubborn and tenacious leader with a touch of fanaticism, who was perhaps at his best in conducting a defensive battle, his name is chiefly associated with the 29th Division, which he commanded in Gallipoli and France.

Henry de Beauvoir, son of Richard F. V. de Lisle, a descendant of an ancient Channel Island family, was born in Guernsey on July 27, 1864. After being educated in Jersey he entered Sandhurst in 1881 and was gazetted to the Durham Light Infantry. He joined the 2nd Battalion at Gibraltar, whence that regiment was sent to Egypt. Having shown himself to be a good horseman, de Lisle was selected for service with the mounted infantry of the Frontier Field Force, and thus served in the Sudan during 1885-86, participating in the campaign against the dervish amir of Dongola, including the affair at Ambigole Wells, the action at Ginnis, and the pursuit of the dervishes to Absarat. He was awarded the D.S.O. and mentioned in dispatches.

Shortly afterwards the battalion was transferred to India. There de Lisle received his promotion to captain in October 1891 and was appointed adjutant. But it was at polo that he was soon to earn a remarkable reputation. For 10 years he acted as captain of the Durham Light Infantry polo team. He taught his team to play the game as a science, and as it had seldom been played before. All young officers were at once "entered" to polo on joining; they attended riding school under de Lisle's own supervision. The result was the repeated capture by the Durham Light Infantry not only of the Infantry Polo Cup but, in one memorable year, of the Regimental Polo Cup, when they beat the crack teams of all the British cavalry regiments then serving in India.

But de Lisle was a keen and practical soldier, polo being an expression of his spirit in peace time. He passed into the Staff College and graduated in 1899, at the beginning of the South African War. He was now able to secure employment on the staff with mounted troops in a form of warfare to which his talents were well adapted. In January 1900 he was given the command of a mounted infantry battalion, then of a mobile column, of a cavalry brigade, and eventually of an Australian mounted brigade. He arrived at the Cape in time to serve under French and Colesberg, and was later severely wounded at Venterskroon.

Being a horseman by nature and a successful leader of mounted troops by reputation, it was not surprising that he should now have sought a transfer to the cavalry arm; in October 1902 he went to the 5th Dragoon Guards. In February 1906 he succeeded to the command of the Royals, who had then been for some two years in India, and gained the brevet of colonel in August.

The First World War found him on Salisbury Plain in command of the 2nd Cavalry Brigade. Included in the British Expeditionary Force, de Lisle's brigade was the first to make contact with the enemy, and was prominent at Elouges, the day after the Battle of Mons, and again during the Battle of the Aisne. In October 1914, when the Cavalry Corps was formed, de Lisle was given command of the 1st Cavalry Division. After the move to Flanders in October his dismounted division held its own splendidly at Messines, holding off three German cavalry divisions. Fierce fighting continued, but the stubborn resistance of de Lisle's cavalrymen was never broken.

De Lisle was now selected to command the 29th Division on the Gallipoli peninsula. Arriving from France, he reached the already famous 29th on the evening of June 4, during the third attempt to break through the Turkish front near Krithia. Six weeks later the 29th Division was moved to Suvla and de Lisle assumed temporary command of IX Army Corps there, and fought the hopeless Battle of Scimitar Hill.

After the evacuation of Gallipoli the 29th Division proceeded first to Egypt, thence to be transferred in the spring of 1916 to France, where de Lisle set about training and refitting the division in preparation for the coming offensive. On July 1 when the battle opened de Lisle was set the heart-breaking task of capturing Beaumont Hamel; and after this failure the 29th Division did not reappear upon the Somme until October.

In April 1917 the 29th Division went through a fortnight's heavy fighting at Monchy, during the Battle of Arras, and later went north again to fight in the third Battle of Ypres, at Langemarck, and Broodseinde, where the general himself was flung into the mud by the burst of a heavy shell, but picked himself up unhurt and unmoved. On October 9 and 29 the division was heavily engaged in the Battle of Poelcapelle, and it played a conspicuous part in the Battle of Cambrai.

In March 1918 de Lisle left the division to assume command of the XIII Corps. For over two and a half years he had commanded the 29th through some of the most stubborn fighting of the war. He had won the respect and confidence of all ranks. Abrupt, reserved, and little disposed to suffer fools gladly, his energy and keenness never failed. The 29th suffered very heavy loss on many occasions; de Lisle was always its "recreator", forming it anew, and impressing the reinforcements with his own sense of duty and of discipline.

After being with the XIIIth Corps for a month de Lisle, now temporary lieutenant-general, was transferred to the XVth Corps which he commanded until after the end of hostilities. In 1919 he was appointed G.O.C. Western Command with headquarters at Chester, where he remained until the end of September 1923. He was promoted general in January 1926, and retired from the Army in October of that year. In 1928 he was appointed Colonel of The Durham Light Infantry, which he remained until 1934.

General de Lisle was created K.C.B. in 1917 and K.C.M.G. in 1919. He was also a Grand Officer of the Order of Leopold and had the Belgian Croix de Guerre; he was commander of the Legion of Honour, and held the French Croix de Guerre and the Grand Cross of the Serbian Order of the White Eagle.

He published two books on his favourite sport, *Polo in India,* and *Tournament Polo,* and also *Reminiscences of Sport and War* in 1939.

He married, in 1902, Leila Annette, eldest daughter of Wilberforce Bryant, of Stoke Park, Stoke Poges, Buckinghamshire, who died in 1938. They had one son.

July 18, 1955.

Cecil B. de Mille died in Hollywood on January 21, 1959. He was 77.

His death marks the end of an era in American film-making, and breaks one of the last direct links with the earliest days of Hollywood. Most Hollywood stars have been claimed as the discoveries of any of a dozen people; to de Mille belonged the unique distinction of being, beyond a shadow of a doubt, the discoverer of Hollywood itself.

Cecil Blount de Mille was born at Ashfield, Massachusetts, on August 12, 1881. His father, Henry C. de Mille, who came from an old New York family of Dutch origin, was a notable popular dramatist, and worked for some years in close collaboration with David Belasco, the American master of stage spectacle (an important formative influence on the future master of spectacle on the screen). Cecil and his brother William, who later himself became a playwright, were brought up in an atmosphere compounded of theatre and strict, Episcopalian, Christianity (another influence to remain important throughout his life), and though de Mille attended the Pennsylvania Military College for a while, he soon entered New York Academy of Dramatic Art with the intention of becoming an actor.

He acted in New York for several years (and in 1902 married an actress from the same company, Constance Adams) and tried his hand at play-writing before he met two other aspiring young men, Jesse L. Lasky and Samuel Goldfish (later Goldwyn*) and decided to go into the new entertainment craze, motion pictures.

Starting with a working capital of $20,000, the Jesse L. Lasky Feature Play Company was formed and de Mille set out westward in search of a location for filming; finding Arizona unsuitable, he hit upon a barn in a little-known country suburb of Los Angeles called Hollywood, transformed a barn into an improvised studio, and made the first American feature film, *The Squaw Man,* from a stage play by Milton Royle; this was a great success, making the extraordinary amount, for those days, of $225,000, and one of the longest and most fruitful careers in films was begun.

Two years later, in 1915, he put the opera star Geraldine Farrar* under contract, and he created for himself other stars, among them Wallace Reid and Sessue Hayakawa. In 1918 the Lasky Company merged with Adolph Zukor's Famous Players Corporation to form Famous Players-Lasky Corporation, and de Mille was made director-general. From this position he was able to experiment in various directions, and became for a time the most advanced director in Hollywood in his treatment of sex on the screen; with a former Mack Sennett [q.v.] bathing beauty, Gloria Swanson, as his star he made a number of sex-comedies and dramas, perhaps the best-remembered being *Male and Female,* based, somewhat improbably, on Barrie's *The Admirable Crichton.* But it was not until 1923 that he found his true bent, and the sort of film with which his name is always associated, in *The Ten Commandments.*

Much has been said of de Mille's religious films, pointing out the adroitness with which themes of sex and violence are mixed with more high-toned elements, and there is no denying that many of his films in this genre have tended to dwell, intermittently at least, on passages of physical violence and extravagant sexual detail (the long parade of elaborate bathing scenes and whippings without which no de Mille film really seemed complete).

On the other hand there seems no doubt of the sincerity of his intentions, and his own apologia may serve as comment: that if his films present religion made palatable with more readily saleable elements, better palatable religion than no religion at all. *The Ten Commandments* exemplified all his faults as well as his virtues; the mastery of spectacle in particular remains memorable, and many would claim that the parting of the Red Sea in his new version (1957) offers no improvement on the original of over 30 years before.

This was followed in 1927 by the most severe and restrained of his religious films, *The King of Kings,* a filmed Passion Play which still circulates in church halls today and remains, despite moments of bathos, a surprisingly impressive achievement. The coming of sound found de Mille eager to experiment with the new possibilities of the medium, and his first talking picture, *Dynamite,* was released in 1928. In 1931 he made a sound version of his old silent success *The Squaw Man,* and in the next year returned to religious themes with *The Sign of the Cross,* made forever memorable by Claudette Colbert's bath in asses' milk and Charles Laughton's* splendid performance as the Emperor.

There followed a number of diverting, if not specially remarkable, costume spectacles, such as *Cleopatra* (1934) and *The Crusades* (1935), before in 1936 he turned to indigenous American material with *The Plainsman* and *The Buccaneer.* A Western, *North West Mounted Police,* went back for its material to a play from his acting days, *The Royal Mounted,* and *Reap the Wild Wind* (1942) featured storms, shipwrecks, high-running passions, and a terrifying giant squid.

His most notable films of recent years were a further return to the Bible (more or less), *Samson and Delilah,* a spectacular circus story, *The Greatest Show on Earth,* and his new version of *The Ten Commandments,* a new treatment of Moses's early life which cost the unprecedented amount of over £5m, and had more than earned back its cost in the first few months of its run.

De Mille was well known by sight to his audiences, as it became his habit in later years to introduce his films himself from the screen; his last film work was the making of an introduction to a new version of *The Buccaneer,* produced by himself but directed by his son-in-law, Antony Quinn. Just before his death he was planning to film the life of Baden-Powell.

Cecil B. de Mille was more than just a director: he was an institution. Reputed to have made over 70 films in his time, he had an unparalleled grasp of the wants and needs of the public, and perhaps made fewer commercial failures than any other director. A deeply religious man, he believed implicitly in the religious importance of his films, and laid aside all the profits of *The King of Kings* and the new *Ten Commandments* for religious charities. Not perhaps, aesthetically speaking, a great director (his handling of the medium remained to the end rather stiff and theatrical), he was nevertheless a truly great personality and one of the real founders of the American film industry.

January 22, 1959.

Lord Denman, formerly Governor-General of Australia, died on June 24, 1954 at Hove, Sussex, at the age of 79.

The Right Hon. Sir Thomas Denman, third Baron Denman, of Dovedale, in the county of Derby, in the Peerage of the United Kingdom, G.C.M.G., K.C.V.O., was a great grandson of the first Baron Denman, the famous lawyer and judge. Born on November 16, 1874, he succeeded his great uncle, the second Baron, when he was 19 years old. He was educated at Sandhurst and was gazetted to The Royal Scots. He saw active service in the South African War with the Middlesex Squadron of Imperial Yeomanry. In South Africa he distinguished himself by his care and considerate treatment of the men under his command. But his interests lay in politics rather than soldiering, and at an early age he made his mark in the House of Lords on the Liberal side, soon taking a prominent place in the party councils, officiating as a whip and also as Deputy Speaker.

In 1903 he married Gertrude Mary, daughter of the first Lord Cowdray. Lady Denman [q.v.] died little more than three weeks before him. On the entry of the Liberal Government into power in 1905, he became a Lord in Waiting and afterwards Captain of the Honourable Corps of Gentlemen-at-Arms.

In 1911 he was appointed Governor-General of the Commonwealth of Australia, in succession to Lord Dudley. His term of office coincided with the first Labour Government in the Commonwealth. His relations with the Labour Ministers were not only correct, but cordial, and he retained the complete confidence of all parties. Conscientious in the discharge of his public duties, he won regard by his geniality and sincerity and his consistent advocacy of the national aims and of Australian ideals. During his period of office as Governor-General three events of outstanding importance were the inauguration of the new federal capital at Canberra, the completion of which was delayed by the 1914-18 War and which was finally opened in 1927 by King George VI [q.v.], then Duke of York; the commencement of the trans-continental railway to Western Australia; and the initiation of the compulsory military service scheme. In defence matters the Commonwealth made great strides during Lord Denman's term of office.

He took great interest in all forms of sport. In particular he organized a Government House polo team which was very successful and popular. He was himself devoted to shooting and hunting and all field sports, and was at one time one of the most successful amateur steeplechase riders in the country. The Governor-General was greatly helped in all that he did by Lady Denman, whose winning personality made her extremely popular among all sections of the Australian populace. In particular she devoted herself to the interests of music and the drama, being herself a good musician and a talented amateur actress. She formed a great friendship for Mme. Melba, who was at that time at the height of her powers and popularity. In 1914 Lord Denman was obliged to resign the office of Governor-General, owing to ill-health.

On the outbreak of war in 1914 Lord Denman was appointed lieutenant-colonel, 1st County of London Yeomanry, and later served on the staff in France. After the end of hostilities he again interested himself in politics, taking part in debates in the House of Lords on any subject, especially in relation to oversea affairs, which evoked his sympathy. In 1931 he initiated a debate in the House of Lords on the subject of the new position under the terms of the Statute of Westminster of the Governor-General of the Commonwealth as the representative of his Majesty only, and urged the appointment of a High Commissioner in Australia to represent the Home Government.

He never lost his interest in things Australian and to an advanced age made pungent and witty comments on a wide variety of affairs both in the House of Lords and in letters to the press.

He leaves a son and a daughter and is succeeded in the family honours by his son, the Hon. Thomas Denman, who was born in 1905.

June 25, 1954.

Lady Denman, G.B.E., chairman of the National Federation of Women's Institutes from its inception in 1917 until 1946, died in London after an operation on June 2, 1954.

She was the Hon. Gertrude Mary Pearson, only daughter of the first Viscount Cowdray, and she married Lord Denman [q.v.] in 1903 when she was still under 20 years of age. An early interest in politics led to her election to the executive committee of the Women's National Liberal Federation in 1909, but she resigned in the course of the next year a little while before her husband took up office as Governor-General of Australia. During her husband's term of office in Australia she earned golden opinions not only as a gracious hostess but as a patroness of many good causes, and there were many in Australia who regretted the departure of the Governor-General and his wife when his term came to an end in 1914.

Back in England, she turned her attention to the Agricultural Organization Society and became the chairman of the first Women's Institute Sub-Committee. When the Ministry of Agriculture took over the institutes she accepted the post of assistant director of the women's branch of the food production department and thus became responsible for the promotion of the Women's Institute movement. She was all her life attached to, and proficient in, most of the old English sports and pastimes, and was above all a good housewife. Her great ambition was to make England "merrie" again and to this end she bent her great energy and organizing ability to link together the thousands of countrywomen in all kinds of useful as well as entertaining pursuits.

Under her guidance the movement went from strength to strength and became a real power for good throughout Britain. With such a record behind her she was clearly the right person to organize the Women's Land Army when the Ministry of Agriculture decided just before the outbreak of war in 1939 that every effort to increase the production of food in the United Kingdom would be one of the major factors in strategy. She lent her home, Balcombe Place, in Sussex, for use as the headquarters of the organization of which she became honorary director, and started the Women's Land Army Benevolent Fund, of which she became chairman.

It was a thousand pities that the exclusion of the members of the Women's Land Army from participation in the gratuities given to women who had served in Civil Defence and in the Armed Forces led her to sever her official connexion with the Government in 1945. Her work for the Women's Institutes, however, was suitably commemorated in 1948 by the founding of Denman College, the first national college for countrywomen, and home of the Women's Institute movement, at Marcham Park, in Berkshire.

Though her greatest work was the development of the women's institutes, she also found time to work from 1934 to 1939 as a member of the executive committee of the Land Settlement Association and as chairman of the Family Planning Association. She was also a life trustee of the Carnegie United Kingdom Trust.

In her youth she was often to be seen in the hunting field, but later her principal pastime was golf and she was president of the Ladies' Golf Union from 1932 to 1938.

She is survived by her husband, a son, and a daughter.

June 3, 1954.

Queen Alexandrine, Queen Mother of Denmark, died on December 28, 1952 in hospital in Copenhagen, after a long illness.

She was born at Schwerin on December 24, 1879, the Duchess Alexandrine Augustine, elder daughter of the Grand Duke Friedrich Franz III of Mecklenburg-Schwerin by his marriage to the Grand Duchess Anastasia of Russia. The Duchess Alexandrine was married at Cannes on April 26, 1898, to the Crown Prince Christian, eldest son of King Frederik VIII of Denmark. The Crown Prince succeeded his father in 1912 as King Christian X. Her Majesty leaves two sons, King Frederik*, who was born in 1899, and married in 1935 Princess Ingrid of Sweden, and Prince Knud, who married in 1933 his cousin, Princess Caroline Matilda, daughter of the late King Christian's brother, Prince Harald.

It is for her strong and devoted sense of duty that Queen Alexandrine will always be remembered by the Danish people. By nature very reserved and longing for that privacy which the consorts of constitutional monarchs cannot know, she yet entered heart and soul into all those public duties devolving upon a queen. When King Christian visited the Faroes or Iceland or Greenland, Queen Alexandrine was at his side, in spite of the fact that at least in her later years she had by no means robust health. Queen Alexandrine was fond of outdoor life. She always accompanied the King to Cannes, where they could be seen daily on their cycling tours. The summer was invariably spent at the Skaw in North Jutland. Here Queen Alexandrine threw off some of that reserve which characterized her in Copenhagen, and mixed freely with the local population of this charming Danish village.

Queen Alexandrine was a keen music-lover, and she was always to be seen at important concerts in Copenhagen. Wagner's music in particular she admired, and it was her custom to go to Bayreuth for the Wagner festivals. It was a great joy to her that her elder son, King Frederik, had inherited this love of music from her and had indeed become a conductor of distinction.

But it was the home and its quiet appeal which was closest to the Queen's heart. It was for this that the Danes, who are essentially a home-loving people, so much admired her. And they will think of her as a wife who stood by her husband in all things (especially during the occupation of Denmark by the Germans), and as a mother who watched devotedly over the welfare of her sons.

December 29, 1952.

Sir Maurice Denny, BT., K.B.E., president of William Denny and Brothers, of Dumbarton, builders of the *Cutty Sark* and patentees of the device against rolling, the Denny-Brown stabilizer, died on February 2, 1955, little more than a week before his sixty-ninth birthday.

Maurice Edward Denny was the eldest son of Sir Archibald Denny, first baronet, and grandson of Peter Denny, one of the founders of the family firm. Born at Dumbarton on February 11, 1886, he was educated at Tonbridge School, and after spending two years in Switzerland and one in Germany went to America, where he studied for four years at the Massachusetts Institute of Technology. On his return he was for a time with Messrs. William Doxford and Sons at Sunderland, and then gained further practical experience in the family shipyard at Dumbarton. In 1911 he became a partner in the firm, and when it was converted into a limited company in 1918 he was appointed a director, becoming vice-chairman in 1920 and chairman in 1922. During the 1914-18 War he served in the Machine Gun Corps, and was created a C.B.E. in 1918.

He was elected in 1935 president of the Institute of Marine Engineers—a position held by both his father and his grandfather—and also of the Shipbuilding Employers' Federation. Five years later he was elected president of the Shipbuilding Conference. In 1952 he and his two cousins who had been the architects of the company's success since 1911 retired, and a cousin of a younger generation became chairman; Sir Maurice became president.

He then, though continuing to take a lively interest in the progress of the business, had the opportunity to pursue the studies of birds upon which he had already spent much of his spare time, and to indulge in his other hobbies of golf and model-making. He had already, many years before, presented to the Science Museum, South Kensington, a model made with his own hands of what was perhaps the firm's greatest achievement, the Cutty Sark.

Lesser achievements there were, among them not only the Denny-Brown Stabilizer, but also the first helicopter known to aeronautical science, and Sir Thomas Lipton's Shamrock II and Shamrock III. During the Second World War the firm launched 12 destroyers, 10 sloops, two merchant aircraft-carriers, and 10 other vessels for the Royal Navy. He retained his places on the boards of the many enterprises who sought the benefit of his wisdom and experience.

Sir Maurice Denny, who succeeded to the baronetcy in 1936, married, in 1916, Marjorie, daughter of the late W. R. Lysaght, C.B.E. There were two sons and a daughter of the marriage and the baronetcy devolves upon the elder son, Mr. Alistair Maurice Archibald Denny, who is married and has a son.

February 3, 1955.

The death of **Professor Edward Dent** which took place at his home in London on August 22, 1957 at the age of 81, robs Cambridge University of a distinguished scholar of English music, one who made an unusually varied contribution to the cause of opera; it robs the wider field of contemporary European music of an international counsellor and mediator.

Edward Joseph Dent came of a family of Quaker origin which for many generations had been settled at Ribston Hall, in Yorkshire, where he was born on July 16, 1876. His father was John Dent Dent, and Edward was the youngest of a large family. He was educated at Eton, where he had the good fortune to be taught music by C. H. Lloyd. He proceeded to King's College, Cambridge, and continued his musical studies under Stanford and Charles

Wood. But it may not be fanciful to suggest that Dent learnt as much, at least in matters of taste, from Oscar Browning, who may well have been responsible for fostering the enthusiasm for eighteenth-century music, and especially for Mozart, which bore such excellent fruit in later years.

He was elected to a fellowship of his college in 1902. This was a rare, if not unprecedented, honour for a musician, which was to have a profound effect upon the status of music in the university. He fully justified his election, not only by his thesis *Alessandro Scarlatti, his Life and Works,* which was published in 1905, but by the manner in which he gathered together the young musicians in Cambridge and inspired them with his own ideals of scholarship and thoroughness. Without Dent's influence, it is difficult to believe that either research work or musical performances in Cambridge would have reached the high level which they have shown. For besides his work as an historian of music Dent turned to the practical side of his art.

He set himself to the production in Cambridge of a neglected masterpiece, which had fallen out of the repertory in England and had, in any case, never been worthily performed—Mozart's *Die Zauberflöte.* He made an English translation of the libretto, and the opera was performed at Cambridge in December 1911. The result was twofold. There was a quickening of interest in the work, which was subsequently revived in London at the Old Vic by Sir Thomas Beecham*, and a sudden realization of the wrong attitude, which had turned Mozart's operas into mere opportunities for the display of star singers. In the second place it turned Dent's attention to the study of Mozart's work as a whole, and the results were embodied in his next book *Mozart's Operas.*

From Mozart Dent passed back to Purcell, whose *Fairy Queen* was in preparation at Cambridge when the war broke out in 1914, so that the performance was delayed for six years. By that time a younger generation of musicians had grown up, and the task of producing Handel's *Semele* (1925) and Purcell's *King Arthur* (1928) passed out of Dent's hands, though his generous advice was always at the service of those who had been his pupils.

In the meantime he had completed translations of *Figaro* and *Don Giovanni,* which were used for productions at the Old Vic—translations which raised the standard of opera translations to a level never attained before. Later he made translations of *Fidelio, Rigoletto* and *Il Trovatore* for Sadler's Wells. His practical interest in Purcell bore in its turn fruit in yet another book, *Foundations of English Opera,* which is a study of the development of that form in England down to Purcell's death.

During the years immediately after the first German war Dent spent a large part of his energies in the encouragement of young musicians both in England and abroad, and, as the chairman of the International Society for Contemporary Music, for the foundation of which he was largely responsible, furthered a better understanding between the musicians of all European countries. In spite of his expressed desire to pass his office into other hands, the society insisted again and again on electing him to the chair, which he occupied from its foundation in 1922 until 1938.

In 1926 Dent was elected Professor of Music at the University of Cambridge in succession to his old teacher, Charles Wood, and held the chair till 1941. In 1947 Cambridge made him an honorary Doctor of Music. Oxford and Harvard—where he had accepted invitations to give special courses of lectures—had bestowed corresponding doctorates on him some years earlier.

Always an advocate of research, Dent was president of the Musical Association from 1928 to 1934. He served on the board of directors of the reopened Sadler's Wells and later became a governor. The Quaker in him made for that intense intellectual honesty and the equal intolerance of all that was sham and ready made, which sometimes laid him open to misunderstanding. His attitude towards the music and the musical criticism which was submitted for his judgment was that what was good in it might be taken for granted, while his keen intellect was exercised in piercing through to any latent faults.

Although, as his handling of the difficulties which constantly arose at the polyglot meetings of the International Society gave ample proof, he had an infinity of tact, he gave his consultants the credit for wanting not smooth praise, which might have been easy to give, but a genuine criticism. So it came about that his friends would say: "When Dent is all smiles, look out for trouble!" It was the same with his attitude to the great musicians of the past. When everyone else was eulogizing Beethoven on the occasion of his centenary Dent was so severely critical that some honest folk seriously regarded his pronouncement as a stab in the back of genius. In truth he was alive to Beethoven's greatness, far more keenly so than most of the eulogists, but he was not interested in what was common knowledge. He wanted to get at something which the rest of the world had not seen.

Such a mind was bound to produce critical work far above the ordinary, and Dent's books are not only models of accurate scholarship but are distinguished by exceptional clarity of style and conciseness of thought. He could pack into the 90 small pages of *Terpander* a fairly complete history of the development of music, and into his "Penguin" a comprehensive study of opera. His brief life of Handel is another masterpiece of compression.

As a lecturer he was both erudite and entertaining. To the world Dent was known for his wit and great learning, but his numerous friends found unstinting generosity behind his somewhat dry manner. No trouble or expense was too great if someone appealed to him in difficulty or illness, and of recent years the victims of political upheaval abroad made additional calls on his time and purse.

In 1945 there appeared *A Theatre for Everybody,* an account of the origins of the Old Vic and Sadler's Wells.

August 23, 1957.

Alfred Denville, a pioneer of the modern repertory theatre in the provinces, and for many years the "actors' M.P.", died on March 23, 1955 at his home at Harrow, Middlesex, at the age of 79.

Born at Nottingham of a theatrical family, Alfred Arthur Hinchcliffe Denville first appeared on the stage as a baby in arms at the old Prince of Wales's Theatre, Greenwich, in a vintage melodrama of the time. For some years thenceforward he was not to know any settled place of abode, for he travelled with his parents in the touring companies of which they were members, and played a number of children's parts. He had some respite from this life when he attended Ushaw College, Durham, but he was soon back with his family, helping to supplement their slender income, sometimes by acting, sometimes by working in the mines, in the quarries, and in factories. For a brief and glorious period he was a professional footballer.

All the while, however, he was acquiring valuable experience which stood him in good stead when in 1900 he took the great risk at the age of 24 of acquiring the lease of a small theatre at Swansea, there to start the only repertory then, and for some time after, existing in the British Isles. In those days there were not the distractions of the cinema and broadcasting, but there was still the potent force of Welsh nonconformity with its bias against the theatre. Denville's ability and energy, however, soon made the venture a success and he began to organize and send out touring companies on such a scale that at one time he had as many as 23 on the road at the same time.

Denville, himself, in addition to the cares of management, undertook principal roles in the plays presented by his companies. The productions ranged from Shakespeare to pantomime and from the eighteenth-century comedy of manners to *The Miracle.* He also turned his hand to writing plays, among them *Annie Laurie, Reported Missing,* and *The Jewess.* He was happy to remember that he had given many a young actor and actress a start and valuable experience which most of them gratefully turned to account; and he was proud that he once had Sir Frank Benson as a member of the Denville Players at the Prince of Wales's Theatre, Cardiff. He was the last lessee of the New Oxford Theatre before it was pulled down and produced there a rewritten version of *A Royal Divorce.* That was in 1926.

By then he had become very much an elder statesman of the theatre. Without deserting the theatre, he determined to play his part on a larger stage and in 1928 stood for Parliament at Hanley, Staffordshire, in the Conservative interest. He was defeated, but in 1931 he was elected for the Central Division of Newcastle upon Tyne and retained the seat until his retirement in 1945. He built the Coliseum Theatre, at Harrow, which was opened in 1940 under the patronage of Queen Mary [q.v.]. Ever mindful of the needs of members of his profession, he founded 28 years ago Denville Hall, a home for aged actors and actresses at Northwood, Middlesex.

March 24, 1955.

André Derain, who was knocked down by a motor car near his home at Chambourcy on July 19, died in hospital at Garches, outside Paris, on September 9, 1954. He was 74.

In his early years Derain was an artist of extraordinary promise. With Matisse [q.v.], Marquet, Braque* and others, he invented Fauve painting and his work in this style—several of his Fauve landscapes were painted in London—was at least as distinguished as that of any of his contemporaries. It was not long before he abandoned the brilliant colouring and flat patterns of this movement and began to use subdued though often rich colours and to model in the round. Of all the painters of his time he was the most obviously inspired by the old masters, and during this period he produced a number of strong but extremely sensitive studies of heads and nudes painted directly from the model.

Up to about 1920 he would certainly have been considered among the four or five most eminent painters in France, but after that date he produced a number of works in which his remarkable facility seemed to get the better of him. He was a born painter, forceful, by no means intellectual, and perhaps rather uncritical; as a result his work was uneven and his reputation to-day is not quite what it was in the past, though the best of his pictures are still very highly esteemed. He designed the scenery and costumes for Diaghilev's ballet *La Boutique Fantasque* and in these there is a delightful vein of fantasy which also appears in a few of his earlier pictures.

André Derain was born at Chatou (Seine-et-Oise) on June 10, 1880. At the age of 15 he gave up his preparations for the *école polytechnique* in order to study painting at the Académie Carrière. There he met and was much influenced by the young Matisse; and a little later became firm friends with Vlaminck [q.v.], with whom he once shared a studio at Chatou, painting the Ile de France landscapes which characterized his early period.

In 1905, after a trip with Matisse to Collioure, he exhibited at the Salon de l'Automne the series of Roussillon landscapes which first established him in the public eye as one of the leaders of the Fauve movement; and this reputation was confirmed by the paintings of Paris suburbs which he exhibited at the Salon des Indépendants the same year.

During the next few years he worked in many places, including Montreuil-sur-mer, Cagnes, Spain (with Picasso* in 1910), Martigues, and Avignon, each new move marking a further step in the development of his style. From service in the 1914-18 War Derain brought back a striking series of drawings and sketches; and then resumed his travels in the south of France, his work being recognized by retrospective exhibitions in Paris in 1916 and 1921, and by the Carnegie prize in 1928.

This was the period when he was most widely recognized as one of the leaders of modern French painting. From 1930 his inclination increasingly led him back towards orthodoxy of form and drawing; and this withdrawal from the main stream of modern painting was symbolized by his retirement in the early 1930s to the village of Chambourcy (Seine-et-Oise), where for more than 20 years he lived in seclusion. Nevertheless, he continued to paint actively in his new style and produced in 1945 a series of coloured engravings for an edition of *Pantagruel.*

September 11, 1954.

James de Rothschild—See **Rothschild.**

Thomas Derrick, an artist of distinction and note, died at his home at Cold Ash, near Newbury, Berkshire, on November 18, 1954. He was 69.

He was a scholarly and versatile decorative artist of the older school, his range including portraits, mural paintings, stained glass windows, and book illustrations. He was also an experienced lecturer on art, and was for five years instructor in decorative painting at the Royal College of Art, South Kensington.

Thomas Derrick was born at Bristol in 1885, and received his early education at the Somerset village of Sidcot. He studied art at the Royal College, where he duly gained his diploma of A.R.C.A. Derrick was not attached to any society or group, but he exhibited fairly frequently at the Royal Academy, the International Society, the New English Art Club, and in Paris and New York. His Academy contributions were all portrait drawings or paintings in watercolour and tempera, the drawings including one of John Galsworthy, exhibited at the Academy in 1934 under the title of "Final Call."

Derrick illustrated several books, including *The Prodigal Son and other Parables Shown in Pictures*; *The Nine Nines*, with Hilaire Belloc [q.v.]; *Everyman*; and *Kennet Country*, with text by Fred S. Thacker. Of these books the first, printed at the Shakespeare Head Press, and the fourth, printed at the Alden Press, were included in the 1935 Exhibition of British Art in Industry at Burlington House. He also contributed humorous drawings and cartoons to various journals, including the *London Mercury, Punch,* and *Time and Tide.*

A characteristic drawing by Derrick, "Cologne: The Guards Crossing the Rhine," in which the chief preoccupation of the artist was with the contrast between the rigid lines of the lattice of the bridge and the shadowy bulk of the Cathedral beyond, was shown at the 1924 British Empire Exhibition at Wembley, and *The Times* of October 25, 1937 reproduced a three-light stained glass window designed by him for the church of Bugthorpe, Yorkshire, in memory of the second Viscount Halifax who was father of the first Earl [q.v.].

As an artist Derrick was curiously restrained and markedly linear in style, with a liking for the regular patterns made by uprights and horizontals. He was distinctly an artist "with brains," exacting of space-relations in the layout of the design, and his work was rather cold on the emotional side, though his *Punch* drawings show that he was not deficient in humour. In painting, tempera seemed to be his most congenial medium. He was a successful teacher, and after giving up his appointment at the Royal College he was for some years lecturer on art at the London Day Training College.

He married Margaret Mary, younger daughter of the late Sir George Clausen, R.A. She died in 1946. They had three sons and a daughter.

November 20, 1954.

Professor Gaetano De Sanctis, the celebrated Greek and Roman historian and, in recent years, president and editor of the *Enciclopedia Italiana,* died on April 9, 1957 in Rome.

He was born in 1870 in Rome, where he took his doctorate in letters in 1892. The favourite pupil of the scholar G. Beloch, he taught ancient history at the University of Turin from 1900 until 1929, when he was called to succeed Beloch in teaching Greek history at the University of Rome. He was removed from this position in 1931 for having refused to take the fascist oath, but was reinstated after the liberation in 1943. A distinguished scholar and master, he studied classical antiquity in all its branches, focusing his learning on the reconstruction of the history of ancient civilization. He carried out epigraphic researches in Thessaly and took part in the archaeological exploration of the island of Crete and of Cyrenaica.

Among his principal published works are *Atthis, Storia della Repubblica Ateniese,* a history of the Athenian Republic; *Per la Scienza dell'Antichita; Problemi di Storia Antica; Nuovi Studi e Scoperte in Gortina,* and various papers on inscriptions in Thessaly, and other epigraphic discoveries published in the *Rivista di Filologia Classica,* of which he became editor in 1923. De Sanctis's greatest work was, however, his *Storia dei Romani,* successive volumes of which have appeared since 1907.

Evidence of De Sanctis's great industry, courage and zeal is afforded by an incident which occurred in 1947 when the sole existent typescript of a great new volume of his Roman history was, together with his publisher's car, stolen on the road from Rome to Milan and never recovered. With great fortitude—the greater since for some years he had been blind—De Sanctis set to to write, or rather dictate, it afresh, almost completing within a few months a version even finer than the first.

This was, in itself, a notable feat for a blind man of nearly 80 years of age; but was the more remarkable considering that at the same time he was teaching regularly at the university in the mornings, devoting his afternoons to his duties as president and editor of the Italian Encyclopaedia (a dual office in which he succeeded Professor Federzoni, the former president, and Professor Giovanni Gentile, the former editor), and was also editing the *Rivista di Filologia e d'Instruzione Classica.*

Frail in appearance, white-bearded, extremely modest, but of remarkable energy and mental activity, De Sanctis was a distinguished figure in the international world of learning.

Honorary doctorates were conferred on him by the Universities of Oxford, Cambridge, Paris and Louvain.

He was made a life Senator in 1950.

April 10, 1957.

Hugh de Selincourt—See **Selincourt.**

Shaw Desmond, the Anglo-Irish author and journalist who in his later years interested himself greatly in spiritualism, died in London on December 23, 1960. He was 83.

As a writer Desmond was fluent, versatile, and often forcible and pungent in a controversial style. He was largely self-educated—he had been taught, he liked to say, by "Irish monks and life"—and he had a varied commercial career before turning to literature and journalism. These circumstances are reflected only a degree less plainly than his adventurous Anglo-Irish temperament in the general character of his writing.

Shaw Desmond was born in Ireland on January 19, 1877, the son of an Irish father and English mother. He left school at the age of 15, engaged in a variety of commercial jobs in London and elsewhere, farmed for a short time in Ireland, and seemed settled in a reasonably successful business career when, in 1909, he definitely turned to journalism. Travel and politics—he had by this time loosely identified himself with the socialist movement—kept him liberally supplied with subjects; he also lectured a great deal in Britain, Ireland, Denmark, and the United States.

Desmond's first serious book was *The Soul of Denmark,* which appeared in Danish in 1917 and in English in the year following. Then came a volume in characteristic vein on *Democracy* (1919), and after that a novel entitled *Passion,* the story of a superman obsessed by a lust for power, in which the effect of the author's stupendous and at times genuinely powerful Wellsian notions was all but undone by the loudness and melodrama of his style. A year later still came *Labour—The Giant with Feet of Clay,* in which Desmond recorded his disenchantment with current socialist thought, condemning the Labour Party for its materialism and somewhat rhetorically proclaiming the need of a "spiritual democracy".

Desmond was always a believer in physical fitness and kept himself in training as an athlete by arduous exercise and by abstaining from tobacco and alcohol. A voyage round Cape Horn—from Vancouver to Durban—in a four-masted barque, and a journey of 7,000 miles in Africa—through the Rhodesias and up the East Coast—during 1930-31 were experiences that he put to good advantage in *Windjammer* (1932) and *African Log* (1935). But the most singular volume he produced in this period of his life was *We Do Not Die* (1934), the first book in which he set down his psychic experiences and his belief in survival after death. Here he testified to his friendship for 3,300 years with a wife of Amenhotep III, denounced (in full-blooded terms) the professors of science on the one hand and the professors of theology on the other, and provided copious information of a general nature about "the astral".

Desmond kept up writing until almost the end; among his later books are *The Edwardian Story,* containing many nostalgic reminiscences, *Irish Moon,* a novel which appeared in 1953, and *Healing: Psychic and Divine* (1956).

In 1911 Desmond married Kaen Ewald, a Danish writer, by whom he had one son and one daughter. His wife died in 1954.

December 24, 1960.

Marshal de Lattre de Tassigny—See **Lattre.**

Anthony Devas, A.R.A., the artist, died suddenly in London on December 21, 1958. He was 47.

His early and great success as a portrait painter was all the more remarkable because he was neither orthodox nor sensational. Though he exhibited at the Royal Academy he could hardly be called academic, and on the other hand he did not, like Sargent, get that reputation for ruthlessness which, like the diatribes of a fashionable preacher, attracts those who profess to be shocked. Perhaps the simplest way of putting it is to say that Devas brought to portraiture a breadth and freedom of treatment already tolerated in landscape and subject pictures but until recently barred from the likeness, and it is no reflection on his talent to say that he was fortunate in the time of day.

Anthony Devas, son of Thomas Gronow Devas, was born on January 8, 1911. He was educated at Repton, and from 1927 to 1930 studied at the Slade School. For some time Devas was associated with Claude Rogers and his colleagues in what has become known as the Euston Road Group, but his work had not much in common with the discreet and intimate realism which distinguishes them.

One-man shows of paintings and drawings by Devas, including portraits, landscapes, figure and still life subjects, were held from time to time at the Cooling, Agnew, Wildenstein, and Leicester galleries. They made it clear that he was a true painter, so certain of his values that he could allow his drawing to be taken for granted. He had an individual style of soft colour and outline which enabled him to be precise without harshness, and his portraits carried conviction not only as good physical likenesses but as understanding and sympathizing with the characters of the sitters.

Though it was in portraiture, including "conversation pieces", that Devas made his chief reputation, his first appearance at the Royal Academy, in 1940, was with a still life painting, "Flowers in a Yellow Jug", and he continued to paint still life subjects and landscapes, but most of his academy pictures were portraits. Devas was a member of the New English Art Club, and in 1945 he was elected a member of the Royal Society of Portrait Painters. His three contributions to its exhibition that year were singled out by *The Times* as the most interesting in the show; not so much, it was added, because of their intrinsic merit as because they showed that a painter trained in other methods and well acquainted with the main tradition of modern painting had set himself to imitate the typical shiny portraits for which there seemed to be a constant demand, while at the same time drawing and laying on his paint as conscientiously as the circumstances would allow.

As these remarks would suggest, Devas was a painter who tried seriously and with a great measure of success to reconcile artistic with social demands in portraiture, and he risked a good deal in doing do. It was only occasionally, in portraits of women, that the need for ornament led him to put in a glitter that falsified his values.

In 1942, when Devas was engaged in civil defence, his still life painting of "Pansies and Sorrel" was bought by the Queen from an exhibition of works by civil defence artists held at the Berner Street Jewish Settlement, Stepney.

Since the war Devas had been a regular exhibitor at the Royal Academy, mainly of portraits, and these included his likenesses of T. S. R. Boase*, President of Magdalen College, Oxford, in 1953, the Rev. John Shirley, D.D., headmaster of King's School, Canterbury, in 1954, and Viscountess Hambledon in 1956. In 1957 he was commissioned by the Honourable Artillery Company to paint a portrait of the Queen. He became A.R.A. in 1953.

Other works by Devas have been purchased out of the Chantrey Bequest Fund for the Tate Gallery and by C.E.M.A., the Contemporary Art Society, and the War Artists Advisory Committee.

December 22, 1958.

Professor Henry Van de Velde—See **Velde.**

Maurice de Vlaminck—See **Vlaminck.**

Bernard De Voto, who collapsed and died on November 13, 1955 at the age of 58, shortly after appearing in a television programme in New York, was a scholar who did not believe in remaining in the study.

Bernard Augustine De Voto was born at Ogden, Utah, on January 11, 1897, and was educated at the University of Utah and Harvard. His studies were interrupted by the entry of the United States into the 1914-18 War and he served in the Army as a musketry instructor. Having graduated from Harvard in 1920, he worked for a time as a schoolmaster and then as assistant professor of English at Northeastern University. In 1929 he joined the teaching staff of Harvard and remained there for some five years. For the next 20 years he was editor of the excellent feature in *Harper's Magazine,* "The Easy Chair".

As befitted his origin, he was intensely interested in "The Frontier" and his greatest work, a trilogy which appeared between 1943 and 1953, stands in the forefront of vivid historical writing. The pioneers, Verendrye, Michaux, Mackenzie, Bill Burrows, Lewis and Clark, move lifesize across the broad canvas, vital and imposing. The Pulitzer and the Bancroft prizes awarded to him were due recognition of, perhaps, the greatest historian of America, who has done for the settlers of the West what Trevelyan* has done for the men of the *Risorgimento*. The three volumes, *The Year of Decision, 1846, Across the Wide Missouri,* and *Westward the Course of Empire* look a formidable task to read; they are, however, so gripping that once the reader has begun there is only pleasure. The material on which they are based is not only documentary, though all seems to have been consulted. What makes De Voto's writing so vivid is the fact that not only was he born in the territory he describes, but constantly visited the scenes he depicted.

His other works on the Middle West, though on a smaller scale, are of high merit and his understanding of the quaint genius of Mark Twain is deep and communicable. In lighter vein, he wrote a number of "thrillers" and popular magazine fiction under the *nom de plume* John August. Indeed, when the extent and gravity of his historical writing are considered, his output, serious and gay, was immense and of fine quality.

November 16, 1955.

Nicolaas Jacobus De Wet, P.C., former Chief Justice of South Africa, died at his home at Pretoria on March 16, 1960. He was 86.

Nicolaas Jacobus De Wet was born in 1873 at Aliwal North, Cape Colony, the eldest son of N. J. De Wet, who was a farmer in the district. He was educated at Victoria College, Stellenbosch, and Cambridge University. He was at first a member of Downing College and obtained a second class in the Law Tripos, Part I, of 1894, when Smuts of Christ's was senior. Having become a non-collegiate student, he obtained a first class in Part II of the Law Tripos of 1895 and was bracketed equal for the Chancellor's medal for English law. After returning to South Africa he was admitted advocate, in 1896, of the Supreme Court of Cape Colony, and also of the High Court of the South African Republic. At Pretoria he attained by his own merits a considerable practice in a very few years.

In the early part of the South African War he was Chief Censor in the Transvaal, and also Assistant-State Attorney, in the latter capacity having General Smuts as his Chief. After the occupation of Pretoria by Lord Roberts, De Wet joined General Botha in the field, and was his military secretary until the end of the war. He was in General Botha's closest confidence. They were being hard pressed by the British troops in the Piet Retief district when Lord Kitchener's letter which opened the peace negotiations leading up to Vereeniging was handed to General Botha on Sunday, March 20, 1902—it is said during a religious service. Dr. Engelenburg, in his life of Botha, records that the Boer General read the dispatch and turning to De Wet, exclaimed: "The war is over". De Wet was doubtful, and said so. Botha's emphatic reply was: "Not one will refuse".

De Wet was also present—with General Smuts and General Schalk Burger—at the poignant meeting following the outbreak of the 1914 War, when General Botha, having called General De la Rey to Pretoria, endeavoured to dissuade—but in vain—his old comrade-in-arms from going into rebellion for the recovery of the lost republic.

As member for Middelburg West in the Transvaal Legislative Assembly from 1907-10, De Wet was among the group of able young men whom General Botha gathered round him when the Dutch resumed the government of the ex-republic. He was legal adviser to the Transvaal delegates to the National Convention (1908-09), which brought about the union of the four colonies and drafted their constitution as endorsed by the Imperial Parliament in the South Africa Act.

In General Botha's first Union Government, General Hertzog was his Minister of Justice. When the Generals parted company, in 1912, over Hertzog's "two streams" policy for the two races, the latter was left out of the reconstructed Cabinet. De Wet succeeded to the vacant office, which he held for more than 10 years. He made a good Minister of Justice, though some of his friends were rather disappointed that he seemed unable to resist party pressure in some of his appointments. Although he spent well over 20 years in Parliaments and Cabinets, De Wet had never been moved by any strong political inclination. Party strife and intrigue were distasteful to him. He seems rather to have entered, as he remained in, politics from a sense of duty to Generals Botha and Smuts, both of whom set a high value on his judgment and professional ability, and warmly esteemed him as a friend. The latter period of his political career (1921-29) he passed in the serener atmosphere of the Union Upper House, in which he sat as a Senator of the Transvaal.

In 1932 he was appointed to a judgeship of the Transvaal Provincial division of the Supreme Court and in 1937 Judge of the Appellate Division of the Supreme Court. Two years later he was made Chief Justice of South Africa and sworn of the Privy Council. After the death of the Governor-General, Sir Patrick Duncan, in July 1943 he became Officer Administering the Government and continued in this appointment until January 1946. In September 1951, he joined the War Veterans Torch Commando and became its patron but he resigned in May 1953, giving as his reason the action of the national chairman of the commando, Kane Berman, and other prominent members, in helping to form a new political party.

On the Bench De Wet, painstaking, patient, and erudite, showed himself an excellent judge. As a man of character and of a marked intellectual type, he dated back to the previous era in which judges of the calibre of De Villiers notably, and Rose-Innes and Solomon, lent distinction to the South African Bench. In private life De Wet was much liked for his modest and kindly disposition. He was a strong Dutch Reformed Churchman.

March 17, 1960.

Professor John Dewey, Professor Emeritus of Philosophy in Columbia University, New York, died there on June 1, 1952 at the age of 92.

He was the foremost philosopher of recent times in the United States, and his writings and work were known in all parts of the world. In a way he carried on the tradition of William James and Josiah Royce, to both of whom he owed much, though he did not study directly under either, but he went far beyond their philosophical theories and also covered in his writings a wider range of philosophical study, reflection, and experiment. There was, indeed, hardly any branch of philosophical study on which he had not written at one time or other, and he was equally at home in ethics, logic, psychology, politics, and education. His practical work in education led to many far-reaching changes in the methods of teaching followed in schools in every part of the United States and had considerable effect elsewhere. His political writings also had a profound influence upon his fellow-countrymen.

John Dewey was born on October 20, 1859, on a farm in the state of Vermont, near the town of Burlington, where his family had lived for generations. He was brought up in hard surroundings, in an atmosphere of plain living and hard thinking. His writing even on the most abstruse problems of philosophy was clear, direct, and simple. He was free from all formalities and complacency, and showed little of the academic temper, for he remained a son of the soil, a rebel against traditionalism, and he might be ranked as a pragmatist, though he moved in his own orbit quite apart from the main stream.

After attending the University of Vermont, where he graduated in 1879, he continued his studies at Johns Hopkins University, in Baltimore, where he took his doctor's degree in 1884. He was then appointed assistant to the Professor of Philosophy in the University of Michigan, where he remained for four years before going for a year to the University of Minnesota as professor. In 1889 he returned to Michigan and was Professor of Philosophy there until 1894. By that time he was well known for his writings on psychology and ethics, and he was appointed Professor of Philosophy and head of the Department of Philosophical Studies in the University of Chicago. He remained there until 1904, and during the last two years of his stay he also acted as director of the School of Education.

With his daughter, Evelyn, he carried out a number of experiments in various schools of the Middle West and published the results in a book entitled *Schools of Tomorrow*. He regarded his task in education as the breaking down of the barriers between the school and the realities of life. In 1904 he went to Columbia University, New York, and remained there for more than 30 years, lecturing to successive generations of American students from all parts of the country, who were strongly imbued with his teaching and carried his message into many spheres of life. He travelled abroad at times, and was familiar with conditions in Mexico, China, and Russia.

All through his teaching life he poured out a regular stream of books on almost every branch of philosophy. His first published work was *Psychology* (1886). Among the best known of his other works were *A Critical Theory of Ethics* (1894), *A Study of Ethics* in the same year, *How We Think* (1909), *Democracy and Education* (1916), *Human Nature and Conduct* (1922), *Experience and Nature* (1925), *The Public and Its Problems* (1927), *The Quest for Certainty* (1929), and *Art as Experience* (1935), as well as his Gifford Lectures on *Philosophy and Civilization,* which were published in 1931. He continued to bring his lively mind to bear on contemporary problems almost to the end of his life, and as late as 1949 collaborated with A. F. Bentley in a philosophical volume under the title *Knowing the Known.*

In his early days he was educated in the German-English metaphysical tradition, but he soon broke away and was one of the first to recognize the importance of the experimental study of behaviour and to refer to physical and biological inquiries. He regarded thought as an activity of a harassed animal living in a changing world. Thinking originated in perplexity and had its consequences in behaviour. His whole system of philosophy was related to life and experience, to those "doings and sufferings", of which he often spoke, out of which thinking emerges. Morals he held to be a matter of social responsibility. True democracy was a society of a free and intelligent community of human beings. He was described as the philosopher of America come of age. He based his hopes for the future of mankind largely on experimental science, but he found a place for art as a better understanding of the highest form of living and for religion as an aspiration of mankind towards the highest common ideals.

In 1886 he married Miss Alice Chipman Fenton, of Flint, Michigan, who helped him in his experimental school while he was in Chicago. Two sons of the marriage died young and a son and two daughters survive. After the death of his first wife he married Miss Roberta Grant and they adopted two children.

June 3, 1952.

Sir Eustace Tennyson d'Eyncourt—
See **Tennyson.**

Dr. Grantly Dick-Read, M.D., who devoted his medical career to spreading the theory and practice of "natural childbirth", died in Norfolk on June 11, 1959. He was 69.

He was the son of Robert John Read, went to school at Bishop's Stortford College, and received his medical training at Cambridge University and the London Hospital. Soon after qualifying he joined the R.A.M.C. in 1914, and three years later became D.A.D.M.S., Indian Cavalry Corps. After release from the Army, he joined the resident staff of the London Hospital in 1919 before going into general practice at Woking, where his life-long interest in childbirth developed.

His authoritative, yet kindly, personality soon gained for him a reputation as an *accoucheur,* and he established himself in Harley Street in this capacity. Witnessing, as he did, the sufferings of women in childbirth, he became increasingly convinced that such suffering was unnecessary, and was due to distortion of a normal physiological process; and that as a normal process it should be free from pain. As his experience mounted his creed developed, which has made his name known throughout the world, that fear causes tension, and tension causes pain. He held that the elimination of fear was the key to physiological labour.

These views were elaborated, and formed the theme of his first publication entitled *Natural Childbirth* in 1933. Controversy always surrounded him, and his views were incapable of scientific proof. He himself held to his views with an almost religious fervour, and a measure of recognition by his medical colleagues was accorded when he was asked to contribute an expression of his theories to a well-known text-book on the care of the expectant mother.

He acquired a large, and often vociferous, following in non-medical circles, but his views were never wholly accepted by his colleagues. Nevertheless, to Dick-Read clearly belongs the credit of having revived the belief that childbirth, and indeed the whole of reproduction, is a normal physiological occurrence; and countless thousands of women throughout the world have benefited from his work. In France, in Russia, and, more recently, in the United States of America, his views have to some extent gained acceptance, and in Great Britain there can hardly be a doctor or a midwife who does not, in some measure, accept them. Like many a prophet Dick-Read tended to overstate his views, and his enthusiasm at times caused him to neglect other advances along allied lines.

In 1948, depressed by the lack of wholehearted and enthusiastic support by his colleagues, he went to South Africa to carry on his work, but he was never happy there, and returned to Britain to retire from medical practice in 1953. He then devoted himself to spreading his gospel, by means of lectures, articles in the public press, and by television appearances.

He was a man of compelling personality, and a fluent writer and speaker, and there can be no question that his views, though extreme, as well as his life's work, have contributed much to the comfort and happiness of expectant mothers. He published many books on his theories in both English and foreign languages, and contributed to numerous medical journals.

He married first in 1921 Dorothea Cannon, by whom he had two sons and two daughters. In 1952 he married Jessica Bennett, *née* Winters.

June 12, 1959.

Lieutenant-Colonel H. R. P. Dickson, chief local representative of the Kuwait Oil Company Ltd., and known and honoured by the Arabs of the area as "Abu Saud", died in Kuwait on June 14, 1959 at the age of 78.

He won the confidence of the Beduin by his understanding of their language, way of life, and traditions and his simple and direct manner with them. ("Abu Saud" means father of Saud, the name of his only son.) Beduin coming to town from the deserts of southern Iraq or Saudi Arabia made straight to his house for a gossip, and no one left without some small token carefully wrapped up by Mrs. Dickson.

Dickson lived in the former political agency for over 30 years. Many visitors to Kuwait will recall the solid, simple old Arab home built in traditional fashion of dried mud and coral on the harbour front with dhows moored almost under its walls. Dickson was a master of story telling and could hold an audience entranced for hours about Kuwait and Arabs.

His books *The Arab of the Desert* and *Kuwait and Her Neighbours* are a mine of information on desert life and Arab tradition, and will be read by people interested in those parts for many years to come.

Harold Richard Patrick Dickson was born on February 4, 1881. His father was Consul-General at Jerusalem. From St. Edward's School and Wadham College, Oxford, he joined the 1st Connaught Rangers in 1903 and served in Ireland. He went east in 1904 and made his career there—or rather made three careers. The first was service in the Indian Army 29th Lancers (Deccan Horse) and in Mesopotamia in the 1914-18 War with 33rd Q.V.O. Light Cavalry. The second was as a political officer in Southern Iraq, Bahrain, and Kuwait which ended when he retired from the Indian Army in 1934. There followed his nomination by Sheikh Ahmed al Jabir as the Kuwait Oil Company's first chief local representative, which continued until his death. He played an important part in the signing of the oil concession and in smoothing out the difficulties which surrounded the planting of a western-manned oil company in the midst of what was then a primitive desert community. He had a command of Beduin Arabic which few British have achieved. He was made C.I.E. in 1917.

He is survived by his widow, Violet Penelope, daughter of Neville Lucas-Calcraft, whom he married in 1920. They had a son, who is a political officer in British Somaliland, and a daughter.

June 15, 1959.

Christian Dior, the famous French couture designer, died suddenly on October 24, 1957 at Montecatini, Italy, at the age of 52. Never strong, Dior had been in ill-health for some time and his death, although so sudden, was not entirely unexpected.

A master of his craft, a rare genius, Dior's name will stand high in the records of fine achievement in the field of couture design. Even more than this he will be honoured for the help that he, with the Marcel Boussac organization, was able to give France just after the war when it was so greatly needed. Then, the great textile industry, the third most important in France, was nearly at a standstill, but following the tremendous success of his first collection in January 1947, with its full-skirted styles each requiring many yards of fabric, orders began to flow into the French mills.

Today thousands of workers throughout the world owe their living directly to his inspiration, not only as a result of his couture showings, but also through the success of the wholesale houses and accessory businesses built up under the umbrella of the central organization in Paris, with officers in London, New York, and Caracas.

Born on January 21, 1905, at Granville, in Normandy, he was the only son of Maurice Dior, a wealthy chemical manufacturer. As a youth he enjoyed designing clothes for his sisters, and a costume representing Neptune, which he designed and wore at a fancy dress ball, won him the first prize. The Diplomatic Corps, however, not dress designing, was originally planned as a career for the intelligent, rather delicate, youth. He studied political science at the Sorbonne, but the French financial crisis of 1930-31, which crippled the family business, enabled him to escape from the prospect of a career which had never greatly attracted him. Always interested in art, with the collaboration of friends he set up a small salon in the Rue la Boétie, in the centre of Paris, and helped to launch Christian Bérard among other young painters. Later Bérard was always to be seen sitting on the floor of the large salon at the première of Dior's collections, until the former's death in 1949.

Forced to give up his art gallery for reasons of ill-health, Dior was sent to the mountains to recover. Returning eventually, he took up couture designing in earnest, first of all with Agnes, for whom he designed hats, and later with Robert Piguet.

Shortly after the outbreak of war Dior retired to the country where he remained for some time with a sister who had a market garden business. On his return to Paris he became one of Lelong's designers, and remained with Lelong until the fortuitous meeting with a friend of his youth, Marcel Boussac. At this time Boussac was, in fact, looking for a designer in order to set up a couture house, and a partnership was arranged culminating in the widely publicized first collection in the spring of 1947.

Christian Dior's very real affection for England and things English stemmed from his first visit at the age of 19 when, to assist his recovery from a serious illness, his father gave him a sum of money and suggested it should be spent exploring Britain. He had, indeed, many English friends and always made a practice of having at least one English mannequin in the house on the Avenue Montaigne. And he always gave sympathetic attention to the products of British fabric manufacturers.

His feeling for line was allied to a wonderful appreciation of colour and texture, and whatever the "line" the result was always feminine clothes designed to flatter the wearer. His early death at this moment is not only a tragedy for the house of Dior, but could have serious consequences for the French industry as a whole, following as it does the death or retirement of a number of other important French designers in the past few years.

October, 25, 1957.

The Hungarian composer **Ernst von Dohnanyi**—he preferred the German form of his name—died on February 11, 1960 in New York in his 83rd year.

Although born (at Pressburg) and trained (at the Budapest Royal Academy of Music) in Hungary, and in spite of a career pursued there until 1948, Dohnanyi was no nationalist. His affiliations were with Vienna and his music stems from the cosmopolitan Liszt rather than the Hungarian nationalists, Bartok and Kodaly*. He is most widely known for his *Variations on a Nursery Song* for piano and orchestra, which he wrote in 1913, and which was for many years a Promenade favourite in Britain. The nursery song is "Ah, vous dirai-je, Maman", or "Baa, baa, black sheep", and some find its humour a little heavy, but it survives on its charm and banter.

He was born on July 27, 1877, back in the days of Franz Josef's Austro-Hungarian empire, and began to work both at piano and composition in 1885. As a student he turned out a number of works in the larger forms which culminated in a symphony performed in Budapest in 1897. In the same year he appeared, after some lessons with Eugen d'Albert, as a concert pianist in Berlin and Vienna, and a year later at a Richter concert in London. In the following year (1899) he toured the United States of America.

Having established his international reputation, he was appointed professor of piano at the Berlin High School. In 1915, after seven years, he returned to Budapest and in 1919 was made Director of the Conservatoire and became conductor of the Budapest Philharmonic Orchestra. He took this orchestra to London in 1928 soon after the famous visit of the Berlin Philharmonic Orchestra and won favourable opinions for its rather different merits. His performance of Brahms was highly praised and this sympathy was sufficiently marked in his own compositions to cause them to be described, though not in a pejorative sense, as Brahmsian. Thus the piano quintet at Edinburgh was a reminder that there is no Magyar influence in his music. His *Ruralia Hungarica*, a suite for piano that also exists in an orchestral version, he invested with a kind of local colour that he had employed in the opera *The Tower of the Voivod*, but not with anything drawn from first-hand study, like Bartok's of the various kinds of indigenous Hungarian folk song.

He retained his command of the piano into old age, for his last visit to Britain was paid in order to perform at the Edinburgh Festival of 1956, when he gave a sonata recital with Campoli and took part with the New Edinburgh Quartet in a performance of his own piano quintet in E flat minor—and of course played the Nursery Rhyme Variations. He had on a previous visit in 1947 played a piano concerto of his own recent composition with Sir Thomas Beecham* at a concert at Drury Lane, where his skill and zest were noted.

He has three operas and three symphonies, and a substantial body of chamber music to his credit, but his international reputation is chiefly founded on his piano music. He left Hungary in 1948 and settled in the United States, where he enjoyed the position of composer-in-residence at the Florida State University.

February 12, 1960.

Sir Frederick Widdowson Doidge, K.C.M.G., High Commissioner for New Zealand in the United Kingdom, died on May 26, 1954 at his home in London after a long illness. He was 70.

He was a man of outstanding personality and integrity, who not only added dignity and accomplishment to any task he undertook but brought distinction to himself in his private affairs and credit to his country in his public services, in which he was courageously unsparing of himself.

Before his appointment as High Commissioner in September 1951 he had been Minister of External Affairs and Island Territories, Broadcasting, and Minister in charge of the Tourist and Publicity Department. He took a leading part in the consultations on the Colombo Plan, the Pacific Security Treaty (Anzus) and the peace treaty with Japan, and led the New Zealand delegations at United Nations meetings at Lake Success in 1950 and Paris in 1951.

The son of Edwin Doidge, of Bere Ferrers, Devon, he was born at Cootamundra, New South Wales, on February 26, 1884, and after being educated in Australia left for New Zealand, where he worked for a time on the wharves at Auckland. Following the example of his father, who edited several country newspapers, he entered journalism, and by the time he was 18 he was doing all the reporting, and much of the typesetting on a small country newspaper, the *Patea Press*. He next joined the *Auckland Star* as shipping reporter and a few years later, although only 21, he was appointed to represent the journal in the Dominion Parliament's Press Gallery. While on the *Auckland Star* he took a leading part in the formation of the New Zealand Journalists' Association, and was elected its first president.

Early in the 1914-18 War he was one of the four finalists in the competition for the position of official war correspondent, but, failing to obtain the appointment, he joined the Army as a private and went to France, serving with the New Zealand Division.

Towards the end of the war he was invalided to Britain, and, while a patient in the Walton-on-Thames Hospital, in response to a London Ministry of Information request for a journalist with knowledge of conditions in Australia and New Zealand, he was seconded for special duties.

He held this post till 1918, and in the process impressed Lord Beaverbrook*, at whose invitation he joined the circulation department of the *Daily Express.* He became associated with the control of the *Sunday Express* and the *Evening Standard* in London, and was appointed a director of the Express group of publications. When Lord Beaverbrook launched his historic Empire Free Trade crusade, Doidge, as organizer and honorary secretary, was his right hand man.

In 1935, however, after 17 years in Fleet Street, Doidge decided to relinquish newspaper work and returned to New Zealand. There he found a new interest in politics with the objective, as he later said, of "assisting in tightening the bonds of Empire". After standing unsuccessfully as an Independent candidate at Rotorua, he helped to form the National Party, and though beaten in the Manukau by-election of 1936 he was elected in 1938 as the member for Tauranga. In the 1943 election he was not only successful but increased his previous majority. In 1949 he was again elected to represent Tauranga, and on the National Party's return to power was appointed a member of the Cabinet.

After serving as Minister of External Affairs he relinquished his Cabinet post to become High Commissioner in London in 1951. In 1952 he became a liveryman of the Worshipful Company of Butchers and soon afterwards he received the freedom of the City of London. He was appointed a K.C.M.G. in the New Year Honours of 1953 and, in addition to representing New Zealand at the funeral of King George VI [q.v.], carried the New Zealand standard at the Coronation.

He married in 1910 Lyle Eirene, daughter of the late Captain Hugh Clark, of Auckland, who survives him. There were no children of the marriage.

May 27, 1954.

Canon F. L. Donaldson, formerly Sub-Dean of Westminster Abbey, who died on October 7, 1953 at the age of 93, was for many years one of the most influential men in the Anglican Church among the many who have served it for more than a generation.

Frederick Lewis Donaldson was born at Ladywood, Birmingham, on September 14, 1860, the son of F. W. Donaldson, into a musical family whose interests were destined to shape his future life. He had an excellent voice, and as a boy became a member of Oxford Cathedral choir, receiving his early education at the Cathedral school. It was no doubt in part the atmosphere of Oxford in his early days which led him to the Church, and he entered Merton College with the intention of taking Holy Orders. He had been reared in the tradition of Birmingham Radicalism, and it was while at Oxford that he launched into the social reform movement of the second half of the nineteenth century which brought him in direct line of succession to men like Kingsley and Maurice. As he himself said later, he made a long and detailed study of social questions in an endeavour to see how their solution could be united with the Christian faith.

Ordained in 1884, he saw something at first hand of the seamy side of life while serving in London curacies in the City and in Hammersmith, and then for a year or so as rector of the colliery village of Nailstone, in Leicestershire. In 1896 he became Vicar of St. Mark's, Leicester, a working-class parish of 17,000 people, where he remained for over 20 years, during which much of his social work was accomplished.

He is especially remembered in the Midlands as an organizer and leader of the march in 1905 of 500 unemployed from Leicester to London and back. It has often since been said that this well-conducted and well-ordered demonstration had an important influence on the social legislation of the Liberal Government in its years of office from 1906 to the outbreak of the 1914-18 war, but in those days his activities were widespread and unceasing. He was an original member of the Christian Social Union and was for 10 years chairman of the Leicester branch. He was also for four years chairman of the Church Socialist League which he had helped to establish. In spite of his responsibilities as vicar of one of the largest parishes in England, he was unsparing in his work of arousing the social conscience and organized, wrote, and spoke incessantly.

In 1918 he was transferred by his appointment as Rector of Paston with Walton, in the diocese of Peterborough, to the comparative quiet of the countryside, and was successively honorary canon, and then canon residentiary of Peterborough until, in 1924—through the influence, it was said, of his old friend the late Ramsay MacDonald, who had been M.P. for Leicester during Donaldson's term at St. Mark's—he was made a canon of Westminster. He became Steward in 1927, Treasurer of Westminster in 1931, Archdeacon in 1937, and Receiver-General in 1938. These new duties, and advancing years, naturally restricted the scope of his activities, especially when, in his 80's, he was appointed Sub-Dean of the Abbey, but the cloistered life at Westminster by no means silenced him. He remained to the end passionately devoted to social reform, and a member of the Labour Party, and he was one of the most outspoken supporters of the old Imperial Alliance for the Defence of Sunday. He held consistently that the Sabbath was made for man, and not man for the Sabbath; that there must be Sunday leisure to sing and to dance, as well as to pray and to read.

Canon Donaldson was as devout a Churchman as he was a zealous social reformer. As long ago as 1913 he led the deputation of Church of England clergy to the then Prime Minister, Asquith, on the question of women's suffrage. He had been Select Preacher at Cambridge University and was in 1918 a member of the Archbishop's Committee on Public Worship.

Canon Donaldson steeped himself in the history and traditions of the Abbey, and when approaching the 90's could often be seen piloting around it little groups of visitors who had no idea of his identity. For a man who was neither a great preacher nor a profound ecclesiastical scholar, his influence upon the Church was remarkable; but it sprang from his humanity, his driving force, and his capacity for friendship. He retired only some two years ago with the title emeritus.

He married in 1885 Louise, daughter of Alderman Eagleston, of Oxford. She died in 1950 and he is survived by two sons and four daughters.

October 8, 1953.

Robert Donat, who died in London on June 9, 1958 at the age of 53, was an actor of great ability and of remarkable versatility.

He had a fine presence and a beautiful speaking voice, and if there were times when it lacked vigour and fire this may have been due to the absolute necessity for him to guard it very carefully. He gave two particularly outstanding performances: as Becket in *Murder in the Cathedral* and as Gideon Sarn—which he regarded as one of his best contributions to the theatre—in the adaptation of Mary Webb's novel *Precious Bane.* For his portrayal of Mr. Chips in the film *Goodbye, Mr. Chips* (from the novel by James Hilton [q.v.]), he received an award of the American Academy of Motion Picture Arts and Sciences for the best achievement by a male actor in 1939.

Frederick Robert Donat was born at Withington, Manchester, on March 18, 1905. He was educated at the Manchester Central School and studied for the stage under James Bernard in Manchester. He made his first stage appearance at 16 in Birmingham as Lucius in *Julius Caesar* and joined Sir Frank Benson's company in 1923. He was associated with it until 1928 but during that period he also played in a number of modern repertory seasons. Towards the end of 1928 he was playing juvenile leads with the repertory company at the Liverpool Playhouse and in the following year he was the leading player at the Cambridge Festival theatre where his parts included Jack Absolute in *The Rivals* and Angelo in *Measure for Measure.* Back at Liverpool he gave a delightful performance as Simon and Harry Blake in *Mary Rose* and then, with so much varied experience at his back, he took the road to London. His first appearance in the West End was in a small part in *Knave and Queen* at the Ambassadors in 1930. In a season at the Embassy which followed he made his first big success as Gideon Sarn in *Precious Bane.*

The production of James Bridie's [q.v.] play *A Sleeping Clergyman* at Malvern in 1933 finally established Donat's reputation as one of the leading actors of his generation. His part was that of a consumptive medical student, fiercely egotistic, intractable, loose-living and brutal, characteristics which he suggested with unfaltering skill. Perhaps his best scene was in the dying consumptive's bedroom, for there the spark of genius contending with bodily and temperamental disabilities was indubitably present. From that time he never looked back, although there were times when his friends wondered whether he could stand up to the physical strain.

In 1936 he went into management at the Queen's and produced J. L. Hodson's [q.v.]

war play *Red Night,* and in 1939 he joined the Old Vic company with which he appeared at the Buxton Festival. Perhaps because he had been playing in a number of films in the interval, his performance in *The Devil's Disciple* as Dick Dudgeon did not entirely satisfy the critics, who gained the impression that he had temporarily lost his normal fluency in the drawing of character. It was not a very good stage performance but rather a series of close-ups with dead stretches between them. But it was recognized that it would be an excellent performance when he got into the skin of the part, and this feeling was fully confirmed when the production went to Golders Green in the first summer of the war.

In 1943 he was a dryly amusing Captain Shotover in *Heartbreak House*, and in the autumn of that year he again went into management, this time at the Westminster Theatre. He produced, but did not appear in, a revival of *An Ideal Husband* and played in Walter Greenwood's* comedy *Cure for Love*. His part made negligible demands upon his powers but it was always one of his favourites and later he played it on the screen.

In 1946 he opened a season at the Aldwych with a production of *Much Ado about Nothing,* in which he was a pleasant Benedick with a humour not untouched by poetry. He was back at the Old Vic in 1953 and scored perhaps the greatest artistic success of his whole career in T. S. Eliot's* *Murder in the Cathedral.* The warm humanity of his Becket shone attractively through his ecclesiastical dignity and, although at moments of crisis there may have been a certain lack of vocal power, his commanding presence always seemed to become his setting.

Donat began his film career in 1932 and his name is associated with many notable British pictures, including *The Private Life of Henry VIII, The Thirty-nine Steps,* and *The Ghost Goes West,* but his greatest success was undoubtedly *Goodbye, Mr. Chips,* which seemed to please the general public more than it did the critics, who said that although he was effective in the early scenes he did not in the end fully impart to the beloved schoolmaster, grown old in the service of the school, the dignity associated with the part because there was a slight grotesqueness which impaired the appeal to sentiment.

In *The Citadel* he played the part of the young Welsh doctor with enthusiasm and candour; in *The Young Mr. Pitt* he succeeded in presenting something of the singlemindedness of the Prime Minister when England was involved in war, although there was nothing of the "unendurably cold and repellent demeanour" (to quote Lord Rosebery*) of the early days of power; he gave a distinguished performance as William Friese-Greene in *The Magic Box,* the picture which was specially produced to mark the Festival of Britain and as a tribute to the pioneers of the film industry; and in *The Winslow Boy* he looked very like the first Lord Carson when he defended the young Osborne cadet accused of stealing a postal order.

When he appeared in *Lease of Life* in 1954 *The Times* declared that he was not seen often enough on the screen, but perhaps it was as well that he should preserve about him an atmosphere of intelligent exclusiveness, for he was not the kind of actor to be content with giving an endless series of repeat performances of himself. *The Times* added: "It is legitimate to infer that he takes great pains with the details of his parts, and he knows how, scrupulously and decently, to subdue himself to his part, to adapt his personality without abandoning it". That, in a single sentence, was the reason for Donat's success.

As on the stage and on the films, so on broadcast programmes, he was an actor whose integrity was immediately apparent, and his was a voice that had been heard with especial pleasure during the B.B.C. Christmas programme which precedes the Sovereign's broadcast.

June 10, 1958.

Professor F. G. Donnan, C.B.E., F.R.S., sometime Professor of General Chemistry at University College London, died in hospital at Canterbury on December 16, 1956 at the age of 86.

Frederick George was the youngest son of William Donnan, of Hollywood, co. Down, and was born on September 6, 1870. He was educated at Queen's University, Belfast, and afterwards studied at the universities of Leipzig and Berlin. He was a pupil of Sir William Ramsay, and also studied under Professors Ostwald, van't Hoff, and Letts. In 1898 he was appointed a junior fellow and examiner of the Royal University of Ireland, and in 1902 he went as assistant professor to University College London. In 1903-4 he lectured in chemistry at the Royal College of Science in Dublin, and in the latter year he was appointed to the chair of physical chemistry in the University of Liverpool. He was also director of the Muspratt laboratory of physical and electro-chemistry there. He remained nine years at Liverpool and the fact that one of the new laboratories there is named after him is testimony to the regard in which he was held in the university.

He was appointed to the chair of chemistry at University College London in 1913, at a time when building was under way at the college. New laboratories were put up in the early years of his professorship, and in 1928 he became director of the chemical laboratories. He retired from his posts at University College in 1937.

He had been elected a Fellow of the Royal Society in 1911 and in 1924-26 he served on the council. In 1928 he was awarded the society's Davy Medal for his contributions to physical chemistry, particularly his theory of membrane equilibrium. He also received the Longstaff Medal of the Chemical Society in 1924. He was honoured by many foreign universities and scientific societies: he was a foreign member of the Royal Academy of Sciences at Amsterdam, of the Royal Society of Sciences at Upsala, and of the Royal Physiographical Society at Lund.

He was however, pre-eminently a teacher. High positions in science are held by his students in many parts of the world, and many learnt from him the arts of living as well as the rigours of scientific method. He continued to infuse others with enthusiasm long after he had passed his prime as a scientist, and his popularity was wide both in his university and in the Royal Society. He was a man of remarkable vigour and, although he had lost the sight of an eye, he was a keen tennis player and went on playing well into his sixties.

He was unmarried. His sister, Miss Jane Eileen Donnan, who was his devoted secretary and working companion, died three days before him.

December 17, 1956.

Ossian Donner, the first Finnish Minister to the Court of St. James's, died on August 2, 1957 at his home in Hampshire at the age of 91.

He was one of a group of men, including Field-Marshal Mannerheim [q.v.], President Svinhufud, Baron Wrede, and others, that was instrumental in establishing Finland as an independent and viable State. He persuaded the British Government to recognize Finland's independence in 1919 and by his efforts ensured the confirmation of Finland's sovereignty over the Aaland Islands in 1921.

He was born on March 24, 1866, into a family prominent for generations in politics, shipping, banking and academic life in Finland. His father, Senator Otto Donner, Professor of Sanskrit in Helsingfors University, served as Minister of Education and on occasion as acting-Prime Minister.

Ossian Donner was educated in Helsingfors, graduating as an engineer. He did not practise, but after a period with his uncle, a large shipowner, he saw the need of a textile industry in Finland. In 1892 he opened his first woollen mill at Hyvinge and in a few years created a great and prosperous industry, today one of the largest in Northern Europe. He did not confine himself to textiles, but started his own insurance company and also became chairman of numerous industrial, banking, and shipping companies.

During the First World War Donner was a staunch supporter of the British and allied cause. After the Russian revolution in 1917 he naturally became a leader in the Finnish drive for independence. The main difficulty was to find the money for arms and supplies, and Donner, who had wide contacts in Sweden, went to Stockholm. At the request of his great friend Field-Marshal Mannerheim he set to work to raise money on a large scale for the Finnish patriots. He backed his appeals in Stockholm by pledging his personal credit and his entire private fortune. Thanks largely to the confidence of leading Swedes in him he obtained both the money and the supplies. Without these it is doubtful if the cause could have succeeded. Had it failed he would have been ruined.

After the Finnish Declaration of Independence in 1919 he was chosen for the post of Minister in London. It was an appointment after his own heart, as he had long and intimate associations with this country. He had married in 1892 Violet Marion, daughter of G. B. McHutchen, a Scottish banker, and they had made a habit of spending some months here every year. His diplomacy in London was an outstanding success. He spoke perfect English, he soon knew everybody, and his personal popularity helped to make the new independent State of Finland a welcome member of the comity of nations.

One important diplomatic achievement—and it was almost entirely a personal triumph—was the confirmation of Finland's sovereignty over the Aaland Islands. After the 1914-18 War the fate of these strategically important islands was in the balance. Sweden was anxious that they should be allotted to her. The matter was in the hands of the Peace Conference and it seemed certain that the decision would be in favour of Sweden.

Donner had had an opportunity of putting Finland's case before Sir Esme Howard (later created Lord Howard of Penrith), whom he knew well in Stockholm and who was chairman of the Baltic Commission. After much thought the Peace Conference transferred the matter to the Baltic Commission, who reviewed all the circumstances and concluded that a decision of such importance must be taken by the League of Nations. Donner set to work to ensure a decision for Finland. It was an uphill task as Sweden, with well-established legations in various capitals, would influence a large body of opinion. During this vital period—1920 to 1921—he was the Finnish representative to the League on the Aaland Islands question. How well he succeeded is now a matter of history.

A single example of his efforts must suffice. In July 1920 he called on Lord Northcliffe at Printing House Square to enlist his help. He asked that a leading article supporting Finland's case might appear in *The Times* when the matter came before the League of Nations. Lord Northcliffe assured Donner, "We are on the side of Finland". On July 10, 1920, the article appeared and evoked favourable comment. It was in line with the policy of the British Government, which was to build up a strong Finland.

Donner continued to serve his country with distinction until he retired in 1926. He held Finland's highest decoration, the White Rose of Finland (First Class) with the sash. In retirement he bought the well known Hurstbourne Park mansion and estate. Here Donner, who took British nationality, settled down to the life of an English country gentleman, but he retained the liveliest interest in politics and finance, British, Finnish, and international, and to the last his exceptional knowledge, ripe experience, and shrewd judgment rewarded the many who sought him out.

He was always a generous host.

Mrs. Donner died in 1944. He leaves one son, Sir Patrick Donner, Conservative M.P. for Basingstoke from 1935 to 1955, and one daughter.

August 5, 1957.

George H. Doran, for many years one of the most prominent and successful book publishers in America, died at Toronto, Ontario, on January 7, 1956 at the age of 86.

Born at Toronto in 1869, he began his career there at the age of 15 as a clerk with a firm of religious publishers and booksellers, and having learnt the elements of his trade migrated to Chicago at the age of 21, where he joined another publishing house with a religious bias. He found the Chicago of those days, the nineties of last century, with its raw materialism uncomfortable, and within a few years he had sailed into the open seas of New York, finally launching his own business, with a capital of $10,000, in 1909, 25 per cent of which had been put up by Hodder and Stoughton.

His first success was with Ralph Connor's novel, *The Foreigner*, of which he quickly sold 125,000 copies. Soon afterwards Doran's wife induced him to secure the American rights of Arnold Bennett's *The Old Wives' Tale,* which began by selling slowly. Its eventual great success in America greatly enhanced Bennett's reputation in England, and he and Doran became close friends. Doran's loyalty to the nationalities of his birth and his adoption—he had to become an American citizen—to, in his own phrase, "the Anglo-Saxon hegemony", led him to espouse the allied cause early in the 1914-18 War.

Doran soon became the official publisher in America for the Ministry of Information. Direct profits apart, the fact that the firm's imprint appeared on several million subsidized title-pages during the years before and after the entry of the United States into the war was an invaluable advertisement.

When the war was over its resulting literature inevitably came Doran's way and among many other works he published Lawrence's *Seven Pillars of Wisdom* and its shortened version, *Revolt in the Desert.* He also published *My Four Years in Germany,* by J. W. Gerard, who had been United States Ambassador in Berlin—a book which sold half a million copies.

By 1925 Doran's publishing house was strong enough to buy out Hodder and Stoughton, and it merged three years later with Doubleday Page & Co. Doran became president of the joint enterprise, which achieved an output of five million volumes a year. He retired in 1930 after some dissensions in the firm.

His reminiscences, which were published in 1935, give a racy account of his relations with his authors; of the three who were proved plagiarists; of threatened proceedings in connexion with the alleged immoral character of *Antic Hay*; of his friendship with Arnold Bennett and Sir Hugh Walpole; of Edgar Wallace, whom he described as the busiest man he had ever known; and of hundreds of others, including Somerset Maugham*, H. G. Wells, Sir Charles Cochran [q.v.], Lloyd George, Lady Oxford, and Frank Harris. Yet, though the accounts of his friendly relations with these and many others are entertaining, they none of them reveal the critical insight which must have informed his professional consideration of their work. The one exception is his tribute to T. E. Lawrence. "Never", he said, "was better publishing publicity conceived, but", he goes on, "I never could understand the stampede for it [*The Seven Pillars of Wisdom*]. Interesting and somewhat spectacular, yes, but great or permanent, decidedly no."

January 9, 1956.

Jimmy Dorsey, the American band leader, died in hospital in New York on June 12, 1957. He was 53.

Jimmy Dorsey was born in 1904 at Shenandoah, in the hard-coal mining region of Pennsylvania. His father was a miner who, self-taught, played in brass bands and taught music. Before they were old enough to go to school, he made Jimmy and his equally successful brother Tommy, who died in 1956, learn instruments—Jimmy the clarinet, and Tommy the trombone.

The struggles of their early years were fully described in a film, *The Fabulous Dorseys,* made in 1947. When Jimmy was 16, and already a coalminer himself, the two brothers started playing in various local bands, working up so successfully that by 1927 they were members of the famous Paul Whiteman* orchestra in New York. It was a time when the Negro jazz of New Orleans and Chicago was at the height of its vogue, and white musicians evolved various styles which modified its authentic simplicity to suit the widest possible market.

The Whiteman band was large, smooth in style, and mainly for dancing; it was when recording for the gramophone with a smaller white group, Red Nichols and his Five Pennies, that Jimmy Dorsey first began to show himself to be one of the first great virtuosi of the alto saxophone.

In 1928 the Dorsey brothers felt themselves able to start their own band, at first for recording only, and later for other engagements. They were an immediate and resounding success, playing at first in a jazz idiom, and later using their talents as soloists to be among the pioneers of the swing style.

In 1935, however, temperamental differences between the two brothers came to a head over a question of tempo; Tommy walked out of rehearsal to found his own band, and the Dorsey brothers' band, for which many later famous instrumentalists had been playing, ceased to exist for 18 years. They were later reconciled and in 1953 they came together again and remained favourites with the American public until Tommy Dorsey's accidental death in November 1956.

Separately and together they made records of which 110 million copies were sold. Large as his commercial triumphs were, Jimmy Dorsey's greatest claim to be remembered was his mastery as a solo saxophonist, one of a generation whose virtuosity enabled jazz to move out of the somewhat rigid limitation of the "traditional" style.

June 13, 1957.

Clifford Hugh Douglas, who evolved the economic theory known as Social Credit, died in Perthshire on September 29, 1952 aged 73.

He was born on January 20, 1879, the youngest son of Hugh Douglas and Louisa Arderne Hordern. After completing his education at Pembroke College, Cambridge, he trained as a mechanical engineer, and held important posts in charge of electrification contracts on the Tyne and in India under the Westinghouse company. In the 1914-18 war he held the rank of major in the R.F.C. and subsequently the R.A.F. It was reputed to be his experience in costing accountancy during the war, when he was sent by the Air Ministry to reorganize production and costing at Farnborough, that first turned his interests to the workings of the money system.

His first book, *Economic Democracy*, appeared in 1919 and this was followed a year later by *Credit-Power and Democracy*, for which A. R. Orage provided a commentary. This was a better argued work than the first, and developed his case which—in the broadest terms—may be described as the need to balance every issue of goods with an equivalent issue of purchasing power. The manufacturer would sell "below cost", the difference being made up to him by grants of credit. The natural objection that this would flood the country with paper money was met with the argument that those credits would not be in respect of goods to be produced in the future but in respect of goods already existing. The credits issued, he argued, would balance the expense of the "intermediary products", which were themselves the basis of future industry, but which were reckoned in the price of the articles put out for sale, thus raising their cost above the purchasing power of the community. In support of this Major Douglas, as he was then known, and Orage developed the idea of a miners' bank, which would seek not to dispossess the existing owners but build up beside them a structure that would be enabled to join them in the task of price-fixing according to the general nature of the plan.

Social Credit, though it attracted supporters, did not develop into an influential party in Britain, and Douglas's work was possibly most important as a stimulant to more rigorous thinkers. In Canada, however, it drew worldwide attention when, in 1935, the party won the general election for the Alberta provincial legislative assembly. In the course of a world tour the year before, Douglas had stopped in Alberta and addressed the Alberta Legislature, and after the election he was appointed Chief Reconstruction Adviser to the Government of Alberta. He resigned in March 1936, when it was stated that he had lost the confidence of the people of Alberta. The Government's attempts to enact his economic creed were later either disallowed by the Canadian Federal Government or declared unconstitutional by the Supreme Court of Canada. He gave evidence before the Canadian Banking Inquiry in 1923, and seven years later in Britain before the Macmillan Committee on banking, finance and industry.

Douglas's arguments were reinforced and developed by others, and his ideas found expression through various monetary reform groups. His later written works include *Social Credit, The Monopoly of Credit,* and *The Alberta Experiment.* In his spare time he was a keen fisherman, and he ran a shipyard at Swanwick, near Southampton, which built yachts.

He was twice married; first to Miss Constance Mary Phillips, and secondly to Miss Edith Mary Dale, by whom he had a daughter.

October 1, 1952.

Norman Douglas, the novelist and essayist, died at Capri on February 9, 1952.

George Norman Douglass (to give the full name which he never used) was born on December 8, 1868, at Tilquhillie, on Deeside, of ancient Scottish lineage, and spent his infancy in the castle of his forefathers.

He was sent to Uppingham, then under Thring, where he found, in his own words, that "the herd-system and team-life, congenial to many, went against my grain". He was taken away in 1883 and sent to the *Gymnasium* at Karlsruhe. There he worked, more or less happily, learning German, Russian, and a little French, making friends of his own kind, and cultivating scientific studies to such good effect that, at the age of 18, he was able to publish a series of articles in the *Zoologist.* A holiday in 1888 gave him his first sight of Capri, which he was later to know and love well. In March 1893 he entered the Diplomatic Service and after a year in London was appointed to St. Petersburg, where he was shortly promoted Third Secretary. For a young man the Russian capital of those years provided all the pleasure that might be desired, and there was little, it appears, that Douglas chose to pass by. At the end of 1896, however, he left Russia.

He had now finished with office work, except for a short period just before the war of 1914-18, when he was assistant editor to Austin Harrison on the *English Review.* He had published several small zoological treatises in the early nineties, and, after a visit to India and Ceylon at the turn of the century, he worked at this subject and at geology. His first excursion into fiction—a collection of short stories entitled *Unprofessional Tales*—was published in 1901. It sold precisely eight copies. Capri held him. For a dozen years or so before 1915 he made his home on the island, delighting in the freedom he had discovered for himself. His first full-length book, *Siren Land,* was vainly sent from publisher to publisher during 1910; then Edward Garnett and Joseph Conrad took an interest and helped to find a publisher for it. *Old Calabria,* issued in 1915 was a mixture of travel, history, and scholarship, and revealed a stylist of brilliantly individual flavour.

It was with *South Wind,* which came out in 1917, that Douglas established his literary reputation. *The Times Literary Supplement,* reviewing the novel on its first appearance, spoke of the author in the same breath with Peacock and Wilde. The wit, the erudite high spirits, the conversational verve and colour of this account of society on the island of Nepenthe were at once recognized by various good judges. The work was less original, no doubt, than it seemed to some, drawing as it did much of its form and temper from Latin models ancient and modern (Anatole France among them), but that scarcely affected the pleasure it gave to a receptive mind. No worse moment, however, than the war-racked summer of 1917 could have been found for the issue of such a book. Its turn of fortune was to come, but in the meantime Douglas, pressed for money, sold outright for £75 the copyright.

In 1920 he published *They Went,* which was only a degree less cynically entertaining than *South Wind.* Then came *Alone* (1921), which he afterwards described as his favourite. Thereafter Douglas produced *Together* (1923), a book about the Tyrol; *Experiments* (1925), a miscellany; *Birds and Beasts of the Greek Anthology* (1927); and *In the Beginning* (1928), an ingenious invention, ironical in temper, of a new mythology. *How About Europe?* (1930) was written as a counterblast to Katherine Mayo's *Mother India,* and in it he expressed a deep scepticism regarding the values of western civilization. In the following year appeared a series of papers of considerable learning on Capri, *Materials for a Description of the Island,* and, a few months later, he exhibited in *Paneros* a no less remarkable degree of learning on the subject of aphrodisiacs. Later came autobiographical works *Looking Back* and *Late Harvest!*

A woman who met Douglas in the twenties spoke of "the terrifying intelligent humorous gleam in his eye". He was a restless and unconventional character, and an uninhibited hedonist. His range of antipathies was wide and included the Christian religion, puritanism in any form, and Socialism.

He married, in 1898, Elsa, daughter of Augustus FitzGibbon, of Mount Shannon, County Limerick, by whom he had two sons.

February 11, 1952.

James Dowd, the illustrator and painter who made his reputation as a lively and sympathetic draughtsman of children, died on March 16, 1956 in hospital at Epsom at the age of 72.

James Henry Dowd was born at Sheffield and studied at the Sheffield School of Art, where he won the King's Prize for anatomical drawing. At 15 he started work as an illustrator for the *Sheffield Telegraph.* Going to London in 1914, he quickly made a name for himself as an illustrator of periodicals.

He was a capable portrait painter in oil, with a keen sense of character, but it is by his drawings, etchings, and drypoints of the unregenerate child that he will be remembered. The word "unregenerate" is intended, because Dowd was not greatly interested in children as domestic pets or as little men and women aping the manners of the Olympians. He was not so much against the Olympians as oblivious of them in his freemasonry with boys and girls of all classes in their own right and about their own affairs. He was not above drawing them washed and tidy, engaged in such legitimate occupations as "The Sand-design Competition," "Watching the Breakers", or lined-up before "Punch and Judy", but he really preferred them when, to recall the judge's famous remark, they were about some form of "instead-of-whiching", as in "The Wood Purloiners". He did not despise either the drawing-room or the nursery, but his true province was the playground of the street.

Dowd was a fairly regular exhibitor at the Royal Academy, where he showed portraits in oil, including one of himself, and drawings and etchings of his spiritual contemporaries, who did not exclude such comparatively respectable figures as "The Boy Scout", and he also showed at the Royal Society of Portrait Painters. But it was as an illustrator of books and periodicals, including *Punch*, for which he was the first to do the lightning sketches for the weekly film review, keeping it up for 30 years, that he reached his larger and more grateful public.

Dowd was essentially a "graphic" artist, in the sense that his expression was in the line itself rather than in the forms enclosed by it, which would not bear close criticism. He drew, so to speak, recklessly, with a broad, free line, and his work was remarkable above all for the suggestion of rapid movement. It seemed to be the natural expression of the games of children. Three volumes of his drawings were published, *Important People, People of Importance,* and *Serious Business.*

He was unmarried.

March 17, 1956.

The Most Rev. Richard Downey, Roman Catholic Archbishop of Liverpool, who died in a nursing home at Liverpool on June 16, 1953 at the age of 72, had been since 1928 perhaps the most vital figure in the hierarchy of Great Britain. For posterity his name will be chiefly associated with the foundation of Liverpool Cathedral; to this generation he was better known as a brilliant and forceful public figure.

Dr. Downey was born in Kilkenny in 1881, and when he was seven years of age his parents settled in Liverpool. He had no social advantages and the educational ones that he enjoyed were won by his talents, which showed early promise of brilliance. From a Roman Catholic elementary school in Everton he proceeded to St. Edward's College where he received a secondary education.

His religious vocation developed early; he made his theological studies at Upholland Seminary, where he was ordained priest in 1907, and at the newly founded Beda College, an English institution attached to the Gregorian University of Rome. His scholarship gained him doctorates in divinity, philosophy, and letters; a sound theologian, he was particularly attracted to philosophy.

He was sent from Liverpool to the Archdiocese of Westminster in 1911, and remained in London from that year until 1926, writing numerous pamphlets and some longer works. He was an accomplished open-air speaker with a happy gift of wit, and during the last six years of his work in London he taught theology to the novices of three religious orders, and in addition undertook, in 1923, the duties of Professor of Philosophy and Psychology at the Sacred Heart College, Hammersmith. In 1922 he visited the United States, where he preached and lectured. In the world of scholarship his lectures and contributions to the secular Press brought him membership of the British Psychological and Aristotelian Societies, and the honorary fellowship of the Philosophical Society of England. He was an external examiner to the National University of Ireland. Liverpool reclaimed him in 1926. He was appointed Vice-Rector of Upholland Seminary, to which he felt a warm and lifelong loyalty, and there engaged actively in the teaching of philosophy and theology.

Dr. Keating, the second Archbishop of Liverpool, died in 1928. The appointment of Dr. Downey as his successor, at the age of 47, came as a surprise to all, including himself; for his reputation had been won in the field of scholarship rather than administration; nor were there recent precedents for the promotion of a priest directly to an archbishopric. He soon showed that he had the qualities of an inspiring leader and sound organizer. His new contacts brought him many friends without, as well as within, his own communion; the hospitality of Archbishop's House combined a proper dignity with a refreshing absence of pomp. Among his own people he won affection and a wholehearted obedience. He made frequent appearances in the houses and streets of his subjects as well as on religious and civic platforms. He had not long been Archbishop before taking a step that created some surprise among Roman Catholics. He forbade the term "The Catholic Party" as the title of the party on the Liverpool City Council which had acted under the auspices of the United Irish League; he also forbade candidatures of priests for the City Council. The result of these strong measures was an accession of strength to the Labour party; but also a strengthening of Catholic influence within that party, which had national as well as local repercussions. Keenly interested in education, Dr. Downey was ceaseless in his efforts to obtain from the Government what he regarded as fair play for Catholic schools.

In 1930 an unhappy public controversy arose between Dr. David, the Anglican Bishop, and Dr. Downey on the question of pressure brought to bear by priests on Catholic parties to mixed marriages. Rowdy elements seized with delight on the dispute; missiles hurled at Roman Catholic churches and at the Archbishop himself prompted Dr. Downey in 1931 to a warning against the revival of the "Stone Age" of Liverpool rioting which he remembered in his boyhood. Controversy, however, was generously stilled on the day of Pentecost, 1933, when Archbishop Downey laid, amid solemn ceremonies and before a distinguished congregation, the foundation-stone of the Roman Catholic Cathedral; the presence of Dr. David that evening at a banquet to Cardinal MacRory, the Papal Legate, and the bishops who attended from many lands, and his delightful speech, marked the ending of the troubled period. Archbishop Downey deserves a great deal of the credit for ending the hostility between Catholic and Protestant that so long embittered the political life of the city.

The cathedral was the great work of the Archbishop's later years. He secured from the City Council for £10,000, a price that reflected their view that such a building would be an ornament to the city, a site on Brownlow Hill. Sir Edwin Lutyens was chosen as the architect; thus, a Roman Catholic architect (Sir Giles Gilbert Scott) [q.v.] was building the Anglican, while an Anglican was to be responsible for the Roman Catholic cathedral. Lutyens designed in the Renaissance style a stone and brick building which was to be the largest cathedral in the world after St. Peter's in Rome.

Though Dr. Downey seldom made a speech without referring to the cathedral, he did not neglect his schools, enlarging and improving many buildings, and keenly supporting the efforts of his priests to meet the spiritual needs of the new residential districts of Liverpool. He was in close touch with national movements of opinion, a vigorous and skilful opponent of anti-Catholic moral teachings, and always ready by apt word and dignified speech to express the views of his Church on major questions. He denounced communist teachings and the encroachment of the state on the sphere of the family. His knowledge of Italian helped him, it is believed, to represent at Rome the point of view of English Roman Catholics. He did much, in his own diocese, to make those members of his flock who were of Irish origin realize their privileges and responsibilities as British subjects, and to put an end to the self-consciousness to which minorities are ever prone. With this end in view it was his annual custom to celebrate St. George's Day with every solemnity; making it an occasion for urging Roman Catholics of all shades of political opinion to take an honest and active share in the public life of the city and country. "A man wrapped up in himself", he used to say, "makes a very small parcel".

A character of such decided views and of such bold leadership was naturally the subject of divided views, both within and without this own communion. But no one who knew him in his informal and delightful private life could resist the brilliance of his mind or the charm of his manner.

June 17, 1953.

Ruth Draper, HON.C.B.E., the American *diseuse,* whose remarkable dramatic gift won her renown all over the world, died in New York on December 30, 1956. She was 72.

She had long been known as a soloist of genius. In her extreme youth she essayed to act in an ordinary play, with ordinary actors and actresses; the result was a minor disaster. It was only by slow degrees and effort after this rebuff that she found and perfected for herself her unique method of expression, which ranged from the thistledown of mirth to imponderable tragedy; and by which she drew her audiences into friendship and opened to them by speech and by suggestion the peopled rooms of her imagination. It took years of concentration before Ruth Draper attained to the interpretation of character which as an artist she demanded of herself; and she was shaken throughout her career by her mistrust of her own conceptions, so that each new study was achieved by scrupulous, hard work. For some years, too, her method appealed to the few rather than the many; in New York and later in London (in 1920-21-22) her audiences were small, and a general appreciation came only from 1925 onwards.

Ruth Draper was born on December 2, 1884, the youngest daughter of Dr. William Draper, a distinguished physician of New York. One of a lively and gifted family, she found for her powers of mimicry an early scope in those childish episodes which were afterwards transmuted with brilliance into such sketches as "The German Governess". She had a home in which work and merriment were friends, and she had an education which depended upon cultivation rather than upon amassing facts. She early learnt French, German, and Italian. She spent periods in Europe and in England; she knew by right among her parents' friends men and women who were eminent in learning, art, and in social service.

She inherited a power of diagnosis which, medically remarkable in her father and her brother, became in her case the foundation of her art. And it is accurate to say *her* art, rather than to use a more general term. For Ruth Draper falls into no category; her work was neither mimicry nor caricature; it was scarcely to be called acting—it partook of all these, but it was apart. She was a penetrating, at times a cruel, critic of men's failings. But at the moment when a certain pitilessness seemed about to repel the listener, she would turn to some human grace which gave the balance of beauty to an incisive portrait. The tourists making babble in the Florentine church, for example, fade like breath on a window-pane, in the face of the silent woman who kneels to pray.

It was Miss Draper's genius that she gave balance to such a contrast, never exaggerating the vapid, never sentimentalizing the enduring. Many such examples must rise in the minds of her immense audiences, together with the recollections of pure mirth provoked by her scenes in an English garden, a New York luncheon room, a dressmaker's studio; and of her human tenderness in such studies as the railway accident, and the Dalmatian peasant in the New York hospital. There are indeed countless points in her work with which memory can play. They reflect those countless points in her character—sensitive, keen, constant, rich in intelligence and pity—which rise in the minds of her friends at the thought of her, as lilies rise and open and are reflected in a clear pool.

Ruth Draper paid regular visits to London. The last was earlier in 1956. Her last performance in England was given in Holloway Prison in August and was one of the fortnightly series of entertainments organized for the London prisons by Xenia Field. In June 1926 she went to Windsor to appear before King George V and Queen Mary [q.v.] and their guests for the Ascot week. On this occasion the Queen made her own selections from a number of pieces in Ruth Draper's repertory.

In 1951 she went to Buckingham Palace to receive at the hands of King George VI [q.v.] the honorary C.B.E. she had been awarded shortly before.

She was honoured by several American universities and was an honorary LL.D. of both Cambridge and Edinburgh. At Cambridge, the Orator, not inaptly, remarked *Unus agit multas vitae per tempora partes.*

December 31, 1956.

Admiral Sir Frederic Charles Dreyer, G.B.E., K.C.B., one of the foremost experts in naval gunnery of his time, died at Winchester on December 11, 1956. He was 78.

Sir Arthur Wilson, Sir Reginald Bacon, and Lord Jellicoe were among the distinguished officers who bore testimony to his skill and energy in improving the mechanism of naval guns, especially in regard to range finding and the control of fire. At Jutland he was Jellicoe's Flag Captain, and later he was among the officers who accompanied the admiral to Whitehall when the latter was appointed First Sea Lord.

Dreyer, who was of mixed Danish and Irish descent, was the son of Dr. J. L. E. Dreyer. He was born on January 8, 1878, attended the Royal School, Armagh, and entered the Britannia in 1891. He served in the Anson and the Barfleur, was promoted to lieutenant in 1898, and in 1899 joined the Excellent to specialize in gunnery. Having passed with honours the advanced course he became a fully qualified gunnery lieutenant in 1901 at the age of 23, and was appointed to the instructional staff at Sheerness gunnery school.

In 1903 he was selected for the battleship Exmouth, flagship of Admiral Sir Arthur Wilson, Commander-in-Chief of the Home Fleet. Sir Arthur Wilson had presented two cups to the Fleet for the winning battleship and cruiser at battle practice, and the former was won by the Exmouth. Dreyer remained in the ship until 1907, when he was selected for special duty in the Dreadnought, then newly completed. Later in that year he was concerned in experiments with Pollen's aim corrector, an instrument designed to improve the control of fire of a ship's armament. Admiral Sir Reginald Bacon, in his biography of Lord Fisher, refers to Dreyer as "the most accomplished gunnery lieutenant of that time". Dreyer was promoted to Commander in December 1907, a few days before he was 30, and appointed to the Naval Ordnance Department.

He resumed sea duty as commander of the Vanguard in 1909, and in December 1910 as Flag Commander to Vice-Admiral Sir John Jellicoe, Commanding the Atlantic Fleet. In January 1913 he received his first independent command, to the light cruiser Amphion, and six months later was promoted to captain. In October 1913 he joined the new battleship Orion, as Flag Captain to Rear-Admiral Sir Robert Arbuthnot in the Second Battle Squadron. Here he served for two years, which included the first year or more of war service.

In October 1915 Admiral Jellicoe obtained his transfer to the Iron Duke, flagship of the Grand Fleet, as Flag Captain, and he was thus employed at the Battle of Jutland on May 31, 1916. The official dispatch of the engagement stated that Captain Dreyer "commanded and handled the Fleet flagship most ably during the action. The rapidity with which hitting was established on ships of the enemy's fleet was the result of long and careful organization and training of the personnel". Dreyer had been made a C.B. (Civil) just before the war for his services to gunnery. After Jutland he was appointed a C.B. (Military). In December 1916 Admiral Jellicoe relinquished the post of Commander-in-Chief. Captain Dreyer accompaned his chief to the Admiralty and, on March 1, 1917, was appointed Director of Naval Ordnance. In that capacity he saw to the introduction of a new design of armour-piercing projectile, with a new type of burster and an altered fuse, for heavy guns, which Jellicoe declared "certainly doubled their offensive power".

As part of the measures taken for suppressing the submarine menace, Captain Dreyer ordered during the first three months of his term as D.N.O. some 4,200 guns for the defensive arming of merchant ships. During 1918, after there had been certain changes in the organization at the Admiralty, Captain Dreyer held the new post of Director of Naval Artillery and Torpedoes, Naval Staff. He remained at the Admiralty until after the conclusion of hostilities, and in the New Year honours, 1919, was made a C.B.E.

After the war his first duty was to accompany his old chief, Lord Jellicoe, on his mission to India and the Dominions, being appointed to the battle-cruiser New Zealand as Commodore and Chief of Staff in February 1919. On his return he resumed his former post at the Admiralty in April 1920, but with the title of Director of the Gunnery Division, for two years. In April 1922 he commanded the battle-cruiser Repulse, and in December 1923 he was promoted to rear-admiral. After the customary period on half-pay and in attending courses he was appointed in October 1924 a member of the Admiralty Board as Assistant Chief of the Naval Staff. In May 1927 he hoisted his flag for the first time as Rear-Admiral Commanding the Battle Cruiser Squadron, in the Hood, and it was during his two years there that he was made a vice-admiral, in March 1929. On June 30, 1930, he returned to the Admiralty Board as Deputy Chief of the Naval Staff, and from April 1931, in addition to his duties in that post, served as Admiralty representative on the League of Nations Permanent Advisory Commission. He was promoted to admiral and to K.C.B. in 1932, and early in 1933 took up the appointment of Commander-in-Chief on the China Station. Four years later he was promoted G.B.E.

Dreyer was placed on the retired list in May 1939, but was later re-employed in the war, first as Commodore of Convoys from 1939 to 1940 and as Inspector of Merchant Navy Gunnery from 1941 to 1942. In the following year he was appointed Chief of Naval Air Services and held this post until 1943, when he became Deputy Chief of Naval Air Equipment.

Dreyer married in 1901 Una Maria, daughter of the Rev. J. Hallett, and there were three sons and three daughters of the marriage.

December 12, 1956.

Lord Drogheda, who died on November 22, 1957 at the age of 73, had been Lord Chairman of Committees in the House of Lords since 1946, and he served with distinction as a temporary Civil servant during the Second World War.

The Right Hon. Henry Charles Ponsonby Moore, K.C.M.G., tenth Earl of Drogheda, Viscount Moore, of Drogheda, Baron Moore, of Mellefont, all in the peerage of Ireland, and Baron Moore, of Cobham, in the county of Surrey, in the peerage of the United Kingdom, and a Representative Peer for Ireland, was born in 1884, the only son of the ninth earl and of Anne Tower, daughter of George Moir, Sheriff of Stirlingshire. He was educated at Eton and Trinity College, Cambridge.

He entered the Foreign Office in 1907 and remained there until 1918. But like many of his colleagues he chafed at his retention in civilian employment during the war. The authorities at the Foreign Office, however, steadily refused to release so valuable an official, until, in 1918, he got his way and obtained a commission in the Irish Guards; but the war was at its end, and he saw active service for a very short time. Drogheda, who succeeded his father in 1908, was elected an Irish representative peer in 1913.

After the 1914-18 War Drogheda, having resigned from the Foreign Office, attended the House of Lords regularly. But he did not at first make it his career, preferring the Bar, to which he was called by the Inner Temple. He practised mainly in the Divorce Court and took a prominent part in furthering divorce reform in the House of Lords.

At the outbreak of war in 1939 he entered the Ministry of Economic Warfare. When the Churchill* Administration was formed in 1940 Hugh Dalton* was made political head of the department, and one of his earliest appointments was to make Drogheda joint director in charge of operations. He was, in Dalton's words, "a live wire and a war wager". In 1942 he was promoted to be director-general. After the war his influence was widely felt; in the cinema industry, where he served as chairman of the Cinematograph Films Council from 1944 to 1954 and chairman of the Films Selection Board from 1946 to 1954; in broadcasting, through his chairmanship of the committee of inquiry into the overseas information and broadcasting services; as chairman of the Home Office advisory council on the treatment of offenders since 1954.

The Drogheda committee to inquire into overseas information services was set up in October 1952. They accomplished their task with dispatch and made their report to the Government a year later. The Government, however, were disinclined to publish it on the grounds that it contained much confidential matter. But they were strongly pressed and in the following spring issued a summary of the report as a White Paper. It was enough to show that the committee had based their proposals on sound principles and a good grip of the facts. They concluded that the overseas information services were inadequate for their job, criticized the series of cuts imposed at short notice, and made recommendations which would cost nearly another £2m. a year.

Drogheda became Lord Chairman of Committees in 1946. Although he was afflicted with asthma in recent years, he was an assiduous attender at the House of Lords, where his rather slight, grey-haired figure was a familiar sight. He had inherited a fine place in Ireland, Moore Abbey, co. Kildare, and he was Lieutenant for co. Kildare from 1918 to 1921; but he ceased to live regularly in Ireland after the separation of the two countries.

He was a keen sportsman—a good shot but perhaps a better golfer.

He was created K.C.M.G. in 1945, was sworn of the Privy Council in 1951, and was created a baron in the United Kingdom peerage in 1954.

He married first, in 1909, Kathleen, youngest daughter of Charles M. Pelham Burn, of Grange Park, Edinburgh. She was appointed C.B.E. for her work in the 1914-18 War. The marriage, of which there was a son, and a daughter who died in 1947, was dissolved in 1922. He married secondly, in the same year, Lady Victor Paget, daughter of Mr. George Meatyard; she died in 1947.

His heir, Viscount Moore, who was born in 1910, is managing director of the *Financial Times.* He married in 1935 Joan, daughter of the late W. H. Carr, and there is a son of the marriage.

November 23, 1957.

Sir James Eric Drummond—See **Perth.**

John Van Druten—See **Van Druten.**

Dr. Wynfrid Laurence Henry Duckworth, Master of Jesus College from 1940 to 1945 and Emeritus Reader in Human Anatomy in the University of Cambridge, died at Cambridge on February 14, 1956 at the age of 85.

He was born at Liverpool on June 5, 1870, the son of Henry Duckworth, and after attending Birkenhead School and l'École Libre des Cordeliers at Dinant he entered Jesus College, Cambridge, in 1889. A brilliant undergraduate career, which included rowing in the college boat as well as academic distinctions, was followed by election to a Fellowship, and shortly afterwards the College appointed him Director of Studies in Natural Sciences and Medicine.

As soon as his Tripos examinations were completed he threw himself enthusiastically into work in the anatomy school, making dissections of the gorilla and other apes and carrying out measurements on skulls from the great collection built up by Humphrey and Macalister. Within a few years he had become a recognized authority on physical anthropology, and in 1899 a university lectureship in that subject was established for him. Meanwhile he had been going on with his medical studies, and he was approved for the doctorates of medicine and of science in 1905.

In 1904 he published an important textbook, *Morphology and Anthropology.* Beginning with a systematic comparison of the structure and development of man with those of the animals most nearly related to him, it proceeded to an account of the anatomical differences which distinguish the various races of mankind and concluded with an outline of the then existing knowledge of human paleontology. No other book covered the same ground and its merits were widely appreciated. He brought out Volume I of a new and enlarged edition in 1915. In 1920 the University showed their appreciation of his services to the Anatomy School by giving him the status of Reader in Human Anatomy. He represented the University on the General Medical Council for the period 1923 to 1926.

Duckworth's interests extended far beyond his own special subjects. From boyhood he had been strongly attracted to natural history and zoology. An expedition to Greece and Crete in 1903 to compare the skeletal characters of their past and present inhabitants brought him into direct contact with classical archaeology.

He had held a variety of administrative offices. He served as Proctor in 1904-5; he was Steward of his college from 1895 to 1920 and again from 1929 to 1945; and Bursar from 1933 to 1945. Thus in many fields he could meet biologists, medicals, archaeologists and men of affairs on their own ground, and the learning with which he could discuss almost any subject from medieval history to automobiles was the cause of perpetual wonder to his colleagues.

Possessed of much quiet humour and with a retentive memory stored with this varied knowledge, he was well fitted to fulfil the social duties which fell to him as President and later as Master of his college. In manner he was somewhat formal, and he was insistent on order and precision, but he was always distinguished by a fine and gentle courtesy and unvarying kindness, and these qualities won him the deep regard of his colleagues and the affection of his pupils.

He was elected Master of Jesus after the death of Arthur Gray in 1940. The five years of his mastership fell within the war period and the college well realized how much it owed to his vigilant care in meeting the difficult problems which then so frequently arose. He retired under the age limit in 1945 but continued to reside in his college rooms, devoting his time mainly to work amid his unique collection in the School of Anatomy. During these later years he placed much of his valuable material in the newly created Duckworth Laboratory in the School of Anthropology and Archaeology. His Huxley Memorial Lecture for 1947 on

Some Complexities of Human Structure directed attention to unsolved problems in anatomy and stressed the need for more intensive study of form and structure in man and the primates.

He was president of the Anatomical Society of Great Britain and Ireland in 1943-45, and Linacre Lecturer at St. John's College, Cambridge, in 1948.

He married in 1902 Eva Alice, widow of Lieutenant Charles Cheyne, and daughter of the late Frederick Wheeler. She died on February 14, 1955.

February 15, 1956.

Sir Arthur du Cros, BT., one of the pioneers of the pneumatic tyre industry, died on October 28, 1955 at his home at Oxhey, Hertfordshire, at the age of 84.

Formerly chairman and managing director and later president of the Dunlop Rubber Company, he was at one time a man of great wealth which he used to support numerous good causes. He was also deeply interested in art and architecture.

His home, Craigweil House, near Bognor Regis, was specially designed to take every advantage of the clear, bright light and pure air of that part of the south coast, and he put it at the disposal of King George V when the latter was recovering in 1929 from a severe illness. His greatest interest, however, was in the development of the pneumatic tyre industry and he made the name of Dunlop known throughout the world. Unfortunately, the highly geared finances of the parent company were not able to stand the strain of the difficult economic conditions of the late twenties and early thirties and he was personally involved in the failure of his intricate financial operations.

Arthur Philip du Cros was born in Dublin on January 26, 1871. Of Huguenot descent, he was the third son of William Harvey du Cros, of Howbery Park, Oxon, who died in 1918. Though Arthur du Cros trained for the Civil Service it did not appeal to him and in 1892 he joined his father and brothers in the newly founded Dunlop Pneumatic Tyre Company. He himself had been the amateur cycle champion of Ireland and France, riding at the Queen's College, Belfast, sports in 1889 with the new tyres, dubbed "pudding tyres" by the spectators. Though for the next quarter of a century he devoted most of his time and energy to the development of the pneumatic tyre industry he entered the House of Commons in 1908 as M.P. for Hastings in the Conservative interest.

Du Cros had always been interested in art, and was an honorary member of the National Art-Collections Fund and an Associate of the National Gallery of British Art. In 1916 he offered to give about £3,000 to secure for the nation the famous collection of Rossetti paintings owned by the late George Rae, of Liverpool.

Among other examples of du Cros's generosity were his contributions of £7,000 to the London School of Medicine for Women (Royal Free Hospital), the sum of £6,000 towards the purchase of the first national airship, and his presentation to the War Office during the 1914-18 War, at the cost of £50,000, of three motor ambulance convoys, which he undertook to maintain at his own expense for the duration of the war. He also raised an infantry battalion, and worked in an honorary capacity for the Minister of Munitions. In 1909 he had formed the Parliamentary Aerial-Defence Committee, of which he was honorary secretary. This committee was formed to secure the inclusion of aeronautics in the Navy and Army estimates.

In 1916 du Cros was created a baronet, and two years later he was representing the Clapham division of Wandsworth instead of Hastings, where he had been the Unionist member for 10 years. In 1922 he resigned. One of his great interests was the Junior Imperial League, of which he was a founder and first chairman of its committee. He was also at one time honorary colonel of the 8th Battalion, The Royal Warwickshire Regiment.

Sir Arthur du Cros married, first, in 1895 Maude, daughter of the late William Gooding, of Warwickshire, and by her had two sons and two daughters. This marriage was dissolved in 1923. He married in 1928 Florence May, daughter of the late James Walton King, of Walton, Buckinghamshire. She died in 1951, and he then married Miss Mary Louise Joan Beaumont.

He is succeeded by his elder son, Philip Harvey du Cros, who was educated at Harrow and served in both world wars. The new baronet, who was born in 1898, married in 1922 Dita, only daughter of Sir Claude Coventry Mallet, who was Special Ambassador to Argentina in 1922 and to the Uruguayan Republic in 1923. They have a son and two daughters.

October 31, 1955.

Gertrude Lady Dudley (in private life), who was **Gertie Millar,** one of the most famous actresses of the Edwardian musical comedy stage, died at her home at Chiddingfold, Sussex, on April 25, 1952 at the age of 73.

Her last appearance on the stage was in 1918; but the charm of this most piquant and accomplished of players in musical comedy is cherished by all old enough to remember her at the Gaiety and at Daly's in the early years of this century. She was tall, slender, and notably graceful; and though she made no pretension to rival the famous beauties of the lyric stage, her small and dainty face sparkled with fun, and her smile was enchanting.

She was born at Bradford, Yorkshire, on February 21, 1879. Gossip in her heyday said that she had been a mill-hand and worn the clogs; but the records state that in December 1892, at the age of 13, she was the female Babe in the pantomime *The Babes in the Wood* at the St. James's Theatre, Manchester; that in December 1899 she was Dandini in *Cinderella* at the Grand Theatre, Fulham, and that during the intervening years she was appearing in pantomime and musical comedy in provincial towns. By the spring of 1901 she had won an admirer who was a man of influence in musical comedy, her first husband, Lionel Monckton. He and Ivan Caryll wrote the music for George Edwardes's new production at the Gaiety, *The Toreador.* Gertie Millar was engaged for the part of a bridesmaid, Cora Bellamy, and thus made her first appearance in London in June 1901. She sang "Keep Off the Grass" and "Captivating Cora", and her fame was made.

At the Gaiety she stayed for seven years; but the house in which she next appeared was not the old Gaiety but the new one built by George Edwardes and opened in October 1903 with *The Orchid,* the music again being by Monckton and Caryll. In that piece she sang "Oh! take care of Little Mary!" a song inspired by Barrie's "uncomfortable play" at Wyndham's. Next came three more pieces with music by Monckton and Caryll—*The Spring Chicken* (1905), *The New Aladdin* (1906), and *The Girls of Gottenberg* (1907).

There came a break in her connexion with the Gaiety when she went, in March 1908, to the Hicks (now the Globe) Theatre to take part in *A Waltz Dream,* an operetta by Oscar Strauss [q.v.]; and with this and *The Girls of Gottenberg* she went in the autumn of that year to win the heart of New York.

Back at the Gaiety at the beginning of 1909 she made one of the greatest of all her hits in *Our Miss Gibbs* with "We never do that in Yorkshire", and the most popular of all, "I'm such a silly when the moon comes out". The music of *Our Miss Gibbs* was by Monckton and Caryll, and Monckton was again her composer in *The Quaker Girl* at the Adelphi in 1910 (it was in this that she sang "Tony from America"). The summer of 1912 saw her in *Gipsy Love* (music by Lehar) at Daly's; then in the autumn back to Monckton's music for *The Dancing Mistress* and for the revival of *The Country Girl.* No one could fit her with songs quite so happily as Monckton; and it was he who wrote for her "Neville was a Devil" in *Bric-a-Brac* at the Palace in September 1915, and composed some of the music of *Airs and Graces* at the same theatre in 1917. Her last appearance in musical comedy was in *Flora* at the Prince of Wales's Theatre in 1918.

Lionel Monckton died in February 1924, and she then married the second Earl of Dudley, who died in 1931. She never lost her interest in the stage and until quite lately was often to be seen in London. A serious illness in 1950 incapacitated her, and latterly she had been obliged to use two sticks or a wheeled chair to get about.

April 26, 1952.

Few modern artists can have had a more recognizably individual style than **Raoul Dufy,** the French painter and designer of textiles and ceramics, who died at his home in the south of France on March 23, 1953 at the age of 75. His style was calligraphic; a style of considered slightness and extreme elegance, gay in feeling and witty in allusion.

Dufy, a Norman, was born on June 3, 1877,

at Le Havre. He was a fellow townsman and close friend of Othon Freisz, who died in January 1949, and whose early artistic education Dufy shared. They studied together under the sound Impressionist painter Charles Lhuillier at Le Havre, where Dufy was employed in the office of an exporting company, and together they went to Paris and entered the studio of Léon Bonnat at the École des Beaux-Arts. Later they studied under the less narrowly academic and more imaginative Gustave Moreau, whose studio is now a museum in the keeping of Georges Rouault [q.v.], who was Moreau's favourite pupil in a brilliant company that included Matisse [q.v.], Derain [q.v.], and Vlaminck [q.v.].

It was mainly out of Moreau's pupils that the group of painters styled *Les Fauves* was formed. Dufy took part in the first *Fauves* exhibition in 1905. After that, though they remained friends, he and Freisz parted company in their art, and Freisz travelled the world while Dufy remained in Paris to share the excitement of the times. He became a member of the *Jeune Peinture Française* and took part in the second exhibition of the society in 1920. In spite of his enjoyment of life and the gaiety of his style, Dufy took his art very seriously. It was about the year 1909, he explained afterwards, that he first had the idea of taking up textiles. He was then engaged in illustrating the work of Apollinaire, and while cutting his designs on wood and studying the different ways of engraving he came to the conclusion that the same thing might be done on fabrics.

For a year he worked with a chemist, making a close study of dyes, and his designs attracted the attention of Paul Poiret, who used them extensively. Dufy continued to paint pictures, in oil and water-colour, which inclined more and more to the decoratively arabesque, deceptively casual in drawing and charming in colour. There is a general similarity in style between his pictures and his decorative designs, but in the pictures the needs of representation are not ignored. In this connexion the story is told of a young woman at an autumn salon who loudly denounced a picture by Dufy as "trivial and childish" and who was observed to be wearing with all too evident pride a frock made of material designed by him.

Dufy's painting is a clear manifestation of the literary axiom that easy reading involves hard writing. Some French critics have complained that his earlier water-colours were a little too easy and "commercial" in character, but at his best he was a very sensitive draughtsman, and if it be the function of art to give pleasure he certainly succeeded. A feature of his work was the apparent separation he effected between drawing and painting. He himself had a theory that when objects are in movement line is displaced more quickly than colour. Occasionally, as in "Le peintre et son modèle" of 1930, an interior with figures, Dufy recalls Matisse, though he had not Matisse's uncanny ability to fix objects in space by colour values alone and needed line to suggest the dimensions of depth. In both his pictures and his decorative designs he was attracted by places and scenes of sport and recreation, such as Epsom and Longchamp, and by such subjects as tennis, dancing, and fishing. Besides designing textiles and ceramics he did a good deal of decorative and illustrative work. He made lithographs for Mallarmé's *Madrigaux* and designed the scenery for Cocteau's* ballet *Le boeuf sur le toit.* At the Paris International Exhibition of 1937, for which Picasso's* "Guernica" was painted, Dufy was responsible for a large decoration, "The History of Electricity", for the Palace of Light.

Dufy paid at least two visits to England, in 1930 and 1935, and among other subjects he painted Hyde Park, the Houses of Parliament, the Changing of the Guard, and "Epsom; the Derby Parade". Exhibitions of his work were held at the Claridge Gallery in 1928, Tooth's Gallery in 1929, the Lefevre galleries in 1936, and the Hanover Gallery in 1949. In a review of the 1936 exhibition it was said: "M. Dufy plans his picture in areas of colour, flatly applied, and then 'writes' the details and incidents upon it, swiftly and surely in dark lines. It is a reduction of painting to the simplest terms, but it is not nearly so easy as it looks, because everything depends upon the justness of the colour relations in the first place, and the sureness and significance of the calligraphy in the second". This gives a good general idea of his procedure and suggests the deceptive ease of his style.

In his old age Dufy renounced the multiplicity of colours which marked his previous work and adopted "tonal colours"—using variations of a single colour, as in his "Red Violin". A crippling arthritis of the hands for several years prevented him from working, but after cortisone treatment in the United States he was able to resume painting in 1950, and shortly before his death he completed a notable portrait of Maître Maurice Garçon in Academician's uniform.

In 1952 his work received crowning recognition in the award of the Grand Prix of the Venice Biennale. On the advice of his doctors, Dufy retired on his return from America to Forcalquier, in the Basses-Alpes. He survived an attack of pneumonia in January, but his system was weakened by it, and he succumbed to a heart attack there. His wife survives him.

March 24, 1953.

Roger Martin du Gard, the distinguished French novelist and winner of the Nobel prize for literature in 1937, died on August 23, 1958 at his home at Bellême in southern Normandy, after a long illness. He was 77.

He was a writer on the grand scale and in the great French realistic tradition; together with Jules Romains* and Georges Duhamel* he was one of the main exponents of the multi-volume *roman-fleuve* during the inter-war years.

"Gide", [q.v.] he once wrote, "is a man of letters from morning till night.... The only aim of his life is to enrich his work". The description will seem to apply no less well to Martin du Gard himself, although his attitude in many ways was the antithesis of Gide's. Nothing was allowed to break the thread of his concentration. He avoided distractions and worldly pitfalls which beset the path of the successful writer. His long working life had in its consistency, its simplicity, its detachment, a dignity that inclines one to echo the words of Luce, the free-thinking philosopher, to Jean Barois, afflicted by remorse at the end of his rebellious life: "Je trouve votre vie très belle".

Roger Martin du Gard was born in the Paris suburb of Neuilly on March 23, 1881, into a well-to-do family of lawyers with origins partly in Loraine and partly in Burgundy. After an education at lycées in Paris he spent three years at the École des Chartes, where he won a palaeographic diploma and wrote an archaeological thesis on the Abbey of Jumièges. This training with its insistence on precise documentation and exactness of detail was to mark all his literary work. In spite of his brilliant qualities as a novelist he was extremely severe on himself: one of his earlier novels, *L'Un de Nous* (1910), he destroyed during the First World War because he was not satisfied with it, and similarly he destroyed the seventh volume of his masterpiece, *Les Thibault.*

His first novel, *Devenir,* appeared in 1909, but he did not achieve wide recognition until his old college friend Gaston Gallimard* published his *Jean Barois* in 1913. In this novel Martin du Gard analysed some of the great intellectual problems of the pre-war years: the value of science, the future of Roman Catholicism, and in particular the problems of conscience posed by the Dreyfus affair. Martin du Gard was always interested in religious problems, but from the age of 15 had ceased to be a practising Roman Catholic, and in *Jean Barois* he expressed his faith in a rationalist intellectual progress. Between 1922 and 1940 appeared the volumes of his greatest work, *Les Thibault,* which traces the inter-related fortunes during the first decades of the century of two bourgeois Parisian families, one Roman Catholic and one Protestant.

The work has dramatic power and vivid characterization, and is especially interesting as a social document portraying the gradual disappearance of an epoch and way of life based on the old family values. When the 1914 War comes neither of the two Thibault brothers, who are the two main characters, is able to survive it morally. One thinks of Galsworthy's *roman-fleuve* about the Forsytes as perhaps the closest English parallel, but Martin du Gard was a greater writer than Galsworthy.

Martin du Gard also wrote several plays on country life, in which he showed an interest in the psychology of abnormal people. One of these plays, *Un Taciturne,* was made famous on the Paris stage by the late Louis Jouvet [q.v.] in 1931.

His "album of village sketches", *Vieille France,* cynical and sharply focused, originally published in France in the 1930s, was translated into English by John Russell and appeared in 1954 as *The Postman.*

Martin du Gard was a friend of Gide—his *Notes sur Gide* was published in England in 1952—and Alain-Fournier, and a leading contributor to the *Nouvelle Revue Française.* Yet he lived rarely in Paris, preferring the seclusion of his villas at Bellême and Nice, and during the later years of his life he rarely received visitors. He had published very little since 1940, save in 1949 a translation of Dorothy Bussy's short novel about a French finishing school, *Olivia*. But he is said to have spent these years working on a new long novel about France during the occupation and liberation, which he has asked should not be published until 30 years after his death.

He was a Companion of the Legion of Honour.

In late June 1958 it was announced by André Malraux that the Government had decided to ask the three French winners of literary Nobel prizes, François Mauriac*, Albert Camus [q.v.], and Martin du Gard, to form a committee which would, with Government accreditation, visit Algeria "to see things for itself".

August 25, 1958.

T. C. Dugdale, R.A., the well-known portrait painter, died in hospital in London on November 13, 1952 at the age of 72.

To make a distinction that is convenient rather than watertight, he was a good painter rather than a great artist. That is to say, he was a brilliant executant in oil pigment, but though he was perceptive both visually and emotionally (and consequently deft in catching the likeness of his sitter) his vision lacked that profundity, that wealth of overtones and associations which make the work of a great artist so various and evocative. Thus, the subject of Dugdale's pictures is on the whole of more importance than the composition and this is rather odd because he had a good deal of experience as a decorative designer, for textiles in particular, and was art adviser to Tootal Broadhurst Lee, the famous firm of textile manufacturers. His apparent inability to carry into his pictures what he had learnt as a designer must be put down to his having been brought up in the tradition which separates the "decorative" from the "fine" arts and pursues the latter too much from the imitative and too little from the decorative point of view.

When this reservation has been made Dugdale was an excellent painter, broad and fluent in execution, with a very good sense of tone, not only as regards factual relationships but also as a means to emotional expression. Thus, he painted the nude very skilfully, with a keen enjoyment of the substance of flesh. Two pictures of his that are remembered with special pleasure are "The Red Jacket", a half-length of a handsome woman, presented to the Tate Gallery by Francis Howard in 1935, and "Mr. Kersey of Iken", a rustic figure exhibited at the Academy in 1940. Primarily a portrait painter, Dugdale excelled in compositions of small figures in landscape surroundings; rather on the lines of the "conversation piece" as practised by Arthur Devis and by Gainsborough in his earlier days; a kind of picture in which likeness itself depends a good deal on certainty of tone and deftness of touch. In this manner Dugdale produced some lively small portraits of brother artists in their home surroundings. Among the eminent people painted by him at full-scale and exhibited at the Academy were Princess Margaret, the late Lord Oxford and Asquith, the Duchess of Gloucester, and Archbishop William Temple.

Thomas Cantrell Dugdale, who was the third son of Alfred Dugdale, an engineer, of Manchester, was born at Blackburn on June 2, 1880. He was educated at Manchester Grammar School and studied art at the Manchester School of Art, the Royal College of Art, and in Paris at Julian's. He was a member of the Royal Institute of Oil Painters and the Royal Society of Portrait Painters, and exhibited fairly regularly at the Royal Academy from 1901 onwards, being elected A.R.A. in 1936 and R.A. in 1943. He also exhibited at the New English Art Club and in Paris, Vienna, Düsseldorf, Venice, Cape Town, Pittsburgh, Wellington, Sydney, and many provincial cities. He received a silver medal for his work at the Paris Salon in 1921 and a gold medal at the Paris Exhibition of Decorative Art in 1925. Works by him were purchased by the Manchester Corporation and the Imperial War Museum, and they also form a part of the permanent collections in many other galleries at home and abroad.

During the war of 1914-18 Dugdale served in a yeomanry regiment in Egypt, the Dardanelles, the Balkans, and Palestine, being mentioned in dispatches in 1915. In 1940 he was active in the organization of Local Defence Volunteers in Suffolk, and a letter from him on the subject of the corps appeared in *The Times* of June 4 of that year.

Though Dugdale continued his work as a portrait painter with undiminished vigour, he yet found time and energy to play a prominent part in the affairs of the Home Guard for the remainder of the war, an achievement of which he was justly proud.

Dugdale, whose work and appearance seemed those of one far younger than his years, was an impulsive, emotional man, greatly liked by his associates. His generosity to brother artists, in material ways as well as in appreciation, was famous.

He married, in 1916, Miss Amy Katherine Browning, an excellent painter in a style that might be called the feminine counterpart of his own. She has exhibited regularly at the Academy and elsewhere under her maiden name.

November 14, 1952.

Ashley Dukes, who died on May 4, 1959 in a London hospital at the age of 73, had been active in the theatre for the greater part of half a century in the capacities of dramatic critic, playwright, producer, and theatrical manager, and the quality of his work in these successive fields was such as to encourage and effectively support the trends and causes in which he most believed.

He had a taste for a number of things in life beside the theatre, and cultivated it deliberately, humorously, and convivially; but he had to a remarkable, perhaps to an unfortunate, extent the power of standing aside from his own work, preferring that it should take its chance and run its course without too much paternal backing from his own fastidious yet sociable self. This feeling on his part that where his plays and productions were concerned they should be left to win their spurs, while he stood by and looked on critically, perhaps explains why such a strong personality never became widely associated in the public mind with the distinctive contribution to the theatre that he unquestionably made. Individualist though he was, it was as a member of a group that he exerted influence. He was a servant, a proud servant, of the theatre, rather than a man of it.

Dukes was in his late teens when he was first converted to the theatre at the beginning of this century, and the conversion was that of an intellectual. It was not only the eminence of Ibsen, Shaw, and the younger dramatists of Granville Barker's Court Theatre, but the Puritan, sociological, political trend of their work that attracted the attention of Dukes, himself the son of a clergyman—the Reverend E. J. Dukes— an *alumnus* of Silcoates School and a graduate in science of Manchester University and a member of the Fabian Society, towards the drama. Even then, however, he felt dissatisfied with the mere "lifelikeness" of the style of Barker's productions at the Court ("the acting standard was high, but the staging rather commonplace in its naturalism"), and when the discovery of Maeterlinck, D'Annunzio, and Hauptmann (*Hannele*) in the theatre joined with the Fabian Society and the Highgate hospitality of Prince Kropotkin, who had known Marx, Engels, and Lassalle, to arouse Duke's interest in contemporary Europe, he soon resigned his post in London as university lecturer in science and, combining private tutoring with the prospect of a post-graduate course at Munich, left England for Germany, where he arrived in September 1907.

He was abroad for two years only; the end of 1909 saw him installed in London as dramatic critic of A. R. Orage's weekly review *The New Age*—he was to claim in later years that his weekly 10s. was the only fee ever paid by Orage to a regular contributor—but Dukes was by now a European and was to remain one. By now he was also a full-time professional writer, having abandoned science as a vocation while he was in Germany, and seeing a play of his—*Civil War*—produced for the first time by the Stage Society in 1910. He continued also to be a playwright to the end, and 1958 saw the publication of his own comedy *Return to Dane's Hill* and the production—by Sir Donald Wolfit*—of two adaptations by him of German plays: *The Broken Jug* from Kleist and *The Maestro* from Wedekind.

His European citizenship and his love and knowledge of the theatre were inextricably combined in Dukes's career as a playwright. He not only adapted many plays from the German and the French: *From Morn to Midnight, The Machine Wreckers, Such Men are Dangerous, Jew Süss, Elizabeth of England, Vintage Wine, The Masque of Virtue* are examples of the first; *The Man Who Married a Dumb Wife* (from Anatole France), *Mozart* (from Sacha Guitry [q.v.]), *A Woman of This World* (from Becque) are examples of the second. *Mandragola,* from Machiavelli, showed him at work on an Italian model. But even his original plays, including the most popular of them, *The Man with a Load of Mischief*, would have turned out differently if their author had not been a European of the kind that Dukes was: the understanding friend as well as the translator of the communist Ernst Toller, the British Delegate of the Critics' Circle at the International Congresses of Critics in Paris (1926) and Salzburg (1927), the Theatre and Music Adviser, Main Headquarters Control Commission for Germany (British Element) after the late war.

In Dukes's case cosmopolitanism meant above all things tolerance: that is, self-restraint in the making of moral judgments and a limited self-indulgence in the enjoyment of human diversity. *The Man with a Load of Mischief, The Fountain Head, A Song of Drums* grew out of a soil for which these attitudes had supplied the top-dressing. They testify with never an exaggerated word to Dukes's belief in the power of human beings to work out their own destiny in the most varied and sometimes unpromising ways.

Do they sometimes act stupidly or viciously and have to pay for it? Let them, he seems to say; they can afford to. Don't interfere with them. Sit back and observe what a good job they still make of it, when you might have supposed they would go under and be forgotten.

It is characteristic of Dukes's work in the theatre at its best that he should have made use of his winnings as a playwright to construct and open the Mercury Theatre, Ladbroke Road—not far from his home—in 1933. He intended it as a workshop for the production—both public and semi-private—of plays and ballets. Beginning with *Jupiter Translated*, by W. J. Turner after Molière, the Mercury plays included—in addition to works by W. H. Auden* and Christopher Isherwood—those of T. S. Eliot* and Ronald Duncan at times when the two latter poets had not been introduced—nor had sought introduction—in the West End.

The Ballet Club, after an experimental season in 1931, soon settled down to Sunday performances, and for nearly 10 years contributed something of distinction to the London theatre. "The enterprise was entirely dependent", wrote Dukes, "on the artistic direction and integrity of Marie Rambert, who undertook complete responsibility back-stage as I undertook it in front [at the Mercury]. There were no guarantors and no committee: we lived within our own joint incomes and had nothing to limit our personal authority and independence". The joint incomes, as his readers knew, were those of husband and wife. In so far as the marriage between Dukes and Mme. Rambert, who first danced in London with Diaghilev's company before 1914, had an aspect of professional partnership, it was of a piece with the pattern, subtle and unobtrusive but clearly marked and rich, of his long, smiling, and persistent career in the theatre.

He is survived by Mme. Rambert, whom he married in 1918, and by two daughters.

May 5, 1959.

Best known as an illustrator of fairy tales and, more recently, as a designer of postage stamps, **Edmund Dulac,** who died in hospital in London on May 25, 1953 at the age of 70, was an interesting case of artistic development affected, if not determined, by early impressions.

Naturalized an Englishman in 1912, Dulac was born on October 22, 1882, at Toulouse. The first works of art of any kind that he saw as a child were contained in the collection of an uncle, who was an importer from the Far East, and this early contact with Oriental art was to influence his work, whether in portraiture or illustration, throughout his life. No doubt Dulac started with a natural instinct for two-dimensional design, but it is hard to believe that early acquaintance with the Orientals did not give him confidence in its possibilities, more especially because there is little evidence in his work of direct imitation in style.

After graduating from Toulouse University as bachelor of science and philosophy Dulac studied law "unwillingly" for two years, and then for three years attended classes in drawing and painting at the Toulouse School of Art. For three weeks only he studied at Julian's in Paris, which suggests that he found the teaching there little to his purpose. His first works to be exhibited, at the Paris Salon in 1904 and 1905, were portraits, and he continued to paint occasional portraits in water-colour of a charmingly decorative kind, particularly when the subjects were children. The flow of line in these portraits recalls not so much the Orientals directly as Botticelli, who, as a Japanese critic has reminded us, had distinct affinities with Far Eastern art. One of Dulac's most successful portraits was of the congenial subject, Madame Wellington Koo, wife of the former Chinese Minister in London.

Dulac began to illustrate books in 1905, and for a good many years from 1907 onwards the original drawings for them were exhibited annually at the Leicester Galleries. The books were not all fairy tales, but it was in that connexion that Dulac did his most characteristic work. He may be said to have run neck and neck in well-deserved popularity with the late Arthur Rackham, and there was a convenient division of labour between them; Dulac excelling on the poetical and decorative sides, while Rackham was a master of the grotesque. Preference between them was likely to be according to whether the spiritual home of the reader was the world of Hans Andersen or that of the Brothers Grimm, with the Little Princess or the Witch as the heroine.

The list of books, stories, and plays illustrated by Dulac includes *The Arabian Nights* (1907), *The Tempest* (1908), *The Rubaiyat of Omar Khayyam* (1909), *The Sleeping Beauty and other Tales* (1910), *Hans Andersen's Snow Queen and other Tales* (1912), *Princess Badoura* (1913), and *Sinbad the Sailor* (1914). In addition, he published *Edmund Dulac's Book for the French Red Cross* (1915), *Edmund Dulac's Fairy-Book* (1916), *The Kingdom of the Pearl* (1920), *Treasure Island* (1927), *Gods and Mortals in Love* (1936), *The Golden Cockerel* (1950), and *The Marriage of Cupid and Psyche* (1951).

Dulac had a talent for caricature of a special kind, in which the general effect of the design counted for more than exaggeration of feature. During 1919 he contributed weekly cartoons to the *Outlook*, and it was at one of the fortnightly staff luncheons which were a pleasant feature of its proprietorship by Faith Moore that he revealed to the company his remarkable gift for caricature dolls. The coffee stage had been reached when Dulac quietly produced from his pocket two small dolls and placed them on the table, setting to partners, as it were. One represented a famous art critic and the other a lady equally well known in the musical world. Without a word said about their identity the company roared in immediate and delightful recognition.

Dulac's connexion with the Mint began in 1935, when his design for the Poetry Medal was approved. Publication of a description and illustration of the medal in *The Times* of July 3 brought on the following day a gently reproving letter from Sir George Hill, of the British Museum, for the absence of any mention of the name of the designer. After observing that efforts by the Deputy Master of the Mint and his advisory committee to encourage the medallic art in this country had not always been approved, Sir George Hill went on: "But on this occasion, I believe I am right in saying, the committee agreed unanimously that Mr. Dulac's design was one of the most, if not the most, beautiful that it had been their good fortune to have submitted to them; and I think that instructed opinion generally endorses their verdict".

The Coronation stamps of 1937, bearing the heads of both King and Queen, were the first to be designed by Dulac, and they met with general approval, though the design was criticized by [Sir] Jacob Epstein [q.v.] as a "conglomeration of objects", which brought a witty retort from Dulac in an evening paper. The range of stamps, from the 7d. to the 5s., printed in 1939 were designed by Dulac and the late Eric Gill in collaboration. Dulac's success with postage stamps was due to his fine sense of scale and of balance in the design and the delicacy of his drawing. He rose admirably to his opportunities when invited in 1940 to design the stamps and banknotes of the Free French movement.

There were not many branches of design, from stage settings and costumes to the backs of playing cards, that were not touched by Dulac at one time or another. He lectured on art and music, and among his hobbies were casserole cooking—like a good Frenchman from the Midi he was a gourmet—and the making of bamboo flutes of the eastern type to be played by breathing from the nose, of which he would give occasional performances. He professed to find western music coarse in both tone and intervals, and all his tastes were on the side of subtlety. Sallow and inclined to be plump, he had something Asiatic in his appearance, with an "inscrutable" expression which may have been cultivated. It was not difficult to imagine him in mandarin's robes.

Dulac was very good company, exceedingly polite and particularly happy with children. He was witty, but seldom unkind except to pretentiousness. In one book of reference he put down as his favourite sport "revolver shooting", which entry may or may not have been a warning to critics.

May 28, 1953.

Prince Duleepsinhji, the former Sussex and England cricketer, died at Bombay on December 5, 1959 at the age of 54. His cricketing career was cut short by illness, but it lasted long enough to establish him as one of the great batsman of his generation.

Kumar Shri Duleepsinhji was born on June 13, 1905. He was a nephew of Ranjitsinhji, with whose style his wristy elegance and attacking spirit had some affinity. When he went to England to be educated, he made his mark on the cricket field almost at once. He was in the Cheltenham XI in 1921 when he was only just 16, and in his last season at the college he was probably the best school batsman of the year. For the Lords schools against the Rest, he scored 108 and took five wickets for 41 runs.

He went up to Cambridge in 1924, and was awarded his Blue the following summer, making 932 runs during the university season, with two centuries. In 1926 he became qualified for Sussex, and showed himself as great a run-getter in county as in all other classes of cricket. It was in 1927 that the first interruption took place, for early in the season he was pronounced to be seriously ill, and after May he played no more. A winter spent in Switzerland set him up, and he returned to England with restored health. Then began an even more notable run of success. His highest score for Sussex, which he captained with tact and ability, was 333 against Northamptonshire at Hove. He scored two separate hundreds in a match three times, and a hundred and two hundred once in a match against Kent in 1929. He made four hundreds in successive innings in 1931. Outside the county game he was particularly effective in Gentlemen and Players, making three centuries. And finally, in the first of his 12 Test matches, against Australia at Lord's in 1930, he distinguished himself with a splendid innings of 173. In his three golden years of 1929-31 he scored over 2,500 runs each season.

The curtain fell all too soon. In 1932 his health again gave way. This time his visit to Switzerland did not have the desired effect, and the pulmonary disease from which he suffered grew worse. In 1933 he retired from the Sussex captaincy, and towards the end of the summer he knew definitely he would not play first-class cricket again.

He joined the Indian foreign service in 1949 and was appointed High Commissioner for India in Australia and New Zealand. After his return to India in 1953 he became chairman of the public service commission in the state of Saurashtra of which his brother was Rajpramukh. He married in 1936 Shrimati Jayaraj Kumari, who survives him.

December 7, 1959.

John Foster Dulles, who died on May 24, 1959, was President Eisenhower's* Secretary of State for more than six years and the first Republican to direct American foreign policy after the United States became the leader of the free world.

A distinguished churchman, he was a staunch anti-communist, deeply convinced that freedom would eventually triumph inside the great communist empires, and determined that the west must stand firm until Russia and China abandoned the use of force to spread their doctrines—he was convinced that was their intention—throughout the world. History may conclude that he was very often right in strategy, but wrong in tactics. These caused much controversy and ill-feeling, and often set back causes in which he deeply believed. Some of his troubles were due to the difficulty of coordinating the policies of allies while steering clear of offence to Congress, which was always capable of wrecking his best-laid plans, especially in his first years of office. Others sprang from his willingness, on occasion, to bend foreign policy to the uses and internal necessities of a political party which had been long in opposition and was still divided on the part America should play in the world. Throughout, however, Dulles enjoyed the complete confidence of Eisenhower, who proclaimed him the greatest Secretary of State he had ever known.

He was the most enduring, the most professional and the hardest-working member of the Cabinet appointed by a president who liked to delegate authority. Eisenhower once revealed that he had considered the creation of a new post—that of First Secretary to the Government—for Dulles. Although this was never proposed publicly, it closely described the position which Dulles came to occupy in the administration.

Even his enemies and critics had to pay reluctant tribute to Dulles's wide experience, his ability and skill as a negotiator, his energy, and his dedication to his task. Yet in foreign countries he never commanded the affection and confidence won by Democratic predecessors whose technical skills fell so far short of his own. He spoke often, and felt deeply, about the need of applying moral principles to foreign affairs, but he was a hard-headed realist and was often accused of opportunism and lack of moral courage.

As a Republican Secretary of State, Dulles laboured under the political necessity of differentiating his foreign policies from those initiated under President Truman*. Yet, judged by his actions rather than by his campaign oratory, a great part of his achievement was to secure the acceptance of responsibilities and policies introduced by his predecessors and endangered by partisan quarrels in the United States. In his fondness for stirring phrases, on the one hand, and his care, on the other, not to involve the United States in war, many commentators found a reflection of the conflicting desires of America itself, which, when Dulles took charge of the State Department, was sick of the Korean conflict but frustrated by the apparent stalemate in the cold war.

No Secretary of State had a more thorough preparation than John Foster Dulles, to whom the State Department represented the height of ambition. Foreign policy was in his blood. One grandfather had been Secretary of State under Harrison, an uncle had served Woodrow Wilson in the same capacity.

Dulles was born on February 25, 1888, the son of a Presbyterian minister, and remained all his life an articulate advocate of the application of Christian principles to everyday life and to the affairs of nations. His first contact with foreign affairs came at The Hague Peace Conference in 1907; the failure of the Versailles Treaty, in which he took a minor part, to secure the peace by providing for the inevitability of change and for the self-enforcement of its provisions, made a great impression upon him. On his return to America he practised law, specializing in important foreign cases for the firm of Sullivan and Cromwell, of which he became the senior partner; at one time he was thought to be the most highly paid corporation lawyer in the world.

Dulles's re-entry into foreign affairs came by way of the churches. In 1941 he was appointed chairman of the Commission on a Just and Durable Peace of the Federal Council of Churches, a Protestant body. In the 1944 campaign he became adviser on foreign affairs to Governor Dewey*, then running against Franklin Roosevelt for the Presidency, and approached the Administration with proposals for keeping the foreign policy of the United States on a bi-partisan basis. His recognition that it would be dangerous to let foreign countries imagine that there would be a great change of policy if Dewey won, and his efforts to combat the isolationists in his party, led to his appointment as one of the group of consultants to the American delegation to the San Francisco conference which created the United Nations, and to an acknowledged position as the Republican spokesman on foreign affairs. Few international conferences took place without the presence of Dulles, who accompanied James F. Byrnes*, George Marshall [q.v.], and Dean Acheson* abroad. In 1950 he was appointed by Truman to negotiate the peace treaty with Japan.

Dulles's only personal experience of politics came when he was appointed in 1949 to fill out the Senatorial term of Wagner, of New York. In the subsequent election for the seat he was beaten despite a resort to partisan invective which Truman found offensive in a man who had enjoyed the confidence of the administration, and despite a public reconciliation with his Roman Catholic son which critics felt to be inspired by political motives.

After this rebuff Dulles continued to serve the Government until the campaign of 1952, in which he became adviser on foreign policy to General Eisenhower. The foreign affairs statement in the Republican platform, the work of Dulles, reflected a desire to heal the split between the supporters of Senator Taft [q.v.] and those of Eisenhower; it also showed that foreign affairs were to be aggressively exploited in the campaign. Impatience with the policy of containment, a demand that

America "seize the initiative", and "unleash Chiang*", the doctrine of liberation for the Soviet satellites, seemed to America's nervous allies to amount to a foreign policy likely to bring on a third world war.

In fact, although Dulles took office with the promise to "rethink" American policy, his bark proved worse than his bite. Appeasement of Congress, and particularly of such right-wing Republicans as Senators McCarthy [q.v.] and Knowland, went on longer than it should, but, as Dulles saw it, this was part of the task of rebuilding confidence in the State Department and providing a firm foundation in Congress for his foreign policy. Civil servants were warned that they must display "positive loyalty" and McLeod, a henchman of the McCarthyites, was appointed security officer to the department. Diplomats whose real crime was that they had affronted the China lobby were dispensed with. However, the "unleashing" of General Chiang Kai-shek, to which the China lobby attached such importance, proved more a matter of words than reality. Formosa was "deneutralized" by withdrawing the fleet placed between the island and the mainland by Truman, but the attack on the mainland which might have set off a world war never materialized.

A similar transformation overtook the doctrine of liberation, which appealed so deeply to Americans anxious for a more active policy and to those with relatives in the oppressed countries. To those who had not read the fine print of Dulles's lawyer's brief, the risk of a war of liberation seemed real. In fact, his policy had always stopped short of war, and although he never wavered in his belief that the strains and stresses inside the Soviet Empire must in time inevitably work toward greater freedom and in the interests of the west, no official steps were ever taken to encourage discontent.

Long before he became Secretary of State, Dulles, in his famous reply to the "Fortress America" speech of Herbert Hoover*, had insisted that solitary defence could never be impregnable and that "a nation which sheds its allies elects a dangerous course". Yet Dulles's attitude to America's allies and to the neutrals in the cold war caused constant criticism. His first big step in office was to announce that unless the European Defence Community were ratified, the United States would have to begin an "agonizing reappraisal" of its foreign policies, which had been centred on Europe.

This brutal frankness, so different from the tone of Marshall or Acheson, sprang partly from the knowledge that the restoration of German sovereignty could not be longer delayed, but also from a long-held conviction that without political and economic unity Europe could never wield the power to which its spiritual and material resources entitled it. In this Dulles proved himself a good friend of Europe; unquestionably he spoke for an impatient Congress and the American people.

Far more controversial was the doctrine of deterrence through the threat of "massive retaliation" at times and places of America's own choosing. This method of escaping from the static containment of the cold war, which gave the aggressor every advantage, and over-extended the resources of the free world, had its roots also in Dulles's conviction that often in the past miscalculations of American intentions had led to war. He had to look no farther than Korea for an example. Yet America's allies were racked with anxiety lest a trigger be pulled in the Pacific which would plunge the whole world in war.

Much of the criticism of Dulles was caused by his Far Eastern policy. To many Europeans it seemed unrealistic and extremely dangerous, based as it appeared to be upon a refusal to accept the communist victory on the Chinese mainland and a hope that Marshal Chiang Kai-shek might some day seize power again in a friendly China. Dulles argued, however, that the United States did not refuse to recognize the existence of Communist China—in fact it conducted long negotiations with emissaries from Peking.

In his view, diplomatic recognition would bestow quite unnecessarily very considerable advantages upon a hostile Power. If the United States abandoned Marshal Chiang the oversea Chinese would have no alternative but to follow the policies of Peking, and this might help to undermine friendly Governments in the Pacific. Moreover, any retreat before communist threats might convince America's small allies in the area and elsewhere in the world that they could not count on American support and that they had better come to terms with the communists.

In 1955, after the Chinese communists had shown aggressive intentions towards Formosa, Congress passed almost unanimously the so-called Formosa Resolution giving the President authority, in advance, to use force to defend Formosa if this became necessary.

Eisenhower always insisted that he would never go to war without congressional sanction, and in the Far East, where an emergency might arise, he was given a blank cheque. The resolution left it to the President and his advisers to determine whether an attack on the smaller off-shore islands formed part of a larger attack on Formosa. This authority, which was to play a large part in the crisis of 1958, occasioned qualms even in 1955, on the part of some far-sighted senators.

In the summer of 1958 the bombardment of Quemoy and Matsu and the dispatch of American naval forces to help supply the islands made many Americans and many of America's allies fear that a world war might break out over these inconsiderable islands, but Dulles insisted that far wider principles were at stake. What was unquestionably true was that the Nationalists had marooned a large number of their best troops on the islands.

At a famous press conference Dulles appeared to be prepared to make considerable concessions; he said that the United States had considered the reinforcement of Quemoy unwise and admitted that Marshal Chiang was unlikely ever to return to the mainland unless a revolt broke out there first. If Communist China would renounce the use of force against Formosa, a negotiated settlement might be possible. In fact, on a personal visit to Formosa, Dulles wrung from the reluctant Nationalists a commitment not to use force against the mainland, and the bombardment—both of the islands and of Dulles—subsided.

The risk of war also seemed acute in 1954 when the French fell back in Indo-China. Dulles returned from Europe convinced that he had secured British agreement to intervention under certain conditions. Sir Anthony Eden [Lord Avon], however, insisted that the understanding had been to consider intervention only after a genuine effort to negotiate had failed. When Dulles returned to Europe there were bitter words between him and the Foreign Secretary over the failure to rescue Dien Bien Phu. This failure to talk the same language was to culminate, two years later, in disaster over the Suez crisis.

Where Indo-China was concerned, however, the President's veto of such hotheads as Vice-President Nixon and Admiral Radford avoided a split with Britain and prevented an initiative which would have divided Americans as well as America's allies. It seems now that the fears expressed at that time were not exaggerated. Inspired revelations in 1956 pictured Dulles as glorying in his journeys to the brink of war and boasting that he had brought pressure upon Peking three times in this manner.

An outstanding feature of Dulles's diplomacy, and the source of many jokes at his expense, was his determination to keep all the threads in his own hands. He was convinced of the value of personal contacts, and no Secretary of State was more indefatigable in pursuing them. In part this was simply the reverse side of his impatience with administration. But it had other serious drawbacks. The importance of ambassadors on the spot was devalued if Dulles might fly in at any moment. Failures of communication between America and its allies seemed to increase and reached their peak in the Suez crisis. Dulles also proved unwilling to delegate authority for policy at home; he was said to carry the State Department in his vest pocket. In his absence, the State Department hardly knew what America's foreign policy was. The Policy Planning Staff which had flourished under Acheson fell almost into disuse.

The Suez crisis displayed Dulles's qualities at their best and at their worst. He had long appreciated the strategic importance of Middle Eastern oil to Europe and the free world; unlike Democratic Secretaries of State he was free of political obligations to Jewish groups and hoped to play an impartial role between Arab and Jew in the Middle East. Moreover, he had long believed that it was an error on Truman's part to neglect the peoples of Asia and Africa and their national ambitions, a course which favoured the success of communist penetration.

The reasons behind the brusque withdrawal of the American offer to help finance Egypt's Aswan Dam, which precipitated the Suez crisis, will long be disputed. A recent book, written after many interviews with Dulles, contends that this was a move calculated to show up the emptiness of Soviet offers of economic aid. Some observers believe, on the contrary, that the humiliation of President Nasser*, who had offended many Republican members of Congress by accepting arms from the communists and recognizing Communist China, was a characteristic piece of appeasement of Congress by the Secretary of State.

Dulles's hasty flight to London to prevent the use of force after the Egyptian seizure of the Suez Canal, and his enthusiasm for the idea of a users' association testified to his energy and resource in the cause of peace. But the British Government, which had been on the point of taking the dispute to the Security Council of the United Nations, put off this step only upon assurances that the association would be a strong one, powerfully supported by the United States; it was understandably embittered as weeks went by and Dulles in his press conferences found more and more reasons why the users' association could not be truly effective.

When, finally, Dulles stated that America must be careful not to associate itself too closely with "colonial" policies, the British Government not unnaturally concluded that Dulles's word could not be relied upon. Sir Anthony Eden was exasperated beyond endurance.

The truth may be that Dulles, like the great lawyer he was, had drafted his proposals with care so that they could bear many interpretations. But the damage to relations with Britain and France had been done. At home the critics of the Secretary of State regarded his assurance that peace had been saved as a transparent piece of campaigning for President Eisenhower, but the man at the polls was thankful not to be at war and asked no questions.

The attack on Egypt, just as Americans were preparing to re-elect Eisenhower, swept any doubts away. Americans as a whole felt that the demand for an unconditional withdrawal was just and one that could not have been avoided; Dulles himself felt that any sign of favouritism towards old friends would have tarred the United States with the colonial brush and destroyed Arab faith in American impartiality.

The Suez crisis was still at its height when Dulles suddenly underwent an operation for what proved to be cancer. Many concluded that he would now be forced to retire. But with that vitality and tenacity which characterized him, he continued to direct policy from his hospital bed and by the beginning of 1957 he had evolved the Eisenhower Doctrine for the Middle East. To carry this new departure through a Congress controlled by Democrats deeply resentful of what they considered to have been his political role in the campaign would have been an ordeal for a younger and stronger man.

Under the Eisenhower Doctrine the United States pledged itself to respond to a request for military support from any middle eastern country which was attacked by another that was under the control of international communism. Dulles's aim, as it was in the Far East, was to preserve the *status quo* and to prevent countries with friendly or neutral governments from falling to the communists. But the only Arab country prepared to throw in its fortunes with the west was Lebanon. Moreover, the formula provided no defence against indirect aggression or against aggression by a Power not controlled by international communism, such as Eygpt—two of the greatest threats to stability in the area.

Finally, many critics felt that what was needed was massive economic aid, not the threat of military intervention. In this respect, however, they did less than justice to the administration, which in 1955 had propounded a far-sighted scheme combining economic aid with settlement of the refugee problem and the boundary issue.

The dispatch of American troops to Lebanon and of British ones to Jordan in 1958 was a response to the *coup d'état* in Iraq as well as to the troubled state of Lebanon, and was undertaken reluctantly, as a last resort, in the knowledge that the step would be regarded as one more affront to the Pan-Arab movement. But it showed that the United States was prepared to stand by its friends and to oppose external attempts to undermine existing Governments. The withdrawal of the troops from Lebanon after the election of a successor to President Chamoun proved that the United States had no aggressive intent.

Russian eagerness for a summit meeting in 1958 found Dulles at first completely unresponsive. He believed that if the west stood firm long enough Russia would abandon its expansionist policy, but this required unity and tenacity on the part of the free world. The summit meeting in 1955 had endangered this firmness of purpose and Dulles, bitterly disappointed, insisted that it was impossible to negotiate with the Russians because they treated promises like pie-crust "made to be broken".

The relief of the State Department was great when Khrushchev* refused an invitation to attend a "summit meeting" of the United Nations Security Council. Some progress in reducing tension was made during the year, however, at the meetings between Russia and the west on means of banning tests of atomic weapons and outlawing surprise attacks.

The fear that concessions might undermine the will of the west underlay the inflexibility which many of Dulles's critics felt was prolonging tension unnecessarily and risking a catastrophic war. The other chief criticism of his policy was that while during the crisis the Secretary of State's behaviour was cool and courageous and usually succeeded in attaining his objectives, little was done between crises to solve the underlying problems and prevent them from erupting at a later time.

Over Berlin, where the Russians attempted to force a decision late in 1958, Americans were more united than they had been over either Lebanon or Quemoy. But when Dulles conceded that free elections were not necessarily the only means of reuniting Germany, hopes revived that this might not be one of his characteristic and meaningless legal truisms, but a response to the changing political climate in America. Among the many Democrats elected to Congress in November 1958 were a number prepared to take some risks in the search for solutions and to consider a measure of disengagement as part of a German settlement.

Only Dulles himself could hope to induce Dr. Adenauer* and General de Gaulle* to accept a measure of flexibility in allied policy and he undertook the vital journey to Bonn and Paris in February although he was already suffering great pain from what proved on his return to be inoperable cancer. How indispensable he had become could be judged by the alarm and concern felt even by his critics. He had been the strong man of the alliance, with all the threads in his fingers.

After a hernia operation in mid-February he was given radiation treatment and went to Florida to convalesce, but the discovery that the malignancy had attacked the lower neck made it clear that his resignation could not long be postponed. Finally on April 15 President Eisenhower sorrowfully announced that Dulles had decided that he must lay down his charge.

He is survived by his wife, the former Miss Janet Avery, whom he married in 1912, and by two sons and a daughter.

May 25, 1959.

Sir Andrew Duncan, G.B.E., whose capacity for organization was of great benefit to Britain as President of the Board of Trade and Minister of Supply during the 1939-45 war, died in his sleep on March 30, 1952 at the age of 67.

Beginning without influence or position, he rose to become the holder of many offices of power and influence in commerce and finance. He served on a number of royal commissions, and made himself master in turn of such big industries as shipping, coal, and electricity, as well as acting as a director of the Bank of England.

He was one of those able young men whom Lloyd George discovered during the 1914-18 war, and brought from purely commercial life into relations with the government of the country. His biggest reputation was made as an arbitrator; and he dealt with a number of big and acrimonious disputes in such a way as to settle the immediate issue and form a basis for permanent agreement between the contending parties. Politics did not form one of his major interests, organization and administration being his strong suits; and it was not until Neville Chamberlain appointed him to the Board of Trade, at the beginning of 1940, that he entered Parliament, though he had made two previous attempts. He was a Scot of the industrious, highly efficient type which has been always such a strong asset in the governance of a great Empire; he had the rich accent and dour determination of his race and he had his place in the kirk on Sundays.

Andrew Rae Duncan was born at Irvine, Ayrshire, in 1884, the son of a social worker, and was educated at Irvine Academy and the University of Glasgow. He began to earn his living by teaching English at Ayr Academy, but he was studying law in the meantime and before long was admitted a solicitor. Before he was 30 he had risen to be a partner in the Glasgow firm of solicitors, Biggart, Lumsden and Co., where he specialized on the industrial side and was brought into close relationship with some of the chief shipbuilders and engineering firms on the Clyde. His senior, Sir Thomas Biggart, was honorary secretary to the Shipbuilding Employers' Federation; and when that body moved to London during the 1914-18 war Duncan took over as full-time secretary. Sir Joseph (later Lord) Maclay [q.v.] then appointed him secretary to the Merchant Shipbuilding Advisory Committee to the Shipping Controller; and Sir Eric Geddes (the First Lord of the Admiralty) made him joint secretary to the Admiralty Shipbuilding Council. Lloyd George, Bonar Law and Lord Birkenhead all saw uncommon ability in him, and his rise was now assured.

At the General Election of 1918 Duncan put up for the Cathcart division of Glasgow, which he had been nursing for some time, standing in the Liberal interest; but the intervention of a Conservative so split the vote that Labour won the seat by a majority of 33. (Duncan tried again for Parliament at Dundee, to be beaten by the late E. D. Morel). Already at the age of 35 he had acquired a considerable reputation as a tactful conciliator in industry; and in 1919 he was given the opportunity to use his powers in a large national field, being appointed Coal Controller in succession to Sir Evan Jones. It was his duty to supervise the changeover of the mines from public control back to private ownership; and in spite of protests from Labour that he was a "bosses' nominee" he worked successfully on the task until 1921, in which year he was knighted.

This occupation would have been a full-time job to most men, but Duncan had the energy to pursue his legal studies and was called to the Bar by Gray's Inn in 1920, and was later elected a Bencher. In 1920 also he became chairman of the newly formed Advisory Committee of the Coal Mines Department (serving till 1929) and permanent vice-president of the Shipbuilding Employers' Federation (till 1927). These first seven years of the decade were full of service on various commissions and committees. In February 1924, Duncan served on the dock strike inquiry; in July of the same year he began two years' work on the Royal Commission on National Health Insurance; and in October 1925 he went out to Nova Scotia as chairman of the Royal Commission to inquire into the coal industry there. Bitter feelings were rife, but Duncan composed the quarrel and followed this up by settling the grievances of the maritime provinces the next year. While in Nova Scotia he was given the honorary degree of LL.D. by Dalhousie University, Halifax.

With the setting up of the electricity grid the Central Electricity Board was founded in order to reconcile the claims and interests of the many parties inside the industry. The chairman was to be chosen from outside Parliament, and the Minister of Transport appointed Duncan to the post in January 1927. He handled this complicated undertaking with conspicuous skill. He became a director of the Bank of England in January 1929. During 1931-32 he was a member of the Industrial Court representing the Chancellor of the Exchequer for the purposes of Civil Service arbitrations; and from the end of 1933 to 1935 he was chairman of the Sea Fish Commission.

In 1934 the Government transferred Duncan from the Electricity Board to be independent chairman of the executive committee of The British Iron and Steel Federation. Here his function was to coordinate the conflicting interests of the various concerns comprised in the federation. With the oncoming of war in 1939 the federation became merged in the Ministry of Supply, as the Iron and Steel Control. In January 1940 Chamberlain appointed Duncan to the Cabinet post of President of the Board of Trade. He was elected unopposed to Parliament the following month for the City of London, as a National Government candidate; and Churchill retained him in office in May. Later in the year, however, he was transferred to the Ministry of Supply, where he served until the summer of 1941, when, in the course of another Cabinet reshuffle, he found himself back at the Board of Trade. In the course of the next year he again became Minister of Supply and retained the office until the end of hostilities. After the Labour victory in 1945 he remained in Parliament and was the principal Conservative spokesman in opposing the nationalization of the iron and steel industry. He was well fitted for the task, for he had, on going out of office, resumed the post of chairman of the British Iron and Steel Federation which he had held before the war and had all the facts at his finger ends.

As will be seen, Duncan made his way into the high councils of the nation through a long succession of important administrative tasks. He had an agile and supple mind, with a firm grasp of detail and a remarkable power of assimilation. He was a good speaker, and in arbitrating on disputes was cool, level-headed, and impressive in his ability to take a broad view of the whole situation. He was a good staff controller, choosing his men with care and allowing them considerable scope for initiative within their respective functions. Duncan was a technical assessor of the Permanent Court of International Justice at The Hague (Labour section), member of the Economic Advisory Council and of the Industrial Development Committee, High Sheriff of the County of London, and one of H.M. Lieutenants for the City of London. He was created G.B.E. in 1938 and held the Order of St. Maurice and St. Lazarus of Italy.

In 1916 he married Annie, daughter of the late Andrew Jordan. There were two sons of the marriage, the elder of whom fell in action in June 1940.

March 31, 1952.

Rosetta Duncan, the comedy member of the famous Duncan Sisters and the "Topsy" in their popular presentation of "Topsy and Eva", died at the age of 58 in December 1959.

Rosetta Duncan was born at Los Angeles, California, in 1901, and she and her sister, Vivian, who is 18 months younger, made their stage *début* in 1913 with George Jessel, Walter Winchell* (then a dancer) and others in Gus Edwards's *Kiddies Revue* in New York. Their Broadway *début* was in May 1917 at the Fifth Avenue Theatre, New York. In May 1921 they made their first London appearance in Albert de Courville's [q.v.] revue *Pins and Needles,* which ran at the Royalty Theatre for 248 performances.

After the closing of *Pins and Needles* the Duncan Sisters stayed in Great Britain for a further two years, topping variety bills at the London Coliseum, the Alhambra, Victoria Palace, and other halls.

On their return to New York they co-starred with George M. Cohan, Frank Tinney, and Fanny Brice in the George M. Cohan revue, and in December 1924 they appeared as Topsy and Eva in their own production of the same name, at the Sam H. Harris Theatre, New York. At this high spot of their career the Duncan Sisters commanded a salary of £1,500 a week for their appearances in vaudeville at the Palace Theatre, New York.

On December 1, 1927, the sisters reappeared in London as stars in *Clowns in Clover,* which ran for 508 performances at the Adelphi Theatre. Then they presented their successful *Topsy and Eva* production at the Gaiety Theatre, where they opened in October 1928. In the third week of the London run Rosetta Duncan was taken seriously ill and Gracie Fields took over her role of "Topsy" but the production was doomed to failure.

The sisters returned to Great Britain in October 1937, and appeared in leading music halls until the following spring, when they went back to America again to revive *Topsy and Eva.* In the past 10 years they have been appearing in night clubs in Los Angeles, San Francisco (where they made their home), and Chicago.

December 9, 1959.

The Very Rev. A. S. Duncan-Jones, Dean of Chichester, died in hospital at Chichester on January 19, 1955 at the age of 75. He had a heart attack on January 12 and his condition steadily worsened.

By his death the Church of England loses one of its most active and useful servants. In his cathedral at Chichester, in Convocation and Church Assembly, on his many visits to the Continent as a sort of ecclesiastical ambassador, he knew his own mind and had his own forceful and effective way of eliciting agreements. He was a notable spokesman of the Church on foreign affairs and on the Christian attitude to war, and he touched life at many points, but always with one motive—the service of the Lord Christ "according to the Use of the Church of England".

Arthur Stuart Duncan-Jones was born at Oldham on April 25, 1879. Both his father, the Rev. D. L. D. Jones, and his mother, whose maiden name was Griffiths, were Welsh. He was educated at Pocklington School and Gonville and Caius College, Cambridge, where he won a scholarship in Hebrew. There he spent four joyous years, winning the Stewart of Rannoch University Scholarship in Hebrew, and was devoted to cricket and other athletic pursuits, in which however he was singularly unskilful.

It was a disappointment to him and to his teachers that he was placed in the second class of the Oriental Languages Tripos. He then read theology, but sudden illness prevented him from sitting for the Tripos, in which he would have gained high honours. In spite of this double disappointment, it was generally recognized that his was no common intellect. In fact, after a year at the Deanery, Westminster, together with R. H. Malden and R. M. Gwynn*, under the care of Armitage Robinson and R. B. Rackham, and a short spell at Ely Theological College, he was recalled to Caius as Fellow and Junior Dean. It was the beginning of the period when dons were gradually ceasing to be aloof seniors and becoming *coheredes gratiae vitae*, only a little older, and a good deal wiser, than the undergraduates. In this he was a pioneer. He had his inner, ascetic, life and outwardly he was everybody's friend. "D.-J.", as he was universally called, was a popular man in a difficult office. He was an eager member of a group which included H. L. Pass, Will Spens*, S. C. Carpenter [q.v.], Gordon Selwyn, Geoffrey Clayton [q.v.] and John How, who were sometimes spoken of as "the younger school of Cambridge theologians".

In 1912 he left Cambridge for the college living of Blofield, Norfolk. There, like Figgis at Marnhull, he had the difficult task of trying out his academic ideas in a country village. But he was always and essentially the pastor, and that gave him the wisdom that was needed. In 1916 he was invited to succeed Percy Dearmer at St. Mary's, Primrose Hill. There he established his reputation as an ecclesiologist. He had laid the foundations of his theological learning at Cambridge; at St. Mary's he became one of the leading champions of the "English Use", as contrasted with what is euphemistically called "Western". He was appointed Hulsean Lecturer at Cambridge in 1916, and his book *Ordered Liberty* is a cogent and scholarly defence of Anglicanism. From St. Mary's he was moved after 11 years to St. Paul's, Knightsbridge. His thoughtful and forcible sermons interested his large congregation, and he was diligent in all the pastoral and social duties of the west end parish. Nevertheless, he found time to be not only assistant editor of the *Guardian* but also an ecclesiastical adviser of *The Times.* He wrote for the paper a number of articles on church subjects, and assisted to guide its ecclesiastical policy.

Ramsay MacDonald made him Dean of Chichester in 1929. His work there was threefold. He ordered the worship of the cathedral on a stately and splendid scale. There was traditional English warrant for everything that was done. Nothing that even faintly suggested modern Roman developments was ever allowed to creep in. Chichester Cathedral became the model for all followers of what may be called the 1549 tradition, of which the *raison d'être* may be found in the publications of the Alcuin Club, of which he became chairman in 1935. Another field of work was international. He had a good knowledge of German and French and made many continental contacts including some with Finland and Estonia. He once flew to Berlin to interview Hitler, and his book *The Struggle for Religious Freedom in Germany* is a masterly piece of work.

His third province was in Convocation and Church Assembly where he spoke often and was heard with close attention. He did much for the Church of England Council on Foreign Relations. In fact the Bishop and the Dean of Chichester were the two leading Anglican experts on continental affairs; and in sermons and in publications he addressed himself to defining the Christian attitude to war.

He was the author of some nine books and a contributor to others. They included studies of Archbishop Laud and of Church music. His interest in the latter subject was marked by his chairmanship of the Church Music Society in 1946. But of all that he wrote the thing that perhaps reveals the man best is an essay he contributed in 1924 to a symposium called *The Necessity of Art.* When, with some misgivings, he read his essay on "The Art of Movement" to his colleagues, he was relieved when a distinguished art critic said: "Yes, I think you've got it".

He married in 1907 Catherine, daughter of the Rev. E. S. Roberts, Master of Gonville and Caius College. It was a most happy marriage of which there were six sons and two daughters. The eldest son is now Professor of Philosophy in the University of Birmingham. He leaves behind him the memory of a loving husband and father, a warm-hearted friend, a many-sided intelligence and profound Christian faith.

January 20, 1955.

Sir Thomas Dunhill, G.C.V.O., C.M.G., M.D., F.R.C.S., who died at Hampstead on December 22, 1957 at the age of 81, had been Serjeant Surgeon to King George VI [q.v.], and an extra surgeon to the Queen since 1952. He enjoyed a world wide reputation as an authority on the thyroid gland.

Thomas Peel Dunhill was born at Tragowel, Victoria, Australia, in 1876, the son of John Webster Dunhill. He was educated at Melbourne University, whence he graduated with first class honours in surgery and won exhibitions in anatomy, physiology, medicine, and gynaecology in 1903-04 and obtained the M.D. degree in 1906. For a time he practised privately in Melbourne and was appointed surgeon to St. Vincent's Hospital. In 1914, on the outbreak of war, he volunteered for service and was appointed colonel in the Royal Australian Army Medical Corps. He served in France and by 1919 had reached the rank of consulting surgeon to the British Expeditionary Force.

At the end of the war he accepted an invitation to act as an assistant in the surgical unit of Professor George Gask at St. Bartholomew's Hospital. The selection was a happy one and Dunhill soon made so great a reputation, especially in connexion with the surgery of the thyroid gland, that he was appointed full surgeon to the hospital. He was also surgeon to Queen Alexandra's Military Hospital at Millbank and consulting surgeon to the London County Council. He was appointed surgeon-in-ordinary to the King in 1933 and after the death of Wilfred Trotter in 1939 he became one of the serjeant surgeons. He became head of the surgeons attached to the Royal Household and he was one of the physicians by whose advice King George VI underwent operations for lumbar sympathectomy in March 1949, and for lung resection in September 1951.

He was created C.V.O. in 1919 and promoted to K.C.V.O. in 1933, and G.C.V.O. in 1949. At the Royal College of Surgeons, of which he was an honorary Fellow, he delivered the Arris and Gale lectures in 1931 and 1934. He was Lettsomian lecturer at the Medical Society of London in 1937 and its Fothergillian gold medallist in 1941. In 1948 he was awarded the Cecil Joll Prize for outstanding work on surgery of the thyroid.

Dunhill was an outstanding surgeon and he had many famous patients. He was also a good teacher, and with his quiet voice, courteous address and friendly manner he was widely liked.

He married in 1914 Edith Florence McKellar. Lady Dunhill died in 1942.

December 24, 1957.

Charles Avery Dunning, who died in a Montreal hospital on October 2, 1958 at the age of 73, was a former Federal Finance Minister and Premier of Saskatchewan.

He was born on July 31, 1885, at Croft, Leicestershire, where his father was a small tenant farmer, was educated at a local school and went to work as an apprentice with an engineering firm at the age of 15. He was a fine swimmer and it was while swimming that he strained his heart. He was advised to try an outdoor life, and in 1902, when he was 17, he took a steerage passage to Canada and went west to Saskatchewan. There he obtained employment with a farmer at a wage of $10 a week. He stayed until he had acquired a knowledge of western farming methods and then in 1904 took up a free homestead of 160 acres at Beaverdale in the Yorkton district of Saskatchewan.

He found himself in a real pioneering atmosphere. There was no railway within 30 miles, the roads were prairie trails and many of the settlers were peasants from Europe who spoke nothing but their native tongues. Dunning built a shack and set himself to transform the virgin prairie into fertile tilth. But his scant savings were his only capital and he could not buy expensive implements. However, he acquired some oxen and began breaking up his land and cropping it. But some years of frost or rust brought ruin to his hopes, and when he did raise a crop the price was poor.

The settlers were at the mercy of the elevator companies and other business interests, and Dunning, like most of his neighbours, had to be content with a bare living. But under these conditions agrarian discontent became rife and found expression in the organization of a body called the Graingrowers' Association of Saskatchewan.

Dunning joined the local branch and took an active interest in its work. He became an apostle of cooperative marketing and at the age of 25 was elected a director of the association. Within a year he was vice-president and from this post of vantage he was able to push his cooperative idea so successfully that the Saskatchewan Cooperative Elevator Company came into existence. The farmers took shares in it through local units and the provincial government lent its credit for the balance of the funds required to build elevators and other parts. Dunning was made general manager in 1911.

Under his direction the fortunes of the new company prospered, business steadily expanded, and within a short time it was marketing about half the wheat grown in Saskatchewan. As head of this organization Dunning became one of the leading figures in the Canadian grain trade and acquired a thorough acquaintance with large-scale business practices.

Charlie Dunning, as he was generally known, had become a popular hero with the prairie farmers, and the Liberal politicians, who ruled the roost in Saskatchewan, knew it. So in 1916 he was invited to join the provincial government of Saskatchewan and as the provincial treasurership was made the bait he accepted it.

It was wartime and a heavy burden fell upon his shoulders; not only did he take over the Department of Railways in 1917 but he served also as director of Food Production for the whole of Canada.

In 1922 William Martin resigned the Premiership of Saskatchewan to take a judicial post, and Dunning became, without any opposition, Premier of the third largest province of the Dominion. By this time the agrarian revolt of which the party politicians had been apprehensive had broken out as the result of the post-war agricultural depression. The Progressive Party, founded in 1919, had swept the three prairie provinces at the Federal election of 1921 and had ejected from office Liberal provincial administrations in Manitoba and Alberta. Dunning, as Premier of Saskatchewan, had to encounter its full floodtide, but where his neighbours had been swamped he weathered the Progressive storm largely by carrying out a programme which remedied the more pressing grievances of the farmers.

At any rate, he came to be recognized as the chief bulwark of Liberalism in western Canada, and when, in the spring of 1926, the Liberal Government of Mackenzie King, bereft of a majority in Parliament, found itself involved in grave difficulties, a Macedonian cry for help was sent to Dunning at Regina.

He brought to the councils of Liberalism at Ottawa a fund of vigour and experience which had a most salutary effect, and he played a large part in the revival of Liberal fortunes at Ottawa and the victory at the general election of 1926, which gave the party another lease of power. The party realized the value of his services, and at one time there was a distinct movement to depose Mackenzie King from the leadership in favour of his young western lieutenant.

After three years at Ottawa he was admittedly one of the strongest figures in the King ministry, and when J. A. Robb, the Finance Minister, died suddenly his claim to the vacant portfolio, the second most important in the ministry, could not be denied. So at the age of 44 Dunning found himself in control of the financial destinies of Canada. But his tenure of office on this occasion was brief, for less than a year later the Government was defeated and Dunning returned to his considerable business interests. It was not until the autumn of 1935 that Mackenzie King called him back to take once more the Finance Portfolio.

Dunning had worked full stretch all his life and by 1938 it seemed that his health was failing. He had a heart attack and was told to rest, but it was not until 1939 that he found he could not carry on his official duties and hope to regain his health and he offered his resignation to Mackenzie King. His withdrawal from public life was widely regretted.

October 3, 1958.

Lord Dunsany, who died in a Dublin nursing home on October 25, 1957 at the age of 79, was an original and imaginative writer with an acknowledged mastery of the art of fantasy.

In prose he was a virtuoso—and a prolific one—with the defects as well as the merits of his type. A self-confessed "dreamer", his eastern allegories and artificial mythology were not to all tastes; but he had the faculty of first intriguing and later surprising his readers, and once at least—in the traveller Jorkens—he created an inimitable character. Although his work as a dramatist was unequal, several of his earlier plays have hardly received the recognition they deserve.

The Rt. Hon. Edward John Moreton Drax Plunkett, 18th Baron of Dunsany, of Dunsany Castle, in the county of Meath, son of the 17th Baron and Ernle, daughter of Colonel F. A. P. Burton, was born on July 24, 1878. He was educated at Eton, where in turn Cornish and E. L. Vaughan were his housemasters, and at Sandhurst, and succeeded to the barony on his father's death in 1899. A few days later he joined the 1st Battalion, Coldstream Guards, in Chelsea Barracks, and soon afterwards went out to Africa to serve as a second lieutenant in the Boer War. He did not stay long in the Army; for a time he settled down to the life of a country gentlemen in Ireland, hunting with the Meath and becoming Master of the Tara Harriers. He took a dilettantish interest in politics, being adopted as Conservative candidate for West Wiltshire in 1903, but failing to win the seat at the election of 1906.

In the meantime, in the autumn of 1905, he had published his first book of stories, *The Gods of Pegana,* which, like its successor, *Time and the Gods,* had a slight touch of preciousness, but was enriched by its detail, of which he was always a ready inventor. *The Sword of Welleran* (1908) was a considerable improvement on both these early efforts. It was followed by *A Dreamer's Tales.*

In 1911 *The Gods of the Mountain,* a remarkable mixture of humour, irony and grotesque horror, was successfully produced at the Haymarket Theatre, both this and the one-act play *The Golden Doom* owing a good deal to incidental music by Norman O'Neill; in the same year the Irish Players acted *King Argimenes,* in some ways an equally striking piece, but one that began rather better than it ended—a not uncommon fault in Lord Dunsany's work. During the next few years his large output included *The Tents of the Arabs, The Queen's Enemies, A Night at an Inn,* and *The Laughter of the Gods*—all of them good, and the first named perhaps the most entirely satisfying of his plays. He also wrote many sketches and short stories. Early in September 1914 Dunsany joined the 5th Battalion, The Royal Inniskilling Fusiliers, reaching the rank of captain, and in April 1916 he received a severe wound in the head during the fighting in the streets of Dublin. In 1918 he published his *Tales of War,* but did not seem quite at ease with the war for a subject.

On the whole the plays that Dunsany wrote after the war lacked the inspiration and distinction of language of those which preceded it, though *If,* a fantastic comedy, had a long run in London in 1921. His other work, however, showed a great advance; he published several novels full of that delightful blend of actuality, humour and fantasy which was so characteristic of him; he created a fascinating story-teller in the person of Joseph Jorkens; and he achieved new success with a series of short plays and stories specially written for broadcasting. Collections of his verse—some of it ephemeral but much of it charming—were published in 1929 and 1938. In 1933 he received the Harmsworth Literary Award for his novel *The Curse of the Wise Woman.*

Throughout his life Dunsany remained a keen sportsman, some of his prowess as a rider to hounds and a first-class shot being modestly reflected in *My Ireland* and an autobiography, *Patches of Sunlight.* Later volumes of reminiscences were *While the Sirens Slept* (1944) and, in the following year, *The Sirens Wake,* the latter volume recounting some of his experiences during the recent years of war, in the earlier phase of which he held for a time the Byron Chair of English Literature at Athens University. Mention must be made, too, of a war novel, *Guerrilla,* published in 1944, which mingled a plain tale and something of fairy-tale with eloquent and truly poetic effect.

For the remaining years of his life Dunsany's imagination continued to stimulate his pen. His translation of the Odes of Horace came out in 1947, *The Man who Ate the Phoenix* in 1949, *The Strange Journeys of Colonel Polders* in 1950, and *His Fellow Men* in 1952. In the same year he published *The Little Tales of Smethers,* a collection of short crime stories, and in 1954 some more of the popular Jorkens, *Jorkens Borrows Another Whiskey.*

Dunsany was an excellent chess-player, and was president of the Irish Chess Union and of the Kent County Chess Association. He was a

Deputy Lieutenant for the county of Meath, a member of the Irish Academy of Letters, and an honorary member of the Institut Historique et Héraldique de France.

He married in 1904 Lady Beatrice Child Villiers, youngest daughter of the 7th Earl of Jersey. His heir is his only son, Colonel the Hon. Randal Arthur Henry Plunkett, born in 1906.

October 28, 1957.

Maurice Duplessis, the Premier of Quebec, died on September 7, 1959 at Schefferville, Quebec, at the age of 69.

Probably no other Canadian politician has been so widely criticized in his country and yet so successful in office. Apart from a period during the last war his party, the Union Nationale, dominated politics in Quebec since the day it came to power in 1936. With Duplessis firmly and forcibly at the helm, French Canada moved slowly out of the depression years of the thirties into a more prosperous period of industrial expansion from 1939. The transition created all kinds of strains on a society and its institutions, governed by hard tradition and by the Roman Catholic Church, and still having an innate suspicion of English-speaking Canada. Duplessis, himself deeply religious and a traditionalist in most things, succeeded in pursuing a policy that encouraged economic development in his province while at the same time keeping a close, and even restrictive, hand on the political and social consequences—although towards the end his hand seemed not so sure.

His main planks of policy could be said to be the industrialization of the province in the interests of its people, and the preservation of Quebec's political autonomy within the framework of federation. He resisted hotly what he called the encroachment of federal powers, keeping his province out of the national hospital insurance plan, tax-sharing agreements, the system of federal grants to universities, and the trans-Canada highway programme. His methods of government were considered by many as questionable. Such legislation as the controversial "Padlock Law" (which gave the Attorney General—a portfolio Duplessis reserved for himself—authority to lock up any premises he believed were being used for the propogation of communism, and which was invalidated in 1958 by the Supreme Court of Canada) struck many people as an insult to democratic government and an encroachment on civil liberties; but since such thoughts never seriously bothered the average Quebec voter they did not therefore bother Duplessis. His political patronage was conspicuous and unabashed.

Duplessis was born at Trois Rivières, Quebec, on April 20, 1890. Brought up in a family with a political background, he entered the legal profession and was first elected to the Quebec legislature as a Conservative for his home town in 1927. Six years later he became provincial leader of his party, but in 1936 he formed his own party, the Union Nationale, made up of Conservatives and discontented Liberals, and was triumphantly returned to power, putting an end to the long Liberal reign.

In 1939 he made his only really bad misjudgment of the political state of Quebec in trying to turn to account latent French Canadian isolationism at the outbreak of war. The federal Liberal party under Mackenzie King threw all its resources into the provincial election of that year and the Union Nationale was defeated. But Duplessis returned to power in 1944 and since then, in three further elections, had consolidated his hold on his party and the province.

Duplessis was a bachelor, witty and well informed in conversation, hospitable and generous. He was also a dedicated politician, in no doubt about the ends he wished to attain, and none too delicate about the means he chose to attain them.

September 8, 1959.

Dr. Pierre Dupong, Prime Minister of Luxembourg, who was admitted to hospital after breaking his leg by a fall in his office, died on December 22, 1953. He was 68.

Pierre Dupong was born on November 1, 1885, at Luxembourg, received his college education there, and studied law at the universities of Berlin, Fribourg in Switzerland, and Paris. After gaining his LL.D., he began practice as a lawyer in his native city in 1911. He was appointed Director-General of Finances and Social Welfare in 1926, and subsequently was given the portfolio of Labour in Dr. Bech's Cabinet. By then he had for 11 years been a member of the Luxembourg Parliament, and played a part in developing the country's resources, by its Custom Union with Belgium, and the creation of the international iron and steel cartel with headquarters at Luxembourg, where highly efficient iron and steel plants were working. Under the Roman Catholic, Liberal, and Conservative coalition which held the majority in the Chamber, Dupong assumed the premiership in 1937, and had stayed in office ever since. When his country was invaded by the Nazis in 1940 he and his Cabinet escaped together with Grand Duchess Charlotte and her family, and soon afterwards they moved to London.

Dr. Dupong, as head of the Luxembourg government, was an impressive personality and a good speaker; he played a dignified part in the Allied councils all through the war years, and made a number of personal friends among his hosts and among his colleagues from other invaded countries. In the course of his career he was awarded a number of high distinctions, among them the Grand Cordons of the Netherlands and Belgium's highest orders, and that of a Grand Officer of the French Legion of Honour.

He returned with his government to Luxembourg immediately after the liberation of the country, though, towards the end of 1944 Rundstedt's [q.v.] last counter-offensive endangered and severely damaged a large part of the small country. He had planned to stand for re-election in 1954 to push forward large reconstruction plans, including new bridges and "European" roads in the Grand Duchy. He was also determined to give Luxembourg a more adequate scheme of social welfare and old age pensions.

In his private life Dr. Dupong was a keen student of history and social welfare; he wrote a good deal about both these subjects in the Luxembourg press as well as in foreign periodicals. Widely read and travelled, he was an efficient linguist, able to conduct international negotiations without the help of interpreters, and with that quiet dignity which seems characteristic of the leading statesmen of our "smallest ally", and he was one of the most determined exponents of the idea of a more closely integrated Europe, and to this end constantly recommended that Luxembourg should amend her constitution to bring it in line with the needs of the European Defence Community.

December 24, 1953.

The Very Rev. F. W. Dwelly, D.D., first Dean of the new Cathedral of Liverpool, died at his home at Liverpool on May 9, 1957 at the age of 76. He had retired two years earlier.

Frederick William Dwelly was born on April 10, 1881, son of Robert Dwelly, a Somerset carriage builder, a religious and forceful character. The lad, at a late stage in his education at Chard Grammar School, was a frequent truant, with the excuse of listening to music. Though the headmaster was indulgent, the facts eventually came to the father's knowledge, whereupon the admonitions were so severe that (it appears with his mother's connivance) young Dwelly left home for London. For some years he earned a livelihood by working in a large draper's shop, devoting his spare time to religious and social work in slums, and adding to his knowledge of the arts, though not in systematic study of them. Through the advice and intervention of a business man he went to Queen's College, Cambridge, and became reconciled to his father, of whom he always spoke with admiration.

Dwelly was ordained deacon in 1906 on a title to St. Mary's, Windermere, five years later moving to become curate at the parish church of Cheltenham, where he remained until 1916, when he was appointed vicar of Emmanuel, Southport, a parish then comprising one of the wealthiest square miles in the north of England. Here his gifts and independence found full scope, and he filled to overcrowding that large modern church. He was one of the inner circle of the Life and Liberty movement but, like Iremonger, Sheppard and others, became disappointed with what resulted from it. He had also become known for his knowledge of church music and as a man of keen aesthetic appreciation.

On the approach of the time for the consecration of Liverpool's new cathedral, the Bishop (Dr. David) sought his help in framing the series of great services which were to mark so unusual an occasion. He soon became the controlling influence and master of ceremonies in all the preparations and their performance. He achieved an acknowledged outstanding success. Thereupon the Bishop made him a residentiary canon of the provisional Chapter, and from that time onwards the formation of all that has become distinctive of Liverpool Cathedral has been due to him. For many years he had a hand, often the major share, in preparing services for special occasions in the Church of England. He had a considerable though not an orderly or academic knowledge of liturgiology, and a great flair for combining material from ancient sources with that of his own and others' devising. On the inauguration of the Dean and Chapter in 1931 he was nominated to the deanery as the Bishop desired.

Dwelly was a man of contrasts. He could be irritatingly vague yet suddenly disconcertingly precise. He could assume the manner and hesitating speech of a simpleton with impenetrable art, yet few who tried to take advantage of him were not outwitted. A failure in punctuality in anything to do with the Cathedral nettled him, though he could hardly have kept any appointment without a vigilant secretary. Most of his correspondence was conducted by long telegrams (reply prepaid) and by telephone; and he was never more set on attaining his purposes than when appearing to yield them. His kindness and help to his friends were unlimited, and most of his troubles arose through assuming those of others as his own. Except occasionally and with trusted friends he was reserved; nevertheless he succeeded in bringing to his cathedral for special services a large number of representatives of all sides of public life, not infrequently its leaders. That, on great festivals, former choristers to the number of 100 would voluntarily muster for processions or any other duties—many of them men in middle life—was a tribute to his power of evoking enduring loyalty in the young. He was less successful, and also less interested, in making the cathedral the central church of a diocese.

However long Liverpool Cathedral stands it can hardly have a more devoted Dean. He knew every stone of it and supervised with meticulous diligence all that went on in it. Since the beginning of the last war it was actually his residence. He would deeply resent that any tribute to his success should not mention how much he owed to the capable and limitless help given him unceasingly by the lady who became his secretary during his years at Southport and upon whom, in his declining years, he depended more and more.

Dwelly retired and became Dean Emeritus in 1955. He was select preacher in Cambridge University in 1937 and Hulsean preacher in 1947-48.

He was chaplain of the Order of St. John of Jerusalem, and in 1954 he was made Hon. LL.D. of Liverpool University.

He married Mary Bradshaw, daughter of Major Darwin, M.D., of Didsbury. She died in 1950. There were no children of the marriage.

May 10, 1957.

E

Stephen Early, secretary to President Roosevelt, and later Under-Secretary of Defence, died at Washington on August 11, 1951, aged 62.

A well known and widely popular journalist and publicity director in Washington D.C., he acted as press agent when in 1920 Roosevelt ran for the Vice-Presidency of the United States. He remained Roosevelt's friend, and in 1933 accompanied him to the White House. There he took general charge of the President's relations with the public and the press, and consistently displayed a tact, knowledge and understanding which made him invaluable. No President of the United States could in tense and difficult times have been more devotedly or ably served.

At the White House it was Early's duty to arrange for the press conferences which were so remarkable a feature of Roosevelt's régime, and in the absence of the President from Washington to give out statements and answer questions on his behalf. Thus "Steve" Early became a power as well as a personality in the official life of Washington and never failed to command wide and sincere respect. After President Roosevelt's death in 1945, Early spent some years in business but returned to Government service in 1949 as Under-Secretary of Defence.

Stephen Tyree Early was born at Crozet, Virginia, near the border of the District of Columbia, on August 27, 1889, the son of Thomas Early, and was brought up in a Southern tradition. He began his education at public schools in his native state and completed it at the high school in Washington, D.C. Then, as a boy of 19, he joined the Washington staff of the United Press as a reporter engaged in general work. Thus it was that as a young man he came into contact with the government offices and made friends in many branches of the public service.

The United Press had won a high reputation for its short and pithy reports of events of the day and Early soon learned the secrets of speed in journalism. Consequently by 1913 he had become one of the best informed newspaper men in the capital. He later joined the staff of the Associated Press, the oldest of American newsagencies, and worked on it from 1913 to 1917 and again from 1920 to 1927. It was while he was with A.P. that he discovered that President Harding was dead, and Early telephoned the news several minutes before a physician made the official announcement.

When, in 1917, the United States entered the war, Early decided to play an active part in it and enlisted in the Army. Eventually he went to France and was soon in the front line where he acquitted himself so well that he was awarded the American Silver Star and received a citation for meritorious service with the artillery. At the time the armistice was signed he was a captain, working on *Stars and Stripes.*

On his return to the United States he came into contact with Roosevelt, whom he had known both as Under-Secretary of the Navy in Washington and during Roosevelt's wartime activities in England. Consequently, when Roosevelt was nominated at the Democratic National Convention of 1920 as the party candidate for the office of Vice-President he asked Early to join him as his press agent. Thus the two men formed a friendship which was to endure until the President's death.

After Roosevelt's inevitable failure at the election, Early returned to Washington as publicity director for the Chambers of Commerce of the United States and at the same time resumed his work for the Associated Press; but the strain of the two posts proved too great and he had soon to confine himself to journalism. In 1927, however, he became Washington representative of the Paramount Public Corporation and of the Paramount News Reels, which entailed lobbying in Congress and general publicity for these concerns, and also the direction of news reels in Washington. When, in 1932, Roosevelt was nominated for the Presidency, Early immediately gave up this work in order to assist in the campaign and proved a substantial contributor to its success.

On his inauguration the new President appointed three secretaries of whom his old friend Louis Howe was the principal, with Early and Marvin McIntyre as assistants. At first Early's chief duty was to be a liaison officer between the President and the press. Later Howe died and the two assistants carried on, to be helped for a time by the President's son. Then McIntyre was taken ill and until the appointment of General Watson Early acted alone. His was naturally an arduous and responsible task, for the President had a tremendous capacity for work. No one could, however, have discharged it better.

After President Roosevelt's death in 1945 Early remained for several months as a special assistant to President Truman* and then, having been awarded the Distinguished Service Medal, he left Government employment to become a vice-president of the Pullman Company. There he remained until the spring of 1949, when he accepted an invitation from President Truman to become Under-Secretary of Defence to act as deputy-secretary to Louis A. Johnson*. He thus had a large share in building up the new department designed to coordinate all defence activities. He left this post shortly before General Marshall [q.v.] became head of the department in 1950. When President Truman's press secretary died suddenly in December 1950, Early returned to the White House temporarily to fill the gap.

He married in 1921 Miss Helen Wrenn, of New York City, who survives him together with two sons and a daughter.

August 13, 1951.

T. W. Earp, the art critic, died on May 8, 1958 in hospital at Alton, Hampshire. He was 65. Earp will be remembered as a writer on art of rare individuality, sound in judgment and contained in expression.

Thomas Wade Earp, who was the son of Thomas Earp, M.P., was born in 1892 and educated at Magnus Grammar School, Newark, and Exeter College, Oxford, where he was a Charles Oldham Scholar. He was not a prolific writer, and everything he published seemed to be the outcome of profound reflection by an original mind on life as well as on literature and art. During his younger days Earp carried out much social and antiquarian research in Paris and London, and the connexion between art and society, the one reflecting changes in the other, was his constant preoccupation.

His first book, *Contacts,* was published in 1916, to be followed two years later by *The Gate of Bronze.* Then there was a gap until 1928, when *Flower and Still-Life Painting,* with an introduction by Earp, was published by the *Studio* and made the subject of a discursive column in *The Times Literary Supplement. Augustus John* and *Van Gogh* both came out in 1934, and the more substantial *Modern Movement in Painting* a year later.

It is in *French Painting,* published in 1945 by the Avalon Press and the Central Institute of Art and Design, established shortly after the outbreak of war with its headquarters at the National Gallery, that Earp's qualities as a writer, his complete digestion of his material, and his ability to express his conclusions with lucidity and conciseness are best appreciated.

Earp was for some years art critic of the *Daily Telegraph* and wrote a good many prefaces to catalogues of art exhibitions and books about art, including one, edited by Lilian Browse, on the drawings of Augustus John*, who was his intimate friend. In a sense, and though he had an intimate knowledge of modern painting in particular, he was the least "professional" of art critics. He seemed to come to painting with a full mind enriched by ruminating on things in general, and in this respect he was in the tradition of Hazlitt, Baudelaire, Pater and Ruskin rather than in that of Reynold or Roger Fry.

The affectionate esteem in which Earp was held by his colleagues is well indicated by the circumstances that he was generally referred to as "Tommy" Earp. Modest and shy, and almost embarrassingly diffident in speaking to older writers, he was a true Bohemian, equally at home in the Paris café or the London pub, but without a trace of conscious unconventionality. Earp was a man of striking appearance, almost startlingly rubicund, who might have been taken for anything but a writer. There is a good portrait of him by Augustus John.

In the ordinary affairs of life he had a charming simplicity. Once he turned up late at an exhibition in Glasgow. "You see", he said in his slow, hesitating manner, "we have a cat", and he went on to explain that his wife had to be out when he should have been catching his train, and so it was necessary for him to delay his departure.

May 9, 1958.

Sir Norwood East, formerly a Commissioner of Prisons and director of the Prison Medical Service, and a leading authority on criminal psychology, died at his home at Crowthorne, Berkshire, on October 30, 1953 at the age of 80.

William Norwood East was born on December 24, 1872, the son of the late W. Quartermaine East, and was educated at King's College School and King's College, London. He qualified at Guy's Hospital in 1897, and while still a young man he entered Her Majesty's Prison Service as a prison medical officer. He was for many years the senior medical officer at Brixton Prison, and in 1924 was appointed medical inspector of His Majesty's prisons of England and Wales. Some six years later he was appointed a Commissioner of Prisons and director of the Prison Medical Service. He had also been an inspector under the Inebriate Acts of 1879-1900, and had served on the departmental committees on the persistent offender and on prison diets. After his retirement he was appointed a lecturer in forensic psychiatry at the Maudsley Hospital—a school of the University of London.

East's contribution to the study of criminal psychology was marked by his long experience in the Prison Medical Service. He was always more of a "realist" than many other medical and psychological writers on the subject, and was often impatient of those who sought to replace the present legal means of dealing with crime by psychological methods of dealing with criminals. He was acutely aware that whereas "the medical aspects of criminal conduct are concerned with individuals, the legal point of view [is] with the protection of society"—and he would never have claimed any superiority for the first over the second.

His writings—including *The Medical Aspects of Crime* (1936) and *Society and The Criminal* (1949), which was published with the official imprimatur of H.M. Stationery Office—were packed with the fruits of first-hand as well as close statistical observation, the observation of one who, apart from his career in the Prison Medical Service, was also one of the assessors who gave his opinion on the sanity or otherwise of murderers after conviction. One of his finest conclusions was that there was more flexibility in the administration of the law than its critics supposed: for example, that though the rules on insanity are behind medical and even popular opinion the interpretation of them by judges is less open to criticism.

Some might find complacency in his judgment that "experience in the criminal courts proves that the judicial authorities and others concerned with criminal conduct usually arrive at reliable conclusions in regard to the motives and intentions of law-breakers", but it was based on careful and well documented observation. The basis of his attitude was a conviction that though scientifically carried out psychological investigations could help greatly in explaining various factors associated with social maladjustment, it was dangerous, especially at the present stage of ignorance and inexperience, to base law, or a theory of punishment, on any psychological and speculative formulae.

In 1900 he married Selina,only daughter of the late Alfred Triggs, who survives him.

November 2, 1953.

Florence Easton (Mrs. Florence Easton Rogers), who died in New York on August 13, 1955 at the age of 70, was for many years prima donna of the Metropolitan Opera.

Florence Gertrude Easton was born at Middlesbrough on October 24, 1884, and studied at the Royal College of Music and in Paris.

In spite of her English origin, her career was made principally in the opera houses of Germany and America. Her early career with the Moody-Manners Opera Company led to her first marriage—to Francis MacLennan, a tenor in the company. She and her husband then joined the Berlin Royal Opera where they stayed from 1907 to 1913. After a short time with the Hamburg Municipal Theatre she went to New York and in 1916 began her long and fruitful career with the Metropolitan Opera, which lasted without interruption until 1929.

Her pure tone, sound technique, and admirable musicianship singled her out even among the brilliant company of singers collected by Gatti-Casazza, and it is doubtful whether any manager has ever possessed a more useful member of a company. Her repertory was enormous, ranging from Brünnhilde to Carmen, and her enunciation in four languages exceptionally clear. She could appear at a moment's notice in well over 100 parts, including sometimes several in the same opera, for example *Der Rosenkavalier* and *Die Walküre.* London heard her but rarely—in 1911, 1928 and 1932, singing notably as Turandot and Isolde.

In 1929 she announced that she would sing in opera no more and for a time retired to a house in Hampstead, but her reappearance in 1932 was followed by a recital over the air in the next year and in 1934 she sang as a guest artist at Sadler's Wells in the part of Tosca. She rejoined the Metropolitan in 1936 and though she had officially retired before the outbreak of war in 1939 she continued to give occasional performances, the last occasion being last year.

Her second husband, whom she married in 1931, was Robert Stanley Rogers, a New York banker.

August 15, 1955.

Dr. Hugo Eckener, whose development of lighter than air aircraft and skill in pilotage brought him, among many other honours, the gold medal of the Royal Aeronautical Society in 1936, died at Friedrichshafen on August 14, 1954 at the age of 86.

Born at Flensburg on August 10, 1868, and educated at Munich, Berlin, and Leipzig Universities, his first connexion with airships was as a severe critic of Count Zeppelin's early attempts, which, like most experiments in scientific novelties, resulted in a number of failures. Then the critic visited the works at Friedrichshafen, and became a convert. In 1906 he joined the Zeppelin company, and four years later, in 1910, he became manager.

During the 1914-18 War he acted as instructor of airship commanders, and among others, trained Captain Ernst Lehmann, who was afterwards his first officer on many flights of the Graf Zeppelin. He also supervised the training of the crews, as well as continuing to manage the works of the Zeppelin company. After the war many of the Zeppelins were destroyed in their sheds by their crews, and the remainder were handed over to the victorious allies. Dr. Eckener then built two small commercial airships, the Bodensee and the Nordstern, the former of which carried out a very successful air service between various German towns for some months, but then both ships were claimed by the allies.

In 1921 the United States arranged for the Zeppelin company to build an airship and fly it across to America. The result was the ship Los Angeles, of 2,500,000 cubic ft. gas capacity, and she was flown across the Atlantic from Friedrichshafen to Lakehurst, New Jersey, in October 1924, with Dr. Eckener in command. This airship proved very successful, and was used by the United States Navy for eight years without mishap. Dr. Eckener arranged with the Goodyear Company to acquire the American rights of the Zeppelin patents, and this company, with the help of German designers and inspectors, built the airships Shenandoah, Akron, and Macon in America.

In due course the ban on airship building in Germany was lifted, and an improved Zeppelin was laid down at Friedrichshafen, afterwards to be known as the Graf Zeppelin. The chief novelty in the ship was the use of blauw-gas as fuel for the engines, so that the ship did not get lighter as fuel was consumed, and so the valving off of hydrogen to compensate for this was obviated. With this airship Dr. Eckener for several years gave a notable and impressive demonstration of the commercial possibilities of airships when handled by a captain of his great experience and judgment, backed by a well-trained crew. In October 1928, the Graf Zeppelin, with Dr. Eckener in command, flew from Friedrichshafen to Lakehurst and back again. Then, after a brief series of cruises round Europe, she flew to Lakehurst a second time in August 1929, and from there, heading eastward, she flew right round the world. This notable flight, the first of its kind by an airship, occupied 21 days in all, but the actual flying time was only 11 days, 23 hours, 33 minutes. The trip covered about 28,000 miles.

Dr. Eckener then planned a flight into the Arctic, but it was not found practicable to insure the lives of the crew, and so the plan was abandoned. In April 1930 Captain Lehmann took the Graf Zeppelin to England, and landed her at Cardington. Dr. Eckener, who was already in England, went aboard and took command for the return flight. The following month he took the airship on her first flight to Brazil. Stub mooring masts were sent ahead and erected at Seville and Pernambuco. The airship visited Rio de Janeiro and New York before returning to Europe. After that, regular flights to South America were carried through each summer, with intermediate cruises over Europe.

However, in 1937, with the explosion of the Hindenburg at Lakehurst, airship aviation was virtually ended. In 1931 Dr. Eckener went to England to give his opinion on the disaster to R 101 before the court of inquiry presided over by Sir John Simon [later Lord Simon, q.v.].

In 1936 Eckener fell into disgrace with the Nazis and while in Brazil with his new airship Hindenburg, the Nazi Propaganda Ministry forbade his name to appear in the press, but the ban was soon lifted when the Nazis realized that Eckener's visit in his airship to the United States could not be ignored or, still worse, could be used as ammunition by political opponents. When the 1939-45 War broke out he was an old man and technical developments in heavier than air aircraft tended to obscure his achievements in the earlier medium.

After the war he resumed his old connexion with the American Goodyear Company and spent some months in the United States directing experiments before returning to Germany in November 1947. In that year, the Zeppelin Foundation funds were transferred to the town of Friedrichshafen. Dr. Eckener opposed this, saying that the money should be devoted to international scientific research, and later resigned his honorary citizenship of Friedrichshafen. In 1952, however, he consented to become an adviser in the administration of the funds, and accepted back his honorary citizenship. In March 1951 he was elected vice-president of the airship club in Edinburgh. Two years ago he was awarded the Grand Cross of Merit, one of West Germany's highest honours.

He was married and had a son and a daughter.

August 16, 1954.

T. L. Eckersley, F.R.S., died on February 15, 1959 at the age of 72. He had been in ill health for a number of years.

Thomas Lydwell Eckersley, a grandson of Thomas Henry Huxley, was born on December 27, 1886. He was educated at Bedales School where he first became interested in the then new science of wireless communication. He subsequently took his B.Sc. at University College London and followed this with some notable research work at the National Physical Laboratory, Trinity College, Cambridge, and the Cavendish Laboratory, Cambridge. He was a member of the Egyptian Government Survey in 1913-14.

During the First World War he served in the Royal Engineers in Egypt and Salonika, where his theoretical and experimental work on "night effect" and coastal refraction served to lay the foundations of his subsequent career.

Eckersley joined the Marconi company in 1919 and began research into the resistance of transmitting aerials, one result of which was a notable increase in radiation efficiency, brought about by his use of earth screens. This work, when published in 1922, earned for him the Duddell Premium of the Institution of Electrical Engineers, a forerunner of the many premium awards he received during his career.

In 1922 the Marconi company sent an engineering team to Australia to carry out an intensive study of long wave propagation. Eckersley was responsible for the analysis of their findings, which was presented in a classic paper in the *Journal* of the I.E.E.

With the advent of the Marconi-Franklin beam system of radio transmission he turned his attention to the propagation of high frequency electromagnetic waves, and in the period 1924 to 1939 directed a research team that carried out many pioneer ionospheric investigations. In further I.E.E. papers he laid down the basis for the prediction of the performance of high frequency radio services, which was brilliantly confirmed in practice.

Eckersley's genius led him to apply the phase integral method, familiar in quantum mechanics, both to the magneto-ionic theory of ionospheric propagation and to the problem of the effect of the earth's resistivity on the diffraction of radio waves round the earth. This work was communicated in several papers published by the Royal Society and has been extended to the tropospheric propagation of very high frequencies. On much of this work the present-day systems of forward scatter transmission are based. He was made a Fellow of the Royal Society in March 1938. The list of new Fellows included also the name of Sir Julian Huxley* another grandson of the great T. H. Huxley.

In 1940 Eckersley joined the staff of the Air Ministry, was engaged on secret work, and in 1942 became Chief Scientific Adviser to the Interservices Ionosphere Bureau, established at the Marconi research and development laboratories at Great Baddow. The techniques of radar owe much to his diffraction theory, while another of his theories helped in the location of submarines which were masked from radar detection by rough seas which scattered the radar pulses.

Though ill-health compelled him to retire in 1946 he continued as a consultant to the Marconi company and published scientific papers from time to time. In that year (1946) he was awarded a Fellowship of the American Institute of Radio Engineers and this was followed in 1951 by the award of the Faraday Medal for achievements in the field of radio research and, in particular, for outstanding contributions to the theory and practice of radio-wave propagation.

His life's work is well summed up by the citation on the occasion of his election to Fellowship of the American I.R.E. This stated, *inter alia,* "Both his approach to the problems from the standpoint of practical communications and his invention of mathematical tools useful in the computation of radiated fields are achievements of lasting value, acclaimed by the whole world, and form a monument of which he may be justly proud".

He married in 1920 Eva, daughter of Barry Pain, by whom he had a son and two daughters.

February 17, 1959.

Brigadier-General Sir James Edmonds, C.B., C.M.G., who died at Sherborne, Dorset, on August 2, 1956 at the age of 94, was well known as the historian of the First World War and must rank as one of the greatest of military historians. The method of recording operations from the three sources of the documents, the memories of survivors, and information from the former enemy and from allies, had been practised before, but he brought it to a science.

James Edward Edmonds was born on Christmas Day 1861. At the age of nine he went as a day boy to King's College School, then in the east wing of Somerset House. He said that he learnt languages at the breakfast table; they had been handed down from father to son since the days of Sir Thomas Edmonds, French Secretary to Queen Elizabeth I and the Ambassador of James I. In 1879 he passed first into the Royal Military Academy, to pass out again first, after winning the Pollock medal, the Sword, and most of the prizes. Gazetted to the Royal Engineers, he specialized at first in submarine mining, then an R.E. and not a naval function.

In 1885, during a Russian scare, he was sent to Hongkong in command of the 33rd Company, R.E., obtaining independent command at an early age because the other officers were on the sick list. The defences had been completely neglected. After three years of hard work, with three months' sick leave in Japan, he came home by way of the United States, where he studied the battlefields of the American Civil War. On promotion to captain in 1890 he became instructor in fortification at Woolwich. There he spent six happy years, using the long vacations to travel and learn more languages, including Russian.

In 1895, the year of his marriage, he entered the Staff College, as usual passing first. On completing the course, he was ordered to Port Royal, Jamaica, where yellow fever was raging. There he found the unpreparedness worse than at Hongkong, and the Spanish-American war developing. In 1899 he was appointed to the Intelligence Division at the War Office and later accompanied his chief, Major-General Sir John Ardagh, to South Africa, charged on behalf of the Foreign Office and War Office to advise Lord Kitchener on questions of international law. When Ardagh went home in 1902 Edmonds took his place, and after the end of the South African War was lent to the civil government under Lord Milner to complete the work.

In 1904 Edmonds returned to the Intelligence Division, now in charge of a section to follow the Russo-Japanese War. Next he was promoted to take charge of M.O.5 (later called M.I.5), and was able in 1908 to convince the Secretary of State for War, Mr. (later Lord) Haldane, of the existence of a complete German espionage system in the country. In this period, with his brother-in-law, W. B. Wood, he wrote a history of the American Civil War which became a text-book in the United States, and with Dr. L. Oppenheim, Whewell Professor of International Law at Cambridge, the official manual, *The Laws and Usages of War.* He also devised the Double Playfair cipher. He contrived to spend a few weeks of each training season with troops, generally on Salisbury Plain, as an extra staff officer.

In 1911 Edmonds was appointed G.S.O.1 of 4 Division, and participated in the war training of the B.E.F. When the division went to France in 1914 its training was of the highest standard. Edmonds, however, broke down for want of sleep and food during the retreat from Mons. He remained at G.H.Q. in the Engineer-in-Chief's department for the rest of the war, during the latter part of which he was Deputy Engineer-in-Chief, with the rank of brigadier-general, and much in the confidence of his old class-mate at the Staff College, by then Field-Marshal Sir Douglas Haig. Had he been a stronger man he might well have become chief General Staff officer of one of the Armies, a post for which he was fitted in many respects.

In 1919, with Haig's approval, he was appointed Director of the Historical Section (Military Branch) of the Committee of Imperial Defence, to produce the official history of the Army in the war. He remained in charge until he was 87. He wrote the narrative of the Western Front, while others under his direction dealt with the other theatres. There was little colour in his style, but it was lucid and economical, and he was master of the art of compression. He knew all the chief actors and had their confidence; his judgment and sense of proportion were excellent. He possessed a prodigious memory and great knowledge of warfare through the ages. His mind was, in fact, a storehouse of information on military matters.

This erudition, together with his engineering skill, earned him the nickname of "Archimedes", over which pseudonym a number of letters appeared in the columns of various newspapers and periodicals. The official history has had its critics, but it has never been excelled. Hampered by shortage of staff, he was caught by the outbreak of another war in 1939, which stopped printing. He continued the compilation, so that by 1945 there was little left to do but to see five volumes through the press and start a new team of historians on its task. After his retirement in 1951 he wrote *A Short History of World War I.*

Edmonds was sarcastic and impish in humour. He would tear reputations to shreds in private talk, while he seldom gave praise higher than to say that so-and-so was "very adequate". To those who satisfied his standards he was, however, a kindly and considerate taskmaster. It might take them long to realize that they were trusted, but when they did they gave him their affection. He called himself a pessimist when things went well and an optimist when they went ill. He was essentially a happy man, and looked back on a long life without a regret, certainly none that he had not risen in his military career to the height foretold by its start.

He was created a C.B. in 1911 and a C.M.G. in 1916. In 1928 he was knighted. He received the knight's cross of the Légion d'Honneur and other foreign decorations. In 1936 he was given the honorary degree of D.Litt. by the University of Oxford.

He was also awarded the Chesney gold medal by the Royal United Service Institution. He was president of the Institution of Royal Engineers from 1931 to 1935, chairman of the council of the Society for Army Historical Research for over 20 years, and a member of the council of King's College Hospital. After the death of Sir John Capper in May 1955 he was extremely proud of the fact that he became the oldest living R.E. officer.

He married in 1895 Hilda, daughter of the Rev. M. Wood. She died in 1921, and he is survived by an only daughter.

August 7, 1956.

F. W. Edridge-Green, C.B.E., M.D., F.R.C.S., who died in a nursing home at Worthing on April 17, 1953 at the age of 89, was a leading authority on colour vision and colour blindness.

He was the inventor of the colour perception spectrometer and colour perception lantern which are used in the official tests of the Royal Navy and by railway and other bodies throughout the world, and he also devised the "bead test", the official test of the National Service Boards. He was for many years special examiner and adviser to the Ministry of Pensions on vision and colour vision, ophthalmic surgeon to the London Pensions Board, and chairman of the Ophthalmic Board of the Central London Medical Boards for National Service.

Frederick William Edridge-Green was born on December 14, 1863, the son of Thomas Allen Green. He received his medical training at St. Bartholomew's Hospital, at the University of Durham, and at St. John's College, Cambridge. He obtained the conjoint qualification in 1887 and in the same year secured first class honours in the London M.B. examinations; he proceeded to the M.D., winning a gold medal, in 1889, and in 1892 he became F.R.C.S. He was Hunterian Professor (1911) and Arris and Gale lecturer (1921-22) at the Royal College of Surgeons of England and a Beit Memorial Research Fellow.

In 1930 he was president of honour at the annual meeting of the Ophthalmological Society of Paris and in 1936 he received the Thomas Gray Memorial Prize for his invention of the colour perception lantern. He was a member of the International Code of Signals Committee and was a former president of the Durham Medical Graduates Association.

Edridge-Green's principal writings were his books on *Colour Blindness and Colour Perception* (1909), and on *The Physiology of Vision* (1920) and his Hunterian lectures on *Colour Vision and Colour Blindness* (1911).

He married in 1893 Minnie Jane, daughter of Henry Hicks, M.D., F.R.S., the well-known geologist. His wife died in 1901 and there were no children of the marriage.

April 18, 1953.

Alfred Edwards, who died on June 17, 1958 at the age of 70, represented East Middlesbrough in the House of Commons for 15 years, first as a Labour member, then as an Independent and finally as a Conservative.

His opposition to the proposals to nationalize the iron and steel industry led to his expulsion from the Labour Party, and he joined the Conservatives in 1949. He lost his seat in the general election of February 1950, and was unsuccessful in his attempt to win the Eastern Division at Newcastle upon Tyne the following year.

Born in Middlesbrough in March 1888, the son of Thomas and Sarah Edwards, Alfred Edwards was educated at an elementary school and then started work as a labourer in a local foundry. By ability and sheer hard work he rose to become a director of an old-established local ironworks, and was connected with many other business enterprises. One of his interests was agriculture, and he farmed successfully at Hemble Hill, Guisborough, Yorkshire.

Before entering the House of Commons he was active in local municipal politics, and sat on the Middlesbrough Town Council from 1932 to 1935. He had joined the Labour Party in 1931, and in 1935 was chosen as parliamentary candidate for the Eastern Division of his native city. He won a notable victory at the 1935 general election, wresting the seat from the Liberals. His majority was only 67 over the Conservative candidate, but the sitting Liberal member was at the bottom of the poll. He increased his majority in 1945 to 8,075 in a straight fight with a Conservative.

But he was not altogether happy in the 1945-50 Parliament. He had little patience with the left wing intellectuals in his party, and preferred to follow a "middle of the road" policy. He became increasingly uneasy at the spate of legislation which was poured out session after session, and eventually took an uncompromising stand against the Iron and Steel Bill. He carried his opposition so far as to incur the wrath of his official leaders and he was expelled from the Labour Party. He continued to sit from 1948 as an Independent and in 1949 he joined the Conservatives.

He showed his courage when, at the 1950 general election, he decided to fight his old constituency under his new colours. The result was a foregone conclusion, particularly as Hilary Marquand* was the Labour nominee. Edwards was beaten by 16,783, though he came second of four candidates. At the general election of October 1951 he failed to wrest Newcastle upon Tyne East from the Labour Party, though he reduced the majority from 5,828 to 2,771 in a straight fight.

In spite of political differences with old colleagues, he had made few enemies. He was greatly respected for his integrity, although his independent outlook was not well suited to party politics. He was a shy, modest man, not always easy to understand, but those who knew him intimately were sure of his friendship for life.

Edwards was never one to wear his heart on his sleeve, and few of his magnanimous acts were ever revealed to the general public. He had a deep and unshakable religious faith, and was a convinced believer in Christian Science.

Edwards married in 1917 Annie Rains Hoskison. She, with their two daughters survives him.

June 18, 1958.

Sir Alfred Egerton, F.R.S., who was Professor of Chemical Technology in the Imperial College of Science from 1936 to 1952, died in France on September 7, 1959 at the age of 72.

Alfred Charles Glyn Egerton, fourth son of Colonel Sir Alfred Mordaunt Egerton, K.C.V.O., was born on October 11, 1886, and educated at Eton and University College London, where he graduated in chemistry in 1908.

He subsequently studied at Nancy under Professor Ganz and at Berlin under Professor Nernst. In 1923 he was appointed reader in thermo-dynamics at Oxford and in 1936 Professor of Chemical Technology at the Imperial College of Science and Technology (University of London). He was elected Fellow of the Royal Society in 1926 and was one of the secretaries of the society from 1938 to 1948.

Egerton's interest in science dated from his school days, when he founded the Eton College Scientific Society, and continued unabated throughout a long life. He was one of the last research students to work with Sir William Ramsay and later he established a school of combustion research, first at Oxford and then at London, which rapidly acquired international prestige. As a research worker he was indefatigable; many of his old students can testify to the enthusiasm with which he conducted his work and all of them owe a great debt to his inspiration and wise counsel. It was a great pleasure to them when he was awarded in 1946 the Rumford Medal of the Royal Society.

But Egerton's activities were not confined to the laboratory. The list of his public services is long.

He served on the War Cabinet Scientific Advisory Committee, was chairman of the Fuels and Propulsion Committee of the Admiralty, the Committee for Heating and Ventilating, the Scientific Advisory Council of the Ministry of Fuel and Power, and was director of the Salters' Institute of Industrial Chemistry. His services to science were recognized by a knighthood in 1943 and by the award of honorary degrees by the universities of Birmingham, Cairo, Nancy, and Helsinki. Apart from his scientific work, he was a talented artist, particularly happy in landscape paintings which admirably expressed his vivid sense of colour and form.

Although he retired from the chair of chemical technology in 1952, he continued his researches at the Imperial College and maintained his interest in his old department. He also took an active part in advising the Government of India on scientific education and on the invitation of Nehru* undertook a review of the work of its 16 national laboratories.

He married in 1912 the Hon. Ruth Cripps, only daughter of the first Baron Parmoor. It was a union marked by a happy community of interests. Their delightful hospitality, their very real interest in the problems of young people, and their innumerable acts of kindness will long be remembered by friends all over the world.

September 9, 1959.

Professor Albert Einstein, the greatest scientist of modern times, died in hospital at Princeton, New Jersey, on April 18, 1955 at the age of 76. He had lived a secluded life for some years, though he had been a member of the staff of the Institute for Advanced Study in Princeton University.

Albert Einstein was born at Ulm, in Württemberg on March 14, 1879. A year later his family moved to Munich, where they remained until he was 15. His parentage was Jewish, but few Jewish usages were observed in his home. He was slow in learning to talk, and at the Catholic elementary school which he first attended was known as *Biedermeier* ("Honest John") from his ponderously accurate way of speaking. Both there and at the Luitpold Gymnasium, where the educational system was rigid, he saw little difference between school and barrack.

His father, Hermann, had a small electro-chemical factory, but he had a greater genius for living than he had for success. Failing in Munich he moved to Milan and later to Pavia. The son, left unhappily at the gymnasium, was well on the way to manoeuvring his departure from it when he was unexpectedly asked to leave as being "disruptive" of his class.

Italy gave him as great an interest in art and music as he already had in Schiller, and the affairs of his father enforced him to seek a career. He had speculated at the age of five on the movement of a compass needle, and he knew that his mathematics, if not his other subjects, were well beyond the usual examination requirements. Combining interest and ability, he arrived at theoretical physics as the field that would most attract him, but, partly because of his father's work, and partly from his own lack of formal attainment, he thought that technological training would be his best approach. He therefore proposed to study at the Swiss Federal Polytechnic School in Zürich, but was at first rejected. He had to qualify for the diploma in modern languages and biology at a cantonal school at Aarau. There he lost his dislike of schooling, and from the age of 17 until the age of 21 he conscientiously followed the course prescribed at Zürich for a teacher of physics and mathematics. In 1901 he became a Swiss citizen—a reflection of his dislike of authority.

Partly on account of his ancestry, he had difficulty in finding a teaching post, but by the influence of a fellow student he was appointed as a technical assistant in the Swiss Patent Office at Berne in 1902. This was the "cobbler's job", which he maintained later was the way that scientists should earn their living. In the next year he married Mileva Maritsch, a fellow student at the Polytechnic. Two sons were born in quick succession, but there were differences of temperament and interest, and the marriage was dissolved after some years.

Einstein's first contribution to theoretical physics was made in the same year that he obtained his Patent Office job. Three years later was his *annus mirabilis*, 1905. Then he burst without warning into an extraordinary range of discovery and new ideas, of which the "Special Theory of Relativity" was one part, not at the time the most comprehensible by his colleagues. In his earliest work he had simplified Boltzmann's theory of the random motions of the molecules of a gas, and in 1905 he applied this method to the "Brownian movement"—the impetuous, irregular motion of microscopic particles, suspended in a fluid, that is produced by molecular bombardment. Einstein showed how the number of molecules per unit of volume could be inferred from measurements made of the distances travelled by the visible particles which they hit. Such measurements, made later by Perrin, verified Einstein's theory so well that the Brownian movement has ever since been regarded as one of the most direct—and impressive—pieces of evidence for the reality of molecules.

In the same year Einstein advanced a revolutionary theory of the photo-electric effect, which has exercised a decisive influence on the modern quantum theory of light. The essence of this effect is that the speed with which electrons are liberated from a metal surface illuminated by ultra-violet light depends only on the colour of the light and not on its brightness. Einstein suggested that the light (from which the escaping electrons must derive their energy) is not continuously distributed in space, but is like a gas with a discrete molecular structure—the "molecules" being photons or units of radiant energy of amounts proportional to the frequency of the light. This assumption gave a concrete physical mechanism for the quantum theory of white light advanced by Planck in 1900, and it provided satisfactory estimates of the speed of photo-electrons. But the importance of Einstein's theory of photons far transcended the occasion of its suggestion. Its real significance is that it accustomed physicists to accept the dual character of light, which sometimes behaves like a continuous train of waves, and sometimes a hail of bullets, and that in 1924 it suggested to de Broglie that matter itself had a similar "dual personality" and could behave either as a wave or a corpuscle. These conceptions have dominated all subsequent speculations about the ultimate elements of matter and light.

Although Einstein's researches in the quantum theory were of vital significance and, in one direction, seemed to show a clearer grasp of its implications than was possessed by its originator, it is with the theories of relativity that his name will always be associated. The "Special Theory of Relativity" was published in the same extraordinary year. It expressed in a simple and systematic form the effects produced on the basic instruments of physics—the "rigid" scale and the perfect clock—by relative motion, and thus codified the earlier mathematical investigations of Voigt, the physical speculations of Larmor and the pioneer work of Lorentz. For the first time the optics of moving media received a satisfactory formulation, and Newtonian dynamics itself was generalized so as to express the effect of motion on apparent mass. In particular, Einstein's deduction that mass and energy are proportional became the basic law of atomic transformation. Apart from its spectacular demonstration in atomic energy, it is supported also by a host of experiments in nuclear physics, in which it is used daily as a tool with which nuclear physicists work. Equally, the design of large engineering machines, such as "synchrotrons", in which nuclear particles are accelerated to high energies, depends directly on its use.

In this group of varied and important publications he showed at once qualities of imagination and insight which were even more vital to his work than mathematical ability, which indeed was a necessary qualification but was not (by the highest standards) exceptional. It was also well for his immediate career that he had more than one contribution to offer.

As soon as the remarkable researches published by Einstein in 1905 became known many attempts were made to secure for him a professorial post. As a result of these efforts he became a *Privatdozent* at Berne in 1908 and *Professor extraordinarius* at Zürich in 1909. In 1911 he became Professor of Theoretical Physics at Prague, but returned to Zürich to the corresponding post in 1912. During 1913 Planck and Nernst persuaded Einstein to go to Berlin as director of the projected research institute for physics, as a member of the Royal Prussian Academy of Science and as a professor in the University of Berlin—with no duties or obligations. He occupied this post until 1933.

The "General Theory of Relativity", published in 1916, was the fruit of many years of speculation by Einstein on the questions: "Can we distinguish the effects of gravitation and of acceleration?" and "Are light rays bent by gravity?" To answer these questions he was led to build a great and complex theory, which needs for its systematic expression a new mathematical discipline invented by Ricci and Levi-Civita. The divergences between the predictions of the planetary theory based on Einstein's theory and those based on the classical theory of Newton are all extremely small, but in one case (the slow changes in the orbit of Mercury) Einstein's theory provides an explanation which had never been found on Newtonian principles. Moreover, it successfully predicted the deflection of light from distant stars as it grazed the sun's disc—an effect subsequently verified by British astronomical expeditions in 1919—and also the reddening of light from very massive stars—which was much later confirmed by observations on the dark companion of Sirius. The success with which "general relativity" gave quantitative predictions of the new phenomena has created a presumption in its favour which has substantially survived.

The application of general relativity to cosmology was implicit in Einstein's original theory, but became explicit through a modification which he introduced into it in 1917. His contribution in this field was an attempt to provide an answer to an old and "insoluble" problem: "How can the universe of stars be uniform in density, fill all space and yet be of finite total mass?" The subsequent relation of observational evidence of "the expanding universe" to the possible forms of theory that might be developed was done mainly by others, including Lemaître, de Sitter, and Eddington, to whom Einstein served as a stimulus.

During the 1914-18 War two other notable events occurred in his life—he refused to sign the "Manifesto of Ninety-two German Intellectuals" which identified German culture and German militarism, and he contracted a second marriage, with his cousin Elsa. In 1921 he appeared publicly as a supporter of Zionism and he actively collaborated with Weizmann [q.v.] in the establishment of the University of Jerusalem. During the post-war years he travelled and lectured in Holland, Czechoslovakia, Austria, the United States (where he not only lectured on relativity but took part in Weizmann's campaign for the Jewish National Fund), and England (where he lectured at King's College, London, and calmed the fears of the Archbishop of Canterbury that relativity was a threat to theology). In 1922 he lectured in Paris, Shanghai, the Kobe, returning home *via* Palestine and Spain.

In the same year he was awarded a Nobel prize, strangely enough for his work in quantum theory, as the committee were not sure whether his theory of relativity was technically a "discovery"! He was awarded a Copley Medal by the Royal Society in 1925. He visited South America in 1925 and lectured at Pasadena (California) during the winters of 1930-31, 1931-32, and 1932-33. In the summer of 1932 he lectured at Oxford, and was made an honorary Doctor of Science. The great purge of Jewish scientists began under Hitler in 1933 and Einstein decided not to return to Germany, where scientific freedom had ceased to exist. He lived for some months at La Cocque in Belgium and resigned from the Prussian Academy. In the winter of 1933, at the invitation of Flexner, he emigrated to America and became a Professor at the Institute for Advanced Study at Princeton, a post which he held until 1945. His second wife, Elsa, had died in 1936.

In his later years he was venerated—and loved—but became somewhat isolated in his work from the main stream of modern physics. Remembering his early contribution to the quantum theory, it might have been supposed that he would have accepted readily the principle of indeterminacy, which came to play so large a part in it; and that, in his quest for a further unification of the laws of Nature, he would have tried to weld together the discontinuous and indeterminate picture given by the quantum theory with the continuous and determinate picture of relativity. But for Einstein physics was firmly rooted in causality; God did not play at dice, and he would not admit the ultimate validity of any theory based on chance or indeterminacy. The quantum theory remained therefore, for him as a passing phase, however important to working physicists. Instead, he attempted further generalizations of relativity, which should incorporate both gravitation and electromagnetism, together with the nuclear fields of force. This work, however, has received no better reception than have all other "unified field theories".

When we consider the basic character of the problems he attacked, the vast cosmical scale on which he worked, and his immense influence on physical cosmology as well as physics, we can only compare Einstein with Newton. If Newton's central achievement was to establish the reign of gravitation in its full simplicity and universality, the essence of Einstein's work was to reveal gravitation as a phenomenon expressible in terms of world geometry.

April 21, 1955.

"Elephant Bill"—See **Lieutenant-Colonel James Howard Williams.**

Queen Elizabeth, Queen Mother of Greece—See **Greece.**

Benno Elkan, O.B.E., the sculptor, died in a London hospital on January 10, 1960. He was 82.

He was a sculptor with a wide range and he was responsible for some important monuments in Germany before he went to Britain as a refugee. In Britain his subjects included many famous persons, among them Toscanini [q.v.], Lord Keynes, Lord Beveridge*, Sir Winston Churchill*, Lord Samuel*, and Mr. Yehudi Menuhin.

Elkan, who was of Jewish descent, was born in Dortmund on December 2, 1877. He received his earliest artistic training at Karlsruhe, and at the age of 28 went to Paris, where he was deeply affected by the work of Rodin and also received some influence from Bartholomé, the sculptor of the familiar Monument to the Dead in the cemetery of Père Lachaise.

From Paris Elkan went to Rome, where in 1908 he made something of a sensation with his polychrome figure of "Persephone". This, draped from the waist, with the arms crossed on the breast and the head bent forward to inhale the perfume of roses held in the hands, was in Carrara marble associated with gold, bronze, onyx, alabaster, malachite, chrysoprase, jasper and agate, the general colour effect being violet, green and yellow. It was an extremely elaborate piece of virtuosity rather than a great work of art. Works executed by Elkan after his return to Germany in 1911 included three bronze panels of the "Sermon on the Mount", a bronze "Flute Player", various plaques and medals and a few public monuments in stone, which last were destroyed by the Nazis.

Elkan went to Britain in 1933, and the following year he was represented at the Royal Academy by a bronze head of Mr. John D. Rockefeller. Subsequently he exhibited regularly at Burlington House, his works, except for a marble torso in 1937, being all in bronze or other metal and ranging in subject from portrait heads to medals in bronze, silver and silver gilt.

In 1936 there was a one-man show of Elkan's recent sculpture at Knoedler's Galleries. It included portrait heads of the King of Siam and Walter Rathenau, photographs of monuments in Germany, and also the first of the bronze candelabra for which Elkan was to become famous. This, designed for Buckfast Abbey, South Devon, was a standard candelabrum, 9ft. high, with a foliated head—rather like that of a stylized tree—providing for 15 candles to illuminate figures of the four cardinal virtues. It was a Gothic conception, recalling the marginal decoration of illuminated manuscripts in the convention effectively revived by Eric Gill in his wood-engravings.

Recognized to be a superlatively good craftsman in metal, Elkan was commissioned by an anonymous donor to design and execute a pair of similar candelabra, to be known as "The Great Biblical Candelabra", for presentation to Westminster Abbey. The Old Testament example, which stood 7ft. high and branched to 6ft. wide, and provided for 33 candles to illuminate more than 30 small bronze figures and groups of warriors, prophets, kings, and heroines, was shown in the Central Hall at the Royal Academy in 1939. It was dedicated by the Dean of Westminster in May 1942.

Similar but smaller candelabra were made by Elkan for the chapels of King's College, Cambridge, and New College, Oxford, and a seven-branched example was executed for the Parliament of Israel. There can be little doubt that the form, which gave opportunities to both his imagination and his craftsmanship, was particularly well suited to his powers. He was appointed O.B.E. in 1957.

He married in 1907 Hedwig Einstein, by whom he had a son and a daughter.

January 12, 1960.

Walter Elliot, P.C., C.H., M.C., F.R.S., M.P., for many years a prominent figure in British political life, who held office as Minister of Agriculture from 1932 to 1936 and as Minister of Health from 1938 to 1940, died on January 8, 1958 at his home, Harwood, Bonchester Bridge, near Hawick. He was 69.

Entering Parliament at the general election in 1918 as Coalition Unionist member for Lanark, Elliot soon impressed his personality upon the House of Commons. He gained a reputation which was steadily enhanced as years went on and he filled one Ministerial post after another. Fresh from his experiences in the European war of 1914-18, in which so many of his contemporaries perished, he brought to the House intense sincerity, zeal for ordered reform, and a mind at once robust and fertile. His grasp of subject, his wide outlook, and his gift of ready and forceful speech marked him out at the time as a coming man. A flexible and supple quality served him well in debate. If there was one criticism to be made it was that Elliot's wealth of ideas and the eagerness with which he poured them out as he turned rapidly from point to point, detracted from the full power of his argument. It was written of him in his early days in the House that he had none of the airs and graces of debate, that he "attacks instead of wooing his subject", and that "his speech has the jerky, breathless movement of thought". This was true, but the style was the man, and time did not change it, although ministerial responsibility may have abated its exuberance.

Walter Elliot Elliot was born in 1888 and educated at Glasgow Academy and University and graduated as B.Sc. in 1910, as M.B., Ch.B in 1913, and as D.Sc., 1923. He served in France between 1914 and 1918 and was awarded the M.C. and bar. In December 1918 he was elected Unionist M.P. for Lanark.

Office came to Elliot early in his political career. It was appropriate that his first experience of it should have been as Parliamentary Under-Secretary of Health for Scotland (to which Bonar Law, then Prime Minister, appointed him in 1923), since he had the best characteristics of the Scot and a firm faith in the contribution which Scotland could still make to the world. His medical studies had also given him a special interest in all that pertained to health. He returned to that office in 1924 in the Conservative Government which in that year succeeded the first Labour Government, and he held it (the title became in 1926 Parliamentary Under-Secretary of State for Scotland) until the general election brought the second Labour Government into office. In 1924 he had been elected member for the Kelvingrove division of Glasgow, which continued to return him until 1945.

The next phase of Elliot's ministerial career opened in 1931, when he became Financial Secretary to the Treasury in the National Government of that time. This office proved to be to him, as to others, the stepping-stone to Cabinet rank. In 1932 he was appointed Minister of Agriculture at a time when fiscal and other measures were being taken to place British agriculture on a better footing. In this office Elliot found his first real opportunity as an administrator.

He entered it with high hopes and with resolute purpose to make agriculture a nationally organized industry. He appealed to the towns to realize that their interests were not antagonistic to those of the countryside, that their well-being was interdependent, and above all that an economically sound agriculture was of primary importance to the country. He set up machinery to give effect to his ideals. If he did not achieve all that he desired, Elliot certainly earned the confidence of the agricultural community, who recognized that he was their, admittedly candid, friend. While he was in this office Elliot was elected in 1933 Lord Rector of Aberdeen University, and in the course of a stimulating rectorial address he dealt with the theme of planning for consumption.

From 1936 till 1938 Elliot was Secretary of State for Scotland. When the shadow of imminent war was falling heavily, Elliot was appointed, in 1933, Minister of Health, and he applied his administrative talents and energy to preparation for war emergency, including the organization of special hospital services and plans for evacuation and billeting. After the Churchill* administration was formed Elliot, who then ceased to be a minister, devoted himself to various forms of public service. In 1941 he succeeded Major-General John Hay Beith [q.v.] as Public Relations Officer at the War Office.

In the general election of 1945 he lost his seat by 88 votes, but he returned to the House of Commons in the following year as member for the Scottish Universities (Sir John Boyd Orr* had resigned) with a majority of 18,421 over Dr. C. E. M. Joad [q.v.]. In October 1947 he was elected Rector of Glasgow University.

On the abolition of the university seats he returned to Kelvingrove and got in in February 1950 by a majority of 1,224.

His appointment as Lord High Commissioner to the General Assembly of the Church of Scotland in 1956 gave much satisfaction to both Church and lay circles, The remaining years of Elliot's life were no less full than those that had gone before; he was to be found on Parliamentary delegations going to distant places with the zest of a man half his age. His penetrating mind and affable personality made him a popular broadcaster and there will be many who listen regularly to "Any Questions" who will miss his thoughtful contributions, sharpened as they were with dry humour.

In 1919 Elliot married Miss Helen A. Hamilton, eldest daughter of Lieutenant-Colonel D. L. Hamilton, R.A.M.C. While they were in the island of Skye on their honeymoon and were walking on the mountains, a mist arose and Mrs. Elliot fell down a mountain side and was killed. Her husband, who also fell, was seriously injured. In 1934 Colonel Elliot married Miss Katharine Tennant, second daughter of Mrs. Geoffrey Lubbock and the late Sir Charles Tennant.

Elliot held the degree of LL.D. from the universities of Aberdeen, Leeds, Glasgow, Edinburgh, and Manchester, and was a D.Sc. of the University of South Africa. He was made F.R.S. in 1935 and F.R.C.P. in 1940.

January 9, 1958.

Madge Elliott, who died on August 8, 1955 in hospital in New York after a long illness, for many years delighted large audiences in England, America, and Australia as an actress and dancer.

Of Australian descent, she was born in London on May 12, 1898, and was educated in Queensland. During the grand opera season organized by Dame Nellie Melba at Sydney in 1912 she appeared as a child dancer and subsequently played the part of Water in a production of *The Blue Bird.* She quickly made her name as a dancer on the Australian stage, and stayed there as principal dancer in a number of successful musical comedies until she returned to England in 1925. She made her first appearance on the London stage in that year at the Hippodrome in *Better Days*. Later in the year she was engaged to play in *Bubbly*, at the Duke of York's, where Cyril Ritchard, whom she married in 1935, was making his first appearance in London.

Their appearance together in *The Midnight Follies* at the Metropole during 1926 and in the next year in *Lady Luck* at the Carlton manifested all the signs of what subsequently proved to be a fruitful partnership in the light comedy vein. By then she had already shown ability in acting which matched her graceful and expressive dancing, and by the time she returned to Australia in 1932 she had become an established actress.

Her partnership in Sydney with Cyril Ritchard again showed remarkable sympathy and after they had appeared together in *Blue Roses,* they took part in revivals of such old favourites of the musical comedy stage as *Our Miss Gibbs* and *The Quaker Girl.* They were also together at that time in *Blue Mountain Melody, Roberta, Gay Divorce* and *High Jinks.* Married now, they appeared together at the Saville, in London, in the revue *Spread it Abroad* in 1936 and the next year at the "Q" in *The Constant Sinner.* After a visit to Australia in 1938 she returned to England after the outbreak of war in 1939 to play the Prince in *The Sleeping Beauty* at the Palace, Manchester.

She naturally had a sympathetic part in *The New Ambassadors' Revue,* produced by her husband in 1941, and from 1943 to 1945 partnered him in *The Merry Widow* in a series of tours for troops at home, and in Egypt and Italy. They were in Sydney in 1946, playing in *Family Album, Ways and Means* and *Shadow Play* ("To-night at 8.30"), and returned to England in 1947 to play Sir Novelty Fashion and Berinthia in *The Relapse* at the Lyric, Hammersmith, which they later played at the Phoenix and in New York. While there they also appeared in *The Country Wife.*

Miss Elliott had been ill for some 18 months and she and her husband returned to New York, a week before she died, from a long holiday in Jamaica. During the journey she took a turn for the worse and was admitted to hospital soon after she had arrived in New York.

August 10, 1955.

Lincoln Ellsworth, the polar explorer, who died in New York on May 26, 1951, was one of those unorthodox persons who choose to do all the things which by upbringing and circumstances they might have been excused.

He went pioneering with railway constructors in Canada, gold prospecting in Alaska, making geological surveys in the Andes, flying to the Poles, and navigating beneath the ice of the Arctic seas. None of these things was demanded of him except by his own nature, which always chose the solitude and the hard places rather than the cities and the comfortable ways of their business.

The urge which seemed always to have filled him was that of the romantic to whom the unknown is a fascination. He once defined it himself as "a desire to get beyond the barriers of the known world", a taste which could not have been satisfied simply by enriching the store of human knowledge, but which had to find expression in the physical sensation of going to unknown places and enduring the trials which isolation imposed.

He was born in Chicago on May 12, 1880, and as a youth he spent two years at Columbia, but his studies were broken off by the chance to accompany the first survey party sent out across Canada to prepare the way for the Grand Trunk Pacific Trans-Continental Railroad. This party, in which he held the imposing position of axeman, got lost in the wilds of Ontario and had to live on horseflesh until a way back to civilization was found. Later he went with the first of the pioneers to survey the western part of the route between Edmonton and British Columbia, and then for five years was a resident engineer on construction work for the C.P.R., living in a railway caravan which was pushed forward over every new mile of track as it was laid.

His next step took him into the goldfields and then into the Arctic Circle, just after the time of the gold rush. He was assistant engineer to a company which worked from headquarters 110 miles north of Nome. There he spent a whole year surveying timber and mining claims, and afterwards he served as field assistant to the Biological Survey, with a collecting area which stretched from the Gulf of California to the Yukon boundary.

During the 1914-18 war he served with the Air Corps of the United States Army. In 1924 he undertook an expedition in Peru to make what he called a geological cross-section of the Andes from the Pacific to the headwaters of the Amazon. Two years later, when he was about to continue this work, he learned that Roald Amundsen was in America fruitlessly seeking support for his projected air exploration of the Polar seas. The Andes expedition was abandoned and Lincoln Ellsworth persuaded his father to back the new idea. The expedition had two phases. In the first, aircraft were used and the explorers nearly lost their lives. In the second one, the airship Norge carried them across the North Pole from Spitsbergen to Alaska in three days.

When Ellsworth resumed his adventuring in 1931, it was to go under the icefields over which he had flown five years earlier. With Sir Hubert Wilkins [q.v.] he made the voyage in the submarine Nautilus under the Polar ice, an expedition which offered all the possible opportunities for unusual adventure. The submarine was equipped with drills for cutting through the ice and with apparatus for blasting holes in the ice crust from below if this should become essential to the safety of the party. Of the risks that it promised none, fortunately, was realized, and the submarine explorers came back with their task at least half done but without any narrow escapes to report.

Two more years elapsed before Ellsworth, now 53 years of age, broke out again into Polar exploration. This time he went south, again with Sir Hubert Wilkins as his companion, intending to fly across the South Pole from the Ross Sea to the Weddell Sea, while Wilkins carried out submarine exploration in the same area.

The projected flight was not made until two years later, when, in the company of Herbert Hollick-Kenyon, Ellsworth took off from the Bay of Whales in an attempt to cover the 2,140 miles across the South Pole to Little America, the base from which Rear-Admiral Byrd [q.v.] made his flight to the Pole. After a silence of 55 days the party was found marooned.

May 29, 1951.

Sir Arthur Elvin, founder of Wembley Stadium, died at sea on February 4, 1957. He had left Britain on a health cruise the previous week. Though scarcely known, even by name, to many thousands of those who flocked to Wembley Stadium for international, as well as national, sporting events he was the man to whom they owed the establishment of one of the finest arenas in the world.

His dream of making it the leading Empire centre for every kind of athletics and spectacular game was fully realized, and he possessed an instinct for being one jump ahead of others in assessing the possibilities of new developments in the world of sport. Greyhound racing and motor cycle racing gained lasting popularity in Britain largely as a result of Elvin's foresight and the facilities he provided. It was no small satisfaction for him to find that, in spite of the fact that speedway events were unaccompanied by gambling, they attracted even greater crowds than "the dogs". His greatest ambition was achieved in 1948, when he took the leading part in staging the Olympic Games at Wembley.

He had seen the arena become the undisputed venue for Britain's football finals, it had been used for religious mass assemblies and impressive concentrations of ardent young people belonging to welfare organizations with world-wide memberships, and, indeed, it was virtually the only suitable British setting for the historic Games. Moreover they proved a resounding success. Awarded to London in 1939, they should have been held in 1944, but the war made that impossible, and it was not until 1948 that the world's finest athletes were brought to Wembley.

Born at Norwich, on July 5, 1899, the son of a policeman, and educated at a local elementary school, which he left at the age of 14, he sold newspapers and tried many other jobs before being caught up in the 1914-18 War while still in his early teens. He joined the Royal Flying Corps as an observer, and was one of the crew of an aircraft shot down near Douai. Thus, though only 17, he found himself a prisoner of war. When at last he regained his freedom at the end of hostilities his first thought was to get a job, and he remained on the Continent demolishing war materials for the Ministry of Munitions.

Having saved £300, he returned to London, but his small fortune was exhausted before he obtained a post, through an ex-officers' employment organization, as a salesman at a tobacco kiosk at the British Empire Exhibition at Wembley. His salary was £4 10s. a week, little enough even at that time, but more disturbing was the knowledge that it would cease when the exhibition ended. The blow fell about 12 months later, liquidators being appointed to sell the stadium, by general consent a "white elephant". Elvin had never been a gambler—throughout his career he left betting to other people—and the price asked staggered him. But on this occasion he gambled. He secured an option to purchase the stadium, his first idea being to turn his experience of demolition work to good account. Indeed, he actually obtained a contract for the removal of several small buildings. Reflection, however, produced other ideas. Greyhound racing, just introduced to Britain, was gaining popularity, and it occurred to Elvin that the stadium would be an ideal setting for the sport, and subsequently for other outdoor attractions.

By that time the late "Jimmy" White, the financier, owned the stadium, and Elvin went to him to discuss the prospects. White wanted £122,500 for the building, but agreed to take £12,500 down and wait for the balance for 10 years. But as Elvin could not produce the first payment he was helpless. Soon afterwards White, whose affairs were in a hopeless tangle, died by his own hand, and the liquidators presented Elvin with an ultimatum. In his dilemma he went to the City, and was so persistent and persuasive that a group of business men agreed to finance the purchase of the stadium. Within a fortnight the success of the deal was assured.

Elvin sold the stadium to a company, receiving a block of shares, and being subsequently appointed managing director. The first greyhound meeting was held in December 1927 and Wembley Stadium was established on sound foundations. In later years speedway racing and ice hockey became regular attractions, the latter sport being presented in a magnificent new building housing a swimming pool.

Elvin was made M.B.E. and an honorary Freeman of Wembley in 1945, and received the honour of knighthood the following year.

February 5, 1957.

George Herbert Ely, who died in a Reading hospital on September 11, 1958 was survivor of a two-man partnership which, under the name of "Herbert Strang", produced 48 full-length tales of adventure and many historical stories and short pieces for annuals. He was 83.

Charles James L'Estrange was the weaver of plots, the manipulator of events, and Ely, with his ripe scholarship and wide historical knowledge, wrote the books as they actually appeared. He could so immerse himself in a story that he could write for hours without pausing for a word. He had a gift for neat versification, as those who read "The Masquerader", which appeared in the *Herbert Strang Annual,* and the story of the "Failed B.A." at the end of *Settlers and Scouts* will remember. Above all, Herbert Strang had humour, not a common quality in writers of books for boys.

Ely began his career as a reader in the Clarendon Press at Oxford, and served with Blackies in Glasgow before going to the Oxford University Press in London. At one time he was organist at a Scottish church, and one of his choirboys used to say that he read manuscripts and proofs during sermons.

The pen name of Herbert Strang came from combining Ely's Christian name with a simplification of L'Estrange's surname. Their partnership began in Glasgow in 1903, and was actually more than a literary partnership, since both later joined the staff of the Oxford University Press, where they played leading parts in the development of the Juvenile Department. In the middle of the first decade of the century L'Estrange was feeling his way towards an annual for boys. The first number appeared in 1908 as *Herbert Strang's Annual,* and it was the first of what the authors of *1066 and All That* would no doubt have called a wave of annuals. At that time the only boys' annuals were the yearly volumes of the *Boy's Own Paper* and other magazines, but many others soon came into being.

The Herbert Strang partnership, which Ely and L'Estrange claimed to be the longest in history of literature—it lasted 36 years—came to an end at the beginning of the Second World War, when L'Estrange retired to Worthing and Ely to a house he bought in the Cotswolds. L'Estrange died in January 1947. Ely worked for Oxford University Press for 33 years and L'Estrange for 31 years.

In 1937 the honorary degree of M.A. was conferred on both men, who were presented by the Public Orator, Dr. C. Bailey [q.v.], as *Gemina Preli Clarendoniani columina.*

September 13, 1958.

Joseph Emberton, F.R.I.B.A., who died on November 20, 1956 at the age of 66, was an influential pioneer of modern architecture in Britain.

Although of later years his work was not of great account, historically his position as a pioneer is secure by reason of the outstanding contributions which he made in the 1930s to the evolution of modern architecture. He was hampered in his large-scale plans (as are most forward-looking architects) by lack of finance, and by the deep-rooted conservatism of clients; yet he had from time to time his opportunities, and made the very most of them. One of his most striking and important buildings was the clubhouse for the Royal Corinthian Yacht Club at Burnham-on-Crouch.

Joseph Emberton was born at Audley, Staffordshire, on December 23, 1889, the son of Samuel Emberton, and had his architectural training at the Royal College of Art. He began his career in the office of Sir John Burnet & Partners, and in 1922 went into partnership with P. J. Westwood, continuing this association until 1926. The Wembley Exhibition furnished one of the first occasions for larger experiment in forthright ferro-concrete architecture. Westwood and Emberton were commissioned to design several pavilions, which they did with great credit.

In 1926 Emberton dissolved partnership and set up practice on his own account. The Royal Yacht Club pavilion at Burnham, a building which had a definite nautical flavour about it, clean in its lines and economical in its use of space, was one of his early successes. It won the bronze medal of the R.I.B.A. for the best building of the year. It may not be altogether fanciful to detect some nautical feeling even in the Empire Hall, Olympia, for the great plain superficies fronts on to the Hammersmith Road like the side of a ship, with the small windows like portholes. In the middle thirties

Simpsons commissioned Emberton to design their Piccadilly shop; and once more he produced a building eminently suited to its purpose. The Casino at Blackpool was a further big job, as was the Olympia garage for 1,200 cars. For the Gramophone Company Emberton designed new shops and showrooms, with the whole frontage above street level in coloured glass. This building was especially ingenious in useful interior devices and ably surmounted many problems in lighting and acoustics. More recently he designed a group of tall blocks of flats in Finsbury on the northern boundary of the City of London; and he was nominated as architect of the new Queen's Hall and prepared his design, but it was eventually shelved with the plan to rebuild the hall.

In the controversy between the advocates of houses and those favouring flats he was strongly on the side of flats. He held that the small house or cottage was an out-of-date unit, partly because of the virtual impossibility of building it to let at a really low rental, and partly because of waste of space and distance from the place of business. He believed too, in making the most of the new materials which science and engineering had made available, notably ferro-concrete and stainless steel. He was one of the earliest architects in Britain to make abundant use of glass, and once said: "We don't seem to realize that one-eighth inch glass on the top of one and a half inches of cork is far better protection from the vagaries of weather than a ten-inch brick wall". Like all pioneers he was perhaps prone to make too positive a theoretical case (there are obvious social and personal arguments for the small house, for example); but in a pioneer extreme views may be forgiven. And the debt of British architecture to Joseph Emberton may be measured by the discerning in their walks about London and various provincial cities. In person he was spruce, quiet, softly spoken, and friendly.

He married in 1926 Kathleen Marie Chantrey, who survives him with two daughters.

November 22, 1956.

Georges Enesco, who died in Paris on May 4, 1955 at the age of 73, achieved distinction in four departments of music to an extent that has become increasingly rare since the eighteenth century and the ever-growing specialization of more recent times. He was composer, conductor, violinist, and teacher. In the last capacity he won wide fame for what he did for Yehudi Menuhin.

He was born in Romania on August 19, 1881, and very early revealed such exceptional talent that at the age of seven he was sent to the Vienna Conservatoire. He went on in his teens to Paris, where he worked at composition with Massenet and Fauré and continued to train for a virtuoso career as a violinist, upon which he was soon launched with success. He had an easy, fluent style and, though he did not often play in Britain, his record of Bach's D minor Double Concerto, which he made with Menuhin, revealed that although in all outward respects a French musician he was a splendid interpreter of Bach. This sympathy with Bach was made further apparent when in later years he gave some remarkable performances of the Brandenburg Concertos with the Boyd Neel Orchestra.

The Romanian was not altogether lost in the French musician, since some of his compositions were based on his native folk music. Best known of these is the highly coloured Romanian Rhapsody for orchestra, but the Third Violin Sonata has also a basis in Romanian popular music. So, too, has his opera *Oedipe,* which was produced at the Paris Opéra in 1936. Whereas as an interpreter Enesco was a classicist, in his compositions he showed himself in a more romantic light. His later years had been devoted more to teaching and conducting than to the violin and composition. He was a welcome visitor to the Bryanston Summer School in Music, and even when his health compelled him to sit when conducting and not to leave the platform from the beginning to the end of a concert his direction of an orchestra remained firm and his interpretation distinguished.

May 5, 1955.

Sir Robert Ensor died in a Beaconsfield nursing home on December 4, 1958. He was 81.

Robert Charles Kirkwood Ensor was born on October 16, 1877, at Milborne Port, in Dorset. He was a scholar at Winchester and passed from there to Balliol, where he obtained firsts in classical Moderations and *Literae Humaniores* and won a Craven Scholarship and the Prize for Latin Verse. But already in his school and university days he manifested the wide curiosity and passion for exact knowledge which characterized him and delighted his friends throughout his life.

His first publication was a booklet on the butterflies of the Winchester district. But this precocious naturalist was also an ardent Socialist; there must be many Wykehamists of an earlier generation whose first introduction to Marxian theory was through Ensor's speeches in the school debating society. His volume of extracts from Socialist writers, published in 1903 under the title of *Modern Socialism,* has never been superseded as a reference book for the evolution of socialist thought up to the end of the last century. At Oxford his political interests carried him to the Presidency of the Union.

Having, somewhat surprisingly, failed to win an All Souls Fellowship, he joined the staff of the *Manchester Guardian,* but, after a short stay in Manchester, moved to London, where he was called to the Bar by the Inner Temple in 1905. During his early years in London he made his home in Poplar and represented that borough on the London County Council from 1910 to 1913.

His main activity throughout these years was, however, in journalism. From 1909 to 1911 he was a leader-writer on the *Daily News* and then for 18 years (1912-30) he occupied the post of chief leader-writer on the *Daily Chronicle.* His close knowledge of Continental politics and intellectual movements, which was kept alive by the fact that, after his father's death, his mother went to live in Brussels, stood him in good stead in the war years and was used to particularly good effect in a volume on Belgium—a model of its kind—contributed to the Home University library in 1915. When the *Daily Chronicle* and the *Daily News* were amalgamated in 1931 Ensor retired from regular editorial work, though his services were thereafter in constant request in Fleet Street, both as an editorial writer and as a reviewer. In 1941, after the death of Herbert Sidebottom, he took his place as "Scrutator" in the *Sunday Times.*

Meanwhile comparative leisure had given him the opportunity of returning to academic pursuits, which had always been congenial to his temperament. He was invited to contribute the volume covering the years 1870-1914 in The Oxford History of England series edited by Professor G.N. Clark. No choice could have been more fortunate, for it provided Ensor with a mould into which he could pour the rich store of knowledge and experience gathered during an exceptionally busy and observant life. The result, published in 1936, was a masterpiece in which the narrative of great affairs, recounted with scrupulous exactitude, is set off by a series of chapters on the literature, the arts, and the manners and customs of the period; even the changes in masculine and feminine attire find their due place and appraisal. Especially noteworthy are the chapters devoted to foreign policy, with their account of the events leading up to the war of 1914.

In 1931-32 Ensor lectured at the London School of Economics, choosing comparative politics as his theme, and in 1933 he published a volume on *Courts and Judges in France, Germany and England,* in which his close knowledge of the working of institutions in the three countries was used to great advantage. Meanwhile, the development of social studies had made a place for him in his old university. He was elected in 1937 to a Research Fellowship at Corpus, which he held together with a research lectureship at All Souls. The university, young and old alike, was not slow to discover how much it had to learn from his combination of ripe scholarship and Fleet Street experience.

He very soon became a prominent figure in the new Faculty of Social Studies and his lectures on political institutions were one of the features of the Modern Greats' course. He regularly acted as Deputy for Sir Arthur Salter during the latter's absence and examined several times for the School, showing a determination to maintain a standard comparable with that of *Literae Humaniores.* It was natural, therefore, that when Nuffield* College was founded as a centre for bringing together theory and practice in the social studies Ensor should be one of the leading spirits in its organization: this led to his appointment as one of the first group of Nuffield Faculty Fellows.

In addition to his other activities Ensor maintained his interest in pure literature. He published several volumes of poetry. The first of these, *Modern Poems* (1903), contains some vivid pen-pictures of working-class life, as he had experienced it on leaving Oxford. To a later volume, *Catherine*, a romantic poem in five cantos, he prefixed a preface in which he expressed characteristically clear-cut opinions on the composition of the *Iliad* and on literary form in general.

He married soon after leaving Oxford Helen, daughter of W. H. Fisher, of Manchester, and, when his family was growing up, left London to settle at Upper Sands, near High Wycombe, where, with his two sons and three daughters, he could indulge his taste for country life, especially gardening and bird-watching. He was knighted in 1955.

He will be widely remembered as one of the many-sided and best-informed minds of his generation and as a wise counsellor, a loyal colleague, and the best and most unselfish of friends.

December 5, 1958.

Professor William James Entwistle, who died suddenly at Oxford on June 13, 1952 at the age of 56, had been King Alphonso XIII Professor of Spanish studies in the University of Oxford since 1932, and Director of Portuguese Studies since 1933.

Those were his titles, but they scarcely do justice to a scholar who, though the Peninsula was the centre of his researches, found languages so trifling a barrier that when he published his most ambitious work, *European Balladry*, he felt obliged to apologize for his lack of proficiency in the outlying dialects of Europe like Breton; a Professor of Spanish Studies who (in collaboration with Dr. W. A. Morison) provided the first exhaustive account in English of the Slavonic language-group; and (with Eric Gillett) wrote a history of English literature; a man of learning who could communicate to his readers his own enthusiasm for his subject, and whose books, however scholarly, retained a warm and sometimes vivid humanity.

Entwistle was the son of the Rev. W. E. Entwistle of the China Inland Mission and was born at Chen Yang Kwan. Educated at the China Inland Mission Schools at Chefoo, Robert Gordon's College, Aberdeen, and Aberdeen University (where, after a distinguished career, he graduated in 1916), he served with the Royal Field Artillery and the Scottish Rifles during the remainder of the 1914-18 war.

After the war he turned his attention from classical to romance studies. He won a Carnegie research scholarship to the University of Madrid for the year 1920-21, and while he was there gathered material for his first book, *The Arthurian Legend in the Literatures of the Spanish Peninsula*, which was published in 1925. This volume extended the early research of Henry Thomas in *Spanish and Portuguese Romances of Chivalry*, and was the first complete survey of novels of the Breton Cycle in Spain, Portugal, and Catalonia. He credited the Plantagenets with introducing Arthurian material into the Peninsula in the thirteenth and fourteenth centuries, and upheld the priority of Spain over Portugal. In this work he displayed the flexible and idiomatic style that distinguishes all his writing.

From 1921 to 1925 he was lecturer in Hispanic Studies at the University of Manchester, and from 1925 to 1932 Stevenson Professor of Spanish at the University of Glasgow. From there he went to Oxford, where he replaced Dr. Salvador de Madariaga as King Alphonso XIII Professor of Spanish Studies. A year later he added the title of Director of Portuguese Studies. In these 10 years Entwistle broadened his knowledge of the Hispanic field so that it embraced the most widely separated corners, as his next three books demonstrated. *The Spanish Language* (1936) is a summary of the linguistic development of the Castilian, Portuguese, Catalan, and Basque languages.

Next came his most ambitious book, *European Balladry* (1939), a magnificent, sweeping survey of the folk-ballad on the entire Continent and in the British Isles. Nothing so inclusive had ever been attempted before; only a master linguist and a stylist of the first order could have compressed within 400 pages such a mass of material and make it live and glow with the colours of the true folk epic. By this time Entwistle had learned to read nearly all the tongues of Europe, and his extraordinary memory enabled him to connect themes that had never before been related.

In the following year appeared *Cervantes* (1940), a brief personal appreciation and estimate of the great Castilian novelist. In addition to these separate volumes Entwistle contributed chapters to *Spain, a Companion to Spanish Studies* (1929), and to the *Handbook to the Study and Teaching of Spanish* (1938), both edited by E. Allison Peers [q.v.]. In 1940 he was to be a delegate to the University of Pennsylvania at its bicentennial conference, but the 1939-45 war prevented him from attending, and his address, "The Search for the Heroic Poem", was read for him. Printed in *Studies in Civilization* (1941), this address cast an eagle-glance over the heroic epic from Homer to Walt Whitman. For Entwistle an epic had to be based on fact, and it succeeded only so far as the poet found symbolic inspiration in historical narrative.

In 1943 came the short history of *The Literature of England,* A.D. 500-1942, in which both he and his collaborator, Eric Gillett, strove to relate English literature to foreign influences. His last work, written with Dr. W. A. Morison, was *Russian and the Slavonic Languages* (1949). This provides an illuminating as well as an exhaustive treatment of its subject, and once again some of the excitement of the story of language is communicated to the reader in a book where perhaps few would look for it.

In 1921 he married Jeanie Drysdale, daughter of J. Buchanan, of Kirkcaldy, who survives him with one son.

June 16, 1952.

Sir Jacob Epstein, K.B.E., perhaps the outstanding sculptor of his generation, and certainly the most controversial, died at his London home on August 19, 1959. He was 78.

So many battles raged round him that it has often been difficult to give a just estimate of his rank and powers as an artist. That most of the controversies have been irrelevant, on religious, moral, or political rather than artistic grounds, does not make the task any easier, because, whether an artist is over-blamed or over-praised on the wrong grounds, the effort in the cause of truth is likely to be strained in either case. So many silly things were said in denunciation of Epstein that it became almost a duty to say more in his defence than was really believed.

It can be said with some confidence, however, that Epstein was the most important portrait sculptor of his time with the possible exception of Charles Despiau, the Frenchman, and the difference between them helps to distinguish positively Epstein's peculiar powers. To call Despiau "classic" and Epstein "romantic" may not be exact, but it will serve, because what strikes one in Despiau is the subtlety of expression he can contain within the formal statement, while in the case of Epstein it is his formal control of exuberant expression, his plastic command of enormous vitality.

Epstein was born in New York in 1880. In books of reference he is described as of Russian-Polish parents, but the artistically relevant fact in his ancestry is that he was a Jew. It is impossible to judge his work fairly without reference to its racial flavour. Not only was he at his best and most sympathetic in dealing with compatriots but he tended to give a Semitic character to Gentile subjects, and a good deal of what aroused hostility in his work was due to his racial preferences in physical types—his large-eyed and heavy-lipped young women, for example. No doubt he owed something to his admiration for Negro sculpture, but Shem rather than Ham presided over his work in general. As a young man in America Epstein was employed in heavy manual work—including coal heaving, he once said—an experience not without value to a sculptor. He was able, however, to draw and paint at the school of the Art Students' League of New York, modelling in the evening classes.

By 1902 he had gone to Paris, where he worked for a short-time at the Ecole des Beaux-Arts, but found more to his profit in the sculpture collections of the Louvre and other museums, Chaldean, Egyptian, and other primitive sculpture in particular. Epstein went to London in 1905. His first important commission was for 18 figures on the new building of the British Medical Association at the corner of Agar Street and the Strand, a commission that he owed mainly to its enlightened architects, Adams, Holden and Pearson. These figures, carved directly in the building blocks of stone, and completed in 1907-08, aroused a storm of abuse, apparently on the score of their alleged ugliness and indecency, but they were stoutly defended by competent judges of many professions, as well as by *The Times*, as the first serious attempt in Britain since the Gothic period at a true relationship between sculpture and architecture, with the single exception of Alfred Stevens.

As may be remembered, the figures came into prominence again in 1935, when the building was taken over by the Southern Rhodesian Government. It was then proposed to remove the figures as "unsuitable". Since they symbolized human life in general the implication was that Southern Rhodesia was outside the pale of humanity. Again influential people rallied to the defence and in *The Times* of May 10 appeared a letter signed by Sir Kenneth Clark and eight other artistic authorities, including the late Lord Crawford*, Sir William Reid Dick* the sculptor, and H. S. Goodhart-Rendel [q.v.], the architect, pointing out that the statues were an integral part of the design of the building and could not be removed without injury to its effect as a whole and danger to themselves.

Richard Sickert resigned from the Royal Academy, to which he had been elected as Associate in 1924, as a protest at the absence of the president from the list of signatories, and Epstein removed his name from the list of candidates for election. As a result of the agitation the statues were allowed to remain, but the matter was only shelved, and in 1937 their removal was again proposed, this time on the grounds of danger to the public from falling pieces of stone. On this occasion, in the issue of June 23, Epstein himself wrote a dignified letter to *The Times*, explaining the cause of the disintegration of the stonework and offering to advise on its repair. Finally, as a result of negotiations between the Royal Fine Arts Commission and the Southern Rhodesian Government, a compromise was reached by which six of the statues were to be removed and the rest repaired.

Epstein's next important commission, in 1909, was the monument to Oscar Wilde in the cemetery of Père Lachaise, Paris, which was seen before removal in his studio. It is an impressive sphinx-like figure on Assyrian lines, carved directly out of a block of Derbyshire marble, but it is rather overcharged with symbolism of a literary kind. It was followed by another controversial work: the memorial to W. H. Hudson for the bird sanctuary in Hyde Park. Obvious illustrative aptness is not the final test of sculpture—or what would be the verdict on Michelangelo's "Night"?—but it is worth recording that when a small model of the memorial was shown at an exhibition of the Architecture Club, the subject of "Rima" was immediately recognized without any more information than that the memorial was to Hudson. The composition of the carving in Portland stone is not perfect, and with its emphatic shadows, it would gain in effect if the wings of the architectural support, designed by Lionel Pearson [q.v.], F.R.I.B.A., of the firm responsible for the British Medical Association building, had been given depth by panelling, but it is a work of high imagination, gaining in appreciation as time goes on. The memorial was unveiled by Ramsay MacDonald, then Prime Minister, in May 1925, and there followed a most violent storm of criticism. Nor did criticism stop at words, for several times the carving has been defaced with paint, a swastika in March 1937, giving a clue to the nature of the opposition.

The same kind of criticism was applied to Epstein's group of "Day", which, with his "Night", decorates the base of London Transport headquarters, designed by Adams, Holden and Pearson. His attack upon the senses was often violent, but his admirers—and they were legion—held strongly that among contemporary major sculptures his alone were the purely formal artistic values subservient to humane ends.

The last 20 years brought him no respite from the rumpuses that his work seemed to attract as a solitary tree attracts lightning. There was "Adam", carved from a block of Derbyshire alabaster, weighing three tons, and standing over 7ft. high, which fetched eventually £7,000; "Ecce Homo" (the subject of recent controversy and still without a home); "Consummatum Est", a giant reclining figure of Christ crucified; and "Lazarus", carved out of a block of Hopton Wood stone. His skill and ability to produce the startling and the stimulating showed no signs of waning, as was revealed when in April 1957 "Christ in Majesty", executed for Llandaff Cathedral, was shown for the first time: a towering 16ft. figure cast in aluminium seen by the sculptor himself as his greatest act of faith, it indeed was a creation of tremendous power.

Making every allowance for the merits of the monumental works, their dignity and their force in execution, it is possible that Epstein's fame will rest upon his bronzes, his portrait bronzes in particular, works of often astonishing virtuosity. He produced some fine figures and groups in bronze, such as the touching "Visitation" in the Tate Gallery, and the "Madonna and Child", from Indian models, which was shown at Knoedler's in 1930, and their superiority to his carvings on a similar or larger scale confirms the belief that not only was his genius "plastic" rather than "glyptic" but that his sense of form was organic rather than crystalline. As an executant he was at home in all materials, but he did not conceive so happily in stone as in bronze, in which he was prolific. His subjects ranged over nearly the whole field of human endeavour: they include Einstein [q.v.], Cunninghame, Graham, Lord Fisher*, Conrad, all works of staggering vitality, Lord Beaverbrook*, Dr. Weizmann [q.v.], Maisky*, Bernard Shaw, Yehudi Menuhin, and William Blake. Blake's bust, executed to commemorate the bicentenary of his birth, was unveiled in 1957 by Sir Geoffrey Keynes, chairman of the Blake Trust. It stands in Poets' Corner in Westminster Abbey.

Commissions for his work continued to flow in in his last years. The Ministry of Works appointed him sculptor of the memorial for Field-Marshal Smuts, in bronze, for Parliament Square. There was another commission for a memorial bust of Sir Stafford Cripps [q.v.], now in St. Paul's Cathedral, and in July 1957 he was appointed sculptor of a memorial statue of Earl Lloyd-George to be erected in the Inner Lobby of the House of Commons.

Epstein published two books, *The Sculptor Speaks,* which came out in 1931, and *Let there be Sculpture,* published in 1940, an autobiography which was revised and extended in 1955. He was created K.B.E. in 1954.

In person Epstein was a powerful, stoutish man of dusky complexion and markedly Jewish appearance. In personal contact he gave the impression of childlike simplicity—a "great overgrown baby" he was once called with some truth—though he talked well and wisely about all artistic matters. That he sometimes lent himself to controversy is probable, but the truth is that he was the kind of artist who is easily "badgered" into saying foolish things.

Epstein was twice married, first in 1906 to Margaret Gilmour Dunlop, who died in 1947. They had one son and one daughter. In July 1955, he married Mrs. Kathleen Garman, who had been his secretary and model for many of his statues.

August 22, 1959.

The Archduke Eugene of Hapsburg, Archduke of Austria and Grand Master of the Teutonic Order, died on December 30, 1954 in a nursing home at Merano in the Italian Alps where he had been convalescing after pneumonia. He was 91.

He was born at Gross-Seelowitz on May 21, 1863, the third son of the Archduke Charles Ferdinand and the grandson of the famous Archduke Charles, Duke of Teschen, Generalissimo of the Imperial forces in the Napoleonic Wars and the victor of Aspern. His elder brother was the Archduke Frederick, who at one time was the Commander-in-Chief of the entire Austro-Hungarian forces during the 1914-18 War, and his sister was Queen Maria Christina of Spain, so that he was the uncle of King Alfonso XIII.

As befitted the grandson of the hero of Aspern, the Archduke Eugene adopted a military career, which he followed seriously. He joined the noted Tyrolean Kaiserjäger Regiment in 1877 and was promoted major-general in 1893. In 1894 he was elected Grand Master of the Teutonic Order in succession to his uncle, the Archduke William, thus becoming the fifty-seventh holder of this dignity, which dates from 1190. After the loss of the last remnants of the Crusader States in Palestine in 1291, the Teutonic Order, which like the other crusading orders had been founded in the Holy Land, transferred its activities to the Prussian marches, and ruled as sovereign over Prussia until 1525, and over Livonia until 1561.

It then reverted to the position of an ecclesiastical principality of the Holy Roman Empire until in 1805 it lost its independent status and became a fief of the new Austrian Empire. But its chiefs, who were chosen henceforth from the members of the Austrian Imperial House, retained their title of "Hoch und Deutschmeister" and administered what remained of the ancient properties of the order, now confined to those situated within the frontiers of Austria-Hungary. The order then turned its attention again to hospital and ambulance work, which had been among its original objects.

The Archduke held several increasingly important commands before the 1914-18 War and during the war gave evidence of military qualities which were possibly higher than those of his elder brother and which won for him in due course the baton of field-marshal. At first he commanded Austrian forces in the Balkans and after Italy entered the war he assumed command of Austrian forces on the Italian front and led his troops at the Battle of the Isonzo.

According to a law passed after the fall of the Empire by the new Austrian Republican Government in 1919, no members of the House of Hapsburg were permitted to remain in the country unless they abandoned all pretensions to their rank and titles. The properties of the Crown were confiscated to the state and the greater number of the Archdukes went into exile, among them the Archduke Eugene. He settled in Switzerland, and for the ensuing 15 years lived in complete simplicity in two rooms of an hotel in Basle, without even a gentleman-in-waiting. He soon became the most popular personality in the town.

In 1934 certain members of the Dollfuss Government, in understanding with their colleagues, informed him that if he desired to return to Austria and to resume his active Grand Mastership of the Teutonic Order, the Government would offer no objection. The Archduke accepted the suggestion, which he had done nothing to invite, and in the spring of 1934 returned from exile and received on his arrival in Vienna a reception whose warmth betokened the revival of sympathy with the monarchical idea.

At Gumpoldskirchen, one of his estates, the Archduke now established himself quietly and modestly, administering the affairs of the order and appearing from time to time at annual reunions and similar ceremonies of regiments with which he had been connected.

His military rank of field-marshal just prevailed sufficiently with the Germans over his disqualifications of Austrian patriot, Archduke, and anti-Nazi, to secure him a reluctant toleration from the German forces in Austria during the *Anschluss* and the 1939-45 War. In 1939 he resigned the active Grand-Mastership of the Teutonic Order.

In 1953 he celebrated his ninetieth birthday, an event which aroused great enthusiasm throughout Austria. Representatives of the Church, the nobility, the former Imperial Army, and the provincial Government congregated in Innsbruck to present their compliments to the aged Archduke, almost the last survivor of a vanished epoch.

As a professed member and Grand Master of the Teutonic Order the Archduke Eugene was a celibate. He was a fine figure of a man, of great height and admittedly the best looking member of a family renowned for its good looks. He possessed, in common with his sister, the Spanish Queen-Mother, that characteristic Viennese geniality and wit which made him extremely popular with the masses.

December 31, 1954.

Dr. August Euler, one of Germany's earliest and most active aviators, died on July 1, 1957 at his home on the Feldberg in the Black Forest.

August Euler, a descendant of the eighteenth-century mathematician and physicist Leonhard Euler, and a relative of the Swedish Nobel Prize winner of 1929, the chemist Hans von Euler-Chelpin, was born at Oelde in Westphalia, on November 20, 1868. He was educated there and at public schools at Cologne and Aachen, where his father was a higher Civil Servant, and from 1885 followed an engineering career.

While with the Dresden sewing-machine, later cycle and car, constructing firm of Seidel & Naumann he took up cycle-racing and from this progressed to motor-racing. In 1908 he founded an aircraft works where he built machines under licence from Gabriel Voisin, of France. In 1909 he set up a flight duration record by staying in the air for 4 minutes 54 seconds. On December 31, 1909 he obtained the German Pilot's licence No. 1 and in the following years began to take a leading part in planning mail services by air. For a time he was an instructor and many well-known German pilots passed through his hands in the early stages of their careers.

A few years before the First World War he moved his factory to Frankfurt and was the prime mover in the setting up of a German aircraft manufacturers' association. His services both as an aircraft constructor and as authority on flying were fully employed by the German Government during the war but his career reached its peak when, after the armistice, the provisional government of the Weimar Republic appointed him Secretary of State for Air and entrusted him with creating a ministry of transportation, simultaneously embracing air and road transport, but under the terms of the Versailles Treaty his office and its tasks became practically obsolete, and Euler resigned in 1920 when the Treaty was ratified.

The Nazis made several attempts to enlist his support for the revival of German air power but he resisted them all. Since his age was considered to offer sufficient pretext for his attitude, he remained unmolested in his self-chosen retirement.

July 3, 1957.

Alfred John Evans, M.C., who died in London on September 18, 1960, was a great player of games in his time. He was an Oxford cricket Blue and got his half-Blue for both racquets and golf; and once he appeared in an English Test team against Australia. He had a distinguished record of service in the Royal Air Force during the First World War, but won even more renown by his prowess in escaping from enemy prison camps.

During the Battles of the Somme, on July 16, 1916, while on an early morning reconnaissance, he made a forced landing behind the German lines near Le Transloy. First sent to the prisoner-of-war camp at Gütersloh, he was transferred to Clausthal, in the Harz mountains, where he soon found an opportunity to escape. The camp was not particularly well guarded, and he and a Belgian officer seized their chance to cut the barbed wire at night and make a dash for liberty. The fugitives travelled by train, separately by way of precaution and, although his companion was recaptured en route, Evans managed to reach Düsseldorf. From Düsseldorf he went on by tramway to Crefeld, whence he started to walk into Holland, but had the misfortune to be caught when he was actually approaching the Dutch frontier.

Soon after his recapture he was removed to Fort 9 at Ingolstadt on the Danube. The fort, which presented a very difficult problem to prison-breakers, was a "strafe camp" where only Allied officers who had shown themselves confirmed "escapers" were confined. Here Evans found himself in congenial company. Many attempts were made by him and his fellows. A daylight rush across the frozen moat of the fort, which he attempted with two others, failed. A similar effort, undertaken in the dark, gained the open country beyond, but he and his companion were recaptured before daylight. Later he assisted in a tunnelling scheme which was discovered when a thaw caused a subsidence of earth.

However, Evans was eventually included in a party to be transferred to Zorndorf. On the way there he and Lieutenant S. E. Buckley, M.C., with the connivance of their fellow prisoners, made an opportunity to jump from the moving train in the darkness. They were in the vicinity of Nüremberg, and made for the Swiss frontier travelling by night through Bavaria and Württemberg, and "hiding up" during the day. They had enough German to serve them at a crisis, and after 18 days and nights of real hardship they crossed into safety at Barzheim.

Later Evans—he had become a squadron commander—served on the Palestine front. On March 19, 1918, he was returning after a bombing raid on Kutrani station on the Hedjaz railway. Engine failure resulted in another forced landing, and he fell into the hands of Arabs, who handed him over to the Turks. At El Afule he dashed out of a Turkish encampment during the night and got clear away, but became so exhausted in his effort to reach the coast and thence the British lines that he was glad to give himself up. He was sent to Constantinople and remained in captivity for over seven months. However, by bribing a doctor, he got sent to Smyrna just before the armistice with a party of invalid officers for exchange.

He was transferred to the unemployed list early in 1919, the year of his marriage to Miss Marie Galbraith, and in December received a bar to his Military Cross.

Evans was the son of Alfred Henry Evans, who was a master at Winchester. Born on May 1, 1889, he was in Blore's house at Winchester and played in the Lords XI in 1906-07-08, being captain in the last named year. He won the school racquets in all three years; the fives singles, also, in 1908; and the golf in 1905-06-07, and 1908. Going up to Oriel, as his father had done, he played cricket and golf for his college, and was awarded his cricket Blue as a freshman in 1909. The match was drawn that year, but A. J. Evans scored 79 and 46, and took two wickets for 16 runs in the first innings of Cambridge. In 1910, when Cambridge were beaten in a single innings, he failed to score, but took four wickets for seven; and in 1911, which saw Oxford victorious by 74 runs, he made 43 in the second innings and secured four wickets for 76. A stylish hard-driving batsman and a medium paced bowler, he was always of county class and played for Hampshire in 1911.

He had represented Oxford against Cambridge at racquets in 1910, and was in the golf team in that year and the year before, winning his singles matches on both occasions. In 1912 he took a second class in history, and in 1914 joined the firm of Edward Lloyd Ltd.

He relinquished his commission in September 1921 and in the same year was published his book, *The Escaping Club*, which vividly describes his adventures in Germany and among the Turks. During 1921, too, he was playing cricket for Kent and the M.C.C. He had to his credit a good innings against the formidable Australian eleven, and so was selected to play for England in the Lords Test match.

In 1946 Evans published *Escape and Liberation 1940-45.*

September 19, 1960.

David Evans, the sculptor, died on March 14, 1959 after a heart attack at his home in Welwyn Garden City. He was 65.

Evans was most widely known as the sculptor of the Guildhall Giants, Gog and Magog, which replaced in 1953 those destroyed by bombing during the Second World War. Although Evans tried to recapture some of the feeling of the old grotesques by putting "movement" into his sculpture, he claimed that he had steered away from "modernism". Nevertheless, after exhibiting at the Royal Academy more or less regularly for about 25 years, he found these statues rejected.

Evans's artistic position was in fact not easily defined. In a book of reference he has been described, presumably with his own consent, as a "modernist", but much depends on the interpretation of the word. He did not follow the path of geometrical abstraction which makes of sculpture a kind of architecture without function, or even produce works as remote from nature as those of Henry Moore. He might be called modern in his interpretation of the nominal subjects of his art, but otherwise, like most Rome scholars, he fitted comfortably for the most part into the Academy tradition.

He was born at Manchester in 1894 and received his earliest training at the Manchester Municipal School of Art. He won scholarships successively to the Royal College of Art, South Kensington, the Royal Academy schools, and the British School at Rome and made his first appearance at the Royal Academy in 1931 with a portrait bust and a relief of "The Road to Calvary".

Evans was an all-round sculptor, his work including portrait heads and busts—those of John Galsworthy, Sir Hugh Walpole, Sir Arthur Evans, Thomas Ashby, and Eugénie Strong among them—statues and statuettes, in bronze, marble, and wood, but it was in the illustrative relief that he excelled. His work was not conspicuously architectural in itself, but he had a very good understanding of architectural application, and he carried out several important schemes on public buildings.

Evans, who was a member of the Royal Society of British Sculptors, was more remarkable for general competence, good taste, and technical skill than for great originality in formal invention. A noteworthy characteristic of his work was nice adaptation in style to purpose and position. A good example of this is the sharply linear treatment, recalling Eric Gill, of his Nurses Memorial in the Lady Chapel at Liverpool. This treatment is not only most in accord with a Gothic building but also the most effective for interior lighting.

Evans was, in fact, a typical product of the British School at Rome—for which, incidentally, he designed and executed a fountain—which aims not only at good craftsmanship in the particular arts but also at a scholarly understanding of the relationships between one art and another, with a view to the collaboration of architects, painters, and sculptors.

March 16, 1959.

John Evershed, C.I.E., F.R.S., who died on November 17, 1956 at his home at Ewhurst, Surrey, was a distinguished solar spectroscopist, and had been director of Kodaikanal and Madras Observatories in India. He was 92.

He was the fourth son of John and Sophia Evershed and was born on February 26, 1864, at Gomshall, Surrey, in which county his family had lived for many generations. He was educated at private schools, and it was in those days that his interest in astronomy was kindled.

His career falls into three distinct phases. In the first, he carried out solar observations at Kenley, Surrey, as an amateur, in those hours not occupied with earning a living in the chemical industry. He joined the British Astronomical Association on its foundation in 1890 and for a time directed the association's section of solar spectroscopic observers—an enthusiastic band inspired by the great discoveries of Lockyer, Janssen, and later of George Ellery Hale. Evershed succeeded not only in observing and photographing solar prominences with very modest equipment of his own design, but kept continuous observations so long as time permitted. He did in fact, independently of Hale, hit upon the fundamental idea of the spectroheliograph, and "Evershed spectroscopes" are still in use at some observatories.

In this period he found it possible to travel to four eclipses—Norway 1896, India 1898, Algeria 1900, and Spain 1905. At the 1898 eclipse he obtained particularly fine results, which included the discovery of a bright hydrogen continuum in the ultra-violet whose interpretation and rediscovery in some stars came some years later. Moreover, his improved measures of solar wavelengths were quoted for their accuracy by the standard German handbook of spectroscopy. In 1900 he had the rare courage to choose an observing station near the edge of the shadow-track, since this suited the observations that he had planned; again he was successful, in spite of an error in the predicted path owing to which he found himself slightly outside totality.

In 1906 he entered the second phase of his career on appointment as assistant director of Kodaikanal Observatory, South India. He threw himself energetically into the opportunity of working professionally with apparatus more suited to his abilities, greatly improving the standards of efficiency in the routine work of the observatory. In 1909 came the discovery of radial motion of gases in sunspots for which he will perhaps be best remembered. This and other work of Kodaikanal earned him the Gold Medal of the Royal Astronomical Society in 1918. A further noteworthy contribution was the continuance of his prominence observations in great detail over a whole sunspot cycle of 11 years, which was published under his name and Mrs. Evershed's as a memoir that remains probably the most complete of its class.

During these years he was officially charged with the task of selecting a site for the Cawthron Observatory, New Zealand. Further, an expedition to Kashmir convinced him of the superiority of observing conditions there over Kodaikanal. Unfortunately, the plan to establish a new solar station there could not be carried out. His directorship set a high standard and laid the foundations for consigning the Observatory work entirely into Indian hands. On retirement in 1923 he was succeeded by Dr. T. Royds, the last British member of the staff, and returned to England, where he received the honour of C.I.E.

At this stage he might have followed the example of many and retired into a quiet and inactive old age. Instead he embarked with unflagging enthusiasm on a new programme of private observations. He erected a solar observatory in an underground pit at his new home at Ewhurst, among the Surrey hills. It was equipped with some of the most powerful apparatus in the world, some of it his own property, and some of it lent by the Royal Society, of which he had been elected a Fellow in 1915. With this he carried out further systematic observations of prominences, sunspot spectra, and of the "red-shift"—the one of the three tests of Einstein's [q.v.] relativity theory whose confirmation remained the least satisfactory. Impressed by the power of liquid prisms he continually experimented with fresh apparatus, demonstrating that given his skill results comparable with those of the 150ft. tower telescope at Mount Wilson, California, could be obtained. In later years he devoted more of his time to the study of magnetic fields in sunspots.

Evershed was a fine example of the practical craftsman, unfortunately increasingly rare in these days, who could design, construct and use with his own hands delicate apparatus for probing nature's secrets. One might say that with those hands he thought and acted simply and effectively.

Although astronomy, and particularly solar physics, formed his prevailing interest in life, he was a keen follower of many problems in natural history. Moths and butterflies proved to be an important sideline and during his Indian days he made a noteworthy collection of tropical specimens. With these and other topics he could delight an audience with a characteristic boyish enthusiasm.

Evershed married twice. His first wife, Mary Acworth Orr, shared his astronomical interests during a happy married life for 43 years, and wrote *Dante and the Early Astronomers* while in India. She died in 1949; and the next year he married Miss Margaret Randall, of Cranleigh, Surrey, who survives him.

November 19, 1956.

Dr. Arthur James Ewins, F.R.S., formerly director of research to May and Baker, Ltd., died on Christmas Eve, 1957. He was 75.

Ewins will be best known for his important work in discovering the first effective drug for curing pneumonia. About 1933 the German workers Domagk and Mietsch showed that a certain sulphonated azo-dye called prontosil was effective in curing infections of streptococci such as puerperal fever of women following childbirth. Shortly afterwards the Frenchmen Trefouel and Bovet showed this action was really due to the sulphonamide groups which had been attached to the dye molecule in order to make it more soluble, and that a comparatively simple molecule, sulphanilamide, was equally effective. Chemists all over the world then set actively to work to modify this molecule in the hope of obtaining greater and wider activity. But no significant advance was made until Ewins and his colleagues attached a pyridine group to sulphanilamide. This compound, the famous M & B 693 or sulphapyridine as it was later named, was tested by Sir Lionel Whitby [q.v.], who found it was very successful in curing experimental infections of pneumococci. The new compound was quickly applied to human infections and proved to be brilliantly successful. For the first time in medical history lobar pneumonia could be cured by a simple drug; and countless valuable lives have since been saved in this way.

Previously Dr. Ewins had discovered many other compounds of medical value, especially the diamidine series of compounds which are curative for trypanosomiasis and leishmaniasis. One of these compounds, pentamidine, will protect a man against African sleeping sickness for six months after a single intra-muscular injection; and this procedure has been applied to millions of people in tropical Africa in order to safeguard them against this deadly disease.

[A long tribute to Dr. Ewins's researches followed this obituary, in the same column.]

December 30, 1957.

F

Émile Fabre, for over 20 years administrator of the Comédie Française and a playwright of distinction in a particular *genre*, died on September 25, 1955 in Paris at the age of 86.

The son of a well-known stage manager, he was born at Metz in 1869 and his youth was spent in the various cities where the professional interests of his father took him. His early education was, therefore, to say the least of it, irregular—schooling in Alexandria, Constantinople, and Pau being followed by a somewhat longer period at Marseilles, where the family settled for several years. At the age of 15 he was already acting small parts in his father's company, but later studied law, supporting himself by working as a newspaper reporter.

He was naturally drawn to the theatre and when only 13 he acted in his own little play for children, *La Mandragore.* In his early twenties his *Comme ils sont tous* was staged. Then, luckily for him, he sat at the feet of Henri Becque, who, pleased and flattered by young Fabre's obvious hero-worship, introduced him to Antoine, the guiding genius of the Théâtre Libre. In 1895 the latter put on Fabre's second adult play to be staged, *L'Argent.* It was on a theme—the power of money in French political and social life—to which Fabre was to return. Indeed it was one which continually haunted him as it did many other figures, including Clemenceau, of the middle and latter days of the Third Republic.

Encouraged by his success Fabre then wrote *Timon d'Athènes*, which was produced at Marseilles in 1899, and *La Vie Publique*, brought out by Gémier at the Théâtre de la Renaissance in 1901. It was Gémier who finally prevailed on Fabre to settle in Paris, where he spent the remainder of his life. By 1905 Gémier had moved to the Odéon and played there the Baron de Thon in Fabre's *Les Ventres Dorés.* In this powerful play, about the life-and-death struggle of two rival company promoters, the power of money is again the theme; and the social circles of these two autocrats of *la haute finance* are etched in a series of *tableaux de genre* of telling and merciless detail. *Les Sauterelles,* produced at the Vaudeville in 1911, carried Fabre's private war into colonial administration by representing colonial officials, the financiers of colonial loans, *et hoc genus omne,* as a swarm of locusts who prey upon the natives and, notwithstanding the babble about a higher civilization, make the last state of the inhabitants worse than the first.

In 1915 Albert Carré, then administrator of the Comédie Française, retired and Fabre was named temporary administrator in his place, an appointment which was confirmed soon after the end of the 1914-18 War. Thereafter he gave up writing plays and consecrated himself to the guidance of an institution which since its foundation in 1680 has been sometimes the inspiration and sometimes the despair of all those who care for the French theatre. Fabre's reign, which continued until 1936, was notable in that the house of Molière continued to draw large audiences not merely to witness the plays of the classical repertory but to see the new works which had passed the scrutiny of one who was perhaps the most penetrating, if not the most broad-minded, dramatic critic in France.

With his high, bald forehead, sharp eyes twinkling behind old-fashioned *pince-nez*, and goatee beard, he was a formidable figure, and quick to deflate pretentiousness with the icy politeness he could command so well. On the other hand, genuine talent could be sure of a warm welcome from him, and his laborious days spent in the multifarious duties of administering France's national theatre had only one object—to keep alive and develop the French drama.

When he retired in 1936 he was named honorary director of the Comédie Française. He was an honorary member of the Society of Authors and a Commander of the Legion of Honour. Three of his plays, *La Vie Publique, La Rabouilleuse,* and *Un Grand Bourgeois* (the last two adapted from Balzac), received awards from the Académie Française.

September 27, 1955.

A. A. Fadeyev, the Soviet novelist and author, was reported to have committed suicide on May 13, 1956 in Moscow, at the age of 55. He was a member of the Central Committee of the Communist Party until a few months earlier, and a deputy to the Supreme Soviet of the U.S.S.R.

Born near Moscow in 1901, the son of a *feldscher* (a semi-trained medical assistant), Alexander Alexandrovich Fadeyev passed his childhood in Vilna and his youth in the Urals and in the Far East Maritime Province. He received most of his schooling in Vladivostok and subsequently spent some time at the Moscow Mining Academy. Soon after the October Revolution he joined the Communist Party and at the age of 17 enrolled in a detachment of partisans in Eastern Siberia, of which large areas were controlled by Kolchak. Twice wounded in the fighting, with the virtual cessation of hostilities he was sent as a communist delegate to Moscow.

There he began to write. His first two essays in fiction, *Razliv* (The Flood) and *Protiv Techeniya* (Against the Stream), showed undoubted promise, but they could scarcely have prepared a reader for the narrative power and mature feeling of *Razgrom* (Defeat), in which he gave vivid and illuminating shape to his partisan experience in the Siberian *taiga.*

During 1924-26 Fadeyev had edited a daily newspaper, *Soviet South,* in Rostov. He returned to Moscow and assumed a partly editorial, partly administrative responsibility for one of the leading monthly literary periodicals in the capital. In 1929 he published the first of the four volumes of a novel, *The Last of the Udegs*, which was designed to illustrate, on lines that followed the theory of Engels, the transition from a primitive communism to a modern, scientific communism—an ambitious, adroitly sustained but rather lifeless exercise in ideological orthodoxy. It was completed in

1940, by which time Fadeyev had served as a member of the praesidium of the Union of Soviet Writers, of which he later became general secretary.

Fadeyev wrote two or three volumes of literary or sociological literary criticism on conventional party lines. During the Soviet-German war he was engaged, like every other Soviet writer of note, in war reporting and patriotic propaganda; his impressions of life in Leningrad during the German blockade—a graphic little volume, though excessively heroic and sentimental in temper in the manner of almost all such wartime work—were published in an English translation under the title *Leningrad in the Days of the Blockade.* But his principal effort during the war years consisted of a heroic novel, *The Young Guard* (published in volume form in 1945 and thereafter hung with every kind of official garland), and the chairmanship of the committee attached to the Council of Ministers of the U.S.S.R., which awarded the Stalin prizes for art and literature.

Holding such prominent official positions he, in common with many others similarly placed, followed the Stalinist line and when he attended the Cominform-sponsored International Cultural Congress for Peace at Wroclaw (Breslau) in 1948, he launched a full-scale attack on western (and particularly American) literature, which, he claimed, was "giving off the stench of decay".

Soon after Stalin's death signs of a revaluation of Soviet literature began to appear and Fadeyev apologized, in six columns of the Soviet *Literary Gazette,* for giving publicity to a number of "ideologically defective" works, the most prominent of which was Vassily Grossman's novel *For the Right Cause,* a story with the Battle of Stalingrad for background.

At the last Communist Party Congress he was dropped from the position of full member to that of candidate member of the Central Committee, but remained on the board of the Writers' Union, of which he had formerly been chairman.

May 15, 1956.

Eleanor Fagan—See **Holiday.**

Sir Richard Fairey, M.B.E., founder and executive chairman of the Fairey Aviation Company, died in a nursing home in London on September 30, 1956 at the age of 69.

Charles Richard Fairey was born on May 5, 1887, and educated at Merchant Taylors' School and Finsbury Technical College, where he studied electrical engineering and chemistry. He had a brilliant career before him as an electrical engineer, but he chose aviation as a profession and became chief engineer to Short Brothers in 1913. Two years later he founded the Fairey Aviation Company, and from then on both he and his company were in the forefront of many new developments in the industry.

Nearly 40 years after his first venture into what was then an industry whose future seemed uncertain, he was still exploiting ingenious inventions. His interest in light aircraft knew no bounds and he contributed substantially to the vast improvements in their structure and performance over the years. For the invention and development of the wing flap he was awarded the Wakefield Gold Medal by the Royal Aeronautical Society, and he created astonishment mingled with admiration when he demonstrated how speed could be added to the other qualities of the helicopter. The firm also produce guided missiles and in February 1956 announced that their Fireflash had destroyed a radio-controlled target aircraft.

Anti-submarine devices particularly attracted his attention, and he worked long and effectively on the creation of aircraft specially designed to detect and destroy them. He had supreme confidence in his own judgment and skill, and seldom did either prove faulty. Among the many famous aircraft built by Fairey Aviation under Sir Richard's leadership were the Swordfish, Flycatcher, Fox, the long-range monoplane, the Battle bomber, Firefly fighter, Barracuda, and the Gannet anti-submarine aircraft which went into service with the Royal Navy in 1954, and the Fairey Delta II, the first aircraft to fly at over 1,000 miles an hour, when it averaged 1,132 miles an hour in level flight in March 1956.

He was chairman of the Society of British Aircraft Constructors from 1922 to 1924, and a member of the Aeronautical Research Committee from 1923 to 1926. He was also a member of the council of the former organization, and of the Grand Council of the Federation of British Industries. He served during the 1939-45 War on the British Supply Council in Washington and from 1942 to 1945 was Director-General of the British Air Commission in that city, being attached in addition to the joint aircraft and combined aluminium magnesium committees. He was twice elected president of the Royal Aeronautical Society, holding office in 1930-31 and again in 1932-33.

Fairey's first-class yacht racing experience was begun in 1929 with the 12-metre Flica, of which one of the famous Diaper family was the professional skipper. With the establishment about 1928 of the so-called "J"-class—great racing cutters of about 80ft. waterline and 175 tons—Fairey acquired Shamrock V, which he raced regularly with this class until its decline shortly before the 1939-45 War. In the interim, up to the outbreak of war, he returned to the 12-metre class with a new vessel named Evaine. Fairey was at one period Commodore of the Royal London Yacht Club, and he had also served on the council of the Y.R.A. (now the Royal Yachting Association).

October 1, 1956.

King Faisal II—See **Iraq.**

Lilian Mary Faithfull, C.B.E., Principal of Cheltenham Ladies' College from 1907 until 1922, and a pioneer in the movement for the higher education of women, died on May 2, 1952 at Cheltenham. She was 87.

Lilian Mary Faithfull, daughter of Francis G. Faithfull, Clerk of the Merchant Taylors' Company, was born at Hoddesdon in Hertfordshire on March 12, 1865. Her uncle, the Rev. Charles Chittenden, kept a preparatory school for boys near by, and she received educational advantages rare for a girl at that period in being allowed to join many of the school classes. In 1883 she entered Somerville College, Oxford—it had 25 students—and took a first class in English literature, which was not yet a recognized school of the university. The next two years were spent in Oxford, first as secretary to the Principal of Somerville, Miss Shaw-Lefevre, and later as a mistress at the Oxford High School under Miss Soulsby. In 1889 she became lecturer in English literature at the Royal Holloway College, then in its early days; and after five years there was appointed Vice-Principal of the women's department of King's College, London.

Perhaps Miss Faithfull's 13 years at King's College were the happiest and most creative period of her life. The women's department had originally been opened as a centre for lectures to ladies, and she set about making it a real university college. She was successful in her main ambition, and King's College for Women took its place in the foremost rank of women's colleges with a keen corporate spirit it had hitherto lacked. While she was Vice-Principal the heavy debt which had hampered the department since its foundation was cleared off. In the field of domestic science she was a pioneer, and it was largely due to her initiative that the scientific study of this subject later found a recognized place in the university.

Miss Faithfull was an enthusiast for games and a notable hockey player; she was first president of the All England Women's Hockey Association, and largely responsible for the success of the association, and she always recognized the value of games in the corporate life of school or college.

In 1906 Miss Beale, the great founder of Cheltenham Ladies' College, died, and in the following year Miss Faithfull was elected to succeed her. She began with characteristic thoroughness to master the details of the large and complex organization, which consisted then of the upper, middle, lower schools, and kindergarten, as well as training departments for elementary, secondary, and kindergarten teachers, and a university department in which students worked for the London University examinations. No one who had not known the Ladies' College in the days of her predecessor could have been more quick to appreciate the great work of Miss Beale, or more anxious to develop the college in the best and highest spirit of its founder. In due course the music and art departments were reorganized and compulsory medical inspection was introduced. She was alive to new educational theories without becoming obsessed by any one. Valuable elements from the systems of Dalcroze, Montessori [q.v.], and others were introduced into the college curriculum, and so too were post-school courses for elder students in art and music, and training as librarians and Sunday School organizers. Long before the

1914-18 war voluntary aid detachments were formed in the college.

In 1922 she retired but remained active in other fields for many years. She was a magistrate for Gloucestershire—one of the first women to be appointed to such a post—a member of the Church Assembly, and she did valuable work on various educational bodies. She lectured in Canada, and in 1937 ran an experiment in communal catering by opening at Marylebone a cookshop which served cheap, well-cooked meals. During the last war she was chairman of the Food Advisory Group of the Women's Voluntary Service in Gloucestershire.

Perhaps her principal interest during her later years was in housing, of which she made a detailed study in London and other large cities. She was struck by the need to provide homes for the elderly where they could live simply and with dignity, and the Old People's Housing Society at Cheltenham was founded by her with this end in view. It was in one of these homes, Faithfull House, that she died. She was sound in judgment and rapid in decision, with quick sympathies and an unusual power of expression. Her rich and generous nature radiated vitality, while a lively sense of humour kept her fresh and human.

Various honours came to her in the course of her career; in 1904 she was made a Fellow of King's College, M.A. of Dublin University in 1905, Hon. M.A. of Oxford in 1925, and C.B.E. in 1926.

May 5, 1952.

Bernard Falk, who died on October 9, 1960 at Hove, was for some 30 years a familiar and notable figure in Fleet Street, where at different times he occupied important editorial posts and was conspicuously successful as a freelance, and afterwards the author of a number of entertaining and instructive volumes with an historical interest. He was 78.

In spite of a constitution none too robust he stood the pace of active journalism until the age of 50 with a gusto and an assurance that are reflected in telling fashion in the first of his books, the autobiographical *He Laughed in Fleet Street.* This had a sale greatly beyond expectations and made Falk's name familiar to a wide public.

Born in Manchester on August 11, 1882, Bernard Falk was brought up in straitened circumstances. From an elementary school he won a scholarship to Manchester Grammar School, which he left in his mid-teens, spending a short time in commercial office work before he was then taken on by A. T. Spalding, the golf expert, as a beginner in journalism on the *Urmston and Flixton Telegraph.* Six months later he migrated to the Hulton office in Withy Grove to serve as a reporter for five years on the *Manchester Evening Chronicle.* He had an excellent apprenticeship there, and at the age of 21 enjoyed his first taste of foreign travel, going on leave to Canada and the United States.

Round about 1905 Falk went to London and was engaged by Kennedy Jones to work at Carmelite House on space. He led a strenuous life, reporting for the *Evening News,* writing also for the *Weekly Dispatch,* and doing a daily police court column in the *Daily Mirror.* In 1910 he ventured into proprietorship with John Cowley and C. T. Watney, starting the *Week-end,* a paper designed, it appears, to cater for a public midway between those of *The Spectator* and *Answers.* A prominent feature consisted of racing tips by Edgar Wallace, and after a short run the *Week-end* was transformed into the *Week-end Racing Supplement.* In the same year the three men started the *Evening Times,* on which Falk acted as news editor, chief sub-editor, make-up man and leader writer. Though the paper was of a high standard and compassed miracles of economical running, it failed by a narrow margin to pay its way.

In 1912 Falk approached R. D. Blumenfeld and was offered a post on the *Daily Express*; but almost immediately he had the better offer, from Sir Henry (later Lord) Dalziel, of the editorial chair of *Reynolds News.* He was not at ease there, however, and before long had set up a freelance office in Fleet Street. Just before the outbreak of war in 1914 he was reporting on space for the *Pall Mall Gazette,* and with the beginning of hostilities he returned to Carmelite House, working on the *Weekly Dispatch* and the *Daily Mail.*

Attesting under the Derby Scheme early in 1916, he was placed in a low medical category and exempted from service. He was sent to the Far East for the *Daily Mail* in 1918 to report on the Czech legions, and was recalled by Northcliffe to cover the "khaki election" and to succeed Hannen Swaffer* as editor of the paper, now renamed the *Sunday Dispatch.* He remained in this post for 13 years, this long tenure being exceptional on a paper noted for its frequent changes of editorship. He was in close touch and on friendly terms with Lord Northcliffe during the last years of Northcliffe's life, and on the latter's death tried to take up shares in the *Daily Mail,* only to be outbid by Lord Rothermere.

A serious illness in 1929 left Falk less able than before to cope with the rough and tumble of his profession, and in 1932 he retired to write books, not without many an affectionate reminiscent glance backwards. *He Laughed in Fleet Street* (1933) was, with good reason, one of the most successful autobiographies of its kind in the thirties. It was followed by *The Naked Lady* (1934), a biography of Adah Menken; *Rachel the Immortal* (1935); *Old Q's Daughter* (1937)—the title refers to Maria Fagnani, wife of the third Marquess of Hertford; and *Five Years Dead* (1938), another book packed with good stories about journalists, politicians, newspaper owners, and artists. Then came a series of "candid" family histories—*The Naughty Seymours* (1940), *The Bridgewater Millions* (1942), *The Berkeleys of Berkeley Square* (1944), *The Way of the Montagues* (1947) and *The Royal FitzRoys* (1950)—in which a lush use of words and a florid outlook on the past are redeemed by genuine research and a real enough feeling for history.

In 1909 he married the daughter of A. C. Lamplough, and there was one son of the marriage.

October 10, 1960.

Yves Farge, a prominent leader of the French resistance movement during the war, who died on March 30, 1953 from injuries sustained in a motor accident in Georgia, one of the constituent republics of the Soviet Union, had gone to the Soviet Union from France in order to receive the "Stalin peace prize" which had been awarded him in December 1952.

Born at Salon-de-Provence in 1899, of a family of school teachers. Farge turned to journalism as a career, starting at the age of 20 on a small local paper at Isère, and in 1931 joining the staff of the *Progrès de Lyon,* of which he was successively foreign news editor and editor. After the occupation of the "free zone" of France on November 11, 1942, the paper ceased to appear and Farge devoted himself almost exclusively to the resistance, in which he worked under the pseudonyms of "Bonaventure" and "Gregoire". Some time before the liberation he was responsible for calling a meeting of the "clandestine prefects" of the Rhône and Alps regions to study the problem of assuring continuity of food supplies when the Germans withdrew. Afterwards, as Commissioner of the Republic at Lyons, he became widely known for the sternness and thoroughness with which he carried through successive "purges", including the expropriation of the famous Berliet motor factory which he handed over to the control of a council of its workers.

In 1945 he was offered the post of Minister of Food, but declined the office when the Ministry of Justice refused to allow the death penalty to be imposed for "black market" offences. The following year, after representing the French press at the atomic explosions at Bikini, he accepted the Ministry of Food in Bidault's Government and represented France at the Copenhagen conference in September.

Bidault resigned the premiership at the end of 1946, when the constitution of the Fourth Republic came into force, and Farge, whose political leanings tended more and more to the extreme left, published in the following year *Le Pain de la Corruption,* a work denouncing scandals in the wine industry, which attained great celebrity and was the cause of protracted legal proceedings between the author and Gouin, the former Prime Minister. In 1948 he became head of the "fighters for peace and liberty", on whose behalf he launched a weekly paper entitled *Action.* From that period, although nominally "progressive", he was in open political alliance with the communists. In addition to *Le Pain de la Corruption* Farge, who was himself a talented painter, published an essay on Giotto. He also wrote numerous polemical works, including *Témoignages sur la Chine et la Corée* on the subject of the alleged American germ warfare.

April 1, 1953.

Joseph Jefferson Farjeon, for many years well known as a novelist, journalist, and playwright, died at Hove on June 6, 1955, two days after his seventy-second birthday.

The son of the late Benjamin Leopold Farjeon, who was also well known as a writer of fiction, he was born on June 4, 1883, and was educated privately and at Peterborough Lodge. From 1910 to 1920 he was engaged on editorial work for the Amalgamated Press, and during his long career as a writer of fiction he published more than 80 novels. Many of these were of the detective and mystery *genre* and enjoyed a deserved popularity for their ingenious and entertaining plots and characterization. He was a regular contributor to *Punch*, the *Evening News*, and the *Evening Standard*.

As a playwright Farjeon's skill was best shown in the field of light comedy and crime dramas where, although the occasional thinness of his material showed his fantasies at a disadvantage, he could always be relied upon to provide good entertainment. His first play, *No. 17*, a melodramatic mystery revolving round an empty house, was produced at the New Theatre in 1925 with Leon M. Lion and Nicholas Hannen* playing the principal parts. *The Hours Between*, a period romantic comedy, appeared at the "Q" Theatre in 1929 and failed to enjoy the success it might have deserved. It was followed in 1930 by *Enchantment*, a touching and amusing fantasy, which was staged at the Vaudeville Theatre. Another period piece, this time a musical comedy, entitled *Philomel*, with music by Dr. Martin Shaw and lyrics by Clifford Bax*, was produced at the Ambassadors Theatre in 1932 and enjoyed a considerable success. His latest play, a light comedy, entitled *Having Parents*, was put on by the Repertory Players in 1937.

He married in 1910 Miss Frances Antoinette Wood. There were a son and a daughter of the marriage.

June 7, 1955.

Henry Farman, the veteran aviator and aircraft designer, died in Paris on July 17, 1958 at the age of 84.

Though he was not the first to fly in a heavier-than-air machine, Henry Farman first showed Europe that the problems of flight had been mastered. Those whose memories go back to 1907 and 1908 will remember the sensation created by the astonishing feats of the black-bearded Anglo-Frenchman in getting off the ground in his Voisin biplane and flying for ever-increasing distances at a height of a few feet off the ground. Stories of the successes of the Wrights had begun to filter through to Europe, but as they had not been taken seriously even by the American press they naturally received even less attention in Europe. The public had not yet heard of A. V. Roe, who was struggling in England to get off the ground in a machine of his own construction; and the eyes of all the world were turned on the French experimenters. Louis Blériot and the Brazilian Santos-Dumont had both succeeded in getting into the air, but had very little control over their machines, and were quite unable to turn. Farman was the first to display a mastery of his machine in the air.

Henry Farman was born in Paris on May 26, 1874, the son of an English journalist who had settled there and brought up his sons as French citizens. Henry began as a painter, then became a champion cyclist, and later a racing motorist and dealer in cars. The brothers Voisin and Delagrange invited him early in the century to join them in the development of aircraft. The Voisins had studied the theory of flight which had been thoroughly set forth on paper by Sir George Cayley, while the experiments of Lilienthal and Pilcher with gliders, to say nothing of the successful flying model of John Stringfellow, had added practical experience. The Voisins designed an aircraft and set Farman to learn to fly it.

It was the best aircraft in Europe at that time, a cambered biplane with a tail carried on booms to the rear and with an elevator projecting in front. A measure of lateral stability was provided by vertical strips of fabric stretched between the upper and lower planes, much in the manner of a box kite, but there was no means of controlling lateral movement until Farman himself fixed movable flaps to the rear of the planes. These flaps were the precursors of the now universal ailerons, and proved a much sounder system of obtaining lateral control than was afforded by the wing-warping device of the Wrights. Nevertheless, the machine was deficient in stability, and to fly it was an exercise in balancing which was acquired only by considerable practice. The first engine with which Farman achieved much success was a 50 h.p. Antoinette, which was all too heavy for its power. The advent of the rotary Gnome made all the difference to the prospects of successful flight.

None the less, it was with the Antoinette that Farman performed the then astonishing feat of flying a closed circuit of one kilometre under official observation, and by doing so he won the gold medal of the Aero Club of France and a considerable sum in prizes.This flight was made in January 1908. Later in the same year he went on an exhibition tour in the United States, which gave rise to law suits. He returned to France, and on October 31 he and Blériot made the first cross-country flights on record in Europe. Farman flew 27 kilometres from Châlons-sur-Marne to Rheims in 20 minutes. Blériot's flight was not quite so long.

In 1909 Farman crossed to England to compete at the Blackpool meeting, and won the prizes for the longest flight, about 48 miles, and also for the greatest speed, 36.38 m.p.h. He did not thrill the crowd as Latham did by flying in a gale of wind, and his steady lapping round the course was considered rather dull. Farman was always a careful pilot, and never took an unnecessary risk. He was quite right, for the inevitable risks were quite heavy enough.

Having established his reputation as a pilot, and having also made a small fortune in prize money, he began to design machines from his own experience. He concentrated on biplanes, in spite of the brilliant successes of Blériot and Latham with monoplanes. His brother, Maurice Farman, also became a designer, and the latter's "long-horn" and "short-horn" machines were used at flying training schools by the Royal Flying Corps during the war. Henry Farman's designs were flown over the lines in Flanders by both French and British. He set up his own factory and flying school in France and presently gave up active flying himself. In due course a company was formed to carry on his work, producing both civil and military machines.

The Farman passenger machine, the Goliath, served the cross-Channel route for many years, carried many thousands of passengers, and in its day proved the most economical of commercial aircraft. When the French aircraft industry was nationalized in 1937 the Farman brothers declined to stay on as employees, and retired.

July 19, 1958.

Jeffrey Farnol, a full-flavoured romantic novelist, who entertained and endeared himself to a happily more innocent younger generation than the present, died on August 9, 1952 at Eastbourne at the age of 74, after a long illness.

The pleasure in novels like *The Broad Highway* or *The Amateur Gentleman* may be recaptured once again, but for the moment the taste for the romance flamboyant seems to have been superseded—and not necessarily by a taste for anything better. Even those who sniff patronizingly at his novels admit that he achieved something more than the costume and prose style of Wardour Street, for in a pulsing, youthful way he was a genuine enough storyteller. Whatever else his tales lack—usually a quality with which he had no wish to endow them—they flow with untroubled zest and assurance.

Farnol knew what he was doing, and knew —who better?—how it should be done. He told stories which any father—did he but command Farnol's vocabulary, humour and invention—would wish to tell his daughter; and if the daughter goes to bed dreaming herself a heroine as young, rich, haughty, beautiful and tyrannous as Lady Elizabeth Carylon, where is the harm?

John Jeffrey Farnol was born on February 10, 1878, the eldest son of Henry John and Katherine Farnol, and was educated at a private school. He began writing short stories at an early age, went to New York in 1902, varied his literary efforts there with a couple of years spent as a theatrical scene painter, and returned to England in 1910, when he published what was apparently his third book, *The Broad Highway*. It was a winner all the way: it could hardly have been otherwise. Everything the goddess romance could ask for was here—set in a rustic Georgian setting: the rich but thoroughly disreputable nephew of Sir George Vibart and the poor but unexceptionable nephew; the reigning toast, Lady Sophia Sefton, whose hand had to be won—the poor but unexceptionable nephew settling down as a blacksmith's man in the same village as Lady Sophia and giving shelter to a damsel in distress who is, of course, fleeing from the rich but thoroughly disreputable nephew.... But it is unfair to go on; there may be someone's daughter somewhere who has not yet read the book.

In 1913 came *The Amateur Gentleman* (hero: Barnabas Barty, recipient of a surprise legacy of £700,000, aged 22; heroine: Lady Cleone Meredith, heiress, aged 19). The literary reviewers searched for a word to describe it and stumbled on "romantico-Dickensian." But why take the trouble? The story was joyful, the zest still tremendous, and the moral? That even Regency Bucks and Corinthians had to be severely tested before carrying home their heart's desire.

Two years later Farnol published in England *The Chronicles of the Imp*. This, without question, was his most attractive piece of work. It is the glorification of "Let's pretend". The Imp, a boy of nine, may be Little John pursuing "caddish barons or caitiffs", or a Roman standard-bearer leaping into a stream after reeds, who are Ancient Britons, or running up the Jolly Roger—but all the time he remains an engaging hero, and the reason, surely, is that Farnol does not smile at his amusements but shares in them.

Beltane the Smith (who wins back his fair inheritance from Ivo, the "black usurper", after a severe trial by battle, siege, and ambuscade), was published in the same year, and was followed three years later by *Our Admirable Betty*, in which the lovely Lady Elizabeth leads her faithful major a terrible dance, what time she helps her brother, a fugitive after the '15, out of hiding.

From then on, for many years, the books continued to flow. The titles were different (and what titles! *The Geste of Duke Jocelyn, Black Bartlemy's Treasure, The Jade of Destiny, Charmian Lady Vibart*), the periods varied, but the ingredients remained the same and were mixed with the same skill and to the liking of those for whom they were written.

Farnol must have smiled as broadly as anyone else when one reviewer was moved to praise one of his romances as "better than *Ivanhoe*". He may have worn his heart upon his sleeve when he was writing, but his tongue was in his cheek at the same time. He would have asked no higher praise than that a generation which in its childhood read happily every word he wrote can now look back and still recall the joy they then brought. S'blood, they were good. As good as the meals whose preparation and cooking he described with such care and excitement that the most love-sick daughter quickly recovered her appetite.

Farnol married, first, Blanche, younger daughter of F. Hughson Hawley, of New York, by whom he had a daughter. The marriage was dissolved in 1938. In the same year he married, secondly, Miss Phyllis Clarke.

August 11, 1952.

Negley Farson, the author and journalist, died suddenly at his home near Georgeham, north Devon, on December 12, 1960. He was 70.

For something like 40 years he was a recording spectator and sometimes, willy-nilly, a participant in the turmoils of an era of upheaval which began in 1914. Wherever there was history in the making, there, by good luck or by good judgment, was he. Yet he was never merely the hard-bitten reporter content to write flinty dispatches and then pass on to the next revolution, the next war. He had an outward-looking feeling for the underdog and the oppressed, a great sensitivity to natural beauty—he was country bred—and pity for the misery that international folly brought in its train.

All these good qualities were abundantly displayed in his writings, in particular in *The Way of a Transgressor*, which was published in 1935 and which was a best seller of best sellers.

He was born on May 14, 1890, at Plainfield, New Jersey, eldest son of Enoch Farson, grandson of Major-General James Negley, and was educated at Andover and Pennsylvania University. He did not begin his life as a writer but as a businessman, and in that capacity went to Britain, by that fatality that was to mark his progress, in 1914. A month after his arrival he went to Tsarist Russia to secure contracts and in Russia he stayed three years. Having sampled the corruption and inefficiency of the regime, he watched the Kerensky revolution without surprise. Becoming impatient with American policy he proclaimed himself a Canadian and joined the R.F.C. He served for a year, ran a scout aircraft into the sands of Egypt and lamed himself for life. After his marriage to Eve Stoker in 1920 he spent a two-year honeymoon on the shore of a Vancouver lake, living, as he later wrote, by means of a shotgun, two trout rods and a typewriter.

After a successful return to business in Chicago he decided to make his way describing his wanderings for an American newspaper. With this in mind he and his wife bought a boat and sailed across the rivers and canals of Europe studying "a more realistic face of Europe than could be seen in the capitals" and seeing often the worst side of nationalism. There followed a period on the staff of the *Chicago Daily News*, both as London correspondent and as a roving reporter, and when this came to an end he went to Yugoslavia to write *The Way of a Transgressor*.

He was in Africa just before the outbreak of the Second World War and wrote of what he saw in a masterful if unequal book, *Behind God's Back*.

The war, during which he served as an A.R.P. warden and also went to Russia for the *Daily Mail*, produced *Bomber's Moon*, a plain-speaking, closely observed and often moving account of Britain—and, in particular, London—in wartime. The 1940s and 1950s saw the appearance of *Last Chance in Africa*, written after a tour of Kenya; *Caucasian Journey;* and *A Mirror for Narcissus*, a second instalment of autobiography.

He had been living for some time in Devon and though not in good health did a good deal of freelance journalism in his last years. He is survived by his wife and his son, Daniel.

December 14, 1960.

Jacques Fath, the Paris dress designer, died in Paris on November 13, 1954 as the result of an illness which had been threatening his life for some time. With his death the Paris *haute couture* loses one of its leading creators and a personality who has contributed widely to French fashion throughout the world.

Born in September 1912, Fath was intended by his father for a business career, and after attending a commercial institute entered a stockbroker's firm. He had, however, other ideas—perhaps inherited from a great grandmother who designed dresses for the Empress Eugénie—and his real vocation proved too strong. By 1936 he had established himself, with a partner, in a modest courtyard flat in Paris, and it was here that the following year he showed his first collection.

A talented designer, who established a style of his own in a comparatively brief time, Fath was by 1945 one of the greatest names in fashion creation, a position he held until his death. He created special collections for the United States and his models have been shown in many oversea capitals, not always merely for business ends but often for charity benefits. In September 1954 a Fath collection was shown at the Dorchester Hotel in London in aid of child polio victims.

Despite his failing health during his last two years, he continued to take a keen interest in his business, which, it had been announced, would be carried on with the full staff of some 600 employees under the management of his widow, Geneviève Fath, who had always been closely associated with the business, and attended in person the showing of a mid-season collection which was presented only on November 9.

Ultra-modern in his designs, Jacques Fath's early training made him a connoisseur and keen collector of antiques and works of art. His salon, hung with eighteenth-century paintings, and his two homes, a flat overlooking the Seine in Paris, and the Château de Courbeville, where he staged a series of outstanding fancy dress parties, are furnished throughout in period furniture, a lasting proof of his excellent taste.

November 15, 1954.

With the death of the Cardinal-Archbishop of Munich, **Cardinal Michael von Faulhaber,** on June 12, 1952, modern German political and spiritual life lost one whose influence had a profound effect on popular thought in Germany.

Born on March 5, 1869, at Heidenfeld, a small town in Lower Franconia, Michael von Faulhaber was ordained in 1892, but selected a teaching profession. In 1899 he was appointed a lecturer at the University of Wuerzburg, and in 1903 Professor of Old-Testamentary Exegesis at that of Strasbourg, in Alsace. During that period he published several learned books in Latin and German on Christian history. He was consecrated Bishop of Speyer in 1911 and continued to write, especially during the 1914-18 war, with a view to stimulating the social conscience and the sense of collective responsibility of the nation. Two of his books, written in strong and fluent language, *Zeitfragen und Zeitaufgaben* and *Das Hohelied der Kriegsfuersorge,* both appearing in 1915, attracted considerable attention; thus, in 1917, at the early age of 48, Faulhaber became Archbishop of Munich, the most important archiepiscopal see in Germany, and four years later was elevated to the Sacred College.

Because of the close relations between the staunchly Roman Catholic Bavarian dynasty and its highest church dignitary, Faulhaber was, in the early republican period, suspected of reactionary leanings and, indeed, continued openly to associate with Prince Rupprecht and his family; but his upright character, his evident devotion to social tasks, and his established, strong, if by no means uncritical, patriotism prevailed and kept his position unassailed until the Nazi movement triumphed. His great day came when Hitler started his persecution, first of the Jews, then of the Churches. Shortly before Christmas 1933 the Cardinal preached a series of sermons, soon afterwards published under the title *Judentum, Christentum, Germanentum*—virtually the best-seller of the time in many lands. In them he stood up for the values of the Old Testament against the neo-paganism of the Nazis; for toleration against racial pride; and for humanity against nationalism.

The story goes that the Gestapo tried to arrest him at the time, penetrating into his palace; that he told their officer to wait until he had dressed, and then appeared in full regalia, with mitre, pallium, and crozier. Fearing that a revolt of the people of Munich would result from his being taken away thus apparelled, the bewildered Gestapo officer asked him in vain to change to mufti. The Cardinal refused: "This", he said, "is an official procedure demanding my appearance in my official capacity." After a telephone consultation with headquarters the attempt was given up and never renewed. Faulhaber went on fighting, preaching in the great churches of Munich and elsewhere in Bavaria to overflowing congregations, while many waited outside to hail him, and occasionally the former royal family, which regularly attended in the face of Nazi and Gestapo. Later he was made Papal Legate.

During the persecution of the Evangelical Church in 1934 he was the instigator of an arrangement by which Roman Catholic funds were utilized to aid Bavarian pastors who had been deprived of their livings on political grounds, and to this extent figured as the champion of Christian solidarity against the new paganism.

His further publications, *Licht und Finsternis,* 1934, and *Die Sittenlehre des Evangeliums,* 1936, &c., show the same fighting spirit combined with considerable political wisdom. A certain moderation, even in his untiring struggle against the persecution of his clergy, confiscation of convents and monasteries, and mass arrests, was the result less, apparently, of the Cardinal's temperament than of consideration for the difficult situation of the Vatican; for Faulhaber had been on terms of close friendship with Pope Pius XII ever since the days when the latter was Papal Nuncio in Germany.

After the breakdown of the Nazi régime Faulhaber played an important role as an unofficial adviser to the allied authorities. He was a true Bavarian; a good German; and a great priest; and it was fitting that in January 1952 President Heuss* should have conferred upon him the Grand Cross of the Order of Service.

June 13, 1952.

Douglas Fawcett, who died on April 14, 1960 at the age of 94, led an adventurous life both in thought and in action. He was a notable mountaineer, and it was among the mountains of Switzerland, where he lived for many years, that he reflected and wrote upon a variety of philosophical idealism that became known as "Imaginism".

Edward Douglas Fawcett was the elder son of E. Boyd Fawcett, an equerry to the Prince of Wales (King Edward VII), and was the brother of Colonel Percy Fawcett, who disappeared in the interior of Brazil.

He was a Queen's Scholar of Westminster School and gave early evidence of imaginative power and precocious erudition in his first published epic poem, *The Wrath of Ana,* written at the age of 13. For fun and a bet, he surprised his headmaster a few years later by winning a gold medal for Latin verse. But his passion for adventure dominated his youthful scholarship and from journalism he turned to science fiction. He was well ahead of H. G. Wells: his *Hartmann the Anarchist* (1891) described the bombing of London from the air and his *Secret of the Desert* (1894) was, surely, fiction's first account of an armoured fighting vehicle in the modern sense.

His first marriage took him to Switzerland, where he became a well-known mountaineer and pioneer skier. After showing his prowess in England as a racing motor cyclist, he made the first (and probably only) motor-car ascent of the mule track from Chamonix to the Mer de Glace, in a De Dion of 8 h.p. That was in 1904 and it opened a new era of motor roads and tourism in Switzerland.

Living on in Switzerland after the death of his first wife, Fawcett devoted himself to his two favourite pursuits in combination and became a mountaineer-philosopher. His two major philosophical works, *The Zermatt Dialogues* (1934), a cosmology, and *The Oberland Dialogues* (1939), a study of the soul, are in a mountain setting. The distinctive mark of Fawcett's philosophy is the discussion of imagination as the fundamental reality of the universe, and this was first clearly displayed in his *Divine Imagining* (1929) and epitomized in his final epic poem, *Light of the Universe* (1957), which he wrote at the age of 91.

Fawcett was ever adventuring. When at 66 he was making his annual ascent of the Matterhorn he had a heart attack and, with his companion, had to lie up for the night in snow. Next morning the two men went to the summit. But that was Fawcett's last climb on foot. At 68, pining for the peaks, Fawcett learnt to fly and thereafter, year by year (excluding the war years) until he was 84, he would battle with the turbulent air among the Alpine heights, flying his light aeroplane and plying his camera. No more allowed to renew his flying licence, Fawcett became a player in chess congresses at national level. He played his last match at Hastings a few months before he died.

Straight-backed, six feet two inches, monocled, Douglas Fawcett combined a universality of mind with a gentle modesty. He married again, in later life, Mrs. Vera Dick-Conyngham, daughter of Mostyn Price, and was accompanied in all he did by his artist wife, who survives him.

April 18, 1960.

Sir Luke Fawcett, O.B.E., chairman of the Southern Regional Board for Industry since 1952, died on October 25, 1960 in a London hospital. He was 79.

As general secretary of the Amalgamated Union of Building Trade Workers from 1941-52, Luke Fawcett played an influential part in the reconstruction programme after the war. During his life numerous changes took place in the methods of building and these caused the old craft traditions to break down and called for many adjustments, in the course of which his ultimate aim remained to provide the building worker with stable employment whatever the weather and the time of year. As a socialist he held strong views on what he considered were the chaotic conditions inside the industry, being in favour of building being treated as a social service with a good measure of centralized control. A large man and an effective speaker, he was one of the trade union movement's most popular figures.

Luke Fawcett was born in 1881 and was a native of the village of Thoresby in Lincolnshire. At an early age he was apprenticed to the trade of bricklayer, following in the steps of his father and grandfather. As a young man he served on the local organization of his union in Leeds and Lancashire and became secretary of the Manchester branch and of the old Manchester Federation of Building Trades Operatives. His experience as a union official during the period of economies and unemployment around 1931 convinced him that the building worker's biggest grievance was casualization and that until he was granted regular employment whatever the weather he would always be at a disadvantage compared with workers in other industries. This later found expression in Fawcett's work for the plan by which workers could be insured against wet-time, contributions being made partly by the employers and partly by the workers themselves.

Together with his trade union activities went a strong consciousness of the industry's responsibilities to the rest of the community. He frequently maintained that the lack of town planning would lead to the creation of new slums and that the dreary new estates, which broke all the canons of architecture and were spoiling the countryside, had few of the necessities for a contented community. In 1934 he had been elected the union's president and when in 1940 George Hicks was appointed Parliamentary Secretary to the Ministry of Works and Building, Fawcett was made acting general secretary, being confirmed in the position the following year. At first he was mostly concerned with wartime building problems, such as the living quarters for his members working on Government projects. In 1941 he was appointed a member of the Central Council for Works and Buildings and chairman of its sub-committee dealing with apprenticeship.

During his time with the union the building industry underwent many technical changes, each of which called for readjustments in the building workers' outlook; thus a new method of stone cutting, though it made for increased efficiency, meant new systems of assessing work and unemployment for a percentage of stonemasons. His union's long opposition to the bonus system of payments as a means of increasing output arose because it not only complicated the wage structure but lowered standards of building and represented a dilution of strong craft traditions. Fawcett was active in many other bodies besides his own union, in particular the National Federation of Building Trades Operatives. In 1941 he gained a seat on the general council of the T.U.C. and remained a member until 1952. In 1946 he sat on the joint committee which the Labour Party set up to consider the political activities of the unions, and their responsibilities under the various schemes of nationalization. In 1936 he had visited Russia as part of a workers' delegation, and throughout his career he was a supporter of Socialism, believing that the working-class movement alone had the power to save civilization.

In 1947 he was appointed to the County Courts Committee to examine the possibilities of cheaper lawsuits. He was also a member of the Department of Overseas Trade's committee on Exhibitions and Fairs.

He was made an O.B.E. in 1943 and was knighted in 1948. From 1954 to 1958 he was a part-time member of the Atomic Energy Authority.

His first wife, Easter Ellen, daughter of Mr. John Plows, died in 1949 and in 1958 he married Phyllis May Tanner, of Worthing.

October 26, 1960.

The Rev. Dr. E. H. Fellowes, C.H., M.V.O., minor canon of St. George's Chapel, Windsor, who died in a nursing home at Windsor on December 21, 1951 at the age of 81, made the greatest contribution of all the scholars and musicians whose efforts have brought it about to the restoration and revival of the English polyphonic music of the Tudor period.

By scrupulous editorial methods he provided reliable texts of all the Elizabethan vocal music, madrigals, church music, and solo songs to the lute. He also enlarged knowledge of the lives of the composers by his assiduous historical researches. Fellowes worked in a limited field and sometimes said half regretfully that he had sacrificed much musical experience to his life's work upon the Elizabethans. For he began as a keen amateur violinist and an assiduous attender at the St. James's Hall concerts, and it was only a casual suggestion made by a friend at a tennis tournament that set him upon the vast labour of producing his great standard editions of the music of the English Golden Age. The editorial work of scoring madrigals led him on stage by stage to historical investigation, literary editorship, critical biography, and practical music-making with choir, violin, and lute, which he learned to play himself. Within his chosen field he won for himself a place of unique authority, and when in 1943 he became president of the Musical Association he brought to that office not only his specialist knowledge but a wider background of musical culture and a first-hand acquaintance with the methods of historical research. During his years of office he secured official recognition of this, the oldest European society devoted to musical research, which has now become the Royal Musical Association.

Edmund Horace Fellowes was born in London on November 11, 1870, and was educated at Winchester and Oriel College, Oxford. He adopted the Church as his profession and was ordained in 1894. In 1897 he was appointed a minor canon and Precentor of Bristol Cathedral. It was here that his attention was drawn to the poverty of the cathedral repertory and to the lack of adequate texts used by the Bristol Madrigal Society, one of the few bodies in the country still interested in that type of art. These two interests, the music of the Church and of the Elizabethan composers, which were to supplement each other very usefully in his researches, may have caused division in the mind of authority, since he never received the preferment in the Church for which he was qualified. Possibly his zeal for reform towards better service music in his early days and a certain angularity in personal relationships, though he was friendly enough at heart, may also have been partly responsible for his remaining at Windsor as a minor canon from 1900 to the end of his life. He was not, however, without honours, since the King made him M.V.O. in 1930 and in 1944 C.H., and the universities of Dublin, Oxford, and Cambridge conferred honorary doctorates of music upon him.

The work actually done in musicology by Fellowes comprises the English Madrigal School in 36 volumes, the English School of Lutenist Songwriters in 32 volumes, editorial collaboration in the 10 volumes of Tudor Church Music published by the Oxford University Press for the Carnegie Trustees, and the collected works of William Byrd in 17 volumes. These editorial labours have been supplemented by several books—*The English Madrigal Composers, English Cathedral Music,* a definitive Life of Byrd and a shorter biography of Orlando Gibbons. He also published *English Madrigal Verse,* an anthology of the Elizabethan poetry enshrined in the vocal music of the period, and a historical monograph on Windsor organists. Among the brief biographies therein assembled Fellowes has included a strictly objective one of himself in so far as he held the office of choir master during the interregnum between Parratt (1924) and Walford Davies (1927).

Another office which he discharged with characteristic thoroughness was that of governor and librarian of St. Michael's College, Tenbury. Here he compiled a catalogue of its rich collection of manuscripts, which was published by the Lyrebird Press in 1934. His interest in history was not limited to music, since he was the author of, among other works, *The Knights of the Garter, The Military Knights of Windsor,* and a *History of Winchester Cricket.* He was indeed a zealous games player all his life and never missed an Eton and Winchester match. He published an account of his rich and varied life in 1946. *Memoirs of a Musical Amateur* contains a chapter on yet another of his interests, heraldry and genealogy.

It is not merely the quantity and importance of his work as scholar, editor, and author that made Fellowes an important factor in the English musical renaissance, but its quality of scrupulous accuracy and his endless pertinacity. He ransacked libraries all over the country to verify a detail; he scored with his own hand thousands of pieces of music recorded only in part-books; he corrected many errors in previous work in his field and enormously extended our certain knowledge therein. It was through his characteristic vigilance that he discovered the clues that led to the restoration after three centuries of oblivion of Byrd's Great Service. This was the spectacular crown of years of patient and persistent endeavour carried through in spite of the interruption and difficulties of two major wars.

December 22, 1951.

Air Commodore Peregrine Forbes Morant Fellowes, D.S.O., who died on June 12, 1955 at Pietermaritzburg, in Natal, at the age of 71, will be specially remembered as leader of the expedition which made the first flights over Mount Everest in 1933. He was also associated with the development of British airships, the pioneering of the Cairo-Baghdad air route, and had a distinguished flying career in the 1914-18 War.

The son of the late Captain Peregrine Henry Thomas Fellowes, formerly chief constable of Hampshire, he was born in Victoria, Australia, in 1883 and was educated at Winton House, Winchester. In 1898 he entered the Royal Navy as a cadet by way of H.M.S. Britannia, and in 1910 he retired. He returned to active service on the outbreak of war in 1914 and in 1915 he transferred to the R.N.A.S. He saw a good deal of service in the Dunkirk sector during 1917, being twice mentioned in dispatches and awarded the D.S.O. In 1918, while in command of No. 61 Wing, he received a Bar to his D.S.O. for a particularly courageous bombing attack on the lock gates at Zeebrugge in the course of which he completed his mission after he had been seriously wounded by anti-aircraft fire and was ultimately shot down into the sea. He was rescued by the Germans and remained a prisoner for the last six months of the war.

Given a permanent commission as wing commander in the R.A.F. in 1919, he flew at every opportunity although his wounds had left him with a crippled leg. In Iraq and Egypt between 1920 and 1923, he had a part in surveying the plough line across the Iraqi Desert, which service and commercial pilots followed for several years until improvements in navigational aids made it superfluous. He also commanded the R.A.F. element during the Chanak crisis and was highly commended for his services. For five years from 1924 he was in charge of airship development at the Air Ministry and at Cardington while the two biggest airships Britain ever built, the R100 and R101, were under design and construction. In 1929 he was promoted air commodore and became Director of Personal Services at the Air Ministry. From 1924 to 1929 he was Air A.D.C. to King George V.

From 1930 to 1932 he commanded No. 23 Group at Grantham and at the end of the latter year he was nominated by the Air Ministry to lead the Everest expedition which the late Lady Houston financed, and of which the pilots were Lord Clydesdale (now the Duke of Hamilton*) and Flight Lieutenant (now Group Captain) D. F. McIntyre, and the chief observer was Colonel L. V. Stewart Blacker*. On that expedition the authority, experience and tact of Fellowes proved of the utmost value in binding together an extremely varied party.

His responsibilities included flying the chief members out to Karachi in three small aircraft, himself and Mrs. Fellowes leading in a Puss Moth; getting the two Westland aircraft assembled and taken to the base at Purnea about 250 miles north of Calcutta; arranging for daily reports from the Indian Meteorological Office; undertaking reconnaissance flights each day to supplement these; setting up a photographic dark room at the base bungalow; and even forbidding bathing in the pool alongside the expedition's airfield until two crocodiles found in occupation had been disposed of.

At one period he had trouble with the controlling committee at home after the pilots had got into difficulties in the fierce downdraught on the lee side of Everest. At that stage the committee would have called off the attempt. Fellowes declined to be stampeded and in the end his steady persistence was justified, for on the second flight over the mountain the pilots secured a complete photographic strip record of their approach to the unsurveyed south face of Everest.

Fellowes himself did not fly over Everest but on the day after the successful flight flew over Kangchenjunga. The whole expedition and all its equipment except one small aircraft that was destroyed on the ground in a hurricane came safely through the adventure. He had made the task one of great enjoyment for all who took part in it, despite the risks and the awkwardnesses involved in working from an improvised base. World rights in this expedition had been secured by *The Times*. On the return of the party a commemorative medal was struck in silver and presented to each member at a luncheon given by *The Times*.

Fellowes retired from the R.A.F. in 1933. In 1914 he married Eleanor Mary, daughter of the late Colonel C. W. Long, M.P. There was one son of the marriage.

June 14, 1955.

Harry Ferguson died from an overdose of barbiturate tablets at his home at Stow-on-the-Wold on October 25, 1960 after a short illness. He was 75. There was no evidence to show whether the tablets were self-administered or ingested accidentally.

Ferguson was born on November 4, 1884, on a farm in co. Down.

As a boy, his main interest was machinery, and at the age of 16 he made his first venture into the field of practical mechanics. In 1900 he set up a small works in Belfast for the sale and servicing of motor cars and motor cycles. He soon began to race his own motor cycles, and later motor cars, winning several hill-climbs and similar sporting competitions. Later he designed and built a small monoplane and flew it for the first time on December 31, 1909. This was the first heavier-than-air machine to be flown in Ireland. In 1911 he returned to the automobile industry and organized a distributing agency in Belfast.

On the outbreak of war in 1914 Ferguson was asked by the Irish Department of Agriculture to supervise the operation and maintenance of all tractors and implements in the country. This was the turning point in his life.

He could see that the existing methods of farm production throughout Ireland—and indeed, the whole world—depended chiefly on animal power, requiring the use of large acreages simply to feed the draught animals. He could see that the animal was a definite impediment on the road of human progress.

By 1920 he had evolved a linkage for attaching a plough to a popular make of tractor. The Ferguson-Sherman Corp., Evansville, Indiana, U.S.A., was formed in 1922 and this company built and sold thousands of Ferguson hand-lift ploughs with automatic depth control. These were all linked to a tractor as an integral unit. In 1935 Ferguson produced what he called the "Ferguson System"—a combined linkage and hydraulic control system applicable to a wide variety of farming implements.

An ease of implement operation, automatic depth regulation of soil-engaging implements, and automatic protection of implements against breakages by hidden obstructions were salient features of the system.

Harry Ferguson then designed a light tractor, incorporating his own ideas. In 1936 the tractor was being manufactured in Huddersfield, England, by the David Brown Company and marketed as the Ferguson tractor.

A thousand or so of these machines were made under this arrangement but the approach of the Second World War brought production to an end on the British side of the Atlantic, as all available factories were needed for armaments. Ferguson went to America and in 1939 concluded the famous "handshake agreement" with Ford. From 1939 to 1947 Ford and Ferguson worked together to make farming a more efficient and profitable operation. The tractor was produced by the Ford Motor Company and distributed by Ferguson on a nationwide basis. Altogether 306,221 tractors were marketed under this agreement.

The break in the relations between the Ford Motor Company and the Ferguson Company actually occurred in November 1946, although production of the tractor was continued under an interim agreement until the end of June 1947. When this agreement ended Ferguson was left with no source of manufacture in America and a shattered distribution organization.

In spite of this, Ferguson managed to arrange for enough capital to begin work on a tractor plant in Detroit. At the same time he made an agreement with Sir John Black* of the Standard Motor Company, to begin manufacture in Britain, and they formed their own British company, Harry Ferguson Ltd., also at Coventry. This enabled his American dealers to be supplied from Coventry while the new Detroit plant was being built.

The new 72-acre factory in Detroit was completed in the record building time of 116 days, and in October 1948 Harry Ferguson returned to the United States to drive the first tractor off his new production line.

In the spring of 1951 the hearing began of a £90m. action brought by Ferguson against the Dearborn Rotor Corporation, a Ford affiliate, and others, alleging infringement of his tractor patents. Ferguson claimed that Dearborn had broken an agreement with Henry Ford and had tried to destroy his business in the United States. A year later it was announced that the suit had been settled by a payment by Dearborn of approximately $9,250,000 (£3,300,000).

By this time Ferguson was beginning to turn his attention to a wider sphere than that of agriculture. Increasingly he was interesting himself in the problems of transportation of all kinds.

To free himself from responsibility for the running of his by now world-wide farm machinery business, in August 1953 he concluded an agreement with the Massey-Harris Company of Toronto to merge the interests of the two organizations. He became chairman and biggest shareholder of the new Massey-Harris-Ferguson Company and maintained his direction of the engineering design of the Ferguson machinery, which was continued as a separate line distinct from the Massey-Harris equipment. But his crusade for a price reducing economy and the development of his ideas for motor vehicles were absorbing Ferguson's time and energy, and in 1954 he resigned from the chairmanship and sold out all his interests in the company.

Since that time there have been many rumours about the projected Ferguson car and its various components. These have been developed by a small company, Harry Ferguson Research Ltd., in which the other directors are the Duke of Richmond and Gordon, Major

A. P. R. Rolt and A. J. Sheldon. In addition to a complete car, an automatic transmission and an unusual type of supension are claimed to offer advantages over current design, but no public demonstrations have been given of their capabilities nor have any official descriptions been issued. Negotiations with the leading firms in the motor industry are known to have taken place with a view to their adopting the Ferguson designs, but Harry Ferguson himself did not live to see any of these plans come to fruition.

He married in 1913 Mary Adelaide, daughter of Adam Watson, of Dromore. There was one daughter of the marriage.

October 26, 1960.

The death of **Rachel Ferguson,** which occurred on November 26, 1957 at the age of 64, removed from our midst a writer of charm, fine balance, and pretty wit, who though she never reached the larger public, national or international, scored considerable success with such novels as *The Brontës went to Woolworth's, A Harp in Lowndes Square,* and *A Footman for the Peacock.*

Rachel Ferguson was born at Hampton Wick on October 18, 1893, the younger daughter of Robert N. R. Ferguson, a Treasury official, and his wife, Rose Geraldine Cumberbatch. She was the granddaughter of Dr. Robert Ferguson, physician extraordinary to Queen Victoria. After an infancy spent at Teddington, Rachel Ferguson was taken at 13 to that Kensington whose annals she was later to write with such wit and polish. She was educated at two private schools there and "finished" with two years at an English school in Florence. She had been writing from her earliest years, but her first public activity, as a girl, was an enthusiastic collaboration in the woman suffrage agitation. She knew all the Women's Social and Political Union leaders, made banners, marched in processions, and at 17 wrote a one-act play with Irene MacLeod for the militants. In the same year she was co-founder of the juvenile branch of the W.S.P.U.

After studying secretarial work at Kensington College she entered the Academy of Dramatic Art in 1911, and after two years there left with the certificate of honour and went on the stage. She played at His Majesty's with Tree, at the Court Theatre with the Irish Players, and had a taste of both revue and grand opera; but after some three years abandoned the stage, as it seemed to offer no future. During the First World War she made bandages daily at a local depot, worked in three canteens, and was a member of the Women's Volunteer Reserve. She wrote a sprightly skit in dramatic form on these feminine activities, and when produced it made even the victims laugh.

During 1919-20 Miss Ferguson was co-dramatic critic for the *Sunday Chronicle,* writing as "Columbine". She became a specialist in play parodies, for which she proved to have a wicked and delightful talent. Her one-act play, *The Pridlington Touch,* was produced at an all-star matinée before Queen Mary in 1923. She began to contribute to *Punch* in 1925, and continued this work until the end of Sir Owen Seaman's editorship, becoming well known and much appreciated as "Rachel". Some of her best work in this kind was collected into volume form as *Nymphs and Satires* in 1932.

Miss Ferguson's first novel, *False Goddesses,* appeared in 1923, and thereafter she produced a very considerable amount of fiction, including *Popularity's Wife, Alas, Poor Lady,* and *The Brontës went to Woolworth's,* which last, published in 1931, really established her in public regard. She had a quiet, gentle, and utterly feminine touch, specializing in the depiction of the well-to-do late Victorian family and in domestic comedy in general. Much of what she wrote was suffused with an all-pervasive humour that could be by turns acrid and tender. She was not a deep philosopher, but had a quality of inspired common sense that was singularly attractive. This appeared above all in her book *Passionate Kensington* (1939), the title of which derived from *Punch's* "Passionate Brompton" joke of the nineties. The volume took the reader through a year's life in the royal borough; but it had, in fact, far more than a local interest, being a splendid "dipping" book, full of mellow wisdom on circuses, ghosts, clubs, the acting of George Arliss, books, plays, and a hundred other subjects. She wrote again of Kensington in *Royal Borough* (1950), which was a popular success.

Her later published works included *Sea Front* (1954), a half-satirical, half-affectionate account of a seaside town, Whitecliff, a hybrid in which something of Brighton, Hastings, Eastbourne, and Folkestone was recognizable.

Miss Ferguson was an accomplished pianist, and amused herself by the drawing of caricatures. Politically she was an intelligent Conservative, fearing regimentation and undue mechanization, and holding fast by the more generous and spacious aspects of our national upper middle-class life. She was devoted to the cause of the decayed gentlewoman (the novel *Alas, Poor Lady* showed one way in which decay set in) and to the welfare of performing animals, writing a pamphlet, *Kindness or the Goad of Fear?* for the Performing Animals' Defence League in 1924.

December 2, 1957.

Professor Enrico Fermi, whose work in the nuclear field contributed much to the harnessing of atomic energy and the development of the atomic bomb, died on November 28, 1954 in Chicago aged 53. He had been for the last eight years Professor of Physics at the University of Chicago's institute for nuclear studies.

He had been ill for some time but his death came as a shock to the members of the Atomic Energy Commission and to his associates in the institute. In mourning his loss the chairman of the commission, L. Strauss, spoke of him as one of the world's greatest atomic scientists, and in a message to Mrs. Fermi President Einaudi*, of Italy, said that Fermi had linked his name for centuries to come with the progress of science.

He was quiet and unassuming in his ways and rarely made any statements about public issues, but two months before he died he engaged in spirited public defence of Dr. J. R. Oppenheimer* (whom the Atomic Energy Commission had denied further access to restricted information on the ground that he was a bad security risk) and of the staff of the Los Alamos atomic laboratory in New Mexico, of which Oppenheimer was the wartime director. His statement was provoked by allegations in a book, just then published, that the laboratory deliberately delayed work for the development of a hydrogen bomb.

Enrico Fermi was born at Rome in September 1901, and studied at Göttingen, Leyden, and Pisa, where in 1922 he took his Ph.D. Two years later he started his career as a lecturer in theoretical physics at the University of Florence, and in 1926, at the early age of 25, he was called to the chair of physics of Rome University as a full professor. In that capacity Fermi investigated the theory and mechanics of the quantum, and contiguous subjects in the field of theoretical and mathematical physics, such as atomic structure and behaviour. He demonstrated the fact that the bombardment of elements by neutrons causes transmutations; thus he synthetized transuranium, the element No. 93, by bombarding uranium with neutrons. He became internationally known by his transformation of statistical mechanics—based upon the quantum theory—and by elaborating a system since called "Fermistatistics".

Consequently scientific awards and honours began to come to him at an early age. In 1929 he was made a member of the Italian Academy; the academies of Turin and Leningrad conferred their corresponding membership upon him; and when, after 12 years, he gave up his chair in Rome and went to the United States he had already turned from his previous main endeavour, the making of artificial radioactive substances, to that other, subsequently vitally important, one of harnessing atomic energy. In the same year, 1938, he received the Nobel Prize in physics, and in 1939 he was made professor of physics at New York's Columbia University.

Apart from his teaching and research work there, he was soon to play an important role in the development of the atomic bomb. During the war he was responsible for the first nuclear reactor that was built in the United States, and in 1945 he was appointed a member of the group of scientists who served as post-war atomic advisers to the Government. He was later transferred to Los Alamos as chief of the advanced physics department.

Fermi received in 1942 the Hughes Medal of Britain's Royal Society, and in 1947 the Franklin Medal was conferred on him by the Franklin Institute. The culmination of several awards and honours bestowed on him was the announcement by the American Atomic Energy Commission earlier in November 1954 that its first special award in the nuclear field would go to him. In recent years Fermi had been investigating the nature of elementary particles, particularly the nature of the meson, a particle of approximately 200 times the mass of the electron, that transmits the forces binding the nucleus together.

He married in 1928 Laura Capon, by whom he had two children.

November 29, 1954.

Kathleen Ferrier, C.B.E., the contralto singer, died in hospital in London on October 8, 1953, at the early age of 41, cutting prematurely short a career of the greatest distinction which contributed much, but still had much to contribute, to the musical life of Britain and indeed beyond it.

Her work was interrupted by illness a year or two ago but it was not till her performance of Orpheus at Covent Garden in February 1953 that a recurrence compelled her to give up the opera after two performances. Her career was romantic even by story-book standards. She was born in Lancashire on April 22, 1912, the daughter of a schoolmaster, and began her working life as a telephonist in Blackburn Post Office. Her music at this time was centred on the piano, at which she was sufficiently proficient to win prizes at competition festivals, and for nine years she was in demand as an accompanist.

At a local festival she listened to a singing class and lightheartedly said she could do better than any of them. A wager was laid and she entered for the next Carlisle Festival and won. The adjudicator called her aside and advised her to take up singing as a career. She worked for a time with Dr. J. E. Hutchinson, of Newcastle, and began to sing in oratorio. She was advised by Sir Malcolm Sargent* to take the big step of going to London, where she put herself under the tuition of Roy Henderson and sang as her first engagement in *Messiah* in Westminster Abbey in 1943. In a very short time she found herself at the top of the tree.

The qualities that took her there were a voice of great natural beauty, a patent sincerity of character which was reflected in her art, intelligence in study, and conscientiousness in executing whatever music she undertook to sing. She was lucky in her teachers, for teachers often destroy natural art even when they do not spoil the voices they attempt to train, for one of the most pleasing features of her singing was its apparent naturalness—she could thus sing folk-songs acceptably, as few trained professionals can do.

The bulk of her work was of course oratorio, and her singing of the Angel in *The Dream of Gerontius* will not be forgotten by any who heard it. But she entered also the fields of opera and recital. In 1946 she sang Lucretia in Britten's [d. 1976] *The Rape of Lucretia* and the next year Orpheus in Gluck's opera—both in the Glyndebourne Theatre. At the first Edinburgh Festival she sang in Mahler's *Das Lied von der Erde* with Dr. Bruno Walter* conducting. That great Mahlerian (indeed he acclaimed her as "one of the greatest singers of all time") was so impressed by her performance that he invited her to New York to repeat it and joined with her as accompanist in a number of Lieder recitals. By now she had become an "international celebrity" who appeared at the big Continental festivals—Amsterdam, Salzburg, Vienna, Milan—as well as regularly at the English festivals. She had sung at all the Edinburgh Festivals until the last, when she was prevented by illness. Her singing of Orpheus at Covent Garden was the crown as, alas, it was the end of her career.

In few executant musicians have qualities of mind and character been combined to produce so fine an art. She was unspoiled by success, and her attitude to the composers whose music she was interpreting was that of a servant. Her singing had not the ponderousness that often besets contraltos: it was vibrant and illuminated by insight.

Her contribution to our music for hardly more than a brief 10 years was such that its recognition by her appointment as C.B.E. in the 1953 New Year Honours was acclaimed as most just and timely, as also was the award in June of the Gold Medal of the Royal Philharmonic Society.

October 9, 1953.

Lion Feuchtwanger, the novelist, died in hospital in Los Angeles in December 1958. He was 74.

Feuchtwanger's death removes a memorable literary figure from the European scene. In an age when the historical novel was suffering under a profound slump Feuchtwanger found means to revivify it by a new technique and a finer colour, so that *Jew Süss* burst upon the English-speaking world as a manifestation of something wholly exceptional.

Born at Munich in 1884, of Jewish parentage, Feuchtwanger had what he described as "a dreary schooling", little related to after needs in life. While at school he wrote, and had performed, a boys' play celebrating the birthday of a prince. He pursued higher studies in philosophy and literary history at Munich and Berlin, under Erich Schmidt, Müncker, and Count Hartling, eventually taking his Ph.D.

In 1912 Feuchtwanger married Martha Löffler, of Munich, and the couple went to live abroad, spending much time on the Riviera, in Calabria, and in Sicily, living well when some successful literary work provided the wherewithal, and cheerfully putting up with poverty at other times. The declaration of war in 1914 found them in Tunis, so Feuchtwanger was interned. His wife soon contrived to smuggle him out through Italy to Germany, and he went into the Army, but not for long.

His play *Warren Hastings* (1916) was more popular in neutral countries than in Germany; *Prisoners of War* found its way to France, where it was published by Paul Reboux in the *Journal du Peuple;* a courageous adaptation of Aristophanes' *Peace* to modern conditions also aroused storms in Germany; but, on the other hand, an Indian play, *Vasantasena,* was played in that country more than 2,000 times.

For some time after the war Feuchtwanger pursued his literary career in his native Munich. He was largely preoccupied by political themes, taking up an ultra-radical attitude. Nevertheless he offended not only the military-minded section of the populace but the radicals as well, and they several times intervened to prevent the performance of his play *Thomas Wendt.* This play had considerable influence on the younger school of German writers. Feuchtwanger was perpetually involved in controversies, and made so many enemies in Munich that he eventually removed to Berlin. *Jew Süss,* his first novel, was published in Munich in 1925 and in London towards the end of 1927 finely translated by Willa and Edwin Muir [q.v.].

The critical world in Britain at once decided (and with good reason) that a new writer of splendid endowments had appeared, and the book was five times reprinted in its first four months.

Its effects were obtained more by narrative than by dialogue, and its method alternated between a wide bird's-eye view and a closely detailed description obviously founded on long and deep historical research. *The Ugly Duchess,* which followed in English in 1928, was rather less successful.

Meanwhile Feuchtwanger was going on with his dramatic work. *The Petroleum Islands,* produced at the Deutsche Schauspielhaus, Hamburg, in November 1927 was a kind of modernized *Ugly Duchess* in the expressionist manner, played to a ragtime accompaniment. *Calcutta, May 4* (which was *Warren Hastings* under another title), made the most of the dramatic events of that statesman's career when played at the State Theatre, Berlin, in June 1928. (It was eventually seen at the Cambridge Festival Theatre in October 1930). *Jew Süss* was given as a play at the Duke of York's Theatre in 1929, with Matheson Lang in the name part, and *The Ugly Duchess* (adapted by Vera Beringer) at the Arts Theatre in the following May.

Another novel of the highest interest was *Success,* the English translation of which appeared in November 1930. This book applied to the Germany of 1920 to 1923 the methods used for the eighteenth century in *Jew Süss,* and was a picture of political corruption and intrigue and social upheaval and unrest during the period of the inflation. Here again personal histories of obscure or eminent characters were very skilfully interwoven with the general tapestry of the time. The whole thing was realized with the utmost particularity and actuality. *The Oppermanns* (1933) continued the modern German social commentary, while *Josephus* (1932), *The Jew of Rome* (1935), and *The False Nero* (1937) went back into the classical past.

As could be well seen from *Success,* Feuchtwanger was no friend to the rising Nazi power, not only because of his race but because of his liberal opinions. Early in 1933 he was in America, where he made sundry disparaging pronouncements about Hitler. He returned to Switzerland to find that the Nazis had visited his Grünewald villa, stolen his car and the manuscript of a sequel to *Josephus,* destroyed his library, and had even gone to the extent of killing his domestic pets and trampling his flowerbeds. He was thenceforward a refugee. Deprived of his German citizenship in August

1933, he lived first in Switzerland and then in Paris, producing in the latter place the novel *Paris Gazette* (1940), an unidealized version of the life of the intellectual refugees, grimly sincere but too much dominated by a thesis.

After a period of imprisonment in the South of France Feuchtwanger reached the United States in 1942, and at once resumed an activity which, though still both scholarly and imaginative, never again touched the heights of his earlier years.

To sum up, he was a well-balanced intellectual writer whose fiction was built up from profound and careful historical research. There have been, of course, many others equally conscientious; but seldom has the past been recreated so vividly not as a matter of text-books but of striving, intriguing, loving human beings, as by this German Jew.

December 23, 1958.

Isobel Field, the stepdaughter of Robert Louis Stevenson, died at her home in California on June 26, 1953 at the age of 94.

She was the daughter of Fanny Osbourne, who, after her divorce from her first husband, married Stevenson. In her autobiography, *This Life I've Loved,* which was published in 1937, Isobel Field described the first appearance of Stevenson in her life at Grez-sur-Loing, an artists' holiday haunt: "standing in the opening, the lights from the hanging lamps showing up his figure like a portrait painted against a black background, stood a young man, slender, dark, with a high colour and yellow hair worn rather long. He was leaning forward, staring with a sort of surprised admiration at Fanny Osbourne".

This event would appear to have occurred in 1879, when Fanny Osbourne, having left her husband in America, had come to Europe with her three children, and, after the death of her youngest child at Antwerp, had migrated to Paris. Not long after this, Isobel Osbourne, herself an artist, married another artist, Joe Strong, against her mother's wishes. She and her husband left for San Francisco, where they were welcomed by her father and began "a happy-go-lucky, jolly life".

They left San Francisco, however, to avoid too much society and went to live in Honolulu, making a great friend of King Kalakaua and his family. Stevenson arrived there some years later, during his voyage on the Casco, and persuaded her, much against her will and tears and arguments, to meet him at Sydney. There she went to find that Stevenson's instructions on her behalf had not reached the bank, and she and her son Austin were stranded. She found a friend, however, and survived until, when the Stevensons eventually arrived, she was persuaded finally to make her home with theirs at Vailima. "I want a home", Stevenson said to her in a heart-to-heart talk at Sydney, "and a family, *my* family, round me".

Her second husband was Salisbury Field.

June 29, 1953.

Marshall Field, grandson of the founder of the famous department store in Chicago, and a prominent Liberal and friend of Great Britain, died on November 8, 1956 in hospital in New York at the age of 63.

He was born in Chicago on September 28, 1893, at a time when the name of Marshall Field was almost the best known in the city for the vast store in its heart, the Loop, supplying the wants of all on an extensive scale and dealing only in the highest class of goods. Yet most of his early life was spent in Britain, where he had many friends and some relatives. And it was there that he received his education.

His father, who was known as Marshall Field, Junior, had died suddenly and the son was then sent to England, where he went to Eton and Trinity College, Cambridge. His aunt was at that time the wife of Sir David Beatty, who later became the first Earl Beatty. During those years he learnt to love England and its people and might well have been content to settle there. But the claims of the family business and the interests of the Field family demanded his presence and continued residence in the United States.

When the United States declared war in 1917 he joined up at once, being one of the first to do so, and became a private in the 1st Illinois Cavalry. He was then transferred to the 122nd Field Artillery, of the 33rd Division, and was soon promoted to the rank of captain. He crossed to France in March 1918 and it was not long before his unit was up at the front. He took part in the extensive operations carried out by the American Army, after it took over a sector of its own, in the St. Mihiel salient and on the Meuse-Argonne front. There he was in the rapid advance which immediately preceded the Armistice. He was discharged in February of the following year.

With his English connexions he had for many years proved one of the best friends Britain had in the United States. He showed that in a variety of ways, without surrendering in the least any of his pride in being an American, but his great opportunity came when war broke out in 1939. During the summer and autumn of 1940 young British children were being sent out to America to live in homes there while the war continued and the air bombing attacks on the cities and towns became more intensive. He undertook the chairmanship of the committee in New York to look after these children when they arrived. He performed his duties in no perfunctory fashion, for he was always early at hand when the ships arrived with the children.

He had for long been troubled by the isolationist and anti-British attitude of the *Chicago Tribune,* Colonel McCormick's [q.v.] powerful newspaper, and decided in 1941 to make a strong challenge by founding a rival newspaper, the *Chicago Sun,* pro-British and Liberal in its principles. The first number was published on December 1, 1941, with a strong staff. Field had already had some experience of newspaper publishing with the New York afternoon paper *P.M.*, and it was something of a triumph that his *Chicago Sun* succeeded in establishing itself against the great resources and enterprise of the McCormick interests. The *Sun* went from strength to strength and Field succeeded in 1948 in buying the *Chicago Times* and merging the two papers. Meanwhile the New York *P.M.* had got into difficulties and Field sold the controlling interest. Two years later he resigned from the presidency of the *Chicago Sun-Times* in favour of his son, who had been assistant to the publisher of the paper.

November 9, 1956.

Marjorie Fielding, the actress, died in London on December 28, 1956. She was born in Gloucester in 1892, the daughter of John Fielding, and she was educated at Cheltenham Ladies' College, where she studied voice production. In 1913 she began in a tour of *His House in Order* a career that was to mark her out as an accomplished player of a particular line of part, a line of high comedy even where the play as a whole, Charles Morgan's [q.v.] *The River Line* for example, had a strongly dramatic pattern. There, as in Douglas Home's *The Chiltern Hundreds* and in a tiny part in the film version of Maugham's [q.v.] *Sanatorium* she spoke up admirably in defence of sanity, practising the tolerance she believed in but never preaching it, a woman as disinclined to exert herself in her own interests as she was ready and determined to protect those of her friends. After the first World War, in which she was engaged in munitions work, she spent some time touring and then in 1924 joined the company of the Bristol Little Theatre. Two years later she joined the Repertory Company at the Playhouse, Liverpool, and stayed there until 1934.

She first appeared in London in July 1932 as Mrs. Phelps in *The Silver Cord.* Later she accompanied Gladys Cooper* and Raymond Massey in a tour of Canada and the United States, playing Hannah Linden in *The Shining Hour* in Toronto, New York and, on her return, at the St. James's Theatre, London. In the 1930s she was constantly in demand on the West End stage, but she is perhaps most generally remembered for her performances as Mildred Royd in both *Quiet Wedding* and *Quiet Week-End.*

The completeness with which Marjorie Fielding could bring characters to life was probably the chief cause of her success in these parts, of whatever size the parts might actually be. The woman before us seemed to be engaged in her daily round, rudely or absurdly though it might be interrupted. The events of the play were things that befell her, things that marked the course of a notably difficult or hilarious evening. They did not make up the whole of it or deflect her more than the breadth of one grey hair from her normally direct and well-controlled course. She would, other things being equal, survive those incidents, and on the following day would have little to say about them and even less about her own part in them or about her own feelings at the time.

In other words the woman of integrity, as

Marjorie Fielding could represent her, was a figure of real importance and a touchstone both in drama and in farce. What she said seemed to have occurred to her without a lot of thought being needed to produce it. It was, her voice and her manner suggested, what anybody with a head on their shoulders would have thought, provided a fair number of years on this earth with perhaps a term of service on the bench as a justice of the peace was behind her. She left the stage as coolly but as firmly as she entered it. The character knew her own mind, but she preferred not to speak it unless it were quite necessary.

She appeared in a number of films, including *Quiet Wedding, Demi-Paradise, Quiet Week-End, Fame is the Spur, Portrait of Clare, The Lavender Hill Mob, Rob Roy,* and *Laughing in Sunshine.*

December 29, 1956.

Princess Arthur of Connaught, Duchess of Fife, died on February 26, 1959 at the age of 67.

Princess Arthur was born on May 17, 1891, the elder daughter of the late Duke of Fife by his marriage to the late Princess Royal, eldest daughter of King Edward VII. She was christened Alexandra Victoria Alberta Edwina Louise, and two years later her only sister, Maud, was born, the future Countess of Southesk. They were granted in 1905 the title of Princess and the style of Highness; with special precedence after the members of the Royal Family styled Royal Highness.

The sisters grew up together, inseparable companions in the nursery, in lessons, in play, and in travel. They shared the home-keeping tastes of their mother, and were happy in their various pursuits and interests at Mar Lodge, at Brighton, and less often in London. They were seldom seen in general society and, indeed, it was not long before Princess Alexandra's marriage that they paid their first country house visit.

The end of 1911 and the beginning of 1912 brought to the Princesses an unnerving experience and a great bereavement. They were travelling with their parents to Egypt, the climate of which had been recommended to the Princess Royal, in the P. & O. liner Delhi. About 2 a.m. on December 13, 1911, in a stormy night, the vessel ran ashore near Cape Spartel. The landing was extremely dangerous, but the Princess Royal, as well as her husband and children, showed admirable courage. Indeed, she refused to leave the ship until all the women and children had been disembarked. The ladies had to be dropped from a considerable height into a boat from H.M.S. Duke of Edinburgh, and caught by members of the crew. The boat carrying the royal party filled and sank before it quite reached the shore. They were all wearing lifebelts, but were severely buffeted by the waves, and Princess Alexandra actually disappeared beneath the surface for some moments.

However, with the sailors' help, the party struggled on land, but their troubles were not then over. Wet through, and pierced with cold, they had to walk four miles in a fierce gale, amid torrents of rain, along the rocky shore to Cape Spartel lighthouse. At the lighthouse they were warmed and dried by the staff, who did all they could in the scanty accommodation. The party then had to set out on mules, sent by the British Minister at Tangier, for a 10-mile ride through the storm to the British Legation, which was not reached until 6 p.m. From this exhausting experience the whole party appeared to make an excellent recovery.

The royal party soon afterwards went on to Cairo, and thence up the Nile to attend the consecration of Khartoum Cathedral. On the way, however, the Duke of Fife caught a chill, which developed into pleurisy, and he died at Aswan on January 29, 1912, at the age of 63. At his death his dignities of Earl Fife, Viscount Macduff, and Baron Braco, in the peerage of Ireland, became extinct or possibly dormant. His dignities of Baron Skene (1857), Earl of Fife (1885), and Duke of Fife and Marquess of Macduff (1889), in the peerage of the United Kingdom, became extinct; but, in virtue of the special remainder attached to a later creation of 1900, his elder daughter succeeded him as Duchess of Fife and Countess of Macduff.

In July 1913, the engagement was announced of Princess Alexandra and Prince Arthur of Connaught, only son of the Duke of Connaught. The marriage was celebrated in the Chapel Royal, St. James's, on October 15, 1913.

In June 1920 Prince Arthur was appointed Governor-General of the Union of South Africa and High Commissioner. It was a happy choice, for the Prince's father had opened the first Parliament of the Union in 1910. When the Prince and Princess with their young son, Lord Macduff, arrived at Cape Town in the following November they received a most enthusiastic welcome, which was repeated at Pretoria. The success of Prince Arthur's term as Governor-General is now part of the history of South Africa, but it is perhaps not so generally known how admirably the Princess seconded him and how fully she shared his popularity.

The Princess at once showed her keen interest in hospitals, especially those for women and children. She was herself a trained nurse. She had passed her examinations as "Nurse Marjorie", and had done regular duty at University College Hospital, assisting at operations and taking her share of ward duty. During the War of 1914-18, also, she helped to nurse the wounded soldiers at St. Mary's Hospital, Paddington, where again she worked under the same conditions as the other nurses. She thus brought to South Africa an exceptional knowledge of hospital administration, and on her visits to these institutions all over the Union, usually paid with an entire absence of official formality, she was able to make many practical suggestions.

In the social duties of her position Princess Arthur showed a combination of tact and friendliness which won for her the admiration, and one might say the affection, of the warm-hearted South Africans. She was very fond of dancing, and in addition to the official balls at Cape Town, Pretoria, and Johannesburg she liked to give quite informal little dances for the younger people. She was herself an excellent dancer, and she saw to it that her partners were not limited to the official set. She was also fond of lawn tennis, for which she used to give afternoon parties. She was a good swimmer, and often enjoyed the exercise at public baths with no more ceremony than if she had been an ordinary member of the public.

In 1939 Princess Arthur became matron of her own nursing home in Bentinck Street. On the outbreak of the Second World War she became sister-in-charge of a casualty clearing station. On one occasion, after she had attended a small girl, the father pressed a sixpence into the Princess's hand, whispering: "'Ere you are, Miss, get yourself a cup of tea or a packet of 'fags'". The sixpence became one of Princess Arthur's valued possessions.

Prince Arthur had died in 1938, and in 1943 his widow suffered further bereavement: her only child, a subaltern in The Scots Greys, who had seen considerable active service in Egypt, died in Ottawa a year after succeeding his grandfather as second Duke of Connaught. The dukedom of Fife, of which he was heir apparent, now passes to Princess Arthur's nephew.

He is Lord Carnegie, son of her sister Maud and the Earl of Southesk. He married in 1956 the Hon. Cicely Dewar, elder daughter of Lord and Lady Forteviot.

February 27, 1959.

Paramount Chief of Fiji – See **Sir Lala Sukuna.**

Gerald Finzi, who died on September 27, 1956 in a nursing home at Oxford at the age of 55, after a short illness, was a composer whose work, already highly esteemed by musicians, was beginning to impress its merit upon a wider public.

Quiet and unobtrusive in style, his music is characterized by high craftsmanship and an individuality which is none the less umistakably his own, for all its evidence of the influence of such two diverse minds as those of Vaughan Williams [q.v.] and Elgar. Bach was also a formative influence and there can be no doubt that Finzi's early association with that wayward, but remarkably sensitive teacher, R. O. Morris, taught him how eclecticism could be bent to his purpose. He was, himself, peculiarly sensitive to the music as well as the meaning of words and this proved to be his strength as a composer, for though he brought the same fine craftsmanship to bear on all his works, it is the vocal works which manifest that extra sensitiveness which makes them so distinctive and so satisfying.

He was still developing when he was struck down by illness and there is no knowing what he might have done. Nevertheless, on what he has already shown there can be no doubt that he was most felicitous in his setting of words to music and was especially happy in interpreting Thomas Hardy – that most difficult of all poets to interpret in musical terms. No other musician has reached Finzi's standard in setting Hardy to music in the two song cycles, "A Young Man's Exhortation" and "Earth and Air and Rain"—a total of 22 settings.

Gerald Finzi was born in London on July 14, 1901, and after attending private schools studied under Sir Edward Bairstow from 1918 to 1922 and then in 1925 under R. O. Morris for a few months. A sufficient competence permitted him to follow his own bent in composition, and his work in this way was interrupted only twice in his life. The first time was when he was a member of the teaching staff of the Royal Academy of Music in 1930-33 and the second time was during the last war when he worked as a temporary civil servant in the Ministry of War Transport. He first became known as a composer by the publication in 1924 of his *Severn Rhapsody* by the Carnegie Trust, but this work he later disowned. Then came a long series of vocal works showing ever increasing mastery of the medium and culminating in the Hardy settings already mentioned.

Meanwhile instrumental works were appearing ranging from solos to works for full orchestra. Since the end of the war his principal works have been choral and include a festival anthem for choir and organ, "Lo the Full Final Sacrifice" and a ceremonial ode for a St. Cecilia's Day concert in London in 1947. He also produced the incidental music for a radio production of Shakespeare's *Love's Labour's Lost.*

His last appearance as a conductor was at the Three Choirs Festival in 1956 and his recently composed cello concerto was broadcast by the Hallé Orchestra on September 26, with Christopher Bunting playing the solo part.

He married in 1933 Miss Joyce Black, who survives him together with two sons.

September 28, 1956.

Luis Angel Firpo, the Argentine heavyweight boxer who met Jack Dempsey for the world championship in 1923, died on August 7, 1960. He was 65.

The Wild Bull of the Pampas, as Damon Runyon called him, was a big, rough fighter who made no scientific contribution to the game. Yet his incredible bout with Dempsey on September 14, 1923, will never be forgotten. For sheer excitement there had never been, and may never be, anything like it in the history of the world's heavyweight championship.

Firpo (6ft. 3in. tall and weighing about 215lb.) and Dempsey boxed—if that word can be used—for only three minutes 57 seconds. First Dempsey was knocked down, then he floored Firpo seven times—standing over him during the counts. Then, just when it looked as though Dempsey was in for a quick victory he was caught by a desperate right to the head from Firpo which sent him through the ropes and out on to the pressmen sitting below the ring.

Dempsey struggled back in time and Firpo, slow to react, missed his chance of following up before the bell. In the second round Dempsey, still dazed but at his greatest now that he was at bay, managed to put Firpo down twice more, and the second time for good.

It was Firpo's finest hour in the ring, but the 150,000 dollars he gained from the contest sent him on to another career as a successful man of business. He had eight more professional bouts, five in 1924, and one in 1926, and there was a brief comeback in 1936.

In boxing's colourful history this wealthy Argentine rancher will be remembered as the giant heavyweight who would come out of his corner, snorting and tossing his great head, covered with its shock of unruly hair, as though he was an infuriated bull about to charge.

August 8, 1960.

Canon John D'Ewes Evelyn Firth, Master of the Temple, died at Winchester on September 21, 1957. He was 57.

"Budge" Firth was born on February 21, 1900, the only son of J. B. Firth, for many years chief leader writer of the *Daily Telegraph.* He was a scholar of Winchester and Christ Church, later returning to teach at Winchester under Dr. Rendall, whose life he published in 1954. He was house master of Trant's from 1939 until 1946 and continued as Chaplain and in charge of Parallel Division until his appointment as Master of the Temple in 1954. Here, unhappily, his work was much frustrated by ill-health. He was made an honorary Canon of Winchester Cathedral in 1952 and had been Canon Emeritus since 1955.

Firth's most obviously enduring monument will perhaps prove to be his *Winchester College*, published in 1949. But underlying that consummately skilful analysis of what he loved to call the *res Wiccamica* was a lifetime of passionate, though never heedlessly uncritical devotion to the past, present, and future of Winchester.

His personal and professional equipment for schoolmastering was of a quite unusually high order. With his great intellectual range, infectious humour, and at times dazzling expository powers he had also an intuitive sense of the mysterious, individual identity of his pupils that usually made them his friends for life. A good classical scholar, his main teaching work lay with the best historians and modern linguists in the school to whom he would discourse on Gladstone, Bismarck, Romanticism, Samuel Smiles, Carpenter's *Church and the People,* or Isabella II with erudition, wit, and a remarkable flair for the dramatic incongruous. It was perhaps during the post-war years that his work as chaplain made a unique contribution to the life of Winchester. Acutely conscious of the movement of the times—his temperamental, even Johnsonian conservatism ever at grips with a genuine sensitivity to radical ideas—he would often in his exquisitely composed sermons achieve a note of almost prophetic urgency as he exhorted his youthful congregation to examine their Christian and Wykehamical convictions in terms of the authentic contemporary situation. But on the need for such convictions he never wavered.

As a friend he was incomparable; contemporaries, pupils, and Trantites know this. In trouble he would give you all his time and all his love; in happiness he was a fountain of gaiety and wit. What fun it was to play cricket with him, and to remember that he had once taken all 10 wickets against Eton. How good it was to dine with him and his devoted wife, for they were greatly given to hospitality. How splendid a travelling companion he was—one remembers him enchanted by the Restaurant Foyot, because Alphonse Daudet took Léon there after prize days at Louis-le-Grand; one sees him crawling excitedly and myopically along the Pont du Gard; one hears his "bravo" at the conclusion of Offenbach's *La Vie Parisienne.* A friend has written: "There never will be anybody like 'Budge', such a combination of wisdom, fun, and innocence. To know all the tricks of the trade and yet not practise them yourself, and to be so sympathetic to those who do, you have there a Christian charm quite without rival."

Firth married, in 1939, Josephine Priscilla, daughter of the late Bishop of Lichfield.

September 24, 1957.

Professor Emeritus J. R. Firth, O.B.E., who was Professor of General Linguistics at London University from 1944 until 1956, died suddenly on December 14, 1960 at Lindfield, Sussex, at the age of 70.

During his 12 years' tenure of the chair Firth created what has become known as the "London School of Linguistics" and he acquired a well merited and international reputation as a leading British figure in his chosen field of study. Firth's outstanding work during the Second World War in language training for members of the Armed Forces was officially recognized by the O.B.E. in 1946.

John Rupert Firth was born on June 17, 1890. He graduated in 1911 at the University of Leeds, with First Class honours in history, and proceeded to the degree of Master of Arts in 1913. In the same year, after a brief period as lecturer in history at the City of Leeds Training College, he joined the Indian Education Service, where he continued to serve until 1928 (with a break for war service in East Africa, India, and Afghanistan). During the years 1920-28 he was Professor of English at the University of the Punjab.

In 1928 Firth was appointed Senior Lecturer in Phonetics at University College London, From 1929 to 1931 he was also assistant in the sociology of languages at the London School of Economics, and from 1930 to 1938 special lecturer in the phonetics of Indian languages at the Indian Institute, Oxford.

From 1932 he was connected with the School of Oriental and African Studies in the University of London, first as a part-time lecturer in linguistics and from 1938 onwards as Senior Lecturer in Linguistics and Indian Phonetics.

In 1940 the title of reader was conferred upon him by the university and in 1941 he became head of the department of linguistics at the school. In 1944 the Senate created a chair of general linguistics at the school and Firth was appointed as its first occupant, a position he continued to hold until his retirement in 1956.

Firth was a particularly vigorous and inspiring teacher and, though his written output was comparatively small, it was marked by great originality of thought. His services to his subject and to the university were recognized by the conferment on him of the title of professor emeritus; his equally outstanding services to the School of Oriental and African Studies, where his vigorous and forthright contributions to discussions in committee were particularly notable, brought his election to an honorary fellowship.

In retirement Firth's interest in his subject was undiminished and in 1957 his *Papers in Linguistics,* a collection of his writings between the years 1934 and 1951, was published. They again made clear Firth's continuing excitement with the living language, never scorning the practical or empirical, and eager to investigate and ponder the social and situational implications of all linguistic material.

During his retirement Firth also did some part-time teaching in the University of Edinburgh, which in July 1960 conferred on him the honorary degree of LL.D.

Firth was a vehement, controversial, vivacious man, often exasperating, always lovable, always worth listening to. His contributions to the study of phonetics and general linguistics and to oriental and African studies in general, were of the first order and will not quickly be forgotten.

December 16, 1960.

Sir William Firth, formerly chairman and managing director of Richard Thomas and Company, the steel and tinplate manufacturers, and for many years an outstanding figure in that industry, died on November 11, 1957 at Kloof, Natal. He was 76.

William John Firth was born in London on July 21, 1881, the son of Richard Firth. He entered the tinplate trade when he was 20, and before he was 30 was, with the late Henry Folland [q.v.], controlling the Grovesend group of works, which later amalgamated with Richard Thomas and Company. In the following years he took a leading part in building up the industrial organization of the Welsh tinplate industry.

Having built up the tinplate output of Richard Thomas and Company, he quickly recognized the importance both for the tinplate industry and for making sheets for the motor car industry of the wide strip mill, first introduced in America in the late twenties. This offered great economies through labour-saving and also provided a better quality product for stamping. Firth at first hoped to build a strip mill in Lincolnshire or Northamptonshire, using the cheap home ores which Stewarts and Lloyds had begun to use successfully for tubes, but there were strong protests from South Wales, then in the grip of depression, and these had political support.

The decision was taken late in 1935 to build the new works at Ebbw Vale. The existing steelworks there was wholly replaced. The financing of this development, which did not meet universal support in the industry, proved more difficult than was expected, partly because of unexpected difficulties, partly because of rising prices.

By the middle of 1938 it had become evident that a large amount of additional money was required, and, as this was difficult to find by normal means, arrangements were made, with the help of the Bank of England, to raise a further £6m. But the price of this was that effective control of the company passed out of the hands of Firth and his board. As part of the arrangement control was vested in a special committee consisting of the Governor of the Bank of England or his nominee, Firth himself, a representative of the steel industry at large, and a nominee of the trustees for the debenture-holders. Three chairmen of competing steel companies were appointed to the board of directors—against Firth's vigorous and outspoken opposition. There followed a period during which relations between Firth and his new fellow-committee men and directors became more and more strained. He himself used to complain that his new colleagues in the running of the continuous strip mill were largely those who had wrongly argued originally that the strip mill was unnecessary. This period ended with his involuntary retirement from Richard Thomas in 1940.

Working with Firth clearly involved difficulties, but his removal meant the removal from the steel industry of one of its most distinguished and farsighted leaders. The technical change which he was the first among the industry's managements to recognize as inevitable has now revolutionized the whole sheet and tinplate industry.

He was an individualist, used to being his own master, and did not work easily in harness with others who had been either unenthusiastic or actually antagonistic to the project which was essentially his creation. But he was endowed with great charm as well as great vigour and imagination, and outside the committee room or the board room he was irresistibly convincing when he ridiculed the idea that he was "a difficult man to work with". Certainly he was always extremely popular with his employees and subordinates, in spite of a tongue which could be cutting on occasion.

Firth and his friends made several efforts to regain control of Richard Thomas as the success of the new works was clear, and he tried to prevent the amalgamation with Baldwins in 1944, but he lacked the necessary support.

Firth, who was knighted in 1932, had been chairman of the International Tinplate Cartel, president of the Swansea Metal Exchange, and a member of the International Tin Committee. He married in 1909 Helena Adelaide, daughter of Joseph Garrett, by whom he had two sons.

November 12, 1957.

Pierre Étienne Flandin, a former French Premier and a leading *Munichois* among the politicians of the Third Republic, who was arrested in North Africa after the Allied landings in December 1943, and subsequently tried by the French Haute Cour as a "collaborator", died on June 13, 1958 at his home at St. Jean Cap Ferrat. He was 69.

At his trial, finally held at Versailles in 1946, he was acquitted of the charge of intelligence with the enemy after Sir Winston Churchill* had given written testimony in his favour. In July of that year he was condemned to a term of "national indignity" for five years, but was granted an immediate reprieve. Subsequently a special law was passed after his acquittal, declaring him and three other former members of the Pétain [q.v.] Government to be ineligible for Parliament in the future. Apart from this, the stigma he had incurred as "the French statesman who congratulated Hitler on Munich" remained indelible. That act bore melancholy witness to an outlook on affairs which during the previous few years had become increasingly evident in Flandin.

A member of the clan commonly described as "the 200 families of France", son of a Resident-General in Tunis, Pierre Étienne Flandin was born in Paris on April 12, 1889. The material advantages he enjoyed followed him at the Sorbonne and in his law studies, and not only there: in 1914, shortly before the outbreak of war, he was elected, at the age of 25, deputy for the Yonne department (he took his place among the Républicains de Gauche, a Right-Centre group), mayor of one of its small towns, and Conseiller-Général of the constituency. In August, waiving his parliamentary privilege and filled with patriotic emotion, he went into the Army and showed a lively interest in military aviation, but did not stay long in uniform. In 1915 he was in charge of the aeronautical section at the Ministrie de la Guerre, and two years later was appointed director of the inter-allied aeronautical service. At the beginning of 1920 he was made Under-Secretary for Air in the Millerand Administration. He was not unpopular then in the Chamber, where at the start of his political career he had been somewhat indulged as an *enfant terrible.*

To his task, in both the Millerand and Leygues Ministries, of assisting in the organization of the French air force, he added the responsibilities of president of the French Aero Club. But Flandin had larger ends in view. His first portfolio as a full Cabinet member—as Minister of Commerce under François-Marsal in 1924—gave him little scope, for that Ministry lasted precisely five days. The affinity he seems to have discovered, however, during the next few years with large-scale industry and high finance bore more substantial fruit. He reappeared as Minister of Commerce and Industry in both the Cabinets of Tardieu during 1931-32, serving as Finance Minister under Laval in between; was Minister of Public Works in the Doumergue Cabinet in 1934; and at last, in November of that year, became Prime Minister. His Premiership lasted only until the following June, but in that time the Rome Agreement, the Stresa Pact, and the

Franco-Soviet Pact were all negotiated.

In one sense these disguise rather than reveal Flandin's ambitions as Prime Minister and as Minister of Foreign Affairs under Sarraut during the first six months of 1936. [See tribute June 19, 1958.]. He was concerned to buttress the Banque de France and to consolidate the position of those who had long used it as an instrument of political power and privilege, to widen the range of industrial and financial interests common to France and Germany, to liquidate France's Balkan alliances, and, as a form of insurance, to withdraw behind the apparently impregnable security of the Maginot Line. In all this he took the line of a French *Realpolitiker.* Far from professing admiration for the Nazi scheme of things, he added to his somewhat demonstrative show of English sympathies in clothes and country pursuits the reiterated hope of an Anglo-French *entente.* At the same time, however, he drew nearer and nearer to urging in public the need for friendship with both Germany and Italy.

These public declarations date from the beginning of 1937 and left no doubt of the political choice he had made. Yet Flandin could not have bargained for what in fact followed Munich. His ambitions and material interests notwithstanding, he was in many ways a patriotic Frenchman and he felt the shock of Hitler's assault upon France keenly enough. Nor could he have been thinking of his material interests, or of these alone, when in December 1940 he accepted the invitation of Pétain, after the latter's sudden dismissal of Laval, to serve as Foreign Minister at Vichy.

He did so, it would appear, with diminishing illusions, and in the two months during which he held office he was not wholly without effect in preserving French dignity in disaster. He did, in fact, as the evidence at his trial revealed, help to steer the policy of the Vichy Government towards a covert understanding with the allies; and it was German pressure that forced his resignation. Neither that sign of contrition, however, nor his subsequent aid to the Resistance movement saved him from arrest in December 1943 and from a long period of detention before he was provisionally released and then brought to trial.

In 1948 he published in *Politique Française, 1919-40,* which he had written during imprisonment in Algiers, a defence of his pre-1939 policy in the guise of a general survey of French foreign policy between the wars.

His parliamentary ineligibility limited his political activity after the war; but he by no means abandoned politics. He formed an association called, "Représentants de la IIIe République" of the former Senators, 250 in all, and former members of the Chamber of Deputies, 500, who had been declared ineligible after the Liberation; and he remained chairman of his political group, the Alliance Démocratique.

In May 1952 he announced that he would be a candidate for election to the Council of the Republic to be held on May 18 in the department of the Yonne which he had represented in Parliament for many years. His announcement raised a difficult constitutional point in view of the law passed rendering him ineligible for membership. The judicial committee of the Assembly had decided in March 1952 that that law should be repealed. On the other hand, the amnesty Bill, which provided for this, had not yet been debated. At all events Flandin, though technically ineligible, stood, and suffered a marked defeat.

June 14, 1958.

Sir Alexander Fleming, D.SC., M.B., F.R.C.P., F.R.C.S., F.R.S., the discoverer of penicillin, died suddenly on March 11, 1955 at his home in London of a heart attack at the age of 73.

Alexander Fleming, the son of a farmer, was born at Lochfield, near Darvel, in Ayrshire, on August 6, 1881. He received his early education at the village school and at Kilmarnock Academy. At 13 years of age he was sent to live with his brother in London, where, for the next two or three years, he continued his education by attending the Polytechnic Institute in Regent Street. At that time he displayed no particular scientific ability nor felt any urge to be a doctor. For some years he worked in a shipping office in Leadenhall Street, but he found office routine deadly dull and after four years in the City a small legacy enabled him to escape. The brother with whom he was living had already taken his medical degree and he encouraged his younger brother to take up medicine.

Thus at the age of 20 he became a student at St. Mary's Hospital Medical School, winning the senior entrance scholarship in natural science. He showed that he had found his true bent by winning almost every class prize and scholarship during his student career. He qualified in 1906 and at the M.B., B.S. examination of London University in 1908 he obtained honours and was awarded a gold medal.

In 1909 he became a Fellow of the Royal College of Surgeons. In 1906 he had begun to assist Sir Almroth Wright in the inoculation department at St. Mary's Hospital, and this association led to his taking up the study of bacteriology. Under the stimulating influence of Wright, who was at that time engaged in his researches on the opsonic theory, he acquired great experience and skill in bacteriological technique and in clinical pathology.

For recreation he attended the drills and parades of the London Scottish, which he had joined as a private in the year before he resigned from his post with the shipping company. For some years he went to the annual camp and, being a fair shot, to the meetings at Bisley. On the outbreak of war in 1914 he resigned from the London Scottish so that he could go to France as a captain in the R.A.M.C. He worked in Sir Almroth Wright's laboratory in the Casino at Boulogne and received a mention in dispatches.

At the end of the war he returned to St. Mary's as assistant to Sir Almroth Wright and was also appointed lecturer in bacteriology in the medical school. He subsequently became director of the department of systematic bacteriology and assistant director of the inoculation department. For some years he acted as pathologist to the venereal disease department at St. Mary's and was also pathologist to the London Lock Hospital. In 1928 he was appointed Professor of Bacteriology in the University of London, the post being tenable at St. Mary's. He retired with the title emeritus in 1948, but continued at St. Mary's as head of the Wright-Fleming Institute of Micro-Biology. Though in 1954 he formally handed over the reins to Professor R. Cruikshank* he continued his own research work there and only the day before he died was at the institute discussing plans for the lecture tour in the Middle East he had been asked to undertake by the British Council.

Fleming's first notable discovery, that of lysozyme, was made in 1922. He had for some time been interested in antiseptics and in naturally occurring antibacterial substances. In culturing nasal secretion from a patient with an acute cold he found a remarkable element that had the power of dissolving bacteria. This bacteriolyte element, which he also found in tears and other body fluids, he isolated and named lysozyme.

Penicillin was discovered in 1928 when Fleming was engaged in bacteriological researches on staphylococci. For examination purposes he had to remove the covers of his culture plates and a mould spore drifted on to a plate. After a time it revealed itself by developing into a colony about half an inch across. It was no new thing for a bacteriologist to find that a mould had grown on a culture plate which had lain on the bench for a week, but the strange thing in this particular case was that the bacterial colonies in the neighbourhood of the mould appeared to be fading away. What had a week before been vigorous staphylococcus colonies were now faint shadows of their former selves. Fleming might have merely discarded the contaminated culture plate, but fortunately his previous research work on antiseptics and on naturally occurring antibacterial substances caused him to take special note of the apparent antibacterial action of the mould.

He made sub-cultures of the mould and investigated the properties of the anti-bacterial substance. He found that while the crude culture fluid in which the mould had grown was strongly antibacterial it was non-toxic to animals and human beings. The crude penicillin was, however, very unstable and was too weak and too crude for injection. Early attempts at concentration were not very successful, and after a few tentative trials its clinical use was not pursued, although it continued to be used in Fleming's laboratory for differential culture.

The position in 1929 was that Fleming had discovered and named penicillin, had investigated its antibacterial power, and had suggested that it might be useful as an antiseptic applied to infected lesions. Attempts to produce a concentrated extract capable of clinical application were not successful and had been abandoned. In the light of later knowledge Fleming's original paper of 1929 was remarkable. It covered nearly the whole field, realized most of the problems and made considerable progress in solving them. The resuscitation of penicillin as a chemotherapeutic agent was due to the brilliant work of Sir Howard [Lord] Florey* and his colleagues at Oxford, notably Dr. E. B. Chain.

After the establishment of penicillin as a life-saving drug Fleming was overwhelmed with honours. He was knighted in 1944 and in the following year he shared the Nobel prize for medicine with Sir Howard Florey and Dr. E. B. Chain. He was William Julius Mickle Fellow of London University in 1942, and received an award of merit from the American Pharmaceutical Manufacturers Association in 1943. He was elected F.R.S. in 1943 and F.R.C.P. in 1944, under the special by-law. His other honours included the Moxon medal of the Royal College of Physicians (1945), the Charles Mickle Fellowship of Toronto University (1944), the John Scott medal of the City Guild of Philadelphia (1944), the Cameron prize of Edinburgh University (1945), the Albert Gold Medal of the Royal Society of Arts (1946), the honorary Gold Medal of the Royal College of Surgeons (1946), the Actonian Prize of the Royal Institution, and the honorary freedom of the boroughs of Paddington, Darvel, and Chelsea. He had innumerable honorary degrees from British and foreign universities, and in 1951 was elected Rector of Edinburgh University. In the weekend before he died thieves stole property from his flat in Chelsea worth about £1,000, and an appeal was made to them to return a gold seal of great sentimental value.

Fleming was president of the London Ayrshire Society and of the Pathological and Comparative Medicine Sections of the Royal Society of Medicine. Apart from the papers describing his great discoveries, he contributed to the Medical Research Council *System of Bacteriology*, to the official Medical History of the 1914-18 War, and to many other publications. He was a keen amateur painter, and he had many friends among artists. He was also very fond of motoring and of gardening. He remained quite unspoiled by the publicity and acclaim that came to him, and no one was more aware than he of the indispensable part played by other investigators in the development of penicillin. Animated by the spirit of the true scientist, he looked ever forward.

He was twice married, first to Sarah Marion, daughter of Mr. John McElroy. She died in 1949, leaving a son. In 1953 he married Dr. Amalia Coutsouris, of Athens, who had been a member of his staff at the Wright-Fleming Institute.

March 12, 1955.

The Right Rev. A. L. Fleming, D.D., the first Bishop of the Arctic, died suddenly at Toronto on May 17, 1953 at the age of 69.

His diocese was the largest in extent of any in the world—2,250,000 square miles, one-third of the area of Canada. His people numbered about 10,000, including traders, Indian and Eskimo. He first went to Baffin Land in 1909 with another young man, both of them eager to work as missionaries to the Eskimo and the American Indians. They followed the Eskimo on their hunting expeditions, travelling by dog-sleigh and boat, and living like them in snow huts. Fleming learned to speak the language of the Eskimo or Inooeet, as they prefer to be called. He found them eager converts to the Christian faith and he established missions wherever possible and followed them with residential schools and hospitals.

Archibald Lang Fleming was born at Greenock on September 8, 1883. After attending Greenock Academy he entered the drawing office of John Brown & Company, the Clydebank shipbuilders. In 1905-06 he took a special course in naval architecture and marine engineering at Glasgow University and then entered the scientific department of his firm. At an early age, however, he had harboured a strong ambition to become a Christian missionary and at 25 threw up his promising career as a naval architect and entered himself as a student at Wycliffe College, Toronto, to prepare himself for work in the mission field. He took orders in 1912 and was for a time financial secretary of Wycliffe College. Later he was rector of St. John's, New Brunswick. From that post he resigned in 1926 to fill the new post of Archdeacon of the Arctic, though he had not been in good health and the change involved personal financial loss. In 1933 he was consecrated the first Bishop of the Arctic.

In summer he travelled some 10,000 miles, visiting his flock in the ice-breaking ship s.s. Mascopie, moving sometimes only 3 miles in five hours, or flying over frozen lakes. Like St. Paul he wrote long letters and descriptions after those journeys. His letters to the "Fellowship of the Arctic" which he had built up to 3,000 members in Great Britain, Canada, and the United States, amounted to small, illustrated and thrilling books of adventure such as *The Hunter-Home, Dwellers in Arctic Night,* and *Perils of the Polar Pack.*

Looking back when he was forced to retire in 1949 because of the condition of his heart, he said that in spite of all the dangers, disappointments, poverty, and privation, he had had "the joy of achievement; he had been able to bring help and succour to many souls in spiritual as well as physical need". The Eskimo repaid him in affection.

Dr. Fleming was twice married, first in 1913 to Helen Grace, daughter of Walter Gillespie. She died in 1941 and he then married Elizabeth, daughter of Lewis Lukens. Twice his second wife accompanied him on his journeys to the Arctic. There were no children of either marriage.

May 19, 1953.

Sir Arthur Fleming, C.B.E., the distinguished electrical engineer who did much to advance technical education in Britain, died on September 14, 1960, aged 79.

Arthur Percy Morris Fleming was born at Newport, Isle of Wight, in 1881, and educated at Portland House Academy in his native town and at the Finsbury Technical College. After occupying positions with the London Electric Supply Corporation and a firm of instrument makers he went in 1900 to America where, at the works of the Westinghouse Electric and Manufacturing Company, East Pittsburg, he underwent a course of training, before joining the British Westinghouse Company, later the Metropolitan-Vickers Company, at Trafford Park, Manchester. On his return to England in 1902 he was first engaged as an insulation specialist, and then became chief transformer designer and superintendent and chief engineer of the transformer department.

At an early stage in his career he realized the complementary needs for scientific research in industrial problems and for the effective technical training of personnel, and his influence in these matters became far reaching. He was instrumental in founding the research department of the Metropolitan-Vickers Electrical Company at Trafford Park and much of the work carried out by the research department under his guidance had important results, for example, the development of a technique for high-vacuum high-voltage equipments and demountable large-power thermionic valves, which played an important part in making the first radar possible. Fleming was also a pioneer of broadcasting in Britain, and the transmitting station established under his direction at Trafford Park was the second in the country to send out regular daily programmes. He also helped in the work which led to the establishment of the Department of Scientific and Industrial Research.

His standing as an engineer, his personal qualities and his devotion to and knowledge of technical education made him a man much in demand and he gave generously of his time, his knowledge, and himself. He held for some time a position with Associated Electrical Industries similar to that he had held with Metropolitan-Vickers. He was president of Section L, British Association in 1939 and 10 years later of Section G; chairman in 1939 of the Electrical Engineering Committee of the Central Register of the Minister of Labour; a member of the governing body of the Imperial College of Science and Technology; of the delagacy of the City and Guilds College; of the War Cabinet Engineering Advisory Committee; and of the Board of Education Committee on the Training of Teachers and Youth Leaders.

After the Second World War, as chairman of the Federation of British Industries overseas scholarships committee, he led an engineering training mission to Latin America and returned much impressed with the potentialities of the young republics. Later he was made president of the British Association of Commercial and Industrial Education and at his death was vice-president.

He first served on the council of the Institution of Electrical Engineers in 1932, being elected a vice-president in 1935 and president in 1938. He has read many papers at meetings of the institution and gave the Students' Lectures in 1934, in 1935 and again in 1946. He delivered the Faraday Lecture in 1937, his subject being the "Evolution of Electrical Power" and was awarded the Faraday Medal in 1941. He was later elected an honorary Fellow. The

Institution of Mechanical Engineers awarded him the Hawksley Medal in 1937.

For his work on submarine detectors in the 1914-18 War Fleming was made C.B.E. in 1920, and he was knighted in 1945. His written work ranged from accounts of original research to discussions of apprentice training organization.

For his services to education and research Manchester and Liverpool Universities conferred honorary degrees upon him.

He married Rose Mary, daughter of William Ash, of Newport, Isle of Wight, by whom he had two sons and a daughter. His wife died in 1948.

September 15, 1960.

Not many men can have made such a wide and solid reputation with a single book as did **Sir Banister Fletcher,** past-president of the Royal Institute of British Architects, with his *History of Architecture on the Comparative Method.* Fletcher, who died at his home in London on August 17, 1953, was a man of many parts, a barrister as well as a practising architect, surveyor, and writer, but nothing else that he did compares in importance with this indispensable work. It is his monument.

The book has been described as an architectural library in a single volume. So far as the claim of the title is concerned that is true, for the work is essentially a history. Any technical information that it contains is purely descriptive, and it scrupulously avoids any expression of opinion. Except by inference it would be difficult to find in it any indication of the author's preferences in style or period.

The *History* began as a modest volume of some 300 pages with 100 illustrations, written by Fletcher in conjunction with his father, the late Professor Banister Fletcher, and published in 1896. It was an instantaneous success, and a second edition was called for within the year. Other editions quickly followed, the fifth edition published in 1905 was reprinted six times, and by the ninth edition in 1931 the book had been translated into Russian and Spanish and arrangements were being made for its appearance in French, Italian and German. With each successive edition the book has been enlarged and improved, with more and clearer illustrations and a closer following up of contemporary architecture. Besides the historical styles the book deals with Indian, Chinese, Japanese, ancient American and Saracenic architecture, it is known all over the world, and no special work of reference can be more frequently consulted.

Fletcher, who was the eldest son of Banister Fletcher, Professor of Architecture at King's College, London, and sometime M.P. for North-West Wilts, was born in London on February 15, 1866. After leaving University College he was articled to his father, and then studied architectural design for six years at the Royal Academy Schools under Norman Shaw, Alfred Waterhouse, Sir Arthur Blomfield, J. L. Pearson, and Phené Spiers. He also studied at the Architectural Association and in the architectural and antique and life drawing schools at King's College, besides gaining practical experience in the carpentry and wood-carving workshops. In order to have direct knowledge of the French system of training he entered the studio of M. Fasnacht, of the *École des Beaux Arts,* Paris. As a student Fletcher gained many prizes, including the Architectural Association medal for design; the Godwin Bursary and travelling studentship; the Tite Medal for architectural design and the Essay Medal of the R.I.B.A. After working as assistant in the office of Mr. William Henman and Colonel R. W. Edis, and in the architectural department of the Metropolitan Board of Works, Fletcher, in 1889, entered into partnership with his father and brother, the late Major H. Phillip Fletcher, D.S.O., who was killed in a flying accident in 1916. Most of his work was done in the name of the firm of Banister Fletcher and Sons.

As might be expected, Fletcher's buildings reflected his learning rather than displayed great originality or a highly developed sense of form in the abstract. He was, indeed, rather inclined to quote "features" for their literary or sentimental associations. There is an amusing instance of this in a house which happens to be familiar, "The Dormers", Portishead, Somerset. The general impression of this house, of the bungalow type, and pleasantly situated above a sloping lawn commanding the Bristol Channel, is that it is all dormers. But Fletcher had a wider range than country houses. Besides houses and flats in London he designed St. George's Hall and School, Old Kent Road; St. Aidan's Church, Stratford; alterations, additions, and new laboratories at King's College, London; King's College School, Wimbledon Common; banks at Harrow, Hythe, Stamford Hill, and Maidstone; factories and warehouses in London; and several war memorials. A recent building of which he was very proud, on account of its "functional" design, was the Gillette factory on the Great West Road.

Fletcher had a high reputation as a lecturer at King's College—where for a short time after his father's death he acted as Professor and where he formed the architectural museum of photographs, casts, and drawings, besides a collection of 15,000 lantern slides for use at lectures—and London University, the British Museum, the Victoria and Albert Museum, and the Central School of Arts and Crafts. He was president of the Polytechnic School of Architecture and director of the Trade Training Schools. Though Fletcher's name will always be associated with the *History of Architecture* it was not his only publication. The others in book or pamphlet form include *Andrea Palladio: His Life and Works, Architecture and the Humanities, The Influence of Material on Architecture, The English Home, Architectural Hygiene,* and *Carpentry and Joinery.* An account of his architectural work by Mr. W. Hanneford-Smith was published by Batsford in 1935. In order to collect material for his *History* Fletcher travelled extensively in all parts of Europe and in North Africa, Egypt, and Palestine, filling many sketchbooks. Greece he visited five times, and for 19 consecutive years he went on the annual sketching tours of the Architectural Association. He also visited the United States to study the methods of teaching architecture on that side of the Atlantic.

Elected A.R.I.B.A. in 1889 and F.R.I.B.A. in 1904, Fletcher was for several years on the council. In 1925 he became vice-president and was president from 1929 to 1931. Senior Sheriff of the City of London in 1918-19, and Master of the Worshipful Company of Carpenters in 1937, Fletcher took an active part in civic affairs. A member of the Court of Common Council, he was chairman of the City Lands Committee in 1921 and chairman of several other committees. The preservation of the 19 City churches proposed to be destroyed was largely due to him, and he stongly opposed the St. Paul's Bridge, which he believed might affect the foundations of the Cathedral. At the request of the late Neville Chamberlain he became chairman of the Greater London Regional Planning Committee, and in 1941 he was appointed a member of the reconstruction committee to consider and formulate the policy of the R.I.B.A. on the subject of post-war reconstruction and planning.

Fletcher was called to the Bar by the Inner Temple in 1908 and knighted in 1919. He was an honorary member of the British Academy at Rome, honorary member of the American Institute of Architects, and honorary corresponding member of the Société Centrale des Architects Français. A tall, distinguished looking man, of legal rather than artistic appearance, with genial manners, Fletcher was twice married: in 1914 to Alice Maude Mary, daughter of Edward Bretherton and widow of Sir J. Bamford-Slack, M.P. She was a brilliant pupil of Miss Beale's at Cheltenham and an active member of the Women's National Liberal Federation. She died in 1932: and in 1933 he married Mrs. Howard Hazell, who died in 1949.

August 19, 1953.

Sir Frank Fletcher, Master of Marlborough College from 1903 to 1911 and Headmaster of Charterhouse from 1911 to 1935, died on November 17, 1954 in a nursing home at Hindhead, Surrey. He was 84.

He was born on May 3, 1870, the eldest son of Ralph Fletcher, of Atherton, near Manchester. The family had for 100 years been colliery owners, and were among the first in the country to introduce life-saving services and pit-head baths. Their name was, and remains, a synonym for fairness and justice, for simplicity of life and for a sense of responsibility for all in their employ. From this home atmosphere, at little more than 12 years old, he went as a scholar to Rossall, to remain there for seven years, first under the headmastership of James and later under the more human Tancock—former masters, by a curious coincidence, at Marlborough and Charterhouse respectively, the two schools which he was later to rule.

At 17 he was head of his house and from then

until at 65 he retired he was to know, except for the interval of his years at Oxford, that responsibility for others which was the family characteristic. The appearance of calm and ease with which he bore it was unconsciously—and unselfconsciously— deceptive, although when once he had taken a decision he would not allow its subject, however intricate or painful, to disturb his mind. In the holidays and after his retirement his evident relief at no longer having to decide matters of such importance to individuals or to a community gave a truer picture.

From Rossall Fletcher went as a classical scholar to Balliol, under the mastership of Jowett, and in due course there came to him first classes in Honour Moderations and Greats, and the Craven, Ireland, and Derby scholarships. The clearness and analytical quality of his mind might seem to have marked him out for a legal career, but his heart was set on schoolmastering and after two terms as Mods. tutor at Balliol he went to Rugby at Percival's invitation. Perhaps there his experience in teaching a low form was even more valuable to himself than his work with the Upper Bench of the VI. His distinguished pupil William Temple's description of him as a "supreme teacher" was to remain true for 40 years, not least in his expositions of Plato, of St. Paul, and of Robert Browning.

Not personal ambition but a desire to use his powers to the full caused him early to seek a headmastership, and in 1903 he was, to his own surprise, appointed Master of Marlborough, the youngest headmaster of his day and the first lay headmaster of a great school—"one lay apple in the clerical dumpling", as *The Times* of the day described him. Doubts as to the preaching of a layman were soon resolved by the quality of sermons which are a lasting memory of Marlburians and Carthusians alike.

There were, of course, difficulties: needed changes were carried out in face of criticism neither charitable nor just, not least from able contemporaries on his staff. Throughout his life Fletcher was often unconscious of susceptibilities he had wounded and suffered fools with more gladness than appeared. How much he and Marlburians at the Lodge and Carthusians later in Saunderites and at Northbrook owed to the tact, sympathy, and unobtrusive work of his wife (he had married in 1902 Dorothy, daughter of William Pope, of Crediton) both he and they have acknowledged with lifelong gratitude.

The call to Charterhouse in 1911 was too strong to be resisted. An illustrious but overlong headmastership had been succeeded by an unfortunate appointment; experience and perhaps ruthlessness were needed. But there was in Brooke Hall—something more than a typical masters' common-room—a welcome for the new headmaster and a readiness to cooperate on which in after years he often commented. Soon there were changes in curriculum: the old "modern forms" disappeared: specialization in history, in science and in modern languages was encouraged (though not at the expense of classics); superannuation became a fact.

In spite of the interruption of the First World War the 24 years of his headmastership saw steady improvements in classrooms and laboratories, in additions to houses and to grounds: and the opening of the memorial chapel in 1927 he probably regarded as their greatest event. Nor did games suffer, for apart from his interest in cricket and football he had been a keen runner, hockey player and climber.

In 1935 he was exploring the possibility of the admission to public schools under Government auspices of boys whose parents could not afford the cost. Again and again he was chairman of the Headmasters' Conference. In 1924 he had been made an honorary Fellow of Balliol and after his retirement honours and duties accumulated—knighthood in 1937, presidency of the Classical Association in 1946—and diocesan and educational work in Devon, and membership of governing bodies occupied his time. His reminiscences were published in 1937 under the title of *After Many Days.* In 1947, in spite of illness, he was present throughout the delayed centenary celebrations at Rossall.

His return in 1948 to the neighbourhood of Charterhouse, most courageously engineered by Lady Fletcher, both made him accessible again to hosts of friends and gave those friends the inspiration of seeing for themselves the quiet determination and fortitude with which he overcame to the very limit of possibility the after effects of his illness.

November 18, 1954.

Hanslip Fletcher, who died on February 21, 1955 at the age of 80, was an accomplished and exceedingly popular draughtsman of architectural subjects, of London streets and buildings in particular.

Hanslip Fletcher, who was the son of G. Rutter Fletcher, F.S.A., solicitor, was born in London in 1874 and educated at Merchant Taylors' School. For a good many years he exhibited drawings in watercolour, pencil, pen and wash, and other mediums, including subjects in Rome and Paris, at the Royal Academy, but his work was most familiar in the form of illustrations in the *Sunday Times,* the *Daily Telegraph,* the *Manchester Guardian,* and other newspapers.

Fletcher's drawings in newspapers had been familiar for a good many years when in 1927 the trustees of the London Museum did him the honour of showing his *Changing London* as the first of a series of temporary exhibitions representing the arts, crafts, and industries of Greater London.

In 1942 an exhibition of photographs and drawings of London's historic buildings before and after war damage was organized jointly by the Ecclesiological Society, the Society for the Protection of Ancient Buildings, the Art Workers' Guild, and the London Society, and held at the St. Martin's School of Art, Charing Cross Road. This exhibition, opened by Lord Esher, was accompanied by a series of talks by eminent ecclesiastical and architectural authorities which were published in the *Transactions* of the Ecclesiological Society under the title of "Historic London Under Fire".

Two collections of Fletcher's drawings were published in book form: *Changing London,* in 1934, and *Bombed London,* with an introduction by Professor A. E. [Sir Albert] Richardson, R.A.,* in 1948. He is represented in the Guildhall Art Gallery by watercolours of London purchased by the Contemporary Art Society; in the Guildhall Library by drawings purchased by the Library Committee; and in the National Museum of Wales, Cardiff. His etching of "Exmouth Street" is in the permanent collection of the Walker Art Gallery, Liverpool. Fletcher, who had a great deal of antiquarian knowledge, was a member of the Art Workers' Guild and of the committee of the Society for the Protection of Ancient Buildings.

February 23, 1955.

Sir Murchison Fletcher, K.C.M.G., C.B.E., who died in London on April 9, 1954 at the age of 75, had a long and distinguished career in various parts of the Colonial Empire.

Arthur George Murchison Fletcher was born on September 27, 1878, the son of Dr. George Fletcher of Highgate. He was educated at Cheltenham, and passed on to Trinity College, Oxford. In 1901 he was successful in the competitive examination for Eastern cadets (Colonial Service) and was appointed to Hongkong, where he served for the next quarter of a century. He was seconded for work in connexion with famine relief in the Kwang-Si province of China in 1903. He was assistant to the Attorney-General of Hongkong in 1909, and was promoted to be Assistant Colonial Secretary in 1913, a post which he held until he left Hongkong for Ceylon.

The responsibilities which Fletcher was called upon to shoulder in his new appointment were far heavier than those which had fallen to his lot in Hongkong. There was much political unrest in the island, and in 1927 a Royal Commission was appointed to investigate matters on the spot and to report as to the changes which it might consider necessary in the existing administration. Eventually in 1930 a form of self-government was approved and introduced. In 1929 he was appointed Governor of Fiji and High Commissioner for the Western Pacific.

He arrived in Fiji in November 1929, but in June of the following year was invalided to Sydney, returning to the colony in August. In June 1931 he left Fiji in H.M.S. Laburnum on a tour of certain of the Islands under his jurisdiction. At the beginning of 1932 he visited New Zealand with a view to promoting an increase in the volume of trade between that Dominion and Fiji.

On May 1, 1936, Sir Murchison Fletcher left Fiji to take up his new appointment of Governor of Trinidad. At a striking farewell ceremony the Fijian chiefs, who had assembled from all parts of the Colony, testified to the affectionate esteem in which he was held by the native race. It was uniformly acknowledged that, in spite of the years of depression, there had been greater progress during his administration than the colony had ever before experienced. In the latter part of 1936 he assumed the Government of Trinidad, but serious troubles awaited him in the following year. There had been for some time unrest among the employees on the oil-fields due to the rise in the cost of living. On June 19 a sudden strike began among the workers. Violent speeches were made and when the police attempted to arrest the ringleaders riots broke out.

In July a Royal Commission, with John Forster as chairman, was appointed and sent to the colony to investigate the matter on the spot and make recommendations. It returned to the United Kingdom at the beginning of November; but later in that month the Governor found it necessary to ask for troops to preserve order and a company of The Sherwood Foresters was sent. No further serious trouble occurred; but on January 11, 1938, the Colonial Office announced in the Press that Sir Murchison Fletcher had tendered his resignation on the ground of ill-health and that it had been accepted by the King.

He married in January 1915 Violet Dorothy, daughter of Lieutenant-Colonel Rogers-Harrison. Of their two sons, one was killed in action in 1944.

April 12, 1954.

Dr. Abraham Flexner died on September 21, 1959 at the age of 92.

He began his working life as a high school teacher in Louisville, Kentucky; in the course of that life he succeeded in making a definite contribution to higher education in the United States, his success deriving in no small measure from a unique capacity to extract large funds from successful men of business for the putting into effect of his ideas.

Flexner was born in Louisville on November 13, 1866, being the sixth of the nine children of Morris and Esther Flexner. His father had emigrated from Bohemia in 1853 and lost his money in the financial panic of 1873. One of his brothers, the late Simon Flexner, successfully directed the Rockefeller Institute for Medical Research.

While at high school Abraham Flexner supported himself by taking a part-time post at the Louisville Library. He was enabled to proceed to Johns Hopkins University through the bounty of his eldest brother, and after graduating in 1886 he took a post as a high school teacher in his native city. He quickly developed his own notions as to how a school should be conducted and in 1890 opened his own school, the success of which brought him to the notice of the educational world.

Further, this venture brought him the means to pursue his later studies. In 1905 he closed his school and proceeded with his wife to Harvard, where he graduated in the following year. He continued his studies in Berlin and Heidelberg and in 1908 published his first book *The American College—A Criticism.* This book brought Flexner to the notice of Dr. H. S. Mitchell, president of the Carnegie Foundation for the Advancement of Teaching. Flexner joined its staff, his first assignment being a survey of American medical schools published in 1910.

It was followed two years later by *Medical Education in Europe.* Flexner's criticisms of the system of medical education as he found it in America created something of a sensation and was productive of a movement for reform. In making his survey Flexner visited every one of the 155 medical schools in the United States and Canada. One of the reforms which he succeeded in bringing about was a substantial reduction in their number. From 1925 to 1928 Flexner was director of the Division of Studies and Medical Education of the Carnegie Foundation.

In the meantime he had become associated with the General Education Boards of the Rockefeller Foundation and thereby was able to realize some of his plans for reorganizing American medical education. At his suggestion John D. Rockefeller gave $40m. for this purpose, and vast additional sums were given by the foundation between 1919 and 1928. Flexner tapped other sources too. In 1920 he induced George Eastman to give $5m. for the establishment of a medical school at Rochester University; the Whitneys gave him $8m. for Cornell and J. P. Morgan $2m.

In 1928-29 Flexner was the Rhodes Memorial Lecturer at Oxford, and his lectures were published in 1930 as *Universities—American, English, German.* In 1928 he was Taylorian lecturer at Oxford. Flexner was particularly critical of the preoccupation of American universities with vocational education and the variety of techniques in which they gave instruction, though it was not always easy to visualize the exact path which in his opinion they ought to have followed. His sojourn at Oxford was productive in the shaping of his most original creation, the Princeton Institute for Advanced Study, which he modelled on All Souls, and which may be taken as indicative of his ideal of a university. Louis Bamberger, the owner of a Newark, New Jersey, department store, provided an endowment of $8m. and the institute opened in 1930 with Flexner as director. Persecutions in Germany helped Flexner in his task of recruiting distinguished scholars to the institute, Albert Einstein [q.v.] being the most notable acquisition. Flexner retired from the directorship in 1939 and was subsequently appointed director emeritus.

He was a short man, Punch-like in appearance. While his wisdom was acknowledged, he tended to express his views with an undue emphasis which evoked dislike. In 1898 he married Anne Crawford; they had two daughters.

September 23, 1959.

F. S. Flint, who died on February 28, 1960 in Berkshire at the age of 74, was a sensitive and original poet and in another sphere an expert on international labour statistics.

Though T. E. Hulme is the putative father of the Imagist movement, which created some stir in English literary circles (and a far greater one in American) in the second and third decades of the century, it owed a great deal to Flint's encyclopaedic knowledge of the French Symbolists and of Rimbaud, and his search for a new mode of poetic expression. Flint's own production was all too small. The death of his first wife in 1920 left him so utterly disorientated that he wrote virtually nothing of moment thereafter; but he continued a vigorous and useful career as Chief of the Overseas Section, Statistics Division, Ministry of Labour, for five years after the usual retiring age, under the exceptional conditions ruling after the Second World War.

Frank Stuart Flint was born in Islington on December 19, 1885, the son of a commercial traveller. His boyhood was passed in squalid poverty and even before he left elementary school he spent many evening, Saturday and Sunday hours working as a barber's lather-boy. Sundry blind-alley jobs followed, but during his adolescence Flint began to buy cheaply from bookstalls, began to travel in the realms of gold, and laid the foundations of what was to grow into a wide and deep culture. At 19 he was admitted to the civil service. He attended night classes, studying Latin and French, and made such progress in the latter tongue that he eventually became almost bilingual, and within 10 or 15 years was actually writing in the *Mercure de France.*

Flint published volumes of verse entitled *In the Net of the Stars* (1909), *Cadences* (1915) and *Otherworld* (1920). He wrote extensively on poetry and French literature in the *Chapbook,* the *Egoist,* the *Poetry Review, The Times Literary Supplement* and elsewhere, and he was the friend of many of the notable literary men of the day. A convinced socialist, he also knew many men in the Labour movement, and W. H. Stevenson, the pioneer editor of the *Daily Herald,* was a close and lifelong friend who shared his love of all things French and made many journeys to France in his company.

Flint's poetry, much of it in "unrimed cadence" (a term invented by him), showed a keen sense of pathos, great humanity, a wide philosophic sweep, and a Wordsworthian faculty for keeping his eye closely fixed on his subject and using something very near "the real language of men". "Courage" and "Otherworld" are perhaps his best-known pieces. He excelled likewise in his official task, taking part in sundry delegations to study foreign labour conditions, presenting masterly reports on such subjects, and keeping his eye on foreign studies. Apart from French, he was able to use Italian, Spanish, German and Russian for such purposes. He was awarded the Imperial Service Order when he retired from the Ministry of Labour nine years ago.

People who met him casually in later life, and many friends of varying ages and callings, will remember with affection and regret the tall, massive frame, the fine domed forehead skirted by long white locks in professorial disorder, and above all the sparkling stream of gay conversation about persons, trends, places, theories, authors, which might range in one session from mathematics to Casanova, from

Avignon to the East End, with occasional quotations from Heine, Dante or Catullus—a conversation which made all interlocutors aware of the impact of a fine, free personality, full of good nature for all but the fool or the knave, who were frostily ignored.

February 29, 1960.

Errol Flynn, the actor, collapsed in Vancouver on October 14, 1959 and died soon afterwards. He was 50.

Flynn's early life sounds more like something out of one of his films than sober fact. Born in 1909 in Tasmania, the son of a biologist, he went to school in London and Paris before embarking on a period of wandering which included, as well as a brief appearance in repertory at Northampton and writing (an activity he kept up throughout his career, writing a novel among other works) diving for pearls in Tahiti and hunting gold and head-hunters in New Guinea.

His introduction to films was quite by chance; a company working on a short film about the mutiny on the Bounty in the South Pacific hired his schooner, some of the material in which he appeared fell into the hands of a talent-scout, and in 1935 he was offered a contract with a Hollywood company, his first professional appearance being in *Don't Bet on Blondes.*

It must be admitted (he admitted it often enough himself) that his early films showed little sign of acting ability, but fortunately he seldom appeared in a role which required much acting: his great popularity was based on a series of swashbuckling adventure stories, such as *Captain Blood, The Charge of the Light Brigade, The Adventures of Robin Hood,* and *The Sea Hawk.* If these parts did not require any very remarkable acting ability, however, they did call for other qualities—a colourful personality, a striking presence, considerable grace and agility, and the ability to look well in period costumes—all of which he possessed in abundance. He also began to show signs of acting ability after five years or so, for he was not so over-shadowed as might have been expected in *The Private Lives of Elizabeth and Essex,* in which he played opposite Bette Davis as Elizabeth.

The war years produced few films of any great interest for him, except perhaps *Objective Burma,* which has never been forgotten in Britain as "the film in which Errol Flynn took Burma single-handed". After the war he made a group of emotional dramas in which he seemed rather less at home, such as *Never Say Goodbye, Need for Each Other,* and *Escape Me Never,* but was soon back in the action roles which he played best, with films like *Gentleman Jim, Against All Flags, The Master of Ballantrae,* and *Crossed Swords.*

He also appeared, rather improbably, as Soames in *The Forsyte Saga,* though plans for him to appear on the London stage in *Jane Eyre* never materialized.

During the early 1950s his career seemed to be taking several wrong turnings while the amount of personal publicity he received only increased. A film he was producing and starring in, based on the life of William Tell, foundered for lack of funds, and the two films he made in Britain with Anna Neagle, *Lilacs in the Spring* and *King's Rhapsody,* were not really suited to his talents. He had already almost been written off by the film industry when he was offered a leading role in *The Sun Also Rises,* based on Hemingway's* novel. His performance as the cheerily dissolute Englishman in this film was a revelation of hitherto unsuspected talents (he maintained that this was the first opportunity he had ever had to play himself on the screen) and made him a leading star again. It was followed by an excellent portrayal of John Barrymore, whom he had known well, in *Too Much, Too Soon,* and the leading role in Huston's *The Roots of Heaven.* In the Cuban revolution he fought on the side of Castro, and shortly before his death he had completed his autobiography.

Errol Flynn's career provides the perfect example of the old actor's adage that short of a couple of years in a repertory company there is nothing like 20 years of top stardom for teaching a performer how to act.

October 16, 1959.

H. P. Folland, O.B.E., one of the pioneer designers of the British aircraft industry, died on September 5, 1954 on the eve of the Farnborough Air Display, at his home at Nottingham after a long illness. He was 65.

It was in the very early days of flying that Folland, who had served his apprenticeship with pioneer motor car manufacturers, decided to throw in his lot with the infant industry, and to that end joined the Royal Aircraft Factory (now the Royal Aircraft Establishment) at Farnborough, where he was assistant to Sir Geoffrey de Havilland*. He played a notable part in the design of the famous F.E. and S.E. series of machines, one of which—the S.E. 5A—was one of the best fighting scouts at the end of the 1914-18 War, and established air superiority over the Germans on the Western Front. His later successes included the great Gloster series, the first of which—the Bamel—won the Aerial Derby of 1921, and a number of machines for the Schneider Trophy races, besides the Gloster fighter aircraft which did so well in the earlier phases of the 1939-45 War.

Henry Phillip Folland was born on January 22, 1889, and served his apprenticeship with the Lanchester Motor Company. Soon after he was out of his time he joined the designing staff of the Swift Motor Company, and then went to Daimlers, where he remained until he joined the staff of the Royal Aircraft Factory in 1912. He remained there until 1917, when he went to the newly formed British Nieuport Company as chief engineer and designer. He was thus responsible for the Nieuport Nighthawk, which was ordered by the Air Ministry in large numbers for the 1919 war programme. The collapse of Germany in November 1918 however, led to the orders being cancelled, and the machine was never used in quantity by the R.A.F. He also designed a twin-engined triplane bomber, the Nieuport London and the Nieuport Goshawk, which broke the then British speed record with a speed of 166 miles an hour.

In 1921 he joined the Gloster Aircraft Company and was first chief engineer and designer and later chief designer and technical director. His first success there was the Bamel which won the Aerial Derby on its first flight in 1921. The machine won again in 1922 and 1923 and walked over in 1924, besides making various speed and height records. In the last-named year he produced his first machine for the Schneider Trophy, but it was prevented by an accident from taking part in the race. In the next year his Gloster Napier III was second, but though he designed several more machines for this competition none of them ever achieved the leading place.

The long line of aircraft for the R.A.F. designed by him while he was still with the Gloster Company included the Grebe, Gamecock, Gauntlet, Gladiator, and the F5/34. His long and fruitful association with Gloster aircraft came to an end in 1937 when he founded his own manufacturing company, Folland Aircraft Limited, with a factory at Hamble, near Southampton. He was managing director until ill-health compelled his resignation in 1951, but continued to serve on the board with his successor, W. E. W. Petter*, the designer of the Canberra.

An aircraft which bears his name—the Folland Midge—a "pocket-sized" jet fighter, was being shown at Farnborough during the display.

Folland leaves a widow and two sons, both of whom are following in their father's footsteps in aviation.

September 7, 1954.

Cathleen Sabine Follett—See **Mann.**

Dr. Mont Follick, Labour member of Parliament for Loughborough from 1945 to 1955, and an ardent advocate of English spelling reform and a decimal currency, died in hospital in London on December 10, 1958.

His advocacy of spelling reform was an absorbing passion. Though he never lost his sense of humour, or his temper, even when subjected to ridicule, he declined to be daunted by opposition, and refused to relax his crusade for the simplification of the English language.

His first Bill—described in its long title as a Bill "to set up a committee to introduce a rational system of spelling with a view to making English a world language and to eliminate unnecessary drudgery and waste of time at school"—was published in February 1949 but was rejected on second reading by only three votes after a lively debate in which I. J. Pitman read some pungent extracts from a commendatory letter from George Bernard Shaw.

Follick was by no means cast down and in

February 1953 introduced the Simplified Spelling Bill, which empowered the Minister of Education and the Secretary of State for Scotland, first, to institute research into new methods likely to improve the teaching of reading to young children; and, secondly, to lay before Parliament a scheme for facilitating the teaching of reading based on the results of the investigation, which the local education authorities would be free to adopt or not, as they thought fit.

This time Follick had better success, for the Bill survived a second reading (by 65 votes to 53). But subsequently he and his fellow promoters withdrew it after the Minister of Education, in a written reply to a question by Follick, expressed her interest in and good will for any proposal designed to investigate improvements in the teaching of reading.

In 1955 he introduced a Decimal Currency Bill, which proposed the setting up of a commission, with the powers of a royal commission, to find out how best decimal currency could be introduced, but he had no success with it.

Born in Cardiff in 1887, he spent most of his life in the study of languages and in addition to speaking seven, he had a working knowledge of 14. He was educated at the Sorbonne, Paris, the University of Halle—of which he was Doctor of Philosophy—and the University of Padua. For four years he was Professor of English at the University of Madrid. Founder and proprietor of the Regent School of Languages, he evolved his own system of teaching, which, he claimed, minimized substantially the difficulties of foreigners in acquiring a knowledge of English.

The destruction of the building by enemy action in the late war represented a setback to his prestige, as well as to the methods he had so long practised. At various times he served as secretary to prominent personalities, including the Aga Khan [q.v.], Sir Robert Philp (Prime Minister of Queensland), and Muley Hafid (Emperor of Morocco).

Follick made his first bid to enter Parliament in 1929, when he stood at Ashford, Kent, but failed to get elected, and his other candidatures, in 1931 for East Surrey and in 1935 for West Fulham, were also unsuccessful. In the general election of 1945, however, he successfully contested Loughborough and retained his seat in the elections of 1950 and 1951. He did not stand for election in 1955.

He was the inventor and patentee of the Geodok system of teaching geography, a governor of Uppingham School and of Nottingham University, and the author of a number of books, one of which, in particular, an English grammar for foreigners, achieved great popularity.

December 11, 1958.

Isaac Foot, P.C., died in his sleep at his home at Callington, Cornwall, on December 13, 1960. He was 80. He had been ill for about two months and confined to his bed for a fortnight.

Isaac Foot was born on February 23, 1880, of comparatively humble origin. A Devon man, by birth and upbringing, he showed the county of his origin in his speech, in his walk and in a spirit which was robust and adventurous.

His education was brief, and he started his career as a clerk in the civil service, earning 15s. a week. He transferred to the law, building up a highly successful solicitor's business in Plymouth. But the law could not contain his energies, and as a young man he was striking out vigorously in national and local politics, and winning deserved plaudits for his eloquence in many a Wesleyan chapel. Although no man of his generation gave more steadfast devotion to Liberal politics, it is probable that he reserved his very best for the Church in whose service he gave himself without stint. He was vice-president of the Methodist Conference in 1937-38.

At the age of 30 he fought his first election, and he fought four more before he won a resounding victory at a by-election in Bodmin in 1922. He sat in Parliament for 2½ years, having to fight in that period four elections. Few members of the House of Commons can have had a poorer return in point of time for the number of contests. Yet Foot quickly made his mark in Parliament. He was decidedly Asquithian in his sympathies and his qualities quickly attracted for him the warm friendship of Asquith's closest councillors—Sir Donald Maclean, W. M. R. Pringle, Vivian Phillips and Harcourt Johnstone. Although Isaac Foot had the somewhat severe opinions associated with his puritanical sympathies—he was, for example, a leader of the temperance movement—these were relieved and illuminated by flashes of wit and learning which delighted his friends and startled those who merely knew of him by hearsay. He was a deft user of the quick shaft and aside; an example, which was much enjoyed by the House of Commons, was when a raw Labour Minister tried to excuse himself by referring to the Law's delays, Foot completed the quotation "and the Insolence of office".

After five years' absence from Parliament he was again returned for Bodmin in 1929, holding the seat until 1935. He served on the Indian Round-Table Conference with conspicuous success, and when the National Government was formed he was Secretary for Mines. After holding this office for little more than a year he resigned with his Liberal colleagues over the Ottawa agreements. Although it might be easy to dismiss Foot's political career as disappointing—and certainly he made great sacrifices for the sake of principle—he yet filled a position respected and coveted by men of all parties and not achieved by his more successful but less adamant Liberal colleagues who remained in the National Government. His political career was a triumph of courage and character, which lent lustre to the eclipse of that great party to which he was proud to belong. In 1937 he was made a Privy Councillor, but he never returned to Parliament.

Apart from the deep consolations of his religious faith, he sought his recreation in books. On leaving Plymouth he went to live in a delightful country house near Callington in Cornwall and the walls were rapidly lined with books. As cases of books came down from the London auction rooms his first wife, who guided him without ostentation, forbade him to buy any more. He went to elaborate subterfuges to avoid this *diktat* and during the war, when he was a member of the Security Executive, his room resembled nothing so much as a bookshop on stocktaking day. He was a colossal reader, teaching himself French, German and modern Greek. The fruits of his scholarship were seen in his speeches, and although something of the fire was spent, he commanded the enthusiasm of audiences when, as president of the Liberal Party in 1947, he spoke in all parts of Great Britain. In 1943 he paid a highly successful visit to America of four months' lecturing. He was Deputy Lord Mayor of Plymouth in 1920-21 and Lord Mayor in 1945-46.

Though Foot might have been more at home in the service of the Lord Protector, on whose career he was an outstanding authority—he was president of the Cromwell Association—or as the colleague of John Bright, he brought to the twentieth century something of the force and fervour of those earlier days. Though morality and spiritual matters may have been out of fashion, he was determined to show that for him at any rate they still counted. The feeling, to which he gave frequent expression in his speeches, that the Liberal Party, even in its decline, was the custodian of a great tradition in English public life, the belief in a moral foundation for party politics, helps to explain how his gifts and oratorical power shed round him:

"A constant influence, a peculiar grace".

His first wife, Eva, daughter of Angus Mackintosh, M.D., by whom he had five sons and two daughters, died in 1946, and he married secondly in 1951 Mrs. Catherine Elizabeth Taylor, daughter of Frederick Dawe, of Liskeard.

The distinction of the father was passed on in good measure to his sons, Sir Hugh Foot (later Lord Caradon), formerly Governor of Cyprus; [Sir] Dingle Foot, Q.C. [d. 1978], Liberal member for Dundee and later Labour member for Ipswich; and Michael Foot, who was recently elected to Aneurin Bevan's [q.v.] seat, Ebbw Vale, and who represented Devonport in the Labour interest from 1945 to 1955.

December 14, 1960.

Admiral of the Fleet Sir Charles Morton Forbes, G.C.B., D.S.O., who died on August 28, 1960 at the age of 79, held in turn most of the important commands at sea or positions at the Admiralty open to one officer.

His career was for many years similar to that of the late Admiral of the Fleet Sir Roger Backhouse, whom he followed in one appointment after another—Director of Naval Ordnance, Controller of the Navy, Second-in-Command of the Mediterranean Fleet, and Commander-in-Chief of the Home Fleet. He held the last-named command at the time of the international crisis of September 1938, and at the outbreak of the war with Germany a year later. In May 1940 he was promoted Admiral of the Fleet and in November of that year he was appointed Commander-in-Chief, Plymouth. This was his last command, which he held until August 1943.

There was nothing spectacular about Forbes, nor, on first acquaintance, did he give the impression of possessing outstanding personality. In modesty he much resembled his predecessor and lifelong friend, Roger Backhouse; but he also resembled him in being a master of his profession, in the faculty of recognizing instantly all the factors in any problem with which he was faced, and in grappling with all difficulties with competence and quiet confidence. No man ever saw him "rattled"; he had full confidence in himself, and he inspired it in those under his command. Those who were in closest contact with him knew best the reserves of power in the man, the clear vision, sound judgment, and strong sense of proportion which were a tower of strength to those who, working under him, shared his burdens though not his reponsibilities.

After his flag was struck at Plymouth, in 1943, he lived at Cawsand Place, Wentworth, Surrey.

Sir Charles was twice married, in 1909 to Agnes Millicent Ewen, of Potters Bar, by whom he had one daughter and one son; and in 1921 to Marie Louise, daughter of the late Axel Berndtson, of Stockholm, by whom he had one daughter.

August 30, 1960.

Paul Fort, who was often referred to as the "Prince of Poets" because of his vast output of charming little poems in ballad form, died at his home at Montlhéry on April 20, 1960. He was 88.

Born at Reims in 1872, Paul Fort was destined for a military career, but devoted himself instead to poetry, letters, and the theatre. When no more than 18, he assembled a company of out of work actors who gave to the Parisian public a number of plays which were reputed to be unactable, the work of Maeterlinck, Rémy de Gourmont and Catulle-Mendès. He also organized performances in Paris theatres of *chansons de gestes.*

Obsessed by the spirit and expression of the Middle Ages, Paul Fort's earliest ballads made their first appearance in book form in 1897, with a preface by Pierre Louys. In the next 40 years new volumes followed until, in 1950, a definite edition was established, of some 40 volumes. Some of their lines have become famous all over the world.

As a poet and artist he was deeply imbued with the symbolism of his time, and his influence was certainly very great among the poetic movements of the beginning of this century. Mistral once called him "the cicada of the north", and it was an apt title for a man whose poetry, full of individual rhythms, metre and assonance, caught very closely the tone and colour of his native land.

Fort, who was a Commander of the Legion of Honour, in 1956 received the Grand Prix Littéraire of the city of Paris. This was one of the last occasions on which his familiar figure was seen in public, with his walking stick and his black beret sitting on his white locks.

The work of Paul Fort belongs to a period which, in the passage of time, has gained in picturesque charm something of what it has lost in vitality. Fort was a member of the symbolist movement. He can be named in the same breath as Georges Rodenbach and Stuart Merrill, and perhaps most closely of all with a better poet than any of the three, Francis Jammes. His *Ballades françaises* still survive—written in a very personal form of poetic prose; and his special art was to bring into French poetry something of the Virgilian spirit. Rustic and tender, he was able to reconcile with a slightly affected innocence of outlook the disquieting impressionism of Verlaine. Much of his output is too remote from the preoccupations of poetry during the past fifty years to carry more than a certain curiosity interest; but once the tide of fashion turns it is likely that room will be found for his charming minor talent.

He was a *chansonnier* in the world of the *Chat Noir,* and in the nineties he briefly acted as a vivifying force in the Paris theatre. In 1905 he founded the quarterly, *Vers et Prose,* which, through publishing works by Gide [q.v.], Claudel [q.v.], Apollinaire, Colette [q.v.], and many of the better writers of the day, laid the path which eventually led to the *Nouvelle Revue Française.*

April 22, 1960.

Hubert J. Foss, who died suddenly in London on May 27, 1953 at the age of 54, touched life at many points, but probably his chief work was the establishment of the music department of the Oxford University Press.

A man of great energy, his whole aspect was vivacious. Behind an exuberant and rather worldly manner he had a ready and well-stored mind, flair, enthusiasm, and high ideals. Publisher, editor, author, pianist, composer and arranger, he made by no means a negligible contribution to the musical life of the country in each of these fields, and as though this were not enough he was a connoisseur of fine printing and played a considerable part in the production of the Oxford Lectern Bible.

Hubert James Foss was born at Croydon on May 2, 1899, and was educated as a classical scholar of Bradfield College, but he did not proceed to university. He was for a short time in the Army towards the end of the 1914-18 war and then went into journalism as assistant editor of *Land and Water.* He went to the Oxford University Press in 1921 and in 1924 founded its music department. Over a period of more than 20 years he built up a flourishing business of general music publishing, initiating series of church and educational music on the one hand and acting for Vaughan Williams [q.v.], Walton, and Rawsthorne*, among contemporary composers, on the other.

He devised and edited the musical volumes in the *Oxford Heritage* series. He was the author of *Music in My Time* (1933) and of a monograph on Vaughan Williams (1949); in 1952 he reissued Warlock's study of Delius with substantial additional chapters from his own pen. Composition was a side-line with him, and his chief works are songs, including seven settings of Hardy. Between the wars he founded the Bach Cantata Club and on occasion conducted its concerts.

During the last few years of his life he was a freelance journalist, broadcaster, and lecturer, turning out excellent concert programme notes and miscellaneous work for the furtherance of music on a broad front. His taste was catholic, but he had a special feeling for the music of Warlock, Moeran, and Van Dieren, to whom he was bound by ties of friendship, and he was a profound admirer of Vaughan Williams. In 1952 he had a serious illness, but recovered sufficiently to enjoy another year of active musical work.

He married Miss Dora Stevens, the singer, who survives him, together with a son and a daughter of the marriage.

May 28, 1953.

John Fothergill, who died in Rugby on August 26, 1957 at the age of 81, was what used to be called "a character". At the age of 46 he abandoned classical archaeology for innkeeping, and made the Spreadeagle at Thame an hotel remarkable for its furnishing, cuisine, wines, and general amenity.

He approached innkeeping as an art, and devoted great resources of labour, good taste, humour, and care for detail to the task of producing a hostelry which should be something far from the ordinary. His day-by-day record of guests and happenings and conversations was seen by C. H. C. Prentice, of Chatto and Windus, who brought it out in 1931 as *An Innkeeper's Diary.* The book quickly went through four printings and had great success as a lively, witty, caustic, self-revelatory document as unique as the Spreadeagle itself. Shortly afterwards Fothergill left Thame for Ascot, and later still moved to Market Harborough, but it was in his Oxfordshire days that he best succeeded in expressing his personality by the creation of an environment.

John Rowland Fothergill was born on February 27, 1876, the son of the late George Fothergill, of Allan Bank, Grasmere, and was educated at Bath College and St. John's College, Oxford. He then spent some time at Leipzig and later took a course at the Slade School. He became the friend of Robert Ross, Henry Tonks, Sir William Rothenstein, P. Wilson Steer, and others prominent in the domain of art; and he always retained a keen interest in matters aesthetic, liking to surround himself with good furniture, pottery and silver, and with people capable of appreciating such things. Twelve years of his early career were spent on archaeological work, chiefly in Greece; and he collaborated with his friend, E. P. Warren, in forming the collection of classical antiquities of the Boston Museum of Fine Arts.

In 1922, Fothergill had to abandon the leisured life of a connoisseur, artist, and archaeologist and take up some remunerative occupation. He had a certain capital, and so decided to keep an inn. After investigating various properties he took over the Spreadeagle, Thame, at a valuation. On the face of it there was no special advantage in the site (unless, perhaps, its proximity to Oxford be considered such) and the trade was that of the ordinary small country town. Fothergill had an uphill task in fashioning his longed-for inn in this place. He was never a tactful man, and managed to fall out with a number of local people because they required (in his view) too much for too little. It took time, much thought and work, and infinite patience before the Spreadeagle began to show a profit and to assume the aspect he envisaged for it. "I've determined", he wrote in his diary, "not only to have proper and properly cooked food but to have only either intelligent, beautiful or well-bred people to eat it".

This high aim involved points of policy and procedure which gave Fothergill's combative and tactless nature full rein. He would refuse guests because he disliked their notepaper or style of letter-writing; far from taking the standpoint that "the customer is always right", he rebuked guests for various peccadilloes; he had a wary eye on the man who is out for something for nothing; and if he suspected the morals of a couple he would call the young man into his office next morning and firmly request him not to come again. On the positive side he showed energy and artistry in various ways. His furniture was old and good; so were his wines (he was very learned on this subject and stocked a huge cellar); he made the utmost efforts to provide unusual dishes worthy of the epicure; and he even sent abroad, to France, Italy, Norway, Greece, or Palestine, for specialities he had enjoyed in those countries. His social and literary connexions were most valuable to him; parties of Oxford dons got to know the resources of the Spreadeagle, and in due course the visitors' book presented a galaxy of famous names in art, politics, literature, the stage, and the aristocracy.

An Innkeeper's Diary is an excellent bedside book, for it can be read in short spasms, forward or backward, and a "dip" anywhere in its pages will bring up some piquant anecdote, some witty piece of worldly wisdom or some caustic observation on human nature. Fothergill, in white coat and buckled shoes, presiding over the thing he had made, let nothing escape him. If he was often uncharitable in his judgments and over-inclined to snobbery, he was capable of sporadic generosities and understanding courtesies that helped to offset these other qualities. This book and the *Confessions of an Innkeeper* (1938), by virtue of their wit, their bluntness, their pellucid honesty (with a vein of real idealism running through all), rank among the healthier literature of their type and time. *My Three Inns,* his last book, came out in 1949.

A fruit of Fothergill's archaeological days was his translation from the German of E. Löwy's *The Rendering of Nature in Early Greek Art.* He got a number of his literary friends to collaborate in the pleasant *Fothergill Omnibus,* while his *Gardener's Colour Book* gave counsel in a field which he had assiduously cultivated. His own garden at Thame was a model, and he was an adept at flower arrangement and blending. Leaving Thame in 1932, he ran the Royal Ascot Hotel for two years and then in 1934 took over the Three Swans, Market Harborough. Here he remained until 1952.

Fothergill was twice married; first to Doris Gillian Herring, and secondly to Kate Headley Kirby, having two sons by the second marriage.

August 29, 1957.

Giles Fox-Strangways — See **Ilchester.**

J. O. Francis, the distinguished Welsh dramatist, died on October 1, 1956 in London at the age of 74.

He reached the heart of the Welsh nation and its characteristics, and put them into dramatic form starkly and divertingly, with a depth and intensity of few other playwrights who have won recognition beyond the bounds of Wales. In his own way he stood alone, and was pre-eminent, with that touch of near genius which set him beside Sean O'Casey*, for his capacity to bring forth laughter and tears in alternate moments. His greatest work, which was presented in 1913 under the title *Change*, is a powerful drama of the industrial scene in Wales and won for him the drama prize instituted by the late Lord Howard de Walden, who was his lifetime friend, patron, and admirer.

John Oswald Francis was born at Merthyr Tydfil on September 7, 1882, a son of Davis Francis. He was educated at Merthyr County School and at the University College of Wales, Aberystwyth, where he graduated, and at the Sorbonne. He then became a school teacher in London but from the beginning his interests and activities were dominated by his acute sense of the dramatic, and his passion for the theatre. This was stimulated by his contact in his mid-twenties with the Irish school of dramatists then making its mark, and with his friends he set out to create a Welsh school as a parallel rather than imitative venture.

Many critics would no doubt say that he was most successful in his high comedies. *Birds of a Feather,* which, during the years of the 1914-18 War, had a remarkably successful run at the London Coliseum, and *The Poacher,* which was in some respects his greatest achievement, proved him much more the man with the finest command of creating character than his massive historical piece *Howell of Gwent,* which was introduced to both the Welsh and the London stages by the Welsh National Theatre Company. On more than one occasion he sought to explain that in the Welsh pioneering years there was a tendency to rely upon observation and experience rather than to range imaginatively over history and legend. The fact remains, however, that he himself was at his happiest, and certainly his most revealing, when he created those irresistible characters of the Welsh countryside with the humour of *The Poacher* or with the conflict of struggle in *The Dark Little People,* which, next to *Change,* was his finest work. He wrote charming, unaffected prose, including a collection of essays, *The Legend of the Welsh.*

He was a man of simple habits and delicate perceptions who never sought recognition and was always surprised—perhaps a little baffled—when from time to time his work was praised. For some years after forsaking schoolmastering he was an official of the National Savings Movement and, although it was always difficult to think of him among the money-changers, he was a successful and popular figure among his colleagues there. He was also held in the highest regard by the intimate circle in which he moved at the National Liberal Club. To the last it was his greatest surprise that for some years his one-act plays and sketches, written at the height of his powers, should have won emphatic success on the British music-hall stage.

October 2, 1956.

Sir George Franckenstein, formerly Austrian Ambassador to Britain, was killed, with his wife, in the crash of a Sabena two-engined aircraft near Rhine-Main airport on October 14, 1953.

Sir George, who was 75, was one of the most distinguished members of the Diplomatic Corps in London during the period between the two wars. He was the envoy chosen by the Austrian Republic to represent it in London when diplomatic relations were resumed with Great Britain after the 1914-18 War, and he held the post uninterruptedly until Austrian independence was destroyed by the German Reich in 1938. When his post was suppressed he became a British subject and was created a Knight Bachelor. The previous year he had had conferred upon him the G.C.V.O.

Franckenstein was born in 1878, the son of a diplomatist of the old Austro-Hungarian Service, Baron Karl Franckenstein and of his wife, who had been by birth a Countess Schoenborn. As a young man he served as attaché and secretary in several of the larger Austro-Hungarian Embassies abroad before becoming private secretary to Count Aehrenthal, then Foreign Minister. He was afterwards frequently sent on special missions abroad, which included a visit to India and another to the Caucasus.

The most painful duty he had to perform was to go to Paris after the War of 1914-18 to receive the terms of peace imposed upon the new and dismembered Austria. He used afterwards half-humorously to recall how he—whom all agreed to regard as one of the gentlest and most cultured of men—was confined behind barbed wire and never allowed to go for a motor drive without an armed guard. He combined dignity with tact in his difficult position, and the Vienna Government had no hesitation in choosing him to reopen the house in Belgrave Square where he had served before 1914 under Count Mensdorff—now to be a Legation instead of an Embassy. He made his Legation a centre of London life, where politicians, artists, journalists, and general society mingled without ceremony, and where first-rate concerts were performed by Viennese virtuosi.

Franckenstein made a great success of his mission. He negotiated the loan raised for Austria under the League of Nations scheme, a large part of the money being found in London. He was also responsible for the idea of holding an exhibition of British art in Vienna in 1927, and furthered every project for encouraging British travellers to visit Austria. He drew the bonds of the two countries very close together, culturally as well as politically, and when the Nazis seized his native land it seemed a natural transition for him to become a British subject. The normally rather complicated formalities of naturalization were waived, and he immediately became known as Sir George, instead of Baron, Franckenstein. He was active during the 1939-45 War on a committee which prepared the case for an independent Austria after the end of hostilities. He published his reminiscences in a volume called *Facts and Features of my Life* (1939).

In 1939 he married Editha, daughter of the late Captain N. Keppel King. There is a son of the marriage.

October 15, 1953.

Gilbert Frankau, the author, died at his home at Hove on November 4, 1952 at the age of 68.

A fluent, lavish novelist, with a genuine gift for story-telling in an idiom conspicuously larger than life, he commanded a wide public in Britain and the United States. Combative by temperament, thrusting in habit and expression, unsentimental where worldly standards were concerned—though by no means lacking in sentiment in his writing—he early fixed his mind on success and quickly achieved it. Like almost everything that he wrote, *Peter Jackson, Cigar Merchant,* which brought him reputation and prosperity, made up for some failings in literary style by the vigour, colour, and aggressive shrewdness of its narrative quality. Frankau lived as abundantly as he wrote, and on all sorts of matters, politics and literature among them, held very positive and often unpopular opinions which he expressed with a verve that was stimulating to some and, to say the least, unwelcome to others.

Born on April 21, 1884, he was the son of Arthur Frankau, a partner in the firm of J. Frankau & Co., wholesale cigar merchants, and of his wife, Julia who in her day enjoyed great popularity as a novelist under the pseudonym of "Frank Danby". From St. Michael's, Westgate-on-Sea, he went to Eton (H. V. Macnaghten's house) by scholarship, and there founded the *X Magazine* and began to write verse. At 17 he left school and was sent to live in Germany to acquire the language. He was taken into the cigar business in 1904, and in the following year became managing director of the concern, now reconstituted as a private limited company.

Frankau remained in the cigar business until 1914, showing some commercial ability and living in reasonable prosperity. He went to Havana and the United States in 1906 and 1907 and made a world tour between 1912 and 1914. He began to take writing seriously about 1910, and before the outbreak of war in 1914 he had published *One of Us* and *Tid'apa*—"novels in verse" of somewhat Kiplingesque sentiment done in the *ottava rima* of Byron's *Don Juan,* which Frankau managed with extreme facility. In October 1914 he was granted a commission in the 9th Battalion, The East Surrey Regiment, and in the following March he was transferred to the R.F.A., became adjutant of his brigade, and proceeded to France. In October 1916 he was appointed staff captain for special propaganda duties in Italy, and carried out his duties for 10 months. Then delayed symptoms of shell-shock and neurasthenia declared themselves, and in February 1918 he was invalided out of the service.

Even during the war Frankau had contrived to continue writing. *The Guns* came out in 1916, *The City of Fear* a year later, when he also published *The Woman of the Horizon,* a first novel, or first prose novel, which was based upon the experiences of his world tour. *Peter Jackson, Cigar Merchant,* appeared in 1919, and thenceforward Frankau was fairly established. His novels followed one another in quick succession, and he was much in demand for newspaper articles, speeches, reports of trials, and so on. For the theme of his novels he was always inclined to turn to what was nearest at hand in his personal experience. Thus *The Seeds of Enchantment* (1921) provided occasion for a vigorous onslaught on the intellectuals, while *The Love Story of Aliette Brunton* in the following year joined melodrama to a considered plea for divorce law reform.

In 1924 Frankau, who had been impressed by the window-dressing of Italian fascism, had taken to political speaking for the extreme Right, and was busily engaged in writing, lecturing, dining out, and running a large establishment in London and a house in the country. His one failure had been a dramatization, made jointly with Aimée de Burgh in 1920, of his mother's novel, *The Heart of a Child.* He never attempted the stage again. In 1926 his *Masterson,* the story of the trials of "an Englishman of the open spaces" in a fashionable and vicious smart set, was bought for America, and he undertook a long and strenuous publicity tour all over the United States. Hollywood did not take to him, nor he to it, though several of his novels were at various times translated to the screen.

The year 1928 brought Frankau an unfortunate adventure in journalism. He had been appointed editor of a new sixpenny weekly, *Britannia,* originally designed as an illustrated magazine of imperial or imperialist sympathies, and the scale of fees paid or offered to the editorial staff and to contributors became a legend in Fleet Street. After Frankau was removed from the editorship and the board, an action brought by him in the Chancery Division was settled out of court. He then returned to novel writing, though it was not long before the magazines renewed their hospitality. He also kept up his political interests, but failed to secure nomination as a Parliamentary candidate. An apostle of the closest collaboration of the English-speaking nations as a means of policing the world, he expressed a violent detestation and horror of socialism and of socialist writers. The course of events during the years before 1939 served only to confirm him in his views, but on the outbreak of war he received a commission in the R.A.F.V.R. and was promoted squadron-leader in April 1940. His later novels were large, lavish, and somewhat hasty, a little dimmed in energy. The most recent was *Oliver Trenton, K.C.,* published in 1951.

Frankau was three times married: first, in 1905, to Dorothea Drummond Black; secondly, in 1922, to Aimée de Burgh; and thirdly, in 1932, to Susan Lorna, only daughter of the late Walter Harris. The first two marriages were both dissolved on the petition of the wives; by the first of them Frankau had two daughters, one of whom, Pamela Frankau*, herself became a well-known novelist.

November 5, 1952.

David Fraser, who for many years was one of the most valued contributors to *The Times* on the affairs of the Far East, died on May 19, 1953 in Washington at the age of 83.

David Stewart Fraser was born on August 16, 1869, at Invergordon, and was educated at Chanonry House, Aberdeen, and at the Edinburgh Institution. He had some experience of commercial life in London with the Bank of New Zealand before accepting employment with the Bank of Bengal in Calcutta. For most men the life of a clerk is one of subjection to routine; in Fraser's case it was an apprenticeship to adventure, for he discovered that he could write, and he began to contribute articles to a local paper. For the most part they were narratives about horses and horse-racing.

In 1900 mind and body responded instantaneously to the call for volunteers to serve in South Africa in Lumsden's Horse. The bank clerk burgeoned swiftly into Regimental Quarter-Master Sergeant, a transformation which sloughed off banking for ever.

The war over, Fraser savoured the pleasures of freedom in London until savings were found to be dwindling with unexpected speed. His adventurous spirit impelled him to present himself to *The Times.* Though the management did not think the expense of a second and untried special correspondent was necessary, Fraser so impressed the official correspondent, under orders to start for the Far East in a few days, that the latter arranged to take him with him as his servant.

He was sent first to Wei-hai-wei, to supervise the erection with all speed of a station equipped with a mast to receive wireless messages from the steamer Haimun, chartered by *The Times* for the special purpose of sending them. The sapper sergeant who designed and erected the mast is still alive and retired in 1931 with the rank of major. "Expedite forestry", "expedite forestry" was the repeated exhortation which Fraser received from his chief. Then fortune poured into his lap the utmost favour she can shower upon a journalist who has wooed and won her. For while his chief made himself responsible for "covering" the war at sea, Fraser, attached to General Kuroki's invading army, sent *The Times* an account of the Battle of the Yalu River which was quoted throughout the world. Remaining with General Kuroki's army until the Battle of the Shako (October 9-17, 1904), Fraser was recalled to London and then commissioned.

Turkey and Persia in Revolt, the outcome of other studies undertaken for *The Times,* published in the following year, marks in retrospect transition from Middle to Far Eastern work for the paper. Fraser the traveller in Turkey, Mesopotamia, Persia, and India became Fraser relatively static in Peking. True, there was a pre-Peking period of two years during which Fraser sat uncomfortably in the editorial chair of the *Peking and Tientsin Times.* Nor did Fraser by any means spend all his time after 1912 in Peking. In 1915 he visited Japan; in 1918 he was sent to Siberia to report on international intervention in Russian affairs; later he travelled in Manchuria primarily to study Sino-Japanese railway rivalries. But in the main he lived and worked (he had become a married man) in Peking.

He brought to Peking, not exactly a preconception but an attitude of mind acquired during his Middle Eastern days, a wary though by no means immutable scepticism as to the capacity of the Orient, whether Young Turkey or Young China, to shake off its unregenerate past, combined with an awareness that what he had learnt about Germany from her Baghdad railway scheme might presently prove applicable to Japan, notwithstanding the alliance, as in fact it did.

Often urged to put together a book on China, he retired to Vancouver in 1940 without doing so. During the 1939-45 war he moved to Washington, where he undertook work for the Government of India Information Service, and since the war had been living there in retirement.

May 21, 1953.

Lady de Frece—See **Tilley.**

Barnett Freedman, C.B.E., the artist, died on January 4, 1958. He was 56.

Freedman's history was a striking instance of the triumph of the ruling passion over difficulties. Born in Stepney on May 19, 1901, he had hardly any schooling, owing to ill health. Four years of his childhood were spent lying on his back in the London Hospital, and it was then that he began to teach himself drawing to relieve the monotony of his existence. His first job was as an office boy, and then for a time he worked as junior draughtsman to a monumental mason. In the evenings he attended the St. Martin's School of Art, where he worked hard, progressed rapidly and finally won a scholarship to the Royal College of Art, then under the direction of Sir William Rothenstein.

Undoubtedly Freedman owed a good deal of his success to the help and encouragement of that admirable teacher. Incidentally, under the title of "A Student", he is the subject of one of Sir William Rothenstein's best portraits. It was at the Royal College, too, that Freedman met his future wife, Miss Beatrice Claudia Guercio, a Sicilian lady of great ability as a book illustrator and decorator. They married young, and besides helping to "produce" him professionally his wife had some influence upon his development in a decorative direction. Freedman left the Royal College in 1925, and for a time, as he put it laconically, starved.

He was true to his race in having an early interest in the theatre. At his first exhibition in 1929 at the oddly named Literary Bookshop—later the Bloomsbury Gallery—some designs for a "London Ballet" were included, and in his interpretations of the life he knew best it was always its dramatic possibilities that appealed to him.

Freedman's next exhibition, at the Zwemmer Gallery in 1931, was mostly of lithographic illustrations to *Memoirs of an Infantry Officer,* by Siegfried Sassoon*, which were later included in the 1935 exhibition of British Art in Industry at the Royal Academy, together with a design for the binding of *Prefaces,* by Bernard Shaw.

By the nineteen-thirties Freedman was well established as a decorative designer. For London Passenger Transport he produced a great deal of work, including a memorable series of posters representing the indoor recreations of London, with chief reference to the theatre, and a cut out and telescopic advertisement on the lines of the toy stage setting, and he also worked regularly for Shell Mex, the B.B.C., and the Post Office.

It was in 1935 that Freedman showed a new side of his talent when his design for the Silver Jubilee Stamp was chosen, with the approval of King George V. In view of the freedom of his work in general his immediate mastery at a first attempt of a symmetrical and formal design came as a surprise.

Freedman was visiting master at the Ruskin School, Oxford, and instructor at the Royal College of Art. Besides *Memoirs of an Infantry Officer* he illustrated Borrow's *Lavengro,* Tolstoy's *War and Peace, Oliver Twist, Wuthering Heights*, and Walter de la Mare's [q.v.] *Love.* He staged and produced plays by Israel Zangwill at the Scala, Little, and Fortune Theatres. Works by Freedman were purchased for the Tate Gallery and the Victoria and Albert Museum.

In 1940, on the recommendation of the advisory committee presided over by Sir Kenneth Clark, Freedman was invited by the War Office to be one of the official war artists. He was with the B.E.F. in France and was evacuated from Boulogne.

From 1941 to 1946 he was an official war artist to the Admiralty.

January 6, 1958.

Dr. Douglas Southall Freeman, the American historian, whose vast and scholarly biographies of General Robert E. Lee and George Washington have few parallels in this century, died of a heart attack at Richmond, Virginia, on June 13, 1953. He was 67.

He was born at Lynchburg, Virginia, on May 16, 1886, and graduated from Richmond College in 1904. He became one of its fellows in 1906 and spent some years in advanced historical studies at Johns Hopkins University in Baltimore. In 1909 he joined the editorial staff of the Richmond *Times-Despatch* and in 1912 joined the staff of the Richmond *News Leader* as associate editor, becoming editor two years later. He remained editor until his retirement in 1949.

Yet in these years he managed not only to edit a newspaper but at the same time to establish himself as one of America's leading historians and to serve on a number of boards, committees and trusts all of which were time-consuming. The achievement was remarkable, but only because the organization of his day was equally so. Rising at 4.30 a.m., he made his own breakfast, reached his office at about 5.20, waded through the news dispatches and typed three columns of leading articles by 8 o'clock, held an editorial conference at 8.10, crossed the street to give a 15-minute broadcast on the news of the day (without a note), returned to his office to transact business until one o'clock, and then gave his second news broadcast. After lunch at home he had a short sleep, and then started his day as an historian, reading and writing until 6.30, when he had supper and went to bed at 8.45. The schedule would alter slightly, but the hours were always as long and every minute of them purposefully occupied.

In spite of his increasing national and international reputation as an historian, Freeman always considered himself a "tramp" newspaperman. He watched his paper closely, setting and demanding high standards of writing. In Richmond he was an institution. Everyone who could listened to his news broadcasts. He was actively associated with every body in the town which worked for the good of the community, and outside Virginia he was a member and trustee of the Rockefeller Fund and the General Education Board, and a trustee of the Carnegie Endowment for International Peace.

Freeman's first major effort in biography—the life of *R. E. Lee*, in four volumes—was the product of 20 years' work. It won him the Pulitzer Prize in 1934. It fully justified its scale. He took care to let the reader see the campaign through Lee's eyes, with only the knowledge Lee had at the time he had to take decisions. He so thoroughly investigated every fact that, in historical value, his biography surpassed even Henderson's classic life of *Stonewall Jackson.* He never let his critical faculty desert him—Southerner though he was—though the very method of writing he chose (following the campaign through Lee's eyes) limited the value of his interpretations. In the virtue of his method lay the defect of the book. Nevertheless it remains a remarkable contribution to military history.

There followed many other studies of the

Civil War, on the military history of which he was now the leading authority, lecturing year after year at the Army War College in Washington. The most important were the three volumes on *Lee's Lieutenants*—"A Study in Command", as he called it in the sub-title—where the same scholarship and incisiveness as before were perhaps marred by his too obvious feeling that Lee, his hero, never received the support he deserved from his subordinates.

Between 1948 and 1952 appeared the first four volumes of Freeman's second great biographical work. A Virginian himself, he approached the greatest Virginian of them all—*George Washington.* Scholarship, objectivity, the amazing mastery of a mass of material: they are all there, preventing a piety proper in a Virginian from becoming blind. The book provides, for the period it covers, almost all that the student or general reader could wish.

In 1914 he married Miss Mary Virginia Geddie, of Richmond, and he had a son and two daughters.

June 15, 1953.

Air Chief Marshal Sir Wilfrid R. Freeman, BT., G.C.B., D.S.O., M.C., who died suddenly in London on May 15, 1953 at the age of 64, took a leading part from 1936 in guiding and developing the aircraft industry of Great Britain. He was closely connected with the vast expansion of the industry to meet the needs of war and the creation of the shadow factories, and was during the 1939-45 war Chief Executive at the Ministry of Aircraft Production.

Wilfrid Rhodes Freeman was born on July 18, 1888, in London, the son of W. R. Freeman. Educated at Rugby and Sandhurst, he was gazetted to The Manchester Regiment in 1908. He learned to fly as a lieutenant in France on a Maurice Farman biplane, taking his certificate in 1913, and was at once selected for the R.F.C. on probation and to join the Central Flying School early in 1914. On completing his course there later in the year he was seconded to the R.F.C. as flying officer. When war broke out in the summer he accompanied No. 2 Squadron to France, where in March 1915 he gained the M.C. and was promoted to flight commander. He returned to England in May, received further promotion to squadron commander in October, and from January to June 1916 commanded No. 14 Squadron in Egypt. In November 1916 he was awarded the D.S.O.

In June 1919 he was accepted for the first naval staff course held at Greenwich after the war; two months later he received a permanent commission in the R.A.F. as wing commander and resigned from the Army. From 1920 he commanded a flying training school at Royston, and from 1922 to 1925 was an instructor at the R.A.F. Staff College, being promoted to group captain in 1923. From 1925 to 1927 he commanded the Central Flying School; from 1927 to 1928 was Deputy Director of Operations and Intelligence; and from 1928 until after his promotion to air commodore in July 1929 commanded the training base at Leuchars, Fifeshire. After a year as chief staff officer at Inland Area headquarters, Stanmore, he was appointed to command the R.A.F. in Trans-jordan and Palestine, and during his three years there from November 1930 was created C.B. in 1932 and promoted to air vice-marshal in July 1933.

He was Commandant of the R.A.F. Staff College from December 1933 to January 1936. Three months later he joined the Air Council as Air Member for Research and Development. In June 1938 when there was a reorganization of the duties of members of the council, he became responsible for production as well as for research and development, and was styled Air Member for Development and Production, the period of his appointment being extended for two years. He had been promoted to air marshal in January 1937 and was promoted to K.C.B. in June of that year. In May 1940 he was promoted to the temporary rank of air chief marshal. He was attached to the Ministry of Aircraft Production under Lord Beaverbrook* from its formation in 1940.

In 1942, with the approval of the Prime Minister, the Minister of Aircraft Production appointed him to be Chief Executive at the Ministry of Aircraft Production, to coordinate and direct the production and the research and development sides of the department. On taking up his new appointment he retired from the R.A.F. and from the Air Council, and the King approved his promotion to G.C.B. in recognition of his outstanding services. He remained as Chief Executive until March 1945, and after relinquishing the post continued to be a member of the Air Supply Council. In the 1945 Birthday Honours he was created a baronet.

He married in 1915 Gladys, third daughter of J. Mews. There were two children, a son and a daughter, of the marriage, which was dissolved in 1935. He married secondly Elizabeth, younger daughter of E. T. Richmond, F.R.I.B.A., and had two daughters. The baronetcy devolves upon his only son, John Keith Noel Freeman, who was born in 1923 and married in 1946 Patricia Denison, younger daughter of the late C. W. Thomas. There is a daughter of the marriage.

May 18, 1953.

Walter Freitag, formerly chairman of the West German Federation of Trade Unions, and a Social Democratic deputy, died at his home at Herdegge on June 7, 1958. He was 68.

Freitag was born in Remscheid, where he was apprenticed as a toolmaker, and joined the trade union movement and the Social Democratic Party while still in his teens. His early political career was stormy, leading in 1918 to a seat on a Workers and Soldiers Council. He returned to trade union work after the revolution and occupied a number of organizing posts until 1932, when he was elected to the Prussian Landtag.

He was one of the first to be arrested after Hitler seized the trade unions, and was imprisoned in concentration camps until 1935. He was savagely treated, and because of ill-health was unable to work until the third year of the war, when he was employed as a watchman. At the end of the war he returned immediately to political work and in 1946 became a deputy in the North Rhine-Westphalia Landtag. But his special interest in the trade union movement remained, and he helped to form I. G. Metall, the largest and most militant union in the Federal Republic. He shared the chairmanship of the union with Brümmer, and was a deputy in the first Bundestag, where he was a fierce critic of Dr. Adenauer's* social policies.

In 1952 differences over the workers' share of control in industry led to the resignation of Fette as chairman of the federation of trade unions, and Freitag was elected. His lifelong militancy did not survive, perhaps because of his increasing ill-health, and within the year he was regarded as a moderate.

As much as anybody he was responsible for the good industrial relations of that period, and passively accepted the formation of the Christian trade unions, a ramshackle organization favoured by church and industry to divide and weaken the movement. His judgment proved good; the Christian trade unions remain small and powerless. He was re-elected in 1955, but retired the following year. Since 1955 he had been a member of the administrative council of the west German national railways.

June 9, 1958.

Thomas Fremantle—See **Cottesloe.**

Francesca French, who died on August 2, 1960 at the age of 88, was a member of the China Inland Mission who in the course of her evangelizing work crossed and recrossed the Gobi desert.

She was the last survivor of a celebrated trio, the other members of which were her sister, Evangeline French, [who had died on July 8, 1960], and Mildred Cable [q.v.]. For 15 years they travelled in and around the Gobi desert distributing Bibles and preaching the Gospel. Although they had but one aim on their journeys—to spread the message of Christianity—they gathered a great deal that was of unique interest to geographers, anthropologists, and philologists.

Francesca French, who had spent her youth on the continent of Europe, was 34 before she began work as a missionary. Her sister Evangeline, who as a child was adventurous, restless, and of wild ideas, had already been a missionary in China for 15 years. Francesca, who was of a quieter disposition, had remained at home to care for her widowed mother. When the two sisters and Mildred Cable joined forces in China they became convinced that they should respond to a need in central Asia. They accordingly obtained a roving commission from the China Inland Mission in 1926 to adapt themselves to what they found. Thus began a partnership to which the Chinese attached their proverb "A threefold cord is not easily broken".

They went to the edge of the Gobi desert and whenever they heard of an oasis in uncharted country they went there taking the Gospel message, their portable harmonium, their hymn sheets, and their stock of Bibles. They crossed the length of the Gobi desert five times with many detours. Discomforts and dangers they underwent in a spirit of indomitable cheerfulness. They wore Chinese dress, spoke Chinese and Turki, and lived the life of nomads, retracing their route again and again to see that the seed of Christianity had taken root.

After returning to England Francesca and Mildred Cable started voluntary work for the British and Foreign Bible Society in 1939. Working together as usual, they spoke at conferences of workers and at public meetings, and played a leading part in building up the organization of women's work for the Bible Society in Britain. In 1945 Miss French was made an honorary life governor of the society in recognition of the services she was rendering to it.

In 1947 "The Trio", as they were called, made a tour of Australia and New Zealand for the Bible Society on the occasion of the society's centenary in New Zealand. On the way home they visited India, gaining inside knowledge of the country and people from the missionaries working there, and giving their own experiences at Bible Society meetings. In 1950 they set out on another tour, of South America, at the invitation of the Evangelical Union of South America.

A book by Francesca French and Mildred Cable followed each of their journeys: they include *Something Happened, A Desert Journal, Through Jade Gate and Central Asia, The Gobi Desert, China, Her Life and Her People,* and *Journey with a Purpose.*

August 3, 1960.

Peter Freuchen, the Danish Arctic explorer and author, died on September 2, 1957 after a heart attack at the Elmendorf air base, Alaska, while on his way to the polar regions with a group of explorers. He collapsed and died after carrying his luggage up a steep flight of stairs.

He left New York on August 31 with Donald Macmillan, a member of the Peary polar expedition of 1908, Sir Hubert Wilkins [q.v.], Colonel Bernt Balchen, who headed the Arctic search for Amundsen and Ellsworth [q.v.] in 1925, and Lowell Thomas, writer and explorer. The party were intending to make a colour film for television.

The word "Thule" is associated, for most people, with that vague, mythical place in the extreme North where, according to the Greek sailor Pytheas, the Sun goes down. But Thule is a very real place, an Eskimo settlement in North-West Greenland and one of the oldest seats of their old civilization; centre of a whole school of Arctic exploring and centre of several expeditions. The Danish traveller and scientist Knud Rasmussen and Peter Freuchen made it known the world over. Through both of them, associated since 1906, and the archaeologist of their expeditions, Mathiasen, the existence of an old, rich, highly developed Eskimo culture of neolithic origin, and reaching well into the seventeenth century, has been established.

Peter Freuchen, youngest of the three, was born in 1886 and studied at Copenhagen. He was a raw, country youth of 20 when the first results of the Danish Literary Greenland Expedition Mylius-Erichsen became known and captivated his imagination. He joined Rasmussen, a member of that expedition, when he organized another on his own which took them, between 1906 and 1908, to Eastern Greenland. From then onwards the Arctic held him: he took part in the famous Thule Expeditions of 1910 to 1912, 1913 to 1920, 1921 to 1924; he explored Greenland on his own in 1927 and 1928, Arctic Russia in 1928, Alaska in 1932 and 1933, and the extreme south of South America in 1935. He was physically equipped for such extreme exertions; he was very tall, was possessed of great physical strength, and had a gift of winning the sympathy of those archaic tribes of the supreme North which few others ever possessed. He suffered a hard blow when Navarana, his Eskimo wife and comrade, died during the Thule enterprise of 1921 from influenza.

The relationship had been highly successful, and to picture him as the white man of fiction consoling himself with a local woman would be unjust and untrue. He described in one of his many fascinating books how she was refused Christian burial because she had thought too little of the morals of Christian traders and missionaries to undergo baptism.

He was wont to say that Greenland made him and certainly it was a hard making, for death in various guises was a companion with whom he became tolerably familiar. Not the least miraculous of his deliverances from death was when he was travelling alone in a storm, dug himself a rough shelter, covered it with his sledge, and woke to find himself locked immovably in ice. As a result of this experience he lost a foot and later adopted a wooden leg.

The results of his explorations which kept him, for three consecutive years, among the Eskimos of the archipelago between Greenland and America, and for seven years in uninterrupted sojourn among other Eskimo tribes, were laid down in a number of successful and interesting books: *Eskimo* in 1928, *Sea Tyrant* in 1929, *Ivalu* in 1935, *Arctic Adventure* in 1936, *It's All Adventure* in 1937, *Siberian Adventure* in 1939, and *Vagrant Viking* in 1954. Apart from these books Freuchen was a regular contributor to the Danish liberal newspaper *Politiken*, and a director of a Hollywood film company, where he staged several films of scientific as well as entertainment value. Among those was the film version of *Ivalu,* in which an Eskimo friend, unsophisticated and practically untrained, played the hero with success; above all, Freuchen was a scientist of real ability.

He was made a member of the council of the Royal Danish Geographical Society, a Fellow of the American Geographical Society, and a Maître of the French Académie des Beaux-Arts, and had read many scientific papers on ethnological, meteorological, geographical, and archaeological subjects before learned bodies.

During the Second World War Freuchen was a member of the Danish underground and helped Allied parachutists to escape from Denmark. He was captured by the Nazis and sentenced to death, but before the execution could be carried out the prison in which he was shut up was bombed and he escaped.

In July 1956 he won $64,000 in a television quiz programme in New York answering questions on "the Seven Seas". Waving his prize cheque he exclaimed: "Now I can buy two peg legs—in plastic". Five months later he won a further $16,000 in a similar programme.

In January 1957 he was awarded the gold medal of the Benjamin Franklin Society "for service to mankind in opening new frontiers".

September 4, 1957.

Dr. F. E. Fritsch, D.SC., PH.D., F.R.S., Emeritus Professor of Botany in the University of London, died on May 23, 1954 at the age of 75. He occupied an outstanding position as an authority on the *algae,* especially the green *algae* of fresh water.

Felix Eugen Fritsch was born in 1879, the son of a schoolmaster. He graduated at London University and subsequently studied at Munich. For seven years he was on the botany staff at University College London, and from there went to take charge of the botanical department at East London, now Queen Mary, College.

In spite of the handicap of severe asthma Fritsch soon established himself as an authority on the seasonal changes in the algal periodicity of fresh waters, and his two volumes on *The Structure and Reproduction of the Algae,* published in 1935 and 1945, are monuments alike to a lifetime of fruitful endeavour in the study of this group and to the painstaking thoroughness which characterized all his work.

It was to Fritsch's initiative that the British Freshwater Association owed its formation; and as chairman of its executive committee he guided it through its early years and laid the foundations of its success. As Dean of Science at Queen Mary College and in the counsels of London University his sound judgment was greatly valued, while his genial personality and steadfast purpose endeared him to his colleagues. Apart from walking, for Fritsch was a real lover of the countryside, his main recreation was music and the quartets or quintets in which Fritsch played the violin were not the least attractive feature of the charming hospitality dispensed by Professor and Mrs. Fritsch at weekends prior to the last war.

Having studied under Selereder, it was appropriate that he should have collaborated with Dr. Boodle, the then Keeper of the Jodrell Laboratory at Kew, in the translation of the Systematic Anatomy of Dicotyledons. Fritsch was also invited by Sir Edward Salisbury to collaborate with him in a series of botanical text-books that have passed through a number of editions. Fritsch was elected to the Royal Society in 1932 and was president of the botanical section of the British Association in 1927. He was awarded the Darwin Medal in recognition of his work on *algae*.

He married in 1905 Hedwig, daughter of M. Lasker, who survives him, together with a son of the marriage.

May 24, 1954.

Captain C. B. Fry, who died on September 7, 1956 in London at the age of 84, was known in his school and university days as the finest all-round athlete of the time.

Strong and well built, he was a perfect type of youthful vigour, and he excelled at those pursuits where quickness of eye and activity of limb are required. In the opening years of the present century he became one of England's leading cricketers, and captain of its team in Test matches against Australia and South Africa. To his fondness for sports and games he added a wide range of intellectual interests.

Charles Burgess Fry was born on April 25, 1872, of a family long settled in Sussex, but when he was born his mother happened to be living temporarily in Surrey, and for most of his boyhood his parents lived in Kent.

He went to Repton in 1885 and to Wadham College, Oxford, six years later. At both places he gained many distinctions in both work and play and at Wadham he was a contemporary of F. E. Smith (later Lord Birkenhead) and John Simon (later Viscount Simon) [q.v.]. He was second in the Sixth form at Repton, won a senior scholarship at Wadham, took a first in Classical Moderations, but owing to other distractions, only a fourth in Greats. At school, where he was in the cricket eleven with the brothers Lionel and Richard Palairet, names of almost equal renown in that sphere, he was captain of both cricket and football, as well as twice winner of the aggregate prize at the athletic sports.

At Oxford he was a triple Blue, and in his third year was elected captain of cricket and Association football and president of the athletic club, a combination of offices which is understood to be without parallel. At the inter-university sports of 1892 he set up a new record in the long jump with a distance of 23ft. 5in., a record which stood for 21 years. In 1894, the year of his captaincy, he scored 100 not out against Cambridge, and at Association football he was a good enough full-back to be chosen for England. He would have secured a fourth Blue, for Rugby football, but for an accident a few days before the university match.

The development of Charles Fry as a cricketer came later. He made plenty of runs at Oxford and always looked difficult to get out, but his style was stiff and his scoring strokes few. After he went down he first played for Surrey, but later Sussex claimed him. In the winter of 1895-96 he visited South Africa with Lord Hawke's team. In the summer of 1898, with increased opportunities of first-class practice, he blossomed out into international form, and those who had watched him play since he was a boy now saw a batsman of a completely different class. While his defence remained as good as ever, the freedom of his strokes and the power of his driving had advanced out of all knowledge. The number of runs made for Sussex in the ensuing seasons by Fry and that brilliant batsman Prince Ranjitsinhji must be read to be believed. In the eight summers from 1898 to 1905 Fry was twice first in the English batting averages and four times second. In one season he totalled over 3,000 runs, and in five others over 2,000.

He never toured Australia with an English side, and for a time he met with little success in Test matches in England, but in 1905 he established himself with a fine innings of 144 at the Oval. In the following year an accident kept him out of cricket, but later he recovered his form, and transferring his support from Sussex to Hampshire under a residential qualification, made more good scores. He captained England in 1912 against Australia and South Africa. He finished his career in first-class cricket in 1921, retiring when he was in his fiftieth year. Altogether he made 94 centuries, and holds the record among English batsmen for consecutive centuries, scoring in 1901 six three-figure innings in succession.

Some of his contemporaries at Oxford thought that Charles Fry, with his energy and ability, might have taken a more prominent part in other spheres of public life. But, though he failed in more than one attempt to enter the House of Commons, he did much valuable work unconnected with either politics or athletics. From his early days he occupied himself with literature and journalism. He edited *Fry's Magazine* and contributed to other periodicals articles on subjects about which he was well qualified to speak. He wrote in a lively style, and was full of theories on the whole art of batsmanship or kindred matters. In 1939 he published *Life Worth Living,* an autobiography which, though sometimes inaccurate in details, is an interesting record of a varied and vigorous career.

The best section of the book is the description of the work carried on for many years by the author and his wife at Hamble in connexion with the Mercury, a training ship for the Royal Navy and the Merchant Navy. The success of this establishment reflects every credit upon the industry and devotion of those who directed it, and made it their life's work. Many opinions are to be found in the narrative on the upbringing of boys and young men, opinions based on the study of education in many places and from many points of view. These opinions are propounded with the fervour of an enthusiast, and it was in the practical application of them that Fry found not only his life's work, but his happiness. To those who knew him it will seem that it was the work for which both by character and by temperament he was best fitted.

He directed the training ship Mercury for over 40 years, from 1908 to 1950, but he continued to take a close interest in the affairs of the ship right to the end of his life. He retained, too, up to the end his bright and intelligent interest, not only in public affairs but also in the intellectual pursuits he had learnt to love at his school and university. A stimulating talker, he attracted, whenever he visited Lord's, a circle about him drawn from every walk of life, and the conversation was always lively, he himself contributing to its liveliness in no small measure. Indeed, the freshness and force of his mind gave the impression that he was a far younger man than he was, and few who heard his brilliant sallies could believe that his first-class cricketing days had been over since 1921.

His writing also had this quality of liveliness and freshness, and he wrote a good deal all his life. Besides the autobiography mentioned above, he wrote (with his wife) *A Mother's Son* (1907), several books on cricket, the first, a compilation edited by him, *The Book of Cricket,* in 1899, and *The Key Book of the League of Nations.* To this output was added a stream of prose and verse contributed to a wide range of magazines and journals.

He married Miss Beatrice Holme-Sumner. She died in 1946, and he is survived by two daughters and a son, Stephen Fry, who has made a considerable reputation in broadcasting.

September 8, 1956.

Margery Fry died in London on April 21, 1958. She was 84.

Penal reform was her life work—or rather, the one among her innumerable interests to which she devoted most of her public time. But to her friends the label of "penal reformer", usually attached to Margery, seemed cold and inadequate. She cared passionately about prisons because prisoners were people, and she loved her fellow men and all their works, above all their painting, their music, their talk, and their discoveries. She used the facts and figures of penology as a battering-ram to convince governments and public opinion of what she believed to be wrong and knew could be put right.

But side by side went on constant help for individuals—lame dogs and healthy dogs alike. A wider audience knew her as a public speaker on many occasions and for many causes, and in recent years millions came to recognize that fine profile, framed in a huge halo of grey hair, and the musical and persuasive voice, through the B.B.C. Brains Trust.

Sara Margery Fry was born on March 11, 1874, the daughter of the Rt. Hon. Sir Edward Fry, G.C.B., a distinguished judge, and Mariabella Hodgkin. She was one of a remarkable family. Her brother Roger was the painter and critic whose home she shared for many years, and whose interests were always her own. Her sisters included Dr. Agnes Fry, a noted natural scientist, and Isabel, the educationist, who died just a month before her. Margery sometimes grew a little tired of explaining that her connexion with Elizabeth Fry was only a distant one, and that there was nothing hereditary in her inclination to penal reform.

Margery Fry was educated at Roedean and then at Somerville College, Oxford. She became Librarian at Somerville in 1898 and left after six years to run a small students' hostel in connexion with Birmingham University. This developed into University House, of which she was Warden until the beginning of the War of 1914-18. She was born a Quaker and in 1915-17 she worked with the Quakers' War Victims Relief Mission in France.

After the war her real life interest began to take shape; she became in 1919 hon. secretary of the Penal Reform League. The first thing she did was to unite the society with the Howard Association, which had been founded in 1866 to reform the penal system. It took about two years but it was a big thing to do, for although the two societies had much the same object, they were unlike in temperament and method, and she brought her great gift of diplomacy to bear upon the situation.

When she retired from the secretaryship in 1926 her colleagues presented her with a silver flute, an instrument which gave her much pleasure to play. She travelled widely and she visited prisons wherever she went, even when on holiday. A close friendship with Sir Maurice Waller, who was chairman of the Prison Commission in the 1920s, enabled her to see many of her ideas translated into practice at home.

In the international field it was she and Gertrude Eaton who, as representatives of the Howard League at Geneva, succeeded in getting the question of penal reform on to the agenda of the League of Nations: and to-day the United Nations as a matter of course have an organization dealing with the prevention of crime and the treatment of offenders.

She accepted the appointment of principal of Somerville College in 1926, but made it very clear that it was to be only temporary. Nevertheless, during the five years she was there she made a very considerable contribution to the life of the women's colleges. Her students enjoyed her. There was nothing eccentric about her; she was essentially sensible and practical, and was the kind of person to whom they felt inclined to go for advice. She was quick thinking, very witty, entirely free from mental superiority, and had enormous courage. More than her own students sought her out.

After retiring from Somerville she was sent on a mission to China in order to establish good relations between English and Chinese universities, and she always kept her interest in the Chinese students, particularly those in Britain.

She was a Governor of the British Broadcasting Corporation from 1937 to 1939 and a member of the Treasury Grants Committee from 1919 to 1948. She remained on the executive committee of the Howard League and was appointed a member of the Home Office Advisory Council on the Treatment of Offenders. She was also a member of the University Grants Committee.

She had not the same flair for writing as she had for speaking. Nevertheless, *Arms of the Law,* her only book, was an exceptionally penetrating study of the development of crime and punishment, from the primitive tribe to the modern industrial society, and provided a useful account of what the English penal system could, and could not, do for the offender.

The more public activities Margery Fry took on the less, by some miracle, she became institutionalized. She was a person of almost infinite compassion and understanding, who could switch her attention from the woes of the world to the comfort of a cat, from the private affairs of her relations and friends to those of complete strangers—and achieve something for all of them. She never interfered, but there can hardly have been a person with whom she came in contact whose life she did not adorn.

April 22, 1958.

Sheila Fry (Mrs. Theodore Penrose)—
See **Kaye-Smith.**

Professor John F. Fulton, who died at his home in New Haven, Connecticut, on May 29, 1960 at the age of 60, held in succession the Sterling Chairs of Physiology and of the History of Medicine at Yale University.

Few medical men of this century have enjoyed such a truly international reputation or possessed so many friends in so many lands. His connexions with Britain were particularly long and close, and it was indeed his going to Oxford as a young Rhodes Scholar that may be said to have set his feet upon the paths which he was to tread with such distinction. In the medical field the two great interests of his life were the physiology of the nervous system and the history of medicine, and in these two directions the influence of his Oxford days was profound and lasting.

John Farquhar Fulton, son of Dr. J. F. Fulton, was born at St. Paul, Minnesota, on November 1, 1899, and was educated at St. Paul's Central High School and at Harvard University, where he graduated B.S. in 1921. A Rhodes Scholarship took him to Magdalen College, Oxford, where he graduated B.A. with first class honours in 1923. From 1923 to 1925 he held a university demonstratorship in physiology and his work in the laboratory of the late Sir Charles Sherrington [q.v.] confirmed his bent towards experimental physiology.

Very soon he was publishing the results of his researches in the Proceedings of the Royal Society and other journals, and much of his work on the physiology of the muscle—a subject which was to remain one of his major interests—dates from this period.

Although Sir William Osler, the great medical humanist, had died just before Fulton's arrival at Oxford, his old home at 13, Norham Gardens was still maintained by Lady Osler as an "Open Arms" for young scholars. Fulton became one of the leading members of the Oslerian group and took an important share in the preparation of the great catalogue of Osler's library which was published in 1929. This experience confirmed his bibliophilic tendencies and resulted in his becoming one of the greatest book collectors of modern times.

After proceeding to the M.A. and D.Phil. degrees at Oxford in 1925 he returned for a short time to Harvard, taking his M.D. there in 1927, and holding the post of Associate Neurological Surgeon at the Peter Bent Brigham Hospital, Boston. At this hospital he worked under the great neuro-surgeon, Dr. Harvey Cushing, whose pupil, intimate friend, and official biographer he was in turn.

As a Fellow of Magdalen from 1928-30 he continued his research in neurophysiology, and in 1931 he was appointed to the Sterling Professorship of Physiology at Yale. During Fulton's tenure of this chair his department attracted students and post-graduate workers from all parts of the world and it came to exert a unique influence in medical education. That this was so was almost entirely due to John Fulton's breadth of outlook, humanistic approach and personal example.

Fulton's physiological work, as reported in some 400 books and papers, was mainly concerned with neurophysiology, electro-cardiology, endocrinology and the physiology of aviation.

His wartime work in the last-mentioned subject was of the greatest importance. Fulton's experimental work on apes provided the basis for the development for the operation of prefrontal leucotomy in the treatment of mental disorders.

Fulton's colossal output on neurological and physiological subjects did not prevent him from devoting more and more attention to history and bibliography. He was no mere bibliomaniac—all his books were collected in accordance with a definite plan which was to preserve all the great literary landmarks in medicine and to make them available to students.

In conformity with this plan Fulton was mainly responsible for arranging the triple benefaction by which his own great private library and the libraries of Harvey Cushing and Dr. Arnold Klebs were presented to Yale. In 1951 Fulton resigned his professorship of physiology on being appointed Sterling Professor of the History of Medicine. From this time forward he devoted his energies almost entirely to the history and bibliography of medicine and science. Latterly he had been greatly handicapped by ill-health but it was a source of the deepest satisfaction to him that he lived to see his library and department properly established within the university.

Quite recently a second chair, of the History of Science, had been created and there is no doubt that the existence of the two chairs and of the magnificent historical library at Yale will make this the greatest centre of organized historical medical and scientific study in the world. That this has come about is almost entirely due to the vision, the drive and, it may be added, to a considerable extent to the private generosity of John Fulton.

Among the most important of Fulton's published writings in book form were his monograph on *Muscular Contraction* (1926), his textbook *Physiology of the Nervous System,* which reached a third edition in 1949, his massive *Life of Harvey Cushing* (1946), and his bibliographies of Robert Boyle and Servetus.

Fulton was honoured by many universities and academic bodies and he received decorations or awards from no fewer than 18

Governments. Among the honours which gave him greatest pleasure were the hon. O.B.E. conferred upon him for his war work, much of which was carried out in Britain; the Hon. D.Litt. of Oxford; the Fellowship of the Royal College of Physicians of London, conferred under its special by-law; and the Honorary Fellowship of the Royal Society of Medicine.

Fulton was a great traveller; there were very few countries of the world which he had not visited as a lecturer or for the purpose of attending medical congresses. His circle of friends and correspondents was vast. He had an enormous zest for life and no one who ever came into contact with him—and especially those who were privileged to enjoy the hospitality of his beautiful home—could fail to be inspired by his example and his personality. Nowhere will his passing be more deeply regretted than in England, the country with which he had such long associations and which he loved.

Fulton married in 1923 Lucia Pickering Wheatland, who was his helpmate and companion in all his work and who was equally well known and loved in many lands. One of Dr. and Mrs. Fulton's innumerable good works was the adoption of three British children in the early days of World War II, and it was typical of them that they went to London for the express purpose of attending the wedding of one of these children in 1955.

May 31, 1960.

Dr. Walter Funk, the former Reich Minister of Economics and President of the Reichsbank, died at Düsseldorf on May 31, 1960. He was 69.

Funk was a financial journalist who, in recognition of his ability as a collector of party funds, was elevated by Hitler first to an important position in the Propaganda Department and then to the control, under Göring, of German economy. He had neither the forceful personality nor the knowledge of Schacht*, whom he succeeded at the Reichsbank; but since he was an opportunist rather than a theorist, he proved more amenable, and seemed able to carry out Hitler's and Göring's requirements to their continuing satisfaction. He had, too, the shrewdness to surround himself with able men and to be governed by their judgment.

Walter Funk was born in 1890 at Trakehnen, in East Prussia, and came of a substantial merchant family. He was at school at Insterburg and then went to the Universities of Berlin and Leipzig. He took to journalism and worked at first on provincial papers; but at 26, on the introduction of the Pan-German Party, whose interests he was expected to serve, he joined the staff of the *Berliner Börsenzeitung.* Then he married the daughter of a wealthy manufacturer, and soon enlarged his acquaintances among the heavy industrialists. These, together with his own family connexions in East Prussia, provided him with useful relationships and information, which he turned to good account. He was, of course, on the side of the capitalists and was little interested in labour questions. By 1926 he was editor-in-chief.

In 1930 owing, it was said, to an office scandal which reflected on his virility rather than his integrity, he was forced to retire. He had, however, valuable friends and Schacht, who at that time joined forces with the Nazis, recommended him to Hitler as economic adviser. He had had some affinities with the party's economic attitude and had already rendered it considerable services by acting on its behalf as an intermediary with the Rhenish industrialists.

It was indeed largely due to his successful efforts that Hitler had the funds to achieve his election successes of 1928. Funk had hesitated to join it at a time when its future was doubtful; but by 1930 its prospects were brighter, and he had no hesitation in entering its economic department. In it he continued his efforts to obtain financial support and generally supervised its finances. Once Hitler was in power, however, the party had all the economic resources of the state at its disposal.

In the new regime Funk, who had earned Hitler's gratitude and confidence, was appointed Chief of the Press but, since this raised some difficulty with Goebbels, he was made State Secretary to the Ministry of Public Enlightenment and Propaganda. In this capacity he acquired a number of remunerative chairmanships which allowed him to indulge his artistic tastes and enjoy a comparatively easy life.

In 1937, however, he was appointed to the Ministry of Economics in succession to Schacht, who had disagreed with Göring in regard to the Four-Year Plan. It was in this position that in 1938 he undertook an economic tour of South-Eastern Europe as a result of which it was claimed that he had made the resources of the Danubian Basin available to Germany.

In January 1939 Hitler dismissed Schacht, whose views had become inconvenient, from the Presidency of the Reichsbank and appointed Funk in his place. Funk was not a banker, but he had the assistance of Brinkman, Under-Secretary of State at the Ministry of Economics, a highly competent man. Hitler gave him explicit directions for his guidance, among them that of opening up the capital market and placing it in an increased degree at the disposal of the private demand for money. It was a difficult period because there were Treasury difficulties which, combined with the slump in foreign trade, raised doubts in regard to Hitler's ability to continue rearmament on the scale which it had attained. He began by seeking to create confidence in German stability and upholding the sanctity of private property and expressing his intention of making posterity pay.

His utterances during the war appeared to reflect unbounded confidence in the future of Germany, and he was wont to dilate on the economic order the Nazis had in mind for Europe: Russia was to be included in the Ostraum (eastern economic region), for which Funk, himself an East Prussian, had great plans.

At Nuremberg Funk was found guilty of planning and carrying out war and of crimes against humanity, but was acquitted of the charge of conspiracy against world peace. He was sentenced to life imprisonment. During the trial Funk claimed that he knew nothing of the terrorist measures against Jews, and thought that property of murdered Jews deposited with the Reichsbank belonged to concentration camp inmates. He was imprisoned in Spandau with other convicted Nazi leaders, but his health deteriorated and he underwent several operations.

June 4, 1960.

The death of **Dame Katharine Furse,** G.B.E., R.R.C., which occurred in hospital in London on November 25, 1952, two days after her seventy-seventh birthday, leaves a gap in the ranks of the pioneers of women's services that all will regret.

The story of the rise of the Voluntary Aid Detachments to the splendid heights they achieved in the relief of suffering during the 1914-18 war, and the organization, later in the same war, of the Women's Royal Naval Service, is one that cannot but bring the warmest feelings of admiration for the woman who above all others made these things possible. Official discouragement meant nothing to her; yet she achieved her ends not by a display of force, though she could be forceful, but by the exercise of a quiet persistence backed not only by an inflexible purpose but by a charm of manner and of nature, which she partly inherited from her father but mostly cultivated herself. Widely read, critical and deft with hand and brain, she was a delightful companion. Those who won her confidence and friendship will ever cherish the memory of loyalty that knew no bounds.

She was the daughter of John Addington Symonds and Janet Catherine North and was born on November 23, 1875. She inherited her father's sensitive, critical mind and her mother's passion for flowers, mountains and solitude and as a child delighted in the life the family lived in the Alps and in Italy. As a young woman she learned wood-carving to such purpose that she did a great deal of work for the decorators of the period; and, after her marriage to the late C. W. Furse, R.A., in 1900, actually carved the frames of some of his Academy pictures. His death after only four years of an ideally happy union was a great blow to her and it was long before she was able to face life again.

One fortunate day in 1911, when the Red Cross organization was calling for volunteer nurses to serve in case of invasion, she went to the London Scottish Drill Hall to enroll. There she met Miss (now Dame) Rachel Crowdy* and with her took the pioneering path. The volunteer nurses had not originally been intended for service abroad, but Mrs. Furse followed the British Expeditionary Force to France and, rebuffed by the authorities, gained with a few friends a foothold in some trucks on a railway siding at Boulogne. There, by refusing no tasks, they became a laundry depôt, a dispensary, a left-luggage office, and grew flowers to make their "rest station" attractive. This was the small beginnings of what in a remarkably short time became a major factor in care for the wounded. As Sir Frederick Treves was able to say when inspecting them: "30,000 ministered to in five weeks . . . a fine piece of Red Cross work". When it began to be seen that the V.A.D.s at home would be wanted Mrs. Furse was sent back to organize a central department, which she did with energy, efficiency, and tact.

Her work from then onwards has gone into history and not least her resignation in 1917 and her recall to public life by the Admiralty to replace men by women in shore jobs. The war had little more than a year to run, and the "Wrens" were dispersed as quickly as possible at its end to make room for men returning from active service. The firm foundations laid by Dame Katharine Furse (she had been created G.B.E. in 1917) were manifest when early in the course of the 1939-45 war the "Wrens" were got together again to do the same good work as before, but on a larger scale and for a longer time.

Though she had little taste for public life, she achieved her place in history out of the purest sense of duty, and once her task was done she retired to other and to her more worthy pursuits. One other public office she held; from 1928 to 1938 she was the Director of the World Bureau of Girl Guides and Girl Scouts. Her engagingly written autobiography was published in 1940 under the title *Hearts and Pomegranates.*

November 26, 1952.

The Right Rev. M. B. Furse, K.C.M.G., D.D., formerly Bishop of St. Albans, who died at Wantage on June 18, 1955 at the age of 84, had won for himself a peculiar position in the Church of England, as he had in his younger days at Oxford while he was a resident don at Trinity. He owed his successive promotions in the Church not to learning but to native force of character and a power, which he developed early, of mixing well with men of all kinds and being accepted by them as their guide and elder brother. He must have known many with whom he had intellectual differences, but few who did not at once acknowledge his sincerity, his loyalty, and his firm and friendly determination to lead others towards a right way of living.

Michael Bolton Furse was born on October 12, 1870, the fifth son of the Ven. C. W. Furse, Archdeacon of Westminster. He was a brother of Charles Furse, whose premature death was a great loss to English painting, and of Lieutenant General Sir W. T. Furse, R.A. He was born and bred in a Tractarian atmosphere and very early came to know Charles Gore intimately. To these two influences he remained loyal throughout his life. He always acknowledged his gratitude to the large family of brothers and sisters among whom he grew up, and indeed his capacity for making friends with all sorts of people was largely due to the fact that they had knocked the corners off him in boyhood.

As befitted a nephew of William Johnson (afterwards Cory), author of *Ionica,* he went to Eton as a colleger and then to Trinity College, Oxford, as a commoner. He was one of those who are marked out from boyhood by character, personality, and physique (he was over six feet) to take the lead. He rowed twice in the Trials but failed to get his Blue, and he produced and took part in the O.U.D.S. presentation of *The Frogs.* He knew everybody, was at home in any company, and was universally known as "Mike". His interests were manifold, but the chief was religion, and he made no secret of it. "Sorry to keep you waiting", he said to a friend who had called on him before Hall, "but I was saying my prayers. I'm always so sleepy when I go to bed". It was a typical remark. He never saw any reason to hide his own views, and was able to speak about religious subjects with an unshy naturalness rare among young Englishmen.

His strength and influence were so valuable that while, soon after he had graduated, he was taking a trip round the world, the college asked him, for the sake of discipline, to return as fellow dean and chaplain. It was an unconventional appointment, and there were elderly dons elsewhere who shook their heads. Furse was no scholar and did not pretend to be one; and a fellowship shorn of academic distinction was unknown in those days. He understood that point of view, and though he accepted and for several years was a great success, he was too wise to stay overlong.

The Bishop of Oxford had ordained him from Cuddesdon in 1896. In 1902 he took part in a mission of help to South Africa and made such an impression that Bishop Carter, who had long known him, asked him to return permanently. He went out in 1903 as Archdeacon of Johannesburg, having first married in Trinity Chapel Frances, daughter of the late Captain James Redfield, of Charlottesville, Virginia. The only child of this marriage, Jane Diana, who early displayed unusual gifts, died at the age of 14 in South Africa. This was a perpetual grief to the Bishop and to Mrs. Furse.

When the bishopric of Pretoria fell vacant in 1909 Furse was chosen for it by the almost unanimous vote of the elective assembly. It looked as if he had found his sphere and might end his days as a bishop in the Church of the Province of South Africa. Its tradition, as well as its model administrative form and synodical government, exactly reflected his own interpretation of the true genius of his Anglican inheritance. He knew that he was a leader; he felt strongly on the native question, and he had characteristics which appealed greatly to those among whom his work lay. But in 1920 he was transferred to St. Albans.

For 16 years his work had lain out of England; he came back to a changed and changing land. It was a good time for him; he was full of ideas and new methods. Unconventional in manner and speech, easy of approach, and utterly free from any trace of pomposity, he steadily made his way into the affections of his diocese. Those whom he shocked succumbed to his friendliness when they came to know him. A strenuous worker himself, he required of his clergy a high degree of industry; the easy-going found his hand a little heavy on them. Perhaps he "spurred too fast betimes" and roused opposition from the slower-going sort, whom he could have won by gentler methods. But even those who thought him a prejudiced traditionalist paid tribute to his exacting sense of justice.

His attitude to the problems connected with marriage and divorce was not that of the easy-going majority, which he showed especially in the debate in Convocation in January 1937, when he and the Bishop of Ely were alone in the minority, and his churchmanship was of a very definite type. He did not enjoy being in opposition, still less being unable to agree with his brother bishops to whose findings in Convocation he adhered as a matter of loyalty, even when he disagreed with them. But he dreaded the result of blurring distinctions which seemed to him vital, and was ready to face any unpopularity in defence of his principles.

To his clergy he was a real Father in God; to the laity of his diocese a great spiritual force. He was greatly interested in church tutorial classes and urged his clergy to promote them. The business of the diocese was admirably done, and his diocesan conference was a revelation of what such gatherings can be. Men of purely academic standards sometimes underrated his abilities. He had, however, a shrewd and logical mind, and was not easily defeated in argument, even if in later years he tended to repetitive prolixity. His opinions were reached slowly; once his mind was made up no one was left in any doubt about it. At one of his regularly held schools of prayer for clergy, one senior and devout priest rose from his knees and remarked aloud: "I will not be bullied into saying my prayers like that". "All right, old boy", laughed Mike, "you go on in your own bad way". But the bishop had a genius for friendship. His friends will remember him as a strong man, with unexpected depths of patience and humility, from whom, whether they shared his opinions or not, they never failed to draw inspiration, for his own life was founded on the discipline of constant prayer.

The Bishop was elected an honorary fellow of his old college in 1921 and in 1936 he was appointed by the Crown to be Prelate of the Order of St. Michael and St. George, which appointment he held until 1951.

After his retirement from the see of St. Albans in 1944 Bishop Furse made his home at Wantage, where he rejoiced to be able to minister to the Community of St. Mary the Virgin.

He was made a Knight Commander of the Order of St. Michael and St. George, of which he was still Prelate, in 1947. As a bishop he could not carry his "title", nor could his gracious and devoted wife.

He published *A School of Prayer, God's Plan,* and *Stand Therefore!* The last, which came out in 1953, is less of a biography than a confession of faith in which he proclaimed the divine vocation of the Church of England.

June 20, 1955.

Dr. Wilhelm Furtwängler, the eminent German conductor whose career was gravely disturbed by Nazi politics, died in a sanatorium near Baden-Baden, in Bavaria, on November 30, 1954 at the age of 68. He had been ill with pneumonia for some days.

The son of Professor Adolf Furtwängler, of Berlin, the distinguished archaeologist, Wilhelm Furtwängler was born in Berlin on January 25, 1886, and had the advantage of growing up among people of artistic mind trained to scientific study. His musical proclivities appeared early, and there were those among his father's wide circle of friends who prophesied his success in the art from the age of eight, and who were able to watch with pleasure the gradual fulfilment of their prophecy. Among the teachers of Furtwängler's youth was Joseph Rheinberger, the famous composer of organ music. Later he studied under Max Schillings, and then entered on the usual series of appointments in the minor German theatres, which then provided an unrivalled training in the practical requirements of a conductor. When, in 1920, he succeeded Richard Strauss as director of the symphony concerts for the Berlin State Opera, he was marked out as one of the leading men of the younger generation. Two years later the death of Nikisch gave him the succession to the concerts of the Leipzig Gewandhaus and the Berlin Philharmonic. In 1927 he was appointed conductor of the Vienna Philharmonic Orchestra.

Furtwängler first appeared in England as conductor in 1924 at a concert of the Royal Philharmonic Society, when his command of his players and his forcible handling of Brahms's Symphony in C Minor made an immediate impression. Subsequently he was "guest conductor" of several concerts given by the Royal Philharmonic and the London Symphony orchestras. The two visits of the Berlin Philharmonic Orchestra in 1929 showed Furtwängler's art in controlling a highly disciplined body of players completely accustomed to his methods, which were unorthodox and to the onlooker's eye confusing. Some felt that his interpretation and style left something to be desired, that discipline of the players was made too much an end in itself, and that Furtwängler's treatment of the larger classics sometimes tended towards heaviness and exaggeratedly slow *tempi.* Nevertheless, those concerts gave some memorable moments, and there was more to come in the next 25 years.

Throughout the German-speaking countries Furtwängler's reputation stood high for work at once thorough and inspiring, though he was never admired in Britain as much as in Germany. Yet his interpretation of *The Ring* was accepted in London and in Vienna as in the great tradition. He was in demand, too, as an interpreter of Beethoven and went with the Vienna Philharmonic Orchestra to London, after the 1939-45 War, to give the symphonies in cycle. He was also a frequent guest conductor for London concert-giving organizations. His last appearance in London was in March 1954, when he was the guest of honour with the Philharmonia Orchestra at the Festival Hall in a Beethoven programme. In Germany his last appearance was at the West Berlin Festival in September 1954. A little volume of his essays, entitled *Concerning Music,* was published in Zürich in 1948 and was made available in England in 1953.

Furtwängler's association with the Berlin Philharmonic Orchestra began in 1922 and it was his principal concern. When the Nazis came to power in 1933 they began to interfere with its members, but its conductor resisted and relations with the authorities became strained. By 1935 a reconciliation had been effected and Furtwängler's loyalty to his orchestra subsequently landed him in trouble on the question of "collaboration". After the war denazification courts cleared him, but he had lost the Berlin orchestra and became a travelling virtuoso conductor until reappointed to his old post in 1952.

The sad and complex story, which illustrates how the Nazi virus infected every aspect of German life, is told by Furtwängler's former secretary and agent of the Berlin Philharmonic Orchestra, Dr. Berthe Geissmar, in *The Baton and the Jackboot,* from which it is clear that Furtwängler was one of the few people who stood up to Hitler in the early days, but was, inevitably, engulfed subsequently.

He was twice married.

December 1, 1954.

Hamilton Fyfe, a journalist of unusually versatile stamp and great experience, who had been well known in Fleet Street over a period of 50 years, died in a nursing home at Eastbourne on June 15, 1951 at the age of 81.

Hamilton Fyfe occupied at different times a large number of posts on newspaper staffs and engaged in a great many ventures as a freelance writer. He had been reporter, sub-editor, literary critic, dramatic critic, and special correspondent as well as editor; his profession had taken him all over Europe and over much of the American continent; he probably saw as much of the war of 1914-18 as any newspaper correspondent; and even in his later and less active years he retained an excellent news sense and a sound instinct for the relative importance of various classes of news. He wrote in a clear, straightforward, and thoughtful fashion that always became the eminently practical journalist he was and that gave consistent point and interest to the books he wrote.

Henry Hamilton Fyfe was born in London on September 28, 1869, the eldest son of James Hamilton Fyfe, barrister and journalist, who had at one period been the Parliamentary Correspondent of *The Times.* He was sent to Fettes, whence at the age of 17 he passed into the office of *The Times.* He was soon put to reporting and then to sub-editing, and in the course of time took on more responsible duties as editorial secretary to the editor of the day, G. E. Buckle. In 1902 he accepted an offer from the Licensed Victuallers' Association to edit and reorganize their daily journal, the *Morning Advertiser.* His innovations were striking enough to catch the eye of Alfred Harmsworth, afterwards Lord Northcliffe, and within a year he had joined the *Daily Mirror,* thus beginning an association with Northcliffe of a most cordial character which was to last until after the war of 1914-18.

In 1907 he was transferred to the *Daily Mail,* for which he wrote copiously over many years, "covering" Russia in 1911, the Duke of Connaught's tours in South Africa and Canada, and the early experiments in aviation made by Graham-White, Blériot, and Paulhan. For *The Times* (then controlled by Northcliffe) he went to Mexico in 1913 to report on the Carranza revolution. From Mexico he went to Ireland, where Ulster sentiment seemed scarcely less inflammable, and so straight out to France, where in common with other correspondents he worked under the special difficulties imposed by the military authorities.

Fyfe's account of the retreat from Mons in *The Times* made journalistic history. He was censured in some quarters as an "alarmist", but he had told the plain truth, and the interpolation by the press censor of dots at various points in the dispatch did more harm than good, leading the public to suppose that facts of special gravity had been suppressed. Fyfe went to Russia in 1915, moving from Petrograd to Galicia, and later to Bucharest. Returning to Russia, he was able to give the British public the first account of the career and murder of Rasputin.

In 1917 Northcliffe sent him first to Spain and Portugal and then to the Italian front, whence he was recalled by telegram to go to New York as honorary attaché to the British War Mission to the United States. He finished the war in Crewe House, where he gave notable assistance in devising propaganda for distribution among the German soldiers and people.

After the Armistice Fyfe's Labour sympathies became more pronounced and he found himself at odds with the editorial policy of the *Daily Mail.* In 1922 Arthur Henderson persuaded him to take over the editorship of the *Daily Herald,* and during the four years he remained in that post he was instrumental in raising its circulation quite considerably. He was, however, never altogether happy, it appears, with the T.U.C. editorial board, and eventually offered his resignation. He was next with the *Daily Chronicle,* which he served until that paper's amalgamation with the *Daily News,* and from 1930 onwards was a valued contributor to *Reynolds News.*

Increasingly he turned to political work in the Labour interest and to authorship. He had been Labour candidate for the Sevenoaks division in 1929 and he stood for Yeovil in 1931, but on each occasion suffered, as he had indeed expected, defeat.

Hamilton Fyfe wrote novels, plays, biographies, sociological and other volumes. His play, *A Modern Aspasia* (produced in 1909 by the Stage Society and later in Prague), was praised by Bernard Shaw and other good judges, and several other stage pieces were well spoken of; so were the novels, which belong to the early 1920s. He produced a study of Twells Brex, biographies of Northcliffe and T. P. O'Connor, travel and political books, and several engaging volumes of reminiscences.

In 1907 he married Eleanor, daughter of the late William Kelly, of the War Office. It was a singularly happy union.

June 19, 1951.

Rose Fyleman, a prolific writer of verse for children, died in a nursing home on August 1, 1957. She had great facility in rhyme and rhythm, an unusual understanding of the child mind, and was known to the wide body of *Punch* readers for her gay and delicate verses published under the initials R. F. She it was who wrote the immortal line: "There are fairies at the bottom of our garden".

Miss Fyleman, like D. H. Lawrence, Laura* and Harold Knight, and sundry others eminent in the arts, was a native of Nottingham. She was born there of Jewish parents in 1877, brought up at a private school, and went on to University College, Nottingham, but academic success was not for her. She was ploughed in Greek and mathematics, and left without a degree.

Teaching, which she had envisaged as a career, was now debarred to her. However, her amateur efforts as a singer revealed that she had an unusually good voice, so it was decided that she should study singing in Paris. She worked there for some two years under Sir Henry Wood, went to Berlin for further instruction, and finished at the Royal College of Music in London, becoming A.R.C.M.

In 1903 she made her first professional appearance as a singer at the Queen's Hall. Thenceforward she was for a considerable period exclusively occupied in this profession. She came to journalism casually, with sporadic articles and verses in various journals; but when *Punch* opened its columns to her in 1916, and her fairy verses there scored almost immediate success, she began to think of writing, rather than singing or the teaching of singing, as her main concern. Her first book was *Fairies and Chimneys* (1918).

It was followed by *The Fairy Green* (1919), *The Fairy Flute* (1921), *Eight Little Plays for Children* (1924), and a long series of successors, the titles of which fill several pages of the British Museum catalogue. She founded, and for two years, edited, a children's magazine called the *Merry Go Round.* As time went on she devoted more and more attention to dramatic form. *Nine Small Plays* (1934), *Six Longer Plays for Children* (1936), and *The Magic Pencil, Eight Plays* (1938) were fruits of this interest. She had a Christmas play produced at the Old Vic in 1926, and with Thomas Dunhill staged a children's opera at Guildford in November 1933.

An inveterate traveller, a linguist who translated from French, German, and Italian, a humorist and facile lyricist, she was in truth the modern laureate of the fairy world, moving easily in the land over the rainbow with a sure step.

August 2, 1957.

G

Clark Gable, for many years one of Hollywood's most consistently successful actors, died in Hollywood on November 16, 1960 at the age of 59. He had a heart attack on November 6 and had been in hospital ever since.

Gable was born at Cadiz, Ohio, on February 1, 1901, and came to the cinema in the mid 1920s after a period of theatrical touring, playing mostly bit parts. His rise in the film world was by no means meteoric; for some years he took only small parts in Westerns, until his first major role came in *The Painted Desert* in 1931.

In a number of subsequent films he became typed as a brooding villain or an aggressive lover, but Gable's first real chance came through one of those ironies which often intervene in Hollywood. His company, believing his popularity to be fading, lent him to a small company for an inexpensive film. That film was *It Happened One Night,* which started a whole cycle of crazy comedies, brought Academy Awards to Clark Gable, his co-star Claudette Colbert, and the director, Frank Capra, and established Gable as the masculine ideal of his generation (so much so that, we are told, when he revealed in *It Happened One Night* that he did not wear a vest, there was at once a disastrous slump in the sales of vests throughout America).

The character of the good-natured, extrovert man of action which he established in this film recurred, with variations, throughout the next decade in such films as *Red Dust* and *China Seas* (both with Jean Harlow), *Mutiny on the Bounty, Boom Town* and *San Francisco.* In 1939 he played the most famous of all his roles, that of Rhett Butler in the film version of *Gone With the Wind,* which confirmed once and for all his right to his Hollywood nickname "the King".

During the Second World War he rose to the rank of major in the U.S. Army Air Force and was awarded the Air Medal for his part in bombing missions over Europe. His postwar films successfully maintained his popularity, if they made few demands on his acting ability; most notable, perhaps, was *Mogambo,* a remake of his prewar success *Red Dust.* In 1954, after 23 years under contract, he left M.G.M. to work independently on such films as *Soldier of Fortune, The Tall Men,* and—a very happy return to comedy—*Teacher's Pet.* Recently Gable continued his success, playing opposite Sophia Loren in *It Started in Naples,* and had just completed a new film with Marilyn Monroe*, *The Misfits,* immediately before his death.

Gable had little ambition to be regarded as a great actor: his parts seldom required much subtlety or penetration, and indeed differed very little through the years. What they did require was a dynamic personality and a virile physique, qualities which he possessed in abundance. To give him the coveted part of Rhett Butler was obviously a classic piece of type-casting, but it is difficult to think of any other actor who could have assembled all the qualities required and used them to such advantage.

Neither should Gable's real skill as a comic actor go unpraised; his timing was perfect—a legacy, no doubt, of his stage training—and his face remarkably expressive. In his younger days the model American he-man, Gable was touched little by the passing years, and gradually matured into the perfect Claudius for some eventual Hollywood *Hamlet.* Not a great actor but a great personality and a great star, he will be hard to replace.

His marriages to Josephine Dillon, his dramatic coach; Rhea Langham; and Sylvia Lady Stanley of Alderley were all dissolved by divorce. His third wife, Carole Lombard, the film actress, was killed in an air crash in 1942. He is survived by his widow, Kay Williams Spreckles, whom he married in 1955.

November 18, 1960.

Grigore Gafencu, who was Romanian Foreign Minister at the outbreak of war in 1939, died in Paris in January 1957.

A person of many gifts and much charm of character, an excellent linguist, a brilliant student of history, in exile from his own country a political observer of exceptional acumen and intellectual integrity, Grigore Gafencu in recent years had impressed all who knew him by the clarity and penetration of his grasp of affairs. In two notable books published in English translation after the close of hostilities in 1945, he had insisted that the division of Europe into zones of influence could not ensure lasting peace. Nobody with experience of the practical conduct of diplomacy during 1939-41 had a better right to proclaim that opinion from the roof-tops.

Grigore Gafencu, who was born in Bucharest in 1892, had Scottish blood in his veins; his grandfather was a Saunders, and his father, after adding the name of Gafencu—which was that of his mother—to Saunders, dropped the latter only after marrying a Romanian lady of noble birth, Ralu Costache, and becoming a naturalized Romanian subject. The son studied in Geneva and in the canton of Argovie, proved a scholar of exceptional attainments, and took the degree of Doctor of Laws. He joined the Romanian Air Force when Romania went to war in 1916, serving as observer, and distinguished himself for bravery and was decorated with the Order of Michael the Brave, the highest decoration in the Romanian armed forces.

After the conclusion of hostilities he took up journalism, founding the *Revista Vremei (Review of the Times)* and then becoming owner of the leading economic journal in Romania—the *Argus.* In 1927 he founded an independent daily paper called *Timpul (Time),* which in the year before 1939 was one of the foremost organs of the Romanian press. Journalism apart, Gafencu specialized in economics and practised as an economic consultant, and was for many years an active member of the National Peasant Party. He held office in several Cabinets before he was appointed, in the difficult and threatening circumstances of December 1938, Minister for Foreign Affairs. He had made no secret of his sympathies in the columns of *Timpul.*

The appointment was well received by the Romanian public—and not by the Romanian public alone, for in the west, after the shock of Munich, it seemed of good augury so far as affairs in south-eastern Europe were concerned. In pursuit of the maintenance of peace, the task Gafencu set himself as Foreign Minister, and the methods by which he sought to realize it, may be studied with advantage in the volume he completed in 1945, translated into English three years later under the title of *The Last Days of Europe.*

For the failure of his policy of practical accord with the Western democracies Gafencu himself can scarcely be blamed. He remained at the Romanian Foreign Office until June 1940, when he was removed as an act of appeasement towards Germany, and in the following month was appointed Minister to the Soviet Union. He continued at his post in Moscow until issue was joined on the eastern front, and spent the rest of the war period in Switzerland.

Then, at the beginning of 1943, he completed the earlier and more important of the two volumes mentioned, *Prelude to the Russian Campaign,* published in Britain in 1946. It is a fascinating study, exhibiting a brilliant historical sense and commanding power of lucid and objective analysis of the course of Russo-German relations from the conclusion of the Soviet-Nazi pact of August 21, 1939, until the opening of hostilities in Russia on June 22, 1941.

Gafencu continued to live in Switzerland, though he left it from time to time to assist in advocating the cause of closer European union. In November 1947 he was sentenced *in absentia* by the communist régime in Romania to a term of 20 years' imprisonment for high treason.

January 31, 1957.

General Maurice Gamelin, Chief of the General Staff of the National Defence, and Generalissimo of the Allied Armies until superseded by General Weygand in the midst of the German invasion of France in 1940, died in hospital in Paris on April 18, 1958 at the age of 85.

There is inevitably a tendency to doubt the qualifications of the commanders of defeated armies, but it cannot be denied that the career of Gamelin had been brilliant or that in the 1914-18 War he had been one of the best, if not the very best, soldiers of his seniority and standing in the French Army. Perhaps his tragedy was that he was a soldier of that war who had not kept himself up to date or followed the logical development of offensive tactics.

There seems little doubt, however, that he had become too old for his task, and older in mind than in body. He had the gift of self-expression which is so useful to the soldier who is brought into constant touch with the politician, but sometimes proves to be a weapon that turns in the hand. In such conversations he would calmly and effectively keep the business under discussion close to the political plane which left the politician thinking how able and broad-minded was the Government's professional adviser, but did nothing to instruct him in genuine military problems. And that is one of the most important functions of the soldier occupying Gamelin's position before the outbreak of the Second World War.

Maurice Gustave Gamelin was born in Paris on September 20, 1872. His first ambition was to become a painter, and his skill with brush and pencil served him well in one of his earliest military employments, on the survey in French North Africa. Educated at the College Stanislas and the Military Academy of Saint-Cyr, from which he passed out first, he was then posted to the 3rd Tirailleurs at Constantine. At the age of 27 he entered the School of War as a lieutenant, probably its youngest pupil, at the time when Foch was an instructor there. At 30 he was promoted captain and posted to the Staff of the XV Corps. Then came two years' service with the 15th Chasseurs-à-pied, after which he served General Joffre successively as orderly officer in the 6th Division and as staff officer in the II Corps. Shortly before the outbreak of war in 1914 and just after he had been appointed to the command of the 2nd Chasseurs Alpins he was again summoned to the staff of Joffre, Commander-in-Chief designate of the French armies.

The part played by Commandant Gamelin, of the Third (Operations) Bureau, at the Battle of the Marne is too complicated to deal with here. It may simply be said that he was taken from his office and placed, literally as well as figuratively, beside the Commander-in-Chief, and that it was he who drafted the most vital of the "directives" to the armies. Those few days were the finest of Gamelin's career, and nothing that afterwards happened can rob him of the honour he then acquired.

Promoted lieutenant-colonel and placed at the head of the Third Bureau he was concerned with the earlier planning for the Somme offensive, but his part in the battle was to be that of a fighting commander. Early in 1916, with the rank of colonel, he took over command of a brigade of Chasseurs Alpins in the 47th Division. His divisional commander used to say afterwards—but long before Gamelin had become famous—that he was the best brigade commander he had ever known. He greatly distinguished himself in the Battle of the Somme.

Once more, now with the rank of Général de brigade, Gamelin was recalled in December to the Grand Quartier Général. But this last cooperation with Joffre lasted only a few days. At the end of the month Joffre departed, to be succeeded by Nivelle, and Gamelin became Chief-of-the-Staff to Micheler. This strange compound of scientific soldier and monk was placed by Nivelle at the head of the Group of Reserve Armies, which was to carry out the great offensive on the Aisne. It must have been a difficult role for a chief of the staff; for his general was at loggerheads with both his superior, Nivelle, and his subordinate, Mangin. The "Nivelle Offensive" failed, and the blighting of hopes rocked both the Army and the country to their foundations.

Gamelin, however, was not one of the many scapegoats. At the age of 44 he was given command of the 9th Division, which he led with admirable skill through the evil days and the good of 1918. With hostilities at an end he was sent to Brazil to organize a French Military Mission in that country. In 1925 he was dispatched to Syria with the rank of Army Corps Commander and did good service in the subjugation of the great revolt. His three years' sojourn in the Levant greatly enhanced his prestige and made it certain that, barring accidents, he would rise to the top.

He took a step on the ladder when he was given command of the famous XX Corps (the command held by Foch in 1914). In 1931 he became Chief of the Staff of the Army, in 1935 Inspector-General of the Army and Vice-President of the War Council. Finally, in January 1938, he was appointed to a new post, Chief of the General Staff of National Defence, a post which gave him wide coordinating powers. No one who reads the retrograde French equivalent of our "Field Service Regulations" can doubt that Gamelin looked back rather than forward, or that the doctrine by which he was inspired was at once timid, and risky by reason of its very timidity. On the other hand, the weakness in French equipment, and especially that of the air arm, which he had probably no means of remedying, hampered him at every turn.

On the outbreak of war Gamelin became supreme Generalissimo, the field command of the armies facing Germany and on the northern frontiers, including that of the B.E.F., being exercised by General Georges. His inanition during the German offensive was astounding. Superseded in the midst of the battle in May, he was shortly afterwards placed under detention and eventually charged with "incapacity owing to lack of energy and with having taken disastrous decisions which weakened the spirit of the French Armies".

After 18 months of internment he was brought by the Vichy Government before the high court sitting in Riom, but refused to defend himself, declaring: "My higher duty is to keep silent".

His trial was adjourned and in March 1943 the General was deported with several other political personalities to Germany and held in Buchenwald concentration camp. The American armies freed him in May 1945.

He later defended himself in three volumes of memoirs, capably but tendentiously. The nearest to being a military record is *Servir: Les Armées Françaises de 1940.* The rest is mostly political; some of it valuable.

In his retirement he lived with his wife in a flat in the Avenue Foch, near the Arc de Triomphe. In his later years he could be seen, small and dapper, strolling with his dog or sitting on a park bench.

Gamelin was a man of attractive personality, extremely well read in military history, and a hard worker. His service with Alpine troops had left him with a love of winter sport, and he was until late in life an ardent skier. Riding and skiing kept him remarkably fit, but he aged rapidly just before the war. There can be few better examples of the need of the age limit, from which he was specially and unfortunately exempted.

April 19, 1958.

The Right Hon. and Most Rev. C. F. Garbett, D.D., Archbishop of York, died on December 31, 1955, at his home in York two days before publication of the Birthday Honours which indicated that the Queen had intended to confer on him a barony. Dr. Garbett was 80, and had announced his intention to resign early in 1956.

Cyril Foster Garbett was born in 1875 at Tongham, near Aldershot, his father being at that time the vicar of the parish, and both home and parish, with their simple life and piety, provided a background to which he always looked back with gratitude. His mother lived to a great age, and from his Portsea days onwards he made a home for her and his sister. He was educated at Portsmouth Grammar School and Keble College, Oxford. In his undergraduate days he was always known as a keen student of social problems and as a forcible speaker, and he became President of the Union. In 1898 he took his degree with a second class in history, and, after training for holy orders at Cuddesdon, was ordained in 1900 to a curacy at Portsea.

His was the unusual experience of remaining in one parish from the time of his ordination as a deacon to the time of his consecration as a bishop. For nine years he was a curate at Portsea and for the next 10 its vicar. Portsea provides a brilliant example of a system which has been used too seldom in the Church of England. As its neighbourhood grew and its population increased, new churches were built to supply their needs. But, instead of following the usual method, which is to develop each district and chapel-of-ease into a separate parish, the policy adopted at Portsea was to retain all the supplementary churches—seven in number—as constituent parts of a single parish. Each with its district was placed in the charge of a member of the staff, who obtained in this way initiative and experience, while the vicar kept a watchful eye on the whole parish, and was ready to mobilize all its resources to aid any one part where special help was needed.

The vicar and the curates—16 of them in Garbett's day—lived together, a happy celibate brotherhood, in the vicarage. At one time its dining-room wall was adorned with the precept: "A good life is better than a good living". Obviously, a parochial organization of this type can prosper only if at its head is a man with great powers of leadership, able at once to control and to maintain a genial relationship with his staff. But Portsea has been fortunate in its vicars. The vicar under whom Garbett went to work as a deacon was Cosmo Lang. A year later he was appointed to the Bishopric of Stepney, and Bernard Wilson succeeded him at Portsea. When, after another eight years, Wilson died, the unusual step was taken of promoting the senior curate, Garbett, to be the vicar.

The appointment was fully justified. During his nine years as curate he had studied with keen sympathy the problems of a large industrial parish. As vicar he developed great administrative powers and was always an indefatigable worker. In the pulpit he could not match the brilliance of Cosmo Lang, but his sermons were marked by force and strong common sense. Always he had something to say and the knack of saying it so that there could be no doubt of his meaning. His robust mind appealed particularly to men, and his men's services and meetings were a great feature of his Portsea ministry. On moral questions, on such matters as housing and slum clearance, while some hearers might criticize the vicar's opinions, none could allege that he had not made those opinions clear. On his curates he impressed his own exacting standards of pastoral duty and organization; and if younger men on first joining the clergy house found the vicar somewhat formidable, they looked back in later years to a training of unusual thoroughness.

A man who had worked for 19 years with marked success in a great industrial parish seemed well qualified to serve as bishop of what is, to a great extent, an industrial diocese, and Garbett's consecration in 1919, as Bishop of Southwark, in succession to Hubert Burge, was generally welcomed. He occupied the rather depressing house at Kennington which was the episcopal residence and threw himself into his new work with characteristic energy. Characteristic also was an announcement he issued at once to his clergy—that he would neither open bazaars nor dedicate memorial windows and tablets, having his time filled by other and more important duties. These duties were many-sided. Bishop Garbett quickly showed himself to be a great administrator.

On the pastoral side he was a strong believer in synodical action, and he referred to his diocesan synod such questions as reservation and various problems of pastoral work. Even those clergy who feared him, as some did, admitted that his administration was fair as well as firm. The success of the "Twenty-five Churches Fund", which he inaugurated for the spiritual needs of new housing areas, was a tribute to his powers of organization. At the same time he applied himself with vigour to the social problems of his great diocese, particularly in regard to housing, on which he became an expert. Older contemporaries among the bishops quickly came to regard him as an outstanding example of what a pastoral bishop should be.

His keen interest in town workers and their problems did not cause the new Bishop of Southwark to neglect the rural areas in his diocese—far more numerous at that time than to-day. Following the example of Bishop Woods [q.v.] of Peterborough, Dr. Garbett made pilgrimages on foot, from village to village, frequently taking with him one or two of his younger clergy, who thus had a close insight both into a bishop's work and into the vigorous quality of their own bishop's mind. At each village he conferred with the clergy, preached in the parish church, spoke to wayside gatherings, visited the schools, called on sick folk. To *The Times* of August 19, 1922, the Bishop himself contributed an account of this work, and it was a method which he continued to employ after his translation to Winchester.

This took place in April 1932, when Garbett was 57. It was a much reduced diocese to which he returned. His former parish of Portsea was now in the new diocese of Portsmouth; Farnham Castle, the historic abode of Bishops of Winchester through long centuries, had passed into the possession of the new Guildford diocese. Dr. Garbett never ceased to regret the drastic readjustment of territory which his diocese had suffered. Any diocese, he maintained, should be so delimited as to contain a proportion both of large town parishes and small rural cures. Only thus, he said, could a bishop place suitable young men, full of energy, in large urban centres where they would have full scope, or, on the other hand, remove men worn out by long toil in a town parish to some rural benefice. Except for Southampton and Bournemouth, there were no really large urban centres in the reshaped Winchester diocese.

There is no doubt that the quieter pace of the Winchester diocese had a mellowing effect upon his mind and character. He was a great gardener, and with the help of his friend, Sir Arthur Hill, then Director of Kew Gardens, he laid out the Wolvesey gardens to great advantage. He valued also the many peaceful evenings he was now able to have at home without constant telephone calls. Though he was in no sense academic—indeed he had almost a "blind eye" for scholastic and academic interests—he was a great reader, and there seemed to be few books or reports of interest which escaped him. On the administrative side Dr. Garbett carried his own responsibilities easily, and expected others to discharge their responsibilities with an equal thoroughness, once he was satisfied as to their efficiency.

A good example of Garbett's methods and driving power was supplied by the Bournemouth Church Congress of 1935. The Congress had not been held for five years. Many people were against reviving it, believing that its usefulness was over. More than one Bishop declined a request that it should meet in his diocese. But Garbett readily agreed. With Archdeacon Daldy as his able lieutenant, he organized every detail of the Congress, without a trace of fussiness but with tremendous energy. The result was completely successful.

Dr. Garbett's capacity for work was severely tested with the advent of war in 1939. His chauffeur was called up, and for two long periods he was without a chaplain. But, though now 65 years of age, he learnt to drive his car himself, and, while driving was never a pleasure to him, he was quickly on the spot where he was needed, as, for example, when Southampton was bombed. He had to spend much time, moreover, in London, where he served on committees dealing with town and country planning and with rural housing. He spoke fairly often on social questions in the House of Lords, and his speeches commanded respect by their knowledge, sincerity, and common sense. He had also been for some years chairman of the Religious Advisory Committee of the B.B.C., in which he took great interest.

It was with much personal reluctance that in 1942 Dr. Garbett accepted the Archbishopric of York, vacated by the translation of Dr. Temple to Canterbury. "A most difficult decision to make", he wrote at that time to a friend. "I am 67, and I do not want to leave Winchester". Hampshire was indeed to an unusual degree his home, for with the exception of the years in Southwark he had spent his entire life there. But he felt that duty called him to undertake the larger work, and in a remarkably short time the strength of his character, his business-like efficiency, his measured yet forcible utterances on social questions endeared him to the north country people: forthright outspokenness was a quality appreciated on both sides; and he himself soon came to love the cities and villages, dales and moors, of his archdiocese. Though often called away by engagements elsewhere in his province or in London, and not least by long journeys oversea, both east and west, the care of his diocese was his most cherished task. Among many other activities he gave much attention to the chairmanship of the Archbishops' Commission on Canon Law, which held its first meeting in 1943 and reported in May 1946.

Between 1943 and 1946 Dr. Garbett became probably the most travelled ecclesiastic in the world. Already in 1938, as chairman of the Missionary Council of the Church Assembly, he had visited India and Ceylon to attend the meetings of the International Missionary Council at Tambaram, where, both in committee discussions and in the full sessions, he brought his strong common sense to bear with great effect. During this journey he visited northern India, including Kashmir and the North-West Province, where he was the guest of Sir George Cunningham, and the United Provinces, where he stayed with Sir Harry Haig.

At Travancore he met leaders of the Jacobite Church, and was the guest of the Maharaja of Mysore, whose Hindu piety deeply impressed him. The first of his journeys as Archbishop was in 1943, when he visited Moscow as the guest of the Patriarchate. He was much struck by the crowded services in the churches and the religious fervour of the worshippers. When Russian ecclesiastics visited York in 1946 they presented the Archbishop with a pectoral cross which had been worn by the Patriarch Sergius, lately deceased, a token of friendship which the Archbishop greatly appreciated. In the spring of 1944, accompanied by the Rev. G. A. Ellison, who had now returned to him as chaplain, he visited the United States to take part in the consecration of Bishop Dun of Washington, and to carry the good will of the Church of England to the Protestant Episcopal Church of America. Among his many speeches and addresses was a notable sermon in the Cathedral Church of St. John the Divine in New York on the basis of a just and durable peace.

Early in 1945 he visited Field-Marshal Montgomery and the troops of 21 Army Group in the Netherlands, where he gave a number of addresses to gatherings large and small. April saw him embarking on a still more arduous journey to Italy and Greece. In March 1946 the Archbishop visited Palestine, Egypt, Abyssinia, and the Sudan. At Addis Ababa, where he went to carry the felicitations of the Church of England to the Emperor* and the Church of Abyssinia on the restoration of their freedom, he had a long conversation with the Emperor, visited schools and hospitals, and was received ceremonially in the Cathedral of St. George. At Khartoum on the homeward journey he attended a great united service, and, after visiting the troops at Benghazi and Tobruk, flew home by Malta. On this trip he covered 12,000 miles, of which 11,000 were by air.

In October 1947 the Archbishop visited Czechoslovakia and Yugoslavia; 1949 found him in America; and in the winter of 1951-52 he made a prolonged journey to the Pacific Islands, Australia, New Zealand, New Guinea, Borneo, and Singapore and Malaya. This visit was one of arduous work and he found constant interest and stimulus in all he saw.

These years after Dr. Garbett's appointment as Archbishop of York were marked also by a succession of public addresses in York Convocation and elsewhere, by occasional weighty and witty speeches in the Church Assembly (his wit seemed to grow with his years), and by a series of books of increasing scope and importance which set forth the character and the tasks of the Church in the present age with notable learning and freshness. Such issues as the Church's position in the matter of marriage and divorce, of Christianity and Communism, of war and peace, and (prompted by the Roman Catholic dogma of the Assumption) of doctrinal authority, were handled with a wisdom and a clarity that were recognized by all; and all of them showed how well he knew the mind of clergy and laity alike and the pace at which it moved.

In 1947 his vigorous book *The Claims of the Church of England* embodied those practical reforms which he felt necessary to the Church's effectiveness. In 1950 appeared his *Church and State in England,* which is not only a plea for reform but also an admirable summary of Church history; and in 1952 followed *In an Age of Revolution,* which gathered and focused with great force his experience of the Church's work in relation to social problems. And in 1955 he broadened his canvas still further in *World Problems of To-day.*

It is not given to many men to write their best works after the age of 70; but Dr. Garbett was enabled to do it by the remarkable consistency of faith, outlook, and discipline which governed his ministry throughout a long and devoted life. He was a living example of the greatness of his calling and its influence and potentialities. Without the initial advantages often said to be necessary for position—wealth, family connexion, outstanding scholastic success—Dr. Garbett showed how the simple and wholehearted consecration of a man's gifts in the church's ministry may lead him to places of the widest influence and scope in church and nation. That is, no doubts, the lesson which above all others he would have wished to leave behind him; and there could be none of greater moment to our generation. His mind never ceased to look forward; his sympathy with younger men and their thoughts and feelings lasted to the end; and the single word *Prospice* might well form the text upon his grave.

Dr. Garbett, who was unmarried, was sworn of the Privy Council in 1942. It is announced in the New Year Honours to-day that a barony was to have been conferred on him.

January 2, 1956.

Roger Martin du Gard—See **du Gard.**

Clive Gardiner died on May 15, 1960 at his home in Chelsea. He was 69.

Alfred Clive Gardiner, the son of A. G. Gardiner, was born at Blackburn, educated at University College School, and studied at the Slade under Tonks.

Equally successful as designer and teacher, the former Principal of Goldsmith's College School of Art at New Cross will always be remembered by his colleagues as the author of one of the best sets of posters ever done for the greatly regretted Empire Marketing Board. The circumstances are worth recalling for the moral they contain for all advertisers, Government or private, who employ artists. The subject of Gardiner's posters was machinery, and when the "roughs" of his designs were under discussion doubts were expressed as to whether the posters would be sufficiently attractive to the general public.

In the result the posters were among the most successful of the series, and the warmest congratulations to the board came from engineers. This was not because Gardiner had spread himself on mechanical technicalities, but simply because he had given artistic expression to what the designers of machinery feel about their work. Inside information enables the appropriate conclusion of this revealing episode to be told. When, on the winding up of the board, the original designs of its posters were offered for sale, the set by Gardiner, which had been exhibited in fear and trembling, was the first to be snapped up.

On the retirement of the late Frederick Marriott, Gardiner was appointed Principal at New Cross. Here he became an inspiring influence, and made several important changes in the system of teaching. One, that both coordinated and gave direction to the various departments of the school and lent interest and entertainment to the annual exhibitions of students' work, was to assemble the term's activities round some central idea, such as that of a particular commodity. By this means every variety of talent, architectural, decorative, pictorial, illustrative—and even literary—was roped in and given an opportunity to contribute on its own lines to the common purpose. Some of the students would design the form or decoration of the commodity itself; others the packages or containers; others the advertisements, both pictures and "copy"; others the shop in which the commodity was to be sold; and others again the window display. Thus unity and coherence were brought into a scheme that still encouraged the individual student to do the sort of thing that he could do best.

Gardiner's abilities did not go unrecognized in the rather belated awakening to the importance of the visual arts which followed the outbreak of the Second World War, and in 1942 he was appointed by the Ministry of Food as art adviser for British Restaurants, to assist local authorities on questions of design and interior decoration. A successful scheme to provide British Restaurants in Greater London with pictures had already been organized for the British Institute of Adult Education and C.E.M.A. by Lady Clark, wife of the Director of the National Gallery, and Gardiner was called in to continue and collaborate in the scheme.

Between teaching and advising, Gardiner had not much time left for individual work, but his decorations at the Rubber Pavilion at the Wembley Exhibition—a series of designs in the production of rubber—should certainly be mentioned for they attracted considerable attention at the time. More recently he painted a mural for the Students' Union of London University.

In 1936 a one-man show of his paintings and watercolours was held at the French Gallery. It included both figure studies and landscapes. The former, under such titles as "La Penseuse" and "Sleeping Woman", were distinguished by a peculiar dignity, as if they belonged to a larger, calmer world than ours. In landscape Gardiner followed the example of Cézanne pretty closely, using colour constructively and concentrating on permanent rather than fleeting effects. This exhibition was enough to demonstrate Gardiner's powers as an original artist, but it was towards the artistic improvement of everyday surroundings, domestic and commercial, that he did his most valuable work. He anticipated an employment of the highly trained artist that is likely to be general in the future.

He married in 1921 Lilian Lancaster, herself a talented painter. They had two sons.

May 20, 1960.

Lieutenant-Colonel A. T. Goldie Gardner, M.C., who died at Eastbourne on August 25, 1958, was a well-known racing motorist who specialized in breaking speed records. In 1939 he made motoring history by exceeding 200 m.p.h. in a light car. He was 68.

Alfred Thomas Goldie Gardner was born on May 31, 1890, at Woodford Green, Essex. He was educated at Uppingham and started work in a broker's office in Ceylon. In the First World War he served in the Cavalry and Royal Artillery, and was severely wounded in the leg in 1917. He was mentioned in dispatches in 1915 and won the Military Cross the following year. He began racing in the 1920s, competing at Brooklands with an Austin Seven in 1924, and winning a novices' race with a Salmson in 1928. His next mount was an Amilcar, with which he had several successes.

In 1931 he acquired his first M.G., a make with which his name was to be linked closely for the rest of his career. With this M.G. Midget he became the first driver to lap Brooklands at more than 100 m.p.h. in a 750 c.c. car.

In the 1932 Tourist Trophy race at Belfast Gardner had a serious accident, his M.G. overturning several times. The leg wounded in the war suffered further injury, and in 1934 he decided to restrict his racing to Brooklands, where he won many races. In 1935 he decided to concentrate on record breaking and in the following year he broke the 1,100 c.c. outer circuit lap record at Brooklands at a speed of 124 m.p.h., driving a single-seat M.G. Magnette. In 1937 he broke some international class G records on the Frankfurt-Darmstadt *Autobahn,* to which he returned the following year with a new streamlined M.G. record breaker, raising the class record to more than 180 m.p.h. In the following spring he made his historic 203 m.p.h. run with this car on the new Dessau *Autobahn.* A few months later he rejoined the Royal Artillery for the duration of the Second World War, in which he spent a considerable time in north-west Europe with 21 Army Group.

For him the war merely interrupted his record breaking hobby, and in July 1946 he took the M.G. to Italy in an unsuccessful attempt to break records in the 750 c.c. class. A few months later he found a more suitable track in the form of the Jabbeke-Aeltre motor road near Ostend and raised the class record to almost 160 m.p.h. Further modifications to the engine enabled him to raise the 500 c.c. record to more than 150 m.p.h., and yet further alterations enabled him to break the 350 c.c. records at more than 120 m.p.h.

With an experimental Jaguar he broke records at 180 m.p.h. in 1948. Gardner's main objective had for long been the one-hour record for cars up to 1,500 c.c., and in 1951 he took his M.G. to the Bonneville Salt Flats, using a supercharged edition of the standard M.G. T.D. engine. He succeeded in raising the record to 137.4 m.p.h.

Altogether, during his racing career, Gardner established 116 speed records, including 35 international class records. He thrice won the British Racing Drivers' Club's Gold Star.

He married Una Eagle-Clark and they had one daughter.

August 28, 1958.

Dr. Maxwell Garnett, C.B.E., died at Seaview, Isle of Wight, on March 19, 1958 at the age of 77.

James Clerk Maxwell Garnett was born on October 13, 1880, the son of William Garnett, D.C.L. From St. Paul's School he went up in 1899 to Trinity College, Cambridge. He was already seen to be a man of parts and his academic career revealed his true merit. He was a Major Scholar, Smith's Prizeman, and Sheepshanks Astronomical Exhibitioner. He took a 1st Class in the 1st Division of Part II of the Mathematical Tripos in 1903 and in 1905 was elected a Fellow of his college. But Garnett was more than a "brain", he was a better than average oar who rowed in the University trial eight and was a lover of mountains and a regular visitor to Zermatt.

He lectured on applied mathematics at the University of London for a brief period and then in 1904 became a Board of Education examiner. Four years later he was called to the Bar by Inner Temple.

Between 1912 and 1920 he was Principal of the Manchester College of Technology and Dean of the Faculty of Technology in the University of Manchester. He was in some ways born before his time, looking ahead where others could not or did not choose to see, and his views on the college's development did not always accord with those put in authority over him. The controversy over the principal's policy of raising the educational status of the college came to a head in the summer of 1920 and Garnett decided to resign after the education committee decided to limit the number of degree students and to admit a certain number of senior technical school boys as whole-time students.

It was in the years of hope and despair between the two world wars that Garnett's practical idealism revealed itself in another sphere of action. In 1920 he was appointed secretary of the League of Nations Union and from then until 1938 he brought to bear all his powers, mental and physical, on the task of inculcating the ideals of the League.

Ever a man of principle and intellectual honesty, he resigned the post in July 1938, believing, as he said in a letter to Lord Lytton, chairman of the L.N.U. executive committee, "that I have come to be regarded by some ... as the principal obstacle to the union's being used as an instrument of political propaganda". This he could not agree to and said so.

He was the author of *World Loyalty* (with Nowell Smith); *The Dawn of World Order; Knowledge and Character;* and *The World We Mean to Make;* and of many papers on mathematical and physical subjects in the *Philosophical Transactions of the Royal Society.*

He was appointed C.B.E. in 1919.

If Garnett was a keen climber his main love was the sea. From an early age he used to spend his summers sailing in Spithead and his old red-sailed dinghy and his Canadian canoes, the first of which he had shipped from Canada when he was still at Cambridge, are well-known sights at Seaview. Garnett continued to paddle his canoe into Seaview village until he was well over 70, and at 74 he competed for the last time in the canoe race in the annual Seaview regatta.

He married in 1910 Margaret Lucy, second daughter of Professor Sir Edward Poulton, F.R.S.

He had a very happy family life and is survived by his wife, six children, three daughters and three sons, and 18 grandchildren.

[A tribute appeared on the same day].

March 20, 1958.

Sir Robert Garran, G.C.M.G., Q.C., who was the first Solicitor-General of the Commonwealth of Australia, died at Canberra on January 11, 1957. He was 89.

He was a distinguished legal and constitutional authority, and enjoyed a reputation both within and without the Commonwealth that extended much beyond his office. In 1930 he presided over the drafting sub-committee which framed proposals for legislation on the lines recommended by the Imperial Conference. The sub-committee's report later served as the basis of the Statute of Westminster.

Among the most notable of his services to the Commonwealth was his work for federalism. He was secretary to the committee which drafted the Federal Constitution of Australia, and joint author with Sir John Quick of the standard *Annotated Constitution of the Australian Commonwealth.*

Robert Randolph Garran was born at Sydney on February 10, 1867, the son of the late Andrew Garran who emigrated to Australia from Britain in the middle of the last century and became editor of *The Sydney Morning Herald* and a member of the New South Wales Legislative Council. His career at school and university was brilliant. He was captain of the Sydney Grammar School in 1884, and won several scholarships at Sydney University, where he graduated B.A. in 1888, and took his M.A. with first class honours in philosophy. He was called to the Bar, and practised for a short time, but, coming under the influence of Edmond Barton, he occupied himself more and more with semi-political activities, especially in the cause of federation.

In 1897 Garran published *The Coming Commonwealth,* a work intended for the ordinary reader, which perhaps did more to form a public opinion on federation than any other of the books and pamphlets issued at that time. In the same year he was appointed secretary to the drafting committee of the Federal Convention. In 1901 he became first parliamentary draftsman of the Commonwealth and secretary to the Attorney-General's Department. In 1916 W. M. Hughes [q.v.], the Prime Minister, made him the first Solicitor-General of the Commonwealth, and the two began a remarkable association. By virtue of the wide powers conferred on the executive by the War Precautions Act, Hughes had little to do but issue regulations under the Act in order to assume almost dictatorial control during the last two years of the war. In this Garran was his right-hand man. The two worked in complete harmony, and their collaboration, in Hughes's phrase, made possible government "by a fountain pen" during a critical period. After the war Garran accompanied the Prime Minister as an adviser to Europe.

In 1932-33 he was chairman of the Indian Military Expenditure Tribunal which met in London, and he was later chairman of the Commonwealth Book Censorship Committee. From 1930 until 1953 he was chairman of the council of Canberra University College. He was appointed C.M.G. in 1901, and in 1917 he was knighted. In 1920 he was promoted to K.C.M.G., and again to G.C.M.G. in 1937.

He brought to his official business a broad intellectual outlook. He was a cultured man who never found the routine of the civil service a bar to the pursuit of humane interests. Many will remember with appreciation the volume of translations from Heine which he published shortly after the 1914-18 War; and in 1946 he brought out *Schubert and Schumann, Songs and Translations.*

He married, in 1902, Hilda, third daughter of John Shield Robson, of Monkwearmouth, Durham. She died in 1936. There were four sons of the marriage.

January 12, 1957.

Apsley Cherry-Garrard—See **Cherry-.**

Dr. H. W. Garrod, C.B.E., Fellow of Merton, Professor of Poetry at Oxford from 1923 to 1928, and later Norton Professor of Poetry at Harvard, died on Christmas Day 1960, at the age of 82.

Heathcote William Garrod was born, the son of a solicitor, at Wells, Somerset, on January 21, 1878. He liked to describe himself as "self educated", but he dedicated an early work to his headmaster at Bath College, T. W. Dunn, "to have known whom is a kind of religion".

At Balliol afterwards his distinctions included the Hertford, the Craven, the Gaisford and the Newdigate. A short period of teaching at Corpus Christi followed his fellowship (1901) at Merton, which proved to be his lasting and beloved retreat. At one period he was regarded at Oxford as the coming Professor of Latin, and his memory as a master of the classics will live in his editions of Manilius, Statius, and Horace (the last a revision of E. C. Wickham's text) and still more in the *Oxford Book of Latin Verse* (1912) and the smaller *Book of Latin Verse* (1915). His stature in Latin studies is best noted in an anecdote. After the 1914-18 War he was known to deplore the declining state of Latin scholarship in his university, saying that it was redeemed only by A. C. Clark and F. W. Hall. Upon this a good judge remarked, "And by Garrod".

His love of ancient literature in no way lessened his sense of the modern, and in 1912 he himself appeared among the poets with a volume entitled *Oxford Poems.* Its qualities were those of a lover and artist of the beautiful, perfecting sweet melodies for gracious thoughts and fancies; some contrast may be noticed in a second book of his verse, brought out in later days and an altered world, *Worms and Epitaphs.* With these volumes those who look beyond fashions in poetry will range his *Poems from the French,* published in Benn's former sixpenny series of "Augustan Books"; for these translations convey almost as surely as Garrod's original compositions the romantic dreams and the delicate idolatries of his inmost nature. But he could turn to mundane and practical matters with ability. During the 1914-18 War he was employed under the Ministry of Munitions and visited America as a member of a special mission headed by C. W. Bowerman and J. H. Thomas. These services were recognized in his being made a C.B.E.

Returning to post-war Oxford, Garrod became more and more conspicuous in the field of English literature, and a succession of critical studies made him known to many others besides the vigilant reader of new poetry and the lover of the classical muses. Such publications as *Wordsworth* (1923), *Keats* (1926), *The Poetry of Collins* (1929), and again *The Profession of Poetry* (1929), *Poetry and the Criticism of Life* (1931), and *The Study of Poetry* (1936), with several subsidiary undertakings, distinguished him as a critic of bold views and pointed utterances. From 1923 to 1928 he was Professor of Poetry at Oxford, an admirable successor to W. P. Ker. In 1929 he occupied the corresponding chair at Harvard; he lectured also on poetry before the University of Toronto.

Through all this his veneration for Matthew Arnold may be perceived as an incentive, and he had extensive editorial intentions concerning the writings of his favourite great Victorian. Yet it was Keats who brought him out as a consummate editor of a British classic. The edition of Keats's poems with variant readings which Garrod published at Oxford in 1939 did what might have been supposed highly improbable, perhaps impossible; it superseded the labours of H. Buxton Forman. Nothing could have been better in its way than Garrod's net-casting for every possible detail affecting the text of Keats, and as he proceeded he indulged in some enlightening digressions. This responsibility did not exhaust him. The severe but congenial task of completing the edition of the *Letters of Erasmus* by his friend P. S. Allen, in collaboration with Mrs. Allen, devolved upon him. In the intervals of such far-spreading yet minute application he found time for such attractive things as his Taylorian lecture on Tolstoy.

Garrod would say smilingly that he was a good journalist, and his reviews of books, such as sparkled in the pages of the *Oxford Magazine,* amply justified this claim—almost the only one he ever made for himself, besides that for his having been first to give the true text of *Wuthering Heights* when he published an edition of the novel in 1930.

Apart from literature, one of his most obvious characteristics was his zeal for antiquities—those at least which won his attention because they were part of the places he loved. His Mertoniana are numerous and valuable. If it occurred to him that, for example, the ancient painted glass of his college called for a more exact history and explanation, he would prepare himself to provide the required pamphlet by intense study of the authorities on the subject at large. He transcribed the archives as perhaps no one else could; and the visitor to Merton has the benefit of his genius in a leaflet on the older buildings, lit up even in its masterly conciseness with flashes of Garrodian irony as well as learning. The east window which Price painted towards 1702 no longer keeps its place, except in the leaflet; and it may now be suggested that H. W. G. was the prime mover in dislodging it in favour of his fourteenth-century beauties.

Something of Birrell, something of Lamb might be recalled to define the conversation of Garrod, which abounded in paradox, challenge, and aphorism. He could appear sometimes abrupt and even wanton, testing his listener, but in quiet vein he soon reconciled those whom he had disconcerted. He was really the soul of the courtesy which means benevolence; and his sympathy with the young generation, possibly when he most seemed to be execrating innovation and irregularity, was almost perfect.

In the working of his college he frequently took a powerful part, produced a wise solution of a perplexity, or introduced an improvement. His phrase "the good life" unified his apparent contradictions; he liked it himself, he wished it for the rest of mankind. Recluse as he affected to be, he would ever lay aside his own business to entertain, assist, and inspirit the many who climbed his stair each day. In brief, for many years he dominated the life of his home—the college, which formed itself about him as about no other; "he was the college", so that when he retired from his research fellowship in 1955 he was elected as honorary fellow, but retained his rooms.

Garrod, who for years was one of the editors of the *Journal of Philology,* was an honorary LL.D. of Edinburgh and an honorary D.Litt. of Durham.

December 28, 1960.

Professor John Garstang, C.B.E., the distinguished archaeologist, died on September 12, 1956 at Beirut. He was on a cruise to southern Turkey in the course of which he visited Mersin, the site of his most celebrated work. He was 80.

He was born in 1876, the youngest son of Dr. Walter Garstang, and was educated at Blackburn Grammar School and Jesus College, Oxford, where he was a mathematical scholar. His archaeological researches began in 1897 while he was still an undergraduate, and his first academic appointment in that field followed in 1902, when he was made honorary reader in Egyptian archaeology in the University of Liverpool. Five years later he was appointed Professor of the Methods and Practice of Archaeology at Liverpool and he remained in the chair until his retirement in 1941.

His first excavations were of Roman sites in Britain, at Ribchester, Melandra Castle, Richborough, and Brough, and they made an important contribution to the growing knowledge of the Roman occupation of the island.

Between 1900 and 1908 he excavated sites in Egypt, Nubia, and Asia Minor, and then for four years turned his attention to the ancient Ethiopian capital, Meroë. His work there, which he described periodically in articles for *The Times*—a practice that was kept up for over 50 years—revealed a number of temples, palaces, and public buildings, including a royal enclosure in which was found a bronze head of Augustus, later deposited in the British Museum; and it produced evidence of occupation of the city by Roman troops. His digs elsewhere had meanwhile thrown light on the Hittite civilization in Asia Minor, on which he became a leading authority. His book, *The Land of the Hittites,* first published in 1910 and brought up to date under the title *The Hittite Empire* in 1929, became a standard introduction to the subject.

During the 1914-18 War he served in France as a Red Cross delegate and was appointed to the Legion of Honour. For a year after the war he was honorary adviser on antiquities to the Military Administration of Palestine, and in 1920 he became director of the British School of Archaeology in Jerusalem and first director of the Department of Antiquities of the Government of Palestine. The latter department was virtually his creation and he was responsible for the model Antiquities Ordinance and for the organization of excellent national and local museums. A skilful administrator and experienced field archaeologist, he superintended the work of the department with distinction until he retired in 1926.

In 1929 he led an archaeological expedition to Jericho, where excavations were carried out for several years. Four separate and successive defensive systems were disclosed, corresponding to recognized phases of Bronze Age culture. Strong evidence was also found that the normal life of Bronze Age Jericho ceased abruptly about 1400 B.C. as a consequence of earthquake and fire—a date that corresponded with the entry of the Israelites into Canaan. Garstang had already turned his attention to bringing the fruits of archaeology to bear on Biblical history in a work published in 1931, *The Foundations of Biblical History: Joshua and Judges.*

His most important work, however, was still to come. In 1936 he was made director of the Neilson Expedition to the Near East which concentrated on the excavation of Mersin, a site in Cilicia astride a historic trade-route linking east and west, which was believed in Turkey to be where the Garden of Eden was. Before the Second World War cultural links there between Europe and Asia were discovered, dating back to 3000 B.C. Later 10 more occupation levels were disclosed below the level where work had ceased in 1939. The discoveries of this excavation were of the first importance, though Garstang's method of presenting them in *Prehistoric Mersin* (1953) was criticized by other scholars.

Garstang was appointed the first director of the British Institute of Archaeology in Ankara when it was opened in 1948. The following year he became president of the institute. He was made a C.B.E. in 1949 and was a member of the Order of St. John of Jerusalem. He was also an honorary D.Litt. of Aberdeen University, a Fellow of the Society of Antiquaries, and a Correspondent of the Institut de France.

He married, in 1907, Marie Louise Bergès, of Toulouse, who shared his interests fully and was his constant companion during his excavations. She died in 1949. There were a son and a daughter of the marriage.

September 14, 1956.

Edgar Gascoyne-Cecil—See **Cecil of Chelwood.**

Hugh Gascoyne-Cecil—See **Quickswood.**

Alcide de Gasperi—See **de Gasperi.**

José Ortega y Gasset—See **Ortega.**

Professor James Brontë Gatenby, who held for many years the Chair of Zoology at Trinity College, Dublin, and was well known in the biological world as a prolific and controversial writer on the fine structure of the animal cell, died on July 20, 1960 at Galway at the age of 67.

Gatenby was born in New Zealand in 1892 and received his schooling there. He read zoology at Jesus College, Oxford, and spent a few years after his degree as Senior Demy of Magdalen in post-graduate work in Goodrich's laboratory. In 1919 he went as lecturer to University College London, and two years later, while still in his twenties, he was appointed to the chair at Dublin, which he held for 36 years, exchanging it in 1959 for a research Professorship of Cytology.

From Goodrich at Oxford and J. P. Hill in London he had received an excellent training in histology and embryology respectively, and these two disciplines occupied a prominent place in his teaching. He edited and wrote some useful works on staining and other microscopical techniques, but his main interest lay in the field of cytology, and especially in the elucidation of the nature and function of the so-called Golgi apparatus.

For a while his interpretation was unquestioned; but in later years rival schools appeared, based possibly on less technical skill and experience but with a more sophisticated chemical background than Gatenby's—for he was never happy with the physiological approach of what he regarded as the wild young men of Cambridge. The anathemas launched from Dublin against these heretics, first in Paris and later, by the unkindest cut, at Oxford, never lacked in vigour.

Gatenby's reputation stood higher abroad than at home. He attracted to Dublin students from many distant parts of the world, and he spent some time in Belgium, Egypt, and the United States as visiting professor. In Dublin his relations with his colleagues were at times strained, for his controversies were apt to extend beyond the technical field, but he was a popular figure in the professional world. Beneath all the thunder lay a fund of simple, jovial bonhomie which, coupled with his extreme opinions on many questions of the day, made him an entertaining companion for a day's fishing or an evening's setting the world to rights.

He was twice married and had four children by his first marriage. Gatenby's son, Dr. Peter Gatenby, was on July 20 appointed Professor of Clinical Medicine at Trinity College, Dublin.

July 22, 1960.

Harold Charles Gatty, an outstanding aerial navigator, who flew with Wiley Post, the American pilot, in the record-breaking round-the-world flight in 1931, died at Suva, Fiji, on August 30, 1957.

Although he achieved much in the United States and was for long associated with American aeronautical schemes, he was born in Tasmania, went to Jervis Bay as a youth, took a naval course, and then for some years served in coastal merchant ships on the Australian and New Zealand coasts. In 1927 his family decided to seek their future in the United States, and on arrival Gatty at once went to sea as chief officer of a luxury yacht. His heart, however, was in flying, and lacking the means to satisfy his ambitions he set up as an aircraft compass adjuster. That, at least, meant getting off the ground. He gained air experience by bartering navigational instruction for flying time, and from these experiences sprang his idea for a Los Angeles air navigational school. Here, among others, came Roscoe Turner, Harold Bromley, Colonel Lindbergh* and Mrs. Lindbergh—she to learn navigation and he to do a little "post-graduate" study.

Subsequently Gatty took part with Bromley in a hazardous attempt to fly the Pacific. They found a beach in northern Japan a mile long. For their overloaded, underpowered, single-engine machine they needed a mile and a quarter to take off and with local help set about making the beach the required length. They were 25 hours over water and for 21½ hours flew blind in cloud and fog. Mechanical trouble forced them back and fumes nearly incapacitated Bromley. They had left the coast near a red-and-white striped lighthouse and to this landmark they returned, made a forced landing on some sand dunes, and collapsed. "Not navigation", said Gatty afterwards, "maybe luck, or some sort of instinct". Yet, all the same, it was almost certainly his excellent navigation that got them back to land.

In 1931 Wiley Post (later killed tragically with Will Rogers, the great humorist, in an air crash) asked Gatty to accompany him in a proposed global flight. This feat they accomplished by masterly skill and stoic endurance, taking eight days 15 hours and 51 minutes. They were met on their return to Roosevelt Field by a large crowd, were accorded a triumphal procession up Broadway, and were both awarded the American Distinguished Flying Cross.

Shortly before they set out Gatty had devised a new type of ground speed and drift indicator, and the first model—almost home-made in appearance—was used in Post's machine. After the flight the United States defence authorities bought the licence for the manufacture of the instrument.

For some years Gatty was with the United States Air Corps in charge of navigation research and training, and played a large part in the planning and establishing of the Pacific air routes for Pan-American Airways.

In the war of 1939-45 he served with the Royal Australian Air Force for a time, later becoming Director of Air Transport in the United States Air Corps in Australia. At the time of his death he was the owner of Fiji Airways.

Gatty was author of an ocean survival handbook, *The Raft,* which was adopted by United States defence authorities, and of many technical papers, and was the joint author with Wiley Post of *Around the World in Eight Days.*

Shortly before his death he had completed *Nature is Your Guide* which incorporates his own experiences of the value of natural observation in air navigation.

August 31, 1957.

Brigadier Andrew Hamilton Gault, D.S.O., who was Conservative member of Parliament for Taunton from 1924 to 1935, died at Montreal on November 28, 1958 at the age of 76.

He was a wealthy Canadian manufacturer and business man from Montreal who settled in England after the War of 1914-18, for which he raised and equipped the famous Princess Patricia's Canadian Light Infantry, commonly known as "The Princess Pat's" [Lady Patricia Ramsay*]. He commanded it in France even after he had been wounded several times and lost a leg, and he was awarded the D.S.O. and mentioned many times in dispatches. At the end he was one of the few survivors of the original battalion, mostly men who had served the Empire in previous wars.

Gault was born in England on August 18, 1882, the eldest son of A. F. Gault who had large interests in woollen and cotton factories at Montreal and in many other Canadian enterprises. He was brought up in Montreal, going to school at Bishop's College at Lennoxville and then to McGill University. Like so many of the English-speaking residents of that city he had learnt from his earliest days an intense love for the Empire and when he grew up there was no more imperially minded loyalist. At the age of 18 he interrupted his studies to join the Second Canadian Mounted Rifles as a subaltern and served throughout the South African War, earning the Queen's Medal and three clasps.

On his return to Montreal and the completion of his studies he entered on the industrial and financial work in which his father had been interested and soon became one of the leading businessmen in the city. He was Consul General for Sweden in Canada in 1909-1911, at the time when immigration was at the highest and the work most arduous. From 1911 to 1913 he was a member of the Montreal Board of Trade.

On the eve of the outbreak of war in 1914 he made up his mind to equip a regiment of men who had previously served the Empire on the field of battle. He got into touch with Colonel Francis Farquhar, who was secretary to the Duke of Connaught, then Governor General of the Dominion. Together they secured his consent and that of the Government, and Princess Patricia agreed to give her name to the regiment. That was on August 3. By the 19th of the month they were 1,100 strong. By October 18 they were encamped on Salisbury Plain and by December 22 in France. Colonel Farquhar was then in command but Gault soon succeeded him.

The Princess Pat's won attention and praise wherever they went. General French, then Commander-in-Chief, said "I have never seen a more magnificent looking battalion, Guards or otherwise". They were at St. Eloi, the second battle of Ypres, Sanctuary Wood, the Somme, Vimy Ridge, Passchendaele, Amiens, Jigsaw Wood, Tilbury, and finally the first advance on Mons. In later days it was a great joy to Gault that the regiment was kept in being, and when it returned to England in 1939 many of the men were sons of those who had served in France. Gault became honorary colonel of the regiment.

After the war Gault made his home at Hatch Court, near Taunton. He kept up many of his business interests in Canada and undertook others over here. He often visited the Dominion, where he had a home in St. Hilaire in the province of Quebec. But his chief interests lay in farming which he did much to encourage and develop in Somerset, and in flying to which he was devoted, often piloting his own aircraft on trips over the Continent.

He entered Parliament in 1924 from a desire to promote closer Empire relations through ties of trade. He was most popular in the county, doing much for the farmers and being a good shot and fearless rider to hounds. In 1932 he was presented with the freedom of the borough of Taunton.

In 1935 he gave up his seat in Parliament, saying that his ideals and purposes had been realized at the Ottawa conference. He was recalled to service in the Second World War and was promoted to brigadier.

He married first in 1904 Marguerite, daughter of the Hon. G. L. Stephens, a former Canadian Cabinet Minister; and when that marriage was dissolved he married in 1922 Dorothy Blanche, younger daughter of C. J. Shuckburgh.

December 1, 1958.

Reginald Moxon Armitage, better known as **Noel Gay,** the composer of "The Lambeth Walk" and many other popular tunes, died on March 4, 1954 at his home in London. He was 55.

The son of the late Harry Armitage, of Wakefield, he was born on July 15, 1898, and became choirmaster at Wakefield Cathedral while still a boy. His original intention was to devote himself to classical music and after holding the appointment of assistant organist at the Chapel Royal, St. James's, he became organist and director of music at St. Anne's Church, Soho, at the age of 18. After going up to Cambridge, where he was at Christ's College and took the degree of Mus. Bac., he discovered that he had the indefinable but unmistakable touch which the writing of popular songs requires. This gift he developed by study of the Gilbert and Sullivan operas.

The secret of his popularity was the employment of simple repetition, exemplified in his greatest success, "The Lambeth Walk", in which both words and music are constantly repeated. It did, indeed, as was said by Lupino Lane [q.v.], who launched it as a dance as well as a song, embody the cockney spirit to a remarkable degree. Other examples may be cited; for instance, "There's something about a Soldier that is fine, fine, fine", where the repetition of the word "fine" has a kinship with genius. "Around the Marble Arch" and "The Fleet's in Port" are yet further examples of the method.

In 1925 a revue of his composing, called *Stop Press,* was accepted for performance. After that success, more successes followed, with *Merry Mexico* in 1926; *Jumbles,* of which he was part-composer, in 1927; *Clowns in Clover,* of the same year; and *Hold my Hand* in 1931. In 1930 he wrote the song "All the King's Horses", for Cicely Courtneidge's musical comedy *Folly to be Wise,* and in 1933 he provided the music for Stanley Lupino's farce *That's A Pretty Thing.* Later he wrote the music for the musical play *Jack o' Diamonds,* which was performed at the Gaiety Theatre in 1935. In the same year *Love Laughs—!* another musical comedy, with music by Gay and starring Renée Houston, was produced at the London Hippodrome.

His greatest success came in 1937 with *Me and My Girl,* for which he wrote the music and composed the song "The Lambeth Walk", which was made famous by Lupino Lane. *Me and My Girl* ran for more than 1,500 consecutive performances and Gay's tune soon found its way into the nation's heart. In 1938 he wrote the music for *Wild Oats,* another long-running production. He also wrote songs for *The Little Dog Laughed,* which was first performed in 1939.

During the war years he wrote the music for a number of light-hearted revues, which included *Lights Up* and *Present Arms* in 1940, *Susie* in 1942, *The Love Racket* in 1943, and *Meet Me Victoria* in 1944. He continued in a similar vein after the war with *Sweetheart Mine* in 1946 and *Bob's Your Uncle* in 1948. In 1949 he composed the music for the pantomime *Aladdin* which was performed at Richmond.

March 5, 1954.

Lord Geddes, who died on January 8, 1954 in hospital at Chichester at the age of 74, had a truly remarkable career.

A Professor of Anatomy who in 1914 was teaching at McGill University in Montreal, he was swift to join the Army, and having served in it in England and France was in 1916 appointed Director of Recruiting and a little later Minister of National Service. He then served in Lloyd George's Government as President of the Local Government Board, Minister of Reconstruction, and later as President of the Board of Trade.

Having during his absence from McGill been appointed Principal of the University, he had intended to return there, but instead was sent in 1920 to Washington as British Ambassador. At the time he went there Anglo-American relations were "sicklied o'er" with the uncertainties and asperities of an unhappy period. When he left the chief points of contention had been eliminated and for his part in removing them, and surmounting many of the minor difficulties, his term of office was not only memorable but his place in the line of British Ambassadors became established as one of great and unquestioned distinction.

After his return from the United States Lord Geddes turned from a public to a business career, but in the earlier part of the 1939-45 War rendered valuable services as a Regional Commissioner. His last years were clouded by the loss of the sight of one eye, but he dictated a most informative family history which was published only in 1953.

The Right Hon. Sir Auckland Campbell Geddes, first Lord Geddes, of Rolvenden, in the County of Kent, in the Peerage of the United Kingdom, G.C.M.G., K.C.B., M.D., LL.D., was born on June 21, 1879, the son of Auckland Campbell Geddes, a Scotsman who for 40 years was engaged in railway construction in India. He was one of a remarkable family, for his elder brother, Sir Eric Geddes, became during the 1914-18 War First Lord of the Admiralty; and his sister, Mrs. Chalmers Watson, was the first woman to be a medical graduate of Edinburgh University and took a prominent part in the struggle for the recognition of the rights of women.

Having been taken at the age of six to Edinburgh he was educated first at George Watson's College and then at the University. On the outbreak of the South African War and with some difficulty because of the defective eyesight which was to afflict him at other stages of his life, he joined the army as a private. His experience left him with a strong belief in the educational value of military training. Back at Edinburgh he took his full span in student life, played Rugby football for the university and was prominent in the volunteer movement. He graduated in medicine and then went, to pursue his studies, to Freiburg, Berne, and Vienna. Having completed them, he returned to his own University to be Demonstrator and Assistant Professor of Anatomy. His next post was that of Professor of Anatomy at the Royal College of Surgeons, Dublin; but after only a year there he went in a similar capacity to McGill University.

Geddes, who had long taken an interest in strategy, became convinced that a European war was inevitable and had taken the precaution of arranging with McGill that when it came he could take leave immediately. No sooner, therefore, did the news of the outbreak reach him than he cabled an offer of his services. It was accepted and he was attached to The Northumberland Fusiliers, who were stationed on the Yorkshire coast. In the Army he rose rapidly and was soon second-in-command of his battalion. A bad fall from a horse prevented him from accompanying his regiment to France, but after a short time he was sent to the front for staff training and was in due course appointed D.A.A.G. He did extremely well, and after the passage of the second Military Service Act in 1916 he was recalled to the War Office to become Director of Recruiting with the rank of Brigadier-General. In this capacity he attracted Lloyd George's attention and when in the next year his department was transferred to civil control he was appointed Minister of National Service, and thus placed in charge of the manpower of the country. His new office entailed his standing for Parliament, and in 1917 he entered the House of Commons as Unionist Member for the Basingstoke and Andover Division of Hampshire, a seat which he held for three years.

When in the autumn of 1918 his task drew towards its close Geddes was given the additional duties of President of the Local Government Board, which was soon afterwards to become the Ministry of Health, and in 1919 he undertook the heavy duties of Minister of Reconstruction.

Meanwhile he had not abandoned his intention of returning ultimately to McGill, and, the posts of Vice-Chancellor and Principal of the university having fallen vacant, he had accepted an invitation to fill them. He had good reason to feel that he had done his duty and a political career offered no great attraction to him. In April 1919 he conveyed to the Prime Minister his desire to return to Canada, but Lloyd George, in a highly appreciative letter, asked him to continue his services for a little longer. In May, however, he was transferred to the Board of Trade at an important juncture in the national affairs and while in office uttered a grave warning against individual extravagance. Then, in March 1920, his appointment as British Ambassador at Washington was announced. It spelt the end of his academic career.

Geddes's appointment to a position of such immense importance provoked considerable criticism in the press and among the public. He had no diplomatic training, nor had he yet disclosed that he possessed the many gifts essential to success at Washington. On the other hand, he had his recent experience at the Board of Trade to help him and some direct personal knowledge of the Empire. It was, however, obvious that he would have to make his own reputation and to do so in circumstances of much difficulty. At the time friendliness begotten of Anglo-American cooperation in the war was already chilling under the shadow of disagreements in regard to Ireland, naval armaments, the Anglo-Japanese alliance, and war debts. There were also many minor difficulties to test an amateur diplomatist with no great gift of personal magnetism. The new Ambassador was not, however, deterred, and he set to work in a quiet self-effacing way to ease the many strains. He succeeded far beyond the general expectation, and when, in 1922, he returned to London on a visit he was welcomed as one who had rendered eminent services not only in regard to the recent Washington Conference but in his general conduct of his office. The fact, indeed, that Anglo-American relations were by the end of his term considerably better was due in no small degree to him and to his sympathetic understanding of life and conditions in the United States. In May 1923 he developed serious eye trouble. In July he returned to England and at the close of the year resigned, to be much regretted in the United States where he had won golden opinions.

After his return to England his health began steadily to improve, and he was able after a time to accept a number of directorships, including, with the chairmanship of several investment trusts, that of the Rio Tinto Company and of the Rhokana Corporation.

In 1924 he was appointed chairman of a royal commission to investigate food prices, but, though he used to speak from time to time at public gatherings, he made no attempt to return to public life. In the winter before war broke out in 1939 he helped Sir John Anderson (now Lord Waverley [q.v.]) in his national service recruiting campaign by speaking at the national service rallies in the big centres; then in the following June he resigned his position in the campaign in order to concentrate upon the duties as Regional Commissioner for Civil Defence, a post to which he was appointed first in the South-Eastern and later in the North-Western regions.

He underwent a delicate, but successful, operation for cataract in 1941 and in January 1942 he was raised to the peerage. In the following July he resigned his commissionership. He continued his work in the City until his health compelled his resignation from his directorships in 1947.

In 1906 he married Isabella Gamble, third daughter of W. A. Ross, of Staten Island in New York City, and leaves four sons and a daughter. His eldest son, the Hon. Ross Campbell Geddes, now succeeds to the title.

January 9, 1954.

Sir Arthur Gemmell, M.C., T.D., M.D., a past president of the Royal College of Obstetricians and Gynaecologists, died at his home in Liverpool on September 24, 1960 aged 67.

Arthur Alexander Gemmell was the eldest son of the late Dr. John E. Gemmell, himself a well-known Liverpool gynaecologist. He was educated at Uppingham, King's College, Cambridge, where he graduated M.A., M.D., and Liverpool University. On the outbreak of war in 1914 he interrupted his medical studies to join The Liverpool Scottish Regiment. He was wounded at Ypres, and was afterwards adjutant in The Queen's Own Cameron Highlanders at Salonika. For his services there he was awarded the Military Cross and the Greek Military Cross.

Gemmell became so enamoured of the military life that he continued as a professional soldier for a short time after the end of the First World War. And even though he then completed his training in medicine he remained a Territorial officer and commanded The Liverpool Scottish Regiment during the years 1923-27, being given the brevet of colonel. Meanwhile he had followed in his father's footsteps and by the late 1920s was established as a consulting gynaecologist in Liverpool, having taken his F.R.C.S. (Edinburgh) in 1924.

For 30 years until his retirement in 1957 he was on the staff of the Women's Hospital, Liverpool, the David Lewis Northern Hospital, and the Liverpool Maternity Hospital, playing an ever increasing part in their work and management. As lecturer in obstetrics and gynaecology in the University of Liverpool he was outstanding as a clear and conscientious teacher.

It is no surprise that Gemmell should have had a large practice, for his care of patients, in hospital or in nursing home, was characterized by assiduous personal attention as well as by exceptional technical skill. His great sense of service, honesty of purpose, clear thinking, fairness and lack of malice ensured him a large place in the administration first of his own hospital and later of the medical services in general. He served on the Liverpool Regional Hospital Board, the board of governors of the Royal United Liverpool Teaching Hospital and the Central Health Services Council. He was until the time of his death chairman of the obstetrical and gynaecological advisory committee of the Liverpool region; and he was at one time treasurer and later vice-president of the Liverpool Medical Institution.

He was president of the section of obstetrics and gynaecology of the Royal Society of Medicine in London during 1957-58; but the body to which he devoted himself above all was the Royal College of Obstetricians and Gynaecologists. Of this he was a foundation member and he served on its council in its early days. For seven years he was honorary treasurer and it was largely through his efforts that in 1947 an appeal for money for a building worthy of the college was launched. It is fitting that he should have lived to see his early enthusiasm justified by the opening of the new college house in Regent's Park by the Queen earlier in 1960.

Much of his time during his later years was spent in London because in 1952 he was elected president of the Royal College of Obstetricians and Gynaecologists, an office which he held with distinction for three years. For his services to medicine both locally and nationally he was knighted in 1955. He was also an international figure in gynaecology and had travelled in Australia, New Zealand, and the United States. He was an honorary fellow of the American Gynaecological Society and the American Gynaecological Club.

Wherever he was, in Liverpool or London, Gemmell was for ever striving to help both individual patients and the maternity services in general. So many demands were made on his unfailing help and guidance that he had little leisure. Such as this was, it was devoted entirely to his family. At the height of his powers and achievements his life was clouded by the serious and incurable illness of his wife. During her many years of invalidism before her death in 1957 he nursed and tended her with the meticulous care and kindliness so characteristic of the man.

He married in 1919 Gladys Freda, daughter of W. A. Reading, and he leaves a son and two daughters.

September 26, 1960.

King George VI died at Sandringham at 10.45 a.m. on February 6, 1952. The King, who retired to rest on the previous night in his usual health, passed peacefully away in his sleep, a statement from Buckingham Palace, London, announced.

Prince Albert Frederick Arthur George was born at York Cottage, Sandringham, on December 14, 1895. The then Prince of Wales, afterwards King Edward VII, had only one surviving son—the Duke of York, afterwards King George V. The birth of a second son to the Duke of York established beyond doubt the succession to the Crown in the direct male line.

The young Prince with his elder brother, younger sister, and three younger brothers had in his childhood a life of simplicity and happiness in which the official activities of their parents and their own busy future were allowed to make themselves felt as little as possible. When it was necessary for them to be in London they lived in early days at York House, St. James's Palace, moving to Marlborough House after Queen Victoria's death. Otherwise they divided the year, according to the migrations of the Edwardian Court, between York Cottage at Sandringham, Frogmore at Windsor, and Abergeldie in Scotland.

After the usual routine of nurses and governesses Prince Edward and Prince Albert were handed over to a tutor. Their parents chose Mr. Hansell, who encouraged in his charges the normal interests and healthy outlook of country-bred boys, but was less successful in giving them a good educational grounding. Both the Prince and his elder brother delighted in the company of their grandfather, finding his easy, chaffing manner perhaps more congenial than that of their father.

For at least two generations it had been a tradition in the Royal Family that the second son should go into the Navy. Queen Victoria's second son, the Duke of Edinburgh, had a long and distinguished career at sea, and in pursuance of that tradition Prince Albert's father had received a naval training during the lifetime of his elder brother. Accordingly Prince Albert was entered at the Royal Naval College, Osborne—once the home of his great-grandparents—in January 1909. From Osborne he went on to Dartmouth, and his career at those two training colleges was marked by a real understanding of his profession and a zest to acquit himself well. The Prince had inherited some of his mother's shyness, which was accentuated by an impediment in his speech. This never entirely left him, and in the rough and tumble of the Naval Colleges proved a difficulty in relations with his fellows.

Passing out from Dartmouth at the end of 1912, he went in January of the following year on a training cruise in H.M.S. Cumberland, spending six months in the West Atlantic. He thoroughly enjoyed the various excursions on shore, playing football for the cadets of the Cumberland at Teneriffe and riding in a gymkhana at Barbados. In the following September he was appointed as a midshipman to H.M.S. Collingwood. He was serving in this ship when war broke out in 1914. Throughout these early days of naval training it is no exaggeration to say that the rank of the Prince was naturally and completely merged in his naval rank, and that he thoroughly enjoyed the normal and unprivileged life of a cadet and midshipman. It was unfortunate that during the first two years of the 1914-18 war the prince should have been dogged by a series of troublesome complaints. In September 1914 he had to be hurriedly operated on for appendicitis and could not return to duty till February 1915. In the following November he was on sick leave for several months suffering from an obstinate gastric disorder. He was again at sea in May 1916, just in time to experience active service at Jutland and to receive (as all who were with him will testify) well deserved commendation for his conduct in action.

In the following September he was finally invalided from the Navy and spent several months of unrelieved ill-health—a gloomy period though somewhat brightened by his twenty-first birthday, when he was invested with the Order of the Garter by his father. On November 30, 1917, he was seriously ill and was operated on for a duodenal ulcer. After that operation the Prince's health steadily recovered. At this period of his life the Prince owed much—both in character and health—to Sir Louis Greig, who had originally known the Prince at Osborne, where he was the medical officer. Greig was in close attendance on the Prince for some years. His father decided that he should be given training in flying, and throughout the spring of 1918 he received instruction at the station near Boulogne, flying an Avro biplane. He was given his wings. In this branch of the fighting Services the future King took much pride, showed great proficiency, and always until his accession appeared on ceremonial occasions, such as Trooping the Colour, in Royal Air Force uniform—the first Prince of the Royal House to do so.

When the war was won Prince Albert was singled out for a gratifying experience. He represented his father at the triumphal entry of the Belgian Royal Family into Brussels. Riding on horseback beside King Albert, the Prince received a popular welcome as the representative of a powerful ally and a relation of the Belgian King.

At the age of 24 the Prince, like many of his contemporaries, found himself untrained except in those spheres which it was devoutly hoped would never again be of practical use. In spite, therefore, of being four years older than the ordinary freshman, the Prince went up to Cambridge in October 1919, going, like his uncle the Duke of Clarence before him, to Trinity College. At Cambridge he read a special course of history, economics, and civics, worked hard (but not too hard), enjoyed riding a somewhat noisy motor-bicycle, and appeared at country houses in the neighbourhood for the civilizing influence of tea and lawn tennis. He lived with his brother, the Duke of Gloucester,* and Sir Louis Greig in a private house off the Trumpington Road. This arrangement, which somewhat resembled the life of their grandfather at Madingley Hall some 60 years previously, was unfortunate since it deprived them of the easy companionship with their own generation which would have been derived from life in college, or even in ordinary university lodgings.

The following year his father's old dukedom of York was revived in his favour and he took his seat in the House of Lords on June 23. Thenceforward he was able to take his part in the many duties and ceremonial functions which befall a Royal Duke. In his own generation there was, at that time, only his elder brother to fill this role, so that an extra heavy crop of foundation-stone laying, opening ceremonies, and speech-making fell to his lot. One of his most interesting experiences during these early years was in 1922, when he travelled to Belgrade to act as "koom", or sponsor, at the wedding of King Alexander of Yugoslavia. During 1921 he supervised the arrangements for the first of his boys' camps, which were composed of 200 public school boys and 200 boys from working-class homes. It is difficult to exaggerate the success and importance of these camps, run under the aegis of the Boys' Welfare Association, of which he had become president in 1919. Nor can there be any doubt that in those days, when strikes and discord between the classes were figuring largely in the national life, the Duke's encouragement was invaluable for the smooth running of the experiment.

At first the scheme seemed slightly odd to many people who could see in it nothing likely to be of lasting value. The boys, however, soon made the camps into a fellowship rich in leavening consequences and to-day, 30 years later, the founder—for the original idea was entirely the Duke's—could have had no clearer proof of the success of his experiment than the number of schools and firms which have organized similar camps. The Duke was only once prevented (in 1934 by indisposition) from visiting the camp; it was an annual engagement which he thoroughly enjoyed. The boys always treated him as one of themselves, and, as though indeed he were, he joined wholeheartedly in their bathing parades, their games, their "rags", and the customary sing-song round the camp fire.

At the beginning of 1923 came the welcome news of the Duke's betrothal to Lady Elizabeth Bowes-Lyon, younger daughter of the fourteenth Earl of Strathmore. The marriage of a son of the Sovereign to a British subject roused great public rejoicing and enthusiasm. It was solemnized on a fitfully sunny April day in Westminster Abbey, and was almost the last State occasion graced by the presence of Queen Alexandra.

His marriage was not only, as all the world knows, ideally happy, it was also a source of great strength to the Duke, both in his public work and in deepening the public's affection for him. The circumstances in which the children of King George V had passed their youth were somewhat unusual; though friendly with several contemporaries among the aristocracy, they inevitably could not mingle with them on terms of absolute equality. Moreover, the war had cut them off from the society of their friends and relatives among the Royal Families of the Continent, so that they lacked something of the discipline of manner which the friendly rivalry of equals alone can give. In the Duke's case this was heightened by the inevitable diffidence of all who stammer, so that his circle of friends was extremely narrow. Those who knew the Duke intimately realized how greatly his character was broadened and rounded off by his wife, and how greatly she strengthened his confidence in himself.

In spite of their great position, the Duke and Duchess were some years in settling down to the comforts of a permanent home. At first they lived at White Lodge in Richmond Park, where Queen Mary [q.v.] had been brought up. This was, however, too far from London to be wholly convenient, and though countrified it lacked the privacy and retirement of a true country home. Subsequently they lived in various houses in London, and Princess Elizabeth was born three years after their marriage in the house in Bruton Street from which her mother had been married. A few months later the Duke and his family moved into 145 Piccadilly—a large Victorian house which was one of a group of houses known in the nineteenth century as Rothschild Row. After renting one or two houses in the country, the Duke was given by his father the Royal Lodge in Windsor Great Park, and he moved there in 1933, three years after the birth of the Princess Margaret. The Duke, both as Duke of York and King, was ideally happy here planning improvements to the house and developing a really beautiful garden. He was extremely interested in the history of the Royal Lodge and had amassed details of all the previous owners and of their alterations to the house. There, in the society of his family, undisturbed by affairs of State and unrestrained by the formalities of Court life, the Duke gave full bent to his zest for life and his naturally high spirits.

That side of the Duke's life was inevitably seen by only a few of his intimates, and the public largely knew him as a distinguished representative of his father in Australia and a zealous worker for charitable objects, and in particular those connected with industrial life. In the year following his marriage he was chairman of the committee for the Wembley Exhibition, and in 1925 he was president of the exhibition, so that he and the Duchess were frequent visitors there. The Duke was not, of course, so widely travelled as his elder brother, but he wisely decided to see something of the Empire before the ties of family life made protracted absence from home a difficulty.

At the end of 1924 he went on a long holiday with the Duchess to Kenya and two years later, in January 1927, he started with the Duchess on his great imperial mission to Australia for the inauguration of the Parliament House in Canberra. Though the programme was extremely exacting, the Duke and Duchess carried it through triumphantly, arousing the greatest enthusiasm in Australia and feelings of proud satisfaction in all who watched their progress from these shores. On his return, in a memorable speech at Guildhall, he spoke of himself as "a thorough optimist", not only as regarded the strength of the Imperial ties between Great Britain and Australia and New Zealand, but as regarded the future prosperity of those two countries. Well known as a minute and patient inquirer into all that he wanted to understand, the Duke made a considerable impression with his speech and may be said to have been justified by events.

After his return from Australia, in the summer of 1927, a visit which had cost the Duke and Duchess six months of the society of their daughter at a very entrancing age, the Duke made no further tours in the Empire before his accession, and his work was thenceforth concentrated at home. Perhaps the work in which he was most interested was his presidency of the Industrial Welfare Society, which was founded to impress on employers that the wellbeing of their workpeople was primarily the concern of industry and not of Parliament or any outside body. As the Duke himself said: "I get a great deal of pleasure as president of the Industrial Welfare Society, for it has brought me into touch with numbers of men and women whom otherwise I should never have met and I have been able to see nearly every industry in the country." The other side of the picture was shown by the manager of a large business who after one of the Duke's visits observed: "Of all the many visitors we have had here, I never met one who asked more sensible questions or showed greater understanding of our fundamental problems. He does like getting to the bottom of things."

Those 13 years which lay between the Duke's marriage and his Accession were years in which he was enabled to lay the foundations of systematic application to work and genuine understanding of his fellows which were to characterize him as King. In addition, the Duke found plenty of time for the enjoyment of his hobbies—especially those outdoor pursuits which he had enjoyed since his earliest days. He was a keen and accomplished lawn tennis player and he was also a good horseman and a good golfer. Of all King George V's sons he inherited most of his father's skill with the gun, and he was perhaps never so happy as when flighting duck or shooting at Sandringham. Yet, as was both natural and inevitable, he was neither so well known nor so popular with the people as was his elder brother. In part this was explained by the shyness, which gave him on first impressions the appearance of being somewhat aloof and distant in manner. Nothing could have been more deceptive, for five minutes' private talk with him revealed that he was well informed, anxious to serve his fellow-men, to comprehend their difficulties and to maintain in the fullest degree the high traditions of his family and position.

The death of King George V at the beginning of 1936 threw open large fields of new work and new opportunities to the Duke as Heir-Presumptive to the Crown. He succeeded his eldest brother in many of his important offices, but he was given no real opportunity to settle down to these new responsibilities before the Abdication of Edward VIII called him to the Throne. One of the most remarkable phenomena of English royal history is the number of times that the dukedom of York has been created only to merge with the Crown. Indeed, Queen Victoria considered it such an unlucky title that she preferred to create her second son Duke of Edinburgh rather than of York. The twentieth-century creation of the peerage proved no exception.Like his father, the new King had been trained to support the Throne rather than to fill it. In both cases the removal of an elder brother, one by death and the other by abdication, demanded great private sacrifices and great personal endeavour from a successor who had always expected to fill the second place. In both the cases of King George V and King George VI the demand was met with an application and resolution which may have surprised even those who knew them best, but which endeared them to their subjects.

Certainly no King has ever succeeded to the Throne in circumstances of greater difficulty. As he said himself, his brother's going deprived him "of a close friendship which I value highly". In a message to Parliament four days after his Accession the new King expressed in simple and moving words the magnitude of his task and the determination with which he met it:—

> "I have succeeded to the Throne in circumstances which are without precedent and at a moment of great personal distress, but I am resolved to do my duty, and I am sustained by the knowledge that I am supported by the widespread good will and sympathy of my subjects here and throughout the world. It will be my constant endeavour, with God's help, supported as I shall be by my dear wife, to uphold the honour of the realm and to promote the happiness of my peoples."

A few days after his Accession the King travelled to Sandringham to spend Christmas there with his family. He remained there until the early days of 1937, while Buckingham Palace was being got ready for the reception of his family. During the early months of his reign the King was not seen a great deal in public, for the pressure of work was exceptional. At the best of times the stream of audiences, discussions, and decisions which envelop a Sovereign after his Accession are exacting, but they can always be spread over the year which divides the Accession from the Coronation. In the case of the King all those events had to be crowded into a brief and hurried five months. However, as all who surrounded the King observed, he seemed to thrive on hard work and was in the best of health and spirits when he had to undergo the great ceremonies of the Coronation.

On May 12, 1937, George VI was crowned King. In one respect there was a new departure—the Coronation Oath was altered to embrace the changes introduced by the Statute of Westminster. The enthusiasm and loyalty which marked the whole of Coronation week proved to all observers and emphasize for posterity the store which, after more than 1,000 years, Britain and the Empire still set by a monarchy true to its traditions. In his broadcast speech on the evening of the Coronation, the King, after thanking the people for their loyalty, spoke of kingship as service, and said "the highest of distinctions is the service of others, and to the Ministry of Kingship I have in your hearing dedicated myself, with the Queen at my side, in words of the deepest solemnity. We will, God helping us, faithfully discharge our trust". He ended by saying, "The Queen and I will always keep in our hearts the inspiration of this day. May we ever be worthy of the good will which, I am proud to think, surrounds us at the outset of my reign." This speech, no less than the one which the King delivered to the Dominion Prime Ministers and the chief representatives of India and the colonies on the day before his Coronation, showed that to him kingship meant service and called for great exertions and high endeavour on his part in return for the confidence so freely given to him.

The year 1938 marked a personal triumph for both the King and the Queen in their visit to France, which after a postponement began on July 19. By his speech at the banquet at the Elysée, which took place on the night of their arrival, and by his bearing in public and his obvious enjoyment of all the festivities arranged for him, the King turned conventional cheers into a deeper and more significant note.

It was known that his Majesty had long been watching with concern the alarming trend of events abroad—his visit to the Continent had done nothing to mitigate these feelings—and even through the formal language of official messages to the head of the German State his allusions to the necessity of peace for the development of both countries had not been overlooked. During the September crisis his Majesty was at Balmoral, but he returned at once to London for consultation with his Ministers. It was known that he himself was anxious to send a personal message to Herr Hitler, but this course was not thought constitutionally advisable.

In his speech on the Prorogation of Parliament the King gave expression to the dominant thought in the minds of all his subjects when he said:—"The desire of all peoples not to be drawn into war with one another is manifest and significant, and everywhere men and women share with me, I am convinced, a feeling of deep thankfulness that the imminent peril was thus averted. I pray that with the passing of this peril a new era may have opened for Europe."

Inspired with the hope to which he had given expression, the King announced in the autumn his intention to visit Canada. There had been some natural disappointment when it was announced earlier in 1938 that the King—partly on general grounds and partly because he was reluctant to lay additional burdens on the revenues of India—had decided to postpone the visit to India which had been provisionally arranged for that winter. The news of the intended visit to Canada gave great pleasure—particularly when it was known that it would be linked with a journey to Washington—and it was quickly noted that his Majesty would be the first British Sovereign to visit the New World.

For the King the spring of 1939 was inevitably filled by preparations for his journey to the

New World. He went at a time when the storms of war were black and threatening, but the King's project served to show how well and truly the foundations of peace had been laid in that quarter of the globe where the British rule of law was supreme. In spite, however, of ominous signs in Europe the King went steadily ahead with his plans, which were all carried out to schedule with the exception of the substitution of a liner for the Repulse, a change forced on the Government owing to the exigencies of the European situation.

The departure of his Majesty for Canada on May 6 brought into effect an interesting and important constitutional departure. In historic times it was always customary for the Sovereign to delegate his royal authority to Lords Justices when he was obliged to leave the country. In 1821, when George IV went to Hanover, it was first laid down, and subsequently followed, that communication in Europe was so simple as to preclude the necessity for any delegation of authority when the King was travelling in Europe. When, however, King George V visited India it was felt that some delegation of authority was essential, and certain Counsellors of State were appointed, as was also done when the same Sovereign was incapacitated through illness in 1928 and 1936. By the Regency Act of 1937 this and other matters were for the first time prescribed and defined by Act of Parliament. That Act named the Sovereign's Consort and the first four adult members of the Blood Royal to act for the King as Counsellors of State in the event of illness or absence from the United Kingdom. On the day before he sailed for Canada the King consequently appointed the Dukes of Gloucester and Kent, the Princess Royal, and Princess Arthur of Connaught to execute a number of royal functions during his absence abroad. In accordance with the terms of the Regency Act the Queen was also named as a Counsellor of State, though it was realized that she could not perform the functions of the office because she was to accompany the King to the New World.

On May 6, a perfect spring day, the Empress of Australia sailed from Portsmouth with King George VI and Queen Elizabeth on board. On May 17 she berthed at Wolfe's Cove, a mile from Quebec, and there Mr. Mackenzie King, the Canadian Prime Minister, boarded the ship and greeted his Sovereign with the words "Welcome, sire, to your Majesty's Realm of Canada". In the morning of May 19, for their time was strictly limited, they left French Canada and later in the day reached Ottawa. They were greeted by the Governor-General, Lord Tweedsmuir. The visit was marked by a historic ceremomy at which the King, seated on a throne in the Senate House, addressed its members and those of the House of Commons, and also gave the Royal Assent to Bills passed by the Canadian Parliament.

From Winnipeg, where the King and Queen arrived on Empire Day, the King broadcast to the Empire. He said that the journey had been "a deeply moving experience" and, speaking of the Empire, reminded his peoples that the aim it served was "freedom, justice, and peace in equal measure for all, secure against attack from without and within it". The simple dignity and unaffected kindliness of the royal pair had made a profound impression not only upon Canadians but also upon many thousands of Americans who had crossed the border to see them. On the night of June 7 the royal train crossed by the Niagara Suspension Bridge into the United States. Thus King George VI entered as an honoured guest with floodlights, music, and cheering the territory from which the last representatives of George III had withdrawn in the bitterness of defeat more than a century and a half before. Mr. Cordell Hull [q.v.], the Secretary of State, met them at the American end of the bridge, and at Washington they were greeted by their host and hostess, President and Mrs. Roosevelt.

The programme in New York included visits to the World's Fair and Columbia University. The route was lined by over 3,000,000 people, and the royal progress was well called a triumph. When, indeed, after their three days on American soil the King and Queen returned to Canada they had registered a resounding personal success and made a unique contribution to good will between the British Empire and the United States.

Within 24 hours of their return to London on June 22, the King and Queen were guests of the City at Guildhall. In his speech there the King said he had brought back an impression of the abiding power of the long English tradition of justice and liberty, still bearing fruit not only across the ocean but outside the British Dominions. Thus he sought to deepen the understanding and fortify the spirit of his subjects who during his absence had confronted the darkening menace of events in Europe.

Soon the menance had turned to reality, and on the first night of the war the King broadcast. "We are called", he said, "to meet the challenge of a principle which if it were to prevail would be fatal to any civilized order in the world", and he asked his people to stand "calm, firm, and united in their time of trial". From that moment, he, the symbol of the Empire's unity, devoted himself unsparingly to the Empire's cause. Inspections with him were no mere form, and he sought, as he always had, to obtain a complete understanding of all he saw. While neglecting no other arm, for he was of them all, he seemed particularly sedulous in regard to the Royal Air Force, with which he always felt a special comradeship.

In early December he crossed to France to visit the British forces. He went up to the front line, tramped through the mud, inspected troops, talked to the officers and men and tested the signal system of the Royal Air Force. On December 19 he was with the Navy at Portsmouth. On Christmas Day he made a broadcast to the Empire. In spirit and in matter it was excellent.

During the critical months of 1940 when the Nazi war machine was thundering across Europe few of his subjects appreciated the seriousness of the situation better than he; but he was able through all that terrible and anxious time deeply to understand the nation's mood, and by his own calm and confidence to steady, and encourage it. On Empire Day, confronting a situation of great gravity, he broadcast to his people. "Let us go forward", he said, "as one man, a smile on our lips and our heads held high and with God's help we shall not fail". It was a tragic moment indeed for him when in July he had to tell his subjects in the Channel Islands that it was necessary to withdraw the armed forces. He was, however, as undismayed in defeat as he was calm in victory.

Coupled with these dire national anxieties, he had the additional strain of a change of Government. Excluding the first few months of his reign, Mr. Chamberlain had been his Prime Minister since he came to the throne. In him the King placed great confidence and they had been further drawn together through the strains and stresses of those days. As the Queen expressed it "during these last desperate and unhappy years, you have been a great support and comfort to us". Like all who were brought into close contact with Mr. Chamberlain—aloof and reserved as he was—the King shared with Chamberlain's Cabinet colleagues feelings of respect and affection for him, mingled with admiration for his singleness of purpose. In fact Neville Chamberlain used to tell the King everything. Naturally with Mr. Churchill*—the principal critic of Chamberlain's policy and one who had pursued an independent line at the time of the Abdication—the King's relations were at first more formal, but they gradually merged into friendship which was deep and sincere.

Inevitably in time of war the King, whose public appearances are shrouded under the cloak of security, must suffer some eclipse in the public eye, especially when the Prime Minister is a personality of outstanding colour and vigour. As King George V found when Mr. Lloyd George was Prime Minister, some of the fierce light which beats upon the Throne withdraws itself from Buckingham Palace and sheds its beams upon Downing Street. Mr. Churchill, fully conscious of this, was determined that the King should not be pushed into the background, and when confidence between them was fully established he showed every consideration to the King and lost no opportunity of publicly praising his steadfastness and his devotion to duty. On his side the King treated his Prime Minister with complete confidence, marked with a strain of deference for one who had been in the service of both his father and grandfather. At regular intervals the King went to dine with Mr. Churchill in Downing Street. This, which was a constitutional innovation, gave him the chance of meeting the leading members of the Coalition in a gathering of friendly informality which generally lasted till the early hours of the morning.

During the great air raids on London the King and Queen did everything in their power to comfort and inspire those who had suffered, and survived. Buckingham Palace itself was bombed twice in a week. The King, who himself saw some of the bombs drop from a low-flying aeroplane, and the Queen escaped harm; but three members of their staff were injured. "We have now had a personal experience of German barbarity", he said in a message to the Prime

Minister, "which only strengthens the resolution of all of us to fight through to final victory".

On September 23, 1940, the King broadcast, and announced his creation of a new mark of honour, the George Cross. There were few better judges of the appropriateness of such a decoration. Despising danger and disregarding air-raid warnings, he and the Queen continued to move about London, to visit stricken areas outside it, and to be, as the *New York Herald-Tribune* said, Ministers of Morale. In November he toured the ruins of Coventry for five hours. Later in the month he opened a new Session in person. Then there were visits of sympathy to be paid to Southampton, Birmingham, and Bristol. On Christmas Day he gave his usual broadcast in "sober confidence".

In March 1941, the King broke all precedent by going to meet Mr. Winant, the new American Ambassador, on his arrival in London. Then he and the Queen went north, and visited Edinburgh, Clydeside, Aberdeen, and Dundee. The records of his activity at this time show how fully he kept abreast of all the developments of the war effort, and how well he planned to be wherever he was needed most.

All through 1942 the endless round of duties went on. Things had gone very badly in the Far East, and, broadcasting in March, he acknowledged that there had been many searchings of heart. He called, however, on his peoples to profit by it, and claimed that the country had never been so united or worked so hard. In May he and the Queen visited the West Country, and saw the damage done to Bath. Then, back in London, he heard from Newmarket, as if from another world, that his horse Big Game had won the Two Thousand Guineas, and he completed the double with Sun Chariot in the One Thousand Guineas. Later the latter was to win the Oaks and the St. Leger. In that year he headed the list of winning owners.

In 1946 he again won the One Thousand Guineas with Hypericum, a filly bred in his own stud. Yet another filly from his stud, Above Board, won the Cesarewitch in the Royal colours in 1950.

King George had always taken a close personal interest in the Home Guard and, on its second anniversary, assumed its Colonelcy-in-Chief. Personally interested as he was in many spheres of national activity, it was incumbent on the King to set an example in all of them. Thus Windsor Great Park was, at his command, given over to corn-growing, and two-thirds of his farm lands there went under the plough. The strictest economy was at his command practised in the Royal Palaces and—to give one instance—lines were drawn at a five-inch level round all the baths. On Christmas Day 1942 he broadcast, and his speech was marked by a strong note of optimism. The Eighth and First Armies were converging in North Africa, the Red Army was rendering a magnificent account of itself; in consequence the prospect was brightening rapidly. Quoting "a former President of the United States", the King told of a boy carrying a smaller boy up a hill. Asked whether the heavy burden was not too much for him, the reply came, "It's not a burden, it's my brother!"

In May came the celebration of victory in Africa and a thanksgiving service at St. Paul's which the King and Queen attended. It was also the occasion of a notable exchange of telegrams between the Monarch and his Prime Minister. Encouraged by the deep cordiality of the King's congratulations, Mr. Churchill took the opportunity to acknowledge the help he had received from his Sovereign and permitted himself to convey a hint of how much the King's advisers owed to his Majesty's counsel. In June, on his official birthday, the King snatched a few hours' respite in order to take his daughters to their first evening performance of a play. It was one of many reminders at this period that both the Princesses were rapidly growing up.

In the summer of 1943 the King took the opportunity of a visit to the armies in Africa who were in the first flush of their victory over the Axis forces. He was attended on this tour by Service Ministers, Sir J. Grigg* and Sir A. Sinclair [Lord Thurso*]; the tour stretched from Gibraltar to Cairo and included Malta. As the tension of the Mediterranean fighting was thus rising to its climax the King had the chance of seeeing his soldiers and their allies and, as he expressed it on his return to England, "of being the bearer of the congratulations of all the peoples of the Empire on a victory which will shine in military history". What made this journey memorable for the King, and peculiarly enjoyable, was the easy relations quickly established between him and all ranks. Many of them, long parted from England and their homes, saw in the King a link with home and gave him a ready, boisterous welcome. He, freed from the formalities and restrictions necessarily surrounding much of his work at home, returned their welcome in the same easy style. It was on this occasion that an American observer said of his work, "How much lustre he gives it, how much warm humanity."

On June 25 he was home again after what he called "a magnificent trip". In July the King and Queen made a tour in Scotland and in August he was with the Home Fleet. On Christmas Day he broadcast and spoke with a new assurance of "our coming victory".

January 1944 inaugurated yet another crowded, though a less anxious, year. In February he and the Queen went to the Yorkshire coalfields and a little later took the Princesses with them on an inspection of the invasion troops. On June 17, 1944, the King himself crossed to Normandy in the cruiser Arethusa and attended a conference at General Montgomery's headquarters. A little more than a month later he paid a longer visit to Italy, and to the units of the Royal Navy, Army, and Air Force who were hotly engaged there. In Italy he travelled many hundreds of miles by air and road, meeting the commanders, inspecting the forces in the field, and decorating some of those who had won the Victoria Cross and other distinctions. It was far more than a formal visit, for during his busy days there he saw things thoroughly for himself.

Thus the long-drawn years of war ran down, and the closing months of the struggle saw the King sharing with his people the final ingenuity of the enemy in the shape of rocket and flying bomb. Again at Christmas 1944 he spoke to his people showing his steadfast faith not only in the approach of victory but in the establishment of happiness and concord to which "these years of sacrifice and sorrow have brought us nearer". Five months later he broadcast again a message of thanksgiving for the overthrow of Nazi Germany and of "remembrance for all those who will not come back". This theme was again uppermost when in the following week after the armistice with Germany he spoke to both Houses of Parliament in reply to their Addresses of Congratulation on the end of the war.

Then three months later the King again broadcast to his people on the occasion of the collapse of the last of the great triumvirate of enemies ranged against them. He emphasized that the four short words—"the war is over"—had for him and the Queen the same significance, "simple yet immense", which they had for all his people. He asked in particular—and the events which were to follow the war showed how wise this was—that there should be no falling off from the high endeavour which had carried the country to victory in the face of trials which appeared insupportable. On August 20 the King, accompanied by the Queen and their two daughters, drove in semi-state to St. Paul's Cathedral to offer thanks to God for the triumph of the allied cause.

The unremitting activities of the war period—it was difficult to remember that in addition to his constant journeyings he was always under the pressure of great affairs of State—gave him a unique knowledge of the way of life of Great Britain. Others may have been greater experts in the affairs of this or that branch of the armed or civilian services, or in particular processes of national production and organization; but the King had seen virtually everything with his own eyes and had investigated it in his own painstaking way. He seemed, therefore, to those who came into official contact with him much more than a mere figure-head of State. Wise, sensible, and observant, he was as competent to give as he was always ready to receive advice which was both sound and apposite.

In his first important engagement after the end of the war King George attended the centenary celebrations of the Imperial College of Science. He emphasized his pride in the connexion between the Royal Family and the college which had been virtually founded by the Prince Consort, but again he was largely concerned to urge that there should be no relaxation in the task of tackling the problems of reconstruction. At the beginning of 1946 the King gave expression to his hope for a firm foundation of peace on which the world—refashioned and reconstructed—could be firmly built. He entertained all the delegates to the General Assembly of the United Nations at a state banquet in St. James's Palace, and in the course of the important speech with which he welcomed them he said: "You may determine whether that lifting of the darkness that brought us strength and hope in the year that is past is to broaden into a true dawn, or whether the clouds are to descend once more upon a world that craves for light".

The anxieties of the year 1946, both national and international, pressed heavily upon the King, and he was known to be looking forward eagerly to the complete change of scene which was planned at the beginning of 1947 in his tour to South Africa.

The end of the war made it possible to resume the series of state visits to the various parts of the Empire which the tour of Canada, the senior Dominion, had been intended to open. Since India, Pakistan, and Ceylon had not yet attained full Dominion status, the Union of South Africa was the only self-governing nation of the Commonwealth with which the King was not yet personally acquainted; and in March 1946 General Smuts, the Prime Minister, tendered on behalf of his Cabinet a formal proposal for a visit in the following year. The King accepted not only for himself and the Queen but for both the Princesses, and on February 1, 1947, embarked (in a blizzard) at Portsmouth in H.M.S. Vanguard (Captain W. G. Agnew) [q.v.]. On February 17 he was received at the Duncan Dock, Cape Town, by the Governor-General (Dr. Brand van Zyl), the Prime Minister and the Cabinet, and made a processional entry into the legislative capital of the Union. Although the Nationalist Party, which was the official Opposition, contained a powerful republican element, he was received with the utmost enthusiasm, which was maintained throughout the length and breadth of the Union to the end of the tour.

It was the first time that a reigning Sovereign had set foot on South African soil. The principal event of the four days' stay in Cape Town was the state opening of the new session of Parliament, the King, with the Queen at his side, occupying the throne and reading the speech defining the programme of his South African Government. The same day he set out on his long and strenuous tour of the Union by rail. A special train had been built for the occasion, which was the dwelling place of the royal party for the greater part of the tour, and in which the King was at all times accompanied by a member of the Union Cabinet as Minister in Attendance and preceded (in a pilot train) by the Administrator of the particular province through which he was passing. The train was in touch by telephone with the United Kingdom, but the constitutional responsibility for all the King's actions and movements in the Union remained, of course, with his South African advisers. The journey occupied just two months, and in the course of it the trains traversed 10,000 miles. All the greater towns of the Union were visited, and at some of the most important, including Pretoria and Bloemfontein, the executive and judicial capitals, and the great port of Durban, the Royal Family left the train and stayed for several days. From Pretoria they paid a number of visits to Johannesburg and the mining towns of the Rand. One of the most moving ceremonies of the tour was the reception of the King and Queen by the *Oudstryders,* veterans of the republican side in the South African war, at the foot of Botha's statue at Pretoria, which echoed the sentiments with which a mounted commando of the old style turned out at the Natal frontier to escort them into the Transvaal.

There had been some apprehension of disharmony arising from the fact that acute friction then existed between the Union and Indian Governments over the position of Indians in Natal; indeed, the Natal Indian Congress had called for a boycott of all royal ceremonies. At Ladysmith, however, most of the Indian colony lined the streets, and when at Durban 10,000 Indians paraded to cheer it was clear that the boycott had been repudiated by the rank and file. The native Bantu peoples, and the coloured, everywhere crowded to pay their homage to their overlord.

The King's Flight of Viking Aircraft had accompanied the tour and its presence made it possible to make a quick journey from Pretoria to Salisbury, the capital of Southern Rhodesia, 600 miles away. Here the King again opened Parliament in state, and went on to make a brief tour of the protectorate, including two days in Bulawayo, whence the Royal Family made the pilgrimage to the grave of Cecil Rhodes at "World's View" in the Matopo Hills. They were able to see the mighty Victoria Falls, and, escorted by the picturesque state barge of the Paramount Chief Imwiko of the Barotse, to cross the Zambesi into Northern Rhodesia and remain there long enough to attend the Governor's garden party. The return journey to the south was made by way of Kimberley and Mafeking, famous fortresses of the South African war, and the trains reached Cape Town again in time for the celebrations of the coming of age of Princess Elizabeth to be held there. After affecting scenes of farewell the Vanguard set sail for England on April 24. It was universally acknowledged that the visit had had a profound effect on the minds of all South Africans, and, in a country in which it had hitherto been easy to represent the monarchy as a symbol of alien rule, an appreciation had been created of the King as a warmly human figure, deeply and personally interested in the welfare of all races of his subjects in Africa, which nothing could eradicate from the minds, especially the younger minds, of those who had seen and heard him in their midst.

From this time forward the King, on that side of his arduous life which consisted in the ceremonial representation of his people, began to enjoy more and more the regular help of his Heiress-Presumptive. Hitherto, the Duke of Gloucester had been the principal royal deputy; now Princess Elizabeth was taking over many of the functions traditionally associated with a Prince of Wales. In the July following the return from South Africa the King, with expressions of great happiness, announced his consent under the Royal Marriages Act, 1772, to an engagement which had been generally believed to be imminent before the Vanguard sailed. Princess Elizabeth was to marry her cousin, the former Prince Philip of Greece, who during her absence in South Africa had become a naturalized subject of the King, surrendering his foreign dignities and assuming his maternal grandfather's surname of Mountbatten. On November 20, in the midst of popular acclamations which constituted perhaps the first really untrammelled rejoicings since the war, the King drove to Westminster Abbey to give the Princess away to her bridegroom, whom earlier in the morning he had raised to the peerage as Duke of Edinburgh.

Two great ceremonies marked the following spring. On St. George's Day the 600th anniversary of the Order of the Garter was marked by a Chapter and a service of great splendour in St. George's Chapel, Windsor. The King, who had already ended the bad old custom of political appointments to this most famous order of chivalry, had nominated a dozen war leaders and statesmen of both parties to the companionship, and now presided over the induction into their stalls of this distinguished company, with his daughter and her husband at their head. Three days later, on April 26, he and the Queen knelt in St. Paul's Cathedral to give thanks for 25 years of happy married life. The scenes of popular gratitude at this silver wedding recalled those attending the silver jubilee of King George V.

In June the King's office underwent an important constitutional change: he formally surrendered the great title of Emperor of India, which Queen Victoria had assumed on Disraeli's advice 72 years before. In the two new Dominions of Pakistan and Ceylon he remained the ceremonial head of the State; to India his relation was henceforth more distant, in that her Government had assumed a strictly republican form, although that republic freely adhered to the Commonwealth of Nations and acknowledged the King's person as the symbol of the unity of the group.

A new stage in the restoration of peace conditions was symbolized in October, when the King opened Parliament in full state, robed and crowned; and plans were being laid to continue the series of Imperial progresses with an expedition to Australia and New Zealand, in which he was to be accompanied by the Queen and Princess Margaret. But in the following month, while the King awaited the birth of his first grandchild, it was known to his doctors and a very narrow circle of his intimates that he himself had been in constant pain for months. His left leg, which had given him trouble in boyhood, was now threatened with a failure of the blood supply through the contraction of the arteries. Princess Elizabeth's son Charles—made a Prince under letters patent issued by the King a few weeks before—was born at Buckingham Palace on November 14; and in order not to cut short the national rejoicing the King concealed his own indisposition for a full week afterwards. Then, however, it had to be announced that he was seriously ill, and the Commonwealth tour would not take place. There was in fact serious danger that the limb would wither for lack of nourishment, and after anxiety which continued through the winter it was found necessary in March to perform an operation on the sympathetic nerve. This gave relief. Thereafter it was always a possibility that the arterial trouble would recur, but in fact it never did so, and it was an entirely different complaint that struck the King down three years later.

The King never entirely laid down his responsibilities; and, although during 1949 the Heiress Presumptive and the Royal Family did everything possible to take burdens off his shoulders while he rested at Windsor or Sandringham, for most of the time he attended assiduously to his heavy routine work at his desk and even made a number of public appearances—generally seated. By the autumn the normal round of his outward life was fully restored, and in 1950 he was travelling as freely as usual about the country to do honour to civil and military occasions. In March of that year he was able to play host at the state visit of the President of the French Republic, thereby both returning the hospitality lately shown in Paris to Princess Elizabeth and Prince Philip, and saluting on behalf of all his subjects the recovery of France and the rebuilding of the Entente Cordiale in a larger European context.

So far was the King's health now restored that it was possible to contemplate the resumption of the plans for the Commonwealth tour. But lying immediately ahead was the centenary of the Great Exhibition of 1851, to be celebrated by the Festival of Britain; and by agreement with the Governments of Australia and New Zealand it was decided to postpone the visit so that the King could take his proper place, at the head of the oldest of his peoples, throughout the celebrations. He took the closest interest in all the proceedings from the beginning, visiting the principal sites more than a year before the event, and in May 1951 going to St. Paul's to offer solemn prayer for the success of the festival and delivering a moving address to the people and the world from the cathedral steps. This, in the midst of the crowding troubles and dangers of the post-war world, was a declaration of faith in the future of the victorious yet burdened people; and he himself, all who heard him felt, was in full measure the representative of their great achievement in war and their high hopes of triumph over the anxieties that beset them. After 15 years under incessant pressure, however, he was a very tired man; and when an attack of influenza prostrated him later in that same month of May he lacked the resilience to throw it off. The doctors prescribed a prolonged period of rest; he removed to Windsor and most of his official engagements were cancelled. His partial recovery was marked at the end of June by the holding of a Privy Council; and it was hoped that his usual summer holiday in Scotland would sufficiently set him up in health to enable him to leave for the Commonwealth tour on January 22, and perhaps even find a tonic in the long sea voyage. These hopes were disappointed. Early in September the doctors in attendance at Balmoral advised the King to come south by air for examination and treatment which could be given only in London. He found time to receive the Prime Minister and accept his advice for the dissolution of Parliament; then, after anxious consultation and bulletins which gave intimations of serious disease in the lung, an operation was performed at Buckingham Palace on Sunday, September 23.

A large crowd waited outside the palace all day, and that night a slow-moving file of people passed the railings to read the bulletin announcing that the King's condition continued satisfactory. His illness led to the postponement of the tour of Canada by Princess Elizabeth and the Duke of Edinburgh, but as his health continued to improve they finally left on October 7, nearly a fortnight later than they originally intended. On the Thursday after his operation the King signed a warrant authorizing the appointment of five Counsellors of State to act temporarily on his behalf, but by December 10 his health was so far recovered that he felt justified in bringing the arrangement to an end.

The operation had been serious and the King's apparent quick recovery was a magnificent example of the grit and willpower he had displayed in overcoming the ill-health that had dogged him throughout his life. On October 20 it was disclosed that for a week previously he had been up for a few hours each day, and on October 25 he sat up late to hear the early results in the General Election broadcast. Although he was unable to open Parliament on November 6, his health continued to improve and he left Buckingham Palace on the last day of the month for the first time since the operation to drive to Windsor for the week-end.

The following Sunday was observed throughout the country as thanksgiving for the King's recovery. The fifteenth anniversary of his accession fell on December 11 and was observed with the customary ceremonies; his Majesty, however, wisely spent the day quietly at Buckingham Palace. It was on Saturday, December 22, that the King and Queen left London for what proved to be their last Christmas together at Sandringham. With them went Princess Elizabeth and Princess Margaret, and later they were joined by others to make this the largest gathering of the Royal Family since the war.

The King, ready as always to put his duty to his people before his own comfort, had before he left London painstakingly recorded his Christmas broadcast, sentence by sentence, although his doctors had ordered him to use his voice as sparingly as possible. Thus he maintained the tradition begun by his father 19 years previously and he was able to listen to the simple and moving message he had devised to give renewed faith and hope to his people.

The royal Christmas party began to break up during the first week in January, but the King and Queen remained at Sandringham, where the King pursued his love of shooting for a few weeks longer. They returned to London on January 28, where the King was very busy receiving people in audience and helping to prepare a Commonwealth tour by Princess Elizabeth and the Duke of Edinburgh. They left London Airport on the last day of January and the King, though his lined and drawn face revealed the extent of his severe and long-continued suffering, saw them off standing erect and bareheaded in the biting wind. The next day the King and Queen, with Princess Margaret, left Buckingham Palace for Sandringham. This was to be his last journey from London to the home he loved so well.

February 7, 1952.

Prince George of Greece, who died in Paris on November 25, 1957 at the age of 88, was the second and last surviving of the seven children of George I, King of the Hellenes, and his wife, the Grand Duchess Olga of Russia. He was an uncle of the Duke of Edinburgh and the Duchess of Kent and a godfather of the Duke of Cornwall.

Born in 1869, he trained at the naval college at Copenhagen in his father's homeland. Upon his return to Greece he joined the Greek navy, also serving as his father's A.D.C. Some years later in company with the Russian Crown Prince, later the Tsar Nicholas II, he circumnavigated the world. While in the Far East he saved the life of the Japanese Crown Prince when a Japanese anarchist made an attempt on his life.

Prince George played his main role in Greek politics in Crete at the beginning of this century and in circumstances strangely reminiscent of the Cyprus dispute. When in 1898 Turkish forces were compelled to evacuate Crete, the island came under the protection of the Allied Powers, who appointed Prince George High Commissioner. He set up his residence at Chanea.

He soon found himself at variance with Eleftherios Venizelos, his principal adviser, who was then directing the Ministry of Justice in Crete. On his own initiative, against the counsel of Venizelos, Prince George set off for Europe to ask the Powers to allow Crete's union with Greece. He met strong resistance and returned to Crete empty handed. His rift with Venizelos had widened and in 1901 he dismissed him from the Cretan administration. This aroused protests and diminished the Prince's popularity until in 1905 the revolutionary Assembly, led by Venizelos, decreed union with Greece. But the Powers remained adamant and in 1906 the Prince resigned, went to Athens for a short time, and then moved to Paris. Crete was officially taken over by Greece in 1913 after Venizelos had become Greece's Premier.

It was in Paris in 1907 that Prince George met and married Princess Marie Bonaparte, daughter of Prince Roland Bonaparte and a qualified doctor. They had two children, Prince Peter, well known for his anthropological and sociological studies, and Princess Eugenie. Prince George, tall, slim, with long white moustaches, was to the Greeks personification of the "pallikari", the youthful, dauntless, affable Greek. In the Second World War, after the German invasion, he followed his nephew, King George II, and the Greek royal family to Crete, then to South Africa, where he was living in Field-Marshal Smuts's residence.

November 26, 1957.

W. F. George, a former chairman of the Foreign Relations Committee of the United States Senate and an influential exponent of bipartisan foreign policy, died on August 4, 1957 at his home in Georgia. He was 79.

The important senatorial appointments in the United States come to a man by seniority. In the case of George, 34 years senator from Georgia, seniority was joined with authority, persuasive eloquence, and a sense of public duty which disregarded party advantage. The temptation to take political tricks must have been strong when from 1953 he was Democratic chairman of the Senate Foreign Relations Committee during a Republican presidency. Instead, George, believing in the advantages of a bipartisan foreign policy, was an invaluable ally of the White House by his advocacy of the President's policies in the Senate. At the same time his influence on those policies was considerable and beneficial.

Walter Franklin George was born at Preston in the state of Georgia on January 29, 1878. He was reared on a farm in the Webster County, and showed an early aptitude for oratory. He was sent to Mercer College, where he graduated in 1900 and went on to take a law degree in the following year. He became prosecuting attorney of the Cordele district court, and in 1912 he was appointed a district court judge. He was later an associate judge of the Georgia Supreme Court until, in 1922, he resigned.

In that year Tom Watson, the demagogic senator from Georgia, died, and George decided to contest the vacant seat. It was the heyday of Republican isolationism, and in that spirit George entered upon his long Congressional career. He was, typically of the Southern Democrats, a conservative. "He cannot be classified as belonging to the liberal school of thought," F. D. Roosevelt once declared, and the two men came into collision over some of the New Deal measures. George was not opposed to all that Roosevelt carried through under the New Deal, but he did kick against Roosevelt's moves to make the Supreme Court more amenable. In 1938 he was an intended victim of Roosevelt's "purge" of the party, but the electors of Georgia thought otherwise: George was re-elected and the Roosevelt candidate defeated.

In 1940 he succeeded to the chairmanship of the Senate Foreign Relations Committee. In spite of their recent dispute George worked well with Roosevelt and was in accord with the policy of fullest aid to Britain in the war against Germany. He piloted the Lend-Lease Bill through the Senate, and looked back on that task as one of the most important in his career. Until the Japanese attack on Pearl Harbour he was opposed to American entry into the war. Before that date, however, he had passed from the Foreign Relations Committee to the chairmanship of the Finance Committee, which he held throughout the war.

In January 1953, with the return of a Democratic Senate, he exercised his right of seniority and again became chairman of the Foreign Relations Committee. President Eisenhower* and John Foster Dulles [q.v.] had more to fear from the isolationist or bellicose extremists of their own party than from their political opponent who now occupied so influential a position in Congress. George endorsed the main lines of the Administration's policy, and was sometimes even ahead of the White House. Early in 1955, for instance, he was advocating a four-Power meeting, which was arranged later that year. He also spoke in favour of direct exchanges with Peking, though that was a less productive proposal. Some of the Administration's more controversial actions in the field of foreign affairs were only made palatable to Congress by the skilful advocacy of Senator George. Fastidious in his dress, a little aloof, an effective debater, he had a shrewd knowledge of foreign affairs and also of the means of carrying the Senate up to the limits of its acquiescence. Nor had anyone in Congress more influence in the Administration's counsels. He provided an example, rare during that presidency, of how the checks and balances between the executive and legislative branches can be made to function smoothly by the personal relationship of a senior committee chairman with the White House.

In 1956 the local politics of Georgia began to work against him and he decided to stand down from the Senate elections in the autumn. When his intention was announced President Eisenhower offered him the post of his special representative with N.A.T.O. It was a mark of the value which the President placed on his services; it was also a reminder of the distance George had travelled from isolationism in 1922 to the heart of America's European alliance 35 years later.

George married in 1923 Lucy Heard. They had two sons, one of whom was killed on active service in 1943.

August 5, 1957.

Charles March Gere, R.A., R.W.S., the landscape painter, died on August 3, 1957 at the age of 88.

Gere was one of several Birmingham artists who descended upon the Cotswolds and made the place their own. He was born at Gloucester in 1869, and received his first artistic training at the Birmingham School of Art under the late E. R. Taylor, and he subsequently taught there himself. Then he went to Italy, where he studied tempera painting, and was for a time associated with William Morris as illustrator for the Kelmscott Press, and later with St. John Hornby at the Ashendene Press. Among the books illustrated by him were *Fioretti* of St. Francis, Dante, and *Morte d'Arthur.* At this time Gere practised a full range of arts and crafts, painting portraits and designing for stained glass and embroidery, as well as illustrating; but he gradually became known almost exclusively as a painter of landscapes, or of landscapes with figures, in oil, tempera and water colour.

It was in 1904 that he settled at Painswick, in the Cotswolds, dividing his time between there and north Italy. He also painted in Wales. His earliest paintings to attract attention were of peasant life in the Italian mountains, beautiful in colour and full of poetry, if a little sentimental, at the New English Art Club and the Royal Society of Painters in Water Colours, of both of which bodies he was a member. He was made A.R.A. in 1934 and R.A. in 1939. At the Academy in 1941 Gere broke away from his usual class of subjects with "The Last Stand at Calais Cathedral, May 1940", dedicated to the immortal memory of those who stood at Calais, and by their sacrifice saved the B.E.F. at Dunkirk.

He was deeply conscious of the charm of the simple life and what may be called the sacramental significance of everyday actions, and his pictures of domestic incidents in the Cotswolds have a truly Wordsworthian appreciation of the "treasures of the humble". His limitations as an artist were seen when, after his election to the Academy, he enlarged the scale of his pictures. It was apparent then that, as in "The Tidal Severn" of 1940 and the earlier "The Mouth of the Severn", though he realized the structure of the Cotswold escarpment with great fidelity he did not so surely realize the structure of the picture itself. His pictures, in fact, were open windows with the subject cut by the frame instead of being composed in relation to it, and on the small scale of his best period this was less apparent.

Gere is represented in the Tate Gallery by a water-colour entitled "Provence", purchased out of the Duveen Drawings Fund in 1927, and by an oil painting, "The Wye at Lancaut", a Chantrey purchase of 1934.

He was unmarried.

August 6, 1957.

Former Crown Prince William of Germany—See **William.**

Ghulam Mohammad, Governor General of Pakistan from 1951 to 1955, died in Karachi on August 29, 1956 on his sixty-first birthday. He will have an abiding place in history for the courage and resolution with which he guided the ship of state through the shoals and quicksands of party strife and outbreaks of unrest. There were some remarkable similarities between him and the first Governor-General, the Quaid-i-Azam.

While M. A. Jinnah and the late Liaquat Ali Khan [q.v.], the first Prime Minister, were campaigning for the creation of Pakistan, Ghulam Mohammad was holding high offices, first as a servant of the Government of India and then as Finance Minister in the Hyderabad State. The Great Leader and his successor in the Governor-Generalship were men of strong determination and unflinching courage and both were hampered in their high office by serious and chronic illness. They were hard workers caring little for recreative pleasures. Usually on his public appearances after the first year of office in Pakistan "G.M.", as he was called by his intimate friends, was supported by two attendants and only his penetrating eyes showed that his subtle mind and swift, clear judgment remained unimpaired. Conversation with him was difficult, owing to the frequency with which by reason of physical infirmity his voice was reduced to a whisper.

He was born on August 29, 1895, and educated at the Aligarh Muslim University, where he graduated in Arts and Law. In 1920 he passed the stiff examination for the Indian Audit Service. His industry and thoroughness were soon noticed, as when, to check the widespread practice of travelling on the railways without tickets, he more than once assumed the garb and work of a ticket collector. His services were lent to the Bhopal State as Commissioner of Development; and two years later he was called to Delhi to be Financial Adviser on Communications. Early in the 1939-45 War he was made an additional secretary of the Supply Department. In 1942 he was called to the Nizam of Hyderabad's Executive Council as Finance Member. In 1945 he left the public service and became a director of Tata's, the largest iron and steel works in India.

In 1946 he was knighted, having been made C.I.E. in 1941. He had become an active member of the Council of the All-India Muslim League and soon after leaving official life renounced these honours. On the creation of the State of Pakistan in August 1947 he was made Finance Minister, and some months later the portfolios of Commerce and Economic Affairs were added. Unlike the Indian Government at New Delhi, Pakistan was unprovided with an adequate and specially built capital and a fully equipped working secretariat. Every requirement had to be improvised against the background of the communal strife, with its tale of slaughter and streams of refugees. Financial breakdown would have been inevitable if charge of the Exchequer had not been in such experienced hands, especially as important assets to be distributed in an agreed ratio were not provided from India, at least in anything like the measure decided on. Happily the intellectual gifts of the Finance Minister were of a high order, and included the combination of broad views with astonishing mastery of detail.

In the wider international field the Finance Minister was an able negotiator, dealing successfully with eastern and western statesmen. Next to promoting the prosperity of his country he sought to build up the Middle East into a sound and viable economic unit, and so to make Islam a factor in shaping world prosperity.

Ghulam Mohammad was fluent in Persian, a master of Arabic, and his English was simple and direct. A great reader and fond of homely quiet, a teetotaller and a non-smoker, he dispensed a generous hospitality in official life. The outlook for the new state at this time was far from encouraging, and the second Governor-General was not destined to enjoy for long the helpful friendship and assistance of Pakistan's first Prime Minister, for Liaquat Ali Khan was assassinated in October 1951.

In little more than 18 months the Governor-General, to use his own words in a proclamation to the people, stated that he had "watched with growing uneasiness the exceedingly difficult conditions" with which the country was faced. He added that there was a grave food shortage and that the maintenance of law and order needed firm handling. He had been driven to the conclusion that the Cabinet of Kwaja Nazimuddin* had proved inadequate to the discharge of its functions. He had therefore dismissed the Ministry and had invited Muhammad Ali*, the Ambassador in Washington, to form a new Government.

Kwaja Nazimuddin protested against this action and argued that it was illegal, but soon accepted the inevitable. A general election in East Pakistan resulted in the crushing defeat of the Muslim League by the United Party under the leadership of Fazlul Huq, the veteran former Chief Minister of United Bengal. A period of further anxiety for the Governor-General ensued and again he took strong action by dismissing the new Ministry and giving the Governor, Major-General Iskander Mirza*, plenary powers. These powers were effectively exercised, and law and order were restored.

Still more drastic action was to follow in October 1954. While India had formulated a detailed constitution which came into effect in January 1950, the nominated Constituent Assembly of Pakistan had gone through seven years of disputation without fulfilling the duty for which it had been created, that of drafting a constitution. Meanwhile, it had been the only federal legislature.

The Assembly had sought to limit the powers of the Governor-General under the Indian Independence Act 1947, so as to prevent his dismissing any future Ministry. His response was to announce the dissolution of the Assembly and to declare invalid such measures as it had passed which had not received his assent.

The Prime Minister, Muhammad Ali, who was in Washington at the time, hurried home and had some heated arguments with the head of the state. He was given the choice of either accepting dismissal or forming an entirely new Cabinet approved by the Governor-General. He chose the latter course. The new Ministry brought into the Government important elements in the body politic which had been disregarded when the Constituent Assembly was formed at the time of separation from India. It now contained a number of prominent men who had in various ways been opposed to the Muslim League, but it had behind it the support of the Army and the Civil Service. It was understood that the state of affairs under which the Governor-General exercised such drastic powers would be replaced as soon as circumstances permitted by an elected legislature and Constituent Assembly.

An important measure designed to reassure East Pakistan as to its future influence was the decision to abolish the provincial governments of West Pakistan and thereby place the two separated portions of the countries on an equal footing, each with a local Parliament, under a federal constitution. The validity of this action of the Governor-General and the new Cabinet, and still more of his dismissal of the Constituent Assembly, was challenged in the Courts, but was ultimately confirmed in the spring of 1955 by the Federal Court sitting at Lahore, though with certain reservations.

A feature of the career of this resolute, ailing man was the frequency with which he travelled abroad in the interests of his country. He was in London in the summer of 1949 at the conference of Commonwealth Finance Ministers to consider problems of the balance of payments between the sterling and dollar areas. In the following year he was in Ceylon for the conference of Commonwealth Foreign Ministers which brought to birth the Colombo Plan. He was frequently at other international gatherings, and in 1953 he visited many countries, including Britain, the United States, Saudi Arabia, Iraq, Egypt, and Turkey.

The Governor-General never lost an opportunity to further good relations, both with the democracies of the west and with the Islamic States. He was the founder and first president of the International Islamic Economic Organization. His procurement of American military aid was much criticized by Nehru*, but Ghulam Mohammad never abated his aim to settle by friendly agreement the many matters of conflict between Pakistan and India. It was an admirable gesture on his part to accept the invitation of the President of the Indian Union to be his guest on the occasion of the Republic Day celebrations in January 1955. He stated on returning to Karachi that his object to promote good will had been achieved. This assurance was the more welcomed as trouble was arising in the north-west. The Afghan authorities were advancing the untenable claim that the tribal areas, including Baluchistan, should be given complete independence in a new state of Pakhtoonistan, in disregard of the settlement reached as far back as 1892 by the creation of the Durand Line inherited from the British Government. Pakistan took a strong, clear line in discussions with Kabul, and the Governor-General had the satisfaction of re-establishing good relations with Afghanistan shortly before his resignation.

Ghulam Mohammad belonged to the triumvirate which saved Pakistan from collapse at birth, and after the death of the Quaid-i-Azam, and the first Prime Minister, he became its foster father. In spite of failing health, he dealt with successive crises with determination, courage, and clear vision. His repeated use of emergency powers caused no more than moderate resentment and indeed was welcomed not only by the Army and the Civil Service, but also by important sections of public opinion which had been neglected by the Muslim League in the earliest days of its triumph in pursuing the two-nation theory of Jinnah.

The last occasion on which the Governor-General exercised in a dramatic way his overriding powers was that of the dismissal of yet another Prime Minister, Muhammad Ali, who returned to the Washington Embassy, from which he had been called in the spring of 1953, to be the head of the Cabinet. He was now replaced by his name-sake Chaudhri Muhammad Ali, who had the financial portfolio.

A few days after this event the Governor-General went to Europe for treatment first at the London Clinic and then in Switzerland. His proposal that there should not be an acting appointment was unwelcome in Whitehall as forming an undesirable precedent, but was accepted on the understanding that in Karachi Major-General Iskander Mirza would be his *de facto* deputy. Ghulam Mohammad returned to Karachi early in September, and in the middle of the month tendered his resignation, which was accepted, and on the advice of the Pakistan Government he was succeeded by Major-General Iskander Mirza.

The retiring Governor-General made a stirring appeal in a broadcast by his private secretary to the people of Pakistan to "develop strength through unity, courage through loyalty, and service through sacrifice". He moved from his official residence and had since lived in the home of his married daughter in Karachi.

August 30, 1956.

Sir Alexander Gibb, G.B.E., C.B., F.R.S., founder of the firm of consulting engineers, Sir Alexander Gibb and Partners, died on January 21, 1958 at his home at Hartley Wintney. He was 85.

His career provides a noteworthy example of a contractor who transferred his activities to professional consulting work. He was born on February 12, 1872, at Broughty Ferry, the eldest son of Alexander Easton Gibb, of Beamsley Hall, Skipton, Yorkshire, head of the firm of Easton Gibb and Son Ltd. Gibb's grandfather, who was engineer of the Great North of Scotland Railway and of Aberdeen Harbour, was trained under Thomas Telford. His great-grandfather, John Gibb, built the first railway in Scotland, and his great-great-grandfather, William Gibb, had a hand in the completion of the Forth and Clyde Canal towards the end of the eighteenth century.

He was educated at Rugby and at University College London and was subsequently a pupil of Sir John Wolfe Barry. Some of his earliest engineering experience was gained during the construction of the Tower Bridge, and on the Glasgow Central, the Lanarkshire and Dunbartonshire, and the Western Highland Railways, and the Barry Docks. Later he was appointed resident engineer on the Metropolitan Railway portion of the Great Central Railway, and on the Whitechapel to Bow Railway, during extensions. He was soon able to join his father as managing director of Easton Gibb and Son, Ltd., and in 1900 in that capacity he was engaged upon such contracts as the King Edward VII Bridge at Kew, the Alexander Docks, and a deep-lock entrance at Newport, Monmouthshire.

The decision in 1903 to provide on the east coast of Scotland a dockyard large enough for any ship of the Fleet resulted in the creation of the naval establishment at Rosyth, for the main works of which the tender of Easton Gibb and Son was accepted in February 1909. The scheme included a main basin, a basin for submarines, a dock and lock, and other works, as well as local reclamation, dredging, and pumping. Meanwhile the German Government had in hand and had completed by July 1914 the deepening of the Kiel canal to enable them to transfer warships rapidly between the North Sea and the Baltic, leaving their prospective enemies the longer and more difficult passage through the Kattegat and Great Belt. The situation at Rosyth on August 4, 1914, was therefore serious, for the work was only two-thirds complete, and no part was available for H.M. ships.

Although the basin for submarines was finished, it was at that time blocked by a dam of clay. In 1926 it was publicly announced at the Institution of Civil Engineers "that it was due to the sagacity, fortitude, and enthusiasm of Sir Alexander Gibb that the works had been completed in time to be of immense use to the Fleet during the vital period of the War".

By the combined effort of the contractors and the Navy the basin for submarines was in fact brought into service by August 20, 1914: by September 2, 1914, it was possible for H.M.S. Aquarius to enter a berth alongside one of the jetties, and by March 25, 1916, the approach channel to the main dock was completed in time to accommodate such vessels as the Dreadnought, Invincible, Princess Royal, Tiger, and Lion, in their hour of need. The total expenditure upon this new dockyard was £6,920,000.

In 1914 Gibb joined the Royal Engineers and became Chief Engineer for Ports Construction to the British Armies in France and Belgium, and Deputy Director of Docks. He carried out accordingly reconstruction work at Ostend and Zeebrugge. The rapidity with which he was selected for further appointments was remarkable. In 1918 he became Civil Engineer-in-Chief to the Admiralty, and in 1919 Director-General of Civil Engineering to the Ministry of Transport. He settled down in 1921 to private practice and became associated with a wide range of engineering institutions and a director of the Dunlop Rubber Company. He gave special attention to what various engineers had put forward concerning a Severn Barrage Scheme.

His professional advice was sought by governments and large private concerns all over the world. He had been consulting engineer to the Admiralty for the Singapore Naval Base, consulting engineer to the Government of Columbia and to the Persian Government. In 1937 he signed a contract with the Ish Bank in Istanbul whereby he became technical adviser for public works and industrial development in Turkey. In 1941 he was called in as consulting engineer for the new dock at Sydney, Australia. In October 1955 his firm signed a contract with the Egyptian Government in connexion with the construction of the High Dam at Aswan.

His catholic knowledge and engineering skill recommended him to an imposing number of public and professional bodies whom he served long and well. He had, for example, been technical adviser to the Treasury under the Trades Facilities Act, joint consulting engineer to the Dean and Chapter of St. Paul's Cathedral, a member of the Royal Fine Art Commission, a vice-president of the Kipling Society, and a member of the Council and executive committee of Princess Helena College.

He was the author of *The Story of Telford—The Rise of Civil Engineering* (1935). He was made C.B. and K.B.E. in 1918 and promoted G.B.E. in 1920. In 1936 he was elected a Fellow of the Royal Society.

He married in 1900 Norah Isobel, youngest daughter of Fleet-Surgeon Lowry John Monteith, R.N. There were three sons of the marriage. His wife died in 1940.

January 22, 1958.

Sir Claude Gibb, K.B.E., F.R.S., who died suddenly on January 15, 1959 at Newark, New Jersey, while travelling on a business trip in the United States, took a leading part in the rapid development of nuclear power after the Second World War. Combining, as he did, a practical flair for engineering with a scientific outlook and a keen business sense, he was one of the few who foresaw the immense possibilities, and wasted no time in putting British engineering in the leading position. He was 60.

Though he rose to the peak of his profession as a mechanical engineer, and became chairman of the famous turbine firm which Sir Charles Parsons, O.M., founded, he would still, on occasions, take off his jacket and wield a file or scraper. His frank report, a few years ago, to the Institution of Mechanical Engineers on the failure of two electrical generators made a deep impression on his professional colleagues and enhanced his company's reputation among electric power authorities.

Claude Dixon Gibb was born at Queenstown, South Australia, on June 29, 1898. He was educated at the South Australian School of Mines, where he studied mechanical and electrical engineering, and at Adelaide University, where he took the bachelor's and master's degrees in engineering. During the same period, from 1914 to 1917, he was gaining practical experience of installation work with Australian firms; in the latter year he joined the Australian Flying Corps as a mechanic and was later commissioned as a pilot.

After the war he was appointed senior assistant and demonstrator to Sir Robert Chapman, professor of engineering at Adelaide University. In 1923 he decided to gain further experience by going to England. He joined C. A. Parsons and Company Limited as a fitter, but in 1925 his ability had been quickly recognized and he was made the senior superintendent in charge of the company's London district. Promotion followed rapidly for him, as assistant outside manager, manager of the Heaton Works test house, and then chief operating and test engineer before Sir Charles Parsons, in 1929, appointed him chief engineer and a director. From then until the Second World War he took a leading part in steam turbine research and design. He became general manager in 1937 and joint managing director in 1943.

The outbreak of war found Britain woefully behind in armament quality and quantity, and Gibb was one of the dynamos who laboured to make up the deficiencies. One who was close to him in those desperate days referred to him as a one-man shock troop. First, in 1940, he was engineering assistant to the director-general of munitions production and then deputy to the director-general.

As director-general of weapons and instrument production from 1941 he accelerated the output of guns; and as director-general of armoured fighting vehicles from 1943, and chairman of the Tank Board from 1944, he did the same for tank production.

On his return to Parsons, in 1945, as chairman and managing director, he set about the task of peacetime production with the same sense of urgency as he had displayed during the war. Calling a meeting of all the 3,000 employees on the day shift, he outlined his board's aims and policies to them. Success followed for him and his men: the number of employees rose from 4,000 to 7,000, the acreage of the works from 43 to 61, and the annual production of turbo-generator plant from 280,000 to one million kilowatts.

During this period the size of individual steam turbo-generators increased very rapidly, and in 1958 his company was awarded the contract for the largest machine of this kind in the world—550,000 kilowatts for Thorpe Marsh power station.

By any standards, the British development of nuclear power has been one of the greatest engineering achievements, and Sir Claude took part in the early planning at a time when many sober authorities were openly sceptical of the whole idea. The result was Calder Hall, to which C. A. Parsons made a substantial contribution.

Nuclear power advances which followed this flying start, and with which he was associated, included the formation in 1958 of the Nuclear Power Plant Company, of which he was chairman; the contract awarded to that company for the construction of the first commercial nuclear power station, at Bradwell, Essex; the conclusion of an agreement in 1958 between the company and an Italian state authority to build the world's first exported nuclear power station; and the decision to build a nuclear research centre on a site adjacent to the Heaton Works, Newcastle upon Tyne.

Though his business responsibilities prevented him accepting the presidency of the Institution of Mechanical Engineers, he served as vice-president for eight years and was twice awarded that institution's Thomas Hawksley Gold Medal.

He was made C.B.E. in 1942, knighted in 1945, and advanced to K.B.E. in 1956. The Royal Society elected him a fellow in 1946.

He married in 1925 Margaret Bate Harris.

January 17, 1959.

Robert Gibbings, who died on January 19, 1958 at the age of 68, had for long occupied a place of distinction among our native wood-engravers, and for some 10 years, during the "boom" in fine books, directed the Golden Cockerel Press, which in its day brought out a number of beautifully illustrated editions, laid out and printed with every refinement of taste.

He was also a moving spirit in the foundation of the Society of Wood-Engravers, which took into its membership Eric Daglish, Gertrude Hermes, Clare Leighton, and many other of the best practitioners of this art. Gibbings also became widely known from various works of travel and natural description which he wrote and illustrated, going for his material—among other places—to the South Seas, where he went under water to study coral formations and tropical fish.

Robert John Gibbings was born at Cork on March 23, 1889, son of the Rev. Edward Gibbings, Canon of Cork Cathedral, and his wife, Caroline Rouvière, daughter of Robert Day, of Cork. He once said that he was "educated in the snipe bogs and trout streams of Munster", but at the appropriate age he found his way to University College, Cork, proceeding from there to the Slade School and the L.C.C. Central School of Arts and Crafts, where he received his training in art. Not much was heard of Gibbings before the Four Years War, throughout the whole of which he served in the armed forces, taking part in the Gallipoli campaign.

The war over, Gibbings returned to his art, and became a prolific producer of wood-engravings, many of which were used for book illustrations. In 1924 he settled at Waltham St. Lawrence, Berkshire, and there took over from Harold M. Taylor the Golden Cockerel Press. Under his direction this press brought out some singularly beautiful issues of classic texts. There were no big financial resources. Gibbings stuck to Caslon Old Face until in the spring of 1930 he introduced a complete new fount designed by the late Eric Gill, exclusive to the Press, for which the Caslon Letter Foundry cut the punches and cast the type. Gibbings showed great perspicacity in choosing illustrators, the chief of them being Eric Gill, who did some of his finest work for the Golden Cockerel *Troilus and Criseyde* and the *Canterbury Tales.*

Gibbings himself also carried out some splendid jobs of illustration for the Press, among the most memorable being the *Song of Songs,* in which the rich blacks and luscious curves he affected were very telling. The method was to run off proof sheets with spaces for illustrations, and the engraver worked with these proofs in front of him, thus having the best conditions for the production of work fitting intimately with the typography.

Meanwhile Gibbings was illustrating for other publishers and taking prominent part in the various West End exhibitions of wood-engravings. Representative collections of his work were acquired by the British Museum and the Victoria and Albert Museum, and no book dealing with the wood-engraving of the period is without examples. The financial crisis of 1931 did irrevocable harm to the fine book market; and in 1933 Gibbings gave up the struggle and confined himself to private practice.

He was now able to satisfy a long-standing ambition to visit the South Seas, being sent out by the Boston publishers Houghton, Mifflin and Co. to do woodcuts for James Norman Hall's book on Tahiti. Later he made another journey, to Bermuda, the Red Sea, and elsewhere, going below in a diving suit and making drawings on xylonite for the book *Blue Angels and Whales,* which appeared in 1938.

The whole submarine panorama had a fascination for him, and he did some sensitive, decorative, and at the same time accurate, renderings of coral formations, seaweeds and "queer fish". Just before war broke out in 1939 Gibbings turned to less spectacular aquatic scenes in *Sweet Thames, Run Softly.* His other published works included: *Iorana, a Tahitian Journal, The Seventh Man, Coconut Island,* and *John Graham, Convict.* In 1942 appeared *Coming Down the Wye,* and in 1944 *Lovely is the Lee,* neither a formal guide book but each containing a rich store of anecdote, folklore, natural history, and above all good talk not often to be found in topographical works.

He was an unashamed digressor but his prose had an easy rhythm that carried the reader over the shallows. *Over the Reefs* came out in 1948, *Sweet Cork, of Thee* in 1951, *Coming Down the Seine* in 1953, *Trumpets from Montparnasse* in 1955, and *Till I End my Song,* something of an auto-biographical calendar of the seasons in Berkshire where he lived and where he died, in 1957.

Gibbings held the honorary degree of M.A. from the National University of Ireland, and from 1936 to 1942 was lecturer in wood-engraving and typography at the University of Reading, where Professor Allen W. Seaby had long fostered a virile tradition in wood-engraving. Gibbings was an excellent draughtsman, with a real appreciation of the potentialities of the wood, and he will undoubtedly have his place in the history of this art. His typographical achievements, too, will long be remembered, though the Golden Cockerel books had, of course, nothing like the resource and fertility in invention shown by the products of some other presses.

Gibbings was twice married, first to Mary Pennefather, by whom he had three sons and one daughter, and secondly to Elisabeth Empson, by whom he had a son and two daughters. He was a big, massive, bearded man, handsome and of impressive mien.

January 21, 1958.

Carroll Gibbons, who died in a nursing home in London on May 10, 1954 at the age of 51, after a short illness, was one of the first dance-band leaders to broadcast from Savoy Hill in the days of 2LO.

His usual opening "Hallo everybody", spoken in his low, drawling voice, for years was the signal for the good things to come; good not merely as dance music, but good as an expression in music of a charming and lovable personality, who made an immense number of friends in all classes. Though his fame was principally founded on his work as a band-leader, he was an excellent pianist and a composer of merit, as manifested by his work for Metro-Goldwyn-Mayer.

Carroll Gibbons was born at Clinton, Massachusetts, on January 4, 1903, and began his musical education at the Boston

Conservatory of Music. With that precocity which is so often evident in musicians, he first appeared in public at the age of 10 as a pianist. In 1924 he went to London with the well-known saxophonist Rudy Vallée, with a view to continuing his studies, and was offered and accepted an engagement at the Berkeley Hotel in the band under the direction of Howard Jacob. Some 10 years later he had his first experience in leading an orchestra with the Savoy Sylvians, which he formed himself, and was so successful that a few months afterwards he accepted an invitation to direct the Savoy Orpheans in succession to Debroy Somers.

He left the Savoy Hotel in 1928 to become director of light music with His Master's Voice, where his work with the New Mayfair Orchestra became very popular. Then came a short period at Hollywood as composer for Metro-Goldwyn-Mayer. In 1931, however, he returned to London and immediately took over the Savoy Orpheans again. He then remained in the employment of the Savoy Company until his death. He was appointed director of entertainments for the firm in 1950, an exacting post, but there was, nevertheless, seldom an evening when he was not to be found playing the piano in the Savoy Restaurant.

May 11, 1954.

Dr. Armstrong Gibbs, who died in Chelmsford Hospital on May 12, 1960 at the age of 70, was a composer who contributed songs of abiding worth to the long tradition of settings of English poetry.

He wrote a substantial amount of choral music, especially secular cantatas, that choirs of moderate abilities could sing with pleasure. Many of them, as also his large number of part-songs, were written with the competition festival movement in mind. For Gibbs, a practical musician, was known throughout the land as an expert adjudicator. He served the Federation of Festivals for many years in committee and high office.

Cecil Armstrong Gibbs was an East Anglian by birth (at Great Baddow on August 10, 1889), and lived most of his professional life at Danbury. A farewell concert was recently given there in his honour since he was proposing to leave Essex and go to live with his daughter in Gloucestershire. He was educated at Winchester and at Trinity College, Cambridge, where he was a contemporary of Rupert Brooke and Steuart Wilson and a pupil of Edward Dent [q.v.]. He went on to the Royal College of Music and subsequently taught composition there for a number of years. He soon found a special affinity in the realm of English poetry with Walter de la Mare [q.v.]. His setting of "Five Eyes" caught the popular fancy as well as the admiration of musicians. His exquisite setting of "Silver" is one of the great songs in English music, though not easy to bring off in performance. Another song that enjoyed wide favour was "The Fields are Full" (Shanks). Slightly more elaborate in that strings are employed are "Nod" and "Before Dawn" for mixed chorus. All these came early in his career and though he never lost his felicity of touch nothing that he wrote later chimed so well with the public mood. His instrumental works were deliberately of light weight; two symphonies and a concertino for piano and strings were traditional in form and manner, but sounded a spontaneous and usually a lyrical note. His largest choral work, *Odysseus,* which the composer described as a symphony in four movements, was a war casualty.

A few small works for the stage began with incidental music for de la Mare's *Crossings* (1919) and for Maeterlinck's *The Betrothal* (1921) and proceeded to a comic opera, *The Blue Peter* (libretto by A. P. Herbert*), and *Midsummer Madness* (1924), a comedy with music, by Clifford Bax*. A children's opera, *The Great Bell of Burley,* and *Twelfth Night* came 25 years later, but are not known. He wrote three string quartets and a Lyric Sonata for Violin and Piano.

In all those works the lyrical impulse that made his songs distinctive is present, but does not successfully lend itself to extended development in any very original manner. His part-songs will continue to be sung and a handful of his solo songs are a permanent enrichment of an already rich tradition but most of the rest of his work served its time and generation without claim to immortality.

Gibbs was a man of wit and charm, possessed of a genial personality that endeared him to competitors and audiences at festivals; he will be remembered with affection by his old pupils and fellow musicians.

May 13, 1960.

George Gibson, C.H., who died suddenly on February 4, 1953 at his home at Manchester, was for more than 30 years a prominent figure in the Labour and trade union world, and had become a considerable influence in wider spheres when a series of circumstances cut short his career and resulted in his retirement shortly after he had been appointed to the board of the Bank of England.

George Gibson was born at Glasgow on April 3, 1885, one of the nine children of a drysalter, and left his elementary school at the age of 12 to become a tailor's messenger boy at 3s. 6d. a week. He had other occupations in Scotland of a blind alley type—which enriched his knowledge and experience— until industrial depression compelled him to seek work elsewhere. He found it in Lancashire, and settling near Manchester he became an attendant in an asylum. Working conditions in such institutions at the opening of the century were not ideal, and Gibson threw himself into the task of organizing the staffs to secure improvements. In 1910 his efforts had been so successful that the Mental Hospital and Institutional Workers' Union was launched, and in 1913 he was elected its general secretary, a post he was to hold for the following three decades and more.

He was quickly recognized as an extremely energetic, able, and shrewd spokesman of the workers, and in his capacity as secretary of the union was called in 1925 to give evidence on staff conditions and the treatment of patients before the Royal Commission on Lunacy. He spoke and wrote frequently on institutional problems, and although he was accustomed at times to use the language of extremism, he was nevertheless gradually becoming a considerable influence in the trade union world, for his knowledge and capacity were widely recognized.

In 1928 Gibson was elected to the General Council of the Trades Union Congress and eight years later was its fraternal delegate to the annual conference of the American Federation of Labour. In 1940 he was elected chairman of the T.U.C. Upon his election, Gibson declared: "The main job facing the trade union movement is to prosecute the war to a successful conclusion, and to prepare for meeting the legitimate aspirations of the working classes of all lands". To these tasks he applied himself with great vigour not only throughout the term of his office but until victory had been won.

Gibson had already many other fields of activity. He was for some years a member of the Overseas Settlement Board, of the Trade Union Advisory Committee to the Ministry of Food, and for three or four years during the war he was vice-chairman of the National Savings Committee, for which he worked strenuously and with marked success. He was a member of the war-time Children's Overseas Reception Board and was on the Lancashire Industrial Development Council.

After the war he became a member of the National Investment Council and in 1946 he was appointed to the board of the Bank of England. He was also appointed to the North Western Board of the British Electricity Authority.

Gibson was established in all these posts, and at the height of his career, when in the autumn of 1948 his name became involved in the circumstances which led to the setting up of the tribunal over which Mr. Justice [Sir George] Lynskey [q.v.] presided. As a consequence of its findings, Gibson shed himself of all his public offices and retired into private life at his Lancashire home.

He had served in the 1914-18 war, first as gunner in the R.G.A. and finally as a major, and was mentioned in dispatches. In 1945 Manchester University made him an honorary LL.D.

February 5, 1953.

Hugh Gibson, the American diplomatist and director of the Inter-Governmental Committee on the Movement of Migrants from Europe, died in Geneva on December 12, 1954 at the age of 71.

Hugh Simons Gibson was born at Los Angeles, California, of Scottish ancestry on August 16, 1883, and was educated in Paris and at the Universities of Louvain, Brussels, and Yale. His long and adventurous diplomatic career began in 1908, when he was appointed a secretary at the American Legation at

Tegucigalpa in Honduras. In the following year he was sent to London as second secretary at the American Embassy and after a year he was recalled to Washington to become private secretary to the assistant Secretary of State. From 1911 to 1913 he was at the American Legation at Havana, and after a tour of special duty observing the progress of the elections in Santo Domingo, was sent to Brussels as First Secretary of the American Legation in early 1914.

On the outbreak of war he assumed personal responsibility for the safety of the thousands of Germans then resident in Belgium and had them transferred to their own country. After a few weeks he saw the entry of the German troops into Brussels and became the intermediary between the burgomaster and the German military authorities. There fell on him the care of those Britons still in the occupied territory, and he also saw and recorded the destruction of Louvain. Eventually he made his way to London and Le Havre, where the Belgian seat of government was then situated. Gibson later made great and prolonged efforts to save the life of Nurse Edith Cavell, who was shot in 1915 for aiding the escape into Holland of wounded Belgian and British soldiers, but his negotiations and representations were all fruitless.

After further service in London and with the Belgian War Mission to the United States he was, in early 1918, appointed First Secretary at the American Embassy in Paris. After the armistice he served with Herbert (later President) Hoover* on relief work, and was appointed a member of the inter-allied mission to the countries of the former Austro-Hungarian Empire. In 1919 he was made American Minister to Poland, and after serving in Poland for five years was appointed American Minister to Switzerland. While in Geneva he served in 1925 as vice-chairman of the American delegation to the International Conference for Control of the Traffic in Arms and later as chairman of the American delegation to the preparatory commission for the Disarmament Conference.

In 1927 he returned to Belgium as Ambassador, and from then onwards played an important part in the League of Nations conferences at Geneva. He also attended the London Naval Conference in 1929. In 1933 he went to Brazil where he spent four years as Ambassador before returning briefly to Brussels before his retirement from the Diplomatic Service in 1938. However, he was too active a man to give up all his European interests and in 1940-41 he was director-general for Europe of the Commission for Polish Relief and the Commission for Relief in Belgium. In 1952 he became director of the newly formed Inter-Governmental Committee on the Movement of Migrants from Europe which was established to coordinate and plan the oversea resettlement of European emigrants and refugees.

During his long and varied career he took part in all the major international meetings and projects, and he also fought hard to raise the remuneration and expense allowances of American diplomatists. At one time he was said to have declined President Hoover's offer to appoint him Ambassador to Britain owing to his own limited income.

Gibson was the author of several books, of which the earliest was his *Diplomatic Diary*, published in 1917. In 1944 he published his views on American foreign policy and the need for more interest to be taken in foreign affairs under the title of *The Road to Foreign Policy*. Together with Herbert Hoover he wrote another book *The Basis of Lasting Peace*, which was published in 1945.

He married in 1922 Mlle. Ynés Reyntiens, of Brussels. She died in 1950. There was one son of the marriage.

December 13, 1954.

William Pettigrew Gibson, Keeper of the National Gallery from 1939, died in London on April 22, 1960 at the age of 58.

He was the elder son of Dr. E. A. Gibson, and was educated at Wilkinson's in Orme Square, at Westminster, and at Christ Church, Oxford. He took a degree in physiology, but soon after he came down from the University in 1924 he abandoned his medical studies at considerable sacrifice to himself, and turned to the history of art; and in 1927 he joined the staff of the Wallace Collection as lecturer and assistant keeper.

He was at the Wallace Collection for nine years; then moved to Portman Square as reader in history of art to the University of London, and deputy director of the Courtauld Institute of Art; and from there to the National Gallery, where he remained for the rest of his career. He married in 1940 Christina Ogilvy, and thus became the brother-in-law of Sir Philip Hendy, his contemporary at Westminster and Christ Church, his predecessor at the Wallace Collection, and afterwards his Director at the National Gallery.

Gibson was a sensitive writer, but did not publish more than an occasional article in the learned periodicals, chiefly on French eighteenth-century art, for which his long service at the Wallace Collection had fitted him. Three of his lectures on French painting were published in 1930; but his administrative duties as Keeper of the National Gallery prevented him from continuing direct participation in the catalogues of the collection.

If for this reason he was less well known to the art world in general than some of his colleagues, his abilities were sincerely respected by a long succession of trustees. He was conscientious and exact in keeping before the board the rules of the gallery and the terms of the trusteeship, and his good manners, combined with independence of judgment and a certain robust common sense, lent weight to his advice. He was determined, sometimes to the point of obstinacy, on what he considered a matter of principle. During the war he spent long periods on duty in the National Gallery by day and night; and when the bombs fell on and around the building, his sense of duty and characteristic imperturbability made him the ideal man for the emergency.

He did not seek a wide circle of acquaintances, but to those who enjoyed his confidence and affection he was most loyal. When Sir Charles Prescott, one of his greatest friends, died in 1955, Gibson collaborated with others in producing a memoir of him; and the essay which he himself published in that book, an excellent example of his elegant style as a writer, reveals something of his truly affectionate nature and also of his own tastes.

Perhaps he was happiest when entertaining, with his talented and charming wife, in his home at Wyddiall Hall in north Hertfordshire, where he settled soon after the end of the war. Though not a countryman by upbringing, he had his own quite personal and unconventional appreciation of country things; and in his own house he liked to live according to his own ideas, without a telephone, or a wireless set, or even (if he could help it) the electric light, in large well-proportioned rooms with no affected nonsense about them, with beautiful lawns and cedars—and a game of croquet—outside.

April 23, 1960.

André Gide, the distinguished French author, died in Paris on February 19, 1951 at the age of 81.

André Gide attained in European letters a far higher eminence than the mild interest he aroused in England would suggest. Beginning as an essayist almost in the tradition of Montaigne, he went on to poetry, biography, fiction, drama, criticism, reminiscence, and translation, and then, after 26 years of comparatively obscure authorship, suddenly emerged, about 1917, as a prophet. Thereupon, for a period of six years or more, he held the ear of French youth, and even after a new generation had stepped forward and adopted other favourites, his work continued to be endlessly debated and attacked. In 1933 his decision to embrace communism provided literate Paris with a nine-day sensation. In 1944, while he was in North Africa, the publication of certain comments of his on the quality of French patriotism led to a violent protest in the Algiers Assembly, and Clemenceau's octogenarian niece thereupon wrote in his defence.

The "message" which, during and after the 1914-18 war, attracted to him, both in France and elsewhere in Europe, so wide and enthusiastic a following, exciting at the same time so many hostile views, was simply an endorsement of escapism, of self-fulfilment, of indulgence and not abstention—a message in line with Blake's proverb that "the road of excess leads to the palace of wisdom", but delivered with exceptional literary elegance and subtlety. This doctrine of escapism might have been expected to appeal to a section at least of English youth in the atmosphere of disillusion that succeeded victory in 1918. In fact, it made little impression in Britain. Outside France, it was in Germany that Gide became best known—the liberal Germany of, for instance, Ernst Robert Curtius [q.v.]. Yet the foreign literature which he admired above all was our own. It was this admiration which led him to translate *Antony and Cleopatra, Hamlet, The Marriage of Heaven and Hell,* and works of Rabindranath Tagore, Conrad, and T. S. Eliot*.

Why, then, having these English affinities, did he fail to stir the English public? In England he was not, of course, altogether ignored. As early as 1912 Edmund Gosse had written an article about him, and in the course of time several of his books appeared in translation. But such faint and sporadic recognition was very different from the English welcome given, for example, to André Maurois*. What was there to account for the difference? In the first place, there was certainly the fact that in England we had already had Walter Pater. Next, there was Gide's extreme Frenchness—which, to liberal Germans, strange though it may perhaps seem, was less alien than it was to English people. Finally, there was in nearly all his writings a persistent heterodoxy which in France itself disqualified him for official honours and erected a formidable barrier between him and the body of English readers. Nevertheless his standing as an author led in 1947 to the award of the Nobel Prize for Literature.

André Paul Guillaume Gide was born in Paris on November 22, 1869, the son of Paul and Juliette Gide. His father was professor of law at the Sorbonne. A delicate as well as an only child, André Gide had an irregular schooling, mainly at the Ecole Alsacienne, the Protestant secondary school in Paris. Both parents had Protestant forebears, although Gide's mother's family, which belonged to Rouen, had lately become Roman Catholic. Gide's father died in 1880, when the boy himself was not quite 11, and he grew up in the care of his mother, to whom he was chiefly indebted for his understanding of music. Had it been necessary for him to earn his living, he once remarked, he would have liked to teach the piano. Although his father had depended on his own exertions, he left the boy provided for, while Mme. Gide's family were well-to-do. So at 22 Gide published a first book at his own expense.

From French Protestantism, indeed, Gide never completely cut free. He could analyse the deficiencies, as he saw them, of its moral psychology in his novel *La Porte étroite* (1909); he could view its effects with irony in another tale, *La Symphonie pastorale* (1919). But nevertheless, he remained in its grip, as is evident alike in the slim volume, *Numquid et Tu?* where the divinity of our Lord is held to be disclosed in the sublimity of his words, and in the account of his own boyhood and early manhood, *Si le Grain ne Meurt* (1924). Yet all the time he continued in revolt against Calvinism, and it was an attempt to assure himself that Blake and, still more, Whitman were right that in 1926 he wrote *Les Faux-Monnayeurs,* a work in the guise of fiction and of great technical interest which he called his first novel.

In 1909 Gide had become one of the founders of the *Nouvelle Revue Française*—a periodical which, after the 1914-18 war, came to be read all over Europe and in both the Americas—and thereby contributed substantially to the diffusion of contemporary French literature. But it might be said that, until 1926, he seemed to restrict his distinctive share in that literature to the reflection of his own self. In that year, however, a new vista was opened to him through a visit to the French Congo, in the course of which he discovered what was involved in the exploitation of the African Negro. The indignation which he voiced in *Voyage au Congo* (1927) was a prelude to the awakening of a social consciousness and to his conversion to communism. The conversion, however, was followed by a visit to Moscow which produced not merely a normal degree of disappointment with conditions in Soviet Russia but an expression of impassioned disenchantment with the Soviet scheme of things. In 1939 he admitted to his *Journal* (of which two volumes have recently appeared in English translation) that in calling himself a communist he means that he had become Christian, a Christian without faith. Certainly his newly acquired awareness of social injustice was too vivid ever to grow dim.

Of Gide's drama, which he kept up intermittently from the publication of *Le Roi Candaule* in 1901, it is probably enough to say that it never securely held the stage. From about 1930 onwards his most distinctive production consisted of the successive volumes of his *Journal,* in which penetrating self-analysis was threaded with acute literary, social, and political criticism. In 1946 his *Thésée* retold in novel form the story of the events that led up to the drama set out in the *Hippolytus,* and must remain a masterly exposition of its author's psychological theories.

Gide married in 1892 a cousin, who predeceased him in 1939. There were no children of the marriage.

February 20, 1951.

Walter Gieseking, the most eminent German pianist of the day, died in hospital in London on October 26, 1956 at the age of 60. He had gone to England from Germany a week earlier, and was taken ill suddenly on October 24.

The loss, great as it is, cuts off no future promise, for Gieseking matured early, concentrated on all the classics of piano literature, has recorded much of it, and was not identified with any modern movements. His playing, however, was a miraculous compound of delicacy and strength and as such was unique, so that his international repute was securely founded.

Walter Wilhelm Gieseking was born on November 5, 1895, at Lyons, the son of a German doctor and entomologist then living in France. During his boyhood the family travelled about a great deal, and it may well be that his sympathy with the music of Chopin and Debussy, unusual in a German, was due to a cosmopolitan upbringing and a private education. He went to Hanover, his mother's home, for formal musical instruction in 1911 and in 1915 made his first public appearance. Conscription for military service soon followed and he spent the last years of the 1914-18 War as a regimental bandsman.

In the Second World War he was *persona grata* with the Nazi authorities and suffered some hostility afterwards as a result, though it was not long before resentment was extinguished by the recognition of the artistic contribution he could make to the whole world. His leisure between his tours was spent on his hobby of entomology, an interest he had inherited from his father along with a large collection, to which he was continually making additions. He has a few compositions, notably a set of variations and a sonatina for flute and piano, to his credit.

As a pianist he first revealed his exceptional quality to London in 1923, when his command of the finer shades of tone was immediately noticed. His physical height and bulk served to reinforce the impression of delicacy in his playing. He would sit bunched but still towering over the keyboard and from his fingers would pour ripples of Scarlatti, diamond-like Mozart, and multi-hued washes of exquisite tone in Debussy. But he was more than a miniaturist and could command breadth and intellectual grasp, though compared with his elder contemporary Schnabel [q.v.] he was a romantic who did not rely on Beethoven and Brahms for his recital programmes so much as on the composers with whom sensibility was the predominant consideration.

His wife was killed in a road accident near Stuttgart in December 1955, when Gieseking himself received head injuries, as a result of which he was in hospital for six weeks. He is survived by two daughters.

October 27, 1956.

Beniamino Gigli, the Italian tenor singer, died on November 30, 1957 at his villa in Rome. He was 67.

It is about two years since Beniamino Gigli retired from stage and concert platform, but his voice and style of singing will be familiar not only to those who remember his performances in the flesh but to younger generations who are only familiar with his gramophone records. For he was a sort of Platonic idea of the Italian tenor in his qualities and limitations—his was a voice of pure gold, lyric rather than heroic in quality, so perfectly controlled that he worked it hard for 41 years; this was *bel canto* if ever there was such a thing; and though he had intelligence he had not enough imagination to make a great artist. Few singers have all the gifts.

He sang opera in all Italian houses, at the Metropolitan in New York for a dozen years, made occasional appearances in German and Iberian theatres, and at Covent Garden. He covered a wider geographical area as a recitalist. Though he visited South America and South Africa he never gave himself enough time to go to the Far East or to the Antipodes. Nevertheless, his reputation was world-wide. In 1957 he published a volume of memoirs in which he told with becoming modesty and pride the story of his success.

Beniamino Gigli was born on March 20, 1890, the youngest of six children of poor parents, at Recanati, near the Adriatic coast of northern Italy. His father was a cobbler, who on being put out of work by factory competition became bell-ringer at the cathedral, which thus exercised an influence, musical as well as emotional and instructional, on a six-year-old boy. Gigli sang from his earliest youth in the cathedral choir and here, there, and everywhere as his *sfogo,* as he called it, his outlet.

It secured his exemption from active service in the First World War, and though his apprenticeship was hard and hungry his obvious destiny as a singer secured him the right friends and the right opportunities at the right time. He won a scholarship at the St. Cecilia Academy in Rome and first place in an international competition at Parma in 1914. In the autumn of that year he made his *début* in *La Gioconda* at Rovigo. In 1915 he sang Faust in Boito's *Mefistofele* for Serafin [q.v.] at Bologna and for Mascagni at Naples. His career went forward through his lengthy association with these conductors, and *Mefistofele* was to bring him to the climax of his early career at home when he sang at a memorial performance conducted by Toscanini [q.v.] at La Scala on December 26, 1918, six months after the composer's death.

His first success abroad was in Spain in 1917. In 1919 he went to South America and in 1920 he arrived at the Metropolitan in New York, where he made his home until the depression of the early thirties caused him to sever his connexion with the Metropolitan (an act widely criticized and admitted by him subsequently to have been tactless) and to return to Italy. He appeared first at Covent Garden in 1930 in *Andrea Chénier, Tosca, Marta,* and *La Traviata,* and thereafter sang in a number of "grand seasons", including the 1939 season in which he sang in *Aida* under Beecham*, and after the war in a performance of *La Bohème* in which his daughter Rina sang Mimi with him.

For a period of 25 years with seven years out during the war, he appeared at intervals in solo recitals at the Albert Hall, and more than once toured the English and Scottish provincial cities. His programmes on these occasions contained mostly operatic arias, drawn from his wide range of roles, which ultimately totalled 60, and trivial songs, sometimes with the addition of an English song as an intended compliment to his audience but by reason of its poor musical quality the reverse of complimentary in actuality.

People liked to hear him sing "Amarilli" or Neapolitan trifles, which he did beautifully, but the lack of true songs, in which Italy is by comparison with Germany and England poor, made these occasions demonstrations of *bel canto* rather than song recitals of artistic worth. Yet it was reassuring to discover that singing was not a wholly lost art. He had no special methods and recommended none, since each voice has its own requirements. He could be slovenly, when intrusive aspirates would mar his line, but he sang by the light of nature and training had kept him on the right lines. He knew what to avoid, so that, for instance, he never attempted Verdi's *Otello.* Though a limited artist he was a great singer.

December 2, 1957.

Christopher Herman Gilkes, who died suddenly on September 2, 1953 at the age of 54, was appointed Master of Dulwich College in 1941.

He went there from Stockport where he had been Headmaster of the Grammar School since 1929, and it was particularly fitting that he should return to Dulwich where he had been born and educated and where his father, the Rev. A. H. Gilkes, had been Master from 1885 until 1914, during some of the most formative years of the school.

He had been teaching since he left Oxford in 1922, first at Uppingham and then at Stratford, his subject being the classics, of which he had a wide knowledge built up on a solid grounding. He had also been an active player of school games in his younger days—he won his school colours in the first XV—and realizing their value in the school curriculum gave ample scope for their play and every encouragement to the boys.

During the war of 1914-18 he served for some years in India and that had broadened his sympathies and outlook and in all his school work he tried to give all members of the staff and of the school the full benefit of his experience and bring them to a fuller understanding and appreciation of current world affairs.

As he was only 43 years of age when he took charge he could look forward to a long term there, which has now been unhappily and unexpectedly cut short. He followed the old traditions largely but at the same time realized the value of many recent theories and practices in education and was not slow to introduce changes which he felt would benefit the school in its work. The boys were in his day drawn from a much wider field of the population than had been usual in his younger days, but he sought to impress on all the Dulwich stamp of character, devotion and comradeship as well as sound learning.

When war broke out in 1939 Dulwich suffered greatly as a result of many of the boys being evacuated, but when the severe air raids of 1940 and 1941 passed, boys gradually drifted back and, along with those who had remained, the school began to assume its former proportions. But some were still absent. It was in these circumstances that Gilkes took charge.

The work was not easy, but he quickly surmounted all difficulties by his courage, his faith in the school, and his willingness to make changes and adapt the work of the school to the circumstances. The staff was much depleted by the departure of younger men to the services and boys were leaving earlier to take up their duties in the war. He made it his aim to give them every preparation that might fit them for the tasks to which they would be called.

Gilkes was born on November 10, 1898. When he left Dulwich in 1917 he did not go up to the university but enlisted and was given a commission in the Indian Army Reserve of Officers. He served during 1917 and 1918 with the 109th Infantry of the Indian Army on the North-West Frontier. After his discharge on returning to England he went up to Trinity College, Oxford, where he took a second class in Classical Moderations and in Literae Humaniores. He was up for four years and played each year in the University Rugby Football trial matches and came near to gaining his Blue. On leaving Oxford he was appointed an assistant master at Uppingham, where he remained till 1928, when he was appointed to Stockport Grammar School.

In 1921 he married Miss E. O. Benson. She died in 1938, leaving no children. In 1939 he married Miss Josephine Gaston Murray, who survives him with their two sons and one daughter.

September 4, 1953.

Basil Gill, the Shakespearian actor, died at his home at Hove on April 23, 1955, at the age of 78.

He made his first appearance on the stage in 1897 and from then until 1944 played a great variety of parts. A man of commanding appearance and with a rich, resonant voice he was popular wherever he went. It is probable that he appeared in more productions of *Julius Caesar* than any other actor of his day.

Born at Birkenhead on March 10, 1877, he first appeared at Bury in *The Sign of the Cross* in 1897, thus at the outset of his career coming into touch with Wilson Barrett. His first work on the London stage was in Barrett's production of *The Daughters of Babylon* in 1898. With him he toured in England, America, and Australia as Marcus Superbus in *The Sign of the Cross,* returning to London in 1902 to play at Drury Lane in the spectacular production of *Ben Hur.* Later in his career he was to be seen at Drury Lane again in *The Last of His Race* in 1907, *Marriages of Mayfair* in 1908, Forbes-Robertson's production of *The Merchant of Venice* in 1913, and *The Garden of Allah* in 1920. His great opportunity came in 1903 when he was invited by Sir Herbert Tree to join his company at His Majesty's Theatre. He remained there for four years and accompanied his chief to Berlin in 1907. He played a whole series of Shakespearian parts as well as Kara in *The Darling of the Gods,* Harry Maylie in *Oliver Twist,* and Clive Newcome in *Col. Newcome.*

Probably the play which he loved above all others was *Julius Caesar,* in which he played Brutus with his life-long friend Lyn Harding [q.v.] as Cassius. Their rendering of the quarrel scene captured London, and for many years it formed a part of special performances in aid of charity. In later productions Gill played either Brutus or Cassius, and it was a great achievement when in 1920 he played the two parts at alternate performances, with Godfrey Tearle [q.v.] as his partner, when scenes from the play were presented at the Coliseum.

He returned to His Majesty's on many subsequent occasions and played Joseph Surface in a notable revival of *The School for*

Scandal in 1909, James Steerforth in *David Copperfield* in 1914, Pygmalion in *Pygmalion and Galatea* in 1916, and Rafi in *Hassan* in 1923. Whenever he had the opportunity he returned to Shakespearian plays. With Lyn Harding he appeared in *Macbeth* at the Knickerbocker Theatre in New York in 1929 as Macduff, a production which ran for seven and a half months.

When Sydney Carroll founded the Open Air Theatre in Regent's Park, Basil Gill played in a number of his favourite Shakespearian parts. In the autumn of 1933 he played Orsino in *Twelfth Night* at the Old Vic, following this by a season at the old Alhambra as Orsino, Brutus, and Antonio. One of his last appearances on the stage was in *Hatter's Castle* in 1944.

April 25, 1955.

E. W. B. Gill, O.B.E., Emeritus Fellow and sometime Domestic Bursar of Merton College, Oxford, died on December 20, 1959 at Oxford. He was 76 and had been ill for some time.

Ernest Walter Brudenell Gill was born on August 12, 1883, the son of Canon E. Compton Gill, and was educated at Bristol Grammar School and Christ Church, Oxford, Having taken a first class in physics, he was appointed a demonstrator in the electrical laboratory and a Fellow of Merton College. Except for the period of two wars he retained both positions until his retirement from the former in 1949, the latter in 1954. Between the wars he was Bursar of Merton College, and a member of Hebdomadal Council and the University Chest. During the 1914-18 War, in which he joined up as a private, skilfully avoiding the medical examination which would have excluded him, he served in R.G.A. 20th Heavy Battery, and in R.E. wireless intelligence, in Egypt, Cyprus, and Salonika.

In the late war he worked first in secret wireless intelligence and later in operational research, where he was one of the original inventors of "Window", the device to protect bombers from location, and of a method of guiding tanks which was used soon after D-Day. Later he went to Germany to discover the achievements of German academic science in the war, which he found to be negligible. His peacetime studies covered a wide range (conductivity through gases, wireless, the magnetron, static electrification, &c.) and he published numerous papers.

Gill was a man of great mental vigour, a fresh and antiseptic clarity of mind, a disinterestedness which inspired devotion among those who served and appreciated him, and a dry wit which made him an *enfant terrible* wherever there was cant or humbug. Utterly indifferent to status, vanity (or indeed comfort), he neither expected nor received any recognition for the numerous services which he always gave as a matter of course. His generosity could be heroic. In 1941, in recognition of American help to Britain, he quietly gave to the American Library of Congress a copy of the second folio of Shakespeare which had come down to him in his family. He hated all fuss. Describing his own activities as university representative on the Oxford City Council, he once wrote, "I had no ideals of public service. I only went on because I was infuriated over the price of electricity and I hoped to 'kick' the company out". With this rough empiric philosophy he continued in fact to give unobtrusive public service throughout his life.

He married in 1921 Mary Harriss, daughter of the Rev. J. A. Harriss, and is survived by three sons and one daughter.

December 23, 1959.

Sir William Gilliatt, K.C.V.O., M.D., M.S., F.R.C.P., F.R.C.S., F.R.C.O.G., the eminent obstetrician, who died after a road accident on September 27, 1956, was consulting obstetric and gynaecological surgeon to King's College Hospital and consulting surgeon to the Samaritan Free Hospital for Women. He attended the Queen (then Princess Elizabeth) at the births of Prince Charles and Princess Anne, and he also attended Princess Marina, Duchess of Kent* at the births of her three children. He was 72.

William Gilliatt, son of the late William Gilliatt, was born at Boston, Lincolnshire, in 1884, and received his medical training at the Middlesex Hospital. He had a brilliant career as a student, winning the Hetley clinical scholarship, the junior Broderip scholarship, the Leopold Hudson scholarship and the Lyell gold medal and scholarship, and qualifying as M.R.C.S., L.R.C.P. and M.B., B.S. London in 1908. At the Middlesex Hospital he held the posts of house physician, house surgeon, obstetrical house physician, and obstetrical and gynaecological registrar and tutor, and he took the higher qualifications of M.D., winning a gold medal in 1910, M.S. and F.R.C.S. England in 1912.

He was elected a Foundation Fellow of the Royal College of Obstetricians and Gynaecologists in 1929 and served as president of the college in 1946-49. He was elected assistant obstetric and gynaecological surgeon at King's College Hospital in 1916, became senior surgeon in 1925, and retired to the consulting staff in 1946. He had been a member of the committee of management of King's College Hospital since 1932 and in 1945 he was elected vice-chairman. His other appointments included those of gynaecologist to St. Saviour's Hospital, consulting gynaecologist to Bromley Cottage Hospital and to the Maudsley Hospital, and examiner in midwifery and diseases of women to the universities of Cambridge, London, and Bristol, and to the Conjoint Board.

His eminence in his profession was such that he was appointed to the medical staff of the Royal Household more than 20 years ago and he had been surgeon-gynaecologist to the Queen since 1952. Sparely built and with iron grey hair, he had the characteristically long tapering fingers of the born surgeon and he was taciturn to a degree. He contributed to various textbooks on obstetrics and gynaecology and he edited the standard work on the subject, *Ten Teachers,* but he was not a voluminous writer.

He was created C.V.O. in 1936 and promoted K.C.V.O. in 1948, and he was elected president of the Royal Society of Medicine in 1954.

He married Anne Louise, daughter of the late John Kann, of Lyne, Surrey. Of this marriage there was a son (who is a member of the medical profession) and a daughter.

September 28, 1956.

Sir Harold Gillies, C.B.E., F.R.C.S., the most eminent of plastic surgeons, died in hospital in London on September 10, 1960 at the age of 78.

Harold Delf Gillies was born in Dunedin, New Zealand, in 1882. His father, Robert Gillies, was a member of the House of Representatives of New Zealand. Gillies was educated at Wanganui College, where he was captain of cricket, and from there went to Cambridge, where he rowed for the university in 1904 and represented it at golf for three years. From Cambridge he proceeded to St. Bartholomew's Hospital, where he qualified in medicine in 1908 and took the F.R.C.S. Eng. in 1910. He was awarded the Luther Holden Scholarship at Bart's and also held the posts of house-surgeon to the general wards and to the department for diseases of the nose, throat, and ear.

The 1914-18 War, which caused the mutilation of so many men, at once gave Gillies the opportunity and showed where his genius lay. Early in 1916 as a major in the R.A.M.C. he began to do plastic surgery at the Cambridge Hospital, Aldershot, and later he worked at the Queen's Hospital for Facial Injuries, Sidcup. At the latter place he, in company with a group of other surgeons from Canada, Australia, New Zealand and America, continued to develop this almost new branch of surgery with astonishing ingenuity. From this time plastic surgery became Gillies's lifework and it was chiefly due to his skill, energy, enthusiasm and influence that it gained its permanent and prominent position. In 1920 he was made a C.B.E. and in the same year he published his epoch-making book on *Plastic Surgery of the Face,* which until the publication in 1957 of his comprehensive *Principles and Art of Plastic Surgery,* written with Dr. Ralph Millard, remained the leading textbook in its field.

After the war Gillies was elected plastic surgeon to St. Bartholomew's Hospital and became consultant to the Ministry of Pensions, while at the same time he conducted a large private practice in his speciality.

The outbreak of war in 1939 made further opportunities of service for Gillies; he was made consulting adviser to the Ministry of Health and in this capacity organized various plastic surgical units in different parts of the country; he also personally supervised the largest unit at Park Prewett Hospital, Basingstoke. In addition to these duties he was consultant in plastic surgery to the R.A.F. and civil consultant to the Admiralty, and was chief plastic surgeon to the London County

Council. After the war he was chiefly responsible for planning the plastic surgery services in the National Health Service.

Along with his many professional activities Gillies for many years managed to maintain his position in the world of golf. He played for England against Scotland in 1908, 1925, and 1926, and won the St. George's Grand Challenge Cup in 1913. Golfers will remember the stir caused by his temporary adoption of a freakish hightee. Gillies was also a highly skilful fly-fisherman.

Plastic surgery as practised by Gillies was indeed an art, a kind of living sculpture, and during the 1914-18 War at least one professional sculptor, the late F. Derwent Wood, R.A., collaborated with Gillies in cases when the manipulation of living tissues needed to be supplemented with modelling in some artificial substance, such as wax. In view of this artistic aspect of plastic surgery it is hardly surprising that Gillies was a talented painter. His paintings were first seen in the exhibitions of the Medical Art Society at the Royal Society of Medicine, Wimpole Street, when he showed watercolours of Iceland, broad and free in style. He also painted in oils, and held two one-man exhibitions in London, the second in 1959.

As a surgeon Gillies had a flair, nay a genius, for his speciality. It was a joy to see him operate and a great lesson to note his patience and minute attention to detail. Men came from all over the world to see his work and they were never disappointed. All through his career he had the gift of imparting knowledge to others and he trained a splendid band of younger surgeons who spread the knowledge of plastic surgery far and wide; he had a great gift for lecturing and was much in demand in all parts of Britain and America for this purpose.

Gillies received several distinctions from abroad including the Commander of the Order of the Dannebrog in 1924, the Order of St. Olav in 1948, and honorary fellowship of the American College of Surgeons. He was elected first president of the International Plastic Society at its foundation meeting in Stockholm in 1955.

Gillies was twice married, first to Kathleen Jackson, by whom he had two sons and two daughters. She died in 1957, and he married, secondly, Marjorie E. Clayton.

[A tribute followed this obituary on the same day].

September 12, 1960.

Gertie Gitana (Mrs. Don Ross), for many years a popular music-hall performer, died in London on January 5, 1957, aged 69.

Gertrude Astbury (for such was her real name) was born at Hanley, Staffordshire, in 1887. When she was only four she appeared with Tomkinson's Gypsy Choir, a concert party which used to tour the Potteries. Less than five years later she was acting as a single turn, under the name Little Gitana, at the Tivoli, Barrow-in-Furness, where her salary was £3 a week—of which she was allowed 5s. for herself. She made her first London appearance in 1900. When she was about 15 she substituted "Gertie" for "Little", and so took the name by which she was afterwards so widely known.

Small, dark-haired, with ringlets falling on one shoulder, and dressed in a white pierrot costume, Gertie Gitana at the height of her career was an immense favourite with the less sophisticated type of audience, especially in the suburbs and provinces.

Billed as "The Star that Never Fails to Shine", she gave a great deal of harmless pleasure with a turn which included singing, a little step dancing, and playing upon the saxophone. Her songs—always of the sentimental kind—included "Silver Bell", "Never Mind", and, above all, "Nellie Dean", which became one of the most familiar of all such compositions. She retired in 1937.

In 1948, when her husband, Don Ross (whom she married in 1928), organized "Thanks for the Memory", a programme of artists of the old music-hall, she reappeared (though no longer in the old pierrot dress and ringlets), singing "Nellie Dean" to audiences that were still word-perfect in the chorus, and taking part in the Royal Variety Performance at the Palladium.

Three years ago a street in Hanley, running near the Theatre Royal, where Gertie Gitana had appeared as a girl, was renamed Gitana Street.

January 7, 1957.

Fyodor Gladkov, the Russian author, died at the age of 75 in December 1958.

Gladkov was known in Britain as the author of *Cement,* one of the earliest Soviet novels to salute the transition from the heroic phase of the Russian Revolution to the practical tasks of economic reconstruction—one of the earliest and in some ways perhaps the most celebrated. Not by any means a literary masterpiece, *Cement*—which appeared in Russia in volume form in 1926—nevertheless sustained its burden of sober and selfless aspiration with robust narrative energy.

Its mood of high, unromantic resolution was nicely attuned to the domestic ends of Soviet policy after the ravages of the years of "war communism", and the novel had a vast circulation in the Soviet Union and was translated into a good many foreign languages. Gladkov never again wrote anything that commanded signal official favour and consequent wide popularity, but his reputation as a leading representative of specifically proletarian literature was not allowed to suffer eclipse.

Born in 1883, the son of a peasant who had turned industrial worker, Fyodor Vasilevich Gladkov passed his childhood in circumstances of harsh poverty and was at an early age engaged in revolutionary activity. As a school teacher in Siberia during 1902-05 he came under the watchful eye of the authorities, and as a result was exiled to the Lena region for four years.

From 1911 until 1919 he continued as a schoolmaster, chiefly in Novorossisk. With the encouragement of the veteran Korolenko, and also of Gorky, he had been writing stories and plays during this time, mostly in the prevailing realistic vein of social protest. They attracted no great attention. He took a predestined part in the Civil War and, at its conclusion, became a member of the literary group known as *Kuznitsa* (The Forge). Besides *Cement,* the only novel of his during the 1920s that made any impression at all was *The Fiery Steed,* though this was an all too obviously halting performance.

In the violent critical controversies that attended the enlistment of art and literature in the service of Socialist construction and the "cultural revolution" generally, Gladkov was for a time among the moderating influences. But his own novel of the Five-Year Plan, *Power* (1933), a long and laboured piece of work, must be considered unsatisfactory from whatever aesthetic or propagandist standpoint the critic may adopt. After that the obligatory code of Socialist realism literature was not without its effect upon Gladkov, as upon other writers of his generation. Apart from his assignments during the war against Germany, he published, in 1945, a volume of short stories, *The Oath,* most of which are lifelessly orthodox in tone and temper.

Gladkov held both the Order of Lenin and the Order of the Red Banner.

December 22, 1958.

The death took place in Hollywood on April 13, 1959 of **James Gleason,** the character actor, at the age of 72. He had been in poor health for some months.

James Gleason was born in New York City on May 23, 1886, and was one of the old school of vaudeville players; born in the proverbial trunk, he came of a theatrical family and, it is recorded, made his stage *début* at the age of three months. By the time he was five he was touring regularly in drama and variety, and in his twenties he worked as actor, writer, director, stage manager and general theatrical jack-of-all-trades in stock companies and touring units. Before long, however, he had established himself on the New York stage, though curiously enough perhaps more as a writer than actor. He wrote several successful comedies, acting in some of them himself, the most notable being *The Fall Guy, The Shannons of Broadway* and *Is Zatso,* the last of which he also produced.

With the coming of the talking film he was imported to Hollywood along with a large number of Broadway actors and writers possessing the vital qualification of knowing how to deal with words. His first jobs in films were as a writer; he was responsible for the script of the original *Broadway Melody,* which set the pattern of film musicals for a number of years, *The Bowery,* and *Change of Heart.* His very first film, however, was an adaptation of his stage success *The Shannons of Broadway* (1929) under the title of *Goodbye, Broadway,* and part of his contract was to recreate his original stage role, so that Hollywood soon became aware of his acting talent as well as his skill in writing dialogue.

Already in his mid-forties when he made his first film, James Gleason changed little in appearance through the years: a small, long-faced man with a dry, even dour manner but a twinkle in his eye, he was from the early 1930s until his death one of the most frequently seen character actors on the American screen. He generally played in comedy or light drama, ranging from Norma Shearer's *A Free Soul* (1931) to his most recent film, *The Last Hurrah,* and among his most memorable appearances were as the father of an old-established vaudeville family in *On Your Toes* and as the fight-manager in *Here Comes Mr. Jordan* (1942), perhaps his best-remembered role.

Other notable films in which he appeared included Capra's *Meet John Doe, Arsenic and Old Lace* and *Riding High* (with his very individual appearance and canny good humour he was a perfect Capra character), Duvivier's* *Tales of Manhattan,* Kazan's *A Tree Grows in Brooklyn,* Charles Laughton's* *Night of the Hunter* and Ford's* *What Price Glory* and *The Last Hurrah,* in which his characteristically sharp and precise performance as Cuke Dillon provided an apt and touching final glimpse of his distinctive talent.

April 14, 1959.

Albert Gleizes, writer as well as painter, who died on June 23, 1953 at his home in the south of France at the age of 72, was one of the most consistent of the Cubists. Like his friend and collaborator Jean Metzinger he specialized in what R. H. Wilenski has christened conveniently "flat-pattern" Cubism in order to distinguish it from the more or less representational art which Picasso* and Braque* had developed from the geometrical hints of Cézanne.

The son of an industrial draughtsman, Albert Léon Gleizes was born in Paris in 1881, that is to say in the same year as Picasso, Braque, and Léger [q.v.]. He was not, however, so quick as they were to follow the call of geometry but began as an Impressionist, exhibiting regularly at the "Old" Salon of the Société Nationale des Beaux Arts, and it was not until 1909, when he was 28, that he joined the Cubist group. Once converted he proceeded to clarify and rationalize the aims of the movement. In 1912, with Metzinger and the three Duchamp* brothers, he opened the "Golden Section" gallery—named after the pleasing Pythagorean division of space—as an exhibition centre for Cubist art in Paris, and in the same year he and Metzinger published the first book on the movement, a small illustrated work entitled *On Cubism.*

Quoted by C. J. Bulliet in *The Significant Moderns,* the description of Cubism as understood by Gleizes and Metzinger is very clear and concise. "Painting is the art of giving life to a flat surface. A flat surface exists only in two dimensions. It is true only in two dimensions. To pretend to give it a third dimension is to deny its own nature. Painting should be in two dimensions: only sculpture has three". But a year after this the poet and critic Guillaume Apollinaire published his more comprehensive and recondite *Cubist Painters: Aesthetic Meditations,* in which, though he did justice to Gleizes, he concentrated more particularly on the versatile genius of Picasso, who was carrying Cubism far beyond the "flat-pattern" phase.

The result was that Gleizes tended to become a back-number in the excited discussions of the times. Gleizes was certainly not one of the most renowned of the Cubist painters, and his work has been dismissed as not more than decorative. His "Composition, 1932", reproduced by Herbert Read* in *Art Now,* has a very graceful "music" of both line and tone.

In general Gleizes's work lends itself very well to architectural decoration and avoids the extravagances of the later manifestations of the movement. It may, indeed, be questioned if the more abstruse developments of Cubism are not in themselves critical red herrings so far as painting is concerned.

June 25, 1953.

Dr. Reinhold Glière, the distinguished Russian musician, died on June 23, 1956 at the age of 81.

The son of a maker of wind instruments of Belgian extraction, he early evinced musical gifts, and his childish compositions were performed in his father's house at Kiev, which was a meeting place for musicians.

Study in Kiev and Moscow followed as a matter of course and he emerged as a composer of international reputation in the first few years of this century. His Belgian descent coupled with his upbringing in the eclectic school of Moscow undoubtedly contributed to his early success in western Europe at a time when the works of the nationalists of the St. Petersburg school, under the leadership of Balakirev, were still too strong a draught for many western audiences to stomach. His first symphony, written in 1899-1900, was first performed in England at a promenade concert at the Queen's Hall in 1906, and his symphonic poem, *Les Sirènes* (dating from 1908) was first performed in London in 1912. Thereafter he was recognized for many years as a contemporary representative of the school of Russian composers who looked to the western tradition in music which was headed by Tchaikovsky, Arensky, Glazonov, Taneyev, and Alexandrov.

After the revolution of 1917 Glière, whose whole interest was in music, showed notable administrative gifts as the head of the musical section of the Moscow Department of People's Education. He undertook many tours to study the folk music of his native Ukraine and of Azerbaijan, Uzbekistan, and other constituent republics of the Soviet Union, and based many of his later works on the knowledge he thus acquired. One of the most notable works of this later phase of his career was the opera *Shah Senem,* founded on the folklore of Azerbaijan, which was completed in 1925, revised in 1933-34, and produced at Baku in the last-named year. It was given in Moscow in 1938, during a festival there of Azerbaijan art. Later works in the same *genre* included the music-drama *Hulsara,* based on Uzbek folklore, and the symphonic poem, *Zapovit,* which was performed on the 125th anniversary of the birth of Taras Shevchenko and dedicated "to the memory of a great people's poet".

Reinhold Moritzovich Glière was born at Kiev on January 11, 1875. He learnt to play the violin as a child and all his early works were for stringed instruments. At the age of 16 he entered the Kiev Music School, where he stayed for some three years studying the violin and composition. He then went to the Moscow Conservatoire, where he continued his training on the violin under Sokolovsky and Hrimadi, and worked at harmony under Arensky and Konius, counterpoint under Taneyev, and composition and instrumentation under Ippolitov-Ivanov. He graduated from the Conservatoire in 1900 with his diploma work, a one-act opera-oratorio, *Earth and Heaven.* After graduation he taught at the Gneissen School of Music in Moscow and produced in rapid succession several collections of songs, the second and third concertos, a number of pieces for pianoforte, and his second symphony, which he dedicated to Kussevitsky. In 1905-07 he studied conducting in Berlin under Oscar Fried, and soon after his return to Russia in 1908 he made his first appearance as a conductor. The symphonic poem *Les Sirènes* of that year was followed in 1910 by his third symphony.

He returned to Kiev in 1913 and took charge of the composition class in the music school there. In the course of the next year he became director of the institution. When his administrative duties allowed he made concert tours and other travels in connexion with the study of folklore. He went back to Moscow in 1920, where, as head of the musical section of the Department of People's Education, he directed the organization of concerts in workers' clubs and acquired the authority of an able organizer. In 1937 he was elected chairman of the management committee of the Moscow Union of Composers, and two years later he became chairman of the Union of Soviet Composers. He was awarded the Order of the Red Banner in 1937 and the next year received the Order of Merit and the high title of People's Artist of the U.S.S.R.

His earlier work, produced under the influence of Tchaikovsky and Taneyev, and his later work, based on regional rather than on general nationalism, produced a manner personal to Glière himself, which has produced a tradition which he has handed on to numerous pupils, among the most brilliant of whom have been Prokofiev, [q.v.], Miaskovsky, and Khachaturian [d. 1978.]

June 27, 1956.

Former Bishop of Gloucester—See **Woodward.**

Mary Glynne, who under this stage name was at the beginning of the century one of the most beautiful young actresses on the London stage and continued her stage career until a few years ago, died on September 19, 1954. She was 56.

She was born on January 25, 1898, the daughter of a doctor, the late Charles Aitken, and the grand-daughter of the late Deputy Surgeon-General William Aitken, of the East India Company's service. Although she had appeared on the stage before, she first made her name at the age of 11, when she appeared at the Strand Theatre as Little Rosalie in *The Merry Peasant.* The piece itself was not a great success, but the crowds flocked to hear the duet between Florence St. John and the little Mary Glynne.

Her next appearance was a few months later at the same theatre in a child's pantomime, and in 1910 she made her *début* at the Duke of York's Theatre as Curly in *Peter Pan.* In the following year she went to the Coliseum to act as Jacqueline in *Joan of Arc,* with Ellaline Terriss* in the role of Joan. Her next success came later in 1911 when she played Cinderella in *The Golden Land of Fairy Tales* at the Lyceum.

When she was still only 14 Mary Glynne was chosen to personate the Dauphin in *The Women of France* at the Lyceum, and it was in the winter of that year that she confirmed her reputation when she succeeded Hilda Trevelyan [q.v.] as Wendy in *Peter Pan,* giving a rendering which captivated London. This was followed by another success as Felicia Lady Grandison in *Lady Noggs* at the Coventry Theatre. When the 1914-18 War broke out she was still only 16, and being spoken of as a future Portia and Ophelia.

But this was not to be. Although Mary Glynne was to appear on the stage for another 30 years and more, to have some successes—notably as Louisa in *The Aristocrat,* at the St. James's Theatre in 1917; as Tilly in Ian Hay's [q.v.] *Tilly of Bloomsbury,* at the Apollo in 1919; as Annabelle West in *The Cat and Canary,* at the Shaftesbury Theatre in 1922; as Simonetta in *Carnival,* at the New Theatre in 1923; as Mary Redmayne in *The Terror,* at the Lyceum in 1927; and as Helena Warwick in *Family Affairs,* at the Ambassadors Theatre in 1934—she never fulfilled her early promise.

She married, first, Dennis Neilson-Terry; and, secondly, John Mannell, who survives her.

September 22, 1954.

General Sir Alexander John Godley, G.C.B., K.C.M.G., who died in Oxford on March 6, 1957 at the age of 90, was a distinguished soldier whose gifts were for practical work in the field. Always known as an excellent horseman and judge of a horse, he acquired a considerable reputation in the early stages of his career as a trainer of mounted infantry and commander of irregular troops. In the First World War he did well at Gallipoli and was uniformly successful as a corps commander on the Western Front.

Born on February 4, 1867, the eldest son of Lieutenant-Colonel William Alexander Godley, he came of the Irish Godleys of Killegar, co. Leitrim. He was sent to the Royal Naval School, but proceeded to Haileybury to commence his preparation for an Army career, eventually passing into Sandhurst from the United Services College. In August 1886 he was gazetted lieutenant in the Royal Dublin Fusiliers.

At the close of 1898 he received a nomination for the Staff College where he was later elected Master of the Draghounds. His studies, however, were interrupted in July 1899 owing to the growing tension with the South African Republics, for he was then selected as one of the special service officers to go out to the Cape on intelligence duties. His mounted infantry experience was soon utilized, as at the outbreak of the South African War he became adjutant of the Rhodesian Protectorate Regiment which formed part of the garrison of Mafeking under Baden-Powell.

During the siege Godley was, for a time, in command of the Western Defences, and later served on Baden-Powell's staff. After Mafeking was relieved in the middle of May 1900 he served on the staff of Colonel (afterwards Field-Marshal Lord) Plumer. From August 1900 to February 1901 he commanded the Rhodesian Brigade, but was then brought home to assist in training mounted infantry drafts, becoming Deputy Assistant Adjutant-General for M.I. at Aldershot. His services in South Africa had been mentioned in dispatches, and he had received the brevet of lieutenant-colonel in November 1900.

In October 1900 he transferred from the Dublin Fusiliers to the newly formed Irish Guards, and he was promoted major in that regiment in September 1901. In May 1903 he took up the very congenial appointment of Commandant M.I. School at Longmoor in the Aldershot Command.

He received the brevet of colonel in February 1905, and in March 1906 went back into Aldershot, first as A.A.G. and then G.S.O.1 of the 2nd Division. Here he remained until February 1910 during a busy period, for the reforms and reorganizations instituted after the South African War were taking shape. In March 1906 he had reached the substantive rank of colonel, and in 1910 was created C.B. In October of that year he was appointed to command the New Zealand Military Forces, and when, after the outbreak of the First Great War, New Zealand proceeded to put a contingent in the field his selection to command the New Zealand and Australian Division—to which Australia contributed one brigade—was viewed with satisfaction in the Dominions. He had been created K.C.M.G. earlier in 1914 and was promoted major-general in October.

His division was brought to Egypt in Birdwood's [q.v.] Anzac Corps and, after being employed on defending the Suez Canal early in 1915, served all through the Gallipoli campaign from the April landing until the evacuation of Anzac at the end of the year. In the latter operation Godley was in command of the Anzac Corps, having succeeded Birdwood when the Dardanelles Army was designated a part of the Mediterranean Expeditionary Force and Birdwood appointed to command it.

The Australian and New Zealand Forces were expanded and reorganized in Egypt at the beginning of 1916, and Godley was then given command of the II Anzac Corps, formed at first of one complete New Zealand and one Australian division. The corps was sent to France and went into the line during the early summer in Flanders; but the New Zealanders were detached to take part in the Battles of the Somme. Being in the Second Army it was not until 1917 that Godley's command took part in a big offensive. In June of that year, however, the corps—then consisting of the New Zealand, one British, and two Australian divisions—took part in the successful Battle of Messines, and it had desperate fighting near Polygon Wood during "Third Ypres".

Godley, who had been created K.C.B. in 1916 and promoted lieutenant-general in June 1918, was mentioned 11 times in dispatches during the war. He proved himself a reliable and active corps commander, his tall, spare figure being well known to his troops. In March 1919, when demobilization was proceeding, he was given a corps command in the Army of the Rhine, but was brought home in November to take up the appointment of Military Secretary at the War Office. In March 1922, however, he obtained far more congenial employment as G.O.C. Rhine Army, coming home again two years later when the British forces in Germany were reduced. He had been promoted general in February 1923 and in June 1924 was given the Southern Command, an arduous and responsible appointment as Salisbury Plain was the chief centre of experimental training with mechanized forces. He was appointed A.D.C. General to his Majesty in July 1925.

After his tenure of command at Salisbury expired in June 1928 he was unemployed until October, when he went to Gibraltar as Governor and Commander-in-Chief, being created G.C.B. It says much for his mental alertness that in the summer of 1932, at the age of 65, and being the senior General in the Army, he passed the preliminary examination in Spanish, one of his fellow students being his own A.D.C. He vacated the Gibraltar command in October 1932.

Godley had been Colonel of the Royal Ulster Rifles since July 1922, and his New Zealand associations were preserved by his Colonelcies of the Otago Mounted Rifles and the North Auckland Regiment. He married in 1898 Louisa Marion, daughter of Robert Fowler, Rahinston, co. Meath, and sister of Lieutenant-General Sir John Fowler who was Director of Army Signals at G.H.Q. in France during the First World War.

Lady Godley died in 1939. There were no children of the marriage.

March 8, 1957.

Dr. G. J. van Heuven Goedhart—See **Heuven.**

Walter Goehr, a composer and conductor of high accomplishment and versatility, died at the age of 57 on December 4, 1960, shortly after conducting a performance of *Messiah* by a combined choir of Sheffield Philharmonic Chorus and Sheffield Choral Society with the Hallé Orchestra in Sheffield City Hall.

Concert audiences in Britain got from Goehr distinguished conducting in his chosen specialist fields of early orchestral music and the works of contemporary composers, British as well as foreign. Among the composers particularly in Goehr's debt here Michael Tippett stands out, with first performances including the Concerto for Double String Orchestra and *A Child of Our Time.* The modern works that he tirelessly presented appeared, moreover, always in a close relationship to the great traditions of the past.

Goehr was also responsible for the first performances of Britten's *Serenade* and Seiber's [q.v.] *Ulysses;* his London concerts during the Second World War were famous for their enterprise as for the fiery performances that Goehr gave as conductor.

Born in Berlin on May 28, 1903, as the son of a prosperous businessman, Goehr studied at the Berlin Academy of Fine Arts, where for a time he was a pupil of Arnold Schönberg [q.v.].

After his arrival in England from Germany Goehr spent the years from 1933 to 1939 as musical director of the Columbia and His Master's Voice gramophone companies. From 1945 to 1948 he was conductor of the B.B.C. Theatre Orchestra.

During the thirties and forties Goehr cultivated a special talent for good light music with the Orchestre Raymonde, which he formed and conducted under the pseudonym of George Walter. Since that time Goehr's services had been much in demand by leading orchestras all over Europe and America. His appearances in London of latter years often followed lengthy and highly successful conducting tours abroad.

Together with the works of many modern composers who stand in his debt, the renewed understanding in this country of Monteverdi's work owes much to Goehr's devoted performances of the *Vespers* and the opera *L'Incoronazione di Poppea.* Here Goehr's talents were also applied as a musicologist, showing a lively scholarship in the version of the *Vespers* he specially prepared which was first performed in Rome in 1956.

This version was undertaken after several performances of the *Vespers* which Goehr had conducted in London during and after the war. Goehr was also a keen and imaginative interpreter of Bach; these performances were marked by knowledge of eighteenth-century practice mingled with lively heterodoxy. A broadcast of Bach's B minor Mass under his direction is still remembered for its abundant surprises, always stimulating and always arrived at for musicianly reasons, however disputable. Earlier Goehr had collaborated with Matyas Seiber in an orchestral transcription of *The Art of Fugue* which was published and several times performed. He joined distinguished company with an orchestration of Mussorgsky's *Pictures at an Exhibition.*

His own music assimilated much of his master Schönberg's teaching into a personal style of taut intellectual vigour and integrity. He had begun composing back in his Berlin days while at the Reinhardt Theatre, and it ranged from chamber music to works of symphonic proportions. He reached perhaps the widest public with his music to the British film *Great Expectations,* which he not only composed but conducted.

Goehr did not hold any official teaching post, but not a few young musicians became his disciples, later to tell how much of musicianship, both practical and theoretical they owed to him. His son, Alexander, is himself a young composer of remarkable achievement.

December 5, 1960.

Dr. Walter Goetz, the historian, died in Germany a few days before his ninety-first birthday in November 1958. He was active until the last months of his life. His autobiography, *Historiker in Meiner Zeit,* appeared in 1957, with a delightful introduction by President Heuss*.

Walter Goetz was born in Leipzig on November 11, 1867. He established his reputation as editor of the *Beiträge Zur Geschichte des Mittelalters und der Renaissance* (1907 ff.) and of the *Archiv Für Kulturgeschichte* (1911 until his death). His studies of the Italian Renaissance encouraged him to relate what was his favourite period to the history of world civilization.

In 1915, as successor to Lamprecht, with whom he had no great sympathy, Goetz became head of the Institute of Historical Research in Leipzig, where he remained until 1933. Between 1920 and 1930 he was a member of Reichstag, standing for the Democratic Party. In 1927 he became president of the German Dante Society, which he piloted through the Nazi period.

Like Acton, Goetz sought to expound his concept of universal history and, aided by the brilliant scholars he gathered at Leipzig, he became editor-in-chief of the *Propyläen Weltsgeschichte* (10 vols. 1929-33). In volume one the inspiration of the Cambridge Modern History was freely acknowledged. Unlike the pioneer in this field, the German universal history was richly illustrated with both documents and pictures, many in full colour, all superbly printed by the Berlin house of Ullstein.

After the Nazis came to power in the 1930s Goetz was forced to withdraw from his academic and political activities. In retirement he collected material for his last major work, a biography of the Emperor William II, his principal sources being the former Secretary of State, Richard von Kühlmann, and the Crown Prince Rupprecht of Bavaria. The manuscript is ready for publication and will be seen through the press by Dr. Helmut Goetz, an historian like his father.

The Nazi régime having collapsed, Goetz and his lifelong friend, Friedrich Meinecke, [q.v.], aged 80, made gallant and successful efforts to salvage the historical associations from the wreck of German academic society. As the only German historian available in whom both the British and American authorities placed absolute trust, he became president of the Historical Commission of the Bavarian Academy, and was put in charge of the *Monumenta Germanica Historica.* German historical scholarship owes its survival to the combined efforts, in Berlin of Meinecke, who died in 1954, and in Munich of Goetz.

November 18, 1958.

Dr. Oliver St. John Gogarty, a surgeon who held a high place in his profession and a moving spirit in Irish literary and artistic circles from the early days of the Irish literary renaissance at the beginning of the century, died in New York on September 22, 1957. He was 79.

Poet, novelist, wit, classicist, a member of the Irish Free State Senate, Dr. Gogarty, it is fair to say, was famed above all else for his Celtic exuberance and high-spirited contrariness. The lavish, witty, and delicately malicious force of his personality and the brilliantly intimate part he played over many years in the social and intellectual life of Anglo-Irish Dublin are to be discovered in the pages of *Hail and Farewell* and of the other volumes covering the period of George Moore's residence in Dublin, and also, though less transparently, in James Joyce's *Ulysses* which he enters disguised as Buck Mulligan; while to the sum of this and other evidence from literary sources Gogarty himself added a revealing and most amusing self-portrait in a celebrated *chronique scandaleuse, As I Was Going Down Sackville Street.* This was probably the best as well as the most entertaining book he wrote. The rest of his work, elegant or brilliant though it is in patches, is more significant in illustration of the author's vivacious personality than as literature.

Oliver St. John Gogarty was born on August 17, 1878, and was educated at Stonyhurst, and at Trinity College, Dublin, where he studied medicine. A notable athlete, he held a great many cycling records and preserved throughout his life a keen appetite for physical exercise and adventure; in his fifties he learned to pilot an aeroplane. He took his M.D. degree, became F.R.C.S.I., and practised both in Dublin and in London. In politics, or in Irish politics, he was a Nationalist of distinctly moderate views; the establishment of the Free State was darkened for him by the lengthening shadow of de Valera*, and in time he came to look back to the Union with unaffected wistfulness. A lifelong friend of Arthur Griffith, he was nominated to the new Senate in 1922 and served until its dissolution in 1936.

He had published a volume of *Poems and Plays* in 1920, but had to await a lucky misadventure in 1923 before a degree of literary as distinct from social fame descended upon him. Early in that year he was kidnapped outside his house in Dublin by armed Republicans and, in darkness and to the accompaniment of shooting, escaped by plunging into the flooded Liffey. In doing so he made the Liffey the Socratic vow of two swans should he land in safety on the opposite bank. *An Offering of Swans,* a slim volume of lyrical poems, their graceful sentiment diversified by a nice distillation of experience, appeared in the following year.

There was another book of poems, *Wild Apples,* in 1930, but not until 1937 was the celebrated Gogartian turn of wit and anecdote presented to the world at large in *As I Was Going Down Sackville Street.* Gay, paradoxical, mischievous, mildly Rabelaisian, and exuberantly instructive, the book (which became the subject of a libel action in Dublin) made entertaining enough reading. Next year Gogarty brought out a volume of travel, historical commentary, and idiosyncratic argument, *I Follow St. Patrick,* and another book of poems, mostly of a rhetorical cast, *Others to Adorn.* In *Tumbling in the Hay* (1939) he recalled, in effervescent high spirits and with characteristic digressions, his student years in Dublin. After that he lightly turned his hand to fiction, producing in *Going Native* (1941), *Mad Grandeur* (1944), and *Mr. Petunia* (1946), entertaining if not altogether harmonious exercises in lavishly romantic and buoyantly discursive narrative. In 1954 he issued a second instalment of his rambling and slightly outrageous memoirs, *It Isn't this Time of Year at All.*

He married, in 1906, Martha, daughter of Bernard Duane. There were two sons and a daughter of the marriage. For the last 10 years or so he had lived in New York.

September 23, 1957.

The death on July 28, 1952 in London of **Sir Harcourt Gold,** O.B.E., at the age of 76 is a loss which will be felt keenly by oarsmen throughout Britain and, indeed, by many in other lands.

Harcourt Gilbey Gold was born on May 3, 1876, and was educated at Eton and Magdalen College, Oxford. "Tarka", as he was to all rowing men, stroked three Eton crews to victory in the Ladies' Plate in 1893, 1894, and 1895. From 1896 to 1899 he stroked Leander in the Grand, winning three times, and he also won the Stewards' twice, for Leander in 1898 and for Magdalen in 1899. At Oxford he won the Boat Race three times, and was president of the O.U.B.C. in 1898.

This brilliant, if not long, active rowing career was followed by a longer period as a coach, of which the peak was, perhaps, his coaching of the famous Leander crew which beat the Belgians in the Olympic Regatta at Henley in 1908, and by a still longer period as administrator. He became a steward of Henley Royal Regatta in 1909 and a member of the committee of management in 1919. In 1945 he succeeded His Honour C. M. Pitman as chairman of the Henley Stewards, and in 1952 became the regatta's first president. For many years he represented the O.U.B.C. on the committee of the Amateur Rowing Association and became its chairman in 1948. In 1949 he was knighted for his services to rowing. He will be remembered as one of the most approachable and sympathetic of rowing's elder statemen.

He married in 1902 Helen Beatrice, the only daughter of Dr. T. J. Maclagan, who survives him together with a son and a daughter.

July 29, 1952.

Avrom Goldbogen—See **Todd.**

Louis Golding, the novelist and essayist, died in hospital in London on August 9, 1958 at the age of 62.

He was best known to the general public as the author of *Magnolia Street* and of the *Tales of the Silver Sisters,* but he was rather more than a "popular novelist" for some of his work is of more than a transitory interest. He was among other things an apt interpreter of British Jewry to its friends and neighbours. An eager and sensitive observer, he wrote with much skill and frequently considerable power. At times he could be delightful, at others almost painful in his realism.

His zest for life was equalled by his prolific output and the catholicity of his interests. He lectured, wrote travel sketches, scripts for films—including that of *Theirs is the Glory,* which was about the Arnhem operations—verse, short stories, and books on boxing. In sport, indeed, he had more than a passing interest and in 1955 wrote a charming piece for *The Times* on cricket on Corfu, and the Lord Byron C.C.

Louis Golding was born in Manchester in November 1895, the third son of Jewish parents, Philip and Yetta Golding, who had recently arrived from Cherkassy, on the Dnieper. He was educated at the Manchester Grammar School, and at Queen's College, Oxford, where he had won scholarships. In his early days he travelled a great deal in the Mediterranean countries and Near East. He began to write while still at the university.

In 1919 he published a book of poems on the war, and in 1920 his first novel, *Forward from Babylon.* It was the story of a Russian Jew exiled to a northern town in England, and was a strong if somewhat unpleasant book. *Sea Coast of Bohemia* (1923) was a satirical novel, humorous, fertile in invention, and well written. After *Sunward* (1924), which was a book of travel sketches, came *Day of Atonement* (1925), another novel, and the best up to that date. It was again on a Jewish subject and showed quick, sensitive psychology and deep feeling.

Store of Ladies and *Miracle Boy,* which both appeared in 1927, were unusual, and well up to the author's standard. They were followed by *The Prince or Somebody* (1929) and *Give up Your Lovers* (1930). The latter was upon the old theme of love between Jew and Gentile, and was concerned with the further adventures of Philip Massel, the main character in *Forward from Babylon.*

In 1932 he published *Magnolia Street.* It was his most remarkable work, the story of a typical street in a provincial city inhabited on one side by Jews and on the other by Gentiles. He viewed it as a beehive is sometimes inspected, through glass. It was lavish and virile, and while markedly pro-Semitic in sympathy, provided much entertainment to the reader. In 1934 it was produced as a play at the Adelphi Theatre. Golding and A. A. Rawlinson, who collaborated with him, were almost overwhelmed by the abundance of their material; but the impression of crowd vitality which was essential to it was conveyed successfully. It was his only play; but he continued to write one or even two books each year.

Five Silver Daughters (1934) was followed in the same year by *The Doomington Wanderer,* a collection of short stories. *The Camberwell Beauty* (1935) was a holiday book, and *The Pursuer* (1936) also fell below the usual level. *The Dance Goes On* (1937) was set in Russia. In 1938 *The Jewish Problem,* a Penguin book, appeared. It was a scholarly work, and traced the process by which anti-Semitism has worked into the fabric of European thought. It showed him deeply concerned about the influence of German propaganda beyond the Reich.

Mr. Emmanuel (1939) had another Jew-Nazi theme and was made into a film in which Felix Aylmer gave a fine performance. In the following year there appeared *The World I Knew* which, though not designed as an autobiography, disclosed much about himself.

In the 1940s and in the present decade he continued to show his versatility; *We Shall Eat Again,* for example, was a wine and food anthology which he edited jointly with André Simon, and *The Glory of Elsie Silver* (1946) was a novel which had the destruction of the Warsaw Ghetto as its theme.

Then in 1955 came *Goodbye to Ithaca.* All his love for the classical world shone out in this modern Odyssey; a labour of love, it won high praise. It was often said of Golding that he wrote too much; that he should have ridden his talent with a tighter rein, but probably the truth was that with his particular gifts, his temperament, and his warmth of feeling it was a case of "write he must".

He married in 1956 Annie Wintrobe.

August 11, 1958.

By the death on February 18, 1954 of **E. P. Goldschmidt,** at the age of 66, the international antiquarian book trade has lost one of its most distinguished members, and certainly its most learned.

Ernst Philip Goldschmidt, of Dutch nationality, was born in Vienna on December 1, 1887. He passed from the K.u.K. Akademisches Gymnasium to Trinity College, Cambridge, in 1905. There he came into the orbit of Gustave David, the well-known bookseller, and the ardent group of young book collectors who were at Cambridge during the first decade of the century. When he went down in 1909 Goldschmidt had already acquired the passionate love of old books and manuscripts which he retained throughout his life, and he printed privately an annotated catalogue of 75 of his best books as a leaving present to his fellow collectors.

On his return to the Continent his talents came to the notice of Konrad Haebler, the incunabulist, and at intervals between 1913 and 1917 Goldschmidt visited the monastic libraries of Austria, collecting material for the *Gesamtkatalog der Wiegendrucke.* Through the systematic handling of thousands of fifteenth-century books he gained valuable experience, and the connexions which he made with librarians and collectors proved of great service when he later turned bookseller: for some of his finest purchases were made from the Austrian monasteries, in particular from Melk.

After some war work with the Dutch Red Cross he acquired in 1917 the Viennese bookselling and auctioneering business of Gilhofer and Ranschburg. Goldschmidt raised the business to a status which could compare with that of any bookseller in Europe. He was able to take advantage of the favourable situation which arose when the Soviet Government, in search of foreign currency, put on to the market the confiscated libraries of the aristocracy, but Goldschmidt's personal fortune was hard hit by the inflation. In 1923 he resolved to return to England and to set up a bookselling business there. In this project he was encouraged by his life-long friend and customer, Sir Stephen Gaselee. He acquired premises at 45, Old Bond Street, from which address he issued over 100 scholarly catalogues, many of which have found a permanent place on the reference shelves of libraries.

In 1928 appeared his best known book, *Gothic and Renaissance Bookbindings,* a great advance on any work hitherto published on the subject, full of original material and ingenious conjecture. In 1943 his *Medieval Texts and Their First Appearance in Print* was published by the Bibliographical Society, of which he was a vice-president and member of the council. His *Printed Book of the Renaissance,* 1950, related humanism to the spread of the printing press, a theme which he had elaborated in the Sandars Lectures in Bibliography which he was to have delivered at Cambridge in 1954 on the First Cambridge press in its European setting. These lectures amount to a critical estimate of early humanism, in which subject Goldschmidt took a keen interest. The text, fortunately, was completed and will be published shortly. He was a contributor to bibliographical journals and frequently wrote for *The Times Literary Supplement.* Goldschmidt's scholarship sometimes suffered from the degree of haste in which he often wrote; but if not always impeccable in matters of detail, it was distinguished by enthusiasm, new ideas, breadth of vision, and a truly international approach.

He had other interests beside bookselling. As a member of the banking family which had joined in the Dutch banking firm of Bischoffsheim and Goldschmidt, he easily took to the study of currency and international commerce. In 1942 Goldschmidt, under the pseudonym of "Sarpedon", published through Macmillan *England's Service,* a statement of Britain's trading situation and a forecast of its economic future. The publication brought correspondence, to the unknown writer's pleasure, from Dr. William Temple, Archbishop of Canterbury, Lord Keynes, with whom Goldschmidt had been on close terms since Cambridge days, and officials of the Bank of England.

Most of his work was done at night, fortified by draughts of black coffee. He was an unorthodox bookseller. "Bookselling", he said, "would be an ideal existence if there were no customers". His ideal customer was one who "lived 2,000 miles away and occasionally ordered by postcard a very expensive book". No bookseller's catalogues were given more care than Goldschmidt's. His learned annotations contributed much to the education of librarians all over the world. A highly unorthodox item was his *Catalogue No. 100,* which was a list, with notes, of all the rarest books that had passed through his hands, and were now on the shelves of discriminating collectors and libraries.

Goldschmidt was a lover of good talk. His friends were always assured of a warm welcome at Bond Street, where they would be regaled with a flow of fascinating reminiscence. He possessed in a high degree the typically Viennese qualities of gaiety, wit, and cynicism, tinged in his case with a strain of the melancholy to which intellectual Jews are particularly prone. He was unmarried.

February 19, 1954.

Stephen Gooden, C.B.E., R.A., perhaps the most accomplished of the several artists of his generation who took part in the revival of line engraving, died at his home at Chesham Bois, Buckinghamshire, on September 21, 1955 at the age of 62.

Most of his work was in the form of book illustration and decoration, with special attention to the bookplate. Gooden, for example, was responsible for the bookplates for the Royal Library at Windsor, the designs for which, in duodecimo, folio, and quarto sizes, were shown at the Royal Academy exhibition of 1938, the year after his election as A.R.A. He later designed the bookplate of Queen Elizabeth.

From the nature of his gift and its usual application, Gooden's name was more familiar to booklovers, particularly collectors of fine editions, than to frequenters of art galleries, where small things are apt either to be overlooked or else, in mixed collections, left to the last, when attention has become jaded by adjustment of the eye to works on a larger scale. He was, however, a member of the Royal Society of Miniature Painters, Sculptors, and Gravers, which has been called a "Royal Academy in Little", and at its exhibitions, as at those of the Royal Society of Painter-Etchers and Engravers, of which he was also a member, where everything is on more or less the same scale, the high quality of his work could be, and was, properly appreciated.

Gooden was a "literary" artist in a better sense than that usually intended. He had not only a keen sense of the form of the book and the possibilities of its page for decoration but also a nice appreciation of the quality, as distinct from the factual meaning, of its content. Whether by choice or good fortune his name became associated with literature of the better kind, and he had a special turn for the packed significance of the fable. Among the books he illustrated were Aesop's and La Fontaine's Fables.

He was particularly happy interpreting the mood that is called "elegiac", and a charming example of his work in this vein is to be found facing the dedication of George Moore's *Ulick and Soracha,* one of the books he decorated for the Nonesuch Press. Another great success of his was with the *Book of Revelations,* two designs for which, "John at Patmos" and "The Rider on the Pale Horse", appeared in the Academy exhibition of 1939. Gooden was not a particularly expressive draughtsman, being inclined to literalness in his rendering of form, but he made up for this by his imaginative grasp of the subject to be illustrated, inventiveness and concentration in design, feeling for the page, and purity of execution.

Gooden, who was a descendant of the engraver Henry Linton, was born in 1892 and educated at Rugby and the Slade School. He started as an etcher, and an early and semi-humorous work of his, "The Ark", executed in 1912, is remembered from an overheard train conversation between Sir Sydney Cockerell* and the late Sir Edwin Lutyens. Sir Sydney had been praising Gooden, and Lutyens asked: "Can he do timber construction?" The answer was, emphatically, "Yes", with the etching produced as evidence. During the 1914-18 War Gooden served as a trooper in the 19th Hussars and R.E. sapper.

He began to engrave, as distinct from etching, in 1923, and made his first appearance at the Royal Academy in 1935 with a line engraving of "St. George". Two years later he was elected A.R.A., becoming full R.A. in 1946. In 1942 he was created C.B.E.

An Iconography of the Engravings of Stephen Gooden, with a preface and introduction by Campbell Dodgson, was published in 1945. The engravings are classified, with chronological order preserved within each class, and there is an appendix of "Juvenilia and Miscellanea". Gooden is represented at the British Museum, the Victoria and Albert Museum, and the Fitzwilliam Museum, Cambridge.

He married in 1925 Mona, daughter of Dr. G. Price, of Bray, Wicklow, who survives him.

September 22, 1955.

Harry Stuart Goodhart-Rendel, C.B.E., the architect and critic, died in London on June 21, 1959, at the age of 71.

It is not easy to decide whether Goodhart-Rendel was most distinguished as architect, critic, or wit. He came into architecture almost by accident. He was studying music at Cambridge when his grandfather, Lord Rendel, showed him the design of a building in which he was interested, expressing dissatisfaction with it. The young man sketched out a new design, which was adopted, and the pleasure he had found in the performance caused him to change his profession. He set up in practice as an architect at the age of 23 and quickly made a reputation which, in 1937, led to his being the youngest architect then to have filled the office of President of the Royal Institute of British Architects.

He was born in 1887, the son of Harry Chester Goodhart and the Hon. Rose Ellen, eldest daughter of Lord Rendel, of Hatchlands. He assumed by royal licence the additional name of Rendel in 1902. From Eton he went to Trinity College, Cambridge, where he studied music with Sir Donald Tovey. During the 1914-18 War he served in the Grenadier Guards, and again in the last war when his duties at Caterham Barracks prompted him to write *The Squad Drill Primer* (which is just what its title declares it to be). He felt a strong attachment to the Brigade of Guards.

He was on the council of the R.I.B.A. from 1926 and was president from 1937 to 1939. An excellent portrait of him by Augustus John*, painted for the council room of the R.I.B.A., was one of the outstanding works in the Royal Academy exhibition of 1940. In 1936 he was appointed Director of the Architectural Association School of Architecture, but resigned a year or two later. From 1933 to 1936 he was Slade Professor of Fine Art, Oxford University. An accomplished musician and author of several light compositions, Goodhart-Rendel was vice-president of the Royal Academy of Music. He was also a governor of Sadler's Wells from 1934, and president of the Guild of Catholic Artists and Craftsmen (1946-52).

Goodhart-Rendel was an illuminating critic not only of architecture but of the other arts and of life in general. His addresses as Slade Professor were full of suggestions that were not the less valuable for being open to question, and his public utterances always gained attention by their combination of wisdom and impish asides. Firm as he was on the side of tradition and for preserving the architectural beauties of the past, he was alive to the danger of sentimental revivals. A man of exceedingly graceful manners, he delighted in lulling an opponent and then pouncing suddenly with a critical objection in an epigrammatic phrase. His appearance lent itself to this manoeuvre. Some chronic disorder gave him a startlingly grey complexion, so that he looked at the point of collapse, which left the unwary unprepared for his vivacity and agility when he got up to speak.

As an architect he was perhaps most successful in his churches, a class of building in which he had a great deal of experience, both in designing and in restorations and additions. Two important examples may be quoted: the church of St. Wilfrid, Elm Grove, Brighton, and the new Prinknash Abbey church, near Gloucester, of which the foundation stone was laid by Cardinal Hinsley in 1939. Both churches are highly original without seeming to aim at novelty.

On the analogy of "stripped Classic", Prinknash Abbey church, of which little more than the foundations have yet been built, may be described as an essay in "stripped Gothic". It has the unusual feature of a circular central tower, and the lines of the building are subtly curved in sympathy in a truly "musical" design.

A good example of Goodhart-Rendel's secular work is Hay's Wharf, near the south end of London Bridge. Other works of his that deserve mention are the Eton Boys' and Old Boys' Club, Hackney Wick, the Princess Elizabeth Hospital for Children, Banstead, and the cloister which forms the Brigade of Guards war memorial in Birdcage Walk.

Among his publications *English Architecture Since the Regency* (1953) is the most important, founded on lectures delivered in Oxford in 1934.

He was working on his memoirs shortly before he died.

June 22, 1959.

Eugene Goossens, senior, who died on July 31, 1958 in hospital in London at the age of 91, was the second of a dynasty of conductors who came from Belgium and settled in England.

The son of the first Eugene Goossens, who was born at Bruges in 1845 and died at Liverpool in 1906, and the father of Sir Eugene Goossens* and of Leon, the oboist, and of Marie and Sidonie, the harpists, Eugene the second was an operatic conductor who served many companies for more than 30 years round the turn of the century. He was to be seen in London concert halls up to this year, a venerable and affectionately regarded figure, whenever Sir Eugene Goossens was visiting this country or introducing one of his own compositions. Sir Eugene's autobiography *Overture and Beginners* gives a graphic picture of the family's musical life in Liverpool and London about 1900.

Eugene Goossens, senior, was born at Bordeaux on January 28, 1867, and went to England with his father in 1873. He received his musical education partly at the Brussels Conservatoire and partly at the Royal Academy of Music in London which he entered in 1891 after a period of service under his father with the Carl Rosa Opera Company, as violinist, répétiteur and sub-conductor. From 1899 to 1915 he was principal conductor of the Carl Rosa Company and with them established his reputation as an operatic conductor of sterling merit.

Earlier he had conducted for other touring companies, including the Moody-Manners, and in 1926 he joined the British National Opera Company as conductor.

He married a Carl Rosa singer, Annie Cook, who was the daughter of a well-known bass singer, T. Aynsley Cook. She died in 1946.

August 2, 1958.

Sir Home Gordon, BT., who died suddenly on September 9, 1956 at his home at Rottingdean less than a month before he would have celebrated his eighty-fifth birthday, was the historian *par excellence* of the cricket of his time.

His time, indeed, was long, for his memory went back to the match between the Gentlemen of England and the Australians, played at Princes' (now Cadogan Square) in June 1878. The feature of a low-scoring struggle, in which no batsman made more than 30, was that the crowd surged into the playing space and, as Sir Home Gordon wrote in *The Times* in May 1956: "I, a startled child in his seventh year, was removed. It was an odd commencement to my prolonged career of an unwearying onlooker". The last phrase is the keynote for it has been said of him that he had done everything connected with first-class cricket except play it, and he claimed that he had seen every Test match ever played at Lord's.

He took to cricket journalism immediately after he left Eton in 1887 and Lord Hawke once described him as "the greatest statistician of the day, nay, of all time".

As a small boy he was privileged to hear the pronouncements of recognised pundits on matches at Lord's, and his modest address and charming manners ensured that all doors were open to him. He was the guest of Ranjitsinhji at the Delhi Durbar, and sat with Ferguson as official scorer in a big match. He was a member or honorary member of many clubs, and for his services to Sussex he was awarded a county cap—an old one belonging to Arthur Gilligan [d. 1976]. From him even Sir Pelham Warner* had something to learn—about the wicket-keeping of Murdoch. Sometimes even the selectors deferred to him, for as he said in his *Background of Cricket,* which was published in 1939: "It is an admitted fact that my persistent advocacy had a good deal to do with Arthur's [A. E. R. Gilligan's] obtaining the captaincy to Australia".

An intimate friend of Lord Hawke, Sir Home Gordon collaborated with him in his numerous and effective efforts for the well-being of professional players. Indeed, the catalogue of his services to cricket is almost inexhaustible.

Almost the last thing he wrote about cricket was the article, to which reference has already been made, and which appeared in *The Times* on May 10, 1956. Its pleasing style and its condensation of an immense amount of information into a small space is a fitting swan song to a life dedicated to all the facets of a single recreation.

Home Seton Charles Montague Gordon was born on September 30, 1871, the only son of Sir Home Seton Gordon, eleventh baronet. He was educated at Eton and succeeded his father as twelfth baronet in 1906. He was for many years chairman of the publishing firm of Williams and Norgate, and a director of the Electric Supply Corporation until the industry was nationalized. During the 1914-18 War he worked in the Ministry of National Service and later in the Air Ministry. He was president of the London Club Cricketers' Conference in 1917-18 and chairman of the Sports Conference in 1919. In the same year he was elected to the committee of the Sunday Games Association. His long association with Sussex culminated with his election as honorary match secretary in 1943, honorary secretary in 1944, and president in 1948.

His earliest book on cricket came out in 1902 and was entitled *Cricket Form at a Glance.* He published a biography of W. G. Grace in 1919, *Cricket Form at a Glance in this Century* in 1924, *Eton v. Harrow at Lord's* in 1926, the *Sussex Cricket Handbook* in 1929, *Lancashire Cricket* in 1930, *Notts Cricket Annual* in 1932, *Kent Cricket Annual* in the next year, *Essex Cricket Annual* in 1935, *Cricket Form at a Glance for Sixty Years* in 1938, *Background for Cricket* in 1939, *Facts and Figures about Essex Cricket* in 1948, *Sussex Cricket Annual* in 1949, a *History of Sussex County Cricket* in 1950. He also contributed to the *Encyclopaedia Britannica* and many periodicals.

He married first in 1897 Edith Susan, daughter of R. J. Leeson-Marshall. She died in 1945 and he married secondly in 1953 Katharine, the youngest daughter of the late J. E. Hornsby. There were no children of either marriage and the baronetcy becomes extinct.

September 10, 1956.

Sir Gordon Gordon-Taylor, K.B.E., C.B., F.R.C.S., one of the most brilliant surgeons of his generation, died in hospital in London on September 3, 1960 after a road accident. He was 82.

He came from Aberdeen, where he received his early education at Gordon's College, and later at Aberdeen University where, in 1898, he took his M.A. with honours. In after life he used to look back with pleasure to his early study of the classics and often quoted them in his writings and addresses. His continuing familiarity with them brought him in later life to the chairmanship of the Horatian Society.

His family moved to London and he took up the study of medicine at the Middlesex Hospital at a time when Henry Morris, Bland-Sutton, and Pearce Gould were at the height of their reputation. No wonder that surgery drew him like a magnet. He took the Gold Medal in Anatomy at the Intermediate M.B. Examination and qualified in 1903. Then, while doing other duties, he worked in his spare time and took the B.Sc. Lond. with first class honours in anatomy in 1904. In 1906 he achieved the M.S. Lond. and the F.R.C.S. Eng.

His first hospital appointment was that of surgeon to outpatients at the Royal Northern Hospital but when a vacancy occurred on the surgical staff of the Middlesex Hospital he was chosen to fill it. Soon his bold yet careful surgery and his great operative skill became widely known. He seemed to live for surgery and spent his holidays in visiting surgical clinics on the Continent and in other parts of Britain ever on the look-out for new techniques and new ideas, and ever ready to adopt what was best in any of them.

In the 1914-18 War he served as a major in the R.A.M.C. and for a time acted as consulting surgeon to the Fourth Army in France. His remarkable skill in successfully carrying out multiple resections of intestine was noteworthy. Gordon-Taylor spent the next 20 years in extremely busy surgical practice. His reputation drew many to the Middlesex Hospital to watch and profit by his operative technique, and also caused him to be much in demand in private practice. He was main consulting surgeon to many outlying smaller hospitals round London. He also examined in anatomy at the primary examination for the F.R.C.S. and even travelled to Australia to officiate at the examination held there. When war broke out in 1939 Gordon-Taylor offered his services to the Royal Navy and was appointed consulting surgeon with the temporary rank of surgeon rear-admiral. In that capacity he did invaluable work.

In 1932 Gordon-Taylor was elected to the council of the Royal College of Surgeons and from that time onward took a great interest in its deliberations and work, acting as vice-president in 1941-43. In 1929 and again in 1942 and 1944 he was a Hunterian Professor at the college. Though a quiet man and a good listener he could, when occasion demanded, speak eloquently and forcibly, and he was much in demand for ceremonial addresses. In 1938 he gave the Balfour lecture at Toronto, and in 1940 delivered the first Moynihan lecture at Leeds, and in 1942 gave the Bradshaw lecture at the College of Surgeons. He also gave at various times the Thomas Vicary, Harveian, Lettsomian, Hunterian, Cavendish, and Mitchell Banks lectures; and he gave the Sheen memorial lecture in the University of Wales in 1949, the John Fraser memorial lecture at Edinburgh in 1957, and diamond jubilee oration of the Royal Australian College of Surgeons in 1958.

Both during and after the Second World War he travelled much, especially to North America and Australia. In 1941 he visited and lectured in the United States and Canada, was made an honorary fellow of the American College of Surgeons and honorary LL.D. at Toronto, and later an honorary LL.D. of Melbourne and honorary Sc.D. of Cambridge.

In 1943 he was one of the representative British surgeons chosen to visit Russia and on that occasion was delegated to confer the honorary fellowship of the College of Surgeons on the famous Russian surgeons Judin and Burdenko. He took the chair of surgery at Harvard for two complimentary periods, and in 1947 he visited Australia to deliver the Syme oration to the Royal College of Surgeons there and to participate in conducting a special course of post-graduate surgery at Melbourne. He was president of the Medical Society of London in 1941-42, of the Royal Society of Medicine in 1944-46, and of the Association of Surgeons of Great Britain and Ireland in 1944-45; and an honorary member of many foreign medical academies.

Two signal honours which came to him later in life were the gold medal of the Royal Society of Medicine in 1956 and, in March 1958, a special issue of the *British Journal of Surgery* to mark his eightieth birthday.

He did not write voluminously but something of his skill may be judged by reading his monograph on *The Dramatic in Surgery.* He inspired those who worked with him and many of his former house-surgeons and registrars are now well known. Though his main work was abdominal he was in the best sense of the term a general surgeon. He was a good friend and a generous host. His name is one of the few which are known and spoken of with admiration and respect wherever surgeons meet together.

He married Florence Mary, F.R.S.A., F.Z.S., eldest daughter of the late John Pegrume. She died in 1949.

September 5, 1960.

Lady Mabell Gore—See **Airlie.**

The Right Rev. N. V. Gorton, D.D., Bishop of Coventry since 1943, died in hospital on November 30, 1955 at the age of 67.

He had been a schoolmaster for nearly 30 years when he was called upon to take up the heavy task of a bishop in circumstances which would have daunted many less stout-hearted men. Yet if to some his views appeared simple, and even naive, they manifested not only the strength of simplicity but also the firmness of a man of integrity and courage. He had learnt in his handling of boys that clarity of expression, based on absolute sincerity, was the most telling quality in anyone seeking to guide, and these qualities he had cultivated through his long experience in helping the young.

There was never any mistaking his meaning, and if sometimes he appeared to over-simplify the problems that all, lay and clergy alike, have to face during their lives, there could be no doubt that the opinions he expressed were the outcome of anxious thought by a man who had gone beyond the confines of conventional theology, even if he had not arrived at a consistent system that could effectively modify it.

One of his most strongly held tenets was that the breakdown of marriage was one of the greatest evils of the day, and he was unequivocally opposed to the remarriage of divorced persons in church. On the other hand he went so far as to ridicule as fantastic nonsense the popular idea that churchgoers ought not to drink, or swear, or put a shilling on a horse. The greatest grief of his last years was the inception of commercial television, in which he saw the Government handing over "an instrument of power to irresponsible and vested interests".

Neville Vincent Gorton was born in 1888, the son of the Rev. C. V. Gorton, a canon of Manchester. He was educated at Marlborough and from there he went with a classical exhibition to Balliol College, Oxford, where he won an Aubrey Moore scholarship. Ordained in 1914, he was appointed assistant chaplain at Sedbergh, where he remained until 1934, in due course becoming a housemaster. He was then appointed headmaster of Blundell's School, Tiverton, a later foundation than Sedbergh, but of very much the same character, so that his 20 years' experience in Yorkshire stood him in good stead in his new work in Devon.

His scholastic achievements, apart from theology, had been in the classics, and these he taught in a clear and attractive manner to the great benefit of his pupils. Valuable though this was, it was secondary to his influence over his boys in his character as a minister of the Church of England. As a chaplain he had always given much time and thought to the preparation of his sermons in chapel, which were short and to the point, giving encouragement to his listeners and impressing on them the simple virtues of loyalty to one another, sympathy with the less fortunate, courage, and devotion. He also gave much of his time to private talks with his boys, helping them to face their difficulties and giving advice which, though it might appear to be only for the occasion, turned out often to be a guiding light for the rest of their days.

Under his guidance Blundell's maintained all its old and proud traditions and, while other schools were suffering from reduced numbers and the need for retrenchment, it went on much as it had before. When war came in 1939 the school even increased its numbers, but difficulties arose through the departure of the younger members of the staff for war service and the difficulty of finding servants to carry on domestic work and gardening. The headmaster therefore introduced a system whereby all the boys had to take a regular share in domestic and gardening work. To facilitate this he had the whole school take meals in hall instead of in separate houses, so that the work of cooking and catering could be lessened by centralization.

He was consecrated Bishop of Coventry in St. Paul's Cathedral in 1943 and was enthroned in the ruins of Coventry Cathedral, which had been destroyed by enemy bombing some three years before. The cross carried in the bishop's procession was made of three large nails salvaged from the débris of the cathedral, and an oak seat placed on blocks of fallen masonry was his throne. The gaunt skeletons of the outer walls, the tower and the spire formed a grim reminder of the horrors England had faced and the hazards which lay ahead. As the new bishop entered the ruins, the provost told him that the edifice had been laid waste and its outward glories had departed. The bishop's typical reply was: "Our Lord has said: 'In the world ye shall have tribulation, but be of good cheer. I have overcome the world!' " It was a reply full of faith and hope—two words which summed up the bishop's whole outlook.

He was, as his career as a schoolmaster had already shown, no theoretical idealist. He spoke out plainly on the problems of the day. His views on marriage, on commercial television, on public houses, on betting, and on housing conditions were clear if at times they seemed a little simple. Yet he was firm that a great deal of accepted theology was abstract, inconsequent, and irrelevant and that the clergy as a whole required to do much new and anxious thinking.

When in 1944 he announced the proposals for the new cathedral, which had been designed by Sir Giles Gilbert Scott [q.v.], there were two striking innovations. The first was that the altar was in the centre of the building and the second was that the cathedral should be a Christian centre of service to the community in full partnership with the Free Churches. Of the altar he said: "It does not belong only to the clergy: it also belongs to the people. Therefore set it up in the middle of the church and let the people gather round it". His words on the Christian centre proposal were: "Eighty per cent of the people of Coventry are without membership of church or chapel . . . if they could see the cathedral standing for a new Christian leadership in an attack on all the problems we have to face together, they could be brought into the circle of Christ's action in Coventry".

His views in these matters met with a great deal of opposition. In [Sir] Basil Spence's [d.1976] later design the altar is in a more orthodox position. Gorton had the firmness born of utter conviction and was not prepared to modify his opinions in essentials, though he well understood the need for compromise and concession so long as the central principles were not impugned.

He married in 1926 Ethel Ingledew, daughter of Dr. Daggett, of Boroughbridge, and there were two sons and a daughter of the marriage.

December 1, 1955.

Klement Gottwald, President of the Czechoslovak Republic, died on March 14, 1953 at the age of 56.

Gottwald's career demonstrates the careful preparation and ruthless action manifested by the Moscow-trained communists. From the first Gottwald set himself against the bourgeois state created by Masaryk and Benes, and though when the crisis came at Munich he was one of the few to counsel resistance he later proved himself rather the tool of Moscow in Prague than a genuine Czechoslovak patriot, in spite of such "deviation" as his acceptance of an invitation to go to Paris in 1947 to consider the Marshall [q.v.] Plan and negotiate a Franco-Czechoslovak treaty. That move was vetoed by Moscow and in the course of the next year Gottwald succeeded Benes as President and thus eliminated the most illustrious of the survivors of the founders of the country. He had his troubles within his own party, as his quarrel with Zapotocky [q.v.] abundantly manifested. Finally, apparently to bolster up his position with Russia, he decided to sacrifice his old friend Slansky, who together with 13 alleged co-conspirators was arraigned. Eleven were executed and by this piece of judicial murder Gottwald demonstrated at once his subservience to a foreign Power and that Power's determination to dominate the affairs of her smaller neighbours.

Klement Gottwald was born of a peasant family at Dedice, Moravia, on St. Clement's Day, November 23, 1896. As a child he worked as a farm labourer and at the age of 12 he was sent by his parents to relatives in Vienna, to learn carpentry; there he joined the Czechoslovak Social Democratic Youth organization. He returned to Moravia in 1914 to follow his trade at Lipnik and later at Hranice until he became a conscript in an artillery regiment in Upper Austria in 1915. He was later transferred as "politically unreliable" to the Carpathian front, where he was wounded, and on his discharge from hospital in Vienna he was sent to Italy to take part in the campaign on the Piave; shortly afterwards he deserted while on leave.

Having joined the new Czech army at Brno in October 1918, he became attached to the "left" political movement, and on finally leaving the army he worked as a labourer in a factory, where he became a shop steward and secretary of the local branch of the left-wing Social Democrats. He was profoundly influenced by Lenin's book *State and Revolution.* Towards the end of 1921, when the schism in the Social Democratic Party resulted in the foundation of the Czech Communist Party, headed by Smeral, Gottwald forsook his trade and joined the "Marxist Left".

This was the beginning of his active political career. He became manager and later editor of the Slovak paper *Hlas Ludu* (Voice of the People), and acquainted himself with all the complexities of contemporary Slovak politics. He was a founder of the Slovak Communist Party, and in 1924 was appointed editor-in-chief of the Slovak paper *Pravda,* published at Ostrava. In 1925 he was elected to the central committee of the Czechoslovak Communist Party and in the following year left for Prague to become a member of the Politbureau and chief of the agitation and propaganda department of the party. He became the chief spokesman of the left in the executive committee of the Comintern in 1928 and in the following year was elected to the Czechoslovak Parliament. In the course of the next year he became general secretary of the Czech Communist Party. The discontent which followed the world depression was exploited to the full by Gottwald, as head of the Communist Party, to foment disturbances throughout Czechoslovakia, particularly among miners and peasants. In 1936 he played a part in organizing international brigades to fight in the Spanish Civil War.

During the tense days before Munich he was outspoken in the Czech Parliament in rejecting the solution of the British and French Governments, and in October he declared "the country must not be led to the shame of capitulation without a fight". In the same month he and other communist leaders withdrew to Moscow, while the remaining Czech political leaders later sought refuge in England.

As head of the Czech exiles in Moscow he supervised broadcasts in Czech and was employed in the Comintern until its dissolution in 1943, directing the translation into Czech of Marxist literature and he himself edited the translation of Stalin's [q.v.] *Problems of Leninism.* In Moscow in 1943 he met and conferred with the Czech Ambassador and Dr. Benes. In the coalition Government at Kosice in 1945, after the liberation of Czechoslovakia, in which communists were represented for the first time, Gottwald was Vice-Premier, and after the elections in 1946 he became Prime Minister. After a series of intricate political manoeuvres, resulting in the fateful days of February 1948, the former carpenter Gottwald was duly "elected" President of the Republic to succeed Dr. Benes.

March 16, 1953.

Sir Henry Leveson Gower, who captained the cricket teams of Winchester, Oxford, and Surrey, died at his home in London on February 1, 1954 at the age of 80.

It would be difficult to name a cricketer who was more widely known than Leveson Gower, in his younger days as a capable player and the best of captains, and in later life as an administrator of cricket affairs. A member of a great cricketing family, he served for many years as a member of every sort of committee, he arranged all kinds of matches, choosing the right class of team for each, and remained as popular as he was enthusiastic.

Henry Dudley Gresham Leveson Gower was born on May 8, 1873, and received his early education at Winchester, where he was three seasons in the eleven, and captain in his last summer there. Of his three matches against Eton, the first was left unfinished owing to rain, but the other two were won easily by Winchester. The school was very strong about that period, having among other representatives J. R. Mason and R. P. Lewis, the future Oxford wicket-keeper. From Winchester Leveson Gower went up to Magdalen College, Oxford, and got his Blue as a freshman. There was never much doubt about his finding a place in the team, or in his keeping it either, for he was always getting runs, and was a hard-working field. In his fourth year he was elected captain of the Oxford side, and it was while holding that office that he had what may, perhaps, have been the greatest moment of his active career.

Of the matches which he played against Cambridge, Oxford won two and lost two. In two of these games, his first in 1893 and his last in 1896, there was an odd similarity, connected with the follow-on rule. At that time the side which led on the first innings by the necessary number of runs had not, as it has to-day, the option of putting in its opponents again, but was obliged to do so whether it wished to or not. In both the university matches referred to, the Oxford team were within a few runs, when their ninth wicket fell, of a score that would save the follow on, and in both cases they wanted to follow on, while Cambridge did not want them to do so. The sequel was a short period of farcical cricket, with the bowlers purposely sending down wides or no-balls in order to swell the Oxford total to the requisite amount. When Cambridge came in after attaining their object, they were greeted with hoots of disapproval, and for some days there were angry letters in *The Times* lamenting this desecration of the glorious traditions of cricket.

Though the preliminaries were the same in 1896 the results were very different. In 1893 Oxford collapsed hopelessly, but in 1896 the tactics provided what one always thinks must have been the supreme moment in Leveson Gower's active career. His side were left with 330 to win, and thanks mainly to a superb 132 by G. O. Smith, the last choice, they won by four wickets, thus completing an achievement which had never been approached in the University match. Forty years afterwards the Oxford captain contributed to *Wisden* some reminiscences of this historic struggle, the best of which was that before the match he was accosted by a stranger who asked him which side was going to win, and he replied in an abrupt manner that of course Oxford would. A few days later he received by post a sapphire pin, with a letter saying that the writer had collected a nice sum, but he knew it was pretty safe, as it came from the "horse's mouth".

Leveson Gower represented Surrey, and captained them from 1908 to 1910, but he never seems to have played much county cricket. He visited the West Indies under Lord Hawke in 1896-97 and America in 1897 under Sir Pelham Warner*, and captained the M.C.C. eleven which toured South Africa in the winter of 1909-10, having already visited that country as a member of the 1905-06 team. As an administrator he was president of the Surrey C.C.C. for 20 years from 1929. He was often a Test match selector, being chairman in 1924 and also from 1928 to 1930. Leveson Gower was knighted in the New Year Honours of 1953, and in 1950 was given the freedom of the borough of Scarborough. He published a volume of reminiscences in 1953.

Much more might be added to this notice, if space allowed, of the great work which he did for cricket, his management of the Scarborough and Eastbourne festivals, the trouble he took to collect teams to meet the universities in their trial fixtures, and his services in other ways. It is needless to say that he was always immensely popular, with countless friends who were attracted by his kindliness and humour. There is an impression that having a nickname is a sure sign of popularity; if it is so, then Leveson Gower, to name him formally, meets the condition. From his schooldays he was called Shrimp, and it is as Shrimp that his loss will be felt by many.

February 2, 1954.

Sir Robert Gower, K.C.V.O., O.B.E., died on March 6, 1953 at his home at Tunbridge Wells at the age of 72. A lawyer of distinction, for more than 20 years a prominent member of the House of Commons, and throughout most of his career closely associated with local government in Kent, he will, however, always be remembered for the work he did for animals. His lifetime of service to them was fittingly crowned in the summer of 1951 when, having for 23 years been chairman of the Royal Society for the Prevention of Cruelty to Animals, he was unanimously elected its president.

Robert Vaughan Gower was born on November 10, 1880, the elder son of the late J. R. Gower, of Tunbridge Wells. He was educated privately and in 1903 obtained honours in the Final Examination of the Law Society. For half a century he was closely engaged in his profession. He began his career in municipal affairs in 1909 as a member of the Royal Tunbridge Wells Corporation, was for nearly 30 years an alderman, several times deputy Mayor, and from 1917 to 1919 he occupied the mayoral chair. In 1925 he was made a freeman of the borough, and for 15 years he was on the Kent County Council, during which time he also became a freeman of the City of London. For some years, too, he was Commissioner of Land Tax for Kent, was Appeals Military Representative on the Kent Tribunals during the 1914-18 war, and as a keen supporter of the Territorial Army he was Honorary Colonel of the 88th (City of London) A.A. Regiment, R.A., and president of the 129th Squadron of the A.T.C.

Gower entered Parliament for the Central Division of Hackney in 1924 as a Conservative. A great deal of his work in Parliament was done outside the debating Chamber—in committee, in tactful negotiations, and in gentle influence with his friends, who were legion in all parties. It was, indeed, at Westminster that his many-sided interests were represented, and his efforts concentrated for more than 20 years. In 1925 he became a member of the Ministry of Health departmental committee on the superannuation of municipal and other government officials, which sat for over two years. In 1930, having by that time left Hackney and been elected for the Gillingham Division of Rochester, he became chairman of the Naval Dockyards Members' Committee of the House, and was afterwards chairman of the committee of members representing the evacuation areas, as well as of the Solicitor-Members' Group, all of which offices he held until he retired from Parliament in 1945.

It was, however, his association with animal welfare that made him the outstanding parliamentarian which he undoubtedly became. From 1929 until his retirement he was chairman of the Animal Welfare Committee, and from the moment he entered the House there was never an occasion when the care of dumb creatures arose that he was not in his place as their counsel. He introduced and piloted through all stages the Protection of Animals (Cruelty to Dogs) Act of 1933, the Protection of Animals Act of the year following, which deals with the training and performance in public of animals, the Cinematograph Films (Animals) Act of 1937, and the Dogs Act of 1938. He introduced other measures, including one for the protection of pit ponies; he helped to establish and was president of the Pit Ponies Protection Society. Apart from his lifetime of association with the R.S.P.C.A., whose silver medal he was awarded in 1932, he had been chairman and honorary treasurer of the National Canine Defence League since 1920, and in 1931 he received from the President of the French Republic a Sèvres vase in recognition of his animal welfare work in France. During the 1939-45 war he was chairman of the R.S.P.C.A. War Animals (Allies) Fund as well as of the Aid for Russian Horses Fund.

His other honorary posts were innumerable. For many years he was president of the Property Owners' Protection Association, president of the Kent Law Society, a leading member of the Royal Institute of International Affairs, and of the council of the Psychical Research Society and several friendly and benevolent societies. Gower had also been master of several City companies, including the Turners, the Pattenmakers, and the Needlemakers. It was always a matter of wonder to his friends how he contrived to fill all the obligations which he so cheerfully—indeed, eagerly—undertook, and there is no doubt that he wore himself out in his service to good causes. His handsome presence, with his fine features and his steel-grey hair, his infinite charm, and his never ceasing patience were the essential qualities that won him friends everywhere.

Honours bestowed upon him were many. He was knighted in 1919, in which year he had been appointed an O.B.E., and in 1935 he was created a K.C.V.O. He held many foreign decorations, together with the honorary degrees of D.C.L. of Budapest and LL.D. of Szeged, and was a Fellow of the Societies of Antiquaries and Genealogists. The study of genealogy was one of his chief hobbies, together with archaeology, and he made many contributions on these subjects to the journals of the learned societies.

He married in 1907 Dorothy Susie Eleanor, daughter of the late M. McClellan Wills, of Exeter. She died in 1936. There were two daughters of the marriage.

His second wife, whom he married in 1944, was Vera, daughter of the late C. H. Thomas, M.R.C.S., L.R.C.P., of Argyll, and widow of R. A. Daniel, M.D., F.R.C.S., of Fort View, co. Wexford.

March 7, 1953.

Lord Gowrie, V.C., G.C.M.G., C.B., D.S.O., Governor-General of Australia from 1936 to 1944, died on May 2, 1955 at his home in Gloucestershire at the age of 82.

Few representatives of the Sovereign in a self-governing Dominion have achieved as great a success, and none has sustained it over so many years. From 1928, when he was first appointed Governor of South Australia, until he returned home in 1944, he was almost continuously in office there, in New South Wales, or at Canberra. It would have been hard indeed to find a man with qualifications better calculated to endear him to a people of good soldiers and sportsmen. His record as a fighting officer could scarcely have been equalled. His V.C. had been won with spectacular gallantry, and was doubly underlined by the bar to his D.S.O. He had served with Australians and had been in Australia. He was, too, a friendly and approachable man with great tact and the easiest of good manners.

In addition he came to acquire great experience and with it a certainty of touch which enabled him to handle the many problems of his high office unfalteringly. He was, indeed, that rare combination, a soldier-statesman, which in times of peril and emergency can, as it did in his case, prove of special value. It was not for nothing that he had obtained direct personal knowledge of Papua and the mandated territory of New Guinea and had himself visited the Dutch East Indies in 1938.

The Right Hon. Sir Alexander Gore Arkwright Hore-Ruthven V.C., G.C.M.G., C.B., D.S.O., first Earl of Gowrie, Viscount Ruthven of Canberra, Baron Gowrie, of Canberra, and of Dirleton, East Lothian, was born at Windsor on July 6, 1872, the second son of the eighth Lord Ruthven, head of an historic Scottish house. His mother, Lady Caroline Annesley-Gore, was a daughter of the 4th Earl of Arran. He was educated at Eton and at 19 joined the 3rd (Militia) Battalion, The Highland Light Infantry. In 1898 as a captain he was attached to the Egyptian Army in the Sudan and commanded the Camel Corps Detachment at the Battle of Gedaref and in later operations, including the final defeat of the Khalifa. He won the Victoria Cross—the first militia officer to do so—for snatching a wounded Egyptian officer away from advancing Dervishes and carrying him to safety. He was also awarded the 4th Class of Osmanieh, the British and Egyptian medals with clasp, and was three times mentioned in dispatches.

He was mentioned again in connexion with the White Nile operations of 1899 and in the same year was gazetted to The Cameron Highlanders. In 1903-04 he was Special Service Officer in Somaliland, was present at the action of Tidballi and received a medal and two clasps. From 1905 to 1908 he was military secretary and A.D.C. to two successive Lords-Lieutenant of Ireland, Lords Dudley and Aberdeen. In 1908 he was promoted captain with the 1st Dragoons and in the same year married Zara, daughter of the late John Pollok, of Lismanny, co. Galway. Then, until 1910, he was for the second time Military Secretary to Lord Dudley, who had become Governor-General of Australia.

In the early months of the 1914-18 War he was a brigade major, and in 1915 became a major in The Welsh Guards and G.S.O.2. In Gallipoli he was severely wounded and was awarded the D.S.O. In 1916 he became a temporary lieutenant-colonel and G.S.O.1, in 1917 temporary Brigadier-General, General Staff, and in 1918 he commanded the 29th Infantry Brigade. For his services in these capacities he was appointed C.B. and C.M.G., and was awarded a bar to his D.S.O. He was also mentioned five times in dispatches. From 1920 to 1924 he commanded the Welsh Guards, and from 1924 to 1928, the 1st Infantry Brigade at Aldershot.

His brilliant career, his gifts as "a good mixer", and his previous knowledge of the Commonwealth made him an ideal appointment to the Governorship of South Australia when in 1928 he succeeded an old friend, Lieutenant-General Sir Tom Bridges, K.C.B. He was warmly received, and took up his duties with great energy. Though in 1930 some strictures which he passed on "a small active and noisy element of hotheads" stung the Australian Trade and Labour Council to a protest, his term was extended in 1933 on the recommendation of a Labour Government and to the general satisfaction.When, in 1934, he and his wife left for England there was a remarkable demonstration of the esteem in which they had been held.

He was not to be long at home, for a few months later he was appointed Governor of New South Wales. At Sydney he received a hearty welcome as a proved "lover of Australia". He was not, however, to hold the office long, for in 1935 he was appointed Governor-General of the Commonwealth in succession to Sir Isaac Isaacs. Shortly afterwards he was raised to the peerage as Lord Gowrie, of Canberra and of Dirleton, and was created a G.C.M.G. In January 1936 he was sworn in at Melbourne. In the following summer he made an extensive tour of Western Australia, returning to the eastern states by way of Darwin. The next year he went farther afield. He began with Papua. The natives decorated their villages with palms and frangipane and declared their grateful loyalty. He went on to the mandated territory of New Guinea, then recovering from the volcanic eruptions of the earlier part of the year.

In 1938 the Government of the Netherlands East Indies, learning that he was returning for a holiday at home, invited him to visit their territories on his way. He accepted, and made tours of Bali and Java. He was received with cordiality and open hospitality. It was a notable incident at a time when international friendships were becoming rare indeed. In the summer of 1939 his tour of duty was almost at an end and on a farewell tour of the Commonwealth he prepared the way for his intended successor, the late Duke of Kent. On September 9, however, it was announced that in view of the Duke of Kent having assumed a naval appointment for the duration of the war, he was to continue in office.

Thereafter Lord Gowrie's appointment was extended from year to year. It therefore fell to him to preside in his official capacity over the immense war effort of the Commonwealth, and to be the link between it and its Sovereign throughout the period in which for the first time it stood in direct and imminent peril. When in 1944 he was succeeded as Governor-General by the Duke of Gloucester*, he and Lady Gowrie were almost overwhelmed by the tributes of regard and affection showered on them by the people who had known and loved them for so long. The earldom that was then conferred upon him was richly deserved.

Return home did not mean retirement, for early in 1945 he was appointed Deputy Constable and Lieutenant-Governor of Windsor Castle, an office he retained until 1953, when he finally retired from public life. In the meantime, in 1948 he was elected president of the M.C.C. and, as such, made a presentation to Don (now Sir Donald) Bradman, then captain of the visiting Australian team.

He had two sons, of whom the younger died an infant and the elder was killed on active service in 1942. The family honours therefore devolve upon his elder grandson, Viscount

Ruthven of Canberra, who is 15.

[A tribute followed the obituary at this point.]

May 4, 1955.

Sir Harold Graham-Hodgson—See **Hodgson.**

Claude Grahame-White, who died on August 19, 1959 in a Nice hospital, would have been 80 on August 22.

Many of the most intrepid airmen whose exploits have made aerial history over-reached themselves at last and came to violent ends. Cody, Gustav Hamel, Hawker, and a dozen others of equal repute, gave their lives in the furtherance of aviation. For Claude Grahame-White a happier fate was reserved. Though his early flying was done in machines which now seem to us like box-kites he lived on to witness the enormous expansion in the utility and performance of aircraft which he had envisaged as long ago as 1910.

At that remote-seeming period, and for many years thereafter, he was an outstanding world personality in aviation. He believed fervently in the future of flying from the outset, and by his own exploits, by organization, by design of models, by the promotion of meetings, and by pen and voice he exercised a powerful influence in making aircraft a practicable, speedy, and tolerably safe form of transport.

Claude Grahame-White was born at Bursledon Towers, Bursledon, Hampshire, on August 21, 1879, the second son of John Reginald Grahame-White, a yachtsman and a founder-member of the Royal Automobile Club. He was educated at Crondall House School, Surrey, and Bedford Grammar School, showing mechanical leanings and aptitudes at an early age and possessing a motor car while still at school.

After completing his schooling he was put in the office of an uncle, a Yorkshire woollen factor, where he interested himself in the engineering side of the business and introduced motor lorries to replace horse vans. While in Yorkshire he also inaugurated at Bradford a motor vehicle service in competition with the electric tramways. He next spent some time as steward of a large Sussex estate; and in 1906 made a long journey big game hunting in South and Central Africa. On his return he went into the motor business in London on the commercial side and did some racing at Brooklands.

It was Blériot's Channel flight in 1909 that impressed Grahame-White with the possibilities of aviation. France was then the chief centre of experimentation, so he went there, bought an aircraft and learnt to fly. At a flying meeting at Rheims he met Farman [q.v.], Blériot, the two Voisins, and other prominent workers in the field; and he was able to spend a most valuable three months in Blériot's Paris factory watching the construction of a machine designed for his use. On January 4, 1910, he received the pilot's certificate of the French Aero Club, being the first Englishman to do so. He started a British flying school at Pau, and spent a great deal of time in the air, having more than one narrow escape from death.

Grahame-White sprang into world reputation in 1910 by his gallant attempt at the *Daily Mail* £10,000 prize for a flight from London to Manchester. He had bad luck, and lost the prize to Paulhan, but his persistence in flying part of the way in total darkness struck the public imagination and he was awarded a gold medal by the French Aero Club and a trophy by the Motor Union. Later in the same year he won valuable prizes at Wolverhampton and Bournemouth, covering the then remarkable distance of 91 miles at the latter meeting. He made a flight over the Fleet at Penzance and another over the Tower at Blackpool, and while at this Lancashire resort he was the first English airman to carry mails.

In September 1910 Grahame-White went over to the United States, where he carried all before him. At the Harvard-Boston Meet he won £2,000 for a flight of 33 miles round the Boston Light; at Washington he flew from the Bennings race track to the White House, to call on President Taft; at Belmont Park, New York, he won the Gordon Bennett Cup in the international speed races and the International Aeronautic Federation's £2,000 prize for a flight round the Statue of Liberty. On returning to England in December Grahame-White was the recipient of a special gold medal from the Aerial League of the British Empire, Earl Roberts making the presentation.

Early in 1911 Grahame-White established the London Aerodrome at Hendon and set up there the Grahame-White Aviation Company, Ltd., which actively engaged in the training of pilots, and which, in the September of that year, carried the first English official delivery of mails (from Hendon to Windsor) by permission of the Postmaster-General. Grahame-White was quick to see the potentialities of aircraft for war, and on May 12, 1911, gave a demonstration at Hendon for the Parliamentary Aerial Defence Committee. In August he made a second successful tour in America, being undefeated at Boston and Nassau Boulevard, New York, and creating five world or American records, one of which was the greatest speed with a passenger—the speed being 63.232 miles an hour.

When the Royal Flying Corps was founded, in 1912, Grahame-White at once wired Lord Haldane offering his services in any capacity. That same April he inaugurated weekly flying meetings at Hendon, and these meetings, at which hundreds of passengers were carried without mishap, were powerful aids to the production of "air-mindedness" in the public. The aerial "Derbies" at Hendon in 1912, 1913, and 1914 created great interest, and in spite of the Jonahs who prophesied financial disaster, Grahame-White eventually made his meetings pay. Meanwhile, ceaseless improvement and experiment were going on in his workshops, which turned out various prize-winning models.

On the outbreak of the 1914-18 War Grahame-White was commissioned as a flight-commander in the R.N.A.S. In February 1915 he took part in an air raid on the enemy occupied coast of Belgium, making a forced descent into the sea off Nieuport and being rescued by a French minesweeper. He was not amenable to discipline and took unkindly to routine; and in any event the Government soon saw that he would be most valuable in the sphere of design and manufacture; so in August 1915 he resigned his commission and devoted himself for the rest of the war to constructional work at Hendon.

In December 1925 the Government took over the airfield at Hendon and all the factories belonging to the company. By this time Grahame-White's effective work as an airman and manufacturer was done; but he continued to watch with the keenest interest the fulfilment of his early prophesies. As long ago as 1919 he was speaking of speeds up to 200, 250, and 300 miles an hour; way back in 1910 he foresaw the use of aircraft-carriers at sea.

He wrote numerous books on aviation, some of them popular works for boys, and others, like *Flying: An Epitome and a Forecast* (1930), well-considered and judicial surveys of the subject.

August 20, 1959.

Grand Duchess Marie of Russia—See **Marie.**

Grand Duchess Olga of Russia—See **Olga.**

P. P. Graves, for many years a valued correspondent of *The Times* in the Near East, and an acknowledged authority on the politics of the Balkans and the Arab world, died at his home in Ireland at the age of 77 on June 3, 1953.

Philip Perceval Graves, a member of a family which took root in Ireland nearly three centuries ago and has flourished there, putting out vigorous literary blossoms in successive generations of churchmen and members of the Services, was born on February 25, 1876, and was educated at Haileybury and Oriel College, Oxford, where his cricket prowess might well have gained him his Blue. Partly as a result of the representation of his family in the Levant branch of the Consular Service, Graves went to the Near East and began to lay the foundations of that knowledge of the political and religious complexities of the Ottoman Empire which was soon to prove so valuable to him and those for whom he worked. In the process he acquired useful experience of practical journalism in Egypt and in 1906 was invited to join the staff of *The Times.*

For two years he was correspondent in Cairo, where he shared a flat with Mr. (afterwards Sir Ronald) Storrs*, the Oriental Secretary. Graves was transferred to Constantinople in time to witness on the spot the overthrow of Sultan Abdul Hamid II by the Young Turks. After that he recorded from day to day the often dramatic and sometimes sanguinary events of the stormy period which saw the failure of the policy of "Ottomanization" (in which he was one of the first to detect the flaws), the collapse of the Ottoman Empire in the first Balkan war, and its partial recovery under cover of the second; and he remained at Constantinople until the doomed Empire found itself precipitated into the 1914-18 war on the side of the Central Empires.

During that war Graves served as an intelligence officer with the rank of captain in Egypt, Arabia, and Palestine, where he was a particularly useful member first of the Arab Bureau in Cairo and then (in company with his consular uncle, Sir Robert Graves), of the Political Mission under Sir Gilbert Clayton at Bir Salem, Allenby's G.H.Q. in Palestine.

After the armistice Graves returned to Turkey, still in his military capacity and served there until demobilization, late in 1919, enabled him to resume his duties as correspondent of *The Times* in Constantinople. The arrival, soon after the overthrow of the Empire, as an important Kemalist official, of a Turk with whom Graves had previously had a marked difference of opinion made any further residence in Constantinople in its decay distasteful, and a successor was appointed as correspondent. Graves was then repeatedly employed as special correspondent in Ireland, in India, and in various countries in the Levant, the Aegean, and the Balkans, where the troubles of that unsettled period simmered and at times boiled over. After having travelled far and wide and put his great knowledge of the Near and Middle East to good use, he returned to the Foreign Department at Printing House Square. There his services as mentor on the affairs of the Middle East and as a writer of special and leading articles were invaluable. In conversation as well as in writing he had an engagingly terse and epigrammatic style, which carried reader and hearer through the dangerous cross-currents of Asian politics with apparent ease.

One of the pieces of historical research of which Graves was proud was his work in helping to prove that "The Protocols of the Learned Elders of Zion" were forgeries, at a time when they were being widely exploited for anti-Jewish purposes. After a critical inspection of the results of the earlier stages of Zionist enterprise in Palestine, for which he was particularly well fitted by his previous experience of that troubled country, Graves published a thoughtful and entertaining account of *The Land of Three Faiths.* The fact that he was thereafter hailed as a "pro-Zionist", because of the favourable opinions expressed in that book about some of the activities of the Zionists which had appeared to him to be praiseworthy, was far from pleasing to Graves who, as an honest and very well informed observer, resented any suggestion that he might have strayed from the straight and narrow path of impartiality prescribed for a correspondent in the Near East into the spacious meadows of propaganda on behalf of any nation, creed, party, or interest in the quarrelsome and suspicious bailiwick.

His taste for the sober history of that part of the world later found expression in a book on *The Question of the Straits,* which covers its different phases throughout some 3,000 years.

Soon after the beginning of the 1939-45 war Graves succeeded his old friend, Sir Ronald Storrs, in one of the most difficult tasks with which an historian can saddle himself. This was the writing, quarter by quarter, of the record of a war actually in progress. It is highly creditable to his skill that Graves was able to produce so satisfactory a succession of volumes under the grievous handicap of knowing that the information available at the time of writing was necessarily incomplete.

Since his retirement from the staff of *The Times* at the end of 1945 he had lived at Bantry, co. Cork, and almost to the end of his life maintained a lively interest in the political developments of the Arab world and the Balkans. His last work was the editing of the memoirs of King Abdullah of Jordan [q.v.], which appeared in 1950.

Apart from his interest in the past, present, and future of the races and religions of the Near East, Graves was fond of delving into the meagre records of the dark period during which the Roman occupation of Britain ended and the Saxon invasions began, and into an examination of the military organization, equipment and tactics of the various peoples which vexed not only Britain but most of Europe with their wars during the fifth and sixth centuries. From these studies, in the pursuit of which he used to argue with convincing eloquence, and was so earnest as to learn a good deal of Welsh in order to help in his search for the "historical Arthur", he would at times turn aside for relaxation to entomology and fly-fishing, and sometimes to the writing of verse. He was elected to the Royal Irish Academy four years before he died.

He was twice married, first in 1912 to Leila Millicent Knox, daughter of Gavin Gilchrist, by whom he had a daughter. After the death of his first wife in 1935 he married Mrs. Katherine Dewar, daughter of the late W. H. E. H. Palmer.

June 4, 1953.

Richard Massie Graves, C.B.E., who spent many years of government service in the Levant and Egypt, died in hospital in London on August 14, 1960 at the age of 79.

He was the son of the Irishman Alfred Perceval Graves, writer of Irish ballads ("Father O'Flynn" among them) and an inspector of schools in England, by his first wife Jane Cooper, of Cooper Hill, co. Limerick. He was thus a younger brother of Philip Graves [q.v.], who was for many years a correspondent of *The Times* in the Middle East, and a half-brother of the authors Robert Graves and Charles Graves. From Haileybury he went to Magdalen College, Oxford, and then, as Oriental languages at Oxford in those days did not come up to Foreign Office standards, to King's College, Cambridge, and in 1903 he entered the Levant Consular Service. Six years later he was vice-consul in Cairo and he then transferred to the Egyptian Civil Service. From 1930 to 1939 he was director of the labour department in the Egyptian Ministry of Commerce and Industry. In 1940 he was appointed labour adviser to the Palestine Government and in 1942-46 he was director of the Palestine Department of Labour.

He had scarcely retired before the Colonial Office appointed him to the unenviable post of chairman of the municipal commission, or mayor, of Jerusalem, then torn by the conflict between Arabs and Jews. During his period of office, June 1947 to April 1948, he was powerless to prevent the steady fall of the city into anarchy; and, for all his impartiality, his life, like those of others occupying less conspicuous positions in Jerusalem at that time, was often in danger. He later published a diary of his year's office in Jerusalem, *Experiment in Anarchy.* For three years after his return he was adviser on social affairs to the International Administration of Tangier.

"Graves Supérieur" was a nick-name attached to him by his colleagues in Cairo: and there was an air of authority about him, as well as his immaculate appearance, that lent point to the witticism. He had also a due measure of his family's wit; and late in life he communicated to the public one of that family's many accomplishments when he brought out a little book on *Singing for Amateurs* (1954). It consists of genial exhortation and advice, and reminiscences of the days when English drawingrooms made their own music—and few more charmingly than his father's.

Graves was also a felicitous translator from French and German, and he was a prime mover in the action recently taken by translators to improve their lot. Latterly he lived at the Savile Club, where he will be sadly missed.

He married in 1912 Eva, daughter of Major H. C. Wilkinson, of Oswald House, Durham. He is survived by his daughter.

August 15, 1960.

Marshal Rodolfo Graziani, Marchese di Neghelli, who died in Rome on January 11, 1955 at the age of 72, was a successful colonial soldier who found that his tactics were outclassed when he was opposed by a European enemy.

Born near Frosinone in 1882, he began his colonial career early. He served in Eritrea from 1908 to 1913, in Libya in 1914, and then took part in the 1914-18 War, during which he was wounded and won his majority. Returning soon afterwards to Africa, he participated in the fighting for the reconquest of the colonies of Tripolitania and Cyrenaica. The real test of General Graziani's genius for colonial warfare came with his transfer from Tripolitania to Cyrenaica and with his assumption of the task of crushing the Senussi rebellion so long and so ably conducted by the wily and treacherous veteran, Omar el Muktar.

Graziani soon realized that Omar el Muktar, in spite of his losses, was able to keep his troops on a war footing because he compelled the native population to furnish him continually with fresh supplies of men, material, and money. Graziani therefore created vast concentration camps along the coast into which he herded the nominally peaceful natives, thus cutting them off from the Senussi. At the same time he constructed along the Cyrenaican-

Egyptian frontier a continuous line of barbed-wire entanglements which prevented the passage of supplies to the rebels from their sympathizers in Egypt.

Recalled home to a high military command in 1934, Graziani was not left long in charge of the Udine Army Corps but was sent out in the following year to be Governor of Italian Somaliland and commander-in-chief of the forces there. When the Abyssinian war broke out he was entrusted with the operations on the southern front. These operations, which he described in a book entitled *Il Fronte Sud,* turned out to be less spectacular than and subsidiary to the operations in the north, conducted first by Marshal (then General) De Bono and afterwards by Marshal Badoglio [q.v.], the captor of Addis Ababa.

Graziani's campaign, however, was highly important, since the occupation of Harar deprived the Emperor Haile Selassie of Ethiopia* of his second capital, and the cutting of the Addis Ababa-Jibuti railway line robbed him of his only source of supply from abroad. Graziani's services were rewarded by his promotion to be a marshal and later by the marquisate of Neghelli.

At the outbreak of the war between Germany and the allies Graziani was at once given charge of a group of armies, and, on the death of Marshal Balbo soon after the entry into the war of Italy, Graziani was made commander-in-chief of the Italian forces in North Africa. Like many another colonial general, however, Marshal Graziani failed when brought face to face with a European adversary. Before the close of 1940 he had been heavily defeated by General Wavell (as he then was) and early in 1941 he was superseded.

When Mussolini, dismissed by the King, set up his new Republican Fascist Government in northern Italy under the protection of German bayonets he chose Marshal Graziani as his Minister of Defence.

Graziani had never been on good terms with Marshal Badoglio and he immediately made a vitriolic attack upon his rival, accusing him and the King of treachery because they had sought an armistice. If the Germans were sincere in pinning their faith to Marshal Graziani they were doomed to disappointment. His efforts to reorganize a Republican Fascist army were unsuccessful, and in April 1945 he was captured by the victorious allies. The Italian Government promptly requested that he should be tried by his own countrymen.

He was brought to trial in 1948, and in 1950 a military court sentenced him to 19 years' imprisonment. The time he had already spent in prison was deducted and he had a further remission of 13 years and eight months. This left him 14 months to serve. He was released under an amnesty after serving only three months of this term.

January 12, 1955.

Prince George of Greece—See **George.**

Princess Nicholas of Greece—See **Nicholas.**

Queen Elizabeth of Greece, who was the consort of the late King George II, King of the Hellenes, died on November 14, 1956 in a nursing home at Cannes. She was 62.

Princess Elizabeth Charlotte Josephine Victoria Alexandra was the eldest daughter of King Ferdinand and Queen Marie of Romania, and a great granddaughter of Queen Victoria. She was born at Pelesh Castle, Sinaia, a residence of the Romanian Royal Family in the Carpathian mountains, on October 12, 1894. She was singularly beautiful in her youth. As a girl she was brought up in an English atmosphere. The family language of the Crown Prince's Court at Bucharest and Sinaia was English, and she had an English nurse and an English governess. Her tastes were simple, and it was commonly said that she refused the hand of Prince George when he came to court her as Diadoch (heir to the throne), but accepted him later when his father lost his throne and was an exile in Switzerland. By the time they were married, however, Prince George was again heir to the throne.

The marriage was solemnized in Bucharest in 1921, and the bride's great-uncle, King Charles of Romania, made her a wedding present of four million lei (approximately £13,500). She went to reside in Athens, but she was persuaded to go to Smyrna at the height of the Greek campaign against the Turks in Asia Minor.

She was expecting the birth of her child, and it was hoped an heir to the throne would be born on Asian soil. Most unfortunately the Princess fell seriously ill in Smyrna, and from the grave operation which had to be performed she never entirely recovered. Nor was her beauty ever quite restored; and although her graciousness and charm remained, she and the Diadoch, who in the meantime became King and then again an exile, gradually drifted apart.

Queen Elizabeth occasionally went to England, but Romania was the home of her choice. Her marriage was dissolved in July 1935, four months before King George was restored to the throne, and she resumed Romanian nationality in order to permit her to own an estate in Transylvania, where she liked to live.

She had established a new hospital and a home for children in Bucharest, to which she devoted much attention. In 1952 she went to live in a villa at Cannes.

November 16, 1956.

F. W. Edridge-Green—See **Edridge-.**

Lord Greene died in a nursing home on April 16, 1952 at the age of 68, after a long illness. His career was in some respects one of the most remarkable in the legal annals of recent times. At Westminster, at Oxford, through the war of 1914-18, at the Bar and on the Bench of the Court of Appeal, which he reached at the early age of 52, it was one long record of success.

The Right Hon. Sir Wilfrid Arthur Greene, Baron Greene, of Holmbury St. Mary, Surrey, in the Peerage of the United Kingdom, P.C., O.B.E., M.C., was born on December 30, 1883, son of the late Arthur Weguelin Greene, of Beckenham. Though a Roman Catholic, he was educated in the stately Anglican atmosphere of Westminster School and of Christ Church, Oxford, where he was a scholar and took a first in Classical Moderations in 1904 and a first in *Lit. Hum.* in 1906. He also won the Craven scholarship in 1903, the Hertford in 1904, and the Vinerian in 1908; and he was awarded the Chancellor's Prize for Latin Verse in 1905, taking for his subject *Artes Magiciae.* In 1907 he was elected a Fellow of All Souls. He entered the chambers of the late Philip Stokes and in 1908 was called to the Bar by the Inner Temple; but Lincoln's Inn was really to be his home, and for several years he shared chambers with the future Lord Maugham [q.v.].

When war broke out in 1914 Wilfrid Greene, though but of six years' standing, was already looked upon as one of the most promising juniors practising in the Chancery Courts, and the change from the lawyer's gown to the soldier's jacket was but to open the path to renown in another field. Within a few weeks of the declaration of war he was gazetted a second lieutenant in The Oxfordshire and Buckinghamshire Light Infantry, T.A., and he served in France, Flanders, and Italy. In due course he became G.S.O.3 on the staff of the Fifth Army, and after 1917 he was G.S.O.2 on G.H.Q. staff in Italy, and in 1918 G.S.O.2, British Supreme War Council. He ended the war as an O.B.E., and with an M.C.

In 1919 Greene resumed his practice at the Bar. While many who had been to the war had to wait for the return of work absorbed by those who had stayed at home, for Greene there was no waiting. Solicitors had not forgotten the brilliant young junior of 1914, and in 1919 they welcomed him back by loading him with briefs. By 1922, at the age of 39, when he took silk, he had one of the largest junior practices in Lincoln's Inn and from the first he was overwhelmed with briefs in the best class of work. In the history of the Bar there are few examples of such unqualified success in so short a time.

The most intricate cases seemed to present no difficulties to Greene's acute mind, accustomed to approach a problem from a scholarly as well as from a legal point of view, and his clear powers of exposition made it a pleasure—which the Bench fully appreciated—to listen to his arguments, lightened up as they were by flashes of elegant humour and learning. Apart from his work in the Courts, the cases sent for his opinion must at the height of his fame have exceeded those of any other leader of the day.

Towards the end of his practice at the Bar he was forced to confine his practice principally to the House of Lords and the Judicial Committee of the Privy Council, and in the Law Reports between 1923 and 1935 probably the names of few leaders appear more frequently in important cases before the final tribunals, apart from those of a purely common law or commercial character. How he managed to bear the strain caused wonder among his friends, and by 1935 the limit seemed to be reached.

When leaving the building on the day in July 1935 when the Privy Council closed its sittings, Greene—who had appeared in nearly every important appeal from the Dominions heard during the term—confessed to an official there that he was "really done", and his doctor agreed with him. The next October, on the promotion of Lord Justice Maugham to be a Lord of Appeal in the place of Lord Tomlin, who had died a few months before, Greene was appointed a Lord Justice of Appeal in his place. It was realized that this preferment, high as it was, was but the stepping-stone to something of greater importance later on, and so it proved to be.

Before leaving Greene's career at the Bar, a tribute must be paid to the considerable amount of unpaid public work that he performed at the height of his practice. In 1925 he was chairman of the Committee on Company Law; in 1930 he was chairman of the Committee on Trade Practices; in 1931 he served as chairman of the Advisory Committee to inquire into the position of Imperial and International Communications Limited, in connexion with the cable merger; and in 1934 he did good work as chairman of the Committee on the Beet Sugar Industry.

On the resignation of Lord Blanesburgh, in April 1937, of his office as a Lord of Appeal, Lord Wright* (who in 1935 had consented to take the Rolls as a stopgap) resumed his place as a Lord of Appeal, and Greene, though one of the junior Lords Justices, was appointed Master of the Rolls in his place.

The same charming courtesy which characterized him at the Bar was extended from the Bench to all who practised before him. As Master of the Rolls Lord Greene was the head of the Record Office and the custodian of the national muniments, and this branch of his duties naturally appealed strongly to his scholarly mind. The responsibilities of his office were increased a thousandfold by the 1939-45 war, and it was due to his zeal that a great number of local records of the utmost value were saved from destruction and placed in proper custody. He was chairman of the National Buildings Record, formed at the beginning of the war to preserve by means of drawings and photographs the memory of damaged buildings; and to the work of this body, which had its habitation at All Souls, Greene brought both enthusiasm and labour.

In June 1942 Lord Greene was appointed chairman of the board of investigation of the coalminers' wage claim and the machinery required by the proposed national wages board, whose report in April 1943 was welcomed by both sides, who in a joint statement declared that for the result they were "indebted in a large measure to the unique powers of persuasion and wealth of experience of Lord Greene himself". After his resignation from the office of Master of the Rolls in 1949 he served for a few months as Lord of Appeal in Ordinary, but resigned for health reasons in 1950.

Greene, who had been standing counsel to the University of Oxford, was made an honorary D.C.L. by the University in 1935 and in the same year an honorary student of Christ Church; and in 1936 Birmingham did him a similar honour by making him a LL.D., as did St. Andrews later on. From 1936 he was principal of the Working Men's College, St. Pancras, and he was appointed a trustee of the Pilgrim Trust in 1941.

He married in 1909 Nancy, daughter of the late Francis Wright. Before her marriage Lady Greene had had some experience on the stage, and she was an early translator of Pirandello's plays into English. There were no children of the marriage.

April 18, 1952.

Arthur Greenwood, P.C., who died on June 9, 1954, was one of the most able and most popular leaders of the Labour Party. His integrity and humanity won for him the affection of men and women of all classes and all parties.

Although he came from a comfortably off middle-class home, there was no more loyal or sincere Socialist, and the support which he had in his own party was demonstrated at conference after conference. He was acting as leader of the Labour Party at the time of the outbreak of war in 1939, and the part which he played in those dark days of crisis will not quickly be forgotten. At the moment of its greatest danger after the war, in 1952-53, the Labour Party looked to him as the man who was most likely to be a successful mediator between its two wings.

He was born at Hunslet, Leeds, on February 8, 1880, the son of William Greenwood, head of a firm of painters and decorators. He went first to a dame's school, and from there to a Church of England school, where he won a scholarship to Leeds Higher Grade School. A few years later he went, again with a scholarship, to Victoria (now Leeds) University. After graduating, he was a school teacher for a short period and then became lecturer in economics at the university and head of the economics department of the Huddersfield Technical College. While holding these posts he took an active part in the development of the Workers' Educational Association.

Shortly before the outbreak of war in 1914 he went to London as general secretary of the Council for the Study of International Relations. During the war he was appointed to Lloyd George's "secretariat", serving in 1917 as assistant secretary to the Reconstruction Committee and from 1917 to 1919 as assistant secretary of the Ministry of Reconstruction. The Minister, Dr. (later the first Viscount) Addison [q.v.], had a high opinion of him and placed great reliance on him.

At the 1918 election Greenwood fought Southport unsuccessfully as a Labour candidate. He had been released from his official duties for the period of the election, and was reappointed the day after his defeat. But he soon left the Ministry, to become in 1920 secretary of the research department of the Labour Party. Two years later he was elected as Labour member for Nelson and Colne, a constituency which he continued to represent until the election of 1931. About this time he played an important part in founding the University Labour Federation, and he remained its president until January 1940.

In the first Labour Government he was appointed Parliamentary Secretary to the Ministry of Health. He was then 43 years old. In the second Labour Government, formed in 1929, he became Minister of Health. It was a post for which he was almost ideally suited; his economic training and his humane interest in the lot of ordinary men and women made him particularly well fitted for dealing with such questions as widows' pensions, housing and slum clearance, and town and country planning. His Widows, Orphans and Old Age Contributory Pensions Act (1929) both increased the grants to widows and lowered the age of eligibility.

When the National Government was formed in 1931, Greenwood was an unhesitating opponent of Ramsay MacDonald's policy, and at the general election of that year he lost his seat, like so many of the Labour leaders. The following year, however, he won Wakefield at a by-election with a majority of 344 in a total poll of more than 30,000 votes. He continued to represent Wakefield for the rest of his life, and at the 1950 general election his majority was more than 10,000. It was typical of him that shortly after the split in the Labour Party he displayed none of the bitterness that characterized some of his colleagues. "I have parted company with men who were in the Labour movement when I was a child", he said. "Nothing will ever tempt me to say a word against the men who built up that movement".

In 1935 he was elected deputy leader of the Labour Party, and from then until 1939 was an outspoken critic of the Government's foreign policy and earned for himself the tribute of a personal attack by Hitler at Weimar in 1938. In the summer of 1939 Attlee* was ill and Greenwood acted as Leader of the Opposition during the critical weeks which preceded the outbreak of war. The night of Saturday, September 2, was, perhaps, his "finest hour". Poland had been attacked the day before and the hesitation of the British and French Governments had excited, in many circles, suspicions that they were unwilling to accept Hitler's challenge. His speech that night was cheered by members of all parties, and no one who was there will forget its impact on an anxious House and Amery's [q.v.] call to him: "Speak for England".

He spoke only from 7.48 p.m. to 7.56 p.m., but the speech was a model of a performance suited to its occasion—"this grave moment". He made no attempt to vilify or pillory Neville Chamberlain: "No one would care to be in his shoes to-night". He spurned all false heroics: "I am not prepared to say what I would have done had I been one of those sitting on those benches". He merely stuck to the simple point that "An act of aggression took place 38 hours ago"; and so far neither France nor Britain had acted. That delay might have been justifiable, he went on, "but . . . I wonder how long we are prepared to vacillate at a time when Britain, and all that Britain stands for, and human civilization, are in peril". Then followed his plea to the French: "I hope these words of mine may go further". When he sat down the whole House was relieved. He had done what Amery had asked. The voice of England had been heard and no one could misunderstand its intonations.

In November 1939 Greenwood, Dalton* and Morrison* were nominated for the position of Leader of the Labour Party, but they stood down, allowing Attlee to be re-elected unanimously. A few days later Greenwood was himself ordered to rest by his doctors, and from then on ill-health constantly interrupted his work. When Churchill* formed his Government in 1940 Greenwood became Minister without Portfolio and Leader of the Parliamentary Labour Party, and in January 1941 was put in charge of the Government's reconstruction plans. It was he who invited Lord Beveridge* to make the inquiry which resulted in the Beveridge Report. In February 1942 he was dropped from the Administration and from then until 1945 acted in fact as a sort of Leader of the Opposition—though there was, of course, no such post as long as the coalition lasted.

After the general election of 1945 he returned to office as Lord Privy Seal, and was charged with the responsibility of coordinating all the departments concerned with national insurance. In April 1947 he was succeeded as Lord Privy Seal by Lord Inman but remained in the Cabinet as Minister without Portfolio. He resigned from the Government five months later at the request of the Prime Minister to make way for "some of the younger members of the party".

Greenwood was for many years treasurer of the Labour Party and, as such, an *ex-officio* member of the National Executive. In 1953 Morrison, who had lost his seat on the Executive in the previous year, was nominated for the post of treasurer in opposition to Greenwood. If other factors had not intruded, Morrison was clearly the fitter man for the post. But one of the factors was the warmth of the party's feeling for Greenwood as a person, and it was partly in recognition of this that Morrison stood down. Greenwood had been chairman of the party from 1952 to 1953.

Greenwood's outstanding qualities were his loyalty to colleagues, his modesty, and his utter integrity. There was a complete absence of self-seeking which won him the respect of all who knew him. His ministerial record was undistinguished: although his achievements as Minister of Health from 1929 to 1931 showed unusual promise for the future, he was not a success in either Churchill's or Attlee's Government. He was a man of more than usual ability, with a love of the highest standards of public service and it must be accounted one of the tragedies of British political life that his own weaknesses prevented him from achieving more; nevertheless his services to his party were considerable. An "intellectual", he was always on the best of terms with the trade unions, and he represented in the party counsels the humane and undogmatic tradition which has been the inspiration of the Labour Party's social—as distinct from its economic and industrial—policies. To the end of his life he maintained an interest in working-class education; and perhaps he will be remembered best as a teacher of human values.

He married in 1904 Catherine Ainsworth Brown, a childhood friend, who survives him. They had two children. His only son, Anthony Greenwood, is a Labour member of Parliament.

June 10, 1954.

Sir Walter Wilson Greg, bibliographer and Shakespearian scholar, who died on March 4, 1959, was 83.

Walter Wilson Greg was born at Wimbledon on July 9, 1875, the son of the essayist and economist, William Rathbone Greg. He was named after his grandfather, the Rt. Hon. James Wilson, founder of *The Economist,* and Walter Bagehot, its most distinguished editor, who had married his mother's eldest sister. He did not rise above the fifth form at Harrow, but he shot in the school VIII at Bisley and fenced sometimes with Winston Churchill*.

At Trinity (1894-97) he read modern English and German in the Modern and Medieval Languages Tripos, and there came to know R. B. McKerrow, for his future the most formative influence of his life. Together they founded a short-lived English Society, the minute-book of which survived to become the minute-book of the Malone Society. Here appear the names of Skeat, Gollancz*, Verrall, and G. M. Trevelyan*. It was intended that Greg should become editor of *The Economist,* a family concern, and he did become a trustee until the paper was sold in 1928; but when he should have been studying monetary theory he was already collecting material for a book on the pastoral and for a bibliography of English drama. His book on the pastoral appeared in 1906 and is still a standard book; but the bibliography of English drama published by the Bibliographical Society in 1900 brought him on the council of that society and under the inspiring influence of A. W. Pollard, and for the rest of his life he gave himself up to the studies in which he excelled. Like Edmond Malone—and no man since Malone has had so profound an influence on the textual study of Elizabethan drama—he was able to work without working for a living, and like Malone he was industrious and single-minded.

Of his skill in palaeography and Elizabethan theatrical history the edition of Henslowe's Diary is an outstanding example; of his work as a formal bibliographer the splendid *Bibliography of the English Printed Drama to the Restoration* (vol. I. 1939: vol. II. 1951); of his knowledge of Elizabethan printers and printing-houses the spectacular exposure of the false dates on the "Shakespearian" quartos of 1619; and of his high standards of accuracy the many plays edited by him or under his supervision for the Malone Society, of which he was general editor for more than 30 years until, with his blessing, the headquarters of the society moved to Oxford in 1938. But his greatest contribution was to bibliography in its widest sense, the critical analysis of texts in manuscript or print with reference to their documentary transmission.

On this problem, with much penetration of mind and with a happy blend of caution and daring, he focused his knowledge of dramatic manuscripts, printed texts, and the history of the theatre in *The Editorial Problem in Shakespeare* (1942). While he never produced an edition of a Shakespearian play, he established principles and standards of textual criticism which no editor may ignore. Of his later works, a monumental work on Marlowe's *Dr. Faustus* appeared in 1950, *Jonson's Masque of Gipsies* in 1952, and *The Shakespeare First Folio,* a large, lucid, and authoritative account, in 1955. In 1956 his lectures, given at Oxford in the previous year as James P. R. Lyell Reader in Bibliography, were reprinted as *Some Aspects and Problems of London Publishing between 1550 and 1650.*

As a reviewer he was severe but just, and he took extraordinary pains to help young scholars. Among the many honours which he received one which gave him special pleasure was his election in 1941 to an honorary fellowship at his old college, of which he had been librarian from 1907 to 1913. In 1950 he was knighted.

In 1913 he married his cousin Elizabeth Gaskell Greg, a mountaineer like himself; she survives him with three children.

March 6, 1959.

Sir Richard Gregory, F.R.S., who died on September 15, 1952 at his home at Middleton-on-Sea, Sussex, at the age of 88, was an excellent organizer and administrator who did work of great value both for science, especially as editor of *Nature,* and also for education. On June 22, 1933, he received the rare honour of election to the Royal Society under Rule XII, which empowers the admission of persons who have rendered conspicuous service to the cause of science or whose election would be of signal benefit to the society.

Richard Arman Gregory was born at Bristol on January 29, 1864, and educated at Queen Elizabeth's Hospital, a famous educational establishment in that city, and after three years as a laboratory assistant at Clifton College, became a student at the Royal College of Science in London, where he took most interest in physics, chemistry, and astronomy. He had his way to make, and on leaving the College of Science he became demonstrator in H.M. Dockyard School, Portsmouth, and a year later computor to the Solar Physics Committee and assistant to Sir Norman Lockyer.

Lockyer, with the support of the Macmillans, had founded *Nature,* and had made it the organ of British science. He secured a remarkable body of contributors, from Darwin, Huxley, and Tyndall to all the rising scientific men. There were original articles, reviews, reports of lectures, notes on research, and a correspondence column so well edited that a letter to *Nature* on a scientific matter had the same distinction as a letter to *The Times* on public affairs. In 1893 Lockyer made Gregory assistant editor, and gradually left more in his hands until, in 1919, the year before his death, he retired and Gregory became editor. It was a fortunate succession. Gregory continued *Nature* on the same general lines, but improved it as a scientific newspaper, increased its circulation, and continued to secure contributors of the highest scientific rank.

Gregory was also deeply interested in the general problems of education and an ardent supporter of the view that, whatever might be the merits of classical studies, a training in some form of experimental science and a knowledge of the main facts of science were vital necessities for all grades of the population, from statesmen to labourers. In the *School World* and the *Journal of Education,* of which he was joint editor, in articles in *Nature,* and in many public addresses he continually propounded that view, and, probably as much as any single person, advanced the educational aspects of science. His own textbooks on physical geography, physiography, experimental science, physics, and chemistry were admirable in their directness and clarity.

Elected President of the British Association in 1939, when he had been connected with the association for about 40 years, Gregory remained President until 1946. At the first meeting held after the war by the British Association, he delivered his presidential address on "Civilization—the Pursuit of Knowledge". It was in this address that he made his famous attack on atomic warfare.

"There can never be moral sanction for the mass destruction of human life by atom bombs", he said, "It is an offence against the light, for whatever cause it is taken". In politics, he was always a radical, with a strong leaning to the left wing. He was a vice-president of the Association for the Cultivation of Cultural Relations with Soviet Russia, and was always disposed to see the best side of every new movement.

Although for a time Gregory was Professor of Astronomy at Queen's College, London, and also lectured under the Oxford University extension scheme, his large contribution to the progress of science was not due to professional work or to laboratory research. He was in the first place a man of affairs, and, as this became more and more realized, he had endless duties thrust on him. He was chairman of the organizing committee of the British Scientific Products Exhibitions, 1918-19; almost the founder, and chairman, of the committee of management of the British Science Guild; and president of a large number of congresses, branches of congresses, and societies, ranging from the educational section of the British Association to the Royal Meteorological Society.

Probably he had a wider personal acquaintance with men of science than any other man of his time, and his delight in new knowledge, eagerness to support and make known the results of research, and warmth of heart made him universally respected and liked.

He was twice married. His first wife, who died in 1926, after a very long illness, left him a son and a daughter, who have both since died, and in 1931, to the pleasure of his friends, he married again. He was created a baronet in 1931.

September 16, 1952.

The death on May 6, 1958 of **Sylvia Grey,** who would have been 93 on May 18, severed perhaps the last remaining link with the Gaiety Theatre in the great days of John Hollingshead, George Edwardes, and Nellie Farren, for it is over 70 years since she first established her position as the principal dancer of the theatre and became the toast of the town.

Her task then was no easy one, for she was joining the company as the successor of one of the greatest dancers of the period, Kate Vaughan, and Nellie Farren was firmly established as the queen of the musical comedy stage.

Her first appearance at the Gaiety in 1885 was in *Little Jack Sheppard,* the last burlesque which John Hollingshead accepted for production. She was immediately hailed as a delightful dancer who could worthily carry on Kate Vaughan's tradition and practically the whole of her career was spent at the original Gaiety Theatre. She was re-engaged for the next production, *Monte Cristo,* in a company which included Nellie Farren, Fred Leslie, and E. J. Lonnen, and then for *Frankenstein,* in which as the Goddess of the Sun, supported by the Gaiety Girls as minor goddesses, she wore wonderful costumes which became the talk of the town.

A world tour which lasted for 18 months followed and it is recorded that when she reappeared at the Gaiety in *Ruy Blas and the Blasé Roué,* one of the greatest successes in the history of the theatre, she was greeted with salvoes of cheers.

This was the last entertainment in which Nellie Farren appeared at the Gaiety. Before the next production she had been stricken with illness and one of Sylvia Grey's most cherished possessions was a letter written to her by Miss Farren, who, although herself very ill, wished Miss Grey a speedy recovery from an illness from which she was suffering. Miss Grey regained her health and made a considerable success in *Cinder Ellen Up-Too-Late,* which included a burlesque of the T. W. Robertson farce *School,* which gave her a good opportunity to act as well as to dance in her usual inspired fashion.

In the autumn of 1892 she migrated to the Prince of Wales's Theatre to appear with Arthur Roberts and Florence St. John in *In Town,* which soon moved to the Gaiety and became a great success. One of the few complaints which the critics made against it was that Sylvia Grey was not given enough dancing.

She was also seen in *Don Juan* before she retired from the stage, but to the end of her long life she retained her lively interest in the theatre and the players. W. J. Macqueen-Pope [q.v.] in his history of the Gaiety Theatre recalls the fact that on the occasion of the last "first night" at the New Gaiety the audience included "a very gracious lady to whom everyone paid the greatest deference". For she had been a star of the Gaiety prior to her retirement, and her name was Sylvia Grey. It was fitting that one of the stars of the old Gaiety should come to the last first night of the New Gaiety.

When she was entertained at a Foyle's luncheon to mark the publication of the book, Sylvia Grey had an honoured place at the top table. In spite of her great age she resolutely refused to grow old and to the end she retained a wide circle of friends who delighted in her anecdotes of the halcyon days of Gaiety burlesque.

May 7, 1958.

Sir Herbert Grierson, Emeritus Professor of Rhetoric and English Literature at Edinburgh University, died in a Cambridge nursing home on February 19, 1960. He was 94.

A scholar and critic of both wide and deep learning, at once careful and enterprising in judgment, a true lover of poetry, a teacher of unfailingly enthusiastic temper, a Scotsman possessed of a native bent for theology and a perhaps equally native capacity for original ideas, Sir Herbert Grierson brought uncommon grace and stimulus to English literary studies during the past half-century. He will be remembered in the first place for his virtual re-discovery of Donne for an earlier generation of readers; for his studies in seventeenth-century literature and of the metaphysical poets in particular; and for his admirable 12-volume edition of Scott's Letters, a labour no less impressively rounded off by a new "Life" that supplements Lockhart to revealing purpose.

Herbert John Clifford Grierson, a native of Lerwick, Shetland, was born in 1866, the second son of Andrew J. Grierson. He attended Chanonry School, Old Aberdeen, before entering Aberdeen University, where he specialized in literature and philosophy, graduating in 1887 with first class honours in philosophy and winning the Bain gold medal. For two years he served as English master at the Collegiate School, Aberdeen, and then proceeded to Christ Church, Oxford, where he continued his studies in literature.

In 1893 he was appointed Lecturer in English Literature at Aberdeen University, and in the following year was made first Chalmers Professor of English Literature. Until then the teaching of English at Aberdeen had been included in the duties of the Professor of Logic. Grierson undertook the responsibility of organizing and developing a separate department of the Faculty of Arts, and during the 21 years in which he held this chair at Aberdeen he created a notable school of English studies.

In 1915 he succeeded George Saintsbury in the chair of Rhetoric and English Literature at Edinburgh University, where he taught for 20 years more. At his retirement his reputation had spread far beyond the borders of Scotland, and as a tribute to his work a committee representing British and foreign universities issued an appeal for subscriptions to a fund to commemorate his services to education and literature. On Grierson's own suggestion the money subscribed was used to endow a prize, called the Grierson Prize for English Verse, to be presented annually to a matriculated student of the University of Aberdeen or the University of Edinburgh. He was then 70, but it was said of him at the time that he was intellectually much more adventurous than the brightest of the younger generation. The students of Edinburgh University paid tribute to him a year after his retirement by electing him Rector in succession to Field-Marshal Lord Allenby.

Grierson's published work is of a high order of criticism and interpretation. Before he left Aberdeen he had achieved no little distinction with an edition of *The Poems of John Donne,* a work of careful scholarship and fine critical intelligence, which has contributed perhaps as much as any volume to the present recognition, after years of relative neglect, of Donne's true standing among English poets. Among other works a selection of *Metaphysical Lyrics and Poems of the Seventeenth Century* (1921) and an edition of Milton's poems (1925) prepared him for the labour of love, undertaken in collaboration with Geoffrey Bullough, of editing *The Oxford Book of Seventeenth Century Verse* (1934). In *Cross Currents in English Literature of the Seventeenth Century* (1929), he examined the workings of the Puritan temper upon literature, and in the result proved engagingly controversial while never failing to quicken and enrich the historical imagination of the reader. His splendid edition of Scott's Letters appeared in 1937, the new Life in the following year. There were several volumes of collected papers; translations of Dutch poetry (seventeenth-century and contemporary), of which he probably knew as much as any English professor; literary-historical essays such as *Carlyle and Hitler* (1933). In 1942 appeared a most spirited and lightly erudite *Critical History of English Poetry*. written by Grierson in association with J. C. Smith. *Rhetoric and English Composition* appeared in 1945; *And the Third Day* in 1948; and *Criticism and Creation,* a further collection of essays and addresses, in 1950.

Grierson, who received his knighthood in 1936, was an honorary LL.D. of St. Andrews and Aberdeen Universities and an honorary D.Litt of Oxford, Cambridge, and Manchester Universities and of Trinity College, Dublin. He married, in 1896, Mary Letitia, daughter of the late Professor Sir Alexander Ogston, K.C.V.O. She died in 1937. There were five daughters of the marriage.

February 22, 1960.

His Eminence Cardinal Bernard Griffin, Archbishop of Westminster since 1944, died on August 20, 1956. He was 57.

At the time of his elevation to the Sacred College Pope Pius XII [q.v.] described Cardinal Griffin as the Benjamin of the College; and his comparative youth gave promise of a long and important chapter in the history of the Archdiocese of Westminster. His appointment to succeed Cardinal Hinsley, who had won a remarkable measure of affection from Catholic and non-Catholic alike, was generally unexpected, although his brilliant scholastic career at the English College, Rome, coupled with the administrative skill he had shown as auxiliary Bishop for Birmingham, had made it clear that he was destined for higher office.

Unfortunately his active mind, warm sympathies and driving energy caused him to overtax his strength; unlike Cardinal Hinsley, who enlisted the help of able subordinates, clerical and lay, he was reluctant to delegate authority; and a series of important visits oversea added a further strain that it was beyond his constitution to bear. Notable among these visits were his journey to Poland after the 1939-45 War, his cross-continental tour in Canada, undertaken with Cardinal McGuigan, Archbishop of Toronto, and during which they were joined by Cardinal Gilroy, Archbishop of Sydney, and his participation in the celebrations that followed the restoration of Cologne Cathedral. It was characteristic of his indifference to physical and mental strain that before travelling to Cologne he insisted upon intensive coaching in German in order to avoid preaching to his German hearers in a foreign language.

A breakdown in health occurred suddenly in January 1949 and was followed by prolonged convalescence. He recovered sufficiently to preside as Papal Legate at the hierarchy centenary congress in the autumn, but he was still obviously a sick man, limping visibly and denied the free use of his right hand. The strength of will that enabled him to preside at the numerous ceremonies, culminating in the open-air Mass in Wembley Stadium, could be assessed fully only by those in the Cardinal's curia; but it was sufficiently evident to the great crowds attending the conference to arouse widespread sympathy.

The effects of a second breakdown were so grave that the Cardinal received the last Sacraments. Until September 1951 he underwent a further period of convalescence, during which the affairs of the see were administered by his senior auxiliary, Bishop Myers, who was appointed to a titular archiepiscopal see and named as coadjutor, though not with right of succession. After his return to Westminster, Cardinal Griffin was obliged to restrict the number of his public engagements and to rely more than in the past upon the administrative help of others. Outwardly his health was remarkably improved, but it was clear still that he needed to husband his strength and to avoid prolonged effort and overwork. Nevertheless he was able to take part in numerous national and diocesan events, during which his addresses and impromptu speeches gave little evidence of a precarious state of health. Indeed many of those who met him on these occasions, and in whose individual activities and problems he showed a lively interest, began to look forward to a complete recovery. In May 1952 he flew to Barcelona to attend the International Eucharistic Congress; and thereafter he continued his annual pilgrimages to Lourdes, and other visits abroad, including an important one to Rome this year for an audience with Pope Pius XII, his journey to Norway, and his journey to Holland for the funeral of the Cardinal Archbishop of Utrecht.

Bernard William Griffin was born at Birmingham on February 21, 1899, the son of the late William Bernard Griffin, who manufactured bicycles at Sparkhill and served on the city council for many years. As a small boy Griffin was sent to Cotton College, in North Staffordshire, the oldest Roman Catholic college in England, and on leaving there passed to Oscott, the seminary of the Archdiocese of Birmingham. He soon left, to serve as a rating in the Royal Naval Air Service during the closing stages of the 1914-18 War. Immediately after the war he returned to Oscott, where he showed such brilliance in his studies that he was sent to the English College at Rome, then under the rectorship of Monsignor Arthur Hinsley, whom he always regarded with affectionate veneration and whom he was destined to succeed in the archbishopric of Westminster. He was ordained in 1924 at the college, but remained in Rome for three years longer, taking distinguished degrees as a Doctor of Divinity at the Gregorian University and as a Doctor of Canon Law at the Apollinare.

In 1927 he went back to England to serve as secretary to Dr. McIntyre, the Archbishop of Birmingham. When Dr. McIntyre retired from the see in 1929 his secretary continued in office under Dr. Thomas Williams. Though the Cardinal was never a parish priest, he filled many and most varied ecclesiastical offices in Birmingham and won admiration and popularity in them all. He was chancellor of the archdiocese, director of studies for the Catholic Evidence Guild, president of the Birmingham Catholic Youth Council, and a member of the religious advisory committee to the B.B.C. In 1937 he became the resident administrator of Father Hudson's Homes, the largest charitable institution in the country for the care of children. Within a couple of years he had added an extensive range of new nurseries and a church to the buildings at Coleshill. When he was only 40 years of age, in 1939, the Pope appointed him auxiliary Bishop of Birmingham with the title of Bishop of Abya. The announcement of his appointment as Archbishop of Westminster was made on December 22, 1943, and caused considerable surprise, not merely on account of his youth but also because his name had not been mentioned in any of the current speculations about the successor to Cardinal Hinsley.

Dr. Griffin lost no time in entering into possession of his see, and was enthroned at Westminster Cathedral on January 18, 1944, the feast of the Chair of St. Peter at Rome. The ceremony was much briefer than usual, because of his previous consecration as Bishop of Abya and also because the *pallium,* owing to conditions of war, could not be forwarded in time from the Vatican. Though few of his new subjects could have had previous acquaintance with their archbishop, he was received with much enthusiasm by the Roman Catholics of London, who had acquainted themselves with the main facts of his distinguished career and were much attracted by his youth, his vitality, and the radiant geniality of his disposition. In his brief inaugural allocution, delivered in a ringing, manly voice, he stated that he intended to direct his mission specially towards the poor, declaring that: "When Our Lord first went to the Temple to teach, He opened the Book of the Prophets and read this rather amazing prophecy about His mission: 'The Spirit of the Lord is upon Me. Wherefore He hath sent Me to preach the Gospel to the poor'. When St. John the Baptist seeks evidence of Christ's mission, the sign, among others, that Christ gives him is 'That the poor have the Gospel preached to them' ". Throughout his life Dr. Griffin was a man of the Gospel; an evangelical. A lasting memorial of his archiepiscopate is the new translation of the Bible which he encouraged Mgr. R. A. Knox [q.v.] to complete; and a collection of his addresses, entitled *Seek Ye First,* which was published in 1949, affords impressive evidence of his apostolic abilities. On his forty-seventh birthday, when he had been at Westminster for little more than two years, he was elevated to the Sacred College as the youngest of the Cardinals.

He was always a believer in the policy of strengthening through personal contacts the bonds that unite Roman Catholics throughout the world, and until his health broke down in January 1949 he showed phenomenal energy in a series of official visits which he paid to the hierarchies of many countries. In 1944, within a month of the liberation of Rome, he flew to Italy to visit the allied troops; in 1945 he made a tour of France, Belgium, Holland, and Germany to re-establish relations with the bishops of those countries and to learn at first hand of their post-war problems; in 1946, in addition to his visit to Rome for the Consistory, he made an extensive tour of the United States of America; in 1947, following another visit to Rome, he travelled on to Lourdes, where he led a great English pilgrimage to pray for peace; and in the June of that year he made a wide tour of Poland, where he was received with immense enthusiasm.

On his return, after a few months of great activity in his own diocese, he went with his two brother Cardinals of the British Empire, Cardinal McGuigan of Toronto and Cardinal Gilroy of Sydney, on a triumphal tour across Canada from coast to coast. Before the year was out he paid a brief visit to Denmark. In February 1948 he was again in Belgium, and later visited Cologne to take part in the celebration of the seventh centenary of its cathedral, going on from there to visit the Roman Catholics of the British troops in Germany. In September 1948 he travelled to Lisieux to bless a great bell for the Basilica of St. Teresa of the Child Jesus, for whom he had a deep devotion. He went to Norway and he visited Germany again as guest of Cardinal Frings and Cardinal Feltin.

He took few and brief holidays. He was the most accessible of prelates. Nearly every weekend found him addressing large gatherings either in his own diocese or in the provincial cities. He was punctilious and self-sacrificing in fulfilling such engagements, and every speech he made was the product of close meditation and reflection. He revelled in the society of men, and had a keen sense of the ludicrous. Those who marvelled at the extent of his activities were not surprised when in January 1949 his health collapsed.

After several months spent in the Hospital of St. John and Elizabeth and a subsequent spell of convalescence, his doctors decided that he was able to return to Westminster and resume his archiepiscopal duties. His cure was apparently complete and he found himself able to direct and control Roman Catholic policy concerning the problem of education, which was then becoming acute; but at the end of September 1949 he suffered a severe and sudden relapse. From this he recovered with surprising quickness and, before the year was out, was well enough to sustain the long and elaborate ceremonies he undertook on important occasions.

In 1950, as active as ever, he was nominated Papal Legate for the celebrations marking the first centenary of the reconstitution of the Roman Catholic Hierarchy in England and Wales.

It was, however, clear when he presided at the long ceremonies in Westminster Cathedral and Wembley Stadium that he needed assistance in walking and that one arm had been affected by his illness, and the strain brought on a relapse. Nevertheless, he led the Holy Year pilgrimage of the Hierarchy of England and Wales to Rome later in the year, but soon after his return in November he was ordered a complete rest by his doctors. After a long-overdue holiday in the country he returned to Westminster a few days before Christmas. In the circumstances it was extraordinary that in addition to his activity in the administration of his diocese, and in the manifold duties of the permanent chairman of the Hierarchy of England and Wales, he presided at the meetings of societies, took a keen interest in their work and presided and preached at many great functions.

Another heart attack supervened, but he again recovered and continued his busy life almost to the end. As Archbishop Gerald O'Hara*, Apostolic Delegate to Great Britain, has truly said: "During the past five years all England and hundreds of thousands of others beyond these shores have stood in admiration before the unflinching courage of Cardinal Griffin in his gallant fight to continue his work as the chief shepherd of the archdiocese of Westminster in the face of prolonged and serious illness".

Only in May the Cardinal, displaying that acuteness of mind and anxious concern for his flock, sent out a pastoral letter putting forward proposals to help young married couples to embark on families with less anxiety. His last public appearance was on June 28 when he presided and preached at the High Mass in Westminster for the centenary of the Victoria Cross.

He was suffering clearly from fatigue after a long series of engagements which had culminated a week earlier in his attendance at the fifth centenary celebrations in Rouen of the rehabilitation of St. Joan of Arc. He was unable to attend a reception after the Mass for Roman Catholic M.P.s; and in the evening a speech he was to have made at a Mansion House dinner was read for him by his private secretary, Mgr. Worlock. On that occasion, the Duke of Norfolk*, presiding, stated that the Cardinal had been ordered to rest.

He stayed for some time at Torquay before going to Cornwall, where he died.

August 21, 1956.

Edward Grigg—See **Altrincham.**

Sir Arthur Grimble, K.C.M.G., who achieved distinction in the Colonial Service and later became a most popular and beguiling broadcasting raconteur, died on December 12, 1956.

Grimble was born in 1888 in Hongkong, where his family had business interests. He was the son of Frank Grimble and was educated at Chigwell School and Magdalene College, Cambridge. After taking his degree he pursued post-graduate studies in France and Germany and became a good French and German scholar. In 1914 he joined the Colonial Service in the Pacific as a Cadet and was posted to the Gilbert and Ellice Islands, where he remained in various positions until 1933. For his last seven years there he was the Resident Commissioner, that is to say, the head of the administration of the colony under the High Commissioner for the Western Pacific. He was then transferred to St. Vincent in the Windward Islands as Administrator, remaining there until he became Governor of the Seychelles in 1936. In 1942 he was promoted to be Governor of the Windward Islands, whose Government he had administered temporarily from time to time while in St. Vincent.

In spite of the fact that for 19 of the most formative years of his life Grimble was relegated to the most remote and least visited part of the British Colonial Empire (a milestone at Tarawa shows the distance from London as 16,001 miles), those lonely Gilbert and Ellice atolls which are the only territory in the world to straddle both the Equator and the International Date Line, he remained a suave, cultivated and polished man of the world and a good European.

At the same time his linguistic gifts enabled him to get to know his attractive charges, the Micronesian Gilbertese and the Polynesian Ellice Islanders, as few white men have got to know them. He became an almost perfect Gilbertese scholar and was said to have been the only white man not married to a native to have been initiated into some of the Gilbertese societies.

In the Seychelles his good knowledge of French proved useful, while in the West Indies his interests took another turn—namely, the encouragement of wider political responsibilities for the coloured people and the pursuit of the goal of West Indian Federation, towards which the federation of the Windward and Leeward Islands was the first logical step.

He became C.M.G. in 1930 and K.C.M.G. in

1938. In 1948 Grimble retired on pension from the Colonial Service and, not long after his return to England, discovered a new bent and, in fact, a new career. In his leisure he began to jot down in narrative form some of his more personal experiences in the Gilbert and Ellice Islands, took them to the B.B.C., and was found to possess not only the gift of telling a good story but an admirable broadcasting voice. The result was a series of talks which became extremely popular and achieved equal success in their published form as *A Pattern of Islands,* which was published in 1933. A film based on the book had its first showing this year.

Grimble married in 1914 Olivia Mary Jarvis, daughter of Lewis Jarvis. There were four daughters of the marriage.

December 13, 1956.

Hans Grimm, the German writer, died at the age of 84 in September 1959.

Born on March 22, 1875, at Wiesbaden, the son of a professor who, as co-founder of the German Colonial Association, influenced the course of his son's career, Hans Grimm had a public school education and studied at Lausanne and at the Colonial Institute of Hamburg before choosing overseas trade as a career.

He went first to Nottingham, then to Port Elizabeth, where the life and landscape of South Africa got hold of him, and, after four years there, moved to East London. He returned to Germany in 1912 to study politics and economics at Munich, and began to write. His first volume of "South African Novels" appeared in 1913, though sketches *Die Grobbelaars* had, without attracting attention, been printed in 1907.

A better novel, *Der Gang durch den Sand,* written before the First World War, was published in 1916 while its author was serving with the German forces. *Die Oelsucher von Duala* (1918) achieved considerable success. But not until 1926, when his two-volume tale *Volk ohne Raum* appeared, did Grimm become a well-known literary figure. He was awarded an honorary Ph.D. by Göttingen University, made a member of literary societies and lionized. *Volk ohne Raum* told the story of German colonization, its rise and fall. Its title implied propaganda for the recovery by Germany of her lost colonies, but it was propaganda written with knowledge and skill. It had enormous sales.

In the meantime he had acquired a country estate once belonging to his family, on the river Weser, and he made another extensive journey in 1927-28 to South Africa, this time for a study of the former German colony S.W. Africa. The fruits were *Thirteen Letters from S.W. Africa* (1928), *The German South-Wester's Book* (1929), and further novels, such as *Der Richter in der Karu* (1930).

His subsequent literary activity was devoted mainly to essays, speeches, and short stories and the creation of a circle of poets who assembled, once a year, on his estate for intellectual exchange. *Der Schriftsteller und seine Zeit* (1931), *Von der bürgerlichen Ehre und bürgerlichen Notwendigkeit* (1931), *Was wir suchen, ist alles* (1933) were the results of a philosophical, essentially nationalist, but not chauvinist thinker. Though the Nazis found *Volk ohne Raum,* in particular, much to their taste, Grimm never, it seems, joined the party. Nevertheless, *Answer of a German* (1952) made it clear that he had more than a sneaking sympathy with their aims.

He emerged politically undamaged from the United States examination of his conduct, in 1945, although for a short period he had been vice-president of the Chamber of Literature during the Nazi period.

In 1955 he resigned his membership in the German Schiller Society in protest against the selection of Thomas Mann as the main speaker at a Schiller memorial ceremony.

September 29, 1959.

Beatrice Grimshaw, whose death at Bathurst at the age of 82 took place in June 1953, was an intrepid traveller among the Pacific islands.

Making her home in that region for many years and exploring dangerous tracts of country in which no white woman had previously set foot, she constructed from her experiences in the South Seas a long sequence of novels and short stories that achieved high competence, and a number of travel books that came nearer to the truth than many of the more highly coloured narrations which the public had learnt to expect from those distant and exotic quarters.

She was born at Cloona, co. Antrim, the third daughter of the late Nicholas Grimshaw, and educated at Caen, Normandy, at the Victoria College, Belfast, and at Bedford College, London. By the date of her graduation her family were settled in Dublin, and she took to journalism there, acting first as sub-editor of a sporting paper and later as editor of a Society sheet. Never a girl to "sew a fine seam", she welcomed the slight lessening of restraints on feminine conduct which began in the nineties. The bicycle was the sign and symbol of this partial emancipation, and Miss Grimshaw used the vehicle with such enthusiasm that she created a new women's 24-hour world record on the road.

From Dublin she made her way in due course to London, where she continued her journalistic occupations. Like many before her, she had conceived a passionate desire to see the world, and especially the South Seas. Having no money to finance such an expedition, she thought of a scheme that was admirably simple but needed *aplomb* (not to say impudence) for its achievement. This was to approach the shipping companies, offering newspaper publicity against free passages, and the newpapers, tempting them with good "copy". By a miracle she convinced both parties, went off on a six months' series of voyages, and was so successful as to realize her dream of living among the islands.

About 1906 Miss Grimshaw began her residence in the South Seas and her career as an author. Over a long period of years she visited Fiji, the New Hebrides, the Solomon Islands, the unknown cannibal country of Papua, New Guinea, the Celebes, Borneo, the Moluccas, New Britain, Burma, the Straits Settlements, New Caledonia, Java, and Dutch New Guinea. The jewel-like colour of these lands attracted her—their almost unsullied summer, their leisured life, endless conversation, and light-hearted spirit. Undaunted by fever, mosquitoes, great heat, rough country, and the presence of tribes known to hunt heads and eat human flesh, she avidly pursued her investigations and travels, and became an authority on tropical colonization. She was the first white woman to visit the great Sepik and Fly Rivers in New Guinea. She had a plantation in that country for some time, but sold it just before 1922 (in which year she paid one of her brief visits to London).

Her first three books all appeared in 1907. Two of them, *From Fiji to the Cannibal Islands* and *In the Strange South Seas,* were works of travel; the third, *Vaiti of the Islands,* was her first exercise in fiction, which promised well in spite of constructional weakness. She followed these volumes up with a long series of novels, collections of short stories, and travel books, which showed genuine knowledge of the native mind and considerable power in creating atmosphere.

Though far from insensible of the picturesque aspects of life in the South Seas, Miss Grimshaw deprecated the exaggerated romanticism which has often represented the islands as being given over to alcoholic libations, passionate dalliance and garlands of flowers. In *Isles of Adventure* (1930) she wrote that the sensual waster would go to the devil there more quickly than elsewhere, but that he was far from being a typical product. Miss Grimshaw faced all situations with courage, and declared that she had never felt herself in danger from cannibals. When she retired 14 years ago to Australia she had found enough material on her tours in the Pacific to fill nearly 40 volumes. Her last book, *Wild Mint of Moresby,* was published in 1940.

July 1, 1953.

Grock, the celebrated clown, perhaps "der König der Clowns", the King of the Clowns, as he was so often billed, died on July 14, 1959 at Imperia, Italy. He was 79.

"There are clowns and there is Grock", wrote A. B. Walkley. "For Grock happens to be an artist, and the artist is always an individual. After all, as an individual artist he must have invented himself. It was a remarkably happy invention". Indeed it was, for everywhere he went—and he had been almost everywhere—he reduced people to helpless laughter at the mere idea of a being so grotesque as the one before them. Reading of his death those whom he so often enchanted will recall, with joy, his deprecating manner as he waddled in with an enormous portmanteau containing a tiny fiddle; the dress clothes into which, on the hint of his partner, he changed; the roar of delight with which he grasped the idea of moving the chair to the piano instead of the piano to the chair; his sliding down the lid to the floor and thereafter playing with his feet; his collapse through the seat of the chair, only to play the concertina with extraordinary brilliance in white cotton gloves; his mastery over all kinds of musical instruments.

They will remember how they longed to rush to help him when his fiddle and bow got into the wrong hands and defied all his efforts to change them over, and to comfort him when his hat came off and the exposure of his bald head brought him to the verge of tears.

He was born Karl Adrien Wettach, the son of a Swiss watchmaker, at Reconvilier, a little village in the French-speaking part of the Berner Jura, on January 10, 1880. His father, a noted athlete, rifle shot, and yodeller, came from Reichenbach, near Frutigen, in the Oberland, and his mother, from Neuchâtel, was of Huguenot stock. From the moment when, at the age of seven, Adrien saw his first circus through a hole in the tent, he determined to become a clown. His father applauded his decision and taught him music. He made his first clown's dress sitting on a dog kennel. At the age of 15 he toured Switzerland with his sister as a tight-rope walker and acrobat.

Thereafter his life, until he became established as "Grock" (he took the name because the Brock partner of a comic couple, Brick and Brock, to whom he was recommended, had to leave to do his military service, so that for three years the firm was Brick and Grock; he made his first appearance under that name in the arena at Nimes), was one long series of adventures. Among other occupations he was, in his time, stable boy, waiter, cook, piano-tuner, conductor, tutor in foreign languages, box-office keeper, watch-maker, gardener, fencing master and water finder. He even, according to his own account, added on one occasion that of assistant *accoucheur*. For when the ship in which he was crossing the Atlantic came into collision at a moment when he was making up for an entertainment he so much frightened a lady who, like himself, had rushed into the corridor that, with the assistance of the doctor, Grock, and a steward, she gave birth to twins.

His American tour was not a success. His train was wrecked in the middle of the night between Halifax and New York and 10 passengers were killed. His taxi-cab turned upside down on the way from the station. He had shingles, a heart attack and influenza. But he was also too simple for the New Yorkers—just as in his first four performances in Berlin he was—extraordinary though it may seem—too "broad" for the Germans, who wanted "variety", not "circus".

He went to England before the First World War, finding the audiences "wonderful, quick, and subtle", with German audiences their only equal. But he left Britain in 1924 after a disagreement with Sir Oswald Stoll, manager of the London Coliseum, saying he would never return. He never did. There was also a dispute with the Inland Revenue—which he never forgot—over an income tax claim on earnings during a previous visit.

After the Second World War he had his own travelling circus in Germany and in Hamburg in 1954, having three times in 28 years retired "definitely and irrevocably", he retired for good. He held an honorary doctorate of Budapest University.

In the last few years he occasionally performed on Italian television. During his final appearance at Milan in March he fell ill in front of the cameras, but managed to finish his act before collapsing.

Grock, "a talking film with the famous clown as the central figure", was produced in Berlin in 1931, and in the same year he published *Grock: Life's a Lark,* a book of reminiscences. Twenty-five years later he published his autobiography.

July 15, 1959.

Sir Hugh Grosvenor—See **Westminster.**

George Grosz died in Berlin on July 6, 1959. He was 65.

He was the *enfant terrible* of modern German art, though he eventually became an American citizen. A brilliant caricaturist, merciless in his castigation of society at large, Grosz was frowned upon equally by the Imperial, Weimar, and Nazi authorities in his native country. Much of his work was pornographical, and it is difficult to say how far this was due to personal inclination and how far to the nature of the vices he attacked, but it is worth recalling that when in 1917 Grosz was arrested and condemned to be shot on the charge of sacrilege, it was the Roman Catholic faction that took up his cause and secured a remission of the sentence.

George Grosz came of a middle-class family and was born in Berlin on July 26, 1893. He began life as a song-and-dance artist in music halls, dancing eccentrically to his own guitar, and chanting satirical monologues of his own composition on the vices and subservience to the military caste of the bourgeoisie from which he sprang.

From 1909 to 1911 he studied painting at the Dresden Academy and other centres in Germany. Later he took part in the Berlin phase of the Dada movement, that "sickness of the world", as it has been called, which began at Zürich in 1916 and was christened by the simple method of slipping a paper-knife at random into a dictionary; the word "Dada" meaning a child's hobby-horse. Besides reducing all art to nonsense in a fit of despair, Dada aimed at obliterating the individuality of the artist. Max Ernst [d. 1976] and Hans Arp* signed each other's drawings, and Heartfield worked under the direction of Grosz.

It was during his Dada period that Grosz narrowly escaped with his life. He had already published the series *Ecce Homo,* satirizing the Junkers, and was under official surveillance, but had been able to establish in Munich a journal called the *Neue Jugend.* In it he attacked the Kaiser personally, and a warrant was issued for his arrest. He escaped, but from his hiding place sent two paintings to an exhibition, one of which represented the crucified Christ wearing a gas-mask. He was caught and condemned to the firing squad for sacrilege, but through Roman Catholic intervention he was paroled and sent to the front line trenches.

After the war Grosz continued to attack authority under Ebert and Hindenburg, and he was constantly under threats of arrest, but by this time he seems to have realized that the evils he satirized were not peculiar to any particular political régime, and his caricatures became more general in their target and at the same time gentler.

In 1924, however, his cartoons were tried for "wounding the moral susceptibilities of normal people". Max Osborn, the art critic, and Maximilian Harden, who were the experts consulted, were unanimous in their tribute to the genius of Grosz. The report of the trial, the judge "severe with suppressed moral indignation", and Grosz "shy, sensitive, awkward, and hardly knowing what to say", makes interesting reading, because it suggests that Grosz's pornographic leanings gave a handle to his political enemies. The result was a verdict of guilty; Grosz and his two publishers were fined 500 marks each, the series of *Ecce Homo* was confiscated, and all the plates were ordered to be destroyed.

Early in 1933 Grosz anticipated Hitler, who also had burnt albums of *Ecce Homo* along with the books of Freud, Krafft-Ebing, and Magnus Hirschfeld, and emigrated to New York as a teacher at the New School for Social Research and T. B. Newmann's New Art Circle, and in due course he was naturalized as an American citizen.

Of the technical ability of Grosz there could be no question, his paintings being carried out in a combination of freely handled incisive line and rather "smoky" gradations of subdued colour, slightly reminiscent of the Japanese Foujita.

Grosz illustrated many albums and books for German and French publishers. He is represented in the Jeu de Paume, Paris, in the museums of Moscow, Antwerp, Basle, Grenoble, Prague, Vienna, Oslo and Venice, and in the principal museums of the United States. In England he is represented in the collection of the Contemporary Art Society. His autobiography, *Ein kleines Ja und ein grosses Nein,* was published in 1955. He returned to Berlin in June.

July 7, 1959.

Brigadier-General P. R. C. Groves, C.B., C.M.G., D.S.O., died in Mombasa on August 12, 1959.

The son of J. Groves, formerly of the Public Works Department of India, Percy Robert Clifford Groves was born in 1878 and educated at Bedford. He joined the King's Shropshire Light Infantry in 1899, served through the war in South Africa and in 1903-04 was employed with the West African Regiment. In 1914 he joined the R.F.C., served in France and the Dardanelles, trained as an observer, and later qualified as a pilot, doing much active flying. For nearly two years he was Chief of Staff, R.F.C. Middle East, an organization which then embraced four theatres of war, and in 1918 he was made Director of Flying Operations at the Air Ministry. In 1919 he was appointed British Air Adviser to the Supreme Council and the Council of Ambassadors, and at the same time to the Council of the League of Nations.

Just before he retired in 1922 with the rank of Brigadier-General he was British Air Representative on the Inter-Allied Military Committee of Versailles, which, under the presidency of Foch, was primarily responsible for ensuring the execution of the disarmament clauses of the peace treaties.

His years of active service made an indelible impression on his thinking; the development of aviation had fundamentally altered the character of war and like others he viewed with alarm the trend of British post-war air policy, believing it to be based on the narrowest traditional military ideals and lacking in vision. He proceeded to campaign at once for the creation of an effective striking force and for a proper regard for the patent realities of civil aviation. He attracted the interest of Northcliffe, and shortly before Northcliffe's death in 1922 a series of articles on "Our Future in the Air" was published in *The Times.*

For two years in the late 1920s he was honorary secretary-general of the Air League of the British Empire and editor of *Air;* and early in 1934 appeared *Behind the Smoke Screen,* in which he was revealed as an able and angry man, passionately concerned about the state of Britain's air defence, and as a forceful campaigner for an immediate expansion of the R.A.F. to parity with the largest European force within striking distance.

In the climate of opinion that then prevailed his book was not universally welcomed—and perhaps his angry arraignment of those in high places did not endear him to many who had been associated with British air policy since 1918, but he wrote illuminatingly of the new problems of strategy, and the book was seen by many as a salutary and revealing document.

In 1939 he returned to active service, was Deputy Director of Intelligence at the Air Ministry until April 1940, and was then seconded for duty at the Foreign Office.

He married in 1920 Suzanne, daughter of E. Steen, of Oslo, by whom he had a son.

August 17, 1959.

General Heinz Guderian, who had one of the most creative military minds of the 1939-45 War, has died at Füssen, in Bavaria, at the age of 65.

He was born at Kulm, in west Prussia, later the Polish "Corridor", in 1888, the son of an army officer. Kurt Schumacher, the late Socialist Democrat leader, came from the same small town, and though Guderian was older the two men knew each other from youth. His father expressed the wish that he should become an officer and he was sent, with his brother, to the Karlsruhe cadet school in Baden. From there he was later transferred to the chief cadet school at Gross-Lichterfelde, near Berlin.

During the 1914-18 War his career alternated between regimental and staff duties, and by 1922 he had a wide knowledge of the army and its organization which stood him in good stead when he came to build up a formidable new arm of the service. It was Hitler, in the 1930s, who gave him the opportunity to put into practice the idea of a mobile armoured army which will stand as his contribution to the theory of war. Other men had the same idea, or a similar one: General Fuller*, General Martel [q.v.], and Captain (Sir Basil) Liddell Hart* in Britain, and General de Gaulle* in France, to all of whom he made acknowledgment. Some are apt to say, therefore, that he owes his place in military history merely to the fact that he alone found a political ruler to back him.

But there was more to it than that. He joined to his creative imagination a dynamic energy and opportunism. As chief of staff to the inspectorate of motorized troops, and later as chief of staff to the armoured troops command, he was given the authority and the resources to build up a powerful mobile armoured force. Then, in 1938, he was appointed chief of mobile troops and promoted general of Panzer troops, and within a year could test his new model army in battle—in the invasion of Poland. The accuracy of his conception was immediately proved by the speed with which he broke through the Polish "Corridor" and drove through Wizna to Brest.

But it was the campaign in the west which was his most remarkable achievement. Here his unorthodox method of leading his armoured and motorized forces—giving them the "green light to the very end of the road"—was as successful as the original conception. In the Russian campaign the Panzer army was at first even more successful. But soon they had to contend with a new and dangerous enemy—space and depth. "The very end of the road" was now a very long way away. Moscow did not fall—and he fell out of favour.

When he was finally reinstated, after the conspiracy of July 20, in which he had no part, he was given the wholly unsuitable post of Chief of Staff, in which his fighting qualities could not help him. This last phase of the war was the phase, too, through which it was difficult for a high German officer to pass with moral credit, unless with risk to his life. He remained attached to Hitler, though not without hesitation and doubts, for which he had to pay in the last months of violence and defeat with utterances which did him no credit. Yet it must be said that he had dared to oppose Hitler when his sense of decent soldierly behaviour was affronted.

As his volume of recollections, *Panzer Leader,* showed, he was a typical product of his Prussian traditions. He never pretended to have conspired against Hitler or to have quarrelled with him, except to prevent him making mistakes. But the German general who in 1944 extorted from Hitler permission to withdraw two S.S. brigades which had committed monstrous atrocities in Warsaw—and it was not an isolated act—deserves the tribute as well as the blame for the qualities nourished by his upbringing and his background.

May 17, 1954.

Lord Haden-Guest—See **Haden-.**

Sacha Guitry died in Paris on July 24, 1957 at the age of 72.

The special technique of writing for the theatre seems to present little difficulty to Frenchmen who can write at all. Perhaps the clarity and constructive quality of the French mind predisposes them to it. Sacha Guitry could make a play out of nothing; he did so, again and again; and he could fill a Paris theatre with those light trifles, which began late, were divided by a long interval, and occupied hardly more than an hour of acting time. But he could also make something more solid. There was that pitiless study of feminine character *Mon père avait raison.* There were his biographical plays, such as *Pasteur,* and *Jean de la Fontaine,* and *Mozart.*

To be sure, he always, or nearly always, took the principal part in his plays himself: and many people thought that it was his charm and skill as an actor which made them, rather than his accomplishment as a dramatist. It will be interesting to see whether the truth of this opinion will ever be tested by revivals of his work. Perhaps the simplicity or the effrontery—which was it?—of his habit of putting on the stage the petty details of his own daily life and that of the Paris of his time will date it so definitely as to make revival impossible until the pieces become period pieces.

Guitry was born into the theatre. His mother was an actress, and his father was the famous, and one might almost say the great actor, Lucien Guitry, who began in the flamboyant and tempestuous school of Sarah Bernhardt—he was long her Armand Duval in *La Dame aux Camélias*—and ended as the founder of a quiet and restrained school of passionate acting.

Sacha Guitry first saw the light on February 21, 1885, at St. Petersburg—hence his Russian first name. His parents were acting there in a French stock company. He was brought back to Paris at the age of six, and eventually went to school at the well-known Lycée Janson de Sailly in the fashionable sixteenth *arrondissement.*

He did not stay there long, however, and was sent in succession to eight other schools—one that of the Dominican Fathers—before he threw up school altogether at the age of 16, and started out on his career as a playwright. This was with a little musical piece called *Le Page.* He had already made his first appearance on the stage when he was five years old, at St. Petersburg with his father; and when he was 17 he joined the company of the Renaissance Theatre in Paris.

However, nine years later, he gave up acting in plays other than his own, and continued writing them for himself at the rate of one, and sometimes two, a year, almost continuously until the war of 1939. His total output was more than a hundred. He had begun as an impertinent infant prodigy; and he really may be said to have kept up that character until the end of his life. In 1920, when he was 35, he was already well enough known to take a company to London and appeared in *Nono, La prise de Berg-op-Zoom, Jean de la Fontaine, l'Illusioniste* (in which he took the part of a conjurer, and displayed his ability, of which he was very proud, to do certain tricks), *Le Grand Duc,* and *Monsieur attend une dame*—all plays of his own. A year earlier he had become the manager of his own theatre in Paris, though he had always in fact directed his productions. This theatre was the little newly built Mathurins, which he opened. He afterwards moved in succession to half a dozen other houses, some large, but usually small, for he preferred a small stage and intimate, indeed confidential, effects.

Away from the theatre he was still a personality. He had considerable talent as a caricaturist and some as a sculptor, and was a very typical member of that undefined social body le Tout-Paris, in which he loved to shine—for he was an excellent talker, and was attractive, if never really sympathetic. Guitry was a collector of pictures, objets d'art, manuscripts, and autographs. His hobby, as listed by himself in a book of reference, was roulette.

After the war of 1939-45 Guitry was arrested together with many other Frenchmen who were thought to have been unduly sympathetic towards the Germans. But it was later decided that he had no case to answer and he was released.

Since 1951 he had been in indifferent and failing health, but none the less managed to make a number of films, including *Si Paris nous était conté* and *Si Versailles m'était conté* both of them historical extravaganzas of dubious taste. His last film was *Assassins et Voleurs.*

He was married five times—"Most men have had as many women in their lives", he said, "but I marry them".

Sacha Guitry's first wife was Charlotte Lyses, a society woman older than himself, who became an actress when he married her, and appeared with him in most of his early plays.

This marriage, like all the others except the last, ended in divorce. He then married his best-known wife and acting partner, Yvonne Printemps [d. 1977]; a charmingly pretty but then unknown singer with a good voice, whom he schooled into being a really accomplished actress (he taught all his wives to act, but never so successfully). Guitry's next wife was Jacqueline Delubac, another charming actress. When divorce had also brought this union to an end, he chose a lady of some social position, Geneviève Serréville, and the wedding was celebrated in church with considerable pomp. His fifth wife was Laura Marconi, whom he married in 1947, and who survives him.

July 25, 1957.

Calouste Gulbenkian, who died in Lisbon on July 20, 1955 at the age of 86, was one of the pioneers of oil development in the Middle East, and the possessor of a vast fortune derived from his holdings in the Iraq Petroleum Company and other companies. He had also made one of the finest private collections of paintings in modern times.

Gulbenkian's death removes the last of the great pioneering figures who gave the oil industry outside the United States substantially the shape that belongs to it to-day. Like his contemporaries, Henri Deterding and Marcus Samuel (first Lord Bearsted), Gulbenkian was primarily a negotiator and organizer. Like them he became involved in the oil industry more or less by chance, but he shared their belief in the dominating part which oil was destined to play in the world, and like them he lived to see his belief justified.

To-day the incredible richness of Middle Eastern oilfields is taken for granted. The fact that half the known reserves of oil in the world lie in the lands above and around the Persian Gulf is a main consideration of international politics. But 40 or 50 years ago it required unusual foresight and persistence to convince financiers and the sluggish Ottoman authorities that oil concessions in the Turkish Empire were something worth worrying about.

His entrenched 5 per cent gave Gulbenkian a unique position in industrial diplomacy. When negotiations affecting his interests were undertaken he ranked on an equality with Governments. He could—and after the Second World War did—hold up arrangements which had been agreed by the other parties concerned. Gulbenkian belonged to the select company of men—Rhodes and de Lesseps being also among them—who built up commercial kingdoms of their own which gave them international standing in their own rights.

Calouste Sarkis Gulbenkian was born in Scutari, Istanbul, on March 24, 1869, into a family of prosperous Armenian merchants. His connexion with England began when he was sent to King's College, London, whence he graduated with distinction from the department of engineering and applied sciences as an associate of King's College in 1887.

Through family business connexions he visited the Baku oilfields and, much impressed with the possibilities of this nascent industry, published a book and several articles looking to a future in which petroleum would be one of the world's main sources of power. One of these articles (in the *Revue des Deux Mondes* in 1892) came to the attention of the Turkish Minister of Mines and led to a request that the young Gulbenkian write a report on the petroleum resources of the Turkish Empire (especially Mesopotamia) and the possibilities of their development. German economic penetration in the wake of the advancing Anatolian Railway, whose objective was Baghdad and the Persian Gulf, also lent topicality to the information in Gulbenkian's report, since the Germans were seeking oil and other mineral exploration and exploitation concessions in the areas adjacent to the railway.

About 1895 Gulbenkian went to London representing some of the Russian oil producers who were exporting kerosene to the United Kingdom and other countries. Gulbenkian prospered, and it was during these last years of the nineteenth century that he established the close contacts with the leading figures in the oil industry, including Frederick Lane, Henri (later Sir Henri) Deterding, Marcus Samuel (later first Viscount Bearsted), J. B. Aug. Kessler, Sir Ernest Cassel, and others.

During these years the oil concession which was later taken over by the Anglo-Persian Oil Company was offered to Gulbenkian for a mere £15,000 by an Armenian friend of his who was at that time Director of Persian Customs. Gulbenkian, after consultation with Lane and Deterding, decided that this was too speculative a venture, and it was turned down, to be taken up at the turn of the century by William Knox D'Arcy. It was during this period that Gulbenkian really established himself in the oil world and laid the foundations of his fortune. The international oil industry was beginning to take shape, and Gulbenkian's skill and energy as a negotiator and financial expert played an important part in the organization of the Royal Dutch Shell Group and in the development of its relationships with the United States oil industry, on the one hand, and Russian oil interests, on the other.

Following the Young Turk Revolution (1908), a pro-British régime was established in Turkey, and the National Bank of Turkey was founded in 1910 in order to facilitate economic development in Turkey under British auspices. The capital of the bank was subscribed privately in England by, among others, Lord Revelstoke, Lord Faringdon, and Sir Ernest Cassel. Gulbenkian, who had just been appointed Financial and Economic Adviser to the Turkish Embassies in London and Paris, was also made a director of the Bank, and was soon in negotiation with the German interests in Turkey regarding mineral rights. By 1912 the Turkish Petroleum Company, Ltd., came into existence with Sir Henry Babington-Smith as chairman, Hugo Baring and Gulbenkian as British directors, and three German directors. Of the £80,000 capital of the T.P.C., 25 per cent. was allotted free of charge to the German interests, and the remainder was subscribed in cash as follows:—

National Bank of Turkey	35 per cent.
Royal Dutch Shell . .	25 per cent.
Gulbenkian	15 per cent.

For some years, however, the newly established Anglo-Persian Oil Company had been trying to extend its concession area from Persia into Turkey, and to that end first H. E. Nichols, then A. L. Marriot, had been negotiating unsuccessfully in Istanbul. The Turkish Petroleum Company, starting nearly 10 years later, but with the advantage of Gulbenkian's local connexions and negotiating ability at its disposal, and with the help rather than the opposition of the powerful German interests in Turkey, was making good progress. The Anglo-Persian Oil Company accordingly began to press, with the support of the Foreign Office, for the National Bank of Turkey's holding in T.P.C. to be transferred to them. Strong pressure was also brought to bear—quite unsuccessfully—on Gulbenkian to place his 15 per cent. at Anglo-Persian's disposal.

In the years 1913-14 an arrangement was eventually negotiated between the oil and financial interests concerned, and with the approval of the British, Turkish, and German Governments, whereby the Turkish Petroleum Company was reorganized so that the shareholding was divided between the Anglo-Persian Oil Company, the Royal-Dutch Shell Group, and the German interests, with a 5 per cent. interest for Gulbenkian. Gulbenkian, in the course of these negotiations, had voluntarily agreed to the reduction of his 15 per cent. holding to 5 per cent. in order to facilitate a general agreement. He resisted most strenuously, however, the attempts that were made to squeeze him right out.

Within less than six months of the achievement of this settlement between the conflicting oil interests in Turkey, conflict broke out on an infinitely larger scale, and the outbreak of war in 1914 brought the activities of the Turkish Petroleum Company to a stop before they had really started. The German holding was seized by the Custodian of Enemy Property, and before the end of the war the company was in such low water financially that it did not have sufficient funds to defray its very small office expenses in London. Moreover, the outlook was so pessimistic and uncertain that at that time the other shareholders refused to bear these expenses, and they had to be met out of funds advanced personally by Gulbenkian and Deterding. Before the outbreak of war, however, the combined efforts of the oil interests, and of the German and British Governments, had obtained a letter, dated June 28, 1914, from the Grand Vizier to the German and British Embassies to the Sublime Porte promising the Mesopotamian oil concessions to the Turkish Petroleum Company. It was on the basis of this *lettre Vizirielle* that the T.P.C. successfully claimed confirmation of its concession in Northern Iraq 11 years later.

During the 1914-18 War Gulbenkian worked in close collaboration with the French High Commissariat for Liquid Fuels, headed by Henri Berenger, and was very active in the negotiations which reorganized the oil refining industry in France and established it on a sound financial footing by the end of the war. Arising from these connexions with the French oil industry, Gulbenkian put forward the suggestion to the British and French Governments that French interests should take over the German holding in the T.P.C., and eventually Gulbenkian's advocacy of this policy at the Foreign Office and at the Quai d'Orsay led to its acceptance and subsequent ratification by the Treaty of San Remo.

The end of the war brought the break-up of the old Turkish Empire, and the Mosul area was now part of the new Iraq. Gulbenkian was involved—though less directly—in the negotiations between the British, Turkish, Iraqi, and other Governments, to determine the final frontier between Turkey and Iraq, and also in the discussions between the T.P.C. and the Iraq Government leading to the granting of a concession in 1925.

The beginning of this inter-war period was also the beginning of American interest in Middle East oil, and inevitably this interest was first focused on Northern Iraq, where oil affairs had received so much public attention because of the international political factors involved. Gulbenkian, characteristically, realized that an attempt to keep the American interests out would upset the applecart generally in the Middle East, and he urged Royal-Dutch Shell, Anglo-Persian Oil, and their new French partner to make room for the Americans. He also pressed this point of view on the Foreign Office where he found powerful support from Sir William (later Lord) Tyrrell. His advice was eventually accepted, and after protracted negotiations agreement was reached whereby shareholdings in the T.P.C. were again reshuffled with the following results:—

Anglo-Persian Oil	23.75%
Shell-Royal Dutch	23.75%
Cie Française des Petroles . .	23.75%
Near East Development, consortium of six leading U.S. oil companies	23.75%
C.S. Gulbenkian	5 %
	100 %

Thus, in 1928 was established the now familiar set-up for the development of Iraqi oil resources for the next 20 years, which gave Gulbenkian the nickname of "Mr. Five Per Cent".

In the course, however, of these negotiations Gulbenkian fell out with Deterding, never an easy man, over certain differences concerning the conduct of the negotiations in the Middle East, and also over the conduct of Venezuelan Oil Concessions Ltd., an affiliate of Royal Dutch Shell, in which Gulbenkian had a large holding. This quarrel brought the long partnership between these two men to an end.

The discovery (October 14, 1927, at Baba Gurgur) of oil in large quantities in the Kirkuk field of Northern Iraq (the area which the young Gulbenkian had nearly 40 years before pointed out to the Turkish Government as being of special interest) led to the building of the first two pipelines to the Mediterranean coast, which were completed in time for Iraq oil to reach world markets in October 1934.

The Second World War brought many new problems, not only in the technical and administrative field, but also politically, and in the relationships between the various oil interests concerned. Gulbenkian regarded the development of the oil resources of Saudi-Arabia by the Arabian American Oil Company (Aramco) without their British and French partners and without himself as being contrary to the 1938 "Red Line" agreement, whereby the oil companies (including the American interest in the Near East Development Corporation) had undertaken to develop all oil resources in the Middle East within the "Red Line" area (*i.e.*, the whole of the Middle East, except Persia and Kuwait) only jointly with their Turkish Petroleum Company (now Iraq Petroleum Company) partners. This difficult situation led to further protracted negotiations in which the now nearly octogenarian Gulbenkian played a leading part, and which eventually resulted, in November 1948, in a settlement which, among other things, led to the disappearance of the "Red Line".

As an art collector, Gulbenkian is known best through his collection of European paintings which was on loan to the National Gallery in London from 1936 to 1950 and was then moved to the National Gallery of Art in Washington, where it is at present on loan. This collection of 40 pictures (including the Rembrandts, Rubens's full-length portrait of his second wife, and Fragonard's "A Fête at Rambouillet") represents only a selection from Gulbenkian's collection, which is regarded as one of the finest individual collections of paintings in the world, and ranges in time from the early Primitives to the end of the nineteenth century. Gulbenkian's artistic interest has not, however, been confined to pictures; he has been a collector of wide range and eclectic taste. His collection of Egyptian sculpture, after being on loan to the British Museum, is now in the National Gallery of Art in Washington. His other collections include Oriental and Middle Eastern ceramics, illuminated manuscripts, fine bindings and incunabula, Syrian glass, furniture, carpets, and tapestry.

Gulbenkian's collection of sculptures comprises several pieces from the Hermitage collection, including the well-known "Diane", commissioned by Catherine the Great from Houdon. Lalique jewellery has been another of Gulbenkian's interests, and his collection in this field must be one of the most complete in the world. In recent years Gulbenkian's interest has been specially concentrated on numismatics, in which field he has specialized in early Greek coins.

During his many years as an active collector, Gulbenkian has moved from one branch of art to another. His attention has been focused on one thing at a time, but he has always been interested in paintings. Gulbenkian is not the typical wealthy collector who is guided entirely by experts. Himself a connoisseur, he has, of course, had advice in plenty, but his various collections bear the stamp of his own individuality and his taste is understandably a reflection of the period in which it was formed.

As a philanthropist Gulbenkian has been mainly concerned with two things: to avoid publicity as far as possible and to give help to those for whom nobody else catered. As a result of this attitude, a great deal of his philanthropic work was in the form of financial assistance to individuals whose need took such a form as to fall outside the scope of existing private or public welfare organizations. This type of philanthropy attracts little or no public attention, but nevertheless there is a very large number of people of all nationalities and in all parts of the world who have good reason to be grateful for the help that came to them in their need—sometimes even without any direct requests from them, but because their benefactor had heard in some indirect way of their plight.

A typical example of this type of assistance occurred when, four years ago, Gulbenkian had his attention drawn to a news item reporting extensive storm damage suffered by the fishermen of the little island of Houat, off the coast of Brittany. The village rector was pleasantly surprised to receive a useful contribution towards making good the storm damage from a hitherto unknown friend. This example, incidentally, illustrates Gulbenkian's special sympathy for victims of marine disasters. Further evidence of this interest can be seen in his contributions to the funds for the victims of the disasters to H.M. Submarines Thetis and Affray. In the case of similar disasters to two French submarines Gulbenkian arranged to give help to the families of the victims through the French Ministry of Marine in the absence of any public fund.

Naturally, in view of his Armenian origin, Gulbenkian was a generous contributor to Armenian philanthropic organizations, as well as to individual needy Armenians. As a devout member, Gulbenkian has given considerable material assistance to the Armenian Church. He built and has maintained for over thirty years the graceful little church of St. Sarkis in Iverna Gardens, South Kensington. This fine example of classic Armenian ecclesiastical architecture was erected and endowed as a memorial to Gulbenkian's parents, and serves the Armenian congregation of Greater London. In October 1952, on the occasion of the 1,500th anniversary of the Battle of Vartanantz (when the Armenian Christians resisted compulsory paganization) the Archbishop of Canterbury entered the church of St. Sarkis in procession and delivered the address.

Gulbenkian has always shown a special interest in the Armenian Patriarchate in Jerusalem. Apart from the handsome Gulbenkian Library, which he constructed in 1930 and endowed, he has regularly contributed to the funds of the Patriarchate, particularly when it has encountered special difficulties as, for instance, since the partition of Jerusalem in 1948. Elsewhere in the Middle East Gulbenkian has contributed to the building of Armenian churches in Kirkuk, Baghdad, Fao, and Tripoli. The Gulbenkian Infirmary on the campus of the American University in Beirut, with its all-embracing dedication "For students of the Arab lands", is another example of his benevolent interest in the Middle East.

In addition to these philanthropic activities, Gulbenkian's name is to be found on the subscription lists of a large number and variety of philanthropic organizations all over the world. It is characteristic of him, however, that in these cases he has not been content merely to contribute financially but has generally taken an active personal interest in the work of the organization and the use to which his contribution has been put.

He married in 1892 Miss Nevarte Essayan who died three years ago. They had a son, Nubar Gulbenkian*, and a daughter, Rita, who married Kevork Essayan.

July 21, 1955.

Professor J. A. Gunn, C.B.E., died on October 21, 1958 in Oxford at the age of 76. He was Professor of Pharmacology at Oxford from 1917 to 1937 and Nuffield* Professor of Therapeutics from 1937 to 1946. He was made Professor Emeritus in the latter year. Between 1935 and 1946 he was Director of the Nuffield Institute for Medical Research.

James Andrew Gunn, son of John R. Gunn, was born at Kirkwall on January 26, 1882. He received his early education at Kirkwall School, where he learned, *inter alia,* to write well and to tell a story well; in both these directions he showed considerable artistry throughout his subsequent life. From Kirkwall he went on to Edinburgh University, where he had a very brilliant student career. In 1901 he graduated M.A., in 1903 B.Sc. (with distinction in anatomy, anthropology, and physiology); in 1905 M.B., Ch.B. (with first-class honours in medicine); in 1907 M.D. (gold medallist); and D.Sc. in 1909; he also gained various other distinctions. Among his teachers was Edward Schafer, who had gone to Edinburgh in 1899 to be Professor of Physiology.

Those who look through the list of Gunn's publications will see that he must have been influenced in no small degree by the discoverer of the physiological activity of the suprarenal medulla. But it was to pharmacology rather than to physiology that Gunn turned after graduation, and it was in Thomas Fraser's laboratory that he effectively began his original researches. He took his D.Sc. in pharmacology in 1909, and during this period he worked on harmaline and harmine, snake-poisons, and various other drugs, in spite of the severe inroads that routine teaching made upon his time.

In 1912 Oxford University decided to make more adequate provision for the teaching of pharmacology, and Gunn was appointed first Reader in the subject. For a laboratory he was given a single long room high up on the west side of the Museum building, and in this room, in spite of the smallness of his departmental grant, he instituted a practical pharmacology course that was much appreciated by the students and preceded similar developments in a number of other schools.

Gunn's lectures were very popular, and he published a number of papers within a short time; he also went out of his way to interest the more promising students in original research. It is not, therefore, surprising that the University, in 1917, decided to create a chair of pharmacology and that Gunn was appointed to it.

The years following the Great War saw a gradual increase in the number of medical students in Oxford and in the middle twenties the Sir William Dunn Trustees gave a large sum of money for the building of a new School of Pathology and for the transfer to the old pathology building of the Department of Pharmacology. About the time of the transfer Gunn was struck down by a virulent streptococcal infection that was all but fatal, and that left him permanently blind in one eye. Such a loss of binocular vision would cause most practising scientists to complain against fortune; Gunn, however, did not utter a word of self-pity but set out to recapture, with monocular vision, the experimental dexterity for which he had previously had a considerable, and well-deserved, reputation; and he continued to play golf with success.

In 1934 he served on the committee that planned the conversion of the eighteenth-century Radcliffe Observatory, given to the Medical School by Sir William Morris, into the Nuffield Institute for Medical Research. In the following year he became its first director, though, as there was little money available for running the institute, he continued as Professor of Pharmacology. With the increase in the institute's activity he found the dual work too much and in 1937, when the institute's finances were put on a more secure footing, he gave up the chair of pharmacology that he had held for 20 years. With the directorship of the institute he thereafter combined a new Nuffield Professorship of Experimental Therapeutics, devoting his attention in the main to a comprehensive study of the actions of adrenaline and related compounds.

The above summary does not exhaust the list of Gunn's scientific activities. He was joint editor for many years of Cushny's standard textbook of pharmacology, and also author of a small *Introduction to Pharmacology and Therapeutics* that was by way of being a best seller. He was a member, and later chairman, of the Pharmacopoeia Commission, and he served for periods as president of the Therapeutics Section, Royal Society of Medicine, of the Pharmacology Section of the British Medical Association, and of more local societies. He was responsible for the suggestion that led to the founding of the British Pharmacological Society. In 1935 he was Dohme Lecturer at the Johns Hopkins University, and in 1939 Oliver Sharpey Lecturer at the Royal College of Physicians, of which he had been elected a Fellow in 1931. He interested himself in the history of medicine, though the number of his publications in this field was not so great as one could have wished.

The picture would be incomplete without reference to other aspects of Gunn's activities. Like so many of his countrymen, he was an enthusiastic golfer and fisherman. Like so many of them, also, he was a most generous and entertaining host. A further way in which he showed himself typically Scottish was in his prowess as an after-dinner speaker. Socially, he was the best of company and in Balliol Senior Common Room he was affectionately styled "The Chief Poisoner", presumably to differentiate him from his successor in the Chair of Pharmacology, who was also a member of that Common Room. He was made C.B.E. in 1947.

He leaves a widow, one daughter, and two sons.

October 22, 1958.

Sir Henry Gurney, whose murder in a Malayan ambush by communist terrorists occurred on October 6, 1951, had been High Commissioner for the Federation of Malaya since September 1948.

He succeeded in this post Sir Edward Gent, who had been killed in an aircraft accident in Britain two months before, at a time when the situation in Malaya was difficult and dangerous. Having spent much of his earlier career discharging the comparatively routine duties of the Colonial Service in Africa, and after two years as Chief Secretary to the Palestine Government, he found himself called to a position requiring initiative, judgment, and vision, and he proved himself worthy of the task entrusted to him. He set about mobilizing the resources of the Federation to fight alien communist tendencies with vigour and determination. He recognized that it was not enough to increase the strength of the police and military forces, but that it was also essential to unite the Malayan peoples—Malays, Chinese, and Indians—and to gain their fullest support in fighting banditry. Towards this end he strove, and the steadily increasing cooperation that the Federal Government has received is, in no small measure, due to his work.

His devotion to duty, and his tact in facing the problems of the emergency, won first the esteem and then the confidence of all good Malayans. He preached with sincerity the gospel of a united Malaya, and watched with sympathy and understanding the recent emergence of the Independence of Malaya Party. Fearless and imperturbable, Sir Henry Gurney travelled widely in the Federation, seeing things for himself. A fortnight ago, accompanied by the Director of Operations, Sir Harold Briggs, he covered 150 miles in a single day, touring the resettlement areas in south-west Selangor.

In Palestine in September 1946, as later in Malaya, he took up his duties at a time when terrorist outrages were increasing. When the High Commissioner for Palestine, Sir Alan Cunningham, went to Britain for consultations early in 1947, Sir Henry Gurney was left in charge of the administration until his return. Through the difficult months that followed until the end of the mandate and the evacuation of British troops, he and the other members of the civil administration worked, sometimes in danger, and often in the face of calumnies and imputations of partiality. The Prime Minister, in a message to them on leaving Palestine, spoke highly of their behaviour and of their "loyal public service".

Henry Lovell Goldsworthy Gurney was born on June 27, 1898, the only son of G. H. Gurney, of Bude, Cornwall, and of Florence, daughter of Edwin Frances Chamier. He went to Winchester College in 1912. After leaving school he was commissioned in 1917 into the King's Royal Rifle Corps and was wounded shortly before the Armistice. On his return to civilian life he went up to Oxford as a scholar of University College, and represented the university at golf. In 1921 he entered the Colonial Service and was posted to Kenya, where he was to work for the next 14 years. In 1935 he was appointed assistant Colonial Secretary in Jamaica. Three years later he was appointed chief secretary to the conference of East African Governors, and secretary to the High Commissioner for Transport in Kenya and Uganda. He was transferred to the Gold Coast in 1944, succeeding Sir George London as Colonial Secretary, and in September 1946 came his appointment as Chief Secretary to the Palestine Government. A knighthood had been conferred on him in 1947. He was created C.M.G. in 1942 and promoted K.C.M.G. in the year he was appointed High Commissioner.

He married in 1924 Isabel Lowther, daughter of T. Hamilton Weir, of Bude. There are two sons of the marriage. Lady Gurney escaped injury in the ambush but had to shelter in a culvert into which her husband's body had fallen.

October 8, 1951.

Sir Henry Guy, C.B.E., F.R.S., chairman of the Mechanical Engineering Research Board of the Department of Scientific and Industrial Research in 1947, and secretary of the Institution of Mechanical Engineers from 1942 to 1951, died at his home at Bournemouth on July 20, 1956 at the age of 69.

Born on June 15, 1887, the son of the late R. Guy, of Penarth, Henry Lewis Guy was trained at the University College of South Wales and the College of Technology, Manchester, and was a pupil of T. Hurry Riches on the Taff Vale Railway. In 1910 he joined the technical staff of the British Westinghouse Company, which later became the Metropolitan-Vickers Electrical Company, and in 1918 became chief engineer of the mechanical department, a position he retained until his resignation in 1941. Among the outstanding machines constructed under his direction were the great 100,000kW. turbo-alternators at Battersea power station, and units working at unusually high steam pressures for Moscow and Brimsdown.

A paper on the economic value of increased steam pressure won him the Hawksley gold medal of the Institution of Mechanical Engineers in 1927, and another notable paper on tendencies in steam turbine development was read by him before the same institution in 1929, while he embodied much of his own work on the efficiency of the nozzles of steam turbines in the Parsons Memorial Lecture of which he was the author in 1939. He was elected a Fellow of the Royal Society in 1936, and served on the council of that body in 1938-39. In 1941 the Royal Society invited him to join the executive committee of the National Physical Laboratory, and later he succeeded the late Sir Nigel Gresley as chairman of the engineering research committee of the National Physical Laboratory.

Just before the outbreak of the 1939-45 War he was appointed a member of the Advisory Council on Scientific Research and Development of the Ministry of Supply, and later became chairman of its gun design committee and of its static detonation committee (bombs). Early in the war he was made chairman of the committee on technical organization of the Army and chairman of the committee on aircraft armament, in addition to serving as an associate member of the Board of Chemical Warfare. In 1944 he became a member of the advisory council to the committee of the Privy Council for scientific and industrial research, and from 1944 to 1947 he was chairman of the Armament Development Board of the Ministry of Supply.

He was appointed a trustee of the Imperial War Museum in 1946. From 1926 to 1941 he served on various committees of the Institution of Mechanical Engineers, being a member of council from 1929 to 1941 and a vice-president from 1938 to 1941, in which year he was appointed secretary. He retired for reasons of health in 1951. He was made a C.B.E. in 1943, and was knighted in 1949.

He married in 1914, Margaret Paton, daughter of S. B. Williams, and there were two daughters of the marriage.

July 25, 1956.

Edmund Gwenn, the actor, who died at Hollywood on September 6, 1959 at the age of 81, established himself as a character actor who was equally well known on both sides of the Atlantic and was as successful in the cinema as in the theatre.

He was born in London on September 26, 1877, and educated at St. Olave's and at King's College, London. As a young actor he excelled in parts that required him to be vulgar, rough, and often noisy; but his acting was best enjoyed by those who saw the polish with which he portrayed the unpolished. He had all the resources of a "low" comedian; but after two separate periods with Willie Edouin and three years in Australia and New Zealand under J. C. Williamson, he made his fame first in a notably intellectual and even sophisticated setting at the Court Theatre under the Vedrenne-Barker management.

There in 1905 to 1907 he was invaluable in smaller parts, among them "Enery" Straker, the board-school-educated chauffeur of John Tanner in Bernard Shaw's *Man and Superman*, and the Cockney gangster in *Captain Brassbound's Conversion*; and in plays by Granville-Barker, Hankin, Galsworthy, and others he gave every part he played its full worth. In Barrie's *What Every Woman Knows*, under Charles Frohman, at the Duke of York's Theatre in 1908, he acted James Wylie, the youth who goes nearly mad on election day, and rushes maniacally shouting on to the stage. Frohman engaged him for his repertory period at the same theatre in 1910; and there he was seen as the newly made knight in *The Twelve-Pound Look,* and in several other first-rate performances.

He was the central figure in *The Bear-leaders,* by R. C. Carton, at the Comedy in 1912; and after that he joined with Hilda Trevelyan [q.v.] in the management of the Vaudeville Theatre, and produced *Little Miss Llewellyn.* Out of scores of other parts which he played in England and in America, the best remembered are probably Hornblower in Galsworthy's *The Skin Game,* the Viennese paterfamilias in *Lilac Time,* and Samuel Pepys in Fagan's *And So to Bed* in 1926. Some years later in his constantly busy career it fell to him to play Samuel Pepys again in another play, *Thank you, Mr. Pepys,* at the Shaftesbury

Theatre. Among his other successes was his performance of George Radfern, the old forger, in J. B. Priestley's *Laburnum Grove.*

He appeared in several silent films during the 1920s—his first was *The Skin Game*—and made his debut in a talking picture called *How He Lied to her Husband,* a British film made at Elstree in 1931. Numerous other parts in early British sound pictures followed, best known of which, perhaps, was that of Jess Oakroyd in *The Good Companions;* and his old part in Sir Carol Reed's [d. 1976] picture of *Laburnum Grove.*

Gwenn first went to Hollywood in 1935, quickly made a reputation for himself, and was thereafter in constant demand, but he continued throughout his career to divide his time between the stage and the cinema. As a film actor, he will principally be remembered as a dumpy amiable figure beaming with toleration and good will (he was awarded an Oscar in 1948 for his real life Santa Claus in *Miracle on 34th Street*) but the seemingly effortless air of geniality masked a skilled and careful style of film acting which was based not only on wide experience, but also on a complete understanding of the film medium. Nor was he capable only of suggesting good humour, as he revealed in the well-known Hitchcock thriller *Foreign Correspondent*, where he tried to push the hero off the tower of Westminster Cathedral; and he also appeared in another Hitchcock thriller, *The Trouble with Harry.*

During the war of 1914-18 Edmund Gwenn was temporarily commissioned in the Army Service Corps and for some time he was employed as an instructor of officer cadets at Aldershot, where he reached the rank of captain. In his earlier years he was a keen Rugby footballer and was a member of the Harlequins. The study of ships and the men who sail in them was another of his hobbies.

Gwenn married a member of his own profession, Minnie, a daughter of Charles Terry and a niece of Ellen Terry. The marriage was dissolved.

September 8, 1959.

Sir Maurice Gwyer, G.C.I.E., K.C.B., K.C.S.I., who died suddenly on October 12, 1952 at his home at Eastbourne, at the age of 74, was the first Chief Justice of the Indian Federal Court and for many years Vice-Chancellor of Delhi University.

A brilliant career in law and education is thus ended. His scholarship and legal and administrative abilities combined to make him an outstanding figure from his entry into Whitehall in 1912, and when, in 1936, the difficult post of Chief Justice of the Indian Federal Court had to be filled it was generally recognized that a wise choice had been made, though he had had small success at the Bar and no previous judicial experience. It was felt, moreover, that no one was more fitting to construe the India Act of 1935 than its principal draftsman.

Maurice Linford Gwyer was the eldest son of the late John Edward Gwyer and was born on April 25, 1878. He was educated at Westminster (he had served as a member of its governing body since 1936), and at Christ Church, Oxford, where he was a Fell exhibitioner. He took a first in Classical Moderations in 1899, and a second in *Literae Humaniores* in 1901.

In the following year he was elected a Fellow of All Souls. This election was remarkable inasmuch as the two competitors, Gwyer and the late Raymond Asquith, were both thought so highly of by the examiners that, though only one fellowship was actually in competition, the exceptional step was taken of awarding one to each candidate.

Gwyer was called to the Bar by the Inner Temple in 1903, obtaining a first class in the final examination and the Council of Legal Education's prizes for constitutional and criminal law, evidence, and procedure. He was a pupil of the late F. D. (afterwards Lord Justice) Mackinnon. Later he was in chambers with the late F. T. Barrington-Ward, a future metropolitan magistrate, and joined the Western Circuit, but he never succeeded in acquiring any large practice. Though in after years, if given the right topic, he could make a graceful after-dinner speech, he had little forensic ability.

In 1912, when a solicitor was required for the Insurance Commission, he entered official life. In 1917 he became legal adviser to the Ministry of Shipping, and at the end of the war—what is not generally remembered—he returned to the Bar, and obtained a certain amount of work in the Commercial Court. In the meantime he had been appointed to the Lectureship in Private International Law at Oxford. He became the legal adviser to the Ministry of Health in 1919. On the death of Clive Lawrence, in 1926, he succeeded him as Solicitor to the Treasury and King's Proctor, taking silk in 1930. He succeeded the late Sir William Graham-Harrison in the arduous and responsible post of First Parliamentary Counsel to the Treasury in 1933.

In this capacity it fell to him to draft the great India Bill. Though in no way responsible for the policy underlying the measure, which was the subject of keen controversy in Britain and in India, Gwyer was understood to have played a very important part in framing its final form, and for such success as the 1935 Act had he is entitled to a large share of the credit. It was on the basis of the 1935 Act that India and Pakistan became independent in August 1947, for it remained in force, subject to amendment, pending the framing of the constitutions of those countries, a process which in respect of India occupied the Constituent Assembly nearly three years. Behind an apparently rather indolent manner and method of work lay a power of grasping at sight the essentials of a subject and expressing it in the clearest language, and Gwyer will certainly be remembered as one of the greatest draftsmen of his generation. He was a member of the Indian States (Financial) Inquiry Committee in 1932, and in 1930 had been the first British delegate at The Hague Conference on the Codification of International Law.

Gwyer had in the course of his official career assisted the Government on many commissions and inquiries. He was a member of the Royal Commission on London Squares in 1927. He assisted in 1928 at the inquiry held into the conduct of a prominent member of the staff of the Foreign Office with allegation of improper speculations in German marks, and in 1936 he was a member of the board which was set up, after the libel action of Lambert v. Levita, to inquire into the administration of the staff of the B.B.C.

It cannot truly be said that Gwyer's reputation was greatly increased by his tenure of the post of Chief Justice of India; but for this he can hardly be blamed, as for the first few years of its creation the Federal Court had practically no work to do and Gwyer was able to devote his interest to Indian education and especially to the affairs of the University of Delhi, of which he had been appointed Vice-Chancellor. By the time that Gwyer's successor, Sir Patrick [later Lord] Spens*, had been selected in November 1942, the Defence of India Rules, passed owing to war conditions, had done something to justify the existence of the Federal Court and give its members something to do.

Gwyer retired from the Federal Court in April 1943 under the age limit of 65—some 10 or 15 years later than it was customary for British members of the services to leave India. He was already a martyr to arthritis and might well have sought the temperate climate of his native land instead of further enduring the heat of the Delhi plains. But, having accepted the post of Vice-Chancellor of Dehli University, he remained in India another seven years to press to completion his plans to make the university in every way worthy of its all-India claim as the metropolitan seat of learning. He had already rescued it from the neglect and obscurity into which it had fallen, and the task he fervently pursued was helped by the great influence he had with the Indian leaders as an undeviating friend of the ideals of independence.

He set his face against student pressure for the lowering of standards and the tendency to indiscipline which have hampered the work of some Indian universities. As a septuagenarian Vice-Chancellor he had the satisfaction of seeing spectacular building progress on the new site in the grounds of the old Viceregal Lodge, and St. Stephen's College already transferred there.

Returning to Britain in the spring of 1950 he lived at Eastbourne, and as he had to use an invalid chair could seldom travel far to meet old friends. His publications included the twelfth to the sixteenth editions of Anson's *Law of Contract*, and of volume I of the same author's *Law and Custom of the Constitution.* He was also responsible for the seventh edition of Pollock and Mulla's *Indian Contract Act.*

He married in 1907, Alsina, the eldest daughter of the late Sir Henry Burdett, K.C.B., K.C.V.O., and sister of the late Osbert Burdett, the author. They had a son and two daughters. Miss Barbara Gwyer*, who was Principal of St. Hugh's College, Oxford, is his sister.

October 13, 1952.

H

King Haakon—See **Norway**.

Lord Haden-Guest died on August 20, 1960 at the age of 83.

His death is a considerable loss to British public life. He was very much a man of parts: a doctor of medicine, in his young days both a health and a socialist propagandist, member of Parliament, traveller, investigator and, for many years in his later life, an administrator. To all his work he brought a sense of urgency and, indeed, dedication. Some of his most useful work was done after he became a septuagenarian and had been elevated to the House of Lords. He was regular in attendance and often made useful and important speeches in debate. He made an important contribution to the public welfare as chairman of the National Medical Manpower Committee of the Ministry of Health, and for many years was connected with the Leverhulme Foundation, acting as secretary of the Leverhulme Research Fellowship Committee.

The Rt. Hon. Leslie Haden Haden-Guest, M.C., first baron Haden-Guest, of Saling in the county of Essex in the peerage of the United Kingdom, was born at Oldham, Lancashire, on March 10, 1877, the son of Alexander Haden-Guest, a surgeon and physician of Manchester, who was himself an active worker for the left in the north during the second half of the nineteenth century. Indeed, the son could scarcely have been other than a rebel and a fighter, for his father kept open house at Hulme for such thinkers as Annie Besant, Herbert Burrows, H. M. Hyndman, J. M. Robertson, the Fabian pamphleteers and essayists, and odd exiles and travellers from abroad. But young Haden-Guest was also deeply impressed by his own experiences of poverty and distress in the cotton towns, and at an early age lectured on social problems and Labour politics. He was educated at William Hulme's Grammar School, and Owen's College, where he studied medicine. On the death of his father he moved to London to complete his medical studies at the London Hospital. After qualifying he went to South Africa, where, after serving in the war, he practised for two or three years.

When he eventually returned to London he began his pioneering work as a children's doctor with headquarters in Southwark, the constituency he later represented in Parliament. For years, during the earlier part of this century, and often with little encouragement or help, he developed what was really the beginning of the school clinic movement in London, which housed the first dental clinic for school children. As his work expanded and progressed, it attracted much attention, and the premises in Pocock Street received a constant stream of visitors, many of whom modelled their own schemes of child welfare upon Haden-Guest's. This work was temporarily interrupted by the outbreak of war in 1914. For the subsequent four or five years he was engaged in organizing and running hospitals and Red Cross work, mostly overseas, and he was awarded the Military Cross for great gallantry in rescuing wounded men under fire at Passchendaele Ridge.

When the war was over he returned to his medical and political work in London, and in 1920 he went with a number of his friends and colleagues to Russia as secretary and medical officer of the Labour Delegation, the first of its kind from this country after the Communist Revolution of 1917. There he met Lenin, Trotsky, Tchitcherin, and other leaders of the new order, and came back to write the results of his searching investigation, which proved to be a biting indictment of Bolshevism.

From 1919 to 1922 he served as a Labour member of the London County Council representing Woolwich (East), and a year later he was elected Member of Parliament for North Southwark. That seat he held until 1927, when he resigned from the Labour Party over its attitude to the Government's Chinese policy. He applied for the Chiltern Hundreds and at the ensuing by-election stood as an Independent Constitutionalist. He was backed by the local Conservative association but was defeated in a three-cornered contest. E. A. Strauss, the Liberal candidate, topped the poll, beating George Isaacs by a thousand odd votes. In June 1928 Haden-Guest wrote to Stanley Baldwin offering himself as a member of the party, and was warmly welcomed.

There followed a somewhat uneasy spell in the ranks of the Conservatives (he fought North Salford in 1929 and was again defeated) and by 1931 he was again within the Labour fold. During the memorable general election of that year he was decisively beaten at High Wycombe and again four years later when at Brecon he opposed his namesake (but no relation), the Hon. Ivor Guest. His return to the House came two years later, when he was elected in a by-election for North Islington. He held the seat until 1950, when he went to the House of Lords.

He was the founder of the Labour Party Commonwealth Group, and a few years after his Russian visit he went with the Empire Parliamentary Delegation to Newfoundland and Canada. He was appointed a member of the commission which the Leverhulme Research Fellowship Committee sent to investigate conditions in West Africa shortly before the outbreak of war in 1939, and he was appointed a member of the Parliamentary Committee on the Evacuation of the Civil Population. He sat also on the West Africa Commission which visited Nigeria, the Gold Coast, and neighbouring countries in 1938-39. Not least of his activities for which he will still be remembered was his foundation of the Anglo-French Committee of the Red Cross Society and the Order of St. John, and for many years he was vice-chairman of its medical group. He was a Lord-in-Waiting to King George VI [q.v.] in 1951 and, for several years subsequently, was Assistant Opposition Whip in the Upper Chamber. He had written a good deal, particularly for the medical and scientific journals and the newspapers, during the course of his long career, and had also published a number of books on international questions, child life, and education.

He married, first, in 1898, Edith, daughter of Max Low, of London, by whom he had two sons. The marriage was dissolved by divorce in 1909, and, in 1910, he married Muriel Carmel, daughter of the late Colonel Albert Goldsmid, M.V.O. They had two sons and one daughter. After his second wife's death he married, in 1944, Dr. Edith Macqueen, of Braintree. The heir to the peerage is the Hon. Stephen Guest, the elder son of the first marriage, who was born on June 7, 1902.

August 22, 1960.

W. W. Hadley, editor of *The Sunday Times* from 1932 to 1950, died on December 16, 1960 at his home in Hindhead, Surrey.

William Waite Hadley was born on January 18, 1866, and trained on the *Northampton Echo*, to which he was to return in later life as managing editor. He served his apprenticeship in the stirring days of Bradlaugh and Labouchere. After a period on the *Rochdale Observer*, during which he reported one of John Bright's last speeches and took his turn in keeping vigil outside the home of the dying statesman, he served as the editor of the *Merthyr Tydfil Times* in 1892-93, returning in 1893 as editor of the *Rochdale Observer*, the affairs of which he conducted with notable success for 15 years. Wherever he went Hadley won the affectionate esteem of the townspeople, who recognized his sterling worth not only as a journalist of conspicuous ability but as a public-spirited helper in any deserving cause.

In 1908 he went back to Northampton as the managing editor of the *Northampton Echo* and the *Northampton Mercury* and became a director of the company which controlled them. He was such a keen feminist that two years later he accepted the suggestion of a Northampton girl that she should join his editorial staff as a very junior reporter at a time when the woman journalist was almost unknown in the provinces. Fifty years later she described how she was given a cubby hole to herself on a landing with stairs leading down to the composing room and Hadley would give her practical help with suggestions for the weekly woman's page. Another of Hadley's apprentices was the late Richard Capel, a local boy who later became the music critic of *The Daily Telegraph*.

Hadley's shrewd appreciation of the political field was recognized by the leaders of all the parties but it came as something of a surprise to his friends when in 1924, at the age of 58, he accepted an invitation to London as parliamentary correspondent and leader writer of the *Daily Chronicle*, a position which he held until the paper was merged with the *Daily News*. In 1931 he was appointed assistant editor of *The Sunday Times* and a year later became editor on the death of Leonard Rees. *The Sunday Times* was fortunate in finding in him both a writing and an administrative editor and though the bulk of his work was unsigned it was fully equal to the best in modern journalism.

Hadley was a firm friend of Neville Chamberlain and a warm supporter of his policy. Towards the end of the Second World War he wrote a short book *Munich: Before and After,* in which he brought out the aims of Chamberlain's policy, the courage with which he pursued them, and the wide measure of support which he enjoyed. In his earlier career he had written in 1920 a book to mark the bicentenary of the *Northampton Mercury*. It was an excellent biography of that newspaper and included an amusing series of extracts from its earlier numbers.

Until the end of his life Hadley took a lively interest in *The Sunday Times,* in journalism generally, and in the welfare of the working newspaper man. He was a keen supporter of the Institute of Journalists and of its activities, having also been a member of the National Association of Journalists, the forerunner of the Institute.

December 17, 1960.

General Sir Robert Haining, K.C.B., D.S.O., who died on September 15, 1959 at the age of 77, was, to use an adjective popular in the General Staff, an "educated" officer. He knew the War Office thoroughly; he knew Whitehall, and how to get things done in both; he had an extensive acquaintance with foreign military affairs. His judgment was good; his experience was wide; he succeeded in most of his undertakings. He was hard-working and expressed himself clearly. These qualifications may not always suffice to form a great staff officer, but they are likely to form one who becomes indispensable.

Robert Hadden Haining was born on July 28, 1882, the eldest son of Dr. William Haining. He was educated at Uppingham and at the Royal Military Academy, Woolwich, from which he entered the Royal Artillery in 1901. He distinguished himself in the First World War, going to France as Staff Captain, R.A., 2nd Division, and ending as G.S.O.1 at the Tactical School at Camberley. He was awarded the D.S.O. and six times mentioned in dispatches. He then steadily mounted the ladder, mainly by staff rungs. Between 1933 and 1940 he was Deputy Director Military Operations and Intelligence, Commandant of the Imperial Defence College, Director Military Operations and Intelligence, G.O.C. Palestine and Trans-Jordan, G.O.C. Western Command, and V.C.I.G.S. It was a record of success.

In May 1941 Haining was appointed "Intendant-General of the Middle East Army". It hardly needs to be said that this grandiloquent rank was disinterred from the past by the Prime Minister and Minister of Defence. The object was to lighten the administrative burden on General Wavell. Haining was instructed by the C.I.G.S. to report on administration in the command and then by the Secretary of State for War to relieve Wavell of some of his administrative responsibilities, organize vehicle maintenance, and economize in manpower. Anyhow, he realized that he was first of all to explore, and did so. He concluded that the administrative problem stretched far beyond the Army; to carry out the duties allotted he would need power over the administrative activities of the Navy, the R.A.F., and British Government departments.

This was a large order indeed. He received no answer, for the good reason that the Government had decided on a measure which must affect his status. This was to appoint a Minister of State to represent the War Cabinet in the Middle East. Among his jobs was to be that of "supervising" the Intendant-General. Oliver Lyttelton [Lord Chandos*], arriving late in June, set up a War Council and made Haining a permanent member. He was now to organize shipping, ports, railways, roads, supplies, and to collaborate with the R.A.F. and Fleet Air Arm over repairs. He was to advise on the economical use of manpower.

The next move was the appointment of a Principal Administrative Staff Officer to the Commander-in-Chief, a high post because it combined, contrary to British practice, the functions of "A" and "Q". Haining's role was defined anew. He was relieved of all duties "in the Army sphere proper", whatever that meant, and directed to coordinate such matters as the Minister of State should desire. It was becoming a comedy, with Haining as an unhappy actor. Finally baffled, he told the Minister that the Intendant-General's appointment was redundant.

Shortly after his return to England Haining went on retired pay on attaining the age of 60. It was sad that the last appointment of a man with his capabilities should have been hopelessly impracticable, but he had many useful years ahead of him and lived an active life. He had become Colonel Commandant R.A. in 1939 and held that office until 1950. He took a deep interest in every activity of the Royal Regiment and worked hard for its charities. He was Lord Lieutenant of Surrey from 1949 to 1957, a Justice of the Peace for the county, and a county alderman.

He married, first, in 1913, Dora, youngest daughter of Richard Barnwell. The marriage was dissolved by divorce in 1922 and two years later he married Hilda, daughter of Towry Piper.

September 17, 1959.

Dr. Norman Haire, who died on September 11, 1952 in London at the age of 60, was a physician who courted unpopularity by his determined advocacy of birth control and sex education.

Born at Sydney in 1892, he was educated at the Fort Street School in that city and proceeded to medical studies at Sydney University and Sydney Hospital, graduating Ch.M. and M.B. There followed a course at the Institut für Sexualwissenschaft in Berlin. Between 1915 and 1919 Haire was a captain in the Australian Army Medical Corps. He held various hospital appointments in Australia, at the Hospital for Sick Children, Brisbane, at the No. 4 Australian General Hospital, the New South Wales State Mental Hospitals, the Sydney Royal Hospital for Women, and the Newcastle Hospital, New South Wales.

In 1919 he determined to burn his boats and went to London. From the date of his establishment in England Haire threw himself vigorously into the movement for sex education and rational birth control. He was forced by the facts that came to his notice in the course of his practice to the conclusion that the happiness of thousands of homes was destroyed by sexual maladjustment and overlarge families, badly spaced and owing their size to ignorance rather than to philoprogenetive tendencies. He therefore began to study, teach, and write about sexual hygiene and contraception, basing his teaching on what seemed to him sound medical and social principles.

In 1921 he was one of the founders of the Walworth Welfare Centre—the first British welfare centre to give advice on contraception; and in the same year attended the Amsterdam Birth Control Conference as British delegate. In the following year he published the first of many books, *Hygienic Methods of Family Limitation,* and was president of the contraceptive section of the fifth International Birth Control Conference, held in London. In 1925 he made a tour through the United States and Canada, lecturing to universities and medical societies on this topic, and served as English delegate at the sixth conference in New York. A year later he was in Berlin, at the first International Congress for Sexual Research, and in 1929 organized the third International Congress of the World League for Sexual Reform.

Haire was a widely travelled man whose peregrinations extended to all five continents, less for relaxation than for the gleaning of new data relative to his paramount interest. His publications included *Birth Control Methods, Sex Life and Sex Ethics,* and an *Encylopaedia of Sexual Knowledge*; but he was also attracted by the possibilities of rejuvenation, and in 1924 published an account of the work of Steinach, Voronoff, and others in that field. He was connected with numerous medical and other bodies concerned with sex education, being co-president of the World League for Sexual Reform, president of the Sex Education Society, and general editor of the International Library of Psychology and Sexology, assistant editor of *Sexus,* and member of the international editorial board of *Anthropos.*

Working as he did in a domain open to the blasts of bitter controversy, it was to be expected that Haire should not only meet opposition but incur a certain degree of personal enmity—the more so because of his extreme outspokenness and because in the matter of theology he was to be found in the rationalist camp. Yet those who were admitted to his friendship (and they were many, drawn as often from artistic and literary as from sociological circles) found him a charming companion, light-hearted, witty, sympathetic, cultured, and loyal. His unconventionality extended even to furnishing and decoration, in which his tastes ran to an opulent *chinoiserie* that did not always find favour with visitors and patients at Harley Street.

The theatre was one of his passions, and he was a connoisseur of acting and stage craft. A big, massively made man, he somewhat oddly combined teetotalism with a nice gastronomic palate. He was unmarried.

September 13, 1952.

Sir William Halcrow, an engineer who had a varied experience in the construction of docks, tunnels and hydraulic works in many parts of the world, died on October 31, 1958 at Folkestone at the age of 75.

William Thomson Halcrow was born on July 4, 1883, and educated at George Watson's College and Edinburgh University. He was articled to P. W. and C. S. Meik and acted for them as assistant and resident engineer on works in Spain and Italy and also on the Kinlochleven water-power scheme in Scotland. He then went out to the Far East for the contracting firm of Topham, Jones and Railton as chief engineer on the construction of the King George V graving dock at Singapore and later, from 1919, as agent in charge of the first stages in the building of the Johore Causeway and Ship Lock. In 1921 he returned to England to become a partner of C. S. Meik.

Among the works for which the firm of C. S. Meik and Halcrow (the style was subsequently changed to W. T. Halcrow & Partners) were engineers, and for which he assumed chief responsibility after the death of Meik in 1923, were improvements at the port of Beira, and the Lochaber power scheme, by which water is brought from a large catchment area including Lochs Laggan and Treig to the aluminium works at Fort William, through a 15-mile pressure tunnel under Ben Nevis.

He was also consulting engineer to the Grampian Hydroelectric Company for works which included 14 miles of tunnels and many dams, and he was engineer for the Caledonian and Glen Affric water-power projects. As consulting engineer for the London Passenger Transport Board's tube railways, jointly with the late Sir H. H. Dalrymple Hay, whom he succeeded as consulting engineer to the G.P.O. for tunnels, he carried out the extensions of the Bakerloo line to Finchley Road and of the Highgate line to East Finchley, and he also designed the flood protection works on the underground railways.

During the 1914-18 War he had been engaged on the construction of submarine and land defences and underground magazines at Scapa Flow, and his work during the last war included deep tunnel shelters for the Ministry of Home Security and munition factories for the Ministry of Supply. He was a member of the War Cabinet Engineering Advisory Committee and chairman of the panel of engineers who designed the Mulberry harbour.

In 1944 he was appointed by the Minister of Fuel chairman of a panel to report on the Severn Barrage tidal power scheme, and in 1951 he reported in a similar capacity on the Kariba and Kafue hydroelectric projects in the Rhodesias. He was a past chairman of the Association of Consulting Engineers, a past president of the British section of the Société des Ingénieurs Civils de France, and a former member of the Royal Fine Art Commission.

He was knighted in 1944.

November 1, 1958.

Sonnie Hale died in hospital on June 9, 1959. He was 57.

Sonnie Hale was born in London on May 1, 1902, his full name being John Robert Hale-Munro, and educated at Beaumont College, Old Windsor. In deciding to go on the stage he was only following a family tradition, since his father, Robert Hale, was a star of pantomime and musical comedy, while his sister Binnie Hale made her first stage appearance five years before him and had already established herself as a notable comedienne and revue star. He, therefore, had to face comparison with his father and sister, and for some time he tended to be overshadowed a little by them, but soon his individual comic style won him an independent reputation.

His first job on the stage was in the chorus of the revue *Fun of the Fayre,* at the London Pavilion in 1921, but he rapidly worked his way up to the position of a featured player in musical comedy and revue, his talents encompassing quite happily singing, dancing, clowning and playing a straight romantic lead (though never too seriously). His most memorable performances were in the spectacular London Pavilion shows of the late 1920s, among them *One Dam Thing After Another, This Year of Grace,* and *Wake Up and Dream,* and in the musical *Evergreen* with Jessie Matthews, to whom he was married at the time. Like many stage actors he was drawn into films with the introduction of the talking film in the early 1930s, and after making his film début in *Tell Me To-night* (1932) one of his first important appearances on the screen was in the filmed version of *Evergreen.* He rapidly became even more popular in the new medium than on the stage, which he virtually deserted during the next decade, acting in numerous films, among them several Anglo-German co-productions with the UFA company, like *Happy Ever After,* in which he fought Jack Hulbert for Lillian Harvey's hand while Cicely Courtneidge simmered in the background—directing *Head Over Heels, Gangway,* and *Sailing Along,* which he also wrote.

At the beginning of the war he returned to the stage, but found some difficulty in re-establishing himself. In 1940 he appeared in his own comedy *Come Out and Play*; two years later he played Tonio in a revival of *The Maid of the Mountains,* and in 1944 he played in his first pantomime as Widow Twanky. He proved to play pantomime dames to the manner born, and was in later years seen as dame at the Palladium in *The Babes in the Wood* (1950) and *Dick Whittington* (1952). He also appeared in a number of his own plays, among them *Pardon My Claws* at the Q Theatre, *The French Mistress* at Wimbledon and Windsor, and *Nest of Robins* at Canterbury. A very happy teaming with his sister resulted in a revue, *One, Two, Three* (1947) and several series of the two-person radio show, which they also wrote, *All Hale.* At the time of his death he was about to return to the West End stage in his play *The French Mistress.*

Sonnie Hale was an excellent light comedian in his early days, combining flawless timing and the sort of crystal-clear musical comedy diction which seems to-day a lost art, with an unusually engaging personality; though his roles sometimes allowed him to behave a little caddishly, one always knew that under it all he would not harm a fly. In later years he turned to the older comedy techniques of the pantomime with equal success, playing pantomime dames with that air of decayed gentility, that feeling that if they are not quite ladies it is only by a very narrow margin and some unkind quirk of fate, which is essential to a proper pointing of the joke. His tour in 1956-57 in a revival of Gershwin's *Lady Be Good* left many theatregoers with a wholly delightful last glimpse of an almost forgotten comic attack, coming from an earlier, simpler, but, on this showing, far from negligible tradition.

His first two marriages, to Evelyn Laye and Jessie Matthews, were dissolved, and he married thirdly Mary Kelsey.

June 10, 1959.

One of the best known and most successful British aero-engine designers, **Major F. B. Halford,** C.B.E., F.R.AE.S., chairman and technical director of the de Havilland Engine Company, died suddenly at his home at Northwood, Middlesex, on April 16, 1955. He was 61.

Halford's work was characterized by original thinking and by a marked ability to anticipate developments in aviation. Having produced a long series of successful piston engines, he early appreciated the significance of the aircraft gas turbine pioneered by Whittle and realized the potentialities of a somewhat different conception of jet engine having a single-sided centrifugal impeller combined with "straight-through" combustion. These features were incorporated in the Goblin engine which powers the Vampire fighter and trainer and in the larger Ghost turbo-jet employed in the Comet I, the world's first jet airliner, and the Venom series of fighters. Halford had a tremendous capacity for work and an unflagging enthusiasm for his calling. He was responsible for every de Havilland engine from the little Gipsy piston motor originated in 1926 to the still secret Gyron axial flow gas turbine, one of the most powerful engines yet produced in any country. The team which he built up initiated a series of liquid fuel rocket engines.

A son of the late H. B. Halford, sometime Sheriff of Nottingham, Frank Bernard Halford was born on March 7, 1894, and was educated at Felsted. He graduated in engineering at Nottingham University. Having learnt to fly at Brooklands—his aviator's certificate was No. 639—he became an instructor at the Bristol School of Flying there. Being interested in engines, he took a post as engine examiner in the newly formed Aeronautical Inspection Department at the Air Ministry. In the first month of the 1914-18 War Halford joined the Royal Flying Corps and went to France, but early in 1915 he was brought back to design a larger engine than the Austro-Daimler. This became the B.H.P. (Beardmore-Halford-Pullinger) 230 h.p. unit, which was used in the early D.H.4s and afterwards, in production form, as the Siddeley Puma, was built in quantity for the D.H.9 and other aircraft. It was in connexion with the D.H.4 that Halford first had close contact with Captain (now Sir Geoffrey) de Havilland* and other members of the old Aircraft Manufacturing Company, from which the de Havilland organization grew.

A V-12 development of the B.H.P. engine, the 500 h.p. Atlantic, was the forerunner of the Siddeley Pacific, for which large orders were placed for aircraft which were to bomb Berlin, but this was forestalled by Germany's capitulation. Halford then collaborated with H. R. [Sir Harry] Ricardo* on one of the first "blown" engines, the Ricardo Supercharger, which embodied, with several B.H.P. features, Ricardo's ingenious system of introducing supplementary air on the working piston to defeat the effects of altitude. This engine was tall and obscured the pilot's view, and it was then that Halford originated the idea of inverting an in-line engine. When the war ended he was assistant to A. E. L. Chorlton, who was in charge of engine production at the Air Ministry.

Halford joined Ricardo and spent two and a half years in the United States negotiating licence agreements. On his return he assisted in developments such as the Ricardo-Triumph motor cycle engine, with which at Brooklands he established a 500c.c. hour record at just under 70 miles an hour. In 1923 Halford set up in business on his own account as a designer and consultant. He had begun to realize the value of high rotational speeds in small engines to get power with the advantages of compactness, and this idea, which he explored in a 1½-litre six-cylinder racing car engine running at 6,000 r.p.m., was put to use in the H-type aero-engines which he designed later for the Napier company. With the 1½-litre engine, fitted in a Halford Special car, he won many races at Brooklands.

Between 1924 and 1927 he worked for the A.D.C. Aircraft Co. on the Airdisco, Cirrus and Nimbus engines. From the Airdisco V-eight air-cooled engine a four-cylinder light aircraft engine was evolved—the 60 h.p. Cirrus which made possible the famous Moth aircraft. The de Havilland company's decision to build their own engines led Halford to design the Gipsy as a Cirrus replacement. This engine has been progressively developed ever since. A version was used in the Comet racer which won the England-Australia race of 1934.

Relinquishing his connexion with the A.D.C. Company in 1927, Halford concentrated on the Gipsy engine and on a new motor for Napier in which he applied his lessons of high-speed rotation by employing a large number of small cylinders, accommodating them by gearing two crankshafts together. This engine, the 305 h.p. 16-cylinder Rapier, was the first H-type engine and the first commercial application of the double crankshaft. The design was developed in the Dagger and Sabre engines. When Captain de Havilland wanted the Gipsy engine inverted, for use in the Puss Moth in 1929, Halford's original idea of 1917 came into its own. In 1935 the Royal Aeronautical Society awarded its silver medal to him for his work on aero-engines.

He had become technical director of Napiers in 1935, a position which he relinquished before the de Havilland Engine Co. was formed under his technical direction in 1944.

During the last war Halford's main efforts were devoted to the design and development of the Napier Sabre engine, which powered the rocket-firing Typhoon aircraft, and to the new field of gas turbines, which he entered in April 1941. The features subsequently incorporated in the Goblin and Ghost jet engines were actually decided before April 1941. He was also responsible for de Havilland airscrew development from 1941 to 1943.

A paper read before the Royal Society of Arts in May 1946 earned Halford the society's silver medal. He was elected a Fellow of the Royal Aeronautical Society in 1927, a member of the council in 1949, a vice-president in 1950, and president for 1951-52. For his work on aero-engines Halford was appointed C.B.E. in 1948. He had been a director of the parent company, the de Havilland Aircraft Co., since 1945.

He leaves a widow, a daughter, and a step-daughter.

April 22, 1955.

Lord Halifax, the first Earl, who died on December 23, 1959 at his home at Garrowby, near York, at the age of 78, held many Cabinet appointments and for two momentous decades exercised a marked influence on international affairs. His chief positions were those of Viceroy and Governor-General of India, Foreign Secretary in fateful years, and wartime Ambassador in the United States. A man of many gifts and strong Christian idealism, he was held in deep respect. He was one of the few men in our parliamentary life whose speeches sometimes change intended votes or lead to the withdrawal of unfortunate proposals. His part in the evolution of Indian independence was great: his influence on the Indian mind was not equalled by any of his predecessors on the Viceregal throne, with the possible exception of Lord Ripon.

Like others in responsible positions at the time he was fated to be judged in the light of the failure of the policy which led to the Munich agreement. When he went to the United States as British Ambassador in wartime his strength of character and unswerving devotion to high principles made a deep impression on Americans and this was reflected in his own country, so that when he laid down his high office in 1946 he had achieved the position of an elder statesman, to which his high character and record fully entitled him.

The Right Hon. Sir Edward Frederick Lindley Wood, first Earl of Halifax, third Viscount Halifax, of Mount Bretton, in the West Riding of Yorkshire, first Baron Irwin, of Kirby Underdale, in the county of York, in the peerage of the United Kingdom, and a baronet, K.G., P.C., O.M., G.C.S.I., G.C.M.G., G.C.I.E., was born on April 16, 1881, at Powderham Castle, Devon. He was the fourth son of the second Viscount Halifax, and of Lady Agnes Elizabeth Courtenay, only daughter of the eleventh Earl of Devon. He was a great-grandson of Earl Grey of the Reform Bill. His father was for many years president of the English Church Union, and Edward grew up to be a staunch Anglo-Catholic, but one always ready to encourage cooperation between the Anglican Church and the Free Churches. He was from early years a member of the House of Laity. In youth he contributed to the "Leaders of the Church" series a biography of John Keble, which was reissued in 1932.

While still a boy he became his father's heir by the death of his three elder brothers. From Eton he went to Christ Church, Oxford, where he gained a first in Modern History. One of his most cherished distinctions was election in 1933 as Chancellor of Oxford University; he became Chancellor of Sheffield University in 1946.

In 1909 he married Lady Dorothy Evelyn Augusta Onslow, daughter of the fourth Earl of Onslow, and she throughout life was an ever present help to him. His election in the following January as Conservative member for Ripon began more than four decades of service in public life. The 16 years he spent in the House of Commons included a time of absence on the Western Front in the 1914-18 War, serving with The Yorkshire Dragoons, which he had joined some years before war broke out. He rose to the rank of major and was mentioned in dispatches. He was later made honorary colonel of the regiment. Immersed as he became in great affairs, he set store on periodical relief from them at his home at Garrowby. Though he had a withered left arm from birth he was a keen and practised rider in the hunting field, and after his return from India was Master of the Middleton Foxhounds.

His ministerial career began in 1917 as assistant secretary to the Ministry of National Service. When in 1921 he was made Under-Secretary for the Colonies he was sent on a tour of the West Indies. His chief was Churchill* who was later to be so critical of some of his actions as Viceroy and of his share in the policy of appeasement towards Hitler and Mussolini. He reached Cabinet rank in 1922 as President of the Board of Education, and was sworn of the Privy Council. In the following year he was made Minister of Agriculture and Fisheries. Himself a practical farmer, he sought to rescue agriculture from the depression of that post-war period. His plan for a conference to this end, of landowners, farmers, and labourers, was lost by the refusal of cooperation by the labour trade union, so he turned to the less ambitious plan of conferring separately with each section of the industry.

In October 1925 Wood accepted with some misgiving the offer to succeed Lord Reading as Viceroy of India, and was created Baron Irwin of Kirby Underdale. He had a hereditary interest in India as his paternal grandfather was the prominent Whig statesman, Sir Charles Wood, who was one of the last Presidents of the Board of Control and from 1859 to 1866 the second holder of the Secretaryship of State for India. He was also the author of the famous Wood dispatch which recognized Governmental responsibility for the promotion of education in the sub-continent. Irwin's arrival in Bombay at the beginning of April 1926 was on a Good Friday, and the Indian intelligentsia were impressed by his decision to postpone the elaborate state reception to the next day, in order to observe the fast and take part in the three hours' service in the church on Malabar Hill.

Irwin found a state of political restlessness which the events of his period of office including the cleavage on Indian policy in the Conservative Party at home tended to accentuate. The wheels of the dyarchial system in the provinces drove heavily, and non-cooperation policies of the Congress as well as terrorism in Bengal gave the Viceroy grave concern. His first important speech, made at Simla in July, comprised an earnest appeal for the ending of communal clashes between Hindus and Muslims—a theme to which he had often to return. Though accepted in theory, his advice to this end met with scant practical response. But little more than 18 months after his assumption of office men of all parties, other than terrorists, were united in condemnation of the wholly British composition of the Statutory Commission of Inquiry into political reforms. In response to vociferous demands from India the inquiry was set up two years before the expiry of the decennial period laid down by the 1919 Act. With Sir John (later Lord) Simon [q.v.] as chairman it was a wholly parliamentary body, and on it Lord Attlee* had his first direct contact with the Indian problem.

The absence of Indian representatives was held to be an insult to the people most directly concerned. The decision of the main parties to boycott the inquiry was endorsed by the Legislative Assembly at Delhi, but not by the Upper House—the Council of State. With his zest for compromise and reasoned discussion, Irwin obtained Whitehall approval of the appointment of an Indian Central Committee, to sit with the commission and scrutinize the evidence and memoranda; but it could not share in the responsibility of reporting direct to Parliament.

By way of counterstroke an "All Parties" Conference was held under the chairmanship of Pandit Motilal Nehru (1861-1931), father of India's first Prime Minister. The conference outlined a plan of Dominion status, but some features of its report aroused opposition from Muslim and other minority interests. Irwin's leave home in the summer of 1929 coincided with the fall of the Baldwin Ministry and the formation of Ramsay MacDonald's second Labour Government. Irwin found Wedgwood Benn (now Lord Stansgate) [q.v.] more ready to listen to plans of Indian political advancement than his Conservative predecessors at the India Office. In correspondence published on October 31 Sir John Simon suggested that after his commission had reported H.M. Government should confer with the leaders both of "British India" and of the princely States for the purpose of seeking the greatest possible measure of agreement for the final proposals the Cabinet would lay before Parliament. Irwin had returned to Delhi and a few hours later announced that in the judgment of H.M. Government it was implicit in the Montagu declaration of August 20, 1917, that the natural goal of India's constitutional progress, as there contemplated, was the attainment of Dominion status. While the announcement gave great satisfaction to the Indian moderates, it was strongly criticized in Conservative quarters in Britain, and also by Lord Reading, the ex-Viceroy, and was much resented by Sir John Simon as pre-judging the findings of his commission. The report, published in the following summer, turned out to be a "best seller" among Stationery Office papers. While the phrase "Dominion status" found no place in the report it contained implications of the ultimate need to take that road.

Irwin stood high in the affections of the people of India and there was general relief when on December 23, 1929, travelling in his special train near Delhi, he and Lady Irwin narrowly escaped destruction by a terrorist bomb. On his return home in the spring of 1931 he was made K.G.; in 1948 he was appointed Chancellor of the Order. Behind the scenes he exerted his influence in the direction of the real political advancement of the sub-continent and on occasion crossed swords with Churchill and the section of the Conservative Party under his lead in this matter. Irwin shared in the heavy labours of the Joint Parliamentary Committee which gave shape to the federal plan, assisted Sir Samuel Hoare (later Lord Templewood) [q.v.] in drawing up the famous White Paper, and furthered in every way he could the enactment of the India Bill of 1935. Altogether he had a profound influence on the march to independence.

Attached as Irwin was to his home at Garrowby and to country pursuits he did not now seek office, but office sought him. In 1932 he was called back to his former post as President of the Board of Education. It was a time of depression and unemployment, and financial stringency stood in the way of the reforms he hoped to make. For a few months in 1935 he was Secretary for War and then was Lord Privy Seal. He was Leader of the House of Lords for three years from 1935, and again in 1940. He succeeded to the viscounty on the death of his venerated father at the age of 94 in 1933. He was made Lord President of the Council in 1937 and early in the following year, on the resignation of Anthony Eden [Lord Avon, d. 1977], became Foreign Secretary. He had been closely associated with international affairs as Neville Chamberlain's lieutenant in the policy of appeasement.

At the end of 1937, in his capacity as Master of the Middleton Hunt, he had accepted an invitation to a hunting exhibition in Berlin. The unfavourable comments this action evoked in some quarters were intensified by reports of the warmth of his reception by Hitler, Goering, and Göbbels. In November 1938 he went with the Prime Minister to Paris. In the following January they were in Rome for discussions with Mussolini. Halifax's desire for peace was stimulated by a keen consciousness of Britain's unpreparedness for war, but he found it his duty to convince the world that his country would stand by her obligations and resist further aggression. In the light of history it may be said that Halifax lent himself too readily to Chamberlain's optimism as to the results of Munich. When, on the eve of hostilities, the last desperate efforts of the Foreign Secretary to engage Hitler in negotiations had failed, he was in the position to reassure the House of Lords that "our consciences are clear".

When Chamberlain's Government fell in May 1940 Churchill kept Halifax at the Foreign Office, and, with Chamberlain himself, called him to the small inner War Cabinet. At the end of the year Lord Lothian, our Ambassador at Washington, died, and with the hearty acquiescence of President Roosevelt, Churchill offered Halifax the appointment.

Halifax had been in Washington less than a year when on December 7, 1941, the attack of the Japanese on Pearl Harbour brought the United States into full comradeship with the British Commonwealth in its bitter struggle against the Axis powers. There were to follow many dark months of suffering and disaster in the field, on the ocean and from the air, but the Grand Alliance had been formed to save the western world from enslavement. Halifax rose to the great change of the United States from the "fetch and carry" policy to complete cooperation and unfaltering comradeship in the struggle. His touch became more certain and his influence on American opinion more assured. In recognition of his outstanding services to the allied cause he was advanced to an earldom in 1944. He remained in Washington 12 months after the collapse of Germany, and then retired at his own request. The Order of Merit was conferred upon him. In 1957 he was appointed Grand Master of the Order of St. Michael and St. George and at the same time was created G.C.M.G. In that year appeared *Fulness of Days*, his autobiography.

Lord Halifax was D.C.L. or its equivalent of more than a dozen British, Canadian, and American Universities. In 1947 he was appointed High Steward of Westminster. He was made honorary R.A. in 1941. He was a Knight of the Order of St. John of Jerusalem. His second son, Major the Hon. Francis Peter Wood, late R.H.G., was killed in action in Egypt in 1942. The Earl is succeeded by Lord Irwin, Charles Ingram Courtenay Wood, late R.H.G., who was born on October 3, 1912, and was M.P. for York from 1937 to 1945. He married in April 1936 Ruth Alice Hannah Mary, only child of the late Right Hon. Neil Primrose, M.P., and granddaughter of the seventeenth Earl of Derby. They have a son and two daughters. The second surviving son of the late Earl is the Hon. R. F. Wood, M.P. for Bridlington since 1950, and since the last general election Minister of Power. The only daughter married the Earl of Feversham, D.S.O.

December 24, 1959.

Sir Arthur Hall, M.D., F.R.C.P., whose name will always be associated with the development of provincial medical schools, died at Sheffield on January 3, 1951 at the age of 84.

At the beginning of this century a candidate for the medical profession whose parents lived away from a metropolis, and could not afford several years' boarding fees, was severely handicapped. Both in material equipment and in personnel the provincial schools were rapidly becoming inadequate for the training of a profession which was in process of becoming scientific in outlook. During that critical period, when universities were being established in a number of provincial centres, it was of mutual advantage both culturally and practically that the local medical schools should become firmly built into the new structures. In Sheffield the practical arguments in favour of the establishment of a university lay mainly along the lines of the steel industry. But without the backing of a profession whose tradition was firmly rooted in the past a technical institute might well have been considered adequate by the business community.

Arthur John Hall was the son of John Hall, a surgeon, of Sheffield, and was born on July 27, 1866. He therefore had intimate family connexions with the business community when he returned with the wider outlook given him by education at Rugby, Cambridge, and St. Bartholomew's Hospital. It is possible that no one will ever know the full extent to which Hall was responsible for modifying the parochialism of that time, but the testimony of those who had a hand in the foundation of Sheffield University points to him as one of the most important influences.

Turning to the medical school, the task of expanding a small non-examining body into an important university department with scope for modern research was of Herculean dimensions. All was at first inadequate. A staff had to be attracted from outside, and at the same time local students must be trained to take responsibility when their time should come. An introduced stranger would find it difficult to initiate new departures, while fitting himself to local ways. Hall adopted the plan of himself occupying a newly established chair for a year or two, and then vacating it in favour of someone appointed from outside. It is evident that this could only be done by one who held the complete confidence of staff and student alike. He early established a club for the pooling of medical literature among the budding consultants, and later a combined staffs club with the motto "Floreat Amicitia".

In the profession as a whole he was best known through his work on *encephalitis lethargica.* When this disease appeared in Britain in 1918 he was among the first to publish a clear description of the symptoms, and unlike others at that time he was careful to steer clear of premature theoretical considerations which were later proved to be unfounded. Such a combination of progressive and original outlook with keenly critical discipline was typical of the man, and applied not only to his own work but to his encouragement of the efforts of his colleagues. Largely on this account he was much sought after as an examiner in the final examination for medical degrees. In this capacity he acted for the universities of London, Oxford, and Cambridge, as well as for the majority of provincial universities. The Royal College of Physicians utilized his gifts first as examiner, then as councillor, and finally as censor. This was the first occasion on which a provincial physician had been elected to that honour.

He married in 1900 Hilda Mary, daughter of Charles Vickers. She died in 1945 and he is survived by a son and a daughter of the marriage.

January 5, 1951.

Marie Hall (Mrs. Edward Baring), who was one of the great names among English violinists in the early years of the century, died in hospital at Cheltenham on November 11, 1956 at the age of 72.

She was born on April 8, 1884, the daughter of a harpist in the Carl Rosa Opera Company, who wanted her to take up the harp. She showed such pronounced mastery of the violin that, after coaching by a local teacher at Newcastle on Tyne, she played at the age of nine to Emile Sauret, who pressed her parents to send her to the Royal Academy of Music. This was not done, but she received instruction from time to time from such distinguished musicians as Elgar, at Malvern in 1894; from Wilhelmij, in London in 1896; from Max Mossel, at the Midland Institute at Birmingham in 1898; and from Kruse, in 1900. She actually won a scholarship to the Royal Academy of Music in 1899, but could not take it up. Nevertheless, her career was much advanced through the help and friendship of P. Napier Miles.

In 1901 Jan Kubelik heard her play and on his advice she went to Prague to study under Sevčik, who coached her at intervals until 1903. Her playing in Prague in 1902 led to her engagement to play in Vienna early in 1903 and later in the same year she appeared at the St. James's Hall, London. She gained immediate successes at all these centres and was well placed for a triumphant career when she suffered a long illness.

In 1905 she reappeared and proved in numerous tours all over the world that she was able to hold her own as one of the best women violinists of her time in any country. She introduced several new works for violin to the public, including Dr. Vaughan Williams's [q.v.] "The Lark Ascending", sonatas by Rutland Boughton [q.v.] and Percy Sherwood and a suite by Gordon Bryan.

She married in 1911 Edward Baring, who died in 1951. Recently she had given recitals on the B.B.C. accompanied by her daughter, Pauline Baring, the pianist.

November 14, 1956.

Vice-Admiral Sir Theodore J. Hallett, K.B.E., C.B., who died at Aldingbourne on June 1, 1957, was particularly connected with the development of combined operations in the 1939-45 War, and with the specialized training that their preparation demanded. He was then a retired officer in the sixties, and rendered valuable service. Although denied opportunities for personal distinction he was regarded with respect and affection by all those who passed through the establishment he organized and commanded. His career covered the long span of 54 years.

Theodore John Hallett, who was born in 1878, was the son of the Rev. J. T. Hallett. He entered the Britannia as a naval cadet in September 1891 and went to sea two years later as midshipman of the Anson in the Mediterranean. In 1896-97 he was in the cruiser Volage, in which he was present at the Diamond Jubilee Review. He became a sub-lieutenant in July 1897, and a lieutenant in December 1899. After serving in the sloop Phoenix in China from 1900 to 1903 he was selected to qualify in gymnastics, as physical training was then known, and between 1904 and 1908 he was P.T. officer in the battleship Albion, flagship of the second-in-command in China, and at the R.N. Colleges at Greenwich and Dartmouth. He went to sea again in December 1908 as first lieutenant of the Bellerophon, and was promoted to commander in June 1912.

During the next five years, including three years of the First World War, he was executive officer successively of the battleships Cornwallis, Neptune, and Royal Sovereign in the Home Fleet. The Royal Sovereign was commanded by Captain Allen T. Hunt and after both officers had been promoted in 1917 Hallett served as Flag-Captain to Rear-Admiral Hunt in two light cruiser squadrons—the third, in H.M.S. Chatham in the Grand Fleet, and the seventh, in H.M.S. Southampton on the South American Station. From 1922 to 1924 Hallett was naval assistant to the Second Sea Lord, Admiral Sir Henry Oliver*. The next two years he spent in the Mediterranean as Captain of the Fleet under two commanders-in-chief, Admirals Sir Osmond Brock and Sir Roger Keyes. From 1927 until his promotion to flag rank in April 1928 he commanded the battle cruiser Repulse. For two years from July 1929 he was Rear-Admiral and Commanding Officer, Coast of Scotland, at Rosyth. In January 1933 he was promoted to vice-admiral, but not having hoisted his flag in command at sea was placed on the retired list.

Returning to active service when the Second World War broke out in 1939, he was at first employed in the Naval Intelligence Division, but from the spring of 1940 became associated with inter-Service training and development. From 1941 he was Flag Officer-in-Charge of the Combined Training Centre at Inverary, and from 1942 to 1944 Director of Combined Training. In March 1944, in readiness for the invasion of Normandy, he was appointed Chief Staff Officer (Administration) to the Commander-in-Chief at Portsmouth. From October 1944 until after the end of the war in Europe he was Naval Officer-in-Charge at Newhaven.

He was made a C.B.E. in 1919 for valuable services in command of H.M. ships and as Flag-Captain in the Third Light Cruiser Squadron. In 1931 he was made a C.B., and in June 1944 he was promoted K.B.E. He married in 1908 Helen Blanche, daughter of Colonel F. Dakeyne. They had a son and a daughter.

June 3, 1957.

Fleet Admiral William F. Halsey, the acclaimed hero of the Pacific in the war against Japan, died suddenly on August 16, 1959 at a holiday retreat on Long Island Sound, apparently from a heart attack. He was 76 and had been in excellent health during a prolonged stay at Fishers Island country club.

Halsey's exploits as commander of the United States Third Fleet have already rung down to history; in the words of Admiral Burke, Chief of Naval Operations, he was a pillar of inspiration to the entire nation during the war years, which saw the American Navy surge from a crippled, battered fleet after Pearl Harbour to an overwhelming victorious, able force in 1945. He recalled that throughout the embattled seas and skies of the vast Pacific, Halsey led his fleet into many actions which contributed to one of the greatest victories of sea power in history. From a foothold at Guadalcanal in the Solomons he directed the air-sea-land campaign in the South Pacific which cleared the enemy from the lifeline to Australia and New Zealand and isolated the Japanese bastion at Rabaul.

Under his aggressive leadership, the liberation of the Philippines was accomplished months ahead of the most optimistic expectations. Halsey then probed the South China seas and the coast of the Malayan peninsula so effectively that these waters became untenable to shipping supplying Japan's oversea garrisons, which were driven back, hopelessly weakened, pending the final onslaught on the home islands.

Others recall Halsey as a master of hit-and-run tactics. His formula was to "kill Japs, kill Japs, and kill more Japs; sink ships and sink more ships". Hit hard, hit fast and hit often, he said. Ever a "sailor's sailor", he had a way of appearing in the most unexpected places at sea or ashore and early in 1942 took his forces deep into Japanese waters for a strike at the Marshall and Gilbert Islands, the first big naval offensive of the Pacific war.

Between July 10 and August 15, 1945, forces under Halsey's command destroyed or damaged 2,804 enemy aircraft, sank or damaged 148 warships, and accounted for nearly 1,600 Japanese merchant vessels. He sometimes recalled that when he took command his force was "only a little shoe string"; after Guadalcanal he had available one damaged carrier, one damaged battleship, one cruiser, and very few destroyers, but "the Jap had been given such a drubbing he didn't come back".

Among these stirring exploits which won him his full admiral's stars, Halsey, in April 1942, took the aircraft carrier Hornet within sufficient distance of Japan to enable Army bombers under Colonel Doolittle, as he was then, to make their raid on Tokyo, and before Guadalcanal he defeated the Japanese in the battle of Santa Cruz. Towards the end of the war he was shelling the enemy's coastal positions and late in 1945 he hauled down his flag at the age of 63 after having been at sea since 1938—the end of 45 years of naval service.

Halsey, the son of a naval captain, came from Elizabeth, New Jersey. After attending the University of Virginia he graduated in 1904 from the United States Naval Academy, where his name was engraved on a trophy as the midshipman who had done the most among his class to promote athletics. He advanced through his grades to the rank of rear-admiral, which he attained in 1938, and on retirement took an appointment in one of the big business corporations.

August 17, 1959.

Mark Hambourg, the famous pianist, who died on August 26, 1960 at Cambridge, was the son of a musician, Michael Hambourg, who had studied with Nicholas Rubinstein, brother of Anton and the "great artist" to whose memory Tchaikovsky dedicated his Elegiac Trio. He was 81.

Though the father made no outstanding reputation for himself in Russia, where he combined with music the teaching of Hebrew as a means of supporting his family, he was a fine judge of artistic talent and knew how to further the careers of his children. Mark was the eldest of three sons who entered the musical profession; his younger brothers, Jan the violinist and Boris the violoncellist, played with him in London as "the Hambourg Trio" some 25 years ago, but Mark's reputation as a pianist was achieved in England at a much earlier age.

He was in his tenth year when in 1889 his father first brought him to England. He had already attracted attention as a wonder child in Moscow, and in his entertaining book of reminiscences *From Piano to Forte* he has described how they arrived at Victoria Station knowing no word of English save an address, painfully conned, which they recited to a driver of a four-wheeler as "Dwenty-voor Ouppair Bedvoord Phlarsee". They were without English introductions, yet in a surprisingly short time the child had played all over England and had been received into that brilliant artistic society of which the studio of Felix Moscheles in Kensington was the focal point.

It was due to the generosity of Paderewski and the interest of Hans Richter that he was presently sent to Vienna to pursue the higher branches of his art under Leschetizky. He arrived there escorted by his father in 1891 and settled down to a course of serious study under the famous teacher and to the enjoyment of all the delights of musical Vienna. His career there culminated in a concert of the Philharmonic Society at which he played Liszt's Hungarian Fantasia with orchestra under Felix Weingartner. He had had his health proposed at a supper party by Brahms himself. Richter, Mahler, Busoni, and a dozen others had become his friends when he left Vienna in June 1895 to start on his first world tour.

World tours were not the commonplace of an artist's career in the 1890s that they are today. Mark Hambourg started from London for Australia, where he found audiences to whom such art as his was a new experience. He returned to London to join Joachim and Piatti at the Monday "Pops" in St. James's Hall, and after a German tour of which Berlin was the chief objective, and a return to his beloved master Leschetizky in Vienna in time to meet Brahms once more, he next set out to discover America and set foot in New York for the first time in October 1898.

Henceforward the strenuous life of the travelling virtuoso was his, but England was his point of departure, and to it he always returned. The days of "Dwenty-voor Ouppair Bedvoord Phlarsee" were long past. His father and he had become naturalized British subjects in 1896. He gave a series of concerto concerts in London, with Henry Wood conducting, in 1901; he had become thoroughly acclimatized to English life and his principal tours subsequently, other than those to America, were to the more distant parts of the British Empire. In 1906 he paid his first visit to South Africa, and on his second two years later he was accompanied by his English wife, the Hon. Dorothea Frances, second daughter of the first and last Baron Muir Mackenzie, P.C., G.C.B., whom he had recently married. All these circumstances considered, it was certainly a rashness on the part of a London newspaper to suggest during the first months of the war that Mark Hambourg had once "considered himself a German", and an action in the High Court secured him substantial damages.

It may be questioned whether it is possible for any artist to pursue so strenuous a career of performance before all kinds of audiences in every part of the world and retain the freshness of outlook and resilience of mind which is essential to a great interpretation of great music. In his later years undoubtedly Mark Hambourg's performance suffered from these conditions. His control became erratic and the old delicacy of touch and the poetic sense only appeared in brief flashes amid extravagancies of execution. But he had the love of travel which is stimulated by an interest in many sides of life and in meeting many kinds of people; he had an enormous vitality and, above all, a keen and kindly sense of humour. He used his remarkable musical gift as a means of gaining a wide experience of life, and the book alluded to above, which he published in 1931, lightly written though it is, shows that not one of his experiences was wasted.

One of his four daughters is Miss Michal Hambourg, the concert pianist.

August 29, 1960.

Cicely Hamilton, author, playwright, and journalist, and a noted figure in the women's suffrage movement during the years before 1914, died at her home in London on December 6, 1952 at the age of 80.

Of versatile taste and accomplishment, Cicely Mary Hammill (she adopted the name of Hamilton when she went on the stage, and retained it afterwards) was born in London in 1872, the child of an Anglo-Scots father who commanded a Highland regiment, and an Irish mother. She went to school in Malvern, then in Homburg, in Germany, and, the family fortunes having declined seriously, started to earn her living at an early age as a pupil-teacher in the Midlands. From this she passed to the writing of novelettes and serial detective fiction, and for a dozen years managed to combine journalism and literary hackwork with a busy career as actress and stage director in touring companies in the provinces (one of her professional names was Elfreda Salisbury). Her most striking performance in London was as Mrs. Knox in *Fanny's First Play.*

Her first piece for the theatre was a one-act play, produced in 1906. Two years later she achieved success with an entertaining if slightly rough-edged comedy, *Diana of Dobson's.* Though she had precipitately sold the rights of the play for £100, her reputation from this time onwards enabled her to write what she pleased. She wrote some 20 plays in all, but, although more than once she came very near to success on the grand scale, conspicuous good fortune in the theatre just passed her by. *A Matter of Money* (1913) made a taking impression, as also did *The Brave and the Fair* (1920), but the play of hers that was best received was *The Old Adam* (1925), a clever, amusing and pessimistic piece arguing the psychological inevitability of war. Asquith is said to have gone to see the play three times. This pre-occupation with the aggressive instinct and war, together with her strongly feminist bias of mind, gives substance to a great deal of her other writing.

She had first proclaimed her feminism in a witty and acutely reasoned book, *Marriage as a Trade* (1909), and up to 1914 she was a familiar figure on suffragette platforms, eloquent though also nervous and excitable, not least when she was condemning the excesses of militants. During the 1914-18 war she served in a British women's hospital in France.

For a short novel, unaffectedly tragic in temper, which she produced in 1919, *William—an Englishman,* she was awarded the Femina-Vie Heureuse prize. In another novel, *Theodore Savage,* which she published in 1922, she envisaged the desolation in England left by a future war waged with all the resources of air bombardment and poison gas. A work of a different and more rewarding kind was the history of the Old Vic she wrote, in collaboration with Lilian Baylis, a very lively contribution to the story of the English stage.

Miss Hamilton had always been a tireless traveller, equally fond of walking and cycling, and in 1931 she published *Modern Germanies,* the first of a long series of descriptive and travel volumes. Italy, France, Russia, and Austria followed, and then came separate volumes on Ireland, Scotland and England, and in 1951 a volume on Holland, all of them observant and often unexpectedly informative. They were fair-minded, too, in a way that may have surprised some who knew only one aspect of her ardent and combative temperament.

Pale and expressive of face, with intelligent eyes, a witty and frequently acid conversationist—she was not always a good listener—Miss Hamilton was a genuine individualist, who hated and feared what seemed to her to be the growth of irresponsible democracy. She wrote an engaging volume of informal autobiography, *Life Errant,* in 1935. In 1938 she was awarded a Civil List pension.

December 8, 1952.

Sir Frederic Hamilton, who died at his home at Tadworth, Surrey, on January 29, 1956 at the age of 90, was formerly editor of the *Johannesburg Star.* He was largely interested in mining in South Africa, Australia, and elsewhere, and was a director of several finance and mining companies.

Frederic Howard Hamilton was born in London in 1865, and was educated at Mill Hill School and at Caius College, Cambridge. After reading for the Bar at the Inner Temple he went to South Africa in 1889. Attracted by the possibilities of the Northern Transvaal, where the search for gold reefs was being extended, he made his way to Pietersburg. Hamilton decided to settle down in a town which provided a special fascination for a young "adventurer", for it stood on the fringes of white South African civilization. Instead of prospecting for gold, however, he took up journalism.

He founded and edited the *Zoutpansberg Review.* Soon after the periodical was established the weekly coach brought him a letter containing what he later described as "the astonishing offer" of the assistant editorship of the *Johannesburg Star.* It astonished him because the *Zoutpansberg Review's* "one title to fame was that there was no newspaper in South Africa to the north of it, and its editor and staff, who were indistinguishable, were devoid alike of training and experience". The man who made the offer—the late Francis Joseph Dormer—must have known his man, however, for, after working on the *Star* for some years, Hamilton succeeded Dormer in the editorship of the paper.

Hamilton took over the editorship at a difficult period. Local grievances were accumulating and the policy of the Republican Executive in granting concessions of all kinds was handicapping the development of trade and the expansion of mining. The reform movement attracted the Rand population and the early idea of "progressive republicanism" began to lose ground. Hamilton backed the Reform Party. The situation became more and more critical and ended in the Jameson Raid. Hamilton was one of the 65 members of the Reform Committee, all of whom except one were arrested and imprisoned by the Boer Government. Before the raid and his arrest Hamilton and Charles Leonard went to Cape Town to see Rhodes and urge that Jameson should not cross the border.

He could have sailed for England after the raid but chose, instead, to return to Johannesburg in time, as it happened, to take the train to gaol in Pretoria. President Kruger evidently bore him no ill-will for he allowed him personal parole to say farewell to his wife. It is said that while in gaol he never became despondent and did his best to raise the spirits of his colleagues.

After paying his fine of £2,000 Hamilton resigned the editorship of the *Star* and left for England. He edited the *African Review* until 1899 and then turned his attention to mining and finance, becoming a director of the London office of the Anglo-Transvaal. In 1936 he was knighted. To the end of his long life he maintained a shrewd and lively interest in world affairs, particularly in Britain's economic problems. He served for a time as chairman of the executive committee of the Liberal National Council.

Hamilton was a discriminating collector of pictures, appreciating early the French Impressionist school. He was also a man of great simplicity and kindness, who seemed almost to disclaim responsibility for his natural generosity.

He married first Helen Mary, daughter of the late H. Didcot, of South Africa. She died in 1941. He married secondly Mary Alice Forster, daughter of A. L. Smith, late Master of Balliol, who survives him.

January 31, 1956.

Lt.-Col. James Stevenson-Hamilton—
See **Stevenson-.**

Oscar Hammerstein II died at Doylestown, Pennsylvania, on August 23, 1960. He was 65.

By his death Broadway loses one of its best-loved figures, and what was perhaps the most fruitful and successful theatrical partnership America has ever known is brought to an end, a partnership which gave pleasure the world over. This was the collaboration between Richard Rodgers and Hammerstein which produced the extremely successful musical plays *Oklahoma, South Pacific,* and *The King and I.*

Oklahoma ran on Broadway for 2,248 performances and *South Pacific* for 1,925 performances. They were no less successful as films.

Oklahoma, as a musical comedy, was revolutionary in technique, and the authors, as a critic wrote, "aimed at making every song, dance, ballet, and joke a means of advancing the story and of holding the mood which they had evoked in the very first words of the opening song "O, What a Beautiful Morning". Rodgers and Hammerstein claimed, with justice, that their songs were organic growths from the theme of the play and that they never gave a twist to the story in order to drag in irrelevant brilliances. The impact on London of *Oklahoma* with its drive, its pace, its zest, and its colour was immediate and lasting; it ran for over 1,500 performances.

Hammerstein will long be remembered as the writer of "Ol' Man River", "Lover Come Back to Me", "O, What a Beautiful Morning", "People Will Say We're in Love", and "All the Things You Are".

For a number of years no Broadway season was complete without a Rodgers and Hammerstein musical, the last being *The Sound of Music,* in which Mary Martin, who had earlier made a hit in *South Pacific,* was the star.

Hammerstein belonged to a famous American theatrical family. His grandfather was the operatic impresario, Oscar Hammerstein I (who built the Stoll Theatre); his father was a theatrical manager, and his uncle was Arthur Hammerstein, the producer, and it was Arthur who gave him his start on Broadway.

He was born in New York city on July 12, 1895, attended the Hamilton Institute and then went to Columbia University, where he took his B.A. in 1916. He entered a law office in New York and studied at the Columbia Law School. At the end of a year he met Miss Myra Finn and asked his employer for a pay increase so that he could marry. The rise was refused and he went to his uncle Arthur and asked if he could work in the theatre. He said later: "If they'd given me another 20 dollars a week I'd have stayed on and probably become a lawyer".

His uncle, a practical man of the theatre like all the Hammersteins, told him to eschew writing (he had made his mark in university theatricals as a "book and lyrics" man) for the moment and learn something of production. He did so well that he was later promoted general stage manager, supervising all Arthur Hammerstein's shows on Broadway and on tour. He now began to write again.

His first real success came in 1922 with *Wildflower,* written with Otto Harbach, and was followed two years later by the tremendous hit *Rose Marie,* for which Rudolf Friml* wrote the music. There followed shows that have become household names, *The Desert Song* and *The New Moon* (with Sigmund Romberg) and (with Jerome Kern) *Show Boat.* This, an adaptation of Edna Ferber's* novel, gave him what he called his "big emancipation". In it he introduced the freshness, reality, and vigour he had been seeking within himself. It was an immense success.

The 1930s were for Hammerstein lean years, the golden touch escaped him—he called it sardonically his "formative period"—but then one day Theatre Guild told him that they were undertaking a new production of the Lynn Riggs play *Green Grow the Lilacs,* using a score by Rodgers, and invited him to write the book and lyrics. The finished show was presented in March 1943 and was called *Oklahoma.*

The partnership with Rodgers lasted the rest of Hammerstein's life. After *Oklahoma* came *Carmen Jones* (*Carmen* in modern dress and a real *tour de force*), *Carousel, Allegro, South Pacific,* and *The King and I,* based on the book *Anna and the King of Siam,* in which starred the late Gertrude Lawrence [q.v.].

Hammerstein was a big, slow-moving man with a rough-hewn, philosophical face and a shy manner.

In a small book called *Lyrics* he wrote: "The song is the servant of the play . . . it is wrong to write first what you think is an attractive song and then wedge it into a story. The most important thing in a song is sincerity. However important, however trivial, mean it, mean it from the bottom of your heart and say what is in your mind as carefully, as clearly, as beautifully as you can". In this can perhaps be seen the seeds of his successes, for in all the plays in which he collaborated there were a ring of sincerity and the mark of careful workmanship.

He twice won a Pulitzer prize for his work, first for *Oklahoma* and then for *South Pacific.* He also won a Motion Picture Academy Award (an Oscar) for the film *The Last Time I Saw Paris.* He was an honorary Doctor of Humane Letters of Dartmouth College.

He was twice married, first to Myra Finn in 1917, by whom he had a son and a daughter. This marriage was dissolved in 1929 and the same year he married Dorothy Blanchard, of Melbourne, Australia, by whom he had a son.

August 24, 1960.

Nina Hamnett, sculptress, painter, and authoress, died in hospital in London on December 16, 1956 at the age of 66. On December 13 she had [accidentally] fallen from the window of her flat in Paddington.

It is an open question whether the world gained or lost by the partial sacrifice of Nina Hamnett, the painter of portraits and landscapes and illustrator, to Nina Hamnett, the Bohemian, but readers of her book of reminiscences, *Laughing Torso,* will have no doubt that in the latter role she contributed to the gaiety of nations. Her friends will know something more: that whatever she might have done ultimately in painting if she had stuck to it more closely, Miss Hamnett was a complete success as a person; generous, good-humoured, loyal, and witty. There are several sorts of Bohemian, of different heights of brow, and she was of the robust kind more likely to be encountered in London "locals" than at cocktail or sherry parties in Chelsea or Bloomsbury. One effect of her genial personality was to reconcile differences, and she was equally popular among artists of generally hostile camps. Thus, Miss Hamnett painted Sickert, and she was the subject of one of the most successful portraits by Roger Fry.

Nothing could have been more conventional than her start in life. A daughter of Colonel George Edward Hamnett, she was born at Tenby, South Wales, on St. Valentine's Day, 1890, and educated at the Royal School, Bath. She studied art at the Dublin School of Art and the London School of Art, where she won a silver medal. Her first opportunity to exhibit was with the Allied Artists' Association, founded by Frank Rutter, at the Albert Hall, and she was one of the young artists inspired by Fry's Post-Impressionist exhibitions at the Grafton Galleries. For a time she joined the Fry circle of decorative designers at the Omega Workshops.

Her first one-man show in London was held at the Claridge Gallery in 1926. It consisted largely of portraits, which seemed to show that her general attitude to humanity was that of amused boon-companionship. Apparently she had no illusions and few prejudices, and such as she had found sub-satirical expression. A sort of wondering tolerance appeared to be characteristic. Her exhibition at the Claridge Gallery the following year contained drawings of the Crystal Palace and illustrations to a first novel, *The Silent Queen,* by Seymour Leslie. A comment on these drawings was that satirical was not quite the right word for them, and that they expressed rather a glad astonishment that such things as the subjects could exist.

Probably her happiest artistic experience was her collaboration with Sir Osbert Sitwell* in *The People's Album of London Statues,* published in 1928, the drawings for which were exhibited at Tooth's Gallery in the same year. The sympathetic humour of her work was well suggested by Sir Osbert Sitwell's remark that "translated into the medium of drawing many of these statues manifest a charm that has been overlooked, and he who came to scoff may yet stay to bless". The general approach was that of affectionate awe, and some of the monuments, the Foundling fountain in Guilford Street, for example, were drawn with real tenderness. Apart from illustrations her artistic remains are rather fragmentary. For the Canadian War Memorial she painted a portrait of General Lindsay, and other eminent people painted or drawn by her were W. R. Sickert, W. H. Davies, the poet, and Sir Edmund Gosse. For a time she taught at the Westminster Technical Institute.

In 1932 Miss Hamnett published *Laughing Torso,* reminiscences of her Bohemian life in London and Paris. Her own adventures are frankly told, and the book is full of amusing anecdotes of celebrated or notorious people, gaining in effect by the apparent artlessness of the writing. The publication of the book had a sequel which caused great excitement in literary and artistic circles. Aleister Crowley brought an action for libel against Miss Hamnett and her publishers and printers for the statement that he had a temple at Cefalu, in Sicily, where he was supposed to have practised black magic. On the fourth day of the hearing before Mr. Justice Swift the special jury stopped the case and returned a verdict for the defendants. Crowley brought an appeal, which was dismissed. She brought her autobiography up to the present decade with the publication in 1955 of *Is She a Lady*? This book, too, was filled with lively reminiscences.

December 17, 1956.

Knut Hamsun, the Norwegian novelist, who died on February 19, 1952 at the age of 92, was one of the great Norwegian authors whose reputation, like that of Ibsen and Sigrid Undset, reached far beyond the Scandinavian countries.

The author of *Hunger* and *Growth of the Soil*—his two most important books—was once known and admired all over the world, but in Norway, and even to many people outside Norway, Knut Hamsun died on April 9, 1940, when on the German occupation of Norway he became a traitor to his own country, a spiritual collaborator with the Nazis, and so much the more dangerous as he was the only European author of high international reputation who supported the Nazi cause. It was then that the Norwegian people mourned for Hamsun, not now.

Knut Hamsun was born on August 4, 1859, in the Gudbrandsdal, where his father was a farmer and a tailor. After a childhood of strenuous hardship in Nordland, his adolescent period was spent in various parts of the far north as a shop assistant, an itinerant merchant, a sheriff's deputy, a teacher's assistant, an apprentice to a shoemaker, and a vagabond. But all the time he was constantly reading, and knew that he wanted to become a writer. His first book, a love story from Nordland, was published in 1877, but had no success.

After a vain effort to find a publisher for a novel, Hamsun settled down in Christiania (Oslo), and this was a period of actual hunger and suffering. He could neither live by his literary efforts nor by his journalism. After a period as a labourer Hamsun went to America, where he joined a Norwegian colony and lived by manual work, until a Norwegian clergyman employed him as his secretary; he was sent home to Norway in 1884, seriously ill. After another hopeless effort to live by his pen in Christiania, he again went to America, taking odd jobs, as a tram-conductor in Chicago, and a farm-hand in various places. His impressions of the American civilization were very unfavourable.

In Copenhagen, where he lived for a period, Hamsun wrote the novel which was to give him his great fame, *Hunger* (1890). This book, with its impressionistic style and its penetrating, human appeal, at once made his literary reputation and Hamsun was suddenly universally recognized as a great genius. The novel is to a great extent autobiographical and deals with a young unknown author's fight against hunger and poverty; its style was so fresh and penetrating that no one could read it without being greatly moved by it. With the vehemence of a young talented writer Hamsun now turned against "the big four" in Norwegian literature, especially against Ibsen, and, influenced by Nietzsche's theories, also against "the average man" and "the mob".

Among his many novels the most outstanding, apart from *Hunger,* are: *Pan* (1894), *Victoria* (1898), *Segelfoss Town* (1915), *Growth of the Soil* (1917), *The Women at the Pump* (1920), *Vagabonds* (1927), and *August* (1930). All these, and several more, have been translated into English. Hamsun also wrote some plays, several short stories and poems, and innumerable articles and pamphlets.

The fertility in narrative and the artistic and stylistic genius of Hamsun have no doubt made many among his readers and critics overlook the fact that his philosophy was always fundamentally anti-social and reactionary. From a cult of the eccentric psychological types in life, the outcasts and vagabonds, Hamsun more and more obviously turned against society as such. His greatest novel, *Growth of the Soil* (which brought him the Nobel Prize for literature in 1920) was not only a fine description of the hard fight of Isak and Inger to transform the wilderness into the Sellenraa farm, but it was also a desperate challenge of modern civilization altogether, and seen on the background of *Segelfoss Town,* Hamsun's most bitter and angry denunciation of town life, progress, and modern culture, it reveals Hamsun as the deeply reactionary author whose last resort was a suicidal alliance with German nazism and Norwegian quislings.

On the liberation of Norway, Knut Hamsun, who had lived, since 1918, on his own farm of Norholm, in south Norway, was arrested and interned as a traitor. The supreme penalty was not exacted because doctors had testified that he was suffering from deterioration of mental powers and he escaped with a heavy fine. Once home again, he began to write the record of his impressions during the three years his case was being considered. *Paa Gjengrodde Stier* is no novel, nor is it a defence of his conduct; rather is it an explanation and guide to a spiritual experience, often brilliantly evocative and of high literary quality. It utterly belies the plea of a deterioration of mental powers.

February 20, 1952.

William Christopher Handy, the Negro composer and music publisher, who wrote some of the best loved tunes of the century and did perhaps more than anyone else to give form and popularity to the blues music of his race, died on March 28, 1958 in New York. He was 84.

"The blues were all born humble", Handy once wrote. His own origins were as humble as those of his music. He was born near Florence, Alabama, on November 16, 1873. His father and grandfather were both stern Methodist ministers, who regarded all secular music as immoral; but his grandfather was born a slave, and several of his family were severely punished—one actually shot—as runaways. Handy grew up in a world where music was ubiquitous. Spirituals in the chapel, work-songs in the quarry and the iron foundry in which he worked as a young man, street bands, and saloon pianos, all provided him with material and steeped him in the dynamic, eclectic tradition which suggested his music and which he was largely to influence.

He became a musician early in life, and led his own quartet at the Chicago World Fair in 1893. Later he was bandmaster to a succession of itinerant brass bands in the southern states. But he had his ups and downs; even if we discard the legend that the three-note germinal phrase of his most famous composition, the "St. Louis Blues", was suggested by the whistling of passing locomotives when he was sleeping out at night, it is clear that Handy went through periods of hardship.

At some time he attended the Kentucky Musical College, and he had been studying harmony by himself out of a hard-bought primer. He was thus able to write down and arrange the traditional music of his race. Most of the compositions attributed to him were folktunes which he picked up and arranged, and for some of them he expressly disclaimed actual authorship. But for all their talent, most of his contemporaries in the south were musically illiterate, and without Handy's skill their songs would have perished unremembered.

In 1912 Handy wrote the "Memphis Blues" for $50 as a campaign song for the notorious Boss Crump, and in the next few years, now established as a music publisher in Memphis, he poured forth a stream of fine blues tunes. They had rigid form. A pithy, usually pessimistic couplet was set, with the first line repeated, to a 12-bar melody on a set harmonic pattern, elegantly embroidered with excursions into the melancholy minor key. But, even early on, Handy took liberties with this traditional form; and later in his life wrote more ambitious works—a blues symphony, the "Aframerican Hymn", and a march, "Hail to the Spirit of Freedom". His patriotism also found expression in a musical setting of the Gettysburg oration.

In 1920 he moved to New York, where, in spite of gradually increasing blindness, he continued successfully to publish music, anthologies, and an autobiography, *Father of the Blues.*

He remained active until he suffered a stroke, three years ago, and he had the satisfaction of knowing that the "St. Louis Blues" became the subject of academic study by European intellectuals, and was adopted as a march for the Ethiopian Army on the command of the Emperor*.

March 29, 1958.

Hans Christian Hansen, the Prime Minister of Denmark, died in Copenhagen after a long illness, on February 19, 1960. He was 53.

He was born in Aarhus, Jutland, on November 8, 1906. The son of a bootmaker, he was to become the first Danish Foreign Minister to have had only a primary school education.

Hansen and his boyhood friend, Hans Hedtoft [q.v.], took over the leadership of the Social Democratic Party after the death, during the German occupation, of their formidable leader, Stauning. The two young men reshaped the party, abandoning the old disarmament policy, and after the war came out strongly for a pro-N.A.T.O. attitude and for a strong defence policy, a reversal of the old Social Democrat line of neutrality.

Hansen became in 1929 secretary, and a few years later chairman, of the Danish Social Democratic youth organization. Ten years later he became leader of the Danish Social Democratic Confederation. He was also the first Danish chairman of the Socialist Youth International.

During the German occupation both Hedtoft and Hansen were obliged to go underground. But together with two leading conservative politicians they formed a close connexion with the freedom council, and Hansen was the link with the Government, consisting of higher civil servants, who provided millions of kroner to aid the underground movement's activities.

In the first Government which was formed after the liberation by the Social Democrat, Buhl, he became Minister of Finance. It was a coalition Government which included members of the resistance movement, and he skilfully carried through a revised monetary policy greatly to the advantage of the Danish economy. He continued as Minister of Finance in Hedtoft's first Cabinet from 1947 to 1950, but in Hedtoft's second Government he became Minister of Foreign Affairs. In 1955 Hedtoft died suddenly in his early fifties during a Nordic conference in Stockholm. Hansen formed his first Government and took the posts of both Prime Minister and Minister of Foreign Affairs. After the general elections in May 1957 he formed a new Cabinet made up of nine Social Democrats, four Radicals, and three members of the Single Tax Party. Subsequently he gave up the foreign affairs portfolio.

During the dispute with Great Britain in June 1958, the local Faroese Government passed a Bill extending the fishing limits from three miles to 12 miles, thus abolishing the 10-year Danish-British agreement signed in 1955. Hansen acted swiftly, issuing a statement saying that the question could not be decided by local government: it was one which concerned Parliament in Copenhagen, since the Danish Government represented the Faroe Islands in all foreign affairs.

Hansen was an experienced and witty debater, a realist with the courage of his convictions. He had an abiding love of lyric poetry, and himself published a small volume of verse.

February 20, 1960.

Admiral Sir Cecil Harcourt, G.B.E., K.C.B., who died suddenly on December 19, 1959, commanded cruiser squadrons which helped to clear the Axis forces from North Africa and Sicily, and also an aircraft carrier squadron in the Far East, where he was Commander-in-Chief at Hongkong after the Japanese surrender. As captain of H.M.S. Duke of York he conveyed Winston Churchill* as Prime Minister on one of his wartime missions to the United States. He was 67.

Cecil Halliday Jepson Harcourt was the son of Halliday Harcourt and Grace Lilian, daughter of Dr. Jepson, and was born on April 11, 1892. He entered Osborne College as a naval cadet in September 1904, had two years there and another two at Dartmouth College, and after the training cruise in the Cornwall passed out as midshipman in May 1909, taking first prize of his term in mathematics. He became a sub-lieutenant in May 1912, and a lieutenant in October 1913.

When the First World War broke out in 1914 he was unemployed, and in October 1915 was placed on the retired list, but in May 1916 he was reinstated on the active list, and joined the battleship Centurion in the Grand Fleet a fortnight before the Battle of Jutland. He remained in her until March 1919, and for the next two years was at the R.N. Barracks, Chatham.

After serving in the flotilla leader Mackay in 1921-22, he commanded the destroyers Wivern and Vidette in the Mediterranean and Atlantic Fleets until his promotion to commander in December 1926. In this rank he had two years in the Operations Division, another two as executive officer of the cruiser Shropshire in the Mediterranean, and from December 1931 until just before his promotion to captain in June 1933 he commanded the destroyer Wessex in the Home Fleet.

After attending senior officers' courses, including one at the Army School, Sheerness, he commanded the Pangbourne as senior officer of the Reserve Fleet mine-sweepers at the Jubilee Naval Review in 1935, and for two years from August of that year was lent to the Commonwealth Government as Captain (D) of the Australian destroyer flotilla.

In September 1938 he joined the Operations Division as Deputy Director. About the time that the Second World War broke out he became Director of this Division and so remained until early in 1941. For his services in this responsible post during the critical days in 1940 he was made C.B.E. His next appointment was in command of the new battleship Duke of York in the Home Fleet, in which he served until after his promotion to flag rank in July 1942.

In addition to various other operations, the Duke of York conveyed Churchill to the United States and back in December 1941 and January 1942. Between October 1942 and the beginning of 1944 Harcourt commanded in succession the 10th, 12th and 15th Cruiser Squadrons in the Mediterranean. He took part in the landings in North Africa in November 1942, for which the United States Government awarded him the Legion of Merit for exceptionally meritorious conduct. "Admiral Harcourt", said the citation, "commanded the British cruiser squadron which provided close support for the landings in North Africa. His unfaltering support in the face of heavy odds did much to make possible the success of that operation".

For further services in the operations leading to the clearance of the enemy from Tunisia he was made C.B. in September 1943. He also took part in the capture of Pantellaria and Lampedusa, the landings in and capture of Sicily, and the landing at Salerno. In February 1944 he was appointed Naval Secretary to the First Lord, and held the post for a year. He was then selected to command the 11th Aircraft Carrier Squadron, which he took to the Far East to join the British Pacific Fleet.

After Japan capitulated he proceeded to Hongkong, where on September 16, 1945, he received the surrender of the Japanese. He remained as Commander-in-Chief—virtually Governor—until June 1946, earning golden opinions from all for the wisdom, insight and sympathy he displayed during a difficult and critical period of reconstruction.

He was promoted to vice-admiral in February 1946, and in December 1945, for distinguished services throughout the war, was advanced to K.C.B. In January 1947 he went to the Mediterranean as Flag Officer (Air) and Second-in-Command, and was there for a year, when he was recalled to the Admiralty to become Second Sea Lord, taking up the post in March 1948. It was again a difficult period in naval administration owing to the decision of the Government to reduce the strength of the Navy to 147,000 from the previously planned strength of 178,000, but thanks to the measures adopted the dislocation was overcome comparatively quickly. Harcourt was especially zealous in the building up of the reserve forces which became of increased importance after the reduction in the active strength, and in March 1949 made a personal appeal to 200,000 former naval ratings and marines to join one of the reserve formations. He was promoted admiral in June 1949 and in May 1950 his appointment as C-in-C. The Nore was announced. In 1953 he retired and in that same year was advanced to G.B.E.

He was chairman of the London and Greater London Playing Fields Association Thames Youth Venture Council; the Joint Commonwealth Societies' Conference; and a past chairman of the Victoria League.

He married first in 1920 Evelyn, widow of Gerald Gould and daughter of Brigadier-General W. H. Suart, C.M.G., and a well-known concert pianist. She died in 1950. Harcourt's second marriage, which took place in 1953, was to Mrs. Stella Janet Waghorn, widow of Air Commodore D. J. Waghorn. There were no children of either marriage.

December 21, 1959.

Martin Hardie, C.B.E., formerly keeper of the department of engraving, illustration, and design in the Victoria and Albert Museum, died at his home at Tonbridge, Kent, on January 20, 1952 at the age of 76.

Besides being a civil servant for 37 years, Hardie exercised his administrative abilities in several voluntary directions. He was, for example, the energetic honorary secretary of the Royal Society of Painter-Etchers and Engravers, and in 1935 he was appointed honorary treasurer of the Artists' General Benevolent Institution, being only the eighth holder of that office since the institution was founded in 1814.

The eldest son of the late James Hardie, M.A., head master of Linton House School, he was born in London in 1875. He was educated at Linton House, St. Paul's School, and Trinity College, Cambridge, and in 1898 joined the staff of the Victoria and Albert Museum as an assistant in the department of engraving, illustration, and design. He was promoted assistant keeper in 1914 and keeper in 1921, remaining in that position until he retired under the age limit in 1935, when he was created C.B.E.

As nephew of both John Pettie, R.A., and C. Martin Hardie, R.S.A., Martin Hardie may be said to have had an artistic ancestry. He studied etching under Sir Frank Short, R.A., at South Kensington, began to exhibit at the Royal Academy in 1908, and continued to do so regularly as well as at the Royal Society of Painter-Etchers and Engravers and the Royal Institute of Painters in Water Colours, of both of which bodies he was elected a member.

Under Hardie's keepership the department of engraving, illustration, and design at South Kensington deepened in interest and extended in scope to cover the whole range of the graphic arts, not only in the more obvious forms of drawing and engraving, but also in applications which had hardly been considered before. The collections of poster designs and of the art of the theatre, for example, are now famous. Upon the history of the British school of water-colour painting Hardie was a recognized authority.

Hardie's publications, in addition to the museum guides and catalogues which he compiled or edited, included *English Coloured Books, Engraving and Etching* (translated from the German of Dr. Lippman), *John Pettie, R.A., The British School of Etching,* and *Charles Meryon and his Eaux-fortes sur Paris,* the last two being special publications of the Print Collectors' Club, of which he was honorary secretary.

January 22, 1952.

Sir Edward Harding, G.C.M.G., K.C.B., who died at Guildford on October 4, 1954, was Permanent Under-Secretary of State for the Dominions from 1930 to 1939, and was then for a short time High Commissioner for Basutoland, the Protectorate of Bechuanaland and Swaziland, and also High Commissioner for the United Kingdom in the Union of South Africa.

A distinguished civil servant of great experience, he was one of the principal secretaries or advisers to the United Kingdom delegation at all the imperial conferences held in the inter-war period, and was executive head of the Dominions Office at the time when the Statue of Westminster was passed. He once said that all those who carry on administrative work in the Dominions should regard themselves as men with a mission, and as explorers in a new country, almost a new universe, of political method. Few servants of the State have, indeed, played a part in greater developments than those which were crowded into his years at the Colonial and Dominions Offices, where in his quiet and effective way he rendered invaluable services to the Empire.

Edward John Harding was born in 1880, the only son of the Reverend John Harding. He was educated at Dulwich College and at Hertford College, Oxford, of which he was a scholar and later an honorary fellow. Having obtained a first class in Moderations and a second class in *Lit. Hum.*, he entered the Board of Trade in 1903. The next year he was transferred to the Colonial Office, and in 1912 became Assistant Private Secretary to Lewis Harcourt when Secretary of State. In the same year he was called to the Bar by Lincoln's Inn.

From 1912 to 1917 Harding, who became a first class clerk in 1916, was Secretary of the Dominions Royal Commission and was then Junior Assistant Secretary of the Imperial War Conferences of 1917 and 1918. In this former year he was created a C.M.G., and in the last year of the war he obtained a commission in the Royal Garrison Artillery. Then in 1921 he became Assistant Secretary in the Colonial Office and acted as Deputy Secretary at the Imperial Conference of 1923, an office which he was to fill again three years later. In 1925 he was appointed Assistant Under-Secretary of State at the Dominions Office, and Registrar of the Order of St. Michael and St. George. In 1926 he was created a C.B. and in 1928 was advanced to K.C.M.G. In 1930 he was promoted to be Permanent Under-Secretary of State for the Dominions, a position which he filled with great distinction until 1939. In this capacity he went in 1936 on the invitation of the Government of South Australia to attend the centenary celebrations at Adelaide, and visited New Zealand on his way there.

In 1939 Harding was appointed to succeed Sir William Clark [q.v.] in the positions of his Majesty's High Commissioner for Basutoland, the Bechuanaland Protectorate, and Swaziland, and of High Commissioner for the United Kingdom in the Union of South Africa. He left for South Africa at the end of 1939. Early in 1940 he went to Basutoland to install the new Paramount Chief, Seiso Griffiths, grandson of Moshesh, who arrived to meet him at the head of 2,000 men. The event was celebrated by the slaughter of 175 oxen which were roasted on camp fires on the hilltops round Maseru.

Unfortunately, however, he was not to stay long in South Africa, for in January 1941 it was announced that his doctors had ordered him a complete rest for several weeks, and in February continued ill health compelled him to retire. However, from 1942 until 1944 he acted as Representative of the High Commissioner for the United Kingdom in Cape Town.

He was also for some years a governor of Dulwich College, a member of the Royal Commission for the 1851 Exhibition, and a member of the Council of the Royal College of Music.

In 1929 he married Marjorie Huxley, elder daughter of the late Henry Huxley, of Boar's Hill, Oxford, who died in 1950.

October 5, 1954.

Gilbert Charles Harding, whose conduct in such B.B.C. programmes as *Round Britain Quiz, Brains Trust, Twenty Questions, We Beg to Differ,* and *What's My Line*? often gave rise to unfavourable comment, which was not always just, died on November 16, 1960 after making recordings at the B.B.C. in London.

Born at Hereford on June 5, 1907, Gilbert Charles Harding was educated at the Royal Grammar School, Wolverhampton, and Queen's College, Cambridge. He began to study with a view to entering the Anglican ministry, but gave it up and became a Roman Catholic. In 1931 he went to Canada to teach English, and the following year found him teaching English in France. After a few months he joined the Bradford City Police but a broken knee forced his retirement and he returned to teaching, this time in Cyprus, where he also acted as *The Times* Correspondent.

He returned in 1936 to read for the Bar at Gray's Inn, meanwhile keeping himself as a "crammer" in Chancery Lane. Before he could take his final examination the clouds of war had darkened the horizon, and as he had a reasonable knowledge of French, German, modern Greek, and Turkish Harding was engaged by the monitoring service of the B.B.C. After a brief period with the Director of Outside Broadcasts he was sent to the Toronto office of the B.B.C., and soon after the end of the war he was appointed Overseas Director.

In 1947 he returned to Britain to make his first big public success in the *Round Britain Quiz.* Thereafter his appearances in the *Brains Trust, Twenty Questions, What's My Line*? and in numerous television programmes thrust him into a prominence which only a handful of people of exceptional talent and stamina could enjoy—or endure.

There is no doubt that the psychological strain of his sudden immense success produced in him a mental distress, which manifested itself by an extreme irritability and emotional disturbance. Popularity was thrust upon him by a medium of mass entertainment and he was convinced, and rightly so, that it was evanescent. This led to moods of determination to exploit the situation, quite cynically, to his own advantage, alternating with extreme depression, which, with illness, caused his frequent incapacity to fulfil his engagements.

The sensitive side of the man, so resolutely masked for public appearances, was revealed in his *Face to Face* interview with John Freeman on B.B.C. television in September, 1960. Harding was clearly moved under questioning whether he had ever been with a dying person, and the impression made upon him. He never married and his evident emotion was taken to refer to his mother's death. In two autobiographical books, *Along My Line* and *Master of None,* Harding showed an equally frank and astringent view of his own personal success.

A well stored mind and a ready wit he had, and he could be one of his own severest critics. Behind the mask of grumpiness there was an ardent being who cared very much about the things that matter, and one who often wished there were some other way in which he could have played his part in setting this right. But his success defeated him, even though it never killed his hopes.

November 17, 1960.

Lyn Harding, the veteran actor and friend and colleague of Sir Herbert Tree, died in hospital at Southend on December 26, 1952, at the age of 85.

Though in his long and distinguished career he played a very wide variety of parts, notably in the rip-roaring melodramas of the nineties, it is on his interpretations of Shakespeare that his reputation chiefly rests. He had already had some experience in Shakespeare when nearly 50 years ago he joined Tree's company at His Majesty's Theatre and thus began a friendship which ended only with Tree's death. During that association he proceeded through almost the whole gallery of Shakespeare's male characters and was particularly memorable as Owen Glendower in part I of *King Henry IV,* as Bolingbroke in *Richard II,* and as Henry VIII. Tree himself said of him in the last-named part: "I think there never will be one like him again".

Age but deepened his emotional grasp and broadened his experience, and though there was always a delightful breath from a more gracious past in his performances he was versatile enough late in life to adapt himself to modern plays. His playing of Dan Pachard in *Dinner at Eight* had a symmetry and poise which many a younger actor must have envied, while his fine presence and dignified utterance gave the part of Baron Lydyeff in *Glamorous Night* a greater distinction than the piece might otherwise have had. His versatility was also shown to advantage on the screen in *I, Claudius, Knight Without Armour* and in several adaptations of the Sherlock Holmes stories.

Born at St. Bride's, a village near Newport, Monmouthshire, on October 12, 1867, he was christened David Llewellyn and attended the village school. After leaving school he worked on a farm and was later a shop assistant at Cardiff. In that period he was a member of a local amateur dramatic society but his first professional appearance was at the Theatre Royal, Bristol, in 1890 in *The Grip of Iron.* He then toured in the same play and gained valuable experience in stock companies in the provinces and in a number of foreign tours during which he visited India, Burma, China, and Japan. Towards the end of the last century he almost decided to go back to farming and indeed for some four years combined farming with acting, spending a season each year playing in Shakespearian revivals at Manchester.

He played at the Shakespearean Theatre, Clapham, in 1898, but his first really successful appearance in London did not occur until 1902, when he played in *The Prophecy* at the Grand Theatre, Fulham. The play did not prove a success when transferred to the Avenue Theatre (now the Playhouse) and Harding returned disappointed to his farm in Monmouthshire. His appearance in 1903 at the Royalty Theatre in *The Snug Little Kingdom* proved a turning point in his career, for so soon as the run ended he was engaged by Tree. While with Tree he not only played in the latter's numerous Shakespearian productions but such pieces as Comyns Carr's adaptation of *Oliver Twist*, in which he was the brutally realistic Bill Sikes.

By then it was patent that he had a flair for "villain roles" and was destined to be a masterly interpreter of the grim and the tragic. The rest of his long career was a series of such personal triumphs as *The Admirable Crichton,* Sir Francis Drake, Ilam Carve in *The Great Adventure,* Svengali in *Trilby,* Scarpia in *La Tosca,* Dr. Grimesby Roylott in *The Speckled Band,* Weston in *White Cargo,* Henchard in *The Mayor of Casterbridge,* Sullen in *The Beaux' Stratagem,* the King in *The Miracle,* and a host of others in which he proved as popular on the other side of the Atlantic. During all this time he continued to take part in revivals of Shakespeare's plays, and since 1936 had given equally notable performances in the cinema.

December 27, 1952.

Lord Hardinge of Penshurst, who had been Private Secretary to King Edward VIII and King George VI, died at his home, Oakfield, Penshurst, Kent, on May 29, 1960. He was 66.

When appointed private secretary by King Edward VIII he had already had 16 years of training first under Lord Stamfordham and then under Lord Wigram as Assistant Private Secretary. Son of Lord Hardinge of Penshurst, the great diplomatist, he had inherited many of his father's gifts. The Private Secretaryship to the King is a most exacting post which demands not only a wide knowledge of men and affairs but a balanced judgment and an unfailing tact. Its occupant must follow every national activity of importance, the life and interests of the British Commonwealth, and the trend of events in the outer world. In Hardinge's case, moreover, the Second World War imposed many additional responsibilities. He had, however, the necessary abilities and in the early years of the reign of George VI rendered services to his royal master which, though inconspicuous, were none the less valuable.

The Rt. Hon. Alexander Henry Louis Hardinge, P.C., G.C.B., G.C.V.O., M.C., second Baron Hardinge of Penshurst, was born on May 17, 1894. He was the second son of the Hon. Charles Hardinge, the distinguished diplomatist who became Viceroy of India and first Lord Hardinge of Penshurst, K.G., by his marriage to the Hon. Winifred Sturt, second daughter of the first Lord Alington. He was educated at Harrow and at Trinity College, Cambridge.

Entering the Indian Army, he subsequently transferred to the Grenadier Guards. In December 1914 his elder brother died of wounds received in action and he became heir to his father's title. He served in the European War from 1915 to 1918, was wounded and awarded the Military Cross. For some time between 1915 to 1916 he was A.D.C. on the personal staff in India. Again after the Armistice he was A.D.C. on that of the British Military Mission to Berlin, and from 1919 to 1920 was adjutant of the Grenadier Guards.

In 1920 King George V appointed Hardinge an Equerry and Assistant Private Secretary to his Majesty, an office which he held with the addition in 1935 of that of Assistant Keeper of His Majesty's Privy Purse until 1936. Created an M.V.O. in 1925, he was advanced to C.V.O. in 1931 and in 1934 created a C.B. In July 1936 King Edward VIII [Duke of Windsor*] appointed him to the important post of Private Secretary, and thus he was inevitably cast to play a part in the events that led up to the Abdication.

In an important article which he wrote for *The Times* in November 1955 (Dame Irene Ward and Lady Davidson subsequently tabled a motion in the Commons proposing that the article should be printed as a White Paper "for the purpose of a correct historical record") Hardinge told his story. Nothing could be further from the truth, he stated, than the account that the King was the victim of a conspiracy on the part of a number of persons to remove him from the throne.

"By the first week in November there was scarcely a leading figure in the political or religious life of the country whose postbag was not flooded with protests from British subjects in every corner of the globe asking why no denial was given to the outspoken press forecasts of the coming marriage of the King and Mrs. Simpson. In order that the King should be under no illusion about public opinion overseas I saw that he was kept aware of those that came to Buckingham Palace".

On November 12 Baldwin told Hardinge

that on the following day a meeting of senior Ministers was to be held to discuss matters. "During a sleepless night", Hardinge decided it was his duty to inform the King what was afoot and to make clear to him the gravity of his position.

The following day Geoffrey Dawson, who had earlier warned Hardinge that the press could not be held in restraint much longer, called and showed the leading article he had written. In the strictest confidence Hardinge showed him the letter he had composed. Dawson found no fault with it.

In it Hardinge told the King that the Press might break silence at any moment; that the resignation of the Government ("an eventuality which can by no means be excluded") would result in his Majesty having to find someone else capable of forming a government: this he believed "hardly within the bounds of possibility". The remaining alternative was a dissolution followed by a general election "in which your Majesty's personal affairs would be the chief issue".

Finally Hardinge suggested that the one step which held out any prospect of a dangerous situation being avoided was for Mrs. Simpson to go abroad "without further delay".

The letter was not seen by Baldwin but was shown to a member of his staff. "There was never any question", wrote Hardinge, "at any time, of my composing it with, or at the instigation of the Prime Minister, Geoffrey Dawson, or anybody else . . . the one thing that everybody was trying to do was to keep the King on the throne".

Although, wrote Hardinge, the King had just chosen him, after many years' service to George V, to be his principal personal adviser, he never once took him into his confidence over his personal dilemma. "He never at any time told me he wished or intended to marry Mrs. Simpson—nor did I, in my letter, express any personal opinion on the merits or demerits of such a proposition".

After the accession of King George VI [q.v.] Hardinge was reappointed. He had been constantly on duty at Buckingham Palace throughout the crisis of the Abdication and consequently the new King granted him an immediate three months' leave. During this time Lord Wigram, who, having been Private Secretary to King George V since 1931 had been made Permanent Lord-in-Waiting, a post which entailed acting in an advisory capacity to the Sovereign, acted for him. Hardinge retired in 1943 and the following year, on the death of his father, became the second Baron Hardinge of Penshurst.

He had been sworn of the Privy Council in 1936, advanced to G.C.V.O. and K.C.B. the following year, and to G.C.B. in 1943.

In 1921 he married Helen Mary, only child of the late Lord Edward Cecil and the late Viscountess Milner. She, a son, and two daughters survive him. The son, the Hon. George Hardinge, who was born in 1921, now succeeds to the barony.

May 30, 1960.

Henry Harrison Hardy, C.B.E., formerly headmaster of Cheltenham and Shrewsbury, and in 1946-48 Director of Studies at the Royal Military Academy Sandhurst, died on December 24, 1958 at his home near Cheltenham. He was 76.

He was born on January 2, 1882, the youngest son of Canon A. C. Hardy. From Rugby, where he was one of the best classical scholars of his time, he went up to New College, Oxford, and there took a first class in Classical Moderations and a second class in *Literae Humaniores.* In 1905 he returned to Rugby as an assistant master and remained on the staff until 1919, but for most of the last five years he was absent on leave on service in the Army. He was one of the busiest and most active of Old Rugbeians and acted as secretary of their association from 1908 to 1913, and was president in 1946. In 1911 he wrote a *History of Rugby School,* a work which throws much light on the public school theories of education and gives a sympathetic appreciation of its methods and aims.

Soon after the war he was appointed headmaster of Cheltenham and after 13 years there he moved to Shrewsbury. He was a headmaster of broad sympathies who constantly encouraged his boys to think for themselves and interest themselves in matters outside the usual scope of the school curriculum. Self-reliance and close personal observation were qualities he instilled into them, and as the war loomed near his experience in the Army proved to be invaluable in preparing the boys for the tasks to which they were shortly to be called. Both at Cheltenham, where the Army tradition had always stood high, and at Shrewsbury he always maintained close and cordial relations with the War Office.

His interest in soldiering went back to the time when he left Oxford and took up his duties at Rugby. He then received a commission in the 2nd Volunteer Battalion of The Warwickshire Regiment and was promoted to captain in 1908. In 1913-14 and again in 1919 after his return from active service he commanded the Rugby contingent of the battalion.

In 1914 Hardy was appointed a captain in the 8th Battalion of the Rifle Brigade and was promoted to major in 1918. He served with the General Staff of the Fifth Army of the B.E.F. in France from 1917 to 1919 and was mentioned in dispatches. He served right through the war and at its close was general staff officer for education in the Southern Command.

In 1946 he was made Director of Studies at the R.M.A. Sandhurst, a new post created as part of the amalgamation of Woolwich and Sandhurst. His retirement after 1948 was full of activity. He was a member of the Admiralty Interview Board, chairman of the Royal College for the Blind, Dean Close School, and Malvern Girls' College, and a member of the Church Assembly's central advisory council for training for the ministry.

Besides his history of Rugby he published two books for his own and other schoolboys, *The Shorter Aeneid* in 1914 and *The Shorter Iliad* in 1927, both textbooks used in public schools.

Soon after going to Shrewsbury he began to take a more prominent part in the work of the Headmasters' Conference and after the retirement of Sir Frank Fletcher [q.v.] he was one of its leading members, being president in 1936-38. In 1939 he was appointed to the Secretary of State for War's committee on the supply of offices, and he was on the Minister of Agriculture's harvest camps committee from 1942.

His first wife was Eleanor Mary Colbeck, who died in 1916. In 1917 he married Edith Jocelyn Dugdale. There were two daughters of his first marriage and three sons of his second.

December 27, 1958.

Major Jocelyn Lee Hardy, D.S.O., M.C., who died in hospital on May 30, 1958, will be remembered as an "escaper" whose inextinguishable spirit was matched by his audacity and determination. He was 63.

He was born on June 10, 1894, and gazetted to his regiment, The Connaught Rangers, in January 1914. It was his misfortune to be captured by the Germans during the retreat from Mons, less than a week after the first shot had been fired by the British Expeditionary Force. He was with the detachment of the 2nd Connaught Rangers at the affair of Le Grand Fayt on August 26, 1914, and was taken that night at Maroilles, a young subaltern barely 20 years of age and a keen Regular soldier to whom a tame existence in a German prison camp was unthinkable.

Sent to the prisoners-of-war camp at Halle, near Leipzig, he was concerned, early in 1915, in an attempt to escape by breaking through a brick wall into an adjacent ammunition factory. After five months' work the project proved impracticable. Later, when he had been 10 days at the Augustabad camp, near Neu-Brandenburg, he broke away in company with a Russian officer from a very careless guard during a bathing parade outside the camp.

The pair started for the Baltic coast, some 50 miles distant, with the intention of stowing away on a Scandinavian ship. It was a difficult journey. They swam a river and a stream and were nearly recaptured once, but eventually reached Stralsund. Here they almost succeeded in persuading the crew of a Swedish schooner to give them a passage, but were arrested at the last moment.

Lieutenant Hardy was sent back to Halle, where he joined in the unsuccessful attempt of a group of Russian prisoners to tear down a wall and get away. His next effort, undertaken alone, involved the picking of locks, breaking through a skylight, and sliding down a rope from the roof into the street. In this manner he made good his escape in darkness and pouring rain. As he spoke German with sufficient fluency he was able to use the railway, making a roundabout journey which eventually brought him to Bremen, and then to Delmenhorst, Holland being his objective. He got no farther, being so overcome with cold and hunger that his recapture here was easy.

He was next confined at Magdeburg, whence he escaped with a Belgian officer by a mixture of elaborate subterfuge, audacity, and good fortune. The fugitives reached Berlin by train and went on to Stralsund, then crossing to the island of Rügen, where they were apprehended before they could discover a fishing boat to take them to Sweden.

Soon afterwards Hardy was sent to Fort Zorndorf, from which escape appeared to be almost impossible. Nevertheless he took part in several attempts. On one occasion, with two others, he nearly succeeded in getting out in the disguise of a German soldier. Once he was concerned in a break-away from the guards while being marched to the Kommandatura, which was outside the camp, and was recaptured after he had taken the train.

About nine months later, soon after his arrival at Schweidnitz, in Silesia, he made his final and completely successful escape in company with Captain Loder-Symonds, of The Wiltshire Regiment. Carrying police "passes" which they had cleverly forged, they climbed a wire fence and negotiated a high wall topped with broken glass. When daylight came they took train and travelled almost the whole breadth of Germany, through Dresden, Leipzig, and Cologne, to Aachen. They went on by tramway towards Richtericht, and within two days of leaving Schweidnitz had crossed safely into Holland.

They reached England by the middle of March 1918 and Captain Hardy—he had been promoted captain in his regiment in January 1917—was soon at the front again. He was attached to the 2nd Leinster Regiment in April whence he was transferred to the 2nd Royal Inniskilling Fusiliers, and saw nearly six months of war. On August 1, 1918, he was wounded in a patrol encounter on the Ypres front, but brought in under heavy fire his severely wounded sergeant. For this exploit he was awarded the Military Cross.

On October 2, during the final victorious advance through Belgium, Hardy gallantly led a counter-attack which drove the Germans out of a farm near Dadizeele after they had recaptured it from our troops. He was severely wounded during the fighting and lost a leg. His D.S.O. was awarded in the *London Gazette* of January 30, 1920.

In 1927 appeared his book *I Escape,* which is as thrilling as any novel of adventure. It is a simple, straightforward story wholly deserving of the eulogistic foreword written by Sir Arthur Conan Doyle.

Among Jocelyn Lee Hardy's other publications were *Everything is Thunder; The Key,* a play with Robert Gore-Browne; *Never in Vain; Recoil; The Stroke of Eight;* and *Pawn in the Game.*

He married in 1919 Kathleen Isabel, daughter of Alec Hutton Potts.

June 2, 1958.

Oliver Hardy, the fat partner in the Laurel and Hardy film comedies, died in Hollywood on August 7, 1957. He was 65.

The partnership between Lancashire born Stan Laurel* and the American Oliver Hardy went back to the days of silent films, and their technique was, even in the last days of their film-making (now some years ago), visibly derived from the silent two-reeler. Yet the coming of the "talkies" did not spell disaster for them, as it did for so many other film actors.

The voices, tentative at first, were soon attuned to the wellworn, but somehow always fresh, action, and the asinine schemes of Laurel, the perennial lad from the farm, delivered with a wealth of irrelevant detail, were welcomed by Hardy with "That's a very good idea!" and a portentous nodding of the head to signify a sagacity that was wholly absent. It was good honest slapstick, unqualified by the pathos that often accompanies the antics of the clown, appealing, as the success of their films showed, to the simple comic sense of millions of people in many countries of the world.

Hardy was born near Atlanta, Georgia, and was destined for a military career; but he left college to join a troupe of minstrels. He gravitated into early motion pictures with the old Lubin films at Jacksonville, Florida, and he went to Hollywood offering himself for the role of scowling villain. There he met his partner, Laurel, when they were cast in the same film. Though film making became their chief occupation they did not lose touch with the stage, and they made several tours in Britain, where Hardy always took the opportunity to play a lot of golf. He was tall as well as fat, and he had a handicap of 10.

August 8, 1957.

H. Wilson Harris, who edited the *Spectator* from 1932 to 1953, and whose sound judgment and wide political experience played a large part in maintaining and enhancing the responsible tradition of that journal, died in a nursing home at Hove on January 11, 1955 at the age of 71. He sat as M.P. for Cambridge University from 1945 to 1950.

Henry Wilson Harris, the son of Henry Vigurs Harris, was born at Plymouth on September 21, 1883, and was educated at Plymouth College and at St. John's College, Cambridge, where he was a foundation scholar and just missed taking first class honours. In 1905 he was elected president of the Cambridge Union. On leaving Cambridge, he ate his dinners at the Middle Temple, but was never called to the Bar. For a time he lived at Toynbee Hall and thought of making teaching his career. In 1908, however, he joined the staff of the *Daily News,* of which paper he became successively news editor, leader writer, and diplomatic correspondent. He never forgot what he owed to A. G. Gardiner, the editor under whom he served.

Being a Quaker by upbringing and a Liberal—the word came to mean more to him as a principle of conduct than as a political label—he found himself thoroughly at home in Bouverie Street, where his work as diplomatic correspondent established his reputation as a writer of principle and integrity. It was already clear in 1917, when he published a book on *President Wilson: His Problems and His Policy,* that he had made up his mind on the road which humanity must take in the attempt to avoid another war. He was actively interested in the League of Nations from its beginning and from the Peace Conference in 1919 onwards he attended many international gatherings on behalf of the *Daily News.* Harris argued the cause of international friendship and disarmament in several books and pamphlets, and soon devoted himself to speaking and writing on behalf of the League of Nations Union. From 1923 until 1932 he served as a member of its staff at Grosvenor Square. The Union's journal, *Headway,* which he edited, and his small book, *What the League of Nations Is* (1925), between them did much to educate the public on the meaning of the League.

Having long laboured in the same fields of international fellowship as Sir Evelyn Wrench* it was natural that Harris should have been chosen to succeed him as editor of the *Spectator* when Wrench decided in 1932 to confine himself to the role of chairman of the company. The selection of his articles which appeared under the title *Ninety-Nine Gower Street* in 1943 shows how well he fulfilled his trust. Topical journalism must be of a very high standard if it is to bear critical examination after a lapse of years, but Harris's reasoned and moderate articles, many of them containing character sketches of the public men of the time, are of the kind that historians of the future will value. The *Spectator* bore the impress of his personality to an unusual degree; his hand could be detected not only in editorial comment but also in book reviews, while he made his pseudonym "Janus" well known as that of a witty and incisive commentator on public affairs.

During the restrictive years of the 1939-45 War, Harris found time to return to authorship. He was responsible for a critical and informative little book, *The Daily Press* (1943), and for a sensible, short survey of the *Problems of the Peace* (1944). A fellow Quaker, Caroline Fox, also engaged his attention; her famous journal had long been out of print, and he contrived to give it fresh currency by basing a biography on the best of its material. In 1945 he finished a life of J. A. Spender, the famous editor of the *Westminster Gazette.* The biography was founded on the mass of letters which Spender had received from the great men of the time, rather than on the files of the *Westminster Gazette,* but it was none the less effective on that account.

In the spring of 1945 Harris accepted the invitation of a representative committee of Cambridge graduates to stand as an Independent candidate for the University at the forthcoming general election, and was elected after a close contest with J. B. Priestley for the second seat. He proved a diligent representative of the University and an acquisition to the debating strength of the House. He spoke whenever he could on foreign affairs, on education, and on matters concerning the press, while his intervention in the debate on the abolition of the death penalty—of which he had long been an earnest advocate in the *Spectator*—was the more effective because of its studied moderation. As an Independent member there is no doubt that he was a great success, while his occasional appearances as a broadcaster made him known to the general public as one whose opinions and point of view deserved respect.

It is no secret, for Harris has confessed it in his characteristic autobiography *Life So Far* (1954), that he regretted that his parliamentary career came to an end with the disappearance of the university seats. He regretted the conclusion of his editorship of the *Spectator* no less, and indeed carried his pseudonym "Janus" into the columns of *Time and Tide*. A man of remarkable and somewhat restless energy, he found an ideal outlet for his abilities as the editor of a weekly review, and being by nature a teacher, and something of a preacher, he was able to give the *Spectator* a moral authority that was admired even by those who disagreed with its opinions.

Wide as his interests ranged in politics, religion, and literature, Harris's outlook on artistic matters was strictly limited. He could be stubborn, and he was not unduly self-critical. Yet he undoubtedly inspired the affection of his friends, and there was in him a broad and consistent philosophy—founded on his classical training, reinforced by a forthright nonconformist conscience, and tinged with considerable dry humour—that made him and his *Spectator* a notable force in twentieth-century journalism.

In 1910 he married Florence, daughter of Dr. A. M. Cash, of Torquay. They had one daughter. In 1953 he received the honorary degree of LL.D. from the University of St. Andrews.

January 13, 1955.

Sir Percy Harris, BT., who died in London on June 28, 1952, was a veteran of the Liberal Party who devoted a great part of his life to the administration of London. He was 76.

The Right Hon. Sir Percy Alfred Harris, first Baronet, of Bethnal Green, in the County of London, was the second son of the late Wolf Harris, sometime warden of the New West End Synagogue. He was educated at Harrow (Small Houses) and at Trinity Hall, Cambridge, where in 1897 he took honours in history and economics. Afterwards he studied law and was called to the Bar by the Middle Temple in 1899. Before beginning his political career he travelled round the world three times and lived for three years in New Zealand. There he studied the labour question and the land laws of the country. One result of that visit was his publication *New Zealand and its Politics.*

His first attempt to enter the House of Commons was in 1906, when he contested the Ashford Division of Kent, reducing the Conservative majority by about 3,000 votes. He was also unsuccessful at Harrow in 1910, but meanwhile he had become a Progressive member of the London County Council in 1907, the year in which the Moderates won a surprising victory. He played an increasingly important part in local government in London, becoming chief Progressive whip in 1912, deputy chairman of the L.C.C. in 1915 and 1916, and continuing to represent South-west Bethnal Green for 28 unbroken years. Although a party man and recognizing the advantages of members working in groups, he disapproved of party manoeuvring in the L.C.C. The matter was brought strongly home to him in 1949 when for a time he held the balance between the two main parties. Labour and Conservative held 64 seats each; Harris was the only Liberal. Still he shunned the party line, devoting his efforts only to the better administration of the capital. His work *London and Its Government* is considered a standard work of its kind.

It was a by-election in the Harborough Division of Leicester in 1916 that gave Harris his Parliamentary opportunity. Standing as a Coalition Liberal and supporter of the Government then led by Asquith, he championed the cause of married men who were called up, urging that more should be done to meet their liabilities and keep their homes together. He was an enthusiastic supporter of the volunteer movement, and was honorary secretary of the Central Association Volunteer Regiments in 1914, which provided training for men over military age or who had undertaken to join the Regular forces. He became honorary assistant director of volunteer services at the War Office in 1916.

In 1918 Harris failed to secure the "coupon" from Lloyd George and lost his seat, but in 1922 he was returned as Liberal member for South-west Bethnal Green, and held the seat until 1945, when he was defeated by the Labour candidate. His secretary in the 1922 election was Winifred Holtby. For 23 years he watched his party shrink in the House of Commons, but he did not falter in his belief in Liberal principles. After 1935 he became Chief Whip for the Liberals, and on him fell the task of seeing that his party's point of view was expressed on all important issues. He was chairman from 1940 to 1945 of the All-Party Panel in the House.

A great social reformer, he took a special interest in housing and education, and held strong views on the question of unemployment. He was an advocate of strict economy in all departments of the state, and did valuable work during the war as a member of the Select Committee on National Expenditure. After the war he continued to work for the Liberal Party outside Parliament. He was an active member of the party committee and chairman of the British Liberal International Council. Earlier in 1952 he decided not to stand again for the L.C.C., which he had rejoined in 1946. He was created a baronet in 1932.

He married in 1901 Frieda, second daughter of John Astley Bloxam. There were two sons of the marriage. The elder, Jack Ashford Harris, born in 1906, succeeds to the title. He is married, has a son, and is living in New Zealand, where he is chairman of the family manufacturing business.

June 30, 1952.

Captain Henry Harrison, O.B.E., M.C., who died in Dublin on February 20, 1954, was one of the old guard of Irish Nationalist members who supported Charles Stewart Parnell in the House of Commons.

Shortly after he first entered the Commons there came the split in the Nationalist Party and, within a few more months, the death of Parnell himself. Harrison withdrew from Parliament in the following year. After that he was to remain interested in but take little active part in Nationalist politics. For the rest of his life his mission was to defend the personal honour and political reputation of Parnell—which he did with remarkable success.

Henry Harrison was born into a County Down family, the son of the late Henry Harrison. He went to Westminster School as a Queen's Scholar, was captain of games, and in 1886 went up to Balliol College, Oxford. He fell under the spell of Parnell as an undergraduate and became honorary secretary of the Oxford University Home Rule Group. In 1889, in the company of his tutor at Balliol, Godfrey Benson, later Lord Charnwood, he crossed to Ireland to visit the scene of the Gweedore evictions. It was on this visit that he first came into conflict with the authorities and his name first came before the public. The incident caused some stir in Parliament and John Morley sharply criticized the alleged brutality of the Irish police towards "this stripling". Harrison himself took a much less sensitive and grave view of the affair. A stripling he might be in years, but in years only. He was a burly 6ft. 2in. and was content to boast of the "damage" he had done to two policemen.

Shortly afterwards, when the Nationalist seat of Mid-Tipperary fell vacant, Parnell offered it to Harrison, who left Oxford and entered the House of Commons. A few months later came the disastrous split. Throughout the dramatic and tragic meeting in Committee Room 15, Parnell found Harrison a devoted personal adherent. After Parnell's death in the following year he supported Redmond, but in 1892 he withdrew from Parliament and never sought to enter it again.

In the 1914-18 War Harrison, in spite of his age, joined the Royal Irish Regiment, obtaining his commission in March 1915. He went out to France with the regiment in January of the following year, and was awarded the M.C. and bar and created an O.B.E., before being invalided out in 1919. His son, who had obtained a commission in an infantry regiment just before his father, lost a leg in Gallipoli in 1915 and later joined the Royal Flying Corps. After the war Harrison temporarily returned to Irish politics, organizing and acting as secretary of the Irish Dominion League. He supported the Anglo-Irish Treaty and the adoption of Dominion status as an acceptable basis of reconciliation between Ireland and the British Commonwealth, though to the end of his life he stated that he was a convinced opponent of partition.

Through the 62 years following Parnell's death, Harrison took it upon himself to encounter "the calumny and falsehood that darkened Parnell's last days", as, in the earliest days, he had defended the honour of Mrs. O'Shea. He regarded it as a crowning victory when, in an appendix to the second part of Volume IV of the *History of The Times,* it was acknowledged that the account of "Parnellism and Crime" given in Volume III was substantially incorrect. The correction which followed was the result of a memorandum prepared and submitted by Harrison after he had been given facilities to study the sources at Printing House Square.

His published works included: *Parnell, Joseph Chamberlain and Mr. Garvin,* published in 1938, and, in the previous year, *Ireland and the British Empire,* a plea for Anglo-Irish collaboration under the menace of impending war.

February 22, 1954.

Dr. Herbert Spencer Harrison, anthropologist and former Curator of the Horniman Museum, died suddenly on July 31, 1958, at the age of 85.

His first employment was in a bank at Birmingham, but preferring an academic career he obtained a science degree in London University, and after a period as a research student in Germany was appointed an Assistant Lecturer in Biology at the University College of South Wales at Cardiff from 1897 to 1904.

Here he met Dr. A. C. Haddon, who suggested his applying for the curatorship of the recently founded Horniman Museum at Forest Hill. Harrison was duly appointed to this post in 1904, and remained there until his retirement in 1937. Like several others, notably T. H. Huxley (some of whose lectures Harrison had himself attended), and Dr. Haddon, he thus approached anthropology by way of biology, with a strong evolutionary outlook.

The best part of his life was devoted to the development of the ethnological section of the Horniman Museum and the arrangement of its collections on comparative and evolutionary lines. In this task he succeeded so well that the museum came to be widely appreciated as a model of its kind and played an important part in the educational schemes of the London County Council. No less admirable was the series of museum handbooks which he prepared on primitive tools and weapons, and the evolution of the domestic arts, &c., of which a second edition was published in 1924.

Much of Harrison's spare time was devoted to the Royal Anthropological Institute, of which he became a Fellow in 1904, and for which he rendered long and valuable service in various capacities: as a frequent member of its council, as acting hon. secretary during the First World War, as hon. editor of its journal from 1916 to 1926, and finally as president, 1935-37.

Some years later Harrison was actually nominated as recipient of the Huxley Memorial medal, but to his colleagues' regret he declined this honour. He had also been president of Section H (Anthropology) of the British Association in 1930 at Bristol.

Harrison was not a prolific writer, but everything he wrote bore the stamp of scientific integrity and balanced judgment; the exposition of his ideas was always lucid, and often enlivened with delightful touches of whimsical humour. He took a special interest in primitive technology, on which he was an unrivalled authority.

His most recent work appeared in Dr. Charles Singer's [q.v.] *History of Technology,* Vol. I, 1954, to which he contributed lengthy articles on "Discovery, Invention, and Diffusion", and "Firemaking, Fuel, and Lighting".

Harrison's other publications included a volume on "Anthropology", in *Science and Modern Life,* 1908, and "Pots and Pans: The History of Ceramics" (in *The Beginning of Things,* Vol. 8, 1928), an extremely readable introduction to a subject which had always attracted him. He contributed many short articles and reviews, notably of French and German books, to *Man* and other journals.

He had a thorough knowledge of both these languages; indeed he used to say that his first familiarity with Shakespeare was acquired through reading the plays in Schlegel and Tieck's German translation. His suggestive analyses of the processes of discovery and invention in terms of such biological concepts as variation and mutation were the fruit of much original thought.

He held strongly that the discipline of accurate observation and measurement of concrete objects ("material culture") was an essential component of any balanced training in anthropology. As he put it: "Without a technological laboratory a school of ethnology is incomplete".

Harrison was of a modest and retiring disposition, disliking the limelight, but without shirking the responsibilities of office. His caution and common sense, and his courteous manner, not untempered by firmness when the occasion required, made him an admirable chairman of committees. For those who had the privilege of his closer acquaintance his kindly and companionable nature, his complete sincerity, and the philosophic qualities of his mind inspired a deep and affectionate regard.

His son, Geoffrey B. Harrison, is a director of research at Ilford, the photographic manufacturers.

August 21, 1958.

Kay (Mrs. Rex) Harrison—See **Kendall.**

Air Marshal Sir Raymund Hart, K.B.E., C.B., M.C., who died on July 16, 1960 after an accident at home with an electric lawnmower, played a leading part in the introduction and operational development of radar before and during the early part of the Second World War.

Born at Merton, Surrey, on February 28, 1899, and educated at Simon Langton School, he joined the Royal Flying Corps in 1917 and flew with No. 15 Squadron on the Western Front. He won the Military Cross for his part in one of the most remarkable air combat victories of the First World War. On April 11, 1918, he was flying an R.E. 8 on artillery observation patrol over Bouzincourt when his aircraft was intercepted by four enemy fighters. Caught in such circumstances, the slow and unwieldy R.E. 8 would normally have had little chance of escape. An early burst of fire from one of the fighters shot away the R.E.'s elevator controls and Hart started to bring it down in a side slip. Unperturbed, the observer (Second Lieutenant L. F. Handford) brought his gun to bear on the fighters, shooting down three of them in quick succession—two were later found to have fallen within 25 yards of each other. The R.E. 8 crashed and both occupants were wounded.

After the war Hart gained his Associateship of the Royal College of Science in physics, and in 1926 rejoined the R.A.F.

In 1936 he began a long association with radar development at Bawdsey, near Felixstowe, where the first experimental radar station was built.

In April 1941 he went to the Air Ministry as Deputy Director of Radar, and in December 1942 to Fighter Command as Command Signals Officer. Later he joined the "Overlord" Staff to plan the air signals for the invasion of Europe, and in 1944 he was appointed Chief Air Signals Officer at S.H.A.E.F. where he was concerned with planning the destruction of the enemy radar system and devising means of misleading remaining stations as to the Allied intentions during the D-Day landings.

As a signals officer of Fighting Area, Hart had been involved as a result of the report by Professor Wimperis [q.v.] on the need to strengthen preparations for air defence—then virtually non-existent. No method of warning approach existed, except the crudest acoustical mirror-type apparatus.

Prior to the development of R.D.F. [radio direction finding]—then anything but proved—he joined in the task of seeing how early warning and interception could be established and what was expected of it. In 1936 Air Marshal Hart was directly concerned with the experiments conducted at Biggin Hill, where the rudiments of an air defence system were developed. He was the first R.A.F. officer to be intimately associated with Sir Robert Watson-Watt* and, in fact, was responsible for injecting the Service requirements—as opposed to the scientific ideals—into the creation of a practicable system. His most important personal contribution was perhaps his realization that the type of information that could be got out of early R.D.F. stations was not sufficiently accurate to be easily interpretable, and he therefore evolved the principle of the "filter room", by which information from a number of R.D.F. stations was compared and turned into a picture which was intelligible to those who had to take decisions and initiate action to intercept the enemy.

Although the highly centralized filter room system was his particular brain-child, he was at the same time conscious of the vulnerability of such a centralized system, and always pressed for decentralization which could only come about as the standard of information from the individual radar stations became intelligible on its own account. He had therefore to build up this centralized system knowing full well that as soon as possible it had to be broken down in order to get the best results. He visualized from an early stage the desirability of conducting interceptions direct from the cathode ray tubes of the radar stations themselves rather than from second-hand information derived from his filter rooms. He was a pioneer in the establishment of the Ground Control Interception stations which played such a vital part in the night war following the Battle of Britain.

He was also deeply involved with Lord Dowding* in the evolution of Service operational requirements for airborne radar devices, which were the only means of closing the gap between the accuracy of control that could be derived from the Ground Control stations and the need for visual contact between the night fighter pilot and his target.

From 1949 to 1951 he was A.O.C. 90 Group and from 1951 to 1955 Director-General of Engineering, Air Ministry. He was A.O.C. 41 Group for a short spell in 1955-56 and then took up the final appointment of his service career, that of Controller of Engineering and Equipment, Air Ministry. Soon after his retirement in January 1959 he succeeded Vice-Admiral J. W. S. Dorling as director of the Radio Industry Council.

He was married and had one son.

July 19, 1960.

A. C. Hartley, C.B.E., president of the Institution of Civil Engineers, died in a London hospital on January 28, 1960. He was 71.

Arthur Clifford Hartley, the son of a Hull surgeon, was born on January 7, 1889. After a general education on the classical side at Hymers College, Hull, he began his engineering studies in 1906 at the Hull Technical College, and was later at the Imperial College of Science and Technology, the City and Guilds (Engineering) College, London. In 1910 he obtained his A.C.G.I. and graduated B.Sc.(Eng.), London University, with Honours.

Hartley then became a pupil of the late T. M. Newell, Chief Engineer of the North Eastern Railway, Hull Docks, and until 1912 was engaged upon designing and superintending of works at the company's docks at Hull, Hartlepool and Middlesbrough. Afterwards he obtained mechanical engineering experience with Rose, Downs and Thompson, of Hull, and management experience with the Limmer and Trinidad Asphalt Company.

During the War of 1914-18 he was commissioned into the Royal Flying Corps and later the Royal Air Force. He graduated as a pilot, was later promoted substantive major, appointed O.B.E., and twice mentioned in dispatches. He was responsible for the development of the Constantinesco synchronizing gear to enable machine guns to be fixed between the blades of tractor aircraft propellers. Over the period 1919-24 he was a partner in the consulting engineering firm of Maxted and Knott, specializing in the design and erection of cement works.

Hartley began his long association with oil engineering when he became assistant manager in the engineering department of the Anglo-Persian Oil Company in 1924. In 1934 he became chief engineer of the company—then the Anglo-Iranian Oil Company—and held that post until his retirement in 1951. Since his retirement he had been in private practice, and also a consultant to Rendel, Palmer and Tritton.

During the 1939-45 War he was lent by the company for the development, in 1940, of a stabilized automatic bomb-sight, and in 1942 contributed largely to the development of "Pluto", the oil pipeline which later ran across the English Channel.

The supply of oil for the armies that were to liberate Europe was one of the great problems that faced the High Command. What was needed was an uninterrupted delivery of millions of gallons at the places and the times needed, in other words, bulk supply across the beaches. Some experts declared this demand could not be satisfied. Hartley had other ideas. He suggested that it might be possible to make a pipeline something akin to a submarine electric power cable, without the cores and insulation, to lay across the Channel. A full-scale order for several hundred yards of this pipeline, which was later known as H.A.I.S. (Hartley, Anglo-Iranian, Siemens), was placed, and within a fortnight the trial length was laid in the Thames. The results were so promising that Geoffrey Lloyd, Minister in charge of the Petroleum Warfare Department, reported the initiation to the Prime Minister and was told to press ahead. As is well known, "Pluto" was a triumphant success, and later 1,000,000 gallons a day were being pumped from the Mersey to the Rhine. Hartley was subsequently recommended by the Royal Commission on Awards to Inventors for an award of £9,000.

In 1942 he was appointed Technical Director to the Petroleum Warfare Department, and was responsible also for the development of the "Fido" airfield fog clearance system, and for flame weapons. He was appointed C.B.E. in 1944, and awarded the United States Medal of Freedom for his work on "Fido".

In 1936 he became a Fellow of the City and Guilds of London Institute, and in 1953 an honorary Fellow of Imperial College. He was elected president of the Institution of Mechanical Engineers in 1951. Among other positions he held was vice-president of the Institute of Petroleum, whose Redwood Medal was awarded to him in 1959.

Hartley was elected an Associate Member of the Institution of Civil Engineers in 1916 and was transferred to the class of members in 1928. He served as a member of council from November 1946 to November 1951 and from November 1952 to November 1955, in which month he was elected vice-president. In November 1959 he took office as president, choosing as the subject of his presidential address the history of civil engineering in its relation to the oil industry.

He married in 1920 Dorothy Elizabeth Wallace, by whom he had one son. She died in 1923. He married secondly in 1927 Florence Nina Hodgson, by whom he had two sons.

January 29, 1960.

Sir Ernest Harvey, BT., formerly Comptroller and then Deputy Governor of the Bank of England, died at his home at Marlborough, Wiltshire, on December 17, 1955. He was 88.

His working life was spent in the service of the Bank of England and his unaffected modesty never asked for recognition. Yet those who met him as a senior official of the Bank noticed at once his competence and his independence of judgment, and his election later as Deputy Governor was warmly welcomed in the City. His ability, experience, and, above all, his complete devotion to the public interest made their mark in this high position, and his name will long be remembered in the City of London.

Ernest Musgrave Harvey was born in 1867, the third son of the Reverend C. M. Harvey, then rector of Acton and later Prebendary of St. Paul's. He was sent to Marlborough, where he gained some distinction as an athlete but gave little promise of later ability. When barely 18 he received a nomination to a clerkship in the Bank of England. In those days the Bank had scarcely begun to realize its continuing responsibility for the welfare of the financial system, and though Walter Bagehot had published *Lombard Street* 12 years before, the phrase "central banking" was not to be coined for nearly 30 years. Harvey applied himself diligently to the Bank routine, came under notice as an exceptionally capable clerk, and at the early age of 35 found himself appointed Deputy Chief Cashier. From the start he had set himself to find an explanation of many operations which were treated purely as matters of routine, and for which many of his older colleagues could give no reason. This frame of mind persisted, and in the years 1902-14 Harvey acquired, as deputy to the chief executive officer of the Bank, an invaluable knowledge of the London Money Market and Government finance. During this period he even lived at the Bank, and one of his children was born there.

The necessities of war finance laid an almost intolerable burden at that time upon the Bank of England and upon its regular staff, depleted by the claims of active service. A full share of work and responsibility fell upon the Deputy Chief Cashier, particularly in the flotation of Government loans. For his services he was made C.B.E. in 1917 and Chevalier of the Legion of Honour and of the Begian Order of Leopold. In 1918 he succeeded Sir John Gordon Nairne as Chief Cashier on the latter's taking up the newly created office of Comptroller. The post-war years presented many financial problems at home of the first importance, such as the consolidation of the National Debt. In addition the Bank, under the leadership of Montagu Norman, was occupied with the financial reconstruction of various foreign countries and the development of relations with reserve banking institutions elsewhere. The art of central banking, now accepted as a natural feature of the economic landscape, was in development, and Harvey's sagacity and resource, based on a profound knowledge of practice, had ample scope. The post of Comptroller fell vacant in 1925 and Sir Ernest—he was promoted to K.B.E. in 1920—was the natural choice. While Comptroller he visited Australia to advise on questions connected with the banking system, and he also went to several European countries in the interest of central banking cooperation.

Among the reforms introduced during Norman's governorship, one of the most important was the change in the composition of the Court of Directors. Men well versed in the needs of British industry at home and abroad came to sit side by side with the City merchants from whose ranks the directorate had been in the past exclusively recruited. The election of Sir Gordon Nairne in 1925 and of Sir Ernest Harvey in 1928 marked the emergence of the full-time "central banker" and the recognition of the expert knowledge possessed by the staff of the institution.

A much greater break with tradition was made in March 1929 by Harvey's election as Deputy Governor, an office previously held for a usual period of two years, but which he was to hold for seven. Thus it fell to his lot to give evidence before the Macmillan committee on finance and industry in 1929 and 1930 on the nature and working of the Bank of England. It may be said that his candour, no less than his grasp of the subject, greatly impressed those members of the committee who had been most critical of the Bank's constitution and policy. The evidence, which occupied seven days of the committee's deliberations, is regarded by students as a principal source for the study of British banking practice. The crisis that preceded the formation of the National Government in 1931 laid a heavy burden on a man with over 45 years of service behind him; and the abandonment of the gold standard in September 1931 opened up an unknown future of fluctuating exchanges from which even a less weary man might well have shrunk.

Harvey was gazetted a baronet (of Threadneedle Street in the City of London) in the New Year Honours of 1933. Among the gifts he received on his retirement in 1936 was a copy of the silver tankard presented in 1696 by the directors of the Bank of England to Sir John Houblon, the first Governor, "in token of his great ability, industry, and strict uprightness at a time of extreme difficulty". To this tribute, first paid in the infancy of the Bank, should be added a mention of Harvey's courtesy, his decision, and his concern for the welfare of his subordinates.

He was a Lieutenant of the City of London, but had little time for outside interests, and after his retirement refused to burden himself with the many directorates that were offered. He was, however, still occupied with public work for some years as independent chairman of R.M. Realisation Company and E.D. Realisation Company, formed to complete the liquidation of the Royal Mail shipping combine. He was also a director of the British India Steam Navigation Company, the P. & O., and the Union-Castle Line. During the 1939-45 War he was a member of the General Claims Tribunal.

Harvey, whose nephew, H. C. M. Mynors, is the present Deputy Governor of the Bank of England, married in 1896 Sophia, daughter of Captain Catesby Paget, who died in 1952. They had, with three daughters, one of whom has died, a son, Richard Musgrave, born in 1898, who succeeds to the baronetcy.

December 19, 1955.

Fryn (Mrs. H. M.) Harwood—See **Jesse.**

H. M. Harwood, a playwright of notable accomplishment, who had maintained the favour of a notoriously fickle public in the commercial theatre during the past 30 years, died on April 20, 1959 at the age of 85.

Possessed of a shrewd and adroit gift for light or lightish comedy, less dependable but often happy enough in his feeling for character, a skilful and practised craftsman, at all times very much a man of the theatre (he was in management, as lessee of the Ambassadors' Theatre, for many years before 1932), H. M. Harwood had to his credit a respectable number of plays of quality which enjoyed popular success.

Of necessity he had his failures also; not an original dramatist, and seldom given to any form of experiment, he fell back from time to time upon a patently "made" story without the stuff of character, and in the result paid the obvious penalty. But few writers for the theatre showed greater fertility over so long a period in devising neat dramatic situations and telling lines.

He had had a varied and interesting career before definitely turning to the theatre. Born in Eccles, Lancashire, on March 29, 1874, the son of George Harwood, member of Parliament for Bolton, and Alice Marsh, Harold Marsh Harwood was educated at Marlborough and at Trinity College, Cambridge, where he took a medical degree in 1900, and at St. Thomas's Hospital. He was house physician there for a time, but then entered business and became managing director and chairman of Richard Harwood and Sons, cotton spinners, of Bolton. In the War of 1914-18 he was a captain in the R.A.M.C. and served in France and Egypt. In 1919 he went into theatrical management.

He had already made a conspicuously successful start as a playwright. After a couple of one-act plays, of which the first, *The Mask,* was written with Fryn Tennyson Jesse [q.v.] (whom he married in 1918 and who died last year), came *Interlopers* (1913), a bright and entertaining piece, and in 1916 his farce *Please Help Emily* enjoyed the good fortune of having Charles Hawtrey and Gladys Cooper* in the principal parts. Next year saw the production of *Billeted,* written in partnership once more with F. Tennyson Jesse, a comedy marked by amusing dialogue and cunningly varied situations—it was scarcely a "war play"—which was happily revived nine years later.

The Grain of Mustard Seed, which is probably Harwood's best known play, followed in 1920. A serio-comedy on the theme of politics, with an idealist contending for light against the dark powers of the cynical-minded, it was very handsomely received by the public, and was revived more than once afterwards.

With this play Harwood was firmly established in the normally uncertain affections of the West End theatre-going public. He strengthened his hold with *A Social Convenience* (1921), a bright, light, witty, if rather artificial comedy on the theme of the bogus correspondent; *The Pelican* (1924), once more the fruit of collaboration with F. Tennyson Jesse; *The Transit of Venus* (1927), a very entertaining piece which for a moment held a glimpse of something more than entertainment; and a number of adaptations from the French.

A rather uneven period followed. On the disappointing side were *The Golden Calf* (1927) and two comedies written in collaboration with R. Gore-Browne, *Cynara* (1930) and *King, Queen, Knave* (1932). To make up for these, however, were *A Girl's Best Friend* (1929), a play of little substance but of infectious gaiety and sparkling feminine animation; *So Far and No Father,* which had some very good lines for Marie Tempest; and *The Old Folks at Home* (1933), again with Marie Tempest, a comedy handled with immense professional skill and finish, in which Harwood was very nearly at his best.

He had little to offer to the theatre during the years of the 1939-45 War, when he returned to his business interests. In 1948 the play which he and Tennyson Jesse had written round the Thompson-Bywaters case, *A Pin to See the Peepshow* (it was adapted from a novel of hers under the same title), was refused a licence for public performance. However, Peter Cotes, whose intention it had been to put the piece on at the Central Library Theatre, Manchester, later achieved his aim at the New Boltons, London, in 1951 where, with Joan Miller in the leading part, the play ran for six weeks. There followed five offers from West End managements, but the Lord Chamberlain remained adamant. The play then went briefly to Broadway.

April 21, 1959.

W. K. Haselden, whose humorous drawings in the *Daily Mirror* and in *Punch* delighted a large public for many years, died on Christmas Day 1953 at the age of 81.

The distinctive mark of his work as a cartoonist was its unfailing amiability. His own gentleness of character, his native benevolence, pervaded the long succession of his ingenious daily "reflexions". He was essentially the "family cartoonist", content to illustrate the small humours, vexations, and incidents of ordinary life. He had little of the taste or temperament of the born satirist; none of the satirist's acidity. He cared nothing for politics and wisely refrained from the derision of controversial ideas.

Apart from his admirable theatrical sketches for *Punch,* his only memorable achievement in personal caricature was his mockery, during the 1914-18 War, of Kaiser Wilhelm and the former Crown Prince Wilhelm [q.v.]. These two he pilloried for ridicule, as knights errant of Hudibrastic stature, under the labels of "Big Willy" and "Little Willy". Even this taunting series, which very cleverly reduced grandeur to paltriness, is said, however, to have diverted the elder of the two victims.

When Walter Sickert told Haselden that he would live "like Aristophanes as the most important historian of England in our age", he paid him a high compliment, but selected the wrong pattern. There was no Aristophanic bitterness about Haselden's observation, which, in the words of another admirer, "sweetened life for young and old" and gave offence to none.

William Kerridge Haselden was born at Seville in December 1872. His father, Adolphe Henry Haselden, was director of the Seville Gasworks, as it was named at that time. In the summer of 1877 William Haselden paid his first visit to England. Here, a year later, his father died, the main part of the mother's interest in the Spanish property had to be sold, and she, with her five young children, had to face a period of severely restricted means; with the result that the future cartoonist's education was confined to a private school in St. John's Wood, supplemented only by occasional private tutors appointed to "strengthen him in the weak points", as he used afterwards to put it. He was inclined modestly to say: "If you put me down as uneducated, you would not be far wrong".

The boy had to seek early employment, and before he began his career as a draughtsman he worked at Lloyd's: to him a humiliating occupation, for he had no talent for business, and declared in consequence that he was "not interested". One day he happened to see a weekly publication called the *Sovereign* which specialized in pen-and-ink drawings of business men. Haselden contributed one of a man prominent in Lloyd's. The model was offended, but the drawing was approved, and Haselden was asked to join the staff of the *Sovereign* which, however, ceased publication a few months later. Undiscouraged by this mishap the determined cartoonist succeeded in getting several of his drawings accepted by the *Tatler* and by the *St. James's Gazette,* but no permanent appointment offered itself until, in December 1903, he boldly approached Alfred Harmsworth. The Mr. Harmsworth of those days replied that he had "nothing to do with the black and white work" in his papers, but referred Haselden to one of his pictorial editors, who offered the young man a salary of £5 a week on the staff of the *Daily Mirror,* which, beginning disastrously as a feminine daily, soon became a success as a "daily illustrated". A large part of that initial success was undoubtedly due to Haselden's contributions, collected in the 29 volumes of *Daily Mirror Reflections* which were published between 1906 and 1935. He retired from the *Daily Mirror* in 1940, having completed over 35 years of rarely interrupted work.

No account of his career would be complete without reference to the theatrical sketches which he contributed for 30 years to *Punch.* He had, as Sir Max Beerbohm [q.v.] told him, an extraordinary talent for portraying "the figures and faces of even the people who, until one sees your drawings of them, seem to have no distinct appearance whatsoever". Seaman as dramatic critic and Haselden as caricaturist were thus regular and inseparable attendants at first nights: the most taciturn, and, in appearance, the most gloomy of humorists. Increasing deafness made this part of his work a burden to Haselden, who, for years before he relinquished it, had been forced to judge actors and actresses merely as "masks and faces", deprived of voices; visible, but inaudible.

In 1907 Haselden married Eleanor Charlott Lane, daughter of W. E. L. Bayliff. She died in 1944, and he is survived by a son and a daughter.

December 29, 1953.

Hashem Bey Atassi, the veteran Syrian nationalist and former President of his country, died on December 6, 1960 at his home at Homs. He was 85.

Born in 1875 and educated at Istanbul University, he became a member of the Syrian General Congress in 1919 and was elected its president the following year.

In 1928 the French abolished martial law, reintroduced certain civil liberties, asked Taj ud-Din el-Hasani to form a government, and on March 10 announced elections for a constituent assembly. The elections in April brought an overwhelming victory to the nationalists, and in June the assembly was opened in Damascus. Hashem Atassi was elected president of the assembly and by August the draft of the constitution was ready. The assembly was finally dissolved in May 1930: but the Syrian constitution, with a transitional clause for the duration of the mandate, was proclaimed on May 14.

There followed six years of turmoil but in 1936 growing tension in the Mediterranean obliged the French to adopt a more liberal attitude. A delegation under Hashem Atassi was invited to Paris where, on September 9, a treaty was signed providing for a perpetual treaty of friendship between Syria and France. The Syrian Parliament ratified the treaty but the French, faced with considerable opposition at home, did not. This failure by France to honour the obligations led, in 1939, to the resignation of Hashem Atassi, who had been elected President after the signing of the treaty, and also of the Government.

After the *coup* of August 1949, in which Marshal Zaim, the President, and the Prime Minister, Barazi, were given a summary trial and executed, Hashem Atassi, who had been living in retirement, was invited to form a provisional government. He became temporary Head of State after the December elections and under the new constitution of September 1950 again President.

His term was not to be a long one; after the clash of opinions that followed the submission of western plans for Middle East defence in the autumn of 1951 he found himself in an impossible position and in December gave place to Colonel Fawzi Silo. A man of stature and of long political experience, even in extreme old age he could not be disregarded as a stabilizing force and after the fall of the Shishakly* régime in 1954 he was again restored to the presidency, being succeeded by Shukry Kuwatly* after the election of August 1955.

December 7, 1960.

Clara Haskil, the Romanian born pianist, died on December 7, 1960 in Brussels, where she was to have given a sonata recital with the violinist Arthur Grumiaux, a favoured partner over a number of years, with whom she recorded the complete set of Beethoven's violin and piano sonatas. She was 65.

Clara Haskil was born in Bucharest on January 7, 1895, but undertook most of her studies first as a child in Vienna, and subsequently at the Paris Conservatoire, where she won first prize at the age of 14. Much of her most valuable musical inspiration nevertheless came from her compatriot, the violinist Georges Enesco [q.v.], with whom she would often go to the Castle of Peles to play for Queen Carmen Sylva of Romania, a great music lover and patron of the arts. For a while the south of France became her home until the German occupation compelled her (as a Jewess), to seek asylum in Switzerland, and soon after the war she was granted Swiss nationality. Incidentally she made the 30-mile journey across the border on foot only a short time after a serious brain operation, showing the same fortitude then that characterized her life-long conquest of a slight physical deformity of a hunchback.

She travelled widely as a younger woman, but it was only in post-war years that her gifts won international recognition. England was one of the first countries to recognize her true stature, notably in a recital organized by the International Arts Guild in December 1946 at Wigmore Hall, and in a series of seven Scarlatti recitals for the Third Programme of the B.B.C. at about the same time. In preparation for the latter programmes she went for a special course of study with a well-known Swiss pedagogue, Anna Hirzel-Langenhan, even though she was then herself a mature artist of over 50.

She subsequently became a regular visitor to the Festival Hall for the Philharmonia Concert Society, and played many concertos with the Philharmonia Orchestra. Her repertoire was not extensive, for she had neither the physique for grandiloquent displays of romanticism nor the sympathy for many of music's more recent developments. But to classical composers, and Mozart and Beethoven in particular, and to some of the more intimate romantics, such as Chopin and Schumann, she brought exceptional keyboard clarity and finesse, as well as a penetrating musical insight mellowed by the wisdom of her advancing years.

December 8, 1960.

Minnie Louise Haskins, the author, died on February 3, 1957.

Her work was not widely known, but was brought suddenly to the attention of the general public in 1939, when King George VI [q.v.] concluded his Christmas Day broadcast with a quotation from one of her books: "I said to the man who stood at the Gate of the Year, 'Give me a light that I may tread safely into the unknown'. And he replied: 'Go out into the darkness, and put your hand into the Hand of God. That shall be to you better than light, and safer than a known way' ". The passage had appeared in *The Times* of September 9, that same year, in "Points from Letters". It had been thought by Mrs. J. C. M. Allen, of Clifton, Bristol, to be appropriate at a time when the nation was at war. The quotation, not then identified, had been found written on a postcard among the effects of a Bristol doctor after his death. His daughters had it printed on greetings card in 1938 and one of these came to Mrs. Allen. The King, struck with the aptness of the passage, had not sought to trace its origin. It was finally identified by the author a few days after the 1939 Christmas broadcast. She had written the lines as an introductory passage to a poem entitled "God Knows" before the First World War.

She was born in 1875, the daughter of Joseph Haskins, and she was educated at Clarendon College, Clifton, and at the London School of Economics. Early in life she did educational work in India. Later she became Tutor and Assistant Lecturer in the Social Science Department of the London School of Economics. She retired in 1939 but was reappointed in the following year. She wrote *The Desert,* a book of verse which was printed privately in the first decade of this century; a novel *Through Beds of Stone* (1928); *A Few People* (1932); and *The Gate of the Year* (1940); and *Smoking Flax* (1942), both books of verse.

February 6, 1957.

Dame Caroline Haslett, D.B.E., who died on January 4, 1957 at Bungay, Suffolk, at the age of 61, was a distinguished engineer and administrator, and a feminist who advanced her cause less by propaganda than by the attainment of high qualifications and responsible positions.

Dropping into an engineering career almost by accident, at a time when a woman engineer was a rarity, she excelled in her profession, and aspired to make posts in lighter engineering available to women generally. She founded the Electrical Association for Women, was secretary of the Women's Engineering Society, and founder and editor of its journal, *The Woman Engineer,* as well as of the *Electrical Age.* She carried out an educational programme for the Central Electricity Board, and after nationalization of the industry became a member of the British Electricity Authority. She was not a brusque or aggressive character and did not appear or behave like the typical woman executive of fiction. She was a person of methodical mind, who yet contrived to avoid being enslaved by system. Her work was her life. She shone as an organizer, and knew the virtues of judicious delegation, so that her time was not cluttered up with detail. Her valuable service and example were publicly recognized in 1931 by the conferment of the C.B.E and by her promotion to D.B.E. in 1947.

Caroline Harriet Haslett was born at Worth, Sussex, on August 17, 1895, the eldest daughter of Robert Haslett, a railway signal fitter and a pioneer of the cooperative movement. After education at Haywards Heath High School she was offered a start in the engineering industry as a secretary with the Cochran Boiler Company. Before long she asked to be transferred to the works, and from 1914 to 1918 worked in London and Annan, qualifying first in general and then in electrical engineering.

In 1919 there was founded the Women's Engineering Society, and Miss Haslett became its secretary, and for many years edited its journal, *The Woman Engineer.* Some of her most valuable work for this society was in breaking down the prejudices of employers against taking on female labour, and above all in persuading the various engineering institutions to allow women to qualify. She herself worked chiefly in the electrical sphere, perceiving that this form of energy was best adapted to household tasks. She edited the *Electrical Handbook for Women* and *Household Electricity,* and showed another kind of solicitude for the well-run house by becoming chairman of the home safety committee of the Safety-First Association and vice-president of the Royal Society for the Prevention of Accidents.

In November 1924 she founded the Electrical Association for Women. Starting in a small way, in a one-room office, it was to grow in a quarter of a century into an organization having over 90 branches and 10,000 members, including housewives, educationists, and domestic science teachers. It founded the Caroline Haslett Trust, providing scholarships and travelling fellowships for these teachers. In 1925, meeting Sir Andrew Duncan [q.v.], chairman of the newly formed Central Electricity Board, she persuaded him that a big educational programme was necessary if best advantage was to be had from the new facilities provided by the grid. The board duly provided the necessary finance to enable the Electrical Association for Women to go ahead.

In 1930 Miss Haslett was the only woman delegate at a power conference in Berlin. During the next 20 years her public activities became legion. She became member of council of the British Institute of Management, of the Industrial Welfare Society, of the National Industrial Alliance, of the Administrative Staff College, and of King's College of Household and Social Science; a governor of the London School of Economics and Political Science, of Queen Elizabeth College, and of Bedford College for Women; a member of the Central Committee on Women's Training and Employment; a member of council and vice-president of the Royal Society of Arts; and president of the British Federation of Business and Professional Women. She was a member of the Women's Consultative Committee and the Advisory Council of the Appointments Department, Ministry of Labour; a member of the Correspondence Committee on Women's Work of the International Labour Office; a vice-president of the British Electrical Development Association, and the first woman to be made a Companion of the Institution of Electrical Engineers.

In September 1947 came an appointment which crowned a many-sided career, the main part of which had been devoted to the electrical industry. Dame Caroline Haslett was named by the Minister of Fuel and Power a part-time member of the British Electricity Authority, formed to conduct the industry under national ownership. Another opportunity of public service in the post-war planning of Britain was her appointment to the Crawley New Town Development Corporation. In the last year or two ill health had obliged her to resign her more onerous posts.

January 5, 1957.

Sir Patrick Hastings, Q.C., who died at his home in London on February 26, 1952 at the age of 71, had for many years, until his retirement from practice early in 1948, enjoyed one of the largest practices at the Common Law Bar, and few advocates in his time were better known by name to the public. He was the Attorney-General in the first Labour Government, formed by Ramsay MacDonald in 1924, and he had the unique distinction, as a busy advocate, of being the author of several plays.

Patrick Hastings, the son of Gardiner Hastings, a solicitor, was born on March 18, 1880, and educated at Charterhouse. Family misfortune clouded his early years, and for a time he worked in a subordinate capacity as a mining engineer. He served in the Yeomanry in the South African war and was severely wounded. Invalided home, he began reading for the Bar, at the same time working as a journalist for a London paper, and as a dramatic critic he made an early acquaintance with the stage.

He was called by the Middle Temple in 1904, and soon after his call he was fortunate to get work in the chamber of Sir Charles Gill, then at the height of a very large criminal practice. After devilling for him he went into the chamber of the future Mr. Justice Avory, and when Avory went to the Bench Hastings took on the chamber. Two years later he married, and he used to say that at the time the joint fortune of himself and his wife amounted to £20.

A contemporary of his, a solicitor who then had a large insurance practice, seems to have launched Hastings on his career with briefs, and in time he acquired what might be described as a "rough and tumble" practice. In a few years he became one of the busiest juniors on the Common Law side, and when, in 1919, he took silk, his success as a leader was equally pronounced and immediate.

In 1922 he was elected Labour member for Wallsend, and when Ramsay MacDonald formed his Government in January 1924, as Labour lawyers were scarce, Hastings was the most obvious choice as Attorney-General.

Through no fault of his own his term as law officer closed with the most unfortunate incident of his professional career, the famous Campbell case, which was indeed the immediate cause of the fall of the Government. Sir Patrick defended his action with considerable skill, but on the Government's defeat MacDonald advised the King to dissolve Parliament, and at the ensuing election, in October, the Conservatives returned with a clear majority. Hastings, with some reason, considered that his treatment by the Prime Minister had been ungenerous and the whole incident, as he afterwards said in his biography, left him with a sense of bitterness that remained for many years.

Again returned at Wallsend, Hastings held the seat until his retirement in 1926, when he found that his health was unequal to the strain of Parliament and a heavy practice as well. With the close of his career as a law officer, Hastings's real ascent to the leadership of the Common Law Bar began. He constantly appeared in the criminal courts as well. Carson (who had a high opinion of Hastings's ability and character) and Duke had gone to the Bench, and Marshall Hall died in 1927, so for several years Hastings and Norman Birkett [Lord Birkett*] divided the best of that class of litigation largely between them.

A few only of Hastings's cases need be recalled. He appeared for Rouse in the sensational "blazing car" murder case in 1931, and the following year he successfully defended at the Central Criminal Court Mrs. Barney, charged with the murder of W. S. Stephen. In summing up that case Mr. Justice Humphreys described Hastings's final speech as "one of the finest speeches" at the Bar he had ever heard. The only murder case in which he ever prosecuted was that of J. P. Vaquier, the Frenchman who was found guilty in 1924 of the murder of the landlord of the Blue Anchor Hotel at Byfleet. Shortly before his retirement he successfully appeared for the defendants in the action for libel brought by Professor Laski.

The task of placing Hastings in relation to the leading advocates of his time is no easy one. He was quick-witted and had a great dramatic sense; moreover, he possessed both courage and audacity. He was at his best with juries in *nisi prius* work rather than in the Court of Appeal, though it is fair to say that as Attorney-General he was placed high by the Revenue authorities for his capacity for putting abstruse technical points succinctly and clearly. He was recognized at the Bar as a dangerous, but always honourable, opponent, and his somewhat aggressive manner was known to cover a warm and generous heart.

At least six plays stand to his credit. *The River,* in 1925, achieved no great success, but *Scotch Mist,* in 1926, ran for 117 nights at the St. Martin's Theatre. In this play Godfrey Tearle [q.v.] and Tallulah Bankhead* played the principal parts. Then came *The Moving Finger* at the Garrick in 1928 and *Escort* in 1942. In 1947 he achieved his greatest success as a dramatic author with *The Blind Goddess,* concerned with a subject he knew well, a *cause célèbre,* which ran for five months at the Apollo Theatre. He also achieved some success as a writer for the films.

During the last four years Sir Patrick Hastings had completely retired from public life. During this time he completed two more books, *Autobiography* and *Cases Famous and Infamous.* His autobiography had a considerable success. It told of his early struggles frankly and of his successes modestly. In 1950 he visited his son, who is farming in Kenya, and while there was taken ill. He returned home but his health did not improve.

Sir Patrick Hastings married in 1906 Mary Ellenore, third daughter of Colonel Grundy, and he leaves one son and three daughters. Another son was killed in the last war.

February 27, 1952.

Ichiro Hatoyama, former Premier of Japan and president of the Liberal Democratic Party, died suddenly at Tokyo on March 7, 1959. He was 76. He had been in retirement from active politics since 1956, though continuing to hold a seat in the Diet and play an important part behind the scenes as a respected and often-consulted adviser to succeeding Governments until his death.

Ichiro Hatoyama was born on January 1, 1883, in Tokyo, the son of distinguished parents. His father had achieved eminence in the academic field before becoming Speaker of the Lower House. His mother was a dominant figure of the Meiji scene. She won fame as a pioneer of women's education, and founded Kyoritsu Women's College in Tokyo. After graduating from the Imperial University in 1907 he opened a law office, but soon turned to politics. Elected to the Tokyo Municipal Assembly in 1912, he became a member of the Lower House of the Imperial Diet three years later.

Thenceforth his political ascent was swift. Cabinet Secretary under Prime Minister Tanaka in 1927, he was Minister of Education in the Inukai and Saito Cabinets in 1931-32. His tenure of office was marked by the dismissal of many teachers and professors considered politically unreliable. Accusations of corruption forced his temporary retirement from the political scene. He had in the meantime become secretary-general of the Seyukai Party in 1927.

When his brother-in-law, Kisaburo Suzuki, expressed his desire to retire from the party presidency on account of ill health in 1939, Hatoyama was regarded as a strong candidate for his succession. But the progressive wing of the party, backed by the all-powerful military, succeeded in keeping him out. It was his first setback.

Throughout the war his attitude was courageous. He opposed the dissolution of the party system by Prince Konoye, and the expulsion of Takao Saito, a member of parliament, for a speech on the reduction of military forces. Such was his popularity with Tokyoites that he was later returned to the Diet in spite of police vexations and without the backing of the Yokusankai, the Imperial Rule Assistance Political Council, which replaced political parties. He retired later to the mountain resort of Karuizawa and took no active part in politics until the end of the war.

In 1945 he founded the Liberal Party, which, in the elections of the following year, emerged at the head of the polls. An unfortunate passage in praise of Hitler and Mussolini contained in a book which he had written before the war on a world tour was resurrected just in time to lead to his "purging" by S.C.A.P., and to prevent him from assuming the leadership of the party, which he then turned over to Yoshida*.

Five years later, in 1952, he was "depurged" and tried to persuade Yoshida to hand over the reins of power. But he had in the meantime suffered a stroke which left him partly paralysed and this was argued as a reason for his inability to serve as Prime Minister. In the elections of August 1952, however, Hatoyama polled the largest number of votes in the country. Failing to make good his claims against Yoshida, he formed a splinter party, but his following was so small that he rejoined the Liberals a few months later.

The growing unpopularity of the Yoshida Government, which had been in power seven years, was at last to give him his chance. At the end of 1954 the Progressive Party merged with a number of Liberal dissidents to form the Democratic Party with Hatoyama as President. When Yoshida resigned in December, Hatoyama became Prime Minister in his stead. The elections of February 1955 consolidated his victory. Swept forward by popular slogans urging the restoration of relations with China and Russia, and "independence" in foreign policy, his party became the first in the Diet with 185 seats. There followed the merger of the conservative forces in November of the same year, when the Liberal and Democratic Parties dissolved to form the Liberal Democratic Party. In April 1956 Hatoyama became its first President, having emerged after the sudden death of his only possible rival, the former Liberal Party President, Ogata, as an unchallengeable figure.

He had already begun, however, to show signs of serious weakness, and to lose his popular following. His tendency to indulge in irresponsible statements, and his failure to control the rival factions of his own party, led to discussion of his retirement from politics. But he was helped by lack of any obvious successor who could control a majority of conservative votes.

The last chapter in his career saw the slow physical breakdown of a man once renowned for his vigour and asperity in debate. He achieved the restoration of relations with Russia by journeying to Moscow in October 1956 to sign a joint declaration giving Japan few of the satisfactions which, under his leadership, she had originally claimed. For Hatoyama it proved a Pyrrhic victory. Two months later he relinquished the Presidency of his party and the Premiership: he had outlived both his strength and his support.

March 9, 1959.

The death of **Nicolaas Christiaan Havenga** at Cape Town on March 13, 1957 robbed South Africa of a much-loved elder statesman who was trusted no less by his political opponents than by moderate men in his own political camp. He was 74.

He belonged to the generation that carried into mature life vivid memories of the Anglo-Boer War. But his loyalty to the old republics left him quite free from any bitterness against his fellow countrymen of British stock. His vision was much wider than that of the backveldt. He saw South Africa as a unit in international affairs and not merely as a remote and self-contained country on the far south of the map. Persistent ill-health had not dimmed his natural geniality. He was a sociable man and a welcome figure in all South African gatherings. If politics divided those present, they were all united in wanting to know his opinion—which was known to be sound and based on long practical experience—of racing form. Everyone from Cape Town to Pretoria knew "Klassie"—and liked him as a man.

Nicolaas Christiaan Havenga was born on May 1, 1882, in the Luckhoff district of the Free State. He was a boy of 17 at Grey College, Bloemfontein, when the South African War broke out. He enlisted and, after serving for a while with De Wet [q.v.], became Military Secretary to General Hertzog, of whom he remained a devoted disciple for the rest of his life. Havenga was seriously wounded, and he used to say in later years that he carried much British lead in his body but no rancour. After the war he followed Hertzog into politics and in 1915 entered the South African Parliament as member for Fauresmith.

When the Nationalists came into power in coalition with Labour in 1924 Havenga was appointed Minister of Finance—a portfolio he held for an aggregate of 21 years, during which he presented 25 Budgets to Parliament. He earned the reputation as a "safe" Minister of Finance by rigidly sticking to orthodoxy. This led South Africa into grave difficulties after Great Britain devalued in September 1931, and Havenga insisted on sticking to the Gold Standard. Farmers, already heavily hit by drought, were all but broken by the low price for wool, and the gold mines were unable to compensate the national economy for its losses on agriculture. A financial crisis followed, which was resolved by devaluation under a coalition Government led by Smuts, Hertzog, and Havenga.

When war broke out in 1939 Havenga with Hertzog pressed for a preliminary policy of neutrality, benevolent however to Britain. But Smuts urged immediate participation in the war and Parliament gave him a majority. Havenga and Hertzog thereupon reunited with the diehard nationalists who under Doctor Malan [q.v.] had held out against coalition. They were unable, however, to agree with the Malanites on a formula for cooperation with English-speaking people, and their reunion ended in 1949. During the war Havenga devoted most of his time to farming.

Later, having taken over the leadership of the Afrikaner Party on the death of Hertzog, he became more active politically, and before the general election in 1948 entered into coalition with the Malanite Nationalists. This combination defeated the United Party under Smuts, and the Nationalists for the first time came into power on Afrikaner strength alone (Hertzog's two Governments were in coalition with Labour). Havenga went automatically to his old portfolio of finance and maintained his former system of almost monotonously recording surpluses by the simple expedient of underestimating revenue. During this period he introduced fiscal policy new to South Africa of loading taxation so that substantial revenue surpluses could be used for capital expenditure. Previously, capital had been sought almost exclusively by loan. The new system has been continued by his successors.

While he remained in the Government Havenga undoubtedly exercised restraining influence on the racial policies of his colleagues. He stood out, for example, against flouting of the entrenchment of coloured franchise in the constitution. When Malan decided to retire towards the end of 1954, it was generally assumed that Havenga would succeed him as Prime Minister, to be followed after due interval by Strydom [q.v.]. The full story of the intrigues of that time are not yet known, but the upshot was that Strydom was chosen as Prime Minister by the Nationalists and Havenga retired from politics and devoted himself to farming and to horse breeding, in which he was passionately interested.

Since his retirement Havenga had kept studiously clear of politics although occasional unguarded *obiter dicta* suggest he was not happy about the present direction of national affairs. Although firmly Nationalist and a devoted follower of so doughty a controversialist as Hertzog, Havenga was always regarded as on the side of moderation. Although he was capable of retaliation if stung in Parliament, the more full-blooded exchanges wherein his colleagues and opponents delighted were not his style. He thus built up a reputation for moderation. But that reputation has to be assessed in light of the fact that it was his coalition with Malan which enabled the Nationalists to get into power and consolidate their position, and thus led to the present more uncompromising Nationalist régime under Strydom.

March 14, 1957.

One of London's most distinguished servants, **Sir Harry Haward,** died on September 8, 1953 at Bournemouth, at the age of 90.

Haward was Comptroller of the London County Council from 1893 until 1920. He thus watched and helped its early development (the L.C.C. was established only in 1889) at the very centre, where its problems were most acute—that is, in questions of finance. His volume of recollections, *The London County Council from Within,* is indispensable to any study of the council's development and structure. It is also a fascinating record of an early and hopeful experiment in democratic local government—albeit of a county which, in the popular mind, does not exist. Not even W. G. Grace, Haward acutely observed, was able to make a county of London.

Harry Edwin Haward was born on January 3, 1863, the son of the late Henry Gilbert Haward, and was educated at University College School. After graduating at London University, he joined the staff of the L.C.C.'s predecessor, the Metropolitan Board of Works, in 1883. Part of the value of Haward's recollections lies in the comparison he makes between the work of the M.B.W. and the L.C.C., just as part of their fascination lies in his memories of a London in which trams were still drawn by horses, the rates were only 5s. in the pound, and Captain Shaw still ruled the Fire Brigade.

The county council came into existence after the passage of the Local Government Act of 1888, and in 1893 (at the age of 30) Haward was appointed Comptroller—the permanent official in charge of finance—of the new body. Finance lay at the heart of its problems, for from 1889 until the almost violent election of 1907 the Progressives enjoyed power. Their schemes for London—the united London of their dreams—called for money, and in the end it was charges of reckless finance which brought them down in 1907—never to return to power again.

Through this early difficult period Haward worked away as the council's servant and financial adviser, and to him must go much of the credit for keeping the council financially on its feet during years of trial and experiment. The major schemes of the L.C.C. throughout his 30 years' association with it—education, housing, tramways and so on—as well as its major failures—the adventure of the Thames steamboats (abandoned by the Municipal Reformers when they were returned in 1907) and the attempt to set up its own Works department (which also was closed by the Municipal Reformers)—called for the establishment and then the maintenance of serious principles of finance.

In this task the presence of so able a financial officer as Haward, through almost 30 crucial formative years, ensured a continuity of advice at a time when it was essential. His advice was all the more valuable because Haward, for all his financial cares, was devoted to London and interested in its improvement. He had entered its service when the hopes for improving the new county were high and (as his recollections reveal again and again) these hopes never altogether died in him. (One of the countless interesting facts in his recollections is the comparison he draws between the average of £400,000 a year which was spent on street improvements by the old Metropolitan Board of Works between 1855 and 1889 and the average of £320,000 a year spent by the L.C.C. between 1889 and 1935). His recollections, published in 1932, did not include these later figures, but he made the point.

In 1920, when he left the L.C.C., Haward was appointed one of the original five Electricity Commissioners under the Electricity (Supply) Act, 1919. It was work for which he was well suited, since as Comptroller of the L.C.C. he had carried out many investigations of the various aspects of the finance of public utility undertakings in London. He retired from this position in 1930, though continuing, at the Commissioners' request, to advise them in a consultative capacity. During the 1914-18 War and after it he served on a number of Government committees dealing with financial and administrative matters. He was knighted in 1917.

He was three times married. His first wife died in 1891. His second wife died in 1925. In 1933 he married Vera Morris, daughter of the late Robert Morris-Parker, of Clough, Rotherham, and widow of Captain W. S. Hopper.

September 10, 1953.

J. M. Hawthorn (Mike Hawthorn), one of the most brilliant racing motorists Britain has ever produced, was killed in an accident later found to have been caused by the speed of his car on the Guildford by-pass on January 22, 1959. He was 29.

John Michael Hawthorn was born at Mexborough, Yorkshire, on April 10, 1929. The son of a motor engineer who himself had racing experience both as a driver and mechanic, he naturally took up motor racing as soon as he was old enough. After several minor races in 1951 with a pre-war Riley, he was extraordinarily successful in 1952 at the wheel of a Cooper-Bristol. On his first appearance with this car at Goodwood on Easter Monday it was evident that Britain had a new champion in the making. He went on to win races at Silverstone and Boreham and achieved some good placings in other races at home and abroad. His obvious talent brought him to the notice of Ferrari who invited him to join their team.

In 1953 he was the only Ferrari driver at the Silverstone meeting in May, and won both the Formula 2 and sports car races. The following week he won the Ulster Trophy. He took part in all the *grandes épreuves* that summer, and achieved a fine performance by winning the French Grand Prix at Rheims.

Driving with Farina*, he won the Belgian 24-hour sports car race, and with Maglioli the Pescara 12-hour race. He wound up a splendid season by driving the Thinwall at Goodwood and defeating the 16-cylinder B.R.M.s, one of which was driven by Fangio. This list of successes brought him the gold star of the B.R.D.C.

The 1954 season began badly for Hawthorn because he had a crash at Syracuse in April. The Ferrari team was over-shadowed by the return of Mercedes to Grand Prix racing that year, but it was Hawthorn who inflicted one of the few defeats on them in winning the Spanish Grand Prix at Barcelona.

Hawthorn began the 1955 season as the leading driver for Vanwall in Grand Prix races and as a member of the Jaguar team in sports car races. He won the Sebring 12-hour race with Walters and the tragic Le Mans race, in which some 80 spectators were killed, with Bueb, both for Jaguar, and was second in the Monza 1,000-kilometre race with Maglioli in a Ferrari.

At Le Mans Hawthorn once again got the better of Fangio (driving a Mercedes-Benz), as he had done at Rheims the year before, and set up a fantastic new lap record at 122 m.p.h.

Hawthorn drove another Maserati (the car used by Sir Alfred Owen* to develop the new B.R.M.) in races in South America at the beginning of 1956, finishing third in the Argentine Grand Prix, and at Goodwood on Easter Monday he drove the B.R.M. for the first time. That year he was again more successful in sports cars, winning the Monza 1,000-kilometre race with Peter Collins [q.v.] in a Ferrari, finishing second at Rheims with Frère in a Jaguar, and third in Sweden in a Ferrari he shared with Hamilton and the late de Portago.

In 1957 Hawthorn returned once more to Ferrari, and he showed that he was capable of reproducing his finest form when he finished second to Collins in the Naples Grand Prix after being delayed for more than two minutes.

Yet 1957 was not his most successful year and he finished fourth to Fangio, Moss and Musso in the final placings. But in 1958 at his determined best he won the French Grand Prix, and took second place in the European race, and in the British, Lisbon, and Italian events.

Finally at Casablanca on October 19 he achieved the highest honour ever attained by a British racing motorist by beating Stirling Moss by one point and winning the world championship for drivers of Formula 1 cars. His record of consistent and sustained brilliance made him a worthy successor to Fangio as the holder of the world title. In October 1958 he was awarded a B.A.R.C. Gold Medal and two months later he confirmed reports that he was to retire from Grand Prix racing.

January 23, 1959.

Ian Hay—See **Beith.**

Helen Haye, the actress, died on September 1, 1957 in a nursing home in London, at the age of 83. She made her first appearance on the stage in 1898 and gave one of her most notable performances more than 50 years later in *Anastasia.*

Her many parts during her long career ranged from the Queen in *Hamlet* to Nellie Denver in *The Silver King,* and from Mrs. Higgins in *Pygmalion* to the Mother Superior in *Marie-Odile.* She played them all with consummate skill but she was undoubtedly at her best when called on to portray the aristocrat of any generation, for her imposing figure and her incisive manner of speech were a great asset. The theatrical profession is under a great debt to her for the way she would willingly undertake to play a part for a single Sunday performance if she felt that by so doing she was helping young players to establish themselves.

Born in Assam on August 28, 1874, she was educated at Bedford High School and in Germany and made her first stage appearance in *School* at the Pier Theatre, Hastings, in 1898, and for the next 12 years she appeared mainly in the provinces. She was a member of two Shakespearian repertory companies, those of Ben Greet and Sir Frank Benson, and the experience she gained stood her in good stead throughout her career. Her first notable success in London came in 1910, when she joined Sir Herbert Tree at His Majesty's to play the Queen in *Hamlet* and Olivia in *Twelfth Night,* crossing the road later in the year to play the Grand Duchess in *Priscilla Runs Away* at the Haymarket. During the ensuing years she played a great variety of parts and Barrie, Bernard Shaw, Frederick Lonsdale [q.v.], Galsworthy and Somerset Maugham* were among the dramatists in whose work she appeared. In 1921 she played in Canada with Marie Löhr* and four years later had a New York season during which she appeared in *The Last of Mrs. Cheyney* and *John Gabriel Borkman.* She played in a number of musical comedies including *The Dubarry* and *Paprika,* and she gave a pleasurable performance as Mrs. Higgins in *Pygmalion* at the Haymarket in 1939. At the end of 1935 she joined the Old Vic Company to play Lady Sneerwell in *The School for Scandal* and Queen Margaret in *Richard III.*

Neither advancing years nor new developments in the field of entertainment presented to her the slightest terrors. She appeared in several British films and towards the end of her career on television as the aged Dowager Empress of Russia in Marcelle Maurette's play *Anastasia.* She repeated her success in this part when *Anastasia* was transferred, soon after the television performance, to the stage of the St. James's Theatre.

As a teacher at the Royal Academy of Dramatic Art she had counted among her pupils Flora Robson, Celia Johnson. Charles Laughton* and Sir John Gielgud.

September 3, 1957.

Arthur Garfield Hays, the prominent New York lawyer whose sympathy and activity in cases involving civil liberties made him well known not only in all parts of his own country but also in other countries, died in New York on December 14, 1954 at the age of 73.

He was born at Rochester, in New York State, on December 12, 1881, and graduated at the Columbia Law School in 1902, taking his LL.B. degree in 1905 and setting up practice in New York City in the same year. He became best known in Britain at the time of the Reichstag fire trial, soon after the Nazis came into power in Germany, when he hurried across from the United States to attend the trial proceedings both in Berlin and at Leipzig, and sought to do all in his power to assist the accused men, though difficulties were frequently raised on the opposite side on account of statements which he was said to have made. Later he took part in proceedings in London which were designed to show the methods and system followed in the German trial.

Hays had been earlier in Britain, for he went to London in 1914 soon after the outbreak of war and took up a number of cases of international law. He remained for over a year at that time and many associations were made by him with others in the legal profession and other walks of life who had ideas and principles like his own.

It was after the 1914-18 War that he took up cases in general in all parts of America which appeared to him to involve some principle of human rights or the citizen's place in the community. Thus in 1922 he was engaged in securing the opening up of towns which had been closed during an extensive coal strike in Pennsylvania. In 1925 he appeared in a case in Detroit which sought to lay down a principle of Negro segregation. In the same year he was engaged in perhaps the most famous case of its kind—the trial of John Thomas Scopes, a school science teacher in Tennessee, who was accused of breaking the state law in teaching the principle of evolution, which did not accord with the fundamentalist view of the Bible as upheld by the law. In this case he had with him his friend and associate, the late Clarence Darrow, and the leading counsel on the other side was the politician William Jennings Bryan.

In the same year, too, was the trial of Sacco and Vanzetti, whose sentence aroused deep feeling in widespread parts of the world among many who knew little of the merits or facts of the case. Other cases in which Hays took part were that of Senator Burton Wheeler, of Montana, later famous as an isolationist leader, also in 1925; the case of the *American Mercury* in 1928, and the case of Countess Cathcart with the immigration authorities in 1929. In most of those cases he acted as counsel or adviser more for the sake of the cause than for hope of reward and in most of them there was no fee. He was also counsel in the United States for the Dionne quintuplets, but that was one of the engagements which paid him, he used to say.

In 1946 he was a member of the commission of inquiry of the Committee for the Fair Trial of the Yugoslav resistance leader, General Mihailovich. He was the author of a number of books, including *Enemy Property in America* (1923), *Let Freedom Reign* (1925), *Trial by Prejudice* (1933), and, in collaboration with others, *Don't Tread on Me* (1926). He also contributed to many magazines and periodicals.

He was twice married, first, in 1908, to Miss Blanche Marks, of New York, and, secondly, in 1924, to Miss Aline Daisy Fleisher, also of New York. He had a daughter by each marriage.

December 15, 1954.

Will H. Hays, Postmaster-General in the Administration of President Harding, and president of the Motion Picture Producers and Distributors of America from 1922 to 1945, died at Sullivan, Indiana, on March 7, 1954. Hays was 74.

In this latter appointment Hays exercised control over the making and exhibition of all American films, being the censor chosen by the members of the industry themselves. At the time he took up these duties there was much scandal connected with many of those employed in Hollywood, and many of the films then being produced were being criticized for the unfavourable reflection they cast upon the American way of life.

A lawyer who held a high place in his profession and in the councils of the Republican party, Hays was widely trusted and respected. An elder in the Presbyterian church and one of its foremost laymen, he was also a mason, and these were additional qualifications of value in the eyes of the public. He had, however, to develop his position and build up his authority for himself. From the first he made it his aim to foster a sense of responsibility among those engaged in the film industry.

During the years he was engaged in this work Hays forbade the filming of more than 200 books and plays, and in 1930 drafted a code of ethics for the industry. When films about gangsters were enjoying wide popularity he issued an order that crime should not be portrayed on the screen in such a way as to excite admiration. This led to the introduction of the "G men" to the films, and they became the successors of the criminal hero. Yet he himself admitted freely that the rate of progress was slow and depended largely on public standards.

In another sphere of his work, by publishing the actual facts in regard to employment in the film industry, he kept many from flocking to Hollywood in a vain search for work. From 1945 until 1950 Hays served as adviser to the Motion Picture Producers and Distributors of America, having been succeeded in the presidency by Eric Johnston*.

In the political career he gave up when he took over his duties relating to the film industry, Hays served on the national committee of the Republican Party, of which he was chairman from 1918 till 1921.

March 9, 1954.

Hazza al Majali, who was assassinated by a bomb that exploded in his office in Amman on August 29, 1960 was twice Prime Minister of Jordan. He held the office for five days in December 1955, when he tried unsuccessfully to steer his country into membership of the Baghdad Pact, and again from May 1959 to his death.

Although trained as a lawyer, politics was his career, and he followed it with courage, good humour, and courtesy. If he was underrated at the start of his second term of office as Prime Minister, when many forecast the imminent collapse of Jordan, he proved that in power he could be as strong as his predecessor, Samir Rifai. With King Husain, to whom he was always a most trusted Minister, he worked to relieve the political tension that grew near to breaking point after King Faisal [q.v.] had been assassinated in July 1958. He maintained the authority that Rifai had built on the stability provided by the presence of British troops at Amman airport, but at the same time he was able to release a number of political detainees and slightly loosen the strait-jacket that had been put on all political activity.

Maintaining an atmosphere of calm in Jordan in the last two years has not been easy. The King and his Government have been subjected to much personal abuse and threats by Cairo Radio, and a number of plots have been uncovered, one a *coup d'état* while the King was touring foreign countries, and another, in March 1960, which had as its aim the assassination of the Prime Minister. This Hazza Majali referred to as "an amusing play", and in a broadcast after the plot had been uncovered said: "The murder of a person or his disappearance from the political stage will never weaken this country's determination to protect and safeguard its existence nor discourage it from carrying out the mission of the great Arab revolution and from standing up to its enemies. Such things would rather foster its resolve and strength. We have many loyal persons who can easily carry out this country's mission and steer the ship to the best advantage, thus frustrating the ambitions of the enemies of Arabism and the covetous ones".

It is a brave epitaph for a courageous man, and all who respect Jordan will hope that it is true, even though Hazza's death must inevitably threaten the stability he worked hard and successfully to achieve.

Hazza al Majali was born 44 years ago in Kerak, "a small rude town" in Jordan, as Charles Doughty described it. Doughty also met some of Hazza's ancestors, members of a well-known semi-nomadic tribe, the chief of whom he described as a "peasant duke". Hazza inherited much of the desert Arab's easy manners and charm, and his courteous and friendly attitude often belied his political astuteness. He obtained his legal training at Damascus, graduating from the University of Syria.

After practising for some years in Jordan he gave up the law in 1947 to become Chief of Protocol for the Royal Palace. This was the start of his intimacy with the Jordanian court and ruling circles that lasted until his death, though his stay in the palace at this time did not last long. In the following year he became Mayor of Amman, and it was soon after this that he became obviously in the running for political office. His career, which until now had been unsettled and rather aimless—he was evidently prepared to accept almost any offer that came along—was finally settled.

After a short period of office as Minister of Agriculture he was appointed to his first Cabinet post, that of Minister of Justice. As tends to be customary in Arabian countries he did not hold the office for very long, soon transferring to the Ministry of Economics. During this first part of his political career Hazza threw himself wholeheartedly, and courageously, behind the movement to bring Jordan into the Baghdad Pact. After the signing of the pact between Iraq, Turkey, Pakistan, Iran, and the United Kingdom in 1955 the question of Jordan joining in was more actively considered by the political leaders in the country—King Husain was himself in favour, and on December 13 Said Mufti's Government announced that Jordan would join the pact.

In the outburst of hostility that followed, much of it provoked by Egypt, the Government fell. In spite of the obvious unpopularity of the idea, and the riots which it had caused, Hazza Majali agreed, at the King's request, to form a Government committed to trying to bring Jordan into the pact. He formed his Government on December 15. On December 20 Parliament was dissolved after a series of strikes and riots had forced the new Prime Minister to resign.

For nearly two years, a long time for Arabia where political memories are short, Hazza Majali was out of office. He became chairman of the Jordanian Development Board for a time, but finally returned to active politics in 1958, when he returned once more to the palace as Minister of the Royal Court in Samir Rifai's Government. In May 1959 he was asked by King Husain to succeed Rifai, who was retiring because of ill-health. Though sneered at in Cairo as "an agent of the British", Hazza Majali this time made clear from the start that his Government's policy was to refrain from aligning itself with "any foreign political or military pact", and that Jordan would remain free of any such ties except for its commitments under the Arab League collective security pact.

The murder of Hazza Majali removes from Jordan an able politician who was proving himself an astute leader, well able to protect his country from the machinations of other Arabian countries. Perhaps, had he lived, he might have been able to turn their still frustrated anger into an acceptance of Jordan as it is. His enemies were not prepared to let him try, or even to continue with his task of strengthening the country through peace and economic growth. Their grim act is a tragic compliment to his unfinished work.

August 30, 1960.

Rose Lady Headfort (Rosie Boote), widow of the fourth Marquess of Headfort, died at home in London at the age of 80, on August 17, 1958. At the turn of the century she was the toast of the town when, as Miss Rosie Boote, she had a brief but eminently successful stage career at the old Gaiety Theatre.

She was born at Tipperary, the daughter of a gentleman of independent means, and she worked her way up to stardom from the ranks of the chorus which she joined at the Gaiety during the run of *The Shop Girl* in 1895. Her delightful appearance, her charm both as a singer and a dancer, and her readiness to take on any amount of hard work brought her quickly to the notice of George Edwardes, of whose company she was a member for the whole of her theatrical career. When *The Runaway Girl* was presented at the Gaiety in 1898 Rosie Boote became one of the principals in the part of Marietta, the flower girl. Then in 1900 came her great chance when she played the part of Isabel Blyth in *The Messenger Boy,* in which she was entrusted with the main song of the show, "Maisie", for which Lionel Monckton had composed the music.

She retired from the stage when she married the fourth Marquess of Headfort in 1901, and she never sought to return to it, although she continued to take a lively interest in affairs of the theatre. There were two sons and a daughter of the marriage. The elder son is the present Lord Headfort.

August 18, 1958.

Sir Ambrose Heal, the furniture maker and designer, died on November 15, 1959 at Beaconsfield at the age of 87.

He was, perhaps, one of the great artists and craftsmen of his time. His introduction of strong but simple and beautiful lines to the modern world of furniture did probably as much of importance and significance as did the great masters of the eighteenth century. He was not unlike them, also, in his love of working with the rarer and more exquisite woods. Yet in spite of this important contribution which he made towards the new orientation in the world of cabinet-making, he had a respect which almost amounted to veneration for the beautiful productions of Britain, France, and Spain before ugliness overtook us, and he was as happy to deal in such work as he was to see people admiring and buying his own pieces, which were the products of his fine perception and understanding.

Ambrose Heal was born on September 3, 1872, the son of the late Ambrose Heal and great-grandson of the founder of the famous business which has been at 196, Tottenham Court Road since 1840 and was established in Rathbone Place in 1810. While at Marlborough he was injured in a house match and was sent to recuperate to a tutor who kept an establishment at the seaside. There he was soon joined by his cousin Cecil Brewer, who had been similarly invalided from Clifton. The two became close friends, and Heal to the end of his life acknowledged his debt to Brewer's genius for design, which but for his early death during the 1914-18 War would have carried him to the top of his chosen profession of architecture.

After leaving school Heal spent some six months in France and was then apprenticed by his father to a cabinet-maker at Warwick. There he spent three years, first at the bench and later in the drawing office, and then in 1893 returned to London to join his father in the family business. Through Brewer he met Lethaby, Selwyn Image, Voysey, and others of the Art Workers' Guild, and he just overlapped William Morris, who died in 1896, the year in which Heal first exhibited at the Arts and Crafts.

Morris and his followers had indeed lit a candle, but its beam as yet shone fitfully if at all in the naughty world of Tottenham Court Road. When Heal attempted to introduce his simply-designed pieces among the florid scrolls of "Queen Anne cabinets" and "Old English tables" with elaborately bobbin-turned legs and stretchers, he was asked by the salesmen how he could expect them to sell "prison furnishings". The craftsmen in the workshops, too, rebelled. As luck would have it, just about that time Ashbee decided to move his Guild of Handicrafts from the fine old house in the Mile End Road, where he had founded it, to Chipping Campden. His foreman, Adams, a fine craftsmen, and a few of the cabinet-makers, were unwilling to uproot themselves from London and joined Heal's staff. Even so, Heal admitted in later life, with characteristic under-statement, that his venture in simplicity in design was not "an instantaneous success". Yet he persisted because he was primarily interested in expressing himself as a worker in wood and only secondarily in reforming the ornate and meretricious designs about which nobody then seemed to mind.

It was indeed an uphill struggle. In 1900 he scored a notable *succès d'estime* by winning a silver medal at the Paris Exhibition for a bedroom suite, part of which was shown at the Victorian and Edwardian Exhibition of Decorative Arts held at the Victoria and Albert Museum in 1952. Increasing certainty of touch in design produced the early products of his gifts, which became recognized by an ever larger number of people of taste as "Heal pieces". His early training at the bench gave him a sound feeling for the relationship between craftsmanship and design and keen appreciation for the possibilities as well as the limitations of woods and other raw materials. The beauty of wood was a passion, and like a true craftsman, in the tradition of Chippendale who constantly used the phrase "very fine wood" in his bills, Heal was capable of designing a piece of furniture, useful and practical to be sure, but the main artistic merit of which was its display of particularly finely marked timber.

After the death of his father in 1913 he was elected chairman of the business and remained in control for practically 40 years, retiring in favour of his elder son, Anthony S. Heal, in January 1953. He remained a director, however, for the remainder of his life. He had helped in 1915 to found the Design and Industries Association and in 1939 he was appointed a Royal Designer for Industry. He had long been a member of the Art Workers' Guild and a Fellow of the Society of Antiquaries and he was knighted in 1933.

His period in control of the family business saw an immense widening in scope as well as reputation. The original firm was concerned only with the making of feather-beds and mattresses; a cabinet-making department was added in 1840, but for long afterwards beds remained the mainstay of the business and the catchwords "Heal's beds" were current until well into this century. Sir Ambrose Heal eventually added departments for the sale of almost all household requirements, and displayed a notable gift in selecting the right men to conduct these new enterprises. Earliest and most important was the department of antique furniture. Pottery was added later and made a notable contribution to the fame of the business, as also did the textile and carpet departments. More modest were the departments for kitchen and bathroom requirements, but even in these, as in the larger and more important departments, Sir Ambrose Heal's fine and catholic taste was observable. When the premises were rebuilt and enlarged some 30 years ago, a great gallery was made in the top floor of the building which was the scene of many notable exhibitions of pictures and furniture, which did much to add to the reputation as well as the turnover of the business.

Though Heal's main interest was in the business he had done so much to build up, it was not his sole interest. First and foremost came his study of his predecessors, the cabinet-makers and upholsterers of London from 1660 onwards. Their trade cards fascinated him and in 1925 he had already collected sufficient to publish a substantial volume. As time passed the collection, to which were added old street directories, grew enormously and in 1953 Heal was able to publish what surely must be the definitive work on the subject, beautifully indexed and illustrated.

His passion for craftsmanship also found expression in his great work on the London goldsmiths in which he was able to add no fewer than 3,600 names to the 2,800 already known. Calligraphy, again a craft, also greatly interested him and his book, *The English Writing-Masters and Their Copy-books, 1570-1800,* to which Stanley Morison* contributed a preface on the development of handwriting, is a notable contribution to the knowledge of a little studied subject. Last but not least may be mentioned his volume on the signboards of old London shops, which appeared in 1948. In 1954 he was awarded the Albert Medal of the R.S.A. for services to industrial design.

He was twice married, first in 1895 to Rose, daughter of Alexander Rippingille. She died in 1901 and in 1904 he married Edith Florence Digby, daughter of Dr. John Todhunter. She died in 1946 and he is survived by two sons and a daughter.

November 17, 1959.

William Randolph Hearst, who will be remembered for his exploits in mammoth newspaper proprietorship and for his achievements in carrying sensational journalism to new lengths, died at Beverly Hills, California, on August 14, 1951 at the age of 88.

Up to a point he was an able man; but for all his skill in the direction of newspaper properties he lacked the consistency of principle and purpose essential to true leadership and, while he knew how to interest a great section of the American public, he failed as a rule to convince it in serious affairs. Thus in spite of exploiting his own unequalled means of self-advertisement to the full, he never succeeded in gratifying even his more moderate ambitions of public office. It was, moreover, this refusal on the part of his fellow-countrymen to take him at his own valuation which moderated the extent of the damage his almost consistent anti-British policy was calculated to cause.

William Randolph Hearst was born on April 29, 1863, the son of Senator George Hearst. In 1882 he went to Harvard, but he did not remain there long, for his university career was abbreviated by a mildly mischievous escapade. While there, however, he is said to have studied the methods of Pulitzer and to have developed some of the ideas in regard to newspapers and the presentation of news which he was afterwards to put into practice. He is also said to have subscribed to *The Times,* and, though the results were never obvious, to have studied it as well. On his return to San Francisco from Harvard Hearst refused to join his father in his mining business. Instead he asked him for a present of the San Francisco *Examiner,* a newspaper which was part of the elder man's political apparatus and had served as a mouthpiece of the San Francisco magnates. His request granted, he proceeded to bring the paper into line with the more sensational press of New York. The *Examiner,* therefore, blazed forth into livid presentations of crimes and scandals and made personalities its speciality. Polite San Francisco was shocked, and the elder Hearst was by no means pleased; but he did not withhold supplies, and, since the general public were amused by the new departure, the *Examiner* began to make profits of which until then it had not dreamed.

Hearst had reached the age of 33 when he decided to repeat his San Francisco successes in New York. He began, therefore, by buying a somewhat second-rate sheet called the *Journal* and turning it into a rival to Pulitzer's *World.* The *Journal* had at first no settled aim, and no principle except to enlarge its circulation at any cost. The result of its methods was, however, that the *World,* although it still preserved its influence, began to appear almost mild and dull. Having thus introduced "yellow journalism" of a deeper shade than any America had seen, Hearst proceeded to spread it over the United States. He multiplied the *Journal* into a couple of score of others in many cities and under many names until eventually he became the largest newspaper proprietor in his country. There was something to be said for his methods, even though they violated all the canons of good feeling and good taste, for his search for iniquities of every kind had to some extent a deterrent effect upon corporate and individual malpractices. Thus he served upon occasion as a public watchdog.

Hearst had very real, even though they were in some cases unattractive, abilities. He was, for instance, a shrewd and excellent judge of men. He was also a generous employer, but keen, enterprising, and resourceful though he was, he was completely lacking in stability and even in fidelity to the ideals he professed. In politics he was nominally a Democrat; but in fact he was a Radical, and his aim during the years in which he nurtured political ambitions—they reached even to the White House—was to gather a personal following in order to enable him to hold a balance of power. In 1905 he ran unsuccessfully for the mayoralty of New York as an Independent, and scored heavily over Tammany. In 1906 he was in alliance with Tammany, and was the official Democratic candidate for the Governorship of the state. Then in 1907 he withdrew from his Tammany alliance, and "fused" with the Republicans. In 1922 he failed once more to be nominated for the Governorship by the Democrats. In politics, indeed, as in journalism, his methods were inconsequent and brazen, but at no time did they carry him further than the position of a representative in Congress.

Whatever his own private sentiments in the matter, it suited Hearst as a fisher in all the troubled waters of the United States to pursue for many years an anti-British policy. It enabled him to appeal with confidence to Irish America and to every element which nurtured historical or other prejudices against this country. But even in this he was inconsistent, and there were times when he suggested that he was prepared to work for Anglo-American friendship, upon, however, his own terms.

In 1937 Hearst, who was approaching 75, began to draw in his horns, and plans emerged for placing his newspapers and allied interests on a permanent footing, independent of him except in editorial policy; and also for disposing slowly of unprofitable buildings and estates and of most of his huge and heterogeneous art collection. He had, in fact, a strange variety of interests, which included land in New York, fruit ranches, vast estates and a palace in California, and also a gold mine in Idaho. To all this in 1925 he had added St. Donat's Castle in Wales, which he had enlarged at vast expense and at the price of despoiling old buildings elsewhere in Great Britain. He therefore appointed a committee and a trustee in order to effect the disembarrassment, and as one result an avalanche of old masters and bric-à-brac descended upon the antique markets of London and New York.

Both before and after the outbreak of hostilities in 1939 Hearst had remained an isolationist. In July 1940, however, he declared that the entry of the United States into the war was "a calamity", and that the eventual winner would be neither Great Britain nor Germany but Russia. Then in March 1941 he wrote a leading article in which he accepted the declaration of President Roosevelt—he was by no means always in agreement with him—of all-out aid for the democracies.

He married in 1903 Miss Millicent Willson, by whom he had five sons.

August 15, 1951.

F. A. Mitchell-Hedges—See **Mitchell-.**

Dr. Sven Hedin, who died on November 26, 1952, at the age of 87, was one of the world's most distinguished and most adventurous explorers of Central Asia, whose eminence in his own country had long been recognized by a place among the 18 members of the Swedish Academy.

His knowledge of Central Asia, of Sinkiang, Mongolia, and above all Tibet, was profound—not less profound, it should be said, because he was apt to dismiss the geographical fruits of all discoveries other than his own—and was widely, indeed universally, recognized. Only the oldest generation to-day will realize in full measure the historic character of Sven Hedin's crossing of the Taklama desert, or of his discovery of the sources of the Indus and the Brahmaputra, or of his successful journey, begun from Kashmir, to Lhasa. Geographical societies the world over honoured him for his achievements, and many universities, including those of Oxford and Cambridge, conferred honorary degrees upon him.

In 1902 his own country granted him a title of nobility, and in 1909 the Government of India invested him with the K.C.I.E. He was a man of arresting physical and temperamental qualities, endowed with a vitality that the years seemed to leave unimpaired. On the eve of his seventieth birthday he undertook an extensive survey of Sinkiang on behalf of the Chinese Government, and at the age of 82, after having recovered the sight of one eye as the result of an operation (he had lost the sight of an eye in the early 1890s and for several years had been practically blind), he planned a journey to Argentina.

He had experienced so many dangerous adventures, and had had so many hairbreadth escapes from seemingly certain death, that his good luck had become proverbial. During and after the war of 1939-45 his vehement protestations of sympathy with the Nazi cause, which sprang from a lifelong admiration for the nationalist and militarist impulse of German *Kultur* (and from a no less firmly rooted Russophobia), earned him bitter reproaches among his own people.

Born in Stockholm on February 19, 1865, Sven Anders Hedin, the son of an architect, was educated at the Stockholm High School and Upsala University, and later at Berlin University, where he went into resolute and methodical training for a career of exploration under Baron von Richtofen. At the age of 20 he went out to Baku as one of Nobel's employees, and in the same year he made his first journey through Persia, Mesopotamia, and the Caucasus. In 1890 he was attached to King Oscar's embassy to the Shah of Persia, and three years later he set out on his first great expedition, which lasted for three and a half years and which he described in a classic volume, *Through Asia* (1898), that marks the beginning of his fame as an explorer. His march through the Taklama desert in the summer of 1895 created a tremendous stir in Sweden when the full details became known. Still more important, it was on this occasion that he first entered Tibet, exploring an extensive part of the northern regions.

His second expedition into Tibet, by way of Sinkiang, followed in 1900, and on this occasion, after heroic and stirring efforts, he only just failed to penetrate Lhasa in disguise. He triumphed at the next attempt, in the expedition of 1906-08, when he started out from Kashmir, reached his goal in part at least owing to the excellent understanding established by Sir Francis Younghusband at Lhasa four years earlier. He crowded into the whole expedition an astonishing variety of perils, adventures, and hardships, which evoked constant anxiety as to his precise whereabouts and destiny. Throughout these first eight years of the century Hedin made discoveries of the highest geographical and geological importance. A prodigious map-maker, he uncovered in careful and illuminating detail the physical landscape of vast areas of Central Asia. His books on the subject—notably the three volumes of *Trans-Himalaya: Discoveries and Adventures in Tibet* and the nine volumes of *Southern Tibet*—are massive, learned, fascinating, though they underrate the merits of brevity and are at times needlessly assertive in temper.

In the war of 1914-18 Hedin, doubtless stimulated by the passion of his anti-Russian bias, swallowed the German case whole, visited both the Western and Eastern fronts, described what he saw, declaimed what he felt at prodigious length, and proved to be Germany's arch-propagandist among the neutrals. It is not, however, for his political views, which sprang into renewed and virulent life with Hitler's accession to power in Germany—Hedin confessed, incidentally, that he was "one-sixteenth non-Aryan"—that he will be remembered.

Asia was the light that continuously beckoned to him. He organized the very fully equipped scientific expedition to Northern China launched by the Swedish Government in 1927—a much more costly and elaborate affair than any he had himself projected—and over a period of six years directed the work of an international team of specialists who between them have revolutionized our knowledge of Eastern Turkestan, Mongolia, and North China. This task was picturesquely crowned by his survey, undertaken at the request of the Nanking Government, of the ancient caravan silk road to the Mediterranean. His virtual blindness restricted Hedin's activities in subsequent years, but his energies of mind were apparently undiminished, and almost to the end of his life he spent much time and effort in issuing immensely detailed accounts of the scientific results of his many journeys in Central Asia. Indeed, the results of the expedition backed by the Swedish Government run to no fewer than 35 volumes and occupied Dr. Hedin for some 12 years up to 1949.

November 27, 1952.

Hans Hedtoft, who was found dead in bed from heart failure in a Stockholm hotel on January 29, 1955, aged 51, had been Prime Minister of Denmark twice since the end of the last war.

The son of a tailor, he was born at Aarhus, the capital of Jutland. He was largely self-educated, but having a passion for history, especially the history of the Socialist movement in Europe, he quickly made a career for himself in the Danish Social Democratic Party. He was elected chairman of the party at the early age of 36 in 1939, but he was forced to resign in 1941 on account of his outspoken opposition to the German invaders. He was already a figure in the resistance movement, but his open clash with the Nazis gave him an even greater reputation among all Danes who refused to compromise with the destroyers of their liberty. Among his other activities on behalf of the resistance was his conduct of an underground newspaper.

Two years after the end of the war he became, at 43, one of the youngest Prime Ministers in the history of Denmark. Ousted by the Conservative-Agrarian coalition in 1950, he was returned three years later as head of a minority Government. A sincere democrat—"better a democracy without socialism than socialism without democracy", he once said—he was the principal exponent of the Nordic Council, formed nearly three years ago by Denmark, Norway, Sweden, and Iceland. His feeling for international organization had an even wider scope, for it was by his unremitting efforts that Denmark became a member of the North Atlantic

Treaty Organization. Broad-shouldered and with twinkling eyes, he had a singularly attractive personality, a fine asset in a public man. His sincerity was patent to all, and though he had had heart trouble for years he maintained his fantastic vitality to the end.

His last days, however, were clouded by the death of his wife. They had known one another since he was 14 and she 12, and her loss only some six weeks before his own cast a shadow over his naturally sunny nature which he had not been able to shake off.

January 31, 1955.

Professor Sir Ian Heilbron, D.S.O., F.R.S., distinguished for his contributions to science in both academic and industrial spheres and for notable service to his country especially during two world wars, died at the age of 72 on September 14, 1959.

Born in Glasgow on November 6, 1886, he was educated at its high school and then at the Royal Technical College; the award of a Carnegie Fellowship enabled him to spend two years with Hantzsch at Leipzig. Appointed a lecturer at the Royal Technical College in 1909, he had already published some interesting research by 1914; but having already been commissioned in the A.S.C. in 1910 he went overseas in 1915, eventually becoming Assistant Director of Supplies in Salonika with the rank of lieutenant-colonel. He was mentioned three times in dispatches and awarded the D.S.O.

After a brief spell with the British Dyestuffs Corporation at Manchester and back at Glasgow as Professor in the college, he held the chairs of organic chemistry at Liverpool (1920-33), Manchester (1933-38), and at the Imperial College of Science and Technology, London (1938-49), leaving in every case laboratories which were well organized and equipped and lively in both teaching and research.

Retiring somewhat early from the academic life he became the first director (1949-1957) of the Brewing Industry Research Foundation and built up its fine laboratories at Nutfield. His scientific activities embraced many fields but he made his most valuable contributions to the chemistry of natural products and he was a pioneer in Britain of the application of chromatography to their purification, and of ultra-violet light absorption to the determination of their structures. At a time when natural product studies were almost the monopoly of scientists in Germany and Switzerland, Heilbron successfully initiated researches in this country on polyenes and steroids, and the interest in these fields manifest in many departments of chemistry in Britain to-day can be traced back to his inspiration.

His most notable contributions were to the chemistry of the vitamins of the A and D groups, to the determination of the structure of squalene (from shark liver oil), which has now assumed great biochemical significance, and to the chemistry of penicillin, especially the recognition of its existence in a multiplicity of forms.

His scientific contributions, though considerable, are not to be measured solely in terms of his published works. He had a flair for inspiring others with his own great enthusiasm; he was quick to recognize outstanding ability among those who worked with him, and spared no effort to further the interests of his many collaborators whose contributions were always generously recognized. Quite a number of the chairs of organic chemistry in Britain to-day are held by his former colleagues, as also are many important posts in industry. The name of Heilbron is most likely to be remembered by future generations of organic chemists in connexion with his valuable *Dictionary of Organic Compounds,* first published in association with H. M. Bunbury in 1934-37, the third edition of which is now in preparation.

During the Second World War he was, from 1939 to 1942, scientific adviser to the Department of Scientific Research of the Ministry of Supply, and from 1942 onwards he was one of the three scientific advisers to the Minister of Production. Probably his most important work during this period was the recognition of the potential value of the insecticide D.D.T. and the vigorous steps which he took to ensure that it became available in quantities sufficient for the Italian and Far Eastern campaigns. From 1950 until 1954 he was the chairman of the Advisory Council for the Department of Scientific and Industrial Research.

His public services and scientific contributions have been widely recognized: by a knighthood in 1946 and awards of the Longstaff Medal of the Chemical Society and Royal and Davy Medals of the Royal Society. In 1945 he was the first recipient, outside the United States, of the Priestley Medal of the American Chemical Society.

He married Elda Marguerite Davis, daughter of H. J. Davis, of Liverpool, in 1924 and nobly sustained a great loss on her sudden death in 1954. They had two sons.

September 15, 1959.

Reuter reported the death in Stuttgart on January 30, 1958 of **Dr. Ernst Heinkel,** the aircraft designer and manufacturer. He was 70.

Heinkel was born on January 24, 1888, the son of a tinker, and went to the Stuttgart Institute of Technology. As a student in 1910 he designed and built his own aircraft, which in the following year he flew and in which he later crashed and was injured.

By 1914 he was chief construction engineer and technical director with the Hansa and Brandenburgische Flugzeugwerke, and during the war that broke out that year was responsible for the design and construction of some 30 different types of aircraft for the Austrian forces. The war over, he founded his own firm and between 1922 and the overthrow of Nazi Germany about 100 different types came from his factories. Machines of his design at various times held many records for speed and distance. In June 1938 the famous pilot Ernst Udet flew a single-engined Heinkel He.112U fighter at over 400 m.p.h., and in April 1939 an improved He.112U did slightly over 463 m.p.h., breaking the world speed record. Within a month the record was pushed higher by a Messerschmitt 109R which achieved 469 m.p.h.

Heinkel did much development work on catapults, and in 1938 had a rocket plane flying. In an interview in 1951 he claimed to have tested and approved his first jet aircraft, the He.178, in August 1939 without the knowledge of Göring's Air Ministry; this was almost two years before the first Gloster-Whittle machine took the air in May 1941.

During the early part of the war of 1939-45 the Heinkel III was in constant use in the big air attacks on British cities. Another of Heinkel's brain-children was the He.162 fighter, which came into action late in the war.

In 1948 a denazification court at Ansbach fined him 2,000 Reichsmarks, but on appeal in 1949 he was cleared of the designation "Nazi follower". A year later he started to develop and produce motors for road vehicles. In 1955, when west Germany was again allowed to undertake aviation work, he started developing new aircraft and jet engines.

His death comes on the heels of reports that he and Willi Messerschmitt had agreed to team up to design and develop new aircraft.

January 31, 1958.

Grand Duchess Helen—See **Nicholas.**

Fred Henderson, the Socialist writer who achieved international readership for his works on socialism, died in his sleep at his Norwich home on July 18, 1957.

To celebrate his ninetieth birthday in February 1957, the national executive of the Labour Party later entertained him at dinner at the House of Commons. The tribute was well deserved, for over the past 60 years he had contributed much towards shaping the party's thought. *The Case for Socialism,* which has been translated into every major language, was followed in 1931 by *The Economic Consequences of Power Production* and *Capital and the Consumer.* When in his sixties Henderson undertook strenuous lecturing tours in America and Canada, where *The Case for Socialism* had become the accepted Socialist Party textbook. Almost to the last he retained his powers and he still sat as an alderman on Norwich City Council, which he joined in 1902 as the first Socialist member. He and his wife, who died in 1933, were the first married couple to sit on a local authority together after women's full civic rights were granted.

James Frederick Henderson—he always used the plain Fred—was the son of James Alexander Henderson and was educated at the Old Presbyterian School, Norwich. His early career in journalism included a spell on the London *Star*, during which he met T. P. O'Connor, Bernard Shaw, and others like-minded at the home of William Morris, who had earlier fired his Socialist enthusiasm while on a visit to Norwich. Henderson's enthusiastic espousal of the cause of the underdog soon led him into serious trouble. Having accompanied a deputation of unemployed to Norwich Corporation in 1887, Henderson found himself later charged with incitement to riot after the mob had got out of hand and raided foodshops. During a four months' sentence served in the old Castle gaol he was put to work on the treadmill. His indignation at this archaic survival led him to campaign for its abolition and this was later achieved through Parliamentary action.

Meanwhile Henderson was writing poetry, some of which attracted wide attention. The Poet Laureateship was vacant at the time and Henderson used to tell how he was among those sounded by Gladstone, whom he met at dinner. Nothing came of it and it is doubtful if Henderson's talent would have found its best expression in occasional poetry. He first achieved fame as a writer almost by chance. When a Labour church was established in Norwich to propagate on Sundays a political gospel, he preached a course of sermons which combined the eloquence of the poet with the zeal of a propagandist. In 1911 the Independent Labour Party published these addresses as *The Case for Socialism.* The book quickly attained national and then international renown.

July 19, 1957.

R. B. Henderson, who died on October 20, 1958 at the age of 78, was formerly headmaster of Alleyn's School, Dulwich, and later lecturer in historical theology at University College of North Staffordshire. He was a man of many parts and his life was dedicated to education.

Ralph Bushill Henderson was the son of the Rev. L. J. Henderson and was educated at Bristol Grammar School and New College, Oxford, where he took a double first in mathematics. "Henders", as everyone called him, was a man with many interests, with that now disappearing versatility to excel in most. He taught at King Edward's School, Birmingham, in 1901 but his most formative teaching years were at Rugby School, where he was a master from 1902 to 1911. He then became headmaster of the Strand School. He served in the 1914-18 War in the R.G.A., was promoted to lieutenant-colonel, and was commandant of the 2nd Army College at Cologne in 1919. He was appointed headmaster of Alleyn's School in 1920, and his 20 years there will be remembered not merely for his inspiring teaching and an efficient administration but because of his wide vision. Bred on the classics which he never ceased to love, trained in mathematics, he moved in his interests towards theology, and a Lambeth B.D. was conferred upon him in 1934, the first to go to a layman for many years.

When he retired in 1940 he was appointed reader in religious education at Oxford. He was also chairman of the council of the Modern Churchmen's Union from 1937 to 1945. Leaving Oxford in 1945 he continued to devote his time to several schools until in 1950 he became head of the department of historical theology at the University College of North Staffordshire, from which he retired in 1954 at the age of 74.

Henderson was the author of many books and articles, some popular, some scholarly. He was devout but intolerant of uncritical orthodoxy. Yet he was no iconoclast. His sermons in many colleges inspired his hearers to search for the deeper truths. He was a man of lasting enthusiasms: for climbing hills, especially in Wales; for riding horses; for the Tal-y-Llyn railway; for music; and for playing the double bass.

But teaching in both religious and secular subjects was his love. He often held the children enthralled in Sunday school telling them moral stories from the Scriptures or from Greek mythology. When he announced voluntary lectures on ancient Greek religion he had large audiences of undergraduates. His interpretations of Greek drama, philosophy and religion, made unassumingly as a layman, pointed the way to many scholars. When he died he was working on a commentary of St. Mark's Gospel. He was indefatigable; within three weeks of his death he asked to be allowed to teach in his bedroom since he was then confined to bed. He was without pretension and in spite of an uncompromising nature he had many friends who will sincerely miss him.

October 24, 1958.

Leslie Henson, one of the outstanding comic actors of the first half of this century, died at his home at Harrow Weald, Middlesex, on December 2, 1957. He was 66.

As actor, manager, and producer, he dominated musical comedy and farce on the British stage for many years. His acting was essentially unmonotonous, carrying the freshness of first nights through the longest runs—and he had little experience of short runs.

He travelled in the realms of absurdity with two highly personal attributes—his temperament and his face. The temperament was bland and benign, compelling his audience to good humour and reassuring it in moments of embarrassment and danger. In his autobiography *Yours Faithfully* he describes how by long practice before the mirror he obtained entire control of all his facial muscles while he was still a young man. The result was frequently unforgettable, and in moments of anguish or ecstasy he has been variously described as resembling a mandarin about to sneeze or a moth that has eaten too much tapestry. His success was based, however, on the more solid foundations of conscientious hard work and a fertile imagination. As all great comic actors must, he took his humour most seriously.

Leslie Lincoln Henson was born at Notting Hill, London, on August 3, 1891, the son of Joseph Lincoln Henson and his wife Mary. After attending Cliftonville College and Emanuel School he was destined for his father's tallow business at Smithfield. It soon became obvious where his talents lay, and his parents sent him, at the age of 17, to dramatic school where he was taught by Ernest D'Auban and Cairns-James. His first professional engagement was with a concert party called *The Tatlers* in 1910, and this, with variations, continued to be his life for the next five years.

From an early age he showed two qualities which served him well throughout his career—a capacity for making friends and a zest for the theatre, which drove him to make the best of every situation and, where necessary, improve on it. Even a one-line part as a waiter in his first play he enlivened by taking on some knitting. The incident built up into a 10-minute gag scene, with Henson replying, when asked what he was doing: "I'm sewing my wild oats!" However good the book, he was likely to make it better. Eventually, he secured a part as understudy in Laurillard and Grossmith's *To-night's the Night.* It was this musical comedy which, after a run in New York shortly after the outbreak of the 1914-18 War, gave him his first West End chance at the Gaiety, but it was as Pony Twitchin in *Theodore and Co.,* a year later, that he scored his first considerable personal triumph.

While acting in this show he joined the Royal Flying Corps. He was sent to France, commissioned, and given the work of organizing shows for the 5th Army. This culminated in his appearance with the "Gaieties" at the main theatre at Lille in 1918. Back in London the following year he found a part as Bibi St. Pol in *Kissing Time,* the first of a series of long runs at the Winter Garden. From then his reputation grew rapidly. *Sally, The Cabaret Girl, The Beauty Prize, Primrose* and *Kid Boots* were the principal plays in which he performed until 1926, when he left the Winter Garden and went on tour in the last named. There followed *Lady Luck, Funny Face, It's a Boy, It's a Girl* and *Nice Goings On.*

In 1935 Firth Shephard and he took the lease of the Gaiety Theatre and produced the first of four big successes with what became, in effect, a West End repertory company. The first of these, *Seeing Stars,* gave him full scope for his own particular brand of comic genius, for he played in them an insolvent hotel proprietor, a pseudo-magician, a Teutonic messenger mangling the English language into preposterous caricatures of meaning, and an undertaker's mute. The other three, *Swing Along, Going Greek,* and *Running Riot* kept him occupied until 1939, when the Gaiety was closed and he took the company to South Africa.

When war broke out he hastened back and with Basil Dean was responsible for the formation of E.N.S.A., the title of which was attributed to him. Once again Henson, with a vastly enhanced reputation, was entertaining the Forces in France in 1940, the Middle East

1943, Belgium and Holland 1944, and the Far East 1945. In 1940 he produced *Up and Doing* at the Saville until the theatre was closed, and subsequently bombed. After the war came *Bob's Your Uncle, Harvey, And So To Bed,* in which he appeared in a full-bottomed wig as Pepys, *Relations are Best Apart,* and *The Diary of a Nobody,* in which he appeared as Mr. Pooter.

For most of these years he worked as producer and manager as well as actor. Soon after the end of the 1914-18 War he went into management with the late Tom Walls, one result of which was their putting on the resoundingly successful farce *Tons of Money* which ran for 737 performances. It was in this play that Ralph Lynn* made his name, and Henson subsequently presented him in three other Aldwych farces. Other successful projects with which he was associated in one capacity or another were *Skin Deep* (1928), *Follow Through* (1929), *A Warm Corner* (1929), *Night of the Garter* (1932), *Living Dangerously* (1934), *Aren't Men Beasts*! (1936), *A Spot of Bother* (1937), and after the 1939-45 War, *1066 and All That.* All this left him with little time for films, but some of his more successful were *Alf's Button, Tons of Money, A Warm Corner,* and *The Sport of Kings.* He was president of the Royal General Theatrical Fund, and was on several occasions a staunch campaigner in favour of the Sunday opening of theatres.

He married first in 1919 Madge Saunders, the actress. The marriage was dissolved in 1925 and he subsequently married Gladys Gunn. This marriage was dissolved and in 1944 he married Mrs. Harriet Martha Day.

December 3, 1957.

Cecil Hepworth, one of the pioneers of the British film industry, died on February 9, 1953 at his home at Greenford, Middlesex.

Born in London in 1874, the son of an ardent amateur photographer, he was fascinated as a boy by the scientific exhibits at the Royal Polytechnic Institution, which preceded the present Polytechnic in Upper Regent Street. He was particularly drawn to the magic lanterns in the theatre there and learned to operate them with skill. He was asked to work one of the cameras for a film of Queen Victoria's Diamond Jubilee but the machine jammed and no pictures were taken. In the next year, however, he successfully took a panoramic picture of the University Boat Race and in 1899 set up in business with a partner at Walton-on-Thames. They produced a number of short films about 50ft. in length which had some success, and in 1901 began a series of "phantom rides" taken from the front of a railway engine.

Meanwhile they had begun to cultivate the "news film", the first of which showed men of the C.I.V. boarding the liner Garth Castle on their way to the South African war. His greatest triumph in this *genre* was the film of the funeral procession of Queen Victoria, which was halted by King Edward VII in Grosvenor Gardens just opposite the camera and so gave a magnificent chance to Hepworth to get moving portraits of the chief mourners.

The year 1905 saw the most famous of Hepworth's early dramatic films, *Rescued by Rover,* in which he, his wife, their baby, their collie dog, and two professional actors took part. The professionals were paid 10s. 6d., out of which they had to find their fares from London. Hepworth built his first indoor studio in that year, but after only two years the place was gutted by fire. The insurance company was generous and he was able to rebuild.

At about this time Hepworth experimented with a gramophone synchronized with the projector and christened the apparatus the "vivaphone". It had some success, but synchronization was not always achieved by the exhibitors and the invention gradually lost popularity. The 1914-18 war was an embarrassing period, for most of Hepworth's younger helpers left to join the services and American competitors were able to gain a much larger share of the market for films in this country.

Hepworth, however, felt able to expand after the war and in 1919 floated his enterprise as a limited company. Perhaps the most successful film which came from the Walton studios at this time was *Alf's Button,* based on a story by W. A. Darlington. In spite of this and other successes Hepworth's enterprise eventually failed, but he never gave up his love for and interest in the industry he had done so much to create, and he continued until a year or two ago to advise on technical questions, to make short outdoor sound films in colour, and to make "trailers".

February 11, 1953.

Joseph Hergesheimer, the American novelist, died at the age of 74 on April 25, 1954.

He settled down to writing when he was 21; his first novel was published when he was 34; *The Three Black Pennys,* always his bestknown book, when he was 37. Thus he broke into print with great difficulty, scored a comparatively rapid success, and, perhaps in consequence, had to suffer an undeserved reaction of critical, and to a lesser degree of popular, opinion.

He was born in 1880 in Philadelphia, where he was brought up in his grandfather's house, a home of strict Presbyterian observances but also of "flowers and space and quiet". His father at sea, his mother ill with no other children, and kept from school by his own ill-health almost into adolescence, he passed a lonely childhood, reading, dreaming, "absorbing the seasons". After a short period at a Quaker school he became a student at the Pennsylvania Academy of Fine Arts, but his ambitions as a painter were never very serious.

At this time he had no notion what he wanted to be or do; it was a period of restless, seemingly ill-spent, idleness. Then, when he was 21, following an extravagant trip to Europe and ignominious return, an accidental contact with the English novelist "Lucas Cleeve" (Mrs. Adeline Kingscote) turned his thoughts to literature. For more than 10 years he wrote persistently, without the least encouragement from family, friends, editors, or publishers. In 1907 he married Dorothy Hemphill, of West Chester, Pennsylvania, and for a year or two came again to Europe. His first article appeared in print in 1913, his first book, *The Lay Anthony,* in 1914.

Frequent attention has been called to the effect upon his work of the long years of seemingly hopeless striving, combined with his student training, in producing an over-careful and over-conscious attention to style, form, and detail. In the earlier works, especially, the characters are felt to move almost doll-like against the luxury of their minutely pictured backgrounds, to be impelled by the necessities less of passion than of pattern. It was charged against him that in writing of the American past he sought the merely picturesque.

Some of his "period" pieces—*The Three Black Pennys, Java Head, The Bright Shawl,* the shorter stories of *The Happy End* and *Gold and Iron,* cannot be wholly exculpated, but in *Linda Condon* he revealed more directly the depths of his apprehension of life, his attention to qualities not simply romantic, and *Balisand* at least suggested that even in his "romances" he was really looking beneath the surface to more permanent realities. He turned to the past because he found the qualities he admired displayed there more vividly and dramatically than anywhere to-day.

It might be doubted whether in the earlier stories he yet realized quite clearly in his own mind what he wanted to say, but from *Balisand* forward that ceased to be so. *Balisand,* like the later *Tampico* and *The Party Dress,* was too long. His simple inspiration was better, more economically, expressed in the shorter tale than the long novel, and *Quiet Cities* and *The Limestone Tree,* both collections of short stories, were among his very finest work.

His most personal books, apart from the little known but exquisite autobiographical *Presbyterian Child,* were the travel volume *San Cristóbal de la Habana,* and *From an Old House,* a description of his home at West Chester. (He was an enthusiastic collector of early American furniture; to many people, he once said, he was known not at all for his books but as the owner of the Paca hunting board.)

April 26, 1954.

The death in Lyons on March 26, 1957 of **Edouard Herriot** breaks one of the principal links between the authentic traditions of the Third Republic of France and the ideals of the Fourth.

The last President of the Chamber of Deputies in the one, virtually the first President of the National Assembly in the other, Edouard Herriot had held a position of unique and uncontested moral authority in French parliamentary life since the liberation of his country in 1945. In later years, it is true, his attitude on foreign policy and the German question in particular suggested that the great European had allowed prejudice to displace reason. But for a generation—indeed for half the life of the Third Republic itself—he had as parliamentarian, as Mayor of Lyons (his fiftieth anniversary as mayor was celebrated in October 1955) and as a man of letters, claimed a place among the foremost sons of the Republic. That claim was reinforced by his courage and loyalty during the years of France's humiliation in defeat, and by the characteristic faith and good will he brought to his responsibilities under the new Republican régime. Frenchmen mourn and honour a man who, through a period of turbulent stress and difficulty, won an esteem and affection seldom accorded to parliamentary leaders. He was in fact that rare breed, a man of action and a man of contemplation.

His early reputation was academic, which rested not only on his early *Philon le Juif* but also on *Mme. Récamier et Ses Amis* and the *Précis d'Histoire des lettres françaises.* A powerful and polished speaker in public, he had in private the art of good conversation made all the more telling by a charming and sympathetic manner.

Born at Troyes on July 5, 1872, Edouard Herriot graduated at the École Normale Supérieure in 1894, taught at the Lycée at Lyons, and was appointed Professor of the Rhétorique Supérieure class (the senior arts form, which prepares students for the École Normale Supérieure) at the Lyons lycée, when the storm of the Dreyfus case was raging in France. He won national reputation first as a scholar (his *Philon le Juif,* of 1897, was crowned by the Academy of Moral and Political Science), and then as as a local administrator, for he became Mayor of Lyons in 1905. His energy and enterprise made the city of Lyons one of the best governed towns in France, and its people kept their loyalty to him to the last.

Before 1919 Herriot was in the wings of national politics. He became Senator for the Rhône Department in 1912, and Minister of Supplies in Briand's Ministry of 1916. His experience of both local and national administration turned his energies towards problems of economic development and reconstruction after the 1914-18 War. He was already urging the planned technical development of French resources in his wartime books, *Agir* (1917) and *Créer* (1919). By the end of 1919, when he entered the Chamber as Deputy for the Rhône, his record and his eloquence brought him into the centre of the stage of parliamentary politics as leader of the Socialist-Radicals.

Thus began the great central period of his career, as one of the leading figures in national and international politics. It was the tragedy of his life that his main role was cast in a time of violent controversy at home and recurrent crisis abroad, for the professor in politics had neither the partisan vehemence nor the political ruthlessness of many of his rivals in those years. He remained one of the most lovable of politicians, even when he proved ineffective. He led the opposition to the policy of Poincaré which culminated in French occupation of the Ruhr in 1923 and the shaking of national credit which caused the franc to totter, and when the elections of May 1924 swept Poincaré from office power fell to the *Cartel des Gauches* led by Herriot.

The demands of the Socialist groups of the *Cartel,* however, brought a constitutional crisis. They demanded the resignation of the President, Millerand, and confronted Herriot with the dilemma which was to haunt his whole Ministry: that of reconciling his followers. Millerand gave way and resigned, but this unconstitutional pressure and the anti-clerical programme which followed turned public opinion against Herriot. Amid these troubles he had to tackle the thorny problems of reparations and disarmament. He welcomed the Dawes [q.v.] Plan because it was based on international guarantees, and the Geneva Protocol because he believed it would provide security for France within a wider framework. But in domestic affairs the pressure of the extremists was steadily splitting his supporters, and in April 1925 he was outvoted in the Senate and resigned. The frustrations of his first Ministry lay partly in the financial legacy of his predecessors, and in the very nature of French party politics: but partly, too, in a certain lack of driving power and parliamentary skill in the character of Herriot himself.

Herriot was more at home as Minister for Education between 1926 and 1928, and as President of the Chamber, an office which he filled with dignity and trust intermittently throughout the 1930s. His second Ministry of 1926 lasted only one day, and his third in 1932 lasted but six months. But in those years he won international repute and esteem. An incident of those times serves in some measure to explain why. The Hoover* moratorium on war reparations proved in fact to mark the effective end of all German payments, a development not likely to be appreciated by French electors or politicians. At the same time the servicing of the French war debt to the United States fell due at the end of 1932, and there was nothing that the outgoing President Hoover or the President-elect Roosevelt could do to alter the arrangement. Herriot appealed to the Chamber to honour France's word by paying the instalment due of $19m.; when his appeal was rejected he resigned and was deaf to the entreaties to change his mind. His visit to Washington in 1933 was a personal triumph, but a political failure. His constant support of close Anglo-French cooperation made him well known in Britain, and Oxford University conferred upon him the honorary degree of D.C.L. in 1935.

In the debacle of 1940 he remained steadfast in republican loyalty and courageously defied the forces of collaboration. He protested against the suspension of Parliament, and was placed under house arrest—and finally complete arrest—for refusing to promise that he would not attempt to leave France. After the return to power of his old rival Laval in April 1942 his protests multiplied. When Laval abolished the bureaux of Senate and Chamber, he wrote a letter of protest to Marshal Pétain [q.v.] "in the name of the sovereignty of the nation". He renounced his *Légion d'Honneur* when that decoration was awarded to collaborators. After he had been transferred as a prisoner to Germany there were frequent German reports that he had died; but in April 1945 he was liberated by Soviet troops from a prison camp near Berlin. He received a tumultuous welcome on his return to his native city, of which he was promptly re-elected Mayor, was similarly re-elected for his old constituency to the new Constituent Assembly, and crowned a brave and honourable career by being chosen to succeed Vincent Auriol*, on the latter's election to the Presidency of the Republic in January 1947, as President of the National Assembly of France's Fourth Republic. This post he held until the end of 1953 when by his own wish he retired, explaining that his age and health no longer permitted him to discharge his duties; for the same reasons he refused to allow his name to go forward as a candidate for the Presidency of the Republic, for which the election was held in December 1953. He was elected Honorary President of the National Assembly, and his rare appearances there, as an ordinary Deputy, never failed to evoke, even from those who disagreed with his views, a manifestation of personal respect and affection.

For there was no doubt that during these years the intensity of Herriot's opposition to German rearmament in general and the European Defence Community Treaty in particular sometimes led him into extreme attitudes which inevitably caused some embarrassment. At the League of Nations in 1924 he had coined the formula "arbitration, security, disarmament", and the same year his Government had extended *de jure* recognition to the Government of the U.S.S.R. Thirty years later the memory of these policies seemed to obsess him, blotting out all the changes that time and circumstance had wrought. It was not simply that he opposed German rearmament—many brave, sincere, and eminent Frenchmen did that—but in an epoch when, however undesirable and unpleasant it was, the division of the world into two blocks had to be admitted as a matter of fact, Herriot seemed to think it possible to eat one's cake and have it. He became, in part unwittingly, the delight of the "neutralists".

Herriot virtually opened the campaign against the E.D.C. treaty, at the Radical Congress in October 1952, in a speech in which his distrust of Germany and his desire to "have another try with the Russians" found full and effective expression. He was back on the same theme at the party congress in September of the following year. His arguments backed up by all the weight of his reputation and great experience, seemed impressive: how indeed, he said, could German fidelity to treaties be trusted when "Germany believes only in evolution and in the future?" But his only alternative policy was to talk with the Russians. By March of the following year

(1954), he was signing, along with Daladier* and "Vercors", the Communist-sympathizing author, a manifesto calling for demonstrations and echoing Soviet proposals for a "union of all European nations".

The dramatic intervention of Herriot in the debate in the National Assembly in August 1954, which led to the outright rejection of E.D.C., was credited at the time with too much significance. The adverse vote was in fact a foregone conclusion, and Herriot's somewhat rambling utterances, infused with the flavour of "neutralism", probably had little, if any, effect upon the final voting figures. Four months later Herriot, who had always implied that his attitude would have been very different if Great Britain had been in E.D.C., was telling the Chamber that he could not vote for the London and Paris agreements (to which Britain was a signatory) because they caused him "insoluble problems of conscience".

In June 1955 Herriot was presented with the gold medal of the international peace prize (the former Stalin prize). The award was, he said, "not only perhaps the last I shall receive", but the most precious to him. Then, throwing his mind back over his long life and noting, evidently, the disapproval which had greeted his acceptance of the prize, he said that he had not solicited it, but accepted it as a tribute to a man who all his life had striven for peace; "I have no right to criticize those who have failed to understand my gesture", he added, "but I pity them". It was a remark typical of the man—a liberal in thought and tradition but a bigot for what he believed to be true.

In 1946 Herriot was elected a member of the Academie Française.

March 27, 1957.

Dr. G. J. van Heuven Goedhart, the United Nations High Commissioner for Refugees, whose sudden death occurred on July 8, 1956 at the age of 55, was a man whose outstanding characteristic was courage. He collapsed while playing tennis at Vandoeuvres with J. M. Read, the Deputy High Commissioner.

Gerrit Jan van Heuven Goedhart was born at Bussum on March 19, 1901, and studied law at the University of Leyden, where he took his degree in 1926. In the same year he was appointed editor of the independent newspaper *De Telegraaf,* of Amsterdam, and conducted it with distinction for several years. Then came a test of his courage. The proprietor wished the newspaper to adopt a pro-Hitler line, which van Heuven Goedhart was not prepared to follow. As a result he was dismissed in 1933, and then established the *Utrechtsch Nieuwsblad,* which made up for its small size by its outspoken opposition to Nazism. Leading Dutch and foreign politicians contributed to its columns.

In 1938 he visited Czechoslovakia, where he met Dr. Benes, and afterwards wrote *Unrest in Masaryk's Country,* in which he exposed Nazi methods in countries bordering on Germany. He went to Finland after the Russian attack in 1939, and in newspaper articles and in his book *Finland As I Saw It* he pleaded the cause of the heroic Finns. He was also a member of a committee formed to raise funds for the Finnish forces and people. With the invasion of his own country in May 1940 he ceased his activities as a journalist and joined the commission for the care of victims of the war, holding an honorary post responsible for housing. He resigned when the Germans imposed the rule that no houses should go to Jews.

At the end of 1941 van Heuven Goedhart became co-editor of the underground newspaper *Het Parool,* which eventually had a circulation of between 55,000 and 60,000. Thirty-seven members of its staff were executed and many others were arrested and interned in concentration camps. He himself managed to escape, notwithstanding that the Germans offered a reward for his capture. In February 1944 after an adventurous journey through France and Spain, he reached London, where he reported to the Netherlands Government on the resistance movement, and was asked to become Minister of Justice. After the liberation he was appointed editor-in-chief of *Het Parool,* which to-day is one of the most important newspapers in the country. He was also elected to the Senate, but resigned both posts when the General Assembly of the United Nations chose him as High Commissioner for Refugees for three years from January 1951—a mandate later extended to the end of 1958.

To the office of high commissioner he brought all his qualities of vigour and vision, espousing to the very end of his life the cause of the most hapless of the war's victims. He was resolute in his dealings with Governments, and sometimes made himself unpopular by his insistence that the final solving of the problem was the responsibility of the international community and could not be left to the state in which the refugees still find themselves. Nothing touched him more deeply than the fact that his own countrymen and women raised the equivalent of $1m. voluntarily to help his work. He continued to the end to work with unremitting vigour, but latterly he had found it increasingly difficult to raise funds, so that about a month ago he told a press conference that perhaps he ought to give up and let someone else try to grapple with the intractable problem of the refugees.

When the twenty-second session of the United Nations Economic and Social Council opened in Geneva yesterday Hans Engen, its president, referred to Dr. van Heuven Goedhart's many services in peace and war, and especially to the vigour, honesty, and singleness of purpose with which he served the cause of the refugees. The sitting was suspended in honour of the High Commissioner's memory. Dr. van Heuven Goedhart received the Wateler peace prize for 1955, and in the same year the Norwegian Storting awarded his office the Nobel peace prize for 1954.

July 10, 1956.

Sir Leonard Hill, F.R.S., a distinguished physiologist, whose researches contributed greatly to medical knowledge, died on December 17, 1959 at Corton, near Lowestoft, at the age of 85.

Leonard Erskine Hill was born on June 2, 1866, and was educated at Haileybury and University College, London, obtaining his first medical qualification in 1889 and his London M.B. in 1890. He came under the influence of Sir Edward Schafer of University College, and proved to be an apt pupil of that distinguished physiologist. Hill became Assistant Professor in University College, London, and later Professor of Physiology in the London Hospital Medical School. He had early shown his gift at expressing himself by the publication in 1899 of his *Manual of Human Physiology,* but it was not only for his medical students that Hill could write in a pictorial and pleasant style. He was always so eager to apply the results of physiological experiments to the affairs of ordinary life, and for him physiology was essentially an applied science. He therefore wrote papers and memoranda and later books for a much wider audience, as for example his contribution on *Common Colds* published with Mark Clement in 1929.

Some of Hill's earliest work had been on "caisson disease", the dreaded occupational risk of those working in compression chambers, and his publications in the early years of this century showed how by special decompression chambers this work could be made safe. It was probably in the course of these studies that he became interested in ventilation, a study which was to keep his attention in various ways for many years. He pointed out the dangers of trains and dormitories as regards infection, and in the course of his studies on the loss of heat from the body he devised the "katathermometer" which he claimed gave a good impression of the efficiency or otherwise of ventilation. His work with the instrument led him to advocate strongly and insistently the value of fresh air and exercise.

In later life he became Director of the Department of Applied Physiology at the National Institute for Medical Research, Hampstead, and on retirement from this found time to become Director of Research of the St. John Clinic and Institute of Physical Medicine.

Hill's services as a physiologist who knew how to apply physiological knowledge to practical problems were in great demand. He had been at various times a member of the Medical Advisory Board to the Navy and the Army and of the Medical Administrative Committee of the Air Board. Many distinctions came his way. He was a F.R.S., and LL.D. of Aberdeen University. He was Oliver Sharpey lecturer of the Royal College of Physicians and a Hunterian Professor of the Royal College of Surgeons of England. He was knighted in 1930.

He was fond of painting, particularly animals and landscape, and was a true amateur in art since he always declared that he liked to paint for the fun of the thing. At one time his pictures took on an impressionist quality, and Hill also went through a phase when he painted almost nothing but turkeys.

He married in 1891 Janet, daughter of Mr. Frederick Alexander, who survives him together with four sons and two daughters of the marriage.

December 19, 1959.

Air Chief Marshal Sir Roderic Hill, K.C.B., M.C., A.F.C., died suddenly in London on October 6, 1954 at the age of 60. He had been ill for several months.

His career as a scientific air officer was outstanding. Nearly half of his 32 years with the Royal Flying Corps and the Royal Air Force had been spent in technical posts, starting as experimental officer at Farnborough during the 1914-18 War and ending as Member for Technical Services on the Air Council. Coupled with his engineering and scientific knowledge, he had a high reputation as a pilot—an unusual combination. Added to this he had literary and artistic gifts of no mean order. He became Rector of the Imperial College of Science and Technology on retiring from the R.A.F. in 1948, and was elected Vice-Chancellor of the University of London in 1953, but resigned his appointment in June 1954 owing to ill-health.

Roderic Maxwell Hill was born on March 1, 1894, the son of Professor M. J. M. Hill, M.A., D.Sc., F.R.S., of London University. He was educated at Bradfield and at University College, London, of which he was afterwards elected a Fellow. His career began as an artist with the Temple Press, and much good work of his appeared in motor cycling and aviation journals. Soon after the outbreak of the First World War in 1914 he enlisted in The Royal Fusiliers, and in December 1914 was commissioned in The Northumberland Fusiliers. He was seconded to the R.F.C. as a flying officer in June 1916 and served with No. 60 Squadron in France, for which he was mentioned in dispatches and awarded the M.C.

In 1917 he was recalled to take charge of the experimental flying department at the Royal Aircraft Establishment, Farnborough. There he did valuable work, for which he was awarded the A.F.C. and Bar, and remained six years, a permanent commission as squadron leader being granted him in August 1919. He was the first pilot deliberately to fly a specially protected machine into a balloon cable during investigations of balloon defences in 1918, and was among the first to experiment with radio telephone receivers in aircraft. He also took part in many experiments at Farnborough relating to radio control of aircraft, flight testing of exhaust-driven superchargers, new types of parachute, and investigation of wing "flutter". In 1921 he was awarded the R. M. Groves Memorial Aeronautical Research Prize.

On leaving Farnborough he graduated at the R.A.F. Staff College in 1924, and was employed on air staff duties at Inland Area headquarters until posted to the command of No. 45 (Bomber) Squadron in Iraq in September of that year. At this time the Cairo-Baghdad mail service was operated by the R.A.F., and Hill gained much valuable experience of desert flying, which he incorporated in a book, *The Baghdad Air Mail* (1929). In November 1926, as a wing commander, he was transferred to Middle East headquarters for technical staff duties, but in the following June was recalled to become an instructor at the R.A.F. Staff College.

In 1931-32 he was chief instructor to, and for a time, commanding officer of, the Oxford University Air Squadron. Promoted to group captain in July 1932, he was appointed Deputy Director of Repairs and Maintenance two months later, and served at the Air Ministry for four years until his promotion to air commodore in July 1936. For two years from August 1936 he was Air Officer Commanding in Palestine and Transjordan. He returned to the Air Ministry in August 1938 as Director of Technical Development, and in 1939 was promoted to air vice-marshal. He was made an acting air marshal in 1940, but did not attain substantive rank until 1945.

Few officers had a more varied round of service in the higher appointments during the Second World War. In 1940-41 he was Director-General of Research and Development in the Ministry of Aircraft Production, and during the Battle of Britain took charge of a working party to pass the new 20mm. cannon through its initial tests. He himself undertook part of the flight testing of the cannon in a Spitfire. After that he went to Washington as Controller of Technical Services with the British Air Commission. He returned in September 1942 to become Commandant of the R.A.F Staff College, but in July 1943 his services were needed as A.O.C., No. 12 (Fighter) Group. When at the end of 1943 Fighter Command and Army Cooperation Command were combined with the American 9th Air Force into a new organization called the Allied Expeditionary Air Force, for the liberation of Europe, he took command of a force, for which the old title of Air Defence of Great Britain was revived, which became responsible for the day and night defence of the islands.

In the summer of 1944 he became A.O.C.-in-C., Fighter Command. During the flying bomb attacks he was a well-known figure on many airfields in southern England, flying his own Tempest aircraft in order to study at first hand the correct use of weapons and interception tactics. In May 1945 he was appointed Air Member for Training on the Air Council. In December 1946 he took up the new post of Air Member for Technical Services on the Air Council, in charge of a new Air Ministry department responsible for all aspects of the technical work of the R.A.F.

In January 1947 he was promoted to air chief marshal. He retired from the Air Council and the R.A.F. in June 1948 and was appointed by the governing body of the Imperial College of Science and Technology as Rector of the college from October 1 of that year, in succession to Sir Richard Southwell. From May 1946 until his retirement he was Principal Air Aide-de-Camp to King George VI. He was made a C.B. in 1941 and promoted K.C.B. in 1944. In person he was lean and active, seldom given to standing upon ceremony, and possessed of great charm of manner. His mind was quick and alert, and he was popular with all ranks.

He married in 1917 Mabel Helen Catherine, daughter of Lieutenant-Colonel E. R. Morton, Indian Army. There were a son and two daughters of the marriage. The son was killed in action in 1944.

October 7, 1954.

James Hilton, the novelist, died at Long Beach, California, on December 20, 1954, aged 54.

He was born at Leigh, in Lancashire, on September 9, 1900, the son of a schoolmaster, and was educated at The Leys School and Christ's College, Cambridge. The *Manchester Guardian* accepted his first journalistic work and for a time he reviewed fiction in the *Daily Telegraph.* His chief business was, however, writing it, and for this he found material from his travels in Europe and from a period of residence in Vienna. He wrote his first book, *Catherine Herself,* while he was still an undergraduate, but the years that followed the war were difficult for him and it was not unitl 11 years later, in 1931, that he had a considerable success with *And Now Goodbye.* Two years later came *Knight Without Armour,* a tale of adventure, and shortly afterwards *Lost Horizon,* which was awarded a Hawthornden Prize. The success of this fanciful story of a remote corner of Tibet where time stands still owed a good deal to the film version which came later.

It was in 1934 that *Goodbye Mr. Chips* arrived, and with it his first resounding success. The story appeared first in serial form in a weekly magazine and was said to have taken him only four days to write. With this simple tale of the old schoolmaster Hilton added to the stock of popular symbols and perhaps softened the criticism of public schools and their masters which has come from both within and without. The improbability of Mr. Chips did not prevent him and the gentle sentimentality of his story being taken to the hearts of thousands of readers on both sides of the Atlantic. The stage version was produced in 1938 and a year later came the film.

By this time Hilton had left England for California, and from then on his work became more and more closely connected with the Hollywood film industry. From the first he had shown talent for storytelling in a smooth and accomplished style, and for the sharp delineation of character, two qualities which sell a novelist's works and help to turn them into films. He possessed also the kind of imagination that can make characters as different as Fabian-minded schoolmistresses, Soviet diplomats, and Hollywood film stars seem equally plausible, and can make a scene in a South American forest seem as likely as one in an English schoolroom. Films were made of most of his novels, and he worked on many scenarios, outstanding among which was that for *Mrs. Miniver.*

In 1941 he had another wide success with *Random Harvest,* which was also filmed. After that he continued writing novels with no less facility but without the high quality that marked his best-known works. They included *The Story of Dr. Wassell* (1944), *So Well Remembered* (1945), *Nothing So Strange* (1947), and *Morning Journey* (1951). His last, *Time and Time Again,* was published in 1953.

A modest and retiring man for all his success, he was a keen mountaineer and enjoyed music and travel. He was twice married.

December 22, 1954.

Francis W. Hirst, editor of the *Economist* from 1907 until the conditions produced by the prolongation of the 1914-18 war led to his decision to lay down his office in 1916, died on February 22, 1953 in his eightieth year after an attack of influenza.

A distinguished writer on economics and politics, he might be described as one of the last of the school of Mill, Cobden, Bright and Gladstone, who in season and out preached the old Liberal doctrines of peace, economy and free trade. In his later years, indeed, he was something of a Cassandra prophesying to his generation the disasters that would ensue from a departure from those principles. He was a fervent disciple of John Morley, whose life he wrote, and his lucid thought and power of expression gave him an exceptional position in the public life of his time.

When he succeeded Edward Johnstone as editor of the *Economist* in 1907 he took over a stereotyped paper, then in the seventh decade of its life, designed primarily to instruct the business community, and by drastic reorganization he set out to regain the wider field of public affairs that Bagehot had made his province. He wrote his own policy leaders and began the building up of a competent and ample staff of assistants inside the office, among them Walter and Gilbert Layton, J. E. Allen, Dudley Ward, Hilton Young, Mary Agnes Hamilton*, and C. K. Hobson. It was a poignant tragedy that an editorship begun so brilliantly should have been frustrated and undone by the shattering in 1914 of the stable, rational, and peaceful world which Hirst took as his postulate.

Francis Wrigley Hirst was the son of Alfred Hirst, a cloth manufacturer of Huddersfield, and was born in June 1873. On his mother's side he was a second cousin to the first Lord Oxford and Asquith. He was educated at Clifton, and in 1891 went up to Wadham College, Oxford, winning there a scholarship in company with Lord Simon [q.v.], who was his exact contemporary there, along with F. E. Smith, Lord Roche [q.v.], and C. B. Fry [q.v.]. In 1894 he took a first in Moderations and in 1896 a first in Greats, and the same year he was elected successively librarian and president of the Union. In 1899 he was called to the Bar by the Inner Temple.

While at Oxford politics and economics were the magnets that had attracted him. He did some coaching there after taking his degree, and he lectured at the then youthful London School of Economics, where he had gained a Russell Studentship and the Cobden Prize. He had already, in 1897, published, with J. E. Phillimore, Belloc [q.v.], Simon, and J. L. Hammond, what seems to have been his first essay in political literature, *The Historic Basis of Liberalism.*

During the next few years, the South African war, in resistance to which Hirst played a busy part, much writing in the *Speaker* (afterwards the *Nation*), editing a series of political and economic books for Harpers, and a *Life of Adam Smith* for the "English Men of Letters" series, occupied his attention until his appointment as editor of the *Economist.*

In this notice it is impossible to do justice to the numerous books that Hirst published bearing upon the economic problems that arose between the two world wars and beyond and little more than mention of the principal titles must suffice: *The Life of Thomas Jefferson: The Political Economy of War* (1915); *Safeguarding and Protection* (1928); *Gladstone as Financier and Economist* (1931); *Consequences of the War in Great Britain* (1934); *Liberty and Tyranny* (1935); *Armaments* (1937); *Problems and Fallacies of Political Economy* (1943), and others. All are the work of a scholar and an independent thinker.

In 1948 he published the pleasant volume of recollections *The Golden Days,* recalling at length his Oxford days, when he helped to build up a Young Liberal movement, which made no small contribution to the party's triumph in 1905. Of his contemporaries, of none does he recall more vivid or more friendly memories than of his Tory opponent, F. E. Smith. Though a keen controversialist and a hard-hitter throughout his career, Hirst never allowed his politics to cloud his personal friendships, and his sincerity was respected by all.

He married in 1903 Helena, daughter of Charles Cobden and a grand-niece of the apostle of free trade, who survives him.

February 23, 1953.

George Hirst, who died on May 10, 1954 at Huddersfield at the age of 82, was generally regarded as the greatest all-round cricketer that England had known since the days of "W. G."

The greatness of George Hirst is to be measured by something beyond his record of achievements, tremendous as they are, for he was without doubt the most popular cricketer of all time, popular in that he was esteemed and loved on every ground that he graced. His short and thick-set body, his buoyant and cheerful personality, and his obvious and perpetual pleasure in every game in which he played made cricket well worth the watching. In Yorkshire he was an unchallenged hero, elsewhere he was greeted as a welcome and tremendously powerful visitor.

George Herbert Hirst was born at Kirkheaton, Yorkshire, on September 7, 1871, and made his name in local cricket at the age of 14, but it was not until he was 18 that he became associated with Huddersfield, and it was then that his real career may be said to have been begun. In 1891 he played for Yorkshire against M.C.C. at Lord's, the late Sydney Pardon, than whom there was no more astute judge of coming greatness, being impressed by the energy with which he bowled at William Barnes. Three seasons of quiet competence followed, until in 1896 Hirst scored 1,122 runs and took 104 wickets and established himself among the leading professionals of the day. There was then a suggestion that his batting was improving at the expense of his bowling. He was a member of A. E. Stoddart's team which went to Australia in 1897, but he then failed to do himself justice, his bowling being ineffective on the Australian pitches.

His first really great season was in 1901, when he made 1,950 runs and took 183 wickets; and from 1903 until 1913 he never failed to achieve the "double", establishing a record in 1906 by making 2,385 runs and taking 208 wickets, a feat which has never been equalled. He again went to Australia in 1903 as a member of P. F. (Sir Pelham) Warner's* team, and in all he played in 12 Test matches against Australia in England, but for some reason he was never the success in representative cricket that he was when playing for his county. In one match against Australia at the Oval in 1902, however, he and G. L. Jessop [q.v.] made history. This was the match in which Jessop put England in sight of victory with a thrilling 104, while Hirst scored an invaluable 58 not out, snatching with Rhodes* the last 15 runs required for victory in singles.

Who it was who first discovered a controlled method of making the ball swing, swerve, or bend in the air has never been satisfactorily established, but certainly Hirst was one of the first and most effective bowlers of this type. A shade faster than medium in pace, he flicked the ball across the pitch with a curl disconcerting enough even without the haste that it made off the ground. He was never quite so antagonistic a bowler as F. R. Foster, from whom E. J. Smith was entitled to expect a tickle on the leg-side more often than the great David Hunter, but like Foster he was deadly accurate and a menace to any batsman who refused to drive a ball over mid-on's head in the manner of C. B. Fry [q.v.].

As a batsman he was brave and quick to realize that the hook when properly developed and controlled was a stroke to which it was exceedingly difficult to place a field. He played this stroke so well that some bowlers complained it to be almost impossible to bowl any ball short of a "yorker" which was not treated by Hirst as a rank long-hop. As a fieldsman he has always been considered one of the greatest mid-offs that ever lived—A. E. R. Gilligan [d. 1976] and George Brown in later days were perhaps his equals. He was, indeed, the standard mid-off, helped to a great extent by the fact that he was left-handed, and the report that he declared that he always moved back a few feet when Kenneth Hutchings came in to bat established that resplendent young Kent cricketer as a driver of more than ordinary power.

No why or wherefore, no explanation of his great ability, not even his record which adorns the pages of *Wisden* can adequately describe to those who had not the fortune to see him play the rich quality of George Hirst, the type of professional cricketer to which all would like to aspire. He played during the golden age of cricket, and he was one of the most illustrious of his time. His last full season in the Yorkshire team was that of 1921, but he made an occasional appearance until 1929.

It was by no means the end of his cricketing career, however, for he acted as coach at Eton, where his professional capacity earned him the respect of the boys and his natural good humour and good manners gained him the love of all. Up to the end of his life he displayed the keenest interest in the game of which he was so bright an ornament, coaching and encouraging the young aspirants of Yorkshire, and he attended the England v. Australia match at Headingley last summer. His health had begun to fail only in his last few weeks.

May 11, 1954.

Sir Samuel Hoare—See **Templewood.**

Major-General Sir Percy Cleghorn Stanley Hobart, K.B.E., C.B., D.S.O., M.C., died at his home at Farnham, Surrey, on February 19, 1957. He was born in 1885, the son of R. T. Hobart, I.C.S., and educated at Temple Grove, Clifton College, and at the R.M.A.

In 1923 Hobart, then an instructor at the Quetta Staff College, joined the new Royal Tank Corps, following in the footsteps of other distinguished Royal Engineers who had played a leading part in the earlier development of the tank. He became an outstanding leader in the subsequent development of armoured forces and their mobile technique after being appointed commander of the first permanent Tank Brigade in 1934. It was his combination of long-range vision with practical thoroughness, as well as his capacity for generating enthusiasm, that brought the new conception out of the womb of theory into active fact. No one, however, more generously acknowledged what was due to the previous prophets and planners in creating the embryo that he delivered into life as a sturdy infant. His mind at once turned to the question of breaking away from the restricted role of close cooperation with infantry to which the tanks had been confined in the 1933 training season, and trying out their wider possibilities.

It may be difficult for a later generation, familiar with the sweeping victories of armoured forces in the Second World War, to understand what a startling innovation the Tank Brigade exercises were at the time, and how far-fetched they appeared to the majority of orthodox soldiers. The enthusiasm that prevailed in the 1st Tank Brigade has rarely been equalled and never exceeded. Strategy and tactics became the staple food of ordinary conversation. Passing through the camp after lights-out, one might hear the men discussing tactics in their tents. In the officers' mess such argument was still more predominant. The story is still told how, during a momentary pause, an officer leant forward across the table and gently asked: "Do you mind, sir, if we don't talk shop for five minutes?"

Late in 1937 Hobart was appointed to succeed Alan Brooke* as Director of Military Training in the War Office. In the crisis of September 1938, he was sent to Egypt, on Hore-Belisha's [q.v.] initiative and insistence, to form and command an armoured division there. On the results, it is worth recalling the verdict of General O'Connor, who commanded the Western Desert Force in the first, and brilliantly victorious, North African Campaign during the winter of 1940-41. He saw the division in the autumn of 1939 barely a year after its formation, and wrote at that time: "It is the best trained division I have ever seen". The test of war confirmed that judgment. The "Armoured Division, Egypt" achieved immortal fame under its new title of "The 7th Armoured Division".

The only shadow on the triumph, as many members of the division felt, was that the man who had originally trained it to such a high pitch of manoeuvring ability had been removed from command a year earlier—because his ideas of how armoured troops should be handled, and what they could achieve on their own, had been regarded with doubt and dislike by more conservative superiors.

In the dark months of May-June 1940, when the German armoured forces broke through the Allies' front in the west and split their armies asunder, applying the methods that Hobart had strikingly demonstrated, he was living in retirement—though he became a private in the Home Guard. But on Churchill's* insistence he was brought back to service later in the year to form and train the new 11th Armoured Division. He trained it so well that, besides being himself recommended for command of an army if an opening came, the division eventually proved, by general acknowledgment, the best of those that took part in the advance from Normandy into Germany.

Meanwhile, the Dieppe operation in 1942 had shown the need for armour-protected breaching devices, vehicles and troops, specially designed and organized for assault on a fortified coast. After this lesson had come to be more clearly realized, the vitally important task of developing such specialized armour was entrusted to Hobart. He had been told that he was considered too old to command in the field, being now 57, but had instead been given the newly formed 79th Armoured Division to command and train. In March 1943 he was summoned to London to see the C.I.G.S., Alan Brooke, who asked him to undertake the new task of preparing what might be termed the "tin-openers". The 79th Armoured Division was to be the organization to handle these instruments, but was greatly expanded and changed in the process. It became the first and only all-armoured formation in the British Army.

In the initial stage there were four main forms of specialized armour—the D.D. (swimming tank), Crab (with flail for minesweeping), the A.V.R.E. (assault engineer), and the C.D.L. (searchlight tank with dazzle device). Later additions to Hobart's mechanized menagerie—commonly called "the funnies"—included the Crocodile (flame throwing tank), Buffalo (armoured amphibian), and the Kangaroo (armoured personnel carrier). This organ of new devices, still officially called a "division", played a vital part in the success of the Normandy landing, but a still bigger part in the final stage of the war. Quantitatively, it far exceeded the scale of any division. Qualitatively, it became the tactical key to victory.

February 21, 1957.

Professor William Herbert Hobbs, who was engaged in the teaching of geology at the universities of Wisconsin and Michigan for more than 40 years, died at Ann Arbor, Michigan, at the age of 88, on January 1, 1953.

He was one of the leading geologists of the United States. Several of his books were translated into other languages soon after they appeared, for he was a recognized authority on earthquakes and glaciers and also on winds and weather and the origin of storms. He led expeditions to Greenland and formed the conclusion that any bad weather which reached Europe had its origin there, and he was one of the first to suggest the establishment of meteorological stations in Greenland by means of which it would be possible to know in advance what kind of weather was likely to be experienced soon in the north-western districts of Europe. He put this theory forward in an interesting lecture at Copenhagen many years ago, and some of his suggestions have been followed with good results.

He was born at Worcester, Massachusetts, on July 2, 1864, and was educated at the polytechnic there, taking a degree in science in 1883. He immediately took up geology and did considerable work for the United States Geological Survey, for which he worked at intervals between 1896 and 1906, being then appointed assistant geologist of the United States. He also spent some time in post-graduate study at Johns Hopkins University, Baltimore, and at Heidelberg. In 1889 he was appointed curator of the geological museum of the University of Wisconsin. He became Assistant Professor of Mineralogy and Metallurgy in the university in 1890, and some nine years later Professor of Mineralogy and Petrology. In 1906 he moved to the University of Michigan, where he was appointed Professor of Geology and director of the geological laboratory, and he worked and lectured there until 1934, when he retired with the title of professor emeritus.

He led expeditions to Greenland in 1925 and 1930 and acted as adviser to other explorers at later dates. He was vice-president of the International Glacier Association from 1930 till 1933, a Fellow of the American Academy of Arts and Science, and its vice-president in 1932. He was president of the American Geological Association in 1931, and a leading and active member of the Geological Society of America and of the American Philosophical Society, as well as of other learned societies.

Most of his books were read by a wider circle than those interested in geological studies. They included *Earthquakes,* published in 1907, of which a German translation appeared in 1910, *Characteristics of Existing Glaciers* (1911), *Earth Features and their Meaning* (1912), *Earth Evolution and its Facial Expression* (1921), *Glacial Anticyclones* (1926), and *Exploring about the North Pole of the Winds* (1930).

Other books, of more general interest, were a study of General Leonard Wood as administrator, soldier, and citizen (1920), *Cruises along the Byways of the Pacific* (1923), and a life of Admiral Robert E. Peary, the first man to reach the North Pole, which appeared in 1936.

In 1896 he married Miss Sara K. Sale and had a daughter.

January 5, 1953.

Sir Harold Graham-Hodgson, K.C.V.O., who died on August 21, 1960, was one of Britain's leading authorities on the diagnostic use of X-rays. He was 69.

He had been Director of the X-ray Department at the Middlesex Hospital, and among the many other important posts he had held were those of Consulting Radiologist to the Royal Navy, and to the British Red Cross. In 1929, while still a young man and practically on the threshold of his career as a consultant, he was called in by the late Lord Dawson of Penn to make radiological examinations during the serious illness of King George V. He rapidly established himself as one of the leading exponents of diagnostic radiology and acquired a large consulting practice. He was chairman of the Medical Committee 1952-53, and a member of the board of governors of the Middlesex Hospital.

Harold Kingston Graham-Hodgson was born on December 5, 1890, the second son of the late Dr. George Graham-Hodgson, of Eastbourne, and was educated at Mulgrave Castle, St. Edward's School, Oxford, and Clare College, Cambridge. He received his medical training at the University of Durham and at St. Thomas's Hospital, and qualified as M.B., B.S., Durham, in 1916. He held the posts of house surgeon, house physician, and assistant resident medical officer at the Royal Victoria Infirmary, Newcastle-upon-Tyne. Before qualification he had served as a dispatch rider in France from August to December 1914, and after taking his medical degrees he held a temporary commission in the R.A.M.C., again serving in France as a regimental medical officer and being wounded. In 1918 he was appointed X-ray specialist to the 2nd Northern General Hospital at Leeds. He obtained the diploma of D.M.R.E., Cambridge, in 1923, and shortly after became radiologist to King's College Hospital, to the Hampstead and North West London Hospital, and to the Ministry of Pensions.

In 1934 he was appointed physician-in-charge of the department of X-Ray Diagnosis at the Middlesex Hospital and university teacher in radiology, his title later being changed to that of Director of the X-Ray Department. Hodgson had also been consulting radiologist to the Central London Throat, Nose and Ear Hospital, to Cray Valley Hospital, to St. John's Hospital, Twickenham, and to the Brentwood District Hospital. He was admitted M.R.C.P., London, in 1932 and was elected to the Fellowship in 1937; he was a foundation Fellow of the Faculty of Radiologists on its establishment in 1939.

He was a past president of the radiological section of the Royal Society of Medicine, a Fellow of the British Association of Radiologists, and president of the Holborn and Westminster branch of the British Medical Association. He made important contributions to the literature of his speciality, especially in connexion with the early diagnosis of cancer and with the study of bone injuries and sinusitis.

For his services during the illness of King George V he was created C.V.O. in 1929, and in 1950 he was advanced to K.C.V.O.

He was twice married; first in 1917 to Winifred Elizabeth, daughter of George Jenkins, of Newcastle-upon-Tyne, and secondly in 1943 to Rosa Dorothy, widow of Frank L. Hallam. There were a son and a daughter of the first marriage.

August 22, 1960.

Sir Robert Hodgson, K.C.M.G., K.B.E., died in hospital in London on October 18, 1956 at the age of 82.

He went to Russia in 1919 as Commercial Counsellor, and in 1924 his post was changed to that of British Agent and Chargé d'Affaires, a post he held until 1927. After an interval as Minister to Albania, he was sent to Spain as the first British representative to General Franco*; and that he should have made a success as a representative to Governments so widely different in ideologies and methods entitles him to honourable distinction in the diplomatic annals of his time.

Robert MacLeod Hodgson was born on February 25, 1874, the eldest son of the Venerable Robert Hodgson, Archdeacon of Stafford, and was educated at Radley and Trinity College, Oxford. On entering the Consular Service in 1901, his first post was that of Vice-Consul at Marseilles, and he was there until 1907, when he was transferred in a similar capacity to Vladivostok. He was promoted Consul in 1911. There he remained until 1919, when he entered upon the most important phase of his career as head of the British Trade Mission to Russia. He found himself in charge of a heterogeneous collection of Englishmen, over a dozen in all, most of whom had little in common, save some previous knowledge of the country. The fact that his wife was Russian probably eased social relations to some extent with her countrymen. Considerable tact was required to keep his staff relatively content and efficient during those years, in the capital of communism, where there were no ordinary society and few possibilities of recreation.

Hodgson's common sense, a sense of humour, and a power of quiet irony, were equal to the task, and those who served him will bear grateful tribute to his memory. More unexpected and strange was the appreciation of Hodgson's indisputable honesty by the leaders of Soviet Russia with whom he had official contact. But he had no easy task. His movements and those of his staff were closely watched and his house and office were always under the observation of spies. Indeed, the espionage practised on his visitors became so serious that when the Russian Mission was in London in 1924 the British Government felt constrained to draw official attention to the matter.

That year Hodgson was promoted to be Chargé d'Affaires. At the time of the break in diplomatic relations in 1927 Hodgson issued a long statement forcibly repudiating the allegations emanating from Moscow of illicit practices by members of the British Mission. These included a charge that the Vice-Consul was involved in plots to blow up the Kremlin and the Grand Theatre, and were so grotesquely absurd that no good purpose could be served by attempting to disprove them.

The purpose of Hodgson's mission to Russia having been served, he was appointed Minister Plenipotentiary at Durazzo, Albania, and there he remained until 1936, when he had intended to retire from the service. However, in November 1937 he was appointed to be the first Chief British Agent to Nationalist Spain, and took up his headquarters at Burgos; and he was made Chargé d'Affaires in February 1939, thereby establishing normal diplomatic relations with the Spanish Government. These were formally cemented shortly by the appointment of Sir Maurice Peterson [q.v.] as British Ambassador; and Hodgson, his mission completed, returned to England in final retirement from diplomacy.

For 18 months he had worked for a better understanding between the British Government and the Nationalist authorities. The task was one of extreme difficulty, not only because his official position was unusual, but also because he was the representative of a nation which, though neutral as regards the civil war then raging, yet was sharply divided upon the merits of the struggle. As in Russia, his tact and good sense contributed to the success of his mission, and he left the country with the good wishes of all with whom he came into contact.

With General Franco his personal relations

seem to have been rather more cordial than Lord Templewood [q.v.] experienced later on. On his return to England he was made a K.C.M.G. in recognition of his services, having been made a K.B.E. in 1925. He was Foreign Office adviser to the Censorship service from 1941 to 1943 and chairman of the council of the School of Slavonic and Eastern European Studies from 1942 to 1944.

He married in 1920 Olga, daughter of Paul Bellavin, and they had one son.

October 19, 1956.

J. L. Hodson, O.B.E., whose novels and plays delighted a large public for many years, died on August 28, 1956 in London, the day after his sixty-fifth birthday.

James Lansdale Hodson was born at Hazlehurst, Lancashire, on August 27, 1891. At the age of 22 he joined the staff of the *Daily Mail,* but his career there was interrupted by the 1914-18 War in which he served first in the ranks of the 3rd Public Schools Battalion, then as a sub-lieutenant in the Royal Naval Division, and finally in the special intelligence branch of the Ministry of Munitions. Having rejoined the staff of the *Daily Mail* after demobilization he quickly made his way, so that in 1924 he was appointed news editor for the northern editions of the paper.

While in the post he took advantage of the opportunity not merely to widen and deepen his knowledge of his native Lancashire, but also to gain a wonderful store of learning concerning the whole industrial north. This bore fruit in his first play, *The Boom,* which was presented at Manchester in 1925 by the Rusholme Repertory Theatre, a merciless satire on the ugly figures thrown up by the post-war boom in Lancashire. If nothing else, the play exhibited Hodson's remarkable talents as a reporter.

The novel *Grey Dawn—Red Night,* largely autobiographical, appeared in 1929, followed by another in 1932, *North Wind,* in which the autobiography is almost as marked. By that time Hodson had left the staff of the *Daily Mail* and had begun to contribute to a number of newspapers, for which he continued to write for many years. Among these were the *News Chronicle* and the *Sunday Times. Harvest in the North* (1934) was in a sense the counterpart to *The Boom,* for it depicted the depression which overtook Lancashire after the boom, and Hodson quickly adapted the novel to the stage. The play was produced at the Embassy Theatre in London. He returned to the theme in *God's in His Heaven* (1935) and then in 1936 an adaptation for the stage of *Grey Dawn—Red Night* was presented at the Queen's Theatre, London.

Our Two Englands, which was published in the same year, was an admirable piece of reporting, which contrasted not Disraeli's "two nations" but the conditions of the depressed northern industrial areas with the more hopeful southern and western regions of England. By this time Hodson had become a practised and sympathetic novelist with a true eye for character and a fine sense of construction. His next two novels, *Carnival at Blackport* and *Jonathan North,* exhibited his quality to advantage.

Then another war supervened and provided him with material for a vivid diary of events culled not only from his own experiences as a war correspondent but as one of the journalists employed in the making of official films and publications for the Ministry of Information.

The war over, he turned again to the novel and in *English Family* presented a slightly idealized picture of England at the time of Dunkirk. *Morning Star* appeared in 1951 and an adaptation of the novel is due to be broadcast by the B.B.C. television service next Sunday. In *Return to the Wood* he portrays an old soldier who goes back to France to visit the battlefields of the 1914-18 War and describes to his companions the slaughter he had lived through. It appeared just 18 months ago and was an appropriate swan-song for one to whom the experiences of two wars remained vivid to the end.

August 29, 1956.

Gerard Hoffnung died suddenly on September 28, 1959. He was 34.

The son of Ludwig Hoffnung, he was born on March 22, 1925, and educated at Highgate School and the Harrow School of Arts. He taught art for a time first at Stamford and then at Harrow, and then spread his wings in the world of magazines and newspapers, contributing to *Punch* and to other British, Continental, and American publications.

Hoffnung's lineage as an artist was derived from the German graphic artists he admired as a very young man, contributors to the German satirical magazine *Simplicissimus,* such as Gulbranson and others of the pre-Hitler war. The artist of his own *genre* that he respected most deeply was Walter Trier. Their styles were different, Hoffnung had much higher spirits and was less lyrical but many of their affections were the same. Children and animals both drew out their happiest creations. Trier once told young Hoffnung that he would never make an artist, a story that Hoffnung always told rather wistfully.

In fact Hoffnung was one of the very best of his generation. His range was considerable. Although he never made serious studies he touched every humorous mood from the sly chuckle, through the belly laugh (his own was highly individual) to something rather hysterical and strange.

His first drawings in print were markedly Teutonic, a world of laughter close to nightmare. These bizarre creations changed over the years into a more habitable world. The mushrooms were still there, but the little people jumped out from under them less often. The line relaxed until it became an unselfconscious act, like laughter. No man could more easily create laughter. Cartoonists are usually rather doleful company. Hoffnung in private was inseparable from his public self.

Of a private passion for music, Gerard Hoffnung came close, in his last years, to making a second career. His instrument was the tuba, and this he played at various times in public, in Vaughan Williams's [q.v.] tuba concerto and in a piece which Francis Chagrin wrote for him to play in a television programme. But beyond the act of making music, Hoffnung had an extensive knowledge of the repertory of music in general.

The inspiration of this knowledge was carried into his drawings, at first spasmodically, then in the various books of musical cartoons, beginning with *The Maestro,* in which an old theme by Wilhelm Busch was reworked, altogether freshly, and culminating in *The Hoffnung Musical Festival.* This book itself inspired a new project in which Hoffnung brought the spirit of his musical cartoons to life in the concert hall, with the help of composers and performers who shared his vision of fallible humanity in the service of an art too noble even for its creators. The first Hoffnung concert in the Festival Hall in 1956 was much preoccupied with the humour of strange musical instruments; it was immensely successful, so much so that its successor in 1958 had to be given four times, and in this Hoffnung inspired a wider view of wit and humour in music.

Hoffnung was among other things an artist, a musician, a linguist, a raconteur, a Quaker, a *bon viveur,* a prison visitor, and a mime. It is usual to say that a man has left behind a gap that cannot be filled. For Gerard Hoffnung there would be needed a handful of men, all of them greatly gifted.

September 29, 1959.

Josef Casimir Hofmann, the pianist and composer, died in a Los Angeles nursing home on February 16, 1957.

The death of this Polish-American pianist at the advanced age of 81 recalls the great age of piano playing that began with Liszt and continued for the rest of the nineteenth century. We do not lack virtuosity today but the older pianists of the central European tradition combined a prodigious technique with a grand manner that lent a touch of the fabulous to their playing. Hofmann began as a prodigy and for more than 50 years maintained an international reputation as "one of the top pianists of the world".

Josef Casimir Hofmann was born at Kracow on January 20, 1876. He was taught by his father; as a boy was commended by the great Anton Rubinstein; appeared with the Berlin Philharmonic Orchestra at the age of nine; and went on to a tour of Europe. He went to America in 1887 and played at the Metropolitan Opera House. Fifty years later he gave a jubilee recital on the same stage and a few months later went to London where he gave a jubilee concert at Queen's Hall, playing the A flat Valse and the E flat Nocturne of Chopin which he had played at his first recital.

The Society for Prevention of Cruelty to Children had intervened at the end of his first American tour on the ground of the strain incurred by giving 52 concerts in 10 weeks. The family then returned to Europe and settled in Berlin, where the boy concentrated on serious study. He worked at the piano with his father, with Moszkowski, and in 1892 with Anton Rubinstein. In 1894 he went to the United States again and lived there till his death, becoming naturalized in 1926. In that year he became director of the Curtis Institute of Philadelphia, a post which he retained till 1938. It was the orchestra of the Curtis Institute which accompanied him in his master Rubinstein's D minor Concerto which he played at his American jubilee. At his English jubilee in April 1938 he played Beethoven's Fourth and Schumann's Concertos, and he had not been heard in Britain since. He had lived for the last 20 years in California in retirement.

An outstanding feature of his playing was an almost unbelievable variety and subtlety of tone-colour, which made his Chopin bewitching. He had an individual rhythm too, so that with these two factors he could lift together the more austere classics like late Beethoven and Brahms's Handel Variations to a kind of sublime power and beauty. He could also achieve transcendence with his dazzling virtuosity which he would fling at his audience in such a *tour de force* as Godowsky's paraphrase of *Die Fledermaus* or Chopin's A flat Valse in thirds. Nevertheless he had small hands, and so never attempted Rachmaninov's Third Concerto, which was dedicated to him.

As a composer Hofmann published under the pseudonym of Michel Dvorsky. Of his works *Chromaticon* (1916) was a dialogue for piano and orchestra which he played at his New York jubilee concert. He also had two sonatas, two suites and a set of variations for piano to his credit.

As a teacher he published a couple of handbooks. Among his pupils at the Curtis Institute was Shura Cherkassky. Among his hobbies was the devising of motor car accessories.

February 19, 1957.

Josef Holbrooke, the composer, died at his home at Hampstead on August 5, 1958, a month after his eightieth birthday.

One of a family of six children, he was born at Croydon. His musical ability was evident when he was a child and at the age of 15 he was sent to the Royal Academy of Music where he studied under Corder for composition and Westlake for pianoforte.

When he left the academy he had something of a struggle to make his way; his father was a musician who used to play the piano at music halls; Holbrooke in deputizing on occasions for his father became acquainted with many comic singers and some of his first earnings came through setting comic verse to music.

Composition, not interpretation, was what he set his heart upon and he did his best to avoid executive work, though this meant that he was often hungry, in order to have more time to write music. His chief public appearances as a pianist occurred in the several series of chamber concerts he gave in London and elsewhere to introduce British music. In this cause he was untiring and generous, for he gave the concerts through many seasons for the benefit of his contemporaries' work as well as his own.

He first came prominently before the public as a composer for orchestra, and his symphonic poem "The Raven" (after Edgar Allan Poe, whose works he found much to his taste) was played at a Crystal Palace Saturday concert in 1900. His grasp of the orchestra as a means of expression attracted immediate attention and other pieces followed. Those which may be classed as landmarks were "Queen Mab", performed at Leeds in 1904; "The Bells" (where he drew again on Poe), played for the first time at Birmingham two years later; and "Apollo and the Seaman", first heard at Queen's Hall in 1908. This was a symphony on a poem by Herbert Trench and at the first performance the poem was shown to the audience on lantern slides. The occasion is amusingly described by Sir Thomas Beecham* in *A Mingled Chime.*

Holbrooke first became known as composer of opera when his *Pierrot and Pierrette,* with words by Walter Grogan, was conducted by himself at His Majesty's Theatre on November 11, 1909. There followed a more ambitious plan, a trilogy concerned with Welsh legends, *The Cauldron of Annwyn,* with libretto by T. E. Ellis (Lord Howard de Walden, who was an enthusiastic patron of Holbrooke's art). Two of the three works appeared early. *The Children of Don* was first given at the London Opera House in June 1912, and *Dylan, Son of the Wave,* at Drury Lane two years later. The third, *Bronwen,* was not performed until 1929. *The Children of Don* was given performances at the Volksoper, Vienna, under Weingartner's direction, and at Salzburg in 1923.

Holbrooke's was an exuberant, versatile talent, and his output particularly of chamber music was huge. Though widely performed, his music never became widely familiar, but "Prom" audiences have always had a special affection for his variations on "Three Blind Mice".

August 7, 1958.

Dr. Charles Holden, who died on May 1, 1960 at the age of 84, was by general consent one of the most distinguished English architects of the period between the wars. He left more of his mark on the appearance of London than any other architect of modern times has done.

His principal works are the London University buildings in Bloomsbury and the headquarters of London Transport at St. James's Park. He combined sanity and moderation in design with a spirit of adventure, and as an assessor in competitions his judgment was widely respected.

Holden was a short, serious and quiet man. He was born at Bolton in 1875, educated at Manchester Technical School and Manchester School of Art, and articled to E. W. Leeson of that city. Returning to Bolton he worked with Jonathan Simpson, mainly designing, as he said, "public houses and private houses". About 1898 he went to London as assistant to C. R. Ashbee, and also studied at the Royal Academy architectural school, entering into partnership with Percy Adams a few years later.

Most, if not all, of Holden's work was done as a member of the firm of Adams, Holden and Pearson, of which he became senior partner on the death of Adams. In such cases it is not easy to define the individual contribution, but it may be said that Holden was preeminently the designer of the firm and that the aesthetic quality of their work was mainly due to him. He excelled above all in preserving the spirit of classical architecture when circumstances required that the letter, in the shape of classical features, should be disregarded. Nobody better than he could strip a classical design to its essentials without leaving it looking naked.

The earliest work in which he was engaged was hospital building, examples of which are the Newcastle Royal Infirmary and the King Edward VII Sanatorium, Midhurst. Then followed two important buildings in Bristol—the Royal Infirmary and the Central Reference Library—to which was added later the Clifton College Memorial Gateway. The infirmary, on a hilly site with terraced gardens, was one of the earliest examples in Britain of the simple block-like structure, relying for its architectural effect on mass and proportion, which has become characteristic of the urban scene.

The Bristol library is remarkable for its effective solution of an exceedingly difficult problem: to reconcile direct provision for the practical requirements of a modern reference library with architectural recognition of the Norman gateway of the Cathedral, with a late Gothic superstructure, to which the library is actually attached.

The first work of the firm to excite national interest, partly retrospective on account of the controversy which followed, was the British Medical Association Building (later the offices of the Southern Rhodesian Government) at the corner of Agar Street and the Strand. It was also the first work to illustrate what came to be characteristic of Holden as a designer: his bold and independent employment of sculpture as an integral part of the architectural scheme. The controversy, it need hardly be said, raged round the figures by [Sir] Jacob Epstein [q.v.] representing the different ages of man.

Holden's first architectural triumph in the wider sense was the Underground, now London Passenger Transport, headquarters, St. James's Park, which in 1929 was awarded the London architecture medal of the Royal Institute of British Architects. This building was also the first to demonstrate Holden's peculiar genius as a planner and one of the earliest, if not the earliest, in Britain to adopt a form of plan, the cruciform, abolishing the central well in favour of the maximum of light and air in the re-entrant angles, which has now become common for large city blocks.

That the Underground building helped in forming a tradition cannot be questioned. Holden's association with London Transport was particularly happy, as may be seen in such reconstructions as Piccadilly and Knightsbridge, and in the new stations on the Tube extensions, which are as charming in detail as they are convenient to the movements of those using them.

The crowning achievement of Holden's career was the University of London building, for which he was appointed architect in 1931. The foundation-stone was laid by King George V—who described the design as "exactly like a battleship"—in 1933. In recognition of purpose, complete advantage of site, relationship to the British Museum, and simple dignity of design, this great building sums up all that Holden had of knowledge, judgment and taste.

In a talk to the R.I.B.A. in 1938, Holden described the meaning and evolution of the design. In this work, he said, was written a faith, a philosophy, and an aesthetic principle, combined. Many plans were tried out and abandoned, and it was finally decided that the best form in view of future requirements was that of a "spine with ribs", with the central axis of the spine in line with that of the British Museum, leaving open spaces on the two flanks. This arrangement had the practical advantage of isolating the university buildings, and thus greatly reducing traffic noises and vibrations. It was most exciting, said Holden, when the elevation was first projected up from the plan, to find that the building "had almost designed itself". That, granted enlightened control of the natural growth, is certainly the effect of the building, which is as full of subtleties in detail, in the fenestration for example, as it is imposing in the general mass.

Holden was architectural and planning consultant to Edinburgh University and to the London County Council for its development of the South Bank site. He also prepared, with Sir William Holford [Lord Holford*], a reconstruction plan for the City of London which was later incorporated, with modifications, in the London County Development Plan.

His designs in later years did not always escape professional criticism—his design, for instance, for the offices of the English Electric Company on the site of the old Gaiety Theatre, which was chosen by the company in preference to the winner of the competition.

He became associate of the R.I.B.A. in 1906, fellow in 1921—having won the Godwin Bursary in 1913—and vice-president for the years 1935-37. In 1936 he was awarded the Royal Gold Medal of the R.I.B.A., which is the highest professional honour that can be given to an architect in Britain. He was a member of the Royal Fine Art Commission from 1933 to 1947, and in 1918 he was appointed principal architect to the Imperial War Graves Commission, being responsible for the layout of war cemeteries at Boulogne, Wimereux, Corbin, Louvencourt, Forceville, and elsewhere. He received honorary doctorates of Manchester and London Universities.

He married Margaret, daughter of J. C. Macdonald. She died in 1954.

May 2, 1960.

Billie Holiday, the distinguished coloured jazz singer, died in New York on July 17, 1959. She was 44.

She was born at Baltimore, Maryland, on April 7, 1915, and her real name was Eleanora Fagan. She was an illegitimate child, and went through a youth of extraordinary difficulty and privation (chronicled in the early chapters of her autobiography *Lady Sings the Blues*) before she started singing in a New York bar at the age of 15. She was an instantaneous success, and from that time on became a popular performer in a number of Harlem clubs, until she was signed to make records in about 1934. Her first records were with Benny Goodman, but in 1935 she made a number as vocalist with Teddy Wilson's band. They brought her fame throughout America, and from that time on she always recorded as a star vocalist.

In 1937 she made a number of appearances with Count Basie's band, and the next year with Artie Shaw's. At the same time she took up acting in a small way, playing in "soap-opera" series on the radio and in a number of short films, but by the end of the 1930s she had established herself as one of the really outstanding jazz vocalists of her generation, and so she remained, in spite of a troubled and tempestuous private life, for the next 20 years. In 1954 she made her first trip to Europe, touring eight Continental countries with a group of American jazz musicians before going as a solo performer to Britain, where she scored one of the biggest triumphs of her career.

Her manner of singing was highly individual and much imitated in its inclination towards the instrumental rather than the vocal in technique, but she never established herself with the more strictly theoretical of jazz enthusiasts.

Rather, one might say, did she resemble that otherwise quite dissimilar artist, Ella Fitzgerald, in that she was at her best not so much in the field of jazz itself, but in bringing the best qualities of jazz technique to bear on the better type of popular music: her versions of songs like *Night and Day, The Man I Love, Some Other Spring* or *Travellin' Light* have the rhythmic tension and precision of jazz and the vibrant intensity of the blues, but are not themselves jazz in any real sense.

In later years she had little voice left, by conventional standards, but her technical mastery was complete, and many of her most accomplished and moving records date from this time.

July 18, 1959.

Lieutenant-Colonel Henry Lewis Hollis, secretary of the Cutty Sark Society, died suddenly in London on November 15, 1959. He was 70. As a young man he was a well-known cricketer and Rugby football player.

He was born and educated at Blackheath, and at the beginning of the First World War he joined the Artists' Rifles, later receiving a commission in The Green Howards. He left the Army at the end of the war and for a short period was on the Stock Exchange. He early became interested, however, in the encouragement of the traditional English forms of sport for the younger generation and was connected first with the Westminster Boys' Club and then with the National Association of Boys' Clubs. During the Second World War he returned to the Army, becoming second-in-command of one of the War Office selection boards, and holding the rank of lieutenant-colonel.

When the war ended he resumed his duties as Chief Officer of the London and Greater London Playing Fields Association, to which he had been appointed in 1939. He gave up this appointment in 1951 and went on the executive committee, on which he sat until his death.

Hollis became a member of the National Playing Fields Association Council and Executive in 1948, and in 1950 was appointed chairman of their general purposes sub-committee.

In 1953 Hollis became secretary of the Cutty Sark Society and played a leading part in the organization of the society and the raising of the funds necessary for the restoration of this historic tea clipper and her preservation at Greenwich. It was he who made all the arrangements for the Queen's visit when she opened the ship to the public on June 25, 1957.

He was a keen cricketer and captained Kent Second XI for many years. He also played for Blackheath, and one of his proudest possessions was a cricket ball, appropriately inscribed, recording his prowess in taking all 10 wickets for 20 runs in a club match. He was a great Rugby football enthusiast, played for the County of Kent and also for Blackheath, and, though he never got his cap, he was reserve for England in a Rugby match against Scotland.

In his later years he played golf, was a member of the County Cricketers' Golfing Society, and at the time of his death was captain of the Royal Mid-Surrey Golf Club.

He was the most lovable of men, with a kindly good nature and dry sense of humour that endeared him to his wide circle of friends in all walks of life. Quietly competent in all he undertook, he sought not the bright lights of publicity for himself but found his reward in the inner satisfaction of a good job well done. The Cutty Sark Society owes much to his devoted service, and the ship herself remains a silent tribute to his work.

Hollis, who was married in 1925, leaves a widow and two sons.

November 17, 1959.

Sir Valentine Holmes, Q.C., died at his home in London on November 19, 1956 at the age of 68. He had in his day one of the largest practices at the Common Law Bar, and occupied an almost unique position there. Had it been his wish, after some 10 years' service as Junior Counsel to the Treasury, he could certainly have attained the judicial ermine, which, with his wide and accurate knowledge of law and practice, he would undoubtedly have worn with distinction.

Valentine Holmes was the son of that distinguished Irish Judge, Lord Justice Holmes, who died in 1916. He was born on July 24, 1888, and educated at Charterhouse and Trinity College, Dublin; and he was called to the Bar by both the Inner and Middle Temples in 1913. His progress was at first slow, and he used to say that from his early days he was handicapped by nervousness in court, which throughout his career he was ever fighting against. However, when once started, he soon acquired a reputation for sound legal knowledge, especially in respect of the settlement of pleadings and the interlocutory steps to be taken before the hearing of the action, and his practice was soon one of the largest at the Common Law Bar.

It was therefore no surprise when in 1935 the Attorney General nominated him as Junior Common Law Counsel to the Treasury, a post which has almost invariably carried the reversion to a seat on the Bench. At the same time he continued to carry on a large business for private clients.

However in 1945, rather to the surprise of the Bar, Holmes resigned the post and took silk. He quickly became one of the most sought-after leaders of his day, and during his last years at the Bar, especially in libel cases, few advocates were more prominently in the public eye. In these actions, when brought against the press, he usually appeared for the defendants. Soon after he took silk he appeared for that ancient newspaper *The Justice of the Peace* in an action for libel brought by a photographer on *The Daily Mirror* staff, arising out of the plaintiff forcing his way into a private house on the occasion of a wedding. Holmes's cross-examination was a brilliant performance, and the judgment of Justice Hilbery for the defendants laid down with emphasis the standard that decency required from press reporters and their editors.

His practice was by no means confined to any class of litigation or any branch of the courts, and he was even retained to appear in police courts in matters involving legal rights of importance. He must have refused as much work as he was able to undertake. He lived for it, and weekends and Bank Holidays would find him in chambers, sometimes for 18 hours a day.

Holmes was by no means a showy advocate; indeed, at first sight, perhaps owing to the handicap referred to, he might have appeared unimpressive, but his wide knowledge of law, the thoroughness with which his cases were prepared, and the absolute integrity with which he presented them, made him an advocate of a high order and a dangerous opponent. As a cross-examiner, there was nothing theatrical about him, and without bullying he would neatly get from a witness just what he wanted, and leave it at that. His retirement from the Bar, stated to be for reasons of health, in 1949 was a matter of real regret to his many professional and lay clients, and to his fellow members, among whom he was deservedly popular.

Holmes's arduous profession left little room for recreation, but after a hard day's work he and his clerk would often be seen going to "the dogs" at the White City, and during the vacations he found amusement in the casinos at Deauville and other Continental resorts.

In 1947 he made an inquiry for the governors of the B.B.C. into allegations of bribery and corruption against certain members of the staff, and as a result he found that, though a woman official had acted very unwisely, there was no solid basis for the general bribery charges.

He was a Bencher of the Inner Temple, and was knighted in 1946. By a happy coincidence his brother, Sir Hugh Holmes, who had been Procurator of the Mixed Court of Appeal in Egypt, received the accolade of knighthood at the same investiture.

He married in 1914 Gwendolen Armstrong, of Dublin. There were a son and daughter of the marriage.

November 20, 1956.

Dr. Eric John Holmyard, who had a distinguished career as a teacher, historian, and interpreter of science, died at Clevedon on October 13, 1959 at the age of 68.

He was born in Somerset—a county which he loved and where he spent a great part of his life—and was educated at Sexey's School, Bruton, and Sidney Sussex College, Cambridge. He early felt that teaching was his vocation: for a short time (1917-19) he was science master at Marlborough and then was appointed Head of the Science Department at Clifton College, where he remained until shortly after the outbreak of the last war. In 1926 he was chairman of the Science Masters' Association.

He not only established a very successful school of science at Clifton but, through a series of textbooks of a then novel type, had a powerful influence on the teaching of science generally: there can be few students of science, and especially of chemistry, who have not at one time or another read his books, several of which are still widely used. All these books, and indeed virtually all his extensive writings, reflect his deep interest in the history of science, for he was a firm believer in the value of the historical approach. In this field he rapidly established an international reputation, especially as an authority on alchemy in Islam, to study which he taught himself Arabic. Much of his learning in this field was distilled into his *Alchemy,* which appeared as a Pelican book in 1957. The University of Bristol acknowledged his important contributions to scholarship by the award of its D.Litt. degree in 1928.

Until recently he was chairman of the Society for the Study of Alchemy and Early Chemistry and he was Membre Correspondant de l'Académie Internationale de l'Histoire des Sciences. His success as a writer on science led to many calls upon him as a consultant; among such appointments was that of science editor to *Everyman's Encyclopaedia.*

A new phase in Holmyard's career began in 1940, when he joined Imperial Chemical Industries to become the first editor of its international scientific review *Endeavour,* remaining in that capacity until his retirement in 1954. That this quickly established itself throughout the world as an authoritative scientific journal is due in large measure to his wise guidance from its early stages. He took great pride in *Endeavour,* and maintained an active interest in it, as consultant, until his death. From 1950 he made a further major contribution to international scholarship as a joint editor of the five-volume *History of Technology*, the result of a collaboration between Imperial Chemical Industries and the Clarendon Press, Oxford. The final volume of this appeared in 1958; the success of this work owes much to his wide knowledge and scrupulous attention to detail.

Holmyard was of a modest and retiring disposition, and for this reason was better known through his literary work than through personal contact. To those privileged to enjoy his friendship he was an excellent host and an entertaining and knowledgeable, though never dogmatic, conversationalist. To those who sought his advice, whether on scientific matters or personal problems, he was unfailingly helpful. To the end he maintained a keen interest in the careers of his former pupils and nothing gave him greater pleasure than to learn of distinctions gained by them: that so many of them have achieved eminence in the scientific world is due in no small measure to his inspiring and vigorous training at a formative stage in their career. He will be widely missed.

In 1916 Holmyard married Ethel Elizabeth, elder daughter of Egbert C. Britten, of Midsomer Norton, by whom he had two sons; she died in 1951.

October 15, 1959.

J. M. Hone, who died on March 26, 1959 at the age of 77, had established for himself a foremost place among Irish biographers and critics. In many ways a characteristic product of the historic Anglo-Irish tradition and outlook, which he traced through Swift and Berkeley, he contributed as editor and biographer to the renaissance of Irish letters in this century. All his critical studies, except his book on Henry Tonks, dealt with the Anglo-Irish figures.

Joseph Maunsell Hone was born on February 8, 1882, the son of William Hone, of Killiney, co. Dublin. He came of a family which has given Ireland four outstanding artists. The eighteenth-century and nineteenth-century Nathaniel Hones were landscape painters, and Horace Hone was a miniaturist. In our own day his sister, Evie Hone, was well known outside Ireland for her stained-glass windows, especially that in the chapel at Eton College.

Hone was educated at Cheam, Wellington, and Cambridge. These years brought out in him the family love of cricket, which lasted throughout his life. Playing for Wellington as a bowler, he became better known in Irish cricket as a batsman, particularly with the celebrated Woodbrook club. A history of Irish cricket published in 1957 by W. P. Hone draws largely upon his brother's recollections and experience.

As a young man Hone was for a time a partner in a Dublin publishing house and edited a periodical, *The Shanachie*, one of a number of lively journals appearing before the First World War, when Irish occasional writing had a courage and independence not easy to parallel to-day. Shaw, Yeats, Lord Dunsany [q.v.], "George A. Birmingham", and other Irish writers were among his contributors. An expedition to Persia and the Caucasus with Page L. Dickinson in the early years of the century led to a travel book, *Persia in Revolution.*

Hone, the biographer of the eighteenth-century golden age in Ireland, settled down to live in Dublin in that second golden age, when a group of brilliant writers tried, in his words, to bring the aristocratic and Protestant tradition of Swift, Berkeley and Burke into line with modern "Gaelic" nationalism. Ireland had not seemed too small a stage for their endeavours.

The Irish contemporaries of whom Hone wrote all left their mark on Irish letters, but the new Ireland in no way corresponded to their hopes. Writing in 1932, with 10 years of self-government as his theme, Hone was conscious of loss. Ireland no longer exercised political influence as the centre of a great empire, and her strategic importance was diminishing. At home there was no union of hearts.

Hone must have started with some misgiving on his life of George Moore, for Moore's autobiographical trilogy is a scarcely rivalled masterpiece of self-portraiture as well as a day-to-day chronicle of the Irish literary renaissance. Yet Hone's biography and its sequel, *The Moores of Moore Hall,* are works of art in their own right. With what tenderness and justice has he delineated that lonely incorruptible figure, Colonel Maurice Moore, the Irish Senator, who was at once too Irish and not Irish enough to suit his fastidious and tyrannical brother George!

To some his biography of Yeats is not so satisfying a work. When Hone published it in 1944 insufficient time had elapsed for the character and achievement of the poet to be seen in perspective. Yet as a friend and contemporary Hone has depicted better than any other writer is likely to do the stormy Irish background of Yeats's life.

As his older friends passed from the scene Joe Hone became an isolated, though always a highly respected, figure. His tall distinguished frame, the chiselled features and the ageless blue eyes, were familiar in Stephen's Green and at the Kildare Street Club. His critical articles, written with care and constant revision, reflected the classical balance of his mind. He had been a friend of d'Annunzio, and sometimes, like Yeats, he girded at the drab respectability of Irish democracy. Yet, in spite of his occasional rantings, it would have been difficult to call him a reactionary.

He was simply an Irish gentleman, who feared the tired and timid simplifications of the recently emancipated. His own considered judgments were seldom influenced by class or creed, and admittedly he owed his good sense in part to the good fortune of his upbringing. This he knew and he never had any hesitation in acknowledging it.

Hone married in 1911 Vera Brewster, an American of great beauty, and famous both for her caustic wit and for her tireless devotion. He is survived by two sons and a daughter.

March 28, 1959.

Arthur Honegger, who died at his home in Paris on November 27, 1955 at the age of 63, was a composer who first became prominent as a member of the group known as *Les Six,* but, as he developed, his mind moved away from the aesthetic tenets of the group to a deeper expressiveness.

Arthur Honegger was born at Le Havre on March 10, 1892, the son of a Swiss business man established in that French port. He began his musical training in Paris with R. C. Martin for harmony and Capet for the violin. He then spent some two years at the Conservatoire at Zürich and returned to Paris in 1912 to study harmony, counter-point, and fugue under Gédalge and Widor and conducting under Vincent d'Indy. This mixture of Gallic and Germanic influences enriched his personality and gave distinction to his art, but, as in the somewhat similar case of Busoni, it was also a source of distraction. He was primarily an abstract musician expressing himself most amply in chamber music and a few essays in the form of symphony and concerto. But he is best known outside France for his oratorio *Le roi David* and his piece of programme music, "Pacific 231", inspired by a railway engine.

In much of his abstract music an austere contrapuntal style, which he derived from his master, Vincent d'Indy, is offset by movements that have been described as witty and charming and expressed sometimes in the insubordinations and paradoxes of *Les Six.* An important side of his work unknown outside France is his incidental music for plays—*Le roi David* was first conceived as such for the play by the Swiss playwright René Morax—by Rolland, Gide [q.v.], Cocteau*, and others.

This last is the category to which *Jeanne d'Arc au Bûcher* belongs, another, and larger, essay in the form of *Le roi David* involving spoken dialogue and, in this case, spectacle. This was given in London, in broadcast and concert forms, by the B.B.C. in 1947 and 1948, when the impression it made was rather of cleverness than of the compassion which Joan of Arc should evoke, though the ultimate responsibility for this hybrid art rests no doubt with the author, Paul Claude [q.v.]. Cleverness is the mark, too, of the three symphonic pieces, "Pacific 231", "Rugby", and "No. 3" (which is without programme), but Honegger's stature is greater than is implied in the label "clever French".

Although he started out with *Les Six* he soon, after marrying one of their adherents, the composer Andrée Vaurabourg, discarded their aesthetic tenets and allowed his feeling for traditional forms and a deeper expressiveness to find expression. His output, therefore, contains even a chorale and fugue for organ, as well as pieces for piano in conventional forms or with characteristic titles in the romantic manner.

The last war drove him to seek the expression of deeper feelings specifically in the *Symphonie liturgique* and by implication in the *Symphony for Strings.* If not all of this could be called successful in the sense of capturing public attention, nor proclaim itself clearly as the work of a single, immediately recognizable, mind, it reveals a personality of broad sympathies, representative of his times and contributing much of value to twentieth-century music.

November 29, 1955.

Professor Ernest Albert Hooton, the well-known anthropologist, died suddenly at his home in Boston, Massachusetts, on May 3, 1954, at the age of 66.

Born at Clemansville, Wisconsin, on November 20, 1887, he was the son of a Methodist Minister, and showed from early years the promise of that originality of mind which his later career brought to fruition. He graduated at the Lawrence College, Appleton, in 1907, and then proceeded to Wisconsin University, whence he was selected as a Rhodes Scholar in 1910 just before he obtained his Doctorate in Philosophy. He entered University College, Oxford, where he gave up his classical studies in favour of anthropology, to which the rest of his life was to be devoted. He showed such remarkable promise on the physical and the cultural sides of this branch of learning that even before he had taken the Oxford Diploma and his B.Litt. he was selected by Harvard University as an instructor. For the remainder of his life he was to work there, in posts of ever-increasing responsibility.

He was a painstaking and scientific field investigator. His study of the ancient inhabitants of the Canary Islands was followed by his remarkable investigation of the Pecos Indians; but all the time he was accumulating material which he was to use in the wider fields of sociology and anthropometric measurement. The fame which at length came to him throughout the United States as "Hooton of Harvard" was due quite as much to his wicked wit, which shocked and delighted generation after generation of his students, and convulsed with indignation the more sedate members of the general public, as to his outstanding services to the organization of scientific anthropological studies throughout the country.

He was a prolific, though not a facile writer, and all his publications bear the mark of sound reflection, even when their serious purpose was partly disguised by the whimsical mode of expression which he favoured as a vehicle for some of his profoundest observations. *Up from the Apes* (1931) and *Men, Apes and Morons* (1937) were widely sold, and brought his theories home to many to whom current anthropological literature would otherwise have been a sealed book. His provocative titles, such as *Why Men Behave like Apes and Vice Versa* (1940) and *Man's Poor Relations* (1942), were mistaken by some as manifesting a flippancy of mind unworthy of so distinguished a scholar; but in fact they were deliberately chosen to attract attention to truths which he believed to be vital for the wellbeing of his country, and, indeed, of the whole human race, and in fact his style has influenced the writing of most of the younger anthropologists. His last essay, *Physical Anthropology of the Irish,* a report on a Harvard expedition to Ireland in the 1930s, is in process of publication.

Hooton never retired from the active control of the great department which he had done so much to build up for Harvard: he died, as he would have wished, in harness. The heart attack which killed him came on just as he had returned to his home from lecturing. He will long be remembered with affection by his many American and British friends, to whom his constant kindness of heart, his wit, and his impish humour have been for many years a perpetual joy. Cambridge, Massachusetts will not seem the same now that that long, shambling figure, with the eyes which twinkled so brightly behind the great spectacles, no longer treads its streets.

He married in 1915 Miss Mary Beidler Camp, who survives him, together with two sons and a daughter of the marriage.

May 5, 1954.

Victor Hope—See **Linlithgow.**

Sir Rhys Hopkin Morris—See **Morris.**

By the death of **Lord Horder,** which occurred on August 13, 1955 at the age of 84, a severe loss is sustained not only by the profession of medicine but by British public life in general; for, though a consulting physician of the highest rank, and chairman or president of numerous medical societies, Horder did not allow his interests to be circumscribed within the bounds of his calling.

He was an accomplished and forthright speaker on a wide variety of topics, an author who wrote not only on medical matters but on larger aspects of experience. He saw very clearly the social implications and obligations of medicine; the amelioration of public health was always prominently in his mind; and he held broad, humane and modern views on the considerations of ethics necessarily involved in controversial matters like birth control, noise abatement, and cremation. A remarkable aspect of his wide outlook was shown by the publication in 1945 of a book written jointly with Dr. Harry Roberts, *The Philosophy of Jesus.*

Horder stood in that clinical tradition which, since the days of Sydenham, has been the conspicuous merit of British medicine. The tradition demands, in addition to powers of observation and deduction, a sense of a special kind which is as difficult to describe as it is easy to recognize, and which constitutes the difference between the ordinary practitioner and one whose advice and help are sought eagerly by his colleagues. The quality is compounded of shrewdness and the capacity to profit by experience; but there is in addition a faculty of understanding which, in the greatest doctors, amounts to genius.

Horder possessed the faculty of understanding and because of that possession rose to the front rank of his profession. He was a supremely good doctor; the fact that he was also business-like and quick and methodical added to rather than detracted from his merit by inspiring confidence not only in his patients but also in his professional brethren. There was nothing undependable or vague in his character and he could be counted on, at all times, to express an informed and reliable opinion. Thus, what he lacked in creative power was made good in respect of experience and wisdom.

His career was successful rather than brilliant and the key to it is to be found in his work *Essentials of Medical Diagnosis.* He knew these essentials as a craftsman knows his tools and they had become so much a part of his nature that he remained, in all his many activities, a doctor among doctors as well as a doctor among laymen. His pride was in his profession and in the great hospital with which he was so closely identified throughout his working life. Horder was pleased, certainly, by the honours, including his peerage, which were showered upon him; but these gave him less satisfaction probably, than the fact that he was a "Bart's man". He called himself a Bart's man in the tones which Scotsmen often use when speaking of their nationality. Bart's dominated his life and his thought and it is certain that his greatest joy was the reflection that he had been able to add in some measure to the lustre of his beloved hospital.

The Right Hon. Sir Thomas Jeeves Horder, first Baron Horder, of Ashford, in the county of Southampton, G.C.V.O., M.D., F.R.C.P., was born at Shaftesbury on January 7, 1871. He was taken to Swindon as a one-year-old child and spent his early years there being privately educated. His scientific and medical education took place at the University of London and at St. Bartholomew's Hospital; and he supplemented his formal biological studies by a University College correspondence course in which his papers were marked by a young tutor named H. G. Wells.

He graduated B.Sc. in 1893 and M.B. in 1898. In the following year he proceeded to the degree of M.D. and soon established himself in Harley Street. In due course he was appointed to the visiting staff of St. Bartholomew's Hospital and rose to the position of senior consultant. Quite early in his career he was called in to attend King Edward VII. An acute diagnosis then greatly enhanced his rising reputation and began his long connexion with the Royal Family which lasted for the rest of his life. He was, in addition, Physician in Ordinary to the Prince of Wales (now Duke of Windsor*) and, afterwards, to King George VI [q.v.]. During the 1914-18 War he was a captain (acting major) in the R.A.M.C. (T). He was knighted in 1918, and created baronet in 1923, the year in which he was appointed medical adviser to the Prince of Wales. Created K.C.V.O. in 1925, he was advanced to G.C.V.O. in 1938, and he was raised to the peerage in 1933.

Horder saw public health as one whole, tending towards the larger end of public happiness. Welcoming every advance in preventive medicine, he envisaged the general problem in much wider terms, and looked forward to a world which should provide certain basic things for everyone. He once summed up these desiderata as good and sufficient food, ready access to fresh air, shelter of the right type at an economic rent, leisure for recreation, freedom from noise, pre-natal care, and disposal of all bodies by the method of cremation. He was chairman of council of the Cremation Society, and a convinced opponent of ordinary burial on grounds of public health. When the Anti-Noise League was founded he became its chairman; and he often spoke out on the folly of tolerating unnecessary noise, with its devastating effect on the nervous system.

In January 1936 he retired from St. Bartholomew's Hospital under the age limit, but he remained as active as ever in his various spheres. In 1937 he published his general addresses as *Health and a Day* and spoke against the Euthanasia Bill in the House of Lords. The next year he delivered the Conway Memorial Lecture, which was published under the title of *Obscurantism.* In October 1939 he was appointed honorary consulting physician to the Ministry of Pensions, and in September 1940 he became chairman of the Committee on the Use of Public Air Raid Shelters.

Horder's work in connexion with air raid shelters was of first class importance. His native shrewdness enabled him to see not only what was wrong but also how remedies might be applied with a reasonable degree of speed. And his courage was not found wanting in the expression of his opinions. He was listened to, just as he had been listened to in his consulting room, because he spoke with an authority which needed no advertisement. In consequence he achieved a really great work which will remain one of his substantial titles to fame.

Another important wartime activity was connected with the Ministry of Food. In 1941 Lord Woolton* appointed Lord Horder as his personal adviser on medical aspects of food problems and thus he could rightly be granted a share of the praise which has on many occasions been accorded to Lord Woolton's great work during the war, when in spite of monotony the standard of the nation's diet was remarkably maintained. Lord Horder also represented this country at international conferences on food and nutritional subjects.

In spite of his very real concern for the social aspects of medicine, nowhere better manifested than in his absorbingly interesting volume of reminiscences, *Fifty Years of Medicine,* published at the end of 1952, he was an individualist of individualists in his conception of the medical man's professional status. With such an attitude, it is not surprising that he should be, as indeed he was, a determined opponent of the National Health Service, as originally outlined by Aneurin Bevan [q.v.], and his advisers. Throughout the protracted negotiations between the Ministry of Health and the medical profession, Lord Horder succeeded in exacting numerous concessions, but always regretted that they were neither numerous enough nor wide enough in scope. His chairmanship of the Fellowship for Freedom in Medicine was a method of carrying on the battle and he continued to speak and write to the end of his life in opposition to the service, which he considered could only have the effect of lowering professional standards in medicine.

In his home near Petersfield he was a gracious host, and many will treasure memories of visits to this small, dark man, with his dark moustache and twinkling, quizzical eyes, whose wide interests illuminated his quiet conversation. Nothing pleased him more than a walk round his garden, in the course of which he could expound the qualities and idiosyncrasies of the trees and plants, especially his magnificent carnations. He took a keen interest in local affairs and was especially pleased to place his small open-air theatre at the disposal of amateur players. When he was dying there was a production of *As You Like It* in progress, and he expressed the wish that it should go on.

Among his many hospital appointments were those of consulting physician at the Cancer Hospital, Fulham, chairman of the advisory committee of Mount Vernon Hospital, member of the governing body of the British Post Graduate Hospital, consulting physician to the Royal Orthopaedic Hospital, the Royal Northern Hospital, and the hospitals of Beckenham, Bury St. Edmunds, Finchley, Leatherhead and Swindon. He was a member of the Central Council of Recreative Physical Training, president of the North West London Child Guidance Society and the Fellowship of Medicine, and chairman of the Empire Rheumatism Council and the Greater London Provident Scheme for District Nursing. His interest in nursing was also shown by his chairmanship of the Nursing Reconstruction Committee set up by the Royal College of Nursing, and he showed his interest in another aspect of nursing by acting as chairman of the Society for Wireless for the Bedridden.

In 1902 he married Geraldine Rose, only daughter of Arthur Doggett. She died in 1954. They had two daughters and a son, the Hon. Thomas Mervyn Horder, born on December 8, 1911, who now succeeds to the family honours. He married in 1946, Mary Ross, younger daughter of the late Dr. W. S. McDougall.

August 15, 1955.

Lord Hore-Belisha, who died at Rheims on February 16, 1957 at the age of 63, first made his mark as Minister of Transport from 1934 to 1937, and then went to the War Office, where he initiated a series of far-reaching changes.

A man of great energy and vivid personality, Hore-Belisha reached his political zenith while he was in his forties. After his removal from the War Office in 1940 his influence was not again restored. He had frequently been at the centre of discussions of public policy and aroused strong partisan feelings. His supporters claimed for him high qualities of initiative, energy, and drive, and always thought of him as an indefatigable cutter of red tape. His detractors, on the other hand (and they were many), blamed him for taking too great a share of the limelight, for self-advertisement, and for frequent indiscretions and mismanagement.

The Right Hon. Leslie Hore-Belisha, first Baron Hore-Belisha, of Devonport in the county of Devon, was the son of J. I. Belisha, who died when the boy was five months old. He was born on September 7, 1893. In 1912 his mother made a second marriage, to Sir Adair Hore, Permanent Secretary to the Ministry of Pensions, and on this event Belisha added the new name to his own. He was educated at Clifton College and in 1913 he went up to St. John's College, Oxford. In October 1914 he enlisted as a private in the Public Schools Battalion, from which he was commissioned to the R.A.S.C. He served throughout the war, in France, Salonika, and Cyprus, being mentioned in dispatches and rising to the rank of major.

On coming down from Oxford Hore-Belisha read law, began to cultivate politics, and took up journalism, specializing in political *reportage* and gossip in the *Daily Express* and the *Sunday Express.* His political ideas were of the radical order of Liberalism, and in 1923 he won the erstwhile Conservative seat of Devonport for that party. He continued his press work successfully, and operated (with far less success, however) in the City of London, sitting on the boards of sundry companies, most of which had short and unprofitable lives. The formation of the National Government in 1931 presented him with a political opportunity which he was not slow to seize. By this time his radicalism was much abated. He led a mutiny against Lloyd George, and became the first chairman of the National Liberal Party, which supported the Government.

In July 1934 Hore-Belisha was made Minister of Transport, and it was his work in this department that made him prominent with the public. Road casualties had become a serious social problem, and Hore-Belisha set himself energetically to its solution. His measures included a new Highway Code, driving tests for motorists, a speed limit in built-up areas, and the "Belisha beacon". In October 1935 the Ministry was raised to Cabinet status and Hore-Belisha was sworn of the Privy Council.

On the resignation of Duff Cooper [Lord Norwich, q.v.] from the War Office in May 1937 Neville Chamberlain made Hore-Belisha Secretary of State for War. The menacing international situation demanded drastic measures, and Hore-Belisha, in fact, carried out some root-and-branch reforms. Younger blood was introduced into the high command; he promoted Lord Gort from far down the list to the post of C.I.G.S.; the importance of the Territorial arm, which he greatly expanded, was underlined by the appointment of its Director-General, Sir Walter Kirke, to the Army Council; and recruiting was stimulated by improvements in soldiers' pay and working conditions. He pressed forward with a policy of *la carrière ouverte aux talents,* embarking on a policy of democratization and providing opportunities for any able man to rise from the ranks to a commission. He was a good deal criticized for what was called the "purge" of the Army Council, for his conduct of the Duncan Sandys case, and for his alleged slowness in providing anti-aircraft defences. Yet he risked unpopularity, and even dismissal by urging on the Prime Minister the necessity of conscription.

With the outbreak of war in September 1939 the burden of his office increased. Under his control and direction a British Expeditionary Force was sent to France in a very short period of time. Yet on January 4, 1940, to the general surprise, Hore-Belisha resigned from the Government. Chamberlain, in fact, removed him from the War Office and offered him the Board of Trade, which he refused. The Prime Minister stated in the House of Commons that no conflict of policy had occurred. In a letter written at the time he said: "Hore-Belisha has very exceptional qualities of courage, imagination, and drive. . . . He has done more for the Army than anyone since Haldane. Unfortunately he has the defects of his qualities—partly from his impatience and eagerness, partly from a self-centredness which makes him careless of other people's feelings. . . . Nothing could be worse than perpetual friction and want of confidence between the Secretary of State and the commander-in-chief in the field".

After that Hore-Belisha resigned his chairmanship of the National Liberal Parliamentary Party in order not to implicate his party in his independent criticism of the Government's conduct of affairs. He became an advocate of an early second front to relieve pressure on the Russian armies.

In 1945 he was brought back into the Government as Minister of National Insurance in the "Caretaker" Administration, but in the general election in July he lost his seat in Parliament. In the following month he joined the Conservative Party, but his next appearance in Parliament was not to be for another nine years, when in 1954 he was created a baron. In his maiden speech in the House of Lords he suggested, with some prescience, that an alternative to the Suez Canal was required to relieve too great a dependence on a single artery of commerce.

He married, in 1944, Cynthia, daughter of Gilbert Elliot. There were no children of the marriage.

February 18, 1957.

Alexander Hore-Ruthven—See **Gowrie.**

Louis Jay Horowitz, builder of some of the best-known American sky-scrapers, died on December 3, 1956. He was 81.

Among the famous buildings for which his firm, Thompson-Starrett, were given contracts were the Woolworth Building in New York, for many years the tallest building in the world, the Lincoln Building, Gimbel Brothers' department store on Broadway, and the Hotel Waldorf Astoria.

The erection of such high buildings called for much faith and enterprise. There were times when the designs were ridiculed but Horowitz was one of the first to have faith in the possibility of tall office buildings. He himself had seen the need and set himself to supply it.

Louis Jay Horowitz was a native of Poland and was born on New Year's Day in 1875 in the small town of Chenstochowa. His parents were poor, yet he contrived to spend some time at the university there before he emigrated with his family to New York at the age of 17 in 1892. He began his life in the new land as an errand boy at a small wage but this occupation did not long satisfy him and he found greater scope for his energy and enthusiasm first as a sales clerk in a boot and shoe shop, then in a furniture business and later in an upholsterer's. His ambition and enterprise were unbounded and he was soon in business for himself.

Horowitz was quickly attracted by the possibilities of the building trade. The coming of quick means of transportation from the heart of the city to its outlying parts made him realize that much might be done in the development of empty fields often of little value near the outskirts of the city for building homes. This kind of building then started on a large scale. Horowitz saw that as the city expanded more room would be required in the commercial and business areas. That was one of the major problems of New York, for Manhattan, where all the commerce and trade of the city were concentrated, was a long narrow island shut off by wide rivers from the nearest places and the only way to extend there was upwards. Horowitz, with others, set himself to solve that problem and began the building of high blocks.

The Thompson-Starrett company, of which he became the president in 1910, was one of the biggest construction companies in the United States and carried on work in many other cities as well as in New York. Horowitz remained its president until 1928, when he became chairman of the board. While he was president he had supervised the erection of great buildings in lower Manhattan in the financial district before the war of 1914-18, but after the war the same kind of work went along on even more ambitious lines in the upper parts of the city around Forty-second Street and beyond.

During the war of 1914-18 he acted as assistant to the Chief of Ordnance of the United States Army, and in that capacity took charge of the construction of tanks for use at the front. At the same time he was director of the department of foreign relief for the American Red Cross.

He married in 1903 Miss Mary H. Decker, of Torrington, Connecticut.

December 4, 1956.

Admiral Nicholas Horthy, former Regent of Hungary, died at Estoril, Portugal, on February 9, 1957. He was 88. He had lived in Portugal since 1949 after spending the immediate post-war years in the American zone of Germany.

Born in 1868 at Kenderes, the young Horthy entered Fiume Naval College in 1882, and eight years later he was appointed a midshipman to the cruiser Taurus. At the time of the Balkan mobilization in 1912 Horthy was commanding the Habsburg and two months later he took command in the Novara, in which vessel he was destined to perform several brilliant exploits of war. His greatest exploit was the battle of Otranto, fought in May 1917. Although his squadron numbered only five vessels he bore down straight upon the large enemy convoy and succeeded in singking altogether 22 patrol boats, two destroyers, three transports, and one flying-machine.

After suppressing the naval mutiny at Cattaro in February 1918, Horthy was promoted to flag rank and later became Admiral of the Fleet. The Bolshevik seizure of Government at Budapest in 1919 gave him his next opportunity. He joined the Nationalist Government formed at Szegadin as Minister of War and on July 14 was appointed Commander-in-Chief. His position was difficult enough. If the Entente looked with horror on Bela Kun's Government it disliked the idea of a Magyar military revival. Many of the young nobles and landed gentry in the Army were hard to discipline, and when the Bolshevik Army collapsed under the Romanian attack on the Theiss many regulars and irregulars indulged in reprisals not only on communists but on those merely suspected of having supported them, while the Admiral and his better-disciplined troops chafed at Szegadin. Not until the Romanians had evacuated Budapest could he enter the capital and reorganize the shaken State.

His proclamation as Regent by no means put an end to his difficulties, but Kaiser Karl's two unsuccessful attempts to seize the throne in 1921 lightened the burden. The support which Horthy received from large sections of the populace of Budapest showed him that he had chosen a national policy. His cautiously correct attitude was not without its rewards. After the ground swell of indignation had subsided among the Czechs, Yugoslavs, and Romanians a more neighbourly spirit towards Hungary slowly grew up, and in their negotiations with the Entente Powers over such questions as reparations the Magyars were able to profit by the admitted mistakes which had been committed in Austria and Germany.

Horthy came of an old family which ranked among the smaller Hungarian nobility and it may well be that his Transylvanian origin inclined him to find in his first Prime Ministers his most sympathetic advisers in such men as Count Paul Teleki and Count Stephen Bethlen.

It was significant of Horthy's success in the guidance of his country's affairs after 1921 that in that time there was no major dispute with any of the succession states, although they were naturally ever on the lookout for the least sign of Hungarian irredentism. In March 1930 the tenth anniversary of his election to the Regency was made the occasion of popular demonstrations throughout Hungary, and a Bill expressing his country's gratitude was passed by Parliament.

In the mid-thirties Horthy made several visits abroad. He went to Austria in August 1936, the first time he had left Hungary since becoming Regent, and later journeyed to Berchtesgaden to see Hitler. In November Horthy was given a royal reception when he made a state visit to the King of Italy. The following March Hitler presented him with a splendid Mercedes car of great power.

Hungary, which dreaded and detested Soviet Russia, signed the anti-Comintern Pact in February, 1939. In June Horthy, obviously growing anxious, made a speech in favour of a conference to settle the disagreements which were bearing Europe to the edge of catastrophe and suggested the Pope as convenor. Like other proposals of this kind, however, nothing came of it, and in September the war engulfed Europe. At first Hungary, under his shrewd guidance, shocked though she was by the German attack on Poland and the Nazi pact with Russia, kept cautiously aloof. He and his Government had repeatedly made clear that they did not regard Hungarian claims as having been fully satisfied, but they allowed it to be known that while in no way abandoning their territorial demands upon Romania they had no intention of taking advantage of war conditions to try to satisfy them by force. They therefore indicated that they would hold their hand until the time came for general settlement.

In September 1940 he rode once again at the head of his troops into the Transylvanian town of Szatmar Nemet (Satu Mare). On April 6, 1941, Hungarian forces invaded Yugoslavia. On November 20 Hungary signed the German-Italian-Japanese Pact, thus siding definitely with the Axis Powers. On December 7 she, like Finland and Romania, was at war with Great Britain.

Life was indeed growing increasingly difficult and depressing for him. A direct sailor who had commanded universal confidence, Hitler's methods were entirely foreign to his character. In the spring of 1943, for instance, he met the Führer again and with him approved the text of a joint announcement to be published simultaneously in both countries. At the last moment, however, it was discovered that the version for Germany added "and its British and American allies" to a declaration to fight Bolshevism to a final victory. Hungary would not agree to this unauthorized bracketing, and issued another more laconic text of her own. In a month the strain was intensified as a result of Hitler's peremptory reiteration of a previous demand that Horthy should strictly fulfil his obligations to Germany—and particularly that he should provide her with recently recruited troops for the Russian front. This the Regent flatly refused, and he also debarred transit for German troops and material both on his railways and the Danube. In regard to the latter he had to yield; but in so far as the railways were concerned he held firm.

Hitler, however, facing a situation which was rapidly growing desperate, occupied Hungary in March 1944. Summoning Horthy to his headquarters, he demanded full military cooperation with Germany, entailing a general mobilization, the placing of it under German command, and control of communications and all other services connected with the security of his troops returning from Russia. Horthy said that the Hungarian Army was ready to do its duty and to defend Hungary, but refused the other demands. While, therefore, he was still with Hitler, the orders to seize his country went forth. Seven months later, on October 16, he issued an order of the day announcing that Hungary had asked for an armistice. Immediately there were indications that the Budapest radio station was under the control of either the Hungarian Fascists or the Germans themselves.

The following day a statement was broadcast to the effect that Horthy had "retired from the direction of the affairs of State". A few weeks later he was said to be in Germany and thereafter there was no certain news of his whereabouts until he was captured by the advancing Americans in a castle at Weilheim and taken into protective custody. He appeared at Nuremberg in March 1948 as a witness for the prosecution in the Wilhelmstrasse case, and denied that he had ever agreed to the occupation of his country by the Wehrmacht. Nine months later he left for Portugal.

February 11, 1957.

Admiral Sir Max Horton, G.C.B., D.S.O., Commander-in-Chief Western Approaches from 1942 to 1945, died in London on July 30, 1951 at the age of 67.

He probably knew more about submarines, our own and the enemy's, than any other officer of his time. In the war of 1914-18 he was the commander of submarine E.9, which in the first year of hostilities had a remarkable record of success in the destruction of German war vessels in the North Sea and Baltic. In the war of 1939-45 he was the flag officer who at a critical stage was taken from the post of head of the Submarine Service to wage war on the U-boats as Commander-in-Chief, Western Approaches.

From the organization and development of British submarine flotillas he turned to destroy those of the enemy. It was a relentless battle, with new weapons and tactics constantly being introduced on both sides. Into it Horton put all his skill and energy, and his reward came when in 1945 he formally accepted the surrender in a remote stretch of water in Northern Ireland of the remnant of the vast U-boat fleet. He retired soon afterwards, and in January 1946 was appointed to the office of Bath King of Arms, in succession to the late General Sir Walter Braithwaite.

Max Kennedy Horton was born on November 29, 1883, the son of R. J. Horton, of Minster, Thanet. He passed into the Britannia in 1898 and went to sea in 1900 as midshipman of the Majestic, Channel flagship, but from 1901 to 1903 served in the Eclipse in China. His connexion with submarines began as a sub-lieutenant in 1904, and from 1907 he commanded C.8, D.6, and E.9. In the last-named he was the first to sink a German cruiser, the Hela, in the Heligoland Bight on September 13, 1914. Three weeks later he sank the German destroyer S.116 off the River Ems. For these services he was the first submarine commander to win the D.S.O., and in December 1914 was promoted to commander. In 1915 he took E.9 into the Baltic, where he sank the German cruiser Prinz Adalbert. When the war ended he was in command of the 4th Submarine Flotilla, having gained two bars to his D.S.O.

Besides being noted for his courage and enterprise, Horton was a capable organizer. He was promoted to captain in June 1920, and appointed Assistant to the Rear-Admiral (Submarines), afterwards commanding the 1st and 5th Flotillas. In 1926 he became Assistant Director of the Mobilization Department, Admiralty, and in 1928 Chief of Staff in the Portsmouth Command. He resumed sea service in 1930 in command of the Resolution in the Mediterranean, until promoted to rear-admiral in October 1932. Three flag commands followed: Rear-Admiral in the 2nd Battle Squadron in 1933-34, command of the 1st Cruiser Squadron in 1935-36, and Vice-Admiral Commanding the Reserve Fleet in 1937-39.

When war broke out he was appointed Admiral (Submarines). In November 1942 he was made Commander-in-Chief, Western Approaches, with headquarters at Liverpool, and devoted his energies to the conduct of the battle of the Atlantic. The measures he took for the safety of convoys and for the organization and disposal of escort groups were a material factor in breaking the back of the U-boat menace during 1943. He held the command until it was disbanded in August 1945. Three months later he retired at his own request to facilitate the promotion of younger officers.

Max Horton was made C.B. in 1934 and promoted to K.C.B. in 1939 and G.C.B. in 1945. He also held a number of foreign decorations, and the Board of Trade silver medal for gallantry, awarded him as a lieutenant in 1911 for saving life when the P. & O. liner Delhi was wrecked off Cape Spartel.

July 31, 1951.

Sir Robert Ho Tung, K.B.E., the millionaire and philanthropist, whose outstanding career marched with the growth of Hongkong, died there on April 26, 1956 at the age of 93. He had been suffering from pneumonia and had lain in a deep coma for two days.

Robert Ho Tung was representative of those happier times when British merchants and Chinese, working in harmonious partnership, brought prosperity and riches to Hongkong, and jointly laid the foundations of great enterprises. Ho Tung was all that was best in a Chinese: thrifty, honest, and persevering, yet generous, entirely without arrogance, and always ready to take a worthwhile business risk. Conservative as regards all that was best in Chinese customs, he nevertheless put the whole weight of his influence on to the side of reform, where reform was needed. His travels abroad—his dignified figure clad in the silken robes of a Chinese gentleman of the old school was a familiar figure in many of the world's capitals—gave him a broad outlook on men and things, and a good understanding of western methods and thoughts.

He preferred to make his great influence in Hongkong felt in the capacity of a private citizen, rather than to play any active part in official life. His power for good, both moral and financial, was nevertheless great—once in 1922 by a combination of arbitration and philanthropy he saved the colony from a general strike which threatened it with total paralysis. Out of the immense wealth that his business acumen acquired for him, he subscribed in the course of his long life several million Hongkong dollars to many worthy causes in Hongkong as well as in China and the United Kingdom. Education was, perhaps, the favourite object of his benefactions; he had contributed more than a quarter of a million dollars to Hongkong University before the 1939-45 War, and after it was over gave a further million for the construction of a new hostel for women. He also greatly assisted the building of the King George V school for European children.

Robert Ho Tung was born in December 1862, the eldest son of a rather poor Chinese family. He received his early education from Chinese teachers and then spent five years at the Central School, Hongkong, which is now Queen's College. He was the only candidate selected from a competitive examination for a post on the outdoor staff of the Chinese Maritime Customs in 1878, but he left after two years and made what was a vital step in his career when he joined the staff of Jardine Matheson and Company as junior assistant to the comprador (Chinese agent).

His pleasant face, and attitude of quiet calm which inspired confidence in those in authority, combined with his undoubted financial abilities, quickly earned him promotion at a time when the great potentialities of Hongkong were becoming apparent. His first great opportunity came when, in the face of the keenest competition from much older and experienced men, he acted as broker in a large property deal which earned him what was in those days a small fortune. By the time his association with the firm came to an end in 1900 he had for six years held the extremely important position of chief comprador, and he was already reputed to be a millionaire. Since then Ho Tung had gone financially from strength to strength; he was a director and shareholder in many great business, financial and banking houses, and there were, indeed, few large concerns, British or Chinese, registered in Hongkong with which he was not in some way connected. His interests ranged, too, far beyond the colony. Sir Robert Ho Tung had received decorations from a large number of countries and was knighted by King George V in 1915 and travelled to England in 1955 by air to receive the insignia of a K.B.E. from the hands of the Queen.

When the Japanese declared war in 1941 he was in Macao, where he had a house. In spite of Japanese pressure he remained there throughout the war—a loyal British subject. He returned permanently to Hongkong only in December 1945, in the company of Admiral Sir Cecil Harcourt [q.v.], the then Military Governor.

Sir Robert married in 1880 Margaret Mak, who died in 1944.

April 27, 1956.

The Rev. E. J. W. Houghton, D.D., Headmaster of Rossall School for nearly a quarter of a century, died on March 2, 1955 at Oxford at the age of 87.

Edward John Walford Houghton was born on August 11, 1867, the eldest son of Canon E. J. Houghton, and was educated at Sherborne and Christ Church, Oxford, where he held a Classical scholarship, as did his father before him and his son after him. At Oxford he read Classical Moderations and *Literae Humaniores,* and also distinguished himself on the cricket and football fields as well as on the running track. He was ordained in 1892, and after seven years as an assistant master at Bromsgrove School was appointed headmaster successively of King Edward's School, Stratford-on-Avon, St. Edmund's, Canterbury, and in 1908, of Rossall School.

It is particularly his 24 years' work at Rossall that entitles him to a place among the great headmasters of his time. He was a man of fearless determination whom no opposition could deter from a course which he decided to be right. In general he would to-day be regarded as old-fashioned. He was wont to say that he considered that the first duty of a school was to teach boys to do as they were told. Although inevitably he did at times tread on some toes, he was always held in the highest respect by all—boys, masters, parents, and Old Boys. He was a great believer in hard work. However little promise might be apparent in some fourth form boy, he was always confident that hard work would bring him to a reasonable standard of education, and very seldom did this confidence prove misplaced.

The classics of his VIth form, in the teaching of which he always took a share, became eminent and there were few years in which his pupils did not appear in good number in the scholarship lists, the record being reached in 1923-24 when the school obtained 16 open awards at Oxford and Cambridge. The teaching of Scripture and the services in Chapel he always put in the foreground of his interests, including the training of the choir, and nothing but the best would satisfy him in these matters. He was examining chaplain to the Bishop of Sodor and Man from 1925 to 1929 and an honorary canon of Blackburn from 1927 to 1932.

He was a keen supporter of interests outside the classroom, particularly cricket (he himself played for Worcestershire and was a member of M.C.C.) and football and the Officers' Training Corps. Largely on the grounds of difficulty in finding appropriate opponents, he decided in 1913 to change the school football game from association to Rugby, a move that not unnaturally roused fierce opposition from a section of the Old Boys of the school. Entirely undaunted, he pursued his course and soon laid the foundations of the fame which later came to Rossall as one of the leading Rugby schools of the north.

He was a great administrator and his keen interest in, and intimate knowledge of, the minutest detail of the work not only of boys and masters but also of the Bursar's multifarious departments, enabled him to keep his finger on the pulse of all activities and maintain the efficiency of the school through all emergencies, not least during the years of the 1914-18 War. By his very character he could not but give the impression to many of being a hard man, and probably only a few of his intimates knew how deep was his sympathy, and in consequence how severe a strain upon him were the years 1914-18, with their constant succession of news of the school's tragic losses, which numbered seven masters and nearly 300 Old Boys.

Like all great headmasters, he had a wonderful memory, and many an Old Boy, whose contacts with the headmaster had been few, was astonished to find himself remembered at once when on a visit to the school perhaps years later. He was a great headmaster to serve under: he could be relied upon to forget nothing that had to be done, always to support his colleagues, and, while expecting hard work from them, never to spare himself in setting an example.

In 1895 he married Ethelwynne, the eldest daughter of the Rev. H. H. Chamberlain. They had four sons, of whom to their great grief three died tragically in the prime of life.

March 4, 1955.

Sir Hubert Houldsworth, Q.C., chairman of the National Coal Board, died at his home in London on February 1, 1956 at the age of 66. He was due to retire from office in July of that year.

He was as near as could be the perfect example of the self-made man who achieved the highest distinctions in his profession, and wore them without self-consciousness. He was for years one of the two or three leading authorities on mining law. He was a physicist of standing, an ardent educationist, but above all, perhaps, he excelled as public servant and administrator, especially in his work with the coal industry, first during the 1939-45 War before nationalization, and afterwards when the mines had come under public ownership. He brought his great knowledge of the coalfields, his wide and patient understanding of production and labour problems, and a great humanity into his work, and in the Midlands and the North he was universally popular and respected—a respect and popularity which were repeated in the larger, national field in the last five years. He had had, however, to face considerable criticism in the last 12 months because, in spite of all his efforts, the output of the industry had steadily fallen.

Hubert Stanley Houldsworth was born in 1889, the son of Albert Edward Houldsworth, of Heckmondwike, Yorkshire. His father, who had a post in one of the local factories, died when his son was seven, and his mother, a woman of rare resource and capacity, had to rear him. When she died in December 1947 at the age of 87, Houldsworth paid her a tribute which should go on the records of the devotion of sons to their mothers. "I owe everything to her", he said. "To keep me she had to go to work as a rug-binder in a Heckmondwike factory, and her efforts enabled me to go to a secondary school, and then to Leeds University. She continued to work until I graduated and began to teach". This indicates much of Houldsworth's background. He won a scholarship to Heckmondwike School, where he was at once recognized as a precociously brilliant pupil, and a further scholarship took him on to the university, where he took science. In 1911 he graduated B.Sc. with first-class honours in physics. His M.Sc. came a year later, and his doctorate in 1925.

After a few years of school teaching he became assistant at his own university, with which he was afterwards to have such a distinguished association, and he was, in fact, a member of the physics staff when, in 1926, he was called to the Bar by Lincoln's Inn. For a while Houldsworth seemed to hesitate between an academic and a legal career. He was probably apprehensive about life at the Bar when he had no association with the legal profession, but eventually he took the plunge, and within a year or two began his long association with the mining industry. In 1936 he became the independent chairman of the coordinating committee of the Midland Amalgamated District under the coal mines scheme of 1930, and that post he held until July 1942; for three years, however, before the outbreak of war in 1939, he combined with it the duties of joint coal supplies officer for the Midland Area of the Mines Department, and then he was successively fuel and power controller of the North-Eastern Region under the Board of Trade, and regional controller for South and West Yorkshire under the Ministry of Fuel and Power.

In 1943 Houldsworth went to London as controller-general of the Ministry, and there he remained until he was made chairman of the East Midland Division of the National Coal Board. Up to that time he had maintained a home in his native town in Yorkshire, but with this appointment he transferred himself to the Grange, at Eastwood, in Nottinghamshire, and entered completely into the life and labours of the vast coalfields in his charge. Within a year or two his area held the national record in production a man, and its harmony became proverbial.

In the autumn of that year occurred the grievous disaster at Creswell. He was deeply distressed, but on the spot at once he tirelessly led investigations and rescue work and won the admiration of everybody who saw him in action. It was said by those who knew that there was not a point about the processes or the laws of mining that Houldsworth had not mastered—all the more surprising because he had no family association with the industry, and had himself made no study of it until his first mining appointment in 1936. He used to say, however, that his early studies as a physicist greatly helped him to master the intricacies of the working of the mines, and some of his first work at the Bar was associated with the industry.

Throughout his life Houldsworth, a man with a genuine love of learning for its own sake, was passionately devoted to the cause of education. He rendered great service for more than 30 years to his old school at Heckmondwike, becoming chairman of its board of governors and helping to make it one of the finest secondary institutions in the North, with an impressive record of scholastic distinctions at the universities. His association with Leeds University continued uninterruptedly from his entry as a student in his late teens. He had been graduate, don, member of the council and court, and for some years chairman of its finance committee, when, in 1949, he became Pro-Chancellor in succession to the late Dr. Veale.

He was a lifelong Liberal, following in the tradition of his parents in the Spen Valley division, and his friends at one time thought that he would combine a political and a legal career, but his only attempt to enter Parliament—at Pudsey and Otley in 1929—failed. After the party split of 1931 he gave his personal support in his own division to Viscount (then Sir John) Simon [q.v.], and to successive members and candidates until he left Yorkshire for Nottinghamshire. If he had remained in the legal profession there is little doubt that high promotion would have come to him, but he made it plain that he preferred to retain and to develop his association with industry. Lincoln's Inn made him a Bencher in 1943—he had taken silk six years before—and for some time he was Recorder of Doncaster.

He married in 1919 Hilda Frances, daughter of Joseph Clegg, who, with an only son, survives him. The baronetcy conferred on Sir Hubert Houldsworth in the last New Year Honours now devolves upon his son.

February 2, 1956.

Clemence Housman, a sister of A. E. Housman and Laurence Housman [q.v.], and herself an artist and writer of individual talent, died in December 1955 at the age of 94.

She was the third child of a family of seven and was born in 1861. Her father was a solicitor, of Bromsgrove. Her life was linked with that of her brother Laurence. The two went to London in 1883 to study art, and Clemence, in addition, wood-engraving. For a time she did commercial work for the *Graphic,* until "process" killed the hand industry, and then for some years was engaged in cutting the illustrations for her brother's fairy tales. Her technique gradually took on a finer and finer cast until at the end it reached a pitch which enables one to claim for her (she would have been the last to claim anything for herself) that her work was the flower of that great English school of wood engravers which had flourished in the sixties.

She also wrote, slowly and at long intervals, but her books are as remarkable in their way as her engravings. Her first story was a tale of horror, *The Were-Wolf,* which appeared first in a Christmas number of *Atalanta* in the 1880s and was afterwards re-published in book form. It is said that she wrote it in 1884 to amuse her fellow students. This was followed by *An Unknown Sea,* and much later by the best of her three, *The Life of Sir Aglovale de Galis,* a psychological reconstruction of a story in *Morte d'Arthur.* It was found rather shocking by the age to which it was first given. But there was a chance to reappraise its excellence when it was issued again in 1953.

When the suffragette movement was in its throes, Clemence Housman threw aside her veil of shyness and joined the throng, serving a short term in Holloway gaol for refusing to pay the inhabited house duty unless she had a vote. Her latter years were spent in the Somersetshire village of Street, where she no longer wrote or engraved, but gave herself up to the peaceful pursuit of gardening, and the encouragement and companionship of her brother.

December 15, 1955.

Laurence Housman died on February 20, 1959 in hospital at Glastonbury. He was 93.

As writer and artist—and as personality also—Housman was a figure of versatile and idiosyncratic distinction. Poet, playwright, essayist, novelist, writer of fairy-tales, polemical satires, dramatic dialogues, he was perhaps best known to the present generation as the author of the *Little Plays of St. Francis* and of another and equally engaging series of Victorian "Palace Plays"—"chamber plays" as they have aptly been called—in which he revealed a nice and individual gift for biography.

But neither his significance in the English literary and artistic scene of a generation or more ago, nor his identification with various artistic, social, and other causes of those years will be widely familiar to-day. Death has made so many gaps in the intellectual circle of which he was once an active member.

Laurence Housman was born on July 18, 1865, the youngest but one of a family of seven, five sons and two daughters, of whom the eldest was the late A. E. Housman, and the third his sister Clemence [q.v.], also an author and a wood-engraver, who lived with him until her death in 1955. Their father was a solicitor, of Bromsgrove. Laurence went to London in 1883 to study art at Lambeth and at South Kensington. His earliest work was book illustration, notably for Christina Rossetti's *Goblin Market.* He was also a contributor to the once famous *Universal Review,* which harboured the early efforts of Ricketts and Shannon as well. But he soon took to writing, and produced, besides a volume on *The Writings of William Blake* (1893), a long line of queerly original fairy tales, of which the sometimes queerer illustrations by himself were engraved by his sister Clemence.

A venture in a more modern or more popular style was *An Englishwoman's Love Letters* (1900), in some sort a psychological study, which appeared anonymously, which was variously ascribed, it seems, to Mrs. Meynell [q.v.], Marie Corelli and Oscar Wilde, which had a wide and all but sensational success, and which Housman himself afterwards described as "the worst book I ever wrote".

He had a distinct fondness, even a passion, for freaks of psychology; to his friends it often seemed that his own mind was essentially freakish. Certainly many of his books carry introspective glimpses of his own soul of a disturbing oddity. They may be discovered in the earliest of his volumes of verse, *Green Arras, Spikenard, A Modern Antaeus,* as well as in his later poems, in his satires, and even in his imaginary conversations and dramatic dialogues.

Such self-revelation was not altogether unconscious. It belonged to an ebullient humour which was very characteristic of the man, which overflowed in his intimate correspondence, and which salted a view of the world at large as something to be shocked and pin-pricked and teased into lively apprehension.

As dramatic author Housman's career was an unlucky one. The plays he chose to write were on religious subjects or on domestic or other aspects of the history of the Royal Family—and this at a time when the conduct of the censorship of the stage was not conspicuously intelligent. The censorship, indeed, loomed large upon Housman's horizon. His first effort was a Nativity play, *Bethlehem,* which was privately produced by Gordon Craig* in 1902 and, banned for a long period, was eventually approved for performance without the alteration of a single word. *Pains and Penalties,* a play about Queen Caroline, effective in theatrical terms but of dubious historical judgment, suffered a similar fate for 15 years; in this case the sole requirement was the excision of a single word, the word "adultery". The only piece of his which escaped condemnation was the charming if funambulesque pierrot play, *Prunella,* written in 1904 at the request of, and in collaboration with, Granville Barker.

In the early 1920s Housman burst into a degree of fame with the general public (with which he was seldom famous for long) through the earliest of his *Little Plays of St. Francis.* Written round the stories and legends of the saint, whose example was a very real influence upon Housman's thought, with the figure of Brother Juniper, the inspired simpleton, to lighten and enrich their dramatic texture, these little plays (which were performed sporadically at Glastonbury and elsewhere) had genuine charm and attractive warmth of moral persuasion.

His Victorian historical pieces in *Angels and Ministers* and *Dethronements* were in a not altogether dissimilar vein of drama, though here the satirical note was dominant. The Queen and the Victorian era generally provided the themes of a large number of historical one-act plays, slight of substance but bearing a pleasant air of authenticity; and Housman had his reward at last when his full-length play *Victoria Regina,* a skilful, affectionate, and, indeed, brilliant pageant, received the Lord Chamberlain's licence and was publicly performed in 1937.

The satirist had been very much in evidence in his essays in fiction since *John of Jingalo* (1912). Sometimes, as in *Trimblerigg* (1924), a pseudonym which scarcely concealed the figure of Lloyd George, the satire—brilliantly cruel—excluded everything else; more often, as in *The Duke of Flamborough* (1928), a name which similarly did little to obscure the features of the old Duke of Cambridge, it was not unmixed with kindliness. On the whole the admixture of satire both in Housman's prose works and in his dramatic dialogues and plays grew steadily more pronounced and gave a still more characteristic flavour to the expression of his essentially romantic idealism.

What "explanation" of Housman may be necessary is not far to seek. A born radical under a conservative skin (a family inheritance), clothed in the formidable traditions of the Victorian era, he proceeded by degrees and at intervals to shed the clothing. In a volume of reminiscences published in 1937, *The Unexpected Years* (so called because he had made up his mind to die at the age of 67, which was his "lucky number"), much of his attitude towards life and towards himself is made clear. The belligerent suffragist, the pugnacious pacifist, the intellectual nihilist, the dubious Socialist, the lover of cats, the romantic moralist, the English anti-nationalist, the all but Christian critic of institutional Christianity—all were of a piece; whether as idealist or iconoclast, it was hard for him to be moderate. An uneasy cuckoo in the nest, he nevertheless regarded himself, as indeed he was, as a Victorian. Nothing would have pleased him better than to have it said of him, as it has been said of so many in the past two decades or more, that he was "the last of the Victorians".

February 21, 1959.

Lieut.-Col. Wilfred Davidson-Houston—
See **Davidson-.**

Clarence Howe, one of Canada's most distinguished Liberal politicians, who held a succession of Ministerial posts in Federal Cabinets for more than 20 years, died in Montreal on New Year's Eve 1960, at the age of 74.

Clarence Decatur Howe was born an American at Waltham, Massachusetts, on January 15, 1886, the son of William Clarence Howe and educated at Massachusetts Institute of Technology where he graduated B.Sc. He taught there for a year but in 1908 went to Canada as professor of Civil Engineering at Dalhousie University, Halifax. He taught in this post until 1913, the year Howe became a Canadian citizen. At that time, too, the late Dr. Robert McGill, who had been appointed chairman of the Board of Grain Commissioners, induced Howe to become their consulting engineer and he moved westward to Fort William, Ontario. In his new post Howe quickly became familiar with the construction and working of elevators and after a few years he decided to go into business as a builder of grain elevators, forming C. D. Howe and Company, with headquarters at Port Arthur. Improvements which Howe wrought in these appliances proved so valuable that his business prospered and he was to build elevators for farmers all over Canada and in many foreign countries.

It was not until 1935, however, that Howe, at the age of 49, took the step of contesting Port Arthur for the Liberals and so, after election, began the political career which was to last unbroken down to the historic defeat of his party at the polls by the Conservatives under Diefenbaker in 1957.

Mackenzie King immediately had the measure of Howe's stature and abilities and brought him into the Cabinet as his Minister of Railways and Canals and Minister of Marine (the two departments being later merged into the Department of Transport). Within a year Howe had decided to appoint one national harbour board in place of the political boards formerly attached to the various harbours across the country, a measure which brought considerable economies. He went on to institute a national board of railway directors, and to bring about a far-reaching reorganization of railway finances.

No less important for Canada proved to be the launching of the Canadian Broadcasting Corporation, for which Howe was the responsible Minister. His sense for the unity of Canada in economic things as much as in cultural forces he showed when he set about devising the first Canadian trans-continental airline system and the founding of today's Trans-Canada Air Lines.

When the Ministry of Munitions and Supply was formed shortly after the outbreak of the Second World War, it was an obvious choice that the most experienced man of business in the Federal Cabinet should be placed in charge of it. Accordingly, Howe became one of the key figures in the direction of the Canadian war effort. His knowledge of engineering stood him in good stead and his abundant fund of initiative and driving power enabled him to gear up Canada's industrial machine to a scale of production far beyond what anybody had then thought possible. Howe was sometimes criticized for the exuberant optimism of his statements but the record of his ministry's achievements spoke for itself. His American origin also greatly helped cooperation with the authorities in Washington, occupied with similar problems to his own. It was Howe who helped, in large measure, to get the air training scheme going in Canada by obtaining on his own initiative aircraft engines in large quantities from the United States.

At his wartime post Howe survived the torpedoing of the liner Western Prince in the Atlantic in December 1940, when he was crossing to England. His party spent eight hours in an open boat, taking turns at the oars, before they were eventually picked up.

In 1944 he assumed the additional responsibility of Minister of Reconstruction, the department which had the task of ensuring that Canada's transition from war to peace should be effected as quickly and smoothly as possible. In January 1946 Howe's two portfolios were merged. He became Minister of Trade and Commerce in 1948 and Minister of Defence Production in 1951. In June 1946 he had been appointed a member of the Privy Council.

Howe, although he liked the rough and tumble of political life, could not be described as a good House of Commons man, for he was a little insensitive to its atmosphere and became easily exasperated with its procedures. If he felt some measure was good for the country he pursued his objective relentlessly. His attitude was perhaps summed up in his remark: "Who's to stop us?" an observation that typified the old liberal administration which had become too arrogant after decades in power.

Yet his political adversaries considered him a great man, and he never allowed criticism to rankle outside the Chamber. With his tough, broad frame, hunched like a bulldog on the front bench, many felt him head and shoulders above his colleagues, particularly in regard to his great vision for Canada. If anything went wrong they sent for "C.D., the man with the oilcan".

In 1916 Howe married Alice Worcester, of Boston. There were two sons and three daughters of the marriage.

January 2, 1961.

Dr. Edwin Powell Hubble, who died on September 28, 1953 of a heart attack at the age of 63 at San Marino, California, was generally recognized as one of the foremost astronomers in the world in recent times.

His work on the nebulae published in book form in 1937, the result of long and patient study and observation over a period of 10 years, was probably the most notable work in astronomy of his time. By means of many photographs and accounts of careful watching he showed conclusively that these were external stellar systems. His book was a remarkable contribution to the knowledge of a subject that had been little known before. When he was awarded the Gold Medal of the Royal Astronomical Society in 1940 it was said that Dr. Hubble's work was outstanding for the power and originality of its method, his observational skill, the objective character of his deductions, and the general brilliance of his results.

After that research he went on with the aid of the 200in. telescope at Mount Palomar to make yet further outstanding discoveries which confirmed by observation the theory of the expanding universe. His work and the discoveries he made became widely known through various lectures he delivered in Britain and in the United States, which were prominently reported at length in the press.

Born at Marshfield, Missouri, on November 20, 1889, he was educated at the University of Chicago where he graduated in science in 1910. He was then awarded a Rhodes scholarship and went into residence at Queen's College, Oxford. It was then his intention to take up the profession of the law and he read jurisprudence, in which he took a first class in 1913. In the same year he returned to the United States and was called to the Kentucky Bar, but he never practised, for he was called to the University of Chicago to undertake research work at its observatory.

That finally decided him to seek a career in astronomy and he continued to work there until the United States entered the war in 1917. He at once volunteered for service oversea and went for training to the first officers' training camp at Fort Sheridan in Illinois. He soon rose to command a battery in the National Army but he did not get to France till the last month of the war and he had then to wait for another year for his return. He was then appointed to Mount Wilson Observatory and his work there attracted such wide attention in all parts of the world that he was soon provided with better and better equipment to continue his work.

He was a Fellow of the Royal Astronomical Society, of the American Astronomical Society, the American Philosophical Society, and many learned societies. He was awarded many medals for his work and was called on to deliver many lectures such as the Silliman course at Yale and the Halley lecture. But the most notable was his course under the Rhodes Trust delivered in Oxford in 1936 and afterwards published in book form under the title *The Observational Approach to Cosmology*.

During the 1939-45 War he was in charge of the American supersonic wind-tunnel laboratory, in which post his knowledge of ballistics was of great use to the allied cause. It is, however, as an astronomer that he will chiefly be remembered and his election as an Honorary Fellow of Queen's College, Oxford, in 1948 was a due recognition of his eminence in that science.

September 30, 1953.

Max Huber, the distinguished Swiss international jurist, died in hospital at Zürich on January 1, 1960 at the age of 85. He had been president of the International Court of Justice, and as president of the International Committee of the Red Cross from 1928 to 1945 he gave outstanding service to the movement.

Hans Max Huber was the descendant on both his father's and his mother's side of old patrician Swiss families. His father was an engineer and industrialist and a colonel of the Swiss Militia, who gave the best available education to his children. Max Huber studied at Lausanne, Zürich, and Berlin, where he gained his LL.D. in 1897. He then started as secretary of the Swiss Chamber of Commerce and, from 1899 to 1901, undertook a world tour for the study of political jurisprudence which took him to Britain, east Asia, the Dutch East Indies, Australia, and the Americas.

On his return he was appointed to the chair of international law in Zürich University, which he held from 1902 to 1921. Long before he abandoned academic life his authority as an international jurist had found recognition: in 1907 he acted as Swiss delegate to The Hague Conference; from 1913 to 1921 as legal adviser to the Federal Government; as judge of the Swiss supreme military court during the 1914-18 War; and as soon as the League of Nations got going in 1920 he became a subsidiary delegate of Switzerland in its assembly.

At the same time he undertook, together with the German jurist Dr. Friedrich Gaus, the elaboration of a new system of treaties of arbitration which, in 1921, produced the German-Swiss treaty that was to serve as model for many arbitration agreements. He served as arbitrator, or as expert, in many international disputes: in the Aaland conflict between Sweden and Finland (1920), and on the blockade commission created by the League of Nations in 1921. His main interest, however, during that period was concentrated on the Permanent Court of International Justice, to which he was appointed a judge from its start in 1920. On September 4, 1924, he was made its President. Simultaneously he acted as a judge of that other great legal body at The Hague, the Permanent Court of Arbitration, founded in 1899.

As an author, Huber was not fertile. Only three of his books go beyond the scope of a special study, or a comment upon problems of the day: *Staatensukzession* (1898), *The Sociological Bases of International Law* (1910), and *International Politics and the Gospel* (1928). But they exercised a lasting, probably a decisive, influence upon the concept of international justice, and the second in particular, of which new editions appeared in 1928 and later, ranks as a classic in its domain.

The year 1928, when Huber relinquished the presidency of the International Court, marked a turning point in his life. Humane, and of a gaiety of heart clearly mirrored in his features, he took to the task of a missionary. Made president of the International Committee of the Red Cross in the same year, he had ample facilities for learning about the alternative to a world ruled according to the principles of international justice; one that needed charity for the healing of self-inflicted wounds. His contributions to the development of the Red Cross movement included the redrafting of its constitution; a new convention for the treatment of prisoners of war; the wider extension of the central prisoners of war agency; and planning the convention for the protection of civilians in time of war. He remained president all through the onerous years of the war, retiring in 1945.

Huber was elected vice-president of the Ecumenical Conference held at Oxford in 1938. He received many academic distinctions in theology as well as law, including an honorary D.C.L. of Oxford and LL.D. of Edinburgh. Yet, like his great fellow-countryman and precursor, Henri Dunant, he remained to himself and those around him a plain Swiss citizen, unaware of having contributed a more than ordinary share to the cause of humanity.

January 2, 1960.

Lord Hudson, the first Viscount, who was Minister of Agriculture during the last war, and before his elevation to the peerage for more than 20 years Conservative member of Parliament for Southport, died on February 2, 1957 in Southern Rhodesia. He was 70.

Before the war he had begun to play a vigorous and useful part in the commercial diplomacy of the country and in encouraging and supporting the efforts of British exporters. Able, masterful and energetic, he made up for a somewhat brusque manner by the force of his intelligence. At the Ministry of Agriculture he was that rare phenomenon, a success. During his time there the demands upon the agricultural industry were immense and kept on increasing with formidable rapidity. As Minister he asserted all his rights of leadership, organizing, innovating, directing and encouraging. He spoke plainly, and was respected for it. He worked strenuously and others emulated him. Although the support he received, and was always ready to acknowledge, was great in quality and extent, there remained a measure of personal accomplishment for which he richly deserved the gratitude of his fellow countrymen.

The Right Hon. Robert Spear Hudson, P.C., C.H., first Viscount Hudson, of Pewsey, in the county of Wiltshire, in the peerage of the United Kingdom, was born in 1886. He was the eldest son of Robert William Hudson, head of a family which had been enriched by the manufacture of soap. He was educated at Eton and Magdalen College, Oxford, where he obtained a second class in modern history. In 1911 he entered the Diplomatic Service and was posted successively to St. Petersburg, Washington, Athens, and Paris, retiring as a first secretary in 1923. In the same year he contested the Whitehaven Division of Cumberland, and was returned for it the year after. He continued to represent this seat until 1929. In 1931 he was elected for Southport, which he represented until he became a member of the House of Lords in 1952. In recognition of his services Southport conferred upon him the honorary freedom of the borough.

From 1931 to 1935 he was Parliamentary Secretary to the Ministry of Labour. Then for a short period he was Minister of Pensions. In 1936 he became Parliamentary Secretary to the Ministry of Health and from 1937 to 1940 to the Department of Overseas Trade. It was in this office that his reputation began to extend beyond Westminster and Whitehall, where he was already known for his competence and capacity for hard work. He soon proved himself particularly useful in connexion with the British Industries Fair and other activities for the promotion of British trade.

At the end of 1938 Hudson associated himself with other junior Ministers in representations to Chamberlain about the defence programme, and early in the New Year he tendered his resignation. It was not accepted. If it had not been for the uncertainty of the international situation 1939 would have been a good and hopeful year for British trade and, ironically enough, it saw a satisfactory agreement between the coal industries of Germany and Great Britain. In March he started on an official mission of inquiry which took him to Warsaw, Moscow, Helsinki, and Stockholm. The object was to secure an improvement in British trade relations with the countries which he visited, and was successful in so far as it created good will and opened the way to further discussions.

In July 1939 a rumour ran through London to the effect that he had discussed with Dr. Wohltat, a German economic adviser who was a visitor in London, a settlement with the Reich on the basis of disarmament and a loan. It was true that Hudson had had an informal and personal talk with Dr. Wohltat, but Chamberlain was able to deny that there was any proposal of a loan. There turned out to be no cause for censure, though there was reason to regret the unscrupulous use made by the German press of what would otherwise have been a harmless incident.

In April 1940 he was appointed Minister of Shipping, and a month later he succeeded Sir Reginald Dorman-Smith [d. 1977] as Minister of Agriculture in the Churchill Government. Few Ministers have enhanced their reputation in this difficult and invidious office. However excellent their intentions and ability, they have in peace time only too often been caught and crushed between the pressure of the consumer for cheap food and that of the producer for a livelihood. Hudson was, however, to prove an exception, and gained steadily in reputation. It is true that good harvests helped him, and that in wartime expenditure is less closely guarded—more food must be produced at home, cost what it may. The energy and judgment he brought to bear produced remarkable results. Moreover the agricultural community was out to help, prepared not only to organize but, if necessary, to police itself. In his New Year's message for 1942 he stated that it would be the toughest year in the history of British farming, but was able to claim three growing assets: new mechanical power on the land; increased knowledge (he had been responsible for the Agricultural Improvement Council); and the Women's Land Army.

Remarkable though the production of 1942 was, the shrinkage of shipping was, as time went on, to create ever increasing demands. There were, too, fresh mouths to feed. Nevertheless by the end of July Hudson was able to inform the House of Commons that the country was then self-supporting in food to the extent of two-thirds. The progress of two years had been spectacular. He had in fact been the leader of an agricultural revolution. It may also be said of him that engrossed though he was in the urgent and intensifying problems of his time, he never failed to bear in mind the post-war future of the industry he had in charge. He was made a Companion of Honour in 1944.

After the war, when Hudson was out of office, he devoted his energies increasingly to the affairs of the Royal Agricultural Society of England, and the British Friesian Cattle Society, of which he became president. His pedigree cattle, with British Friesians and Ayrshires, on his Wiltshire farms have earned a great reputation in the stockbreeding world for him and Lady Hudson, who shared his interests, political and agricultural, in full. He was also chairman of the Board of Governors of the Imperial Institute from 1953, and was much concerned in the negotiations about the future of the institute's building in South Kensington. And as Britain's representative in the United Nations Trusteeship Committee he spoke up vigorously for his country's colonial record and defended it against much ignorant misrepresentation.

He married in 1918 Hannah, daughter of Philip Synge Physick Randolph, a member of a prominent Philadelphia family. She survives him with their son, the Hon. Robert William Hudson, who succeeds to the viscounty.

February 4, 1957.

Dr. S. W. Hughes, one of the great Nonconformist leaders of this century—perhaps the last of his type—died in a Northampton nursing home on September 16, 1954 at the age of 80.

Samuel William Hughes succeeded Dr. John Clifford in the famous Baptist pastorate at Westbourne Park, London, in 1915. Dr. Clifford had done more than any other single man to make Nonconformism militantly articulate on social and political issues at the end of the nineteenth and the beginning of this century. It was he who gave the "Nonconformist conscience" an unprecedented political power, forcing from F. E. Smith a famous protest after the Liberal victory of 1906.

Hughes had to work in very different conditions. With the decline of Liberalism, Nonconformism ceased to be identified with any political party; with the decline of radicalism, it ceased to find any natural political expression. Moreover, many of the Nonconformist radical's battles had been won, and as the churches generally lost their hold on the industrial working class, and the denominations ceased to be so jealous of each other, the "Nonconformist conscience" became more and more muted.

It was Hughes's achievement in his long life that the voice of Nonconformism was, nevertheless, still to be as firm and unequivocal as ever. His battles were fought less spectacularly than Dr. Clifford's, and for less spectacular ends. The evils to be destroyed were different, gambling becoming gradually more prominent than drink. The denominations were to begin to cooperate, and the tension between them gradually became relaxed. But Hughes kept alive the inner fire of the old militant Nonconformist tradition—the belief that a man's first duty is to his conscience.

He was born at Walgrave, in Northamptonshire, on July 11, 1874. After a short business career in a lawyer's office and private training under the Rev. Dr. Owen, he accepted the pastorate of the Baptist church at Walgrave, where he remained for three and a half years. The Baptist church at Market Harborough then called him, and his power of utterance first began to be noticed, especially in his men's meetings, which were never small. In 1904—when Dr. Clifford was at the height of his power—he received a unanimous call from the Christ Church, Birmingham.

Here during the years when Nonconformism was a remarkable power in the land, Hughes established himself as one of the greatest personal forces in the industrial area round Birmingham. The choice of him to succeed Dr. Clifford at Westbourne Park in 1915 was unchallengeable. He remained there until 1932, when he was appointed general secretary to the National Council of the Evangelical Free Churches, a post which he held until 1940. He was vice-president of the Baptist Union from 1948 to 1949, and president from 1949 to 1950.

In 1903 he married Miss Edith Annie Walker, who died in 1940. In 1942 he married, secondly, Miss Winifred Walker. There were two sons and one daughter of the first marriage.

September 18, 1954.

By the death of **William Morris Hughes,** at the age of 88, on October 28, 1952 the Commonwealth lost one of the founders of Australian nationalism who was yet an ardent supporter of the Imperial connexion.

There was never anything narrow about Hughes's political outlook. If there was inconsistency in upholding Australia's claims to recognition in the councils of the Allies, and then opposing, 10 years later, a conception of the Empire which conceded to the Dominions formal autonomy, it did not trouble him. Throughout his career, he saw no future for the Commonwealth of Australia except as an integral part of an Empire where sentiment was reinforced by as many ties of material interest as could be devised.

The crisis of the 1914-18 war provided just the occasion for which his restless genius was best fitted. A supreme capacity for administration, an aggressive will, and, above all, an inspiring confidence in the rightness of the country's decision to fight, made him one of the greatest leaders which the war produced. He was secure in a virtual dictatorship at home: he governed Australia, he said, "with a fountain-pen". In Europe, he spoke for his country with an authority and vigour which won him respect and—even more important—an attentive hearing.

After the war, deprived (like Lloyd George in Britain) of the support of a party which could give him power, much of his career seemed an irrelevance. The Labour Party came to denounce him as a betrayer of the workers' cause. The Nationalist Party, of which he was the first leader, cast him off as a tyrant. Nothing, however, can remove the impression of greatness which the perspective of history is already beginning to confirm. He saw and loved Australia as a nation, but he never suffered from the parochialism which was the weakness of some other Australian politicians in those early years.

He was born at Llandudno on September 25, 1864, and after becoming a pupil-teacher at St. Stephen's Church of England School, Westminster, embarked, at the age of 19, for Australia, without means or prospects. For three years in Sydney he wandered from job to job, and at last found his chance in the trade union movement. He organized the waterside workers of Sydney, became secretary of the Sydney Wharf Labourers' Union, president of the Carters' Union, and later president of the Waterside Workers' Federation.

He was first returned to the New South Wales legislature as a Labour member in 1894, and remained a member until his election to the first federal Parliament in 1901. The Labour Party was already the best organized in Australia, particularly in Hughes's own state. As a member of its most extreme section, he had a hand in drafting and exacting the pledge by which every Labour candidate was forced to surrender his independence to the party caucus—a development of great importance in the history of Australian politics.

Hughes held office for the first time in the Watson administration, which lasted for a few months during the summer of 1904. In the previous year he had been called to the New South Wales Bar, and when Andrew Fisher, who had succeeded Watson in the party leadership, became Prime Minister in 1908, Hughes was appointed Attorney-General. The Government lasted only seven months, but the Labour Party won an electoral victory in 1910, and Fisher again took office, again with Hughes as Attorney-General and the ablest man in the administration.

Hughes was the driving force behind the Government's attempt to extend federal powers—particularly with a view to controlling trade, regulating great corporations, and nationalizing monopolies. This policy was, however, rejected by the people when submitted to them in 1911 and again in 1913 by the device of the referendum. After being defeated in 1913 the Labour Party was again victorious in the following year, and soon after the outbreak of war Fisher was again Prime Minister with Hughes as his right-hand man.

In the opportunities provided by the war, Hughes showed his quality as a statesman. He succeeded Fisher as Prime Minister in 1915. By temperament, by his grasp of the world-wide nature of the conflict in Europe, by his willingness to adopt bold and imaginative policies, he gave the leadership which Australia needed and his predecessor could never have provided. Like Lloyd George in Britain, he had made numerous political enemies before the war, but so vigorously did he uphold Fisher's famous pledge to "stand by our own kin . . . to the last man and the last shilling" that he was soon leading a united House and a united nation.

Restless and dynamic, Hughes retained for himself all responsibility and initiative. In 1916 he visited England to discuss metal and grain supplies. He immediately caught the imagination of the British people, who could not hear enough of his trenchant and impassioned speeches on the conduct of the war—"war with the gloves off", as he said. He attended a meeting of the Imperial Cabinet, cities united to do him honour, and Oxford led other universities in conferring degrees on him. He also attended the Allied Economic Conference in Paris as a delegate.

On his return to Australia Hughes had at once to face the problem of conscription. He faced it courageously and was to pay a severe political price for his boldness. Conscription had already been enacted in Britain and New Zealand, and Hughes was convinced that Australia should do the same. He could not, however, convince either the whole country or his party. Conscription was rejected at the referendum of September 1916 and he was expelled from the party he had served so loyally and so well.

In February 1917 he formed a coalition with the Opposition, and at the head of this Nationalist Government was again returned to power in May. A second conscription referendum held in December produced the same result as the first. In June 1918 Hughes returned to England to attend meetings of the Imperial War Cabinet. He remained for a year, attending in the last few months the peace negotiations in Paris. In his book, *The Splendid Adventure,* he has recounted the attempt he made with Sir Robert Borden to obtain for the Dominions separate representation. He also vigorously opposed a "racial equality" clause in the League covenant—he had entered politics just at the time when the "white Australia" policy was put into practice—and successfully asserted his claim that Australia should have a mandate over German colonies captured by Australian troops in the south Pacific.

In spite of the tumultuous welcome which he received when he returned to Australia, the next years were to be difficult for Hughes. It seemed almost that he had no friends. His bitter tongue alienated not a few and he was accused of autocratic tendencies. Moreover, his Socialist policies were not popular with many members of the Nationalist Party which he now led. A new Country Party was formed, and when it gained the balance of power at the elections of 1922 its leader refused to support Hughes and he retired in favour of his treasurer, S. M. Bruce [Lord Bruce of Melbourne*].

There followed, during the years between the wars, a growing estrangement from those he had formerly led. He was out of sympathy with much of Bruce's policy, and in 1929 led an open revolt in the Nationalist Party, when Bruce proposed to abolish federal arbitration in industrial disputes in favour of the states. In the next Parliament, following the defeat of Bruce's Government, Hughes's connexion with the Nationalist Party was finally severed, and he founded a new party—the Australian Party. Old political feuds were soon, however, to be forgotten in the financial crisis of the next two years, and during this period Hughes, by his critical independence of judgment, did something to restore his reputation.

He held various posts from 1934 until the return of the Labour Party in 1941. On the outbreak of war in 1939, the voice of the Imperial statesman was heard again. He vigorously defended Britain and attacked her critics, declaring that for 150 years Australia had owed her immunity from attack to British command of the sea. Believing national unity to be vital, he gave his support to the Labour Government when it took office.

It was a comparatively peaceful ending to a violent career, in which, though he was often dictatorial and sometimes descended to devices of political pettiness, he also rose to greatness. His personality contained strange contradictions. He made enemies, but he retained the affection of the Australian people. He was more a phrase-builder than an orator, but could sway Parliaments and the populace alike.

October 28, 1952.

Cordell Hull, Secretary of State under President Roosevelt for more than 11 years—longer than anyone else in American history—died on July 23, 1955 in the Bethesda Naval Hospital, near Washington, after the last of a series of strokes which had caused him to be bedridden for some time. He was 83.

Cordell Hull was one of the greatest of the

many famous men who have held office as Secretary of State of the United States. Through all three of President Roosevelt's administrations he was in charge of the foreign policy of his country, and continued to command a measure of public respect and confidence beyond that accorded to any of his fellow Ministers. Such was his intellectual integrity and high purpose that, while his political associates regarded him as a party and national asset, there were times when the praise of his opponents became almost an embarrassment to him.

He left a deep impress on the history of his time, for, apart from the statesmanship of his outlook and the wisdom he displayed in the handling of the innumerable problems of the war period, he was the builder of the new structure of inter-American cooperation through which the "good neighbour" policy was realized. In the crisis of the war, as indeed in the preceding years, Hull was a great support to President Roosevelt, for he was a master of the difficult art of satisfying Congressional committees. He strove during his last months of office to lay the foundations of an international security system in which the United States would play its part. But he had retired before the inauguration of the United Nations in 1945. His contribution to that achievement has not gone unrecognized.

Cordell Hull was born in a little farmhouse between Byrdstown and Willow Grove, in Overton County, in the State of Tennessee, on October 2, 1871. Since he proved a bright and promising scholar his father sent him to Mountvale Academy at Celina. Then after a term or two at the Normal School at Bowling Green, Kentucky, he went on to the National Normal University of Lebanon, Ohio. By this time he was 18 and had decided to be a lawyer. He was, therefore, sent to Cumberland University in his own State, and obtained his LL.B. degree there in 1891. A year later he was admitted to the Bar.

Almost from boyhood he was interested in politics. When he was barely 19 he was elected a delegate to the State Democratic Convention, and at 22 to the State Legislature. Resigning when the Spanish-American war broke out, he formed a company of volunteers, was commissioned a captain, and went to Cuba. In 1906 he was elected to Congress for the Fourth District of Tennessee by a large majority. His chief interest in those days was the question of income and inheritance taxes. When, therefore, in 1913 the Democrats came into power President Wilson entrusted him with the difficult task of drafting a system of federal income-tax. Such a tax had a number of years before been declared unconstitutional; but Wilson and Hull were satisfied that it was fiscally necessary to offset the reduction in tariffs which was a part of Democratic policy, and in the end their proposals were carried into law with singularly little protest.

In 1917, once the United States was in the war, the task of financing it became Hull's chief preoccupation. The retirement of Woodrow Wilson in 1920 spelt disaster for the Democratic Party; Hull himself was defeated for the only time in Tennessee. The party was in serious financial straits. In these circumstances he was chosen to be chairman of the Democratic National Committee and succeeded in restoring both its fortunes and vitality. In the Presidential election of 1924 the Tennessee Legislature put forward his claims, but he discouraged the move and resigned his chairmanship. Hull was then to pit himself against the tariff policy of the Hoover* administration, but in vain. In 1929, however, the stock markets collapsed and a new and pregnant situation arose. Hull had been long perturbed about the state of the American nation and had even meditated retirement to Tennessee. Instead, however, he stood in 1930 for the Senate and was easily elected.

In 1933 President Roosevelt offered Hull the post of Secretary of State. After some delay he accepted. It was a daring appointment for he had had no diplomatic training. Yet, although almost untravelled, he had been a close and thoughtful student of international affairs, especially in their bearing on finance and trade; and after his appointment to the State Department he lost no time in inaugurating the policy of reciprocal trade treaties, which was his major achievement before the world was plunged into war in 1939. He was also keenly alive to the dangers inherent in the European situation, and was prepared to employ his good offices in seeking to avert them.

The World Economic Conference was fixed for June, and seemed to him to offer possibilities. Consequently, he went to London as chairman of the American delegation. On his arrival there he found that stabilization of currency was considered generally to be an essential first step. This was opposed both to his own opinion and to the official American point of view. He was, nevertheless, prepared to feel for an accommodation. While, however, he was doing so Moley, the Assistant Secretary of State, went swiftly to London with, as rumour alleged, instructions from the President, and proceeded to engage in discussions of his own. As a result of them he put to the President views much the same as those which Hull was forming. The President, however, rejected them flatly, and Hull had to read to the delegates a Presidential message which amounted to a rebuke to the whole assembly.

On Hull's return to the United States the President summoned him in a most appreciative telegram to Hyde Park. At the time there were widespread rumours that he would retire, but he went back in silence to Washington and his work. There, defeated for the time being in the Old World, he decided to turn to the New, where he saw a possibility of establishing under simpler economic conditions the foundations of an enduring, even if localized, peace. Consequently he went in November to Montevideo to the seventh International Conference of American States, and attained at it a measure of success which restored his self-confidence.

In the Presidential election campaign of 1936 Hull took no very prominent part and immediately after it went to Buenos Aires for a conference of the American Republics, to which the President also paid a brief and spectacular visit. Then came the discovery that the neutrality legislation did not cover civil wars and the necessity for adjusting its provisions to the civil war in Spain. Meanwhile, events elsewhere in Europe were marching on, and Hull began to make more pointed references to the bullying methods of the Nazis and their violations of treaties. American opinion remained, however, for the most part unperturbed, and even the annexation of Austria caused no serious alarm. Munich brought, of course, a temporary relief, but Hull had too clear a view of the whole European situation to be deceived into any measure of optimism, and worked on the theory that it was no more than a respite. When, therefore, in the autumn he attended the Pan-American conference at Lima he went there in search of a measure of mutual protection for the member States and succeeded in securing a reassertion of the principle that a threat to the security of any American Republic would be regarded as a threat to all of them. He also won approval for arrangements for consultation in the event of a threat of war anywhere in the world.

When in the summer of 1939 Congress adjourned, the vital matter of American foreign policy in the event of war was largely undetermined owing to continued difficulties with the isolationists. War came before the Legislature met again, and the President, after formally declaring American neutrality, had to summon them to repeal the arms embargo. It was only, however, after the invasion of the Low Countries that American opinion began to swing decisively in favour of the President. During the pre-election period of this year there were suggestions that Hull himself might run, for no man was more widely esteemed and trusted; but he neither desired to do so nor to accept the nomination to the Vice-Presidency which he was offered. In the summer, therefore, he went to Havana for a consultative meeting of the Pan-American Foreign Ministers and returned with valuable reassurances.

From his early days at the State Department Hull had laboured patiently and not without hope to strengthen the hands of the moderates in Japan. By 1940, however, it was obvious that the tide of militarism was to prove too strong for him. Thereafter negotiations became of less and less use. The arrival of Kurusu in the United States in November 1941 was merely an effort on Japan's part to keep discussions going until the appointed hour. On December 7 Kurusu and Admiral Nomura presented the reply to a memorandum which the United States had addressed to Japan shortly before. Hull read it in their presence and found that the broad suggestions he had made for a non-aggression pact and a Far Eastern settlement had been not only flatly but insultingly turned down. He burst forth, as when he believed he had been tricked he sometimes did, and characterized the contents of the documents as "infamous distortions". Immediately afterwards he left for the White

House, to learn there of the attack on Pearl Harbour.

As Secretary of State in war Hull's deep understanding and ripe experience were of immense value to the Administration. Then, as he had done in the period before Pearl Harbour, he threw all his weight into advocacy of all-out help for the allies. He was not in agreement with his British allies in every particular during their joint prosecution of the war. There was, for instance, sharp disagreement over the status of the Free French. When, in 1941, General de Gaulle* wrested two islands from the Vichy Government against the advice of the State Department, Hull was affronted, and made his annoyance known in a declaration in which he referred to the "so-called Free French". Later his reluctance to accord recognition to the French Committee of National Liberation was overcome only after prolonged persuasion by the British Foreign Secretary.

In August 1943 he attended the Quebec Conference with the President, Winston Churchill* and Mackenzie King, and shortly after his return categorized the basic foreign policy of the United States under six headings, which he regarded as of universal application. In the same speech he carried his foreign policy considerably farther by stating that international cooperation must be based "on the willingness of the cooperating nations to use force if necessary to keep the peace". Then in the following October he left for the Three Power Conference in Moscow, accompanied by a powerful American delegation, and on the way joined Eden [Lord Avon, d. 1977] at Teheran. It was his first flight in an aeroplane, and he was then over 70. From Churchill it earned the phrase "that gallant old eagle". On his return to Washington he found that he stood higher than at any period of his career in the regard and confidence of his fellow countrymen, and was promptly invited to address both houses of Congress.

In the early spring of 1944 Hull was pressed for and gave a fuller definition of American foreign policy, but it consisted chiefly of a summary of his own declarations during the war. In April, however, he made a most important broadcast in which he asked "with insistence" that the neutrals should cease to provide essential war materials to the enemy, and went on to propound the principles of American policy. They included the keeping of the peace through agreement between the four great allied Powers, an effective international organization to uphold international law, and further cooperation for the increase of world prosperity. His last months in office were occupied in laying plans for an international security system in which the United States would join. He did not remain Secretary of State, however, long enough to witness the inauguration of the United Nations Organization for which he had worked. Yet President Roosevelt gave symbolic recognition to Hull's achievement when he left a space for his signature on the United Nations Charter. He called him the "father" of the United Nations.

The strain of 12 arduous years of office had told heavily on one no longer young when first appointed, and when President Roosevelt, after his reelection in November, came to reconstruct his Cabinet Hull, on medical advice, laid down his heavy burden. It was, he said in his letter of resignation, a supreme tragedy to him that he was unable to continue making his full contribution to the development of a full and complete structure of world order under the law. Thus ended the career of one who, in the words of Lord Halifax's [q.v.] moving tribute to him, was "a great public servant to his country and a great example to statesmen of any country—universally respected, known, and trusted". He was awarded the Nobel Peace Prize for 1945.

He published his memoirs in 1948. They had been written during the two preceding years, much of which he had spent in hospital. The book was a disappointment: the heavy hands of collaborators were in evidence, the style was portentous, and there was little of the pungent and salty comment which relieved his conversation, especially when he was roused.

He was in middle life when in 1917 he made a happy marriage with Miss Rose Frances Whitney, of Virginia, who died in 1954. He leaves no children.

July 25, 1955.

Sir Travers Humphreys, P.C., who when he retired in 1951 was the senior and the oldest Judge of the King's Bench, died in London on February 20, 1956 at the age of 88.

Before his elevation to the Bench he had been one of the most noted criminal advocates of his day, and as standing prosecuting counsel to the Crown at the Central Criminal Court he had appeared there in most of the important criminal trials across a number of years. He was also one of the very few examples in the annals of the Bench of a stuff-gownsman from the criminal courts receiving judicial preferment.

Travers Humphreys was the fourth son of Charles Octavius Humphreys, head of the well-known firm of solicitors, C. O. Humphreys, Son and Kershaw, then of High Holborn, who in addition to a large general practice appeared frequently in criminal matters.

He was born on August 4, 1867, and educated at Shrewsbury School and Trinity Hall, Cambridge, where he was a contemporary of Lord Maugham [q.v.] and Lord Romer, and on several occasions he stroked the boat of that famous rowing college. He was called to the Bar in 1889 by the Inner Temple, which Inn, five years before he became a Judge, did him, as a junior counsel, the unusual honour of electing him a Bencher. Humphreys, as has been seen, started with the advantage of a close family connexion with a leading firm of solicitors, and he was a nephew by marriage of Lord Halsbury.

After passing his examinations, he went for a time into the chambers of Thomas (afterwards Sir Thomas) Willes Chitty, then the leading junior at the Common Law Bar and later Senior Master of the King's Bench, and after his call he went into the chambers of E. T. E. Besley, a great name at the Central Criminal Court in those days, and after devilling for him and for the future Sir Archibald Bodkin [q.v.], in the same chambers, Humphreys quickly acquired a practice of his own and became a familiar figure at the Central Criminal Court and the Sessions, and also in licensing cases, in which branch of law he also acquired a substantial practice. He appeared with the late Sir Charles Mathews as Sir Edward Clarke's junior for Oscar Wilde in all three trials in 1895, and 10 years later, in 1905, he was appointed Counsel to the Crown at the Middlesex Sessions and North London Sessions and, in 1908, Junior Counsel to the Crown at the Central Criminal Court, and Senior Counsel in 1916.

During the years that preceded Humphreys's elevation to the Bench there were few notable trials at the Central Criminal Court in which he was not engaged. He appeared in the Crippen case in 1910; in the Sedden case in 1912; in 1913 he prosecuted Arthur Newton, the well-known Marlborough Street solicitor, who was sentenced to penal servitude for fraud; in 1914 he was engaged in the sensational trial of G. J. Smith ("Brides in the Bath" case), and in the prosecution of Sir Roger Casement in 1916. In 1918 he appeared in the Pemberton Billing case. In 1922 he achieved perhaps his greatest forensic triumph when, as leader for the prosecution, he obtained the conviction of Horatio Bottomley, who had previously eluded the skill of several distinguished counsel. In after years he modestly disclaimed this distinction and maintained that it was "Drink" that had "floored" that crafty rascal, who was by 1922 so drink-sodden as to become careless. In the same year he was concerned for the prosecution in the Bywaters and Thompson case. In 1924 he appeared for the Crown in the case of one Norman, which was argued before the Court of Criminal Appeal, composed of 13 Judges, and laid down the law as to the defence open to a prisoner charged with being an "habitual criminal".

Humphreys was an admirable Crown Counsel, impartial, lucid and concise, with a wide knowledge of every branch of the criminal law, to which must be added the valuable quality in an advocate of restrained humour. His fairness in conducting prosecutions is exemplified in the remark of a distinguished defender of prisoners: "He is so damned fair that he leaves nothing for the defence to say!" He was in private an admirable mimic and would probably have been as successful on the stage as in the Courts. (It may be mentioned, by the way, that he was a nephew of Corney Grain, the popular entertainer). At the Bar there were few more popular figures. He was Recorder of Chichester from 1921 until 1926, and of Cambridge from the latter year until he was made a Judge. In February 1926, to meet the emergency created by the sudden death of Mr. Laurie, the deputy chairman of the London Sessions, Humphreys—

who had been knighted the previous year—was appointed to act temporarily in his place for the current Sessions.

In February 1928, pursuant to an Address from both Houses of Parliament, two new Judges had to be appointed in the King's Bench Division, and Lord Cave's nominations fell upon Sir Travers Humphreys and E. B. Charles, K.C. The former was certainly unexpected; but in the circumstances was recognized as sound. The only criminal expert on the bench, Sir Horace Avory, had served for over 17 years and was in his seventy-seventh year, and a successor in his special branch of the law was considered to be desirable; the more so because of recent years the Commercial Court had perhaps provided rather more than its due proportion of Judges, who were, of course, largely without criminal experience and whose handling of the criminal business on circuit had not always met with the approval of the Court of Criminal Appeal. Sir Horace Avory's own nomination by Lord Loreburn was not so pronounced a departure from precedent as was Sir Travers Humphreys's, for the former, after he took silk in 1901, had before his appointment as a Judge in 1910 acquired a large general business in the Courts; whereas the latter could hardly have seen a statement of claim since his student days. The first days of his judicial career were by an odd fate spent as the Judge in Chambers. In 1932 he tried Mrs. Barney, who was acquitted of manslaughter after a trial that attracted great public interest. He also presided the following year at the trial, which lasted for 31 days, of the fire-raising gang who for years had defrauded the insurance companies of very large sums.

Some remarks he made in sentencing Irishmen convicted on charges of causing bomb explosions in 1939 were the subject of a protest by the Eire Government, and a man was later charged and pleaded guilty on a charge of grossly libelling the learned Judge in connexion with the same series of crimes.

From the first he showed himself to possess the qualities that made him one of the most successful Judges in his own line of his generation, and the contribution made by him to the development of the criminal law, both as a Judge of first instance and in the Court of Criminal Appeal, will long be remembered. The extreme fairness with which he conducted his Treasury prosecutions characterized his deportment on the Bench and, whether innocent or guilty, no prisoner could ever complain that his case had not been put fairly to the jury. His handling of the plea of insanity in the Haigh case at Lewes Assizes in 1949 was particularly notable in this respect.

Though punctilious in requiring cases to be presented in proper form, and severe in any failing in this respect, he was considerate to counsel and always anxious to meet their convenience. He believed in capital punishment, and occasionally in crimes of violence he ordered flogging. His sense of humour, previously alluded to, was severely restrained, and neither jokes nor irrelevant observations at large ever impaired the dignity which characterized the trials over which he presided.

In 1946, being then one of the two senior Judges of the King's Bench Division, he was made a Privy Councillor. In the same year he published an interesting and pleasantly written book, *Criminal Days,* which enjoyed great popularity. Its scope was limited by his proper feeling "that a Judge while on the active list should not express in public his views upon matters that have come, or may come, before him in his judicial capacity", nor did he "think it desirable that he should comment upon members of the profession still living".

After his retirement in 1951 he published *A Book of Trials,* which exhibited similar qualities. The genial tone and wise precepts of these volumes go far to explain Humphreys's great success on the Bench and the great regret with which the news of his death will be received.

The late Judge married in 1896 Zoe Marguerite, daughter of Henri P. Neumans, a well-known artist, of Antwerp. She died in 1953. His only surviving son is a member of the Bar in a large criminal practice, and has been a senior Treasury Counsel since 1942.

February 21, 1956.

Sir Robert Hutchinson, BT., who died on February 12, 1960 at his home at Thurle Grange, Streatley, Berkshire, exercised a profound influence on the British school of children's physicians and was an authority on diet. He was 88.

Born at Kirkliston, Midlothian, in 1871, he had a brilliant career at the University of Edinburgh, where he was Vans Dunlop Stark and Ettles Scholar, and was Leckie Mactier Fellow. He was senior President of the Edinburgh Medical Society, graduated with first class honours in 1893, and took the M.D. and the M.R.C.P.Ed. three years later. He then served as house physician at the Edinburgh Hospital for Sick Children and house surgeon at the Royal Maternity Hospital, proceeding afterwards to Strasbourg and Paris for postgraduate study.

Returning to Britain he was appointed Demonstrator of Chemical Physiology in the university and went to London as house physician to the Hospital for Sick Children in Great Ormond Street, where he was successively assistant physician, physician and consulting physician. He joined the medical school attached to the London Hospital as Demonstrator of Physiology, was elected as assistant physician, became full physician, and resigned in 1933.

At the Royal College of Physicians in London he was admitted a member in 1897 and was elected a Fellow in 1903; delivered the Goulstonian lecture in 1904; was Harveian Orator in 1931; and was elected president, in succession to Lord Dawson of Penn, in 1938. This he held until he retired in 1941. In 1939 he received a baronetcy. He was president of the Royal Society of Medicine in 1934.

Hutchinson will be greatly missed by a wide circle of friends, for he inspired real affection in those with whom he worked. "Bobbie" to his colleagues and juniors at the London Hospital, and "Robert" at Great Ormond Street, he lived in an atmosphere of almost reverential admiration. His shafts of wit sent home his teaching points and his powers of instruction inspired a large number of physicians and children's specialists. But most of all he taught general practitioners to think clearly. "To clear their minds of cant" is one of his epigrams, and through them he helped many a patient over a difficult time.

February 13, 1960.

Baroness von Hutten, (Bettina von Hutten), who with her first novel *Pam* attained instant popularity, died in London on January 27, 1957.

She was born Bettina Riddle, of Irish-American parentage, at Erie, Pennsylvania, in 1874. At the age of 17 she paid her first visit to Europe and began her literary career by writing for the *English Illustrated Magazine.* Her family settled in Florence, and there she studied music under the best masters. Her voice was so beautiful that at one time she seriously considered training for grand opera, but her strongest desire was to be an author.

After her marriage in 1897 to Baron von Hutten zum Stolzenberg she devoted herself to writing at her home, Schloss Steinbach, in Bavaria. Here *Pam* was written, that entrancing story with a charming and original heroine from childhood to womanhood. It was so unusual in method and treatment that it created something of a sensation. Bettina von Hutten was frank and outspoken at a time when sentimentalism and conventional morality were still respected. What could now be considered mild to the point of primness was then called a "bold breakaway". Kingsmead, her next book, was an admirable study of youth; the hero, Tommy, Earl of Kingsmead, was one of those attractive, gay and yet wistful young men with whom Bettina von Hutten excelled.

Sharrow and *Mothers-in-Law* were of a more ambitious type, and in both books there was much of the wit and the brilliancy peculiar to the author. *Sharrow* is almost diabolically clever, conveying as it does the suggestion that beneath the calm and beauty of the tale an upheaval is being stealthily prepared. *Mothers-in-Law* shows two strongly contrasted types: the pretty, gay, and intelligent American, whose daughter marries the son of a narrow, rigid Italian, widow of a nobleman. The young people, Sappho, the American, and Nino, descendant of the house of Gamba, are far less interesting than their respective mothers. *What Became of Pam* was written in answer to many urgent entreaties from those eager to know more of that young woman. It was so successful that it was followed by a sequel, *Pam at Fifty.*

Her marriage, which began under such happy auspices, ended in divorce in 1907. The German feudal atmosphere at her husband's castle in Bavaria, the rigidity of the etiquette at the court, where her husband was Chamberlain, wearied and irritated the high spirited, brilliant girl, who from childhood had been a prodigy to her adoring circle and who was indeed greatly gifted. Separation followed estrangement, and finally by mutual consent a divorce was arranged.

She then settled in England to enjoy her freedom and the admiration freely given her. She had personal beauty of a strange and compelling charm, and her height alone—she was nearly six feet—would have made her a striking figure. She appeared at His Majesty's Theatre, under the management of Sir Herbert Tree, in *Pinkie and the Fairies*, and at one time was inclined to leave writing for the stage. But, as she herself confessed, nothing could absorb her as did story writing. With each novel her popularity increased; she made a great deal of money, which she spent with the reckless generosity that was one of her characteristics, but with the war her vogue ceased. In the first fierce hatred of the enemy no one wanted to read books by a German, and though Bettina von Hutten had as much, indeed more, reason than most people to dislike the Germans, she was classed as one of them.

Treated as an enemy alien, forbidden to travel more than five miles from her registered place of residence without a permit, impatient of such supervision and bitterly resenting the fact that though she was wholeheartedly devoted to England she should be regarded as a foe, she on more than one occasion defied the law. Finally in 1916 she was summoned to appear at Westminster Police Court, and was fined five pounds and ordered to pay five guineas costs for trying to evade the regulations.

But her courage and gay sense of humour never forsook her; she worked untiringly and her books came into favour again. She made a great deal of money, but as usual she spent so lavishly that there was little left for the rainy day that came in the shape of serious and recurring illnesses, when to work was impossible. In 1925 a receiving order was made against her, but because of her continued ill health her public examination was not held till April 1930. The honest and straightforward manner in which she had dealt with her liabilities—all her royalties on her various books going to her creditors—was warmly commended when she applied for and was granted her discharge. She was free once more after efforts to meet her obligations that had cost her much in health and peace of mind. She regained her American nationality in 1938 and lived in California until 1948. Subsequently she went to live in Europe.

Personally Bettina von Hutten was even more interesting, more fascinating than her books. She had the power of making both men and women who began by disapproving of her end as her devoted and uncritical friends. What might be wrong for others seemed to her adoring circle right for Bettina. Her beauty, her charm disarmed the most fault-finding. Even in old age she kept the fascination of her youth. Her snow-white hair and pure, colourless skin gave her indeed a loveliness she had not possessed in her girlhood. She was a unique being, with her power of making all who came within her orbit love and excuse her. She gave happiness to others because she possessed it herself, a sheer joy in life that always lifted her above the many troubles and trials that beset her.

January 29, 1957.

Lady Hutton, C.B.E., **(Dr. Emslie Hutton),** wife of Lieutenant-General Sir Thomas Hutton, K.C.I.E., C.B., M.C., died on January 11, 1960 at her London home.

Isabel Hutton, only daughter of James Emslie, of Edinburgh, Deputy Keeper of the Privy Seal of Scotland, was educated at Edinburgh Ladies' College and Edinburgh University, and was determined at an early age to become a doctor. She passed her examinations with distinction and in spite of the prejudices prevailing at the time received the warm approbation of her professors.

Her first appointment was as pathologist at the Stirling District Asylum at Larbert. Subsequently she became a resident at the Royal Sick Children's Hospital, Edinburgh, from which she accepted the appointment of physician in charge of the women's side of the Royal Mental Hospital, Morningside, Edinburgh, under Dr. G. M. Robertson, who had seen something of her work when he was medical superintendent of Larbert. This post had never before been held by a woman. She had already gained her M.D. with honours while still at Larbert.

It was while she was at the Children's Hospital that Dr. Charles Mayo, who was visiting the hospital, invited her to join the staff of the famous Mayo Clinic—a unique distinction not so far enjoyed by any other British doctor, male or female. However, receiving at the same time the offer of the post at Morningside, she decided to make psychiatry her career.

In August 1915, in spite of every effort to deter her, she joined the Scottish Women's Hospitals which, having been refused by the British Government, had been accepted with enthusiasm by the French, Russians and Serbians. After a few months' service in France her unit went with the Armée d'Orient to Salonika and she remained in the Balkans until the end of the war.

She was C.O. of the unit which volunteered to accompany the Serbian Army in its victorious advance in 1918, and this was in fact its only hospital. As such it had to contend with malaria, typhus and Spanish "flu" in addition to the surgical requirements of the Army, Bulgarian prisoners and the civil population. She did most of the operations herself. This was perhaps the highlight of her career. Subsequently she published an account of her experiences under the title of *With a Woman's Unit in Serbia, Salonika and Sebastopol.*

After closing her hospital in Serbia Dr. Emslie took charge of Lady Muriel Paget's unit, which was serving in the Crimea with General Wrangel. She was one of the last to leave and brought a number of orphan children down to Constantinople in a destroyer. Here she took a prominent part in organizing relief for the starving Russian refugees.

On return to Edinburgh she was reinstated in her post at West House but resigned it on her marriage to Major T. J. Hutton, whom she had met in Constantinople. In 1921 Dr. Emslie Hutton, as she then styled herself, took up her residence in London. She obtained in succession a temporary research post at the Maudsley Hospital as a result of which she published a joint paper with Sir Frederick Mott; an appointment as honorary consultant at the new out-patient clinic at the same hospital; a similar post at the West End Hospital for Nervous Diseases; and finally one at the British Hospital for Nervous and Mental Diseases.

This last was in effect an out-patient clinic for early mental cases. It was largely that experience, against the background of her earlier work in mental hospitals, that persuaded her to publish her book *Mental Diseases in Modern Life.*

It was partly the result of her clinical experience with patients that she decided to write *The Hygiene of Marriage.* This undertaking was one which at that time required great courage and much anxious thought. However, its simplicity, frankness and good taste earned the universal approval of the medical profession and its press. At a later date she wrote *Women's Change of Life* (Heinemann), also published in the U.S.A.

In 1938 Dr. Hutton's husband was appointed to command the Western Independent District, India, and she followed him there in the autumn in order to install him in his new house in Quetta.

At an early stage in the war she offered her services as a consultant to the Government of India, but in spite of her qualifications and experience, and the shortage of medical staff, they were not interested. She took up therefore such useful activities as occasion offered—*e.g.*, in organizing the Thrift Shops, which not only met a crying need but also provided large sums for war charities; in broadcasting through All-India Radio on music, poetry and other subjects; in translating secret dispatches for the External Affairs Department; and in holding clinics in connexion with Miss Copeland's Coolie Welfare Scheme in Simla. Eventually she was offered and accepted the post of Director of the Indian Red Cross Welfare Service, which she occupied until she went home in 1946.

In that year Lady Hutton became senior consultant at the British Hospital and continued to serve in that capacity under the National Health Service until, after a year's extension, she was retired under the age rule and appointed Consultant Emeritus.

She received many decorations from the French, Serbs and Russians for her services in the First World War, and was appointed C.B.E. for her work as Director of Indian Red Cross Welfare in the War of 1939-45.

January 12, 1960.

I

Major-General Sir Ibrahim, Sultan of Johore— See **Johore.**

Harold L. Ickes, United States Secretary of the Interior from 1933 to 1946, who died in Washington on February 3, 1952 at the age of 77, was perhaps the most contentious figure in President Roosevelt's Administrations.

A Republican for most of his life, he was at last given his chance of high office by a Democrat and he used the power thus conferred upon him to protect with passionate fervour what he believed to be the rights of individuals against those who, he thought, had gathered too much power. A man of combative tendencies with a sharp tongue and a zest for controversy, he made a number of enemies: but there was no doubt of his efficiency and the many duties which fell to him were ably and conscientiously performed. Both in regard to the New Deal and the civil organization of the United States for war he did work of exceptional value. He resigned from office in 1946 with a characteristic gesture on the ground that he could not support certain men selected by President Truman* for inclusion in the Administration.

Harold L. Ickes was born on a farm in Frankstown Township, Blair County, Pennsylvania, on March 15, 1874. He came of Scottish-Irish and German stock. At 16 he was sent to school in Chicago and went on to the University of Chicago, where he paid his way by teaching in night schools. He was then for four years a reporter on local newspapers including the *Chicago Tribune* but returned to the university again to study law and in 1907 took the degree of Doctor of Law there. He then settled down in Chicago to practise as a lawyer.

From 1914 to 1916 he was a member of the Progressive national committee and in the latter year of the national executive committee. Then in 1916, after the break in the Republican Party had been healed, he took a prominent part in Charles E. Hughes's national campaign for the Presidency. In the 1914-18 war Ickes went to France and worked for the Y.M.C.A., and after this intermission entered politics again.

Ickes was Illinois manager of Hiram W. Johnson's Presidential campaign in 1924. He also continued to take part in municipal contests and on a later occasion refused an offer to run for the mayoralty of Chicago. Until 1932, indeed, he was as a rule to be found on the minority side, employing his remarkable energies on behalf of doomed causes and candidates who proved unacceptable. Then, however, he gave his support to Franklin D. Roosevelt's campaign.

On Roosevelt's election to the Presidency, Ickes went to Washington with an introduction to him from Senator Hiram Johnson, and, it was said, the hope that he might be appointed Indian Commissioner. At the time the President-elect was looking for a suitable head for the Department of the Interior. Ickes had the kind of political background he required, and, as there was no other promising candidate, he was given the position. The appointment came as one of the several surprises of the time, for he was little known outside Chicago, and Washington was at first in some doubt about the pronunciation of his name. Once again, however, Roosevelt, with his remarkable flair for human personality, had found the man he required.

Ickes was by nature a fighter. He was also a hard and effective worker. At the Department of the Interior, however, he found an office which taxed even his remarkable energies to the full. Not only was he virtually the equivalent of the British Home Secretary; from the middle of 1933 he was also Public Works Administrator, and in that capacity responsible for great public relief works in many parts of the country. At any time a large number of public services are under the supervision of the Secretary of the Interior; but at the time Ickes entered the Administration the New Deal was on the point of materialization and naturally added immensely to his labours. He was, however, full of zeal and activity, and on taking over his department was said to have hit it "like a small typhoon".

With the entrance of the United States into the war Ickes's duties were still further increased. He became, for instance, war-time Petroleum Coordinator and in 1942 Petroleum Administrator. It was naturally an invidious post. Later he was placed in charge of the coal mines and miners and was both firm and plain-spoken in the exercise of his authority. The more unpopular tasks of the Administration seemed indeed to fall largely to him. He appeared, however, to be unperturbed by criticism and attack, although he reserved his right to reply to it as pungently as he chose.

In spite of his official preoccupations Ickes found time to write some books—one was the *Autobiography of a Curmudgeon*, another *America's House of Lords*—to contribute articles to magazines, and to pursue his taste for gardening. For all his hard hitting he was a sensitive man, jealous of his own perogatives, delighted to be consulted, and angry if ignored. Although he had himself been a journalist, he became in his later years a sharp and persistent critic of the press.

In 1911 he married Miss Anna Wilmarth Thompson, who died in 1935; he married, secondly, Miss Jane Dahlman, of Milwaukee, in 1938. There was a son of the first marriage and a son and daughter of the second marriage.

February 5, 1952.

Courtenay Ilbert, who died on March 19, 1956 in London at the age of 67, was recognized without question as the leading expert in Britain, and perhaps over most of the world, on the history of horology.

Courtenay Adrian Ilbert was born on April 22, 1888. He was educated at Eton and King's College, Cambridge. He subsequently trained, and for a time practised, as a civil engineer, but the greater part of his life was given up to the study of the history of horology, and the perfection of his unrivalled collection, which he started while still at Eton. The collection includes not only typical instruments of all periods and nationalities, but many rare or unique specimens as well, and these are backed up by a library which probably has no equal.

All this was matched by his apparently limitless knowledge, in which he had the added advantage of a quite exceptional memory. Much as he disliked doing so, he was most generous in lending from his collection to horological exhibitions, both in England and abroad, and he accepted with remarkable equanimity the damaged condition in which his precious pieces were sometimes returned to him.

For the last five years of his life he was much occupied as the senior editor of the seventh edition of *Britten's Old Clocks and Watches and their Makers,* the standard British horological reference work, but hitherto many years out of print and out of date. It is indeed fortunate that a good part of his knowledge has been put on permanent record in this way.

In 1954 he was admitted honoris causa to the freedom and elected to the Livery of the Worshipful Company of Clockmakers. He had been a most patient invalid since November 1954.

March 23, 1956.

Lord Ilchester, the 6th earl, died in London on October 29, 1959 after an illness of several months. He was 85.

Though he had played no part in politics, nor was his voice often heard in the Great Council of the Nation, he will yet be long remembered for his wide culture, and for his life-long devotion to art and literature, borne witness to by his services (among others) as a trustee of the British Museum, as chairman of the National Portrait Gallery, and as president of the London Library.

His more permanent claim to remembrance lies, however, in his admirable historical works, of which the best known are: *The Life of Henry Fox, First Lord Holland*; *The Home of the Hollands*; and *Chronicles of Holland House*, which in a dignified and elegant style shed a real light on the political and social life of England, and especially of the Whig Party, during 100 years, and indeed raise their author to the ranks of the literary historians of his time.

His versatility is also shown in his services to the turf, and as a great landlord in the west of England much of his time was absorbed in the conscientious performance of the duties of local government.

The Rt. Hon. Giles Stephen Holland Fox-Strangways, G.B.E., sixth Earl of Ilchester, Baron Ilchester and Strangways, Baron Ilchester and Stavordale, and Baron of Redlynch, was the eldest son of the 5th Earl of Ilchester and was born on May 31, 1874. His mother was Mary, daughter of the first Earl of Dartrey. He went to Eton in 1887, to Marrindin's house, and later to Dalton's. His first tutor was Marrindin, and a later one H. V. Macnaghten.

He went up to Christ Church, Oxford, in 1892; but in the light of his subsequent scholarly interests he strangely did not take his degree, but instead hunted, joined the Bullingdon Club, and was gazetted to the Coldstream Guards. He did not remain long on the active list and went into the Reserves of Officers in 1897. He saw no more of military service until the war broke out in 1914, when he rejoined his old regiment and was appointed a King's Messenger, and carried continuously dispatches, not only between London and G.H.Q. in France, but to places as wide apart as Archangel, Salonika, India, and Cairo. He was created O.B.E. (Military) and received the Legion of Honour for these services.

Lord Ilchester's first published work, *The Life and Letters of Lady Sarah Lennox* (whom George III wished to marry) appeared in 1901, to be followed by the editorship of the 3rd Lord Holland's *Further Memoirs of the Whig Party*, and he also edited the *Journals of Elizabeth Lady Holland.* A work on a larger scale, *Henry Fox, His Family and Relations,* appeared in 1920. This was suggested to him by the late Lord Rosebery, and although primarily a biography, was indeed a political history of England from 1739, when Henry Fox obtained his first office, till his death in 1774. A life of his relative Sir Charles Hanbury-Williams, together with an edition of the correspondence of that Ambassador and Catherine II of Russia, appeared in 1929.

Eight years then elapsed before, in 1937, Lord Ilchester published what is really one work, though in two volumes, entitled respectively *The Home of the Hollands, 1605 to 1820,* and *Chronicles of Holland House, 1820 to 1890.* These volumes, as their name implies, had for their inspiration and centre Holland House, Kensington, whose destruction by enemy action in October 1940 was one of the chief minor tragedies of the war. (The property was sold to the L.C.C. in 1951).

Letters of Lady Holland to her Son was published in 1946 and *Lord Hervey and his Friends, 1726-1738,* of which Lord Ilchester was the editor, in 1950. In June 1948 he sent to *The Times Literary Supplement* an interesting letter that he had found among the saved Holland House MSS, addressed by Madame du Deffand to Horace Walpole, giving an account of the fall of the Duc de Choiseul.

Mention must also be made of Lord Ilchester's long membership of and service to the Walpole Society, which is devoted to the history of the arts (especially painting and sculpture) in England, and which he joined in 1916. He became a member of its council in 1923, and for many years acted as chairman of its two sub-committees, finally succeeding the late Earl Bathurst as its president in 1943. Lord Ilchester played a decisive part in guiding the society through the difficult years of its reconstitution after the late war. He also contributed to its volumes, his most important publications in the series being the analytical *Index* to Volumes I-V of the *Vertue Notebooks,* 1947 (a model of its kind), and the text and index of the *Supplementary Vertue Volume,* 1955.

His wide knowledge of art and history, stimulated by the possession of the collections at Melbury and Holland House (fortunately removed before the destruction of the latter), led to his appointment in 1931 as a trustee of the British Museum, and later as a trustee and in 1941 chairman of the National Portrait Gallery. From 1940 to 1952 he was president of the London Library. From 1943 to 1957 he was chairman of the Royal Commission on Historical Buildings, and for many years he was president of the Royal Literary Fund and of the Roxburghe Club.

He was considered, as this record of service shows, an ideal chairman of a committee, combining firmness and business capacity with a pleasant manner. At the British Museum in particular he was recognized as one of the most conscientious of the trustees, who never missed a meeting unless detained by one of his numerous other activities, and who had made himself acquainted with the work of every department and knew its officials, with whom he was on most friendly terms.

Reference should also be made to Lord Ilchester's interest in, and services to, the turf. As an owner he had no great success. His two best known horses were, perhaps, Jack Snipe and Misfit. But he had been a member of the Jockey Club since 1907, and he was a Steward in 1937, 1938, and 1939, and Senior Steward in 1939. He will be best remembered as the chairman of the Racing Reorganization Committee, the idea of which he proposed and the late Lord Derby seconded, which presented a report to the Stewards of the Jockey Club in 1943, and he was for many years chairman of the Rules Committee.

Lord Ilchester succeeded to the sporting estate of Melbury, on the borders of the Blackmore Vale country, where in his youth his father kept what must have been the last, or nearly the last, pack of roedeer hounds in England. Abbotsbury, another of his estates, has the famous swannery of which Lord Ilchester was very proud.

Natural history was also among his hobbies, and an appendix to *Chronicles of Holland House* is an interesting account of bird life in London.

Much of his time was spent on his property in the west, where he was active in local government. He had been Vice-Lieutenant and Deputy Lieutenant for Dorset, a Justice of the Peace, and a county alderman.

In the Second World War, though over 65, he was an active member of the Home Guard. He was created a G.B.E. in 1950, and he was given a D.Litt. degree by Oxford University the year before.

Lord Ilchester married in 1902 Helen, the daughter of the sixth Marquess of Londonderry. She died in 1956. There were two sons and two daughters of this marriage. He is succeeded by his elder son, Lord Stavordale, who was born on October 1, 1905, and married in 1931 Helen Elizabeth, twin daughter of Captain the Hon. Cyril Ward, R.N. They have a son and a daughter.

October 30, 1959.

Lord Iliffe, who died on July 25, 1960 in a London hospital at the age of 83, was probably associated with newspapers and periodicals for a longer period than any of his contemporaries in the same field.

The Rt. Hon. Edward Mauger Iliffe, G.B.E., first Baron Iliffe, of Yattendon, was born on May 17, 1877. All his life he was steeped in the newspaper tradition. He was the younger son of William Isaac Iliffe, a Coventry printer, who founded publications serving the cycle and motor industries in their very early days.

His long career in newspapers began when he was 17 in the *Coventry Evening Telegraph* which his father had established. On his father's death he and his brother W. Coker Iliffe were responsible for a very large expansion of the periodical publishing side of the firm. The business went to London and throve exceedingly.

Subsequently Iliffe became associated in a successful partnership with Lord Camrose [q.v.] and Lord Kemsley* in newspaper interests extending to many parts of the country and from 1928 to 1937 he was part-proprietor of the *Daily Telegraph.* In 1937 the partnership between Iliffe, Lord Camrose, and Lord Kemsley was dissolved. Apart from the *Daily Telegraph* he disposed of his shares and relinquished the deputy chairmanships of Allied (later Thomson) Newspapers and the Amalgamated Press (now Fleetway Publications). He kept control for a time of Kelly's Directories, which had acquired all the Iliffe periodicals, but finally sold out, retaining until 1943—when he acquired the *Birmingham Post,* the *Birmingham Mail,* and the *Birmingham Weekly Post*—the family paper in Coventry as his only publishing interest. At his death he was president of the Birmingham Post and Mail Ltd.

Iliffe had a remarkable capacity for crowding a wide range of business interests into a life already fully occupied with the affairs of newspapers and periodicals. He served as controller of the Machine Tools Department of the Ministry of Munitions in 1917-18 and represented the Tamworth division of Warwickshire as a Conservative from 1923 to 1929, when he resigned in order to give a seat to Sir Arthur Steel-Maitland, a former Minister of Labour, who had been unseated in the election.

For many years he did splendid work for the Association of the British Chambers of Commerce and was the association's president in 1932. He had considerable insurance interests, was chairman of the Guildhall Insurance Company and a director of the London Assurance. He was also a member of Lloyd's.

Iliffe had been Master of the Company of Stationers and Newspaper Makers, the Coachmakers and Coach Harness Makers' Company. and of the Clock Makers' Company. He had also been president of the Periodical Proprietors' Association. He gave Allesley Hall, with about 52 acres of land, to Coventry City Council and was a benefactor of Sherborne School. He was president of the Trustees of the Shakespeare Memorial Theatre, Stratford-on-Avon, from 1933 to 1958.

As a young man Iliffe was a fine lawn tennis

player and his interest in the game continued all his life. From 1945 to 1959 he was president of the International Lawn Tennis Club of Great Britain. His services as chairman of the Duke of Gloucester's Red Cross and St. John Fund in the Second World War—over £50m. was raised—were rewarded by his advancement to G.B.E. He had been made C.B.E. in 1918, knighted in 1922 and created a baron in 1933.

He married, in 1902, Charlotte Gilding, who survives him with one son and daughter. The heir to the barony is the Hon. Edward Langton Iliffe, chairman of the Birmingham Post and Mail Ltd. and of the *Coventry Evening Telegraph.*

July 26, 1960.

Sir Godfrey Ince, G.C.B., K.B.E., who died on December 20, 1960 in hospital in Wimbledon, was one of the outstanding figures of the Civil Service of his time. In the Second World War from 1941 he held the post of Director-General of Man Power in charge of the National Service, Labour Supply, and Military Recruitment, and from 1944 to January 1956 he was Permanent Secretary to the Ministry of Labour. Shortly after his retirement from the Civil Service Ince became chairman of Cable and Wireless and its associated companies. He was 69.

Not long after Ince became Permanent Secretary to the Ministry he had to concern himself with the vast problems of the oncoming demobilization after the war. He carried out the task with a skill and judgment which were in striking contrast to the confusion of policy after the First World War. Under the postwar Labour Government he had to face the problems of manpower shortages and dealt with them in an orderly and efficient way. He had to handle the reintroduction of a limited direction of labour. With a much stronger personality than the Minister of those years, George Isaacs, he was the man mainly responsible for the success of the department's policy as well as of its administration.

He was perhaps a planner by nature, a master of statistics of the future as well as the past, and under him the Ministry played an important part in the shaping of the nation's life. His orderly approach was perhaps less attuned to the confused problems of labour relations than to those of manpower supply, but to them also he gave much careful thought. Early in 1954, at a time when there had been some loss of confidence in arbitration machinery, he made a speech in which he said that the negotiating machinery in all industries should make provision for finality in a dispute by way of arbitration. This attracted a lot of attention and the Minister of Labour put the suggestion to his National Joint Advisory Council, but they took the view that while it might be good for some industries it was not necessarily good for others. Labour relations continued to defy all attempts to introduce system and order into them.

Godfrey Herbert Ince was the elder son of G. A. R. Ince, J.P., of Reigate, and was born on September 25, 1891. He was educated at Reigate Grammar School, and then at London University, gaining a Surrey County scholarship. His career there was exceptionally brilliant. He was Sherbrooke University Mathematical Scholar in 1912; Mayer de Rothschild Scholar in Pure Mathematics in 1913; Ellen Watson Memorial Scholar in Applied Mathematics in 1913; Joseph Hume Scholar in Political Economy in 1914; Senior Mathematics Prizeman in 1913; Senior Physics Prizeman at University College in 1914; and he took his B.Sc. with First Class Honours in Mathematics.

In the 1914-18 War he held a commission in the Yorkshire Regiment and was later transferred to the East Lancashire Artillery, and saw service in France, where he was wounded and where his mathematical knowledge was utilized by the field survey of the Royal Engineers, to whom he was attached. After being demobilized in 1919, Ince entered the Ministry of Labour, where, with his brilliant academic record, he was at once made an assistant principal. At that time the Ministry of Labour was regarded as rather the Cinderella of the Departments, though it was soon to produce a number of remarkable men, among them Lord Beveridge*, Sir Horace Wilson*, Humbert Wolfe, and C. E. M. Joad [q.v.], besides Ince himself.

In 1920 he was appointed Private Secretary to the Chief Labour Adviser, Sir David Shackleton, and he was later Private Secretary to successive Ministers of Labour, including the first woman Cabinet Minister, Margaret Bondfield [q.v.]. In 1933 he was made Assistant Secretary to the Ministry and Chief Insurance Officer under the Unemployment Insurance Act. In this last post, he had the unusual experience for a civil servant of spending a year or more in Australia and New Zealand, to assist the Governments of the Commonwealth and Dominion to work out their own social insurance systems. He later published a report on Unemployment Insurance in Australia.

On his return in 1938, he was made Principal Assistant Secretary to the Ministry. Then, the following year, came the war, which was to launch Ince into the main current of the work for which he will be remembered. In January 1940 he was made Under-Secretary to the Ministry to be specially concerned with National Service matters, and the following year he was seconded to the War Cabinet Office to take charge of the Production Executive Secretariat, whose chairman was Ernest Bevin [q.v.]. He and Ince were old acquaintances, for the latter had been the secretary to the dock enquiry presided over by the late Lord Shaw (afterwards Lord Craigmyle) in 1920, where Bevin scored his personal triumph as "the Dockers' K.C.". In June 1941 at the age of 49 Ince was appointed to the new and very responsible post of Director-General of Man Power: charged with the supply of men to the factories and recruiting for the Forces, and adjudicating upon the endless questions arising on the schedules of reserved occupations.

There is no doubt that Ince was one of the men who behind the lines and out of the glare of publicity did much towards winning the war. He was possessed of the clearest of brains and a phenomenal memory. His mathematical genius enabled him to reel off figures for hours without the aid of a note. All the details of manpower were at his finger-ends, and it was said that he could tell off-hand how many people had registered in each age-group. For the remarkable smoothness with which the nation was mobilized and after the war demobilized, he should receive a large share of the credit. The departments he controlled would run like clockwork; he was popular with his staff, who knew that they could trust him to deal with them fairly, and also in the industrial world for the same reason.

Ince was a civil servant who needed as Minister a man of the imaginative strength of Bevin, under whom he served during the war, but under lesser men he was still able to ensure that his Ministry was one of the most efficient.

Quiet and retiring and shunning publicity, a non-smoker and almost a teetotaller, Ince could yet surprise a dinner-table with a witty speech, and his athletic record was by no means undistinguished. He organized and captained the first University of London football team, the first English team ever to play at Moscow and subsequently at Prague, where the future President Benes was on the other side, and his average batting in University College cricket was respectable.

Ince was made a C.B. in 1941 and a K.B.E. in 1943. In October 1960 he was installed as a Knight Grand Cross of the Order of the Bath.

Ince married in 1918 Doris, second daughter of the late C. Maude, of Northallerton, Yorkshire, and he leaves three daughters.

December 21, 1960.

The Very Rev. W. R. Inge, K.C.V.O., D.D., Dean of St. Paul's from 1911 to 1934, died on February 26, 1954 at his home in Berkshire at the age of 93, after being ill for some time with bronchitis.

Of independent mind, fortified by the courage of his convictions and by the formidable graces of a first-class controversialist, he was often at issue not only with others of his cloth but also, and at times more seriously, with large sections of the public. The rightness of his views apart, he was one of the most effective polemical writers of his day. Vigorous thought found expression in vigorous language. When he was already over 90 he wrote a new preface to his controversial book, *England* (first published in 1926), which, in the directness of its style and views, would have been remarkable even from a man 30 years younger.

Essentially a philosopher rather than a theologian, a Christian Platonist prizing mystical experience above all else, Inge was unorthodox in some of his religious beliefs and was too forthright by nature to temper any wind.

Over most of his life his political views were sharply at variance with the easily popular currents of opinion. He maintained, with increasing emphasis, that progress, democracy, socialism were mere nineteenth century fetishes. In these as in other respects, however, he had the force as well as the singularity of a prophet, and if he did not always persuade, he compelled consideration of the religious aspect of problems which, without his intervention, would have been conceived in purely material terms.

Inge was, indeed, by no means the least active intellectual influence in the succession of the Deans of St. Paul's. His ability as an administrator was also proved by his handling of the problem of preserving the structure of the cathedral, which was found to be perilously insecure. It was in association with him as head of its Chapter that *The Times* was privileged to raise the funds to save it.

William Ralph Inge was born at Crayke, in Yorkshire, on June 6, 1860. He was the eldest son of the Reverend William Inge, D.D., Provost of Worcester College, Oxford, and Mary, daughter of the Ven. Edward Churton, Archdeacon of Cleveland. He was educated at Eton and King's College, Cambridge, and his long list of academic honours included the Bell, the Porson, and the Craven scholarships, a first class in each part of the Classical Tripos, and the Senior Chancellor's Medal and the Hare Prize.

From 1884 to 1888 he was an assistant master at Eton, from 1886 to 1888 a Fellow of King's, and from 1889 to 1904 a Fellow and Tutor of Hertford College, Oxford. In 1889 he was Bampton Lecturer at Oxford. Later, in 1906, he was Paddock Lecturer in New York, and in 1925 Lyman Beecher Lecturer at Yale. From 1905 to 1907, on the nomination of Canon Henson, he was Vicar of All Saints', Ennismore Gardens, and from 1907 to 1911 Lady Margaret Professor of Divinity and Fellow of Jesus College, Cambridge.

In the latter year Asquith chose him to be Dean of St. Paul's. At the time of his appointment he was already known as a religious teacher and a writer of independent temper. His contributions to the volume of essays by Oxford tutors entitled *Contentio Veritatis* (1902) and to a volume of Cambridge Biblical essays had drawn deserved attention to him. He had also published the earliest of his studies in mysticism, had followed the work of various German and other writers on eschatological themes, and had provoked a number of attacks by High Church thinkers and theologians. It was obvious from the first that the new Dean intended to take a prominent part in the intellectual life of his time, and he began with a series of vigorous and often pungent addresses to the Women's Diocesan Association.

Always frank and lucid, he was prepared to give and take blows on almost any subject. It was not for nothing that, in 1946, on the occasion of a literary celebration of the ninetieth birthday of his friend Bernard Shaw, Inge described himself as "the last surviving Whig". He had no use for socialism—or for that matter for modern capitalism—distrusted the masses, and stood for strong and austere government. His running comments, often penetrating and sometimes reactionary, on current affairs led him to be nicknamed "the gloomy Dean", a soubriquet he always maintained he did not deserve.

In 1915 he published his *Types of Christian Saintliness*, a book which illustrated in telling fashion his courage as a teacher and his penetration in criticism. Then, having given himself to further meditation during the war years, in 1919 he brought out his two volumes of lectures, *The Philosophy of Plotinus*. This, the most important of Inge's works of religious interpretation, was the most sympathetic attempt that had yet been made to present the spiritual aspect of its subject to English readers. Inge was intellectually and imaginatively absorbed in Plotinus as a saint and as the exponent of a mystical way of life, and his commentary is a sincerely felt and illuminating contribution to neo-Platonic thought. In the following year, as Romanes and Hibbert Lecturer, he examined the popular belief in progress not as a task for humanity but as a law of nature. His thought here owed not a little to Bury, but was not less characteristic on that account. Equally characteristic was his Galtonian faith in eugenics, which he proclaimed tirelessly from this time onwards.

Lucid, incisive, and not seldom mordant in style, with a remarkable breadth of reading, Inge was a busy author and journalist. It is impossible to do more than note some of his more arresting volumes. In his *Victorian Age* (1922) he maintained that that period and the Elizabethan were the greatest England had known. *Lay Thoughts of a Dean* (1926), a collection of his contributions to the press—for 30 years he was a most versatile, live, and stimulating contributor to the *Evening Standard* (earning the sub-acid description, "a pillar of the Church of England and two columns of the *Evening Standard*")—ranged over a vast and varied field of comment and inquiry.

In June 1934, at the Classical Association, he spoke on "Greeks and Barbarians". He was several years beyond the allotted span but as fresh and vigorous as ever. A few months later, however, he retired after nearly a quarter of a century at St. Paul's: his farewell sermon ended with the words, "I have finished the work that Thou gavest me to do". Almost simultaneously his *Vale* appeared. Dr. Inge went to live at Brightwell, near Wallingford, but continued almost as busily as ever to lecture and to write. His *Freedom, Love and Truth* (1936) was a remarkable anthology of the Christian life; *A Rustic Moralist* (1937), *Our Present Discontents* (1938), and *A Pacifist in Trouble* (1939) were volumes of miscellaneous writings; in *The Fall of the Idols* (1940) he confessed his satisfaction that he would not have to live in an England from which all the things that his upbringing had led him to prize—the English country house, the public school, the scholar and scientist of independent means—were banished. Except for an occasional reference to his advanced years, the volume bore few signs of his age.

Mysticism in Religion was a sort of summary of his literary effort, a recapitulation of the themes and interests nearest to his heart. For many years in his later life he had preached annually in Pusey House Chapel—his father was one of the original founders of Pusey House—and when he visited there as recently as May 1949, and preached on the text, "Now we see through a glass, darkly", he spoke with undimmed energy, throwing off characteristically brilliant flashes, and made a deep impression upon an unusually large congregation. Advancing years were only manifested by increasing deafness which, greatly to the regret of his friends, deprived them of the mental stimulus of the cut and thrust of conversation which had earlier been so great a pleasure.

In 1918 he was created a C.V.O. and in 1930 a K.C.V.O.

In 1905 he married Mary Catherine, daughter of the late Ven. H. M. Spooner, Archdeacon of Maidstone. She died in 1949. Of the three sons of the marriage the youngest died on active service with the R.A.F. in 1941, and Dr. Inge is survived by two sons and a daughter.

February 27, 1954.

Professor Sir Charles Inglis, O.B.E., F.R.S., Vice-Provost of King's College, Cambridge, from 1943 to 1946 and Professor Emeritus of Engineering in the University of Cambridge, died on April 19, 1952 at the age of 76.

Charles Edward Inglis was born on July 31, 1875, the son of Dr. Inglis, of Redhall and Auchindenny, Midlothian. Educated at Cheltenham College—in the activities of which school he took the keenest interest and was since 1929 enabled to play an active part as a member of the College Council—he was elected to a scholarship at King's College, and went into residence in 1894. In 1897 he was classed as twenty-second Wrangler in the Mathematical Tripos, and in the following year gained a first class in Mechanical Sciences. After taking his degree he joined the famous consulting firm—and training ground of so many engineers who have since reached eminence in their profession—Sir John Wolfe Barry and Partners, serving his time as a pupil and later becoming assistant engineer on public works of importance, including the construction of a section of the London Underground Railway.

It was during this period that he turned his attention to the study of mechanical vibration and, starting as a pioneer in a field of which few but he can at that time have foreseen the ultimate importance, he continued throughout his life with unabated interest, vigour, and freshness of imagination to lead in scientific contribution to this subject, now recognized to be at the root of a wide range of problems facing the engineer. It was this interest also which in a sense dictated his later career, since his early work gained him his Fellowship of King's College and led to his return as a university lecturer to Cambridge, where, interrupted only by the war of 1914-18, his life work lay, though in the widest sense.

In 1914 he was commissioned in the Royal Engineers and served with distinction and the War Office, where his originality and ingenuity found scope in the invention and design of military bridges, culminating in the notable Inglis bridge which at that time became an accepted standard of sapper equipment. In 1918 he retired with the rank of major, was appointed O.B.E., and returned to Cambridge, now as Professor of Engineering.

Nevertheless he found time to maintain an active contact with his profession and to establish a distinguished reputation as a consultant, as shown, for example, by his work for the bridge stress committee of the Department of Scientific and Industrial Research, his appointment to the committee set up by the Secretary of State for Air to inquire into the loss of the airship R101, and more recently by his chairmanship of the Railway (London Plan) Committee, which reported to the Minister of War Transport in 1946 with a bold scheme for development of the whole of the railway systems of London to fit the future needs of the metropolis. In 1944 he retired from the Chair of Engineering at Cambridge, though continuing to devote himself to consulting, and in the summer of 1945 he was awarded the honour of knighthood for his distinguished services to the country in war and peace. Lady Inglis, daughter of the late Lieutenant-Colonel Moffat, whom he married in 1901, died a few weeks before him.

Such is a brief outline of the life of a man who was bound to achieve distinction in any career which he had chosen to adopt, since his gifts of personality, character, and intellect passed far beyond the limits of any specialist attainment. Of his contribution to science much will remain to be written by the many whom he served (he himself would have chosen the word); by the firms who came to him as a consultant and found an engineer with an intensely practical outlook as well as a depth of knowledge and, where required, a rare mathematical skill to bring to their aid; by the London Midland and Scottish Railway, of whose research committee he was for many years an inspiring member; by the Institute of Naval Architects and the Institutions of Mechanical, Structural, and Waterworks Engineers, on whose councils he served, and of the latter of which he was elected president in the year 1935; by the Royal Society, into whose Fellowship he was admitted in 1930; and by the Institution of Civil Engineers, who first recognized the value of his work by their award of the Telford Medal in 1924, and into the presidency of which—perhaps the greatest honour which can be paid to an engineer—he was elected in 1941 after many years of service on their council.

In a life of such width of activity it is not easy to single out a particular feature, but since technical and scientific achievements will come to be recorded in their lawful places it may be proper here to refer to two other aspects which must rank him as one of the great men of his generation. The first is as a teacher, and here, although following in the tradition laid down by his one-time chief at Cambridge, Sir James Alfred Ewing, he was no mere follower but an inspired disciple whose influence on engineering education throughout the country was profound. It is the engineer's business to build first of all a solid foundation upon which the stability of whatever structure may later be required must rest, and it was upon this that Inglis based his creed—that the first essential of an engineer's education is a solid groundwork of scientific first principles upon which the specialized knowledge and technique required later can be firmly built.

The other aspect is personal. What characterized Inglis above all can only be described as his joy in living; his intense pride, but humility, in the profession which he had chosen, and an enthusiasm for the achievements of men in any sphere of human activity provided it was true and honest.

April 21, 1952.

Melbourne Inman, who held the professional billiards championship six times between 1908 and 1919 and was one of the greatest match players the game has ever produced, died in Farnborough Hospital, Kent, on August 11, 1951 at the age of 73.

He was in his prime when ivory balls were in use and when the big matches were played by points instead of by time. In those days safety play was engaged in to such an extent that the scoring of a sessional number of points, perhaps 666 or 750, would take anything up to three hours to complete and the result was that games were often decided as much by defensive play as by large breaks or consistent scoring. In this particular form of play Inman was in his element, and although he was a very fine all-round player it was sometimes felt that other more stylish opponents and perhaps more skilful players might have beaten him if they had possessed the same temperament. It was in this respect that Inman was such a difficult player to beat.

One of his oldest opponents was T. Reece, but although they must have played more matches together than any other two players in the history of the game Inman was usually the winner. Again and again he showed that temperament can play an enormous part in the game. Inman relied to a great extent on all-round play. He knew little of, and seemed to care less for, close-cannon play and he devoted little attention to the top-of-the-table game, but as a losing-hazard and long-range-cannon player he was second to none. Nothing seemed to ruffle him and although he might have fallen considerably behind his opponent he usually won the match in the end.

Inman was declared champion of the game when there was no contest in 1908, and after that he had many stern matches with such players as H. W. Stevenson, T. Reece [q.v.], and later with W. Smith, T. Newman, and C. Falkiner, who were making sound progress during this stage. Inman won the championship in 1909 and was then beaten in the final twice by Stevenson.

Inman renewed his hold on the championship in 1912 and held it, with the war intervening, until 1919, after which the younger generation began to carry off the chief honours.

August 13, 1951.

Cardinal Innitzer, Archbishop of Vienna, died there on October 9, 1955, having undergone an operation a month earlier. He was in his eightieth year.

The Cardinal's name is most clearly remembered outside Austria in connexion with the German occupation of Austria in 1938, and with reports, which were published at the time, of his apparent eagerness to recognize and assist the invaders. Much was made of the "Heil Hitler" in his own handwriting which he appended to his covering letter to Herr Bürckel, the Plebiscite Commissioner. It was certainly true that he issued a statement as head of the Austrian hierarchy calling for compliance with regulations issued by the *de facto* authorities. But parts of this statement were suppressed by the German censorship, in particular a qualifying reference to the need for guarantees of the "rights of God and of the Church". Read today the statement seems to have amounted to little more than an expression of thanksgiving that there had been no bloodshed and an appeal to Catholics in Austria to comply with orders "voluntarily and with good grace".

Nevertheless, the Holy See, through the *Osservatore Romano*, made it clear that the action then taken by the hierarchy was without previous consultation of, or approval by, the Vatican. Subsequently Cardinal Innitzer was summoned to Rome, where Pope Pius XI, in audience, warned him of the dangers confronting Germany and Austria (the Cardinal was of German birth), adding, as Cardinal Innitzer himself stated after the liberation of Austria by the Allies, that Hitler was a warlike man who would lead the German nation into war.

On his return to Vienna the Cardinal met Hitler, who promised a generous attitude to the Church in Austria. "He promised me everything in religious matters. . . . But all Hitler's promises were lies." Within a few months the pattern of Nazi policy had become clearer. The Cardinal and his fellow bishops issued a pastoral protesting strongly against the new laws secularizing marriage and excluding priests and religions from schools, hospitals, and public institutions. Later a mob, rather hastily and vaguely disowned by the Nazi authorities, attacked the Cardinal's palace, doing considerable damage. More rioting and looting occurred in the next few months; and part of the damage has been left unrestored ever since by Cardinal Innitzer's orders, as a reminder of the outrages suffered.

Whatever may be thought of his immediate attitude to the annexation of Austria, there can be no doubt that he was swift in protesting against each further encroachment on liberty and that he commanded throughout the war and afterwards the sincere devotion of his people, as well as the respect of the leaders of other denominations.

Theodor Innitzer was born on Christmas Day, 1875, at Weipert Neugeschri in Bohemia, the son of a lace maker of moderate means. Although obliged to leave school in 1890 to find work, he continued what studies he could until his parish priest succeeded in raising the money needed for his entrance to a seminary. His years of comparative hardship gave him an understanding of working class conditions, which showed itself during his episcopacy in his practical application of social principles for the relief of the unemployed and of deprived children.

His ordination in 1902 was followed by his appointment to a seminary in Vienna. Subsequently he became a lecturer on New Testament exegesis at the University of Vienna, and in later years he became well known as an archaeologist. In 1918 he was appointed rector of a college specializing in the scientific instruction of theological students. Following the death of Cardinal Piffl in 1932, the Papal Nuncio consulted Mgr. Ignaz Seipel on the choice of a successor. Mgr. Seipel himself was being considered for the see, but offered reasons of ill health for declining and proposed the name of Dr. Innitzer, who was consecrated in that year and in March of the following year was elevated to the Sacred College of Cardinals.

October 10, 1955.

Lord Inverchapel, formerly British Ambassador to the United States, died in hospital at Greenock on July 5, 1951 at the age of 69.

He was one of the ablest and most successful of the British diplomatists of his day. Having served in many parts of the world and been Minister in Guatemala and at Santiago, he was posted in 1931 to Stockholm, where he rendered considerable service to Anglo-Swedish relations. In 1935 he was appointed Ambassador to Iraq, and two years later succeeded Sir Hughe Knatchbull-Hugessen* in China. From China he was transferred in 1942 to Russia, an even more important post. At the height of the common war effort of the two countries against Germany it was for him to be the resident expositor in Russia of British policy.

When he arrived in the United States in May 1946 he was generally considered to be the only person who could follow Lord Halifax [q.v.]. During his first two months in Washington the British loan—the last attempt to re-create the pre-war world—was passed by Congress. Before he left, two years later, he had seen Congress pass the European Recovery Programme by a much larger majority.

Between the middle of 1946 and the middle of 1948 he had watched the United States lose hope of Soviet good will and decide to build a new western world strong enough to resist Russia. By then those who had known Lord Inverchapel in previous posts recognized that he was a tired man and one robbed of the hopes he had brought from Moscow. Economic problems of the kind with which his Embassy was now preoccupied did not interest him or suit his temperament, and it was no surprise when he decided to retire rather than undertake to stay through the whole four years of the Marshall [q.v.] Plan.

Sir Archibald John Kerr Clark Kerr, P.C., G.C.M.G., first Baron Inverchapel, of Loch Eck, in the County of Argyll, in the Peerage of the United Kingdom, was born on March 17, 1882, the fifth son of the late John Kerr Clark, of Crossbasket, Hamilton, Lanarkshire, by his marriage with the late Kate Louisa, daughter of Sir John Struan Robertson, K.C.M.G. Having been educated privately and nominated an attaché in the Diplomatic Service in 1905, he passed a competitive examination in 1906 and was posted to Berlin.

In 1913 he was appointed British secretary to the British and American Claims Arbitration Tribunal and a little later was transferred to Rome. Promoted to second secretary in 1914 he was transferred to Teheran. In 1916 he was recalled to the Foreign Office, and in 1918 enlisted in the Scots Guards. Returning after the war to his own service he was promoted to first secretary in 1919 and appointed to H.M. Agency at Tangier. Thence in 1922 he went to Cairo as counsellor to the Residency and in this capacity was second to Lord Allenby, the High Commisioner, between the departure of the Hon. E. S. Scott, the Minister, in September 1923 and the arrival of (Sir) Nevile Henderson just after the Egyptian crisis in November 1924. In 1925 Clark Kerr, who had been promoted acting counsellor in 1923 and counsellor in 1924, was appointed Minister to the Central American Republics, a position which he held until 1928, when he was transferred to Santiago de Chile. While there he married Maria Teresa Diaz Salas, daughter of Javier Diaz Lira of that city.

His next mission was to Stockholm. In 1935 he was created a K.C.M.G. and in the same month left to become British Ambassador to Iraq. He was at Baghdad for nearly two years, and then went to China as successor to Sir Hughe Knatchbull-Hugessen, who had been seriously wounded in an attack by low-flying Japanese aircraft upon his motor-car.

His was indeed to become a perilous post; and in his tenure of it he was to show not only great courage but remarkable ability. At a time when Great Britain was compelled to conceal the real feeling of her people towards the Chinese by closing the Burma Road and limiting supplies through Hongkong, he succeeded without any disloyalty to the official attitude in conveying their sentiments by his own bearing. His bomb-scarred house in Chungking has been described as a moral landmark, and he is said to have remarked on one occasion: "The Foreign Office have ordered me to move the Embassy, but they cannot order me to move my body". Thus he and his Russian colleague were the only foreign representatives who faced out the daily bombings with the Chinese officials. When, therefore, he left in January 1942 to succeed Sir Stafford Cripps [q.v.] at Moscow he had won the admiration of the Chinese and there was widespread regret at his going. Shortly before he had been promoted G.C.M.G. and also received the Order of the Brilliant Jade from the Chinese Government.

His four years in China were naturally a valuable qualification for his new post, which, at the time he went to it, was of vital importance to Great Britain and the allied cause. On his way to take over his duties he stopped at Teheran and saw the development of the supply route to Russia, for his first task was to assure the Soviet Government that the assistance which was then being rendered to the Russian armies would be continued. In April he went from his temporary headquarters at Kuibyshev to the Kremlin where he had a long and most friendly talk with Stalin [q.v.]. The result of it and of his conversations with Molotov was to better the understanding between the allied Governments.

There was general regret in Moscow when he was withdrawn early in 1946 to go on a special mission to the Netherlands East Indies to try to effect a settlement of the tangled politics there which were an aftermath of the Japanese occupation. Only a very limited time was available, for he had already been nominated to succeed Lord Halifax as Ambassador to the United States, and in May he took up his onerous duties in Washington. There he made many friends during his too short stay, for he resigned his post in 1948 and at the same time retired from the Diplomatic Service.

July 6, 1951.

Lord Inverforth, P.C., who died at his home in London on September 17, 1955 at the age of 90, was a great shipping and commercial leader, and was at his prime when the British shipping industry was rich in men of outstanding ability.

His career may be divided into three main parts. In the first, which preceded the war of 1914-18, he built up the business of Andrew Weir and Co., shipowners and merchants, of London, Glasgow, and elsewhere, of which he was senior partner. He saw to it that the foundations of this business were soundly laid and the methods practised highly efficient. When Lloyd George formed his Government in 1917 Andrew Weir, as he was then, was spoken of in the shipping industry as a possible Shipping Controller. Lloyd George, however, chose Lord Maclay [q.v.], who proved signally successful in the position, and Lord Inverforth assumed other important duties in the national interest, first at the War Office and then as Minister of Munitions from 1919 to 1921. His public work during that war formed the second stage, although a short one, in his career. The third began soon after the end of the war when he returned to his own business, and, although during this period he did not often appear before the public, he exercised great influence in the different commercial spheres in which he concerned himself.

A native of Kirkcaldy, Andrew Weir, who was born in 1865, started life in comfortable circumstances. But what he owed most to his parents, if this outstanding characteristic was attributable to them, was an absorbing interest in commerce. This continued to be the dominating force with him throughout his life. He was the main architect of the fortunes of Andrew Weir and Co., managing owners of the Bank Line, which included many large motor vessels and well-designed and well-equipped steamships engaged in general trading; Invertanker, Limited, owning several oil tankers; and the Inver Transport and Trading Company, Limited, owners of a number of large motor ships. The interests of his companies extended to the Baltic coasts—he was concerned in the United Baltic Corporation—to the oil industry, and to the nitrate trade of Chile.

Lord Inverforth made his first appearance in public life in March 1917, when, on the invitation of Lord Derby, then Minister of War, he reported on the commercial organization of the supply branches of the Army. He recommended the appointment of a Surveyor-General of Supply who would be a member of the Army Council, with authority to take over from the different departments of the War Office all the work related to supplying the Army with stores and equipment other than munitions. This recommendation was adopted, and Lord Inverforth was invited to become the new Surveyor-General of Supply. He accepted the appointment and was made a member of the Army Council.

Accompanied by Sir John Cowans and Sir Crofton Atkins he visited the battlefields on the Continent, and there followed the organization of far-reaching schemes of salvage in all theatres of war as well as at home. His outstanding success in this work led to his appointment after the Armistice as Minister of Munitions, whose task it was to liquidate the immense commitments, running into hundreds of millions sterling, authorized by his predecessors in the office during wartime. These duties involved the examination and disposal of hundreds of thousands of contracts and accounts. He held this position until March 1921. He then became the first chairman of the Disposal and Liquidation Commission, which was concerned with the sale of vast quantities of military stores in the British Isles and in war areas throughout the world.

After his retirement from Government work Lord Inverforth became actively associated with the Marconi group of companies. He was president of Marconi's Wireless Telegraph Co. Ltd., and joint president of the Radio Communication Co. Ltd., Marconi International Marine Communication Co. Ltd., and the Marconi Sounding Device Co. Ltd. In 1929 he became president of Cable and Wireless (Holding) Ltd., and in June 1945 was appointed president of all the associated enterprises. His other directorships included the chairmanship of the Anglo-Burma Rice Company and of the Wilmer Grain Co. Ltd. He was on the board of Lloyds Bank.

His love for commerce and close application to it, which amounted to genius, meant that he was absorbed in it, whether at home or in the City, morning, afternoon, and night. He had no hobbies apart from a little interest in yatching and affection for his home and grounds.

During the war of 1939-45 he often thought of possible fresh openings for enterprise to be carried out when peace was restored, and he consulted his lieutenants on the prospects. Like a number of other commerial leaders he was a good judge of character, and the men appointed to important positions in his large organization were carefully chosen. Once satisfied that those selected were worthy of full confidence he trusted them implicitly. He was a model employer and concerned himself with the welfare of members of his staffs during their active working lives and afterwards in retirement. He was easily approached.

He was created Baron Inverforth, of Southgate, and made a Privy Councillor in 1919, and he received the American D.S.M. in the same year.

In June 1941 he suffered a heavy loss through the death of his wife. She was Anne, younger daughter of Thomas Kay Dowie. The marriage took place in 1889. His heir is the Hon. Andrew Morton Weir, who was born in 1897. He is also survived by four daughters.

September 19, 1955.

King Faisal II of Iraq was shot dead in his palace at Baghdad on July 14, 1958, with his uncle, Crown Prince Abdul Illah [q.v.] and Nuri es Said [q.v.], Prime Minister of the Arab Federation.

Faisal ibn Ghazi ibn Faisal el Hashim, who was 23 at the time of his death, belonged to the forty-first generation of the Hashemite family, which claims descent from the Prophet Mohamed. Among his ancestors were the Abbassid caliphs who ruled Baghdad from the eighth to the thirteenth century.

He was born in Baghdad at Qasr al-Zuhur, the Palace of Roses, on May 2, 1935, the only son of King Ghazi and Queen Aliyah.

His parents were first cousins, so that on both sides he was great-grandson of Hussein ibn-Ali, the grand sherif of Mecca, who became the first King of the Hejaz in 1916 after joining the Allied cause in the First World War, and founded the modern Hashemite dynasty. On the paternal side his grandfather was King Faisal I, who fought against the Turks with Lawrence of Arabia and emerged as the first King of modern Iraq.

In April 1939 King Ghazi, driving his own car, crashed into an electric power standard near his palace and died of his injuries within a few hours. His son, then only three years old, was proclaimed King Faisal II and the Emir Abdul Illah, King Ghazi's first cousin and brother-in-law, was appointed Regent and heir to the throne.

As a child King Faisal had an English nurse and a Scottish governess. His first schooling was under a tutor who conducted classes for him and five or six Iraqi boys of his age who had been chosen to provide him with companionship.

At the age of 12 the young King left for Britain to enter Sandroyd Preparatory School, near Salisbury, where he stayed for two years before going to Harrow. His father was an old Harrovian and he proudly sported his father's straw hat. His English education had from the beginning its national counterpart, and Arab tutors followed him to Britain. He was taught his mother tongue Arabic, as well as the geography and history of the Middle East. He also learned Turkish, Kurdish, and French.

In 1950 he suffered a great blow when his mother, Queen Aliyah, who had been supervising his studies and watching over him in Britain, died at the age of 38.

After completing his studies at Harrow in the summer of 1952 the young King left for an extensive tour of the United States with his uncle, Abdul Illah. On May 2, 1953, Faisal acceded to the throne as third king of modern Iraq, on the same day as his cousin Hussein became King of Jordan. Wearing a field-marshal's uniform, he drove through cheering crowds to take the oath to the constitution before a session of both Parliaments and officially began his reign.

In 1954 Faisal, accompanied by his uncle, paid a state visit to Pakistan. Later he went to London and on his way back stopped in Amman for talks on Arab affairs with King Hussein of Jordan. This was followed by an official visit to Lebanon.

The next year he attended King Hussein's wedding in Amman, paid a state visit to Turkey and stayed privately in Britain. It was during that year, too, that his Prime Minister, Nuri es Said, took part in the founding of the Baghdad Pact. In the spring of 1956 he paid an official visit to Spain, followed by another to the Sultan of Morocco. In July he was again in Britain, on his second state visit.

Almost a year later Faisal and King Saud met in Baghdad, declared their determination to safeguard their independence and their spiritual and Islamic heritage and their opposition to foreign intervention, Zionism and imperialism "which were threatening the Arab nation". In July the King went by air to Istanbul to begin a summer holiday. There was a meeting with King Hussein on board the Turkish presidential yacht Umur, and in September it was apparent that the royal stay on the Bosporus had been concerned with matters other than holiday-making, for it was announced that the King was to marry Princess Fazilet, daughter of Prince Thehmet Ali Ibrahim of Egypt.

In February 1958 he arrived in Amman, at the invitation of King Hussein, to take part in discussions on the federation of Jordan, Iraq, and Saudi Arabia. Three days later at a ceremony held at 7.30 in the morning the two kings proclaimed the union of their kingdoms in the "Arab federation", with King Faisal as head of State and King Hussein as his deputy. The two young men had sat up all night putting the finishing touches to the agreement and it was signed before breakfast.

From an early age Faisal showed exceptional promise. His perspicacity was evident in his grasp of detail and his intelligence was shown to advantage in his lively conversation with an endless succession of visitors.

July 23, 1958.

Crown Prince of Iraq—See **Abdul Illah.**

Field Marshal Lord Ironside died on September 22, 1959 at Millbank Military Hospital, London, at the age of 79, after an accidental fall at home.

His achievements in North Russia gave him a place in the imagination of the public, and he held it with his massive presence, friendly manner, and the reputation for endurance and adventure in out of the way parts of the world.

The Right Hon. Sir William Edmund Ironside, first Baron Ironside of Archangel and of Ironside, in the County of Aberdeen, in the Peerage of the United Kingdom, a Field-Marshal in the Army, G.C.B., C.M.G., D.S.O., was born on May 6, 1880, the son of Surgeon Major William Ironside, R.H.A., of Ironside in Aberdeenshire. His father died a few months after his birth and he was brought up by his mother, who was Emma Maria, a daughter of William Haggett Richards, of Martock, Somerset. She continued to be a great influence in his life until her death in 1939 at the age of 94.

Ironside was educated at Tonbridge and the Royal Military Academy, Woolwich, and was commissioned in the Royal Artillery in 1899. He was soon in South Africa, with a Field Battery, the 44th, and saw continuous and hard campaigning in Cape Colony, the Orange River Colony and the Transvaal.

He had a facility for acquiring languages and in very early days in South Africa had mastered Cape Dutch. This had enabled him, while still a very junior subaltern, to carry out a fine piece of intelligence work in German South-West Africa. Impersonating a disaffected young Boer, he drove a wagon and span of oxen to the frontier and became a transport driver to the Germans. He was able to obtain information on the conduct of operations by the Germans and their treatment of the inhabitants before suspicion was aroused and he had to leave hurriedly.

Qualifying for the Staff College at Camberley in 1913, he was thus in the Senior Division when war came in 1914.

He was selected in January 1918 as Commandant of the Small Arms School in France. Then came the German offensive against the fifth and third British Armies. Instructors, students, batmen, cooks were all brought from the schools as reinforcements, and Ironside, with his contingent, joined the IV Corps at Bucquoy. He was at once put in command of the 99th Infantry Brigade of the 2nd Division, which had been badly mauled. His first task was to absorb the large drafts of reinforcements, and refit and train his command. He led the brigade in the offensive through the actions at Albert and Bapaume, the early stages of the final advance. He returned to staff work as Brigadier-General, General Staff, and was then selected to command the allied expeditionary forces at Archangel.

The expedition to North Russia had been sent at the request of the new Russian Government to stem any German pressure in that part, but on the conclusion of the treaty of Brest Litovsk it became more and more an effort to prevent the spread of Bolshevism. A formidable task faced Ironside. His own allied command of 18,000 men from 16 nations was made up of men of low physical category, ill-suited for service on any active front, let alone the Arctic in mid-winter. He raised their spirits and welded them into a reasonable whole. His main concern was to make something of the Russians available, and he set about training and arming some 25,000 of them, into whom he instilled some enthusiasm though, as the best had been killed, he was hampered by the lack of officers of good quality. As winter wore on and spring came, he had to meet three serious attacks, and it was clear that enthusiasm for action lay with the Bolsheviks whom his Russians became less and less willing to attack or oppose. The culmination was a series of mutinies. Although two seasoned infantry brigades had reached him, it was clear that a second winter was impossible, and Sir Henry Rawlinson was sent out to supervise the withdrawal from Archangel and Murmansk.

His next post was Chief of the British Military Mission to Eastern Hungary, which was concerned largely with the frontier with Romania. After a short time in Mesopotamia, he was put in command of the force in the Ismid peninsula, on the Asian shore of the Bosporus, in support of the Greeks who had been entrusted by the allies with the protection of Anatolia and Asia Minor against any incursion by Mustapha Kemal.

He next took over the small North Persian Force whose task was to prevent the Bolsheviks from penetrating into Central Persia from the Caucasus and the Caspian. He returned to England in 1921 and in the following year was appointed Commandant of the Staff College at Camberley where he remained until the spring of 1925. He succeeded Sir Peter Strickland as commander of the 2nd Division at Aldershot and in 1928 went out to India to command the Meerut District and the 3rd Indian Division, a command much more to his taste than Aldershot. He was promoted lieutenant-general in 1931, ended his command the next year, and went on half pay. At the same time he was appointed Lieutenant of the Tower of London.

In 1933 he returned to India as Quartermaster-general at Army Headquarters to Sir Philip Chetwoode, the Commander-in-Chief. The mechanization of part of the transport of the Army in India was in progress and he dealt energetically with the many problems of choice of vehicles, of organization, and of logistics which the change produced. He was promoted general in June 1935, but remained as Q.M.G. until the following year. He returned to England to be General Officer Commanding in Chief, Eastern Command.

The choice of Lord Gort (who was Military Secretary to the Secretary of State for War, Leslie Hore-Belisha [q.v.]), to be Chief of the Imperial General Staff seemed to suggest that General Ironside might not be selected for further high appointment; and this view seemed to be confirmed when it was announced that he was to become Governor of Gibraltar. Then came the Munich crisis and a new future seemed to open for him. He went to Cairo to take over the new Middle East Command.

The appointment was, however, provisional, and he arrived at Gibraltar to take over only a fortnight after the date originally planned. He at once set about improving the defences of the fortress, a process which was to continue during the years of the war. He was appointed Inspector-General of Overseas Forces and left Gibraltar in the following June. He was in Poland for discussions for the last weeks in July and came back with a somewhat optimistic view of the capabilities of the Polish Army. On the declaration of war Lord Gort became Commander-in-Chief of the British Expeditionary Force and Ironside, the senior General on the active list, took his place as Chief of the Imperial General Staff.

His first concern was to carry through the arrangements for the dispatch of the Expeditionary Force to France. Preparations for the reception of further formations, both of the Army and the Royal Air Force, were pushed forward during the winter, which foreshadowed a large increase in the British commitment and involved a huge amount of reserve material and stores being sent across the Channel. The German invasion of Norway demanded intervention and drew to that front the few formations immediately ready in the British Isles, and even an Infantry Brigade from France. When the Germans next attacked in the Low Countries, the Chief of the Imperial General Staff had no reserve to hand with which to influence the battle. He told the Government that a withdrawal to the coast which had been adumbrated in a conversation he had had earlier in the day with General Pownall*, Lord Gort's Chief of Staff, could not be accepted, and advised a movement to the south through Amiens to link up with the French left. They agreed and he went at once to France with orders to Lord Gort to carry this plan into effect. On arrival he found that events had overtaken him and he could but agree with the Commander-in-Chief that to save as many men as they could through Dunkirk was the only possible course of action.

In May 1940 he handed over as Chief of the Imperial General Staff to Sir John Dill and was appointed General Officer Commanding-in-Chief Home Forces. He at once set about raising a Defence Force, which later became the Home Guard, sorting out and re-equipping the troops returning from Dunkirk, and preparing a G.H.Q. Defence Line. It was not a task well suited to his temperament. In July he was succeeded by Sir Alan Brooke [q.v.] and promoted Field-Marshal. In the next New Year's Honours List he was created a Baron.

He married in 1915 Mariot Ysobel, daughter of the late Charles Cheyne, who survives him with the son and daughter of the marriage. The son, Edmund Oslac Ironside, R.N. (retd.), born September 21, 1924, succeeds to the title. He married in 1950 Audrey Marigold, younger daughter of Lieutenant-Colonel the Hon. Thomas Morgan-Grenville, D.S.O., O.B.E.

September 23, 1959.

Sir James Irvine, K.B.E., F.R.S., who died at his home at St. Andrews on June 12, 1952 at the age of 75, had been Vice-Chancellor and Principal of the University of St. Andrews for more than 30 years.

He brought to his duties a knowledge of the work and needs of the university gained during his 12 years' work there as Professor of Chemistry and director of the research laboratories, and four years as Dean of the Faculty of

Science. The number of students increased greatly, and work both at St. Andrews and at University College, Dundee, expanded rapidly. He also found time for much external work for education.

As chairman of the Forest Products Research Board and of the Prime Minister's committee for the training of biologists, as well as of the Colonial Office inquiry into the training of forestry officers, he did much to help other universities and industry. He was chairman of the Adult Education Committee of Scotland and of the Scottish Universities' Entrance Board, and for several years served on the advisory committees of the Scottish Education Department and of the Department of Scientific and Industrial Research. For these services he was created an honorary Fellow of the Educational Institute of Scotland in 1933. His reputation as an adviser on educational matters led to his appointment to the Viceroy's Committee on the Indian Institute of Science in 1936; to the Commission on Higher Education in the Colonies, and as chairman of the Inter-University Council convened to deal with colonial education from 1946 to 1951. He was also in 1944 appointed chairman of the Committee on Higher Education in the West Indies.

His work as a chemist was well known and appreciated throughout the world, and was concerned in the main with the constitution and chemistry of sugar, in which he continued the researches of Emil Fischer and evolved new processes for industry relating to these natural products. During the 1914-18 war there was a scarcity of sugar for certain vaccines which had been formerly procured from Germany. The stocks had become exhausted and a fresh supply was urgently needed for medical use in the armies. He set about the task of preparing it synthetically, and after persistent efforts was able to produce it in such quantities as were required in temporary sheds erected on the lawns of the university at St. Andrews, and much more cheaply than it had been purchased from Germany before the war.

James Colquhoun Irvine was born at Glasgow on May 9, 1877. Educated at the Allan Glen's School and the Royal Technical College there, he went on to St. Andrews University, where he took the degree of B.Sc. in 1898. He then proceeded to the University of Leipzig, where he took the degree of Ph.D. in 1901. Two years later he took his doctor's degree in science at St. Andrews and was attached to the chemical department as research student and assistant before he became professor. His work for education and for chemical studies brought him many honours. He was elected a Fellow of the Royal Society in 1918 and was awarded its Davy medal in 1926. In 1920 he was created a C.B.E., knighted in 1925, and promoted K.B.E. in 1948.

He married in 1905 Mabel Violet, the youngest daughter of John Williams. There were two daughters and a son of the marriage. The latter died on active service in 1944.

June 13, 1952.

J

Dr. L. P. Jacks, the founder and editor for 45 years of the *Hibbert Journal* and for many years Principal of Manchester College, Oxford, died at his home at Oxford on February 17, 1955 in his ninety-fifth year.

A profound and original thinker, he stimulated thought in others throughout a long career extending over two generations. There was never any doubt about his own predilections and his liberal convictions, but although it may be said that he engaged himself mainly in propagating throughout his long life, fearlessly and persuasively, the view that a fundamentally spiritual way of existence was in the strictest sense rational, he was no narrow bigot, and his long record as preacher, teacher, editor, and writer long ago revealed a breadth of view and a tolerance for which even some of his friends only tardily gave him credit. No man who ever proclaimed the Free Christian doctrine was more understanding of those whose faith rested upon dogma and authority, and no Unitarian leader ever had a wider range of fast friends within all the schools of religion and philosophy.

Lawrence Pearsall Jacks was born at Nottingham on October 9, 1860, one of a numerous family who were left fatherless at an early age. As a boy he went to the University School, Nottingham, but as a youth he had to provide for himself by teaching, an experience giving him an insight into educational problems with which he was to be so much concerned in later years. Deciding to study for the Unitarian ministry, he entered Manchester College, then situated at University Hall, London. He took his London M.A. degree in 1886, and studied theology under the great Dr. Martineau, whose lines of thought he so closely followed. Later, Jacks spent some months at Göttingen, and then made his first acquaintance with the United States as Hibbert Scholar for a year at Harvard.

He was fortunate enough in 1887 to become assistant at Bedford Chapel to the Rev. Stopford Brooke, whose secession from the Anglican Church in 1880 was still a topic of the day in religious circles. Jacks became son-in-law to his chief by marrying his daughter, Olive Cecilia, in 1889 and later wrote his father-in-law's biography. Subsequently he was appointed minister at Renshaw Street Chapel, Liverpool, in succession to the distinguished preacher and theologian, Dr. Charles Beard, and in 1896 he went to the Church of the Messiah, Birmingham, as a successor to Dr. Crosskey. There he remained until 1903, when he was appointed lecturer in philosophy at Manchester College, Oxford. In 1915 he was appointed Principal, in succession to Dr. Carpenter, and held that office until 1931, when he retired, having reached the age of 70.

Dr. Jacks was a many-sided man; he possessed great business capacity, as was shown in his management of the *Hibbert Journal.* This review was begun by him with the financial support of the Hibbert Trust, and he held the editorship for 45 years. It started as an obscure theological quarterly, but its circulation soon rose to 7,000 copies a quarter, and its contributors had leading names in various schools of philosophy and religion.

Another side of Dr. Jacks's varied character is seen in such well-known stories as *Mad Shepherds* and *The Legends of Smoke-over.* In his stories he was not a satirist, scourging the follies of his age; he was not a wit, making fun of them; he was not the philosopher, confuting them; or the preacher condemning them. His method was, on the whole, a kindly irony. Queer characters, queer thoughts, appealed to his sympathies without convincing his intellect. He disliked above all the conventional.

As a biographer, in his life of his father-in-law, Stopford Brooke, and in that of the Rev. Charles Hargrove, entitled *From Authority to Freedom,* Dr. Jacks showed great insight into character and instinct for the essential. There was practically no end to the many-sided character of his life, which all who knew him, old and young, will always like to think of as singularly happy and urbane, even when beset by his inward struggles and his concern for the state of the world. A wonderful domestic partnership was severed by the death of his wife in 1945 after 56 years as a devoted and admiring help-meet, and, as one of his friends so aptly said, his family of five sons and one daughter were all of them worthy of that remarkable home from which they came.

He had great practical capacity. He bought a fine estate at Shotover, where he built himself a house in 1912. He lived there until 1928, when he moved to another home, "Greatstones", which he built on a brick field, and round some old brick kilns, in a lower and more secluded part of Shotover. Like Sir Walter Scott, he was a great planter of trees. He had much skill in planning and laying out an estate, and considerable knowledge of farming. To make two blades of grass grow where one grew before seemed to him more worth while than to be the author of many books. This underlying scepticism about writing probably gave his writing more power.

One of the enduring memories for those who had known him in the last 30 or 40 years of his life will be of his patience, his industry, and his enormous energy when most men of that age go about in a wheelchair. Not only was he speaking and writing, but at his home near Headington, in which he settled late in life, he was taking long walks, working in his orchard, and with his clear, alert mind, entertaining his family and friends with reminiscences and with his brilliant and suggestive comments on men and affairs as a nonagenarian saw them.

February 18, 1955.

Dr. John Jackson, C.B.E., F.R.S., died in hospital in Epsom on December 9, 1958. He was 71.

He was born on February 11, 1887, and after a brilliant career at school he proceeded to Glasgow University to study chemistry and botany with a view to making a career in chemistry, but his interest was soon attracted to astronomy, which he studied under Professor

Ludwig Becker, who considered him to be the most brilliant student he had ever taught.

In 1909 he proceeded to Trinity College, Cambridge, and was placed among the Wranglers as the result of the Mathematical Tripos Examination in 1912, obtaining special distinction in Spherical Astronomy and Celestial Mechanics, and was awarded the Tyson Medal and Sheepshanks Exhibition.

In 1914 he received the First Smith's Prize at Cambridge and was awarded the Mackinnon Studentship of the Royal Society for research on the motion of Jupiter's eighth satellite, but in that year he was appointed Chief Assistant in the Royal Observatory, Greenwich, succeeding (now Professor) Sydney Chapman*.

He remained at Greenwich until 1933, except for a period during the First World War, when he served in France as holder of a commission in the Survey Section of the Royal Engineers.

In 1933 he was appointed H.M. Astronomer at the Royal Observatory, Cape of Good Hope, succeeding Dr. (now Sir) Harold Spencer Jones [q.v.] on his appointment as Astronomer Royal. He held that position until his retirement in 1950 when he returned to Britain to take up residence.

Throughout his career his astronomical work was concerned with many problems in celestial dynamics and in fundamental and positional astronomy, branches of the subject which are unfortunately now somewhat unfashionable, as they do not have the glamour attached to modern astrophysical research, but which are of great importance because they provide the foundations on which the whole of astronomy is based.

His first important work at Greenwich was concerned with the observations of binary stars that had been made at Greenwich with the 28in. refractor over a period of many years. These he collected and discussed, determined the orbits of a number of binary stars and inferred the parallaxes of 556 visual binary stars. With the introduction of the Shortt free-pendulum clocks at the observatory as the standards of time, he discussed their performance, particularly with regard to the possibility that their accurate time-keeping might give trustworthy determination of the variability in the earth's rotation.

He concluded that clocks of this type would be unlikely to serve this purpose, a conclusion which later proved correct, the variations in the earth's rotation having later been fully established through the use of quartz crystal and atomic clocks. He showed, however, that as a result of the nutation of the earth's axis, sidereal time was not uniform and, in consequence, astronomers have had, as a result of Jackson's work, to distinguish between apparent and mean sidereal time.

He was an assiduous observer with the Airy transit circle at Greenwich, and on one occasion during the First World War he continued observing quite unperturbed when a Zeppelin dropped a bomb in the observatory grounds, commenting that the purpose of the observatory was to secure observations.

Among the dynamical problems to which he devoted attention were the motion of Jupiter's eighth satellite, retrograde satellite orbits, and the figure and rotation period of Neptune. He concluded that the rotation period of Neptune was much longer than the period accepted at that time, based on visual observations. This conclusion, based on a dynamical investigation, has since been confirmed by spectroscopic observations.

He collaborated with Dr. Harold Knox-Shaw, the Radcliffe Observer at Oxford, and with his assistant, in a careful re-reduction of the observations of the sun, moon, planets, and stars, which had been made by Hornsby with the transit instrument and quadrant at the Radcliffe Observatory, Oxford, in the years 1774-98. These observations, which, for their time, were of high accuracy, are of value in connexion with the determination of the proper motions of the stars and for the investigation of the orbits of the sun, moon, and planets.

During the 17 years while he was director of the Royal Observatory, Cape of Good Hope, work was continued mainly on the lines laid down by his predecessor, the principal programmes being the determination of positions and proper motions of stars, the parallaxes of southern stars, and the preparation of a photographic catalogue of southern stars between 30deg. S. declination and the South Pole.

At that time the photometry of the southern stars was in an unsatisfactory state and, under his direction, Dr. R. H. Stoy, who on Dr. Jackson's retirement succeeded him as H.M. Astronomer, undertook the determination of the magnitudes of southern stars, which has resulted in the provision of accurate standards of magnitude.

Among other interests of Jackson was the observation of total eclipses of the sun. He obtained successful observations at the total eclipse of 1927 at Giggleswick, at Parent, in Canada, in 1932, and at Calvinia, in Cape Province, in 1940. He also led an eclipse expedition from Greenwich to Alor Star, Kedah, Malaya, for the observation of a total eclipse in 1929, when the clouds unfortunately prevented observations being obtained.

Jackson was elected a Fellow of the Royal Astronomical Society in 1913 and served as secretary 1924-29. He also served at various periods as a member of council and as vice-president and in 1953, after his return to England, he was elected president of the society for the period 1953-55. He was elected F.R.S. in 1938.

In 1952 he was awarded the gold medal of the Royal Astronomical Society for his work on stellar parallaxes and his contributions to the general problems of star positions and proper motions.

He was elected president of the Royal Society of South Africa in 1949 and in 1958 was awarded the recently instituted Gill Medal of the Astronomical Society of South Africa for his important contributions to astronomy during his period as H.M. Astronomer. He was appointed C.B.E. in 1950.

In 1920 he married Mary Beatrice Marshall, who survives him. They had no children.

December 12, 1958.

Mr. Justice R. Jackson, an associate Justice of the United States Supreme Court, and chief war crimes prosecutor for the United States at the Nuremberg tribunal of 1945-46, died suddenly in Washington on October 9, 1954 at the age of 62. He was United States Attorney-General in 1940-1941.

Robert Houghwout Jackson was born at Spring Creek, Pennsylvania, on February 13, 1892. He studied for his profession at the Albany Law School, and after being called to the Bar in 1913 set up in practice at Jamestown, New York, in the same year. As his business grew he became vice-president and counsel for the local street railway, another local railway system and various other public utility corporations operating in the town and surrounding country. He was appointed a member of a state commission to investigate the administration of justice, and served on many other legal committees concerned with the work of the profession and its relations with other sections of the community. From 1928 till 1930 he was president of the New York State Bar Association and in 1933 he was chairman of the national conference of Bar Association Delegates.

His legal work frequently took him to the capital of the State, Albany, to appear both in the Supreme Court and before committees of the Legislature and there he came into contact with Roosevelt, then Governor of New York. The two became fast friends, finding themselves in accord on many of the questions of the day, yet neither thinking that in years to come they would be brought together in Washington on more momentous occasions to put their theories into practice. During his visits to Albany he also came into contact with many lawyers from other parts of the state and so, when he was summoned to Washington in 1934 from a small country town, he was already well known to the legal profession as a whole and had already won their regard.

He had always been an active Democrat in politics and there was, therefore, no surprise when he was called to Washington and appointed general counsel to the Bureau of Internal Revenue. That work included much investigation and research on behalf of the President. In 1936 he was appointed assistant Attorney-General to Homer S. Cummings [q.v.], and his duties were then chiefly concerned with the drafting of new legislation, the defence of that already passed by Presdent and Congress before the courts, and the prosecution of business companies who failed to observe the provisions of the law.

When he became Solicitor-General in 1938 his duties were to put the Government's case before the Supreme Court in all cases in which the Government was involved when actions came up there for decision. The subsequent change in the attitude of the Court towards the New Deal, whereby legislation which would previously have been annulled was sanctioned, was largely due to his ability as an advocate. He was a clear thinker, a lucid exponent of a case and an enthusiast for the causes he had made his own, and while his methods may not at all times have been those usually associated with a Supreme Court they were none the less effective. He knew more than any one else of the New Deal's legal ramifications, having contributed much at its origin and having assisted in drafting the legislation which made it effective.

In January 1940 he was appointed Attorney-General in President Roosevelt's Cabinet. He had long been deeply concerned about the question of maintaining international order, and strongly supported the President's action in sending 50 over-age destroyers to Great Britain in that year. In the following year, 1941, he was appointed an Associate Justice of the Supreme Court. There his decisions stamped him as an original and independent thinker. His long and consistent record as a defender of human rights made him a natural choice as chief United States prosecuting counsel on the tribunal set up at the end of the war to try war criminals, and his appointment in this capacity was announced by President Truman* a week before the war in Europe ended. At the Nuremberg tribunal he opened the case against the leaders of Nazi Germany in a lengthy statement which was considered by all who heard it as a *tour de force* and a magnificent exposition of the American case. In it he traced the whole history of the Nazi conspiracy against the world, and also gave a masterly dissertation upon the law of the case and the propriety of the trials.

During the trials he showed himself to be quick-moving and quick tempered, as the German defence counsel often had cause to rue. Indeed, at times he was not above threatening to cut off the documents of German counsel if they persisted in tactics that he felt to be deliberately dilatory—an attitude that sometimes, not without reason, gave doubt about the fairness of the trials. Although his major speeches were models of diligence and idealistic law, in some of the individual cases his brief gave an appearance of skimping, for he was not the master of German affairs and Nazi crimes that some of his juniors made themselves. This was never more apparent than during the cross-examination of Göring, who was generally considered to have secured most of the points.

Both during and after the trials he vigorously upheld new legal conceptions of making war and of international crime, in spite of various criticisms in the United States. His optimism that war was outlawed at Nuremberg was, no doubt, modified by growing experience of communist tactics. He was elected an honorary bencher of the Middle Temple in 1946.

He married in 1916 Miss Irene Gerhardt. There were a son and a daughter of the marriage.

October 11, 1954.

David Jagger, who died on January 26, 1958, was not one of those artists who frequently come into the news, but among those who valued a capable portrait likeness he was held in high esteem.

Jagger sought after beauty not only in treatment but in his subject itself, disregarding any possible accusations of "prettifying". His handling of paint was suave and spirited; he appreciated character, and knew how to indicate it in a portrait. At the same time, without going in for elaborate backgrounds or accessories, he created a decorative effect which could be appreciated quite apart from one's knowledge of, or interest in, the sitter.

David Jagger came of an old Yorkshire family, and his father was a colliery manager living a few miles out of Sheffield. His brother was the late C. Sargent Jagger, one of the most vigorous sculptors working between the two wars, who produced the Artillery Memorial at Hyde Park Corner; while his sister, Edith Jagger, also won credit as an artist.

In his early days Jagger acquired a love of music that was to remain always with him, and also began to draw and paint; and, like many another boy whose parents look for a practical form of satisfying this desire, he was apprenticed at 14 to a firm of commercial lithographers. He worked for a short period at this trade in Sheffield, but found himself so discontented that his father bought out his indentures. David then began to paint the beautiful moors which surround Sheffield, and to produce pastel portraits at a modest £5 each. He had some minor success with these, and at least paid his way, so in due course he decided to attempt the London field, arriving in the capital with a collection of head-and-shoulder portraits of attractive girls.

Jagger sought out the commercial houses, and almost at once had two offers of employment, one of which he accepted. Yet commercial art was with him but a means to an end, and in his spare evening hours he began to paint heads by artificial light. Some of these were hung in the Royal Academy. Jagger's real success, however, began when Lord Beaverbrook* purchased his picture, *The Bolshevik*, for presentation to the National Gallery of Canada. Thereafter Jagger made steady progress. He was able to abandon commercial work, and gradually acquired a practice as a portraitist, including among his sitters Queen Mary [q.v.].

A study of the Duke of Edinburgh, commissioned by the Welsh Guards, of whom the duke is Colonel, was unfinished at the time of his death.

He became a regular exhibitor at the Royal Academy, the Salon, the London Portrait Society, and the Royal Institute of Oil Painters. He was a member of the council of the last-named body. Controversy had no part in his quiet and industrious career, and in spite of indifferent health he had a prolific output.

January 28, 1958.

Alex James, the Scottish international, Preston North End, and Arsenal footballer, who made his name in the late 1920s and early 1930s, died in hospital in London on June 1, 1953 at the age of 51. He had been ill for a long time.

Although capped eight times for Scotland, James will be remembered principally for his association with Arsenal, whom he joined in 1929 and, before retiring in 1937, had helped to win the F.A. Cup twice and the Football League championship four times.

James was one of the cleverest inside-forwards of his time. Compact in build, he had a smiling, chubby face which added to the picture of a player who looked quite unconcerned about the fortunes of a match, but the appearance of James belied his ability. He was always on the watch for an opening; he could get off the mark in a flash; he had a powerful shot; could beat much taller men in the air; and, above all, possessed an extraordinary knack of tricking opponents merely by feinting and swerving. The Arsenal forward line of Hulme, Jack, Lambert, James, and Bastin was, perhaps, the best which has represented the club.

James was born at Mossend, near Glasgow, and played at school with another boy destined to become a great Scottish footballer—Hughie Gallacher. Raith Rovers was the first big club James played for, and he stayed three seasons with them before going to Preston.

After James retired from the Arsenal team he took up a position with a football pools firm. Later he went in for sports reporting and also did pig-farming. He never lost his interest in soccer and in recent years coached Arsenal youngsters in the finer points of the game.

James leaves a widow, two sons, and a daughter.

June 2, 1953.

R. A. Scott-James—See **Scott-**.

Elsie Janis died on February 28, 1956 in Hollywood at the age of 66.

Her death will recall to older playgoers many happy recollections of the period just before the outbreak of war in 1914 when she made such an outstanding success in her first London appearance at the Palace Theatre in *The Passing Show*. Her reputation as a charming dancer, a capable singer, and a brilliant mimic had preceded her from America, and from her first appearance her popularity in England was never in doubt.

Born at Columbus, Ohio, on March 16, 1889, she was only eight years old when she made her first stage appearance as a small boy in *The Charity Ball*, and a year later she was playing in a stock company in *Little Lord Fauntleroy* and *East Lynne*.

Just after her tenth birthday she arrived in New York and played on the vaudeville stage, using the name of "Little Elsie". For the next three years she toured the United States, and in the summer of 1905 she scored her first real success in *When We were Forty-one* at the New York Theatre Roof Garden. Her powers of mimicry surprised her audiences, who found it difficult to believe that a girl who was still in her teens could so exactly depict the mannerisms and foibles of her fellow-artists. Thereafter she played in a number of musical comedies, and in 1914 went to London for *The Passing Show*.

Macqueen-Pope [q.v.] said of her in his book *Ghosts and Greasepaint*: "Announcing the name of the victim to be imitated, she would pick up a hairpin, give her locks a few twists, stick the pin in and, lo and behold, she not only talked and walked and sang like the objects of her imitation but looked like them, too". She was fortunate in her stage partner, Basil Hallam, the young English actor who created the song "Gilbert the Filbert", and who was later killed on war service. Their duet "You're here and I'm here" swept London, and when war broke out a few months later it was very popular with the troops. *The Passing Show* ran for nearly 400 performances, and when *The Passing Show of 1915* was presented Miss Janis went back to London from America to appear in it.

Early in 1918 she went to France to entertain American troops and returned in the autumn to London in *Hullo, America!* at the Palace. Two years later she went into management on her own account at the Queen's with *It's All Wrong*, of which she was author and part composer, and this was followed by her first appearance in Paris in *La Révue de Elsie Janis*. For three years Elsie Janis was absent from the London stage but she reappeared in June 1924 in *Elsie Janis at Home*. She then played for a short time at the Adelphi in *Clowns in Clover* in the autumn of 1928, the last time she was seen on the London stage.

She was always a prolific worker and in addition to her stage work she appeared in many films and was the author of one, *Close Harmony*. She wrote about 50 songs as well as three books, including an autobiography.

February 29, 1956.

D. R. Jardine died in Switzerland on June 18, 1958. He was 57. He became ill in 1957 while visiting Southern Rhodesia, and never completely regained his health.

Douglas Jardine was an instance of heredity in cricket skill, for his father, M. R. Jardine, was for four seasons, from 1889 to 1892, in the Oxford XI. In his last year, when Oxford under the captaincy of Lionel Palairet won the University match by five wickets, M. R. Jardine batted brilliantly, scoring 140 and 39. After leaving Oxford he entered the Indian Civil Service and was lost to English cricket. His son, Douglas, who was destined to become one of the most famous players of a later generation, was born at Bombay on October 23, 1900.

Douglas went to Winchester, and finished his school career about the time that the first European war came to an end. He was a member of the school XI for three seasons, and was captain of it during his last summer. He did well in some of the one-day wartime matches, which were arranged against various other schools, for in 1919, his last year at Winchester, he made 25 and 89 against Eton and 135 not out against Harrow.

He went up to New College, Oxford, and in accordance with expectation got his Blue as a freshman. He was thought by some good judges to be the best batsman on the university side, for he was constantly making runs. At Lord's he did nothing noteworthy against Cambridge in a game which was ruined by bad weather. In 1922, his third year, an accident to his knee obliged him to stand down in the inter-University match, but he rejoined the side in 1923 and made 39 against Cambridge.

After leaving Oxford he played little first-class cricket for some time, but as the years went on his appearances became more frequent, chiefly for Surrey, who welcomed his assistance. His batting gained in power and freedom, so that he came to be regarded as one of the best amateurs of the day. His qualities as a leader were also recognized; he was appointed captain of the Surrey team and filled the same office at other principal matches.

In the winter of 1928-29 he paid his first visit to Australia, as a member of the side captained by A. P. F. Chapman*. The last two English tours in Australia had ended in the loss by England of nine Test matches out of 10, and the conspicuous success of Chapman's XI came as a welcome change to this depressing record, for they won four out of their five Tests. The third match proved the most remarkable victory of the series. England were left with 332 runs to win, a task formidable enough in itself, but rendered more difficult by the damaged condition of the wicket. However, Hobbs* and Sutcliffe [d. 1978], our famous opening pair, faced the position with vigour, and brought up the hundred before they were parted. At the suggestion of Hobbs, Jardine was sent in first wicket down, and supported Sutcliffe so effectively that the game was to all intents and purposes won before another wicket fell. Our margin was reduced by some careless play at the finish to three wickets.

Four years later Jardine was invited by M.C.C. to undertake the leadership of the English team that visited Australia in the winter of 1932-33. The trip from the point of view of winning matches was again a great success, for four out of the rubber of five Tests went in England's favour, but unfortunately this satisfactory result was to some extent obscured by the amount of controversy which was created.

The subject of dispute was what was termed "leg theory" bowling. For many years it had been the occasional practice of various bowlers to pack the on-side with fieldsmen, and to bowl at the batsman's legs, or outside them. Nobody had ever dreamed of objecting, or of saying anything about it, except that it was rather a dull form of attack. But on this tour England had a fast bowler, Larwood, of Nottinghamshire, who was in a class by himself, being much faster than anyone else and more accurate. When his field was set for leg theory the Australian batsmen were far from endorsing the dullness of the attack. It was the pace at which it was bowled that made the difference.

The sensation caused in Australia was considerable. The batsmen ducked their heads, or retreated to short leg, so that all might see the severity of the ordeal they were undergoing. The crowd kept up a chorus of insulting cries; the press concocted stories of differences of opinion among the English players as to Larwood's bowling; somebody invented the epithet "Body Line" to emphasize the physical menace of the method employed. This confusion was followed by an exchange of cable messages between the Australian cricket authorities and M.C.C. The latter body met the complaint with the cold reply that if the Board of Control so desired they would consent with reluctance to the abandonment of the rest of the tour This suggestion was promptly declined.

These difficulties connected with this tour in Australia have been treated at some length, because they form an important part of Jardine's cricket career. Supported as he was by the complete loyalty of his own men, and fortified, it must be owned, by the approval of many critics not only in England but also in Australia, he stuck to his guns with a tenacity which nothing could disturb. Tall and fiery in appearance, austere and aloof in expression, he became the centre of cricket's fiercest controversy; and on his return to England he published a book of his experiences.

Jardine played subsequently in only four more Test matches, two of them as captain against West Indies and two in India, where he took an M.C.C. side in the winter of 1933. In the second of the two matches against West Indies Constantine* and Martindale gave him, as it were, a taste of his own medicine by making him the main target of a body-line attack. Jardine's reply was his first century in Test cricket, and in the words of Wisden for 1934 he played this form of bowling "probably better than any other man in the world was capable of doing".

But by 1934 his playing days were virtually over. An occasional broadcast and some part-time journalism continued to keep his name before the public, and he always took a lively interest in Surrey and Oxford cricket, being President of the Oxford University Cricket Club from 1955 to 1957.

Jardine qualified as a solicitor in 1926. He was chairman of the N.S.W. Land Agency Ltd., and a director of the Scottish Australian Company, Ltd. In the war of 1939-45 he served with The Royal Berkshire Regiment in France, Belgium, and India.

In 1934 he married Irene Margaret, daughter of Sir Harry Peat, by whom he had a son and three daughters.

June 20, 1958.

Major C. S. Jarvis, C.M.G., O.B.E., who died at his home in Hampshire on December 8, 1953 at the age of 74, had been one of Great Britain's most successful administrators in the Middle East, where he had been Governor of the Sinai Peninsula for some 15 years, and, on his retirement, he became well known to a large public through his books on the desert, special articles in *The Times*, and for his writings on country subjects, such as the feature he contributed to *Country Life* under the title of "A Countryman's Notes".

Claude Scudamore Jarvis was born on July 20, 1879, the son of John Bradford Jarvis. His career as a soldier started in the South

African War when he served as a trooper in the Imperial Yeomanry, and in 1902 he was gazetted to the 3rd Battalion, The Dorsetshire Regiment (Special Reserve). In the 1914-18 War he served in France, Egypt, and Palestine, and in 1918 entered the service of the Egyptian Government. He was appointed to the Frontiers Administration, and was first sent to the Western Desert, where he remained for two years. He then became Governor of the Oases of the Libyan Desert, with his headquarters at Kharga, for another two years, and, in 1922, was appointed Governor of Sinai, a post which he held until his voluntary retirement in 1936.

Jarvis brought great knowledge of the Arabs and Beduin law to his task; also, being himself a keen agriculturist, he devoted much time in settling the nomad Beduin on the land. In Sinai he dammed up the stream which the Israelites knew as Kadesh Barnes, and thus provided some 300 acres of rich land to be worked and owned by the Beduin. He also succeeded in settling all the blood feuds between his people and the Arabs of Trans-Jordan and Arabia. He also put a stop to raiding and made Sinai safe for the wayfarer.

Jarvis's books were usually written with a satirical humour which was emphasized in his criticism of the Victorians in his autobiography *Half a Life*.

He also disclosed in this book that at the age of 17 he joined the Merchant Navy as an apprentice, and sailed from Shadwell to Sydney and back by way of Cape Horn on his first and only voyage. Readers of his weekly feature in *Country Life* will remember him for his knowledge of rural pursuits and pastimes, interspersed with sound views on agriculture and with delightful anecdotes; he also had an intimate knowledge of the natural history of the desert.

Among his other books were— *Yesterday and To-day in Sinai*; *Three Deserts*; *Deserts and Delta*; *The Back Garden of Allah*; *Arab Command*; *The Biography of Lieutenant-Colonel F. G. Peake Pasha, C.M.G., C.B.E.*; *Scattered Shots;* and *Innocent Pursuits,* which appeared only a few weeks before he died.

Jarvis married, in 1903, Mabel Jane, daughter of Mr. Charles Hodson, who survives him together with a daughter of the marriage.

December 10, 1953.

Jules Jeanneney, a veteran Parliamentarian of the French Third Republic, who was President of the Senate when disaster came in the summer of 1940, and who was one of the principal figures to urge the removal of the Government to North Africa and the continuation of the struggle, died on April 27, 1957 in Paris at the age of 92.

Jeanneney was a widely respected figure in French political life. A member of the small group known as the Gauche Démocratique, closely associated in the thirties with the Socialist-Radical Party, a man of firm principle, averse from publicity and with little inclination to practise the politician's art of pleasing, he consistently refused to take office during those years between the wars in which so many of his fellows in both the Chamber and the Senate seemed to pursue no other ambition. This, while it could not but impress a somewhat cynical electorate, gave him a perhaps exaggerated reputation for austerity, for Jeanneney was of simple and friendly enough temperament. But it also demonstrated, beyond all doubt, his independence of mind and integrity of political purpose.

Born at Besançon on July 6, 1864, Jules Jeanneney made the law his profession and practised at the Court of Appeal. He entered local politics in the Haute-Saône department in 1896 and was president of the general council of the department from 1905 until 1927. Elected deputy for Vesoul in 1902, he served in the Chamber until 1909, when he was translated to the Senate. He was for many years a member of the finance committee of the Senate, and eventually—in 1931—became its president. Except for one or two minor appointments in the earlier phase of his career, the only government post that Jeanneney held under the Third Republic was that of Under-Secretary of State for War in the Clemenceau administration of 1917-19. He was elected vice-President of the Senate in 1930, lost by a narrow majority to Lebrun in the election for the Presidency in the following year, but was the only candidate a year later. He continued in the office of President of the Senate until 1940.

In the hour of catastrophe Jeanneney displayed courage and resolution, voicing firm opposition to the proposal to sue for an armistice. He remained in France all through the occupation and gave further evidence of his quality in the letters he and Edouard Herriot [q.v.] jointly addressed to Pétain [q.v.] protesting against the latter's subservience to Germany. On the liberation of his country he was appointed Minister of State by de Gaulle*, but at the age of 80 he was, though active in mind and body, ill prepared for the political exigencies of the new French régime in the making.

April 29, 1957.

Dr. Claude Jenkins, D.D., F.S.A., Regius Professor of Ecclesiastical History at Oxford, and Canon of Christ Church since 1934 and Subdean from 1943 to 1957, died on January 17, 1959 at Tunbridge Wells. He was 81. By his death the university and church lose a scholar of almost legendary learning, and Oxford a character whose idiosyncrasies lent variety and amusement to its society.

Claude Jenkins was born on May 26, 1877, the eldest son of Oswald and Sarah Jenkins of Little Aston, Staffordshire, and educated at King Edward's School, Birmingham, whence he went up to New College as open classical exhibitioner. In the schools he did not attain the highest distinction, being placed in the second class successively in Mods, Greats, and theology; but he obtained a Liddon exhibition in 1900, and the Denyer and Johnson scholarship in 1902. Practically the whole of his life was to be spent in academic work; for, after a year as assistant master at Magdalen College School, Dr. Headlam, with his flair for discerning youthful talent and promise, took him in 1903 to King's College London as the academic equivalent of the bishop's deacon.

With this college Jenkins was to remain associated with over 30 years in a steady ascent of the *cursus honorum,* becoming lecturer in ecclesiastical history for women in 1905, lecturer in patristic texts in 1911, and succeeding to the college chair of ecclesiastical history in 1918, when Dr. J. P. Whitney went to Cambridge. He was professor in the University of London from 1931 until his appointment to the regius chair at Oxford on the resignation of Dr. E. W. Watson in 1934. From 1925 he was also Reader in Greek and Latin Palaeography in London University.

On going to London he took Holy Orders, and entered the *familia* of Archbishop Davidson as Lambeth librarian in 1910, and chaplain in the year following, an association which enabled him to add to his ever-growing knowledge of past ecclesiastical history an invaluable acquaintance with problems and persons of contemporary Anglicanism. From 1929 to 1934 he was also a residentiary canon of Canterbury, a preferment richly merited and greatly enjoyed; though his residence at Canterbury involved the resignation of one of his London offices held since 1903, that of assistant curate of St. Martin-in-the-Fields and assistant chaplain of Charing Cross Hospital, the combined duties of which were a source of great pleasure to him.

The number and variety of his interests illustrated a salient feature of Jenkins's character, his prodigious appetite for committees. He confessed once to being a member of more than 50 such bodies simultaneously, and to the proceedings of each he brought unflagging interest and even enthusiasm. But they consumed a great deal both of time and of energy; and it is little surprising therefore that his own contribution to the writing of Church history was disappointingly meagre. It is difficult to exaggerate the loss thereby sustained by historical scholarship, for the comparatively few small books which he published, *Ecclesiastical Records* (1920), *The Monastic Chronicler and the Early School of St. Albans* (1922), and *F. D. Maurice and the New Reformation* (1938) are models of erudition compressed into brief compass, though it is only upon second or even third reading that they yield to the careful reader their full measure of learning; while his memorable 37-page review in *The Journal of Theological Studies* for October 1922 (republished in 1935 by the Church Historical Society as a pamphlet entitled *Bishop Barlow's Consecration and Archbishop Parker's Register),* of Mgr. A. S. Barnes's *Bishop Barlow and Anglican Orders* was a brilliant and devastating exposure of a pretentious work and a model of documentary historical criticism. *The Church Quarterly Review* (in the editorship of which he shared from 1903 to 1927) and other periodicals contained sundry learned articles from his pen; but all these were but the firstfruits of an anticipated harvest. His *Origen on I Corinthians* remains as a fragment only of the *magnum opus* intended on that author; of his extensive studies in Puritanism nothing was published; and the same is true of other projected books. His very omnivorousness as a reader was a bar to writing, and a prudent restriction of range might have resulted in more publication.

It was difficult, therefore, for those not brought into close personal relations with him to appreciate the range, depth, and accuracy of his learning. But with fellow-students admitted to the privilege of his friendship, astonishment at his erudition vied with gratitude for the prodigality of his kindness and his inexhaustible patience in answering questions, giving counsel, correcting manuscripts, proof-reading, and placing all the stores of his knowledge at their disposal.

Jenkins greatly enjoyed lecturing; and as a lecturer was unusual, for from any single lecture or course the sapient student might take away a mine of curious information, not always related to the advertised theme, provided he shared the lecturer's indifference to the chronological limits which the course was designed to cover but rarely achieved. His sermons displayed the same facility for turning aside from an initial theme to pursue reflections arising *currente calamo* (for lectures and sermons alike were carefully written in full); and this element of surprise gave to them interest and spontaneity. His churchmanship was reminscent of the austerity and sobriety of the old High Church and early Tractarian tradition, and nothing gave him greater satisfaction during his career than the canonries which he occupied at Canterbury and Christ Church, since he found in these cathedrals the workshop of his craft as an ecclesiastical historian.

But it is as a character that he will be remembered by many who knew only slightly his historical and ecclesiastical lore. In the colleges of which he was a member he was always a notable figure, generally with a particular seat in the circle which he preferred to occupy; his conversation was witty and liberally spiced with anecdote; he had a remarkable memory for historical events and allusions, a considerable store of wise saws and modern instances (culled from Lambeth), and an equal curiosity about persons and things; and the whole was punctuated by frequent replenishing of one or other of the several pipes which he extricated from a remarkably capacious pocket and which exuded a fragrance unknown to the generality of smokers. During term-time in the High, or the Strand, he was recognizable by his unvarying muffler (for he claimed to be indifferent to extremes of both cold and heat and to scorn the conventional changes of wardrobe), mackintosh, and old-fashioned clerical hat.

In vacations he escaped from the quasi-eremitical privations of his lodgings in Tom Quad to indulge at Tunbridge Wells or Malvern Wells his zeal, specified in *Who's Who*, for walking and the milder forms of climbing. There he appeared in grey flannel trousers, alpaca coat, cloth cap, and a stout ashplant in hand; and in the hotels in which he stayed he became a legendary figure of learning and eccentricity. He carried a ton of books with him on holiday and had collected a remarkable library. At a dinner given by his colleagues to celebrate his entry on his eightieth year he described himself as "of modest, if not of a retiring, disposition"; and in his later years his eccentricities became more pronounced, finding (as was generally believed) a kindly yet penetrating record in the portrait of Dr. Stringfellow in *The Guardians.* His death makes both University and Church the poorer in learning and *pietas,* and his pupils will lament the loss of a true friend and a master in Israel.

He was unmarried, having an equal aversion to matrimony and to cats.

January 19, 1959.

Mary Jerrold, the actress, in private life Mrs. Hubert Harben, died at her home in London on March 3, 1955 at the age of 77.

She used to say that her only recreation was the theatre and this undoubtedly was not an over-statement, for during her long stage career of nearly 60 years there were very few occasions when she was not at work. She rarely missed a performance and long runs presented no terrors for her. Indeed, in *Arsenic and Old Lace*, which ran for three and a half years at the Strand Theatre, the number of occasions that she was absent from the theatre was negligible. The present generation will remember her frail appearance, her quiet charm, and gentleness of manner, and yet with all an assured competence, which enabled her to play a beneficent old lady, or to commit a murder with equal facility. But older playgoers will recall also the many delightful performances of her younger days.

Born on December 4, 1877, the great-granddaughter of Douglas Jerrold, she gained much of her early experience in repertory work. First, for more than three years, she was with the Kendals then at the Royalty, Glasgow, and finally in 1910 in a memorable season at the Duke of York's, where she was seen in, among other plays, *The Sentimentalist, The Madras House,* and *Trelawny of the Wells.* In the original production of *Milestones*, and again in a revival two years later, she had a charming part in Rose Sibley, of which she took full advantage. There followed a number of other successes, including Lady Beaconsfield in *Disraeli,* Mrs. Morland in *Mary Rose,* Susan Throssel in *Quality Street,* and Mrs. Purdie in *The Sport of Kings.*

Her greatest success came with the production of *Arsenic and Old Lace* at the end of 1942, when Lilian Braithwaite and she played the two imbecile old ladies who were the most charmingly sincere of poisoners. Of her more recent appearances she gave much pleasure in a double bill at the Lyric, Hammersmith, in which she played Lady Wrathie in *Shall We Join the Ladies?* and, in Christopher Fry's *The Boy with a Cart,* the part of the mother of Cuthman the saint.

Mary Jerrold never allowed her art to grow stale and entered with zest into any new form of entertainment. She began her film career in 1931 and appeared in many pictures; then came broadcasting and many memorable appearances on television. She gave an outstandingly beautiful performance in the televised version of Pinero's short play, *A Private Room.*

She was the widow of Hubert Harben, the actor, who died in 1941.

March 4, 1955.

Fryn Tennyson Jesse, novelist and playwright, who in private life was the wife of H. M. Harwood [q.v.], died at her home in London on August 6, 1958. She was 69.

Born into a literary tradition—her maternal grandmother was the Emily Tennyson, a sister of the poet, who had been engaged to Arthur Hallam—and possessed of an individual poetic fancy and alert and nicely disciplined sensibilities, Tennyson Jesse had the not too common advantage of writing out of a great diversity of interests. The plays she wrote either by herself or in collaboration with her husband were for the most part light entertainment, but they bore witness to a shrewd instinct for the theatre and seldom failed in craftsmanship.

It was as a novelist that she exercised the full range of her abilities, which were various enough to enable her to make a point of never saying the same thing twice. Hers was a strong and assured romantic imagination; she had the great gift, as one critic remarked, of enjoying romance without being its dupe. Like other authors of genuinely imaginative temperament in this age of increasing silence, she had written relatively little fiction in recent years.

Fryn Tennyson Jesse was born in 1889, the daughter of the Rev. Eustace Tennyson d'Eyncourt Jesse. In her early years she travelled a great deal in Europe. She was 10 when her father became chaplain to the wine-growers at Marsala, in Sicily; she was afterwards at school in Paris; and at the age of 17 she went to study painting under Stanhope Forbes, R.A., at Newlyn. She exhibited a picture or two, illustrated a book, wrote poetry, came to feel more confidence in her writing than in painting, did some reporting work for *The Times* and book-reviewing for its *Literary Supplement,* and was a newspaper correspondent and carried out commissions for the Ministry of Information and other bodies in the war of 1914-18. In 1918 she married H. M. Harwood, the dramatist.

They had collaborated very happily in an amusing light comedy, *Billeted*, produced in the previous year, which seemed to find them well matched in devising neat situations and telling lines, and which was successfully revived (it was hardly a "war play") nine years afterwards. By that time Miss Tennyson Jesse had also written two plays of her own—*Quarantine* (1922), an airily entertaining piece, and *Anyhouse* (1925), in which she paid the penalty of describing a *milieu* she could scarcely have known well—and had again collaborated with her husband in *The Pelican* (1924), a workmanlike and theatrically effective piece, which was very well received and was revived in 1931. She had, too, published *The Sword of Deborah*, a vivid account of the war work done by British women in France, and a volume of poems, *The Happy Bride,* of notable accomplishment.

Her earliest mature essay in fiction appears to be *The White Riband* (1921), in which she immediately strikes her most individual and characteristic note. The setting is Cornwall, the period early Victorian, and from this conjunction of time and place her fancy evokes most ingeniously what is almost the libretto of a gay and fetching ballet. A touch of Cornish in her hero similarly releases the romantic poetry of her novel of the sea and sailing ships, *Tom Fool* (1926); while her fancy soars delightedly in another and more sinister direction in the brief *Moonraker,* or *The French Pirate and Her Friends,* published in the following year. Two years later came *The Lacquer Lady,* without doubt her best novel, a tragicomedy of the last days of an earlier phase of Burmese independence. Not the least impressive feature of a book of richly evocative and dramatic quality is the persuasive force of its detailed picture of court life in the Golden Palace at Mandalay during the brief reign of King Thibaw.

Among the books that followed was *A Pin to See the Peepshow* (1934), a solidly planned but slightly old-fashioned essay in realism—a story that followed fairly closely the details of the Thompson-Bywaters case, with a heroine methodically cast in the same mould as Emma Bovary. It enjoyed considerable success, though its interpretation carried less than complete conviction. It was adapted years afterwards, in collaboration with her husband, as a play.

Act of God (1937) was a delicately imaginative little commentary on the nature of miracles. Not a great deal came from her pen during the years of the Second World War, though in 1946 she produced an informed and well-written volume on *The Story of Burma.* Her two most recent novels were *The Alabaster Cup* (1950), slight but perhaps over-intense in style, and *The Dragon in the Heart* (1956), vivid as always, but in dramatic content somewhat inconclusive. A serious student of murder trials and of criminology in general, Tennyson Jesse had edited several volumes in the *Notable British Trials* series, among them *The Trial of Madeleine Smith* and *The Trials of Timothy John Evans and John Reginald Halliday Christie,* published in 1957.

August 7, 1958.

Gilbert Laird Jessop, who died on May 11, 1955 at Fordington Vicarage, Dorchester, in Dorset, a few days before his eighty-first birthday, was the most famous hard-hitting cricketer in the annals of the game.

"It was difficult", Sir John Hobbs* has said, "to bowl a ball from which he could not score and he made me glad that I was not a bowler." He started with two principles—to play in his own way and never to lose sight of the fact that a half-volley is a half-volley whether it comes along on a county ground or on a village green.

He could, in the course of a few minutes, alter the whole aspect of a match. There have been batsmen who hit the ball farther and higher than he did—for instance C. I. Thornton, or G. J. Bonnor, the Australian—and a few who hit it as hard. No one has ever equalled Jessop for the number of balls he scored off, for the consistent pace of scoring off bowlers of all kinds and in all sorts of conditions of wicket and with a greater variety of strokes. For Jessop was much more than a driver; he had wonderful pull shots; he had a splendid square cut; he had a "wind and water" stroke—he could cut past third man when apparently jumping in to drive. The better the bowling the more likely did it seem, at the height of his fame, that he would get runs off it. He was a terror to the faint-hearted bowler and a source of endless interest to the courageous. Rather under medium height, he was lissom and yet splendidly knit and strong. The enormous concentration of weight and power—much of it came no doubt from the back and loins—which he put into his batting was astonishing. To see Jessop "come off" was as exciting a spectacle as cricket has provided.

In his younger days he was a fast bowler of considerable merit, and as a fieldsman at cover point he was of the class of those who only appear once in a generation. He had a wonderful pace of movement and a return which, though it was slightly more overhand than that of some cover points—his pick up and return were in almost one motion—was incredibly fast and deadly straight.

Born at Cheltenham on May 19, 1874, the son of Dr. Henry Edward Jessop, cricket was his early love. He began it with a soft ball and a hard nurse; he learned fielding by long stopping to a fast and erratic bowler on a bumpy pitch. As a boy he carried his bag eight miles to a match. He went to Beccles College and then up, in 1895, to Christ's College, Cambridge. He played in the University matches of 1896-99, being once on the winning side and losing twice, the last match, when he was captain, being drawn. He was by then already one of the most talked-of players in England, having first played for Gloucestershire in 1894.

At this early stage he was heard to say that with bowling at all low, he was apt to get out quickly. But the advice given to him in the nineties to be more careful never affected what was called his "annihilating unorthodoxy". And when it came off it was so well worth watching that the hope of seeing Jessop at the wicket sent crowds to any ground almost as certainly as did the advent of his county captain, "W.G." So quick was his eye that he was able to treat Richardson as though that terrible Surrey man was no more than ordinary medium pace.

From the time he went down from Cambridge until war broke out in 1914 he was the mainstay and for many years—from 1900 onwards—the captain of his county team. It was for them that many of his wonderful hitting feats were done.

His first of many Test matches was at Lord's, when he was still at Cambridge, in 1899. He appeared in four of the five Test matches in 1902, and in the last game that year at the Oval he played one of the most famous innings of all time. Australia had already won two matches and two had been drawn, so the "Ashes" were not at stake. But an English defeat at Old Trafford by three runs—Jessop had been left out of the team—called for reply. It did not seem to be coming. The follow-on was only narrowly avoided. England were left in the fourth innings to make 263 on a rain-damaged wicket. Maclaren, Braund [q.v.], Palairet, Hayward, and Tyldesley were all out for 48 20 minutes before luncheon. Then Jessop joined F. S. Jackson. He started by giving two chances of being stumped and caught. He survived and immediately after the interval went beserk for the bowling. When out at last, caught at square leg, he had made 104 out of 139 in 75 minutes. The postscript to this great innings made cricket legend as well remembered as Jessop's whirlwind hitting. For it was after he had gone back to the pavilion that Rhodes* joined his fellow Yorkshireman Hirst [q.v.], who has so often been quoted as saying: "Wilfred, we'll get 'em by singles"—as they did.

He visited Australia in 1901-02 with Maclaren's side, and he went on two trips to America. He represented Cambridge at hockey, and later became a very keen golfer.

His record, measured by figures, includes 53 centuries; and one season (1900) in which he scored 2,210 runs and took 104 wickets. At Harrogate against Yorkshire in 1897 he made 101 out of 118 in 40 minutes; at Hastings in 1907, playing for the Gentlemen of the South, he made 191 out of 234 in 90 minutes, reaching 50 in 24 minutes, 100 in 42, and 150 in 63. Against Braund at Bristol in 1904 he took 28 off one over, and he repeated this against Burrows, of Worcestershire, at Stourbridge in 1910.

A lively descriptive writer, his books include *A Cricketer's Log,* in 1923, and, in the same year, *Cresley of Cressingham,* and, in 1925, *Cricket and How to Play It.* He also contributed to the press.

He married Miss Millicent Osborne, of Moss Vale, New South Wales, who died in 1953. There was one son of the marriage, the Rev. G. L. O. Jessop, who has played for Dorset in the Minor Counties Championship.

May 12, 1955.

Henrietta Jex-Blake, for many years Principal of Lady Margaret Hall, Oxford, died at Gerrards Cross, Buckinghamshire on May 21, 1953 at the age of 90, after several years of failing health.

She was the daughter of the late Dr. T. W. Jex-Blake, Dean of Wells, and formerly headmaster of Rugby School. Educated at home, she received like her sisters a classical training from Rugby masters; she studied also modern languages and music, and continued her musical studies at the Leipzig Conservatoire, Dresden, and Vienna, becoming an accomplished violinist. She was always a voracious reader and a graceful dancer, skater, and swimmer, and at Oxford she delighted in canoeing. She was a believer in games for girls.

In 1898 Miss Jex-Blake joined her friend Maud Daniel, the head of St. Margaret's School, Polmont. Miss Daniel had been a classical lecturer at Girton, and she aimed at making another school for Scottish girls on lines somewhat like those of St. Leonards School, but with rather lower fees. Miss Jex-Blake was second mistress, taking an active part in teaching, and house-mistress of an additional house, Netherfield. On Miss Daniel's sudden death in 1899 she was appointed to succeed her.

In 1909 Miss Jex-Blake succeeded Dame Elizabeth Wordsworth, who had been Principal of Lady Margaret Hall, Oxford, for 30 years. It was a critical time in its history and in that of women's education in Oxford. In 1910 the establishment of the Delegacy for Women Students brought them into direct relation with the university. In the hall there was a steady growth in numbers, and the governing body had decided to build a library, dining hall, and kitchens as the necessary preliminary to providing rooms for more students. The work was well advanced in 1909, the buildings being opened the next year by the Chancellor of the University; and it was followed up in 1914 by the addition of Toynbee Building.

The war years from 1914 to 1918 put a term to the steady growth of the hall, Nevertheless, life and work continued as far as possible on normal lines, and the great majority of students completed their course and went out to do their part in the struggle. This steadiness in face of the temptation to rush off to the first war-work that offered was greatly the result of the principal's precept and example.

The strain of these years told heavily on Miss Jex-Blake; she had long spent the vacations in caring for her mother and rarely took a real holiday. The end of the war period brought the added anxiety of the influenza epidemic of 1918, while the growing numbers and the grant of retrospective degrees in 1920 meant increased correspondence which fell heavily on the principal when there was no secretarial assistance. Her health had suffered and in 1921 she tendered her resignation.

May 22, 1953.

Dr. C. E. M. Joad, civil servant, author, university teacher, controversialist, and entertainer, died at his Hampstead home on April 9, 1953 at the age of 61.

If his achievement in the intellectual life and habit of his time can be summed up in a phrase, it would be that he was a star performer as a popular educator. He had zest, gaiety, wit, agility, combativeness, and an unfailing lucidity and equally unfailing glibness. They were qualities particularly suited to the "brains trust", devised by the B.B.C. during the 1939-45 war, and Joad (the word is not intended to be unkind) exploited them to the full. Within a few months he had become, in a quite literal sense, a household name.

As a writer Joad drew on the same qualities which always ensured him an audience when he talked. There was a lucidity and springiness in his writing which gave interest to his expositions of other people's ideas. He had no original contribution to make as a philosopher, and the most interesting development of his ideas came late in his life. After a life-time of agnosticism he was moved by the greatest war in history to recognize the all-pervading nature of evil. This fundamental change in his outlook to a theistic explanation of the universe was announced to the world in 1943 in *God and Evil.* It was clear from this book that theism could not be his permanent resting-place, and nine years later, in 1952, he published *The Recovery of Belief*, in which he stated his reasons for accepting the Christian faith as it is held and practised in the Church of England.

The Recovery of Belief is certainly the most interesting and important of his books. It is marked by a humility which contrasts notably with the intellectual arrogance of his earlier writing. It follows the arguments which led him from agnosticism to Christianity with a fearless honesty, and it equally fearlessly faces and rejects the claims of science as "a stick to beat religion". It concerns itself with the fundamental problems of the universe and human nature, about which he had previously been so superficial. True, the conclusions he reaches are the traditional Christian view, often stated before, but the story of his journey to belief gives the book an intellectual vitality and freshness surprising in this age of unbelief. Not least interesting are the reasons why, having accepted Christianity, he then went on to find his true home in the Church of England.

Cyril Edwin Mitchinson Joad was born in 1891, the son of a schoolmaster in Barbados and afterwards an inspector of schools in this country. He was educated at Blundell's School, Tiverton, and went with a scholarship to Oxford. He took a first in Greats, was John Locke scholar in moral philosophy in 1914, and in the same year entered the Civil Service, serving first in the Board of Trade and afterwards in the Ministry of Labour. His interests, however, were always outside his official work and, in retrospect, it is surprising that it was not until 1930 that he left the Civil Service to become head of the department of philosophy and psychology at Birkbeck College, London. His books already published had included, besides a novel and a volume of short stories, *Mind and Matter,* 1925, an introduction to metaphysics, and *The Future of Life,* 1928, in which he elaborated a rather eclectic theory of vitalism. The books which followed included *Philosophy for Our Times,* in which he emphasized the non-religious standpoint of his value-philosophy, and many on more topical subjects—about war, science, education, and pacifism. He was chairman of the National Peace Council in 1938.

Joad was a passionate lover of the English countryside. He once described England as having the ugliest towns in the world and the most beautiful countryside, and his horror at any desecration of the country was perhaps summed up in the title of his book, *The Untutored Townsman's Invasion of the Country.* In this, as in so many others of his beliefs, one could discover the underlying sincerity of the man, which was so often obscured by his earlier arrogance. The moving tribute which he paid in his last book to the parish priests of the Church of England provides, perhaps, the clue to a man who never fulfilled his promise but to the end of his life could always claim to have been honest in the views he held and courageous in upholding them.

He was twice married.

April 10, 1953.

Former Bishop of Johannesburg—See **Clayton.**

Sir (William) Goscombe John, R.A., the sculptor, who was responsible for many statues of statesmen and politicians, died on December 15, 1952 at his home in London at the age of 92.

He was once called in jest the sculptor of Parliamentarians but, in fact, he was rather versatile. He was particularly successful with small works combining symbolism and decoration of a kind relating sculpture to the goldsmith's craft. He was commissioned by King George V to design the King's Silver Jubilee Medal, and he was responsible for the insignia and commemorative medals of the Prince of Wales's investiture in 1911, when he was knighted, and for the new Great Seal of King George VI [q.v.] in 1937. His Celtic fancy was expressed in some charming works of an imaginative character, such as *Water* and *The Elf.*

John was born at Cardiff in 1860. He studied there and at the Lambeth School at Kennington, the nursery of many British sculptors under the successive direction of Dalou and W. S. Frith, and later at the Royal Academy Schools, where, in 1889, he won the Gold Medal and Travelling Scholarship for his group called *Parting.* The next two years he spent in Paris, receiving an honourable mention at the Salon in 1892 and a gold medal in 1901. On his return from Paris his scholarship work, *Morpheus,* was bought by the committee of the Cardiff Art Gallery. A good deal of his work was done for his native city. His *St. David Blessing the People* is among the several statues of Welsh historical characters commissioned by Lord Rhondda of Llanwern for the City Hall, and Cardiff also possesses his *St. John* and his statue of Lord Tredegar. Among his other principal works are Lord Salisbury in Westminster Abbey, W. E. H. Lecky at Trinity College, Dublin, Colonel Saunderson at Portadown, King Edward VII at Cape Town, Prince Christian Victor at Windsor, seventh Duke of Devonshire at Eastbourne, Lord Wolseley on the Horse Guards Parade, Sir Arthur Sullivan in St. Paul's Cathedral and also in the Embankment Gardens, Thomas Sutton at Charterhouse, Coldstream Guards' and War Correspondents' Memorials in St. Paul's Cathedral, and the Llandaff War Memorial. He is represented in the Tate Gallery by *Boy at Play*, a Chantrey purchase of 1896, and the

Fitzwilliam Museum, Cambridge. The Glasgow, Liverpool, Manchester, and Preston art galleries also have examples of his work. He was elected A.R.A. in 1899 and R.A. in 1909. He was LL.D. of Wales, corresponding member of l'Institut de France, and Commander of the Order of Leopold II of Belgium. In 1942 he was awarded the Gold Medal of the Royal Society of British Sculptors.

John was a lively little Welshman, entertaining in conversation, and fond of dwelling upon his alleged humble origin, claiming a village cobbler and a village blacksmith among his immediate ancestors. His father, Thomas John, was a sculptor, and it was he who gave him his first training. After he left Cardiff John was for a time assistant to C. B. Birch, continuing his studies in the evening, and visiting Italy and Greece. Thus he had a wide artistic experience. He was an excellent craftsman in many materials, his work being distinguished by play of fancy in a vein of delicate realism rather than by monumental qualities, though his portrait statues are not deficient in form.

He married in 1890 Marthe Weiss and had one daughter.

December 16, 1952.

Lord Webb-Johnson—See **Webb-**.

Dr. Charles Spurgeon Johnson, first Negro president of Fisk University, Nashville, Tennessee, died in November 1956 of a sudden heart attack at Louisville, Kentucky, at the age of 63.

The son of an emanicipated slave, he worked his way through college, first at Virginia Union University and then at the University of Chicago, where he came under the spell of one of the most exceptional personalities of the American academic scene—the famous sociologist, Professor Robert E. Park.

Johnson's future career as one of the most distinguished sociologists of his generation was determined by the ferment which Park added to his own passionate, yet objective, will to work for the welfare of the Negro people; but after graduation he "took time off", as he was always willing to do for other human concerns, to serve with distinction in France during the closing stages of the 1914-18 War. On returning to Chicago he found himself involved in the "race riots" that broke out there as an aftermath of the war; and he gave two years to studying their causes, and the prospects of bringing about greater harmony between whites and Negroes, with the Chicago Commission on Race Relations.

This work proved that a new mind had appeared in the field of American sociology, but adequate academic employment remained closed to him. Therefore, in 1921, he joined the National Urban League, a Negro social welfare organization in New York, as its director of research and editor of its monthly journal, *Opportunity*. In these capacities he not only conducted and guided investigations that made the league an important political force, but he also used *Opportunity* to sponsor the cultural awakening that came to be known as the New Negro Movement of the twenties.

These activities, though valuable and far-reaching, were nevertheless excursions from Johnson's intention to build a school of sociology which would tackle, in basic and cumulative ways, the problems of including the Negro in the main stream of American progress. In 1928 he saw the prospect of hope becoming reality through the offer of an appointment as director of the Institute of Social Studies at Fisk University, which he accepted in spite of the many personal advantages of remaining in New York. The somewhat enervating climate, both moral and meteorological, of Nashville did not reduce the energy he brought to his new task, nor did an insufficient budget and the difficulties of the depression bother him beyond the need to finance the institute himself from funds provided by the philanthropic agencies, especially the Julius Rosenwald Fund, with which he was associated.

Almost from the moment that Johnson settled himself in his offices on the sleepy Fisk campus his department became a centre of sociological industry from which there issued a growing stream of projects, source materials, reports and books, among them such well-known basic works as his own *Race Relations*, *The Negro in American Civilization*, *Shadow of the Plantation*, and *Patterns of Negro Segregation*. It became a fruitful teaching department, too, which demanded zestful application from its students and gave them the equipment for teaching and research on more than a pedestrian basis. In pursuit of this policy he attracted to his department, for varying periods, many eminent or otherwise interesting personalities, including the great Robert Park himself.

Most men would have been happily enclosed by such circumstances, but he kept steadfastly to a larger vision. He gave his services wholeheartedly to the affairs of his university, to other institutions and agencies, both coloured and white, to the Government and to other countries, and to most activities concerned with the improvement of intergroup relations. By 1947, when he was invited to become president of Fisk University, he was a major figure in the world of education and social welfare. He had travelled widely and repeatedly in all the continents, attending conferences, lecturing, or reporting for the Federal Government; he was a member of innumerable boards and official commissions; he had helped in the foundation of Unesco, especially in shaping its intergroup programme; and many millions of dollars had passed through his hands, or on his recommendation, to good causes and needy scholars. In later years many millions more were to be disbursed through his good offices, for he had a respected voice on the Board of Foreign Scholarships under the Fulbright Act, the Ford Foundation, and other bodies.

He was at first reluctant to leave his desk at the institute for the president's office, and was never quite reconciled to abandoning his unfinished sociological projects; but, stifling his regrets, he gave himself wholly to the enormous task of reorganizing and extending the resources of Fisk University, and to revitalizing every department with the "fresh insights" that he was so adept at finding. He gave Fisk a necessary touch of gaiety, too, with more than equal collaboration from his warmhearted and distinguished wife. There had not been much laughter at Heritage House, the presidential mansion, until the Johnsons and their children moved in.

Yet Johnson had none of the attributes so often associated with the brisk American. He was, in fact, an old-fashioned Liberal; modest, cautious, inclined to lean on the side of authority and officialdom, but never afraid to speak bluntly when matters of principle were involved. Typically he said of recent events in the Southern states: "It is a struggle between those who believe in democracy and those who do not".

He was a frequent visitor to Great Britain, where his ready smile and gentle manner made him many friends. His pleasures there, apart from academic gossip and an alert eye for more visiting professors, were a morning spent with his tailor in Savile Row, an afternoon or two of fussy shopping for antiques and gifts for his family, a quiet evening in an English home, and a day in the country. He was delighted, though already well equipped with honorary degrees, with his Glasgow doctorate *in honoris causa*; and he set great store by British opinion—traditionally so, for British opinion, funds, and support for the famous Fisk Jubilee Singers helped greatly to consolidate Fisk University after its establishment in 1866. The attention given by British newspapers in news reports and articles during the past few years to Negro questions were "gratefully welcomed" by him as important tokens of the fact that "the Negro minority is finding a place in the larger brotherhood of man".

November 15, 1956.

John Johnson, C.B.E., Printer to the University of Oxford from 1925 until 1946, died on September 15, 1956 at the age of 74.

Born in a Lincolnshire vicarage in 1882, John de Monins Johnson passed from Magdalen College School to Exeter College, Oxford, where he read "Greats", and in 1906 joined the Egyptian Civil Service. Shortly after the retirement of Lord Cromer [q.v.] he turned to archaeology and from 1908 to 1914 was a member of the Graeco-Roman branch of the Egyptian Exploration Fund. He was still a papyrologist when he became acting assistant secretary to the Delegates of the Clarendon Press in 1915, a heart strain having made him unfit for military service; but his edition of two papyri of Theocritus which he had discovered had then to be laid aside, and was ultimately completed by A. S. Hunt.

Throwing himself into his new occupation with an energy which seemed to some of his friends to be disturbing to the established habits of a university press, he planned new series and in one way or another revealed unexpected capacity for business. As a designer of books he excelled in providing them with illustrations, which were often all chosen by himself.

In 1925 he volunteered to leave the publishing branch of the Oxford Press in order to become its Printer. During his rule—for such it was—he planned structural alterations, decided for a "closed house", and introduced various changes which were to fit the Oxford Press to cope with the great volume of work assigned to it by the Government and the Allied Command during the war. Every man and woman knew on clocking in that the Printer was already in his office and would be there when the day's work was over; he even slept in his office while there was the fear that Oxford would be bombed, and continued to sleep there till the very end of the war.

He became the leading authority on the history of the Oxford Press. His *Print and Privilege at Oxford to the year 1700,* written in collaboration with Strickland Gibson, threw new light on its beginnings, and also on publishing in London in the seventeenth century. But his investigations were not confined to the book trade. Whereas the historical study of printing had hitherto been almost solely bibliographical, his interests spread to all branches of the printer's craft. He collected specimens of every kind of English printing from broadsides and old bank notes to valentines and posters—he called them his "ephemera"—and gradually formed a museum which soon attracted experts from abroad, and is of great value to the social historian. It was the only museum of this kind in the country, and was the property of the university.

His gift of seeing the significance of objects from the past was remarkable, and he was never bound by the tastes and fashions of the moment. As a collector he took no more interest in one period than in another; as a printer he tried to ensure that the work of his press was not mannered, but equally good in different styles. Once his interest was engaged in any project he gave his mind to it with enthusiasm, and his great fund of miscellaneous and out-of-the-way information was always at the service of others. He seemed to think little about himself; and the wide circle of his acquaintances and employees have many acts of kindness to remember.

He was appointed C.B.E. in 1945, was an Honorary Fellow of Exeter College, and was given the honorary degree of D.Litt. on the completion of the *Oxford English Dictionary* in 1925.

He married in 1918 Margaret Dorothea, daughter of Charles Cannan, by whom he had a son and a daughter.

September 17, 1956.

Sir Nelson King Johnson, K.C.B., Director of the Meteorological Office from 1938 to 1953, died in hospital on March 23, 1954 at the age of 61 after taking aspirin while the balance of his mind was disturbed by an illness.

He was born in 1892, the son of J. G. Johnson, of Canterbury, and was educated at the Simon Langton School at Canterbury, and at the Royal College of Science, University of London. After post-graduate research in astrophysics he became assistant to Sir Norman Lockyer at the Hill Observatory, Sidmouth, in 1914, and in 1915 he joined the R.F.C., in which he served as a pilot until 1919. Because no weather forecasts were available he had a bad crash and it was this accident, he said, which turned his thoughts to meteorology and its importance to the future of aviation.

After demobilization he joined the Air Ministry Meteorological Office, remaining there until 1928, when he was seconded to the War Office for duty at the experimental station at Porton and became chief superintendent of the Chemical Defence Research Establishment. In 1938 he returned to the Meteorological Office as Director upon the retirement of Sir George Simpson. As Director he was responsible for the Meteorological Office's large growth to meet the needs of service departments and civilian organizations, and during the 1939-45 War he carried the heavy burden of responsibility for forecasting the weather for the landings in Normandy on D-Day, as well as for the British and American bombing offensives against Germany.

He was president of the International Meteorological Committee from 1946 to 1951, in which year he became president of the World Meteorological Organization. He was made a K.C.B. in 1943 and retired from the directorship of the Meteorological Office in the autumn of 1953, being succeeded by Professor O. G. Sutton [d. 1977].

He married in 1927 Margaret, daughter of J. Taylor, of Blackburn, who survives him together with a son and a daughter.

March 24, 1954.

Major-General His Highness Sir Ibrahim, Sultan of Johore, G.C.M.G., G.B.E., died in London on May 8, 1959 at the age of 85.

Coming to the rulership of the unfederated State of Johore in the south of the Malay Peninsula, he exercised authority over a country 7,380 square miles in extent for a far longer time than usually falls to the lot of an Oriental potentate. The period up to the outbreak of war in 1939 saw remarkable developments in Johore, owing mainly to the rapid growth of the rubber industry and also advances in tin mining.

The Sultan's ownership of many thousands of acres of rubber plantations led to his being spoken of as one of the world's richest men. His relations with the suzerain British Power were generally cordial and from time to time he gave substantial tokens of loyal devotion to his treaty obligations. This attachment stood the searching test of the Japanese occupation of Malaya in the 1939-45 War.

He was born to Sultan Abu Baker on September 17, 1873, and at the age of 17, when he was heir to the Sultanate, he made the first of his frequent visits to Europe. He was proclaimed Sultan in succession to his father on September 7, 1895, and was crowned on November 2. Some three months before the outbreak of war in 1914 the announcement was made that he had agreed to the appointment of a general Adviser instead of a British Agent and General Adviser, and to that official's advice being asked and acted upon in all matters affecting the general administration of the country other than those touching the religion and customs of Malay. The adviser was also to regulate the collection and control of all revenue.

In 1916 the Sultan made a contribution of $25,000 (£2,492 14s. 2d.) to be used by the Army Council as they thought best. He had always been interested in military affairs, and was now Colonel Commandant of the Johore Military and Volunteer Forces and also Honorary Colonel of the Johore European Volunteer Engineers. In the economic crisis of 1931, the Sultan made a gift of £5,000 to the British Exchequer. Four years later, in commemoration of the Silver Jubilee of King George V, he gave £500,000 to his Majesty's Government for the purpose of accelerating the completion of the defence of Singapore.

The Sultan's constitution was not well suited to tropical heat and this fact lead to his preferring life in Britain and paying frequent visits to London. On the outbreak of war in 1939 he was in Johore and made a notable broadcast appeal to his people to rally to the allied cause to the utmost of their power.

A few months later he made a war contribution of £250,000 to the British Exchequer. From the first he scouted the suggestions of his entourage that he should come to Britain, or at any rate find some safer place of residence than Malaya. "Are my people in danger", he asked, "and shall I leave them in the lurch?"

The reality of the danger was soon brought home poignantly by the Japanese occupation of Malaya. The Sultan met the dangers and sufferings of the times with a courage and fortitude which added to the regard and affection of his people he had long enjoyed.

Yet after the war their attachment to him was strained, for he made no bones of the fact that he preferred the past, in which Johore as one of the unfederated Malay States relied on a British adviser as its political executive, to the present which was bringing independence without British advisers in the same sense as before.

This attitude brought him into conflict with Malay politicians in Kuala Lumpur and there was some coolness, especially when he spoke his mind at his Diamond Jubilee. Probably because of this, and his health, he did not offer himself as a candidate for selection by his fellow rulers as Head of State in the new Malaya in 1957, though as the most senior ruler he would have been the first to be considered.

The Sultan is succeeded by his son Prince Ismail Tunku Mahkota.

May 9, 1959.

Violet (Mrs. Edward) Joicey—See **Loraine.**

Professor Frédéric Joliot-Curie, the distinguished French physicist, died in Paris on August 14, 1958. He was 58.

Joliot was trained at the École de Physique, under Langevin, who influenced his ideas in other directions besides science. A decision which, more than any other, affected his career in research was his move to the Institut de Radium in the 1920s; there he met Irène Curie, [see the following obituary], daughter of Pierre and Madame Curie, the discoverers of radium. They soon became friends and partners in work. In 1926 they married. Within eight years—on January 15, 1934—they presented to the French Academy of Sciences a joint paper which a year later brought them a Nobel award. The discovery of radium by the earlier partnership had been succeeded in the next generation by that of artificial radioactivity.

The exciting nature of this discovery appeared even in their formal account to the Academy. "Il a été possible pour la première fois de créer . . . la radioactivité". Rutherford, who had earlier sought to do so, was now generous in congratulation. It had not been a chance discovery. They were engaged at the time on a systematic study of the effects produced on the nuclei of the lighter chemical elements by bombarding them with alpha-particles from the naturally radioactive element polonium. They found that the energy of bombardment caused various already known kinds of particle to be emitted from those atoms. Among these particles were the newly discovered neutron, and the positive electron—which, too, had only recently been discovered. There was nothing unusual in this. But when the source of irradiation was removed they found that "the emission of positive electrons . . . persisted for a time more or less long, being more than half an hour in the case of the boron". They found three examples: the irradiation of boron, magnesium and aluminium was accompanied by the production of radioactive nuclei of nitrogen, silicon and phosphorus respectively.

As well as its immediate interest and value in research, the discovery of artificial radioactivity was an important step along the road which led within a few years to atomic energy. The Joliot-Curies had already done other research which was important. Although they missed discovering the neutron—the particle which maintains the fission process in a nuclear reactor—it was the combination of experiments by the Joliot-Curies in Paris and a suggestion made earlier by Rutherford that led Sir James Chadwick* to the correct solution of a problem which it was still a major contribution to have presented and recognized.

The Joliot-Curies were complementary in temperament as well as training and early experience. The calm insight and persevering work of Irène Curie was allied with the stronger personality and quick-ranging imagination of her husband.

During the war, he found leadership of a new kind in the Resistance movement. Already a member of the French Communist party, he emerged as leader of the Front National. The liberation gave him a new opportunity as head of the Centre National pour la Recherche Scientifique—the main means by which Government resources were made available for research in selected fields in science. Although there must have been some loss to universities from this policy, it has produced results, and owed much to the energy and prestige of Joliot. He was appointed also as High Commissioner for Atomic Energy and, in that capacity, laid foundations which provided a good basis for expansion when that came. Together with university work and politics, he was immensely busy. The combination was, however, open to criticism—and the more so as emphasis on the exclusively peaceful objectives of French research in atomic energy was appearing to lose something in conviction. In April 1950 he was dismissed from the commission.

In January of the following year his wife also was dropped. Little more than five years later she died, as her mother had done before her, from the effects of life-long research into radio-active bodies.

Joliot-Curie's name became widely known in the early years of this decade through his enthusiastic support of the World Peace Council, of which he became president, and he was involved in a dispute with American scientists over the alleged use of germ warfare in Korea. He was awarded the Stalin Peace Prize.

August 15, 1958.

Irène Joliot-Curie, wife of Professor Frédéric Joliot-Curie [see the previous obituary], died on March 17, 1956 in hospital in Paris at the age of 60. The doctors in attendance announced that her death was the result of leukemia resulting from the work on radiation to which she had devoted her life.

The daughter of the late Pierre and Marie Curie, the joint discoverers of radium, she was born in 1896 and proved to be a remarkable example of inherited genius. In 1918 she began to act as her mother's assistant at the Institut du Radium. It was a hard school in which to learn. Completed only in 1914, the institut had lost its staff by dispersion, and most of the value of its endowments, during the war years. To this difficult period, and especially to her mother, Irène owed a thorough knowledge of the chemistry of the natural radio-elements and of methods of separation and analysis applicable to small quantities of materials.

By the 1920s things were looking up, and Frédéric Joliot came to the institut. He had been trained by Langevin at the École de Physique. In personality as well as in training the two were complementary: Irène, calm, pertinacious, and farseeing, by training a chemist; Joliot, forceful, imaginative, and a physicist. They soon became friends and partners in work, and in 1926 they married. On January 15, 1934, they reported to the French Academy of Sciences the discovery which only a year later brought them a Nobel prize. This was the discovery of artificial radioactivity, or of "induced" radioactivity, as at the time they preferred to call it. In their own words, "il a été possible pour la première fois de créer . . . la radioactivité".

The occasion was remarkable in several ways. There was first the coincidence that whereas radium had been discovered by Mme. Curie and her husband, Pierre, the discovery of artificial radioactivity should have been made by their daughter Irène and her husband. There have been examples of family successions in the history of science; there is no other case like this one. Also unusual—but remarked rather in England than in France—was the fact that H. G. Wells had forecast something of the kind in his novel *The World Set Free,* published in 1913, and had got the year of discovery right. It was perhaps not surprising that some two years later Mme. Joliot-Curie should have been appointed by Léon Blum, Under-Secretary of State for Scientific Research.

The discovery was not only a stimulus to research; it offered the possibility of a new era in which radioactive materials, artificially prepared and similar in all other respects to the normally stable chemical elements, could be used in research and possibly in medicine. Within a few months Irène was in London; and, in a few minutes after a meeting, gave an exact but imaginative survey of what have proved since to be the main lines of development.

The experiments of the Joliot-Curies were also notable in another way. Although many examples of the artificial transmutation of one element into another had been recorded in the Cavendish Laboratory, the evidence had involved in all cases an element of deduction. There had been no case supported by evidence which would satisfy a chemist. Nor could there have been at this time; so long as the elements produced were known only as stable atoms, the quantities were too small for them to be separated chemically. But now that the elements produced were radioactive, it was possible to mix the radioactive element with a small quantity of the corresponding stable element.

The discovery of artificial radioactivity by the Joliot-Curies was both preceded and followed by other scientific work of importance. In 1932 they had come close to discovering the neutron—the existence of which had been postulated by Lord Rutherford in 1920, and which had led by 1939 to the discovery of the fission process, and thence to the release of atomic energy. Towards the discovery of the neutron, the Joliot-Curies contributed a critical observation. They saw that a new phenomenon was needed to explain it. But they did not know about Lord Rutherford's suggestion—or they might have concluded, as soon afterwards did Dr. (later Sir James) Chadwick*, that they had evidence for the neutron.

There was no chance about their discovery of artificially produced radioactivity. They were engaged at the time in a systematic study of the effects produced on the nuclei of the lighter chemical elements by bombarding them with alpha-particles from the naturally radioactive element polonium. They found that the energy of bombardment caused various already known kinds of particles to be emitted from these atoms. Among these particles were the newly discovered neutron, and the positive electron—which, too, had only recently been discovered. There was nothing unusual in this. But when the source of irradiation was removed they found that "the emission of positive electrons . . . persisted for a time more or less long, being more than half an hour in the case of boron". They found three examples: the irradiation of boron, magnesium and aluminium was accompanied by the production of radioactive nuclei of nitrogen, silicon and phosphorus respectively.

The discovery of artificial radioactivity, together with that of the neutron, led directly to atomic energy. It was, as it were, the last ingredient necessary in order that the fission of uranium atoms should be discovered. Professor Fermi [q.v.], then working in Rome, showed that exposure to neutrons was an especially fruitful method for the production of further radio-elements—radioactive isotopes as they would now be called—and among other elements he tried uranium. As is now known, the effects which he observed were due to the fission of uranium atoms. But the fission process was quite unexpected at the time. For the correct interpretation to be arrived at, it was necessary that the very small quantities of new elements produced should be identified chemically. With a colleague at the institute—P. Savitch—Mme. Joliot-Curie made the first analysis of the kind; it was work of the kind that she had made her own. The final solution to the problem depended on research in other laboratories and a return to physical methods. But, as earlier in the discovery of the neutron, so again in the discovery of fission, the contribution of Mme. Joliot-Curie was important. She will be remembered as a great woman and a great scientist—and a level partner with her husband.

He had for years been a member of the French Communist Party, which Mme. Joliot-Curie was not, though she was far from unsympathetic. It was therefore not surprising in view of the eminence of both of them in their scientific field that after the last war they should have been members of the French Atomic Energy Commission. That they should both have been dismissed from it, the one in 1950 and the other in 1951, is also intelligible.

March 19, 1956.

The death in hospital on February 11, 1958 of **Dr. Ernest Jones** removed from the world of psycho-analysis its most eminent figure since the death of Freud. He was 79.

Ernest Jones came of Welsh stock. He received his university education first at University College, Cardiff, then at the University of London. He completed his medical studies at University College Hospital (where he died).

In 1901 he obtained the degree of M.B., B.S. of the University of London, with two gold medals, and when he later proceeded to the degree of M.D. he was again awarded a gold medal. He was elected Fellow of the Royal College of Physicians in 1942.

After filling a number of hospital posts in London and carrying out some research work on the Continent he was appointed Professor of Psychiatry at the University of Toronto, and Director of the Ontario Clinic for Nervous Disorders.

During these early years of the century, Jones became progressively more interested in the work of Freud, whose first major writing introducing the beginnings of psycho-analysis appeared in 1895. While in Canada, Jones introduced the study of psycho-analysis both there and in the United States. Before his return to England in 1913, Jones again visited the Continent, and his friendship with Freud became consolidated. Since that date Jones continued working in London up to the time of the Second World War.

He quickly collected around him a group of physicians and others who were interested in the work of Freud on the psychoneuroses, and soon after the First World War he founded the British Psycho-Analytical Society. It soon became clear that in addition to its function of scientific discussion the Society must also take responsibility for the training of psycho-analysts, and in 1924 the Institute of Psycho-Analysis was set up, another of whose functions was to take over responsibility for the *International Journal of Psycho-Analysis,* which had been founded by Jones in 1920 and was edited by him until 1939.

The institute also undertook the publishing of books in conjunction with the Hogarth Press, and 50 volumes have appeared in the International Psycho-Analytical Library under Jones's editorship.

In addition to all this pioneer work in England, to which was added the burden of an extremely busy private practice, Jones played a very active part in the organization of psycho-analysis on an international basis. The International Psycho-Analytical Association was set up in 1910. Jones was its president from 1920 to 1924, and again from 1932 to 1949; since then he had been honorary president, and remained its invaluable counsellor until his death.

In England Jones was the natural and undisputed leader from the beginning, and remained president of the British society until his retirement in 1944; when he became honorary president. At that time the British society decided to commemorate his work and achievement by establishing the Ernest Jones Lectures, delivered yearly by persons distinguished in various sciences and arts related to psycho-analysis.

Besides all this organizing activity, Jones maintained a steady output of scientific contributions of the highest order, from 1907 up to his last illness. Amazing in quantity, these covered a remarkably wide range of subject and were by no means limited to the clinical and theoretical aspects of psycho-analysis proper; some of them, for instance, dealt with education, art, literature (where his study of Hamlet is outstanding), religion, and anthropology. Some of these papers were collected in his *Papers on Pyscho-Analysis* and his *Essays in Applied Psycho-Analysis.* Finally, he turned biographer and his three-volume *Sigmund Freud, Life and Work* has been widely acclaimed as a masterpiece. At the time of his death he was engaged upon his autobiography.

It was not only in the world of scientific achievement that Jones was outstanding. He had qualities of leadership, courage, and strength of character which showed themselves at their most brilliant when the Nazis invaded Austria, and Freud himself and the large group of analysts in Vienna were in the gravest danger.

It was Jones's superhuman efforts which led to a happy outcome and enabled Freud to end his life peacefully in London, and also enriched British and American psychiatry by the influx of refugee analysts. This had been preceded by a similar migration from Germany after 1933, in which Jones had also played a leading part.

It would require a large volume to do justice to Jones's many-sided achievements; even at his hobbies he was outstanding. One of these was figure-skating, and he wrote a text-book on the subject. He was also an expert and very keen chess-player.

As is so often the case when a man is able to make a rich contribution to the world, he was magnificently supported, helped and encouraged by his wife, Katherine Jokl, whom he married in 1919; he is survived by her and by two sons and a daughter.

The passing of Ernest Jones will be mourned and his memory honoured not only in the world of psycho-analysis but by all for whom the proper study of mankind is man.

February 12, 1958.

Sir J. Lennard-Jones—See **Lennard-**.

Sir Harold Spencer Jones, F.R.S., Astronomer Royal from 1933 to 1955, died suddenly on November 3, 1960. He was 70.

Harold Spencer Jones was born in Kensington on March 29, 1890. He was educated at Latymer Upper School, Hammersmith, and Jesus College, Cambridge, where he gained high distinction in both mathematics and physics. He was elected a Fellow of Jesus College in 1914, but a year before had been appointed Chief Assistant at the Royal Observatory, Greenwich, thereby embarking on what was to prove an outstanding astronomical career.

His chosen profession was, however, interrupted by the 1914-18 War though his skill in optics and instrumental design was appropriately used by the Ministry of Munitions. He returned to Greenwich after the war and remained there as chief assistant until 1923, when he was appointed H.M. Astronomer at the Royal Observatory, Cape of Good Hope.

During the early years at Greenwich Spencer Jones was developing the qualities which later made him both an individual research worker of high merit and an outstanding administrator. It is a characteristic of British science that these qualities are often combined in the same individual, and Spencer Jones was a striking example of this happy tendency. It was soon clear that he was to become a leading authority on astronomy of position, and that he was especially interested in the accurate determination of the fundamental constants of astronomy. His analysis of the observational results obtained at Greenwich for the movement of the earth's poles showed both painstaking thoroughness and originality. But it also became clear that his interests were catholic and embraced the whole field of modern astrophysics. It was this catholicity of interest which led him to write his valuable book *General Astronomy,* the first edition of which appeared in 1922, a second and considerably revised edition appearing in 1934.

Spencer Jones's tenure at the Cape Observatory (1923 to 1933) was marked by a violent outburst of activity. He applied himself with zest and skill to the analysis of observational raw material which had been accumulated at the Cape, and his researches included determinations of the constant of aberration and the mass of Venus, as well as analyses of the moon's motion and of the variations in the rate of rotation of the earth. Astrophysics was represented by a valuable investigation of the system of the double star Procyon, and by a comprehensive memoir on the spectrum of the "new star" Nova Pictoris. But perhaps his outstanding contribution to the fine record of the Cape Observatory was his institution of a programme of the direct measurement of stellar distances, which was continued by his successor Dr. J. Jackson, F.R.S., [q.v.], and which, by 1945, had yielded determinations for some 1,400 stars.

In 1933 Sir Frank Dyson retired as Astronomer Royal and Spencer Jones succeeded him at Greenwich. It was not long before he had to face a major crisis in the history of our national observatory. The conditions at Greenwich had been worsening for some time owing to its proximity to London, and in the years following the First World War the process was accelerated. The transparency of the sky became so bad that many programmes of observational work were no longer practicable. The future of all photographic observations was threatened by the increasing brightness of the night sky arising from modern street lighting. And the deposition of solid matter on optical and other surfaces began to inflict serious damage on instruments. Spencer Jones was deeply attached to the historic site at Greenwich, but this attachment did not prevent him from recommending the removal of the observatory, a step absolutely necessary if it was to continue its contributions to astronomical knowledge.

The 1939-45 War intervened, however, and it was not until 1946 that approval was given for the removal of the Royal Observatory to Herstmonceux Castle in Sussex. The task of moving a large observatory is, naturally enough, a heavy administrative burden, and it was a fortunate circumstance that the move should have materialized during the tenure of office of a man whose abilities were admirably suited to such demands. Spencer Jones was also concerned with the initial plans for the Isaac Newton telescope, which is to be sited at Herstmonceux and to be available to university astronomers. Both ventures went forward, however, at a pace conceivable only in an organization dependent on penny-wise public accounting, and in his later years as Astronomer Royal he gave the impression that the frustrations of this period, following on the difficult wartime years, had left him perhaps a tired man.

Before Spencer Jones left the Cape he had commenced the major research which eventually led to the award, in 1943, of the Royal Astronomical Society's Gold Medal, the highest honour the society can bestow. One of the most important of the fundamental constants of astronomy is the mean distance of the earth from the sun. It was realized that the opposition of the minor planet Eros in 1930-31 would provide an extremely favourable opportunity for the accurate determination of this constant, and in 1928 an international commission was appointed to organize the work with Spencer Jones as president.

The observations were secured at many of the world's observatories but circumstances favoured the Southern Hemisphere, and by far the greatest amount of material was actually secured at the Cape under Spencer Jones's own direction. After the observations had been obtained, it fell to him to assemble and analyze the material, a very heavy task which took some 10 years. In 1943 he announced the final result, a value of 149,670,000 kilometres for the mean distance of the earth from the sun. Other products of the investigation were determinations of the ellipticity of the earth and of the constant of nutation. It is not too much to say that this work will become one of the landmarks in the history of astronomical science.

It was characteristic of Spencer Jones that his devotion to this major research was not allowed to interfere with his efficient administration of Greenwich Observatory. He was keenly interested in the work of every department and his catholic knowledge was at the disposal of every member of the staff. He took a particular interest in the development of improved methods of determining and distributing time, and under his direction the time department of the observatory was considerably expanded.

The expansion was necessitated by developments in radio and allied work involving the setting up of substandards of frequency which had to be controlled by the observatory, and the necessities of the public service thus called for the use of new and improved methods. But in addition to the utilitarian aspect of this work there is a purely scientific one: increased accuracy in timekeeping opens the road to a direct check on the variations in the rate of rotation of the earth, and this consideration intensified his determination to make the best possible provision for an increasing public need. His interest in this work had been further justified by the big increase in accuracy made possible by the advent of atomic clocks.

Spencer Jones was elected F.R.S. in 1930 and knighted in 1943. In 1955 he was created K.B.E. He was President of the Royal Astronomical Society in 1937 and 1938 and from 1945 to 1948 president of the International Astronomical Union, where his tact and administrative skill were of great value in the post-war reorganization of international cooperation.

In the year after his retirement as Astronomer Royal Spencer Jones became secretary-general of the International Council of Scientific Unions, a post which he held until 1958. He was always ready to give his time to individuals and organizations whom he thought it worth while to help. Thus he became president of the British Horological Institute in 1939 and did his best to draw attention to its work, and in a similar spirit he became president of the newly formed Institute of Navigation in 1947. Other bodies which gained from his experience included the Royal Institution and the Society for Visiting Scientists, of which he was an original member of the council and president for six years.

Spencer Jones was a rather quiet but determined man with great personal charm, full of the joy of life, and a valued friend to his colleagues. In 1918 he married Gladys Mary Owers. There were two sons of the marriage.

November 5, 1960.

Group Captain James Ira Jones, D.S.O., M.C., D.F.C., M.M., who won an enviable reputation as a fighter pilot of great dash and distinction in the First World War, died on August 29, 1960 in a Swansea hospital. He was credited with the destruction of 28 enemy aircraft, three balloons, and with the sending down of 10 aircraft out of control. He was said to have escaped from 28 crashes.

Jones was born in 1896, educated at Carmarthen Grammar School, and went straight into the Welch Regiment when war broke out in 1914. A year later he transferred to the Royal Flying Corps. His autobiography, *An Air Fighter's Scrapbook,* recreates with considerable success the grim but roaring days and nights of the first fighter pilots. Emotional, highly strung, the offensive spirit burned fiercely within him but it was matched by a deadly skill that enabled him to fight another day and yet another. He was many times decorated for bravery.

He served in the R.A.F. until 1936, when he retired, but he offered himself for duty in the Second World War, in which he commanded an operational training unit. But his heart was in flying and he could with difficulty be kept on the ground.

On one occasion when he was commanding an R.A.F. station in Wales a Junkers 88 was reported in the area. Jones took off in an aircraft armed with only a Very pistol, and chased it firing his pistol. The bomber made off.

In addition to his autobiography he wrote a biography of the great fighter pilot Edward ("Mick") Mannock, with whom he had fought.

August 31, 1960.

Dr. M. G. Jones, who died on September 1, 1955 at her home at Cambridge at the age of 75, was for many years Director of Studies in History, Law, and Economics at Girton and a notable scholar and teacher.

Mary Gwladys Jones, the daughter of the architect John Price Jones, was born at Cardiff on April 28, 1880. The easy circumstances of her childhood, diversified by foreign travel with her parents, were brought to an abrupt end by her father's early death in 1892, when heavy domestic responsibilities devolved upon her as the eldest girl in a family of 10 while she was still attending Howells School, Cardiff. Thus it was not until 1905 that she was able to go up to Cambridge to read history at Girton, where her maturity of judgment and powers as a speaker gave her a leading position among her contemporaries, and where she formed a close and lasting friendship with her fellow student Eileen Power. She came out top of the lists in the Mays examinations of 1906, though she failed to obtain a first class in the Tripos.

After a year's training under Miss Powell at St. Mary's, Lancaster Gate, she went in 1909 to the Ladies' College, Cheltenham, at first as Lecturer in History, and later as head of the Secondary Training Department. In 1914 she was appointed head of the Training Department for Women Teachers at Dublin organized jointly by Trinity and Alexander Colleges, and in 1920 she succeeded Eileen Power as Director of Studies in History at Girton College, a post she held for 20 years. Under the new University Statutes of 1926 she was appointed a University Lecturer in the Faculty of History, and she was a member of the Board of Studies for many years, serving also as examiner for the Historical Tripos and manager of the Mays examinations on many occasions. Her lectureship, which would normally have ended in 1940, was extended for five more years by the Faculty Board, and during the war years, while continuing her lectures on international law for Part II, she took on heavy additional work in order to fill the gaps caused by the temporary absence of colleagues.

In Ireland Miss Jones had begun work on the history of the Charity Schools founded in that country by the Society for Promoting Christian Knowledge in the eighteenth century. Twenty years of research in the archives of the S.P.C.K. and in local school records throughout the length and breadth of the British Isles bore fruit in *The Charity School Movement,* published in 1938 by the Cambridge University Press, justly described by G. M. Trevelyan* as "a remarkable book". Eminently readable, and a monument of scholarship, it threw new light on the religion and society of the eighteenth century.

The history and practice of education was indeed a leading interest with Dr. Jones throughout her life. She was a member of the Cheltenham Borough Education Committee, of the Council of Cambridge Training College, and a manager of many schools, both provided and non-provided. In 1919, when holder of the Frances Mary Buss Travelling Scholarship, she studied the educational systems of Canada and the United States on the spot; she made use of her Sabbatical leave from Cambridge to visit schools in China and Japan. Generations of her former pupils who entered the teaching profession can testify to the tireless and discriminating concern with which she watched and guided their careers. She was herself a brilliant teacher, both in the study and the lecture room, with exacting standards of thoroughness and a remarkable clarity of exposition, combined with quick perceptiveness and keen interest in personality.

Her interest in international affairs coloured both her politics—she was a convinced Liberal of the best freedom-loving humanitarian tradition, and a firm supporter of the League of Nations—and her studies. Her lectures on international law and relations for Part II of the Tripos, constantly rewritten to keep pace with the current happenings of the period between the wars, will be remembered by all who heard them for their lucidity, solidity, and underlying moral conviction. A Tolstoyan pacifist in her youth and doubtful as to the inevitability of the war of 1914, she had come by 1938 to rank justice as a greater good than peace, and from 1939 she taxed herself beyond her strength in such war work as research for the naval intelligence division, registration work for the Ministry of Labour, lectures to Polish officers for the British Council, and to cadets on short courses at the university.

In earlier and less strenuous days her many-sided social interests had fuller scope. From the days of her babyhood when, according to family tradition, her beauty made her the toast of Cardiff, she was at her happiest and most vivid as hostess or guest. She was a hockey international in her youth and played tennis for her college, and was throughout her life an ardent music lover and student of drama, acting herself and producing plays with great spirit. She could do nothing by halves; she was of those who would rather wear out than rust out.

As Fellow, member of council, and Vice-Mistress of Girton she gave ungrudgingly of her time, energy, and wisdom for 20 years to the service of the college whose welfare was her dearest interest and who has never had a more faithful daughter.

September 6, 1955.

Dr. Thomas Jones, C.H., who was Deputy Secretary to the Cabinet from 1916 to 1930, and later secretary and then chairman of the Pilgrim Trust, died on October 15, 1955 in hospital in London. He was 85.

The 14 years during which he was a member of the Cabinet secretariat and so at the centre of governance formed the most important period of his life: they covered not merely the critical war years (during which he was personally concerned, and very closely concerned, with the numerous domestic issues that arose out of war conditions) but also the anxious years of the early post-war period, and throughout his unselfish influence played its part. They may not have been the happiest years of his life, for his highly sensitive nature must have felt from time to time the jar that (rather often in politics) follows failure to persuade others that what is good must be done and done now.

He was a fine colleague during those busy years. Known already to many as "T. J.", it was not long before that was what he was called by an ever-widening circle. Naturally without any desire for publicity, he experienced no difficulty in absorbing those traditions of the Civil Service that call for self-effacement and anonymity, and he was satisfied to play a part behind the scenes. Like those with whom he worked—and he worked as hard as any—he was content to master the facts of the problem in hand, to weigh up and state impartially the pros and cons, to offer what seemed to be the best solution or the best advice, and then (suppressing any personal view) loyally conform to the decision of Ministers, putting forth all his energy again to see that that decision was adequately carried into practice.

Thomas Jones was born in 1870 at Rhymney, a Monmouthshire village famous for its iron works. His father was manager of the shop and farm of the Rhymney Iron Company. He himself on leaving school at 14 began work as a timekeeper with the company. Determined, however, to continue his studies, he saved his wages with this end in view. He had ambitions for the Civil Service, but there seemed no opening in sight, and under the influence of his Methodist environment he was encouraged to become a candidate for the ministry in 1890. With the money he had saved and with the help of his father he was enabled to enter University College, Aberystwyth (to which he returned as president towards the end of his life), and subsequently to go to Glasgow University, where he was Clarke Scholar. He was Russell Student at the London School of Economics, and Barrington Lecturer in Ireland from 1904 to 1905. He became assistant to the Professor of Political Economy and Lecturer in Economics in Glasgow University, and in 1906 was appointed a special investigator for the Poor Law Commission. Three years later he was appointed Professor in Economics in Queen's University, Belfast, but left the next year to be secretary of the Welsh National Campaign against Tuberculosis. In 1912 he was appointed secretary to the National Health Insurance Commissioners (Wales), in which position he remained until 1916, when he became Deputy Secretary to the Cabinet. Here he served during critical years as colleague of Sir Maurice (Lord) Hankey*, and he was also Secretary of the Economic Advisory Council.

It was characteristic of T. J. that, though a man of strong convictions, and of great intellectual and personal independence, he was adaptable and able to work closely and on terms of friendship with Prime Ministers of widely differing types—Lloyd George, Bonar Law, Stanley Baldwin, Ramsay MacDonald—though his intimate friends sensed at times how he was discouraged and depressed at what he thought was mistaken action or policy, or at what appeared to be weakness. He differed from many of his Civil Service colleagues in having a very wide range of contacts throughout the unofficial world: he had the gift of making people talk freely to him, as if to a friend, and it was this faculty for gaining the confidence of all sorts of men that enabled him to play so well an unobtrusive part in the negotiations about the labour disputes that characterized the inter-war years—including the General Strike of 1926. There were those who thought him unduly anxious to see that the views of the miners, railwaymen, and others were brought to the notice of higher authority; but if he was insistent that full regard should be paid to the merits of the men's case, it was only because he realized that on a long view political and social stability would best be served if, even though beaten in a strike, the men could know that at least the Government had been impartial.

T. J. read widely and deeply and his love for literature—without which little of a book remains in mind—gave him a fine store of knowledge of a phrase; hence his facility for easy yet forceful writing, for finding just the way to express a view that would best commend it to the reader or the audience. He wrote smoothly and gracefully, drawing upon his knowledge of what had been written before for the quotation that supplied just the last turn of the petal that forms the perfect flower. He once said that he "had made a second fortune" (his first was made up, he said, of friendships) "out of contents of books, and had collected and scattered books all through his life—theology, economics, politics, history, poetry. What enjoyment it had been to grow rich without robbing or hurting anybody!"

When he left the Civil Service in 1930 T. J. became the first secretary of the Pilgrim Trust, a post that was most congenial to him. With trustees like Hugh Macmillan, Stanley Baldwin, John Buchan—already his friends—he found himself in a position to aid just those forms of activity that were dear to his soul. Indeed, the contents tables of the reports of the trust (printed at the Gregynog Press, in Newtown, another of the children of his spirit) probably form the epitaph that he himself would have wished—social service (youth camps, welfare of the physically disabled, settlements and clubs for the unemployed, &c.), preservation of national treasures (countryside, ancient buildings, archives) research (social, medical, scientific). After his resignation of the secretaryship in 1945, he was elected a trustee and for two years, 1952-54, he was chairman.

In 1934 he was appointed a member of the Unemployment Assistance Board, and once again (though now he had to conserve his health) he was able to utilize his sympathetic wisdom, this time to the problem of what to do about those who had been so long unemployed that they were outside the normal field of industry. Here, characteristically, and because he well knew the frailties of men, his colleagues found him fully ready to advocate a policy which, while helping fairly the cases that needed help, would frown upon any who might think idleness a claim to generosity. Yet even when he frowned officially, it was with a benignity that showed the idler that much would be done for him could he but again take off his coat and buckle to.

Indifferent to social advancement, T. J. yet mixed as readily with the great as with those who were not. He revelled in some weekend gatherings in noble houses, believing as well as feeling that the atmosphere and historical background of an old English home added something to a discussion of some social problem that was to form the subject of the conversations. And if on Monday morning his notes on the need for action about unemployment, or housing, or education were trenchant, they were at least in perspective, and, as he wrote them he was fired with his desire for progress in the nation's social life, while at the same time steadied by his knowledge of the lessons of history.

He both loved learning and appreciated it; what is more, he worked to ensure that others might both love and appreciate it. Hence his interest in adult education and his efforts to found Coleg Harlech. Ten years after it was founded he had the satisfaction of receiving from the staff and past students of the college a volume of essays entitled *Harlech Studies.*

Naturally he took a special interest in Wales and in things Welsh, and many were the journeys he paid to his native land. He possessed in a large degree the Welsh love of the beautiful; his heart was saddened by the physical desolation of the South Wales valleys, as is manifest in his charmingly nostalgic volume, *Rhymney Memories.* There was no project for the improvement of those casualties of industry that did not find in him a sympathetic well-wisher. He had a great love for Welsh literature, and worked hard for the encouragement of Welsh culture. The splendidly produced translation of the *Mabinogion,* which appeared in 1948, is a lasting monument of his work in this field. He spoke Welsh fluently, and was always glad of an opportunity of doing so. He was a member of the Court of the University of Wales, a Governor of the National Library, and of the National Museum of Wales, and his signal services to Welsh learning and culture were recognized in 1945 by the award of the Cymmrodorion medal.

Yet he was in no sense parochial. During his 14 years in the Cabinet Office, and for some years afterwards, he was brought into contact with imperial and international affairs, and with imperial and foreign statesmen. Here, again, his attractive friendliness gained for him the confidence of many, and each fresh contact widened the scope of his correspondence. So he had sources of information as wide and varied geographically as in subject matter. These widely ranging friendships and acquaintances were turned to good account in his volume, *A Diary with Letters,* published in 1954. With its day-to-day account of the movements behind the scenes in politics in the period 1931-50, it is an important historical document.

Three years before he had published a life of Lloyd George which he modestly described as an "interim, unofficial contribution". Though brief, it was a valuable biography, written with sympathy and shrewdness and based on an intimate acquaintance with its subject.

On a different level was his address to the Double Crown Club on the Gregynog Press, of which he had been chairman. This, luxuriously published in the penultimate year of his life, was a lively and succinct account of the production of fine books between 1923 and 1940. In these manifestations of his latest flowering he exhibited an affinity with both Horace Walpole and Charles Greville.

He married, in 1902, Eirene Theodora, daughter of the late R. J. Lloyd, D.Litt. She died in 1935, and he leaves a son and a daughter, Eirene White [Lady White], member of Parliament for East Flint. Another son was killed in a motor accident in 1928.

October 17, 1955.

King Abdullah of Jordan was shot dead in Jerusalem on July 20, 1951 as he was entering a mosque.

With his death Britain lost one of the oldest and most faithful of her allies. The brother of the late King Feisal I of Iraq, he became Emir of Transjordan, a British mandate, after the first world war, and during the second world war sent his troops, the famous Arab Legion, to fight for Britain in both the Syrian and Iraq campaigns.

After the cessation of hostilities in 1946 Transjordan achieved its independence, and Abdullah was proclaimed King, entering at the same time into alliance with Britain. After the termination of the British mandate in Palestine in May 1948, the Transjordan Army occupied Jericho and an agreement was signed in Amman, King Abdullah's capital, between Syria, the Lebanon, Transjordan, and Iraq as a prelude to organized hostilities with Israel. At the same time King Abdullah remained the most moderating influence in the Arab camp, while furnishing its only effective army, the Arab Legion. His relations with the extremists of the Arab League, and particularly with Egypt, were consequently often strained.

During this period he pursued two ambitions of his own. The first was the creation of a Greater Syria, composed of Transjordan, Iraq, Syria, and the Arab parts of Palestine, with himself as leader. This project probably never had much chance of success, owing to the hostility of the other Arab countries, Secondly, he wished to annex the Arab parts of Palestine, which were in any case largely controlled by the Arab Legion in the latter stages of the war with Israel. He declared himself "King of Jordan" in 1949 and these areas gradually became *de facto* incorporated in his kingdom, though formal annexation was proclaimed only in April 1950.

King Abdullah had several times travelled to England, his most recent visit being in the summer of 1949. His eldest son, Emir Talal, recently had a breakdown and is undergoing treatment in Geneva. The second son, Naif, has been appointed Regent.

Abdullah, who was born in 1881, the second son of the Sherif of Mecca, afterwards King Hussein of the Hejaz, began his political career in 1907 as the representative of Mecca in the Ottoman parliament and played a considerable part in the beginnings of the Arab nationalist movement. Shortly before August 1914 he had conversations on this subject with Lord Kitchener, but these were inconclusive. The outbreak of war, however, caused the British Government to reopen negotiations with his father, and in these Abdullah again played his part. When they resulted in the unfurling of the Arab standard at Mecca, in July 1916 by his father, the newly-established King of the Hejaz, Abdullah commanded the Arab forces in the first stage of the campaign. In the space of three months, Mecca, Jedda, and Taif were captured and their Turkish garrisons expelled.

In 1921 Abdullah, whose military attainments had hitherto been slight, set out from Mecca, his declared object being to attack the French, who had deposed his brother Feisal in Syria. It so happened that at this moment Winston Churchill*, then Secretary of State for the Colonies, was in Jerusalem on official business connected with the settlement of Middle Eastern affairs; and a conference was arranged between him, the High Commissioner, and Abdullah, at which an arrangement was made whereby Abdullah undertook to assume the administration of Transjordan under the general direction of the High Commissioner for Palestine. In return for his recognition he was to abandon his hostile intentions as regards Syria.

In July 1921 the British Parliament voted a grant-in-aid of £180,000 for the assistance of Transjordan; and in July 1922 the Council of the League of Nations formally approved the mandate for Palestine and Transjordan, whereby the international status of Transjordan was placed on a regular basis. The next stage in the constitutional development of Transjordan under Abdullah was a declaration issued by the High Commissioner for Palestine in 1923 to the effect that, subject to the approval of the League of Nations, Britain would recognize the existence of an independent Government in Transjordan under the rule of the Emir Abdullah, provided that such Government was constitutional and placed Britain in a position to fulfil her international obligations in respect of the territory by means of an agreement to be concluded with him. This agreement was signed in Jerusalem in 1928.

Abdullah was the possessor of attributes which marked him out in many ways as the epitome of the Arab warrior-prince. He was a master of the Arabic language, which added immensely to his prestige in the religio-literary setting of the Arab world. With a taste for poetry he combined an enthusiastic interest in the chase and in Arab bloodstock; he was an outstandingly good rifle shot. He retained to the end of his days his grasp of international affairs and also of the most up-to-date developments in military science. The efficiency of the Arab Legion owed much to his personal interest, and he insisted that its officers should he attached to the Long Range Desert Group in order that it should be able to take the fullest part in active operation when war broke out. At the same time he had a thorough appreciation of the English way of life and sent his eldest son to Sandhurst.

July 21, 1951.

Dr. H. E. K. Jordan, F.R.S., Director of the Zoological Museum, Tring, from 1930 to 1939, and previously Curator of Entomology from 1893 to 1939, died in a Hemel Hempstead hospital on January 12, 1959. He was 97.

Heinrich Ernst Karl Jordan was born on December 7, 1861, near Hildesheim in Hanover, the seventh child of a small farmer who died when Karl was five. But for the generosity of an uncle which enabled him to attend high school at Hildesheim, entomology might never have known him. In 1886 he graduated with highest honours in botany and zoology at the University of Göttingen. After a year of voluntary military service, which he enjoyed, though because he had to pay for his own food and lodging he often went hungry, he took up a teaching post in the School of Agriculture at Hildesheim. During this period his remarkable qualities were recognized both by Professor Metzger, of the Academy of Forestry, and by Count Berlepsch, a well-known local naturalist. It was at the latter's house that he met Ernst Hartert, then recently appointed Director of the Zoological Museum which Walter Rothschild (later Lord Rothschild) was building up at Tring. In 1893 he accepted an invitation to Tring and was given the task of reducing to order the immense but chaotic collection of insects which had already accumulated there.

At Tring Jordan found precisely the material suited to his outlook. He had long been impressed by the way birds and insects varied geographically, but the nature and manner of this variation could not be studied in the type of collection then popular, which consisted of selected specimens; large random samples were needed, and these were available in full measure at Tring.

About two years after Jordan's arrival at Tring there was published Rothschild's Revision of the Oriental Swallow-tail butterflies, in which the hand of the master is already everywhere evident. So far ahead of contemporary thought was Jordan that, as one writer has said of this work, though "written 10 years before the rediscovery of Mendel's laws, and 40 years before the modern synthesis of taxonomy and population genetics, it can be read virtually without reservation to-day".

At one stroke the butterflies were shown to provide not only an attractive amusement for the amateur, but material of the highest importance in the scientific approach to the study of evolution. Further similar monographs appeared during the next 15 years which gave Jordan further scope to develop his conceptual contributions in the field of taxonomy and evolutionary thought. In this field he foreshadowed the "new systematics" outlook of the last quarter of a century, leaving to its sponsors only the credit of supplying the appropriate tools and techniques. Though, understandably, Jordan's earlier philosophical contributions have been modified, his taxonomic work has proved indeed basic and remains unchallenged.

About 1898, through assisting Charles Rothschild with his studies of parasitic insects, Jordan became intensely interested in fleas. An inquiry into the genus *Xenopsylla* led to the discovery that the genus contained a number of very similar species, only one of which, *X. cheopis,* transmitted to man the bacillus of bubonic plague. It was then found that the distribution of plague and of this particular flea coincided—a valuable practical outcome of taxonomic research. Since those days medical entomologists throughout the world have been outspokenly grateful for the constant inspiration they received from their "dean of siphonapterists".

Not only did he provide them with a sound basis of classification and identification, but every query sent him met with a generously helpful reply. In his studies of the morphology, classification, and evolution of the fleas Jordan's descriptive and artistic skill, his acumen in evaluating the taxonomic importance of anatomical features, his faculties of analysis and synthesis, are to be seen at their best.

Always international in his outlook, Jordan believed that even a small international agreement on a purely scientific subject was a worthwhile advance towards the ideal of universal political sanity. Reasons of this nature led him to initiate the International Congresses of Entomology which, starting in Brussels in 1910, have been held at intervals, largely under his guidance, ever since.

Similarly he felt it his duty to preside later over the International Commission on Zoological Nomenclature. Of both organizations he was later honorary life president. In 1911 he became a naturalized British subject. In 1932 he was elected a Fellow of the Royal Society, and in 1929 to the Presidency of the Royal Entomological Society of London. The latter society took the occasion, unique in its history, of publishing in his honour and on his ninety-fourth birthday a Jubilee volume of their Transactions.

To most entomologists Jordan was the distinguished author of very many important works on entomology. To those who had the boon of knowing him personally he could be father and mentor, happy companion and even pupil all at once, and all with a vein of original, puckish humour that was a constant source of surprise and delight.

January 14, 1959.

Sir William Jordan, K.C.M.G., P.C., High Commissioner for New Zealand in London from 1936 to 1951, died in Auckland on April 8, 1959. He was 79.

By his sincerity and unassuming ways he won the good will of all who met him, and represented New Zealand with dignity and ability. His was a record term in more than one sense.

Born at Ramsgate, Kent, on May 19, 1879, William Joseph Jordan was the son of Captain William Jordan, who had been a member of both Ramsgate and Margate lifeboat crews. The coming of the steam trawler caused distress among the fishermen and the Jordan family migrated to London. Jordan used to remark that it was fortunate that he and a sister were accepted by St. Luke's Parochial School, Old Street, which provided clothes and other forms of help. His scholastic career, however, was short for he left when 11 years old to become an errand boy for a Clerkenwell jeweller, and was not a little disappointed when after some months he was compelled to return for a further year. He left finally in 1892, and after a short spell at a type foundry became an apprentice to a coach painter in Old Street.

His next venture was in the engineering section of the postal service, but in spite of some success he was restless and dissatisfied, and he joined the Metropolitan Police, serving as a constable in Limehouse and Forest Gate. Still discontented, for the routine of police work did not attract him, he took the most important step in his life and emigrated to New Zealand.

On arrival he took a job in the Pohangina Valley. After strenuous exertions in stumping, grass seeding, milking, fencing, road-making, and other tasks, he yielded to the lure of town life, and worked successively in Nelson and Wellington, where he took part in the formation of the New Zealand Labour Party, and became its first secretary.

Leaving Wellington later, he started in business in the gold mining town of Waihi and also traded in the Waikato township of Ngaruawahia. Here he married Winifred, daughter of Louth Bycroft. When the war broke out in 1914 Jordan was among the early volunteers. He went to France with the New Zealand forces, saw much heavy fighting, and was severely wounded. He did not return to his business at the end of hostilities, but accepted a post as grader and blender with the New Zealand Honey Producers' Association. He had retained his interest in Labour politics, however, and resumed his activities on its behalf. In 1922 he was elected to the New Zealand Parliament for the Manukau division and represented the constituency until his appointment in 1936, as High Commissioner. He was chosen to represent the Parliamentary Labour Party at an Empire Conference in Canada in 1928, and in 1933 he was elected president of the Labour Party.

When in 1935 the Labour Party attained power Jordan was offered the choice of membership of the Cabinet or the High Commissionership in London. M. J. Savage, the new Prime Minister, advised him to take the latter course. In his official capacity he became a member of the Council of the League of Nations, and two years later its president, officiating at the opening of the Assembly. Jordan represented his Dominion at the Coronation of King George VI [q.v.], and carried the New Zealand Standard in the procession in Westminster Abbey. He accompanied Savage, the New Zealand Prime Minister, to the Imperial Conference in London in 1937, and the next year was the New Zealand representative at the Nine Power Conference in Brussels to discuss Japanese aggression in China.

When New Zealand entered the Second World War the work of the High Commissioner was much concerned with the members of New Zealand's three fighting services who came to the United Kingdom, and he made it his personal business to keep close contact with every New Zealand unit in the country. Indeed one would imagine that he came to know every New Zealand service man personally and was concerned with his welfare. In 1946 he was New Zealand's representative at the Paris Peace Conference.

Jordan was a Freeman of the City of London, a distinction which, in view of his having spent his boyhood there, gave him satisfaction almost equal to that he felt at being made, in 1937, a Freeman of his native town of Ramsgate. Amid all his activities he found time to work as a layman for the Methodist Church in New Zealand, where his services as a local preacher were much in demand, while in London he served as a churchwarden of St. Lawrence Jewry. He saw no inconsistency in the two offices, and would remind any who raised the subject that Charles Wesley remained a member of the Church of England until his death.

In 1946 he was made an honorary LL.D. of St. Andrews University, and a similar honour was conferred on him by Cambridge University in 1951.

He was a member of the Girdlers' Company and after the War of 1939-45 gave the company a Master's chair of white kauri upholstered in blue leather, to take the place of the chair lost when the Girdlers' Hall was destroyed in the war. He was also a member of the Butchers' Company.

He was much sought after as an after dinner speaker for he had an infectious humour typical of his London upbringing. He was wont to remark after he had been sworn of the Privy Council that there had been a time when the letters P.C. went before his name. He had known poverty and hardship in early life and perhaps because of this never lost his sympathy for those in need.

He was created K.C.M.G. in 1952.

His first wife died in 1950 and he married secondly in 1952 Mrs. Elizabeth Ross Reid, who, with a son and a daughter of his first marriage, survives him.

April 9, 1959.

Michael Joseph, one of the most enterprising publishers of his day, died in a London hospital on March 15, 1958 after a short illness. He was 60.

Joseph was born in London on September 26, 1897, and educated at the City of London School and at London University.

He served throughout the First World War first with The Wiltshire Regiment, in which he was commissioned, and later in the Machine Gun Corps. He was a writer long before he was a publisher, his first book, *Short Story Writing for Profit* (to which Stacy Aumonier contributed a foreword), coming out when he was in his mid-twenties. There was a sharp precision about the title which reflected the astringent qualities of the book itself. He was to write again about the pains and pleasures of writing for profit.

He founded the publishing business that bears his name in 1935, a decade in which many well-known firms were compelled to close their doors and others to pass through a time of great anxiety. As he was to say in *The Adventure of Publishing,* he held on by "the skin of his teeth".

But in the ensuing years he more than held his ground. The firm prospered and the names of many outstanding writers appeared in his lists, among them those of C. S. Forester* and H. E. Bates*. Joseph was wont to describe his recreation as cats, but they were something more than a recreation, for he wrote about them with charm and feeling.

He was three times married.

March 17, 1958.

Louis Jouvet, one of France's greatest actors and producers, died on August 6, 1951 at the age of 64.

Louis Jouvet, who was born in Brittany in 1887, was one of a number of French actors of our time who have become famous not by the traditional methods of a training at the Conservatoire and a career at the Comédie-Française but after the knockabout of provincial touring companies, followed by association with various modest artistic ventures in Paris.

He was a junior member of Robert d'Humières's company at the Théâtre des Arts in the early years of the century. When Jacques Copeau founded the Vieux-Colombier in 1913 Jouvet joined him as his working stage manager and also as a comedian whose range seemed at first to be severely limited by his lanky and ungainly figure, his large staring eyes, his staccato diction, and his sepulchral voice. Under Copeau he gave an admirable performance as Sir Andrew Aguecheek, and a memorable one as Autolycus.

His association with Copeau was broken by his being called up to the colours in 1914, but he accompanied him to New York in 1917, and remained there for two years. Eventually he left Copeau in 1922, when Copeau himself retired to the country, and became sole director of the Comédie des Champs Elysées in 1924.

His first really successful production, which led to his becoming a manager, was Jules Romains's* comedy *Knock, ou le triomphe de la médicine,* a study of a successful quack country doctor. During his management of this theatre he produced other plays by Jules Romains and early works of several other playwrights who have since become widely known. After *Siegfried* in 1928 he produced every one of Girandoux's 10 plays, and he declared that if he had done nothing else in the course of his career he would have been satisfied with this title to be remembered.

In 1934 he left the Comédie des Champs Elysées to take over the management of the Athenée, in the very centre of Paris, and in 1936 he became a professor at the Conservatoire. In the same year Bourdet, the dramatist, was appointed administrateur of the Comédie-Française, and invited Copeau, Baty [q.v.], Dullin, and Jouvet in 1936 to occupy the newly invented posts of "stage directors". This only meant producing a play occasionally, because each of them except Copeau had his own theatre; Jouvet's only production was a revival of Corneille's neglected comedy, *l'Illusion,* which was not a success.

During the 1939-45 war, Jouvet took a company to South America, with which France has always maintained close cultural relations, and gave what was then Girandoux's latest play, *Oudine,* as well as a revival of Molière's *École des Femmes.* In this latter play he gave a remarkable performance as the elderly, violent, and deceived husband, Arnolphe.

Jouvet was best known in Great Britain as a film actor—in *Carnet de Bal, La Kermesse Héroique, Entrée des Artistes,* and other pictures; but he was at his best in the theatre, as actor—often content with a modest part in his own productions—as a director who could get fine acting out of his company and could make fruitful suggestions to his author, and as a designer of simple but very effective scenery. It was perhaps in his mastery of stage lighting that he showed the greatest originality. Those who knew him personally can testify that he took his profession very seriously; he never did anthing—even speaking a few words over the wireless—without full rehearsal. His little book, *Réflexions du Comédien,* contains much wisdom on the art of acting.

August 17, 1951.

Lord Jowitt, the first and last Earl, who died at his home near Bury St. Edmunds on August 16, 1957, was in his day an outstanding and brilliant advocate. He was 72.

Apart from his private practice at the Bar he was Solicitor-General in Sir Winston Churchill's* Government in 1940, though he first held office as Attorney-General in 1929. On accepting that post he changed from the Liberal Party to the Labour Party, a decision giving rise to strong criticism and acute controversy which was a long time in being forgiven if not forgotten. Nevertheless, as was to be expected, he fulfilled those offices with high skill, and the crown of his career was reached by his expected and, indeed, inevitable appointment as Lord Chancellor in the third Labour Government which came into office in July 1945 with, for the first time, a clear majority over all other parties.

The Rt. Hon. William Allen Jowitt, P.C., first Earl Jowitt, Viscount Stevenage, of Stevenage, Viscount Jowitt, and Baron Jowitt, of Stevenage, in the county of Hertford in the Peerage of the United Kingdom, was the only son of the late Rev. William Jowitt, rector of Stevenage, and was born on April 15, 1885, and educated at Marlborough and New College, Oxford, where he took a first in jurisprudence in 1906. He was called to the Bar by the Middle Temple in 1909, and became a pupil of A. J. Ashton, K.C. Subsequently he became a Bencher of the Middle Temple and was Treasurer in 1951. He was later in chambers with the future Mr. Justice Charles and Sir Holman Gregory, afterwards the Recorder of London.

His rise was rapid and within a few years of his call he was seen in the best class of commercial work, as well as in that class of litigation which captures the public imagination and is widely reported in the press. It is interesting to recall that among his pupils was the future Attorney-General, Sir Donald Somervell [q.v.], under whom in later years Jowitt was himself to serve as Solicitor-General. When he took silk in 1922 he was regarded as one of the best all round juniors at the common law Bar. For his career he was well endowed by nature; to a fine presence were added a rich, resonant, and well-modulated voice, a persuasive manner, free from truculence, and a method depending more upon subtlety and lucid statement than emotional appeal.

It was said that the quality of his arguments seemed to place a case on a higher level. As a leader his reputation was more than maintained, and in the years before, and between, his periods of office he was retained in many cases of first-rate importance on the common law side.

In a £200,000 suit between two radio companies he once spoke in the Court of Appeal for over 17 days and was said to have delivered over half a million words; and another of his cases, a dispute over the export of whisky to New South Wales, involving many thousands of pounds, occupied the Privy Council for several weeks. These give some idea of the extent of his practice. As Attorney-General it fell to him to prosecute Lord Kylsant for issuing a prospectus with intent to induce persons to advance or entrust property to the Royal Mail Lines, and his skilful handling of that very intricate case was considered a masterpiece of forensic ability.

Jowitt's political career, which was later to involve him in rough water and bitter controversy, began in 1922, the year he took silk, when he was elected as Liberal member for the Hartlepools, winning the seat from the sitting Conservative by some 600 votes. In the House the logical and unemotional expressions of his views, generally in support of the more advanced Liberal opinion, created a good impression, and his future, should his party ever require a Law Officer, was promising. He was one of the few Liberals who supported the Labour Government in the Campbell case, which brought about its downfall. At the following General Election, in May 1924, he lost his seat, and for the next five years he was out of Parliament.

In the meantime, in 1929, he had been appointed a member of the Royal Commission on the Lunacy Laws. In the General Election on May 30, 1929 (which resulted in the return of the second Labour Government) Jowitt was returned as one of the Liberal members for Preston. He and Ramsay MacDonald had long been friends and the latter was anxious when he formed his Ministry to find satisfactory Law Officers; he therefore proposed to Jowitt that he should come over to Labour and accept the office of Attorney-General. Jowitt did so, and explained that he had come to the conclusion that it was to the Labour Party that Radicals like himself had now to turn for achieving the objects which they had at heart; at the same time he offered the Liberal Association to resign his seat and stand again as a Labour candidate. The association made no request for his resignation, but a lively controversy arose in political and legal circles on the integrity of Jowitt's change of front, and a vigorous correspondence justifying or condemning his action raged for some days in the columns of *The Times.*

In the end Jowitt resigned his seat and submitted himself again to the electors of Preston as a Labour candidate. On July 31, 1929, he was elected by a majority of 6,440. He proved, as was expected, a valuable addition to Labour's debating power in the House, and when, in 1931, the National Government was formed he elected to join it and was thereupon expelled from the Labour Party. When the General Election came in October 1931 he stood as National Labour candidate for the Combined Universities (though having previously advocated the abolition of the University franchise), but he failed to secure election, and it being found impracticable to find him a seat he shortly afterwards resigned the office of Attorney-General and remained out of Parliament and office for some seven years.

Jowitt was thus free to resume his practice at the Bar and solicitors were glad to welcome back one who in his own lines was certainly one of the foremost advocates of his day. The Second World War broke out before he returned to Parliament. In 1936 he had been readmitted to the Labour Party and in October 1939, on the death of the sitting member, F. B. Simpson, Jowitt was returned unopposed for Ashton-under-Lyne, which constituency he represented until he was raised to the Woolsack in 1945.

When Churchill formed his Government in 1940 Jowitt was appointed Solicitor-General, serving as has been said, under his former pupil, the Attorney-General, Lord [then Sir Donald] Somervell. In May 1942 he was made, in succession to Lord Hankey*, Paymaster-General, an office which is usually an unpaid sinecure, but to which he was appointed at a salary of £5,000 to carry on some of the work in preparation for post-war reconstruction which had formerly been under Arthur Greenwood [q.v.], and in January 1943 he was made Minister without Portfolio and carried on his existing duties with regard to post-war reconstruction as before.

In October 1944 he was appointed Minister of Social Insurance. The scheme of social insurance and family allowances outlined in the Government's White Paper was put to the test in the House of Commons on November 2, 1944, on a motion inviting the House to welcome the scheme, which was commended to the House by Jowitt in an admirably lucid speech; but the whole question of social insurance passed into the hands of another Government as the result of the general election in July 1945, and the discussion of the Coalition Government's White Paper has now only an academic interest. As was expected, when Clement Attlee* formed his Government after that election, Jowitt became Lord Chancellor, which position he occupied till 1951, when the Conservative Party was returned to power. During his tenure of that office he presided at the hearing of the House of Lords of the appeal of William Joyce (more familiarly known in his broadcasts from Germany as "Lord Haw-Haw") against his conviction of treason.

When the House of Lords debated the Criminal Justice Bill in April 1948, Jowitt, as Lord Chancellor, moved its second reading. He referred to that highly controversial question the suspension of the death penalty, and, though he declared himself opposed to its suspension, said that, having agreed to a free vote in the House of Commons, he must rely on the decision of that House, and advised that the experiment of suspending the penalty should be tried.

While Lord Chancellor he made a number of visits abroad. In August 1947 he sailed for America and addressed official bodies in Canada and the United States. He went to Paris in February 1948, where he delivered a lecture at the Sorbonne on "The English Conception of the Rule of Law". In the following month he visited Italy. He was received by the President and also had a private audience with the Pope. While in Rome he delivered two lectures, the first on "Liberty and the law", the second on "Legal training in England". His visit aroused widespread interest.

Early in the following year he suffered slight trouble with one of his eyes because of some overstrain and on medical advice obtained a month's leave of absence during which he went to Malta. In the Long Vacation of that year he was the guest of the Brazilian Government. The highlight of his journeys abroad came in January 1951, when he inaugurated the new permanent supreme Court of Appeal for Eastern Africa, which included Aden, the Seychelles, and Somaliland. The importance of the occasion was recognized by the formalities of the colourful proceedings. The Lord Chancellor, who was accompanied by a pursebearer and attendants, wore court dress, full-bottomed wig, and gold-braided damask robe of black silk.

Jowitt, unable to resist the lure of authorship, certainly chose a difficult subject when he wrote his study of *The Strange Case of Alger Hiss,* published in May 1953. He himself wrote that the materials which would enable him to attempt a sketch of the character of Alger Hiss were not to hand—all he had was the impression which had been formed in his mind by recording in cold print the evidence which Hiss gave both before the House Committee and at the second trial. Never having had the opportunity of seeing Hiss or of judging from his demeanour what manner of man Hiss was, his impressions must, he said, be purely tentative. The book was an objective and detached analysis of the case and reactions to it must be a matter of personal opinion. It raised acute criticism in certain sections of America.

Indeed, when the American publisher withdrew copies already distributed to bookshops and reviewers there appeared to be a *cause célèbre* in the making, since it was alleged in some quarters that political pressure had been brought to bear to secure the withdrawal. This was subsequently denied by the publishers, who explained that the copies of the book had been recalled because it was found that some inferences drawn by Jowitt from the evidence of Whittaker Chambers were "not warranted by facts"; there had also been misunderstandings of American legal practice and Jowitt had been invited to revise the relevant passages. Finally a revised edition was announced for July. Originally the book should have appeared in May.

A second book, *Some Were Spies,* was published in December 1954. As Solicitor-General, Jowitt was responsible for the conduct of trials in the early days of the late war of persons accused of espionage. No doubt, with regard to the chapters of the book on those matters, which were heard in camera, the author obtained permission from the authorities where necessary for the disclosure of material otherwise secret.

The rest of the book refers to notable trials in which Jowitt was briefed and were widely reported in the newspapers, such as the Kylsant, Hatry*, and Youisoupoff cases. The method in which the facts of the various cases were presented gave the book its particular interest, and the author was on more familiar ground than in the book on Alger Hiss.

Jowitt, who had been Leader of the Opposition in the House of Lords since 1952, decided in November 1955—he was then 70—to retire from that onerous leadership at the end of the year. He was succeeded by Lord Alexander of Hillsborough*. But as a former Lord Chancellor he continued to give valuable service in the hearing of appeals both in the House and in the Judicial Committee of the Privy Council.

Jowitt's acute intelligence was brought to bear on the controversy in 1955 over the proposed ban on the manufacture of heroin. During the debate in the Lords in December, on Jowitt's motion to extend licences for manufacture, the Government announced that licences would be issued for 1956. Earlier Jowitt had startled the House by casting doubts on the legality of the proposed ban.

He had received a barony in 1945, was raised to a viscounty in 1947, and made an earl in 1951.

At the Bar Jowitt had neither sought nor obtained wide popularity. In the political sphere he had laid himself open to charges of inconsistency and self-seeking, and the recollection of such charges echoed through the years. Of his sudden change over to Labour there is, however, this to be said; his type of Liberalism was much akin to Labour and the dyke to be crossed was a narrow one. Moreover, there is no doubt that his acceptance of the Attorney-Generalship at the time was a distinct public advantage, as he was universally held to possess all the necessary learning and prestige for the office, and as Head of the Bar he maintained all its best traditions. Jowitt was a man of fine appearance and stately manners.

He married in 1913 Lesley, second daughter of J. P. McIntyre, and he leaves one daughter.

August 17, 1957.

K

Count Michael Karolyi, President of Hungary in the short-lived republic which succeeded the 1914-18 War and was superseded by the régime of Bela Kun, died at Vence on March 19, 1955 at the age of 80.

Born in 1875, he had the usual upbringing of a Hungarian magnate. Imagination and vision, genuine reforming zeal, and a knowledge of the conditions and tendencies of western democracy, made a rebel of him and he led the Opposition in the Hungarian Parliament before and during the 1914-18 War. After the collapse of the Dual Monarchy in 1918 he became Prime Minister and later President of his country, but resigned in the following year when the extremists of the left attained power.

He then went to England and later, after the opposition of the immigration organization of the United States had been overcome, he visited that country. During the 1939-45 War he was prominent in the "Free Hungarian" movement and in 1946 he returned to Hungary, where his anti-fascist activities were recognized by an Act of Parliament. Some months later he was appointed Hungarian Minister to France, but resigned his post in 1949, ostensibly on account of age. Very shortly afterwards the Hungarian Government issued a statement attacking Karolyi's motives in resigning. On that occasion he was referred to as "a dotard of 75".

Since 1950 he had been living a retired life at Vence, not far from Nice, with his wife, a member of the Andrassy family. His last wish was to be buried in the Isle of Wight beside his son, Adam, who at the age of 20, in 1939, was killed in an aircraft accident while working as a test pilot.

March 21, 1955.

Henry Edward ("Ted") Kavanagh, whose scripts for the B.B.C. radio programme *Itma,* in which Tommy Handley played the leading part, became remarkably popular during the Second World War, died after a short illness in a London hospital on September 17, 1958. He was 66.

Henry Edward Kavanagh was born in 1892 at Auckland, New Zealand, and educated at the Sacred Heart College, Auckland, and Auckland University. He went to England in 1914 to study medicine and later joined the New Zealand forces. After demobilization in 1918 he resumed his medical studies in London, and later in Edinburgh, but did not sit for his final examinations. Instead he decided to devote himself to free-lance journalism and to sketches and lyrics for the stage.

During this time he acted as London correspondent for New Zealand papers, prepared editorial material for firms concerned with medical supplies, and wrote for various reviews, including the *New Witness* and its successor *G. K.'s Weekly,* to which he contributed editorial notes and articles, in addition to playing an active part in the weekly meetings held by Chesterton's supporters.

Meanwhile he had foreseen the enlarging opportunities presented by the development of broadcasting. He recognized radio in its early formative stages as something that, going beyond a mere improvement of acoustics, was really a medium that imposed its own special limitations on performers, while offering scope to his own special talents. Before the British Broadcasting Corporation came into being he began to write humorous monologues for his friend Tommy Handley, following them, in 1927, with the broadcast revues which prepared the way for the remarkably successful *Itma* programmes. Kavanagh had the ready flow of ideas, sharp sense of character and powers of satire and irony to which Handley could add a skill in delivery and timing that he had perfected by long experience on the stage. Yet it would be a mistake to regard them as two persons: for the shaping of a script from its original form to the quick-witted, fantastic version heard by listeners owed so much to collaboration with the producer, Francis Worsley, as well as between themselves, that no one really knew where Kavanagh began and Handley ended.

This much is clear, however, that the invention of a host of characters and situations and the playing on words and sounds that distinguished the *Itma* programmes owed a great deal to the fertility and wit of Kavanagh. He insisted always that he could find jokes only in serious subjects, and he carried into his scripts a personal sympathy with and understanding of others that excluded malice from anything he wrote. It was largely for that reason that his characters won widespread popularity, so that the phrases they used were repeated *ad nauseam* in general conversation. *Itma* was accorded signal honour when the company gave a command performance at Windsor Castle. In December 1947 the Royal Family, during a visit to Broadcasting House, joined the studio audience while the programme was being broadcast.

In addition to his scripts for *Itma* Kavanagh prepared material for a number of other B.B.C. programmes, none of which achieved anything like the same popularity, in spite of the skill and humour they displayed. Nor could it be said that he was really successful as a film scenarist. His first venture in the cinema, indeed a visual re-creation of the most popular *Itma* characters, provoked the criticism that he had failed to give reality on the screen to people of whom each listener had a different mental impression.

In 1944 Kavanagh formed his own company of writers, artists, and producers, which, under the title of Ted Kavanagh Associated, was interested in numerous broadcast programmes and in ventures in the general field of entertainment.

Apart from his professional work Kavanagh was well known among Roman Catholics for his devoted work on behalf of a number of vocational and other lay organizers, including the Catholic Stage Guild, of which he was chairman after its revival in 1946, and the Catholic Writers' Guild of St. Francis de Sales.

He played an important part also in the organization of the Hierarchy Centenary Congress in 1950 and of subsequent rallies and pageants, besides being in constant request as a speaker at Roman Catholic meetings.

For the past six years he had contributed a popular feature "Ted Kavanagh's Roundabout" to the *Universe.* In 1952 he was awarded a knighthood of St. Gregory by Pope Pius XII.

His published works included the biography of Tommy Handley, a serious work on dieting, *Why Die of Heart Failure*? and *The Memoirs of Colonel Chinstrap.*

He married in 1919 Miss Agnes O'Keefe, of Edinburgh, who, with their two sons Kevin and Patrick, survive him.

September 18, 1958.

Sheila Kaye-Smith, the novelist, who in private life was Mrs. Theodore Penrose Fry, died at her home in Sussex at the age of 68 on January 15, 1956.

She had as genuine and intimate a feeling, perhaps, for her own county, Sussex—its landscape, people, crafts, history—as any of the "regional" novelists among her contemporaries had for theirs, and probably as sound a knowledge of farming and farming ways. Robust in feeling rather than in any conventional sense earthy, the best of her books have a quietly challenging veracity and are done with controlled feminine vigour and sincere warmth of personal sentiment. Many of the earlier books received, unfortunately, somewhat extravagant praise and were made the subject of far-fetched critical comparisons, so that their real virtues were apt to be obscured.

Availing herself for the most part of simple materials and turning again and again to the theme of innocence trapped by passion, Sheila Kaye-Smith brought off an effect of tragedy with admirable directness and unsentimental clarity.

This high mood of imaginative simplicity did not last, however; though she retained both skill and sympathy her tragic material in time became somewhat threadbare and was overlaid by more conventional stuff. She continued now and then to reproduce something of her old form—*Susan Spray,* for instance, published in 1931, was on only a slightly lower level than *Joanna Godden,* to the theme of which, indeed, it bore some resemblance—but her later fiction lacks the truth and the power of her best work. Nevertheless, in sum hers was a notable performance as novelist.

The daughter of Edward Kaye-Smith, a medical practitioner at Hastings, where she was born in 1887, Sheila Kaye-Smith spent much of her childhood with her sister in farmhouses in Sussex and Scotland, and remained firmly anchored at Hastings until her marriage in 1924. From a very early age, it seems, she had been in the habit of inventing endless stories for herself and of declaiming them aloud, and at the age of 15 she took up her pen. Apparently she wrote no less than 13 novels during her last two years at school, and was hardly more than a school-girl when her first published novel, *The Tramping Methodist,* appeared in 1908. There were two more Sussex novels, *Isle of Thorns* and *Three Against the World,* in 1913 and 1914, and then, two years later, came *Sussex Gorse,* which attracted and deserved notice. The portrait of a farmer of stubborn and formidable temperament, covering the changes in farming method and the law of land tenure during the nineteenth century, this was a telling feat of imaginative realism, giving admirable promise for the future.

Two more books came from her slightly over-fluent pen before *Tamarisk Town* appeared in 1919. A growing preoccupation with matters of religious belief was already apparent in this spirited story of the transformation of a Sussex fishing village into a prosperous seaside town, and was still more marked in its successor, *Green Apple Harvest,* which appeared in the following year and which Miss Kaye-Smith herself was afterwards inclined to think the best of her novels.

A year later still came *Joanna Godden,* with a heroine driven to the exercise of a coarse, unscrupulous and almost freakish masterfulness by her determination to farm in her own way the land she has inherited. The more than ordinary merits of this novel, which was lit by a generous humanity and truthfulness, were at once recognized, but financial success still eluded the author. It came, as so often happens, with a much less satisfactory book, *The End of the House of Alard* (1923), in which the picture of the English squirearchy in decay was rather untidily diversified by the expression of the author's social and economic opinions and by her Anglo-Catholic cast of religious sentiment. With her next novel, *The George and the Crown* (1925), she was back in her best form.

She continued to produce a new book almost every year, sometimes oftener. They varied in quality and tended to show something of a decline in power; most of the later ones were, perhaps, in a more frankly popular vein than might have been expected. But there was excellent work in *Shepherds in Sackcloth* (1930), in which she reverted to a favourite theme, and in such essays in historical reconstruction as *Superstition Corner,* a story of Sussex in the days of the Armada, and *Gallybird,* both published in 1934.

Other books of hers that deserve to be mentioned are *Three Ways Home* (1937), a volume of informal autobiography; *Tambourine, Trumpet and Drum* (1943), an accomplished and readable enough specimen of her later fiction; *Talking of Jane Austen* (1944), written in partnership with G. B. Stern* (the theme was returned to in 1950 in *More Talk of Jane Austen*). *The View from the Parsonage Window,* published only in 1955, sketches, perhaps a little too succinctly, the thoughts of a gentle, intelligent, bachelor parson, as he watches the dissensions in the local squire's family while he rears his daughters in an atheistic philosophy into which he has carried over all the ethical principles engrained by a Christian upbringing. Her two delightful novels about children, *The Children's Summer* and *Selina is Older,* should not be forgotten.

Though far and away the most important part of her work consists in her novels, Sheila Kaye-Smith contributed to the "Regional Books" series *The Weald of Kent and Sussex,* and she wrote from time to time accomplished verse inspired by her love of the corner of Sussex in which she lived all her life. She broke new ground in *Quartet in Heaven,* published in 1953, in which she studied the lives of four Roman Catholic heroines, three of whom have been canonized, while the fourth may be some day. Two, Caterina Fiesca Adorna and Isabella Rosa de Flores, belong to the Renaissance, and two, Cornelia Cornelly and Thérèse Martin, to the nineteenth century. The theme of the book is that "Grace follows Nature" and it may well be that here Miss Kaye-Smith's insight has received its highest expression.

She married in 1924 the Rev. Theodore Penrose Fry, the eldest son of Sir John Fry, Bt. At the time of the marriage he was assistant priest at St. Stephen's, Gloucester Road, a well-known Anglo-Catholic church. Later he resigned this appointment and in 1929 both husband and wife announced their conversion to the Roman Catholic Church. They settled at Northiam, about 15 miles from Hastings, and there built a Roman Catholic chapel, dedicated to one of the saints about whom Miss Kaye-Smith has written, Sainte Thérèse de Lisieux.

January 16, 1956.

Lady Curzon of Kedleston—See **Curzon.**

Sir Frederick Keeble, C.B.E., SC.D., F.R.S., who died on October 19, 1952 at his home in London at the age of 82, was Sherardian Professor of Botany in the University of Oxford from 1920 to 1927 and Fullerian Professor in the Royal Institution from 1938 to 1941.

Frederick William Keeble was born on March 2, 1870, and received his early education at Alleyn's School, Dulwich. Always interested in natural history and plants, he turned to the serious study of botany when he went up to Caius College, Cambridge, from Dulwich School, becoming Natural Science Scholar and Frank Smart Student of Botany in the university. German influence on the systematic science of botany was predominant at the close of the last century, and on leaving Cambridge Keeble went to Germany to study for a time under Professor Pfeffer. A year in Ceylon followed before he returned home to join the teaching staff of Owens College, Manchester, as Assistant Lecturer in Botany. After two years at Manchester Keeble went south again to take up the posts of Professor of Botany and Dean of the Faculty of Science at University College, Reading, and it was during his 12 years' tenure of those offices that he came under the eye of Sir Isaac Bayley Balfour, King's Botanist for Scotland and Regius Keeper of the Botanic Garden at Edinburgh.

In 1913-14 that brilliant savant's advice had been sought by the Council of the Royal Horticultural Society, the members of which felt the need for some readjustment of the society's activities to meet the changing horticultural spirit of the times; and it was on Balfour's advice that Keeble was appointed Director of the Wisley garden, which it was then intended should be developed as a station for the many scientific problems connected with horticulture. Unfortunately, war supervened to prevent the realization of Balfour's scheme for the reorganization of Wisley and its equipment as a research station, and soon after Keeble's appointment as director he was made controller of the department of horticulture and food production in the Board of Agriculture, a post that he held concurrently with that of head of the Wisley garden, relinquishing both positions in 1919 on his promotion to assistant secretary in the Board of Agriculture.

His official tenure of the Whitehall post, however, was brief, as on the resignation by Vines of the Professorship of Botany in Oxford University at the end of 1919, Keeble, mainly on the advice of Bayley Balfour, who had previously held the post himself, was elected to succeed him. His occupation of the Sherardian Chair lasted for seven years, and was distinguished by the happy union of practice and theory in the study of botany, for, as those who knew his garden at Boar's Hill are aware, Keeble was a keen gardener.

On his retirement from the university Keeble joined the staff of Imperial Chemical Industries as adviser in agriculture, and had much to do with the development of that side of the company's operations which relates to fertilizers and their effect on farm and garden crops.

The establishment of the company's experimental station at Jealott's Hill, near Bracknell, in 1929, was an outcome of Keeble's labours, and in the three years during which he directed the station it acquired a wide reputation as a centre of research, especially on the effect of fertilizers on grazing land. Keeble also initiated a valuable series of experiments on the conditions that make for success or failure in smallholdings. When he was 62 Keeble relinquished his original post with I.C.I. but remained a member of the executive council of the company.

Apart from his work on the *Gardeners' Chronicle,* of which he was editor from 1908 till 1919, Keeble wrote much on botanical and horticultural subjects. His text-book *Practical Plant Physiology* was followed by a volume entitled *Life of Plants,* and his book *Fertilisers and Food Production* is an important contribution to a subject on which he was a recognized authority. Keeble was a fluent and ready speaker, and his powers of lucid exposition were such that his lectures were never dull. His work, both verbal and written, was savoured with the first-hand knowledge that removed it from the sphere of the purely academic.

His autobiography *Polly and Freddie,* published in 1936, is charming reading, and *Science Lends a Hand in the Garden,* which appeared some three years later, is full of wise guidance by a scientist who knew the strengths and the limitations of scientific method.

Keeble was elected Fellow of the Royal Society in 1913, in 1917 was appointed C.B.E., and was knighted in 1922. He was twice married, first in 1898 to Mlle. Mathilde Maréchal. She died in 1915, and in 1920 he married Miss Lillah McCarthy [q.v.], the well-known actress, who survives him, together with a daughter of his first marriage.

October 21, 1952.

Lillah Lady Keeble—See **Lillah McCarthy.**

Sir Hugh Keeling, C.S.I., M.I.E.(INDIA), who died on February 3, 1955 at his home in London at the age of 89, will have a place in history as the chief constructor of New Delhi close to the last seat of the Moghul Emperors, to replace Calcutta as the winter seat of the British Raj and destined to become the all-the-year-round capital of the Government of the Indian Republic.

Hugh Trowbridge Keeling was born on April 14, 1865, the son of E. T. Keeling, of London, and, after attending Marlborough, he entered the Royal Indian Engineering College, Coopers Hill. He was, perhaps, the oldest survivor of the long line of members of the Indian Public Works Department and the Forestry Department trained at that institution. As long ago as 1887 he joined the Public Works Department in the Madras Presidency. He was engaged in the Periar Dam project, and irrigation works from the Krishna, Kauveri, and other great rivers of the presidency. He also had a share in training Indians for employment in the department, as for a short time he held a professorial chair at the Madras Civil Engineering College and was for a year its principal.

After the announcement by King George V at the Coronation Durbar early in 1912 that the winter capital of the Government of India would be transferred from Calcutta to a city to be built near Delhi, Keeling was appointed to be Chief Engineer of the great undertaking, and secretary to the Chief Commissioner of the enclave created for the purpose. He was made a member of the Imperial Delhi Committee appointed in 1913. Various points of importance had to be considered in fixing the actual site of the new city, and Government had to be provided with temporary accommodation on and about the ridge outside the walls of the old city.

The progress of construction of the new capital was delayed by the 1914-18 War, by controversies on questions of important details, by financial considerations, and by the fact that the two distinguished architects, Sir Edwin Lutyens and Sir Herbert Baker, were not always in agreement. In any event New Delhi, like Rome, could not be built in a day. Cool, clear judgment and tact were called for on the part of the Chief Engineer, and Keeling displayed these qualities to the full. So it was not surprising that when the normal date for his retirement from the Public Works Department came in 1920 he should be reappointed and continue in charge for another five years.

During his 13 years at Delhi, Keeling had had no real holiday, for when home on short leave he had had to be in touch with the India Office and contracting firms. On his retirement he took a leisurely world tour on his way home.

He had many amusing stories to tell of his experiences to fellow members of the East India and Sports Club, of which, for several years, he was an alert octogenarian chairman.

He married in 1893, Edith, daughter of Colonel T. O. Underwood, of Heath Park, Birnam, Perth, and they had a son and daughter.

February 5, 1955.

Alexander Keiller, F.S.A., who died at his home at Kingston Hill, Surrey, at the age of 65, on October 29, 1955, was well known as the archaeologist who was responsible for the important discoveries at Avebury.

A member of the wealthy Keiller family of Dundee, he purchased the tract of land in which the original discoveries were made in 1925 and as the work progressed made other purchases. Though much of the work was carried out in conjunction with the Office of Works, the whole cost of the undertaking was borne by Keiller, who was able in 1943 to transfer the whole of the Avebury property to the National Trust with the help of the Pilgrim Trust and I. D. Margary, F.S.A.

The great monument of Avebury was built some 3,500 years ago in the first phase of the Early Bronze Age. Here prehistoric man put forth one of his mightiest efforts, but for centuries the site was allowed to decay. Thanks to Keiller and his creation, the Morvan Institute of Archaeological Research (named after the Keiller estate in Aberdeenshire), these important remains have been preserved. The settlement was clearly inhabited for a long period, as is indicated by the quantity of human, animal, and pottery remains—the most spectacular being an almost complete specimen of the skeleton of a dog of greyhound build, claimed as the first known domestic dog.

The great circle has been accurately determined, as has also the West Kennet Avenue of stones, though through deterioration and removal not all the stones are now to be seen.

October 31, 1955.

Sir Arthur Keith, F.R.S., died on January 7, 1955 at Downe, Kent, at the age of 88. He had been pruning fruit trees only the previous day.

Natural science grows slowly. Original investigation yields detached results often expressed in highly technical language contributed to the transactions of learned societies which are rarely read by the public. It is difficult, therefore, for men of ordinary education to know what advances have been made or where to find an account of them. Once in a generation a great popularizer is produced, one who has not only taken part in the work but has the balanced judgment to estimate its value, the literary skill to make it interesting, and imagination sufficient to point the way to further knowledge. Such a man was Thomas Henry Huxley, the exponent of Darwinism, and such a man was Sir Arthur Keith, whose loss we now deplore. Keith, perhaps, was endowed with a more original mind than Huxley for he had many of the traits which made John Hunter famous as a Master of Medicine, but he was not pugnacious and was not so good a hater as Huxley.

Born in 1866, he was the son of John Keith, of Turriff, Aberdeenshire, and was educated at the University of Aberdeen, where he graduated M.B. with first class honours in 1888. He then studied at the University of Leipzig and going to London he worked at University College with Professor Thane, the anatomist. In 1894 he was admitted M.D. of the University of Aberdeen and gained the Struthers medal and prize in anatomy for a valuable essay on the ligaments of the Catarrhine monkeys. In the same year he became a Member and a few months later a Fellow of the Royal College of Surgeons of England and was immediately appointed Senior Demonstrator of Anatomy at the London Hospital Medical College, a post he filled with increasing reputation to himself for the next 12 years.

He was appointed Conservator and Arnott Demonstrator at the Royal College of Surgeons in Lincoln's Inn Fields in 1908, succeeding Professor Charles Stewart. In this post he had charge of the magnificent museum collected by John Hunter in the eighteenth century, and here he soon gathered round him a band of ardent workers which made the museum a centre of good work both in anatomy and pathology. Keith himself specialized in anthropology and his work became so conspicuous that he was elected president of the Anthropological Institute in 1912. In 1913 he was elected F.R.S. and in 1917 he was appointed Fullerian Professor of Physiology at the Royal Institution, where his lectures did much to popularize the branches of science in which he was more especially interested. His eminent services to science were recognized in 1921 when the honour of knighthood was conferred upon him to the great satisfaction of his numerous friends. He married in 1899, Cecilia, the daughter of Thomas Gray, the artist, but had no offspring.

He wrote *An Introduction to the Study of the Anthropoid Apes* in 1896; *Human Embryology and Morphology* in 1901; *Ancient Types of Man* in 1911; *The Antiquity of Man* in 1914; *Menders of the Maimed* in 1919, which was based upon a lecture delivered at the Royal College of Surgeons in 1918 entitled "Bonesetting Ancient and Modern"; and *Engines of the Human Body* in 1920. In addition to these books he contributed countless papers to the scientific journals which were all marked by originality and sound common sense. On December 4, 1922, he was elected secretary of the Royal Institution in succession to the late Colonel E. H. Grove Hills, C.M.G., C.B.E., F.R.S.

In 1927 Keith was president of the British Association for the Advancement of Science when it met at Leeds. As president he made an appeal for the preservation of Downe House, in Kent, where Charles Darwin had lived for many years and had written the series of books which made him famous. The appeal met with instant response, and Sir William Bragg, the next president, was able to announce at Leeds that the property had been bought by Sir Buckston Browne, F.R.C.S., who had transferred it to the association under the most liberal conditions and with an endowment sufficient to maintain and preserve it for all time. When later Sir Buckston Browne bought and endowed an estate and building near by for use as an experimental surgical institute, Sir Arthur Keith saw one of his own dreams realized and in his retirement from active work in London went to live at Downe as Master of the Buckston Browne Institute.

Sir Arthur Keith's reputation increased steadily until it became worldwide. Bones of prehistoric times were referred to him from all parts for examination and report, and his findings were accepted as final. He was acknowledged, too, as a master in the science of anthropology. The subject which more especially interested him was the evolution of mankind, for which he postulated enormous periods of time and showed that several abortive types had been developed, *homo sapiens* being the sole survivor. In this relation the distribution of modern man came under review. He also did much good work on the development of the brain, showing how the cerebral hemispheres had gradually dominated the older brain not only of man but of many animals. When the jaw and skull of the "Piltdown Man" were first under discussion Keith thought they might be the remains of two creatures—a man and an ape—but he allowed himself to be persuaded of their genuineness. Late in 1954, however, when told that investigations had proved that the remains had been faked, he replied: "I think you are probably right, but it will take me some time to adjust myself to the new view".

As a man Keith was above the middle height, with a stoop of a scholar. He had clean-cut features with piercing eyes and was always clean shaven. He spoke slowly and softly, hesitating slightly, and with the least suspicion of a Scottish accent. As a lecturer he talked in detached sentences as if thinking what he was about to say. He used no notes but had so deep a knowledge of his subject and such a faculty for clear exposition that it was both pleasing and instructive to listen to him. His quiet manner, however, belied the force of his arguments, which were cogent and at times challenging, as when in 1931 during his address as Rector of Aberdeen University he caused a great public outcry by his statement that war was Nature's pruning hook. Yet he was not the preacher of a hopeless gospel, for much of his later research work was concerned with what he somewhat fancifully described as "the secret processes of Nature by which she brought about the ascent of Man and, having mastered her methods, Man can use them for his own improvement". "That", he continued, "is one of the goals towards which science is reaching".

His three books, published since the war, show still a lively and inquiring mind and the last, his *Autobiography,* recalls vividly his original doubts about the Piltdown remains not only on structural characteristics but also because they did not fit in with the chronology he had worked out for the evolution of man.

January 8, 1955.

Major-General R. F. L. Keller, C.B.E., who commanded the 3rd Canadian Division in the assault on Normandy on June 6, 1944, died suddenly in London on June 21, 1954. He was 53.

Rodney Frederick Leopold Keller was born at Tetbury, Gloucestershire, on October 2, 1900, the only son of Dr. H. L. A. Keller, of Kelowna, British Columbia. He was educated at Chesterfield School, Kelowna, and at the Royal Military College, Kingston, Ontario, from which he graduated in 1920. After being commissioned he transferred in 1921 to Princess Patricia's Canadian Light Infantry. He graduated from the Staff College at Camberley in 1936.

Soon after the outbreak of war in 1939 he was posted oversea to England, and in 1940 was appointed G.S.O.1, 1st Canadian Division, with the rank of lieutenant-colonel. He became Officer Commanding, Princess Patricia's Canadian Light Infantry, in August 1941, and in the following month was promoted brigadier, commanding the 1st Canadian Infantry Brigade. A year later, with the rank of major-general, he was appointed to the command of the 3rd Canadian Infantry Division.

On July 3, 1943, General McNaughton* informed the Commander of the 1st Canadian Corps that the 3rd Canadian Division had been "selected for assault training with a view to taking part in the assault in Operation 'Overlord' ". From December 1, 1943, Keller and his troops passed for "operational direction" under I British Corps, which was to command in the actual assault. The force eventually embarked under the command of Keller—whose headquarters ship was H.M.S. Hilary, which had served the 1st Canadian Division in the same capacity during the assault on Sicily—consisted of just over 15,000 Canadians, with over 9,000 British troops attached.

The immediate task of Keller's force was to hold the central sector of the front occupied by the Second British Army, with the 3rd British Division on its left and the 50th (Northumbrian) Division on its right. By midday of June 6 the situation was sufficiently in hand to enable Keller to take his divisional headquarters ashore—and it was set up in an orchard in Bernières. By the evening of June 6, with the day's objectives only partly attained, Keller had lost nearly 1,000 of his men—killed, wounded, or missing.

But the beachhead had been established. There followed the weeks of desperate and violent fighting in the Caen area, which the Germans had chosen to make the pivot of their defence, and in this fighting the Canadians, along with their British comrades, won for themselves immortal fame. Before the final entry into Caen, in the second week of July, II Canadian Corps (which in the build-up during June had already taken the 2nd Canadian Division under its command) took over a section of the front and with it the 3rd Canadian Division.

It was during the fighting to close the Falaise trap that a tragic incident ended Keller's personal contribution to the allies' victory in Normandy. While American Fortresses were providing air support, some of their bombs fell on Canadian troops. The tactical headquarters of the 3rd Canadian Division was showered with fragmentation bombs and Keller received several severe wounds. He was unable to continue his command from that day. He was therefore forced out of the battle just at the moment when victory in Normandy was about to be achieved. But he and the Canadians under him had played a gallant part in establishing their section of the beachhead. Keller had led the Canadian spearhead in N.W. Europe.

He leaves a widow and two sons.

June 23, 1954.

Sir David Kelly, G.C.M.G., M.C., who died on March 27, 1959 at his home in Ireland, was 67.

Although best known as British Ambassador to Moscow and, after his retirement in 1951, as an authoritative commentator on Soviet affairs, he had in fact an exceptionally varied as well as a long and distinguished career in the British Foreign Service. He represented the transition between the "old" and the "new" diplomacy. Of other colleagues contemporary with him the same, of course, could be said, but he, more than any of them, gave conscious and public expression to the fact.

He came of Ulster landowning stock and was a son of the Protestant Anglo-Irish "ascendancy" on both sides of his family. Later he became a Roman Catholic and he always kept his ties with Ireland. But in education and outlook he was thoroughly English. He was born in Adelaide, South Australia, on September 14, 1891, during one of his father's fits of emigration, but on his father's death his mother took him as a child to London and sent him to Colet Court and then to St. Paul's School. Of his years there, and in particular of the influence of its celebrated High Master, Frederick Walker, Kelly gave an account in his autobiography, *The Ruling Few,* published in 1952. But it was Frederick Walker's son, R. J. Walker whose friendship and eventual relationship (since he married the widowed Mrs. Kelly) played a really important part in the direction of Kelly's tastes and talents. That brilliant, erratic and versatile personality deepened young Kelly's interest in history, and in 1911 he went up to Magdalen with a history scholarship.

The "indolence and luxury" which Kelly ascribed to Magdalen in those days did not disturb the habit of diligent and wide study which he had acquired as a boy, and the judgments and impressions he formed during a tour of Europe and North Africa which R. J. Walker organized were turned to good account when he joined the Diplomatic Service. This he did in 1914, when, having got a First at Oxford and encouraged by Sir Herbert Warren, President of Magdalen, he secured a nomination to the Foreign Office. In spite of what he later described as the handicap to entry which candidates from day-schools then encountered, he passed the Selection Board, but before he could take the examination the First World War had broken out and he had obtained a commission in The Leicestershire Regiment. He served in France, mainly as Intelligence Officer to the 110th Infantry Brigade, and in 1917 was awarded the Military Cross.

Immediately on demobilization, in March 1919, Kelly was accepted for the Foreign Office and served two years in Buenos Aires. The social changes caused by the war, which came eventually to influence the British Foreign Service, had not by then penetrated the Argentine circles with which Kelly was brought into contact, but he was by no means unaware of them, or the necessity for diplomacy to concern itself more with economics and finance. His views on this and on the true functions of the professional diplomat—to serve his Government as a barrister serves his client, and to keep on good terms with the "ruling few"—are lucidly explained in his autobiography, which still affords profitable, if sometimes provocative, reading for young diplomats. Kelly was always a keen defender of his chosen profession.

Before leaving Argentina in 1921 Kelly married Isobel Mills who died in 1927. A not very agreeable spell at the Foreign Office, and in Portugal and Mexico, preceded his appointment to Brussels, and here, in 1929, he married Marie Noelle, daughter of the Comte de Jourda de Vaux. The same year he was transferred to Stockholm, and after another turn at the Foreign Office as head of the American Department he was appointed in 1934 as Minister in Cairo under Lord Killearn*. This contact with Egyptian affairs, which he continued in 1938 and 1939 as Head of the Egyptian Department in London, was evidently congenial to him; it gave him a series of fascinating concrete political problems and brought him into touch with the

British Empire's broad strategic interests. But at the end of 1939 Kelly was promoted to be Minister in Berne, where he was, among other things, concerned with the abortive "peace-soundings" of Prince Hohenlohe.

In 1942 he was again advanced in rank, to be Ambassador in Buenos Aires, where he saw the triumph of General Perón*. Both this and British relations with the United States at that time put the British representative in a position of some delicacy, and although Kelly, in his own words, "avoided the dangers of a negative and thankless mission", his appointment in 1946 as Ambassador to Turkey was clearly welcome to him, as it was to Lady Kelly—Kelly had been made a K.C.M.G. in 1942. Both threw themselves with zest into Turkish official and social life; they travelled widely about the country, made contacts with most of the provincial governors and with the press. They played no small part in maintaining Turkish confidence in Great Britain in the post-war years when the British economy was under such severe strain.

Although Kelly had, with R. J. Walker, made a tour of Russia in undergraduate days, and had come under its spell, he did not welcome his appointment as Ambassador to Moscow in 1949; he would have preferred Madrid. The Soviet Union, he complained, gave no opportunity for that expression of personality in diplomacy which he considered was his special gift. Nevertheless, in spite of the severe and keenly felt frustrations of the Stalinist [q.v.] period, Kelly and his wife managed to see more of Russia than did most of their colleagues, and Lady Kelly wrote two books, illustrated with her own photographs, which are a notable record of the time. In 1950 Kelly was advanced to G.C.M.G., and in 1951 he left Moscow and retired from the Foreign Service.

With relief, it would seem, he now devoted himself to writing and lecturing, and public service. He was a regular writer in the press on Soviet policy; in 1952 he published the outstanding volume of reminiscences, already mentioned, *The Ruling Few*; in 1955 he gave expression to his Christian conservative humanism in the book *The Hungry Sheep*. His public duties included the chairmanship of the Anglo-Turkish Society, and of the British Council from 1955. He was also prominent in the British Atlantic Committee, being profoundly convinced of the necessity for an Anglo-American alliance and the maintenance of European unity, spiritual no less than economic and political, in the face of growing dangers.

March 28, 1959.

Admiral Sir Howard Kelly, G.B.E., K.C.B., C.M.G., M.V.O., who died on September 14, 1952 at the age of 79, served with distinction as a captain and commodore during the 1914-18 war, and is best known to the general public for his services in command of the Gloucester in chasing the German battle cruiser Goeben and light cruiser Breslau. His sound judgment combined with stern resolution were well exemplified in that episode, as they were on other occasions during his long career, particularly as Commander-in-Chief in China in 1931-33.

William Archibald Howard Kelly, born on September 6, 1873, was the son of Lieutenant-Colonel H. H. Kelly, Royal Marine Artillery, and a younger brother of the late Admiral Sir John Kelly. He entered the Britannia as a cadet on January 15, 1886, and two years later went to sea in the battleship Temeraire. He passed for the rank of sub-lieutenant in September 1892, but in his courses for lieutenant he did not do particularly well, gaining only one first-class certificate, in pilotage, so that he remained a "sub" for two and a quarter years, until December 1894. His time, however, was well occupied in gaining practical experience in a good school, that of small ships, for he was navigator of the gunboats Firefly and Onyx, at Harwich, and of the Hebe, in the Mediterranean, to the last-named of which he was reappointed as a lieutenant.

In May 1896 he joined the Cruiser, a sailing sloop for the training of ordinary seamen in the Mediterranean, so that he was quite familiar with the handling of a ship under sail. From January 1899 he was navigator of the cruiser Calliope, also employed in the training service. A few months in H.M.S. Spartiate were followed by his selection in July 1903 to be first and navigating lieutenant of the Hyacinth, flagship of Rear-Admiral G. L. Atkinson-Willes, Commander-in-Chief in the East Indies. In her he served during the campaign in Somaliland, and received the General East Africa Medal, with Somaliland 1902-04 clasps. It was while in the Hyacinth that he was promoted to commander in December 1904 and reappointed as navigator. During his last few months in her the Hyacinth flew the flag of Vice-Admiral Sir Edmund Poë, whose daughter, Nora, he married in 1907.

Service in the battleships Russell and Nile was followed by his appointment to the Naval Intelligence Department. He had already qualified as an interpreter in French. In February 1910 he resumed sea service in command of the light cruiser Barham in the Mediterranean, and a year later was selected for the post of naval attaché in Paris. Here he served for three years, during which time he was promoted to captain and did very useful work. On the occasion in June 1913 of the state visit to King George V of Poincaré, the French President, to whose suite he was attached, Kelly was made M.V.O. It was on his return from Paris that he was appointed, in March 1914, in command of the Gloucester.

H.M.S. Gloucester located the Goeben and Breslau at Messina on the afternoon of August 5, 1914. At 5 p.m. on August 6 the German ships steamed out of harbour, expecting to encounter one or more British battle cruisers, but they were otherwise engaged. Kelly in the little Gloucester, a 4,800 ton ship with two 6in. and 10 4in. guns, shadowed the Goeben, a ship of 22,640 tons with 10 11in. and 12 5.9in. guns, all that night and until late in the afternoon of the next day. The Goeben could have caught and sunk her at any time had she dared to turn upon her, but she was apparently deterred by the boldness of the Gloucester, which gave the impression of support close at hand.

In spite of the danger, Kelly hung on to the heels of the Goeben for over 24 hours, and only relinquished the chase under the direct orders of the Commander-in-Chief. The German ships, it will be recalled, fled to the shelter of the Dardanelles where their arrival was a primary cause of the entry of Turkey into the war against the Allies. In the official record of Kelly's services when he was awarded the C.B., it was stated that "the combination of audacity with restraint, unswerving attention to the principal military object, namely, holding on to the Goeben without tempting her too much, and strict conformity to orders, constitute a naval episode which may justly be regarded as a model".

After further service in the Mediterranean and East Indies, the Gloucester at the end of December 1914 joined the 2nd Light Cruiser Squadron, Grand Fleet. In January 1916 Kelly was recalled for service in the Intelligence Division at the Admiralty. He resumed command of the Gloucester in March 1916, but a few months later was selected for duty as Naval Liaison Officer in Paris between the Admiralty and the French Ministry of Marine. This duty he relinquished in August 1917 to become commodore of the 8th Light Cruiser Squadron in the Adriatic and Mediterranean. The submarine menace was then at its height in this theatre of the war, and under his command Kelly had British, French, Italian, and American light forces, together with a British air force, with his headquarters at Brindisi. Under his direction, the Straits of Otranto were blocked by a mobile barrage, thus preventing the free egress of enemy submarines from the ports of the Austrian coast.

On his return to England in April 1919 Kelly was selected to proceed to Greece as the head of the British Naval Mission asked for by Venizelos. He left for Athens in H.M.S. Canada in June, with the rank of vice-admiral in the Royal Hellenic Navy. He served there until October 1921, and in the following May was promoted to rear-admiral in the Royal Navy, after a few months in command of the battleship Emperor of India. On May 3, 1923, he hoisted his flag in H.M.S. Revenge as rear-admiral in the 1st Battle Squadron. On completing the tenure of this command a year later he was appointed in charge of the Signal Books Committee, to re-edit and bring up to date the fleet signal books. On May 15, 1925, he again hoisted his flag—this time in the Curacoa in command of the 2nd Cruiser Squadron, Atlantic Fleet—a two-year appointment. Promoted to vice-admiral on July 2, 1927, he was appointed to relieve Admiral Sir Aubrey Smith as British naval representative at the League of Nations, and he served at Geneva until April 1929.

A month later he again hoisted his flag in H.M.S. Revenge, this time as Vice-Admiral

Commanding the 1st Battle Squadron, and Second-in-Command, Mediterranean Station. In December 1930 he was appointed Commander-in-Chief in China, where he served until March 1933, and while there he was promoted to admiral. This was a troublous time in the Far East, culminating in the Sino-Japanese dispute and the landing of Japanese marines and troops at Shanghai in January 1932. A small and inconclusive war was waged, without any declaration of hostilities, between Japan and China in the area north of Shanghai, and the International Settlement was endangered. Comparative quiet was restored early in March, and armistice proposals were made at a conference on board Sir Howard Kelly's flagship, H.M.S. Kent, although peace was not signed until May 5. He hauled down his flag in March 1933.

When Kelly was placed on the retired list in 1936 he had served 50 years in the Royal Navy—a rare achievement nowadays. He was recalled to active service in 1940—at the age of 67—and went to Ankara as personal representative of Admiral Sir Andrew Cunningham, Commander-in-Chief Mediterranean [Admiral of the Fleet Lord Cunningham of Hyndhope*]. He stayed there until July 1944, and during this time his imposing personality became something of an institution. He was one of the few persons, and certainly the only foreigner, who had free access to the unapproachable Field-Marshal Fevzi Chakmak, former chief of the Turkish general staff, and he became very popular with the Turkish public. On his return to England, Kelly threw some light on the achievements of his mission when he said that, "though the entry of Turkey into the war would have been for us a diplomatic victory, it might also have proved a military disaster". On his return—at the age of 71— he was again placed on the retired list.

Sir Howard Kelly was left a widower when his wife died in 1951. They had one son and one daughter.

September 15, 1952.

Guy Kendall, who died on September 28, 1960, made his mark in the educational system of Britain by his wise conduct of a modern public school over a period of 20 years. At University College School he was the right man in the right place, for his freedom from conventional ideas and his skilful blending of traditional and modern systems made him a most suitable headmaster for a foundation conceived on liberal and tolerant lines.

Kendall was the fourth son of H. J. B. Kendall, partner in a firm of South American merchants, and was the nephew of Admiral Ommaney. Born at Bush Hall, Hatfield, in 1876, he passed his infancy there and had started Latin and Greek by the age of nine. In 1889 he entered Eton as a King's Scholar, under Warre's headmastership. He won the Newcastle Medal and the Wilder Divinity Prize, rowed in the Boats on the Fourth of June in his last three years, and in 1895 (after tutoring the sons of the Prime Minister, Lord Rosebery, for some weeks) he went up to Magdalen as a demy. He took part in Union debates, where he met Hilaire Belloc [q.v.], John Simon [q.v.], F. E. Smith, and E. C. Bentley [q.v.]; and he was one of the earliest members of the University Fabian Society, in due course becoming its secretary and vice-president. He took firsts in both Mods. and Greats, after which he read theology, again winning a first.

Doubts on doctrinal points (especially the immaculate conception) led Kendall to refuse ordination. For some months in 1900 he was tutoring; then at the invitation of Alice Crompton he succeeded E. T. Campagnac as Warden of the Manchester University Settlement at Ancoats, working also at Ruskin Hall and as a substitute master at Manchester Grammar School. His first contact with industrialism and poverty made an abiding impression on him; but after a year he decided that he would be a schoolmaster.

Of three possible posts an appointment at Charterhouse was the only one which put no obstacle in the way of his marrying; so to Charterhouse he went in 1902. Beginning as a classics master, he gradually widened his interests to embrace history, geography, and English, and eventually became head of the modern side of the school. More and more did he come to believe in the prime importance of the mother tongue and the native literature as instruments of education. He formed a poetry society (to which Robert Graves belonged) and did useful work with it. His own poems, which were felicitous and thoughtful, came out in volumes entitled *The Sunlit Way* (1908), *Castle-building* (1912), and *The Call* (1916).

Kendall was not the man to confine his attentions to matters within the school walls. He got to know Fabian Ware, and wrote for him regular anonymous articles on educational subjects in the *Morning Post.* This work led him to visit and investigate modern schools, thereby accumulating information which he was able to correlate with the practice of the older public schools. He also contributed to the *Westminster Gazette,* and a sympathetic review of Dr. Montessori's [q.v.] first book led to his being co-opted to the committee of the British Montessori Society, though he never became a Montessorian *pur sang.* His collected educational articles appeared in 1913 as *The New Schoolmaster,* by "Fourth Form". Some leading arguments were against compulsory Greek and in favour of the training of all teachers and the universal inspection of schools. He registered for military service under the Derby scheme in 1915 but was rejected on medical grounds.

In 1916 Kendall was appointed to succeed Dr. H. J. Spencer as headmaster of University College School, Hampstead. He was neither a narrow authoritarian nor a crank, and steered a happy medium course for U.C.S. He was entirely free from social and educational snobbery. He aimed to get rid of shibboleths and make the school a real training for the wide life; and his average product was a hard-working, broad-minded, useful citizen; while some of his more able boys have become men of great eminence in the professions and in public life. His wide culture, fundamental common sense, and gift of happy compromise were shown by his encouragement of music, drama, the graphic arts, and handwork in the school, by his liberal approach to religious training, by his use of corporal punishment very rarely, as a last resort, and by his attitude towards games. He faced the obvious fact that many excellent boys dislike football or are bored by cricket, and so only insisted that some form of healthy exercise should be taken. He formed a rowing club (first on the Welsh Harp and later at Richmond) which did well in the public schools competitions.

Kendall served for a year as chairman of the Incorporated Association of Headmasters in Secondary Schools and for several on the committee of the English Association. In 1933 he published *A Headmaster Remembers,* an account of his life-work in education. He retired from U.C.S. in 1936, and the following year wrote *A Headmaster Reflects.*

He was tutor at Ripon Hall, Oxford, in 1938, and during his retirement wrote *A Modern Introduction to the New Testament* and *Christianity and the Future Life* (both 1938). *Robert Raikes* appeared in 1939, *Charles Kingsley and his Ideas* in 1947, in which year he brought out also *Religion in War and Peace.* His last book was *Application of Christianity.*

Kendall married, in 1902, Ada, daughter of J. Sampson, of Withington, Manchester, and had one son and one daughter.

September 30, 1960.

Kay Kendall, who died in London on September 6, 1959 at the age of 32, was not an actress of great range; but on her chosen ground of sophisticated comedy she had a personal elegance and incisiveness, which rapidly established her as one of the cinema's few outstanding comediennes.

She was born in Yorkshire on May 21, 1927, of a theatrical family; Marie Kendall*, the singer, was her grandmother. From the first she had her heart set on a theatrical career and it is recorded that she ran away from her convent school at the age of 12 to go on the stage. Her first job was with George Black revues on tour, and when she was 14 she and her sister Kim Kendall joined a variety act touring the halls. They appeared together in several films during the war. Her first big opportunity came with *London Town,* an attempt by Rank* Organization to break into the American market with a large-scale musical. In spite of a large budget and a number of talented performers the film was a disastrous failure, and though Kay Kendall's performance had considerable youthful charm, her career suffered something of a setback as a result.

From 1946 to 1949 she was back on the stage, appearing in plays and revues in the West End or on tour and entertaining troops abroad. Then in 1950 she returned to the screen, with small parts, showing a distinctive gift for comedy; but it was not until *Genevieve* in 1953 that she was really given a notable chance to show her skill. Here her own combination of style and grace and appearance, and a strong feeling for grotesque characterization came into full play – who will forget her, a blasé model slightly drunk after a veteran car ride to Brighton, announcing that she could play the trumpet better than the man in the band and promptly, electrifyingly, doing so?

After a splendidly energetic comic performance in the film version of *Simon and Laura*, she went to America, where she married Rex Harrison, with whom she had previously appeared in *The Constant Husband*. Her first Hollywood film, *Les Girls*, produced perhaps her best performance. In 1958 she starred with her husband in *The Reluctant Debutante*, from William Douglas Home's comedy, and made a less successful appearance on the West End stage in *The Bright One*, produced by Rex Harrison, which ran for only 10 days. Earlier in 1959 she was taken ill while filming *Once More, With Feeling* in Paris, but recovered sufficiently to complete the film. However, her illness was traced to a serious blood condition, and though she continued to plan future appearances on stage and screen, its recurrence was not long delayed.

September 7, 1959.

Frank Kendon, the poet, died on December 28, 1959 at the age of 66.

Frank Samuel Herbert Kendon (but he preferred to be just Frank Kendon) was born in 1893. His father kept a school at Goudhurst, a remarkable institution at which the late Lord Stamp and the late E. A. Benians received their early instruction. Frank was, of course, a member of the school and has enshrined his memories of it in *The Small Years* (1930), which deserves to be remembered as one of the minor classics of English autobiography.

In the war of 1914-18 he served with the Royal Engineers in Egypt and after the armistice went up to St. John's College, Cambridge. It was a period full of experiment and liveliness, especially in the field of literature. The English Tripos had only recently been established and Frank Kendon, in company with J. B. Priestley, Gerald Bullett, Edward Davison, and other eager young writers were quick to seize the opportunity of reading for an honours degree in something less rigid than classics or history. Frank, like the rest of them, was soon busy writing and it is characteristic that of his first two books (published in 1924) one was *Poems and Sonnets* and the other *Mural Paintings in English Churches*. After applying unsuccessfully for a post at the Victoria and Albert Museum he joined the staff of *John o'London's Weekly*, and here he had his first experience of the marketing of literature. Here he learnt to be a copy-writer and an editor as well as a poet, and in 1935 he joined the staff of the University Press as an assistant secretary.

The work was immediately congenial to him and he brought to it not only a persistent industry but an acute literary judgment and a highly individual sense of artistry in the layout and decoration of books and of their supporting publicity. In the design of book-jackets particularly he showed himself a master. His "blurbs" were not just puffs or paraphrases of an author's preface but brief and intelligent appreciations of the author's purpose; and he could use a drawing or a photograph with the sensitivity of a true artist. Side by side with his office work his own writing went on, together with the rewriting of other people's. Small volumes of poems appeared from time to time and he maintained the tradition of Christopher Smart in winning a succession of Seatonian Prizes for a poem on a sacred subject.

He lived at Harston, a few miles out of Cambridge. In good weather he bicycled to and fro at an incredibly slow pace, missing nothing of the progress of the seasons and constantly storing appropriate images in his poet's mind. He was, in his own phrase, "a man busy with mesh of words", and he liked to disentangle his words in the peace, or the storm, of the countryside. To those who could appreciate his observant quietism he ranked high as a poet: but when he applied his gifts and his methods to the writing of a novel, *Martin Makesure* (1950), the ordinary novel-reader was inevitably disappointed. On the other hand, those readers who recognized their poet in another setting were delighted with the book.

Notwithstanding his constitutional quietism, he was deeply gratified when he was elected to a fellowship at St. John's in 1948 and he derived genuine pleasure from an evening in Combination Room. Gentle in manner and hampered by increasing deafness, he could take a very firm line in argument when he felt strongly on a subject, whether literary or ethical or political; his insistence on ultimate values, coupled with a keen and quiet humour, made him a most lovable companion.

His marriage to Cecilia Horne in 1930 brought him great happiness; he had three sons and one daughter.

December 30, 1959.

Sir Howard Kennard, G.C.M.G., C.V.O., for nearly 40 years a member of the Diplomatic Service, and British Ambassador to Poland at the outbreak of war in 1939, died on November 12, 1955 at his home at Bath, at the age of 77.

Howard William Kennard was born on March 23, 1878, the only son of Arthur Charles Kennard, and was educated at Wixenford and Eton, where he boarded first at Dr. Carpenter's and, on his death, at Mr. (afterwards Sir Annesley) Somerville's. Mr. Tatham was his tutor. He left Eton in 1896, but did not proceed to a university, spending his time working for the Diplomatic Service which he entered in 1901. After a few months in the Foreign Office he was appointed to Rome. In 1903 he was promoted to be a third secretary, passed an examination in international law, and was transferred to Teheran, where he gained an allowance for knowledge of Persian.

He remained at Teheran for three years, and then after a short spell in the Foreign Office was transferred to Washington, where he remained until 1911. After a few months at Havana he was transferred to Tangier, where he gained an allowance for knowledge of Arabic. He was regularly in charge of the Agency during the absence of Sir Herbert White on leave, and in 1916 returned to the Foreign Office, being promoted to be Counsellor of Embassy at Rome in 1919 where he acted four times as Chargé d'Affaires.

He attained the rank of Minister in 1925 and was appointed to Belgrade. Kennard's mission was a successful one. He was interested in the country, learnt the language well, and spent as much time as he could spare travelling about, often on foot, and getting well acquainted with the people of Yugoslavia. Tactful and discreet, he was able to get on terms of friendship with the Opposition leaders without exciting the suspicions of the Government. Difficulties with Italy and Austria were not unknown and it must perhaps be admitted that the Yugoslavs were not always as patient as they might have been.

After four years at Belgrade Kennard was appointed to Stockholm, also a post of observation, but a very important one, for Sweden offers a valuable point to study the general politics of north-eastern Europe. Then, from 1931 to 1934, he served as Minister at Berne. In the latter year he was promoted to be Ambassador to Poland. The years 1934 to 1939 witnessed the gathering of the storm clouds. Poland made hectic efforts to avoid the clash with Germany which approached nearer and nearer. Kennard, on the instructions of his Government, assured the Poles of British support, but it was obvious that neither England nor France could do much to help Poland against German aggression. The blow fell in September 1939 and within three weeks the Germans had overrun Poland and come to an agreement with Russia. Kennard and the Embassy were able to get out of the country *via* Romania, and at the end of September they reached Bucharest. Thence they made their way to London.

The Polish Government, driven from Warsaw, established itself in France and thither the mission went. They remained in France till the collapse in 1940 and then preceeded to England. Kennard, though he was but 62, retired from the service. It will no doubt be astonishing to most that the Government did not retain his services longer. Kennard knew Poland and knew the Poles, and his retention as Ambassador would seem to have been the obvious course, and doubtless his knowledge would have been of great value.

He had been created a K.C.M.G. in 1929 and was promoted G.C.M.G. in 1938 and sworn a member of the Privy Council on his retirement.

He married in 1908 Harriet, daughter of Jonathan Norris, of New York. She died in 1950 and he is survived by an only son.

November 14, 1955.

Lord Kennet, P.C., G.B.E., D.S.O., D.S.C., died at the age of 81 on July 11, 1960.

The Right Hon. Edward Hilton Young, first baron Kennet of the Dene, was born on March 20, 1879, the third son of Sir George Young, third baronet of Formosa Place, Cookham, Chief Charity Commissioner from 1903 to 1906 and formerly President of the Senate of University College London. He was educated at Eton and at Trinity College, Cambridge, where he obtained a first class in the Natural Sciences Tripos. In 1904 he was called to the Bar by the Inner Temple and practised in the King's Bench and on the Oxford Circuit.

Interested from his early days in finance and economics, Hilton Young became in 1909 assistant editor of the *Economist* and the next year was appointed financial editor of the *Morning Post,* a position which he held until the war. After it he was to be editor of the *Financial News.* In 1910 he stood as Liberal candidate for East Worcestershire and Preston, but was defeated.

In August 1914 he joined the R.N.V.R. and was appointed as an executive officer in H.M.S. Iron Duke. A year later he was posted to the staff of the British Naval Mission with the Serbian Army. It consisted of a small force of naval ratings and marines engaged under Rear-Admiral Troubridge in seeking to prevent the Austrians from using the Danube as a route for traffic to Bulgaria. After this period of service he was invalided home for a time.

At this stage he stood for Parliament again as a Liberal in a 1915 by-election at Norwich. He was successful on this occasion and remained as Liberal member for Norwich—with one hiatus between the 1923 and 1924 elections—for 14 years.

Later in 1915 he returned to active service and was posted back to Rear-Admiral Troubridge's command in the Balkans. This was at the time when the Serbian Army was in retreat under conditions of great misery and hardship. Joining Troubridge at the little port of Medua, he remained there exporting refugees and importing food until January 1916, when they were compelled to evacuate it. He was awarded the Obilich medal and the fourth class of Karageorge Order with swords. Then after a gunnery course and some active service with the Dover Patrol and in the North Sea, he went to the naval guns ashore at Nieuport Bains. For his services with them—it was an uncomfortable and dangerous post—he received the D.S.C. and Croix de Guerre.

At Zeebrugge Hilton Young was in command of two of the six-inch guns in Vindictive, and, just before she reached the Mole, was hit in the right arm. Having made his way as best he could to a dressing station to have it tended he remained on deck throughout the action. Later he lost the limb. He was promoted lieutenant-commander for his services. Recovered by July, he was sent to Archangel and placed in charge of an armoured train which attacked the Bolshevik position on the Khima Brook. For his services in action he received the D.S.O.

After the Armistice he returned to post-war England to devote himself more fully to political life and to his parliamentary duties as member for Norwich. The first of his official appointments came in 1920, when the Government sent him on a financial mission to India. From 1921 to 1922 he was Financial Secretary to the Treasury, and in the latter year was British representative at The Hague Conference on International Finance. In 1922 he was appointed Chief Whip of the National Liberal Party, and was sworn of the Privy Council. From 1923 to 1924 he was out of Parliament; but in the latter year Norwich reelected him and he was to continue to represent it until in 1929 he became member for Sevenoaks. In 1925 and again in 1930 he went on financial missions to Iraq, and in 1926, 1927, 1928, and again in 1932, he was British delegate to the Assembly of the League of Nations. During this period he was also chairman of the Royal Commission on Indian Currency and Finance, and on the Closer Union of the Dependencies in eastern and central Africa.

Early in 1926 Hilton Young had found himself at issue with the Liberal Party in regard to its land policy, which he held to be socialistic, and abandoned it. The Liberals of Norwich decided, however, to take no action in regard to the representation of the city and a little later he joined the Conservatives. In the same year he became the first lay member of the General Medical Council. In 1927 he was created G.B.E.

In September 1931, on the formation of the National Government, he was appointed Parliamentary Secretary of the Department of Overseas Trade, but his tenure of the post was brief, for after the general election he was appointed Minister of Health.

It was a time of great financial stringency; but from the first he was in favour of maintaining the essential health services. Housing was in such circumstances one of his chief problems and he determined to concentrate on the provision of accommodation for the poorest class. In the autumn of 1934 he was in a position to report that there was hardly a considerable town in the country where the local authority was not working at high pressure on slum clearance. In June 1935 he was created a peer.

From 1935 onwards Lord Kennet, as he now was, began to take an important part in business life, and joined the boards of various financial and commercial undertakings, of some of which he became chairman. His services were in still more urgent request when the 1939-45 War brought a great increase in the range of public duties for which men of the highest standing and ability were needed. In 1942 he was made chairman of the Committee on Manpower in Banking and Allied Businesses, in Ordinary Insurance and in Industrial Assurance. A year later he was appointed chairman of the National Savings Committee.

The last and perhaps the most important of many "Kennet Committees" was one of postwar rather than wartime significance. This was the Capital Issues Committee, a body of financial and industrial experts which was set up to advise the Treasury on the operation of the control of new capital issues which the Treasury exercised under the Defence (Finance) Regulations and subsequently under the Borrowing (Control and Guarantees) Act. Lord Kennet was the chairman of this committee throughout all the difficult post-war years when the great pent-up demand for capital had to be rationed and controlled by a careful system of priorities.

All applications to raise fresh capital or borrow money in excess of a small maximum amount came before this committee, and its work in advising on the treatment of these applications and on the terms of capital issues was onerous and protracted. He gave up his chairmanship in 1959.

In 1911 he published *Foreign Companies and other Corporations* and in 1915 *The System of National Finance* (Third edition 1935), in which he set forth his belief in "economy". Later, in addition to a volume of excellent verse which he called *A Muse at Sea* (1919), he wrote *By Sea and Land* (1920), his reminiscences of the war. Then after a long interval came *A Bird in the Bush* (1937), a prose poem in which the birds—he was a great bird-lover and watcher—supplied the undertone. It was illustrated by his step-son, Peter Scott. He was president of the Poetry Society, and was a past President of the Royal Statistical Society and Association of Technical Institutes.

Kennet was also intensely fond of social life and of conversation and discussion of all kinds, and he contrived somehow never to let the weight of his labours deprive him of its pleasures. How he managed to fit as much as he did into a day was always something of a mystery, but he was an exceptionally quick and decisive worker in everything he touched. In private and social life these quick and decisive qualities of mind were mellowed by his inborn friendliness and the immense pleasure which he took in people's company.

In 1922 he married Kathleen, daughter of Canon Lloyd Bruce and widow of Captain Robert Falcon Scott, C.V.O., R.N., the famous Antarctic explorer. By this marriage he had one son, the Hon. Wayland Hilton-Young, who, born in 1923, now succeeds to his title. Lady Kennet died in 1947.

July 13, 1960.

Annie Kenney (later Mrs. James Taylor), who was prominent in the suffragette movement in the early years of this century, died in hospital on July 9, 1953 at the age of 73.

She and Christabel Pankhurst [q.v.] were the first to raise the "votes for women" banner in the militant suffragette movement, in the

Manchester Free Trade Hall in 1905. They interrupted the speeches of (Sir) Winston Churchill* and his chairman, the late Lord Grey, and were sent to prison next day.

Annie Kenney was the daughter of very humble folk who had 11 children. She was the fifth child and was born on September 13, 1879, in the little village of Springfield, in Lancashire.

At only ten years of age she went to work half-time in the local mill and at fourteen she left school and was a full time worker. Very early she was moved by the conditions of down-trodden women and was inspired by the writings of Robert Blatchford. He persuaded her to start a trade union in her mill and later she took a fortnight off and organized the workpeople in other mills. Then she met [later Dame] Christabel Pankhurst.

Although she had only the education of the village school, she educated herself by reading and became a most eloquent public speaker in the suffragette movement. A small woman with large, gleaming, dark eyes, she had a vivid personality which attracted and inspired other women. She went to prison many times as a militant suffragette and was a hunger striker.

Kenney's whole early life was given over to social welfare. When war came in 1914 she helped Mrs. Pankhurst in her recruiting centre and in 1924 published her autobiography, *Memories of a Militant.* Her exploits in the militant suffragette movement were recalled in a radio play broadcast by the B.B.C. in 1952.

After her marriage to James Taylor she took no further part in public life. Their son was an officer in the R.A.F. in the 1939-45 war.

July 11, 1953.

Eric Kennington, R.A., died on April 13, 1960 after a long illness. He was 72.

Kennington was both painter and sculptor, but he was first and foremost a draughtsman, realistic in outlook and forcible and incisive in style; and it was in association with T. E. Lawrence that some of his most interesting drawings were made. Shortly after the end of the War of 1914-18 Kennington happened to see a film dealing incidentally with Lawrence in Arabia which excited his interest, and when two years later he heard that Lawrence had bought two of his drawings he took the bull by the horns and telegraphed to say that he was coming to see him. They met at All Souls College, Oxford, where Lawrence was at that time a Research Fellow, and at the end of half an hour's talk Kennington had promised to accompany his new friend to the East and to paint his Arabs.

At the last moment Lawrence was unable to go with Kennington to Trans-Jordania but, as Kennington said on his return, "The introductions I had from Lawrence were a bodyguard". He added that for the sake of Lawrence many of the Arabs risked their souls by sitting for their portraits against the dictates of their religion. The results of the journey were shown at the Leicester Galleries in October 1921, the introduction to the catalogue of the exhibition being written by Lawrence. Several of the portrait drawings were used to illustrate the 1926 edition of *The Seven Pillars of Wisdom,* of which he was art editor.

The friendship between Lawrence and Kennington lasted until Lawrence's death in 1935, and Kennington, who had drawn and painted many portraits of his hero, was responsible for several memorials to him in sculpture, including the recumbent effigies of Lawrence in Arab dress in St. Martin's Church, Wareham, Dorset, and at the Tate Gallery, the bronze bust in the crypt of St. Paul's Cathedral, and the portrait relief in the High School, Oxford.

Eric Henri Kennington, who was the son of an artist, Thomas Benjamin Kennington (1856-1916), original member and first secretary of the New English Art Club, represented in the Tate Gallery by a painting of "Orphans", was born in Chelsea in 1888. At the age of 10 he was sent to St. Paul's School, where he was generally at the bottom of his class owing to neglect of his studies in favour of carving and scratching figures of navvies and costers on his desk. When he was 16 his father wisely removed him and sent him to the St. Paul's School of Art, and he afterwards studied at Lambeth and Kennington. After trying to earn a living as a black-and-white artist Kennington turned to portraiture and got a fair number of commissions including some from Russia, which he visited at the suggestion of a relative who lived in St. Petersburg.

His first works to attract attention, however, were paintings of London types made in the neighbourhood of Walham Green. In these, of which "The Flower Girl" was an early example, the influence of Italian and Flemish primitives gave a new and exciting flavour to the Cockney subjects, and from this time onward it became clear that Kennington's natural affinity was with the Pre-Raphaelites. "The Costardmongers", painted in 1914, was bought by (Sir) William Nicholson and presented to the Luxembourg Museum, Paris.

During the first year of the war Kennington served in Flanders and France as a private in the 13th London Regiment, the Kensingtons. After about three months he was invalided home, but in 1916 he returned to the Front in order to make drawings for war pictures. The first result was "The Kensingtons at Laventie" which, exhibited at the Goupil Gallery in 1916 for the benefit of the Star and Garter Building Fund, caused a great sensation. Representing a group of 10 men, with one asleep on the ground, standing in exhausted attitudes under the weight of their equipment in a battered village, it is a passionate tribute to the ordinary soldier. All the figures are obviously portraits, as of Tom, Dick, and Harry, and the head of Kennington himself as a reverent observer appears in the background. The treatment, with its precision of detail, recalls that of a Flemish primitive, the sharpness of effect being enhanced by the fact that the picture is painted on glass.

All Kennington's war pictures, which include "The Victims", a company of Canadian-Scottish marching through mud, painted for the Canadian War Memorial and shown at the Alpine Club Gallery in 1920, tell the same tale: detestation of war and intense admiration of the men who take part in it. They are all emphatically celebrations of brave men rather than of important military events, and this, while it gives to Kennington's work a passionate conviction, will suggest its artistic limitations.

For a short time after the war Kennington expressed his reaction from its horrors in portraits of children, serene in mood though incisive in treatment. Then came the meeting with Lawrence which, with its results, has been described already. The first work of sculpture to attract attention was the memorial to the 24th Division, presented by Kennington, in Battersea Park. In all that concerns characterization this is a fine piece of work, infinitely to be preferred to the rhetoric or professional tidiness of most official memorials, but from the point of view of the formal organization which makes sculpture endure it is sadly incoherent.

Possibly from his association with Lawrence, Kennington appears to have hankered after a mystical significance which was foreign to his nature. Some of the best things he did in sculpture are the five figures of "Love", "Jollity", "Treachery or Hate", "War" and "Life and Death" carved in the brickwork of the Shakespeare Memorial Theatre at Stratford-on-Avon.

In the figures the illustrative intention, the Gothic idiom and the texture of the material—the figures were carved *in situ* across the jointing of the brickwork—combine to produce something as racy and original as it is decorative.

In 1940 Kennington was appointed an official war artist to make portraits of generals, and in 1943 there was an exhibition of new pastels by him, chiefly portraits of officers and men of the Army at home, including the Home Guard, the pastels of the older and more rugged types being particularly successful. Even more characteristic were the 52 portrait drawings contained in *Drawing the R.A.F.,* published in 1942.

A shy, nervous, fresh-coloured man, he was rather jerky in conversation, with a trick of humming to himself betwen his remarks. He was elected A.R.A. in 1951 and R.A. in April 1959.

Kennington is represented at the Tate Gallery by drawings in charcoal, chalk, and pastel. They include a portrait drawing of C. M. Doughty, given by Lawrence in 1922, the others being presented by the Contemporary Art Society and various private benefactors. The Tate also has a version in *ciment fondu* of the effigy at Wareham. The Imperial War Museum has a large collection of his works.

In 1922 he married Edith Celandine, daughter of Lord Francis Cecil, and they had a son and a daughter.

April 16, 1960.

Elizabeth Kenny, who died on November 30, 1952 at the age of 66 after an attack of cerebral thrombosis, was a nursing sister who devoted most of her life and energy to the study and treatment of paralysis.

She was born at Warialda, New South Wales, and qualified as a nurse in 1911. With the exception of her service with the Australian Army Nursing Service during the 1914-18 war, her early professional experience was gained in Queensland, where, often under difficult conditions, she acquired her first practical knowledge of caring for patients with infantile paralysis. She became convinced that the medical profession was not treating this disease in the best way, and on this conviction her life's work was based. Having devised and practised physical methods of treatment for infantile and other forms of paralysis, she considered that her methods could, if used early enough in the disease, produce a complete cure. At first her claims were scouted but she pressed them with such energy that they ultimately attracted wide attention.

In 1935 a clinic was opened in Sydney where her methods were applied, and in 1936 a Royal Commission was appointed at her own request by the Queensland State Government to examine the merits of the system. The following year she came to England to demonstrate her treatment in a specially conducted trial lasting a year. The conclusions of the Royal Commission and the report of the doctors at the trial were on the whole not encouraging. The objection made was that the improvement which Sister Kenny undoubtedly obtained could have been achieved equally well by the accepted means of treatment.

Yet while damaging epidemics of infantile paralysis continued, and while orthodox medical treatment remained relatively powerless to reduce the rate of mortality, her optimism and confidence drew many people, doctors among them, to her support. When she visited the United States her views were no more acceptable to the medical profession than they had been elsewhere; nevertheless she was asked to open a treatment centre in Minneapolis, and the Elizabeth Kenny Foundation was established. Her results at that centre were favourably received by many American doctors, and clinics for giving the Kenny treatment were established in many countries, but her methods never gained the general acceptance for which she strove. Sister Kenny's teaching may not have been the important advance that she wholeheartedly believed it to be, but there can be no doubt about the great measure of suffering she relieved or about the value of the vigorous and sustained stimulus which she gave to medical opinion.

She published a number of technical works explaining her methods of treatment, and her autobiography *And They Shall Walk* (written in collaboration with Martha Ostenso) was published in 1943.

December 1, 1952.

Sir Frederic Kenyon, G.B.E., K.C.B., T.D., for 21 years Director of the British Museum, which he served for more than 40 years all told, died on August 23, 1952 at the age of 89.

It is doubtful whether the museum has ever had, or ever will have, a director more variously distinguished or with so striking a combination of qualities. At once scholar and administrator, he was the ideal occupant of a post which, while primarily administrative, calls continually for a sympathy with the world of scholarship and understanding of its problems. By training a librarian, and lacking (as he would doubtless have admitted) any intimate knowledge of archaeology or special sense of aesthetic values, he had nevertheless sufficient adaptability and range of knowledge to appreciate the claims of departments remote from his personal experience; and every keeper could count on his support and sympathetic interest. As an administrator he showed an extraordinary grasp of detail and an equal capacity to formulate the general principles educed from them. Jealous for the honour of the museum and expecting from his staff a high standard of conduct and efficiency, he was ever vigilant to safeguard their interests. Finally, a sense of breeding and tradition, that ease of manner which bespoke "the scholar and the gentleman", lent distinction to his tenure of office.

Frederic George Kenyon was born in London in 1863, the son of John Robert Kenyon, Q.C., D.C.L. He was the seventh of a family of 15 children, and was educated at Winchester, of which he was a scholar, and thence proceeded, again with a scholarship, to New College, Oxford, in 1882. He obtained first classes in Classical Moderations in 1883 and in *Literae Humaniores* in 1886; in 1888 he was awarded a Fellowship at Magdalen; and in 1889 he won the Chancellor's English Essay prize. In the same year he entered the British Museum as an assistant in the Department of Manuscripts. It was a moment at which his classical attainments were particularly welcome. The science of papyrology (though not the name, which was not coined till later) had been called into being by the great discoveries of papyri at Medinet el Fayum in 1877 and following years. A portion of these documents had been acquired by the British Museum, which already possessed a number of papyri from previous finds; and though the earlier acquisitions had been catalogued by Forshall as long ago as 1839, and the Austrian scholar Wessely had worked at some of the later ones, it had seemed advisable to issue a catalogue of the whole collection. For this work Kenyon was obviously the right man.

A more exciting task, however, was to take precedence. In the very year of his appointment the museum acquired an unusually important series of papyrus rolls, which included Aristotle's lost treatise on the Athenian Constitution, the mimes of Herodas (an example of a *genre* hitherto unrepresented among the remains of Greek literature), and a new speech of Hyperides. The publication of the first (1891) ranks as a landmark in modern Greek studies and Kenyon's reputation was established at once.

Several of the other literary texts were edited or (in the case of known works) collated by him in *Classical Texts from Papyri in the British Museum* (1891), and he had to return more than once to the Aristotle, of which he published an English translation in 1891, editing the text afresh in 1904 for the Berlin Academy and in 1920 for the Clarendon Press.

In 1896 the museum acquired a papyrus roll containing 20 odes, complete or imperfect, of Bacchylides. Kenyon's publication of these in 1897 not only added to our stock of Greek poetry a writer previously known by no more than a few fragments, but extended our knowledge of the epinician ode, hitherto represented (apart from exiguous fragments) only by Pindar.

In addition to these publications of newly acquired literary papyri, Kenyon did valuable work on earlier acquisitions. He had himself published in *Classical Texts* the *editio princeps* of Hyperides' *In Philippidem*, which, in 1892, he republished along with the oration against Athenogenes; and in 1907 he contributed to the Oxford series *Scriptorum Classicorum Bibliotheca Oxoniensis* a complete edition of all the extant remains of this orator. It may be assumed that his personal preference was for literary rather than for documentary papyri; and his excellent *Palaeography of Greek Papyri*, which appeared in 1899, was undertaken with a special view to the former, though it necessarily dealt also with documentary hands. He did not, however, neglect the papyri of the latter class. In 1893 he published Volume I of the *Catalogue of Greek Papyri in the British Museum*, which included all the non-literary material, together with the magical texts, acquired up to the end of 1890. The still larger Volume II followed in 1898, and in 1907 appeared Volume III, in which he had the help of a younger colleague. This was his last appearance as an editor of non-literary papyri; his appointment in 1909 as Director and Principal Librarian made further work of the kind impossible.

He had in 1898 been made Assistant (now Deputy) Keeper of Manscripts, creating what is probably a record by passing direct to that position from the status of second class assistant, just as he was later promoted from the post of assistant keeper to the directorship. Henceforth administrative duties occupied much of his time. Both before and after his promotion he took an active share in the ordinary duties of his department.

His interest in the Bible had been shown already at Oxford, where in 1885 he won the Junior Greek Testament Prize. In 1895 he published *Our Bible and the Ancient Manuscripts*. In 1900 appeared, under his editorship, *Facsimiles of Biblical Manuscripts in the British Museum*; and this official publication was followed next year by his *Handbook to the Textual Criticism of the New Testament*.

Greek papyri and Biblical criticism did not by any means monopolize his attention. He was a constant reader both of the Greek classics and of English literature. In the latter it was particularly with the Brownings and their circle that he concerned himself. He was joint editor of Robert Browning's *Poems* in 1896, and he published several books and articles on both Robert and Elizabeth Barrett Browning.

His directorship included the period of the 1914-18 war, when he faced problems such as few of his predecessors had contemplated; he was an active Territorial officer in the Inns of Court Regiment, joined the Expeditionary Force in France for a short time in 1914, and served with his regiment till 1919, becoming a lieutenant-colonel; and in 1918 he was appointed adviser to the Imperial War Graves Commission.

Before and after the war he held many other positions of responsibility which claimed much time. He was president of the British Academy, 1917-21; Professor of Ancient History in the Royal Academy in 1918; president of the Hellenic Society, 1919-24, and of several other societies at various times; and Warden of Winchester College, 1925-30. Yet with all this outside activity he gave to his official duties at the British Museum an attention which never flagged and which neglected no detail.

Honours had come to him in abundance. In 1911 he was created C.B., in 1912 promoted K.C.B., and in 1925 he received the Grand Cross of the British Empire, of which he had been made Gentleman Usher of the Purple Rod in 1918.

Not long before Kenyon's retirement [Sir Alfred] Chester Beatty* had acquired in Egypt a remarkable series of papyrus codices representing many books of the Bible. The editing of these occupied much of Kenyon's leisure after his retirement, and the fruits of this return to an early love were seen in a series of volumes dealing with the textual criticism of the Bible, from his Schweich Lectures, *Recent Developments in the Textual Criticism of the Greek Bible,* 1933, to his small but weighty *The Bible and Modern Scholarship,* published in 1948. His study of the codex form led to the writing of his *Books and Readers in Ancient Greece and Rome* (1932). Almost to the end of his life his services were much in demand by learned societies as president, chairman, or secretary. For a time during the Second World War he served in the Home Guard.

He married in 1891 Amy, daughter of Rowland Hunt, J.P. She died in 1938, having borne him two daughters.

August 25, 1952.

Sir John G. Kerr, F.R.S., formerly Regius Professor of Zoology at Glasgow University, and M.P. for the Scottish Universities from 1935 to 1950, died at his home at Barley, near Royston, Hertfordshire on April 21, 1957. He was 87.

A son of the late James Kerr, M.A., Principal of Hoogly College, Calcutta, John Graham Kerr, who received his knighthood in 1939, was born on September 18, 1869, at Rowley Lodge, Arkley, Hertfordshire, and was educated at the Royal High School, Edinburgh, and at the Universities of Edinburgh and Cambridge.

He was a brilliant student and at an unusually early age won the highest honours in natural science at both universities. When he was only 20 he went to South America, where he spent two years in zoological explorations, especially on the Pilcomayo river, and about five years later he joined an Argentine Government expedition to the Gran Chaco to investigate the habits and life history of the lower vertebrates, particularly the lung-fish, or mud-fish. In that branch of natural science he became a recognized expert. The hardships that beset Kerr in the little-known tropical region of South America were endured with a stoicism that revealed in him physical fitness equal to the demands of his mental brilliance. Struggling at times for bare existence, he continued to make collections and observations which added considerably to the knowledge of South American fauna and flora.

On his return to England in 1897 he became Demonstrator in Animal Morphology at Cambridge University, where he continued his zoological research work and also acted as resident examiner in zoology for the Natural Science Tripos. From 1898 to 1904 he was a Fellow of Christ's College, Cambridge. In 1902 he was appointed Regius Professor of Zoology at Glasgow University, being succeeded in 1936 by Dr. Edward Hindle*. A member of the University Court from 1913 to 1921, he was also associated in Glasgow with the governing bodies of the Royal Technical College, the Anderson College of Medicine, and the Royal Infirmary.

For many years Kerr took a leading part in the Unionist Party in Scotland, particularly in Glasgow, and was rewarded for his substantial contributions to the party's activities by being elected in 1935 as M.P. for the Scottish Universities in succession to the late Lord Tweedsmuir, on the latter's appointment to the Governorship-General of Canada and elevation to the peerage. His close association with the inner councils of the party made him an admirable choice. In 1934-35 he was president of the Scottish Unionist Association, and for five years he was chairman of the Glasgow Unionist Association; his other political offices included the chairmanship of the Glasgow Committee of Scottish University Unionists and the convenership of the Western Divisional Council. He was also an honorary vice-president of the Glasgow Unionist Teachers' Association, and chairman of the Glasgow University Unionist Association.

Kerr was a member of many learned societies. A Fellow of the Royal Society and the Royal Society of Edinburgh, he also served for a time as president of the Royal Philosophical Society of Glasgow and the Royal Physical Society of Edinburgh. He was the author of various papers on zoological and biological subjects, and his publications included *Primer of Zoology, Text-Book of Embryology, Zoology for Medical Students, Evolution: an Introduction to Zoology,* and *A Naturalist in the Gran Chaco,* a remarkable account of the young Kerr's ascetic life 60 years earlier when, stranded on the Pilcomayo muds, he went out to the swamps and forests to observe and to hunt. One reviewer remarked of this book: "It is *Far Away and Long Ago* again, from the same quarter of the world but from a different angle". He was chairman of the Advisory Committee on Fishery Research from 1941 to 1949. In 1955 he was awarded a Linnean gold medal.

In 1914 Kerr originated and communicated to the Admiralty a scheme for the protective coloration of ships in strongly contrasting colours.

He married in 1903 Elizabeth Mary (who died in 1934), daughter of T. Kerr, Writer to the Signet, and had two sons and one daughter. In 1936 he married Mrs. Alan Clapperton of Lochwinnoch, daughter of the late Mr. and Mrs. A. Dunn Macindoe, of Glasgow.

April 24, 1957.

Field Marshal Albert Kesselring, one of the ablest German generals of the Second World War, died on July 16, 1960 at Bad Nauheim, at the age of 74. His *Blitzkrieg* methods in Poland and his long, stubborn campaign in Italy showed that he possessed, rarely among military commanders, an equal understanding of the command of air and land forces.

Albert Kesselring was born on November 30, 1885, of a middle-class family, and was commissioned in a Bavarian artillery regiment in 1906. He served in the First World War, reaching the rank of captain, and was quickly promoted in the post-war Wehrmacht. He served as a major in the Department of the Defence Ministry responsible for training, and as a lieutenant-colonel at Army headquarters. Under Hitler he was promoted in 1935 to major-general and transferred to the Luftwaffe.

The Luftwaffe was not then the effective weapon it later proved to be, and Kesselring was given much of the credit for its high state of training. He was responsible for many of its operations in the early phases of the war when aircraft and armour combined to make *Blitzkrieg* a terrifying and effective weapon. In the Polish campaign he commanded the First Air Fleet, and under his leadership the air attacks against Norway and on the western front were mounted. He was promoted to field marshal for these successes, and in 1942 assumed command of air operations in the Mediterranean and Africa.

He took over the armies in Italy in 1943, where he fought a bitter defensive campaign, and in March 1945 replaced von Rundstedt [q.v.] as Oberbefehlshaber West, and assumed command of all forces on the western front. When the Soviet Army broke through south of Berlin his command was extended to all forces south of the breakthrough. He surrendered to the American armies on May 6, 1945.

Kesselring was held with the other field marshals in Dachau, and in the following year was extradited to Italy to face charges of responsibility for the murder of 335 Italian civilians and issuing orders for the shooting of civilians as reprisals against partisan activities. He was found Guilty by a British military court in Venice and sentenced to death, though it was said in evidence that it was Field Marshal Lord Alexander's* opinion that Kesselring had fought fairly. The sentence was deplored by some of those who had fought against him, and was commuted to life imprisonment. He was released in 1952, and afterwards became the president of the ex-service men's association, Stahlhelm.

July 18, 1960.

Albert W. Ketelbey, who died at Cowes on November 26, 1959, was born in Birmingham in 1875. He was educated at Fitzroy College, Fitzroy Square, and at Trinity College of Music, where he beat the runner-up, Gustav Holst, for a musical scholarship.

He distinguished himself in numerous fields, especially in composition. His first compositions were in the classical style and a Quintet for Strings was awarded the Sir Michael Costa Prize. He developed a talent for descriptive writing, however, and of all his many works it is in those of this genre—"In a Monastery Garden", "In a Chinese Temple Garden", and "In a Persian Market", where he showed an ability to catch atmospheric tone—that he found his public.

He was active in several other fields. He was musical editor to some well-known publishing houses, and for some years musical director of the Columbia Gramophone Co. He was a popular conductor and was well esteemed in the theatre world where he conducted for André Charlot [q.v.] at the Vaudeville. He also conducted many concerts of his own works, in London and the provinces, and as guest conductor with well-known orchestras on the Continent, including the Concert Gebouw Orchestra of Amsterdam. His reputation on the Continent was in fact probably higher than in his own country. He was himself fond of European travel and spoke several foreign languages.

He married first Charlotte, daughter of L. Curzon; and secondly Maud, widow of L. S. Pritchett, who survives him. There were no children by either marriage.

November 27, 1959.

By the death at her home on February 13, 1958 of **Florence Ada Keynes,** widow of the late Dr. J. N. Keynes and mother of the late Lord Keynes, Cambridge loses one of its most remarkable links with the past. She was 96.

Born in 1861, Mrs. Keynes was the daughter of John Brown, a minister at Bedford and a distinguished writer on many aspects of the history of Puritanism. She was admitted to Newham Hall, as it was then called, in 1878. Miss Clough [q.v.] was Principal, and chaperonage was strictly enforced, but at the house of William Bond in Brookside she met John Neville Keynes, a young Fellow of Pembroke, and they were married in 1882. A house was built for them in Harvey Road and in that house Mrs. Keynes lived until her death.

In 1882 the married don was a novelty and a new kind of social life developed in Cambridge—the life so brilliantly depicted in *Period Piece.* Dinner parties were not, however, enough for Mrs. Keynes. From the first she was active in good works of a practical kind such as the Charity Organization Society, and in 1914 she became the first woman member of what was then the Cambridge Borough Council. Later she was made an alderman and in 1932—the year of her golden wedding—she was elected mayor.

Among the schemes which she inaugurated or helped to develop were the Friendly Societies Institute, and the Central Aid Society, of which she was honorary secretary for many years, expanding its work until it became one of the most valuable and active of the town's social services.

She was the first secretary of what is now known as the Papworth Village Colony, for patients suffering from tuberculosis, and acted as chairman of the house committee for many years. On her ninetieth birthday one of many celebrations was the luncheon given in her honour by the National Council of Women, of which she had once been president. In the middle of her admirable speech she apologized for being obliged to put on her spectacles in order to decipher some little obscurity in her notes.

It would be wrong to think of Mrs. Keynes simply as a pioneer of women's rights and activities. To her children (the world-famous Maynard; Geoffrey, distinguished both as surgeon and bibliographer; Margaret, wife of A. V. Hill [d. 1977]) she was both mother and companion, and she constantly renewed her interests in the widening circle of her grandchildren and great-grandchildren.

Readers of [Sir] Roy Harrod's [d. 1978] *The Life of John Maynard Keynes* will have caught something of the atmosphere of 6, Harvey Road, and those who can look back, with affection and gratitude, to 50 years of hospitality in that house preserve a precious memory of a Victorian lady who refused to become a period piece.

February 14, 1958.

Tshekedi Khama—See **Tshekedi.**

Lieutenant Leonard Keysor, V.C., Reserve of Officers, Australian Military Forces, who was awarded the Victoria Cross for conspicuous bravery at Lone Pine, Gallipoli, in August 1915, when he caught the Turks' bombs as if they were cricket balls and threw them back at the enemy, died in London on October 12, 1951 at the age of 65.

Born in London on November 3, 1885, Leonard Keysor went to Canada as a young man, but after spending several years there decided to go to New South Wales to live. He had just begun to settle down when the 1914-18 war broke out. Keysor soon joined up for service and he went out to Gallipoli as a private in the 1st Battalion, Australian Imperial Force. The deeds of valour which won the coveted decoration of the Victoria Cross for him were performed on August 7 and 8, 1915, when the fighting in the south-east corner of Lone Pine trenches had been particularly fierce, and bomb-throwing had been incessant. Keysor not only distinguished himself by his outstanding skill as a bomber, but also found time to smother with sandbags, and even sometimes with his coat, enemy bombs which had fallen into his trench. The Turks at last realized that they were setting their fuses for too long a period, so they cut down the time.

Realizing that if these bombs were allowed to drop into the trench he would not have time to smother them or pick them up and throw them back before they burst, Keysor performed what was probably one of the most spectacular individual feats of the war. As the bombs came over from the enemy, Keysor caught them one after another as if they were cricket balls and, quick as lightning, returned them to the Turks to burst in the enemy trenches. It was not to be expected that Keysor would come through such fighting unscathed. He was wounded twice and ordered to hospital.

Keysor, however, refused to go and, more than that, volunteered to go and throw bombs for another company whose bomb throwers were all killed or wounded. So great was his endurance that for a period of 50 hours he was bomb-throwing continuously. The notification of the award to him of the Victoria Cross was published in the *London Gazette* of October 15, 1915.

After the war ended Keysor returned for a time to Australia and continued the career in civil life which he had scarcely had time to establish before he joined the Army. He did not abandon his interest in military matters, however, for he took a commission, and was placed upon the list of Reserve Officers for the Australian Military Forces. He enlisted for service at the outbreak of war in 1939 but was rejected on medical grounds.

He leaves a widow, Gladys, daughter of F. Benjamin, whom he married in 1921, and one daughter.

October 13, 1951.

Dr. Khan Sahib, who was assassinated on May 9, 1958, was prominently identified with the Indian independence movement and a warm friend of Nehru* from the days when the latter was eating his dinners at the Middle Temple and Khan Sahib was walking the wards of St. Thomas's Hospital. He was destined ultimately to be Chief Minister of West Pakistan when its provinces were merged into a single unit. Quiet and courteous, patient and of deep convictions, he had the stature of a statesman.

Kahn Sahib was born in 1882, a son of Khan Bahram Khan, an influential landowner of Utmanzai in the Peshawar district. His elder brother, with whom he was usually associated in the Indian independence movement, was Abdul Gaffer Khan, the leader of the "Redshirt" movement, who underwent imprisonment under both the British Government and that of Pakistan. Khan Sahib was educated at the Peshawar Government High School and Mission College. He studied medicine at St. Thomas's Hospital, qualifying L.R.C.P. and M.R.C.S., and then competed successfully for the Indian Medical Service.

In 1930 he entered politics and was associated with the Indian National Congress in the struggle for Indian independence. He and his tempestuous brother, Abdul Gaffer Khan, both rose to be Chief Ministers of the North-West Frontier Province. When provincial autonomy was introduced in 1937 but was not applied to the Frontier Province, Khan Sahib headed a new Ministry. On the approach of war he resigned, and, like his brother, was put under detention, returning to the headship of the Ministry when the war was about to end in 1945.

Under his leadership the province embarked on a programme of industrial development and, for instance, the sugar mills at Mardan and Takhbhai were started. A much needed reform was the abolition of the *begar* system of forced labour, whereby the agricultural masses were freed from the undue exactions of landowners. He viewed with misgiving the Muslim League's demands for partition, and it was not to be expected that when partition came Jinnah would wish to include him in either the central or provincial Administration. When, however, in 1954 the Governor-General, Ghulam Mohammed [q.v.], dismissed the Pakistan Cabinet and a new coalition Ministry was formed, Dr. Khan Sahib was given the portfolio of communications.

He remained in that office until April 1955, when the provinces and states of West Pakistan were merged into a single unit, thereby placing West Pakistan on the same footing as East Pakistan. Dr. Khan Sahib now became Chief Minister of a vastly wider area than that of the North-West Frontier Province over which he had formerly presided. When in January 1955 Ghulam Mohammed paid a visit to New Delhi, he tactfully took with him Dr. Khan Sahib. Both were cordially greeted by Nehru, but it was obvious that for the vast crowds assembled the hero of the hour was Dr. Khan Sahib.

Unfortunately there was long-standing rivalry between Dr. Khan Sahib and the Muslim League party, which led to the formation of a new Republican Party by the former. At the end of 1956 parliamentary government in West Pakistan was suspended. When in July 1957 he was reinstated as Chief Minister, he immediately resigned in favour of Sardar Abdur Rashid Khan, to whom he had already relinquished the leadership of the Republican Party.

May 10, 1958.

Sir Hamidullah Khan—See **Bhopal.**

Liaquat Ali Khan—See **Liaquat.**

G. J. Kidston, C.M.G., formerly British Minister to the Republic of Finland, died at his home at Box, Wiltshire, at the age of 81, on December 26, 1954.

George Jardine Kidston was the second son of the late G. J. Kidston, of Finlayston, Renfrewshire. He was born on January 25, 1873, and was sent in 1887 to Eton, where he was in Broadbent's house, and became an n.c.o. in the school Rifle Corps. After three years at New College, Oxford, where he took history honours, Kidston studied abroad, and in 1898 passed the Civil Service examination and was appointed an attaché in the diplomatic service.

His first post abroad, after a few months' apprenticeship in the Foreign Office, was at Rome, where he served for four years under Sir Philip Currie, and witnessed the assassination of King Humbert. There followed appointments at Peking and Teheran. The Legation in Teheran was hard worked, but Kidston found time to learn Persian and to travel through a country that, in those days before the advent of the motor car, was little known to Europeans.

From Teheran Kidston was sent to St. Petersburg. His arrival in Russia coincided, however, with the conclusion of the Anglo-Russian Convention, which, brought about by the common fear of German aggression, interrupted for a time the rivalry of Russia and Great Britain. The stage was in fact being set for the 1914-18 War, and at Constantinople, where he was sent as Head of the Chancery in 1912, Kidston saw further steps taken in the same fateful direction. He was in Turkey throughout the two Balkan wars, when the Turks lost all but the remnant of their European Empire. There were exciting days in Constantinople in October 1912, when the Bulgarian guns could be heard at Tchataldja, and preparations were made for flight across the Straits to Broussa.

On August 4, 1914, Kidston was transferred to Brussels to assist Sir Francis Villiers, and a fortnight later had to accompany the Belgian Government and the legations to Antwerp on the approach of the Germans to the capital. In the beginning of October Antwerp was evacuated, and the flight was resumed to Ostend and finally to Havre. At Havre Kidston was in charge of the Legation during December 1914 and January 1915 and in the following July and August. Later in the war he served in the Foreign Office, reaching the rank of Counsellor in August 1919. A year later he was appointed Minister to Finland in succession to Lord Acton. Kidston stayed only one year in Finland. During this short period he did much to raise British prestige there, at a time when, owing to our failure at Murmansk, and to other causes, it was at a low ebb. He had a strong, straight-forward personality, which won sympathy for British policy where formerly there had been mistrust.

On his return to England in 1921 he retired to his home, Hazelbury Manor, near Box, in Wiltshire. The estate is not far from Bath and since the early Middle Ages the Hazelbury quarries have been a rich source of the Bath stone from which many of the great abbeys and houses of the West Country have been built. Kidston's history of the manor, which was published in 1936, is a splendid manifestation of his fastidious and painstaking scholarship.

Kidston was a generous benefactor to the Wiltshire Archaeological Society and one of its vice-presidents. He was also the first chairman of the records branch of the society, founded in 1937. Besides his *History of Hazelbury,* he was the author of *The Bonhams of Wiltshire and Essex,* printed for private circulation in 1948.

Kidston married, in 1911, Lilian Frances, daughter of Sir George Francis Bonham and sister of Lady (Evelyn) Grant Duff, and he leaves a son and four daughters.

December 28, 1954.

With the death of **Dame Grace Kimmins** in hospital at Haywards Heath at the age of 83 on March 3, 1954 there passed one of the most remarkable women in the field of social endeavour.

It was due to her inspiration, her faith, and her indomitable will and purpose that that most famous of all the modern institutions of its kind—the Heritage Craft Schools and Hospitals, at Chailey, in Sussex—was conceived and established more than 50 years ago. Under her leadership Chailey developed into a model centre for the care and training of crippled children, and to the schools and hospitals came men and women from all parts of the world in order that they might learn, profit from, and follow her example.

Grace Thyrza Hannam, the daughter of James and Thyrza Hannam, was born into a comfortable middle-class family, and she inherited the instinct for social service as a tradition. Even in her early days at Wilton House School she was moved by the neglected suffering of the poor, blind, and crippled in London, and much individual voluntary work on her part in their service brought to her side a number of willing helpers and supporters. On St. Martin's Day, in 1894, when Grace Hannam was still in her early twenties, and inspired largely by Mrs. Ewing's famous book *The Story of a Short Life,* she called the first meeting which led to the foundation of the Guild of the Brave Poor Things, with its motto: *Laetus sorte mea.*

With the aim of bringing together as many maimed people as possible, irrespective of age, creed, or any other limit, to make them truly "happy in my lot", she gathered about her an impressive collection of notable people to aid her in her task. They included Mrs. Henry Fawcett, wife of the blind Postmaster-General, Adeline Duchess of Bedford, Lady Henry Somerset, Emmeline Pethick, later to become Lady Pethick-Lawrence [q.v.], Mrs.

Hugh Price Hughes, Lady Lunn, and many others. From the hall of the West London Mission in Cleveland Street to the headquarters of the Bermondsey University Settlement, and finally to the Chapter House of Southwark Cathedral, moving as it grew, the Guild flourished. Branches were established in many parts of the country, and out of it came Grace Kimmins's dream of establishing her school for crippled children.

In 1903, six years after Grace Hannam had become the wife of Dr. Charles William Kimmins, the noted educationist, she was able to open in the most modest and primitive way at Chailey the first residential school with hospital treatment for cripples. It began with seven boys drawn from the Guild of the Brave Poor Things, housed in buildings which consisted partly of an old workhouse and partly of an industrial school—buildings which had already been condemned as unfit for habitation. In 40 years the numbers had increased to more than 500—boys and girls housed in magnificent modern buildings, trained in the arts and crafts to become intelligent, independent, self-supporting citizens.

Warmly supported and aided by her husband and their friends, Mrs. Kimmins was able for some years to finance the early stages of development and to continue operations by private benefactions, but as the fame of Chailey grew and its commitments increased, public assistance was appealed for and was speedily forthcoming. No great charity in British history has had warmer or more generous support, or a greater variety of well-wishers. Moved by the astonishing energy and driving force of Grace Kimmins, quickly advancing from one achievement to the next and always undaunted, some of the most influential people in Britain and in America gave it their blessing and their money. Queen Mary [q.v.] was an early friend, and for some years Queen Elizabeth the Queen Mother has been its patron, taking the closest personal interest in its welfare and progress. The Duke of Norfolk* was president, and for 45 years, until the Heritage was taken over by the Government under the National Health Service, Dame Grace remained at the administrative helm. Nominally honorary secretary, there she was, well into her seventies, still inspiring and directing the vast operations of this unique centre.

Grace Kimmins was that rarest combination, a masterful, methodical, driving woman with, as one of her candid friends once remarked, "a resolute knowledge of what she wanted and a tremendous belief in her own powers", but her personality was tempered by deep compassion for suffering humanity in every sphere, and an astonishing capacity for making and holding friends who appreciated her candour just as much as her devotion and her ability. Even after the Government had taken over her beloved schools and hospitals, and relieved her colleagues and herself of the reponsibilities which they had so gaily and devotedly discharged, she was still busy, often from a sick bed, devising ways and means by which in her own way she could add to the comforts and happiness of the Chailey children, who adored her.

In 1927 she was made a C.B.E. and in the 1950 Birthday Honours promoted D.B.E. For years she had been a Dame of Grace of the Order of St. John of Jerusalem.

Her two sons are Major-General B. C. H. Kimmins, C.B., C.B.E., and Captain Anthony Kimmins*, O.B.E., R.N., the author and dramatist.

March 4, 1954.

Lord Kindersley, President of the National Savings Committee until 1946, for many years chairman of Lazard Brothers and Company, Limited, and a director of the Bank of England, died in hospital at East Grinstead, Sussex, on July 20, 1954, at the age of 82. Between November 1939 and May 1945 he persuaded the public to save £9,000m.

The Right Hon. Sir Robert Molesworth Kindersley, G.B.E., first Baron Kindersley, of West Hoathley, Sussex, in the Peerage of the United Kingdom, born on November 21, 1871, son of the late Captain E. N. M. Kindersley, was educated at Repton. His career was a striking example of success won in the complicated world of finance by sheer energy and force of character. In winning this success he was certainly helped by his personality and presence. Sprung from a family distinguished on the river and in the football field, his tall figure, topped by a countenance expressing bulldog determination in every line, and made more impressive by a pair of bushy black eyebrows drawn straight across it, commanded immediate respect. Here, at a glance, was a man with whom it would be safe to go tiger-hunting and whom it would probably be unprofitable to oppose. With these advantages, mental and bodily, he won his way from a partnership in a firm of stockbrokers to the position of chairman of the London house of Lazard Brothers, with important international connexions, a seat on the Court of the Bank of England, the Governorship of the Hudson's Bay company, an institution even more ancient than the Bank, and other directorships.

His indomitable energies, however, sufficed for many activities apart from those involved by his rapid climb to the top of the financial tree. His services during the 1914-18 War to his country and to its allies were rewarded by a K.B.E. in 1917, with advancement to G.B.E. in 1920, the Legion of Honour, the Grand Cross of the Order of the Crown of both Belgium and Italy, and other distinctions. The part that he took in civic life brought him the Lieutenancy of the City of London, membership of the Court of the Fishmongers' Company and service as High Sheriff for Sussex. He also did good work as chairman of the Trade Facilities Act Advisory Committee, as a member of the Bankers' Committee on German Finance in 1922 and, in 1924, as senior British representative on the Dawes [q.v.] Committee, which made such a valiant effort, foiled by subsequent political developments, to solve the problem of Germany and her reparation liabilities.

But to the general public Kindersley's name was best known through his untiring work in connexion with the War Savings Committee and with the National Savings movement which grew out of it, one of the few legacies that the 1914-18 War left us which did not prove to be a *damnosa hereditas.* At its birth the Savings Committee was a Parliamentary body, hastily created out of the Parliamentary Recruiting Committee. As its scope widened and its economic importance came to be more clearly recognized, its membership was strengthened from outside and Kindersley was one of its earliest and most forceful acquisitions. The Committee got together and learned to row like a crew. Kindersley and the band of devoted workers whom he led so well saw, and set out to teach the public, confused by doctrines of "business as usual", that feeding the guns and the men behind them was a task that was going to strain the resources of the nation to their limit, and self-denial for victory must be vigorously practised by the non-combatant population. During that 1914-18 war-time period of monetary inflation, rapidly rising wages and unjustifiably large profits, checked too late and too partially by the belated and capricious Excess Profits Duty, many people, especially among those to whom high wages were a bewildering novelty, found themselves with more money than they knew what to do with, and so were an easy prey to sellers of unnecessary luxuries and expensive articles for which they had neither use or accommodation. To such folk and to many in the classes more accustomed to handling surplus funds, the war savings missionaries preached their gospel with extraordinary success and so established the saving habit among millions of the population, with important social effects, all the more valuable afterwards owing to the pressure of direct taxation on the wealthy, by whom the necessary growth of the national capital had hitherto been mainly provided. In this work Kindersley's energy and driving power, first as chairman and afterwards as president of the National Savings Committee, did yeoman service for his country, as he urged the benefits of thrift and wise spending and warned the unwary against the "parasites waiting to prey on the weaknesses of human nature".

On the outbreak of war in 1939 it very quickly became clear that the Government must look to national savings for a substantial contribution to the country's war resources. Here was a great summons to service, and Kindersley again devoted himself to the movement, and his long experience and driving power were placed unreservedly at the service of what soon became a very great war savings campaign. He gathered round him for that purpose a notable company of voluntary workers, whom he inspired with his own fiery enthusiasm and to whom the country owes a profound debt. The farsighted planning, however, without which the immense results could not have been achieved, was Kindersley's own. He worked like a Titan, and the organizers of many a local War Savings or War Weapons Week must have been surprised at the amount of personal interest and help he gave them. He made platform speeches at meetings in connexion with the movement in most of the centres of population, and he even achieved a reputation as a popular broadcaster, for the public were quick to perceive the sincerity and enthusiasm—and the undoubted element of genius— which he brought to this great matter. In recognition of his services, a peerage was conferred upon him in 1941. On his resignation in November 1946 from the position of president of the National Savings Movement the Chancellor of the Exchequer paid warm tribute to his 30 years of devoted service.

His activities were by no means confined to the domestic field. In the fateful August of 1931 he represented the Bank of England in Paris, conferring with the Bank of France concerning measures for the protection of the pound sterling against the panic which led to its fall. Later on he devoted much time and study to the question of the oversea investments of Britain, and the extent to which they were being reduced by the adverse balance of payments which for some years was a feature in its economic position. In the field of statistics he was a pioneer. Formerly his annual estimates in the *Economic Journal* were keenly awaited, and rightly credited with just as much authority as any Government statistics on a matter of comparable importance. Indeed his work met a great and pressing need at a time when statistics of national importance were still left to the private individual to compile unaided. Kindersley's work on this subject was always regarded as something of a classic: indeed the professional world of finance would almost regard it as his greatest achievement.

In 1896 he married Gladys Margaret, daughter of Major-General Beadle, late R. E., by whom he had three sons, the youngest of whom died in 1932, and two daughters. His eldest son, Brigadier the Hon. Hugh Kenyon Molesworth Kindersley, M.B.E., M.C., who served in the 1914-18 and 1939-45 wars in the Scots Guards, and was wounded in France shortly after D Day, married in 1921 Nancy Farnsworth, daughter of Dr. G. Boyd, of Toronto, and has a son and two daughters. Lord Kindersley's second son, Captain the Hon. Philip Leyland Kindersley, Coldstream Guards, was wounded in North Africa in 1942, taken as a prisoner to Italy, and to Germany.

July 21, 1954.

King Abdul Aziz Ibn Saud—See **Saudi Arabia.**

King Abdullah—See **Jordan.**

King Faisal II—See **Iraq.**

King George VI—See **George.**

King Haakon VII—See **Norway.**

Fleet Admiral Ernest J. King, Commander-in-Chief of the United States Fleet and Chief of Naval Operations during the last war, died in hospital at Portsmouth, New Hampshire, at the age of 77, on June 25, 1956.

His long career in his country's Navy, in the course of which he saw service in three wars, was distinguished not only by the high standards of efficiency he maintained but by a characteristic versatility which made him the only American naval officer of high rank who was a specialist in all three spheres of undersea, surface and air warfare. This, which was one of the secrets of his advancement, was to prove an outstanding qualification in the commander who became responsible for directing the arms-length operations of the American Navy in two hemispheres. Known in peacetime for running a "taut ship" he was a man of strong will and hot temper; but he also possessed an innate sense of justice which allowed him to pardon failure in those whom he knew to have done their best.

Ernest Joseph King was born on November 23, 1878, at Lorain, in the inland state of Ohio, the son of a railway master mechanic. He acquired his interest in ships by watching those which plied along the shore of Lake Erie.

After his graduation from high school he entered the United States Naval Academy at Annapolis, and passed out in 1901, the fourth man of his class. At the time a comment on him was: "Temper? Don't fool with nitroglycerine".

As a midshipman in the cruiser San Francisco King saw his first active service in the Spanish-American War, and was promoted an ensign in 1903. He thus started upon the steady climb which was to take him to the top of his profession. From 1916 to 1919 he was Assistant Chief of Staff to Admiral Mayo, the Commander-in-Chief of the United States Fleet, and was awarded the Navy Cross for service in the course of which he stood beside Admiral Jellicoe while Ostend was bombarded. Then, after being head of the Post-Graduate School of Annapolis, he requested transfer to submarine duty and in 1926 was appointed commander of the submarine base at New London. In that year he won the Distinguished Service Medal for successfully directing the salvage operations of the S-51, and two years later won the addition of a gold star to it for salvaging the S-4.

At about this period King began to realize how great a part the air arm was destined to play in naval warfare, and, after completing the senior officers' course at the Naval War College, volunteered in 1927—he was nearly 50—for the course at Pensacola, Florida. There he qualified as an aviator, rose rapidly in the air service, and six years later was appointed Chief of the Bureau of Aeronautics as the only officer of his rank who could fly an aeroplane. Thereafter he continued for the greater part of his time to devote himself to semi-experimental aircraft investigations and did much of the original work in the laying out of the Alaskan bases. He was thus employed until 1936, when he was given command of the aircraft of the Battle Force. Then in December 1940 he was transferred to that of the Atlantic Patrol Force, and a little later promoted to full admiral. It was in this capacity that, guarding the eastern approaches of the United States and patrolling the neutrality zone, he rendered immense help to the Royal Navy by keeping a watch on every activity in the Atlantic sea-lanes.

Soon after the United States entered the war King was designated Commander-in-Chief of the United States Fleet, a post in which he succeeded Admiral Husband E. Kimmel, who had retired after Pearl Harbour. In it he was responsible directly to the President. This appointment marked a sharp break with tradition, for until then the office of Commander-in-Chief had been vested in the commander of the Pacific Fleet. Then, in March 1942, he was given the additional post of Chief of Naval Operations. In taking the oath necessary for this office he said: "It is time to toss defensive talking and thinking overboard. Our days of victories are in the making—we will win this war". With King in command there was general confidence that the air arm of the United States Navy would be used to the utmost advantage, and, in 1943, he said that the Navy's strategy and tactics had always revolved round those weapon-bearers which could hit farthest and hardest, adding that in the war then being waged those bearers were aircraft. The coordination of all striking powers was, however, a cardinal point in his faith.

Throughout the remainder of the war King remained at the head of the Navy, in which position he was also American naval representative on the Combined Chiefs of Staff. He had the reputation of being less cooperative than General Marshall [q.v.] or General Arnold and of viewing the British Fleet with a certain amount of suspicion. In fact, like many American naval officers, he viewed every other service with suspicion, not least the United States Army and Air Force. He ardently desired to win the war in the Pacific without help and, at a time when the anti-British press in America was accusing Britain of being unwilling to do her share in defeating the Japanese, Churchill* had to fight hard to be allowed to send the British Fleet to the East. It was with Admiral King, and his wish not to share the glory, that Churchill had to argue.

Much of his determination to keep the Pacific war to himself was caused by the need he felt for wiping out the memory of the disaster at Pearl Harbour. Though he may have been difficult for the British to deal with, the energy and brilliance with which he set about rebuilding the American fleet after December 1941 won him his reward. Within six months the victory at Midway had put the Japanese on the defensive, and from that time, with Admiral Nimitz* in command of the Pacific Fleet, the destruction of all enemy forces was ruthlessly pursued until the Battle of Leyte Gulf completed the process. Within three years King had built the American Navy from shattered remnants into the most powerful seaborne striking force in history. It was a masterly achievement.

When President Roosevelt created the post of Fleet Admiral at the end of 1944 King was immediately promoted to that rank—on December 17, two days after Admiral Leahy [q.v.], the President's Chief of Staff, who was the first to have the title. With the war over he retired in December 1945, and was succeeded by Admiral Nimitz. The account of King's wartime achievement, based on his reminiscences, communicated to the author, Walter Muir Whitehill, and published in 1952, is rewarding reading.

He leaves a widow, a son and six daughters.

June 26, 1956.

Frank Kingdon-Ward, O.B.E., the eminent traveller, geographer, author, and plant collector, died on April 8, 1958 at the age of 72.

He was born on November 6, 1885, the son of the late Harry Marshall Ward, F.R.S., Professor of Botany at the University of Cambridge, and was educated at St. Paul's School and Christ's College, Cambridge, where he took honours in the Natural Sciences Tripos in 1906. In the following year he accepted a short-term appointment as a school teacher in Shanghai and in 1909, as his first exploratory venture, he joined the late Malcolm P. Anderson on a journey into the interior of China. It was the forerunner of a series extending over nearly half a century. The complicated and remote mountainous regions on the borders of China, India, and Burma, with their intriguing botanical and geographical problems, fascinated him.

As a result of his studies on the distribution of the plants and animals of the area, and in spite of objections from contemporary geographers and geologists, Kingdon-Ward was a forceful supporter of the theory that the Himalayan range is prolonged north-eastwards from the loop of the Tsangpo across south-eastern Tibet and into China. The tremendous gorges which score the country from north to south over a distance of 200 miles he regarded as the eroded valleys of rivers crossing the axis of the main range. From these parts Kingdon-Ward was responsible for introducing many notable plants to gardens in Britain. He had a flair for selecting good flower forms and took great pains to mark plants in the field so that, months later when he returned for seed, he could distinguish his special choice. Rhododendrons, primulas, lilies, gentians, and poppies were Kingdon-Ward's special interest, and the wealth of species of these plants in British gardens is to a large extent due to him. His most outstanding introduction is probably the blue poppy, *Meconopsis betonicifolia,* which he collected in south-east Tibet and which is now one of the most cherished garden plants.

His record of exploratory journeys is remarkable and a tribute to his amazing sustained energy and fortitude. In all he engaged in about 25 large-scale expeditions, mostly to the border lands of south-west China and India. Until his second marriage in 1947 he preferred to travel alone, and organized his expeditions austerely, usually living frugally on the country. He records that in his fiftieth year, when he was exploring the Assam Himalaya, he lived chiefly on milk as he had done in his first year.

He did not employ professional collectors, preferring to select and prepare his own specimens, and thus he was able to give accurate and detailed descriptions of the plants. His field notes reveal keen observation, accurate botanical knowledge, and also his feeling for things of beauty. His efforts on his journeys were prodigious, and in addition to his scientific collecting he kept a voluminous diary in which he recorded day-to-day events. He wrote easily and vividly and his letters to friends were full of interest and lively comment. He had an excellent knowledge of geology which enabled him to interpret the topography of the areas he visited, and the superb illustrations to his score of travel books bear witness to his skill as a photographer.

His exceptional experience of travelling in mountainous, heavily forested country was an asset after Burma was overrun by the Japanese in the last war. Kingdon-Ward organized a jungle-survival school for training people to recognize the plants which could safely be used for food. He was also engaged to track down wrecked aircraft in the Burma-Assam-Tibet frontier areas.

In recent years his travelling had perforce been restricted to areas less rich in material of botanical and horticultural interest. Nevertheless, accompanied by his wife, he explored in Assam and Burma, discovering a number of exciting plants, including a lily which grows perched on the trunks of trees, and another species, *Lilium macklineae,* which commemorates his wife and which is now firmly established in cultivation in Britain.

On August 15, 1950, Kingdon-Ward and his wife were camped a few miles from the epicentre of one of the biggest earthquakes ever recorded in south-eastern Tibet. Mountains were shattered, rivers were choked with rocky *débris*, and the vegetation and appearance of great tracts of country changed overnight. Kingdon-Ward felt the full force of the cataclysm and had immense difficulties in reaching India. He realistically described the aftermath of this experience in the *Geographical Journal* in 1955.

Kingdon-Ward received many honours for his services to geography and horticulture. From the Royal Geographical Society he twice received the Cuthbert Peek Grant, and in 1930 was awarded the Royal Medal. The Royal Scottish Geographical Society honoured him with the award of the Livingstone Medal in 1936. He received the Veitch Memorial Medal from the Royal Horticultural Society in 1933 and in 1932 the Victoria Medal of Honour.

He was twice married, secondly in 1947 to Jean Macklin, who survives him. There were two daughters of his first marriage, which was dissolved in 1937.

April 10, 1958.

Sir Norman Kinnear, C.B., who was a Director of the British Museum (Natural History) from 1947 to 1950 and for many years a well-known ornithologist, died on his seventy-fifth birthday, August 11, 1957.

Kinnear was not academically trained in zoology, but acquired an extensive knowledge of birds, and of other vertebrates, especially those of Britain and India. As a museum official he showed himself a first-rate civil servant—hard working, courteous, and a good organizer—and his appointment as Director of the Natural History Museum was, though his tenure of the post was brief, remarkably successful. He was a sound field naturalist, and much interested in naturalists of past generations, especially Scottish. Though his health was not robust, he was active in many societies, being particularly prominent in the British Ornithologists' Union, of which he was president from 1943 to 1948.

Norman Boyd Kinnear was born on August 11, 1882, the son of C. H. G. Kinnear, an Edinburgh architect, and was educated at Edinburgh Academy and Glenalmond. From 1905 to 1907 he worked as an assistant at the Royal Scottish Museum under William Eagle Clarke. On a Dundee whaler he made a voyage to Spitzbergen where he observed and collected birds and other arctic animals for the Edinburgh museum. In 1907 he was appointed curator of the Bombay Natural History Society's Museum, and he remained there until 1919. While holding that office he became well known to all naturalists—and to many sportsmen—in India. By a special appointment he received a post in the British Museum (Natural History) in 1920; eight years later he was appointed Assistant Keeper, becoming Deputy Keeper in charge of birds in 1936. This position he continued to hold until he succeeded M. A. C. Hinton as Keeper of Zoology in 1945.

On August 11, 1947, Kinnear was due to retire on reaching the age limit. It is an open secret that many members of the staff of the Natural History Museum had then for some time felt frustrated, and that discontent was rife among them. The trustees, perhaps as a consequence, had great difficulty in finding a successor to Sir Clive Forster-Cooper, and it is believed that several eminent scientists, not connected with the museum, refused the post. The day after Kinnear became 65 it was announced that the trustees had taken the exceptional and unexpected step of appointing him Director. He himself regarded his appointment as merely temporary, but he very soon demonstrated that the expedient was well justified. The wheels began to move smoothly again, and the staff, with hardly an exception, recovered its equanimity. This was almost entirely due to Kinnear's personal qualities, and though he held the directorship for less than three years he performed during that time an exceptionally valuable service to the museum. In June 1950 he was knighted—an honour which gave great pleasure to those who had been aware of his work. He had been appointed C.B. two years earlier.

Kinnear was assistant editor of the Bombay Natural History Society's *Journal* from 1908 to

1919, and later, from 1925 to 1930, edited the *Bulletin* of the British Ornithological Club. To those publications, as to the *Ibis* and the publications of the Linnean Society and other scientific societies, he contributed a number of papers, but on the whole he wrote comparatively little and generally in collaboration. He was, nevertheless, a prominent figure in British ornithology, and to inquirers and amateurs in search of advice he was invariably kind and helpful. He was at various times a member of the council of the Zoological Society, of the Home Office Advisory Committee for the Protection of Birds, and of the Council of the National Trust.

He married, in 1913, Gwendolen Beatrice, daughter of Dr. William Millard, of Edinburgh, and they had two daughters.

August 12, 1957.

Dr. Alfred Kinsey, the biologist who became a social anthropologist, died on August 25, 1956 in hospital at Bloomington, Indiana, at the age of 62.

Alfred Charles Kinsey was born at Hoboken, New Jersey, on June 23, 1894. He received his early education at Bowdoin College and in 1919, while attending Harvard, where he gained the Sc.D. in 1920, he was awarded the Sheldon travelling fellowship. After holding teaching posts in both botany and zoology at Harvard he was appointed Assistant Professor of Zoology in the University of Indiana. He became Associate Professor in 1923 and Professor in 1929. He was in charge of a number of biological expeditions to Mexico and Central America in the 1930s and made a considerable reputation as an entomologist, being in fact one of the greatest authorities on the gall wasp.

Meanwhile in 1921 he had married Miss Clara Bracken McMillen, who was one of his pupils in biology, and they had four children, three of whom survive him. He had been married some 17 years when in 1938 he was persuaded to take a course at Indiana University which had as its object fitting students for married life. This turned his attention to problems which had not presented themselves to his mind in such an acute form before and he set out to place the investigation of sexual behaviour on a scientific basis. At first he financed a limited experiment out of his own pocket, and, the results seeming satisfactory to him, he persuaded his university, the Rockefeller Foundation, and the National Research Council to sponsor investigations on a larger scale. These bodies have since 1942 sponsored Dr. Kinsey's researches.

When in 1948 *Sexual Behaviour in the Human Male* appeared, Dr. Kinsey was hardly known outside the narrow circle of biologists, but the material of the book, based on the examination of some 6,000 individuals and presented with a wealth of statistical analysis, proved of great interest to an enormous number of people. Dr. Kinsey drew no conclusions from his wealth of material; he was content to record the facts as they had been found and he left it to others, some well and some ill informed, to place interpretations on them.

The controversy was still in full swing when in 1953 *Sexual Behaviour in the Human Female* appeared, based on a slightly smaller sample than its male counterpart.

It is unlikely that Dr. Kinsey's death will seriously impair the work of the Institute for Sex Research, which recently moved into a new building in Indiana University. When the controversy had died down it will probably be seen that no harm but much good will have resulted in bringing the spirit of scientific inquiry to subjects which have for long been the happy hunting ground of obscurantists.

August 27, 1956.

Major-General Sir Howard Karl Kippenberger, K.B.E., C.B., D.S.O., whose gift for leadership and tactical skill brought him promotion from commander of a battalion to that of a division in two years in the late war, died on May 5, 1957 in Wellington, New Zealand.

He was born in 1897 and was educated at Christchurch Boys' High School in New Zealand. At the outbreak of the War of 1914-18 he was only 17, but before the end he had fought as a private soldier and non-commissioned officer in the New Zealand Division and had been wounded. After the war he studied law but gave much of his leisure to the Territorial Army.

In 1939 he was coming to the end of his period of command of a Territorial battalion. At 42 he felt that a younger man might be preferred to himself to command one of the battalions of the brigade raised in New Zealand as the first echelon of the 2nd New Zealand Division, but Kippenberger got the job. Much of his active service was spent in command of a brigade, though active service is rather too mild a word to describe the bitter fighting, the gruelling soldiering which the New Zealanders experienced in one campaign after another.

Kippenberger, a splendid man of arms, was also a reflective one, and his reflections recollected in tranquillity, though not in themselves entirely tranquil, were published in 1949 under the title of *Infantry Brigadier.* His powers had drawn him steadily upward and he was commander of the 2nd New Zealand Division before Cassino in March 1944, when by cruel misfortune he stepped on a mine and as a result he lost both his feet.

He won a D.S.O. in 1941 and was awarded a Bar to it in 1943. He was appointed C.B. and C.B.E. in 1944 and was promoted K.B.E. in 1948. He was editor-in-chief of the New Zealand War Histories.

He married in 1922 Ruth Isobel, daughter of Joseph Flynn, of Lyttelton, New Zealand.

[A tribute followed this obituary on the same day].

May 6, 1957.

The death of the **Right Rev. K. E. Kirk,** D.D., Bishop of Oxford, on June 8, 1954, was a serious loss to the Church of England.

A brilliant scholar, a divine uniting broad-mindedness with intense conviction, and a man of most attractive personality, he gained a powerful influence on the life of the Church. Specially notable was the knowledge of young people which he showed when taking Confirmations.

The Oxford diocese contains a large number of important schools, including Eton, Wellington, Radley, Bradfield, and the Imperial Service College, and nothing could have been more effective than the Bishop's method of gaining the confidence of schoolboys. For many years he was a Fellow and latterly president of the Woodard Corporation, and he was a life governor of Marlborough College. Remarkable also was his power of getting on easy terms with the village folk of his diocese. By every class he will be profoundly mourned.

Kenneth Escott Kirk, only surviving son of the late F. H. Kirk, director of Samuel Osborne and Co. of Sheffield, was born at Sheffield on February 21, 1886. Educated at Sheffield Royal Grammar School, he went up to St. John's College, Oxford, in 1904 as an Exhibitioner. He gained a First in Classical Moderations in 1906, and a First in *Lit. Hum.* in 1908. He did not remain in Oxford, but threw in his lot with the University of London, becoming Assistant to the Professor of Philosophy at University College in 1909 and Warden of its Hall at Ealing in 1910. In 1911 he took his M.A. degree and went to Cuddesdon to prepare for ordination. Next year he was ordained deacon by Archbishop William Temple, then Archbishop of York, and was licensed to the curacy of the colliery parish of Denaby Main.

In 1913 Kirk was ordained priest by the same archbishop, won the Denyer and Johnson Theological Scholarship at Oxford, and was elected to a tutorship at Keble. Then came the 1914-18 War. Kirk was a temporary Chaplain to the Forces from 1914 to 1919. He suffered from the effects of gas, and they injured his health in all his subsequent years. He remained Tutor of Keble till 1922, being also Fellow of Magdalen from 1919. In 1922 he was elected Fellow and Lecturer of Trinity College, Oxford, and was appointed by Archbishop Davidson a Six Preacher in Canterbury Cathedral. By this time he had become known as a particularly good man of affairs as well as a scholar, and various university appointments fell to him. He was appointed a Select Preacher in 1925, and an Examiner in the Theological Honour School next year.

Kirk had made his name as an authority in the difficult study of moral theology by a book which quickly went into a second edition. He was appointed University Reader in the subject in 1927. At once a student and a most popular and devoted priest, Dr. Kirk (he took his B.D. in 1922, and became D.D. in 1926) was one of the ablest and most hard-worked men in Oxford. He was a first-rate preacher, he was a capital lecturer, and he gave himself without stint to a multitude of good causes. In 1933 he was appointed to the Chair of Pastoral and Moral Theology, which carried with it a canonry at Christ Church; he was the obvious man for the Professorship. On the resignation of Dr. T. B. Strong Dr. Kirk was appointed, amid almost universal acclaim, to the bishopric of Oxford, and was consecrated on St. Andrew's Day, 1937. He had just accepted the Provostship of the Corporation of St. Mary and St. Nicolas, Lancing—*i.e.* the Woodard Schools in the South—and he retained the office with his bishopric until 1945.

He quickly decided to give up occupation of the Bishop's palace at Cuddesdon, which he considered too remote, and to make his headquarters in Oxford itself, a policy to which he owed much of the success that was his during his tenure of the see. Hardly more than a year after his enthronement he contracted laryngitis and while he was recovering was again laid low with pneumonia, complicated by phlebitis. A prolonged convalescence was brightened by the appearance in July 1939 of a volume of essays prepared under his direction and entitled *The Study of Theology*.

While longing for the unity of Christendom, as all good Christians must, he had little sympathy for undenominational services in which several sects could take part, holding that this was merely to attack the symptoms and not the disease of disunity. His defence of the policy of heavy bombing of German industrial targets in 1944, on the ground that the war would thus be shortened, caused some comment, but his views were echoed by many leaders both inside and outside the Church of England and were soundly based on moral grounds.

In 1947 he published a scholarly little book on the Church dedications of the Oxford diocese, which has already stimulated a good deal of study in this neglected field of research, but his busy life as a bishop precluded his wholehearted participation in the scholarship which had distinguished him as Regius Professor. Nevertheless, while he was able to write little himself, he directed the work of others with tact and skill and the book of essays entitled *The Apostolic Ministry*, which also appeared in 1947, is a monument to his sanity and scholarship, as is also *The Coherence of Christian Doctrine*, which appeared three years later.

The Bishop married, in 1921, Beatrice, second daughter of the late Judge Radcliffe, K.C.; they had one son and three daughters. The death of his wife in 1934 was a terrible blow to him.

June 9, 1954.

Lord Kirkwood, who will be best remembered as David Kirkwood, for many years Labour member for the Dumbarton Burghs, died on April 16, 1955 in hospital at Glasgow at the age of 82.

The news will be received with real sorrow by members of all parties at Westminster. When the Clydesiders first burst upon the House, this sturdy, fiery man with the tremendous voice was perhaps the stormiest petrel of them all. But it was not long before his passionate sincerity and his knowledge of working-class conditions, coupled with his genuine friendliness and good nature, in spite of scenes and suspensions, made a deep impression, and as time toned down something of his vehemence while he lost none of his personality, he became one of the notable "characters" of the House. In recent years he had made few speeches, but he was diligent in attendance. As a mellowed veteran of his party and a man of warm friendliness he was held in affectionate respect by all. Sometimes he would bark an interruption at Sir Winston Churchill*; and nothing surprised new members more than to hear these two address each other across the floor of the House as "Winston" and "David". After his elevation to the peerage in 1951, he waited nearly three months before making his maiden speech in the House of Lords, and then made it clear that he caught the ear of that House as he had so long engaged the ear of the House of Commons.

The Right Hon. David Kirkwood, First Baron Kirkwood, of Bearsden, in the county of Dunbarton, was born on July 8, 1872, the son of a labourer who never earned more than 30s. a week in his life. David Kirkwood went to work at Beardmore's, the great Parkhead engineering firm, and became a craftsman to his finger-tips. Against his will he was forced into the position of a shop steward. There arose a strong mutual respect, almost affection, between him and the late Lord Invernairn, then Sir William Beardmore, although they often fought each other. The 1914 strike for higher wages by the Clydeside engineers led to a quarrel with the union itself, as did the passing of the Munitions Act, which forbade engineers to leave the works at which they were employed or to seek work elsewhere. This was an outrage to Kirkwood's Scottish pride and sense of personal freedom, and he fought it valiantly. He was anything but a pacifist, and did all he could to increase the production of munitions. The strike itself he conducted with so much attention to constitutional methods as to lose him the confidence of many of his supporters.

Early in 1916 he was arrested with a number of his fellow shop stewards, deported from his native Parkhead district, and imprisoned in Edinburgh Castle on the charge of organizing the strike at Parkhead. In May 1917 there was a laconic announcement: "The Ministry of Munitions has decided to request the Scottish Command to allow the Clyde deportees to return to their homes". After his release he set about proving the bad faith of the commissioners for the Ministry of Munitions, who, he said, had laid the seeds of having organized the strike. Kirkwood contested the Dumbarton Burghs Council in 1919. Some months before the general election of 1922 he won great local prestige, as Secretary of the Scottish Labour Housing Association, by his persistence and success in fighting rent cases for the unemployed, so that he became known as the "Tenants' K.C." No wonder that he was triumphantly elected.

In 1935 Kirkwood published *My Life of Revolt,* a deeply interesting autobiography which, belying the title, was much more a catalogue of his affections, for the British Empire, for Scotland, for the poet Burns, for pride of craft, for his friends, for his enemies, for Stanley Baldwin, and for the writer of the foreword, Sir Winston Churchill. He gave a vivid account of his struggles in the House, of his gradual parting from his hero, Ramsay MacDonald, and of the Zinovieff letter, and the general strike. He was ungrudging in his appreciation of the men against whom he fought; of Lloyd George alone was he even slightly harsh in his judgment.

Kirkwood was for 12 years a member of the National Council of the I.L.P. In Parliament he was very persistent about the "Stone of Destiny", which was brought by Edward I from Scotland, the theft of which from Westminster Abbey by Scottish Nationalists was a nine days' wonder. But the achievement on which he looked back with the greatest satisfaction was the part which he played in bringing about the building of the liner Queen Mary on Clydeside; in this he spoke not only for his constituents but for the whole of Scotland, and his speeches made a profound impression on the House. His account in his book of the dead shipbuilding yards, the decaying homes and shops and streets, is most moving.

He married in 1899 Elizabeth, daughter of Robert Smith, of Parkhead, Glasgow, who survives him together with two sons and two daughters of the marriage. The heir to the family honours is the Hon. David Kirkwood, the third but elder surviving son, who was born in 1903 and married in 1931 Eileen Grace, daughter of the late T. H. Boalch. There are two sons of the marriage.

April 22, 1955.

Fred Kitchen, whose cry of triumph as the bailiffs' man, "Meredith, we're in!" echoed for years in every music-hall, died on April 1, 1951 in a nursing home at Hampton Hill, Middlesex, at the age of 78.

Descended from a family connected with the stage since the early years of the last century, he was born on June 15, 1872, and made his first stage appearance a few months afterwards when he was carried on to the stage of the old Prince's Theatre, Portsmouth, by his father for the christening scene in *The Dumb Man of Manchester.* He had already appeared in pantomime at the Aquarium Theatre, Westminster, when, while still quite a lad, he made an extensive tour of Europe and North Africa. He had thus gained valuable experience in playing to very varied audiences when he joined Fred Karno, a partnership which lasted nearly 50 years and brought laughter to innumerable music-hall audiences.

Kitchen's first big chance came when he was playing the small part of a pageboy in *His Majesty's Guests,* one of Fred Karno's earlier sketches. The chief comedian had suddenly to be replaced and Kitchen played the part with great success at the Princess's Theatre, Glasgow. Thenceforward he was one of the stars of Fred Karno's company and took a larger and larger part not only in acting but in devising the innumerable sketches presented by the troupe. The famous catchphrase was born, apparently, on a railway platform when Kitchen was thinking over possible names for his fellow bailiff. His eye caught the advertisement of a biscuit manufacturer at the psychological moment.

Like so many comedians, Kitchen harboured an ambition to play in serious parts, but after one unsuccessful attempt he wisely resumed his comic livery. The fact is that the patrons of the old music-hall liked their favourites to be familiar. Departure from routine was reprobated, and Sam Mayo, for instance, was booed off the stage once for daring to appear without his red nose; nevertheless, when once a star had established his particular set of conventions he could do no wrong, and Kitchen, with his lisp and peculiar gait, could keep a large audience wiping away tears of laughter for five minutes on end.

He retired from the stage during the course of 1945 and, except for his own benefit, which took place at the Winter Garden Theatre towards the end of that year, had hardly entered a theatre since, for what little he saw of the modern music-hall he did not like.

His wife died during the 1939-45 war, but a son carries on the family theatrical tradition of more than a century.

April 2, 1951.

The sudden death at Zürich on January 27, 1956 at the age of 65 of **Dr. Erich Kleiber** robs the world of one of its greatest operatic conductors. In Britain he rendered services of great value to the Royal Opera House at a vital stage in its new development as a national, all-the-year-round opera following on its reorganization in 1946.

A Viennese by birth, Kleiber combined the tradition of the classics with an interest in the modern experimental developments of music after the 1914-18 War. His production of Berg's *Wozzeck* at the Berlin State Opera in 1925 made history. Political events in Germany made him a wanderer after 1935, and wherever he went he was both traditionalist and pioneer. He was thus the first to produce Beethoven's *Missa Solennis* and Strauss's *Die Frau ohne Schatten* in South America. He became an Argentine citizen and lived chiefly in Buenos Aires from 1936 onwards, where he found, in the intervals of extensive European tours, plenty of work not only at the Teatro Colon but also as an orchestral conductor all over the South American continent.

He was born on August 5, 1890, in Vienna, but went to Prague for his education at the university and the conservatoire. His first post was as conductor at the Darmstadt Opera, and by a series of quick promotions, through Barmen-Elberfeld, Düsseldorf, and Mannheim, he reached at the age of 33 the top of the tree as Director of the Berlin State Opera, where he stayed till 1935. Here his rigorous standards and go-ahead policy brought him a world-wide reputation. He returned to his old post only a year or so before he died, but soon left it as he found his freedom too much restricted for his benevolently autocratic disposition. Of the benevolence in his autocracy many of the singers and players at Covent Garden can testify, for his concern to help them in technical or artistic difficulties quickly established their confidence.

It was indeed a remarkable thing to observe his decisive down-beat which launched *Der Rosenkavalier* on a performance about which from that moment there could be no flicker of doubt. He was complete master of an opera as a whole and into his conception every detail fitted. His performances of *Elektra, Wozzeck,* and *The Queen of Spades* at Covent Garden were memorable in this respect in the seasons from 1950 to 1953.

Before his return to Berlin in 1954 he spent much time as a visiting and festival conductor all over Europe. He had directed the London Philharmonic Orchestra for a season in 1948 to its advantage and subsequently appeared in concert work in every European capital. After his second departure from Berlin he made his centre in Zürich. His career is one more illustration of Germany's self-inflicted loss being the world's gain at the cost of exile to the individual musician.

January 30, 1956.

Melanie Klein died in a London hospital in her 79th year on September 22, 1960.

Her name may not be widely known to the general public and is only gradually gaining recognition in psychiatric and psychological circles. Yet her work revolutionized psychoanalysis and has directly or indirectly exerted a profound influence on psychiatry, psychology, child upbringing and infant care, and more remotely on such disciplines as sociology, anthropology, and art criticism.

Melanie Klein was born in 1882 in Vienna of Jewish parents. She was trained in psychoanalysis by Ferenczi and Abraham, and she started practising in the Berlin Psychoanalytical Society. Soon her interest centred on the then hardly explored possibilities of child analysis and in 1921 she published her first paper. She gradually evolved a technique in child analysis which gave her access to the deepest layers of the child's mind. She provided the child with small toys and used his free play and spontaneous communications in the same way in which associations are used in psychoanalysis of adults. Both her technique and her findings provoked strong criticism, even from her psychoanalytical colleagues. First of all her technique aroused opposition, since she used Freud's interpretative technique without any concession; she would give neither advice nor reassurance nor any educational guidance.

She used this technique in her work with children, however small, and the youngest was under three years old. Her aim was to analyse the child unconscious and by rendering it conscious to help the child to integrate various aspects of his personality. Secondly, her findings were found shocking and therefore unbelievable; even to those who had come to accept Freud's views about child sexuality Melanie Klein's dicoveries came as a shock. Freud, in analysing adults, had established that many of their feelings, anxieties, and phantasies had their roots in childhood. Analysing children, Melanie Klein discovered that many of the processes described by Freud had their roots already in earliest infancy, for instance, in a patient aged two and a half she found evidence of a superego and an Oedipus complex which had already a long and complex history. She also recognized that aggression and sadism play in a child's mind a role still greater than had been assumed by Freud. The discoveries she made in child analysis enriched her understanding of adults.

In 1926 Ernest Jones [q.v.], one of the first to recognize the potential greatness of her work, had invited her to come to England and work within the British Psychoanalytical Society, and it is in London that she spent most of her working life and did her greatest work—for instance, her study of the depressive and paranoid-schizoid illness and their origins in infancy. In other psychoanalytical societies her work is often referred to as "the English school", not quite correctly, since only some of the analysts of the British Psychoanalytical Society were trained and taught by her and used her technique, though there is no doubt that the whole of the British society is deeply influenced by her work.

To work with Melanie Klein and to come into contact with her was an experience leaving a deep impact. The power and acuity of her intellect had strength and integrity, her originality and abundant creativeness left one in no doubt that one was in touch with an outstanding personality.

September 23, 1960.

Olga Knipper, the celebrated Russian actress and widow of Anton Chekhov, died in Moscow on March 22, 1959. She was 90.

Chekhov first saw her in 1898 at a rehearsal at the Art Theatre of *The Seagull.* In 1900, when he was at Yalta and could not visit Moscow, the company came to him and acted *Uncle Vanya.* The stay turned from a simple friendly visit to a triumphal pageant for Chekhov. As a correspondent of *The Times* wrote later: "Life—cleverest of impresarios—made the brightness of those days still more vivid through love. All Yalta knew that Chekhov was in love with Olga. People whispered about it, shook their heads, were delighted or envious. They watched the lovers and marvelled at the contrast between them. There was a kind of feline sleekness about the actress and something insinuating in the dark, sparkling eyes, the fair skinned, irregular face. . . . Chekhov was tall and thin and his smile was one of gentle irony. . . ."

They were married in May 1901, just over three years before the Russian author died. They were much apart: she continued with her career at his request and desire, but he was devoted to her. Olga Knipper had only a fleeting experience of Britain—Mrs. Pankhurst [q.v.] made an indelible impression on her—but she had acted in America. She played Gertrude in Gordon Craig's* 1911 production of *Hamlet* in Moscow, and she and Craig corresponded until her death.

In 1926 appeared Constance Garnett's translation of Chekhov's letters to Olga Knipper, the first written in June 1899, and the last shortly before he died in 1904, the most intimate letters Chekhov wrote and perhaps the most revealing.

Until her death Olga Knipper remained a considerable figure in Russia, admired and respected, and, indeed, something of an object of pilgrimage by foreigners.

March 23, 1959.

Sir Geoffrey Knox, K.C.M.G., who died in Tobago on April 6, 1958 at the age of 74, was chairman of the Governing Commission of the Saar from 1932 to 1935 and later Ambassador to Brazil.

Geoffrey George Knox was born in Sydney, New South Wales, on March 11, 1884, the son of George Knox and grandson of Sir Edward Knox. When he was still a youth his parents took him to England where his education was completed. In 1906, after a competitive examination, he was appointed a student interpreter in the Levant and two years later was promoted to assistant. In 1910 he became acting consul at Kermanshah and in the following year went in a similar capacity to Shiraz. In 1912 he was again promoted to be vice-consul at Cairo, and was acting consul there in 1913 and 1914. After terms of duty at Salonika and Cavalla he was granted a temporary honorary commission as a lieutenant in the R.N.V.R. for duty with the British Aegean Squadron.

Knox remained with the Navy until the autumn of 1918 and then resumed his position in the Levant. In 1919 he was employed at Bucharest and was acting consul-general for some months. Then, having been certified as a second secretary in the diplomatic service, he was attached in 1920 to the British High Commission at Constantinople. Promoted first secretary in 1923, he was transferred to Berlin where in the following year he acted for a short time as chargé d'affaires. Two years later he returned to Constantinople.

After a period of unemployment Knox was recalled to the Foreign Office as a first secretary in 1930 and was promoted in 1931 Counsellor of Embassy at Madrid.

Then in the following spring he was seconded for service as chairman of the Saar Governing Commission and given the rank of minister plenipotentiary in the diplomatic service. It was, from the first, a difficult position and grew more difficult still as the date of the Saar plebiscite approached. In 1934 a request of his that the League of Nations should approve the recruitment of a neutral police force to superintend the plebiscite met with specially hostile criticism in Berlin. The Governing Commission had, nevertheless, displayed a strict impartiality, to which their action in suspending the publication of two newspapers of the left for insulting Hitler in articles and caricatures bore evidence. Knox set himself firmly against the intrusion of Nazi terrorism into the Saar.

Early in 1935, after the plebiscite had been held, the Saar became German once again, and Knox's invidious task was done. It had been admirably performed in spite of his own indifferent health and of the venomous and defamatory criticism with which he had been assailed. He had distinguished himself particularly in upholding civil rights throughout the territory committed to his charge. In March he was promoted to K.C.M.G.

Knox's next appointment was that of Envoy Extraordinary and Minister Plenipotentiary at Budapest, a position which he filled with characteristic ability until in September 1939 he was promoted Ambassador Extraordinary and Plenipotentiary at Rio de Janeiro. He remained there until the beginning of 1942, when he retired. In the following year his book *The Last Peace and the Next* appeared.

Knox, who was unmarried, combined a philosophical disposition and a sense of satirical humour—he revered both Gibbon and Voltaire—with a sovereign objectivity and unusual force of character. He was a collector of rare books and first editions, and was fond of driving high-powered cars in which he used to do the journey from the Saar to Geneva in a day.

April 10, 1958.

The Right Rev. Monsignor Ronald A. Knox, who died at Mells, Somerset, on August 24, 1957 at the age of 69, was the wittiest churchman in England since Sydney Smith; he was as earnest as he was witty and as devoted as he was diverting.

Born into the purple of the Anglican Church, the son of a great Bishop of Manchester, educated at Eton and Balliol, at the peak of its Edwardian brilliance, converted later to Roman Catholicism, he moved, throughout his life, in the inner circles of the religious and intellectual élite. He was never—he never sought to be—a public figure. But to men of all creeds and of none, who delight in a personality that combines simple unaffected faith with a brain that could cut like a razor, he was regarded as one of the individually great in his generation.

His powers matured early; long before he came down from Oxford he was a legendary figure. Such figures were more common then than they have since become. Ronnie Knox towered head and shoulders above almost all of them. Unlike many of them, he stood up to the test of cold print read by those who did not know him, and so had not fallen for his charm as a companion and in conversation.

His natural setting was the country houses of his friends, Beaufort, Aldenham, Mells, where he could live the regular life he loved. It was one secret of his great and steady output, written and spoken—he never spoke without holding his personally typed manuscript in his hand—that throughout his life he lived in the country so much, and avoided multifarious social life. He never lost a certain shyness with strangers; among close friends he never sought to dominate the conversation or to hold forth. Almost diffidently, pulling at his inseparable pipe, he would contribute his reflective, highly original ideas. One evening, picking up *The Times,* he remarked: "I have always wanted to write a letter to the Editor, answering all the letters of the previous day".

As a satirist and a deeply sincere defender of what he believed to be true, he handled English verse as easily as prose. He dared to make his points by parodying Dryden himself, and by catching the style of the classic masters of pamphleteering. The persistence of his inherited social preferences was marked. They went side by side with depth of spirituality and extraordinary industry, both of which were harnessed in the gigantic task, successfully performed, of translating the Bible. His keen interest in scripture was inherited from his Anglican and Evangelical parentage. He began and ended, as did his brother Wilfred, a finer New Testament scholar, as a student of the Bible.

Ronald Knox was no recluse. He was significant for his Church in England not only because of what he wrote, but because of his influence on individuals, and particularly on those who were capable of influencing other people. For 12 years he was chaplain to the Roman Catholic undergraduates at Oxford. Friendships established there became intimacies for life. No matter how long or distant the physical separation, he had the gift of picking up the conversation where it left off. Some ardent and fastidious minds were converted. Later in life, from Aldenham or Mells, he would make his way to London to preach at the marriages or to christen the children of these his parishoners. Only a few years before his death he travelled over a large part of tropical Africa where others live scattered in veldt and bush.

The tone at the Old Palace, the chaplain's residence, was academic rather than ecclesiastical. Mass was celebrated austerely without incense, acolyte, or organ. The appeal was to the mind, not to the senses. This suited contemporary Oxford.

Ronald Arbuthnott Knox was born on February 17, 1888, fourth of the brilliant sons of Dr. Edmund Arbuthnott Knox, Bishop of Manchester. His mother, a daughter of Dr. Valpy French, Bishop of Lahore, died when he was four years old. He spent his early boyhood with relatives in a country rectory, where he was deeply affected by an atmosphere of learning and simple piety, to which he paid a moving tribute in later life.

By gaining a first Eton scholarship he began a series of scholastic successes that culminated in a first in Greats at Oxford. He won a first

Balliol scholarship, the Hertford in 1907 and the Ireland and Craven in 1908, and he became President of the Oxford Union, which he continued to delight for nearly 50 years as has no other ex-President. As an undergraduate his reputation as a wit became almost embarrassing, since any anonymous epigram or parody that came into currency was attributed immediately to his pen. At the same time his scholastic brilliance was attracting attention throughout the University and he alone, perhaps, was surprised by the offer, on taking his degree in 1910, of a fellowship at Trinity College. He took Holy Orders in 1912 and was then appointed Chaplain of Trinity.

The beginning of his chaplaincy was at the height of the controversy over Modernism in the Church of England that was marked by the publication of *Foundations.* The most spirited reply came from Knox in a book to which he gave the characteristic title *Some Loose Stones.* The book, a notable contribution to religious controversy, established his reputation as a man of letters and an accomplished adversary. With the publication in 1914 of *Reunion All Round,* the idea was expressed that, like Newman, he was turning his steps from Trinity in the direction of Rome. But his resignation in 1917 was not so much with the immediate intention of entering the Roman Church as from the feeling that he should retire for a time to reconsider his position, particularly in the matter of Authority. Decision came later in the same year when he visited Farnborough Abbey and was received into the Roman Catholic Church by the late Abbot Cabrol. In 1919 he was ordained by Cardinal Bourne at St. Edmund's College, Ware, and accepted as his first preaching engagement an invitation to the pulpit of St. Aloysius', Oxford.

The link with Oxford and in particular with Trinity was broken only temporarily by his new allegiance. From 1926, until in 1939 he began his new translation of the Bible, he was chaplain to Roman Catholic students at the University. In 1941 his election as an Honorary Fellow at Trinity (which had paid a like honour to Newman) gave him more pleasure than many another of the public tributes he received. He was appointed a Domestic Prelate to Pope Pius XI in 1936 and in 1951 he became a Protonotary Apostolic *ad instar.* Five years later he was nominated as a member of the Pontifical Roman Academy of Theology, then recently revived by Pope Pius XII [q.v.]. The honour was particularly notable since membership of the Academy is restricted to 40, of whom 20 are resident in Rome and only 10 of whom are nominated from nations outside Italy.

His translation of the Bible was commissioned from him by the Roman Catholic Hierarchy more on account of his classical training and mastery of English prose than because of any claim to qualification as a Biblical scholar. The translation was from the Vulgate, though in places where that text is plainly wrong he sometimes preferred the Greek texts, or in the case of the Old Testament the Hebrew or the Greek of the Septuagint. He was criticized for not admitting to his departures from the Vulgate of the New Testament when his version was published in 1946; his preface to the Old Testament (1949) was more explanatory.

He aimed, he wrote, "at a sort of timeless English that would reproduce the idiom of our day without its neologisms". In this he was eminently successful and his version far surpasses any other modern translation in dignity and clarity. The task occupied him for the greater part of 10 years, which he spent in virtual seclusion at Aldenham Park, which had been placed at his disposal by Lord Acton.

Almost immediately the war came and the Convent of the Assumption was evacuated from Kensington to Aldenham, and he found himself acting as chaplain to a girls' school. He adapted himself with his usual virtuosity and two of his most popular books, *The Mass in Slow Motion* and *The Creed in Slow Motion,* came from this work, which never deflected him from the timetable he had set himself and kept for the Bible.

The most considerable, and by no means the least diverting, of his other books was *Enthusiasm: A Chapter in the History of Religion* (1950). He had pondered long and read widely for this study of manifestations of "ultra-supernaturalism", from the early Church at Corinth to the extravagances of modern American revivalists. With gentle penetration he examined the departures from orthodoxy of the Montanist heretics, Jansenists, Quietists, George Fox, John Wesley, Madame Guyon, and many others who took inspiration for their guide.

The book is a contribution to the psychology as well as the history of religion. The chief mark of his apologetical writings, such as *The Belief of Catholics* (1927) or his letters to [Sir] Arnold Lunn* (the correspondence was published in 1932 under the title *Difficulties*), was clarity and persuasive skill; of his sermons and addresses, precision in the choice of words. Whether expounding the Mass to schoolgirls or delivering a funeral oration on Hilaire Belloc [q.v.], he spoke with a directness and elegance of diction that made fresh the familiar. His last appearance was to give the Romanes lecture at Oxford on translation in June 1957—an engagement fulfilled by a man far from well with unwavering resolution.

It was this same rare sensitivity to language that enabled him to bring off so many *tours de force* of parody and pastiche: his *Barchester Pilgrimage,* his skit on the Shakespearians in which he sought to prove by cryptogram that *In Memoriam* was written by Queen Victoria, or his parody of the German school of Higher Criticism at work on Sherlock Holmes; and, best of all, *Let Dons Delight,* imaginary conversations at the high table of Simon Magus College, Oxford, at which the learned occupants, at intervals through three and a half centuries, discuss the burning topics of their day with all their prejudices about them, oblivious of the final judgments of posterity. The book evokes with delicacy the changing styles of speech and argument and the changing intellectual preoccupations of the University.

He also turned his hand to detective stories, whose ingenious situations were never quite matched by the liveliness of the characters; to broadcasting, which was an art he thoroughly understood—so much so that in a burlesque of a news programme he once persuaded some of his listeners that London really was succumbing to mob rule; to articles, acrostics, and epigrams in English, Greek, and Latin. Chesterton was near the mark when he imagined the surprise of Mary Queen of Scots,

"To see wit, wisdom and the Popish creed
Cluster and sparkle in the name of Knox".

These were his accomplishments, of which the public was aware. Behind them was a serenity of spirit born of a humble love for God and a profound compassion for His creatures.

August 26, 1957.

Theodore Komisarjevsky, whose stage productions of Russian and English classics were sometimes extravagantly praised and sometimes equally extravagantly attacked, died at Darien, Connecticut, at the age of 71, on April 17, 1954.

Medium in height, with a pale face enlivened by a pair of inscrutable brown eyes, he was a formidable man under whom to rehearse, in spite of his quiet voice and restrained though effective gesture. Obviously sincere, thoughtful, and cultured, he never allowed slipshod work to pass even though momentarily he had appeared not to notice it. He had none of the extravagance so often expected of men of the theatre, but to him the theatre was in a very real sense a reflection of a particular civilization, and it was in this realization that his strength lay.

The son of the first tenor of the St. Petersburg Opera and Princess Kourzevich, he was born in Venice in 1882. He was educated at St. Petersburg University and at the Imperial Institute of Architecture, a training which was evident in his stage settings. He first appeared as a producer for the stage in Russia in 1907, and after working for a time with the Moscow Grand State Theatre of Opera and Ballet he went to London to produce opera for Sir Thomas Beecham* in 1919, a partnership of which the outstanding outcome was the magnificent production of Borodin's opera *Prince Igor.*

One of Komisarjevsky's stories of his early days in England producing opera was that, to his horror, he was expected to mount *Parsifal* with only two days for rehearsal. During the first performance he stood in the wings on the prompt side whispering instructions. Only those on his side of the stage could hear, and on the other side chaos ensued. For his later productions he insisted on much—in the opinion of many of the actors who took part in the plays too much—preparation, but the results always justified the immense amount of work involved. This was particularly the case in his productions of the plays of Gogol and Tchekhov, many of them at the famous Barnes

Theatre under the auspices of Philip Ridgeway [q.v.].

Many, for instance, who found the turntable in the middle of the stage in Komisarjevsky's production of *The Government Inspector* disconcerting at first, realized before the evening was over that it had played a notable part in reinforcing the farcical element in that uproarious comedy. Similarly, the great beauty, even if it appeared a trifle mannered, of the groupings in *The Three Sisters* was clearly the result of a deep sensibility to the atmosphere of Tchekhov's most poetic play.

Komisarjevsky became a British subject in 1932, and in the same year began to produce Shakespeare's plays for the Stratford Festival. His productions there again displayed his sensibility to the many-sided genius of Shakespeare, though he seemed more at home with the difficult *King Lear* than with the more readily appreciated *Twelfth Night* and *As You Like It*.

Apart from the great classics he was responsible for the admirable production of *Escape Me Never*, for *The Boy David, Magnolia Street, Musical Chairs*, and many other such pieces. He wrote and produced a remarkable interpretation of Dostoevsky's *The Brothers Karamazov*, under the title *The Brass Paperweight*, adapted Schnitzler's *Fräulein Elsa* for the stage, and was part author of *Russian Bank*, produced in New York. He had visited the United States in 1922 at the invitation of the Theatre Guild. In 1934 he again went to the United States and stayed there until his death.

His early architectural training was manifested not only in his stage settings, for he designed the interiors of a number of new cinemas and theatres in England and the United States. His many sided nature was also expressed in a number of admirable books on theatrical subjects, sometimes autobiographical and always entertaining, of which *Myself and the Theatre, The Costume of the Theatre*, and *The Theatre and a Changing Civilization* are the best known.

April 19, 1954.

Sir Alexander Korda, who died at his home in London on January 23, 1956 at the age of 62, was one of the leading figures in the film industry and signally contributed to its development not only in Britain but in the United States and on the Continent as well.

Born at Turkeve, Hungary, on September 16, 1893, he was the eldest of three brothers, whose father, a land agent, died when he was 14. He at once assumed the role of breadwinner for the family, and became a teacher in order to earn money. His early ambition, however, was to be a newspaper man, and before he reached the age of 20 he joined the *Fuggetlen Magyarorszag* as a reporter. He made rapid progress, was soon a staff writer, and eventually a night editor. The advent of the animated picture, however, captured his imagination, and in spite of the inevitable crudeness which marred its infancy he quickly gauged its possibilities, forsook journalism, and became a picture-maker.

His first venture was on a humble scale. Renting a small, dilapidated building in a suburb of Budapest, he bought a camera, and, unaided, produced films, the scripts for which he wrote himself. Other pioneers were also at work, and, seeking greater opportunities, he went to Vienna, where he obtained a post as director of the then flourishing firm of Sascha Films.

His first picture, *The Prince and the Pauper*, created a new standard in production, and was a conspicuous success. A bold experimenter, with a highly developed artistic sense, he paid particular attention to the improvement of technique, and his patient study of the mechanical processes involved brought its reward. He next went to Berlin, where he directed a number of pictures for the Ufa studios. By that time, however, Hollywood had became the chief centre of film production in the world, and Korda, whose fame had reached the founders of the American industry, was soon demonstrating his capacity as a director. But though his services were in constant demand by some of the leading companies their lack of appreciation of his individual talent quickly reduced him to despair. Finally he decided to leave America, intending never to return. He threw up his job, and, with only a few dollars in his pocket, returned to Europe accompanied by his wife, Maria Farkas, whom he had married in 1919, and his young son Peter.

Continental film companies were by no means prospering, lack of financial resources, combined with high costs, being handicaps from which most of them suffered. Eventually, however, Korda and a few friends, among them Lajos Biro and Steven Pallos, formed a company in Paris, but almost before it began to function he was offered and accepted a post with the Paramount company to direct European versions of their pictures.

This proved to be the turning point of his career, for he was asked to go to London, and at the Elstree studios of the firm he made the film *Service for Ladies*, which was acclaimed by the critics as a triumph and made him famous. That was in 1931, and within a few weeks he founded London Film Productions, with its distinctive trademark of "Big Ben", and from then on the name of Korda meant something in the film world. From well-equipped studios at Isleworth and Denham—Korda founded the latter centre which later became a film colony—were issued many pictures which were hailed as màsterpieces, and established British prestige far and wide. In 1935 Korda became associated with United Artists, and was elected to the board.

Among the outstanding films then made under his guidance were *The Private Life of Henry VIII, The Shape of Things to Come, The Man Who Could Work Miracles, The Four Feathers*, and many others which created a new standard of excellence in the British industry, and caused some misgiving in Hollywood. Even to name his successes which are still being shown in many parts of the world would take up a good deal of space. Suffice it to say that pictures bearing the stamp of Korda have done much to enable the British film industry not only to survive, but to become the most powerful rival of Hollywood.

The outbreak of war in 1939 had a serious effect on Korda's career, for it meant the end of the Denham régime, and, having made *The Lion Has Wings* for the British Government (a miracle of expeditious production), he travelled almost continuously in the next few years between Britain and America. In 1942 he was knighted for his services to the film industry, and in the following year he amalgamated his old company, London Films, with the Metro-Goldwyn-Mayer British Studios, Ltd., and became chairman, managing director, and production supervisor of the new undertaking. When the end of the war came he severed his connexion with "Metro", and once more became head of London Film Productions, securing the cooperation of some of the most eminent producers and film artists in the world. Among his later successes were *The Third Man, Fallen Idol, The Wooden Horse, The Sound Barrier*, and *Seven Days to Noon*.

Korda always kept pace with every development in the art to which he gave his life. From the flickering pictures of the early days, through the disappointing period of the first talking picture experiments, to the present-day successes of Technicolor films, he never lost faith in the capacity of the screen to provide healthy entertainment and as an educational medium. He encouraged the production of pictures to spread knowledge, and lived to see the industry take its place worthily side by side with the theatre.

Throughout his long and chequered career he was on the look out for talented actors and actresses whose gifts he directed with such skill that many who were relatively obscure enjoyed and will continue to enjoy popular favour which they would otherwise never have experienced.

He married secondly Miss Merle Oberon in 1939, and after that marriage was dissolved married in 1953 Miss Alexandra Boycun.

January 24, 1956.

C. J. Kortright, the Essex cricketer, perhaps the fastest bowler who has ever been seen, died at his home at Brentwood on December 12, 1952 at the age of 81.

Even batsmen of wide experience find difficulty in assessing the comparative pace of bowlers when they have once reached and passed a certain measure of ferocity; but over and over again in discussions it has generally come to be admitted that not even J. J. Kotze, of South Africa, Ernest Jones, of Australia, or, of more modern times, H. Larwood were quite so fast as Kortright. Tall and muscularly strong, he had the ideal build of the fast bowler and, with the run up to the wicket which was almost demoniacal in its fury, he was indeed a terrible man for a batsman to face. He had, moreover, great endurance, required little nursing, and could bowl with full aggression for long periods.

He was born at Ingatestone, Essex, on January 9, 1871, and his playing career for Essex extended from 1889 to 1907. It must be remembered that in those days England was rich in bowlers of real pace—not merely quick bowlers but truly fast bowlers. Every county then had a fast bowler, some had two; and with such men then playing as Richardson, Lockwood, Brearley, Knox, and Fielder, it was hard to gain a place in England's team. Even so, it is one of the most remarkable features in the history of cricket that Kortright never once played for England.

He made many appearances for the Gentlemen against the Players, his bowling in the match at Lord's in 1893 being particularly hostile and being said to cause extreme discomfort to the batsmen. W. Gunn, that great and commanding Nottinghamshire batsman, declared that Kortright was yards faster than anything he had ever known, and in an article which Kortright contributed to *Wisden* in 1948 he recalls the occasion at Wallingford, on a pitch best described as "sporty", when he bowled a ball which, after it had struck the pitch, never touched the ground again until it landed over the boundary behind the wicketkeeper. Unlike many fast bowlers of more recent times, who have the advantage of a slightly smaller ball, he had little need to rely on a crowd of fieldsmen at short leg. He relied on beating the bat by sheer pace and shattering the stumps, or having his man caught in the slips.

Moreover, it must be borne in mind that the leading batsmen to whom he bowled in those days were for the most part attacking batsmen; at least they were certainly prepared to attack bowlers of all varieties of pace and skill. When Kortright bowled to A. C. Maclaren or J. T. Tyldesley, to C. B. Fry [q.v.] or Ranji, the intimidation was not confined to Kortright's terrific speed, for it was met with offence. It has been said that on those occasions Kortright was inclined to bowl short. Even so, his pace warranted it, and it is a fact that he alone was able to claim that he could pierce Ranji's defence with his pace, beat his bat, and hit him on the body. That in itself was a magnificent feat.

One of his greatest performances was when he took six Surrey wickets, including those of T. Hayward and R. Abel, for four runs at Leyton, his favourite hunting ground, in 1895. In 1900, also at Leyton, he took eight Yorkshire wickets for 57—a tremendous performance when one remembers the gigantic strength of Yorkshire's batting at the beginning of the century. He caused dismay when bowling against Surrey, at Leyton also, in 1893 when in the two innings he took 13 wickets for 64 runs. Indeed, every county in the land will remember the bad moments they had when facing Kortright in these years, and it is safe to say that not even Larwood made batsmen ponder more seriously on the chance of their life's extension.

He had one great achievement as a batsman when, in 1898, going in last against the Players at Lord's, he stayed with W. G. Grace while 78 runs were scored, and only failed by four minutes to save the match. Of later years he was to be met on Essex golf courses, and strangers were told in a whisper almost of terror: "That's Kortright". Certainly he earned the awful respect of contemporary batsmen.

December 13, 1952.

Serge Koussevitsky, for a quarter of a century conductor of the Boston Symphony Orchestra, died on June 4, 1951 at the New England Medical Centre at the age of 76.

It would be wrong to say that Koussevitsky graduated from a string-bass player to a conductor, for his talents in both directions seem to have developed not only at the same time but at a very early age. He was already a sufficiently accomplished player of his unwieldy instrument at the age of nine to play in the theatre orchestra of his native town and some two years later actually conducted it.

Nevertheless, he first achieved a reputation outside Russia as a double-bass player, and his virtuosity on that instrument was first demonstrated to London audiences in 1907 in a series of recitals at the Wigmore (then the Bechstein) Hall. In the course of the next year, however, he conducted the London Symphony Orchestra in a Beethoven programme which proved to be the precursor of many other fine performances not only of Beethoven but of modern Russian and Finnish music.

Though, when his interpretations were first heard in western Europe, their passionate and romantic aspects were most prominent to audiences, his insistence on clarity of line and meticulous control of speed and dynamics were later recognized as the chief instruments whereby a singularly lofty and penetrating mind achieved interpretations of the great works of orchestral literature of a quality seldom equalled. It is the ideal of the conductor to persuade all the players to perform like virtuosos; then he can feel that his vision can be realized. It was Koussevitsky's greatness that, having the vision, he could persuade those under his direction that their every semiquaver was an essential ingredient in the grand design of the composer.

Serge Alexandrovitch Koussevitsky was born at Tver on July 26, 1874, and studied the double-bass under Rambauseck at the Philharmonic School, Moscow. His reputation as a virtuoso on that instrument dates from 1896, but his attraction to the orchestra caused him to study conducting first in Russia and then under Nikisch at the Berlin High School. Like Berlioz, however, his genius was of the intuitive kind which owes little to teaching and he formed his own orchestra, which toured Russia with great success, interpreting such modern composers as Scriabin and Sibelius [q.v.]. He also founded a music-publishing house, but this was confiscated after the revolution and his orchestra was scattered. Though he accepted the invitation to take charge of the State orchestras, he was not happy in Russia and finally left in 1922.

Between 1922 and 1924 he conducted in London, Rome, Berlin, Paris, and Barcelona, and then became conductor of the Boston Symphony Orchestra. The reputation of that orchestra rose to unprecedented heights during the quarter of a century he had charge of it, and there is no doubt that his work there had a profound effect on the musical life of the United States.

Meanwhile, he had founded the Berkshire Music Centre at Tanglewood, Massachusetts, and continued to direct it after his retirement from his post as conductor of the Boston Symphony Orchestra in 1949. His conducting of Beethoven's Ninth Symphony at the Albert Hall in 1950 was greeted with tremendous enthusiasm, and there must be many who regret that he had to cancel, owing to ill-health, the European tour he had planned.

June 6, 1951.

Lydia Kyasht, until her death at her London home on January 12, 1959, was one of the three surviving principal ballerinas of the old Empire, pre-Diaghilev ballet, the others being Adeline Genée* and Phyllis Bedells.

Kyasht actually succeeded Genée as prima ballerina at the Empire in 1908. She could speak nothing but Russian at that time but she lived and worked in England ever since, contributing her knowledge of the classical style and technique which she gained at the Imperial School in St. Petersburg by the teaching she has given in her own studio and for the Royal Ballet School.

She was born in St. Petersburg in 1885 and trained at the Imperial School under Gerdt, along with Pavlova and Karsavina as fellow-pupils. Incidentally, she claimed to have danced Pavlova's famous *The Dying Swan* before Pavlova at a charity *matinée* held in St. Petersburg during the Russo-Japanese War.

She made her *début* in 1902 and reached the rank of prima ballerina at the Maryinsky Theatre in 1908, when she went to England. Her first part there, which she took over from Genée, was Swanilda in *Coppélia.* Phyllis Bedells describes her as "as pretty as a china doll . . . but we were appalled by the very short *tutu* she wore", and also as being "sensationally successful, dancing as a wild gypsy in the Moscow scene" (in *Round the World*). *The Times* praised her pirouettes. Her partner at the Empire was Adolf Bolm.

One of her principal roles during her five years at the Empire was as Sylvia, in the ballet of that name, which was given its first English presentation in May 1911. In 1912 she was with Diaghilev dancing the Firebird in *L'oiseau de feu* and Colombine in *Carnaval.* In 1913 she visited America but the venture in which she was engaged was a failure and she returned to London, where in 1914 she organized a season of her own at the Coliseum. After the war she was re-engaged by Diaghilev to strengthen his company.

Much later, in 1940, she raised another company, the Ballet de la Jeunesse. She published *Romantic Recollections* in 1929.

January 16, 1959.

L

Francis Laidler, who died in hospital at Bradford on January 6, 1955, the eve of his eighty-fifth birthday, had for more than 60 years been associated with the British theatre, more especially on the lighter side of entertainment.

For the greater part of that time he had been famous to millions of people as a producer of pantomime and revue, in London and in the provinces. Since the beginning of this century he had been responsible for nearly 250 British pantomimes, all of which he staged in the traditional style, but especially with an eye to beauty, and the introduction of child dancers during the 1914-18 War brought a new feature into this art which has since been widely adopted.

Francis Laidler was a Yorkshireman, born in the North Riding on January 7, 1870, the son of Joseph Laidler, M.R.C.S., and was educated at Wharfedale College, Boston Spa. He left school at the age of 16 to join the staff of the National Provincial Bank. Before he was 20 he had moved to Bradford, and left banking for a merchant's office, but he found himself in his early twenties sole lessee and manager of the Prince's Theatre, Bradford, upon the untimely death of his senior partner, Walter J. Piper. It was a strange contrast to his earlier environment—grandson of a banker, and son and brother of well-established medical men—but the theatre had already begun to absorb him, and soon he was making a name for himself with his theatrical productions and stagings.

There were times when he had as many as seven pantomimes running at once in London and the provinces, and many if not most of the stars of this century at one time or another, either in obscurity or in subsequent fame, appeared in his companies. One of his delights was always to make one brief personal appearance in each of his pantomimes. Laidler had an almost uncanny faculty for spotting and bringing out young people with a theatrical flair, and a great many men and women who were to achieve fame within his own time were given their first opportunity by him.

Although he will always be thought of as a master of the spectacular in this world of entertainment, he had also an instantaneous sense of humour and fun of the wholesome type which he provided in such a form that parents were never hesitant in taking their children to the shows which he staged. Some of the greatest comedians over the past 50 years have been among his discoveries. Laidler loved the life of the theatre, and even in his eighties he was as tireless in his personal attention to pantomime as he was when he first entered the business of the stage.

For years he had been governing director of the Alhambra and Prince's Theatre at Bradford, the Theatre Royal, Leeds, and the Hippodrome, Keighley, but he had also produced at Covent Garden, Daly's, the Victoria Palace, London suburban theatres, and many of the leading provincial theatres. In London he is particularly remembered for his staging at the Coliseum during the 1939-45 War of four spectacular pantomimes which survived the air raids at a time when he was also involved in his provincial productions. He was a member of the Theatrical Managers' Association, and of the Independent Theatres Association.

He married Miss Gwladys Stanley, for many years famous as a pantomime principal boy.

January 7, 1955.

Henry Lamb, R.A., M.C., who died on October 8, 1960, was one of the several distinguished British artists—Sir F. Seymour Haden, the etcher, and the late Professor Henry Tonks may be quoted—who combined art with medicine or surgery, though in Lamb's case the practice of medicine was a matter of duty, inspired by the War of 1914-18, rather than of choice. He was 77.

As an artist Lamb comes less easily than most into any classification. In his earlier work some influence can be traced of both Augustus John* and Stanley Spencer [q.v.], with whom he shared a Pre-Raphaelite inclination, but he developed on his own lines and he left no following. A painting by Lamb was immediately recognizable in a mixed exhibition by its colour scheme alone, a scheme in which greenish-gold and violet were prevailing notes. On a small scale, as in flower studies, he often produced effects with the magic of unusual chords in music.

The picture that first brought him into prominence owed some of its fame to the then notoriety of the subject, the late Lytton Strachey, painted in 1914 and afterwards presented to the Tate Gallery by J. L. Behrend. Keeping well on the right side of caricature, it is an infinitely amusing picture, bringing out the old-maidishness that lay behind the scholarly flippancy of the biographer of Queen Victoria. Strachey is represented in a lofty room, with a park-like landscape seen through the glass of the large window; and his trailing legs, ending in red slippers and neatly rolled umbrella propped against a chair upon which is placed a high-crowned hat, are as eloquent of personality as they are apt in serving the compositional requirements of the artist. All that the word "Bloomsbury" conveys of intellectual superiority and valetudinarianism combined is summed up in this picture.

Its success was followed by that of "Palestinian War Picture", painted in 1919 and now in the Imperial War Museum, and "Salonika War Picture", painted in 1920 and now in the Manchester City Art Gallery. The first represents a sudden bombardment in a rocky amphitheatre with scattered men rushing for shelter, and it is so treated as to suggest a momentary arrest of time in which apparently irrelevant details are stamped upon the mind. In the second picture, which represents an advanced dressing station with a group of stretcher-bearers and an orderly giving a wounded man a drink in the foreground, the suggestion is that of the tension of waiting.

These three pictures brought Lamb into public notice, though his talent and originality had been recognized already by artists and critics, notably in the almost embarrassingly moving "Death of a Bretonne", painted in 1910. After the First World War Lamb painted many aspects of life and nature: portraits, genre subjects, landscapes, street scenes, and still life studies. He had a special turn for the family group, as in the famous examples of "The Anrep Family", of 1920, and "George Kennedy and Family", of 1921. In these works precise and humorous observation of individuals is combined with a subtle appreciation of the general family atmosphere. Lamb's first one-man show was held at the Alpine Club Gallery in 1922. After that his work was seen chiefly in periodical exhibitions at the Leicester Galleries, though he also exhibited at the New English Art Club as well as at the Academy, where his later exhibits were mainly portraits.

Lamb, who was a son of Sir Horace Lamb, F.R.S., the distinguished mathematician and physicist, was born at Adelaide, Australia, in 1883, and brought up and educated in Manchester, where his father was Professor of Mathematics at the university. On his mother's side Lamb was Irish. His elder brother was Sir Walter Lamb, secretary of the Royal Academy from 1913 to 1951. He was originally intended for medicine, and he had gone far in his course as a medical student when, at the age of 20, having already worked at the elements of art under Mr. J. Knight, assistant drawing master at the Manchester Grammar School, he left Manchester to become a professional artist, receiving encouragement from Francis Dodd and Augustus John. He also studied at Jacques Emile Blanche's school, La Palette, in Paris. For several years he lived and worked mostly in France, coming back to London in 1911. On the outbreak of war in 1914 he returned to the study of medicine, and served with distinction as battalion medical officer in Macedonia, Palestine, and France, winning the Military Cross for gallantry. In 1934 his painting of "The Artist's Wife" was purchased out of the Chantrey Bequest Fund for the Tate Gallery, where he is represented by four other works, including the remarkable "Phantasy", presented by the Contemporary Art Society in 1924.

At the Manchester City Art Gallery, besides "Salonika War Picture", there is "The Yellow Dress". For the Birmingham City Art Gallery Lamb was selected in 1939 to paint the portrait of Mr. Neville Chamberlain, then Prime Minister, and he is also represented at Belfast, Aberdeen, Southampton and in numerous colleges at Oxford, Cambridge, Manchester and Leeds Universities. He was elected A.R.A. in 1940 and R.A. in 1949. He was a trustee of the National Portrait Gallery from 1942 and trustee of the Tate Gallery, 1944-51. Shortly after the outbreak of war in 1939 he was appointed an official war artist for the Army and is fully represented in the Imperial War Museum.

His intellectual interests were wide, and they were sharpened in youth by his friendship with Lytton Strachey and the stimulating—if formidable—circle of Cambridge friends of that great man. He shared with them a refreshing intolerance of convention, and a deftness in removing what was false both from subjects and persons. Lamb was a man of varied accomplishments—a musician (he played the clavichord) and gifted with a discriminating taste in literature. His private letters had a tense, distinctive style which was delightful. Possessed of the keenest sensibility he was an entrancing companion—his gifts showed to the best advantage as host in his home at Coombe Bissett, near Salisbury.

He married in 1928, after the dissolution of his first marriage, Lady Pansy Pakenham, sister of the present Earl of Longford. They have a son and two daughters.

October 10, 1960.

Admiral of the Fleet Sir Charles E. Lambe, G.C.B., C.V.O., First Sea Lord and Chief of Naval Staff until May 1960, when he resigned these appointments because of ill-health, died on August 29, 1960. He was 59.

Although not widely known to the general public, Lambe was an officer of exceptional gifts who rose to the top of his profession by merit and diligence. He had very few opportunities of service in action, but was most successful as a staff officer, being retained in the Plans Division at the Admiralty, of which he became Director, for most of the Second World War, including the decisive years. Originally a torpedo specialist, he was keenly interested in flying. He qualified as a free balloon pilot as a midshipman of 17, and as a young lieutenant took his pilot's civil A licence; he flew his own aeroplane for many years.

It was natural that he afterwards attained some of the chief posts in the Fleet Air Arm. He had the honour of being appointed a naval equerry to King George VI from the time of his accession, and from 1939 was an extra equerry.

Charles Edward Lambe was born on December 21, 1900, the only son of Henry Edward Lambe. Entering the Royal Navy as a cadet at Osborne College in May 1914, he saw active service in the Grand Fleet as a midshipman in the Emperor of India from 1917 until the end of the war.

In 1922 he was sent to Cambridge University for the special educational course arranged for young naval officers to fill the gaps in their studies caused by war conditions. He went out to the Mediterranean, after completing the course, to join the Benbow as a lieutenant. From her he was appointed for the course in the Vernon torpedo school at Portsmouth, where he qualified as a torpedo specialist in 1926. His next commission was in the flotilla leader Stuart, again in the Mediterranean, and on returning to England he was selected to go to the Naval Staff College in 1930.

In 1932, having graduated as p.s.c. in the rank of lieutenant-commander, he joined the cruiser Hawkins, flagship of Vice-Admiral Dunbar-Nasmith*, Commander-in-Chief in the East Indies, as fleet torpedo officer. In the following year he was promoted commander and went back to the Mediterranean Fleet on the staff of Rear-Admiral A. B. (afterwards Lord) Cunningham [of Hyndhope],* then commanding destroyer flotillas. He returned to the Vernon in 1935 to become commander of the establishment.

Promoted captain in December 1937, he was appointed a year later to his first command, of the cruiser Dunedin. Out of the first 120 days at war up to the end of 1939, she spent 92 days at sea, mostly under the severe conditions of the Northern Patrol. In November 1940 he joined the Plans Division as Assistant Director, and embarked on a period in Whitehall which was to last for the greater part of the war years, until 1944.

Although he was nominally Deputy Director of Plans from July 1941, his duties were largely concerned with the inter-service Joint Planning Committee on the Staff of the War Cabinet. He became Director of Plans in March 1942, and reverted to the more purely naval side, in the Admiralty building, but was still called on to attend occasional meetings in the War Cabinet offices. He was made C.B. in January 1944, and left to take command of the aircraft carrier Illustrious, in which he carried out a series of operations with the Eastern Fleet under Admiral Somerville in 1944 and the British Pacific Fleet under Admiral Fraser in 1945.

In April of the latter year, during attacks by her aircraft on the Loo Choo Islands in support of the American invasion of Okinawa, the Illustrious was hit and damaged by a Japanese kamikaze (suicide) plane but was in action again, with her flying deck cleared, within 20 minutes.

At the end of hostilities Lambe was promoted to the acting rank of rear-admiral and appointed Assistant Chief of Naval Staff (Air). Confirmed as rear-admiral in July 1947, he was chosen for the appointment of Flag Officer Flying Training for the difficult task of building up naval air strength on a new footing after the demobilization of wartime officers and men. Between 1949 and 1951, during which time he was promoted to vice-admiral in 1950, he was Flag Officer 3rd Aircraft Carrier Squadron in the Home Fleet, in H.M.S. Vengeance. From 1951 to 1953 he was Flag Officer Air (Home) at Lee-on-Solent. He had been seconded as Flag Officer Royal Yacht in the s.s. Gothic for the projected Commonwealth tour in 1952. This was abandoned on the sudden death of King George VI [q.v.], and Lambe's flag was struck in the Gothic at Mombasa on February 9.

From 1953 to 1955 he was Commander-in-Chief, Far East Station, and was promoted to admiral in 1954. He returned to the Admiralty from 1955 to 1957 as Second Sea Lord, and from 1957 to 1959 was Commander-in-Chief in the Mediterranean and also N.A.T.O. Commander-in-Chief, Allied Forces there. On May 1, 1959 he succeeded Lord Mountbatten as First Sea Lord and Chief of Naval Staff. He was created K.C.B. in 1953 and advanced to G.C.B. in 1957.

He married in 1940 Lesbia Rachel, the daughter of the late Sir Walter Corbet, Bt. There were two children of the marriage, a son and a daughter.

August 31, 1960.

The death of **Constant Lambert** on August 21, 1951 within two days of his forty-sixth birthday removes a brilliant musician of unusual versatility from English musical life, when further compositions from his pen had once more become a possibility.

For many years his work as musical director of the Sadler's Wells Ballet had absorbed most of his energies, but since he relinquished its conductorship in 1947 he had returned to composition, and as recently as July 1951 he produced the substantial score of the new ballet *Tiresias* with choreography by Ashton and *décor* by his wife.

Constant Lambert was the son of the Australian painter George Washington Lambert and was born in London on August 23, 1905. His early environment was thus artistic and his tastes and talents were not confined to music. He was thus exceptionally well fitted to play his decisive part in collaboration with Dame Ninette de Valois in producing an English ballet, an art which involves the partnership of all the arts.

He was educated at Christ's Hospital and the Royal College of Music, and the first steps in his musical career were taken as a composer. Diaghilev commissioned a ballet from him when he was still a student, which was produced at Monte Carlo in 1926. Later ballets were *Pomona* and *Horoscope,* which were original, and *Comus* and *The Prospect Before Us* for which he edited Purcell and Boyce—the latter's symphonies he also edited for concert use. But his most original, as it was his most successful, work was the *Rio Grande* for chorus, orchestra, and piano solo, in which he incorporated jazz rhythms. He had never despised dance music or light music; he was a champion of Duke Ellington* and a connoisseur of jazz. The music of *Rio Grande* is at once English and exotic: it has atmosphere, is brilliant and seductive by turns, and all the time takes colour from the evocative words of Sacheverell Sitwell.

His other choral work is on a larger scale, a setting of Nashe's *Summer's Last Will and Testament* in four movements, through which the composer by a natural affinity with Elizabethan sentiment and musical language reproduces the pastoral, bibulous and bitter emotions of his author's text. At its recent performance during the London Season of the Arts it was observed that though it has had few performances since 1935 it has not dated but is probably his most significant work. For orchestra alone he wrote *Music for Orchestra,* a substantial symphonic movement but perhaps less distinctive than the vocal works; and the *Aubade Héroique* for chamber orchestra, which was inspired by the circumstances of the hasty evacuation of the Sadler's Wells Ballet from Holland in 1940 at the time of the German invasion. There are also a concerto for piano and chamber orchestra; and a piano sonata, in which the romantic treatment of the instrument is abjured in favour of the percussive treatment that became fashionable in the twenties under the double influence of neo-classicism and jazz.

Though Lambert's compositions are of considerable importance he did first-class work also as a conductor and a critic. What he did for the Sadler's Wells Ballet from its earliest days as musical director was real creative work for it helped to evolve the company's permanent style and technique. During the war, when there was no orchestra for him to conduct, he played the piano for it on its tours, and at all times his advice was sought on matters relating to the ballet outside music, since he had an all-round artistic sensibility.

He was in demand as a conductor of modern music, both in London for the B.B.C. and abroad for the festival of the International Society for Contemporary Music. Though not a frequent occupant of the rostrum at concerts, he helped with the Promenade season of 1945 and appeared for other organizations when programmes that lay obliquely across orthodox taste—Liszt, for instance—were involved.

For a short time Lambert did newspaper criticism for the *Referee,* but his chief critical work was the book *Music Ho*! which he described in its sub-title as "a study of music in decline". It is full of acute observation and is written with the wit that distinguished his conversation. This multiplicity of gifts was perhaps an embarrassment of riches for his career, but it enriched a vivid personality that had no fellow among his contemporaries.

August 22, 1951.

Bishop of Landaff—See **Morgan.**

Lupino Lane, whose immense success with *Me and My Girl* enlivened Londoners in the years just before the outbreak of war in 1939, died on November 10, 1959 at the age of 67.

A small, lithe man with remarkably mobile features, he was an engaging comedian whose perfect timing always disguised the unflagging energy he put into his work. He had, too, a touch of the clown's endearing pathos and, a relic of his early clowning days, he could hold an audience without speaking a word while he mimed his way through some elaborate and usually quite improbable fantasy. He was proud of his descent from a family which had been connected with the stage as dancers and acrobats since the eighteenth century, and was one of the best exponents of that fresh, clean humour which seems to spring without effort from the Cockney on holiday. His stage surname records his connexion with his great-aunt on his mother's side, the celebrated Sara Lane, lessee of the Britannia Theatre, Hoxton.

The son of Harry Lupino, he was born in London on June 16, 1892, and made his first appearance on the stage at the age of four at the Prince of Wales's Theatre, Birmingham, at a benefit performance for Vesta Tilley [q.v.]. In his early days he was known as "Nipper" Lane and appeared under that name at the London Pavilion in 1903. There followed the usual routine of provincial tours but by his early twenties he had already begun to make a reputation in the West End in such parts as Andrew Janaway in *What a Catch*! and Clarence in *Any Lady,* and thereafter provincial tours became less frequent. His playing of Concourdi in *Afgar* at the Palace, Manchester, led to his first visit to New York, the precursor of many others, and he was almost as well known on the other side of the Atlantic as on this, a result to which his film work, which had begun as early as 1913, did much to contribute.

The long list of successes in comedies in the West End, of many of which he was author, either by himself or in collaboration, and some of which he managed, were all eclipsed by his triumph at the Victoria Palace with *Me and My Girl,* which set the town singing and dancing "The Lambeth Walk". The original run was extended more than once and the comedy was repeatedly revived, the public never seeming to tire of the spectacle of Lane's consummate management of his peer's robes even at the disastrous climax on top of the piano on the wrong side of the footlights. A later venture *La-di-da-di-da* was perhaps over-elaborately mounted for the slight satire on the "hunt-the-necklace" play.

Towards the end of the war there appeared a little book from his pen, *How to Become a Comedian,* which is a *tour de force* of delicate satire on the efforts of the many solemn gentlemen who urge the neophyte to "teach himself" in so many pages of dullness. The announcement was made in 1946 that Lupino Lane had bought the Gaiety Theatre for £200,000, but he disposed of the property four years later without having managed to reopen it. The name of Lupino has been connected with the Gaiety for more than 100 years.

He married Violet Blyth, and they had one son, Lauri Lupino Lane, who has kept up the theatrical tradition of the family.

November 11, 1959.

Professor William Henry Lang, F.R.S., a botanist of outstanding distinction and world-wide reputation, died on August 29, 1960 at the age of 86.

He was born in 1874 and entered Glasgow University as a medical student. But after graduating in medicine in 1894, with distinction also in science, he devoted himself to botanical studies under the influence of F. O. Bower, then Professor of Botany. Having been awarded the Donald Robertson Studentship he went to Kew, and worked at the Jodrell Laboratory on the production of sporangia on fern prothalli, a subject of great novelty at that time: the results of this work were so interesting that they were published in the Transactions of the Royal Society.

At this time Dr. D. H. Scott was the Honorary Keeper of the Laboratory at Kew and was engaged on his famous researches on the structure of fossil plants from the coal measures. Thus began a close friendship between Scott and Lang which lasted till the death of the former and stimulated Lang's interest in the study of extinct plants.

At Scott's suggestion he also undertook the investigation of the pollen-bearing structures and the ovules of the living cycad Stangeria, then believed to be a primitive form.

After working at Kew he returned to Glasgow as Lecturer in Botany at the Queen Margaret College of the university. Bower was actively engaged on his lifelong investigation of the problems of evolution and of the origin of the land flora, by the study of ferns and allied forms of living plants; in this he was ably assisted by his two young colleagues, Gwynne-Vaughan and Lang. The three men, known as the Triumvirate, formed an active, powerful and stimulating combination. They had frequent visits from Robert Kidston, the eminent Scottish palaeobotanist, who kept them informed of current research on extinct plants. In 1900 Lang went with A. G. [Sir Arthur] Tansley [q.v.] to Ceylon and Malaya to study the cryptogamic plants of the eastern tropics. He brought back much interesting material which he studied and described in a noteworthy series of papers.

When the Barker Professorship of Cryptogamic Botany was founded at Manchester University in 1909 Lang was chosen for the post. This position gave him time for research, but he also gained a great reputation as a teacher and as a source of wisdom both to students and colleagues. He was elected to the Royal Society in 1911 and served on its council from 1917 to 1918. He was president of the botanical section of the British Association in 1915 and delivered an address of outstanding interest. About this time he began work with Dr. Kidston on Early Devonian plants from the Rhynie Chert. Kidston had previously been assisted in anatomical studies of fossil plants by Gwynne-Vaughan, and after the untimely death of this brilliant plant anatomist Lang took his place. This led to a fine series of papers, published in the *Transactions of the Royal Society of Edinburgh, 1917-21,* which described and displayed the detailed structure of the very ancient plants which they called the Psilophytales. This work forms a landmark in the study of plant evolution and inaugurated a revolution in plant morphology.

Poorly preserved remains of somewhat similar plants had long been known but had received little attention; Lang now began to study and describe this neglected material and to search for other specimens in the older Devonian rocks. By the use of Walton's transfer technique he was able to remove fragments of plant tissue from the rock and to examine its microscopic structure. He was thus able to show that the vegetation of Silurian and Early Devonian times contained a number of types of land-plants of a very simple form. He described such species from Scotland, England and Canada, also from Australia in collaboration with Dr. Cookson, and from Wales with W. H. Croft.

His work was recognized by the award of a Royal Medal in 1931, and by his election to the foreign membership of the Swedish Academy of Science. He was given the honorary degree of LL.D. at Glasgow and in 1956 the Linnean Gold Medal by the Linnean Society of London. After retiring from his Chair at Manchester he went to live in Westmorland. Lang was unusually modest and retiring but he exerted a great influence on those privileged to know him. His interests extended far beyond the science of botany, and he was well read in philosophy and the arts. He had a profound and original outlook, and his conversation was most stimulating.

The friendliness and hospitality of Lang and his wife was of outstanding quality, and through this his influence on some of the most distinguished of his colleagues at Manchester extended to departments of the university as widely spaced as history, classics, and the fine arts. He will be remembered with affection and gratitude by many.

August 31, 1960.

Dr. Irving Langmuir, the distinguished American scientist whose researches on the films of molecules formed on the metal filaments of electric lamps led to the invention of the gas-filled lamp, died in hospital at Falmouth, Massachusetts, on August 16, 1957. He was 76.

With two other scientists he did pioneer work on the creation of artificial rain by seeding clouds with dry ice or silver iodide.

Langmuir, who had been an outstanding member of the staff of the physical chemical research laboratories of the General Electric Company at Schenectady, New York, for more than 40 years, retired in 1950 as Associate Director and thereafter became the laboratories' consultant. His work attracted attention from all parts of the world. Few homes or factories are without some electrical equipment which owes something to his patient study and inventive genius. Many medals and prizes were awarded him by learned societies for special pieces of research and for his work as a whole. In addition to the Nobel Prize for chemistry awarded in 1932 for his work in surface chemistry, he received the honorary degree of Doctor of Science from Oxford University in 1938 and that of Doctor of Laws from Edinburgh University in 1921.

His chief work lay in the development of gas-filled tungsten lamps, electrical discharge apparatus, condensation high vacuum pumps, and atomic hydrogen welding.

During the First World War he worked on devices for submarine detection at the Naval Experimental Station at Nahant, Massachusetts, and in the late war developed a smoke-screen generator. He also supervised a large staff of assistants who were constantly engaged in discovering new devices for improving the manifold electric equipment manufactured by the General Electric Company.

He was born at Brooklyn, New York, on January 31, 1881. After passing through the local schools he went to the Columbia School of Mines in New York, where he graduated in 1903. He then studied for three years at the University of Göttingen in Germany, where he took a Ph.D. in 1906. On his return to the United States in the same year he was appointed instructor in chemistry at the Stevens Institute of Technology in Hoboken, New Jersey, and in 1909 he joined the staff of the General Electric Company, with whom he was to stay for so many fruitful years.

His published work consisted largely in technical contributions to the journals of learned societies, of many of which he was an active member. He was a Fellow of the Royal Society, an honorary member of the Royal Institute of Chemists of London, and was awarded the Faraday Medal in 1943. In his own country he was a Fellow of the American Academy of Arts and Sciences, the American Physical Society, and the American Chemical Society, of which he was president in 1929. In 1941 he was president of the American Association for the Advancement of Science.

More than a score of medals were awarded to him during his career. Among them was the Hughes Medal of the Royal Society, which he received in 1918 for research in molecular physics. Two years later he received the Nichols Medal for researches in atomic structure, and the Rumford Medal of the American Academy of Arts and Sciences for research in thermionic phenomenon. In 1925 he was awarded the Cannizzaro Prize in Rome.

Other prizes awarded him were the Nichols Medal of the New York section of the American Chemical Society for research in chemical reaction at low pressure, which he received in 1913, the Perkin Medal (1928), Chandler Medal (1929), Willard Gibbs Medal (1930), the Franklin Medal awarded by the Franklin Institute (1934), the Holley Medal of the American Society of Mechanical Engineers (1934), an award from the Johns Scott Medal Fund of Philadelphia in 1937, the Medal of Merit from the United States Army and Navy in 1948, and the John Carty Medal, National Academy of Sciences in 1950.

He married in 1912 Marion Mersereau, of South Orange, New Jersey, by whom he had a son and a daughter.

August 19, 1957.

Mario Lanza, the Italian-American singer and film star, died in Rome on October 7, 1959. He was 38.

Mario Lanza was born in New York on January 31, 1921, of Italian parents, his real name being Alfred Arnold Cocozza. He became interested in music as a boy, buying Caruso records with his pocket money and learning to imitate the performances note by note. His first job was connected with music, in the humble capacity of piano-mover, but before long his natural vocal gifts were discovered and he began to train at the Berkshire School of Music (he did not, in fact, learn to read music until he was 25). His first appearance on the concert platform was at the Berkshire Music Festival of 1942, where he achieved an instant success. His career was interrupted for three years by military service, but after the war he returned to music, making records, appearing on the radio, and giving concerts throughout the United States. In 1947 he took part in a concert performance of *Andrea Chenier* at the Hollywood Bowl, and in the next year he made his operatic *début* as Pinkerton in *Madame Butterfly* in New Orleans.

His film career began unspectacularly when he was put under contract by M-G-M and starred in a modest feature, *That Midnight Kiss* (1949), which was followed by *Toast of New Orleans.* His popularity with filmgoers reached fever pitch when he played his idol in a biographical film *The Great Caruso,* and his next film, *Because You're Mine,* was also phenomenally successful. By this time he had begun to put on weight, and a dispute with his studio about this ended in his role in *The Student Prince,* for which he had already recorded the songs, being taken by another actor. After a brief period of eclipse he returned to the screen in *Serenade,* his popularity remaining undimmed (one admirer confessed to having seen it 78 times). Two further films followed, *The Seven Hills of Rome* and *For the First Time,* both made in Europe.

As a singer, Mario Lanza possessed a strong and well-balanced tenor voice and considerable attack in the more extrovert arias of his repertoire, but his insufficient basic training showed in a lack of finesse and, latterly, a concentration of force and volume rather than subtlety of phrasing which was tending to ruin his voice for serious purposes. His popularity as a film star, unmatched by any other operatic singer, depended as much on the appeal of his personality as on his strictly musical talents.

October 8, 1959.

King Sisavang Vong of Laos died in his palace at Luang Prabang on October 29, 1959. He was 74.

Somdech Phra Chau, Sisavang Vong, King of Laos, was born in 1885. He was the son of King Zakarine of Luang Prabang and of his senior wife, Queen Thongsi. Luang Prabang was, at that time, a semi-independent kingdom under French protection. It was later absorbed in French Indo-China and, in 1945, became integrated in the Kingdom of Laos.

King Sisavang Vong was educated under French supervision and passed two years at the Colonial School at Paris. He acquired there an affection for and understanding of the French way of life which was to remain with him all his life, though he never ceased to put first in his loyalties the customs and rights of his people. His hereditary function of High Protector of the Buddhist faith, formerly in Luang Prabang and latterly in the whole of Laos, gave him an authority which no politician could effectively challenge. He succeeded to the throne of Luang Prabang on the death of his father in 1904, and for the next 40 years served loyally under the French administration. He remained loyal even during the Japanese occupation and was deposed for a few months in 1946 by the Japanese-tolerated "Lao-Issara" ("Free Laos") movement.

He had his reward after the return of the French, when Luang Prabang was amalgamated with the two other Lao-speaking provinces of Champassak and Vienttiane, and, as first King of a Laos reunited after more than 200 years, he led his country towards independence. When the Viet-minh invaded Laos in 1951 King Sisavang Vong stood firm in his mountain capital and refused to leave, even when it seemed that his capture by the enemy was otherwise certain.

His confidence was justified; the Viet-minh never reached Luang Prabang and their threat gradually subsided. Though the Communists were long to remain in possession of the two northernmost provinces of Laos, by 1953 King Sisavang Vong was, nevertheless, able to sign the treaty by which a united Laos achieved complete independence within the French Union.

The great span of King Sisavang Vong's reign saw the transformation of Laos from the most remote and feudal principality to a modern state playing a part in the whole field of South-East Asian politics. As a young Asian monarch of the early twentieth century, he enjoyed a very considerable liberty in matrimonial affairs and, in spite of his European education, had 13 wives and close on 50 children. His senior wife died shortly after the war and was succeeded by the present Queen, who is mother of the King's eldest surviving son and heir, the Crown Prince Savang Vatthana. Many other children are still alive to-day, though King Sisavang Vong's reign was darkened by a calamitous canoe accident in which 14 of his sons were drowned.

For the greater part of his reign, having ruled over only one of the three provinces of his present kingdom, and communication between the central administration being at the best tenuous and often non-existent, King Sisavang Vong did not quickly become popular among his subjects. Even to-day it is certain that many thousands among them have never heard his name nor of the existence of a united Laos. Nevertheless, he earned for himself an affection and esteem far more extensive than that enjoyed by any of his predecessors and, as Laos grew in coherence and strength, so his renown spread not only among the Laos themselves, but also among the Kha, Man, Meo, Thai, and innumerable other unrelated tribes which make up the ethnological patchwork of modern Laos.

In part his increase in prestige was the fruit of a deliberate propaganda campaign by a Government anxious to create loyalty towards a central administration with which 99 Laotians in a hundred could otherwise have no contact. But the legend could never have been created save for the outstanding qualities of King Sisavang Vong himself. In appearance a heavy, almost reptilian figure, he bore himself with the absolute dignity of one who, for more than 50 years, had never deemed it possible that he might be other than a king. His honesty, simplicity, and formidable common-sense earned him the special esteem of the French colonial administrators and of all those who had later dealings with him. He showed all the kindness and gentleness which are endemic in his people and, in full measure, the charm and sympathy which is so strongly marked in all the members of his family.

In the last few years of his life King Sisavang Vong was increasingly crippled by arthritis and forced to leave most of the royal functions to the Crown Prince Savang Vatthana. Secluded though his life was, never for one moment could his presence be forgotten, and the knowledge that this grand figure still watched over his people was an inspiration and a rallying-point in all the country.

The kingdom is fortunate that the crown has passed to Prince Savang Vatthana, who, for the past five years, has carried out most of the secular and religious duties of the disabled Sisavang Vong. The new king is well known to his people, and, what is equally important, is popular with the group of young politicians who are now at the helm in Laos.

October 31, 1959.

H. M. Last, formerly Principal of Brasenose College, Oxford, died at Harlow on October 25, 1957. He was 62.

Hugh Macilwain Last was educated at St. Paul's and went up to Lincoln College as a Scholar in 1914. Debarred by ill-health from military service he devoted himself to learning with great thoroughness. He found inspiration in his Greats tutor, Warde Fowler, who, after Last had fulfilled all hopes in the Schools, urged him to add to his reading rather than seek to make an early or narrow mark in the field of research. Thus he became a sound Latinist and at the same time studied the Oriental background of ancient history.

On his election to a tutorial Fellowship at St. John's in 1919 he applied himself with equal zeal to teaching, and became a close ally of Stuart Jones, then Camden Professor, from whom he derived an especial interest in Roman constitutional doctrine and practice. Last's lectures were soon appreciated for their precision and thoroughness, so that his influence spread beyond his own college; for years before he became Camden Professor many Oxford scholars owed him a great debt for the unflagging help he gave them.

For a time Last wrote little, apart from some reviews which were recognized as a positive contribution to learning in their own right, but presently he became a considerable contributor to the *Cambridge Ancient History,* an enterprise of which he was a most loyal though not always uncritical friend. His chapters both on the Roman Republic and the Principate showed his range and quality as a historian. Behind them lay profound study of the epigraphical and literary sources and an independent judgment sceptical of fashionable doctrines and short cuts of any kind, and they were set out in a style somewhat elaborate, weighty, lucid and precise.

They revealed more understanding of the Roman community than emphasis on personalities, and a Roman combination of legal doctrine and practical common sense. In these, as in all his other writings, Last was careful to show what was certain and what was speculative and to practise the *ars difficillima nesciendi.* Together they made clear, what was indeed expected of him, that he could perform with admirable sureness what he taught others to aim at.

Last's interests extended to the work of British scholars outside Oxford and of Continental historians, especially in France and Italy. But beside this widening activity in his subject he devoted himself to the affairs of St. John's, where his careful and prudent counsel was much valued, especially in matters of finance. No trouble was too great for him to take with his pupils whether or not they could show promise of distinction, and he earned and received their constant good will.

In university affairs he took part rarely except in those relating to ancient history and archaeology, but on occasion he would offer uncompromising resistance to policies which seemed to him insufficiently supported by sound arguments. For a short period he was a Delegate of the Oxford Press. On the retirement of Professor J. G. C. Anderson in 1936 he succeeded as by right to the Camden Chair of Ancient History. Thus he became a Fellow of Brasenose, though he retained his affection for St. John's, which was repaid in kind, as also for Lincoln, of which college he was an honorary fellow. He was quickly at home in the affairs and the social life of his new college, and when after 12 years Brasenose lost its Principal he received a notable tribute to his powers and personality in his election to the headship of the college in 1948.

The responsibilities of this office thenceforward had first claim on him, but, while he ceased to be Camden Professor, he generously assisted for a time in the formal teaching of ancient history and remained the unwearied helper of his friends and former pupils. As Principal he combined a natural authority with an understanding of his colleagues and a very shrewd and practical judgment of affairs. The austerity of his intellectual standards showed no decline and where his scholarly conscience was engaged he could be unyielding and even severe. But he was the most unselfish and unselfseeking of men whom it was impossible not to respect.

Besides the diligent discharge of his professorial duties Last had taken a great part in the business of the Roman Society, of which he duly became president. During his tenure of that office he carried through a close alliance between the society and the *Société des études latines.* For he had a firm belief in common effort in learning. For many years he was a very active member of the editorial committee of the *Journal of Roman Studies,* to which he contributed papers and reviews of marked value. The high position which the *Journal* attained and kept was largely due to Last's energy and judgment.

Most characteristic of him was his acceptance of the honorary secretaryship, and, later, treasurership of the Egypt Exploration Fund at a time when his business ability and tactful guidance were of the utmost value to that society. This showed how greatly he cared for competent learning and for the due support of those whose work he admired. He was equally effective as chairman of the Faculty of Archaeology of the British School at Rome.

Apart from scholarship his interests were not especially wide. He enjoyed shooting and was a good shot, and he was knowledgeable about the countryside. He was naturally rather shy behind a manner which for a time gained him a reputation as formidable. But the more he had to do with people the more this notion gave place to liking, and with his especial friends he was always at his ease. He was hospitable and an excellent host whether of a college boat or a foreign *savant.*

He spent his life in Oxford except for most of the 1939-45 War, when he was very successfully engaged in government work of a confidential kind. But he was widely known among scholars and the effect of his personality was deeply felt outside as well as within his own university. For recognition he cared little and preferred to avoid any outward signs of it. He was, however, an Honorary Doctor of Edinburgh and of Dublin, a Corresponding Member of the Instituto Lombardo di Scienze e Lettere and of the Académie des Inscriptions et Belles Lettres, and in 1949-50 president of the Classical Association.

In 1956 Last found himself obliged, because of a serious illness, to resign the headship of Brasenose, to the great regret of the college. For the remainder of his life he lived in the country at Harlow, at times able to pursue his interests in scholarship. His enforced withdrawal from active work made it appropriate to recognize his services to Roman history, to the Roman Society and its *Journal* by the dedication to him of the volume for 1957, to which eminent scholars from abroad added their contributions to those of his British colleagues and former pupils. Though he did not live to have the volume presented to him on his sixty-third birthday, the knowledge that it was in preparation gave him much pleasure.

October 30, 1957.

The death of **Peter Latham** on November 22, 1953 at his home at Chiswick at the age of 88 will be heard of with regret by players of tennis and rackets all over the world. Though it might be said that William Gray before him or Jock Soutar after him were his equals at rackets, or that Jay Gould at his best would have rivalled him at tennis, there can be no question that as a champion of the two games together he was without a peer.

He was born in 1865 and entered the Manchester Rackets Club in his own words as a frail small boy of 11. He quickly grew in strength, and in 1887, at the age of 22, he defeated Joseph Gray at Rugby and Manchester for the world's championship at rackets. In the following year he went as head professional to Queen's Club, and there and at Charterhouse successfully defended his title against Joseph Gray. In 1891 he beat George Standing at Queen's Club and Prince's Club, and from then for six years was unchallenged at rackets. This enabled him to concentrate his powers on tennis, and so rapidly did he improve that in 1895 at Brighton he won the championship from Charles Saunders, hitherto considered unbeatable, by seven sets to three. Shortly afterwards, on the occasion of one of his matches with the Hon. Alfred Lyttelton, he was presented with a testimonial by his admirers on attaining the double honour. This he held for seven years.

Latham's greatest years were 1897 and 1898. In the former year, at the zenith of his career at rackets, came the match with George Standing. Latham won by four games to one at Queen's Club. Crossing to the United States, he won two of the first three closely fought games to retain the championship, but it was agreed to continue the New York match as Standing's many supporters contended that their player could not lose in his home court. Amid the greatest excitement, however, Latham, after being within a point of losing, struggled home by four games to three. In the next year Latham probably reached the height of his skill at tennis with the match against Tom Pettitt, of Boston. So confident were Pettitt's backers that the match was made for £1,000. Latham, playing for the first time against a fast "railroad" service, made splendid use of his prowess at both games and ran away with the match, winning by seven sets to love.

For the next few years there was no one near him at either game. In 1901 when Sir Charles Rose built his tennis court at Newmarket, Latham went there and to Hardwick. In the following year he easily beat Gilbert Browne at rackets, and though he could probably have held the title for some years after—he was rated scratch in professional handicaps as late as 1909—having played five matches and won them all he resigned the championship at the age of 37. His next challenge at tennis came in 1904 when he beat C. Punch Fairs by seven sets to five at Brighton, but in the ensuing year at Queen's Club and Prince's Club he met his one and only defeat in a championship match, Fairs winning by five sets to one. It is fairly certain that for the first time Latham was not at his best, for two years later he regained the title, though much the older man, beating Fairs at Brighton by seven sets to two. After his last triumph at the age of 42 he retired from championship contests. After that Latham went again to the United States, where his play at both games was as much appreciated as it was in England, and he played exhibition matches at tennis with the then youthful Jay Gould, afterwards the greatest of amateur players.

He also played many matches in Paris and visited Bordeaux. In 1916 he returned to Queen's Club and as a player and a teacher was the centre of a post-war revival of tennis. He played two fine matches in 1919 giving half-fifteen to the amateur champion E. M. Baerlein. Two years later, as an instance of his stamina and of how little his powers had abated, he reached the final of the Professional Handicap at Brighton after a match that went to five sets with E. Johnson, and, though of course receiving odds at this age, actually reached match point in the final only to lose in a fading light to G. F. Covey, then champion of the world. As an exhibition of tennis by both players this match was considered as fine a one as has been seen.

It is clear that to have achieved so much Latham must have possessed exceptional qualities. At rackets a wonderful wrist, balance, and footwork gave him a grace and perfection of style and movement, and there was no weak point in his armour. At tennis it took him years of diligence to master the correct stroke, and to this he added all his natural racket strokes and power of hitting. His backhand stroke will be remembered as the classic model of power and grace, and his backhand boast for the *dedans* which "made haste" off the main wall as his *tour de force.*

Beyond this he was a master of match-play in its various phases. He had, first, the ability of a champion to produce his best on the day, and then a remarkable flair for changing his tactics when things were going against him. It was said of him that some things he might disdain—he never used the "railroad" service at tennis—but that there was nothing he could not do if the occasion warranted it. And, lastly, he had a real love of the games which led to the ceaseless application so essential to a champion which was to make him in later days so successful a teacher of players of all standards. For he was equally happy whether tackling a beginner or improving a first-class player.

On his eightieth birthday in May 1945, Peter, as he was known to everyone, was given a luncheon at Lord's which was attended by a large number of distinguished players of various games. Many players and friends will miss a wise counsellor, who up till his last days could entertain them with his rare gift of relating his varied and colourful experiences on and off the court.

November 23, 1953.

Marshal de Lattre de Tassigny, who died in Paris, after two serious operations, on January 11, 1952 [as General, but posthumously created Marshal] had his career cut short at a time when his services were as urgently needed as at any period of his life. He was 62.

He leaves behind him a record of fine leadership and personal gallantry, to which he added in the course of the year 1951 a proof of high statesmanship, perhaps less expected than the military skill simultaneously displayed. He brought to the service of arms the combination of ruthless determination, strategic and tactical ability, and a swift and subtle intelligence. To some observers his character was marred by a difficult temper, by vanity, and by a flamboyant bearing. He was well aware of the first charge and did not seek to rebut it. The third feature was in part deliberately assumed. He felt that the French Army needed the tonic of pride in its leaders and in itself. After the war he considered that it had acquired the right to pride in its final achievements, but that even then its record was not fully appreciated by its own people. The first sentence of his preface to his history of the First French Army runs: *"La France, cependant jalouse de ses gloires et consciente de ses sacrifices, a mal connu le rôle militaire que, grâce à son Armée ressuscitée, elle a tenu dans la coalition des Nations Libres, alliées pour vaincre l'Allemagne nazie".*

Jean-Joseph-Marie de Lattre de Tassigny was born on February 2, 1889, at Mouilleron-en-Pareds, Vendée, the birthplace of Clemenceau, as he was fond of recalling.

Educated at the Jesuit College of Poitiers and Paris, he passed out of Saint-Cyr first of his class in 1910 and entered the 12th Dragoons. The first of his four wounds in the 1914-18 war is said to have been inflicted by a German lance in 1914. Transferring to the infantry, he was awarded eight citations to the Croix de Guerre and ended the war in command of a battalion of the 93rd Infantry Regiment at the age of 29.

His next active service was in the Riff campaign in Morocco, 1921-25, where he was again mentioned and again wounded, this time seriously. His companion in hospital at Taza was Colonel Giraud who in 1927 became his instructor at the École de Guerre. He was posted to the General Staff of the Vice-President of the Conseil Supérieur de la Guerre, General Weygand*, in 1932. Then he resumed the contact with Giraud which was later to prove so valuable. In 1935 he was given command of the 151st Infantry Regiment in Alsace, when Giraud was Military Governor of Strasbourg and Commander of the Army of Alsace, and in 1937 was appointed his Chief of Staff. Some two years later he was appointed Chief of Staff of the Fifth Army, in which General de Gaulle* commanded the armoured forces.

At the beginning of 1940 de Lattre assumed command of the 14th Division. This formation fought with great determination at Rethel, and he kept it well in hand in the subsequent retreat and rearguard actions. At the moment of the final collapse he requested that it should be transferred either to England or North Africa, but this demand was, as can well be imagined, refused. A brief period of service in France under the Vichy régime followed; but the atmosphere was little to his liking and he was happy to be appointed to the command of the forces in Tunisia in 1941. From this post he was, however, recalled in January of the following year, on the basis of well-founded suspicion of sympathy for the allied cause, and given the command of a division at Montpellier. When the allies landed in North Africa in November of that year he foresaw that the Germans would enter unoccupied France. In the hope that an allied landing in southern France would follow he strove to establish a bridgehead near Cette; but his handful of men was overrun and he was condemned to 10 years' imprisonment.

On September 3, 1943, de Lattre broke out of his fourth prison, that of Riom, with the aid of his wife and son. In the early hours of October 18 an aircraft of the R.A.F. picked him up near Mâcon and carried him to England. Reaching Algiers in late December, he received from General Giraud command of the Second Army, later Army B, which he had to organize from the bottom up, in face of considerable political as well as military obstacles. His first operation was the liberation of Elba. On August 15 he landed on the French Riviera, and the capture of Toulon and Marseilles was swiftly carried out. After a rapid pursuit of the retreating Germans up the valleys of the Rhône and Saône during the first half of September, Army B established touch with the "Overlord" armies on the plateau of Langres and from approximately this time became known as the First French Army. Its next great feat was the breaching of the "Gap of Belfort" in mid-November snowstorms.

The German Ardennes offensive brought about a *crise de commandement.* The First French Army was ordered to prepare for withdrawal from Alsace to the slopes of the Vosges, and this order became positive when the Americans on its left were heavily counter-attacked in the region of Bitche. The resistance of de Lattre was fortified by the support of General de Gaulle and the order was cancelled. Between January 20 and February 9, 1945, the First French Army, reinforced by the United States XXI Corps, cleared the "Colmar Pocket", captured 20,000 prisoners, and almost annihilated the Nineteenth German Army. In March it broke through the Siegfried Line and crossed the Rhine north of Karlsruhe. Then came its sweep to the Danube and thrusts southward into Tirol, a magnificent revenge. On May 8 de Lattre signed on behalf of France the act of capitulation of the Reich in Berlin.

After a short spell in command in Germany, de Lattre was appointed to the dual post of Inspector-General and Chief of Staff of the Army. He gave up the second of these appointments in 1948, but on the other hand his inspectorate was extended to that of the Armed Forces. This was the period of his remarkable experiment in the training of young conscripts, the creation of the Light Camps in open country. He was working in the moral at least as much as in the strictly military field because he regarded the two as one. Fresh air, fresh water, bodily and mental fitness, adaptability, liveliness, the cutting out of dead wood in training methods, the replacement of jargon, learnt parrot-wise, by intelligent appreciation of material and machinery—these were his primary aims.

In October 1948 General de Lattre was appointed Commander-in-Chief of the Land Forces of Western Union at Fontainebleau. This was another experiment, and after accomplishing invaluable service it outlived its usefulness. De Lattre and Field-Marshal Lord Montgomery, chairman of the Commanders-in-Chiefs Committee, both positive and strong-minded men, did not always find collaboration easy, but each warmly appreciated the other's high quality and each praised with equal warmth the other's work after their partnership had ended. When de Lattre saw that Western Union would be replaced by, or—perhaps more properly—embodied in, the North Atlantic Treaty Organization, he put himself forward as candidate for what nine soldiers out of 10 would have considered the most ungrateful appointment in the French service, command in Indo-China. In December 1950 he went out as High Commissioner and Commander-in-Chief.

His military achievements in 1951 are well known. They were based upon new dispositions rendering mobile a far higher proportion of the army, upon heavy reinforcement of the native forces of Viet Nam, upon modern equipment, largely from the United States, and above all upon his own far-sighted and vigorous strategy and tactics, his inspiring personality, and his unconquerable will.

Less well known is his enlightened attitude politically, though this was an equally important factor in his success. His work is left unfinished and it is impossible to foretell the future of the attempt to defend Indo-China against communism, but he accomplished outstanding service and brought about an astonishing transformation of the situation.

General de Lattre had plenty of enemies, but also a host of friends and admirers, many of them in Britain. He was served with devotion by his staff. He was a brilliant and inspiring conversationalist and a delightful companion. At table he would sit moodily for a while, then, as if suddenly electrified, break out into a flow of argument and reminiscence. He will be sadly missed as soldier, statesman, and in social life.

He married in 1927 Mlle. Simone Calary de Lamazière, who survives him. Their only son was killed in the Red River Delta at the head of his Viet Nam troops.

January 12, 1952.

Professor Max von Laue, who died in Berlin on April 24, 1960 at the age of 80 (he was involved in a car accident on April 8), was the originator of a new branch of science—X-ray crystallography—which in the hands of the Braggs, father and son*, and their successors has led to a precise understanding not only of the arrangement of atoms in crystals but also of aspects of chemical structure which purely chemical methods had been unable to reveal.

Its continuing vitality is illustrated by the two present extremes of its use: on the one hand as a routine method, mainly in industrial laboratories, for the identification of small quantities of powdered crystalline material; on the other to elucidate the disposition in three dimensions of large molecules, such as the proteins and nucleic acids, which are of key importance in living cells, including our own. Such are the ripples that have spread out from an idea entertained by von Laue in 1912 and from experiments which he instigated to test it. His own part was to initiate. He provided powerful new evidence that X-rays were of the same nature as the waves of light and radio, and that they could be used in principle to show the structure of crystals. He did not develop the experimental procedures necessary to realize the possibilities that were thus opened up. But his contribution was decisive, and in 1914 he was awarded the Nobel Prize for Physics.

Born on October 9, 1879, at Pfaffendorf near Coblenz, he grew to manhood during the exciting period when the discoveries of X-rays, radioactivity, and the electron were inaugurating a new era in physics. A theoretical physicist, he studied at Göttingen, Munich, and Berlin, and received his doctor's degree from Max Planck, the originator of the quantum theory. In 1908 he went as a lecturer to Professor Sommerfeld's department in Munich. This was three years after the publication of Einstein's [q.v.] first or special theory of relativity, and the same year that Minkowski showed that Einstein's theory could be formulated in the language of four-dimensional geometry. In 1911 von Laue wrote a book on relativity, giving it such mathematical elegance that Einstein said in jest of it that he himself could hardly understand it.

One of von Laue's senior colleagues at Munich was Professor William Röntgen, the discoverer of X-rays. Von Laue took the view, in opposition to Röntgen, that X-rays were electromagnetic waves. He wrote about the consequences of this view and was aware of a calculation by his chief, Sommerfeld, which showed that, if this were so, X-rays would have a wavelength only about one five-thousandth of that of light waves. His mind was thus already well prepared when a student in the department came to him in 1912 with a problem which caused him to think about the supposedly regular arrangement of matter in crystals. The volume occupied by an atom was roughly known, so that the distances between atoms could be estimated. Having done this, it at once occurred to von Laue that these distances were of the right order for planes of atoms to act as a diffraction grating for X-rays—scattering them preferentially in certain directions according to their wavelength—just as finely ruled parallel lines act as a diffraction grating for light waves. He therefore proposed that an experiment should be done.

Röntgen and Sommerfeld at first refused permission. But in the end permission was given, and first one and then another experiment were done by Freidrich and Knipping, an assistant and research student in Röntgen's department. The experiments showed that X-rays did indeed interact with the structure of crystals in such a way as to produce patterns of the kind that von Laue had foreseen. The idea and the conviction needed to put it to the test were von Laue's. So also was the working out of the complicated theory of three-dimensional diffraction. When he presented the results of the experiments at a meeting of the Berlin Physical Society on June 14, 1912, he was received with roars of applause.

In the same year he was appointed assistant professor of theoretical physics in the University of Zurich, and in 1914 he went as full professor to the University of Frankfurt on Main. From 1919 onwards he held the chair of physics at Berlin and directed the institute of theoretical physics. He was a poor lecturer, but as an expositor in print was superb, and popular accounts of his own work which he published in 1920 and 1923 rank as classics of their kind.

A happy family life, a grandiose neglect of formalities of dress and speech, a liking for gardening in bad weather, and his careless driving of his open car made him into a characteristic and well-loved figure in Berlin.

Never a politician, he was an early critic of Hitler's government. He spoke openly on behalf of Jewish scientists, and helped them. He also took an early opportunity to arrange a series of lectures for himself at Princeton University, which kept him out of Germany for most of a year. When he received an honorary degree from Manchester University in 1936 he was described aptly as "not merely a great physicist, but also . . . an unbending champion of scientific truth, with a faith as handsome as the yachts he sails, as dynamic as the motors he drives, and as firm as the rocks of his beloved mountains".

April 25, 1960.

Dame Vera Laughton—See **Mathews.**

Marie Laurencin, the French painter, died in Paris on June 9, 1956. She was 70.

She had good claims to be numbered among the most celebrated women painters of our day. The sources of her art were obscure; she had an unmistakably original style; and though she was attached by bonds of friendship to Cubists and Fauves, she really belonged to no school. She had considerable refinement and grace. Her besetting fault was that her talent was monotonous.

She was born in Paris on October 31, 1885, the natural child of an "important personage" whose name is not recorded. Brought up in comfortable bourgeois surroundings, with schooling at the Lycée Lamartine, she showed aptitude for painting and was put to study at an academy run by F. Humbert. Before long it became evident that she would not develop along academic lines. She got to know Picasso* and Braque*, and became closely associated with the Polish poet and critic, Guillaume Apollinaire. She first exhibited at the Salon des Indépendants in 1907. An exhibition at the Galerie Barbazanges in 1912 made her work more widely known. André Salmon and other critics approved; and when Apollinaire brought out his book, *Les Peintres Cubistes,* in 1913, he included her in it, though she could by no means be classified with Braque, Picasso, and Léger [q.v.].

In 1914, just six weeks before the war, Marie married the German painter, Otto von Wätjen; and so, although profoundly French in sentiment, she was perforce an exile during the next few years. Her husband took her to Spain, so she was able to correspond with her old friend, Apollinaire, which she did constantly until his death from wounds on Armistice Day.

Soon after the war her marriage was dissolved and she reappeared in Paris, now associated with the musician Erik Satie. A further big exhibition, held at the Galerie Rosenberg in 1920, consolidated her reputation. In the following year two monographs on her work appeared, one in French by R. Allard and the other in German by H. von Wedderkop. Her paintings began to find their way abroad, and were seen at the Leicester Galleries in London, the Rosenberg and Helft Galleries, and elsewhere. She was prolific, and was mistress of several media, including watercolour, drawing and lithography. She also executed some mural decorations and dress designs for Paul Poiret.

The physical elements of Marie Laurencin's most pronounced style were female figures, elongated and stylized, with pointed fingers, deep black slits of eyes and no noses. But literal verbal description cannot but render somewhat ridiculous a convention that had in fact great charm. The Laurencin ladies seemed to render in flat paint (with elimination of all detail) the grace and refinement of femininity. A beautiful woman, she had no model but herself, so that it has been said that "all nature was to her a hall of mirrors". She had a favoured colour scheme of pinks, greys and pastel blues, and from this she rarely departed. Sober and subtle, her art had no great depth; but through it appeared an unusual and attractive personality.

June 11, 1956.

Sir Hersch Lauterpacht, Q.C., the distinguished international lawyer and a Judge of the International Court of Justice at The Hague, died in hospital in London on May 8, 1960 at the age of 62.

He was born on August 16, 1897, and educated at Lwow and at the Universities of Vienna and London. He was appointed an assistant lecturer at the London School of Economics in 1927 and five years later became reader of public international law in the University of London. He was called to the Bar by Gray's Inn in 1936, took silk in 1949 and became a bencher of his Inn in 1955. For 17 years from 1938 he was Whewell Professor of International Law in the University of Cambridge.

He was also a professor at The Hague Academy of International Law during several years and a visiting professor to universities in the United States. He was a member of the British War Crimes Executive in 1945-46, of the United Nations International Law Commission in 1951-55, and president of the Permanent French-Swedish Conciliation Commission and of the Norwegian-Portuguese Conciliation Commission. He was installed as a Judge of the International Court of Justice in 1955 and was knighted in the following year.

His part in the administration of international justice was therefore already large at the time of his early death, but his contributions to the academic study of the subject were of even greater importance. In an early work, *The Function of Law in the International Community* (1933), he attacked the doctrine that international disputes "are necessarily divided into two categories as 'legal' and 'political', as 'justiciable' and 'non-justiciable', or as disputes as to 'rights' and conflicts of 'interests' "—a doctrine which he argued was juridically unsound.

When the international order was about to be restored after the overthrow of the dictators in the Second World War Lauterpacht published in *An International Bill of the Rights of Man* (1946) a cogent plea for an international bill of rights with constitutional embodiments of the principle. He was thoroughly alive to the practical and theoretical objections to the idea, and his arguments exhibited to good effect his particular combination of legal learning and acuteness with practical sagacity. He had contributed various important articles to *The Times* on such subjects.

He married in 1923 Rachel, daughter of Michael Steinberg, by whom he had a son.

[This obituary was followed, in the same issue, by a long tribute, particularly to his achievement in international law.]

May 10, 1960.

Frieda (Mrs. D. H.) Lawrence, widow of D. H. Lawrence, died on August 11, 1956 at Taos, New Mexico, on her seventy-seventh birthday. She was Mrs. Ravagli.

Seldom, if ever, has a great writer's wife been so intimately involved in his work as Frieda Lawrence was in that of D. H. Lawrence. Certainly none has been depicted with such wonderful fidelity as she was in his poems and novels. Ursula Bragwen, Tanny Lilly, Harriet Somers, Lady Connie—even Kate in *The Plumed Serpent*—these are, to those who knew her, the woman herself, in her gaiety, her independence, her vitality, her glorious disregard of conventions and class distinctions. And readers of those books will realize that her importance to Lawrence was much more than that of having served him as a model. She was an inseparable, and sometimes indistinguishable, part of the life-experience which it was his mission to explore and interpret. His friends were first inclined to chafe at Lawrence's insistence that what was creative in his books came from her as much as from himself; but they came to understand that it was true.

Their life together was at times almost legendary for its tempestuousness; for many years it was one of great hardship and downright poverty. Only a few months ago she wrote, in connexion with a proposal to build a costly memorial to Lawrence in Eastwood: "The irony of it! When I remember what £100 would have meant to us". Yet her happy temperament was such that poverty seemed only to increase the intensity of her pleasure in the small joys of life. A bunch of foxgloves in a jug, in the rather grim Cornwall days, would send her into quiet raptures. No woman ever demanded less to make her happy. And the speed with which she adapted herself to her husband's hereditary domestic skill was astonishing. One felt it was with a sigh of relief that she took to scrubbing and washing and ironing. She came positively to revel in such things and delighted in them to the end of her days.

She was, when Lawrence met her, a very beautiful woman, and her blonde beauty and her lovely green brown eyes remained unscathed for many years. But the quality with which one was immediately and permanently impressed was her entire naturalness. At a first meeting you felt that you had known her all your life. She had a childlike insouciance, rendering herself gaily to the impulse of the moment. Nothing could be more characteristic of her than the story she told of her first husband's surprise when he came upon her sliding down the banisters on the way to a dinner party.

Her capacity for enjoying life, on the simplest terms, was inexhaustible. She was quick to tears and even quicker to laughter. She was the perfect counterpoint to Lawrence's agonized concern for the world, for she seemed to be part of nature, rooted firmly and easily in its abiding life: a haven of warmth and security for a too-often tormented soul. At one moment, it is true, the tight bonds between them came near to snapping when, towards the end of a sojourn in Mexico, Lawrence's pursuit of the "dark God" was more than she could bear, and she fled to Europe. But Lawrence, after some weeks of hesitation, followed her, and she once more accepted her manifest destiny of cherishing the life of the man of genius whom she loved and whom she now knew to be mortally ill.

Frieda Emma Johanna Maria was born in 1879, the daughter of Baron Friedrich von Richthofen, an army officer who had gained the Iron Cross in the Franco-Prussian war. He was, at the time of her birth, acting as civil governor of Metz. The most joyful recollections of her childhood were entwined with that famous city at the time when it was adjusting itself to German rule. She played with her sisters and boy friends about fortifications, or sat on the garden walls of the old house where she lived and pelted the soldiers marching below with cherries. At 17 she spent a glamorous year in Berlin as the guest of a cousin, Oswald von Richthofen, who was Under-Secretary of State.

Not long after her return to Metz she married the late Professor Ernest Weekley, at the age of 19, and went to live in Nottingham. Twelve years later she met Lawrence, who was one of her husband's students. He fell headlong in love with her and she with him. In May 1912 they departed together for Germany, with incredibly little to live on: and an adventure, which will be immortal in our literature, began.

Her marriage with Lawrence took place in the summer of 1914. After his death at Vence in 1930 she settled in New Mexico, and in 1952 she married Angelo Ravagli, an artist. There were three children of her first marriage.

In 1936 she published a volume of recollections, *Not I, But the Wind . . .*

August 13, 1956.

Gertrude Lawrence, who died on September 6, 1952 in hospital in New York, was an actress of high vitality, of keen wit and undoubted style, for many years an ornament of the light comedy and musical comedy stage.

Like many another actress of merit (especially in the lighter field) she was brought up in the theatrical atmosphere from her earliest years. She was born in London on July 4, 1898, daughter of a Dane, Arthur Lawrence Klasen, and his English wife, Alice Louise Banks, and was christened Gertrud Alexandra Dagma Lawrence. Her parents' marriage was dissolved while she was still an infant, and she went to live with her mother, a small-part actress. Such formal education as she had was obtained at the Convent of the Sacré Coeur, Streatham, but she spent much time with her mother on tour in theatrical lodgings, and made her own *début* as a child dancer at the age of nine at the Brixton Theatre.

Later, at Christmas 1911, she was one of 50 girls who appeared at Olympia in Charles B. Cochran's [q.v.] spectacular show, *The Miracle.* She studied dancing under Mme. Espinosa and had instruction in elocution and acting under Italia Conti. Christmas of 1912 found her appearing as principal dancer at the Liverpool Repertory Theatre in *Fifinella.* Thereafter she toured the provinces in various pieces; and in 1916 she was seen by Lee White and Clay Smith, who in June of that year brought her to the Vaudeville Theatre as principal dancer and understudy to Billie Carleton in *Some.* She later toured with this piece in a principal part, and this was her first real stage success.

Miss Lawrence was then much in demand for musical comedy and revue parts, in which she danced (as one observer put it) "with magical lightness". She had a true, clear voice and, though not strictly beautiful, knew how to make the most of her looks. As time went on she made herself "the ideal musical comedy star". She took a leading part in *The Midnight Follies* at the Hotel Metropole at Christmas 1922. André Charlot's [q.v.] revues presented her with sundry good opportunities, and for many years she worked in close collaboration and friendship with Noël Coward*, whom she had met as a boy actor when she was in her early 'teens. In 1930 Coward wrote *Private Lives* especially for her, and in it she gave a brilliant and sustained piece of high comedy acting. Gertrude Lawrence went to New York in 1924 with *André Charlot's Revue of 1924,* and at the Times Theatre endeared herself to the sophisticated American audiences as she had done in London. Her United States tour in *Susan and God* (1935) was accounted a dazzling performance; and she won further laurels in New York in the winter of 1936-37 in Coward's *To-night at 8.30.* Another notable performance was in *The Skylark* in October 1939.

Her great popularity in America, where she played in, among other pieces, *Lady in the Dark* and *Pygmalion,* and her work for Ensa during the war caused her absence from the West End stage for almost 10 years. However, she reappeared in Daphne du Maurier's *September Tide* at the Aldwych in 1948, displaying all her old charm, and then again crossed the Atlantic for, as it happened, the last time. At the time of her death she was captivating New York audiences with her performance of the governess, Anna, in *The King and I.*

Gertrude Lawrence was not only a mistress of light comedy but had a versatile talent which brought her distinction in a number of serious parts. She had verve and *chic,* and a remarkable way of wearing her clothes that caused Captain Edward Molyneux* to give, as his considered opinion, that she was the ideal subject for the *haute couture.* She was both slim and graceful.

She was twice married. Her first marriage (to Francis Gordon-Howley) was dissolved; and in 1940 she married the theatrical producer, Richard S. Aldrich, who was with her when she died.

[This obituary of Gertrude Lawrence was followed by a tribute in the same issue.]

September 8, 1952.

Lady Pethick-Lawrence – See **Pethick-.**

Lady Layton, wife of Lord Layton, who died on March 18, 1959 at the age of 71, was one who shone in two roles, the much-loved wife and mother and the educated, intelligent, politically minded woman, a champion of good causes, national and international. Indeed, she satisfactorily resolved the problem which perplexes many a married woman to-day: how to reconcile marriage and a university education.

She was Eleanor Dorothea, only daughter of F. P. B. Osmaston, of Limpsfield, Surrey, and she was born on October 4, 1887, educated at Prior's Field, and went on to a brilliant career at Newnham College, Cambridge. In 1910 she married Walter Thomas Layton.

Throughout her life Lady Layton devoted a great deal of time and energy to public work. Starting over 50 years ago in the constitutional branch of the Women's Suffrage Movement, she found an outlet for her political activities, after the vote had been won, in the Liberal Party.

Her political career terminated in the presidency of the Women's National Liberal Federation in 1947-49. In this capacity she was chairman of the group which produced *The Great Partnership,* the report which was adopted by the Liberal Party as the charter for married women and which summed up in its title the philosophy behind all her political work.

But Lady Layton's enthusiasms extended far beyond party politics. Inspired by the Brussels Financial Conference of 1920, which was largely organized by her husband, and by the first Assembly of the League of Nations, she threw herself into the newly formed League of Nations Union and in 1925 became a member of its executive committee which stimulated and guided the movement for peace through collective security in Britain between the wars. After the Second World War she continued on the executive of the United Nations Association as long as her health permitted.

In the 1920s she engaged in active propaganda for family allowances in association with Miss Rathbone and Mrs. Hubback and within the Liberal Party.

In 1929 she travelled through India with the Statutory Commission, for which her husband was the financial assessor. As a result she was concerned with the foundation of the Women's Advisory Council on Indian Affairs during the Round Table Conference in London; she became its chairman when the council was reconstituted in 1941, and again in 1949 under the title of "The Women's Council (Co-operating with the Women of India, Pakistan, and Ceylon)". Since 1953 she had continued in office as its president.

Lady Layton's contribution to the movements or organizations in which she was interested always extended beyond committee work and public speaking into some immediately practical form. The wide range of her 50 years of service includes the organizing of a day nursery and of a children's clinic and the chairmanship of a local housing committee. For some 20 years, first as chairman, later as a trustee, she was one of the executives who looked after the thousands of Basque children who were brought to Britain at an early stage of the Civil War in Spain. As chairman of the Clothing and Comforts Committee of the British Fund for Relief of Distress in China (arising out of the Lord Mayor's Fund) she played an active part in the dispatch of material aid to Chinese refugees, in the Sino-Japanese War.

Though her public interests were so manifold they were only the complement to an exceptionally full and absorbing family life in which music played an important part. She leaves seven married sons and daughters and 19 grandchildren.

March 19, 1959.

Fleet Admiral William Daniel Leahy, who served as Personal Chief of Staff to President Roosevelt during the last world war, died in Washington on July 20, 1959 at the age of 84.

He had already ended an outstanding naval career of 46 years, from which he retired in 1939, before being summoned to more challenging tasks in the realm of diplomacy and high policy that had a direct bearing on allied war councils.

As American Ambassador to the Vichy Government after the German occupation of northern France, a post he held for two years, Leahy was in many ways the focal point of Washington's differences with General de Gaulle's* Free French headquarters in London, but events largely vindicated American insistence on the usefulness of maintaining a diplomatic link with the Pétain [q.v.] régime.

The voluminous intelligence he quietly gathered in Vichy, some of it from the far corners of the French empire, was of the utmost value, and he is given much of the credit for the subsequent American landings in North Africa.

Soon after the United States entered the war, Leahy became Chief of Staff to President Roosevelt, whom he accompanied to wartime conferences with Britain and subsequently Russia at Quebec, Casablanca, Teheran and Yalta; he was with President Truman* in the same capacity at Potsdam and continued in his influential post until the end of the presidential term in 1949. As a leading proponent of American sea power, he made an obvious impact at the White House on allied war strategy; the large construction programme which he successfully advocated during his two years as Chief of Naval Operations (ending in 1939) was to reap vital benefits after Pearl Harbour.

Most of Leahy's active senior commands, which included the destroyer scouting force and the battle fleet, were held between the two wars, but after graduating from the Naval Academy in 1897 he had seen much service as a young officer in the Spanish American War, and the naval expeditions at the turn of the century in the Far East and the Caribbean. He served as a commander during the First World War, and for a brief period after his retirement was Governor of Puerto Rico.

High honours were bestowed on Leahy by many countries of Europe and Latin America, and in 1945 he was made an honorary G.C.B.

July 21, 1959.

Gilbert Ledward, O.B.E., R.A., died in London on June 21, 1960. He was 72.

As a sculptor Ledward linked the ideals of two generations. In his formal conceptions he did not depart very far from the classical realism with a symbolical or illustrative tendency which had continued in all Academies since the Renaissance, but he shared the curiosity about materials of the younger men, and, like them, he distinguished between the possibilities of modelling and carving.

His training was orthodox. After studying at the Royal College of Art and the Royal Academy Schools he won, at the age of twenty-five, the double distinction of the Rome Scholarship in Sculpture of the British School at Rome, the first to be awarded, and the gold medal and travelling scholarship of the Royal Academy, and proceeded to Rome, where a close study of Italian art formed his style.

Then came the critical interruption of the war, during which, from 1916 to 1919, he served as a lieutenant in the Royal Garrison Artillery on the Italian front, and it is evident that the enforced abstention from the practice of his art served a valuable purpose in allowing time for his more personal ideas to develop.

Perhaps Ledward's best known work in London is on the Guards Memorial near the Horse Guards Parade, for which he designed and executed the bronze figures and relief panels, the architectural part being the work of the late Harold Chalton Bradshaw, F.R.I.B.A., who had won the Rome Scholarship in Architecture in the same year that Ledward won the scholarship in sculpture. But, though these bronze figures of guardsmen gained for Ledward in 1927 the medal of the Royal Society of British Sculptors "for the best work of the year by a British sculptor in any way exhibited to the public in London", they do not do full justice to his powers.

The whole memorial, indeed, though it has a certain stolid dignity, is a good example of the way in which artistic talent is apt to be cramped in expression by official requirements. Ledward had better opportunities in his reliefs for the Imperial War Museum and in the marble relief which forms the reredos of the altar to the memory of the Marquis of Ormonde, designed by Sir Reginald Blomfield, R.A., in Kilkenny Cathedral.

The son of a sculptor, Ledward was born in London in 1888. As already said, he was trained at the Royal College of Art, the Royal Academy Schools, and in Rome. His early success gained for him several commissions for war memorials, as at Blackpool, Stockport, and Abergavenny. For some years he was Professor of Sculpture at the Royal College of Art, and it was during this period that his interest in carving seems to have been awakened, most of his earlier work being in bronze.

His "Caryatid Figures", a group of two nude women with raised arms, supporting an abacus, carved in Roman stone, excited great interest when it was exhibited at the Academy in 1929. Some criticism of the work was made on the grounds that, being open in structure, it was better suited to bronze than stone, but it was recognized to be a fine piece of direct carving of a kind new to Burlington House. It was followed in 1930 by "Reclining Figure", symbolizing the Earth, also in Roman stone, which Ledward deposited as his diploma work on his election as an academician in 1937.

Upon young carvers his influence was particularly valuable, because he showed that stone could be given expression without the arbitrary deformations that some of the moderns think necessary. Not less valuable was the work he did in association with several other sculptors, including Eric Gill, with the object of improving the design of headstones and other memorials and encouraging the use of native stones instead of Italian white marble in country churchyards.

Other works by Ledward that deserve mention are the memorial plaque in bronze to the late Sir Alfred Gilbert, R.A., in the crypt of St. Paul's Cathedral; the memorial to the late Lord Milner in Henry VII Chapel, Westminster Abbey; the statuettes in stone of King George V and Queen Mary [q.v.] for niches in the restored cloisters of Norwich Cathedral; "Monolith", purchased for the Tate Gallery out of the Chantrey Bequest Fund in 1936; and the three figures, symbolizing the Submarine Branch of the Royal Navy, the Commandos and the Airborne Forces, in the cloisters of Westminster Abbey. These last were unveiled by Winston Churchill* on May 22, 1948. One of the last commissions he executed was a frieze depicting the peoples of Africa above the entrance of the new Barclays Bank D.C.O. offices in Old Broad Street, London. Before carrying out the work he made an extensive tour of Africa in order to see its peoples in their own land.

In 1956-57 he was a trustee of the Royal Academy and from 1954 to 1956 he was president of the Royal Society of British Sculptors. In 1956 he was appointed O.B.E.

His marriage to Margery Beatrix Cheesman took place in 1911. They had a son and a daughter.

June 23, 1960.

E. T. Leeds, F.S.A., who died at his home at Oxford on August 17, 1955, was Keeper of the Ashmolean Museum at Oxford from 1928 to 1945 and a well-known authority on Anglo-Saxon archaeology. He was 78.

Edward Thurlow Leeds, second son of Alfred N. Leeds, F.G.S., was born in 1877 at Eyebury, near Peterborough. From Uppingham he obtained a classical scholarship to Magdalene College, Cambridge, in 1896, graduating in 1898 with second class honours in the Classical Tripos. From 1900 to 1903 he was a cadet in the Federated Malay States service, and spent some time in China, learning Chinese. But his health then broke down and he had to abandon all thoughts of proceeding with his chosen career. This stay in China made a lasting impression on him, and his fondness for the country and for the language, in which he attained a competent proficiency, never left him.

Recuperation from his breakdown came but slowly, and for several years he lived at home at Eyebury and was unable to seek a full-time post. A chance introduction to Arthur Evans brought him in 1908, when he was quite recovered in health, an appointment as assistant keeper in the Ashmolean Museum at Oxford and finally decided what his life work was to be. Shortly afterwards Evans retired from the keepership, and in the reorganization whch followed Leeds became assistant keeper of the department of antiquities under D. G. Hogarth. In 1928, after Hogarth's death, he became keeper of the department and of the Ashmolean.

Leeds's view of his duties in the Ashmolean was a rigid one. His sense of custody was of the highest, and nothing angered him more than visitors and students whose demeanour indicated that they had not the same sense of the museum director's functions and inhibitions.

As assistant keeper Leeds was in a position to give his attention to departmental duties, though he also ably assisted Hogarth in the general administration of the museum. But when he became keeper administrative matters occupied more and more of his time and—to his constantly expressed regret—he was unable to occupy himself with departmental matters in the way he so longed to do. During his keepership several new extensions to the fabric necessitating much internal reorganization were planned and built. In 1937 his health, which had not been good for many years past, broke down completely as a result of two serious heart attacks, and only his indomitable will-power enabled him, after nearly a year's leave of absence, to return to duty and carry on throughout the war. When he retired in 1945 he was a sadly tired man, but his remarkable powers of recovery again availed him and he was able to devote himself for some years to study and research.

When Leeds went to the museum Arthur Evans had just presented his father's great collection of Anglo-Saxon and Dark Age antiquities, and Leeds's first job was to catalogue and arrange it. This happy chance directed his research into a subject which he found thoroughly congenial and in which he rapidly acquired an international fame. His first book, *The Archaeology of the Anglo-Saxon Settlements,* published in 1913, was a pioneer work in assessing the archaeological evidence for the course of the first English settlements in Britain. Thereafter articles from his pen regularly appeared in *Archaeologia,* the *Antiquaries' Journal*, and elsewhere on detailed aspects of Anglo-Saxon archaeology, to be followed in 1936 by his second book on this subject, *Early Anglo-Saxon Art and Archaeology,* based on his Rhind lectures for 1935. This was again followed by further articles, and by *A Corpus of Early Anglo-Saxon Great Square-headed Brooches,* published in 1949.

But Leeds's fame as a scholar does not rest on his Saxon studies alone. His published articles cover all periods of British archaeology and, indeed, some foreign subjects as well. His book *Celtic Ornament in the British Isles down to A.D. 700,* which appeared in 1933, though its detailed conclusions have not always won acceptance from other writers on the subject, is admittedly a basic work; and his papers on seventeenth and early eighteenth-century wine-bottles and on Oxford seventeenth-century tradesmen's tokens are classics. Recently his friends and pupils have been preparing a volume of essays in his honour, entitled *Dark Age Britain.*

Leeds was, both by nature and by his employment, a museum man rather than a field-worker, but he realized that his post in Oxford, in the centre of a rich archaeological district, made it incumbent on him to do what he could, with such help as he could get from undergraduates and others interested, to rescue the archaeological evidence on local sites marked out for destruction by gravel-diggers or house-builders. This led him year by year to a sequence of excavations on sites of all periods, from a neolithic settlement at Abingdon to the Saxon village at Sutton Courtenay and a medieval castle on Faringdon Folly; his numerous papers on the results of these digs laid the foundation of modern archaeological research in the Oxford district. Trained as he was in older methods, and conservative by nature, Leeds never mastered the more scientific methods of his younger contemporaries; but he was a painstaking excavator, who recorded minutely what he saw, and the soundness of his interpretations of the evidence has—with one or two exceptions—stood the test of time.

The honours that came to him were less than his share. Perhaps the two that he valued most were the official fellowship to which he was elected at Brasenose—his adopted Oxford College—in 1938 (a fellowship which on his retirement in 1945 was converted into an honorary one) and the gold medal of the Society of Antiquaries, awarded to him in 1946. He was elected F.S.A. in 1910 and was a vice-president of the society from 1929 to 1932.

He married, in 1925, Alice Marjory, elder daughter of James Blomfield Wright, of Norwich.

August 18, 1955.

Dr. George Martin Lees, M.C., D.F.C., F.R.S., who was for nearly 23 years chief geologist to the Anglo-Iranian Oil Company Limited before his retirement in 1953, died in hospital in London on January 25, 1955 at the age of 56.

The son of George Murray Lees, of Edinburgh, he was born on April 16, 1898, and was educated at St. Andrew's College, Dublin, and the Royal School of Mines. During the 1914-18 War, after attending the Royal Military Academy at Woolwich, he served in France with the Royal Artillery and then transferred to the R.F.C. He was awarded the M.C., and after a tour of duty as a flying instructor in Egypt he saw further service in Mesopotamia, where he was awarded the D.F.C. He then joined the Civil Administration of Iraq and served as assistant political officer in Kurdistan.

Early in 1921 he joined the Anglo-Iranian Oil Company as assistant geologist, and spent the following three years on survey work in the Middle East. In 1925 he took part in the survey of Oman and obtained from the Sheikh of Qatar a two-year option on the oil rights in the sheikh's territory. After a year's study at the University of Vienna, where he was awarded a doctorate of philosophy for a thesis on the geology of Oman, he engaged in further survey work in many countries, and in 1930, at the age of 32, he was appointed chief geologist.

His discovery of oil-bearing sands on the coast of Dorset led ultimately to the Anglo-Iranian Company's prospecting for oil in Britain, the discovery of the Eakring oilfield in 1939 and other fields in 1941-42, and the production of up to 100,000 tons of good oil for the British war effort. During the 1939-45 War he was seconded to the Petroleum Division of the Ministry of Fuel and Power. His services there, in Persia and Oman, and in the discovery of oil in Britain were marked in 1943 by the award of the Bigsby medal of the Geological Society.

In 1948 he was elected a Fellow of the Royal Society, and from 1951 to 1953 he was president of the Geological Society. He was also a Fellow of the Royal Geographical Society, and of the Institute of Petroleum, and was a member of the Geological Survey Board and the Colonial Geological Survey Board. Early in 1954 he was awarded the Sidney Powers Memorial Medal of the American Association of Petroleum Geologists.

He married in 1931 Hilda Frances, daughter of E. B. Andrews, of Birmingham. There was one son of the marriage.

January 26, 1955.

The Right Rev. Spencer Leeson, D.D., Bishop of Peterborough, died in hospital in London on January 27, 1956 at the age of 63.

His remarkable achievement in reaching the episcopate only 10 years after his ordination was an emphatic pointer to the quality of his character. At different times a soldier, sailor, civil servant, and school-master before entering the church, he brought to his vocation a wealth of practical experience of an unusually large number of life's facets. In most of his writings which, considering his busy life, were large in volume and high in quality, he strove to emphasize the place of religion in education, and these volumes will certainly remain to be counted among the major contributions to the arguments against the trend towards secularization. His delightful reminiscences of his time as rector of St. Mary's, Southampton, *The Parish Priest in Dockland,* manifest his deep and wide sympathies.

Spencer Stottisbury Gwatkin Leeson was born on October 9, 1892, the son of J. R. Leeson, M.D., Charter Mayor of Twickenham. From the Dragon School, Oxford, he entered Winchester as a scholar and thence won a scholarship to New College, Oxford, where he took a first in Classical Moderations in 1913. He was granted a war degree in 1916, but by that time he had been given a commission in the Middlesex Regiment, in which he served in Gibraltar and Flanders. Later in the 1914-18 War he served in the Naval Intelligence Division with a commission in the R.N.V.R. After demobilization he worked in the Board of Education as an assistant principal and was private secretary successively to the Parliamentary Secretary and the Permanent Secretary of the Board. He resigned in 1924, but meanwhile in 1922 he had been called to the Bar by the Inner Temple.

He was an assistant master at Winchester from 1924 to 1926 and headmaster of Merchant Taylors' School from 1927 to 1935. His reputation had by then grown to such stature that he was nominated to succeed the present Bishop of Winchester as headmaster of Winchester College. His term there of 11 years proved a most difficult and testing period, for Winchester, within the area of a possible invasion, was seriously handicapped and in spite of all the efforts of its forceful headmaster found its corporate life more than ordinarily difficult to maintain. In these conditions Leeson decided to enter holy orders and was ordained deacon in 1939 and priest in 1940.

So soon as he was qualified he was appointed Wiccamical Prebendary of Wyndham in Chichester Cathedral, and he was Select Preacher at Cambridge in 1941 and 1951 and at Oxford in 1952. Soon after his appointment as headmaster of Winchester he joined the Council of Southampton University College and gave of his best there until 1949. From 1943 to 1949 he lectured there on the philosophy of religion and he was chairman of the Governors of King Edward VI's School, Southampton, from 1946 to 1949. He delivered the Bampton Lectures at Oxford in 1944 and from 1937 to 1949 he was vice-chairman of the council of King Alfred's Training College, Winchester. In 1946 he was appointed rector of St. Mary, Southampton, and rural dean, and for three years carried out his duties with his usual conscientiousness until his consecration in 1949 as Bishop of Peterborough.

His thought in his published works revolved round the twin subjects of religion and education. These he strove to harmonize and did so to a remarkable extent. In this he showed himself to be a true Platonist and his analysis of Nettleship's essay on Plato's educational theory is abundant proof of his endeavour to bring together Greek clarity of thought and Jewish passion in the synthesis of these which became orthodox Christianity in the first three centuries of the Christian era. His Bampton lectures, published in 1947, on Christian education, enlarge not altogether successfully on the theme, while his volume *The Public Schools Question,* published later in the year, suffers from an approach less profound than a consideration of the implications of the Butler Act really deserves. A parallel criticism might be made of *The Church and the Welfare State* published in 1954. Yet, from all these writings there emerges a fine and sensitive nature in which the Greek element in Christianity finds emphatic and not altogether fashionable expression.

He married in 1918 Mary Cecil, daughter of Dr. Montagu Lomax, and there were three daughters and a son of the marriage.

January 28, 1956.

The death occurred at his home near Paris on August 17, 1955 of the French painter **Fernand Léger.** He was 74.

"Tubism" serves well to describe the brand of Cubism that Léger made peculiarly his own. Out of the several possibilities indicated by Cézanne's famous remark about the geometrical basis of natural forms he selected the cylinder, and, though he admitted other forms, a tubular tendency runs through most of his compositions.

Léger was a Norman, the son of a prosperous cattle grazier who came of a family settled on the land for many generations. He was born at Argentan in 1881, the same year as Picasso* and Braque*. He was trained as an architectural draughtsman and gained an early reputation for the delicacy and precision of his work, and he was also interested in geometry and mechanics for their own sake. As a painter he was mainly self-taught, but at the age of 20 he entered the École des Beaux Arts where he studied under Léon Gérôme. His geometrical interests however attracted him to Seurat, and through him he got to know the work of Cézanne. His youthful admiration of the Douanier Rousseau is recorded, and later he came under the influence of Picasso and Braque. By 1911 he was exhibiting as a Cubist.

During the war of 1914-18 Léger served in the army, and like several of the English artists of his generation, the late C. R. W. Nevinson and Percy Wyndham Lewis [q.v.], for example, he found inspiration in the formal effects of mechanized warfare, and after 1919 reminiscences of them began to appear in paintings of his that had no connexion with military subjects, such as *The City* and *Le disque rouge.* A good many of his later paintings were in the form of mural decorations, and he designed the settings for several ballets and films—*La Création du monde* for the Swedish Ballet in 1923; a laboratory scene with machine forms for a film called *L'inhumaine* in 1924; and, in collaboration with the American photographer Dudley Murphy, an abstract film with geometric forms called *Ballet Mécanique.* Léger was one of the 50 painters and sculptors who in 1929 made portraits of the dancer Mme. Maria Lani.

Works by Léger were seen from time to time in mixed exhibitions in London. In 1937 there was a one-man show of 30 of his paintings in oil and gouache at the London Gallery in Cork

Street; in 1950 a large exhibition of his paintings and drawings at the Tate Gallery; and in 1954 a retrospective exhibition at the Marlborough Gallery. In 1953 an important exhibition of his work was shown in several centres in the United States, where on the whole he was more readily appreciated than in England. The impression these exhibitions gave was that he was one of several painters who were trying to find an adjustment between their art and mechanical surroundings, and that he was a good though rather rationalistic composer, the characteristic components of his pictures being mechanical, or at least geometrical, forms in strong colours, with curved planes to give the maximum of colour gradation. But with these forms were combined those of human figures reduced to a robot condition and, particularly in the later works, vegetable forms, as of flowers and large leaves with twining stems, with a slightly surrealistic effect.

Perhaps what specially distinguished Léger from the other Cubists was his preference for concrete mechanical objects instead of abstract geometrical forms in his compositions. In view of his early proficiency as an architectural draughtsman it is not unlikely that his sensibility was really architectural rather than pictorial. In his *Art Now* Sir Herbert Read*, adopting the terminology of William James, divides Cubists into "tough-minded" and "tender-minded", naming Léger as typical of the former and Braque of the latter. The distinction is apt.

It is questionable if complete integration between the emotions of the artist and mechanical surroundings can be achieved in the medium of painting, but Léger got nearer to it than most and, on its own lines, his work is admirably decorative.

August 18, 1955.

Sir John Lennard-Jones, K.B.E., F.R.S., SC.D., D.SC., Principal of the University College of North Staffordshire since 1953, died in hospital at Stoke-on-Trent on November 1, 1954 at the age of 60.

John Edward Lennard-Jones was born on October 27, 1894, and was educated at Manchester University and at Trinity College, Cambridge. He obtained a doctorate of science at both universities, and during the 1914-18 War served as a pilot in the R.F.C. After holding the appointments of lecturer in mathematics at Manchester University and reader in mathematical physics at Bristol University he was, in 1925, made Professor of Theoretical Physics in the University of Bristol. From 1930 to 1932 he was Dean of the Faculty of Science at Bristol, and in the latter year he was appointed Plummer Professor of Theoretical Science in the University of Cambridge, a position which he retained until his appointment as Principal of the University College of North Staffordshire in 1953.

During the 1939-45 War he served in the Ministry of Supply, being for three years Chief Superintendent of Armament Research and later Director-General of Scientific Research (Defence). From 1942 to 1947 he was a member of the Advisory Council of the Department of Scientific and Industrial Research, and from then until 1953 he was chairman of the Scientific Advisory Council at the Ministry of Supply. He was president of the Faraday Society from 1948 to 1950. In 1946 he was made a K.B.E.

His principal contributions to physical chemistry were to the modern theory of valency and molecular structure, and much recent work in this direction is based upon papers he published in 1929. He was elected a Fellow of the Royal Society in 1933 and was awarded the society's Davy Medal in November 1953 for his work in the field of application of quantum mechanics to the theory of valency and to the analysis of the structure of chemical compounds. Two months before he died he was awarded an honorary doctorate of science by the University of Oxford.

He married in 1925 Kathleen Mary, daughter of the late Alderman S. Lennard, of Leicester. There were a son and a daughter of the marriage.

November 2, 1954.

Sir Gerald Lenox-Conyngham, F.R.S., who died at his home at Cambridge, at the age of 90, on October 27, 1956, had a long and distinguished career as head of the Trigonometrical Survey of India before he began his equally distinguished career as University Reader in Geodesy at Cambridge, a post he did not relinquish until his eightieth year.

Gerald Ponsonby Lenox-Conyngham was born at Moneymore, in Northern Ireland, on August 21, 1866. After a distinguished career at Woolwich, he was commissioned in the Royal Engineers in 1885. In 1889, at the age of 23, he joined the Survey of India and remained a member for 31 years. Soon after his appointment he assisted Sir Sidney Burrard in the longitude observations then in progress. Together they elucidated a troublesome discrepancy that had appeared in these observations. For some years after this longitude work Lenox-Conyngham was engaged in latitude observations in Madras. From 1894 to 1896 he and Burrard made a new determination of the longitude of Karachi. This involved visits to Potsdam and Teheran.

In 1896 he returned to India and two years later was employed in arranging the camps for the observation of the total eclipse of the sun, visible in that year in the Central Provinces. Here he met Professor Newall, who was in charge of one of the parties, and formed a friendship that lasted till the latter's death in 1944.

He went back to England in 1902 on leave and spent a large part of the time preparing himself and obtaining apparatus for a new series of gravity observations. The apparatus obtained at this time was used in all his subsequent work in India and now rests in the Science Museum in London.

The initial purpose of the new series of observations in India was the elucidation of the "hidden range" which Burrard believed to be indicated by observations of the deflexions of the vertical. An earlier series of pendulum observations had been brought to a close by the death of Basevi in 1871 while making pendulum observations high in the Himalayas. The reliability of these earlier observations was in doubt as the effect of the sway of the support of the pendulum had been neglected. The series begun in 1902 therefore represented a fresh start and the observations were the first in India to be free from the large errors that have made it necessary to reject most nineteenth-century pendulum work. In 1912 Lenox-Conyngham became Superintendent of the Trigonometrical Survey and was thereafter occupied almost entirely in administrative work. He was promoted colonel in 1914 and retired in 1921, having had a knighthood conferred upon him in 1919.

Almost immediately he was elected to a Fellowship at Trinity College, Cambridge, and in 1922 was appointed Reader in Geodesy by the university. With the cooperation of Sir Horace Darwin he designed the well-known pendulum apparatus made by the Cambridge Instrument Company. With the assistance of students and of the Ordnance Survey and others, a large number of observations have been made with this apparatus in England and in many other parts of the world. In 1931 the university formed a Department of Geodesy and Geophysics with Lenox-Conyngham at its head. The larger income and improved facilities of this department enabled the work to expand in a number of directions and attracted research students interested in many branches of geophysics. The outbreak of war in 1939 temporarily brought this work to a standstill, but, as soon as peace seemed near, he applied himself with the greatest enthusiasm to the problems of reconstruction. He retired from his Readership in 1947 when over 80 years of age.

Impressive as are the two careers in India and in Cambridge, extending together over nearly 60 years, it is not for this alone that he has earned the affection and esteem of his friends and colleagues everywhere. All those who met him at home, at the meetings of the International Union of Geodesy and Geophysics, or at those of the Pacific Science Congress, learned to love and respect his humanity, dignity, and kindliness. At a luncheon held in honour of his eightieth birthday the Master of Trinity said: "He is a scholar, a soldier, and a great public servant, and he looks all three".

He married in 1890 Elsie Margaret, eldest daughter of Surgeon-General Sir A. F. Bradshaw, K.C.B. There was one daughter of the marriage.

October 29, 1956.

Jack de Leon—See **de Leon.**

Lionel Leonard—See **Lonsdale.**

Sir Henry Leveson Gower—See **Gower.**

Surgeon Commander G. Murray Levick, founder of the British Schools Exploring Society, died on May 30, 1956 at Budleigh Salterton, Devon, at the age of 79.

George Murray Levick was born in 1877 and received his medical training at St. Bartholomew's Hospital, where he qualified M.R.C.S., L.R.C.P. in 1902. After gaining experience in a number of hospital appointments he joined the Royal Navy, and in 1910 was given leave of absence to accompany the expedition of Captain Scott to the Antarctic as medical officer and zoologist. He proved himself an efficient medical officer and, as a zoologist, a keen and sympathetic observer. His descriptions of the penguins, the first of which was published early in 1914, quickly became famous, and he returned to the study of these fascinating creatures more than once in his writing.

However, later in 1914 there was sterner work to do, and he returned to active duty with the Navy while the clouds of war were gathering over Europe. During the 1914-18 War he served in the Grand Fleet and at Gallipoli, rising to the position of fleet surgeon in 1916. As a young man he was a keen and skilful Rugger player and was instrumental in founding the Royal Navy Rugby Union. He was, indeed, throughout his life very much interested in methods of maintaining physical fitness and in physical rehabilitation after illness or injury.

After he retired from the Royal Navy he gave most of his attention to this important aspect of medicine, and was at various times electrologist to St. Thomas's Hospital, consultant physio-therapist to the Victoria Hospital for Children, medical director of the Heritage Craft Schools, Chailey, and consultant for physical treatment to the East Sussex County Council. He was also a member of the London University Committee for Physical Education. Ancillary to these activities and in some aspects even more important was his interest in the training of boys. For many years he was on the council of the Lucas Tooth Boys' Training Fund and on the committee of the National Cadet Training Association.

His most famous, and in some ways his greatest, work was the foundation of the British Schools Exploring Society in 1932. For the remainder of his life he was president and took an active part in organizing annual expeditions to unknown parts of the world, except for the period of the 1939-45 War. He volunteered for duty during that war and served for a time in the Naval Intelligence Department and was also concerned with working out schemes of training for the Commandos. The Royal Geographical Society recognized his services to exploration by the award of the Beck grant to him in 1942. As soon as the war ended the British Schools Exploring Society resumed its activities, and, though no longer young, he was as enthusiastic and efficient as ever in promoting each new expedition.

[A tribute followed this obituary, in the same issue.]

June 1, 1956.

Dr. H. Elvet Lewis, poet, preacher, and former Archdruid of Wales, known to all Welshmen by his Bardic title "Elfed", died at his home at Penarth, Glamorgan, on December 10, 1953 at the age of 93.

Indeed for Welshmen there was no such person as Dr. Elvet Lewis. There was only Elfed, the former Archdruid and leader of Eisteddfodau for some 60 years; the preacher whose long-awaited special services at the local chapel would mean extra seats down the aisle and small boys squatting on every window-sill; the writer of Welsh and English hymns which will never die.

Strange that this grand old man of Wales should have spent the greater part of his ministry in England, yet such was the case. Since he had returned to Wales and a busy retirement he had come ever closer to the hearts of his countrymen. Every year, even after blindness had overtaken him, he donned his silver Bardic robes for the National Eisteddfod and the great throng of his countrymen rose in spontaneous tribute as he was led to his place on the platform. Every year, too, his voice had ushered in the New Year for Welshmen over the Welsh Home Service of the B.B.C. That voice is now stilled, but the thoughts and aspirations which it expressed will ever live in the hearts of Welshmen through his noble contribution to Welsh literature.

Howell Elvet Lewis was born in the Conwyl Elfed district of Carmarthenshire on April 14, 1860. Educated at the Newcastle Emlyn Grammar School and Carmarthen College, he accepted a call at the age of 20 to the pastorate of the English Congregational church at Buckley, in Flintshire, where he soon became known as a preacher of unusual eloquence and charm. In 1885 he became pastor of a church in Hull, returning to Wales in 1891 as minister of the Park Chapel, Llanelly. In 1898 he began his long connexion with London; in that year he became the pastor of Harecourt Chapel, Canonbury, and five years later he undertook the last of his pastoral charges, that of the Welsh Congregational Church at King's Cross, where he remained till his final retirement from pastoral work. Although he had been blind for some years, he continued to preach in Welsh pulpits up to the last few weeks.

He was one of the most popular preachers of the day and he had also taken an active part in other spheres of religious work. He had been president of the National Council of Evangelical Churches, chairman of the Congregational Union of England and Wales, and chairman of the Welsh Congregational Union. He had also visited Madagascar and the United States on special missions. Some of this work was undertaken when blindness threatened, and some when it had actually overtaken him, but he never permitted that misfortune to curb his activities or, to all appearance, to dishearten him.

His career as a writer—and he wrote much both in Welsh and English—was an unusually long one. His first success at an Eisteddfod was won as far back as 1888. This was followed by many similar victories, and his poems, unlike some productions for Eisteddfodau, were popular and widely read. Quotations from Elfed are familiar to most Welsh people, and at one time he was probably the most generally read of all contemporary Welsh poets. He was closely identified with the National Eisteddfod and had served a successful term as Archdruid, but he was also a pioneer along new pathways in Welsh writing, and a forerunner of the renaissance that came with the opening years of this century. His hymns, both Welsh and English, have a place in many collections, and some of his poems are assured of a place in most future anthologies of Welsh verse.

It was said that Dr. Elvet Lewis and the late Lord Lloyd George had the best speaking voices in the country; even in Elfed's old age there was no tremor in his voice and he could make himself heard in a large hall or in the open air without apparent effort. He held the honorary M.A. and D.D. degrees of the University of Wales. In 1948 he was made a Companion of Honour.

He was married three times and had two sons and three daughters. One son, Malcolm Meredith Lewis, is Professor of Law in the University of Bristol.

December 11, 1953.

Mabel Terry Lewis, who died suddenly in a nursing home on November 28, 1957 had had a career on the stage that extended over 50 years.

Though closely related to many theatrical personalities her achievements as an actress were by no means a mere reflection of that association. She was not only successful in her own right, but also a gifted painter of miniatures whose work had been exhibited at the Royal Academy and other London galleries. As a niece of such notabilities as Charles, Ellen, Fred, George, and Marion Terry, it was hardly surprising that she should choose the stage as a career. Indeed, in the circumstances the fact that she was 22 before she made her professional *début* seems remarkable. By that time, however, she had gained a good deal of experience in amateur theatricals, and when she appeared at the Garrick, London, as Lucy in *A Pair of Spectacles,* in the distinguished company of John Hare, she needed little coaching.

Born in London on October 28, 1872, she was the daughter of the late Arthur James Lewis and his wife Kate (Terry). She was educated at home. Her appearances in the early part of her career were not frequent. But in April 1898, she was seen in the part of Mary Faber in *The Master,* again with Hare, at a time made memorable by her mother's emergence from retirement, after an absence of 21 years, to act in the same play.

A few years later she played Muriel Eden in *The Gay Lord Quex,* Madeleine Orchard in *After All,* with Martin Harvey, and also understudied Winifred Emery at the Haymarket in *Caste, There's Many a Slip,* and *The Unforeseen,* playing all three parts.

On her marriage to Captain Ralph C. Batley in 1904 she retired from the stage and did not return to it until 1920, after his death when she accepted the part of Lady Sarah Aldine in *The Young Person in Pink,* which was put on for a special matinée at the Prince of Wales's theatre. Soon afterwards she appeared in *The Grain of Mustard Seed* at the Ambassador's and continued her career in earnest.

In 1923 she went to New York, where she played the part of Mrs. Sabre in *If Winter Comes* at the Gaiety, but a month later was back in London, where she remained until late in 1925. During subsequent visits to America she was a member of casts which included Ethel Barrymore [q.v.], Jane Cowl, and Cyril Maude [q.v.], and played for three seasons in such popular pieces as *Aren't We All, Easy Virtue,* and *The Constant Wife.* Other plays in which she took leading roles in London included *The Skin Game, The Importance of Being Earnest* (as Lady Bracknell), *Death Takes a Holiday, Dinner at Eight, The Admirable Crichton, Distinguished Gathering, Victoria Regina, They Came to a City,* and *Lady Windermere's Fan.* She also appeared in films, including *The Scarlet Pimpernel, Dishonour Bright, The Squeaker, Jamaica Inn, The Adventures of Tartu,* and *They Came to a City.*

She considered painting and shooting as her recreations, and was equally absorbed in her hobbies of farming and dog breeding.

November 30, 1957.

Percy Wyndham Lewis, an artist and writer of originality and of strongly individual temperament, died in a London hospital on March 7, 1957 at the age of 72.

To the generation that can recall the climate of the year 1914 Wyndham Lewis will be remembered in the first place as the founder of the Vorticist movement in painting, and editor of its somewhat singular organ, *Blast.* Almost a quarter of century later, during which period he kept a place near the centre of the stage in the intellectual and artistic society in London, he came into the public eye as a painter through the rejection of his portrait of T. S. Eliot* by the Royal Academy. But the public as a whole were probably little aware of his distinction as a controversial writer, a mordantly satirical novelist, a critic of uncommon dialectical subtlety, and a master of English invective.

Wyndham Lewis's was a stormy career because as both painter and writer he was always the man in opposition. Unlike many painters who start new movements, however, his talents were undeniable. He had a harsh integrity of pictorial vision and was an incisive if not perhaps conspicuously sensitive draughtsman. His ideas about life and art, though often launched in unnecessarily startling fashion, were as often distinguished by a genuine force of independence. A champion of intellect in art, and a most formidable critic of the cant of democracy, it was once said of him that he could start more hares in a paragraph than others could in a volume.

Percy Wyndham Lewis was born in America in 1884. Educated at Rugby, he studied art at the Slade School, where he won a scholarship at the age of 16 and was considered the most brilliant draughtsman the school had produced since Augustus John*. After leaving the Slade he travelled and studied in Holland, Spain, and France. He was first noticed publicly in 1912, when he exhibited some symbolical panels and a large painting, "Kermesse", which seems to have been the first English work to show the influence of Cubism. He had already led the secession from the New English Art Club known as the Camden Town Group, which in 1914 was enlarged into the London Group. But Lewis, his band of Vorticists trailing behind him, could not long remain happy in this fold and in 1918 resigned in order to set up the short-lived "Group X".

At this distance of time it is possible to recognize in these artistic alarms and excursions a simpler expression of intellectual discontent than was then apparent. Vorticism, which—though it was not political—had some affinities with Italian Futurism, expressed a sort of "two-fisted he-man" attitude to life and art, running to expletives, both pictorial and verbal. It represented, in fact, the tough element in the general revolt against academic art.

When war broke out in 1914 Lewis was recovering from septicaemia. He employed his convalescence in writing his first novel, *Tarr,* which on its first appearance (it was afterwards revised and was republished in 1951) had a merited success among fellow intellectuals but was above the head of the ordinary fiction-reading public. Ribald, distinctive, and brilliantly decorated, it remains perhaps his best known novel, although *The Revenge for Love* (1937) is often thought a better book. He then enlisted in the Royal Garrison Artillery, and served as bombardier and later as commissioned officer.

The fighting over, he retired, as he said, "underground", making occasional portrait drawings and producing a series of provocative volumes in which, as Whistler said of Wilde, he was sometimes inclined to spell art with a capital "I". In *The Art of Being Ruled* (1926) he attempted an analysis of society which foreshadows his later approximation to an authoritarian philosophy.

In *The Apes of God* (1930), an immense work of fiction charged with a fury of eloquent opposition to almost everything and everybody, Lewis left the impression of a comic novelist overcome by the novelist of ideas. *The Diabolical Principle and the Dithyrambic Spectator* (1931) and *Doom of Youth* (1932), both astringent and stimulating essays, were marked by much tilting against windmills; and *Left Wings Over Europe* (1936) in its anti-democratic bias seemed to come near to exasperated justification of Nazi principle. In *The Hitler Cult,* however, published in December 1939, Lewis set himself the task of refusing to take the Führer seriously.

His sight had been failing for some years before in 1951 he said simply, "I can no longer see a picture". For the last five years of his life he was quite blind. But he continued to write with undaunted intellectual energy. The most significant effort he made towards the end was the second and third parts of the trilogy, *The Human Age,* which had been begun as far back as 1928 with *The Childermass.* The B.B.C. broadcast a version of the novel in 1951 and then commissioned Lewis to write the promised sequel. A version of the whole work was broadcast on three nights in 1955 before the publication of the second and third volumes, *Monstre Gai* and *Malign Fiesta.*

The rejection by the Royal Academy of his portrait of T. S. Eliot, which followed a one-man show of his paintings and drawings in London in the previous year, caused a considerable stir, and was altogether an unfortunate affair. For Lewis, whose drawings, notably the more or less realistic but severely simplified figure studies of his maturity, rank with the best of their time, and whose symbolical compositions rarely fail in power and interest, was probably most impressive in portraiture.

He married in 1929, Anne Hoskyns, who survives him. She is the subject of a number of his paintings and drawings.

March 9, 1957.

The death on November 29, 1952 of **Rosa Lewis,** known to a vast number of friends as Rosa, and to even larger numbers as the proprietress of the Cavendish Hotel, Jermyn Street, for nearly half a century, evokes memories of a society which two wars have done much to destroy.

She was Rosa Ovenden, one of nine children, and married very early in life. Her own story is that she and her husband quarrelled while leaving the church, and she thereupon began to earn her own living in domestic service. A quite remarkable gift for cookery early came to the notice of King Edward VII, when, as Prince of Wales, he was entertained by the fourth and last Lord Ribblesdale, then Master of the Buckhounds. Her fame thereafter spread rapidly, with the result that in the very early years of this century she was able to set up as proprietress of the Cavendish Hotel. Once there, other gifts quickly became evident. First, a remarkably sure and very personal flair for furnishing and decoration, and a delightful, if austere, taste in dress. Few who knew her in her heyday will forget the tall, elegant figure who welcomed them, clad in a dress cut on the severe lines affected by a famous habit maker.

Guests of the hotel were not welcomed unless they were personally known to the proprietress, or came with an introduction from one of her constantly increasing circle of friends on both sides of the Atlantic. A slight air of raffishness might sometimes creep into the parties which Rosa Lewis constantly entertained in her sitting room; this atmosphere somehow seemed to be heightened by the enormous number of portraits and photographs of the famous, and not so famous, and the merely notorious, which lined the walls. On those occasions champagne flowed freely, but any declension from Mrs. Lewis's standards invited the rebuke: "You treat my house like an hotel!" That remark held the secret of her fame; she saw herself the hostess looking after her guests, and many young men will remember her thus with gratitude. The fact that money was later collected (from those who could afford it) by her devoted companion, Miss Jeffrey, and later by others, some of them the sons and grandsons of Mrs. Lewis's first friends and guests, who determined that she should fulfil her lifelong ambition to die in harness, was of very minor importance to her. Thus she remained a welcoming, gracious survivor from another age.

December 1, 1952.

Sinclair Lewis, whose satirical novels of American life in the period between the wars came as something of a shock to the reading public on both sides of the Atlantic, died on January 10, 1951 in a nursing home in Rome at the age of 65.

Sinclair Lewis was born at Sauk Center, Minnesota, on February 7, 1885. His father was a doctor of medicine, and the young Lewis received a representative American education, graduating from Yale University in 1905. He had no doubt, even at the age of 20, that he would one day become a novelist, and when he went to live in New York he began serving his apprenticeship first in journalism and then as reader and adviser to various publishing businesses, more particularly to the house of George Doran [q.v.], who was at that time developing in the United States the reputations of the group of young English novelists which began to attract notice at the end of the first decade of the twentieth century.

His early and comparatively unsuccessful books, such as *Our Mr. Wrenn* (1914), *The Trail of the Hawk* (1915), and *The Job* (1917), were characteristically American in their style and method, written with due attention to the shaping of a story, and designed, it may be inferred, to meet the requirements of the American fiction market. It was not until the publication of *Main Street* in 1920, a book that achieved instant success in the United States, that he broke away from tradition and first exhibited himself as a pungent critic of American life. In this instance his criticism did not make a wide appeal to English readers, since they were unable to realize the finer points of the satire on the society of a typical growing township in the Middle West. They were, however, more appreciative of the next book, *Babbitt,* published some two years later, in which the central figure, an estate agent or "realtor", came much nearer to the popular conception of the American "type".

In these early books, however, the development of American slang to a point amounting almost to a difference of language interposed something of a bar between Sinclair Lewis and a wide English public, a fact that he himself realized after his first visit to Europe, several months of which were spent in England. With a rather characteristic arrogance he blamed us for our "ignorance" in a long interview given on his return to New York in May 1923, but whether as a concession to that ignorance or because his subjects did not necessitate such free use of the American idiom, his later novels did not make the same demand for a glossary.

The more important of these subsequent books were *Martin Arrowsmith* (1925), *Elmer Gantry* (1927), and *Ann Vickers* (1933). In the first of these it is the medical profession, in the second a Baptist minister, and in the third, incidentally, certain aspects of the prison system on which Sinclair Lewis turns his critical attention, the bitterest and most scathing of the three attacks being that upon the hypocrisy of such men as Elmer Gantry. In addition to these books he found time to write such less serious novels as *Mantrap, The Man who knew Coolidge,* and *Dodsworth,* perhaps the least typically American of his books. After *Dodsworth* came an apparent decline in quality, but Lewis staged something of a "come back" with *It Can't Happen Here*—the reaction of the American liberal to the danger of dictatorship. A new aspect of American life was revealed in *Gideon Planish,* published in 1943, that of the moral, philanthropic, and religious clubs which flourish in the United States. In *Kingsblood Royal,* the subject of racial antagonism in the United States is treated with all the author's polemical skill, and he vigorously takes sides with the coloured people. When *It Can't Happen Here* was dramatized Lewis took a sudden interest in the theatre, for which he wrote and acted without much success. The fact was that, like Alexander, he sighed for new worlds to conquer and could not find them.

In November 1930, Sinclair Lewis was awarded the Nobel Prize for literature. This does not inevitably afford a measure of his achievement, but the award certainly stimulated further interest in the general purpose and permanent value of his novels. Like Dickens, Sinclair Lewis was a keen and none too kindly critic of his own times, though the analogy need not be pressed further. He had a gift for seeing the more flagrant weaknesses and abuses of contemporary American society, and pilloried them by presenting an exaggerated figure to represent the things he despised. Nevertheless, he never followed the example of the writer to whom his youthful devotion was given, by holding up his story to analyse the social causes that lay behind the evil or to indicate a remedy. In such a portrait as that of Elmer Gantry, the subject is treated with an excess of spleen. George F. Babbitt, a truer representative of his class, is handled more gently. In *Martin Arrowsmith* and *Ann Vickers,* the chief character is the sufferer, and their creator's satire is directed on the conditions against which they had to struggle. But the qualities that distinguished Lewis's work from the mass of contemporary fiction, whether English or American, were the wit, the richness of invention, and the imaginative insight, which were all an expression of his tremendous vitality. That ebullience of his was in fact characteristic of his personal relations not less than of his writing and at one period he succeeded in achieving a certain unpopularity on both sides of the Atlantic by his outspoken comments on men and manners.

He was twice married, the second time in 1928 to Miss Dorothy Thompson* author of *The New Russia* (1929), a well-known journalist, who was invited by the secret police to leave Germany in August 1934, the reason given being an objection to the tone and substance of an article published by her some four years earlier, after an interview with Hitler.

January 11, 1951.

Liaquat Ali Khan, who was assassinated by shooting while addressing a public meeting at Rawalpindi, West Punjab, on October 16, 1951, was the first Prime Minister of Pakistan and its undisputed leader after the death of its founder, Mohamad Ali Jinnah, in September 1948. He was 56.

He brought to bear on the vital issues confronting the new nation qualities which in some ways contrasted with those of "the Great Leader", and which were sorely needed for the survival and progress of Pakistan after the severe birth-pangs it endured. His conceptions of democracy on a basis of Islamic Socialism were much wider than those of the imperious chief architect of the new state, and it fell to him to influence his people towards patience, tolerance, and moderation, joined with the inflexible purpose for Pakistan to survive and prosper as the greatest Islamic nation in the world. He showed skill in combining a due regard for the orthodox conceptions of the religious leaders with modern ideas of nation building. Early in 1951 he won a moral victory at the conference of Commonwealth Prime Ministers, held in London, by his determination that the question of Kashmir should be discussed. It was well said on that occasion that a great step forward had been made when the Prime Ministers were prepared to make practical proposals which were accepted by all, with one exception. If affairs in Kashmir have since worsened, it is all the greater loss to his country and to the Commonwealth that Liaquat Ali Khan has fallen before his time to an assassin's bullet.

Liaquat Ali Khan, who was born on October 1, 1895, belonged to a family of Punjab landowners founded there by migrants from Persia some five centuries ago. After graduating at what is now the Aligarh Muslim University, he came to England in 1918 and joined Exeter College, Oxford, where he took an active part in the Indian Majlis and was elected its treasurer. After graduation he was called to the Bar by the Inner Temple in 1921. For 14 years from 1926 he was a member of the United Provinces Legislature. He became leader of the Democratic Party, and in the last six years in the House was a Deputy President. He came to London in 1937 as a member of the Indian trade delegation to negotiate fresh agreements on preferences in replacement of the Ottawa pacts. In the preceding year Jinnah, yielding to solicitations to take charge of the moribund Muslim League, had reorganized that body and set it on the road which led to the creation of Pakistan. He selected Liaquat Ali to be the honorary general secretary.

Liaquat Ali never believed in the employment

of force for political ends, and could not have been whole-hearted in the acceptance of the decision of the League in the summer of 1946 to authorize the leader to introduce "direct action" to such extent as he thought appropriate. After a first refusal the league in the autumn came into the interim National Government which had been set up by the late Lord Wavell with Pandit Nehru* as vice-president. The distribution of offices in the composite Cabinet was on a percentage basis, and Liaquat was made Finance Member in one of the most divided of coalitions known to history.

Early in June 1947 the way of escape from an intolerable situation was found by the agreement pressed on the acceptance of the main parties by Lord Mountbatten. The withdrawal of British authority was ante-dated by eight months, and on August 15, 1947 the two Dominions of India and Pakistan came into being. In the latter Dominion Jinnah, now styled the Quaid-i-Azam (Great Leader) took the Governor-Generalship and Liaquat became Prime Minister. Relying in part on the call of Islamic brotherhood, the Karachi Government was able to deal firmly with the disruptive declaration of Abdul Gaffar Khan, the "Frontier Ghandhi", for a separate Pathanistan, and also to reduce greatly the intolerable drain of the cost of frontier defence. While various matters of day to day administration were adjusted between the two Dominions, they were bitterly opposed over the Kashmir dispute, with Indian troops waging war on the Azad (free) Kashmiri fighters and the tribal incursions over the border to assist them. There was also the grave irritant of the Hyderabad issue, ultimately leading to "the five days' war", and the setting up of an Indian military administration as the stepping stone to absorption with the Indian Union.

In all these matters the Quaid-i-Azam, with failing health and fits of impatience over details, had to rely more and more upon the Prime Minister, whose statesmanship grew with increasing responsibilities. Hence the death of the Great Leader, less than 13 months after the creation of Pakistan, was not so shattering a blow as had been feared. There was a Joshua to succeed Moses. With a new Governor-General, Kwaja Nazimuddin*, free of great personal ambition and brought in from East Bengal, Liaquat Ali had no rival in assuming the *de facto* headship of the state, and it was soon clear that he had firmly seized power. Soon after he went with the Begum to London for the Conference of Prime Ministers, and like the two other representatives of Asian Dominions, those of India and Ceylon, was warmly welcomed. To this historic new development of Commonwealth relations he made his contribution with dignity and success.

At a quite early stage in the Kashmir dispute Liaquat Ali made approaches to nations of the Commonwealth with a view to their coming together to settle what he termed "family differences", but Whitehall viewed the proposal with timidity, and India in self-righteous mood referred the issue to the United Nations. There were interminable discussions and one proposal for mediation after another fell to the ground. Not until the beginning of 1949 did a Five-Power Commission from the Security Council induce the parties to sign a "cease-fire" agreement.

The Pakistan leader was not happy over the compromise reached at the Conference of Dominion Prime Ministers in London in April 1949, whereby India remained a full member of the Commonwealth while adopting a republican constitution. Before leaving London he gave the warning that Pakistan should not be taken for granted and treated like a camp follower. Nehru's visit to the United States and Canada as an honoured guest in the autumn of 1949 was followed by the intimation that Liaquat Ali was to be the guest of Stalin [q.v.] in Moscow. It was freely said in Karachi in this connexion that if the dire necessity arose it would be a lesser evil to fall under Soviet rather than under Hindu Indian domination. The Moscow project, however, did not mature, and in the summer of 1950 Liaquat Ali and his Begum were the guests of President Truman* and the Canadian Government, receiving a welcome no less cordial than that accorded earlier to the Indian Prime Minister.

The visit was made on the morrow of a great act of statesmanship by the two Premiers. From the beginning of the year the continuance of the cold war over Kashmir and the aggravation of trading obstacles between the two countries arising from devaluation of the rupee in India but not in Pakistan had led to a renewal of the flight of refugees, especially between the two Bengals, but with further influxes of Muslims into west Pakistan, the press of both countries gave lurid stories of sufferings endured and attacks on defenceless minorities on either side of the border. In the words of Nehru, the two countries were on the brink of the precipice when in April 1950 Liaquat Ali went to Delhi and negotiated with the Indian Prime Minister an agreement on the treatment and rights of minorities and on the prevention of communal strife. This great departure stemmed and eventually stayed the tide of intermigration. Nehru, who paid a return visit to Karachi by way of showing the mutuality of the settlement, lost from his Cabinet the two Bengali members, one of whom had been president of the militant Hindu Mahasabha. In the changed atmosphere at the top other outstanding questions, such as that of exchange of commodities, were settled; but the problem of Kashmir continued until Liaquat Ali's death to be the main cloud between the two sister nations.

October 17, 1951.

Bishop of Lichfield—See **Woods.**

Dr. Scott Lidgett, C.H., D.D., LL.D., who was chosen to be the first president of the United Methodist Church in 1932 after the union of all the Methodist Churches, and who had a strong claim to be considered the greatest Methodist since John Wesley, died on June 16, 1953 at the age of 98 in a nursing home at Epsom, Surrey.

He was also one of the best known Wesleyan ministers; none in this generation had taken such an active part in the public life of London. He was leader of the Progressive Party in the L.C.C. for 10 years, 1918-28, Vice-Chancellor of London University, 1930-1932, and Warden of Bermondsey Settlement from 1891 to 1949. His public offices were innumerable. Yet he never became "important", but retained his almost childlike simplicity. His spirituality was not choked by the cares of organization and in consequence his influence in his own denomination was not lessened but rather enhanced by his public activities. These all grew out of his work at the Bermondsey Settlement for which the Wesleyan Conference set him apart in 1890. There he met problems which had to be solved by public action and he saw to it that that action was taken.

Born at Lewisham on August 10, 1854, John Scott Lidgett came of clerical stock. He was educated at the Blackheath Proprietary School and then at University College, London. He entered the Wesleyan ministry in 1876 and held pastorates at Tunstall, Southport, Cardiff, Wolverhampton, and Cambridge. But all these were only preliminary to the great work of his life in London. In 1891 he founded with the late Dr. W. F. Moulton, head master of The Leys School, Cambridge, the Bermondsey Settlement, of which he was warden for 58 years. For more than a generation he carried on work on institutional lines. In his interesting *Reminiscences,* published in 1928, he records that the object of this settlement was "to bring a force of educated workers to give help to all the higher interests in the neighbourhood, religious, educational, social and administrative". His method was that of settling a community of social workers who by friendship and cooperation would work towards the well-being of the whole neighbourhood. Some of the pioneer work of the settlement has been taken over by the Borough of Bermondsey, including schools for mothers, day nurseries for children, and educational opportunities under the London County Council. The Alice Barlow House, the home of the activities of the women's branch of the settlement, is now used chiefly as a very successful youth centre.

From an early date Dr. Scott Lidgett began to take a deep interest in educational and social problems. In 1897 he became the member for the Southwark division on the London School Board, was an alderman of the London County Council from 1905 to 1910, a member of the L.C.C. from 1910 to 1922, when he lost his seat, but was immediately re-elected alderman, an office he held until 1928. In succession to Sir John Benn he was leader of the Progressive Party in the council for 10 years from 1918. With McKenna and Birrell he fought many a hard battle to secure a better recognition of the Free Churches in education.

In 1913 he was appointed a member of the Commission on Venereal Diseases. He was chairman of the executive committee of the Central Council for Nursing from 1922 to 1928. In 1922 he was elected a member of the Senate of the University of London, with which he had always kept in close contact. In 1929 he was appointed Deputy Vice-Chancellor, and in June 1930 he was paid the honour of being elected by the Senate Vice-Chancellor of the University for two years.

All his life Dr. Scott Lidgett's interests and sympathies were with children and young people. That is why he accepted the appointments of governor of the Royal Holloway College in 1931 and of Queen Mary's College in 1934, and served as chairman of the Universities China Committee from 1933 to 1936. Every young man who entered the Methodist ministry received a word of encouragement from the veteran who had fought a good fight.

He was president of the National Council of the Evangelical Free Churches of England and Wales in 1906-07 and president of the Wesleyan Methodist Conference in 1908-09. In 1909 the University of Aberdeen conferred upon him the honorary degree of D.D. From 1912 till 1915 he was president of the Free Church Commission, and became honorary secretary of the National Council of the Evangelical Free Churches in 1914.

A leading Nonconformist, Dr. Scott Lidgett was frequently consulted on ecclesiastical questions by those outside his own Church. In the many conferences between Anglicans and Free Churchmen on church union, and in the presentation to successive Lambeth conferences of the position of the Nonconformists, his advice was considered of great value. He worked very hard for the reunion of the Methodist churches, and it was a proud day for him when it was accomplished. His appointment as a Companion of Honour in 1933 was in recognition of this service, as well as for his work at the Bermondsey Settlement.

Dr. Scott Lidgett was well known for his literary work, first as editor of the *Methodist Times* for 11 years from 1907, and subsequently as joint editor of the *Contemporary Review*, a position he held from 1911. His own publications were many. He delivered the Fernley Lecture in 1897 and issued it afterwards under the title *The Spiritual Principle of the Atonement.* The book passed through many editions. In 1907 he published an important volume, *The Christian Religion, its Meaning and Proof.* His views of churchmanship and his schemes for a wider union of Christians were proclaimed in the *Apostolic Ministry*, 1909, and *God, Christ and the Church*, 1927.

Dr. Scott Lidgett's most widely read book was *The Cross Seen from Five Standpoints*, published in 1941. He continued writing and having books published every year or so and published his *Salvation* in 1952.

He kept in touch with the leaders of modern thought, and took every opportunity of pressing the claims of the causes he espoused. He was much loved by a host of friends who remember his winsome personality more than the cleverness which carried him through so many enterprises. He was good company, for in his long life he had known many great people and witnessed many important events and his memory and power of conversation remained with him to the end. In Bermondsey he was loved like a father. He had stayed with the people during the heavy part of the "blitz" and he never had any thought of leaving them or his work on account of advancing years. He gave them almost 60 years of active service, and soon after his retirement in 1952 their affection and respect was expressed by his election as an honorary freeman of the borough.

Dr. Scott Lidgett's wife, who was a daughter of the late Andrew Davies, M.D., of Newport, Monmouthshire, died in May 1934. For more than 40 years she managed the domestic affairs of the Bermondsey Settlement, and her husband said of her: "Without her aid my work could not have been done". His only son was killed in the 1914-18 war, and he leaves one daughter.

June 18, 1953.

Roy Limbert, who together with Sir Barry Jackson* founded the Malvern Festival in 1929, and was joint director of the festival until 1938 when he assumed the sole control, died on November 29, 1954 at his home at Malvern. He was 60.

The son of Charles Alberic William Limbert, he was born at Surbiton, Surrey, on December 26, 1893, and was educated at Nelson College, Blackheath, and Bedford School. He began his career of theatrical management in 1911, and in 1912-13 he was general manager for the touring production of *The Girl in the Train.* After touring with his own concert parties in early 1914 he joined the Army on the outbreak of war and served until 1919. After demobilization he engaged in commerce, and in 1923 founded the firm of Ad-Visers, Ltd., of which he became chairman and managing director.

In 1929 he and Sir Barry Jackson founded the Malvern Festival—he was the lessee of the Festival Theatre there—and began a notable series of productions. The first performance of Shaw's *The Apple Cart* was given at the festival in 1929, and this was followed in 1930 by *The Barretts of Wimpole Street.* Among other important productions were Drinkwater's *A Man's House* and Denis Johnston's *The Moon in the Yellow River* in 1934, and Shaw's *The Simpleton of the Unexpected Isles* in 1935.

In 1938 Limbert was invited by the Malvern Council to direct that year's festival, as Sir Barry Jackson had announced that he was unable to accept the responsibility of organizing another. Limbert therefore undertook the entire direction and produced five new plays—Shaw's *Geneva*, J. B. Priestley's *Music at Night*, C. K. Munro's *Coronationtime at Mrs. Beam's*, Lord Dunsany's [q.v.] *Alexander*, and James Bridie's [q.v.] *The Last Trump.* Limbert also revived *St. Joan*, with Elisabeth Bergner playing the part of Joan. At the following year's Malvern Festival he produced six new plays, including Shaw's *In Good King Charles's Golden Days* and Bridie's *What Say They?* After the 1939-45 War he directed one festival—that of 1949.

Apart from his work for the Malvern Festival and the Malvern Company, founded by him in 1932, which has played continuously since then, not only at Malvern but at many other important centres, he was also responsible for many West End productions. These included *Rookery Nook* (with Barry O'Brien) at the St. Martin's Theatre in 1942, *Mr. Bolfry* (with Linnet and Dunfee, Ltd., and Alastair Sim [d. 1976]) at the Westminster Theatre in 1943, *The Anatomist* at the Westminster Theatre in 1948, and *Black Chiffon*, also at the Westminster Theatre, in 1949.

Between 1940 and 1949 he presented 10 special Malvern summer seasons at the Arts Theatre, Cambridge, and in 1944, 1945, and 1946 he presented special Malvern seasons at the Memorial Theatre, Stratford-on-Avon. In 1948 he directed the first Harrogate season of plays by Shaw.

November 30, 1954.

Frederick Alexander Lindemann—
See **Cherwell.**

Walter Lindrum, O.B.E., the greatest of billiards players, died suddenly near Brisbane on July 30, 1960. He was 61.

Lindrum was by general consent the greatest all-round billiards player the game had ever seen. His early achievements in Australia clearly conveyed that he was a player of pronounced merit, but it was not until he paid his first visit to Britain in the winter of 1929-30 that it could be realized how brilliant he was.

The son of a former Australian champion, Walter Albert Lindrum was born at Kalgoorlie on August 29, 1898. He was 30 when he first came to England, and he soon broke almost every record there was to break. His speed of scoring was extraordinary. Lindrum, who was a left-handed player, had developed the close cannon method of scoring to such a pitch that he not only outplayed but also outpointed his opponents so decisively that it soon became apparent that the only way he could be matched with any of the English professionals was by the concession of a very liberal start. Among the many records he established was a break of 4,137, which easily beat the great break of 3,304 made 42 years previously by W. J. Peall, and which then stood as a record except for long runs made by entirely specialist methods.

In 1933 Lindrum, to demonstrate the ease with which he could score by nursery cannons, played the balls two and a half times round the table in a run of 529 consecutive cannons. He made four-figure breaks with almost daily frequency and it can be said of him that he revolutionized the game. Although he scored so freely by this means Lindrum was equally as good in any other department of the game, some of his four figure breaks being made with only an occasional short run of cannons.

Lindrum did not take part in the professional championship until 1933, when he beat J. Davis in the final, this success being repeated the following year. Those were the only two occasions he competed. As the result of these successes the event became the world championship; and another event, the United Kingdom championship, was instituted, this being confined to home players. Lindrum was still world champion when he retired in 1950.

Lindrum was a charmingly modest man and one who never quibbled at a decision. He took the game very seriously as his profession. Even when he was playing apparently at the top of his form, he was known to put in an hour's practice in his rest time in the course of an important match to satisfy himself that some little detail had not been overlooked. After his retirement from competitive play he used his fame and skill to raise large sums of money for charity.

August 1, 1960.

Lord Lindsay of Birker, Master of Balliol College, Oxford, from 1924 until 1949 and latterly Principal of the University College of North Staffordshire, died suddenly on March 18, 1952 at the age of 72. He was Vice-Chancellor of Oxford University from 1935 to 1938.

The Right Hon. Alexander Dunlop Lindsay, Lord Lindsay of Birker, of Low Ground in the County of Cumberland in the peerage of the United Kingdom, was born on May 14, 1879, at Glasgow, and was the son of the Rev. T. M. Lindsay, D.D., Principal of the United Free Church College at Glasgow and a well-known writer on ecclesiastical history. To his father he owed a deep religious outlook on life and a philosophical attitude to its problems. He was educated at Glasgow Academy and proceeded to Glasgow University, where he had a distinguished career and showed a marked aptitude for philosophy. He then determined to go to Oxford and sat for a scholarship at Balliol, but was passed over in favour of a candidate who afterwards edited the *Boys' Own Paper.* University College elected him a scholar, and his career at Oxford was no less distinguished than at Glasgow. He obtained first classes both in Moderations and in Greats and was president of the Union in 1902.

Lindsay's bent for philosophy was now clear and he held the Clark Philosophical Fellowship at Glasgow from 1902 to 1904, followed by the Shaw Philosophical Fellowship at Edinburgh from 1904 to 1909. In 1904 he began his life's work as a teacher of philosophy by his appointment as assistant to the Professor in the Victoria University, Manchester. In 1906 Balliol, which had rejected him as a scholar, called him back to Oxford as Fellow and Classical Tutor to do the philosophy teaching for Greats. This office he held continuously until 1922, succeeding J. A. Smith as Jowett Lecturer in Philosophy in 1910. He lectured regularly on the *Republic* of Plato and in 1907 published a translation of it, but his interests were turning more towards modern philosophy and, in particular, to Kant, whose doctrine became the core of his philosophical thought. He published a small book on Kant in 1913 and had, previously, written also *The Philosophy of Bergson.* His lectures were vigorous and stimulating, and in his private tuition he became a power in the college, even inspiring pupils with no great philosophical capacity with a love of the subject and with the habit of thinking for themselves. In 1907, soon after his appointment at Balliol, he married Erica, daughter of Francis Storr, whose mind and personality counted for much in the rest of his life. They had two sons and a daughter.

During the 1914-18 war Lindsay served with the labour battalions in France. His capacity for organization and his tact in managing men led to speedy promotion. He was several times mentioned in dispatches, attained the rank of lieutenant-colonel and was made C.B.E. His experience with troops of several nationalities undoubtedly widened his horizon and aroused new interests. On his return to Balliol he was of great help to the college in dealing with the large and miscellaneous body of men who came up to continue or begin their university education after service in the Army. It was his sense of their needs which led him to think that the university should provide some course in which men could study philosophy without the classical background. He played a large part in the establishment of the Honours School of Philosophy, Politics and Economics (Modern Greats) in 1922 and also urged the foundation of a school in which philosophy might be studied in conjunction with the principles of natural science.

In 1922 Lindsay was elected Professor of Moral Philosophy at Glasgow, but his stay there was short, for in 1924 on the death of A. L. Smith the Fellows of Balliol recalled him to be Master. It was not an easy task for a "non-Balliol" man, younger than several of his colleagues and known to have advanced political views. During the earlier years of his mastership the college was expanding in many directions. Even when the rush of the end of the war in 1918 had subsided, undergraduate numbers remained fairly steady at 250 and the problem of residence was met through the generosity of old members of the college by the building of Holywell Manor. The number of Fellows too was doubled, partly by the necessity of providing for tuition in new subjects, partly by the assignment to the college, under the Commissioners' Statutes, of a considerable number of professorial Fellows. With all these developments Lindsay grappled with alacrity and with a ready optimism. He characteristically insisted on taking his share in tuition, lectured regularly on philosophical subjects, and heard essays from undergraduate members of the college and from a number of students from the women's colleges. He also preached each term in the college chapel, and a volume of his sermons was published in 1927 with the title *The Nature of Religious Truth.* His outlook was also shown in *The Essentials of Democracy* (1929), *Christianity and Economics* (1933), *The Churches and Democracy* (1934), and in a small but careful and critical study of *Karl Marx's "Capital"* in 1925. A more permanent and directly philosophical work was his larger book on Kant published in 1934.

In 1935 Lindsay was nominated by the Chancellor (Lord Halifax [q.v.]) as Vice-Chancellor of the University. Some members of the university were afraid that he would prove rash and hasty in his designs and inconsiderate of the views of others. Such forebodings were quickly silenced. Though he was clear in holding and stating his own opinions, his perfect fairness and his personal courtesy, combined with an untiring energy, enabled the university in the next three years to carry through many difficult undertakings.

Lindsay was an enthusiast and a pioneer who, as the master of a college, had many critics. They doubted the soundness of his judgment of men and they wished that his interests in the outside world had been less multifarious and less political. There was never any doubt as to the eagerness of his desire to keep Balliol and Oxford as living forces for civilization in a changing world. The eagerness of his vision and his longing that theory should result in action made him something of a prophet; but he had the austerity, not the severity of a prophet, and the simplicity of his character, free from any assumption or affectation, endeared him even to those who differed most from him.

It was no surprise to those who knew his pioneering spirit when he accepted the invitation to become Principal of the University College of North Staffordshire. There, with a quarter of a century in control of an old and famous seat of learning behind him, he began at the age of 70 a new life, bringing his zeal and understanding to the practical men and women of the Potteries. It was not, perhaps, so great a change, for the Workers' Educational Association had always been near to his heart and he seized the opportunity to bring the benefits of education in its widest connotation to those whose main work would necessarily be with their hands. He looked forward to many years' work in this selfless pursuit and had indeed made great strides in organizing the new college on original lines.

He is succeeded in the barony by his elder son, the Hon. Michael Francis Lindsay, who was born in 1909 and married in 1941 Hsiao Li, daughter of Li Wen-chi, of Lishih, Shansi. There are three children of the marriage, a son and two daughters.

March 19, 1952.

Major-General George M. Lindsay, C.B., C.M.G., C.B.E., D.S.O., who died on November 28, 1956 at the age of 76, played a leading part in the development of two of the most important instruments in modern warfare, the machine-gun and the tank, and of the corps which handled them.

An ardent advocate of the machine-gun before 1914, when few soldiers recognized its potentialities, he became the moving spirit in the formation of the Machine-Gun Corps, and the formulation of its tactical technique, in the First World War. After that war he turned, with even more far-reaching vision, from the instrument that had paralysed tactical mobility to one that would revive it, and became one of the foremost advocates of mobile armoured warfare.

His association with the new arm began in 1921, when he was sent out to Baghdad to take charge of the three armoured car companies in Iraq, which were formed into No. 1 Armoured

Car Group, Tank Corps. With this aptly entitled No. 1 Group, Lindsay produced the first extensive practical application of the new gospel of armoured mobility that was being expounded by Fuller* and a few forward-thinking soldiers.

On arrival in Iraq Lindsay set out to explore both the state of the companies and the problems of operating armoured cars in such a country. In overhauling the organization he weeded out a number of inefficient officers, but relied more on making officers and men efficient by infecting them with his own enthusiasm. He was then, as later, the most sympathetic of reformers, with a geniality and a kindness rare in dynamic men. The response it evoked was typical in the way that all who came in contact with George Lindsay found it hard to use his surname without the affectionate coupling of his Christian name. He went on to organize a series of experiments culminating in what was called the "Ramadi Reconnaissance", where an embryonic mechanized force operating in the desert was directed by wireless and maintained entirely by air supply for nearly three weeks, during which it covered some 600 miles, and made several moves of about 70 miles in a day.

When tanks were definitely accepted as a permanent part of the Army, and constituted in 1923 as the Royal Tank Corps, Lindsay returned to England to guide its training—as Chief Instructor at the R.T.C. Centre for two years and then as Inspector of the Corps from 1925 to 1929. Those years were of far-reaching importance, not only for the future of the Corps but also for the future of warfare.

For Lindsay himself it was not altogether an easy decision, and it is worth giving his own account of how he came to it. "One of the things that influenced me in deciding that I would leave my regiment, the Rifle Brigade, to join the Tank Corps was that my own baby, the Machine Gun Corps, had been abolished and I felt a burning desire to get into the most modern and up-to-date service that I could; the Tank Corps seemed the one best suited to that purpose". It is significant that a number of the chief exponents of mobile armoured warfare both in Britain and abroad were men brought up in the quick tempo of rifle or light infantry service and tradition—among them Fuller, Guderian [q.v.], Rommel.

The primary task of those who had grasped the new idea was to spread it. In that mission Lindsay did work still more valuable than what he achieved within the Centre. There he was the chief instructor; outside he became the chief evangelist. His charter to visit other places gave him frequent opportunities of "preaching the gospel", and they multiplied when he became inspector. Being both a good lecturer and a good talker, with a knack of arousing interest and a manner that disarmed opposition, he was able to influence the minds of many soldiers who were not accustomed to read military books and journals. He used to begin by reciting the story of David and Goliath, as an allegory of "a new idea" defeating "brainless brute force", and rubbed it in with aptly chosen examples from subsequent military history, of which he was a keen student.

In a letter of 1925, enthusiastically approving an article which suggested that the all-mobile Mongol armies were the model for modern armies to follow, with the advent of motor power, he wrote: "The Mongol idea of extreme mobility, combined with great fire-power, is not dead, but lives. It is the line on which we must develop our modern Mechanical Force. Yes, go for nerve centres, and make the existence of the enemy field army impossible... the war will be won, or lost, as far as military operations go, by the Mechanical Force in the air, and on the ground, working in combination". That was fulfilled when the next war came 14 years later but, unfortunately, by the Germans in the first place.

In 1929 Lindsay became B.G.S. in Egypt, where he repeatedly urged the importance of creating an armoured force such as eventually proved the decisive instrument in repelling the Axis invasion of Egypt and, later, in throwing the enemy out of Africa. After returning home he was given an opportunity of commanding an improvised armoured division in the final exercise of the 1934 training season, but the trial was not renewed until three more years had passed. Meanwhile Lindsay had gone to command a district in India and had no further opportunity in the field of mechanized warfare before his retirement in 1939. But in a series of other spheres of activity he showed the same unquenchable enthusiasm, remaining a Crusader until the end.

George Mackintosh Lindsay was the son of Lieutenant-Colonel and the Hon. Mrs. H. G. Lindsay, of Glasnevin House, Dublin, and was educated at Radley. In his eighteenth year he was commissioned in the Militia, and in January 1900, during the South African War, he entered the Regular Army, being gazetted second-lieutenant in The Rifle Brigade. He served in Natal, including the action of Laing's Nek, and in the Transvaal, and was mentioned in dispatches. He was selected to be an instructor at the School of Musketry, Hythe, in 1913. After regimental duty on the Western Front he was recalled to England in 1915 on appointment as G.S.O.2 at the Machine Gun Training Centre at Grantham. In June 1916 he crossed to France again to become brigade-major of the 99th Brigade in the 2nd Division, and fought on the Somme, at Ancre, and at Arras. In March 1918 he went to First Army Headquarters as machine-gun officer with the temporary rank of lieutenant-colonel in the Machine Gun Corps. He had been awarded the D.S.O. in 1917 and was mentioned in dispatches six times. In 1919 he was created C.M.G.

Having passed the Staff College in the second post-war course, he was given command, in June 1921, of No. 1 Armoured Car Group in Iraq, having been transferred to the Royal Tank Corps in January. He returned home in March 1923 and in August became chief instructor at the Royal Tank Corps Central Schools. In 1925 he was at the War Office for four years of duty as Inspector, Royal Tank Corps, and he was appointed A.D.C. to the King in November 1928. He went to Egypt as Brigadier-General General Staff in October 1929 and returned in the summer of 1932 to take up the command of the 7th Brigade at Tidworth in July. Promoted major-general two years later, he went to Calcutta in 1935 as commander of the Presidency and Assam District, where he remained until he retired in 1939. From 1938 until 1947 he was Colonel Commandant of the Royal Tank Regiment.

He was recalled at the outbreak of war to command the 9th Highland Division, and in 1940 he was appointed Deputy Regional Commissioner for the South-West Civil Defence Region, and was there throughout the years of bombing. In 1944 he became, for two vital years, Commissioner of the British Red Cross and Order of St. John in North-West Europe.

In 1942 he delivered the Lees Knowles lectures on military history at Cambridge, which were later published as *The War on the Civil and Military Fronts*.

He was vice-president of the Army Boxing Association and had in his youth been Army and Navy middleweight champion.

He married in 1907 Constance, daughter of George Stewart Hamilton, who survives him with a daughter.

November 30 & December 6, 1956.

Dr. Lilian Lindsay, C.B.E., who died on January 31, 1960 at the age of 89, was the first woman to obtain a dental qualification in Great Britain. Throughout an exceptionally long career she had rendered outstanding service to her profession, in which she had long been regarded as an almost legendary figure—an inspiration to all and beloved by all.

Lilian Murray was born in 1871 and was educated at the North London Collegiate School for Young Ladies. At the time when she resolved to become a dental surgeon women were not admitted to the qualifying examination in England and she was obliged to go to Edinburgh. She studied at the Edinburgh Dental Hospital and obtained the L.D.S.Edin. in 1895. It was on the steps of the Edinburgh Dental Hospital, as she recalled many years later, that she met Robert Lindsay, who was to be one of her teachers and her future husband. After the Lindsays' marriage in 1905 they practised together in Edinburgh, but moved to London when Robert Lindsay became the first whole-time Dental Secretary of the British Dental Association.

In 1920 Lilian Lindsay was appointed honorary librarian of the association and the collection of books and journals which she built up—now known as the Robert and Lilian Lindsay Library—ranks as one of the finest in the world. During the time that she was engaged in dental practice Mrs. Lindsay wrote many clinical papers and reports, but latterly she had devoted herself to the historical aspects of medicine and dentistry and had distinguished herself in these fields. She was president of the Odontological Section (1945-46) and of the Historical Section (1950-52) of the Royal Society of Medicine, both unique distinctions for a woman.

She published only two books, *A Short History of Dentistry* (1933) and a translation of the celebrated *Chirurgien Dentiste* of Pierre Fauchard (1946), but the list of her contributions to dental journals is a very long one. As recently as 1955 she published her recollections of 75 years of annual meetings and a long series of biographies of "Personalities of the Past" in the *British Dental Journal.* It was hoped that she would live to bring out the large-scale history of dentistry upon which she had long been engaged and which she was so well qualified to write.

She played a prominent part in the affairs of the British Dental Association for nearly 40 years and her services were recognized when she was elected president of the metropolitan branch in 1933, and president of the association in 1946. On the occasion of the association's annual meeting at Edinburgh in 1946 the honorary degree of LL.D. was conferred upon her, and on the same occasion the women members of the association presented her with a travelling case and a gold watch. In the Birthday Honours of 1946 she was appointed C.B.E. The University of Durham had already conferred the honorary degree of M.D.S. upon her in 1939, and in 1947 she was one of the first Fellows in Dental Surgery of the Royal College of Surgeons of England. The British Dental Association presented her with her portrait in 1951 and in 1958 it gave her the only honour which it had left to bestow, the honorary membership.

Apart from her professional interests, Mrs. Lindsay was a leading light of the Johnson Society, being its vice-president in 1950, and she was a Fellow of the Society of Antiquaries. She was a true scholar and a very remarkable woman, and no-one ever sought her help or advice in vain. In her, shrewdness and great tenacity of purpose were concealed by a deceptively modest and gentle manner, but there was never any doubt as to her great qualities of mind and character.

February 2, 1960.

The name of **Lord Linlithgow,** second Marquess, who died on January 5, 1952 at the age of 64, will live in history as that of the Viceroy of India whose tenure of office was longer and fraught with graver anxieties arising from momentous events than that of any of his 17 predecessors.

It fell to him to establish the full provincial autonomy provided for by the India Act of 1935, to guide and sustain the magnificent war effort in men and materials of the sub-continent against the active opposition of the main political party in the country, and yet to prepare the way for the withdrawal of British authority, which was effected four years after the close of his viceroyalty. Lord Linlithgow played his vital part in allied victory and India's progress to self-rule with steadfast devotion and unfaltering courage.

The Most Hon. Victor Alexander John Hope, second Marquess of Linlithgow, in the county of Linlithgow or West Lothian, eighth Earl of Hopetoun, Viscount Althrie, and Baron Hope of the county of Lanark in Scotland, Baron Hopetoun of Hopetoun, and Baron Niddry, of Niddry Castle, county Linlithgow, in the United Kingdom, and a baronet of Scotland, K.G., K.T., G.C.S.I., G.C.I.E., O.B.E., T.D., was born on September 24, 1887, the eldest son of the first Marquess of Linlithgow, the first Governor-General (1900-02) of the Australian Commonwealth.

He was educated at Eton, and was only 21 when he succeeded his father in 1908. Three years later he married the younger daughter of the late Right Hon. Sir Frederick Milner, seventh baronet, a widely known Yorkshireman. They had twin sons and three daughters.

The young marquess was on the Western Front for almost the whole period of the 1914-18 war, being mentioned in dispatches and made an O.B.E. (military). He was with the First Lothians and Border Armoured Car Company, a territorial unit which he commanded for six years from 1920. In 1922 Stanley Baldwin appointed him a Civil Lord of the Admiralty, and when the first Labour Government was formed in 1924 selected him as deputy chairman of the Conservative and Unionist Party organization. In 1923 he was chairman of a departmental committee on the Distribution and Prices of Agricultural Produce, and later of the Meat Advisory Committee of the Board of Trade. All this time the young marquess was upholding the traditions of his family as feudal laird, sportsman, and host. He was a member of the Royal Fine Arts Commission, Scotland, and for 10 years president of the Edinburgh and East of Scotland College of Agriculture. He was honorary colonel of the Edinburgh University O.T.C., and an ensign of the Royal Company of Archers, in which he was later promoted captain. He was also chairman of the Medical Research Council, and of the governing body of the Imperial College of Science and Technology; and for a time president of the Navy League.

His first direct contact with Indian problems was as chairman of the Royal Commission on Agriculture in India appointed in 1926. No inquiry could have been more thorough and practical, and no chairman could have spared himself less. The massive report was inspired by the aim of a better standard of living for the cultivator. Later, as Viceroy, he had the opportunity to extend the scope and usefulness of the Imperial Council of Agricultural Research which was set up on the recommendation of the committee. His keen solicitude for the health and welfare of the masses was reinforced by Lady Linlithgow's successful inauguration of an anti-tuberculosis fund. After the publication at the end of 1931 of the White Paper on Indian Reforms, based on the work of the three sessions of the Round Table Conference, a Select Committee of both Houses of Parliament was set up, and Lord Linlithgow was elected chairman. The report and the proceedings, published in the autumn of 1934, showed a majority generally favourable to the Government proposals, but opposition by two dissenting sections—the right wing Conservatives who held that they went much too far, and the Labour members, who held them to be inadequate. In the discussions on the resulting India Bill, which ran the gauntlet of strong "diehard" opposition, Lord Linlithgow played the useful part of a fully informed and convinced exponent of the merits of the federal scheme.

He succeeded the late Lord Willingdon as Viceroy in April 1936, with high hopes of establishing the federal plan provided for in the Act. Within a year of his arrival provincial autonomy was launched and Burma was separated from the Indian Empire. The preceding general election, under a vastly increased franchise, gave the Congress Party ascendancy in six of the 11 provinces of British India. By fiat of the party caucus, the Working Committee, acceptance of office in those provinces was made contingent on assurances that as long as the Cabinet acted within the Constitution "the Governor will not use his special powers of interference or set aside the advice of his Ministers". As no such pledge could be given consistently with the statutory obligations of Governors, the Viceroy bent his energies to a compromise settlement. In less than three months he succeeded and the interim Governments were replaced by Congress Ministries.

The plan of All-India Federation, which the Viceroy had so much at heart, dragged at the chain for two main reasons: the hesitations of rulers of important states on the question of the optional accession to the Federation, and the growth of communal dissension arising from the treatment of minorities in Congress provinces. The All-India Muslim League, growing rapidly under Jinnah's leadership, declared its opposition to the scheme for federation, and subsequently demanded the creation of Pakistan on the "two nations" theory.

When the Munich crisis of 1938 came, Lord Linlithgow was home on leave. He saw that a vast expansion of India's defensive preparations brooked no delay, and on returning to New Delhi he took urgent measures to this end. The Indian Press was united in vehement condemnation of power politics in Europe. The Princes once more rallied to the cause of the King-Emperor, but the Congress Party showed an unaccommodating spirit. India, like the colonies, automatically became a belligerent when Britain declared war. The Viceroy discussed the situation with leading Indian politicians of widely different shades of opinion, but the Congress Governments resigned and Governors in these provinces took full charge under Section 93 of the 1935 Act. The efforts of the Viceroy to secure a united front in meeting the common danger were persistent, and the historic "August offer" he made in 1940 accepted for the first time on behalf of H.M. Government the principle that the responsibility for framing a constitution for full self-government should be primarily that of Indians themselves.

Instead of taking the proffered opportunity of representation in the Viceroy's Executive Council the Congress Party adopted Gandhi's plan of individual civil disobedience whereby persons he selected publicly courted arrest by anti-war propaganda. The campaign was lacking in any real momentum and gradually petered out. Meanwhile men of good will were coming into the Government of India, and by successive enlargements the Viceroy's Council was markedly Indianized. In the field of first importance the Viceroy's determined efforts were remarkably successful. Up to the time of his retirement in 1943 an entirely voluntary army of more than two million men, apart from considerable Indian States contingents, had joined the colours. His was the brilliant conception of the Eastern Supply Council, with headquarters at New Delhi. It did invaluable work for the Empire countries composing it, until Japanese onslaughts broke the chain and alternative measures had to be taken.

India's "most dangerous hour" came in 1942. The historic offer in the spring by his Majesty's Government, through Sir Stafford Cripps [q.v.], of post-war self-determination, was rejected by the two principal political organizations. In August the Congress Party embarked on a course of mass civil disobedience. The decision was at least partly attributable to the then unfavourable war situation, with Japan in possession of the greater part of Burma, and a spirit of defeatism was engendered. The Government had no alternative to the prompt and firm measures of prevention which it took.

Some critics dwelt on the alleged aloofness of Lord Linlithgow, on his failing in "the human touch", but this complaint did not tally with the testimony of those who had long known him in ordinary settings. It was partly accounted for by the intensity of his devotion to duty. He was so tied to his desk and in some ways so aloof and self-sufficient that he missed helpful opportunities for contacts and exchange of views. On the other hand at the outset of his Indian rule he took a much needed initiative in breaking down the prolonged estrangement between the Viceroy's House and the Congress Party, which had for years boycotted social and other gatherings initiated by the British authorities. When Lord Linlithgow went home in the summer of 1943 after seven and a half years of Vice-royalty, and after three extensions of office, there were many anxious months of further warfare to pass through, but the tide had turned in favour of the Allies, and his main work of saving India from enslavement to the Japanese aggressor had been accomplished.

Lord Linlithgow, who had been Viceroy under three sovereigns, resumed his Scottish and business activities. He was Lord Lieutenant of West Lothian and from 1944 Chancellor of Edinburgh University. In 1944 and again in 1945 he was Lord High Commissioner to the General Assembly of the Church of Scotland. In February 1945 he was appointed chairman of the Midland Bank and was on the boards of numerous other financial and industrial concerns.

In appearance and manner he was a fine type of British aristocrat. An impression of dignity and poise was conveyed as he walked, and still more when he spoke, after his inborn first shyness had been overcome. A newcomer, awed somewhat by his deep voice and powerful lower jaw, was soon reassured by noting his humorous mouth, kindly eyes, and brow of a thinker. He could administer a rebuff with devastating pungency or disarming mildness. His humour broke out now as light badinage, now as brilliant repartee, and frequently as a lightning-conductor in an atmosphere charged with thunderbolts. The outstanding qualities of his mind were versatility, sound judgment, and tolerance, though in public speech he tended to repetition and over-elaboration.

He is succeeded by the Earl of Hopetoun, his elder twin son, who was born in 1912 and married in 1939 Vivien, daughter of Major R. O. R. Kenyon-Slaney. They have a son and a daughter. The younger son of the late Marquess is Lord John Hope, M.P. for Pentland, and there are three daughters.

January 7, 1952.

Ephraim Lipson, the economic historian, died in London on April 22, 1960. He was 71.

The son of H. R. Lipson, he was born on September 1, 1888. As the result of an accident when a child he was cruelly deformed. His family were not well off and he had to make his own way in the world. He was educated at the Royal Grammar School, Sheffield, won a scholarship to Cambridge and in 1910 went to Oxford to set up as a private tutor.

He was highly successful and from 1921 to 1931 was Reader in Economic History at Oxford. He was a very popular lecturer and in that time "Lipson was economic history in Oxford". In 1931 was founded the Chichele Chair, and Lipson was passed over for the professorship. It was a severe blow which Lipson took very hard. He left Oxford immediately never to return. There were many at Oxford who felt that a great injustice had been done.

Subsequently he spent much of his time between the National Liberal Club and South Africa, though he was Lavell lecturer at Boston in 1932 and visiting lecturer in the University of California the following year. Lipson was one of the few people able to make a good living as an academic author.

He was one of the most productive and influential economic historians of his generation. The most important of his many works was his massive *Economic History of England,* the first volume of which appeared in 1915, when he was only 27, and the two final volumes, on *The Age of Mercantilism,* in 1931. This work, in part a synthesis of a vast mass of published material but also, in many respects, an original work, had a wide success. In later years he devoted much of his time to keeping the successive editions of the work abreast of scholarship and it remains the only modern large-scale treatment of its subject. To attempt single-handed so comprehensive a survey of English economic history at a time when the frontiers of the subject were rapidly advancing was an ambitious and perhaps a risky enterprise, but generations of students have been grateful for Lipson's courage.

In 1949 he published a further economic history, *The Growth of English Society,* which showed the same lucidity of exposition and mastery of detail as his larger work. He was also principally responsible for the foundation of the *Economic History Review,* which he edited, with Professor Tawney*, for the first seven years of its existence. He was a brother of D. L. Lipson, Independent member of Parliament for Cheltenham from 1937 to 1950, and the late Solomon Lipson, Chaplain to the Forces.

April 26, 1960.

Gen. Sir Beauvoir de Lisle—See **de Lisle.**

Sir James Lithgow, BT., a prominent figure in the shipbuilding world and one of Scotland's leading industrialists, died on February 23, 1952 at his home in Renfrewshire. He was 69.

James Lithgow, first baronet, of Ormsary, County Argyll, G.B.E., C.B., M.C., T.D., was the eldest son of the late W. T. Lithgow, of Drums, Renfrewshire. After attending Glasgow Academy he studied for a time in Paris. In 1908 he became a partner of Russell and Co., of Port Glasgow, of which his father was one of the three founders. Later it became the family business, known throughout the world as Lithgows, Limited. Heavy responsibilities fell on him and his brother, the late Henry Lithgow, early in their business careers, and in 1912 James was already president of the Clyde Shipbuilders' Association. Early in the 1914-18 war he commanded a heavy battery, R.G.A., in France, was wounded, mentioned in dispatches, and awarded the M.C. In 1917 he was recalled from the front to become Director of Shipbuilding Production in the Admiralty Controller's Department. During the 1939-45 war he was to fill a similar post as Controller of Merchant Shipbuilding and Repairs. In this connexion he refused a salary of £3,000 a year, and was made a member of the Board of Admiralty.

Between the two wars he played a leading part in the rationalization and reorganization of the shipbuilding industry, particularly after its abnormal expansion in the 1914-18 war, which was found to be much beyond peace-time economic needs. In 1926 Lithgow became president of the Shipbuilding Employers' Federation. He was actively concerned in the formation of the National Confederation of Employers' Organizations, now the British Employers' Confederation, and became its president in 1924. He was British employers' delegate to the International Labour Conference (League of Nations) at Geneva and a member of the governing body from 1922 to 1928 and again from 1933 to 1935.

On the commercial side of industrial enterprise he was president of the Federation of British Industries in 1930, 1931, and 1932, a member of the Central Electricity Board from 1927 to 1930, and president of the British Iron and Steel Federation from 1943 to 1945. He received a baronetcy in 1925, and his services during the last war in directing the great British shipbuilding effort were recognized by his being made in 1945 a G.B.E. In 1947 he was made a C.B.

He always had closely at heart the prosperity

of his native Scotland. In 1931 he became chairman of the executive committee of the Scottish Development Council, which was a forerunner of the present Scottish Council (Development and Industry). Since 1943 he had been Vice-Lieutenant of Renfrewshire. He combined great energy with organizing ability and far-seeing vision. His Scottish individualism made him a pungent and sometimes provocative speaker.

He married in 1924 Miss Gwendolen Amy Harrison. She survives him with one son, William James, who succeeds to the title, and two daughters.

February 25, 1952.

David Litvinov, Russian Commissar of Foreign Affairs from 1930 to 1939, died on December 31, 1951 at the age of 75, after a long illness.

As Deputy Commissar and Commissar for Foreign Affairs, Litvinov conducted the foreign relations of the Soviet Union during the long and comparatively uneventful period which followed the death of Lenin. His policy was a blend of communist propaganda, romantic idealism, and realist imperialism. As often as occasion allowed, and particularly when the Soviet Government announced its intention of adhering to the Kellogg Pact, he introduced into his diffuse Notes to foreign Powers a lecture on the virtues of the Soviet Government; at Geneva he made a proposal for complete and universal disarmament; and during the dispute with Manchuria over the seizure of the Chinese Eastern Railway he protested at this violation of Russian rights in the strongest possible manner. In other fields he did his best to maintain the new standard in diplomatic intercourse set by his predecessors, Trotsky and Chicherin.

Of the sincerity of his opinions there can be no doubt; he had been a revolutionary in his youth, and he remained a revolutionary in the less exacting times which followed the Bolshevist seizure of power. But he stood aloof both from the doctrinal differences and from the personal rivalries which divided the party; and in the long-drawn disputes between Right Opposition, Left Opposition, Trotskyist, Stalinist, and Anti-Stalinist factions his name was never heard, although at one time or other almost every Bolshevist leader of the Old Guard was concerned in them.

David Mordeovitch Wallach—of the many names Litvinov used this was the one to which he was entitled—was born at Bielostok in 1876. After an education in the "modern" secondary school, he enlisted at the age of 17 in the Army. There he first came in contact with Marxist propagandists, and when his term of service had ended he himself undertook revolutionary propaganda among workmen. In 1900 he became a member of the Kiev Committee of the Russian Social Democratic Labour Party, for which he organized a secret printing press. The head of the committee proved to be an *agent provocateur,* and Litvinov and his fellow-members were arrested. After a year and a half of imprisonment he escaped from Siberia to Kiev, and thence abroad. In exile he worked for a time on the staff of *Iskra.* After the split in the Social Democratic Party he joined the Bolshevists, and was sent back as a propagandist to Russia, where he remained until it was evident that the revolution of 1905 had failed. Then he again left Russia, to remain abroad for the next 10 years.

In his second exile Litvinov continued his revolutionary work, attending socialist congresses at Stuttgart and elsewhere, working in the International Socialist Bureau in Berlin, and smuggling arms to the revolutionaries in the Caucasus. He settled in London in 1907 under the name of Harrison, and from that time until 1918 he took an active part in the work of the Bolshevists, and made his living working for a firm of publishers and as a bookkeeper. He helped to conduct the Herzen Circle, a society formed by the Russian colony for the discussion of political and other questions. In 1914 he left the International Socialist Bureau as a protest against the entry of Socialists into the 1914-18 war.

The Bolshevist Revolution gave him his chance. In 1918 Trotsky, then Foreign Commissar, made him Plenipotentiary to Great Britain of the newly formed Soviet Government, and, on giving an undertaking to refrain from propaganda, he was permitted to open what was styled an Embassy in London. It was alleged that he did not keep his undertaking, and he was housed in Brixton gaol as a hostage for [Sir Robert] Bruce Lockhart* and other British subjects then held prisoner in Russia. When the agreement for the exchange of prisoners with the Bolshevists was effected, Litvinov was allowed to leave for Leningrad, where he arrived in January 1919. For the first few years after his return he served in a number of posts, on the *collegium* of the Commissariat for Foreign Affairs, in the Workers' and Peasants' Inspectorate, and on the Revolutionary Military Council. In the intervals of work in the Foreign Commissariat he was sent on missions abroad, to Copenhagen, where he negotiated with the British Government, to the Genoa Conference with Chicherin, and later as leader of the Russian Delegation to The Hague Conference of 1922. His negotiations with the Entente Powers proved fruitless, but he succeeded in concluding the treaty with Estonia which removed the danger of further civil war from that side, and he later concluded trade agreements with Norway and Germany. On his return from The Hague he was formally appointed First Deputy Foreign Commissar, a post which became of some importance owing to Chicherin's frequent absence from his duties. During Chicherin's long illness Litvinov was Acting Foreign Commissar, and in 1930, when Chicherin resigned, he was appointed Commissar.

Litvinov was a conspicuous figure at Geneva, where he went as head of the Soviet delegation to the meetings of the Preparatory Commission for the Disarmament Conference. He put forward drastic proposals for disarmament, but there was a too obvious ingenuity in the way in which he reconciled the need for a strong Red Army with the necessity for universal disarmament. He conducted negotiations in 1932 and 1933 which resulted in non-aggression pacts with France, Latvia, Poland, Finland, and Estonia. He attended the World Economic Conference in London in 1933, and in November of that year went to the United States, and was successful in establishing diplomatic relations between that country and Soviet Russia.

As a result of his efforts the Soviet Union became a member of the League of Nations in 1934, and at Geneva Litvinov constantly supported every measure for the effective application of the League Covenant for the preservation of peace. In September 1938, during the international crisis when the German menace was becoming ever greater, he announced during the closing stages of the discussion on the Secretary-General's report in the League Assembly that his Government was prepared, in accordance with treaty, to afford Czechoslovakia immediate and effective assistance if France did the same. There was considerable surprise when he resigned his post as Foreign Commissar in May 1939, but the move was explained when later Russia entered into a treaty with Germany, for Litvinov's policy had always been collaboration with the Western Powers. After Germany's treacherous attack on Russia in June 1941 Litvinov returned to official life, and his appointment as Ambassador to the United States in December 1941 was a fitting recognition of his talents.

Litvinov remained Ambassador until his appointment as Vice-Minister of Foreign Affairs in 1943. During that period he continually urged the opening of a second front. He also had talks with Roosevelt and with Eden, during the latter's visit to Washington in 1943. He was succeeded in Washington by Gromyko. He remained Vice-Minister of Foreign Affairs until August 1946, when he retired because of uncertain health. A report in *Pravda* states that "owing to serious illness he had not taken part in active work during the last few years".

In 1916 he married Ivy [d. 1977], daughter of Walter Low and niece of Sir Sidney Low. They had a son and a daughter.

January 3, 1952.

Archbishop of Liverpool—See **Downey.**

Sir Richard Livingstone, President of Corpus Christi College, Oxford, from 1933 to 1950, died on Boxing Day 1960 in Oxford, at the age of 80. By his death Britain loses one of its leading Greek scholars and the most active champion of classical studies.

Richard Winn Livingstone was born on January 23, 1880. On his father's side he was descended from a family which had for generations had close links with the Church of England, while through his mother he was, and was always proud to be, Irish. He was educated at Winchester and New College, where he obtained the two classical first classes and won three classical prizes—the Hertford, the Latin Verse prize, and the Arnold Essay Prize. With this record to his credit he was naturally sought after as a classical tutor and there was some disappointment in his old college when he accepted an offer from Corpus. There he spent 20 years, broken only during the 1914-18 War by a year as a master at Eton.

During these years he published the first of a series of books in which he expounded the value of the classics—*The Greek Genius and Its Meaning to Us* and *A Defence of Classical Education*, and edited two other volumes, *The Legacy of Greece*, a collection of essays by various writers, and the *Pageant of Greece*, a volume of selections from Greek literature. But his major energies during these years he devoted to his pupils, many of whom later became lifelong friends. What they remember in him is not simply the exact scholar, with the unfailing literary sense which gave such distinction to everything he wrote, but the man who, to use an expression which he himself was fond of quoting, enjoyed "the habitual vision of greatness". Livingstone was indeed the humanist *par excellence*.

In him the Greek and the Christian inheritance formed a blend so perfect that it was difficult for him to realize how others found contradictions in its composing elements. But he was far from being a mere cloistered scholar. During the earlier years of his tutorship the university was stirred by an agitation ("reform from within" was the battle cry) carried on in the columns of *The Times* and the *Westminster Gazette*, and the subject of a debate in the House of Lords initiated by Bishop Gore. Livingstone was one of the small group of younger tutors who were a drive in this movement, which led, in due course, to an inquiry by the Chancellor, Lord Curzon, and eventually to a royal commission. If Oxford is today no more "the playground of the idle rich" and has a faculty organization and arrangements for postgraduate study which compare favourably with those of other seats of learning, without any sacrifice of its own unique quality, this is due in no small measure to the group of earnest and (as it was then thought) impertinent young men among whom Livingstone and William Temple, later Archbishop of Canterbury, were leading spirits.

In 1924 Livingstone left Oxford to become Vice-Chancellor of Queen's University, Belfast. He found the university in a very vigorous condition, but sadly handicapped by lack of funds: it could not attempt to do what the British universities were doing, thanks to the liberal provision granted to them on the recommendation of the Universities Grants Committee. He was impressed by the fact that Queen's University occupied a unique position in the British Isles as "the University of a people", and he set himself the task of bringing home to the people of Northern Ireland the realization that they were responsible for the welfare of their own university. He persuaded local authorities to add to its income, so that new posts could be created and new buildings provided. He also started a "University Guild", with the object of bringing town and gown closer together. He thus not only secured the sympathy of many of the public but established a body that has from time to time given presents of equipment to the university.

He took an active part in many of the schemes for the health and well-being of the community; and his departure from Belfast caused widespread regret.

In 1933, on the death of Dr. P. S. Allen, Livingstone, who had been knighted in 1931, returned to Oxford as President of Corpus. He threw himself at once into the life of the university and he soon became one of the most important influences there. He was Vice-Chancellor in the difficult years 1944-47. He was a valued member of the Committee for Social Studies during the period when, with the assistance of the Rockefeller Foundation, these were largely developed. He was on more contentious ground when he advocated the appointment of a permanent Vice-Chancellor, and even the modified form of this proposal, which would have given the Chancellor the right, or the duty, to make his own selection among Heads of Houses, was eventually rejected by Congregation.

But in another venture he was more successful. He was the originator of the idea of adopting the Staff College principle for overseas administrators home on leave. This first took concrete shape in a 10-day summer school for colonial administrators in 1937 and 1938, but Livingstone always hoped to see it applied in more extended courses and looked to Nuffield College to see his hope realized. In his own college, which had perhaps been somewhat slow in keeping abreast of the latest academic developments, he was a careful innovator and a resourceful administrator: one of his most successful strokes was the arrangement by which, in collaboration with All Souls, the services of R. C. K. Ensor [q.v.] were secured as a Research Fellow.

But his principal energies were devoted to the cause of classical education. Already in 1920 he had been a member of the Prime Minister's Committee on Classics and had an important share in drawing up its report. He had also from 1920 to 1922 been editor of the *Classical Review*. He was now successively president of the Hellenic Society (1938) and of the Classical Association (1940-41), delivering notable addresses in each capacity; here also his Rede lecture at Cambridge in 1944 with its "modest suggestions as a preliminary to progress" must be mentioned.

Moreover he found a fresh field for his skill as an editor in a new series of Greek and Latin texts in which, by a method of abbreviation and comment all his own, the classical authors are rendered very much more readable and interesting to the modern schoolboy—and not the schoolboy alone. To these years, too, belongs Livingstone's maturest contribution to his favourite subject—*Greek Ideals and Modern Life* (1935).

But his influence now began to extend into a wider field—that of education in general. In 1936 he was president of the Educational Section of the British Association and was able to carry his campaign into the scientific camp. He was also much in request during these years as a broadcaster, both to the general public and for the schools. In 1941 he set forth his educational views in a little volume, *The Future in Education*. It was a plea for part-time education from 14 to 18 (as opposed to the wholesale raising of the age to 16), for the transformation of the "public schools" by subjecting them to public control and admitting only boys of proved capacity, and for a large development of adult education on the lines of the Danish system of residential colleges, together with an exposition under the heading "Adult Education for the Educated", of his favourite Staff College idea. These proposals, set forth with the distinction and the persuasive simplicity of which Livingstone was such a master, at once attracted much attention, among both experts and laymen, and he was overwhelmed with invitations to develop them on the public platform and in private gatherings. He was a renowned figure in the United States, where he was much in demand as a lecturer, and he was a frequent visitor, particularly in his years of retirement.

He was an honorary D.Litt. of Cambridge, Belfast, Toronto, Durham, Manchester, London, Columbia, and Yale, and an honorary LL.D. of St. Andrews and Dublin. Shortly before his death he was created a Knight Commander of the Order of King George I of Greece.

Livingstone was married in 1913 to Cecile, daughter of the late George Maryon-Wilson, of Fletching, in Sussex, and she and their children, two sons (one of whom was killed in action in 1944), and two daughters, made a perfect setting for his activities both at Belfast and in Oxford.

December 28, 1960.

Lord Llewellin, who died in Salisbury on January 24, 1957, was the first Governor-General of the Federation of Rhodesia and Nyasaland. He was 63.

Throughout the federation he was known and liked as a representative of the Queen who, while possessing a natural dignity, was approachable and preferred to unbend among his fellow human beings. He rendered great service to the federation by his shrewd counsel and his long experience of the political game. Nobody was quicker than he to see possible solutions to seemingly insoluble problems. At the same time he was self-effacing, and did not thrust his advice on unwilling hearers—he waited for them to come to him, and in time come to him they did.

A bachelor, he entertained much at Government House, Salisbury, either alone or with his sister. He was naturally gregarious, and the official dinners which might so easily have seemed a duty, in his presence took on the atmosphere of a family party. He took a great interest in the building of the new University College of Rhodesia and Nyasaland, and did much to embellish it by the gift of flowers from the gardens of Government House, for he was a keen gardener. One of his last public acts was to open the arts wing of the College, which is named after him. His tour of duty as Governor-General was perhaps the greatest service he had rendered in a distinguished career.

The Rt. Hon. John Jestyn Llewellin, P.C., G.B.E., M.C., first Baron Llewellin, of Upton in the county of Dorset, was born at Sevenoaks on February 6, 1893, the son of William Llewellin, of Upton House, Poole. He was educated at Eton where he was in "upper Boats", ran, and played football. Later, at University College, Oxford, he kept up his rowing and was in the "University" boat which in 1914 ended Head of the River. In September of that year he was commissioned in the Dorset Royal Garrison Artillery and served in France from 1915 to 1919. In 1917 he was awarded the Military Cross. In 1921 he was called to the Bar.

In 1929 he was returned to Parliament as Conservative member for the Uxbridge Division. In the House of Commons, where he was personally to become very popular, he soon attracted notice. From September to October 1931, he was Parliamentary Secretary to the Postmaster-General. From 1931 to 1935 he was Parliamentary Secretary to the First Commissioner of Works, and from 1935 to 1937 Assistant Government Whip. Later he became Civil Lord of the Admiralty.

In 1939 he went to the Ministry of Supply as Parliamentary Secretary. In August the whole of Supply Organization of the Board of Trade had been transferred to it. The Government had, in fact, been for some time a trader on a great scale quietly conserving and maintaining the supplies which it was calculated would be necessary in war.

In 1940 he became Parliamentary Secretary of the Ministry of Aircraft Production. Lord Beaverbrook* was his Minister and concentrated his tremendous driving power upon his task. There was no question of the need for aircraft, and everything that human energy could do to obtain them was done. In his historic endeavour Llewellin was a competent and most successful assistant.

There were several Cabinet changes in May 1941, and he went as Parliamentary Secretary to the Ministry of Transport, and was sworn of the Privy Council. It had been decided as soon as might be to amalgamate the two departments of Shipping and Transport as the Ministry of War-time Communications, and, pending the completion of the process, Llewellin was to represent both in the House of Commons. In February 1942 he attained Cabinet rank as President of the Board of Trade. He was, however, transferred almost immediately to the Ministry of Aircraft Production in succession to Colonel Moore-Brabazon [Lord Brabazon of Tara*].

Urgent though the need for aircraft had been in his days with Lord Beaverbrook, it was no less so in 1942. A couple of months after his appointment he was able in a broadcast speech to assure the Empire of the immense improvement in British aircraft since his Ministry came into being; and that advances in quality were such as to guarantee its superiority over anything the enemy could bring against it.

In November 1942 Sir Stafford Cripps [q.v.] left the War Cabinet and was invited by Churchill* to assume responsibility for aircraft production. At the same time Llewellin was sent to Washington to fill the new post of Minister Resident in Washington for Supply. When Lord Woolton* was chosen as Minister of Reconstruction Llewellin succeeded him as Minister of Food. He took over at a time when there was no glamour to be had from the post, and when food problems were becoming more difficult as the war neared its end, but here again a job of work was well done.

At the general election in the summer of 1945 he lost his seat at Uxbridge to Frank Beswick, and in the resignation honours list announced in August he was created baron.

On June 24, 1953, *The Times* published an article forecasting Lord Llewellin's appointment as the first Governor-General of the Federation of Rhodesia and Nyasaland, and on the Royal Assent being given to the Enabling Bill later in the summer his appointment was officially announced. At the same time he was appointed G.B.E. (he had been made C.B.E. in 1939). The office was not an easy one. The new Governor-General had not only to advise the Federal Prime Minister on political matters, but also to help maintain relations between the Federal government and the territorial governments, particularly the governors of the two colonial territories of Northern Rhodesia and Nyasaland. This was a task which required the greatest tact and skill. The first federal general elections were held in December, and resulted in a sweeping victory for the Federal Party, led by Sir Godfrey Huggins (now Lord Malvern*). The following years were taken up in all the difficult tasks of forming a federal administration and a federal civil service, subjects which were bound to cause heart-burnings in the different territories concerned and which offered plenty of play for the part of mediator.

During 1956 the demand by local Europeans for "improved status" and the discussions over the federal franchise have occupied the political stage in Salisbury. Here the Governor-General's intimate knowledge of the political temperature in Britain has been of especial value to the federal leaders. Shortly before Lord Llewellin's death Lord Malvern retired and Sir Roy Welensky, who was already well known to the Governor-General as Deputy Prime Minister, succeeded to the premiership.

January 25, 1957.

Frank Lloyd, the Hollywood film director, died on August 10, 1960 in Hollywood. He was 71.

His work was all of a high professional standard, but so varied in form and content as to make it difficult to point to anything which could be regarded as distinctively his. He had a flair for handling action sequences and an enjoyment of colourful period backgrounds and full-blooded drama. He was an excellent technician who made several outstanding films—and when the films are of the quality of *Mutiny on the Bounty* or *Cavalcade* that is no mean achievement.

Frank Lloyd was born in Glasgow in 1889, and early in his life became interested in the theatre, his father being an actor in musical comedy. Before long he went on the stage, acting in repertory companies and later in light comedy, musicals and operettas in London. In 1910 he tried his luck in films, acting for Universal in America. At this period most people in the business were able to turn their hand to almost any job, and Lloyd found himself writing and directing films as well as acting in them. As a director he became noted for his special skill with costume stories: *Les Misérables* in 1918 (the first of innumerable versions), *A Tale of Two Cities* in 1921, *Oliver Twist* in 1922, and *The Sea Hawk* in 1924.

He was one of Hollywood's most versatile directors, switching easily from thriller to romance or from comedy to high drama. His penchant for period pieces continued throughout the 1930s, and over a wide range of subjects. In 1933 came one of the most successful of all his films, from Noël Coward's* *Cavalcade:* with a largely British cast headed by Clive Brook* and Diana Wynyard*, Frank Lloyd managed to recreate Britain convincingly in America, and the piece gained from the added mobility the film medium could give it.

His next success, perhaps his greatest, was *Mutiny on the Bounty*. In this classic adventure story Charles Laughton* gave a savage and overbearing performance as Captain Bligh which provided music-hall impersonators with material for years. The script ingeniously balanced respect, if not sympathy, for both sides, and the film was directed with a fine feeling for the poetry of the sea. It was given the Academy Award for the best film of the year, and confirmed Lloyd's position in the forefront of his profession in Hollywood. More spirited costume films followed: *Under Two Flags, Maid of Salem* and others, as well as an excellent western, *Wells Fargo* and a comedy, *Lady of Chayenne.*

During the war Lloyd's first job was to supervise the whole production and direct some sequences of a Hollywood tribute to Britain, *Forever and a Day.*

August 12, 1960.

Edith Lady Londonderry, D.B.E., who was the widow of the seventh Marquess, died at Mount Stewart, Newtonards, co. Down, on April 23, 1959 at the age of 80.

She was born into politics, married into politics, and for years was one of England's leading political hostesses, notably at Londonderry House, but also at Mount Stewart, in Northern Ireland, and at Wynyard Park, in Durham. She travelled extensively, meeting wherever she went people of note, and often recalling her experiences in vivacious writing. Her friends, whom she retained in spite of her sometimes disconcerting frankness, were numerous and invariably life-long; but she will be best remembered now and in the years to come for her war services from 1915 to 1919 as founder and director of the Women's Legion, a task to which she brought great organizing skill, combined with common sense and understanding, infinite patience, and untiring devotion. It was for these services, and probably also for the part that she played in helping to organize and to sustain the Officers' Hospital which had been set up in Londonderry House, that she became in 1917 the first woman to be appointed D.B.E. (Military Division).

Edith Helen Chaplin was born on December 3, 1879, the second of the three children of that vintage Victorian figure, Henry Chaplin, of Blankeney, Tory leader and sportsman, who afterwards became the first Viscount Chaplin, and his wife Lady Florence Leveson Gower, daughter of the third Duke of Sutherland, who died in 1881. After her mother's death a great part of her early childhood was spent at the Sutherlands' Scottish home, Dunrobin Castle, under the care of her grandmother. In London she lived with her grandparents at Stafford House, later the London Museum, and now called Lancaster House.

It was in November, 1899, when she was 20, that she married Viscount Castlereagh, only son of the sixth Marquess of Londonderry, and she and her husband were among the very last guests of Queen Victoria at Windsor. Castlereagh was then an officer in the Blues, and when on duty they lived in town at Londonderry House, but created for themselves a beautiful little home at Oakham, to which they went whenever possible. She and her husband were drawn into politics, and within a few years of their marriage Castlereagh was elected as Conservative member for Maidstone in the landslide election of 1906. Despite the petition to unseat him for alleged corrupt practices by his supporters, which was dismissed after a week's hearing, he continued to hold the seat until he succeeded to the family honours on the death of his father in 1915, and throughout the nine years his wife was his constant help.

Within a few weeks of the outbreak of war in 1914 she had accepted the post of Colonel-in-Chief of the Women's Volunteer Reserve, which eventually reverted to its old status, and the Women's Legion, developed on much broader and different lines, came into being. She was unsparing and indefatigable in her task, and there is no doubt that the agriculture section of the Legion which did such magnificent work for nearly four years was almost entirely her inspiration and creation.

After the war ended she took an active part for more than 25 years in the political and social scenes. She was hostess at Londonderry House for the first great reception for the Coalition Government of Lloyd George. In Ulster with her husband she gave powerful aid to the newly formed Northern Ireland Government, and with greater leisure and freedom than she had had during the war years she made Mount Stewart and its magnificent gardens one of the loveliest places in the kingdom.

Not least of her many striking characteristics was her capacity to meet easily and affably those with whom on many questions she most fundamentally disagreed. She was a close personal friend of the late Ramsay MacDonald and his family, for whom she was repeatedly hostess during his Premierships, and who was a frequent and always welcome guest at Mount Stewart. Her gaiety, her mental and physical alertness, and her boundless range of interest were proverbial among her friends. She was riding and swimming when well over 70. Her husband died in 1949.

Among her published works were *Henry Chaplin, A memoir; The Magic Inkpot; Retrospect;* and in 1958, a fascinating account of her predecessor in title, the wife of the third Marquess of Londonderry. She also edited with H. M. Hyde *The Russian Journals of Martha and Catherine Wilmot, 1803-1808,* and *More Letters from Martha Wilmot, 1819-1829.*

April 24, 1959.

Marjorie (Mrs. A. L.) Long—See **Bowen.**

Air Vice-Marshal Sir Charles Longcroft, K.C.B., C.M.G., D.S.O., A.F.C., who died in London on February 20, 1958, was one of the early band of Army officers who learnt to fly in 1912 and straightway joined the Royal Flying Corps (Military Wing). He was 74.

All of that band were enthusiasts, and all were young men of high courage, and among them Longcroft won a high reputation for his well-considered daring, and for the high degree of intelligence which he brought to bear upon his work. He was a dashing and skilful pilot; he held high commands in the field and responsible appointments in time and peace; but of many others the same can be said.

Charles Alexander Holcombe Longcroft was born on May 13, 1883, and educated at Charterhouse and the Royal Military College, Sandhurst. In May 1903 he was commissioned as 2nd Lieutenant in The Welch Regiment. In the spring of 1912 he learnt to fly, and in March that year received the Royal Aero Club certificate No. 192. Next month he was attached to the Air Battalion of the Royal Engineers, and in July became a flying officer of the R.F.C. By November he had become a flight commander and a temporary captain, though it was not until August 1913 that he was promoted to a permanent captaincy in his regiment. By May 1914 he had risen to be squadron commander and temporary major.

In the meantime he had had various adventures and had made his mark as a pilot. In September 1912 the Royal Flying Corps took part in Army manoeuvres, and for the first time was able to demonstrate that the aircraft could show a general what was on the other side of the hill. Longcroft, flying a B.E.2, was one of a composite squadron under Captain G. H. Raleigh which was attached to the Red Army under Lieutenant-General Grierson. The R.F.C. proved its possibilities on those manoeuvres, but it had still much to learn. Shortly afterwards Longcroft was appointed to No. 2 Squadron under Major C. J. Burke.

In January 1913 No. 2 Squadron changed station by air, and flew from Farnborough to Montrose, which at the time was quite a notable feat. Longcroft, now a temporary captain, flew a B.E. and had a forced landing near Littlemore and spent the night at Littlemore lunatic asylum. There were not a few people in those days who thought that a most appropriate place for a flying man.

Long cross-country flights seemed to fascinate Longcroft, for in August of the same year he and Colonel F. Sykes (afterwards Sir Frederick Sykes [q.v.], Governor of Bombay) flew in a B.E. from Farnborough to Montrose in 7 hours 40 minutes, landing once at Alnmouth. But a few months later Longcroft did better than that. He had extra petrol tanks fitted in a B.E. which had a 70 h.p. Renault engine, and on November 22 flew non-stop from Montrose to Farnborough, looking down on Portsmouth on the way. This flight was accomplished in 7 hours 20 minutes and earned for Longcroft the award by the Royal Aero Club of the Britannia Trophy.

Longcroft was a temporary major when the war broke out. He still remained with No. 2 Squadron and went to France with it, but was supernumerary to its establishment. On August 20 he made a notable reconnaissance flight with Captain (afterwards Group Captain) U. J. D. Bourke over Louvain, and brought in a report of German forces on the march.

Two days later an Albatross flew over the airfield of the R.F.C. (all four squadrons lived together at that time), and was chased by such British pilots as could get on its track, carrying hand grenades as their only weapon. A witness has put it on record that he thought Longcroft was going to catch the German, but his hopes were disappointed.

Before long Longcroft was given the command of No. 4 Squadron, which formed part of the 3rd Wing, and in this capacity he took part in the battles of Neuve Chapelle on March 10 to 12 and Aubers Ridge on May 9. Meantime it had been realized that the sending oversea of the whole of the R.F.C. had left no organization at home for reinforcements. In response to urgent requests, Longcroft and some other selected officers were sent back to England to start an organization for training pilots.

The Central Flying School could not deal with all the pupils, and other training units had to be improvised. In August 1915 Longcroft was promoted to wing commander and temporary lieutenant-colonel. By the summer of 1916 he was back in France, and commanded No. 2 (Corps) Wing in the 3rd Brigade R.F.C. during the battles of the Somme.

This was a period of great ascendancy for the R.F.C. Its aggressive tactics well-nigh drove the German aircraft out of the sky, and accordingly the British infantry and gunners received the maximum help which aircraft could give in the way of reconnaissance and artillery observation.

Longcroft's wing comprised six squadrons, and was therefore an important command. A very large share of the credit for the complete success of the air campaign at this time must go to those in command behind the lines.

Though promotion came rapidly to all survivors of the original four squadrons, it cannot be said that Longcroft received undue rewards for his work. In August 1915 he received the Russian Order of St. Stanislas, 3rd Class, with swords. In 1917 he was awarded the Croix d'Officier of the French Legion d'Honneur. It was not until January 1918 that he was decorated by his own country, but then the decoration chosen was the Distinguished Service Order, and it was well deserved. The Air Force Cross and companionship of the Orders of St. Michael and St. George and of the Bath came to him after the war was over. He was promoted K.C.B. in 1938.

In 1917-18, before the reorganization of the Royal Air Force into Areas, Major-General Longcroft was placed in command of the Training Division, which had charge of the vast organization for turning out pilots in Great Britain. He set a good example to all ranks by flying a single-seat Camel when he visited the training depôts.

On receiving a permanent commission in the Royal Air Force in August 1919 he was granted the rank of colonel (later group captain), but was promoted a few days later to air commodore. Then commenced four years in command of the R.A.F. Cadet College at Cranwell, a period of great importance as the college was new and was in process of learning to justify itself and to take its place beside the established Sandhurst and Woolwich of the Army. That Cranwell has proved a brilliant success is due in very great measure to the officer who commanded it during those critical early years.

In 1924 Longcroft was appointed Director of Personal Services at the Air Ministry and was promoted to Air Vice-Marshal. Then for three years he was in command of the Inland Area. In November 1929 he was placed on the retired list at his own request.

In November 1932 he was appointed by the King to be Gentleman Usher of the Scarlet Rod of the Order of the Bath, and he held the appointment until 1948, in which year he became Registrar and Secretary of the Order. In 1934-35 he was president of the Aerodrome Board.

February 21, 1958.

Frederick Lonsdale, who died in London on April 4, 1954 at the age of 73, was for long a most entertaining, deft, and successful playwright, an unerring craftsman in his own vein of artificial light comedy.

His was a rare good fortune in the theatre. It was he who wrote the "book" of *The Maid of the Mountains,* which established at the time a record for the run of a musical comedy in Britain, and of other noted confections of the same kind at Daly's; while so far as "straight" plays were concerned there were not a few occasions in the 1920s—the period of *The Last of Mrs. Cheyney, On Approval,* and the rest—when three of his comedies were running simultaneously in the West End of London. He has, as playwright, little variety; the same few epithets serve to characterize all his plays. But his idiom was a very amusing one. Lonsdale's feelings for the theatre, it might fairly be said, matched very closely the circumstances and temper of theatre audiences, or at least of the larger part of the stalls, in the period between the wars. Slight and artificial of substance, rather narrowly concerned with the amorous and other vagaries of the titled and the very rich, his comedies projected, as a rule, a gaily nonsensical or impudent situation and drew much of their effect from a cascade of cynical wit and epigram. At his best Lonsdale had a remarkably sure instinct for "theatre", even for "good theatre", but without the gay and cynical good humour of his verbal embellishments most of his plays would scarcely have held together. Dazzling success in the theatre is notoriously short-lived, but Lonsdale maintained his popularity both at home and in the United States, where he spent much of his time, for the best part of 30 years. His most amusing plays were frequently revived, and adaptations for the cinema gave him still wider favour.

"Freddie" Lonsdale—nobody who knew him called him anything but "Freddie"—whose real surname was Leonard, was born on February 5, 1881, at St. Helier, Jersey, within a mile of the birthplace of Lily Langtry and of Sir Seymour Hicks. He enjoyed an unusual and singularly varied apprenticeship to the playwright's craft, for he was, in turn, a private in The South Lancashire Regiment, an able seaman in a merchant sailing ship, a steward on a liner, a farm worker in Canada, and a great deal more. Apparently the first piece he wrote for stage performance was a one-act play forming part of a barracks entertainment. His professional career, however, dates from 1908, in which he wrote—and sold—*The King of Cadonia,* the libretto of a musical comedy, a play entitled *The Early Worm,* and *The Best People,* a comedy that served as model for almost everything he attempted later. An adroit and witty trifle, bearing no close resemblance to life as it is lived, about the philanderings of the idle rich, it was produced at Wyndham's in the following year, with players no less eminent than Eva Moore [q.v.] and Fred Kerr in the leading parts, and made the happiest impression.

After that came three musical comedies, *The Balkan Princess* (1910), done in collaboration with Frank Curzon; *Betty* (1915), written in partnership with Gladys Unger; and the triumphant *Maid of the Mountains* (1916). Lonsdale's truly spectacular success in artificial light comedy began in 1923 with *Aren't We All?* a witty absurdity held within the bounds of a matrimonial squabble, and, by way of *The Fake* (1924) and *Spring Cleaning* (1925), culminated in *The Last of Mrs. Cheyney* (1925), memorable for its *coup de théâtre* at the close of the first act and the handsome performances of a distinguished quartette of players, Gladys Cooper*, Sir Gerald du Maurier, Ronald Squire [q.v.], and Ellis Jeffreys. All these plays have more than once been revived, *Aren't We All?* as late as August 1953.

Then came the shining frivolity of *On Approval* (1927), the epigrams of *The High Road* in the same year, and the gay, cynical nonsense of *Canaries Sometimes Sing* (1929). The rest was almost of necessity a decline from that high level of professional competence; for fashion in the theatre, or, at any rate, fashion in artificial light comedy, changes rapidly. *Once is Enough* (1938), first performed in New York, was almost, but not quite, the mixture as before; *Another Love Story* (1943) was, a little surprisingly, somewhat unavailingly facetious; while *But for the Grace of God* (1946) mingled a heavy spice of melodrama with rather lame wit. In *The Way Things Go* (1950), however, with its "daring" central scene and quick changes of situation, Lonsdale showed something of the old deftness which had brought him success for so long. A gay companion and a "good mixer", Lonsdale in these later years bore his disappointments cheerfully and turned to writing for the cinema.

He married Miss Leslie Brooke Hoggan, and there were three daughters of the marriage.

April 6, 1954.

The death of **Violet Loraine,** on July 18, 1956 in hospital at Newcastle upon Tyne, a week before she would have celebrated her seventieth birthday, will stir memories of those home leaves from France during the 1914-18 War to which a visit to the Alhambra in Leicester Square to see and hear her in *The Bing Boys* contributed so much gaiety.

Her career as actress and singer was a romance in the old tradition, for she actually did rise from humble beginnings as a chorus girl in pantomime to stardom in musical comedy. Undoubtedly her greatest successes were achieved in the "Bing Boys" shows, which proved so popular that they were followed by spectacular entertainments featuring the "Bing Girls", and with Violet Loraine in the principal part made music hall history. Once she had emerged from the chorus she never looked back, for she had talent as well as charm.

Born in London on July 26, 1886, and educated at Trevelyan House, Brighton, she made her first appearance, at the age of 16, on the stage at Drury Lane Theatre on Boxing Day 1902, in the chorus of the pantomime *Mother Goose.* By the time the run had ended she had been engaged for the part of Tita in *The Medal and the Maid,* which opened at the Lyric in April 1903, and in October of the same year she was seen in *The Duchess of Dantzig.* Steady work followed in the next few years, and in August 1905 she ventured on the variety stage, making her *début* at the Palace. She was then engaged by George Edwardes to tour in *The Spring Chicken,* and was so successful that she was given the part of Mitzi in *The Girls of Gottenberg.*

Her initial appearance as an entertainer on the music hall without benefit of a supporting company, at the long since defunct Oxford, established her as an artist in her own right, and from that time she controlled her professional destiny with conspicuous skill and judgment. Even during the difficult years of the 1914-18 War she maintained her place in the front rank of entertainers, and indeed it was in 1916, when Britain was still darkened by the shadow of mounting casualties in France, that her greatest success was attained.

As Emma in *The Bing Boys Are Here,* at the old Alhambra, now but a memory, she proved an antidote for the sorrows of the period, and became an established favourite with the public. *The Bing Girls Are There*, staged in 1917, was an appropriate sequel to the original show, and *The Bing Boys on Broadway*, produced in 1918, seemed an inevitable completion of an entertaining trilogy.

She was at the height of her success in 1921 when she married and retired from the stage, and it was not till May 1928 that she returned to take the part of Sally Jellyband in *The Scarlet Pimpernel*, put on at the Palace to raise money for King George's Pension Fund. Later the same year she reappeared professionally at the King's Theatre, Edinburgh, and for some years afterwards she was seen at intervals on the stage in London in varied productions. In December 1934 she took her former role of Emma in a revival of *The Bing Boys Are Here*, at the Alhambra, singing again "If You Were The Only Girl in the World" and "Let the Great Big World Keep Turning" with all her original ebullience.

Her last appearance on the stage was at the Royal Albert Hall in September 1945, when she was featured in the R.A.F. pageant, organized by the *Daily Telegraph*, and sang several of the songs with which she had achieved her greatest triumphs. She had grace of movement and a rich mezzo-soprano voice which she knew well how to use. Sentimental and humorous by turns, she displayed her talents in a way peculiarly suited to the moods, sometimes recklessly gay, at others sadly resigned, of those who had escaped for a brief time from the holocaust across the Channel.

Her husband, Captain Edward Joicey, M.C., died in 1955. Only a fortnight before her own death her younger son was awarded the George Medal for his bravery in rescue operations during a fire in a shipyard.

July 20, 1956.

The Right Rev. Neville Lovett, D.D., seventy-first Bishop of Salisbury, died at his home at Droxford, Hampshire, on September 8, 1951 at the age of 82.

Ernest Neville Lovett—in later years he always used the second of his Christian names—was born on February 16, 1869. He was sent to Sherborne, from which school it had been intended that he should go to Oxford, but a last-minute change of plan sent him to Christ's College, Cambridge. Here he took his degree with a second class in the Theological Tripos. He was ordained in 1892 to the curacy of Christ Church, Clifton, and three years later was appointed to the rectory of Bishop's Caundle and the vicarage of Wootton, Dorset, benefices which had long been held by his father. These parishes he was destined later, as Bishop of Salisbury, to have in his diocese. Earlier, as Bishop of Portsmouth, the Isle of Wight was in his territory, and this again was familiar ground to him, for from 1898 to 1908 he had been vicar of Shanklin and, for part of that period rural dean of East Wight.

Next came four years, 1908-12, during which he was rector of Farnham. While there he wrote a play based on episodes in the early history of the town and castle; this was performed by his parishioners. In 1912 he became rector of St. Mary's, Southampton, and rural dean. In this important parish he was very successful. He was a strenuous worker, with considerable organizing powers, while his genial and lovable character made him popular alike with his parishioners and his staff. St. Mary's, with its complete and smoothly running machinery and congregations crowding its great church, became in many ways a model parish. In 1920 Lovett was made a C.B.E. in recognition of his war work; already he had been appointed a chaplain to the King, and an honorary canon of Winchester.

In 1925 Winchester College nominated him to the vicarage of Portsmouth, and Bishop Woods appointed him archdeacon. When, two years later, the subdivision of the Winchester diocese was affected and Portsmouth became a see, the choice of Lovett as its first bishop fulfilled a general expectation, and the choice was fully justified. No new diocese could have had a more successful beginning than that which Portsmouth obtained under its first bishop's energetic, kindly, and sagacious rule. He was popular with all classes in his territory, and not least with the Navy. To its higher command a natural introduction was provided for him by the fact that in 1894 he had married Evelyn, sister of Admiral of the Fleet Sir Osmond Brock. She died on August 22, 1937.

He was beloved, too, by the clergy, and to be with the bishop and his ordination candidates at Bishopswood—the modest thatched residence at Fareham where he lived—was to witness an ideal relationship between the chief pastor of the diocese and the young men at the beginning of their work under him. While forfeiting nothing of the dignity due to his office, the bishop was on terms of easy and genial friendship with his ordinands, and nothing could have been at once more impressive or more full of robust good sense than the addresses he delivered to them.

The cathedral had been the parish church of Portsmouth for 750 years. The Bishop at once resolved to enlarge it, so as to accommodate great congregations on special occasions of national or diocesan importance. Accordingly, he engaged the services of Sir Charles Nicholson, who produced a delightful plan, keeping the old parish church, with its many distinctive features, as the choir of the cathedral, and adding a nave. Then the Bishop worked vigorously to obtain funds in order that the first stages of this transformation might begin, and he was remarkably successful. In fact, he seemed ideally placed, and to be still in the thick of tasks for which he was remarkably well qualified, when his career experienced a complete and most unexpected change.

Dr. St. Clair Donaldson, Bishop of Salisbury, on December 6, 1935, had a conversation by telephone in the late evening with a friend in the Close, remarked that he had never felt in better health, went to bed, and died during the night. There was the usual crop of conjectures about his probable successor. Everyone, however, and not least Neville Lovett, was astonished when the offer of the vacant see was made to the Bishop of Portsmouth. He told his friends afterwards that the pressure put upon him by the Archbishop of Canterbury and the Prime Minister was of a kind which made refusal impossible. Yet the fact remained that in his sixty-eighth year he was transferred from a small and compact to a large and widely scattered diocese, from the charge of 200 clergy to one of 600, from work which he had at his fingers' ends and was doing with conspicuous success, to tasks of a quite different character.

He had reached a time of life when it is still easy for a man to continue with much success work among people and in a setting with which he has become familiar, but when it is difficult to take up quite new and different work among strangers. However, the Bishop could feel that his youthful days had made him well acquainted with the part of his new diocese which lay in Dorset. He was keenly conscious—for no one could be more modest on this point—that his intellectual abilities were not of the kind that had distinguished many previous holders of what is one of the foremost English sees, but he obeyed what seemed to him the call of duty and transferred himself, reluctantly enough, from Fareham to the Palace at Salisbury.

That large, rambling, and picturesque mansion is, whatever its inconveniences from the housekeeping standpoint, one of the most attractive of episcopal homes, and in its garden, as it were, is a cathedral of which the exterior view is among the loveliest things in England. That prospect was an intense daily joy to the new occupant of the palace, and he was fascinated by the old house, its historic associations, its portraits of bygone bishops. It would be idle to pretend that he did not look back regretfully to Portsmouth and the Portsmouth clergy, yet at once he threw himself with his old energy into his new tasks. Thus for the next 10 years he devoted himself to his largely rural diocese with as much success as had attended his untiring efforts at Portsmouth, and in 1946, having continued through the stress of the years of war, he resigned to make way for a younger man, though he was still at the height of his powers. His retirement was met with general regret.

Personally, the late Bishop was wholly charming; in the full sense of the term, an English gentleman. As a preacher he made no claims either to eloquence or to profound thought, but his sermons attracted by their evidently intense sincerity, their practical common sense, and the sympathetic and genial character they revealed. Lovett was specially felicitous in his addresses to young people and holiday crowds, while his strong sense of humour made him always welcome as an after-dinner speaker.

He was a man with whom it was impossible to quarrel, and his wide sympathies made it easy for him to gain the confidence of all types of Church people. Among his contemporaries there may be some more distinguished Bishops, but few indeed whose loss will be more deeply felt. He is survived by five daughters.

September 10, 1951.

The Very Rev. John Lowe, D.D., sometime Dean of Christ Church, Oxford, and Vice-Chancellor of the University in 1948-51, died on August 11, 1960 at his home at Oxford. He was 61.

He was born on January 9, 1899, at Calgary, Alberta. His paternal grandfather, who married a cousin of Lord Acton, was of a Liverpool family and went out to settle in the backwoods of Muskoka; his mother's father, John Carter, a gifted but improvident organist, married a Macnab whose forebears had emigrated from Scotland to Virginia soon after 1700, and had then moved north to Canada with the United Empire Loyalists at the time of the Revolution.

Dr. Lowe's father, a noted preacher and a saintly man, died of overwork just before he was made an archdeacon, and the widow, who had come from Toronto, went east to live with her two sons in the Niagara Peninsula. There was little money and the boys were educated first in the free elementary and secondary schools, then at Toronto University by scholarships and vacation earnings. As Dr. Lowe's brother, Dr. Percy Lowe, got a first and a Ph.D. in physics, there can have been little amiss with the Government schools of Canada about 1900.

By 1922 John Lowe had taken his M.A. at Toronto, after interrupting his course by two years (1917-19) as a signaller in the Canadian Engineers in France and Belgium. He went to Christ Church as a Rhodes Scholar in 1922; rowed and ran for his college; and got first in Greats and theology, and a Liddon Studentship. He served for a time in the New York Theological Seminary, where he helped to acclimatize Oxford methods of honours tuition; and in 1927 went to Trinity College, Toronto, to become in turn lecturer, fellow, professor of New Testament language and literature, dean of divinity and a member of the university senate.

When in 1939 Dean Williams was transferred, after only four years, from the House to the see of Durham, John Lowe accepted the invitation of the Crown to return to Oxford as the first Canadian Dean of Christ Church, and one of the first scholars from a great Dominion to fill an important place in the religious and academic life of England; a year later the distinction of his career was appropriately recognised by his election as a Rhodes Trustee.

He arrived with his wife and young family a few weeks before war began, and to the inevitable difficulties of settling into a large and almost wholly unfurnished house in a new country were added the overwhelming problems of the war and of the children. But the Dean and Mrs. Lowe courageously decided not to despair of the state and send the children, as they so easily could have done, back to Canada: and the example they so quietly set was a fine one.

While the Dean was finding his feet he was inclined to be dry and reserved in his approach and, like his name, monosyllabic; but as the months passed and his devotion and ability and calm showed themselves he inspired his colleagues with complete confidence and was himself buttressed and mellowed by their trust. He was not very intimate with the undergraduates; and his natural reserve and taciturnity were reinforced at first by the impossibility of much entertaining during the war, and by his inevitably limited knowledge of the English scene in general and of the school world in particular. But when he had anything he wished to say he could say it unaffectedly.

The same qualities appeared in his preaching, which was notably good. The New Testament was his chief field of study, and in his sermons he would begin with a theological topic and then lead it to something immediate and practical. The result was firm and satisfying—qualities that appeared in everything he did.

After the war Lowe was fully occupied with the cathedral chapter, the governing bodies of the House and of Westminster, the Rhodes Trust, a major part of the extra-mural delegacy, the theology school, and much travelling and preaching. Then, on top of all this, the accidental death of Dr. Stallybrass in October 1948 and the unavailability of two or three natural successors shot the Dean at two days' notice, and with none of the usual period of training, into the office of vice-chancellor of the university with its inhuman burden of committees. There, his success was immediate and continuous; the cool clarity of his mind made him an admirably lucid expositor of the most tangled questions, and he was always fully master of his material.

After his three years of office he went straight off by air, in 1951, with no time for a proper holiday, to take part in an over-strenuous tour of universities in Pakistan, India, and Ceylon. It was too much and as he waited in Colombo for his boat home he was struck down in January 1952 by illness. His convalescence was long and slow, but he was able for some college work by October. Gradually he got back into full work, but to his colleagues he seemed never quite the same again. He had to cut down on his external work; and though his mind was as clear as ever he got more easily tired and had to rest on what afternoons he could find. It no longer seemed that he would be fit for the preferment for which he had hitherto seemed destined.

His illness recurred late in 1957 and 18 months later he tendered his resignation to the Queen. In May 1959 shortly before his resignation became effective the university took the unusual step of honouring one of its own active members when it conferred on him the honorary degree of Doctor of Divinity.

The duties of his many offices did not allow him to publish the full fruits of his undoubted scholarship, though in 1957 he brought out a short monograph on St. Peter.

He married in 1929 Ruth Maude, daughter of L. J. Burpee, and had two sons and a daughter.

August 12, 1960.

Lord Lyle of Westbourne, president of the sugar refining firm of Tate and Lyle, died at his home at Bournemouth on March 6, 1954 at the age of 71.

An uncompromising exponent of private enterprise, he was ingenious and forceful in his methods of carrying on the fight. "Mr. Cube", comical and more often than not satirical, was a stroke of genius and was taken to the hearts of innumerable housewives up and down the country.

It was, indeed, on Lord Lyle's own part at any rate, a good humoured fight and largely because of this quality its modest and unassuming originator was successful.

The Right Hon. Sir Charles Ernest Leonard Lyle, Baron Lyle of Westbourne, of Canford Cliffs, in the County of Southampton, in the Peerage of the United Kingdom, and a baronet, was a grandson of Abram Lyle, founder of the firm which bore his name. He was born on July 22, 1882, and was educated at Harrow and Trinity Hall, Cambridge. In 1918 he entered the House of Commons as Coalition Unionist member for the Stratford Division of West Ham and sat until 1922. In the course of the next year he was elected for Epping, but remained in the House only until 1924. In 1919 he was Parliamentary Private Secretary to C. A. McCurdy, then Food Controller, and was knighted in 1923.

Though his interest in politics remained always active, he found, after the amalgamation of the family business with that of Henry Tate and Sons in 1921, that his business interests took up most of his energy, and it was not until 1940 that he again entered Parliament as Conservative member for Bournemouth. He held the seat until 1945. He was created a baronet in 1932 and raised to the peerage in 1945.

As long ago as 1937 he was telling his colleagues in business to watch closely any further attempts to control and regulate their trade from Whitehall, and in 1949 began his fight against the nationalization of the sugar-refining trade. "Mr. Cube", whose portrait was printed on every packet of sugar distributed by the firm of Tate and Lyle, became a figure of importance and sometimes of fun in every household. The campaign, of which he was the very effective symbol, was the subject of a ruling in the Chancery Division. Mr. Justice Harman held that the costs of printing "Mr. Cube" on the packets were admissible as deduction from profits for income-tax purposes and dismissed an appeal by the Crown against a decision made by the City of London tax commissioners. The Court of Appeal affirmed the decision in the firm's favour.

In his younger days Lord Lyle was a keen and efficient lawn tennis player and golfer. He represented England at lawn tennis, and in 1922 won the East of England Championship. He was president of the Professional Golfers' Association, and had formerly been president of the Lawn Tennis Association.

He married in 1904 Edith Louise, daughter of the late John Levy. She died in 1942, leaving a son and two daughters. The family honours devolve upon the son, the Hon. Charles John Leonard Lyle, who was born in 1905 and married in 1927 Joyce Jeanne, daughter of Sir John Jarvis, Bt.

March 8, 1954.

A. E. Lynam, who died at Oxford on October 14, 1956 at the age of 83, was for many years one of the most eminent preparatory school masters in the country, with an almost lifelong connexion with the Dragon School, Oxford; for he attended it as a boy between 1883 and 1886, and had an unbroken association with it from 1895 onwards.

Alfred Edward Lynam was born on March 29, 1873, the eighth son of Charles Lynam, F.R.I.B.A., F.S.A., of Stoke-on-Trent. He got his nickname "Hum" from his youngest sister; the name stuck, and was adopted not only by a family addicted to nicknames but by a school where the relationship between teacher and taught has always been the reverse of formal. When he joined the Oxford Preparatory School—as the title of the Dragon School then was—his elder brother "the skipper" was headmaster. "Hum" went on as a scholar to Rossall where he won, among other prizes, the translation prize and Lord Egerton's classical prize, each of them three years in succession. From there, again as a scholar, he went to Exeter College, Oxford.

He was still an undergraduate when, in 1895, he joined "the skipper" as a classical master, and he continued on the staff after he went down. For the next 25 years, as well as taking the top classical form and a set in French, he acted as bursar and, for a period, as editor of the school magazine, the *Draconian;* and when, in 1920, "the skipper" retired officially, he succeeded him as headmaster.

The decade after 1920 was a period of expansion for many schools, and the Dragon School was no exception. When "Hum" took over, the school numbered just over 200; in 1930, 373. The new hall with its classrooms had been opened in the school's jubilee year, 1927, and additional boarding space was acquired. (The Dragon School is unique in that it is the only school of its size and kind to be composed in almost equal numbers of day boys and boarders; "Hum" always held the day boys to be one of its greatest assets).

To lighten the ever-growing burden of administration and to give him more time for his work on outside bodies he co-opted in 1930 his son, Joc, and the late G. C. Vassall ("Cheese") as joint headmasters. He, however, remained firmly in control, for many years after that, until about the middle of the last war. Nor, when he handed over the reins, did this mean a withdrawal from the scene or anything like a complete retirement, for he found much to occupy him in both house and school affairs—in particular arrangements for the Sunday services.

He served for three periods of three years on the Council of the I.A.P.S., retiring in 1934, and on the joint standing committee of the Preparatory Schools' and Headmasters' Conference. There he constantly pleaded for closer liaison between the preparatory schools, public schools, and the universities and—more than once—urged that Latin, at the public schools, should not be compulsory for boys who had shown, at their preparatory schools, their unsuitability for it. Another body on which he served and in which he took a lively interest was the parents' association; and for many years he was, and encouraged the school to be, a good friend to the Oxford and Bermondsey Clubs, who made him their visitor in 1947.

As a teacher of the classics he was thorough, interesting, and alive, often dynamic and brilliant; if he could also be explosive, the underlying humour and kindliness were never far from the surface. He had a sound judgment of classical authors, and insisted always that translation must be into good English; "translationese" was never tolerated. In his earlier period he also demanded an accurate knowledge of grammar, even of the rarer forms, but his views on the importance of this underwent much modification; indeed, in his later days, he was known to argue, with his characteristic vigour, *against* the learning of much grammar in the early stages.

He had a strong belief in physical training, outdoors whenever possible, and in physical education in general; and an equally strong objection to what he called "the tyranny of compulsory organized games", and cricket in particular. This was, in his view, for boys without natural aptitude, an indefensible misuse of their time, and he held that all schools, whether preparatory or public, should provide suitable alternatives. When, in 1935, the Dragon School formed a special group, "the snapdragons", where non-cricketers could play their own peculiar form of the game not only without embarrassment but with positive pleasure, he was personally delighted.

It is with the Dragon School Sunday service that "Hum" Lynam will always be associated by Dragons and by many others outside the school; and the service bore his unmistakable imprint. The whole question of religion in education had for long absorbed him, and the service, which owed its development principally to him, was the outcome of his conviction that religion must be made comprehensible and interesting to the young. He was himself a keen and loyal member of the Anglican Church, but he felt that the Prayer Book services were not suited, as they stood, to the needs of the preparatory schoolboy.

So the Dragon Service evolved: chosen readings (from a diversity of sources), prayers, canticles, and hymns, all linked to a central theme, conducted by "lectors" chosen from the boys, and followed by a short address by a selected speaker, usually a visitor and often a layman. The whole service lasted not more than 45 minutes. There was no organ and no special choir, this at least partly because he considered organs and choirs to be definite obstacles to community worship, and he regarded the service as essentially a corporate act. Latterly, in order to familiarize the boys with the book, a Prayer Book Service was held each term.

His *Hymns and Prayers for Dragons,* which he brought out first in 1923, was another side of this attempt to give the boys religious matter within their grasp, as was *The Shorter Bible* in 1930. This was an abridged edition of the Authorized Version, selected and arranged by Dr. David, Bishop of Liverpool, the Rev. V. L. Brook, of Lincoln College, Oxford, Mr. (later Sir) William Hamilton Fyfe, at that time headmaster of Christ's Hospital, and himself. Two years later *Explanations,* a companion volume of short notes, edited by the Rev. J. S. Bezzant, then Chancellor of Liverpool, was published. It would be idle to pretend that these Sunday services did not have their critics; for all that they were a sincere and notable attempt to make (as he once put it himself) "the central hour of the whole week exert its influence upon every other hour".

In 1945 he celebrated his jubilee as a Dragon master and six years later his golden wedding. "Mrs. Hum"—to generations of Dragons—was Miss Mabel Woods, of Coalbrookdale, Shropshire. His two children survive him: J. H. R. Lynam, who succeeded him as headmaster, and a married daughter.

October 16, 1956.

Dr. G. Roche Lynch died suddenly on July 3, 1957 at the age of 68.

Although Lynch either appeared or provided vital evidence in many murder cases, he never attracted anything like the public attention aroused by such men as the late Sir Bernard Spilsbury and other of his contemporaries. For in spite of his superior qualifications in some fields, and more especially toxicology and chemical pathology, he shrank from dogmatism in his expressions of opinion, and his findings were invariably kept within the limits of demonstrable accuracy. His testimony was always strictly objective and dispassionate. Yet he did not lack personality, and even the most casual observer could not fail to be impressed by his scrupulous regard for exactitude and a noticeable tendency to understatement. Indeed, his demeanour in the witness box savoured of the lecture room rather than the criminal court, and this may have been responsible for his testimony seldom being challenged by the learned members of the Bar watching for a loophole in favour of their clients. He was certainly one of the most talented of a team of brilliant men, which included Professor Pepper, Sir William Willcox, and Sir Bernard Spilsbury, whose skill made it extremely difficult for poisoners to escape the consequences of their misdeeds.

Lynch's association with the Home Office, and indirectly with the work of Scotland Yard's Criminal Investigation Department, began in 1920, when he was appointed official analyst. Eight years later he succeeded to the senior office, which he continued to occupy until 1954. His evidence in the Browne and Kennedy trial at the Central Criminal Court had an appreciable effect in ensuring the verdict, which resulted in both being executed for the murder of P.c. Gutteridge. Among the poisoning cases in which Lynch was an important witness were three in the 1930s in which women were concerned, and all three were hanged.

Gerald Roche Lynch, O.B.E., M.B., B.S., D.P.H., F.R.I.C., L.M.S.S.A., was born on January 12, 1889, the son of Jordan Roche Lynch, M.R.C.S., L.R.C.P., of Notting Hill, and belonged to the fifth and possibly sixth generation of his father's family who chose the medical profession as a career. Educated at St. Paul's School, he entered St. Mary's Hospital about 1906, and, with certain intervals, was there for most of his working life.

In 1908 he began to study chemistry under the late Professor H. E. Armstrong at the City and Guilds Institute, South Kensington, and remained about two years. During the 1914-18 War he served in the Royal Navy as surgeon, and in 1920 became assistant chemical pathologist at St. Mary's Hospital, subsequently being appointed chief of the department of which he was afterwards director for many years. Appointed lecturer in forensic medicine and toxicology at Westminster Hospital in 1924, he secured the corresponding appointment at St. Mary's some 10 years later, and though he resigned from the former in 1945, he retained the latter until 1954.

He was examiner for Branch E for the fellowship of the Royal Institute of Chemistry, of which he was also successively a member of council, vice-president, and, finally, from 1946 to 1949, president. Other examinerships he held included that in forensic medicine and toxicology at the University of London, and for the diploma of public health for the R.S.S. and R.C.P. He was a past president of the Society of Public Analysts and Other Analytical Chemists, and of the Medico-Legal Society, and Privy Council Visitor to the examinations of the Pharmaceutical Society of Great Britain.

July 6, 1957.

Mr. Justice Lynskey, who died in hospital in Manchester on December 21, 1957 at the age of 69, had been a Judge of the Queen's Bench Division since 1944.

Sir George Justin Lynskey was a son of the late George Jeremy Lynskey, a solicitor of Liverpool, and was born at Knotty Ash, Liverpool, on February 5, 1888. He was educated at the St. Francis Xavier College, Liverpool, and Liverpool University, where he took his LL.B. in 1907, and his LL.M. in 1908. He was admitted as a solicitor in 1910, and after practising in that branch of the profession for seven years, was called to the Bar by the Inner Temple in 1920. With so substantial a Liverpool background and great natural ability, he soon acquired a large junior practice on the Northern Circuit. Within 10 years of his call he took silk, and in 1938 was made a Bencher of his Inn. As a leader, his success was immediate on his circuit (of which at the time of his appointment to the Bench he had become the leader, and in the life of which he always maintained a keen interest), and he was associated with most of the important cases, criminal as well as civil, heard at Liverpool and Manchester during the 10 years he was in silk. He was appointed Judge of the Salford Hundred Court of Record in 1937, an appointment which carries with it the right to continue in practice at the Bar.

When in 1944 judicial vacancies arose, there was much speculation how they would be filled, and there was some surprise when Lord Simon [q.v.], then Lord Chancellor, recommended Lynskey for appointment to the Bench, for his name was but little known among solicitors in London and his appearances in the Strand were comparatively rare. But all who were acquainted with him in the north applauded the appointment, for, apart from his legal qualifications, Lynskey's genial demeanour had endeared him to all his brother barristers, who prophesied that he would make both a capable and a popular Judge. There was much, too, to be said for recruiting to the Bench sometimes from among men enjoying a large circuit practice, where specialization is less the rule and where familiarity with criminal law, combined with ordinary *nisi prius* business, is general.

Lynskey was a sound lawyer and a good Judge. He kept firm control of a case and could express himself strongly at times. He quickly saw the essentials of a case, which was accordingly determined without waste of time. These desirable, indeed necessary qualities, together with an unfailing courtesy and patience, not only earned for him the respect and affection of those who appeared before him, but gave him a high reputation among all who knew him.

He will perhaps be chiefly remembered as chairman of what came to be known as the Lynskey Tribunal, appointed in October 1948 to inquire whether there was any justification for allegations that payments or rewards had been given to certain Ministers or public servants in connexion with licences or permissions required under any enactment or in connexion with the withdrawal of any prosecution, and what persons were involved. The committee sat for some 26 days and heard a great number of witnesses. The inquiry was a most difficult one to conduct and keep within reasonable limits. It was generally agreed that Lynskey's handling of it was a masterly combination of fairness and firmness, and the report was accepted without serious criticism. It undoubtedly increased his reputation among the general public, to whom hitherto his name had been little known.

Lynskey took a keen interest in cricket and, when his judicial duties permitted, was to be seen at Lord's. Indeed, in summer 1956 he travelled down from the Northern Circuit to London to see Lancashire playing Middlesex.

He married in 1913 Eileen, younger daughter of John Edward Prendwille, of Liverpool, by whom he had two daughters.

December 23, 1957.

Admiral Sir Lumley Lyster, K.C.B., C.V.O., C.B.E., D.S.O., who died on August 4, 1957 in Dorset at the age of 69, served with distinction in command of naval air formations and as Chief of Naval Air Services in the Second World War.

He organized the attack which crippled the Italian fleet at Taranto at a critical stage of the war in 1940. Though not a qualified pilot himself, he gained the complete confidence of the young officers of the Fleet Air Arm through his instinctive understanding of, and sympathy with, their outlook and point of view as the pioneers of a new branch of the naval service.

Arthur Lumley St. George Lyster was the eldest son of Arthur E. Lyster, M.D., and was born on April 27, 1888. From Berkhamsted School he entered the Britannia as a naval cadet in September 1903, and went to sea in January 1905. After serving in the Drake and Grafton he joined the Excellent in August 1912 to specialize in gunnery, and was retained as an instructor on completing the course. When war broke out in 1914 he was appointed gunnery officer of the battleship Glory, in which he served for two years at the Dardanelles and elsewhere.

In April 1917 he joined the cruiser Cassandra as gunnery and executive officer, and for service in that ship in the Sixth Light Cruiser Squadron in the North Sea and Baltic was awarded the D.S.O. in 1919. After the Cassandra was sunk by a mine in December 1918 he was gunnery officer of the Renown, and took part in the tours of the Prince of Wales to Canada and Australasia. He was promoted to captain in 1928, and in that rank he was naval member of the Ordnance Committee in 1929-30, commanded the cruisers Danae and Despatch in 1931-32, the Fifth Destroyer Flotilla in 1933-35, and Chatham Gunnery School in 1935-36. After service at the Admiralty as Director of Training and Staff Duties, he commanded the aircraft carrier Glorious in the Mediterranean in 1937-39. From January 1939 he was a naval A.D.C. to the King.

Promoted to rear-admiral in August 1939, he served at Scapa and in Norway during the first year of the Second World War, and in August 1940 was appointed Rear-Admiral (Air) in the Mediterranean, with his flag in the Illustrious. Outstanding among his good services in this command was his organization of the attack by Fleet Air Arm squadrons on the Italian Fleet at Taranto on November 11, 1940. Torpedo aircraft from the Illustrious obtained hits on three of the six Italian battleships, while bombers from the ship attacked the cruisers and destroyers.

This stroke, brilliantly conceived and daringly executed, altered the balance of naval power in the Mediterranean overnight, and had far-reaching effects on the morale of the Italian Fleet. In March 1941 Lyster was appointed Fifth Sea Lord and Chief of Naval Air Services, but by July 1942 he was back at sea as Rear-Admiral (Air), Home Fleet, and shortly afterwards was promoted to vice-admiral. He took part in the last convoy which was fought through to Malta before the landing in North Africa.

In April 1943 he was appointed to the new post of Flag Officer, Carrier Training, in which he served until after the end of the war in Europe.

He married in 1916 Daisy Agnes, second daughter of Tankerville Chamberlayne, of Cranbury Park, near Winchester, who survives him with three daughters.

August 5, 1957.

M

Sir Ian MacAlister, who was secretary of the Royal Institute of British Architects from 1908 until 1943, died on June 10, 1957 at the age of 79.

In Ian MacAlister the R.I.B.A. had a secretary of imagination and foresight, who for 36 years gave himself unsparingly to its interests. When he was appointed the breach between the R.I.B.A. and some of its most distinguished members on the question "Architecture, a profession or an art?" had lately been healed. He felt that while it lasted it hurt both sides and benefited neither, and he determined that if he could prevent it such internal friction should never recur. During his secretaryship it never did recur; that it did not was certainly due more to MacAlister than to anyone else. Now and again there were threatening quarrels, but his wise foresight and unruffled mediation succeeded in dispersing the storms. Presidents and councils came and went; with every election institute policy might change, now gently, now with violence. MacAlister would loyally carry out these wishes, but in quiet, often undetected, ways he would get them modified wherever he saw danger to the reputation or influence of the institute.

MacAlister came of a distinguished family. He was the second son of Sir John MacAlister, secretary of the Royal College of Surgeons; and Sir Donald MacAlister, Chancellor of the University of Glasgow, was his uncle. Born in Liverpool in 1878, he was educated at St. Paul's School and Merton College, Oxford, where he was an exhibitioner in modern history and took a second class in classical moderations and *Lit. Hum.* After leaving Oxford he was for two years aide-de-camp and secretary to Major-General the Earl of Dundonald when he was G.O.C. of the Canadian Army, and during the First World War he resumed his commissioned career for three or four years as a lieutenant in the Royal Defence Corps.

It was in 1908 that MacAlister, who was a Fellow of the Chartered Institute of Secretaries, was appointed secretary of the R.I.B.A. in succession to W. J. Locke, the novelist. Organization in itself had no attraction for him, but recognizing that it is necessary to the success of policies, he laboured untiringly towards making it efficient. His work in connexion with the Architects' Registration Acts of 1931 and 1938 was probably the hardest task of his career. While he was secretary the institute grew rapidly in numbers, width of field, and unity. Whereas in 1907 there were 18 allied societies and branches in the United Kingdom, in 1939 there were 73; abroad in 1907 there was one, in 1939 34.

The directing and ordering of this expansion was a job after MacAlister's own heart, and one for which he was peculiarly fitted. His Canadian experience had given him an insight into the attitude and ways of the Dominions, while his faith in relations based upon good will and human decency safeguarded the institute from the dangers of an over-formalized constitution. The Commonwealth relations of the institute have moved from indifference to loyalty and friendship; and of all the influences that have helped to bring this about, MacAlister's genial and genuine welcome to all Dominion visitors stands first. He was similarly bent upon friendship with the American Institute of Architects, of which he became an honorary member; many of its members could tell of his kindness and helpfulness to them in their travels, and this was repaid to him personally in unexpected ways.

For architectural education he worked enthusiastically, especially in the expansion of the R.I.B.A. board of architectural education, which transformed the institute from a merely examining to an educational body. He felt deeply that education took first place among all the functions of the institute. Outside institute affairs he had many interests, among which military and naval history ranked first. For years before his retirement he had looked forward to enjoying these interests, but a street accident, from which he barely escaped with his life, was followed by months of hospital treatment and a maimed arm. This disaster, the deaths of two sons in the war, and a serious accident to the third, though they did not break his spirit, sadly marred the fulfilment of his hopes.

In person MacAlister was attractive, with blue eyes, a high colour, an expressive mouth, and a winning smile, which added charm to the warmth of his greeting. He was a persuasive speaker on public occasions, with a scholarly choice of phrase which gave point to his rare expressions of disapproval.

He was knighted in 1934. He married in 1909 Frances Dorothy, daughter of R. C. Seaton. There were three sons and four daughters of the marriage.

June 11, 1957.

C. G. Macartney, the most brilliant Australian batsman in his day, died on September 9, 1958 at Sydney. He was 72.

Macartney first came on the scene as an all-rounder, but he became a sparkling batsman, hard hitting, confident, resourceful, with a most unorthodox repertoire of strokes. He was prepared to cut even fast bowling off his stumps. "A law to himself—a triumph of individualism—not a model to be copied", said *Wisden* cautioningly in 1922. If players with a less perfect eye tried to reproduce his strokes, they were out. That was part of the fascination he held for the crowd. If it was said "Macartney is in", people left what they were doing and went along to watch.

Charles George Macartney was born on June 27, 1886, at West Maitland, New South Wales. He made his first appearance in first-class cricket for New South Wales at the age of 19. Chosen to go to England in 1909 as an all-rounder, he played in the five Test matches and his medium-pace left-hand bowling contributed much to the Australian victory at Leeds, his 11 wickets costing only 95 runs. He toured in England four times, in 1921 hitting four successive hundreds, while his 345 against Nottinghamshire established two records—the highest innings of an Australian in England (even Sir Donald Bradman was unable to surpass it) and the most runs ever made by a batsman in one day.

He was largely self-taught, with a style all his own—the result of native ability fostered by keen observation; audacious and self-confident, perfect in footwork, he drove with great power and was on the attack from the moment he reached the wicket. His innings of 151 in the Leeds Test match of 1926 passed into cricket history. Off the first ball of the match Bardsley [q.v.] was caught at slip off Tate [q.v.], and off the fifth ball Macartney was dropped by Carr*, also at slip; thereafter he gave a wonderful display and actually reached his century before the luncheon interval, thus equalling the achievement of Victor Trumper many years before at Old Trafford.

In his 35 Test matches he made 2,132 runs with an average of 41, and in his whole career 48 hundreds. In his later period his bowling was of secondary importance, but his name could certainly be joined with those of Miller, Noble, and Armstrong in the company of the great Australian all-rounders. Macartney served abroad during the 1914-18 War. He was associated with W. A. Oldfield [d. 1976], the Australian wicketkeeper, in a sports equipment business, and he had had some experience as a journalist.

September 10, 1958.

Dame Rose Macaulay, D.B.E., an author of lively and ironic intelligence, wide scholarship, and fastidious wit, died suddenly on October 30, 1958 at her home in London. She was 77.

Few writers of this century inspired so quick and so lasting an affection among people of every kind. Whether, at an age when less vigorous observers are usually content to do their travelling from an armchair, she was driving alone down the Mediterranean coast of Spain; whether she was at the centre of a fascinated group at one of the innumerable parties which she managed to reach day after day; whether, with inexhaustible kindness, she was giving a precious fragment of her own courage to someone who had need of it, she never failed to find friends. And out of her friendships there flowered not only a series of novels which have not lost their power to enchant but a natural eagerness for life, which lifted her, at times, from sparkling prose to moments of true poetry.

Everything she touched took on part of her own vitality. Even the hardly tried succession of cars in which she terrified her friends acquired an almost human responsiveness to the dash of her approach. Nothing frightened her. Just as she made a habit of swimming in the coldest water (the Serpentine included) at the most unpromising times of year, she used her remarkable intellectual faculties in every climate of opinion. A certain reticence kept her from speaking much of the things which meant most to her, yet the breadth and generosity of her mind were ready for any test. And although she could be formidable when she wished to be, there were in her springs of affection as transparent as they were rare.

The daughter of G. C. Macaulay and Grace Mary Conybeare, Rose Macaulay was one of a family of six children. Her father, well known in his day for his translations of Herodotus and Froissart and as the editor of the works of Gower, was for some years an assistant master at Rugby and from 1905 until his death in 1915 lecturer in English at Cambridge. Miss Macaulay grew up in a stimulating home atmosphere, read eagerly as a child (to the end of her life *Masterman Ready* remained one of her favourite books), and also widely.

Though her first book appeared in 1906, the earliest of her essays in fiction to make any sort of impression was *Views and Vagabonds*, published in 1912—a gay and entertaining effort, though lacking something of coherence. In the following year she brought out *The Lee Shore*, which had in fact been begun before the other and temporarily laid aside, and which won a £1,000 prize offered by the publishers. This was an unusually promising piece of work, the story of an all too charming hero who drifts from luxury to poverty, which was told with the nicest and strictest detachment and a restrained comi-tragic sense. It promptly established the author in the affections of the intelligent novel-reading public.

In the novels that followed, diverse in quality though they were, her gay inventiveness seldom failed her. In *The Making of a Bigot* (1914) she was inclined to push her turn of comic illustration to slightly fanciful extremes; while *Non-Combatants and Others* (1916) seemed to miss its opportunities through being rather too episodic in style. On the other hand, the irresistibly entertaining *Potterism* (1920) and, a year later, *Dangerous Ages*, which was awarded the Femina-Vie Heureuse prize, displayed her graces of humour and irony at their most attractive. There was more substance in her informal style than was immediately apparent.

It is not possible to do more than pick and choose among her novels of the next 30 years. *Told by an Idiot* (1923) was one of the most ambitious of them, a family portrait, at once witty and sympathetic in style, illustrating the social, political, and religious thought of the previous 40 years or so. In *Orphan Island*, in the following year, she attacked in mischievous spirit a theme not very different from that of *The Admirable Crichton*: how far would the postulates of the Victorian social order hold good if put to the stark challenge of nature? The answer she suggested was not Barrie's.

Keeping up Appearances (1928) exhibited a bitter edge, an almost flippant pessimism; in *Going Abroad* (1934) she set out, in her own phrase, to write a novel of "unredeemed levity"; while *And No Man's Wit* (1940) brought a light and almost excessively cool touch to a picture of Spain in the throes of civil war and a playfully mocking temper to the complacencies of English liberalism. She herself would have professed no political creed other than the liberal one.

Two novels of her later period specially deserve mention. In 1950, 10 years after the appearance of her previous novel, she produced *The World My Wilderness*, a study of the barbarian of our day at odds with civilized society. She had handled the theme more amusingly in an earlier book, *Crewe Train*, but on this occasion she achieved a more contemplative effect and an unexpected note of almost brooding compassion. Her last novel, *The Towers of Trebizond* (1956), was once more gay and fanciful, a paradoxically moving exercise in the digressive and idiosyncratic. It received the James Tait Black memorial prize.

Her fiction apart she was an essayist, critic, anthologist, occasional poet, and travel writer of conspicuously individual character. Her essay *Some Religious Elements in English Literature* (1931) was both lively and instructive. She called herself, it should be said, "a High Church Agnostic", but concealed beneath a surface of light-hearted surprise at the demands of orthodoxy a profound and ever-growing religious conviction. In a very active sense the Grosvenor Chapel was her second home.

She also produced a most companionable anthology of verse and prose, revealing wide literary learning and distinctive tastes, entitled *The Minor Pleasures of Life*; a critical appreciation of the work of E. M. Forster*—a subject highly congenial to her literary taste and temper; and *They Went to Portugal* (1946), an informed, ironical and entertaining commentary on the long procession of English visitors to Portugal. This last work was crowned by *Fabled Shore: from the Pyrenees to Portugal* (1949), in which the traveller and the scholar were deliciously blended. No less absorbing was her *Pleasure of Ruins* (1953), which was compact of wit, learning, and eloquence.

In recent years she had given a good deal of pleasure through her literary journalism and broadcasting. The regard in which she was held by many people who did not know her personally was shown when, her collection of books at her home in London having been destroyed in the blitz, replacements of some of her most cherished volumes reached her from complete strangers. Tall in figure, informal of manner, careless of mere appearances, a gay and spirited conversationalist, she will be greatly missed.

She was one of the group of distinguished English literary figures whose protest to the Writers' Union in Moscow about the treatment of Boris Pasternak [q.v.] appeared in *The Times* [on the day she died].

She was created D.B.E. in the New Year Honours List, January 1958. Cambridge conferred upon her an honorary Litt.D.

October 31, 1958.

James McBey, whose death in Tangier at the age of 75 occurred on December 1, 1959, provides one more example of the grit and pertinacity, allied to great talent, so often found in the sons of Scotland; for, born obscurely in the far north, receiving no encouragement or training in art, he used hand and brain to such good effect that by the age of 30 or thereabouts he was internationally famous as an etcher.

Today his name has, for the time being, largely dropped out of fashionable art talk; but at the height of the boom in contemporary etchings, some 30 or 40 years ago, he was among the few most eagerly collected artists.

McBey was born on December 23, 1883, at the fishing village of Newburgh, near Aberdeen. He went to the village school, and at the age of 15 became a clerk in the Aberdeen branch of the North of Scotland Bank. His interest in the graphic arts had been aroused at an early age by an article in a magazine, and he sought out instructional books at the public library. There he found S. R. Koehler's translation of Maxime Lalanne's *Traité de la Gravure à l'Eau-Forte*, which moved him to such enthusiasm that his first attempts at art work were made in the etching medium. So vital a factor was Lalanne in McBey's education that in 1926 he presented the Aberdeen Public Library with a new copy in exchange for the one he had used as a borrower in his youth. He began etching at 17, using zinc rather than copper for economy's sake, and pulling his earliest proofs in the domestic mangle. The very early print "Boys Fishing" (1902) already shows his distinctive "liny" style and is well composed and well managed in tone.

In 1904 McBey was transferred to an Edinburgh branch of the bank, and while there he etched "The Dean Bridge" and other local subjects. Back in Aberdeen the following year, he now devoted the leisure of two years to drawing and painting. In 1910 he felt enough confidence in himself to abandon bank clerking, and went to Holland, where he etched no fewer than 21 plates during the summer. After a brief period in Aberdeen once more, and visits during 1911 to London, Spain and Carmarthen, he held his first exhibition, in November of that year, at the Goupil Gallery. Three critics of mark—Malcolm Salaman, Martin Hardie [q.v.] and James Greig— at once recognized the unusual quality of his work. All available prints were quickly sold, and publication was taken up by Gutekunst in London and Davidson in Glasgow.

Though now domiciled in London, McBey did not at first take kindly to metropolitan subjects. The remaining years before the war produced sets of etchings from Sandwich, Morocco, Holland, and Cornwall; but when at last, early in 1914, he began to see the beauty of Thamesside, he wrought two of his most imposing and finished plates, "The Lion Brewery" and "The Pool", prints from which brought record prices in the sale-room. At the outbreak of the war the house of Colnaghi took over the publication of McBey's etchings and he subsequently held various "one-man" exhibitions of paintings at their galleries. He went to France in 1916 and made a number of drawings at the front; and this led to his appointment in July 1917 as official artist to the Palestine Expeditionary Force. He remained in the Near East until 1919, doing much notable work (a good deal of which is in the Imperial War Museum), including the memorable "Dawn: The Camel Patrol Setting Out". He found Palestine an attractive *terrain* and returned there in 1921. Holland and Morocco, too, claimed further visits, and McBey also went to Venice. He was now at the height of his powers, and during the post-war "boom" in etchings his prints fetched auction prices hitherto unheard of except for Old Masters. In 1925 Martin Hardie brought out a *catalogue raisonné* of his etched work from 1902 to 1924, and in 1929 Malcolm Salaman (who had previously included him in the *Studio* series "Masters of Etching"), published a finely illustrated account of his life and career as an etcher.

Meanwhile painting was by no means neglected, and McBey did many portraits and landscapes in oils. An exhibition at Colnaghi's in 1937, chiefly made up of subjects from Morocco, was an impressive demonstration of his high status as an oil painter; and from time to time he made watercolours of an individual and delightful quality embodying calligraphic quill pen work.

McBey married, in 1931, Marguerite Huntsberry, daughter of the late Adolf Loeb, of Philadelphia. He was made honorary LL.D. by the University of Aberdeen, and examples of his work have been acquired by the British Museum and other important public collections in England and America.

December 3, 1959.

Joseph McCabe, a pillar of Rationalism as a way of thought and a movement in Britain, died on January 10, 1955 at his home in London at the age of 87.

In his early days Joseph McCabe was a Franciscan monk; but in 1896 he renounced his faith and thereafter became a tireless propagandist of Rationalism. In a long and busy life as writer and lecturer he produced a large assortment of books—biographies, historical studies, semi-philosophical and semi-scientific volumes—in which he directed a steady fire of criticism against revealed religion in general and the Roman Catholic Church in particular. A reviewer described him many years ago as "one of our few surviving Victorians", and of necessity this distinction grew more marked with the passage of time. McCabe was indeed a lonely survivor of the serious, militant but somewhat elementary scepticism which perturbed the closing decades of the nineteenth century.

Joseph McCabe, who was of Irish ancestry, was born on November 11, 1867. In 1883, at the unusually early age of 16, he entered the Franciscan order and was trained at St. Francis' College, Manchester, at St. Antony's, Forest Gate, and at Louvain University. Ordained a priest in 1890, he was forthwith appointed a professor of scholastic philosophy, and in 1895 became Rector of Buckingham College. In the following year McCabe left the Roman Catholic Church. The reasons which persuaded him to this course are set forth in his *Twelve Years in a Monastery,* a book which he published with the help of Leslie Stephen in 1897.

While still a Roman Catholic he had set himself to study various aspects of contemporary science, and after he left the Church he became a successful lecturer on evolution and kindred subjects. His *Evolution of Mind,* which appeared in 1910, contained what was probably his best work in this sphere. A student of German, he translated, among other works of its kind, Haeckel's *Riddle of the Universe,* which in its cheap English edition had a very wide circulation. Other books of his, such as *The Decay of the Church of Rome* (1909) and *A Candid History of the Jesuits* (1913) were violently and at times rawly polemical; but McCabe wrote with conscience, and a saving historical sense acted in some degree as a brake upon a temperamental pugnacity.

In the long series of McCabe's works the biographies of Abelard (1901), St. Augustine (1902), Goethe (1912), Bernard Shaw (1914), G. J. Holyoake (1922), and —in particular— Edward Clodd (1932) are worth recalling. Patient in inquiry and analysis and clear and vigorous in expression, at his best he could provide stimulating reading. Of all his writings his *Biographical Dictionary of Modern Rationalists* (1921), which took him several years to compile, was his most exacting effort. All too plainly, however, it was open to the criticism that his classification was of too general a character to be significant; even at that time, in an intellectual sense, he seemed to have outlived his age. But he was still full of fight. For all its weakness of proportion, *The Golden Ages of History* (1940) displayed all his old confidence and independence of judgment, while *The Testament of Christian Civilization,* published in his eightieth year, breathed defiance to the last.

In 1899, three years after he had left the Roman Catholic Church, he married Beatrice, daughter of William Lee, a foreman of works at Leicester, by whom he had two sons and two daughters.

January 26, 1955.

Senator Patrick A. McCarran, for over 20 years a member of the United States Senate and sponsor in that House of the notorious McCarran-Walter Immigration Act, died suddenly on September 28, 1954 at Hawthorne, Nevada, while addressing a Democratic Party rally. He was 78.

Patrick A. McCarran was born at Reno, Nevada, on August 8, 1876, and he was educated at the University of Nevada, where he graduated in 1900. He was then engaged in farming and stock raising on a considerable scale for five years, but on entering the state legislature, to which he was elected in 1903, he decided to take up the profession of the law. He was called to the Nevada Bar in 1905 and immediately set up in practice at Goldfield and adjoining towns during a mining boom. He prospered while business was active there and in 1907 was elected district attorney for Nye County. In 1909 he returned to Reno to take up practice there and soon became one of the leading lawyers of the city. In 1913 he was elected an Associate Justice of the Supreme Court of Nevada and was promoted to be Chief Justice in 1917. During this time he was also a member of the State Pardon Board and the Parole Board.

For some years he was chairman of the state Board of Bar Examiners. He had represented the state at a national Irrigation Congress in 1904 and in later life he always took a lively interest in such questions as affected the ranchmen and cattle breeders of Nevada. He had long taken a prominent part in politics as a Democrat. In 1926 he stood as a candidate for the party nomination in the primary election for the Senate, but was defeated. In 1932 he won the nomination and was elected when the Democrats swept all before them. From the start of his career in the Senate he fought all attempts to free from Government control the silver mined in Nevada, which, owing to its link with American currency, is one of the main sources of revenue of the state.

After the outbreak of war in 1939 he was a strong supporter of the policy of neutrality and used every effort in 1941 to prevent the passage of the Lend-Lease Bill. An isolationist of the isolationists, he wished the United States to be completely independent in matters of defence and to this end advocated as far back as 1935 a strong air force; yet he opposed compulsory military service, and treaties of alliance were to him mere foreign entanglements. Early in his career he broke with President Roosevelt and indeed he seemed destined to the end of his life to fight the majority of the members of his own party more bitterly than he ever conducted the more conventional party warfare.

He opposed after the end of the war President Truman's* efforts to admit displaced persons from southern and eastern Europe into the United States, and in 1950, pushing this attitude to its extreme conclusion, forced through Congress against the President's veto the notorious McCarran-Walter Immigration Act forbidding foreign seamen to land on American soil unless they submit to an inquisition by immigration officers. The Act came into effect in June 1952 and has done more harm to the relations of the United States with other maritime nations than any other single measure. Needless to say, Senator McCarran was a strong supporter of Senator McCarthy [q.v.], and only the day before he died had vigorously assailed the Watkins Committee for recommending the censure of the Senator from Wisconsin.

September 30, 1954.

Major-General Sir Robert McCarrison, C.I.E., late of the Indian Medical Service, died at the age of 82 on May 18, 1960.

His original investigations into deficiency diseases formed the basis of much of the modern science of nutrition and entitle him to a high place among members of the Indian Medical Service who have contributed to the advancement of science and the good of mankind.

Robert McCarrison was born at Portadown, Ulster, on March 15, 1878, the second son of

Robert McCarrison, of Lisburn, co. Antrim, and was educated at Queen's College, Belfast, and the Richmond Hospital, Dublin. He qualified in 1900 and joined the Indian Medical Service in the following year. Eighteen months later, when he was stationed at a fort in Chitral, he began to investigate a local fever, the distribution of which appeared to correspond with that of the sandfly. He sent for a microscope and improvised incubators, but was unable to complete his researches as he was moved to Gilgit, in Kashmir. His surmise that the disease was transmitted by the sandfly was confirmed in 1906.

As early as 1903 he had begun to investigate the incidence and causation of goitre, and, after serving as Agency Surgeon at Gilgit from 1904 to 1911, he was in 1913 assigned to special duty for the investigation of goitre and cretinism in India. In 1918 the scope of his researches was widened to cover deficiency diseases in general, and from 1929 to 1935 he was Director of Nutrition Research under the Indian Research Fund Association. During the greater part of this time he worked at the Pasteur Institute at Coonor, in Southern India, whence he and his assistants issued a constant stream of reports and memoirs on goitre, cretinism, and deficiency diseases. In all his researches McCarrison combined laboratory investigation with observation in the field, and it was this combined method of approach that made his nutrition work of such practical importance.

McCarrison's principal publications dealt with *The Aetiology of Endemic Goitre* (1913), *The Thyroid Gland in Health and Disease* (1917), *Studies in Deficiency Disease* (1921), *The Simple Goitres* (1928), and *Food* (1929).

His work received wide recognition: as early as 1911 he was awarded the First Class Kaiser-i-Hind Gold Medal for public service in India, and in 1914 he received the Prix Amussat of the Academy of Medicine of Paris for his original researches on goitre and cretinism. He was made C.I.E. (1923), was honorary physician to the King (1928-35), and was knighted in 1933. In 1921 he made a lecture tour of the United States, in the course of which he gave the Mellon lecture at Pittsburgh, the Mary Scott Newbold lecture at Philadelphia, the Hanna lecture at Cleveland, the Mayo Foundation lecture at Rochester, and the De Lamar lecture at Baltimore. He also gave accounts of his researches in the Milroy lectures at the Royal College of Physicians (1913), the Cantor lectures at the Royal Society of Arts (1936), the Lloyd Roberts lecture at the Medical Society of London (1936), the Gabriele Howard lecture (1937), and the Sanderson-Wells lecture (1939).

He was awarded the Stewart prize by the British Medical Association (1918), the Arnott memorial gold medal by the Irish Medical Schools and Graduates Association (1922), the Silver Medal of the Royal Society of Arts (1925), the Arnold Flinker prize of the Julius Wagner-Jauregg Foundation of Vienna (1934), and the Barclay memorial medal of the Royal Asiatic Society of Bengal (1939). Since his retirement from the Indian Medical Service in 1935 he had been living at Oxford. During the 1939-45 War he served as deputy regional adviser in medicine to the Emergency Medical Service and as chairman of the local medical war committee. From 1945 to 1955 he was Director of Post-Graduate Medical Education at Oxford.

He married in 1906 Helen Stella, third daughter of J. L. Johnston, I.C.S., of Guildford, Surrey. There were no children of the marriage.

May 19, 1960.

Sir Desmond MacCarthy, the dramatic and literary critic, died on June 7, 1952 at Cambridge, two days after the university had conferred on him the honorary degree of Doctor of Letters. He was 75.

Known to a wide public as a regular and urbane contributor first to the *New Statesman,* then to the *Sunday Times* and, latterly, as a broadcaster, he was at his best and most individual in writing on the theatre. Indeed, there have been few more discerning dramatic critics and his early work in *The Speaker* on the plays of Bernard Shaw are models of the *genre.* These notices were published in book form in 1951, and reflected with great acuity and fairness the development and decline of Shaw as a philosophic dramatist. MacCarthy brought to the practice of the art of reviewing a very wide range of reading, sensitive judgment, and a perpetual curiosity about new writing. Cleverness and fashion never deceived him and he never grew unsympathetic towards innovation. He treated each book with perceptive interest, searching for good qualities but clearly indicating weakness, and he judged the whole against the liberal background of humane letters in which he had been bred.

Born in 1878, the son of Charles Desmond MacCarthy and Louisa de la Chevallerie, Desmond MacCarthy was educated at Eton and at Trinity College, Cambridge. The possession of some money of his own enabled him to support over a number of years the trials of free-lance journalism. He wrote dramatic criticism for *The Speaker,* contributed to the *Eye Witness* (of which he was, in the end, one of the unpaid creditors) and to the *New Witness,* but entered into relative security only in 1913, when Clifford Sharp appointed him dramatic critic of the *New Statesman.*

The quality of his work as what at the time was called an "impressionist" critic of the drama was such that when, more than 20 years later, he published a selection of his notices in volume form, MacCarthy had little reason to regret his early judgments. During the war of 1914-18 he drove an ambulance and, with the return of peace, engaged for a time in more varied journalism than he had so far attempted. He had attended the trial of Sir Roger Casement and set down his reflections upon it, and, in the process, had found that he had the gift of descriptive reporting. In later years, indeed, he was to confess rather wistfully that he feared he had wasted his talent for this kind of writing. Apart from a visit to Ireland, during the "troubles", for the *Manchester Guardian,* MacCarthy made few excursions into the drama of real life.

Since he wrote so frequently and so well, his published work—other, that is, than collections of reprinted articles and reviews—is disappointingly small. When he did commit himself to a more or less prolonged effort, as in an occasional short story, it was with an oddly marked reluctance, as if an excellent and practised speaker had been brought to his feet against his will. There are, however, volumes of reprinted pieces such as "Portraits" (1932), presented as the first volume of his collected journalism, and "Experiences" (1935), which still make the happiest reading. If they lack the pronounced, too pronounced, efficiency of much good journalism, they provide many of the most fortunate accidents of conversation. MacCarthy's was a wide and carefully cultivated knowledge of literature, though as a critic he was most penetrating and gave the greatest pleasure when he was able to approach his subject by way of his own observation of the actual human being. Hence the revealing quality of his critical appreciation of a figure like Henry James.

He edited *H.H.A.: Letters of the Earl of Oxford and Asquith to a Friend* (1933), and also wrote a small volume on Leslie Stephen (1937).

A Fellow of the Royal Society of Literature, an honorary LL.D. of Aberdeen University, elected in 1945 president of the English P.E.N. Club, he was an influential figure in the contemporary literary scene. The charm of his writing was reflected in his conversation. Few men of letters, powerful in their day as critics, have won so many friends or made less enemies. He was knighted in 1951.

In 1906 he married Miss Mary Warre-Cornish (who as Mary MacCarthy produced, among other volumes, a delightful memoir of her early years, *A Nineteenth Century Childhood*). She survives him with two sons and a daughter, Lady David Cecil.

June 9, 1952.

Senator Joseph McCarthy, who died suddenly on May 2, 1957 in the Bethesda Naval Hospital, where he had been taken at the beginning of the week for treatment for hepatitis, was for some years the most bitterly controversial figure in American political life. Since 1954 he had been in eclipse, his power and influence dwindling with the national mood which fostered that political method to which he had given his name.

As this wave of anger and anxiety subsided McCarthy was left with no other momentum for his political career than he could generate in his capacity as senator, and in that he had been gravely damaged not only by the censure of his peers but also and perhaps more important by the Republican defeat of 1954, which deprived him of the chairmanship of the Senate committee which had been the instrument of his power. So withered was his prestige even with the right wing of his own party that there was considerable doubt whether he would have been nominated again to run for the Senate in 1958.

Joseph Raymond McCarthy was born at Grande Chute, Wisconsin, on November 14,

1909. He was one of the seven children of Timothy and Bridget McCarthy, his father having emigrated from Ireland and his mother from Germany. He went to a country school, helping his father on his farm, and for a time was successful in raising chickens. Then, after working for a time in a grocery store, he decided to study law. At 19 he enrolled in a high school, and crammed enough knowledge to be able to enter Marquette University, in Milwaukee, in 1930.

Supporting himself, he took his law degree in 1935 and then practised for a short time in Shawano. The business which later was to earn McCarthy worldwide notoriety showed itself when at the age of 29, shortly after he had qualified, he decided to seek election as a State circuit judge. His decision to contest the office was received with derision. In the event McCarthy won by 15,000 votes against 11,000, ousting an incumbent of 24 years' standing.

On the entry of the United States into the 1939-45 War, McCarthy temporarily deserted the Bench for active service. He joined the United States Marines and later qualified as an air gunner. That he received a leg injury during his active service is beyond doubt, but how it was occasioned became a matter of political controversy. His enemies claimed that it arose during some horseplay while crossing the Equator, his friends that it was the result of enemy bullets.

In 1945 he was discharged from the service and, without opposition, was re-elected to the Bench of the circuit-court. McCarthy then set about ousting Robert La Follette, junr., from the Wisconsin seat in the Senate, which became vacant in the next year. In the primary election he defeated La Follette (who previously had sat as a Progressive) and won the substantive election without much difficulty.

McCarthy's first three years in the Senate were fairly uneventful, and his rise to fame and the beginnings of McCarthyism are generally dated from February 9, 1950. On that day in the course of a speech at Wheeling, West Virginia, he said: "I have here in my hands a list of 205—a list of names that were made known to the Secretary of State (Dean Acheson)* as being members of the Communist Party and who nevertheless are still working and shaping policy in the State Department".

McCarthy's speech caused a tremendous sensation in the United States, but his charges were denied by the State Department. Later in the month the Senate set up a five-man subcommittee to investigate McCarthy's charges. The committee held its hearings in the full glare of publicity but made little real progress. The Senate made charges against individuals but when pressed for evidence merely assailed the good faith of the committee. While maintaining his attack, McCarthy received the collaboration of certain influential Republican senators and newspapers and, in the atmosphere which he succeeded in creating, to seek evidence was equated with opposing McCarthy, and opposing McCarthy was equated with sympathizing with Communism.

The Senate subcommittee reported in July 1950, clearing all persons named by Senator McCarthy as having Communist sympathies and rebuking him for his "irresponsible" and "untruthful accusations". The report was not unanimous, however, and it became evident that McCarthy had a wide measure of support both in Congress and in the country at large.

In the new Senate McCarthy's influence was greatly enhanced by his appointment on January 30, 1951, to a powerful subcommittee of the Appropriations Committee which had jurisdiction over the State Department, as well as the Departments of Justice and Commerce. In June of that year McCarthy published a 60,000-word speech (most of the Senators walked out of the Chamber as it was being read, but he inserted the remainder in the Congressional Record), in which he charged General George Marshall [q.v.], the former Secretary of State, with being involved in a conspiracy to weaken the United States for its conquest by the Soviet Union, "a conspiracy so immense, an infamy so black, as to dwarf any in the previous history of man". McCarthy kept hammering at his charges; he named individuals; he secured the removal from the foreign service of important officers; and he fostered a sentiment of "guilt by association" which secured the removal from their posts of many people in any walk of life in which they could have any influence on the public.

McCarthyism was well before the public in the election of 1952, which secured the return of a Republican Administration under President Eisenhower* after two decades of uninterrupted Democratic rule. The Senator himself was returned triumphantly for Wisconsin, but the coming into power of a new Administration, headed by a popular soldier, and creating in the public mind the impression that old cobwebs were bound to have been swept away, eventually contributed to the decline of McCarthy's influence.

The year 1953 saw a widening breach between McCarthy and the Eisenhower Administration, and the *dénouement* was precipitated by the Senator's relations with the United States Army. He and one of his staff used pressure and threats to secure a commission for a private who had formerly served on his staff and, at hearings concerning the retention of a dental officer who had been accused of Communist sympathies, the Senator was extremely abusive of General Ralph Zwicker. In March 1954 charges and counter-charges between McCarthy and the Army were going on in public and the Senate decided that they should be investigated. On April 22, 1954, there began 36 days of televised hearings, which did nothing to improve the Senator's credit in the country.

The upshot was the adoption by the Senate on November 8, 1954, of a motion censuring McCarthy—it being the first occasion since 1929 that such a resolution had been passed. By that time the international climate had changed. Stalin's [q.v.] death had brought indications of happier relations between Russia and the West; the fighting in Indo-China had ceased; and, just as important, the Democrats had won the mid-term congressional elections.

Physically McCarthy was a big man and he was extremely energetic. In September 1953 he married Miss Jean Kerr, a member of his office staff.

His career indicates the great, if transient, influence which can be obtained in the life of a democratic country by the loud and persistent repetition of the big lie.

May 3, 1957.

Lady Keeble, O.B.E.,—**Lillah McCarthy,** the actress who made an important contribution to the theatre during the early years of this century when her first husband, Harley Granville Barker, was staging Shaw and Shakespeare—died at the age of 84 on April 15, 1960.

It was in her striking person that several Shavian heroines—Ann Whitefield, Mrs. Dubedat, Margaret Knox, Lavinia—were first seen, and when Barker, continuing the pioneering work of William Poël, marked the beginning of the twentieth century in Shakespearean production with his *The Winter's Tale, Twelfth Night,* and the *Dream,* Lillah McCarthy was the Hermione, the Viola, and the Helena. The break with Barker, followed by the divorce in 1917, came as she was entering on middle age, but she continued her career for a few years and was actress-manageress of the Kingsway for a short season. But her marriage in 1920 to Professor F. W. Keeble, C.B.E., F.R.S., later Sir Frederick Keeble [q.v.], took her to live near Oxford, where he filled the Sherardian Chair in the university, and her professional work ceased in 1922.

The daughter of J. McCarthy, F.R.A.S., she was born on September 12, 1875, at Cheltenham and went to school there before studying elocution and voice production. As an amateur in 1895 she gave a performance of Lady Macbeth which Shaw noticed with favourable jocularity in *The Saturday Review.* She went to see him and he told her to go away and get professional experience. She was engaged that same year by Ben Greet and in 1896 by Wilson Barrett for *The Sign of the Cross.* In the latter play she went to America, then rejoined Barrett and, with intervals, worked with him in England, Australia, and South Africa till his death.

Barrett had intended setting her up in her own company, but she now returned to the West End, and in 1905 again rang Shaw's door-bell. He gave her *Man and Superman* to study, and at Barker's suggestion—Barker had toured with her in Ben Greet's company—meanwhile offered her Nora in *John Bull's Other Island* at the Court. So began her collaboration in a notable enterprise to which native playwrights such as Galsworthy, Masefield*, St. John Hankin and Laurence Houseman [q.v.], to say nothing of Gilbert Murray [q.v.] as Euripides' translator, Schnitzler and Hauptmann contributed.

Lillah McCarthy married Barker in 1906, but did not thereafter appear exclusively in his productions. She worked for Dion Boucicault in plays by Barrie and Somerset Maugham* and for Reinhardt as Jocasta to Martin Harvey's Oedipus. But she was actively associated with her husband at the Court during his joint management with J. E. Vedrenne, at the Little, first appearing with him there in *Anatol* in 1911, at the Kingsway, where they presented *Iphigenia in Tauris,* in Shakespeare at the Savoy (1912 and 1914) and at the St. James's (1913). It is doubtful whether he, with his growing distaste for the theatre, would have gone on working there as long as he did, had it not been for her enthusiasm. She was no match for him intellectually, and this made her unskilful in taking his direction at times; but, apart from the frequent excellence of her stage work, she did much for Barker by finding backers, and enlisting the support of such well-wishers as the Prime Minister, H. H. Asquith.

After the outbreak of war the Stage Society of New York invited Barker to direct a series of productions. Asquith thought the season likely to do good, and recommended him and Lillah McCarthy to go. Their programme included Shaw, Shakespeare, and Greek tragedy. They were in England again in 1915. Barker went back to America alone, and wrote to tell his wife early in 1916 that he did not mean to return to her. It was months before she brought herself to seek a divorce. Meanwhile she more or less maintained her high reputation by her work in London, though her old position was lost, and her attempt to recover it by appearing under her own management quickly failed.

After her second marriage she was Matheson Lang's "leading lady" in two romantic plays. But Shaw would not allow her to present *Heartbreak House* with herself as Ellie Dunn, and when she wanted to return to the stage in *Saint Joan* it had already been entrusted to Dame Sybil Thorndike [d. 1976]. So it happened that Lillah McCarthy did no more regular stage work, though she gave a number of poetry recitals during the 1930s.

She and Keeble, himself a strong personality, understood each other and their marriage—she was his second wife—brought them happiness.

April 16, 1960.

Sir Francis McClean, A.F.C., who died in a nursing home in London on August 11, 1955 at the age of 79 after a long illness, may be said to have been the founder of naval flying as he certainly was the founder of amateur flying in heavier than air machines in Britain.

A civil engineer by profession, he retired from the Indian Public Works Department at an early age and had his first experience of flight in 1907 as assistant to Griffith Brewer in the Gordon-Bennett balloon race from Berlin. In the next year's race from Zürich he was a pilot and in December of that year flew with Wilbur Wright at Le Mans. The following month saw the beginning of his long cooperation with Short Brothers, of Rochester, in developing the heavier than air machine. Leysdown and, subsequently, Eastchurch, in the Isle of Sheppey, were the sites of these early experiments on ground bought by McClean and subsequently let to the Aero Club of Great Britain (now the Royal Aero Club) at 1s. a year. Interest in heavier than air flight grew rapidly and in February 1911 McClean offered to lend aircraft so that naval officers could learn to fly, and the Admiralty accepted the offer. An offer to the War Office to give Territorial officers a similar opportunity was turned down.

Francis Kennedy McClean was born on February 1, 1876, the son of Dr. Frank McClean, F.R.S., and was educated at Charterhouse and Cooper's Hill. He spent only four years in the Public Works Department in India, from 1898 to 1902. To his flying activities he added submarine photography, in which he was also a pioneer, and in cooperation with the late Hugh Spottiswoode took some remarkable photographs of the wreck of the Oceana at Eastbourne. That was in June 1912. In August of that year he was back in the air and created a record by flying up the Thames in a seaplane, passing between the upper and lower parts of Tower Bridge and under London Bridge without touching water.

In the winter of 1913 he flew up the Nile with four passengers. He joined the Royal Naval Air Service on August 6, 1914, and was put on Channel patrol, but later became chief instructor at Eastchurch. On the foundation of the R.A.F. he was given a commission, but resigned in 1919.

He was twice chairman of the Royal Aero Club, first in 1923-24 and again from 1941 to 1944, and he was elected a vice-president in 1945. In July 1954 a memorial was erected on the Isle of Sheppey to record that the island contained the first centres of heavier than air aviation in England. Sir Francis McClean's name is among those of 13 aviators recorded on the memorial.

He married in 1918 Aileen, daughter of W. H. Wale, who survives him together with two daughters of the marriage.

August 12, 1955.

Colonel Robert Rutherford McCormick, editor and publisher of the *Chicago Tribune,* died at Chicago on April 1, 1955, at the age of 74. He had been in failing health for several months. While Colonel McCormick was world famous principally for his dislikes, prominent among which were most things British, he was personally a charming host and many Englishmen who went to Chicago found him a fount of hospitality and thoughtfulness.

The son of Robert Sanderson McCormick, at one time United States Ambassador to Russia, he was born at Chicago on July 30, 1880, and was educated at Groton (where the late President F. D. Roosevelt was at school) and Yale. After graduating in 1903 he became clerk to a lawyer and studied law at Northwestern University Law School. He served on Chicago City Council from 1904, when he was made an alderman, to 1906, and then became president of the Chicago Sanitary District. From 1905 to 1910 he successfully administered a big sewage disposal project for the city of Chicago; and he was meanwhile admitted to the Bar in 1907, becoming partner in the law firm of McCormick, Kirkland, Patterson, and Fleming.

In 1910 McCormick, who had had no previous connexion with journalism, joined with his cousin James Patterson in taking over the *Chicago Tribune,* a property of the family. It was founded in 1847 by his maternal grandfather, Joseph Medill, who was also the first editor. McCormick threw himself with enthusiasm into the rough-and-tumble of the American circulation war, and quickly built up the paper to become one of the most widely sold sheets in the United States. The circulation rose from 188,000 in 1910 to 1,040,000 in 1947. He made the *Chicago Tribune* a journal of power, but not of prestige. Scares, sales promotion stunts, brusque tergiversations in policy made the paper unacceptable to the sober-minded, intelligent American reader; but it had its public, and a large one. In the course of increasing the paper's influence and circulation McCormick introduced comic strips, embarked on a wide variety of campaigns, fought vigorously to outshine W. R. Hearst's [q.v.] rival *Examiner,* bought forest rights in Canada and opened paper mills in Quebec and Ontario.

When the 1914-18 War broke out the *Chicago Tribune* was isolationist, but McCormick went out to the Russian front in 1915, interviewing Asquith and Sir Edward Grey on the way out and the Czar when he arrived in Russia. His organization was early in the field with the use of war newsreels. When, in 1917, the United States became a belligerent, McCormick went to Paris on General Pershing's staff. He later served at the front with an artillery unit, won the Distinguished Service Medal, and attained the rank of colonel. In 1919 he was recommended for the rank of general officer by Pershing. He produced two war books: *With the Russian Army* (1915) and *The Army of 1918* (1920).

After the war McCormick and Patterson founded the New York *Daily News.* They broke their connexion in 1925, Patterson retaining the *Daily News,* which became the most widely circulated daily paper in America. McCormick meanwhile became deeply involved in campaigns concerned with the municipal life of Chicago and with the crime which was an evil by-product of prohibition. He bitterly condemned prohibition, advocated conscription, and used much powder and shot against the Bolshevists. President Roosevelt's New Deal of 1933 aroused his anger, and trade union activities and Great Britain were other *bêtes noires.* Much of McCormick's hostility towards Britain was due to his belief, amounting to an almost religious faith, in "100 per cent. Americanism".

Depreciating both the Nazi menace and the Japanese threat, he showed an almost unexampled capacity for nearly always backing the wrong horse. When lend-lease was introduced during the 1939-45 War he described the measure as a "dictator Bill", and his attitude towards the war caused great acrimony in Chicago. It was only after Pearl Harbour that the *Chicago Tribune* came round to wholehearted support of the war, but even then it maintained raucously that only America was doing anything to win it.

McCormick was devoted to riding and

hunting and had a stable of Irish steeplechasers. Deep-sea fishing was another interest. He initiated many excellent welfare and insurance schemes for the benefit of his employees. A moving spirit in the Freedom of the Press Committee of the American Newspaper Publishers' Association, he wrote *The Freedom of the Press,* which appeared in 1936. Other books were *Ulysses S. Grant* (1934), *How We Acquired our National Territory* (1942), *The American Revolution and its Effect on World Civilization* (1945), *The Founding Fathers* (1951), and *The American Empire* (1952).

He married in 1915 Miss Amie Irwin Adams. She died in 1939. He married secondly in 1944 Mrs. Maryland Mathison Adams. There were no children of either marriage.

April 21, 1955.

Sir Murdoch Macdonald, K.C.M.G., C.B., formerly member of Parliament for Inverness, died at the age of 90 on April 24, 1957.

Murdoch Macdonald was a member of the distinguished group of British civil engineers whose fame rests upon the irrigation works that now control and distribute the waters of the Nile. What he lacked in early professional training and administrative experience he made good by industry and force of character, so much so that Lord Kitchener described him as "a man of granite". His success in launching irrigation projects in Egypt and the Sudan was widely acknowledged and his achievements were recognized by his profession when he was appointed in 1932 president of the Institution of Civil Engineers. In politics he found further scope for his activities as the Liberal, and later Liberal National, member for his native county of Inverness.

The son of Roderick Macdonald, he was born on May 6, 1866, and was educated at Farraline Park School, Inverness. He was apprenticed as an engineer and gained experience while assisting in railway surveys and construction in northern Scotland. During the building of the Black Isle line (1890-1894) and during the widening of the main line between Dalnaspidal and Blair Athol to provide for double-line working (1896-1898), he acted as a resident engineer. This early work foreshadowed his career in miniature, for it included the design of an earthen dam across a burn, the provision of a small power-station operated from it, and the calculation of dimensions for a spillway as a safeguard against floods. To this he alluded on the occasion in 1930 when the freedom of the burgh of Inverness was conferred upon him.

In 1898 he had the good fortune to be invited by Sir Benjamin Baker to proceed to Egypt as an assistant to Sir Maurice Fitzmaurice for the construction of the original Aswan Dam. By 1903 he had secured the position of resident engineer for the protection works downstream of the dam; in 1907 he was Director-General of Reservoirs, Egypt; two years later he became Director of Construction; and in 1911 he was promoted to be Under Secretary of State for Public Works. From 1912 to 1917 he was Under Secretary without an Adviser—the Advisership during those years having been suppressed—and from 1917 to 1920 he was Adviser and Under Secretary. After 1920 he was Adviser alone, and P. M. Tottenham became Under Secretary. In addition, on returning from leave at the end of December 1915 he was appointed temporary and local colonel under the Deputy Director of Works, and he took charge of the works then in progress for the defence of the Suez Canal. His knowledge of road and rail construction, transport, and water supply was of special value, and he was made a C.B. shortly after this service. He had been made a C.M.G. in 1910 and promoted to K.C.M.G. in 1914.

During his work in Egypt, from 1898, he practically lived on the Aswan Dam—until 1902 on the construction of the original dam, in 1902-03 on its maintenance, and from 1903 to 1906 as resident engineer in charge of construction of protective works downstream of the dam. From 1907 to 1911, as Director-General of Reservoirs and later of Construction, he was in supervisory control of the works, of the elaboration of details of the general scheme for heightening and thickening the original dam, of the construction of the Esna Barrage in 1907-08, and of the Minufiya Head in 1910. In those early years he instituted large-scale experiments at the Aswan Dam for the volumetric measurement with extreme accuracy of vast discharges of running water by passing it through sluices of the dam into a derelict tank downstream to determine sluice coefficients. In 1921 he and Dr. H. E. Hurst read a paper on the subject at the Institution of Civil Engineers for which they were awarded respectively a Telford gold medal and a Telford premium.

From 1909 onwards, owing chiefly to the decline in the yield of the cotton crop, projects were prepared for dealing with the drainage of the low-lying lands of the northern Delta. On Sir Murdoch's promotion to the Under-Secretaryship in 1911, Lord Kitchener, who had become High Commissioner in Egypt and the Sudan, decided that the trouble must be attacked in a large and striking way. Powerful pumping stations on the sea coast to lift practically the whole of the drainage water of the Central Gharbia and Western Behera provinces were accordingly to be provided. Before much work had been done, however, the First World War intervened; and when operations were resumed it was upon less ambitious lines.

Lord Kitchener again made use of Sir Murdoch's driving force to start in 1914 the construction of the Gezira Canal and the Sennar Dam. The war retarded progress until 1919-21, when controversy, political events, and rising prices combined to stop operations. Similarly in 1914 a larger and more striking structure was contemplated for the Gebel Aulia Dam than was ultimately found suitable. Again the war, controversy, and political difficulties impeded progress and, though something was done in 1920-21, it was not until 1933 that work on a smaller scale was resumed and the contract finally assigned.

It was during Macdonald's tenure of office as Under-Secretary and Adviser that, owing to various criticisms, special outside opinions were taken concerning the Ministry's works. These commissions were held on various occasions, notably in 1912, 1914, 1917, 1918, and 1920. The commissions of 1918 and 1920 were the outcome of charges brought by Sir William Willcocks in 1918 against the Public Works Ministry in the person of Macdonald for alleged falsifying of data and misleading the public. In consequence, the Foreign Office appointed a distinguished commission to sit in London, which entirely exonerated Macdonald. Nevertheless, because of the impression upon the Egyptian public, an International Commission was appointed in 1920 to report on the Ministry's proposed programme of works and to examine what became known as the Willcocks-Kennedy charges. It was in connexion with this matter that Macdonald compiled a valuable report entitled *Nile Control.* The commission found no defect in the Ministry's programme of undertakings, and repeated the Foreign Office Commission's condemnation of the attacks upon it.

These deplorable controversies, which reached their height between 1917 and 1921, almost monopolized the scientific and intellectual resources of the Ministry, and led to the temporary suspension of most of the works then in hand. Although Macdonald was entirely exonerated, he was naturally aggrieved, and in May 1921 he resigned his appointment of Adviser and decided to practise as a consulting civil engineer in Westminster. In 1939 he was appointed by the Great Ouse Catchment Board to advise in the fight against the flood danger in the Fens. He advised the Portuguese and Greek and Jordan Governments on irrigation problems, and in recent years had been engaged on several schemes in Egypt including two barrages across the Nile.

In March 1922 he was elected for the Inverness Division as a Coalition Liberal and held the seat first as a Liberal, and from 1931 to 1950 as a Liberal National.

April 25, 1957.

Sir Noel Mason-MacFarlane—See **Mason-.**

Major Agnes McGeary, M.B.E., A.R.R.C., formerly of Queen Alexandra's Royal Army Nursing Corps, died on December 9, 1954 at the age of 45. She had a distinguished nursing career, and will be chiefly remembered for her close association with the Chindits in 1943 and 1944.

Agnes McGearey was born on January 24, 1909 at Mossend, Lanarkshire, where she received her early education before going on to the Royal Alexandra Infirmary, Paisley, and the Royal Maternity Hospital, Glasgow. She joined the Q.A.I.M.N.S., as it then was, in April 1934 and served in Malta until September 1939 when she went to France, being evacuated in June 1940. Two years later she went to India; and the chances of war found her in charge of the hospital at Imphal in the spring of

1943, when the survivors of General Wingate's first expedition into Burma were returning from their deep foray beyond the Chindwin.

Matron McGearey put all else aside and devoted herself passionately to the well-being of these officers and men, plundering supply depôts and overriding regulations in order that they should have the best of what little was available. Chief among her patients was General Wingate himself, who reached Imphal to discover that for once he had met his match, and was under a discipline as iron as his own. She protected him in turn from interruption; and it was in a small hut which she provided in the compound of her hospital that he wrote his report on the expedition.

Later in the same year, when General Wingate returned from the Quebec Conference with his command and responsibilities greatly enlarged, he fell desperately ill with typhoid. Lord Mountbatten, newly appointed Supreme Commander, caused Matron McGearey to be flown from Imphal to Delhi to nurse him through the crisis and back to health. Returning to Imphal, it fell to her again to succour many of the wounded from Wingate's second Burma expedition. It is no exaggeration to say that she had by now acquired, for the Chindits, something of the stature of a Florence Nightingale.

After some time at home, she was in Haifa during the worst of the troubles in Palestine, and then in Egypt and England. In May 1953 she took charge of a hospital at Taipang, in Malaya, from which she was flown home seriously ill, in August 1954. It would be idle to deny that Major McGearey was a difficult subordinate and an exacting superior. Scottish by birth, Irish by blood and temperament, she was a bonny fighter by instinct. She loved soldiers and understood them; and she rejoiced in her profession, which has suffered grievously by her early death.

December 10, 1954.

Admiral of the Fleet Sir Rhoderick R. McGrigor, G.C.B., D.S.O., who died in hospital in Aberdeen on December 3, 1959 at the age of 66, had a distinguished record of service in the two world wars. He was a lieutenant in the Grand Fleet at Jutland.

Between 1939 and 1945 his service ranged from China to the Arctic, with an eventful period in the Italian campaigns in 1943. After the war he became Commander-in-Chief of the Home Fleet, Commander-in-Chief at Plymouth, and finally First Sea Lord. He was familiarly known in the Navy as "Wee Mac", for he stood only 5ft. 4in. tall.

Rhoderick Robert McGrigor was born on April 12, 1893, the son of Major-General C. R. R. McGrigor, 60th Rifles, grandson of Sir C. R. McGrigor, second baronet, and great-grandson of Sir James McGrigor, first baronet, Chief of the Medical Staff of the Duke of Wellington's Army in the Peninsular War, 1811.

He entered Osborne College as a Naval Cadet in January 1906 and passed out at the top of his term from Dartmouth College in December 1909 and from the training cruiser Cornwall in August 1910, taking prizes for grand aggregate, mathematics, and French. He was a midshipman in the Formidable and the Africa. In his examinations for lieutenant in 1913 he gained firsts in all subjects and also the Beaufort and Wharton testimonial.

When the First World War began in August 1914 he was sub-lieutenant of the destroyer Foxhound in the Mediterranean, and in 1915 took part in the campaign at the Dardanelles. He was promoted to lieutenant from October 1914. Joining the Malaya in the Grand Fleet in December 1915, he was present at the battle of Jutland five months later. In September 1917 he joined the Vernon to specialize in torpedoes and in June 1918 returned to the Grand Fleet as torpedo officer of the Conqueror. From 1919 to 1921 he was fleet torpedo officer on the East Indies station in the cruisers Highflyer and Southampton. After staff duty in the Vernon torpedo school and Dolphin submarine depôt he was appointed in September 1923 for the course at the R.N. Staff College.

For two years from August 1930 he was staff officer (operations) to the Commanders-in-Chief of the Atlantic and Home Fleets, in H.M.S. Nelson. He then took up his first command, of the destroyer Versatile in the Home Fleet, from August 1932 until promoted to captain in December 1933 at the age of 40. After attending senior officers' courses he was deputy director of the Training and Staff Duties Division, Admiralty, for two years from August 1934; and from September 1936 until August 1938 he commanded the 4th Destroyer Flotilla of the Home Fleet, in the Campbell and Kempenfelt.

He was next appointed as chief of staff on the China Station to Admiral Sir Percy Noble [q.v.], with the rank of commodore, second class. This was the post he held during the first part of the Second World War. He afterwards commanded the battle cruiser Renown in Force H at Gibraltar, including the operations which resulted in the destruction of the Bismarck in May 1941. In the autumn of that year he was appointed an assistant chief of naval staff, having been promoted rear-admiral in July 1941, and served at the Admiralty until the spring of 1943. He then went to the Mediterranean, where he commanded the force at the capture of Pantellaria in June 1943, and took part in the landing in Sicily a month later. He was Flag Officer, Sicily, during the campaign for the conquest of the island, and commanded the naval force in the landing at Reggio in September. During the latter operations he was wounded when blown out of a boat by a bomb, but swam around, was picked up, and carried on his duties. Later he became Flag Officer, Taranto and Adriatic.

In March 1944 he took command of the First Cruiser Squadron in the Home Fleet. Until the end of the war in Europe he commanded cruiser and aircraft carrier forces on several operations off the coast of Norway and on many hazardous convoys to North Russia. He conducted the last offensive operation in the Arctic before the war ended. He was promoted to vice-admiral in April 1945.

From October 1945 he was Vice-Chief of the Naval Staff for two years. He became Commander-in-Chief of the Home Fleet in January 1948, and eight months later was promoted to admiral. After the customary two years in the Home Fleet he was appointed Commander-in-Chief at Plymouth from March 1950. He became First Sea Lord in December 1951 and held that appointment until April 1955, when he was succeeded by Lord Mountbatten. He had been promoted Admiral of the Fleet in April 1953.

He was awarded the D.S.O. in December 1943 for gallant and distinguished services and untiring devotion to duty in the operations which led to the capture of Sicily. A month later he was made a C.B. in the New Year honours; in the 1945 Birthday Honours was advanced to K.C.B., and in 1951 to G.C.B. From April 1952 to May 1953 he was First and Principal Naval A.D.C. to her Majesty.

He married in 1931 Gwendoline, daughter of Colonel Geoffrey Glyn and widow of Major Charles Greville, Grenadier Guards. They adopted twin sons.

December 5, 1959.

Sir Archibald McIndoe, C.B.E., the famous plastic surgeon, died on April 11, 1960 at the age of 59. He was a pupil and inherited the mantle of Sir Harold Gillies [q.v.], and his reputation as an exponent of the art of plastic surgery was world-wide.

Archibald Hector McIndoe was born at Dunedin, New Zealand, on May 4, 1900, the son of John McIndoe and his wife, Mabel Hill. He was educated at the Otago High School and at the Otago Medical School, where he graduated M.B., Ch.B. in 1923, winning a medal for clinical medicine and surgery. He was appointed house surgeon at Waikati Hospital, but in 1924 he was awarded a Mayo Foundation Fellowship which took him to the great surgical centre at Rochester, Minnesota.

He received the degree of M.Sc. in pathology from the Mayo Foundation and University of Minnesota in 1927. In 1928, at the expiration of his fellowship, he was awarded a William White travelling scholarship and was appointed assistant surgeon at the Mayo Clinic. He subsequently went to England and became chief assistant to the plastic department at St. Bartholomew's Hospital, London. He proceeded to the M.S. New Zealand in 1929 and to the F.R.C.S. England in 1932. He was elected a Fellow of the American College of Surgeons in 1934. The 1939-45 War greatly increased the scope of the plastic surgeon's work, and McIndoe's services were in constant demand. He was appointed consultant in plastic surgery to the Royal Air Force and surgeon-in-charge of the famous Queen Victoria Plastic and Jaw Injury Centre at East Grinstead.

Here he did splendid work, treating badly burned aircrew, remodelling faces and reshaping limbs. But he did more than restore them physically, he implanted in them the will to conquer disability and face the world. Some measure of McIndoe's influence on these young men and the faith they had in him can be obtained from the late Richard Hillary's remarkable book *The Last Enemy*. Hillary, shot down and badly burned in 1940, owed much to McIndoe and in *The Last Enemy* acknowledged that debt. One of the most impressive aspects of McIndoe's work was the way he continued to follow the fortunes of the members of the Guinea Pig Club, the organization he founded for 600 of the men he personally operated on at East Grinstead. They turned to him for help and advice and he never failed them.

McIndoe was also plastic surgeon to St. Bartholomew's Hospital, to Chelsea Hospital for Women, St. Andrew's Hospital, and Hampstead Children's Hospital; consulting plastic surgeon to Royal North Staffordshire Infirmary, the Hospital for Tropical Diseases, and Croydon General Hospital. He was Hunterian professor at the Royal College of Surgeons in 1939, was a member of the council, and in 1958 was elected vice-president.

McIndoe's outstanding services to the relief and rehabilitation of the war injured received wide recognition. He was appointed C.B.E. in 1944 and was knighted in 1947. He was a Commander of the Legion of Honour, a Commander of the Order of the White Lion of Czechoslovakia, of the Order of Polonia Restituta (Poland), and of the Order of Orange Nassau (Holland). Sir Archibald was the author of numerous papers on his speciality.

He married, first, in 1924, Adonia Aitken. They had two daughters. The marriage was dissolved by divorce in 1954 and McIndoe married, secondly, the same year, Mrs. Constance Belcham.

[A tribute followed on the same day.]

April 13, 1960.

Group Captain D. F. McIntyre, A.F.C., lost his life in an air crash in the Libyan desert on December 8, 1957.

David Fowler McIntyre was one of the two pilots who first flew over Mount Everest on April 3, 1933. The present Duke of Hamilton*, then Lord Clydesdale, was the senior pilot of that expedition. The two had already been associated as officers of the City of Glasgow Squadron of the Auxiliary Air Force and later McIntyre was to command that squadron. From the beginning he had taken his flying seriously. In preparation for his work in the Glasgow squadron he got himself attached for training to No. 12 Squadron at Andover and during that period had to make a parachute descent from a damaged aircraft at a height of 10,000ft.

It was typical of the man that, when his parachute had safely opened, he allowed himself the comfort of a cigarette during the 20 minutes' slow progress towards the earth. On his way to the top of Everest in 1933 he likewise ran into an emergency in which he behaved with equal coolness. His aircraft on that occasion was carried, because of someone else's underestimation of the wind strength, to the leeward side of the peak where the wind fell over like a breaking wave and sucked the Wallace down 2,000ft. towards the glacier between Everest and Makalu.

Only good piloting got him and his observer, Sidney Bonnett, out of that predicament. McIntyre crept along into the area of quieter air close to the easterly face of Everest and there, making careful figures of eight in the thin air of 27,000 feet, gradually recovered the 2,000 feet of height and cautiously worked his way round to the south side of the mountain to come at last over the summit with a bare 50 feet to spare and the chance for his photographer-observer to take some of the finest pictures of the stony, windswept crest that have ever been taken. Those pictures were reproduced in *The Times* a few days afterwards together with others taken by Lieutenant-Colonel L. Stewart Blacker*, the observer in the Duke of Hamilton's aircraft.

McIntyre enjoyed undertaking a serious job of work, carrying it through to its end and then laughingly dismissing it as "a piece of cake". The full story of his experiences over the Himalayas might never have been told had not another member of the expedition allowed himself a somewhat coloured account of what had happened. Up to that point the Aeronautical Correspondent of *The Times*, who shared a bedroom with McIntyre in the bungalow at Purnea, had got little out of his friend, the second pilot, except on the subject of the survey trip.

His refusal to dramatize his job or even make a fuss of its incidental difficulties chimed in well with Lord Clydesdale's attitude to the expedition. Both would have cut out the publicity if they could, but the expedition had had to go to the late Lady Houston for financial backing and had got it only on condition that there should be plenty of publicity to prove to the world, and to Indians in particular, that the British had not become soft and effete. That was how *The Times* came to be invited to buy the story and the pictures, and to send its Aeronautical Correspondent along as a member of the expedition.

In consequence, it was the sober but graphic account of *The Times* representative that was spread under huge headlines over the pages of newspapers all over the world. Lord Clydesdale and David McIntyre returned to find themselves famous and the pair slipped adroitly out of the limelight to get busy doing something about aviation for the benefit of Scotland. They set themselves to create a first-class airport for Scotland and to organize a flying school and an aircraft works alongside it.

With Clydesdale as chairman and McIntyre as managing director of the company, the project went forward. McIntyre knew of an area only a few miles square in Ayrshire, which was reputed to have an average of only four days in the year of such poor visibility as to prevent flying. In the middle of that area lay the flat acres which are now Prestwick Airport. It was in full use as a training airfield in pre-war days. When war came it was a godsend.

Since the end of the war, Prestwick has grown in importance as a port of call of Atlantic passenger services, and the works of Scottish Aviation have progressed to the designing of their own aircraft, striking out a line of their own with types capable of getting into and out of the smallest airfields with good payloads. David McIntyre was the inspirer and contriver of all this development, bringing to the work his shrewd judgment, intense application, and gay spirit.

December 10, 1957.

As a Scots historian and a learned and devoted student of Scottish life and letters, **Dr. Agnes Mure Mackenzie,** who died in Edinburgh on February 26, 1955, achieved notable distinction.

Her most important work consisted of the six volumes of her *History of Scotland,* published between 1934 and 1941, a study on reasoned "nationalist" lines that combined serious research with an independent and lively judgment. Her interest and cultivation of mind were, however, by no means restricted to Scotland; she was a novelist of genuine accomplishment, a discerning critic of literature and a careful student of Shakespeare and the Elizabethan drama. But Scotland was always closest to her heart. As president of the Saltire Society she watched jealously over the cultural heritage and the contemporary promise of her country and people.

Born in 1891 at Stornaway, in the Isle of Lewis, where her father, Murdoch Mackenzie, was a doctor, she was educated at home and at Aberdeen University, where she graduated with honours in English language and literature. It was for *The Process of Literature,* an acute study of the psychology of authorship, which was published in 1929, that she received the degree of D.Litt. But she had commenced authorship some years before and had attracted notice with her first novel, *Without Conditions* (1923), which gave an entertaining and instructive picture of Aberdeenshire society in the middle of the nineteenth century. *The Half Loaf* (1925), *The Quiet Lady* (1926), and *Lost Kinnellan* (1927) followed, the last of these being completed by a sequel and both parts of the story issued in 1930 under the title of *Keith of Kinnellan. Cypress in Moonlight* appeared a year later and *Single Combat* in 1934. As a novelist Mure Mackenzie, who drew mostly upon Scottish historical subjects, was always intelligent and skilful in manner, though her pages lacked something of vivid and immediate life.

Her critical work during these years included, among other volumes, *The Women in Shakespeare's Plays* (1925), *Between Sun and Moon* (1933), and an admirable historical survey of Scottish literature up to the year 1714. But all this time she had been collecting material for her *History of Scotland,* reading widely, studying neglected records in private libraries and visiting or revisiting the scenes of great and lesser events in the Scottish past. She was led to undertake the whole enterprise, it seems, by the view which emerged from her study of Robert the Bruce, whom she saw as a truly great national figure, wholly innocent of the then conventional charges levelled against him of disloyalty, cowardice, and self-seeking. Certainly her portrait is vivid, spirited, and of telling historical proportion, even although some were startled by the large place she gave in the story to her own Highland people—an intelligible protest against the Lowland emphasis of the run of previous historians.

Robert Bruce, King of Scots, 1286-1329, the second of the six volumes, is the most impressive of them all. Her touch is not quite so sure in most of the others, which bear the titles of *The Foundations of Scotland: to 1286; The Rise of the Stewarts, 1329-1513; The Scotland of Queen Mary and the Religious Wars, 1513-1638; The Passing of the Stewarts, 1638-1748;* and *Scotland in Modern Times, 1720-1939.* Hers is a Tory point of view, which seeks to illustrate the damaging effect of the Union upon Scotland. For the rest, in portraying a Scotland that seemed to her to be still very much in the making against a general background of European history, the occasions when she reveals an imperfect knowledge or a too idiosyncratic bias of mind may be forgiven her, for the work as a whole is live and rewarding reading.

Mure Mackenzie brought out a single-volume history in 1940, a year after she had put forward, in *I Was at Bannockburn,* careful if not wholly persuasive arguments for siting the field of battle some way to the east of the place assigned to it by tradition. In 1942 she gave evidence alike of her deep concern for all things Scottish and of her fundamental good sense in Saltire pamphlets on *The Arts and the Future of Scotland* and *Scottish Principles of Statecraft and Government.* Between 1946 and 1951 she made a selection in three volumes of the best pieces of the contemporary authorities she had consulted for her *History of Scotland,* under the title *Scottish Pageant,* and in 1950 there appeared a novel, *Apprentice Majesty,* based on the regency which succeeded the death of Alexander III while his heiress, the child Margaret of Norway, lived—a period which led to the rivalry of the Bruce and Comyn factions, with the predatory and menacing figure of Edward I of England in the background.

March 1, 1955.

Major-General P. J. Mackesy, C.B., D.S.O., M.C., died suddenly on June 8, 1956 in the Isle of Wight. He was 73.

He was a soldier of wide experience and had a full career of successful achievement as a regimental officer, a staff officer, and a commander before he came into the public eye as the commander of the land forces in the expedition to Narvik in April 1940.

Pierse Joseph Mackesy was born on April 5, 1883, the younger son of the late Lieutenant-General W. H. Mackesy of the Bengal Staff Corps. He was educated at St. Paul's School and the Royal Military Academy, Woolwich, and was commissioned in the Royal Engineers on August 23, 1902. In 1911 he was selected for survey duty under the Colonial Office in the Gold Coast, and carried out surveys in Ashanti and the Northern Territories until appointed Deputy Director of Surveys, Gold Coast in 1913. He was promoted captain in the same year.

On the outbreak of war in 1914 he was immediately given the task of getting together as many horses as he could on which to mount police and others to swell the force that set off to Togoland and the Cameroons. He served with this expedition until he fell sick at the end of the year and was sent back to Accra, where he tidied up the survey office before being invalided back to England. He later served in France with the 15th and 1st Divisions. In the spring of 1918 he went to the staff course at Cambridge but was out again in France soon after the German attack in March, as a G.S.O.2, first at VI Corps and then at General Headquarters.

He was next at Murmansk as a staff officer, and, on the withdrawal of the forces from North Russia, he joined the military mission to Denikin in the Black Sea. Soon after his return home in 1920, he went to the Staff College at Camberley. In the spring of 1935 he took over command of the 3rd Infantry Brigade at Bordon, and took the brigade out when the 1st Division went to Palestine. He was promoted Major-General in 1937. He returned to England early the following year to command the 49th (West Riding) Division of the Territorial Army at York and was created a C.B. In 1939 he was sent to the Defence Conference in New Zealand, and remained, at the request of the New Zealand Government, to advise on their Defence Forces. He returned to Britain, and the outbreak of war found him with his Territorial Division to embody and train.

When the Germans invaded Norway in April 1940 he was designated commander of the land forces destined for Narvik. On April 15, Admiral of the Fleet Lord Cork and Orrery*, the Naval Commander, met Mackesy at Harstad, where the expedition had landed. It was at once evident that the two commanders took opposite views of the task ahead. Lord Cork, who had received his orders in London in talks with the First Sea Lord and a final chat with the First Lord, Winston Churchill* in his car on the way to the House, was quite clear that an immediate assault on Narvik should be staged, shaken as it must be by the action of the destroyers two days before. Mackesy was equally clear that his instructions did not warrant an opposed landing for which, without artillery, mortar ammunition or landing craft, his force was not prepared, and argued stubbornly that in the appalling snow conditions against unsilenced machine-guns the outcome would be disaster.

Lord Cork was placed in supreme command at Narvik on April 21, but, after a personal experience of the snow ashore, accepted the advice of both naval and military officers not to order an attack. An experimental bombardment on April 24, after four days of blizzard, disappointed both Lord Cork and Mackesy, but the same day news came that a half brigade of Chasseurs Alpins was leaving Scapa. This allowed Mackesy to plan his alternative attack, to assault Narvik by land from the north and from the south. Preliminary moves took place, but by the first week of May Lord Cork and he agreed that the Guards Brigade should be sent south to stem the German advance, leaving the Chasseurs Alpins, who were suitably trained troops, to carry out this plan. On May 7 Mackesy considered the time ripe for the attack on Ojford, but Lord Cork put this off to May 12.

When General Auchinleck, who had been appointed as Corps Commander on April 28, arrived at Narvik he exercised the discretion given him by the C.I.G.S. to assume command at once under Lord Cork. Mackesy returned to England and was placed on the retired list in July, although re-employed at the War Office for the remainder of the year. In the spring of 1941 he went to the offices of the War Cabinet and, with a small staff from the three services, carried out a study of possible enemy operations. This was his last official employment. For a year he was Military Correspondent to the *Daily Telegraph,* and then retired to his home at Southwold to busy himself in local government. He was elected to the borough council in 1945 and was Mayor of the Royal Borough of Southwold four years in succession from 1949. He was elected to the East Suffolk County Council in 1949.

A man of trained intelligence, with wide interests, he will be remembered as a loyal and steadfast friend, an entertaining and cheerful companion, and a man of great courage and integrity.

He married, in 1923, Dorothy, the only daughter of James Cook, of Enfield, Cults, Aberdeenshire, who is known as a novelist under her pen name as Leonora Starr. She survives him with two sons of the marriage.

June 11, 1956.

Jean Sterling Mackinlay died on December 15, 1958, just over a year after the death of her husband, Harcourt Williams [q.v.]. She was 76. Her death will be regretted all over Great Britain by adults and by children whom she had amused and entertained in a manner that she invented and developed for herself.

The daughter of an eminent singer, Antoinette Sterling, and her husband, John Mackinlay, she was born in London. On leaving Roedean School she studied for the stage under the notable tragic actress Genevieve Ward. Her first public appearance was with F. R. Benson during his season at the Comedy Theatre in 1901: and almost the last part she played on the stage was the French Princess in Benson's production of *Henry V* at the Shaftesbury Theatre early in the war of 1914-18.

During the intervening years she had found no difficulty in getting engagements at the best London theatres, acting at the St. James's with George Alexander; at the Garrick with John Hare during his final season in 1907-08; in *Arms and the Man* at the Criterion (1911), in *The Voysey Inheritance* at the Kingsway (1912), and in *Romance* at the Duke of York's in 1915.

A few old playgoers who saw her play Juliet at some special performance in the East End of London used to maintain that her regular engagements never gave her the chance that she deserved; but the stage's loss, however serious, was the gain of other arts of entertainment when she struck out in a line of her own and took to folk-song and old ballads. It was always difficult, or impossible, to define her place in the category of entertainments. She called herself a *diseuse,* but only in order to make it clear that she did not profess to be like her mother, a singer. She was not a reciter or an "elocutionist". She had a very sweet voice, and she sang the old tunes beautifully, though holding herself at liberty to desert the air for dramatic effect. She took no liberties with her texts, yet she was not a folk-song expert according to the strict standard of Cecil Sharp House.

It speaks well for both Jean Sterling Mackinlay and for the experts that in spite of her unorthodox ways her recitals were welcomed at Cecil Sharp House and her work in folk-song recognized. That work, the selection and the dramatic interpretation of folk-song and old ballads, French as well as English, involved the study of a great many more than she ever chose to perform in public; and in it she was greatly helped by her beloved brother and accompanist, Kenneth Mackinlay, whose lamentable death by fire in January 1925 was a blow from which neither she nor her art ever fully recovered.

Her range was wide. In a tragic ballad like "Binnorie" she could be terrifying. In a love-song like "I know where I'm going" she revealed depths of tender devotion; no one could sing an old carol with a more engaging simplicity; and in songs of merriment or absurdity her fun was irresistible.

The fun was naturally to the fore in a very important part of her work, the entertainment of children (she claimed to be the originator of the Children's Theatre movement in Great Britain). Every Christmas holiday she would stage, somewhere in London, an afternoon programme more elaborate than her recitals. In these mixed entertainments she was supported by her husband and one or more others and by a small body of singing boys from the London School of Choristers. Here, too, were seen some delightful costumes. The favourite was the ribbon dress that she wore to open the programme with "Boys and Girls, Come out to Play"; but all were designed to show the beauty of her face and figure and the dramatic force of the movement which her tendency to restlessness taught her to keep severely in check.

She married Harcourt Williams in 1908, and had a son and a daughter. He died in December 1957.

December 16, 1958.

Elizabeth Mackintosh, who under the pen-name "Gordon Daviot", wrote a number of plays, the most successful of which was *Richard of Bordeaux,* died in London on February 13, 1952.

She was born and brought up at Inverness and was trained as a physical training instructress at the Anstey Physical Training College, Birmingham. She taught physical training at various schools in England and Scotland, but had not got very far in her chosen calling when she had to return home to look after her father. In the midst of her household duties she began to write and had some short stories accepted by the *English Review* and other periodicals. Meanwhile she began seriously to study the theatre and, after writing a number of plays which she did not feel were up to the high standard she had set herself, she wrote *Richard of Bordeaux,* which was performed at the Arts Theatre in 1932.

The play was so favourably received by the critics that it was produced in the course of the ensuing year at the New Theatre, where it was played to enthusiastic audiences for a whole year and established her reputation as a playwright. Though she was always serious in purpose and displayed an uncommon insight into character, it cannot be said that even *Richard of Bordeaux* attained that depth of penetration that is the hall-mark of the best dramatic writing, yet it merited criticism on a higher plane than most of the plays of its period.

Elizabeth Mackintosh never attained quite the same success with her later ventures in the theatre, though she came near it in *Queen of Scots,* which was produced in 1934 and re-established her title to serious consideration after the not undeserved failure of *The Laughing Woman,* a romanticized dramatization of the relations of the sculptor Henri Gaudier and Sophia Brzeska, though even this contained a more intelligent and persuasive study of an artist than is at all common on the modern stage. *The Stars Bow Down,* the story of Joseph and his brethren, was published in 1939, and had to wait some 10 years before it was produced at the Malvern Festival. Meanwhile another play on a Biblical subject, *The Little Dry Thorn,* and a somewhat bloodless drama having for its subject conditions in Roman Britain towards the end of the second century, were produced and received respectful attention from the critics but little public support.

Best known as a playwright, she published *The Daughter of Time* and other novels and short stories, and under the pen-name, "Josephine Tey", wrote a number of detective stories in which a distinctive quality, usually historical, enhanced the ingenuity which is the main attraction of this kind of fiction.

Her last work was a study of Morgan, the pirate, under the title of *The Privateer.*

February 15, 1952.

Sir Eric Maclagan, K.C.V.O., C.B.E., Director of the Victoria and Albert Museum from 1924 until 1945, died suddenly on September 14, 1951 while in Spain.

Eric William Dalrymple Maclagan, born in 1879, was a son of the late Dr. W. D. Maclagan, Archbishop of York, and his second wife, Augusta Anne, daughter of the sixth Lord Barrington. Educated at Winchester and Christ Church, Oxford, he joined the staff of the Victoria and Albert Museum in 1905. He was attached to the Department of Textiles, and in 1907 produced a useful *Guide to English Ecclesiastical Embroideries.* Shortly after this he was transferred to the department of Architecture and Sculpture, where he worked under A. B. Skinner, and on Skinner's death in 1908 became head of the department. One of his first tasks had been to rearrange the collection of Italian sculpture in a manner which may be accepted as a model of museum display. He also began the large *Catalogue of Italian Sculpture,* which was published in 1924.

In 1916 he was transferred temporarily to the Foreign Office, and later to the Ministry of Information. He became head of the Ministry's bureau in Paris in 1917 and its controller for France in 1918, and was attached to the British peace delegation in Paris in 1919. For his services in this connexion he was made a C.B.E.

On the retirement of Sir Cecil Harcourt Smith in 1924 Maclagan was appointed director and secretary of the museum. He made great strides in humanizing the museum by such developments as the extensive sale of picture post-cards and Christmas cards of museum objects, the issue of a popular series of sixpenny picture books (his own *Children in Sculpture* and *Portrait Busts* are good examples), the arrangement of lantern lectures open free to the public, and the encouragement of guide lecturers. Another valuable step of this kind was the placing on prominent exhibition each Monday of an "Object of the Week", selected from the museum's principal treasures, with a descriptive label combining scholarship with popular appeal: no one could write those descriptions better than himself. In a wider sphere the prestige of the museum was undoubtedly increased among leaders in the art world abroad owing to his personality and scholarship, his powers as a linguist, and his almost unrivalled knowledge of Italian sculpture.

He was, moreover, personally responsible for a number of important public exhibitions held in the museum. Among the most outstanding were one of works of art belonging to the livery companies of the City of London in 1926, the William Morris Centenary Exhibition in 1934, the exhibition of the Eumorfopoulos collection in 1936, and, above all, the exhibition of English medieval art in 1930. Perhaps the most interesting of the exhibitions in 1945 was that of the sculptures from the Henry VII chapel and other parts of Westminster Abbey which had been removed for safety during the war. In these and other directions he proved himself an inspiring and efficient administrator. His own wide knowledge and cultured taste set an extremely high standard for those who worked under his leadership, and led to the acquisition by the museum of many notable works of artistic and historical importance.

Among his personal interests Italian Renaissance sculpture took first place, followed by French Romanesque architecture and sculpture, and by early Christian and Byzantine art; but there were few subjects within the scope of the museum to which he did not bring fresh ideas, as the result of a fine natural taste developed by wide reading and personal contact with works of art. He was a keen churchman, and took a prominent part in the activities of the Central Council which since 1916 has exercised control over the archaeological and artistic aspect of church buildings and their treasures. For many years, before the building of the new Church House at Westminster, the Central Council office, with the support of Sir Cecil Harcourt Smith and later of Sir Eric Maclagan, was accommodated in the museum and depended much upon their advice and encouragement. Maclagan was chairman of the Winchester diocesan committee of the council, as well as an active member of the Lincoln Committee.

His colleagues and, indeed, all who came into close touch with him were impressed by his fundamental honesty, sincerity, and disinterestedness. His mind worked very rapidly—one of his colleagues complained that "Maclagan always sees two moves ahead of me"—and there were in consequence times when he was brusque and impatient; but if he ever spoke in haste, he repented most generously at leisure. When in the mood he was a brilliant conversationalist, and being a Scotsman by birth could relate a good tale with zest and humour. Even to his friends he occasionally seemed stern and reserved, but there was something in his nature which always endeared him to the young; he was full of uncondescending sympathy with their anxieties and ambitions. He took part in no sports or games. A weekly visit to the cinema and the solving of "Torquemada" were his lightest forms of relaxation. He lived in and for his work.

He was a Fellow of the Society of Antiquaries, acting as vice-president from 1932 to 1936; president of the Museums Association, 1935-36; an honorary A.R.I.B.A.; Officier de L'Instruction Publique in France; a member of the Order of St. Sava. He was knighted in 1933 and made a K.C.V.O. in 1946.

In 1913 he married Helen Elizabeth, daughter of Commander the Hon. Frederick Lascelles, R.N., second son of the fourth Earl of Harewood. She died in 1942. He had two sons, one of whom was killed in action in 1942.

September 17, 1951.

Victor McLaglen, British-born film actor, died in Hollywood on November 7, 1959 at the age of 72.

Born at Tunbridge Wells on December 11, 1886, the eldest of a clergyman's eight sons, he joined the Life Guards in 1900, pretending to be 18 in the hope of serving in the Boer War, but was in fact not sent out of England. Instead he became regimental boxing champion before his family found him and brought him home. His father later became a bishop in South Africa, and in 1914 McLaglen was in Cape Town, having meanwhile had experience in music hall, as a professional boxer (he once lasted six rounds against Jack Johnson, the world champion), and as gold prospector in Australia. He quickly returned to England and rejoined the Army, serving in Mesopotamia with the Royal Irish Fusiliers and becoming Assistant Provost-Marshal in Baghdad with the rank of captain.

After the war he tried various jobs before agreeing to appear in a film just for fun. He was an immediate success in *The Call of the Road* (1920), and starred in several more British films before going to Hollywood in 1924. The title of his first American film, *Beloved Brute,* formed an apt summary of his role in the film world. Never conventionally handsome, he possessed a rugged virility and at the same time radiated charm and good nature, so that his popularity was as great with women filmgoers as with men. During the silent era he appeared with great success in a series of action films, though generally with a fair admixture of comedy. Among them were *Beau Geste, The Loves of Carmen, A Girl in Every Port,* and *King of the Khyber Rifles,* in several of which he starred with Edmund Lowe, with whom he had begun a fruitful partnership in his most famous silent film, *What Price Glory*?

Their most successful sound film together was *The Cockeyed World* (1930), but from the beginning of the 1930s McLaglen began to strike out on his own as a dramatic actor in such films as Sternberg's* *Dishonoured,* with Marlene Dietrich, and Ford's *The Lost Patrol* and *The Informer.* In the latter he won the Academy Award for the best acting performance of 1935 with a memorable portrayal of a simple, well-meaning Irish giant betrayed by greed into treachery. His other films of the period were extremely varied, including *Professional Soldier,* with Freddie Bartholomew, *Klondike Annie,* with Mae West, and *Wee Willie Winkie,* with Shirley Temple (another of John Ford's* films).

He continued to act through the 1940s and 1950s, his last film being *Sea Fury,* made in Britain in 1958, and announced that he had no intention of retiring and taking things easy so long as the public wanted him.

He was married three times, leaving a son and a daughter. He became an American citizen in 1933.

November 9, 1959.

Lord Maclay, who died at his home in Renfrewshire on April 24, 1951 at the age of 93, will be best remembered as Shipping Controller during the war of 1914-18. He was in control of British shipping during a critical period in which the most effective possible use of our diminishing resources in tonnage was of vital moment, and he contributed to the final victory of the allies by his skill in organizing the whole shipping industry and securing the hearty cooperation of its leaders.

The Right Hon. Sir Joseph Paton Maclay, first Baron Maclay, of Glasgow, in the County of Lanarkshire, in the peerage of the United Kingdom, Bt., P.C., was born on September 6, 1857, the son of Ebenezer Maclay, of Glasgow, and Janet Paton, and went early into business. In 1885 he established with T. W. McIntyre the firm of Maclay and McIntyre, which prospered so well that at the outbreak of war in 1914 it owned as many as 50 cargo vessels. Sir Joseph Maclay—he was created a baronet in 1914—was for many years the chief partner in the firm. As soon as war broke out in 1914 it was apparent that central control of shipping, on which the food supplies of the nation and the maintenance of the forces oversea depended, would be essential.

In the first two years of the war various attempts were made to exercise partial control, but the decisive step was not taken until Lloyd George formed the Coalition Government in 1916. A Ministry of Shipping was then established, and Maclay was appointed to preside over it as Shipping Controller and was sworn of the Privy Council. He stipulated that he would not enter Parliament, knowing that his whole time would be fully occupied, and the Ministry was represented in the Commons by a Parliamentary Secretary. The choice had not been expected, but when it was announced its wisdom was at once recognized throughout the shipping industry.

Maclay's success in a large measure was due to his personality. His obvious sincerity was allied to native shrewdness, great tenacity, and unshakable courage. His colleagues, whose complete affection he won, never knew him to falter in his confidence in ultimate victory or to lose his cheerfulness. Hardness and gentleness were curiously mingled, but there was always a saving sense of humour and his serenity was of immense value in its influence on his colleagues.

In the spring of 1917 the toll taken of shipping by submarines was at its height, and all the resources of the Shipping Controller were needed to enable the constantly dwindling supply of tonnage to fulfil the steadily increasing requirements. When it became clear that the control of the existing shipping imposed a sufficiently serious strain on the Ministry, apart from the responsibility for new construction, measures were adopted to separate the duties, and finally Lord Pirrie was appointed Controller-General of Merchant Shipbuilding.

It was then the duty of the Ministry of Shipping, over which Sir Joseph Maclay presided, to decide the particular types of vessels that were needed, and the function of the Controller-General to see that the ships were built. After the war Sir Joseph rendered further service to the country by his advocacy of the sale of the standard ships which had been built during the war. In 1921 he was appointed a member of the Business Committee on Finance, but otherwise he did not appear much in public life. In 1922 he was raised to the peerage.

Lord Maclay was a J.P. and D.L. for Renfrewshire, where he had his seat, Duchal, Kilmacolm, and was made honorary LL.D. of Glasgow.

He married in 1889 Martha, daughter of William Strang, of Glasgow, and by her he had five sons and two daughters. The heir to the family honours is his eldest surviving son, Sir Joseph Maclay, K.B.E., who was born in 1899 and married in 1936 Nancy Margaret, daughter of R. C. Greig. There are three sons and two daughters of the marriage.

April 25, 1951.

Yvonne (Mrs. Hugh) McLellan— See **Arnaud.**

Dr. W. F. P. McLintock, C.B., Director of the Geological Survey and Museum of Practical Geology from 1945 to 1950, died in Edinburgh on February 21, 1960. He was 73.

William Francis Porter McLintock was born at Edinburgh on February 2, 1887, educated at George Heriot's School and Edinburgh University. He entered the Civil Service in 1907 as a successful candidate in a special mineralogical examination for the post of assistant curator in the Museum of Practical Geology. While in this post he published works on the minerals of south-west England, and prepared a guide to the collection of gem stones which was later described as a complete introduction to the study of gems. In 1911 he transferred to the charge of the geological collections in the Royal Scottish Museum, Edinburgh. He published the results of research, carried out jointly with colleagues, on the Strathmore meteorite and on the pigment Egyptian blue, but his most detailed research of that period was on the zeolites of the tertiary lavas of Mull, their geneses and transformations. In 1921 he returned to London as curator of the Museum of Practical Geology. Five years later he was sent with Dr. J. Phemister under the aegis of the Anglo Iranian Oil Company to study and report on the utility of gravitational survey in exploring geological structure, and in the following years he organized and carried out such surveys by Eötvös balance and by magnetic variometer in Britain.

From 1930 his time became more and more occupied with the impending removal of the museum from Jermyn Street to South Kensington, and with his director, Sir John S. Flett, he visited many of the national museums of Europe noting largely what to avoid in the new building, clear in his own mind on what the new museum should be and determined to have it. He cooperated with the Ministry of Works to develop a building which should attract the public with a modern style of exhibition, provide facilities for research by the survey and museum staff and open the collections to easy access by responsible outside workers. The Geological Museum was opened in July 1935 by the late King George VI, then Duke of York, and stands as a monument to McLintock's vision and purposeful tenacity.

The years of war 1939 to 1945, during which the museum was dismantled, saw the embryo organization under McLintock as deputy director of the Atomic Energy Division of the Geological Survey. Appointed director in 1945, he repaired the ravages of wartime on the survey organization and on the museum, succeeding so well that the Geological Museum was the first of the national museums to be reopened to the public, and when re-organization of the scientific Civil Service came in 1946 he was completely prepared to table an exact and logical plan for the development of the survey and museum in the new era in terms of both work and staff.

As director he attended the United Nations conference on Conservation and Utilization of Resources at Lake Success in 1949. After 43 years of public service he retired in 1950 and in the following New Year Honours List his services were recognized by his appointment as C.B.

A brilliant, witty, and pungent conversationist, McLintock was always the best of company, but perhaps his friends will remember most his unswerving, though not uncritical, loyalty to the Geological Survey and the Museum of Practical Geology.

February 23, 1960.

Lord Macmillan, the eminent jurist and an original trustee of the Pilgrim Trust, died at his home at Ewhurst, Surrey, on September 5, 1952 at the age of 79.

The Right Hon. Sir Hugh Pattison Macmillan, Baron Macmillan of Aberfeldy, in the county of Perth, a life peer, G.C.V.O., was the son of the Rev. Dr. Hugh Macmillan and was born on February 20, 1873. He studied first at the University of Edinburgh, where he graduated with first-class honours in philosophy in 1893. He then crossed over to the University of Glasgow for his studies in law, and, taking the degree of LL.B. in 1896, he was the chief prizeman of the year. He became an advocate in 1897, and while building up a practice acted as examiner in law at Glasgow University from 1899 till 1904 and as editor of the *Juridical Review* from 1900 till 1907.

His practice grew steadily and he was in great demand in cases which involved municipalities and public bodies, the administration of the existing law, and the promulgation of fresh charters. He was appointed standing counsel for the Convention of Royal Burghs, an association which has for centuries been one of the most powerful influences in Scottish life and history. He took silk in 1912.

For a time during the 1914-18 war he acted as an assistant Director of Intelligence at the Ministry of Information, and in the late war he was Minister of Information for about a year. His work was mainly before the House of Lords in appeals from the Scottish Courts, and before Parliamentary Committees, representing various interests in connexion with impending legislation. He held retainers from all the English railway companies. The most important case he had at the Bar was undoubtedly the litigation between Canada and Newfoundland with regard to Labrador, which was heard by the Judicial Committee of the Privy Council in 1926.

In 1924 the Labour Party came into office for the first time. There was no M.P. on their side with the legal qualifications necessary for holding the office of Lord Advocate. Macmillan was not a member of the Labour Party, nor a Socialist, nor indeed an M.P., yet he was appointed to the office of Lord Advocate. He thus became a member of the Labour Administration without being a member of the party. It was an unusual position, but it worked well enough on the whole, and the innovation had the happy result that it brought Macmillan to the notice of a much wider public. When he had been appointed to the office of Lord Advocate, he was at the same time sworn of the Privy Council and elected an honorary Bencher of the Inner Temple.

Work on commissions of various kinds absorbed most of Macmillan's time and attention during the years that followed his vacation of the office of Lord Advocate. There was hardly any inquiry of note or importance on which he was not asked to serve, and generally he was first choice and designated for the place of chairman to preside over the deliberations. The mere mention of the names and scope of these inquiries bears ample testimony to the manysidedness and abilities of the man.

First came the Royal Commission on Lunacy and Mental Disorder. Then in 1925 followed the long and exhaustive inquiry into the coalmining industry, which did its utmost to avert the disastrous strikes. In 1927 he presided over an inquiry into street offences. In 1919 he took charge of the inquiry into Finance and Industry, one of the biggest undertakings ever set before a Royal Commission. Many other inquiries followed, lesser, perhaps, in scope, but still of great importance. No inquiry in which he took part was slipshod or hurried. Yet the results of his investigations were formulated and made public at the earliest possible moment. He had a remarkable gift for securing unanimity among the members of a commission. This was strikingly demonstrated by the Royal Commission on Finance and Industry which, though composed of representatives of many shades of opinion, presented a practically unanimous report. His work attracted the attention of the Canadian Government, and at their request he acted as chairman of a Royal Canadian Commission which made a close and extensive investigation into Canadian banking laws and financial procedure during 1932 and 1933 and ended in a recommendation for the establishment of a Central Bank.

As the years went on, Lord Macmillan's life became busier and busier. His work and attainments were held in high honour and regard everywhere. His advice, his interest, and his support were sought on every hand and were always willingly and ungrudgingly given. He was elected to the Board of Trustees of the British Museum, of the National Library of Scotland and of the Sir John Soane Museum. Only the barest reference can be made to the many institutions and bodies over which Lord Macmillan was called upon to preside. From 1929 until 1943 he was chairman of the London University Court; he was chairman of the Lord Chancellor's Committee on Advanced Legal Studies, and of what perhaps gave him the greatest pleasure of all, the Pilgrim Trust, of which he was an original trustee, and succeeded the late Earl Baldwin as chairman. In 1937 he was made chairman of the B.B.C. Advisory Council. He was also a member of the Carnegie Trust for the Universities of Scotland and of the council of the National Trust, and president of the Society for Promotion of Nature Reserves. In 1941, he was appointed Honorary Professor of Law in the Royal Academy in succession to the late Sir Francis Newbolt.

He was also much in request as chairman at public dinners and assemblies, where his finished and graceful oratory, with its dry Scottish wit, never failed to charm and (if the occasion demanded) to stimulate generosity. In 1937, he published under the title of *Law and Other Things,* a collection of essays and addresses delivered on various occasions. He was made a G.C.V.O. in 1937.

He married in 1901, Elizabeth Katherine Grace, daughter of the late Dr. W. J. Marshall.

September 6, 1952.

Hector McNeil, who had a stroke while travelling to the United States in the Queen Mary, died in hospital in New York on October 11, 1955.

As Under-Secretary of State at the Foreign Office and later as Minister of State, Hector McNeil can be considered to have played an important part in shaping the peace settlements. Working in the closest association with Ernest Bevin [q.v.], he represented Britain during the troubled period immediately after the war in many of its most crucial dealings with other Powers, through both normal diplomatic channels and many international conferences. In Parliament, where he represented Greenock, he was reckoned to be among the most receptive brains. Burly, fair-haired, a keen soccer player and talking slowly in a Scottish accent, he always remained an undoubted representative of his native Clydeside, an impression that his forthright utterances both in and out of office confirmed.

Hector McNeil was born on March 10, 1907, at Garelochhead, the second of seven children of a journeyman shipwright. A defect in one hand prevented him from following his father's trade, and after attending Woodside School, Glasgow, he went on to Glasgow University with the idea of reading for the Ministry. He made a great name for himself in the university debating tour of Newfoundland, Canada, and the United States. On graduating he gave up the idea of becoming a clergyman and joined the Glasgow branch of the Kemsley newspaper organization, which he left after six months and went over to the *Scottish Daily Express.*

He had already become a confirmed Socialist and was deeply involved in local politics, at 25 being elected as a Labour Councillor on the Glasgow Corporation. In 1935 his employers transferred him to London where he managed to continue with his work on the Glasgow Corporation, sitting on the committees dealing with sanitation, health, and public libraries, finding, like many other prominent politicians before him, that this first insight into the administration of a great city provided him with a most valuable training in the ways of democratic government. In 1937 he returned to Glasgow as the night editor of the *Scottish Daily Express,* but after some months in this capacity he found that he had taken on too much and decided to withdraw from the Corporation.

In 1935 he had only just been beaten by Walter Elliot [q.v.] in an exciting poll for the Kelvingrove seat in Parliament and the following year he was beaten again by Malcolm MacDonald in a by-election for Ross and Cromarty. But in 1941, by which time he had been transferred to the *Evening Standard,* he was returned unopposed as the Member for Greenock. As a back-bencher his brilliance as a speaker and his alert, analytical mind soon attracted attention and after only a year in the House he became Parliamentary Private Secretary to [Philip] Noel-Baker at the Ministry of War Transport. Working under Noel-Baker in almost any capacity, it was almost impossible not to take an intense interest in foreign affairs, and in conversations together McNeil must have learned much of the mysteries of diplomacy.

He was returned again in the 1945 General Election and when in that year Noel-Baker left the Foreign Office for the Air Ministry, McNeil took his place as Parliamentary Under-Secretary. In spite of his brilliance, to give such a vital post to so young a man was one of the Government's most unexpected appointments. With Bevin, who called him his "indentured apprentice", so often away at conferences, McNeil, at 38, became one of the most important of the Government's spokesmen to the House and to the world on foreign policy during some of the most difficult and crucial months history has ever known. But the House began to realize the wisdom of the choice after a dazzling defence of the Government's policy in Poland, which he delivered after only three weeks in office. At question time, when a slight shift of emphasis might have far-reaching effects, he was admirably firm, but, although members of his own party sometimes accused him of being too popular with the Opposition, he also understood the art of being able to give unpleasing answers without putting people's backs up.

At the Paris Peace Conference he played a notable part which was recognized by his promotion in October 1946 as Minister of State. He was also the youngest Privy Councillor in the kingdom. One of his earliest jobs was to make a full report on, and try to help with, the dangerous situation in Greece, to which country he made two arduous trips. Here, as in his relations with other liberated countries, he had to deal with peoples who had not only suffered from the devastation of war and the hardships of the occupation, but were also in the throes of acute changes in their social structure.

Much of his work by its nature, therefore, fell into two parts, even though they were closely interconnected. In the first category came the relief of distress, resettlement, the movement of whole populations, and clearing up the chaos left by the war. He had much to do with Unrra, led the British delegation to the Economic and Social Council of the United Nations at its meetings in New York in 1946 and 1947, and in 1946 opened the plenary session of the Intergovernmental Committee on Refugees. In the second category came the endless misunderstandings with Russia, the difficulties with Egypt and the blunt words to Romania and Hungary. In all this he was of course helping to carry out a policy worked out within the framework laid down by Bevin, but no one could have expressed himself with such confidence and conviction, if they felt that the framework was in any way misconceived.

In the autumn of 1947 he led the British delegation to the General Assembly of the United Nations, and by a speech at an early session, sharply indicting the obstructive and minatory attitude of the Soviet *bloc* in the United Nations, earned the unstinted praise of the majority of the delegates and became an international figure overnight. Early in 1948 he played the chief part in arranging an Anglo-Belgian trade agreement. Speaking in Geneva in March of that year at a United Nations conference on freedom of information he again condemned a system which, by repression, selectivity, and the suppression of facts outraged the very first principles of that freedom. Later speeches in 1948 and 1949 continued the attack on the Soviet Government as "a disturber of the peace and a menace to the independence of a small nation" (namely Yugoslavia). He told the United Nations political committee that "the conscience of the world is revolted by the mechanical cynicism of the Soviet régime".

In the general election of February 1950 McNeil was returned for Greenock with a majority of 8,910 over the nearest of four opponents. There was some surprise when, in March, he was removed from the international field and made Secretary of State for Scotland. Attlee's* action was, as indeed it was intended to be, a high compliment and McNeil was properly responsive. As head of a young team at the Scottish Office, consisting of two law officers, two under-secretaries, and himself, he entered on his new duties with enthusiasm. He was well aware of the urgency of many of Scotland's difficulties and brought his incisive mind to their consideration. His days of office were, however, numbered and he had little chance to implement the various lines of policy he had sketched out in the few months he had his native country in his care. Nevertheless, he did persuade Lord Balfour of Burleigh* to accept the chairmanship of a commission designed to stimulate the more rapid expansion of cattle breeding in the Highlands before the Labour Government was defeated in October 1951. The result of that and the succeeding elections showed that he retained the loyalty of his fellow Scots at Greenock, though his last majority was little more than 1,000.

Even while he was at the Scottish Office he did not feel able to forgo his interest in foreign affairs. In May 1950 he warned the General Assembly of the Church of Scotland that there could be no expectation of an end to the "cold war". A few months later, speaking in Lancashire, he emphasized necessity for the

Atlantic Powers to arm for defence and therefore make it quite clear that the search for a peaceful solution to the problem of Korea did not spring from weakness.

In Opposition he gave full rein to his bent. A devout disciple of Ernest Bevin, he took his stand on the right wing of his party. In a recorded broadcast on the American Broadcasting Company's network, timed to coincide with Attlee's arrival in Moscow on August 10, 1954, he roundly denounced the visit of the delegation of the Labour Party to Russia and Communist China as "highly irresponsible and ill-timed". He afterwards said that he had recorded the talk and that the timing of the release was not his choice. It certainly set the cat among the pigeons and there were those who recalled that, in the generosity of spirit that was his in abundant measure, he had spoken in sudden, passionate praise of Sir Winston Churchill* at a meeting of the United Nations when someone had handled his name lightly. And that at a time when Sir Winston, then leading the Opposition, was not making himself exactly beloved of the Labour Government. Such gestures were of the essence of the man and while such bright integrity exists no one need fear that tyrannical party machines can extinguish the individuality that is the essence of our democracy.

He married in 1939 Sheila, daughter of Dr. James Craig, and there was a son of the marriage.

October 12, 1955.

W. J. MacQueen-Pope, who produced in the course of a life spent chiefly in the active service of the theatre a number of informed and readable accounts of certain aspects and phases of it, died on June 27, 1960 in a London hospital. He was 72.

Born in Devonshire on April 11, 1888, Walter James MacQueen-Pope, though he began to earn his living in a shipping office, had the theatre in his blood. As he pointed out in his book *Ladies First,* Jane Pope, the Mrs. Candour of the original production of *The School for Scandal,* who at the age of 14 had played for Garrick at Drury Lane, was his great-great-great aunt, and he traced his descent as far back as Morgan Pope, owner of the Bear Garden, Bankside, and to Thomas Pope, actor and shareholder of the Globe Theatre, in the late sixteenth century.

He himself was initiated into the affairs of the theatre as private secretary to the late Sir George Dance, playwright, manager, and donor of £30,000 to the Old Vic. MacQueen-Pope was appointed business manager at the Queen's by Sir Alfred Butt*, and he went on to hold this position at other West End theatres in turn, exchanging it for that of general manager at the Duke of York's in 1927 and at the Whitehall on the occasion of its opening in 1930.

But it was as press representative at the Palladium in 1925 that he began to develop his special talent for passing on to others through speech and writing something of his love and knowledge of the theatre generally and in particular of Drury Lane, of the Haymarket ("Theatre of Perfection"), of the Gaiety ("Theatre of Enchantment"), and of the St. James's ("Theatre of Distinction"). He was in charge of publicity at Drury Lane for 21 years, including four years as public relations officer to E.N.S.A., which had its headquarters in the building; and between 1946 and 1958 he brought out lively books on all four of the playhouses mentioned and, a by-product of his long association with the younger man at Drury Lane and elsewhere, *Ivor, the Story of an Achievement: A Biography of Ivor Novello* [q.v.].

Novello and his work had the quality regarded by MacQueen-Pope as all-important not only in the theatre but in life: glamour. He considered that the world had once been rich in this and was now poor, and he expressed this opinion vigorously and provocatively in such books as *Twenty Shillings in the Pound, Back Numbers,* and *Give Me Yesterday.* One of his principal gifts, said a reviewer, was that of over-statement, and indeed, as he employed it, it served his general purpose by helping to raise a laugh. To publish two full-length books a year was not exceptional for him: *Shirtfronts and Sables: A Story of the Days When Money Could Be Spent,* and a biography of Franz Lehar, written in conjunction with D. L. Murray [q.v.], both appeared in 1953. He began in 1955 to give talks on the theatre on television, using his own nickname "Popie" as a title for this series.

By his marriage to Miss Stella Suzanne Schumann, which took place in 1912, he had one daughter.

June 28, 1960.

Lady MacRobert, widow of Sir Alexander MacRobert Bt., (founder of the British India Corporation), and well known for her gifts of aircraft to the Royal Air Force during the 1939-45 War in memory of her sons, died on September 1, 1954 at her home at Tarland, Aberdeenshire.

She was Rachel, daughter of the late Dr. William Hunter Workman, the noted Himalayan explorer, and was born at Worcester, Massachusetts. She was educated at Cheltenham Ladies' College and at the Royal Holloway College, where she took the degree of B.Sc. Later she studed geology and political economy at Edinburgh University, and attended the Royal College of Science and School of Mines where she gained the B.Sc. honours degree of London University. She also took a post-graduate research course in mineralogy and petrology at the Christiania Mineralogisk Institutet.

Her studies led her to undertake considerable geological research work along the Scottish border, in the iron-bearing region of Sweden, and in the Kolar goldfields in India, where she spent much of her married life. In addition to being a Fellow of numerous societies, including the Society of Antiquaries of Scotland, she was a Fellow of the Geological Societies of London and Stockholm, being one of the first three women admitted to the Fellowship of the former society. She was the author of several books on geological subjects.

She married Sir Alexander MacRobert as his second wife in 1911. He was created a baronet in 1922, and died the same year. Upon his death she became a director of the British India Coporation which he had founded in 1920, and played an important part in the corporation's activities for many years. There were three sons of the marriage, of whom the eldest, Sir Alasdair Workman MacRobert, the second baronet, was killed in a flying accident at Luton in 1938. The other two sons, Sir Roderic Alan MacRobert, the third baronet, and Sir Iain Workman MacRobert, the fourth and last baronet, were killed in action during the early years of the 1939-45 War while serving with the Royal Air Force, the former with a Hurricane squadron in Iraq, and the latter while piloting a Blenheim aircraft of Coastal Command.

In August 1941 the Air Ministry announced that Lady MacRobert had given £25,000 for the purchase of a Stirling bomber in memory of her sons. The aircraft, which was named by her wish "MacRobert's Reply", took part in many raids, including a daylight attack in December 1941 on the German warships Scharnhorst and Gneisenau sheltering in harbour at Brest.

In March 1942 Lady MacRobert gave a further £20,000 for the purchase of four "MacRobert Fighters" to operate on fronts where they would be helping Russia's war effort. Three of the aircraft, which were Hurricanes, were named after her sons, and the fourth was named "MacRobert's Salute to Russia". They saw action in the Middle East, and the gift was the subject of many Russian tokens of appreciation and thanks.

In 1943 Lady MacRobert gave her principal country house in Aberdeenshire, Adastrean House, to the R.A.F. as a leave centre for R.A.F. officers. It was destroyed by fire in 1952. In 1945 she founded the MacRobert Reply Association, which inaugurated a scheme for the betterment of members of youth organizations in Scotland. She also made many gifts to organizations in north-east Scotland, and was well known in more recent years as a breeder of pedigree Shorthorns and of Highland cattle.

September 2, 1954.

Crown Princess Maertha, of Norway— See **Norway.**

President Ramon Magsaysay of the Philippines, who was killed in the crash of a Philippine Air Force Dakota near Cebu city on March 17, 1957, had enjoyed a greater confidence among his people than any other Philippine leader since the war. He was 49. No rival seemed likely to displace him in the presidential elections due in October.

Coming of relatively humble country origin, he started life as a garage mechanic and rose to be foreman of a provincial bus company. It was under the Japanese occupation during the war that Magsaysay's quality was revealed as a resistance leader. He worked in company with American officers in command of guerrilla bands; and when the war ended the returning American forces made him military Governor of west central Luzon. For this district he was elected to the lower House of Congress in 1950, whereupon President Quirino appointed him Secretary for Defence. In that office he tackled the Communist-led Hukbalahap rebellion with such success that an armed force that had previously been able to harry even the outskirts of Manila was reduced from over 10,000 to less than a thousand armed men.

His appointment as Defence Secretary had been in response to American urging, and he had some American assistance in his campaign against the Communist rebels. When the 1953 elections were due it was expected that Quirino would make way for another candidate, but Magsaysay's disgust with the nepotism and corruption of the Liberal administration drove him out of the party. His political ambitions were eagerly seized on by the rival Nacionalistas who adopted him as their candidate in place of older leaders such as Jose Laurel and Claro Recto. In elections which were generally agreed to be better conducted than any before, he won an easy victory.

As President his colourful, easygoing personality appealed to a people who inherit many Latin-American characteristics from their Spanish conquerors. Magsaysay was anxious to maintain the American connexion but had lately shown himself sensitive to the criticism that for the Philippine economy to develop fully that connexion was too close. He was equally determined to improve the lot of the poverty-stricken peasantry and his popularity was perhaps greater in the countryside than in the towns, where political intrigue promoted other loyalties. In the last year of his Presidential term feeling against a man with the best intentions but lacking clearly defined policies was beginning to grow in the active political circles of Manila and other towns, but such criticism had made little inroad on his nation-wide popularity.

He leaves a wife and three children.

March 18, 1957.

Roger Mais, the Jamaican painter, novelist, and playwright, died in Kingston, Jamaica, at the age of 50 in June 1955 of an illness which first attacked him while on a visit to France.

Born in Kingston in 1905, he was one of a family of eight children. He attended high school for the "bit of paper"—the Cambridge school certificate—that every West Indian boy must have if he wants a job, especially a Government job. After school Mais followed a variety of occupations, including an appointment in the Education Department and work as a foreman on an estate, riding his rounds of inspection on a mule.

During the last war he worked for a number of West Indian newspapers and periodicals, and was one of the many Jamaicans with West Indian aspirations for more representative and responsible government at that time. Some violence of language led to his conviction and sentence to six months' imprisonment for seditious libel. Soon after his release from prison he took up painting and was so successful in selling his work that he was able to save enough money to visit England in 1952. He lived for a time in London, supporting himself by painting and writing. He wrote quickly, was a regular contributor to the B.B.C., and had a play performed by the Venture group.

The two novels published during this period reveal an acute observer of life with a pronounced gift for dramatic presentation. *The Hills were Joyful Together,* published in 1953, is almost too full of incident and he draws on his own experience in prison with effect, but the characters are not apprehended from within and the action is dissipated because there is no common theme. *Brother Man,* published in 1954, shows a very great advance in technique. Presenting the life of a West Indian slum, the author prefaces each chapter by a "chorus of people in the lane", very reminiscent of Dylan Thomas's [q.v.] method of poetic description.

By describing in turn one group of people, he builds up a powerful impression of a neighbourhood, but (and here is advance indeed) each character is in the round and the story of each has its own unity within the larger pattern. Such a rapid and notable growth augured the emergence of an author of no mean stature, and it is a thousand pities that Mais should have been cut off before he had behind him the solid achievement that undoubtedly would have been his.

June 22, 1955.

Dr. Daniel Malan, who died at Stellenbosch on February 7, 1959, defeated General Smuts in 1948 and became the first Prime Minister of the Union to begin putting into practice the full-blooded policy of *apartheid.* He was 84.

Daniel François Malan, D.D., was born at Riebeek West, Cape Colony, on May 22, 1874, and was educated at Victoria College, Stellenbosch, and at the University of Utrecht, where he took the degree of Doctor of Divinity. Thus prepared he became first a school teacher and later a *predikant* of the Dutch Reformed Church in South Africa at Montagu in the Colony of his birth. There he gave early evidence of his uncompromising spirit, for he began his ministry by preaching strict temperance, if not total abstinence, to a congregation of wine farmers.

From the cure of souls Malan turned to journalism. An unbridgeable gulf had opened between General Botha and General Hertzog, for, while the former stood for cooperation, the latter openly declared himself for separatism. Thereupon the Nationalists launched their own newspaper, *Die Burger,* and Malan became editor. To Malan, however, the press was only a stepping-stone. He had steadily prepared his approach to parliamentary politics and had served a useful apprenticeship as chairman of the Cape Nationalist Party. When, therefore, a timely vacancy arose in the Calvinia Division he took his opportunity and was returned to the Assembly.

The Legislature provided him with yet another pulpit, and he had much to declare and to denounce from it; but there was no doubt about his Parliamentary gifts. When, therefore, in 1924 Hertzog was returned to power, Malan was an obvious choice for office, and he entered the Administration to serve in it throughout its long term as Minister of the Interior, Public Health, and Education. Tielman Roos was his only rival for the second place to Hertzog and, on Roos's acceptance of a judgeship in the Appellate Division, it seemed that the position of the Prime Minister's closest colleague and ultimate successor would be his without further challenge. As a Minister Malan was active in the departments. He gave a more definitely vocational and agricultural direction to education and he reformed the conduct of elections. Under him, however, it seemed a rule that, other things being equal, appointments should go to the adherents of his own party. There was, as a result, much discontent among the British, particularly in Natal. Malan maintained, however, that in fact the Government were only applying the principle of language equality seriously.

The "flag question" which arose in the early days of the Hertzog Government disclosed Malan in his most contentious mood. The policy of the Nationalist Dutch was to exclude the Union Jack as the flag of the Union and to substitute for it the emblems of the extinct republics. Malan introduced a Bill to effect this purpose. The British element on the other hand was strongly opposed. Fortunately for South Africa a compromise was eventually found, which Malan had the statesmanship and good grace to accept with an expression of complete satisfaction.

Much against Malan's will, the Nationalist and South African parties came together to form a coalition Government in 1933. In the election of May of that year, having stood reluctantly as an official Coalition candidate, he found himself in difficulties in his constituency of Calvinia and appealed to General Smuts, who, although he incurred considerable criticism by doing so, came personally to his assistance. Abandoning his previous insistence that the identity of the Nationalist Party should be maintained, he reached an agreement in the next year with General Hertzog in regard to "a new party" to be formed by a fusion between the followers of General Smuts and General Hertzog. In the correspondence, however, which passed between him and General Hertzog in this matter, a heavy emphasis was laid on the "independence" of South Africa and the right of secession was strongly urged.

General Smuts's ideal of a United South Africa had never in fact an appeal for Malan. He and his lieutenants were members of the *Afrikander Broederbond,* which was originally an organization for the advancement of Afrikaan culture. It developed, however, into a secret society and aimed at an independent,

Afrikaner form of Government with its own personal head of the State and a strictly isolationist policy. It would not only have excluded the English-speaking South Africans but also those Afrikaans speakers who supported national unity.

After the passing of Hertzog from the political scene, Malan became the most powerful leader of the now reunited Nationalist Party—the Herinigde Nasionale Volkspartie. He remained unshakenly opposed to South African participation. Even late into the war he kept on declaring that the allied cause was hopeless and that the Union should withdraw, though in 1942 he thought it prudent publicly to dissociate himself from Dr. van Rensburg's pro-Nazi Ossewabrandwag. At the same time he formulated his political demand for a "Christian Nationalist" Republic in South Africa and thus committed himself to opposing not only the growing war spirit of the Union but the tide of world events. The lesson of the heavy defeat which his party sustained in the South African election of 1943 was not lost upon him. Thereafter he began to concentrate on internal politics, particularly on the ever-present racial question.

The policy of *apartheid*, designed to appeal to the fears of most of the white population, whether English- or Afrikaans-speaking, paid him handsome dividends in the election of 1948 and he remained in office until ill-health caused him to retire in 1954.

After the victory of his party had placed him in supreme authority he approached the issues raised in the campaign with a proper respect for Parliamentary institutions which he undoubtedly felt with greater keenness than did many of his supporters. He chose moderate men as his Cabinet colleagues and announced that there was enough common ground between the two white races to eliminate the racial question, so far as it concerned them, from South African political life. At the same time he sought to placate his more narrowly nationalist supporters by his insistence on the sovereign status of South Africa and by the display of hostility to the United Nations.

February 9, 1959.

Sir Dougal Malcolm, K.C.M.G., for many years president of the British South Africa Company, who died in London on August 30, 1955, less than a month after his seventy-eighth birthday, was a leading authority upon South African affairs.

After a brilliant career at Oxford—he was an excellent classical scholar—he entered the Colonial Civil Service and having spent some years in South Africa became a director of the British South Africa Company and thereafter devoted himself chiefly to the tasks of development which the late Cecil Rhodes inaugurated in 1889. An economist and an educationist, he also rendered useful services in connexion with Imperial and public affairs. Shrewd and wise in his judgment and sound in his assessment of facts, he was never dogmatic and was always willing, and indeed anxious, to maintain discussion until all relevant issues had been ventilated. He was a courtly and urbane man, who impressed all who met him by a charm of manner which clearly had its origin in genuine good nature.

Dougal Orme Malcolm was born on August 6, 1877, the son of the late William Rolle Malcolm, of Walton Manor, Epsom, at one time senior partner of Coutts's Bank, and Georgina, daughter of the late Major-General Lord Charles Wellesley, M.P., and sister of the fourth Duke of Wellington, K.G. He was educated at Eton, where he was in Walter Durnford's house, and at New College, Oxford, where he obtained first-class honours in Classical Moderations and *Literae Humaniores.* In 1899 he was elected a Fellow of All Souls and, in 1900, entered the Colonial Office. Having for a time been private secretary to the late Lord Milner in London, he went in 1905 to South Africa as private secretary to Lord Selborne, the High Commissioner, a position which he held for the five years Lord Selborne served as High Commissioner. For a short time he served Lord Grey, the Governor-General of Canada, as private secretary. In 1911 he was transferred to the Treasury, where he was appointed secretary of the Dominions Royal Commission, but retired at the end of 1912 in order to become a director of the British South Africa Company.

The company, one of the last of the old type of company incorporated by Royal Charter, was formed by Cecil Rhodes to exploit the territories of Matabeleland and Mashonaland, now known as Rhodesia. As it turned out the mineral rights, which under its charter the company enjoyed in perpetuity, were far and away its most valuable asset. The movement towards self-government in the Rhodesias naturally called in question the special position occupied by the Chartered Company and after long and complicated negotiations the company surrendered its perpetual rights in 1949 for a term of 37 years, during which it would pay 20 per cent of its net revenue from mining to the Government of Northern Rhodesia, the amount to be regarded as an expense for the purpose of Northern Rhodesia income-tax. In return the Northern Rhodesian Government agreed that no special tax should be imposed on mineral royalties as such within its territories. Sir Dougal Malcolm, who had become president of the Chartered Company in 1937, had the main burden of these negotiations and of recommending their terms to the shareholders.

From 1926 to 1928 Malcolm was chairman of the Committee on Education and Industry appointed by the President of the Board of Education and Minister of Labour, and in the latter year was a member of the British Economic Mission to Australia. In a speech which he made on his return he expressed the view that Australia tended to advance in certain directions "further and faster than was quite wise", and commented upon large projects there which had proved unremunerative.

Malcolm wrote *The British South Africa Company, 1889-1939,* and on September 12, 1940, the jubilee of Rhodesia, contributed a retrospective article to *The Times.* He also wrote *Nuces Relictae,* a light, amusing, and scholarly book, which was published in 1926.

Concerned in the direction of several public concerns, he was vice-president of the British North Borneo Company. He was also honorary treasurer of the Children's Country Holiday Fund and vice-chairman of the Court of Governors of the London School of Economics and Political Science.

In 1910 he married Dora Claire, daughter of the late Hon. John Stopford. She died in 1920 and he married, secondly, in 1923, Lady Evelyn Farquhar, daughter of the fifth Earl of Donoughmore, K.C.M.G., and widow of Colonel Francis Farquhar.

August 31, 1955.

Dr. Joan Malleson, who died [of coronary thrombosis] on May 14, 1956, at the age of 55 while in the sea during a brief visit to Fiji, was one of the pioneers of family planning in Britain.

She was on her way home from New Zealand, where she had spent four months under a professional exchange scheme, and had broken her journey to spend a day in Fiji. She was a most enthusiastic worker for education and enlightenment in sexual matters, but she never allowed her enthusiasm to run away with her. She realized that prejudices were strong and she did her best to overcome them, using great tact and understanding in the process. Quite early in her career she had become friendly with Havelock Ellis and the outlook of that philosophical and tolerant observer and indefatigable research worker was a formative influence in her career.

Joan Graeme Billson was born at Leicester on June 3, 1900, and was educated at Bedales, where she was head girl. She received her medical training at the Charing Cross Hospital and qualified M.R.C.S., L.R.C.P. in 1925. A year later she took the M.B., B.S. London. While still a student she married Miles Malleson*, the actor and dramatist, a marriage which was later dissolved. Her early work as medical officer of the comprehensive clinic of the Holborn Borough Council and as clinical assistant at the West End Hospital for Nervous Diseases determined the direction of her future career, for the constant difficulties she found in the sexual life of her patients, both within and without marriage, seemed to defy classification. Yet, with experience she began to feel her way to various classifications which would aid diagnosis and so aid cure. Though it would be an over-simplification to say that anxiety and ignorance were the principal causes of sexual difficulties, that broadly was the basis of her doctrine, and the cure—though this again is an over-simplification—she considered simply to be education.

As medical officer of the clinic for sexual difficulties of the North Kensington Women's Welfare Centre, and of the contraception clinic attached to the Obstetrics Department of University College Hospital, she did magnificent work. She was very popular with the mothers she advised, and she undoubtedly played a large part in establishing family planning as a recognized procedure, both inside and outside the medical profession. She had written a large number of works on the subject and had frequently broadcast. As a member of the Eugenics Society and of the executive committee of the Family Planning Association, she was recognized internationally as one of the leading authorities on the subject she had made her own.

May 16, 1956.

Former Bishop of Manchester—See **Warman.**

Cathleen Mann (Mrs. J. R. Follett in private life), who died on September 8, 1959 [after taking drugs while mentally disturbed] was a talented portrait painter. She was 62.

Cathleen Sabine Mann was born at Newcastle in 1896, the daughter of Harrington Mann, the Scottish portrait painter, and her work provides an interesting example of hereditary talent developing naturally in accordance with changes in artistic opinion. After working in her father's studio she studied at the Slade School and later in Paris. As early as 1924 she had two portraits in the Royal Academy, and from 1930 onwards she exhibited there regularly. Miss Mann was a member of the National Society, the Royal Institute of Oil Painters, and the Royal Society of Portrait Painters. At the exhibitions of the last-mentioned in particular her work always made a welcome impression by reason of its superior pictorial qualities, reserve in colour, and freedom of handling. Only in November 1958 her "A Group of Writers" attracted notice there. Her work had, above all, the great merit of consistency, the cool colour schemes enhancing the plastic effect of the simplified forms, while the broken touch was nicely adjusted in scale to the design as a whole.

A frankly expressed admiration for Miss [Dame] Ethel Walker [q.v.] was evident in Miss Mann's work, and the influence of Miss Walker upon the grounding in her father's studio would be a reasonable explanation of her general development. Miss Mann had not Miss Walker's exquisite sensibility or her poetical imagination, but at her best in portraiture and flower painting, an important application of her talent, she did not fall far below that admirable artist, though she was always more positive in her pictorial statements.

One-woman shows of Cathleen Mann's work, including landscapes, were held at the Dighton, Lefèvre, and Goupil Galleries, and her last one at the O'Hana in 1952. She is represented in the Victoria and Albert Museum, the Luxembourg Museum, Paris, and the Glasgow Institute, but as she was mainly a portrait painter most of her work is in private ownership.

In 1926 she married the eleventh Marquess of Queensberry as his second wife. They had a son, the present marquess, and a daughter. In spite of a full social life, Miss Mann was an indefatigable worker. Painting, she said, was both her work and her recreation, and if she went away for a weekend visit she took her painting materials with her. As a hostess she was fertile in unobtrusive provisions for the intelligent diversion of her guests.

Her marriage to the Marquess of Queensberry was dissolved in 1946, and she married John R. Follett, who died in 1953.

September 10, 1959.

The death occurred on August 12, 1955 in Zürich, where in recent years he had made his home, of the celebrated German novelist, **Thomas Mann.** He was 80. He had been flown back to hospital in Zürich from a holiday in Holland in July.

Thomas Mann held the leading place among German prose writers of this century. That he was a writer of commanding intellectual power and the highest artistic integrity is incontestable; the evidence of *Buddenbrooks* and *Der Zauberberg*, even of the later *Joseph und Seine Brüder*, is not to be gainsaid: these are monumental works, lit by a studied and searching irony. Yet his appeal in translation to the English-speaking public was never deep enough or intimate enough to match the singular quality of his literary reputation, and this for reasons which are not far to seek. The German novel has always made a heavy-footed and cloud-encompassed showing by comparison with the French, the English, or the Russian, and as a novelist Mann was German, all too German. To an English critic who had lived in Germany and perhaps studied at a German university, or who at any rate felt a degree of genuine sympathy with the intellectual inheritance of German classical philosophy, Mann was a supremely interesting and significant figure in the direct line of German *Dichtung*. To the mere Anglo-Saxon novel-reader, however, his addiction to the symbolism of German thought, the increasing prolixity and self-consciousness of his style, and the general portentousness of his *sensiblerie allemande* were a weariness that often enough counterbalanced the rest.

He was once styled "the German Galsworthy", and the comparison, for what it is worth, can to some extent be sustained. Like Galsworthy, Mann in his best known work depicted a society in decay, a society giving way to the inexorable claims of a new order. And, just as Galsworthy in the years after the First World War came to be regarded abroad as the peculiar representative of modern English fiction, so Mann during those same years and afterwards was looked upon in Britain and in the United States as the most significant force in German letters.

In a brief autobiography issued in 1931 he gave an interesting account of the outward events of his career. He was born in 1875, at Lübeck, where his family had been established for two or three generations. His father was a merchant and a Senator of the Free City, his mother was partly German in origin, partly Brazilian. In all, the family consisted of five sisters and three brothers, of whom Thomas was the second, the eldest being Heinrich, who was for a time to achieve almost equal celebrity as a novelist, though in a different and much more radical vein. When Thomas Mann was 15, by which time the family business was failing badly, his father died, and the house at Lübeck was sold and Frau Mann and her children moved to Munich. These were early experiences which were turned to good account in Mann's long chronicle of family life, *Buddenbrooks*. He had begun to write at an early age, and in Munich, where he was for a time a clerk in an insurance office, he formed congenial literary friendships and was encouraged in his ambitions.

It was the short stories he wrote while living with his brother Heinrich in Rome which first attracted serious attention to him. Then, having retired during the Roman summer to Palestrina, Mann began in 1897 the composition of *Buddenbrooks*. He returned with a large but still uncompleted manuscript to Munich, where he established friendly relations with the group round the famous satirical weekly *Simplicissimus* and was brought into close touch in particular with Ludwig Thoma and Jakob Wassermann. He finished the novel just at the start of the new century. Discharged from military service as unfit, he found himself in a fair position at the end of 1900 to enjoy the considerable fame which his work, after a doubtful start, won for him from critics and public alike throughout Germany.

In many ways, it might be argued, Mann's earliest full-length work, a sustained feat of descriptive energy and psychological penetration, was his best, certainly the freshest and—for the English reader—the most imaginatively satisfying. Until the appearance in 1924 of *The Magic Mountain*, which caused a wider stir, it remained, at all events, the most admired of his books both in Germany and abroad. There were short stories like *Tonio Kröger* (1903), *Early Sorrow (Unordnung und frühes Leid)*, and the sensitively written *Death in Venice* (1908) to mark the more poetical side of his talent; but there was also the novel *Royal Highness* (1906), a fable of the heir-apparent to a small grand duchy and an American multi-millionaire bride, to illustrate, at least to a foreigner, the arch and embarrassingly wordy humour of which Mann was capable in his ostensibly lighter mood. He had married in 1905 (two of his six children, Erika and Klaus, became writers), and it was after he had joined his wife in Davos, where she was taking a cure, that he began, in 1912, *The Magic Mountain.*

A just appreciation of that remarkable work, which seeks to anatomize the intellectual and spiritual motives at work in the Europe that was shattered by the war of 1914-18, necessitates an unprejudiced view of Mann's conservative and nationalist cast of thought until the end of the war—and perhaps of his difficult conversion to an aspiring European liberalism afterwards. The essay he published in 1914, *Thoughts in War*, cannot be described as other than a hymn of praise to the spirit of German nationalism. Even in 1918 his anguished *Betrachtungen eines Unpolitischen,* in which he exalts a *Kultur* from which everything political is excluded above the "pacifist ideal of civilization", affirms that war ennobles Germany but merely degrades other nations. A true interpretation of the war as a turning point in the spiritual history of Europe *The Magic Mountain* may thus be, but only so far as its conception of "a good European" is in line with the lingering nationalist bias which Mann maintained in the early phase of his support for the Weimar Republic.

His dawning democratic faith lacked nothing of courage or consistency as the disruptive forces within the régime gathered strength. Mann was from the first unequivocally hostile to the aims of German National Socialism. He travelled widely in Europe and lectured on literary and literary-historical themes. He used his voice and pen to advocate, as in his *Appeal to Reason* in 1930, the ideal of a Franco-German *rapprochement.* And he continued to write, assured of an attentive public in many lands by the award of the Nobel Prize for Literature in 1929.

An impressive short story *Mario and the Magician,* appeared in the following year, but the outstanding work of Mann's mature years was the tetralogy, *Joseph and His Brethren,* a "prose epic" elaborated from the chapters of the Biblical story. The first volume, *The Tales of Jacob,* was published in German in 1933, and *The Young Joseph, Joseph in Egypt,* and *Joseph the Provider* (1944) followed.

For Mann's warmest admirers this is an epic of scarcely less power and significance than *The Magic Mountain.* The dètached—and foreign—critic, however, while recognizing the *tour de force* that Mann executed here and admiring its enthusiastic scholarship and echoes of Freud and *The Golden Bough,* cannot but be dismayed at times by the diffuseness of thought and language with which the author has inflated the austere chapters of the Book of Genesis. His idiosyncrasy as a storyteller is still more apparent in *Lotte in Weimar* (1940), an oblique psychological portrait of Goethe done with mannered sprightliness, and in *The Transposed Heads* (1941), whose metaphysical symbolism in a setting of Indian legend is sustained on much the same note.

Mann returned in less ambiguous fashion to a key of high philosophic seriouness in 1947 with *Doctor Faustus,* a commentary on what is still the favourite theme of the German romantic imagination. This is perhaps the most notable of his later works, in which he elaborates, in the story of a modern composer and his pact with the devil, a dual symbolism of artistic creation and of Germany's rise and fall. It is profound and poetic in conception, though the intellectual self-consciouness is very apparent. *Der Erwählte* (1951), translated as *The Holy Sinner,* another medieval legend in modern dress, has much learning and virtuosity but little life; while *Die Betrogene* (1954), translated as *The Black Swan,* a study in morbid psychology, leaves an odd impression of misdirected ingenuity. The strange thing is that the farther he retreated from his original German sentiment, the more wilfully Germanic Mann became in style and diction.

From the first it had been plain that he and the Nazi régime could not dwell together. During the era of appeasement he was not the least distinguished of the refugees from Germany who gave explicit warning of the destructiveness of the Nazi creed. He had been deprived of German nationality by the new rulers of his country and in 1937 became a naturalized Czechoslovak citizen. In the following year he left for the United States and signalized his deepened liberal faith in an eloquent statement of "The Coming Victory of Democracy". In 1940 he became a naturalized citizen of the United States. From that year his broadcasts to the German people struck as intellectually intimate a note of anti-Nazi propaganda, it would seem, as anybody's. Mann's progress, indeed, towards the realization that philosophy could not but comprehend politics is well illustrated in the essays and speeches of two decades collected in the volume entitled *Order of the Day* (1943).

He was, at the end, truly a good European and a citizen of the world, though as an imaginative writer he remained firmly rooted in a native tradition of the grandiose. He returned to Germany for the first time since voluntary exile in 1949, on the 200th anniversary of Goethe's birth, when he received the freedom of Weimar and west and east Germany combined in honouring him with the Goethe Prize.

The freedom of Lübeck, his native city, was conferred on him—in spite of long years of resentment at his picture of the city in *Buddenbrooks*—less than three weeks before he died, and he was elected to the German Order "Pour le Mérite" just four days before he died. Oxford University awarded him an honorary D.Litt. in 1949 and Cambridge in 1953.

August 13, 1955.

Field-Marshal Baron Mannerheim, one of the outstanding figures of Finland and a great soldier, died in a hospital at Lausanne, Switzerland, on January 27, 1951. He was 83.

Carl Gustaf Emil Mannerheim was born on June 4, 1867. He was a Swedo-Finn, or "Finlander", of a noble house prominent in Sweden from the mid-seventeenth century and in Finland for some 150 years. His paternal ancestors for three generations had been outstanding figures. The most remarkable of them was his great-grandfather, Count Carl Erik, the eminent statesman who founded the system of free institutions granted to Finland after the Russian conquest of 1808, and who served for some years as Prime Minister of his country.

Gustaf Mannerheim, who was to distinguish himself in five wars, was early apprenticed to the profession of arms, entering the Corps of Cadets at Fredrikshamm in 1881. Six years later he joined the Nicolaevsky Cavalry School at St. Petersburg. At the present day a word of comment on his 30 years' loyal service in the Russian Army may be of interest. Russian rule, with some unfortunate lapses, was mild and almost beneficent in Finland until shortly before the beginning of this century. The less narrowly nationalistic Finns did not desire complete independence for Finland. The Finns were well enough pleased that members of the leading families should enter the Russian Army because the Russian authorities recruited their administrators in Finland from this source.

In 1889 Mannerheim was gazetted ensign in the 15th Alexandrinsky Dragoon Regiment, but transferred soon afterwards to the more fashionable Chevalier Guards. His good looks and a certain rather aloof charm, his brilliant horsemanship, and enthusiasm for life made him a popular figure. In late 1904, a lieutenant-colonel aged 37, he went east to take part in the war with Japan, arriving after the Russians had suffered defeat in the battle of Liao-Yaung. On the losing side an officer of his rank often finds opportunities of proving his worth as good as those which present themselves to the victor, and Mannerheim on that occasion showed that there were in him the makings of an exceptional commander.

Between that war and the next the most important episode in Mannerheim's career was his famous trans-Asiatic expedition, which lasted two years, from the summer of 1906 to that of 1908. In that period, though he made several halts, he averaged about 11 miles a day on horseback, covering over 8,000 miles. The ride started at Andijan, and led through Sinkiang, Kansu, Shensi, Honan, and Shansi to its terminus at Peking. Its official object was to obtain military, and especially cartographical, intelligence, and that was fulfilled. But the scientific and artistic strain in Mannerheim, undeveloped till now, made itself felt; he constituted himself archaeologist and ethnologist, and brought back not only an immense amount of lore but also a notable collection of antiquities, works of art, and manuscripts which is now treasured by his country. Perhaps the most precious was a fragment of manuscript in a north Asiatic language believed to have been in use about the time of the birth of Christ.

In 1910 Mannerheim was appointed to command the Regiment of Uhlans of the Life Guards, and the following year, at the age of 44, was promoted major-general. On July 31, 1914, he led the Guard Cavalry Brigade to the San, with the task of covering the mobilization of a Russian Army at Lublin. From the very first he showed his calibre, carrying out a brilliant flanking movement from Krasnik with a force of all arms and inflicting on the Austrians a sharp local reverse which had a considerable effect upon the main operations. During the next few months he took part in the heavy fighting in Poland, and continued to distinguish himself. In February 1915 he was appointed to the command of the 12th Cavalry Division, and was engaged in all the fluctuating fighting in Poland until the end of 1916. He was then transferred to the Carpathians, where he took over the "Wrancza Group", containing Romanian as well as Russian troops. After the revolution broke out Mannerheim went home. By the time he reached Helsingfors Finland had proclaimed her independence. In January 1918 he was appointed Commander-in-Chief of a non-existent Finnish Army.

In the War of Liberation Mannerheim

displayed military genius, but his first act was one of almost incredible daring, when he attacked well-equipped Russian troops with a few half-trained peasants. The Russians, however, anxious only to get home, made no serious resistance. It was otherwise with the "Red" Finns whom they had equipped and to whom they sold their arms, and these proved most determined foes. Mannerheim, however, looked upon further Russian intervention as possible and was therefore careful to cut communications across the Karelian isthmus as soon as he had made his own base of operations secure.

It is impossible even to outline the course of his campaign or to attempt to unravel the tangle of interests which extended into Finland from the rest of warring Europe and brought German troops to Mannerheim's aid, though not until he had already gained substantial success. By May opposition had come to an end. On the 16th Mannerheim entered Helsingfors at the head of 16,000 men. The aftermath of the war was accompanied by difficult and often distressing problems, and the harsh treatment of the imprisoned revolutionaries, which resulted in thousands of deaths, brought obloquy on the head of Mannerheim, though he had in fact opposed the Government's measures. He served as Regent in the confused days of constitution-making, as mediator with foreign States. His work for child welfare was of particular importance, and he would be remembered for it alone had he accomplished nothing else. With the leisure of retirement he travelled a great deal and was able to indulge his love of sport, especially shooting and fishing. In younger days he had been one of the finest horsemen in Russia and largely instrumental in the development of Russian military show riding, which achieved triumphs at Olympia and elsewhere.

In 1939 came the Russian attack upon Finland, and once again Gustaf Mannerheim took command of his country's forces. Once again Mannerheim, now supported by efficient commanders and staff officers trained under his own eye, displayed remarkable skill. His defence might, indeed, provide matter for a text-book on winter warfare in the far north. The breaking of the "Mannerheim line", however, rendered the Finnish situation hopeless, and it was on his advice that the Government decided to submit to the terms of the Soviet. In Finland's ill-advised second war against Russia, Mannerheim again acted as Commander-in-Chief. In this war the Finns largely confined their efforts to the recovery of what they had lost in the first, and it was not marked by many outstanding incidents. In the end they had to submit to taking action against their former German allies and driving them out of the country.

Mannerheim, who had been President of Finland in 1944, did not have to undergo trial, as at one moment seemed likely, and after residing abroad for some time was able to return home.

At the age of 25 Gustaf Mannerheim married Anastasie Arapov, daughter of a Russian Guard officer. He had two daughters, the elder of whom eventually became a Carmelite nun.

January 29, 1951.

The death of **Dr. Albert Mansbridge,** C.H., on August 22, 1952 at Torquay, in his seventy-seventh year will be sincerely mourned by great numbers of scholars and educationists who knew and worked with him, and by many working men who have owed to him their opportunity for higher education.

Albert Mansbridge was himself an example of the power of education to transcend circumstance and build character. He was born at Gloucester on January 10, 1876, the son of a mechanic. He left Battersea Grammar School at about 15 to become an office boy in the City. At 20 he took a post as desk clerk with the Co-operative Wholesale Society and soon began to take a deep interest in the movement, especially on its educational side. Between 1899 and 1902 he was not only working full time at the C.W.S. but teaching in evening schools into the bargain. From 1901 to 1905 he was cashier in the Co-operative Permanent Building Society.

It was in January 1903 that the *University Extension Journal* published an article by Mansbridge on "Democracy and Education", which, with two succeeding articles, outlined a scheme for a working alliance between Co-operation, Trade Unionism, and University Extension. He decided then to start "An Association to Promote the Higher Education of Working Men", and he and his wife (Miss Frances Jane Pringle, of Dublin, whom he had married in 1900) constituted themselves the first members. A provisional committee was got together by July, and within a month the association had been recognized by most of the British universities. Mansbridge was the first general secretary. The president was Dr. William Temple, later to become Archbishop of Canterbury. The first branch was formed at Reading in October 1904; in the ensuing year the more manageable title of Workers' Educational Association was adopted. The subsequent history of the movement cannot be here followed in detail, but under Mansbridge's most able management it spread all over England, and he accepted invitations from the Dominions to explain the scheme to them. He was very gravely ill with cerebro-spinal meningitis in 1915, and on recovery abandoned his general secretaryship.

Though thus compelled to modify the rapid pace of his life, his grasp and ability in educational matters were not allowed to fall into neglect. Between 1915 and 1918 he was a member of the Prime Minister's Committee on the Teaching of Foreign Languages. From 1919 to 1922 he was a member of the Royal Commission on the Universities of Oxford and Cambridge, and in 1923 he was a member of the Statutory Commission on Oxford. Side by side with these purely educational tasks he had for long made a study of church matters and had served on the Selborne Committee. An enterprise which owed a great deal to his initiative and on which he worked for 17 years was the foundation of the National Central Library. He was also chairman of the Seafarers' Education Service, and had much to do with the organization of ships' libraries. He became president of the World Association for Adult Education, Tutor in Civics at Cuddesdon, and Director of the Co-operative Permanent Building Society.

Mansbridge delivered the Earle Lectures in California in 1926 and a second course of Lowell Lectures in 1934 (the first course he had given in 1922). Early in 1939 he lectured on Oxford and Cambridge at the annual meeting of the Association of American Colleges, in Washington, and made inquiries into American housing conditions.

He was a skilled and ready writer who, besides books on Margaret McMillan and on the Co-operative Building Society, wrote a history of the W.E.A. called *An Adventure in Working Class Education* (1920), and a study of Talbot and Gore (1935). He published his collected essays and addresses of the period 1903 to 1937 in 1944.

He was created a Companion of Honour in 1931, was an honorary M.A. of Oxford, and honorary LL.D. of Cambridge, Manchester, Pittsburgh, and Mount Allison. He is survived by his widow and a son.

August 25, 1952.

The Rev. Dr. Thomas Manson, who died on May 1, 1958, at the age of 64, will be sadly missed by many men and women of all denominations and of none.

A great Christian scholar, he carried his piety and his learning with simple and unaffected lightness of heart. His happiness in following the best ways, spiritual and intellectual, spread itself and was an example to other people. To have been in Dr. Manson's company was to have known how well equipped a really good man is to face—and to enjoy—life.

Thomas Walter Manson, born on July 22, 1893, went from Tynemouth High School to the University of Glasgow (of which he ultimately held two doctorates in Divinity and in Letters). He read Mental and Moral Philosophy. In the war of 1914-18 he served as an officer in the Royal Artillery in France, where he was wounded. From Glasgow he proceeded to Cambridge as a scholar of Christ's College, and after reading for the Oriental Languages Tripos entered Westminster College as a Student for the ministry of the Presbyterian Church of England. His course completed, he remained for three years as Tutor in the college. Leaving Cambridge in 1925, he spent some six years ministering to Presbyterian congregations at Bethnal Green and at Falstone in his native Northumberland. Out of the Falstone manse came his first book, *The Teaching of Jesus, a Study of its Form and Content* (1931), which gained immediate recognition as a substantial contribution to New Testament scholarship. The following year he was appointed to the chair of New Testament Greek and Exegesis at Mansfield

College, Oxford, and in 1936 he found what was to be his main life-work in the tenure of the Rylands Chair of Biblical Criticism and Exegesis in the University of Manchester.

His energy and executive ability, no less than his distinction as scholar and teacher, soon made their mark on biblical and Semitic studies in the university. He was not only largely responsible for developments in the theological faculty, but also identified himself with the general life and work of the university, which he served in various capacities, including the offices of Presenter of Honorary Graduands and of Pro-vice-chancellor in the important period after the late war.

In addition he found opportunities for much public service in war and peace. In 1953 he was Moderator of the Presbyterian Church of England.

Manson's chosen field of study was that of the criticism and interpretation of the Gospels. In his first book, already referred to, he attempted, on the basis of a careful criticism of the documents, to fix the meaning of some of the leading concepts of Gospel teaching, with constant reference to the rabbinical literature (with which he had a close acquaintance), as representing the Jewish modes of thought which must have provided their matrix. At a time when there was something like a deadlock between opposed schools of Gospel interpretation, Manson's book was welcomed by many as helping to break the deadlock by a fresh approach. It exerted considerable influence even where his conclusions were not accepted without reserve.

This book was followed six years later by a commentary on the Gospels in which Manson collaborated with H. D. A. Major and C. J. Wright, under the title *The Mission and Message of Jesus* (1937). Manson's part in it (republished separately later on, under the title *The Sayings of Jesus* (1949)) dealt with the Sayings of Jesus, especially as reported in Matthew and Luke. He carried forward in greater detail the lines laid down in his earlier work.

In later years he found himself in conflict with a newly influential school of thought which would have the Gospels treated as expressions of the faith and insight of the early Church, and decried any serious interest in them as sources of historical information. In numerous articles he insisted that through a rigorous and sober criticism of the documents, backed by a genuine understanding of the Jewish environment, it was possible to build up a coherent and convincing picture of the career of Jesus as a credible episode in first-century history, and that this picture portrayed both the "Jesus of history" and the "Christ of Faith". The picture is sketched in his book *The Servant-Messiah* (1953). Outside this, his main field of study, Manson made numerous contributions to biblical learning, chiefly by way of articles in theological journals, characterized, like all his work, by accomplished scholarship, penetration and caution in judgment, and common sense. His short book *The Church's Ministry* (1948) was accepted as a weighty contribution to the debate then proceeding upon the biblical basis of Church order.

His distinguished work received recognition in the conferment of several honorary degrees at home and abroad, as also in a fellowship of the British Academy. He maintained lively contact with foreign colleagues, both in the United States, where he travelled and lectured widely, and on the Continent. When the international Society of New Testament Studies, after its abortive start in the week of Munich, 1938, was effectively constituted after the war, he became its first British president.

A scholar and divine of high and exacting standards, Manson was also known to many as a genial companion, sharing a wide range of non-professional interests, and delighting in the easy interchange of good talk. His speech, quiet and deliberate, was spiced with a dry humour, and could at need be blunt and forthright. A vein of tenacity underlay his tolerant good nature.

His chief recreation was fishing, and in retirement he found a retreat as he had always desired, beside a good trout stream.

He married in 1926 Nora, daughter of J. R. W. Wallace. There were no children of the marriage.

May 2, 1958.

Walter de la Mare—See **de la Mare.**

The nation will receive with real sorrow the news of the death of her Highness **Princess Marie Louise,** at the age of 84 [on December 8, 1956].

Her life had been one long devotion to the public good; with her name were associated most branches of social service; and her character and ability were worthy of the best traditions of the reigning House. Her pathway through life had been no easy one; indeed, her approach to the sorrows of others had been through many of her own. But her energy never flagged, her sense of public duty never failed, and to the end she retained a cheerfulness that must often have covered a burden of weariness. An agreeable jest once made to her mother, Princess Christian, that the phrase "the rest of the Royal Family" had no meaning, for the Royal Family took no rest, aptly applied to Princess Marie Louise, who was never content merely to be a figurehead but brought a strong organizing power to every enterprise upon which she embarked and to every committee over which she competently presided.

Her Highness Princess Franzisca Josepha Louise Augusta Marie Christiana Helena, V.A., C.I., D.G.C.V.O., G.B.E., R.R.C., was the second daughter of Queen Victoria's third daughter, Princess Helena Augusta Victoria, and Prince Christian of Schleswig-Holstein, and was born on August 12, 1872. She married in 1891 Prince Aribert of Anhalt, who proved of unsatisfactory character, and in 1900 the marriage was dissolved by virtue of a new family law of the House of Anhalt, and the Princess resumed her unmarried name and returned to England. It is interesting to record that the Emperor William, who had suggested and pressed this marriage, afterwards admitted that he had been mistaken as regards the character of the bridegroom.

The death of Queen Victoria, with whom Princess Marie Louise was always a favourite, about the time of the Princess's return to England, added yet further to her sorrows. Thenceforth, she threw herself with zeal into the public service and identified herself with her mother's interests and with many more besides. She was indefatigable in opening and attending bazaars and charitable entertainments of every kind and was always ready to take the place of a brighter Royal star who might fail at the last moment. As a speaker, she was very much at home and could keep an audience, that had come to be bored, amused with a genial humour that they could easily understand. On committees, too, she showed considerable organizing power and displayed a will of her own and took a view which generally proved to be a sound one. Among the many charities with which her name will be especially associated are University College Hospital, the South Eastern Hospital for Children at Lower Sydenham, and the Friends of the Poor; and she was interested in the work of maternity homes and disabled soldiers' associations. In July 1956 a luncheon was held in her honour in London, when she received the "deep love and great appreciation" of an assembly of charity workers. She was a Dame Grand Cross of the Order of St. John of Jerusalem, the Lady President of the Order of Mercy. She was also a keen Churchwoman.

In the spring of 1925 she paid a visit to the Governor of the Gold Coast Colony and made an extensive tour in West Africa. She published the following year her letters written in the course of her journeys to her sister, the late Princess Helena Victoria, amplified by historical information and details of native customs and rites added subsequently. In 1928 she again visited Africa and in the course of her journey took part in the Air Survey of the Zambesi; and she made another visit to the continent in 1955. These tours must have been a pleasant relief from the perpetual calls made upon her good nature in England.

In April 1931 the Princess suffered another loss in the death of her only surviving brother, Albert, Duke of Schleswig-Holstein, to whom she was much devoted. He had succeeded his uncle as Duke of Schleswig-Holstein in February 1921. In March 1948 her sister, Princess Helena Victoria, with whom she had shared a home in Pall Mall, died. Damage to the house was caused in an air raid in the winter of 1940, and the princesses then removed for a time to Sunningdale. Latterly they had lived in a flat at Fitzmaurice Place, Berkeley Square.

Princess Marie Louise moved in general London society rather more than most members of the Royal Family. She was President of the Forum Club and constantly attended the dinners and discussions there. Her especial interest was in the overseas section of the club and in the useful work it carries on in promoting social relations between the wives of officials on their visits to England and those interested in Imperial affairs. Her agreeable personality, a combination of dignity, intelligence and kindliness, will be greatly missed and will for long be remembered. It was well reflected in a volume of her memoirs, *My Memories of Six Reigns*, which was published [a few weeks before she died], and the manuscript of which she wrote in longhand. Princess Marie Louise was an accomplished musician and a painter of agreeable water colours.

She was created a G.B.E. in 1919 and a Dame Grand Cross of the Royal Victorian Order in 1953. She was also a Lady of the Order of Victoria and Albert and of the Order of the Crown of India.

December 10, 1956.

The Grand Duchess Marie Pavlovna of Russia died in Germany at the age of 68 in December 1958.

The Grand Duchess was born on April 6, 1890 (old style). Her father was the Grand Duke Paul, uncle of the last Tsar, and her mother was Princess Alexandra of Greece, daughter of King George and of Queen Olga, who had been born a Grand Duchess of Russia.

She lost her mother before she was two years old, and she was only 12 when her father was exiled by the Tsar for having married morganatically Madame Olga Pistolkors. He was allowed to return six years later, and meanwhile the Grand Duchess and her brother Dmitri, to whom she was devoted, were taken care of by their uncle, the Grand Duke Serge, Governor-General of Moscow, until his assassination in 1905, and their austere aunt, Elizabeth, the elder sister of the Empress.

As she recorded in an interesting volume of reminiscences which she published in 1930, her childhood was passed under conditions of etiquette and restriction which nowadays are almost inconceivable. An atmosphere of intellectual mediocrity tempered by gorgeous Court ceremonies, and occasionally punctuated (though little was said about them in Court circles) by such incidents as the Coronation panic on the Khodinsky Meadows, when thousands were killed and injured, and the strikes and riots raised by the Government's mismanagement of the War with Japan, could not fail to be depressing to a girl with any aspirations, however limited, for a larger life. But happiness was long in coming.

At the age of 17, through the agency of her aunt, she was betrothed, on a few minutes' acquaintance, to Prince William of Sweden, and, in spite of the protests of most of the rest of her family, and of the fact that she definitely disliked the young man, they were married in the spring of 1908. The wedding ceremonies at Tsarkoe-Selo were carried out with the traditional splendour and with the Grand Duchess so heavily weighted by her dress that she was unable to rise from her knees without help.

A son, Prince Lennart of Sweden, was born in due course. But no amount of visits to relations, nor even a six months' trip to the Far East, could relieve the boredom of her life, and the marriage was dissolved by Imperial decree in 1914 just in time for her to return to Russia and to take up war work as a hospital nurse.

Her experiences in this capacity gave her character a chance of developing which it had never had before. She took part in the retreat of the Russian Army from Gumbinnen to Insterburg, and received the medal of St. George for her strenuous work in transferring seriously wounded to the railway station during an air attack on Insterburg.

Meanwhile she became more and more convinced of the coming collapse of the Imperial régime, in which cracks had been visible since the Russo-Japanese War. By the summer of 1916 the word "revolution" was to be heard everywhere. Rasputin's influence over the Empress increased daily, until Prince Yusupov* organized the conspiracy for his removal. Among the participants in that affair was Dmitri, the Grand Duchess's brother. So far as she herself was concerned, matters reached a dangerous pitch when, in the spring of 1917, a wounded soldier whose hand she was bandaging jumped up and struck her hard on the chest. At the front soldiers had begun to kill their officers, and it was clearly time for her to depart.

But during a period closely resembling a blockade at Tsarskoe-Selo she resumed an early acquaintance with Prince Sergey Putiatin, son of the commander of the palaces there, and for the first time she fell in love. They were married at Pavloska on September 19, 1917. Apart from the danger and privations caused by the Bolshevist uprising, she and her husband were not greatly affected by the new order of things, but when one night they went to the ballet and saw the box of the Imperial family filled with sailors and their women she fainted for the first time in her life. One difficulty was to conceal safely the family diamonds, and she hid some at the bottom of a bottle of ink, others in home-made paper weights, and still others in imitation church candles. In July 1918 she gave birth to a son. The increasing strength of the Bolshevists and the fate of many of her relations at length rendered it obviously necessary to flee, and after a nerve-racking experience she and her husband escaped into the hands of the Germans.

They found refuge at the Court of Romania, when few dared to befriend a Romanov. She was forbidden to accompany the Queen to the Paris peace conference, but she made her way there with her husband, and thence to London, where they lived on the proceeds of the sale of her jewels. The money soon went and the Grand Duchess became a needle-woman. A fortunate conversation with a fashionable Paris dressmaker raised her from that lowly occupation to the management of a factory for Russian embroideries. But neither her nor her husband's business talents were sufficient for the enterprise, and in 1930 they moved to America.

December 20, 1958.

Violet Markham, C.H., died at her home in Kent at the age of 86 on February 2, 1959.

Among the many remarkable women whom the great social changes of the last half century have drawn into public life Violet Markham stands pre-eminent, as combining, in a personality of unusual distinction and charm, great administrative ability and wide intellectual interests. From her early days she had studied social and political problems, and after opposing women's suffrage and contesting a Parliamentary election, serving as Mayor of Chesterfield and on innumerable enquiries and committees, and writing several important books between-whiles, in 1927 she was appointed to the responsible post of Deputy Chairman of the Assistance Board.

Violet Rosa Markham was born in October 1872. Her family was interesting on both sides. She was the younger daughter of the late Charles Markham of Tapton House, Chesterfield, part owner of the famous Markham Collieries, among the richest and most up-to-date coal mines in the country. On her mother's side she was a grand-daughter of Sir Joseph Paxton, the famous designer of the 1851 Exhibition and of the Crystal Palace. Mrs. Charles Markham, Rosa, was one of Paxton's younger daughters, and a highly intelligent woman of strong character, from whom her daughter inherited her wide interests, sense of duty, and administrative capacity.

Unlike many women of her own generation, and more of a later, who have achieved distinction in public life, Violet Markham had no brilliant academic career behind her and she used to say that she owed her education almost entirely to her mother; and indeed her only schooling was at an establishment, West Heath, Ham Common, conducted by Miss Buckland (a sister of Frank Buckland the naturalist) and Miss Percival (a sister of Bishop Percival). Later, she was given the D.Litt. of Sheffield and the LL.D. of Edinburgh.

At Chesterfield, where her family were the leading industrialists, Violet Markham almost as a girl acquired her interest in and knowledge of industry and obtained her first insight into the problems of municipal affairs, but it was not until the outbreak of the war in 1914 that through the influence of Sir Robert Morant she moved into a wider sphere and was put upon the executive committee of the National Relief (Prince of Wales's) Fund, and in 1917, when the National Service Department under Neville Chamberlain was established, she was made the deputy director of the women's section. That year she was one of the first recipients of the newly established Companionship of Honour.

As has been said, Violet Markham, like many members of the Liberal Party to which she and her family had always belonged, had opposed the grant of the suffrage to women, and she had been much in request at anti-suffrage demonstrations where she had frequently appeared on the platform in the company of Lord Curzon, Lord Cromer and other opponents of votes to women. However, once female suffrage had become law during the war, she determined at the general election of 1918 to try her luck at the polls, and she contested the Mansfield Division of Nottingham as an Independent Liberal, but was handsomely beaten by Labour, and she never stood again. Indeed, with increasing official calls in many directions, party politics ceased to concern her. It is probable that had she entered the House she might have made a reputation there and in time reached Ministerial rank, for she was a lucid and persuasive speaker and one moreover who always meant what she said.

In the meantime she had married in 1915 Lieutenant-Colonel James Carruthers, D.S.O., M.V.O., though for convenience in her public life she continued to use her maiden name. And that public life was a very full one. She had been a member from its inception in 1914 of the Central Committee of Women's Training and Employment, which in its first 25 years trained nearly 100,000 women, principally for domestic service, and she was for many years to perform these with the other duties which she undertook. From 1920 for many years she had been a member of the Industrial Court, and she was an early member of the Lord Chancellor's Advisory Committee for Women Justices. She was for long a town councillor of Chesterfield and was mayor there in 1927; and she was vice-chairman of the Chesterfield Education Committee.

In 1934 she entered upon the most serious work of her life as a member of the Assistance Board and in 1937 she was made Deputy Chairman of that body; probably the most important administrative post up to that time that had been held by a woman. Violet Markham's interests were by no means confined to Britain and extended to the problems of the Dominions beyond the seas, especially South Africa (where she had met her husband) and Canada. On the former Dominion she published several works: *South Africa Past and Present, The New Era in South Africa,* and *The South African Scene,* and Canada did her the exceptional honour of appointing her in 1923 to represent the Canadian Government on the governing body of the International Labour Office at Geneva.

The outbreak of war in 1939 was sooner or later to draw Violet Markham into fresh activities. In its early stages her duties as Deputy Chairman of the Assistance Board chiefly engaged her attention, but she found time to equip, and largely run an all-night canteen for the needy in South London. She was also on the appeal tribunal on the internment of aliens and others under the Defence of the Realm Regulations, and on an advisory committee on air-raid shelters. In 1942 public opinion was disturbed by highly coloured rumours of immorality in the women's services, and she was appointed chairman of a strong committee of investigation, whose report, dissipating most of the rumours and paying high tribute to the organizations, is a pamphlet that even today may be read with profit, if only for its useful reminder that "virtue has no news value". In 1945 she was engaged on an even greater task of more general interest. With Florence Hancock* she was invited to investigate the post-war organization of private domestic employment. The elaborate report of these ladies, issued in June of that year, aroused much interest and had a favourable reception by the public and the Press. She lectured, too, for the British Council in France and elsewhere.

Besides those mentioned Violet Markham published several other works of a different character. After the War of 1914 she had accompanied her husband to Cologne where he had a command, and the result of her observations were published in a book that attracted attention at the time, *A Woman's Watch on the Rhine,* and expressed far-sighted views upon the German situation which, had they prevailed in high places at the time, might have prevented the greater tragedy of 1939. In 1929 the result of wide travel in France was *Romanesque France,* an informed and well documented account of most of the great churches of that character.

Her most interesting literary effort was however, the life of her grandfather, Sir Joseph Paxton, published in 1935, under the title of *Paxton and the Bachelor Duke* which, with the aid of the Chatsworth papers to which she had access, remains a real contribution to the social history of mid-Victorian days. In 1953 she published a volume of reminiscences, *Return Passage,* telling the tale of a life largely devoted to the public service, with a generosity of spirit and unconcern with self, which is singularly attractive. It presents, moreover, from a remarkably intelligent standpoint, a picture of social and industrial England between the two wars that should be of value to the future historian. She followed this in 1956 with *Friendship's Harvest,* consisting largely of recollections of her numerous friends in public life, among other of Lord Haldane, Mackenzie King, John Buchan, and Sir Robert Morant (an outstanding but now largely forgotten figure in the Civil Service), of whom she supplies a vigorous defence against his detractors, displaying a power of analysis and restrained invective that might be the envy of an experienced advocate.

The tale of Violet Markham's public life has been an easy one to tell, and her name will be remembered for long as one of the ablest administrators of her sex; but the tale would be incomplete without some reference to the personal side of her character, and that is a far more difficult matter to do justice to. Perhaps the qualities that were most marked were complete honesty of purpose, a strict sense of duty, and the widest charity towards others. She had been born to considerable wealth, and she appreciated to the full the things that wealth could procure, but from her girlhood in industrial Chesterfield she had seen the lives of the workers and to the end an improvement of their lot had been her aim.

Her physical energy, aided by a fine constitution, was a marvel to her friends. She could pass from one committee to another and throw herself without apparent effort into the work of each, and at the end of a long day she would be equally ready to take her place in a social gathering where she would shine as the most brilliant talker. And even then the day would not be finished, for as has been indicated, she was a woman of wide general culture, and the latest work of religion, philosophy or metaphysics would claim her attention well into the small hours, perhaps to be followed by a detective story, a branch of literature for which she had an unexpected enthusiasm.

To friends in trouble or who needed advice she was always accessible, however heavy at the time was the burden of public work, and her private charity was boundless where it could be usefully bestowed. Another side of her that perhaps was known to but few of her intimates was the religious background that coloured her outlook on life. It was not obtruded, it was perhaps not very orthodox, but no picture of Violet Markham would be complete without this passing reference.

She suffered the great grief of her life in the death of her husband, who died suddenly on the Ayr racecourse in June 1936 after he had seen his filly Mora win the Castlehill Plate. He had been well known as a racehorse owner, especially in Scotland. It always seemed rather paradoxical that the husband of Violet Markham should own a racing establishment, but it was quite in keeping with her wide outlook on life that she added her husband's pursuits to her own, and supplies yet another reason for claiming her as one of the most interesting and indeed remarkable, women in public life of her generation.

February 3, 1959.

Sir Edward Marsh, K.C.V.O., C.B., C.M.G., for some 40 years a noted Civil servant, private secretary to not a few of the most distinguished Cabinet Ministers of his day, and a discerning and generous lover of the arts, died on January 13, 1953 at his home in London at the age of 80.

Few well known figures of our time can have been so widely popular in cultivated society as Sir Edward Marsh, and few, probably, have lived such full and happy lives. Marsh did not attain the highest eminence as a Civil servant, although throughout his career he rendered devoted and all but unfailingly valued service in whatever department he found himself. His chief claims to remembrance are of a different and subtler kind. They consist, first, of the confidential relationship he established with the great men he served; next, of his diverse and intimate contacts with the art and fashion of his day. Known to a multitude of friends by the affectionate diminutive, "Eddie", he was a pleasant-mannered, conservative-minded epicure who took the liveliest interest in contemporary art, literature, and drama, and who "knew everyone" in a less hyperbolical sense than the use of that phrase generally implies. A translator of French and Latin verse and an anthologist of the poetry of the "Georgian" era, though otherwise without serious artistic pretentions of his own, he was a perfect audience for others. His death will leave very many with a sense of personal loss.

Edward Howard Marsh was born on November 18, 1872, the son of Howard Marsh, Professor of Surgery in Cambridge and Master of Downing College, and, on his mother's side, a descendant of Spencer Perceval. He went to

Westminster at the early age of 10 as a day boy and in 1891 went up with a scholarship to Trinity College, Cambridge. During his five years in residence there he was contemporary with Bernard Russell*, made a particular friend of Maurice Baring, and got to know older men like Bridges [Lord Bridges*], Colvin, Gosse, and Henry James. He took a first class in the first part of the Classical Tripos in 1893 and a first with distinction in the second part two years later, also winning the senior Chancellor's medal for classics in 1895. In 1896 he entered the Civil service as a second-class clerk and began work at the Colonial Office as junior in the Australian department. His long secretarial career began in 1900, when he was made assistant private secretary to Joseph Chamberlain. Promotion to the grade of first-class clerk followed in 1905, and in that year began an association with Winston Churchill* that was to continue for many years.

Marsh accompanied Churchill on an official tour to Cyprus, British East Africa, Uganda, the Sudan, and Egypt during 1907-1908, and in the latter year went with him to the Board of Trade. The misgivings he had felt on first taking up secretarial duties with Churchill were soon dispelled, and the two men worked together in the greatest harmony—so happily indeed that Marsh followed the Minister to the Home Office in 1910, to the Admiralty in 1911, and later to the Duchy of Lancaster and to the Ministry of Munitions.

Meanwhile his social life had been as full and active as his official career. His friendship with the Lytton family meant much to him, and it was Neville Lytton, the painter, who towards the turn of the century gave him the idea of collecting pictures. Beginning with classical English masters, he turned, about the year 1911, to contemporary paintings, and in course of time assembled a collection which covered every inch of wall-space at his rooms in Gray's Inn. He had excellent native taste, and many painters now highly esteemed, Duncan Grant, Stanley Spencer [q.v.], R. O. Dunlop, and Richard Wyndham among them, are indebted to him for early encouragement that took the practical form of purchase. Marsh was never converted to the refinements of abstract art, but his judgment of "representational" painting came to be regarded with sincere and merited respect. He eventually took the chair of the Contemporary Art Society, which he held until 1952, and in 1937 was made a trustee of the Tate Gallery.

His interest in literature and in the stage retained until the end a quality of youthful generosity. The appearance of the initials "E. M." over the volumes of *Georgian Poetry* during 1911-22 did genuine credit to his poetic sympathies, whatever flights the whirligig of fashion has made since then. He included among his literary friends a great many whose names were famous—Bernard Shaw, Sir James Barrie, D. H. Lawrence, T. E. Lawrence, and others. The death of Rupert Brooke in 1915 was a heavy blow to Marsh, who commemorated his friendship with the poet with a memoir published in 1918. Marsh also produced a set of well turned translations from La Fontaine in 1931 and went on to a complete version in English of the Fables, and brought out an urbane, almost too urbane, volume of reminiscences, *A Number of People*, in 1939. For many years he was to be seen at the first night of any new play of note.

After the war of 1914-18 Marsh did duty at the War Office, again with Churchill, and then returned in 1921 to the Colonial Office, where he served successively under the Duke of Devonshire and J. H. Thomas, visiting South Africa with the latter in 1924. In the same year, after the fall of the Labour Government, he worked at the Treasury with his old chief, Churchill, once more.

He had been created C.M.G. in 1908, C.B. in 1918, and C.V.O. in 1922, and on his retirement from the Civil service in 1937, when he was private secretary to Malcolm MacDonald at the Dominions Office, he received additional honour by his creation as K.C.V.O. In retirement he produced a vigorous and accomplished translation of the Odes of Horace (1941), a volume of verse translations from the French, parodies and epigrams, *Minima* (1947), the accumulated minor poetical baggage of half a century, and a translation of Eugène Fromentin's novel *Dominique* (1948).

"Eddie" Marsh represented a type that lent grace to English society before 1914 and that is not often encountered to-day. He had tact, humour, a great talent for friendship, an unfailing appreciation of the good things of life, and a genuine zeal for the encouragement of the arts. His generosity and flair as an art patron were truly remarkable, and all sorts and conditions of needy artists and men of letters have cause to remember his discriminating taste and his kindness of heart.

He never married, but lived a hospitable bachelor life in chambers for many years at Gray's Inn and latterly in Chelsea, surrounded by his pictures and the mementoes of widespread friendship and good will. His eightieth birthday was suitably celebrated by numerous tributes in the press and a gathering at the Travellers' Club which reflected the many facets of his broad sympathies.

January 14, 1953.

General of the Army George Catlett Marshall, who had been Chief of Staff of the United States Army from 1939 to 1945, Secretary of State and Secretary of Defence, died in the Walter Reed Army Hospital on October 16, 1959 at the age of 78.

He was the creator of the greatest military force ever known in the New World and the directing brain which trained, equipped, and deployed it. But the organizer of victories had moral qualities, above all an invincible integrity, which were recognized and respected by Americans in both political parties and which enabled him to play an even more notable part as a civilian in the reconstruction of Europe and in the leadership of the free world during dangerous years. To President Truman*, who sent Marshall as his special envoy to China in 1946, who made him first Secretary of State and then Secretary of Defence, Marshall was always "the greatest living American".

Many brilliant and perceptive minds contributed to the Marshall Plan, which between 1947 and 1950 rescued Europe from economic disintegration and helped to restore its self-respect and confidence. But Marshall's moral authority played a key part in persuading Americans to embark, at this fateful turning-point, upon a course of generous and fruitful cooperation with the free world which was in keeping with their power and responsibilities.

During the Truman Administration, which overlapped with the McCarthy [q.v.] era, Marshall's selflessness, courage, and high sense of duty constituted a standard of public behaviour of which Americans could be proud and which millions in other countries felt represented much of the best in the American character. As Secretary of Defence during most of the Korean War Marshall, the former soldier, helped to make certain that the civilian authority would prevail and that the interests of the alliance of free nations would not be jeopardized by MacArthurism.

He was a rock of good sense and disinterestedness in years when extremists threatened to engulf the Truman Administration. The deep sense of shock when McCarthy dared to attack Marshall as a front for traitors was a measure of how impregnable his position had seemed to be and of the decay of American public life at that unhappy time. It was entirely fitting that he should have been awarded a Nobel Peace Prize in 1953.

George Catlett Marshall was born on December 31, 1880, the son of a father of the same names by his marriage with Laura Bradford, and came of the family of Chief Justice Marshall. He was educated at the Virginia Military Institute—later he was to pass through both the Infantry-Cavalry School and the Army Staff College—and in 1901 was commissioned as a second lieutenant of infantry. He served in the Philippines and was an instructor at the Army Staff College. In 1917, after the United States entered the war, Marshall went oversea as Chief of Operations on the Staff of the First Division. For his services, which impressed Pershing, he was awarded the United States Distinguished Service Medal and the Victory Medal with five bars and the Croix de Guerre with palms.

Between the wars Marshall's promotion was not unusually rapid, but by 1938 he had become Chief of the War Plans Division of the General Staff and the next year, on his return from a successful military mission to Brazil, he was appointed acting Chief of Staff and promoted General. In September 1939—just as the Germans were sweeping through Poland—Franklin Roosevelt recognized his quality and made him Chief of Staff over the heads of more senior officers. At that time the Army consisted of only 200,000 men and it fell to Marshall to modernize, to build, and to equip.

His growing reputation and the confidence which Congress had in him, as a strategist and an organizer, enabled him to set about this task vigorously. He is credited with having persuaded Congress to retain conscription by a single vote. It was primarily due to Marshall that the

United States entered the war with a formidable striking arm of 1,800,000 men.

As early as 1938 it had been decided that if the United States should become involved simultaneously in wars in Europe and in the Pacific priority should be given to the European conflict. On this point there was no wavering, despite the popular emotions bound up in the Pacific War.

Marshall had no doubt that the war in Europe must be tackled first; his disagreements with the British sprang, instead, from his conviction that an assault across the Channel should be launched with the least possible delay. In 1942 he went to London to press the American view, which to the British seemed so premature as to invite a massacre. Unfortunately Marshall went home believing he had a firmer promise of early action than had, in fact, been given. Other disagreements sprang from Marshall's veto of an attack on the Balkans and his support of Operation Dragoon, the attack through southern France.

Lord Alanbrooke's* memoirs make it clear that the British Chiefs of Staff had little opinion of Marshall as a strategist. But without his constant urging the attack on Europe might well have been postponed until 1945 and Britain might have suffered severely from German rockets. Until his death Sir John Dill, who was stationed in Washington, and for whom Marshall had great respect and affection, helped to bridge the differences.

Throughout the war Marshall accompanied President Roosevelt to his meetings with the British and the Russians, and although he never allowed himself to speak save as a professional soldier, this experience unquestionably gave him a broad view of the war and the peace which was of great value when he became Secretary of State. At an early stage, Marshall had picked General Eisenhower* to lead the European assault and supported Roosevelt's decision that the Army's Chief of Staff should remain at the centre. No doubt Marshall would have much preferred to be in Eisenhower's shoes. When General Eisenhower ran into difficulties with General Montgomery [d. 1976], Marshall was, however, available to smooth them over. At home he had to act on many occasions as the spokesman of military policy before Congress, and showed that he had the clarity and force of mind to make an impressive and convincing witness.

In 1945 Marshall, who had been made General of the Army the year before, had reached 65 and expected to retire. Truman had other plans for him. At the President's urgent personal request, Marshall reluctantly accepted the task of attempting to end the Chinese civil war and bring the two sides together in a government which the United States could support. He went as the President's Special Envoy with the rank of Ambassador. After eight months he had to admit failure and outspokenly condemned the extremists both of the Communist Party and the Kuomintang; not long afterwards he recommended that the efforts to mediate be abandoned as hopeless and that American military units be withdrawn. This was the seed of that bitter whirlwind of which Dean Acheson [q.v.] five years later was to bear the brunt, for the Republicans decided that the State Department and the Administration—at Marshall's recommendation—had abandoned Chiang to the Communists.

In January 1947 Marshall succeeded J. F. Byrnes* as Secretary of State—again in response to the President's urging and out of a sense of duty. It was an immensely popular appointment; he was confirmed by the Senate unanimously in a matter of minutes, although he was the first military career man ever to serve as Secretary of State.

One source of his strength was his statement—which not even the most cynical Republican could doubt—that he cherished no political ambitions of any kind. Marshall's courage, directness, and selflessness were invaluable at this cross-roads of history. In the United States Henry Wallace* was calling for accommodation with the Russians which smacked of appeasement. Marshall, at the frustrating Moscow conference, took a strong line and on his return insisted there could be no "agreement for the sake of agreement", no compromise of great principles. But he also insisted that "action cannot await compromise through exhaustion" and that "the patient is sinking while the doctors deliberate".

It was not long afterward that Marshall, at the graduation exercises at Harvard University, on June 5, made the speech which brought hope to a continent facing disintegration, hunger, and growing economic paralysis. He recognized that there could be no recovery for one country without the recovery of all; he pledged action against no country and no doctrine but only against chaos, hunger, and desperation; and he demanded that the European nations should band together to help themselves. It is not too much to say that in this speech there was the kernel of such economic unification as western Europe has already seen and perhaps more that is to come. The response was electric.

The genesis of the Marshall plan owed much to such men as Acheson, Bohlen*, and Kennan. But its passage through Congress and the grant of interim aid to help Europe through the bleak winter of 1947-48 would not have been possible without Marshall's moral authority and his firm insistence that the United States must meet the need. At one point he said sharply to Congress, which was threatening to pare the amount of aid, "Undertake to meet the requirements of the problem or do not undertake it at all"; there were even hints that if thwarted he would retire to Leesburg.

By the spring of 1948 the Russians had taken over Czechoslovakia and such prodding was unnecessary. In the next three and a half years over $12 billion was made available as Marshall aid; "the most unsordid act in history" had accomplished its purpose of restoring confidence and economic health to the free nations of Europe. And once the United States had set itself on a course of cooperation it could not draw back.

In 1949 Marshall, who had had a serious operation the year before, retired. His successor, Acheson, had great abilities, and technically was far more proficient than Marshall, who never pretended to possess either diplomatic experience or a diplomat's temperament. What Acheson lacked, however, was Marshall's immunity—or so it seemed—to political attack from the extremists now rallying for an assault upon the State Department, its staff and its policies.

Marshall, in his retirement, made no public move to support Acheson, just as the next year he made no defence when he himself was attacked by Senator McCarthy. But in June 1950 the Administration took the historic step of going to the defence of South Korea; the attacks on Acheson increased, and many of them were encouraged by Louis Johnson* the Secretary of Defence. In September Truman turned once more to Marshall, asking him to return as Secretary of Defence.

As by law this post could not go to anyone who had held an active commission during the last 10 years, Congress had to be asked to grant Marshall a special exemption. Marshall's greatest services to his country may well have been performed during these two years. His displacement of Johnson brought unity back to the Cabinet. But, more important, his appointment was a guarantee that the civilian authority would remain supreme and that the extension of hostilities which other members of the free alliance so much feared would not be authorized unless it became unavoidable.

Marshall's towering reputation made him the only man who could safely discipline the legendary General MacArthur* who was continually tugging at the leash and whose exploits and personality fascinated Congress and the country. Marshall stood squarely behind the President when Truman finally decided that General MacArthur must be recalled. And when General MacArthur returned to make his case to Congress, it was Marshall who calmly and convincingly took the MacArthur legend to pieces and made an overwhelming case for patience, intellectual honesty, and good sense.

Marshall, although a kindly man, was reserved and dignified and entered little into Washington society; it has been said that he had "no enemies—and no nickname". When he was finally able to retire he lived quietly in Leesburg. In 1953 he was awarded a Nobel Peace Prize.

In 1902 he married Elizabeth Carter Coles, of Lexington, Virginia. She died in 1927 and in 1930 he married Katherine Boyce Tupper Brown, of Baltimore, Maryland.

October 17, 1959.

Sir Guy Marshall, K.C.M.G., F.R.S., Director of the Imperial Institute of Entomology from 1913 to 1942, died in London on April 8, 1959. He was 87.

Guy Anstruther Knox Marshall, the distinguished entomologist, was born in India on December 20, 1871, and educated at Charterhouse. Having been unsuccessful in entering the Indian Civil Service, he joined a firm of mining engineers in Salisbury, Rhodesia, in 1895. At that time little was known of the fauna, particularly the insects, of that part of Africa, and his residence there gave ample scope for the development of his marked taste for natural history and acute powers of observation.

Moreover, at this time he came into communication with a most inspiring teacher in the person of the late Sir Edward Poulton, F.R.S., Hope Professor of Zoology at Oxford. Their collaboration produced the most fruitful results, as is evidenced by their joint paper published in the *Proceedings of the Entomological Society of London* in 1902 and entitled "Five Years' Observations and Experiments on the Bionomics of South African Insects".

This work was largely devoted to Marshall's experiments and observations relating to mimicry and warning colours, but also includes a vast number of valuable field notes as well as the proof of his own theory, published some years before, that some of the supposed distinct species of the genus *Precis* are in fact only the seasonal phases of a more limited number of these butterflies.

Marshall returned to Britain in 1906 fired with the determination to devote himself to entomology. In the following year he was appointed Curator of the Sarawak Museum but, by an apparently unkind stroke of fate, was taken seriously ill literally at the very last moment, only a few hours before he was due to sail, and had to give up the idea.

Actually, this apparent disaster was a blessing in disguise both to himself and entomology, since it made him available for much more important work. In 1909 there came into being under an honorary committee of management appointed by the Secretary of State for the Colonies, the Entomological Research Committee (Tropical Africa). Of this body, which began in a very small way, Marshall was appointed Scientific Secretary.

One of his first acts was to start the publication of the now well known *Bulletin of Entomological Research*. By 1913 the work of the committee had developed on such successful lines that its activities were extended to the whole Empire and it became the Imperial Bureau (subsequently Institute) of Entomology with Marshall as its first director, a post that he held until 1942.

During this long period the work of the institute steadily expanded, a fact that was of considerable importance as its success justified the bringing into existence of a number of similar bureaux, first of mycology, and subsequently of all those dealing with various aspects of applied biology now administered by the executive council of the Imperial Agricultural Bureau.

During 1913, the first year of the existence of the bureau as an imperial organization, Marshall had to carry a heavy burden single-handed, including the first issue of the now famous *Review of Applied Entomology*, but was joined at the beginning of 1914 by Dr. Sheffield Neave, who had been representing the Research Committee in East Africa since its inception, as assistant director, and who eventually followed him as director in 1942.

During this long period, 1914-42, Marshall devoted himself mainly to the important identification branch of the institute's activities, while acting at the same time as adviser on Entomology to the Colonial Office. He was able in addition to find time to carry on his specialized work on the classification of Curculionidae or Weevils. He became the recognized authority on this very large family of beetles, especially on the African and Oriental species, and he published a very large number of papers on them. He was also an authority on problems connected with tsetse flies in Africa.

Marshall was made an Honorary Doctor of Science of Oxford University in 1916 and elected to the Royal Society in 1923. He was made C.M.G. in 1920, was knighted in 1930 and was advanced to K.C.M.G. in 1942 on his retirement. A man of rather retiring disposition, he could never be persuaded to become president of the Royal Entomological Society, though pressed to do so on several occasions.

He married in 1933 Hilda, daughter of the late David Alexander Maxwell, and widow of James ffolliott Darling.

April 10, 1959.

Sir John Hubert Marshall, C.I.E., who was Director-General of Archaeology in India from 1902 to 1931, died on August 17, 1958 at the age of 82.

It was due to the initiative of Lord Curzon that Marshall was appointed Director-General of Archaeology in India. In an eloquent lecture addressed to the Asiatic Society of Calcutta in 1900, the great proconsul insisted on the preservation of the relics of the past as a duty weighing on the Government. A first requirement was to find a scholar to organize and direct the Archaeological Survey of India which since the retirement of Dr. James Burgess in 1889 had been without a head. The choice of Marshall was a singularly happy one.

Born at Chester on March 19, 1876, and educated at Dulwich and King's College, Cambridge, where he was Porson prizeman in 1898, John Hubert Marshall had received an excellent training in classical archaeology. He was attached to the British School at Athens between 1898 and 1901, and he took part in the excavations at Knossos and other ancient sites in Crete. He was no doubt very young to assume a post of such great responsibility, but he was full of enthusiasm for the important task awaiting him. This task was more comprehensive than it had been in the days of his predecessors who could devote their energies entirely to research without being troubled by questions of preservation. For Marshall the preservation of the ancient monuments became the foremost duty of his department, and this entailed an ever-increasing correspondence and a large office staff.

In the early spring of 1902 Marshall arrived in India; on March 15, 1934, he left the country for good. The amount of exploratory work accomplished by him during those 32 years testifies to his untiring energy. He was the first to carry out excavations on strictly scientific lines in India. Among the ancient sites explored were Charsadda on the Swat river, identified with Pushkalavati, the ancient capital of Gandhara (1903); Rajgir, ancient Rajagriha, the mountain-girdled capital of Magadha (1905); Sarnath near Benares, famous as the scene of Buddha's first sermon (1906-08); the site of the ancient city of Sravasti and the adjoining Buddhist monastery Jetavana (1908-09); and Bhita near Allahabad (1911-12).

The three places which will most closely remain associated with Marshall's fame as an explorer are Sanchi in Central India, with a fascinating group of early Buddhist monuments, Taxila in the Punjab, and Mohenjo-daro in Sind. Taxila, the cosmopolitan city of the North-West, open to Hellenistic and Iranian influences, was a site attractive to a scholar like Marshall. His long campaign of exploration, begun in 1913 and lasting more than 20 years yielded discoveries of great historical interest.

His ambition to find monuments of an earlier period than the inscribed pillars of Asoka which then made up the first chapter of Indian archaeology was realized by the discovery of Mohenjo-daro. The excavations under his direction in 1925 brought to light a large city of well-built brick houses belonging to a period between 3250 and 2750 B.C. The early civilization thus revealed was the most notable discovery made during Marshall's term of office. His magnum opus *Mohenjo-daro and the Indus Civilization* (in three quarto volumes) appeared in 1931.

It was followed in 1940 by the magnificent monograph on the monuments of Sanchi. The publication of the excavations of Taxila was delayed by the war. It appeared in 1952, in three volumes, and presents a fascinating account of the Indian city associated with memories of Alexander the Great, the Buddhist Emperor Asoka, the Parthian king Gondofares who figures in the legend of St. Thomas, and Apolonius of Tyana.

The name of Sir John Marshall will doubtless be connected in the first place with the explorations described in these three imposing monographs. Yet most of his energies were devoted to the preservation and repair of the many decaying monuments of India and Burma. A feature of this work of conservation in which he took a special pride was the restoration of the ancient gardens which surrounded many of the Mogul monuments and the designing of new ones to enhance the beauty of the architecture.

In his work Marshall was keen, clear-sighted, and inflexible, rather austere in manner, exacting in his demands as he was on himself, yet considerate and kindly when his assistance was sought. He had to win effective cooperation from viceroys, members of council, governors, princes, and officials of many departments. During his first 20 years in India he directed a remarkably cosmopolitan team, while towards the end the senior men were nearly all Indians. He turned easily from the cares of business to show a light-hearted charm; and his former associates remember his courtesy, friendship, and hospitality, his brilliant conversation and glowing enthusiasm for the promotion of Indian archaeology.

He was knighted in 1914, and was awarded many honorary degrees and was an honorary member of many foreign oriental societies. He held the gold medals of the Royal Society of Arts, of the Royal Asiatic Society, and of the Bombay branch of that society. He was elected an honorary Fellow of King's College, Cambridge, in 1927, and a Fellow of the British Academy in 1936.

He married in 1902 Florence, youngest daughter of the late Sir Henry Longhurst. They had a son and a daughter.

August 18, 1958.

Lieutenant-General Sir Giffard Martel, K.C.B., K.B.E., D.S.O., M.C., who died on September 3, 1958 at his home at Camberley at the age of 68, fully lived up to his own expressive description, "*Outspoken Soldier*", which was the title he gave his autobiography. Before the Second World War he was probably the best informed, and certainly the most forthright, tank expert in the Army. He always had the courage of his own convictions and stated these vividly and often provocatively. He was no respecter of rank and was equally at home addressing a gathering of miners or arguing bluntly with the Chief of the Imperial General Staff.

Throughout his 37 years of service he was fearless of any possible consequence to his career of his views and his criticism of long-established practices.

Giffard Le Quesne Martel was born on October 10, 1889, the son of General Sir Charles Martel. From a preparatory school he went to Wellington in 1903, where he distinguished himself in boxing and by winning the Wellesley Scholarship awarded annually to the top boy on the modern side. In 1908 he went to the Royal Military Academy and passed out in 1909 with a commission to the Royal Engineers.

Martel went to France in the third week of August 1914 and for nearly two years he carried out the normal duties of a field company officer and commanded his unit for the last year. In September 1916 came an appointment which had a lasting influence on the rest of his Army career. He was appointed G.S.O.2 to General Elles's Tank Headquarters, with Colonel Fuller* as his G.S.O.1.

In that post he had the experience of preparing the tank units at the battles of Arras, Messines, and Cambrai.

He spent the next three years at the Experimental Bridging Establishment at Christchurch, where his inventive genius and technical skill produced the box-girder bridge, a forerunner of the Bailey Bridge, and adaptations of existing tanks for use as bridging, minesweeping, and engineer tracked vehicles. While at the Staff College in 1921 he became convinced of the need for a small and inconspicuous tracked vehicle for the infantry. Being unable to get his ideas accepted, in 1925 he designed and built himself in his own well equipped workshop a vehicle which became the forerunner of the Garden Loyd machine gun carrier. After a spell with the first mechanized field company of the experimental armoured force in 1927, Martel went to India, where he was an instructor at the Quetta Staff College and continued to preach the doctrine of mechanization.

In 1936 he was appointed Assistant Director of Mechanization, and that year accompanied General Wavell to observe the large-scale manoeuvres in Russia. Here he saw the B.T. tank, a variation of the American Christie, and was most impressed with its suspension. On his return he persuaded the Nuffield organization to import a Christie, which was redesigned to become the cruiser tank, so well known in the desert. During his time as A.D.M. Martel was also responsible for the design of the Matilda infantry tank and for the production of the Merrit steer and gear box, which was a great improvement on previous methods.

In February 1939 he was promoted major-general to command 50 Division (Tees and Tyneside), T.A., and took part in the defence of Arras and the counter-attack with the 1st Army Tank Brigade on May 21, 1940. In December 1940 he was promoted acting lieutenant-general and appointed Commander, Royal Armoured Corps. The appointment was an invidious one in that he was under the command of the C.-in-C., Home Forces, and at the same time given direct access to the War Office and the C.I.G.S. His main responsibility was to raise, according to a timed schedule, a large number of armoured units and to develop a technique for armoured warfare.

Martel had never commanded a unit or a formation of armour, and under his control were many senior officers of great and lengthy experience whose views often diverged from his. That he succeeded in formulating a common doctrine was a tribute to his tenacity of purpose. From March 1943 until the following January he was head of the British Military Mission to Russia. In February he lost an eye in the bombing of the Army and Navy Club and was placed on retired pay in 1945.

In 1945 he contested the Barnard Castle Division of Durham as a Conservative, but failed to get sufficient support from the miners, many of whom had fought in his division. In his later years he was a strong supporter of any organization set up to oppose communism in Britain.

Throughout his life he was a keen sportsman and excelled as a boxer, winning the Army and Navy, the Army, and the Imperial Services welterweight championships between 1912 and 1922. He was a useful big-game hunter and a good horseman.

Martel wrote several books of which the best known are *In the Wake of the Tank, Our Armoured Forces,* and *The Russian Outlook.* He was also a regular contributor after the war to service journals and the national daily and evening press. His military books were translated in Russia and circulated widely in the Soviet Army.

He married in 1922 Maud, daughter of D. F. Mackenzie, who survives him with a son.

September 4, 1958.

Sir Charles Martin, C.M.G., M.B., D.SC., F.R.C.P., F.R.S., director of the Lister Institute of Preventive Medicine from 1903 to 1930, died at his home near Cambridge on February 15, 1955 at the age of 89. In the course of a long and varied career he had held professorships in the Universities of London, Melbourne, and Adelaide, and had made many important contributions to medical research.

Charles James Martin, son of Josiah Martin, was born in London in 1866 and received his early education at home. Later he attended King's College, London, St. Thomas's Hospital, and Leipzig. He qualified as M.R.C.S., L.S.A., in 1889 and obtained the M.B. London in 1890, being an exhibitioner, gold medallist, and university scholar in physiology. As early as 1887 he had acted as demonstrator in biology and physiology and as an evening lecturer in comparative anatomy at King's College, and in 1891 he went to Australia to take up the post of demonstrator in physiology at the University of Sydney. In 1897 he was appointed demonstrator and in 1901 Professor of Physiology at Melbourne, and he held this Chair until 1903 when he was offered the post of director of the Lister Institute and returned to England.

During the early years of Martin's directorship the newer specialities of experimental pathology and bacteriology were giving a fresh impetus to medical research and great advances were made, especially in the control of infectious diseases. In 1904-07 Martin acted as chairman of the War Office Committee on Anti-Typhoid Inoculation, and so played a large part in extending the application of Almroth Wright's epoch-making discovery, the value of which had been amply demonstrated during the South African War. At the same period he was a member of the Advisory Committee for the Investigation of Plague in India, appointed jointly by the India Office, the Royal Society, and the Lister Institute, and in 1905 he visited India to organize the investigation.

He was appointed to the Chair of Experimental Pathology in London University in 1912. During the 1914-18 War he served with the Australian Army Medical Corps in Gallipoli, Egypt, Palestine, and France. He held the rank of lieutenant-colonel, was twice mentioned in dispatches, and in 1919 was appointed C.M.G. In 1930 he retired from the directorship of the Lister Institute and from his Chair at London University, but accepted a second call to Australia after an interval of 40 years. From 1931 to 1933 he acted as Professor of Biochemistry and General Physiology in the University of Adelaide and as chief of the division of animal nutrition of the Australian Council for Scientific and Industrial Research.

Martin's great services to the cause of medical research were widely recognized. He was elected F.R.S. in 1901 and received the Society's Royal Medal in 1923. Elected F.R.C.P. in 1913, under the special by-law, he was Dobell lecturer in 1912 and Croonian lecturer in 1930. He was knighted in 1927 and was awarded honorary degrees by the universities of Cambridge, Dublin, Durham, Edinburgh, Melbourne, and Sheffield; he was a Fellow of King's College, London.

He married in 1891 Edythe Harriette, daughter of Alfred Cross, of Hastings. She died in March 1954 and he is survived by a daughter of the marriage.

February 17, 1955.

Glenn L. Martin, one of the pioneers of flying and the founder of one of the biggest American companies manufacturing aircraft, died at Baltimore on December 4, 1955 at the age of 69.

Glenn Luther Martin was born at Mackesburg, Iowa, on January 17, 1886. When he was two years old his family moved to Liberal, Kansas, where his father, a hardware dealer, opened a shop. From very early youth young Martin was attracted by air-propulsion and began his experiments by rigging a sail to propel a small wagon and then a tricycle. He was, too, an inveterate kite-flyer, and finding that the traditional tail tended to drag down the kite, he dispensed with it and then built box type with biplanes. With this device he won a local contest and was able to sell a number of kites of this design at 25 cents apiece.

A few years later the Martin family moved to Salina, Kansas, where the boy took the opportunity afforded by this then small and isolated town to get out into the country and study the flight of birds. He also began to display a pronounced mechanical bent. His interest in flying was fostered by his mother, who read him stories of flying. One day, seeing a picture of an early biplane, he determined that some day he would build one himself. While he was attending high school at Salina he worked in a bicycle shop in his spare time. Then he took up a course in business methods at the Kansas Wesleyan College, but found it too dull and dropped it within a year. The first garage in Salina had meanwhile been opened and he was given employment there as a mechanic and learned his trade to such good purpose that when the family again moved, this time to Santa Ana, California, he felt qualified to begin in business on his own account as a motor engineer. The enterprise was a success from the start.

The success of the Wright brothers at Kitty Hawk, North Carolina, in getting their newly built biplane into the air and staying aloft for nearly a minute, covering 852ft., rekindled Martin's early ambition. His first move was to build himself a biplane glider and practise gliding from the hills round Santa Ana. By 1908 he was ready for his own experiment—the construction of a powered aircraft. He was still working at his garage during the day, but at night he used an abandoned church building, which gave him the necessary space to build his new machine.

After rather more than a year of work he managed to complete his first powered biplane. The power was provided by a Ford 15 h.p. motor-car engine and Martin carved the wooden propeller himself. He had to remove part of the wall of the church to get the machine out, and in August 1909 he made his first flight, covering 100ft. at an altitude of two feet. Shortly afterwards he built a second machine and then with the money earned from his garage and motor-car sales he organized one of the earliest aircraft factories in the United States, employing three men. Meanwhile his activities were beginning to be noticed by the newspapers, which were, however, still sceptical of his ability to build reliable machines.

By 1910 Martin considered that he could fly as well as the Wrights and two years later decided to begin touring as an exhibition flyer, and he even made some "stunt" flights for the cinema. By these means he managed to gain enough money to keep his factory working and he kept his name before the public by such exhibitions as carrying a sack of mail for a few miles in California. Later he took a parcel of newspapers 24 miles in 25 minutes, and on May 10, 1912, he attracted wide attention by flying the 38 miles from Newport Bay, near Los Angeles, where by then he had established his factory, to Catalina Island and back. This flight was accomplished in a "seaplane" of his own manufacture, equipped with floats and an inflated tyre to keep the pilot afloat in case of a forced descent. Exactly 25 years later, on May 10, 1937, he re-enacted his flight to Catalina, this time flying with his mother in his China Clipper, then regarded as one of the world's best aircraft.

In 1913 the Glenn L. Martin Company built its first military aircraft for the United States Army, and after the outbreak of war in 1914 production was greatly accelerated. After a brief partnership with the Wright Company, Martin established a new factory on his own account at Cleveland, Ohio, in 1916, and within a few months brought out the Martin Bomber, a prototype of most of the bombing machines made for the next 10 years or so. From the Cleveland factory there also came the first machine built specifically for mail service, the first American metal monoplane and the first bomber with an alloy steel fuselage.

A new plant at Middle River, near Baltimore, was established in 1929 from which in 1932 emerged Martin's greatest engineering achievement, the first of the big all-metal monoplane-bombers of what was then immense range, load, capacity, and speed. This earned him the Collier Trophy. Other achievements were the great JRM-MARS flying boats, the B-26 Marauders, and the production at the Martin plant at Omaha, Nebraska, of hundreds of B-29 bombers. The immense organization built up by Martin continued after the end of the last war to be in the forefront in the production of military aircraft, guided missiles and other warlike devices, but also has contrived to develop passenger and load carrying aircraft for peaceful purposes with a large margin of safety and the best possible aids to pilotage and navigation.

Martin himself controlled the company as president and general manager until 1949. He then became chairman of the board and three years later resigned from that position, though he remained the principal shareholder and retained a seat on the board until his death.

December 6, 1955.

Hilda Martindale, C.B.E., who died on April 18, 1952 at her home in London, had held positions of great responsibility in Whitehall. After reaching the office of Deputy Chief Inspector of Factories at the Home Office, she was, in 1933, made Director of Women Establishments at the Treasury, a post that she held until her retirement from the Civil service in 1937.

Hilda Martindale was the daughter of William Martindale, a City merchant, and his wife, Louisa Spicer, the eldest child in the large family of James Spicer, the founder of the great paper business. Mrs. Martindale, of whom her daughter gives an interesting and intimate account in her volume of reminiscences, *From One Generation to Another,* was a well-known figure in her day, associated with Liberal politics, the women's cooperative movement, women's suffrage, and in unexpected combination, foreign missions and the British and Foreign Bible Society. At the time of the marriage, William Martindale was a widower, with four children. Of the three children of his second marriage, Hilda was the youngest and was born six months after her father's death in 1875. Mrs. Martindale prepared her daughters by education and travel for that wider life which she envisaged for all women. Before settling down to a career Hilda had thus not only visited for prolonged periods most European countries, but had also travelled as far as India, Australia, New Zealand, and the United States.

After a high school education she passed on to the Royal Holloway College, and later at Bedford College she studied hygiene and sanitary science under the late Sir Thomas Legge. Her entry into the Home Office as a factory inspector, in 1901, was fortuitous and due to Dame Henrietta Barnett inviting her to speak at a meeting on the work for children being carried on in the countries she had visited. Among the audience was the late Dame Adelaide Anderson, the Principal Lady Inspector of Factories, who a few days later offered Hilda a post in the factory department. She remained at the Home Office for 32 years, passing through the grades of Senior Lady Inspector and Superintending Inspector, and reached the post of Deputy Chief Inspector of Factories in 1925.

In 1933 the important post of Director of Women Establishments at the Treasury fell vacant by the death of Hilda Maude Lawrence, and was offered to Hilda Martindale. She accepted it without enthusiasm, as she thought it a mistake to have a separate establishment for women, a view ultimately shared by the authorities, for on her retirement her post was not filled, but a lady of considerable ability was appointed an assistant secretary in the ordinary establishment branch of the Treasury. However, Miss Martindale made a success of the post and was much liked by her colleagues. In 1937, having reached the age of 65, she retired at her own request and received the unique distinction of being given a farewell party by the Civil service at Lancaster House, at which over 600 people were present.

In the course of her long official career, Miss Martindale had served upon numerous committees and inquiries bearing upon, and beyond, matters affecting her sex. In 1916 she was a member of the committee appointed to inquire into excessive drinking among women in Birmingham; in 1928 she was a member of the committee on factory inspection; and in 1934 of the committee appointed by the Secretary of State for Foreign Affairs to review the question of the admission of women into the Diplomatic and Consular service, which it may be remembered could arrive at no agreement, and in which Hilda Martindale found herself in a minority of two in one of the three reports, the only result of the labours of much distinguished talent.

She was technical adviser to the British Government delegates to several sessions of the International Labour Conference at Geneva, and a member of the Industrial Research Board from 1933 to 1937.

Miss Martindale was the author of three interesting volumes, *Women Servants of the State, 1870-1938, Some Victorian Portraits and Others* and her book of recollections.

April 19, 1952.

Lieutenant-Colonel Arthur Martin-Leake, V.C. AND CLASP, V.D., F.R.C.S., who won the Victoria Cross for conspicuous bravery, first in the South African war in 1902, and secondly in the 1914-18 war, died at his home near Ware, Hertfordshire, on June 19, 1953, at the age of 79.

He was born at Marshalls, Ware, Hertfordshire, on April 4, 1874. After receiving his education at Westminster School and University College, London, he qualified M.R.C.S. and L.R.C.P. in 1898. Soon afterwards the South African war broke out and Martin-Leake joined the Imperial Yeomanry as a trooper. It was while serving with the newly formed South African Constabulary that he displayed that conspicuously gallant conduct that won for him his first Victoria Cross. The citation stated that he went out into the firing line to dress a wounded man under very heavy fire from about 40 Boers who were only 100 yards away. After having done everything possible for the man, Martin-Leake went over to an officer who was lying very badly wounded. While he was endeavouring to place the officer in a more comfortable position Martin-Leake was shot three times. He persisted, in spite of his condition, in carrying on with his duties, and it was only when he was thoroughly exhausted that he gave up. Martin-Leake received the decoration from the hands of King Edward VII at Buckingham Palace on June 2, 1902.

Some time was to elapse before Martin-Leake was fit to resume his professional duties, but he was able to study, and as a result, having passed the necessary examination, he was admitted F.R.C.S. in June 1903. A few months later he left England for India to take up the appointment of administrative medical officer of the Bengal-Nagpur Railway. As the railway's chief medical officer he had charge of an excellent hospital which provided him with continual opportunity for the practice of surgery, and in addition he was the medical officer of the two battalions of infantry volunteers formed from the staff of the railway. Though he was given leave of absence to go on active service more than once he retained his post with the railway for 34 years. When Montenegro declared war on Turkey in 1912, Martin-Leake was in England on leave. Eager to go on active service again, he found his opportunity with the British Red Cross, which formed a unit for service with the Montenegrin Army.

The outbreak of war in 1914 found him back in Calcutta attending to the duties of his post. The news did not reach Calcutta until the morning of August 5, but immediately he heard he applied for leave of absence from his railway duties. After an adventurous journey Martin-Leake arrived in Paris on August 30 and was posted to the 5th Field Ambulance with the rank of lieutenant. It was during the first battle of Ypres that he gained the great distinction of being the first man to win a bar to his V.C. His great gallantry was the subject of a special reference by Field-Marshal Sir John French (afterwards the first Earl of Ypres) in his dispatch of January 14, 1915. As a result the announcement of the award to Martin-Leake of a clasp to the V.C. he had won in the South African War was announced in the *London Gazette* of February 18, for conspicuous bravery, especially during the period October 29 to November 8, 1914, near Zonnebeke, in rescuing, while exposed to constant fire, a large number of wounded who were lying close to the enemy's trenches. The clasp was presented to Martin-Leake by King George V at Windsor Castle on July 24, 1915.

With his previous experience in the Balkans in mind, the authorities then sent him there with the "Adriatic Mission". The mission, however, arrived too late to be of much assistance to the retreating Serbian army and Martin-Leake, after spending a short time in Corfu and in Italy, returned to England on March 6, 1916, where he remained but a fortnight before returning to the Western Front. A year later he was given the command of a field ambulance and was promoted to the rank of lieutenant-colonel.

The medical profession had good cause to be proud of so distinguished a member, and as a mark of the high regard in which he was held the British Medical Association awarded him in July 1915 the Gold Medal of the association. The medal is given to those "who shall have conspicuously raised the character of the medical profession".

In 1930 Lieutenant-Colonel Martin-Leake married Winifred Frances, widow of C. W. A. Carroll and second daughter of W. A. Nedham of the Central Provinces Commission, India. Unfortunately his happiness was short lived, for his wife died two years later. There were no children of the marriage.

During the 1939-45 war he commanded a mobile A.R.P. unit at Puckeridge, near his home, which won many prizes for efficiency.

June 24, 1953.

Edith How Martyn, one of the first militant suffragettes, died in a nursing home at Sydney, Australia, in January 1954. She was nearly 90 years of age.

Among the first women to be sent to prison in 1906 during the "Votes for Women" campaign, she gave up her post as lecturer in mathematics at a girls' school in North London to become honorary secretary of the first group of the Women's Social and Political Union in London. She had gained the degree of D.Sc. at the University of London and was also an Associate of the Royal College of Science. Her husband was a science lecturer. In September 1907 she broke away from the Women's Social and Political Union in company with Mrs. Despard and Mrs. Billingdon-Greig and others who did not find it democratic. Mrs. Despard founded the Women's Freedom League and Edith How Martyn became honorary secretary. She remained a member for the rest of her life.

In the struggle for the vote she was an outstanding leader, an extraordinarily good organizer and manager, marvellously quick and competent. She was not an orator, but her speeches were dynamic, provocative, scintillating, and full of ideas. Her arguments were logical and her appeal was to the intellect. Those who worked with her were much attached to her.

In the first Parliamentary election after women had obtained the vote, in December 1918, Edith How Martyn was a candidate for Hendon. She founded and was chairman of the Suffragette Fellowship, which bound together the women who had fought in the "Votes for Women" campaign.

In 1919 she became the first woman member of the Middlesex Council and served for three years. She was hon. director of the Birth Control International Information Centre, and went to India, with Margaret Sanger*, and alone, making contacts with officials and educated Indians on behalf of her crusade. She travelled practically all over the world preaching her gospel, and was the author of a volume entitled *Birth Control Movement in England.* She formed the first Play Centre in Hampstead Garden Suburb where she lived.

After the outbreak of war in 1939 she went to Australia with her husband. She was too ill to return to Britain after the war had ended.

February 4, 1954.

The death of her Majesty **Queen Mary,** which occurred at 10.20 p.m. on March 24, 1953, will be learned with universal sorrow, and she will long be remembered with affection in the hearts of British men and women.

For a quarter of a century as Queen and for many years also as Queen Mother she discharged the duties of her high station with a dignity which was truly queenly and which yet won for her the warm-hearted admiration of the populace. Queen Mary richly deserved the description of gracious—that adjective selected by the compilers of the Prayer Book to typify the virtues and charms of an English Queen. But her graciousness had none of the condescension sometimes associated with that word—it could rather be defined as an inherent instinct for what was fitting. Extremely shy and extremely reserved (with any but the members of her immediate family), Queen Mary found her numerous public appearances far more of a tax than was often imagined by the public. Yet she was always ready to take an active part in helping the work of any charitable or noble cause. This, which was well known to members of the public, endeared her to them. Moreover, her fellow-countrymen felt that Queen Mary typified not only the grace and distinction but the more sterling qualities of English womanhood.

Born in England—she was the first Queen Consort born in this country since Catherine Parr in the sixteenth century—her Majesty had the great advantage of being familiar with the social outlook of all classes since the days of her girlhood. In that connexion the debt which Queen Mary owed to her mother was immense. The Duchess of Teck—King George III's granddaughter—understood the British public and was beloved by it to a remarkable extent. She was the least conventional and the most anxious to understand all classes of any royal personality in the nineteenth century, and she trained her daughter in that tradition. It is well known that Queen Victoria (no mean judge in such matters) had singled out the Duchess of Teck's daughter as the person most suited to marry the heir to the British Throne. Certainly no choice could have been more amply justified by the result or more widely acclaimed by future generations.

Princess Victoria Mary Augusta Louise Olga Pauline Claudine Agnes was born on May 26, 1867, in the same room in Kensington Palace which had seen the birth of her first cousin once removed, Queen Victoria. The latter recorded in her journal how she went to see the baby, "who is a very fine one, with pretty little features and a quantity of hair". Princess Victoria Mary, or May as she was always called from her earliest days, was the eldest child and only daughter of Prince and Princess Francis of Teck. The Prince was a grandson of the King of Württemberg; a few years after his marriage he was created Duke of Teck. It was on a visit to the Prince and Princess of Wales in 1863 that the Duke first met his future wife, Princess Mary of Cambridge. She was the younger daughter of Adolphus, Duke of Cambridge (George III's youngest son), and sister to Prince George, Duke of Cambridge, who was for many years Commander-in-Chief of the British Army.

Princess May was brought up with strict simplicity, partly as her mother's wish and partly through the necessities of economy. Her father had no private fortune and her mother had nothing apart from her Parliamentary grant, from which she contributed lavishly to a large list of charities. It was for that reason that Queen Victoria granted the Duke and Duchess on permanent loan the large but lovely house in Richmond Park known as White Lodge. The childhood and girlhood of Princess May could hardly have been passed in more delightful surroundings than White Lodge and the apartments in Kensington Palace, if a sojourn in London was necessary. Among the valuable lessons which she learned at home was that of punctuality, for her mother, with all her excellent qualities, had an infinite capacity for being late, and the child's suffering from the waste of time and temper involved in waiting for her was the cause of her admirable punctuality in later years. Similarly some thought that Princess May's reticence was due to her mother's extreme volubility, which made small talk on her part unnecessary.

The expenses of a growing family and the cost of keeping White Lodge in royal state proved far beyond the financial resources of the Duke and Duchess. In order to economize they shut up White Lodge in the summer of 1883 and went to live very quietly in Italy, taking with them their daughter, who was then 16, and a very small suite. Princess May was undoubtedly fortunate in having this agreeable opportunity of familiarizing herself with examples of the work of the Florentine school which must form the basis for any serious appreciation of painting. Florence not only stirred the Princess's interest in art, it also stimulated her curiosity about history.

Princess May and her parents returned to England in the summer of 1885, living in a house in Chester Square while White Lodge was being put in order for them. Later that year the Princess was confirmed in the Chapel Royal—having been prepared by her mother's great friend, Carr Glyn, who was afterwards Bishop of Peterborough. In the following year Princess May came out, and there followed a very strenuous period, during which, in addition to being present at a number of State functions and society entertainments, the Princess read steadily for six hours a day. She was an accomplished linguist and 40 years later the facility with which she switched from fluent German to fluent French at a diplomatic reception was admiringly noticed. She accompanied her mother on many visits to English country houses, and nearly every summer to St. Moritz. It was almost inevitable that as Princess May was the only unmarried English princess not descended from Queen Victoria she should have been considered as the most likely bride for the ultimate heir to the Throne—Queen Victoria's grandson, the Duke of Clarence. At the end of 1891 their engagement was announced and was received with widespread approval throughout England and the Empire.

A few weeks before the date fixed for his marriage the Duke died. Prince George of Wales, created Duke of York in 1892, thus became heir to the Throne after his father. The public, nervous for the succession, became insistent that he should marry, and it was generally hoped that he would choose Princess May. The public was not disappointed, and the marriage took place on July 6, 1893, on a memorably hot day. The wedding of the Duke and Duchess was the first wedding of the Royal Family to take place in St. James's Chapel since the death of the Prince Consort. Most of Queen Victoria's own children had been married in the comparative seclusion of Windsor, and the London crowd, for long deprived of a Royal wedding, made up for the past by the warmth of its welcome to the Queen and the bride and bridegroom.

The bride was attended by five grown-up bridesmaids and five children. The Archbishop of Canterbury (Dr. Benson), assisted by the Bishops of London and Rochester and Carr Glyn, took the service. Queen Victoria, after the ceremony was over, made one of her rare appearances on the balcony of Buckingham Palace, where she was joined by the Duke and Duchess. For the Duchess this was the first of many such appearances in times of national rejoicing or emergency. The honeymoon was spent at Sandringham, and immediately afterwards the Duke and Duchess went to Osborne to stay with Queen Victoria.

It is well known that Queen Victoria was especially fond of both the Duke and Duchess. They were homely, domestic, and simple—delighting to live the kind of happy, unpretentious life which the Queen and Prince Consort had enjoyed and made fashionable. It contrasted strangely with the lively, restless life favoured by the Prince of Wales, which influenced society in the nineties and in Edwardian days. In London they lived in the suite of apartments in St. James's Palace which had formerly belonged to the Duchess's grandmother, the Duchess of Cambridge. In honour of their new occupants these apartments were raised to the dignity of a house and called York House. It was subsequently lived in by the eldest son of the Duke and Duchess when Prince of Wales, [the Duke of Windsor*], who was born a year after their marriage, and it is now the home of the Duke* and Duchess of Gloucester. For a country home the Duke and Duchess lived at York Cottage, close to Sandringham, and it was there in December 1895 that King George VI [q.v.] was born. In April 1897 the Princess Royal* was born, and the Duchess was able to take part in the rejoicings for the Diamond Jubilee in the following June.

Shortly after the Jubilee the Duke and Duchess paid a visit to Ireland. After a rough crossing the party landed at Kingstown in brilliant sunshine and were received by the Viceroy, Lord Cadogan, Lord Roberts, and many eminent Irishmen. The Duchess wore a dress of Irish poplin, which combined with the sincerity and charm of her demeanour to arouse what *The Times* described as "a pitch of national enthusiasm which cannot be surpassed".

The position of the Duchess in the early years of her married life was not easy, and those attached to the Court formed the highest opinion of the courage and tact with which she faced her difficulties. The family of King Edward VII was singularly close knit and self-contained, a fact of which a newcomer to the circle was quickly made conscious. For example, the Duchess was not able to arrange the furniture at York Cottage or plant the garden without previous consultation with her husband's family. The smallest change or innovation aroused immediate distrust and criticism. Moreover, the Duchess was irked by the absence of any intellectual interests in her husband's family. In her home she had to efface herself, and this was not the best background for one whose shyness was a serious handicap in the ceremonial duties which were beginning to loom large in her life.

The closing years of the old century were ones of sorrow and anxiety for the Duchess. In October 1897 her mother died after a sudden operation, and three years later her father died. The outbreak of the South African war saw the Duchess's three brothers on active service. The death of Queen Victoria in 1901 was a further blow to the Duchess, because a very strong tie, based on a real understanding and appreciation of each other's character, had sprung up between them. The only bright spot in that gloomy period was the birth of a third son—the Duke of Gloucester—in 1900.

At the end of her reign Queen Victoria had shown keen interest in the formation of the Commonwealth of Australia and had deputed her grandson to deliver the royal message at the opening of the first Federal Parliament. It was the wish of the new Sovereign, King Edward VII, that this programme should be adhered to in spite of royal mourning. The Duke and Duchess did not at once become Prince and Princess of Wales, but set out on their Empire tour as Duke and Duchess of Cornwall and York. On March 16 they started in the Ophir on a seven and a half months' cruise which was to embrace the greater part of the British Empire. It was a strenuous tour, and the royal travellers visited Gibraltar, Malta, Aden, Ceylon, and Singapore. The only times of real rest for the Duchess were when she was on board ship, and, as she was an extremely bad sailor, she found the journey excessively tiring. The Ophir arrived at Melbourne in May, and the Duchess was given a warm welcome by the Governor-General (Lord Hopetoun)—one of her mother's closest friends. The opening of the Federal Parliament—the chief object of their visit—took place on May 9. They returned to England by way of South Africa (where the war was still dragging on) and Canada. In both Dominions they were received with the utmost enthusiasm, and it was noticeable that, with increasing experience, they gained greatly in the confidence with which they confronted crowds. As soon as they returned home the King created his son Prince of Wales.

On their return the Prince and Princess found considerable alteration in their lives. The modest cosiness of York House was exchanged for the formal splendour of Marlborough House. King Edward VII also gave them Abergeldie, near Balmoral, and Frogmore, a rambling and inconvenient house in Windsor Great Park. For 40 years Queen Alexandra had been the wife of the heir to the Throne, and the eclipse of Queen Victoria by mourning made the Princess of Wales's position at once more arduous and more important than is usually the case. She was, indeed, the leader of society. When Queen Alexandra became Queen the new Princess of Wales naturally took a less influential position than had her mother-in-law, at least so far as society was concerned. At the end of 1902, a few months after the Coronation, the Princess gave birth to a fourth son, Prince George, the late Duke of Kent. For the next few years her time was much occupied in entertaining at Marlborough House and in accompanying her husband on numerous engagements (including a trip down a tin mine in Cornwall) throughout the British Isles. As the Prince was the Sovereign's only son these engagements were especially heavy.

In 1905 the Princess had a fifth son—Prince John, who died in 1919—and at the close of that year came the memorable tour in India by which the Prince and Princess were to complete their journeys through the Empire. Although King Edward VII as Prince of Wales had been to India, this was the first time a Princess of Wales had ever been to that country. She and the Prince embarked at Genoa on board H.M.S. Renown and landed at Bombay, where they were received by the Viceroy (Lord Curzon) on the King's birthday, November 9. They spent about 18 weeks in India, and during that time explored the vast country from end to end—from Bombay to Burma, from the North-Western Frontier to Mysore. The Princess, with her eager desire to see beneath the surface and her inexhaustible energy, employed the intervals of state receptions in seeing as much as possible of the actual life of the people. She had prepared herself by careful study at home; and her excellent memory enabled her to retain for years afterwards with singular vividness the deep impression which India made upon her mind.

King Edward VII died on May 6, 1910, and while still in their early forties the Prince and Princess became King and Queen. The Queen had always been officially called Victoria Mary, out of compliment to Queen Victoria, but on becoming Queen she dropped the former name and was known simply as Queen Mary. After a year of strict mourning for King Edward the new Sovereigns then started on a series of brilliant and important functions.

These began in 1911 with the unveiling of the memorial to Queen Victoria, for which the German Emperor and Empress were entertained at Buckingham Palace. This was followed a few weeks later by the Coronation. At the end of the year they went out to India for the Durbar. In 1913 they journeyed to Berlin for the marriage of the Kaiser's only daughter with the Duke of Brunswick—the last occasion on which the Royalty of pre-war Europe was gathered in its full splendour. After this visit the Queen paid a flying visit to her Aunt Augusta at Strelitz, a remarkable lady of over 90 who was devoted to her niece and was a large influence in her life, since she was the last link between the old Royal Family of George III and modern times. After the visit to Berlin the King and Queen paid a state visit to Paris, where the grace and dignity of the Queen's bearing made a deep impression on the French.

In those years before the 1914-18 war the ceremonial side of the Queen's life—brilliant and strenuous as it was—did not interfere with her less spectacular but no less important duties in the home. The task of bringing up a large family is rendered more than usually difficult when its members have to face the prospect of great responsibility in the future, and cannot, even as children, escape the dangers of publicity and flattery. Queen Mary was determined that her children should at any rate enjoy that which she had enjoyed but which had too frequently been denied to other Royal children—a real home life. She made certain that, at least in Sandringham and in Scotland, her children should enjoy the simplicity and discipline of family life. The second Lord Esher drew in his book a forceful contrast between Court life at Balmoral under King Edward VII and under King George V. The whist and the fashionable life of the former reign gave way to picnics with the children and quiet evenings spent by the Queen in knitting. This even, domestic life of King George V and Queen Mary was greatly appreciated by the bulk of the nation, particularly during the stern and anxious days which were lying just ahead.

The four years of the war brought inevitably their own train of personal difficulties and personal anxieties for the Queen—not the least of which was the restricted field open to women's service. Queen Mary at once showed one way in which every woman could be useful in the early weeks—the traditional one of providing the fighters with warm clothing. She transformed the Needlework Guild, originally founded by the late Lady Wolverton, into a central organization, with headquarters at Friary Court, St. James's Palace, for the distribution of the thousands of parcels collected from every corner of the Empire. As the struggle was prolonged and the need for greater exertion by all classes became more necessary, the Queen quietly but effectively played her part. The Royal households were among the first to set an example in the rationing of supplies by limiting the use of light, fuel, and food. In the summer of 1917 the Queen accompanied King George V to France. Naturally her Majesty did not visit the front line, but she went up as far as Haig's headquarters, where she met King Albert and Queen Elisabeth of the Belgians*. Her chief work in France was the inspection of hospitals, and this task she did with a sympathy and thoroughness which will never be forgotten by those who saw her.

At a moment when the behaviour of the Women's Army Auxiliary Corps was being freely criticized, the Queen allowed herself to be appointed Commander-in-Chief of the organization, thereby enabling a high ideal of conduct to be set before Queen Mary's Army Auxiliary Corps. Among other institutions in the founding of which the Queen played an important part were the workshops at Roehampton, the hospital for Indian soldiers at Brighton Pavilion Hospital, and Queen Mary's Hospital, Sidcup, for the treatment of facial injuries. She established the Maternity Home, Hampstead, as "an enduring memorial to the efforts of many women of the Empire who gave their aid during the war". Of Queen Mary's Hospital for the East End at Stratford she became a patron in 1916. Her appreciation of the work done by women in the war was signalized at the end of it by messages to the women of the Empire and of India.

In 1918 the King and Queen celebrated their

silver wedding and gave public thanks for their 25 years of happy married life in St. Paul's Cathedral. The Armistice set the seal on their happiness, though early in the following year they had the great grief of losing their youngest son. The years immediately following the war were crowded with public rejoicings, with state visits from the heads of the allied States, with the Wembley Exhibition, and with the marriages of the Duke of York (later King George VI) and Princess Mary (now the Princess Royal). During those years, when the upheaval caused by the war had given a very raffish twist to social life, the Queen strictly adhered to her own rigid standards.

It may well be the verdict of historians that the work done by King George V and Queen Mary was never fully appreciated until the end of the King's reign. From the time of King George's serious illness in the winter of 1928 the affection of the public for their Sovereign and his Consort took on a deeper note. Queen Mary's dignified bearing during those anxious days no less than the constancy of her care for her husband struck a chord in the public imagination which stimulated and strengthened the feelings of affection for her. This sentiment was particularly marked when, during the darkest period of the King's illness, her Majesty went to unveil the War Memorial to the officers and men of the Merchant Navy and Fishing Fleets, whose epitaph was, as she said, that "they have no grave but the sea". During the fluctuations of that long illness and weeks of convalescence the Queen's courage and spirit never flagged. One of the doctors, on being asked who had really saved the King's life, answered at once "The Queen".

For the seven years of the King's life that remained those qualities were needed by the Queen in full measure. She accompanied King George on all his public appearances, but only those in close touch with Court circles were aware of the shadow of anxiety concerning the King's strength which marked that work, and must have added immensely to its strain. The culmination of public affection was marked by the wonderful scenes of the Jubilee of 1935, and, in the midst of her grief for King George's death, which occurred but eight months later, the Queen made special reference to that manifestation in her message to the nation.

It is necessary to go back in English history to Queen Charlotte, wife of George III, for a Queen Consort who was on the Throne for a longer period than was Queen Mary. Oddly enough, neither Queen was what might be called fashionable in the sense of being a society leader. Yet historians of the future will probably agree that Queen Mary's example had a deep and abiding influence over the national life. Certainly her natural good taste, her genuine interest in furniture, pictures and *objets d'art,* and her wide knowledge of the subject played a great part in the general improvement in taste in the country which coincided with the period when she was Queen. More than that, her late Majesty rearranged the furniture and decorations of the royal palaces so that they can to-day be seen to the best advantage. She was not, however, content that enjoyment of these things should be confined to the privileged few who were entertained by their Sovereign. She encouraged and personally supervised the publication by Clifford Smith of his book on the contents of Buckingham Palace, and she did the same for Mr. Roberts's book on the history of the Brighton Pavilion.

After King George V's death Queen Mary moved into Marlborough House. This had stood empty for the 12 years since Queen Alexandra's death, and Queen Mary had it renovated throughout. It was not, perhaps, with its Victorian additions, an exactly elegant house, and its enormous wall paintings inside made it difficult to furnish. However, all who were privileged to see it would have agreed that her Majesty furnished it with an admirable blend of homeliness and dignity. Queen Mary soon made it clear—and the public showed every sympathy with her—that she had no intention of leading a life of exclusive and lugubrious widowhood—such as had been usual in a past age. Her presence at the Coronation of King George VI (a new departure for a Queen Mother), no less than her many public appearances for charitable and beneficial objects, made that abundantly clear.

In the early summer of 1939 Queen Mary had a dangerous accident when she was motoring through Wimbledon. Her car was badly damaged and overturned, and she herself was severely bruised and received an injury to an eye which affected her sight. She bore herself with characteristic courage—so much so that the family privileged to offer her a temporary asylum had no idea of the extent of her injuries. This accident was particularly untimely because the King and Queen were away in Canada and America, and Queen Mary had in consequence many extra burdens and duties thrust upon her. But that summer marked the close of an era, and in September, on the outbreak of war, Queen Mary, who had lived in and loved London all her life, was obliged to leave for the country. She went to live at Badminton, the house of the Duke of Beaufort, whose wife was her niece. Here she spent all the war years.

In the more circumscribed life of the provinces she maintained her activity, paying frequent visits to Bath, Bristol, Gloucester, and Salisbury. At Badminton she spent her free afternoons cutting down overgrown shrubs and battling with ivy, for which she had a lifelong aversion. She was punctilious in offering "lifts" to service men, and she greatly enjoyed the informal conversations to which they gave rise. Eventually she had a metal disc made and inscribed "For Luck, M.R.", which she always gave to all who chanced to travel with her. At Badminton one evening she heard the news of the death on active service of her accomplished son, the Duke of Kent. She was able to attend his funeral service at Windsor, but she was naturally extremely crushed and broken by his untimely and unexpected death.

Though she always saw personal questions in their due proportion, she felt acutely her enforced banishment from the capital. In all her war-time messages to the Lord Mayor at the time of her birthdays she emphasized her happiness at being still remembered by Londoners, her admiration for their courage, and her recollections of the happy years passed in their midst. She loved the bustle of London, the theatre, the cinema, and picture galleries, and the chance of forwarding the great variety of societies and causes in which she was interested. She attended the great thanksgiving service in St. Paul's for victory in Europe and within a fortnight of the signing of the Armistice she was back in Marlborough House.

Two years later, in 1947, she celebrated her eightieth birthday, and although the occasion was saddened by the death of her son-in-law, Lord Harewood, she met with a resounding ovation when she appeared on the balcony of Buckingham Palace. During all these recent years she maintained a round of public engagements which at her age was truly remarkable. Her capacity for standing and walking—sometimes commented upon rather ruefully by her attendants—was unimpaired. So far back as 1939 it was calculated that she had completed her 100 miles in touring the British Industries Fair, in which she had always shown the liveliest interest since it started.

Even her leisure was turned to the interests of her country, as was evidenced by the tapestry covers for chairs which she worked and sold to the United States for a substantial sum in dollars. An even more striking example of her taste and industry was the wonderful carpet in *gros point* which took her some eight years to complete and, after exhibition in Britain and in Canada and the United States, realized $119,651 collected by the Imperial Order Daughters of the Empire of Canada.

The death of her beloved son, King George VI, could not but be a severe blow to her then well past her eightieth birthday, but she met that catastrophe with characteristic fortitude, and though she bowed to the decision of her doctors, who thought that the strain of attending the funeral would be too great, she accompanied her son, the Duke of Windsor, to Westminster Hall and, hardly noticed by the mourning throngs, thus shared in the people's tribute to their well beloved Sovereign.

Queen Mary's place in the hearts of the British public was deep and will be abiding. To explain the reason for that is not wholly easy. She lacked the graces and the captivating charm of her mother-in-law, Queen Alexandra—in fact her shyness made her austere and even formidable in those necessarily brief encounters on which the popularity of famous persons must ultimately rest. Yet the familiar figure of Queen Mary, invariably dressed in the gayest colours, with the close fitting hat and carrying the tight furled umbrella or sunshade was calculated to draw a deeper throated cheer from a London crowd than almost any other famous personality.

The explanation of her popularity perhaps lay in the appreciation by the public that she filled an extremely difficult position not only with complete decorum but bore herself with a courage and individual distinction which compelled the admiration of all. Her services to the British monarchy and her devotion to the highest ideals of kingship have never been fully revealed, but it will not be forgotten that when King George V paid public tribute to her at the time of the Silver Jubilee he said to those helping him to prepare the speech, "Put that paragraph at the very end, I cannot trust myself to speak of the Queen when I think of all I owe her".

March 25, 1953.

Lieutenant-General Sir Noel Mason-MacFarlane, K.C.B., D.S.O., M.C., formerly Governor of Gibraltar, died at his home at Twyford, Berkshire, on August 12, 1953 at the age of 63.

Frank Noel Mason-MacFarlane was born on October 23, 1889, the son of the late Colonel David Mason-MacFarlane, and was educated at Rugby and the Royal Military Academy, Woolwich. He was gazetted to the Royal Artillery in 1909 and served in France, Belgium, and Mesopotamia during the 1914-18 war, earning two mentions in dispatches, the Military Cross and two bars, and the French War Cross. In 1919 he served in the third Afghan war and after graduating from the Staff College, Quetta, in 1920 held a number of staff appointments in India. From 1931 to 1934 he was military attaché in Vienna with responsibilities not only in Austria but in Switzerland and Hungary as well, and in 1935 he graduated from the Imperial Defence College. For a brief period he commanded a mechanized field artillery brigade, but was soon drawn back into staff work, in which he had shown great gifts, as military attaché in Berlin and Copenhagen.

For a brief period in 1939 he was Brigadier, Royal Artillery at Aldershot, but was soon appointed Director of Military Intelligence with the British Expeditionary Force in France. He was then spoken of as the best D.M.I. the Army had ever had. After the German break-through in 1940 MacFarlane was ordered to ensure the safety of valuable equipment lying at Arras and hastily brought into being a miscellaneous force of something like the strength of a division which fought its way through to the coast with its precious charge. For his brilliant handling of "MacForce" he was awarded the D.S.O.

His next important assignment came in the summer of 1941 as head of the British Military Mission to Russia. His particular work was to learn what kind of military equipment would be of greatest help to the Red Army, and to this end he visited the fighting areas to see how tactics were developing, so that he would have a clear idea of the quality and quantity of equipment necessary to stem the German advance. Just before he left, early in 1942, he wrote an article in *Izvestia,* giving his impressions of the Red Army. Later that year he was appointed Governor of Gibraltar and remained in the post until early in 1944 when he became Chief Commissioner of the Allied Control Commission in Italy.

Unfortunately he held the post only a few months, for in July it was announced that he had to undergo a prolonged course of medical treatment. Later it became clear that he could not expect to return to active service and in 1945 he retired from the Army, having in the previous year been appointed a Colonel Commandant, Royal Artillery. After his retirement he joined the Labour Party and won North Paddington in opposition to Brendan Bracken [Lord Bracken, q.v.], but his health did not permit him to sit in the House of Commons for long, and in 1946 he applied for the Chiltern Hundreds. Latterly he had lived at Twyford, in Berkshire.

He married in 1918 Islay, daughter of the late F. I. Pitman. She died in 1947, and he is survived by a son and a daughter of the marriage.

August 13, 1953.

H. J. Massingham, who died at his home in Buckinghamshire on August 22, 1952 at the age of 64, brought both power and charm to his descriptions of the English country scene.

As various as Cobbett, with something of Cobbett's obstinacy but without his acerbity, Massingham was a passionate advocate of the spiritual value of living close to nature. Like George Sturt, he knew what "the world looked like in the heart of a tree", and as his sojourn with nature was prolonged he became ever less patient with those who turned their backs on old ways and old truths, and though in a sense the life he lived was consciously a background for the finely wrought literature he poured forth in abundance, it was, nevertheless, a deep and firm foundation for a life led in the light of, and with the aspiration to, the highest ideals of the spirit. What some critics mistook for an occasional affectation in writing turned out on closer and more profound study to be an expression of spiritual struggle. In his later years, feeling that he must lose no time in delivering his message, he undoubtedly wrote too much and too hurriedly, but the main body of his work remains of impressively high quality.

Harold John Massingham was born on March 25, 1888. He was the son of Henry William Massingham, the distinguished Liberal journalist. His mother was Emma, daughter of John Snowdon, and, like her husband, came from Norwich. He was educated at Westminster School and at Queen's College, Oxford, where he was an exhibitioner and followed his father into the profession of journalism. Between 1912 and 1914 he was a staff writer on the *Morning Leader,* the National Press Agency, and the *Athenaeum.* From 1916 to 1924 he was a weekly contributor to the *Nation and Athenaeum* on literary subjects and natural history. He also wrote occasionally for other journals.

In 1919 his *Letters to X* appeared. It comprised a correspondence with a non-existent person to whom he afforded no right of reply, and for this and other reasons was unimpressive. In the same year he published an anthology of seventeenth-century verse. Then followed a series of books which, though in various forms, were chiefly concerned with birds. He loved wild life and could write interestingly and fancifully about it. In the early 1920s he began his rambles about England and began to develop the type of book by which he was to make his name. In *Downland Man* and *The Heritage of Man* he turned his attention for a time to archaic civilization. It was all, however, grist to his particular mill.

In 1925 he edited *H. W. M.,* a selection from the writings of his father. In 1932 he collaborated with Hugh Massingham in presenting a collection of studies by different types of mind, then living, upon a collection of authors and thinkers of the period 1837 to 1901. These were, however, diversions, for he was increasingly to settle down to his best work of describing England in his own way. *Wold Without End* was perhaps his ablest effort; but *Country, English Downland,* and *Shepherd's Country* were pleasantly typical of his aims and methods. His *Old Rural Crafts* of 1939 was also admirable, and his knowledge of its subject was reflected in his *Chiltern Country. The English Countryman,* which appeared in 1942, was a true and timely delineation of rural types, and was regarded by some critics as his best and most important work. Books and articles, far too numerous to mention here, flowed in an increasing stream from his pen and, a work dear to his heart, he edited the Nonsuch edition of Gilbert White. He frequently employed admirable illustrations. There was much in modern life which he disliked and would have altered if he had only known the way. He was against enclosures and mass efforts, and his ideal of a rural community was one in which the husbandman should own the soil he tilled. He believed indeed in a spiritual rather than an economic basis for life. In 1939 he met with an accident which necessitated the amputation of a leg and put an end to his country ramblings. It did not, however, interfere very much with his active participation in working the garden in the wooded western slopes of the Chilterns, for which he harboured a warm love and pride.

He married in 1933 Anne Penelope, daughter of the late A. J. Webbe, who survives him.

August 25, 1952.

Dame Vera Laughton Mathews, D.B.E., Director of the Women's Royal Naval Service throughout the Second World War, died at her home in London on September 25, 1959 on her seventy-first birthday.

Her father, Sir John Laughton, R.N., was well known as a naval historian. His daughter was educated at the Convent of St. Andrew at Streatham, and Tournai, in Belgium, and at King's College London. Her career with the W.R.N.S. began in 1917, when she volunteered on the day the formation of the service was announced. She was selected for the first officers' training course and was in charge of a training depôt at the Crystal Palace, H.M.S. Victory VI. In six months' time she had reached the relative rank of lieutenant-commander and had built up a successful unit of 250 women. She was made an M.B.E. for this work.

When the W.R.N.S. was demobilized she was one of the enthusiasts who formed the Old Comrades Association, and for many years she edited *The Wren,* the journal of the association. She also at this time worked in general journalism, with *The Ladies' Field* and *Time and Tide.*

In the years between the wars she helped to start the Sea Ranger branch of the Girl Guide movement and directed the organization in London which comprised some 20 companies. In 1924 Vera Laughton married, in Japan, the late G. D. Mathews, an engineer, whom she bore two sons and a daughter. They lived for some years in Japan, and while she was there she was international commissioner for Girl Guides throughout the islands. Later she was for eight years Guide division commissioner for a large and very poor area in London.

In 1939 the Admiralty for the second time decided that a women's service auxiliary to the Navy was essential, and appointed Mrs. Laughton Mathews Director, and the late Miss E. M. Goodenough Deputy Director, to work out the details and prepare the way. After a committee had inquired into the welfare conditions in the three women's services, Mrs. Cazalet Keir, a member of the committee, said of Mrs. Laughton Mathews in the House of Commons: "She seems to me to combine two very important qualities in a leader, great humanity and sound common sense. These qualities have assisted to build up complete harmony and confidence between Wrens of all ranks".

She gained the affection of officers and ratings alike. It was said that she knew every one of her officers, and her memory was remarkable. She had the gift of wise selection. She was a big woman physically and mentally; her deep musical voice and cheery laugh were expressive of a kindly, generous nature.

She was created a D.B.E. in 1945 and in November 1946 she retired after seven and a half years as Director of the W.R.N.S. Yet she pursued an active and many-sided public life. She was appointed chairman of the Domestic Coal Consumers' Council when it was set up in 1947. She was president of the National Smoke Abatement Society in 1949-51; president of St. Joan's International Social and Political Alliance, which was but one of the organizations through which she worked to improve the status of women and their career prospects; adviser on women's affairs to the Gas Council; a member of the South East Gas Board; and life president of the Association of Wrens.

September 28, 1959.

Henri Matisse, one of the most outstanding representatives of the modern French school of painting, died on November 3, 1954 at his home at Nice. He was 84.

Partly, if not chiefly, because they were both subject to the same indiscriminate abuse from artistic "diehards" in England, Henri Matisse and Pablo Picasso* were closely connected in the public mind. In reality they had not very much in common, though they were associated in their first departure from academic art. To some extent they were complementary, and Matisse was weak where Picasso is strong, and the other way about. Of the two, Matisse was the less intellectual, and he had not the range and depth or the inventiveness and versatility of the Spaniard, but it is questionable if he had not more of the special sensibility of the painter as distinct from other kinds of creative artist. His colour was enchanting and his handling of paint was masterly.

Matisse was a Picard, the son of a grain merchant in a small way, and was born at Le Cateau Nord, on December 31, 1869. His father wanted him to become a lawyer, and put him into the office of a legal friend to pick up what knowledge he could before entering a law school. But after about a year the boy got appendicitis, and during his long convalescence at home he took up painting at the suggestion of a neighbour who had seen him sketching. The result was that when he was 20 Matisse went to Paris, where he entered the École des Beaux Arts and studied under Bouguereau. When he was 28 he married Mlle. Amelie Noellie Parayre, and before long he had a young family of a daughter and two sons. Times were hard, but besides being an excellent housewife Mme. Matisse opened a small millinery shop to help out the family income.

Then Gustave Moreau, the "mystical" painter, who may be said to have started the cult of "Salome", saw Matisse working in the Louvre, making copies of pictures there, and invited him to study in his own studio at the École des Beaux Arts which was designed to become a nursery of young rebels, the fellow pupils of Matisse. In 1897 he met the veteran Camille Pissarro and for a time worked as successfully as an Impressionist as he had as a copyist of old masters in the Louvre. On the advice of Pissarro in 1898 Matisse visited London to study Turner. Matisse was not greatly impressed by Turner, which was not surprising, because the acute interest in Paris had shifted from Impressionism, but he heard about Whistler and his Japanese prints. On his return to Paris he began to study oriental art systematically, and after a visit to Corsica, where he stayed a year, he went to Munich to see an exhibition of Moslem art, which confirmed his impression of the decorative values of the East.

Up to now, though he was experimenting, Matisse had not kicked over the traces. He was exhibiting regularly at the official Salon, and in 1904 the dealer Vollard, from whom he had bought Cézanne's "Bathers" to hang in his studio, gave him a one-man show of nearly 50 pictures. The explosion came at the Autumn Salon of 1905. For this exhibition Matisse organized a collection of works by the more advanced painters, including himself, Derain [q.v.], Braque*, Rouault, and Vlaminck [q.v.], and these were hung in a room by themselves. An indignant critic, Louis Vauxcelles, writing in *Gil Blas,* called the room a *"cage aux Fauves"* or "cage of wild beasts", and the name stuck. Beyond distortion or deformation of natural appearance in the interests of design and vehemence in statement, the Fauves had no common doctrine. Fauvism, in fact, might be described as a violent wrenching away of the picture from literal representation.

A picture that came in for special abuse was Matisse's "Woman with a Hat". This, for which Mme. Matisse was the model, was bought by the American writer Gertrude Stein, who was doing useful propaganda for the rebels. In 1906 she introduced Matisse to Picasso, who was then painting her portrait. Matisse was now celebrated. The Galerie Druet gave him a big one-man show, and in 1908 he was introduced to the American public by Alfred Steiglitz.

Fauvism in Paris was followed by Cubism, which was originated by Picasso and Braque. Matisse is credited with the invention of the name, but he does not appear to have more than flirted with Cubism, though it was he who introduced Negro sculpture to Picasso. The truth seems to be that Matisse was too much of a painter in the special sense of the word to be greatly interested in geometrical abstraction. After 1908, when, refusing to take any fees, he taught for a short time at a school in Paris opened by his friends and supporters, Matisse did not greatly change his style. He spent two years in Morocco, stayed various times at Saint Tropez, Cassis and Colliure, and travelled in America, Tahiti, Italy, and Russia. In 1917 he took a villa at Nice, where he remained more or less for the rest of his life.

On his first visit to America Matisse was violently attacked and accused of obscenity in his work, so that he begged an interviewer, "Oh please do tell the American people that I am a normal man; that I am a devoted husband and father; that I have three fine children; that I go to the theatre, ride horseback, have a comfortable home, a fine garden that I love, flowers, &c., just like any man", and this self description tallies with the impressions of an English observer who described Matisse as a quiet, sensible, bourgeois gentleman, without pose or affectation. America, too, revised its opinion, for in 1927 Matisse received a first prize at the Carnegie International, and a year or two later the Carnegie Institute invited him to be a judge in its competition.

Besides being a painter Matisse was an etcher, lithographer, and wood-engraver, and he produced a good many works of sculpture. He illustrated the poems of Mallarmé and an edition of James Joyce's *Ulysses,* published by the Limited Edition Club, New York, in 1935. His work is known all over the world, the largest collections being in the Moscow Museum of Western Art and the Barnes Foundation, Pennsylvania. Matisse, who is represented at the Tate Gallery by "Le Forêt" and "Nude", both bequeathed by C. Frank Stoop in 1933, was included in both the Post-Impressionist exhibitions at the Grafton Galleries in 1910 and 1911, and in 1937 there was a very extensive exhibition of his work at the Rosenberg and Helft Gallery in London.

Though he was already well known in artistic circles in London, it was not until 1945 that Matisse really got "into the news". In the December of that year an exhibition of works by Picasso and Matisse, arranged by La Direction Générale des Relations Culturelles and the British Council, was opened by the French Ambassador at the Victoria and Albert Museum. Criticism began mildly enough with a letter to *The Times,* signed by Professor Thomas Bodkin* and Dr. D. S. MacColl, to the effect that the war-diminished space in our galleries and museums should be devoted to the exhibition of their own historical treasures rather than to the works of two contemporary foreign painters of highly disputable merit. There followed in *The Times* a spate of correspondence for and against, many of the blows aimed at Picasso falling upon Matisse. Red herrings were strewn, but the discussion as a whole ranged round the perennial question of the distortion of natural appearance under emotion and in the interests of pictorial design.

In 1947 Matisse offered to design and build a chapel for the Dominicans of Vence, and this was consecrated in 1951. An architect built it on a plan suggested by the artist and inside Matisse painted three large compositions in black on white ceramic tiles. Last year there was an exhibition of his sculptures at the Tate Gallery, and he was honoured by the National Arts Foundation in New York as an "outstanding artist of 1953". Matisse was a member of the French Communist Party, but his standing with the communists in recent years was unclear. Criticism came from Russia of his chapel at Vence, and in 1952 the French Communist Party was reported to be considering his expulsion for not falling into line with Moscow's instructions that art must be "realistic and depict Communist ideals".

There can be no doubt about Matisse's technical competence as a painter, but graceful as they are, his innumerable "Odalisques" in Mediterranean interiors may to some minds end by becoming rather boring. Matisse himself said: "While working, I never try to think, only to feel". That is enough to explain his distortions, perhaps also his defects. As a colourist he was something more than decorative, because he had in high degree the rare capacity to establish the position of objects in the depth of the picture by the relations between colours, without the aid of linear or atmospheric perspective.

November 5, 1954.

A. E. Matthews, O.B.E., the distinguished actor, and very likely the oldest member of his profession still to rank as a leading man in the theatre and as a featured player in films and on television, died on July 25, 1960 at his home at Bushey Heath, Hertfordshire.

Alfred Edward Matthews was born at Bridlington, Yorkshire, probably on November 22, 1879. His father, William Matthews, was one of the Matthews Brothers of the original Christy Minstrels, and his great uncle, Tom Matthews, was a pupil of Grimaldi, "Matty" he had always been to his friends and "Matty" he became in time to the whole profession. Love of his work, refusal to take himself or his celebrity seriously, and enjoyment of the open air, of exercise and of the garden of his cottage helped him to keep active till the end of his long career. In his middle twenties he played and looked the part of a 17-year-old Eton boy in Barrie's *Little Mary*, just as, at the age of nearly 80, he could play and look the part of a hale and upright man of 50.

An attempt to earn his living as assistant to a city bookseller at a salary of 3s. 6d. a week was one of his few failures. Carved on his desk in the office was the name of one of his predecessors, a lad who also gave up bookselling for the stage and whose success thereon may have inspired young Matthews. The name was—then—Henry Brodribb. Matthews began his stage career as callboy at the Princess's Theatre in Oxford Street (where Waring and Gillows now stands) when he was 17. The following year, while stage manager at the Grand, Islington, one of his duties was to instruct the "supers" in their entrances and exits in George R. Sims's drama *In The Ranks.* A bright lad, a couple of years his junior, applied for such a job—at the salary of 1s. a night—and thus began a lifelong friendship. The lad's name was Seymour Hicks.

It is impossible to enumerate all the parts Matthews took, but among those that stand out are the midshipman (Ellen Terry's stage son) in *Alice Sit By The Fire;* Jack Barthwick in *The Silver Box;* Algy in *The Importance of Being Earnest,* in New York, London, and Paris; and Jerry in *Peg o' my Heart,* which he played over 700 times at one theatre alone, the Comedy.

In his early days Matthews went with Lionel Brough to South Africa, playing 43 parts in a twelve-month, and he went later to Australia in *Charley's Aunt* and *The Private Secretary*. He became as popular in the United States as he was in England, and during the 20 odd years separating the two wars he was constantly backwards and forwards across the Atlantic.

Thus he appeared in both countries as Sapper's Bulldog Drummond and as the philanderer in Lonsdale's [q.v.] *Spring Cleaning;* he was the leading man in America in such British plays as *The Last of Mrs. Cheyney, The First Mrs. Fraser, The Breadwinner,* and *Spring Meeting;* and he occasionally introduced to London an American play like *Beggar on Horseback.* He was in England, in J. B. Priestley's *They Came to a City* among other plays, almost all through the Second World War, and he paid one more visit to New York in 1949 as Lord Lister in the biggest of his post-war successes, *The Chiltern Hundreds.* He had refused to take a holiday during the play's long run in London. Or rather—he had laughed at the idea of taking a holiday, and it was dropped.

His work was the admiration of his fellow actors. He may have given the appearance of lounging through a part as Charles Hawtrey used to do, but everyone who worked with him knew there never was a more careful rehearser, more meticulous in detail, and more concerned to present a character as a whole. At the same time, this preparation did not impair his freedom of movement; colleagues indeed were sometimes disconcerted to find him never quite the same two nights running. In this he was more like a French than an English actor, though nothing could have been more upper middle class English than his manner and appearance—not to mention the deerstalker hat, which he would "forget" to remove indoors, the white silk cravat, the Norfolk jacket, the comfortable brogues. He fostered the legend of his absent-mindedness, barefacedly protesting that he never studied his lines, and that he could not remember whether he was 90 or merely 80, and that he would not and could not ever appear in the classics. When it was suggested that a chance of entering the classical field "under the banner of Molière" in *The Gay Invalid* had at last, in 1951, turned up, he replied by telegraph "Never heard of the fella but will do anything you suggest". His attempts to learn his part of Mr. Crock (Argan) were anguish to him, and he gave it up after the third performance at Manchester, but on officially rejoining the company later he was, and he remained thenceforward, word-perfect.

Matthews was twice married: first to Miss May Blayney, by whom he had twin sons and a daughter; secondly to Miss Pat Desmond. His autobiography *Matty* was published in 1953. He was appointed O.B.E. in 1951.

July 26, 1960.

Cyril Maude, the veteran actor, died at his home at Torquay on February 20, 1951 at the age of 88. He had been ill for several weeks.

Playgoers of long memory will testify to many hours of pleasure conferred upon them by the air of happiness that radiated from him. No matter how bad-tempered the character he was assuming, it was plain that he enjoyed his work and his success in his profession; and though not in the first flight of light comedians he had talent and was accomplished enough to carry his personal charm and his familiar mannerism.

Cyril Francis Maude, the eldest of the six sons of Captain C. H. Maude, of the 14th Madras Regiment, H.E.I.C., was born in St. George's Square, Pimlico, on April 24, 1862. At Charterhouse his bent for theatricals declared itself, and after a few months at an Army crammer's he went to London and studied under Charles Cartwright and Miss Le Thiere. Before he was ready to try his fortune on the stage he was pronounced to be suffering from some incurable disease. A voyage to Australia and back did not cure him; and he was sent to live an outdoor life in Canada.

At 21 he gave up farming and went to the United States, where he obtained a small engagement in the travelling company of Daniel Bandmann. A year later he was in England again and spent several years in provincial companies. He was one of the young men of good family for whom the Bancroft management had made the stage a respectable profession; but he was anxious not to be mistaken for an amateur, and he faced his portion of the drudgery which the profession in those days involved.

In 1888 he married Winifred Emery, a member of an old theatrical family and herself a fine and successful actress. Engagements came from Wyndham, Mrs. Langtry, and Comyns Carr, with whom he spent three years at the Comedy Theatre. He had parts at the Avenue Theatre in Henry Arthur Jones's *The*

Crusaders and *Judah;* and he was Cayley Drummle when Alexander produced Pinero's *The Second Mrs. Tanqueray* at the St. James's Theatre in May 1893.

In 1896 began the partnership in the Haymarket Theatre of Cyril Maude and Frederick Harrison. After 13 years on the stage he found himself joint manager of the leading comedy theatre in London, only lately vacated by Beerbohm Tree. And for nine years the Haymarket and Cyril Maude did very well for each other. The list of his parts and productions in those nine years includes Gavin Dishart in *The Little Minister,* Heath Desmond in Davies's *Cousin Kate* (and that play and that part—with Ellis Jeffreys as Kate—form one of the choicest of mature playgoers' memories), White in W. W. Jacobs's *The Monkey's Paw,* and James Barley in the same author's *Beauty and the Barge.* Besides these new plays there were some revivals of classics, with Maude as Old Hardcastle in *She Stoops to Conquer,* as Bob Acres in *The Rivals,* as Sir Peter Teazle in *The School for Scandal,* as Lord Ogleby in *The Clandestine Marriage,* and as Eccles in *Caste.*

Maude left the Haymarket in July 1905, his last part there being Joseph Lebanon in Pinero's farce *The Cabinet Minister.* He had acquired the old Avenue Theatre, next to Charing Cross Station, and it brought him little luck. In December the roof of the station fell and wrecked the theatre, which he was rebuilding; and he was a nomad for more than a year. During that year, however, he had found *Toddles,* and it was with this pleasant, popular little piece that in January 1907 he opened his new Playhouse (as he had renamed it), which showed London how charming the inside of a theatre could be with quiet decoration, mellow lights, and really comfortable armchairs in the stalls. He stayed at the Playhouse for six years; but they were not like the years at the Haymarket, and in September 1913 Cyril Maude set sail for Canada and the United States. Touring in those countries and in Australia occupied nearly all his time until the war was over. November 1919 was the date of his appearance at the Criterion in *Lord Richard in the Pantry.* With Connie Ediss as the cook, the play was a great success; and another of Maude's props in his later years was *Grumpy,* a play which he had produced in Glasgow on the eve of his first visit to Canada.

Engagements in London and the United States kept him at work until 1927, when he went to live in Devon. During his management of the Haymarket a history of that theatre had been published bearing his name, and in 1925 he had published a lively novel, *The Actor in Room 931.* In 1927 the first fruits of his leisure were an equally lively book of memories, *Behind the Scenes with Cyril Maude.*

By his first wife, who died in 1924, he was the father of a son John Maude, K.C., M.P., and of two daughters, one of whom, Margery Maude, had a brief but brilliant career on the stage which she reliquished on her marriage. In 1927 Cyril Maude married Beatrice Mary, widow of P. H. Trew.

February 21, 1951.

Lord Maugham, formerly Lord Chancellor and both as advocate and as Judge one of the brightest ornaments of the Chancery Bar, died on March 23, 1958 at his home in London. He was 91.

In the history of the Lord Chancellors of England Lord Maugham is remarkable for having achieved the Woolsack by legal attainments alone without the aid of party politics. Apart from his tenure of the office of Lord Chancellor, he will rank high among the judges of his generation; indeed, his career from his call to the Bar is one long tale of continuous success, and, unlike many successful advocates, he more than fulfilled on the Bench the hopes of those who in his early days had foreseen for him high judicial office. He was born into a legal world. His grandfather was one of the founders, and was for 35 years secretary, of the Law Society, and his father, Robert Ormond Maugham, practised as a solicitor in Paris, and was for many years legal adviser of the British Embassy there, a post afterwards held by his son, the late judge's elder brother. His younger brother is Mr. Somerset Maugham*, the novelist and dramatist.

The Right Hon. Sir Frederic Herbert Maugham, first Viscount Maugham, of Hartfield, Sussex, in the peerage of the United Kingdom, was born on October 20, 1866. He was educated at Dover College and Trinity Hall, Cambridge, of which he was a scholar, and where he was a Senior Optime in the Mathematical Tripos in 1888. This was the heroic era of Trinity Hall rowing, and in 1887, the year in which Cambridge won every event at Henley and the Hall succeeded in the unprecedented task of winning five trophies, Maugham rowed in the 2nd College Eight, which carried off both the Ladies' Plate and the Thames Cup. He rowed in the University Eight in 1888 and 1889. He was president of the Union in 1887, and later an Honorary Fellow of his College. Lincoln's Inn called him to the Bar in 1890, and he was a Bencher there long before he obtained the judicial ermine. He soon acquired a large practice and took silk in 1913. In the meantime, in 1896, he had married Helen Mary, daughter of the late Sir Robert Romer, Lord Justice Romer "the Elder", and father of Lord Romer, whose colleague in the Court of Appeal and in the House of Lords Maugham was later destined to be. As a silk Maugham was an immediate success, and as a "special" he appeared before the House of Lords in most of the important equity appeals of his day, and he was constantly briefed before the Judicial Committee of the Privy Council.

While the election of 1922 was in progress he received a message from the Conservative "shadow cabinet" that if he could obtain a seat the Prime Minister would offer him the position of Solicitor-General. However, much to his disappointment, no seat could be found for him, so his career for a time took a course away from politics. When Mr. Justice (afterwards Lord) Russell was promoted to the Court of Appeal in 1928 Lord Hailsham's nomination of Maugham for the vacant judgeship was expected and applauded, and it proved an unqualified success. At the Bar Maugham's manner had been slightly supercilious and never very genial, but during most of his career there he had been thoroughly overworked, to which his occasional irritability may in fairness be ascribed. All this, however, seemed to disappear on his elevation to the Bench, where from the first he added courtesy and consideration to great rapidity in the disposal of his work.

His knowledge of case law was immense, but he never allowed it to cramp his breadth of view and independence of mind, and as a Judge of first instance he contributed a large number of decisions of first-rate importance to the reports. He seldom reserved a judgment, and not an instance can be recalled where one of his decisions of importance was reversed. The grave economic crisis through which Britain was passing at the time brought before him many schemes for the reorganization of public companies, and in sanctioning or refusing these he showed himself the vigilant guardian of the rights of shareholders, who as a rule understand little enough of what is being proposed with regard to their property.

On the resignation of Lord Justice Lawrence, in January 1934, Maugham was nominated to fill the vacancy, with the full approval of the profession, tempered with regret that the strongest judge in the Chancery Courts would function there no longer. He remained in the Court of Appeal under two years, for on the death of Lord Tomlin during the long vacation of 1935 Maugham, though one of the junior members of that Court, was nominated as a Lord of Appeal in Ordinary, again with the full approval of the Bar.

In the House of Lords Lord Maugham not infrequently intervened in debates on legal measures, and he took a prominent part in the discussions of the Matrimonial Causes Bill in 1937. His was the amendment embodied in the Act reducing the period during which a petition for divorce cannot be entertained from five to three years after marriage, subject to the discretion of the Court to reduce this period in cases of exceptional hardship. Shortly before his appointment as Lord Chancellor he introduced in the House of Lords the Law of Evidence Bill, in the drafting of which he had been prominently concerned, and soon afterwards, as Lord Chancellor, he had the satisfaction of having the Royal Assent given to that valuable measure.

But a combination of unexpected circumstances was soon to call Lord Maugham to a position of far greater importance in the debates of the Upper House. In March 1938 Chamberlain decided partly to reconstruct his Government, and it was obvious that in any such reconstruction the position of Lord Chancellor would have to be considered. For some 18 months Lord Hailsham had, through ill health, been unable to sit judicially and it was only with difficulty and often with obvious discomfort that he had been able to preside on the Woolsack, so he was willing to assume the less onerous position of Lord President of the Council. The appointment of his successor as Lord Chancellor presented some difficulty. For various reasons no suitable candidate in the ordinary line of legal promotion was available, so the Prime Minister decided upon what amounted to a non-political appointment, and naturally the Lords of Appeal in Ordinary presented a brilliant field for selection. Though 71 years of age, Lord Maugham was by no means the senior Law Lord in point of service, and it was rumoured at the time that more than one of his colleagues considered that they had a higher claim; but Chamberlain's choice was, at any rate by the legal profession, cordially approved, and was certainly justified.

The new Lord Chancellor was plunged at once into the rough waters of the highly contentious Coal Bill, of which he was principally in charge for the Government. In the earlier stages of its discussion his somewhat direct speaking, perhaps due to his unfamiliarity with the atmosphere of political polemics, gave rise to some acrimonious criticism by opponents of the Bill; but before the debate closed handsome tributes were paid to him for his able conduct of the measure. In spite of Lord Maugham's great intellectual qualities his tenure of the Woolsack will hardly be remembered as the most successful phase of his career.

In the early days of the war, when the assistance of the Lord Chancellor was constantly invoked by the Departments in connexion with the drafting of emergency legislation, he was not always easy to work with, and it was complained that he would often take a too narrow and unpractical view of a question and adhere to it with uncompromising obstinacy—faults to which great lawyers are sometimes prone. When he assumed office it had been understood that he regarded himself only as a stopgap, and when Chamberlain reconstituted his Government in September 1939 Maugham relinquished the Great Seal, and resumed for two years his post as a Lord of Appeal in succession to Lord Macmillan [q.v.], who became Minister of Information. He was, as is now customary, created a viscount.

Maugham was a widely cultivated man, interested in many things, and in congenial society he was an agreeable companion. As has been shown, his rowing was of a high order, and when those days were over he shot and played golf; in his younger days at the Savile Club he played a good game of billiards.

He was widely travelled on the Continent, and he spoke French with ease. The literary aptitude of his family found expression not only in his judgments but in his masterly study of *The Case of Jean Calas*, the mysterious murder at Toulouse, which since the days of Voltaire has engaged and intrigued the curiosity of the learned, and in his much longer work on the Tichborne case, published in 1936. In 1944 he published what was regarded—whether agreed with or not—as a masterly defence of the Munich agreement, *The Truth about the Munich Crisis*.

In 1951 he published *U.N.O. and War Crimes*, criticizing the drafting of the Charter of the International Tribunal, and raising grave doubts as to the justification of the sentences pronounced at Nuremberg under international law. In 1954, at the age of 88, he published his autobiography. On the whole it was a disappointing work, at least to lawyers.

Lady Maugham died in 1950. Their son, Robin Maugham, a novelist and barrister-at-law, succeeds to the title.

March 24, 1958.

Rear-Admiral Loben Edward Harold Maund, C.B.E., who served with distinction in the Royal Navy in both world wars, died on June 18, 1957 at Fittleworth, Sussex, at the age of 64. Maund was in command of the legendary aircraft carrier H.M.S. Ark Royal at the time when she was sunk by German torpedoes in November 1941.

He was born on September 26, 1892, and showed something of his mettle early in life, gaining the King's Medal at Osborne and Dartmouth in 1905-09. Passing for lieutenant just before the First World War, with three "firsts", he served in destroyers during hostilities and commanded one, H.M.S. Scorpion, from March 1918. He graduated at the Staff College in 1923 and was afterwards staff officer with Sir Herbert Richmond in the East Indies. In 1929-30 he was Naval Assistant Secretary to the Committee of Imperial Defence and from 1931 to 1933 was executive officer of the aircraft-carrier H.M.S. Courageous. In June 1935 Maund was appointed Assistant Director of Plans and after a spell in this appointment was, in 1936, placed in command of the Danae, which had been in reserve at Devonport.

In 1938 he was appointed Commandant of the Combined Operations Development Centre and thus began his connexion with the theory and practice of amphibious warfare under modern conditions. He was Naval Chief of Staff in the Narvik expedition and served either in Combined Operations headquarters or training establishments, or in amphibious operations themselves, for the greater part of the rest of the war. The long transition from the ill-fated Narvik campaign to the efficiency of the Sicilian, Calabrian, and Normandy landings of the later war years had two sides—the evolution and production of amphibious craft suited to modern conditions and the training of officers and men in the art of waterborne assault. Maund had a share in both tasks and told the story of them fully and comprehensively in *Assault from the Sea*.

Maund's command of the aircraft-carrier Ark Royal began in the year after Narvik, and he took part in the operation against the Bismarck and in three hazardous convoys to Malta. He was the Ark Royal's last captain. Though not perhaps a beautiful ship, to the lay eye even a top-heavy one, lacking the terrier dash of the destroyer and the Olympian might of the battleship, Ark Royal had, nevertheless, long since captured the imagination of the British people. The gibes and prognostications of doom emitted by "Lord Haw-haw" did but serve to win for Ark Royal a greater affection, but in November 1941 German torpedoes did what German propaganda had failed to do. At Gibraltar, after the sinking, Maund paid striking tribute both to ship and crew, and a few days later kicked off at a football match at Gibraltar between the Ark Royal team and one from The Black Watch.

In 1942-43 Maund was Director of Combined Operations Middle East and India and from 1944 to 1945 Rear-Admiral Landing Ships and Craft. He was made C.B.E. in 1941.

June 20, 1957.

Major-General Sir Frederick Maurice, K.C.M.G., C.B., who died on May 19, 1951 at his home at Cambridge, came under popular notice in somewhat sensational fashion during the 1914-18 war when, in 1918, he challenged in all sincerity the good faith of the Prime Minister and by this act ended his own military career.

His talents and disposition were admirably suited for work upon the staff, and he held a long succession of staff appointments. Those with whom he served were impressed by his efficiency, loyalty, and capacity for friendship; he never held any important command either in peace or war. After leaving the Army, however, he wrote prolifically and attained considerable academic distinction. He was also keenly interested in the British Legion, of which he was president from 1932 until 1947.

Frederick Barton Maurice was born on January 19, 1871, the eldest son of General Sir Frederick Maurice and grandson of Frederick Denison Maurice. He chose the Army as a career and was gazetted to The Derbyshire Regiment (now The Sherwood Foresters) in 1892. After a brief period as A.D.C. to his father, he served in the Tirah Expedition. On the outbreak of the South African war he was sent out as a special service officer. For his services in South Africa he was promoted brevet major (at the age of 29) and was mentioned in dispatches. He passed into the Staff College in 1902, and was successively brigade major to 19 Brigade, IV Corps, 11 Brigade, Eastern Command, and a G.S.O.2 at the War Office in the Directorate of Staff Duties under Major-General Douglas Haig. In 1913 he went as an instructor to the Staff College, where his distinguished father had been Professor of Military History some 20 years earlier.

For the first nine months of Maurice's service at the Staff College, Major-General, later Field-Marshal, Sir William Robertson was Commandant, and a close friendship began which was maintained through all the ensuing years. This friendship had a marked influence on Maurice's future career. When the war broke out in 1914 he went to France as G.S.O.2 on the staff of 3 Division (Major-General Hubert Hamilton) and before the end of August succeeded Colonel Boileau as G.S.O.1 in the division. Sir William Robertson became Chief of the General Staff, British Expeditionary Force, at the end of January 1915, and in April selected Maurice to be head of the operations branch with the rank of Brigadier-General, General Staff. Maurice thoroughly understood his chief's method of work and served him admirably. Sir William Robertson became

Chief of the Imperial General Staff in December 1915, and he at once appointed Maurice to be Director of Military Operations. Maurice's last promotion came in 1916, when he was made major-general at the age of 45. Until Sir William Robertson relinquished his appointment in February 1918 Maurice worked with him in the complete accord which had marked their association in France. Early in May Maurice was giving up his War Office Directorate and about to take up an appointment in France. At this moment he wrecked his career by an act of indiscipline which could not be ignored by his military superiors, however much they may have appreciated his motives.

Early in April 1918 the Prime Minister (Lloyd George), defending the Government against the charge of having contributed to the March disasters by refusing to strengthen the Army in France with drafts that were available at home, said in the House of Commons that on January 1, 1918, the Army in France was "considerably stronger" than it had been on January 1, 1917.

On May 7 a letter signed by Maurice appeared in the London newspapers giving the direct lie to this and other similar statements made by the Prime Minister and Mr. Bonar Law. Maurice described himself as actuated by his duty as a citizen, which he felt must override his duty as a soldier, whatever the consequences to his career; yet it was a grave breach of the Regulations. Maurice was right in fact. The figures employed by the Prime Minister had been supplied to him by the appropriate department of the War Office and, as they supported his case, he used them to the full, but a change in the methods of calculating the strength in fighting troops of the Army in France had made it appear that there had been an increase instead of a substantial decrease in the fighting strength by the beginning of 1918. The end was swift. The case was considered by the Army Council and Maurice was removed from the active list in May. Earlier in the year he received his last war honour, when he was created K.C.M.G.

Later Maurice became Military Correspondent to the *Daily Chronicle*, changing later to the *Daily News*. From 1922 to 1933 he was Principal of the Working Men's College, St. Pancras, which his grandfather had helped to found in 1854. He was given the honorary degree of LL.D. at Cambridge in 1926, and became a D.Litt of London University four years later.

In 1927 he was appointed Professor of Military Studies at London University, and a year later became chairman of the Adult Education Committee, Ministry of Education. He was honorary treasurer of the British Legion from 1930, and became its president in 1932. In 1930 also he was appointed a trustee of the Imperial War Museum (from which he resigned in 1945) and elected a member of the Senate of the University of London. He was Principal of the East London College (University of London) from 1933 until 1944, and he was appointed an honorary Fellow in 1946. He also became an honorary Fellow of King's College, Cambridge, in 1944.

A prolific writer, his published military historical studies have embraced the Russo-Turkish war, 1877-8, and Robert E. Lee. He also wrote a life of his father, and collaborated with Sir George Arthur in a biography of Lord Wolseley. His *Life of General Lord Rawlinson of Trent* appeared in 1928. Among his other books are *Governments and War, British Strategy*, based on a series of lectures, and *The 16th Foot. Forty Days in 1914* is an excellent study of the B.E.F. in the opening campaign; *The Last Four Months* is hardly on the same level. Sir Frederick was a contributor to many magazines and reviews, and also to the *Cambridge Modern History*.

He married in 1899 Helen Margaret, daughter of the late Professor Howard Marsh, Master of Downing College, Cambridge, and had one son and four daughters. She died in 1942.

May 21, 1951.

The death at Tours on November 16, 1952 of **Charles Maurras,** the French royalist leader, removes a strange and wayward figure who, whatever his faults and follies, added spice if not much substance to the public life of France. Maurras lived in—and, perhaps, for—controversy. He died as he would have wished: a provocation to controversy.

He was born at Martigues, in Provence, in 1868. His father was a minor Civil servant of republican sentiments; he died when Charles was still a child. His mother, a devout Catholic, went to great pains to see that the son received a strict religious education at the Catholic College of Aix. Curiously, two of the priests to whom it was entrusted became bishops. He himself, when his schooling was ended, accepted the positivism of Comte. It was typical of his temperament. He began by writing on literary subjects in the reviews, and joined Moréas to found what they called l'École Romane; but he soon found his *métier* in political journalism, and entered upon a career of restless and passionate activity. His polemics were pugnacious and violent—and on occasion even virulent and vicious; but his brilliant literary gifts were unquestioned. At first he fulminated in various papers, including the *Figaro;* but it was as joint editor, with Léon Daudet, of the *Action Française*, that, from 1908, Maurras found his real platform, from which to propound, at first bi-monthly and then daily, the eternal virtue of monarchy. His following, mainly among Gallican and almost anti-Papal Catholics, grew; and the *Action Française* became not only a newpaper but, as its name implied, an active and noisy propagandist association of young Royalists.

What led Maurras to espouse royalism was simply explained. "Democracy is evil, democracy is death", he preached with endless variations. One besetting sin of France, and the source of all her supineness, was her disorder. In hereditary government—that is, through monarchy—she would find strength and stability and, hence, salvation. This was his obsession, and in the case of Maurras it had all the excesses of obsession. His longing for the renewal of the greatness and glory of France was genuine enough, but it assumed odd forms. He was prepared to accept an admitted injustice to Dreyfus rather than have the good faith of France brought into question. He attacked Caillaux during the 1914-18 war, but he also assailed Briand after the war because he brought about Locarno. He began a campaign against the Catholic hierarchy because, among other things, it blessed the efforts to achieve a French-German *rapprochement*—a campaign that had a certain vileness about it and ended in the *Action Française* being put on the Index.

He was on sounder ground in castigating the financial scandals of Stavisky and others which disgraced the French Parliamentary régime. In 1937 he was sentenced to a term of imprisonment for incitement to murder Blum, then Prime Minister of France, who had, in fact, been severely beaten up in the Paris streets by a group of young *Action Française* members four months before he became Premier. Yet, when Maurras was elected to the Academy, notwithstanding thunder on the Left, which is not strong in that eminent body, most people were ready enough to acknowledge that his literary work, for all its non-conformity, merited the homage of his country.

After the collapse of 1940 he probably reflected mournfully that if only his warning words had been heeded France would have been spared her unhappy fate of being at a foreign country's mercy. He was anti-British, but hardly pro-German. He was a Pétainist [q.v.], but Laval was not a leader he could follow. After the liberation of France Maurras was arrested and condemned in 1945 for collaborating with the enemy; but he continued to carry on much of his polemical writing from his prison cell. He was released from prison in March 1952 on the ground of ill-health and ordered to reside near Tours. In captivity he also wrote a book of poems and an *Apologie de Socrate*. He had been excluded from the Academy after his condemnation in 1945.

Maurras published about 20 books. The earlier ones were poems and philosophical and literary studies—his *Amants de Venise* was a penetrating analysis of the George Sand and de Musset love affair, and his *Avenir de l'Intelligence* a bitter attack on the enslavement of brains by money. The later books were almost all aggressively political. As a vigorous personality, Maurras possessed an undoubted power of attracting support and arousing enthusiasm; and enthusiasm he never himself lacked until the day of his death. One could not help being animated by him, however much one disagreed with him. In his later years he became so deaf that one could only converse with him by placing one's mouth close to the centre of his forehead and shouting, for he would never use hearing aids. But that hardly diminished his vivacity and the stimulating quality of his talk.

November 17, 1952.

Osborne Henry Mavor—See **Bridie.**

Professor Sir Douglas Mawson, O.B.E., F.R.S., the eminent Antarctic explorer and Emeritus Professor in Geology in the University of Adelaide, died in that city on October 14, 1958. He was 76.

Mawson ranks high among Antarctic explorers less by reason of arduous adventure or epic marches, though he had his share of those, than for the dominantly scientific character of his work. He was, first and foremost, a geologist and mineralogist who regarded Antarctic exploration from a frankly utilitarian point of view. On his return from his first visit to the Antarctic, when he accompanied Shackleton's expedition of 1907, he set himself to persuade the Australian people of the potential wealth of the seas and continent to the south.

Exaggerated hopes of realizing that wealth have long since been dispatched, but it is now a commonplace that Australia cannot afford to neglect the field of meteorological, biological, and mineral research opened up in Antarctica, and this change in outlook is almost entirely to the credit of Mawson. At the same time, his solid achievements were transcended for the public by his enterprise, courage, and endurance. His death now, however, will be recognized as a great loss to Australian science. In his vigour and initiative he typified the best traits of Australian character; in his intellectual powers he was among the first of the brilliant group of geologists who have followed up so thoroughly the earlier explorations of the interior of Australia. And in his work in the Antarctic he was never carried away by success to embark on showy projects; he lent his support to nothing which he did not sincerely believe to be in the interests of scientific knowledge.

Mawson had had an early introduction to scientific inquiry under rigorous conditions. Born at Bradford, Yorkshire, on May 5, 1882, he went to Australia as a boy with his parents, and graduated in science at the University of Sydney. With a reputation already as a mineralogist and geologist, he then joined a Government expedition which was to report on the geology of the New Hebrides. The expedition at first worked under armed escort, but presently pushed on alone into the interior among head-hunting tribes, where white men had never been, and obtained data which was the material for several brilliant papers and reports by Mawson. Soon after his return to Australia he was appointed, in 1905, lecturer in mineralogy and petrology at the University of Adelaide, the beginning of a long connexion. (He was Professor in Geology from 1920 to 1952).

Only two years later he was granted extended leave to accompany Shackleton to the south. From the records of this expedition the world first learnt of his great gifts for organization and intrepid leadership. He was one of the first party to climb Mt. Erebus (13,370ft.), where he took the measurements of the crater; and he was one of the northern party of three who, under the late Sir Edgeworth David, left the base in October 1908—while Shackleton was on his great southern journey—to find the South Magnetic Pole. The party sledged hazardously up the Ross Sea on the sea-ice, struck inland on to the ice-plateau and arrived over the daily fluctuating Pole, according to Mawson's reckoning, on January 16.

The journey to the Magnetic Pole and back covered about 1,260 miles. Mawson did an immense amount of work, including a triangulation survey. Once he fell through a snow lid into a crevasse, and hung there dangling at the end of his sledge harness, the fastenings of which were worn. His companions let down an Alpine rope, and, with great difficulty, hauled him up again; while he was swinging between the walls of the crevasse, he coolly picked some ice crystals and threw them up for examination.

On the very day of the party's return to the coast they were sighted and picked up by the relief ship.

The Australian Antarctic expedition of 1912-14, under the auspices of the Australian Government, was organized by Mawson himself.

Its objects were to explore the coastline of Antarctica lying due south of Australia between South Victoria Land and Kaiser Wilhelm II Land, to study the mineral resources of the land enclosed by that arc, and, especially, to investigate the meteorology of the region in the light of its relation to Australian weather.

In all these essentially practical aims the expedition was successful. The coastline was recharted and new land discovered, a report was drawn up on the considerable mineral wealth found, and results of the greatest utility were achieved by the meteorological investigators. For the first time in Antarctic exploration wireless telegraphy was used, constant communication with Australia being maintained through the station on Macquarie Island set up on the way south.

It was on November 9, 1912, that Mawson, Dr. X. Mertz, a Swiss zoologist, and Lieutenant B. E. S. Ninnis, of the Royal Fusiliers, started on the most memorable of the many sledge journeys undertaken by the expedition, eastwards from the base, across the margin of the ice-plateau. On December 13, when they had gone 280 miles, Ninnis with his dog team and nearly all the food fell into a crevasse and was seen no more. For nine hours the other two looked down into the ice-chasm, hoping against hope. They then set out on the return with 10 days' food for themselves and none for their dogs, whom they were soon reduced to eating. Mertz rapidly weakened and on January 7 died, 100 miles from the base.

Mawson wrote in his diary: "I read the burial service over Xavier [Mertz] this afternoon. As there is little chance of my reaching human aid alive, I greatly regret inability at the moment to set out the detail of the coastline met with for 300 miles travelled, and observations of glacier and ice-formations, &c., the most of which latter are, of course, committed to my head".

He struggled on, narrowly escaping death in a crevasse himself. When only five miles from the base, illness and bad weather confined him in an ice-cave for a week. He reached the base at last on February 8, after a month of such loneliness and strain as only an iron resolution and endurance could survive.

He had been nearly given up for lost, and the Aurora had sailed for home a few hours before. She was recalled by wireless, but could not make communication again with the shore. Mawson and those who had remained behind for him had to spend another winter in Adelie Land. It was not a wasted year, for the previous winter's scientific programme was repeated with useful results.

Home once more, Mawson found himself famous while still a young man. In Britain, which he visited late in 1914, his name was acclaimed with those of Scott and Shackleton. He was knighted and awarded the Founder's Medal of the Royal Geographical Society and the King's Polar Medal. With little respite, however, he had to set to work to clear off the deficit of several thousand pounds in which the miscarriage of the relief plans had involved the expedition.

With characteristic energy he did a great deal towards this by personal appeal and by lecturing. Outside help and the success of his book, *The Home of the Blizzard*, did the rest. During the latter part of the war he was employed on military service in Great Britain as an embarkation officer, but he presently returned to Australia and resumed his work at Adelaide University. This had already established him as perhaps the leading mineralogist in the Commonwealth. In 1909 he won his doctorate for a study of the Broken Hill mineral field. Two years later he had surveyed in the same area the first radium deposit found in Australia. He was indefatigable in field work and was accustomed to visit for long periods the metalliferous region in the north-east of South Australia, where his good comradeship and enthusiasm made him a welcome guest in the hut of more than one boundary-rider or out-station overseer.

He was not again in the Antarctic until 1929, when he organized and led a scientific party in the Discovery, Captain Scott's old ship, for the purpose of charting parts of the Southern Ocean and the Antarctic seaboard, and investigating marine and bird life. The ship made two voyages from Australia and a great deal of data was collected. Mawson's own lively narrative of the incidents of the voyage appeared in *The Times*.

The ship left Cape Town in October 1929 and entered the pack early in December in 60deg. south latitude, and it became impenetrable at only 65deg. south until a gale gave an opening south-westwards to 67deg. in 72deg. east longitude. Land sighted to the south-east from a seaplane was named after MacRobertson, a principal benefactor of the expedition. Later a large bay was discovered west of Enderby Land. Shortage of coal compelled Discovery to return in April 1930, but after refitting she left Tasmania again in November 1930, and a landing was made on Macquarie Island, south of which a submarine ridge was traced for 100 miles. Seaplane flights showed the trends of the coast west of Wilkes Land; and Banzare Land and Sabrina Land were discovered. Reaching Queen Mary Land the amount of ice was found to be much less than in 1911, and in 67deg. east Discovery was able to sail farther south than the year before so that a new land, named after Princess Elizabeth, was sighted from the air. A large bay between Princess Elizabeth Land and MacRobertson Land was surveyed and named Mackenzie Sea.

In 1934 Mawson took an investigating team into the centre of Australia to examine meteorite craters.

Tall and spare, with long, thin face, high forehead, and serious expression, Mawson suggested at first sight rather the student than the active explorer. But he was strongly built, and his journeys showed that he was possessed of unusual stamina. His character was marked by great strength of purpose and determination to succeed, and few explorers have achieved a higher reputation by the leadership of a single expedition.

He married, in 1914, Paquita, daughter of G. D. Delprat, C.B.E., of Amsterdam and Melbourne, and had two daughters.

October 15, 1958.

General Sir Ivor Maxse, K.C.B., C.V.O., D.S.O., died on January 28, 1958 in a Midhurst nursing home at the age of 95. He was a man of marked originality both in his ways and in his military ideas, and was probably the most dynamic trainer of troops for war that the British Army has known in modern times.

Maxse's powers of training were attested by a signal success in 1916. In the Somme offensive his 18th Division achieved a striking success, penetrating deeply into the German positions at comparatively small loss. Before the offensive Maxse's original training methods had met with considerable criticism and opposition, but the day justified both the man and his methods. The capture of Thiepval, for months an impregnable obstacle, was yet another triumph for the 18th Division. After the spring disasters of 1918 he was appointed inspector-general of training of the British armies in France and, with a band of enthusiastic disciples, he preached the new gospel of infiltration and manoeuvre until it permeated the Army. The effect contributed in no small measure to our economical victories in the autumn.

After the 1914-18 War, when he became G.O.C.-in-C., Northern Command, it was under his influence and encouragement that these principles were developed and embodied in the post-war official doctrine, and the infantry freed from the rigidity of trench-warfare methods which, for a time, were upheld by a strong rival school of thought. Further, when he finished his command in 1923, he left as legacies of his work the reorganization of the system of depôt training, and the foundation of a great new military training centre at Catterick, foreseen by him as the Aldershot of the North.

A man of extreme quickness of thought and action, he did not suffer fools gladly, and his manner often frightened subordinates of weak character. Looking back, one may hazard the opinion that it was designed as a test of character, for no man was more generous to those who did not flinch, or more free from pettiness. And his manner covered the kindliest of hearts, as well as a rare unselfishness in helping younger men of promise. In the Army, as in other professions, many will recognize youth to the extent of "picking its brains", but few will give full credit and take none, while even concealing their own kind actions. Of this kind was Ivor Maxse, and it is but one of many reasons why he is held in such enduring affection by those who served him.

Frederick Ivor Maxse was the eldest son of Admiral Frederick Augustus Maxse, the friend of George Meredith. Admiral Maxse's mother was Caroline FitzHardinge, a daughter of the fifth Earl of Berkeley. Maxse's brother, Leo, was famous as the founder and editor of the *National Review,* and his younger sister is the widow of Lord Edward Cecil and of Lord Milner [Viscountess Milner, q.v.]. He was born on December 22, 1862, and educated at Rugby. From Sandhurst he was gazetted to the (7th) Royal Fusiliers in 1882. Seven years later, after being promoted captain, and stimulated thereto by his relatives, he applied for an exchange into the Foot Guards and was transferred to the Coldstream in May 1891. During 1893 he served as A.D.C. to Lieutenant-General Sir A. J. Lyon Fremantle, commanding the Scottish District, and in January 1894 went to Malta with his chief, who was appointed Governor and Commander-in-Chief. This post, however, was not altogether to Maxse's liking, as he preferred regimental duty, and also London life, so he resigned.

It was unfortunate for Maxse that at this period he should not have turned his thoughts towards the Staff College. But military ambition was to prevail. Two years later, in January 1897, he applied to be seconded for service with the Egyptian Army and went to Cairo. He was first employed on the personal staff, and in that capacity went through the summer campaign of 1897, being present at the action of Abu Hamed. In December of that year, after receiving his majority, he became a brigade-major with the Egyptian forces. Very soon afterwards he received command of the 13th Sudanese Battalion. The 13th participated in the battles of the Atbara and of Khartoum and were employed in the final overthrow of the Dervish forces during 1899. A brevet of lieutenant-colonel resulted for its commanding officer.

As he was still serving in Egypt, Maxse, in spite of his wishes, could not reach South Africa at the outbreak of war—in fact, it was only owing to Lord Kitchener's recommendation that he was allowed to leave Egypt when he did. On arrival at Cape Town in December 1900 he was at once selected for the duty of transport officer during Lord Roberts's forthcoming advance, and was appointed a D.A.A.G. He was thus present at the relief of Kimberley, the action at Paardeberg, and the remaining operations culminating in the occupation of Pretoria. In November 1903 he became a regimental lieutenant-colonel, and a brevet colonel in January 1905. He commanded a battalion of the Coldstream for nearly four years. His advancement had hitherto been rapid. But at this period he began to feel the results of not possessing the Staff College certificate and of not having held any more important position in the South African campaign. In August 1910, however, he was elected to command the 1st (Guards) Infantry Brigade at Aldershot and held that command for four years.

He was due to leave his brigade when the 1914-18 War broke out. Consequently, in August 1914 Maxse took the first brigade to France, in the 1st Division of I Corps under Sir Douglas Haig. This division did not come into action at Mons or Le Cateau, but on August 26 at Etreux Maxse's rearguard, consisting of The Munster Fusiliers, became isolated from the brigade and was badly cut up. This was his only action in the retreat. At the Battle of the Marne, on September 8, the 1st Brigade found the passage across the stream Le Morin at Sablonnières, but otherwise was not seriously engaged. At the Battle of the Aisne Maxse took a prominent part in the fighting of the 14th, the great day of the battle. Meanwhile Maxse's promotion to major-general had been gazetted. Consequently, on October 1, he was sent home to command the 18th Division of the New Armies, and he thus missed all the fighting at Ypres. In fact he remained at home until the following autumn.

At the front Maxse's 18th Division was not highly tried until the following year. Then, at the beginning of the Battle of the Somme, the 18th Division captured the whole of its objectives on the first day. Later, moved to the valley of the River Ancre, it captured Thiepval and the Schwaben Redoubt, a really brilliant achievement. At the beginning of 1917 Maxse received the command of the XVIII Army Corps, with the temporary rank of lieutenant-general. In March 1918 the Corps became involved in the Fifth Army's retreat before Ludendorff's great offensive. Maxse's troops managed to survive some of the worst trials of the retreat, but suffered grievously. In April, after the reorganization of his broken divisions, he was nominated to act as Inspector-General of Training in France, and continued in that appointment until after the Armistice.

In May 1919 he was selected for the appointment of G.O.C.-in-C., Northern Command, and remained at York until the end of October 1923, shortly after being promoted full general. He was not employed again, and retired in the autumn of 1926, when he went to his Sussex home, where he devoted himself to horticulture.

Maxse received the D.S.O. in 1898. He was made a C.B. in 1900 and a C.V.O. in 1907, and was promoted to K.C.B. in 1917. He was appointed Colonel of The Middlesex Regiment in 1921. For original exploration on the River Sobat, in the Sudan, he was elected F.R.G.S. in 1899. He was the author of *Seymour Vandeleur* (1906).

In December 1899 he married the Hon. Mary Caroline Wyndham, daughter of the second Lord Leconfield and author of *The Story of Fittleworth.* They had two sons and one daughter. Lady Maxse died on January 21, 1944.

January 29, 1958.

William Maxwell, who died on October 12, 1957 at the age of 84, was for many years managing director of R. & R. Clark, the Edinburgh printers.

William Maxwell was born at Leith, the port of Edinburgh, in 1873. His parents were Orcadians, "children of the sea and soil of Scotland", he used to say. He was put to school before reaching five years of age and by the time he was 12 he had passed through all its classes, including the "ex-seventh". Having learnt all that the school could teach him, which was little more than the three R's, he spent a year as unpaid amanuensis to his headmaster, his chief duty being to collect, count and stack the pennies which pupils contributed to the cost of a board school education.

Without consulting his parents he got a job as office boy to a wholesale grocer when he was 13, and five years later he was cashier and correspondence and confidential clerk to the proprietor. In 1892 he secured a post as correspondence clerk in the office of R. & R. Clark and then began the association with printing that lasted until his retirement as managing director of the firm in 1949.

Clark's printed—they still print—the papers of the Court of Session, and young Maxwell's duties occasionally took him there. He was not long in discovering that the official court reporters had a staff of devils who worked at night transcribing from dictation the day's proceedings which had to be produced in court the next morning. After a nine-hour day at Clark's Maxwell began a regular eight hours shift with these reporters, taking and transcribing 1,500 words an hour, thus earning 25s. a night.

He had been hired by James Kirkwood, joint managing director with Edward Clark, the only son of Robert, founder of the firm. Gradually he came closer to Edward and eventually became his confidant, not only in business but in private affairs. In 1910 he presented Edward Clark with a complete scheme of reorganization of the Brandon Street Works, a scheme that was accepted and carried out by 1914, when Maxwell became secretary of the company. In 1912 the firm sent him on an American tour; and in 1920 he became a director. Edward Clark, who died in 1926, nominated Maxwell in his will as managing director. Maxwell was already a considerable figure in the printing trade. Vice-president of the Edinburgh Master Printers' Federation since 1923, he declined the presidency in 1926 only because he became president of the Scottish Alliance in that year.

That was the year of the general strike; and even after work was resumed great bitterness informed the relations between the employers and the operatives. As chairman of the negotiating committee Maxwell's moderation was hindered by the obduracy of some of his colleagues. A "ranker" himself, he might well have been suspect on both sides. The measure of his success may be gauged by his subsequent election to honorary membership of the trade union; and he would conclude the telling of this story by saying that if anything would get him into heaven it would be the production of his union card. In 1929 this side of his career culminated in his election as president of the Master Printers' Federation.

Clark's have never employed a traveller. In the 1850s Robert Clark, the founder of the firm, made his first journey to London to enlarge his scope from law printing to book work. Ever since, it has been the firm's practice to send a director to London regularly to take personal instructions from publishers and other clients. In this way the firm's unique relationship with Shaw began in 1898 with the printing of *Plays Pleasant and Unpleasant.* James Shand has recorded and annotated the details of this relationship as they relate to Maxwell in an illustrated article in No. 8 of *Alphabet and Image.* In a letter to "My dear William" in 1946 Shaw wrote of this collaboration with Clark's that it had been for nearly 50 years "as natural a part of my workshop as the pen in my hand". And while he remembers Edward Clark "it was with you that our business relations developed into a cordial personal relationship which has been of inestimable value to me as an author". Maxwell rightly regarded his work and friendship with Shaw as the consummate triumph of his career. His personal files show how early Shaw grasped the importance of Maxwell's expert sympathy in solving typographical problems; and the story of Shaw's reluctant conviction that machine-setting had superseded hand composition is only one of many examples of the very individual and particular association between the two men.

In 1949 Maxwell celebrated his retirement by a lengthy visit to relations in the Antipodes. The Australian printers saw to it that the presence of so notable a colleague did not pass unhonoured, and Maxwell complained that official functions interfered with fishing.

Maxwell carried on a great tradition and gave it new lustre. In Robert Clark's day Stevenson had already communicated direct with him as a printer, giving detailed instructions on the production of his work. Maxwell extended this practice, notably with Shaw, but also with Hardy, Kipling, the Sitwells**, Hugh Walpole, James Stephens, and Charles Morgan [q.v.], whom he regarded as a model author in his careful preparation of a typescript and the minimal extent of his proof correction. He encouraged authors to consult him and to interest themselves in the typographical presentation of their work. The shelves of his extensive library and his correspondence files teem with evidence of his success. It would indeed be difficult to exaggerate the degree of his influence in Britain in a period that is not the least remarkable in the history of fine printing.

Maxwell was made a Fellow of the Royal Society of Edinburgh in 1932, and in 1947 he was given the degree of Doctor of Laws by Edinburgh University.

He married Agnes Macniven, who died in 1941. He is survived by a daughter. His only son was killed in 1918 while on active service with the Royal Flying Corps.

October 14, 1957.

Louis B. Mayer, formerly the head of the Metro-Goldwyn-Mayer film company, died in Hollywood at the age of 72 on October 29, 1957.

His career was one of outstanding achievement in an industry which has always been able to offer great wealth and much power to those who can fully comprehend its peculiar requirements. Louis Burt Mayer was probably the most successful of all film producers because he combined the exceptional business acumen needed to organize so vast a concern as the M.G.M. studios with a basic simplicity of outlook which made him at one with the ordinary, average filmgoer of the world.

It is said that he was deeply sentimental and could quickly be moved to tears by the emotional scenes which occurred in his films. The importance of this lay not so much in the fact that he *was* so moved, but that what moved him was almost certain to move film audiences as well, for the most valuable quality in any film producer is the ability to gauge public taste and public requirements.

This accuracy of judgment was revealed not only in the stories which he chose but also in the players whom he discovered and whom he raised to stardom. Just as he disliked and distrusted all violent, controversial and propaganda subjects, so also he disliked complicated or frustrated personalities. He delighted in warm-heartedness, tears and happy endings. His aim was a simple, emotional film, expertly made and elaborately exploited. As a business man he was often despotic; and his belief that sentiment had an important place in business, as well as on the screen, tended to be theoretical.

It was his good fortune to reach the height of his power in Hollywood during the pre-war period when the American film industry was also at its zenith. Television was then still an unconsidered and unimportant rival, and the future prosperity of the big film companies seemed to stretch out endlessly before them. He left the M.G.M. company in 1951, when the halcyon days were already past.

In the early 1940s he had been the highest-paid American. In the fiscal year 1942, according to the Securities and Exchange Commission, he received a salary of $949,765 (about £237,000). He did better in 1943, in which year he was paid $1,138,992 (about £284,000).

His career was as sentimental as he could have wished—a story of immense wealth achieved out of humble beginnings. He was born at Minsk, in Russia, on July 4, 1885, and was taken to Canada as a child. His career started in his father's scrap metal business in 1907, but he soon turned his attention to the American film industry, then in its infancy. He built up a chain of cinemas in New England, and obtained the New England rights for the distribution of D. W. Griffith's *Birth of a Nation* in 1914. With this he sowed the seeds of his fortune. He formed his own distribution company in 1915, and in 1924 the Metro-Goldwyn-Mayer amalgamation came into being. It was destined to become the most successful film company in Hollywood.

The stars whom he created, and the films which he made, are too numerous to mention in full. Marie Dressler, Greta Garbo, Clark Gable [q.v.], Myrna Loy, Robert Taylor*, Spencer Tracy*, Mickey Rooney, and Judy Garland* were but a few of those whom he made famous. His films included *Ben Hur, Trader Horn, The Thin Man, Mutiny on the Bounty, Mrs. Miniver,* and *Gone With the Wind.*

Another "star" he was said to have discovered was Leo the lion—whose roaring head became the trade mark of M.G.M. films. He saw the beast in a Los Angeles zoo and was struck by its "photogenic qualities".

From 1931 to 1936 he was president of the Association of Motion Picture Producers. In 1950 he received a special award from the Motion Picture Academy in honour of his 44 years' leadership in the film industry. Few showmen have ever been endowed with a closer insight into the mind of the general public.

He married in 1904 Margaret Schenberg, who died in 1955. This marriage had been dissolved. In 1948 he married Lorena L. Danker. He had two daughters by his first marriage, Edith, who married William Goetz, a film executive, and Irene, who married the producer David O. Selznick*.

October 30, 1957.

Major Robert Hobart Mayo, O.B.E., designer of the Short-Mayo composite aircraft, died in London on February 26, 1957. He was 66.

He was born on September 25, 1890, the son of Dr. James Mayo, and educated at the Perse School and at Magdalene College, Cambridge. He took a first class in the Mathematical Tripos, Part I, in 1910 and two years later took another first class this time in the Mechanical Sciences Tripos. Mayo early turned his attentions and his undoubted talent to aircraft design, and in 1914 he was appointed head of the experimental department, Royal Aircraft Factory. The following year saw him in action in France with the R.F.C. and in 1916 he became senior flight commander of the Testing Squadron. The following year he was made Head of Design (Aeroplane) Section, Air Ministry, and this post he held until 1919, when he joined Oglivie and Partners, consulting engineers.

In 1925 he took up the appointment of consulting engineer to Imperial Airways. Eleven years later he was made technical general manager. In the late 1930s his invention the Short-Mayo composite aircraft made its appearance. This consisted of a float seaplane, Mercury, which was borne on the back of a flying boat, Maia, until the latter had reached an agreed height. There the device uniting the two was released and Mercury rose clear of the mother aircraft and went on its way with enough fuel for a journey of 3,500 miles and a payload of 1,000lb. The prime consideration of his invention was the big load. The argument underlying it was that an aircraft could be made to carry much more in the air than it could take off the ground. The first launch in mid-air was accomplished in February 1938. In July 1938 Mercury, piloted by Captain D. C. T. Bennett (now Air Vice-Marshal Bennett), flew 3,240 miles from Foynes, co. Limerick, to New York in 25 hours 8 minutes, including a stop of 2½ hours at Montreal. Returning in easy stages, it touched water at Southampton a week and 12 minutes after leaving Foynes, having flown 8,000 miles and spent only 48 hours in the air. Later Captain Bennett established in Mercury the long distance record for seaplanes, Scotland to South Africa, which still stands.

In November the same year the composite aircraft undertook its first duties as part of the mail-carrying fleet of Imperial Airways and flew over a ton of mail non-stop to Alexandria.

In December 1938 Mayo became technical adviser to Imperial Airways. He was a former chairman of the Records, Racing, and Competitions committee of the Royal Aero Club, a past chairman of the Air League of the British Empire, a member of the National Civil Aviation Consultative Council, and a vice-president of the Fédération Aeronautique Internationale. He was also a director of Airtech, Ltd., and Superflexit, Ltd.

He married in 1924 Thorva Eyres Merrylees. There was a daughter of the marriage.

March 15, 1957.

Philip Mead, who died in hospital in Bournemouth on March 26, 1958, broke the hearts of first-class bowlers through more than 30 seasons, and kept the affection of all cricketers and of the crowds who watched him. He was 71.

The stalwart figure, left-handed, unhurried, hard as a rock in defence, having all the strokes when he had a mind to use them, saw Hampshire through many a crisis and did sterling work for England. He could be got out—all innings are mortal—but he never looked like getting out. Other batsmen came and went; he went on for ever, or as nearly so as Father Time allows. His record, measured in terms of the score book, was tremendous. A century made in 1931 put him level with Grace and he lived to score several more.

But he will be remembered above all for integrity and reliability in the field. Nothing seemed to tire him, nothing hurried him, nothing flurried him. No batsman has ever been more fairly described as having a barn door for defence. When he was fielding it was a rash stroke that put the most awkward ball within his reach. He kept in form until well down the thirties, and when it was known later that he had gone blind a shadow darkened all cricket grounds.

Charles Philip Mead was born on March 9, 1887. He started on the staff at the Oval, but Surrey, to its lasting cost, turned a blind eye on the promise of this youngster. He migrated to Hampshire and with his first game in 1905, before he had qualified, was allowed to show his form against fast bowling by a spirited 41 taken off the Australians. His first county match, against Yorkshire in 1906, gave him a century while more experienced batsmen were falling to George Hirst [q.v.].

By the outbreak of the First World War he had established himself in the first flight. His record before 1914 included a 132 against the West Indians; a memorable 223 for the Players against the Gentlemen at Scarborough; 2,000 runs in a season on an M.C.C. Australian tour (1911-12); top place in the first-class averages (in 1913), and centuries in Test matches in South Africa.

The renewal of the game after the war brought more triumphs. He was first in his county's averages in 1919. He cleared the 3,000 run mark for the first time in 1921, when he again headed the first-class averages with 69.1. That year was memorable for his highest score, 280 against Nottinghamshire at Southampton, a ground that was one of his happiest hunting grounds. He also brought off a pair of centuries, 224 and 113, against Sussex at Horsham. He was left out of the first three Australian Test matches but came in for the last two at Old Trafford and the Oval. A solid 47 in the first was followed by a characteristic effort of non-stop defence in the second.

For five hours he kept the Australian bowlers at bay and, when Tennyson [q.v.] declared, he was 182 not out. That was not all the Australians heard of him; he made a lovely 129 against them for his county. His bag was 10 centuries in that season. Next year his total fell to 2,391, but it included eight centuries in county matches, with two doubles against Worcestershire and Warwickshire. In 1922-23 he visited South Africa for the second time, taking over eight hours to make his only century. That was in the Durban Test. Runner-up to Hendren* in the first-class averages in 1923, he finished with an average of 59.18 and 2,604 runs, with a 222 against Warwickshire and six other centuries.

The middle twenties saw Mead—so it was thought—passing his peak. But those who expected that it was to be a steady decline were proved false prophets. At home he continued to be in the first few in the lists of averages, and in the spring of 1928 he gathered four centuries in five innings when he went out to Jamaica with Tennyson's team. In 1928 his average went up to 75.67, helped by 10 not outs in more than 3,000 runs. When he was over 40 he made his second visit to Australia in 1928-29. But he played in only one Test and got only one century. Next year an injury set him back, but not so far that he did not end fourth in the averages. The 1930s began badly for him and again some people believed that he had passed his best. But again he fought back and in 1931 (in which year he joined Hobbs* as the only cricketer who up till then had passed Grace's record for century making) he topped the county averages.

During the following season he made 104 not out against Derbyshire at Southampton and had then scored a century against every county. In 1934, then 47, he finished second to Walter Hammond* in the first-class averages, scoring 2,576 runs, including 10 centuries.

He came only third in the county averages of 1936, with 1,084 runs and a highest innings of 126 to his credit, but 1,084 runs is no bad total for a man of 49.

This was his last season, for at the end of it the Hampshire executive did not renew his agreement and thus ended the connexion with the county for which he had done so much.

In number of runs scored Mead still stands fourth to Hobbs, Woolley, and Hendren with 55,060, and an average of 47. In 27 out of his 28 seasons he reached a four-figure aggregate. In two he made over 3,000, in nine over 2,000, and in the remaining 16 over 1,000. In the list of makers of hundreds he is again fourth, that great batsman Hammond being above him in place of Woolley. Mead made 153 hundreds in England and eight abroad.

March 27, 1958.

Air Chief Marshal Sir Charles Medhurst, K.C.B., O.B.E., M.C., Head of the Air Force Staff, British Joint Service Mission in Washington from 1948 to 1950, died on October 18, 1954 in hospital at Lymington, Hampshire. He was 57.

It was in the field of Intelligence and in the Royal Air Force's relations with the air forces of other countries that Sir Charles made his greatest contribution to his service. His ease of manner and quiet charm made him an excellent "mixer" and brought him a wide circle of friends in London, Washington, Cairo, and many of the European capitals.

Charles Edward Hastings Medhurst was born at Smethwick on December 12, 1896, the second son of the late Rev. C. E. Medhurst, of Collingham. He was educated at St. Peter's, York, and Sandhurst, and was commissioned in The Royal Inniskilling Fusiliers in June, 1915. Two months later he was seconded to the Royal Flying Corps for flying duties. Before the end of the year he had joined No. 13 Squadron in France and in 1917 he went out to the Middle East Brigade, seeing service in Salonika in 1918, and being awarded the M.C. He served with No. 111 Squadron in Palestine in 1919 and returned to England the following year.

He was selected for technical engineering training and took the technical course at Chiseldon before going to the Air Ministry for air staff duties in October 1923. In 1925 he took the R.A.F. Staff College course and the following year the senior officers' course, after which he went out to Iraq for two years' air staff and operational duties. In 1929 he was selected for the Imperial Defence College course and during 1930 he commanded No. 4 Squadron. Then followed three years as instructor at the Staff College. By this time it was clear that it was in the direction of air staff duties rather than in the technical field that his bent lay and in 1934 he returned to the Air Ministry with the rank of wing commander, in the Directorate of Operations and Intelligence. He became a Deputy Director in 1935.

In August 1937 he went out to Rome as Air Attaché and remained there until 1940 when Italy entered the war. He then returned to England to become R.A.F. Secretary of the Supreme War Council. Later that year he became Director of Allied Air Cooperation, and after a short time as Director of Plans he was appointed Assistant Chief of Air Staff (Intelligence) in 1941. He was made an additional member of the Air Council in October 1941 while acting as temporary Vice-Chief of the Air Staff, and in the following year he was appointed Assistant Chief of Air Staff (Policy). For the last two years of the war he was Commandant of the R.A.F. Staff College.

In October 1945 he became Air Commander-in-Chief, Mediterranean and Middle East Command, of which the headquarters were in Cairo. Later he faced the difficult task of carrying through the move of his headquarters and the major part of his forces from the Nile to the canal zone. He was succeeded as Air Commander-in-Chief by Sir William Dickson in March 1948, and in May he went to Washington as Head of the Air Force Staff, British Joint Services Mission, being promoted air chief marshal shortly afterwards. In Washington he moved with a sure step at a time when a quick understanding of the American mind and scene was indispensable. He retired in 1950.

He married, in 1919, Christabell Elizabeth, daughter of the late Canon T. E. B. Guy, of York. Their only son was killed in action with the R.A.F. in 1944; there are two surviving daughters.

October 19, 1954.

Dr. Kenneth Mees, F.R.S., whose death occurred at Honolulu on August 15, 1960, devoted his life to research into and the development of the photographic processes. He was 78.

Charles Edward Kenneth Mees was born at Wellingborough on May 26, 1882, the son of a Wesleyan minister. He was educated at Kingswood School, Bath, and at St. Dunstan's College, where he met Samuel E. Shepherd, also a student. The two formed a lifelong friendship terminated only by Shepherd's death in 1948.

The two worked together at University College London, on the theory of the photographic process under the guidance of Sir William Ramsay. On the basis of their study they received the degree of B.Sc. by research in 1903 and of D.Sc. in 1906. Their theses, published as a book *Investigations on the Theory of the Photographic Process,* were thereafter known to photographic workers as "Shepherd and Mees".

For the next six years Mees was a partner and joint managing director of an English photographic firm, Wratten and Wainwright, Ltd., of Croydon. During his first year there he manufactured a successful series of panchromatic plates, light filters, and darkroom safelights. He later developed special plates for photo-engravers and spectroscopists, and did research on the theory of photography, including the first measurements of the resolving power of photographic materials.

Mees accepted George Eastman's invitation to join the Kodak company in 1912 on the condition that the firm of Wratten and Wainwright was purchased at the same time and he went to the company's Kodak Park Works, Rochester, New York, to organize and direct a research laboratory.

After the First World War he became Director of Research and Development for the company. Through his efforts and under his guidance the research laboratories grew enormously in extent and in the scope of their operations. In 1923 he was made a director of the company.

From the beginning of his early experimentation in photography Mees held to his aim of adding to the knowledge of the scientific theory of photography. A milestone on this course came in 1942, with the publication of *The Theory of the Photographic Process,* a compendium of photographic science. It was completely revised in 1954. At the same time one of the clear goals of his applied research was to bring to as many people as possible the best in simplified cameras and good films for easy picture-taking. From the laboratories under his direction came outstanding research achievements, including home movies, panchromatic films, and processes of colour photography. Mees was one of the pioneering businessmen who early grasped the significance of science in industry.

He was the author of about 150 publications, more than one hundred of which are scientific papers. *The Path of Science,* published in 1946, is an account of science for historians and of world history for scientists. With Dr. John A. Leermakers, he was co-author of *The Organization of Industrial Scientific Research,* published in 1950, a complete revision of his book published in 1920, which was the first of its kind.

Mees was elected a Fellow of the Royal Society in 1939 and his achievements were recognized by numerous other scientific awards. Among the more important were the Progress medal of the Royal Photographic Society of Great Britain received in 1913 and again in 1953; the John Scott medal and award of the City of Philadelphia in 1921; the Janssen medal of the Société Française de Photographie in 1923; the Progress medal of the Society of Motion Picture Engineers, and the Henry Draper medal of the National Academy of Sciences in 1936; the Rumford medals of the American Academy of Arts and Sciences in 1943; the Adelskold medal of the Swedish Photographic Society and the Progress medal of the Photographic Society of America, both in 1948; and the Franklin medal in 1954.

In 1910 he was made a Fellow of the Royal Photographic Society and in 1926 an honorary Fellow; in 1921, a fellow of the American Association for the Advancement of Science; in 1934, a Fellow of the Society of Motion Picture Engineers: and in 1937, a member of the American Philosophical Society: he served as a member of the council of the society from 1942 to 1945. In 1950, after he became an American citizen, he was elected a member of the National Academy of Sciences.

Mees married in 1909 Alice Crisp (she died in 1954), by whom he had a son and a daughter.

August 17, 1960.

Arthur Meighen, Q.C., who was Prime Minister of Canada for two brief periods in the 1920s, and leader of the Canadian Conservative Party, died at Toronto on August 5, 1960. He was 86.

There was an element of tragedy in the public career of Arthur Meighen, in that the Canadian people made so little use of his first-rate political abilities. He combined the tastes of a scholar whose knowledge of history and literature was wide with a shrewd practical mind, and he was a vigorous man of action. In the opinion of some he was the greatest master of the spoken word who ever sat in the Canadian Commons. In his younger days he held radical views which were modified as he grew older, but he also became dubious about the value of high tariff protection for Canada. He was a staunch believer in the value to Canada of close connexions with Britain and the rest of the Commonwealth and never had any patience with the creed of the extreme nationalists. No other Canadian politician of his time was so steadfast in his principles: opportunism was foreign to his nature and he never curried favour with the voters by promises that he did not intend to fulfil. But his judgment of men was often poor and loyalty to old friends sometimes had disastrous results.

Arthur Meighen's strain of blood was Scottish-Irish from Ulster, and he was born on June 16, 1874, on a farm near St. Mary's in Perth county, Ontario, the son of Joseph and Mary Meighen. After receiving his early education at St. Mary's Collegiate Institute he entered the University of Toronto, where he helped to finance his progress by delivering milk twice a day.

He had established a law practice in the country town of Portage La Prairie in Manitoba when he was nominated Conservative candidate for the Federal constituency of which the town was the centre, and won it in the election of 1908. His competence as a debater led his leader, Sir Robert Borden, to make frequent use of him, and after the election of 1911, which enabled Borden to form his first Ministry, he appointed Meighen to office.

He was still a junior Minister when in 1917 the parliamentary battle over the Military Service Act developed, and because Borden's membership in the Imperial War Cabinet kept him in London and his senior Ministers had no heart for vigorous advocacy of the Bill, Meighen had to shoulder the main burden of piloting it through the House of Commons. But, while his success in this difficult task increased his prestige in the English-speaking provinces, it earned for him the lasting enmity of the French-Canadians, which ultimately proved fatal to his career.

When Borden retired in 1920 Meighen was elected leader of the Conservative Party. When he became Prime Minister the coalition broke up and he formed a purely Conservative Ministry and was sworn of the British Privy Council. He attended the Imperial Conference of 1921 as head of Canada's delegation, to find the Lloyd George Ministry seeking approval for the renewal of the Anglo-Japanese alliance. This he opposed with what the late Lord Horne, then Chancellor of the Exchequer, described as the most powerful piece of political advocacy which he had ever heard. His main argument was that Canada in view of her close relations with the United States could never be a party to a treaty which was so objectionable to Washington, and his threat to contract out of it made British Ministers abandon their project. Undoubtedly, if the treaty had been renewed, it would have created a strain in relations between Britain and the United States in the decades between the two world wars.

When Meighen, having returned from the conference, sought a fresh mandate from the Canadian people, a postwar depression and an agrarian political revolt produced conditions unfavourable for his party, and in a bad defeat, which reduced its strength to 50, he lost his own seat. But when he assumed the leadership of the Opposition he proved almost single-handed a match for the whole front bench of the Liberal Ministry. He became the acknowledged master of the House of Commons, before whose attacks Mackenzie King often used to quail. He also achieved such a revival of confidence in the Conservative Party that in the election of 1925 it made a net gain of 66 seats and was only seven short of a clear parliamentary majority.

The precarious hold of the Liberals was badly shaken by a parliamentary committee's revelation of grave scandals in the Department of Customs, but, when Mackenzie King asked for a dissolution Lord Byng, the Governor-General, refused to grant it; and when King resigned Meighen was invited to form a Government. His acceptance of office entailed in those days reelection to Parliament, and in his absence the maladroit conduct of his lieutenants resulted in the early defeat of his Government by one vote. Meighen then appealed to the country, but in the election, which was fought on a constitutional issue raised by Lord Byng's action, Mackenzie King fanned the new nationalistic spirit of Canada so successfully that the Conservative strength fell to 91. Meighen, who had again lost his seat, was convinced that until his party could recover substantial support in French Canada, which seemed impossible as long as he was leader, it could never regain power at Ottawa, and so he resigned his leadership.

The late Lord Bennett, who succeeded him, won the election of 1930, and when he formed his Ministry persuaded Meighen, who had engaged in financial business in Toronto, to join it as Government leader in the Senate and Minister without Portfolio. In his new role he proved a tower of strength to the Bennett Ministry and as his skill as a parliamentarian was unimpaired he became the dominating personality in the Senate. After the Liberal Party returned to power in 1935 he led the Opposition in the Senate until 1942, when he again assumed the leadership of his party. He did not find a seat in the Commons, however, and took leave of politics. Resuming his business activities he became a leading figure in the financial world of Toronto.

His demeanour in public, and a strain of caustic irony, gave the Canadian people the false impression that he was a cold, austere intellectual, for in reality he was a friendly, warmhearted man.

He married in 1904 Jessie Isabel, daughter of Charles Cox, by whom he had two sons and a daughter.

August 6, 1960.

Dr. Friedrich Meinecke, the distinguished German liberal historian, died in Berlin in February 1954 at the age of 91. Of great industry and capacity, he poured forth a large number of major historical studies and remained clear and active in mind almost to the end of his long life.

Friedrich Meinecke was born on October 30, 1862, at Salzwedel, in the heart of the province of Saxony. He studied history and philosophy, and at the age of 25 entered the Prussian Civil Service as an archivist. He stayed in that office from 1887 to 1901, gaining inside knowledge of scientific documentation and acquiring the skill in sifting written evidence which distinguished all his subsequent research work. In 1901 he was offered the Chair of History in the University of Strasbourg on the strength of several publications, including a two-volume *Life of Field-Marshal Hermann von Boyen.* In 1906 he got a call, in the same capacity, to Freiburg, where he taught until 1914.

With a handful of contemporary historians, notably the late Hermann Oncken, Meinecke by this work established a liberal tradition in historical studies, as against the more nationalist school of Treitschke—whose work, however, he studied closely and was later to sum up and, in his own distinguished way, to criticise in *Die Idee der Staatsraison,* after having collaborated with him from 1896 to 1914 as co-editor of the *Historische Zeitschrift.* Meinecke particularly stands out for his success in combining political work with cultural history; in fact, it was this side of his work which established his strongest claim to the leadership of modern, pre-Hitlerite historians. He reached the peak of his career when, very shortly before the 1914-18 war, he accepted a call to Berlin University, where he was to teach until 1928.

Only a small part of his great output can be mentioned here, for he continued to write to an advanced age and his volume published in 1946, *Die Deutsche Katastrophe,* shows no sign of a weakening of power. Among his other outstanding works are *Das Zeitalter der Deutschen Erhebung* (1906), *Von Stein zu Bismarck, Radowitz und die Deutsche Revolution, Preussen und Deutschland im 19 und 20 Jahrhundert,* and *Geschichte des Deutsch-Englischen Bündnisproblems.* He was co-editor with Oncken of the huge *Classics of Politics,* and from 1903 until shortly before war broke out in 1939, he edited an *Encyclopedia of Medieval and Modern History,* of which 20 volumes appeared.

After the Nazi defeat he returned to a Berlin suburb, still active and of unbroken spirit.

February 9, 1954.

Sir Edward Mellanby, G.B.E., K.C.B., F.R.C.P., F.R.S., who died suddenly on January 30, 1955 while gardening, had a long and distinguished career as a research worker in medicine, with particular reference to nutrition. He was 70.

He was one of three distinguished brothers all of whom have left their mark on the world of science or technology; Professor Alexander Lawson Mellanby was Professor of Civil and Mechanical Engineering at the Royal Technical College, Glasgow, and Professor John Mellanby was a distinguished physiologist. Edward Mellanby, who was born in 1884, received his medical education at Cambridge and St. Thomas's Hospital, London. He early showed his interest in the scientific side of medicine, for he became a demonstrator in the Department of Physiology at St. Thomas's in 1909 and in 1913 became first lecturer, and later Professor of Physiology at King's College for Women, London. But Mellanby was essentially interested in the application of scientific research in the field of curative medicine, so that it was with great pleasure that in 1920 he became Professor of Pharmacology in the University of Sheffield and Honorary Physician to the Sheffield Royal Infirmary.

During his earlier work in physiology Mellanby had been particularly interested in the developments foreshadowed by the discovery of the vitamins. He realized that a particularly useful study of the effects of Vitamin D could be made by observing the growing bones of the puppy, and he pointed the way to the modern method of the cure and prevention of rickets in the early 1920s. Mellanby made a detailed study of the action of Vitamin D with particular reference to what he termed anti-vitamin effect of certain cereals, and if his denunciation of oatmeal in this respect roused a certain amount of displeasure across the Border, it was with gratitude that in later years the Scottish physicians were able to apply Mellanby's work in the conquest of rickets in their big cities. Mellanby also interested himself in the function of Vitamin A.

It seemed right, therefore, that on the death of Sir Walter Fletcher, Mellanby should be appointed as secretary of the Medical Research Council, for it is this body above all which serves to correlate research which ultimately has as its object the prevention and alleviation of sickness. Mellanby held the post with tact and efficiency, encouraging the young worker, cutting out the dead wood from reports, and serving usefully and intelligently the many committees which sought his aid. He was elected F.R.S. in 1925, and F.R.C.P. in 1928.

During the 1939-45 War his services were much in demand for chairmanships of essential committees where scientific research of a medical kind was involved. Later he became involved in the work of the British Council and in this sphere helped to develop international relations in the medical field. His retirement in 1949 from the secretaryship of the Medical Research Council was not before the new buildings at Mill Hill had been erected, and right up to the end of his term of office his interest in active research was maintained, as was shown in his most important discussions on the effect of "agenized" flour on dogs. Right up to the end of his official position Mellanby maintained also his personal interest in the many research workers under his "command" and in his pensioners—many of them scattered throughout the British Isles—whom the Medical Research Council had at some time supported. It was this personal interest which endeared him to his staff and undoubtedly brought out the best of many otherwise shy and retiring men and women. He was elected an honorary member of the British Paediatric Association in 1945, a gesture which gave him special pleasure, for, as he said, he had been telling children's physicians how to cure rickets for 20 years.

He married in 1914 May [d. 1978], daughter of George Tweedy, who shared in her husband's interests and his research work to the full, receiving honorary doctorates of science from Sheffield and Liverpool.

January 31, 1955.

H. L. Mencken, the American author and former editor of the *American Mercury,* whose death occurred on January 28, 1956 at the age of 75, will be remembered for his classic work *The American Language* and for the leading part he took in the critical debate on American life and letters during the first half of the century.

"The Sage of Baltimore" or "The Disturber of the Peace", according to fancy, the writer who, in Walter Lippmann's* phrase, "denounced life and made you want to live", H. L. Mencken was time after time compared with Bernard Shaw. It is an obvious comparison, but no less true for that like Shaw (on whom he wrote one of his first books) he did much to shake complacency. His fierce treatment of the Dayton Fundamentalist trial helped to modernize Southern opinion and he fought with all his power against lynch law. Though he was close on 70 he returned to the arena in 1948 to write on Henry Wallace's* candidature at the Democratic Convention, with all the fire and incisiveness of his youth. Through his writing he became both hated and loved, but never was a critic so difficult to dislike personally once his open countenance and blue eyes were upon one.

Henry Louis Mencken was born on September 12, 1880, in Baltimore. The son of a cigar manufacturer, he was descended from a long line of professors of law and history at Leipzig, Halle, and Wittenberg. After being educated at a private school and the Baltimore Polytechnic, he became, on the death of his father in 1899, a reporter on the *Baltimore Morning Herald.* He was city (that is, news) editor from 1903 until 1905, and in 1906 became editor of its evening edition. A year later he joined the *Baltimore Sun,* with which he maintained his connexion till the end of his life. He was also for several years literary critic and joint editor of the *Smart Set,* and a contributing editor to the New York *Nation.* In 1924 he founded, in collaboration with George Jean Nathan [q.v.], the *American Mercury,* which he edited until 1933. He then resigned so that he could devote himself to the task of revising *The American Language,* which originally appeared in 1918, to writing other books, and to his work for the *Baltimore Sun* and the *Evening Sun.*

Mencken's importance in American letters was for long obscured by his form and style of expression. Superficially his writing exhibited some of the characteristics of popular journalism in the United States. He relied, for instance, on the use of provocative titles, the freest American vernacular, wild and wilful exaggeration, and a slap-bang verbal gusto. But the style, with Mencken, was very much the man. If, in the end, it was the sheer energy of his diction, rather than the substance of his thought, that gave him his popular standing, the thought itself still mattered, and it had a deep and pervading influence on American literary standards. It was as a pioneer of the modern American literary idea that Mencken deserved—and secured—recognition.

In 1908, as literary critic of the *Smart Set,* he began his self-appointed task of removing the undergrowth which concealed the living body of an authentically American language and literature. Until the beginning of the century a self-conscious critical temper had rarely made itself felt in American life and letters. The ball had been set rolling, perhaps, by Paul Elmer More, who in 1904 published his *Shelburne Essays.* Mencken (whose earliest volumes had dealt with the plays of Bernard Shaw and the philosophy of Nietzsche) pushed the ball in another and unexpected direction when in 1918 he published his *Criticism of Criticism of Criticism,* later republished in his first volume of *Prejudices.* Here, together with the verbosity into which he sometimes slipped, was the seed of his long campaign against what he called Puritan prejudice, academic sterility, and the cant of a spurious democracy. From then onwards he went ahead with his revaluation of American literature.

It was to further this aim that in 1924 he founded the *American Mercury.* He made of it a genuinely national literary review. At the same time he gave it his own formidably individual stamp. He attacked every feature or aspect of the American scene which seemed to him pretentious, and under his onslaught many traditional ideas and habits of thought were shaken. The controversies of his years of loudest and fiercest energy have now largely receded into literary history, but Mencken doubtless felt with justice that part at least of an important mission had been accomplished when in 1933 he resigned the editorship of the *American Mercury.*

Among the books he published, chiefly of criticism and satire, are the series of six volumes of *Prejudices* (1919-27), *Notes on Democracy, A Book of Burlesques, In Defence of Women, Treatise on the Gods, Treatise on Right and Wrong,* and the several volumes of *Americana,* reprinted from the *American Mercury.* There are also his three volumes of memories, *Happy Days, Newspaper Days,* and *Heathen Days,* published between 1940 and 1943. They are a vivid essay in autobiography, which, after a period of partial eclipse, restored him to a position of significance in public estimation. His greatest work remains *The American Language,* a treasury of learning, wit and fun, first published in 1918, which was revised for the fourth time in 1936 and to which supplements were added in 1945 and 1948. Only in the week before he died he announced the forthcoming publication of a new book, to be entitled *Minority Report,* which he had written in 1948 and then forgotten until his secretary recently found the manuscript among a pile of his papers which were being sent to a museum.

Until his fiftieth year Mencken was one of America's most famous bachelors. In 1930, to the surprise of his friends and his reading public, he married Miss Sara Powell Haardt, a Baltimore school teacher and a contributor to the *American Mercury.* She died in 1935.

January 30, 1956.

Erich Mendelsohn, who died on September 15, 1953 at San Francisco at the age of 66, was one of the most original and important architects of the century.

First in his native Germany, and later in this country of his adoption, he designed a large number of public and private buildings, which not only made full and frank use of steel, glass, and ferro-concrete, but were executed in a style, compact of austerity and grace, which pointed the way towards a real twentieth-century architecture. With Oud, Gropius*, Poelzig, Tony Garnier, Le Corbusier*, and others he may be called one of the chief exponents of the modern movement.

His Schocken stores at Chemnitz and elsewhere had a beneficent influence on the architecture of department stores all over the world—not least in our own country, where it is seen in the Peter Jones building (London) and other big shops. Other important works are the Luxor Palast (formerly Universum Cinema) in Berlin, the Government Hospital at Haifa, the University Medical Department at Jerusalem, and the De la Warr Pavilion at Bexhill.

Mendelsohn was subjected to classical influences in early life, and his architecture, though it rejects all the conventional classical apparatus, has the integrity and sweetness of the classical spirit, and its measure and balance. A special feature of his style is its preference for long horizontal masses, often broken by projecting semicircles.

Erich Mendelsohn was born at Allenstein, East Prussia, on March 21, 1887, the son of a German-Jewish merchant. His mother was profoundly musical, and the culture of this art soaked so deeply into Mendelsohn's mind that in after life he would make architectural sketches with such titles as "Brahms Concerto" or "Bach Cantata". In 1907 he made a false start at the University of Munich, studying economics, but a year later he entered the Berlin *Technische Hochschule* as an architectural student.

After two years there he worked for a further two at the Munich *Technische Hochschule,* graduating as an architect in 1912. As early as 1910 he had written: "I believe that a new civilization is beginning, based upon the great conceptions of ancient times". Up to the 1914-18 War he was playing with the Expressionist idea, and engaged on building projects, stage designing, and painting.

At the outbreak of the war Mendelsohn joined the Engineers. He was on the Russian front until 1917, and thereafter in the west, being demobilized in November 1918, and setting up in practice within two days. In the spring of 1919 he staged an exhibition called "Architecture in Steel and Reinforced Concrete" at Paul Cassirer's Gallery. His first important work, built in 1920-21, was the Einstein Tower, at Potsdam, an astro-physical laboratory and observatory designed specially to further Professor Einstein's [q.v.] researches.

As early as 1919 he was invited to lecture in Holland, and did so again in 1923. Up to the latter year some major tasks were the hat factory for Friedrich Steinberg, Hermann and Co., at Luckenwalde, a set of semi-detached houses at Charlottenburg, a silk store at Gleiwitz, and additions to the *Berliner Tageblatt* building in Berlin.

In 1923 Mendelsohn made his first visit to Palestine, to design a power station at Haifa. The next year brought his first trip to America. In 1925 the Soviets invited him to design a factory for the Leningrad textile trust, and he spent some time in Leningrad in that year and the next. The period from 1924 to 1928 saw the completion of many big shops and town-planning projects, including the Herpich fur store, Berlin; the Schocken stores at Nuremberg, Stuttgart, and Chemnitz; the Jews' cemetery at Königsberg (blown up by the Nazis in 1938); and a street of shops, a cinema, flats, &c., for the Woga Company in Berlin.

In 1929 he was an invited competitor for the design of the Palace of the Soviet, at Moscow, but was unsuccessful. His Universum Cinema (1928) was an important attempt to conceive a building really suited to the nature of the cinema—as shown in details like the setting back of the screen, so that it should be at some distance even from the front seats.

In 1931 Mendelsohn visited England as the guest of the Architectural Association, and went to Corsica on a French project. In March 1933, in view of the anti-Jewish activities of the Nazis, he settled in England, going into partnership with Serge Chermayeff. At first he had only permission for a short stay, but, largely through the instrumentality of Professor C. H. Reilly, Sir Giles Gilbert Scott [q.v.], and Sir Ian MacAlister [q.v.], he received a five-year permit, and became a naturalized British citizen in 1938.

Meanwhile in 1934 Mendelsohn and Chermayeff had scored an initial British success by winning the competition for the De la Warr Pavilion at Bexhill; and that beautiful, seemly, spacious building remains an example of what sea-front architecture should be and a standing reproach to the iced-cake mock-baroque of the usual seaside pavilion. The partnership went on until the end of 1936.

Between 1934 and 1938 Mendelsohn carried out a great deal of work in Palestine, including the Government Hospital at Haifa, the University medical building at Mount Scopus, Jerusalem, a big private house for Salman Schocken, and sundry gardens, which last he designed very intelligently to carry on the lines of the houses. He also got out a grandiose plan for the development of the White City site at Shepherd's Bush, and a fine scheme for a garage, hotel, and shops at Blackpool.

Mendelsohn was a man of enormous, restless energy, and very great creative capacity, who had a clear view of the social implications of architecture and firmly held ideas as to the lines along which twentieth-century work should move. His procedure in individual cases was first to make a careful examination of the site and then to produce perspective drawings, leaving the plans till the last. He was a tireless and prolific maker of drawings, filling many sketch-books with vivid schemes for buildings.

In 1915 he married Luise Maas, a cellist. They had one daughter.

September 17, 1953.

Jules Menken, who achieved an envied reputation as a writer on world affairs and problems of defence, died in London on July 20, 1957.

He was born in 1900 in New York where his family, of German-Danish origin, had been settled for some time. He took his degree at Columbia University and was expected to enter the family law business, but he decided to come to Britain to continue his studies at Emmanuel College, Cambridge, where he took a double first in Economics. On coming down from Cambridge he was a member of Lloyd George's secretariat and on his shoulders fell much of the burden of economic research and advice for the famous "Yellow Book". Later, he turned to business life and was economic adviser to a famous London store, but his interests were always in the academic field where he felt he could influence men's minds, and, when he was offered the post of head of the Department of Business Administration in the London School of Economics, he welcomed the chance to return to that field. The department was largely his personal creation, and it was a blow to him when personal issues intervened and he resigned five years later. In 1932 he visited the Soviet Union and heartily disliked what he saw.

He had become a British subject in 1929 and, after leaving the school, he turned to politics, and although he twice narrowly missed a chair and a return again to the academic life it was in politics he remained. He was one of the protagonists of increased armaments against the Hitler menace: he played a part in Duncan Sandys's "First Hundred Thousand", but the war ended these activities, and he took a post in the B.B.C.'s European Service for which he continued his work after the war as a freelance journalist.

It was after 1945 that he became known to the small public which is concerned directly with government and defence, and he gradually built up a considerable reputation as a writer on military affairs and on the politics of defence. That reputation was founded on many articles in periodicals, general and technical, in Britain and in the United States, which he visited two years ago and where he had considerable success as a lecturer. He wrote articles for *The Times* and *The Times Literary Supplement;* he helped Lady Milner [q.v.] during the latter years of her editorship of the *National Review;* for a time he was with the *Observer;* he was a regular contributor to *Brassey's Annual;* he produced an excellent little book on *The Economics of Defence;* and his last work which appeared in technical journals like *Ordnance* and *Engineering* was concerned with the new nuclear weapons and with the transformation of war which they made inevitable.

He had under contemplation a major work on defence which he saw as the defence of western civilization against the communist menace from the East, and it was into this that he intended to put not only the facts of the case but his own philosophy of life. A strong Conservative and an Imperialist of the type which is now considered old-fashioned, he had little patience with the exponents of "sweetness and light", for first and foremost he was a fighter. If his writings were distinguished by their scrupulous accuracy, his advocacy of the causes he had at heart was uncompromising. It was in his conversation rather than in these that the real man came out, the forthright Anglican churchman who saw in the battle between the Christian ethic and dialectical materialism, between selfishness national and personal against sacrifice, the old battle which had again become the battle of our times. Simple in his faith but strong in it he saw no alternative but to resist the evil he felt was winning too many victories. To those who shared his beliefs and were honoured by his friendship his too early death is a hard disappointment, for with the possibility before him of entering the House of Commons, they felt that he might at last obtain the platform he wanted. But it is also a very personal blow. To him, as to Dr. Johnson, keeping friendships in repair was a duty and there are very few of his friends who do not owe much to him for material help and generously given counsel. Their thoughts go out to his wife.

July 23, 1957.

Eugene Meyer, owner of the *Washington Post,* who died on July 17, 1959, at the age of 83 left the mark of strong principles on banking, government service, and journalism during three distinct phases of his career.

Meyer's recipe for success was that a man should know more than anyone else in the same business, work harder than anyone else, and be absolutely honest. By his early forties he had made a fortune as a banker and Wall Street broker, specializing in railway, chemical, copper, oil, and other industrial investments—new and "dangerous" ventures that finally had J. P. Morgan saying: "Watch out for that fellow Meyer, because if you don't he'll end up having all the money on Wall Street".

Another of Meyer's precepts was that any man who had achieved success in business owed a period of public service; and so it was that he held a succession of financial and economic posts in Washington under seven Presidents. His knowledge of the copper market made him a valuable adviser in 1917 to Woodrow Wilson's administration; also during the emergency he directed the War Finance Corporation, the forerunner of contemporary government lending agencies, and he served under President Hoover* both as governor of the Federal Reserve Board and the first chairman of the Reconstruction Finance Corporation, a novel system, largely devised by himself, for relieving distressed business and industrial enterprises by federal loans. In 1946 Meyer came back for six months as the first president of the newly created World Bank, which in the main still follows the course he set.

His career provides a familiar pendant to the American success story. He was given the start in life denied to his father, a penniless orphan who emigrated to California from Alsace 100 years ago—a Yale education, boxing lessons from James L. Corbett, and two years in Europe with the banking house of Lazard Frères, of which his father had become a partner. In 1933, at an age when most wealthy Americans are thinking of retirement Meyer bought the foundering *Washington Post* at public auction for less than one million dollars (£357,000), and by new money and new blood during the years of recovery made it one of the most influential newspapers in America, largely through the independence and strength of its editorial opinions. Northcliffe had once said that the *Post* was the one American journal he would wish to own because it reached the breakfast table of members of Congress; and this position was reinforced when the newspaper absorbed Colonel McCormick's [q.v.] *Washington Times Herald.*

Meyer's successful venture in journalism was guided by his belief that the first function of a newspaper was to inform; it must be the conscience of its community, and the opinions of the *Washington Post,* he held, must appear on its editorial page and not in the news columns. For six years he worked actively as editor and publisher before handing the management to his son-in-law Philip Graham, but his influence as chairman of the board did not diminish. A few years ago he presented stock worth half a million dollars to long service members of the staff.

July 20, 1959.

Esther Meynell, the author, died at her home at Ditchling, Sussex, on February 4, 1955.

A writer of versatile and graceful talent, Mrs. Meynell's range of interest extended from literary and historical biography to music and country life and ways. Music and country things were her chief love. The first served as the real subject of a number of individually attractive and sincerely felt novels. The other enabled her to demonstrate how truly her roots were in the country—above all, in Sussex, where she had lived continuously since her childhood. Mrs. Meynell was neither a writer of exceptional force or originality nor a best-selling author, but there was little she produced that was without charm or genuine literary quality.

Esther Hallam was the eldest daughter of Samuel Moorhouse, a Yorkshire Quaker of a prosperous commercial family; she left her native county for Sussex at the age of 10. Her health as a child was delicate, and she was educated at home with results that she herself in later life had no doubt were to her advantage. She read unusually widely, was drawn to naval history among other subjects (a book review of hers led to a long friendship with Admiral Lord Fisher), and published her first book in 1906, *Nelson's Lady Hamilton.* Books on Pepys, Wordsworth, Nelson in England, Hans Andersen, and other subjects followed, and her love of music is first clearly evidenced in *The Little Chronicle of Magdalene Bach* (1925). She married Gerard Tuke Meynell, a nephew of Alice and Wilfred Meynell, in 1911, and they had two daughters. She was received into the Roman Catholic Church in 1931.

From that time onwards her books succeeded one another at intervals of a year or a little more. In a novel of somewhat homely sentiment about music, entitled *Grave Fairy-Tale,* she took for her principal character an historical figure reminiscent of Beethoven, choosing by turns to follow the facts of his life and to devise situations of her own. *Quintet* (1933), with a world-famous pianist for hero, is more happily contrived, betraying no hint of self-consciousness in the expression of emotions which are roused by music; while *Time's Door* (1935) is better still, the story of an Italian violinist, a pupil of Paganini, who on a visit to Leipzig captures a vivid sense of the past and re-creates for himself the atmosphere of the Bach household.

In *Sussex Cottage* (1936) and *Building a Cottage* (1937) Mrs. Meynell celebrated the building, or the circumstances attending the building, of a small house in Ditchling (until then she had lived near Pulborough); *Country Ways* (1942) was a pleasantly discursive and rambling book on Sussex; *Cottage Tale* (1946) introduced, among other things, cottage economics; while in the following year Mrs. Meynell produced a volume on Sussex, the first in a new English County series, into which she poured all the wealth of her knowledge of its past and present, all the intimate lore of her personal observation. In 1953 she published yet another book on her favourite county, *Small Talk in Sussex.*

February 7, 1955.

Wilhelm Miklas, President of the Austrian Republic from 1928 until the country was occupied by the Nazis in 1938, died in the early hours of March 20, 1956 in Vienna, at the age of 83.

He was born in 1872, one of a family of eight children, of lower middle-class stock, at Krems in Lower Austria, not far from the great monastery of Melk that, on its rock above the Danube, is familiar to every traveller to Vienna. After education at the local national school and at the University of Vienna, he became a schoolmaster, teaching at Trieste and at Horn, which place he represented in the Austrian Parliament from 1907 to 1918 and again from 1920 until he was elected President.

What turned him from the scholastic profession to politics seems to have been originally his outstanding oratorical talent, which together with an interest in public affairs led him into local and later into national politics.

Miklas was a man of shrewd judgment and he soon made a mark in Parliament, serving in succession on the committees of budget reform, railways, and public education.

Miklas, who had been secretary of the last Assembly convened in Vienna under the Dual Monarchy, was, in the chaos of the disintegrating Hapsburg Empire, a valuable servant of the weak and impoverished new Austrian Republic. Standing outside the crowd of political quacks to whom the revolution gave an hour of notoriety in Vienna, he was one of the few responsible and experienced public men available to take control when the first clamour had spent itself. His provincial canniness was shocked by the powerlessness of the ultra-democratic President of the Republic, and his first service to the infant State was to propose in June 1922, and to secure the passage of, a Bill giving the President more power and responsibility.

In this he was supported by all the parties of the Right as well as by a large number of Socialists who had become alarmed at the increasing confusion in the Republic, and the antagonism between the provinces and the unwieldy capital. By the same votes in 1923 he was elected president of the National Assembly, a position which he held for five years until December 5, 1928 when by 94 votes to 26 he was elected President of the Republic.

Under the Austrian constitution the Federal President is elected for four years. Dr. Hainisch, the first holder of the office, had, after his first term, been re-elected President by a referendum as laid down in the constitution. This procedure was dispensed with in the case of Herr Miklas. His re-election was affected in October 1931, before it became due, by the combined action of the bourgeois parties in defiance of the Socialists, it being feared that in the strained situation engendered by the acute financial crisis in Austria political conflicts might arise if the referendum were resorted to.

The financial crisis was followed by a political crisis which caused the bourgeois parties to close their ranks even more tightly. The President, provincial, clerical and conservative, was their man and under the new federal constitution of 1934 his term of office was prolonged indefinitely. His term of office came, however, to an abrupt end in 1938 when his country was invaded by the Nazis. He could not approve of the annexation of his country by Germany and retired from politics. He was one of the few Austrian political leaders not imprisoned by the Nazis and since his retirement from politics had lived quietly in Vienna.

March 21, 1956.

Audrey Mildmay—See **Christie.**

Sir Humphrey Milford, for many years Publisher to the University of Oxford, died on September 6, 1952 at the age of 75.

Humphrey Sumner Milford was born on February 8, 1877, the youngest of the ten children of Canon R. N. Milford, of East Knoyle, and Emily Sumner, and so a grandson of Charles Sumner, Bishop of Winchester from 1827 to 1869. He was in College at Winchester, and was a scholar of New College, Oxford, where he took first classes in Classical Moderations and in Greats. In 1900 he was appointed assistant to Charles Cannan, who had lately become secretary to the Delegates of the University Press and was already rousing it from the torpor of the nineties. There Milford quickly made his mark as a publisher, especially with books concerned with the writers of the early nineteenth century. In 1906 the delegates sent him to their London office to assist their publisher, Henry Frowde. The intention was that he should succeed Frowde who, though a great Bible publisher, had no academic background and was not in touch with Oxford scholarship. This intention was realized in 1913, and Milford remained Publisher to the University until his retirement in 1945.

The Oxford University Press in London moved from Amen Corner to Amen House (in Warwick Square hard by) in 1924, and in Milford's reign greatly expanded its premises and its business in London and overseas, notably in New York, Toronto, Melbourne and Bombay.

His principal achievement had three aspects. The Press of the nineteenth century had been firmly established on the sale of Bibles and prayerbooks. This was too narrow a basis in altered times, though Milford strengthened the old foundations by his skilful promotion of new hymnals; he was able to widen them by many fresh enterprises in general literature (notably the "World's Classics"), by better marketing of the parallel products, more specifically Oxonian and distinguished as "Clarendon Press books", and by adding fresh departments in medicine and music. Secondly, he had to overcome certain prejudices in strengthening the staff, at home and abroad, with young men and women from the university. Finally, he achieved remarkable though hardly complete success in making the Press, in London and even overseas, a real function of the university.

He certainly made the staffs in London and New York feel themselves to be an Oxford from Oxford. The university *intra muros* remained incompletely converted to this reciprocity. In these activities Milford was helped by his frequent visits to Oxford, by his entertainment of delegates and of his colleagues from Oxford at Amen House, and by occasional visits (with the Oxford secretary) to America. But his success was due primarily to personal qualities. The mild despotism of his rule (which made him "Caesar" to Charles Williams and his colleagues at Amen House), his unfailing catholicism, his nose for a good book on any subject, and a rare sense of the practicable brought him to the head of his profession.

Though unremitting in attendance at his office six days in the week, Milford found time for literature, games, and society. He was a good cricketer in his youth, and later an accomplished player at lawn tennis. He edited, to admiration, the poems of Cowper and Leigh Hunt.

He was the chief editor of *The Oxford Book of Regency* (now *Romantic*) *Verse* and the prime mover in the *Oxford Dictionary of Quotations.* From 1919 to 1921 he was president of the Publishers' Association.

On the completion in 1928 of the *Oxford English Dictionary,* Milford and others were made honorary doctors of letters of the university. He was knighted in 1936 and his portrait was painted for the delegates in 1938 by William Coldstream.

He married first, in 1902, Marion, youngest daughter of Horace Smith, metropolitan magistrate. She died in 1940 and he married, secondly, in 1947, Rose, widow of Sir Arnold Wilson, K.C.I.E., D.S.O., M.P. He had two sons and a daughter by his first wife.

September 8, 1952.

Gertie Millar—See **Dudley.**

Cecil B. de Mille—See **de Mille.**

Carl Milles, one of the most distinguished European sculptors of this century, died in Stockholm at the age of 80 on September 19, 1955.

Not since Rodin has any sculptor (with the possible exception of Sir Jacob Epstein [q.v.]) won such universal suffrage among art critics as Carl Milles, and none has acquired so widespread an international reputation. The general increase of interest in this branch of art had assisted his progress, no doubt, but he owed his renown chiefly to the grandeur of his conceptions, to his unusual sense of fitness in setting, and to a truly sculptural mode of looking at his work, reinforced by genuine humour, tenderness, and imaginative grasp. His celebrated garden at Lidingö, now a possession of the Swedish people, has become a place of pilgrimage for such connoisseurs as have been able to include Sweden in their travels, and his country has been enriched by the public mónuments he had set up in many places.

Carl Wilhelm Emil Milles was born on June 23, 1875, son of Mille (or Emil) Anderson (who had fought on the French side in the war of 1870-71 and thereafter called himself Milles) and his wife, Valborg Tisell, a lady who included a French paternal grandmother in her lineage. Carl's mother died when he was four, and he was taken from a country home to a town flat in Stockholm and educated at the Nääs Sloyd School. Wood sculpture and various handicrafts early aroused his interest; but he was not happy in an urban school and at the age of 14 attempted to sign on aboard a sailing ship, only to be sent home by the skipper. His father then apprenticed him to a cabinet-maker and he attended a technical institute in the evenings. His independent craftwork brought him a prize of 200 crowns, and in 1897, with this modest financial provision, he set off for Chile to join a friend of his father's who was conducting a school of Swedish gymnastics. Arriving in Paris *en route,* he found the attraction of the artist's life so great that he abandoned the emigration project and stayed in the French capital for eight years.

Milles took a small studio and attended classes in sculpture at the Académie Colarossi. For some two years or more he experienced poverty that reached the point of privation; but after he had received an honourable mention for a marble Hylas in the Salon des Artistes Français in 1900 he found himself able to sell small bronzes from time to time to the firm of Collin et Blot, and thereby make a living.

While in Paris he made the acquaintance of such men of mark as Pasteur, Flammarion, and Rodin, and for a considerable period his sculpture was strongly influenced by that of Rodin, and, to some extent, by Constantin Meunier.

The German, Bernhard Hoetger, whom he met in Paris, became a friend, and also influenced his early work in some degree. In 1901 he entered a competition for a monument to a Swedish national hero, Sten Sture, His sketch won only fourth prize, but the students of Upsala were dissatisfied with the verdict and nominated a new jury. Early in 1903 Milles produced a simpler design; but it was not until 1912 that he definitely received the commission, and only in 1925 was this great bronze group, on its huge granite base, at length set up at Upsala.

Leaving Paris in 1906, Milles stayed for a longish period at Munich, where he met Adolf Hildebrand, sculptor, and author of a pamphlet, *Die Problem der Form,* the argument whereof, tending to place sculpture in an ancillary relationship to architecture, made a profound impression on the mind of Milles. At length he returned to Sweden, taking with him as bride an Austrian artist, Olga Luise Granner, of Graz.

Once back in his own country, Milles rapidly cast off all traces of extraneous styles, moved farther away from naturalism, and showed an increasing realization of architecture and sculpture as an *ensemble.* Animal subjects appealed to him from the first. He began to cultivate the gigantic, studied reconstructed prehistoric skeletons, and made an elephant group and a family of *pleiosauri.* He collaborated in various projects with the architects, Liljeqvist and Boberg, and executed figure groups for Tengbom's Enskilda Bank. The volume of commissions became gradually greater, and by 1910 he was busily working on monuments and fountains for public bodies and private concerns.

Milles used all materials, with a special preference for bronze, and carried out most kinds of sculpture, excelling especially in great basin fountains. The first of these was the Fountain of Industry, in green bronze, 15 feet high, at the Stockholm Technical School. The most ambitious in scale and conception were the Poseidon at Gothenburg and the memorial to Folke Filbyter, at Linköping. A smaller fountain, Susanna, won a *grand prix* at the International Exhibition of Decorative Art, Paris, 1925; and another small subject, Diana, in the courtyard of the Swedish Match Company, was light, graceful, and pleasantly diversified in design by the addition of animals and birds. He carried out portrait models like Swedenborg and Lee, and huge stylized figures like the Gustavus Vasa in the Northern Museum.

From some time in the twenties Milles worked more and more in America, where critics, art societies and public bodies united to do him honour and tried hard to induce him to make his home permanently in the United States. He went so far as to spend three months each year at Cranbrook University, Michigan, but would not give up the domain at Lidingö. In spite of the obvious difficulty and expense of arranging sculpture exhibitions his work was shown in some quantity in foreign cities.

Carl Milles was perhaps the greatest, the most versatile and the most profoundly original sculptor produced by our generation. In his early years of work various currents of influence could be detected—French, German, Egyptian, and Oriental—but by the time he had reached his middle thirties he had synthetized all this into a personal style that is not readily susceptible to definition. In its imaginative stylization of real and mythical animals and legendary characters it is strongly Nordic; it contains an element of humour that is rare in sculpture; and its tritons, naiads, and fauns are treated with a wonderful fantasy which, however, never takes away from their monumental solidity.

The architectural sense shown in his planning of large schemes and his placing of individual pieces was remarkable. Fountains in particular showed his genius well, for the interlacing of water jets, the size of pools, the disposition and reflection of figures in them, were all most carefully thought out, so that sculpture and still or moving water combined to form complete designs. Never did his productions seem mere objects for display in a museum. They were strongly rooted in life, in history or in folk-lore, and in their physical aspect they were deliberately designed to be viewed against sun and sky.

In person Milles was short and stocky, with the blond hair so often seen in Sweden. He was quiet and soft-voiced, a man of enormous capacity for work, fond of animals and flowers, reigning in his garden, as a French critic put it, *comme un dieu au centre de sa création.* In a full and happy life one great regret was that his marriage brought him no children.

September 21, 1955.

Dr. R. A. Millikan, who died at his home near Pasadena, California, on December 19, 1953 at the age of 85, was formerly chairman of the Executive Council of the California Institute of Technology and a holder of the Nobel Prize for Physics.

He holds an assured place in the history of science from his determination of the charge of the electron, one of the fundamental constants of physics. Since the ratio of the charge to the mass of the electron had already been determined by J. J. Thomson, and by others after him, Millikan's careful determination of the charge of the electron led at the same time to a more accurate measurement of its mass. For this work, and for his photo-electric determination of Planck's constant, he was in 1923 awarded the Nobel Prize in Physics. He was the first American-born physicist to receive this honour, and the example of experimental skill, imagination, and energy, which he showed during his long working life was of outstanding value in the development of American physics. From 1921 to 1945 he was Director of the Norman Bridge [physical] Laboratory, and chairman of the Executive Council of the California Institute of Technology. On his retirement he became vice-president of the Board of Trustees. Among the many honours that he received was the Hughes Medal of the Royal Society.

Robert Andrews Millikan was born at Morrison, Illinois, on March 22, 1868, and was educated at Maquoketa (Iowa) High School and at Oberlin College. He spent two years in research at Columbia University, obtaining his Ph.D. in 1895, and he studied also at the universities of Berlin and Göttingen. On his return to the United States in 1896, he began an association with the Department of Physics in the University of Chicago which lasted until 1921. It was during this period that he did the research which brought him his Nobel award, and for which he will be chiefly remembered.

Millikan's work at Chicago was begun at that stimulating period when the problems of modern physics were beginning to take shape. In 1897, the year following his return to the United States, J. J. Thomson published his classical experiment on the magnetic and electrostatic deflexion of a beam of cathode rays (electrons), and in the same year J. S. E. (Sir John) Townsend [q.v.] published the first attempt at a direct determination of the charge of the electron through experiments on a cloud of electrically charged droplets of water. The problem was one of great difficulty, and neither Townsend's experiments, nor others which followed, led to reproducible results.

Millikan's work on the electron began in 1906 with a repetition of one of these earlier experiments. Being unable to do better, he developed his own methods which, one by one, eliminated the main possible sources of error. The effect of his improvements was to make it possible to make all measurements on individual droplets, so that statistical uncertainties would be eliminated, and to get rid of unwanted effects from evaporation. These aims he secured by using an electric field strong enough to balance exactly the force of gravity upon the cloud and, in his later experiments, by working with droplets of oil instead of water. His earliest measurements on individual water droplets were reported as an additional paper presented at the Winnipeg meeting of the British Association in August 1909, and by 1917 he had arrived at a value for the charge of the electron which differed by little more than one-half of one per cent. from that now accepted. These experiments formed the kernel of his book *The Electron,* which was first published in 1917, and is as much a classic of exposition as the experiments described are a model of careful and accurate measurement.

His insight into what was important in contemporary physics led him in 1925 (by that time he was at the California Institute of Technology) to begin work in the then relatively new field of cosmic rays. He contributed to the final establishment of the reality of these "rays" and to the recognition that they include at sea level a component more penetrating than the *gamma-rays* emitted by radioactive elements. With I. S. Bowen and H. Victor Neher he was responsible for a high-altitude geographical survey which yielded much valuable information. The evidence was not available at that time which would have made it possible to draw final conclusions as to the nature of the primary "rays"—those which enter the earth's atmosphere from surrounding space—much less as to their origin, which is still uncertain. Millikan had his own ideas on both points, and, through his own work and that of others, stimulated further observation and research. If his interpretations in this field were not supported by later evidence, he has been amply justified on the most important issue: that cosmic rays were a field of work important to modern physics, and promising of results which could not otherwise be obtained. To this work the California Institute of Technology, under his direction and since, has contributed brilliantly.

He married in 1902 Miss Greta Ervin Blanchard. There were three sons of the marriage, one of whom, Clark B. Millikan, has been in charge of aerodynamic research at the California Institute of Technology.

December 21, 1953.

Annette Mills, famous for her association with the "Muffin the Mule" puppet, and one of the most popular entertainers of children on television, died in hospital in London on January 10, 1955. She was 60.

The daughter of Lewis Mills, she was born in Chelsea and was educated at King's Lynn High School and the Convent of Notre Dame at Norwich. Her younger brother is John Mills, the actor.

Her original intention was to become a concert pianist and organist. She turned, however, to dancing and won fame first as an exhibition dancer in Britain and oversea. Her career in entertainment was twice interrupted and altered by accidents, the first being a fall in which she broke a leg. This put an end to her career as a dancer, and she then began writing popular songs, with some success. Of these "Boomps-a-daisy" and "Home, Sweet Home Again" will probably be best remembered. She later returned to the stage in cabaret and revue, and it was during the 1939-45 War, when on her way to entertain troops, that ill-luck again overtook her. She was severely injured in a car accident, and her success in television came after a courageous fight back to health necessitating three years in hospital.

Her first broadcast had been from Savoy Hill in 1930. She also took part in the first "In Town To-night" programme and had made several other broadcasts before her appearances with "Muffin the Mule" and the other puppets manipulated principally by Anne Hogarth, as well as the "Prudence the Kitten" programmes, brought her outstanding success. Her first appearance on television was in June 1946, before she created the "Muffin the Mule" programme with Miss Hogarth. In addition to her work for the programme, she wrote a number of "Muffin" song books, made records, and published a reading book about the adventures of the puppet.

She was twice married, and her second marriage, to Robert Sielle, was dissolved. She is survived by her daughter, who was born of her first marriage, and was the illustrator of the "Muffin" books.

January 11, 1955.

W. H. Mills, F.R.S., Fellow and President of Jesus College, Cambridge, 1940-48, and Emeritus Reader in Stereochemistry in the university, died on February 22, 1959 at the age of 85.

William Hobson Mills, son of W. H. Mills, went up to Jesus College, Cambridge, from Uppingham in 1897, and read medicine and natural sciences, taking first class in both parts of the Tripos. But chemistry soon became his main interest and he commenced research directly after taking his B.A. In 1899 he was elected to a Prize Fellowship at his college and shortly after left for Germany, where he studied at the University of Tübingen under von Pechmann and where he graduated Sc.D., *summa cum laude.*

On the expiry of his College Fellowship in 1902 he left to become head of the Chemical Department at the Northern Polytechnic Institute, a post which he held for 10 years. In 1912 he returned to Cambridge to take up the duties of Fellow and Lecturer in natural sciences at Jesus College and demonstrator to the Jacksonian Professor (Dewar), in succession to the late H. O. Jones.

The Cambridge school of stereochemistry was founded by Jones, and greatly extended by Pope and by Mills, but it is to Mills and his pupils that its greatest achievements were due. All Mills's published work was characterized by originality, elegance, and great thoroughness. Perhaps his most outstanding contributions to this branch of chemical science were his demonstration of the configuration of the ammonium salts in 1925, in which he showed that in these compounds the groups around the nitrogen atom are arranged tetrahedrally; his proof in 1935 that the valencies in certain platinous compounds are in one plane; and his realization in the same year with Maitland of optical isomerism in an allene, which had been predicted theoretically by van't Hoff.

During the First World War Mills became occupied with a variety of technical problems, of which the most important were the cyanine dyes. These compounds have the property of rendering photographic plates sensitive to yellow and red rays, and research on their preparation and properties for preparing panchromatic films for aeroplane photography was an urgent matter. In collaboration with his pupils, Mills subsequently published the results of these and of further investigations on the same subject between 1920 and 1922. He was elected a Fellow of the Royal Society in 1923.

After holding a university lectureship for a number of years, he was appointed to a specially created Readership in Stereochemistry—a post which he held until his retirement. He held the George Fisher Baker Lectureship in Chemistry at Cornell University in 1937, but contrary to the usual custom he never published his course of lectures. He was President of the Chemical Section of the British Association in 1932, and of the Chemical Society in 1943 and 1944. From the Chemical Society he received the Longstaff Medal in 1930, and the Royal Society awarded him the Davy Medal in 1935.

Mills fulfilled with great distinction the office of president of Jesus College. He was in every sense of the word a scholar, and was a brilliant lecturer. His abler research pupils found him most stimulating. With weaker men he was less successful, indeed his problems were beyond their grasp. He was a very "well-read" chemist, with an extensive knowledge of many branches of the science altogether remote from the one in which his greatest interests lay. This scholarly attitude of mind led him to distrust the ever-increasing tendency to premature specialization.

But not only was Mills widely read as a chemist; he was in addition a most accomplished field botanist and ornithologist. There are, indeed, few who excelled him in knowledge of the distribution and habitat of fen and Breckland plants, and he was an expert on the brambles. No one knew him fully who did not know him as a naturalist. His love of the English countryside found expression, too, in his activities on the local committee of management of the National Trust properties at Wicken Fen, of which committee he was for many years treasurer and then chairman.

Mills had too a delightful and kindly sense of humour and a fund of good stories to which his excellence as a *raconteur* enabled him to do full justice. People of many different interests found him most excellent company, for his range of knowledge and interests was so wide that there were few who would not find some point of contact.

In 1903 Mills married Mildred Gostling. There were four children of the marriage, a son and three daughters.

February 23, 1959.

The death of **A. A. Milne,** which occurred on January 31, 1956 at the age of 74 at his home in Sussex, after a long illness, marks the loss of a gifted and conspicuously successful playwright and of an essayist, novelist, and writer of light verse of witty and whimsical accomplishment.

His was very much a gift for light comedy. Yet the wit, the good humour, the graceful ease of his plays, while for the most part they afforded only innocent pleasures and sustained a restricted range of illusion, were turned to genuine dramatic effect by his skill and resource in craftsmanship. What he attempted to do in the theatre he nearly always did uncommonly well, but it is for his nursery books that his name will be chiefly remembered. Pooh has become an international figure and stands out from countless animals of nursery literature as a classic. There must be in such a classic something that appeals to grown-ups, a quality that makes them wish to introduce the work to their children. The gentle philosophy, the pure nonsense, and the skill and grace of the writing which are to be found in the Pooh books provide this quality abundantly. To the reproach, for such it often seemed to be, that he had always been successful, Milne very sincerely replied in his autobiography, *It's Too Late Now,* published in 1939, that he had always written precisely what he had wanted to write. It was a characteristic apologia for his sense of personal good fortune.

Born of Scots parentage on January 18, 1882, the youngest of three sons of John Vine Milne, preparatory school master in London, Alan Alexander Milne was educated at Westminster and at Trinity College, Cambridge. He was prominent in undergraduate journalism, edited *Granta* for a year, and immediately went into professional journalism in London. From 1906 until 1914 he was on the staff of *Punch.* Three volumes of essays and papers published during those years largely made up of his contributions to *Punch* exhibit a pretty wit and a pleasant, half-deprecatingly bookish vein of reflection. In 1915 he enlisted in The Royal Warwickshire Regiment and served in France.

His first piece for the theatre, a short play entitled *Wurzel Flummery* (1917), was slight and somewhat laboured in farcical idea. It was amusing in performance, did not lack a neat and whimsical sense of character, and gave unmistakable evidence of a natural bent for the theatre. The presiding influence of the five plays Milne had written by 1919 was, without question, Barrie, though as yet it was an influence imperfectly assimilated. Then, in the following year, came *Mr. Pim Passes By,* and the trumpets sounded for Milne for the first and by no means the last time in Shaftesbury Avenue. Adroit, amiable, nicely scored with fun, the play is a shrewd and entertaining trifle, which bore revival more than once in succeeding years. In the same year also playgoers had their first opportunity of seeing *The Romantic Age.* The following year was marked by the production of *The Truth about Blayds.* The play has a wonderfully good first act, which almost destroys the balance of what follows, and there will be many to remember the superb acting of Norman McKinnel, who was assisted by Dion Boucicault, Irene Vanbrugh, and Irene Rooke [q.v.] in the original performance.

Henceforth one had a fair idea of what to expect from any new play of Milne's. At his best he was spirited in fun and lively in dialogue. *The Dover Road* (1922) and *The Great Broxopp* (1923) were both pieces of light and fetching nonsense; *To Have the Honour* (1924) was Milne at his lightest; and *The Fourth Wall* (1928), a most ingenious essay in the logical deduction of murder, was an exceptionally skilful piece of craftsmanship. Of the plays that followed, the frequently revived *Toad of Toad Hall,* a graceful and charming adaptation of Kenneth Grahame's *The Wind in the Willows,* is in a class by itself. But *Michael and Mary* (1930), though it misses conviction in the theatre, carries off its effects with romantic zest, and *Other People's Wives* (1932) manifests a pleasant farcical accomplishment.

Outside the theatre there was a special audience, consisting of a widening multitude of children and grown-ups, that Milne had made his own, and it was here, perhaps, that he scored his greatest success. In *Winnie-the-Pooh* and *The House at Pooh Corner* he caught and held for a moment in his hands that enchanted moment of childhood when to do nothing is to do everything. The idea of bringing his child's toys to life belongs to his wife, and to the task he brought an exquisitely careful craftsmanship and a properly serious appreciation of the work involved. Pooh and his playmates have been taken to heart by children everywhere, and the whimsical bear is assured of a lasting place in the nursery, not only in Britain but in the many countries into whose language they have been translated, including Japanese and Bulgarian.

It was the same combination of craftsmanship and comprehension that gave charm to his books of children's verse, beginning in 1924 with *When We Were Very Young.* None of these verses had quite the carefree, nonsensical quality that was to be found in the Pooh books, and although many of Christopher Robin's moods were perfectly mirrored, Milne stumbled at times from sentiment into sentimentality as he never did in the woodland. Yet, generally, he was surefooted and nimble.

Milne wrote two detective novels and two "straight" novels, *Two People* (1931) and *Chloe Marr* (1946). In *Peace with Honour* (1934) he gave expression to a sincere and thoughtful attitude towards the menace of a revived militarism in Germany. His autobiography, which appeared on the eve of the War of 1939-45, is good reading. In his last years he turned to writing short stories and found in America, as always, an appreciative audience. *Birthday Party* and *A Table Near the Band,* collections of short stories which appeared in England in 1949 and 1951, showed him to have lost none of his versatility, including as they did the adventurous, the sentimental, the cynical, and the purely frivolous. His last published work was *Year In, Year Out,* a collection of urbane pieces in verse and prose.

In 1952 he underwent an operation on the brain which left him an invalid. His courage, and a remarkable piece of surgery, brought him through that crisis, and he returned to his home at Hartfield, Sussex. He was a man of cultivated taste, a friendly companion at golf and at his clubs in London, and a lover of cricket and of country pursuits.

He married Miss Dorothy de Sélincourt in 1913. There was one son, Christopher Robin Milne, of the marriage.

February 1, 1956.

Lady Milner, who died at her home near Hawkhurst on October 10, 1958, was cast in the heroic mould. All her long life—and she was 86 when she died—she was a valiant fighter.

Many who did not know her well may have thought of her chiefly as an intransigent exponent of strong Imperial views. Certainly when she took over the editorship of the *National Review* from her brother Leo Maxse she made it one of the hardest-hitting periodicals in Britain, always highly individualistic and by no means orthodox in its conservatism. It gave warnings against German militarism before 1939 when such warnings were not fashionable. It attacked the South African Nationalists—and many of the United Party for good measure. It decried the League of Nations, the Socialists, most of the Liberals, and could criticize both Neville Chamberlain and Sir Winston Churchill* in the same number.

Yet there were many other sides to her strong and deep character. Although she was brought up in the settled Victorian years, and lived among the greatest in the land, she was never—even towards the end of her life—anything but a contemporary, passionately interested in all the changes and all the events of the day. The life she had known was gone, but she never wasted time in repining for the privileged past. Courage was her stay, and she would always use her piercing intelligence to analyse every political and social trend and every international happening. As she withdrew through age from political life she kept alive her friendships and was never happier than when meeting younger people and hearing of their hopes and problems. To them she was loyal, generous, warmhearted, wise and patient in giving advice, unsurpassed in courtesy, grace, and understanding.

Few ladies of her years had such a fund of tradition and experience to draw upon, and in talks at her home at Great Wigsell she drew upon it freely to enlighten the problems of the day—or just for the pleasure of remembering things past. She seemed to have known everyone: Queen Victoria, Rhodes, Meredith, Clemenceau. Her first marriage, to Lord Edward Cecil brought her into the great world of Hatfield when Lord Salisbury was Prime Minister, and Cabinet Ministers and visiting foreign statesmen gathered. Having known so many people, then their children, and then their grand-children, and having watched traits running through families, she was a brilliant reader of character. Often she would foretell how a man would develop, how he was likely to face a crisis, or whether he would persevere or waver on a long uphill road—and she was uncannily right almost always.

She had herself been brought up in a different world from Hatfield. Her father, Admiral Maxse, had carried dispatches through the Russian lines in the Crimean War. His marriage was not altogether happy, and the five children spent part of their time with their father in the country and part in London with their mother. As a girl Lady Milner—Violet Georgina Maxse then—studied art in Paris, went with her mother to private views of the Academy pictures, heard Joachim play at afternoon parties, and met many writers. Lord Salisbury, before her marriage to his son, seems to have wondered how, with her artistic and literary pursuits, she would fit into the political life at Hatfield; she would recall how he once drew her aside and said in the kindest possible way: "Never forget, my dear, Hatfield is Gaza, capital of Philistia!"

They were happy and enthralling years. Lord Edward Cecil, her husband, and Sir Ivor Maxse [q.v.], her brother, gained the D.S.O. on the same day in 1898 for services in Egypt and the Sudan. After a distinguished career, first in Egypt, then in South Africa and again in Egypt and the Sudan, Lord Edward died in 1919. Their only son had been killed in the early days of the fighting in France in 1914 while serving with the Grenadier Guards; it was a blow all the heavier to bear because Lady Edward, with her Maxse family, had for years been giving warning of German preparedness for war. Their daughter, Helen, married the second Lord Hardinge of Penshurst [q.v.] in 1921.

Lady Edward, who had met Lord Milner during the South African War, was married to him very quietly in 1921. Her second husband, who was in his sixty-seventh year at the time of his marriage to her, died, full of honour in 1925. Soon afterwards his widow gave their home, Sturry Court, Canterbury, a beautiful Jacobean house standing in a garden which had been Lord Milner's delight in his closing years, to The King's School, Canterbury, and the junior school, formerly in the precincts of the cathedral, is still housed there.

In 1929 Lady Milner, by a further act of generosity, handed over to the Public Record Office various documents relating to the famous Doullens Agreement of 1918, under which Lord Milner, on behalf of the British Government, agreed to the unity of command of the allied forces in France under Marshal Foch. She gave the rich accumulation of Milner Papers to New College, Oxford, which she often visited.

During the illness and after the death in 1929 of her brother Leo Maxse, Lady Milner took over as a pious duty the editorship of the *National Review* and continued his work of writing the "Episodes of the Month", the chief and most characteristic feature of the periodical. She upheld the trust with untiring energy until in 1948 she met with a serious accident, from which she happily recovered, but which curtailed her activities for some time. The editorship was then taken over by Lord Altrincham [q.v.].

It was truly said when she gave up her work for the paper that her memorable editorship would stand on its own feet as part of the history of the times. Yet she would have been the last to claim it as such, for she always maintained that she merely carried on the work of her beloved brother. She shared to the full his vehement political opinions, his distrust of German policies, his implicit faith in all things French. (Only in her later years did the state of France sadden her.)

During the Second World War she met General de Gaulle* several times, and one of the last books which she read, only a few weeks ago, was his account of his mission during the war years—"a great book", she said. She had an immense knowledge and love of literary and historical works, French as much as English, and, when talking, could always produce a quotation very much to the point from Saint Simon, Lenotre, Dickens, Meredith, or Kipling. To the very end her mind kept its incisiveness. She remained eager to meet people, and fretted only because increasing age stopped her going to Paris and made her visits to London less frequent than she wished.

In 1951 she published *My Picture Gallery*—a freshly told account of her life and of the people she had known in Victorian days.

October 11, 1958.

Dr. F. C. Minett, C.I.E., M.B.E., D.SC., M.R.C.V.S., Director of the Animal Health Trust's farm livestock research station at Houghton Grange, died on Boxing Day 1953 at Hartley, near Dartford, Kent, at the age of 63.

Francis Colin Minett was born on September 16, 1890, and was educated at King Edward's School, Bath, the Royal Veterinary College, London, and the Institut Pasteur, Paris. From 1914 to 1924 he held a commission in the Royal Veterinary Corps and soon after resigning his commission he was appointed director of the research institute in animal pathology at the Royal Veterinary College. He became Professor of Pathology there in 1933 and retained the post until 1939 when he went to India as Director of the Imperial Veterinary Research Institute at Mukteswar. After the end of British administration in India he was engaged by the Government of Pakistan as Commissioner for Animal Husbandry. His contract expired in 1949 and for the next two years he was veterinary adviser to the Government of Turkey.

During his career he published upwards of 50 original research papers, mostly on the pathology and bacteriology of disease conditions of farm livestock. He also contributed a number of more popular articles for educational purposes; among the latter may be specially mentioned articles annually from 1928 to 1938 on prevention of animal disease in the *Farmer's Guide to Agricultural Research,* published by the Royal Agricultural Society; the article on mastitis in the *Encyclopaedia of Veterinary Medicine,* edited by Professor G. H. Wooldridge; and the article on glanders in the *System of Bacteriology,* published by the Medical Research Council.

Either alone or in collaboration he had conducted researches into bovine tuberculosis, including experiments on the vaccination of cattle, using bacilli from man and birds; Johne's disease; and foot-and-mouth disease. The last-named work was undertaken on behalf of the Foot-and-Mouth Disease Committee. His other work included investigations of mastitis in sheep, black-quarter, anthrax, strangles in horses, mortality wastage among livestock in India, animal health as affected by climatic conditions, and various public health subjects.

He married in 1919 Iza, daughter of Mr. W. Stitt, of Belfast, who survives him with a son of the marriage.

December 31, 1953.

Mistinguett died on January 5, 1956 at her brother's house on the outskirts of Paris. When spending Christmas with him she suffered a heart attack and pneumonia developed.

More people will regret the disappearance of Mistinguett from the scene than ever saw her. Superior in this even to film stars, whose appearance at least is known to thousands, she was a member of that little band of legendary figures which for some reason or other appeal to the imagination of the world although the world might be hard put to say what it is in them that is appealing. For Parisians, no doubt, Mistinguett will be mourned partly as a music-hall performer whose remarkable vitality, frank vulgarity and sympathy with the popular part of her audience made her notable.

Yet even Parisians will mourn her as something else, as the topic of innumerable anecdotes and the subject of, as it might be, an individual folklore. London, which did not see her on its own stage until 1947, when she was certainly over 70, beheld with fascinated attention the spectacle at last of a personage whose music-hall reputation became for our week-ending fathers one of the symbols of Parisian gaiety. Beneath an immense mushroom of feathers and somewhat precariously balanced on very high thin heels, she sang in a voice that was still pleasantly firm a few songs that cynically, if a little conventionally, linked love with money. Flourishing a long cigarette-holder, she visited the stalls in search of a millionaire. And then, at the second line of her well-known song "Mon Homme", she burst into tears and said she would not go on. Her manager came forward with the explanation that, for all her long experience, Mistinguett was suffering from "first night nerves".

Behind and beyond her performances were the adventures, the little ebullitions of unconventionality, which appear so captivating to the conventional rest of us. "Miss", as Parisians had for so long called her, had the power, not always to be envied, of causing things to happen. When over 60 she had a narrow escape from a too-ardent admirer from the provinces who turned up at her flat in Paris to press his suit with the aid of a revolver and a whip. He rushed from room to room in search of her, but "Miss", who was used to admiration from her public, had locked herself in her boudoir and stayed there until help arrived. In the United States between the wars she seems to have stepped into the shoes of Bernhardt so far as glamour was concerned, and there, too, she had adventures, now among the manufacturers of patent medicines, now with the promoters of a new religion which needed the boost of a "female pope".

Mistinguett's real name was Jeanne Bourgeois. She was the daughter of a Belgian and a French Jewess who kept a small furniture shop at Montmorency, near Paris. She was given what was to be her stage name at the age of 15 by the companions who daily took the train from Enghien, a neighbouring suburb, to Paris with her, when she went up to town to take violin lessons. They chose it for her because they considered that her profile and her prominent front teeth made her look English—or at any rate like the Englishwoman of the French cartoonist of the period. So she had to be "Miss". At first the name was Mistinguette; but when she went on to the café-concert stage a year or two later she dropped the final "e" to make it, as she thought, more English than ever. She won her earliest successes during an eight years' engagement at the most famous of the old café-concerts, the Eldorado. She left it to take part in light musical plays, then joined the Moulin-Rouge, where her "Valse Chaloupée" became the rage of Paris. Afterwards she appeared in farce at the Gymnase and the Palais-Royal, and returned to musical plays as a member of the famous company at the Variétés.

In 1911 she made her first visit to the United States, and on her return began her appearances in the long series of spectacular *revues* at the Folies-Bergère and afterwards at the Casino de Paris and the Moulin-Rouge, where for half the show she wore magnificent costumes and enormous hats and for the other half played low-life sketches, usually with Maurice Chevalier* as her partner. It was during this period that songs of hers, like "Mon Homme", became famous. It was also during this period that it was said that her perfect legs were insured for a fabulous sum. In 1921 she returned to the dramatic stage by taking the principal part—originally played by Réjane—in a revival of Sardou's *Madame Sans-Gêne*. But she soon returned to the Casino de Paris and its revues.

Though she did not often appear outside Paris she was persuaded to undertake a number of tours after the end of the last war. Besides her appearance in London in 1947, she appeared in Rome in 1950, and in the course of the next year she again visited New York. Soon after her return to Paris the city learnt with consternation that she had collapsed with a heart attack while attending a first night at the Théâtre Edouard VII. She, herself, made light of it and indeed not long after was showing her famous legs at the "Kermesse aux Étoiles", the annual fête of the theatrical profession in Paris.

Soon afterwards she wrote an autobiography which was less revealing than many people had hoped and added little to her *Confessions* which had appeared in 1938. It certainly did not give away her age, her fierce concealment of which had for years been the origin of many jokes widely current among her compatriots. But the jokes were good humoured for, to the French, and in particular to the Parisians, she was indeed what King Edward VII once called her: "The Spirit of Paris".

January 6, 1956.

Lucila Godoy Alcayaga—Gabriela Mistral to use the name under which the Chilean poet and educationalist wrote—died in hospital in New York on January 10, 1957.

The national poet and author as the representative figure of a country's overall aspirations is a rare phenomenon; yet that precisely is the part played for decades by Gabriela Mistral for Chile, land of her birth. She played it in a dignified and impressive way, steadily increasing her international stature and it is not easy to decide in which sphere she shone the brightest, as the Nobel Prize-winning writer or the humanitarian reformer and educationist.

She was born on April 7, 1889, at Vicuña in Chile. She received a good education and studied child welfare, labour and education while working for a teacher's degree. After working at several rural and secondary schools she was appointed to the Liceo de los Andes at Punta Arenas, in the far south of Chile, in 1912, subsequently becoming its director. Ten years later she was sent under a Government mission to Mexico, there to act as adviser and to study the public library system. She stayed from 1922 to 1924 and, by this work as well as by her literary activities which had started in 1908, so impressed her authorities that she was pensioned off as a teacher on the grounds of "her outstanding cultural work" in 1924, and, a year later, appointed as Chilean delegate to the League of Nation's Institute of International Intellectual Cooperation at Paris. In that capacity she had the opportunity of travelling widely and of representing Chile, together with Ecuador, at the International Congress of Universities at Madrid in 1928, and of lecturing as a guest professor at American universities and colleges.

Gabriela Mistral was head of the Committee of Letters of the Paris Institute of Intellectual Cooperation, and of the League of Nations' Committee for Arts and Letters, both from 1926 to 1939. Simultaneously Chile, in order to regularize her role as the country's "spiritual ambassador", appointed her as consul, first in Madrid in 1934, and from 1935 as "Consul for Life", by a special law, with far-reaching particular privileges. Among them was that of choosing where she should serve. Exercising her privilege, she was Consul at Lisbon, then at Nice, Rio de Janeiro and Petropolis, Brazil, Los Angeles, and Santa Barbara, and finally in Mexico.

Apart from her journalistic work Gabriela Mistral wrote *La Voz de Elqui* (1908), *La Muerte, Desolació* (1922), *Lectura para Mujeres* (1923), *Nubes Blancas* (1923), *Tala* (1938), *Ternura* (1946), and a *Life of S. Francis of Assisi,* as well as some remarkable poetry, in which the influence of Buddhist thought is often to be traced. Most of her novels have since found their way into French, English, and other foreign literature, although they do not lend themselves easily to translation. Their lasting importance, however, received the highest recognition by her winning, in 1945, the Nobel Prize of Literature, Honorary degrees were conferred upon her by many foreign universities, among them Florence, California, Guatemala, and Santiago.

Of great personal charm and sincerity, she benefited from the frame and the means of her official capacity as Consul of her country for the creation of a wide and varied circle of friends and of guests of all nationalities, mostly in her home at Santa Barbara, in California. She left her imprint, however, upon a much wider circle; possibly, upon her whole period.

January 11, 1957.

F. A. Mitchell-Hedges, explorer and author, died on June 12, 1959 at his home near Newton Abbot. He was 76.

Frederick Albert Mitchell-Hedges, son of John Hedges, was born on October 22, 1882, and educated at Berkhampstead and University College School, London. He came to manhood at a time when if there were no new continents to conquer there were still "faraway places with strange-sounding names" to be visited and the going was still good. In his autobiography, *Danger my Ally,* which was published in 1955, he described how before he was 20 he had been on an ill-fated geological survey on the edge of the Arctic and had some success playing the New York stock market, later fighting under a series of leaders in various South American countries.

Central America, indeed, came to be something of a spiritual home to him; he found there what his adventurous nature sought, and he returned to it again and again, disappearing for a year or more at a time to emerge laden with the trophies of the chase, bird, beast, and fish, and the household gods of ancient civilizations which were a lifelong interest of his.

In the early 1920s he was several times in Panama fascinated by the way of life of the Chucunaque Indians who live in a remote part of the isthmus. The fruits of these travels, a large ethnographical collection including necklaces, wood carvings, and brightly painted woven cloth, were given to the British Museum.

He was in British Honduras in 1925 with Dr. T. W. F. Gann exploring the Maya city of Lubaantun, and in the following year did some digging there. Four years later he led an expedition from the United States into the Republic of Honduras, where ancient ruins were explored and a quantity of pottery which was brought home was given to the Museum of the American Indian. His later travels took him to Islas Bahia, off Honduras, from which he again presented a collection to the British Museum; to the Seychelles, where the atolls south of Mahe were explored; and to the southern province of Tanganyika, where he examined Islamic ruins in the Kilwa Masoko region.

For many the name Mitchell-Hedges will always be associated with big game fishing. He fished much in the Caribbean, often, it would appear, at some risk to himself and his companions; tiger sharks, sting rays, sawfishes all fell to his line and what he caught he brought home and exhibited at one of the large London stores.

He was a romantic—the titles of some of his books, *Battles with Giant Fish, Land of Wonder and Fear*—bear witness to that. They were writ large, perhaps a little too large for some scientific authorities who felt that his conclusions were too dogmatic and imperfectly substantiated.

Himself brimful of enthusiasm and initiative he praised them in others, and it was typical of him that in 1947 he should present a solid silver bowl (132 years old—he had a fine collection of old silver—) to the mining industry to be awarded as a prize in a national coal output competition.

In 1947 he offered to finance a British Museum expedition to British Honduras, but the difficulties of post-war reorganization at the museum made it impossible for his offer to be accepted.

June 13, 1959.

Dimitri Mitropoulos, who died in a Milan hospital on November 2, 1960 after a heart attack while rehearsing the orchestra of La Scala, was Greece's greatest conductor, a convinced and eloquent champion of new music, and an orchestral trainer of outstanding brilliance, whose work with the New York Philharmonic Symphony Orchestra made a deep impression on his two visits to Britain as their conductor.

It was not to conducting that Mitropoulos aspired in his youth, but to composition—and to a monastic life. His family and forebears included several monks and priests, and Dimitri, who was born in Athens on March 1, 1896, fully intended from boyhood to devote his life to the Orthodox church, giving back to God the musical talent which had already shown itself in him. The world claimed Mitropoulos's musicianship, but he remained a deeply religious man, spartan in his daily life and mystical in his thought, though remarkably practical in his music-making.

In Athens he studied pianoforte and musical theory, graduating in 1918 with a gold medal for his piano playing. Two years later his first and only opera, *Sister Beatrice,* was produced in Athens and roused the interest of Saint-Saëns, who proposed that Mitropoulos should go to study with him in Paris; the young composer had, however, already made plans to study composition in Brussels with Paul Gilson, where he also trained as an organist. He was by now a pianist of high promise and from Brussels he went to Berlin as a member of Busoni's pianoforte master class, at the same time earning his living as a *répétiteur* at the Berlin State Opera. In 1924 he returned to teach in Athens, but also to conduct there.

From 1927 his direction of the Athens Conservatory Orchestra began to attract a more than local reputation, both for the sheer quality of the orchestral playing and for Mitropoulos's championship of new music and of neglected classics. In 1930 he was invited to conduct the Berlin Philharmonic Orchestra, and when his soloist failed to appear, caused a stir by performing Prokofiev's [q.v.] third piano concerto himself, as well as conducting the orchestra.

The success of this dual role encouraged Mitropoulos to make it a feature of his repertory. After tours of Europe and Russia he was invited by Sergei Koussevitsky [q.v.] in 1936 to conduct the Boston Symphony Orchestra, and from then on he worked principally in America, first as conductor of the Minneapolis Symphony Orchestra from 1937 to 1949, and subsequently of the New York Philharmonic Symphony Orchestra with which he visited London and the Edinburgh Festival. In recent years he had conducted fairly regularly at the Metropolitan Opera in New York, and in 1958 brought Samuel Barber's opera *Vanessa* to Salzburg Festival for its European premiere. He was often to be heard at other European music festivals, and it is to be regretted that he visited London so rarely.

Mitropoulos's performances were characterized by white-hot intensity. In the classics his impulsiveness and ardour sometimes resulted in lopsided or unstylish interpretations, but the impulsiveness sprang from no inner uncertainty, but from profound knowledge of the music and from convictions that he could not restrain. In romantic music, particularly of the Russian school, he was a thrilling interpreter; but it was in contemporary works that he excelled, from Richard Strauss to the serialists of today.

He conducted without a baton and from memory, even at rehearsal—American musicians were dumbfounded by his command of every detail in the score of Berg's *Wozzeck* when he prepared and conducted the concert performance which was recorded for the gramophone (it has yet to be issued in Britain). His memory was not, however, photographic; he learned his scores the hard way, by scrupulous analysis. British audiences will best remember him for the magnificent reading of Vaughan Williams's [q.v.] fourth symphony which he conducted at the Edinburgh Festival in 1951 and again in 1955. We are slow to accept foreigners' interpretations of British music, but many musicians who thought that they knew this symphony well found themselves capitulating utterly before this revelatory performance by an American orchestra under its Greek conductor.

November 3, 1960.

Hadj Mohammed El Mokri, who was Grand Vizier of Morocco for nearly 50 years, died at Rabat on September 9, 1957 at the reputed age of 116.

His delicacy, subtlety of wit, experience of affairs, and the facility with which he assimilated ideas and information enabled him to keep a place of power at the foot of the throne for nearly half a century, and to accomplish much for his country's benefit. In the end even his age, piety, and dignity did not preserve him from falling before the new force of independence. Early in his long career he led a Moroccan delegation to the court of Napoleon III: two years ago he led another, by aircraft, to negotiate with a Government of the French Republic a settlement which soon led to the end of the French protectorate which he had been instrumental in arranging 43 years earlier.

El Mokri was born in Fez. His father was a building contractor and left him a considerable fortune. The son entered the service of Sultan Moulay Hassan and, during the reign of Sultan Moulay Abdul Aziz, represented Morocco at the Conference of Algeciras in 1906. On his return he was appointed Minister of Finance, in which capacity he undertook a mission to Paris in 1908 and returned to become Grand Vizier for the first time. On the accession of Sultan Moulay Hafid in 1909 he once again became Minister of Finance, and during the same year was sent to Paris for the purpose of signing a financial treaty. In 1911 he succeeded Si Madani Glaoui as Grand Vizier—a position which he held at the time of the outbreak in Fez which led to the proclamation of the Protectorate in 1912.

From that time onwards he loyally supported the new ruler, Sultan Moulay Yussef, and the Resident-General, Marshal Lyautey, and helped them to survive a difficult period in which the future of the country lay in the balance. At the end of 1913 he asked to be relieved of his duties but in 1917 he was recalled to Rabat and made Grand Vizier once again. He often acted as mediator between the Sultan and the Resident-General, urging moderation on both sides.

He was still at the centre of affairs during the disturbances in Morocco which preceded its attainment of independence in 1956, holding his office before and during the exile of Sultan ben Ussef; and he was a member of the regency council when the Sultan ben Arafa withdrew to Tangier in September 1955. But he had been too long identified with the French administration to survive on the political stage when the forces of independence prevailed, and his power, together with his office, was abolished under the new regime.

September 10, 1957.

J. A. Mollison, M.B.E., who died on October 30, 1959 at the age of 54, will be remembered chiefly as a pilot who made many long-distance flights in light aircraft in record time in the years between the wars.

To Jim Mollison record-breaking flights were both a passion and a profession. He loved adventure and travel, and he loved to pit his own skill—he was a fine navigator, indeed he had to be—and his remarkable powers of endurance against the great distances of the world.

He was born in Glasgow on April 19, 1905,

and was educated at Edinburgh Academy. When he was 18 years of age the Lord Provost of Glasgow nominated him for a short service commission in the Royal Air Force, and he learnt to fly at the Flying Training School at Duxford, Cambridgeshire. In 1925 he was sent to India and took part in the air operations against the Mahsuds. For a time he was test pilot at the Aircraft Park at Lahore. On being transferred to the Home establishment he went through a course at the Central Flying School at Wittering, and was posted as flying instructor at the Flying Training School at Sealand, near Chester.

Subsequently, his Air Force service behind him, Mollison went to Australia and became instructor to the Adelaide branch of the Australian Aero Club. Later he became a pilot of the company formed by Kingsford Smith, Australian National Airways Ltd., which carried on air services between Brisbane, Sydney, and Melbourne.

In 1931 he determined to try to establish a new record for a solo flight in a light aircraft from Australia to England. Lord Wakefield presented him with a Gipsy Moth, but in endeavouring to take off from Darwin he crashed and wrecked the machine. Lord Wakefield then gave him another Moth, and on July 30 he took off from Wyndham. Flying with a minimum of sleep and rest, and navigating with extreme accuracy, he reached England and landed at Pevensey Bay after a flight of 8 days 19hr. 25min.

On March 24, 1932, he made a start for the Cape in a Puss Moth with a Gipsy 3 engine, and arrived at Cape Town after a flight of only 4 days 17hr. 22min. Again he allowed himself only a minimum of sleep, and when he arrived over Cape Town airfield about 8 p.m. he was so exhausted that he suffered from duplicated vision, and the aerodrome lights bewildered him. Accordingly he landed on the beach near by, ran into the sea, and turned over.

At Cape Town he again met Amy Johnson, the airwoman, and shortly afterwards they became engaged. The marriage took place at St. George's, Hanover Square, on July 29, 1932. Colonel Shelmerdine, Director of Civil Aviation, was best man, while the bride was given away by Kathleen Countess of Drogheda. They flew in two light aircraft to Scotland for the honeymoon.

Mollison had already decided to fly the Atlantic from east to west in a light aircraft, and he did not let his honeymoon interfere with his plans. He procured a Puss Moth with a 120 h.p. Gipsy 3 engine, and named the machine "The Heart's Content", after, he said, a town in Newfoundland. On August 18, 1932, he took off from Portmarnock Strand in Ireland. After 19hr. 5min. he struck the coast of Newfoundland, only 20 miles north of the spot at which he had aimed. Then he turned southwards hoping to make New York, but ran into very heavy fogs, and in the next six hours covered only 136 miles. As he realized that his remaining petrol would not take him to New York he landed in New Brunswick in a field.

When he reached New York a few days later he was given a great reception. This flight was the first crossing of the North Atlantic in a light aircraft; it was the first solo crossing from east to west; it was the fastest crossing from east to west, and it was the longest duration flight at that time in a light aircraft.

On February 6, 1933, Mollison started off from Lympne in "The Heart's Content" with a Gipsy Major engine and flew across the South Atlantic to Brazil, which he reached on the evening of February 8. His course was across France and Spain and down the west coast of Africa to Thies, where he started off across the ocean. He did the 2,000-mile crossing in the record time of 17hr. 40min. He went on from Natal to Rio de Janeiro, and toured about before returning home.

Then Mr. and Mrs. Mollison decided to do a great dual flight by husband and wife, and had an ambition to beat the long-distance record by flying eastward from New York to Baghdad. They got a D.H. Dragon with two Gipsy Major engines and flew out to America in it on July 22-24, 1933, making for New York. About 60 miles short of that city they realized that their petrol was short, and so landed in the dark at Bridgeport. The Dragon ran into a swamp and overturned, and both the occupants were slightly injured. The machine was seriously damaged.

In March 1934, Mollison was awarded the Britannia trophy in recognition of the flight from England to Brazil. With his wife he took part in the famous Melbourne Centenary Air Race of that year and in competing (in a D.H. Comet) they broke the record for a flight to India, which they reached in less than a day.

In the Second World War he joined the Air Transport Auxiliary and then served with "Atfero", the organization set up to assist in ferrying American machines across the Atlantic. During the war he delivered over 1,000 aircraft of almost every type used by the R.A.F. For these wartime services—his earlier flying triumphs had not been officially acknowledged—he was made M.B.E.

His marriage to Amy Johnson had been dissolved before the war. She also served with the A.T.A., and so serving lost her life in January 1941. The year following, a film was made describing their famous flights; entitled *They Flew Alone* it had as its stars the late Robert Newton and Anna Neagle. Mollison's second marriage, in 1938, was to Phyllis Hussey, and, after this had been dissolved in 1948, he married thirdly Maria Kamphuis.

November 2, 1959.

W. Nugent Monck, C.B.E., founder of the Norwich Players in 1911 and Director of the Maddermarket Theatre from 1921 to 1952, died on October 21, 1958 at his home in Norwich. He was 80.

Walter Nugent Bligh Monck was born at Welshampton, in Shropshire, on February 4, 1878, the son of the Rev. George Gustavus Monck and Hester Isabella Nugent, an Irishwoman of wit and remarkable character. From the one he inherited a puritan strain and from the other a Celtic temperament which mingled oddly at times in his life but effectively in his stage work. Most of his boyhood was spent in a Liverpool dock-side parish, where he went to the Royal Institution School. From the age of six he was brought up to be a musician and when he was 15 he entered the Royal Academy of Music. Those who ever heard him read a part at sight will have realized that his eyes and brain were not well coordinated. This handicap made a career either as a singer or violinist extremely problematical, so he transferred in 1895 to the dramatic side of the Academy and trained under William Farren.

From 1898 to 1900 he was on tour and then in the early years of the century he met William Poel and became his stage-manager and disciple. He absorbed Poel's ideas on costume, colour, simplicity, and, above all, many of his ideas on producing Shakespeare, which had led to the formation of the Elizabethan Stage Society. It was left to the disciple to build the first Elizabethan theatre since Commonwealth days and put Poel's theories to the test of practical demonstration on a permanent stage.

In 1908 the Precentor of Norwich Cathedral, the Rev. Rex Rynd, who had been a fellow student of Monck's at the Royal Academy, suggested him as a suitable producer for some historical tableaux to be given in St. Andrew's Hall, Norwich, in January 1909. Monck was appointed and paid his first visit to the city he was to make still more famous. The tableaux were produced in the grand manner and there was a 32-page programme, handsomely printed, with a foreword by Rider Haggard and a two-colour cover by A. J. Munnings [q.v.]. The show was a success. Monck liked Norwich and was offered a house well within his means, so he decided to come back as soon as he could.

In the summer he returned and gave the first of the many masques he produced at Blickling Hall. He went again the following summer to produce a water-frolic at Blickling and brought Poel's assistant stage manager, W. Bridges Adams, as his designer, who before the days of Diaghilev's visit to London astonished people with the richness and vividness of his colour. Each month till the following June he produced a play or plays with various groups of amateurs. With the Old Girls of Norwich High School he produced *The Countess Cathleen.* Yeats went over to see it and was so pleased that he returned to see an adaptation of *Job* played in the Blackfriars Hall. Still more impressed, he persuaded Monck to go to the Abbey Theatre, Dublin, for the autumn and winter while the first company was touring in the United States. In the spring he was back in Norwich rehearsing the first of his big pageants, the Mancroft Pageant, which was to raise money for the restoration of St. Peter Mancroft, that magnificent church which dominates Norwich Market Place. So successful was this pageant that the grounds, known as the Spring Gardens, became a pleasure resort for the next 20 years. That winter he toured with the Irish Players in the United States.

He had grown tired of producing masques, water-frolics, and graceful entertainments for such strangely assorted beneficiaries as the N.S.P.C.C., the Aylsham Cricket Club, the Aylsham habitation of the Primrose League, and church restorations, so in 1911 he had founded the Guild of the Norwich Players. There were eight of them. They had no money, a few costumes, much enthusiasm, and Monck's large drawing-room (with two staircases) into which on occasions 70 people were strenuously packed. Here were performed with a moving simplicity mysteries and moralities which evoked by their colour, grouping, and costumes constant recollections of the Old Masters. Here, too, they listened to the music of Palestrina, Archedelt, and Farrant, and elsewhere, in his Shakespearian productions, to the later Elizabethan composers. From his earliest and stormiest days Monck insisted that dresses, dances, and music of an Elizabethan play should be Elizabethan.

During these months Monck was slowly gaining a regular audience which he trained as rigorously as his actors, and in 1914 he felt secure enough to take the Music Room, an old banqueting hall of the Pastons in King Street, as his permanent theatre. Here, on a tiny stage, where the actors at the sides bumped their heads against the rafters and clumsy halberdiers knocked the tiles off, with an auditorium licensed for only 99 seats, he began regular productions, till war broke up the company.

Monck joined the R.A.M.C. and from 1915 to 1918 was in Egypt, where he produced five of Shakespeare's plays with the troops. One production was in the Opera House at Alexandria, for which he "borrowed" some searchlights from the naval ships to increase his lighting effects.

He was in Salonika from 1918 to 1919 but was demobilized in time to open the Music Room in September 1919 with a production of *Much Ado about Nothing*. At the end of two seasons the audience had outgrown their little theatre and Monck spent the summer of 1921 doing a small pageant called *Revelry* and looking for larger premises. In the Maddermarket he found what he wanted: a plain rectangular building with a gallery running round three sides. It had been built in 1794 as a Roman Catholic Church, became a warehouse in 1900, and a Salvation Army Citadel in 1908. With Noel Paul as his architect he converted it into a simple Elizabethan playhouse, with most of the characteristics of the private theatre and, illogically but most effectively, the pillars and heavens of the public theatre. There were no footlights and very few top lights: the main lighting came from the front of the house.

Here, with no money, no bar, no smoking, no names on the programmes, no curtain calls, no professionals but a group of very ordinary amateur actors and a small but loyal audience, he built up an international reputation. Here for 32 years he ruled as an autocrat, a daemon king of energy, ideas, intuitions, tantrums, producing only the plays he liked, in the way he wanted to do them. He produced Toller's *The Machine Wreckers* for the Stage Society in 1923, *Cymbeline* in 1946, and *Pericles* in 1947 for Sir Barry Jackson* at Stratford-on-Avon. He lectured for the British Council in Germany and the West Indies, where he produced *The Merchant of Venice* at Kingstown in 1950.

At the Maddermarket he produced the whole of Shakespeare, most of the English classics, many of those of France, Germany, Greece, Italy, Norway, Russia, and Spain; some Noh plays from Japan; Sakuntula from India; and the first performance in England of 40 plays. He produced in all 280 plays.

Amateur actors come and go, their standards rise and fall, but are seldom consistently and uniformly high, so Monck concentrated on the visual side of his productions, achieving not a series of static beautiful groupings but a constantly moving composition of loveliness. He seldom missed a moment of dramatic intensity or suspense and found many usually overlooked. He played Shakespeare at a great pace but with no feeling of uncomfortable haste. The First Folio version of *Hamlet*, with only moderate cutting, took two hours and three-quarters.

He retired in 1952, exhausted but still full of ideas.

Monck was made O.B.E. in 1946 and advanced to C.B.E. in 1958.

October 23, 1958.

Mrs. Lionel Monckton—See **Dudley.**

Lord Francis Montagu-Douglas-Scott—See **Scott.**

Dr. Maria Montessori, who evolved the Montessori educational system, died at Noordwijk, Holland, on May 6, 1952, aged 81.

An Italian, she was for many years an important influence on the trend of educational practice. Her aims and technique have at times been travestied and misunderstood, yet she forced educationists everywhere to take stock of their ideas and was a powerful agency in the broadening of curricula and the humanization of instructional method. Moreover, her work has very wide social and philosophical implications.

Born at Chiaravalle, Ancona, on August 31, 1870, Maria was the only daughter of Cavaliere Alessandro Montessori. She entered the University of Rome as a medical student and was the first Italian woman to win the degree of M.D. She then became an instructor in the psychiatric clinic of her university, taking a special interest in pedagogical anthropology and the training of the mentally deficient child. The methods which she found the most congenial basis of experiment were those which Edouard Séguin had begun to apply some 50 years earlier in France. She rapidly came to the conclusion that for the cure of mental deficients the pedagogical approach was more important than the medical; and from her practical work at the clinic on these lines was to grow up the whole structure of her wider educational method. In 1898 she was appointed directress of the Scuola Ortofrenica in Rome. After due training she put several eight-year-old defectives in for the State examination in reading and writing. They not only passed, but gave better results than the normal children.

At last, early in 1907, came the great opportunity which enabled her to elaborate and test her method on a large scale. The Roman slum district of San Lorenzo had become a byword for filth, insanitary housing, overcrowding, and misery. The Instituto Romano di Beni Stabili now took it in hand and attached to each block a *Casa dei Bambini*, a kind of crèche. Dr. Montessori was put in charge. She set out to discover whether principles that had worked so well with defectives would be equally efficacious with normal children. The infants went ahead by leaps and bounds under her system of free discipline. The Montessori method was established, and in 1909 its author issued her *Metodo della Pedagogia Scientifica.* A further two or three years of experimentation followed, and in 1912 she published her *Autoeducazione nelle Scuole Elementari.* In the previous year the method had been widely introduced into the Swiss state schools, and began to be employed in other schools, not only in Italy but in England, America, and elsewhere. At the Fielden Demonstration School, controlled by the University of Manchester, notable results were obtained with children aged from four to six.

In subsequent years many societies and institutions were founded for the study and exposition of the method, and Dr. Montessori travelled widely, observing, lecturing, and demonstrating. A research institute was founded at Barcelona in 1917. In 1919 she gave the first of her London training courses, which were afterwards repeated biennially, under the aegis of the British Montessori Society. A teachers' training college was opened in Italy in 1928 and a year later a similar college began operations in London. From 1931 onwards annual congresses have been held. Besides controlling these various bodies and presiding over congresses. Dr. Montessori acted from 1922 as government inspector of schools in Italy. In 1923 she was awarded the honorary degree of D.Litt. by the University of Durham. Her books have been translated into many languages.

Her method is empirical, being built up on the observed results of actual teaching rather than conceived as a philosophical entity and imposed from above. Its two main principles are non-interference with the child's freedom and individuality, and the use of sensory training in the earliest stages of education. Her claims to originality lie in the application of sensory training to normal children, in the working out of a systematic scheme, stage by stage, and in the provision of a set of didactic materials for handwork.

She believed that the best kind of education is provided by learning for oneself; and from this it follows that the teacher is a guide and observer, strongly adjured not to impose her personality on the pupils. In the *Casa dei Bambini* work for its own sake was never imposed. Toys and common objects were provided, and it was left to the child to decide what his occupation should be. Ordinary household tasks like brushing, washing, and darning played a large part in the training. Discipline arose naturally out of the teacher's personality and the spontaneous interest of the children in what they were doing. Rewards and punishments were utterly abolished, and there was no insistence on remaining quiet and still.

Legitimate criticisms of Dr. Montessori's method are that it tends to over-stress the manual side of education at the expense of the intellectual, that it gives insufficient scope to the natural imaginative faculty, and that its empiricism has not been confirmed by a philosophically coherent body of theory. There can, however, be no doubt as to the high status of this great woman in the line of educational reformers. The final judgment on the system may well be based not so much on the degree to which it has won integral acceptance in the schools as on the measure wherein its principles have been assimilated into the general consciousness of the race.

May 7, 1952.

Eva Moore, who died at her home near Maidenhead on April 27, 1955 at the age of 85, had a long and honourable career on the stage which began under the management of J. L. Toole and extended over half a century, during which time she played leading parts with many of the great actor-managers.

In her early days she had a rare beauty and no one who saw her performance with Sir George Alexander in *Old Heidelberg* will forget her wistful and bewitching performance as the innkeeper's daughter who fell in love with the student prince. Under the title *Exits and Entrances* she wrote her reminiscences 30 years ago. To the end of her life she retained her charm and her sense of humour, and she must certainly rank as one of the outstanding actresses of her generation.

Born on February 9, 1870, she was the eighth child of Edward Henry Moore, of Brighton. Two of his other children, Bertha and Decima (who became Lady Guggisberg), were also on the stage, and the beauty of the three sisters was almost legendary. Most of her early stage experience was gained with Toole, and many of the theatres in which she appeared are now only names, among them Terry's, Toole's, and the Opéra Comique. At the age of 21 she married the handsome young actor Henry V. Esmond, and for 30 years they were one of the most successful married couples on the stage. Esmond was also a playwright of considerable promise and they appeared together in his successful comedy *Eliza Comes to Stay*, produced at the Criterion in 1913. A year later came a second success in *The Dangerous Age* at the Vaudeville.

This popular partnership was brought to an end, however, by Esmond's death in 1922. Eva Moore refused to allow her grief to interfere with her work for the stage, which she continued for another 20 years. She was one of the founders of the Stage Guild, and in 1924, while touring with a comedy, *Mary, Mary Quite Contrary,* which afterwards went to the Savoy, she was the victim of a libel which forced her to take legal action, in which she succeeded.

The list of her performances is far too long for reproduction here. Nevertheless, a few of those which are particularly memorable ought to be mentioned. Outstanding as was her characterization of Aunt Ottillie in *Delicate Question* at the Embassy in 1931, it had been rivalled by her charming *vignette* of Mrs. Watson in *The Holmeses of Baker Street* at the Lyric in 1927. Few, too, will forget her Lady Catherine de Bourgh in *Pride and Prejudice* at the St. James's in 1936. One of her last stage appearances was in *It Happened in September,* which was produced at the end of 1942 at the St. James's Theatre, the scene of her great success as a young actress.

There were two children of the marriage, both of whom followed their parents in adopting the stage as a profession.

April 29, 1955.

C. H. C. P. Moore—See **Drogheda.**

Professor G. E. Moore, O.M., Emeritus Professor of Philosophy in the University of Cambridge, died on October 24, 1958 at the age of 84.

George Edward Moore was born in London on November 4, 1873, the son of Dr. Daniel Moore and his wife Henrietta Sturge, and a younger brother of T. Sturge Moore, the poet. He went to school at Dulwich under A. H. Gilkes, and in 1892 entered Trinity College, Cambridge, where he first read Classics, being placed in the first class of Part I of the Classical Tripos in 1894 and being Craven Scholar the following year. Acting largely on the advice of Bertrand Russell (Lord Russell)* two years his senior, he then turned to philosophy, and obtained a first in Part II of the Moral Sciences Tripos of 1896.

He was elected to a prize fellowship at Trinity College two years later, and during his tenure of this fellowship published, in 1903, two works which made his reputation as a philosopher—*Principa Ethica* and an article in *Mind* with the provocative title, "The Refutation of Idealism". Moore had some private means, and spent the next few years in Edinburgh and Richmond reading philosophy and writing articles and his Home University Library book on *Ethics* (1912). In 1911 he returned to Cambridge as University Lecturer in Moral Science. He lectured in Cambridge three times a week (and sometimes more) during every term for the next 28 years, and very soon became the dominating influence in Cambridge philosophy. In 1925 he succeeded James Ward in the Chair of Philosophy, becoming a Professorial Fellow of Trinity College. After his retirement from the Professorship in 1939, under the age limit, he gave lectures at Oxford and from 1940 to 1944 at various universities in the United States. In 1921 he followed G. F. Stout in the editorship of *Mind*; and the high repute of that journal is largely due to his conscientiousness. He resigned the editorship in 1947.

He was a Litt.D. of Cambridge, an Honorary LL.D. of St. Andrews, and was elected a Fellow of the British Academy in 1918. In 1951 he was appointed to the Order of Merit.

Moore was a philosopher's philosopher: besides his *Principia Ethica* and his *Ethics* he published only articles and lectures (some of which were collected in his *Philosophical Studies* of 1922 and in *Some More Problems of Philosophy* in 1954), and his writings were too exact and too much lacking in any *Weltanschauung* to have a popular appeal. But his way of thinking had an enormous influence on philosophers in Britain and America, and a volume in the "Library of Living Philosophers" was devoted to *The Philosophy of G. E. Moore* (1942).

Moore's "Ideal Utilitarianism" (the name given by Sir David Ross* to the system of *Principia Ethica*) has been a focus of ethical discussion in Britain, and his writings on the philosophy of perception have made historians of contemporary philosophy name him, along with Lord Russell, as the begetter of Anglo-American "New Realism". The most influential work of his maturity was his contribution to the second series of personal statements in *Contemporary British Philosophy* (1925). In this essay, called "A Defence of Common Sense", Moore insisted upon the distinction between understanding the meaning of an expression and being able to give a correct analysis of this meaning. The business of a philosopher is not to cast doubt upon the facts unreservedly accepted by common-sense judgment but to provide analyses of these facts. Moore's lectures at Cambridge were principally devoted to examining analyses propounded by other philosophers, and to suggesting analyses of his own. None of these ever completely satisfied him.

In his "Reply to my Critics" in *The Philosophy of G. E. Moore* (1942) he had to admit that on each of the two problems of the objectivity of good and of whether or not material objects are directly perceived—problems about which he had thought for 40 years—he was entirely unable to make up his mind between two incompatible views, the reasons for both seeming to him equally strong. Thus Moore's philosophical thinking raised questions rather than provided answers: the German historian of British philosophy (Rudolf Metz) called him "the greatest, acutest and most skilful questioner of modern philosophy".

But none of his pupils is likely to forget his patient and persistent method of inquiry, never satisfied with specious solutions. In the informal discussions which followed his lectures, and at conferences of philosophers, Moore's single-minded devotion to clarity and truth were an inspiration to all, not least to those who failed to follow the intricacies of the argument. In these discussions Moore was no respecter of persons: the freshest undergraduate would find a germ of truth in a remark he had made being disclosed and elucidated by Moore, while the most eminent person present might find himself being told that what he had just said was utter nonsense, Moore banging the table or jumping up from his chair to emphasize the point.

Moore's influence has thus been far greater than could be inferred from his published writings. As a young man he played a great part in Lord Russell's intellectual development, and affected such writers as G. Lowes Dickinson, Lord Keynes, and I. A. Richards. In his maturity his method of philosophizing was spread throughout the English-speaking world by students who had come to Cambridge to sit at his feet, and his ideas have been incorporated into the books of many of them.

At Cambridge he continued the requirement of Henry Sidgwick that a philosophic question should be precisely stated before an answer is attempted; and, by infecting his pupils with his own excitement, proved himself one of the great teachers of philosophy.

In 1916 Moore married Miss Dorothy Ely, who bore him two sons.

October 25, 1958.

Dr. R. W. Moore, who had been head master of Harrow since 1942, died suddenly on January 10, 1953 at the early age of 46.

Though he had not himself gone to one of the leading public schools he had spent some years on the teaching staff at Rossall and Shrewsbury, and was familiar with the traditions which they represented, and had already done much to preserve them. He was a man of high principles and sound ideals and had the gift of imparting them to others in the same way as he could communicate to those who studied under him his thorough scholarship and taste. Right to the end of his incredibly busy life he was able to give a clear lead not only to those under his charge but as a writer and broadcaster, and his address to Harrovians last Speech Day, with its insistence on high courage and high ideals constitutes a message which must rank as one of the most hopeful and encouraging utterances made by any head master for many years.

Ralph Westwood Moore was born at Wolverhampton in 1906. At Wolverhampton Grammar School he was quickly recognized as a classical scholar of promise and won an open scholarship at Christ Church, Oxford. There he took firsts in Classical Moderations and in *Literae Humaniores* and also won an honourable mention for the Hertford Scholarship. Soon after taking his degree in 1928 he was appointed assistant master at Rossall and in 1931 went to Shrewsbury, where as sixth-form master he followed in the train of many famous classical scholars. In 1938 he was appointed head master of Bristol Grammar School.

Such a post seemed at the time a strange choice for one who had, in spite of his youth, already begun to be known as a classical scholar of no mean order. Moore, however, quickly demonstrated that at least one of the uses of a classical education was the development of sound and vigorous views on education in general. He always believed that the school master's prime function was to teach, and at Bristol, as later at Harrow, he refused to be submerged by mere administration and insisted on taking as many classes as possible himself. In the short time he was at Bristol he made a lasting impression, and though it was, perhaps, too much to hope that he would stay there, there was keen disappointment at Bristol, tempered by pride that the school had had a head who was found to be worthy to fill the post of head master of one of the great public schools of the country at the early age of 36.

Harrow in 1942 shared the difficulties of the country in general at that time. The school buildings had suffered from bombing, numbers were reduced and some houses had been closed. Accommodation had to be found for the staff and boys of Malvern, whose school had been requisitioned. Moore entered on his task with courage and confidence and won the trust of staff and boys by his high purpose, courage, and hard work. The aftermath of war had its problems, too, but these were gradually being surmounted when the illness from which he eventually died first manifested itself.

Early in 1951 he had an attack of bronchial pneumonia, and when later in the year a mass-radiography unit visited the school he was one of the first to be examined in order to encourage the boys to undergo the X-ray examination. Within two months he was operated upon and by last summer was back at work. His health, however, again deteriorated and only two days before his death the announcement was made that he was too ill to continue.

For many years he was a member of the council of the Classical Association and from 1936 till 1938 of the Joint Committee of the Classical and English Associations. In the midst of his work he found considerable time for writing and was a frequent contributor to *The Times* (his first connexion with the paper was when he was at Shrewsbury) and *The Times Literary Supplement.* From 1935 till 1937 he acted as editor of *The Threshold,* an annual anthology of prose and verse from the schools of England. In 1933 he brought out *Prose at Present,* in 1934 *Greek and Latin Comparative Syntax,* in 1937 *Idea and Expression,* in 1938 *The Romans in Britain. The Roman Commonwealth,* and *Education To-day and To-morrow* followed. All were works which revealed much of his teaching experience and methods as well as his wider interests. At times he gave talks for the B.B.C., many of them short religious pieces of a devotional character, the product of a mind of wide experience and sympathy and a modern outlook with a deep reverence for all that was best in the past.

In 1931 he married Elsie Barbara, daughter of W. H. Tonks, of Wolverhampton, who survives him together with two sons of the marriage.

January 12, 1953.

Charles Morgan, who died suddenly on February 6, 1958 at the age of 64, achieved success as a novelist, a dramatist, and a critic.

His capacity for work and his versatility as an artist still left him time to impress himself as a social figure in more than one walk of life and to be a man of many friendships. After a brief and distasteful experience as a young naval officer and the bad luck to be interned in Holland early in the First World War, he first found himself as an undergraduate at Oxford. There he became a pillar of the O.U.D.S. and one of the best-known personalities of his generation. Immediately on coming down he made his mark as a dramatic critic. His distinguished figure and careful, almost dandyish style of dressing marked him out as a familiar character at first-nights in the twenties and thirties. But he did not reach his full capacity until he turned to novels.

Charles Langbridge Morgan was born on January 22, 1894. He was the eldest son of Sir Charles Morgan, C.B.E., a past president of the Institution of Civil Engineers. In 1907 he entered the Royal Navy as a cadet and served in the Atlantic and China. In 1913 he resigned, but on the outbreak of war he joined the Royal Naval Division. From 1921 he was on the editorial staff of *The Times* as assistant dramatic critic under A. B. Walkley, whom he succeeded in 1926.

As a novelist Charles Morgan was in an almost unique, and in some ways unenviable, situation. He began by writing two novels, *The Gunroom* and *My Name is Legion,* which reflect the utterly different facets of his art. In the first, which was based upon his naval experience, he displayed at once his gift for holding the attention by a direct narrative with moral implications. It was a young man's book, indignant, vivid and urgent. Six years later his approach to fiction was already changing. A brooding preoccupation with the values of the heart had begun to slow his pen.

With each succeeding book it became truer that Morgan found it hard to reconcile the modulations of a questing spirit with the ordinary exigencies of story-telling.

In German, or in French, his concept of his art would have appeared perfectly familiar, and this must account in part for the high esteem in which he was held abroad. He was a member of the Institut de France.

At home, however, he walked alone. The philosophical idealist never seems wholly at ease in the guise of an English novelist; beauty of diction, dignity of thought, fineness of intuition—all of which must be accorded Morgan in a high degree—cannot compensate for the throb of life which our greatest novelists have contributed to the art of fiction. Hence one of Morgan's earlier novels, *Portrait in a Mirror,* remains the most satisfying of them all. For here, allied to technical skill, he had not only an idea to adumbrate but a story to tell. In successive volumes—*The Fountain, Sparkenbroke, The Voyage, The Judge's Story* and *Challenge to Venus*—the same merits persist and the mastery of prose deepens.

As the years went by, Morgan's name as novelist receded into a backwater. Readers of Graham Greene, Angus Wilson and the like had little patience with a view of life so obstinately elevated. Just as in the 1930s his reputation had mounted to the very first rank of contemporary novelists, so, in the last 10 years, he has been unjustly decried. For, although he was not prepared to make concessions in order to keep a public, he was well aware of the bleak questions which demand an answer in the modern world. Only, unlike exponents of contemporary realism, he put his faith in the power of the individual, supported by a guardian rank of old-fashioned virtues and deliberately turning away from the fascination of new-fangled vices.

During the Second World War, week after week, he contributed to *The Times Literary Supplement* a series of papers afterwards republished in the two volumes of *Reflections in a Mirror,* and it is here that his literary personality emerged most clearly.

The play in which Morgan most fully expressed himself will probably turn out to be the first. In *The Flashing Stream,* written in 1938, he successfully married mathematical integrity and physical passion in a lively stage action which actors obviously enjoyed acting and a serious public found intellectually provocative and entertaining. It ran for six months.

The River Line, presented at the Edinburgh Festival of 1952 and later in London, contains a central episode of escape along one of the underground routes of occupied France. An atmosphere pervaded by danger, suspense, and suspicion is powerfully worked up to the shock of sudden violence—a superb stroke of melodrama reminding playgoers how surely Morgan worked until he found it necessary, as later in the play he inevitably did, to sublimate melodramatic action into spiritual significance.

In his last play, *The Burning Glass,* he produced, in the Prime Minister, probably his best stage character.

For some 18 years Morgan's notices of current plays were familiar to readers of *The Times.* Unsigned, they had their own individuality. His style was never flurried. It grew with the years more polished and urbane, and—as he shook off the slightly literary solemnity of his nonage—came ever more flexibly to terms with theatrical trivia, often offering a witty threnody on the imminent demise of some poor little piece.

In his general dealings with drama Morgan had, of course, his preferences. His critical enthusiasm was less easily fired by Shakespeare than by Strindberg at his most tormented, or by Ibsen in his last phase of doomsday reckoning with himself. Morgan's sympathies were with characters knotted up inside with mysterious tensions.

He sometimes surprised playwrights by the beautiful lucidity with which he wrote about the spiritual implications of self-struggles at which they had hinted but had not imagined with sufficient clearness. But however much his mind might occasionally overflow the given subject he was more careful than most in his conscientious treatment of actors.

His opinions were his own and he kept them to himself until he came to set them down on paper. When he struck out he struck out hard—as in the notice which made the transliteration *Wee-der-dee* the current symbol for the managerial folly of engaging foreign actresses, with hardly a word of English, to play Shakespeare.

He married in 1923 Hilda Vaughan, by whom he had a son and a daughter who in 1948 married the Marquess of Anglesey.

February 7, 1958.

The Most Rev. Dr. John Morgan, D.D., Archbishop of Wales, who died in hospital in London on June 26, 1957, was only the fourth prelate to hold that office, but 97th Bishop of the Diocese of Llandaff.

He combined, on the one hand, a sense of history and tradition with a realization of the needs and the demands of modern times and, on the other, was an ecclesiastic with a wide knowledge and a keen experience of organization and administration. In him were met simple piety, eloquence, and a keen and genial sense of humour.

Morgan was born into the Welsh Church at Llandudno on June 6, 1886, a son of John Morgan, at that time rector of the North Wales holiday resort. He was a chorister and soloist at Llandaff Cathedral, and was a pupil at the Cathedral School, then conducted by Ernest Owen, with whom he later went to Stancliffe Hall, Matlock. From Matlock he went to Llandovery College, and then as an exhibitioner to Hertford College, Oxford, where he graduated in 1910.

For a while he was at Cuddesdon, and proceeded to his M.A. in 1914. For a while he was in North Wales as curate of Llanaber, Barmouth, in the diocese of Bangor, with which he was already familiar (his father had been Archdeacon of Bangor), and then from 1912 to 1916 was resident chaplain to Bishop Burrows at Truro. In 1916 he was appointed a temporary Chaplain to the Forces, served until after the end of the war, and at the same time acted as vicar-choral of St. Asaph Cathedral and vicar of St. Asaph. In 1919 he was appointed curate-in-charge of Llanbeblig with Caernarvon. A year later he became vicar of the parish. Those were the years of his most intimate parish experience, expanded by his work as chaplain to the town prison, and the organization of the movement and the raising of funds which led to the renovation of the fabrics of the two local churches.

In 1933 he was appointed rector of Llandudno, there following the footsteps of his father, and a year later he was elected as the second Bishop of Swansea and Brecon in the new dispensation of the Welsh Church. It was his first administrative experience in a diocese largely industrial and prepared him for his translation, in 1939, to the see of Llandaff. In his new duties his remarkable gift of administration and organization, his integrity and his humanity were displayed to their best advantage; there was little doubt, in 1949, as to who was to succeed Dr. Prosser in the Primacy, and Morgan's election was applauded both within and without the Principality.

He was probably outstanding among all the recent products of the Welsh Church for the variety of his attainments, his interests, and his endeavours. He was in the line of great pulpit figures Wales has been producing for centuries, for to his erudition and his presence he added a fine voice. He was Select Preacher at Oxford in 1951 and 1952.

He was a considerable musician, and an accomplished organist. It was largely a consequence of his energy that the Choral Festival in the Arfon Deanery flourished years ago, and there were many occasions when he could be found in the organ loft of one of his own cathedrals. He had been chairman of the provincial committee entrusted with the difficult task of preparing a new Welsh hymn book for the Church in Wales. He was made a Lambeth Doctor of Divinity in 1934, and he was given the same degree (*honoris causa*) by the University of Wales in 1952.

June 27, 1957.

Brigadier-General John Hartman Morgan, Q.C., Emeritus Professor of Constitutional Law in the University of London, died at Wootton Bassett, Wiltshire, on April 8, 1955 at the age of 79.

He was a widely recognised authority upon his subject, who had already begun to make his name when in the war of 1914 to 1918 he placed his services at the disposal of his country and did valuable work on the staff of the Adjutant-General in France, and afterwards in connexion with the Commission of Control for the Disarmament of Germany. From 1947 to 1949 he was legal adviser to the American War Crimes Commission at Nuremberg. An excellent lecturer on legal themes, he wrote a number of books on them and also on other subjects. He was British Member of the Académie Diplomatique Internationale.

John Hartman Morgan was born on March 20, 1876, the son of the Rev. David Morgan, Congregational Minister of Ystrad Rhondda, and Julie, daughter of Felix Wethli, of Zurich. He began his education at Caterham Congregational School and afterwards entered the University College of South Wales, whence at the early age of 20 he took the London M.A. degree in mental and moral science, political science, and economics. In the same year he obtained a scholarship at Balliol College, Oxford. While at Oxford he earned distinction as a speaker at the union and made a considerable reputation as an original student in modern history, especially by his researches in the archives at Paris into diplomatic records.

On leaving Oxford Morgan studied at the London School of Economics under Professor Hervins, was elected to an economic research scholarship at the University of London, and under its terms went to Germany to study the operation of trusts under the Tariffs. From 1901 to 1903 he was on the literary staff of the *Daily Chronicle,* and from 1904 to 1905 a leader-writer on the *Manchester Guardian.* In 1908 he was appointed to the Chair of Constitutional Law and Legal History at University College London. In January 1910 he contested the Edgbaston Division of Birmingham in the Liberal interest, and West Edinburgh in December of the same year, but in neither case was he successful. In 1913 he was appointed Rhodes Lecturer to the University of London in the Law of the Empire.

At the outbreak of war Morgan offered himself for combatant service, but was attached to the Adjutant-General's staff as Home Office representative with the British Expeditionary Force to inquire into the conduct of the Germans in the field. His report on his investigations was published by the Parliamentary Recruiting Committee and was widely in demand. After the war he went as A.A.G. to Paris to represent the Adjutant-General at the peace conference, and was later sent to Cologne to report on the British occupation of the Rhineland. Then he became British military representative on the Prisoner of War Commission. Later still he served for some four years in Germany on the Inter-Allied Council of the Commission of Control for the Disarmament of Germany, retiring from the Army in 1923 as a brigadier-general.

During the First World War period Morgan published *The German War Book* (1915), a literal translation of the handbook on the usages of war issued by the German Army; *War, Its Conduct and Legal Results* (1916), and also *Leaves from a Field Note Book* (1916), which contained his experiences as Home Office Commissioner. In 1924 he added to them his *The Present State of Germany* and *Viscount Morley, an Appreciation.*

In 1926 he was appointed Reader in Constitutional Law to the Inns of Court and took silk. He was by then well established as one of the greatest authorities upon constitutional law. He had before the war written some books on constitutional questions—Lord Loreburn had supplied a preface to his *The House of Lords and the Constitution* (1910)—and in 1925 he published his *Remedies against the Crown.* He was also legal editor of the *Encyclopaedia Britannica.* From 1934 to 1937 he was counsel to the Indian Chamber of Princes and in 1935 appeared for Western Australia at the hearing before Parliament of the Succession Petition.

Between the wars he made a study of the disarmament and rearmament of Germany. In 1945 he published the result of his researches in *Assize of Arms,* which disclosed in detail the manner in which the German officer corps evaded the provisions of the Treaty of Versailles. From 1942 to 1945 he was counsel to the Parliamentary Post-War Policy Group, and later to the American Commission at the Nuremberg trials, where he was also a witness.

April 21, 1955.

Christopher Morley, the American writer, who was perhaps best known in Britain as the author of the lively and altogether charming *Thunder on the Left,* died on March 28, 1957, at Long Island, New York. He was 66.

Christopher Morley turned his hand successfully to almost every form of literature, or at least of light or lightish literature, and brought to them all the happiest flow of whimsical humour and discreet sentiment. Novelist, playwright, poet, critic and a great deal besides, in all these capacities he retained something of the quality of the essayist in the tradition of Lamb and Stevenson. This was his principal and engaging virtue alike as a writer and as a conversationalist; gently curious, humorously urbane, lightly fanciful, delicately allusive, he could be relied upon in almost all circumstances to please—and, from his prodigious memory, to reinforce his own sentiments with an apt quotation from his literary masters. To these essayists' characteristics he added a turn of fantasy somewhat in the prettier manner of Barrie—demure, unexpected, yet threatened by a too conscious charm, a too practised wistfulness. He had, as novelist, a large public in the United States and was also a broadcasting favourite in the "quiz" type of programme, in which his voice was well known in this country, where he was always a welcome visitor.

The son of Frank Morley, of Woodbridge, Suffolk, a Cambridge don before he settled in the United States, and Lilian Janet Bird, Christopher Darlington Morley was born at Haverford, Pennsylvania, on May 5, 1890. He took his degree at Haverford College in 1910 and spent the next three years as a Rhodes Scholar at New College, Oxford. On returning to the United States he engaged in publishing and journalism and was successively a member of the staff of the *Philadelphia Public Ledger* and of the *New York Evening Post.* From 1924 until 1940 Morley was a contributing editor of the *Saturday Review of Literature* and a critical voice of no little authority in the United States.

His earliest volumes consist of collections of verse, of essays, of one-act plays, many of the latter done in collaboration with another hand. From the first there was no mistaking his indebtedness as an essayist to classic English models, however ingeniously, as in *Safety Pins and other Essays,* he might borrow from—or add to—the American vernacular. Fame came to him with the publication in 1926 of *Thunder on the Left,* a fantasy of childhood translated to a grown-up world that was delightfully contrived as a comedy of sentiment. The novel proved enormously popular and was effectively adapted to the stage. Success, not unnaturally, stimulated Morley's confidence as a writer. He produced, in rapid sequence, a volume of inconsequent and charming travel notes on France and England, *The Romany Stain*; a book of three fantastic stories, *The Arrow*; a book of stories for children, *I Know a Secret*; and a very happy, and at times wholly delightful scrapbook, *Off the Deep End.*

In the years that followed Morley's whimsical fancy invaded all that he wrote to very pleasant effect. He never set himself a task that lay beyond his powers, but was content, as in *John Mistletoe,* for instance, or *Swiss Family Manhattan,* to cultivate still further his natural gifts and to provide entertainment that was light, witty, satirical, fanciful, and delicately and discursively sympathetic to a fault. In 1940, however, he earned fresh laurels with a novel, *Kitty Foyle,* that displayed his characteristic merits to unusual advantage. The story was, in point of fact, a sentimental one, but it was unfolded with a wealth of parenthetical humour and of slangy invention that was irresistible. Equally enjoyable, though in a rather different way, was *Thorofare* (1943), the nostalgic story, only fitfully illuminated by specifically American pride, of a small boy in Suffolk who became a citizen of the United States. A book of mainly light verse, *Spirit Level and Other Poems,* published in 1947, exhibited his polished ease of craftsmanship and his flair for literary and local allusion. This was followed by *The Man Who Made Friends with Himself* (1949) and *The Ironing Board* (1950), the one snatches of the life and opinions of an imaginary literary agent, the other a farrago of essays, skits, and pieces of literary detection, both in his familiar vein.

Morley married in 1914 Miss Helen Booth Fairchild. There were a son and three daughters of the marriage.

March 29, 1957.

Sir Rhys Hopkin Morris, Q.C., M.P., Deputy Chairman of Ways and Means in the House of Commons and a former Independent Liberal member who opposed Lloyd George's leadership in the 1920s, died on November 22, 1956 at his home in Kent. He was 68.

He was born in 1888, at Maesteg, Glamorgan, where his father, the Rev. John Morris, was minister of a Congregational church. He was a student at the University College of North Wales, Bangor, and a graduate of the University of Wales and of the University of London. Called to the Bar by the Middle Temple, he joined what was then the Oxford and South Wales Circuit. He served through the 1914-18 War and was mentioned in dispatches.

He first came into prominence in Welsh public life during the Cardigan by-election of 1921. Llewellyn Williams, M.P., had quarrelled with Lloyd George over compulsory military service and was not placated by the offer of high office. In the 1918 general election the "coupon" went to another man and Williams was defeated. At the by-election in 1921 he entered the fray again, and again Lloyd George brought all his force against him. Williams had the able and whole-hearted support of Hopkin Morris, then a young barrister. The election was all-important to Lloyd George, as an entry in Lord Riddell's diary of that date shows. Lloyd George's candidate won, but there sprang out of the contest an enmity between Lloyd George and Hopkin Morris that remained throughout their public lives.

In 1923 Hopkin Morris was returned for Cardigan after a fierce contest as an Independent Liberal. In the House of Commons and outside the two men continually clashed. Hopkin Morris openly opposed Lloyd George's offer in 1926 to put his political fund at the disposal of the Liberal Associations. "Accept the creed [of Lloyd George's Land and Nation League]", he said, "and you get the money; your principles can be purchased for the price of your election expenses".

Hopkin Morris kept his seat in Parliament in the elections of 1929 and 1931. By that time he had begun to be looked upon as the future Welsh Liberal leader. There was therefore much disappointment and some surprise when he decided to accept the offer of a post as a Metropolitan magistrate. On the bench he won a reputation not only as a good lawyer but also for fairness and courtesy.

In 1936 he took yet another new direction by becoming B.B.C. Regional Director for Wales. He went to Cardiff at a critical moment in the history of Welsh broadcasting; he brought to his task a wide general culture, a keen and resolute mind, and a full and sympathetic knowledge of Welsh life and needs. It is to his guidance and support of those who were working out the practical side of the programmes that Welsh broadcasting owes much of its reputation. He took a discerning delight in Welsh literature, but confessed that he was handicapped by a lack of musical sense. He used to tell how he had fallen foul of his commanding officer once, when his battalion had been brought out of the trenches, for not marching to attention when the band played the regimental march, "Men of Harlech". He had not recognized it.

In 1945 he resigned his post with the B.B.C. and returned to politics and the Bar. He won the Carmarthen Division for the Liberals in 1945 when the tide was flowing strongly in Labour's favour. His popularity in Wales was high, in spite of an aloofness over questions like Home Rule. One of his greatest triumphs was at the chairing ceremony of the 1948 Eisteddfod (it used to be Lloyd George's special occasion) when, by his eloquence, out of keeping in so quiet and meditative a politician, he fired his audience to enthusiasm. It earned him the title "Member for Wales".

In 1951 he became Deputy Chairman of Ways and Means. A dry sense of humour, combined with an ability to understand every point of view, made him an admirable guardian of the rights and privileges of private members of the House of Commons. Like the Speaker himself, he had a keen legal brain, and this enabled him to go straight to the heart of the many arguments and points of order raised when he was in the Chair. He never allowed himself to be drawn into a hasty ruling and preferred to rely on the good will and common sense of his Parliamentary colleagues rather than on stricter methods. It probably came as no hardship to him, but rather a relief, to be compelled from 1951 onwards to stand aloof from politics. He was knighted in 1954.

The main characteristic which struck everyone who came into contact with Hopkin Morris was his absolute integrity. Most men have an inner core of rectitude; with him it was the whole man. With his rather gaunt face and deep-set eyes he had an air of sternness. But to those who knew him well he could unbend into the most charming of companions. With all his passion for principle he was also a tolerant man; the one thing he could not abide was humbug.

He married in 1918 Gladys Perrie Williams, O.B.E., Litt.D., who survives him with a daughter.

November 23, 1956.

George Morrow, the humorous artist who delighted innumerable readers of *Punch* for so many years with his historical fantasies, died at his home at Thaxted, Essex, on January 18, 1955 at the age of 85.

He was the soul of modesty and unpretentiousness, but it was his special gift to pencil his comments on the margin of life. His route was essentially the by-way. Comment on politics, on domestic experiences, and on the teeming life of the streets he left to others. His game was humbler, more idiosyncratic, the record of his own quaint ruminations—ruminations quite unlike those of anybody else. Caran d'Ache was technically more brilliant and more carelessly witty; and Caran d'Ache was as certainly George Morrow's predecessor as Wilhelm Busch was Caran d'Ache's. Morrow must indeed have seen a great deal of Caran d'Ache's work when he was studying in Paris in Toulouse-Lautrec's heyday. But Morrow's strong originality soon asserted itself and his style was unmistakable by the time he began to contribute to *Punch* in 1906.

He was probably the most consistently comic artist of his day. Time after time it is possible to return to his drawings and see some subtle detail that had escaped notice before. However crowded the picture, every part received due consideration. A good example in his vein of historical fantasy is the early "A Supper with the Borgias", in which not only are the guests adopting every possible subterfuge to avoid eating or drinking anything, but even the dogs look suspiciously at the fare surreptitiously passed to them under the table.

After contributing to *Punch* for some 18 years Morrow joined the staff in 1924 and thus attended the weekly luncheons round the famous *Punch* table. He was art editor of the paper from 1932 until 1937. If in his later years his style became a little stereotyped, imagination had not flagged and the kindly humour that endeared him to his friends still shed a warm glow which kept the circle of his admirers constant. His work appeared regularly in *Punch* until about a month before he died, and within the last fortnight he made a valiant attempt to finish one of his drawings.

January 20, 1955.

Lieutenant-General Sir Leslie James Morshead, K.C.B., K.B.E., C.M.G., D.S.O., who was G.O.C. Australian Forces in the Middle East in 1942-43, died in hospital at Sydney on September 26, 1959. He was 70.

He was the son of William Morshead, of Ballarat, Victoria. During the 1914-18 War he served in Gallipoli and France, commanded a battalion for the last two years of the war, was awarded the D.S.O., and mentioned in dispatches six times. He was a regular soldier, and when war broke out again in 1939 he was in command of an infantry brigade in Australia. His brigade formed part of the Australian force which went from England to the Middle East in 1940, and early in 1941 Morshead was promoted to command the 9th Australian Division. When the Germans had advanced across Cyrenaica in the spring of 1941 Morshead was left in command of beleaguered Tobruk with a garrison of 31,000 men, including four Australian brigades. "The defence of Egypt", General Wavell instructed him, "now depends largely on you holding the enemy on your front. . . . I know I can count on you to hold Tobruk to the end."

The Germans, after their initial assault, made two more attempts to overrun Tobruk in May, but they were beaten off. Morshead countered by continuous raids on the German lines. In September and October, at the insistence of the Australian Government, the 9th Australian Division at Tobruk was relieved, the contingents moving out during moonless nights.

Morshead commanded the 9th Division at Alamein, although he had earlier succeeded General Blamey [q.v.] as G.O.C. Australian Forces in the Middle East. In 1943 he returned to Australia to command the Second Australian Corps. He then transferred his attentions to the Japanese and was G.O.C. New Guinea Force in 1944 and commanded the combined Australian and American Forces in the Borneo operations in 1945.

Having retired from the Army Morshead embarked on a no less successful career in business and commerce. He was president of the Bank of New South Wales, chairman of the Sydney department store company David Jones, Ltd., and a former general manager in Australia of the Orient Line.

September 28, 1959.

The Rev. A. C. Moule, LITT.D., Professor of Chinese Language and History in the University of Cambridge from 1933 until 1938, died on June 5, 1957 at St. Leonards-on-Sea. He was 84.

Arthur Christopher Moule was born at Hangchow, China, on May 18, 1873, the youngest son of George Evans Moule, Bishop in Mid-China. He was educated at the King's School, Canterbury (where he lost his last year owing to an attack of pleurisy which, thanks to the doctor's blunder, nearly cost him his life and permanently deprived him of the use of one lung), and at Trinity College, Cambridge. In spite of setbacks he took a second class in the Classical Tripos of 1895.

Though hampered by ill health he worked for some time in the office of the architect Walter Shirley (afterwards Earl Ferrers), who became his life-long friend and once described him as a very shy and retiring parson who instinctively saw the sort of things the pure in heart see. In 1900 he was building a church at Tientsin for the Society for the Propagation of the Gospel when the Boxer Rising took place, and in 1904, after offering himself to the Church Missionary Society and being rejected on medical grounds, he was ordained as a missionary of the S.P.G. and was in charge of one or other of their stations in North China till he left for England in 1909.

In England he served in various curacies and livings, the most notable being Trumpington from 1918 until 1933, when he was appointed Professor of Chinese Language and History at Cambridge. At the same time he proceeded to the degree of Litt.D., and four years later was elected a fellow of his own college. He held his chair until he reached the retiring age of 65, and after war broke out he had the living of Mundford in Norfolk for a few years.

Wherever he was he investigated and threw light upon countless matters—Chinese pigeon whistles, Chinese musical instruments, the exact history and meaning of the famous Nestorian Inscription at Sianfu, other traces of early Christianity in China, everything connected with Marco Polo, the Sacred Mountain of Tai-an, the history of Trumpington Church, gingko nuts, silky fowls, the earliest "taxi-cab", early references to goldfish . . . and he contributed innumerable articles to learned journals. On a larger scale are his book *Christians in China before 1550* (1930), which, to his amazement, won him the Stanislas Julian Prize from the French Academy, and his share, with the late Professor Pelliott, in the magnificent edition of Marco Polo, planned and financed by Sir Percival David. He wrote to the last years of his life, and two works by him, *The Rulers of China, 221 B.C. to A.D. 1949*, and *Quinsai, with other Notes on Marco Polo*, came out in his last 12 months.

Moule was first and foremost a convinced and earnest Christian. His most outstanding characteristic was an invincible love of truth; he seemed incapable, except when praising others, of exaggeration: everything was measured and counted. Equally strong was his courage, moral and physical, displayed, though he did not know it, on numbers of occasions, among others at the siege of Tientsin when his life was in great danger. At that time he nursed the future Admiral Jellicoe to health when the Chinese had shot him through the lung. Another marked characteristic was his modesty; unaware of possessing any ability he would have disputed hotly with anyone who called him a scholar. Yet he spoke Pekinese like a native and showed time after time the scholar's almost uncanny power of divining the meaning of some impossible Chinese sentence or the bearing of a hitherto unnoticed hint on the true solution of some ancient historical or geographical puzzle. His penetrating mind and determination to follow the evidence worked wonders.

He married in 1904 Mabel Wollaston, a missionary of the S.P.G., who survives him.

June 6, 1957.

Lady Mountbatten of Burma, C.I., G.B.E., D.C.V.O., wife of Admiral of the Fleet Lord Mountbatten of Burma, died in her sleep at Government House in Jesselton, north Borneo, on February 20, 1960. She was 58.

Tall, fair-haired and blue-eyed in the English tradition, she was the heiress of great wealth and made a brilliant marriage to one closely allied by blood and marriage to the Royal Family. Lady Louis gave early promise of the part she would play as the last Vicereine of India by her dedication to the interests of all those who care for the sick and helpless. No one did more to help that cause during and after the Second World War than she, and her devotion was amply repaid by the love of the people of the sub-continent of India. Her influence there was immense and it was suitably acknowledged by Jawaharlal Nehru in 1948, when he recalled how she had moved from camp to camp in the stricken Punjab to bring help and cheer to the refugees.

She was the elder daughter of Lord Mount Temple, a grandson of the seventh Earl of Shaftesbury, and his first wife Amalia Maud, only child of Sir Ernest Cassel. King Edward VII stood sponsor at her christening and she was named Edwina Cynthia Annette. Though the heiress to great wealth, she was brought up strictly and up to the age of 21 she had a dress allowance of only £100 a year. Her grandfather's close personal friendship with King Edward VII and her father's prominent position in the House of Commons before he was raised to the peerage, ensured to her an *entrée* into the best circles, and it was at a Cowes Week soon after the end of the 1914-18 War that she was introduced by the Duke of Windsor*, then Prince of Wales, to the first Marquess of Milford Haven's younger son, then Lord Louis Mountbatten, and serving in the Royal Navy. Their marriage was one of the great social events of the season of 1922 and was graced by the presence of King George V and Queen Mary [q.v.]. Both were young and full of life and they became by sheer force of character the leaders of the young fashion of the time. Sir Ernest Cassel had died in 1921 and had left between his two granddaughters the income from his immense fortune, subject to a number of provisions which were soon to become embarrassing. Only five years after his death Brook House, the great mansion in Park Lane, which Sir Ernest Cassel had built and filled with an immensely valuable collection of objects of art, was sold and a block of flats was built on the site, with a penthouse on the roof to accommodate the Mountbattens. They also had a house at Bosham, a castle in the west of Ireland, and later Broadlands, near Romsey, once the home of Lord Palmerston.

Yet amid all this luxury neither of them forgot the more serious things of life. Lord Louis pursued his career in the Navy which his father had served with devotion throughout his life; Lady Louis took the greatest interest in dockland settlements and other charitable causes, but above all in hospitals and nursing. She became president of the London County branch of the St. John Ambulance Brigade in 1939 and after the outbreak of war was indefatigable in the work of recruitment and organization. When her husband became head of Combined Operations in 1941 she added to her duties by organizing most efficiently the welfare branch of that immense inter-service body. Later on she proved a valuable stimulus in the same field in the even larger sphere of the South East Asia Command.

She had become Superintendent-in-Chief of the Red Cross and St. John war organization and as such made an immense number of inspections of hospitals, welfare centres, schools, and clinics all over the world, but particularly in the Middle and Far East. In a three-month tour in 1945 she travelled some 34,000 miles, visiting many parts of India, Ceylon, Chungking, and the Burma front. Later in the year she visited Palestine and Jordan, and after the collapse of Japan she did sterling work in Java in the early days of the organization for the recovery of allied prisoners of war and internees (R.A.P.W.I.). She was gazetted D.C.V.O. in the New Year Honours of 1946, a recognition richly deserved. In the spring of that year she visited Australia and in Sydney was invited to march with the veterans of both wars to the Sydney cenotaph for the dawn service, a unique honour in recognition of her and her husband's work for service men.

She was therefore no stranger to India, Burma, and Malaya when she went to New Delhi as Vicereine in 1947. The staff at Viceregal House quickly found that she was determined to get to grips with the problems of Indian life. When her husband flew to the riot-torn Punjab she went with him, travelling thousands of miles by aircraft, car, and on foot in heat and dust, to bring hope and solace to the despairing refugees. She was no great lady standing at a distance, but a mother and a nurse who took their soiled and trembling hands in hers and spoke quiet words of womanly comfort. In the short and difficult term of office of the last Viceroy of India she won the hearts of all, and nobody contributed more to the warm ties of friendship between the British and Indian peoples than she.

In 1947 she was made C.I. She had been appointed C.B.E. in 1943 and in the New Year Honours of 1948 she was advanced to G.B.E.

The year 1949 saw the introduction of a private Bill into the House of Lords with the object of varying the terms of her inheritance. Taxation had risen so steeply that her income had shrunk to less than a tenth of its original amount and some relief from the provision of Sir Ernest Cassel's will forbidding the anticipation of capital was urgently necessary, otherwise she and her husband would be compelled to curtail the public work they had so long and so devotedly performed. An Act giving relief from onerous provisions of settlement of married women's property had been passed in 1935, but it was not retrospective and as Sir Ernest Cassel had died in 1921 its provisions did not apply to Lady Mountbatten's case. The Bill passed through all its stages in the House of Lords, but there was considerable opposition from both sides of the House of Commons. After debate, the private Bill was withdrawn and a public Bill having similar force was eventually passed into law in November.

At the time of her death Lady Mountbatten was connected with a dozen and more bodies devoted to the welfare of youth, the sick and the underprivileged; among them the St. John Ambulance Brigade (of which she was Superintendent-in-Chief), the Westminster Hospital, the Girl Guides Association, Save the Children Fund, the Royal College of Nursing, and the W.V.S. Yet her interest was never passive; she had an inquiring mind and it was never enough for her to be just a name on a letter heading. Once her sympathies had been roused she gave generously both of her time—she was often oversea—and her organizational experience.

Of the two daughters she bore Lord Mountbatten, the elder, Lady Patricia, is married to Lord Brabourne; and the younger, Lady Pamela, was married in January 1960 to David Hicks.

February 22, 1960.

Alexander Albert Mountbatten—See **Carisbrooke.**

Admiral Lord Mountevans, who died on August 20, 1957 while on holiday in Norway at the age of 75, was perhaps the naval officer whose name was more widely known to the public than any other of his generation. For this he was himself largely responsible, for he was never one to hide his light under a bushel; he revelled in publicity and enjoyed being in the public eye. But there was nothing spurious in the light which he delighted in displaying.

His qualities were as real and admirable as his achievements. The Royal Navy traditionally dislikes self-advertisers, but his brother officers loved "Teddy Evans" as much as did the men who served under him, and found no fault in him for characteristics that they would never have tolerated in a lesser man. He had a knack of sensing the impression he produced on any audience or person to whom he talked, and almost instinctively adjusting his behaviour so as, without any surrender of his own vehement individuality, to gain their sympathy and assert his influence over them. These qualities were particularly valuable when he reached the higher ranks.

The Rt. Hon. Sir Edward Ratcliffe Garth Russell Evans, K.C.B., D.S.O., first Baron Mountevans, of Chelsea, in the county of London in the Peerage of the United Kingdom, was born on October 28, 1881, the son of Frank Evans, of the Chancery Bar.

He was within the canon of the boy's adventure story—from which, man of action that he was, he might well have sprung—when at the age of eight he tried to run away to sea accompanied by his two brothers, aged seven and nine. They walked from St. John's Wood to Barking, but were arrested by a "not too cheerful policeman . . . taken home by our mother and properly chastised".

He was educated at Merchant Taylors' School and in H.M.S. Worcester, the Thames Nautical Training College, whence in 1896 he passed into the Royal Navy, becoming a midshipman the following year, a sub-lieutenant in 1900, and a lieutenant two years later. While still a sub-lieutenant he was selected as navigating officer of the steam yacht Morning, which was sent out by the Royal Geographical Society in 1902 to the relief of Captain Scott's first Antarctic expedition, in the Discovery, when that ship was frozen in MacMurdo Strait. The expedition was revictualled, and in 1903 the Morning made a second voyage of relief, accompanied by the Terra Nova; on this occasion the Discovery got clear and the ships returned together.

In 1910 he was again selected by Scott to join the latter's second Antarctic expedition, this time as navigator and second-in-command of their ship the Terra Nova. In that capacity he acted as navigator of the polar party in their journey south until 150 miles from the Pole, when that duty was transferred to Lieutenant H. R. Bowers and Evans turned back with two companions, Able Seamen Lashley and Crean, to return over the Great Ice Barrier to the ship. Evans was the last of living men to speak to Scott when, on January 4, 1912, he said goodbye to him and turned north. When near the end of the journey he developed scurvy, and owed his life to the devotion of his two companions, to whom in after years he paid generous tribute in many lectures. They brought him back to the ship in February 1912, whence he was invalided home.

In June 1914 he returned to naval duty in command of the Mohawk, destroyer, of the 6th Flotilla, and was actively engaged in the Dover Patrol throughout the war. He had many distinguished services to his credit, including, besides engagements with the enemy, four successful salvages. But the best known of his services there was the occasion when he was in command of the flotilla leader Broke, in company with the Swift, Commander Ambrose Peck, his senior officer, on the night of April 20, 1917, on which they engaged the German 5th half-flotilla of six destroyers which was returning north-eastward after bombarding the harbour and castle of Dover. The two forces met on opposite courses east of the Goodwin Sands. Peck and Evans attacked with guns and torpedoes and turned to ram.

The Swift was unsuccessful, passing through the enemy line, but the Broke rammed G.42, and G.55 was disabled by a torpedo and set on fire; both German ships sank later. The Swift had one killed and four wounded; the Broke, which had come under heavy fire while lying entangled with G.42, had 40 casualties, and both ships had much material damage. But the Germans made no more surface raids on the Dover area for many months. The commanders of the Swift and Broke received special promotion to captain from the date of the action. From October 1917 Evans was Chief of Staff to Sir Reginald Bacon, the Vice-Admiral, Dover, remaining in that capacity with his successor, Sir Roger Keyes, until April 1918, when he resumed duty afloat in command of the Active for the remainder of the war.

After a period of half pay, he was appointed to command the cruiser Carlisle on the China Station, and again came into the public eye for the salvage of the steamer Hong Moh which, with over 1,000 passengers on board, had gone ashore near Swatow and broken in two. Heavy seas made it difficult and dangerous to get boats near the remains of the ship, but Evans himself took charge of the cruiser's one small motor boat, and finding that there was no other way to rescue survivors, himself swam to the wreck with a line, established communication, and was able to save 221 out of 350 who still survived on board when the Carlisle arrived on the scene. For this service he was awarded Lloyd's Gold Medal for saving life, he and two of his officers received the Board of Trade silver medal for gallantry, and three ratings received the bronze medal.

Evans's next employment was for two years from July 1923 as Captain of the Auxiliary Patrol, an appointment afterwards known as Captain of the Fishery Protection and Minesweeping Flotilla, with his headquarters at Portland. In June 1926 he assumed command of the battle-cruiser Repulse, one of the plums for senior captains, in the Atlantic Fleet, and held it until a few months before his promotion to rear-admiral in February 1928.

As a flag officer, his first command was that of the Australian Squadron, with his flag in H.M.A.S. Australia, which he held for two years from May 1929. He was extremely popular in the Commonwealth, and on leaving he took an unconventional farewell of the naval personnel by entertaining some 2,000 officers and men and their wives at a cinema, which he thought "much better than marching round in awful majesty, in cocked hat and all the dingle-dangle of braid, on the quarterdecks of the various ships". In March 1933 he succeeded Vice-Admiral H. J. Tweedie as Commander-in-Chief on the Africa Station, with his flag first in the Cardiff and later in the large cruiser Dorsetshire.

In the Union of South Africa, too, he was universally popular, though he was the object of some trenchant criticism for his handling, when acting High Commissioner during the absence on leave of Sir Herbert Stanley [q.v.], of the case of Tshekedi [q.v.], the Regent of the Bamangwato tribe of Bechuanaland, in September 1933. Tshekedi was accused of having exceeded his authority by flogging a European on the grounds that he was associating with African women in tribal territory. Evans, accompanied by a substantial force of naval ratings, travelled to Bechuanaland in state and publicly suspended Tshekedi from his chiefship, at the same time expelling the European from Bechuanaland. Tshekedi was admitted to have been, on the whole, an enlightened and capable chief, and after a few weeks Evans cancelled the suspension and reinstated him. It was thought by many that the whole affair might have been more happily handled with less ostentation and publicity.

In February 1934 Evans briefly renewed his acquaintance with the Antarctic. Shifting his flag to the 1,060-ton sloop Milford, he visited Bouvet Island in order to check its position, but was unable to continue on to the south as the Milford's fuel supply had been depleted by the heavy weather encountered.

In 1936, now Admiral Sir Edward Evans, he was elected Rector of Aberdeen University by a majority of three to one, and he was again chosen in 1939. He received the Freedom of Chatham and of Dover and numerous other distinctions. He relinquished the Nore Command in January 1939 and three months later was nominated as a Regional Commissioner for London under the civil defence scheme. He held this post honourably and energetically throughout a most harassing period and his personality and bearing stimulated all ranks of the C.D. services.

Evans married first Hilda, daughter of T. G. Russell, of Christchurch, New Zealand, who died in 1913; and, secondly in 1916, Elsa, daughter of Richard Andvord, of Christiana (now Oslo), by whom he had two sons. He was made C.B., Civil Division, in 1913, and Military Division in 1932; he received his D.S.O. in 1917 and was promoted K.C.B. in 1935. In 1945 he was made a peer.

August 22, 1957.

Edwin Muir, C.B.E., poet and critic, died in hospital at Cambridge on January 3, 1959 at the age of 71.

The major landmarks of the world of writing are not those men who stand at its busy centres but those whose personal vision, integrity, and creative resource fit them rather for the calm and opportunity of comparative isolation. Edwin Muir was among these. His last years, spent in a beautiful Cambridgeshire village, serenely completed a life which had always been nearer to distinction than to celebrity. Here at Swaffham Prior, Muir's study looked out on a scene (a graveyard on a hill, a ruined church, a ruined tower) which might well have come from his own verse; and it was in this room that some of his best work was done. Indeed, he became at 70 perhaps the foremost poet in English to be writing actively week by week. Starting late in life as a poet, he died at an advanced age; but it was his prime. Old age and declining powers were things that he did not experience.

Muir's life began in a remote croft on the main island of Orkney, where he was born in 1887. Both his father's and his mother's family had been crofters for generations: but it was not a period in which crofting could flourish and in 1902 the Muirs moved to modest quarters in Glasgow. Then, in drab works and offices, Muir became to some extent the victim of that more brutal side of modernity which later he was so humanely and yet so searchingly to indict.

Already he was reading widely, thinking deeply, and beginning as a writer himself: contributing, under A. R. Orage, for example, to the *New Age.* But the true beginning of his literary career was his marriage in 1919 to Willa Anderson (in her turn a Shetlander), whose more emphatic personality, and also perhaps quicker practical sense, contributed profoundly to his life and in large measure made it possible for him to do what he did.

Muir began to write verse only in the 1920s. Even then his prose was at first more important. His early criticism (*Latitudes* 1924; *Transition* 1927) is remarkable for, among other things, almost the first wholly outspoken recognition of D. H. Lawrence as the major genius of his generation. *The Structure of the Novel* (1927) is a lucid and thoughtful book; it may owe a little to Stevenson but it reveals unmistakably the fresh mind of its author. Other and later critical pieces were published as *Essays on Literature and Society* (1949). Muir's social insight shows also in *Scottish Journey* (1936). Yet these works have been less influential than the translations from German fiction which he and Willa Muir, over a number of years, produced in collaboration. Of these *Jew Süss* may once have been the best known; but the most important in the end proved certainly to be those from Kafka (*The Castle,* 1930; *The Trial,* 1935, &c.). Before their appearance Kafka was almost unknown in Britain. The Muirs virtually created his literary reputation among us. Their translations are still standard and have recently been reissued.

It is not difficult to see how Kafka's intense yet sedate anxieties would have had their appeal for Muir; and the partial kinship of his mind with Kafka's sometimes appears in his verse. But the strongest influence on that verse is undoubtedly Muir's own life and his endeavour to come to terms with life. The remote and spacious islands where he was born have left their image throughout his work. Yet it is perhaps two things together, the archaic simplicities and enduring strength of his background, and also his interest in other literary models than the fashionable ones (his decisive tribute to Dante comes here to mind), which brought it about that his poetry was always a poetry more of things than of words, a poetry with little place for a rich language because what it sought was a plain reality.

The potentialities of his style, one assessed with difficulty through the critical ideas most current to-day, were not indeed fully apparent in his earlier volumes (for example, *First Poems,* 1926, or *Journeys and Places,* 1937), although here as always there is much to praise. Not until *The Voyage,* 1946, and *The Labyrinth,* 1948, was it apparent that his serene but subtle gravity of cadence and power to transmit in a naked minimum of words a single poignant, insistent, inescapable image could produce work of altogether outstanding quality. Moreover, after the war he had returned to Prague as head of the British Institute, and the fall of Czechoslovakia to communism had affected him deeply. Poems like "The Combat" or "Adam's Dream" now proved that he was not drawing on the good and evil in his early life merely in order to retreat into a private landscape. These pieces, with *Collected Poems* 1952, *One Foot in Eden,* 1956, and later substantial poems (like "The Last War"), which were published in periodicals up to within a few months of his death, revealed him as now, of all living English poets, the one most immediately and profoundly concerned to confront, and surmount, the challenges of his time.

After Czechoslovakia and a short period of work in Rome, Muir returned to Scotland, became Warden of Newbattle Abbey College, outside Edinburgh, and in 1955 was appointed Charles Eliot Norton Visiting Professor at Harvard. This, the award of literary prizes, the conferment of a C.B.E. in 1953, and the growing list of his honorary doctorates (Prague, 1947; Edinburgh, 1947; Rennes, 1949; Leeds, 1955; Cambridge, 1958) show that his achievement was being widely recognized.

But those who knew him during his last years will recall more his ineradicable modesty than his growing fame. The latter did not disturb or even preoccupy his days. In the first place he lived for a world of poetry, and seemed, purely and easily, to know its essence where others knew only its decoction. But he was happy also in the simplicities of life, the quiet meal, the short stroll, the calm, relaxed conversation where he always showed a gentleness without weakness, and that charity of mind which comes from a deeper clarity.

Ignorant, for a long time, of the slow-moving efforts being made in many quarters to secure him from financial anxiety, he worked on even into his last illness as a reviewer. What he found to praise was always what marked out the writer, never what merely tallied with the critic's yardstick. Young people who met him at this time (last year, for example, he was the first Churchill Professor at Bristol) instantly saw through his unassuming manner to the integrity and strength within; and when he chose that line of work he was a fine and ennobling teacher.

These are incidentals. His family and friends will remember him as a good and in some ways almost a saintly man. Others will remember him after them, for now he is among the English poets.

January 5, 1959.

Professor Sir Robert Muir, F.R.S., the eminent pathologist and bacteriologist, died on March 30, 1959 at the age of 94. He was Professor of Pathology at the University of St. Andrews in 1898-99, and at Glasgow from 1899 to 1936.

The son of the Rev. R. Muir, of Allars Church, Hawick, he was born on July 5, 1864, and was educated at Hawick Academy and at Edinburgh University. He graduated M.A. (1884), M.B., C.M., with first class honours (1888), and M.D., winning a gold medal (1890). He became lecturer on bacteriology at Edinburgh in 1892, and was shortly afterwards appointed assistant to the Professor of Pathology and Pathologist to the Royal Infirmary. After holding for one year the Professorship of Pathology at St. Andrews, he was appointed in 1899 to the corresponding chair at Glasgow. This office he held until his retirement in 1936, when he was made professor emeritus. While holding the Glasgow professorship he was also Pathologist to the Western Infirmary.

Muir's own researches were mainly concerned with immunology and culminated in the publication of his *Studies on Immunity* (1909). His greatest reputation was, however, gained as a teacher and author of standard textbooks. His *Manual of Bacteriology* (written with the late Professor J. Ritchie) first appeared in 1897 and reached a tenth edition in 1937; his *Text-Book of Pathology* (1924: 5th edition, 1941) is generally regarded as one of the finest expositions of the subject ever written.

Muir was elected a Fellow of the Royal Society in 1911, was a member of its council in 1926-27, and was awarded a Royal Medal for his work on immunity in 1929. Many other honours came to this doyen of pathologists. He was knighted in 1934; received honorary degrees from the Universities of Bristol, Dublin, Durham, Edinburgh, Glasgow, and Leeds; was an honorary Fellow of the Royal Colleges of Physicians of London and Edinburgh, of the Royal Faculty of Physicians and Surgeons of Glasgow, and of the Royal Society of Medicine.

He was for many years a member of the Medical Research Council.

April 1, 1959.

Cardinal-Archbishop of Munich—
See **Faulhaber.**

Sir Alfred Munnings, K.C.V.O., President of the Royal Academy from 1944 until 1949, died on July 17, 1959 at the age of 80.

He made his chief reputation as a painter of horses, but he ranged over country life in general and did not neglect pure landscape. Nor did his celebration of the rural scene end with painting, for, a keen rider to hounds himself, he could compose and deliver a rousing hunting ballad. His work as a painter had the merits and the defects that are common when love of the subject for its own sake is the chief inspiration.

Alfred James Munnings came of East Anglican country stock, and was born on October 8, 1878, at Mendham Mill, on the Waveney, in Suffolk, the son of John Munnings. The river and the horses which as a boy he loved to look after, to ride, and to study, remained all his life his abiding joy and almost a necessary part of his environment. The drawings of Randolph Caldecott excited his boyish emulation, but from copying and drawing from the imagination he progressed, under good advice, to drawing from nature, one of his first models being the white pony which he used for the exploration of the flat countryside.

Leaving Framlingham College at the age of 14, Munnings was apprenticed to a firm of lithographers in Norwich. Though his hours were from nine to seven he spent two evening hours studying at the Norwich School of Art, and to the end of his life gratefully acknowledged the good early grounding given by his headmaster, Walter Scott.

For his firm he did a number of posters (including work for Caley's and Colman's). One of them won him a gold medal. His private work began to commend itself to local collectors in this artistically minded town, and several bought sketches and pictures from him. One Norwich business man took him on a tour of Holland and Germany.

In 1898, at the age of 20, Munnings finished his indentures and set up a studio at his native Mendham, in a former carpenter's shop. He had already begun to show at the Norwich Art Circle, and even at the eclectic Royal Society of Painters in Water Colours. This year, without telling any of his friends, he submitted three paintings to the Royal Academy, and characteristically celebrated the acceptance of two of them by going to Bungay races. It is worthy of note that neither of the pictures hung was a horse subject.

A disaster soon befell the young painter. He was pushing through a hedge with some dogs when a thorn snapped back and totally blinded his right eye. He was forbidden to paint for six months, and then started again; and it is an extraordinary reflection that the whole great output of this prolific painter was produced with the use of only one eye.

Munnings remained in the Norwich district for six years. He had a studio in the town itself for part of the time, but he moved about the countryside a great deal, painting gypsies, horse-fairs, race-meetings and so forth. He spent an especially fruitful period at the "White Horse", Crostwick, where there was a common growing the gorse he loved, and where, as he recalled in some recollections published in the *Studio* in 1945, he could live comfortably, hire a horse and gypsy models, and buy all the small comforts he required for less than £300 a year. When Preston Corporation purchased "The Last of the Fair" Munnings was able to go over for a period of study at the Académie Julien, in Paris.

In 1904 Munnings moved his studio to Swainsthorpe, near Norwich, where he took a farmhouse. Always in and out of the saddle, he hunted regularly, attended many race-meetings, and had his own collection of pony models, his own caravan for transport of work, and even his own particular set of gypsy models. He would often start out in May with a man, a gypsy boy, a caravan, and his string of ponies, paint in the open air all the summer, and then sell his ponies in September or October.

After six years at Swainsthorpe Munnings transferred himself to the well-known artistic colony at Lamorna, in Cornwall; but he never became either a studio painter or, to any great extent, a marine painter. He still rode every day and hunted in season with Bolitho's hounds.

It was his hunting pictures that first brought him into public esteem, since they treated a well-worn subject in a fresh and lively way. And for lovers of the horse who desired to be painted in the saddle he was the ideal portraitist, who could be relied upon to produce not only a faithful and spirited version of man and beast alike but also such a landscape setting as would grace the walls of a town or country house.

Munnings held his first one-man show at the Leicester Galleries, London, in 1913. During 1917 and 1918 he was attached as official artist to the Canadian forces in France, working with the Cavalry Brigade and the Forestry Service, depicting various scenes from their activities and making many equestrian portraits of officers. With the ending of the war he found himself a gracious home by a river—namely, Castle House, Dedham, Essex, near Constable's Stour.

The year 1919 also saw an exhibition of 45 of his war pictures in the Gem Room at Burlington House and his election as A.R.A. In 1920 he married Violet, widow of William McBride, a lady who shared his open-air and hunting tastes and herself rode to hounds for many years.

Munnings was elected A.R.W.S. in 1921; and in the following year he won a gold medal at Paris with the picture "Changing Horses". A big exhibition at the Alpine Club Galleries, London, in 1923 was very successful.

By this time Munnings was one of the best known of British artists. His election to the full rank of Royal Academician occurred in 1925 and the Royal Society of Painters in Water Colours made him a full member in 1929.

In 1941 Castle House, Dedham, was requisitioned by the military, remaining in their hands until 1946. During most of this period Munnings was at Exford, on Exmoor, chiefly painting rapid and brilliant sketches of the half-wild moorland ponies, which, of course, had to be sought out on horseback.

In 1944 Munnings was knighted and elected President of the Royal Academy in succession to Sir Edwin Lutyens, who had recently died. In 1947 he was created K.C.V.O. In the same year he was admitted to the honorary freedom of the City of Norwich. In 1949 he retired from the presidency of the Royal Academy because he thought that the president should be someone who lived in London and could always be consulted, and also because he wanted to attend the Two Thousand Guineas at Newmarket, which is always run on Academy Private View day.

In 1956 the Academy honoured him with an exhibition of over 300 of his works in the Diploma Gallery.

Munnings was essentially an outdoor painter. He would rough out the main lines of his composition in a few rapid sketches, transfer this to the canvas, and then paint direct on the spot. His studios, whether at Dedham or at Chelsea, were chiefly used for finishing touches. Munnings believed in putting on bright colours first, and then overpainting—a process that gave a singularly glowing quality to his work. Though the horse was Munnings's main subject he was no narrow specialist. There is the splendid, monumental "Friesian Bull", for example, and some of his rapid studies of hounds, from all angles and in all stances, are among the finest things he did.

Munnings's works are to be found in many notable public and private collections. His general manner and attitude were breezy—even brusque. There was "no nonsense" about him, as the saying goes, and he was a profound believer in the virtue of hard work. Much has been made of Munnings's periodical attacks on some tendencies in modern art, as in his explosive speech at the Royal Academy banquet in 1949.

In reality the case was quite simple. For Munnings the merits of a work of art were chiefly in proportion to the accuracy with which the appearances of nature were represented in it, and he was constitutionally incapable of understanding any art in which accuracy of representation was not an aim. He had the courage of his limitations and did not hesitate to name the objects of his disapproval. Unfortunately, in his bewilderment he was apt to accuse artists like Matisse [q.v.], Picasso*, and Henry Moore of incompetency, and this exposed him to ridicule.

He wrote three volumes of autobiography, *An Artist's Life, The Second Burst,* and *The Finish,* sprawling, exuberant books reinforced by a wealth of illustration.

July 18, 1959.

Sir Keith Murdoch, one of the most prominent figures in Australian journalism and newspaper production for many years, died at his Melbourne home early on October 5, 1962 at the age of 66.

As managing director and managing editor of the Melbourne *Herald* he created a newspaper "chain" during the years between the wars which extended to all but one of the capital cities, and which introduced an entirely new element into Australian newspaper production. The final results of this policy are a matter of opinion, but there can be no question of the profound influence which the *Herald* amalgamations and acquisitions, closely following models in Britain, have had on journalism and public opinion in the Commonwealth. During the early days of the war Murdoch's outstanding position was recognized by his appointment as Director-General of the Australian Department of Information, and in 1946 he became the first Australian trustee of Reuters.

The son of a clergyman of Camberwell, near Melbourne, Keith Andrew Murdoch was born there on August 12, 1886. After attending the local grammar school, he continued his education at the London School of Economics. He found his first opportunity as a young man of 30 while on the staff of the Melbourne *Age*.

With the rank of captain he was sent on a special mission in 1915 to the Australian forces in Gallipoli. He conceived his duties as journalist in an independent spirit and though without military experience or accredited status as war correspondent formed strong opinions of his own on the Dardanelles policy. Having regard to the interests of the Australian troops, he concluded that immediate evacuation was essential. His views in this respect coincided with those of Sir Ellis Ashmead-Bartlett, the official British correspondent, and on his departure for Imbros in September he was entrusted by the latter with a secret uncensored letter to the Prime Minister urging that course. The existence of the letter became known, Murdoch was detained on his way back at Marseilles, and the letter taken from him. He contrived, however, to take another copy with him into England.

At the same time he had written a letter himself to the Australian Prime Minister containing immoderate criticism of the Dardanelles policy and of the officers and troops, other than Australian, then serving on the peninsula. A copy of this was sent also to Asquith, who, in the words of the Official History of the War, "though subsequently admitting that many of its allegations were untrue", took the "unusual step of printing it as a State paper". There is no doubt that the fact, if not the substance, of the letter played a part in the Cabinet's eventual decision to evacuate.

During the remaining war years Murdoch served as one of the Australian correspondents on the Western Front, his dispatches being always vivid and provocative. For some time after the war he represented the Sydney *Sun* and the Melbourne *Herald* in London, as London editor and manager of the United Cable Service (Australasia), now the Australian Newspapers Cable Service. In 1921 he returned to Melbourne as editor-in-chief of the Melbourne *Herald*. He travelled back as Special Correspondent of *The Times* on the Renown, which was carrying the Prince of Wales* [later Duke of Windsor] on his visit to Australia and New Zealand.

Under Murdoch the Melbourne *Herald* achieved the height of its influence and prosperity, and the paper together with the numerous publications which were quickly absorbed into the organization came to represent the complementary side, in enterprise and news efficiency, to the soundness and solidity which has long been a recognized feature of the Australian Press. The financial conditions for the success of the Melbourne *Herald's* venture in newspaper control were not all of Murdoch's provision, but his gifts of organization and his wide vision and ambition were essential, and these were amply used in the post of managing director and later as chairman and managing director. He was the founder of the newsprint industry in Australia. When the Australian Newspapers Conference decided to establish a permanent secretariat in 1936 Murdoch was appointed first president, and in June 1940 Menzies announced his appointment as Director-General of Information. Murdoch's remarkable gift of organization was never more clearly manifested, for by November he was able to say that the newly formed Department of Information was thoroughly established and running so smoothly that his services were no longer necessary except in an advisory capacity.

He resigned from the position of managing director of the Australian Associated Press, which he had held for some years, in 1944, and in 1946 and again in 1950 was chairman of the Australian delegation to the Imperial Press Conference. Appointed a trustee of the National Gallery of Victoria in 1933, in which year he was knighted, he was elected president in 1936 and was largely instrumental in financing the first loan exhibition in the gallery in 1935.

Murdoch married, in 1928, Elisabeth, daughter of Rupert Greene, of Melbourne. There were four children of the marriage—a son and three daughters.

[A tribute followed this obituary on the same day.]

October 6, 1952.

Professor Gilbert Murray, O.M., D.LITT., D.C.L., LL.D., who died at his home, Yatscombe, Boar's Hill, Oxford, on May 20, 1957, was one of the outstanding figures of his generation. His reputation as a classical scholar was world-wide, and to many who are not scholars his translations of Euripides have given, on the stage or in the study, their first introduction into the character and methods of ancient tragedy. In recent years, after a record of devoted service to the ideals of the League of Nations, he brought his personal faith and energy to the cause of the United Nations, and at his death was joint president of the United Nations Association.

George Gilbert Aimé Murray was born at Sydney on January 2, 1866, the third son of Sir Terence Aubrey Murray, who was president of the Legislative Council of New South Wales. Going to England at the age of 11, he went to Merchant Taylors' School, and in 1884 he entered St. John's College, Oxford. Besides first classes in Honour Moderations and *Lit. Hum.* he won the Hertford and Ireland scholarships in 1885, a Craven scholarship, the Chancellor's Prize for Latin Verse, the Gaisford Greek Verse Prize in 1886, and the Gaisford Greek Prose Prize in 1887. In 1888 he was elected a Fellow of New College, and was awarded the Derby scholarship in 1889. With such a record it was not surprising that he was at once elected to succeed S. H. Butcher as Professor of Greek at Glasgow. He was 23 at the time. In the same year he married Lady Mary Howard, the eldest daughter of the ninth Earl of Carlisle; the marriage ceremony was performed by Jowett in the chapel of Castle Howard.

At Glasgow Murray proved himself a great teacher and a striking lecturer, and in his *History of Ancient Greek Literature* (1897) showed an unusual range of knowledge and a capacity for handling an old theme with freshness. During these years he laid the foundations of his special study of Euripides. The three volumes in the Oxford Classical Texts were produced successively in 1901, 1904, and 1910. The critical apparatus showed the extent of his learning, and the text the soundness of his judgment and the brilliance of his occasional conjectures. But to Murray a Greek drama was primarily a play to be acted, and in many places in the text the assignment of lines in choruses to different persons and the frequent supposition of breaks, interruptions, and aposiopesis have proved stumbling-blocks to readers of less vivid imagination. It was probably the same wish to realize the dramatic purpose of Euripides that led him to produce the series of the now well known verse-translations. They were quickly seen to offer a unique opportunity for presenting Greek drama to an English audience; many of the plays have been performed. It is possible that Murray occasionally read too much into Euripides; to drive the theme home in its English dress he sometimes pressed a parallel unjustifiably; but his genius was more at home in the human and sceptical Euripides than in the static beauty of Sophocles or the tense grandeur of Aeschylus, though he translated several plays of each. He also published versions of *The Frogs* and *The Birds* by Aristophanes.

At the time of his death about 396,000 copies of his translations had been sold. *Electra* (60,000) headed the list, followed by *The Trojan Women* (40,000), *Iphigenia* (37,000), and *Alcestis* (31,000).

In 1899 he returned south and taught privately at New College. In 1908, on the resignation of Ingram Bywater, he was, as had been generally expected, nominated by the Crown as Regius Professor of Greek. The contrast was marked. Bywater was an Aristotelian, a precise and minute interpreter, a little suspicious of the appeal of the classics as literature. Murray believed profoundly in this appeal; his lectures drew crowds, and in the brilliance of his generalizations the audience was apt to forget the immense detailed knowledge on which they were based. His private classes became a feature in the classical course.

To the years from 1899 to 1914 belong the greater part of the Greek play translations and at least two other of his most important works. He had long been attracted by the speculations of the anthropologists as to the thoughts and ways—and especially the religious thoughts and ways—of primitive and early man, and had applied them to his Greek studies. In *Andromache,* published and acted in 1900, the year after his only modern play, *Carlyon Sahib,* had been favourably received in London, he attempted to show how the events which gave rise to a classical story might have happened among a prehistoric people. The same reconstructive imagination lay at the back of *The Rise of The Greek Epic* (1907)—an attempt to survey the "Homeric Question" in the light of anthropology. Accepting the view that the Homeric poems, as we have them, cannot be regarded as the work of a single author, he contended that they were a "traditional book", built up by the additions and modifications of a succession of poets and reciters. Behind this book he saw a primitive civilization, barbarous and savage, which he depicted with a master hand. Turning next to tragedy, he expounded a theory of its ritual origin in the struggle, death, and resurrection of the "year-god".

Murray was, during these years, much in sympathy with the speculations of Jane Harrison and F. M. Cornford, and shared their belief that the genuine Greek religion was to be found, not in the cult of the Olympians, but in an older and more primitive chthonic cult, of which traces remained in classical times. This view found expression in the first chapter of *Four Stages of Greek Religion* (1913), republished in 1925 as *Five Stages of Greek Religion* and in *Stoic Philosophy* (1915).

The full development of his activities was cut short in 1914. In 1900 he had contributed to a volume called *Liberalism and the Empire;* later he had taken an active part in the movement for woman suffrage. Naturally a lover of peace, he was distressed and horrified by the European cataclysm, but had no doubt in his own mind as to the rightness of Britain's choice, and his study of *The Foreign Policy of Sir Edward Grey* (1915), written as it was from a detached and independent point of view, confirmed many waverers. Throughout the 1914-18 War, while fulfilling his obligations as professor, he assisted the Government in a variety of ways in London. When the war was over he threw himself heart and soul into the work of the League of Nations. For the League of Nations Union, of which he was chairman from 1923 until 1938, he worked with the zeal of a missionary; he thought no local branch too small to address, no detailed committee work too dull to attend to; in writing and speaking alike his purpose was to inform public opinion of the aims and achievements of the League and to ensure that its supporters did not allow vague sentiment to be a substitute for accurate knowledge. He stood three times as a candidate for Parliament in the University of Oxford, but never succeeded in breaking through the Conservative tradition.

In the domestic politics of the University Murray took no great part, though he was a leader in the movement for the retention of compulsory Greek in Responsions and always a strong supporter of the cause of women's education. He served on the council of Somerville College, and was its president from 1916 to 1919, and always showed a great interest in the work of women students who were reading classics. He was a Fellow of the British Academy and a trustee of the British Museum. He also served as president of the Society for Psychical Research in 1915; he followed the society's investigations with enthusiasm, and had himself powers as a "thought-reader". His last published work included the skilful reconstruction of the *Perikeiromené* and the *Epitrepontes* of Menander, a volume of *Greek Studies* (1947), and *Hellenism and the Modern World* (1953).

In 1926 he was professor of poetry at Harvard; and he retired from the Greek Chair at Oxford in 1936. The honour of the Order of Merit was conferred upon him in 1941.

After the last war his voice through many broadcasts on literary and political subjects became known and revered by a wide public; particularly memorable was an occasion in which he took part in a broadcast with Bertrand Russell* and Max Beerbohm [q.v.]. His work on the classics continued unabated; as recently as 1955 there appeared a revised text of the Oxford *Aeschylus* and in 1956 a translation of *The Knights,* by Aristophanes.

A short while ago Dr. Ritter, Counsellor at the German Embassy, went down to Yatscombe and conferred the honour of Pour La Mérite upon him. Only recently he had been asked to receive the Freedom of the City of London.

Murray was a man of singular grace and charm. Well built and lissom, with a long swinging gait, a high domed brow, and long delicate hands, he looked what he was—a scholar with a wide outlook and a strong sense of humour. His speeches were amusing, closely reasoned, and persuasive, made the more effective by a melodious voice. He was the friend of almost all sorts and conditions of men, and his hospitable house at Boar's Hill was hardly ever without a visitor and often thronged with scholars, undergraduates, Liberal M.P.s, poets, and guests from abroad. Lady Mary Murray's welcome and her own strong and sympathetic personality helped to make a visit to Yatscombe a memorable experience. He was a brilliant talker and liked to hear the views of others. Yet there was about him a certain detachment, as though his truest life was lived with his books and his thoughts; something of this comes out in his short Apologia, *Religio Grammatici* (1918).

He had three sons, two of whom predeceased him, and two daughters—Rosalind, who was formerly married to Dr. Arnold Toynbee*, and won distinction as a novelist; and Agnes, who devoted great gifts to the service of international understanding after the 1914-18 War and died in 1922. Lady Mary Murray died in 1956.

May 21, 1957.

Philip Murray, the American labour leader and president of the Congress of Industrial Organizations, the large amalgamation of various unions opposed to the American Federation of Labour, died on November 9, 1952 at San Francisco.

He was a native of Scotland, where he was born at Blantyre, in the Lanarkshire coalfields, on May 25, 1886. He emigrated at the age of 16 to the United States, and there found work in the coalfields near Pittsburgh. In 1911 he became a naturalized American and soon became one of the leaders in the miners' union, the United Mine Workers of America. He was appointed in 1912 a member of its international board, which took under its wing miners in Canada as well as those in the United States. In 1916 he became president of district No. 5, which included the area round Pittsburgh and parts of adjoining states, such as West Virginia, where there are extensive coalfields. In 1920 he became vice-president of the union under John L. Lewis*, who was for many years president. He gave effective service to the country on the Pennsylvania Board of War Labour in 1917 and 1918 and as a member of the committee for the production of bituminous coal.

Some years later when Lewis founded the Congress of Industrial Organizations in opposition to the American Federation of Labour, in order to extend union influence into many industries, such as steel, motors, and rubber, in which workers had hardly been organized, he joined and at once took a leading part in its work. As opposed to the federation their purpose was to organize great unions by industries in place of by crafts, as had long been the practice, and the organizers had visions of vast unions in the large industries all over the country.

In the autumn of 1940 when Roosevelt was re-elected President for the third time Lewis, who had previously been his friend and collaborator, carried out a threat made during the election campaign to give up his position with the congress if Roosevelt became President again. Murray was appointed congress president in his place, and not long afterwards, when war production began to assume vast proportions under the Lease and Lend Act, he was appointed by Roosevelt one of labour's representatives on the Labour Mediation Board. Unlike Lewis, Murray was a firm believer in all-out aid to Britain, and had little accord with the isolationists, of whom Lewis was one.

In the summer of 1941 when a coal strike broke out in mines owned by the steel companies over the question of the "closed-shop" Murray, under the influence of Lewis, still president of the miners, resigned his place on the mediation board. He had so far been a restraining influence among the miners, and had helped the settlement of many labour disputes by curbing the extremists, but this time he found Lewis too strong for him. In the course of the next year they composed their differences.

The feud, however, broke out again shortly afterwards with increased violence and during the Presidency of Harry Truman* the industrial scene was marred by a series of large coal strikes. Murray found himself progressively less sympathetic to Truman's Administration, which he more than once accused of yielding in "abject cowardice" to the refusal of industrialists to engage in collective bargaining. The fall in the purchasing power of wages, and its remedies, would have been high on the C.I.O. agenda he was preparing when he died.

November 10, 1952.

John Middleton Murry, O.B.E., the author and critic, died on March 13, 1957 in hospital at Bury St. Edmunds. He was 67.

As a critic Middleton Murry aroused in his readers, or perhaps in many of them, feelings of a curiously personal kind. Those who agreed with his opinions of the moment, or who were in sympathy with his way of expressing them, tended to become, in some sort, his active disciples; those who, on the other hand, were not temperamentally drawn to his views on life and literature or who deprecated his fondness for a mystical or mystificatory idiom were inclined to feel distaste for whatever might be his particular message. One of the earliest of his books is entitled *The Evolution of an Intellectual,* and Murry's considerable output as a writer represents, it might be said, the unceasing effort of an intellectual to dicover an absolute of satisfaction or assurance which seemed to be denied to him by his critical faculties. In this dilemma he sought to turn the lessons of literature, Christianity, communism, pacifism, and a great deal more to his own peculiarly charged necessity.

A writer of notable ability, widely and in many respects deeply read, resourceful in argument, with an impassioned and poetic feeling for metaphysical mystery, Murry was, by turns, rewarding and provoking in his later and more emphatically didactic stage. He was undoubtedly at his best as a literary critic, although even here his mannerisms grew markedly on him. Still, allowing for his distinctive bias of mind, he said much in his own way that was acute, discerning, and well worth saying about the genius of Shakespeare, Keats, Blake, Chekhov, and others.

John Middleton Murry was born at Peckham on August 6, 1889, the child of parents in modest circumstances. It was suggested by those who had known him as an undergraduate or afterwards that his intellectual anxieties as a young man of brilliant attainments arose in part from an uneasy and self-conscious preoccupation with his lower middle class origins, and it is certain that in the early part of his career he was much beset by the desire to forget his childhood environment. He made his way by scholarships from an elementary school to Christ's Hospital and Brasenose College, Oxford, where he took his degree in 1912. In that year, having first considered political journalism as an appropriate stepping-stone for a career, he joined the staff of the *Westminster Gazette.* Next he became an art critic, while throughout the period of the War of 1914-18 he was a leading contributor to *The Times Literary Supplement,* proving himself a literary critic of acute temper and graceful distinction of style. During 1916-19 he served in the political intelligence department of the War Office, and in the latter year was chief censor. He then became, for the last two years of its separate existence—1919-21—editor of the *Athenaeum.*

By then he had published several volumes in a vein, self-critical, romantically intense and aspiring, that could be plainly recognized as characteristic. The first was a novel, *Still Life* (1916), with a strongly autobiographical flavour, the portrait of a young man tormented by the desire to discover the meaning of things. In the following year came a study of Dostoevsky—a personal, romantic and "mystical" interpretation. Then, in 1919, came a volume of poems, in which the poet's rare intellectual apprehensions obscured the more enduring texture of poetry, and the year after saw the publication of the essays on life and literature entitled *The Evolution of an Intellectual,* a poetic drama called *Cinnamon and Angelica,* and the critical essays of *Aspects of Literature.* There were, similarly, three books in 1922—another novel, anxious, clever, tenuous, *The Things We Are;* and two volumes of criticism, *The Problem of Style* and *Countries of the Mind,* which are among his soundest and most perceptive work.

After he came down from Oxford Murry had been a notable figure in an intellectual and artistic group in London who included among its members D. H. Lawrence and Katherine Mansfield.

Murry had married Katherine Mansfield in 1913. Her death 10 years later, after prolonged ill-health, at the early age of 33, appears to have called forth in Murry a mystical experience, an illumination of mind or spirit, a crisis of faith or of being, to which he attached profound significance, particular and universal, but which he found it rather difficult to communicate. Not that he easily tired of trying to communicate it. His articles in the *Adelphi,* which he founded in the same year as Katherine Mansfield died, were but the first of many attempts to put this inner experience of his into words. They appeared in volume form, under the title of *To the Unknown God,* in the following year, during which he also published a wispy sort of novel, *The Voyage,* and a volume of brief literary essays, *Pencillings,* which had originally appeared in the columns of *The Times.*

After that most—indeed, all—that Murry wrote was directly coloured by the mystical revelation which had thus been vouchsafed him. His personal illumination was translated into a public gospel, in the propagation of which his literary criticism acquired a more noticeable edge of dogmatism. He wrote a *Life of Jesus* in 1926 in order to satisfy an inner need; he produced in *God* (1929) what he described as an introduction to the study of metabiology; in *Son of Woman* (1931) he gave his own version of the personality and message of D. H. Lawrence; and in 1932 he preached *The Necessity of Communism.*

From this point, by way of a life of Katherine Mansfield, a volume of intellectual autobiography entitled *Between Two Worlds,* and a work on Shakespeare, he progressed towards the formulation of an individual Christian pacifism. His initial standpoint, as that was revealed in *The Necessity of Pacifism* (1937), was elaborated and modified in some half-dozen volumes before he finally renounced pacifism as a philosophy in *The Free Society* (1948), in which he virtually advocated a preventive war against Russia.

Murry's critical biography *Jonathan Swift* was published in 1954 and his *Unprofessional Essays* in 1956. These included a defence of Henry Fielding and an excellent piece of writing on T. S. Eliot's* verse plays. His latest book, *Love, Freedom and Society* was published on March 11 [two days before his death].

March 14, 1957.

Sir John Myres, Emeritus Professor of Ancient History in the University of Oxford, died on March 6, 1954 at his home at Oxford, at the age of 84.

John Linton Myres was by birth a Lancashireman, the son of the Rev. W. M. Myres, of Preston. His long life was devoted to his love and study of Greece, both ancient and contemporary. Few students of antiquity have made themselves so fully equipped or so versatile, and with this equipment he resolutely refused to allow his varied interests to obscure his main objective as an historian. For it was as an ancient historian that Professor Myres achieved his reputation, although he took an honoured place as anthropologist (he was for many years the editor of *Man*), archaeologist, geologist, and geographer. Myres coordinated numerous interests to the main task of interpreting the history of Greece; and it was as the Wykeham Professor of Ancient History in Oxford that he will be remembered.

He was born on July 3, 1869, at Preston, was a scholar at Winchester and at New College, and took a first in the Classical School. In 1892 he was elected to a prize fellowship at Magdalen, and to a Craven fellowship for travel in Greece, and also (an early tribute to his versatility) to the Burdett-Coutts scholarship in geology. After these years of travel he held a studentship at Christ Church from 1895 until 1907, and then went to Liverpool as Gladstone Professor of Greek, and was at the same time lecturer in Ancient Geography. While at Liverpool he won the Arnold prize at Oxford for an essay on "The Place of the Greek Islands in the Early History of Greek Civilization". In 1910 he returned to Oxford as Wykeham Professor and took up the fellowship at New College annexed to it. He vacated his professorship in 1939, but remained on the Governing Body of New College till 1946, when he was elected an Honorary Fellow. He was elected an Honorary Fellow of Magdalen College in 1944.

His early travels had taken him to Cyprus, Asia Minor, and Crete, as well as to the mainland of Greece. He travelled with Evans in Crete at the time when Evans's great surmise was taking shape; he made lasting contributions to the topography of south-western Asia Minor; and of Cyprus he made his own particular province; he twice excavated in Cyprus, and compiled the catalogue of the Cyprus Museum. Later at the invitation of the Metropolitan Museum in New York he catalogued the important Cesuola collection of Cypriot antiquities there. These catalogues set the standard for their day; Cyprus, lying on the horizon of so many great civilizations, with vistas in so many directions, was an excellent field for Myres's genius. For Myres had more than a touch of genius.

Myres's mind was romantic, but his eye was for the actual and concrete. His medium of expression was a prose style wonderfully supple, clear, and firm. He was an omnivorous reader and delighted in what he read. Much of his work is buried in periodicals, in the *Journal of Hellenic Studies,* the *Geographical Journal, Folklore,* the *Journal of the Royal Anthropological Society.* and elsewhere. His largest and most important book was *"Who Were the Greeks?"* This massive work, the fruit of a year's leisure in the beautiful climate and surroundings of the University of California, does in fact incorporate most of a lifetime's preoccupation with the problem of what factors had caused the Greek people of the first half of the first millenium before Christ to be so remarkable. How much of its conclusions will endure is not yet clear, nor indeed of primary relevance in a scholar like Myres, whose function was to open new vistas of thought.

The 1914-18 War gave Myres the rank of lieutenant-commander and later commander in the R.N.V.R., and a roving commission among the Southern Sporades and the islands off the Turkish coast. His task was to obtain information about the disposition of the Turkish forces and to harry the Turkish villages by any means in his power. One of his enterprises was to organize Anatolian peasants into bands, well armed, which were landed in darkness on the Turkish coast and instructed to drive back or slaughter the cattle of the enemy. This Homeric sport afforded discomfort to the Turkish garrisons and fresh meat for the British Navy. For his services in Greek waters against the enemy he was awarded the Greek Order of King George I of the first class.

Myres was for many years general secretary of the British Association, and during his last years, both before and after his retirement from his professorship, he was chairman of the managing committee of the British School of Archaeology at Athens. The 1939-45 War prevented this from being what he would have wished, a work mainly of organizing and encouraging younger workers in his chosen fields: it presented instead some harassing and difficult problems to which, in spite of increasing infirmities, he devoted himself. The British School at Athens has played some part in forming the singular bond which through all political change so firmly attaches Greece and England to each other, and Myres himself was regarded with warm affection in many villages and islands of the Aegean.

He remained an active and productive scholar to the end. Indeed, his last three books, *Scripta Minoa II, Geographical History in Greek Lands, Herodotus: Father of History,* all appeared within the last two years or so. In 1953 he was awarded the Victoria Medal of the Royal Geographical Society. He received his knighthood in the Birthday Honours in 1943.

He married in 1895 Sophia Florence, younger daughter of Charles Ballance, of Clapton, and they had two sons and a daughter. The younger, and only surviving son, the present Bodley's Librarian, followed his father as a scholar at Winchester and New College and as a student of Christ Church.

March 8, 1954.

N

Imre Nagy, Hungarian Premier during the ill-fated Hungarian rising against the Soviet Union, whose execution after a secret trial was announced on June 17, 1958 first from Moscow and later from Budapest, was the youngest son of a poor peasant, a member of the Calvinist minority in Hungary.

He was born in 1896. After a brief attendance at an elementary school he was apprenticed, at the age of 10, to a locksmith, earning a shilling a week as a mechanic when he was called up to serve in the Austro-Hungarian Army in the 1914-18 War. Wounded on Polish soil, he was taken prisoner by the Tsarist Army. On the outbreak of the Bolshevik revolution he went straight from hospital to join the Communist Party and the Red Army. To convince the new régime of his faith in the revolution he renounced his Hungarian citizenship and became a Soviet citizen.

At the time of the Bela Kun revolution in Hungary he returned to Budapest and was given a minor job, but with the collapse of the Bela Kun régime he was forced to seek asylum in France, and plotted against Horthy's [q.v.] Government. In 1923 he returned to Hungary, where he helped to organize the clandestine Communist Party working in close contact with the Comintern. He was arrested in 1927 but managed to escape and found his way back to Moscow, where he remained for a period of 15 years, returning again to his native Hungary in 1944 when the Soviet forces reached Budapest.

While in Russia he studied agriculture at the Moscow Institute and for a time was a member of the managerial committee of a collective farm near Moscow which was also used as a training centre for Hungarian and other communists from abroad. When the first communist government was formed in Hungary, Nagy was given the post of Minister of Agriculture with the task of collectivizing the land and organizing farming on the Soviet system—a task which he carried through with force, although not with the same ruthlessness as in Russia.

An ardent communist and still retaining his Soviet citizenship Nagy, like Gomulka in Poland, never abandoned completely his national sentiments. This brought him quickly into conflict with other members of the Hungarian Politburo and with Moscow. In 1949 he was criticized by Stalin [q.v.] for holding "incorrect views" on the question of agriculture and was dismissed from his post and Politburo, but was forgiven a year later and restored to the Cabinet and made a Deputy Premier under Rakosi.* When Rakosi lost favour in Moscow, Nagy succeeded him as Premier, and after Stalin's death was the first communist leader to permit the peasants to contract out of collective farms, admitting their failure. This was the Malenkov spring in Russia and Nagy's liberal policy was hailed by the Hungarians.

But this period was short lived and in 1955 Nagy was forced to resign and deprived of his party membership. A few months later, in October 1956, he was swept back into power on a peak of anti-Soviet feeling and the revolt against the iron fisted policy of Geroe and his associates. Nagy again became Premier of Hungary and for 10 days was the national hero who was bringing back freedom to his people and liberation from Soviet oppression. For this he now paid with his life. He was arrested by Soviet troops after he had left the Yugoslav Embassy, where he had been given asylum, and taken to Romania. According to reports he was brought back to Budapest in 1957 and tried in secret, the trial lasting for over a month, and much evidence against him having been supplied and prepared in Moscow.

While he was in prison there appeared in the United States what was described as Nagy's "Liberal Testament", in which the ill-fated Hungarian communist leader put down his amended thoughts and views on communism and its system of government. In it Nagy, writing from experience, showed that in the communist system there is no room for freedom and—as proved by yesterday's tragic news—no escape from oppression and total extinction even for those who served it all their lives.

June 18, 1958.

Sir Lewis Namier, who died on August 19, 1960 in a London hospital at the age of 72, was an historian, a trainer of historians, and a character of rich idiosyncrasy.

Namier had a remarkable career, quite apart from the quality of his work. The son of a well-to-do landowner in the Ukraine, he was born in June 1888 and was given the education of a Polish gentleman, Roman Catholic and cosmopolitan. Not yet of age, he shook off this character and returned to the Jewish allegiance of his ancestors. To emphasize his change he broke, too, with central Europe and went to Balliol College, Oxford, for his university education. He regarded himself as a Jew by nationality, not in religion; and he combined his Jewish character with a sturdy British Imperialism, being naturalized shortly before the 1914-18 War.

During the 1914-18 War, in which he served for a time as a private in the 20th Royal Fusiliers, Namier was one of the brilliant team who provided the Foreign Office with a true Political Intelligence Department. He had a profound knowledge of the national conflicts in Austria-Hungary and was insistent that the Habsburg monarchy should be replaced by national states. His influence counted for something in the British refusal to answer Count Andrassy's note of October 27, 1918.

After the war he tried unsuccessfully to establish himself teaching history at Oxford. He was a brilliant teacher and lecturer. He was also a formidable conversationalist, tireless and persistent; and he expected everyone to be as interested as himself in the topic that occupied his mind at the moment—whether that topic was the secret-service accounts of the Duke of Newcastle, land-holding in Galicia, Zionist politics, or the diplomacy of Georges

Bonnet*. As a result the fellows of more than one college asked themselves, in Namier's own words: "What would he be like after dinner?" and the answer kept the Oxford that he loved barred against him.

For many years he lived from hand to mouth, while writing his great book; and found security only when elected Professor of Modern History at Manchester University in 1931. Though he lectured brilliantly here also and inspired some devoted pupils, he was not as happy as he would have been in Oxford: he liked to live on the edge of the political world and never found himself in Manchester society. Oxford relented later on, when secure against having Namier as a permanency. An honorary degree, an invitation to deliver the Romanes lecture and—what he treasured most of all—an honorary fellowship at his old college quietened whatever bitterness Namier felt in his heart. In a strange way he achieved fulfilment only after passing the official retiring age. For then, as one of the editors of the *History of Parliament*, he set up headquarters in the Institute of Historical Research, and directed a nationwide search for biographical material.

By this time, too, Namier had almost forgotten his Zionism. Earlier he had sacrificed much time and some academic reputation to it. He lacked, and longed the more for, a secure, unconscious background; hence his admiration, almost envy, for the English governing class. Even his Zionism was something he had deliberately acquired; and he hoped that future generations of Jews would find in Palestine the national home and the settled tradition which he had missed. He twice left the life of scholarship to serve as a Zionist political officer in London. Some of his best books remained unwritten as a result; and narrower academic minds condemned this devotion to the cause of his people.

Still, the work which he accomplished made him the outstanding modern history scholar of his generation in England. Only one other foreigner, Vinogradoff, has so established himself in English history; and Vinogradoff's chosen field of feudalism had more European parallels. British political society in the eighteenth century, Namier's topic, was unique: it could not be explained by reference to anything else. This, however, was Namier's advantage: he did not attempt to explain the eighteenth century in terms of the Victorian constitution. He asked the practical question: Why did men go into politics? and he gave unadorned, often non-political answers. His great work, *The Structure of Politics in the Eighteenth Century*, was revolutionary when it first appeared. Historians shook their heads at it; and its teaching was being digested only a generation later. By then perhaps Namier had been almost too successful. Having started by demonstrating that high principle was not the only thing that counted in political life, he got near to implying later that it did not count at all. He himself was not afraid of the accusation that he had taken the mind out of history. This is only to say that he had a view of history intensely personal, intensely creative, and occasionally overdrawn. A new edition of his masterpiece came out in 1957.

Namier wrote, too, some masterly essays on the history of Europe in the nineteenth century. He brought the same high standards to contemporary history; and his *Diplomatic Prelude*, dealing with the origins of the 1939-45 War, combined scholarship and wit. He had a relentless accuracy. This did not make him popular, for he never understood that others did not welcome correction so readily as himself. Although he spoke English with a marked accent, he wrote it flawlessly in the plain English style. His writing, though scholarly, was deeply personal: every sentence reflected his mind, ponderous yet clear, overbearing yet truthful, loaded with thought yet with its meaning unmistakable. He had one defect as an historian: he was incapable of prolonged narrative. He could draw a brilliant sketch of a country or of a century; he could make a detailed analysis, meticulous and profound; he could not capture the movement of history. His writing recalled his stance when lecturing: motionless, with an occasional relentless hammer-blow of his clenched right hand. And, indeed, the effect of his writing was so powerful that it would have exhausted and battered both him and the reader had it been sustained for hundreds of pages. Even as it was, many found Namier overwhelming—in print and still more in person. Like Dr. Johnson, he wielded a bludgeon; and the crushing blow was the more unexpected from being delivered with a special Jewish dexterity. He had defects of sensibility and he wasted much of his ability. All the same, he was in the first flight among his contemporaries in accuracy of scholarship, in brilliance of style, and in clarity of vision; and he will take his place with the great English history scholars of the past.

Namier, who was knighted in 1952, was an honorary D.Litt. of Durham (1952), Oxford (1955), and Rome (1956), and in 1957 Cambridge conferred on him an honorary Litt.D. In June 1960 the Prime Minister, at his first Encaenia as Chancellor of Oxford, conferred on Namier the honorary degree of Doctor of Civil Law.

Namier married in 1947 Julia de Beausobre.

August 22, 1960.

George Jean Nathan, the American dramatic critic and author, who brought to an inexhaustible passion for the theatre exceptional acuteness of mind, a rich and unfailingly trenchant use of the American vernacular, and a devotion to the impalpable essence of the American genius that he shared with his friend and colleague H. L. Mencken [q.v.], died on April 8, 1958 in New York at the age of 76.

A man of many interests, of individual taste, and of a cultivated frankness of speech, Nathan gave himself for almost half a century to the business of dramatic criticism with undiminishing zest. With the exception of A. B. Walkley—who keenly relished Nathan's quality—one can think of few men so variously endowed who have been content over anything like so long a period of time to confine themselves as writers, as Nathan did or very nearly did, to criticism of the theatre. He was, at different times, dramatic critic of an extraordinary variety of leading American journals and periodicals. In his earlier phase in particular, when the peculiar need for what he had to offer was most strikingly evident, a special value of his criticism lay in the forthright and challenging independence of his aesthetic opinions. Walkley once described him as "the devotee of taste and the arts checked and baited by what we in England call Podsnappery".

Born on February 14, 1882, at Fort Wayne, Indiana, the son of Charles Nathan and Ella Nirdlinger, George Jean Nathan was educated at Cornell University, where he took his degree in 1904. In the following year, after some time spent abroad at the University of Bologna, he joined the editorial staff of the *New York Herald* under James Gordon Bennett, and a year later became dramatic critic of the *Bohemian Magazine*. In 1908 began his long association with Mencken. Together the two young men founded and edited the *Smart Set*, which was always willing to introduce young writers of performance or promise to a more or less sophisticated American public and which provided a brave platform for Nathan's provocatively styled criticism until 1923. Next year Mencken and he founded the *American Mercury*, blessed among American monthlies of the period. Nathan's criticism of the theatre appeared there and, at various times in later years, in *Vanity Fair, Life*, the *Saturday Review of Literature, Scribner's*, and many other magazines.

Nathan liked to maintain that the theatre offered a writer wider scope and opportunity than any other entertainment, art, or institution. Certainly he himself strove mightily to demonstrate the truth of this maxim. His books, setting aside the two or three he wrote in collaboration with Mencken, are necessarily fragmentary in character, since they consist for the most part of collections of reprinted essays, articles, and notices, all of them bearing in one way or another on drama and the theatre. But they teem with *obiter dicta*, speculations, digressions, rhapsodic fancies, and prejudices of the liveliest kind that have little or nothing to do with the theatre (except, of course, that the theatre, as Nathan saw it, comprehended the whole of life), and with a vigour, vivacity, and raciness of American language that seems to generate its own distinctive commentary on what Nathan styled the American consciousness. The titles of his volumes—*The Critic and the Drama, Another Book on the Theatre, The House of Satan, Testament of a Critic, Since Ibsen, The Mornings after the First Night*, and so on—scarcely matter. It is always the explosive vitality of mind, the violent integrity of feeling, the roaring American friendliness of his criticism that one looks for and discovers in his books.

As a critic he took his stand on the doctrine that the theatre is above all else a place of amusement; it was the illusion of the lighter side of life that he looked for, he said, on the stage. This was a doctrine in harmony with the professedly hedonist philosophy that gave colour to his zest for living, friendship, and conversation. The doctrine did not, however, prevent him from writing with great acumen as well as knowledge of the world's masterpieces of drama; nor did it deter him from seeking to apply to his most extravagant criticism what he regarded as first principles; nor did it hinder him in appreciation—perhaps too generous appreciation—of the plays of Eugene O'Neill [q.v.], whom he regarded as a specifically American genius, the sole indisputably great dramatist America had produced. For the rest, in denouncing portentousness, pretentiousness, prudery, and humbug on the American stage, he was in his own way pleading for more light in the theatre, greater intelligence, and better craftsmanship. In 1932 his criticisms brought the warning from a Congressional committee that it intended to hold hearings because "dramatic criticism has destroyed the legitimate spoken drama of our country". Nathan offered to attend if the meetings were held in Munich.

In 1955 he married Miss Julie Haydon, the actress.

April 9, 1958.

Julia Neilson (Mrs. Fred Terry), the actress, died on May 27, 1957 in a London hospital at the age of 88.

With the passage of time, Julia Neilson had become the doyenne of English leading actresses, but she had brought her stage career to an end before age made it impossible for her any longer to play the parts in which her noble presence, her splendid vigour, and her great beauty gave her a position which was unrivalled in the theatre. Nevertheless, she was still playing these parts at the age of 60. To say that she was ever a great actress would be to place her in a position to which she never really aspired; but she was a fine actress, gracious and high-spirited, and of an artistic quality which made her popularity well deserved.

Born on June 12, 1868, she came of a Jewish family which has produced several successful players, notably her first cousin, Lily Hanbury, almost as handsome as herself. Like many others, she reached the dramatic stage by way of singing; for she had won several prizes at the Royal Academy of Music when she took her first speaking part, which was an important part, at the Lyceum in 1888. This was in Gilbert's *Pygmalion and Galatea,* and the Galatea to whom she played second was the very beautiful Mary Anderson. Soon afterwards, she had the leading part herself, the Pygmalion being Lewis Waller. She then appeared in several of Gilbert's non-musical plays, but never in his comic operas. The step which affirmed her position as a leading actress was her engagement, in 1888, as leading lady to Beerbohm Tree at the Haymarket.

She was not yet 21 when she created her first new part with him in a melodrama from the French, called *A Man's Shadow*; and she stayed with him for five years, taking the lead in *The Dancing Girl, The Tempter,* by Henry Arthur Jones, and *A Woman of No Importance,* by Oscar Wilde, as well as in other plays. After this first long engagement with Beerbohm Tree, during which, in 1891, she married Fred Terry, then a member of the company, she appeared, in 1895, with Lewis Waller and Charles Hawtrey in another Oscar Wilde play, *An Ideal Husband.* After a tour in the United States with John Hare, she became, for two years, George Alexander's leading lady at the St. James's and here, in 1897, she played her first important Shakespearian part, Rosalind, soon to be followed in 1898 by her Beatrice in *Much Ado About Nothing.* Among modern plays in which she appeared with Alexander was Pinero's *The Princess and the Butterfly.* Towards the end of 1899 she returned to Beerbohm Tree for a year, and played Constance in *King John* as well as Oberon in *A Midsummer Night's Dream,* where her splendid presence and her always admirable diction made her performance an outstanding memory.

However, it was during her joint management with her husband, which began at the Haymarket in 1900, that she and he established their great popularity in comedy melodramas in costume. These productions, which began with *Sweet Nell of Old Drury* and included *Dorothy o' the Hall, The Popinjay,* and particularly *The Scarlet Pimpernel,* did not aim very high artistically, as indeed their titles indicate. But they were happy and healthy. They were good to look at, gay in colour, and historically faithful so far as the visual side was concerned. They were put on the stage with scrupulous care and competence. Above all, they were acted with such spirit and gallantry that they could be enjoyed by spectators with brows a good deal higher than those of the simple public to which they were primarily addressed. Nobody could have been better fitted than Julia Neilson and her husband to carry such plays along with the proper good will. Both had been through the school of Shakespeare, and knew the business of romantic acting from its foundations. Both were physically imposing and of high vitality. Both were good looking; for the husband was as handsome as the wife was beautiful, and he had the Terry charm of his great sister Ellen in addition.

The theatrical partnership of husband and wife continued for 20 years; but after the first 13 of them first the husband, then the wife, and then the husband again were incapacitated by long periods of illness. Her husband, who was more than five years her senior, lived until April 1933, but as a sick man. She herself passed the evening of her days in the house at the top of Primrose Hill which she had first entered, with her husband, in 1911, at the height of their joint success. In 1938 she was honoured by a large company representing all classes of society, when she was entertained at luncheon in London and presented with gifts in commemoration of the fiftieth anniversary of her appearance on the stage.

The gifts, which were presented by Lord Hailsham, consisted of a copy of a James II Monteith bowl and an original George I two-handled loving cup, which was made in London by Edward Peacock about 1725. Each piece bore the inscription: "Julia Neilson Terry. A token of affection from her devoted friends and public, 21st March, 1888, to 21st March, 1938". Her daughter, Phyllis Neilson-Terry [d. 1977], has followed in her mother's footsteps by having been leading lady to Beerbohm Tree, with whom she played a number of Shakespeare's heroines between 1911 and 1913.

May 28, 1957.

Olga Nethersole, C.B.E., R.R.C., who died on January 9, 1951 at Bournemouth, will be remembered not only as an actress of great emotional power, but also as a pioneer in health education.

Of Spanish ancestry on her mother's side, she excelled in such roles as Nedda in *I Pagliacci,* Carmen, and Floria Tosca in *La Tosca,* and it is no accident that one of her greatest triumphs was at the Théâtre Sarah Bernhardt in 1907, when her Latin fire entranced the critical Parisian public. She was not, however, limited to such roles, for she had a sharply analytical turn of mind, and was thus able to give a notable performance of the heroine in Paul Hervieu's celebrated play *Le Dédale.* She could also play such parts as Gilberte in *Frou-Frou* and Agnes in *The Notorious Mrs. Ebbsmith* with an enviable lightness of touch.

Acting was, however, but half her life, and she often said that had she not been attracted to the theatre she would have gone into the medical profession. As early as 1906 she was busy enlisting support for the Women's International Anti-Tuberculosis League, and during the 1914-18 war she worked as a surgical nurse at the New End Military Hospital, near her home at Hampstead. In 1917 she began her campaign to try to improve the general level of health of the people, and her efforts, directed towards the medical profession, their patients, and the Government, bore fruit in the People's League of Health. Her work was recognized by the award of the R.R.C. in 1920 and in the New Year Honours of 1936 she was made a C.B.E.

Olga Isabel Nethersole was the youngest daughter of the late Henry Nethersole, a solicitor, and was educated privately in London and in Holland. Even before her first professional appearance in 1887 at the Theatre Royal, Brighton, she had had some stage experience. She was not destined to remain long in the provinces for in the summer of 1888 she appeared successively at the Strand, the Adelphi, and the St. James's theatres, though the plays gave her little but experience. At the end of the year, however, she returned to the Adelphi as Lola Montez in *The Silver Falls,* and this led to her engagement by John Hare for his production of Pinero's *The Profligate* at the Garrick Theatre in the spring of 1889, in which she had her first success as Janet Preece. An even greater success followed for, owing to the illness of Mrs. Bernard Beere, she was called on to play Floria Tosca in the subsequent production of *La Tosca.* From 1890 to 1892 she toured Australia with Charles Cartwright.

She further increased her reputation in 1893 by her performance at the Garrick of Comtesse Zicka in *Diplomacy,* when the cast included

John Hare, the Bancrofts, Arthur Cecil, Forbes-Robertson, and Kate Rorke. It was the day of the actor-manager and she saw no reason why there should not be an actress-manageress. Accordingly she entered on management at the Court Theatre, where she produced A. W. Gattie's play, *The Transgressor*, playing Silvia Woodville. Her first American tour followed, and after playing Agnes in *The Notorious Mrs. Ebbsmith* at the Garrick she toured the provinces and again visited America. In 1898 she produced *The Termagant* at Her Majesty's and during another tour of the United States appeared as Paula in *The Second Mrs. Tanqueray*.

From the turn of the century her appearances on the London stage became very infrequent for she had become such a favourite with American audiences that she never lacked bookings. She created the part of Mary Magdalene in Maeterlinck's play of that name at Richmond, Virginia, in 1911 and later in the year appeared at San Francisco in the title role of *Sister Beatrice*.

After many years' absence from the stage she appeared for a single performance at Wyndham's in 1923, playing Barbara Lawrence in *The Writing on the Wall*. By that time she was deeply involved in her work for the betterment of the general level of health and she spent the remainder of her life in promoting a cause to which she had given her whole heart.

January 11, 1951.

Professor Max Neuburger, the celebrated historian of medicine, died on March 15, 1955 at his home in Vienna at the age of 87.

The wide range of qualifications required in a professional medical historian of medicine—as distinct from those possessed by many occasional writers on the subject—are found but rarely, and the number of those engaged in this speciality has always been small. Among this select band Max Neuburger had long held the highest rank. In him were combined a thorough acquaintance with practical medicine (he had in his early days held hospital posts and was a brilliant neurologist), wide scholarship which enabled him to master original sources in many languages, prodigious industry, and that general historical training and insight which are so often lacking in the mere dilettante.

Max Neuburger was born in Vienna in 1868 and obtained his M.D. degree there in 1893. He held posts at the Rudolfspital and at the Allgemeine Krankenhaus, and was following an early bent towards specialization in neurology when he came under the influence of Theodor Puschmann, the then holder of the Vienna Chair of the History of Medicine. From about 1898 onwards he devoted himself more and more to historical studies. His earliest important work in this field dealt with the development of neurophysiology. Between 1902 and 1905 he brought out, in collaboration with Julius Pagel, an equally great scholar, a new and revised edition of Puschmann's *Handbuch der Geschichte der Medizin*. This three-volume work retains its place as one of the most comprehensive and authoritative texts on the subject.

Neuburger was appointed Professor Extraordinary of the History of Medicine in the University of Vienna in 1904 and he became full Professor in 1917. Under his direction the department developed into a fully fledged Institute for the History of Medicine comprising a large library and a museum. Neuburger's own history of medicine appeared in its German original at Stuttgart in 1906-11, and Dr. Ernest Playfair's English version of the greater part of it was published between 1910 and 1925. This book is one of the fullest and most learned accounts of ancient and medieval medicine, and it has always been a matter of regret that its author was never able to bring his history down to modern times. That he did not do so was certainly not due to any decline in his interest or application, because books and papers on all periods of medical history poured from his pen. Of special importance were his books on the history of medicine in Austria (1918), on medical practice and personalities in old Vienna (1921), the standard biography of the great clinician Hermann Nothnagel (1922), and the *History of the Doctrine of the Healing Power of Nature* (1926).

After the German occupation of Vienna in 1938 Neuburger went to England and a place was gladly found for him on the staff of the Wellcome Historical Medical Museum. Anxiety for the safety of his beloved institute and its treasures inevitably saddened his years of exile, but his spirit was never broken and he continued to write. In 1943 he published a book on *British Medicine and the Vienna School*, in which he showed the reciprocal influence of British and Austrian medicine throughout the eighteenth and nineteenth centuries and, incidentally, recorded his gratitude to and abiding admiration for Britain.

In 1948, when he had reached the age of 80, he went to live in retirement with one of his sons, a physician practising in the United States. In the same year his eightieth birthday was celebrated by the publication of a *Festschrift* in which medical men and historians from all parts of the world paid tribute to the greatest living historian of medicine. An irresistible urge to return once again to the city of his birth led him to cross the Atlantic in 1952, when he was 84 years of age and it was in Vienna that he died after some months of gradually failing health.

March 17, 1955.

Baron von Neurath, who was sentenced at Nuremberg to 15 years' imprisonment for his part in the Nazi conspiracy but was released from Spandau in 1954 on account of age and ill health, died at Enzweihingen, near Stuttgart, on August 15, 1956 at the age of 83.

A diplomat of the old school, who began his career in the reign of the Kaiser William II, suave, shrewd, adaptable, and far-seeing, he lent the authority of a previously distinguished career to bolster up the reputations and further the policies of a set of men many of whom he could not but despise. At his trial his denial of responsibility for this piece of wickedness or that brutality was refuted by the production of documents proving his guilt. True, he did not, like Heydrich, his colleague in Czechoslovakia, bathe his own hands in the blood of the victims of Nazi brutality, but he directed a policy which had as its avowed aim the utter destruction of the Czech people.

Konstantin von Neurath was born on February 2, 1873. He studied law at Tübingen and Berlin, and after taking his degree entered the German Consular Service. From 1903 to 1907 he was vice-consul in London. Having served for a time in the German Foreign Office, he was transferred to the Diplomatic Service and from 1914 to 1916 was Counsellor at Istanbul. Recalled to Germany in 1917, he was appointed *chef de cabinet* to the King of Württemberg. After the end of hostilities he served for a time as Minister to Denmark and in 1921 was appointed Ambassador to Italy. He was transferred to London to be Ambassador to the Court of St. James's in 1930, but two years later was recalled to Germany to fill the post of Foreign Minister, under von Papen*. He remained Foreign Minister through the successive Cabinets of von Papen, von Schleicher, and Hitler until 1938.

According to his own account, he held on—through the "blood bath" of 1934, the reoccupation of the Rhineland, the abandonment of the Disarmament Conference and of the League of Nations by Germany, and the occupation of Austria—in order to try to restrain Hitler, whose policy Neurath clearly saw must lead to war. He seems to have been singularly ineffective. Even when he was superseded by Ribbentrop, some little time before the Munich crisis, he remained in Hitler's entourage as head of a new "secret cabinet council", still enjoying the honorary rank of *Gruppenführer* in the S.S., conferred upon him in 1937.

Enough has already been said of the blackest part of his career, his term from the spring of 1939 to the autumn of 1941 as "Protector" of Bohemia and Moravia, the territories of Masaryk's Republic of Czechoslovakia. Neurath was then 68 and asked for long leave to restore his health. He also asked for a deputy to be appointed to act until he was well enough to resume his duties. The deputy was Heydrich. That was really the end of Neurath's career; he retained office, nominally on leave, until 1943, when he was replaced by Frick as "Protector".

August 16, 1956.

Sybil (Mrs. Clive) Neville-Rolfe, O.B.E., who was a pioneer of education in eugenics and for many years secretary-general of the British Social Hygiene Council, died on August 3, 1955 after a long illness. She was 69.

Widowed as a young woman of 20, she concentrated her considerable determination and ability in order, in her own words, "to study prostitution and venereal disease and try to get rid of them". Undismayed by the disapproval with which the efforts of one of her sex and age to ventilate these unpalatable subjects was greeted, she persevered in her plans for education of the public and action by the authorities, and was rewarded with a great measure of success.

Sybil Katherine was the daughter of Admiral of the Fleet Sir Cecil Burney. She was educated privately, and at the age of 19 married Lieutenant A. C. Gotto, R.N. Within a year of their marriage her husband was killed in a coaling accident in the Mediterranean. It was after that that she determined upon her reformatory purpose and first sought experience at the "shelter for fallen girls" established in Shaftesbury Avenue by Madame Ruspini, who was in charge of the rescue work of the London diocese. She became acquainted with members of the Sociological Society who were interested in eugenics and, with the blessing of Sir Francis Galton, was instrumental in forming the Eugenics Education Society. In 1913 pressure grew for the appointment of a royal commission to report on the problem of venereal disease. Mrs. Gotto (as she then was) and her associates joined in the demand, and also insisted that the proceedings of the commission should be fully reported in the Press. There was some resistance to this, but it was overcome when Mrs. Gotto gained the ear and the support of Lord Northcliffe.

In 1914, after some difference of opinion within the Eugenics Council, a new body was formed with Mrs. Gotto as honorary secretary, the National Council for Combating Venereal Disease, whose title was changed in 1926 to the British Social Hygiene Council. For a short time during the war she worked in the Treasury with the War Savings Committee, and for her service there she was made O.B.E. In 1917 she returned to the executive of the National Council and in the same year married Commander Clive Neville-Rolfe, D.S.O.

By 1918 the work of the National Council had prospered, £15,000 had been taken in voluntary contributions, and 54 branches established abroad and at home. It was at this time that Mrs. Neville-Rolfe decided to make a personal investigation of rumours that the police in certain districts of London were conniving at prostitution. She purchased a red wig, practised the art of make-up and took a room in Bloomsbury where, armed with a card of identity from the Chief Commissioner of Metropolitan Police, she observed the habits of the women whom she was simulating, and found the rumours justified.

The necessity of tackling the scourge of venereal disease by international measures brought the National Council, often in the person of Mrs. Neville-Rolfe, into association with the Red Cross and the League of Nations. The Council also extended its activities to the colonies and during her long period as general secretary Mrs. Neville-Rolfe made several extensive tours abroad. In the course of the Second World War she resigned her post as general secretary of the British Social Hygiene Council after some of its functions had been taken over by the Central Council for Health Education.

She had also been associated from the beginning with several other organizations with broadly similar aims including the National Council for the Unmarried Mother, the Professional Classes Aid Society, and the Union Internationale contre le Péril Vénérien. Another cause she served was the British Rheumatic Association and, as its general secretary since 1949, she helped to build it up from very small beginnings. Herself a victim of rheumatoid arthritis, she worked tirelessly to bring to the notice of the public the large numbers of severely incapacitated rheumatic sufferers. She also inspired the campaign for the critical examination of the work of Remploy which resulted in the appointment of the committee to discuss the problems of disabled persons, under the chairmanship of Lord Piercy*.

In 1941 she was awarded the American Snow Medal "for distinguished services to humanity"—the first non-American and the first woman to gain the award.

Mrs. Neville-Rolfe was a forceful—though always a friendly and a likeable—manager, adept at lobbying, "pulling strings", and persuading influential (and possibly only half-convinced) people to help in her good causes. At times her tactics were irritating; but they were so patently employed only to further the welfare work to which she was devoted, never for personal ends, that irritation soon gave way at least to amused tolerance, often to keen collaboration.

August 5, 1955.

Evelyn (Mrs. H. W.) Nevinson—See **Sharp.**

Ernest Newman died on July 7, 1959 at his home at Tadworth, Surrey. He was 90.

His death deprives musical journalism in Britain of its most prominent figure. He began life in business at Liverpool, but his interest in music and his gift of facile penmanship soon marked out the direction of his career, and encouraged thereto by the friendship of Granville Bantock, he did some music teaching at Birmingham and soon made a name for himself as a trenchant and thoughtful essayist.

His real name was E. N. Roberts and the name of "Ernest Newman", which he presently adopted in private as well as in public life, was originally a pen name chosen to suggest the character in which he saw himself, a new man who meant serious business. He ranged himself on the side of what was then the new music, and his collected essays, *Musical Studies* (1905), contained a vigorous defence of "programme music", a study of the "Faust" music of the great nineteenth-century composers, in which he examined the psychological approach of the composers to a dramatic subject, and other matters then rather outside the view of the more academically minded musician. A book on Hugo Wolf, whom he regarded as the most penetrating of song writers, raised a controversy at the time but remained the one authority on the subject in the English language until 1951.

Newman's journalistic career was for many years pursued in the provinces chiefly because he was unwilling to shackle himself with the necessity for attending and reporting immediately on daily concerts, many of them of slight artistic importance, which is the condition of work for the London daily Press. He was critic to the *Manchester Guardian* and the *Birmingham Daily Post* in succession, and it was only after the 1914-18 War that he settled in London, as critic first to the *Observer* and then to the *Sunday Times,* which he served without intermission until he reached the age of 90.

These Sunday papers gave him the conditions he required. He could pick out the more interesting musical events of the week and discuss them in conjunction and with an air of comparative leisure. His weekly articles soon became a valued feature which all musically minded people had to read. Leisure, however, was a thing of which Newman gave himself very little. Besides journalistic work he always had several books on hand, and somehow he accomplished the tasks of translating Schweitzer's* big book on Bach into English as well as the text of *The Ring, Meistersinger* and *Parsifal* for the edition of Breitkopf and Haertel. Much of his best writing was devoted to the inexhaustible subject of Wagner. His enormous admiration for the artist and his contempt for the man were set out in *Wagner as Man and Artist* (1925), a powerful book exasperating to the devout believers in the cult of Bayreuth.

But even that did not exhaust his interest in that subject or his labours in that field. His four-volume life, which was only concluded in 1945, is likely to remain the standard biography of Wagner in the English language, in which anything of the slightest value or interest has been preserved after a patient sifting of the prodigious bulk of available material. A by-product of the process was a book on Liszt which, following Wagnerian precedent, appeared before the conclusion of the parent work. Berlioz was another of his heroes.

Though he professed to look forward to an objective, almost a scientific kind of criticism, his own practice was that of an artist using criticism as his medium. Consequently Newman became the leading exponent of the personal type of signed criticism that is now much more common than it was when he took up the craft. This standpoint made him a strong bulwark against the notion that criticism exists primarily to advertise the art and the artist. Undoubtedly personal considerations swayed his judgment at times, both in directions of excessive praise and disparagement. He could not always resist the temptation of his own cleverness. But his general contention that the critic should stand by his own opinion, without thought of its consequences to the persons or institutions about whom it was formed, was salutary.

His refusal to encourage the young composer because he is young, of British music because it is British, brought him into conflict with certain tendencies in his middle age. From having been the "earnest new man" in days when he championed Strauss, Elgar, and Delius, he came to be regarded as something of a reactionary who dealt hardly and satirically with the bright young spirits of the 1920s. But the book *A Musical Critic's Holiday*, in which he set out his principles of criticism, showed that this was not merely the increasing conservatism of age. He continued to look for the big impulse in creative art and found little of it in modern experimentalism. Nor was he much interested in earlier music. His sympathies were fastened upon the late romantic developments of the nineteenth century. His was a naturally keen mind, burnished by constant study and very little, if at all, blunted by the hackwork of journalism.

Two volumes of reprinted articles, edited by Felix Aprahamian, ranged over 30 years and showed besides a consistency of view on his favourite topics how catholic his mind was and how penetrating it remained into old age. Three books, *Opera Nights, More Opera Nights,* and *Wagner Nights,* were analytical and expository; they employed the same kind of minute scholarship that had applied to the biography of Wagner, but were also immensely readable. They did much to promote the cause of opera among the public in Britain and in America which was sceptical of the aesthetic basis of an art to which Newman was devoted.

July 8, 1959.

Sir Frank Newnes, BT., C.B.E., the bearer of a great name in the publishing world, died on July 10, 1955 in Perth, Western Australia, at the age of 78.

His long service in the family business, for he entered it on coming down from Cambridge and only resigned the chairmanship of George Newnes Ltd. in 1954, was recognized by the board by the creation of a special post for him, that of president. It was an unusually touching compliment and was due not only in recognition of faithful service but also to the sad realization that there is no son to carry on the family tradition.

Sir Frank Newnes was never one to seek the limelight, though, having inherited the Liberal principles of his father, he did once sit in Parliament, but that was long ago and when he was defeated in 1910 he never sought election again. Apart from his interest in George Newnes Ltd., he was also interested in C. Arthur Pearson Ltd. and Country Life Ltd., and he was a member of the boards of a number of insurance companies, investment trusts, and industrial undertakings. His greatest interest, however, outside publishing was in hospitals.

Frank Hilliard Newnes was born in Manchester on September 28, 1876, the elder but only surviving son of the late Sir George Newnes, Bt., the well known newspaper proprietor and publisher, and Priscilla, daughter of the Reverend J. Hilliard. He was educated privately and at Clare College, Cambridge, where he graduated in 1897. In 1898 he was called to the Bar by the Inner Temple and in the next year became a director of the publishing business of George Newnes Ltd. In 1906 he was elected to the House of Commons in the Liberal interest as Member for the Bassetlaw Division of Nottinghamshire, but was defeated in 1910 and did not stand for Parliament again. In 1915 he became a sub-lieutenant in the Royal Naval Volunteer Reserve, but two years later transferred to the Army and was a captain in the 12th Battalion, The Bedfordshire and Hertfordshire Regiment.

In addition to his interest in the family business Sir Frank Newnes was for many years a director of Country Life Ltd., of C. Arthur Pearson Ltd., and of Newnes and Pearson Printing Company Ltd. He was also from 1908 to 1921 a director of Westminster Gazette Ltd. As a member of the council of the Empire Press Union he took an active interest in its affairs and was a delegate to the Imperial Press Conference at Melbourne in 1925. He also interested himself in Press charities and in the hospitals, being a member of the Voluntary Hospitals Committee for London and of the committee of management of the Royal Free Hospital and the Royal Free Hospital Medical School, chairman of the committee of the Post-Graduate Institute of Dental Surgery and of the Eastman Dental Hospital. He was president of the Printers' Pension Corporation in 1948-49, a vice-president of the Periodical Proprietors' Association and of the National Liberal Council.

Newnes, who succeeded his father as second baronet in 1910, was twice married, first in 1913 to Emmeline Augusta Louisa, daughter of the late Sir Albert de Rutzen. She died in 1939, and in 1946 he married Dorothy, widow of Stephen Delmar-Morgan and daughter of E. Firebrace Darlot, of Perth, Western Australia, who survives him. There were no children of either marriage and the baronetcy becomes extinct.

July 11, 1955.

Princess Nicholas of Greece, widow of Prince Nicholas of Greece, mother of the Duchess of Kent [Princess Marina*], and aunt by marriage to the Duke of Edinburgh, died at her home near Athens on March 14, 1957 at the age of 75. She was born on January 17, 1882, the Grand Duchess Helen, only daughter of the Grand Duke Vladimir of Russia, uncle of the Tsar Nicholas II who was murdered during the Bolshevik uprising.

She married in August 1902 Prince Nicholas of Greece, third son and fourth child of King George I of Greece and the Grand Duchess Olga. They were in Russia paying an annual visit to his mother-in-law when the First World War began and it took them more than a fortnight to return to Greece. There followed the acute conflict between King Constantine and Venizelos as to the part to be played by Greece in the war. The King ultimately decided to leave the country and Prince and Princess Nicholas were obliged to follow him shortly afterwards. They stayed first at St. Moritz and during the summer of 1918 were at Lausanne and elsewhere in Switzerland. After King Constantine had gone into exile for the second time Princess Nicholas and her husband lived with him at Palermo until his death.

After the new king George II had, in his turn, been driven from Greece Prince and Princess Nicholas took up residence in France. During the London season of 1923 the eldest of their three daughters, Princess Olga, married Prince Paul, later Regent of Yugoslavia [d. 1976]. Princess Elizabeth, the second daughter, married Count Törring-Jettenbach in 1934, and Princess Marina, the youngest daughter, married the Duke of Kent in November 1934.

Prince Nicholas died in 1938. During the late war Princess Nicholas remained in occupied Greece, living in a villa on the outskirts of Athens.

She worked tirelessly in Greek hospitals for the International Red Cross and her philanthropic work and help to resistance groups is still remembered with affection and gratitude in Greece.

March 15, 1957.

Charles Nicholson, O.B.E., one of Britain's leading yacht designers, died on February 27, 1954 at his home near Fareham, Hampshire, at the age of 85.

Charles Ernest Nicholson was born in Gosport on May 12, 1868, the third son of the late Benjamin Nicholson. He was educated at Mill Hill School and afterwards in Brussels. His first design, the Lucifer, was launched when he was only 18, but his first success came a few years later with the design of two smallish vessels Gareth and Dacia. Gareth, a 2½-rater, enjoyed a successful career, season after season, for many years. Dacia was bought by Lord Dudley, who challenged any Clyde-built 5-rater for a match with a stake of £500 a side. The challenge was taken up, the match being sailed in Torbay, where Dacia won two races out of three.

Nicholson's name was now made, and in 1912 he designed Istria for Sir Charles Allon. Istria, a 15-metre boat, popularized what in her day was sometimes called the "Marconi-rig". Instead of a fidded topmast, Istria had her topmast stepped inside the lower-mast, obtaining thereby a greater height of hoist. It is not too much to claim for this vessel that she did most to reintroduce the Bermuda-rig, now well-nigh universal. In her first season Istria won 35 prizes in 36 races.

In the next season, 1913, Nicholson produced an even faster boat—Colonel S. G. L. Bardley's Pamela—as well as another 15-metre called Paula III, perhaps equally good. Coming after Istria, they "placed Nicholson in the fore-front of naval architecture". Attaining such eminence, it naturally followed that he was soon entrusted with the design of a challenger for the America's Cup. Shamrock IV, designed by him for Sir Thomas Lipton, was on her way out across the Atlantic when war broke out in 1914. The contest was held in 1920, when the challenger was defeated; and although many held that she should not have been, Nicholson accepted the reverse with characteristic equanimity. He came even nearer success with Sopwith's Endeavour in the contest of 1934.

The design of Endeavour—which experts have said was "the most beautiful racing yacht ever built"—Nicholson presented to the Americans. This unheard-of generosity was turned to good account, for it was acknowledged that the design of the incomparable Ranger, the successful defender in 1937, was evolved in the main from a study of the first Endeavour's "lines".

Any list of Nicholson's other creations reads like a chant of famous names—Endeavour II, Margherita, Nyria, Brynhild, White Heather, Creole, Sylvia, Vynara, and Shamrock, the noble 23-metre. Nicholson himself, however, took proper pride in the pioneer part played by the firm of Camper and Nicholson's, Ltd., in the evolution of the motor yacht. Indeed the name of the first motor yacht he designed—and she was the first in the world of her size and type—was the Pioneer, a vessel whose success was the largest single factor in the decay of the large steam yacht, and further resulted in the bulk of orders for large tonnage going to the south of the kingdom rather than as formerly to the Clyde. It was in recognition of this that he was made the first Freeman of Gosport in 1934.

Nicholson designed in 1937 Philante, which at 1,629 tons was the largest motor yacht built in Great Britain. In 1948 she was converted to Norge, the Norwegian Royal Yacht. During the 1914-18 War his two newly-designed diesel-engined yachts were both on war service and 12,000 tons of yachts of his design were again on service during the 1939-45 War, with the naval auxiliary services.

In 1947 American yachtsmen asked him to represent their interests on the technical committees of the International Yacht Racing Union. He was a member, and an honorary member of the council, of the Yacht Racing Association, and a liveryman of the Worshipful Company of Shipwrights.

In 1895 he married Miss Lucy Ella Edmonds, who during their long married life took a prominent part in social work at Gosport and founded the Gosport mothercraft centre. She died in 1937, leaving two sons and two daughters of the marriage.

March 1, 1954.

Admiral Sir Percy Noble, G.B.E., K.C.B., C.V.O., who was Commander-in-Chief, Western Approaches, during 1941-42, and from then until 1944 leader of the British Naval Delegation in Washington, died on July 25, 1955 at his home in London at the age of 75.

Percy Laxland Harnam Noble was born on January 16, 1880, the son of Colonel Charles Noble, and entered the Navy as a cadet the day before his fourteenth birthday. Two years later he was appointed to the cruiser Immortalité (Captain [afterwards Admiral Sir] Edward Chichester) on the China Station, in which he served for three and a half years, being rated midshipman after six months. On returning home he served for six months in the sailing training squadron before being promoted to sub-lieutenant. While undergoing sub-lieutenants' instructional courses at Greenwich and Portsmouth he was detailed for the naval guard of honour which was mounted at Windsor at the funeral of Queen Victoria, a duty for which he was made M.V.O.

As a sub-lieutenant he served in the battleship Hannibal, in the Channel Squadron, remaining in her on promotion to lieutenant in 1902. After two years in the battleship Russell, in the Mediterranean as a watch-keeper, he became Flag-Lieutenant to Rear-Admiral A. L. Winsloe, commanding flotillas at home. When Admiral Winsloe was relieved in that command, Noble served for a year in command of the destroyer Ribble in the 1st Destroyer Flotilla, after which he joined the Signal School at Portsmouth and qualified as a signal officer. From January 1910 until October 1911 he was again Flag-Lieutenant to Admiral Winsloe, then Commander-in-Chief on the China Station, a post which he left on his appointment to the Royal Yacht Victoria and Albert.

He succeeded to the position of First Lieutenant of the yacht the following year, and in August 1913 he was promoted commander. Four months later he became executive officer of the armoured cruiser Achilles, in the 2nd Cruiser Squadron, Home Fleet. In September 1916 he was transferred in the same capacity to the new cruiser Courageous (Captain Arthur Bromley), flagship of Rear-Admiral—later Vice-Admiral—T. D. W. Napier, Commanding the Light Cruiser Force of the Grand Fleet, where he was still serving when he was promoted to captain at the end of June 1918. Four months later he took over his first command, when he became Flag-Captain to Rear-Admiral Sir Allen Everett, in the Calliope, 4th Light Cruiser Squadron, Grand Fleet. In March 1919 he transferred to the Calcutta, on Admiral Everett becoming Rear-Admiral Commanding the 8th Light Cruiser Squadron, America and West Indies Station, and served there for two years, in the course of which he became C.V.O.

After a period of unemployment, Noble became for some 18 months Chief Staff Officer to Admiral Sir H. L. Heath in the Scottish Command, and in October 1922 he returned to the sea for two years in command of the battleship Barham.

After a period of committee work at the Admiralty, he became captain of the Ganges, the training establishment for boys at Harwich, and captain-in-charge of the port. When he had held that command for two years he was selected as the first commanding officer of the new boys' training establishment, H.M.S. St. Vincent, at Forton, Gosport, in the inauguration of which his experience at Harwich was invaluable. As soon as the new establishment was running smoothly, Noble was relieved after being in command of it for nine months, and took over the highly responsible post of Director of the Operations Division of the Naval Staff at the Admiralty. He was promoted rear-admiral in October 1929.

A year of unemployment followed, and in January 1931 he became Director of Naval Equipment at the Admiralty. He did not hold that post for the full two years, however, as in December 1932 he was selected for the command of the 2nd Cruiser Squadron, Home Fleet, with his flag in the Leander. After two years in that command he returned once more to the Admiralty, this time as Fourth Sea Lord and a member of the Board of Admiralty. He was promoted vice-admiral two months after taking up duty, and remained on the Board for two years and eight months, when he was selected to succeed Admiral Sir Charles Little* as Commander-in-Chief on the China Station. He was made a C.B. in 1932 and was advanced to K.C.B. in 1936.

The anti-British attitude of the Japanese forces in China was at its worst when he assumed command, and to uphold British rights and British dignity in the face of Japanese intrigue and often insult, with little or no material forces at his back, called for qualities of firmness, good sense, tact, and restraint of the highest order in the Commander-in-Chief—qualities which he possessed in abundance. He was promoted admiral in 1939. In July 1940 he was recalled from his command-in-chief in China after two and a half years, and in March 1941 he took up the appointment of Commander-in-Chief, Western Approaches.

In November 1942, after 18 months directing the struggle against enemy submarines in the Atlantic with ever-increasing success, he was appointed Head of the British Admiralty Delegation in Washington in succession to Admiral Sir Andrew Cunningham (now Admiral of the Fleet Lord Cunningham of Hyndhope*). He lost no time on his new appointment in making clear to the American public the seriousness of the U-boat menace, and during his two years in Washington succeeded notably in his duties as representative of the Royal Navy with the combined chiefs of staff. For his services he was made a G.B.E. in 1944.

From 1943 until his retirement in 1945 from the Active List on reaching the age limit he was First and Principal Naval A.D.C. to King George VI [q.v.], and after his retirement he was appointed Rear-Admiral of the United Kingdom and of the Admiralty, an appointment which carries no duties except in attendance on the Sovereign.

He married in 1907 Diamantina Isabella, only daughter of Allan Campbell. She died in 1909. There was one son of the marriage. He is Commander A. H. P. Noble, D.S.O., D.S.C., R.N. (retd.), Conservative member of Parliament for Chelsea since 1945, and Parliamentary Secretary to the Admiralty from 1951 until the general election of May 1955.

Admiral Sir Percy Noble married secondly, in 1913, Celia Emily, daughter of Robert Kirkman Hodgson. There was one son of the marriage.

July 26, 1955.

Lieutenant-General Edward Felix Norton, C.B., D.S.O., M.C., Colonel Commandant, Royal Artillery, since 1941, and a member of the Mount Everest expeditions of 1922 and 1924, died on November 3, 1954 at his home at Morestead, near Winchester. He was 70.

The son of the late Edward Norton, of Fareham, Hampshire, he was born on February 21, 1884, and was educated at Charterhouse and the Royal Military Academy, Woolwich. He was gazetted to the Royal Artillery in 1902, and during the 1914-18 War he saw service in France as brigade major, R.A., with the Canadians and as Staff Officer to the Artillery Commander of the Canadian Army Corps. In 1914 he was awarded the M.C., and in 1918 the D.S.O. He was also three times mentioned in dispatches.

In 1922 he took part in the second attempt on Mount Everest, which was commanded by Brigadier-General the Hon. C. G. Bruce. The climbing party included G. Leigh-Mallory, Dr. T. H. Somervell*, and Captain [later Professor] G. I. Finch*, the oxygen officer. On May 20 Norton, Leigh-Mallory, and Somervell climbed to a height of 26,895ft. from their camp at 25,000ft., above the North Col, and a week later Finch and Bruce, using oxygen equipment, reached 27,300ft. by a different route.

In 1924 Norton was second in command of a further expedition, also commanded by Brigadier-General Bruce. The party included Leigh-Mallory, Somervell, Captain J. G. Bruce, J. de V. Hazard, A. C. Irvine, and N. E. Odell, and the assault was directed by Norton as Brigadier-General Bruce had fallen ill. A steeper route was found up the North Col, and Leigh-Mallory and Captain J. G. Bruce pitched camp at 25,000ft. Norton and Somervell climbed to a height of 28,200ft.—within 1,000ft. of the summit—on June 4 before turning back. Four days later Leigh-Mallory and Irvine set out to attack the summit and were never seen again. In 1925 the official account of the expedition, written by Norton and other members of the expedition, was published under the title of *The Fight for Everest, 1924.* In 1926 Norton was awarded the Founder's Medal of the Royal Geographical Society.

After this Himalayan interlude he resumed his military career, being promoted colonel in 1927, and acting as an instructor at the Staff College, Quetta, from 1929 to 1932. He then returned to England to take up the post of Commander, Royal Artillery 1st Division, at Aldershot, and from 1934 to 1938 he was Brigadier, General Staff, Aldershot Command. In 1937-38 he was an A.D.C. to King George VI, and he then returned to India to take command of the Madras District, with the rank of major-general. He was made a C.B. in 1939.

In August 1940 he went to Hongkong as acting Governor, remaining there until 1941, after which he commanded for a time the Western (Independent) District of India. He was placed on the retired list in 1942 and returned to England, where he commanded the North Hampshire Group of the Home Guard. He was appointed Colonel Commandant of the Hongkong-Singapore Royal Artillery in 1941, and from 1947 to 1951 he was Colonel Commandant, R.H.A.

He married in 1925 Isabel Joyce, daughter of the late Dr. William Pasteur, C.B., C.M.G. There were three sons of the marriage.

November 6, 1954.

King Haakon VII of Norway, who died on September 21, 1957 at the age of 85, had a double claim to historical fame. He was the first sovereign of an independent Norway for five centuries, and during the last war he became the living symbol of his country's resistance to German aggression.

From the beginning of his reign, when he was elected by direct vote of the people of Norway, he identified himself wholly with the independence of his adopted country and with democratic government, which had been a Norwegian tradition for more than 1,000 years. This, together with his integrity, his grave charm, his kindliness, and his unostentatious self-sacrifice, made him both respected and loved by his people.

His nationalism caused him to insist on complete independence and self-determination even within the Baltic block. But, though he kept his country neutral in 1914 and he tried to do the same in 1939-40, he was well aware of Norway's influence in world affairs, built up by her great merchant navy, and of the responsibilities that that influence entailed. In 1944, speaking from London whither he had gone when his country was invaded, he gave a lead to the smaller nations of the world when he said that he realized that neutrality was a failure and that neither Norway nor any other country could stand alone in the future.

King Haakon saw himself as the chief permanent official in the public service and his court dispensed with much of the pomp and ceremony which usually surround monarchies. A true people's King, he was often to be seen walking in Oslo, and when the hour of peril came in 1940 he showed that he had all the traditional kingly virtues. His leadership and example inspired his people to resist the invader and maintain an uncompromising attitude until the defeat of Germany.

He was unusually tall—nearly 6ft. 3in.—and his erect, spare figure increased the impression of height. A high forehead, deepset eyes, and prominent patrician nose gave him a distinguished and grave look. But when he was amused his face would light up into the most winning smile. He had an acute sense of humour and when he laughed he did so wholeheartedly, rocking back and forth on his legs. He lived very simply, ate little, and kept to a strict time-table. A tireless worker, he attended personally to his correspondence, which included many letters from ordinary citizens. He followed closely events and public opinion and read newspapers representing the views of all parties every day.

In State matters his Government, through the long years of his reign, learnt to appreciate and respect his opinions, and not least his tactful manner of expressing them. He had a remarkable memory. At the weekly Cabinet meetings held at the Palace in Oslo he often surprised Ministers by his understanding of complicated points and his pertinent questions.

From his early days as a naval officer in the Danish Navy he retained throughout his life a great love of the sea. He was fond of visiting ships and spent much of his time in the summer months cruising in the royal yacht Norge, given him by his subjects on his seventy-fifth birthday. Often he had his yacht moored in the harbour at Oslo and lived in her, while continuing to attend to the affairs of state at the palace. He loved and practised many sports, particularly, like all true Scandinavians, winter sports. The cinema was also one of his favourite interests. He frequently had films shown at his palace and during his wartime exile in Britain would often slip unnoticed into a local cinema.

The oldest king in Europe at the time of his death, King Haakon was born Christian Frederik Carl Georg Waldemar Axel, Prince of Denmark, at Charlottenlund, Denmark, on August 3, 1872. He was the second son of the Crown Prince Frederik of Denmark, later King Frederik VIII, and of Princess Louise of Sweden and Norway. As was customary with the second son in the Danish royal house, Prince Carl, as he was known, was destined for the Navy, which he entered at the age of 14.

On July 22, 1896, when he was 23, Prince Carl married at Buckingham Palace, in London, his cousin Princess Maud, daughter of the Prince of Wales—the future King Edward VII—and Princess Alexandra of Denmark. He was therefore the grand-uncle by marriage of Queen Elizabeth II of England. The royal couple were given as a wedding present by the bride's father a fully furnished home, Appleton, near Sandringham, in Norfolk, where their only child, Crown Prince Olav of Norway, was born on July 2, 1903.

Prine Carl, who spoke English perfectly and was known in the British royal family as "Uncle Charlie", became so attached to England, an attachment which, he said, lasted all his life, that there was once talk of his settling here and entering the British Navy.

Events decided otherwise. On June 7, 1905, the Norwegian Storting voted unanimously in favour of dissolving the union with Sweden which had lasted since 1814. The Norwegian people ratified the decision in a plebiscite held in August, and in October a treaty was signed by which Sweden recognized the dissolution. Norway, once again an independent nation after more than 500 years, was without a king and the Storting offered the throne to Prince Carl of Denmark. The Prince accepted it; but only on condition that he was chosen by the free vote of the people. Although there was a good deal of republican sentiment in Norway at the time, a plebiscite in November 1905 gave him a four to one majority.

A few days later Prince Carl, who had chosen the name of Haakon after the kings of Norway of the Viking Age, arrived in his new kingdom with Queen Maud and his small son and declared his allegiance to the Norwegian Constitution, choosing as his motto "All for Norway". The following June the king and queen were crowned in the ancient cathedral of Trondheim. From the beginning King Haakon endeared himself to his people by his quiet, unobtrusive life, his love of winter sports and his great strength—he could bend a poker with his bare hands. His hold upon the loyalty and affection of his subjects remained unshaken even when the Labour Party came to be the strongest in the land.

After the outbreak of war in 1914 King

Haakon, King Christian of Denmark, and King Gustav of Sweden met at Malmö, in Sweden, and declared their intention of maintaining absolute neutrality, a decision they reiterated in 1917 in Oslo. Between the wars Norway played an increasing part in world affairs as her maritime influence grew.

In 1937 King Haakon showed his belief in the importance of small nations when he unequivocally rejected a Dutch proposal that the Scandinavian countries should approach Britain and France for recognition of the Italian conquest of Abyssinia. A year later he suffered a grievous loss when his wife, Queen Maud, died in a nursing home in London. He had hurried to London a few days earlier and he returned to Norway in the British battleship Royal Oak, escorting the Queen's remains.

When war broke out in 1939 King Haakon, after a meeting in Stockholm with the other Scandinavian kings and the President of Finland, emphasized in a broadcast the determination of Norway and her neighbours to preserve strict neutrality and full independence. In November 1939 he associated himself with the appeal of Queen Wilhelmina of Holland [later Princess Wilhelmina of the Netherlands*] and King Leopold of the Belgians to the combatant nations to stop fighting and accept mediation. In the ensuing months Norway's neutrality was sorely tried for no neutral country suffered as badly as she from Germany's destruction of neutral shipping. Hundreds of her seamen were drowned in ships which were torpedoed, bombed, or mined. At the opening of the Storting in January 1940 King Haakon made a moving speech on Norway's sufferings and her determination, if possible, to keep the peace.

Three months later, on April 9, the Germans invaded his kingdom without warning, and in spite of overwhelming odds the Norwegian people, heartened by a determined broadcast appeal from the king, bravely resisted. With his Cabinet and Parliament King Haakon and the royal family left Oslo to avoid capture. On April 10 the King refused a demand by the German Minister to Norway that Abraham Vikdun Quisling, whose name became a symbol of treachery, be appointed Prime Minister. He told the German envoy that as a constitutional monarch he could not appoint a Prime Minister who had not the confidence of the people. This decision was confirmed by the Government.

The next day the Luftwaffe bombed the town to which the King and his Cabinet had retreated and went on harrying the aging monarch at every halt on a strenuous journey northward through the deep snows of the Norwegian mountains. The King, the Cabinet, and the Crown Prince finally reached Molde, on the western coast. The town was in flames from German bombing when they eventually sailed in a British cruiser for Tromsö, in the extreme north. They remained in Tromsö while Narvik was recaptured by Allied forces. The respite lasted but a month. On May 30, after the German break-through in the Low Countries and France, the Allies decided to evacuate Norway and on June 7, 35 years to the day after Norway gained her independence, King Haakon, accompanied by the Crown Prince, members of the Government, and a few officials, sailed for Britain in the British cruiser Devonshire.

King Haakon's presence in Britain at the head of his Government became a rallying point for all Norwegians working for the deliverance of their homeland. During his years of exile he devoted his whole time to helping the organization of "Free" Norway's war effort, the growth of its Army, Navy, and Air Force, and the welfare of its 25,000 merchant seamen. In frequent broadcasts he comforted and encouraged his enslaved people and made a point of receiving personally all Norwegians—and there were many—who escaped to Britain. Throughout his exile he lived at Foliejohn Park, in Berkshire.

When he returned to Norway after the German capitulation in 1945 he was welcomed by a nation which looked upon him as the personification of Norway's will to resist oppression and restore democratic liberty. He landed in Oslo on June 7—a date which has in some mysterious way been the most important all through his life—and was hailed as no king had ever before been hailed in Norway.

During the war the Norwegian home-front kept close contact with the King and government in London. The home-front never took decisive steps without consulting the Government and on its side the Government kept the home-front well informed of its policy. The King therefore returned to a Norway which was without serious conflicts between home-front and "exile" governments which in some cases were of so great disturbing effect after the war. Normal elections took place in Norway within a few months after the king's return.

In 1947 King Haakon went to London to attend the marriage of Princess Elizabeth—now Queen Elizabeth II—and the Duke of Edinburgh, and in 1948 he was one of the sponsors at the christening of their son, Prince Charles. His life had now spanned five generations of the British Royal Family, beginning with Queen Victoria, who, more than half a century earlier, had witnessed his own wedding. He paid a state visit to Britain in his yacht Norge in 1951 and the following year returned to attend the funeral of his nephew, King George VI [q.v.].

His eightieth birthday in August 1952 brought further tributes to his popularity, the most significant of which came perhaps from the Norwegian Communist newspaper *Friheten,* which said: "There is scarcely a king to-day who enjoys such popularity as King Haakon. This is due to his personal qualities which have won respect even from those who are far from being supporters of the monarchy".

On August 23 King Haakon became a great-grandfather when a son was born to Princess Ragnhild, who had married the shipowner Erling Lorentzen. He was christened Haakon.

The incidents in the golden sunset of a great reign are soon told. In the spring of 1953 King Haakon paid a state visit to Sweden, where he was greeted by King Gustaf Adolf* and Queen Louise*, sister of Lord Mountbatten, and received the heads of the diplomatic missions in Stockholm. Then in the summer he visited Holland and in the course of a crowded three days went to Stavenisse, on the island of Tholeur, which was badly damaged by the floods of February 1953. There he opened "King Haakon Street", where 255 Norwegian houses, presented by Norway after the disaster, had been built.

In the summer of 1955 he welcomed Queen Elizabeth II and the Duke of Edinburgh and showed them the hospitality he could dispense not only as the head of a friendly nation but also as a close relative by blood. In spite of his age he carried out the exacting programme with infectious enthusiasm. He attended the theatre, spoke at the state banquet, and, when the time of departure came, he changed his programme and, as though loth to say farewell, sailed with his guests in the royal yacht Britannia as far as the outer lighthouse of Oslo harbour. When a few days after their departure he fell in his bathroom and sustained a fractured thigh he went to hospital for the first time in his life.

He made a satisfactory recovery but it was of necessity not a quick one and he was still in the state hospital to which he had been taken after his accident when he celebrated the fiftieth anniversary of his arrival in Norway. A royal salute was fired and flags were flown but official celebrations were postponed until the King's health should further improve.

September 23, 1957.

The death of the **Crown Princess of Norway,** which occurred on April 5, 1954, caused a wave of sorrow to sweep over the country.

Princess Maertha Sophia Louise Dagmar Thyra was the younger daughter of Prince Carl, younger brother of the late King Gustaf V of Sweden and Princess Ingeborg, sister of King Haakon VII of Norway [q.v.]. Born at Stockholm in 1901, she imbibed the democratic traditions of the Scandinavian royal families and it was no surprise when Prince Olav, King Haakon's only child, asked for his cousin's hand and was accepted. The wedding, on March 21, 1929, was the first royal wedding celebrated in Oslo since King James I, while still King James VI of Scotland, married Princess Anne of Denmark there in 1589. As though to strengthen still further the British connexion, Prince Olav's best man was his first cousin, King George VI [q.v.], then Duke of York. The marriage was also interesting in that it connected the Swedish and Norwegian royal families 24 years after the separation of the two countries.

After the wedding the young couple, unable to face the cost of reconditioning the palace of Oscarshall, accepted from Baron Wedel Jarlsberg the estate of Skaugum about 20 miles from Oslo, as a wedding present. They had been there but a few months when the picturesque wooden manor house was badly damaged by fire and many of their wedding presents were destroyed. The Vasa diadem and the ancient Norwegian drinking horn, Hoel's Hornet, were saved.

Three children were born of the union,

Princess Ragnhild, Princess Astrid, and Prince Harald. The quiet and useful lives of the Crown Prince and Crown Princess were rudely disturbed by the invasion of their country by the Nazis in 1940. The Crown Princess with her three children took refuge in Sweden and thence went to the United States, where she remained until she went to London in 1942 to take part in the celebrations of the seventieth birthday of her father-in-law, King Haakon. During the difficult period of enforced exile she remained steadfastly at her husband's side and with him visited and heartened Norwegian forces in the United Kingdom and in Canada training for the great day when they should liberate their country. When that day arrived they were well rewarded by the unstinted enthusiasm and admiration of their normally undemonstrative subjects.

Not long afterwards, however, the Crown Princess's health began to fail, and in spite of a series of operations by American surgeons and long periods of convalescence in Florida and elsewhere little improvement occurred. The progress of her illness was watched with anxiety throughout Norway, and when it became clear that the liver complaint from which she had suffered acutely since a visit to northern Norway in 1950 might prove fatal there were few in Norway who had not some personal reminiscence of her kindness and her public spirit, so that the loss they feared seemed a peculiarly intimate and individual sorrow.

April 6, 1954.

Nevil Shute Norway, whose best-selling novels appeared under the name of **Nevil Shute,** died in a Melbourne hospital on January 12, 1960 at the age of 60. He was a novelist of intelligent and engaging quality, deservedly popular, and at the same time a notable figure in the aeronautical world.

Born on January 17, 1899, the son of Arthur Hamilton Norway, C.B., and Mary Louisa Gadsden, he was educated at the Dragon School, Oxford, Shrewsbury School, the R.M.A., Woolwich, and, after a short period in 1918 as a private in The Suffolk Regiment, at Balliol College, Oxford, where he took his degree. Having decided, in his boyhood, on an aeronautical career, he began by working for the de Havilland Aircraft Company for nothing, and in 1922 entered the firm as a calculator. He rose to be deputy chief engineer in 1928 and two years later twice flew the Atlantic, as representative of the Vickers company, which had built the great dirigible, in the R.100.

Norway, who had held an amateur's licence as pilot since 1925, founded Airspeed Limited in 1931 and was joint managing director until 1938. During the war of 1939-45 he was commissioned in the R.N.V.R., was appointed lieutenant-commander in 1941, and was assigned to a variety of special duties.

Norway was pursued by an inherited talent in writing while he made his way as an engineer. His grandmother had written children's books. His father had turned out travel books of good literary quality. He was accustomed from his earliest years to the ways of writers and their dealings with publishers; yet he wanted so badly to become an engineer that for most of one term he played truant from an uncongenial master in Hammersmith and spent his days in the Science Museum. The itch to write went along with him. At Shrewsbury he was writing poetry. At Hendon, with de Havilland's after he left Oxford, he spent all his leisure writing novels.

That nobody wanted what he wrote made no difference to his industry or his bent. He accepted the verdicts of publishers then as modestly as he accepted the fame of a best seller 20 years later, put his reject on a shelf and settled down to write another. Meanwhile he was making things as an engineer that brought him the real satisfactions of his life. There at Hendon he enjoyed the romance of those relatively early flying days. He went flying with pilots who were to become famous, like Alan Cobham* and Hubert Broad, and worked on design with men who were bound to distinguish themselves, Geoffrey de Havilland* and C. C. Walker* among them.

Work on new aircraft came to test and fruition in those days with an interval of perhaps only nine months between conception and completion. Norway found his keenest interest in creation. In later years, when he saw looming ahead of him at the Airspeed company years of production and business management, he gratefully slid out and was never again tempted back to the more complicated and prolonged labours of development associated with modern aircraft.

Something more than six years with de Havilland gave him a good grounding in design and particularly in the engineering and mathematics of aircraft structures. That experience led to his being offered the post of assistant to Barnes Wallis in the building of the R.100; and before he left Hendon for Howden, in the wilds of east Yorkshire, to turn his attention to airships, he had actually had a novel accepted. From then on the two aspects of his life were to march together, except for a spell at the Airspeed company, when he had persuaded a good many people to invest what he called "risk capital" in an undertaking that had to struggle most of its days, and he felt obliged not to divert any of his energies from it.

At Howden he was happy to be wrestling once again with unknown aeronautical quantities and resolving new propositions in stress and strain, making his contributions to the ingenious ideas that yielded a successful airship at a fraction of the cost of the R.101, which the Government built at the same time. He was afterwards to recall the "almost religious experience" of finding at last the calculations come right out of the mass of unconventional girders, polygonal frames and web suspension wires, after weeks of re-checking.

That was the way too that he wrote his novels. Every one was written twice. Some were written four times. Some of his friends got the impression that he found the same deep satisfaction in "engineering" his novels that he got from bringing to successful design a difficult structure closely beset by weight limitations. When the R.100 had flown to Canada and back and then been doomed by the disaster to the R.101, Norway, at a loose end, sank all he had, £1,000, in his new Airspeed company, which started in an old garage in York and afterwards moved to Portsmouth.

For the next seven years, 1931 to 1938, he was striving, in the midst of a depression, to put his new industrial child on its feet, much more the business man and administrator than the engineer, coming gradually as the price of stability more under the control of government departments and obeying the behests of Civil servants, against whom he cherished feelings of disapproval in industrial matters after seeing how the venture of the R.101 had gone. In 1938 the prospect for Airspeed Ltd. was years of turning out the Oxford trainer.

Norway took the solatium offered him and left. The other side of his life had given him his freedom. Rights in the latest novel of Nevil Shute had just been bought by a film company for £5,000. It was not quite the end of engineer Norway. There was a war to come and Norway, in the modest rank of lieutenant-commander, was to make his contribution to it in the matter of unorthodox secret weapons for the Navy. But he had had his fill of industry; and aeronautics was becoming too much a long-term team job to offer him any repetition of life's earlier joys.

By the time the war ended he had firmly found his new sphere and with it a measure of prosperity he had never expected. That prosperity never made much difference to his way of life. Indirectly it drove him to emigrate, once again to escape the dead hand of the state. He had marched far into the supertax class and resented the highest rate of taxation. He found that by going to Australia to live he could avoid the 19s. 6d. in the pound and be liable for only 13s. 4d. in the pound. That, he said frankly, was his reason for going.

He settled happily on a 200-acre farm 30 miles from Melbourne, had an aircraft of his own for convenience and pleasure, went sailing again as he had as a youth, found himself getting on well with the Australians and never regretted his change. He paid visits to England or the United States only when business demanded it, but he made those visits occasions for meeting all his old friends. He was as easy and welcome a companion in the days of his prosperity as he had been in the years of his arduous endeavours in one of the chanciest of industries.

Throughout his life he suffered from a stammer. It worried neither him nor his friends, for there were never any pretensions about Norway. At the height of his popularity he was incapable of posturing as a literary man. He brushed off his achievements with the explanation that he "happened to have the knack of writing"—a disclaimer that ignored the care he invariably took to create a situation and fit characters and plot into it with all the precision he once built into his structures.

As novelist his virtues are in the first place those of the storyteller. He had a narrative ease and liveliness that made him never less than readable, a fund of sympathy, especially with the young, that warmed the reader, and a quiet air of veracity that enabled him to communicate excitement and danger without ever shocking the reader's sense of probability. Nevil Shute was, in brief, the sort of novelist who genuinely touches the imagination and feeling of the book-borrowing public.

He did not acquire his sureness of touch all at once. He had already written three novels before he secured attention in 1938 with *Ruined City,* an entertaining story of the grandeurs and miseries of high finance. Early in 1939 came *What Happened to the Corbetts,* in which he pictured, in serious enough fashion though in a characteristically light tone, the effect of an unheralded air bombardment of Britain. Then followed *An Old Captivity* (1940), the tale of an archaeological expedition to Greenland, which was weakened by a conventional turn of fantasy, and, later in the year, *Landfall,* a most persuasive and moving little story of the misadventure of an R.A.F. pilot. *Pied Piper* (1942) was, once more, admirable storytelling, though a shade sentimental, on the subject of France in disaster, while *Pastoral* (1944) was altogether delightful—perhaps his happiest work, *Most Secret* (1945), *Vinland the Good* (1946), and *The Chequer Board* (1947) were followed by *No Highway,* which was concerned with metal fatigue in a large airliner, and *A Town like Alice,* a moving story of the effects of the Japanese occupation in Malaya, which had immense success when made into a film. Norway's autobiography *Slide Rule* came out in 1954, *Requiem for a Wren* the following year, and in 1957 *On the Beach,* which described the possible effects of global war; the northern hemisphere annihilated, the southern still uninhabited but under sentence of death by radioactive dust. A film based on this novel and with a cast including Gregory Peck and Fred Astaire was given its first showing in London and other capital cities in December 1959.

Norway married in 1931 Frances Mary Heaton, who had qualified as a doctor. She, with the two daughters of the marriage, survives him.

January 13, 1960.

Lord Norwich, still better known as **Duff Cooper** even 18 months after his creation as a viscount, died suddenly on January 1, 1954 aboard the French liner Colombie, at the age of 63.

The Right Honourable Sir Alfred Duff Cooper, Viscount Norwich, of Aldwick, in the county of Sussex, in the peerage of the United Kingdom, P.C., G.C.M.G., D.S.O., was born on February 22, 1890, the eldest son of the late Sir Alfred Cooper, a surgeon who came of an old Norwich family, and was educated at Eton and New College, Oxford, where he obtained honours in modern history. He was a nephew of the late Duke of Fife through his mother, Lady Agnes Duff; and a son-in-law of the eighth Duke of Rutland through his marriage in 1919 to Lady Diana Manners.

He served with distinction in the Grenadier Guards during the war of 1914-18 and won the D.S.O. for an exceptionally gallant action. His war service interrupted the career which he had just begun at the Foreign Office, and to which he returned on demobilization. But, financial considerations apart, he was as well equipped for a political as for a diplomatic career, and after his marriage he entered Parliament in 1924 as Unionist member for Oldham. Recognition of his gifts was not long delayed, and in 1928 he was appointed Financial Secretary to the War Office.

Next year, however, he lost his seat at the general election which resulted in the formation of the second Labour Government; and it was not until 1931 that he re-entered politics. The re-entry was, however, dramatic. At the time there was something very like a split in the Conservative Party. Criticism of Baldwin's policy was rampant, and the newspapers controlled by Lord Beaverbrook* and Lord Rothermere took the lead in this criticism. The test came at a by-election in St. George's, Westminster, when an anti-Baldwin candidate was found to stand as an Independent. Duff Cooper was chosen as the official Conservative candidate and won the seat after a hot fight by nearly 6,000 votes. This victory ensured his return to office on the formation of the first National Government, and three years later he became Financial Secretary to the Treasury—a post then considered as the ante-room to Cabinet office.

So it proved to be, and Duff Cooper was successively Secretary of State for War and First Lord of the Admiralty during the years when re-armament was beginning. He was, however, never happy with the line of policy pursued by Baldwin and later by Chamberlain, and was known to be more inclined to the views expressed by Churchill*. This uneasiness may explain why he won no great reputation as an administrator in the Service Departments which he controlled. Matters came to a head at the time of the Munich settlement, when he resigned office because, as he said, the terms of the settlement "stuck in his throat".

At the outbreak of war in 1939 Duff Cooper undertook a lecture tour of the United States during which he had the not unusual experience of arousing sharp controversy. He had, however, returned by the time that the battle opened on May 10, 1940, and accepted Churchill's invitation to become Minister of Information. It might have been thought that this post would be congenial to his talents; but it hardly proved to be so. The Ministry had been subjected to consistent and justifiable criticisms throughout its earlier existence. But as some already suspected, Duff Cooper's talents did not include the gift of setting right faults in administration. His voice was, moreover, not a good broadcasting voice, and he cannot be said to have become a public figure nor to have changed materially the unpopularity of his department.

In the summer of 1941 Duff Cooper, after ordering what became known as a "Cassandra" broadcast on the B.B.C., ceased to be Minister of Information and, as Chancellor of the Duchy of Lancaster, was dispatched on what appeared at first to be a somewhat vague visit to the Far East. On his way through New York he announced that the Government expected great developments there. In early September he arrived at Singapore. There he held various conferences, gave a broadcast in which he spoke of the isolation of Japan, and then went on to Burma, India, and Australia and New Zealand. It was in fact his intention to coordinate British political, diplomatic, and other activities throughout the whole of the Far East and to provide facilities for reaching speedier decisions on important questions as they arose, and so urgent did he feel his task to have become that in November he dispatched a member of his staff from New Zealand to London with a preliminary report.

In December he was back in Singapore, and it was soon announced that he had been appointed Resident Minister of Cabinet rank there for Far Eastern affairs and would preside over a war council. Meanwhile, however, events were moving apace, and the British retreat in north-west Malaya had begun when, on December 21, he made an anxious broadcast. Early in January 1942 the Government were pressed to define his position and duties—General Wavell had by then become Commander-in-Chief in the south-west Pacific—and after only three weeks of office he was recalled. Back in London in March he strongly defended the men and women of Singapore from charges of levity which had been made against them. In June he took over the chairmanship of the Home Defence (Security) Executive, known generally as the Swinton* Committee.

In May 1943 Duff Cooper gave the public a reminder of his literary abilities by publishing *David,* a most skilful presentation of the Psalmist as man, statesman, and soldier. In November he resigned his Cabinet post in order to become Great Britain's diplomatic representative with the French Committee of National Liberation at Algiers. In it he had the personal rank of Ambassador. He thus relieved Harold Macmillan, who had been appointed British representative on the Advisory Council for Italy, of some of his burdens, and filled the need for a full-time representation with the French National Committee.

In June 1944 he accompanied General de Gaulle* to England in order to help in discussions with Churchill and Eden. In the following September he arrived in Paris to assume the duties of British Ambassador and to establish residence at the British Embassy, which Sir Ronald Campbell [q.v.] had vacated on the fall of France. He remained Ambassador until 1947.

During his term as Ambassador he did much to improve Anglo-French relations, especially in the fields of the arts, but, though a good friend of France, his range of contacts was perhaps too small to make him the ideal Ambassador.

The reason why Duff Cooper failed on the whole to realize the high hopes entertained for him can probably be found in a streak of dilettantism which made him good at many things but not in the first rank at anything. For example, he could be a brilliant and incisive speaker, and he had the gift of following up an ordered argument without notes. But he was not a great success in the House of Commons. Again, he could be a brilliant writer, and the first of his works—a biography of Talleyrand published in 1932—was a most stimulating book. But his official biography of Lord Haig was generally considered to be far less brilliant. In his writing, as in his politics, he was better in a spirited and challenging controversy than at the sober balancing of views upon controversial questions; and would probably have found himself more at home in the eighteenth than in the twentieth century. He was no reactionary, and both his courage and sincerity were beyond dispute. But his keen enjoyment of life gave him a rather "grand seigneur" flavour and an unwillingness to suffer either fools or sober-sides gladly.

His last book, published a few months ago, was his autobiography, *Old Men Forget.* It was—tragically, it now seems—his most entertaining and instructive work. It had a frankness about himself and a freedom from pomposity which are not always to be found in the autobiographies of the distinguished. Moreover his revelations of Neville Chamberlain's methods of conducting foreign policy before the war form one of the most searing indictments of Chamberlain which have been made. The book, which was informed by his zest for life, ended with an appropriate epitaph: "... life has been good to me and I am grateful. ... I love the sunlight, but I cannot fear the coming of the dark".

He is survived by his widow, and the title passes to his only child, John Julius Cooper, who was born on September 15, 1929, and married, in 1952, Anne Frances May, eldest daughter of Sir Bede Edmund Hugh Clifford, of Jacob's Well, near Guildford.

January 2, 1954.

Sir Cyril Norwood, who died on March 13, 1956 at the age of 80, by his commanding personality and forceful practical idealism acquired an exceptional influence with all educationists and teachers.

Cyril Norwood was born on September 15, 1875, the son of the Rev. Samuel Norwood, of Whalley, Lancashire. He was sent in 1888 to Merchant Taylors' School, then under Dr. Baker's headmastership. He was three years in the cricket XI, was head monitor, and was elected in 1894 School Tercentenary Scholar, Pitt Club Exhibitioner, and Scholar of St. John's College, Oxford, where he took a first in Classical Moderations and a first in *Lit. Hum.* On going down from the University, he passed first into the Home Civil Service and worked for some years in the Admiralty, until, realizing that teaching was his real vocation, he resigned and in 1901 accepted the Classical VI at Leeds Grammar School. Five years later he was offered his first headmastership.

Bristol Grammar School, of which Norwood became headmaster in September 1906 at the age of 30, had reached the height of its reputation in the second half of the nineteenth century. A succession of rich years had produced a band of scholars who were to make their mark in academic life, in the professions, and in commerce. In the same period the school itself had been moved to spacious buildings on the outskirts of the city; it is near the centre now. Then had followed a period of relative stagnation; the stream of boys who were to win distinction was reduced to a trickle, and the spacious new buildings became half empty. The problem was to attract once more to the school boys of the old type, and to rekindle the spirit of endeavour which had animated them.

Norwood's influence at once ran throughout the school like an electric shock. The headmaster's presence, obtruded nowhere, was felt everywhere. In the arrangement of the time-table short periods of concentrated effort took the place of long periods of listlessness sinking into sheer boredom. Athletics, which had only survived at all through the energy of a few enthusiastic masters and boys, school societies of all kinds, and the cadet corps, of which he took command himself, became active. The school, which to masters and boys alike had been merely their daily task, became in a few months their absorbing interest. At the same time, with the help of Mrs. Norwood's social gifts, parents and even strangers to the school were made to share in the newly awakened keenness.

When he left Bristol for Marlborough in 1916 the number of boys in the school had risen, in his 10 years of office, from 207 to 528 and the number of masters from 13 to 27. In the same period new buildings at a total cost of nearly £20,000 had been presented to the school, as well as ample new playing-fields and a pavilion, and two valuable scholarships had been endowed. It is a commentary on the fallibility of human judgment that he had been the governors' second choice, and became headmaster only because the man who was first appointed withdrew.

The nine years at Marlborough constitute the zenith of Norwood's career. Bristol had been a brilliant prologue, Harrow was to prove a disillusionment, and Oxford an honourable epilogue to a life of service to education. The Master of Marlborough, however, was generally conceded to tower above his contemporaries, and quite apart from the finer points which an intimate study of his reign might reveal, the school's meteoric record in scholarship—in 1925 it won 30 open scholarships and exhibitions to Oxford and Cambridge—and sport during this period silenced critics. Not that his path was easy at the first. The same suspicions and prejudices, which were later to balk him at Harrow, met him in a lesser degree at Marlborough.

The appointment of a grammar school headmaster, however distinguished, was resented by boys, masters, and Old Marlburians alike, and Norwood, whose methods during this period of his career were nothing if not despotic, did little to assuage their feelings; he set out to overwhelm opposition by the measure of his achievement. That he was successful, when at Harrow he may be said partially to have failed, was due to the different constitutions of the two schools. The government of one was a system of checks and balances, whereas at Marlborough the Master was singularly untrammelled by the governing body and could exercise more or less unrestricted control over his staff, a control of which Norwood was prepared on occasions to make ruthless use.

The general lines of his policy remained much the same as at Bristol. He enlarged the sphere of modern studies, giving languages, geography, and science a partnership, if a junior one, in the curriculum with classics. At the same time the Classical Sixth, under the tutelage of the late G. M. Sargeaunt, never had a more brilliant period, combining a liberal education with a remarkable capacity for snapping up the major scholarships. A modernist so far as the training of the mind was concerned, Norwood made little attempt to modernize the somewhat crude domestic conditions in which the 750 boys under his charge lived.

Marlborough remained much as it was when Bradley planted the Arnold tradition on the banks of the Kennet, and if parents sometimes looked wistfully at the up-to-date accommodation of more recent establishments the Master found an *exiguo adsueta juventus* more responsive to the lesson he had to teach. This response he found in full measure. Under his leadership the intellectual and athletic life of the school quickened to a Periclean vitality. He had the great gift of never imposing petty restrictions, and was bold enough to encourage tendencies to liberal thought which lesser schoolmasters repress through fear of not knowing how to deal with its consequences. He could repress drastically when necessary, and never tolerated idlers. He was a great believer in short, sharp periods of hard work, leaving the boys plenty of spare time in which to digest in their own way the lessons they had learned in the classroom.

As the years passed the school acquired a steady self-confidence in its own powers such as comes to those corporate bodies in which the limbs are sound and the organism in harmony. It came as a shock when one evening the Master walked on to the stage in the Memorial Hall and announced his almost immediate departure for Harrow. His sense of duty told him that his task at Marlborough was completed and that his hand was required elsewhere; but the school never felt happy at the decision. They felt that Marlborough and her Master were well wedded and that neither would fare so happily without the other.

Norwood succeeded Lionel Ford as headmaster of Harrow in January 1926. The appointment was greeted with applause in the educational world and was regarded as placing him in his due position in English education. But the situation bristled with difficulties. An ancient school must necessarily be bound by many traditions, and Dr. Norwood refused to be shackled by those he found at Harrow. He had his way in the end, but only at the expense of alienating the senior masters, boys, and many parents. His first move was the reform of the curriculum. He found the school organized as a stage preliminary to the universities; he made it his aim to shape an education that was complete in itself. While he faithfully carried out, on the lines laid down by his predecessor, the mission imposed on him by the Governors of raising the standard of the classics in the school, his real sympathy lay with progress. He placed modern studies on a sound basis, and introduced the newer subjects of geography and economics. He encouraged intellectual hobbies, and gave the quiet student greater freedom than was usual in public schools. Educational experiments of all kinds gained his approval, and during his régime Harrow became a national centre for conferences of schoolmasters and other educational activities.

But he was not content with bringing Harrow into line with his theories of modern education; his ambitions tended towards spreading them to all the schools of the country. To this end he strove in the daily Press to influence opinion, and in the summer holidays of 1928 he compiled, perhaps too hastily, his volume *The English Tradition in Education.*

His voluntary duties outside Harrow became immense. Every important educational body, including the Board of Education, sought his counsel. Scarcely a week passed but he expounded his educational creed at some prizegiving, and he found time to preside over the headmasters' conference, the investigation into the school certificate examinations, from which the famous "Norwood Report" issued in 1943, and innumerable other committees.

When he left Harrow in July 1934 it was with relief at his escape from the social duties connected with the school and from forces of tradition with which he had grown weary of battling. His term as president of his old college at Oxford came as something of a relief, and it continued from 1934 until his resignation in 1946 on account of his wife's ill-health. He mellowed with the years and found in the Oxford to which he returned a balm to his spirit, in spite of the distractions or war and the disruption of academic life.

He married Catharine Margaret, daughter of Dr. W. J. Kilner. She died in 1951, and he is survived by three daughters of the marriage.

March 14, 1956.

The death of **Ivor Novello,** after playing in *King's Rhapsody* at the Palace Theatre, London, on March 6, 1951, was to be widely felt, not only among the thousands of theatregoers for whom his musical plays, in particular, long meant a welcome holiday from the humdrum, but also among the many members of the theatrical profession to whom his kindnesses were endless.

Perhaps few other theatrical figures of the age are so likely to leave behind a legend. Novello was one of those exceptional people in connexion with whom the phrase "a man of the theatre" acquires meaning and virtue. He really was a man of the theatre. As actor, playwright, and composer he occupied a position with the public in general which even Noël Coward*, his friend and rival, could scarcely challenge; and in the course of time his pieces, with or without music, came to prove that the tentative theatricality of even his earliest play, *The Rat,* had developed into a sure and conscious aptitude for such strokes and situations as come to life only upon the stage. Where barren playwrights, also enamoured of the theatre, fail because they merely duplicate the effects they have admired in other men's plays, Novello succeeded because he did not imitate but had instead a genuine sense of "those colours that show best by candlelight".

He could tell to a nicety, as time went on and his constant practice in theatrical writing again and again brought him success, what fell within the romantic view of the theatre, which was his own view. His romanticism went happily hand in hand with a genial and rather farcical sense of humour, and in such plays as *Party* and *We Proudly Present* he showed that he was quite capable of laughing at the theatre itself and at the profession he loved. His latest musical play, *Gay's the Word,* disarmed those who were from time to time constrained to criticize him, for in it he cheerfully parodied the very Ruritanian romances to which he owed his most triumphant successes. As a romantic, he was seldom to be tempted into the soberly sustained examination of a character, but now and again he was led by the very intensity of his absorption in the theatre to make the effort. In *Proscenium,* for instance, in 1933, he concentrated the dramatic interest of the piece on the relationship, made difficult by age and ambition, of an actor and an actress who love each other; and in *Comedienne,* 1938, with the admirable assistance of Lilian Braithwaite, he drew the full-length portrait of an actress.

It is probably by the spectacular musical romances of his latest period that Novello will be popularly remembered. *Glamorous Night, Careless Rapture, Crest of the Wave, The Dancing Years, Arc de Triomphe, Perchance to Dream, King's Rhapsody*—their very titles cunningly suggest the succession of spacious and highly coloured scenes which their author found for the great stages of Drury Lane and similar theatres. Princes and prima donnas, millionaires and royal mistresses, aristocrats and struggling composers, were the natural inhabitants of that world, and their affairs were arranged so serviceably by the experienced playwright as really to earn the description of "musical play" instead of "musical comedy", which is so often a title of playwriting incompetence. In any case, though they had their passages of amusing dialogue, they were seldom chiefly comic, their principal elements being a highly agreeable nostalgia for time past, or time perhaps that never was, and a perennially youthful insistence on the interest and dignity of romantic love. With their opportunities for decorative dressing and particularly of course at Drury Lane for the spectacular employment of stage machinery, and with music that was unfailingly graceful, these big productions of Novello's may be reckoned as unique in their kind. With the death of their author a whole spring of popular entertainment will have dried up.

Ivor Novello was born at Cardiff on January 15, 1893, the son of David Davies and Clara Novello Davies. He was educated at Magdalen College School, Oxford, became a chorister at the college in 1905, and remained there for six years. Even in early youth he had a flair for song writing, in which he was encouraged by his gifted mother, and one of his songs was published when he was only 15. His most famous was "Keep the Home Fires Burning", which became one of the popular marching tunes of the troops in the 1914-18 war. At the outbreak of that war he joined the Royal Naval Air Service and remained with it until the Armistice. In 1921 he made his first appearance on the stage, in *Deburau* at the Ambassadors Theatre. By 1924 he had become an actor-manager, presenting *The Rat,* his first play, written in collaboration with Constance Collier [q.v.]. His next venture in management was in partnership with Frank Curzon at the Queen's for the run of *Down Hill,* also written in collaboration with Constance Collier [q.v.]. He resumed management on his own account and produced *The Truth Game* and *Symphony in Two Flats,* both written by himself. The latter piece, which ran for 12 months, was presently made into a successful film.

In 1930 he went to New York and appeared at the Ethel Barrymore [q.v.] Theatre in *The Truth Game.* The following year he was acting and writing in Hollywood, where he played opposite Miss Ruth Chatterton* in the film *Once a Lady,* made a film version of *The Truth Game,* and wrote dialogue for, among others, *Tarzan of the Apes.* On his return to England he appeared in his comedy *I Lived With You,* and throughout the 1930s the West End was seldom without a play by Novello. Though he usually acted only in his own plays, he made two striking appearances in those of others. At Drury Lane in 1938 he played King Henry V in Shakespeare's history, and at His Majesty's in 1936 he was Lord George Hell in an adaptation of Sir Max Beerbohm's [q.v.] story, *The Happy Hypocrite.* The success of his own musical plays was due in large measure to his own polished performances and meticulously careful production. In August 1944 he took a company to Normandy, where he presented *Love from a Stranger* for the entertainment of the allied forces. In 1947 he took *Perchance to Dream* to South Africa.

When all Novello's manifold achievements have been taken into account, however, he will still be missed for more than his talents and his brilliant successes as author and actor. He inspired in all who knew him personally, however slightly, a genuine liking, and in those who worked closely with him or enjoyed his friendship their liking quickly passed into a real and lasting affection.

March 7, 1951.

Alfred Noyes, C.B.E., who died in hospital in the Isle of Wight on June 28, 1958, was a prolific, versatile, and notably talented writer, whose work had been prominently before the public since the beginning of the present century. He was 77.

He turned to authorship at an early age (he was arranging the publication of his first book when he should have been taking his schools at Oxford) and made his mark quickly—so quickly that he soon became that rare bird, a poet who lived comfortably by the earnings of his poetry. As a poet his natural piety and musical fluency were in the direct English line, and indeed he was very English in sentiment, with a strain of liberalism that made the Catholicism of his later years sit somewhat uneasily upon him.

Noyes was a poet of considerable distinction, although not of the highest order. The time-spirit, it might perhaps be said, somehow failed to take him under its wing. He was in a conspicuous degree chary of experiment and inclined to look askance at what was new. Yet some of his shorter lyrics have a rare felicity of sentiment, while in "The Torch-Bearers" he hit upon a splendid theme for a modern epic and treated the great moments of scientific discovery with insight and dignity. He was of our age, too, in his rejection of the classical apparatus and his frequent use of something like "the real language of men". His criticism was at its best and most humane when it dealt with issues not easily twisted to literary or religious controversy; yet the volume on Voltaire, if once its extraordinary original premise could be swallowed and digested, was a singularly interesting, well-argued and well-documented piece of special pleading. Thoughtful, melodious (whether in prose or verse), endowed with an attractive personality that looked out from all he wrote, Noyes served the art of letters with single-hearted devotion.

Alfred Noyes was born at Wolverhampton on September 16, 1880, the son of another Alfred Noyes and his wife, Amelia Adams Rowley. His boyhood was largely spent by the sea, where he learnt to row and to swim—exercises which, coupled with much country walking, helped to produce in him a physical robustness that he was always to prize. From 1898 to 1902 he was at Exeter College, Oxford. He rowed in his college boat for three years, and in 1901 was No. 6 in the Exeter eight at Henley. He read widely at Oxford, where he began to write verse; some of his earliest writing appeared in a university publication called *The Jester*. In 1902 he had a book of verse in the hands of a publisher and went to London to discuss details of publication at the very moment when he should have been sitting for his finals.

Noyes thus left Oxford without a degree. But his initial volume, *The Loom of Years* (1902), secured a word of praise from Meredith; *The Flower of Old Japan*, in the following year, similarly attracted notice; and in 1905 *The Forest of Wild Thyme* established him among the more interesting of the younger English poets. His Elizabethan preoccupations were apparent in *Forty Singing Seamen* (1908), a volume produced under the marked influence of Swinburne, and in the same year drew from him an epic poem, "Drake", which first appeared serially in *Blackwood's Magazine*.

He had married in 1907 an American lady, Garnett, daughter of Colonel B. G. Daniels, and in 1913 he paid his first visit to her native land, delivering the Lowell lectures at Boston, lecturing at Princeton and other universities, and being made an honorary Litt.D. of Yale. He made an immediate impression in the United States. In the following spring he paid another visit to the United States, and in April was appointed visiting Professor of Poetry at Princeton. He continued in that post until 1923. Debarred from military service by defective eyesight, Noyes was not inactive during the war of 1914-18. He returned home in May 1916 for temporary attachment to the Foreign Office, and later worked in France. He wrote a series of articles for *The Times* on various aspects of the war at sea and also published two or three volumes.

Early in 1922 appeared the first part of "The Torch-Bearers", Noyes's most ambitious work in the epic form (the remaining two parts came out in 1925 and 1930 respectively). The poem was inspired by the sentiment that, while kings and conquerors had never gone short of praise in verse, the more important and lasting conquests of science had been neglected: reparation should now be made. In the result Noyes's blank verse achieved less than a line-by-line perfection or even than a firm poetic consistency. Yet it bore something of genuine visionary power and a great many impressive moments.

But Noyes during these years had not confined himself to epic poetry, lyric, and ballad, though no doubt it is chiefly on these forms that his reputation is likely to rest. Apart from a play or two, he published collections of critical essays from time to time, of which in particular *Some Aspects of Modern Poetry* (1924) and *The Opalescent Parrot* (1929) revealed him as a supporter of "tradition" in Western literature and a foe to "novelty" in most of its fashionable or less fashionable guises. Modern developments in English poetry Noyes was inclined to regard as "downright insanity". In fiction, besides a volume of short stories, *The Hidden Player* (1924), he produced *The Sun Cure* (1929), a light and unpretentious effort, and *The Last Man* (1940), an experiment in fantasy.

Mrs. Noyes had died in September 1926. A year later Noyes married Mary Angela, eldest daughter of Captain J. G. Mayne and widow of Richard Shireburn Weld-Blundell, of Ince Blundell Hall, near Southport. They had a son and two daughters.

Later he was received into the Roman Catholic Church, and much that he subsequently wrote was coloured by a convert's zeal. The largest and perhaps strangest of Noyes's contributions to Catholic apologetics was his *Voltaire* (1937). Here he set out to show that, far from being anti-Christian, Voltaire remained a believer—though an unorthodox believer—in God, and that the objects of the Voltairean criticism were superstition and the venality of the French clergy of his day. A rather complex controversy followed, in which the attitude of the Holy Office was involved and in which Noyes, Cardinal Hinsley, and others exchanged charge and counter-charge. Eventually it was explained that there had been errors in translation into and from Italian, and in March 1939 a statement was issued from Archbishop's House, Westminster, to the effect that all difficulties had been happily composed. In an earlier book, *The Unknown God*, Noyes developed cogently and eloquently the argument that the world's need was religion, and directed a sustained attack on the foundations of materialism.

Other prose works by Noyes ranged from a volume on William Morris in the English Men of Letters series to a book about gardens and the Isle of Wight called *Orchard's Bay*. The work of his later years included *The Edge of the Abyss* (1944), a recall to Christian philosophy; *Shadows on the Down and other Poems* (1945); an autobiography, *Two Worlds, for Memory* (1953); and a final book of poems, *A Letter to Lucian*, published last year.

An incident which occurred early in his life greatly troubled him in later years. He was one of the select handful of people who were shown, during the trial of Roger Casement, pages or copies of pages purporting to be taken from a diary of Casement illustrating the latter's sexual perversion. At the time he accepted them as genuine evidence, but later came to believe that they were a calumnious forgery, and he was to feel remorse for unwittingly assisting what he thus suspected was a piece of base deception. The last book he wrote was an attempt to clear the character of Casement from these charges.

June 30, 1958.

General Nuri es Said—Nuri Pasha es Said—who was 70 at the time of his death in the Baghdad rising on July 14, 1958 with King Feisal II of Iraq [q.v.] and the Crown Prince Abdul Illah [q.v.], was the most eminent Iraqi since the foundation of that kingdom.

A man of unusual vigour, intelligence, and charm, he found himself in conflict in his later years with some of the currents of nationalism in his own country and in the Arab world at large. Yet he was a sincere and devoted Arab patriot and at the same time a firm friend of Great Britain. He was in large part an architect of the Baghdad Pact, but his services to his country were equally great in the impetus he gave to its economic development based on the oil revenues.

The only son of an inconspicuous official of the Ottoman empire, he was born in Baghdad in 1888: the eldest of his sisters was later to marry Ja'far al Askari—Prime Minister of Iraq in 1926 and later years—whose sister, Na'ima, Nuri himself married. His early education was at the local primary school, followed in 1903 by the Military Academy in Istanbul. He returned to Iraq, a newly commissioned officer, in 1908, and went again to Turkey for the Army Staff College two years later. Between 1910 and 1914 he made his first contacts with the infant Arab nationalism of the time, and became a member of the secret al-Ahd (Covenant) Society. Captured by the British early in the War of 1914-18, he elected, like many Arab brother officers, to join the Arab Revolt with Feisal and Lawrence, and there showed unusual ability and force.

In postwar Damascus he stood close to the Emir Feisal both before and after the latter was elected King of Syria in April 1920; he acted as his personal escort or envoy on critical occasions, and accompanied him to Europe when Feisal was expelled by the French in July 1920. He joined his prince in Iraq in 1921 soon after the latter had been placed on the throne of that country, and quickly established his position by successful tenures of the highest commands in the police and the army. His first Cabinet appointment was as Minister of Defence in November 1922, and he held the same post in three subsequent Cabinets in 1923-28 under Muhsin al Sa'dun, Ja'far al Askari, and Naji al-Suwaidi. He succeeded to the premiership in March 1930 and quickly effected the signature of the Anglo-Iraqi Treaty on June 30, which was destined, unlike many others, to survive for its whole intended life of 25 years. His Cabinet maintained itself, against growing opposition, until March 1932, by which time Iraq's emancipation from the mandate, and its entry into the League of Nations, had been accomplished. Nuri had meantime visited Turkey and signed a comprehensive good will treaty with that country.

In the period 1932 to 1936 Nuri appeared in a number of short-lived Cabinets as Minister for Foreign Affairs, was in Switzerland with King Feisal when he died in August 1933, and accepted office under Yasin al-Hashimi (1935-1936), in an administration which was ended by the sudden *coup d'état* of General Bakr Sidqi in October 1936. He saved himself from a probable fate similar to that of Ja'far Pasha, who was murdered, by a hurried departure from the territory in an R.A.F. aircraft. He could return when some months later Sidqi was assassinated and normal government restored: but he preferred for a time to accept diplomatic posts abroad. He was at this period concerned with plans for closer Arab unity, and sought to influence the British Government towards a non-Zionist policy in Palestine. He again accepted the premiership in December 1938 and attended the London Conference on Palestine.

In the first year of the Second World War Nuri stoutly upheld the British connexion, but difficulties internal to Iraqi politics compelled him to resign office early in 1940, though he occupied posts in succeeding Cabinets. The sudden usurpation of power by four Generals (the "Golden Square") in the German interest, the flight of the Regent, Abdul Illah, [later Crown Prince], and the ensuing Anglo-Iraqi thirty-day hostilities, led again to Nuri's withdrawal from Iraq; but he was recalled to the premiership in October 1941, retained it for nearly three years, caused Iraq to declare war on the Axis powers, and moved towards an organization for greater Arab unity.

He took a leading part in negotiations regarding the status of Palestine, and satisfied a life-long ambition by his initiatives which led to the foundation of the Arab League in 1954. For three years thereafter he was alternatively in and out of office, led a mission to Turkey, supported Iraq's intervention in Palestine early in 1948, visited Great Britain annually, and was among the Ministers who, signatories of the Anglo-Iraqi Treaty of Portsmouth, which was rejected by mob-rioting in Baghdad, wisely stayed out of Iraq for 12 months. In spite of fatigue and some ill-health in 1949 he again became Prime Minister, founded his Constitutional Union Party, and disengaged Iraqi troops from the Palestine fiasco. His efforts to establish better terms with Syria during the latter's period of military dictatorship were, not through his fault, unsuccessful.

In the period 1950-1957 Nuri became, in spite of uncertain health, more than ever a dominant figure; unpopular with those who looked to Egypt under Nasser* as the focus of Arab nationalism, the support which his personality and outstanding services attracted was mainly from the upper-middle classes, the non-political masses, the tribes, and elements of the Army. In 1952 he was compelled to withdraw from office by student rioting on electoral procedure, but his Constitutional Union Party swept the board in 1953, and as Minister of Defence he could pursue his firmly anti-Communist policy.

Next year, in spite of Egyptian advances, he led his country, as Prime Minister again, towards a policy of broader defensive alliances, and visited Pakistan and Turkey; and in 1955 he broke off relations with the U.S.S.R., and signed the Baghdad Pact with Turkey, later joined by Pakistan, Persia, and Great Britain, weathering the storms of Egypt's wrath and the consequent splitting of the Arab League. A new Anglo-Iraqi agreement, covering defence, was made in March 1955 as an outcome of the pact. The outspoken hostility of Egypt, joined by Syria and, for a time, Saudi Arabia, did not prevent his expressing support for Egypt over the nationalization of the Suez Canal; relations with France, but not with Britain, were broken off, and the blow to Nuri's pro-western policy, always heavily criticized in Baghdad political circles, was indicated by rioting in Mosul and Baghdad. The need for rest determined Nuri to resign the premiership (his sixteenth tenure of that office) in June 1957, and he again visited London.

In March 1958, in response to the union of Egypt and Syria, he formed a new cabinet in Baghdad and began discussions shortly afterwards to bring about a federation between Iraq and Jordan. In May he resigned as head of the Iraq Government preparatory to becoming Prime Minister of the newly formed Federation. He was again a visitor to London in June for health reasons but found time for meetings with the British Government and expressed his concern over the situation in the Lebanon where he thought western intervention might be necessary.

July 23, 1958.

Tazio Nuvolari, in the opinion of many the greatest racing driver the world has yet seen, died at Mantua on August 10, 1953 at the age of 60. In the years between the wars he won a host of admirers for his ability to carry off astonishing victories by dash and skill in handling his car against more powerfully mounted opponents.

Born on November 16, 1892, the son of a small farmer near Mantua, he first achieved distinction after the 1914-18 war in motor-cycle races, also driving an assortment of cars in minor events. In 1925 he attracted the attention of the Alfa-Romeo management, but his trial run for them ended in a crash and, on leaving hospital, he returned to motor-cycle events to win the Grand Prix des Nations at Monza.

He then acquired a Bugatti car with which, racing independently, he carried off the Rome Grand Prix and the Garda Circuit in 1927, and the Tripoli Grand Prix and Alessandria Circuit in 1928. As a result the Alfa-Romeo team were again disposed to enlist his services, and for them he won in 1930 the R.A.C. Tourist Trophy in Ulster and (with Giudotti) the Mille Miglia; in 1931 the Targa Florio, the Coppa Ciano, and (with Campari) the European Grand Prix at Monza; and in 1932 the title of Champion of Italy, with victories in the French and Monaco Grands Prix, the Targa Florio, the Coppa Ciano, the Avellino Circuit, and the Coppa Acerbo. Next year he won the Grands Prix at Carthage and Nimes, the Alessandria Circuit, the Eifel race, and (with Compagnoni) the Mille Miglia, and (with Sommer) the Le Mans 24-hour race. Then he had a difference with Alfa-Romeo and drove a Maserati in the Belgian and Nice Grands Prix and the Coppa Ciano, and an M.G. Magnette in the Ulster Tourist Trophy, winning all four. In 1934 he won at Naples and Modena with a Maserati; but after narrowly escaping an accident at Rheims he had a bad crash in the Circuito Bordino and broke a leg.

This reverse was followed by a *rapprochement* with Alfa-Romeo, for whom at the end of the year he broke international class records at 200 m.p.h., with a twin-engined car. In 1935, racing an Alfa-Romeo for the Scuderia Ferrari, he won the Grands Prix of Pau and Nice, the Coppa Ciano, the Modena, Biella, and Turin Circuits, and—in a brilliant race against the State-subsidized teams of Mercedes-Benz and Auto-Union—the German Grand Prix. This was undoubtedly Nuvolari's finest race. In 1936 he won the Grands Prix of Peña Rhin, Hungary and Milan, the Coppa Ciano, the Modena Circuit, and the Vanderbilt Cup in the United States.

By the next year Alfa-Romeo were plainly being outstripped technically by the German teams, and after winning again at Milan, Nuvolari joined Auto-Union, for whom he won the Donington Grand Prix in England, the Italian Grand Prix in 1938, and the Yugoslavia Grand Prix in 1939. After the war he won the 1946 Grand Prix de l'Albigeois with a Maserati, and he followed this up with an epic drive in the 1947 Mille Miglia, finishing second in the general classification in a Cisitalia.

He found, however, that age and failing health did not permit him any longer to stand the effects of exhaust fumes. Apart from very occasional appearances at race meetings he retired to live on the property in which he had invested his winnings over the years.

August 12, 1953.

O

The Very Rev. Monsignor John O'Connor, who died in a nursing home at Leeds on February 6, 1952 at the age of 81, was a familiar and much-loved figure in Roman Catholic literary circles, and a close friend of the late G. K. Chesterton, who had him in mind in his characterization of the omniscient "Father Brown".

Born at Clonmel in 1870, he was educated by the Christian Brothers in Ireland, and at St. Edmund's, Douai, whence he went to Rome to study further for the priesthood, and was ordained at St. John Lateran in 1895. After serving on several missions in Yorkshire he was appointed parish priest of St. Cuthbert's, Bradford, where the present church was opened in 1935.

It was probably not until 1901 that Father O'Connor showed the world at large that he had other qualities than those usually expected of the successful parish priest; for in that year was published the *Arundel Hymnal*—an excellent collection of Catholic hymns edited by Charles Gatty, to which O'Connor contributed 12 original compositions and 15 translations from the Latin and Italian. In the same year Gatty introduced Fr. O'Connor to Sir Robert Hudson, who became his life-long friend, and through whom he came to know men like Augustine Birrell and Lord Rosebery—the nucleus of a band of literary enthusiasts whose object of admiration at that time was Bramah's *Wallet of Kai Lung.*

As Chesterton brought out in his autobiography, the priest made an immediate impression on him at their first meeting in the spring of 1904, and "Father Brown" was planned soon afterwards. As to his part in the creation of the famous detective, O'Connor confessed in his *Father Brown on Chesterton*—a charming, discursive account of their friendship published in 1937—that his "native talent for detection was of the slenderest". On the other hand, he admitted that he often carried brown paper parcels, that "the flat hat was true to life, but it perished in its prime", and that "the large and cheap umbrella was my defence against wearing an overcoat".

It may be that at the time Chesterton regarded Fr. O'Connor as a typical parish priest, as indeed he was in essential respects; overlooking the fact that Fr. O'Connor's acquaintance with arts and sciences was rather more extensive and deeper than the average priest is likely to enjoy. The point of the "Father Brown" stories was that the priest would range from subject to subject if required to do so, and the point of the particular identification was that Fr. O'Connor was at home in so many subjects that, as Chesterton remarked, he "never knew a man who could turn with more ease than he from one topic to another".

If he did not really introduce Paul Claudel [q.v.] and his work to Chesterton, at least he interested an English-speaking public to Claudel's major work, *The Satin Slipper,* an intricate drama on the workings of grace which is unlikely to be performed until the stage combines with the cinema and possibly broadcasting to secure its own effects. Shortly after translating *The Satin Slipper* Mgr. O'Connor wrote translations of several essays by Claudel and of his poems, to one of which, on a penitent, he added his own complement in verse, "The Priest Replies".

In May 1951 illness prevented him from continuing active parochial work, and his death now will be much felt, not least in Bradford, where he had a deep and lasting influence.

February 8, 1952.

C. K. Ogden, originator of Basic English, died on March 20, 1957. By his death the world of scholarship loses an unconventional but deeply learned and profoundly original thinker.

To the wider general public Ogden was best known for his invention of Basic English, a "boiled down" version of English which he put forward as an international language, and the furthering of which became the main interest of his life. Among his other works *The Meaning of Meaning* (written in collaboration with Professor I. A. Richards) was a very serious, solid, and enlightened attempt to go more deeply into the psychological basis of linguistics than any earlier scholar had gone.

Ogden was born in 1889, son of C. B. Ogden, and was educated at Rossall School. He was later a Magdalene man, and did most of his work in Cambridge. The explorations which at length resulted in *The Meaning of Meaning* were begun as long ago as 1910. The book itself appeared at the beginning of 1923 and aroused considerable attention in scholarly circles, especially in America, where it was very soon put into the official university curriculum at Columbia and elsewhere. It had reached a fourth English edition by 1936. Profound and subtle in analysis and synthesis, abstruse in argument, logical in method, it was the first serious attempt to consider the central linguistic problem of meaning in the light of modern psychological research. The volume was published as one of the "International Library of Psychology, Philosophy, and Scientific Method", of which Ogden acted as general editor. The series was planned to give in convenient form, and at a moderate cost, a set of authoritative works on psychology and allied studies. Its scope was wide (a random choice of titles would cover, for example, telepathy, Greek philosophy, human speech, and the development of the sexual impulses); and in addition to expository works it included highly original (and in due course famous) works like Jung's* *Psychological Types* and Lange's *History of Materialism.*

Out of certain considerations put forward in *The Meaning of Meaning* arose Ogden's great invention of "Basic English", the book of that name appearing in 1930. Having in view the desirability of an international tongue, Ogden argued that English, or rather a severely simplified version of English, had manifest advantages over purely artificial languages like Esperanto and Ido. The first and greatest of these was that English is already the native tongue of many millions in the British Commonwealth and America, and that it is widely known in Germany, Scandinavia, and elsewhere. The fewness of inflexions is another point in its favour. After long and careful thought Ogden produced a Basic vocabulary of only 850 words which, he claimed, would serve for all ordinary purposes. He even made the curious claim that Basic had "no verbs"; but it has, in fact, 18, like "be", "come", "get", and "put", described as "operators". From the Orthological Institute, which he founded at Cambridge, there came forth a long series of books on Basic and translations thereinto. The whole idea was one of the most interesting educational notions of our generation.

Another absorbing interest of Ogden's was the mind and work of Jeremy Bentham, on which he wrote more than one book. His *The Meaning of Psychology* (1926) was a profound study of the relationship between mind and expression. With Professor Richards he also wrote *The Foundations of Aesthetics* (1922). Ogden was a man of remarkably wide interests and the brightest intellectual endowments. Psychology and linguistics by no means absorbed all his time and energy. He was an expert photographer, familiar not only with technical procedures but with the laws of light; he had considerable knowledge of electricity and acoustics, and could and did invent machines in this line of study. A restless, fanatical, lucid expositor of his ideas, he was a witty, devastating and indefatigable controversialist, especially when launched on his favourite subject, Basic. Ogden was a sensitive and kindly man, a connoisseur of good living, and an excellent host.

March 23, 1957.

The Grand Duchess Olga Alexandrovna of Russia, youngest daughter of Tsar Alexander III, died in Toronto on November 24, 1960 at the age of 78.

The Grand Duchess Olga was a remarkable example of courage, fortitude, and the spirit of forgiveness. She was the youngest sister of the last Tsar of all the Russias, Nicholas II, who was shot dead in July 1918 with his wife and five children in a cellar at Ekaterinburg. Though she had witnessed herself the brutal side of the revolution, her faith in the Russian people was never shaken, and her country came first and foremost in her thoughts and feelings.

The Grand Duchess was born on June 1, 1882, at Peterhof, the summer residence of the Russian court, built by Catherine the Great on the model of Versailles. Languages played a great part in the education of the two daughters of the Tsar, and the Grand Duchess Olga had completely mastered Russian, English, French, and German at an early age. She was brought up in the faith of the Greek Orthodox Church and, if part of her religious education was formal, it had a deep spiritual side. Sport was not neglected and she early became an excellent horsewoman.

The Grand Duchess was only 12 when her father died and her brother came to the throne. When she grew up the time of the splendid receptions was over, as the new Tsaritsa was inclined to a secluded life. The last big ball in the Winter Palace, where all the guests had to wear the Russian dress of the sixteenth century, was held in January 1903. There was less and less intercourse between the Tsar Nicholas and his people, and a cloud of sadness hung over the reigning family.

In July 1901 the Grand Duchess was married to Duke Peter of Oldenburg, a man whose chief interest in life was the management of his vast estates. She entered with zeal into the activities of her father-in-law, who was the only member of the family to take an interest in social work. He was the chief of the Russian medical aid service, and had done much to improve sanitary conditions and to combat infectious diseases in Russia. Her married life, however, proved to be unhappy, and in 1916 the Tsar and the Church dissolved her marriage.

When the First World War broke out the Grand Duchess devoted herself to Red Cross work. From 1915 she was at the head of her own hospital at Kiev, where she shared the hard daily work of the trained sisters. Many of her wounded found it difficult to believe that this cheerful, unassuming woman, with her friendly smile and shining grey eyes, was the sister of the Tsar. In November 1916 the Grand Duchess married morganatically a captain of the Guards Cavalry, Nicholas Koulikovsky, a member of the Russian nobility. She went to a priest at Kiev and asked him to celebrate the marriage at once, although it was Lent, during the leave of her fiancé, who was going soon to the front.

The Revolution found her at Kiev with her mother and her sister, the Grand Duchess Xenia [q.v.] who died in April 1960. At first they were treated with respect and suffered no personal discomfort, but soon she, like all members of the Imperial family, were declared "the enemies of the revolution and the Russian people". The Dowager Empress and her daughters made efforts to join the Tsar at Tsarkoe Selo, but were not allowed to do so. Then an order was given to them to leave Kiev and to retire immediately into their Crimean estate. There they lived for several months under menace of death.

Ultimately the Dowager Empress and the other members of the family were rescued by H.M.S. Marlborough. The Grand Duchess, however, did not want to leave Russia, and she and her husband stayed in the south with the White Army. Like the families of those whose men were fighting in the civil war, she had often to live in a railway van or a peasant cottage. The 10 officers attached to her person by the General Command to protect her from a sudden Bolshevik raid were not always able to find her and her family other accommodation. When the end came—she was found by American Red Cross workers living in a railway van with other refugees—the Grand Duchess sailed from Novorossisk with her husband and her two sons for Denmark, where she settled.

A few years later the Grand Duchess bought a farm near Copenhagen with money inherited from her mother, and thus was able to give a proper education to her two sons and to shelter some of her old servants. She was full of energy and herself undertook a great part of the management of the farm. Since 1948 she had lived quietly in Cooksville, near Toronto.

The Grand Duchess had an undoubted gift for painting in both oil and water-colours. Her favourite subjects were flowers, Russian landscapes, and character studies of Russian soldiers. An exhibition of her work in London in May 1936 pleased the critics and brought a substantial sum for the Russian refugees. She had a second show in London just before the outbreak of the Second World War.

Over the Anastasia controversy, which has come alive of recent years, the Grand Duchess had early taken her stand. She strongly denied the claims of the woman now living in seclusion in southern Germany to be the Tsar's daughter, Anastasia Nikolaievna, finding no resemblance to the girl whose aunt and godmother she had been. She is reported to have remarked on one occasion when interviewed by the press: "This affair will plague me all my life". The Grand Duchess was, however, resigned, believing the dispute would continue if only because people love a mystery.

Those who met the Grand Duchess fell under the spell of her charm. Brought up in the seclusion of an old-fashioned court, she remained the typical Russian gentlewoman so well pictured by the novels of the great Russian writers, with their culture, refinement, and calm heroism in time of adversity.

November 26, 1960.

Dr. F. W. Oliver, D.SC., F.R.S., Professor Emeritus of Botany in University College, London, died suddenly at his home at Limpsfield, Surrey, on September 14, 1951 at the age of 87.

Francis Wall Oliver was born at Richmond in 1864 and, as the only son of Daniel Oliver, F.R.S., the Keeper of the Herbarium at the Royal Botanic Gardens, Kew, he was brought up in an atmosphere of botany and was wont to recall how he delighted to show the squirting cucumbers to distinguished visitors whom he induced to poke the ripe fruits that were appropriately orientated. He was educated at the Friends' schools at Kendal and York, at University College London, and Trinity College, Cambridge, and never lost his boyish charm or enthusiasm to the end of his life. Whether he was indulging in his favourite recreation of climbing in the Alps, surveying a salt marsh or investigating a palaeobotanical specimen, it was all an intriguing pursuit in which it were better to travel hopefully than to arrive. Appointed to the Quain Professorship of Botany in University College London at the early age of 24, Oliver occupied the chair for 41 years. In two directions his botanical work was of a pioneer character.

Oliver was the first to obtain incontrovertible proof that the fern-like plants of the coal measures were in fact seed-bearing species, a piece of first-class detective work that was so revolutionary in its implications that he invited Dr. D. H. Scott to collaborate with him so that the account of *Lagenostema Lomaxi* could have the authority of his senior's experience. Oliver's later accounts of the seeds *Physostema elegans* and *Polylophospermum,* and those by him and his pupils of other reproductive and vegetative organs of the Pteridosperms, placed our knowledge of this group of extinct plants on a broad and firm foundation.

The second direction in which Oliver played a conspicuous pioneering role was in the dynamic approach to ecology at a time when the subject was in danger of becoming purely descriptive. He played an important part in the promotion of the study of ecology in Britain, and in the early years of the century he initiated practical field classes in this subject by taking his senior students to investigate salt marsh vegetation in relation to the habitat conditions for a fortnight each year in Brittany, and later in Norfolk, a mode of instruction that has now become generally adopted.

After leaving University College Oliver was for a few years Professor of Botany at the Egyptian University at Cairo and then retired to live at Burg-el-arab. He was elected to the Royal Society in 1905 and was awarded the Linnean Medal in 1925. Oliver edited various works, of which the best known is the English translation of Kerner's *Natural History of Plants.* He was also for some years editor of the *Annals of Botany.*

He married in 1896 Miss Mildred Alice Thompson, who died in 1932. There were two sons of the marriage.

September 18, 1951.

The death at 58 of **Adriano Olivetti,** the head of the famous office equipment firm which bears his name, robs Italy of one of its most remarkable individualists. He suffered a stroke on the Milan-Lausanne express on February 27, 1960.

Olivetti was a highly successful industrialist, whose wide range of views and activities in the cultural, political, and social fields suggested something nearer the ideal of the complete man of an earlier age and time. There was something of the Renaissance in the breadth of his interests and in his patronage, and something of the eighteenth and nineteenth century progressives in his approach to his work—and to his workers.

To the British mind he recalled in certain ways Josiah Wedgwood, in his sense of beauty and consideration for his employees. And yet the products of his factories, such as typewriters, office furniture, and electronic equipment, were essentially of the modern world. He was considered a model employer. Moral issues played a part in many of his schemes, not only for the welfare of all those connected with the firm, but also in such truly humanitarian ventures as his decision to take industry to the under-developed southern regions of Italy. His comparatively new factory outside Naples, for instance, was not only an excellent example of design but a centre for assessing the abilities of the southern worker on the basis of thorough investigation. He gave a lead to the consciences of other Italian industrialists in his several southern projects, and some hard-headed encouragement as well by his carefully documented conclusion that the maligned southerner was as skilful as the Milanese or other experienced workers of the north in tackling the finer points of engineering.

He was born in April 1901 at Ivrea, where his main factories are now a national showpiece. After obtaining a degree in industrial chemistry he took a job as a worker in the family business. He followed this with a visit to the United States to study the development of industry there. After this experience he became in 1929 director-general and in 1938 chairman of the Olivetti company. Under his guidance it was built up as one of the most successful Italian concerns both at home and in the international market. At the same time he developed his views on design for which the firm is famous, on the comprehensive requirements of industrial and artisan communities, and on politics.

It is typical of him that he could see no way of applying his progressive political views through any existing political party. Instead he overcame more cautious counsels and formed his own, investing large sums of money in his Community Movement, with which he entered the last general election in 1958. The results were undoubtedly disappointing, bringing him only one seat in the Chamber, which he occupied himself until he resigned his mandate in 1959.

February 29, 1960.

Eugene O'Neill, whose death occurred at Boston, Massachusetts, on November 27, 1953, became between the wars America's leading dramatist.

His technical variousness, his adventurous agility among ideas, his high purpose and his large vitality carried his name round the world, and all but one or two of his plays have been performed, published, and widely discussed in Britain. They are for the most part powerful and defective. How far the best of them survive their own defects is a question that has always divided, and continues to divide, opinion. The highest of his titles to permanent fame beyond a doubt is the vast and lowering trilogy, *Mourning Becomes Electra,* a translation of the *Oresteia* into terms of American life at the end of the Civil War.

If O'Neill had been able to define his ideas in precise and pregnant language he would have a place among the immortals, but his literary powers were unequal to his dramatic genius. He sought to compensate for this essential lack by experimenting with various stage conventions, with the use of masks and of the chorus, with the "aside", and with the division of a single personality into two moral aspects, each represented by a different actor, and by using now one theatrical style, now another. But though he could create life in his characters and had something of value to reveal, the plays most fully charged with imaginative energy and tragic purpose (not excepting the Oresteian trilogy) are those which suggest most clearly that he was fundamentally at cross-purposes with his chosen medium. The theatre asked for memorable words; he, impotent to satisfy this insistent requirement, impatiently demanded of the theatre effects which it was incapable of giving him or anyone else. This conflict was never wholly resolved, and the plays suffer accordingly. They are nevertheless remarkable as the record of a passionate mind's restless, thrusting endeavour to express its own constantly changing vision of life through many different theatrical forms.

Eugene Gladstone O'Neill was the son of an actor and was born in New York on October 16, 1888, but by nature a rover and adventurer, he spent his youth knocking about the world in a variety of occupations. It may be that while he was observing life he should have been learning to write about it, and certainly his failure to form a style was to become his chief handicap as a dramatist. On the other hand, his imagination was training itself in these impressionable years to work freely outside the small and stale world framed by a proscenium arch, and it was not perhaps in his nature, richly gifted as it was, to make words a disciplined instrument of lucidity. The only formal training he received was in Professor G. P. Baker's playwriting class at Harvard, and in 1914 he wrote his first play, *Thirst.*

Access to the theatre was made easy in the next few years by his discovery of the Provincetown Players and their discovery of him. They produced a number of short plays of the sea subsequently given the general title of *S.S. Glencairn.* His association with these amateurs was possibly not an unmixed advantage. True, they provided the budding dramatist with a stage on which he could study his own work, but this admiring docility may well have encouraged him in the dangerous belief that the enlarged freedom he instinctively sought was to be gained by more violent means than by practising a more subtly exact obedience to the theatre's own laws. He was for the rest of his career to claim for the stage the liberties that are the natural inheritance of the novel.

His first full-length play, *Beyond the Horizon* (1920), won him the Pulitzer Prize. It revealed the two O'Neills that were to become familiar—the experienced observer setting down accurately and vividly what he had seen and the aspiring symbolist driven by a genuine poetic impulse but often betrayed into making an evidently forced poetic parade. *The Emperor Jones,* an exciting piece of expressionism not wholly dependent on the stage device of the persistent drum beat, was produced in the same year, and the plays that followed in the next three years established O'Neill's reputation abroad as well as in America. They were *Anna Christie* (1921), *The Hairy Ape* (1922), *All God's Chillun Got Wings* (1924), and *Desire under the Elms* (1924). The realist was the senior partner in the writing of these plays and his strength was impressively shown, especially in the dark and brutal story of New England peasants driving fiercely and ignorantly at the satisfaction of their primitive desires. But the symbolist regained the ascendancy in *The Great God Brown* (1926) and *Lazarus Laughed* of the same year. These attempts at philosophic drama fell into confusion, but the fierce attack on materialism represented by *The Great God Brown* was renewed in the mordant satire of *Marco Millions* (1928).

In the same year the faith of O'Neill's more ardent admirers was greatly fortified by *Strange Interlude,* a play devoting nine acts to a history of the seven ages of woman and holding the episodes together in tragic unity. It was in this play that extended soliloquy was used on a hitherto unexampled scale. With *Dynamo* (1929) the symbolist reasserted himself unsuccessfully, and it was in 1931 that O'Neill made his closest approach to genuine tragedy in *Mourning Becomes Electra.* Whether it be in fact tragedy or only a magnificently presented case-study of a family living under a perpetual curse, it cannot be gainsaid that the presence of evil is completely communicated. The play is alive in the sense that it gives life to the spectator's imagining and causes it to become the dramatist's ally. At all events, it is vastly superior to anything that came before or after. *Ah, Wilderness* (1933), a little comedy of family life, surprised by its gentleness and good humour; *Days Without End* by showing O'Neill, the ardent and versatile free-thinker, returning to more orthodox ways of thought; and *The Iceman Cometh*—heralded as the first of a great cycle of dramas studying modern America—by its emptiness.

O'Neill was awarded the Nobel Prize for Literature in 1936.

November 30, 1953.

Max Ophüls, the German-born French stage and film director, died in hospital in Hamburg on March 26, 1957. He was 54.

Born in Saarbrücken on May 6, 1902, he went on the stage at the age of 19 in Aachen, and at the age of 23 became a producer—the youngest ever to be on the staff of the Vienna Burgtheater. Later he turned his attention to film direction and made a name as a producer of witty, sophisticated pieces. His first big successes were for the German Ufa concern—*Die verkaufte Braut* and *Liebelei.* He left Germany in the thirties and directed films for French, Italian, and American companies. In Hollywood he was responsible for two films of unusual interest, *The Reckless Moment,* a story of blackmail and sudden death, and *Letter from an Unknown Woman.* In other hands this was a film that might well have been dismissed as a crude exercise in sentimental melodrama, but Ophüls's sensitive direction made it throughout an exact and moving description of the emotions and mental processes of a woman whose life is wholly dedicated to a musicianly philanderer she met by accident when he lodged in the house in which she lived as a young girl. This was a part admirably played by Joan Fontaine.

To the great mass of the British cinema-going public, with its craving for "stars" and its ignorance of directors. Ophüls was not well known until *La Ronde* came to London, there to equal an American musical show with its staying power. Here Ophüls brilliantly exploited a theme of lovers playing an amorous form of musical chairs. He had a remarkable cast including Anton Walbrook*, Odette Joyeux, Simone Signoret, Simone Simon, Serge Reggiani, Danielle Darrieux, Daniel Gelin, Jean-Louis Barrault, and Isa Miranda, and he made a memorable film.

As he demonstrated in *Le Plaisir* and *Madame de* . . . . the former film made up of three of de Maupassant's short stories and the latter based on a story by Louise de Vilmorin, Ophüls showed himself to be something of a master in the difficult art of transferring to the screen the anecdote or short story that relied for its main effect on the careful mingling of the ironic and the tender.

His last film, *Lola Montès*, with Peter Ustinov and Martine Carol, was the subject of a dispute between the director and the producers, Gamma Films. Ophüls originally edited *Lola Montès* in the form of a complicated series of flashbacks, in which episodes in the life of the dancer alternated with their reconstruction in a circus. This bizarre version was a commercial disaster in France, in spite of its Cinemascope and lavish costumes, since the public found it far too obscure and undramatic. So the producers had it re-edited in a chronological form that is simpler to understand but neatly kills the irony and subtlety of the original.

March 27, 1957.

Paul Oppé, C.B., who died on March 29, 1957 at the age of 78, was a remarkable example of a man who achieved distinction in two different spheres of activity—as an official of the Board of Education, and as a connoisseur and art historian.

Adolph Paul Oppé, a son of the late S. A. Oppé, was born in London on September 22, 1878. He was educated at Charterhouse, at St. Andrews University, and at New College, Oxford, where he was an exhibitioner and took first classes in Classical Moderations and in *Literae Humaniores.* After brief periods as lecturer in Greek at St. Andrews and in Ancient History at Edinburgh, he entered the Board of Education in 1905 and remained there until his retirement on reaching the age of 60 in 1938. From 1930 he had been a principal assistant secretary, and in 1937 was appointed C.B. It was as an official of the Board that he served from 1910 to 1913 as Deputy Director of the Victoria and Albert Museum. He was eventually head of the branch dealing with the training of teachers, a subject in which he had a deep personal concern.

Oppé's artistic interests were always strong, and as early as 1909 his book on Raphael appeared, to be followed by one on Botticelli in 1911. His love of Italian painting remained keen through his life, but it was with English art, and especially with English watercolour and other drawings, that his name became principally associated. In 1923 he published a finely illustrated volume on Rowlandson, and the same year also saw a book on Cotman. Two years later came one on the watercolours of Turner, Cox, and de Wint. In 1934 a remarkable long essay on early Victorian painting in the composite volume on Early Victorian England (edited by G. M. Young [q.v.]) drew the attention of a wider public to Oppé's work as a critic.

After his retirement Paul Oppé was able to devote himself entirely to his artistic work. One of his most important tasks was the critical study and recataloguing of the earlier English drawings in the Royal Library at Windsor; his *catalogue-raisonné* of the drawings of Thomas and Paul Sandby at Windsor, which was published in 1947, cleared away a great deal of untenable legend from the biographies of the brothers; and his similar volume, published in 1948, on the drawings of Hogarth, which, though it drew largely upon the Windsor collection, was not limited to it, proved immensely valuable in supplying a basic *corpus* of drawings firmly established as by Hogarth, and in cutting away much that had been falsely attributed to him. The catalogue of the *English Drawings, Stuart and Georgian Periods,* at Windsor, issued in 1951, threw most interesting light on the origins and growth of the Royal Collection. The latest of Oppé's critical works, dealing with Alexander and John Robert Cozens, was published in 1952.

It contained the conclusions of many years' detailed and careful study of these two great draughtsmen, and was more easily and readably written than, for example, the very difficult introduction to his Hogarth catalogue.

The strength of Oppé's work lay in his combination of a delicate aesthetic perception with a searching mind which was unwilling, without serious examination, to accept unsupported statements as facts. He did much to free the history of English drawing from the cloud of myth that had settled upon it. As a collector he was, upon his own lines, one of the most percipient, and again and again bought important drawings without any reference to current fashion. Many artists (notably Francis Towne and his amateur pupil, John White Abbott, to each of whom he devoted a pioneer article in the publications of the Walpole Society) owe their present reputation very largely indeed to Oppé. Apart from his English drawings, those in his collection by Italian masters were notably fine.

In spite of an occasional capriciousness, which his friends were inclined to attribute to uncertain health, Paul Oppé's judgment about old drawings, whether British or foreign, was held in the very highest regard by fellow scholars. For many years he had advised the National Gallery of Canada about the purchase of works of this kind. The chief treasures of his collection were frequently to be seen in important loan exhibitions, and he often showed great kindness to other students. No man was more careful and assiduous in watching, and taking notes of, whatever passed through the principal London sale-rooms, where his slight, rather stooping figure, sallow complexion, and black, curling hair, which remained almost unsilvered to the end, will be much missed.

He married in 1909 Valentine, daughter of the late Rev. R. W. L. Tollemache. She died in 1951. They had a son and a daughter, who survive them.

April 1, 1957.

Sir Ernest Oppenheimer died suddenly at his home at Johannesburg on November 25, 1957. He was 77.

Oppenheimer was one of a well-known family of brothers, distinguished by personal popularity, who had all been more or less closely associated with mining and finance in South Africa. One of the brothers will be recalled in connexion with the efforts that were made—unfortunately without enduring success—to establish a diamond cutting industry at Brighton (in which ex-soldiers were to be largely employed) shortly after the war.

It used to be said that Ernest Oppenheimer "got into the limelight" *via* politics. Precisely the converse was correct. It was because he had attained by spectacular strides to a position of dominance in diamond and gold mining—with their related finance—that it became virtually a necessity to follow up his vast trusteeship into the Legislature. Arriving there after the general election of 1924 as member for Kimberley—Rhodes's old constituency—Ernest Oppenheimer was at once accepted as the authoritative spokesman not only of the diamond industry but also of the highly important and complex interests involved in the South African mining industry as a whole. In doing this Oppenheimer filled a position that was strangely and, considering the vast interests to be cared for, rather obviously vacant.

Outside Parliament, too, a similarly peculiar situation was apparent about the time when Oppenheimer was asserting his claim to leadership and power in the great mining enterprises on which the South African fabric rests. There were vacant chairs in *the* industry. Outstanding leaders of the early days also had founded "houses" and become "Rand magnates", had passed on, or retired, leaving no comparable successors. Ernest Oppenheimer fitted—and filled—some of those vacant chairs. It was perhaps fortunate for him, but it was just as well for the industry. In politics Oppenheimer had both ambition and ability. He was one of the leaders of the South African Party and a political friend of General Smuts. It is probable that on a return of the South African Party to power, and assuming Oppenheimer's business interests would allow him to give the requisite time, General Smuts would have made the member for Kimberley his Minister of Finance.

He was born at Friedberg, Hesse, on May 22, 1880, the son of Edward Oppenheimer. At the age of 16 he followed an elder brother to London to work in a firm of diamond merchants—Dunkelsbuhlers—where his abilities were soon recognized, and he went to Kimberley in 1902 as a representative of the firm. Always a man who took, or seemed to take, great risks, he quickly established himself as a leader in the diamond trade. Side by side with his business activities, he occupied himself in the municipal affairs of the diamond capital. He was Mayor of Kimberley in 1913-15, and in that capacity had a main part in raising the Kimberley regiment at the outbreak of the Great War. In 1917 Oppenheimer formed the Anglo American Corporation of South Africa, of which he was chairman and a permanent director until 1953, in which year he became an ordinary director while retaining the chairmanship. Two years later the corporation acquired important holdings in South West Africa. With these in hand Oppenheimer brought into being what was in effect an amalgamation of his own powerful interests with those of De Beers in the amazingly rich ex-German territory which passed under mandate to the Union *via* the Treaty of Versailles.

Towards effecting his purpose Oppenheimer had held two very strong cards: he had succeeded in enlisting the powerful Morgan finance from America in South African mining; and this, coupled with the ability of the potentially profuse diamond output of South West Africa to flood the market, naturally disposed the great diamond corporation of De Beers to appreciate the strength of Oppenheimer as a new factor in this sphere—an appreciation which, duly translated into business terms, established the diamond monopoly as it exists to-day. There could be no better proof of Oppenheimer's personal force and commanding financial ability than the fact that—a condition precedent to this achievement—he had succeeded in impressing his ascendancy on the wealthy Barnato group, and so acquiring the chief shareholding and directional control of De Beers, with their allied mines, the Premier, Jagersfontein, and the Consolidated South West Africa enterprise.

The Anglo American Corporation, inspired by Oppenheimer's leadership and foresight, made rapid progress, becoming heavily interested in the gold, diamond, and copper mining industries, and, in general, occupying a position of great prominence in the mining and finance of South Africa. In the diamond world in particular the extent of Oppenheimer's range and success may be gauged by his chairmanships, which included those of the Consolidated Diamond Mines of South West Africa, the Diamond Corporation, and the Premier Diamond Mine.

His mastery in the great diamond monopoly was finally consolidated in his election to the chairmanship of De Beers in 1929. As a gold-mining house, the Anglo American controls such great producers of the Far East Rand as Brakpan, Springs, West Springs, and Daggafontein; and, in concert with Lewis and Marks and the Union Corporation, is interested in Grootvlei. In 1926 Anglo American began to concern itself in the "coming" mineral of South African—copper. To consolidate its important holdings in Northern Rhodesia, Rhodesian Anglo American was formed in 1929. Of this company Sir Ernest—he was knighted in 1921—was chairman, and he was also one of the vice-chairmen of the Rhokana Corporation.

Oppenheimer was eminently a man of the happy life. With all his wealth he was unpretentious, of simple tastes, and fond of his home.

In the midst of his multifarious activities he found time for golf. Success came to him early, and easily; or so it seemed. Actually he was destined for success by his commanding grasp, understanding of men, strong concentration, and untiring zeal in all that he undertook. He had great charm of manner—"like all the Oppenheimers", people would say; and it was another familiar remark that "Oppenheimer always gets his own way".

He was really popular, had many friends, and no enemies. With these gifts, and a way of doing business which won and held the confidence of all who had dealings with him, he was clearly marked out for leadership and the handling of great enterprises. Although his companies concerned in diamonds and copper sustained vast losses by depreciation in the world slump which culminated in 1932, their foundations had been laid too strongly for the essential fabric to be endangered. It was generally held that, given such a reasonable improvement in world conditions as would allow diamonds and copper to "come into their own", Ernest Oppenheimer would take rank as the biggest man in minerals in Europe, rivalling even the mighty Guggenheims in the American field.

Oppenheimer's philanthropy was stealthy and imaginative. His work for the improvement of African living conditions was carried out without ostentation or fuss. Queen Elizabeth House at Oxford was founded in June 1954 under the joint auspices of Oxford University and the Colonial Office with a gift of £100,000 from Oppenheimer and a grant of £50,000 from the Colonial Development and Welfare Fund for capital expenditure. He took a deep interest in Commonwealth studies at Oxford and helped to open up a number of new branches of work in this field. His family had had many connexions with Oxford and he himself was made an honorary Doctor of Civil Law of the University in 1952.

In the Union Parliament—in which he sat until 1938—Oppenheimer was accounted a good speaker. He used a remarkably cogent, though non-rhetorical, style, never committing himself to a statement which could not be strictly squared with the facts. So that, in this critical sphere also, the Oppenheimer habit of "getting his own way with everybody" generally held good. Certainly he was by far the most impressive and acceptable "magnate" that the "big interests" had ever had to represent them in the Union Parliament. He both liked and was liked by the Dutch.

Sir Ernest married in 1906 Mary Lina, daughter of Joseph Pollak. They had two sons, of whom Harry Oppenheimer survives. Lady Oppenheimer died in 1934. He married secondly in the following year Caroline Magdalen, daughter of Sir Robert Grenville Harvey, second and last baronet, and widow of Sir Michael Oppenheimer, second baronet.

November 26, 1957.

Vittorio Orlando, last of the "Big Four" of Versailles and Prime Minister of Italy in the latter part of the 1914-18 war, died in Rome on December 1, 1952 at the age of 92.

An eminent jurist and parliamentarian who contributed largely, as Prime Minister in 1917, towards rallying the broken Italian spirit after the defeat of Caporetto, Orlando was above all a fanatical and unrepentant nationalist. As the Italian representative at the Paris peace conference in 1919—he was, with Clemenceau, Lloyd George, and Wilson, a member of the Council of Four—his nationalism became the expression of his countrymen's hunger for what they considered the just rewards of having fought the war on the side of the allies. Nearly 30 years later, when the Italian peace treaty was signed, Orlando, then nearly 90, was able to marshal again, with scarcely diminished frenzy, the old arguments about the injustices done to Italy by those with whom she had fought. Though many Italians deplored or ridiculed his Sicilian emotionalism and bombast, his integrity and his unrivalled span of public life gave him a unique and revered position as the doyen of the Italian political scene.

Vittorio Emanuele Orlando was born at Palermo in 1860 and after a period as Professor of Constitutional Law, entered public life in 1898, when he was, as a Liberal, elected deputy for Palermo. He was made Minister of Public Instruction in the Giolitti Cabinet of 1903. His appointment caused a considerable sensation, for the portfolio had usually gone to a deputy who had at one time been an Under-Secretary of State, whereas Orlando had been in the Chamber for only five years and had never held office before. Giolitti, however, had no reason to regret his choice, and when he formed his fourth ministry in 1907 he appointed Orlando Minister of Grace and Justice, which portfolio was again entrusted to him in the Salandra Ministry of March 1914.

From the outbreak of war in 1914 Orlando was wholeheartedly on the side of the allies, and in the National Defence Ministry of Boselli he held the most important portfolio, that of the Interior.

In 1917 he became Prime Minister. It was a crucial moment. The Italian Army, riddled with Bolshevist and pacifist propaganda and badly led, had crumpled at Caporetto, and the morale of the country was at a low ebb. Orlando organized the Unione Sacra, a form of patriotic national front, and was able by the following year so far to restore the situation that, with substantial French and British help, the Italians routed the Austro-Hungarian Army at Vittorio Veneto.

The armistice brought political difficulties to Italy as to the other allied countries, and the enthusiastic welcome given to President Wilson in January 1919 did not, unfortunately, mean that the country was united in its peace policy. After a number of heated Cabinet meetings Nitti and Bissolati resigned from the Government and public opinion was turning against Orlando before he went to Paris as head of the Italian peace delegation. Much of the blame for Italy's failure to win support in Paris was doubtless due to Baron Sonnino, the

Foreign Minister, but the general public naturally reproached the Prime Minister.

The role of the Italian delegation to the peace conference, which Orlando led, was in many ways an impossible one from the start. As [Sir] Harold Nicolson* has shown, the clash of principle between the secret treaty of London, by which Great Britain and France stood pledged to reward Italy in the Adriatic for having entered the war on the side of the allies, and the Wilsonian concept of self-determination, was complete and irremediable. Furthermore, Italian public opinion, fired with war and nationalist propaganda of the brand of D'Annunzio, was expecting much more of the spoils than ever looked like being accorded. Nevertheless, nothing of this can justify the depths and heights of sophistry and obstruction to which Orlando and Sonnino treated the conference, and which culminated in Orlando leaving Paris in tears. He would have done his country better service and perhaps achieved better results by adopting a less intransigent attitude. On his return to Rome he was greeted with the wildest enthusiasm, but when it was found that the gesture had in fact achieved nothing it was clear that a change of government had become imperative. Italy was convinced that her claims were just; President Wilson was convinced that they were not. The clash of principle was abrupt and final. In June 1919 Orlando resigned and was replaced by Nitti. After the general elections of 1919 Orlando was elected president of the Chamber of Deputies, and this post he held with scrupulous fairness and real success until the fall of the Nitti Government.

After a courageous but unsuccessful attempt to reconcile Fascism with the democratic process, Orlando retired as a resolute anti-Fascist into private life in 1925, not to emerge again until after the liberation of Rome in 1944. Thenceforward his role was that of the respected elder statesman who, as heir to an earlier democratic tradition, exercised a considerable influence during the formative period of the new Italian Republic. Increasing years in no way abated his nationalism, which at times became a bitter xenophobia; he formally resigned his seat in the Constituent Assembly as a protest against the signing of the peace treaty in 1947, and in May 1950, within a few days of his ninetieth birthday, made, in the Senate, an impassioned attack lasting two hours upon the Government's foreign policy, in which he implied that it would be better for Italy to withdraw from the Atlantic Pact rather than suffer the treatment accorded her by the allies over Trieste and other questions. It was on this occasion also that he gave vent to his mortified feelings with the startling slogan of "Io odio l'Europa!" (I hate Europe). For all the intemperance of the sentiments, however, Orlando's power of oratory and his venerable white-haired figure evoked a feeling of respect and affection which was shared by virtually all Italians.

Although he will be best remembered as an elder statesman of Italy, it should not be forgotten that he had a lifelong and distinguished career in the law and until shortly before his death he continued to appear as an advocate in the Court of Cassation in Rome.

December 2, 1952.

José Ortega y Gasset, one of the most prominent Spanish philosophers of the century, died in Madrid on October 18, 1955 at the age of 72.

A humanist in the tradition of Goethe, he had a wide-ranging intellect and a surprising fecundity, but he also had a pragmatic talent for illuminating the problems of contemporary civilization. This is not a talent which in any country brings official popularity, and Ortega, like so many other Spanish intellectuals, knew exile. His *Revista del Occidente* achieved a position which set it in the same category as the *Nouvelle Revue Française,* but the freedom of expression he permitted himself and his contributors often offended his more orthodox compatriots. Yet he had the rare ability to perceive in what essential elements truth can be called the same in all places by men of the most varied traditions and beliefs; and his teaching as a whole must be acknowledged to possess a value to our time which is both apposite and rare.

Printers' ink flowed into the veins of José Ortega y Gasset from both sides of the family, and he himself said he was "born in a printing press", as either of his parents' surnames might suggest to persons versed in the history of Spanish journalism, for the signatures of Ortega Munilla and Eduardo Gasset were well known in their day. The birth of Ortega's son and Gasset's grandson occurred on May 9, 1883, in Madrid, though it was at Málaga that the boy attended a Jesuit college before entering Madrid University. Later he finished his education in Germany, where he was deeply influenced by those German philosophers who were to set so clear a mark on all his writings from the age of 26 until the end of a long distinguished literary career. On his return to Spain in 1909 he taught at the Senior Law School, which had just been founded, and the following year he was elected to the Chair of Metaphysics in his old university.

Ortega y Gasset's first book, *Meditations on Don Quixote,* was published in 1914; it impressed the critics as remarkably mature, and was succeeded at brief intervals—for, like most Spanish authors, Ortega was wonderfully prolific—by a series of lucid essays and full-length commentaries on human behaviour, which included such important works as *Politics Old and New, The Spectator* (eight volumes, of which the first two appeared in 1916 and 1917), *People and Things* (1922), *Invertebrate Spain* (1923), *The Theme of Our Times, Atlantidas* (1924), *The Dehumanization of Art, Ideas on the Novel* (1925), *The Theory of Andalusia* (1927), *The Revolt of the Masses* (1929), *Mirabeau the Politician, Kant, Goethe, Systematic History,* and *Studies of Love* (1944), among many others.

For the most part Don José was his own publisher, since he had founded a highly selective magazine, *La Revista del Occidente.*

Contemporary problems were Ortega y Gasset's chief interest; he was naturally attracted to politics as a progressive thinker who made no secret of his Republican ideals, in spite of his personal acquaintance with King Alfonso XIII. He was a contributor to the Liberal newspaper *El Sol,* and there is no doubt that he helped to bring about the King's downfall by publishing in its columns an historic accusatory article entitled *Delenda est Monarchia.*

When the Second Spanish Republic was declared Ortega y Gasset rejoiced with his intellectual friends—Pérez de Ayala*, Marañón, García Valdecasas, and others—at the dawning prospect of democracy in Spain. He took his seat as a deputy in the Constituent Cortes which met to organize the new régime; but he soon found himself in disagreement with the majority and therefore formed his own party, to which he gave the unwieldy name "At the Service of the Republic". Subsequently his high hopes were dashed, and in practice the freedoms which he had advocated struck him as "sour and sad".

He returned to Spain from voluntary exile after the Civil War, and took up residence again in Madrid, but devoted himself solely to the non-political pursuits of philosopher and historian. In 1948 he criticized certain of Professor Arnold Toynbee's* ideas in a series of lectures, and in the following year he visited Germany on the occasion of Goethe's bicentenary.

Ortega y Gasset's chief works have been translated into half a dozen languages. More popular in style, less mystical in thought than his great contemporary, Unamuno, and better known as an interpreter of the Spanish genius than Ganivet, who died while Ortega was still at school, he ranks with them, whom he survived, among the foremost of modern prophets honoured in their own country and reckoned of universal significance abroad.

October 19, 1955.

Dr. C. S. Orwin, who died on June 30, 1955 at his home at Blewbury, Berkshire, was well known to agriculturists throughout Britain as a pioneer in the important subject of agricultural economics, and to a wider public for his studies of the open-field system and his bold policy for the future of British farming.

Charles Stuart Orwin was born at Warnham, Sussex, in 1876, the only son of F. J. Orwin. He began his education at Dulwich College and in the summer of 1894 went with his father to see the new agricultural college at Wye, being the first prospective student to the college. But it was unfinished and his father decided against entry that year, so he waited till October 1895. After completing the course he worked with a land agent in Tunbridge Wells, then had a brief engagement in the City but soon gave it up and returned in 1903 to Wye as lecturer in estate management. In 1906 he left to take charge of the Turnor estates in Lincolnshire, in a purely farming region; there he closely studied farm accountancy and drew up systems of book-keeping that the ordinary farmer could himself practise and from which he would obtain helpful information about the financial results of the various branches of the farm. In this he was largely influenced by the late A. D. Hall, under whom he had studied at Wye, and with whom he afterwards established a deep personal friendship.

Hall had always insisted on the need for putting farming on a quantitative basis, and making costs one of the chief branches of agricultural teaching: Orwin set out to devise methods and assemble data. He did this so effectively that when, in 1913, the Development Commission set up the Institute for Research in Agricultural Economics in the University of Oxford, he was the obvious man to take charge. The subject was entirely new, and he had to work out methods of investigation and of assessing the value of the results obtained. He wisely kept to quantitative data: he developed methods of costing suitable types of British farming and enlisted the support of numerous practical farmers who allowed him to keep their books and to make full use of all the figures obtained. So he was able to build up for the first time a mass of definitely ascertained data relating to the operations and processes of the farm.

The results enormously widened the possibilities of agricultural teaching. Strange as it may appear, lecturers on agriculture at that time could rarely furnish definite examples of costs; they had to confine themselves to rather vague general statements. The work assumed new importance during and after the 1914-18 War, when prices of agricultural produce had to be fixed, and the whole agricultural community, therefore, became deeply interested in costs of production. Orwin's data were of great value both to agriculturists and to the various Ministries in the difficult negotiations preceding the settlement. The high respect in which he was held was shown in 1917 when he was appointed a member of the Agricultural Wages Board; he served on this for four years.

He maintained his interest in the technical side of agriculture and, in spite of growing demands on his time, he held for 25 years the editorship of the *Journal* of the Royal Agricultural Society which he had undertaken in 1912. When in 1922 the Agricultural Tribunal of Investigation was set up, composed of three eminent economists, Sir William Ashley and Professors Adams and Macgregor, he was appointed agricultural assessor, and played an important part in the drawing up of their report, one of the best surveys that has been made of the position of agriculture in Britain; it was issued in 1924. A little later, in 1925, he became a member of the Food Council, on which he served for eight years.

Meanwhile his institute was prospering, for he succeeded in attracting a band of able, level headed young people, free from the prejudices and unbalanced views sometimes associated with agricultural politics. Among them were A. W. Ashby [q.v.], Keith Murray, A. Bridges and others, who became widely known for their excellent work. A steady stream of useful publications was issued. The first surveys were on a county basis, but after the surveys of agriculture of Oxfordshire and of Berkshire had been completed this method was given up; it necessitated the inclusion of so many subjects that the treatment could only be on broad general lines; moreover, county treatment meant a good deal of repetition because agricultural systems do not follow county boundaries. So a more fruitful method was adopted that allowed of much more detailed study: the surveys were narrowed down to specific subjects, *e.g.*, milk marketing, open-air dairying, rural industries, economics of small holdings. It is no detraction from this work that the method of surveying was afterwards fundamentally altered by the investigations of [Sir] R. A. Fisher* and F. Yates at Rothamsted; Orwin has the credit for first using surveys extensively in the study of agricultural economics. A summary of the work of the institute was published after it had completed its twenty-fifth year.

Orwin was deeply interested in agricultural history and perhaps his most important book was *The Open Fields* (1939), which he wrote in conjunction with his second wife, and in which he gave a detailed account of the system as exemplified by the open fields of Laxton. Here he used his standard method of taking a concrete example and developing it. He had earlier (1929) published an excellent account of reclamation on Exmoor Forest, a book written *con amore* as he was deeply interested both in land reclamation and in Exmoor, where he had made many delightful journeys from his comfortable house in Minehead. He accepted enthusiastically Hall's thesis that the traditional small units in English farming were uneconomic, that much larger units were needed, but that these could be achieved only if the Government acquired the whole of the agricultural land of the country and parcelled it out into fewer and larger farms. This he expounded with considerable skill in *Speed the Plough* (1942), a Penguin volume.

Both at Wye and at Oxford he enjoyed a great measure of respect and quiet popularity.

He married in 1902 Elise Cécile, daughter of Edward Renault, of Cognac, who bore him three sons and three daughters. She died in 1921. In 1931 he married Christabel Susan, daughter of the late Charles Lowry, sometime headmaster of Tonbridge.

July 1, 1955.

Mosheh Oved died on September 16, 1958. Mosheh Oved, to call him by the name by which he was best known—this was the name by which he was known in the Polish Ghetto; his real name was Edward Goodack, shortened by a London signwriter to Edward Good—was long an interesting personality. Connoisseurs visited his shop, overflowing with objects of antiquarian art, in Museum Street, London, and he will be much missed by a large circle, many not only customers but friends.

This circle ranged through all classes of society, for in his volume of reminiscences *Visions and Jewels* he mentions more than one collector who patronized him, even although apparently on the verge of starvation, and at the other extreme Queen Mary, always an eager collector, was a not infrequent visitor. The prices he used to place on his treasures were also adapted to any pocket, from a few pence to some hundreds of pounds.

Mosheh Oved was born in a small Polish town in the year 1885. He went to England to seek his fortune as a lad of about 17 at the beginning of the present century. He had had some training in watch-making in Poland and after two or three experiences in other occupations in London he found employment with a watch repairer and after a year or two set up business for himself on a very small scale in Museum Street.

This tiny shop whose contents were at its opening probably worth less than £10 developed until it reached its present status and size. From a cheap watch repairer he proceeded to deal in second-hand watches and other trumpery jewelry, and from them to more artistic objects, especially of antiquarian interest. This shop early took the name of Cameo Corner and for a time the owner was known as The Cameo King. These designations arose out of the purchase by him of four cameo brooches for two shillings, neither he nor the vendor knowing what they were. Their quick sale turned his attention to cameos, which he began to study, and he became one of the outstanding authorities on this minor art. His illustrated catalogue *Cameos and Inspiration Jewellery* was accepted as one of the authorities on the subject and attained the distinction of being translated into Chinese at the instance of the National Museum of Peking.

From cameos Mosheh Oved turned to antique watches and especially watch cocks—artistically carved plates taken from the interiors of these early watches, often illustrated with the portraits of the owners or makers. His collection of these plates at one time reached a total of 17,000.

Mosheh Oved was, however, not only a shopkeeper, collector, and antiquary. He was also a writer—first in Yiddish, later in English—a poet and to some extent a philosopher. His first autobiographical work, *Visions and Jewels,* published in 1923, has already been mentioned. It was followed two years later by another, *Gems and Life.* His first book, *Out of Chaos,* was of a philosophical character. *Liebenslieder* (1923) is a volume of light poetry. *Book of Affinity* (1933), which was illustrated by Sir Jacob Epstein [q.v.], is for the most part in verse but can hardly be classified. Other of his books are *For the Sake of the Days* (1940) and *In Chedararein* (1945).

It is difficult to describe his style. It is personal to himself. He cannot be said to belong to any school. His writings are all autobiographical in greater or less part. They show a light-hearted humour, always with flashes of optimism. As a reviewer in *The Times Literary Supplement* said of him: "Mr. Oved is a mystic, a man to whom every facet of human experience is, or should be, symbolical of a deeper hidden meaning . . . he translates these experiences from matter-of-fact and every-day life into another world".

September 17, 1958.

Will Owen, familiar to several generations as a humorous draughtsman and in particular as the illustrator of the novels and short stories of W. W. Jacobs, died on April 14, 1957 at his flat in Charterhouse Square. He was 88.

Will Owen was born at Malta in 1869, the son of Thomas Owen, an engineer in the Royal Navy, and went to England when he was a year old. He was educated at the Mathematical School at Rochester. As a young man he worked in the Post Office Savings Bank, as did W. W. Jacobs. Owen long afterwards told how their collaboration began when they went on a Saturday afternoon walk in Epping Forest, as a result of which Jacobs wrote a humorous article which Owen illustrated. It was offered to various papers, but always rejected. Soon, however, luck changed. Jacobs had work accepted by J. K. Jerome for the *Idler* and *To-day,* by the *Windsor Magazine,* and finally—in the middle nineties—by the *Strand Magazine.* Here for many years Jacobs and Owen became firmly established favourites, the one as author, the other as illustrator. Owen, indeed, recorded that he made between 300 and 400 drawings for Jacobs's stories.

The most characteristic of Owen's illustrations appear, in reproduction, like pure pen-and-ink drawings, though in fact he usually drew over a preliminary sketch in pencil. In this he resembled Phil May, to whom Owen's draughtsmanship owed a great deal, especially in the years before the First World War. But, though his lively and fluent pen outlines and vigorous diagonal hatching remind one of May, yet Owen was very far from being a mere imitator. He lacked the slightly bitter or satirical undercurrent of which one is conscious in Phil May, and substituted his own much more genially humorous personality. For many thousands of readers during the past 60 years Jacob's characters, especially his elderly seamen and the celebrated Night Watchman, who told so many of their adventures, were perfectly embodied in Owen's drawings. He recorded, in fact, with a truth which his humour infused without destroying or even much distorting, one phase of English life, small, perhaps, but highly idiosyncratic and characteristic.

Moreover, it was not only the persons, but the scene that he recorded—the back streets, the small old shop-fronts, the comfortable low-ceilinged bar-parlours of the little seaports. His frontispiece to *Salthaven* is a sensitive landscape drawing in pen-and-ink that admirably suggests the setting of the tale. When, as in the plates for *Captains All,* he seems to have worked up the drawing in watercolour, much of the individual flavour of his work is lost.

Owen was a frequent contributor of drawings to *Punch* and to many other English periodicals. His work was also known in America. His poster-designs include the earlier of the "Bisto Kids" series. He was, too, known as a lecturer and as a writer whose books included *Mr. Peppercorn,* a study of an amiable domestic philosopher, published in 1940.

In 1897 Owen married Margaret Florence Porteus. They had two daughters.

April 16, 1957.

P

By the death of **Juho Kusti Paasikivi,** which occurred in Helsinki on December 14, 1956, Finland has lost a statesman of exceptional distinction and a figure of unique authority in her national life since she became an independent and sovereign State in 1920. Sorrow at his death will be felt by almost every section of the Finnish public. He was 86.

Elected President, in succession to Marshal Mannerheim, in 1946 for the period until 1950, and re-elected by a handsome majority in 1950, Paasikivi had done more than any other man in Finland to establish stable and friendly relations with Russia. He remained President until his term of office expired in 1956. It was he who had led the Finnish delegation which negotiated the Treaty of Tartu with Soviet Russia in 1920, and he had taken part in almost all important Soviet-Finnish negotiations since then. From the outbreak of war in 1939 his attitude towards the Soviet Union, which the majority of his countrymen learnt to adopt through bitter experience, was firmly realistic: since Finland and Russia would always be neighbours, Finland could not afford to pursue a foreign policy which might lead her into conflict with Russia.

It was Paasikivi accordingly who sought to avoid war with Russia in 1939, who negotiated peace in the following March, who again opened armistice negotiations early in 1944, and who formed a Government in November of that year on the basis of a policy of peaceful cooperation with the Soviet Union. And the most striking tribute to his statesmanlike qualities of mind and force of personality lies in the fact that he, a Conservative and uncompromising apostle of economic liberty, could apparently make himself better understood and inspire greater confidence in Moscow than any other leading representative of his country.

Recognizing the clamant fact that Finland could not escape from her geographical position, he used all his considerable ability to retain the friendship of Russia and at the same time to prevent any attempt by communists in his own country to usurp power by unconstitutional means. Powerfully built, broad-shouldered, with a square, cropped head, a masterful nose, and commanding chin, he looked, which in fact he was, a strong and eminently dependable character.

Born on November 27, 1870, in the textile town of Tampere, Juho Kusti Paasikivi came of a family originally named Hellsten, which he himself, in denying that it was Swedish, traced back to pure Finnish peasant stock in the sixteenth century. He learnt Russian in youth, studied history, was an athlete and a singer, and engaged successfully in commerce and banking. For a brief period in 1918, after the Bolshevik revolution had allowed Finland to declare herself a sovereign and independent State, he was Prime Minister. He turned diplomatist when he was sent to Moscow in 1920 to negotiate terms of peace in confirmation of Russian recognition of Finnish independence. Thereafter he took no part for many years in public affairs.

Paasikivi's hour of opportunity did not come again until 1939. In October he headed the Finnish delegation that had been invited to Moscow to discuss the Soviet request for a revision of the frontier and the acquisition of the naval base of Hangö. A series of talks with Stalin [q.v.] and Molotov held out the hope of a satisfactory and peaceful issue: but, to his bitter disappointment, Paasikivi had in the end to acknowledge failure, and the Soviet invasion began on the last day of November. Nevertheless, it fell to him once more in the following March, when he was serving as Finnish Minister in Stockholm, to proceed to Moscow in order to negotiate terms of peace. Appointed Minister in the Soviet capital a month later, he held that post until May 1941, when his reluctance to be involved in any way in a possible war against Russia for the second time impelled his resignation.

He withdrew from affairs until the position of Finland as an ally of Germany in the war against the Soviet Union became patently desperate. In the autumn of 1943 there had been an abortive Finnish attempt to establish contact with Moscow, but even indirect peace negotiations were not opened until the following February, when Paasikivi paid what was ostensibly a private visit to Stockholm. At the end of March he was in Moscow, whence he returned a month later to Helsinki with the Soviet terms for an armistice. This was not concluded until September, and Finnish hesitations, which were overcome only when in August Marshal Mannerheim [q.v.] became President with the express purpose of getting the country out of the war and negotiating peace with the Allied Powers, undoubtedly cramped Paasikivi's style. He had, nevertheless, acquitted himself with characteristic resource and realism in his dealings with Moscow.

In November 1944 he became Prime Minister of a Government pledged to peaceful cooperation with Russia. In the following April, after the general election of the previous month, he resigned and formed a new Government, in which the Communists were included and from which only the Conservatives—the party with which he himself had been identified—were shut out. Then, in March 1946, on the resignation of Mannerheim, he succeeded to the Presidency. No one in Finland was better qualified than the new President to understand and to serve the country's immediate needs. He took every step to ensure that the obligations laid upon Finland by the peace treaty with the Soviet Union—which came into force in September 1947—were faithfully and scrupulously fulfilled; but he firmly resisted Communist pressure and penetration, notably after the communist *coup* in Prague in the spring of 1948. He remained in Helsinki during the negotiations in Moscow for the pact which Russia sought and which was signed in April, but evidently was in control at every stage of the proceedings. The presidential election of 1950 was marked by vigorous efforts by the communists in Finland to discredit Mr. Paasikivi. They did, in the event, increase slightly the proportion of the total votes cast for them, but Mr. Paasikivi was re-elected for a further term of six years, receiving 171 votes out of the total of 300 of the Electoral College, the next highest vote being the People's Democrat candidate, Pekhala, with 67.

In September 1954 Paasikivi was presented with the Order of Lenin by the Soviet Ambassador in Helsinki. This award of a high Soviet distinction to the President who did not sympathize with communism came as a surprise to the capital.

His term of office as President expired in 1956 and in the ensuing elections Kekkonen, the Prime Minister, was successful by a narrow majority.

December 15, 1956.

Eugenio Pacelli—See **Pius XII.**

Sir Leo Page, whose studies in the problems of crime and punishment have had a wide influence, died on August 31, 1951 at his home near Faringdon, Berkshire, at the age of 61.

Leo Francis Page was the youngest son of the late W. H. Page and was born on April 2, 1890. He was educated at Beaumont and University College, Oxford, and attended the Royal Military Academy, Woolwich, before being commissioned in the Royal Flying Corps, and served in France until 1916 as a flight commander, when he was invalided out of the Army. He then enrolled as a student of the Inner Temple and was called to the Bar in 1918. For many years thereafter he practised on the South-Eastern Circuit. In 1925 he was appointed to the Commission of the Peace for Berkshire and assiduously attended the sittings of the justices. As the years went by he formulated in his mind the body of principles in the administration of the criminal law and the punishment of offenders on which his reputation chiefly rests.

His first work on the subject, *Justice of the Peace,* was published in 1936 and received wide attention, and a second edition appeared in 1947. Whether viewed as a handbook for magistrates or as a programme for reform, it was a temperate and lucid treatise and had considerable influence on thought on a subject to which too little attention had been given. In *Crime and the Community,* published in 1938, he drew on his experience as a visiting magistrate to build up a view of the psychology of men in captivity and suggested that there should be three classes of prisons, the first emphasizing reclamation, the second deterrent, and the third for proven incorrigibles. *For Magistrates and Others,* which followed closely in 1939, was a series of addresses summing up the doctrine he had evolved up to that time.

His status as an authority on his subject was recognized in 1940 by his appointment as secretary of the Commissions of the Peace, a post he held until 1945. For the remainder of his life his help and guidance were in great demand as a member of the various official and unofficial committees set up to study the whole field of the administration of justice in courts of summary jurisdiction and the treatment of criminals. In 1947 he published *The Problem of Punishment* and in the next year *The Sentence of the Court.* Both were based on the discussions of the committees of the Home Office and elsewhere in which he had played an important part.

His last work, *The Young Lag,* published in 1950, reviewed the treatment of the young criminal in a humane and understanding manner. As an advocate of the reform of the penal system he was temperate and persuasive and there is little doubt that his ideas have greatly altered the views held not only by lawyers and officials, but also by the general public.

He was High Sheriff of Berkshire in 1937 and was knighted in 1948.

He married in 1916 Violet, daughter of Captain F. C. Loder-Symonds, who survives him together with two sons and a daughter of the marriage.

September 1, 1951.

Dorothy Paget, for many years a leading racehorse owner, died on February 9, 1960 at the age of 54.

The Hon. Dorothy Wyndham Paget was the second daughter of the first and last Baron Queenborough, G.B.E., sixth son of General Lord Alfred Paget, and a grandson of the first Marquess of Anglesey, by his first marriage to Pauline, daughter of William C. Whitney, sometime Secretary of the United States Navy. She was educated at Heathfield School, Ascot.

From her father Dorothy Paget inherited a love of the Turf—his horse St. Louis won the 2,000 Guineas in 1922—and from her mother's side a pretty fortune. Perhaps her most triumphant successes were brought her by the peerless Golden Miller, who won five Cheltenham Gold Cups and in 1934 the Grand National.

In the 1930s she became a leading buyer of bloodstock, eclipsing at one time even the Aga Khan [q.v.], but her purchases were not always fortunate. In 1936 she paid 15,000 guineas for the yearling Colonel Payne, who, 10 years later, was sold for only 250 guineas. Tuppence, also, did not fulfil her hopes. He cost 6,000 guineas as a yearling and the night before the 1933 Derby it was thought that he would win. His price came tumbling down from 100 to 1 to 10 to 1 but he finished nearer last than first, and in 1935 was sold for £300.

She made many attempts to win the Derby but success eluded her until 1943, when Straight Deal, ridden by T. Carey, won an exciting race by a head from Umiddad, with Nasrullah third. Miss Paget bred her winner herself—at her Elsenham stud—and, as a splendid supporter of racing and breeding for so many years, her win was an extremely popular one. Straight Deal was trained by Walter Nightingall and was only the second Derby winner to be trained at Epsom.

During the war she interested herself in the W.V.S. and had an ambulance built fitted with a refrigerator and cots, and this was used exclusively to evacuate babies from London to the country.

Miss Paget was a figure whom everyone knew on the racecourse. Dressed almost invariably in the same old tweed coat which she wore because she suspected that it brought her luck, she came with an entourage whose job was not only to keep her company but to find out the prices, carry messages, and place bets. More than one motor car was always taken to convey her in convoy to the course in case of a breakdown. Horses had been her hobby since childhood, and she had been an accomplished rider in the showring. Her first big successes as an owner were after she bought Golden Miller and Insurance. In the same year, 1932, they won the Gold Cup and the Champion Hurdle respectively, trained by B. Briscoe, the first of the many trainers she employed during her life. Insurance won the Championship again the following year, while Golden Miller proceeded to win the Gold Cup five times in all. When this great steeplechaser won the Grand National as well, in 1934, Miss Paget was worried about the crowds and the celebrations usual afterwards, for she had an antipathy to the public gaze and used her wealth to live as retired a life as could be managed. Her Roman Hackle won the Gold Cup in 1940, and Mont Tremblant won it once again for her in 1952. Solford might have emulated Insurance in the Champion Hurdle in 1939 but for falling at the last fence, and in 1940 he confirmed this view by beating the 1939 winner, African Sister, in it.

Distel was yet another Champion Hurdler for her in 1946. Her horses won many races on the flat, but her record there, with the exception of her Derby winner, Straight Deal in 1943, was not so magnificent, Miss Paget dearly loved a bet, and in particular she liked to raid small meetings like Folkestone or Windsor in an attempt to take three or four prizes in one afternoon. Her character was highly individualistic and among her eccentricities was a tendency after a failure to hold *postmortem* inquiries with her trainer in a draughty part of the racecourse, sometimes lasting for hours. When particularly put out she would address all her remarks to him through a third party. Her arrangements for future events often would begin after midnight on the telephone. Some of her trainers after Briscoe were O. Anthony, D. Snow, F. Walwyn, H. Jelliss, J. Rogers, W. Nightingall, and Sir Gordon Richards. Because of her anxiety to keep away from people she made few friends and did not take the place she deserved in racing.

February 10, 1960.

Dame Leila Paget, G.B.E., widow of the Rt. Hon. Sir Ralph Paget, P.C., K.C.M.G., C.V.O., the first British Ambassador to Brazil, died on September 24, 1958 at Kingston upon Thames. Quiet and self-effacing, she was much loved by her friends; but her claim to public remembrance will rest upon her devoted labours as nurse and matron in Serbia during the war of 1914-18. The tributes to her heroism and skill at that time came not only from allies but from Austrian and Hungarian soldier prisoners, many of whom owed their lives to her. In the Second World War her home became a convalescent home and she worked on Red Cross and welfare committees.

Louise Margaret Leila Wemyss Paget, the daughter of General Sir Arthur Paget and his wife, Minnie Stevens, of New York, was born in 1881. Her mother was a gay figure in Edwardian society, but Leila was delicate in health and had no taste for social amusements. In 1907 she married Ralph Paget, the diplomatist, a distant cousin many years older than herself. Sir Ralph Paget (as he became in 1909) was sent to Belgrade in July 1910, and both he and his wife came to love and understand the Serbians and to sympathize warmly with their national aspirations. During both the first and second Balkan wars Lady Paget ran a military hospital in Belgrade, receiving public thanks for her work.

This experience prepared her for the more onerous and hazardous task for which she volunteered in 1914. The Lord Mayor's Serbian Relief Fund organized a hospital unit, and Lady Paget (living for the moment in London) was put in charge of it, leaving England at the end of October. The promptness of this aid made it doubly valuable. At Skoplje she took over a gymnasium converted into a hospital of 330 beds and at once began to cope with an inrush of terribly wounded men.

Conditions of sanitation, victualling and supply were in the last degree appalling. There were times when the water was cut off for hours on end; public authorities had to be urged to attend to drains that cried out for attention; and there was a general shortage and primitiveness of equipment almost comparable to that which Florence Nightingale found at Scutari.

In spite of all, Lady Paget and her splendid staff worked wonders. Yet very soon typhus became a worse enemy than actual wounds. Spreading rapidly, it menaced the whole town, until by Lady Paget's efforts an isolation hospital was established. By the beginning of May 1915 Skoplje was cleared of typhus, but in the meantime the matron herself had caught the dread complaint and had gone to England to recuperate and report to her committee.

As soon as she was better Lady Paget returned to Serbia. She was with her unit in Uskub in October 1915, when that town was taken by the Bulgarians; and since by a misunderstanding there was insufficient transport to evacuate the patients the nursing staff remained with them. The British were for four months under the Bulgarians, kindly and courteously treated. Indeed, Lady Paget went with a mission of 32 members to Sofia as the guest of the Bulgarian Red Cross Society and was received by Queen Eleonore. In March 1916 the whole nursing unit was accommodated with a special train to Bucharest, honourably welcomed there, and repatriated the same month by way of Petrograd. On her return to England Lady Paget was appointed by King George V a Lady of Grace of the Order of St. John of Jerusalem.

In August 1916 the Pagets moved to Copenhagen, on Sir Ralph's appointment as British Minister there; and two years later to Rio de Janeiro, when the Legation in that city was raised to the status of an Embassy. In 1917 she was made G.B.E.

For her work in Serbia Lady Paget was invested by King Peter with the Grand Cordon of the Order of St. Sava, the country's highest decoration for which a woman is eligible. Her name was venerated in the country, and was given to one of the streets of its capital. In *The Times* there appeared in December 1918 a moving letter from Countess Michel Karolyi, Government Commissioner of the Hungarian Red Cross, which formed one more loving testimony to her care for enemy wounded, no less than for the Serbs. The Hungarian prisoners said of her: "She has been a mother to us; she was God's angel among us"; and that high tribute may well be her best epitaph.

September 25, 1958.

Sir Michael Palairet, K.C.M.G., successively British Minister and Ambassador to Greece, died in his sleep on August 5, 1956 at his home at Bossington, near Minehead, Somerset, at the age of 73.

Born on September 29, 1882, the second son of the late Captain C. H. Palairet, of Ledbury, Herefordshire, he was educated at Eton and joined the Diplomatic service as an attaché in 1905. Appointed to Rome in the ensuing year, he was promoted to third secretary in 1907 and in 1908 was transferred to Vienna. Soon after his transfer to Paris in 1913 he was promoted to second secretary and in 1917 went to Athens. He thus saw the Greek capital in both wars.

After working at the Paris Peace Conference in 1918-19, he was transferred to the Foreign Office staff, but in 1920 returned to Paris as first secretary. He went to Tokyo on promotion to Counsellor in 1922 and was serving there during the disastrous earthquake of 1923. Transferred to Peking in 1925, he did not remain there long, for he was brought back to the Foreign Office in 1926. After serving for a few months in Rome in 1928, he was appointed Minister to Romania in 1929 and remained there until called on to fill a similar post in Stockholm in 1935. Some two years later he succeeded Sir Walford Selby* as Minister to Austria and withdrew after the Nazi invasion.

He was appointed Minister to Greece in 1939 and, after the Nazis had invaded the mainland, he accompanied the King and the Government of Greece to Crete and escaped with them when the island was attacked. He remained accredited to the Greek Government until 1943, being promoted Ambassador in 1942. For the last two years of the 1939-45 War he served as an Assistant Under-Secretary of State in the Foreign Office.

He married in 1915 Mary de Vere, daughter of the late Brigadier-General H. W. Studd, C.B., C.M.G., D.S.O., who survives him together with a son and a daughter of the marriage.

August 6, 1956.

Professor Friedrich Adolf Paneth, F.R.S., Director of the Max-Planck-Institute for Chemistry, who died in Vienna on September 17, 1958 at the age of 71, was one of the first to realize the value of radioactive materials as indicators or "tracers" which could be used to solve scientific problems of many kinds.

For this work, done in collaboration with Professor G. Hevesy, he will hold an assured place in the history of science. It was more remarkable that it was begun 20 years and more before the discovery of artificial radioactivity by the Joliot-Curies [q.v.]. Yet in these early experiments, done at a time when only two of the more familiar chemical elements—lead and bismuth—were available in radioactive form, Paneth and Hevesy arrived at the main principles which govern the uses of radioisotopes in research up to the present time.

In his own right Paneth was an expert also in the handling and measurement of very small quantities of gases, and applied the method of dating the edges of rocks by their content of helium gas to make estimates of the ages of meteorites—a field of work which he made very much his own.

Like many chemists of his generation he was internationally educated. The eldest son of Dr. Joseph Paneth, Lecturer in Physiology in Vienna University, he was born on August 31, 1887, and educated in the universities of Vienna, Munich, and Glasgow, where he worked in the laboratory of Professor (later Sir Frederick) Soddy [q.v.], who had been responsible for working out the chemical side of the chains of radioactive breakdown followed by radium and thorium. It was this period at Glasgow which determined the course of Paneth's later work. He obtained his Ph.D. at Vienna in 1910, and two years later became an assistant in the Institute for Radium Research, Vienna. He worked with Hevesy on the uses of radioisotopes of lead and bismuth formed during the breakdown of natural radio elements. In 1918, at the early age of 31, he was appointed to a Chair at the Prague Institute of Technology. An appointment to Hamburg University followed a year later. After three years there he moved to Berlin, and in 1929 was appointed Professor and Director of Chemical Laboratories at Koenigsberg University.

The rise of Nazism took him to England as a refugee in the 1930s. He was found accommodation at the Imperial College of Science, London, where he built his own apparatus for measurement of small quantities of helium gas. He spoke English fluently, and soon extended his circle of English friends. In 1938 he was appointed Reader in Atomic Chemistry in London University, and a year later to the Chair of Chemistry in Durham University.

With his training and experience in radioactive material, he was a natural recruit to the chemical side of atomic energy, and for two years—from 1943 to 1945—he was head of the chemistry division of the joint British-Canadian atomic energy team in Montreal.

After the war he returned to Durham, where a radio chemical laboratory was built for him.

Here he founded a school of research in what, in Britain, was substantially a new subject, and resumed his earlier interest in the ages of meteorites. When a meteorite fell on a hotel in Beddgelert he was as quick and keen to investigate as any young research student. He cooperated also in an American experiment, done with rockets, with the object of discovering how far up in the atmosphere mixing of the air continues to take place.

In 1952 he reached the age of 65 and the next year accepted the directorship of the Max-Planck-Institute for Chemistry. His laboratory remained an absorbing interest for him and he was glad at all times to receive visitors and discuss freely what work was being done.

As an example of an early use of radioisotopes, Hevesy and Paneth in 1913 published the results of an experiment in which they used a radioactive isotope of lead to measure the solubility of lead chromate, one of the most insoluble chemical salts known. They also used radioactive isotopes to discover where elements go in chemical reactions—a beginning of the "tracer" method as it is now called.

Paneth was interested, too, in the chemical classification of the elements, and was a recognized and sternly impartial authority on certain planes to the discovery of new elements which had led to controversy. In his own work he was meticulous in method and measurement yet at the same time an enthusiast. He had great charm of manner and a gift for a simple statement of principles.

Apart from his election as a Fellow of the Royal Society, his outstanding ability was recognized by the award of many other honours by foreign nations. He was Liversidge Lecturer of the Chemical Society in 1936, Halley Lecturer at Oxford in 1940, and Schoenheimer Memorial Lecturer at New York in 1951.

His published works include *Radio Elements as Indicators and other Selected Topics in Inorganic Chemistry* (1928); *Manual of Radio-activity* (with Professor Hevesy); and *The Origin of Meteorites* (1940).

In 1913 he married Else, daugher of Dr. L. M. Hartmann, professor of history in Vienna University. They had a son and a daughter—who work in England—and in his later years the life of his family oscillated between the three countries in which he had most work.

September 19, 1958.

General Pangalos, whose short-lived dictatorship in Greece in 1926-27 is hardly now even a memory, died at the age of 73 on February 27, 1952.

Theodore Pangalos was born in 1878 in the island of Salamis and, after completion of his studies, he entered the Military School "Evelpides" in Athens, in 1895. With the rank of second lieutenant he was admitted to the Military Academy of Saint Cyr, Paris. In 1916, while holding the rank of major, he commanded a regiment on the Macedonian Front and in the course of the next year he became Chief of Staff at the War Ministry. He took over the command of a division in 1918 and in 1919 he became Chief of Staff of the Greek Army in Asia Minor, which post he held up to 1920 when he was placed on the retired list.

After the revolution of 1922, led by Plastiras [q.v.] and Gonatas, he was again placed on the active list, and was president of the special court which tried and condemned to death the then Premier, the Generalissimo in Asia Minor, and other prominent military and political figures held to have been responsible for the Asia Minor disaster, which culminated in the sack of Smyrna. In December 1922 he became Minister of War and in 1923 Commander-in-Chief of the Greek Army in Thrace.

He was elected member of Parliament for Salonika late in 1923 and became leader of the Liberal-Republican Party. He was nominated Minister of Public Order in the first Republican Cabinet under Papanastassiou and later replaced General Kondylis, a rival Republican leader, as Minister of War in the same Cabinet.

In June 1925 he headed a new revolution which succeeded without bloodshed and declared himself Prime Minister and Minister of War. Admiral Konduriotis, who had been Head of the State since the abdication of King George II, resigned his office in April 1926 "for reasons of ill-health and fatigue" and General Pangalos was elected President in his place. By August, however, it became clear that General Pangalos had been displaced in the confidence of the army by General Kondylis, and after the latter had engineered a military *coup d'etat,* Pangalos fled in a warship.

He was, however, intercepted and after trial was banished to Crete. For the next six years or so his partisans were active and caused a good deal of embarrassment to successive Greek governments, but by 1932, when after a period of freedom he was confined on Corfu, his movement had lost most of its force.

He made a brief reappearance after the liberation of Greece, when he was charged in 1945 with collaboration with the Germans and Italians, but the charge could not be pressed because the police officers who had arrested him fled during the ensuing civil war and no evidence could be produced.

February 28, 1952.

Dame Christabel Pankhurst, D.B.E., who with her mother, Mrs. Emmeline Pankhurst, founded the Women's Social and Political Union, which in the years before the First World War campaigned for women's suffrage, and who was the driving force behind the militant section of the movement and possibly its most brilliant orator, died on February 13, 1958 at Los Angeles. She was 77.

From the start of the campaign her power sprang from what was, in a very real sense, a magnetic personality. A most attractive young woman with fresh colouring, delicate features, and a mass of soft brown hair, a graceful figure on the platform, she spoke with a warmth, a passion, and a highly effective *raillerie,* which few who were prepared to give her a hearing could resist. Though the crowds in Hyde Park did not always spare her, the most familiar cry they set up in the neighbourhood of the W.S.P.U. platform there was "We want Chris". Courageous and resourceful in her extreme fashion in the years before 1914, she was a force to be reckoned with.

On the outbreak of war she and the other leaders declared a truce and lent their organization to the cause of national service. She made one or two attempts after the conclusion of hostilities to enter Parliament, but then abruptly abandoned public life and in her later years assumed the part of religious propagandist and proclaimed her belief in the imminence of the Second Advent.

Christabel Harriette Pankhurst was born on September 22, 1880. Her father, Richard Marsden Pankhurst, a man of some ability who had been the friend of John Stuart Mill, was a barrister and an ardent social worker. Her mother, Emmeline Pankhurst, was the daughter of Robert Goulden, a calico printer. Until she was 13 she was educated at home and then, after a spell at Manchester High School at the age of 16, was sent to complete her education in Switzerland. Both parents were keenly alive to politics and both were what a generation ago would have been called feminists—her father had helped to form the original Woman's Suffrage Committee in 1865.

From an early age Christabel herself grew absorbed in political questions. Her father died in 1898, leaving the family in straitened circumstances, and for some time she helped her mother, over whom she at all times exercised a strong influence, by acting as a deputy registrar of births and marriages. She shared—and deepened—her mother's sympathies with the Independent Labour Party, and in 1901, when she was appointed to the executive committee of the North of England Society for Women's Suffrage, she also became a member of the Women's Manchester Trade Union Council. In 1903 mother and daughter jointly set up the Women's Social and Political Union, which promptly began to carry resolutions on the suffrage question in trade councils all over the country.

In the following year, having studied law at what was then the Victoria University, Manchester, where later she took an LL.B. degree with honours, she sought admission as a student at Lincoln's Inn and was refused. This refusal, against which she entered an impassioned protest, marked what was perhaps the real starting-point in her career of militancy. Not, however, until her arrest in 1905, together with Annie Kenney [q.v.], after their determined interruption of a meeting at Manchester addressed by Sir Edward Grey (Christabel had spat in a policeman's face, and, after refusing to pay the fine imposed, went to prison for a week) was the militant movement formally inaugurated. Mrs. Pankhurst and other members of the W.S.P.U. gave it a start with their pilgrimages to the House of Commons, and long conflicts with police followed.

All that was most dramatic in Christabel Pankhurst's career is bound up with the history of the militant phase of the "Votes for Women" campaign during the nine years before the outbreak of war in 1914. As organizing secretary of the W.S.P.U., she was tireless and purposeful. In February 1907 she was arrested and served a term of a fortnight's imprisonment. Not long afterwards she was charged with her mother and Mrs. Drummond with inciting to riot and received a sentence of 10 weeks. During her trial she called the Home Secretary (Herbert Gladstone) and the Chancellor of the Exchequer (Lloyd George) as witnesses and with her legal training ably cross-examined them. In 1912, at the height of the window-breaking campaign, she escaped to Paris, where her mother, temporarily released from prison, joined her.

On the outbreak of war they both declared an immediate suffrage truce. With the announcement that as militant women she and her associates might be able to do something to arouse the spirit of militancy in men, she set herself the task of furthering national service and encouraging recruiting. From this point she planned somewhat vaguely to make of the body of future women electors a national, Imperial and international force.

In November 1918 she was adopted by the "Women's Party" (into which the W.S.P.U. had translated itself in the previous year) as a candidate for Parliament. At the "khaki election" she stood as a Coalition candidate for the Smethwick division and was only narrowly defeated. Later she became prospective candidate for the Abbey division of Westminster. But her interest in politics waned rapidly, and the preoccupations of her later years are illustrated in various small volumes in which she turned to, among other sources, the Apocalypse of St. John of Patmos for support for her belief in the imminence of the Second Advent.

She had been created D.B.E. in 1936.

February 15, 1958.

Sylvia Pankhurst, who was one of the chief figures among the militant suffragettes in the years before 1914, died in Addis Ababa on September 27, 1960.

A woman of ardent temperament, devoted without emotional or any other reserve to the causes she made her own, Sylvia Pankhurst found in the women's suffrage movement an outlet for her somewhat tempestuous energies more satisfying than she was able to find afterwards. Her mother, Mrs. Emmeline Pankhurst, and her elder sister, Christabel [q.v.], were the chief forces in the Women's Social and Political Union; but she, as its honorary secretary and, later, in secession from the W.S.P.U., was not the least dramatic personage in the movement as a whole.

An unqualified and vehement militant, she came frequently into collision with the law and suffered imprisonment on numerous occasions under the rigours of the "Cat and Mouse" Act. When in 1914 her mother and sister, together with most of the other militant leaders, called a truce in their campaign and lent their organization to the cause of national service, Sylvia Pankhurst took her stand upon violent opposition to the war. She was drawn towards the extreme Left and continued upon occasion to find herself in serious trouble with the police. In later years, when the glory of the militant campaign had been dimmed, she devoted herself above all else to an all but private crusade against Fascist Italy and on behalf of Abyssinian independence.

At the time of her death she was editing the *Ethiopian Observer.*

Estelle Sylvia Pankhurst was born in Manchester in 1882. Her father, Richard Marsden Pankhurst, who had been a friend of John Stuart Mill, was a barrister and a sincere and high-minded social worker. Her mother, Emmeline Pankhurst, was the daughter of Robert Goulden, a calico printer. She was educated at the High School for Girls, Manchester; the Municipal School of Art; and the Royal College of Art, South Kensington. She won medals and scholarships and during her student days went to Venice, where she took a diploma at the Accademia. In 1903 her mother and her sister, Christabel, founded the Women's Social and Political Union, and in the course of time she became honorary secretary.

In 1912 and 1913 Sylvia Pankhurst formed branches of the W.S.P.U. in East London, which, developing upon other lines than the parent body, became a separate organization, under the name of the East London Federation. Thus she came to pursue her own feminist and other ideals, working in isolation from her mother and sister. In 1914 she established the *Workers' Dreadnought,* in which her pacifist attitude of mind was supported by a vaguely revolutionary social philosophy.

She was active all through the war years in organizing the work of a number of clinics and a day nursery in East London, though not in work of that character only; in October 1918 she was fined £50 on a charge of attempting to cause mutiny, sedition, or dissatisfaction among His Majesty's Forces or the civilian population. Two years later, having in the meantime embraced with passion the cause of the Russian revolution, she paid a visit to Russia and on her return figured prominently among the communists in Britain. Later in the year she was arrested again on a charge of publishing subversive matter, notably an article entitled "Discontent on the Lower Deck", and was sentenced to six months' imprisonment—a conviction that was upheld on appeal. She was expelled from the Communist Party in the following year after having refused to hand over to it the *Workers' Dreadnought.*

Abyssinia represented her chief devotion before, during, and after the war of 1939-45, and there she settled finally in 1956. For her services she received from the Emperor* the decoration of the Queen of Sheba, first class.

She wrote many books, most notably a history of the suffragette movement (1931), an interesting enough volume, though characteristically it displayed little knowledge of the non-militant movement; a Life of her mother (1935); and in the last year of her life a number of works concerned with various aspects of Ethiopian life.

September 28, 1960.

Field-Marshal Alexander Papagos, Prime Minister of Greece, died suddenly at his home on the outskirts of Athens on October 4, 1955 at the age of 71, after a long illness.

A brilliant military record was interspersed by adventures in politics, but it was only some three years ago that he emerged unmistakably as the strong man able to save Greece from her economic plight and political sterility. His great popularity helped to bring about his triumph at the polls in 1952, but afterwards he showed an administrative ability that was unexpectedly high. He early announced that the pivot of his foreign policy would be: "Close cooperation with Great Britain, France, and the United States".

With Germany, the chief market for Greek exports, he laboured to secure an understanding and in this he succeeded. He was, therefore, well set on a sound policy when the movement in Cyprus for union with Greece found a deep emotional response among the Greek people, which he could not ignore. This strained his relations with Great Britain considerably as he knew it must, and his interview with Sir Anthony Eden in 1953 left him in no doubt of the British attitude.

Yet he continued to press at least for a liberal constitution for the island if not for immediate self-determination. An unforeseen consequence was the violent reaction of the Turkish people, who had no wish to see their cousins in Cyprus at the mercy of Greek irredentists. The situation is still critical and Stephen Stefanopoulos, the Foreign Minister, whom Field-Marshal Papagos appointed acting Prime Minister only yesterday, in response to the urgent request of King Paul*, inherits a major problem.

Born in Athens on December 9, 1883, the son of General Leonidas Papagos, he joined the Military Academy in Brussels at the age of 19, and, later, the Cavalry College at Ypres. He saw action as a lieutenant in the Balkan Wars of 1912-13 while serving as equerry to King Constantine, then Greek Commander-in-Chief. After holding several staff and field appointments he was promoted to lieutenant-colonel in 1920 and distinguished himself during the Greek Army's abortive venture in Asia Minor.

He had his first experience in politics in 1935 when, as a lieutenant-general, he was appointed Minister of War in the Kondylis Cabinet which restored the monarchy in Greece. After a brief spell as Inspector-General of the Army he was reappointed Minister of War until August 1936, when he became Chief of the Army General Staff, a post he held throughout the dictatorship of General Metaxas from 1936 to 1940.

This period of Papagos's career has been overshadowed by his subsequent successes as Commander-in-Chief during and after the last war. Very few appreciated the magnitude of the task then assigned to him. However, with his outstanding military qualifications, his long experience in the army and excellent administrative ability, he succeeded, within those four years, in reforming the Greek Army, which consisted of 150,000 undisciplined soldiers in civilian clothes who had just defeated one of the frequent political revolutions in Greece.

By 1940 Papagos had silently built up an armed force of 500,000 men of the highest order and morale and, at the same time, had elaborated a mobilization plan so that, when the war broke out, the Italian General Staff was taken by surprise. Within a few weeks Papagos had reversed the tide of events by assuming the initiative in the field.

But Greece's valiant defence was doomed to collapse before long. When the Wehrmacht overran the country in April 1941 Papagos shared the fate of the Greek soldier and retired to his country house near Athens. In 1943 he was arrested and deported to Germany, and after being confined in various concentration camps was freed by the United States Army in March 1945. In recognition of his services to the nation, the Greek Parliament promoted him in 1947 to the rank of General on the retired list. He was then head of the military household of the King.

The following years were crucial for the future of Greece. Early in 1949 the communist rebels, aided and abetted by Greece's northern neighbours, had got a stranglehold on the country. It was then that Parliament recalled Papagos to active service and appointed him Commander-in-Chief of the Armed Forces, with wide powers. Within a very short period of time, helped by able collaborators he, himself, had chosen (and to a great extent by Tito's defection from the Soviet orbit), he led the army to victory against the rebel forces. In August 1949, nine months after his recall, the Greek Communists admitted total defeat. On October 28, 1949, the ninth anniversary of Greece's rejection of the Italian ultimatum, Papagos was promoted to Field-Marshal—a rank never before held by a commoner in Greece.

An unfortunate disagreement with the Palace led to his resignation from the post of Commander-in-Chief on May 31, 1951. The King had then denied him the right of vetoing military appointments to the Palace. Taking advantage of his immense popularity and without his apparent knowledge, some senior officers loyal to him staged on the night of his resignation a *coup d'état* to seize power. Papagos himself drove to Athens from his country house at Ekali and ordered the rebel officers to go home.

At that time the political parties had resumed their petty professional rivalries and political instability was jeopardizing the economic recovery of Greece, which had been so delayed by the rebel war. The lack of leadership was making itself felt. To a people as individualistic as the Greeks the qualifications for leadership were: a successful past, great popularity and, above all, integrity. Papagos, they found, possessed these qualities. When in August 1951 Papagos announced his decision to break into the exclusive domain of the professional politicians he invited the Greek people to rally round him, regardless of politics, "to save the country".

The elections of November that year returned his "Greek Rally" party as the most powerful single party in Parliament with 114 out of a total of 256 seats. The lack of an absolute majority and Papagos's belief that coalition cabinets were the root of Greece's political evils kept him in the Opposition. His aim was to force new elections at the earliest possible date with a more favourable electoral system. He and his principal adviser, Markezinis, were therefore accused of indulging in non-constructive opposition within and without Parliament. However, they succeeded.

The Chamber would only produce short-lived "centre" coalitions; so, a year or so later, King Paul dissolved it and new elections were proclaimed for November 1952. By that time all popular fears about Papagos's loyalty to the principles of democratic government (expertly fanned by the other parties) had been allayed. The majority system favoured the Greek Rally and Papagos stormed the polls. His party gained 241 seats out of the 300. This ensured, at least in theory, political stability until 1956.

The first measures adopted by the Papagos administration were unpopular but, according to *bona fide* observers, necessary, if Greece's economy was ever to be detached from its almost absolute dependence on foreign economic aid. Although his relations with the Palace improved steadily, Field-Marshal Papagos had retained much of his military mentality which could not, in many cases, be reconciled with the requirements of a political career. After what was described as a "clash of personalities" with Markezinis, the latter resigned from the Government and withdrew from the Greek Rally party, taking with him 22 deputies.

In 1912 he married Mary, daughter of General Andrew Kallinsky. They had a son, who is a member of the Greek foreign service, and a daughter.

October 5, 1955.

Richard Pares, C.B.E., F.B.A., Fellow of All Souls College, Oxford, and formerly Professor of History in the University of Edinburgh, died at Oxford on May 3, 1958 at the age of 55. His outstanding position among contemporary English historical scholars was at once an achievement of intellect and a triumph of spirit.

Richard Pares was born at Colchester on August 25, 1902, and was the elder son of a remarkable father, the late Sir Bernard Pares. He was successively scholar of Winchester and of Balliol, and gained a first in *Lit. Hum.* in 1924. He then began to read for the school of modern history, but in November 1924 he was elected to a prize fellowship at All Souls; he then abandoned the school but energetically continued his study of history. For a time he thought of journalism as a career, and spent some months on the staff of the *Liverpool Daily Post,* but he retained his interest in history and soon returned to academic pursuits. In 1926 he spent several months on an archaeological journey in Asia Minor. Already, too, he had begun to work on British colonial records in the Public Record Office.

As an historian, therefore, he was formed in no "school" and paid allegiance to no "master". In 1927 he became assistant lecturer in history at University College London, and his teaching there was in the field of modern English history. In 1928-29 he spent a year as Rockefeller Memorial student in the United States, and on his return he was appointed lecturer at New College, Oxford. For the next 11 years he took an active part in college teaching in the schools both of modern history and of "Modern Greats", and served as Proctor in 1938-39. During the same period he published his first two books, *War and Trade in the West Indies, 1739-63* (1936) and *Colonial Blockade and Neutral Rights* (1938): these were highly specialized studies based on extensive research in English, French, American, and West Indian manuscript sources, and they were received with respectful appreciation both by historians and by international lawyers.

From 1940 to 1945 Pares was a temporary Civil servant at the Board of Trade. He rose to be a principal assistant secretary and principal priority officer of the department, a position the duties of which he afterwards described in an essay contributed to the volume entitled *Lessons of the British War Economy,* edited by D. N. Chester (1951). His commanding intellectual powers, personal detachment, and complete integrity gave him great influence, and he won the affection as well as the respect both of the Ministers under whom he served and of the colleagues with whom he worked. During this period of almost overwhelming official activity, he read widely on such subjects as nineteenth-century African exploration, and took his full share in carrying on the *English Historical Review,* of which he had become joint-editor in 1940. But already a pauseful finger was being laid upon his life. While he was still at the Board of Trade there had appeared what proved to be the first symptom of the grave illness which gradually crippled him into almost total physical incapacity.

Meanwhile, however, he had taken up the appointment of Professor of History in the University of Edinburgh: he held it from 1945 to 1954, and in spite of the darkening shadow of ill-health he achieved striking success both as a teacher and as a head of department, and found much happiness in his work. He kept to the Scottish tradition whereby the professor in person lectures to the large first-year class, and as his lecturing had a virile distinction of style which reflected the wide-ranging interests of his own mind, his lectures made a great impression. His good sense and good speech were much in demand by Senatus and Court committees, and he took an active part in their proceedings until attendance became too difficult for him.

He then replanned his life as a scholar, deciding that he must depend upon the materials which he had already collected and on the resources of the libraries to which he had access. He continued his illuminating studies of the West Indies in *A West Indian Fortune* (1950), based upon the family papers of the Pinneys, in *Yankees and Creoles* (1956), and in an essay on "A London West Indian Merchant House, 1740-69" in the volume of *Essays Presented to Sir Lewis Namier* [q.v.] (1956)

jointly edited by Pares himself and A. J. P. Taylor. His more general interests were reflected by *King George III and the Politicians* (1953), embodying the Ford lectures which he had delivered to delighted audiences in Oxford in 1951-52, and by the very remarkable review in the *English Historical Review* (1956) of Dr A. J. Toynbee's* 10-volume *Study of History* both of which illustrated the precision and range of his historical scholarship, his strongly marked personal approach, and his formidably alert and critical mind. The same qualities were apparent in an essay on *Limited Monarchy in Great Britain in the Eighteenth Century*, issued in summer 1957.

He was appointed C.B.E. in 1945. He was elected Fellow of the British Academy in 1948, an honorary Fellow of Balliol College in 1953, and LL.D. *honoris causa* of Edinburgh University in 1956.

He married in 1937 Janet Lindsay, younger daughter of Sir Maurice Powicke*: she survives him with the four daughters of the marriage.

May 5, 1958.

Eric Parker, a well-known writer on field sports and the countryside and an active campaigner for the protection of wild birds, died at his home near Godalming on February 13, 1955 at the age of 84. He was editor of the Lonsdale Library and a former editor-in-chief of the *Field.*

Frederic Moore Searle (Eric) Parker was born at The Grange, East Barnet, in 1870, the eldest son of Frederick Searle Parker and Elisabeth, daughter of William Wilkieson, of Woodbury Hall, Bedfordshire. He was a King's Scholar at Eton and a Postmaster at Merton College, Oxford. He took a second class in Hon. Mods. in 1891, and a fourth class in *Lit. Hum.* in 1893. He entered journalism in 1900, when he became junior assistant editor to Theodore Cook on the *St. James's Gazette.* While still on the staff of the *St. James's* he started to write for the *Spectator* under St. Loe Strachey, and when St. Loe Strachey bought the *Country Gentleman* Parker was appointed editor of that paper, coupling it with regular writing for the *Spectator.*

The Country Gentleman ceased publication in 1907. By that time Parker had written one book, *The Sinner and the Problem,* and illustrated another, A. K. Collett's *British Inland Birds.* He was always a great Surrey man, and lived in that county for most of his life, and so it was fitting that he should then have been asked to contribute the volume on Surrey to the Highways and Byways series of Macmillan. He had a thoroughly enjoyable, though strenuous, time in prowling about the nooks and crannies of the county, and the result, illustrated by Hugh Thomson, was by no means the least attractive of an attractive series.

In 1911 he became shooting editor of the *Field* in succession to James Harting. For the next few years he was hard at work writing *Eton in the 'Eighties,* the first of several books he wrote about Eton—or rather about College at Eton. "Mr. Parker is only an Etonian in the second place", a reviewer wrote. "In the first place he is a Colleger, and to the death a member of the Election that came to Eton in the winter half of 1883".

After the First World War, in which he served with The Queen's Royal (West Surrey) Regiment, Parker returned to the work of rebuilding the shooting department of the *Field,* and in 1920 he published *An Angler's Garland,* an anthology which gave him more pleasure than any of the other anthologies which he compiled. His books and anthologies came out regularly in the years that followed. One of the most delightful was *Field, River and Hill,* in which the subjects of the articles varied from Norfolk partridges to Highland grouse, and from pike in an Irish lough to trout in a Thames backwater.

In 1928, on the death of Theodore Cook, Parker became joint editor with Lord Lonsdale of the celebrated Lonsdale Library of sport, and 15 months later succeeded Cook as editor-in-chief of the *Field.* Four years later Parker began his great fight for the protection of wild birds. What he wrote about the common practice of trapping and caging linnets, goldfinches, and other birds contributed in no small measure to the passage of the Wild Birds Protection Act of 1933.

In December 1937, after holding the appointment for eight years, Parker resigned from the editorship of the *Field* to devote more time to his literary work and to broadcasting. He had been associated with the *Field* for 30 years, and was offered and accepted a seat on the board. His last days as editor were marked by the organization of the British Section of the International Big Game Exhibition in Berlin.

He married in 1902 Ruth Margaret, daughter of the late L. Messel. She died in 1933. They had four sons and two daughters. Two sons were killed in the 1939-45 War.

February 14, 1955.

John Parker, whose death occurred on November 18, 1952, was the founder of *Who's Who in the Theatre,* and he edited that invaluable work of reference from 1912 until the eleventh edition, which appeared in January 1952.

Born in New York City on July 28, 1875, he began to contribute to the *Illustrated London News* at the age of 17, and subsequently joined the staff of the *Era.* He was appointed London correspondent of the *New York Dramatic Mirror* in 1903 and in the same year became London correspondent of the *New York Dramatic News,* a post he held until 1920.

His passion for accuracy pervaded his mind even in those early days and, greatly daring, he wrote to Clement Scott to point out certain errors of fact in the latter's theatrical articles. Scott wisely made use of Parker's talent for research and tried to persuade a publisher to undertake a work of reference to supplement and eventually to supersede Pascoe's *Dramatic List,* originally published in 1878 and still a valuable historical document, but of little current interest.

Meanwhile Parker, who had edited the *Green Room Book* in 1908-09 and had begun to contribute to the *Dictionary of National Biography,* forged ahead with his plans and the result was the publication in 1912 of the first edition of *Who's Who in the Theatre.* In comparison with the latest, the eleventh, edition, it was a small and unpretentious affair and, in contrast with Pascoe's work, contained no critical notes. Its strength lay in the absolute accuracy of the severely factual contents and on this merit it has made its way over the years on both sides of the Atlantic. The compilation of so encyclopaedic a work single-handed, for Parker always maintained that accuracy could only be attained by writing each entry by hand—typewriters with the extra hazard of literals were barred—might seem to be more than enough to absorb the editor's energy.

Parker, however, had many other interests in the theatre, as honorary secretary of the Critics' Circle since 1924 and as honorary editor of the *Critics' Circular* since 1923. He was, moreover, head of a busy shipping and export firm in the City and so in theatrical matters an amateur in no pejorative sense of the term. Indeed, his position in the world of the theatre was suitably manifested by his election as president of the Critics' Circle in 1937, the year of its silver jubilee, and in this capacity he represented Great Britain at the International Congress of Critics in Paris.

He was twice married, first to Edith Maud, the youngest daughter of the late M. B. Pizey, by whom he had a son and a daughter. After her death, in 1942, he married secondly, in 1944, Doris Mary, the youngest daughter of George Sinclair.

November 20, 1952.

Elizabeth (Mrs. G. R.) Parks—See **Robins.**

Thomas Frederick Parnell—See **Fred Russell.**

Anne Parrish (Mrs. Josiah Titzell in private life), the American novelist, died at Danbury, Connecticut, on September 5, 1957. She was 68.

She returned again and again in her novels to the exposure of egoists, with a delicate irony and an acute discrimination that found the weak joints in the harness of her readers. In her early novels—*The Perennial Bachelor* (1925), which won the Harper Prize, first brought her a wide public—she stood a little apart from the other American novelists of the day. Piercing and impertinent, clever and astringent, the conventions of social realism sat lightly upon her. By 1936, when *Golden Wedding* appeared, her talent had matured. There were passages of beautiful writing, of moving restraint, and of sensitive dissection of human selfishness. The rhythm and homogeneity of that novel she did not recapture. In her last book, *And Have Not Charity* (1954), the mood alternates uncertainly between irony, farce, and violence.

She was born at Colorado Springs in 1888 and educated at private schools. She wrote in all more than 20 books, some of them for children.

She was twice married, first to Charles Albert Corliss, who died in 1936, and then to Josiah Titzell, who died in 1943.

September 7, 1957.

Sir John Parsons, C.B.E., F.R.S., who had been consulting surgeon to the Royal London Ophthalmic Hospital and consulting ophthalmic surgeon to University College Hospital, died in hospital in London on October 7, 1957. He was 89.

John Herbert Parsons was born in 1868 and received his education at Bristol University (where he won the Gilchrist Scholarship and other distinctions), at University College London, and at St. Bartholomew's Hospital. He early showed his scientific bent by attaining the B.Sc. Lond. with Honours in Physiology when he was only 22 years of age. Two years later he qualified in medicine at London University and in 1900 took the B.S.Lond. and the F.R.C.S.Eng.

From the first he showed great interest in the physiological aspects of vision and in 1901 was granted a British Medical Association Scholarship. In 1903 he gave an Arris and Gale lecture at the Royal College of Surgeons and in 1904 gained the Middlemore Prize in Ophthalmology. In 1907 he was awarded the Nettleship Gold Medal.

After his appointment to the staffs of University College Hospital and the Royal London Ophthalmic Hospital Parsons had ample opportunity to proceed with his researches, though an extensive private practice made it more difficult for him to find the necessary time. His special knowledge also caused him to be much in demand for service on departmental committees of various Ministries dealing with such matters as factory lighting, sight tests, and prevention of blindness. He also served on the Glass-workers Cataract Committee of the Royal Society. In the War of 1914-18 Parsons served as Consulting Ophthalmological Surgeon to the Armed Forces with the temporary rank of Colonel A.M.S.

In 1919 he served on the Advisory Medical Council for the Air Ministry and in 1922 acted in a similar capacity for the Admiralty. In 1919 he was appointed C.B.E. and in 1922 was knighted. From 1928-32 Parsons was a member of the Medical Research Council. His distinction as a man of science was recognized by his being elected a Fellow of the Royal Society in 1921. Parsons wrote several well-known books on the physiology and pathology of the eye. His popular text-book on *Diseases of the Eye,* first published in 1907, reached its tenth edition in 1942. His large work in four volumes on the *Pathology of the Eye,* published in 1904-08, remained for long a standard text-book and is still a work of reference. His books on colour vision and on the theory of perception enhanced his reputation as a scientist and philosopher. In the latter work he made an attempt to correlate what is known of the growth of the nervous system with the evolution of the intelligence, and to show how structure and function have developed together.

In 1936 his position of eminence in the profession was shown by his being elected President of the Royal Society of Medicine. Other honours which came to him were the Fellowship of University College, the Hon. LL.D.Ed. and the Hon. D.Sc. Bristol.

Parsons was a philosopher and scientist who was able to apply his ophthalmological erudition in a practical manner for the advancement of his own branch of medicine and the social betterment of his fellow citizens. He held his opinions tenaciously but, a quiet man who spoke with a kind of drawl, he was by nature undemonstrative in manner so that at first one might not fully recognize his great ability. The better one knew him the more one appreciated his true worth and greatness.

After his retirement from active practice Parsons still continued to take interest in the advancement of ophthalmology.

October 8, 1957.

The death of **Gabriel Pascal,** the film producer and director in New York on July 6, 1954 at the age of 60, removes from the world of the cinema a dynamic and forceful personality who, in his time, roused the most lively and acrimonious controversy.

His great achievement as a man was to "capture" for the film the most famous and formidable of modern dramatists, Bernard Shaw, who refused to have anything to do with cinematographic versions of his plays until he was round about the age of 80. Then, in the mid-thirties, Pascal won him over, and was able to persuade Shaw that he was a man of genius who was worthy to be the only director of Shavian films. Pascal's work in this capacity, in the opinion of the general body of critics, by no means matched up to the great opportunity. *Pygmalion* won good praise in 1937; *Major Barbara,* in 1940, earned rather less; but *Caesar and Cleopatra,* shown at the end of 1945, provoked a storm of abuse and denigration such as few major films have produced in the whole history of the cinema.

Gabriel Pascal was a Hungarian, born at Arad, in Transylvania, on June 4, 1894, the son of a farmer. He had a military training in a hussar regiment, studied for a brief period at an agricultural college, then went on the stage, being trained in acting by Josef Keinz at the Hofburg Theater, in Vienna. His early years as an actor were spent at the Vienna Volkstheater, but he never made more than a beginning on the legitimate stage, throwing in his lot with the infant film industry as early as 1914. With the Hungarian producer, Urban Gad, he went to London in that year as assistant producer and as actor, playing lead with Gad's wife, Asta Nielsen. Political events made this a brief episode also. Pascal returned to Hungary and served through the 1914-18 War with his hussar regiment.

After the war Pascal recommenced film work, this time in Italy, acting in *Populi Morituri* and other films. This was his last period of acting, for he now began to acquire cinema theatres and to direct his own films, the best-known of which was *Frederika.* In 1932 he went to the United States, but did not make a long stay there, soon going to England. It was about this time that he conceived the idea of filming works by Bernard Shaw, and, succeeding where others had failed, he brought out *Pygmalion* in 1937. Both this and the ensuing *Major Barbara* (1940) not only won the attention that was natural because of the fame of the author but put Pascal into the limelight as a director and brought him good financial reward.

In 1943 Pascal began work on *Caesar and Cleopatra,* but it was not shown until the end of 1945. Not only had it taken nearly three years to produce, but it was commonly reputed to have cost something like £1,300,000 (though four months after production Shaw said that £700,000 to £800,000 was nearer the true sum). Critics used phrases such as "boring", "lavish but limping", and "the tinsel vulgarity of the production". Hardly a dissentient voice relieved this chorus of disapproval, nevertheless the film (which had certain merits as a spectacle) was a box-office success. In April 1946 the Association of Cine Technicians in London took the unprecedented step of passing a resolution that Pascal should not be allowed to make further films in England "unless subject to special control".

The Shaw-Pascal alliance continued, and the director was *persona grata* at Ayot St. Lawrence, where he spent a good deal of time. In the summer of 1946 Mary Pickford at last prevailed upon Shaw to allow some of his works to be filmed in America, and arrangements were made for the Artists' Alliance to produce *The Doctor's Dilemma, The Devil's Disciple* and *The Shewing Up of Blanco Posnet,* with Pascal as director.

Pascal also formed his own company, and in 1947 began work in Italy on *Androcles and the Lion,* which was shown in 1951.

With his own production unit he was responsible for various films in Italy, France, Germany, and England.

July 8, 1954.

Boris Pasternak, who at the age of 70 died on May 30, 1960 at his country home outside Moscow, was born in 1890 of a highly cultivated Jewish family. His father, Leonid Pasternak, was an admirable painter of the Impressionist school and the friend of Tolstoy; his mother was an accomplished musician.

Boris Pasternak was bred in an atmosphere of passionate devotion to the arts and kept this faith all his life. After studying music with Scriabin and philosophy at Marburg he turned, with some hesitation, to poetry, but found that it was his life's work and never abandoned it. His first work shows the marks of the Russian Futurists and undoubtedly owed something to his great admiration for Vladimir Mayakovsky. Amid certain violences of expression, which he soon abandoned, Pasternak already showed his delicate eye for physical nature, his capacity for concentrating a powerful experience into a few, telling words, and his profound belief in the goodness of life.

An injury received in childhood prevented him from fighting in the First World War, and he was free to develop his talents. The result was his astonishing *Sister, My Life,* written in a spate of creative excitement in 1917. In this and in *Themes and Variations,* published in 1922, Pasternak showed himself as a poet of a powerful and original genius. He had rejected his early extravagances and wrote in the traditional verse-forms of Russian poetry, although he varied them with unusual rhymes and half-rhymes and still maintained his elliptic, allusive way of expressing himself. The two volumes cover a wide range of experience. Though they are strictly personal and lyrical they not only cover Pasternak's deep love of natural beauty and of his favourite authors, Pushkin and Lermontov, but touch with great power on love and even on politics. His love-poems have a great dramatic power and, though not always pleasant to read, are always impressive and moving.

His political poems are intensely personal, the record of what a sensitive, detached, humane man felt about the earthshaking events of those eventful years. His imagery is always strikingly original and effective, and no poet of our time knew how to do much so much in so small a space. In 1929 Pasternak tried an experiment in narrative poetry with his *Year 1905,* which contains two long poems about revolutionary themes. Though they have many beautiful passages they seem to lack his intensely personal touch and not to be the right medium for his genius, and it is significant that, after one or two other experiments in the same kind, he returned to lyrical poetry.

In *Second Birth* (1932), *On Early Trains* (1944), and *Terrestrial Space* (1945) he showed how his lyrical gifts had matured and mellowed. These poems are less concentrated and less explosive than his earlier work, but they have an even greater power of description, notably in his splendid pictures of the Caucasus, and they are more tender and more human. He wrote some notable poems on the Second World War and showed how even the most contemporary of themes can take on a universal significance when it is handled by a master. He also translated from foreign languages; his versions of Kleist, of poets from Georgia, and of *Hamlet, Antony and Cleopatra,* and *Romeo and Juliet* show how a translation can be both exact and a real work of poetry. Of his prose, *Safe Conduct* is a fine account of his own early life, and his *Letters from Tula* an imaginative and beautiful love story. At a time when much political pressure was put on Russian writers to make their work "socially useful". Pasternak kept his independence and artistic integrity and served no end but his own high standards of art and craftsmanship. Life was not easy for him. He was continually attacked and disparaged and suffered almost everything except open persecution. He was never afraid to say what he believed, or to preach his doctrine that an artist must tell the truth as he himself sees it. When other poets gave themselves up to political claims and produced work of purely ephemeral interest, Pasternak, with a greater courage and finer insight, wrote of things as he really saw them and transformed into poetry the creative excitement which he found in his own age.

Such a devotion to his art won favour neither with the Soviet authorities nor with Pasternak's fellow-writers. Even the "thaw" after Stalin's [q.v.] death did little for him, and his reputation in his own country was much more that of a translator than of an original writer. However, he was not in any way broken or discouraged by the treatment given to him. He worked hard after the war at his only long novel, and in 1958 *Dr. Zhivago* appeared, first in an Italian and then in an English translation. It made at once an enormous impression on the whole western world and was welcomed for the great work that it was. At last Soviet Russia had produced a work which could be compared with the great works of the past, and the events of the revolution and afterwards were portrayed with impartial insight and understanding. Except that it deals with political events *Dr. Zhivago* is not a political novel and certainly contains no political message. Its central theme is the story of a gifted man who loses his confidence and happiness because circumstances are too much for him. But he keeps his artistic integrity, and writes poems, which are printed at the end of the book and are the ripest fruits of Pasternak's art. To this degree *Dr. Zhivago* has an autobiographical element, and we may see in some of its episodes Pasternak's own experience.

The book won Pasternak the Nobel Prize for literature, and this unhappy stroke of fortune caused him much anguish. He would have liked to take the prize, but his fellow-writers denounced and disowned him, and he was forced to refuse it. That he fully deserved the prize cannot be denied; indeed he should have had it earlier, without the political complications which it brought when it was offered to him. In it he shows that he was as great a master of prose as of poetry, and indeed no Russian novelist, not even Turgenev, has put so much authentic poetry into a novel.

The plan of the book may at times seem too loose for a strict critic, and realists complain that it relies too much on coincidence. But throughout it there breathes the powerful spirit of a true poet, passionately interested both in humanity and in nature, and able to give to both the full creative attention of his outstanding genius.

June 1, 1960.

The Nawab of Pataudi, who died at New Delhi suddenly on January 5, 1952 from a heart attack while playing in a polo match, will be long remembered for the pleasure he gave to countless spectators in various parts of the British Commonwealth by his cricketing prowess.

Nawab Muhammad Iftikar Ali Khan Bahadur was born in March 1910 and at the age of 19 succeeded to the rulership of Pataudi, a small state in the Gurgoan district of what is now East Punjab. He went to England in 1926 to go up to Oxford. He was coached by Frank Woolley, the Kent and England batsman, who forecast a brilliant cricket future for him, and gained his Blue in 1929, scoring 106 and 84 against Cambridge. Two years later he established a new record by making the highest individual score in these university matches in remarkable circumstances. In the Cambridge first innings A. Ratcliffe scored 201, so breaking the record which had been held for 27 years. Ratcliffe's honour lasted only a few hours, however, because Pataudi obtained 238 not out for Oxford. It is said that before going in to bat Pataudi declared his intention of trying to pass Ratcliffe's score.

Pataudi went to Australia as a member of D. R. Jardine's [q.v.] team in the 1932-33 tour. He scored a century in his first Test but, after one more game for England, was left out of the side. He reappeared for England when Australia visited in 1934, by which time he was playing for Worcestershire, but his next Test appearances came in 1946, when he led the Indian Test team to England and played in all three Tests. On that tour Pataudi did not enjoy the best of health and he disappeared from first-class cricket after his return home, but in autumn 1951 he returned to England for a visit after finding a school in Switzerland for his 11-year-old son. When he was in England Pataudi made contact with his former county and Worcestershire successfully applied to the Advisory County Cricket Committee for him to be regarded as still qualified to play for them. He hoped to turn out for them occasionally in the 1952 season when visiting his son at school.

After a long engagement arising from tardy consent by her father, the Nawab of Bhopal [q.v.], one of the most important Muslim-ruled States in India, he married the second daughter of that prince in 1936, and he leaves a son and three daughters.

January 7, 1952.

Sir William Paterson, M.I.MECH.E., designer of the "Anderson shelter", died on August 9, 1956 in London, less than a week after his eighty-second birthday.

William Paterson was born on August 5, 1874, the son of James Paterson, of Roslin. He was educated in Edinburgh and, after technical training at the Heriot Watt College, Edinburgh, served six years' apprenticeship as an engineer in the workshops and drawing office of a firm of paper mill engineers. From early days he realized the importance of water purification and in 1902 he decided to form his own company, the Paterson Engineering Company, for the development of this branch of engineering. In the course of his career he filed over 70 British patents and many of these foreshadowed improvements which were not developed on a practical scale until years later. The history of water purification in the first half of the twentieth century conforms closely to the pattern of the developments initiated and made possible by his knowledge and foresight.

In 1939 Paterson was urgently asked by Lord Waverley [q.v.], then Sir John Anderson, Home Secretary and Minister of Home Security, to devise a form of air raid shelter suitable for protection against blast and flying débris and capable of rapid production in very large numbers at a minimum cost. The accepted design—known as the Anderson shelter—was patented to prevent its commercial exploitation and Paterson presented the patent to the nation.

In 1944 he was knighted and in recent years had the distinction of being elected to honorary membership of the Institution of Water Engineers and the Royal Society of Health, to an honorary fellowship of the Heriot Watt College, vice-presidency of the Junior Institution of Engineers, and life membership of the American Water Works Association. In January 1956 he retired from the chairmanship of his company after having been in control for 53 years.

During the whole of his life he was a man of great foresight and imagination, with a directness of purpose and an integrity of thought, a generosity of disposition, and a thoughtfulness for others which not only controlled all his actions but also served as a pattern and stimulus to those who had the privilege of being in contact with him.

He married Dorothy, daughter of Mr. H. F. Steedman, who survives him, together with a daughter of the marriage.

August 10, 1956.

Admiral Sir Wilfrid R. Patterson, K.C.B., C.V.O., C.B.E., who died on December 15, 1954 at his home in London, was in command of the battleship King George V at the sinking of the German battleship Bismarck in May 1941, and later played a prominent part in preparing for and supporting the allied invasion of Normandy.

Wilfrid Rupert Patterson was the son of W. R. Patterson, of Belfast, and was born on November 20, 1893. He entered Osborne College as a cadet in September 1906, left Dartmouth College four years later, and after making the training cruise in the Cornwall was a midshipman from May 1911 in the Drake, flagship in Australia, and other ships. During the 1914-19 War, as a sub-lieutenant, he was second-in-command of torpedo boat No. 32 and of the torpedo gunboat Jason, in 1914-15. He won the bronze medal of the Royal Humane Society in 1915 for gallantry in saving life. After his promotion to lieutenant in July 1915 he served in the cruiser Lowestoft and the flotilla leader Saumarez in the Grand Fleet up to February 1918, when he was appointed to specialize in gunnery. From July 1920 he was gunnery officer in the cruiser Centaur and battleship King George V, in the Mediterranean, the cruiser Dauntless, in which he made the cruise round the world with the special service squadron, and the battle-cruiser Hood. From 1925 to 1927 he was on the staff of the gunnery school.

Promoted to commander in June 1928, he was reappointed to the Hood as squadron gunnery officer in the battle-cruiser squadron, and from April 1929 held a similar appointment in the Revenge in the 1st battle squadron in the Mediterranean. From May 1931 until after his promotion to captain in June 1933 he was executive officer of the cruiser Kent, flagship in China. He returned there in 1935 in command of the sloop Folkestone, and from 1936 to 1938 was flag-captain to the Vice-Admiral Commanding the Reserve Fleet, in the Effingham and Hawkins. For his services in connexion with the Coronation naval review at Spithead on May 20, 1937, he was made a C.V.O.

From April 1938 he was lent to the Commonwealth Government in command of the cruiser Canberra and as chief staff officer to the Rear-Admiral Commanding the Australian Squadron. This command he held during the early months of the Second World War. From July 1940 until 1942 he commanded the new battleship King George V in the Home Fleet, and for his services in the chase and destruction of the Bismarck was appointed a C.B.

He helped to plan naval anti-aircraft defence against flying bombs, and was concerned with the original planning of the Mulberry harbours when Assistant Chief of Naval Staff (Weapons) at the Admiralty. Shortly after D-Day he was commanding cruisers in the bombardment of the Normandy coast. From March 1945 he commanded a cruiser squadron of the East Indies Fleet in the concluding operations of the war against Japan, for which in June 1946 he was awarded the C.B.E. He was promoted to vice-admiral in 1946, and in the birthday honours of 1947 was made a K.C.B. He was appointed Admiral Commanding Reserves in October 1947 for the customary period of two years, and on retirement in 1950 he was promoted admiral.

He married in 1923 Maureen, daughter of James Mahon, of Belfast and New York, and had one son and one daughter.

December 17, 1954.

Friedrich Paulus, the former German Field-Marshal, who surrendered his army before Stalingrad in January 1943, died in east Germany in January 1957. He was 66.

The disaster that befell his armies was not of his making. His position was rendered first desperate, then hopeless by the insensate demands of his master, Hitler. As Sir Winston Churchill* has said in *The Hinge of Fate:* "The lure of Stalingrad fascinated Hitler; its very name was a challenge. . . . It became a magnet, drawing to itself the supreme effort of the German Army and Air Force". And later in the same book: "This crushing disaster to the German arms ended Hitler's prodigious effort to conquer Russia by force of arms and destroy communism by an equally odious form of totalitarian tyranny".

In the years of his captivity after Stalingrad there was much speculation about Paulus's fate and status. At one time he was said to be raising, together with von Seydlitz-Kurtzbach, an army of converted Germans, numbering many hundreds of thousands; at another, he was seen as a leader of a "Free Germany". These reports he denied when he emerged suddenly, and to the general surprise, at the Nuremberg trials as a witness.

Thereafter his whereabouts were again uncertain until the autumn of 1953, when the east German radio stated that he had gone to live in east Germany. The following July he re-emerged to give a press conference in east Berlin in which he attacked the Bonn Government and indicted the Government of the United States for its "attempt at world dominance". To work for the unity and sovereignty of Germany was, he said, the "most honourable field of endeavour for former German officers". Later he was said to be an instructor at the Military Academy of the Soviet Zone (People's Police).

Paulus, the son of a Civil servant, studied law at his university and joined the German Army in 1910. In 1935 he was a colonel in the Reich Defence Ministry and by 1939 had become a major-general. The following year he was promoted lieutenant-general and in 1942 he went to the Russian front. As Paulus was to say at Nuremberg, Hitler was set upon taking the oilfields at Grozny and Maikop in the Caucasus mountains, and this was one of the prime objects of operations in the summer of 1942. Hitler's directive of July 23 divided the Southern Army Group into subsidiary groups. Group A was to capture the eastern shore of the Black Sea, advance inland, and seize Maikop; thereafter, a mobile force was to take Grozny. Subsequently the Baku area was to be captured by an advance along the Caspian Sea. Group B, having established a defensive flank along the Don, was to advance on Stalingrad, "smash the enemy forces being assembled there, and occupy the city".

The switching of forces delayed the attack on Stalingrad, resistance grew stiffer, and the outskirts of the city were not reached until September 15. Tremendous assaults were mounted by the Germans and some ground was gained at terrible cost to attackers and defenders, but the Russians hung on. Paulus, who led the Sixth Army, was in bad case; his men were exhausted, his flanks were covered by allies of uncertain quality, and the weather became daily worse. Hitler was implacable, there was to be no withdrawal. On November 19 came the long-awaited Russian counter-offensive, directed against the German flanks with the object of encirclement. Four days later the pincers met and Paulus was trapped between the Don and Volga. He planned a breakout, but again Hitler overruled his local commander and ordered Paulus to hold his ground. For seven more weeks Paulus and his army held out in an impossible position with little hope. Efforts to supply him by air were made but little got through. The weather was no less hostile than the Russians: food and ammunition were scarce and typhus broke out among the German troops.

Finally, German units began to surrender wholesale. At the moment of defeat, when

Paulus was about to be run to earth in the cellar of a general store, Hitler promoted him Field-Marshal. Over a year after the Stalingrad disaster Moscow radio broadcast what purported to be an appeal by Paulus to the German people to rid themselves of Hitler. The Russian armies were on the borders of East Prussia. The allies had broken through in France. Germany, said the broadcast voice, had lost the war.

February 4, 1957.

Sir Charles Peake, G.C.M.G., M.C., British Ambassador at Athens until his retirement early in 1957, died in London on April 10, 1958 at the age of 61.

Peake had for many years a special place in the thoughts of members of the Foreign Service and of journalists who knew him in his many posts at home and abroad. He had a lively, imaginative, and intelligent mind, and great shrewdness. He loved expounding the intricacies of a given problem, and he would do it always in a way that was both lucid and agreeably flattering to his hearer, as though there was nothing really new in it all, but a reminder of known facts might be useful. The adroit combination of old-world diplomatic language and sudden flashes of modern slang made it all the more agreeable.

His own colleagues, and journalists, always learned a great deal from him, and he was never shy of giving advice—in the same courteous, pungent way—to the Secretaries of State under whom he served. Especially to young journalists he gave help and confidence through his easy, friendly manner, broken only by his habit of breaking off a little disconcertingly to day-dream.

Off duty he was a delightful companion. He had an unending fund of stories and reminiscences, and he was never so happy as when telling one of his old favourites, which with his gift of quick improvisation he would refurbish on most occasions with a piece of fresh embroidery. He had read extensively and his memory was retentive. But what mattered most to him was his religion. He held his faith firmly and consistently. His pronounced sympathies were with the Anglo-Catholic branch of the Church of England, and he could discuss Church matters with knowledge and authority.

Charles Brinsley Pemberton Peake was the son of Colonel W. P. Peake, of Hildenborough, Kent. He was at school at Wyggeston, Leicester, and from there went straight into the Army in 1914 and he served throughout the war as an officer in The Leicestershire Regiment. He was mentioned in dispatches and awarded the Military Cross. He was badly wounded in the leg and, although the leg was saved, he suffered from the wound for many years after the war and had to undergo several operations. After the 1914-18 War he went to Magdalen College, Oxford, where he took his degree in 1921, and in the following year entered the Diplomatic Service.

During his early years in what later became known as the Foreign Service Peake held a series of appointments abroad, which included Sofia, Constantinople, Tokyo, and Berne, until he was transferred to Paris in 1933, a few months before he reached the rank of first secretary.

Peake served in Paris very happily for two years and profited greatly from the opportunities offered by what was at that time the most important and stimulating post in the service, but having by this time spent so many years abroad he was anxious to get back to the Foreign Office, of which he had hitherto had little experience. The post in the News Department which he had asked for entirely suited his temperament and his abilities, for he greatly preferred to deal with people rather than with official papers. Peake entered on his task with enthusiasm, and after three years found himself head of the department when war came in 1939 and the press section of the Foreign Office was transferred to the Ministry of Information building.

While serving in the Foreign Office Peake had attracted the attention of Lord Halifax [q.v.] and in 1941, when the latter was appointed Ambassador at Washington, he asked Peake to accompany him as his personal assistant. Though the appointment was by its very nature short-lived it cemented a firm and lasting friendship between the two men and helped greatly to extend the younger man's circle of acquaintances. On returning to London in 1942 Peake was appointed British representative to the French National Committee, when he needed all the tact and diplomacy at his command in smoothing the frequently ruffled feelings of General de Gaulle* in the ups and downs of his relations with the British Prime Minister. In 1944-45 he was political adviser to the Supreme Commander of the Allied Expeditionary Force.

At the end of the war Peake had his first experience as head of a diplomatic mission abroad, first at Tangier, where in spite of the title of Consul-General the work was mainly political in character, and then a year later when he was appointed to Belgrade. Here he served for five years during the period when Marshal Tito's relations with the Soviet Government were at their worst. This gave Peake an opportunity, of which he made full use, for establishing a more personal relationship with the Yugoslav dictator than would have been likely in different circumstances. With the utmost tact and skill he explained British policy to the Marshal and the Yugoslav predicament and needs to London. Several difficult corners were turned during his mission.

Though Belgrade offered much of interest it could not provide anything comparable to Athens in the amenities of life. This was Peake's last appointment in the Foreign Service, and it was also his longest, for he remained Ambassador at Athens for five and a half years. During the early part of his time there the traditional friendship between Britain and Greece had not been disturbed by the subsequent bitterness over Cyprus. Ably assisted by his charming wife, Peake was able to make the British Embassy the most popular and frequented centre in Athens. It was all the more bitter and frustrating therefore when the storm over Cyprus reached such an intensity that the Embassy was virtually boycotted by the Greeks: only a small faithful remnant were willing to be seen entering its doors.

Many Greeks were puzzled to know how it was that his own friendly personal manner was not reflected, as they saw it, in British policy. But he could, and did, speak firmly to the Greeks. He had to leave with the problem unsolved, but he and Lady Peake were given a warm send-off when he retired from Athens and the Foreign Service early in 1957. In his retirement he acted as special adviser to the Colonial Office on Cyprus.

In 1926 he married Catherine, daughter of the late W. G. Knight. There were four sons of the marriage, one of whom took Holy Orders in the Church of England.

April 11, 1958.

Sir George Pearce, K.C.V.O., who died on June 24, 1952, had a long and honourable career in the Australian Federal Parliament.

He was one of the ablest of the group of Labour members who entered the Commonwealth Parliament at the beginning of the Federation, and although he afterwards accompanied W. M. Hughes [q.v.] in breaking away from the Labour Party during the 1914-18 war, he remained characteristically a Labour politician of the type which has had so much influence on the development of the Commonwealth, honest, serious, and capable. After the war he was indispensable in every Nationalist Government. He was best known in Britain as the able delegate of the Commonwealth to the Washington Conference of 1921 and to the League of Nations Assembly in 1927, when he was appointed K.C.V.O.

George Foster Pearce was born in South Australia on January 14, 1870, and, like many other Australian politicians of his type, he was educated in the school of experience. He began his working life as a carpenter and joiner and at the age of 22 went to Western Australia. In the gold rush of the nineties he walked from Perth to Coolgardie to try his luck, but made no money, and returned to the coast to become a labour organizer. In 1901 he was elected as a Labour Senator for Western Australia to the first Federal Parliament. His earnestness and debating powers made their mark, and he was given the portfolio of Defence in the second Labour Government to be formed. The important Defence Act of 1910, which first organized the defence services of the Commonwealth, was not entirely of his inception, but it was he who carried it successfully into practice.

Pearce was early convinced that voluntary enlistment would not maintain sufficient reinforcement for the army corps on active service during the 1914-18 war, and he was Hughes's right-hand man in the embittered campaign that began in 1916 for the institution of conscription. When the break came with the Labour Party in 1917 even Hughes's expulsion by the party executive was not accompanied with greater personal acrimony, for the party regarded Pearce if not as a brilliant leader at any rate as a steadfast follower. But he was as steadfast in what he believed to be in the best interests of the country, and he was not afraid to risk political extinction for his belief. He remained Minister of Defence, as it fell out, until 1921, his last important service in that capacity being the representation of the Commonwealth at the Washington Conference. In 1919 he visited Britain to take control of the demobilization of the Australian troops, and he signed as the representative of Australia the Treaty of St. Germain.

From 1922 to 1926 he was Minister of Home Affairs, retaining the portfolio when Hughes was succeeded by S. M. Bruce [later Lord Bruce of Melbourne*], from 1926 to 1929 Vice-President of the Federal Executive Council, from 1931 to 1934 again Minister of Defence, and from 1934 to 1937 Minister for External Affairs. In all these Administrations he was the leader of the Government in the Senate, where his long membership, his personal integrity and his shrewd handling of debate had given him an undisputed position of influence.

After his retirement from the Senate in 1938 he became a member of the Commonwealth Grants Commission, and in 1940 his experience of defence measures was well utilized by his appointment as chairman of the Defence Business Board.

To the public he was not so well known as his political eminence merited, and an awkward and over-serious demeanour lent him sometimes more readily to caricature than respect; but all who knew him recognized him as essentially a man to be trusted and a loyal and willing colleague.

He married in 1897 Eliza Maude, daughter of A. J. Barrett, and there were two sons and two daughters of the marriage.

June 25, 1952.

Lionel Pearson, F.R.I.B.A., who died at his home at Roehampton on March 19, 1953 at the age of 73, was a member of the firm of Adams, Holden and Pearson, the architects of some of the most important recent buildings in London, including the Underground headquarters at St. James's Park station.

Lionel Godfrey Pearson was born at Liverpool on October 29, 1879, and was educated at Manchester Grammar School. He was articled to Woodhouse and Willoughby, of Manchester, and also took a two years' course at the Liverpool University School of Architecture. He went to London in 1901 and acted as assistant to Professor E. S. Prior and W. Flockhart until 1903, when he entered the office of Adams and Holden, who were already famous as the architects of, among other works, the old British Medical Association building in the Strand.

Throughout the war of 1914-18 Pearson served in France with the R.A.M.C., resuming practice as an architect in 1919. A long list might be made of the buildings with which, whether as assistant or partner of the firm, Pearson was associated, but it is enough to say that, besides the Underground headquarters—which in 1929 was awarded the London Architecture Bronze Medal of the R.I.B.A.—they included the Bristol Royal Infirmary, the Bristol Central Reference Library, and several hospitals and country houses.

On his own account Pearson was responsible for the architectural support of the Artillery War Memorial at Hyde Park Corner, with its sculpture by the late Charles Sargeant Hagger, A.R.A., and the layout and structure of the Hudson Memorial in Hyde Park, with its carving of "Rima" by Sir Jacob Epstein [q.v.]. The architecture of these monuments did not come in for the criticism, violent in action as well as words in the case of "Rima", to which the sculpture was subjected.

Among the hospitals for which Pearson was mainly, if not wholly, responsible were the new Westminster Hospital and its additions of nurses' home and school in St. John's Garden, Horseferry Road, the Royal Westminster Ophthalmic Hospital, the Southern Hospital, and, with A. Taylor, the new Mineral Water Hospital at Bath. In 1933 Pearson had an interesting commission to design the model of a miniature hospital to be exhibited in aid of King Edward's Hospital Fund. For this purpose Queen Mary [q.v.] gave the architect every facility, allowing him and the model maker to make a private inspection of the Queen's Dolls' House.

Pearson, who was elected F.R.I.B.A. in 1921, was a very attractive personality, with the always pleasing combination of tallness and shyness. About his own work in architecture he was modest, and when asked what was his particular share in the hospitals designed by his firm he said that he looked after the drains—thus improving upon Bernini's boast that as an artist he could not be bothered with drains.

In 1932, at the comparatively late age of 53, when he was looked upon as a confirmed bachelor, Pearson married Miss Melinda Elizabeth Osborne, who was many years younger than himself, and there was a daughter of this extremely happy marriage.

March 20, 1953.

Sir Robert Pearson, for many years chairman of the committee and subsequently of the council of the London Stock Exchange, died on February 12, 1954 in London at the age of 82.

There can be few more striking approximations to the old ideal of *mens sana in corpore sano* than Pearson. Formidably tall and still a striking figure in his old age, he was in youth a notable all-round athlete—oarsman, golfer, footballer, and cricketer. He won his Oxford Blue for golf and had the rare distinction of holding a Harlequin cap and a trial cricket cap in the same year, 1894. His career at the Scottish Bar, though brief, was not undistinguished and, after a short flirtation with party politics, he employed his considerable mental powers in learning and finally greatly influencing one of the most powerful financial institutions in the world, the London Stock Exchange.

In his 11 years as chairman, first of the committee and then of the council which replaced it, he insisted on the highest degree of probity in the conduct of business. The general public owes him a particular debt of gratitude because under his chairmanship the Stock Exchange consistently took investors into its confidence concerning its decisions and methods, and the reasons for them. He evinced the quality of leadership all his life, kindly and genial to everyone, yet sometimes with a word of firm restraint for the perhaps too exuberant youth.

Robert Barclay Pearson was the youngest son of the late David A. Pearson and was born on November 20, 1871. At Loretto he was in the XI and XV, and in 1891 went up to Brasenose College, Oxford. Those were the days when a college was assessed by its standing on the river, and Pearson threw himself heart and soul into this effort. He rowed twice in the B.N.C. torpid which was head of the river, and in the college VIII when second and third, and got his "trial eight". He was also tried for the University XI and XV, but in fact got his Blue for golf. He was captain of the Oxford golf team in two successive years, and owing to the poor condition of the Royal Wimbledon course on account of the weather during his first year's captaincy succeeded in getting the match transferred to the Royal St. George's in the next year. How unlucky he was in barely missing his cricket Blue in 1894 may be judged from the fact that he was awarded his Harlequin cap in that year.

Such prowess in the field and on the river generally goes with a "pass" degree. Pearson, who among his other accomplishments was a gifted violinist and piper, in fact took a creditable second in *Lit. Hum.* Having read law with some success, he was called to the Scottish Bar in 1898. He was well qualified to serve on the Royal Commission on Physical Training in Scotland in 1902-03, and for a year or so afterwards he was legal secretary to the Lord Advocate. The associations of his family with Kincardineshire led him to attempt to win the constituency for the Conservative interest in 1909 and 1910, but the Liberal Party was then too strongly entrenched. He then decided to go into business and joined the well-known firm of London stockbrokers, Laing and Cruickshank.

He had then little or no knowledge of the affairs of the Stock Exchange, but his training at Oxford and his experience as an advocate in Scotland, allied with native aptitude, made him a quick learner. He made a careful study of financial affairs generally and was intent to make stockbroking more a profession than a business. Within three years he was admitted to membership of the London Stock Exchange and to a partnership in his firm. Within 16 years he was elected to the Stock Exchange Committee and five years later became deputy chairman. In 1936 he was elected chairman, a position from which he retired in 1947, full of years but still full of vigour.

His 11 years of office were eventful. The war and its aftermath radically changed conditions throughout the world, and the repercussions of these changes were naturally acutely felt at the hub of international business in the City. Sir Robert Pearson (he had been knighted in 1944) brought a cool head and clear judgment to the many problems that arose first on account of the strains of war and then on account of Socialist policy. Under his wise guidance the Stock Exchange, while never failing to carry out the requirements of official policy in its own ordinances, equally never abrogated its independence and on more than one occasion won over a reluctant Government to its own point of view. The unification of the most important functions of the committee and the trustees in 1945 in the newly established council was largely due to his clarity of thought and skill in negotiation, and there is no doubt that the country in general and the investing public in particular greatly benefited from his insistence on the highest standards of probity in the conduct of stock and share business. He retired from his partnership in Laing and Cruickshank in 1932.

He married in 1898 Margaret Ethel, daughter of the late James Stewart, who survives him with the three sons and two daughters of the marriage.

February 13, 1954.

Edward R. Pease, one of the founders of the Fabian Society, of which he was secretary from 1890 until 1913 and honorary secretary for the next quarter of a century, died on January 5, 1955 at his home in Limpsfield, Surrey. He was 97.

Edward Pease, though neither his name nor his personality was known to many, was a figure of not a little consequence during the formative phase of the Labour movement in Britain. He contributed much of practical value to the development of Fabian Socialism, assisting the Webbs in their earliest researches and furthering their policy of "permeation" with remarkable modesty and address, and had almost as intimate a knowledge as anybody of the early history of the Labour Party. It was in his rooms in Osnaburgh Street that the Fabian Society was born. It grew out of a body known as the Fellowship of the New Life, of which the principal aim was to assist in the cultivation of a perfect character. That preoccupation illustrates the ethical ideals, deriving from both his Quaker ancestry and the conscience-ridden temper of the age, which ever afterwards informed Pease's Socialism.

He was born on December 20, 1857, the son of Thomas Pease, of Bristol. Educated at home, he entered a merchant's office in that city at the age of 17, stayed there for four years, and after an interval of uncertainty in 1880 became a member of the London Stock Exchange. He continued there for some six years, but with increasing uneasiness; the responsibilities of wealth, moderate though that wealth was, sat uncomfortably upon him, and the whole business of the Stock Exchange went against his conscience. An amateur carpenter and lover of good furniture, he spent the years from 1886 until 1889 as a cabinet-maker in Newcastle, where he gained a first-hand experience of trade unionism.

In 1890 he was appointed secretary of the Fabian Society and in 1913 became honorary secretary, a post he retained until 1938. Members and visitors to the offices at Clement's Inn and, later, in Tothill Street, Westminster, will remember his kindness and courtesy sometimes masked by a gruffness of manner. He had lived in retirement in Limpsfield for many years, absorbed in his garden and carpenter's workshop, but sadly afflicted by deafness. When in July 1954 the Fabian Society celebrated its seventieth birthday, Austin Albu, M.P., the chairman, presented to Pease specially bound copies of the *New Fabian Essays* and [Lord] Attlee's* memoirs.

Pease was a member of the executive of the Labour Party from 1900 until 1913, and a governor from its foundation of the London School of Economics. He produced a Fabian pamphlet, *The Case for Municipal Drink Trade,* but more important was his *History of the Fabian Society,* written in quiet vein and with a remarkable air of detachment—a most illuminating piece of work, invaluable as a source of reference, published in 1916. His last work was his contribution to *The Webbs and Their Work* on the Webbs' association with the Fabian Society. The volume was published in 1949.

He married, in 1889, Marjory, the daughter of the Rev. G. Davidson, of Perth. She died in 1950 and he is survived by two sons of the marriage.

January 7, 1955.

Sir Charles Reed Peers, C.B.E., F.B.A., who was for 20 years Chief Inspector of Ancient Monuments in the Office of Works, died in Surrey on November 16, 1952.

He was the son of the Rev. William Hanbury Peers and was born on September 22, 1868. Educated at Charterhouse and at King's College, Cambridge, he entered as a pupil in 1893 the office of the late Sir T. G. Jackson, R.A. He was for a time architectural editor of the Victoria County Histories until, in 1910, he became an inspector of ancient monuments in the Office of Works. For 20 years, from 1913 to 1933, he was chief inspector, and in that position he built up an organization and created a tradition which came to be regarded as a model of its kind for the whole world. Under his guidance the old quarrel between the "restorers" and the "preservers" practically died out. Only a fanatic could criticize the work that he did for the old buildings and monuments entrusted to his care, and his unique reputation in this field culminated in his presidency of the International Congress of Prehistoric and Protohistoric Sciences held in London in 1932.

After his retirement from the Office of Works he became surveyor of Westminster Abbey in 1935, and consulting architect of York Minster and Durham Cathedral. He was largely responsible for two important Acts passed by Parliament to protect ancient buildings and monuments, and there were few historic buildings and sites in the British Isles which did not owe something to his skilful care. He was architect-in-charge of the Durham Castle restoration scheme from 1933 to the completion of the work, and was responsible for the restoration of three interesting early groups of figures at New College, Oxford.

The variety of his activities and of the honours bestowed on him illustrates the scope of his professional career. His association with the Society of Antiquaries was a long and intimate one, for he was secretary from 1908 to 1921, then director until 1929, when he became president for five years. In 1938 he was the society's gold medallist. In 1933 he was elected a trustee of the British Museum and in the following year of the London Museum. He was appointed a member of the Standing Committee on Museums and Galleries in 1931, and two years later became Antiquary to the Royal Academy. In 1929 he had been elected a Fellow of the Royal Institute of British Architects.

Created C.B.E. in 1924, he was knighted in 1931. He held the degrees of Litt.D. and D.C.L., and was a governor of the Charterhouse. He wrote widely on his special subjects, contributing papers to *Archaeologia,* the *Proceedings of the Society of Antiquaries,* the *Antiquaries Journal,* and the proceedings of a number of learned societies.

In 1899 he married Gertrude Katherine Shepherd, by whom he had three sons.

November 17, 1952.

Professor E. Allison Peers, who as Gilmour Professor of Spanish in the University of Liverpool made that university one of the most important centres in England of Hispanic studies, died in hospital at Liverpool on December 21, 1952 after a long illness.

The Iberian peninsula, surrounded on three sides of its great area by the sea and cut off from the rest of Europe by the barrier of the Pyrenees, has developed a characteristic life of its own, sharing sometimes in the cultural movements of the continent of which it is a part, but more often standing somewhat aside from the main European stream. It has thus repelled some students, but upon others it has exercised the strong attraction that attaches to the mysterious and esoteric. It is, perhaps, the strong strain of mysticism in the Spanish character that has so often proved the lodestone to those students who have not turned away from this species of thought.

Professor Peers, who while still an undergraduate at Cambridge was strongly attracted to the romantic aspects of English and French literature, soon came under the spell of Spanish mysticism. He had already published a penetrating study of Elizabethan drama and its mad folk, and a work on the origins of French romanticism, when in 1923 he published his fine study of the Duque de Rivas, pointing the latter's part in the romantic movement in Spain. Another study of Rivas and a volume on Spanish mysticism quickly followed and established Professor Peers's reputation as an authority on Spanish thought whose work could not be neglected.

A stream of scholarly works of a similar character, together with translations of the work of such prominent Spanish thinkers as St. John of the Cross and St. Theresa, followed and consolidated a reputation already high. Professor Peers was a founder member of the Modern Humanities Research Association, and his interest in Catalan history, institutions, and literature was deep and life-long.

Meanwhile his propagation of Spanish studies was fostered by the publication of numerous books on Spain of a more popular character, among which may be mentioned *Royal Seville, A Companion to Spanish Travel,* and *Spain, the Church and the Orders.* Modern Spanish politics also came within his purview and his trilogy *The Spanish Tragedy, The Spanish Dilemma,* and *Spain in Eclipse* are redolent of a mind stored with the historical and cultural origins of the conflict which convulsed Spain in the years before the outbreak of war in Europe in 1939.

Lastly Peers, who as a teacher in one of the more modern universities was concerned to see that the fabric of higher education in England should be enlarged and strengthened to meet the changed conditions which were the aftermath of war, wrote under the pseudonym of "Bruce Truscot" some wise and useful little volumes pleading not for a lowering of the standards of the ancient seats of learning but for a recognition of the potentialities of the modern universities. "Oxbridge" and "Redbrick" (to use his graphic barbarisms) each has its vital part to play in the scheme of education, and few can quarrel with his conclusions.

Edgar Allison Peers was educated at Dartford Grammar School and at Christ's College, Cambridge, where he took a first class in the Medieval and Modern Languages Tripos in 1912. He also won the Winchester and the Harness prizes and had a double distinction in the Teachers' Diploma. After working as modern languages master at Mill Hill, Felsted and Wellington, he was appointed to the Gilmour Chair of Spanish in the University of Liverpool in 1920 and remained there for the rest of his life.

He held at various times a number of visiting professorships in Spain and America, and was Taylorian Lecturer at Oxford in 1940. From 1943 to 1946 he was educational director of the Hispanic Council.

He married in 1924 Marion Young, daughter of D. Grange, of Exeter, who survives him.

December 24, 1952.

Dr. F. W. Pember, D.C.L., who died on January 19, 1954 at the age of 91, was Warden of All Souls College, Oxford, from 1914 until 1932.

Francis William Pember was the son of Edward Henry Pember, K.C., of Vicar's Hill, Lymington, by his marriage to Fanny Richardson. He was born on August 16, 1862. After a happy and brilliant career at Harrow he went up to Balliol as a scholar in 1881. He took first classes in Honour Moderations and *Literae Humaniores,* won the Craven, Ireland, and Eldon scholarships, and was elected to a fellowship in law at All Souls in 1884. He was called to the Bar in 1889, and in later years became a Bencher of Lincoln's Inn. He practised as an equity and Parliamentary draughtsman and conveyancer, and served from time to time as a temporary assistant legal adviser at the Foreign Office.

In 1895 he married a woman of remarkable character and gifts, the Hon. Margaret Bowen, daughter of Lord Davey of Fernhurst, a Lord of Appeal in Ordinary. Their elder son, Edward, who would have gone up to Balliol from Harrow as an exhibitioner, joined the R.F.C. during the 1914-18 War, and was killed while flying. Their second son died in childhood. Their daughter, Katherine, is the wife of Sir Charles Darwin*.

In 1910 Pember was elected Estates Bursar of All Souls and maintained a lively interest in that department for the remainder of his association with the college. After the death of Sir William Anson in 1914 he was chosen by the Fellows to succeed Sir William as warden. No better choice could have been made. The new warden's interest in law was always more that of a scholar than a practising barrister, and he was better fitted by temperament for an academic career than for bureaucratic routine or the conflicts of the courts. Warden Anson had been practically the second founder of All Souls, and had achieved the most difficult task of transforming the character and activities of the college and at the same time keeping not merely the good will and respect but the deepest affection of the Fellows of both the old and the new foundation. His successor was admirably suited to carry on this tradition, to maintain this unity and once again to lead All Souls, as the only college of graduates in the University, to adapt itself to the changed conditions and needs of Oxford after the 1914-18 War. Warden Pember worked steadily, as Warden Anson had done a generation earlier, to secure this end, and at the same time to maintain the essential structure and fruitful vigour of his college. The new statutes of All Souls, drawn up in accordance with the recommendations of the Universities Commission after the 1914-18 War, show the success of his work.

Dr. Pember was vice-chancellor of the University from 1926 to 1929. None of those who were present will forget the dignity with which he welcomed his lifelong friend, Lord Grey of Fallodon, as chancellor in 1928. The quietness of these years in the history of the university bears witness to Pember's power of conciliation and the soundness of his judgment in affairs. In the sharpest controversy of the time—the discussion on the future of the Bodleian Library—he made no secret of his own views. Yet, although he was personally in favour of a large and far-reaching scheme of library development and coordination, he busied himself primarily with the discovery of a compromise which would meet on essential points the wishes of the two main parties in the university; to his work was largely due the agreement upon which it was possible for Oxford to approach a benefactor. In addition to his university and college work, Dr. Pember was chairman of the Governors of Harrow School from 1910 to 1944, and took the utmost care to foster and support the interests of the school.

He was a man who possessed in the highest degree the graces of friendship, and that rare gift of the years which bridges the gulf between old and young. He and Mrs. Pember took the greatest delight in the entertainment of their friends, and fulfilled the heavy social obligations of the vice-chancellorship with a distinguished and unselfish hospitality. No one could work with him or meet him without taking pleasure in the charm and ease and gentleness of his mind, the tolerance and sincerity of his opinion. He read widely in the arts and sciences as well as in his own subject of law. His memory was remarkable, and his conversation was furnished with a store of knowledge rare in these days of specialized study. He excelled in classical scholarship and in the felicitous expression which this scholarship teaches.

He was physically a strong and well-built man, a good cricketer, a tennis-player, and a fisherman. He took a wise man's delight in gardens, in the planting of trees, and in all the work of the fields. During his wardenship he and Mrs. Pember bought and restored Broncroft Castle, near Craven Arms. Here in the library and the garden, or in walking on the hills above Corvedale, they spent their days of leisure.

After his wife's death in 1942 Pember's own fine health began to fail. He gave up Broncroft Castle and had latterly lived with his daughter and son-in-law at Cambridge. To the end of his long life he remained for his friends a pattern of that serenity and natural goodness known to the ancient authors whose writings he loved to read.

January 20, 1954.

The name of **Sir George Pepler,** who died on April 13, 1959 at the age of 77, was almost a synonym for town and country planning. His career broadly spanned not only the growth of official town planning from birth to full maturity but also the parallel growth of the town planning profession. He was intimately concerned with both.

His official career began when he was called into the Local Government Board in 1914 to succeed Thomas Adams, the first town planning inspector to be appointed to attempt to get into operation the first, adoptive Town Planning Act of 1909. He remained in the same central department (which changed its name several times and is now the Ministry of Housing and Local Government) as technical head of planning from 1919 until his retirement in 1946. His last major work before leaving was the policy and machinery embodied in the planning sections of the 1947 Act, which established comprehensive and obligatory town and country planning as a normal function of local and central government. Throughout the inter-war years, when planning was neither liked officially nor understood by the local authorities who had to administer it, he worked steadily away stimulating thought and action all over the country. His contribution to the eventual acceptance of planning as obviously necessary may well outweigh that of any other single individual.

Unofficially he was both a founding father of the Town Planning Institute and a foster father to many of the young men who subsequently entered the new profession. Adams, Unwin, Lutyens, Geddes, Adshead, and a few others, including Pepler, were the leading spirits in launching the institute. The inaugural meeting's agenda in 1913 described Pepler as "honorary secretary and treasurer *pro tem*". He retained the post until his death, never regarding it as merely honorary, working all through for the advancement of his developing profession. For many years one of the institute's external examiners, he will be remembered by generations of architects, surveyors, and engineers for the way in which he could put students at their ease and draw the best out of them. He had no time for humbug, "long-haired behaviour", or doctrinaire opinions. He was the institute's president in 1919 and again in 1949, and was, in 1953, the first to receive its gold medal, an honour shared only with Sir Patrick Abercrombie [q.v.] and Lewis Mumford.

George Lionel Pepler, son of Harry Pepler, was born at Croydon in 1882 and educated at Bootham and Leys Schools. He was then articled to Walter Hooker, and in 1903 started in private practice as a surveyor and planner with Ernest Allen. They were pioneers in the modern layout of villages and towns on garden city lines, as instanced in their work at Fallings Park (for Sir Richard Paget), at Knebworth (for Lord Lytton), and other similar projects for owners of large estates.

Having built up a flourishing practice, and having got the institute launched, he allowed John Burn, then president of the Local Government Board (who had attended the institute's inaugural dinner) to entice him into the Civil service as a planning expert in 1914. There, under various designations, he remained as the nation's technical planning chief from 1919 onwards. He showed inspiration, patience, assiduity, and tact in getting an unfamiliar and controversial function eventually accepted as normal. His approach to planning was strategic, in the social-geographical tradition initiated by Geddes. His concern was with the pattern and distribution of settlements and industry, the communications between, land-use zoning, and the layout of developed areas—all the elements he helped to establish as the commonplaces of contemporary planning.

He had a fine capacity to visualize a region as a whole. This stood him in good stead, early in his career, in his work on the South Wales Regional Survey of 1920 and Neville Chamberlain's Committee on Unhealthy Areas in 1921, as in his outline plan (with Mr. P. W. MacFarlane) for the North East Development Area and his advisory work for Singapore at the end of his career, and in a diversity of similar projects in the years between. Between the wars, with little official support, he showed great skill in coaxing local authorities into forming regional groupings and preparing regional advisory plans to constitute an orderly framework for local planning decisions. Here it was his negotiating tact and awareness of psychological factors, as much as his technical competence, which made him so valuable an agent of his department. He was chairman of the Inter-Allied Committee for Physical Planning and Reconstruction in 1942-45 and of the Institution of Professional Civil Servants in 1937-42, and was president of the International Federation for Housing and Town Planning in 1935-38 and in 1947-52. He was knighted in 1948.

His kindness and humanity were irrepressible. Official retirement meant a return to private practice and a new range of interests—Singapore, membership of the Royal Commission on Common Land, work for the National Playing Fields Association and for rural preservation, advocacy of nursery schools and space for children. He coined the phrase "adventure playground" for one recent new development.

In 1903 Pepler married E. Amy (who died in 1942), and in 1947 Elizabeth Halton. He is survived by his second wife and by the son and two daughters of his first marriage.

April 15, 1959.

Lord Percy of Newcastle died at his home at Etchingham on April 3, 1958 at the age of 71.

The seventh son of the seventh Duke of Northumberland, Lord Eustace Sutherland Campbell Percy, P.C., was born on March 21, 1887, and educated at Eton and Christ Church, Oxford. He won the Stanhope History Essay Prize in 1907 and in the same year took a first class in Modern History. He began his career in the diplomatic service in 1911 and had the reputation of having gained more marks in the entrance examination than had ever been gained before.

He retired from the service in 1919 and two years later was returned as Conservative-Unionist member for Hastings, which continued to return him until he resigned the seat in 1937.

He had a foretaste of the Board of Education, on which he was to leave a mark not yet erased, when he was Parliamentary Secretary to the Board for a short spell in 1923 before passing over to the Ministry of Health, again as Parliamentary Secretary. Percy was one of the original members of the 1924 Royal Commission on Lunacy and Mental Disorder; over 30 years later he presided over the Royal Commission on the Law Relating to Mental Illness and Mental Deficiency, which proposed radical changes in the law affecting mental patients and suggested that the occasions for compulsory treatment should be less frequent.

In 1924 he returned as President to the Board of Education and was soon seen to be a power in the land. A whole man himself, he desired that others should be and believed that much could be done to create them by giving them education of the right sort in the right way. He had his own ideas on the leaving age, on sizes of classes and of training teachers, and did not hesitate to express them (though they did not always accord with those of his fellow Conservatives), for he felt that democracy was on trial and good education and good democracy were one flesh.

As he said some years later: "Excepting Russia, there is no dictatorship which did not arise out of the failures of democratic education. Let us be very careful lest we by undue smugness about our freedom and by our educational mistakes should prepare the way for a dictatorship in some form in this country". He was ever forward looking; he wrote in 1930: "The most desperate need of English education to-day is a common university policy"; he conceived of local colleges which would combine technology, commerce, art, and other activities, and also the manifold educational efforts that were grouped under the name of adult education, colleges presided over by men of the same intellectual rank as the head of an Oxford or Cambridge college, and he saw them in partnership with the universities giving humanism to an entire nation.

When the National Government was reconstituted in June 1935 Percy entered the Cabinet as Minister without Portfolio. Speaking a little later Stanley Baldwin declared it was essential to have a Minister entirely free from departmental duties who could help them in various investigations. He particularly wanted Percy, he said, with his trained, clear mind, to help him and the Cabinet in the consideration of many questions, particularly in relation to the social services and unemployment.

There was general disappointment when it was found that Percy would have no staff and that as he would not be in charge of any department it would be impossible to address questions to him in the Commons. The appointment lasted less than a year. In April 1936 he resigned: he felt, he said in a letter to Baldwin, that it would be difficult to justify the continuance of his post into a new financial year.

He remained in Parliament until 1937, when he resigned after his appointment as first Rector of King's College, Newcastle, which had been previously Armstrong College. During his stay—he remained until 1952—notable advances academically and structurally were made.

Percy's keen intellect and profound experience of education made him an obvious choice to preside over the committee set up in 1944 by R. A. Butler, President of the Board of Education, [Lord Butler of Saffron Walden] to report on future collaboration between universities and technical colleges on higher technological education in relation to the needs of industry. It was a subject close to Percy's heart and his name was given to the committee.

From 1953 to 1956 he was chairman of the Burnham Committee. A gifted and lucid speaker, he was no less gifted with his pen, and his writings cover a wide range of subjects. His published works include: *The Responsibilities of the League* (1920); *Education at the Crossroads* (1930); *Democracy on Trial* (1931); *Government in Transition* (1934); *John Knox* (1937); and *The Heresy of Democracy* (1954). For several years he edited the *Year Book of Education.*

He was sworn of the Privy Council in 1924 and in 1953 received a barony. He took the title of Baron Percy of Newcastle, of Etchingham in the county of Sussex.

He married in 1918 Stella, only daughter of Major-General L. Drummond, C.B., C.B.E., M.V.O. There were two daughters of the marriage.

[A tribute followed this obituary on the same day].

April 5, 1958.

Esmé Percy, the actor and producer, died in his sleep on June 16, 1957 at Brighton, where he was about to play in a new production, *The Making of Moo.* He was 69.

He was one of the last links on the English stage with Sarah Bernhardt, whom he ran away from school to see and under whom he studied. He made a speciality of Shaw's plays and was the first to accomplish the feat of staging the whole of *Man and Superman,* and it was a fitting election when he was made president of the Shaw Society in 1949. But though he is chiefly remembered as a Shavian he by no means confined himself to those roles, or even to the stage, for he appeared frequently in films and on television. His last appearance in the West End was in Wycherley's *Country Wife* in 1957.

Saville Esmé Percy was born on August 8, 1887, and was educated at Windsor and Brussels, where he decided on a stage career. He had the good fortune to study for the stage first at the Brussels Conservatoire and later in Paris, under Georges Berr, Maurice Leloir, and Sarah Bernhardt. His first appearance in England was in February 1904 at the Theatre Royal, Nottingham, with F. R. Benson's Shakespearian company. In the following year he took the part of Romeo in *Romeo and Juliet* at the Royalty in London, appearing under the auspices of the Elizabethan Stage Society. Though he had no difficulty in obtaining engagements in London, he spent several years touring with well-known companies here and in South Africa, and then joined Miss Horniman's company at the Gaiety, Manchester, where he found congenial occupation in important roles in carefully selected modern as well as classical plays.

In 1913 he himself formed a travelling company in partnership with Miss Kirsteen Graeme, and produced many pieces including several plays by Shaw and Wilde. When the 1914-18 War broke out he was making his name on the stage, but in 1915 he joined the Army and was commissioned in The Highland Light Infantry, with which he served in France until the end of hostilities. He made no attempt to return to civil life for some years, but remained with the Army of Occupation in charge of the Army-of-the-Rhine Dramatic Company, producing no fewer than 140 plays.

In 1923 he joined Reandean as assistant producer, and in the following year he became general producer for Charles Macdona's Bernard Shaw Repertory Company. In 1932 he went to America where he made such an impression that he remained for several years, producing and playing leading parts in Shakespearian and other plays.

In 1940 he joined Robert Atkins's* Open-Air Theatre in Regent's Park, and he continued to produce and to play in the West End until his death. Twenty years ago he lost the sight of his left eye when a Great Dane which he was stroking snapped at his face.

June 18, 1957.

Dr. R. C. L. Perkins, D.SC., F.R.S., the distinguished entomologist, best known for his work on the fauna of the Hawaiian Islands, died on September 29, 1955 at Bovey Tracey, Devon, at the age of 88.

Robert Cyril Layton Perkins was born on November 15, 1866, at Badminton, Gloucestershire, the second son of the Rev. Charles Matthew Perkins. He was educated at the King Edward VI Grammar School, St. Albans, where his father was headmaster, and also at Merchant Taylors' School. In 1885 he won an open classical scholarship to Jesus College, Oxford. He had, however, always been intensely interested in natural history and after reading classics for two years (by which time he had already made contributions to natural history journals) he was inspired by a lecture on the colours of insects by E. B. Poulton (afterwards Hope Professor and later Sir Edward Poulton) to give up classics and study science, though he had had no grounding of science at school.

In 1891 he was chosen by a committee appointed by the Royal Society and the British Association for the Advancement of Science to investigate the land fauna of the Hawaiian Islands; and he left England early in the following year. For nearly 10 years he worked for this committee, most of the time collecting material in the islands, but also, during visits to England, studying the subject at Cambridge. From March 1899 onwards began to appear his classic papers on the insect groups and birds in the *Fauna Hawaiiensis;* this work continued to appear until 1913, when he completed the general introduction to the whole series. This brought him world fame, and in 1912 he was awarded the Linnean Society of London's gold medal for eminent services rendered to zoology.

From 1902 to 1904 he worked for the Agricultural Department of the Hawaiian Islands in various capacities. In 1904 the Hawaiian Sugar Planters' Association added an insect department to their experimental station and took over the entomologists of the territorial Department of Agriculture with Dr. Perkins as the first director. His work there with O. H. Sweezey and F. Muir was mainly concerned with controlling the pests of the sugar cane, by introducing their natural parasites from their native countries. This involved making collecting expeditions to as far away as Australia. He was also concerned with Albert Koebele in the first attempt to control weeds with the insects that feed on them. In this case they controlled Lantana plant, which was covering large areas of sugar plantation with impenetrable thickets, by introducing some of its natural enemies from Mexico.

He was forced to retire through ill-health in 1912, and he settled at Newton Abbot in Devon, where he continued to work on his collections of Hawaiian insects and to write about them for more than 20 years. In England he furthermore made outstanding contributions to the knowledge of British insects, mainly bees and sawflies. In 1920 he was elected a Fellow of the Royal Society, and in 1954 an honorary Fellow of the Royal Entomological Society, of which he had been an ordinary Fellow for more than 50 years.

He married in 1901 Zoe, daughter of A. T. Atkinson, Superintendent of Public Instruction, Honolulu, Hawaiian Islands. She died in 1940. There were three sons of the marriage. He married secondly in 1942 Mrs. Clara Senior, of Highweek, Newton Abbot. She died in 1949.

October 5, 1955.

Eva Perón, acknowledged by both friends and enemies to be the most remarkable woman in Argentine history, whom Congress proclaimed the "spiritual chief of the Argentine nation", died on July 26, 1952 at the presidential residence in the presence of General Perón*, members of the Cabinet, and leaders of the General Confederation of Labour. Eva Perón, wife of the President of Argentina, was second only to her husband in power and influence in their country.

The republics of South America have in their brief histories abounded in men rising from obscurity like comets, to pass across the political horizon and to set again with equal speed. Señora Perón is the first woman to have had so spectacular a career in a part of the world where the tradition of feminine domesticity is still strong. True, she had a colourful personality, good looks, charm, and determination, but these gifts do not in themselves explain the hold she gained over her countrymen as well as her countrywomen, and though her marriage to the popular and forceful President of Argentina certainly contributed to her power, she was already a personality in her own right before her marriage. She thus remains something of an enigma, an enigma which her account of her political and social ideals published in 1951 under the title *La Razón de mi Vida* does little to resolve. Perhaps the secret of the influence of this young and attractive girl of humble origin, who could, while wrapped in furs and sparkling with diamonds, address the workers of Buenos Aires as one of themselves, was that they saw in her all their cherished ambitions and aspirations fulfilled. To them she was Cinderella in real life and if she could make the grade so could they.

Eva Maria Duarte was, according to

Argentine works of reference, born at Junin in the province of Buenos Aires on May 7, 1922, of relatively humble stock. The facts of her early life are obscure, but she seems to have gone to the capital before she was 20 and, aided by striking good looks and a vivacious manner, to have made something of a career for herself on the stage and in the cinema. Greater success attended her as a radio artist, in which in a number of historical serials she was cast for the heroine, generally encouraging and comforting South American liberators whose fortunes were temporarily in eclipse. Thus for millions of Argentines she became "Señorita Radio" and so was one of the people of nation-wide popularity on whom Colonel Perón, then Minister of Labour and Welfare, called when he wanted to make a great appeal for a national fund to help the victims of the San Juan earthquake. The attraction was mutual and together they set out to win support.

When her husband fell from power in October 1945 and was arrested, she it was above all others who roused the workers to paralyse the country until he was released and placed on the way to supreme power. When that was attained, she organized the women workers, made female suffrage a live issue, and was behind every step taken to lend aid to the aged, succour the children, and alleviate distress—especially if these things could be done in such a way as to flout the former ruling classes—the "oligarchy", as Señora Perón called them. She had, indeed, little or no sympathy with those who sought salvation outside the ranks of "Peronismo". The tangible results of her vast work as an organizer exist in the great social aid fund—an institution whose enormous financial resources have never been estimated and whose income and expenditure could not be audited. The fund became under her guidance the most important single influence in Argentine life. Every form of out-relief, children's playgrounds, aid for earthquake victims, toys for destitute children, clothes for the needy—all were available under "Evita's" banner, and this fact explains much of her power and popularity in her own country.

Her popularity, however, received a check in 1951, when her candidature for the Vice-Presidency caused such opposition in the Army that she felt obliged to announce over the radio, in a voice shaken with emotion, that she had taken the irrevocable decision to renounce the high honour by her own free will. For this her husband awarded her the Grand Extraordinary Peronista Medal, "in recognition of her noble gesture".

Her health was, in fact, already failing and in November she underwent a serious operation which led to a temporary recovery. She reappeared in public several times, but she was never able fully to resume her former activity. Masses for her recovery were said throughout Argentina, but it seemed unlikely that a fatal issue to her long illness could be far off. With her characteristic courage she accompanied her husband in the ceremonies of the inauguration of his second presidential term on June 4, and stood beside him in an open motor-car. This was her last public appearance.

July 28, 1952.

C. W. Dyson Perrins died at his home, Davenham, Malvern, on January 29, 1958 at the age of 93.

The death of Charles William Dyson Perrins means the loss of a generous benefactor, who also combined a wide variety of artistic tastes with exceptional means for gratifying them.

He was born on May 25, 1864. His father was a member of the firm of Lea and Perrins, retail chemists, in Malvern. They obtained—tradition said from a retired officer who had served in India—the recipe of the "Worcester Sauce" which through a long period has been famous throughout the world. All the immense fortune gained was derived from the sauce alone; its manufacturers placed no subsidiary articles on the market. One of its early results was to enable Dyson to be educated at Charterhouse and Queen's College, Oxford. In later years he bestowed a large endowment for research on his university, which conferred on him the honorary degree of D.C.L.

After four years (1888-1892) in the Highland Light Infantry, Dyson, who had married in 1889, entered the family business, living in Malvern and journeying daily to the factory in Worcester. At no time did his artistic tastes hinder him from being also a most astute and successful business man. He became Mayor of Worcester in 1897 and High Sheriff of Worcestershire in 1899. By this date he had begun to acquire those illuminated manuscripts and early printed books which were ultimately to form one of the most valuable privately owned collections in England.

There seemed no limit to his resources. When the famous collection of Richard Fisher, of Midhurst, was to come under the hammer, a number of bibliophiles and agents from the United States hastened to cross the Atlantic. On reaching Liverpool—this was before the days of wireless—they found that there would be no auction; to avoid their undesired competition, Perrins had stepped in and bought the entire library.

In 1946 he began to disperse his collection of printed books. The first sales began in November 1946, and the final auction took place in June 1947. In all the books realized £147,627. He retained his famous illuminated manuscripts.

Perrins proposed to use most of the sum derived from the sale for the development on a very large scale of what for long had been another of his principal interests. He was a first-rate authority on Worcester china, and had a possibly unique collection of it. When, in the "slump" of the 1920s, the china works were in great difficulties and their closing seemed imminent—resulting in a great increase of local unemployment—Perrins took over the management, and kept the historic factory in operation at heavy loss to himself. During the first part of the 1939-45 War it had to produce utilitarian china for the Government, and afterwards to manufacture parts for aeroplanes. On the return of peace Perrins determined to spend a large part of his private fortune in re-equipping the Worcester china works on the largest scale, and to give its products an artistic standard of the highest kind.

He had got together also a remarkable collection of eighteenth and early nineteenth century drawings and caricatures. Indeed, the number of his hobbies was remarkable. He was a keen sportsman. For upwards of 20 years he owned Ardross Castle, in Ross-shire, which provided him with deer forest, grouse moors, salmon fishing, and a number of lochs.

Perrins's benefactions were a pattern of their kind. He was no indiscriminate giver or scatterer of charitable largesse. Careful investigation had to convince him that the cause fully deserved support, but when convinced he gave munificently. Personally, he was among the most modest of men, and, with all his great wealth and wonderful possessions, he consistently avoided publicity with striking success. But the memory of his personal friendship will indeed be treasured by those who were fortunate enough to gain it.

January 30, 1958.

Lord Perry, for many years head of the Ford organization in England, died on June 17, 1956 suddenly at his home in the Bahamas at the age of 78.

The Right Hon. Sir Percival Lea Dewhurst Perry, Baron Perry, of Stock Harvard, in the County of Essex, in the Peerage of the United Kingdom, K.B.E., was born at Bristol on March 18, 1878, but spent his childhood at Birmingham, where he won a scholarship at King Edward's School. He began his working life in a lawyer's office in that city, but as soon as the opportunity arose left to try his luck in London. There he renewed association with several friends of his youth and after a number of tentative business ventures he finally entered the motor trade, being instrumental in introducing the Ford car to England in the early years of the century.

Recognizing the possibilities of cheap motoring, he concentrated the greater part of his energies on the American firm's interests. He visited the United States, met Henry Ford, the founder of the firm, and returned keener than ever on promoting its success. In 1909 he formed the Ford Motor Company (England) Limited and in 1911 the company took over a factory at Trafford Park, Manchester. He handled the reorganization of the Ford interests in England and Europe in 1928, which resulted in the formation of the present Ford Motor Company Limited with a capital of £7m. (later £9m.) and the great new factory built on the Thames at Dagenham. He was chairman until his retirement at the age of 70 in 1948. In addition he was chairman of the Ford Motor companies of Belgium, Denmark, Finland, the Netherlands, Italy, Spain, and Sweden, a director of the National Provincial Bank Limited, and president of the Motor Trade Association from 1914 to 1916.

Other extensive business concerns founded

by him included the Slough Estates, which he organized in 1920 on a basis provided by the purchase of hundreds of acres of land, buildings and surplus supplies of mechanical transport thrown on the market after the end of the 1914-18 War. This conversion of the Slough depôt into an industrial estate was probably one of the most successful transformations of a war-time "white elephant" into a prosperous investment.

During that war he worked with his own staff without remuneration in various Government departments. He was deputy controller of the food production department of the Board of Agriculture in 1916, for two years director of the agricultural machinery department at the Ministry of Munitions, and in the latter part of the war, first, deputy controller of the mechanical warfare department, and then director of traction at the Ministry of Munitions.

He was appointed C.B.E. in 1917, promoted K.B.E. in 1918, and was raised to the peerage in 1938 in recognition of his public service. In the 1939-45 War he served from its outbreak for a year as business adviser to the Ministry of Food, but resigned on the appointment of Lord Woolton*, whose experience made the office virtually redundant.

Lord Perry's chief interest outside the motor industry was farming, and in association with Henry Ford he was responsible for instituting at Boreham, Essex, a remarkable experiment in cooperative farming, known as the Fordson farms. In spite of his material success as a business man he never lost his liking for the things of the mind, and many who expected to discover in him the orthodox hard-headed materialist were surprised at his fondness for poetry, literature, and the arts. He published several books on economics and finance and a volume of verse.

He married in 1902 Catherine, daughter of John Meals of Hull. There were no children of the marriage, and the peerage becomes extinct.

June 19, 1956.

Dr. Bliss Perry, Emeritus Professor of English in Harvard University and for many years one of the foremost men of letters in the United States, died at Exeter, New Hampshire, on February 13, 1954 at the age of 93.

He was widely known as editor, professor, novelist, critic, poet, and biographer. Though he was a busy man with many calls on his time, his literary work seemed hardly ever to suffer through strain or hurry and always manifested a tone of freshness and of refined and delicate taste. He always relished his work and revelled in it, and when he came to retire to private life after many years spent in teaching, the title he chose for his delightful autobiography was *And Gladly Teach.*

Bliss Perry was a native of New England and spent nearly all his life there. Born at Williamstown in Massachusetts on November 25, 1860, he was naturally sent to Williams College and after graduating there in 1881 went on to take post-graduate work at Princeton, Berlin, and Strasbourg. In 1886 he returned to Williams College as Professor of English Literature and after seven years went to Princeton to fill a similar position there. In 1899 he was induced to take over the editorship of the *Atlantic Monthly,* to which he had been a frequent contributor, and during the next 10 years he raised it to a high place among the more serious American magazines. During most of that time he engaged in no teaching, but in 1907 he accepted an invitation to fill the Chair of English Literature in Harvard University.

He took up his duties at once, and continued to edit the *Atlantic Monthly* for the next two years, but in 1909 gave that task up to devote himself fully to his professorial duties. He held the chair at Harvard till 1930 when he retired at the age of 70, having won the respect and love of generations of students. In 1909-10 he was Harvard lecturer at the University of Paris. He received honorary degrees from many American universities, was a member of the American Academy of Arts and Letters, of the Massachusetts Historical Society, and of the Royal Society of Literature in London.

Besides his work for the magazines he acted as editor of many series of books. Some were designed for the use of his students; such are his selections from Burke, Scott, and Emerson, but his notes so enlivened these little books that they soon found a wider public. He also edited a series of "Little Masterpieces" in 18 volumes. He was for a time editor of the Cambridge edition of the poets, standard publications of complete works enjoying a wide circulation all over America.

Of his own original works his novels and stories circulated among an understanding and appreciative circle. They were his earliest work, *The Broughton House* (1890) and *Salem Kittridge* (1894). After that he devoted himself chiefly to criticism. He wrote on poetry and prose fiction always with fine understanding and judgment. His works on Walt Whitman, Whittier, and Carlyle fully justified his appreciation of each, but his chief praise was reserved for Emerson, whom he revered above all the other New England writers. His own writing was generally of a happy, carefree character, but when he found any one detracting from the glories of Emerson he found it difficult to restrain himself. He collected in book form from time to time many of his occasional literary essays and poems, and it is surprising how often some work of his, intended for the moment, evinces a lasting power and freshness.

He married Miss Annie L. Bliss, of New Haven, Connecticut, in 1888. There were two daughters and a son of the marriage.

February 16, 1954.

Henry Seymour (Atty) Persse, a well-known racehorse owner and trainer, and in his younger days a notable amateur rider, died in hospital at Windsor on September 5, 1960 at the age of 91.

He was the son of Henry Sadleir Persse, of Glenarde, Galway, and was educated at Cheltenham and Oxford. He spent his early years in Ireland, where he was master of the Limerick Hunt, won the Conyngham Cup at Punchestown in 1897, and headed the list of amateur riders in 1902. He was also an amateur rider in the United States.

Persse started training in 1903, and his first notable successes were with Bachelor's Double, who won the City and Suburban Handicap and the Royal Hunt Cup in 1910. His classic winners were Sweeper II (1912), Tetratema (1920), and Mr. Jinks (1929) in the 2,000 Guineas; and Silver Urn (1922) in the 1,000 Guineas. The race in which he had most success was the Kempton Park Great Jubilee Handicap, which he won six times. He headed the list of winning trainers in 1930 with nearly £50,000 to the credit of his stable.

Yet he is probably best remembered as the trainer of The Tetrarch, the grey horse who on account of his peculiar markings was popularly known as the "Spotted Wonder". Persse bought The Tetrarch as a yearling for 1,300 guineas on behalf of Major Dermot McCalmont. The colt's performances as a two-year-old were the talk of 1913, and after being retired to the stud he sired three St. Leger winners.

At the time of his retirement in 1953 Persse was training at Kingsdown, Upper Lambourn, Berkshire.

Even to those who had been nearly a lifetime on the racecourse he seemed to have been there for a generation before, and there is no one who knew him who will not feel that a little of the fun of the day's sport is now gone.

A remarkable blend of perspicacity and humour made up his character. As a trainer he was a disciplinarian feared by his Irish lads, but they gave him a loyalty and affection they might not have given elsewhere. What will be remembered equally with the success of The Tetrarch is the unusual ability with which he produced two-year-olds ready to race out of the gate like old hands on their first visit to the racecourse.

With hounds he was in his element, and in Limerick, Galway, or Kilkenny he got across the country second to none. When boots were drawn off on winter evenings his company was much sought, for from his enormous experience he would produce an endless stream of chuckling stories that could keep one up gladly until the early hours of the morning.

He married in 1921 Emily, daughter of the late Sir George Brooke, Bt., who before her marriage had appeared in several successful plays in the West End. She died in 1953. Their only son was killed in action in Italy in 1944.

September 6, 1960.

Lord Perth, Secretary-General to the League of Nations from its formation in 1919 until 1933, and British Ambassador to Italy from 1933-39, died on December 15, 1951 at his home at Rogate, Sussex, aged 75.

As first Secretary-General, he found himself responsible for the creation of the permanent Secretariat of the League, and for its organization as a cohesive body. Heavy responsibilities fell on him at the meetings of the Council, and the League may be said to have owed much of its early authority and successes to his untiring efforts and practical wisdom. During his time as British Ambassador at Rome relations between the two countries were often strained, but he did not lose the qualities of sound judgment and even temper which made him a valuable conciliator throughout a distinguished career.

The Rt. Hon Sir James Eric Drummond, sixteenth Earl of Perth, Lord Drummond of Cargill and Stoball, tenth Viscount Strathallan, Lord Drummond of Cromlix, Hereditary Thane of Lennox, Hereditary Steward of Menteith and Strathearn, and Chief of the Clan Drummond, P.C., G.C.M.G., C.B., was born on August 17, 1876, the second son of James David, eighth (or tenth but for an attainder, according to *Debrett*) Viscount Strathallan. His mother was Margaret, eldest daughter of William Smythe, of Methven Castle. He succeeded to the title on August 20, 1937, on the death of his half-brother, William Huntly Drummond, the fifteenth Earl, born in 1871, elder son of the above James David and Ellen, second daughter of Cuthbert B. Thornhull, I.C.S. He went to Eton in 1890, and was in Philip Williams's house, his tutor being Richard S. Kindersley. He won the Prince Consort's first French prize in 1895, the year in which he left Eton.

He entered the Foreign Office in 1900, and in 1906 was appointed to be private secretary to Lord E. Fitzmaurice, then Under-Secretary of State for Foreign Affairs in Sir Henry Campbell-Bannerman's Ministry. In 1908 there began his association with Sir Edward Grey, to whom he was précis-writer in that year and again in 1910. He was one of Asquith's private secretaries from 1912 to 1915, and private secretary to Sir Edward Grey from 1915 to 1916. He remained private secretary to the Secretary of State for Foreign Affairs after Grey's retirement in 1916, and served in that capacity with Balfour, whom he accompanied on the mission to Washington in April 1917. After the resignation of Balfour he continued for some time as private secretary to the Secretary of State, then Lord Curzon.

In 1919 he accompanied the British delegation to the Peace Conference. In Paris, amid an atmosphere of tension and during the most agitated periods, he brought to the complicated affairs under discussion a detachment the sincerity of which was plain to all. His sound knowledge of procedure and grip of detail were of infinite value to the delegation. Such qualities could not fail to be taken into account when the idea of a League of Nations began to take practical form. It was eventually decided to place a trained official at the head of the League organization, designed to be the constant element in the League, which in the early stages promised to be a centre of turmoil. Balfour suggested to Clemenceau the name of Drummond as Secretary-General. He at once supported the idea and secured the assent of President Wilson. Drummond took office on May 5, 1919.

During the course of the Peace Conference much of the enthusiasm in the British, Dominions, and American delegations for the idea of a League had been damped down, and Drummond began his task of forming the Secretariat in an atmosphere of benevolent scepticism. As he conceived it the Secretariat was to be an expert international organization, the task of which would be to draw up objective statements of the problems to be discussed and indicate the points on which Governments were in agreement, limiting automatically discussions by Government representatives to matters of real divergence, and thus greatly increasing the chances of success.

Having secured the adoption of his point of view Drummond could go ahead with the creation of the neutral-spirited institution he conceived the Secretariat to be. He himself has described how on returning to London he settled down to work in a small back drawing-room in Manchester Square, with Lord Colum Crichton-Stuart (then a second secretary in the diplomatic service), one typist, and an office keeper. At an early stage they were joined by two valuable collaborators, Jean Monnet and Raymond Fosdick, Between them they sketched out the framework of the organization. It grew apace. Soon the staff moved to Caxton House, next to Sunderland House, where it overflowed into annexes, and then to the Hotel National, Geneva. In this manner an international Civil service, unprecedented in history, was brought into being.

The League began under a cloud, for the United States threw over President Wilson and rejected participation, and Drummond himself, for all his faith, doubted greatly whether the League could survive the blow. It went on and in a few months the machinery he had built up was in full action. Within 10 months of the coming into force of the peace treaty there had been held 10 meetings of the council and one of the assembly.

As events developed, two major functions were forced upon him. On the one hand he remained a diplomat, charged with a wider mission than can ever have fallen to any ambassador; on the other he was head of a Civil service and was responsible, in the last resort, for all the detail of its administration and activities. There were few Foreign Ministers who did not consult him on problems connected with the foreign relations of their countries, and not necessarily on matters coming before the League. Throughout the years the Disarmament Conference, first in its preparatory stage and then in all its unwieldy development as an international wrangle, continued to claim his attention. He at least had no illusions as to the scale of the problem, and the president, the late Arthur Henderson, already a sick man, leaned on him for advice in everything. Drummond prepared the entry of Germany into the League during a visit to Berlin in March 1925, when he negotiated with von Schubert and Stresemann.

Drummond took leave of the Secretariat, formally handed over his office to his successor, Joseph Avenol [q.v.], and finally left Geneva on June 30, 1933. On July 7 it was officially announced that he had been appointed Ambassador at Rome in succession to Sir Ronald Graham.

Drummond found an Italy which, though her ulterior motives were not yet apparent to the rest of the world, was working steadily to secure her position in Europe in order to be able to embark on a course of adventure in Africa. The fading of all serious hope of disarmament during the summer of 1934 must have suggested to Mussolini the desirability of coming to terms with Germany over Austria, for in June he met Hitler, and made his first attempt to size up the rival dictator by personal contact. Whatever hopes he may have conceived of striking a bargain were, however, dashed by the murder of Dr. Dollfuss, and the German decision early in 1935 to reintroduce conscription and rearm on a large scale sent Italy into close conclave with England and France.

The formation of the Stresa front was the result, and in the negotiations which led up to the conference Drummond played an important part. Events in Abyssinia were, however, already following the course laid down for them by Mussolini, and presently Drummond found himself the vehicle of anxious inquiries and aggrieved protests evoked from the British Government by Italy's aggression in Africa. Sanctions, which came into force on November 18, 1936, threw Italy into the arms of Germany and paved the way for the creation of the Rome-Berlin axis.

Nothing in the power of the most gifted of ambassadors could have prevented it. Nevertheless, it was during this period that Drummond, by his patience, even temper, good sense, and transparent honesty of purpose, gradually established relations of personal confidence with Mussolini, which enabled him later to negotiate successfully for the re-establishment of Anglo-Italian friendship, the signing of the "Gentlemen's Agreement" in 1937, and, after the setback of Italian intervention in Spain, to the Anglo-Italian agreement of 1938.

Perth was now 62 and had well earned the right to retire. He was anxious to devote himself to the care of the estates which he had inherited, and his health was no longer quite equal to the strain of daily desk work. In May 1939 he retired from the service. On the outbreak of war he gave his wide experience to the newly formed Ministry of Information as chief adviser on foreign publicity until his resignation in 1940.

In 1946 he was appointed Deputy Leader of the Liberal Party in the House of Lords. He was made a C.B. in 1914, a K.C.M.G. in 1916, and a D.C.L. of Oxford in 1930. In 1931 he was awarded the Wateler Prize of £2,000, the proceeds of which he devoted to the International Federation of League of Nations Associations in Brussels. He was promoted G.C.M.G. in 1934.

He married in 1904 the Hon. Angela Constable-Maxwell, youngest daughter of the eleventh Baron Herries. There were one son, Viscount Strathallan, and three daughters of the marriage.

December 17, 1951.

Marshal Philippe Pétain, former Marshal of France, who died aged 95 in the Ile d'Yeu on July 23, 1951—six years to the day after the opening of the trial at which he was sentenced to death—was head of the French State from the capitulation of France to Germany in June 1940 until her liberation in 1944. Twelve years ago he would have been chiefly remembered by the world as the successful defender of Verdun, and as the leader in immediate command of the victorious French armies in the summer and autumn of 1918. To-day he goes down to history as the man whose influence forced on his country the humiliation of surrender. He believed that an early surrender would soften the German terms, and he even dreamed that he could build a France cleansed through suffering. He was tragically mistaken, but clung to his faith in his mission almost to the end.

Henri Philippe Pétain was born at Cauchy-la-Tour, in the Pas de Calais, on April 24, 1856. While peace lasted his career as a professional soldier was not one of outstanding distinction, though he had held the appointment of lecturer at the École Supérieure de la Guerre. August 1914 found him in command of the 33rd Infantry Regiment with the rank of colonel, but he was promoted to command of a brigade at the end of that month, and soon gave proof of his ability in the field. During the battle of Charleroi his brigade covered the retreat of Lanrezac's army across the Meuse with such skill and determination that a month later he was placed at the head of a division. His promotion continued with unusual rapidity, for in October he was given command of XXXIII Corps—a step which he fully justified by brilliant generalship in the Artois fighting early in 1915.

By 1916 his reputation was solidly established, and when the situation at Verdun became critical in February 1916 Joffre had no hesitation in sending him to take over the defence of the hard-pressed fortress. The situation was serious when he arrived at his new post. He began by completely reorganizing the defensive system and then, by his example and bearing, completed his task by restoring the morale of his sorely tried troops. In a short time he had checked the German onrush; and finally he so consolidated his position that after some months of further desperate but fruitless and costly efforts the Germans abandoned the offensive. His famous phrases, "Ils ne passeront pas!", "On les aura!" were slogans which he fulfilled to the utmost.

The victor of Verdun was made a Grand Officer of the Legion of Honour and appointed to succeed General Langle de Cary in command of the Centre Group of Armies. These forces were not heavily engaged in Nivelle's ill-fated plan for a breakthrough in 1917, and when that commander was removed after his failure Pétain, who had from the first condemned the offensive as premature and overbold, was appointed to succeed him as commander-in-chief and found that he had taken over a herculean task. The terrible losses of the Nivelle offensive had driven many of the French troops—already war weary and discontented—into open mutiny. He succeeded in restoring first confidence and then discipline. At the end of the war, on November 21, 1918, he received the corded Marshal's baton in the reconquered city of Metz.

His next appointment was that of Vice-President of the Supreme War Council, and in January 1922 he was also made Inspector-General of the Army—an office which had been re-created to secure closer cooperation between the Army and the Ministry of War. Thereafter, but for a brief period of office as Minister of War in the Doumergue Cabinet of 1934, he lived in comparative retirement.

In March 1939 he came into the public eye again as French Ambassador to Spain—a post which he accepted at the urgent request of Édouard Daladier*, then Prime Minister. But although his personal prestige with the Spaniards was great he was unable to do much to remove the very strong anti-French bias of General Franco* and his followers. He remained in Madrid until May 1940, when he was hastily recalled by Paul Reynaud* to enter the Cabinet as Vice-Premier in the hope that his presence would strengthen the national morale at a moment when the German armies were overrunning the country. The fateful Cabinet meeting at Bordeaux, on the night of June 16, found Pétain leading the majority in favour of capitulation. He formed a Cabinet the same night, and remained head of the State, with a fictitious authority and a questionable title, until his deportation by the Germans. In the so-called free zone the first inclination was to hail him as the saviour of his country from worse calamities. He used his prestige to substitute the words *Travail, Famille, Patrie* for the *Liberté, Égalité, Fraternité* of the revolution, but the movement which they were intended to inspire was still-born.

His relations with his German masters—he himself admitted that they held the leading-strings—were as shifting as his policy. He first got rid of Laval, the unscrupulous apostle of collaboration and a German victory; thereafter he allowed Admiral Darlan, himself by no means backward in "collaboration", to secure a large measure of power; and finally he allowed the return of Laval with an authority which, backed by German bayonets and the cudgels of a motley of French Fascists, made him dictator. In November 1942 came the allied landings in North Africa and the German march into Pétain's free zone. Throughout 1943 resistance inside France waxed and Pétainism waned. In the summer of 1944 the "Head of the State" left Vichy, first for the neighbourhood of Paris and later for the Swiss frontier. Thence he was removed into Germany. Meanwhile Paris was liberated, and the High Court of Justice had declared its intention to try the Marshal *in absentia,* the charge being an "attempt against the internal safety of the State". But before the trial opened Pétain approached the Swiss Government, through the German authorities, for leave to enter Swiss territory, in order to surrender as a prisoner at the French frontier.

This leave was granted, and so opened the last phase, with his incarceration in the fortress of Montrouge, from which, with his wife, he was transferred to the court building in Paris, where his trial opened on July 23. Early in the proceedings Pétain read a statement in which he said that the court did not represent the French people, and that he would not answer any questions. The trial dragged on, with Weygand* giving evidence for the defence on the eighth day and Laval appearing as a witness on the eleventh. Then, early on the morning of August 15, he was sentenced to death, but the Supreme Court expressed the wish that the sentence should not be carried out, because of the Marshal's great age. Before the jury had withdrawn Pétain rose to speak again of the silence he had kept, and of his part in the sufferings of France: "The French people will not forget. They know that I defended them as I did at Verdun". The High Court's recommendation was accepted, the sentence being commuted to detention for life.

In November 1945 it was announced that Pétain had been transferred to the island of Yeu, about 15 miles off the French coast between Nantes and La Rochelle, and it is on this island that he died, remembered not as the defender of Verdun but as the Marshal of Vichy.

July 24, 1951.

Sir Maurice Peterson, G.C.M.G., Ambassador to the Soviet Union from 1946 to 1949, died at his home at Kintbury, Berkshire, on March 15, 1952, less than a week after his sixty-third birthday.

The most obvious traits in his character were calm reserve and economy of words, and he struck many foreigners as the traditional Englishman. He was in fact less insular than he appeared and this was largely due to his Canadian background. He had a remarkably clear mind, and, at any rate, in his confidential reports, took care never to cloud his meaning. This characteristic is particularly noticeable in his volume of reminiscences, where, having at last shaken off the shackles of official reticence, he wrote in forthright style of Soviet domestic and foreign policy.

Maurice Drummond Peterson was born on March 10, 1889, the younger son of the late Sir William Peterson, of McGill University. He was educated at Rugby and Magdalen College, Oxford, and took a first in Modern History in 1911. In 1913 he began his unusually varied career in the diplomatic service and came early into contact with A. J. Balfour, whom he accompanied to the Washington Conference on the limitation of armaments in 1921-22, and with Lord Curzon. For both of these great figures of a past age he cherished a high admiration, which helped to form his strong and decisive personality. His rise was remarkably rapid and by 1934 he was acting High Commissioner in Egypt.

It was not long before he was made head of a mission for in 1936 he was appointed Minister to Bulgaria, but after only some two years in the post he was transferred to Iraq and then to Spain as Ambassador, where it was considered necessary at that time to have a strong man. In the early days of the 1939-45 war, in increasingly difficult circumstances, he defended British interests with such persistence that in the spring of 1940 he was officially congratulated by the then Foreign Secretary, Lord Halifax [q.v.]. A few weeks later he received a letter informing him that he was to be replaced immediately. The situation was not handled with the highest tact, and Peterson took it hardly when he learned that his successor was to be Sir Samuel Hoare, now Lord Templewood [q.v.].

After an unhappy period at the Ministry of Information and the Foreign Office he was appointed Ambassador to Turkey in 1944. He had recovered from his Spanish tragedy and, always happiest in the Near East, he did excellent work in Ankara. Yet another sudden move came in 1946 when he was sent as Ambassador to Moscow. Relations between Russia and the west had already worsened and there was little he could do in Moscow to mitigate the suspicion which had begun to grow up there even before the end of the war. Nevertheless, there were few who could have done better to defend British interests and to match Russian suspicion with British reserve. Unfortunately the latter part of his term in Moscow was clouded by illness, and though he returned to England to recuperate he was compelled to resign from the Diplomatic service in 1949, when he joined the board of the Midland Bank.

He had been created C.M.G. in 1933 and was promoted K.C.M.G. in 1938 and G.C.M.G. in 1947. In 1950 he published a most readable volume of reminiscences under the title *Both Sides of the Curtain,* containing a number of penetrating studies of the men, both British and foreign, with whom he had had to work during his career.

He married in 1927 Eleanor Angel, second daughter of the late Rev. H. W. L. O'Rorke, who survives him together with three sons of the marriage.

March 17, 1952.

Lady Pethick-Lawrence, who died on March 11, 1954 at her home at Gomshall, Surrey, at the age of 86, was a leader with the Pankhursts [q.v.] of the Women's Social and Political Union in the struggle for votes for women.

A true orator with a great power of inducing sacrifice, she had a fertile imagination and a great sense of the picturesque; all the colour, pageantry, and symbolism of the militant suffragist movement were due to her efforts. Beginning as a social worker bent on easing the lot of young women working in industry, she did fine service among the working girls of the East End long before she became interested in seeking political power for women. When that work was added to her other self-imposed tasks, her passion flamed into incandescence and until the battle was won she was a formidable champion. Her great influence on women continued after the vote was won and almost to the end of her life women's societies frequently sought her advice.

Emmeline Pethick was born at Bristol on October 21, 1867, the daughter of Henry Pethick, J.P., and was educated at private schools in England, France, and Germany. Attracted to social work, she became a "sister" at the West London Mission under the Rev. Hugh Price Hughes. With Mary Neal, another "sister" from the mission, she founded the Esperance Club for working girls and originated the first scheme to give them holidays. With the Hon. Lily Montagu and her sister she founded the "Green Lady Hostel" at Littlehampton in 1898 to implement the scheme. This venture was followed by the "Sundial" at Holmwood for holidays for the club children. She also started a cooperative dressmaking firm, Maison Esperance, which had an eight-hour day, a minimum wage and annual holidays, all of them bold innovations at the time.

For years she had been a member of the old and somewhat staid Suffrage Society but in 1906 she joined the Pankhursts in the newer and more militant Women's Social and Political Union. She became honorary treasurer of the union and for the next six years gave all her time, thought and energy to it. Her first arrest was in 1906 in the lobby of the House of Commons; she was imprisoned five times and was a hunger striker. In 1901 she had married Lord Pethick-Lawrence* who at that time was F. L. Lawrence, editor and part proprietor of the London evening paper, the *Echo.* They worked together in the suffrage movement and together they edited the weekly paper *Votes for Women.*

In 1912 she split with the Pankhursts on the question of extreme militancy and in 1914 she joined the newly formed United Suffragists. In that year she was invited to America to promote the Women's International League for Peace. While there she helped to inaugurate the campaign which resulted in the political enfranchisement of women in the United States. After being present at the International Women's Congress at The Hague she became honorary treasurer of the Women's International League in Britain.

The first time women were able to stand for Parliament, in 1918, she was Labour candidate at Rusholme, Manchester. She was president of the Women's Freedom League for years, and in 1953 was President of Honour.

Her notable volume of reminiscences, *My Part in a Changing World,* was published in 1938. Written with deep feeling and intensity of expression, the book is a moving account of the high courage which she brought to her particular mode of dealing with the problems of social betterment. She was indeed in the main stream of Victorian philanthropy, but she brought an individual touch and a sense of mission to the work which gave it permanence and something of greatness.

March 12, 1954.

The Gypsy **Petulengro** died on June 16, 1957 at his home at Littlehampton, Sussex.

"An arrogant, independent being, jack of many trades, master of all" was his description of himself. He was all that popular fancy would have a Romany be: he wandered the country and the world, he fought with his fists, he played the violin, he prepared philtres, told fortunes, culled his meals from the hedgerows. In one way he was untypical: he could read and write—to the great gain of the public.

In his book *A Romany Life* he appears as a grandson of Ambrose Smith, George Borrow's Petulengro. His father traded Welsh ponies in Hungary and Romania, and married and settled down there; and Petulengro's earliest memories were of the town of Galatz and the Danube. When he was still small his family crossed Europe in their caravan and went to England. He learnt odd jobs and the rudiments of horse trading until an encounter with a game-keeper, whose teeth he knocked out, prompted him to take refuge in the militia. He was later a regular cavalryman. Out of the Army, he became a hawker and a herb collector for chemists; he went to America, where he dealt in potions under the name of Professor Thompson-Thompson; he was gaoled in Brazil, where he had gone to play the fiddle; he prospected for diamonds in South Africa; and chatted with Michael Collins in Cork when the "Black and Tans" were out. He was a trick fiddler at a circus and a member of the Queen's Hall orchestra under Sir Henry Wood.

He became a popular broadcaster before the war and his lore found an unexpected application during the worst days of food rationing, as he described dishes which could be made out of dandelions and other wayside plants.

In 1937 he was crowned as "gypsy king" in a recently revived ceremony at Baildon on the Yorkshire moors.

June 17, 1957.

Harry St. John B. Philby, C.I.E., an explorer of the first rank to whom we owe most of our knowledge of the Arabia of today, died in Beirut on September 30, 1960. He was 75.

He was born on April 3, 1885, in Ceylon, where his father, Henry Montague, was a tea-planter. After a very successful career at Westminster and Trinity College, Cambridge, he entered the I.C.S. (1907), served in the Punjab, attained a high standard in several oriental languages, and in 1915 became Secretary to the Board of Examiners at Calcutta. From 1915 to 1917 he was employed on political duties with the forces in Mesopotamia, was made C.I.E., and then finding, as he admitted, that there was not room for him and Arnold Wilson, he gladly accepted charge of a British Political Mission to Ibn Saud.

This gave him the chance to make the 44-day crossing of Arabia from Uqair to Jedda which formed the subject of his first book, *The Heart of Arabia* (1922); it also led to his conclusion that the rising star in Arabia was Ibn Saud [q.v.] and not King Hussein. During the siege of Jedda by Ibn Saud's forces in 1925 Philby, though still a member of the I.C.S., went there as a self-appointed go-between, to the embarrassment of H.M. Government, who were maintaining strict neutrality between Ibn

Saud and King Ali.

Philby now retired from the I.C.S., and in 1926 he set up in business in Jedda as resident director of Sharqieh Ltd. In 1930 he declared himself a Muslim, and thereafter his home was mainly in Arabia, though his plans might have been completely changed if he had succeeded in his aim to enter Parliament. In spite of disappointment at the immersion of the Labour Party in home affairs he offered himself in 1939 as Labour candidate at Epping, but was rejected, and when he stood at Hythe as anti-war candidate he lost his deposit. In about 1945 he moved over to the short-lived Commonwealth Party, but he seems then to have given up home politics, for which he was temperamentally quite unfitted.

Having thrown in his lot with the Muslims, Philby had a unique opportunity to explore Arabia under the protection of Ibn Saud, and sometimes with his financial help. In return Ibn Saud secured a first-class explorer to map his country, and to make it known to the world, and in addition a companion with western knowledge who was prepared to discuss any subject at any hour of the day or night. Absent in England when war began in 1939, Philby returned to Arabia at Ibn Saud's invitation. Usually amused at the quirks in Philby's character, Ibn Saud now became seriously disturbed at the bitterness of his criticisms of Britain. Nevertheless, Philby maintained that it was not disagreement with Ibn Saud which induced him to leave for the United States in 1940, but his own unwillingness to "go on enjoying the complete security of Arabia in wartime". Philby was arrested in Karachi, on the way to America, and deported to England, where he was detained for four months under Section 18b of the Defence of the Realm Regulations. He records in *Arabian Days* (1948) that the tribunal that examined him not only set him free but revoked unconditionally the order of detention.

Philby's assurance of being always right, especially as against the British Government, was a byword. He gave up his posts as Adviser to the Ministry of the Interior in Iraq (1921) and as Chief British Representative in Transjordan, because he disapproved of Government policy. His objection to the backing of the Amir Faisal for the throne of Iraq by H.M. Government had something to be said for it, but Philby must needs allege, without any justification, that Sir Percy Cox decoyed Saiyid Talib (Philby's favourite for the throne) to a tea-party where he could be arrested for deportation. Again, when his unannounced entry into the Aden Protectorate from Yemen (*Sheba's Daughters,* 1939) caused a stir and the Aden Government announced that he was acting without their authorization, he declared that they were inviting his assassination.

For all his oriental leanings, Philby had, in fact, a full share of Anglo-Saxon self-righteousness. This he sometimes ingenuously revealed, as when, in *Forty Years in the Wilderness* (1957), he made a statement of his assets to dispose of the charge that he had enriched himself in Saudi Arabia, but mentioned casually that Ibn Saud had given him a house worth £10,000 but at the time of writing worth £20,000.

It would not be fair to represent Philby as always cantankerously anti-British. He defended the reputation of Lawrence, whom he described as a genius, and spoke highly of Glubb's services to Jordan. Although strongly anti-Zionist, he advised the Arabs to accept partition, though it is true this was because he feared a worse fate for them if they refused. His wholehearted support of Ibn Saud, to whom he would cheerfully have handed over the whole of the Arabian peninsula "with the exception of Aden", did not prevent his inserting some criticisms into *Arabian Jubilee* (1952); and in the preface to *Saudi Arabia* (1955), after the death of Ibn Saud [in 1953], he wrote strongly against the corruption and general degeneration in the country, though in subsequent criticisms he attributed the downfall to corrosive western influences incidental to the sudden enrichment of Saudi Arabia from the exploitation of oil rather than to any weakness in the Arab character or the Muslim religion. The criticisms, exploited, Philby said, by his enemies, led King Saud to expel him. He was invited back after a year, and returned, he said, without accepting any conditions.

When Philby's eccentricities have been forgotten he will still be remembered for his great work as an explorer. The oil prospectors who used his maps and descriptions found them completely accurate. He made large additions to British collections of geological and zoological specimens from Arabia. The British Museum owes to him many new species of birds, including a partridge named after him and a woodpecker named after his wife. He took up the collection and study of early Semitic inscriptions in Arabia, and he claimed to have increased from some 2,000 to over 13,000 the number of known Thamuddic inscriptions.

Philby married in 1910 Dora, daughter of A. H. Johnston, of the Indian P.W.D. She died in 1957. There were four children.

October 3, 1960.

Gérard Philipe died suddenly in Paris on November 25, 1959. He was 36. Philipe could claim to be one of the leading stage actors of the post-war years in France as well as undoubtedly the leading film hero of his time.

He was born in Cannes on December 4, 1922, and studied there at the Institution Stanislas before going to Paris, where, after a brief flirtation with the law, he enrolled at the Conservatoire d'Art Dramatique.

In 1942 he made his *début* on the Paris stage, playing in the companies of Jean Huet and Jean Wahl. Though he owed his later national (and later still international) fame primarily to his film appearances, he never lost his early love of the theatre, and continued to act on the stage from time to time throughout his career, making notable appearances in, among other plays, *Caligula, Ruy Blas, Le Cid* and the *Prince of Homburg.*

He had not been on the stage for long, however, before the cinema claimed him, and he made a deep impression in two of his earliest films, *L'Idiot,* adapted from Dostoevsky, and Autant-Lara's *Le Diable au Corps,* based on the novel of young love by Raymond Radiguet. His performance in the second, as a sensitive schoolboy involved in a tragic love affair with an older woman, exquisitely subtle and sensitive as it was, might well have typed him for a decade as a handsome and soulful *jeune premier,* but his re-creation of Dostoevsky's tormented hero in *L'Idiot* hinted at a talent too deep and adventurous to remain happily stuck in a conventional rut, however lucrative, and his subsequent work only went to confirm this impression.

A list of his film appearances during the past 12 years sounds more like a roll of honour of the French cinema than the work of one man. He was constantly in demand by the leading film-makers of his country, among them René Clair, Claude Autant-Lara, Max Ophüls [q.v.], René Clément, Marcel Carné, Julien Duvivier*, and many more.

In Britain he was probably most familiar for his appearances as the elegant and dissolute count in Ophüls's *La Ronde* and as the hero of three famous films by René Clair: *La Beauté du Diable,* his very personal version of the Faust legend; the graceful dream comedy *Les Belles de Nuit;* and the exquisitely tragi-comic *Les Grands Manoeuvres.* In other films less known in Britain, however, such as Autant-Lara's *Le Rouge et le Noir* (in which he made a perfect Julien Sorel) and *Le Joueur* (another Dostoevsky role) he showed other sides of his talent: an ability to switch from quiet good manners to hysterical frenzy in the space of a short scene, to observe in minute detail the social nuances of a character's speech, dress, and behaviour, and at moments a true tragic stature, very different from his good-natured clowning in diversions like *Fanfan la Tulipe.* His most varied and impassioned performance seen in England was probably the hero in Sartre's *Les Orgueilleux,* otherwise an inferior piece of work.

In recent years his talent had continued to develop and branch out in new directions. He produced a number of plays for the Théâtre National Populaire; he directed, with Joris Ivens, an ambitious film version of *Tyl Eulenspiegel* (which, unfortunately, found little commercial success, in spite of his own presence in the title role); he appeared in films in England (Clément's witty and cynical *Knave of Hearts*) and Mexico (Buñuel's *Le Fièvre Monte à el Pao*), and he even played the lead in a film by a member of *la nouvelle vogue,* Roger Vadim's *Les Liaisons Dangereuses.*

It is rarely that one can say of a film star of Gérard Philipe's eminence and success that he had never ceased to develop his talent and show new facets of his personality, and that he was never afraid to explore new paths, but with Philipe it is undoubtedly true: with his death France has lost an actor not only of known ability but also of enormous potential, as yet it seemed, largely unexplored.

November 26, 1959.

Mabel (Mrs. Hilton) Philipson, widow of Captain Hilton Philipson, and well known both on the stage as **Mabel Russell** and as one of the first women to become a Member of Parliament, died in a nursing home at Brighton on January 9, 1951.

Born in 1887, she was anxious to go on the stage at an early age, but, unable to overcome the opposition of her parents, she took a job in the box office of a London theatre. Her first chance came when one of the principals fell ill, and someone remembered the little girl in the box office who knew all the songs. Soon after she was spotted by George Edwardes. She played the part of Fifi in the original production of the *Merry Widow* in 1907, and took part in several other successes at Daly's Theatre, and later at the Gaiety. She played Nan in the *Country Girl.* While playing in *The Dollar Princess* at Daly's she married Stanley Rhodes, nephew of Cecil Rhodes, who was killed three months later in a motoring accident.

In 1912 she forsook musical comedy for the legitimate stage, and played the part of Aggie Lynch in the play *Within the Law,* which ran for over a year at the Haymarket. While appearing in this play she was offered the part of Eliza Doolittle by Sir Herbert Tree in the original production of *Pygmalion.* But the management could not release her. In 1917 she played with Gerald Du Maurier in the great war-time play *London Pride.* While appearing in this she left the stage and married Captain Hilton Philipson. In 1921 her husband was elected Liberal member for Berwick-on-Tweed, but six months later he was unseated on petition, due to a technical offence committed by his agent, and therefore was not allowed to stand for seven years. At a meeting to select his successor an old farmer proposed Mrs. Philipson, but she refused to stand as anything but Conservative, and in the 1923 by-election she was elected by a large majority as a Conservative, after Berwick had been a safe Liberal seat for 36 years.

In 1927 she introduced the Nursing Homes Registration Service as a Private Member's Bill. She was the first woman to become a member of the Air Committee, and in 1924 she was the only woman representative on a Parliamentary delegation to Italy, where she met and talked privately with Mussolini and the Pope.

She returned to the stage in 1929 and her last stage appearance was in 1933 as Mrs. Tilling in *Other People's Lives* at Wyndham's. She attended the Gaiety actresses' birthday party in 1949 and 1950, and her recorded voice was heard in the broadcast *Farewell Gaiety,* on December 15. She was looking forward to its sequel, *Goodbye Daly's.* She leaves two sons and a daughter.

January 10, 1951.

Wallace B. Phillips, C.B.E., who laboured long and faithfully in the cause of Anglo-American friendship, died in New York on April 14, 1952 at the age of 66.

Wallace Banta Phillips was born in New York City on March 30, 1886, and was early attracted by the culture and history of Europe. As a young man he travelled widely and thus developed that breadth of sympathy and understanding which was so marked a feature of his personality later in life. In 1913 he settled in London as managing director of the Pyrene Company, a position he held until 1951.

When America entered the war of 1914-18 he was appointed chief of circulation, G.2 of the American Expeditionary Force in France. The war over, he settled back in England and set himself to understand and appreciate the English way of life while abating not one jot of his American inheritance. Thus, though the calls on his time and energy of a great and expanding business, providing portable fire-extinguishing apparatus, were ever more pressing, he made opportunities for himself to engage in much social work in England, work in which he was enthusiastically helped by his wife, Miss Ann Lewis, whom he had married in 1915.

He was a founder member of the Royal Society for the Prevention of Accidents and honorary treasurer of the society from 1923 to 1951, and, though he added to his responsibilities in business by accepting a seat on the board of the Avon India Rubber Company in 1931, this made little difference to his keenness in supporting all good causes. He became a member of the executive council of the National Union of Manufacturers in 1936 and that organization benefited much from his sound and ready advice.

The outbreak of war in 1939 gave him still greater opportunities for service and early in 1940 he founded the American Ambulance in Great Britain, of which he became the first director-general. In the same year he was appointed a special assistant to the Director of Naval Intelligence of the United States Navy and in 1941 director of the special information services in the Office of Strategic Services. At the same time he was elected to the council of the English-Speaking Union, work which was particularly near his heart. He was able still further to advance the cause of Anglo-American friendship when he was elected president of the American Chamber of Commerce in London in 1943.

By reason of his intimate association with influential and well-informed circles in Washington and London there was little he did not know of the effort being made by industry on both sides of the Atlantic to provide the sinews of war, and he used that knowledge to bring Americans and Britons together to make greater and greater sacrifices to bring the glittering prize of victory nearer. As treasurer of the International Chamber of Commerce, a post to which he was appointed in 1944, he redoubled his efforts, but even before the prize was won he realized that for Britain a stiff fight lay ahead, when peace should come again, and gave a warning early in 1945 at a luncheon at the Savoy that the war had made American industry an even greater force to be reckoned with in world trade after the war.

Nevertheless, he realized with a clarity, not always evident in America or Britain, that the friendship forged in the furnace of war must last into what might become the arctic climate of peace if western civilization is to survive, and this was his theme for the remainder of his life. He became a member of the executive committee of the Pilgrims in 1946 and president of the American Society in London in 1950. His retirement in 1951 from active participation in all his cherished causes on the British side of the Atlantic to become president of the Pyrene Manufacturing Company in New York was greatly regretted by the wide circle of his friends in London and the presentation in May of an honorary C.B.E. to him by the British Consul-General in New York was a signal honour for one who had laboured long and hard to forge indissoluble links between the two great English-speaking democracies.

[This obituary was followed on the same day by a tribute.]

April 16, 1952.

Eden Phillpotts, who died on December 29, 1960, at the age of 98, at his home near Exeter, was an author of versatile powers and an uncommonly prolific one.

Novelist, playwright, and poet, his literary career spans more than a half-century and was attended by conspicuous though not uniform success. The present generation knew him best as the author of a long series of Dartmoor novels, pleasantly bucolic for the most part or with a crime interest, and of the most popular of his stage comedies of Devon village life, the prodigiously successful *The Farmer's Wife.* But Phillpotts's range was wider than that and his literary distinction notably higher. Although as a novelist, in which capacity he did his best work, he was always some way behind the front rank of his contemporaries, his achievement, more particularly in the earlier phase, has solider merit than is perhaps generally recognized today.

Born at Mount Aboo, India, the elder son of a British political agent in Rajputana, on November 4, 1862, Phillpotts was educated in Plymouth, served for 10 years as a clerk in an insurance office, went to London in 1890 to study as an actor, abandoned the idea, had thoughts of painting as a career, and then abandoned that idea too.

He commenced as author, it seems, in 1888, with *My Adventure on the Flying Scotsman: a Romance of London and North-Western Railway Shares;* but his effective literary beginnings are signalized by the publication in 1897 of *Lying Prophets,* a Cornish novel encompassing the tragedy of a betrayed heroine done with a sombre veracity and power. In the following year came *Children of the Mist,* the first of the novels which were to link Phillpotts's name with the region of Dartmoor and to prompt a humble comparison with Hardy's Wessex. A year later the first of his discursive *Human Boy* diaries appeared, and in the next year *Sons of the Morning,* one of the soundest and most vividly rendered of his early essays in fiction, indeed of all his novels.

To list them all is unnecessary; it may be sufficient to indicate their remarkable variety.

Besides the Dartmoor novels, both serious and light—*The Whirlwind* (1907), *The Thief of Virtue* (1910), and *Widecombe Fair* (1913) are good examples—Phillpotts took in his stride, almost in pioneering fashion, a series of "industrial" novels, in which he described, for instance, the men of the slate quarries, the niceties of oyster-fishing, the craft of the potter; another series of novels, sometimes of a lightly fabular quality, of ancient Greece; crime fiction, the supernatural, and pure fantasy; and a vast mass of short stories of every conceivable kind. Broadly speaking, his virtues as a serious novelist lay in a vigorous and unaffected humanity, a robust dramatic sense, and an unfailing open-mindedness; his defects were apparent in the lack of cohesion of his novels and a rather heavy style of description, even in passages of "poetic" evocation.

The defects, if they did not spring directly from Phillpotts's prolific cast of mind and imagination, were certainly confirmed in him by the sheer volume and pace of his output. Phillpotts wrote far more than any writer of quality should or, perhaps in the long run, could. During the 10 years from 1904 until 1913 he produced 11 of the Dartmoor novels, 18 further novels, and collections of stories, four volumes of plays, three of poetry, and two of belles-lettres—a performance rivalling, say, Dumas's or Edgar Wallace's. In 1923 he made what was apparently a start as a writer of mystery novels with *The Red Redmaynes,* but in point of fact he had already engaged in what was to be a long series of thrillers (chiefly for the American market, where he commanded a steady sale) over the pseudonym of Harrington Hext. There seemed very little, indeed, in the way of words to which he could not turn his hand.

As a poet Phillpotts had a genuine gift of seriousness, a sincere and perhaps essentially pantheistic sentiment for nature, a personal philosophy that was never egoistic, but not the strangeness or the intensity in which poetry so often dwells. His verse is fluent and shows a nice command of traditional usage, though even in the best of it the harmony of sense and form is apt to be only fitful.

It was as a playwright that he won the loudest applause and the most substantial rewards. None of the earlier plays, several of them adapted from his novels, met with any degree of success in the theatre, but Phillpotts, in the midst of all his other labours, nevertheless persevered. In 1912 *The Secret Woman,* which treated the subject of physical passion with patent sincerity but in theatrically laboured and diffuse fashion, was banned by the too cautious censorship of the period, then licensed for six private performances.

Disappointment here may have helped to turn Phillpotts's mind towards the simpler varieties of comedy, but at any rate it was with the innocent and rollicking Devon humours of *The Farmer's Wife* that he found fortune. Produced in wartime, in 1917, at the Court Theatre, the play, after an uncertain start, proved a thumping and celebrated success, and ran for three years.

It was revived many times. Phillpotts had a good many other plays produced in the years following, but the only one that met with a comparable reception was *Yellow Sands,* written in collaboration with his daughter, Mary Adelaide Eden Phillpotts, and of a not dissimilar theatrical character.

When in his seventies Phillpotts turned to broadcasting, finding there a fresh success for his plays and indeed proving a natural radio writer with his strong, lively plots and dialogue. He wrote new plays or would himself take great pains over the adaptation for the B.B.C. of *The Farmer's Wife* and many of his other pieces.

The novels, the plays, the poetry continued to flow from his pen, though in his later years the lighter side predominated and the Devon village humours and the mystery stories tended to oust the rest. As a story-teller, too, he relied increasingly upon the use of dialogue, almost always one of the more practised and less exacting methods of narrative. Otherwise, however, his energies hardly seemed to flag. *The Changeling* (1944) and *The Drums of Dombali* (1945), from among his last books, exhibit, indeed, a rare octogenarian vigour.

Phillpotts was a man of singularly honest mind, kindly unassertive, and with an attractive vein of simplicity.

He was twice married; first, to Emily, daughter of Robert Topham, by whom he had a son and a daughter, and who died in 1928; secondly to Lucy Robina, daughter of Dr. Fortescue Webb, who survives him.

There will be many to regret the death of a veteran writer of very English quality who was a household name.

December 30, 1960.

Wilhelm Pieck, President of the German Democratic Republic, died on September 7, 1960 at the age of 84.

He was the perfect type of communist doctrinaire, and no suspicion of the sin of "deviation" had ever clung to him. He rose at one time to be secretary general of the Comintern itself; he had been an associate of Karl Liebknecht and Rosa Luxemburg; he survived the violent events of 1918, evaded the wrath of Hitler, and in his old age became the President of the Soviet-dominated state of east Germany.

Pieck was born on January 3, 1876, at Guben near Berlin, the son of Friedrich Pieck, a labouring man, and his wife, Wilhelmine Bahrow. He began work as a carpenter at the age of 14, joined the Social Democratic Party in 1894, took a leading part in several strikes, and in 1905 was elected to the Reichstag by Bremen as a Social Democrat. In 1910 he became secretary of the party's central educational committee. Associating with Karl Radek, Rosa Luxemburg, and Karl Liebknecht, he was one of the founders of the Spartakusbund in 1915. In May of that year, having led an anti-war demonstration to the Reichstag, he was expelled from the party and imprisoned, and finally conscribed and sent to the front. Late in 1917 he contrived to desert to Holland, where he ran a pacifist paper in Amsterdam.

Pieck returned to Berlin in October 1918, took part with Liebknecht and Rosa Luxemburg in the street fighting against the Fehme, and, the only one of the trio to escape death, made his way to Russia, where he met Lenin. He became one of the founders of the German Communist Party, was returned to the Prussian Parliament in 1921 as a communist deputy, and the same year became president of the Rote Hilfe. Always well considered by the Russians, he was elected to the executive committee of the Comintern in 1928. He was a member of the Reichstag from 1928 to 1933, served on the Berlin City Council in 1929, and on the Prussian State Council in 1930.

In February 1933 came the Reichstag fire, with its well-known sequel. For some weeks he evaded the police in Germany. Later in the year he fled to Paris, and, after living there for some time, found his way to Moscow. On Dimitrov's retirement from the post of general secretary to the Comintern Pieck succeeded him, until the Comintern was dissolved in May 1943. During the Second World War his main effort was to convert German prisoners to Communism, and he became secretary of the National Committee of Free Germany and the Union of German Officers in the U.S.S.R.

After the fall of Berlin Pieck returned there and recommenced his political activity in Germany. He was the prime mover in the formation of the Anti-Fascist Democratic block, comprising Communists, Social Democrats, Christian Democrats and Liberal Democrats; but after a plebiscite in April 1946 had given a heavy vote by the various Democrats against collaboration with the communists, he and Otto Grotewohl* became co-chairmen of the new Socialist Unity Party, an organization subservient to Soviet policy in the eastern zone of Germany. In March 1948 Pieck was prominent in the "All-Germany Peoples' Congress for Unity and a Just Peace", which nominated a People's Council of 400 members and a praesidium of 29 members. The elections of May 1949, run on the familiar Russian one-party plan, paved the way for the establishment of the Volkskammer in the following October. Pieck became President of the German Democratic Republic by a unanimous vote. He was re-elected for a second four-year term in 1953, and again when an old and ailing man in 1957. He ceased to be co-chairman of the Socialist Unity Party in 1954, when the joint offices were abolished, but remained in the Politburo.

Pieck enjoyed great popularity among the extreme left-wing section of the Berlin working class, to whom he made himself acceptable not only as a political figure but as a personality. He was a ready, but not highly eloquent, speaker. He owed some of his popularity to his status as the sole prominent survivor of the events of 1918, and, in later years, perhaps most of it was due to the fatherly impression which the portly, beaming, and silver-haired old man created on his public appearances and which the east German propagandists readily exploited—with some justice, for he was moderate in speech and manner. If he was not brilliant—Rosa Luxemburg described him as one of her "most loyal but most stupid pupils"—he was not politically vindictive and escaped much of the criticism which other east German leaders incurred in west Germany.

Pieck was first married in 1898 to Christine Hafker, by whom he had three children. She died, and he married again late in life.

In the last years of his life he suffered from a heart ailment, and from 1950 onwards took long holidays in the Soviet Union.

September 8, 1960.

Professor A. C. Pigou, the outstanding British economist of his day, died on March 7, 1959 at the age of 81.

Arthur Cecil Pigou was born at Ryde on November 18, 1877, and, like his father, C.G.S. Pigou, of the 15th Regiment, was educated at Harrow, where he was in Marshall's house (Newlands) and became the first modern head of the school.

In 1896 he went as a history scholar to King's College, Cambridge, where he was awarded a first class in the Historical Tripos in 1899 and in Part II of the Moral Sciences Tripos in 1900, also winning the Chancellor's Medal for English Verse and the Cobden, Burney, and Adam Smith Prizes, and becoming President of the Union. From 1902 until his death he was a Fellow of King's College. His election in 1908, at the age of 30, to succeed his deeply revered master, Alfred Marshall, in the Chair of Political Economy did not give universal satisfaction to the practitioners of a subject which then, as now, was apt to be riven by faction; Pigou, it was held by some, for all his unquestioned ability, was too cloistered a figure, with insufficient contact with the real world, to be a suitable holder of the post.

Be that as it may, for 35 years, until his retirement under the age-limit in 1943, he discharged with supreme distinction the duties of the Chair according to his own interpretation of them. That interpretation included the delivery of a course of lectures on economic principles, splendidly lucid and well-ordered but becoming somewhat stereotyped as the years passed by—he was not one of those who enjoy giving their latest thoughts a trial run in oral delivery.

Nor was he much interested in questions of administration or of curriculum and teaching technique, which he was ready to leave so far as possible in the hands of more restless spirits. In the main he devoted himself to a systematic exploration of one department after another of economic doctrine; and it is on the resulting galaxy of published works that his world-wide reputation rests. From his pre-professorial days date a couple of small books on the tariff problem and one on industrial peace. Then in 1912 came *Wealth and Welfare,* which, in the form into which it was revised and expanded in 1920 under the title of *The Economics of Welfare,* has remained his most abidingly important work.

In this book Pigou, skilfully using and refining the tools of analysis inherited from Marshall, discusses the nature of economic welfare and its relation to welfare as a whole, examines the forces governing the size, composition, and distribution of the national income, and explores the degree and manner in which certain kinds of Government action may be expected to improve on the state of affairs brought about by the unrestricted play of private self-interest.

This great battleship of a book was followed in due course by a number of stately vessels, of which it must suffice to mention here *Industrial Fluctuations* (1927), *Public Finance* (1928), and *Employment and Equilibrium* (1941)—all revised in subsequent editions: as well as by a whole flotilla of smaller works, some of them (*e.g. Lapses from Full Employment,* 1945) on rather specialized topics, others (*e.g., Socialism versus Capitalism,* 1937, and *Income,* 1945) illustrating the author's gift for lucid exposition at a more popular level.

The publication in 1936 of Keynes's *General Theory of Employment, Interest and Money* drew from Pigou a strongly critical review, expressed with an unusual warmth accountable for largely by the fact that he believed the book to contain "unwarrantable strictures" on the work of Marshall.

In a couple of lectures delivered in 1949 there came a more favourable, though still critical, evaluation: "I should say . . . that, in setting out and developing his fundamental conception, Keynes made a very important, original and valuable addition to the armoury of economic analysis".

Unlike some members of his craft, Pigou felt no great urge towards the talking of shop either with fellow-academics or with practitioners in the factory, the board room, and the market place; he was not always easy of access to visitors and was seldom to be seen at conferences and the like. But his concept of professorial duty included the fairly frequent writing of weighty letters to *The Times* on problems of the day, and ready obedience to any summons to definite tasks of public service.

Thus, he was a member of the (Cunliffe) Committee on the Currency and Foreign Exchanges (1918-19), the Royal Commission on the Income Tax (1919-20), and the (Chamberlain) Committee on the Currency and Bank of England Note Issues (1924-25)—this last being the body whose report was the prelude to the much criticized restoration of the gold standard at the old parity of exchange.

Pigou was elected to the British Academy in 1925, but resigned in 1947. He was a foreign honorary member of the American Academy of Arts and Sciences, a foreign member of the Accademia Nazionale dei Lincei, and an honorary president of the International Economic Association.

Pigou was unmarried. Even the briefest account of him would be incomplete without reference to his rugged physical frame, its ruggedness enhanced by a legendary untidiness of costume; to his love for the mountains of Switzerland and Cumberland, and his ascents thereof; and to his great goodness and generosity of heart, poured out mainly on chosen friends among the young.

March 9, 1959.

Oswald Pirow, Q.C., leader for the prosecution in the South African mass treason trial in the late 1950s, died suddenly on October 11, 1959 at Pretoria. He was 68. He had been a member of General Hertzog's government before the Second World War.

Pirow was a notable and disturbing force in South African politics. A man of remarkable organizing talents and a vigorous personality, he seemed to be marked out for eminence as a constructive statesman not only in the Union of South Africa but also in the British Commonwealth. Yet by opposing his country's participation in the war against Hitler, by preaching the "New Order" of National Socialism, and by appearing to seek the destruction of democracy in South Africa, he brought an end to his political career, at least as a Commonwealth statesman.

He was the elder son of Carl Ferdinand Pirow, a German doctor who had settled at Potchefstroom, Transvaal, and become a naturalized burgher of the republic. His father at one time wanted him to serve the Fatherland and endeavoured to gain consent for his entry into the German Navy. The application was rejected on the ground that the elder Pirow was no longer a citizen of the Reich.

Oswald Pirow was called to the Bar by the Middle Temple in 1913, and, having been placed first in the Bar Final examination, he was awarded a certificate of honour and a studentship. On his return to South Africa he practised at Pretoria, and with the efficiency of his race he rapidly worked up a large and lucrative practice. He had the advantage—alike at the Bar and, later, in politics—of the special friendship and guidance of Tielman Roos, later Chief Justice of the Union.

The general election of 1924 gave Pirow a seat in the Union Parliament. General Hertzog immediately invited him to join the Cabinet as Minister of Justice. Later he became Minister of Railways and Harbours in the same Cabinet. When Tielman Roos, having resigned as Chief Justice, launched his memorable attack on the gold standard, which precipitated the formation of the Hertzog-Smuts Government on March 30, 1933, Pirow retained his portfolio, and took in addition that of Defence. On assuming the portfolio of Justice, Pirow had taken in hand the organization of the South African Police, a semi-military force charged with the maintenance of order throughout the Union, and purged it of those officers he considered too old or inefficient.

In June 1936 Pirow went to London to discuss with the British Government the defences of South Africa in the light of developments in Abyssinia. He took pains to proclaim that, apart from her moral obligations to the League of Nations, the Union was absolutely unfettered in her right to decide whether or not to join a war in South Africa or elsewhere. In a statement at Pretoria after his return from London he declared that the colonial question could never be settled unless Germany were granted colonies in Africa.

His next visit to London caused more stir and was made in more stirring times. After launching a £6m. defence programme he arrived in London early in November 1938 to discuss technical details with the Service Ministers. He broke his journey at Lisbon, where he saw Dr. Salazar*, then went to Salamanca and Burgos and visited the battlefronts of the civil war in Spain. He went to Berlin on an official visit and had personal conversations with Hitler and Goering. Later he saw and talked with Mussolini and Ciano in Rome. He went back to London to declare dolefully that Europe was doomed to war unless there was a "complete change within the next month or two". He asserted that this impending tragedy could be averted because there was no principle at stake in the Czechoslovak question and that even the vexed refugee problem could be easily settled by establishing a vast dumping ground (but not in South Africa) for the pariahs of Europe.

When General Hertzog failed to keep the Union neutral when Britain and the other Dominions declared war against Germany Pirow, like his chief, resigned his cabinet office. Hertzog and Pirow were not, however, to remain partners in opposition for very long. Hertzog, after placing every obstacle in the way of the Smuts government, began, as the result of the irreconcilably bitter and foolish conduct of many members of his party, to see some of the errors of his ways and retired from public life. Pirow remained more or less in the limelight, stumping the country to gather converts for his "New Order". By this time the extreme Nationalists were quarrelling among themselves and Pirow found himself the propagator of only one version of the true gospel. His barely concealed adherence to Nazi doctrine (his "New Order" as outlined in an issue of *Vaterland* of October 1940, was, with a few modifications, framed to soothe local susceptibilities, borrowed almost wholesale from the Nazi ideology) alienated many Nationalists, but appealed to many others who were ready for any drastic change so long as it promised them severance from the Empire.

After the war, as leader of his New Order movement, Pirow was less of a political force than a mordant critic of other political parties. He was in London again in 1948 to consult with Sir Oswald Mosley, with whose Union Movement he had links. The two men thought alike about the colour question, and Pirow was a forceful advocate of separate native states in South Africa. At the beginning of 1957 he announced his intention to retire from the Pretoria Bar, where he had had a long and distinguished career. But he later accepted a brief as prosecutor of the 150 men and women who were rounded up in December 1957 and charged with treason.

Pirow was the author of a polemical and personally digressive life of Hertzog published in 1958.

October 12, 1959.

Ludmilla Pitoeff, who died on September 16, 1951 at Rueil, near Paris, was for long one of the most prominent figures on the Parisian stage.

The fact that she could become a leading Parisian actress is one more illustration of the fact that artistically Paris is an international capital. Romanians—more than one—have become Sociétaires of the Comédie-Française; but they went through the training of the Conservatoire, and passed up through all the grades. Caucasian-born Ludmilla and her Armenian husband suddenly set themselves up as Paris actor-managers with no more experience than having run a modest little semi-amateur theatre at Geneva, where they took into their company the son of a local grocer, who has since become the stage and film comedian, Michel Simon*. It says much for the talent of Pitoeff and his wife, but much also for the generosity of the Parisian public and the critics, usually so exacting about the correct pronunciation of their language, that they opened their arms to her, who never lost her Russian accent, and to him, whose Armenian one was so awful as to be a joke.

They were married at Geneva in 1915, when she was hardly 16 years old, and it was only after their marriage that she took to the stage with a passion which never left her, and was only equalled by her passion for her husband—was indeed part of it, for there can hardly ever have been a distinguished actress who gave so much of herself to her art and so much to her husband and her family. She had seven children, whom she adored and who adored her. Two, a son and a daughter, carry on the name in the theatre. The death of her husband in 1939 so broke her that she never afterwards gave any notable performances.

When she and Pitoeff were married he had already been running his Geneva company for three years. He ran it for three more, presenting translations of Strindberg, Chekov, Ibsen, Tolstoy, Wilde, Synge, and D'Annunzio, as well as the early works of such French dramatists as Lenormand, J. J. Bernard, and Claudel [q.v.], in incredibly difficult financial conditions, before he and his wife migrated to Paris in 1919. There they took the Théâtre des Arts, and at once made an artistic success with a version of Andréev's circus drama *He Who Gets Slapped,* where her bird-like and child-like, and at the same time spiritual, personality—"she had an aura", Jouvet [q.v.] said of her—affirmed itself as much as his idealistic stage direction, and the contrasts between brilliant light and deep shadow in his lighting.

Among many other such artistically distinguished, but financially unprofitable, productions were fortunately one or two which took the fancy of the public, such as Pirandello's *Seven Characters in Search of an Author;* and eminent among these was Bernard Shaw's *Saint Joan,* in which Ludmilla Pitoeff made the great acting triumph of her career.

Her Joan, frail, pathetic, sometimes pouting, sometimes wheedling, but glowing with the inner light of the spirit, was a different thing from the rougher and more vigorous interpretation which Shaw himself encouraged in Sybil Thorndike [d. 1976], the creator of the part; but it showed once more that in really dramatic material there may be two quite different interpretations, and both of them right.

Among others of Ludmilla Pitoeff's notable performances were the leading parts in Ibsen's *Doll's House* and *Wild Duck,* in Maeterlinck's *Miracle of Saint Anthony,* and in Lenormand's *Le Temps est un Songe.*

September 18, 1951.

Pope Pius XII, who died early on October 9, 1958 at his summer palace at Castel Gondolfo, after a stroke on the previous day, was known by sight to a wider audience, and knew people by travel to a greater extent, than any of his long line of predecessors. He was the first Pope who could speak with first-hand knowledge of North and South America as well as of Europe. Like his predecessor, Pope Pius XI, he was an exceptional linguist.

When he ascended the papal throne in 1939 he had lived through war and revolution in Germany, visited England and America, and kept closely in touch for nearly 10 years with all the chancelleries of Europe. Almost his entire working life was spent in the diplomatic service of his Church; but he was a canonist as well as a diplomat, largely responsible over a period of 13 years for the codification of Canon Law. It is significant that he begged to be released from the beginning for pastoral work and snatched such opportunities as he could get to give retreats, help parish priests near Rome, and attend the confessional.

His predecessor, Pope Pius XI, elected in 1922, soon after his work at Warsaw, also had close experience of war and revolution, but his long experience as librarian of the Bibliotheca Ambrosiana in Milan and his principal recreation as an alpinist acted upon his mind as a counterpoise to his diplomatic experience and gave him a bias towards the contemplative life. There was, however, a closer affinity between Pope Pius XII and Pope Benedict XV, who ruled the Church during the war of 1914-18. It was Benedict XV who singled out Mgr. Pacelli (as his Holiness then was) in 1917, after the completion of the codification of Canon Law, appointed him to the titular see of Sardis, and sent him to Munich as Nuncio. His recall from diplomacy in Germany was ordered by Pius XI, who raised him to the Sacred College of Cardinals and made him Secretary of State.

Pius XII was a man of outstanding piety and frugal life. An imperturbable ease of manner and a distinguished eloquence in several languages fitted him for his venerable office. So did his tall and slender frame, well suited to stately ecclesiastical robes and vestments, and his serious, alert countenance. He was a master of elocution, and his voice was studiously even, yet clear and ringing. To the meticulous regularity in routine, which all recent Popes have observed, he added a taste for technical efficiency: the aeroplane, by which he had travelled, the fast car, the electric lift, the microphone, were parts of the equipment of the Vatican. Also he took a keener interest than some in its rich heritage. In recent years he authorized excavations and sponsored important archaeological reports.

While the aesthetic aspect of his tall figure deepened the impression of sadness conveyed by his face in repose, the smile that lit his countenance was always vivacious, and at no time did he sacrifice public audiences on account of pressure of affairs. His manner of allowing all sorts and conditions of men and women to crowd round him in public was new to the Vatican. The Pope, in fact, was at home in a crowd, and, as a born Roman, he loved a spectacle. When, on the occasion of the Coronation of King George V, he accompanied as Counsellor the Papal Mission, he was delighted with the Naval Review at Spithead, and often spoke of it to English friends.

Eugenio Pacelli was born in Rome on March 2, 1876, of a noble family from Acqua Pendente, the son of Filippo, an eminent ecclesiastical lawyer, and his wife, the Marchesa Virginia Graziosi. A brother of the future Pope was the Marchese Francesco Pacelli, who followed his father's career and was legal adviser to the Holy See in the Lateran Treaty negotiations. There were two other children. Though the family was "black", with a long tradition of service in the ecclesiastical courts, Eugenio began his education at a State school, from which he passed to the well-known Capranica seminary in Rome for ordinands of noble birth.

On the accession of Pope Pius X the decision was made to carry out the huge task of codifying Canon Law. To assist him in this work Cardinal Gasparri called in the young priest, who made it his principal occupation thereafter. Meanwhile, however, he was chosen to accompany delegates on missions abroad. He visited England for the Eucharistic Congress of 1908 and the Coronation of King George V, but had previously been in England with the Papal delegation for the funeral of Queen Victoria. In 1914 additional responsibilities were added to him with the appointment of Cardinal Gasparri as Secretary of State.

In May 1917 Pope Benedict appointed Mgr. Pacelli to be Nuncio at Munich. For the next 12 years, first in Munich and later in Berlin, the future Pope was diplomatically employed in Germany. He was able to negotiate concordats in Munich, Dresden, and Berlin, and he returned to Rome in 1929 with the reputation of an able negotiator. The Nuncio, however, was little known as a public figure when he received his Cardinal's hat. Gasparri's work was now accomplished with the conclusion of the Lateran Treaties, and the new Cardinal Pacelli, who had followed him step by step, became Secretary of State and Archpriest of the Basilica of St. Peter.

The Church was now beginning to reckon with the prospect which resurgent nationalism in Germany would offer for a continuation of good relations. The National-Socialist régime proffered, and in return obtained, manifestations of cordiality which were given formal shape in the conclusion of a new general Concordat signed in 1933 by the Reich, superseding the Concordats with the federal states.

Any estimate of the part which Cardinal Pacelli, as Secretary of State to his predecessor, had in the gradual hardening of Vatican policy against National-Socialism could only be the fruit of special knowledge; but the vigorous Pontiff, Pius XI, was thoroughly roused by the threats of German neo-paganism, and his personal imprint is stamped upon the encyclical *Mit Brennender Sorge* of March 1937.

On the death of Pius XI in 1939 it fell to Cardinal Pacelli as Chamberlain of the Holy Roman Church to preside over the ceremonies of the funeral and interregnum. The Conclave assembled on March 2, Pacelli's sixty-third birthday. Since the sixteenth century there had been no precedent for election of a Secretary of State. The Cardinals, however, clearly felt that the situation of the world and of the Church demanded an exceptional choice. At 4.30 p.m. the third ballot took place, when all the votes save his own are said to have been cast for Pacelli. The result (little anticipated by the world) was generally well received; Rome in particular delighted in the elevation of a Roman-born Pontiff. The Nazi Press had previously expressed the hope for a "non-political" election and had instanced Cardinal Pacelli as one who was to be regarded as a "politician".

The labours of the new Pope and of his Secretary of State, Cardinal Maglione, to avert the closely threatening war are not as yet publicly available. Vatican diplomatic activity in the summer of 1939 was intense. When Hitler began his undeclared war against Poland on September 1, his Holiness at once extended his public sympathy to the Polish nation in the person of Cardinal Hlond, Patriarch of Cracow. The first encyclical of the new reign, *Summi Pontificatus,* to which in English the significant title "Darkness over the Earth" was given, resolutely took up a position above the mêlée of the combatants.

An exchange of visits between the Pope and the Italian Sovereign in the winter of 1939 symbolized in the eyes of Italy and of the world the strong desire of Vatican and Quirinal alike to save the country from war. This view was conveyed in no uncertain terms to the Italian Ambassador to the Holy See. On both sides, also, an exchange of nobly phrased messages between the Pope and President Roosevelt was expected to introduce a close collaboration between the great spiritual and the great temporal neutrals. Papal messages to the Sovereigns of Belgium, Holland, and Luxembourg, when their countries were invaded, afforded a clear index to the direction in which efforts were still being attempted, but Italy's entry into the war on June 10, 1940, ended the hope of limiting it.

Events brought to the Pope's audience chamber, at various times, Ribbentrop, Suñer, and Matsuoka. The opening of diplomatic relations between the Vatican and Japan after the Japanese occupation of the Philippines was criticized, but the opening of diplomatic relations with Chungking, soon announced, explained the Pope's action. In some quarters the Pope was considered to view Nazi doctrines and deeds with too great detachment. The strong feeling of the Roman Hierarchy against the communist doctrines of Russia was held to have been the occasion of a certain relaxation of the indignation against Germany. On the other hand, the Italian Fascists found it necessary to maintain fierce attacks upon the alleged pro-British clique established in the Vatican in charge of the *Osservatore Romano* newspaper. A steady stream of remonstrances later reproached the Pope with his failure to denounce the Anglo-Russian alliance. The Pope's political efforts were in fact thrown into the formulation of general principles essential to a future successful peace.

While making clear the principles on which a just peace could be based, Pope Pius XII ordered the setting up of spiritual and temporal organizations for the alleviation of suffering. Notable was the institution of the Vatican Information Service which brought together and issued by letter and radio the names of prisoners of war in many parts of the world. In addition large sums of money were sent to bishops throughout Europe for the relief of exiles and the feeding of the destitute. The Pope also gave some £25,000 for the restoration of churches damaged by war in Britain, and in the immediate period before the liberation of Rome the Holy See provided daily meals for some 40,000 people in the harassed city.

After the war there was a great influx of pilgrims, all of whom wished at least for a public audience and all of whom received it. Service men and civilians mingled in unprecedented numbers at the Vatican. On one day alone it was estimated that 8,000 people had gathered to greet the Pope. Yet even greater were the crowds that awaited audience during the Holy Year of 1950, which by special decree Pope Pius XII extended to the world in 1951.

Pope Pius XII was a man who followed traditions, or if need be jumped back centuries to earlier traditions. His encyclical on Scripture, *Divino afflante Spiritu* (1943), while commemorating Leo XIII's *Providentissimus Deus* (1893) and surveying the same ground, did so less from the standpoint of the theologian than that of the exegete. This encyclical will probably rank as the Pope's most far-reaching and enduring contribution to ecclesiastical legislation. In effect Pius was less "fundamentalist" than Leo, whose encyclical resulted in many unhappy restrictions upon Catholic scholars. The Dominican M. J. Lagrange was silenced in 1912, and Catholic scholarship generally was placed at a disadvantage as against non-Catholic, made temporary by Pius XII. That he sympathized with the textual scholar was again manifested in the answers of the Biblical Commission concerning translations (1943), and the Latin version of the Psalter published in 1944. The new encyclical enjoins ("it is absolutely necessary") the proper use of the aids afforded "by history, archaeology, ethnology, and other sciences in order to discover what literary forms the writers of that early age intended to use". In doing so the Pope emphasized the importance of the writings of the Eastern fathers and took occasion to deprecate "over literal Europeanized exegesis". The Pope's serious interest in Eastern Christians, Catholic or Orthodox, led him also to protect the Greek liturgy. During his reign he manifested his insistence on spiritualities by restoring the Easter Vigil to the Roman Liturgy, with its significant introduction of the vernacular for the renewal of the baptismal vows. He followed further the work of Pope Pius X, whom he beatified in 1951, and whose canonization took place in May 1954, by relaxing the rules of the eucharistic fast and permitting the offering of evening Masses.

The changes in the Holy Week liturgy were very far reaching indeed, including the revival of the Easter vigil on the night of Holy Saturday as well as of the historic rights for Maundy Thursday and Good Friday, which restored to them their original spiritual significance and dogmatic splendour. In addition the liturgy throughout the year was revised in one of the measures enacted by the Holy See to further the efforts of the Pope's immediate predecessors for a true liturgical revival. An historic event in his reign, too, was the definition in 1950 of the dogma of the Assumption of the Blessed Virgin.

Until 1946 he had made no fresh appointments to the Sacred College of Cardinals since his election. The number of Cardinals had been reduced to 38, when in a personal broadcast (the first of its kind in the history of the Holy See) he nominated 32 new Cardinals, to bring the strength of the college to its full complement. Another creation in 1953 included the conferment of the Red Hat on Archbishop Stepinać [q.v.], who had recently been released from imprisonment by the Yugoslav Government. The result of this broadening of the basis of the college was considerably to reduce the numerical preponderance of the Italian element in its membership.

The consistories of 1946 were particularly notable because they brought members to the Sacred College from the five continents, with a Chinese Cardinal among the new creations, and emphasized the intention of the Holy See to provide for new ecclesiastical jurisdictions with increasing numbers of native priests. This policy was clearly shown in the setting up of a hierarchy in China and another in British West Africa. Promotion of sees in mission territories and the consequent consolidation of ecclesiastical government throughout the world was one of his major achievements.

Meanwhile he was obliged to cope not only with attacks on the Vatican from European Governments but also with campaigns against the whole body of Christian teaching. His encyclicals and addresses touched frequently on the materialistic arguments that were gaining currency. At the same time he criticized less obvious trends, particularly in an address to midwives on what became known as the "mother and child" controversy. His insistence on the equal value in the sight of God of the lives of mother and child was obscured by faulty translation, as was a later declaration on the dangers of television, which he had in fact described as one of the great achievements of science. Yet it was significant that he instituted a policy of welcoming vocational bodies to Rome for international congresses and offered to them the guidance of a trained philosopher.

In August 1953 Pope Pius XII proclaimed a year of ceremony and commemoration to mark the hundredth anniversary of the dogma of the Immaculate Conception. On December 8 of that year, in one of his rare journeys through Rome—it was only the third of his reign—he drove from the Vatican to the basilica of Santa Maria Maggiore to inaugurate this Marian Year, which brought many pilgrims to Rome throughout 1954 and which he intended to close at a solemn ceremony at the same basilica on December 8, 1954. His intention was, however, frustrated by a recurrence and aggravation of the digestive trouble and fatigue which, in January 1954, first caused a serious modification of his usual intense activity.

Although this illness in the early months of 1954 brought anxiety and repeated suggestions from his doctors that he must take a complete rest, he continued to attend to the most urgent matters brought to him by his two Pro-Secretaries of State. Even so, it was more than two months before he was able to celebrate Mass again in his private chapel, and several weeks more before he was able to resume his habitual heavy programme.

Towards the end of 1954 he was again gravely ill, special prayers were called for his recovery and anxious groups gathered in St. Peter's Square. Yet his extraordinary powers of recovery came once more to his aid and on his seventy-ninth birthday in 1955 he appeared at the window of his study and gave his blessing in a strong clear voice. In spite of ill-health and the advance of old age he continued to face, as he had always faced, the challenge of his times, admonishing and advising his people on the great issues of peace, war and nuclear weapons, and also on what may be termed problems of civilization, on painless childbirth, on music and religion, fashion, anaesthesia, euthanasia and racial conflict.

In the maelstrom of politics and economics and conflicting spiritual views it may seem difficult to form a clear idea of the life and character and mind of Pope Pius XII. To those who saw him, spoke to him, or studied his work he was most certainly a man of learning, understanding, and surpassing piety.

October 10, 1958.

Joyce (Mrs. A. K.) Placzek, widely known as **Jan Struther,** the creator of Mrs. Miniver, died in New York on July 20, 1953.

Mrs. Miniver was, in conception, a product of Printing House Square. In 1937 it was decided that the occasional articles which at that time appeared on the Court page would be the better for an infusion of feminine interest; this, it was thought, might conveniently be accomplished by inventing an imaginary female character, not very different in outlook and background from many of the ladies who (it was hoped) would read of her doings, and allowing her to react to such seasonal vicissitudes as Christmas shopping or the end of the holidays. This delicate task was entrusted to Miss Struther, and it can fairly be said that within the limitations of her medium, she never put a foot wrong. Miss Struther had, in addition to felicity of style, considerable perception and an urbane sense of comedy; and Mrs. Miniver rapidly established herself as a character in her own right. She was too conventional to suit the *avantgarde,* and the epithet "miniverish", with its imputation of smugness and triviality, has on its rare appearances a mildly pejorative connotation. But the fact that it was coined at all is a tribute to the sound craftsmanship with which Miss Struther built up, in a series of thumb-nail sketches, the character of her protagonist.

When a collection of her articles appeared in book form in Britain, it achieved only a comparatively modest sale. But Mrs. Miniver proved greatly to the taste of the Americans, and the lady's immense popularity was the foundation of much useful (and exacting) propaganda work which Miss Struther carried on over there during the last war. Mrs. Miniver was the heroine of at least two films, in the first of which Hollywood paid its own particular type of tribute to the fortitude of the British housewife during the anxious days of 1940. Though not strikingly successful at recapturing the atmosphere of those days in any of its essentials, the film had impeccable intentions and can have done nothing but good to the British cause in war-time.

Miss Struther, who took a detached view of Mrs. Miniver, often said that she was "not a proper writer", and it is true that the facility and assurance of her craftsmanship was not matched by a strong creative urge. But whatever she wrote, whether poetry or prose, had a trim excellence, an agreeable flavour, and a point; and she gave to the English-speaking world a character (or perhaps it would be more accurate to say a type) who, from the unpromising spring-board of the Court page of *The Times,* soared upwards to take her place, at any rate for a generation or so, with the household words of fiction.

Joyce Anstruther was born on June 6, 1901, the daughter of the late Henry Torrens Anstruther and Dame Eva Anstruther. She was educated privately in London, and in 1917, as Jan Struther (an obvious adaptation of her maiden signature) she began a long career as a contributor of verses, articles, and short stories to periodicals which included, at various times, the *London Mercury, Punch,* the *Spectator,* the *New Statesman,* and *The Times.* Her first book of poems, *Betsinda Dances,* appeared in 1931 and was followed by *Sycamore Square* in 1932, *The Modern Struwwelpeter* in 1936, and other volumes. She had a gift for pleasant verse, sometimes amusing, sometimes thoughtful, though not deeply so. Of a later collection of poems, *The Glass-Blower,* issued in 1940, a critic wrote: "Their grace and intelligence leave an impression of not having been tested enough by harsh reality. They are the fruit of a refined rather than a strongly imaginative awareness". Yet within these limitations they had many merits.

It was not, however, until the first of the Mrs. Miniver articles appeared, on October 6, 1937, on the Court page of *The Times,* and was followed by many others in the same vein, that Jan Struther hit a wider public taste. The articles continued to appear at intervals until December 1939. They dealt with the life of a middle-class English lady, her architect husband, their three children, and their neighbours. They chronicled the preparations for the arrival of a new car, the setting off of fireworks on Guy Fawkes Day, holidays in the country, the search for a charwoman in London, and many other such matters. Most readers, particularly perhaps those who saw in the characters themselves as they were or would like to be, found these brief sketches entrancing, but there were others who (as one of them wrote in a letter to the editor) found her exasperating because "she is always so smug, so right, such a marvellous manager, and things always go so well with her". Yet whatever the reaction to Mrs. Miniver, there was never any doubt that she was vividly alive.

Joyce Anstruther married in 1923 Anthony Maxtone Graham, and they had two sons and a daughter. The marriage was dissolved, and in 1948 she married A. K. Placzek, a member of the libraries staff of Columbia University.

July 22, 1953.

General Nicholas Plastiras, leader of the E.P.E.K. Party and a former Prime Minister of Greece, who died on July 26, 1953 at Psychico, near Athens, had lived a long, adventurous, forceful and crowded life in the service of his country both in the Army and in politics. He had seen much active fighting as an irregular on the Bulgarian and Turkish frontiers and as an officer in five wars. His lifelong republicanism included frequent periods as an exile and as head of the State, including (for one day) dictatorship in 1933.

Born at Karditza, in Thessaly, in 1883, he saw in early youth eventful and gallant service, first with a band of Greek *Komitajis* on the Bulgarian frontier and later as an officer in the Balkan wars. In 1916 he joined Venizelos's provisional Government at Salonika. Promoted to the rank of lieutenant-colonel he became known as *Karapiperi* (black-pepper). In 1919 he was with the Greek Expeditionary Force in South Russia and in Asia Minor commanded an Evzone regiment, where he distinguished himself during the retreat to Smyrna. With General Gonatas, he played a leading part in bringing about King Constantine's abdication in 1922, becoming himself leader of the Revolutionary Committee.

At this time he incurred the lasting hostility of the Royalists for the shooting of five former Cabinet Ministers, an act which embittered political life in Greece for many years. He also advised King George II to leave the country, and after the King's departure in December 1923 he invited Venizelos to return to Greece. He then emulated Cincinnatus by returning to his farm in Thessaly. His retirement, however, was shortlived. General Pangalos [q.v.], as dictator, in 1925 ordered his arrest, but for a fortnight he eluded soldiers and police and only after a chase over the roofs of houses was he surrounded. After refusing to surrender except to an officer of his own rank he was given a passport which had been prepared for him and deported to Brindisi.

In 1926, after the overthrow of General Pangalos, he returned to Greece. After the defeat of the Venizelists at the polls in 1933 he seized Athens and enjoyed a 24 hours' dictatorship. The Army failed to support him and he withdrew to the South of France. From exile he bitterly attacked the Metaxos régime. Throughout the German occupation of France he remained studiously aloof from Greek politics, but late in 1944, after the civil war had broken out, General Plastiras flew to Athens at the request of the Prime Minister, George Papandreaou*, and on January 3, 1945, formed a Government. This only lasted three months, but the December communist revolution had meanwhile largely been broken. He then staunchly campaigned for the republican cause against those who supported the return of King George II.

He became suspect to the Nationalists at this period, since he seemed prepared to end the civil war which had broken out again by a policy of appeasement through amnesty for the rebels. In March 1950 he re-entered politics, joining Tsouderos, the former Prime Minister and leader of the Democratic Progressive Party, to form the National Progressive Union of the Centre (E.P.E.K.) which had an immediate success, winning 45 seats out of 250. After some manoeuvring among the centre parties General Plastiras formed a coalition Government but this was forced to resign in August 1950, when the Liberal Ministers withdrew.

Late in July 1951 it became clear that owing to the infinitesimal distribution of parliamentary power among the numerous political parties and groups the Greek Chamber, elected 16 months before, could only produce short-lived coalitions with the Liberals—the strongest party, with one quarter of seats in Parliament—as their basic ingredient. The need, therefore, for fresh elections was felt in all quarters, and General Plastiras, confident that the popularity of his Progressive E.P.E.K. Party had increased enormously, became one of the leading advocates of this solution. His confidence, however, seemed wholly unjustified, particularly after the decision of Field-Marshal Papagos [q.v.], the former C.-in-C., a personality enjoying almost unprecedented esteem and repute, to stand for election at the head of a conservative movement. Moreover, a crypto-communist party, under the name of United Democratic Left (E.D.A.), appeared in the political arena and was certainly bound to attract many of Plastiras's dissatisfied left-wing adherents. These forecasts against the success of the general were so persistent that even his associate, Emmanuel Tsouderos, the E.P.E.K. party whip, broke off with 11 deputies and joined the Liberal Party of Sophocles Venizelos* which then appeared to have a good chance of winning in the elections.

The elections of September 1951 proved that Plastiras's confidence in electoral victory (a word measured by Greek standards) was well founded. His party beat the Liberals and was returned with 74 M.P.'s, while Venizelos gained only 57 seats. As was expected no one party obtained a clear majority, but Papagos's "Greek Rally" had certainly won over the right-wing electorate and was returned with 114 seats out of a total of 258. Papagos's stubborn refusal to cooperate with any other party led King Paul* to ask General Plastiras, leader of the second strongest party, to form the new Government. Negotiations with the Liberals were begun, and although the main stumbling-block was Plastiras's determination to "pacify" the country, agreement was reached through mutual compromise. In mid-November, however, Plastiras, who was over-fatigued from his countrywide pre-election tour, was taken ill with angina pectoris. His physicians recommended a long rest, but six weeks later, at 5 o'clock in the morning of December 23, the General left his bed and drove to the Chamber to cast his vote for the ratification of the revised Greek Constitution, which brought to an end a long constitutional anomaly in Greece.

The Premier recovered rapidly and was frequently seen in town on the coldest days of the last winter without an overcoat. He was busy then trying to have the law on "Pacification and Leniency to former Communists" passed by Parliament. He had taken this task to heart and his greatest ambition is to be referred to in history as "the pacifier of Greece". He therefore deeply resented the dilatory attitude on this subject of his Liberal partner. At long last the debate was fixed for March 11; but on the previous Sunday, while attending the unveiling of the war memorial at Menidi, near Athens, he was suddenly taken ill with palsy. The debate was postponed and on March 11 he signed a decree deputing his powers and duties to Venizelos. The decree was approved by the King on the same day.

Plastiras later went to Paris for treatment and seemed to have recovered sufficiently in the autumn of 1952 to return for the elections of November 11. He toured the countryside delivering speeches, but by that time popular feeling had already shifted to the Greek Rally Party of Field Marshal Papagos, who was brought to power with a large majority. Plastiras himself was not re-elected in Athens, but his party obtained 30 seats. Subsequent rivalries within the party led to the split of E.P.E.K., which was finally left with the present 19 members in Parliament. These internal disputes had deeply embittered Plastiras.

July 27, 1953.

Sir Frank Platt, managing director of the Lancashire Cotton Corporation Ltd., died on July 8, 1955 at his home at Bramhall, Cheshire, at the age of 65. He began life as a worker in the office of a Rochdale mill at the age of 13 and lived to become chairman of one of the greatest commercial combines in the country. He served for the greater part of the 1939-45 War as Cotton Controller.

He was born on June 9, 1890, a son of the late Thomas Platt, of Rochdale, and was educated at the Derby Street Boys' School and the Central Higher Grade School there. He was first employed in the counting house at the Clover Croft and State Mills, and two years later began to learn the technique of manufacturing. In 1914 he joined the Higher Crompton Mills Ltd., at Shaw, as mills manager, and within six years he was a director. He extended his directorial and controlling interests in the Rochdale and Oldham districts, and when the international and economic depression came he set himself the task of meeting the problem by a process of radical readjustment and modernization. He "telescoped" 150 mills into 50, scrapped out-of-date machinery, and within a year converted a £300,000 annual loss into a £10,000 profit, for what had become by then the Lancashire Cotton Corporation.

He remained managing director of the company until the end of 1939, when he was appointed Deputy Cotton Controller, and an executive member of the Cotton Board. In 1940 he became the first chairman of British Overseas Cottons Ltd., in pursuance of the Government's export policy for textiles, and in the next year succeeded to the office of Cotton Controller, which he held until the end of the war. With great foresight and courage he built up raw material stocks, storing great pyramids all over the county, often in open fields, under protection, to beat the German bombing attacks. When the war ended he returned to his duties as managing director of the Cotton Corporation. Immediately afterwards he was appointed vice-chairman and, in January 1954, chairman.

Although he had the reputation in industry and commerce of being an exacting and sometimes ruthless man of action, especially in crises, it could be well said of him that his striking achievements were the justification of his life's work. In his leisure, and his domestic circle, he was a man of much charm and kindliness.

He had owned race-horses, was a keen farmer and horticulturist, and for many years was an active director of the Oldham Athletic Football Club. In his later years he played an excellent game of tennis. He was knighted in 1943.

He married in 1915, Mary, daughter of Benjamin Lord, who survives him together with a daughter of the marriage.

July 11, 1955.

Dr. Albert Plesman, founder and president of the Royal Dutch Airlines (K.L.M.), died in hospital after a sudden illness at the end of December 1954. He was 64.

The son of a small business man at The Hague, he was born in 1889 and joined the Netherlands Army as a boy. In 1911, the year in which he received his commission, he saw a heavier than air aircraft for the first time and from that moment determined to become an airman. He was, however, posted to a cyclist regiment and it was not until 1915 that he was transferred to the young Netherlands Air Force as an observer. He was granted his military flying licence in November 1918 but this was only a step towards the goal at which he was already aiming. Even while the 1914-18 War was still raging he was preaching the potentialities of aviation as a medium for the development of international understanding and early in 1919 he succeeded in organizing an international air exhibition at Amsterdam.

Some idea of his persuasiveness may be gained from the fact that he induced 4,000 people to fly during the exhibition and later in the year succeeded in getting the backing of a group of Dutch financiers to found K.L.M., which came into being on October 20, 1919. The first flight was made from London to Amsterdam in May 1920, with a DH9 piloted by Captain J. Shaw. Before the end of the year 584 trips were made without accident. Thenceforward Plesman and his company went from strength to strength, always in the forefront of developments tending towards safety, regularity, and comfort.

By the summer of 1940 the great organization, except for the West Indian section and a London-Lisbon service, was broken, but Plesman did not give up hope and the German armies were scarcely out of Holland before K.L.M. was flying again from its homeland and developing its regular passenger services throughout the world.

Dr. Plesman's big frame, rugged bony face, and large hands suggested rather a farmer than an airman, an impression reinforced by his slow, deliberate, and simple speech. Though his was a triumph of will devoted to the achievement of a single object, he was by no means a man of only one idea. His interests were wide and his approach to life human.

He is survived by his widow, a son, and a daughter. Two other sons predeceased their father; one was killed on active service with the R.A.F. during the last war and the other was killed in a civil aviation accident.

January 1, 1954.

Professor Robert Henry Aders Plimmer, Emeritus Professor of Chemistry in the University of London, died in hospital on June 18, 1955 at the age of 78. He was a leading authority on protein chemistry and a pioneer in the field of vitamins and nutritional biochemistry.

The son of Alfred Aders, of Manchester, he was born on Apirl 25, 1877, and adopted the surname of his stepfather, Henry George Plimmer, F.R.S. He was educated at Dulwich College, and University College London, whence he graduated B.Sc. in 1899 and D.Sc. in 1902. After further studies at the Universities of Geneva and Berlin he was in 1902 appointed to a two-year research studentship at the Lister Institute by the Grocers' Company and in 1904 he became an assistant at University College. He was elected a Fellow in 1906 and in the following year appointed assistant Professor of Physiological Chemistry in University College.

From 1912 to 1919 he was reader in this subject at the college and in the latter year he became head of the Biochemical Department of the Rowett Institute of Research in Animal Nutrition at Aberdeen, which had been established by the generosity of a former schoolfellow of his, John Q. Rowett, the promoter of the Shackleton-Rowett Antarctic Expedition. At Aberdeen Plimmer was chiefly concerned with the composition and energy value of different foods and with the chemistry of proteins and vitamins.

In 1922 he was appointed to the chair of Medical Chemistry at St. Thomas's Hospital Medical School in the University of London, which he held with distinction for 20 years. He was made Emeritus Professor in 1944. After his retirement he became a member of the Biochemistry Department at the Post-graduate Medical School at Ducane Road, Hammersmith, where he continued actively at work almost until the day of his death.

He was a founder member of the Biochemical Society and its first secretary and treasurer in 1911-12 and honorary secretary from 1913 to 1919. His published works included a well known and internationally famous book, *Organic and Bio-chemistry,* and several other books on associated subjects. In 1922 he and his wife published an instructive little book entitled *Vitamins and the Choice of Food.* From 1908 onwards he was together with the late F. G. Hopkins, of Cambridge, co-editor of the well known series of monographs on biochemistry published by Longmans.

He married in 1912 Miss Violet Geraldine Sheffield. She died in 1949. There were a son and three daughters of the marriage.

June 21, 1955.

Edward Drax Plunkett—See **Dunsany.**

Guy Pocock, who died at his home at Cambridge on March 19, 1955, was endowed with many gifts as author, editor, scholar, and teacher.

Guy Noël Pocock was the second son of the late Noël Lewis Pocock and was educated at Highgate School and St. John's College, Cambridge. For some 10 years he was a master at Cheltenham and then joined the staff of the Royal Naval College, Dartmouth. The atmosphere of the latter establishment led him to the study of naval history, though his first love was the study and teaching of English. This, indeed, remained with him all his life so that at over 70 he was still supervising English studies for the English Tripos at Cambridge.

In 1923 he gave up teaching in order to devote himself to writing and editing. Apart from a number of admirable school books for the teaching of English, he made anthologies of modern prose and poetry and collaborated with Sir Arthur Quiller-Couch in editing the "King's Treasuries of Literature" series. Also in 1946 he made the new "Everyman" selection of Charles Lamb's letters from E. V. Lucas's comprehensive edition, together with Lucas's valuable notes and index.

His original work was a series of light but entertaining and workmanlike novels of a quality to be expected from such a fastidious craftsman and critic. His first novel, *Knight's Gambit,* evokes a pleasantly nostalgic picture of middle-class England from the South African War to after the 1914-18 War. Others followed not at too short intervals, and though his output in this *genre* is not large, it has a consistent, quiet quality that is savoured rather by aroma than by taste. The contrasting picture of the same village seen through the benevolence of Mrs. Clutterbuck and the melancholy acuteness of Dr. Rally is well brought out in *Mrs. Clutterbuck Laughs,* while in *Design for a Staircase, Period Programme,* and *Together We Go* the behaviour of well defined characters cast into unaccustomed circumstances is vividly presented.

In 1934, while continuing his literary work, he joined the staff of the talks department of the B.B.C., becoming acting head of the department. Later he was appointed editor of the supplementary publications. He, however, left the corporation in 1940 and went back to Cheltenham to teach for the remainder of the war. Since 1946, in addition to his work for the English Tripos at Cambridge, he delivered lectures on naval history to naval officers up at the university on short courses. He was an outstanding teacher and made a deep and lasting impression on the many pupils who passed through his hands at Cheltenham, Dartmouth, and Cambridge, many of whom kept in regular correspondence with him over the years.

He married in 1924 Dorothy Allcott Bowers, daughter of the late Bishop of Thetford, who survives him together with a son of the marriage.

March 22, 1955.

Sir Felix Pole, who held successively two key positions in industry—as general manager of the Great Western Railway and chairman of Associated Electrical Industries, died on January 15, 1956 in hospital at Reading, Berkshire, at the age of 78.

Felix John Clewett Pole was born on February 1, 1877, the son of a schoolmaster. He entered the service of the Great Western Railway at the age of 14 in the telegraph department at Swindon. There had always been a peculiar pride in the old Great Western company and Pole had his full share of it. Nevertheless, though the company always had a great reputation for looking after its employees and encouraging keenness and efficiency, it was greatly to Pole's credit that at the age of 44 he should have been selected as general manager of the whole line.

That was in 1921 and he remained in office until 1929. There were few more difficult periods in railway management than these. Many complex problems were involved in the application of the Railways Act of 1921, with the numerous amalgamations and absorptions it required. The Great Western was lucky in that it was easily the biggest fish in the parts of the country it served. Unlike the other proud pioneer lines, such as the London and North-Western, the Great Northern, and the Midland, it was in the upshot the only one to retain its name and all the associations that it carried. The famous "family spirit" of the company was fostered and intensified under the régime of "Pole of Paddington", as he came to be called, and during his eight years as general manager many developments took place. The "Castle" and the "King" classes of locomotives were introduced and drew famous expresses which were then the fastest in the world.

As an experienced railwayman he visited the Sudan in 1923-24 and again in 1930-31 at the invitation of the Sudan Government to report on the railways and steamers there, and in 1924 he served on the committee set up to inquire into claims for pensions by ex-ranker officers. He served on many other committees and commissions at that time and afterwards, and was for a time a member of the Industrial Court.

In the summer of 1929, in a speech at Swansea, he dropped a hint that he might soon relinquish his position as general manager, but added that he hoped still to be associated with the "good old company". The following day his appointment as chairman of Associated Electrical Industries was announced. While in that position he had to find ways of mitigating the effects of the trade depression in the great undertaking he controlled, and when in the middle thirties the trade outlook gradually began to brighten, his enterprise, with its efficiency and morale at the highest level, was in a splendid position to take advantage of the better conditions.

At this period his services were in even greater demand by Government departments than before. He was, for instance, a member of the Colonial Development Advisory Committee and the Coal Commission, and chairman of the Rural Housing Committee in 1936. He also reported in 1934 on transport conditions in Northern Ireland to the Government of Northern Ireland. He remained chairman of Associated Electrical Industries until 1945, but after his resignation continued a member of the board until 1955, though for the past few years he had been blind.

He married in 1899 Ethel Maud, daughter of Horace Flack, of Regent's Park, who survives him together with a son and two daughters of the marriage.

January 16, 1956.

Vladimir Poliakoff, who from the time he settled in Great Britain more than 35 years ago was a trenchant commentator on foreign affairs, died on June 5, 1956 at his home at Welwyn Garden City at the age of 75.

For years it was his amazing fund of vitality that struck all who met him. He was a ready writer, but also a splendid and amusing talker. Those who did not know him well might think him boisterous, but his outward manner was a cover for real modesty and deep sensitiveness. Perhaps the last quality was shown in his reluctance to talk much about the Russia he had known; he put it behind him and threw himself with enthusiasm into each new work he undertook. To those who knew him well he was always the kindest and most unfailing friend.

He was born of a well-to-do family in southern Russia on November 8, 1880, and was educated at the Classical Gymnasium at St. Petersburg (now Leningrad). Choosing to study railway engineering, he attended the Emperor Alexander I Institute of Railway Engineers and while there made a special study of tunnelling. During the earlier part of the 1914-18 War he served as an engineer officer in the Russian Army on the Galician and Polish fronts, winning the St. George Cross, but in the confused period which culminated in the collapse of Russian resistance found himself isolated. Determined, if possible, to keep Russia in the war, he made contact with the British diplomatic representative in Russia. After Lenin's triumph Poliakoff escaped to the United Kingdom.

Like many educated Russians, he had a superb command of foreign languages and so he found no difficulty in settling down in Britain.

He quickly evinced a pronounced gift for writing and as early as 1919 began a series of informative articles in the *Nineteenth Century.* With these his reputation as a commentator on foreign affairs was founded and in 1920 he joined the staff of the *Daily Telegraph.* He continued, however, to contribute to various other publications under the pen-name "Augur", which quickly became the hall-mark of well-informed comment in Poliakoff's special field. When he had served some four years with the *Daily Telegraph* he transferred his allegiance to *The Times* and for the next 12 years or so brought his wide information and strong judgment to bear in the diplomatic comment appearing in its columns during a critical and testing time in international affairs.

During all that period he constantly widened his acquaintance, not only among such journalists as Pertinax and Mme. Tabouis, but among the prominent political figures of the period, including most of the Foreign Ministers of Europe. He was especially friendly with Count Grandi and throughout the period between the wars strove to maintain the traditional friendship between Great Britain and Italy. At his home in London he entertained at one time or another almost every distinguished foreign visitor to the capital and he kept up a vigorous correspondence across the Atlantic. In this way he collected an unrivalled array of authentic information, which he constantly placed at the service of *The Times.*

He was one of the first commentators to point out the danger of a resurgent Germany after the 1914-18 war and this was, indeed, his main theme until war actually broke out again in 1939. It was, however, a theme which became ever less popular until the shock of Munich had its due effect. Meanwhile Poliakoff, feeling that he would have a freer hand to pursue his bent, resigned his post on *The Times* and redoubled his efforts to instruct public opinion in newsletters and syndicated articles under the by then well-known pen-name "Augur". These articles were widely read in provincial newspapers of Britain, in the United States and in a number of countries in Europe.

At the beginning of the war he had moved from London to Welwyn Garden City, where he took up gardening with the same verve he displayed in everything he undertook. It was a great grief to him that he had to give it up a few years ago after a stroke which left him partly paralysed. He went to London at least one day a week, kept in the closest touch with diplomatic circles and continued his writing until a second illness incapacitated him a few months ago.

He married in 1905 Xenia Leon, who survives him with two daughters.

June 6, 1956.

Harry Pollitt, chairman of the Communist Party, died in the liner Orion on June 27, 1960 while on the way home from Australia. He was 69.

Pollitt was often described as what many people regard as almost a freak of nature, a communist with a sense of humour. Short and bald, with a quiet manner and a twinkle in his eyes, he had likable qualities which endeared him to some of his most bitter political opponents.

But Pollitt was the man who, with Palme Dutt* behind him, was chosen by the Communist International in 1929 to bring the British party under the complete control of Moscow. These two men, with the complementary qualities of the workers' leader and the theoretician, maintained the party's subservience, with a break for a series of political somersaults from 1939-41, until Pollitt resigned the secretaryship in 1956 and became chairman.

Though Pollitt remained in favour for so much longer than most of his counterparts on the Continent, apart from his temporary disgrace at the beginning of the war, this was perhaps because little importance was attached to the small and ineffectual British party, for he was never admitted to the inner counsels of the international movement. His life was devoted to an impossible task—that of attracting the mass of the British people to Soviet communism.

Pollitt was born on November 22, 1890, at Droylsden, Lancashire, son of Samuel Pollitt, a boiler shop worker. He entered a cotton mill as a half-timer at the age of 12, working with his mother, who was a weaver. "Every time she wrapped her shawl round my shoulders to keep out the cold, I swore I would make the bosses pay for what she had endured", he wrote later in his autobiography, *Serving My Time* (1940).

At 15 he became apprenticed as a boiler-maker at the Gorton Tank locomotive works. He began to speak at meetings before he was 18, and joined the I.L.P. in 1909, studying industrial history and economics in the evenings.

In 1912 he completed his indentures, procured work at a small factory at Levenshulme, Manchester, and soon became a shop steward. In June 1915, now working in a shipyard, came his first sharp conflict with authority. He actively opposed the war and led the opposition to a request from the Ministry of Munitions that the boilermakers should sacrifice their holidays in the interests of war production. A little later he led an anti-dilution strike and was one of those fined £5 for impeding the war effort.

In 1918 he went to London and the following year became London district secretary of the Boilermakers' Society. He became first national organizer of the Hands Off Russia movement and played an active part in the agitation which led to the "Jolly George" strike, when dockers refused to load arms for the Polish war against Russia.

He was a foundation member of the Communist Party of Great Britain in 1920, and two years later was one of a commission of three (which also included Palme Dutt) to make recommendations for carrying out Comintern instructions for the reshaping of the British party.

In August 1924 he became secretary of the National Minority Movement, which aimed at bringing the trade unions under communist control. In October the following year he was one of 13 leading communists tried for uttering a seditious libel and contravening the provisions of the Incitement to Mutiny Act. He was condemned to a year's imprisonment and served 11 months at Wandsworth.

The British Communist Party was still not pleasing Moscow and, to make matters worse, was losing membership. The British officials, who considered it necessary to adapt their policy to British conditions, were not sufficiently docile, and under pressure from the Comintern there was a long controversy in 1929, during which the British leaders vainly defended themselves before the Comintern in Moscow.

They were forced to call a special congress in November that year, as a result of which Pollitt was appointed general secretary and, with Palme Dutt behind him, began his long period of leadership. "I was appointed to the position of general secretary when the party was, perhaps, at its lowest ebb in membership, organization, morale, and leadership", Pollitt wrote later, "with no clear perspective of what was the line of march immediately ahead. We had 3,500 dues-paying members, no daily paper, and disagreements on policy that required two party congresses in 1929 to sort out". One of his first duties was to arrange for the publication of the *Daily Worker.*

During the following years his views frequently got him into trouble. In 1933 he was deported from Belfast. In 1934 he was arrested in Cardiff, with Tom Mann, for speeches about the treatment of the unemployed, but was released. He visited Spain a number of times during the Spanish civil war.

In September 1939 the central committee met in London and declared their support for the war of democracy against fascism. Pollitt wrote a pamphlet entitled *How to Win the War.* But it soon appeared that the Soviet Union was following a different line. After a fierce debate in the central committee lasting nine days, they decided that the war was an imperialist one. Pollitt and one of his colleagues, who had apparently opposed this decision to the end, were removed from office, though once the decision was taken Pollitt declared publicly that it was correct and that he accepted it. When Germany invaded Russia the war became again an anti-fascist one and Pollitt was restored to office.

He was not again to fall from grace, though there were moments in his later years when it was possible to detect faint traces of cynicism in his attitude to the party he continued to serve faithfully.

He visited Russia late in 1957 for a five-week stay. In 1958 he spent a short time in hospital after suffering a minor stroke. During his tour of Australia, from which he was returning when he died, he appeared on Australian television.

During his career he stood for Parliament nine times without success. His wife, Marjorie Pollitt, contested unsuccessfully the Hendon North Division as a Communist candidate in the 1950 general election. There are two children, a son and a daughter.

June 28, 1960.

Vere Ponsonby—See **Bessborough.**

Pope Pius XII—See **Pius XII.**

Walter J. Macqueen-Pope—See **Macqueen-.**

Sir Robert Brooke-Popham—See **Brooke-.**

Group Captain R. C. Porteous, D.S.O., who was killed on July 9, 1953, when about to land a Vampire fighter aircraft at Wahn, Germany, entered the Royal Air Force, like many officers who gained distinction in the war years, with a short-service commission.

Some three years' service flying before the war broke out had given him enough depth of experience on which to build a valuable and progressively important career. The campaign in North Africa in 1941 and 1942 was a great era for improvisation and resource, and with one of the war's most colourful experiments Porteous's name will always be associated. This was the Hurricane aircraft fitted with two Bofors guns, slung under the wings, and used to attack German tanks. This was only one example of Porteous's concern with the tactical aspect of land-air warfare to which most of the mature years of his service career were devoted.

Roger Cave Porteous was born on March 25, 1913, and between his preparatory school, St. Bede's, Eastbourne, and his going to Sutton Valence School he spent two years at the Alpine College, Villars, Switzerland. He was accepted for training as a pilot in March 1936, and after successfully completing his elementary flying training at Brough was granted a short-service commission in the general duties branch. The war was not a month old when he went oversea on flying duties with No. 13 Squadron in the Air Component of the British Expeditionary Force. It gave him his first experience of what was then termed Army co-operation and from then onwards his experience in this field was extended and developed.

In 1941 he was posted to No. 253 Wing in the Middle East for flying duties, serving for a time with No. 244 Squadron. After a visit to A.H.Q., Iraq, in January 1942 he was given his first command, No. 6 Squadron, and it was in leading his pilots with such resource and ingenuity against the enemy armour in the desert that he was confirmed as a brilliant tactical air commander.

After a year with his squadron he was awarded the D.S.O. for skill, courage, and leadership. To pass on the technique and experience he had won he was given command of No. 74 Operational Training Unit in January 1943, with which he stayed until the late summer, when he was selected for special duty with the British delegation in Washington on the air support side.

At a time when logistics had become the predominating issue it was invaluable to have first-hand advice about the practical aspects of air support when the preparations were being made for D-Day. He was able to see again a British expeditionary force in the field in France, this time more adequately supplied itself and more strongly partnered in the air, as he was posted to the headquarters of No. 2 Group of the Allied Expeditionary Force in June 1944. Within a few months Air Marshal Embry [d. 1977] gave him command of No. 487 Squadron, which he held until he returned to take a course at the R.A.F. Staff College in 1945.

His first post-war posting was as Wing Commander (Organization) at 41 Group in Maintenance Command. Two years later he was again selected for special duties in the United States, being appointed to the U.S.A.A.F. Tactical Air Command, where he spent 15 engrossing months at busy Langley Field. Towards the end of 1948 he was appointed R.A.F. instructor in the Army Tactical School of the School of Land-Air Warfare, Old Sarum. Here his experience and charm won him more friends in both services during the two and a half years he spent there. He went out to Germany in April 1951, first as Wing Commander (Training) at B.A.F.O. headquarters, and then to command the station at Celle.

July 13, 1953.

Lord Porter, a Lord of Appeal in Ordinary from 1938 to 1954, died on February 13, 1956 in a nursing home in London at the age of 79.

The Right Hon. Sir Samuel Lowry Porter, Baron Porter, of Longfield, co. Tyrone, G.B.E., was born in 1877. He was educated at Emmanuel College, Cambridge, and was called to the Bar by the Inner Temple in 1905. Before he specialized in the Commercial Court he was fortunate in enjoying a good general practice, particularly on circuit and in county courts, and the experience thus gained proved invaluable in the varied work which later fell to him as a recorder and as a judge. After some years at the Bar he confined his practice to the Commercial Court, a class of work in which more than average ability is required for success. That he achieved. In 1925 he took silk, and this gamble of life at the Bar further established and confirmed his reputation. When the present Lord Roche [q.v.] became a lord justice in 1934 it was expected that a successor would be chosen from those practising in the Commercial Court and the general opinion was that the vacancy would be offered to Porter.

Of a judicial temperament, a sound lawyer, quiet but forceful in manner, and courteous to all who came before him, he was considered by many to have been one of the ablest of the King's Bench judges. His pale features, slim figure of medium height, and slight scholarly stoop discounted a robust physique, but he was active and wiry, possessing the necessary strength for the arduous life of the Bar.

Porter was not always an easy judge to listen to, but the difficulty sometimes of hearing what he said was not a failing confined to him alone. Another matter, which seems more peculiar to the Commercial Court, was in the preparation of reserved judgments whose reliance for the form of a judgment was sometimes placed in notes and on extracts from the necessary documents rather than on a fully written decision. It is clear that, where difficult points of law were involved, the practising lawyer in search of precedent can find greater assistance in a carefully prepared and closely reasoned judgment than from one which must inevitably be more loosely constructed if it is not first written out. No doubt the mass of documents in a commercial case, the masses of correspondence, and the frequently obscure charterparties with their numerous inter-lineations have unconsciously exercised an influence on the form in which judgments have sometimes been delivered in that Court.

Though not a man much in the public eye—indeed, he was not one to court publicity—Porter came into prominence in 1936 as the chairman of the tribunal appointed to inquire into the question "whether any unauthorized disclosure was made of information relating to the Budget for the present year, or any use made of any such information for the purposes of private gain". It may be recalled that after the tribunal had issued its report J. H. Thomas resigned his office of Minister for the Dominions.

Porter served in the Army during the 1914-18 War, as a captain on the General List. He was Recorder of Newcastle-under-Lyme from 1928 to 1932, and of Walsall from 1932 to 1934, when he was appointed to the High Court Bench.

After the conferment of a life peerage upon him in 1938 he regularly sat with the Law Lords to hear appeals to the House of Lords. Of these the most noteworthy was the appeal of William Joyce ("Lord Haw Haw") in 1946 against his conviction at the Central Criminal Court on a charge of high treason. The appeal was dismissed, but in a dissenting judgment Lord Porter held that there was no evidence that Joyce had kept his British passport for use after September 18, 1939.

In 1948 he became chairman of the Committee on the Law of Defamation and two years later became chairman of the Departmental Committee on Railway Wages, but had to resign on health grounds.

No notice of his life would be complete without some mention of his labours on behalf of the International Law Association, which he addressed in 1946 as president when the association organized a conference at Cambridge, the first conference since that at Amsterdam in 1938. Cambridge conferred on him the LL.D. *honoris causa* in 1947 and he was created G.B.E. in 1951 for his services to the association. He resigned the office of Lord of Appeal in Ordinary in 1954 owing to ill-health.

February 14, 1956.

Former Bishop of Portsmouth—See **Lovett.**

Queen Amélie of Portugal, the widow of King Carlos I of Portugal, who was assassinated in 1908, died at her home near Versailles on October 25, 1951.

Her father was Louis Philippe Albert, Comte de Paris and pretender to the throne of France, and her mother Isabella, an Infanta of Spain. Marie Amélie Louise Hélène de Bourbon-Orléans was born in 1865 at Orleans House, Twickenham, where the greater part of her youth was spent. She was brought up largely on English lines and her girlhood was as happy and carefree as that of the ordinary upper-class English girl. This period, perhaps the happiest in a life that was to be overshadowed by more than one tragedy, left her with a love of England that remained with her all her life. Her future husband, Dom Carlos, heir to the throne of Portugal, is said to have been so attracted by a photograph of her that he chanced to see in Lisbon that he hurried post-haste to Paris, where she was staying, to make her acquaintance.

Not long after the meeting their engagement was announced, and in 1886 the Royal pair were married in Lisbon, with all the pomp and circumstance of the time. The marriage was a very happy one, and when, owing to the illness of his father, Dom Carlos was called upon to act as Regent, her qualities were such that she was able to give him considerable assistance in guiding the destinies of his troubled country. For her own part, she was active in establishing hospitals on up-to-date lines (she took a great interest in nursing) and encouraging, by all means in her power, the development of education. Her private charity was legendary, and she would often visit *incognito* the poorer quarters of Lisbon in order to alleviate distress. Once, on one of these expeditions, near the Tagus, she dived in and rescued a child who had fallen into the river, for which deed she was awarded the medal of the Royal Humane Society.

After the assassination of her husband and elder son in 1908, her younger son ascended the throne of Portugal as King Manoel II, but reigned hardly more than two and half years. Her popularity in Portugal was such that after her son's abdication she could, perhaps, have remained in the country, but she preferred to share his exile.

During the 1914-18 war her interest in nursing found expression in work at the 3rd London

General Hospital at Wandsworth, and after the war she lived in retirement near Versailles, where she remained, apparently unmolested, throughout the German occupation of France. The measure of the esteem in which she was held in Portugal is that to-day and for the next two days the flags fly at half-mast and her remains will be conveyed by a Portuguese warship to rest beside those of her husband.

October 26, 1951.

Emily Post, an acknowledged authority on American manners and deportment, died in New York in September 1960, at the age of 86.

It is remarked that her simple and kindly counsels had eased social problems for thousands of people since her first widely known book on etiquette appeared in 1922; at a time when good manners were elaborate she set about simplifying them to the extent of saying that a hostess might possibly have too many forks if one picked up the wrong one.

Her writings sprang from an innate kindliness and a horror of affectation; they were largely directed to the debutantes, the suitors and newly weds anxious to establish themselves in the world around them, and ranged from passable behaviour in a seven year old to complicated forms of address of the European nobility.

Her book was revised 10 times, and every edition emphasized the basic rule of etiquette—to make the other person feel comfortable. For many years Mrs. Post had her own broadcast programme, and her daily syndicated column was still appearing in 200 newspapers. It is said to have been largely due to her guidance that the chaperone tended to loom less large in society until she disappeared almost completely from Mrs. Post's book; and in 1946 she founded the Emily Post Institute, given to the study of gracious living.

Her own social position was excellent—she came of a Baltimore family—and she travelled extensively in Europe, besides having an intimate knowledge of the social summers of Bar Harbour in Maine. She had some success as a novelist and short story writer but good manners always remained her forte.

September 28, 1960.

Leff Nicolas Pouishnoff, the well-known pianist, was found dead at his London home on May 28, 1959. [It was due to barbiturate poisoning and caused by misadventure.] He was 67.

Pouishnoff was born in Odessa on October 11, 1891, and educated at Kiev. He began to play the piano when he was only three and a half, and at the age of five gave his first public concert. Entering the St. Petersburg Conservatory in 1907 he studied the piano with Annette Esipoff and composition with Glazunov, Rimsky-Korsakov, and Liadov; he left the conservatory three years later, having won the gold medal and the Rubinstein Prize.

In 1911 he went on a concert tour with the violinist Leopold Auer, and from 1913 to 1917 he taught the piano at the Tiflis Conservatory. He left Russia in 1920 with the intention of settling in Paris; there, however, he rashly lent a large sum of money (almost all he possessed) to some Armenians, who absconded with it. But he followed them to London, recovered the money, and with it was able to establish his reputation by giving five recitals. He liked London so much that he decided to make it his home, and in 1931 he became a naturalized British subject.

Meanwhile, in 1923, he had made his first appearance in the United States. In 1926 he gave a week of Chopin recitals in the Wigmore Hall; although these took place during the general strike they were so successful that he repeated them the next year. In 1934 he toured Australasia where, in six months or so, he gave nearly a hundred concerts. Subsequently he undertook several tours round the world, and he was the first professional pianist to be heard in Persia. A frequent broadcaster for many years, he also appeared on television, and he was a favourite artist at the Henry Wood Promenade Concerts.

During the last war he gave hundreds of concerts for the Forces, factory workers, and miners; and at an Albert Hall concert in 1946 he celebrated the fiftieth anniversary of his first public appearance.

With his fluent technique, interpretative gifts, and general air of authority, Pouishnoff won wide acclaim, more especially in the popular classical works; he was also the composer of a number of piano pieces of a light but brilliant character.

His first marriage was dissolved in 1941, and in 1942 he married the pianist Dorothy Hildreth, who survives him.

[Mrs. Dorothy Pouishnoff died three weeks later, also from barbiturate poisoning, after years of illness; an open verdict was recorded.]

May 29, 1959.

Admiral of the Fleet Sir Arthur Power, G.C.B., G.B.E., C.V.O., who died in hospital at Gosport on January 28, 1960, had a distinguished record of service in the Second World War, beginning as captain of the aircraft carrier Ark Royal and ending as Commander-in-Chief of the East Indies Fleet, with intervening periods as a member of the Board of Admiralty and in reponsible commands afloat. After the war he was C.-in-C. Mediterranean Fleet during the delicate period of the withdrawal of the British garrison from Palestine. In February 1952, when C.-in-C. Portsmouth and C.-in-C. Home Station (designate), he was appointed the first Allied C.-in-C. Channel and Southern North Sea, a post within the N.A.T.O. framework. Earlier in his career he was a gunnery specialist and he had rendered good service at the Naval Staff College and Imperial Defence College. He was 70.

Arthur John Power was born on April 12, 1889, the son of E. J. Power, of Etchingham. He entered the Britannia as a naval cadet in May 1904 and went to sea as midshipman in September 1905. Promoted to lieutenant in April 1910, he served in the battle cruiser Indomitable and as first lieutenant of the destroyer Nautilus before being appointed in October 1913 to specialize in gunnery.

During the First World War he was gunnery officer of the battleship Magnificent, the cruiser Royal Arthur, the monitor Raglan at the Dardanelles, and the battle cruiser Princess Royal in the Grand Fleet. He was promoted to commander in 1922 after two and a half years on the staff of the gunnery school.

After serving as assistant to the Director of Naval Ordnance, he attended the course at the Royal Naval Staff College in 1924-25. For two years from July 1925 he was executive officer of the battle cruiser Hood, and for the next two years until promoted to captain in June 1929 he was on the instructional staff at the R.N. Staff College. He was naval member of the Ordnance Committee in 1929-31, and in 1931-33 commanded the Dorsetshire as flag-captain and chief staff officer in the Second Cruiser Squadron, Home Fleet. For the next two years he was naval member of the directing staff at the Imperial Defence College, and from 1935 to 1937 commanded the Excellent, gunnery school.

In January 1938 he took command of the new aircraft carrier Ark Royal, then fitting out at Birkenhead, and commissioned her for service in the following November. He was in the Ark Royal during the early months of the Second World War, when the Goebbels propaganda machine hopefully "sank" her many times. [She was finally torpedoed near Gibraltar in November 1941.] In May 1940, while still a captain and a naval aide-de-camp to the King, he was appointed an Assistant Chief of Naval Staff (Home). A month later he was promoted to rear-admiral.

In August 1942 he was given command of a cruiser squadron in the Mediterranean, but nine months later was appointed Flag Officer-in-Charge, Malta, with acting rank as vice-admiral, in succession to Vice-Admiral Sir Stuart Bonham-Carter [q.v.], who relinquished this post owing to ill-health. The Malta Command was of particular importance at that time, when the invasion of Sicily was being prepared and organized. After the Italian surrender he hoisted his flag afloat in command of the naval force which occupied Taranto, and afterwards held special appointments in Italy until his selection at the end of 1943 as Second-in-Command of the Eastern Fleet, by which time he had been promoted to vice-admiral. He conducted several bombardments and air strikes by battle forces of the Eastern Fleet in 1944, against Sabang, Sourabaya, and other ports in the hands of the Japanese.

In November 1944 on the creation of the British Pacific Fleet under Admiral Sir Bruce (later Lord) Fraser, Vice-Admiral Power became Commander-in-Chief, East Indies Fleet, until December 1945. With his flag in the cruiser Cleopatra he arrived off Singapore on September 3, 1945, signalling the return of the Royal Navy to this base after 3½ years, and was present at the formal surrender of the Japanese a few days later.

From February 1946 to March 1948 he was

Second Sea Lord and Chief of Naval Personnel, and was promoted to admiral from May 1946. In May 1948, he succeeded Admiral Sir Algernon Willis [d. 1976] as Commander-in-Chief, Mediterranean station.

As Captain of the Excellent he was in command of the naval party which drew the gun carriage at Windsor at the funeral of King George V, in January 1936, for which he was made C.V.O. He was appointed C.B. in the 1941 birthday honours, advanced to K.C.B. at the New Year 1944, and to G.C.B. six years later. He had been made G.B.E. in 1946. He was promoted Admiral of the Fleet in 1952.

"Arthur John", as he was affectionately known throughout the Navy in the heyday of his career, was recognized as one of the outstanding officers of his generation. Good looks, a strong character, and a complete mastery of every branch of his profession in which he had served, combined to make him a man of mark alike to those meeting him for the first time and those who, having worked with or under him for long periods, came to apprehend his high merit.

He was twice married. His first wife, Amy, daughter of Colonel D. A. Bingham, by whom he had three sons, died in February 1945, and in August 1947 he married Margaret Joyce (Second Officer, W.R.N.S.), only daughter of A. H. St. C. Watson, of Penfold House, Hendon.

January 29, 1960.

Rhoda Dolores le Poer Power, M.B.E., one of the pioneers of B.B.C. school broadcasts, through whose imaginative scripts many children came to feel that there was more to history than just a list of dates, died in London on March 9, 1957 at the age of 66.

She was educated at Bournemouth High School, Oxford High School, and St. Andrews University. In the first decade of this century she went to Russia as companion to a merchant's daughter.

In 1918 she found herself standing on a platform at King's Cross station with one and sixpence in her pocket, having returned from Russia after no inconsiderable adventures in the 1917 revolution. The following week, for two guineas, she sold an account of those adventures to a newspaper, and on the strength of this set up as a freelance journalist—an occupation which took her to Palestine as a reporter. A few years later she was back in England to find that in her absence broadcasting had been invented, and she was immediately invited to give a series of talks on the new-born air.

It was arranged that she should do six talks on "Boys and Girls in History", the "aim" of the broadcasts being to present historic scenes and events as seen through the eyes of a contemporary child, "Jock the Fenman's son", for example, or the "Villein's Twins". It soon became apparent that she had a flair for presenting history through the new medium.

It soon occurred to her that the atmosphere of a bygone age could be better re-created if the straight talk were enriched by the addition of music, sounds, dialogue and, ultimately, dramatic interludes. The plain talk became an illustrated talk. She had invented a radio technique which has become traditional.

She had, in the nature of things, to condense her subject but she could condense without distorting historical fact; with her history might be popular but it never became potted. Her playlets were good listening, for the writer was one who could get the feel of an historical occasion into her scripts. History lived. She could make even the less sensational episodes in our rough island story attractive and stimulating to children and to adults, to many of whom, perhaps for the first time, history began to have some kind of coherence, meaning, even entertainment value.

She wrote several books, among them *Boys and Girls of History* and *More Boys and Girls of History,* in collaboration with her sister, Dr. Eileen Power, *We Were There, We Too Were There, Ten Minute Tales, Here and There Stories* and a three-volume children's history which has achieved great success.

March 11, 1957.

Tyrone Power, the film and stage actor, died suddenly of a heart attack in Madrid on November 16, 1958, at the age of 44. Playing the leading role of King Solomon in the spectacular film *Solomon and Sheba,* he collapsed during the rehearsal of a dramatic sword duel.

He came of a notable theatrical family. His grandfather was an Irish comedian who migrated to London, his father a Shakespearian actor of some reputation, and his mother, Patia Emma Reaume, was also a talented actress.

He was born at Cincinnati, Ohio, on May 5, 1914, and educated at public schools there and at St. Xavier University. His early attraction to acting was easy to understand but the reason for it did not always help his career. He had to live down being the possessor of an already famous name, and most of his earlier successes were made in the cinema, although later he returned to the stage from time to time. His first screen role was in *Girls' Dormitory* (1936), and his first big success later the same year when he played a leading role in *Lloyd's of London.* Being dark and handsome, he was generally assigned swashbuckling, romantic roles in spectacular costume films during the 1930s: among the best-remembered are *In Old Chicago, Marie Antoinette, Jesse James, The Mark of Zorro,* and *Blood and Sand.* He also played in occasional comedies and drama such as *The Rains Came* and *Johnny Apollo.*

During the war he served in the United States Marine Corps, and did not return to the screen until 1946. In spite of his stage background and training, few of his pre-war films had offered him much real chance to act, but his first post-war film, *The Razor's Edge,* marked a striking change of pace: his creditable attempt at the difficult part of Maugham's* hero, variously inclined to mysticism and drink, made film producers more willing to take him seriously as a dramatic actor. Though he continued to appear in popular costume adventures such as *Captain from Castile, Prince of Foxes,* and *The Black Rose,* he also had more substantial roles in biographical films like Ford's *The Long Gray Line* and *The Eddie Duchin Story,* or dramas like *Seven Waves Away* and *Witness for the Prosecution.* During the decade following the war he also consolidated his reputation as a stage actor with a number of successes in New York and London; he will be remembered best in Britain for his performances in *Mister Roberts* and *The Devil's Disciple.* He also took part in public readings throughout the United States and was one of the founders of Four Provinces Films, a company designed to encourage a native Irish film industry.

Tyrone Power sought throughout his career to achieve a decisive success on the legitimate stage to keep up his family tradition, but in spite of his efforts he was doomed to be accepted in theatre primarily as a visiting film star. In films he perhaps never had a real opportunity to demonstrate his undoubted acting talent to the full; in earlier years his somewhat Mediterranean good looks identified him in producer's minds with passionate Latin roles in romantic extravaganzas, but later in his career he played a much wider variety of roles with considerable success while retaining his firm place in the public's affections.

He was three times married.

November 17, 1958.

George R. Preedy—See **Bowen.**

Maire Price (Maire Nic Shiubhlaigh), who died in hospital in Drogheda, co. Louth, on September 9, 1958, was one of the founder players of the Irish National Theatre, and later one of the best tragediennes of the Abbey Theatre's early days.

The Irish Literary Theatre of W. B. Yeats and Lady Gregory was languishing in the early years of the present century when Maude Gonne, who had then entered the national movement, founded her "Daughters of Ireland". This was a political and cultural club and attached to it was a small dramatic group in which W. G. Fay was producer. Maire Nic Shiubhlaigh joined it and became one of the players of the Irish National Theatre, the small amateur society which was founded in 1903 by the brothers Frank and W. G. Fay. She appeared with Maude Gonne in Yeats's *Cathleen ni Houlihan* when it had its first production in a temperance hall in Clarendon Street, Dublin, in 1902; and in the productions of the Irish National Theatre Society in the Molesworth Hall before it acquired the Abbey Theatre in 1904.

With the sisters Sara Allgood and Maire O'Neill she gave lustre to the Irish stage in the early years of the dramatic revival. Her range was more circumscribed than theirs and her delicate talent was seen at its best in tragic roles. She parted company temporarily with the Abbey Theatre in 1905, for the unusual reason that salaries began to be paid to the players, and she worked for a time with a now forgotten amateur group called The Theatre of Ireland which used to present its plays in Irish.

One of her most celebrated parts was Moll Woods in Seumas O'Kelly's *The Shuiler's Child;* another was Nora Burke in Synge's *In the Shadow of the Glen;* and about that time she played in *The Singer* by Padraic Pearse, the political leader who was executed after the Easter Rising of 1916.

She went on the Abbey company's first American tour in 1911-12 and was on the stage during the riots provoked by *The Playboy of the Western World.* At Philadelphia the members of the company were arrested, though only technically, for producing an immoral play *(The Playboy)* on information laid by a liquor dealer of Irish extraction.

She retired from the professional theatre in 1917, but remained actively interested in the amateur stage and until some years ago she produced plays for drama festivals. Her last appearance on the Dublin stage was in 1947, when she took part in a production of Lady Gregory's *Gaol Gate.* In 1950 she collaborated with her nephew in *The Splendid Years,* a book about the foundation of the Irish Theatre.

Maire Nic Shiubhlaigh was a daughter of Mathew Walker, a member of a family closely associated with the Irish national and the theatre movements. Two of her sisters, Anne and Gipsy, and a brother, Frank, were also early members of the Abbey Theatre Company.

September 11, 1958.

Crown Prince of Iraq—See **Abdul.**

Prince Antoine Bibescu—See **Bibescu.**

Prince Chichibu—See **Chichibu.**

Prince Duleepsinhji—See **Duleepsinhji.**

Prince George of Greece—See **George.**

Princess Arthur of Connaught—See **Fife.**

Crown Princess Maerthe—See **Norway.**

Princess Marie Louise—See **Marie Louise.**

Princess Nicholas—See **Nicholas.**

Sergei Prokofiev, whose death in Moscow at the age of 62 took place on March 4, 1953, was the most gifted contemporary Russian composer, and was nearer to being a world figure than any of his Soviet contemporaries.

In his abundant talent there were several strands, that of the nationalist, the modern, the caricaturist, and the comparatively conventional composer who can work to order. It was the existence of these manners side by side that enabled him to remain a Russian composer, while actually an *émigré* writing for Diaghilev, composing the brittle stuff of his concertos, and turning out acceptable music for ballet and films. His voluntary return to Russia in 1935 after 17 years' absence was a source of wonder to the western world and, as events proved, even his versatility was over-strained by conditions in the Soviet State, but its significance was that he was still a Russian in the nationalist tradition. His sixth and last symphony was a final attempt, apparently more successful than the fifth, which he wrote during the war, to reconcile conflicting loyalties.

Sergei Prokofiev was born in 1891 at Sontzovka, in the Ukraine, near Ekaterinoslav, the son of an estate manager. At the age of five he composed small piano pieces, which were written down by his mother, who gave him piano lessons. When he was eight his work attracted the attention of Taniev who entrusted his musical education to Glière [q.v.]. In 1904 he entered the St. Petersburg Conservatoire, where he studied composition under Rimsky-Korsakov and Liadov, conducting under Tcherepine, and pianoforte under Anna Esipova. His second piano concerto of 1911 created an uproar. The audience left the hall and it was described as "nothing better than cat-calls in a back alley". But when he graduated in 1914 he was awarded the Rubenstein medal for his performance of his first piano concerto, and the first prize in the form of a grand pianoforte. Between 1914 and 1918 he produced numerous piano pieces, the well-known "Scythian Suite", and his opera *The Gambler* based on Dostoevsky; and contemporary music critics admired the freshness and vigour of his work in this period. In 1918 he left Russia, and until 1933 lived in Paris and made many appearances on concert platforms throughout the world.

His operas and ballets achieved great popularity. Among these were *The Love of the Three Oranges* and a comic opera, *The Buffoon (Chout),* both produced in 1921, the former in Chicago and the latter by Diaghilev in Paris. These earned him the reputation of an irrepressible jester, and he began to be regarded as the *enfant terrible* of Russian music. These works were followed by *Le Pas d'Acier* and *The Prodigal Son.* In the former he turned for the first time to Soviet themes. To this period also belong his third and fourth symphonies, the fourth piano concerto, the first string quartet, the opera *The Flaming Angel,* and a cycle of piano pieces. His last ballets were *Romeo and Juliet* and *Cinderella.* During his absence from Russia he was productive and wrote operas, ballets, piano sonatas, incidental music to *Eugene Onegin* and *Boris Godounov,* as well as the splendid music for Eisenstein's film *Alexander Nevsky.* For Stalin's [q.v.] sixtieth birthday in 1939 he wrote the cantata *Zdravitsa* for chorus and orchestra, which was well received officially. In the early years of the war he produced his "Symphonic Suite, 1941", which was followed by the opera *War and Peace* after Tolstoy, for which he was awarded the Stalin Prize. He later wrote the music for Eisenstein's film *Ivan The Terrible.*

Shortly afterwards he began to fall into disfavour with the Soviet Communist Party, and was branded as a "formalist". His "Ode to Stalin" was condemned by Zhdanov as "atonal", and his sixth symphony was likewise pronounced "formalistic". At the conference of Soviet musicians in 1948 the works of Prokofiev, Shostakovich* and Kachaturian were attacked by Zhdanov as "anti-people and divorced from reality . . . marked by formalist perversions". The great reputations of these composers were alleged to have been built up by "a clique of sycophantic critics and racketeers". Prokofiev was "ill" and did not attend the meeting, but later acknowledged his "formalism" in a letter to the union, and promised "to do better in future", blaming foreign influences for his lapses. His opera *The Story of a Real Man,* with which he intended to atone, was criticized as "anti-melodious and modernist . . . lacking in understanding of Soviet heroism and humanity".

Yet Prokofiev was a serious musician who worked successfully in all the big forms, but what was most engaging in him was a boyish gaiety amounting to impudence, a quality found elsewhere only among the French, where, however, it is likely to become sophisticated. The humour of *Peter and the Wolf* never palls, the parody in the pastiche of the Classical Symphony never loses its point, the mock dignity of *The Love of the Three Oranges* is laughable and lovable. He could be dry, and the percussive character of his piano concertos makes them as succulent as dog biscuit. But animating it all are the recognizably Russian qualities that he derived from the "Big Five", Rimsky-Korsakov especially, natural melody, technical resource, and a love of colour. His wit was his own.

March 9, 1953.

Vsevolod Illationovich Pudovkin, whose death was announced by the Soviet Ministry of Culture on July 1, 1953, was one of the most notable of the Russian film directors, with a long and distinguished record.

Born in 1893, he was educated at Moscow University and was one of the earliest directors of the Meshzapouv film studios. He had already to his credit such finely conceived studies as the films *Mother* and *The End of St. Petersburg* when in 1929 he published his first theoretical work on film technique. At that time the principle was still strongly held in Russia that the cinema should dominate the actor, so that there should be no "stars" and consequently none of those essentially theatrical means of expression typified by the term "close up". In place of these, methods within range only of the film should be used.

The example he gave in the book—of the interposing of "shots of a brook swollen with the rapid flow of spring, of the play of sunlight broken on the water, and finally of a laughing child" to express a prisoner's joy on release—seems naive in statement but it is most effective in practice. His second principle is that "the foundation of film art is editing". That is to say that only the director can give the correctly varying emphasis to the work of unskilled actors, photographed at long intervals in time and space.

His later work on film acting, which was published in 1935, reproduced the substance of a course of lectures delivered at the State Institute of Cinematography in Moscow. Here again the actor plays a secondary role and it is the director who makes the artistic unity whereby the art of the actor moves the audience. So much for theory.

In practice the films directed by Pudovkin certainly were moving, and though at first, particularly in such pieces as *The End of St. Petersburg* and *The Descendant of Jenghis Khan,* it is the scope of the historical theme which lingers in the mind, the later work of Pudovkin, perhaps in spite of his theory or perhaps because of a change of emphasis, often brings the actor into the greatest prominence. This happened in both *General Suvorov* and *Admiral Nakimov*. True, the glowing canvas of history was still there, but it was a luminous background against which the Russian heroes stood out with all the greater brilliance.

July 2, 1953.

Sir Arthur Pugh, C.B.E., who was general secretary of the Iron and Steel Trades Confederation for 19 years and chairman of the general council of the Trades Union Congress at the time of the general strike in 1926, died on August 2, 1955 at the age of 85.

Pugh was one of those trade union leaders who, without the spectacular qualities which catch the public eye, have by their integrity, reliability, and administrative skill raised the prestige of the movement to the high level at which it stands to-day. He was the architect of the Iron and Steel Trades Confederation, formed by a group of unions during the First World War, and he devised the ingenious method of gradual amalgamation by consent of individual members, which proved a complete success. He was the first general secretary and held that office until his retirement in 1936. During his term he set the pattern of independent judgment, skilled negotiation, and patient attention to detail, combined with a readiness to accept responsibility, which has been followed in more recent years. His qualities enabled him to build up an attitude of mutual confidence between the employers and the union which still survives. Wages in the industry are high and strikes are rare.

His influence on his successors did not depend only on example. He continued right to the end to keep in touch with the union and to let the existing general secretary know quite clearly whether he approved or disapproved of what was being done. His comments were welcomed for he had an established position as elder statesman and his judgment remained clear.

He belonged, one might say, to the solid right wing of the movement, and it was ironic that he should have been chairman of the T.U.C. general council at the time of the general strike in 1926. There is little doubt that at the time he regretted the decision to call the strike, but circumstances were too strong to be overcome.

Pugh was a Welshman, his father William Pugh, a civil engineer, being a native of Neath, but he was born at Ross in Herefordshire in 1870. He went to the elementary school at Ross and started work at the age of 13, apprenticed to a farmer and butcher. He had lost his parents in infancy, and at the age of 24 he moved to Wales and found work in a steel works at Cwmavon. The industrial organization of iron and steel workers was then getting under way and Pugh joined the British Steel Smelters' Association, which had been formed by John Hodge at Motherwell in 1886.

From South Wales Pugh moved to Lincolnshire and there he began his career as a trade union official, becoming a local secretary and, in 1906, assistant secretary of his union. The union headquarters with Hodge, Pugh, a statistical department, and trained staff was described by the Webbs as the most efficient office in the trade union movement.

In 1915 plans were laid for amalgamating the six principal unions in the industry. Two years later three of the six came together to form the British Iron, Steel and Kindred Trades Association, and Pugh, who was a leader of the negotiations, became its secretary. Shortly afterwards, by an ingenious system of dual existence, all the unions were brought into a new organization, the Iron and Steel Trades Confederation, with Pugh again as general secretary.

Three of the confederation's principal officers were members of Parliament, Hodge becoming Minister of Labour, but Pugh did not nourish political ambitions. He was fully occupied with the work of his own union, the promotion of education among trade unionists, and his membership from 1920 of the general council of the T.U.C. He also sat on several committees of inquiry into industrial disputes, including those of the building trade and tramway services, and on Board of Trade inquiries into the claims of various industries for protection against foreign competition.

In 1925 he was elected chairman of the general council of the T.U.C. He was thus in office at the time of the general strike the following year. His advice before and during the "nine days" was conciliatory and it cannot have been with regret that he reported to the Prime Minister on May 12 that the strike was to be called off "forthwith", and negotiations resumed.

Pugh remained general secretary of the Iron and Steel Trades Confederation until 1936. He was also a member of the economic consultative committee of the League of Nations. In 1939 he was appointed a member of the appellate tribunal formed under the Military Service Act.

His acceptance of a knighthood in 1935 was, as similar actions have been, criticized by some trade unionists and Labour Party members.

In 1952, when he was 82, Pugh published a 600-page history of the steel unions, *Men of Steel,* using the *nom de plume* "One of Them".

He married in 1901 Elizabeth Morris, of Port Talbot, Glamorganshire, who died in 1939. There were a son and two daughters.

August 3, 1955.

Christopher James Purnell, C.B.E., late secretary and librarian of the London Library, died on May 31, 1959 at the age of 80.

Born at Oxford on August 7, 1878, the son of William Purnell, he was educated at the Oxford High School. At the age of 14 he entered the Bodleian Library as an under-assistant. Four years later he was appointed a senior assistant and matriculated as a non-collegiate member of the university, taking his B.A. degree in 1899.

At first his library work consisted chiefly in cataloguing arrears of ephemeral copyright books which had accumulated for very many years. Later he assisted Dr. A. E. Cowley, the sub-librarian, in cataloguing foreign books, including those in Hebrew, Armenian, and Russian. His desire to attain as high a standard as possible is shown by his taking special tuition at his own expense in Hebrew and in Greek accentuation. He also had opportunities for making himself proficient in other branches of library administration.

In 1905 Purnell resigned his post at the Bodleian for that of special assistant of the London Library, where under Dr. Hagberg Wright he quickly made his mark. Four years later, when he applied for the librarianship of the Free Public Libraries, Liverpool, Wright spoke in high terms of his fellow-worker, and said that he considered himself fortunate in having found one so well qualified for assisting in the compilation of the Subject-Index on which he was then engaged. Hagberg Wright's name alone appears on the titlepage, but the preface states that "those who may use this Index should above all others be grateful to Mr. C. J. Purnell. If the Index should happily be found fairly accurate and complete, much of such accuracy and completeness is to be attributed to him".

The Catalogue with the Subject-Index and supplements, which together form a great and famous book of reference, was henceforth to be Purnell's main purpose in life. A new edition of the Catalogue was published in 1913-14 with supplements in 1920 and 1929; supplements to the Subject-Index appeared in 1923 and 1938. On the titlepages of all five volumes Purnell appears as joint author. The third supplement to the Catalogue was published in 1953 and contained 150,000 titles of books acquired between 1928 and 1950. This supplement was the first to bear Purnell's name alone. In 1909 Purnell was appointed assistant secretary and sub-librarian, and in 1940, on the death of Hagberg Wright, secretary and librarian of the London Library, a position he held till 1950, when, on retirement at the age of 72, he was succeeded by S. Nowell-Smith.

Although he retired in 1950 Purnell was invited by his committee to see the third supplement through the press. Then on its completion in 1953 he began, as a labour of love, a revision of the list of books damaged or destroyed by bombing.

He was also honorary librarian of the Royal Society of Literature, to which he gave effective and welcome aid. Purnell kept strictly to his chosen field of cataloguing, but in 1916 he edited for the Japan Society the log-book of William Adams, the first Englishman to establish maritime relations with Japan (1614-19).

His sterling qualities were not fully or even generally recognized until the war period. After the bombing of the library in 1944 he at once organized a body of volunteers who helped him in clearing up and in making lists of damaged or destroyed books. At the end of the war there were further difficulties in connexion with the publication of the third supplement owing to labour conditions, shortage of paper, lack of certain types, and the slow rate of printing. All were met with characteristic determination and confidence. To add to official difficulties his house at Blackheath was rendered uninhabitable by bombing. For a time he and his wife found accommodation in the Library: finally they decided to substitute the hotel for the home.

Brought up with Brethren, Purnell throughout his life lived austerely, though his love of music, poetry and the country and his later years of worship in the Anglican Church gave him a wide spiritual experience; shortly before his death he was appointed churchwarden of St. Jude's, Kensington.

Purnell's contribution to the cause of learning was marked in 1950 by his appointment as C.B.E., and his services to the library by a portrait by Freeth for permanent preservation in the London Library.

He married in 1912 Letitia Lucy Glanvill. There are a son and a daughter of the marriage.

June 2, 1959.

Edna Purviance, whose name must be linked in the history of the cinema with [Sir] Charles Chaplin's earlier work, died in a home for aged actors and actresses in Hollywood in January 1958. She was 61 and had been in retirement for more than 20 years.

Edna Purviance started her career in the film world purely by chance. It is said that as a young typist of 17 she happened to visit the studios on a day when Chaplin was searching for a leading lady for his comedies from among some 500 applicants who had crowded there to be interviewed by him.

It is part of Chaplin's genius that he can recognize talent almost on the instant, particularly the specialized talent which was required for his slapstick comedies. Not many young actresses were ready to become involved in such undignified proceedings—nor indeed had they the ability to portray the simple innocence which he demanded. For although he appeared as a comedian, Chaplin [d. 1977] himself was no more than a downtrodden little tramp, battling against the world, and his leading ladies had to reflect this same forlorn mood of resolution in the face of adversity. From the outside Edna Purviance fitted perfectly into this special pattern and she appeared thereafter in nearly all his short comedies.

A turning point in the careers of both of them occurred in 1923. It was in this year that Chaplin took the revolutionary step of writing and producing a film, *A Woman of Paris,* in which he did not appear himself (except for a brief and anonymous moment as a French railway porter). *A Woman of Paris* was a cynical, sophisticated comedy quite unlike anything he had ever attempted before and was fashioned in the polished style in which Lubitsch was later to make his name. It depended for its success on two performances—that of Adolph Menjou*, making his screen *début*, in the part of a suave man about town, and of Edna Purviance who played a cultured and elegant prostitute. It was in this picture that she proved her considerable versatility, by making the difficult change from simple innocence to the worldly elegance of the demi-monde. Her performance owed much, of course, to Chaplin's masterly direction, but it will always stand as the part by which she will be remembered.

January 17, 1958.

Dr. Herbert Putnam, Librarian of the United States Congress in Washington from 1899 to 1939, when he retired with the title emeritus, died in Washington at the age of 93 in August 1955.

The Library of Congress is far the most important and extensive in the United States and is among the most important in the world, particularly in modern books, for it enjoys the same privilege as the British Museum in London and the Bodleian at Oxford of having the right to claim a copy of every book, pamphlet, or periodical or other printed material published in the country at the time of its issue. It is also the depository for all original documents of the Federal Government of the United States and is thus the chief treasure house for those who are making a study of American history. It has also profited greatly through the large funds placed at its disposal by successive Congresses to purchase older books and it has received many bibliographical treasures through the benefactions of wealthy Americans.

During Dr. Putnam's term of office the library increased greatly and was much improved by offering greater facilities for readers and making its treasures more accessible to students. Dr. Putnam was known throughout the world as one of the foremost librarians and the systems he introduced and the improvements he carried out were followed in many other large libraries. He came from a family which had had a long and distinguished connexion with the publication of books and he brought to his task an enthusiasm, a hereditary love and respect for books, and an experience which few men in the world could rival.

Herbert Putnam was born in New York City on September 20, 1861, the son of George Palmer Putnam. He was educated at public and private schools in the city and then went to Harvard where he took his degree in 1883. He then took a year of his law course at the Columbia Law School in New York. His love of books was even then known to a wide circle and in 1884 he was offered the post of Librarian to the Athenaeum, a centre of culture and study in arts and letters in Minneapolis. After three years he was appointed librarian of the public library of Minneapolis with which the collection of the Athenaeum was incorporated.

At that time the work of a librarian was not looked upon as a regular profession and he still hankered after the law. He had completed his studies in his new home in Minneapolis in 1886 and was called to the Bar of the state of Minnesota. Then in 1891 he threw up his position as librarian and went to Massachusetts, where he was called to the state Bar and set up in practice in Suffolk County, near Boston. He practised there for over three years, but then came another offer in the world of books, which he could not overlook. He became head of the public library of the city of Boston and remained there until 1899, when he was summoned to the biggest position of the kind which America could offer, Librarian to Congress at Washington.

He was always regarded as the leading librarian in the United States. He was president of the Massachusetts Library Club in 1896 and 1897, president of the American Library Association in 1898 and again in 1903 and 1904. He represented his country at the international conference on libraries in London in 1897 and again at the five hundredth anniversary of the birth of Johann Gutenberg at Mayence, at the international library and bibliographical conference at Rome in 1929, and at many other gatherings of the same kind. When America entered the war in 1917 he took charge of the libraries for troops in the United States and oversea.

His work at Washington was highly appreciated by statesmen and members of Congress and many students and professors who worked in the Library of Congress, all of whom found him most attentive and considerate. In 1929 he was awarded the medal granted in memory of President Theodore Roosevelt for distinguished service to the State. He was honoured by many universities and received honorary degrees in recognition of his work from Bowdoin, Brown, Princeton, Illinois, Columbia, now George Washington, Wisconsin, Yale, Williams, Harvard, and New York.

August 16, 1955.

Sir David Pye, C.B., F.R.S., died on February 20, 1960 at Godalming. He was 73.

David Randall Pye was one of the comparatively few men, other than professors, who have held fellowships at both Oxford and Cambridge. He went to Trinity College, Cambridge, from Tonbridge School, in 1905, and was one of three men placed in the First Class of the Mechanical Sciences Tripos in 1908. After a period of practical experience in the firm of Mather & Platt he was invited to join Professor Jenkin in the new Engineering

Laboratories at Oxford in 1909, and was elected a Fellow of New College in 1911. He was the first and only lecturer in the Department of Engineering up to 1914. He shared the burden of teaching in the morning with the professor, and they devoted all the afternoons and most of the vacations to research on the thermal properties of refrigerants, about which little was known at the time. The results of these investigations were published in the Philosophical Transactions in 1913 and 1915. They have stood the test of time.

In 1914 Pye was contemplating leaving Oxford and devoting himself to the practice of engineering. His mind was made up for him by the outbreak of war. He became an Experimental Officer in the Royal Flying Corps and was one of Professor Bertram Hopkinson's chosen men at Orfordness and later at Martlesham Heath, Suffolk.

When he was demobilized in 1919 he returned to Oxford for a time, and then moved to Cambridge as a Fellow of Trinity College and a Lecturer in Engineering. His vacations were at first largely spent at Sir Harry Ricardo's* works at Shoreham, where he studied the self-ignition of fuels when suddenly compressed. Two papers followed in the *Philosophical Magazine;* and a lengthy report on the character of fuels for internal combustion engines, published by the Empire Motor Fuels Committee in 1924, added considerably to the theory of the subject. He never lost his interest in the internal combustion engine, and particularly in the aircraft engine. Much of his working life was spent in encouraging and helping designers of engines. His book on the subject, first published in 1931, was widely read.

In 1925, soon after H. E. Wimperis [q.v.] became the first Director of Scientific Research in the Air Ministry, Pye was persuaded to join him as Deputy Director. He succeeded him as Director in 1937, and bore the heavy responsibility of introducing into the Royal Air Force the new methods and equipment which were to prove of such inestimable value in the war. He held this appointment for six years, and then, as it was clearly too late for the introduction of anything radically new for the remainder of the war, was released to become the Provost of University College London. He held this appointment until 1951.

Pye was elected President of the Institution of Mechanical Engineers in 1952. His presidential address was devoted largely to the higher education of engineers. He felt that there was a tendency in university education to discourage the art of the designer and constructor. And indeed it is remarkable how many of the distinguished designers of the present day were trained at technical schools or colleges, rather than at universities.

Pye's wide cultural interests and charm of manner brought him close friends in many walks of life. He was an enthusiastic mountaineer and rock climber. His memoir on his devoted friend George Leigh Mallory is a gem of its kind.

February 22, 1960.

Q

Queen Alexandrine—See **Denmark.**

Queen Amélie—See **Portugal.**

Queen Elizabeth—See **Greece.**

Queen Mary—See **Mary.**

Lord Quickswood, a brilliant member of a distinguished family, a former Provost of Eton and a powerful influence in the creation of the Church Assembly, died at his home in Bournemouth on December 10, 1956. He was 87.

The Right Hon. Hugh Richard Heathcote Gascoyne-Cecil, P.C., first Baron Quickswood, of Clothall, in the county of Hertford, was born on October 14, 1869. He was the fifth son of the third Marquess of Salisbury and of Georgina, daughter of the Hon. Sir Edward Alderson.

His parents had alike a strong interest both in politics and in theology; and the delicate child, inheriting their tastes, cultivated these with a nervous nicety of dialectic and fervour of moral sentiment that powerfully affected his career, and sometimes betrayed itself in antagonisms. The small boy who, in the armoury at Hatfield, accused Gladstone of being a bad man, and, to the eminent statesman's protest that if that were so Lord Salisbury would not have invited him to the house, retorted with circumstantial assurance, "My father is coming to kill you in a quarter of an hour", was parent to the man of 40 who, as member for Oxford University, led the tumult that greeted the advocacy of the Parliament Bill of 1910 by Gladstone's greatest lieutenant.

Surrounded though he always was at Hatfield (which remained his home after his father's death) by a wealth of family affection, causes seemed to retain for him, who perhaps never thought of marriage, something of their first romantic spell, and men in the dim, religious light of principle to be sometimes seen as causes walking. Neither humour nor friendship nor contact with various worlds of men, though all were his, served altogether to convert a born knight errant into a finished man of the world.

To Oxford—and, like his brothers before him, to University College—Lord Hugh Cecil proceeded after an Eton career devastated by bad health. The place, still greatly affected by the movement to which it gave its name, was congenial to a mind by nature Anglican. Seeing the English Church much in the light in which Newman had once presented it at St. Mary's, and in which Liddon—that great friend of his family—was still depicting it at St. Paul's, as one branch of a larger society cemented by an Apostolic episcopate, he was not less fully convinced that Catholicism in its Roman interpretation was incompatible with liberty; nor did a fruitful friendship with Wilfrid Ward cause him to modify this view. A wide gulf consequently separated him from the late Lord Halifax, and his dismissal of ritualistic vagaries in respect to vestments as "ecclesiastical foppery" was significant both of his habit of mind and angle of vision.

Meanwhile, as those who have heard him plead the claims of the Oxford House (where for a short time he lived) will testify, he had developed a deep interest in the religious life of the poor. This association was not without its humours. "We are obliged to your Lordship for your address", an East Ender, deputed to convey a vote of thanks to him, is said to have observed, "but we feel that not we alone have been the gainers by your presence here, and that your Lordship has spent among us a more profitable evening than among the drinking and gambling aristocracy". In later years this evangelical aspect of his life took more definite shape in the delivery of lay sermons under episcopal licence.

The choice of politics as a profession, encouraged though it was positively by a mother to whom he was always devotedly attached, and negatively by the doubts of his father and of another well-qualified adviser as to his vocation for holy orders, was thus no primary inclination; yet there will probably be little dispute among those who knew him well that the decision was right. He was no ecclesiastic but a layman.

A son of the Conservative leader, emerging from Oxford with first class honours in history and a Hertford Fellowship, could find little difficulty in securing a seat in Parliament, and the less that Conservative fortunes were at that time in the ascendant. In 1895 Lord Hugh entered the House of Commons as member of Parliament for Greenwich. In spite of certain infelicities of gesture, both physical and metaphorical, it was plain that a speaker of promise and distinction had to be reckoned with in the young parliamentarian, whose outstanding ability seemed to justify the wits in styling his political associates as "Hughligans".

It was not until his second Parliament that Lord Hugh Cecil secured a reputation for eloquence as great in the opinion of some judges as that of any speaker at that time in the House of Commons. Two of his perorations were especially admired—that in relation to the Deceased Wife's Sister Bill, in which he concluded his advocacy of a Christian law of marriage with a graceful allusion to the old Saxon simile between the life of men and the passage of a bird across a lighted hall; and that upon the Education Bill of 1902, in which, with unmistakable reference to John Morley, seated attentive opposite, he claimed the alliance of those who accepted Christian morals but not the Christian faith and the chamber of whose mind, as he put it, was hung round with the regalia of beauty yet held in the midst an empty throne. The splendour of his oratory remained thenceforward as incontestable as its limitation. He could fascinate, interest, amuse, delight, inspire; yet he could not persuade.

So far he had confined his efforts almost exclusively to the high region of religious interests. The Tariff Reform movement brought him to earth, and economic studies supplemented ecclesiastical ones. He came out as a strong free trader, had trouble in consequence in his constituency, and at the ensuing general election lost his seat. For three years—from 1906 to 1909—he was out of Parliament. It was during this interlude, when he was said to be contemplating a history of the reign of William IV, that he developed a taste for society, was to be seen at balls, discovered an interest in dress, and entered the hunting field.

His riding, unhampered by experience, was considered intrepid, and showed the presence in his nature of traits which subsequently during the 1914 War brought him a commission in the Royal Air Force.

These spirited adventures were, however, but as blind alleys in his career; and it was fortunate that a vacancy in the representation of Oxford University in 1909 gave him, in spite of his free trade opinions, a seat in Parliament, from which he was in no subsequent danger of being dislodged. His independent reputation as a debater, not less than the acquaintance with college business that had come to him as a Fellow of Hertford, was an excellent qualification for a university member, and by common consent he fulfilled his duties admirably, though, as his speech on the Report of the Oxford and Cambridge Commission in 1923 discovers, with some measure of conservative scepticism as regards "reform".

In an ingenious and interesting little volume, published in 1912, under the title of *Conservatism* will be found his confession of political faith. The book depends to some degree for its effectiveness upon the contention that Burke, whose style and substance were peculiarly congenial to his mind, ought to be reckoned a Conservative, and that in Burke's writings, more really than in the tradition of Bolingbroke and Beaconsfield, the true philosophy of Conservatism is to be found.

The book contains the characteristic statement that "the championship of religion" is the most important of the functions of Conservatism", and it was all in keeping with this conviction that political discontents in the post-war period drove Lord Hugh Cecil back upon ecclesiastical interests. Exasperated by the administration of Lloyd George, and anxious to stand by his brother, he "crossed the floor" of the House in conjunction with Lord Robert Cecil in the winter of 1921. This step illustrated his habitual detachment of mind and independence of action, but was no indication, as perhaps it may have been in his companion, of some deep-set difficulty in the acceptance of traditional party divisions. Whether he would have been able to throw his mind into the common stock for purposes of Cabinet government is another question. He, like others, had long had his own doubts upon the point, but he was never in fact offered office, and by 1922 recognized, and possibly others knew, that his health, not at all improved by his time in the air force, would not have allowed of his accepting it.

Only in the Church Assembly, which he had done much to create, was he perfectly at home; only there was his influence equal to his talent and his eloquence. It was thus the tragedy of his political career that he failed to recommend the Revised Prayer Book, which the Church Assembly had brought forth, to the favour of the House of Commons. To persuade a composite legislature that the introduction of alternative forms is in keeping with the genius of common prayer was doubtless no light undertaking; yet, even so, his championship of the cause disappointed expectations; nor did some recovery of power, when the attempt was repeated, altogether mitigate the severity of his rebuff.

His interest in the kind of questions that now inevitably occupied the House was, moreover, relatively small; and his attendance grew to be infrequent. Yet on the rare occasions upon which he spoke he found a younger generation eager to hear him, for his reputation as a speaker had become almost a tradition. Meantime the Church Assembly remained a supreme interest to him; and there, as chairman of the general purposes committee, he showed, together with a mastery of procedure, a talent for conciliation and counsel. The old uncompromising firmness, however, where matters of principle seemed to him to be involved, remained; and in his controversy with the Bishop of Liverpool in 1933-34 over the admission of the Unitarians to the pulpit of Liverpool Cathedral his dialectic was as forcible as it was amusing. His intervention proved completely successful, and, the Upper House of the York Convocation having passed a resolution in this sense, he withdrew his petition for the exercise of the archiepiscopal jurisdiction in the affair. The incident may be said to have established his position as the most influential Anglican layman of his generation.

In 1936 the Provostship of Eton fell vacant, and the Prime Minister invited the governing body to submit their views for recommendation to the Crown. At this juncture, it is said, a friend, who happened to be sitting next to Lord Hugh Cecil at dinner, asked him whether he had any views on the subject, and received the reply, not perhaps in the first instance intended to be taken very seriously, that it was just the sort of job that he should like himself. Others thereupon inquired whether the sentiment expressed his real feeling, and, finding that this was indeed the case, proceeded to bring his name forward. The suggestion was approved by the governing body, and to the very general satisfaction the Prime Minister accepted it, and Lord Hugh Cecil was appointed. The change, which necessitated the resignation of his seat in Parliament early in 1937, gave him a house of his own, which he had never yet had, and a position as nearly that of the Dean of a cathedral as a layman could aspire to. He was perhaps at no time of his career a happier man.

He remained at Eton until 1944. In a farewell to the boys he remarked that there was nothing more pleasurable than the laying-down of office, for at the age of 75, and he suspected also at 15, duties seemed unattractive.

For the rest, he continued to be a brilliant figure in the social life of his time; his presence welcome, his conversation witty, his views original, his candour entertaining, his power of exposition remarkable, his charm unaffected. No sketch can hope to give the peculiar flavour of his personality, nor is it easy to disinter even from the vast chambers of the dead a parallel for him. Yet a Plutarch, in search of his compeer, might find in Montalembert—the Montalembert of Sainte-Beuve's portrait—enough points of resemblance to justify a comparison between two ardent devotees of liberty, and, according to their respective interpretations, of Catholicism.

Lord Quickswood was created a Privy Councillor in 1918 and a baron in 1941.

He received honorary academic honours from the universities of Cambridge, Edinburgh, and Durham. He was an Honorary Fellow of New College, Oxford, and of Keble College, and was a Trustee of the London Library.

December 11, 1956.

Roger Quilter, composer of songs and of children's music, died at his London home on September 21, 1953 at the age of 75.

His vein was delicate and distinguished, but he achieved a wide popularity with the lyrical grace of his settings of English poems by Shakespeare, Herrick, and Tennyson, and by the simple-heartedness of his *Children's Overture* and the incidental music to *Where the Rainbow Ends.*

Quilter was born at Brighton on November 1, 1877, was educated at Eton and then at the Frankfort Conservatoire, where he had as fellow-students Cyril Scott*, Norman O'Neill, and Balfour Gardiner, who were all working under Iwan Knorr for composition. He first made his mark with his three Shakespeare songs published in 1905, which appealed to concert singers and amateurs alike.

Quilter followed up his success with his cycle of "To Julia", four of Dowson's "Songs of Sorrow", a set of seven Elizabethan lyrics, and a round dozen or more of separate songs, of which "Now Sleeps the Crimson Petal" and "To Daisies" achieved the widest favour.

Herrick's Julia seemed to bring out the essence of Quilter's melodic and harmonic idiom and to Julia he returned for the name of his light opera, produced during a winter season at Covent Garden in 1936. This was a pretty comedy of a countess and a composer and the music was pretty to match. The adjective "pretty" can be applied without any derogatory suggestion to all Quilter's music. It sounds no great depths nor seeks to do more than charm by its euphony, grace, and craftsmanship.

Nor did his talent grow in range—two Shakespeare songs published in 1939 did not differ in style, treatment or idiom from those of 1905.

The incidental music to *Where the Rainbow Ends* and the *Children's Overture* based on Crane's book of nursery rhymes, *Baby's Opera,* show the same manner in an orchestral guise, and are attractive in the same ingenuous way as the songs.

But the ingenuousness is not simplicity; it was part of the man himself, while his music had all the romantic sweetness, not to say richness, of the late nineteenth-century tradition in which he grew up.

Quilter sometimes appeared on the concert platform to accompany his own songs and his musical interests extended beyond the narrow plot of ground which he himself was content, and rightly content, to cultivate. He took no part in musical politics, but he was a founder member of the Musicians' Benevolent Fund and served on its committee, where his gentle nature found expression for its quick sympathies.

September 22, 1953.

Dr. Quo Tai-Chi, the first Chinese Ambassador to Britain, died in California on September 21, 1953.

Born in Anhui Province in 1889, he was educated in America at the University of Pennsylvania. After his return to China in 1916 he became private secretary and interpreter to President Li Huan-Hung. He attended the Paris peace conference in 1919 as one of the Chinese delegates, who walked out when it was disclosed that the allies had agreed that Japan should keep the German possessions in Shantung. After the victory of the Chinese nationalists in 1928 Quo was for a time mayor of the Chinese district of Shanghai.

In 1932 he was sent to London as Minister, and in 1935 became Ambassador when the Legation was raised to an Embassy. The kindness he had received from the American family with whom he lived as a lonely youth gave him a lifelong love of America; but there is no doubt that before long this was matched by equal regard for England, where both he and Madame Quo soon became widely popular. Probably his worst recollection of those days was the annual journey that he had to make to Geneva for the thankless task of pleading China's case against the rising aggression of Japan.

He was especially prominent in connexion with the memorable Chinese art exhibition at Burlington House in the winter of 1935-36. As president of the China Society he raised that somewhat dry-as-dust organization to a high pitch of liveliness and activity. The honorary D.C.L. conferred on him by Oxford University was felt by all to be well deserved.

In 1941 Quo was recalled to become Foreign Minister, and in 1946 he represented China on the United Nations and served a term as chairman of the Security Council. A year later he was forced to resign through ill-health, but shortly after he was appointed Ambassador to Brazil.

He had a lovable nature and was cultured and gentle in manner as in speech. At some time in his later years he became a Christian, and in a recent letter to a friend in Britain spoke of his undying faith that China would ultimately triumph over communism.

Quo married a Shanghai Chinese, who survives him, together with two sons, the elder now an assistant director in the Dupont Television Company of New York.

September 22, 1953.

R

Basil Radford, who died on October 20, 1952 in hospital in London at the age of 55, was a versatile actor best suited, on the stage and on the screen, to the medium of light comedy.

He endeared himself to theatrical and film audiences as the Englishman of a popular romantic convention. No great shakes as a thinker, this Englishman never lost his sense of values, and in the thick of fearful hazards was less dismayed by the likelihood of imminent capture than by the news that England had collapsed in the second innings. These parts showed the eternal small boy twinkling through the wrinkles of middle age; but Radford's range was much wider than is suggested by his successful hold on a single type. Indeed, versatility was, perhaps, his foible.

He believed that an accomplished actor should be capable of dealing effectively with emotional as well as comic situations. As the distraught Salathiel in John Drinkwater's Biblical play, *A Man's House,* and in other pieces, he made good his theory; but when he chose to represent men of the world, eminent lawyers and the like, a sense of strain sometimes appeared and the emotional effects came by contrivance rather than through a complete identification of self with part. There was always something irrepressibly boyish in his playing, and he was happiest in those comedies which helped him to exploit this amiable quality.

The first film in which Radford appeared was *Barnum was Right* in 1929, but it was not until several years later that his real chance came on the screen, and good use he made of it. In such films as *The Lady Vanishes* and *Dead of Night* he portrayed, in partnership with Naunton Wayne*, the dim-witted but dogged and amiable sportsman with a good effect, which was less easy to sustain when transferred to the medium of broadcasting. That his place in film comedy was secure is shown by his appearance latterly in such successful productions as *Passport to Pimlico* and *Whisky Galore.*

Basil Radford was born at Chester on June 25, 1897, and was educated at St. Peter's, York. He was on active service from 1915-18, and on his return to civil life studied for the stage at the Royal Academy of Dramatic Art, making his first appearance on the London stage in July 1924 in *Collusion* at the Ambassadors'. From 1927 until 1931 he was abroad, first touring New Zealand in *The Ghost Train,* and thereafter at San Francisco and Los Angeles. For nearly two years he played with the British Guild Players at Vancouver and then, returning to England, reappeared at the Strand, in May 1932 in *The Love Pirate.* From then on he appeared in a great variety of plays, notably *Night Must Fall* and *Spring Tide.* Since the last war he has played in *Clutterbuck, Blind Goddess,* and *The White Falcon.* In the summer of 1951 his health began to give trouble and he decided to take a holiday. He made several gallant attempts to resume acting, but after several collapses, the last of which occurred in August, he was compelled to relinquish his career.

In 1926 he married Miss Shirly Deuchars. They had one son.

October 21, 1952.

Grand Admiral Erich Raeder, Commander in Chief of the German Navy from 1928 until 1943, and the chief architect of the Navy with which Germany faced the sea-power of Britain in 1939, died on November 6, 1960. He was 84.

He was released from Spandau prison in September 1955 after serving nine years of the life term to which he had been sentenced for war crimes at Nuremberg in 1946. The reasons given for his release were his advanced age and his state of health.

The verdict on him at his trial stated that in the 15 years of his command he had built and equipped the German Navy; that the conception of the invasion of Norway had been his and not Hitler's; that he had participated in planning and waging aggressive war; and that he had tried to dissuade Hitler from attacking the Soviet Union and had urged as an alternative an aggressive Mediterranean policy. The most serious charge was that he had carried out unrestricted naval warfare on neutrals.

Both at the trial and in his memoirs, published in a single volume English translation in 1959 (but earlier in Germany in two volumes), Raeder admitted the violation of the Versailles Treaty. In his view it was the duty of a German naval officer to do his utmost to keep a Navy in being. His defence of the steps taken in the days before Hitler was that he worked for nothing more than a defensive force capable of meeting a possible attack by Poland which, he contended, would have been supported in the Baltic by French warships. He welcomed the coming of Hitler because of the Führer's assertion of Germany's right to rearm, combined with his apparent agreement with Raeder's view of the hazards of challenging British sea-power. He justified the attack on Norway on the grounds that German intelligence knew well of British plans under "Operation Stratford" to occupy Norwegian bases and that, under international law, Germany had a right to forestall them.

Raeder was born at Wandsbek in Silesia in 1876. In 1894 he entered the Navy but at first failed and was side-tracked into the editorial staff of the German naval journal, *Marine Rundschau.* In 1910, however, he was appointed navigating officer of the Hohenzollern, the Kaiser's yacht. While thus employed he met the future Admiral Hipper who recognized his abilities and in the war made him his Chief of Staff. Thus it was that when Hipper was in command of the German cruiser fleet, Raeder was present with him in the Lützow at the Battle of Jutland. During the course of the engagement the Lützow was so badly damaged that Hipper and Raeder had to transfer by destroyer to the battle-cruiser Möltke.

When in 1928 Raeder was appointed Commander-in-Chief of the German Navy there was little enough of background to so proud a title. Germany was impoverished and public opinion had long been lethargic in regard to naval matters.

It was Raeder's consistent view that Germany's needs were for fast cruisers and submarines rather than for large battleships and aircraft carriers. In accordance with this general conception he was responsible for the pocket battleships, the first of which was commissioned in 1933. His idea was that they should be able to outpace anything that could destroy them and destroy anything that could overtake them.

Whether his protestation that he did not want war with Britain be accepted or rejected, it is certain he did not want it in 1939. His aim was to have a powerful and well-balanced force by 1945; thus the German Navy went to war with an inadequate surface fleet and too few submarines. The influence of Göring ("his main peculiarities", wrote Raeder while in Russian hands, "were unimaginable vanity and immeasurable ambition, untruthfulness, impracticability, and selfishness") on Hitler had caused the Luftwaffe to thrive and the Fleet Air Arm to languish.

With what he had his strategy was sound; British sea communications were attacked but encounters with large British units avoided. Raeder rightly saw the use to which Norwegian bases could be put and he it was who urged Hitler to invade Norway.

He was less fond of the projected invasion of Britain, believing that German naval and air forces would be better employed in starving Britain into surrender.

As Alan Bullock has written in *Hitler: A Study in Tyranny,* Raeder urged Hitler to consider the Mediterranean as a fruitful field of operations. Here, he argued, was the most vulnerable point in Britain's imperial position: the weak link against which Germany ought to concentrate all her strength.

At two conferences with the Führer in September 1940 Raeder made concrete proposals; Gibraltar and the Canary Islands should be secured and the protection of north-west Africa strengthened in cooperation with Vichy France. At the same time Germany, with Italian cooperation, should begin a major offensive against Suez and from there northwards through Palestine and Syria to Turkey. Raeder was to revive his demand for action in the Mediterranean more than once, notably in the autumn of 1941 when Allied fortunes in the Middle East were low.

By 1943 Raeder believed his opinions carried no further weight with Hitler and after a typical tirade (again Raeder saw the malign influence of Göring at work) in which the Führer found no health in the German Navy, he gave place to Dönitz.

November 7, 1960.

Louis Raemaekers, the biting anti-German cartoonist of the 1914-18 War, died on July 26, 1956 at Scheveningen, near The Hague, at the age of 87.

It has been said of Raemaekers that he was the one private individual who exercised a real and great influence on the course of the 1914-18 War. There were a dozen or so people—emperors, kings, statesmen, and commanders-in-chief—who obviously, and notoriously, shaped policies and guided events. Outside that circle of the great, Louis Raemaekers stands conspicuous as the one man who, without any assistance of title or office, indubitably swayed the destinies of peoples.

At the outbreak of war in 1914 Germany made enormous efforts to win Holland to her side by attempts to purchase the sympathy of the Dutch press, and by endeavouring to influence the minds of the Dutch people through the pens and platform speeches of a whole corps of professors. That the effort was a failure was chiefly due to the courage of the *Telegraaf,* of Amsterdam, in which Raemaeker's cartoons were published, and especially to those cartoons themselves. In those early months of the war Raemaekers's influence was confined to Holland; but gradually the power and passion of his drawings in the *Telegraaf* began to attract the attention of the editors of newspapers in other countries, and early in 1915 albums of reproductions of his first cartoons, published in Holland, were already beginning to make their way in the Allied and neutral countries of Europe. By the end of that year the name of Raemaekers was coming to be well known in most civilized countries, and that winter the first exhibition of the cartoons was given in London at the Fine Art Society's Galleries in New Bond Street, and created a profound impression. Immediately afterwards Paris gave itself up to a "Manifestation Raemaekers", when for a week the French Government, the city of Paris, the press, the artistic community, and the people of the capital vied with each other in doing honour to the Dutch cartoonist.

From the beginning of 1916 Raemaekers made his home in England as being the most central point for the distribution of his drawings to the press of Holland, France, and Great Britain simultaneously. Throughout the war he worked with unflagging energy and unfailing enthusiasm for the Allied cause. There were very few weeks in the course of the war in which he did not make at least four cartoons for publication in the press, besides making an immense number of drawings for posters, programmes, &c., for charitable purposes in connexion with the war effort.

It was impossible that all could be of the same high standard as the best of his earliest cartoons, but the level sustained was extraordinarily high, and among the drawings of the last months of 1918 were some of the very finest that he ever made. He remained in England for some years before returning home and received many honours. In 1919 he was the guest of honour at a great luncheon party given by the Lord Mayor of London at the Mansion House to signalize the Allied triumph, at which representatives from all sections of the community were present.

Glasgow University gave him its LL.D. He was made an honorary member of the Royal Society of Miniature Painters, of the Free Arts Club, and Honorary Fellow of the Royal Society of Literature, and an honorary member of the First Edition Club. France in 1916 made him a Chevalier of the Legion of Honour, and he had received honours and decorations from most European countries, including his own, where he was an officer of the Order of Orange Nassau.

Except when giving utterance to his detestation of Germany, Raemaekers was a man of a singularly modest, sweet, and gentle nature, a man of transparent integrity and good impulses. He greatly loved England, spoke its language perfectly, knew well its literature, and was something of an authority upon its history.

He was born on April 6, 1869, at Roermond, in Limburg, the son of Josephus C. H. Raemaekers, an editor and publisher of that town. He was educated at Roermond, and studied art in Amsterdam, later making frequent visits to both France and Germany. His home before the 1914-18 War was at Haarlem, Holland, where, though he also did some drawing for the press, he followed his profession as a landscape painter. He began drawing for the press in 1907, when he contributed to the *Algemeen Handelsblad,* and in 1909 he became the political cartoonist of the *Telegraaf.* He had lived in strict retirement for many years.

He married in 1902 Johanna Petronella van Mansvelt, by whom he had a son and two daughters.

July 27, 1956.

Dr. H. R. Raikes, who died in hospital at Johannesburg on April 13, 1955, had been associated with Johannesburg since 1927, when he was appointed Principal of the University of the Witwatersrand in succession to Sir William Thomson.

Humphrey Rivaz Raikes, born on July 14, 1891, was the third son of the Rev. Canon W. A. Raikes, of Goudhurst, Kent. He was educated at Tonbridge and Dulwich College, then at Balliol College, Oxford, where he was Williams exhibitioner in 1910 and Abbott scholar in 1911. In the following year he took first-class honours in the final honours school in natural science (chemistry), having in the meantime been granted a commission in the Army Supplementary Reserve. On the outbreak of war in 1914 he served with The Buffs until he was wounded in France in May 1915. He then transferred to the Royal Flying Corps for experimental work, and he gained his pilot's certificate. He became chief experimental officer, R.F.C., in January 1918, and six months later was a member of the Royal Air Force Mission to the United States.

After the war Raikes became a lecturer at Balliol, and subsequently was elected a Fellow of Exeter College, where he was later appointed sub-rector. In October 1925 he rejoined the R.A.F. as chief instructor to the Oxford University Air Squadron, being granted the rank of wing commander.

His personality and academic qualifications admirably fitted him to be Principal of the

Witwatersrand University. He regarded the university not only as a place of academic training but was insistent on its value for business and commercial life. In this respect his judgment was regarded as of great value by many industrial firms. Not only was he an excellent tutor and a sound governor, but a most efficient organizer as well as a leader.

He held decided views on the relationships of white and black in South Africa, urging that the white race could not prevent the advance of the native races, although it might delay progress. Endeavours to maintain white ascendancy should be directed towards further development of the white race, at the same time helping the native to develop. His views on education were equally outspoken. He declared that South Africa had to destroy the matriculation fetish, and to substitute tests which would meet the varied needs of commerce, industry, and so on, as well as providing an adequate test for university entrance. During a visit to Rhodesia he established educational contacts with neighbouring territories, and commented on the valuable work that might be done in the Union by an organization similar to the Beit Trust.

His energy and determination were shown after the fire which destroyed the university library, including the fine collection of Africana. He did not accept this as a loss, but used it as a stepping stone for the new and finer library that was built. His appeal aroused interest, and contributions of books and money were received from universities in many countries.

During the 1939-45 War his attitude was that, while students in their last two years should finish their courses, all others who were fit and over the age of 19 should join up. He made several forceful speeches on the subject. He retired from office just over two years before he died.

April 22, 1955.

C. E. Raimond—See **Robins.**

A. B. Ramsay, successively Lower Master of Eton and Master of Magdalene College, Cambridge, and for many years Cambridge University Correspondent of *The Times*, died at Malvern on September 20, 1955 at the age of 83.

Allen Beville Ramsay was the son of Beville Ramsay, of Croughton House, Brackley, and was born on August 3, 1872. He was elected a King's Scholar at Eton in 1886, and going into College in 1887 began an Eton career which lasted until 1925. As a boy he was always popular for his quiet humour, and was fairly successful at games, playing for College at the Wall in 1890. Luxmoore was his tutor and he was in the Select for the Newcastle Scholarship in 1891. He went up to King's College, Cambridge, as an Exhibitioner and took a first class in the Classical Tripos of 1894, when two subsequent headmasters of public schools were in the same class, Dr. Nairn and F. B. Malim. He was Browne's medallist for the Latin Ode in 1893 and for the Greek Epigram in 1894.

In 1895 Dr. Warre appointed him as an assistant master at Eton. There he soon had a full pupil-room, and in due course a successful house. As a tutor he followed the Luxmoore tradition, exacting from his pupils, as from himself, the highest standard of industry and accuracy. He would amend a boy's faulty verse with unerring skill, and his corrections—written always in a beautiful hand—inspired many generations of pupils with a feeling for scholarship.

In 1916 he was chosen from his colleagues to be Lower-Master when Frank Rawlins became Vice-Provost. In this office he fulfilled all expectations and, in particular, he left his mark in Lower Chapel, where he took infinite care to render the services worthy and helpful to the boys. In 1919 he formed among the lower boys the first troop of boy scouts in a public school. Everyone at Eton liked him, and in the holidays he kept up his Cambridge friendships. He was one of those who often bicycled with Dr. Montague James on the Continent at Easter and celebrated Christmas with him at King's.

In 1925 he went back to Cambridge as Master of Magdalene in succession to Arthur Benson. As Benson had succeeded Dr. Stuart Donaldson, the office of Master was thus occupied by three ex-Eton masters since the death of the sixth Lord Braybrooke. Like other Heads of Houses, besides devoting himself to the society of Magdalene he had to take his share of work on the boards and committees which deal with the domestic affairs of the University, and on others which deal also with external matters, as, for example, the Colonial Services Probationers' Committee. When, in 1928, the Cambridge Preservation Society was formed, Ramsay at once took the lead on the part of the university in cooperating with the town.

From boyhood he was always something of a poet in English, Greek, and Latin, and he published five very charming small books of verses and translations, *Inter Lilia, Ros Rosarum* (the titles allude to the arms of Eton and King's), *Frondes Salicis, Flos Malvae,* and *Ros Maris,* which are full of delicate versification and neat scholarship. His language, written or spoken, was always distinguished.

His happy use of story and quotation made him an admirable host and after-dinner speaker. Eton and Cambridge life gave ample scope for the exercise of his genial gifts and he was a fine judge of what he would affectionately describe as "a noble wine". He was Vice-Chancellor in the years 1929 to 1931; so the election and installation of Stanley Baldwin, as he then was, as Chancellor of the University fell in his period of office. A close and easily understandable friendship arose out of this association. For many years he was president of the Cambridge University Cricket Club, a position which he much enjoyed and in which he worked actively for the maintenance and endowment of Fenner's. His friends will remember his love of the three Cs: classics, cricket, chess.

He succeeded the late Sir Arthur Shipley, Master of Christ's College, as the Cambridge University Correspondent of *The Times.* Having reached the final statutory age he retired from the Mastership of Magdalene in 1947; and leaving Cambridge with his sister, Eva Ramsay, his well-remembered hostess at Eton and Magdalene, he made his home at Malvern.

His churchmanship was a deep and formative influence in his life; his effect on Lower Chapel at Eton has been already noted; and Magdalene men will recall his presence, grave, reverent, and unfailing, in the Master's stall in Chapel. He had a singular capacity for identifying himself with the societies to which he belonged, yet there was no loosening of any attachments already made. His love and his loyalty were equally given to Eton, King's, and Magdalene.

September 22, 1955.

Lord Ramsden, O.B.E., died at his home at Gomersal, near Leeds, on August 9, 1955. He was 72.

The Rt. Hon. Sir Eugene Joseph Squire Hargreaves Ramsden, O.B.E., first Baron Ramsden, of Birkenshaw, in the West Riding of Yorkshire, and a baronet, was born on February 2, 1883, the only child of James Ramsden, principal of James Ramsden Ltd., one of the foremost woollen and worsted merchanting houses in the north. He was educated in England, France, and Germany, and then for many years devoted himself almost exclusively to the family interests, succeeding, on the death of his father, to the control of the merchanting business. He also became associated with the Conservative Party, both nationally and in the Spen Valley division in which he lived, although his career was interrupted by a period of war service, from 1914 to 1919 in France and Egypt, during which he was mentioned in dispatches and appointed O.B.E.

The call of politics became so insistent on his return that, because his control of the family business was making such a heavy demand upon his time, he disposed of his interests and for many years devoted himself almost entirely to public life. Years before he had been president of the Junior Unionist Association in the Spen Valley division, and in 1923 was the unsuccessful candidate for the party against Viscount (then Sir John) Simon [q.v.]. A year later he was elected for the northern division of Bradford, and then began an association with Westminster which lasted, with a break of only two years, until his death. In the general election of 1929 he was defeated by Sir Norman Angell*, the Labour candidate, but he regained the seat in the Labour landslide of 1931 and held it until 1945, when he was raised to the peerage and went to the Lords. He had been knighted in 1933 and created a baronet five years later.

Few men have done more in the political sphere without catching or cultivating the public gaze. He was a plain, and sometimes blunt, public speaker, but he attracted and held attention, especially in Yorkshire, by his persuasive logic, his reliance upon facts, and his manifest command of all the intricacies of British business. In the Conservative Party these qualities, combined with his organizing capacity and his almost passionate devotion to work, quickly made him one of its outstanding honorary officials. And as a member of Parliament he served with distinction on numerous committees dealing with trade and commerce.

Long before he achieved general prominence in the Conservative Party he had spent many years in its service in the north. He was Yorkshire area chairman, and presided over the Yorkshire coordinating committee of the National Government Party, which came into existence after the 1931 election. He was also chairman of the publications sub-committee of the National Union of Conservative and Unionist Associations, sat on the executive committee of the finance and general purpose sub-committee, and was a Governor of the Bonar Law College at Ashridge. In 1935 he became a vice-chairman of the Conservative National Union, succeeded to the senior office in 1938, and for five years was chairman of its national executive committee.

His many journeys abroad were induced not only by his political activities but also because in later years he returned, largely under the pressure of his many friends, to the world of trade and commerce. For years he was chairman of A. and S. Henry and Co. Ltd., a director of the Monotype Corporation, the Yorkshire Electric Power Co. Ltd., British Insulated Callenders Cables Ltd., and others. He was also on the board of Lloyds Bank and an underwriting member of Lloyd's.

He was often in the United States. He went also to South America, Canada, the West Indies, China and Japan, and Africa, and he knew practically all the European countries well. Before the 1939-45 War he was chairman of the British Trade Mission to Poland, led a visit of members of the Empire Parliamentary Association to Tanganyika, and took part in a Government trade deputation to Scandinavia. A great advocate of higher education, he was especially interested in the development of technical training and in the promotion of the study of foreign languages, and amid all his preoccupations he had spent much time and effort as chairman of the education committee of the British Council.

In 1919 he married Margaret, daughter of Frank E. Withey, of Michigan, United States, and widow of Major George W. Farwell, of the United States Army. There were no children of the marriage, and the peerage becomes extinct.

August 10, 1955.

Frederick Ranalow, who for long delighted a large public in the character of Captain Macheath in the *Beggar's Opera* at the Lyric Theatre, Hammersmith, died on December 8, 1953 in a nursing home in London at the age of 80.

An old trouper (he would have been pleased by the phrase), he had a pronounced gift for welding together a company on tour and turning it into something more than a collection of people travelling from town to town to earn their livings. A great gift this and infrequently recognized, it is yet of paramount importance, and in Ranalow it amounted to something akin to genius. When to it was added a fine and flexible voice (who, having heard it, could ever forget the superb *nuance* of his rendering of "When the Heart of a Man is Depressed with Care" in *The Beggar's Opera*?) and excellent histrionic talent, the sum total could not but be impressive. Modest and unassuming to a degree, he would have scouted any suggestion that, either professionally or personally, he was an outstanding figure. His abiding passion for the game of billiards (incidentally it was Mozart's favourite pastime) gave him constant opportunities to remark, with an uncomfortably close approximation to truth, that he was "the worst player of billiards in the world". Nevertheless, this hobby played its not unimportant part in making him the good companion he was for so long.

Frederick Baring Ranalow was born in Dublin on November 7, 1873, and was educated at Westminster School, whence, having already evinced a pronounced talent for music, he went to the Royal Academy of Music to study under Randegger. He became a Fellow of the Royal Academy of Music in 1906. At the turn of the century he was appointed a lay vicar of Westminster Abbey and retained the post for some eight years. He had, however, already appeared on the stage as Father O'Flynn in *Shamus O'Brien* with the Ben Greet Opera Company at the Pavilion at Rhyl in 1898; by the time he laid down his appointment at the Abbey he had become an experienced opera singer.

Equipped with a baritone voice of sympathetic quality and great flexibility, he was for long a great asset to the Quinlan, Denhof, and Beecham opera companies in such parts as Hans Sachs, Falstaff, Figaro, and Papageno. To his musical gifts were added a quite exceptional *flair* for acting, and a literary judgment which was constantly used to smooth away the difficulties of translated *libretti*—a gift which has received graceful and cordial acknowledgment in Sir Thomas Beecham's* autobiography, *A Mingled Chime.* In 1916 he created the part of Ned Travers in Dame Ethel Smyth's opera, *The Boatswain's Mate.*

When the late Sir Nigel Playfair embarked on the revival of *The Beggar's Opera* in 1920 Ranalow, with his mature artistry, did much as Captain Macheath, the principal male part, to ensure the outstanding success which the venture became. He played the part of Macheath over 1,000 times in the original run and was in every revival of that 200-year-old masterpiece, entering fully into the spirit of the producer.

Ranalow played Macheath with a stylized gesture and beauty of vocal tone that enchanted all audiences. Moreover, so perfect was his diction, that even in the patter songs no word was ever lost by the audience. He never again attained quite such a success, even in other eighteenth-century English operas, in the same vein, such as Arne's *Love in a Village,* but to everything he did he brought a fine sensibility and rich artistry and so was able to invest the productions of pieces which were far from masterpieces (in which as a professional entertainer he sometimes had to take part) with a lightness and grace to which, but for his presence, they could hardly have attained. For many years the Guildhall School of Music and the Royal Academy of Dramatic Art had the advantage of his services as a teacher of singing.

He married in 1909 Lilian Mary, daughter of the late W. E. Oates, who survives him together with a daughter of the marriage.

December 9, 1953.

J. V. Rank, one of the chief figures in the British milling industry and a well-known racehorse owner, died in a nursing home in London on January 3, 1952 at the age of 70.

He was the eldest of the three sons of Joseph Rank, the founder and for many years head of the milling organization bearing his name with branches in Hull, London, Cardiff, Liverpool, Glasgow, and many other cities in the British Isles. [The youngest son Joseph became Lord Rank*.]. When the father grew older James Rank took over the management of Rank's milling business and several other subsidiary concerns. By that time it was one of the largest milling combinations in the world, but he was thoroughly familiar with the details of every department in the organization, for he had worked through most of them at some period in his career, and under his management the business flourished as it had never done before. He became president of the National Association of British Millers in 1928 and worked out a scheme for the rationalization of the industry which involved radical changes. It worked so well that he continued in office for another year and was re-elected president again 10 years later.

James Voase Rank was born at Hull in 1881 about the time that his father was making his first ventures with rolling mills and erecting new structures which were to be the basis of his future expansion and success. He was educated at Hull and Harrogate. His first job was with a firm of wheat merchants with whom he learned the technique of the market and practical buying and selling. He then joined his father and after working for a time at the mechanical side of milling he turned his attention to the commercial side of the business. After serving for some years at Hull he went to new mills which had been opened at Barry in South Wales, and when the headquarters of the firm were moved to London he joined his father and was soon well known on the exchanges such as the Baltic and Mark Lane. When new mills were opened at Birkenhead he made his headquarters at Liverpool for a time. He made many visits to Canada, the United States, and Argentina to study the grain markets there. In time, when the Birkenhead mills had been firmly established and the firm was extending its activities in other directions, he returned to London, and after the 1914-18 war assumed the management of the whole concern. During the 1939-45 war he was Director of the Imported Cereals Division of the Ministry of Food.

His interests in horse racing are referred to on another page of *The Times* by the Racing Correspondent, but before he took up racing extensively he bred both horses and dogs at his large estate, Ouborough, near Godstone, Surrey. Not far away, near Edenbridge, he maintained an establishment for the breeding of shorthorns for beef, and had won many prizes with members of his herd, including the championships of the Royal Agricultural Show. He was a director of the International Horse Show at Olympia, chairman of the Great Dane Breeders' Association, and a member of the committee of the Kennel Club, and held many other offices of a similar kind. All his sporting activities were managed by experts, and while he followed them closely he never allowed sport to interfere with his chief work, the prosperity of the flour milling industry.

He was a man of open handed generosity, and he gave away without ostentation to numerous hospitals and charitable institutions large sums of which few people ever heard. His chief interest, however, was in the Alexandra Orphanage. For many years he was its honorary treasurer, and he arranged for its transference from Hampstead to a new home near Reigate. Every year the children would have an outing at Ouborough and Rank was always present and enjoyed himself to the full with the children.

He was twice married and leaves a daughter by his first wife.

January 4, 1952.

Professor A. O. Rankine, O.B.E., D.SC., F.R.S., Emeritus Professor of Physics in the Imperial College of Science and Technology, South Kensington, whose experiments led to the system of fog dispersal on airfields known as "Fido", died in a nursing home in London on January 19, 1956 at the age of 74.

Alexander Oliver Rankine was born at Guildford in 1881, and was educated at Guildford Grammar School and University College London. He graduated with first class honours in physics in 1904, and was thereupon appointed an assistant in the physics department of the college. He was awarded the London degree of D.Sc. in 1910, chiefly for his research work on the viscosity of gases, and was elected a Fellow of University College in 1912. During the latter part of the 1914-18 War he was attached to the anti-submarine division of the Admiralty.

In the same year he was appointed a Professor of Physics in the Imperial College of Science and Technology and continued his teaching and research work there until 1937. He was elected a Fellow of the Royal Society in 1934. In 1927 he became interested in the subject of applied geophysics, especially in relation to the search for oil, and became adviser on such matters to the Anglo-Persian (now Anglo-Iranian) Oil Company. In 1937 he accepted an invitation to become chief physicist to the Anglo-Iranian Oil Company, and resigned his post at the Imperial College with the title of emeritus professor.

During the 1939-45 War Professor Rankine was released by the company to serve in various capacities in the Admiralty, the Ministry of Aircraft Production, and the Petroleum Warfare Department. His chief work was an experimental investigation of the conditions required for the effective dissipation of fog on airfields by the application of heat—known in its practical operation by the popular name of "Fido". He resumed his work with the Anglo-Iranian Oil Company in 1945. At the end of 1947 he resigned full-time service with the company, but continued to act in an advisory capacity, until his health broke down some three years before he died.

He married in 1907 Ruby Irene, daughter of Samuel Short, who survives him together with two sons and a daughter.

January 21, 1956.

Samuel Kerkham Ratcliffe, who died in a London hospital on September 1, 1958 at the age of 90, was one of the last, as he was one of the ablest, of the old type of Radical journalist, a former acting editor of the daily Calcutta *Statesman*, and a much respected writer and lecturer on Indian and American affairs.

For many years he devoted himself to expounding (though always of his own Liberal and independent judgment) the British view of world affairs to the American public, and the American view to the British public. His strong interest—typical of the school to which he belonged—in moral problems and religious freedom, made him an ideal author for the history, published in 1955, of the South Place Ethical Society—of whose panel of lecturers he had been a member for more than 40 years.

Short and thickset in figure, he had a strikingly handsome head, with smooth silver-grey hair, and a clear-cut profile. In Liberal journalistic circles he was one of the most familiar personalities—enthusiastic, kindly, and full of encouragement to young writers.

He was born of East Anglian stock in 1868, spent his earliest years in Manchester and finished his school days in London. After working in his early teens for two City firms he turned to journalism. He gained a footing on the staff of the halfpenny evening *Echo* and in 1900, after the death of the proprietor and editor, Passmore Edwards, was given editorial charge.

In 1902 he went out to Calcutta as assistant editor of the *Statesman*, then under the diligent charge of two sons of the founder, Robert and Paul Knight. Some two years later he became acting editor while the brothers returned to Britain nominally for "a short holiday". They stayed three years and procured the first rotary presses and linotype machines to be used in India.

Ratcliffe was back in London in 1907 and became a constant contributor, often of leading articles, to the *Daily News* and *Manchester Guardian*. Vigorous, conscientious, and resourceful, blessed with a capacious memory and an exceptionally clear mind, he was at all times—perhaps most of all during the years of the First World War—a model editorial colleague. "S.K.'s" accuracy in matters of detail was deservedly celebrated. He wrote also for periodicals, and his frequent contributions to the *Contemporary Review* extended over more than 40 years. An active member of the Fabian Society, he was always at heart a liberal rationalist rather then anything else. From 1910 until 1917 he edited the *Sociological Review*. He contributed frequently to the *New Statesman* and to the *Observer*. In the last named he on occasion took the late J. L. Garvin's place as author of the principal article of the week.

In 1914 Ratcliffe made a lecture tour in the United States and thereafter his services were in constant request in the great republic and Canada. It would be difficult to rate too highly their value to this country. In all he spent 28 winter seasons on the other side of the Atlantic, and spoke in nearly all the 48 states of the Union and in all parts of Canada. He gained a great reputation for unprejudiced exposition and for the force and balance with which he answered questions on British imperial affairs in particular.

His vigorous rebuttals of anit-British calumnies by professional Indian propagandists came with the greater effect because of his known sympathy with the cause of Indian self-government. This sympathy was very evident in his biography, published in 1923, of Sir William Wedderburn, one of the I.C.S. adherents to the Indian National Congress in its early years.

Books were few in Ratcliffe's vast output of print, but besides the two already mentioned he wrote *The Roots of Violence* in 1934. His outstanding merit on the platform and as a broadcaster was that of clear, animated and sincere exposition. In his eightieth year he joined the staff of the *Glasgow Herald* as leader writer and remained there for two and a half years.

He had warm friends in many lands and, as hosts of fellow members of the National Liberal Club knew well, he was a most likeable and far-ranging conversationalist with the happiest gift of anecdote. In his last year or two he had borne failing eyesight with philosophy and cheerfulness.

He married Miss K. M. Jeeves, and leaves a son and two daughters.

September 2, 1958.

William Ratcliffe, who died in London on January 6, 1955 at the age of 84, was with the exception of Walter Bayes [q.v.] the last survivor of the original Camden Town Group of artists who, under the leadership of Harold Gilman, and with the blessing of Sickert, may be said to have domesticated Post-Impressionism in England, as Impressionism had been domesticated by the original members of the New English Art Club.

Ratcliffe's connexion with the group gives

him a certain historical importance, and, in view of what was to come, the circumstances of its origin are interesting enough to demand some description. The Camden Town Group started as a small secession from the New English Art Club, and it has been said that it would never have come into existence if the New English had accepted the work of Gilman and Wyndham Lewis [q.v.]. After the death of Spencer Gore (1878-1914), who was one of the small group gathered round Sickert in Fitzroy Street, and consequently a link between him and the Camden Town Group, it was decided to enlarge the group and change its title.

The result was the London Group, formed by the junction of the Sickert circle and the Vorticists under Wyndham Lewis, with Gilman as its first president. Gilman died in 1919, Wyndham Lewis resigned, and Roger Fry became the strongest influence in the group, which later welcomed the more extreme developments of Cubism and Surrealism. So that, seen in historical perspective, Ratcliffe may be said to have been in at the birth of the movement away from Impressionism in England, which, with increasing variety of aims, has continued until the present day.

William Whitehead Ratcliffe, who was the son of Johnson Ratcliffe, was born at King's Lynn in 1870. He first studied art at Manchester and until his mid-thirties earned his living as a wallpaper designer. He then studied at the Slade School and under Harold Gilman. Besides with the Camden Town Group and the London Group, of each of which he was a foundation member, Ratcliffe, who painted in both oil and watercolour, exhibited at the New English Art Club, the Modern Watercolour Society, and various provincial galleries, and also at the Chicago Art Institute and at Boston in the United States. Recognition of his work was slow in coming. It took the shape of purchases by several public galleries and examples of his work were illustrated in the *Studio*.

Ratcliffe was a man of retiring disposition, and he did not for long continue to exhibit his work in public. When, in 1946, a one-man show of his paintings was held at the Roland, Browse, and Delbanco Galleries, it was stated that none of the works had been executed after 1921. Ratcliffe revealed himself in that exhibition, and at a one-man exhibition in 1954 at the Letchworth Museum, as a very conscientious artist, careful in design and construction, with a rather delicate and gentle sensibility.

Ratcliffe had not the force of Gilman (who, as the spokesman of the Camden Town Group, coined the description of their general aims as "Neo-Realism", which avoided both intellectual abstraction and distortion), or the poetry of Gore (who was the genius of the group), but his patient method was compatible with a feeling for light and atmosphere.

Like the other members of the group, Ratcliffe applied his pigment in small touches, which, however, differed fundamentally from the dotting of the French "Neo-Impressionists" in that they did not break up the light or disregard local colour. The aim, apparently, was to enhance the decorative richness of the colour effect. It is as a modest link in the development of "modernism" in British painting that Ratcliffe will be remembered. Incidentally, his personality reminds us that so-called "revolutionaries" in art are sometimes mild-mannered men.

January 8, 1955. (4-star edition).

Gregory Ratoff, the well-known Hollywood director and character actor, died in hospital at Solothurn, Switzerland, on December 14, 1960 at the age of 63.

He was born in Petrograd (as it then was) on April 20, 1897, and was at first intended by his family for a safe commercial position; with this end in view he studied at the Imperial School of Commerce. Though this training may have come in useful later, when he became a film producer with a grasp of practical finance as astute as it was eccentric, he was not immediately called upon to use it, but instead took to acting, making his first stage appearances at the Imperial Theatre, Moscow; and then followed the path trodden by so many Russians in the 1920s to the United States and American show business. There his picturesque English and distinctive gift for comedy soon found him regular work as an actor (in such shows as *Blossom Time, Tenth Avenue,* and *Wonder Boy*), and before long he had branched out into stage production with *The Kibitzer, Candlelight* and other plays.

At the end of the twenties the talking picture took him to Hollywood, and he rapidly became known as a reliable character actor for any film which included a voluble and temperamental Russian. A career of modest distinction as an actor included *What Price Hollywood, George White's Scandals,* and *Let's Fall in Love;* while as a director he was responsible for several agreeable unmemorable pieces like *Something to Shout About, Where Do We Go From Here*? and Mae West's last film, *Tropicana,* as well as that famous contribution to America's wartime pro-Russian propaganda *Song of Russia.*

After the war he achieved more and more freedom as an independent producer-director, and consequently was seen as an actor less and less frequently, playing only parts which held some special appeal for him (notably in *All About Eve* and the O. Henry omnibus *Full House*).

He was a pioneer of the American film-maker's move to European locations with the bizarre *Black Magic,* a fictionalized account of Cagliostro's career, starring (and directed in collaboration with) Orson Welles; dabbled in rosy location realism with *Taxi;* and starred opposite Kay Kendall [q.v.] in his own irreverent middle-eastern romp *Abdullah the Great.* In the 1950s he returned occasionally to the theatre, directing *Nina, The Fifth Season,* and *Black Eyed Susan* in New York.

His most recent acting appearance was in Stanley Donen's film *Once More With Feeling* in 1959, and his most recent directorial work in the cinema was by general consent his best: *Oscar Wilde,* with Robert Morley playing the title role.

His only marriage, to Eugenie Leontovich, was dissolved.

December 15, 1960.

Sir Narsing Rau, C.I.E., who died on November 29, 1953 in a nursing home at Zürich at the age of 66, was, like his younger brother, Sir Benegal Rama Rau (with whom he was sometimes confused in newspaper reports), one of a select band of Indian members of the former Indian Civil Service whose wide experience of administration and knowledge of affairs were of incalculable value to the Republican Government at Delhi in the very difficult initial years.

Benegal Narsinga Rau was the eldest son of Dr. Benegal Ragavendra Rau, and was born on February 26, 1887. From the Presidency College, Madras, he went to Trinity College, Cambridge. He was a wrangler and retained through life a warm attachment to his Cambridge memories. He passed the I.C.S. examination in 1909 and was listed for Bengal, doing district work both in that province and in Assam. He gravitated to the judicial side and became a district and sessions judge. After some experience in the Legislative Department in Assam he went to New Delhi at the close of 1934 as additional joint secretary of the Legislative Department.

He was made a Judge of the Calcutta High Court in 1938 and in the following year was on special duty with the Central Government for the heavy labour of revision of the Indian statute book. He was chairman of the committee which in 1941 codified Hindu law, and also of a commission to adjudicate on inter-provincial and state claims on the Indus water supply for irrigation purposes. Retiring from his substantive appointment on the bench of the Calcutta High Court in 1944, he was for a year or so Prime Minister of Kashmir. Then as Constitutional Adviser to the Constituent Assembly at Delhi he had at the outset a considerable share in the shaping of the detailed constitution which came into force in January, 1950. He had previously helped in framing the constitution of republican Burma.

He was appointed a member of the Indian delegation to the United Nations in 1948, and became the permanent representative of his country in the following year. He proved a fully informed, eloquent and sincere interpreter of the somewhat intricate foreign policy of Nehru*. His Kashmir experience equipped him the better for his part in the protracted arguments on the future of that Himalayan State, and Sir Zafrullah Khan, the Pakistan Foreign Minister, found in him a doughty opponent. His chairmanship in July 1950 of the Security Council was in striking contrast to that of his Russian successor, Jacob Malik, for he was gentle, quiet and scholarly, as well as firm.

He was in closer touch than any other non-communist delegate with the head of the mission of the Peking Government. When in the autumn of that year Trygve Lie's* term of office as Secretary-General was closing, the name of Sir Narsing Rau was widely canvassed as that of a suitable successor. But he was more needed to exercise his responsibilities as a representative of India, particularly in connexion with the Korean war. Earnestly seeking a peaceful settlement, he took an active part in the discussions of the political committee of the Assembly, and in drafting resolutions aimed at reaching a peaceful solution. It was inevitable when in 1951 a ceasefire commission was appointed, that he should be one of its three members. The commission prepared the way for the long-drawn discussions at Panmunjom in respect of the repatriation of prisoners of war.

He became a Judge of the International Court of Justice at The Hague in 1952 and went to India on a few weeks' leave before taking up his new duties. However, he entered a nursing home at Zürich and earlier in November was reported to be very seriously ill.

December 1, 1953.

Frieda (Mrs. Angelo) Ravagli—See **Lawrence.**

Gwendolen Raverat, whose sensitive wood-engravings won her wide praise, died in Cambridge on February 11, 1957. She was 71.

To say that she was a pioneer in the revival of original wood-engraving is true in the matter of date but slightly misleading with reference to the character of her work. Of all the members of the Society of Wood Engravers who have made this one of the most satisfying minor arts of our time, she was the least suggestive of a revivalist. In both choice of subject and style of execution her work was completely free from self-consciousness and from the effect of any intention but that of giving expression to her feelings in terms of a traditional craft that had never declined.

To all appearances Mrs. Raverat carried on in ignorance that, since Bewick, there had been a period in which wood-engraving was employed only as a means of reproduction, presently superseded by the photographic process block. Her work was both decorative and illustrative, but as if by the way, as natural consequences of the fusion of theme and craft, and it was above all imaginative in the sense of expressing her intense reaction to the inner meaning of the subjects she chose to engrave, without the aid of fancy. The pitiful irony of her "David Old" is a case in point. In technical matters Mrs. Raverat was a superb craftswoman, with both the knife and the graver, but the means were so strictly subordinated to the end that "virtuosity" was the last word that would occur in any description of her work.

Gwendolen Mary Raverat came of a very distinguished family which in the younger generation has developed the artistic talent only hinted at in one of the greatest British men of science. Born in 1885, she was the daughter of the late Sir George Darwin, K.C.B., Plumian Professor of Astronomy and Experimental Philosophy at Cambridge, and consequently granddaughter of Charles Darwin. Gwen Raverat received her artistic training at the Slade School, but it was her sister-in-law, Mrs. Elinor Darwin, the painter and sculptor, whose talent has descended to her son, [Sir] Robin Darwin*, who taught her the rudiments of wood-engraving when she was about 20. In 1911 Gwendolen Darwin, as she was then, married Jacques Raverat, who pre-deceased her, leaving her with two daughters.

She was one of the two artists for whom the Royal Society of Painter-Etchers and Engravers, of which she became a full member in 1934, altered its rules to permit the inclusion of prints from wood, a concession that has been amply rewarded by the increased variety and decorative appeal of its exhibitions. She was also one of the earliest members of the Society of Wood-Engravers, founded in 1920. Perhaps the best way to suggest the general character of Mrs. Raverat's engravings is to recall what an American writer said *à propos The Times* new roman type: "Good typography should be as invisible as a clean window-pane". You look "through" an engraving by Mrs. Raverat, not so much at the facts of the subject represented, as into its meaning as felt by a mind distinguished by imagination, sympathy and humour, just as you look through good typography into the meaning of a poem. For this very reason, in comparison with the decorative emphasis and extreme virtuosity which are now common in wood-engraving, a print by Mrs. Raverat is apt to look "ordinary" in a mixed exhibition at a casual glance. It is only when attention is concentrated on one of her prints that its remarkable fullness of content is felt.

To speak of her work as "poetical" might convey the wrong impression unless it be understood to mean that her work is concerned with poetical as distinct from literal truth. This is very well illustrated in her series of "Little Rivers". To anybody susceptible to the spirit of peace a little river, such as the Windrush or the Roding, is not merely the diminutive of a great river but has a positive "personality" of its own, like that of a child as compared with a grown-up person, and this character Gwen Raverat conveyed to perfection.

In 1952 there appeared her delightful *Period Piece*, a discursive reminiscence of a Victorian and Edwardian youth.

February 13, 1957.

Dr. Grantly Dick-Read—See **Dick-.**

Lord Reading, who died in Rhodes hospital on September 19, 1960, was Minister of State for Foreign Affairs from 1953 to 1957. He was 71.

The Rt. Hon. Gerald Rufus Isaacs, P.C., G.C.M.G., C.B.E., M.C., Q.C., second Marquess of Reading, Earl of Reading, Viscount Erleigh, Viscount Reading, Baron Reading, all of Erleigh in the county of Berkshire in the Peerage of the United Kingdom, was born on January 10, 1889, the only son of Rufus Isaacs—later first Marquess of Reading—who by his own exertion and talents came to hold some of the highest offices of State and who received in turn every degree of the peerage save a dukedom.

Gerald Rufus Isaacs was educated at Rugby School and Balliol College, Oxford, where he graduated B.A. After leaving Oxford he followed his father's footsteps in entering the Middle Temple and was called to the Bar in 1912.

When the war broke out in 1914 he joined The Royal Fusiliers and served throughout the war, where he distinguished himself, being mentioned in dispatches and gaining the M.C. and the French Croix de Guerre. On the conclusion of the war he returned to England, becoming in 1920 lieutenant-colonel and C.O. of the Inns of Court Officers' Training Corps. He resumed his work at the Bar and took silk in 1929—in which year he unsuccessfully contested Blackburn as a Liberal. He became a bencher of his Inn in 1936, and in 1938 he was appointed to be chairman of the Coal Valuation Board, which carried out its work in the long vacation of that year.

From the outbreak of war in 1939 until 1941 he commanded a Pioneer Corps Training Centre, later served on the staff as a colonel, and in 1943-44 was brigadier, Director of Labour at the headquarters of the 21st Army Group. For his good work he was made C.B.E. in 1945.

In the years that followed the war his services were in constant demand. He was chairman of the Departmental Committee on London Government; of the Appeal Tribunal under the Further Education and Training Scheme; of the Central Valuation Board Panel of Arbitration and Panel of Referees under the Coal Industry Nationalization Act; of the Joint Select Committee on Consolidation Bills; and of the Departmental Committee on Copyright Law. This period of very full employment coincided with a deepening interest in politics.

He was regular and active in his attendance at the House of Lords, sitting on the Liberal benches and criticizing Clement Attlee's* administration in a number of forceful and eloquent speeches. His point of view led Conservative peers to regard him as a welcome ally. Reading was particularly concerned with the expanding number and power of the bureaucracy and with the protection of the courts of justice from encroachments on their functions.

In 1950 Reading joined the Conservative Party and a year later became joint Under-Secretary of State for Foreign Affairs. He specialized in the affairs of South-East Asia and Latin America, and in particular was from the first a warm supporter of the Colombo Plan. In 1952, when the return of a Conservative Government was none too popular in India, Reading travelled to Delhi on one of his numerous visits to Asian countries. He was faced with a press conference in an atmosphere charged with suspicion and even hostility, but it was typical of him that his candour and friendliness speedily disarmed those who had come to heckle. In November he was again on a good-will tour to Brazil, Uruguay, Argentina, Chile, and Peru, before attending the annual conference of British representatives in South Asia at Bukit Serene.

In 1953 he was promoted to be Minister of State, Foreign Office, and for several months in 1954 he served Sir Anthony Eden [later Lord Avon] on the British delegation to the Korean and Indo-China conferences at Geneva. Later in 1954 he was himself in the Far East, leading the British delegation to the South-East Asia conference at Manila, and there the unaffected informality with which he sat through humid sessions in the flimsiest of coloured shirts won him many a new friend in that highly variegated throng. In the following year Reading attended the consultative committee of the Colombo Plan in Singapore and paid a visit to Indonesia.

During the Suez crisis much added responsibility at the Foreign Office fell on him. Selwyn Lloyd, then Foreign Secretary, was for long hours at No. 10. Downing Street, or in New York, or Paris. Reading had to expound and defend Government policy in the House of Lords and on him fell too the burden of Government hospitality at Lancaster House and a watching brief over the Foreign Office machine.

It was certainly a sad disappointment to Reading when he was dropped from the Government in January 1957. His five years at the Foreign Office had endeared him to the Ambassadors of the South-East Asian countries. Much to his delight they gave him a dinner at Claridge's shortly after his retirement. He was made a K.C.M.G. but was perhaps more pleased when he was chosen to lead the British delegation to the meeting of the Colombo Plan Consultative Committee at Saigon in October 1957.

In 1958, in which year he was advanced to G.C.M.G., Reading became chairman of the Council on Tribunals, to supervise the working of administrative tribunals and inquiries under the Tribunals and Inquiries Act. It was a task for which he was well suited through his interest in preserving personal liberties and wide knowledge of public administration. He was also pleased towards the end of his career to become Treasurer of the Middle Temple.

Reading's wit, good humour, and approachability won him an affectionate respect as a member of the House of Lords and among a wide circle of the senior and junior officials who served with him in the Foreign Office.

He had leanings towards literature and published various books and articles. In 1930 he wrote an article on Rupert Brooke and not long after he published an account of the South Sea Bubble. But his best known work was a life of his father in two volumes. For a son to write his father's life is no easy task, for, as Reading said in his preface, "to give praise may be thought uncritical and to withhold it unfilial", but he managed to overcome these difficulties and the result proved a complete success.

He was deeply moved by the persecution of the Jews in Germany and joined with his brother-in-law, Lord Melchett, in his endeavour to assist them. In this work he was much aided by his wife, Eva Violet, Lady Reading*, elder daughter of Sir Alfred Mond, first Lord Melchett. Lady Reading was as enthusiastic in the Zionist cause as her husband and brother and published several articles on the subject.

Reading is survived by his widow, one son, and two daughters. The family honours now pass to the son, Viscount Erleigh, M.B.E., M.C.

September 21, 1960.

Sir Richard Redmayne, K.C.B., who died at his home in Hertfordshire on December 27, 1955 at the age of 90, had a wide experience of the coalmining industry in its technical and economic aspects and was for 12 years Chief Inspector of Mines.

Although he will be best remembered as one of the most prominent experts on safety in mining, a man who did much more than anybody else to bring comparative security to the colliers below ground, this was only one of his many interests. He was a great mineralogist; an industrialist, as a director of companies; he knew much about agriculture; he was a graceful writer; and, what few people outside his own circle ever knew, a talented amateur artist. Above all he had a great zest for life. He was as keenly interested in affairs when well over 80 as he was when he was a young man, and he had that strong northern characteristic, a keen sense of dry humour, which was present almost as much and as often in his lectures as it was in his private conversation.

Richard Augustine Studdert Redmayne was born at South Dene, Gateshead-on-Tyne, on July 22, 1865, the fourth son and one of the eight children of John Marriner Redmayne, J.P., of Low Fell. His father had strong ideas about education, and Redmayne was educated by private tutors and at Durham College of Science, Newcastle upon Tyne. Originally intended for the Army, his interests were switched completely to mining through his early studies in geology, and when he was only 17 he won the first prize at the college in this subject. At the age of 18 he began what was to be a lifelong association with mining when he was apprenticed at the Hetton Collieries, Durham. He still continued his studies while learning the technique of mining, and he was under 25 when he became an under-manager. A year or two later an opportunity came for him to extend his knowledge by going out to Natal, where he spent two years in managing collieries and making reports and surveys on mining properties. Returning to England, he was appointed in 1893 resident manager of the Seaton Delaval Collieries, Northumberland. Nine years later he became consulting mining engineer and Professor of Mining in the then new University of Birmingham. It was certainly a great honour for a man only 37, but the appointment was soon justified by the work he did not only in organizing plant and laboratories but also in pursuing his investigations towards perfection in safety apparatus.

In 1908 he was chosen to be the first holder of the post of His Majesty's Chief Inspector of Mines, and it was in this office that he was able to indulge to the full his campaign for safety in mines. He presided over the Royal Commission appointed to investigate accidents in shafts, underground haulage, and falls, and, thereafter, sat on committees dealing with the use of electricity, testing of safety lamps, spontaneous combustion, drainage, support of workings, and so forth. During the 1914-18 War he was also assistant to the Controller of Coal Mines, and with his knowledge of all branches of the industry, as well as of the miners, he rendered great national service in maintaining and then increasing output.

At the end of 1919 he resigned his post as Chief Inspector to become chairman of the Imperial Mineral Resources Bureau, a post which he held until 1925, when he became chairman of the Advisory Council on Minerals to the Imperial Institute, of which, for a while, he was acting director. In 1934 he was appointed independent chairman of the National Joint Conciliation Board for Road Motor Transport, but practically throughout this period, after his departure from Government service, he was in private practice as a consulting mining engineer, engaged in duties which took him all over Great Britain and abroad.

In earlier years he was a director of the Stafford and Florence Coal and Iron Companies and of the Blaina (South Wales) Colliery Company. Later he joined the board of the company of Dixon Corbitt and Co. Ltd., a large firm of rope manufacturers at Gateshead, was elected chairman, and became immersed not only in the technique of rope-making but also in the company's welfare schemes for its workers. From the outbreak of war in 1939 he rendered considerable service to the state in various capacities, while still being chairman of the Road Haulage Wages Board, a member of the Southern Region Valuation Board under the Coal Commission, and chairman of the Agricultural Wages Committee for Essex. He had been re-elected for the thirty-third year president of the Institute of Professional Civil Servants, a position he had held since shortly after the body was formed in 1921.

He was until recently still writing, adding to the long and impressive list of books and papers on colliery working and management, on the ownership, valuation, and rating of coal and mining properties, and taking a keen interest in the many technical societies and institutions with which he had been associated since his early years. In 1916 he was president of the Institution of Mining and Metallurgy, and in 1934 of the Institution of Civil Engineers. He was also a Fellow of the Geological Society.

In 1898 he married Edith Rose, the eldest daughter of the late Thomas Picton Richards, of Swansea; she died in 1942. There were one son and two daughters of the marriage.

December 29, 1955.

Tom Reece, the famous billiards player, who compiled the world record break of 499,135 by means of the "anchor" stroke, died at his home at Lancing, Sussex, on October 16, 1953 at the age of 80.

Reece played a large part in the development of modern billiards. One of the greatest ambitions of his life was to win the professional championship, but in this he failed, although he must have taken part in the event on a greater number of occasions than any other player. He was contemporary in the game with such players as H. W. Stevenson, M. Inman [q.v.], George Gray, C. Falkiner and later in his career with W. Smith, T. Newman, and others. A stockily built man, he was gifted with a most delicate sense of touch. No one has played the close cannon game with greater attractiveness.

W. Lindrum [q.v.] developed it later in the history of the game, but much of the credit belonged to Reece. He did not make big breaks, as understood by more modern players, with the same frequency, but no one has shown greater skill in maintaining the required position. He was always ready to try an experiment and he showed that, while almost unlimited scoring could be achieved by a certain type of specialist play, it could also be detrimental to the real interests of the game.

Many years before the game was developed on its present lines—in 1907—Reece made a break of 499,135 unfinished by means of what was known as the "anchor" cannon. The two object balls were played into a position between the shoulders of a top pocket and the stroke was made gently on to the first ball, the cueball being kissed backed into its original position off the second object. It was made with great delicacy and it is doubtful if many other players could have accomplished so much. The break took nearly six weeks to complete but, clever though it undoubtedly was, it showed the danger of allowing unrestricted specialization, and led ultimately to legislation so far as this kind of scoring was concerned.

Reece also developed the "pendulum" cannon, another most ingenious method, but this too merely helped to show that the game would not benefit if unlimited scoring was permitted by entirely specialist means. In all respects he was a most delightful player to watch, and perhaps his greatest achievement was when before the 1914-18 war he beat G. Gray, the Australian red ball player, and H. W. Stevenson in turn in the professional championship, only to be beaten in the end by his old rival, M. Inman.

October 17, 1953.

Austin Reed, who died on May 5, 1954 at his home at Gerrards Cross, Buckinghamshire, in his eight-first year, was a pioneer in modern business methods.

The founder and director of Austin Reed, Ltd., he entered his father's men's wear business at Reading in 1888. Before the close of the century he went to the United States, where he made a close study of the organization of the great departmental city stores. He returned with a vision of service to the public.

Fired with the idea of establishing a store where a man could be fitted out in a few hours with everything he needed in the way of clothes for anywhere in the world, Reed, in 1900, founded the business of Austin Reed in a small shop in Fenchurch Street, E.C. It proved remarkably successful, and eventually led to the opening of the big men's wear store in Regent Street. There Reed achieved his ambition. He was able, for instance, to make suits for men unable to afford Saville Row prices—"Service for the middle-class man", he would say, "the backbone of the nation".

The secret of Reed's success was to be found in his personal character. He inspired trust and enthusiasm wherever he went and in whatever he did. He combined an acute business intellect with high ideals of simplicity, sincerity, and service. He had a deep spiritual faith, and was an active Free Churchman. In 1933 he met Dr. Frank Buchman*, the founder of "moral rearmament", with whom he formed a lasting friendship. Through this contact he developed his philosophy that the true function of business was to distribute the resources of the world for the benefit of all and the exploitation of none.

He married, in 1902, Emily Wilson. She died in November 1953, after more than 50 years of wonderfully happy married life. They had six children, two sons and four daughters. His younger son, a fighter pilot, was killed in North Africa during the war.

May 6, 1954.

Major-General Thomas Wynford Rees, C.B., C.I.E., D.S.O., M.C., conqueror of Mandalay in the War of 1939-45, collapsed and died in London on October 15, 1959. He was 61.

Rees was a soldier of forceful personality and unconventional mind. He spent most of his career with the Indian Army, earning the respect and affection of his men by his qualities of leadership and by his skill in speaking many of their languages.

He was the son of a Welsh clergyman, the Rev. T. W. Rees, and was born at Barry in January 1898. He passed through Sandhurst, taking his commission in November 1915, and spent the rest of the war years with the British Expeditionary Force in France. He was mentioned in dispatches, was wounded, and won the Military Cross and the D.S.O.

His next activities were with the Indian Army, with which he served in Waziristan in 1920 and from 1922 to 1924 (earning another mention in dispatches in the second campaign). There followed a spell as instructor at Sandhurst in 1926-27 and a period as Private Secretary to the Governor of Burma from 1928 to 1930. Rees was D.A.Q.M.G. for the Waziristan District in 1937-38 (having received two more mentions and a brevet-lieutenant-colonelcy in the Waziristan campaign of 1936-37). The outbreak of the Second World War found him Commandant of the 3rd Battalion, the 6th Rajputana Rifles (Napier's). He had been created C.I.E. in 1931.

Rees took part in the North African fighting with the 4th Indian Division, and was at the victory of Sidi Barrani. On the second day of the battle he found himself only a thousand yards from the Italian guns, in a wireless truck. The enemy were firing over open sights, but Rees and his operator remained thus exposed for three hours without being hit. This gallant episode won him a bar to his D.S.O.

Rees was later transferred to the Burma front and in May 1942 promoted to the acting rank of major-general. His chief distinction was won in command of the 19th ("Dagger") Division, which first went into action in November 1944, crossing the Chindwin at Sittaung and the Irrawaddy east of Shwebo, thus being the first division of the Fourteenth Army in central Burma to cross, and stay across, both rivers.

In the spring of 1945 Rees's troops made unexpectedly rapid progress in their southward drive. Rees watched the final assault on Mandalay from a point two hundred yards away; and in mid-March the city was taken, and the Union flag that the general had personally prepared and hoarded was broken at last.

Later he commanded the Punjab Boundary Force at the time of the transfer of power in India and was head of Lord Mountbatten's military staff during the troubled times which followed. He retired in 1948, but continued to lead an active life.

In 1949 the Government of Nyasaland, seriously concerned about the possibility of a bad harvest, appealed to the Home Government for a large quantity of agricultural tractors and implements to cultivate the land surrounding some of the smaller lakes in the Lake Nyasa region. Lord Trefgarne, chairman of the Colonial Development Corporation, sought a man of energy to run through an emergency convoy from Tanganyika; the Controller of Operations, Lieutenant-General Sir Ernest Wood, knew Rees, put his name forward, and Rees did the job, taking the convoy from Lindi to Mbamba on Lake Nyasa. The journey of over 500 miles over much singularly unaccommodating country was accomplished by Rees in 11 days.

At the time of his death he was chief executive and general manager of Cwmbran New Town. He was a Deputy Lieutenant for Monmouthshire and an Hon. LL.D. of the University of Wales.

Rees was a man somewhat under middle height, and his short stature earned him various nicknames. Sepoys called him "the *chota* general"; his habit of standing with one hand tucked into his bush shirt prompted the sobriquet of "the pocket Napoleon"; but the most generally used nickname was the affectionate diminutive, "Pete".

In ordinary social intercourse Rees appeared quiet, kindly, and methodical. In the heat of action, however, he was a man transformed, showing a tireless and positively volcanic energy. He was indifferent to danger and was a bold and unconventional tactician. These qualities helped to make him a magnificent leader, and to them was superadded great solicitude for the personal welfare of his men. Though himself a non-smoker, he would take a gift of cigarettes to a sick man in hospital. His abstemiousness extended also to alcohol (though he might take an occasional glass at a social function), but not to very strong tea, for which he had a passion.

Rees was a fluent Welsh speaker, and liked

to have a Welsh-speaking officer on his staff. He was made C.B. in July 1945.

He married in 1926 Rosalie, only daughter of Sir Charles Innes. A son and a daughter were born of the marriage.

October 17, 1959.

George Relph, C.B.E., the actor, who died on April 24, 1960, had started very well in his profession and then for a while lost ground, but he had completely reestablished himself in later years through his association with the Old Vic Company and with Sir Laurence Olivier in particular. He was 72.

Born in Northumberland on January 27, 1888, Relph got his early experience in London, Australia, and America, and at the age of 24 made a success as Joseph in Tree's production of *Joseph and his Brethren* at His Majesty's. Two years later he played Romeo in New York, but he went home to join the Army in 1916 and was badly wounded at Arras when serving as a subaltern in The Yorkshire Regiment.

On his return he resumed his career as a "leading juvenile", appearing in such plays as Somerset Maugham's* *Caesar's Wife* and William Archer's *The Green Goddess.* Later he toured South Africa at the head of a company and was Horatio to John Barrymore's Hamlet at the Haymarket. But his reputation had not increased. He seemed on the contrary to have grown into rather a spiritless, uninteresting type of actor, and in the years preceding the Second World War he was no longer considered eligible for leading parts.

His work acquired distinction again after he had reached middle age and been given the opportunity of playing interesting, secondary parts. The first was that of the unprosperous Dr. Blenkinsop in the successful wartime revival of *The Doctor's Dilemma.* In 1944, when an Old Vic Company was being formed round Sir Laurence Olivier and Sir Ralph Richardson for a season in the West End, Relph was asked to join it. He proved a versatile member of the Old Vic Company during four consecutive years in London—Subtle in *The Alchemist* and Grumio in *The Taming of the Shrew* were two of his best parts—and also on a tour, again under Sir Laurence Olivier's leadership, of Australia and New Zealand. He appeared under the same actor's management in two important modern plays in the West End, and later supported him in John Osborne's *The Entertainer* and on television in *John Gabriel Borkman.* Relph's acting and personality combined to give crisp authenticity to his Billie Rice—an Edwardian once a music-hall artist and still a professional at heart and a "fine figure of a man"—in Osborne's play.

Films provided him with a long succession of minor parts, of which the Roman Emperor in the re-make of *Ben-Hur* was a fair example. He was made C.B.E. in 1959.

He married first in 1911 Miss Deborah Nanson. This marriage was dissolved and he married secondly in 1925 Miss Mercia Swinburne, the actress. His son by his first marriage is Michael Relph, the art director and producer of films.

April 25, 1960.

Colonel José Antonio Rémon, the President of the Republic of Panama, was assassinated at Panama City late on January 2, 1955, having been shot down with six others by sub-machine guns at a race track.

President Rémon was educated at Nassau School and at the Military Academy in Mexico City. In 1932 he returned to Panama, and joined the mounted section of the police, where he soon became captain in charge of training. He was made Deputy Chief of Police by President de la Guardia, and in 1947 he became Chief of Police.

In November 1949 he took part in the *coup d'état* which raised President Arias to power, and he continued to serve the President until 1951, when he disagreed with him on constitutional questions and joined the campaign which led to the President being deposed in favour of Señor Arosemena. At the end of 1951 he retired from the post of Chief of Police to conduct his campaign for election as President. He was elected in May 1952 and in October he was installed in office.

He proved an effective President, combining an easy-going manner that made him popular with the people with a determination that gave Panama a firm and stable anti-communist Government and put her on the road to economic prosperity. His popularity was increased by the conclusions of a new and more favourable treaty with the United States in December 1954.

In November 1953 he received Queen Elizabeth on her way through the Panama Canal to New Zealand, and was presented with the insignia of a Knight Grand Cross of the Order of the British Empire.

January 4, 1955.

Harry Stuart Goodhart-Rendel—
See **Goodhart-**.

Dr. Karl Renner, who died on December 31, 1950, twice brought into being an Austrian Republic, first in 1918 and again in 1945.

Karl Renner was born on December 14, 1870, at Dolni Dunajovice, in Moravia, of peasant stock. His early brilliance won him a scholarship to Vienna University, where he read law, and he entered the Civil service of the Austro-Hungarian Empire. He was appointed librarian of the Austro-Hungarian Reichsrat in 1896. Having joined the Socialist Party he was elected to Parliament in 1907 and soon as leader. As such he fought for a reconstruction of the Habsburg Empire on lines which would have turned it into a federation of autonomous states such as, too late, the Emperor Charles proclaimed shortly before the collapse in the autumn of 1918.

The succeeding Austrian Republic saw Renner as its first Chancellor, heading the first three coalition Governments from November 1918 until June 1920. He led the Austrian delegation to St. Germain in 1919 and, when his Foreign Minister, Otto Bauer, resigned over the prohibition of the *Anschluss* and the loss of Southern Tirol, assumed his portfolio too and signed the peace treaty on September 10, 1919.

At home he had to fight separatist and communist movements and, against strong opposition, insisted upon permanent dethronement of the Habsburg dynasty and banishment of its members unless submitting to the republican régime. The great, if rather expensive, social measures, and especially the Vienna programme of model settlements for workers, were largely due to his initiative; but, as early as December 1919, he had to go once more to Paris in order to beg for a softening of the financial and economic burdens inflicted at St. Germain to prevent a breakdown of the young republic. He had some success and was able to go on with his programme irrespective of the growth on the right wing within the Christian Social Party, his coalition partners, led by Dr. Seipel, of a strength about equal to that of the Socialists.

In June 1920, however, technically over a question connected with the small new army, Renner was forced to resign from the Chancellorship; his ability found recognition inasmuch as he stayed in the Foreign Office until October. As the leader of his party, member of its executive, president of the Cooperatives' central organization, and in 1931 Speaker of the Austrian Parliament, Renner continued to play an important part in the country's public life. After the sanguinary clash between workers and Heimwehr, under Dollfuss, Dr. Renner was imprisoned, accused of high treason, and spent several months in gaol, an experience later repeated under more drastic conditions when the Nazis began to feel Austrian opposition, and, in their war, held the aged Socialist leader in a concentration camp.

This, and his old record, made him the obvious choice for heading an anti-Nazi Government. Thus Renner was appointed at first by the Soviet authorities, but later confirmed by the four Powers on April 29, 1945, Chancellor and Foreign Minister of Austria. After the elections of November 25, 1945—which gave a majority to the People's Party, equivalent of the old clerical one, of 85 against 76 socialists and four communists—Renner's Cabinet resigned and he was succeeded by Dr. Figl*, leader of the Christian Party.

On December 20, however, Dr. Renner was elected unanimously by both Houses of Parliament as the first President of resurrected Austria. Though in a representative rather than an influential position, Renner acquitted himself of its tasks with dignity and fearlessness which were proved during his short-lived Chancellorship, for example, when he protested at the end of July 1945 against Austria's, especially Vienna's, division into four zones, and against unnecessary hardships inflicted upon his people. He had the satisfaction of seeing them mitigated—for example by oil being brought from Russia, coal from Britain and the United States, and food from all of the occupying Powers.

Among his numerous books, partly published under pseudonyms such as "Synopticus", or "Rudolf Springer", *Der Kampf der Nation um den Staat* (1902), *Oesterreichs Erneuerung, Die Wirtschaft als Gesamtprozess und die Sozialisterung, Staatswirtschaft, Weltwirtschaft und Sozialismus,* besides some juridical treatises, deserve mention.

January 1, 1951.

Professor Ernst Reuter, who died suddenly at his home on September 29, 1953, had been Chief Burgomaster of Berlin since 1947.

One of the most eminent German leaders to emerge in his country since the war, no man, save Dr. Adenauer*, enjoyed such popularity at home and so wide a reputation abroad. From the moment he assumed office as chief burgomaster of Berlin he made himself a name by his fearless and merciless denunciations of communist tyranny, and for his eloquent appeals for German unity. He pressed tirelessly for a vigorous allied policy of resistance to the unceasing vexations and arbitrary acts of the east German authorities in Berlin, and took great pride in the city's position as an outpost of the free world and a haven for all the refugees from oppression in the east.

A big burly man, as much a symbol of Berlin as the bear on the arms of the city, he limped slightly from a wound inflicted by a Russian bullet during the 1914-18 War, and his health was permanently weakened by his two terms in Nazi concentration camps. His keen brown eyes looked out from heavy features which had the plasticity of a great actor, and his informal and quiet speech was as effective, both in informal and intimate discussion, as on the platform, avoiding alike the dullness of the professor and the histrionics of the demagogue.

It was during the Berlin blockade that Reuter, together with Frau Louise Schröder [q.v.], showed the true quality of greatness and the metal of his leadership. His natural gifts as an orator sustained the spirit of the citizens of Berlin in fortnightly broadcasts during those long months of hopelessness and privation. He never doubted that the blockade would in the end be broken, just as he never ceased to doubt until his death that Germany would be reunited and that Berlin would resume its rightful place as the capital of the country. He earned during that period the affection of his fellow-citizens, and never lost it until his death.

Ernst Reuter was born on July 29, 1889, at Apenrade, in that part of Schleswig returned to Denmark after the 1914-18 War. He was the son of a captain and instructor in the merchant navy. A liberal education at three universities (where in protest against the beer-drinking customs of his fellow-students he became a teetotaller) laid the foundation of a lively and cultivated mind.

Then in 1912 he horrified his family by joining the Social Democratic Party. Drafted into the German Army, he served in France and in Russia and it was while on the Russian front that he received a wound in the leg which led to his capture and to the limp which permanently affected his walk. The Russians sent him to the Tula coalmines, and after the outbreak of the Russian revolution in 1917 he organized his fellow-prisoners into a Soviet and was sent by Lenin to administer Catherine the Great's German colony on the Volga into an autonomous republic. His immediate superior was Stalin [q.v.], then Commissar of Nationalities. He returned to Germany as secretary of the German Communist Party in 1921, but after the Communist uprising in the central provinces, he went back to the Socialists. In 1926 he was in control of the department for traffic and transport of the Berlin Magistrat, and in 1931 was selected burgomaster of Magdeburg.

He was in opposition from the start to the Nazi régime, and twice suffered imprisonment in a concentration camp. Threatened with a third arrest, he escaped to Turkey, where, at the outbreak of war, he was appointed Professor of Municipal Theory and Practice in the State Institute for Senior Administrators at Ankara. After the end of the war he returned to Germany, and to his former traffic department in the Magistrat. When, in April 1947, Dr. Ostrowski, the then chief burgomaster, resigned, Reuter as his immediate deputy succeeded him. But his appointment provoked sharp opposition in the communist east German press. Formally elected chief burgomaster the following June by 89 votes against 17, he was confronted with the veto of the Soviet Control Commission, and in August the allied authorities reluctantly pronounced his dismissal, while making it clear that they did so only at the request of the Russians. The Berlin municipal elections of December 1948, however, led to his triumphant reappointment as chief burgomaster by the House of Deputies.

From that time onwards he devoted himself without regard to his health or his age to the tasks of administration of the city, of negotiation with the allies in the Kommandatura, and of defending the rights and liberties of west Berlin against encroachments of the east. A fiery tribune by temperament and inclination, he was at times an embarrassing and strong-headed advocate of radical solutions, which discounted international repercussions and brought him more than once into conflict with the allied authorities, for urging both a more rapid emancipation of west Berlin from the leading strings of the occupation and a stiffer attitude towards the Russians. His theory was that a bold front would pay useful dividends in the negotiations with the Soviet Union which he felt convinced would come in time. Meanwhile, he sought to enlist support for the cause of Berlin both at home and abroad (to that end he contributed an article in *The Times* in February 1953) and paid several visits to England. His journey to the United States in March 1953 was an immediate success, and his personality captured the imagination of American audiences. He pleaded with great eloquence for the thousands of refugees streaming into Berlin and was able to collect considerable donations to help in relief work.

The last bold measure with which he was associated was the distribution of food parcels to east Berliners and inhabitants of the eastern zone, who responded in hundreds of thousands, and forced the east German Government into sharp and unpopular counter-measures. He was just about to organize, in cooperation with the American authorities, a scheme for the distribution of warm clothing for the winter when death overtook him. For those who would object the possibly dangerous repercussions of these schemes, he would reply that the more the weaknesses and difficulties of the east German Government were exploited, the sooner Germany would be liberated from the communist yoke—although he never envisaged this liberation by other than peaceful means.

September 30, 1953.

Frank Reynolds, the humorous artist and illustrator, died in a nursing home in Surrey on April 18, 1953 at the age of 77. His most characteristic drawings appeared in *Punch,* to which he was a contributor for more than 40 years; he was art editor from 1921 to 1932.

His work may be said to have formed a bridge between the old and the modern schools of *Punch* artists—between Charles Keene and Pont, Phil May and Emett. He was a realistic draughtsman, and a humorist who went to everyday life for his material. Under his régime as art editor the captions to *Punch* drawings became gradually less wordy; he was prepared to dispense with a caption altogether.

Born in London on February 13, 1876, Frank Reynolds was the youngest child of a large family. His father, William George Reynolds, an Irishman from County Meath, had set up in Notting Hill as a picture framer and restorer; he also painted landscapes in the Constable tradition, which he sometimes exhibited and sold in his own shop. Young Frank Reynolds used to accompany him on his sketching expeditions along the Thames, and he was soon allowed his own colour-box and brushes with a home-made miniature palette. He was sent to a local church school, and in the evenings he learned to make himself useful in his father's workshop.

His father had won local celebrity by his public readings of Shakespeare, and his brother, the late Tom Reynolds, was a member of Sir Henry Irving's company at the Lyceum. Soon Frank Reynolds was contributing regularly to *Pick-Me-Up* and earning about £5 a week—on which a boy could do very well indeed in those days.

Then his father died, leaving his business affairs in some confusion. Frank Reynolds and his brother had to turn aside from their chosen careers, go back to the shop, and stay there for more than a year. It was a time of bitter frustration for both of them. Frank Reynolds managed, however, to attend evening classes at Heatherly's, then presided over by Professor John Crompton; when he was free to return to press work it was with a greatly improved technical equipment.

Reynold's long association with *Punch* started in the summer of 1906, when at the invitation of the then art editor, F. H. Townsend, he contributed a picture of cockney boys struggling for a cricket bat, with the legend, "Precedence at Battersea: 'Garn! The Treasurer goes in before the bloomin' Seckertary!' " As time went on he became particularly well known as a commentator on suburbia, who brought fresh humour to the old idea of the "little man". He did not limit himself to the London suburbs. Perhaps his most famous single drawing was one, published in the 1914-18 war, which showed a German middle-class family enjoying their "morning hate". During that war he served in a coast defence battalion of The Cheshire Regiment and later in a section of the intelligence staff concerned with pictorial propaganda.

Besides his work for *Punch*, Reynolds made frequent contributions to the *Sketch*, the *Bystander*, and other journals. As a young man he illustrated several of Dickens's novels in water-colour; he was elected a member of the Royal Institute in 1903. In more recent years he devoted much of his leisure to painting in oil—usually landscapes or street scenes worked up in the studio from outdoor notes or memories. He loved the medium and, though he had no great opinion of his own ability to handle it, examples of his work were twice accepted by the Royal Academy.

In later life he also took to writing: his two books, *Off to the Pictures* (the pictures being films) and *Humorous Drawing for the Press*, were enhanced by their illustrations; and the writing was racy and amusing.

He was married in 1905 to Anne Winifred, daughter of D. B. Milne, and they had two sons and two daughters. The younger son, John Patrick Reynolds, who died in 1936, was considered one of the most promising young press artists of his day.

April 20, 1953.

Lady Rhondda, who died in hospital in London on July 20, 1958 at the age of 75, was a truly exceptional woman. The only daughter of a captain of industry, she first helped and then succeeded her father in his business interests, and proved by her successful handling of them that she had more than the normal man's capacity for affairs. She gave support by her own achievements to a lifelong belief in the equality of the sexes, for which in the days of the suffragette movement she had undergone imprisonment.

With a lively mind, wide interests, and great concentration of purpose she was prominent alike in business and in political journalism. She had always wished to be an editor and for the last 30 years of her life she actively edited her own paper, the independent weekly *Time and Tide*. Naturally hospitable, she enjoyed good company and good conversation, and her friendships spanned the worlds of politics, business, and the arts. Parties at her country home or her London flat were always the scene of animated and interesting discussions, over which she presided with real and infectious enjoyment. The young were included on equal terms on these occasions, and there must be many to-day, in the risen and the rising generations, who owe their introduction to public life to the generous gatherings over which she, with her friend Theodora Bosanquet, so ably presided.

Margaret Haig Thomas, Viscountess Rhondda, was born in 1883, the only child of David Alfred Thomas, M.P. for Cardiff, who was president of the Local Government Board in 1916-17 and Food Controller in the following year. He was raised to the peerage in 1916 as Baron Rhondda, of Llanwern, co. Monmouth, and in 1918 created a viscount with special remainder to the heirs male of his body, and in default of such issue to his daughter. Her mother was the late Sybil Margaret, D.B.E., at one time chairman of the Women's Advisory Committee and of the National War Savings Committee, who was fourth daughter of George Augustus Haig, of Pen Ithon, Radnorshire, The first Lord Rhondda came of small farmer stock; his wife was of an ancient Border family.

Lady Rhondda once wrote of herself that she was a shy child, devoted to her parents. In spite of all her success in the world she retained this initial shyness to the end of her life, as also her profound family affections. She was educated by governesses until she was 13 years old, when she was sent to Notting Hill High School. There she started a printed magazine called *The Shooting Star*, to which cousins were the chief contributors. Its brief life ended when she went on to St. Leonards School at St. Andrews. Her schooldays over, she was in London for three seasons and then for a time at Somerville College, Oxford. She did not like it, and after leaving married Mr., afterwards Sir Humphrey, Mackworth, seventh baronet, from whom in 1923 she was to obtain a divorce.

In the early months of her marriage she joined the Women's Social and Political Union, and took up its cause with considerable enthusiasm, began to speak in public and to write articles on the suffrage question for provincial newspapers. Other members of her family, including her mother, were strong supporters of the movement. Occasionally she asked questions at meetings addressed by Cabinet Ministers, and once she jumped on the running-board of Asquith's car, but was never quite certain whether she had in fact the courage to say "Votes for Women" to him, as was expected of her. After this incident she was roughly handled by the crowd.

In the days of militancy she followed a practice common among the suffragettes of the day and burnt the contents of a pillar box by dropping tubes of chemicals into it. The crime was traced to her and she was arrested. Found guilty at her trial, she was sent to Usk gaol, where she went on hunger strike but was shortly after released.

Soon after her marriage she began to help her father in his business interests which he directed from Cardiff docks, and became his close and confidential assistant. Among his interests were some Welsh newspaper properties. In 1916 she accompanied him to America. They returned in the ill-fated Lusitania. When the ship was struck she was unable to find her father and being on deck was sucked down with the vessel. On coming to the surface she found a bit of board which, with her lifebelt, kept her afloat. At dusk, after nearly three hours in the water, she was picked up unconscious by a small boat and taken to the patrol ship Bluebell. When, a little later, Lord Rhondda entered the Ministry, she was put on to a number of her father's boards, and thus took control of his interests. In 1918 she accepted an appointment in the Ministry of National Service in connexion with enlistment for the Women's Army Auxiliary Corps. In July of the same year Lord Rhondda died and she succeeded to his viscountcy, though not to his barony, which became extinct.

In 1920 Lady Rhondda, true to her belief in the equality of the sexes, petitioned the King to issue her a writ of summons to attend the House of Lords. The matter was referred to the Committee of Privileges of the House, which at first reported favourably. On the motion of the Lord Chancellor the House referred the report back for consideration, and in 1922 a final report against the claim was carried by a majority of 20 to four.

Meanwhile, owing to her close association with her father in business, Lady Rhondda had inherited a large part of his position, served on a number of important boards, and lived the life of an active business man. But she had preserved her ambition also to be an editor, became chairman of the Time and Tide Publishing Company, and in the years between the wars took over the active editorship of the independent weekly which during the ensuing years was to absorb ever more of her time and interest. She collected about her many outstanding contributors: Evelyn Underhill, Theodora Bosanquet, Rebecca West, Winifred Holtby, E. M. Delafield, Ellen Wilkinson, Norman Angell*, Charles Williams, and many others.

The impress of her strong personality and her intense belief in personal liberty and the rights of the individual gave a distinctive character to a paper which she built up into one of the leading weeklies. She had, however, for most of those years to provide a private subsidy for the paper. Early in 1958, although its circulation was between 20,000 and 25,000, Lady Rhondda stated that the paper would have to cease publication unless financial help was forthcoming. Shortly before she died it was announced that there had been sufficient support to assure its immediate future.

July 21, 1958.

Father William Ignatius Rice, O.S.B., M.A., headmaster of Douai School from 1915 until the end of the summer term in 1952, when ill health forced him to retire, died on April 22, 1955 at Douai Abbey. He was 72.

Born in 1883 in Birmingham, he was educated at St. Edmund's, Douai, at Oxford, and at St.

Anselmo, Rome. He was in the senior school at St. Edmund's when the English Benedictine priory was raised to the dignity of an abbey by Pope Leo XIII in 1898, and he was beginning his studies for the priesthood in 1903 when the Law of Associations compelled the community to return to England and re-establish the abbey, as Douai Abbey, at Woolhampton, Berkshire. His ordination to the priesthood in 1910 was followed five years later by his appointment as headmaster of the Abbey School.

In 1915 Douai School was entering the second phase of its new existence in England. New monastic buildings were being put up, relieving the somewhat cramped circumstances of the school, and development on the lines of a modern public school was made possible for a young headmaster who could expect to hold office for a period of years. Previously, although by no means a seminary, the school had trained a large number of future clergy and had been remarkable as a nursery for prelates. Dom Ignatius was anxious to preserve this tradition, but he was concerned equally to make Douai known as a school for laymen. The success of his policy was shown in later years when Old Dowegians who had been his pupils advanced to high position in the church and also to distinction in the services and various professions.

Dom Ignatius brought varied gifts to his headmastership. A sound classical training had been accompanied by wide reading in English literature. His interest in the work of contemporary authors was quickened by friendship with Alice and Wilfred Meynell and G. K. Chesterton, at whose reception into the Roman Catholic Church he assisted a fellow-Dowegian, Mgr. John O'Connor [q.v.]. He was also a first class cricketer, playing for Warwickshire during the summer holidays—for some years he was the only monk admitted to the pages of Wisden. A tall, well built, and handsome man, he had a distinguished bearing and attractive personality, and while he insisted on all the marks of respect due to his position *in loco parentis,* he was accessible to any boy who wished to discuss any point with him, so that the headmaster's study became a room which none approached in fear unless conscience prompted cowardice.

His aim in education was to make the fullest use of the traditional methods of the Benedictine Order, while studying and possibly adopting new ideas and equipment. He opposed any increase in the number of pupils that might limit opportunity for personal coaching by the teaching members of the community, and he was interested in examination results only in so far as they were necessary to the future careers of his pupils. He contended that the success of boys from public schools in after life was due not to scholastic clannishness and the passport of the old school tie but to the distinctive quality of their educational training.

Under his direction the school was enlarged by the addition of a new senior wing, gymnasia, swimming baths, and a theatre. He was an active member of various educational and literary associations and a contributor to quarterly and other reviews.

In 1950 he accepted an invitation to lecture at American colleges on contemporary English writers, particularly G. K. Chesterton. His visit was extended to include a number of public lectures. After his return he resumed his duties as headmaster of Douai until his retirement in 1952.

In 1954 he was appointed Titular Prior of Gloucester.

April 23, 1955.

Dorothy Richardson, the novelist, who in private life was **Mrs. Alan Odle,** died on June 17, 1957 in a nursing home at Beckenham, Kent, where she had been a patient for some years. She was 84.

In the years that passed since she published, in 1915, the first of the 12 volumes of *Pilgrimage,* in which she projected an illusion of reality solely through the consciousness of the central character, Dorothy Richardson's achievement lost much of its seeming oddity. Only the older generation of readers to-day will appreciate as fully as it deserves her quiet persistence in the austere task she chose for herself; only the historically minded critic will perceive the true measure of her originality. If expressions like "the stream of consciousness" and "the interior monologue" are to-day commonplaces of criticism, it is in no small degree because of Dorothy Richardson's pioneering labours. Her method has obvious limitations and she had exhausted its possibilities long before she reached the last volume in the series. Her insistence upon the incompetence of the male to follow the female mind or the female subconscious sustained her, no doubt, in her task. Her vision of reality has questionable depth; yet the contemporary novel is greatly indebted to her example.

Dorothy M. Richardson was born in 1873, one of four daughters, her father being a man of independent means who slowly dissipated his income by unwise investment. In the middle 1880s, having lived for some years at Abingdon, he took a house at Barnes, where Miss Richardson first met Amy Catherine Robbins, afterwards Mrs. H. G. Wells, with whom she remained on terms of close friendship until Mrs. Wells's death in 1927.

From the age of 18 Miss Richardson had to earn her own living, and was for a time governess to the children of Horace (afterwards Mr. Justice) Avory. Later she sought greater independence in a variety of employments, and for some years acted as daily secretary to a partnership of dentists in Harley Street. In these earlier years she occasionally contributed to *The Saturday Review* and other periodicals short sketches and articles marked by a curious preciosity of style. But it was not until some of her friends had helped in one way or another to give her sufficient leisure in which to write that she was able to publish the first of her novels.

Pointed Roofs (1915) was the opening instalment of a work of fiction under the general title of *Pilgrimage.* It was no secret from Miss Richardson's friends that every detail of the story was autobiographical, although the method of *Pilgrimage* completely disguises the original material. The method is, indeed, *sui generis.* Comparisons have inevitably been made between her work and the work of Proust, of Joyce, of Virginia Woolf. But there is no real likeness; what these writers shared was an imaginative sense of the varying levels of consciousness in human beings rather than a common technique. In *Pilgrimage* everything experienced is related to, and transmuted by, the consciousness of Miriam Henderson. Miriam, and Miriam only, is the medium of communication, and what she communicates is made up almost entirely of adventures of the mind and the less spectacular emotions. In an enthusiastic critical essay on Dorothy Richardson published in 1931 John Cowper Powys* declared: "No other writer, as far as I know, in any country or in any age, has deliberately undertaken to represent the peculiar feminine reaction to life, not only in humour and sentiment but in what might be called cosmic apprehension".

June 18, 1957.

Sir Owen Richardson, F.R.S., who died at his home in Hampshire on February 15, 1959, was Director of Research in Physics at King's College London for 20 years, and the winner of the Nobel Prize for Physics in 1928. He was 79.

He will be remembered for his discovery of the fundamental physical law governing the motion of electrons from hot bodies—before his death it had already been labelled the Richardson Law—which is the basis of the action of the wireless valve, on which wireless telephony and broadcasting depends.

He was perhaps the most modest and self-effacing of all his scientific colleagues who made their mark in the first half of this century for their contribution to physical knowledge. To none but his own immediate circle was he personally known, and to the wider world he was scarcely a name. But to his intimates he endeared himself for the warmth of his affection, freely given, and his generous help to all those who pursued knowledge.

Owen Willans Richardson was born on April 26, 1879, at Dewsbury, Yorkshire, into a family of middle-class industrialists, and at an early age began to show his scientific inclinations and qualities. Much encouraged by his father, Joshua Henry Richardson, he won, while a pupil at the day school of St. John's Church, Dewsbury Moor, a scholarship to the ancient foundation, Batley Grammar School, near by. He did remarkably well in physics and chemistry, and was awarded a scholarship to Trinity College, Cambridge. There he was awarded a fellowship in 1902. At the age of 27, and while still enjoying his Cambridge fellowship, he was elected Professor of Physics at Princeton University.

By the time he left the United States eight years later to take the Wheatstone chair at King's College London, he had already become recognized on both sides of the Atlantic as one of the band of physicists who were busily engaged in laying the foundations of atomic physics. A tremendously hard worker, with little interest beyond his laboratories, Richardson was destined to spend the greater part of his academic career in King's College. For 10 years he occupied his university chair, until in 1924 he was appointed Yarrow Research Professor of the Royal Society, and director of research at the college, upon which he was relieved entirely of teaching and lecturing.

It was quickly seen that the investigations which he had started in his early twenties, continued and perfected, had formulated and verified the laws underlying the evaporation of electricity from heated metallic filaments, and helped to produce the basis of the design of the filament of the modern hard thermionic valve which revolutionized radio communication, and led to his later discoveries in soft X-rays and electrons. It was while Richardson was at the height of his work at King's College, and still a relatively young man, that in 1928 he was awarded the Nobel Prize for Physics. He was a Fellow of the Royal Society, an Honorary Fellow of King's College, an Hon. LL.D. of St. Andrews and London, an Hon. D.Sc. of Leeds and, since 1941, an Honorary Fellow of Trinity College, Cambridge.

When he resigned his Yarrow chair and his directorship of research at King's in 1944 he was made emeritus professor in the University of London. In 1926-28 he was president of the Physical Society and was for many years its honorary foreign secretary, and he was a corresponding member of several foreign academies. In 1932 he returned to the United States as Silliman Memorial Lecturer at Yale.

Richardson's contributions to physical science were confirmed and enriched by his publications. In 1914 appeared his *Electron Theory of Matter,* two years later his famous *Emission of Electricity from Hot Bodies,* and in 1933 his *Molecular Hydrogen and its Spectrum;* he also wrote many articles on theoretical and experimental physics particularly connected with electrons. Although he retired from university life in 1944 at the age of 65, he worked just as hard, indeed possibly harder, in the quietude of his home near Alton, in Hampshire.

Richardson, who was knighted in 1939, was first married in 1906 to Lillian Maud Wilson, sister of his friend and former colleague, Harold Albert Wilson, Professor of Physics at the Rice Institute, United States. By her he had two sons and one daughter. She died in 1945, and he married secondly in 1948 Henrietta Maria Rupp, of Hampstead. His elder son is now Professor of Physics at Bedford College, London.

[A tribute on February 21, 1959, covered interests of Sir Owen Richardson outside the pursuit of physics.]

February 16, 1959.

Philip Ridgeway, well known as a theatrical producer, broadcaster, and radio entertainment producer, died in hospital in London on October 27, 1954, a week before his sixty-third birthday.

The son of Edward Bower, managing director of the Leaf Tobacco Company, he was born in London on November 3, 1891. His mother was formerly Miss Minnie Valentine, a well-known coloratura soprano. He began his stage career, while still a boy, at Miss Horniman's Repertory Theatre. After touring the provinces and gaining experience in many roles, principally as juvenile lead in plays and musical comedies, and also in pantomime, he became an actor-manager in his early twenties. His first production was *Jane Clegg,* by St. John Ervine*, in which he played the part of Henry Clegg.

For a time he had studied for the Bar, being a student of the Inner Temple, and during the 1914-18 War he joined the Duke of Lancaster's Yeomanry and later saw service with a cavalry regiment. In 1918 he decided to stand for Parliament, but the stage called him more strongly than did politics, and in 1925 he opened the Barnes Theatre, where he produced all the plays of Chekhov, and Hardy's *The Mayor of Casterbridge.* Among those actors whom he was the first to "discover" were Claude Rains* and Charles Laughton*.

He was also concerned with many West End productions and Sir John Gielgud and Ivor Novello [q.v.] were among those he presented there. For a while he was connected with the Fortune Theatre, and in 1927 he brought back to the stage Lily Elsie* in *The Blue Train* at the Prince of Wales's Theatre, a production in which Bobby Howes* had his first major West End role.

In 1929 he left the Fortune Theatre for Savoy Hill, to broadcast light entertainment for the B.B.C. There he wrote, sang, composed, produced, and acted in his own entertainments, which were at first Victorian plays with music, then period vaudeville, and finally the series known as "The Ridgeway Parade". This show, which had a great success and became very popular, toured the country for some 10 years.

During the 1939-45 War Ridgeway revived the "Farjeon Revues" and then, at the suggestion of Sir Stafford Cripps [q.v.], he went to the Ministry of Aircraft Production, as the industrial knowledge which he had gained in earlier days was of value to the national interest. After the war he concerned himself with the diamond tool industry, and only recently he decided to return to his greatest interest—the stage—by providing, for many social functions, the "Ridgeway Cabaret".

He married Miss Doris Nathan, who survives him together with two sons and a daughter.

October 28, 1954.

A colourful and interesting personality has gone from the scientific world with the death on October 24, 1956 at 100 of **H. N. Ridley,** C.M.G., F.L.S., F.R.S., who formed a link with the period when the pursuit of natural knowledge was regarded as more or less its own reward.

Henry Nicholas Ridley was born on December 10, 1855, at Bishopstone, in Herefordshire, and had already developed an interest in entomology and particularly the *Coleoptera* while still a schoolboy at Haileybury. After he had graduated from Oxford, Ridley was appointed to the staff of the British Museum, where he took up a post in the botanical department under Carruthers at the time of the move to South Kensington. There he received the munificent salary of £100 a year, but after eight years his chance came when he was selected at the age of 33 to fill the directorship of the botanical gardens in the Straits Settlements, a position which he occupied for 23 years. The rich flora and fauna of the Malay Peninsula and the opportunities for exploration of unknown country appealed alike to his wide interests and adventurous spirit, and he rapidly amassed an extensive knowledge of the country and its products.

Ridley, more than anyone, was responsible for the successful establishment of the rubber plantation industry in Malaya from the plants of *Hevea brasiliense* sent out from the Royal Botanic Gardens, Kew. For his share in this he was awarded the Rubber Plantation Association's gold medal in 1914, while his achievements in plant introduction with this and other species were recognized by the American award of the Frank Meyer Medal in 1928.

Ridley published extensively, but his best known works are his *Flora of the Malay Peninsula* and his *Dispersal of Plants Throughout the World.* If his taxonomic descriptions sometimes lacked critical discrimination, it was perhaps due to his knowing his plants rather as one knows one's friends, as personalities more than as police descriptions.

On his retirement from Singapore in 1911 he was appointed C.M.G. and went to live at Kew. Thereafter his short, stout figure and vivacious face were familiar features at meetings of the Linnean Society, the discussions at which were enlivened from his well-filled mind and wide experience. The society awarded him the Linnean Medal in 1950.

He was an entertaining conversationist never tired of recounting his travels and adventures and fully conscious of the story-teller's art. Until the later years of his life Ridley worked in the Herbarium at Kew, indeed descriptions of new species by him were published in his ninety-first year, and he was also a frequent visitor to the gardens, where he carried on his hobby of bird watching.

He was elected to the Royal Society in 1907 and served on the Council of the Linnean Society.

October 25, 1956.

Mary Roberts Rinehart, the American novelist and writer of mystery tales, died at her home in New York, on September 22, 1958 at the age of 82. She was perhaps first of the "had I but known" school of crime writers.

In her book of reminiscences, *My Story,* she described how her first attempts at writing "happened" almost by accident. She was born at Pittsburgh in August 1876, and was educated at high schools there, and then attended a training college for nurses where she completed her course and qualified for the nursing profession well before she was 20. After some years in practice she married a surgeon, Stanley Marshall Rinehart, by whom she had three sons.

They lived a happy, intelligent family life while he followed his profession. Subsequently she found herself involved in difficulties through illness and her responsibilities to her family. It was then she made her first venture with a short story. It was immediately accepted and she followed it with a regular flow from her imaginative mind and pen and soon many magazines were clamouring for her work.

Her first novel appeared in 1908, *The Circular Staircase,* and this was followed by one more each year till 1911, when she brought out as many as four. Among the best known of her books are *"K", The Breaking Point, Tish, The Book of Tish, Tish Marches On, The Man in Lower Ten, The Yellow Room, This Strange Adventure,* and *Familiar Faces.* She wrote with skilful manipulation of plot, characters, and situation and her output was large; when she died she had 65 titles to her credit.

The Circular Staircase, of which over 1,250,000 copies were sold, was rewritten as a play, *The Bat,* by Avery Hopwood and herself, and it was estimated that it had been performed in seven languages and seen by 10 million people. It was put on at the Embassy Theatre in London in 1937 with a cast that included Ivan Brandt, Michael Redgrave, Max Adrian*, and Heron Carvic.

She wrote several other plays including *Double Life, The Avenger* (with her husband); and *Seven Days* and *Spanish Love* (both in collaboration with Avery Hopwood).

She went to Europe twice in the First World War, on one occasion as the accredited representative of the Secretary for War. She was as intrepid as she was imaginative, and for a woman who was not a professional journalist she got as near to the front as any of the regular war correspondents, and sometimes nearer. She was presented to Queen Mary [q.v.] and interviewed King Albert and Queen Elisabeth of the Belgians* and many other political and military leaders, publishing the results of her observations in a book, *Kings, Queens and Pawns.*

She held a strong brief "for the English at home, restrained, earnest, determined, unassuming; for the English in the field, equally all of these things".

Her husband died in 1932.

September 24, 1958.

Dr. Hubert Ripka, who died in a London hospital on January 7, 1958, at the age of 62, was a former Czechoslovak Minister of Foreign Trade. He led the 12 non-Marxist Ministers who, in February 1948, resigned from Klement Gottwald's [q.v.] four-party administration and thus precipitated the communist coup in Prague.

He was born in 1895, and after graduating in history at Prague University was appointed lecturer in the history of international politics. For some years he combined university work with journalism, and he edited with distinction the *Lidové Noviny,* a Prague daily newspaper. Like Edvard Beneš, he belonged to the National Socialist Party which, when the name had acquired Hitlerite associations, was later changed to the Czechoslovak Socialist Party; but, again like his leader, he concerned himself chiefly with international affairs. He believed that Hitler had always meant to assail Bohemia, and his leading articles from the remilitarization of the Rhineland to the fateful meeting in Munich were models of lucidity and firm warning. He was, moreover, an accessible editor, and few foreign journalists considered their mission in Prague to be complete until they had a long talk with him.

After Hitler's march into Prague, Ripka succeeded in joining Beneš in Paris, where he began to organize propaganda. Next year he made a difficult escape from France, and by the time he reached London he was already chosen to be State Secretary for Foreign Affairs. He was thus deputy to Jan Masaryk, who made long and frequent visits to Washington. His training was Czech and French, and in the summer of 1940 he knew no English. Yet he was to become an effective speaker in London and in Oxford, where his wife, a gifted Frenchwoman, made a most hospitable home.

He gave admiring support to Sir David Ross*, who as Vice-Chancellor arranged that Oxford University should grant full facilities to the exiled students of Prague, Brno, and Bratislava. A love for the English way of life grew upon him, and he became one of the most Anglophil of Beneš's colleagues. Beneš liked his independence of mind and breadth of views and hoped, it was believed in wartime London, that he would be his eventual successor as President of the Republic.

Though Ripka had long argued that a close alliance with Russia was inevitable and could be fruitful, he did not like the way in which he and his colleagues were received in Moscow after their departure from London. His new post as Minister of Foreign Trade enabled him to see how Moscow discouraged the opening of new channels of trade with the West. Like Jan Masaryk, he urged his colleagues to accept the Marshall [q.v.] offer in the summer of 1947. Within two days he and other offending Ministers were summoned to Moscow by Molotov and ordered to reject the offer.

A day of decision was fast approaching, but at Christmas Ripka announced that he would seek new trade with Britain.

When he saw that Gottwald planned to use the trade unions as a lever for full-scale communism, he urged his non-Marxist colleagues to resign with him and thus make it possible for Beneš to appeal to the Assembly, where the communists did not hold a clear majority of seats. He was reckoning without Zorin, the Soviet Vice-Commissar for Foreign Affairs, who hurried to Prague. Zorin arranged with its chairman that the Assembly should not meet unitl Beneš, already a sick man, had accepted the people's revolution. For a second time Ripka was a fugitive from his own country.

His escape from his native country was one of the most exciting episodes in his long and remarkable political career and he himself used to refer to it as almost a miracle.

When the news of Jan Masaryk's tragic death became known the French Government offered to send a special aircraft to fetch Ripka and two other of President Beneš's closest associates, namely, Szramek, wartime Czech Premier in London, and Hala, Minister of Posts. The French plane was to land at a disused airfield at Rakovnik, near Prague, where all three were to be waiting. But on arrival there the French pilot saw that the airfield had already been ploughed up. He therefore began to circle hoping to find an alternative landing place. Thinking that the aircraft was in trouble, the local peasants notified the police, who arrived in force and arrested Ripka's two would-be co-passengers, who later died in a concentration camp. But Ripka himself, being younger and more agile, managed to escape into some woods near by and was hidden by the peasants until he was able to make another attempt to escape; this time he was successful and reached France.

Incidentally, it was the first failure that brought home to Ripka's wife and family their danger, and they made their escape even before he himself was out of the country.

Ripka, who leaves a widow and two sons, was the author of *Munich: Before and After* and *Czechoslovakia Enslaved.*

January 8, 1958.

Arthur Riscoe, who died early on August 6, 1954 at his home in London at the age of 57 after a heart attack, attained a wide and lasting popularity as an actor in light comedy.

The son of J. A. Boorman, he assumed the name of Riscoe early in his career. Born on November 19, 1896, at Sherburn-in-Elmet, Yorkshire, he was educated at Sherburn Grammar School and Leeds Modern School. After leaving school he was first apprenticed to an engineering firm, but at the age of 15 he went to Tasmania and worked there on a farm for some years until in the summer of 1914 he found himself in New South Wales, where he was engaged by a concert party then appearing at Bondi Junction. Soon after his eighteenth birthday he joined the Australian Imperial Forces, was commissioned, and awarded the M.C.

On demobilization he began to look for work on the stage and was lucky enough before 1919 was out to be engaged by a touring company to play Norman in *The Lilac Domino.* He first appeared in London as Rifleman Jenks in *French Leave* in 1920, but though he made some mark then he had to do a deal of touring in the 10 years or so that followed before he could be said to have established himself in the West End. His greatest success was as Jack Crawford in *Jack and Jill,* which opened at the Alhambra, Glasgow, in December 1933. When the play went to the Saville, London, in the ensuing year it was renamed *Jill Darling* and owed much of its attraction to Riscoe's acting.

Technically accomplished, experienced, and with a fine presence and voice, he was thenceforward very much in demand. Though he never attained quite the public reputation his gifts deserved, he was popular in the profession not only because he had learned his work thoroughly and could be relied upon but also because in the presence of his generous nature petty jealousies melted away.

He had acted for the cinema since 1932 and his last engagement was with a touring company playing *And So To Bed* in spring 1954.

August 7, 1954.

Captain Henry Peel Ritchie, V.C., who was awarded the Victoria Cross for conspicuous bravery in the course of the operations at Dar-es-Salaam, East Africa, in November 1914, died on December 9, 1958 at the age of 82.

Born in January 1876, Henry Peel Ritchie was the son of Dr. R. Peel Ritchie, M.D. Not long after the outbreak of war in 1914 he was second in command of H.M.S. Goliath, which was employed on the east coast of Africa in support of those cruisers which were engaged in rounding up the German warship Königsberg. After that had been done, Ritchie was given the independent command of the armed auxiliary vessel Duplex, and went to Dar-es-Salaam with a view to destroying as many as possible of the enemy vessels that might be found there. A number of craft had been operating from the port, keeping the Königsberg supplied, and it seemed probable they were being used for taking provisions down the coast to her, now she was barricaded in the reaches of the Rufigi.

Ritchie realized that it would be quite impossible for the Duplex, by reason of her size, to enter the harbour and examine the adjoining creeks. He therefore armed a small steamboat with a Maxim gun, and having protected the sides of the boat with such material as he could find, he sailed into Dar-es-Salaam Harbour with the support of two tiny boats.

Ritchie and his men were allowed to steam around the harbour without interruption and proceeded to sink or damage irreparably every vessel or craft afloat; not a single shot was fired by the enemy, who, as was obvious a little later, must have been watching what was going on.

Ritchie, suspecting a trap, refused to take any chances. After he had made a thorough investigation of the main creek which ran into the harbour, he took over two steel lighters and lashed one on each side of his steamboat. Having lashed the lighters fast, he then began to back slowly down the creek into the harbour.

When this strange looking craft got into the open, the enemy, who had held back their fire for so long, began to rain projectiles on the British boat from all directions. Fire was poured from field-guns, machine guns, and rifles, and the little boat found shells and bullets coming from houses, huts, the wooded groves and hills above the town, and even from the direction of the cemetery.

Inadequate though the protection provided by the lighters was, it is certain that had it not been for Ritchie's foresight in utilizing them in that manner, none aboard the British pinnace would have been left alive. As it was many of the crew were severely wounded.

One of the first to be hit by the enemy fire was Ritchie himself, though the wound was not severe enough to make him relinquish command of the operations. Shortly afterwards Petty Officer Clark and Able Seaman Upton, who were at the wheel, were so severely wounded that they could not continue with their duties. From that point Ritchie took the wheel himself until on being hit for the eighth time he was knocked out.

But the boat struggled on and it was not until she had reached the mouth of the harbour that Ritchie, who had managed to take the wheel again, finally collapsed unconscious through loss of blood. Then Petty Officer Clark, having been roughly bandaged, took the wheel once more, and steered the boat to safety in the open sea.

In spite of the number of his wounds, after spending six weeks in Zanzibar Hospital he quickly regained his fitness, and by May 1915 he was back on duty.

For the gallant part they had played in the exploit, Petty Officer Thomas James Clark and Able Seaman George Edward Upton were decorated, the former with the Conspicuous Gallantry Medal, and the latter with the Distinguished Service Medal.

Ritchie married Christiana Lillias Jardine, only daughter of James A. Aikman, of Edinburgh, and had two daughters.

December 12, 1958.

Lord Riverdale, G.B.E., LL.D., the well-known industrialist, died at his home near Sheffield on July 7, 1957 at the age of 84.

In the course of many active years he rendered a number of important public services. As Sir Arthur Balfour he was chairman of the Government Committee on Industry and Trade, which was constituted in 1924 and made a series of reports which formed a valuable guide to the broad fields they covered. The committee also tendered advice which time and bitter experience were amply to vindicate. In addition to a knowledge of the practical aspects of the steel industry he had, through close study and wide travel, acquired a thorough understanding of the industrial organization of the country in its relation to the world at large. Fortified by this wide experience, and by his inherent common sense, his judgment was over and over again to prove of the highest value.

The Rt. Hon. Arthur Balfour, first Baron Riverdale, of Sheffield, and first baronet, was born in London in 1873 and educated at Ashville College, Harrogate. He began life as an office boy in Sheffield, and after four years went to the United States, where he obtained his early business training. In 1896 he returned to Sheffield.

In 1899 he married Frances Josephine Keighley, daughter of C. H. Bingham. After his wedding he made a tour of the world with her, visited the oversea branches of Arthur Balfour and Co. Ltd., and opened new ones. In the same year he was appointed Vice-Consul for Denmark at Sheffield. In 1911, when managing director of Messrs. Seebohm and Deckstahls Steel Works, he was elected Master Cutler. In 1913 he was appointed a member of the royal commission on railways, the first of his many public services.

After the outbreak of war in 1914 he became a member of the Advisory Committee on War Munitions, the Industrial Advisory Committee to the Treasury, and, later, the Advisory Council for Scientific and Industrial Research, the Engineering Industries Committee, and Lord Balfour's Committee on Commercial and Industrial Policy.

In 1919 he was elected president of the Sheffield Chamber of Commerce, and four years later of the Association of British Chambers of Commerce. In the three difficult years after the Armistice the Government made frequent use of his services on commissions and committees on economic and industrial problems. In 1922 he went to America and made an exhaustive study of the economic outlook. In 1923 he was a Government delegate to the International Conference on Customs and was made a member of the Board of Trade Advisory Council. In the same year he was created a K.B.E.

In 1924 he was appointed chairman of the Government Committee on Industry and Trade. The final report, which appeared in 1929, was in nine sections. The most important of them dealt with the means of production, conditions of employment, and other factors in relation to competitive power, taxation, and British Customs policy. It called attention to and warned against commercial barriers and economic nationalism. It held that full employment in the exporting industries could be approached only if there were a substantial increase in the export of capital, and that the only real cure for unemployment was the expansion of production and trade. It concluded generally that the first step towards putting British industries in a position to compete successfully in oversea markets should be a thorough process of reconditioning.

While the committee were still sitting he had continued to assist the Government as leading British delegate to the Consultative Committee of the Economic Conference at Geneva. In 1929 he was created a baronet. In 1930 he became a member of the Economic Advisory Council of the Cabinet, of the Advisory Council of the Department of Overseas Trade, and of the Imperial Economic Committee. In 1931 he was chairman of the United Kingdom Trade Mission to Egypt, and of the Budget Committee of the International Chamber of Commerce, of which body he had been appointed a vice-president in 1928.

In 1935 he was raised to the peerage, and in the same year was appointed chairman of the Committee on Fire Brigades. In 1937 he became chairman of the Advisory Committee of the Privy Council for Scientific and Economic Research, and later of the British Air Mission to Canada.

He had been appointed vice-chairman of the

British Council in 1935, and was president from 1947 to 1950.

He was chairman of Arthur Balfour and Co., Ltd., of Sheffield, and of High Speed Alloys Ltd., of Widnes, and sat on other boards. Politically he was a Conservative. A constant traveller, with a wide knowledge of the Continent, he received a number of foreign Orders.

Lord Riverdale had two sons and three daughters. His elder son, the Hon. Robert Arthur Balfour, who succeeds to the title is managing director of Arthur Balfour and Co., Ltd. He was born in 1901.

July 8, 1957.

Sir Hugh Roberton, founder of the Glasgow Orpheus Choir, and its conductor for 45 years, died on October 7, 1952 in Glasgow, aged 78.

He had an undertaker's business in Glasgow when he began to occupy himself with music. He started the choir in a hall in Glasgow in 1906, and discovered in himself a genius for such work, since he evoked from his fingers the feeling for the natural expression of every song. He arranged for choral voices traditional songs, particularly those of Scotland, and, though the choir sang many kinds of music, its repertory and its style were based primarily on national melody. The choir was built up by him until it became known in Britain, Canada, and the United States.

London heard the "Orpheus" in 1921 and was conquered immediately. For many years the choir paid regular visits to the city, and each time the tickets were sold out weeks before the event. In 1928 the choir performed before King George V and Queen Mary. Because of his pacifist views a ban was imposed upon Roberton and his choir by the B.B.C. at the end of 1940, but after the matter had been discussed in Parliament the choir was once more allowed to broadcast, Winston Churchill* remarking, in a statement in the House of Commons, that he did not see why being pacifist should make a man play flat. In 1951, on the retirement of its founder, the choir was disbanded. He felt that he was no longer able to give it the energetic leadership that it needed to maintain its high reputation. A concourse of 80 choirs from all parts of the country assembled to pay tribute to him at the Festival Hall, and a fund to mark his contribution to music was opened, the money from which he proposed to hand to various musical organizations.

Roberton was a man of an agile mind, a facile pen, and a caustic tongue; gifts which can be dangerous when turned in the direction of impulsive politics. Music saved him from a possible misdirection of his energies. He threw himself whole-heartedly not only into teaching his choir and composing and arranging for it, but into successful lecturing and judging at competitive festivals all over the country. In these activities he exerted a powerful and salutary influence on his generation, and in acknowledgment of his influence on popular music-making he was knighted in 1931.

He was twice married, and had seven sons and two daughters.

October 8, 1952.

E. N. Roberts—See **Newman.**

Kenneth Roberts, the American historical novelist, died at his home at Kennebunkport, Maine, on July 21, 1957.

Kenneth Roberts stepped into the front rank of best-sellers in the United States with his novel *Rabble in Arms,* published in 1933. He had served a relatively hard apprenticeship to that feat of good fortune, an apprenticeship in journalism, in authorship, and in assiduous historical research. *Rabble in Arms* was his tenth book. It was written while he was a staff correspondent of the *Saturday Evening Post* (a position he had held since 1919 and continued to hold until 1937) and it made use of material that he had begun to broach to less satisfactory purpose in a novel published three years earlier. Its strictly literary merits apart—and these were, for American readers, of a truly popular order—the book was helped to success by two special circumstances. In the first place the author reaped the reward of his daring in making an authentic hero of Benedict Arnold, whom the American equivalent of Macaulay's schoolboy had until then recognized as the most infamous figure in American history. Secondly, this was the hour of the epic strain in popular American fiction, and *Rabble in Arms* both followed and stimulated a fashion born of the dawning American consciousness of American destiny. Its author, at any rate, never looked back after that first dizzy success.

Kenneth Lewis Roberts was born in Kennebunk, Maine, on December 8, 1885, the son of Frank Lewis Roberts and Grace Mary Tibbets. He took his degree at Cornell University in 1908 and promptly embarked upon a journalistic career. He had a spell of reporting, ran a humorous column in the *Boston Post* from 1909 until 1917, was also on the editorial staff of *Life* during 1915-18, and then, after serving as a captain in the intelligence section of the United States expeditionary force in Siberia, was appointed to the *Saturday Evening Post* and travelled extensively.

His early books are collections or articles written in the course of such travels. *Europe's Morning After* (1921) and *Why Europe Leaves Home* (1922) are both good journalism, vigorous and graphic in transatlantic style, if also a little tiresomely facetious now and then, and full of instruction. The latter volume, in particular, is notable for its shrewdly humane and practical temper. Books on New England and Florida among other subjects followed, and then Roberts set himself a more rewarding task and began to collect material for a novel on Benedict Arnold and his descent upon Quebec.

Arundel: A Chronicle of the Province of Maine and of the Secret Expedition Against Quebec was published in 1930. It bore evidence of considerable research and showed conspicuous skill in the handling of the background colour: the mode of life of the various New England settlements and the relations between the colonists and the Indians were described in vivid detail. But Roberts saddled himself with a mechanical plot and a pedestrian style of narrative and much of the merit of his work was dissipated in consequence.

The Lively Lady (1931), his next novel, made even less impression, but two years later he published *Rabble in Arms* (the phrase was Burgoyne's) and Benedict Arnold's defection to the English cause now shone with the light of an exalted if also perverted patriotism.

Four years later still came *Northwest Passage,* set in the period just before the American Revolution and with an indomitable, swaggering schemer and dreamer for hero; this also was a prodigious success and like others of his novels was made into a film. The narrative style in this novel, as indeed in all the author's novels, was inclined to be conventional and somewhat lifeless, but the first part in particular, recounting an expedition against a French settlement, was otherwise spirited enough.

Roberts continued to exploit the vein he had so handsomely opened up, and *Oliver Wiswell* (1940), another enormously long tale of the Revolution, not only had a loyalist for hero but also scourged the rabble-rousers with whips and scorpions. *Lydia Bailey* (1946), a sprawling picaresque novel with a mixed historical theme, was less expertly done than the earlier books. *Captain Caution,* a modern account of the war of 1812, appeared in Great Britain in 1949, and *Boon Island* in 1956.

July 22, 1957.

Sir George Robey, C.B.E., the comedian, died on November 29, 1954 at his home at Saltdean, Sussex. He was 85 and had been in poor health for some time.

His real name was George Edward Wade, and he was born on September 20, 1869, at Herne Hill, the son of a civil engineer. He recorded in his autobiography, *Looking Back on Life,* that he was educated privately in London and Dresden and was for a short time at Cambridge, until some of his father's speculations went wrong and "the undergraduate dream had to be dropped". His connexion with the university must, however, have been tenuous, for his name is not to be found in Venn's *Alumni.* He made his first appearance in 1891 at the Aquarium Theatre. His first regular music-hall engagement was at the Oxford, on June 15 of the same year.

George Robey belonged to the greatest period of the music-hall. He could not compare in delicacy and subtlety with Dan Leno or with Albert Chevalier in characterization. Nor was his art so closely based on life as that of the elder George Formby. Nevertheless, Robey was a comedian of genius, who had, in addition, that robust quality of character which in the end made him a national figure. His attack and gusto, and his gift of gesture, were superb. From the first moment that he came on the stage, running trippingly to the centre and holding a short cane in both hands, there was no doubt of his absolute power over his audience. It was a constant joy to see him lift those heavily blacked eyebrows in pained surprise when the audience would insist on taking some remark of his in its less innocent interpretation, or raise a solemn hand to bid them "desist from this unseemly merriment". There was a glorious impudence about his bearing at such moments that was far funnier than anything he said; and the "honest vulgarity" of which he was so proud was in truth not always palatable—though a suggestion of jovial roguery, hidden behind his air of unctuous solemnity, was no doubt essential to his humour.

The effectiveness of Robey's turn was greatly assisted by the costume he adopted—the long, collarless frock-coat, buttoned up to the neck, and the little, semi-clerical bowler-hat that looked like a saucepan lid. In this rig-out Robey had a fascinating air as of a genial Stiggins, and he always sang the first song in his turn so dressed. Of those songs one remembers "I Live Underneath", "Archibald, Certainly Not!" "What was There was Good", "Tempt Me Not!" and—perhaps best of all—"In Other Words", one of the songs with which he delighted audiences in *The Bing Boys* during the 1914-18 War.

Robey also sang, upon the music-halls, a number of songs, with patter, dressed in character—"The Prehistoric Man", "The Mayor of Mudcumdyke", "Robin Hood", and so on. Funny as the best of these were, they never seemed quite the essential Robey. Yet his character portraits certainly included one of the most brilliant of all his sketches, that of the delightful old German musician who was surrounded with instruments of all sorts, which he was always just going to play, though in the end he never played anything more difficult than the triangle. In describing Robey's performance, moreover, one must not forget his voice, with its slightly hoarse resonance and sub-cockney accent, and his wonderfully clear diction, which, whether in song or in patter, made every word carry to the farthest corner of the hall.

In revue Robey's greatest successes were in *The Bing Boys Are Here* at the Alhambra in 1916 (his first appearance in this kind of entertainment) and in *Zig-Zag* at the Hippodrome in 1917. In the first of these his artful solemnity was ideally contrasted with the dismal innocence of Alfred Lester, and he showed an unexpected talent by joining Violet Loraine [q.v.] in singing what proved to be the most popular sentimental song of the First World War, "If You were the Only Girl in the World, and I were the Only Boy". Robey also appeared in such operettas as *Helen,* at the Adelphi in 1932, and *Jolly Roger,* at the Savoy in 1933. He played, too, in a number of films, including those of *Chu-Chin-Chow* and *Don Quixote,* in the latter of which he was Sancho Panza to the Don Quixote of Chaliapin.

He made a solitary stage appearance in Shakespeare, taking the part of Falstaff in *Henry IV (Part I)* at His Majesty's Theatre in 1935, an experiment of which *The Times* Dramatic Critic wrote that it was "A very odd and, in flashes of silence, a most diverting performance, but not, it must be confessed, a comfortable one". In the colour film of *Henry V* he played a short scene depicting the death of Falstaff, an interpolation entirely justified by the affecting nature of his performance. In his later years Robey was heard a good many times on the wireless, but (at least to those who knew him as a master of the music-hall) he never seemed to do himself justice in that medium.

The fact was that he depended upon facial expression and gesture. What he said was seldom very witty (and sometimes not funny at all) when divorced from what he did and how he looked. Some of his most ludicrous performances were those in which pure miming had a predominant share—as in the unforgettable revue scene (also played on the Continent by Morton) in which Robey was a country cousin who had taken a box at the Savoy Theatre under the impression that it was a bedroom at the Savoy Hotel.

In January 1939, while acting in pantomime at Birmingham, he met with a serious accident. He recovered completely, however, and even in his eighties the "Prime Minister of Mirth", (as he was described on music-hall programmes) continued to make occasional appearances. In 1952 there was a brief glimpse of him as Old Weller in the film of *Pickwick Papers.*

His hobbies included football, cricket, and the making of violins. At one time he was often to be seen practising at the nets at Lord's. He also wrote a number of short stories and was something of an amateur draughtsman.

George Robey was one of the artists selected to appear at the first Variety Command Performance before King George V and Queen Mary in 1912, and was a great success. He raised large sums of money for wartime charities, and was made a C.B.E. in 1919. Early in 1954 he was knighted.

He married first, in 1898, Miss Ethel Haydon. The marriage was dissolved in 1938. He married, secondly, Miss Blanche Littler, who survives him. A son by the first marriage is E. G. Robey, who served for many years as a barrister in the office of the Director of Public Prosecutions and is now a Metropolitan magistrate.

November 30, 1954.

Elizabeth Robins, who died on May 8, 1952 at Brighton, attained success both on the stage and in literature.

She will be remembered by an older generation of playgoers principally for her interpretation of Ibsen, and by a younger and perhaps wider generation of readers for a series of admirable novels. To her accomplishments were added beauty and social charm that drew to her orbit many friends famous in their day and since, and Henry James's Letters to her were published in volume form in 1932.

Elizabeth Robins was born at Louisville, Kentucky, the daughter of Charles E. Robins. She made her first appearance on the stage in 1885 with the famous Boston Museum Stock Company. She was first seen in England as Mrs. Errol in *The Real Little Lord Fauntleroy* in 1889, and her first appearance in an Ibsen play in England was as Martha Bernick in *Pillars of Society* at the old Avenue Theatre in 1890. The previous year Janet Achurch, with her husband, Charles Charrington, had launched Ibsen on a bewildered public with *A Doll's House* at the old Novelty Theatre. In 1891 Elizabeth Robins played Mrs. Linden when the play was revived at Terry's Theatre, and in the same year she made perhaps the greatest success of her stage career as Hedda in *Hedda Gabler,* a performance which won the warm admiration of Bernard Shaw. Her other Ibsen interpretations were Hilda in *The Master Builder* at the Opéra Comique in 1893, Rebecca West in *Rosmersholm,* Agnes in *Brand,* and in 1897 she closed her regular appearance on the stage as Ella Rentheim in *John Gabriel Borkman* at the Strand. Notable among other parts she played was Countess Zicka in a revival of *Diplomacy* at the Garrick in 1894.

Under the name of C. E. Raimond in 1894 she published her first novel, *George Mandeville's Husband,* which was acclaimed by the critics as showing great promise, and during the next two years came *Milly's Story* and *Below the Salt.* The authorship of these stories, written much in the spirit of the age that had heralded Ibsen and the emancipation of women, was the subject of speculation. *The Open Question,* published in 1898, revealed their true authorship and attracted considerable attention, placing Miss Robins high in the ranks of contemporary fiction. Her next novel, *The Magnetic North,* published in 1903, was the result of a journey by the author to the Klondyke during the gold rush. Into the midst of this mob Miss Robins plunged, and her book is full of the trials she endured and the hardships she survived. It remains probably her finest literary work.

Other of her novels are *A Dark Lantern, The Convert,* frankly propagandist for female suffrage, and *Where are You Going To?* which might be described as a burning (and, indeed, much exaggerated) tract for the times on the white slave traffic. A play by her, *Votes for Women,* founded upon her novel *The Convert,* was produced at the Court Theatre in 1907. In 1940 she published a volume of recollections, *Both Sides of the Curtain,* telling of her early years in England; her friendships with Wilde, Tree, Ellen Terry, and many others.

Her husband, George Richmond Parks, died not long after their marriage and before she came to England.

May 9, 1952.

Lord Robinson, chairman of the Forestry Commission since 1932 and, concurrently, Director-General of Forestry from 1945 to 1947, died in Ottawa on September 5, 1952 of pneumonia at the age of 69. He was chairman of the British Commonwealth Forestry Conference now in session in Ottawa and head of the United Kingdom delegation.

The Right Hon. Sir Roy Lister Robinson,

first Baron Robinson, of Kielder Forest, Northumberland, and of Adelaide in the Commonwealth of Australia, in the peerage of the United Kingdom, O.B.E., was born at Perth, Western Australia, on March 8, 1883. He received his early education at St. Peter's College, Adelaide, where he was a State Exhibitioner and Scholar, and later at the School of Mines, Adelaide, and Adelaide University. Going to England as a Rhodes Scholar, he entered Magdalen College, Oxford, where, in 1908, he gained first-class honours in the School of Natural Science, being also made a Burdett Coutts Scholar. Of exceptionally strong physique, he was a member of the Oxford XI in 1908 and 1909 and of the athletic teams from 1907 to 1909, and the lacrosse team from 1906 to 1909.

Robinson began his career as an assistant inspector with the Board of Agriculture and Fisheries in 1909, and was made an inspector in the following year. In 1912 he was promoted to the office of superintending inspector and was serving in this capacity when war broke out in 1914. During the war he was engaged on important work for the Ministries of Munitions and Agriculture, and when it ended was appointed Technical Commissioner to the newly-constituted Forestry Commission, a position he occupied from 1919 to 1932, being also the commission's vice-chairman during the last three years. He then succeeded to the chairmanship and gave such satisfaction that in 1945 he was made Director-General of Forestry.

In December 1931 Robinson had been appointed vice-chairman of a committee "to investigate and submit proposals for improvements in the utilization of home-grown timber", and it was largely on the results of that inquiry that he based his subsequent advocacy for the proper handling of home-grown timber by the timber trade. In 1947, however, he relinquished the post of Director-General, but retained the Chairmanship, of the Forestry Commission and the same year, in recognition of his "outstanding services to British Forestry", he was presented with a gold medal by the Society of Foresters of Great Britain, of which he had been the first president.

In 1910 he married Charlotte Marion, youngest daughter of the late H. C. Bradshaw. His only son was killed in action in 1942, and he is survived by his widow and two daughters of the marriage. The peerage becomes extinct.

September 6, 1952.

F. Mabel Robinson, who died at her home in Paris on June 18, 1954, was over-shadowed as a writer by her elder sister Mary (Mme. Duclaux), but some of her novels published in the eighties and nineties, though now largely forgotten, attracted and deserved attention in their day.

Her father was G. T. Robinson, F.S.A., an architect of taste, especially in connexion with internal decoration, and a man of wide learning and culture, from whom his daughters inherited their literary talent. The Robinsons' houses—first in Gower Street, and later in Earl's Terrace, Kensington—were pleasant meeting places for many members of the literary and artistic society of the time, and the daughters from their earliest years absorbed all that was best in contemporary culture.

Mabel Robinson at first intended to be a painter and studied at the Slade School under Le Gros, but she early abandoned this for literature. Her first book, *Mr. Butler's Ward,* was published in 1885; *Disenchantment* (a realistic study of the demoralization of character by drink) followed in 1886; *The Plan of Campaign* (an Irish story written under the influence of the Home Rule movement, of which the author was an enthusiastic supporter) in 1887; and she wrote several others between that year and 1895, when she published her last novel, *Chimera.*

At that time they were considered somewhat bold in their treatment of life, and their author probably owed not a little of her realism to the influence of the earlier novels of her friend, George Moore. She was a frequent contributor to the *Athenaeum* when under the editorship of Norman Maccoll, and she also wrote an *Irish History for English Readers.*

For many years Mabel Robinson had lived in Paris with her sister, Mme. Duclaux, and except for an occasional translation from the French her name had long passed out of contemporary literature. But a few may still remember her as a girl of singular beauty, and many more as a woman of intelligence, charm, and wit.

June 22, 1954.

Professor H. R. Robinson, F.R.S., Vice-Chancellor of London University from June 1954 until his resignation at the beginning of the month for reasons of health, died suddenly on November 28, 1955 at his home in London, two days after his sixty-sixth birthday.

He had for many years been regarded as outstanding among his contemporaries in physical science, and for his contributions to the study of rays and atomic structures, but in the wider world he was better known for his services to Queen Mary College, and, for a period of great activity, as Vice-Chancellor of London University. His assumption of this latter office came at a time when the great expansionist movement of the post-war years was beginning to bear fruit; the various departments, particularly in the Faculty of Science, were expanding both in the number of students and in the extent of their influence; and the great new buildings in Bloomsbury were beginning to be populated. It was a matter of regret not only to him but to everybody associated with the university that periods of indifferent health during the latter part of his term as Vice-Chancellor necessarily curtailed his activities, and that eventually, upon urgent medical advice, he had at the end of October to tender his resignation shortly before the installation of Queen Elizabeth the Queen Mother in the office of Chancellor.

He had been closely associated with the late Lord Rutherford. His own work on the effect of X-rays in liberating electrons was of great importance in revealing the details of atomic structure, and his election as a Fellow of the Royal Society in 1929 was a due recognition of his stature in this highly specialized branch of physics. In view of his close association with Rutherford, Robinson was chosen to deliver the first Rutherford Memorial Lecture, which was delivered before the Physical Society in 1942.

Harold Roper Robinson was born on November 26, 1889, the eldest son of the late James Robinson, of Ulverston, Lancashire. He was educated at Manchester University and had the good fortune to come directly under Lord Rutherford's influence at the early age of 19. Rutherford quickly appreciated the quality of his pupil and after Robinson had graduated made the flattering offer of collaboration. Their first joint paper, on the heating effect of radium and its products, came out in 1911 and the two men continued to work together until the outbreak of war in 1914, when Robinson was granted a commission in the Royal Artillery. He served in France and in the Near East and used his knowledge of physics to develop methods of sound-ranging. After demobilization he was granted the Moseley research studentship of the Royal Society and, going up to Trinity College, Cambridge, resumed his association with Rutherford's work, which he carried on after the latter's death. He already had the D.Sc. of Manchester University, and Cambridge granted him a Ph.D. During the period between the wars he was successively Reader and Carnegie Teaching Fellow in the University of Edinburgh, Professor of Physics in University College, Cardiff, and finally, in 1930, Professor of Physics in Queen Mary College, University of London, of which he became Vice-Principal in 1946. He resigned both posts in 1953.

Almost from the beginning of his settlement in London Professor Robinson had taken a great interest in the administration of the affairs of the university. He was for some years a member of the Senate before becoming Vice-Chancellor in 1954. Popular alike with his colleagues and with undergraduates, he discharged his duties with an energy and zest which no doubt helped to cause his breakdown in health. He had a manner to everybody which was both courtly and unaffected, and a remarkable gift for inspiring both respect and affection equally. There was not a trace of pomposity in him, yet he commanded instant attention for his judgments, and had a remarkable faculty for reaching the right conclusion out of difficult arguments; and, with all this, his greatest quality perhaps during these latest years was his courage. He skimped none of his arduous duties in spite of the constant threat of serious illness because of his heart trouble; he never made any excuses and time and again, either at formal functions or when engaged on university business, he went on devotedly, and quite uncomplainingly, despite the inevitable strain. It was this quality, as much as anything else, that made his doctor forbid him to go on with the Vice-Chancellorship up to last week's installation.

A collector of old books and a connoisseur of Burgundy, he was as much at home in the company of humanist scholars as with his scientific colleagues. He was always greatly interested in the arts, particularly the theatre and the ballet, was a member of the Governing Body of the Old Vic, and vice-president and an honorary life member of the Vic-Wells Association.

He married first, in 1920, Marjorie Eve, only daughter of the late T. E. Powell, of Marchamley, by whom he had one son and one daughter. She died in 1939 and in the following year he married Madeleine Symons, J.P., who is well known in political circles and as a social worker.

November 29, 1955.

Dr. Lennox Robinson, the Irish playwright, died in Dublin on October 14, 1958, aged 72. He was little more than a youth when, after the turn of the last century, the Abbey Theatre began to disclose the wealth of dramatic talent which existed at that time in Ireland. Fascinated by its work, he devoted himself and his remarkable gifts to it. For some years he was its manager and all his plays were written primarily for its stage.

So young was he when he took his first call as author that he survived most of those whose works had made its fame and, it would appear, the sources of their inspiration. Whether or no the illumination of those early days was due to sparks from the friction between the step-sister islands, Eire has proved herself far poorer in literary genius than the Ireland she succeeded.

Lennox Robinson never attained to the stature of a Synge; but he wrote numbers of admirable plays, most skilfully adapted to the personalities and capacities of the Abbey Company. His stagecraft was of the highest order, his humour racy and abundant. Even for an Irishman his sensibilities were unusually keen. As in the case of most Irish playwrights his dialogue—the fact that conversations at the Dublin street corners tend to assume dramatic form has been no small help to them—was excellent.

Esmé Stuart Lennox Robinson was born at Douglas, co. Cork, in 1886, the youngest child of the late Rev. A. C. Robinson who, first a stockbroker, became at 50 a clergyman of the Church of Ireland. Much of his childhood was spent at Kinsale; but later the family moved to Ballymoney. In *Three Houses* (1938) he tells the story of these years. He was educated at Bandon Grammar School. While still a youth he saw in Cork the Abbey Company perform *Kathleen ni Houlihan* and *The Rising of the Moon.* He was deeply stirred, and thereafter forsook his family's Unionism to follow the gleam of Irish nationalism.

The Abbey Theatre, which in his early manhood was inspiring indeed to such as he, continued to attract him. He began to write for it and his *The Clancy Name,* a powerful little play, was produced there in 1908; his *The Cross Roads* in 1909. From 1910 to 1914 and again from 1919 to 1923 he was manager of the Theatre, and in the last year became a director of it. From 1915 to 1925 he was organizing librarian of the Carnegie Trust, and from 1917 to 1918 served on the staff of the Irish Convention of which his friend, the late Sir Horace Plunkett, was chairman.

The Patriots was staged at the Court Theatre in 1912. It, like its predecessors, was set in the Ireland that he knew. It was a work of fine thought and feeling and was splendidly acted. *The Whiteheaded Boy,* which first appeared in 1916, was played in London in 1920 and again in 1926. It was a sly, demure little comedy, entirely true to life, and one of his best. Again, the company which he knew so well stood by him magnificently. Then came *The Lost Leader,* an interesting attempt in which he presented a Charles Stewart Parnell still living obscurely 25 years after his supposed death and burial. Dramatic though the notion was, the play contained much preaching which did not greatly move either London or Dublin. *The Round Table*—he published it in 1924—proved once and for all that he had acquired the hand of a true craftsman.

In the next 12 years or so Robinson wrote quite a number of plays. *The Big House* was about "the troubles". *Give A Dog* presented the theme that sooner or later genius must play the part of genius. *The Far Off Hills* was loosely bound and fragile. *Ever the Twain* marked the twenty-first year of his career as a dramatist and was his sixteenth play. It was the outcome of a visit to the United States, and the action was in a liner on its way there and in America itself. *All's Over, Then?* was tense and arresting, though of a type with which the traditional acting of the Abbey Company found it hard to cope. In *Drama at Inish* (afterwards he called it *Is Life Worth Living?*) he studied the impact of the Continental "drama of ideas" upon an unsophisticated audience. In it he was more himself, and extremely amusing. *Church Street* was technically a remarkable piece of stagecraft and was once more purely Irish. *When Lovely Woman* he staged for the first time at the Gate Theatre in Dublin rather than, as had theretofore been his invariable practice, at the Abbey. It was somewhat below his usual standard. With *Killicreggs in Twilight* he returned in 1937 to the Abbey for what proved to be his final first-night. His stagecraft was as good as ever.

Robinson wrote several books, including his own biography, *Curtain Up* (1942). In it he interwove the darker and lighter threads of the life he had known in Ireland. His Golden Treasury of Irish Verse (1925)—it was by no means the first anthology of the kind—included some beautiful versions from Gaelic poetry. His *Poems by Thomas Parnell* (1927) was a competent study of that poet; his *Bryan Cooper* (1931) was the life of an Irish landlord who, once a Unionist M.P., threw in his lot with the new régime in Ireland. *I Sometimes Think,* a collection of essays, appeared in 1957.

Lennox Robinson was made an honorary D.Litt. of Trinity College, Dublin, in 1948.

October 15, 1958.

Lord Roche, a Lord of Appeal in Ordinary from 1935 to 1938, who died on December 22, 1956, was, especially when expounding his own subject, commercial law, one of the most efficient judges of his time. Without the fine scholarship and elegant diction that carry the judgments of a Macnaghten, a Sumner, or a Parker into a class by themselves, Roche will be remembered as a learned and conscientious judge, always prompt to make up his mind, and unambiguous in expressing the result arrived at.

Alexander Adair Roche was the son of William Brock Roche, of Seaton, Devon, and was born on July 24, 1871. The family originally came from co. Cork, and Adair Roche's grandfather, John Roche, was a physician, who practised in East Anglia. Roche was educated at Ipswich Grammar School and Wadham College, Oxford, where he was a contemporary of Lord Birkenhead and Lord Simon [q.v.]. Roche took a first class in classical moderations in 1892, and a first class in *Lit. Hum.* in 1894. He was later elected an honorary Fellow of the College.

He was called to the Bar by the Inner Temple in 1896. He was a pupil of Scott-Fox, a leader in the North-Eastern Circuit and later a County Court Judge. As a junior, his practice in the Commercial Court, at the time when the leaders there were Joseph Walton (afterwards a judge), Pickford (afterwards Lord Sterndale), Hamilton (afterwards Lord Sumner), and the future Lord Justice Scrutton, was very large, and when, in 1912, Roche took silk he soon fell into much of the practice of those great advocates, now safely removed from competition to the Bench.

His mind and manner were exactly suited to the litigation of the Commercial Court, which peculiarly demanded the gift of clear expression and the power to master masses of documents and complicated facts. Had he remained but a few years longer at the Bar he would have reaped the rich harvest of the post-war commercial boom, but he was in silk for only five years.

On October 11, 1917, on the nomination of Lord Chancellor Finlay, he was apppointed a judge of the King's Bench Division in succession to the late Mr. Justice Low. He was a believer in press publicity, and once told a grand jury that nowadays intimate matters are discussed in the press and on the stage without any apparent inconvenience or trouble to anyone, and he did not think plain statement did harm, but a great deal of good. A litigant in person was once informed that he was wasting his time and would go crazy if he did not mind, and was advised to go and read *Bleak House.* In 1925 another litigant in person, of a less ingenuous type, was sent to prison by the Divisional Court for eight months for scurrilous abuse of Roche, who had dismissed an action brought by him against the Royal Liver Friendly Society.

In administering the criminal law he was progressive in his outlook, and his sentences were carefully weighed and never unduly severe. The object of criminal law, he remarked to a grand jury, was reform and not to get rid of offenders with great dispatch.

In August 1934 the Court of Appeal suffered

the loss of the veteran Lord Justice Scrutton, and at the beginning of the October Sittings Roche was nominated by the Prime Minister to follow still further in the footsteps of that master of commercial law. He remained there but for one year. The opening of the legal year in 1935 was one of many changes in the higher Judiciary. At the beginning of the preceding Long Vacation Lord Tomlin had died, and in October Lord Hanworth's continued ill-health had necessitated his relinquishment of the Rolls. To fill this office Lord Wright unexpectedly resigned his Lordship of Appeal in Ordinary, and Lord Justice Maugham [q.v.] was promoted to Lord Tomlin's post. Though not the senior Lord Justice from the Common Law side, Roche was nominated to succeed Lord Wright* as a Lord of Appeal and thus to maintain the standard of commercial learning in the final courts of the Empire.

A few weeks after his appointment Lord De Clifford was tried for manslaughter before the House of Lords and it fell to Roche, as the junior Baron, to express his view first among the assembled Peers. Both in the House of Lords and at the Judicial Committee of the Privy Council Roche completely maintained his previous reputation of 18 years on the Bench.

When he accepted the post he stipulated that his tenure of office would not be a long one, and when, in 1937, Lord Wright resigned the Mastership of the Rolls and returned to the House of Lords and the Judicial Committee, Roche considered that the terms of his contract had been fulfilled and that he was entitled to his leisure. So at the beginning of 1938 he retired.

From 1932 for many years he was chairman of Quarter Sessions for Oxfordshire. After his retirement he performed much public work on committees. He was chairman of the Committee on Justices' Clerks in 1934, and for some years he was chairman of the Agricultural Wages Board in succession to the late Lord Ullswater. A good horseman, he hunted regularly well into his later years, and he rode in the Bar Point to Point. He was also an enthusiastic fisherman.

Roche married in 1902 Elfreda, fourth daughter of John Fewick, of Ledbury. She died in 1955. There were two sons and a daughter of the marriage.

December 24, 1956.

Sir Ernest Rock Carling—See **Carling.**

John D. Rockefeller, jnr., died at Tucson, Arizona, on May 11, 1960. He was 86. He was the father of Nelson Rockefeller, Governor of New York.

By his death humanity has lost one of the truest and most practical friends it has ever known. The son of a remarkable father who, having acquired a fabulous fortune, devoted a great portion of it to the benefit of mankind, he applied his own ability and best energies to discovering the wisest and most effective ways of doing good. In him the business gifts which had created the Rockefeller wealth found outlet in no less businesslike efforts to spend it to the utmost advantage.

Rockefeller was an earnest, self-effacing man of strong though tolerant convictions who never spared himself in his self-appointed task. In outlook as in action he was a true humanist; but he was also a cool and clear-headed thinker. His judgment was both sound and steady and the success of his projects was largely due to his own instinct for selecting the right man to execute them. Disliking ostentation or vulgarity of any kind and ever averse from personal advertisement, he maintained an admirable poise both in thought and action. All that he did was done handsomely but with a restraint which invariably preserved the highest standards of good taste. Whether he was ordering the conduct of research, furthering education, or raising immense edifices like those of the Rockefeller centre, the best only was good enough for him; but there was no undue show and no waste of any kind. At Williamsburg, in Virginia, his great restoration scheme was carried out with a conscientiousness and delicacy of feeling which he, as its moving spirit, inspired, and nothing was more typical of him, or indeed of Mrs. Rockefeller, than the fact that his own small house there was no more pretentious than that of any moderately well-off citizen of the eighteenth century.

John Davison Rockefeller, junior, was born at Cleveland, Ohio, on January 29, 1874, the only son of John Davison Rockefeller, the oil magnate and philanthropist. The family came of continental stock and had been poor settlers at Cleveland in its early days. Four years, however, before the birth of his son, the elder Rockefeller had founded the Standard Oil Company and had thus laid the foundations of the vast fortune he was subsequently to create. As a result the boy was brought up in affluent circumstances, but under a firm and almost austere discipline and with the example of his hard-working and simple-living father, to whom he was devoted, continually before him. He was sent to Brown University in Rhode Island, where there was little temptation to self-indulgence or extravagance, and graduated there in 1897. Brought up as a Baptist he was to remain an earnest but open-minded adherent to that creed.

On leaving the university Rockefeller entered the Standard Oil Office and in due course became a member of the directorate. At the time he entered upon his business life his father had withdrawn from active direction of the affairs of his huge corporation. They had long been the subject of contention and of legal investigation, so much so that in 1898 the Standard Oil Trust which was founded in 1881 had taken refuge under the corporation laws of New Jersey as the Standard Oil Company of the state. Nothing, however, seemed to stem the prosperity of the business and as a result of it the huge profits of the Rockefellers continued to pour in.

The Senior Rockefeller had spoken frequently of the "Benevolent Trust" and had meant by it a body of able business men charged with the prudent distribution of great wealth. In 1901 the idea took shape in the first of his great corporations, the Rockefeller Institute of Medical Research. Then in 1907 there came the General Education Board and two years later the first steps were taken to launch the Rockefeller Foundation with a gift of £20m. which was to be increased by the additions of subsequent years. Of this body the younger Rockefeller became president and in 1910 withdrew from the business direction of Standard Oil though as a large shareholder he continued to influence its policies. As a business man he showed an enlightenment which helped greatly to redeem the ill-repute of Standard Oil in its earliest days.

The distributions of the two Rockefellers—the father had handed over a great store of his wealth to the son—amounted to huge figures, and covered an immense range. The professed object of the Rockefeller Foundation is "to promote the well-being of mankind throughout the world" and the evidence of its efforts to realize this aim are to be found all over the globe. In Great Britain University College and its Hospital Medical School, the Universities of Oxford, London, Edinburgh, and Bristol and the London School of Economics have good reason to be grateful to it. France, too, has profited largely. It has conducted a magnificent campaign against disease in the pestilential areas of the world. It has also educated, trained, and endowed in many countries. The United States itself had naturally been a leading beneficiary; but the foundation has known no frontiers and Rockefeller's own interests were as wide as humanity itself. In 1940, on attaining 65, he retired from the chairmanship and from the board of the foundation.

His gifts were fabulous. The painstaking reconstruction of Colonial Williamsburg in Virginia engaged his keen attention for years and his financial support to the total of $60,000,000. He not only gave The Cloisters to the Metropolitan Museum of Art but he provided about 95 per cent of its original contents. So that the beauty of the area should be preserved he brought 11½ miles of the Palisades on the opposite side of the Hudson River to ensure that no neon lights or any form of advertising should spoil the view from Fort Tryon Park, where The Cloisters was built.

In 1952, feeling anxious about the future of The Cloisters, he asked for a report on what could be done with a million dollars. Before the report could be got ready he had raised the sum to two millions and a little later to "five millions, more or less". When the report was ready he wrote out a simple statement giving not $5m. but $10m. "for the enrichment of The Cloisters in the broadest sense of the term, and for the preservation, housing and presentation of its collection".

Nor was that all. Many years before his death he set his mind and heart on getting a fabulous twelfth century Spanish Romanesque apse for The Cloisters. But it turned out that the building was a Spanish national monument. It took him 23 years to buy it, during which period he bought, in America, six medieval Spanish frescoes to give to Spain and also financial aid in the reconstruction of the church near Segovia from which the apse was to be taken. It arrived in New York early in 1958 and now forms a wing of The Cloisters.

At a time when the United Nations was having difficulties in selecting a permanent home he bought the Turtle Bay area on the East River at New York for $8,500,000 and presented it to the world organization as the site for its permanent home. In 1958 New York City decided to raze old buildings near the south-west corner of Central Park and build the Lincoln Centre for the performing arts. Towards that project Rockefeller gave five million dollars. This was by no means his first gift to advance culture in his native city and change its contours and skyline. In addition to the United Nations site, The Cloisters and Lincoln Centre he, of course, built that amazing collection of buildings known as Rockefeller Centre, and he also built low-rent housing in the negro district of Harlem and another such project on the lower east side. He contributed generously to the building of Riverside Church, which dominates the skyline of upper Manhattan on the west side, and he built International House for the accommodation of foreign students visiting New York.

He was a notable collector of art with a special interest in porcelains. When the Morgan collection of Chinese porcelains came on the market he acquired it all for about a million dollars. He gloried in colour and beautiful craftsmanship, hence his purchases of lovely tapestries, 17th century rugs and Kang Hsi porcelains.

His first wife, Abby Green Aldrich, died in 1948 and he married for the second time in 1951, his bride being the widow of one of his classmates at Brown University. Mrs. Martha Baird Allen, a concert pianist.

May 12, 1960.

Sir Alliott Verdon-Roe—See **Verdon-**.

Bruce Rogers, internationally famous as a typographer and one of the most eminent figures in the field of book production, died at Fairfield, Connecticut, on May 18, 1957. He had celebrated his eighty-seventh birthday earlier in the week.

Rogers had far-reaching influence in Britain and in the United States. He held that the responsibility for the appearance of any book, as to design, presswork, and binding, should belong to one man. This belief was novel in the early years of the century; to-day no reputable bookhouse is without its designer. Much of the merit that may be claimed for the printed book in this country is traceable to influence exercised by Rogers and those indebted to his example. His principles were developed from a fusion of the cult of dilettante printing which John Lane and Elkin Mathews had made fashionable in London with the help of Ricketts, Shannon, and others, with the Arts and Crafts movement. His mind was essentially eclectic and empiric. Thus his work was not deliberately medievalist, like Morris's, nor consciously Renaissance like Ricketts's. His admiration of the great printers of the past extended beyond those of the fifteenth and sixteenth centuries.

Bruce Rogers was born on May 14, 1870, at Binnwood, Indiana, son of George Rogers and his wife, Ann E. Gish. He went to the local public school, learnt drawing from his father, and at 16 entered Purdue University, where he studied drawing and decoration, graduating B.S. in 1890. A year's pictorial journalism on the *Indianapolis News* was a false start. In 1892 he was working in a railway office at Parsons, Kansas, and the following year as a general draughtsman for the Indianapolis Illustrating Company; meanwhile he painted landscapes. He had early acquired the sense of good typography, and while at college already designed one or two title pages for Thomas B. Mosher. In 1895 he first appeared as architect of a Mosher book. Engaged as a designer by L. Prang and Company, proprietors of the quarterly *Modern Art,* he met J. M. Bowles, founder of that magazine, who showed him some Kelmscott books, an episode which definitely turned his attention to book-production as a career.

In this same year *Modern Art* removed to Boston. Rogers followed soon after, now working partly for the magazine and partly independently. He met Daniel B. Updike, and in 1896 also G. H. Mifflin, of the Houghton, Mifflin Company, who supervised the Riverside Press at Cambridge. Mifflin gave him his first regular typographical post, and for four years he produced trade editions, edited book advertisements in the *Atlantic Monthly,* and controlled a department for fine limited editions specially established for him. His first book in a series remarkable for the individual approach to each text was *The Sonnets and Madrigals of Michaelangelo Buonarotti.* He revived the Brimmer type face (later identified as that of John Bell), evolved the Montaigne fount from an original Jenson, and from a 14-point foundry Caslon he designed the "Riverside" Caslon. In 1912 Rogers left the Riverside Press and spent a summer in Europe. While in London he found a kindred spirit in the late Emery Walker, and formed a friendship not severed when he returned to America. He then essayed a free-lance career and worked on ordinary commercial jobs in New York for three years. He found some time for private ventures, however, and in 1914 produced for the Grolier Club one of his most notable works, Luther S. Livingston's *Franklin and his Press at Passy.*

In 1915 Rogers collaborated with Carl P. Rollins, printer to Yale University, in a few books produced at the Dyke Hill, Montague, Massachusetts. For one of these, Maurice de Guérin's *The Centaur,* he designed the fount known as Centaur, later cut by the Monotype Corporation. In the same year he was paid an honour not before accorded to a living printer, when his work was the subject of a paper read by the late Alfred W. Pollard, then Keeper of the Printed Books, British Museum, before the Bibliographical Society.

Emery Walker started his own press at Hammersmith at a rather unavoidable time, and invited Rogers to assist in its management. He began work in London early in 1917, and the impossibility during wartime of finding skilled workmen compelled him for the first time to handle the stick and make ready formes for press, an experience in practical method and achievement of lasting benefit. Shortly afterwards the Syndics of the University Press at Cambridge accepted the recommendation of Sir Sydney Cockerell* and appointed him their typographical adviser, thus creating a new position. He worked at Cambridge until the summer of 1919, destroying bad type faces, resurrecting good ones, and quietly assisting in the creation of that high typographical standard which still marks books with this imprint. At a period when fine printing was still held inseparable from hand setting, Rogers was quick to realize the possibilities of machine composition.

From Cambridge, England, Rogers moved in 1919 to Cambridge, Massachusetts, as a typographical adviser to the Harvard University Press. With this attachment he combined the design of limited editions for the late William Edwin Rudge, of New York. His connexion with Harvard continued till 1934, but in the years 1928-31 he was again with Emery Walker in London, in association with whom he produced in 1931 a sumptuous limited edition of the *Odyssey* that he persuaded T. E. Lawrence to undertake.

He next began work on a superb lectern Bible for the University Press at Oxford. It took four years to produce. It appeared in 1935 and will certainly rank as his supreme achievement.

He married in 1900 Anne E. Baker, of Stockwell, Indiana, who died some years ago.

May 20, 1957.

Florence Easton Rogers—See **Easton.**

Sax Rohmer, author of the Dr. Fu Manchu mystery stories and many other books, died in a London hospital on June 1, 1959.

He was born in the Midlands and his real name was Arthur Sarsfield Ward. Early in life he became greatly interested in Egyptian history and culture and made an unsuccessful attempt to gain a Civil service appointment in the Middle East. He then turned to journalism, and in 1913 created that compelling figure Fu Manchu whose sardonic humour and soft villainy were soon much to the taste of those readers who like their Orient sinister and their Orientals inscrutable.

"When the door opened . . . a veritable miasma of death seemed to come out to meet him, to envelop him", and this miasma of death (to be found in this instance in *The Yellow Claw*) enveloped many readers of many another tale of mystery. Pigtailed diamond thieves, ivory-skinned damsels, repulsive Levantines, stealing across priceless carpets only slightly stained with fresh blood—Rohmer handled them all with ease and skill.

Though he wrote many stories that thrilled and chilled, Fu Manchu was his most popular character. His deeds and misdeeds appeared in 25 languages, were translated to the screen

(Warner Oland—the esteemed Charlie Chan—played him in 1929), were seen on television, and were the subject of broadcast plays.

June 3, 1959.

Ex-King Carol II of Romania died suddenly at Estoril, near Lisbon, on April 4, 1953. He collapsed and died of a heart attack.

Prince Carol of Romania was born on October 15, 1893, at Pelesh Castle, Sinania, the elder son of the heir to the Romanian throne (afterwards King Ferdinand) by his marriage with Princess Marie, daughter of the Duke of Edinburgh and reigning Duke of Saxe Coburg and Gotha. He was, therefore, a great-grandson of Queen Victoria and, through his maternal grandmother, closely related to the Russian royal house. During his childhood and youth his Hohenzollern uncle, King Carol I of Romania, took charge of his education. The combination of the stern discipline and irksome restrictions imposed by this uncle and the influence of a mother who simultaneously spoiled and sought to dominate him drove him increasingly into revolt.

After a palace education and some time studying law and political science at Bucharest University, Prince Carol was given a military training. He went to Potsdam to complete it, but the outbreak of the 1914-18 war forced him to return to Romania. In the same year Carol I was succeeded by King Ferdinand and his sympathies were largely with Germany. But in 1916 the Queen, who was strongly pro-ally, had her way and Romania declared war on Austria. In a military sense the move proved a catastrophe, for the Central Powers occupied Bucharest and the Court moved to Jassy. It was there that Prince Carol, lonely and bored, became infatuated with Zizi Lambrino, a commoner. Not all the threats and cajolery of his parents and the Court could move him from the determination to marry her, which he did at Odessa, after smuggling her into Russia. When the young pair returned to Romania, Prince Carol was ordered into close confinement; the courts declared the marriage illegal; and, though he announced his abdication, Prince Carol accepted defeat and returned to Bucharest alone.

At the age of 28, much to the satisfaction of his family, he married Princess Helen of Greece. In October 1921 a son, Prince Michael, was born; but the incompatible temperaments of the royal couple had driven them apart and reconciliation by now seemed impossible. He had meanwhile revived an earlier friendship with Madame Helena Tampeanu (known after the dissolution of her marriage by her maiden name of Lupescu), and this had become a matter of sharp criticism in Romania. In 1925, after attending the funeral of Queen Alexandra, he went to Italy to meet Mme. Lupescu. There he received a message as a result of which he once again renounced his rights, and when his father died in 1927 Prince Michael succeeded to the throne. His wife divorced him in the following year.

Prince Carol had, however, never regarded the abdication of his claims as final and in June 1930, after a secret departure from France and a dramatic series of adventures, he arrived unexpectedly by air in Romania and within a few hours had control of the armed forces. The Romanian Parliament, called hurriedly together, at once removed his disabilities, and amid tumultuous rejoicings he was proclaimed King Carol II. As a king Carol was not long in making his influence felt, and gradually asserted himself against his many enemies inside the country.

In 1937 he faced a serious crisis produced by the terrorist methods of the anti-semitic and pro-Nazi Iron Guard of his own country, and by a combination of police action and drastic reform destroyed for a time their power. He paid a state visit to London in November 1938 together with Prince Michael, and the Order of the Garter was conferred on him by King George VI [q.v.].

Immediately after this he went to Berchtesgaden and at an interview with Hitler made a bold show of defiance. When war broke out in 1939 he maintained Romania's neutrality. He was, however, subjected to an insistent German pressure and blackmail and, yielding to it, found himself driven from concession to concession in his pursuit of a hopeless policy of appeasement.

He had reached the limit of humiliation when, in the early autumn of 1940, widespread disorders fermented by the Iron Guard occurred in his country and demands for his abdication arose. He therefore asked General Antonescu to form a new Ministry and, after a night of consultation with him, decided to vacate the throne in favour of his son Michael. On September 8 he departed with a suite of 39 persons, including Madame Lupescu. Thereafter he was an exile in many lands, including Switzerland, Spain, Portugal, Bermuda, Mexico, and Brazil.

In 1949, after a civil ceremony some time before, the religious marriage of ex-King Carol and Madame Lupescu was solemnized at his residence at Estoril. She took the title Princess Helena [d. 1977]. In exile he lived a modest and retired life. His last public act was to attend the memorial service for Queen Mary [q.v.] at St. George's Church, Lisbon.

April 6, 1953.

Irene Rooke, the actress, who died at her home at Chesham, Buckinghamshire on June 14, 1958, had virtually retired from the stage more than 20 years ago, but it will be remembered that she made a very definite personal contribution to the work of the progressive theatre in the early part of this century, as carried on by Granville Barker at the Court, by Miss Horniman at the Gaiety, Manchester, and, much later, by her own husband, Milton Rosmer*, and Malcolm Morley at the Everyman, Hampstead.

Irene Rooke trained with Ben Greet, and had already toured in Shakespeare and *The Sign of the Cross,* had played Ophelia to Gordon Craig's* Hamlet (1897), and in the original production of *Quality Street,* before she created the leading part of the charwoman, Mrs. Jones, in *The Silver Box,* John Galsworthy's first play, produced by Barker at the Court in 1906. She was to become associated with characters of this type, quiet but valiant, misunderstood but uncomplaining; but her range was wider, for at various times during her membership of Miss Horniman's company, with which she visited Canada in 1913, she played such parts as Paula Tanqueray, Major Barbara, and Alice in *Alice Sit-by-the-Fire,* not to mention Viola and Portia in Shakespearian comedy.

In addition to Mrs. Jones, she created leading characters in five other plays by Galsworthy: *The Eldest Son, The Fugitive, The Mob, Windows,* and *Old English.* But the part that allowed her to make the sharpest impression during the later years of her career was perhaps that of the hero's mother in John Drinkwater's *Oliver Cromwell* (1923). The gentle, slightly aloof old woman, who loved the cause of freedom but loved poetry still more, became a strong, delightful character in her handling of it. She caused us to share in Mrs. Cromwell's excitement as she dipped into a volume by young Mr. Herrick for the first time.

June 16, 1958.

Dr. A. S. W. Rosenbach, the outstanding American dealer in rare books and manuscripts during the past 30 years, died at Philadelphia on July 1, 1952, aged 75. He had been in poor health for some years, yet only a few days before he died his cabled bid to Sotheby's secured for his firm Bernard Shaw's letters to Mrs. Patrick Campbell.

Abraham Simon Wolf Rosenbach was born in Philadelphia on July 22, 1876. His parents, Morris and Isabella Rosenbach, were educated Jewish people, and his maternal uncle, Moses Polock, was well known as a bookseller. The boy took very early to book collecting, and when only 11, and having but $10 in his pocket, he bid $24 for a copy of *Reynard the Fox,* and was allowed by the auctioneer to pay off the balance by instalments. He graduated from the University of Pennsylvania in 1898, and seemed destined for an academic career. In 1901 he received a Ph.D. and a two-year fellowship to teach English, but finding that he could not, by these means, earn enough money to buy all the books he wanted, he decided to become a dealer.

Two book collectors of the time, Joseph M. Fox and Clarence S. Bement, financed this venture, and he opened a shop in Philadelphia in partnership with his elder brother Philip, who has concerned himself chiefly with the old furniture and silver in which the Rosenbach firm also deals. Abraham Rosenbach soon began making weekly trips to New York, and succeeded in selling Caxtons for what then seemed high prices at a time when it was said that "no one in America buys Caxtons". Before long the new firm was able to pay off its backers and stand on its own finances.

Rosenbach was thus a bookseller of the new kind, with some background of formal scholarship, and he was also himself a collector, especially of early American children's books and of Jewish books. But he was none-the-less an extremely astute business man, with a full understanding and appreciation of money, and of showmanship. He had already made a considerable place for himself in the trade, and had opened sumptuous premises in New York, which to the visitor had all the appearance of a private house and not of a shop, by 1920. His early customers included Henry Elkins Widener, whose library he catalogued in 1913 and 1918. His greatest chance came, however, after the death in 1920 of G. D. Smith, who had hitherto made most of Henry Huntington's purchases for him, and who was the principal figure at the sale of the first part of the Britwell Court Library at Sotheby's. At sales of later parts of this collection it was Rosenbach who carried all before him.

In the twenties Rosenbach was certainly the most spectacular personality in the Anglo-American trade in rare books; his frequent visits to England made his thickset figure, with serious clean-shaven face, familiar in the London bookshops and sale rooms. In the early thirties, as a result of the great financial slump, he seemed to pass through a period of comparative quiescence, and Rosenbach bids were less common in London. But, to some degree at least, the appearance was deceptive, for he had important clients to whom he went on selling quietly behind the scenes. It is probable, however, that during the past 20 years more of his bidding was on commission, and that some of his most sensational sales, such as that early in 1952 of his Shakespearian books to Dr. Martin Bodmer, of Geneva (a transaction credibly thought to have amounted to about $350,000—though a much higher figure has been quoted), were from stock acquired in the twenties.

Rosenbach received various honorary degrees from his old university, at which he founded a fellowship in bibliography in 1930. His publications stretched over a long period, for he collaborated with Austin Dobson in 1898 in an edition of Johnson's Drury Lane prologue, a copy of which Rosenbach had bought at auction for $3.60. In 1917 he issued a collection of short stories, *The Unpublishable Memoirs,* an *American Jewish Bibliography* was published in 1926, and in 1933 came the important catalogue of his own collection of children's books.

His volume of reminiscences, *Books and Bidders,* 1928, was followed in 1936 by *A Book Hunter's Holiday.*

July 3, 1952.

The death of **Dr. Otto Rosenheim,** PH.D., F.R.S., at the age of 84 on May 7, 1955 removes an outstanding figure familiar to biochemists and physiologists for four and a half decades.

He was born in Germany and, having taken his Ph.D. degree at Würzburg under Tafel in Emil Fischer's laboratory, he moved to Geneva to work with Graebe. Realizing that conditions in Germany were not favourable for permanent return for one of his creed, he wrote to W. H. Perkin, who was then at Manchester. Thus it was that in 1895 Rosenheim settled in England and worked temporarily at Manchester University. In 1901 he went to King's College London, to collaborate with Tunnicliffe as research student in pharmacological chemistry, was elected lecturer in 1904, and on Tunnicliffe's departure joined Halliburton as Assistant Professor of Physiology; he was Reader in Biochemistry in the University of London until 1920. From then onward Rosenheim occupied no official post.

During the tenure of his official positions Rosenheim carried out some outstanding work on the chemistry of the brain, following on the work of Thudichum, for whose researches Rosenheim had a great admiration. This was the period when the entity of protagon from brain was the subject of violent controversy. With Locke he collaborated in the classical work on the consumption of glucose by mammalian heart muscle.

Miss Mary Christine Tebb, whom Rosenheim later married, was on the staff of King's College and with Rosenheim had worked on the isolation of spermine phosphate from mammalian fluids. When insulin was being developed in 1924 Rosenheim, who had pre-eminently an inquiring turn of mind, thought spermine and insulin might be connected, so he went as a voluntary worker to the National Institute for Medical Research at Hampstead and collaborated with Dudley in working out the structure and synthesis of spermine. Here also, with Webster, he carried out the fundamental work on the irradiation of ergosterol to produce an antirachitic vitamin. This renewed interest in sterols, which are intimately linked with the chemistry of the brain, led Rosenheim and Dr. Harold King in 1932 to formulate a new ring structure for the sterols which opened up numerous avenues of research which are still being pursued by many workers.

Rosenheim loved to pursue his own research activities—as a rule unaided. He was meticulous in everything he did. He was ever helpful to the young worker; by the more experienced his wisdom, sagacity, and encyclopaedic knowledge were often called upon, and given willingly. He seemed fated from the controversial days of protagon to live among mild controversy, often not of his own choosing as he was the mildest-mannered of men.

He was elected to the Royal Society for his work on brain chemistry in 1917. He was a Fellow of the Linnean Society and an enthusiastic rock-gardener; and in his earlier days he was a mountaineer. He was a born artist and his essays in still-life photography earned high commendation.

May 16, 1955.

Irene (Mrs. Milton) Rosmer—See **Rooke.**

Gertie (Mrs. Don) Ross—See **Gitana.**

Professor Michael Rostovtzeff, a great authority on classical and ancient history, died on October 20, 1952 in America, aged 81.

He made new contributions to the history of Rome and Greece, where he had many distinguished predecessors, yet the most original part of his work is connected with his study of the prehistoric civilization of South Russia, where he discovered material only slightly outlined by other scholars. He tried to define the part played by South Russia in general history and to emphasize its contribution to civilization. A man of extraordinary cleverness and erudition—he was a member of many academies and doctor *honoris causa* of Oxford, Cambridge, and other universities—Rostovtzeff was both cautious and bold in his judgments. His books are masterpieces of historical interpretation, and, although they contain a large number of facts, make pleasant reading even to the layman.

Born in Kiev in 1870, the son of an official in the Ministry of Education, he was a schoolboy in a classical *gymnasium* in Kiev when he wrote his first historical essay, *The Administration of the Roman Provinces in the Epoch of Cicero.*

In 1895 he received from the University of St. Petersburg a three years' grant and went abroad to study ancient history. He was especially interested in excavations and archaeological studies, and formed many friendships with scholars of different countries, whom he also met at the national congresses and scientific meetings which he regularly attended. In 1903 Rostovtzeff was made Professor of Ancient History in the St. Petersburg Imperial University and in the University for Women. These two chairs he occupied for 15 years. He was an excellent speaker, and in his lectures, always delivered extempore, he could make the past live again with extraordinary vividness. He was only 26 when, working in Paris on the *Catalogue des Plombs de L'Antiquité de la Bibliothèque Nationale,* he saw the so-called Scythian Crown of Tissafernes offered to the Louvre as a find from South Russia. Rostovtzeff was the first to discover that it was a "fake", and vainly tried to persuade the director of the Louvre not to buy it. It was proved a counterfeit some years later.

The Bolshevist revolution forced him to leave Russia in 1918, and for two years he stayed at Oxford, where he studied English, and could be seen every day in the Bodleian writing his *Iranians and Greeks in South Russia.* He devoted a part of his energy to politics, and founded, in London, with Dr. and Mrs. Harold Williams, the Russian Liberation Committee, to explain to British public opinion the real meaning of communism.

In 1920 he accepted the chair of ancient history in Wisconsin University, and in 1925 was appointed to the corresponding chair at Yale University, where he was accorded special facilities to go abroad every year for research. At his suggestion Yale University and the French Academy of Inscriptions and Letters took up again in 1928 the excavation on the Euphrates at Dura-Europas started some years before by the eminent French scholar F. Cumont. The Dura excavations brought a new light on the history of the Caravan cities and on many other problems of the past.

His first book printed in English, *Iranians and Greeks in South Russia,* was published in 1922, and was followed by *The Social and Economic Life of the Roman Empire* (1926), *A History of the Ancient World* (1927), *Inlaid Bronzes of the Han Period* (1927), *Mystic Italy* (1928), *The Animal Style in South Russia and China* (1929), *Out of the Past of Greece and Rome* (1932), *Caravan Cities* (1932), many volumes of *The Excavations at Dura,* of which he and P. V. C. Nons were editors, and *The Social and Economic History of the Hellenistic World* (1941). Beside these capital works Rostovtzeff published more than 600 reviews and essays in Russian, English, French, German, Italian, Serbian, and Bulgarian.

Rostovtzeff was a charming man, a fine talker full of spontaneous and cheerful witticism. When his small, grey, deeply set eyes gave a certain twinkle, his friends knew that he would delight the company with some sparkling or sarcastic repartee in French, German, Russian, English, Italian, or Latin.

He married in 1901 Sophie Kultchisky, whose excellent memory was always at his service, and who undertook the responsible work of making indexes to his books. Though far from their native land they led an enriched and enlarged life, which was absolutely unlike the conventional picture of the monotonous existence of professors.

October 22, 1952.

Lady Rothenstein, widow of Sir William Rothenstein and one of the last remaining links with the Pre-Raphaelites and Swinburne, died at Sheffield on June 16, 1957.

She was born in Chelsea on May 31, 1867, Alice Mary, the eldest child of the artist Walter John Knewstub. Her father, a descendant of the Elizabethan divine John Knewstub, was Rossetti's only pupil and an intimate of the Pre-Raphaelite circle, and her mother was a noted beauty several times painted by Rossetti. She thus became familiar as a girl with the artistic and literary worlds of London.

For a short time she was on the stage as Alice Kingsley, when she played with Irene Vanbrugh, with Toole, and with Herbert Tree at Her Majesty's. Her father was indignant when Shaw wrote that she was perhaps better known through William Rothenstein's drawings of her than for her gift as an actress.

In 1899 she was married to William Rothenstein, Max Beerbohm [q.v.] acting as best man, and shortly afterwards her sister Grace married William Orpen.

Of a striking blonde beauty, she was drawn and painted by many artists among whom were Legros, Wilson Speer, and Augustus John* and she figured in her husband's well known painting, "The Doll's House", at the Tate Gallery. Her qualities of wit and high spirits endeared her to a wide circle of friends, especially writers, including Oscar Wilde and W. H. Hudson, who left her some of his manuscripts.

She is survived by her four children. Sir John Rothenstein, director of the Tate Gallery, Michael Rothenstein, the artist, and her two daughters, who married respectively Alan Ward and Dr. Ensor Holiday.

June 17, 1957.

Lord Rotherwick died at his home at Sedgwick Park, near Horsham, on March 17, 1958. He was 76.

He led a full and active life as shipowner, politician, soldier, and sportsman. Although connected with a number of industrial and commercial concerns, including the Commercial Bank of Scotland, of which he was governor, his greatest interest was shipping, and on this he was a foremost authority.

The Rt. Hon. Herbert Robin Cayzer, first Baron Rotherwick, of Tylney, was born on July 23, 1881, and educated at Rugby. He was the fifth son of Charles William Cayzer, who founded the family shipping concern of Clan, Irvine and Company. This venture was typical of the days when a man of integrity and practical experience could start a shipping business backed by a little capital, ability, and enthusiasm, and the financial support of those who believed in him. Charles William Cayzer was such a man. He started as a junior clerk in India with the British India Steam Navigation Company in 1861, at the age of 18. He returned to England in 1873 and five years later entered into partnership with a Captain Irvine, and the Clan Line was launched. Six merchant ships, at 11½ knots, fast by the standards of the day, were built for the Indian trade; when Cayzer died in 1916 the fleet consisted of 60 ships of nearly 300,000 gross tons.

Cayzer, who was created a baronet, was contemporary with Donald Currie, Bruce Ismay, and others who made the latter part of the nineteenth century and the first part of the twentieth a period of remarkable prosperity for shipping. On the death of his father, Lord Rotherwick, then Major Cayzer, became vice-chairman and subsequently chairman of the company. It has always maintained a strong family tradition and the name of Cayzer is borne by several of the directors to-day. Throughout its history the Clan Line has never in normal times employed other than first-class tonnage, built in Britain to its own design. There was an exception during the war, when vessels had to be ordered from America to replace losses.

Lord Rotherwick took a leading part in the fusion of the interests of the Union-Castle Mail Steamship Company with the Clan Line under the title of the British & Commonwealth Shipping Company, and he assumed the chairmanship of the new concern and also that of the Union-Castle Line. Active and vigorous, he was well over 70 years of age when he and Lady Rotherwick paid a visit to South Africa—the first for 20 years—to resume personal contact after the merger with prominent people in the Union. It was a strenuous six weeks' tour, during which he travelled many hundreds of miles, sometimes driving his own car. It was typical of him and his pride in his ships that on the outward voyage he accompanied the master daily on his rounds of inspection.

It was natural that Lord Rotherwick should occupy a leading position in the organizations which represent shipping in this country. It was due to him as much as anyone that the General Council of British Shipping came into existence. The Chamber of Shipping of the United Kingdom (of which he was president in 1941) and the Liverpool Steam Ship Owners' Association represent between them virtually all the shipping companies in Great Britain.

Liverpool, however, has always tended to be independent in thought and action, and it was to secure "full cooperation in matters of policy affecting the industry as a whole" that in April 1941 the two bodies joined to create the general council under Lord Rotherwick's chairmanship, each body continuing to preserve its identity and autonomy. The establishment of the general council was described at the time as "no mean achievement in an industry of individualists".

For many years Lord Rotherwick was chairman of the British Ship Adoption Society, which arranges the "adoption" by schools of ships and thus stimulates youthful interest in the Merchant Navy. He was a director, too, of the Thames Nautical Training College (H.M.S. Worcester) and a past president of the Institute of Marine Engineers. He was one of the British commercial directors of the Suez Canal Company, representing the shipowning interest.

His baronetcy was created in 1924 and he was elevated to the peerage in 1939. He entered the House of Commons as Conservative member for the southern division of Portsmouth in 1918. He was elected again in 1923. As a shipowner it was appropriate that he should become chairman of the House of Commons Shipping Committee, a position he held for seven years, relinquishing it only when he went to the Upper House. He was also chairman from 1936 to 1939 of the House of Commons Naval Committee and he served as a member of the Select Committee on Estimates for two years from 1934.

He was a staunch supporter of the Commonwealth and Empire, and his speeches both in Parliament and outside reflected the strong views he held that the prosperity of Great Britain, and consequently the well-being of merchant shipping in this country, depended on imperial preference and Empire trade.

Lord Rotherwick served with distinction in the First World War. He commanded the 24th Division Mounted Troops in France and was mentioned in dispatches. He was appointed honorary colonel of the Royal Corps of Signals in 1939. He raised and commanded the 25th (Rotherwick) Battalion of the Home Guard in the last war, and his lively interest in war comradeship was shown by his acceptance of the presidency of two branches of the British Legion.

At one time a keen rider to hounds, Lord Rotherwick was Master of the Garth Hunt from 1922 to 1926 and joint Master from 1931 to 1939. He was a Justice of the Peace for the City of Glasgow and also for Southampton, and served as Deputy Lieutenant for Hampshire from 1936 to 1950 and for Sussex from 1948.

Slight of carriage, dapper and debonair, wearing a monocle that gave him a somewhat puckish appearance, Lord Rotherwick concealed a warm humanity behind a rather stern demeanour. He believed profoundly in the causes he advocated and could, and did, advance them with forcefulness, sometimes tinged with a little acidity. But those who knew him intimately found him a kindly, considerate, and courtly man, and guests at the annual garden parties he gave at his attractive Sussex home, Sedgwick Park—parties which brought together almost everyone in the shipping world—saw him as a charming and genial host.

He married in 1911 Freda Penelope, daughter of Colonel W. H. Rathbone, and he had two sons and two daughters. He is succeeded by the elder son, Herbert Robin Cayzer.

March 18, 1958.

James Armand Edmond de Rothschild, who died in London yesterday, was the elder son of Baron Edmond de Rothschild, of Paris, the well-known banker and philanthropist, who from his devotion to the settlement of Jews in Palestine over a period of almost two generations was known as the Father of Jewish Colonization in Palestine.

James de Rothschild was born in Paris on December 1, 1878, and was educated at the Lycée Louis le Grand, Paris, and Trinity College, Cambridge, of which university he was an M.A. Although a French citizen, he entered the British Army on the outbreak of war in 1914, and served throughout that war, rising to the rank of major in the Royal Fusiliers. He served both in France and in Palestine, gaining the D.C.M. Rothschild's inclinations were always strongly in favour of English life, and it is believed that for many years he felt the desire to settle and become a British citizen. His father was, however, for long opposed to such a step, but after the end of the European war he consented.

In England de Rothschild soon settled down to the life of an English country gentleman and public man. He inherited the Waddesdon Manor and estate, near Aylesbury, from his kinswoman Miss Alice de Rothschild, and married Dorothy, daughter of Eugene Pinton, of Gloucester House, Piccadilly. In the country he was an ideal landlord, a squire of the best type. He was also an ardent supporter of the Turf and a popular figure in racing circles.

He had his first important success in the 1907 Manchester Cup; four years later his horse Atmah won the 1,000 Guineas, and in 1919 Brigand won the Cambridgeshire. The notorious Tishy, who "crossed her legs" in the Cesarewitch, raced in his colours after she had been sold by Sir Abe Bailey, and for him she won a long-distance handicap on the July course at Newmarket.

In 1929 he was elected Liberal member of Parliament for the Isle of Ely and represented the constituency until 1945. In the House he spoke occasionally and was always listened to with respect. Among the subjects in which he took a special interest was that of the Colonies. Although only an unofficial member of the smallest party in Parliament, he gained confidence in all quarters and was generally accepted as the representative of Jewish opinion. This was specially noticeable when the subject of the refugees from Nazi cruelties was under consideration, particularly on that historic occasion when the whole House rose to its feet to express its sympathy with these victims.

The great interest of Rothschild's life was probably that of the Jewish settlement in Palestine. This he inherited from his father, who had given a lifetime of devotion and a great fortune to that end. After he had attained manhood he was associated with his father in his Palestine interests. He succeeded him as president of the Palestine Jewish Colonization Association (Pica), which had been formed to take over the administration of Baron Edmond's agricultural and industrial interests and endowments in Palestine. He was also a governor of the Hebrew University of Jerusalem, vice-president of the Economic Board for Palestine, and a director of the Palestine Electric Corporation.

May 8, 1957.

Georges Rouault, the French painter, died on February 13, 1958 at his home in Paris. He was 86.

Appropriately, in view of the explosive character of his work, he was born in a cellar under bombardment in the Belleville quarter of Paris towards the end of the Commune in 1871. But, partly by virtue of his technical expedient of a dark line, the work of Rouault is as firmly controlled as it is explosive, so that the total effect is one of passion contained under great pressure. This distinguishes him from the German "expressionists", with whom at a glance he might seem to have something in common. In 1938 he was included in an exhibition at the Lefèvre Galleries of the "Tragic Painters", and the description was just as applied to him, because he illustrates very well the difference between the tragic and the merely pathetic or sentimental.

Rouault began his career as a worker in stained glass in the tradition of the earlier Gothic windows in Paris churches, and the experience had a permanent effect upon his style in painting: glowing colours enclosed in a framework of heavy dark lines. He studied painting under the "mystical" artist Gustave Moreau (1826-1898), and at the age of 23 won the important Chenavard prize at the École des Beaux Arts with his "The Child Jesus and the Doctors".

Among Rouault's fellow pupils under Moreau were Matisse [q.v.] and Dufy [q.v.], and at the Salon of 1905 he was represented with them in the notorious "Fauves", or "wild beasts", room, as it was called by the outraged Parisian public. Although Rouault was by nature more of an artistic "wild beast" than any of the others he was not interested in the polemics of Fauvism, and retiring to the Moreau Museum he cultivated his own interpretation of the tragedy of life.

The war of 1914-18 gave point to Rouault's satirical powers, which have been compared to Daumier's, and he produced some savage caricatures—of the German Emperor as "*Le Superhomme*" and of the war profiteer as "*Le Père Ubu*", for examples. But this topicality was a passing phase, and Rouault's more characteristic subject of satire was the abiding weakness of humanity in general, expressed in types of universal significance.

Rouault's work is comparatively well known in London. It was introduced by an exhibition at the St. George's Gallery in 1930 which included a "*Tête de Christ*", a poignant realization of "The Man of Sorrows", and "*La Mariée,*" with its irresistible suggestion of the Punch and Judy tragi-comedy, which was bought by the Contemporary Art Society for presentation to the modern foreign collection at the Tate Gallery.

Since the last war Rouault lived virtually in retirement, emerging only twice into the limelight and on both occasions attracting a good deal of publicity. One was in 1946 when he brought an action against the heirs of his former dealer, Vollard, in which he claimed that he still possessed the moral right to retouch or finish his paintings even when they had been sold.

The other was two years later, when it was discovered that he had burnt 315 of his paintings. Both seem to indicate that the artist was putting his finishing touches to a life's work that he considered to all intents and purposes complete.

Retrospective exhibitions of his art have been held in the last 10 years in Europe and in America, but the artist himself made little further contribution. In his last year he lived the life of a hermit in the Paris home he shared with his wife Marthe Le Sidaner, of the family of the well-known painter, and his daughter.

February 14, 1958.

Sir Archibald Rowlands, G.C.B., M.B.E., who retired only in December 1952 after an unusually brilliant career in the Civil service, died very suddenly at his home at Henley-on-Thames on August 18, 1953 at the age of 60.

Though he will be particularly remembered for his work at the Ministry of Aircraft Production in the grim days of 1940-41, when it is not too much to say that the whole outcome of the war depended on the success of efforts of the Minister and his staff to supply the aircraft which finally turned the scale in the Battle of Britain, Sir Archibald Rowlands had his triumphs both before and after these events. As a young private secretary to successive Secretaries of State for War he impressed not only his immediate chiefs but all those with whom he came into contact. Later as adviser to the Viceroy of India and later still as adviser to Jinnah, he showed a vision and judgment which was little short of miraculous in the trying latter days of British rule and in the early days of native rule in the sub-continent. Industry and energy he had in abundance, yet these would have availed him little if there had not been a touch of genius in a mind at once penetrating and kindly—a rare combination.

Archibald Rowlands was the son of David Rowlands and was born on December 26, 1892. He was educated at Penarth, the University of Wales, and at Jesus College, Oxford. He entered the War Office, and by the time he was 28 had reached the rank of an Assistant Principal. In the interval he had fought with distinction in the war in the Army Cyclist Corps, in which he was a captain, was mentioned in dispatches, and was awarded the Military M.B.E. From 1920 to 1922 he was private secretary to Sir Herbert Creedy*, when Secretary at the War Office; and afterwards he was private secretary to successive Secretaries of State for War, Viscount Hailsham, Viscount Halifax [q.v.], and Duff Cooper [Lord Norwich, q.v.]. Lord Hailsham used to declare that Rowlands was the ideal private secretary, and it is said that when he left the War Office to return to the Woolsack in 1935 he left special suggestions about Rowlands's future.

The following year saw the close of Rowlands's connexion with the War Office, as he was seconded as Adviser on Military Finance to the Indian Government. He was there for about two years, and returned in 1939, to be Deputy Under-Secretary of State at the Air Ministry, and in 1940 he became Permanent Secretary to the Ministry of Aircraft Production. In that capacity he accompanied [Sir] Ben Smith*, the Parliamentary Secretary to the Ministry, to the United States and Canada to visit aircraft factories, and was a member of the memorable mission to Moscow headed by Lord Beaverbrook* and Averell Harriman.

At the end of 1943 he returned to India as Adviser to the Viceroy on War Administration. His duties were to supervise the branches and agencies of those departments of the United Kingdom Government which war-time needs had made it necessary to be established in India and at the headquarters of the South-East Asia Command. In this extremely complicated task he was remarkably successful in surmounting the constant emergencies to which the ever-changing military situation gave rise. It was already clear that he had made a deep impression in India, and that fact was signalized by his appointment in 1945 as Finance Member of the Governor-General's Executive Council in succession to Sir Jeremy Raisman [d. 1978].

He had been appointed by R. G. [Lord] Casey [d. 1976], then Governor of Bengal, as chairman of a committee to inquire into the adequacy of the administration of the province, and in the summer of 1945 the report of the committee was published. Rowlands's mind and hand were clearly discernible in the suggestions of a radical overhaul of the machinery of government. His days in India were, however, drawing to a close, for in the summer of 1946 he returned to England on appointment as Permanent Secretary to the Ministry of Supply in succession to Sir (then Mr.) Oliver Franks [Lord Franks], who had become Provost of Queen's College, Oxford.

By then the Ministry of Supply was beginning its post-war contraction and Rowlands's abounding energy sought other outlets. In a little over 12 months he was seconded to serve as special adviser to Jinnah, Governor-General of Pakistan, who had been greatly impressed by his capacity during his early visit to India. It was not long before the fruits of this appointment became apparent. By November 1947 he had put forward radical proposals for the government of the Dominion, which in fact had inherited much of its machinery from the days of British rule. Rowlands's proposal was to sweep away the provincial administrations to unify the government in Karachi. He did, indeed, admit that East Bengal might be a problem but pointed out that the four provinces in the north-west formed a compact administrative unit. He later expressed himself as a believer in the possibility of Pakistan attracting sufficient foreign capital for an adequate programme of industrialization, notwithstanding the predominantly agricultural nature of the economy of the country.

At the end of the year he returned to Britain and again took up his duties not only at the Ministry of Supply but also as a member of the Economic Planning Board, where his industry and clear vision were of inestimable benefit. He retired on reaching the age limit of 60 only eight months before his death and was at once invited to join the board of Express Newspapers Limited, thereby renewing a partnership with Lord Beaverbrook which in the years of war had been particularly close and of great benefit to the nation.

He married in 1920 Constance May, daughter of P. W. Phillips, who survives him.

August 20, 1953.

Benjamin Seebohm Rowntree, C.H., chairman of Rowntree and Co. Ltd., from 1925 to 1941, and well known as a philanthropist and sociologist, died on October 7, 1954 at his home at High Wycombe, Buckinghamshire. He was 83.

The second son of the late Joseph Rowntree, founder of the cocoa and chocolate firm at York, he was born on July 7, 1871, and was educated at Bootham, the Quaker School at York, and at Owen's College, Manchester. The atmosphere of broad religious and social interests and of enlightened philanthropy in which he grew up was eminently conducive to the development of the social betterment schemes and inquiries with which his name is associated.

Inspired by his father's work and by Charles Booth's investigations into "life and labour" in London, Rowntree's first essay in similar directions was his book *Poverty: A Study in Town Life,* published in 1901. This was a survey of social conditions in York based on visits by investigators to every working-class household in the city. He promoted a second and more wide-ranging survey in York in 1936, the findings of which, reviewing "the degree in which a typical provincial city has benefited from the efforts put forth during this century to improve social conditions", were published in *Poverty and Progress* (1941).

It is perhaps chiefly for these classic inquiries that he will be remembered, together with their demonstration that poverty was far more widespread in childhood than in adult life, and with his own conclusion that no feasible improvements in wages could abolish childhood poverty without the addition of family allowances. It is significant of his influence that virtually every one of the many social surveys made in Britain between the two world wars used methods of measuring poverty directly or indirectly derived from the "human needs" standard which he devised for his first York survey. A third very summary survey of York in 1950, *Poverty and the Welfare State,* and a somewhat heterogeneous study of *English Life and Leisure,* both published in 1951, were not characterized by the scrupulous thoroughness of the work of his best years.

Other books associated with his name include *Land and Labour: Lessons from Belgium* (1905); *Unemployment: A Social Study* (with Bruno Lasker, 1911); *How the Labourer Lives* (1913); *The Human Needs of Labour* (1918, revised edition 1936); *The Human Factor in Business* (1921); *The Responsibility of Women Workers for Dependants* (with F. D. Stuart, 1921); and *Industrial Unrest: A Way Out* (1922). He worked in close collaboration for some 20 years, up to 1933, with Lloyd George. In the later years of this association they were both particularly concerned about questions of housing and unemployment.

The quick growth of the York business, of which he was vice-chairman for several years before he succeeded his father as chairman in 1925, was in no small degree due to him. He always viewed his work as a sacred trust, and gave as much scrupulous attention to plans for improving the workers' position as to the other details of the business. His great interest in the Joseph Rowntree Village Trust was not confined to the creation of the garden village at New Earswick, nor were the houses in that village let to employees only. He believed that its chief value was in demonstrating what well planned houses, beautiful in appearance, could be.

What was being done at York, largely under his personal guidance and inspiration, opened a wider sphere of usefulness. After having been a member of the Land Enquiry Committee in 1913-14, he was invited by Lloyd George during the 1914-18 War to become director of the Welfare Department of the Ministry of Munitions, through which reasonable conditions of working were ensured for thousands, especially women. On relinquishing this work in 1918 he became a member of Dr. [Lord] Addison's [q.v.] Reconstruction Committee. In politics he was a Liberal and was a member of various reconstruction committees for the Liberal Party.

He participated to a major degree in the

work of a number of *ad hoc* committees, such as those which produced the following books and reports: *Britain's Industrial Future* (1928, with W. T. Layton, E. D. Simon, Lloyd George, J. M. Keynes, and others); *The Agricultural Dilemma* (1930, with Lord Astor, [the second Viscount*]; *Are Trades Unions Obstructive?* (1935, with John Hilton, Dr. J. J. Mallon*, Sir Arthur [Lord] Salter*, and others); *British Agriculture* (1938, with Lord Astor); and *Mixed Farming and Muddled Thinking* (1946, with Lord Astor).

He was a Trustee of the King George's Fields Foundation, of the Nuffield Trust for Distressed Areas, president of the Outward Bound Trust, and chairman of the important old age survey committee set up by the Nuffield Foundation, the report of which was published under the title *Old People* in 1947. He was also closely identified with the anti-gambling movement and with the movement for obtaining disinterested management of the liquor trade.

An active member of the Committee of the National Institute of Industrial Psychology and of the Industrial Welfare Society, he was the originator of the Lecture Conferences for Works Directors, Managers, and Foremen, started in 1919, and of the Management Research Groups, first started in 1926. Throughout his life he was keenly interested in adult education and, particularly in recent years, in the advances made in this field by Denmark. He was a justice of the peace, and also an honorary LL.D. of Manchester University. He was made C.H. in 1931.

When he resigned his chairmanship of Rowntree and Co. in 1941 and made his home in Buckinghamshire he did not cease to be interested in York matters. These included his close interest in the repertory theatre in York, and his chairmanship of the York Citizens' Theatre Trust. He was also director of the Repertory Theatre at Amersham and president of the Conference of Repertory Theatres.

From his Quaker ancestors and the Quaker surroundings of his upbringing he had learned to look on life as a whole, and he never wished to draw a sharp line of distinction between his activities as being "religious" or otherwise. He was a loyal member of the religious society to which he belonged and took an active part in the extension of Quaker work of all sorts, especially in Yorkshire. He was one of the originators of the Swarthmore Lecture, which precedes the "Yearly Meeting" of the Society of Friends. For a few years, in spite of his many other activities, he undertook the position of "clerk" (*i.e.*, chairman-secretary) of the Industrial and Social Order Council of the Society, putting gladly at its service all the fullness of his own knowledge and experience.

In private life a delightful companion and conversationalist, he was perhaps as much at home as anywhere in group and larger meetings where problems had to be faced and overcome. A man of strong personal opinions, he had the tact, humour, and willingness to see the other point of view, which drew out the best in others, with the result that even if full agreement or solution were not reached misunderstandings were not left to mar further explorations.

He married Miss Lydia Potter in 1897. She died in 1944. There were four sons and one daughter of the marriage.

October 8, 1954.

J. F. Roxburgh, the first Headmaster of Stowe School, Buckingham, died on May 6, 1954 at his home at Great Brickhill, Bletchley, Buckinghamshire, the day after his sixty-sixth birthday.

John Fergusson Roxburgh was born on May 5, 1888, the son of Archibald Roxburgh, of Glasgow and Liverpool, and was educated at Charterhouse and Trinity College, Cambridge, where he won a classical scholarship. After taking his degree he went on to the University of Paris and he held the degree of L. ès L. from the Sorbonne.

His career as a schoolmaster began at Lancing, whose staff he joined in 1911 as sixth form master, an appointment which he held for 12 years, with a short break from 1917 to 1919 when he saw active service in France and Flanders as a subaltern with the Royal Engineers and the Royal Corps of Signals. Within two years of his appointment he was made house tutor of the Headmaster's House, where the bulk of the responsibility for the administration of the house naturally fell upon him, and in 1916 he became Housemaster of Sanderson's.

At Lancing he very quickly built up a great reputation which soon extended beyond the limits of the college and those directly interested in it. He was not only a brilliant teacher and an exceptionally level-headed administrator; he had—and it was the fundamental secret of his success throughout his career—an almost unique gift for obtaining the trust and affection of boys and a capacity for friendship with them which amounted to genius. He had, too, sufficient idiosyncrasy and a touch of the grand manner which inevitably made him a prominent figure in any institution or company.

The official appointment of Second Master had in fact been abolished at Lancing in 1892, but such was Roxburgh's prestige and so large was the part which he played in Lancing's remarkable revival in the years after the 1914-18 War that he was frequently referred to as such and his name was widely and publicly coupled with that of the headmaster, the late Canon H. T. Bowlby, as being jointly responsible with him for the college's increasing efficiency and prosperity. When, in 1922, the highly controversial decision was taken to found a new public school in the disused palace of the Dukes of Buckingham at Stowe, this reputation, won in so comparatively short a time, made Roxburgh almost an obvious choice for the headmastership of this bold venture. He made Stowe his life's work and remained there for 26 years until his retirement in 1949.

The task which Roxburgh undertook when he opened the summer term of 1923 with a school of 99 boys in a still largely derelict and unconverted mansion seemed to many to be well nigh impossible, yet within a very few years he had succeeded in thrusting into the forefront of the educational world a new public school with over 500 boys which was proving itself well able to compete on equal terms with the best of the ancient foundations. There was nothing cranky or modernistic about Roxburgh's approach to the problems of education and, though he disliked the self-consciousness of school "traditions" as such, he maintained the traditional organization, methods, and ideals of the English public school, seeking only to offer a greatly increased freedom within that framework and to develop boys much more as individuals rather than as parts of a system. The happy relationship with boys, the absence of unnecessary restraints, coupled with an exacting standard of performance, which had made Sanderson's the outstanding House at Lancing, were now extended, with apparent effort and with no loss of close personal and individual touch, to the whole of Stowe, where he knew every member of the school intimately, yet without losing his grasp of the larger aspects of educational policy and the formidable administrative problems with which he was continually faced.

The difficulties, financial, technical, and architectural, involved in the adaptation of the house and grounds of Stowe to the needs of a great public school Roxburgh had to meet almost single-handed yet, since there was no department of the school's life on which he did not leave the stamp of his own personality, no boy passed through the school without being decisively influenced by him. Stowe is his monument and it is probably even now still too early to assess his achievement there with precision. Enemies and rivals were apt to attribute too much of the school's success to the skill with which the Headmaster handled its public relations, which was certainly great. The real secret was probably a deep and fundamental liberalism in Roxburgh himself which made him an important pioneer in the movement which set in strongly in the twenties to modernize the public schools and free them from the somewhat hidebound curricula and habits of mind which had resulted from a half-century of prosperous empire building. His views on education, which were enlightened rather than revolutionary, he set forth in a Platonic dialogue written in 1930 under the title of *Eleutheros,* and he also published a small course of lectures on English Literature under the title of *The Poetic Procession.*

Roxburgh never married and the whole of his life and interest were more and more concentrated in Stowe. On such a man the 1939-45 War inevitably imposed exceptional burdens. Apart from the anxieties, financial and otherwise, thrust on all headmasters in those difficult years, every Old Stoic casualty was for him a bitter personal loss. It was the consciousness of his own exhaustion which made him retire at the end of the summer term of 1949, in spite of the persuasions of Governors and friends, when he had successfully guided the school through the difficult transitional years from war to peace and left it securely founded on the position he had won for it.

May 7, 1954.

More widely known under her maiden name of **Dr. Maude Royden, Mrs. W. Hudson Shaw** died at her London home in London on July 30, 1956 at the age of 79.

The daughter of a wealthy citizen of Liverpool, she had been prominent in the Women's Suffrage Movement when in 1917 she became an assistant preacher at the City Temple.

Later she became the joint founder of the "Fellowship Services" at Kensington and then established herself as a pastor at the Guildhouse in Eccleston Square, London. She was, therefore, one of the first women pastors in England, and, being a mistress of pulpit oratory as well as a forceful personality, gained a large following. She was a woman of strong and sometimes unconventional views which she expressed with sincerity and courage both in speaking and in writing. These qualities were nowhere more evident than in her remarkable and revealing account of the great love of her life in *A Threefold Cord.*

Agnes Maude Royden was born in 1876, the youngest daughter of Sir Thomas Bland Royden, Bt., of Frankby Hall, Birkenhead, a former Mayor of Liverpool. She was educated at Cheltenham Ladies' College and at Lady Margaret Hall, Oxford. After working for three years at the Victoria Women's Settlement in Liverpool she went to help the Rev. G. W. Hudson Shaw, the vicar of the country parish of South Luffenham.

She then became a lecturer in English Literature to the Oxford University Extension Delegacy and so developed a natural gift for public speaking. She was a strong upholder of the rights of women and in 1908 joined the National Union of Suffrage Societies. A person of her gifts and personal magnetism was a valuable recruit and in the same year she became a member of the executive committee and editor of the *Common Cause,* positions which she held until 1914 when she resigned from the executive. Her chief interest during her connexion with the suffrage movement was its economic, ethical, and religious aspects, and on these principally she wrote and spoke.

In 1917 Maude Royden, who sought an outlet for her undoubted gifts as a preacher, but as a member of the Anglican Communion was unable to find one within it, obtained a pulpit appointment from Dr. Fort Newton, of the City Temple, London. There she soon began to make her name and to receive invitations to preach elsewhere. Naturally, however, she encountered difficulties. Thus, when her old friend, the Rev. G. W. Hudson Shaw, asked her in 1919 to preach at a "three hours service" at St. Botolph, Bishopsgate, the Bishop of London "prohibited" the service, which was consequently held in an adjoining parish room. Two years later, however, she preached in the church without the approval but also without the inhibition of the Bishop. A little before, she had ceased to be an assistant preacher at the City Temple and with Dr. Percy Dearmer had founded the "Fellowship Services" in Kensington Town Hall. In 1921 Eccleston Square Congregational Church was acquired for the Fellowship Guild and reopened under the name of the Guildhouse, Eccleston Square.

She made a tour of the United States in 1923, spoke in the pulpits of churches of many denominations, and on the whole created an excellent impression. A few years later she went round the world and visited Australia, New Zealand, India, and China. At both Adelaide and Christchurch her appearance in the cathedral pulpit started vigorous controversy. In 1930 she was created a C.H. and in 1931 Glasgow University conferred a doctorate of divinity upon her. She was one of the organizers of the "Peace Army" in 1932, and in 1936 she announced her intention of resigning her pastorate of the Guildhouse in order to devote herself to the promotion of world peace.

In October 1944 she married her old friend, the Rev. G. W. Hudson Shaw, who by that time was over 80 years of age and had retired from his city vicarage of St. Botolph, Bishopsgate. He lived, however, only until the following December. The story of their love, which was shared by Shaw's first wife, with strict regard for the Christian view of marriage, is movingly told in *A Threefold Cord,* which was published just over three years after Shaw's death. Dr. Royden had years before proved herself a writer and thinker of no mean achievement, but in this, her last work, she surpassed herself.

July 31, 1956.

Admiral Sir Percy Molyneux Rawson Royds, C.B., C.M.G., died on March 25, 1955 at the age of 80.

He had served for 40 years, from 1887 to 1927, on the active list of the Royal Navy, and was a captain in command of cruisers throughout the 1914-18 War. An energetic and capable officer, he was also a keen athlete and sportsman, and was one of the first to hold the post of Superintendent of Physical Training in the Navy. His last duty before retirement was as Admiral Superintendent at Chatham Dockyard. After retiring from the Navy he was for seven years Conservative Member of Parliament for Kingston-upon-Thames.

The son of the late Ernest Royds, J.P., of Rochdale, he was born on April 5, 1874, and educated for the Navy at Eastman's Academy, Southsea, passing into the Britannia as a cadet in 1887. He served as a midshipman, was promoted to lieutenant in 1895, and, deciding to specialize in gunnery, joined H.M.S. Excellent. Four years later he was first lieutenant of the Arethusa during the Boxer rising in China, and received the China medal for his services.

After further service afloat he joined Devonport Barracks in 1904 as gunnery officer. A year later he was promoted to commander at the early age of 30, and appointed to the cruiser Europa in reserve at Devonport. He was then in the cruiser Argyll until, in 1908, he was selected for duty as Superintendent of Physical Training, Portsmouth, a branch of naval work in which he had always taken a keen interest. As a young man he had played Rugby football for Blackheath and the Navy, and played in three English international fifteens. In 1910 he was elected as naval representative on the English Rugby Football Union, with which he was connected for many years, serving later as representative for Kent on the selection committee. He also served on the committee of the Royal Tournament, and of the Physical Culture committee and Olympic Council.

On his promotion to captain in 1912 he took a course at the War College, Portsmouth, and in 1913 was given command of the light cruiser Bellona. In this ship and the light cruiser Canterbury he served throughout the 1914-18 War in the Grand Fleet in the North Sea. The Canterbury took a fair part in the Battle of Jutland, and for his part in the action Captain Royds was mentioned in dispatches and awarded the C.M.G.

After the war ended he was appointed Captain in Charge of the R.N. College, Greenwich, until 1920, when he returned to his pre-war interest and was made Director of Physical Training and Sports. From 1921 until 1922 he was captain of the battleship Malaya, relinquishing the command on his promotion to rear-admiral. Later he was appointed Admiral Superintendent at Chatham Dockyard, where he served until 1925. He was made a C.B. in 1924 and three years later was promoted vice-admiral by seniority. Not having hoisted his flag at sea he was retired on the following day. He became an admiral on the retired list in 1932.

He took a keen interest in politics and served as president and chairman of the Kingston-upon-Thames Conservative and Unionist Association for several years before he was elected as its member of Parliament in 1937.

Royds was knighted in the following year, and was a member of the House of Commons until 1945. He also served for some years on the Surrey County Council.

He married in 1898 Florence, daughter of the late Sir Alfred Yarrow, Bt. She died in 1948. There were one son and three daughters of the marriage.

April 21, 1955.

Admiral Sir Guy Royle, K.C.B., C.M.G., collapsed and died on January 4, 1954 while helping firemen to put out a heath fire near his home at Trickett's Cross, near Wimborne. He was 68.

From 1939 to 1941 he was a Lord Commissioner of the Admiralty and Chief of Naval Air Services, and he was then appointed First Naval Member of the Commonwealth Naval Board. In 1946, after retirement, he became Yeoman Usher of the Black Rod, and in 1948 secretary to the Lord Great Chamberlain. He retired from both these posts in November 1953.

Guy Charles Cecil Royle was the second son of Arnold Royle, C.B., of Esher, Surrey, and was born on August 14, 1885. He entered the Britannia in 1900, went to sea as midshipman in 1901, and became a lieutenant in 1906. Responsibility came early to him at the age of 21 in command of a torpedo-boat, No. 52, in the Portsmouth flotilla in 1906-07. After a commission in the cruiser Good Hope he was appointed to specialize in gunnery in 1909. When the 1914-18 War broke out he was gunnery officer of the Marlborough, flagship of the 1st Battle Squadron, Grand Fleet. He was still in her when, as flagship of Admiral Sir Cecil Burney, second-in-command to Admiral Jellicoe, she took part in the Battle of Jutland on May 31, 1916.

Sir Cecil Burney in his report said of Royle: "It was entirely owing to his organization and work that the ship fired so extremely well, quickly, and accurately during the action, especially so after she had been struck by a torpedo and took up a considerable list." For service at Jutland he was promoted to commander. From 1917 to 1919 he was Flag Commander to Admiral Sir Charles Madden. In July 1919 he was appointed C.M.G. for war service in the Grand Fleet. In 1919-20 he was fleet gunnery officer in the Atlantic Fleet, and in 1920-22 executive officer of the flagship Iron Duke in the Mediterranean. During 1923 he served in the Naval Ordnance Department and was promoted to captain at the early age of 37.

For three years from January 1924 he was naval attaché at Tokyo. In 1927-29 he commanded the cruiser Canterbury in the Atlantic Fleet. His next appointment was in command of the Excellent gunnery school for two and a quarter years from May 1930. Then came his first connexion with the Fleet Air Arm, when he was selected to command the aircraft carrier Glorious in the Mediterranean from 1932 to 1934. From September 1934 to May 1937 he was Naval Secretary to the First Lord, and it was while at the Admiralty that he was promoted to rear-admiral in July 1935. In 1936 he was made a C.B. He was Rear-Admiral, Aircraft Carriers, from July 1937 to July 1939 with his flag first in the Courageous and later in the Ark Royal.

Before giving up this command he was nominated as Fourth Sea Lord and Chief of Supplies and Transport from September 15, 1939. Owing to the outbreak of war he did not take up this post, but resumed instead his former appointment as Naval Secretary.

In November 1939 he joined the Board as Fifth Sea Lord and Chief of Naval Air Services, and it was under his direction that the vast expansion of the Fleet Air Arm required by the war was put into effect. In July 1941 he became First Naval Member of the Commonwealth Naval Board, where he served until June 1945. Under his guidance the Royal Australian Navy was greatly expanded and equipped to take its part in the later stages of the war in the Pacific.

He was made a K.C.B. in 1941 and promoted to admiral in 1942. He retired in March 1946. In his younger days he was a keen Rugby footballer and captained the Navy.

He married in 1915 Elizabeth Ellis, daughter of Charles Dunlop Gilmer, who survives him. She was appointed O.B.E. in the recent New Year Honours List.

January 6, 1954.

Ida Rubinstein, the well known dancer, died in October 1960, at Vence, near Nice, where she had lived in retirement for many years. She was 75.

Ida Rubinstein first became famous in 1909 when she appeared for Diaghilev's Russian Ballet in the title role of *Cléopatre* during Diaghilev's first Paris season. An amateur actress and dancer who was a private pupil of Fokine, she combined striking beauty with such natural elegance of movement that she won immediate success with Paris audiences, rivalling even her colleagues from the Imperial Ballet.

Born in St. Petersburg, an orphan of good Jewish family, she was educated by an aunt and early determined to use her gifts in the theatre. To this end she devoted the large inheritance which was hers when she came of age. Diaghilev first saw her in the Dance of the Veils arranged for her by Fokine in Oscar Wilde's *Salome.* Struck by her beauty Diaghilev needed little persuasion by Fokine and Bakst when the chance came to cast her as Cleopatra. Even so it was a daring, if typical, decision to present this untrained dancer among the stars of the great Mariinsky.

Diaghilev, building on the success of *Cléopatre*, gave her the role of Zobeida, the favourite wife, in Fokine's *Scheharazade* the following year.

After this the limitations even of one so beautiful became too marked to keep her longer with the Russian Ballet and she left to pursue her own career. Using her large financial resources and the fame of her beauty, she commissioned several works in which she could appear as a dancer or actress, the most famous being, perhaps, *The Martyrdom of St. Sebastian* in 1911. Subsequently she formed a company which lived from 1928 to 1935, employing many Diaghilev dancers after the great man's death and helping to train others, including the young Frederick Ashton. Several of this company's ballets, like *La Bien Aimée* and *La Valse,* survived their day as memorials in a sense to the good taste which pervaded all Ida Rubinstein's work.

Around her there clung till the end the atmosphere of a period which died in the First World War and was buried in the great slump. Her death sees the passing of a remarkable theatrical personality who became in her own lifetime a voice from the past.

October 18, 1960.

Lord Ruffside, who died on May 7, 1958 at the age of 78, was Speaker of the House of Commons for more than eight years—from March 1943 to October 1951. In that time he was able to realize his three great ambitions—to lead the House of Commons into St. Margaret's Church for the thanksgiving service at the end of hostilities, to sit in the Speaker's Chair when it was re-erected in the new House of Commons, and when peace came to turn on the switch which controls the lantern on the top of Big Ben.

Elected unanimously to the Chair of the House of Commons while the Second World War was at its height, Clifton Brown, as he then was, will probably be remembered as the most unconventional of Speakers. A soldier by profession, and the second only to be First Commoner, he had been a member of the House since 1918 (save for a brief interruption between 1923 and 1924), and had had over four years' experience as Deputy Chairman and Chairman of Ways and Means.

He undoubtedly possessed in abundant measure the rare combination of qualities which the House of Commons demands from the arbiter of its proceedings. He was firm and impartial; but he also had the perfect tact upon which the influence of a Speaker so largely depends.

He liked to be known as "the House of Commons' man", and, above all, as "the back-benchers' man". He emphasized this in the notable speech he made in reply to his re-election to the Chair in 1945. He was not, he said, "the Government's man or the Opposition's man". He always remembered that it was the special duty of the Chair to see that minorities were not brow-beaten and got a fair hearing in debate, and he pledged himself to follow the line of his predecessor in that respect.

Douglas Clifton Brown was born on August 16, 1879, the fifth son of Colonel James Clifton Brown, M.P., of Holmbush, Sussex, by his wife Amelia, daughter of Charles Rowe, of Elm House, Liverpool. He was educated at Cheam and at Eton (Miss Evans's House) and at Trinity College, Cambridge, where he graduated in 1901. Later he proceeded to M.A. In 1900 he had been commissioned in the Lancashire Royal Garrison Artillery (Militia) and in 1902 transferred to the 1st Dragoon Guards, in which he obtained his captaincy in 1908. From 1910 to 1919 he was in the special reserve of this regiment and in 1919 was promoted major in it. From 1914 to 1918 he served in France and Belgium. From 1925 to 1929 he was lieutenant-colonel commanding The Northumberland Hussars Yeomanry, and was awarded the brevet of colonel.

In December 1918 Clifton Brown was returned as Conservative member for the Hexham division of Northumberland. He lost his seat in November 1923, but regained it in October 1924, and continued to represent Hexham until his elevation to the peerage in 1951. From 1920 to 1922 he was Parliamentary Secretary (unpaid) to the Ministry of Pensions, and was a member of the Central Advisory Committee on War Pensions. A popular and much respected member, he was in due course appointed to the panel of Chairman of Committees selected by the Speaker. On the occasions on which he presided over the House of Commons in Committee he made an excellent impression by his conduct of debates.

It was therefore no surprise when on the death in 1938 of Captain Bourne, the Deputy Chairman of Ways and Means and Deputy Speaker, he was chosen by agreement of all parties to succeed him. In this office he enhanced both his popularity and his reputation and proved his capacity to manage the House successfully in all its varying moods. When, in January 1943, Sir Dennis Herbert resigned the chairmanship of Ways and Means and Deputy-Speakership he was again unanimously chosen to fill the vacant place.

In March 1943 Captain Fitzroy, the Speaker, died in office. From the first there was no doubt that Clifton Brown would be acclaimed as not only the obvious but an entirely worthy successor.

In the Chair Clifton Brown was no respecter of persons. Indeed, he was so much a "back-benchers' man" that he frequently crossed swords with some of the Privy Councillors and members of both Front Benches. An outstanding example of this occurred on March 4, 1947. During question-time Winston Churchill*, who was then leading the Opposition, and William Shepherd, a back-bench Conservative, rose simultaneously to put supplementary questions. To the general surprise the Speaker called Shepherd, and added: "The right hon. gentleman must not gate-crash on a back-bencher". There were Ministerial cheers, and Opposition cries of "Shame!" Amid the uproar Churchill protested, stating that he had no idea that Shepherd had risen, and submitting that the use of the word "gate-crash" was wholly unwarranted. The Speaker, however, stuck to his guns, but stated that if Churchill took offence at the word "gate-crash" he was very sorry. The incident ended happily, Churchill, later, smiling as he rose to ask a further supplementary question.

Clifton Brown was plagued, during his later years in the Chair, with many complaints of breach of privilege and he had difficult decisions to take, often with very little time to consider them. He did his best in trying circumstances, but the heavy burden affected his health for a time. Fortunately he made a good recovery, but it was no secret that he desired to retire far earlier than he did. He had hoped that the end of the third Labour Government in February 1950 might mark the close of his tenure of office. But the result of the general election was so close that the Speaker, conscientious almost to a fault, felt that it would be unfair to saddle his successor with the onerous task of holding the scales evenly between two so equally balanced parties. He therefore postponed his retirement until after the next general election in October 1951.

This, happily, allowed him to fulfil his ambition of sitting in the Speaker's Chair in the new House of Commons.

On his retirement Clifton Brown had conferred on him a viscounty, and took the name, style and title of Viscount Ruffside, of Hexham in the county of Northumberland.

In all his work as Speaker he was greatly helped by his wife, who was a frequent occupant of the Speaker's gallery in the House of Commons. She was Violet Cecily Kathleen, only daughter of Frederick Eustace Arbuthnot Wollaston. They were married in 1907, and had one daughter. Both survive him.

His daughter married in 1931 Sir Harry Hylton-Foster*, who became M.P. for York in 1950, Solicitor-General in 1954 [and Speaker in 1959.]

May 8, 1958.

The death of **Ruggero Ruggeri** in July 1953 is a blow not only to the Italian stage but to European drama as well.

In his 64 years on the stage he displayed a fine talent which embraced both comedy and tragedy. Possessed throughout his long career of a rare, beautiful voice, full of light and shade, low, yet distinctly heard all over a large auditorium, he obtained his effects with a quietude very unlike the popular idea of a temperamental Italian. The few gestures he made with his hands were, because they were so sparing, wonderfully expressive, and his whole movement manifested the depth of insight he brought to the interpretation of the parts he played, ranging from Shakespeare to Pirandello and D'Annunzio.

The son of a schoolmaster in Tuscany, he was born in November 1871, and at the age of six was already so interested in the theatre that after seeing a theatrical performance he would mimic the gestures of the actors before a mirror on his return home. Somewhat against his parents' wishes he went on the stage at the age of 17 and made his way in those early years rather slowly. If his progress was slow, his schooling was thorough, and this told to his great advantage in his later career. By 1906 he had acquired sufficient reputation and authority in his own country to organize his own company, and for many years thereafter the company played for 10 months every year. Self-sufficient and contemplative to a degree, he spent much of his annual resting period quite alone.

He had already made a great reputation in Italy as an interpreter of Shakespeare and had electrified his countrymen by his playing of the leading part in the first performance in 1922 of Pirandello's *Enrico IV.* When he went to London in 1926, greatly daring, he opened his season at the Globe with *Hamlet.* To some English eyes it did not seem that the whole character was there; only the intellect, displayed with astonishing flashes of insight, seemed to be exhibited with a strange, perfected coldness in which Hamlet's doubts and passions had no place. Yet the performance called forth the delighted comments of such a discerning critic as Maurice Baring, who recalled then that Duse had never achieved popularity on the English stage until the last few years of her career. Ruggeri never achieved it.

After giving a special performance of *Enrico IV* in Milan in April 1953 he left for London with the plaudits of the great and enthusiastic audience ringing in his ears, to play the same part at the St James's Theatre. Alas, the size of the audiences proclaimed the fact that the number of Londoners who understand Italian is pathetically small. Undefeated, Ruggeri, whose style was enriched by an age which seemed not to impair his vigour, appeared in a television production in which he described "how nice it is to be young".

July 23, 1953.

Former King Carol II of Romania—
See **Romania.**

Field-Marshal Gerd von Rundstedt, who died at the age of 77 at Hanover on February 24, 1953, after suffering heart trouble for many months, was one of the ablest German commanders of the Second World War.

The epithet "brilliant" does not fit him, because he lacked the unconventional qualities which it summons up, but his orthodoxy was never narrow. The Army ranked him high, and since the war the younger school has treated his military reputation with respect. Cautious by temperament, he could act very boldly and lent a sympathetic ear to bold plans put up to him by competent subordinates. He was an accomplished soldier with his profession at his fingers' ends; but his ideas were strategic rather than tactical and, unmindful of well-known advice, he preferred small-scale to large-scale maps. For tactics he relied heavily upon his staff. He served in the principal European campaigns: Poland, France in 1940, Russia, and North-west Europe. He was strongly opposed to war with Russia and feared it would turn out ill. Accused of war crimes, he was, after long delay, released on grounds of ill health, and proceedings against him were dropped. To many people in Britain they had been unwelcome.

Karl Rudolf Gerd von Rundstedt came of an ancient family in the Altmark of Brandenburg. He was born on December 12, 1875, and was posted to the 83rd Infantry Regiment in 1893. In the 1914-18 war he served in France, Russia, and Hungary, ending as chief staff officer of XV Corps. He rose at moderate speed, though he held most of the staff appointments and several commands. The last in peace, in Berlin, was notable because, Fritsche and Beck being recluses, receptions and social intercourse fell to him. Though grim and laconic, he became a man of the world—at least the political and military world—and well known outside Germany. In the autumn of 1938, having angered Hitler over the celebrated Fritsche and Beck "affairs", he retired, but was brought back next year for the offensive against Poland. He was six years the senior of his superior, Brauchitsch, Commander-in-Chief of the Army, though regarded as the more capable soldier and the stronger man.

He next took over Army Group A, which was to attack in the west. The final plan bore little resemblance to the original. The former was the work of Manstein*, his chief staff officer in Poland, who had accompanied him to his new command. Rundstedt supported and slightly modified it. It was adopted, though its author was relegated to the command of an infantry corps in reserve.

The thrust through the Ardennes, the essential feature, was carried out by Rundstedt's group. When Guderian's [q.v.] armour was ordered to halt on the Meuse to await the infantry and that headstrong man proffered his resignation in a passion, Rundstedt sent Colonel-General List to bid him stay at his post; Guderian was allowed to make "reconnaissances in force" and interpreted this directive so vigorously that he drove on to the Channel coast. Rundstedt had clearly been in two minds over the affair. In the last phase the passage of the Aisne and the drive to the Swiss frontier, his group played an equally vital part. The commander was promoted to the rank of field-marshal.

Against Russia Rundstedt commanded Army Group South, which included Hungarian and Italian troops. Farther south lay the Romanian forces, over which he had general strategic control. Experience in the Carpathians in the earlier war had taught him how to deal amicably with foreign troops. He handled the offensive with skill, determination, and success. At the end of November, however, he decided that his worst fears were being realized and that a halt, and even a withdrawal, were necessary to save the army from being engulfed in the Russian winter. On December 1 he was relieved of his command.

In March 1942 he was appointed to a command in the west, extending from Holland to the Italian frontier. By 1944 his chief subordinate, the commander of Army Group B, which would have to face invasion from Britain, was Field-Marshal Rommel. The strategic ideas of the two were opposed. Rundstedt advocated a classic system of defence, keeping the armoured forces well back from the coast and disposed so that they could strike at an invader wherever he might land. Rommel, deeply impressed by the difficulty of movement resulting from the complete British-American command of the air, thought this plan too risky and relied on defeating invasion on the coast. He was supported by Hitler, and Rundstedt does not appear to have fought very hard for his views. He was perhaps by now beginning to feel his years; indeed, henceforward his conduct, admittedly in the most difficult circumstances, seems to have become less vigorous. The upshot was that the armour was committed more or less piece-meal and there was no counter-offensive on a great scale.

Rundstedt was relieved in early July and served as president of the "court of honour" set up after the attempt on Hitler's life, but on September 5 returned as commander-in-chief in the west. His last great action was the counter-offensive in the Ardennes, but he considered the plan extravagant in view of the land and air resources available. He advocated an offensive, but with limited aims. Though this has been called the "Rundstedt offensive", it was Hitler's, and Hitler dealt directly with the group commander, Model. Soon afterwards Rundstedt was relieved once more. He must have got used to the process by then.

On May 2, 1945, he was arrested in the house in which he was living near Munich. From early 1946 till July 1948 he was incarcerated at Bridgend in Glamorgan and Diss in Norfolk. In May 1949 he was released in Germany. Brauchitsch, who was to have stood trial with him and Manstein, was dead, so the last-named was tried alone. Rundstedt represented the old Army and, where he was concerned, its alliance with Hitler was uneasy. Some thought that his opposition to Hitler would take active form, but his temperament and character in fact rendered this unlikely.

February 25, 1953.

Major-General Sir Andrew Hamilton Russell, K.C.B., K.C.M.G., who commanded the New Zealand and Australian Division during the final stages of the Gallipoli campaign and went on to command the New Zealand Division in France from April 1916, right up to the Armistice, died at Hastings, New Zealand, on November 28, 1960.

Born on February 23, 1868, the eldest son of Colonel Andrew Hamilton Russell, of Petersfield, Hampshire, Russell was educated at Harrow and Sandhurst and gazetted second lieutenant in The Border Regiment in September 1887. After five years, mostly spent in India, where he won a great reputation as a polo player and race-rider, he retired from the Service in 1892 and went to New Zealand to join his father, who was sheep farming at Hawkes Bay. He indulged his taste for soldiering, however, by joining the New Zealand auxiliary forces and in 1907 reached the rank of major in the Wellington East Coast Mounted Rifles Regiment.

When the Great War broke out Russell was appointed to the command of the New Zealand Mounted Rifles Brigade which, as part of the Australian and New Zealand Corps, arrived in Egypt in December. The brigade was not employed in the first landing on Gallipoli, but soon saw hard service on the peninsula. In May 1915 it joined the New Zealand and Australian Division at Anzac, where it fought dismounted for the remainder of the campaign.

Colonel Russell (as he then was) commanded the left or northern sector of the Anzac line, "Russell's Top" being the name given to the ridge first held by his New Zealanders. He commanded a column in the August attack on Sari Bair, accounting for the Turkish outposts north of Anzac, and his brigade was hotly engaged in the fighting for Hill 60 later in the month. In November he was promoted major-general to command the New Zealand and Australian Division, and during the final 48 hours of the evacuation of Anzac in December he was in command of all troops.

In Egypt the arrival of New Zealand reinforcements permitted of the creation of a New Zealand Division, which Russell was appointed to command. In April 1916 the division embarked for France. The New Zealand Division's fine record of achievement on the Western Front speaks eloquently of the capacity of its commander. His natural gifts had been developed by study and experience; cool, courageous, untiring, and determined, he was a master of detail and a shrewd judge of men, and he possessed a personality which inspired confidence and genuine regard. The command of a corps could have been his had he not preferred to remain with the division, and he continued to lead it until the Armistice: at the battles of Flers-Courcelette, Morval, and Le Transloy on the Somme in 1916, at Messines Ridge, and in the later stages of "Third Ypres", 1917, during the German offensive in Picardy in the spring of 1918, and in the advance to victory when the New Zealanders, in the Third Army, fought no less than eight successful major actions.

Russell had been created K.C.M.G. in 1915 for his Gallipoli services; C.B. in 1917; and promoted K.C.B. in 1918; and mentioned many times in dispatches. Just after the Battle of Messines his skull was grazed by a sniper's bullet which passed clean through his steel helmet.

The New Zealand Division formed part of the Army of Occupation in Germany, but in February 1919 when demobilization had begun Russell, whose health had suffered, relinquished the command. On his return to New Zealand he was accorded a national reception at Wellington, being hailed, in Maori, as "Ariki Toa", "The Fighting Chief Sent Forward to Lead".

Russell's main interest now became the welfare of the demobilized soldier and he was President of the New Zealand Returned Soldiers' Association from 1921 to 1924 and again from 1927 to 1935. During the Second World War Russell was a member of the New Zealand War Council and Inspector General of the New Zealand Forces from 1940 to 1941.

In 1896 he married Gertrude, daughter of J. N. Williams. There were two sons and three daughters of the marriage.

November 30, 1960.

Sir Claud Russell, K.C.M.G., died at his home, Trematon Castle, Saltash, on December 9, 1959, his eighty-eighth birthday. The grandson of Lord Arthur Russell, M.P. for Tavistock 1857-1885, second son of the sixth Duke of Bedford, he was born on December 9, 1871, and educated privately and at Balliol College, Oxford.

He joined the Diplomatic Service in 1897 and retired in 1935, having been created K.C.M.G. in 1930. To a certain degree his career was disappointing, for his abilities were considerable. It is true that in Lisbon at the end of his service he had reached the rank of Ambassador (then, of course, far less common than nowadays), but Lisbon, though one of the most agreeable posts, had, when he was there, no great political importance.

Russell, a diplomatist of the old school, had much in his favour. Tall, dark, slim, with a slightly etiolated air of well-bred indolence, and fine, aristocratic features which were set off on occasion by a monocle, he looked the part to perfection. His mind was acute and clear; his dispatches and minutes were written in a prose that was fluid but concise and cogent. He possessed the power of reducing complicated problems to their simple basic elements. He had, too, a wide experience of men and affairs. The list of the countries where he served reads like a travel agent's prospectus: Turkey, Egypt, China, France, Russia, Morocco, Argentina, Paraguay, Spain, Greece, Abyssinia, Switzerland, and Portugal. In the Foreign Office itself he had only a brief spell in 1914.

But against these assets was set a complete failure to practise the art of pleasing. He had, indeed, no desire to please. Few men can have done less than Russell to humour the prejudices or study the foibles of his chiefs. This was not due to lack of ambition. Though markedly uncompetitive, he had a legitimate pride of family (he was a grandson of the sixth Duke of Bedford and his mother's father—she was French—had been a Minister of Charles X), and he liked to feel that he was carrying on their tradition of public service.

But he was, unfortunately, incapable by temperament of understanding that other men might, unlike himself in whom the fires of life burned low, be swayed by emotion rather than by reason; that they might regard as important, and expect him to do the same, events and problems which to him were almost trivial. And even if he had understood their point of view he would have been too fastidious to go through motions or affect an enthusiasm which he would have felt to be unnecessary and hypocritical. Thus he laid himself open to accusations of apathy and even of indolence, accusations which were the more vehemently pressed when, as not infrequently happened, the turn of events seemed to prove that Russell's inertia was justified. It was in this way that his tour of duty in the Foreign Office turned out unfortunately for him. He was put into a key department at a time of crisis. In such surroundings Russell's almost oriental belief in the danger of haste, an attitude of mind valuable in a chief but decidedly less so in a subordinate, combined with a reluctance to accelerate his tempo, did little to endear him to an ambitious and harassed head of department.

Russell cared little for entertaining and did not make friends easily. Happily married and self-sufficient, he hardly felt the need for them. But to those whom he knew well he could be a delightful companion. He had a fund of anecdotes which he recounted with a dry humour and a rare, wintry smile in the somewhat over-precise diction common to certain other members of his family. For him a word such as towel, for instance, was a dissyllable. Indeed, his speech might have seemed an affectation had it not been so manifestly an extension—and a likeable one—of a rare and delicately muted personality.

Withal he was a formidable and lucky negotiator. Though he failed when Minister in Addis Ababa to conclude an agreement about the head waters of the Nile, nobody else could have succeeded or indeed come nearer success than he did. In the smaller things, however, he almost always got his way, thanks rather to the awe than the affection which he inspired in the Ethiopian officials with whom he had to deal, and this was no mean feat. In Lisbon, where he is still remembered as a typical if somewhat remote English gentleman, he had a number of substantial if unspectacular achievements to his credit and it was always a disappointment to him that what he had accomplished there was not more generously recognized by the Foreign Office.

Russell had the distinction of being allowed by the Foreign Office to mobilize with his regiment, the Bedfordshire Yeomanry, in August 1914, and went to France on the outbreak of war. It was characteristic of his sense of duty and of the fitness of things that 26 years later, at the age of 69, he should enlist in the Home Guard.

He married in 1920 Athenais, one of the two beautiful daughters—the other is the wife of Sir Pierson Dixon*—of the late S. Clifford Atchley, C.M.G., whose encyclopaedic knowledge of Greece and its affairs was so highly valued by a succession of British representatives in Athens.

December 10, 1959.

Fred Russell, the ventriloquist, as **Thomas Frederick Parnell,** O.B.E., was widely known, died at his home at Wembley, Middlesex, on October 14, 1957. He was 95.

For generations he had enjoyed the esteem and affection of everyone associated with variety entertainment in Britain, and was not less respected in many other parts of the world. He not only possessed to the end of his life all his faculties, but maintained an impressive dignity and mental alertness. His speech at the dinner arranged by his brethren of the Grand Order of Water Rats to celebrate his ninetieth birthday will remain in the memory of all who heard it. It was a *tour de force,* warm-hearted, affectionately reminiscent, yet deeply touching in its simplicity. He had many titles conferred upon him by his contemporaries of the variety stage, and every one of them had a solid basis. He was known, for example, as the "Father of Variety" because of the part he played in the founding of the Variety Artists' Federation. At 90 he became its President.

Russell was born in London on September 29, 1862, and at 20 embarked on a journalistic career. But in his spare time he was a ventriloquist, and in 1886 he began to perform in public. He was occupying the editorial chair of the *Hackney and Kingsland Gazette,* in 1896, when his chance came to take up ventriloquism professionally and he forsook journalism for the music-hall stage. Charles Morton, a famous showman, had been much impressed by Russell's performance, and engaged him at the Palace Theatre, London. Russell introduced his new technique in ventriloquism: instead of the orthodox family of dummies he relied on one, which he named "Coster Joe". The engagement lasted 20 months, and the man and his doll became inseparable partners, growing in favour with music-hall patrons.

It was said that he changed his name to Russell because at the time he was founding his ventriloquial career the name Parnell was thought to have too much of a political flavour for his purpose; he therefore took the name Russell from his local member of Parliament, who was later Lord Russell of Killowen.

Year after year Russell and his "familiar" were seen at every amusement centre of consequence in Britain, and later during three prolonged tours of Australia, New Zealand, and South Africa, and during visits to America and Ceylon, Russell and his quick-witted cockney companion "Coster Joe" were welcome wherever they went. In 1932 they appeared at the Royal Command Performance. His abilities remained undimmed in later years, and occasionally he delighted in demonstrating them. As recently as January 1952, introduced as "the oldest ventriloquist in the world", he appeared in Music Hall on television, and again in August of the same year he gave another televised performance.

A member of the Grand Order of Water Rats almost from its inception, he was King Rat as long ago as 1903. He had the unique distinction of being ruler of the "Rats" for four separate terms, and for 26 years was preceptor of the order. His enthusiasm on its behalf knew no bounds, and it was his proud boast that every movement for improving the lot of variety performers had been initiated in its lodge room.

One of the founders of the Variety Artists Federation, he was active for over 50 years in the interests of its members. At one time there were 14 members of his family in variety. One of his sons is Val Parnell*. In 1948 he was appointed O.B.E. in recognition of his 50 years' service to the variety profession.

He did not forget his journalistic training and in 1906 founded *The Performer,* and was its managing director for 30 years. The journal ceased publication in September.

October 15, 1957.

Sir Thomas Wentworth Russell, K.B.E., C.M.G., widely known throughout the Middle East as **Russell Pasha,** died in London on April 10, 1954 at the age of 74.

For 44 years he served successive Egyptian Governments in the police; and when he retired in June 1946 the tradition, first set up by Valentine Baker Pasha in the reign of the Khedive Tewfik, of strengthening that famous force by British officers in senior posts came to an end. But long before his retirement his achievements as commandant of the Cairo City Police and as director of the Egyptian Government Central Narcotics Intelligence Bureau had become legendary; and he leaves a name that will not quickly be forgotten.

The son of the late Rev. Henry Charles Russell, of Wollaton, Nottingham, and a great-grandson of the sixth Duke of Bedford, he was born on November 22, 1879, and was educated at Haileybury and Trinity College, Cambridge. He joined the Egyptian Civil Service in 1902, and when an inspector of the Ministry of the Interior he formed the Camel Corps which brought discipline and order to the wild desert fringes of the Nile Valley. In 1917 he became commandant of the Cairo Police, a post which he held under no fewer than 32 different Egyptian administrations.

In spite of the anti-western feeling which sometimes made the lot of foreigners very difficult, he was wholly trusted by every Government under which he served. In the policing of a great metropolitan city inhabited by many racial elements he showed himself both efficient and resourceful; while the respect in which he was held even by malefactors often enabled him to disperse a dangerous mob by his mere presence without the use of force. He was made a C.M.G. in 1926 and an O.B.E. in 1920, being advanced to

K.B.E. in 1938.

His international reputation, as contrasted with his reputation in Egypt, was won by his outstanding achievements as head of the Central Narcotics Intelligence Bureau, which was set up by the Egyptian Government at his suggestion in 1929. His reports of the nature and extent of the international traffic in the "white drugs" cocaine and heroin, stirred moral opinion throughout Europe and the Middle East. He waged successful warfare against powerful drug rings for many years, and with the cooperation of the Swiss, French, Turkish, and Bulgarian Governments he brought the entire traffic under something like effective control. His determination and resourcefulness met and matched the most ingenious devices that smugglers could contrive.

In his book *Egyptian Service, 1902-1946,* published in 1949, he left a modest and most readable account of the many strange experiences which had come to him in the course of his career. Some of the episodes which he describes are more exciting than most current fiction, and although he was no great hand with the pen, the complete and simple honesty of the narrative atoned for any lack of literary skill. With his death a great public servant, who made the name of Britain respected in many lands and among many races, has passed away.

He married, in 1911, Evelyn Dorothea Temple, daughter of Francis Moore, who survives him, together with a son and a daughter.

April 12, 1954.

Judge Sir G. Russell Vick—See **Vick.**

Grand Duchess Marie of Russia—See **Marie.**

Grand Duchess Olga of Russia—See **Olga.**

Grand Duchess Xenia of Russia—See **Xenia.**

Albert Rutherston, formerly Ruskin Master of Drawing in the University of Oxford, died on July 14, 1953 at the age of 71 while on holiday in Switzerland.

Albert Daniel Rothenstein (to give him his original name, anglicized at the time of the 1914-18 war) was born at Bradford on December 5, 1881, the son of Moritz Rothenstein and his wife, Bertha Dux. He was the brother of Sir William Rothenstein, former Principal of the Royal College of Art. After attending Bradford Grammar School he entered the Slade School in 1898 and studied for four years under Professor Frederick Brown. He began to exhibit at the New English Art Club in 1901 and remained faithful to that association throughout his painting career. Another group which accepted him was the Royal Society of Painters in Water Colours.

He began with well-observed realistic transcripts from scenes of ordinary life, but he was a man of experimental turn of mind, and he arrived in time at a decorative technique that was very charming and was marked by a highly personal handwriting. Its concomitants were a thin, calligraphic line, with a narrow strip of colour along it, shading off to cream or white, elongated figures, conventionalized but not severely distorted, and stylized clouds, flowers, and vegetation. Pale, delicate blues, greens, and purples predominated, set off by an occasional splash of brilliant red or yellow. Though many Japanese artists paint on silk, the process is not common in the West, and Rutherston was one of the few contemporary British artists to attempt it.

His stage work included sets done in collaboration with Norman Wilkinson for *Comus* and *The Winter's Tale,* and independently for *Androcles and the Lion, Le Mariage Forcé,* and some of Pavlova's ballets. His decorative and symbolical treatment was well adapted to these themes. In book-illustration, too, he made some happy excursions, like Mme. Maeterlinck's *The Children's Blue Bird, Cymbeline* (in The Players' Shakespeare), and the Cresset Press edition of Herrick. When the Nonesuch Press brought out a revised edition of their most popular *Week-End Book* Rutherston was chosen to decorate it.

Rutherston held that all imaginative art should be grounded in a knowledge of natural forms, and his own practice bore out this belief. He was capable, too, of turning out delicate, naturalistic pen and wash drawings in what might be described as the "Slade manner", and his technical accomplishment brought him in 1929 the post of Master of the Ruskin Drawing School at Oxford, a post he held for 20 years. He wrote *Decoration in the Art of the Theatre* and, in collaboration with the late John Drinkwater, a memoir of Claud Lovat Fraser. His editorship of the *Contemporary British Artists* series was marked by sound selective ability.

Broad and humane views in general emerged from a series of wireless dialogues called *Artists at Work* arranged by Stanley Casson in 1932 and published in book form a year later.

He married in 1919 Miss Marjory Holman, who survives him together with one son of the marriage. Their other son died only a few months ago.

July 15, 1953.

Alexander Hore-Ruthven—See **Gowrie.**

Dr. Risto Ryti, President of Finland from 1940 to 1944, died on October 25, 1956 at the age of 67, after a long illness. He had been condemned to 10 years' imprisonment in 1946 as a war criminal, but was released after serving three years of his sentence owing to illness. He had taken no part in public life since his release.

His own tragedy was in some sort the tragedy of his country. Caught up in a quarrel between two major Powers, Finland had a difficult and ungrateful part to play in the war in eastern Europe. The Russo-German Treaty of August 23, 1939, was the starting shot in a war which eventually spread over all the world and countries in exposed positions like Finland were willy-nilly involved. In the uneasy peace which followed the "winter war" in 1939-40 between Russia and Finland, Finland had good reason to fear both the Germans and the Russians. Any move was perilous, but so also was inactivity, as events but too vividly showed in the later stages of the German campaign in Russia. Ryti, by permitting German troops to enter Finnish territory, no doubt bowed to *force majeure,* but his mistake was to pledge his country to the German side without full and open consultation with the representatives of the Finnish people and for this he paid the penalty.

Born in 1889, he was educated at Helsinki University where he read law, and he was in practice as a lawyer from 1909, when he graduated from the university, until 1919. In the latter year he was elected to the Finnish Parliament and two years later became the youngest Minister of Finance in the world. He again made a record in 1923 when only in his middle thirties he became Governor of the Bank of Finland and in his long period of office made an enviable reputation in international banking circles.

When southern Finland was invaded by Russian forces in 1939, Ryti was known to be strongly in favour of the stiffest resistance and he backed President Kallios's policy to the utmost of his capacity. The latter died suddenly in December 1940 and Ryti was elected President in his stead, polling 288 of the electors' 300 votes on the first count. In the uneasy period that followed he retained the confidence of the country, so that he was re-elected in 1943 to try to steer his country through the narrow and tortuous channel it had to navigate between the warring Powers.

At first he maintained correct and neutral relations with both Russia and Germany, but as the tide of war in Russia began to flow against Germany, the Germans sought to use Finland as a base from which they could open up another and diversionary front to draw off Russian troops from the hard pressed German forces in White Russia and the Ukraine. An American offer to mediate between Finland and Russia came to nothing and in the summer of 1944 Ryti, in a personal letter to Hitler, pledged his country not to make a separate peace with Russia.

When news of this leaked out there was an explosion of public indignation and Ryti resigned, being succeeded in office by Marshal Mannerheim [q.v.]. He returned to the Bank of Finland, the governorship of which he had held *in absentia* while he was President, but within a few weeks of the German collapse in 1945 he resigned that office also.

Later in the year he was put on trial with a number of his colleagues, and after protracted hearings and lengthy adjournments was sentenced in February 1946 to 10 years' penal servitude. He was released after he had served for three years, but never re-entered public life.

October 26, 1956.

S

Michael Sadleir, novelist, biographer, bibliophile, and authoritative student of the literature of the Victorian age and of Victoriana generally, and a leading London publisher, died on December 13, 1957 at the age of 68.

A man of many parts, Michael Sadleir was notably successful in almost all that he undertook. As a publisher, a director since 1920 of the firm of Constable, he served the interests of a distinguished list of authors and of the reading public with excellent judgment and practical ability. The firm continued to publish the work of authors whose high reputation it had helped to establish before 1920, but in the following years it also claimed, in no little measure owing to Sadleir himself, a considerable share of the new talent in this country. As a bibliophile and collector—he had collected since his undergraduate days—Sadleir was supreme in his own field.

His private library, based upon a love of first editions, included a superb collection of Victorian fiction of the three-decker period. And, as a writer, he achieved something of fame and fortune as both a best-selling novelist of a romantic and curiously instructive stamp and the author of a standard biography of Trollope and of other volumes that provide an illuminating commentary on Victorian literary history. Altogether Sadleir's was an impressive record of achievement and success.

Born on December 25, 1888, the son of Sir Michael Sadler, K.C.S.I., C.B., who was Master of University College, Oxford, from 1923 until 1934, and Lady Sadler, Michael Sadleir (he adopted that spelling of his name in order to assist in avoiding confusion between his father and himself) was brought up in an atmosphere of scholarly cultivation and wide artistic interests. He was educated at Rugby and at Balliol College, Oxford, where he took second class honours in history and won the Stanhope Essay Prize. He entered the office of Constable and Co. in 1912; served in the War Trade intelligence department during 1915-18; was a member of the British delegation to the Peace Conference at Versailles in 1919; and, for a brief period in the following year, of the secretariat of the League of Nations; and, on returning to publishing, was made a director of the firm of Constable in 1920.

The Stanhope Essay Prize, *The Political Career of Richard Brinsley Sheridan,* had been published in 1912; before then Sadleir had written a novel, *The Anchor,* which in later years he chose to forget. His first considered piece of imaginative work was a novel, *Privilege* (1921), which pictured the old order of existence already in decay before the war of 1914-18—a rich, romantic, well-written if not conspicuously alive piece of story-telling. A year afterwards he produced *Excursions in Victorian Bibliography,* in which his delight in Trollope is specially apparent. Then came two more novels, *Desolate Splendour* (1923), which exhibited a rather perilous fondness for strong and flamboyant drama, and *The Noblest Frailty,* a slighter and on the whole more persuasive piece of work, illustrating the process of decay in mid-Victorian times that ripened into catastrophe in 1914.

Trollope: A Commentary appeared in 1927. Its claim to rank as a standard biography was at once apparent. Sadleir's childhood training in Trollope had flowered into adult enthusiasm and he had given several years to the work of amassing and arranging his material. The result, distinguished by conspicuous skill in narrative, was a triumph of love and admiration. It bore immediate fruit in a revival of interest in Trollope, a revival to which the remarkable popularity of the novels during the years from 1939 onwards was a fitting sequel. A year after the biography came a Trollope bibliography, a model of its kind, to which the author added a series of illuminating notes on the literary history of Trollope's day.

Then, with an interlude for the publication, in 1930, of the first volume in a "Bibliographia" series, issued by Constable, *Evolution of Publishers' Binding Styles, 1770-1900,* which was really a fascinating chapter of the unwritten history of the book trade, came *Bulwer and His Wife* (1931) and *Blessington-D'Orsay* (1933). The first, described as a "panorama", painted a brilliant picture of the picturesque and raffish society which lent gaudy colour to English life during the first 30 years or more of the nineteenth century, and in so doing made a sparkling rococo romance of Bulwer's obstinately second-rate career. The other, described as a masquerade—it is a slighter book—brought gay and likely fancy to the relationship of the "gorgeous" Lady Blessington and the scarcely less gorgeous Count D'Orsay, discovering in it an emblem of a special sort of the chaos of morals and taste of the period.

In subsequent years Sadleir turned his hand again to fiction, this time with signal success. *These Foolish Things* (1937), "a first person experiment in emotional intimacy", does not come off particularly well, but both *Fanny by Gaslight* (1940) and *Forlorn Sunset* (1947) accomplish very well indeed what they are meant to. Each of the studies of the London of the 1870s, or at any rate of the vicious underworld, gilded or plebeian, of the London of the period, is piled high with authentic detail; but in each instance the story, though shrewdly contrived, is artificial and melodramatic, narrowly restricted alike in its range of interest and fidelity to life. Both, however, were enormously popular. Of the former a successful film was made.

In 1949 appeared *Michael Ernest Sadler: A Memoir by His Son,* and in 1951 *Nineteenth Century Fiction,* a bibliographical record based on his own collection. The following year that collection of first editions and other significant editions of nineteenth-century fiction, comprising over 10,000 volumes, was bought *en bloc* by the University of California.

Sadleir married in 1914 Edith, daughter of Canon A. D. Tupper-Carey. There were three children of the marriage, two sons and a daughter. The elder son was killed in action in 1940.

December 16, 1957.

Former Bishop of St. Albans—See **Furse.**

Miss **Christopher Marie St. John,** the author, died on October 20, 1960 at the Priest's House, Smallhythe, where she lived for many years with the late Edith Craig, whose mother Ellen Terry had been their nearest neighbour, and with Clare Atwood,* the painter.

It was with Christopher St. John's and Edith Craig's help that Ellen Terry completed the revision of her autobiography, and it is to the editorial work of Christopher St. John that we owe the publication of Ellen Terry's correspondence with Bernard Shaw. It all began with the writing by St. John of adoring letters to Ellen Terry towards the end of the latter's partnership with Irving at the Lyceum. She went up to Oxford in 1894 and one day in 1896 had an interview with Ellen Terry in her dressing room. In 1899, at a time when she was doing secretarial work in the mornings for Lady Randolph Churchill and her son Winston,* she bicycled over to Fulham, where Ellen Terry was playing. On this occasion she met Edith Craig, who was then a member of her mother's company. The spark of friendship between the two was struck immediately, and later in the year, while Ellen Terry went with Irving on his last tour of America, Edith Craig and Christopher St. John set up together their first house, and their first garden, at 7 Smith Square. Their contemporaries, not suspecting how inappropriate to "Edy" and "Chris" such a nickname would sound to us today, christened them "The Squares".

From Smith Square they moved into a flat close to Bernard and Charlotte Shaw's in Adelphi Terrace House, and thence to 31 Bedford Street, where they admitted during the 1914-18 War a third housemate, Clare Atwood. Meanwhile the two senior partners had taken over the Priest's House, Smallhythe, a stone's throw from the cottage-retreat of Ellen Terry. After Bedford Street was given up, the Priest's House became their home. Ellen Terry died in 1928. Edith Craig founded the Barn Theatre, adjoining the cottage, and organized some sort of annual performance there in her mother's honour till her own death in 1947—the centenary of Ellen Terry's birth. "Chris" and "Tony" (Miss Atwood) went on living at the Priest's House. In particular the kitchen and the garden were "Chris's" province. "You ought to write a history of that *ménage à trois.* It was unique in my experience," Shaw told St. John. But she never did.

She wrote, however, several plays and adapted others. Ellen Terry appeared in the first of her original plays, *Erikkson's Wife,* and toured in England and in America in *The Good Hope,* adapted by St. John from the Dutch of Herman Heijermans. She also adapted *Le Carneval des Enfants* by St. Georges de Bouhélhier, which Edith Craig produced, and she wrote, with Cicely Hamilton [q.v.], on behalf of the Women's Freedom League, *How the Vote was Won.* She accompanied Ellen Terry to America in 1907, chiefly with the object of working with her on her lifestory: a project in which the star lost interest when she married her American-born leading man, James Carew, in the course of the season. Nevertheless the revised edition was finished and published in 1908.

St. John did dramatic criticism for *Time and Tide* from 1920 till 1931, and in at least one contribution to a book of essays wrote discriminatingly of the work of Ellen Terry's great-nephew, Sir John Gielgud.

October 25, 1960.

Former Dean of St. Paul's—See **Inge.**

Cardinal Jules-Géraud Saliege, Archbishop of Toulouse, died on November 5, 1956 at Toulouse at the age of 86.

Cardinal Saliege had reached the age of 76 when he was elevated to the Sacred College of Cardinals. It was generally believed that Pope Pius XII had selected him not only because of his long service as archbishop of an important see, but also in recognition of his conduct during the German occupation from 1940 until 1945. His protests against oppression culminated in the circulation of a pastoral letter in which he denounced racial propaganda with special reference to the persecution of the Jews. This prompted an order for his arrest, but in view of his advanced age and poor state of health he was released from detention and allowed to remain in Toulouse comparatively free from molestation.

He was born at Mauriac on February 24, 1870, and ordained to the priesthood in 1895. His first appointment was to a seminary near Toulouse where he taught mathematics before receiving a professorship of theology. He became a chaplain in the French Army in 1914 and served with distinction throughout the 1914-18 War. His consecration as a bishop in 1926 was followed two years later by his appointment to the archiepiscopal see of Toulouse. A few months before his elevation to the Sacred College he celebrated his sacerdotal golden jubilee.

His pastoral letter condemning the persecution of the Jews, which led to the order for his arrest during the occupation of France, was the more courageous because he had suffered from a stroke in 1931 and was partly paralysed. For that reason he was arrested but not imprisoned, and he continued his opposition to persecution and his personal efforts for members of the French Resistance who sought sanctuary from him.

His infirmities became more marked during the years that followed the war (his speech was impeded) but in no way checked the activity of his mind. He was unable to travel to Rome for the Consistories in which he was elevated to the Sacred College in 1946, and he received the Red Hat a month later from the Papal Nuncio to France.

Later Mgr. Gabriel Garrone, who now succeeds him in the see of Toulouse, was appointed Coadjutor-Archbishop, but Cardinal Saliege continued much of his work, particularly with regard to diocesan organizations and religious communities. He was decorated in 1946 with the Legion of Honour in token of his work during the occupation.

November 6, 1956.

Bishop of Salisbury—See **Lovett.**

Professor Gaetano Salvemini, the distinguished Italian historian and an outspoken opponent of Fascism, died at Sorrento on September 6, 1957. He was 84.

Born in Sicily, he made his mark at the University of Florence, where he studied under Villari. His experiences as a teacher led him into the campaign for the reform of the *Scuole Medie* and for the raising of the status of the profession. He became an influential Socialist, fully alive to the neglect the south suffered under the union. But he was too uncompromising to prosper as a politician, and he fell out with his party over the question of intervention in 1914. He had long uttered warnings against the menace of German aggrandisement, and when the war came he supported, against his party, intervention on the side of the Entente. He was not, on the other hand, a nationalist, and he conducted a spirited opposition to the imperialism of some of his countrymen which laid claim to Dalmatia. He founded, and for many years edited, the weekly newspaper *L'Unita.*

He disliked, making no secret of his dislike, both Fascism and the way it came about; and in 1925 he was arrested on a charge of complicity in the publication of a clandestine news-sheet. Later that year he was deprived of his professorship at Florence.

Abroad, at first in England and then in the United States, he persevered in his hostility to Mussolini's régime. By reason of his scholarship, his sure grasp of fact, and his disinterested Liberal principles, he was one of the most formidable critics of Fascism, notably in two books, *The Fascist Dictatorship* (1928) and *Under the Axe of Fascism* (1936).

He was a historian of sound scholarship who was attracted to historical subjects by the light they throw on the events of the historian's own day. Thus his valuable study of the early history of the Italian communes was undertaken largely on account of its bearing on the politics of Italy before the 1914-18 War; and the course of lectures which he gave in London in 1923 on "The Foreign Policy of Italy from 1871 to 1914", was full of topical reflections. The particular value also of his study of the French Revolution (1925) lay in his sense of the relevance of that eruption to the problems of the day. He also wrote a sarcastic treatise on Mussolini's foreign policy during the 10 years 1922-32, and a diplomatic history of the Abyssinian War entitled *Prelude to World War II.* He returned to Italy in 1954, and was in 1956 awarded the Italian inter-nation prize for history.

In his rectitude of purpose Salvemini resembled Mazzini, whose disciple he was, and whose ideas he analysed in a monograph first published in 1925. He also possessed in full measure the exuberance of the southern Italian, which he combined with humour and warm sympathies.

September 7, 1957.

Albert Sammons, the violinist, died on August 24, 1957 at his home at Southdean, Sussex, after a life fairly evenly divided between orchestral, chamber, and solo playing and teaching. He was 71.

As a soloist he achieved his most memorable distinction as an interpreter of Elgar's concerto—indeed, he has had no successor in this particular work. In chamber music he was associated successively with the London String Quartet, the Chamber Music Players, and William Murdoch in sonatas.

He was born in London on February 3, 1886, and had some lessons from his father, an amateur musician, and very little professional teaching. Yet he acquired an adequate technique from sheer natural aptitude.

He was playing in a restaurant band when, in 1908, he was heard by Sir Thomas Beecham,* who promptly engaged him to lead the orchestra he had formed for his opera seasons. He continued orchestral playing, with excursions into concerto playing, until the war. In 1910 he formed a string quartet with Petre, Waldo Warner, and Warwick Evans, which continued for nine years, during which a number of modern English works were introduced to the public.

After the war Sammons joined a different sort of quartet, the Chamber Music Players, consisting of Murdoch, Tertis* and Cedric Sharp (*vice* Felix Salmond, who went to America). It was this *ensemble,* augmented by W. H. Reed, that gave the first performance of Elgar's piano quintet at a concert at which the string quartet, another product of Elgar's war years, was also introduced. In spite of the heavy commitments of its members to solo work, this consort played together (with a change of cellists) for 22 years.

The later years of his career were spent in teaching at the Royal College of Music. He has one composition to his credit, a Phantasy quartet, which won a Cobbett award.

August 26, 1957.

Professor Gaetano De Sanctis—See **De Sanctis.**

Flora Sandes, who died in November 1956 at the age of 80, served for seven years from 1915 in the Serbian Army as a fighting soldier and was decorated for her bravery in the field.

She was the youngest daughter of the Rev. Samuel Dickson Sandes, Rector of Whitechurch, co. Cork, who later moved to England, where she was born. She was adventurous by nature and learnt to ride and shoot and, in the days when motoring was an adventure and not just a means of transport, acquired an old

French racing car. In such ways she relieved the monotony during the period when she had to earn her living as a secretary in a London office.

At the beginning of the 1914-18 War, having been a member of the St. John Ambulance Brigade for some years, she had a chance to go out to Serbia with a small nursing unit. She later joined the Serbian Red Cross, and when the Bulgarians invaded Serbia she obtained permission to join the ambulance of the 2nd Infantry Regiment as a dresser. The Serbian Army was slowly being driven back by overwhelming odds with their only line of retreat through the Albanian Mountains, and conditions were such that Miss Sandes drifted by successive stages from a nurse into a soldier.

The soldiers with the ambulance took it for granted that anyone who could ride and shoot would be a soldier under such conditions, and it was not unusual for Serbian peasant girls to fight with the army. When, therefore, they reached country impassable to ambulances she took the Red Cross badge off her arm and said she would join the 2nd Regiment as a private. The procedure was simple; the colonel took the little brass regimental figures off his own epaulettes and fastened them on the shoulder straps of his new recruit, and official sanction came a little later. She was regarded as a considerable asset, for the simple peasant soldiers looked on her as a representative of England and a pledge that in the end England would help them. But their personal affection for her soon increased almost to idolatry, for under the stress of war she showed all the qualities they most admired—outstanding courage, cheerfulness, and sympathy.

Her service with the Serbian Army lasted seven years and she experienced the hardest conditions of mountain warfare, with terrible losses, through defeat and victory until the general demobilization in the autumn of 1922. The 2nd Regiment was known as the "Iron Regiment" and spent most of its time in the front line, where she fought in every battle until she was severely wounded by a Bulgarian hand grenade in November 1916. Sergeant Sandes, as she then was, was taken to a British military field hospital for Serbians, where she remained for about two months, and where she was decorated by the aide-de-camp of the Prince Regent with the Order of the Kara-George—a rare decoration given for conspicuous bravery in the field.

She was given sick leave in England, where she raised more funds and collected comforts for the Serbian soldiers, and in May 1917 she returned to her regiment and took part in all further operations. She was given a commission in June 1919 and promoted to lieutenant on demobilization in 1922, and in 1926 she received the rank of captain.

In 1927 she married Yurie Yudenitch, who had been a colonel in the White Russian Army and had escaped from Russia during the revolution. He joined the Serbian army as a sergeant and had been in her regiment. They lived in France for a time and later in Belgrade, where during the last war they were both interned by the Germans.

They were later released on parole. They had little to live on, but she had her army pension and taught English. Her husband died in 1941, and at the end of the German occupation she settled in England in a small cottage in Suffolk, where she lived until her death.

December 1, 1956.

The Rev. Dr. William Edwin Robert Sangster, who died at his home in London on May 24, 1960, was unquestionably one of the outstanding preachers of his day, his reputation reaching far beyond denominational boundaries in either Britain or the many countries which he visited.

Two years before he died he was seized by a wasting muscular illness which necessitated his retirement from the ministry. He had continued his writing until a more rapid deterioration set in a day or two ago.

Born in London in June 1900, the son of Henry George Sangster, and educated at the Shoreditch Secondary School, he had no family associations with Methodism, but the influence of the Radnor Street Sunday School, which was appropriately connected with Wesley's Chapel itself, led him to offer for the ministry after a period of service with The Royal West Surrey Regiment towards the end of the 1914-18 War. He was a student at Richmond College and graduated in the University of London. His earliest appointments were at Bognor and Colwyn Bay and his unusually effective preaching quickly became known to holiday congregations. There followed a term in the Bootle Circuit, and in 1932 he became minister of Queen Street Church, Scarborough, which has always been regarded as something of a Methodist pivotal point.

Visitors as well as residents quickly realized that preaching of an uncommon quality was to be heard and a crowded church was the consequence. Four years later the appointment of Dr. Leslie Weatherhead [d. 1976] to the City Temple created a vacancy at the Leeds Brunswick Church, then in its heyday as a result of the notable Weatherhead ministry. There was deep anxiety that the right successor should be found, and Dr. Weatherhead himself advised that Sangster should follow him. There was no regret at the choice and it was quickly obvious that one outstanding figure had followed another.

Occupancy of this pulpit brought him invitations to address Methodist meetings in many parts of Britain and so did his reputation rise that there was little surprise when in 1939 he was invited to Westminster Central Hall, the principal preaching place of Metropolitan Methodism. This was the pulpit which Dr. Dinsdale T. Young had helped to make famous for many years.

The Sangster ministry could hardly have started under more depressing circumstances, as it began on September 3, and he had hardly faced his congregation before the first air raid warning of the war sounded. That it was a false alarm was not known to the public at that time. Air raids were to play a big part in the earlier part of the Sangster ministry as the crypt became a shelter, housing large numbers of people each night, and Dr. Sangster with his wife lived there throughout the danger years.

Despite wartime difficulties congregations were maintained and, with the war over, the Central Hall remained as one of the few inner-ring churches of any denomination to be crowded to capacity Sunday by Sunday. All this time the minister had been in great demand by the Methodist and other churches for special occasions. In 1950 he was elected President of the Methodist Conference, the distinction coming to him at a much earlier age than had been customary for many years. He contrived to preach at Westminster at least once a month, despite his strenuous itinerary. At the beginning of 1953 a sermon on "What a Religious Revival Might Do for Britain" was widely publicized, creating probably as much attention as any pulpit pronouncement for a decade.

In 1955 he was appointed general secretary of the Methodist Home Mission Department and thus became responsible for development work throughout the country. He organized a series of schools of evangelism to train church workers and adopted many means of invigorating church life. Dr. Sangster frequently visited the United States and also gave the Cato Lecture to the Methodist Conference of Australia. He served on the Methodist delegation which discussed closer relations with the Anglican Church. He was also for several years a member of the Senate of London University.

Vitality was the keynote of his preaching. He had distinctive mannerisms which seemed distressingly obvious at a first hearing but were entirely forgotten at a second. In style he came more nearly to the old pulpit masters, but his arguments were invariably developed with crisp illustration, and he had a lively wit which he kept in constant employment.

He was the author of many books including: *Why Jesus Never Wrote a Book; He is Able; The Craft of Sermon Construction;* and *The Secret of Radiant Life.* He contributed to many journals and wrote innumerable pamphlets on religious topics.

He married Margaret, daughter of John Conway, of London, by whom he had one son and one daughter.

May 25, 1960.

George Santayana, the philosopher and man of letters, died on September 26, 1952 in Rome, aged 88.

His death deprives America and Europe of a thinker who had for long held a position of august if somewhat isolated eminence, and in whom the worlds of philosophy and literature were joined with singular felicity. Santayana—who described himself as a recalcitrant materialist—was not a philosopher's philosopher; he was never given to the pursuit of metaphysical abstractions, and was in closer sympathy with the artist than with the metaphysician. In substance his philosophy, though at once eclectic and intellectually inconsistent, is a restatement of the materialism of Democritus cast in a profoundly humanist mould. What gives it its high creative distinction is its genius of style. With Santayana the style is, very nearly, the philosopher himself. His superb gift of exposition, his fertility of mind, his Latin grace and clarity, his wit and aptness and accuracy of phrase, bring home to the unprofessional student of philosophy and to the reader of literary taste the riches of Santayana's "dogmatic naturalism".

George Santayana—Jorge Agustin Nicolás de Santayana—was the child of Spanish parents, and was born in Madrid on December 16, 1863. At the age of 11 he was transplanted to America, and took his B.A. degree at Harvard in 1886. At Harvard, which was to be his academic, but never his spiritual, home, he made contact with such typically American philosophers as William James and Josiah Royce. From 1889 to 1912 he was first instructor and then professor of philosophy, and his teaching offered a piquant contrast to that of his colleagues. His first important book was a brief treatise on aesthetics, *The Sense of Beauty,* published in 1896, a work which exhibited the penetration and vigour of his intelligence as well as his strictly self-limited horizons. The essays in *Interpretations of Poetry and Religion* (1900) are even today fascinating reading, but Santayana's earlier writings were eclipsed by the publication between 1905 and 1906 of the five volumes of *The Life of Reason,* a work which later dissatisfied him greatly, but which displayed his gifts at their highest development.

The Life of Reason is best described, perhaps, as a review of the conquest of "reason" in the story of mankind, from the point of view of a humanist and a classicist with strongly marked preferences and prejudices of his own. Its five volumes trace the progress of "reason" in "common sense" (that is to say, in the formation of those primary conceptions without which systematic thought is impossible, and which have now entered into the structure of human intelligence), in society, in religion, in science, and in art. It might, perhaps, be called an imaginative autobiography of the Spirit of Man, recalling in a mood of meditation the triumphs, defeats, and aberrations of his historic past. It was, without doubt, the enchantment of his style—somewhat overloaded here and there, but possessing the masculine strength of the best type of Renaissance ornament—that won for Santayana a wide circle of admirers.

As a critic he had a rare depth of discernment and a still rarer power of entering, admittedly with a degree of satirical zest, into the minds of thinkers with whose views he had scant sympathy. A volume published in 1910, *Three Philosophical Poets* (Lucretius, Dante, Goethe), bore witness to these gifts, and helped to extend his celebrity in literary circles.

In 1912 he left Harvard and became a European. He stayed in Oxford, London, Paris, and Rome. During the 1914-18 war, while living at Oxford, he composed those *Soliloquies in England* which contain some of his finest and most subtle critical work, and which are still perhaps the most sympathetic study of the English temperament and English institutions that has been made by a foreigner.

His later years were much occupied by the effort to recast his *Life of Reason* in a fresh form. Between 1923 and 1940 he published *Scepticism and Animal Faith* and the four volumes of *Realms of Being—The Realm of Essence, The Realm of Matter, the Realm of Truth,* and *The Realm of Spirit.* They show no decline in mental vigour, and their style is, if anything, more varied and delicate than that of the *Life of Reason.* In the opinion of many they can hardly be reckoned an improvement on the earlier work, but the whole work was a feat of revision such as only Santayana could have sustained with comparable breadth and brilliance of mind.

Among the works of his later period a special place is held by a vast, entertaining, and highly instructive novel, *The Last Puritan,* published in 1935, when he was 72. This "memoir" of Oliver Alden is a feast of ironical philosophic commentary, graced by admirable comic verve and intellectual fancy. This was followed by two equally enjoyable and instructive volumes of informal autobiography, *Persons and Places* (1945) and *The Middle Span* (1948).

In 1951 there appeared *Dominations and Powers,* another series of soliloquies illustrating his philosophy on questions of liberty, society, and government.

September 29, 1952.

Mary Sargant-Florence, the artist, who was best known for her work as a mural painter, died on December 14, 1954 at the age of 97.

An excellent composer, never at a loss in filling a space, however awkward, effectively, and a choice colourist, she was one of the most learned artists of her day in the various mediums of painting, deriving much of her knowledge from a careful study of old writers, Cennino Cennini in particular, and checking it by the light of modern science. She worked in tempera and watercolour, but her speciality was the difficult medium of "true" fresco, or *buon' fresco,* in which the colours are applied to the plaster while it is still wet, a method which compels decision and directness and allows no alterations. Very few modern artists have mastered this technique, in which Mrs. Sargant-Florence may be said to have challenged the saying of Michelangelo that oil painting is for women and fresco for men.

Mary Sargant, daughter of Henry Sargant, barrister, was born in London in 1857. She was educated at home and at private schools in Brighton and studied art in Paris under Luc-Olivier Merson, one of the first Frenchmen to appreciate the Italian "Primitives", and at the Slade School under Alphonse Legros. In 1888 she married Henry Smyth Florence, musician, by whom she had one son and one daughter, and for professional purposes hyphenated her name as Sargant-Florence.

A member of the New English Art Club, the Mural Decorators' Society, and the Arts and Crafts Exhibition Society, and an honorary member of the Women's International Art Club, Mrs. Sargant-Florence carried out several important schemes of decoration; at the Old School, Oakham, Rutland, and at Bourneville Schools, near Birmingham, both in true fresco; and at her home at Lords Wood, Marlow, in fresco and tempera. Her best known work in London is a panel in tempera in Chelsea Town Hall, part of one of the earliest concerted attempts in the present century to decorate public buildings.

Mrs. Sargant-Florence was only an occasional exhibitor at the Royal Academy, but at the Exhibition of Decorative Art at Burlington House in 1923 she was represented by several works, including a portion of a design for the mural decoration of a hall, *Les Aveugles,* inspired by Maeterlinck, with a study for the same in true fresco, and a design of *Spring* for a tapestry *portière,* executed at the School of Weaving at Stratford-on-Avon. Two of her cartoons for mural decorations, *Suffer Little Children to come unto Me* and *Pentecost,* which had been bought for the nation out of the Chantrey Bequest Fund, were included in the Royal Academy summer exhibition of 1933. A tempera painting, *Children at Chess,* was also purchased by the Academy and shown in the exhibition of 1950.

As an artist Mrs. Sargant-Florence was distinguished by the poetical and imaginative quality of her conceptions, Franciscan in feeling, the sureness of her drawing, and, above all, by her personal and delicate taste in colour. A keen gardener and a lover of animals, she was fond of introducing them into her compositions. Some of her smaller studies were enchanting in their unexpected harmonies of colour.

In 1940 she published a book, begun many years before, on *Colour Co-ordination.* In so far as it was concerned with "establishing the theory of the underlying principle of balance in grouping which shall satisfy the sense of aesthetic design in colour" it was full of valuable suggestions: but the references to music made it unnecessarily abstruse, so that, as *The Times Literary Supplement* remarked, it was a book to be read with a wet towel round the head. But, with its elaborate diagrams and mathematical formulas, the book left a formidable impression of mental power.

There was something irresistibly pathetic in her attempts during later years to interest all and sundry in the "harmony compass" which she had invented. Mrs. Sargant-Florence, of all people, had no need of such aids to colour composition, though no doubt the "compass" might be useful to the less gifted.

December 16, 1954.

King Ibn Saud, of Saudi Arabia, who died at Riyadh early on November 9, 1953, aged about 73, was the greatest figure in the Arab world in this century and for most of his life and for most of his reign was a firm friend of Great Britain.

The Wahabi King, Abdul Aziz Ibn Abdur

Rahman Al Faisal, commonly called Ibn Saud, King of the Hejaz and Nejd and its dependencies, was born at Riyadh about 1880. His father, the Emir Abdur Rahman, was the youngest of four sons of the Emir Faisal who reigned over Nejd from 1834 to 1867. On Faisal's death his two elder sons, Abdullah and Saud, plunged the country into civil war, as the result of which Hasa was occupied by the Turks in 1875 and Riyadh itself by Ibn Rashid in 1891. Abdur Rahman went into exile with his family, first at Bahrein and later at Kuwait, where the young Ibn Saud came under the influence of the astute Sheikh Mubarak Ibn Sabah, at a time when the Persian Gulf was a focus of international rivalries.

From this period Ibn Saud imbibed a conviction that the friendship of Great Britain was essential to the prosperity and independence of Arabia. The lawful pretender to the Wahabi throne was Abdul Aziz, son of Saud, but it was Abdur Rahman who in 1900 took the first step towards unseating the usurping dynasty of Ibn Rashid, Emir of the Shammar. After the defeat of his attempted invasion he formally relinquished his rights and obligations to his son Abdul Aziz, whom he was destined a quarter of a century later to see the recognized king of the greater part of Arabia.

In 1901 Abdul Aziz Ibn Saud launched out into the desert on a desperate venture with a force of 200 men, including his cousin, Abdullah Ibn Jiluwi, who afterwards became his Governor of Hasa. Leaving the bulk of his force a day's journey distant, he entered Riyadh by night in January 1902 with 15 men and forced an entry into a house opposite the fort, the gate of which he watched till dawn. Immediately the Rashidian governor issued from its portals the watchers rushed out and cut him down. Ibn Saud was immediately proclaimed ruler of Nejd, and the next few years were spent in the recovery and consolidation of the outlying provinces. In 1904 the Turks sent a force to assist Ibn Rashid to defend himself against the growing power of his rival, but the battle of Bukairiya, at which Ibn Saud was wounded, decided the issue and the Turkish forces withdrew under safe conduct leaving Ibn Saud master of the Qasim.

At the desert watering of Artawaya there was founded in 1912 the first of the Ikhwan colonies, the prototype of some hundred or more settlements which sprang up during the next 15 years all over Nejd. The nucleus of each colony was a mosque and ecclesiastical establishment subsidized by the state, and the essential features were agriculture and the mixing of hitherto antagonistic tribal elements in a common brotherhood. Each colony became in effect a section of the Wahabi standing army and a monument to the political genius of Ibn Saud. Having thus built up his administration on firm foundations, Ibn Saud turned his attention to Hasa, where the Turks had ruled since 1875, and drove them out.

During the spring of 1914 Captain W. H. I. Shakespeare, British Political Agent to Kuwait, had visited Ibn Saud, and soon after the outbreak of war in Europe he was again sent to Riyadh to secure the Wahabi ruler's co-operation against the Turks. Ibn Saud undertook military operations in the Shammar against Ibn Rashid, who had sided with the enemy, and in January 1915 an indecisive battle was fought at Jarrub, in the course of which Shakespeare was unfortunately killed. The British authorities then decided against further activities in the Wahabi country and Ibn Saud, who concluded a treaty of friendship with Great Britain in December 1915 at Uqair, remained quiescent and increasingly nervous at the position which the Grand Sherif of Mecca, King Husein, was making for himself in the west with the assistance of Lawrence and others.

In spite of all British efforts to foster friendly relations between the Hashimite King Husein and the Wahabi ruler, obvious rivals for the ultimate hegemony of Arabia, the bitterness between the two rulers increased as the 1914-18 War progressed. Early in 1919 King Husein persuaded Lord Curzon and the British Government to adopt his view of the controversy and to authorize him to occupy Khurma.

Then Ibn Saud, with threats of the stoppage of his annual subsidy of £60,000 and of the displeasure of the British Government, was ordered to relinquish the village, but with characteristic energy in defence of his rights against all encroachment he placed himself at the head of his army and marched west. The Hejaz was in a ferment of anxiety and Taif, the summer capital, was evacuated, but characteristically, again, Ibn Saud, having vindicated his position and annexed Turaba, returned to Riyadh. During the next three years Ibn Saud steadily pursued a policy of expansion, adopting the offensive as the best means of defence against the declared designs of the Hashimite Court. Meanwhile the nomination by the British Government of Hashimite Sherifs to the thrones of Transjordan and Iraq came as a bitter disappointment to him.

The stage was now set for a final settlement with the Hejaz, and the first step in this direction was the Conference of Kuwait (1923-1924), convened by the British Government and rendered abortive by the obstinacy of the Hashimite representatives, who demanded the setting back of Ibn Saud's frontiers to the 1915 position. The die was thus cast for war, and in September 1924 the Wahabi army advanced on the Hejaz. Mecca was occupied in October and the siege of Jeddah began in December. During 1925 the whole of the Hejaz was gradually over-run, and in October Sir Gilbert Clayton, on behalf of the British Government, visited Ibn Saud in his camp in Wadi Fatima to negotiate the treaties of Babra and Hadda, by which outstanding questions with Iraq and the boundary of Nejd and Transjordan were satisfactorily settled.

In May of the same year Sir Gilbert Clayton again visited the Wahabi King to negotiate the treaty of Jeddah, by which the complete independence of the dual monarchy of the Hejaz and Nejd was formally recognized. In the winter of 1927-28 the Wahabi King again visited his central dominions and was actively occupied in the task of settling an unfortunate outbreak of Ikhwan fanaticism on the Iraqi-Nejd frontier, caused by the mistaken belief that the Iraqi Government had violated its treaty obligations by building a police post at the desert walls of Busaiya, 70 miles from the frontier. British aeroplanes were sent into Nejdi territory to bomb the Mutair Beduin by way of reprisals for their attack on Busaiya. Throughout this incident the Wahabi King retained his equanimity, endeavouring, by protest against the unnecessary intervention of the British and Iraqi Governments as well as by action to restrain his Beduin subjects from giving further cause for provocation, to transfer the dispute from the battlefield to the conference chamber.

Meanwhile prospectors had been busy in the Arabian peninsula and rich deposits of oil were suspected if not proved. A less far-seeing sovereign might have allowed merely commercial considerations to prevail, especially in view of the keen competition for concessions. Ibn Saud, however, true to the policy he had pursued all his life in his foreign relations, preferred to lease what were afterwards discovered to be very rich deposits indeed to predominantly Anglo-Saxon interests.

As early as 1933 he had awarded the oil concessions of the eastern part of his kingdom to the Standard Oil Company of California, which was later joined by the Texas, Standard Oil of New Jersey, and Socony-Vacuum companies. Production, begun in 1936 with 2,600 metric tons, had risen by 1949 to 23 million metric tons. Thus a ruler whose total revenue in 1917 had been some £100,000 now enjoyed a revenue of not less than £30m. Such an increase was indeed beyond the dreams of avarice, and in 1941 Ibn Saud could tell the American business men who had acquired further concessions that two years before the Germans and Japanese had been bidding frantically for concessions. "The Japanese", he said, "offered me twice as much for one-third of what you now obtain". During the whole period of the 1939-45 War Ibn Saud remained the firmest of the friends of Great Britain in the Middle East, though many attempts were made to undermine his loyalty.

The Zionist claims to Palestine were never admitted by Ibn Saud, though his distrust of the Hashimites led to a rather lukewarm support of the Arab League. The comparative ineffectiveness of the league cannot, however, fairly be placed only on Ibn Saud's shoulders. The question of leadership was involved and there were three claimants, none of whom was disposed to forgo his claim. Ibn Saud could fairly claim that he was by right of achievement the greatest man in the Arab world. The Hashimites could claim that as descendants of the Prophet, and for hundreds of years the guardians of the holy places, they were entitled to lead, whiie Egypt, as the most settled and progressive state, felt that the leadership ought to be hers. In spite of visits of courtesy the rivalry remained and effectively prevented the emergence of any broad body of policy. Nevertheless the league was more than once a useful weapon in the armoury of peace, and the idea underlying it permitted in 1948 the first friendly meeting for over a quarter of a century of Ibn Saud and the late King Abdullah of Transjordan [q.v.], then the most capable living member of the Hashimite house.

These contacts continued under King Abdullah's son and grandson. Towards the close of Ibn Saud's life the cordiality of his relations with Britain was temporarily overcast by his effort to assert his sovereignty over the Buraimi oasis, which the British-protected Sultan of Muscat* also claimed. Fortunately the dispute, which was, on the whole, conducted temperately, seems unlikely to cause a serious breach of good understanding.

Personally a man of commanding presence and of a stature exceptional in Arabia the Wahabi King was remarkable for a gentle and equable temperament capable of sudden transition under provocation to heights of indignation truly majestic. Uxoriously inclined, he took the fullest advantage of the social code of Islam—often for purely political purposes—to marry frequently and to divorce freely. He is believed to have had no fewer than 150 wives, by whom he had a large number of acknowledged children. His fortitude in the field of battle was only equalled by his equanimity in the council chamber, and his long reign bids fair to establish itself in history as the Golden Age of modern Arabia.

November 10, 1953.

Hilary St. George Saunders, C.B.E., remembered for his prowess in telling the story of many of the most fascinating facets of the recent war, died on December 16, 1951 at Nassau, Bahamas, at the age of 53.

Having served for a number of years on the secretariat of the League of Nations at Geneva, and while there published a number of novels in collaboration with a friend under a pseudonym, he suddenly, in 1943, achieved an immense and deserved success with his account, compiled from official sources, of the Battle of Britain. Other pamphlets succeeded this, and all had the hall-mark not merely of the practised writer but also of the careful historian. There is no doubt that the project on which he was engaged at his death, that of writing the history of the historic islands in which he died, would have been carried out in a style befitting the author of some of the most memorable literature inspired by the recent war.

Hilary Aidan St. George Saunders was the elder son of the late Rev. G. W. St. George Saunders and was born at Clifton on January 14, 1898. He was educated at Downside, and at the age of 17 he enlisted as a private during the 1914-18 war, and after six months received a commission in the Welsh Guards. He saw action in Belgium and France, and at the age of 20 was awarded the Military Cross for "conspicuous gallantry and devotion to duty". In 1919 he went up to Balliol and studied history. The following year he went to Geneva to witness the first assembly of the League of Nations, and he joined the staff of the secretariat of the league and remained on it for some 17 years.

From 1921 to 1923 Saunders served as a secretary to Dr, Nansen and travelled with him in England, Holland, France, Belgium, Norway, Sweden, and Germany, but with these intermissions he remained at Geneva until after the death of his first wife in 1937, when he returned to England, and in 1938 was appointed assistant librarian in the House of Commons. On the outbreak of war in 1939 Saunders was seconded to the Air Ministry and in 1940 he went to Paris to act as liaison officer between the British Embassy and the French Ministry of Information. He and his second wife had a narrow escape just before the Germans entered the city.

In March 1941 he published, with the approval of the Government, the first of the remarkable series of books for which he will be remembered, *The Battle of Britain,* of which over 300,000 copies were sold on the first day; *Bomber Command,* being the official account of the British bombing offensive, followed in October 1941; *Coastal Command,* being a companion volume, appeared in January 1942; and *Combined Operations* in 1943. His *Per Ardua: The Rise of British Air Power, 1911-1939,* was published by the Oxford University Press in the autumn of 1944. This remains a work of permanent value to the military historian.

In the meantime Saunders had joined the staff of Air Chief Marshal Sir Trafford Leigh-Mallory, A.O.C.-in-C. of the Allied Expeditionary Air Forces. He had also paid a visit to the United States at the invitation of Elmer Davis, Director of the United States Office of War Information, to discuss methods to make public the British war effort. He was already known there, as his *Combined Operations* had been the selection of the "Book of the United States Book of the Month Club" in June 1943. He published a brisk and candid account of this trip under the title of *Pioneers! O Pioneers!* At the conclusion of the war he returned to the House of Commons and was appointed librarian to the House in 1946, a position from which he retired in 1950. His pen, which had already so successfully portrayed many of the facets of the war effort, was again employed to tell the story of the merchant navy, the Commandos, and the parachute troops. These, respectively, *Valiant Voyaging, The Green Beret,* and *The Red Beret,* were published in 1949 and 1950.

A reference must be made to Saunders's numerous works of fiction, the enumeration of which presents some complication from the fact that, as stated above, they were written in partnership under different pseudonyms. The first, *The Seven Sleepers,* appeared under the pseudonym of "Francis Beeding" in 1924, and was the joint work of Saunders and the late John Palmer, a friend and colleague on the League of Nations staff. This was followed by *No Fury, The Six Proud Walkers, Death Walks in Eastrepps, Eleven were Brave,* and probably others by the same partnership and under the same pseudonym. Later this was changed to "David Pilgrim", and they produced *So Great a Man, No Common Glory,* and *The Grand Design.* Some were detective stories, others historical novels, and their composite author was described in *The Times* as coming into the front rank of those who succeed in making their readers sit up until the book is finished.

Fiction and contemporary history were not the only claimants for his pen, for in 1950 he brought out a carefully documented and well presented history of the Middlesex Hospital, and only last month appeared his history of Westminster Hall.

He married first Miss Helen Foley, who died in 1937, and secondly Joan, daughter of J. P. Bedford, and he leaves one son and one daughter.

December 18, 1951.

Professor Denis Saurat, Emeritus Professor of French Language and Literature in the University of London, died on June 7, 1958 at his French Riviera home. He was 67.

Denis Saurat was born in Toulouse in 1890. He studied English at the Universities of Lille and Paris and taught alternately English in France and French in Great Britain. From the Chair of English at Bordeaux, to which he was elected in 1922, he moved in 1924 to London, where he was Director of the Institut Français du Royaume-Uni until the dissolution of the original Council of the Institute in 1945. In 1926 he was elected to the Chair of French Language and Literature at King's College London.

His scholarly reputation was most firmly based on his writings on Milton, and perhaps the most solid if not the most widely acclaimed part of it rested on his first work, *La pensée de Milton,* presented for the degree of *Docteur-ès-lettres* at the Sorbonne in 1920. Saurat had already singled out the passage on "retraction" in *Paradise Lost* (vii, 170-73) as holding the kernel of Milton's thought; in 1921, studying the *Zohar* for sources of Blake's ideas, he recognized Milton's notion in the Zohar doctrine of divine withdrawal; and his subsequent work on Milton was devoted to investigating occultist elements and tracing their possible sources. *Blake and Milton* (1920) was followed by *Milton, Man and Thinker* (1925) and *Milton et le matérialisme chrétien* (1928); even those readers who felt that the textual bearing of occultist thought was overstressed, or who rejected the suggestion that the contemporary source was Robert Fludd, were grateful to the author for the scope of his intellectual imagination and his sensitiveness to relations between ideas.

Occultism was the link between his main literary interests—Milton, Blake, and Victor Hugo; it also became a personal preoccupation which inspired a number of works poised, sometimes uneasily, often hypnotically, between philosophy and poetry, theology and the more exotic fields of scientific speculation. The most personal of these was perhaps *La Fin de la Peur* (1937). His last books were about the lost Atlantis.

He narrowly escaped with his life when his house suffered a direct hit from a German bomb, and his health never completely recovered from the shock of this experience. In 1948 he was elected a Fellow of King's College; in 1950 he retired from the Chair of French and settled in Nice, where he became

Director of the Centre International d'Études Françaises. All who sat under him, as undergraduates or among the large audiences he drew to his many public lectures, will remember the brilliance of his intelligence and the spell of his personal magnetism.

June 10, 1958.

Dorothy L. Sayers died at her home at Witham, Essex, on December 17, 1957 at the age of 64.

Sudden death would have had no terrors for her. She combined an adventurous curiosity about life with a religious faith based on natural piety, common sense, and hard reading. She made a name in several diverse fields of creative work. But the diversity of her success was founded on an inner unity of character. When she came down from Somerville with a First in Modern Languages she tried her hand at advertising. The directness and the grasp of facts that are needed by a copywriter stood her in good stead as a newcomer to the crowded ranks of authors of detective fiction. During the 1920s and 1930s she established herself as one of the few who could give a new look to that hard-ridden king of novel.

Her recipe was deftly to mix a plot that kept readers guessing, with inside information, told without tears, about some fascinating subject—campanology, the backrooms of an advertising agency, life behind the discreet windows of a West End club. Lord Peter Wimsey came alive as a good companion to the few detectives into whom an engaging individuality has been breathed.

This was not done by chance; she had made a close, critical study of the craft. Lecturing once on Aristotle's *Poetics,* she remarked that he was obviously hankering after a good detective novel because he had laid down that the writer's business was to lead the reader up the garden, to make the murderer's villainy implicit in his character from the start, and to remember that the *dénouement* is the most difficult part of the story.

But it is some 20 years since Miss Sayers wrote a detective story, and, shortly before her death, she said: "There will be no more Peter Wimseys". The detective writer had been ousted by the Christian apologist. Miss Sayers approached her task of making religion real for the widest public with a zeal that sometimes shocked the conventionally orthodox (with whose protests she was well able to deal) and always held the ears of listeners and the eyes of the reading public. *The Man Born to be King* became a B.B.C. best-seller attracting large audiences Christmas after Christmas.

She carried what she regarded as the central purpose of her life on to the stage and into books. Dogma had no terrors for her. She did not believe in putting water into the pure spirit of her Church. Dante, with his colloquial idiom and unselfconscious piety, naturally attracted her. The translations she published of his *Inferno* and *Purgatorio* caught the directness of the original but failed, as Binyon did not, to catch the poetry. But her prose comments have done more than those of any other recent English author to quicken interest in Dante.

Dorothy Leigh Sayers was born in 1893, the daughter of the Rev. Henry Sayers and Helen Mary Leigh. She was in print before she was 21 with *Op I,* a book of verse, and followed it in 1919 by another, *Catholic Tales.* It was a medium in which she could be skilful, flexible, and effective, and readers of *The Times Literary Supplement* will, no doubt, remember her strong poem, *The English War,* which appeared in its issue of September 7, 1940.

Lord Peter made his first appearance in 1923 in *Whose Body?* There followed *Clouds of Witness* (1926), *Unnatural Death* (1927), *The Unpleasantness at the Bellona Club* (1928), and *The Documents in the Case* (1930).

In 1930 Miss Sayers, in addition to producing her *Strong Poison,* yet another detective book, made an interesting departure. Out of the fragments of its Anglo-Norman version she had constructed her *Tristan in Brittany,* in the form of a modern English story, and produced it, partly in verse and partly in prose.

Have His Carcase (1932) introduced a companion for Lord Peter in the shape of Harriet Vane, a writer of detective stories. In *Hangman's Holiday* (1933), a book of short stories, she created another amateur detective, Montague Egg, who was a simpler reasoner than Lord Peter, but almost as acute. In *The Nine Tailors,* though it was of the same *genre,* her theme was built round a noble church in Fenland, and possessed a majesty which disclosed powers the authoress had scarcely exerted until then. *Gaudy Night* (1935) took Lord Peter and Harriet Vane into the serene and serious life of a women's college at Oxford, and psychological problems deeper than those which belong to the detective convention arose.

In 1936 her *Busman's Holiday,* a play which presented Lord Peter married—Miss Sayers called it "a love story with detective interruptions"—was staged at the Comedy Theatre. She had a collaborator in M. St. Clair Byrne, and between them they provided Lord Peter's public with an excellent entertainment. *The Zeal of Thy House* (1937), which was written for the Canterbury Festival and played there and in London, was set in the twelfth century and was a sincere and illuminating study of the purification of an artist, a kind of architectural Gerontius purged by heavenly fire of his last earthly infirmity. *The Devil to Pay* (1939) was also written for the Canterbury Festival. It set the legend of Dr. Faustus, one of the great stories of the world, at the kind of angle most likely to commend it to the modern stage. Later it was played at His Majesty's Theatre. By sheer alertness of invention and the power to fit her ideas into a dramatic narrative she accomplished an extremely difficult task with credit. *Love All* (1940) was an agreeable and amusing comedy.

In 1940 Miss Sayers published a calmly philosophic essay on the war, which she named *Begin Here.* Then, in 1941, she followed it with her *The Mind of the Maker,* in which she analysed the metaphor of God as Creator and tested it in the light of creative activity as she knew it.

Unpopular Opinions, a miscellaneous collection of essays, came out in 1946, *Creed or Chaos,* another series of essays, pungent and well reasoned, in 1947, and *The Lost Tools of Learning* in the following year.

She began her translations of Dante for the Penguin Series with the *Inferno* which came out in November 1949; *Purgatorio* followed in May 1955.

She found the third volume *Paradiso* the hardest, and in August 1956 her translation had reached Canto VII. Her commentary was one of the most valuable parts of her books. After she had finished her second volume she slipped in, as a kind of relaxation, a translation of *Chanson de Roland,* published in 1957.

She was an honorary D.Litt. of Durham University. She married in 1926 Captain Atherton Fleming. He died in 1950.

December 19, 1957.

Otto Moritz Schiff, C.B.E., who devoted the greater part of his life to helping Jews who came to Britain as refugees from war and tyranny, died on November 15, 1952 in London.

He was born in Frankfurt-am-Main in 1875, the son of Philipp Schiff, a member of a well-known Frankfurt Jewish family that had given in an earlier generation a chief rabbi to England and a lay head of the Jewish community to the United States of America. Otto Schiff went to England as a young man and entered the Stock Exchange, soon establishing the firm of Bourke, Schiff and Company.

His introduction to public work was probably due to Hermann Landau, an Anglo-Jewish philanthropist who devoted many years to helping his co-religionists from Russia and Poland who settled in England or passed through England on the way to the New World. The Jews' Temporary Shelter in Mansell Street, London, was the principal instrument through which Landau worked. Here Schiff soon became an indefatigable lieutenant and ultimately his successor.

The outbreak of war in 1914 led to a great influx into London of refugees from Belgium, including some 12,000 Jews. It was to the shelter that these refugees turned and it fell to Schiff, with the support of the leading members of the Anglo-Jewish community, to deal with the influx. A Jewish War Refugees Committee was formed, of which he was the directing force and inspiration. After the war, during a part of which he served as a gunner in the Royal Artillery in France and was wounded, he had the job of repatriating to Belgium most of the Jewish refugees who had sought shelter in England.

In 1933 the task of coping with the influx of Jewish victims of Nazism fell to him, and this influx grew until the outbreak of war in 1939 closed the gates of Britain to refugees from Central Europe. Here new problems arose, for support had to be provided for these homeless and hopeless victims who were for a time forbidden to seek employment. Another task was helping the large number of relatives and friends in England, Christians as well as Jews, who wished to get their friends out of Germany and Austria. At the head of this new work was Schiff. Pressure was so great that not only had he to abandon almost entirely his private business but in the end his health broke down, and he was compelled to give up part of his work.

His later work brought him into contact with Government departments and in particular the Home Office. Here he was in a position of considerable responsibility and some confidence. Decisions had necessarily often to be taken on little more than his recommendation. He soon came to be completely trusted, and his reputation in Government circles proved a great asset to Anglo-Jewry during the latter half of his life.

His principal offices were the presidency of the Jewish Temporary Shelter, and the chairmanship of the German-Jewish Aid Committee, afterwards the Jewish Refugees Committee. For his services to the Belgian refugees he was awarded the O.B.E., and for those in connexion with the refugees from Germany he was created C.B.E. He was unmarried.

November 17, 1952.

The death of **Artur Schnabel** on August 15, 1951 at Geneva is a sad sequel to the disappointment which was caused when it was announced two months earlier that he could not fulfil his engagement to play at the Philharmonia concerts at the Festival Hall, London. He was 69.

Schnabel was a pianist of the greatest distinction for two paradoxical reasons—his interpretative range was more limited than most pianists of the front rank, and he was much more than a pianist, although he never made a composer or a writer. The symphonies he wrote were unintelligible—though he denied in a letter to *The Times* that the one played here in 1948 was composed in the twelve-tone system—and the lectures he published were wordy and perverse, but this intellectual activity fertilized his playing of the products of the greatest minds in music, Beethoven especially, so that it was an illumination. In his earlier days his touch, his approach to the music, and his actual performance had a certain uncompromising asperity, but on his last visits to London his playing had very much mellowed, as though his later years had added wisdom to intellect and tolerance to conviction.

Artur Schnabel was born at Lipnik, in Austria, in 1882. He studied in Vienna under Leschetizy and was a member of Mandyszewski's circle, and thus as a boy became acquainted with Brahms. To his concert work he all his life added much teaching, notably at the Berlin State Academy of Music, where he was professor of piano until 1933, when he left Germany, and latterly in New York (he became an American citizen in 1944). He was a conscientious editor of Beethoven and Brahms.

From him came the idea and the ideals of the Bryanston Summer School, now in session, and his influence has been potent everywhere he went, since he was a man of strong personality and high ideals. He wrote a considerable amount of music, including some songs—his wife was a singer—but he courted no popularity for it.

He found the fullest expression of his own musical personality in the interpretation of the great German masters of the piano.

August 16, 1951.

Dr. Percy Scholes, O.B.E., who died in Switzerland on July 31, 1958 at the age of 81, was a pioneer in the study of musical appreciation, the author of many popular books of musical exposition, and an indefatigable lexicographer.

Percy Alfred Scholes was born at Leeds on July 24, 1877, and retained through life many of the traits of Yorkshire puritanism. He began his educational work as a lecturer for the Country Holiday Association. Through Lord Woolton*, who was at that time joint secretary of this body and the Home Reading Association, he discovered the need of textbooks for guidance of the members of the latter association. His discovery led immediately to the foundation of the periodical the *Music Student,* and ultimately to the writing of a long series of books on music.

He took his degree of B.Mus. at Oxford in 1908 and undertook extensive lecturing not only for his own university but for Manchester, London, and Cambridge as well. When the 1914-18 War came he found opportunities for continuing adult education through the offices of the Y.M.C.A., and as an immediate outcome of the needs of the troops he wrote the first *Listener's Guide to Music,* a masterpiece of intelligible exposition in a small space, written in a fortnight taken off from his organizing. It sold by the thousand for 30 years after.

Scholes was one of the few musicians to realize at once the possibilities of the mechanical reproduction of music for mass education in music, and he was associated with the B.B.C. in its earliest days as adviser and critic. His early work as editor of the *Music Student* led him further into journalism, and after a time with the *Evening Standard* he worked as music critic of the *Observer* from 1920 to 1925. But by this time the claims of authorship and the success of his books enabled him to give up newspaper work and retire to Switzerland, there to prepare his encyclopaedia, *The Oxford Companion to Music,* which is a marvel of organization of a huge mass of information into a single volume.

Scholes's claim to a more scholarly reputation than these merely informative works afford rests upon his books *The Puritans and Music* and *The Life of Dr. Burney.* He broached a new kind of historical writing when he compiled from the pages of the *Musical Times* the survey of a hundred years of musical life in England in *The Mirror of Music* (1947).

During the Second World War Scholes lived at Oxford, where he joined the newly created Faculty of Music and was made a doctor of music *honoris causa:* he had previously been honoured by Lausanne University with the degree of *Docteur ès Lettres.* In 1957 he was rather belatedly given official recognition by the award of the O.B.E.

He married Dora Wingate, daughter of Richard Lean, of Gloucester, who survives him.

August 2, 1958.

Professor Arnold Schönberg, who died on July 13, 1951 at his home at Los Angeles, at the age of 76, was probably the most discussed musician of the twentieth century.

His system of atonality, or, as he preferred to call it, twelve-tone music, though reached by process of evolution from chromaticism, was the most revolutionary movement in musical history since Monteverde in the seventeenth century. It is so subversive of established ways of thought that its general adoption is improbable in the extreme, but it has provided a ferment of far-reaching influence on modern music. In this respect, as in some others, Schönberg is like Stravinsky*; between 1910 and 1930 these two men were the outstanding figures in the history of modern music. Curiously enough, both suffered the same fate. At the height of his fame each was forced to leave his country and to adjust himself to new conditions.

Schönberg was born in Vienna on September 13, 1874. At the age of eight he learnt to play the violin and composed short violin duets for his lessons. Later on he taught himself the cello and composed a string quartet. For several years he worked without any outside help or supervision. Alexander von Zemlinsky (whose daughter he married in 1901), a composer of whom Brahms had a very high opinion, recognized his outstanding talent, gave him his first instruction in composition, and brought him into the musical circles of Vienna. Schönberg's earliest works were written in the style of Brahms, whose technique he admired, and later set as a model to his pupils when he was teaching composition himself.

The first work which Schönberg made known to the musical world was a string sextet, *Verklärte Nacht.* It was an attempt to apply the symphonic form of a tone poem to chamber music. To the same period belong the *Gurrelieder,* a cantata for solo voices, chorus and orchestra written in 1900, a tone poem, *Pelleas and Melisande,* and a string quartet in D minor. A new development began with the Chamber-Symphony in E, opus 9, in 1906. Schönberg's style became concise, his harmonies more daring. It was these works which first roused the opposition of conservative musicians and the admiration of a younger generation who were trying to find new ways of expression. This aim was achieved in the three piano pieces, Opus II, 1909, written in the so-called "atonal style" which aroused much discussion among musicians all over the world.

At this time Schönberg left Vienna and settled in Berlin. Here he wrote *Pierrot Lunaire,* a cycle of poems recited in a kind of song-speech accompanied by instruments. This work established Schönberg's fame as one of the leading modern composers. In 1913 he returned to Vienna to teach composition, and, after the end of the 1914-18 war, he founded a society for the performance of modern music. He embodied his technical principles in the *Treatise on Harmony*, begun in the early years of the century and since revised, but it is only recently in a volume of essays, *Style and Idea*, that he has discussed their aesthetic basis.

The years between 1920 and 1925 were the most prosperous in Schönberg's life. His works were performed regularly at the festivals of the International Music Society, his principal choral work, the *Gurrelieder*, aroused general admiration at a performance in his honour at the Vienna State Opera, and most conductors included his works in their programmes. He had now gained an international reputation. When Busoni died in 1924 in Berlin, Schönberg succeeded him as a member of the Academy of the Arts, a position which should have given him financial independence for the rest of his life. After Hitler came to power, however, in 1933, he lost his position and accepted an offer from the Malkin Conservatory, Boston.

He felt the change as a great shock. His health suffered from the eastern winter and he soon moved to Los Angeles, where he was appointed Professor of Music in the University of Southern California. Here he wrote a suite for string orchestra (1934), the fourth string quartet (1938), a violin concerto, a piano concerto, and the *Ode to Napoleon*.

Schönberg retired from his university post in 1944 at the age of 70, to spend the rest of his life in composing and teaching. He completed the opera *Moses and Aaron*, on which he had been working for many years, not long before he died. He had the satisfaction of seeing a revival of his works after the defeat of the Nazi régime, and the re-establishment of his fame as one of the most inspiring innovators of contemporary music.

His wife died in 1923 and he is survived by a son and a daughter.

July 16, 1951.

Louise Schröder, acting Lord Mayor of Berlin during the blockade of the city, and for many years a leader in the German Socialist Party, died in Berlin on June 4, 1957. She was 70.

Louise Schröder was born on April 2, 1887, at Altona, the daughter of an artisan in the building trade and an official of the S.P.D., the old Socialist Party of Germany. Educated at a secondary school in her home town and at a vocational school at Hamburg, she soon got a job as private secretary in an insurance company, where she stayed for 15 years. She joined the Socialist Party in 1910, and soon proved a brilliant orator and debater. In 1919 she was elected to the Weimar National Assembly, and in 1920 to the Reichstag. Specializing in social problems, she played a prominent though discreet part in all decisions of the S.P.D.

In 1933 she was dismissed by the Nazis from all offices and functions and placed under police supervision. She went back to Altona and tried to make a living with a little bread-shop which failed, however, from a Nazi boycott. In 1938 she moved to Berlin, and there survived the war, ill and suffering when it ended. She recovered and again became active in the Socialist Party. She was elected to its board and, in 1946, to the Berlin City Council. In the same year she became deputy chairman of the party, by then once more the largest in Germany. Elected Burgomaster, Deputy Lord Mayor, of Berlin in December, she became acting Lord Mayor (which, in Germany, is not a one year's honorary office but comprises most of a city clerk's functions as well) when Russian obstruction prevented the Lord Mayor Dr. Ernst Reuter [q.v.], from functioning after his election in May 1947.

Especially during the period of the blockade of Berlin, Louise Schröder displayed energy, initiative, and wisdom such as to earn her the friendly nickname "Mother of Berlin". Unsparingly, though of frail stature and health and seriously ill several times, she pleaded Berlin's cause with the allied authorities and at conferences abroad. She took part in the German Premiers' conferences at Munich, Frankfurt, and Coblenz, and was elected President at the German Cities' Diet at Frankfurt in 1948. She received Anthony Eden [Lord Avon] in July 1948, and was cheered with him by the population. By then she had become an international figure, and a return of her former illness in 1949 drew the attention and the good wishes of people in many countries, who recognized in that brave little woman with the steel-rimmed spectacles a person who had mastered one of the most difficult political and administrative tasks of her time with a smile, feminine common sense, compassion, and a good deal of determination.

She was a member of the Bundestag since 1949 and was a delegate to the Council of Europe at Strasbourg.

June 5, 1957.

Dr. Kurt Schumacher, leader of the German Social Democratic Party, and one of the most forceful figures the German Left ever possessed, died at Bonn on August 20, 1952 at the age of 56.

Born at Kulm, West Prussia, on October 10, 1895, he studied law and economics at the universities of Halle, Leipzig, and Berlin, and won his degree of doctor of political science at Münster, Westphalia. During the 1914-18 war he was on active service with the German Army and lost his right arm, a loss which was to become a political asset later in his career. After a short period in the German Ministry of Labour, his political ambitions drove him to a more active profession, and in 1920 he joined the staff of the main Socialist paper in Württemberg, the *Schwäbische Tagwacht*, and soon made a name for himself as a gifted and intelligent politician. As his reputation spread he contributed to other Social Democratic papers, including *Vorwärts*.

In 1924 he was elected to the Württemberg Diet, to which he belonged until 1931. He was elected to the Reichstag for his Swabian constituency in 1930 at the critical moment when the Nazi party invaded the German Parliament with 107 deputies as against 143 Socialists. In the Reichstag he was one of the youngest members and belonged, together with Mierendorff and Leuschner, to a "ginger" group which thought that the German Republic was doing too little to ward off the Nazi danger. As a result of repeated clashes with the N.S.D.A.P., and particularly with Goebbels, he was arrested after the Nazis came to power and placed in a concentration camp for 10 years. There the inflexible courage of his behaviour made him a figure of legend. His eyesight was badly damaged by ill-treatment at Dachau. On one occasion he maintained a hunger-strike for 29 days. He was released in 1943 and re-arrested in 1944 in the round-up that followed the plot of July 20. Released from captivity by allied troops in 1945, he set himself to reconstitute the Social Democratic Party on an all-German basis and established its headquarters in Hanover.

There were no formal elections in western Germany until 1946, but important decisions had to be made within the party, in particular to what extent the Social Democrats would in future cooperate with the communists. The time seemed ripe for a reconciliation of those two parties, since it had become a widely accepted, though illusory, belief within the German Left that, had the socialists and the communists stood together between 1918 and 1933, Hitler could never have seized power. In addition the whole western world, to which the German Social Democrats felt they belonged, had fought the 1939-45 war as allies of the Soviet Union.

Within the S.P.D. there was a faction led by Otto Grotewohl*, a member of the S.P.D. executive until 1933, which strongly favoured a complete merger between communists and socialists. It was to Schumacher's credit that he opposed this merger, and it was entirely due to his leadership that the Grotewohl manoeuvre (which was strongly backed by the Soviet Military Government) failed.

It may be said that, from the German point of view, Schumacher's other claim to historical merit was that he represented "the other Germany" to the rest of the world. In 1945 Germany was engulfed in hatred. The concentration camps had just been overrun by the liberating armies, and horrors until then unbelievable to many in the western world received the full glare of publicity. Dr. Schumacher's release was a timely reminder that Germans, too, had suffered in these camps. He was the first envoy whom Germany could send abroad, and who could claim with justification to speak to the Allies as a fellow-sufferer from Nazi barbarity. Thin, haggard, and emaciated, Dr. Schumacher appeared in 1945-46 to be alive only by superhuman effort. It was impossible not to be impressed by him, for he seemed to be the incarnation of the years of suffering endured by millions of decent Germans under the Nazi régime.

To an allied observer in 1946 it was encouraging to see how a proven anti-Nazi of Schumacher's calibre, who in spite of some harsh words against the western occupying Powers could be counted on as a defender of western ideas and ideals, could command a large following in post-war Germany. His visit to England at the invitation of the Labour Party was, however, viewed with some misgiving in France and Russia.

The year 1947 marked the beginning of a period in Schumacher's career which was not perhaps such an unqualified success as the first two years had been. A thrombosis in his leg, which ultimately led to its amputation, kept him to his bed for many months, during which time he saw very few people except his closest friends and supporters. He is said to have survived this illness and the operation through sheer will power, but the results of it had a marked effect on his approach to political problems. His attacks on opponents became more bitter than ever and they were designed not only to hurt but to kill. The impression gained was that here was a man fighting for political power with everything he had got and with little time to lose. Schumacher's main struggle was now waged against Dr. Adenauer's* Christian Democratic Union. When that party won the 1949 Federal elections and Dr. Adenauer became Chancellor, Schumacher obviously hated his political opponent with a German intensity. It has been felt among some allied observers that this personal hatred was one of the sadder tragedies of post-war Germany.

A great deal of criticism has been levelled against Dr. Schumacher in the past few years inside and outside Germany. Within his party he undoubtedly laid down the party line and tolerated little opposition, which attracted "yes-men" to his camp as much as it alienated more independent sympathizers. The gravest criticism is, however, laid against the strong nationalist tone he introduced into his recent statements on western Germany's foreign policy. Perhaps the key to Dr. Schumacher's demand for Germany's equal status as a price for German alignment with the west, which frequently led to a charge of "nationalism" against him, may be considered in the following light. Schumacher was haunted by the thought that there could be a repetition of what happened after the 1914-18 war. In this period a Social Democratic Government inherited post-war chaos, had to sign the terms of an exacting peace treaty, and was subsequently made responsible by the extremists of the Left and Right for all the shortcomings that do occur in the first decade after a lost war.

Schumacher was determined that these things should not happen again. Perhaps that is why his policy was loud in condemning any arrangement, however temporary, in which Germany was not accorded equal status, or by which she would sign away territories within her 1937 frontiers. Schumacher felt perhaps that no neo-Nazi movement of the future would ever be in a position to accuse the Social Democrats, as the Nazis had done between 1929 and 1933, the period which had led Germany into the greatest catastrophe of her history.

However exaggerated this fear may seem to those outside Germany's frontiers, it might have been this fear that was responsible for the fervent, violent language of Dr. Schumacher, which from time to time made him the most controversial as well as the most feared personality in German politics since the war.

August 22, 1952.

The death of **Elisabeth Schumann** in New York on April 23, 1952 will stir many memories in all the lands which knew her incomparable art as operatic soprano and interpreter of German *Lieder*.

Her voice had a quicksilver quality, of greater purity than power, but with an indefinable and characteristic ring in it. It was controlled by a musician's sensitiveness to phrasing. With this equipment her singing of Schubert, especially the lighter and prettier songs, was ideally ingratiating. When she sang in opera she brought to it a further dramatic charm, especially in mischievous or saucy parts. Her Susanna in *Figaro* thus served a whole generation as a model of characterization in singing. As a natural consequence of her qualities she was limited in the interpretation of more serious songs which were liable to become arch, and of Bach, which she did not often attempt, though those who heard her in the Beethoven Mass in Vienna at the Beethoven centenary in 1927 are not likely to forget the experience.

She was born in Thuringia, the daughter of an organist, in 1885, according to *Grove's Dictionary*, but she was reticent about her age, and her friends in New York, where she had lived since the fall of Austria, put it at 63. She made her *début* in Germany simultaneously with Lotte Lehmann [d. 1976] at Hamburg in 1908. She was not heard in London till 1924, when she sang Sophie in *Der Rosenkavalier* with a vocal beauty and dramatic demureness that have made the performances of that opera about that time, in which Lotte Lehmann and Richard Mayr were also singing, fabulous.

She joined the Vienna State Opera in 1919 and stayed with it at Richard Strauss's instigation for 20 years. She had already appeared at the Metropolitan Opera in New York in 1914, where the company at the time included Caruso, Destinn, Hempel, Farrar*, and Scotti. Her roles in Vienna included, besides those named, Blonda in *Die Entführung*, Zerlina in *Don Giovanni*, Despina in *Cosi fan tutte*, Eva in *Die Meistersinger*, and Adele in *Fledermaus*. She married Richard Alwin, one of the conductors of the Vienna Opera.

She was a much better singer of Lieder than most operatic singers: her line and intonation were true, and her vocal production was such that even after her voice had lost its youthful lustre she could still make it serve her purposes in the recitals which she has given in Britain since the end of the war—she sang at the Edinburgh Festival for instance in 1947 with Dr. Bruno Walter* at the piano. She wrote a book on German song, which was translated by D. Millar Craig for the illustrated *World of Music* series, in which she unexpectedly showed herself a critic possessed of a historical sense who could appraise the composers whom she so well served with her voice and her art of interpretation.

April 25, 1952.

The death of **Lord Schuster** on June 28, 1956 removes one of the acutest minds in the public service and closes a varied career, culminating in his appointment as Clerk to the Crown and Permanent Secretary to the Lord Chancellor, which important offices he had held from 1915 until 1944.

The Right Hon. Sir Claud Schuster, first Baron Schuster, of Cerne, in the county of Dorset, in the peerage of the United Kingdom, G.C.B., C.V.O., belonged to the famous Jewish family, which had its origin at Frankfurt-on-Main, whose name has been famous in finance, law, science, and many walks of public life. He was the only son of the late Frederick Leo Schuster, of Manchester, and was born on August 22, 1869. He was educated at Winchester and New College, Oxford, where he graduated with a second class in modern history in 1892. He was called to the Bar by the Inner Temple in 1895, and just 30 years later he was made a Bencher of that Inn. He joined the Northern Circuit and the London and Middlesex Sessions, but he seems to have done little or no general practice, for in 1899 he was appointed the secretary to the London Government Act Commission, under the late Sir Hugh Owen, G.C.B., work which occupied him until 1902.

He was then secretary to the old Great Northern Railway Company for a very short time, for in 1903 he was appointed legal assistant to the Board of Education. In 1907 he was promoted assistant secretary, and in 1911 he was again promoted to be principal assistant secretary of the legal branch of that department.

The same year he was made Chief Registrar of Friendly Societies, which post made him an *ex-officio* member of the Insurance Commission. In 1912 he became secretary and legal adviser of the National Health Insurance Commission (England), and in 1913 he was made legal member of that commission and of the National Health Insurance Joint Committee. Schuster held the post until July 1915, when he was called to office still higher and more dignified.

In that month Lord Muir Mackenzie, then in his seventieth year, resigned the posts of Clerk of the Crown and Permanent Secretary to the Lord Chancellor, the former of which offices he had held since 1885 and the latter since 1880. For some time it had been realized that Muir Mackenzie's term of office had been drawing to its close, and the question of his successor had been a matter of some interest and discussion in official and legal circles. The answer of the Lord Chancellor, Lord Haldane, in whose nomination the appointment lay, caused some surprise, and at such a time it showed some courage, having regard to the name and ancestry of the nominee. By all who knew Schuster's acute mind and the record of his work, however, it was realized that it was a fitting climax of his official career, and his long term of office was its complete justification.

Since the Report of the Royal Commission

on the Civil Service which sat between 1912 and 1915, the methods of recruiting for the legal departments have undergone considerable changes, and Schuster's position as regarded patronage was never altogether that of his predecessor. But, apart from this somewhat thankless branch of his office, the Permanent Secretary, it must be remembered, is in the absence of any regular Department of Justice responsible for the administration and supervision of the offices of the Law Courts and the legal departments generally, and here Schuster's long official experience and organizing power were of the utmost value to a long line of Lord Chancellors.

His ideas were in the main sound and practical and, as Lord Hailsham said of him on a historic occasion in the House of Lords in 1934, he had been the author and initiator of a great many of the legal reforms which have been passed under successive Lord Chancellors. His methods of obtaining his ends did not, however, always escape criticism, and with the years an increasing dislike of opposition tended to strain his relations with certain members of the judiciary and heads of departments with whom he was brought into contact.

In 1945 he was appointed head of the legal division of the Control Commission in Austria, and later he spent several months in Rome in a similar capacity. To the last his vigour and rapidity of thought and judgment were the envy of much younger men.

Schuster was a good linguist and a man of wide culture and many interests. As a young man he was a serious mountaineer, and he had the distinction of having been president of both the Alpine Club and the Ski Club of Great Britain. His book, *Peaks and Pleasant Pastures*, published in 1911, has since been reissued, and his *Postscript to Adventure* was published in 1950. He was also the author of some elegant verse, generally upon the theme of his favourite pastime. It may be added that his masterly article on Lord Birkenhead in the *Dictionary of National Biography* is the fairest and most judicial estimate yet made of that remarkable man.

He married in 1896 Mabel Elizabeth, daughter of the late Dr. W. W. Merry, sometime Rector of Lincoln College, Oxford. She died in 1936. His only son was killed in the 1914-18 War, and his only daughter survives.

June 29, 1956.

Lieutenant-Colonel Lord Francis Scott, K.C.M.G., D.S.O., who played a notable part in the development of Kenya, died suddenly at Paddington Station on July 26, 1952. He was 72.

Lord Francis George Montagu-Douglas-Scott was born in 1879, being the youngest son of the sixth Duke of Buccleuch by his wife, Lady Louisa Jane Hamilton, daughter of the first Duke of Abercorn. He was educated at Eton (R. A. H. Mitchell's house) and played in the eleven in 1898, and then went up to Christ Church, Oxford. Gazetted to the Grenadier Guards in 1899, he saw active service in the South African War. In 1905 he went to India as A.D.C. to the Viceroy, the fourth Earl of Minto, whose eldest daughter, Lady Eileen Elliot-Murray-Kynynmound, he was later (in 1915) to marry. He returned to England in 1910 and was on active service throughout the 1914-18 war. At the first battle of Ypres he was wounded and as a consequence he had many years later, in 1933, to have a leg amputated. His gallantry at that battle was mentioned in dispatches and he was awarded the D.S.O.

He retired from the Army with the rank of lieutenant-colonel in 1920, and not long after settled in Kenya. There he soon took an exceedingly active part in the life of the country, being for many years leader of the European elected members in the Legislature. He had unbounded faith in the future of Kenya, which he recognized as occupying an important strategic position in relation to the rest of the Commonwealth, and where he believed large numbers of immigrants from Britain could usefully be settled. He was always insisting strongly on the rights of the settlers to be consulted in matters affecting the administration, and once, in 1936, resigned from the Executive Council on the grounds that he and Captain Schwartze, the other European unofficial member, had not been taken sufficiently into the confidence of the Governor, Sir Joseph Byrne, concerning the organization of defence. The dispute was later settled and Lord Francis Scott and Captain Schwartze were reappointed to the Executive Council. In 1938 Lord Francis Scott suffered a grievous blow in the loss of his wife, a lady of great charm and courage, who had shared his hopes and enthusiasm for the land of their adoption.

In spite of his age, Lord Francis Scott rejoined the Army in 1941 as A.M.S. to the G.O.C., East African Forces, and took part in the Ethiopian campaign, being again mentioned in dispatches. Some two years ago the Duke* and Duchess of Gloucester (whose uncle he was) spent a holiday at Lord Francis Scott's home, Deloraine, in the Rongai district about 120 miles from Nairobi, and the Duke presented to the mayor and council the Royal Charter conferring upon Nairobi the status of a city. No event could have given Lord Francis Scott, with his long years of devotion to Kenya, greater pleasure.

July 28, 1952.

Sir Giles Gilbert Scott, the architect who designed the new House of Commons, Liverpool Cathedral, and Waterloo Bridge, died in a London hospital on February 8, 1960. He was 79.

With every allowance for individual genius, Sir Giles Gilbert Scott cannot fail to be remembered as a striking instance of hereditary prowess in architecture. He was not only the third of his name to distinguish himself, but his work was the logical fulfilment of that of his grandfather, and to consider in succession the buildings of Sir Gilbert Scott, R.A. (1810-77), George Gilbert Scott, F.S.A. (1837-97), and the design of Liverpool Cathedral is to follow an architectural development of extraordinary consistency.

After the eighteenth century there could have been no profitable return to Gothic without the scholastic and imitative phase which Sir Gilbert Scott conducted. To George Gilbert Scott was left the first attempt to adapt the recovered letter of the style to contemporary requirements and conditions of labour. And Giles Scott may be said to have reconciled the spirit of the style with the formal unity of classic design which the two earlier Scotts, each immersed in his own problem, had almost of necessity neglected.

Scott, who was the second son of George Gilbert Scott, F.S.A., was born on November 9, 1880. As a Roman Catholic he was educated at Beaumont College, Old Windsor, and he was articled to Temple Moore, commencing practice on his own account in London in 1902. In the same year—when he was only 22—his design for Liverpool Cathedral was selected out of more than a hundred submitted in competition. It was accepted on condition that he agreed to work in partnership with G. F. Bodley, who had been one of the judges, and the foundation stone of the cathedral was laid by King Edward on July 19, 1904.

When Bodley died, in 1907, there was no question about leaving the entire work in the hands of the young architect.

A study of Liverpool Cathedral brings out the nature of Scott's genius and its limitations. Like Wren, he perceived that the chief requirement of an Anglican cathedral after the Reformation was a large auditorium, and, with its great central space under the tower, supplemented by the eastern and western transepts, and nave and choir of nearly equal length, the cathedral is boldly planned with that in view.

The remark "But if the bones are classic, the flesh in which they are clothed is pure Gothic", in the official handbook to the Cathedral, is a criticism as well as a description, but it is a criticism of something beyond the powers of the individual architect unless he were, as Scott was not, a master of all the circumstances which relate architecture to life as well as of architectural design. With these reservations, Liverpool Cathedral remains nevertheless one of the noblest buildings of the early part of this century: dignified in the general mass, uplifting in atmosphere, and admirably proportioned in detail.

Scott's powers as an architect, his broad grasp of the requirements, monumental feeling, and extraordinary command of mass and plane, were displayed in many other churches besides Liverpool Cathedral. Of these, St. Paul's Church, Derby Lane, Liverpool, and the Church of the Annunciation, Bournemouth, may be quoted as particularly fine examples. He also did restoration work at Chester Cathedral, and he designed an exceedingly beautiful War Memorial Chapel for Charterhouse School.

But though Scott was best known as an ecclesiastical architect he was not exclusively so, and his additions to Clare College, Cambridge, consisting of a memorial archway flanked by sets of rooms, give a good idea of what he could accomplish when his classical instincts could find full expression in style as well as in form. Later in 1933 he designed the University Library, and at Oxford he was responsible for the new Bodleian Library, for additions to Magdalen College and the new Chapel at Margaret Hall. A house in the Queen Anne tradition that he designed for his own occupation in Clarendon Place, Bayswater, in 1928 received the annual medal of the R.I.B.A. for London street architecture.

In his later practice Scott was involved in several rather thankless though important tasks in which the architectural problem was obscured by other considerations, nostalgia for the past, uncertainty about the forms of religion, and differences of opinion about the requirements of town planning. Typical of the first was the rebuilding of Waterloo Bridge, when it was decided that Rennie's bridge was no longer adequate for its purpose. Besides its precarious condition there was much controversy over its replacement, and in the end Scott was commissioned to design a new bridge in collaboration with Rendel, Palmer, and Tritton, the engineers. The result, though not truly expressive of construction, was refreshingly simple and graceful.

The rebuilding of Coventry Cathedral, after it had been practically destroyed during the last war, was a still more complicated affair, and Scott's design came in for much criticism. After some heated discussion Scott decided to resign the commission and the design of a new cathedral was made the subject of an open competition.

But these troubles were as nothing to the storm of protest raised by the proposal to erect an electric power station on Bankside, with Scott, who had already pleased many people with his external treatment of Battersea power station, as architect. The storm was reflected in a lengthy correspondence in *The Times,* in which the grounds of objection kept shifting. They included fears about the architectural competition between the power station and St. Paul's Cathedral and about possible damage to the fabric of the cathedral by fumes from the power station. The final stage of the discussion centred on the alleged undemocratic action of the Minister of Town and Country Planning in persisting with the scheme against the weight of expert and public opinion, but when the station was built little dislike of it was expressed.

After the war Scott, though nearing 70, continued busily in practice. His most notable task was the rebuilding of the bombed Commons Chamber in the Palace of Westminster, which he performed with great skill and ingenuity. Another and happier restoration was that which he undertook for the City Corporation in rebuilding Guildhall. Here he replaced the Victorian timber ceiling by a groined vault in stone, and created thereby a more finely proportioned interior than the one that had been destroyed in the war.

Scott was elected A.R.A. in 1916 and R.A. in 1922, and in 1925 he was awarded the Royal Gold Medal for Architecture. He was knighted in 1924, and received the Order of Merit in the Birthday Honours of 1944. From 1933 to 1935 he was President of the R.I.B.A.

As a man Scott was dignified and modest, somewhat reserved in his manner, but full of quiet fun upon occasion. To students and laymen interested in architecture he was always sympathetic, and he took a keen interest in the activities of the Architecture Club, of which he was an original member; also in those of the Building Centre, of which he was president.

He married Louise Wallbank Hughes in 1914, and they had two sons.

February 10, 1960.

R. A. Scott-James, O.B.E., M.C., journalist and author, who was editor of the *London Mercury* from 1934 to 1939, died on November 3, 1959 after an operation. He was 80.

Rolfe Arnold Scott-James was a journalist of wide cultivation of mind, liberal and humane in politics, and a literary critic of fine and discriminating sensibility. His career in London journalism over nearly half a century was quietly distinguished.

Born on December 21, 1878, the son of the Rev. John Scott-James, he was educated at Mill Hill School and proceeded as a Scholar to Brasenose College, Oxford. After leaving Oxford he lived for some time at the Canning Town settlement and at Toynbee Hall, where the personality of Canon Barnett was not without its influence upon him. In 1902 he joined the staff of the *Daily News* and was literary editor during 1906-12. Appointed editor of the *New Weekly* in 1914, he enlisted two years later, was commissioned in the Royal Garrison Artillery, served in France, and as a captain was awarded the M.C. in 1918.

From 1919 until 1930 Scott-James was a leader writer on the *Daily Chronicle,* and then, during 1933-35, leader writer and assistant editor of the *Spectator.* In 1934 also he assumed the editorship, after the resignation of Sir John Squire [q.v.], of the *London Mercury,* and he remained editor, lending a grace and distinction of his own to its pages, until that admirable literary monthly ceased publication in 1939. From that year until 1945, through all the stress and difficulty of the war years, Scott-James was back once more with the *Spectator,* combining his work there from 1940 onwards with the skilful and attractive editorship of *Britain To-day.*

Well informed and versatile in capacity, Scott-James's most notable talent was, without a doubt, for literary criticism. He was a perceptive and sympathetic reviewer, and was at various times a contributor to *The Times Literary Supplement.* His earliest book, *Modernism and Romance,* published in 1908, gives clear evidence of his instructed taste and balanced judgment, and the evidence is reinforced in *Personality in Literature,* first published in 1913 and reissued in an almost unchanged form in 1931, and *The Making of Literature* (1928), which is a history of literary criticism from Aristotle onwards and a model of instruction for the beginner. He published *Fifty Years of English Literature, 1900-50,* a critical survey, in 1951; *Thomas Hardy* in the same year; and *Lytton Strachey* in 1955.

Scott-James married, in 1905, Violet Eleanor, daughter of Captain Arthur Brooks. She died in 1942. There were one son and two daughters of the marriage. His second marriage, to Paule Honorine Jeanne, daughter of P. E. Lagarde, took place in 1947.

November 4, 1959.

Hubert Scott-Paine, a pioneer in the design and construction of aircraft—in particular, flying-boats—and of sea craft, and himself a fine racer of motor boats, died at his home in Greenwich, Connecticut on April 14, 1954. He was 63.

He was born at Shoreham, Sussex, on March 11, 1891, and after an unconventional boyhood and youth—he ran away from school to sea and earned his living in a variety of ways—he soon began to make his name as an original spirit in the new field of aviation. He first flew in 1910, and from then until 1914 designed and built several land aircraft. Then, still no more than a youth, he began his exciting development of marine aircraft.

In 1913 he constructed the first circular flying-boat hull, and though this was his most important advance he proceeded to patent many original developments in flying-boats. He built the first quadruplane and also one of the first twin-engined land machines in England. Soon after the 1914-18 War he opened the first international flying-boat route, from Le Havre to Southampton, and later opened another route connecting Southampton and the Channel Islands.

Scott-Paine had meanwhile become manager and owner of the Supermarine Aviation Works, Limited, until in 1923 he organized and financed the British Marine Air Navigation Company, which was soon incorporated with Imperial Airways, of which he was a founder and a director from 1924 until 1940. This active and ever originating interest in aviation led him in 1922 to build and finance British Challenger, which won the Schneider Trophy in the same year.

A complementary interest in sea craft developed in Scott-Paine, especially after 1927, when he founded the British Power Boat Company, of which he remained chairman until his death. He designed, built, and raced—still another venture—Panther I, Panther II, Miss Britain I, Miss Britain II, and Miss Britain III. This last was the first all-metal motor boat and the first to use an aero engine. It became the prototype of the Royal Navy's motor torpedo boats and motor gunboats, and of the R.A.F.'s air-sea rescue launches. Scott-Paine handed over Miss Britain III to the National Maritime Museum in 1951.

Shortly before the war he began to design and build P.T. boats in the United States and Canada, where he established—and was chairman of—the Marine Design and Engineering Development Corporation, U.S.A., and the Canadian Power Boat Company, Limited.

Through an astonishingly active career of 43 years Scott-Paine, besides possessing such unusual skill as a designer and constructor, was endowed with an undimmed vision of the possibilities of air travel and fast sea travel. Southampton—to mention only one of his beneficiaries—owes to him its status as the first marine airport in the Commonwealth.

April 17, 1954.

The Rev. Dr. W. G. Scroggie, D.D., the renowned Bible teacher, died on December 28, 1958 at Wimbledon. He was 81.

Born in March 1877, William Graham Scroggie received his early education at Exeter, Malvern, and Bath and then entered Spurgeon's College. He held many important pastorates in England and Scotland, leaving the impress of his character and message on each and all, for he was a formidable man, an arresting preacher and one who "bore witness gloriously".

His ministry and influence extended beyond the Baptist church; that was seen very clearly when for health reasons he was obliged to retire in 1933 from the pastorate of Charlotte Baptist Chapel, Edinburgh. Representatives of the different denominations, of the university, of the municipality and of the laity of the church paid tribute to his influence and his teaching ministry at a public breakfast given in his honour. For 17 years he had been a notable teacher in a city noted for outstanding preachers. Scroggie's Bible School had been an event of the week to a wide circle of people.

His congregation tried to persuade him to withdraw his resignation, but the effect of the Scottish climate on his health would not allow it.

An invitation from Auckland, New Zealand, led Scroggie to undertake a six months' temporary ministry when he left Edinburgh. He had in mind a wider ministry; and to further it, before he left, he had accepted an invitation from the Mildmay Movement, a worldwide evangelical organization, to join their education department. When his six months' engagement in Auckland was completed he visited all the principal cities of Australia and held successful "Life and Service" campaigns. The Mediterranean and Middle East, South Africa and Rhodesia, Egypt and Palestine were included in his travelling ministry. The World Evangelical Movement took him to the United States in the autumn of 1936, first to California and then east to take part in the Moody centenary celebration.

Scroggie, who was a favourite speaker at the Keswick Convention, was known all over the world to Bible students as the writer for many years of the Scripture Union notes. It was his ministry of the pen as well as of the pulpit which caused Edinburgh University to confer upon him the honorary degree of Doctor of Divinity in 1927. He was a prolific writer and had published some 30 books of scriptural exposition.

His marriage to Florence Harriet Hudson, by whom he had a son, took place in 1900.

December 30, 1958.

Margaret Scudamore (Mrs. J. P. Anderson), the actress, who died in London on October 5, 1958, aged 73, first appeared on the stage in pantomime in 1898, but her connexion with the theatre extends beyond her life, as it were, in both directions, since the playwright F. A. Scudamore was her father. Michael Redgrave is her son by her marriage to the actor Roy Redgrave, and Vanessa Redgrave, lately seen in *Major Barbara* at the Royal Court, is thus her granddaughter.

Margaret Scudamore had her first chance in the West End under Arthur Bourchier's management, deputizing for Violet Vanbrugh in Alfred Sutro's *The Fire Screen* at the Garrick in 1912. She understudied and played in four of H. B. Irving's productions at the Savoy during the First World War, and in 1921 joined Bridges-Adams's New Shakespeare Company at Stratford-on-Avon, where she was seen as Mistress Page, Queen Margaret, and Lady Sneerwell.

She took an active part in the formation of a Sunday society for the production of Shakespeare, the Fellowship of Players, once more appearing as Mistress Page under their auspices in 1924, and she had important parts in two revivals staged by William Poel during the last phase of his career: Hamlet's mother in *Fratricide Punished* (1924) and Agrippina in *Sejanus* (1928).

In more modern plays she was often cast for commanding, imperious persons of the type of Lady Bracknell, a character actually played by her in the revival at the Haymarket directed by Allan Aynesworth [q.v.] in 1923. The Victorian mama of the heroine, Fay Compton, in *Secrets* (1922), the veteran actress Mrs. Telfer in Margaret Bannerman's revival of *Trelawny of the "Wells"* (1926), and Lady Britomart in Dame Sybil Thorndike's [d. 1976] revival of *Major Barbara* (1929) all came within this category.

The longest run of any play in which she appeared was probably that of St. John Ervine's* *Robert's Wife,* extending over 18 months during the late 1930s. The parts subsequently taken by her included the mother-in-law in *Home and Beauty,* the hostess in *The Last of Mrs. Cheyney*—both revived during the Second World War—and Miss Ramsden in John Clements's production of *Man and Superman* (1951). Her characters in Shaw included the mother in *Arms and the Man* in a film—her first film—made in the early days of the talkies.

October 8, 1958.

The Right Hon. J. H. Scullin, who died at Melbourne on January 28, 1953, was Prime Minister of Australia in the highly critical years of 1929 to 1931, and though his career as a parliamentarian both before and after was far from undistinguished, his reputation not unnaturally stands or falls by his record during that period. He was an admirable debater and a sincere and personally respected leader, but it was not to him that the country turned when a strong and decisive policy became imperative.

James Henry Scullin was born at Ballarat, Victoria, on September 18, 1876, and after an elementary education began work in the gold mines at an early age, combining this with night-school. His spare time he gave to debating practice.

In 1903 he joined the Labour Party as an organizer and three years later was selected to contest the Ballarat seat against Alfred Deakin, then Prime Minister, but was unsuccessful. He was eventually returned to the Federal Parliament in 1910, as Labour member for Corangamite, but sat for only three years. The 1914-18 war period and until 1923 he spent as editor of a Ballarat evening newspaper. He re-entered the House of Representatives in 1923 as member for Yarra.

On the retirement of Mr. Charlton in 1928 Scullin was elected leader of the Federal Labour Party and a year later, on the victory of Labour at the 1929 election, he found himself Prime Minister. In 1930 he was sworn a member of the Privy Council.

The first impact of the depression was just beginning to be felt by Australia when he took office, and one of the first acts of the new Government was to impose drastic restrictions on imports in an attempt to restore the balance of payments. But this and other remedies were of little avail against the loss of national income, and Scullin, on his departure for the Imperial Conference in August 1930, a sick man, left behind him a state of confusion and uncertainty. His visit to London, however, was a personal success, and he was liked everywhere for his simple manner and obvious integrity. One of his chief tasks was to advise the King that, in accordance with Labour views, the new Governor-General of the Commonwealth should be an Australian.

But in his absence the Parliamentary Labour Party split seriously on economic policy. He returned to find his authority as leader gone and the party torn between the paths of economic orthodoxy and the inflationist remedies sponsored by the New South Wales Labour leader, Mr. Lang. Scullin failed either to reconcile these differences or to convince the country at large that he himself had any definite opinions on what should be done. At the end of 1931 his Ministry was defeated in the House by the defection of the extremist Labour group.

In 1907 he married Marie McNamara, of Ballarat.

January 29, 1953.

The Most Rev. Pedro Segura, Cardinal-Archbishop of Seville and one of the most outspoken prelates in Spain, who had been seriously ill for some weeks, died in a nursing home in Madrid on April 8, 1957.

Don Pedro Segura was born in the province of Burgos on December 4, 1880. He was educated at the Pontifical Seminary at Comillas, in the province of Santander, where he took the triple doctorate in Divinity, Canon Law, and Philosophy.

From his ordination to priesthood in 1910 his rise in the Church was rapid. In 1912 he became a Canon at Valladolid and auxiliary bishop there in 1916; he was made Bishop of Coria in 1920. It was during this period that Cardinal Segura became known also as a social reformer for his outstanding humanitarian work in the inhospitable and most backward region in Spain, Las Hurdes. In 1926 came the appointment as Archbishop of Burgos, and in the following year Pope Pius XI raised him to the dignity of Cardinal and appointed him Archbishop of Toledo and Primate of all Spain.

On the proclamation of the Republic in April 1931 the Archbishop declared in his cathedral: "The Spanish Church is sad and anxious". These words and a pastoral letter in which the Cardinal gave thanks to King Alfonso XIII for his devotion to the Church led in the end to his expulsion from Spain by the Republican Government after he had been arrested and placed *incomunicado.* Against this treatment he protested strongly, saying that only by force would he leave Spain. He was escorted to the frontier by the police and put over the Pyrenees in May 1931.

He then lived in Rome as a Cardinal *in Curia* but remained Primate of Spain until 1935. He voluntarily resigned when, under a moderate Republican Cabinet, a new Primate was appointed. In 1938, during the Civil War, Cardinal Segura was made Archbishop of Seville. He began to show disagreement with certain aspects of the Franco* régime in 1940, taking particular exception to the association with Hitler's Germany; to the identification of church and state; and to the censorship of the press. He roundly denounced the Falangists and prohibited under pain of excommunication the painting of memorial notices to the founder of the party on the walls of the churches of his diocese; he was the only Spanish Bishop to adopt this firm attitude. Later he became preoccupied with the effects of Protestant propaganda, which he roundly denounced in several pastoral letters.

On the occasions of General Franco's visits to Seville the Cardinal did not appear in public; he was represented by his Vicar-General. There was undoubtedly a growing feud between the Cardinal and the head of the Spanish state. He did not welcome the Concordat of 1953 and this and his absence for several years from the meetings of the Archbishops (though complying with Canon Law by sending one of his suffragan Bishops to represent him) caused the Holy See to take an almost unprecedented step in December 1954 of appointing, without the Cardinal's consent, a Coadjutor Archbishop with the right of succession to the see of Seville. Cardinal Segura remained Archbishop of Seville, but the government and administration of the diocese were placed in the hands of the Coadjutor.

He was a brilliant exponent of the spoken and written word, and his short sermons known as "sabatinas" were models of evangelical doctrine; so, too, were his frequent pastoral letters.

A typical Castilian, frugal and austere, faithful to his friends, devoted to the person of King Alfonso XIII, a lover of the poor, he leaves nothing but his pectoral cross and his episcopal ring.

April 9, 1957.

Matyas Seiber, the composer, lost his life in a car crash in South Africa on September 24, 1960. He was 55.

By his death an exceptionally inspiring teacher of composition, and a musician of remarkable and diversified gifts, has been robbed from Britain, his adopted home for a quarter of a century.

There was hardly a sphere of music which he did not enrich in one way or another. He was a composer of symphonic and chamber music, of films and jazz and light music; he wrote an accordion tutor in 10 volumes; he lectured on music, conducted choirs and orchestras both amateur and professional, wrote with distinction in several languages about music, was an able cellist, and a teacher of composition with a capacity to stimulate imagination and transform technique from drudgery into inspiration. Truly he was the general practitioner in music *par excellence,* not because he had no special gift for any branch of the art, but because his mind was musical through and through, his musical vitality was so strong that it could not be confined within any one field of activity.

He was born in Budapest on May 4, 1905, and christened Matyas György. His family was musical, his mother being a piano teacher, and he grew up in an atmosphere of practical music-making. His first instrument was the cello, which he began to learn at the age of 10, and which he later played in a ship's orchestra so as to work a passage to America. At the Budapest Academy of Music he also studied composition with Zoltan Kodaly*, who paid public tribute to Seiber's purity of style as a composer. Kodaly's broadminded approach to musical education must have infected Seiber; it was his outstanding quality when he came himself to ground pupils in the elements, as in the subtleties, of musical language.

After graduating at Budapest he took a post as teacher in Frankfurt-am-Main, where in 1928 he joined the staff of the Hochschule and shocked people by instituting a jazz class, the first of its kind. Ten years later he enlivened a festival of the International Society for Contemporary Music in London with a vivid critical exposition of jazz as music; his analysis of metre and rhythm in jazz, then regarded as so much lunatic fringe, is now accepted as axiomatic. While in Frankfurt, Seiber was also acting as choral trainer, conductor, cellist in the unusually adventurous Lenzewski String Quartet, and musical journalist. This last activity took him to Russia after he left Frankfurt in doom-laden 1933.

Two years later he settled in London, and eventually became a British citizen. In 1942 he joined the musical staff of Morley College, where he taught and conducted. Shortly afterwards he was one of those who founded the "composers' workshop" now known as the Society for the Promotion of New Music. In 1945 he formed a small choir, the Dorian Singers, which specialized in the performance, under Seiber's direction, of pre-classical music, particularly English madrigals, and new works.

When not occupied with these demands on his energy, and enthusiasm, he taught, quietly, with supreme efficiency, opening the pupil's ears to the expressiveness of Morley, the bold effects of Bach, the new paths signposted by Stravinsky* or Schönberg [q.v.], and the latent creative predilections of the pupil himself. His musical enthusiasms were so many, and ranged so wide, that he had no need to bring any dogma into his teaching—except the dogma of musicianship.

His own creative gift might well have taken first claim on his energy, and in fact he went on composing music whatever else demanded his attention.

In Germany he wrote incidental music for plays, in England for films (notably the animated cartoon of Orwell's novel *Animal Farm*) and radio (in which medium his music for a bicentenary broadcast of Goethe's *Faust* remains outstanding). His grasp of all contemporary styles, and ability to write effectively in any of them, seemed to detract, at one time, from truly creative success as a composer. It was only in later years that he found in 12-note music an idiom that he could mould to really individual and expressive purpose. His cantata *Ulysses* (1947), to a text from James Joyce's novel, was not only brilliantly written but evoked an atmosphere, and created a texture, that still sounds completely original and holds the attention spellbound.

Of his chamber music the third string quartet (1951) is a remarkably positive, logical argument that works an imaginative way to an inevitable conclusion. In *The Pezzi,* for cello and orchestra, he went further idiomatically and still deeper in thought. A recent setting of another Joyce text, from *Portrait of the Artist as a Young Man,* boldly attacked the problem of combining speech with chamber music, sometimes naively, but with an acumen and feeling for sheer musical sound that still commanded admiration.

His understanding of words and of the singing voice, felicitously deployed in choral conducting, also gave vividness and gratification to his songs, in Hungarian, German, French (a set of folk songs), and English—his song cycle *To Poetry* is particularly fine.

September 27, 1960.

Hugh de Selincourt, whose delightfully fresh chronicles of village cricket will be remembered, died on January 20, 1951 at his home near Pulborough, Sussex, at the age of 72.

Though not born in Sussex, he had lived there so long that he could claim to be an adopted son, and there can be no doubt that the Tillington which figures in so much of his writing is a Sussex village, nestling under the South Downs in the manner of the villages he knew and loved so well. How he came to be an expert in the kind of cricket he described so vividly he has placed on record in *Over* and in *More Over*, but there he tells only half the story, entertaining though it is. His earlier works, in which he constantly gave himself the severe task of writing a story from the point of view of a small boy, were an exacting apprenticeship, but the novels themselves were no prentice work.

Hugh de Selincourt was born on June 15, 1878, and was educated at Dulwich and University College, Oxford. From 1910 to 1912 he was dramatic critic of the *Star*, and in 1911 joined the staff of the *Observer*, where until 1914 he worked as a literary critic. He continued to review books for the *Observer* for many years. Meanwhile he had written a number of novels, the first of which, *A Boy's Marriage*, was published in 1907. This was quickly followed by *The High Adventure*, *The Way Things Happen*, and *A Fair House*.

The outbreak of war in 1914 turned his thoughts in another direction, and *A Soldier of Life*, *The Sacrifice*, and *Women and Children* strike a deeper note. On the return of peace, however, he resumed his earlier line of thought with greater finish in *One Little Boy*, *Young Mischief*, and *Young 'Un*. After the appearance of *The Saturday Match* in 1937 there was a long silence, and then, in 1948, the author, perhaps in deference to his advancing years, published *Gauvinier Takes to Bowls*, a remarkably successful character, and in much of the writing of that novel can be seen the seeds which grew later into such sturdy plants as *The Saturday March* and the rest.

His plays, though finely wrought and of considerable literary merit, never brought the fame that his novels and essays won for him.

January 22, 1951.

D. S. Senanayake, Prime Minister of the Dominion of Ceylon, who died on March 22, 1952 from an injury received in a fall from a horse in Colombo, was a far-sighted administrator and a wise Commonwealth statesman.

He entered politics in middle life and rendered great service to his country by establishing its claim to independence and by the imaginative schemes he started for the development of the interior and the promotion of agriculture. Himself a Ceylonese, he never allowed sectional interests to predominate in his policy, but worked equally for the good of the Tamils, Burghers, and other racial minorities. For 15 years as Minister of Agriculture, before becoming the first Prime Minister in 1947, he showed himself to be a hard worker, capable of quick decisions. His simple and jovial nature endeared him to his countrymen, who looked on him as "the father of the nation".

Don Stephen Senanayake (the "Don" was a reminder of the Portuguese period in Ceylon's history) was born on October 20, 1884. Though he came of a devout Buddhist family, and remained faithful to that religion, he was educated at St. Thomas's Church of England College, and in due course became a member of its governing body. After a brief period as a clerk in the Surveyor-General's office he turned to rubber planting on his father's estate. His energy in clearing forest and planting rubber and coconuts earned him the nickname of *Kelay* John ("Jungle John"). From 1913 onwards he deeply interested himself in temperance reform. He maintained that the Colonial Government's excise policy was resulting in the multiplication of drink-shops; and he pressed forward the method of local option.

In 1915 Senanayake was imprisoned during the troubles that broke out under the operation of martial law; but far from becoming an irreconcilable he entered the Legislative Council in 1922. When the Donoughmore Constitution gave universal adult franchise to Ceylon in 1931, Senanayake was elected to the State Council and appointed Minister for Agriculture and Lands, a post he was to hold for 15 years. Within two years he had put through the Land Development Ordinance, which brought about great improvement in the condition of the peasantry, and by promoting irrigation schemes for the dry areas of Ceylon brought a great deal of hitherto barren land into cultivation. He condemned the internal security plan of 1940 as "a diabolical scheme", on the ground that it allowed the military to keep law and order without proper public control.

Senanayake took energetic and constructive measures in feeding the islanders when normal supplies had been cut off by developments in the 1939-45 war. Ceylon had so far drawn four-fifths of her rice supply from Burma and Siam. When Japanese penetration removed this source of supply she turned to India, but in 1942 was able to obtain only 172,800 tons as against 583,734 in 1939. Senanayake made it his business to procure rice from Egypt and Brazil, and also (though wheaten flour was not a staple diet in Ceylon) had by 1944 raised flour imports to 10 times the volume attained in 1939. He set the Department of Agriculture to work on researches in chemistry, botany, plant pathology and entomology; and during his tenure of office the production of pulses, sugar, milk and dairy produce greatly increased. In the distributive field he worked more and more through the cooperative societies (he had himself founded the movement in 1923). He refused a knighthood in 1946, but was sworn of the Privy Council in January 1950.

The attainment of independence status within the Commonwealth meant the realization of what he had long worked for. In his message to the people of Ceylon on February 4, 1948 he expressed gratification that freedom had been won without bloodshed or bitterness, and, speaking of the British, said: "We have had our disagreements with them, but we shall always remain grateful for their good will and cooperation which has culminated in our freedom, and I sincerely hope that our relations with them and with the sister nations of the Commonwealth will always be one of perpetual friendship and cordiality". He became Premier of the new Dominion without any rival in the field, having commended himself by his work to all sections of public opinion. He quickly set afoot further measures to improve the economic condition of the island, a notable step being the initiation of hydro-electric installations, which are of cardinal importance in a country producing no coal or oil.

He took an especial concern in the work of clearing great areas of the high jungle, settling land which for hundreds of years had been made uninhabitable by the invasion of the mosquito. With great imagination he looked on the ruins of the ancient cities of the Ceylonese kings—Anuradhapura and Polonnaruwa—with their great dams (or "tanks") and their canals, now largely disused and overgrown; and he saw that if the mosquito could be killed through D.D.T. men could return and the old dams and canals could be repaired. The interior of Ceylon could then have a ready-made irrigation system. With an energy equal to his imagination Senanayake organized the work. Thousands of acres have already been cleared and by 1953 the Government will have established "agricultural colonies" on about 130,000 acres of newly won land. He also took vigorous measures against corruption in public life, and in 1949 set up a judicial inquiry which recommended the dismissal of six high officials.

He married in 1909 Miss Emily Maud Dunuwille and there were two sons of the marriage. The elder one, Dudley, has been Minister of Agriculture in Ceylon since 1947.

March 24, 1952.

Mack Sennett, one of the pioneers of screen comedy, died on November 5, 1960 in a Hollywood hospital at the age of 76.

Sennett's real name was Mickall Sinnott, and he was born at Denville, Quebec, in 1884. He began his film career as an actor, joining the old Biograph Company in New York at the same time as Mary Pickford, working there under D. W. Griffith, the most famous director of the day. But Griffith had his heart in epic historical films, while Sennett was only interested in humour. Above all, he wished to make a series of comedies involving policemen, and since Griffith showed no enthusiasm for the idea, Sennett left Biograph in 1912 to form his own film production unit, which he called the Keystone Company.

As a result the "Keystone Cops" were born, an indefatigable body of men dedicated to the high-powered pursuit of the elusive criminal—for speed and the chase were the very essence of Sennett's work. Many famous players of the silent films learnt their trade under Sennett's direction, including Mabel Normand, Polly Moran, Mack Swain, Harry Langdon, Chester Conklin, Roscoe "Fatty" Arbuckle and Ford Sterling, who, according to film legend, was the first comedian ever to throw a custard pie on the screen, although this missile later became the special weapon of "Fatty" Arbuckle. Subsequently, in order to introduce glamour into comedy, Sennett created his team of Bathing Beauties, among whom were Gloria Swanson, Marie Prevost, and Phyllis Haver.

Ford Sterling's contract with Sennett ended in 1914, and it became essential for a successor to be found. Joseph M. Schenck* advised

Sennett to go and see a young English comedian named Charles Chaplin [d. 1977], who was then on tour of the United States with Fred Karno's Vaudeville Company in a sketch called *A Night in an English Music Hall.* Sennett saw the young man, realized at once his potentialities, and Chaplin was launched on his career as a screen comedian.

If Sennett had done nothing else than this his place in film history would have been secure, but Sennett was, in his way, one of the true pioneers of the cinema. His approach to comedy was simple, and he relied upon slapstick for his effects, but he understood perfectly the requirements, the strength, and the weaknesses of the new medium of film. It is true that his work soon became old-fashioned, even before the close of the silent film era, but many famous directors who followed him—men of far greater wit, subtlety, and sophistication—learnt the basis of their art from Sennett.

During the 1930s, after the coming of sound, he produced a few feature films, and in 1939 became an associate producer with 20th Century-Fox, but Sennett's name belongs to the infancy of the cinema. His handling of these early film comedies can provide an object lesson to screen writers and screen comedians even today.

November 7, 1960.

The death occurred at Lancieux, Brittany, on September 11, 1958 of **Robert W. Service,** the poet, whose *Songs of a Sourdough* and other volumes of verse in similar vein once earned him the popular title of "the Canadian Kipling". He was 84.

It was a title that Service himself probably deprecated, for although there could be no question of the extent to which he had taken Kipling for model—"Kipling", runs a line in his last volume of verse, "to whom I bow the knee"—Service was always modesty itself about his poet's gift. In spite of a jingling facility which was only rarely Kipling's also, he was indeed almost too insistently modest.

All that mattered, he seemed to suggest, about his verse was that he wrote it with ease, and that its success brought him a life of independence, for which he was grateful. Certainly the success, of which the echoes have by this time very nearly died away, was remarkable. And the verse, for all its vigour and fluency, its wide range of rhyme and rhythm, was something less than poetry. Yet Service's ballad jingles were an appropriate medium for the tales he told in them, tales humorous and melodramatic or mock-heroic, all of them drawn from the workings of an active imagination and ready sympathy during years of hard living in the Canadian West and High North.

Robert William Service was born in Preston, Lancashire, on January 16, 1874, the eldest of the 10 children of Robert Service and Emily Parker. His father was employed in a bank at a salary of £200 a year, and the boy's education stopped short at Hillhead High School, Glasgow. It was after he had been employed for some years with the Commercial Bank of Scotland in that city that he decided to emigrate. At 21 he sailed for Canada, travelling steerage. During the next 10 years he wandered up and down the Pacific coast engaging in a profuse assortment of outdoor jobs. For a time he appeared to be settled on Vancouver Island, absorbed in farming. Then, having in 1905 surprisingly joined the staff of the Canadian Bank of Commerce in Victoria, British Columbia, he was transferred to White Horse, Yukon Territory, and thence to Dawson. He spent eight years in all in the Yukon, travelling extensively in the sub-Arctic.

Songs of a Sourdough, a title that invoked the old-time placer-miner and the epoch of gold hunting in the North, during which yeast was an unknown luxury, appeared in 1907. It enjoyed instantaneous and vast popularity. Service had produced a great deal of verse in youth and then stopped; for years he had not written a line. In the Yukon he took his part in the local social round, and from reciting and strumming his banjo he went on to compose ballads of his own. His early training had not been wasted; writing verse now came to him as easily, in his own phrase, "as slipping off a log". Here, in the fluent Kiplingesque rhythms of poems such as "The Shooting of Dan McGrew", "The Spell of the Yukon", and "The Cremation of Sam McGee", were the male verities, the grim humour, the epic human condition that sprang from the great open spaces of the northern wilderness. More important than these, at any rate so far as poetry is concerned, was Service's sincere response to the beauty of nature.

It was said that Dan McGrew was intended originally for recitation at a Yukon church social, but it was never given, as some of the language was thought to be on the strong side for such an occasion. Service, who had scratched out the ballad on the back of old envelopes, let them gather dust until a bonus from his bank put him in funds and enabled him to publish it in Toronto. Later publishers wrote saying the printers were peddling the ballad from galley proofs and offered to bring out his verse at their own expense. By 1940 two million copies of *Songs of a Sourdough* had been sold.

He continued his verse-making in *Ballads of a Cheechako, Rhymes of a Rolling Stone* and other volumes, and his popularity was for many years undimmed. In 1912 he went to live in France. He was a war correspondent for the *Toronto Star* during the war of 1914-18 and also an ambulance driver with the Canadian medical services in France for two years. He was in Russia at the start of the Second World War, managed to reach Warsaw, and left that city as the Nazi bombardment began. After a hazardous journey he reached France with his wife and daughter and ultimately they made their way to Canada.

Besides his books of verse Service also turned his hand to fiction. His most interesting novel is, perhaps, *The Pretender,* published in 1915, the story of a young American novelist who goes to Europe—an uneven and somewhat strained piece of work, though with genuine and vivid passages set in the Latin Quarter of Paris.

The title of his last volume of verse woke a deliberate echo of Kipling—*Bar-Room Ballads,* which appeared in 1940. In 1946 he published a volume of autobiography, *Ploughman of the Moon* (a title taken from Verlaine), which exhibited his remarkable control of phrase and an attractive candour regarding his aspirations and capacities.

September 13, 1958.

Dr. R. W. Seton-Watson, who for over 40 years was recognized as one of the foremost authorities in Britain on the history and politics of Central and Eastern Europe, died at his home on the Isle of Skye on July 25, 1951 at the age of 71.

Robert William Seton-Watson, only child of William L. Watson and of Elizabeth Lindsay Seton, was born at Ayton, Perthshire, on August 20, 1879. In him the characters of both his parents were curiously blended—the cautious shrewdness of a well-to-do Scottish business man and landowner, and the idealism of a lady of ancient lineage. The influence of a female relative to whom his upbringing was entrusted after the early death of his mother accounted, in part, for a shyness and diffidence of manner which he never quite overcame. Behind it lay passionate devotion to what he held to be right and true. Winchester and New College set their stamp on him and made him a scholar. With the approval of H. A. L. Fisher he chose history as his special field, and gained distinction with the Stanhope Historical Essay before taking his degree in 1902. A year later a study of Maximilian I revealed a bent which, after he had translated *The Tombs of the Popes* by Gregorovius, took him to Vienna, where he intended to write a history of Austria since Maria Theresa.

On reaching Vienna in 1905 contemporary political movements rather than history aroused his interest. The Hungarian Parliament had come into conflict with the Crown over an interpretation of the Austro-Hungarian settlement of 1867. Seton-Watson first supported the Magyar view in this conflict, for he regarded the Hungarians as "a nation rightly struggling to be free". These sympathies took him to Hungary where he meant to spend some months. In a few weeks he left Hungary full of wrath against the Magyars. He resented their attempts to mislead him by pretending that the non-Magyar races, and the Slovaks in particular, were really Magyar. He began to study the Magyar tongue and to collect documentary evidence upon the true position in Hungary. The early results of these inquiries he contributed to the *Spectator,* under the name of "Scotus Viator", and in 1907 summed them up in a little work: *The Future of Austria-Hungary.* Next year he published a more ambitious volume, *Racial Problems in Hungary;* and in 1911 *The Southern Slav Question.*

Meanwhile the name "Scotus Viator" had become anathema to the Magyar authorities, and correspondingly popular among the Hungarian Slovaks, Romanes, and Croats, who groaned under the Magyar yoke. To a good knowledge of German, French, and Italian he added sufficient command of Magyar, Slovak, Romanian, and Serbo-Croatian to give him access to literature in those languages. Personal acquaintance and friendship with non-Magyar leaders opened to him special sources of information, though his extreme caution in utilizing them sometimes earned him unmerited suspicion. Once convinced, Seton-Watson made ample and even passionate amends for initial scepticism. Though the soundness of his painstaking erudition was, perhaps, overlooked by those who disliked his conclusions, those who knew as much as he admired and trusted him. Among them was Professor Thomas Masaryk, afterwards President Liberator of Czechoslovakia, whom Seton-Watson first met in 1910. Their friendship enabled Seton-Watson to render outstanding service to the Czechoslovak cause.

Soon after the outbreak of war in 1914 Seton-Watson met Masaryk in Holland and brought back a weighty memorandum for Sir Edward Grey. In 1915-16, when Masaryk had escaped to England, Seton-Watson was foremost in securing for him a professorship at King's College, London. With Masaryk, too, Seton-Watson founded in 1916 an influential weekly review, *The New Europe,* of which he bore the main cost. It was fitting that after the liberation of Czechoslovakia Seton-Watson himself should be appointed in 1922 Masaryk Professor of Central European History in the University of London, and that jointly with Sir Bernard Pares he should have edited *Slavonic and East European Studies.* His qualifications for such work were beyond question. His learning was wide and deep, his industry untiring, his enthusiasm inexhaustible. He held the London Chair until 1945, when he became the first Professor of Czechoslovak Studies in Oxford. He retired from that Chair in 1949.

After helping to organize and direct the Serbian Relief Fund during the war of 1914-18 he entered the Political Information Department of the Foreign Office, and also took charge of the Austrian section of Lord Northcliffe's organization for propaganda in enemy countries. At moments he may have felt tempted to follow a political career, but he yielded finally to the attractions of academic life and of university teaching. Though not a lecturer of compelling power, his grasp of facts and of principles was unsurpassed; and if, as a historian, he tended to blur the outlines of a narrative by over-attention to detail it was because his passion for facts overcame his care for literary artistry. No student of European politics between the years 1905 and 1950 can afford to ignore or to neglect his many works—in particular his great study, *Britain in Europe, 1789-1914*—nor will any lightly challenge the soundness of his antecedent judgment of the course events would take in such essays in contemporary politics as *Britain and the Dictators* and *From Munich to Danzig.*

For popularity he cared little. For the truth, as he saw and ascertained it, he cared much. Had his manner been as confident as his probity was unassailable his outstanding worth might have been more readily and more generally recognized. Abroad, and especially in central and south eastern Europe, it was widely recognized. Academic honours were showered upon him. Statesmen sought his counsel. Throughout the war of 1939-45 he was in constant touch with Czechoslovak and Yugoslav leaders. Among his unpublished records of those years much valuable material will be found. It will be an indispensable source of knowledge of the inner history of more than one European people.

He married in 1911 Marion Esther, daughter of Edward Stack of the Bengal Civil Service. There were two sons and a daughter of the marriage.

July 28, 1951.

Cardinal-Archbishop of Seville—See **Segura.**

H. H. Seyyid Khalifa-bin Harub-bin-Thuwaini-bin-Said—See **Zanzibar.**

Count Carlo Sforza, who through many years powerfully influenced the destinies of his country, died in a nursing home in Rome on September 4, 1952 within a month of his seventy-ninth birthday.

As a public man Sforza suffered from a certain pomposity of manner and an irritating egoism which often made those with whom he came into contact, whether Italian or foreign, feel they were being patronized. These faults, though they could not help to make him popular, were more apparent than real; with his unshakeable opposition to tyranny of any kind, his almost unrivalled experience over more than half a century of foreign affairs and diplomacy, and his lofty sense of internationalism tempered by a knowledge of the possible, Sforza was in every way a great modern European.

His work as Foreign Minister in Italy after the 1939-45 war, when he patiently strove, against frequent opposition from within and without, to reinstate Italy as a full member of the family of free nations should eventually win him a more lasting place in the hearts of his countrymen than he ever seemed to occupy during his lifetime.

Sforza was born at Montignosa, near Massa, in 1873. As a young and middle-aged man his career in the Italian diplomatic service brought him many and varied experiences in different parts of the world, including China and the Balkans. He entered politics in 1919 as Under-Secretary for Foreign Affairs in the Nitti administration, and as Foreign Minister in the Giolitti Government of the succeeding year negotiated the Treaty of Rapallo with Yugoslavia. In 1922 he was Ambassador in Paris when the "March on Rome" took place; Sforza, although pressed by Mussolini to co-operate with Fascism, immediately resigned the Paris Embassy and returned to Italy, where he carried on, so far as was possible in those early days of the new régime, anti-Fascist propaganda.

In 1926, however, the Italian Association for Democratic Control, of which Sforza was a member and which was one of the main weapons of resistance, was dissolved, and all further forms of open opposition became impossible. Two years later Sforza left Italy, which he was not to see again for 15 years.

The exile was spent largely in Belgium, which was his wife's country, though he was also a visitor to the United States where, as the result of a series of lectures on the peace treaties after the 1914-18 war, he was invited to join the committee of the Carnegie Foundation for International Peace.

These years saw also a steady output from his pen, partly in the form of contributions to the Belgian, French, American, and British Press—including the *Manchester Guardian*—and partly in political and international studies, of which *Makers of Modern Europe,* published in 1930, became the best known. From 1940 to 1943 Sforza was in America, having passed through England on the way; while in London he besought the members of the British Government whom he met "never to confound"—the words are his—"either in words or thought, Italy and Fascism".

In 1943, a month after the Italian armistice, Sforza returned to Italy and immediately became, with Benedetto Croce [q.v.], the spearhead of the opposition to King Victor Emmanuel, whom he described at the time as "the Pétain [q.v.] of Italy". This was the period when, with less than one-third of the country in allied hands, Marshal Badoglio [q.v.] was the head of a "Government" which satisfied no one except, it seemed, H.M. Government in London. Although he eventually took service with Badoglio, Sforza became increasingly resolved, as the first year of Italy's new-found democratic life developed and Rome was cleared of the Germans, to get rid of the King (though not the monarchy), because with countless other Italians he saw a man inexcusably guilty of the betrayal of the country's interests to the Fascists.

This attitude finally led, in the autumn of 1944, to serious and unfortunate misunderstandings with the British Government, in which Churchill* and Eden [Lord Avon, d. 1977] accused Sforza of bad faith in working against the Government of which he was a member, and Sforza vigorously defended himself against the charges. Wherever, in these turbulent times, the right and wrong may have lain, certainly an unhappy and by no means justified impression was left in some British minds—indeed, in some quarters it was a confirmation of old suspicions—that Sforza was not wholly reliable.

Prevented by the British veto—the Allied Control Commission were still the virtual rulers of Italy—from becoming Foreign Minister in the second Bonomi Cabinet, Sforza withdrew for a time from the forefront of political life. A year later, in September 1945, he was by a large majority elected President of the *Consulta,* the preliminary parliamentary assembly which was the first attempt at free democratic discussion in Italy for 20 years; the choice of Sforza was a fitting tribute to his long struggle against the Fascists.

In the third De Gasperi [q.v.] Government,

formed in February 1947, Sforza became Foreign Minister and held this post through all succeeding administrations until July 1951 when, a sick man, he was replaced by the Prime Minister himself. One of his first official acts—to address to the allies a Note expressing the hope that the Italian peace treaty, just signed, might be revised—was symbolic of his constant endeavours to win for the new Italy a place of equality among the nations. Greatly helped by the support of his chief, Alcide De Gasperi, with whom he worked always in the closest cooperation, Sforza pursued throughout his reign at the Palazzo Chigi a policy of international collaboration with all who were willing to reciprocate.

His most valuable gift during these years was an imperviousness to criticism. Because he refused to placate nationalist opinion with uncompromising claims for the return of Trieste or the colonies he was dubbed a "*rinunciatario*"; because, with great skill and patience, he led Italy slowly but soundly towards the western side and away from neutrality in the cold war, until she eventually became a full and equal partner in the Atlantic Treaty, he had to bear constantly the force of communist vituperation. One of the major sticking-points of this time was that of Anglo-Italian relations, which were perhaps worse than ever Mussolini had tried to make them. The main issue was the colonial one, and it was certainly not Sforza's fault that the compromise for the disposal of the former colonies which he and Ernest Bevin [q.v.] had so patiently evolved in May 1949, should have failed to secure a majority in the United Nations.

The culminating point for this policy of friendly reinstatement came in 1951, when, with Italy closely linked by formal ties to her friends in western Europe and to the United States, Sforza and De Gasperi met, all within a few months, the French Prime Minister and Foreign Minister at Santa Margherita, the British Prime Minister and Foreign Secretary in London, and Adenauer* the Federal German Chancellor, in Rome. Even then Sforza's ideas—he was a prodigiously hard worker and reader—were reaching farther afield to the vision of Atlantic union and a permanent link between free Europe and the United States.

The range of his thinking no doubt owed much to the fact that he was never a party man in Italian politics; a tenuous association with the Republican Party left him free to write and speak as he chose, and almost to the last he was a regular, if infrequent, contributor of articles to the *Corriere della Sera*.

September 5, 1952.

Edward Shanks, the well known author and journalist, died on May 4, 1953 in hospital in London at the age of 60.

Poet, novelist, critic, essayist, Edward Shanks was a writer of uncommon versatility who maintained a consistently high level of interest and craftsmanship. He has a recognized place among the "Georgian" poets—the expressive charm of his early verse serves in some degree to define the character of the Georgian school as a whole—and he has the distinction of being the first recipient of the Hawthornden Prize for imaginative literature. Poetry apart, he wrote a considerable number of books and for many years combined a busy life in journalism with active authorship, producing much that was both soundly and attractively devised.

Born in London on June 11, 1892, the eldest son of E. L. Shanks, Edward Richard Buxton Shanks was educated at Merchant Taylors' School and at Trinity College, Cambridge, where he was senior scholar in history and took his degree in 1913. In his last year at Cambridge he was editor of the *Granta.* He enlisted on the outbreak of war in 1914 and was soon granted a commission in The South Lancashire Regiment, but in 1915 he was invalided out of the Army and served until the close of hostilities in the War Office.

Shanks had begun to write poetry while still an undergraduate and his first two books of verse were published in 1915 and 1916. They exhibit a precocious maturity and in their verbal ease and control of poetic impulse are characteristic of his poetic output as a whole. In 1919 came what is perhaps his most felicitous volume of poetry, *Queen of China, and Other Poems,* which carries its romantic illumination with unaffected grace and assurance. It was for this book of verse that Shanks received the Hawthornden Prize. In later volumes he was to make a rather more concentrated effort to extract poetic reality from experience, but never to more charming effect.

In 1919, when he also became assistant editor of the *London Mercury,* where he remained until 1922, Shanks published his first novel, *The Old Indispensables,* a light-hearted and indeed skittish commentary on the war in Whitehall. A year later came a novel of very different character, *The People of the Ruins,* a fine and full-blooded essay in prophecy, done in semi-Wellsian vein. *First Essays in Literature* (1923) reveal a critic of thoughtful and often delicate perception with an engaging streak of robustness and a pleasant indifference to the higher and more recondite reaches of criticism. After that the poet, novelist, and critic in Shanks appeared by turns. He produced poetry and criticism chiefly during the early part of the period, 1928-35, when he was chief leader-writer on the *Evening Standard;* but he gave striking evidence of his industry and versatility in publishing a series of accomplished and very readable novels in the later years—*Queer Street* (1932), *The Enchanted Village* (1933), *Tom Tiddler's Ground* (1934), and *Old King Cole* (1936).

In the following years Shanks produced, among other books, excellent critical works on Poe and Rudyard Kipling, the latter "a study in literary and political ideas" and a reasoned commendation, and later still made selections from Swinburne and Browning. In 1933 a volume of *Collected Poems* appeared and his latest verses appeared earlier in 1953 under the title *Poems, 1939-1952. The Universal War and the Universal State,* which was published in 1947, exhibited a view of history, clearly reflecting a naturally meditative temperament, seemingly derived from Spengler and Arnold Toynbee*.

Shanks married, in 1926, Dorothea Maryon, daughter of R. H. Burbrook.

May 5, 1953.

Evelyn Sharp, author, journalist, and crusader for a variety of social and humane causes, and widow of H. W. Nevinson, died on June 17, 1955 at the age of 85.

In a period which must seem strangely remote to all but her contemporaries, she achieved her share of celebrity as a conspicuous figure in the women's militant suffrage movement in Britain. From 1905 until the close of the battle in 1918, women's suffrage, it seemed, was her dedicated end in life, the absorbing passion of her days and nights. She was a tireless campaigner, received a prison sentence more than once, and was a determined hunger-striker. Victory achieved, however, she gave herself almost as generously to other causes and campaigns. And side by side with this resolute and idealistic activity in public affairs went her career as a writer. She wrote novels, biographies, sociological essays, children's books, but perhaps displayed her versatile talents to best advantage as a serious, informed and public-spirited journalist.

Born in London in 1869, one of a large Victorian family (an elder brother was Cecil Sharp, to whom more than any other man credit was due for reviving English folk dance and song), Evelyn Sharp enjoyed a singularly happy childhood and a degree of freedom from parental restraint that was both unusual for the time and beneficent. She was educated privately, began to write at an early age—she published her first short story at the age of 18—and was soon caught up in the literary and artistic devotions of the *Yellow Book* period.

She sent a short story to the *Yellow Book* and a novel *(At the Relton Arms)* to John Lane, and both were promptly accepted. With their publication in 1894 she launched out into an independent life of her own in London, wrote busily, entered into the movements of the day, and soon counted among her friends the Harlands, the John Lanes, Alice Meynell and her family, Stephen Gwynn, H. W. Nevinson, Sir Max Beerbohm [q.v.], William Watson, W. J. Locke, and others. In the next few years she became a welcome contributor to the serious journals and periodicals, and from then onwards, though never affluent, she was always able to maintain herself as an author, journalist, and lecturer.

The struggle for the vote was her stay and inspiration until the end, and the unspectacular circumstances in which it was rewarded in 1918 necessarily came as something of an anti-climax to her as to other militants. The confusions of peace, however, gave her further opportunity, and in 1920 she was engaged in relief work in Germany under Quaker auspices, later in combating famine in Russia. She travelled and lectured a great deal in the early 1920s, then turned to social conditions at home and the particular problem of the adolescent child in the East End of London. *The London Child* (1927) and *The Child Grows Up* (1929) were based upon sympathetic study of working-class life and were at once informative and practical, though perhaps there were also traces in both books of a sentimental temper that belonged rather to the "visiting" of an earlier period.

Apart from the novels, volumes of short stories and children's books, two of Evelyn Sharp's books deserve special mention. One is her memoir, done with affectionate knowledge and admirable judgment, of Hertha Ayrton (1926), the other is *Unfinished Adventure: Selected Reminiscences* (1933), an engaging, alert, and instructive fragment of autobiography. It may be recorded, too, that it was Evelyn Sharp who wrote the libretto of Dr. Ralph Vaughan Williams's [q.v.] opera, *The Poisoned Kiss,* which was produced in 1936. Until the end she maintained her interests, friendships and hobbies. She had worked conscientiously in her time for the Labour Party and for many years she gave her energies to, among other bodies, the National Council of Civil Liberties, the Council for the Abolition of the Death Penalty, and the English Folk Dance and Song Society.

In 1933, after a friendship that dated almost from the very beginning of her career and that had been strengthened by their close association in the suffrage campaign, she married Henry Nevinson, whose first wife had died a little time before. His death in 1941 visibly told on her. In 1944 she edited his essays and poems under the title of *Visions and Memories.*

June 21, 1955.

Sir Percival Sharp, who died at Falmouth on February 8, 1953 at the age of 85, had been associated with education for more than half a century and will be especially remembered, as a member of the Burnham Committee from its inception in 1919, for his strenuous advocacy of improved conditions for teachers.

He was the son of Henry and Catherine Sharp and was born on September 12, 1867. Having been educated at Edward Walton's Endowed (public elementary) School, Bishop Auckland, and the Homerton Training College, he began his career as an assistant master, and was later a head master in elementary schools. In time he became the mathematical master in the Hull School of Science and an Inspector of Schools at St. Helens, Lancashire. In 1905 he was made Director of Education there. He occupied that post until 1919, when he was appointed Director at Sheffield. In a rather surprising collocation with that post he acted as honorary controller of the Sheffield Corporation Printing Department. He had therefore played a prominent part in the civic life there, and on reaching the retirement age in 1932 he was entertained to a complimentary dinner by the Lord Mayor, and presented with an address and gifts from the chief officials of the corporation departments.

From 1925 until 1944 he was secretary of the Association of Education Committees (England, Wales, and Northern Ireland); a member of the governing body of Armstrong University, Newcastle upon Tyne, and a member of the Council and Finance Committee of Sheffield University, which conferred upon him the honorary degrees of LL.D. and B.Sc.

It was in connexion with the Burnham Committee on Teachers' Salaries, in the inception of which in 1919 he took a prominent part, that he will best be remembered. For 30 years he was a member of that body until, in December 1949, on the rejection of the teachers' claim for an extra £3 a week, he resigned in protest, and issued a trenchant statement giving his reasons: "I cannot be a party", he wrote, "to a procedure which shifts from the Minister of Education and the Chancellor of the Exchequer to our shoulders an odious responsibility of denying justice to teachers—a responsibility which, if it must be exercised, should be exercised by responsible Ministers and not by us". He had been a member of the Departmental Committee on Teachers Salaries in 1917, and of the Norwood [q.v.] Committee.

Like many men of strong character, Sharp could be somewhat dictatorial in manner, and his methods did not always escape criticism, but it would be generally conceded that he possessed a most comprehensive knowledge of his subject, great energy and enterprise, and he administered his department with efficiency and left a deep impression on the educational system of Sheffield. Teachers, too, will feel that with his death they have lost a formidable guardian of their interests. He was knighted in 1938 for his services to education.

He married in 1891 Jessie, daughter of Thomas Henderson Maclaren, and he leaves three sons.

February 11, 1953.

Maud (Mrs. W. Hudson) Shaw—See **Royden.**

Joseph Shearing—See **Bowen.**

Admiral Forrest P. Sherman, who died of a heart attack in Naples on July 22, 1951, on arriving from London to visit Allied Forces headquarters in southern Europe, had been United States Chief of Naval Operations since 1949. He was 54.

His early attainment of the highest professional position in the United States Navy was due not only to outstanding competence in his chosen calling but also to a tact and understanding more usually found among diplomats than sailors. His splendid conduct in saving 90 per cent. of the crew of his ship when she was set on fire and sunk in one of the Pacific engagements of the last war is sufficient proof of his skill in seamanship and bravery in command, while his work as Deputy Chief of Naval Operations in helping to bring unity of direction in the defence of the United States is an eloquent tribute to his diplomatic gifts.

The latter gifts were those to which he owed his last promotion. Since the unification of the three fighting services of the United States under the civilian head of the Department of Defence, and America's wide commitments for the defence of the western world, the days were past for the professional head of the United States Navy to have merely professional status and interests. President Truman* had already observed the acute mind and skill in negotiation of the young vice-admiral and promoted him over the heads of several with better professional claims to the post of Chief of Naval Operations. Since his appointment Admiral Sherman had notably fulfilled his promise, and regret at his death will be as deep and widespread on both sides of the Atlantic.

Forrest Percival Sherman was born on October 30, 1896, and received his early education at Melrose High School, Massachusetts. He had already entered the Massachusetts Institute of Technology when he was appointed to the United States Naval Academy in 1914. He passed out second of a class of 199 and received his commission as ensign in 1917. Promoted to lieutenant in the course of the next year, he served in the Atlantic and the Mediterranean during the 1914-18 war. Then, after serving as Flag Lieutenant to Rear-Admiral Newton A. McCully, in the Atlantic, he qualified as a naval aviator at the Naval Air Station at Pensacola in 1922. Service in a number of aircraft-carriers followed and in 1930 he was appointed an instructor in seamanship and flight tactics at the Naval Academy, Annapolis. Soon after his assumption of the command of an aircraft squadron based on the Saratoga, the squadron won the aircraft gunnery trophy in 1932, and in the course of the next year he was appointed to the bureau of ordnance in the Navy Department, Washington.

When war broke out in 1939 he was Fleet Aviation Officer on the staff of Admiral Claude C. Bloch, Commander-in-Chief, United States Fleet. From 1940 to early in 1942 he was in the war plans division of the office of the Chief of Naval Operations. He assumed command of U.S.S. Wasp in May 1942 and was in charge of her when later in the year she delivered a supply of much needed aircraft for reinforcing the air defences of Malta. He was still in command of her when she was sunk by enemy action off the Solomon Islands later in the year. He was awarded the Navy Cross for his handling of his ship during his short but brilliant command, and the Legion of Merit for his work in his ensuing appointment as Chief of Staff to Vice-Admiral John H. Towers [q.v.], Commander of the Air Force, Pacific Fleet. He then became Deputy Chief of Staff to Admiral Nimitz*, Commander-in-Chief, Pacific Fleet, and for his work in the post received the Distinguished Service Medal.

After the collapse of Japan he returned to Washington as Deputy Chief of Staff, Navy Department, and early in 1948 was appointed to command the United States naval forces in the Mediterranean, where he relieved Vice-Admiral Bieri.

He remained there for almost two years, when he was recalled to Washington late in 1949 to become Chief of the Naval Staff. Since his appointment he had visited Europe on a number of occasions to smooth out difficulties which are bound to arise in so large and complicated a conception as the Atlantic Treaty, and had made many friends.

July 23, 1951.

Sir Charles Scott Sherrington, O.M., G.B.E., M.D., D.SC., F.R.C.P., F.R.C.S., F.R.S., the distinguished physiologist, died on March 4, 1952 in a nursing home at Eastbourne at the age of 94, after a short illness.

Born on November 27, 1857, he was educated at Ipswich Grammar School, Gonville and Caius College, Cambridge, and St. Thomas's Hospital, taking the degrees of M.B. in 1885, M.A. in 1887, M.D. in 1893, and D.Sc. in 1904. Though he did some work in pathology Sherrington early devoted himself to physiology, the study of which he pursued with such success that he became the most illustrious of the members of the Cambridge school of physiologists which flourished so notably under the inspiration of Michael Foster. He served as Demonstrator of Physiology at Cambridge for a while, and later became Lecturer on Physiology at St. Thomas's Hospital, Medical School, holding this post till 1895. During these periods he published a number of papers on the nervous system and on other subjects. About the year 1892 he succeeded the late Sir Victor Horsley as Professor-Superintendent of the Brown Institute of Animal Pathology and Brown Professor of Pathology in the University of London. While holding this chair he worked on the subject of rabies. In 1895 he succeeded the late Professor Gotch as Holt Professor of Physiology in the University of Liverpool, taking up his duties in time to organize the establishment of the Thompson-Yates laboratories in a new building.

At Liverpool he took an active part in the formation of departments of psycho-physiology and veterinary medicine, and also introduced a course on school hygiene for secondary school teachers. He delivered the second series of Silliman memorial lectures at Yale University in 1904.

In 1913 Sherrington was appointed to the Waynflete Chair of Physiology in the University of Oxford. He was elected Fellow of the Royal Society in 1893 and served for three terms on the council, being vice-president in 1917-18. In 1920 he was elected president. From 1914 to 1917 he was Fullerian Professor of Physiology at the Royal Institution. He was president of the section of physiology of the British Association at Cambridge in 1904, and president of the British Association at Hull in 1922.

Sherrington's life was devoted mainly to the study of the nervous system. As early as 1884 he published, in conjunction with J. N. Langley, a paper dealing with the anatomy of the nervous system, and this was followed by several other papers on anatomical points. These led on to the very numerous and important papers on the physiology of the nervous system which were remarkable on account of the originality of the ideas they contained and the precision and continuity of thought they manifested. The results contained in the papers published up to 1904 were comprised in the Silliman Lectures, subsequently issued in book form under the title *The Integrative Action of the Nervous System.* This book put the study of the nervous system on a new plane. A reprinted edition, with a new foreword by the author, was issued on the occasion of the International Physiological Congress in Oxford in July 1947.

It was the genius of Sherrington which enabled him to see clearly that the unit reaction of the nervous system was the simple spinal reflex, that this unit could be studied successfully by experimental methods, and that, while the simple reflex is really a purely abstract conception, since in life no one part of the nervous system is isolated from the rest, it could be investigated with fruitful results. He was thus able to apply successfully to the study of the nervous system the principle of advance from the simple to the complex. The recognition of the simple spinal reflex as a definite unit, and the clear conception of the fact that its anatomical basis comprises (1) a receptor organ, (2) a conductor, and (3) an effector organ, mark off Sherrington's work on the nervous system from the vague generalities in which the subject had been previously enwrapped. The thesis of the book on *The Integrative Action of the Nervous System,* which is built up on the results of many ingenious experiments of his own as well as on a wide knowledge of the work of others, is that the role of the nervous system is correlation of the individual activities of all the cells of the body, whereby a new entity results—namely, the animal itself, and that, while other methods of correlation exist, the nervous system is preeminent for speed of response.

After the publication of this book, Sherrington's energy and fertility of thought did not flag. The volume of his work was amazing. He published over 200 papers in 40 years, and the great majority of these were papers of the first importance. His Gifford lectures delivered at Edinburgh in 1937-38 and published in 1940 as *Man on his Nature* were the next of his researches into the philosophy and science of the sixteenth and seventeenth centuries.

While Sherrington's life work was concerned with the physiology of the nervous system, it should not be forgotten that he did good work in other directions. He was a skilful histologist and investigated the formation of scar tissue and the changes in the blood which accompany local inflammation. He also studied the metabolism of the body in cancer and did not leave bacteriology entirely untouched. He was appointed by the Royal Society a member of a commission to investigate Asiatic cholera in Spain in 1886, and was also a member of the Malaria and Sleeping Sickness Commission of the Royal Society. He investigated the effects of chloroform for the British Medical Association in 1902-05. He served on various government committees, including those on sight tests, 1910-12, lighting of factories, 1913, tetanus and surgical shock, 1916-17, and alcohol 1916-17; and was chairman of the Industrial Fatigue Board, 1918, and of the committee on Foot and Mouth Disease, 1924.

Apart from his success as a research worker, Sherrington was a successful man of affairs and, while forming shrewd and decided opinions, had the capacity of getting his colleagues to work together. He also became a successful public speaker. He endeared himself to his colleagues and assistants by his modesty and never-failing consideration. In spite of the great calls on his time he was ever ready to help and advise. No one could hope to work under a finer chief.

Sherrington received honorary degrees from many universities, was honorary or corresponding member of many learned societies, and was made an hon. Fellow of his old college, Caius. He delivered the Croonian lecture before the Royal Society in 1897, the Page May Memorial lecture of the University of London in 1910, and the Croonian lecture before the Royal College of Physicians in 1913. He received the Baly gold medal of the Royal College of Physicians, the Retzius gold medal of the Royal Swedish Academy, and in 1905 a Royal Medal.

In 1922 he was created G.B.E. In 1927 Sherrington received the first award of the Conway Evans prize, jointly chosen by the president of the Royal Society and the president of the Royal College of Physicians. The same year saw him receive the Copley medal of the Royal Society. But his greatest distinction in the scientific field was probably reached in 1932, when he was chosen jointly with Professor E. D. Adrian [Lord Adrian, d. 1977] for the Nobel Prize in medicine. He was appointed O.M. in 1924.

He married Ethel Mary, younger daughter of John Ely Wright, of Preston Manor, Suffolk. She died in 1933 and he is survived by a son of the marriage.

March 6, 1952.

Robert Sherwood, who died on November 14, 1955 in hospital in New York at the age of 59, was not only a distinguished author and playwright but one of the strongest opponents of isolationism in America.

After war broke out in 1939 he devoted a large part of his earnings to causes which would aid the British war effort and help those who suffered through the war in Europe. He also spoke frequently at large public meetings and over the wireless, urging Americans to give ever more increasing aid to Britain. No supporter of Britain's cause in the United States was more outspoken than he, and he showed great courage in speaking out a time when it was by no means certain that American opinion would be so unanimous on the question of helping Britain as it later became.

He spoke from conviction, for he had had experience of fighting on the side of Britain in the 1914-18 War and he knew what Britain was fighting for. He was a student at Harvard in 1917 and had been there for three years when suddenly he became convinced that he ought to take an immediate part in the war and, taking the first train for Montreal, he enlisted there as a private in the Canadian Black

Watch. Before long he was at the front in France and he took part in many of the battles of the Canadian Army before the Armistice, being gassed and wounded at Arras.

Robert Emmet Sherwood was born at New Rochelle, near New York City, on April 4, 1896, and on his return home after demobilization he decided to seek a career in journalism. In 1919 he was appointed dramatic editor of *Vanity Fair* and then came into close contact with the stage for the first time. In the following year he became associate editor of the old *Life* and in 1924 its editor, a position which he held until 1928. By that time he had begun to write plays of his own and when they met with immediate success he decided to give up the more arduous part of editorial work and from that time onward remained only as motion picture critic for a time of *Life* and then of the *New York Herald-Tribune*.

He was a frequent visitor to England, which he loved as his second home, and for a time had a house at Witley, in Surrey, near the places where he had been in camp with the Canadian Army.

For many years he was president of the Dramatists' Guild of America and of the American National Theatre and Academy; to the work of both he gave much time and attention so as to help his fellow writers and those who acted their plays on the stage. His first notable play was *The Road to Rome*, produced in 1927, when he was still under the influence of Bernard Shaw. Gradually he hammered out his own style, which was seen in full power in *The Petrified Forest*, which was a success on both sides of the Atlantic. Then came *Idiot's Delight*, *Tovarich*, *Abe Lincoln in Illinois*, and, perhaps the greatest of all, *There Shall be No Night*.

Much of his work was a literary protest against force and tyranny, but he also had a lighter side and collaborated with Irving Berlin and Moss Hart* in various musical plays. Another and quite different aspect of his talent was his serious historical interests, which were manifested in his study *Roosevelt and Hopkins*. His close friendship with the late Franklin Roosevelt was the basis of this study, and he had access to many private papers.

He won the Pulitzer prize four times—for three of his plays, *Idiot's Delight*, *Abe Lincoln in Illinois*, and *There Shall be No Night*, and for *Roosevelt and Hopkins*.

November 15, 1955.

Ella Shields, one of the best known "male impersonators" of the music halls, died in hospital at Lancaster on August 5, 1952, where she had been taken after collapsing at a holiday camp.

Ella Shields was born at Baltimore, United States, on September 26, 1879, the daughter of Edward T. Buscher. She was educated at South Bend, Indiana, and first appeared on the stage at Altoona, Pennsylvania, in 1898. On October 10, 1904, she made her English debut at the Forester's Music Hall in the East End of London, and from that time onward became thoroughly acclimatized as an English performer, eventually retaining in her speech nothing but a pleasant soft burr—which might almost have been West Country—as evidence of her American origin.

Her performance was in the tradition of Vesta Tilley [q.v.]. With wavy auburn hair, and dressed as a young man in evening dress, nervously fingering his white tie, she made a very charming and gay figure. Her songs included "Just one kiss", "You'll stick to London Town", and, in rather later years, "If you knew Susie". By far her greatest success was in "Burlington Bertie from Bow". This song was written about the time of the 1914-18 war by her husband, William Hargreaves (whom she divorced in 1923), and it is said was originally intended for the comic singer J. W. Rickaby. He, however, thought it too closely modelled on a song he was already singing. Ella Shields then took it over, and though she adopted the tattered clothes and worn top hat of the traditional "broken down swell" act she did so with a difference, making of what might have been ordinary broad comedy something delicate and, in its way, almost moving.

Though she announced her retirement in 1929, she had made a good many appearances since, and in 1948, with other artists of her generation, she took part in the "Thanks for the Memory" programme, which toured the music-halls very successfully.

With this company she appeared in the Royal Variety Performance at the London Palladium—at which music-hall, it was recalled, she had been on the bill when it first opened its doors in 1910.

August 6, 1952.

Sir Thomas Drummond Shiels, M.C., M.B., CH.B., who had an eventful and distinguished career in politics and medicine, died suddenly in hospital in London on January 1, 1953 at the age of 71.

Of comparatively humble origin, he gained a considerable place in public life by his talents and industry. He was born in Edinburgh on August 7, 1881, and after receiving an elementary education he began life as a photographer. Later he became a chemist and was eventually able to study medicine at Edinburgh University. Thereafter he devoted his energies not only to his private practice but also to public health, and was at one time president of the Royal Medical Society. His services during the 1914-18 war as commander of a trench-mortar battery were mentioned in dispatches and he was awarded the M.C.

In 1919 he was elected to the Edinburgh Town Council. He was elected Labour member of Parliament for East Edinburgh in 1924 and in 1929 was appointed Parliamentary Under-Secretary for India. Some two years later he went to the Colonial Office in the same capacity. When it was found that the number of Under-Secretaries in the Commons was one more than allowed by law Ramsay MacDonald offered him a peerage, but he refused the honour.

In debate he could state a case effectively, and he gained general respect by his cool judgment, and popularity for his friendliness and his pawky sense of humour. He was a member of the 1927 Royal Commission on Constitutional Reform in Ceylon which recommended training in local self-government as the prelude to the full autonomy Ceylon gained two decades later. After losing his seat in Parliament in 1931 he took up hospital appointments in London, and was also deputy secretary of the Empire Parliamentary Association under his former chief at the India Office, Lord Stansgate [q.v.] (then Mr. Wedgwood Benn). In 1946 he became a member of the Colonial Economic and Development Council, but his appointment in the same year to be public relations officer at the Post Office was the subject of some criticism. However, he did good service until his retirement in 1949.

He took a sustained interest in the work of the Royal Empire Society, serving most helpfully for many years on the council. He became a vice-president and he was sometime chairman of the library committee, the information bureau, and the colonial group. His knowledge of Empire affairs was turned to good account as editor of *The British Commonwealth: A Family of Nations*, and he secured the cooperation of well-known authorities on the countries concerned, and also on such general topics as the food problems. This work first appeared in Odhams' "New Educational Series" and was brought out in a new and attractive form towards the end of 1952. In all he undertook he was methodical and purposeful.

In 1904 he married Christian Blair, daughter of Alexander Young, of Gilmerton, Edinburgh. There was one daughter of the marriage. He became a widower in 1948 and he married secondly, in 1950, Miss Gladys Buhler, M.B.E., for many years on the Imperial studies staff of the Royal Empire Society.

January 3, 1953.

Mamoru Shigemitsu, the former Japanese Foreign Minister, died suddenly at his home in central Japan on January 25, 1957 at the age of 69. He was Japanese ambassador in London at the beginning of the last war, and Foreign Minister from 1943 until his country's surrender in 1945, and again Foreign Minister from 1954 until Ichiro Hatoyama [q.v.] resigned in December 1956.

Shigemitsu had long diplomatic experience, and during his three years as ambassador in London he enjoyed wide respect for his ability and his evident friendship towards Britain. It was believed that as a member later of the Japanese War Cabinet he used his influence in the cause of peace. This, however, did not save him from conviction as a war criminal. But when he reappeared on the political scene he proved himself a staunch supporter of the western connexion, in spite of the unpopularity this brought him towards the end of his career. Having no strong faction behind him and being less adept than some of his colleagues at political intrigue, his position in the Cabinet became increasingly difficult to maintain.

He was born in Oita Prefecture in July 1887 and graduated in law at Tokyo Imperial University. He entered the Foreign Ministry and was a junior member of the Japanese delegation to the Versailles Peace Conference in 1919. He held posts in Germany and the United States and was then appointed Minister Plenipotentiary to China. While he was there in 1932 he lost his left leg when a bomb was thrown in Shanghai as a demonstration of anti-Japanese feeling.

He was appointed Vice-Minister of Foreign Affairs in 1933 and later Ambassador in Moscow. In 1938 he was moved to London. He was recalled just before Japan's entry into the war in 1941, and was then Ambassador to China until he entered the Government as Foreign Minister in April 1943. He resigned in April 1945 but rejoined the new Government formed in August, and it fell to him to sign the instruments of his country's surrender on board the United States warship Missouri in Tokyo Bay on September 3, 1945.

In 1948 he was sentenced to seven years' imprisonment by the international military tribunal for the Far East. He was acquitted of conspiracy, but convicted of waging a war of aggression and of failing to take adequate steps to have the treatment of war prisoners investigated. His sentence was the lightest which was imposed by the court. It was strongly argued by Lord Hankey* and others that the majority judgment in Shigemitsu's case was unjust, and that he had entered the Japanese Cabinet with the object of promoting peace. In 1952 his sentence, of which there were still three and a half years to run, was terminated, and he at once returned to politics as a member of the Progressive Party, of which he was soon elected president.

In December 1954 he was appointed Foreign Minister in Hatoyama's government. "Our policy", he said, "is immutably based on cooperation, close and cordial, with the free nations of the world, especially the United States". A year later he visited Washington at a time when there was disagreement between the two capitals about the adequacy of Japan's defence plans. He faced heavy criticism on his return for allegedly entertaining the possibility of sending Japanese troops oversea—a charge he denied. About Russia's intransigence and the threat of communist subversion he had no illusions. His inconclusive negotiations with Russia about a peace treaty were resumed by the Prime Minister in autumn 1956 and concluded on the terms which he had been prepared to accept earlier as the best available. The way was clear for realizing his ambition of Japan's entry into the United Nations, but Shigemitsu's political reputation suffered in the course of these exchanges and he resigned with Hatoyama in December.

One of his last official duties was as Japan's delegate at the conference on the Suez Canal held in London in August 1956.

January 26, 1957.

Maire NicShiubhlaigh—See **Price.**

Stanley Howard Shoveller, M.C., who died at Broadstone, Dorset, on February 24, 1959, aged 77, was a leading figure in hockey at the beginning of the present century and until a few years after the First World War. At that time he was the most successful centre forward known to the game, with stickwork, ball control, and speed to outwit most defences, and a deadly shot in the circle.

Shoveller was one of the boys at Kingston Grammar School instrumental in starting hockey there, and a member of the 1897-98 side which defeated most of the leading London clubs. His own club was Hampstead and the first of his 29 England caps was gained in 1902. He was forced to decline many further invitations to represent his country.

He won gold medals on the hockey field in the 1908 and 1920 Olympic Games, and acted as honorary match secretary of the Hockey Association from 1906 to 1912. From 1921 he had been a vice-president of that association.

Shoveller, or "Shove", was the W. G. Grace of hockey. He was ambidextrous and as a centre forward unparalleled and most unselfish. To give one example of his prowess: playing in a match against Surbiton, he stopped the ball from a corner hit and scored a goal, defeating five opponents.

He married Vera, daughter of the late Sir Henry Smith, and resided at Broadstone.

February 26, 1959.

Sir John Shuckburgh, K.C.M.G., C.B., who died at his home in London on February 8, 1953 at the age of 75, had an unusual career as he had served for long periods and with distinction in the India Office and Colonial Office, and after his official retirement in 1942 worked in the historical section of the Cabinet Offices.

Born on March 18, 1877, John Evelyn Shuckburgh was the son of the late Evelyn Shirley Shuckburgh, Litt.D., of Grantchester, who had been an assistant master at Eton and Fellow of Emmanuel College, Cambridge. He was educated at Eton and went up to King's College, Cambridge, where he gained a first class in the Classical Tripos of 1899. In 1900 he was appointed, after competitive examination, to a junior clerkship in the store department of the India Office, and in the following year was transferred to the judicial and public department. About the same time he became joint editor of the *India Office List.*

He was appointed private secretary to Sir Arthur Godley (later Lord Kilbracken), the Permanent Under-Secretary of State, in 1902 and was promoted to a senior clerkship in the political department in 1906. He received further promotion to the secretaryship of the same department in 1917 and held the post until 1921. During the 1914-18 war he was chosen to act as private secretary to a large and important committee appointed by the Government to advise on certain matters which would require consideration when peace was restored. The draft report which he submitted to the committee won high commendation for its lucidity of phrasing, a quality of his thought and expression which was to prove of great value to him in the new career upon which he was soon to enter. The close of the war left Palestine and Iraq under military administration, but at the conference at San Remo in April 1920 the principal allied Powers decided that the two countries should be assigned under mandate to the United Kingdom. This necessitated the introduction of some form of civil administration, and tentative efforts were made in that direction by the India Office, with the cooperation of the Foreign Office, Shuckburgh being placed in charge of the work.

The position remained very unsatisfactory in the two countries, and in February 1921 Winston Churchill* was transferred from the War Office to the Colonial Office to take over (as he tells us in his sketch of Colonel T. E. Lawrence in *Great Contemporaries*) "our business in the Middle East and bring matters into some kind of order". A new department was quickly formed in the Colonial Office to discharge these new responsibilities with Shuckburgh at its head. He was given the provisional rank of an Assistant Under-Secretary of State, but his appointment was placed on the permanent establishment on April 1, 1924. This post he held until 1931, when he was promoted to be Deputy Permanent Under-Secretary of State. Before that date he had visited both Palestine and Iraq to make himself acquainted at first hand with local conditions.

He was appointed Governor of Nigeria in 1939, but did not assume office owing to the outbreak of war in that year.

As might be expected from his academic record, Sir John had a well-trained and cultured mind; his outlook was broad and he had a wide knowledge of men and things. As an official he was efficient and genial and was deservedly popular both with his colleagues and with the outside public. He was fond of sport and in his day had been a good cricketer. Rather surprisingly he was a great authority on Dickens. He was created a C.B. in 1918, and a K.C.M.G. in 1922.

In 1906 he married Lilian Violet, daughter of the late A. G. Peskett, of Magdalene College, Cambridge, and by her he had three sons (one of whom was killed on active service in 1941) and two daughters.

February 10, 1953.

Nevil Shute—See **Nevil Shute Norway.**

Jean Sibelius died at his home, Ainola, at Traeskaenda, outside Helsinki, on September 20, 1957 at the age of 91. No prophet has been more honoured in his own country. Indeed it may fairly be said that his honour in the world followed from that paid to him by the people of Finland.

Next to Finland, England has shown the keenest appreciation of his music, and during the nineteen-thirties at least no living composer was so constantly represented in our concert programmes by his major works; in Sibelius's case seven symphonies and a number of symphonic poems for orchestra. But while English opinion places him firmly in the great symphonic tradition, continental and American critics express surprise that we vigorously sustain so high an estimate of one whom they regard as a survivor of nineteenth-century nationalism, whose work is not for general export or universal consumption. We remain unrepentant.

Jean Christian Sibelius was born, the son of a doctor, at Tavastehus, an inland town to the north of Helsinki, on December 8, 1865. There had been music in the family, but his ancestors had been of the professional classes. His musical nature developed naturally, and it was not until after he was 15 that the habit of family chamber music playing led to chamber music composition. At 20 he went to the University of Helsinki to study law, and thence to the Music Institute to develop his composition under Martin Wegelius, a sound teacher. There he formed a friendship with Ferruccio Busoni, then pianoforte professor at the institute, a friendship useful to him later through Busoni's introduction of certain of Sibelius's works in his Berlin concerts. Meantime periods of study in Berlin and Vienna were undertaken, but it was in his own country that his reputation was made, and when he returned home in 1892 he found it already established through the performance of his works.

He joined the staff of the Music Institute at Helsinki, but was soon relieved of the need to earn his living by teaching through a stipend granted to him by the Finnish Government, which enabled him to earn it more abundantly by devoting himself to composition. Robert Kajanus, his close friend, was then director of the National Orchestra, and he brought Sibelius's works before the public as they appeared, and later disseminated them to the world through gramophone records when that invaluable machine became a major resource of musical propaganda.

Sibelius's First Symphony appeared in 1899, and shortly afterwards Granville Bantock persuaded him to go to England to conduct it at New Brighton, where Bantock was then directing an enterprising series of concerts of modern music. Thus Bantock was his first English friend, and Sibelius sealed the friendship by the dedication of his Third Symphony to him. Henry Wood took up the works of Sibelius, urged thereto by the enthusiasm of Mrs. Rosa Newmarch, and such works as "Finlandia" and "En Saga", heard at the Queen's Hall Promenade Concerts, first made known to many English people the national identity of Sibelius's native country. A wider recognition was gained when Sibelius conducted his Fourth Symphony at the last of the Birmingham Festivals in 1912, and many musicians realized in their hearing of it that the composer was not only the musical laureate of his country but a leading figure in the world's music.

Sibelius went to England again after the 1914-18 War and at one time or another he visited most of the countries of Europe and the United States of America to conduct his own works. Nevertheless he was not eager to propagate his own works by personal efforts. Indeed, he was relieved of any such self-advocacy by his country, which made him, as it were, its figurehead, the symbol of its national life to the world at large.

A considerable proportion of Sibelius's long list of compositions consists of songs and short piano pieces on the one hand and incidental music to a number of plays on the other. A few pieces from both classes have achieved wide general popularity—the "Valse Triste" being the most conspicuous case. Most of the rest are minor works, interesting outside Finland only because they bear his name. It is through the larger works for orchestra that he has impressed himself as one of the outstanding figures of our time upon the world at large, alike in works with subject titles drawn from the legends and epics of Finnish literature, and in those which carry no other description than that of symphony. After the recondite Fourth Symphony the bold and majestic Fifth appeared simultaneously with his fiftieth birthday (1915), celebrated in Finland as a public festival. There was then a pause of nine years before the more intimate Sixth Symphony arrived, and this was followed by the closely knit Seventh and his most famous tone-poem *Tapiola.* After that the Eighth Symphony, actually announced for performance in London at one time, was eagerly awaited, but, though it was generally supposed that it had been written, it did not appear.

The symphonies have shown a continuous development of musical structure. Sibelius was not an innovator in harmony or orchestration, though his music has an unmistakable individuality. But after the Second Symphony his thought moved away from the conventional sonata form that had served music so well for nearly two centuries and devised principles of coherence that were novel and original. The Fourth Symphony shows an almost elliptical terseness, whereas the Fifth is an almost perfect example of a continuously developing organic form. The Sixth is freer, but the Seventh reverts to compression—with a single movement. The other most conspicuously original feature of his style is his propensity to use short motifs and hammer them together instead of taking longer themes to be subsequently broken up in the development section. There is a nationalist element in his thematic material but it has been integrated into the strong, personal style that has been created by a powerful intellect.

For the last part of his life Sibelius lived with his wife and daughters in retirement and privacy at his country home north of Helsinki. He was invited to attend the Edinburgh Festival in 1948 but replied that his physician forbade him to travel. He received few visitors and it was regarded as a surprising concession when in 1953 he permitted a Finnish film company to photograph him for a film they produced in his honour. In 1952 an international prize for music was instituted bearing his name.

His eightieth, eighty-fifth and ninetieth birthdays passed with celebrations in many countries, and to mark his ninetieth birthday, in 1955, Sir Thomas Beecham* conducted a concert of his works at the Festival Hall in London.

He married, in 1892, Aino Järnefelt, by whom he had five daughters.

September 21, 1957.

Professor N. V. Sidgwick, C.B.E., F.R.S., the distinguished chemist, died in a nursing home at Oxford on March 15, 1952 at the age of 78.

Nevil Vincent Sidgwick was born on May 8, 1873, the eldest son of William Carr Sidgwick, who was a Fellow of Merton College. He went to Rugby School in 1886. After an education consisting mainly of classics with a little science he specialized in classics for about a year, and sat for a classical scholarship at Oxford in the spring of 1890. He failed to get an award, and, against the advice of his headmaster, but with the support of his father, insisted on specializing in science. After a further year he was awarded an open scholarship in science at Christ Church in December 1891. He spent three years studying chemistry, and took a first class in Finals in 1895. He then decided to read Greats, and after two further years of work took another first class.

After his final examination in 1897 Sidgwick acted as a demonstrator under Harcourt for a year, and then went to Leipzig to study under Ostwald. He returned to England for a short time in 1899 and then to Germany, this time to Tübingen, where he carried out research under Professor Peschmann. He was awarded the degree of Doctor of Philosophy with the highest honours in 1901. Before he left Germany he was elected Fellow of Lincoln College. He settled down at Lincoln in the autumn of 1901 for the rest of his life. He never married, so he was one of the old school, now fast dying out.

In 1920 Sidgwick started to apply the Rutherford-Bohr nuclear theory of the atom to problems of chemistry. By then it had become clear that the chemical properties of the elements were determined by the arrangement of electrons round the nucleus. Sidgwick set himself to consider in more detail how this theory could be applied to the properties of molecules and compounds. This was a task exactly suited to his interests and ability. Although he was no mathematician he had the physical insight which enabled him to appreciate the real significance and application of a mathematical theory; and his encyclopaedic and orderly mind enabled him to survey and bring together under a single broad conception a mass of disconnected observations. The result, after seven years' work, was the appearance of his well-known book, *The Electronic Theory of Valency,* the publication of which put him at once into the front rank of chemists.

In 1931 he was invited to deliver the George Baker Lectures in Cornell University, which were published in 1933 under the title *The Covalent Link in Chemistry.* He stayed at

Cornell for only four months on this first visit to the United States, but this was long enough for him to fall in love with the country and with its friendly and hospitable people. He frequently returned and travelled widely in the United States: probably there was no British scientist more intimately known to American scientists, old and young.

Sidgwick's many researches, with the help of his pupils, since 1920 were mainly concerned with the structure of molecules and compounds. The more important advances in knowledge were discussed in his presidential addresses to the Chemical Society (1936-37), in his Bakerian lecture to the Royal Society (1940), and in his Liversidge lecture to the Chemical Society (1941).

His last and greatest book, in which are stored the fruits of a long life of study and research, appeared in 1950 under the title *The Chemical Elements.*

March 17, 1952.

André Siegfried, the celebrated political critic and economist, died suddenly on March 29, 1959 at his home in Paris, three weeks before his eighty-fourth birthday. He was active to the last, having just completed one of the political articles for *Le Figaro* which have attracted international attention for their clarity and sound sense since he began to contribute them regularly in 1945. He remained an active member of the board of directors until his death, and only in December 1958 was published *De la Quatrième à la Cinquième République*—a sequel to his work the year before on the transition from the Third Republic to the Fourth.

Distinguished as much for his knowledge of affairs in Britain and the Dominions—indeed, throughout the English-speaking world—as for his grasp of realities in his own country, Siegfried will doubtless be remembered in the first place for the penetrating study of *England's Crisis,* which he published in 1931. That book was open to criticism on more than one count: but no Frenchman of his time brought a better trained mind or more objective temper, greater sobriety or candour to the analysis of the English way of life, and few essays in interpretation of its kind illuminated so clearly the process of historic change in Britain's position in world economy between the wars. Siegfried was a frequent visitor to Britain, where he lectured from time to time (in very good English), and was always a sympathetic though by no means uncritical admirer of English institutions. From the first he held firmly to the view that Britain after the war of 1914-18 could prosper only in close association with the continent of Europe.

Siegfried was born at Le Havre in 1875 and completed his education at the Sorbonne. At the age of 23 he travelled to Australia and New Zealand, and had covered the greater part of the world before he returned to France. Thenceforth he was an inveterate globe-trotter. He was appointed professor of economic geography at the École des Sciences Politiques in 1911 and, having lectured also at the École Supérieure de Guerre and elsewhere during the intervening years, became a professor at the Collège de France in 1933.

His earliest books, *La Démocratie en Nouvelle Zélande* and *Edward Gibbon Wakefield et la colonisation systématique,* were published in 1904, and were followed two years later by *Le Canada, les Deux Races.* An objective commentary on the political and economic history of the Third Republic appeared in 1913, and then came an instructive account of his observations in North America just before the outbreak of war in 1914. During 1918-19 Siegfried was secretary of a French mission in Australia and Canada, and from 1920 until 1922 he headed the economic section of the French service of the League of Nations, representing his country also during that period as an expert at international conferences at Brussels, Barcelona, and Genoa.

In 1924 Siegfried published *L'Angleterre aujourd'hui, son évolution économique et politique*—a book written for Frenchmen, but so well informed, so perceptive and just in temper as to earn prompt translation into English. Although voices in Britain were raised in protest against what was considered Siegfried's too conservative point of view, time has only confirmed the soundness of his argument concerning British export needs. The work that came next, the fruit of many transatlantic voyages, *Les États-Unis d'aujourd'hui* (1927), was a model of comprehensive and unbiased investigation, and was regarded by many critics as the best work on America since Bryce's *American Commonwealth.* Then came a lively and amusing *France: A Study in Nationality* (1930), based on lectures delivered at the Williamstown Institution of Politics in Massachusetts, and in the same year *Tableau des Partis en France,* a brilliant exposition of the psychology of French politics since 1918. *La Crise britannique au XXème siècle,* translated under the title of *England's Crisis,* followed a year later, extracts from the book having appeared in a series of articles in *The Times* before publication in Britain.

Later works were *Amérique Latine* (1933), consisting in the main of notes on an extensive tour a couple of years earlier; *Europe's Crisis* (1935); *La Canada, puissance internationale* (1937 and revised in 1947), in which Siegfried discussed the process of "Americanization" there; *Suez and Panama* (1940); *Europe, États-Unis, Canada* (1946); *Notes de voyage en Afrique du Sud* (1947); *l'Arne des Peuples* (1947); *Savoir parler en Public* (1948); and *La Fontaine, Machiavel français* (1949). In 1955 he brought out a new view of *America at Mid-Century*—an afterthought to his work of 28 years before which in some respects at least reversed his previous impressions. He found the United States changed beyond recognition, and notably expressed the regret common to European observers at the decline in the contemplative spirit. He feared that the ideal American, and therefore the ideal world leader, would be a man of action rather than a man of thought. He continued his travels—*La Géographie Politique des Cinq Continents* came out in 1953—and in 1955-56 he did a season of three months' lecturing at Harvard.

During the last war he restricted his public activities and confined himself chiefly to his professional work at the École des Sciences Politiques, and at Lyons. It is true that Marshal Pétain [q.v.] made him a member of his Conseil National; but this was without consulting him, and he immediately resigned, as he did not wish to be associated with the Vichy Government. The Germans left him alone. After the liberation of France he was a member of the French delegation to the United Nations Conference at San Francisco. In spite of this responsible work he continued his lectures, and only ceased to give those at the Collège de France when he reached the age limit for that institution at the age of 70 in 1945. Those at the École des Sciences Politiques were hardly interrupted by the journeys which he made, after 1945, to the United States, Canada, South America, and India—this last as recently as 1950.

Siegfried was elected to a Fellowship of All Souls in 1927, and had been a member of the Académie des Sciences Morales et Politiques since 1932. In 1944 he became a member of the Académie Française.

March 30, 1959.

Lord Simon, Lord Chancellor from 1940 until 1945, died in a London hospital on January 11, 1954 at the age of 80.

Few of his day possessed so capacious and so clear a brain or so great a power of lucid presentation. In the Law Courts he was preeminent; at the Home Office excellently placed; at the Treasury a somewhat disappointing Chancellor; in foreign affairs, for all his qualities, a failure. It was for the Woolsack to redeem his fading reputation.

He presented, in fact, an almost perfect example of the limitations as well as of the uses of the legal mind. A Liberal by temperament and conviction, he had, in addition to his politician's, a lawyer's love of principle, and carried it into all his offices. He was prepared, as he showed in his earlier days, to imperil his ambitions for its sake; but at a time when nationalism ran riot in Europe and neither principles nor precedents prevailed, he lacked the inspiration which could alone have served to arrest the advancing doom. He had, too, a certain coldness of approach and a reserve which sometimes tended, however unjustly, to suggest that he had hidden motives. It is because so much depended on him then that the appointment of even so brilliant and resourceful a man as Foreign Secretary must be regarded as having been among the graver errors of the period.

The Right Hon. Sir John Allsebrook Simon, Viscount Simon, of Stackpole Elidor in the county of Pembroke, in the peerage of the United Kingdom, P.C., G.C.S.I., G.C.V.O., O.B.E., Q.C., LL.D., was born on February 28, 1873, at Manchester, where his father, a Congregational preacher, had charge of Zion Church. His mother died at the age of 90 in

1936, and the tribute which he then paid to her in *The Times* was later published as *Portrait of My Mother.* It was remarkably moving both in the charm of its simplicity and the power of the emotion. His mother had filled a large place in his life and it was never again to be filled.

At 14 he won a scholarship at Fettes and at 19 another at Wadham College, Oxford. There the first Lord Birkenhead was his contemporary, and a rivalry which was to continue for 30 years of their legal and political lives began. Both were prominent figures at Union debates and both were presidents. At Oxford Simon did more than well, obtaining in 1896 a first in "Greats" and in 1897 he was elected a Fellow of All Souls. For all the rest of his life the college was his second home. In its intimate society his reserved nature thawed to an extent that his associates in law and politics, except, perhaps, the Benchers of his Inn, would have scarcely believed possible, and he was a devoted and munificent son of the foundation. *Si monumentum requiris circumspice,* said the Junior Fellow's annual Latin speech after one of his several embellishments of the fabric; Simon relished the compliment and repeated it back to the author in Hall 30 years later. It was characteristic that at the last two elections to the Wardenship he took upon himself as Senior Fellow the heavy labours of conducting most of the long-drawn discussions in order that the Sub-Warden, who was an obviously eligible candidate, should be spared embarassment.

In 1898 he won the Barstow Law Scholarship and in the following year was called to the Bar by the Inner Temple—he was also a member of the Middle Temple—and joined the Western Circuit.

At this time Simon married Miss Ethel Venables, by whom he had a son and two daughters. The marriage was of brief duration for, to his deep grief, she died three years later. In his profession, although he had no influence, he rapidly became one of the busiest juniors on his circuit. His ambition was, however, chiefly political, and in 1906 he stood successfully in the Liberal interest for the Walthamstow Division. At the same time he took "silk", to become the youngest K.C. In 1910 he was appointed Solicitor-General, and in October 1913, at the age of 40, he succeeded Sir Rufus Isaacs as Attorney-General with, as was usual at the time, a seat in the Cabinet.

In August 1914, he decided to leave the Cabinet with Lord Morley and John Burns; but on the invasion of Belgium he changed his mind and withdrew his resignation. In May 1915 Asquith offered him the Lord Chancellorship. After much hesitation he refused for the sake of his political future, and became Home Secretary instead. It was an office to which, as he was to show more clearly later, his abilities were particularly suited. Thereafter his political career was to suffer a series of checks. On grounds of principle he was strongly opposed to compulsory service, and resigned from the Cabinet on that account. His position in England was not easy and, after a year of kicking against the pricks, he accepted a major's commission in the Royal Flying Corps.

It was not until 1922 after a previous unsuccessful attempt at a by-election there that Spen Valley returned him to the House as its member. He was to represent it until he went to the House of Lords, though in 1938 he announced his intention not to stand for it again.

During the general strike of 1926 Simon delivered a memorable speech in the Commons. In it he distinguished an industrial dispute within the protection of the Trade Disputes Act of 1906 from a general strike, regardless of contracts and ordered by a body which assumed power within the State to coerce not indeed employers in a particular industry but the Government of the realm. It was a new view of the law which dismayed the strike leaders and contributed markedly to the collapse of the movement. Within a week it was upheld by Mr. Justice Astbury in an interlocutory judgment.

In November 1927 he was asked by Stanley Baldwin's Government to become chairman of the Indian Statutory Commission to inquire into the working of the Government of India Act of 1919 and the possibility of extending the principle of responsible government. The commission spent three months in India at the beginning of 1928, returned to England for the hot season, and resumed the inquiry during the winter of 1928 and the spring of 1929. Its historic report was published in two parts in June 1930. As a diagnosis of the situation it was unquestionably a great and scarcely precedented achievement. Before he left India he had announced his retirement from the Bar.

It is, however, for his conduct of foreign affairs in the crucial years from 1931 to 1935 that he is chiefly criticized. Looking back it is easy to say that his tenure of office was disastrous. When he went to the Foreign Office the world was in a state of uneasy peace; Germany was almost totally disarmed; Hitler had not risen to power; Japan had not embarked fully on her course of aggression; Italy was a close associate of Britain and France. When he handed over to Lord Templewood [q.v.] Germany was heavily armed and breaking treaties with impunity, Japan was in full career, Italy was hostile and pouring troops against Abyssinia. France, placing no faith in German undertakings, was preparing to defend herself and seeking external alliances. Disarmament was at a standstill and in spite of an economic recovery in Great Britain and elsewhere, even the hopes of 1932 were submerged beneath the fears of an approaching Armageddon. Simon cannot be acquitted of blame, but the climate of public opinion—in Britain and abroad—has to be brought into the picture. In most western countries the memory of the 1914-18 War lay heavy on all minds. War was the supreme evil that had to be avoided at all costs, and in Europe Germany's actions and ambitions were all too often excused as simple and even honourable reactions to the Treaty of Versailles. The idea of British rearmament was anathema, most of all to the Labour Party.

One of Simon's first tasks was to help in instituting the League of Nations "impartial inquiry" into Japan's aggressive moves in Manchuria. He has been bitterly attacked for not proposing sanctions immediately against Japan. His defence was that China herself did not press for sanctions, and that the United States—associated with the impartial inquiry, although not a member of the League—was, when her standpoint was investigated, no less strongly against any extreme measures. But inept handling of an American suggestion for Anglo-American action created the legend that Simon had rebuffed Stimson's efforts to restrain Japan. He was, however, aware that Britain, which would have had to bear the main burden of sanctions, was not strong enough in arms to do so. He and others—Stimson among them—took refuge therefore in the delusion that "moral disapproval" would halt an aggressor.

Throughout the early part of his term of office his mind was much taken up with the Disarmament Conference. It is fair to remember that he recognized that the low state of British arms was no contribution to peace. The belief that others would be induced to follow the British example was soon shattered, and he then supported the painfully slow British moves to build up a modicum of deterrent strength. In 1935, when Hitler had been in power about two years, Simon paid his visit to Berlin with Eden. This was a vital year in the story of modern Europe. When the two British visitors arrived in March Hitler had just torn up another part of the Versailles Treaty by announcing conscription and, in a series of frank talks, he informed them of many of his ambitions to bring all Germans within the Reich. They were left with few illusions.

Simon went with MacDonald in April to the Stresa conference with Italy and France. The declared aim of the three Powers was to ensure their own solidarity in face of Germany's increased armaments, but also to prepare the way for Germany's return to the League, where she could play, as was said, her proper part in the creation of collective security in Europe. It was a dual policy that was bound to fail. Three-Power solidarity broke down because Italy was already preparing for her invasion of Ethiopia, launched later in the year. At Stresa there seems to have been little or no discussion about Mussolini's plans, first hatched in 1933 and made clear to the world by the Walwal incident between Italian and Ethiopian troops (well inside the Ethiopian border) in December 1934. Mussolini was thereby encouraged to go ahead, and was all the more furious—all the more closely driven into Hitler's arms—when Britain was later to take the lead in advocating sanctions against him.

The Stresa front was more speedily broken when, just after Simon left office, the British Government signed the naval agreement with Germany without collaboration with France or Italy. Although preparatory work for the Anglo-German Naval Agreement of 1935 was done while Simon was still Foreign Secretary, the actual exchange of Notes between Ribbentrop and Sir Samuel Hoare (as he then was) took place on June 18, 10 days after it was announced that Sir John Simon had been appointed Home Secretary. He was succeeded in the Foreign Office by Sir Samuel Hoare [Lord Templewood] who remained Foreign

Secretary until he in turn was succeeded by Anthony Eden [Lord Avon, d. 1977] a few months later. Hitler was to have a naval tonnage equal to a third of the British tonnage, but his number of submarines was to be proportionately much higher. If any treaty was worth while with Hitler, there was something to be said for the strict terms of the agreement; it attempted some regulation of armaments, and no doubt it attracted Simon for that reason. But in effect it condoned a breach of treaty obligations. Both France and Italy were aghast and affronted at the British action.

The chief criticism against Simon at the Foreign Office is that he seems to have been guided by no kind of diplomatic strategy. He was certainly no friend of aggressors, but for too long he believed that they were open to reason, and he was too slow—as many were at the time, it has to be said—in building up an adequate front against them. He sought agreements when none was possible, and when he left the Foreign Office he had not deflected the disastrous course of events, in spite of all his high hopes and his undoubted skill.

As Home Secretary for the second time Simon was a success. He was firm and sensible. The exuberances of the British fascists and their clashes with their communist opponents gave him some trouble, but he handled the situation wisely, and passed his Public Order Bill to the general content. He understood the spirit as well as the letter of British law. His Factory Act of 1937 was a valuable piece of legislation long overdue. At this time he was a Deputy Leader of the House of Commons, and also, by exercise of his great gift for argument, made himself useful to the Administration in the country.

In 1937 he became Chancellor of the Exchequer. His task was to meet the mounting expenditure which rearmament demanded. In 1938 he introduced his first Budget. His chief problem was to decide how far the increased bill should be met by borrowing and how far by taxation. He was anxious to keep as much of his borrowing power as he could in reserve in order to meet the still higher demands of the future, and therefore put sixpence on the income tax and additional imposts on petrol and tea. It was the less popular but more courageous course.

In early 1939, owing to deterioration of the international situation, the Government had to ask for power to increase the borrowing limit for defence from £400,000,000 to £800,000,000. In his Budget statement in April 1939 he announced that he required to raise £24,000,000 by fresh taxation. At this figure he was able to avoid a further rise in the standard rate of income tax and to obtain his money from surtax, death duties on large estates, and tobacco. It was on the whole an exceedingly sensible Budget. In September 1939 he presented an interim War Budget. It was an unimaginative effort, and he did no more than increase existing taxes. He seemed indeed in some particulars to prefer tidiness to foresight.

In May 1940 he became Lord Chancellor and was elevated to the peerage. With his accession to the Woolsack in 1940, both friendly and hostile critics will agree that Lord Simon entered upon the most successful phase of his varied political career since the days when he had led the English Bar. It is a commonplace that great advocates often fail to make even good judges, but the remark has no application to Lord Simon, for he at once revealed the judicial qualities that will place him among the great Lord Chancellors of the first half of the present century. From his early days at the Bar he had been engaged in the best class of litigation confined to no one branch, and a remarkable memory had enabled him to retain the law he had learned across the flurried years of political life. His scholarship he had also retained, and his judgments were always expressed in a finished literary style. In his leisure hours he could with ease turn a legal principle into Greek iambics.

In his early days on the Woolsack it fell to him to deliver some judgments that will rank as landmarks in English law. In Benham v. Gambling the principle was laid down upon which damages as regards expectation of life should be calculated in cases of death by negligence. In Potts v. Hickmann, in a case arising for the first time under the Landlord and Tenant Act, 1709, it was held that a distress for rates under a justice's warrant was not an execution and did not give a preferential claim for rent to a landlord. In 1942, in the case of Fibrosa Spolke Akeyina v. Fairbairn Lawson Combe Barbour Ltd., the law respecting frustration of contracts was put on a new and juster basis, and the famous case of Chandler v. Webster, a decision of the Court of Appeal that had caused much trouble some 30 years earlier, was overruled. In the case of Mancini, one of the few murder appeals that have reached the House of Lords, the principles were laid down upon which a jury should be directed where there is a possible alternative defence of manslaughter.

In December 1943 the Coalition Government decided to set up a Royal Commission to investigate the birthrate and trend of population, and of this Commission Lord Simon was appointed chairman. With the defeat of the Coalition Government at the general election in July 1945 Lord Simon's political career closed, and he was succeeded on the Woolsack by Lord Jowitt [q.v.]. He continued to sit, however, at the hearing of appeals before the House of Lords and the Judicial Committee of the Privy Council.

Oxford, Cambridge, and a number of other universities conferred honorary degrees upon him.

He was active in the House of Lords to the end of his life. On December 17 he had spoken on the negotiations with Egypt, and on the previous day had initiated a debate on capital punishment. Lady Simon [q.v.], his second wife, who was Kathleen Manning, a widow, survives him. She is the author of a work on slavery, a subject in which she has taken great practical interest. For her public work she was created a D.B.E.

The title passes to his son by his first marriage, the Hon. John Gilbert Simon.

January 12, 1954.

Kathleen Lady Simon, D.B.E., died in London on March 27, 1955 at the age of 83.

When in 1917 she married the first Viscount Simon [q.v.] as his second wife she was herself a widow with one son, B. O'D. Manning. She was Kathleen, daughter of the late Francis Harvey, of Kyle, co. Wexford, and was brought up in Ireland, attending various schools in Dublin. From her parents she inherited that love of liberty and hatred of servitude which inspired her every activity. How wide were her sympathies may be gathered from the causes she championed. First in order and in importance was the release of slaves, but much of her time and energy was given liberally to many other causes, among them the combating of anti-Semitism, mothercraft and child welfare, and the Salvation Army.

In addition she readily accepted the burden of individuals in distress and throughout her long life she never left unanswered an appeal for help. At one time she worked as a nurse in the slums of London, after training, because she wanted to see for herself the conditions in which the women in these districts had to bear children. She also taught herself to be a writer and lecturer in order that she might be a more effective social worker.

Her book, *Slavery*, published in 1929, with a preface by the late Lord Simon, caused a sensation by its exposures of slavery existing under the Union Jack. She missed no opportunity of pleading the cause of emancipation and the visit of her husband to India opened the door to discussions with several ruling princes and led later to some years of cooperation with the Aga Khan [q.v.] in humanitarian causes. It is hardly an exaggeration to say that she filled the place in Britain that Harriet Beecher Stowe had earlier filled in the United States, and her friends everywhere were delighted when in recognition of her work she was made a D.B.E. in 1933.

This world-wide activity emanated from a spirit deeply moved by wrongdoing, for, alas, the body was at all times a handicap; few weeks passed without pain or suffering, but never, except under the most vigorously expressed medical injunction, would Lady Simon allow physical weakness to cancel an engagement. In addition to all this public work, there was a wonderful devotion to the husband she so deeply loved. His death was a blow from which she never recovered.

April 21, 1955.

Lord Simon of Wythenshawe, who died on October 3, 1960 at the age of 80, was a great industrialist who had enjoyed an unusually active life, making contributions to a wide range of subjects: housing, slum clearance and town planning, smoke abatement, health, local government, broadcasting and university education.

He gave generously to funds of the City of Manchester and its university, with which he had been intimately associated for considerably more than 40 years. In 1912 he married Shena, daughter of John Wilson Potter, and so started a happy union dedicated to public service.

Ernest Darwin Simon, first Baron Simon of Wythenshawe, of Didsbury, was born in Manchester on October 9, 1879, the son of Henry Simon, who introduced into Britain two new industrial processes. It is probably no exaggeration to state that within 21 years Henry Simon revolutionized both flour milling and the production of coke ovens.

Ernest Simon was educated at Rugby and Pembroke College, Cambridge, where he studied engineering; and, since his father died when he was only 20, heavy responsibility and great opportunity came to him at an early age. In characteristic fashion he faced the challenge and within a relatively short time was appointed chairman (later governing director) of the family business. By vigorous attention to detail, vision, appreciation of the value of research and the wise selection of staff the Simon Engineering Group rapidly expanded and prospered under his inspiration and leadership.

But no business, however progressive and influential, could satisfy Simon: his restless energy, sense of service and phenomenal vigour demanded other outlets. He became a member of the Manchester City Council in 1911, was chairman of the Housing Committee in the significant years 1919-23, and was elected Lord Mayor in 1921, his year of office as chief citizen being a memorable one. From 1923 to 1924 and again from 1929 to 1931 he was member of Parliament, in the Liberal cause, for the Withington division of Manchester. On the latter occasion he became Parliamentary Secretary to the Ministry of Health. In 1932 he was made a Knight.

His longest association was with the University of Manchester. Elected a member of the Court and Council in 1915, he remained a member, except for a brief interlude, until his death. He was treasurer from 1932 to 1941, when he was elected chairman of Council, an office he occupied during the difficult war and postwar years, and continued as chairman until 1957. Even when he ceased to be chairman he remained a member of the Court and Council. In 1944 the university conferred upon him the degree of LL.D., *honoris causa.* In 1959 he was made a Freeman of Manchester.

During the Second World War he was north-west regional representative for the Ministry of Aircraft Production and a member of the Advisory Council for Fuel and Power. He was also chairman of the committee, set up by the Minister of Works, which reported in 1944 on the Placing and Management of Building Contracts.

After the war he joined the Labour Party and was elevated to the peerage in 1947. For five years from 1947 he was chairman of the B.B.C. On appointment to the B.B.C. he resigned from membership of the Royal Commission on the Press, to which he had been appointed a few months earlier.

Simon, physically robust and vigorous in mind, threw himself wholeheartedly into every activity which attracted him, being completely tireless, whether walking in Cheshire or in the Lake District (where for many years he had a country cottage), or following up his most recent interest. He played a useful game of tennis, one of his few relaxations until long after most men have become spectators. The late Professor T. W. Manson [q.v.], when presenting him for the honorary degree, described him as "the embodiment of perpetual youth, inexhaustible vigour, and insatiable appetite for experiment and adventure; who combines the qualities of a volcano in active eruption and a cornucopia in full production".

He not uncommonly failed to realize that others found his pace a trifle exacting; but his enthusiasm and abounding energy was infectious. Sometimes his urge to get things done led to impatience and impetuousness and a manner which appeared strangely autocratic for one who believed so passionately in democracy. A list of his publications conveys some idea of his industry and diversity of interests: *The Smokeless City; A City Council from Within; How to Abolish the Slums; The Anti-Slum Campaign; The Rebuilding of Manchester; The Smaller Democracies; Rebuilding Britain; A Twenty Year Plan; The B.B.C. from Within.* From time to time he would escape to his cottage in Langdale, but not to rest; it was usually to write, to catch up with his reading, and to undertake long walks over the hills.

He enjoyed travel but his journeys usually had a definite purpose, as when he and Lady Simon* toured America to study municipal developments and education. On this occasion they visited no fewer than 20 universities and he was much impressed and influenced by what he saw.

His generosity was lavish, and not always recorded or communicated even to his most intimate friends. The gift of Wythenshawe Hall and Park to the city and the creation of the Simon Research Fellowships for the promotion of research and teaching in the social sciences at the university are probably his two most munificent benefactions, but there were others. His devotion to the university increased with the years and he spared no effort to understand what the individual professors and lecturers were doing and thinking. He was well known to almost every member of the teaching staff and held in high regard by all. Most of them and not a few students and others were familiar with the little black note book in which he recorded any particularly significant statement which occurred in conversation. The development and expansion of the University of Manchester in recent years owes much to his inspiration and encouragement.

He is survived by Lady Simon and the two sons of their marriage. Their only daughter died in 1929.

October 4, 1960.

Sir Francis Simon, C.B.E., F.R.S., who succeeded Lord Cherwell [q.v.] as Dr. Lee's Professor of Experimental Philosophy only a month earlier, died on October 31, 1956 in a nursing home at Oxford at the age of 63.

He was a leading authority in low temperature physics and had already established his reputation in this field before he went from Breslau to Oxford in 1933 and developed there the low temperature physics group at the Clarendon Laboratory. Under his leadership this has grown to be one of the leading groups of its kind in the world. His interests in the low temperature field were wide and included the thermal properties of matter near absolute zero, the alignment of nuclei, and experiments with high pressures at low temperatures. He will, however, be remembered especially for his work on the third law of thermodynamics, and it is largely due to him that this law is now recognized as one of the guiding principles of low temperature physics. It is particularly tragic that Oxford and the Clarendon Laboratory should have lost him at the start of what would undoubtedly have been a fruitful leadership. He was also well known outside Oxford for his interest in technology and his effort to improve the methods of teaching and the number being taught in this subject in this country. He was an expert consultant on questions of fuel efficiency and the conservation of Britain's supplies of coal. He was a man of great friendliness, who much appreciated Oxford common room life.

Francis Eugene Simon was born in Berlin on July 2, 1893, and received his early education at the Berlin Gymnasium. He then attended the universities of Göttingen, Munich, and Berlin and joined the teaching staff of the last named university as *Privat-Dozent* in 1924. Three years later he was promoted Professor Extraordinary of Physics and in 1931 he went to Breslau University as Director of the Laboratory of Physical Chemistry. He had been there scarcely two years when the advent of the Nazi régime made it advisable to leave Germany and he went to England to work on the research staff of the Clarendon Laboratory, Oxford.

He was a vigorous and outspoken commentator on general scientific policy, and a few days before he took over from Lord Cherwell he suggested that Great Britain ought to have a Minister of Science and Technology in the Cabinet if she were to survive until the age of plentiful nuclear power. He had been connected with the atomic energy project from its inception, and had been since 1945 Professor of Thermodynamics in Oxford.

He was elected F.R.S. in 1941.

He married in 1922 Miss Charlotte Muenchausen, who survives him together with two daughters of the marriage.

November 1, 1956.

Oliver Simon, O.B.E., chairman of the Curwen Press, who had been for over 30 years a leading figure in the printing trade, seen in its artistic aspect, died at his home in London on March 18, 1956.

His death at the age of 60 removes from typography a vital influence in the production of fine books, a judicious writer on the art, and the founder and editor of two periodicals that, together, exercised a dominating influence in his generation. Oliver Joseph Simon was born on April 29, 1895, at Sale, Cheshire. His father was a cotton merchant, addicted to the study of philosophy, and his mother a sister of Sir William Rothenstein and Albert Rothenstein (afterwards Rutherston [q.v.]). After his preparatory school he went to Charterhouse, and thence to Jena. Simon never seemed robust, nor was he a great success at books in the scholastic sense. His vocation was decided by the sudden and chance vision of the Kelmscott Chaucer in a Piccadilly shop window. After the usual discouraging preliminaries the late Harold Curwen, then associated with Claude Lovat Fraser and Joseph Peter Thorp, took the risk of employing as pupil one who later became chairman. Thus, in the year 1919, at the age of 24, Simon began his 35 years' continuous connexion with the Curwen Press, the fame of which he so greatly increased.

In 1922 he founded, edited and produced the first volume of a typographical annual *The Fleuron,* the issues of which were limited, according to his decision, to seven. Of these he edited four, his partner in the enterprise being responsible for the remaining three. In 1924 he initiated, with the late Hubert Foss [q.v.], of the Oxford University Press, the Double Crown Club, an association of authors, artists, typographers and others interested in the designing and making of books. The self-criticism inspired by the club, which still flourishes, is largely responsible for the fact that the product of the London publishers stands so high in the estimation of international judges.

In 1936 Simon's energy found new expression in the "quadrimestrial" entitled *Signature*, which he conducted and printed. For 20 years the magazine gave generous space to critical articles on the work of masters, old and new, of the arts of printing and design, of calligraphy and typography; the whole finely printed and sumptuously illustrated. His autobiography, *Printer and Playground,* published a fortnight before he died, set out the principles that underlay his practice of typographical design.

Simon's own style succeeded, as style, because his considerable innate artistry was combined with a sufficiency of painfully acquired scholarship; and, as printing, because he perceived that a piece of typography, like a painting on canvas, changes hands at a price that corresponds with factors distinct from artistry and scholarship. The *Introduction to Typography* that Simon published in 1945 appeared in 1954 in the form of a "Pelican". It is, virtually, his *credo* and aptly bears on its title page the Voltairian commandment that salvation comes from the cultivation of an art throughout one's life.

A natural dilettantism of manner linked to a genuine humility of mind concealed great strength of conviction and strong fixity of purpose. The power he exercised by his example was matched by the influence of his conversation. A wide circle of authors, artists, and publishers benefited from his precepts, and his intimates enjoyed, in addition, the bland hypochondriac pose and attitude of elderly condescension towards seniors in which he persevered. It is doubtful if any member of the numerous group, engaged after the 1914-18 War in establishing typography as an industrial art, contributed as much as he to the liberation of the trade from the habit of archaistic reproduction, and to the evolution of a sound contemporary style.

In 1924 he married Ruth, the daughter of C. H. Ware, of Bromyard, Worcestershire. She survives him with a son and a daughter.

March 20, 1956.

Sir John Lionel Simonsen, F.R.S., who died at his home in London on February 20, 1957, was an organic chemist whose career in research passed with smoothness and success into a second career in administration. He was Director of Colonial Products Research from 1943 until 1952.

Simonsen was born in 1884, the son of a Manchester merchant. He was educated at Manchester Grammar School and University, where he held in turn a research fellowship and lectureship. Six years after graduation, in 1910, he was appointed to the Chair of Chemistry at the Presidency College, Madras, and from then onwards was concerned with the chemistry of plant products. Characteristically, he made time to be interested also in the development of science and industries in India, as well as in research and teaching.

He was honorary secretary of the Indian Science Congress from 1914 to 1926, and was president both of the section of chemistry and of the Congress. During the First World War he was Controller of Oils and Chemical Adviser to the Indian Munitions Board. Later he was appointed as Forest Chemist at the Forest Research Institute and College, Dehra Dun, a position which he held until 1925. To this period there belonged some of his most original research as a chemist. From Indian pines and grasses he extracted and identified the first naturally occurring representatives of new complex hydrocarbons, and elucidated also the course of their formation.

From 1925 to 1927 he was Professor of Organic Chemistry in the Indian Institute of Sciences, Bangalore. By now he was a recognized authority on the terpenes—a group of complex hydrocarbons which are produced in lavish variety by plants. On these he wrote an authoritative treatise, published in 1931 after his return to England. From 1930 to 1942 he held the Chair of Chemistry at the College of North Wales, Bangor.

In 1932 he was elected to the Fellowship of the Royal Society.

When interest in the potentialities of oversea development increased during the war, his combination of qualities and experience made his a natural appointment as the first Director of Colonial Products Research. This post he assumed in 1943 and held until 1952. He threw himself into his new post with imagination and enthusiasm. He saw that the colonial territories could no longer be regarded solely as prime producers, and looked to plant products, and especially to sugar, as the raw materials of chemical industry. He was enthusiastic also over the possibilities of colonial microbiology and a visit which he paid with Sir Robert Robinson* to the Caribbean in 1944 was largely responsible for the decision to open a Microbiological Research Institute in Trinidad.

His wide energies were shown also by the fact that for four years, from 1945 to 1949, he was simultaneously Secretary of the Chemical Society and a member of the Agricultural Research Council. As a chemist he received many honours, among them the Fritzsche Award of the American Chemical Society in 1949, and the Davy Medal of the Royal Society the following year. He was president of the section of chemistry at the first post-war meeting of the British Association in 1947, and at the 1950 meeting at Bristol opened a discussion on colonial plant products.

He was knighted in 1949.

He married in 1913 Dr. Janet Dick, daughter of R. Hendrie, of Nairn.

February 21, 1957.

Lady Simson—See **Ashwell.**

Dr. Charles Singer, Professor Emeritus of the History of Medicine at London University, who died on June 10, 1960 in Cornwall at the age of 83, enjoyed a world-wide reputation as a historian of medicine and science. In Britain his pre-eminence in his chosen field of study was unchallenged.

Charles Joseph Singer, son of the Rev. S. Singer, was born in London on November 2, 1876, and received his early education at the City of London School. He went up to Magdalen College, Oxford, with a scholarship, attended St. Mary's Hospital for his medical training, and took his M.B. in 1905. Immediately after qualification he went on an expedition to Ethiopia, being absent for the best part of a year. On his return he held residential posts at St. Mary's and other hospitals, and then gained further experience of tropical medicine by spending six months as house surgeon at the Government General Hospital at Singapore.

He then travelled in Egypt, Greece and Italy, and, settling in London about 1909, secured appointments at the Research Institute of the Cancer Hospital and at the Dreadnought Hospital for Seamen. In 1910 he married Dorothea Waley, daughter of Nathaniel L. Cohen and granddaughter of Professor J. Waley, of University College London. At this time he began to take up seriously the study of medical history, while still occupied with research work in pathology and with consulting practice. He was admitted M.R.C.P. London in 1909 and proceeded to the M.A. and M.D. degrees in 1911.

Singer's marriage marked a definite turning point in his career, because his wife shared his taste for historical studies in science and was herself anxious to undertake research in that field. The couple soon decided to devote themselves entirely to the history of medicine and science and henceforward they worked side by side in an ideal partnership. After spending some months in preparatory studies at Heidelberg, they took up residence in Oxford in the early part of 1914. By special leave of Bodley's Librarian and the Curators an alcove was placed at their disposal in the Radcliffe Camera. This the Singers fitted up largely at their own expense, and as the Science History Room it became the meeting ground for a select band of Oxford students of the history of science. Singer had his projects well under way and was beginning to publish when war came and he joined the R.A.M.C.

During his war service in Salonika he took the opportunity of acquiring facility in Modern Greek and, later, during a stay in Malta, he undertook anthropological and archaeological researches in collaboration with Sir Themistocles Zammitt. Throughout the war years Mrs. Singer, who was engaged on her great catalogue of early alchemical manuscripts, kept him supplied with photostat copies by means of which he was able to continue his studies. In spite of all difficulties he was able in 1917 to publish the first volume of the magnificent *Studies in the History and Methods of Science,* and to follow it up by a second volume in 1920. After the war Singer returned to Oxford as Lecturer in the History of the Biological Sciences, but he was shortly afterwards appointed to the newly instituted Lectureship in the History of Medicine at University College London. In 1931 his status was raised to that of professor.

Singer's vast literary output included books on *Greek Biology and Greek Medicine* (1922), *The History of the Circulation of the Blood* (1922), *A Short History of Medicine* (1928), *The Historical Relations of Religion and Science* (1928), *From Magic to Science* (1928), *A Short History of Biology* (1931), and *A Short History of Science* (1941). He contributed to *The Legacy of Greece,* and was coeditor, with Dr. Edwyn R. Beran, of *The Legacy of Israel.*

The Christian Failure appeared in 1943, Vesalius on *The Human Brain* in 1952 and *A History of Technology,* of which he was one of the editors, in four volumes, between 1954 and 1958.

Dr. Singer's preeminence in his department of learning was widely recognized. He was president of the Third International Congress of the History of Medicine (1922) and of the Second International Congress of the History of Science and Technology (1931). His FitzPatrick lectures at the Royal College of Physicians in 1923-24 on "The Evolution of Anatomy" form one of his best-known books.

He was Noguchi Lecturer at Johns Hopkins University and Mary Scott Newbold Lecturer at Philadelphia in 1930. During 1931-32 he acted as Visiting Professor at the University of California, and in 1934, on the death of Professor W. H. Welch, he was offered and declined the chair of the History of Medicine at Johns Hopkins.

He was elected a Fellow of the Royal College of Physicians in 1917, was a Fellow of the Society of Antiquaries, and a past-president of the Historical Section of the Royal Society of Medicine. He was president of the British Society for the History of Science from 1946 to 1948 and of the International Society for the History of Science from 1947 to 1950.

His old university of Oxford conferred the honorary degree of D.Sc. upon him in 1936.

Dr. Singer had resided for many years at Par, in Cornwall, where he had a beautiful home and a fine private library.

June 13, 1960.

Lord Justice Singleton, who died on January 6, 1957, had been a Lord Justice of Appeal since 1948. He had previously been a Judge of the King's Bench Division from 1934 until his promotion to the Court of Appeal. He had been Judge of Appeal, Isle of Man, and had represented in Parliament for two years the Lancaster Division of Lancashire.

John Edward Singleton was the third son of the late George Singleton of Howick House, near Preston, and was born on January 18, 1885. He was educated at Lancaster School and Pembroke College, Cambridge, where he took honours in law in 1905, and his LL.B. In 1906 he was called to the Bar by the Inner Temple and joined the Northern Circuit. There and in London he obtained a large practice in the best class of litigation, to be interrupted by the war of 1914, in which he attained the rank of Captain in the R.F.A. and was mentioned in dispatches. He took silk in 1922, and at the general election of that year he was elected Conservative member for the Lancaster division of Lancashire with a majority over Fenner Brockway of 10,000. He did not again contest the seat at the general election of 1924.

In 1928 he succeeded Sir Ernest Wingate-Saul as Judge of Appeal in the Isle of Man, an appointment always given to members of the Northern Circuit and one not precluding practice at the Bar. The same year he was also appointed Recorder of Preston. In November 1934, pursuant to an Address from both Houses of Parliament, two new Judges were required, and Lord Chancellor Sankey's nominations of Singleton and the future Lord Porter [q.v.] for the posts were expected and warmly welcomed.

From the first Singleton proved a success in both civil and criminal cases. It fell to him in March 1936 to preside at Manchester at the trial of Dr. Ruxton for the murder of his wife in a wild ravine at Moffat, Lancashire. The case attracted wide public interest and Singleton's conduct of the trial enhanced his judicial reputation. With juries he was particularly successful. His mind was detached and scrupulously fair, and, without any apparent attempt to drive them, he could generally get from a jury the verdict that he thought would meet the justice of the case. He was a strong upholder of the jury system, and in public on more than one occasion bore tribute to the extraordinary efficiency that both sexes displayed in arriving at the right result in serious cases that had come before him.

He required efficiency also from counsel, and slovenly work or the slightest departure from the correct standards of decorum were apt to recoil unpleasantly on the head of the delinquent. He was the author of a little book, *Conduct at the Bar.*

In 1945 he was made chairman of the Anglo-American Commission on Palestine. He was elected an Honorary Fellow of his college in 1938.

He was unmarried.

January 7, 1957.

Mickall Sinnott—See **Sennett.**

King Sisavang Vong—See **Laos.**

Victor Sjöström, the real father of the Swedish film industry and one of its two leading directors during the silent period, died at the age of 80 on January 1, 1960.

He was born at Varmland, Sweden, on September 21, 1879. His interests were from the first largely bound up with the theatre, and after completing his formal education he decided to enter the acting profession. He soon established himself as a powerful actor and scored a number of successes in both drama and comedy, most notably in *Berg-Ejving och hans hustru (The Outlaw and his Wife)* by the Icelandic dramatist Johan Sigurjonsson. Meanwhile his interest in the production side of the theatre had been growing, and from 1910 onward he became known as a fine director of other actors as well as a versatile player in his own right.

In 1913 he acted in his first film, *De svarta Maskerna,* which was of little interest except that it helped to bring his work to the attention of Charles Magnusson, head of the company which was eventually to become Svensk Filmindustri. Magnusson was little interested in the theatre, but saw the potentiality of the film as a medium for realistic delineation of the life and landscape of his country, and, finding in Sjöström a sympathetic disciple, offered him the opportunity to adapt and direct a film. The result, *Ingeborg Holm,* in which Sjöström did not himself appear, was a strong and severe drama based on the sometimes unjust workings of the poor law. Generally recognized as the first Swedish film of artistic value, it achieved a considerable success with intellectuals and the general public alike.

Sjöström's next cinematic venture, an adaptation of Ibsen's epic poem *Terje Vigen* (1916), allowed him to give the atmospheric background, with its constant play of the wind and the waves on a bleak Norwegian coastline, full value, as well as providing him with a strong role as the intrepid fisherman who runs English blockades in the Napoleonic wars. This film established him as a leading figure among Swedish film-makers (his only rival being Maurice Stiller), and for the first time suggested the potential of Swedish films on the international market.

Its success was confirmed by his next two films, *The Girl from the Marsh Croft* (1917), a simple rustic tale of a girl who sacrifices herself to save her lover from perjury, and a film version of *The Outlaw and his Wife,* in which Sjöström re-created his stage role and offered some of the most striking natural locations yet seen on film as a background to the story of love and jealousy. *The Girl from the Marsh*

Croft also marked his first collaboration with the novelist Selma Lagerlöf. A more spectacular refashioning of a story by Selma Lagerlöf followed in 1918-20, when Sjöström directed an ambitious trilogy based on her long novel *Jerusalem, The Sons of Ingmar,* Pts. I and II, and *Karin, Daughter of Ingmar,* again notable for its subtle and poetic use of natural scenery as well as its famous dream sequence in which a character ascends Jacob's ladder to heaven to consult his ancestors.

His masterpiece was undoubtedly *The Phantom Carriage,* based yet again on a story by Selma Lagerlöf, an allegorical fantasy presenting a sort of variation on the Flying Dutchman theme, in which, too, Sjöström gave one of his finest performances. In 1923 he left for America, to be followed the next year by Stiller. With these two leaders gone, the Swedish film industry went rapidly into decline, but Sjöström continued a most successful career in America, under the name of Seastrom. His first film on arrival was *Name the Man,* followed by *Confessions of a Queen* and *He Who Gets Slapped.* All these were subtle and technically polished pieces of work, but it was not until *The Tower of Lies* (1925), in which he returned to the familiar ground of Selma Lagerlöf, that he regained his stride.

This was followed by two masterpieces, both starring Lillian Gish, who later said "I never worked with anyone I liked better", and between them a Garbo film, *Divine Woman,* in which she appeared opposite another Swede, Lars Hanson. The first, *The Scarlet Letter,* was based on Hawthorne's novel of life among America's early Puritan settlers; the second, *The Wind,* again deals with a group of characters seen against an elemental background, with the forces of nature playing a dominant part in their lives, and, if anything, surpasses *The Scarlet Letter* in its intense poetic feeling for detail and its majestic sweep of narrative.

During the 1930s Sjöström acted in three undistinguished films for other directors and went to England to direct Annabella and Conrad Veidt in *Under the Red Robe* (1936), but it was not until 1941 that he had the chance to do anything notable in the cinema again. During the 1940s Swedish films underwent something of a revival, and between 1941 and 1945 Sjöström acted in a sequence of four films directed by another veteran of the Swedish cinema, Gustav Molander: *Striden går vidare, Det brinner en eld, Ordet,* and *Kejsarn av Portugallien.* The second and third in particular were of interest, *Det brinner en eld* being a revealing exploration of the neutral mentality under the strains of war, and *Ordet* a screen version of Kaj Mund's famous play about a raising from the dead.

In 1958 he scored a major triumph in *Wild Strawberries,* written and directed by the leading Swedish director of the younger generation, Ingmar Bergman. In this film his beautifully modulated performance as an old professor, brought through dreams and new human contacts to a realization of his failures in humanity, won him again an international reputation, as well as a number of awards, including the Best Actor award at the Mar del Plata Festival.

A fortnight before he died American film critics voted him the actor of the year.

January 5, 1960.

Engineer Vice-Admiral Sir Reginald William Skelton, K.C.B., C.B.E., D.S.O., a former Engineer-in-Chief of the Fleet, died at his home at Aldingbourne, near Chichester, on September 5, 1956 at the age of 84.

His career was as varied as it was distinguished. Unlike many officers who have held the post of Engineer-in-Chief, most of his service was spent afloat and not in technical or administrative appointments in the dockyards. He also had rare experience as chief engineer of the National Antarctic Expedition of 1901-04 under the late Captain Robert Falcon Scott. Over 25 years later he presided at a private dinner in London, at which 33 members of nine British Antarctic expeditions and two expedition relief ships forgathered and decided to form an Antarctic Dinner Club. He opened in 1948 an Antarctic exhibition on board the Discovery, moored in the Thames near the Temple.

Reginald William Skelton was born on June 3, 1872, the third son of William Skelton, of Long Sutton, Lincolnshire. He was educated at Bromsgrove School, Worcestershire, and at the R.N. Engineering College at Keyham, where he studied from 1887 to 1892. His first appointment was as an assistant engineer in the Malabar troopship, but in 1894-97 he served in the Centurion, flagship in China, and later in the Majestic, flagship in the Channel Squadron. In 1900 he was selected to superintend the building of the Discovery for the National Antarctic Expedition, and he accompanied the expedition as chief engineer. In addition to his work as engineer officer of the ship he was responsible for a certain amount of scientific work, and had charge of most of the sledging.

We find on referring to Scott's *Voyage of Discovery* no fewer than 30 references to Skelton, all drawing attention to his technical prowess, adaptability, and the invaluable help which he rendered to the expedition in conditions of extreme difficulty; one may venture to quote Scott's own words:—"One of my earliest acts on behalf of the expedition was to apply for Skelton's services, and it certainly was a very fortunate one, as from first to last of our voyage we never had any serious difficulty with our machinery or with anything concerning it. But Skelton's ability extended far beyond his primary duties, and I shall have to tell later of the many ways in which he assisted the scientific work of the expedition, whilst thanks to his ability with the camera in the course of his work as photographer-in-chief he produced the most excellent pictures which have ever been obtained by a Polar expedition".

Many similar remarks appear in Scott's narrative of the expedition, with the result that Skelton was granted the Antarctic Medal and recommended for early promotion.

After his return to England he was in destroyers for a short time, and then from 1906 to 1912 was employed on duties concerning submarines and their machinery. From July 1, 1907, he was promoted to engineer commander. Next he had four and a half years in big ships, the Superb, 1912-14, and the Agincourt, 1914-16. In the latter he was present at the battle of Jutland, and was awarded the D.S.O. for his services. Admiral Sir Cecil Burney, commanding the 1st Battle Squadron, in which the Agincourt served, spoke of him as "a valuable officer whose department during the action reflected credit on his organization". In July 1916 he returned to duty for two years with submarines, on the staff of the Commodore of this branch at Fort Blockhouse.

He went to Archangel in October 1918 as engineer officer on the staff of Admiral Sir John Green, Senior Naval Officer in the White Sea, in the Glory. While there he was promoted to the rank of engineer captain in December 1918. He was responsible for the machinery of the ice-breakers and the service craft, and also for Archangel dockyard and the numerous calls made upon it in connexion with the campaign on the river Dwina. In March 1920 he became Fleet Engineer Officer in the Mediterranean and at Constantinople, on the staff of Admiral Sir John M. de Robeck, Commander-in-Chief, in the battleship H.M.S. Iron Duke.

When, in August 1922, Sir John was appointed Commander-in-Chief, Atlantic Fleet, Engineer Captain Skelton accompanied him to the Queen Elizabeth, in which he served for a year, until after his promotion to the rank of engineer rear-admiral on August 1, 1923. His next appointment, from 1925 to 1928, was as engineer admiral on the staff of the Commander-in-Chief at Portsmouth. He served as Engineer-in-Chief of the Fleet from May 1928 to December 1932 with the rank of engineer vice-admiral, and retired from the active list on being relieved at the Admiralty.

He was made a C.B. for his services in the Agincourt and in submarines in the 1914-18 War, and a C.B.E. for his work in North Russia. He was promoted to K.C.B. in 1931. After his retirement from the Royal Navy he was for many years a director of John I. Thornycroft and Co., the shipbuilders and engineers.

He married, in 1905, Sybil, fourth daughter of William Devenish-Meares, of Christchurch, New Zealand.

Lady Skelton died in 1953 and he is survived by a son and two daughters.

September 6, 1956.

Professor H. W. B. Skinner, F.R.S., Professor of Physics, Liverpool University, died in Geneva on January 20, 1960, aged 59. He had gone to Geneva to attend a meeting of physicists called by the European Organization for Nuclear Research, to whom he had been chief consultant in the building of the 600 million electron-volt synchrocyclotron at Meyrin.

Herbert Wakefield Banks Skinner was born on October 7, 1900, and educated at Rugby and Trinity College, Cambridge. He took a first in the natural sciences tripos and afterwards worked for five years under Rutherford at the Cavendish Laboratory. In 1927 he went to the

University of Bristol, first as a research Fellow and later as a lecturer under Tyndall. In 1932-33 he held a Rockefeller fellowship at the Massachusetts Institute of Technology. It was at Bristol that he developed the method of soft X-ray spectroscopy of solids, and his work in this field was followed in 1942 by his election to the Royal Society.

Professor Skinner was the first man to measure the distribution in respect of energy of low energy X-rays emitted by the lighter metals when bombarded with electrons. Apart from being technically difficult these experiments made an important contribution to the understanding of the properties of metals in terms of wave mechanics. They both confirmed the main predictions that had been made a few years earlier on theoretical grounds—that there should be a spread of energies with a sharp cut off at the upper limit—and added new points not predicted by theory at the time.

During the war he was at first engaged with T.R.E. (Telecommunications Research Establishment) at Swanage and Malvern in work on radar. In 1943 he went to the United States and joined the atomic energy group working in association with Professor Edward Lawrence at Berkeley, California. He returned to Britain in 1946 to the post of deputy chief scientific officer at Harwell, in charge of the general physics division, which was responsible for the building of the Harwell cyclotron and the electromagnetic isotope separator. After four years at Harwell he was appointed to the Lyon Jones Chair of Physics at the University of Liverpool in succession to Sir James Chadwick*.

He inherited from Chadwick a legacy both of opportunity and responsibility. The university had been entrusted with the erection of a 156in. synchro-cyclotron and the erection of a nuclear physics laboratory to contain the machine, and the associated workshops had already been begun. Skinner threw himself into the project with a single-minded energy and enthusiasm which achieved the success which they deserved. When the machine came into operation in 1953 it incorporated a novel method of extracting the beam which produced an intensity markedly greater than anything previously known. The machine has continued in active use, largely employed in studying the properties of the particles responsible for the forces which hold the atomic nucleus together.

The new Chadwick physics laboratory of the university has just been completed, but although Skinner had watched over its building and equipment from the planning stage he did not live to use it. He had no hobbies but lived essentially for his home and his work. Within the university, the laboratory and the leadership there of a team of younger colleagues whom he infected with his own enthusiasm had first claim on his attention. But he was gradually absorbed into the whole life of the university. A forthright and outspoken member of the Senate and an unconventional but effective chairman of committee, he made an impact which will not readily be forgotten. His enthusiasms were almost boyish, his judgment in matters of administration intuitive rather than profound, but whatever the issue his independence and sincerity were never in question.

His death will be deplored throughout the university and the scientific world in which he moved. But the sense of personal loss will be most keenly felt among colleagues in his own laboratory. He might be impetuous and unpredictable at times, but their devotion was unchanging. They knew their chief as he was, fearless but unassuming, generous to a fault and youthful in heart as the newest member of his staff. At a most critical phase in its history and at the height of its dependence upon him the university has lost a man who can with difficulty be replaced.

He married, in 1931, Erna Wurmbrand, by whom he had one daughter.

January 22, 1960.

John Skliros, O.B.E., who died on April 18, 1956 in a nursing home in London at the age of 75, was for 15 years managing director of the Iraq Petroleum Company and played a major part in the development of Middle East oil.

Born in 1880, he went to Mesopotamia soon after the turn of the century, and in commercial life in Basra and Baghdad acquired a knowledge of local conditions and people which was put to good use on the outbreak of war in 1914 by his appointment as assistant to Sir Percy Cox, then Political Resident in the Persian Gulf. In 1915 he became Adviser to the Mesopotamian Expeditionary Force and later A.D.C. to General Maude on his appointment as Commander-in-Chief.

After the capture of Baghdad in March 1917 Skliros was placed in charge of local purchases for the Expeditionary Force, and afterwards organized the department of stores and transport for the civil administration.

In 1922 he became associated with the Anglo-Persian Oil Company in connexion with the projected refinery at the confluence of the Diyala and Tigris rivers to supply the oil requirements of Iraq. He went to the London office of the Anglo-Persian in 1924 as assistant to the late H. E. Nichols, the then chairman of the Turkish Petroleum Company, and was intimately connected with the negotiations which culminated in the Turkish Petroleum Company concession in 1925. In 1930 he became acting general manager of the Iraq Petroleum Company in succession to Sir Adam Ritchie, becoming general manager in 1931 and managing director in 1934. He negotiated in 1931 the revision of the Iraq Petroleum Company's concession and transit concessions for the construction of the pipelines through Trans-Jordan, Palestine, Syria, and the Lebanon, and some seven years later negotiated the Basrah Petroleum Company's concession.

It was largely due to the respect in which he was held throughout the Arab world that oil concessions were obtained in Trans-Jordan, Palestine, Syria, Lebanon, the Trucial Coast, Oman and Dhofar, the Hadhramaut, and western Arabia.

Skliros played a major part in the formation of the companies, organized by members of the Iraq Petroleum Company to operate these concessions. Embracing British, Dutch, French, and American interests, they were a unique example of international cooperation in oil. The evolution of a harmonious company policy was in no small measure due to his genius for compromise.

He always shunned publicity, but to his colleagues and staff was the most accessible of chiefs, to whom the most junior could take personal problems with the certainty of sympathetic understanding. Few men have inspired more personal loyalty, and he took with him into retirement in 1950 the affection and good wishes of the whole of the staff at home and abroad.

Sportsman, amateur, first-nighter, linguist, business man, negotiator and, in his retirement, a landscape gardener and geranium-fancier, he brought to all of these activities an enthusiasm and zest which, in his later years, was the envy of many younger men.

In 1939, two years after the death of his first wife, he married Miss Elizabeth Victoria Dore, who, with their twin daughters and two sons and a daughter of his first marriage, survives him.

April 19, 1956.

Tod Slaughter, the actor, who for many years chilled the spines of his audiences with his melodrama and Grand Guignol, died on February 19, 1956 at Derby, where he had been appearing in *Murder in the Red Barn.* He was 70.

Few actor managers have done more to keep the lamp of melodrama burning in the theatre. During his long stage career, which extended over half a century, he appeared in more than 500 plays and sketches, and a mere catalogue of some of the outstanding titles will recall to older playgoers many hours of horror and suspense which they spent with Tod Slaughter, in the West End, the suburbs, and the provinces.

There was a great period of three years during which he was in control of the Elephant and Castle Theatre, when thousands of playgoers crossed the river to see Tod Slaughter revel in the horrors of *Maria Marten,* or *The Murder in the Red Barn,* in *Sweeney Todd,* or in *Spring-Heeled Jack.* His audience wanted cold-blooded crime and Slaughter made it his duty to provide it in abundance. There was little subtlety in his work, but he never spared himself and he was obviously disappointed if at the end of the evening his audience did not regard him as the greatest criminal to have escaped the gallows.

N. Carter Slaughter (as his real name was) was born at Newcastle upon Tyne on March 19, 1885, and made his first stage appearance 20 years later. In 1912 he began his successful policy of transferring West End plays to variety theatres for twice nightly performances, and in the following year he became the lessor of the Richmond and Croydon Hippodromes, which he retained until he joined the Army in 1914. Later he served in the Royal Flying Corps and the Royal Air Force until he was demobilized in 1919.

Then for four years he was in control of the Theatre Royal, Chatham, as a prelude to his successful management at the Elephant and Castle. In 1927 he added *The Silver King, The Lights o'London,* and *The Face at the Window* to his repertory, and in 1931 he was playing Long John Silver in *Treasure Island* at the Kingsway. In 1944 *Landru* and *Dr. Jekyll and Mr. Hyde* were added to his chamber of horrors, and a year later he launched a season of Grand Guignol plays at the Granville Theatre, Walham Green. Later he turned to the screen, and there is a film of *Maria Marten* in existence to remind future generations of an actor who was steeped in crime on the stage but was a general favourite in his profession and a popular figure at the Green Room and Savage Clubs.

He married Miss Jenny Lynn, who appeared with him in many of his plays, and who survives him.

February 20, 1956.

H. Clifford Smith, formerly Keeper of the Department of Woodwork at the Victoria and Albert Museum, died on February 14, 1960 at the age of 83.

He was a specialist in the study of old English furniture, but he was also a writer of wide historical and antiquarian knowledge on the decorative arts in general, with a special turn for the human side of the subject as reflected in manners and customs. His most important publication was a book on the art treasures of Buckingham Palace.

Harold Clifford Smith, son of the late A. Clifford Smith and grandson of Sir William Smith, D.C.L., LL.D., F.S.A., was born in London on July 7, 1876. He was educated at Bradfield College and University College, Oxford, where he graduated in 1898, afterwards, studying for a year at the Slade School, University College London.

He entered the Museum Service in 1900 as assistant in the National Art Library at the Victoria and Albert Museum. From this he was transferred to the Department of Woodwork, becoming Assistant Keeper in 1922, Deputy Keeper in 1934, and Keeper from 1935 to 1936, when he retired, having served longer than any other senior official of the museum. Outside the museum he was on the governing bodies of several places of historical interest, including Sulgrave Manor, the home of the Washingtons, Northants, and Dr. Johnson's House, Gough Square, E.C. At various times Clifford Smith was member of council of the Society of Antiquaries, member of the executive committee of the National Art-Collections Fund, and member of the executive committee of the Georgian Group. From 1921 he was inspector of furniture and works of art at Chequers, the national home of Prime Ministers, in Buckinghamshire.

Clifford Smith's earliest publications were connected with the smallest of the decorative arts, of which he had made a special study: *Jewellery,* in 1908; and *The Goldsmith and the Young Couple*—a title that well indicates his way of treating a subject—in 1915. He was responsible for several of the official publications of the Victoria and Albert Museum on woodwork: *The Bromley Room,* 1914; *The Inlaid Room from Sizergh Castle,* 1915; *Catalogue of English Gothic Furniture,* 1923; *The Waltham Abbey Room,* 1924; *Catalogue of Late Tudor and Early Stuart Furniture* 1930; and *The Haynes Grange Room,* 1935.

The acquisition of the last was a good instance of the informal way in which things often come to the national collections, as also of Smith's watchfulness, though he said modestly that it was an "accident". The room, a perfect example of early English panelling, was already packed up for delivery to America when Smith mentioned it casually at a luncheon party. The immediate response was a contribution of £250 towards the purchase price, and before the luncheon was over £2,000 had been promised. The remaining £2,000 needed was raised with comparative ease.

Buckingham Palace: Its Furniture, Decoration and History, with introductory chapters on the building and the site by Christopher Hussey, was first published by *Country Life* in 1931. In writing the book Clifford Smith had the assistance of Queen Mary [q.v.], who supplied him with much information and herself corrected the proofs. In 1937 the book was republished at a lower price in a Coronation edition.

Other works by Clifford Smith of a similar kind are *Sulgrave Manor and the Washingtons,* with a foreword by Viscount Lee of Fareham, 1933; and *Marble Hill House, Twickenham,* 1929. As a gift to his old college Clifford Smith prepared in 1943 a private inventory of the works of art of all kinds belonging to University College, Oxford, the first complete inventory of the artistic possessions of any of the Oxford colleges to be compiled.

He was a contributor to the *Proceedings of the Society of Antiquaries,* the *Antiquaries Journal, Bryan's Dictionary of Painters and Engravers,* the *Dictionary of English Furniture,* and many periodicals and art magazines.

Though Clifford Smith had a wide knowledge of art in general and a sound judgment of quality his special concern was the "art treasure", that is to say the work of art which has acquired the value of historical or sentimental associations or has the value of rarity, values which may or may not coincide with high aesthetic value. His private collection included Venetian paintings of the eighteenth century, Tudor portraits, including Henry VIII and Anne of Denmark, and English furniture of the seventeenth century.

His human approach to works of art made Clifford Smith an ideal public lecturer. He was a big, genial man, with a fresh complexion, and looked rather like a country squire. An attractive shyness and hesitation in his manner was likely to leave strangers in ignorance of his vast stores of widely assorted knowledge.

In 1925 he married Gladys, daughter of John Beattie Crozier. They had no children. His wife died in 1957.

February 17, 1960.

Sir Matthew Smith, C.B.E., died in London on September 29, 1959. He was 79.

As a painter of still-life, landscape and figure studies, alike distinguished by their richness of colour and opulence of effect, Matthew Smith gained a special eminence among modern British artists. The growing mastery which first drew the admiring attention of connoisseurs and fellow-artists in 1920 was affirmed and more generally acknowledged as the years passed, and he still seemed a vital figure in the 1950s, as well appreciated by a younger and newly experimental generation as by such old friends and admirers as Sir Jacob Epstein [q.v.], an ardent collector of his works, and Augustus John*, who described him as "one of the most brilliant and individual figures in modern English painting".

Born at Elm View, Halifax, on October 22, 1879, the son of a wire-manufacturer, Matthew Arnold Bracy Smith, after education at Giggleswick, went for a time into the family business but soon left it for the study of art, first at the Manchester School of Art, 1900-04, then at the Slade School, 1905-07. Slow to develop, he was approaching 30 when he went to France for further study, working in Brittany and Paris. A month or two spent in 1911 at Matisse's school on the Boulevard des Invalides (until it closed down) and acquaintance with *Fauviste* art as represented by Matisse [q.v.] and Derain [q.v.] opened his eyes to gorgeous possibilities of colour, already to be seen in the "Lilies" of 1913-14, first of his many contributions to the London Group exhibitions. During the First World War (when he held a commission in the Army), he painted intermittently and until 1920 in the *Fauviste* spirit—as in the excellent series of landscapes painted after the war in Cornwall.

From then onwards he worked much in France, his "second country"; in Paris, at Cagnes, and Aix-en-Provence, though retaining a studio in London; a mature and personal style now appearing in series of paintings of the nude and in French landscapes. His first one-man exhibition in London at the Mayer Gallery in 1926, when he was 47, established his reputation and was followed at intervals by others in which the warmth and fullness of his integration of form and colour were triumphantly asserted.

In 1938 a group of 23 paintings was selected for the Venice Biennale, where again in 1950 he had a one-man exhibition of 26 works at the British Pavilion. The retrospective exhibitions of his works at Temple Newsam, 1941, and at the Tate Gallery in 1953, justly acclaimed the "torrent of beauty" (as it was described on the latter occasion) with which he had enriched British art.

He was appointed C.B.E. in 1949, knighted in 1954, and became Hon.D.Litt. (London) 1956. A quiet and modest man, never enjoying robust health, he lived latterly in seclusion, though still working in his London studio, among his more recent productions being drawings, pastels, and watercolours of a masterly simplicity.

Limitations of repertoire and inventiveness may assign him a secondary place in modern art viewed from an international standpoint, yet these in one way were an asset and, free from all irrelevant matter, his oil paintings were as truly and essentially "painting" as could be wished, showing, as Sir Philip Hendy has said of his work, "the great variety of sensation which can be expressed with a very small variety of theme". He is well represented in the Tate Gallery and the Leeds Art Gallery, Temple Newsam, and pictures by him figure in many other public collections in England, Canada, Australia, and U.S.A.

In 1912 he married Gwendolen Salmond, also a painter, and daughter of Major-General Sir William Salmond. Their two sons were killed while serving in the R.A.F. in the last war. Lady Smith died in 1958.

September 30, 1959.

Sheila Kaye-Smith—See **Kaye-**.

Sidney Smith, who died suddenly in Ottawa on March 17, 1959, abandoned a distinguished academic career in 1957 to become Canadian Secretary of State for External Affairs. He was 62.

Sidney Earle Smith, who was born on a farm at Port Hood, Nova Scotia, on March 9, 1897, was educated at Port Hood Academy and King's College, Windsor, N.S. In the First World War he served with the 9th Canadian Siege Battery and the Royal Flying Corps. After the end of hostilities he studied law at Dalhousie University and Harvard, combining the practice of law with lecturing at Dalhousie Law School, of which he was made Dean in 1929.

In 1934 his appointment as president of the University of Manitoba made him the youngest Canadian head of a university, and his success led to his translation to the presidency of the University of Toronto in 1945.

Administration, rather than erudite scholarship, was his strong point and under his rule the activities of his university expanded; though he had to fight a losing battle against the tendency of students to prefer purely vocational courses to the humanities.

He was no cloistered academic recluse, and his active social conscience moved him to serve on a variety of public bodies.

He had always nourished political ambitions and in 1940, when he was in Manitoba, he reluctantly refused an invitation to stand for the leadership of the Progressive-Conservative Party, but he was to have another chance. In 1957 Diefenbaker, who knew him as a friend and as a man of no ordinary ability, called him to high office. The sudden elevation of a political novice to the Cabinet is not always popular with those who have fought hard election battles, but Smith was a national figure and was soon seen to be a valuable reinforcement to the Ministry.

He was forthright in his views and on leaving the academic life for the political remarked that, Professor or no, he would be known as Mr. Smith. "I'm not going to trail those degrees around with me. Professors are sometimes looked at askance, so I revert to what I was born with", he said.

He was the author, or joint author, of several works on the law "as lucid as they were penetrating", as the Public Orator observed when Cambridge University conferred on him an honorary doctorate in 1948.

A big man with bushy grey hair he was a keen trout fisherman, and his nose bore witness to his love for Rugby football as a young man.

March 18, 1959.

Vivian Hugh Smith—See **Bicester.**

Dr. Frederick Soddy, F.R.S., Emeritus Lee's Professor of Chemistry in the University of Oxford, and one of the pioneers of research into atomic disintegration, died in hospital at Brighton on September 22, 1956, less than three weeks after his seventy-ninth birthday.

Born at Eastbourne on September 2, 1877, he was educated at Eastbourne College, and after attending the University College of Wales, Aberystwyth, he went on to Merton College, Oxford. At about the turn of the century he began to work with Rutherford at McGill University, Montreal, on a classic series of experiments on radioactivity, and in 1903-04 worked with Ramsay in London on a similar kind of research. He was, therefore, very well equipped indeed to take up in 1904 the post of lecturer in physical chemistry and radioactivity in Glasgow University.

Even apart from his natural talent for teaching, the 10 years he spent there were fruitful indeed. The small volume *Radioactivity,* which appeared in 1904, was followed in 1909 by *The Interpretation of Radium,* for long a standard work, which was enlarged in 1920 by a section on the structure of the atom and superseded in 1932 by *The Interpretation of the Atom,* one of the seminal books on the subject in its period.

Soddy, who had been elected F.R.S. in 1910, became Professor of Chemistry in Aberdeen University in 1914, and in 1919 returned to Oxford as Lee's Professor of Chemistry.

He had married, in 1908, Winifred Moller, daughter of the late Sir George Beilby, F.R.S. It was a remarkably happy marriage and her death in 1936 was a major setback to him. He resigned his chair and virtually retired from academic life, emerging only occasionally to ride one of the many hobby-horses he had mounted in his heyday, for he held strong views not merely in his own subject but on education in general and on economics and finance. As early as 1922 he had published a volume called *Cartesian Economics* and his *Wealth, Virtual Wealth, and Debt,* of 1926, proved a stimulant to thought which had its outcome in the "technocracy" movement in America in the early thirties.

After his retirement from his chair, however, only two works of his appeared, one amateur, *The Arch-Enemy of Economic Freedom,* published in 1943, and the other professional, *The Story of Atomic Energy,* which was published in 1949. There were few better qualified to write a popular work on the subject. Soddy had been in at the beginning of things with Rutherford and Ramsay 50 years before. His work had brought him the Nobel Prize for Chemistry for 1921, and his own contribution as early as 1913 was the discovery of the elements with the same chemical qualities but different atomic weights, which he termed "isotopes", without which it is difficult to conceive the uses of atomic energy for peaceful purposes.

Then, after 1936, there was silence and Professor Soddy was somehow missed from the official honours which usually come to men as eminent as he. It is pleasant, however, to recall that in 1953 Mrs. Muriel Howarth issued a memoir in which his work received due recognition, and that in 1955 efforts made by her and Dr. L. E. C. Hughes to have the Albert Medal awarded to him were successful.

September 24, 1956.

Lord Somervell of Harrow, a Lord of Appeal in Ordinary from 1954 until the beginning of 1960, when he resigned, died on November 18, 1960 at the age of 71.

Somervell had been a Lord Justice of Appeal from 1946 until 1954, and was Solicitor General from 1933 to 1936 and then Attorney General right up until the end of the Second World War. In Churchill's* "caretaker" Government from May until July 1945 Somervell served as Home Secretary.

The Right Hon. Donald Bradley Somervell, P.C., O.B.E., Baron Somervell of Harrow, of Ewelme in the county of Oxford, was the son of the late Robert Somervell, the well-known Harrow master, and was born on August 24, 1889. He was educated at Harrow in a Small House and Davidson's, and at Magdalen College, Oxford, where he took First Class honours in natural science (chemistry) in 1911, and had some intention at the time of following a scientific career. The following year he was elected a fellow of All Souls.

On leaving Oxford Somervell went for a time into the office of Coward, Chance and Co., the City solicitors, who were so impressed by his ability that they offered him a partnership if he would qualify for their branch of the profession, but he preferred the more uncertain adventure of the Bar, and before the 1914-18 War had broken out had already passed the Bar examination. He was a Territorial officer and his regiment, the 9th Middlesex, was sent to India, and Somervell saw fighting in Mesopotamia.

He was called by the Inner Temple *in absentia* in 1916. Through the good offices of Chance he was found a seat in the chambers of the future Lord Jowitt [q.v.], who was then enjoying one of the best junior practices in the Temple, and who, a quarter of a century later, was to serve as Solicitor General under Somervell when the latter held the post of Attorney General. A fellow pupil was the future Lord Justice Asquith [q.v.], and both joined the Western Circuit on the same day.

Somervell did not have long to wait for

work, as his friends Coward, Chance and Co. supported him from the first, and he got a flying start with briefs that Jowitt could not hold. So, as he afterwards used to regret, the Western Circuit saw little of him and he never had the invaluable experience of prosecuting and defending prisoners in the criminal courts. Perhaps his most important case as a junior was the famous Bank of Portugal's action against Waterlow and Sons, Ltd., in 1927, when he was led by the late Stuart Bevan. In 1929 he took silk, and until he took office as Solicitor General he enjoyed a large—if not overwhelming—practice in the best class of litigation.

The same year, as a Unionist, he contested Crewe unsuccessfully, but in October 1931 he won the seat with a majority of 6,790. In the House Somervell proved himself an effective debater, and a speech he made in February 1933 on the Government's Indian policy attracted attention, and during the passage of the India Bill he rendered substantial assistance to Sir Samuel Hoare [Lord Templewood, q.v.].

In September 1933, on the appointment of Sir Boyd (later Lord) Merriman* to succeed Lord Merrivale as President of the Probate, Divorce, and Admiralty Division, Somervell succeeded Merriman as Solicitor General, and three years later, in March 1936, at the age of 46, he became Attorney General in succession to Sir Thomas Inskip, afterwards Viscount Caldecote.

In 1938 the unfortunate, and now largely forgotten, Sandys case, in which it was alleged that the member concerned had obtained secret information upon which to base a question, occupied the attention of the House of Commons, and allegations were made that the Attorney General had improperly threatened Sandys with the Official Secrets Act. The majority of the select committee appointed to investigate the matter acquitted Somervell of blame, but a minority draft report was less favourable. So far as the public was concerned the whole business was regarded as more silly than sinister, due, as the committee said, largely to a series of misunderstandings.

The Second World War, and especially the numerous cases of detention of persons whose activities were considered prejudicial to the safety of the realm—of which Liversidge v. Anderson, that caused such an acute division of judicial opinion in the House of Lords, is best remembered—added greatly to the Attorney General's responsibilities, and the mental and physical strain was great. Somervell, however heavy the burden, was never flustered, always accessible, and his invariable courtesy and kindness, both to those associated with him and to those opposed to him, contributed to make him an attractive and popular figure.

His tenure of the office of Home Secretary must have been the shortest on record, and on the formation of the Labour Government Somervell returned to his practice at the Bar. In June 1945 he lost his seat at Crewe. He succeeded Lord Justice MacKinnon as a Lord Justice of Appeal in January 1946. In the Court of Appeal Somervell maintained his reputation as a lawyer, and the kindness and courtesy that had distinguished him at the Bar made him the pleasantest of Judges to encounter on the Bench. As befitted a fellow of All Souls, his judgments had distinction of style, and his scientific training gave them conciseness and precision. In 1954 a life barony was conferred upon him. In 1959 Oxford University made him an honorary D.C.L.

Apart from science, he was interested in the more intellectual side of theology, and especially in the chronology of the Bible, upon which at one time he had had hopes of producing a treatise. He was a trustee of the National Portrait Gallery, chairman of the board of governors of Harrow School, and an honorary fellow of Magdalen College, Oxford.

Somervell married in 1933 Laelia, daughter of Sir Archibald Buchan-Hepburn. She died in 1945.

November 21, 1960.

Cornelia Sorabji, author, social reformer, and the first Indian woman to practise law, died on July 6, 1954 after a long illness.

Cornelia Sorabji was born in 1866, daughter of the Rev. Sorabji Karsedji, an agent of the Church Missionary Society at Poona, converted from Zoroastrianism, and of Franscina Sorabji, a convert from Hinduism to Christianity. Two brothers had died in infancy, and the family of seven girls and a brother was "brought up English"—on English nursery tales with English discipline, and taught to admire all that was best in both British and Indian life. Mrs. Sorabji cared for the sick and poor around her and promoted the education of girls in an age when organized social service was almost unknown to Indians. Under her inspiration Cornelia, before she was nine, dedicated herself to the cause of Indian women secluded behind the purdah. She was the first girl student at the Deccan College, Poona, and encountered in the early days hostile and inconsiderate treatment from the 300 youths of that institution.

She came out first in a degree examination which entitled her to a Government scholarship tenable at a British university. Held to be debarred by her sex, she gained a fellowship in the Gujarat College, Ahmadabad, where, still in her teens, she lectured on English literature and language. The offer of a "substituted scholarship" by certain friends in England enabled her to enter Somerville Hall, Oxford, in 1888. She had the good fortune to enjoy the helpful, stimulating friendship of Jowett, and at his weekend parties she met many famous people and formed some lasting friendships. After she had studied law in chambers in Lincoln's Inn Jowett, as Vice-Chancellor, obtained a special Congregational decree in 1893 "that Cornelia Sorabji be allowed to sit for the B.C.L. examination", and she was the first woman to do so.

In 1902 she submitted to the India Office a plan for connecting lady counsel with the Provincial Governments for the purpose of protecting the legal rights of women landholders under the Court of Wards. The scheme slowly developed, and in 1904 she was appointed Legal Adviser to *purdahnashins* under the Courts of Wards in Bengal, Bihar, Orissa and Assam, and also Consulting Counsel to the Government of Bengal. Her varied and sometimes exciting experiences, her long journeys, her perils, her watchings and her joys as she worked among the purdah women are recorded with inimitable charm in her principal autobiographical work *India Calling* (1934) and supplemented two years later in her *India Recalled.*

Owing to the sex barrier it was not until 30 years after taking her Oxford degree that she was called to the Bar by Lincoln's Inn. Other Indian women had become barristers, but there was only one Cornelia Sorabji, and when she retired from her work for the Courts of Wards the appointment lapsed. By then some 600 wives, widows, minor heirs and orphans had received the benefit of her advice—given without charging fees in cases of undeserved penury. After her call to the Bar in 1923 she settled in Calcutta to practise in the High Court. She organized a League for Infant Welfare, Maternity and District Nursing, and it made headway until nationalist spite, hating her political views, drove it from the field. She was awarded in 1909 the Kaiser-i-Hind Gold Medal, and it was supplemented by the bar of the first class in 1922.

The first of her many studies of those aspects of Indian life she knew best was *Love and Life Behind the Purdah* (1902). Her delightful pensketches of Indian children, *Sun Babies,* came two years later, to be followed in 1920 by a second and illustrated series bearing the same title. She told the heroic story of the life and work of her parents in *Therefore* (1924), and she paid tribute in a short biography, *Susie Sorabji* (1932), to a like-minded younger sister who was an educationalist of wide interest in western India. The middle years brought *Between the Twilights, Indian Tales of the Great Ones, The Purdahnashin,* and *Gold Mohur Time.* She had a deep love for the colour and life of the ancient East and felt that some so-called "progress" was harmful rather than beneficial.

She was a prolific writer of short stories and articles to English and American magazines and reviews, and she contributed letters and occasional articles to *The Times.* She had an exceptional gift of narrative: of transcribing from life in graphic, pointed phrase her experiences and conversations, and she could also resort to apt poetic parables. Her amazing tales of the intrigue, deception, cruelty and oppression accompanying zenana life are relieved by humorous episodes and by instances of serious danger for herself or her clients being out-manoeuvred, or by expressions of a wise philosophy met with in unexpected places.

Her last literary effort, proposed by her and undertaken when she was more than half way through her eighth decade was her editorship of *Queen Mary's Book for India* in support of the Indian Comforts Fund (1943). Her perseverance in this labour of love was the more amazing since her visual powers were severely reduced in the last years.

July 8, 1954.

Austin Spare, an artist of unusual gifts and attainments and of even more unusual personality, died on May 15, 1956 in hospital in London at the age of 67.

A dreamer of dreams and a seer of visions, he had that complete other-worldliness so often depicted in romantic fiction and so rarely found in real life. Money meant nothing to him. With his talents as a figure draughtsman he might easily have commanded a four-figure income in portraiture, but he elected to live quietly and humbly, rarely going out, painting what he wished to paint, and selling his works at three or four guineas each. Even in outward aspect he conformed to type—with his untidy shock of hair, small imperial, and a scarf instead of a collar. But for most of his life he did not mix in what are called "artistic circles". Not Chelsea, Fitzroy Street, Bloomsbury, or Hampstead claimed him, but for years a little flat "in the south suburbs by the Elephant", far removed from the *coteries,* deep-set in the ordinary life of the people.

Austin Osman Spare was born in Snow Hill, near Smithfield Market, London, on December 31, 1888, the son of Philip Newton Spare, a City of London policeman. Leaving his elementary school at the age of 13, he took his higher education into his own hands, working not only at art but at general subjects, in particular the occult. He had some formal tuition at the Lambeth School of Art and the Royal College of Art. He was already exhibiting at the Royal Academy at the age of 16, but in later years ceased to send anything there. In July 1914 he had his first one-man exhibition, at the Baillie Gallery, showing a number of his so-called "psychic" drawings and some very powerful generalizations of animal nature.

Just after the 1914-18 War Spare became friendly with John Austen and Alan Odle, figure draughtsmen differing considerably from him and from each other, but each having certain aims in common with his. From October 1922 to July 1924 Spare edited, jointly with Clifford Bax*, a sumptuously produced quarterly called the *Golden Hind* for Chapman and Hall. It collapsed for lack of support, but during its brief career it reproduced in large scale some really superb figure drawings and lithographs by Spare and others. In 1925 Spare, Odle, Austen, and Harry Clarke showed together at the St. George's Gallery. Two years later Spare showed alone, at the same gallery, a collection of "psychic drawings and others of magical and occult manifestations", one of which, "Druid Rite", was acquired by the National Museum of Wales. He exhibited again, in 1929, at the Lefèvre Galleries, and in 1930 at the Godfrey Phillips Galleries.

Thereafter Spare was rarely found in the purlieus of Bond Street. He would teach a little from January to June, then, up to the end of October, would finish various works, and from the beginning of November to Christmas would hang his products in the living-room, bedroom, and kitchen of his flat in the Borough. There he kept open house; critics and purchasers would go down, ring the bell, be admitted, and inspect the pictures, often in the company of some of the models—working women of the neighbourhood. Spare was convinced that there was a great potential demand for pictures at two or three guineas each, and condemned the practice of asking £20 for "amateurish stuff". He worked chiefly in pastel or pencil, drawing rapidly, often taking no more than two hours over a picture. He was especially interested in delineating the old, and had various models over 70 and one as old as 93.

During the last war, while on fire watching duty, he was blown up and temporarily lost the use of both arms. His memory was also affected, but in 1946 in a cramped basement in Brixton, he began to make pictures again, starting, as he said, from scratch. In 1947 an exhibition of no less than 163 of the pictures he had painted in the previous few months attracted many people to the Archer Gallery, in Westbourne Grove.

Spare's alleged "automatic" and "psychic" drawings tended to lack discipline, and were on the whole inferior to his "straight" work. This last chiefly comprised nudes, which combined strength and delicacy of a high order and had a wonderful three-dimensional feeling. His minute draughtsmanship may have owed something to the Pre-Raphaelite influence, though in general his art was much more human and full-blooded than that of the "brethren". Of his technical mastery there can be no manner of doubt. The collection of his drawings may yet become a cult.

May 16, 1956.

Beatrice M. Sparks, who was Principal of Cheltenham Ladies' College from 1922 till 1936, died on August 6, 1953 at her home at Leamington Spa, Warwickshire.

She succeeded Miss Lilian M. Faithfull [q.v.], who had just retired after 15 years' service, and it was no easy matter to follow in the steps of one who had done so much to build up the school, besides taking a wide interest in the higher education of women and many other causes affecting the lives and careers of women at large. From the first Miss Sparks, who had already had 17 years' experience as a head mistress at Wisbech and at Bristol, devoted herself wholly to the work of the school and laid down a curriculum more adapted to train girls for their future careers at a time when many fresh openings were being offered to them in the professions and in other spheres of life.

With her attention centred on the school and its works, she enforced a stricter discipline, which may at times have seemed hard but was generally recognized in the end to be just, and while she insisted on girls maintaining the standards suited to their age and place in the school she laid stress at the same time on the development of character, of habits, of punctuality and neatness, and a general spirit of comradeship and loyalty. Her principal aim was to promote a spirit of unity, which was not always easy in a school of such large numbers. Under her the school continued to prosper and there were long waiting-lists of girls whose parents wished them to go there.

Outside Cheltenham her activities were chiefly concerned with the teaching profession and she enjoyed the trust, friendship, and esteem of her fellow head mistresses in all parts of the country. She was president of the Association of Head Mistresses from 1925 till 1927 and was frequently consulted by others who had less experience of the work of a head mistress than she. Her advice was always freely and willingly given and invariably proved to be useful and acceptable. She also served as a member of the Departmental Committee on Scholarships and was a member of the Burnham Committee on the payment of teachers.

Her work was recognized among women interested in education and as a mark of appreciation she was elected an honorary Fellow of St. Hugh's College, Oxford, where she had been educated after tuition at home by her father, the Rev. W. R. Sparks. She first became a head mistress when she had barely reached the age of 30 and was appointed to Wisbech High School in 1905. She remained there till 1913 when she was appointed head mistress of the Colston's Girls' School, Bristol. In 1922 she left to take charge of Cheltenham.

On speech day there in the year she retired Lord Askwith, chairman of the council of the college, unveiled a portrait of her by Howard Somerville, which had previously been exhibited at the Royal Academy.

August 7, 1953.

Harold Speed, who died on March 20, 1957 at the age of 85, was an excellent academic painter, his work being more remarkable for correctness of drawing and suavity of execution than for depth of feeling or interest of design.

He was mainly a portrait painter, and though he produced a good many landscapes and a few figure compositions it was in portraiture that he did the best justice to his talent. For many years he exhibited regularly at the Royal Academy, and he was so faithful to its traditions and so well equipped on the technical side that it is rather surprising that he was never elected. He published two sound books, *The Science and Practice of Drawing,* 1915, and *The Science and Practice of Oil Painting,* 1924. They were not only full of good practical advice but they contained some illuminating analyses of compositions by the old masters.

The son of an architect, Edward Speed, A.R.I.B.A., Speed was born in London. It is said that he was only five years old when his parents decided that he should become an artist. He was educated privately, and at the age of 17 won a gold medal in the national competitions, which took him to the National Art Training School, now the Royal College of Art, South Kensington. After a year he entered the Royal Academy Schools, where in 1892 he won the Armitage Prize for composition, having already received his first commission for a portrait, and in 1893 the gold medal and travelling scholarship for his composition of "Joseph interpreting Pharaoh's Dream". Though it is evident from his writing that Speed did not neglect the old masters he seems during his year in Italy to have given most of his attention to landscape, and his future career suggests the not uncommon case of a man kept to the exercise of his real abilities by demand rather than inclination.

Speed was, indeed, much in demand for presentation portraits. His "King Albert of Belgium", exhibited in the Academy of 1916, won great praise; he painted King Edward VII for Belfast; Viscount Grey for the Oxford and Cambridge Club; Dr. W. Crawthorne Unwin for the Institute of Mechanical Engineers; and T. F. Halsey, Deputy Grand Master of the Freemasons of England, for Freemasons' Hall. Among other eminent people painted by him were Sir Henry Campbell-Bannerman, John Burns, John Redmond, Sir Charles Dilke, Holman Hunt, Lilian Braithwaite, Sir Robert Baden-Powell, the Bishop of Durham, the Bishop of Wakefield, and Professor Priestley Smith.

Probably Speed's most successful landscape is "The Alcantara, Toledo, by Moonlight", purchased out of the Chantrey Bequest Fund in 1905 and now in the Tate Gallery. It is an attractive picture, though even here an artificial "glamour" is felt. Speed is also represented at the Walker Art Gallery, Liverpool, and in the municipal collections of Manchester, Bristol, and Melbourne. In 1928 his "May Morning" was purchased for the Wellington Art Gallery, New Zealand. He did at least two mural decorations; in the refreshment room at the Royal Academy and at Wesley House, where he painted two large panels flanking the organ in the Williamson Lamplough memorial chapel.

Speed was a member of both the Royal and the National Society of Portrait Painters, and in 1931 he was elected a member of the Société Nationale des Beaux Arts. At the Anglo-German Exhibition, 1906, and the Panama Pacific Exhibition, San Francisco, 1915, he was awarded gold medals.

For several years Speed was on the teaching staff of Goldsmiths' College, New Cross, where his grasp of principles and clear exposition made him very successful. He was always interested in craftsmanship, and in 1916 he was elected Master of the Art Workers Guild, taking a full part in its periodical discussions.

March 21, 1957.

Sir James Spence, M.C., M.D., F.R.C.P., Professor of Child Health in the University of Durham, who died at his home at Newcastle upon Tyne on May 26, 1954 at the age of 62, was a distinguished paediatrician who also enjoyed a great reputation as an authority on present-day problems of health and medical education.

At Newcastle, in addition to fulfilling the duties of his chair, he was honorary physician to the Royal Victoria Infirmary, the General Hospital, and the Babies' Hospital; in the wider world of medical affairs he gave valuable service as a member of the University Grants Committee, of the Medical Research Council, of the Medical Advisory Committee of the Nuffield Provincial Hospitals Trust, and of the Central Health Services Council.

James Calvert Spence was born on March 19, 1892. He was educated at Elmfield, York, and at the University of Durham, where he graduated M.B., B.S., with honours, in 1914. He then entered the R.A.M.C. and served throughout the 1914-18 War, winning the M.C. and bar. At the end of the war he filled the office of casualty medical officer and house physician at the Great Ormond Street Hospital for Sick Children, and during 1920-22 he held the John and Temple Research Fellowship at St. Thomas's Hospital. In 1922 he was appointed chemical pathologist and medical registrar at the Royal Victoria Infirmary, Newcastle upon Tyne, and he held this post until the end of 1927, when he was elected to a Rockefeller Research Fellowship and spent a year at the Johns Hopkins University, Baltimore. He obtained both the M.D. degree and the M.R.C.P. London in 1921, and he was elected F.R.C.P. in 1930.

In 1943 Spence was selected to fill the newly created Chair of Child Health in the University of Durham; this was the second university chair of the kind to be established in Great Britain, that of Edinburgh having been founded in 1931. With the steady growth in his reputation he was in great demand as a lecturer both at home and abroad. Thus he was Bradshaw Lecturer (1940) and Charles West Lecturer (1946) at the Royal College of Physicians, Interstate Postgraduate Lecturer in Australia (1948), Cutter Lecturer at Harvard University (1949), Blackader Lecturer before the Canadian Medical Association (1949), Dawson Williams Lecturer to the British Medical Association (1949), and Linacre Lecturer at St. John's College, Cambridge (1951).

Spence made his original approach to problems of children's disorders largely through the then newly developing science of biochemistry, influenced no doubt by his contact at St. Thomas's Hospital with the late Professor H. Maclean. His work on rickets and its treatment by irradiated ergosterol, for example, was a development later on of this early interest. But he gradually widened his field, becoming involved first in many clinical problems and later developing what had been undoubtedly a latent tendency, namely, a special interest in the social and humanistic side of the work. He was an original member of the British Paediatric Association and its president in 1950-51.

Within his own field he was responsible for many innovations, one of the most notable being at the Babies' Hospital of Newcastle, where mothers were admitted at the same time as their offspring and were allowed to play their part in the care and nursing of the children. He was knighted in 1950.

In 1945-46 he served as a member of the Interdepartmental (Curtis) Committee on the Care of Children. During his Australian tour in 1948 he was granted the honorary degree of D.Sc. by the University of Western Australia, and he was an honorary member of the Canadian Society for the Study of Diseases of Children.

He married in 1920 Kathleen, the youngest daughter of Robert Downie-Leslie, of Aberdeen, who survives him together with a son and four daughters of the marriage.

May 27, 1954.

Lewis Spence, one of the pioneers of the Scottish literary revival and a leading authority on mythology and folklore, died after a short illness at his home at Edinburgh on March 3, 1955 at the age of 80. Twenty-five years ago he contested unsuccessfully a Parliamentary election as a Scottish Nationalist candidate, the first of his party to do so.

James Lewis Thomas Chalmers Spence was a journalist who took up the study of mythology and became one of the leading authorities on the early history, culture, and religion of Mexico and Central America. He wrote many books on these and kindred subjects which were widely read by scholars in all countries and also by members of the general public, for he wrote in a simple and attractive style and had the knack of making even the dullest subject of interest to his reader. He was a poet, too, and in the years following the 1914-18 War he fulfilled a vow made as a schoolboy that he would strive "to restore the guid Scots tongue as a medium of serious poetic expression".

He was a native of Broughty Ferry, where he was born on November 23, 1874. After attending the collegiate school there and studying privately he went on to Edinburgh University and on completing his studies joined the editorial staff of the *Scotsman* in 1899. In 1904 he became editor of the *Edinburgh Magazine,* but only for two years.

In 1906 he joined the editorial staff of the *British Weekly,* but after three years he returned to Edinburgh to devote himself wholly to his studies of Central American mythology and folklore. He became a fellow of the Anthropological Institute of Great Britain and Ireland and later vice-president of the Scottish Anthropological and Folklore Society. Soon his extensive and prolonged studies made him an authority on the ancient history, religion, and culture of early America with few equals in this country or even in America itself. His first published work on these subjects was in 1907 in the form of a handbook in a popular series on *The Mythologies of Mexico and Peru.* This was followed by many longer and more detailed books on the same and kindred subjects.

Yet this was only a small part of his work. In 1910 he brought out *A Dictionary of Mythology,* covering the whole range of tradition, a book which has proved invaluable to many students. He followed it with other works of the same kind: *A Dictionary of Mediaeval Romance and Romance Writers,* which appeared in 1913, *An Introduction to Mythology* (1921), an *Encyclopaedia of Occultism* (1920), an account of the folklore of Brittany (1917), and many other books on the mysteries of other cultures—British, Egyptian, Babylonian, Assyrian. He made a special study of the Atlantis legend and published several books advancing arguments in favour of the island's reality. He also published volumes of verse, which were brought together in his *Collected Poems* in 1953. In recognition of his large and distinguished output he was granted a royal pension for services to literature in 1951.

His patriotism led him to throw in his lot with the Scottish Nationalist party. In 1929 he came forward as their candidate in a Parliamentary contest for the division of North Midlothian, but in spite of much effort and the support of many able Scotsmen he lost his deposit, gallantly declaring that the money was well spent, since so much interest had been focused on Scottish affairs.

He married in 1899 Helen, daughter of George Bruce of Edinburgh. She died in 1942, and he is survived by a son and three daughters.

March 4, 1955.

Charles Spencelayh, who died on June 25, 1958 at the age of 92 in a Northampton hospital, was an accomplished figure and portrait painter in oil and watercolour, and a miniaturist and etcher.

Not only did he paint very small pictures but he had an unfailing instinct for the kind of subject that could be treated effectively on that scale. The relation between subject and scale in his work was, indeed, so just that a picture of his in a mixed exhibition was felt to be a standing criticism of the larger works with a similar subject surrounding it.

Spencelayh was a member of the Royal Society of Miniature Painters, but, though he painted good miniature portraits, his more characteristic works were not technically miniatures but little oil paintings. They consisted generally of an interior with a single figure, crowded with interesting detail. They were not so much "conversation pieces" as racily English versions of seventeenth-century Dutch pictures of domestic genre. Such "conversation" as there was in them was not between one person and another but between the central figure, generally a man, and the surrounding objects, which were chosen to throw light on his character and interests.

His work was full of the spirit of Dickens, of *The Old Curiosity Shop* in particular. This is not only because Spencelayh delighted in painting the assortment of objects that are found in curiosity shops but also because he had a natural sympathy for the kind of man who keeps one—an old bachelor, in his conception.

Spencelayh, who has been happily called "the modern Meissonier of British domestic life", was the son of Henry Spencelayh, engineer and iron and brass founder, and was born at Rochester on October 27, 1865. He was educated at Dr. Burns's School, Rochester, and studied art at the National Art Training School, now the Royal College of Art, South Kensington, and in Paris. He was a regular exhibitor at the Royal Academy, the Paris Salon, the Royal Institute of Oil Painters, and the Royal Society of Miniature Painters, of which he became a member in 1897. He was also an honorary member of the Royal Birmingham Society of Artists and vice-president of the British Water-Colour Society.

The titles "The Dealer", "Lot Thirteen", "Overdrawn at the Bank", "The New Codicil", "Here's Luck", and "The Empty Chair", some of Spencelayh's little pictures, will indicate his typical subjects and the variety of mood he contrived to express in them. Like most artists who have completely mastered a particular kind of picture he was able to make it allude to current events, and several of his later works reflected the war. The only one-man show of Spencelayh's work was held at the Sunderland Art Gallery in 1936.

June 26, 1958.

Dr. L. J. Spencer, F.R.S., formerly Keeper of Minerals at the British Museum (Natural History) from 1927 to 1935, who died on April 14, 1959, aged 88, was a born collector and an indefatigable and incessant worker, whose curatorial work on the national collections in his department was remarkable for its thoroughness and exactitude. His scientific research was of a high order, but his most outstanding achievement was his complete and detailed mastery of the whole of mineralogical literature, which he had abstracted and indexed since 1894. He devoted all his life to his work, taking few holidays and working excessively long hours.

Leonard James Spencer was born at Worcester on July 7, 1870, the eldest son of the late James Spencer, for many years headmaster of the day school department of the Bradford Technical College. After a very successful career at the Royal College of Science, Dublin, and then at Sidney Sussex College, Cambridge, he was appointed to an assistant keepership in the department of mineralogy in the British Museum in 1893.

Spencer's scientific papers number over 100. He translated from the German two large quarto works, Max Bauer's *Precious Stones* (1904) and Reinhard Brauns' *The Mineral Kingdom* (1908-1912), and he wrote two books, on minerals and on gemstones, which had a wide circulation: *The World's Minerals* (1911) and *A Key to Precious Stones* (1936). He contributed the articles on minerals to the *Encyclopaedia Britannica* (eleventh to fourteenth editions) and to Thorpe's *Dictionary of Applied Chemistry.* He had abstracted papers on mineral chemistry for the Chemical Society since 1894, catalogued the mineralogical papers for the period 1883-1900 for the Royal Society *Catalogue,* and for 1901-1914 for the *International Catalogue of Scientific Literature.* The *Mineralogical Magazine* was edited by him from 1901 to 1955. His friends contributed articles to an editorial jubilee number of the magazine and a dinner was given in his honour to celebrate his completion of 50 years as editor in November 1950. *Mineralogical Abstracts* made its first appearance in 1920, and Spencer wrote most of the abstracts and compiled all the indexes until 1955. His lists of new mineral names which he had published triennially since 1897 were in constant use by mineralogists all over the world: by 1958, when the twenty-first list was published, they included 3,363 names and synonyms.

When he succeeded Prior as Keeper of Minerals in 1927 he carried on his predecessors' work on the great collection of meteorites, making a special study of meteorite craters and of the glass formed by the fusion of the desert sand in the vicinity of the newly discovered craters at Henbury in Central Australia (1931) and Wabar in Arabia (1932). This work led him to investigate other forms of silica glass of supposed meteoritic origin and in 1934 he joined an expedition to the Libyan Desert in an endeavour to discover the source of the remarkable masses of yellow silica glass discovered there by P. A. Clayton in 1932.

His work received frequent recognition both at home and abroad. He was elected a Fellow of the Royal Society in 1925, and was awarded the C.B.E. in 1934. He was an honorary member of the Mineralogical Societies of America and Germany and president of the Mineralogical Society of Great Britain from 1936 to 1939.

He married in 1899 Edith Mary, daughter of Islip J. Close, and had one son and two daughters. Mrs. Spencer died in 1954.

April 16, 1959.

Sir Stanley Spencer, the artist, died on December 14, 1959 in the Canadian Red Cross Memorial Hospital, Taplow, Buckinghamshire. He was 68.

Spencer was one of the few contemporary British artists who could be called with some confidence a man of genius as distinct from a man of talent. He came of a very remarkable family, each member of which was distinguished in a different way, only one of his brothers becoming a painter. Among the others were two musicians, a priest, and a professional conjurer.

Spencer's paternal grandfather was a Cookham bricklayer and builder in a small way, with a passion for astronomy and a love of music which led him to found a local singing club. His son, the father of Stanley, inherited both these interests. He was organist at Cookham church and teacher of music, and his knowledge of astronomy so impressed Lord Boston, who lived near, that he built him a small observatory. His eldest son, William, was an even more talented musician. At the age of seven his playing of Beethoven's sonatas attracted the attention of the then Duke of Westminster, who asked him to play at his house and sent him to the Royal College of Music and finally to Germany, where he became Professor of Music at Cologne.

It will be seen then that Stanley Spencer came of a family with the double advantages of sturdy rural stock and mental powers of a high enough order to excite the interest of influential patrons. Stanley, who was born in 1891 and spent his early years at Cookham, was the seventh son. He attended the village school run by two old ladies and from the age of 14 concentrated on drawing, illustrating fairy tales and making grotesques. An early influence was Edward New's illustrations to White's *Natural History of Selborne,* and an early admiration was Fred Walker's *Harbour of Refuge.* After a year at the Maidenhead Technical Institute, which rather damped his artistic enthusiasm, through the influence of Lady Boston—whose husband had built his father's observatory—and financial help from his brother, the Professor of Music, Stanley was able to go to the Slade School, where he remained for three years, making a great impression with his originality.

The religious bent in Spencer's work seems to have been inherited. It was matter-of-fact and unsentimental, without any trace of propaganda. The dressing of Biblical characters in contemporary costume did not suggest either an imitation of the old masters or a wish to show that the story is true to-day, but simply the natural thing to do. An early example, "The Visitation", painted in 1913 when Spencer was 21, is just a print-clad young Cookham woman coming to an older one with a piece of news, and the effect of urgency is due more to the lines of the composition than to the expression of the faces. In other words the emotional meaning is conveyed by pictorial and not by illustrative means.

The same artistic capacity is shown in the still earlier "John Donne Arriving in Heaven" of 1911, when Spencer was still at the Slade. To the Cookham period belongs the remarkable "Self-portrait" (1913), an "out-size" head, which gives a formidable impression of power. On the one hand the picture is remarkable for technical maturity and on the other for a peculiar "staring" quality, as if the result of visual hyperaesthesia.

With the exception of "The Bed", of 1915, children sheltering from an air-raid, Spencer's war pictures were painted after the war. The most important of them, "Travoys Arriving with Wounded at a Dressing Station, Smol, Macedonia", commissioned for the Imperial War Museum, was painted immediately after his release from the Army. It is an imaginative record of fact, in which violent perspective intensifies the emotional effect. In his later war pictures, which embodied many studies made in Macedonia, Spencer gave more rein to his imagination, with a bolder use of deformations and distortions.

The picture that made Spencer's name with the general public was "The Resurrection", a large canvas measuring 18ft. by 9ft., painted in Cookham churchyard and described as "An allegory of the saving of the black and the white races—the instinctive and the intellectual". This, exhibited at the Goupil Gallery in 1927, was hailed in *The Times* of February 28 as "in all probability . . . the most important picture painted by any English artist during the present century".

Included in the same exhibition were several studies and two of the completed panels for Spencer's most important decorative scheme—mural paintings in the Oratory of All Souls, Burghclere, near Newbury, commissioned by Mr. and Mrs. J. L. Behrend, who already possessed several of Spencer's pictures.

The Burghclere Oratory, which is the central feature of a block of almshouses, is a simple brick building with white interior walls. Upon them Spencer has expressed his full emotional reactions to the war in a series of panels representing incidents in the life of the R.A.M.C.; such as "Scrubbing Floors" and "A new Convoy arriving at the Hospital".

Spencer was elected A.R.A. in 1932. He exhibited nothing at the Academy until 1932, when he was represented by six oil paintings, including the striking triptych, "Souvenir of Switzerland". In 1935, at the request of the Hanging Committee, the President and Council of the Royal Academy asked him to withdraw two of the five pictures he proposed to exhibit, on the grounds that the committee did not think these works "of advantage to your reputation or the influence of the Academy", and Spencer immediately resigned his associateship. Against his wish the three pictures to which there was no objection were included in the Summer Exhibition, and the two banned works, "The Lovers" and "St. Francis and the Birds", were shown at Tooth's Galleries. "St. Francis", at any rate, in which the saint was represented as a bulky earthy man preaching to domestic poultry, was both characteristic of the artist and true to the spirit of the legend.

Many artists and other people protested at the action of the Academy, and Augustus John*, R.A., wrote a letter to *The Times* in which, commenting on the epithet "funny" often applied to Spencer's work, he recalled that Brueghel the Elder, with whom he thought Spencer showed a distinct affinity, was also sur-named "le Drôle". That the Academy, though within its rights, was mistaken is now generally agreed, though it is difficult to resist an amused sympathy with a body embarrassed by the discovery that the kitten of its adoption had grown into a tiger. He returned to the academic fold in 1950, in which year he was elected R.A. In that year also he was appointed C.B.E.

Many people cordially dislike Spencer's work, but it is impossible to ignore it, and his power in representation is universally recognized. Certainly "The Resurrection", "Christ Bearing the Cross", also in the Tate Gallery, "Travoys", "Swan Upping at Cookham", "The Last Supper", "Unveiling a War Memorial at Cookham", and the Burghclere wall paintings, to name no other works, represent a formidable contribution to contemporary British painting.

In a sense Spencer was a Pre-Raphaelite, but what in the members of the group remained illustration was by him turned into pictorial expression both by intensity of feeling and by command of compositional devices. In his expression of religious ideas through homely symbols he reminds one very much of Bunyan. His deformation and distortions do not appear to be arbitrary or theoretical, but rather as if things bulged when he looked at them. His visual intensity, possibly linking him with Bosch, has been observed—*à propos* Augustus John's comment, Brueghel's "The Adoration of the Kings" in the National Gallery is not unlike a Spencer.

Spencer made one of his few public pronouncements about himself when he wrote a preface (which was reprinted in *The Times*) to the catalogue of his big retrospective exhibition at the Tate Gallery in 1955. In this he admitted that something like a failure of inspiration had changed the character of his work after about 1932, and it was, as he explained it, in quest of some deeper "scheme" or "meaning" to substitute for his lost "joy" that he embarked on several elaborate series of religious paintings which occupied him at various intervals to the end of his life. In one of these he took up again the theme of resurrection. The stimulus this time, however, was not Cookham but a cemetery outside Glasgow, where he had been sent in 1940 as an official war artist to record the activities of Clydeside. Another was the grandly conceived "Christ Preaching at Cookham Regatta", episodes of which would periodically appear as they were completed at the Academy or in the galleries.

Spencer, who was a small, eager man, absorbed in his own interests, was twice married; first to Hilda Carline, member of a well-known family of artists. His second wife, professionally known as Patricia Preece, is a talented painter.

December 15, 1959.

Lord Ivor Spencer-Churchill—See **Churchill.**

Sir Harold Spencer Jones—See **Jones.**

Constance Spry, for many years the leading British artist in flower arangement, died suddenly on January 3, 1960 at Winkfield Place, Berkshire. She was 73.

Those who are familiar only with her grander works, whether they were the showpieces which she exhibited at the Chelsea Flower Show or the ambitious creations designed for stately homes and ceremonial occasions, undoubtedly knew only one side of her talent for flower arranging. She was equally at home with the intimate arrangement for a dinner table and indeed delighted in the exquisite miniature confection in an old tea caddy or a Sèvres trinket box.

Her versatility was equalled only by her tolerance of the extremes in flower arrangement fashion which from time to time inevitably swept across the scene in flower arranging as in any other form of art. The essence of her approach was always that one should extract pleasure from the arranging of flowers and her only criterion when judging an exhibit used to be whether it was beautiful or not. Modern line arrangements appealed to her no more and no less than the traditional English style.

Regrettably, many flower arrangers look upon the flowers, fruits, and foliage they use as so much material, but Constance Spry had a passion for living plants, and as she filled her gardens with the beautiful, the unusual, and the rare, she appreciated them as much for their garden value as for their use in her bowls and vases.

Although she was at home in every branch of flower arrangement she was probably at her best in the creation of adornments for the grand occasion. She was responsible for the flower arranging at the wedding of her Majesty the Queen, the Duke of Gloucester*, and of the Duke of Windsor* in France, and on many society occasions. She also was responsible for the flower decorations at gala performances at Covent Garden.

On the occasion of the Queen's Coronation she was adviser to the Minister of Works and was in charge not only of the flower decorations in the Abbey annexe but also on parts of the royal route. She and her staff planted in Parliament Square all the plants sent from Commonwealth countries. For her services at this time she was appointed O.B.E.

Constance Spry was born in Derby on December 5, 1886. She was educated in Ireland and spent much of her youth in that country. During the first war she worked for the Ministry of Aircraft Production and subsequently busied herself with welfare work in the East End of London. In the late 1920s she first began her work with flowers. The late Norman Wilkinson opened a scent shop in the West End of London and, impressed by the flower arrangements which she made for her own home, asked her to undertake the decoration of his shop. Thus began a new interest in flower arranging, and many of her friends asked her to decorate their homes for special occasions.

In 1929 she opened a small shop near Victoria Station which she called "Flower Decorations". Later she opened a larger shop in Burlington Gardens and subsequently moved to South Audley Street. There, before the last war, she opened her school of floristry which, of course, had to close during the war. When, however, it reopened after the war she had many requests to combine "Cordon Bleu" cooking with flower arrangement, but, this proving impracticable, she arranged with Rosemary Hume a separate "Cordon Bleu" cookery school.

These sides of her life work are fairly well known, but the school she opened at Winkfield Place near Windsor was perhaps her most ambitious and successful venture. There she set out to train girls who wanted to be efficient wives in the art of entertainment, flower arrangement, English and French cooking, the appreciation and choice of wines—in short, the creation of a beautiful and well-ordered home.

She published 13 books, the most recent being *Favourite Flowers.* Her works, particularly *A Gardener's Notebook, Flower Decoration,* and *A Constance Spry Anthology,* have been widely read at home and abroad, and *A Gardener's Notebook* gives a delightful glimpse into her character and her approach to flowers. *The Constance Spry Cookery Book,* which she wrote in collaboration with Rosemary Hume, was swiftly recognized as an authoritative work on all present-day cooking.

January 5, 1960.

Sir John Squire, who died on December 20, 1958 at the age of 74 at his home in Sussex, played a leading part in literary, social, artistic, and Bohemian life between the wars. As an editor his influence was potent; as a critic he helped to create many reputations; as a personality he added to the gaiety of his time.

John Collings Squire was born in Plymouth on April 2, 1884, of West Country stock. His Devonshire loyalties he always cherished, and in 1934 he was president of the Devonshire Association. These loyalties were reinforced by his education at Blundell's School, Tiverton, in which he kept a lively interest throughout life. On leaving St. John's College, Cambridge, he went to London and a year before the First World War he was appointed literary editor of the *New Statesman,* of which he became acting editor in 1917. It was during the war years that his literary reputation reached its highest point. His early poems, which included in *Tricks of the Trade* some of the most demurely brilliant parodies in the language, were soon widely known, and he took his place as a leader of the "Georgians".

At the same time his critical essays—especially those written under the name of "Solomon Eagle" and later collected in the three volumes of *Books in General*—gave him a platform which he used with uncommon grace.

To his lasting distress bad eyesight prevented him sharing the war experience of his own generation, so that for some years he was rather a solitary man of letters in London, carrying single-handed a heavy burden of work. Immediately after the war his political interests—at that time he was a Radical—led him unsuccessfully to contest Cambridge University and then, in 1924, Brentford and Chiswick. But much more to the point was a venture carried on until 1934, which may well prove his most enduring memorial: he founded and edited the *London Mercury*—with the *Criterion* and *Life and Letters* perhaps the most enterprising literary monthly of its period in England.

Until 1939 he continued to write books, of which the *Poems in One Volume* of 1926, two autobiographies, *The Honeysuckle and the Bee* and *Water Music,* and several collections of essays are outstanding. His play, *Berkeley Square,* written with J. L. Balderston, was a considerable success, and as editor of enterprises as different as "The English Men of Letters Series", the *Collected Poems* of James Elroy Flecker, and various anthologies, he displayed the range of his curiosity; while at different times he was a most active literary journalist, above all in the columns of the *Observer* and the *Illustrated London News.*

Nevertheless, it is above all as a personality, and not only a literary personality, that Jack Squire deserves to be remembered. In many ways he recalled William Morris. In time his political interests turned away from Radicalism, but activities which Morris would thoroughly have approved were his championship of the City churches, at a time when they were threatened with destruction, and his activity in saving Stonehenge for the nation. He loved all beautiful things, and was a robust defender of causes later made fashionable by Sir Kenneth Clark, H. S. Goodhart-Rendel [q.v.] and John Betjeman. The eighteenth century, the Gothic Revival, and the best work of the Victorians gained his suffrage long before most of his readers troubled to take them seriously.

Similarly, as an editor he showed refreshing catholicity. Even though his private sympathies stopped short of most that has been written in the last quarter century, he did not allow a prejudice of taste to exclude good writing of any school from the *London Mercury,* and he lavished his generosity, both of act and thought, on those who turned to him. Indeed, his weakness was too great a love of the human race. Although he liked to play the part of the tough, he was so easily swayed by a naturally sociable character that it sufficed for Lady Houston, say, to give him a pleasant evening or T. S. Eliot* to dampen his spirits by declining a pint of beer, and he discovered on the one hand a temporary leaning towards fascism and on the other a temporary distaste for Laforgue. Unpractical, lavish and affectionate, he never kept a penny in his pocket, and he never let his better judgment interfere with a kindness. Country things and field sports he loved. He was happiest when shooting, or shooting at, a pheasant, kicking a football about, or taking the field at the head of his incomparable cricket team, the Invalids.

Comic things were always happening to him—partly through his defective sight. A dead bird might fall on his head, cricket balls regularly knocked him prostrate, and in the daily business of life he suffered a constant series of small and endearing accidents. Towards the end of his life he grew the beard of a Blake prophet and retired more and more into the shell of one who was surprised rather than hurt by the apparent neglect of younger people, many of whom were personally devoted to him and had reason to remember his kindness when they were unknown. Of his poems a handful at least will survive—for if they were lit by a romantic glow which modern taste may find too roseate, they were also at their best intense and evocative. His light verse can be mentioned in the same breath as his friend Belloc's [q.v.], and some of this criticism remains provocative. As a friend he was staunch, difficult, and greatly beloved.

Squire was knighted in 1933. In 1908 he married Eileen, daughter of the Rev. A. A. Wilkinson, by whom he had three sons and one daughter. The loss of his youngest boy, Maurice, in the Second World War was one of the great sorrows of his life.

December 22, 1958.

J. H. Squire, who died on September 18, 1956 in hospital at Hillingdon at the age of 76, was for many years a popular broadcaster of light music.

John Henry Squire was born in 1880 and ran away to sea when he was 11 years old. His early musical training appears to have been given to him by one of the seamen on a battered cornet. This training the boy put to good use when in his early teens he found himself involved in a revolution in a South American state, for he served as a trumpeter in one of the opposing forces and was paid a dollar a day and his keep. It was not long before he deserted, and on being captured was sentenced to death. He escaped, however, and took refuge in a British ship.

Before he was 21 he had seen service in the South African War and in the Boxer troubles in China. After his return to England he stayed only three weeks and then went off to the United States, where he found music publishing more profitable than the performance of music.

One of his most successful ventures in this field was the introduction to England of the ragtime song "Yiddle on your Fiddle" and Irving Berlin's work. It was while engaged in music publishing in England that he used frequently to have tea with a "nicely spoken man, rather eccentric in the matter of dress—silk hat, frock coat and brown boots"—who turned out to be Dr. Crippen!

All the time he was in the music publishing business he had the ambition to perform and he achieved this when he formed his octet in 1913. He gave it the name of the "Celeste Octet", and the ensemble gave its first performance some four months before the outbreak of war in 1914. He was quick to see the possibilities of broadcasting and 10 years after the founding of the octet it made its first broadcast. Altogether, between the wars, the octet broadcast over 1,000 times and with the fees thus collected and gramophone royalties Squire enjoyed a very large income.

In the 1939-45 war he visited France under the auspices of Ensa and after Dunkirk performed in war factories, camps and hospitals. Since the war he had broadcast again with the reformed Celeste Octet until the ensemble was broken up a few years ago.

September 19, 1956.

Ronald Squire, the actor and theatrical manager, died in hospital in London on November 16, 1958 at the age of 72.

Squire was a comedian of the du Maurier school. His enviable casualness hid a carefully controlled technique, and for many years his name on a programme has been a guarantee that, whatever the play might be like, the evening would contain one performance that belonged to the category of fine comic art. Frederick Lonsdale [q.v.] was the author who best suited his style. He gave the impression that he had himself invented the epigrams given him to speak, found them so easy to invent that he thought nothing of them, and was gladly surprised at the droll effect they produced.

He had to perfection the trick of letting off verbal fireworks without appearing to notice them. He was also able to judge to a nicety when the moment had come in a heartless comedy to let in a little humanity. By chuckling appreciatively he could convey that he was on the side of young love in distress, and when the tireless epigrammatist subsided temporarily into a brown study it was usually a sign that he was thinking of something that would bring foolish misunderstandings to a happy end. He could often on such occasions introduce into glossy comedy a moment of genuine sentiment. However great a sponger or rascal the character Squire played, it was bound to become sympathetic in virtue of the actor's own sympathetic personality.

People were always best pleased when Squire was "playing himself" in a part in which hard cynicism had to be softened by charm of manner, and lazy affability, and in such parts his technical cunning was never allowed to show; but whenever he played outside his stage self, as, say, the doctor in *A Month in the Country,* he arrived at uncharacteristic effects with the same seeming ease.

Ronald Lancelot Squirl (Squire was the name he adopted for the stage) was born at Tiverton on March 25, 1886, the son of Lieutenant-Colonel F. M. Squirl, of the 93rd Argyll and Sutherland Highlanders, and of Mary, daughter of Charles O'Toole, of co. Wicklow. He was sent to school at Wellington, but in spite of that prelude to following in his father's footsteps, it was the theatre that claimed him. But first he spent some years as a journalist, writing for the *Bystander* and the *Graphic.* He had his first part on the professional stage in 1909 when he appeared in *An Englishman's Home* at Eastbourne. In the following year he acted in London with Gerald du Maurier in *Nobody's Daughter.* In 1911 he went to Liverpool for the opening of the repertory theatre there and played in *The Admirable Crichton* and other productions. He had two seasons at the Vaudeville in 1912 and 1913 and was soon established in the West End. The part of Algy Longworth in *Bulldog Drummond,* which he took at Wyndham's in 1921, was typical of the parts he was playing at that time. In 1916-17 he had his first American tour.

In 1928 Squire took to producing—and acting in his own production. His first enterprise was *By Candle Light,* which he produced in association with Leslie Faber and Lady Wyndham; and in 1929 he produced with Sir Alfred Butt* the Lonsdale comedy *Canaries Sometimes Sing,* in which he appeared with Yvonne Arnaud [q.v.]. He was seriously injured in a motoring accident in Switzerland in 1934 and was unable to act for more than a year. But the Second World War found Squire still in the centre of the stage. One of his best-remembered roles was in those years, as the Duke of Ayr and Stirling in [Sir Terence] Rattigan's comedy of the Grand Alliance, *While the Sun Shines,* which ran for two years at the Globe. He appeared in many films from 1934, including *The Rocking Horse Winner* and *My Cousin Rachel,* and he was one of the many distinguished actors with a part in *Round the World in 80 Days.*

He was twice married. His first marriage, which took place in 1914, was to Muriel Martin Harvey, and was dissolved in 1924. In 1947 he married Esyllt Williams.

November 17, 1958.

H. de Vere Stacpoole, a romantic novelist of an older generation who long enjoyed a household reputation as the author of *The Blue Lagoon,* died in hospital at Shanklin, in the Isle of Wight, on April 12, 1951, a few days after his eighty-eighth birthday.

Islands in tropical seas, the stars in Southern skies, coral strands, forests of palm, with love and adventure encompassing all—such are the elements of tried and familiar magic of which the majority of Stacpoole's 50 or so volumes of fiction are composed. Setting aside the mere romantic formula that he perfected, the chief virtue of his novels lies, perhaps, in the reflected light and colour of his tropical seascapes and landfalls; his descriptions, which commonly owed something to Pacific travel, often communicate a genuine delight and wonder.

Born in 1863, Henry de Vere Stacpoole was the son of the Rev. William Church Stacpoole, D.D., of Kingstown, County Dublin, and Charlotte Augusta Mountjoy, who was also of Irish origin, though born in Canada. All his life Stacpoole was to remain typical of the polite and highly individualized society which in the Victorian era resided along the southern shore of Dublin Bay. Of the Ireland which came later and which largely submerged the other he knew little and seemingly cared less. As a child he travelled a great deal with his mother, was then sent to school at Malvern, and went on to pursue medical studies first at St. George's Hospital and then at St. Mary's. After having qualified he was in general practice for some years.

Irked by this discipline, intent on indulging his love of travel, Stacpoole took to writing and was soon enabled to abandon medicine. Of his early novels, the one he himself liked best was *The Doctor,* a portrait of the old type of practitioner; in much later years he was indeed inclined to think it was the best book he had ever written. It missed the success he looked for, however, as also did his tentative excursions into high farce, but reward for his labours came with the three novels with tropical or exotic settings published between 1907 and 1909. The scene of the first, *The Crimson Azaleas,* was Japan; that of the third, *The Pools of Silence,* was the Congo forest. In between came *The Blue Lagoon.* Told with an engaging and persuasive charm, and with an all but Gauguinesque feeling for tropical colour, the story of the unfolding of life and love for two children dwelling alone amid Pacific enchantments won many hearts.

Even had he wished to do so, which there is no need to assume, the author of *The Blue Lagoon* would scarcely have been permitted by an enraptured public to forsake so beglamoured a scene. The tropical background of *The Ship of Coral* (1911), *The Pearl Fishers* (1915), and *The Reef of Stars* (1916) continued to enchant a large body of readers. Even after he had exhausted his power of springing fresh surprises from his favourite setting, he could, up to a point, still attract. He could even choose a different setting, as in *Goblin Market* (1927)—the island in this instance was only just across the Solent—in which he invested a sentimental story with something of real tenderness.

He had, indeed, a natural sensitiveness of feeling as well as the easy and flowing humour of his Irish blood. Both showed in the informal autobiography, *Men and Mice,* which he published in 1942, when he was nearly 80, and its successor, *More Men and Mice* (1945). Stacpoole—a big, handsome man of fine physique—had a house in the Isle of Wight—Cliff Dene, at Bonchurch—where Swinburne had spent part of his boyhood.

In 1934 he presented the pond at Bonchurch,

a noted haunt of rare birds, to Ventnor as a memorial to his first wife, who had died in that year. She was Margaret, a daughter of the late William Robson, of Tynemouth. In 1938 he married her sister, Florence.

April 13, 1951.

The death of **Joseph Stalin** in Moscow on March 5, 1953, at the age of 73, like the death of Lenin 29 years ago, marks an epoch in Russian history. Rarely have two successive rulers of a great country responded so absolutely to its changing needs and piloted it so successfully through periods of crisis. Lenin was at the helm through five years of revolution, civil war, and precarious recovery. Stalin, coming to power in the aftermath of revolution, took up the task of organizing and disciplining the revolutionary state, and putting into execution the revolutionary programmes of planned industry and collectivized agriculture. He thus equipped the country to meet the gravest external peril which had threatened it since Napoleon, and brought it triumphantly through a four years' ordeal of invasion and devastation.

The characters of the two men present a contrast which corresponds to the different tasks confronting them. Lenin was an original thinker, an idealist, a superb revolutionary agitator. Stalin neither possessed, nor required, these qualities. He was essentially an administrator, an organizer and a politician. Both were ruthless in the pursuit of policies which they regarded as vital to the cause they had at heart. But Stalin appeared to lack a certain element of humanity which Lenin generally maintained in personal relations, though allied statesmen who dealt with him during the war were unanimous in finding him approachable, sympathetic, and readily disposed to moderate the intransigence of his subordinates. As the war drew to its close Stalin, whether for reasons of health or for reasons of policy, became less and less accessible to representatives of the western Powers and so the rift began which was to widen in the counsels of the United Nations and in the policies towards the west of Russia's satellites, until the open warfare broke out in Korea which still festers and poisons the whole international scene.

In Russia and the adjacent communist states, Marshal Stalin at the time of his death occupied a position of personal eminence almost without parallel in the history of the world. His rare public appearances provoked scenes of tremendous enthusiasm; his speeches and writings on any subject—linguistics, the art of war, biology and history, as well as on the theory of communism—were treated as virtually inspired texts and analysed in meticulous detail by hundreds of commentators. A quotation from the works of Stalin was the irrefutable end to any argument. The mere mention of his name at a political conference in any of the satellite states was sufficient to bring all present to their feet by a prolonged ovation. The Stalin legend became an integral part of the chain which united orthodox communists all over the world.

In appearance Stalin was grey; his hair grey and stiff as a badger's; his nostrils and lower cheeks greyish white; his moustache, too, though in youth it had been richly brown and still showed some traces of that colour, was grey. He spoke softly, moved slowly, but his expression was quizzical, like a man enjoying a hidden joke, at times softening into a broad smile. Often as he spoke his look was oddly remote and withdrawn, the look of a man thinking through two or three processes at once. His expression was above all confident, without a trace of nerves; strong, calm or suddenly watchful in an amused kind of way. Tough, yet unathletic, dignified yet self-conscious, he dominated any group of which he formed a part, for all his small stature.

Joseph Vissarionovich Dzhugashvili, known to the world as Stalin, one of his many revolutionary *noms de guerre,* was born at Gori, in Georgia, on December 21, 1879. His father, a cobbler of peasant origin, died when he was 11. Joseph was sent to the church school in his native town, where he remained until 1893. It was here that he learned to use Russian as an instrument of expression, since all ecclesiastical schools in Georgia at that time were the implements of the Tsarist policy of Russification. He emerged from the school at Gori sharply conscious of the suppression of Georgian nationalism and not unaware of the social inequalities and injustices prevailing in his native Georgia. Such feelings were never revealed however to the school staff, and, in view of the fact that he was invariably the best pupil in his form, the head master and the local priest had no hesitation in recommending him for a scholarship at the seminary in Tiflis following upon his matriculation there in the autumn of 1894.

In his early period at the seminary Dzhugashvili was a model pupil, able and diligent at his work, but towards the end of his first year, unbeknown to his tutors, he was already in contact with opposition groups in Tiflis and published some patriotic radical verses in the Liberal newspaper *Iberya.* His contact with radical groups in Tiflis, headed by former seminarists, continued to develop until finally in August 1898 he joined the clandestine Socialist organization known as Mesamé-Dasi. Thenceforward he began to lead a kind of dual existence. His few leisure hours were spent in lecturing on socialism to small groups of working men in Tiflis; discussion in a secret debating society, formed by himself inside the seminary; and the reading of radical books. This state of affairs eventually came to the notice of the seminary authorities and in May 1899 the 20-year-old Dzhugashvili was expelled. He then embarked on a revolutionary career, but was faced with the immediate problem of employment. For a few months he made a little money giving lessons to the children of middle class families, and at the end of 1899 found a job as a clerk in the observatory at Tiflis—an occupation which seems to have afforded him much free time for political activity. He remained in this employment until March 1901, when his political activities forced him to go underground completely.

In November 1901 he was elected to membership of the Social Democratic committee of Tiflis, and a few weeks later was sent to Batum, where he proceeded with the establishment of a vigorous clandestine organization and an illegal printing press. The influence of this organization, under his leadership, on the oil workers of Batum was so remarkable in its manifestations that Koba (as Dzhugashvili was then known) was arrested and imprisoned in the spring of 1902 as a dangerous agitator. From his exile in Siberia he escaped a few weeks later and reappeared in Tiflis to find that the great schism which divided the Social Democratic Party in 1903 had left the Mensheviks in virtual control of the Caucasian party. A few months after his return, with some hesitation "Koba" took the side of Lenin and the Bolsheviks and proceeded to agitate energetically against the Mensheviks and other political groupings.

"Koba's" role during the "general rehearsal" of 1905 was a local rather than a national one. Apart from organizing the "fighting squads" (later to be a subject of considerable controversy within the party) and the editing of the newspaper *Kavkaski Rabochi Listok* (Caucasian Workers' News-sheet), which enjoyed temporary legality, he continued to conduct a vigorous onslaught against the Mensheviks. When he attended the party conference in Tammerfors in December 1905, as a delegate of the Caucasian Bolsheviks (a group of uncertain credentials, since most of the local leaders were Mensheviks), "Koba" emerged for the first time from the provincial arena of Caucasian politics into the atmosphere of a truly national gathering. Here, too, he first met Lenin. In the following year he attended the Stockholm Congress and in 1907 the London Party Congress as a Caucasian delegate, where he encountered Trotsky.

Soon after his return from the London Congress he was elected to membership of the Baku Committee, and it was in the oil wells of Baku that Stalin, on his testimony, first learned to lead great masses of workers. He was arrested in November 1908 and deported to Vologda province. A few months later, however, he escaped and appeared again in the south, under the name of Melikyants. His period of freedom was brief, for he was re-arrested in March 1910 and sent back to Vologda to complete his sentence of 1908. Released in June 1911, he settled in Petersburg at the home of his future father-in-law, Alliluyev, although he had been forbidden to live in most large towns. In consequence, he was again arrested. Reaction was now at its height and the party fortunes at their lowest ebb. A small conference of Bolshevik stalwarts in Prague in January 1912 coopted Stalin as a member of the central executive committee of the party; and on his escape a few weeks later he helped to found the new party journal *Pravda* in Petersburg.

It was in the winter of 1912-13 that Stalin made his only extended visit abroad, spending some months with Lenin in Cracow and some time in Vienna. This was a turning-point in his career. Ten years earlier Lenin, in his famous pamphlet *What is to be Done?* had first stated the case, on which he never ceased to insist, for a centrally directed party of professional revolutionaries, organized and disciplined in thought and deed, as the essential instrument of social revolution. Stalin had all the marks of Lenin's ideal professional revolutionary: he was intrepid, orderly and orthodox. It was a further asset that, though born a Georgian and a member of one of the "subject races", Stalin had had no truck with separatist or "federalist" ideas within the party and was an out-and-out "centralist". Not for nothing therefore did Lenin at this time refer to Stalin in a letter to Maxim Gorky as "a wonderful Georgian" who was writing an essay on the national question. The essay, eventually published under the title "Marxism and the National Question" in a party journal, was an attack on the "national" heresies of the Austrian Marxists Bauer and Renner [q.v.], and a statement of accepted Bolshevik doctrine, steering a cautious middle course between those who regarded any kind of nationalism as incompatible with international socialism and those who regarded nationalism as an essential element in it. It was the first of his writings to be signed by the name under which he was to become famous.

Back in Russia, Stalin underwent in February 1913 his sixth and last imprisonment and exile. The revolution of February 1917 released him, and he was probably the first member of the central committee of the party to reach Petersburg. In this capacity he temporarily took over the editorship of *Pravda.* This was the occasion of a short-lived deviation to which Stalin afterwards frankly confessed. In common with the other leading Bolsheviks then in the capital—excluding Molotov and Shlyapnikov—Stalin believed that the right tactics for the Bolsheviks were to support the provisional Government and rally to the defence of the fatherland; and this line, which would have assimilated the policy of the Bolsheviks to that of the Social-Democratic parties of the Second International, was taken editorially in *Pravda.* Lenin, chafing inactively in Switzerland, denounced in his *Letters from Afar* the weak-kneed Bolsheviks of the capital. When later he reached Petrograd in the sealed train and propounded his famous "April theses" of no cooperation with the provisional Government or with any policy that would keep Russia in the war, he quickly rallied his faltering party, and geared it for the second revolution. Thereafter Stalin remained a faithful and undeviating disciple.

The difficulty for the biographer of this, as of the earlier, period of Stalin's life is to disentangle the authentic contemporary evidence from the mass of more recent and largely apocryphal accretions. It seems that he first became a figure familiar to party *cadres,* at the time of his election to a new central committee of nine members in April 1917, and after the difficult July days, when Lenin and Zinoviev were compelled to retreat to Finland and Kamenev, Trotsky and others were arrested, Stalin emerged to lead the party. On their return to the political scene, he retired again into the shadows. While there is but little information relating to any participation by him in the work of the Revolutionary Military Committee during the actual rising, he nevertheless undoubtedly performed an important function in the editorial office of *Pravda.* He supported Lenin against Zinoviev and Kamenev in the controversy over the preparation and timing of the October revolution and against Trotsky over Brest-Litovsk; and though his interventions recorded in the minutes of the central committee were on both occasions brief and inconspicuous, his fidelity to Lenin in these troubled times must have won the gratitude of the leader and greatly enhanced his status in the party. He was appointed People's Commissar for Nationalities in October 1917, and in this capacity one of his first measures was to proclaim Finland's independence from Russia, at a conference in Helsinki. In spite of the opposition of elements within the party, who regarded this as an unwarranted concession to bourgeois nationalism, the decree was officially signed by Lenin and Stalin in December. He also played an active part in the drafting of the 1918 constitution of the Russian Socialist Federal Soviet Republic, and he was still more closely concerned four years later in framing the federal constitution of the Union of Socialist Soviet Republics.

The civil war provided fresh scope for Stalin's unflagging energy and undoubted administrative talents. That the civil war provided the occasion of Stalin's first open breach with Trotsky; that Stalin and Voroshilov intrigued busily against Trotsky, criticizing both his disposition of his armies and his use of former Tsarist officers; that recriminations flared up to a dangerous point over the defence of Tsaritsin (renamed Stalingrad some years later) against Denikin; that Lenin tried to smooth over these animosities and to retain the services of two invaluable though quarrelsome lieutenants—so much is clear. But the historian of the future may well find it a super-human task to extract the grain of truth from the chaff of subsequent controversy and the haystack of misrepresentation beneath which Trotsky's achievements have been hidden.

For the rest, Stalin's name figures little in the literature of the period. At any time up to 1922 the general impression which he made on his colleagues was apparently one of undistinguished competence; though admitted to the first rank of Bolshevik leaders he seemed the least remarkable of them, the most lacking in personality. But his capacity for hard and regular work more than balanced the more spectacular talents of his rivals, and indeed it could not have escaped the notice of a few that Stalin's influence in the state and his hold on the party machine had grown enormously. At the end of the civil war he filled three significant posts: membership of the Politburo, Commissar of Nationalities, and Commissar for Workers' and Peasants' Inspection (Rabkrin).

In March 1922 he was appointed Secretary-General of the party—a newly created post obviously suited to his rather pedestrian gifts. Though not regarded by anyone as a potential stepping-stone to supreme power, nevertheless this post, considered in conjunction with his other spheres of influence, rendered his personal position most formidable. Although Lenin still held the reins, Stalin's influence was becoming comparable to that of Lenin.

In May of the same year Lenin had a first stroke from which he recovered, temporarily and incompletely, to be finally stricken by a second in March 1923. From this moment, though Lenin lingered on, totally incapacitated, till January 1924 the succession was open.

Had anyone seriously canvassed Stalin's chances, a letter from Lenin to the central committee of the party—commonly, though unwarrantably, known as Lenin's testament—might have seemed a decisive obstacle. Writing at the end of December 1922, with a postscript of January 4, 1923, Lenin, who evidently knew that his days were numbered, passed in review the principal party leaders. He noted that Stalin since he had become Secretary-General had "concentrated in his hands an immense power", and expressed the fear that he might not always use it prudently. He described Stalin as "too rough", and proposed that he should be replaced by someone "more patient, more loyal, more polite, more attentive to the comrades, less capricious, &c." Fortunately for Stalin, the letter also treated Zinoviev, Kamenev, and Bukharin with scant respect, so that there was a powerful interest in limiting its circulation, although it was familiar to all members of the central committee, and its authenticity has never been contested. But Stalin must be credited with extraordinary skill in surmounting so formidable an obstacle. When the twelfth party congress met in April, 1923, Lenin was known, though not yet publicly admitted, to be past recovery. The talk was of a group of three ("troika") to take over his authority; and the names of Zinoviev, Kamenev, and Stalin were freely mentioned. Stalin, with consummate tact, defended Zinoviev and Kamenev rather than himself from attacks jointly on all three. Trotsky was gradually edged on one side. Attacks on him for undermining the unity of the party began in the autumn of that year.

The year 1924 was decisive for Stalin's ascent to power. During this year he for the first time exhibited to the full that amazing political dexterity which made all his rivals look like bunglers and amateurs. In the first place he brought about what may not unfairly be called the "canonization" of Lenin. From the moment of Lenin's death, and almost entirely as the result of Stalin's initiative, every word that Lenin had uttered or written came to be treated as sacrosanct—as Lenin himself had treated the works of Marx and Engels; and everyone who had differed from him was now suspect not merely as a heretic in the past, but as a potential heretic in the future. This weapon was aimed primarily at Trotsky, whose impetuous character and long record of past bickerings with Lenin made him highly vulnerable. But it could also serve against Zinoviev and Kamenev, who had more than once been severely castigated by Lenin for their backslidings. Stalin had been too prudent or not conspicuous enough to come under the lash—except in the unofficial "testament" now being gradually consigned to oblivion. This was a negative asset. But immense pains were taken, both at this time and afterwards, to build up a positive picture of Stalin as Lenin's ablest coadjutor, most faithful disciple, and chosen political executor.

Secondly, Stalin, well aware of the prestige

attaching in the party to the master of Marxist theory, set out to establish his credentials in that field. In the spring of 1924 he delivered at the Sverdlov University in Moscow a course of lectures on "The Foundations of Leninism"—a competent exposition of the development and application by Lenin of Marxist doctrine. He went on to take the offensive against Trotsky. In the lectures themselves he had followed the usual view that the ultimate success of the Russian revolution depended on the spread of revolution elsewhere in Europe. But the revolutionary failures of 1923 in Germany suggested that this consummation was remote; and the new international status of the Soviet Union, which had been recognized in 1924 by all the principal Powers except the United States, made the encouragement of world revolution an increasingly inconvenient policy. At the end of 1924 Stalin issued a revised edition of his lectures in which he proclaimed the doctrine of "socialism in one country". Trotsky could thus be branded as an internationalist, a champion of the outmoded slogan of "permanent revolution".

Thirdly, Stalin strengthened his control of the party machine and discovered how to use it for the discomfiture of his enemies. As Secretary-General he was already master of all promotions and appointments to key positions in the party. Lenin's memory was now honoured by the admission of a large number of new members; and this admission, managed by Stalin and his supporters, brought a mass of recruits to the new orthodoxy. Whatever opinions were held among the leaders, the weight of numbers must begin to tell. Before long Trotsky was being shouted down at party meetings by enthusiastic young Stalinists.

By January 1925 the campaign against Trotsky had gathered sufficient momentum to permit of his deposition from his office as People's Commissar for War. Before the end of the year Zinoviev and Kamenev, taking fright at Stalin's growing power, were seeking a *rapprochement* with Trotsky. But the move came too late to save them. In 1926 Stalin secured a condemnation of Trotskyites and Zinovievites alike both by a party conference and by the Comintern; and in November 1927 Trotsky, Zinoviev, and Kamenev were formally expelled from the party. Two months later Trotsky was forcibly removed from Moscow and sent to Alma-Ata in central Asia. He was finally expelled from Russia in January 1929.

In the struggle thus concluded personal rivalries had been intertwined not only with the issue of foreign policy already referred to but with internal political controversies. Trotsky had always been an advocate of industrialization and planning. Stalin opened the campaign against him with the N.E.P. slogans of conciliating the peasant and with the charge, repeated and illustrated *ad nauseam*, that Trotsky was guilty of "underestimating the peasant". But Stalin soon saw the dangers of going too far, and from the end of 1925 onwards cleverly steered a middle course between the "left" opposition of Trotsky and Zinoviev, who were accused of ignoring the peasant, and the "right" opposition of Rykov and Bukharin, who exaggerated the policy of appeasing the peasant.

After the rout of Trotsky, Zinoviev, and Kamenev, Stalin's position was not yet supreme in the Politburo. He still had to deal with the "right" opposition of Bukharin, Rykov, and Tomsky. Contrary to the prophecies of the recently defeated opposition, the influence of the Bukharin group did not overshadow that of Stalin. The fifteenth Congress elected a new Politburo of nine and in the new line-up Stalin had a majority of votes, among them Kaganovich and Mikoyan. The flaring up of conflicting forces inside the Politburo did not come until 1928, when in view of the grain famine "emergency measures" were instituted by the Politburo, resulting in Stalin's call for "the elimination of the kulaks as a class". Although in the councils of the Politburo these measures were opposed by Bukharin and his group, it was not until April 1929 that Stalin openly denounced Bukharin as the leader of the "right" opposition to his policy in the countryside. Soon after, Bukharin, Rykov, and Tomsky were excluded from the Politburo and other significant posts. Stalin's ascendancy in the Politburo was now complete, and from this moment he was recognized as the virtual ruler of the Soviet Union—a position consecrated by the unusual demonstrations with which his fiftieth birthday was celebrated in December 1929. At the very moment of Trotsky's expulsion Stalin was preparing a powerful swing-over towards industrialization. The first Five-year Plan was launched by him in 1928. Its inevitable concomitant, the collectivization of agriculture, though not seriously taken in hand till 1931, had been on the party agenda since the end of 1927. Throughout this period, though mistakes were made (notably in the estimate of the pace at which collectivization could be carried out), Stalin's sense of timing was on the whole superb. Few, if any, of the policies which he applied were original to himself; but he was unique in his sense of when to act and when to wait.

In the middle thirties, with industrialization well on the way and collectivization a *fait accompli*, the Soviet Union may well have seemed to be sailing out into smoother waters. The second Five-year Plan promised an increased output of consumer goods. Stalin's public pronouncements assumed a more optimistic tone, and he may well have originally conceived the "Stalin constitution", promulgated in 1936, as the crown of his work. Socialism had been achieved; the road to communism, however distant the goal, lay open; increased material prosperity and broader constitutional liberties were a vision of the immediate future. These expectations, if they were entertained, were not fulfilled. In the middle thirties the Soviet Union entered a new period of storm and stress. The murder of Kirov at the end of 1934 was the symptom or starting-point of a grave internal crisis; and in international affairs Germany regained her power in a form particularly menacing to the Soviet Union. The internal crisis was obscure, the evidence relating to it contentious, and it was dealt with by methods which left a lasting cloud on Stalin's name. The growing-pains of collective farming, the liquidation of the kulaks, the need—in face of the Nazi menace—to increase the pace of industrialization had all imposed severe strains on the population and bred discontent, sometimes in high places. Stalin decided to strike hard. In the panic which followed old scores were paid off and new grudges indulged, and things probably went a good deal farther than Stalin or anyone else intended at the start.

In 1935 and 1936 successive trials were held in which all those prominent Bolsheviks who had at one time or another been implicated in "Trotskyism" or other forms of opposition to the régime—Zinoviev, Kamenev, and Bukharin among them—were condemned and shot for self-confessed treason. In 1937 a number of the leading generals were shot on similar charges without public trial. Of the leading Bolsheviks of the first generation, hardly any survived except Stalin, Molotov, and Voroshilov*.

In 1938 the purge was at last stayed. Yagoda, long the head of the G.P.U. and its successor the N.K.V.D., who had been removed from office at the end of 1936, was now himself executed; and Yezhov, his successor, formerly an influential party leader, disappeared from the scene about the same time. Judgment on the purge will depend partly on the amount of credence given to reports and confessions of active treason on the part of the accused; and it has to be admitted that the Soviet polity afterwards survived the almost intolerable strains of war with fewer breaks and fissures than most observers had been prepared to predict. Nevertheless it is certain that the damage done by the purges to Soviet prestige in the west was a fatal handicap to the foreign policy of a common defensive front with the western Powers to which Soviet diplomacy was at that time committed. This was probably the gravest and most disastrous miscalculation of that period.

Soviet foreign policy in the thirties, as much as Soviet domestic policy, was clearly Stalin's creation. He had long been by inclination a Soviet nationalist rather than an internationalist; and now that he was firmly established in the seat of power he was unlikely to shrink from any of the implications of "Socialism in one country". Faced by the German menace, he executed without embarrassment the ideological change of front necessary to bring the Soviet Union into the League of Nations and to conclude treaties of alliance with France and Czechoslovakia. In the end it was not lack of Soviet good will that defeated this project, but the weakness of France and what appeared to Soviet eyes as a dual policy on the part of Great Britain. So long as Great Britain could be suspected of hesitating between a deal with Germany and a common front against her, Stalin on his side would equally keep both doors open. Munich, though a severe shock to prospects of cooperation, was partly offset by British rearmament, and the riddle of British policy was unsolved throughout the winter. On March 10, 1939, at the eighteenth party congress, Stalin gave what was doubtless intended as a note of warning that Soviet policy was "not to allow our country to be drawn into conflicts by war-mongers". But his speech was overtaken by the march of events.

It was Hitler's seizure of Prague in the

middle of March which fired the train. Great Britain now prepared feverishly for war and sought for allies in the east. Two alternatives were still open to her. She could have an alliance with the Soviet Union at the price of accepting Soviet policy in eastern Europe—in Poland, in Romania, in the Baltic States; or she could have alliances with the anti-Soviet Governments of these countries at the price of driving the Soviet Union into the hostile camp. British diplomacy was too simple-minded, and too ignorant of eastern Europe, to understand the hard choice before it. It plunged impetuously into the pacts of guarantee with Poland and Romania; and within a few days, on May 3, 1939, the resignation of Litvinov, and his replacement by Molotov, signalled a vital change in Soviet foreign policy. The British mission which had been sent to Moscow found itself unable to make any progress. Negotiations continued; but unless Great Britain was prepared to abandon the Polish alliance, or put severe pressure on her new ally, their eventual breakdown was certain. When Hitler decided to wait no longer, Stalin for his part did not hesitate. Ribbentrop went to Moscow and the German-Soviet treaty was signed. It is fair to infer that Stalin regarded it as a *pis aller.* He would have preferred alliance with the western Powers, but could not have it on any terms which he would have found tolerable.

Twenty-two months of most uneasy neutrality followed. The German advance in Poland was answered by a corresponding Soviet move to reoccupy the White Russian territories ceded to Poland by the treaty of Riga in 1921. Thus, by the autumn of 1939, Soviet and German power already confronted each other in Poland, on the Danube, and on the Baltic. The war against Finland in the winter of 1939-40 was designed to strengthen the defences of Leningrad by pushing forward the frontier in a westerly direction. It eventually achieved this object, but at the cost of much discredit to Soviet prestige and the formal expulsion of the Soviet Union from the League of Nations.

After the fall of France, Soviet fears of German victory and German predominance grew apace; and military and industrial preparations were pressed forward. Stalin now probably foresaw the inevitability of conflict, but was determined not to provoke or hasten it. In November 1940 he sent Molotov on a visit to Berlin without being able to mitigate the palpable clash of interests. On the other hand Japanese neutrality was assured when Matsuoka was effusively received in Moscow in April 1941. In the following month Stalin, hitherto only secretary-general of the party and without official rank, became President of the Council of People's Commissars—the Soviet Prime Minister. The appointment sounded a note of alarm at home and of warning abroad.

The German invasion of the Soviet Union on June 22, 1941, and the almost immediate threat to the capital placed on Stalin's shoulders an enormous weight of anxiety and responsibility. From the outset, the supreme direction of the war effort and defence organization became vested in the State Defence Committee consisting of five members—Stalin, Molotov, Voroshilov, Beria [q.v.], and Malenkov, with Stalin as chairman, though it was not till March 1943 that he assumed the rank of marshal, and later of generalissimo. During the war his customary public speeches on May 1 and on the eve of November 7 took the form of large-scale reviews of military operations and war policy. He was also active in a diplomatic role. Before the war Stalin had been almost entirely inaccessible to foreigners. Now, apart from regular conversations with the allied Ambassadors, he received a constant flow of distinguished visitors. Lord Beaverbrook* and Harriman were in Moscow in August 1941 to organize supplies from the west; Churchill* came in August 1942, and again, with Eden, in October 1944. In December 1943 Stalin met President Roosevelt and Churchill at Teheran, and in February 1945 at Yalta. The last meeting of the Big Three, with Truman* succeeding Roosevelt and Attlee* replacing Churchill in the middle of the proceedings, took place at Potsdam in July 1945.

Among his diplomatic activities Stalin was particularly concerned with the perennial problem of Soviet-Polish relations. By dint of much patience he eventually secured the recognition of the new Polish Government by his allies, and the acceptance by them as the frontier between the Soviet Union and Poland of the so-called "Curzon line" originally drawn by the Allied and Associated Powers at the Paris peace conference of 1919. He worked untiringly to secure for his country that place of undisputed equality with the other Great Powers to which its achievements and sacrifices in the war entitled it.

Two striking decisions of domestic policy during the war—the disbandment of Comintern and the renewed recognition of the Orthodox Church—were undoubtedly taken by Stalin out of deference for allied opinion; but they were in line with this long-standing inclination, accentuated by the war, to give precedence to national over ideological considerations. The reforms of 1944 which accorded separate armies and separate rights of diplomatic representation abroad to the major constituent republics of the Soviet Union were perhaps partly designed to secure to the Ukraine and White Russia independent membership and voting power in the United Nations.

When the war ended Stalin was in his sixty-sixth year. A holiday of two-and-a-half months in the autumn of 1945 at Sochi on the Black Sea produced the usual crop of rumours, but was no more than a merited and necessary respite from the burden of public affairs. In December he was back in Moscow for the visit of Bevin [q.v.] and Byrnes*. Thenceforward there were few personal contacts between Stalin and representatives of the western Powers. In February 1946 he took part in the elections to the Supreme Soviet, making the principal campaign speech, in which he forecast an early end of bread rationing—a hope which was defeated by the bad harvest. He also declared that it was the intention of the Soviet Communist Party to organize a new effort in the economic field, the aim of which would be to treble pre-war production figures. Although advanced in years, Stalin still continued to hold the reins of power and in March 1946 he was again confirmed as secretary of the central committee of the party. In the same year the State Publishing House began publication of a collected edition of his works.

The unparalleled popularity in the non-communist world with which the Russian people in general, and Marshal Stalin in particular, had emerged from the war thus early gave place to mistrust. It had been hoped that the pre-war doctrine which was associated with Stalin's name, of "socialism in one country", would provide the basis for peaceful coexistence in the post-war period. Stalin's own comments on international affairs sometimes tended to confirm, and sometimes to deny, this prospect. Thus in answer to questions put to him by the Moscow correspondent of the *Sunday Times* in September 1946, Stalin declared that, in spite of ideological differences, he believed in the possibility of lasting cooperation between the Soviet Union and the western democracies, and that communism in one country was perfectly possible. This provoked world-wide interest and was regarded as a welcome statement, contributing much to the easing of growing international tension. A month later, however, in reply to questions sent to him by the United Press of America, he asserted that in his opinion "the incendiaries of a new war", naming several prominent British and American statesmen, constituted the most serious threat to world peace, and thus destroyed the earlier good impression.

Russia's post-war policy towards her neighbours did nothing to confirm Stalin's peaceful protestations. The independent Baltic States, Lithuania, Latvia, and Estonia, had already been incorporated in Russia in 1940. Finland and Bulgaria were compelled to surrender territory to Russia as the price of defeat, and Poland suffered even greater amputations as the reward of victory. In the Far East Russia claimed North Sakhalin and the Kurilles Islands as her price for taking part in the war against Japan. In all the countries which had been overrun by the Red Army it was only a question of time before a Communist régime had been set up and its opponents liquidated. By the middle of 1948 the borders of communism stretched from the Elbe to the Adriatic. A year later communism had triumphed in China. Stalin controlled the destinies of an empire far larger than any Tsar had ever dreamed of.

It was the *coup d'État* in Prague in February 1948 which finally forced western Europe and North America into action for their common defence. The North Atlantic Treaty was signed in April 1949. But even before then the west had successfully met another outward thrust by Russia. It was in June 1948 that the air-lift began which nullified the effects of the blockade of Berlin.

Stalin remained, as always, in the background during this period of dynamic Russian expansion. It was only rarely that he received a foreign diplomat, though leaders of the satellite States naturally had readier access to him. From time to time the suggestion was made for a new conference between Stalin, the American President and the British Prime Minister, but none of them came to anything. It was in 1946 that President Truman disclosed that he had invited Stalin to Washington for a social visit, but that Stalin had found it necessary to decline for reasons of health. In the last interview which he gave to a foreign correspondent (to the representative of *New York Times* in December last year) he indicated that he held a favourable view of proposals for talks between himself and the head of the new American Administration, President Eisenhower*, and that he was interested in any new diplomatic move to end hostilities in Korea. President Eisenhower declared his willingness last month to hold a meeting with Stalin in certain circumstances, and Churchill subsequently told the House of Commons that he did not rule out the possibility of three-cornered discussions.

It was in the last year of his life that Stalin appeared in a role which would have surprised former colleagues, such as Lenin and Trotsky, but which therefore may well have given him most pride—as an economic theorist in the tradition of (and not less important than) Marx, Engels and Lenin. Shortly before the nineteenth congress of the Russian Communist Party, which was held in Moscow in October 1952—the first congress since 1939—Stalin published his *Economic Problems of Socialism in the U.S.S.R.*, which has since become the definitive text-book for communists in all countries. In this work he warned his readers that, for all Russia's successes in building a new society, it was wrong to think that the natural economic laws did not apply as much in Russia as elsewhere. He also forecast a deepening crisis of capitalism, that west European countries would dissociate themselves from the United States, and that war between these capitalist countries was inevitable. He also outlined a programme of basic preliminary conditions necessary for the transition to communism in the Soviet Union. At the congress there was a reorganization of party organs—the Politburo and the Orgburo being brought together in a single body, the Praesidium of the Central Committee, of which Stalin became chairman.

On the occasion of his seventieth birthday in December 1949 there were widespread celebrations throughout the Soviet Union and busts of Stalin were erected on 38 of the highest peaks in the Soviet Union. It marked, too, the inauguration of international Stalin peace prizes, to be awarded each year on his birthday.

On March 3, 1953, it was announced by Moscow radio that Stalin was gravely ill as the result of a haemorrhage, that he had lost consciousness and speech, and that he would take no part in leading activity for a prolonged period.

Only a few details are known of Stalin's personal life. In 1903 he married Yekaterina Svanidze, a profoundly religious woman and the sister of a Georgian comrade, who left him a son Yasha when she died in 1907 of pneumonia. His second wife, whom he married in 1918—Nadezhda Alliluyeva—was 20 years younger than himself and was the daughter of a Bolshevik worker, with whom Stalin had contacts in both the Caucasus and St. Petersburg. She was formerly one of Lenin's secretaries and later studied at a technical college in Moscow. This marriage, too, ended with the death of his wife in November 1932. She left him two children—a daughter, Svetlana, and a son, Vassili, now a high ranking officer in the Soviet Air Force. Late in life he married Rosa Kaganovich, the sister of Lazar Kaganovich, a member of the Politburo.

March 6 & 7, 1953.

Sir Herbert Stanley, G.C.M.G., who died in a nursing home in Cape Town on June 5, 1955 at the age of 82, had a long and distinguished career with many associations with South Africa both by the nature of his appointments and public service and by marriage.

Herbert James Stanley was born on July 25, 1872, and was educated at Eton and Balliol College, Oxford. He entered the diplomatic service, and from 1897 to 1902 he was attached to the office of the British Minister at the legations at Dresden and Coburg. Four years later he was appointed assistant private secretary to the First Lord of the Admiralty and subsequently he became private secretary to the Lord President of the Council. It was in South Africa, however, that his administrative gifts were developed. When, in 1910, Lord Gladstone became the first Governor-General of the Union of South Africa, Stanley accompanied him to South Africa as private secretary, and he was also private secretary to Lord Gladstone's successor, Lord Buxton. He remained with the latter only six months and was then appointed Resident Commissioner of Southern and Northern Rhodesia, an office which he filled for three years.

From 1918 to 1924 he was Imperial Secretary in South Africa. He became Governor of Northern Rhodesia in 1924 and in 1927 he was appointed Governor of Ceylon, an appointment which aroused criticism on the ground that he lacked experience in oriental administration. However, he filled the office with distinction and played a notable part in the framing of a new constitution for Ceylon. He was a popular and able governor and his term of office was extended for three months. In 1931 he returned to South Africa as High Commissioner for the United Kingdom in South Africa. His appointment marked an innovation in administration, for with this post was combined the office of High Commissioner for South Africa, a post formerly held by the Governor-General. He was thus responsible for the administration of Basutoland, Bechuanaland, and Swaziland.

In 1935 he was appointed Governor of Southern Rhodesia. He was due to retire at the end of 1937, but official bodies in Southern Rhodesia petitioned the Colonial Office to extend his period of office. As a result the announcement that the request had been granted and that Stanley would remain in office till the end of 1940 was welcomed throughout the country. In fact he stayed even longer, for his period of office was again extended and he did not retire until the end of 1941.

After his retirement he settled in Cape Town and took an active part in local affairs. He identified himself with the Red Cross and Boy Scout movements. In 1942 he was appointed Chief Commissioner of the Boy Scouts in South Africa.

He married in 1918 Miss Reniera Cloete, a member of an old Cape family, the Cloetes of "Alphen" Wynberg, who was created D.B.E. in 1941. She died in 1950 and he is survived by two sons and two daughters of the marriage.

June 6, 1955.

Lord Stansgate died on November 17, 1960 in a London hospital at the age of 83.

By his death British public life is deprived of one of its most vivid personalities and the House of Lords loses one of its most endearing, irrepressible, provocative, and witty debaters.

"Wedgie Benn", as he was affectionately known, was a fighter to the end of his days. Age seemed only to sharpen the flashing blade of his scorn for injustice, indolence, equivocation, or woolly mindedness in high places. The spell of his charm could, however, vanquish the most acute exasperation which he might provoke, and even his victims soon forgave him. For his integrity of purpose was manifest. His physical bravery was matched by high moral courage, and he stood in awe of nobody.

It is as a parliamentarian that he will best be remembered. Few could rival his knowledge of procedure or match his mastery of the niceties of debate. His sharp brown eyes could pierce to the heart of any sham; they could also blaze with righteous fury and twinkle with fun. He was relentless in exposing shoddy argument, hypocrisy, and inconsistency. With a vivacity which could electrify the dullest debate, he had a galvanic effect on proceedings in the House of Lords.

The Right Honourable William Wedgwood Benn, P.C., D.S.O., D.F.C., first Viscount Stansgate, was born on May 10, 1877, the second son of the late Sir John Williams Benn, Bt., and younger brother of Sir Ernest J. P. Benn [q.v.], the publisher. The boy was brought up to take an interest in progressive thought and in the life of the East End constituency represented by his father. Educated at the Lycée Condorcet, Paris, and at University College London, he graduated B.A. with first class honours in 1898 and later became a Fellow.

He chose a political career on the Liberal side, and early in the century was candidate for St. George's-in-the-East. In 1906 he was returned as Member for the St. George's division of Tower Hamlets, soon becoming parliamentary private secretary to Reginald McKenna, then First Lord of the Admiralty. In 1910 he was appointed a Junior Lord of the Treasury.

After the outbreak of the First World War Benn joined the Middlesex Yeomanry. He was sent to Gallipoli in August 1915, and was in the last attempt to storm the heights at Suvla. He was posted in April 1916 to the Egyptian R.N.A.S. seaplane station as observer, and won the D.S.O. at the sinking of the Ben-my-Chree. His last year of the war brought him the D.F.C. and Chevalier of the Legion of Honour.

He was demobilized with the rank of captain, and in 1919 published an account of his war experiences called *In the Side Shows.*

At the 1918 election Benn was returned as a Liberal for Leith. His affinities were Asquithian; he was uneasy under Lloyd George and in February 1927 resigned his seat and joined the Labour Party, having found, as he said at the time, that he had long been voting with them on big public issues. He was returned for North Aberdeen in August 1928, and the following June MacDonald appointed him Secretary of State for India. He showed genuine sympathy with Indian aspirations and was a successful Secretary; but he found himself unable to support the National Government, and the 1931 election put him out of office and Parliament.

The viscounty conferred on him by the King in December 1941 was one of four peerages created on the advice of the Coalition Government as a special measure to strengthen the Labour Party in the Upper House. When the new Labour Ministry took office in 1945, Attlee* appointed Stansgate Secretary of State for Air. It was not an easy task to discharge, involving as it did the complex and often delicate adjustments attending the transition from war to peace, and the manifold problems created by demobilization. Stansgate tackled the job with characteristic energy. He was also charged in the spring of 1946 with leading, as Ernest Bevin's [q.v.] deputy, the Cabinet mission which went to Cairo to negotiate a revision of the Anglo-Egyptian Treaty of 1936. It was not for lack of effort on his part that the attempt proved abortive.

Meanwhile, the Cabinet had put in hand a reorganization of the defence system involving the formation of a Defence Committee and the creation of a Minister of Defence responsible for unifying policy. Stansgate decided to place his resignation in the Prime Minister's hands. Attlee paid a warm tribute to the excellent work he had done. In April 1947 Stansgate was elected president of the Inter-Parliamentary Union and in 1957 made honorary president.

Free of the cares of office, Stansgate threw himself into the legislative and debating controversies which occupied the Lords. One of the most interesting debates launched by him had to do with the succession to his own title. His eldest surviving son and heir, Anthony Neil Wedgwood Benn (who was first elected Labour M.P. for South-East Bristol in 1950) desired to retain the right to stand for, and sit in, the Commons after his father's death. In April 1955 Stansgate moved a second reading of a Bill to provide that on his death the peerage should be deemed to have gone into abeyance for as long as Anthony Wedgwood Benn was alive, and that on his death it should be fully restored to the next male heir. Although Stansgate pleaded his son's case most persuasively, the Lords turned down the Bill.

Stansgate married, in 1920, Margaret Eadie, daughter of Daniel Turner Holmes. In addition to the new peer, there is a second surviving son of the marriage.

November 18, 1960.

Sir George Stapledon, C.B.E., F.R.S., who died on September 16, 1960 at the age of 77, may be counted among the half-dozen or so who profoundly influenced British agricultural thought in the first half of the century and among the very few who lived to see their thoughts embodied in standard agricultural practice.

Born in 1882, the son of William Stapledon, of Northam, North Devon, he was educated at Westward Ho! and Emmanuel College, Cambridge, and passed into the Indian Civil Service. But his heart was in the English countryside, and in 1907 he decided to abandon his Civil Service career and return to Cambridge to read for an agricultural diploma, which he took in 1910.

His first appointment was at the Royal Agricultural College, Cirencester, where he began at once to specialize in grass. His surveys of the species—coverage of pastures in the district—led him to two main conclusions: the large proportion of inferior species present in all but the very best pastures, and the profound effect of management on the species population of a pasture. These conclusions, commonplace today, were then little appreciated, and they were the foundation on which his later work was based.

In the 1914-18 War he became the first director of the official seed-testing station set up by the Board of Agriculture, and in 1919 he was appointed Professor of Agricultural Botany at University College, Aberystwyth, and director of the Welsh plant breeding station.

These appointments gave him his great opportunity. With a growing organization and staff, he threw himself wholeheartedly into two tasks to which his previous conclusions had pointed. The first was to breed improved strains of grasses—strains that would produce nutritious leaves instead of woody stems running quickly to seed, strains that by early or late growth would extend the grazing season. The second followed on from this, to make productive the millions of acres of inferior grassland that were contributing so little to the nation's food supply. In many cases this could only quickly be done by making a new start and reseeding. From this followed the principle of "taking the plough round the farm".

This was not entirely new. In the north and other districts of high rainfall, the growing of three or four-year leys had been a long-established practice, but it was Stapledon who put it on the map as an integral part of British farming over a wide range of soils and climates. He also did pioneer reclamation experiments on the heather-clad soils of the Welsh mountains.

When the Second World War came his knowledge and experience of grassland were freely utilized in the Ministry's food production campaign, and his survey of British grassland, which he had been compiling for some years, was of great value in apportioning county ploughing tasks—the new Aberystwyth strains of grass and clover seeds proved their worth.

In 1948 Stapledon became director of the grassland improvement station at Stratford-on-Avon, which position he held until his retirement, when he became a director of Dunns Farm Seeds Ltd. His publications were *A Tour in Australia and New Zealand* (1928), *The Land: Now and Tomorrow* (1935), *The Way of the Land* (1943), *Disraeli and the New Agriculture* (1943).

He was made C.B.E. in 1932 and knighted in 1939, in which year he became F.R.S.

He married in 1913 Doris Wood Bourne and leaves no children.

Agricultural science is a comparatively new profession, and Stapledon is perhaps the outstanding personality it has so far produced. Original in thought, overflowing with vitality, completely sincere in his beliefs and relentless in pursuing them, he was a leader inspiring affection as well as enthusiasm among all those with whom he worked.

September 17, 1960.

Prince Starhemberg, who died on March 15, 1956 of a heart attack at the age of 56 while walking at Schruns, in the Vorarlberg, was the youngest and most adventurous of the political leaders and one of the most hotly contested personalities in the public life of Austria between the wars.

He was one of the numerous body of young men in both Germany and Austria who, having had to take their places in the firing line at an immature age, were drawn, partly by temperamental inclination, partly through the unsettlement of their educational careers, into those political and military adventures which could be had almost for the asking in the first turbulent years of peace. It was in keeping with these beginnings when Starhemberg, returning to his native Upper Austria in the early twenties, threw himself heart and soul into the levying, equipment, and training of one of the provincial defence forces known collectively as the Heimwehr.

The Prince became in time an admiring disciple of Mussolini, whom he often visited, and by whom, in the presumed interests of Italian policy, the Heimwehr movement was supported and encouraged. But by a paradox it was the triumph of National-Socialism in Germany, to a far greater extent than the backing, overt or concealed, of fascist Italy, which was indirectly to raise the Heimwehr to established power and influence, and Starhemberg himself to a position of the highest responsibility.

Through all this period Starhemberg had been exerting pressure on Dr. Dollfuss to hasten the counter-revolutionary process which would establish an "authoritarian" or fascist state, but he had also shown patience and restraint in asking only for what was possible. By the time of the promulgation of the future corporative constitution, on May 1, 1934, he was ready to take his place as second-in-command to Dollfuss, as Vice-Chancellor in the Cabinet and Deputy Leader in the Patriotic Front.

His Serene Highness Ernst Rüdiger, seventh Prince of Starhemberg, Count of Schaumburg and Waxenberg, Lord of Wildberg and Lobenstein, was born on May 10, 1899 at Eferding, in Upper Austria, in the principal of his family's 18 castles. The Starhembergs trace their descent from Gundacher of Steinbach, a twelfth-century feudal bailie, whose grandson, also Gundacher, took the name of "Storchenberg", later to become "Starchemberg", after a castle which he had built. The greatest of the line was that other Ernst Rüdiger, Count of Starhemberg, who commanded the heroic defence of Vienna during the second and final Turkish siege in 1683. Starhemberg succeeded to the family honours in 1927.

After passing out of the gymnasium at Gmünden and studying for a time at Innsbrück and Munich, Starhemberg joined the 4th Dragoon Regiment in 1917. He fought in Russia and on the Piave. His adventurous disposition led him to take a part in the reactionary Kapp *Putsch* of 1920 in Berlin, and later to fight as a volunteer against the Poles in Upper Silesia. Returning to Austria, he levied, equipped, and trained at his own expense the irregular Starhemberg Jäger and other Heimwehr formations. In 1929 he became provincial leader of the Heimwehr for Upper Austria, and a year later was chosen as federal leader. By an accident of party politics he was Minister of the Interior in the Vaugoin Cabinet from September to November 1930.

The Heimwehr movement grew steadily more active and aggressive in word and in deed, and rumours of threatened and impending *Putsches* were continually in the air. But when the *Putsch* came in September 1931, under the inspiration and command of the Styrian, Pfrimer, to whom Starhemberg had handed over the federal leadership, it was a miserable fiasco bloodlessly suppressed in a few hours. Starhemberg, who had stood aloof in Upper Austria, thereupon resumed the federal command. In May 1932 it was announced that he had applied to the provincial court at Linz for the appointment of a receiver; through his generous expenditure on the Heimwehr he had run heavily into debt. From this time on, under the Chancellorship of Dollfuss, the influence of the Heimwehr steadily increased; Heimwehr leaders successively joined the Cabinet till they formed one half of it; and on May 1, 1934, Starhemberg himself assumed the Vice-Chancellorship.

Though he supported Dr. Schuschnigg [d. 1977] after the murder of Dr. Dollfuss, it soon became evident that there was not room for both of them in Austrian politics, and the dissensions in the Heimwehr between Starhemberg and Major Fey gave Schuschnigg the opportunity he was seeking to destroy a rival. His triumph was, however, short lived, for the Nazis over the border had been waiting to pounce and Schuschnigg was in due course destroyed himself.

Starhemberg retired to Switzerland and was living in France when war broke out in 1939. He joined the French Army and after the collapse of France his presence in the Free French forces was the cause of some unfavourable comment in the House of Commons.

His memoirs came out in 1942, throwing much light on the long jockeying for position of Hitler and Mussolini with Austria as the prize, finally won by Hitler, though not to be enjoyed by him for very long.

In the latter part of the war he lived in South America. His estates in Austria were restored to him in 1952 and in December 1955 he visited his native country after 18 years.

March 16, 1956.

Dr. James Sullivan Starkey, LITT.D., better known as **Seumas O'Sullivan,** the Irish poet and bibliophile and editor of the *Dublin Magazine,* died in Dublin on March 24, 1958.

For over half a century Dr. Starkey interested himself in the Irish literary theatre—he appeared in a Yeats play on the opening night of the Abbey Theatre on December 27, 1904—and from the earliest days of the literary revival he was one of the most respected men of letters in Dublin, with a reputation that extended far beyond the boundaries of Ireland.

He supported Sinn Fein up to the time of the Anglo-Irish treaty and was an intimate friend of Arthur Griffith and of many other leaders of the 1916 Rebellion. Of the execution of one of them, John McDermott, he wrote: "They have slain you, Sean the gentle, Sean the valiant, Sean the proved". With the late Oliver St. John Gogarty [q.v.], James Joyce, and others he was one of the group of young men at the beginning of the century who surrounded Griffith and who frequented the Old Martello Tower in Sandycove, immortalized by Joyce in the opening chapters of *Ulysses.*

He was a life-long friend, too, of George Russell ("A. E."), and was one of the group who met on Sunday afternoons with A. E. to discuss the arts, literature, politics, poetry, and world affairs.

In 1923 he founded the *Dublin Magazine.* Ireland was emerging from the strains of the civil war and his friends believed he was embarking on a hopeless task. But the *Dublin Magazine* continued in unbroken sequence up to this day, and virtually every writer of note in Ireland and outside contributed to its columns from time to time. Originally a monthly, it became a quarterly and circulated throughout the English-speaking world, its contents in prose and poetry standing at a high literary level. In 1939 when Dublin University conferred the honorary degree of Litt.D. on him, the Public Orator extended to Dr. Starkey "the homage due" to the most notable poet in Ireland since the death of Yeats. In 1957 he was awarded the Lady Gregory Medal, the highest award of the Irish Academy of Letters.

For more than half a century Dr. Starkey's imposing figure surmounted by a wide-brimmed hat could be seen leaning over the second-hand book carts on the Dublin quay, where for a few pence he secured such treasures as the first editions of Goldsmith, Sheridan or Gray, the first edition of an early Yeats, or a rare find, a presentation copy of *Religio Medici.* He had in his home a collection of more than 20,000 books, many of them rare first editions which he collected and preserved with loving care.

Starkey was born in Dublin in 1879. His father, a native of West Cork, was a chemist in Rathmines Road, Dublin. He is survived by his wife, formerly Estella Solomons, a gifted artist and an associate of the Royal Hibernian Academy.

March 26, 1958.

Wickham Steed, who died on January 13, 1956 at his home at Wootton-by-Woodstock, Oxfordshire, at the age of 84, was one of the ablest and at one time one of the most conspicuous men in European journalism. Nor was he inconspicuous physically. An impressive appearance given by his height was rendered the more distinguished by a pointed beard. He looked indeed as if he came of the age of chivalry and there was in fact not a little of the knight errant in his generous, emotional, and challenging personality.

From 1896 until 1913 he was one of the foreign correspondents to whom *The Times* owed the exceptional influence which it wielded in the domain of international affairs before the war of 1914. He next became head of the Foreign Department at Printing House Square, and became Editor of *The Times* during the first and scarcely less troubled years ushered in by a Peace Conference that brought little real peace to the world.

Henry Wickham Steed was born at Long Melford, Suffolk, on October 10, 1871. His early education at the old Grammar School of Sudbury, Suffolk, included a thorough grounding in English and Latin. Steed was intended for the Civil service, but failed the examination owing to a cycling accident. He entered the City office of Sir Cuthbert Quilter (M.P. for South-West Suffolk). There he caught more than a glimpse of City life and his bent for methodical study led him to master shorthand.

A turning point came in 1891 when he heard J. A. Spender lecture at Toynbee Hall on old-age pensions, upon which subject at Long Melford a curate, Frome Wilkinson, was a pioneer. With some knowledge of the question Steed sent a report of Spender's lecture to the *Pall Mall Gazette.* Appearance in print turned his mind towards journalism, and he formed the ambition, unusual in those days, to study economics and sociology at German and French universities. The by-products of this move were significant. Through Quilter, who was interested in Dalziel's news agency, he sent telegrams to the agency. In consequence his name was given by Davidson Dalziel to the then Berlin Correspondent of *The Times,* Valentine Chirol.

In the autumn of 1893 Steed left Berlin to study history at the Sorbonne. Early in 1895 an "interview" with Millerand on the resignation of the French President Casimir-Périer, which he contributed to the *Westminster Gazette,* brought from Joseph Pulitzer an invitation to act as Paris correspondent of the New York *World.* In this capacity Steed in one day "interviewed" seven of the leading French economic authorities, mono-metallist and bi-metallist. A singularly capacious and accurate memory enabled him to write out their statements without taking a note, a feat which so impressed Pulitzer that he sent Steed back to Berlin to make a similar report on the opinion of the German currency experts. While in Berlin Steed naturally resumed his acquaintance with Chirol, and was asked to call at Printing House Square, where he saw Moberly Bell and Donald Mackenzie Wallace, then head of the Foreign Department.

At Berlin in March 1896 Steed found Chirol on the eve of final departure from Berlin. George Saunders, of the *Morning Post*, had already been chosen to succeed him at the beginning of 1897. Since Chirol's assistant Earle, who was to fill the interregnum, fell seriously ill, Bell asked Steed to take responsibility for the Berlin correspondence till the end of the year, and thereafter consider an appointment in Rome. The outstanding incident of his work in Berlin was his detection of the authorship of an anonymous article in the *Hamburger Nachrichten* which unveiled the secret treaty of reinsurance that, until March 1890, had existed between Germany and Russia. The treaty had been concluded behind the backs of Germany's partners in the Triple Alliance. This was now revealed and, at the same time, the refusal of Bismarck's successor to renew it, which until then had been kept equally secret. Steed alone in Germany immediately attributed the disclosure to Bismarck.

At once Steed was recognized at Printing House Square as worthy of promotion and was appointed to succeed W. J. Stillman, then due to retire from his post as *The Times* correspondent at Rome. In 1902 he was transferred to Vienna. Four years' intense study passed before he felt himself at ease. He learned enough Hungarian to appreciate the fact that the Dual Monarchy could be understood only as a dynastic estate whose tenants were its nine or ten different races. Steed visited every part of the Dual Monarchy, and thus organized a prompt and accurate service of information. These years of labour put him in possession of data which he set out in a book entitled *The Hapsburg Monarchy*, published upon his return to England in the autumn of 1913.

At Marienbad in August 1908 King Edward VII (who made a point of ascertaining Steed's views upon a number of international questions) questioned him regarding the outlook in Austria-Hungary. Steed told him that public opinion was being prepared for an early annexation of Bosnia-Herzegovina. The King, to whom the Emperor Francis Joseph had given no hint that such a step was contemplated, thought it impossible; but the annexation of Bosnia-Herzegovina occurred in October of the same year.

Although Steed appreciated the fateful importance of the Serbian problem for the Austro-Hungarian monarchy it was the annexation of Bosnia-Herzegovina, and the European crisis which it brought on, that convinced him that the monarchy was doomed. The salient point of his analysis was his certainty that after the Bosnian *coup* Russia had determined never again to suffer herself or any Slav nation to be humiliated. The "alliance system", as he understood it, forced the conclusion that German and Austro-German policy was such as to leave Britain and France with no alternative but to support Russia. Britain could not afford to stand aside, for, if she did so, France would be crushed and Russia neutralized. Germany would then have no difficulty in attacking Britain at her leisure.

Steed left Vienna in July 1913 and, after a brief spell at Constantinople, he returned to London and Northcliffe soon placed him at the head of the Foreign Department, in the place of Sir Valentine Chirol, who had retired. In so doing he emphasized his belief that Steed understood German policy, and would not be susceptible to the German propaganda which had in recent years gained considerable influence over the British Government and sections of the press. In January 1914 Lloyd George denounced expenditure on the Navy as an "overwhelming extravagance", and affirmed that our relations with Germany were "infinitely more friendly than they had been". Northcliffe and Steed believed the opposite, and held fast to the conviction that Berlin was striving to drive a wedge between England and France.

The international outlook improved until June 28, the day of the assassination of the Austro-Hungarian heir apparent at Sarajevo. Obviously, Steed said, the crime might be used by the military party in Vienna as a pretext for an attack on Serbia, which might well lead immediately to the European war that many observers on the Continent, but few at home, had long feared and prophesied. By July 21 he was so strongly urged by the Austro-Hungarian Ambassador in London to advocate the "localization" of an Austro-Serbian conflict that he concluded that war could be averted only by an immediate announcement by the British Government that it would side with France and Russia against any attempt to transform the Sarajevo tragedy into an attack on the peace of Europe. On July 22, the day before the presentation of the Austro-Hungarian ultimatum to Serbia, *The Times* warned Austria-Hungary and Germany that a European conflict let loose by an attack on Serbia would end only with disaster to both the Central Powers. This leading article was the first of a series which awakened the country to a sense of its imminent danger. Upon Steed, as head of the Foreign Department under Geoffrey Dawson, fell the main responsibility for the paper's policy between June 22 and the outbreak of war on August 4. Throughout the whole period of his editorship Dawson was wont to praise his colleague's deep sense of loyalty.

Early in 1918 Northcliffe accepted the position of Director of Propaganda in enemy countries—on condition that he should lay down the policy which propaganda would serve. Northcliffe instructed Steed to define allied policy as the basis for his propaganda, and sent him to carry it out as the head of a mission on the Italian front. His mission greatly helped to demoralize the Austro-Hungarian front in Italy.

It was at the Paris Peace Conference in January 1919 that personal differences between Dawson and Northcliffe ended in the Editor's resignation. The editorship was then offered to Steed. Steed's policy, acceptable to Northcliffe, was (1) to maintain the independence of *The Times* towards all parties, politicians, and Governments; (2) to work immediately for a settlement of the Irish question both for its own sake and because there could be no stability in Anglo-American relations unless it were settled; (3) to support the just claims of France and the other allies so that admonitions might be addressed to them without offence when it should be necessary in the interests of Great Britain and of Europe; (4) to advocate and support constructively and critically the League of Nations as the chief hope of avoiding future war; and (5) to deal fairly with Labour demands and movements in Great Britain, while resisting any "Bolshevist" tendency.

In one important feature of Steed's policy Northcliffe had no direct share, though it was known that Northcliffe would approve. This was the campaign of *The Times* for the termination of the Anglo-Japanese Alliance, a campaign inspired solely by the facts of the international situation as Steed ascertained them in Canada and the United States during the summer of 1921, when Northcliffe was in Australia. Steed's work at the Washington Conference of 1921-22 formed part of this policy.

In 1922, under pressure from Northcliffe, he attended the Conference at Genoa. Steed's telegram regarding Lloyd George's threats to put an end to the Anglo-French Entente, unless France would come into line with British policy, was contradicted. It was as accurate in substance as it was inconvenient. The incident, however, gravely damaged Steed's reputation for detachment. He had, in fact, not seen himself as a neutral reporter but as a watchdog of British interests which still, he believed, demanded the maintenance of friendly relations with France. *The Times* was an important influence in getting for the Bonar Law Administration a working majority of 78 at the General Election of 1922 and in the last 3½ months of his editorial work Steed wrote nearly 100 leading articles in addition to performing his other duties. His editorship came to an end on November 30, 1922, a little more than a month after *The Times* was taken over by the new proprietorship of Major (as he then was) J. J. Astor [later Lord Astor of Hever*] and John Walter*.

During his editorship of *The Times* and after it Steed lived in a large flat in Holland Park, where his Saturday afternoon entertainments of persons of many countries who were distinguished in politics, diplomacy, literature, and journalism became a feature in the cosmopolitan life of London. His hostess on these occasions was Madame Rose, a woman truly remarkable in virtue of her knowledge of European affairs, who, many years older than himself, had helped in his early days in Rome and continued throughout their long intellectual association to exert a considerable influence upon his outlook. In 1939 he married Violet Sybille, daughter of the late James Francis Mason and of the late Lady Evelyn Mason.

On leaving *The Times* Steed decided to seek another platform and bought the *Review of*

Reviews, which he edited from 1923 to 1930. He also wrote his autobiography, *Through Thirty Years* (2 vols., 1924), and lectured in England, France, Germany, and the United States, working unceasingly upon the problems of international peace. He attended regularly the Assemblies of the League of Nations. As early as 1926 he predicted the impossibility of avoiding a Second World War unless British policy should be firm in opposition to German designs. He expounded in the autumn of 1933 the meaning of Hitlerism. He consistently fought the British policy of "appeasement" and set forth his belief that no mere non-war or any other negative view of peace could hold the minds of men. His *Vital Peace* (1936) was a firm repudiation of neutralism.

Meanwhile his services as a broadcaster were in demand, and it was with considerable satisfaction that from 1938 onwards he attained the position of a chief broadcaster on world affairs in the Empire and Overseas Services of the B.B.C., and thus wielded considerable personal influence upon opinion throughout the British Commonwealth during the war. In this work his gift for forecasting how things would be likely to turn stood him in good stead.

He remained a frequent contributor to the correspondence columns of *The Times* and was, until lately, a frequent reviewer in the *Literary Supplement.* Steed, a lifelong lover of liberty, had no ambition outside journalism, in which he found the fullest freedom of expression. He enjoyed the position of lecturer at King's College, London, on Central European history from 1925 to 1938. He declined titles and decorations, but was happy to accept doctorates from Strasbourg and Cluj universities.

Though primarily a commentator, as a good journalist must be, Steed was also a man of vision and of strong convictions. These characteristics were of the spirit and the method that earned for the paper under Barnes and Delane its dominant position. Editorship, though it imposed new responsibilities on him, some of which were perhaps not too congenial, for they were not what he had been accustomed to as a foreign correspondent, brought out certain aspects of his mind which those who had known him before might not have suspected. It was a common but completely erroneous belief in London society that he was an Englishman so continentalized as to know little or care little for his own country.

Underneath the layers of culture, French, Italian, Viennese, which had set their mark on him, widened his mind, enriched his outlook and often informed his strong literary and artistic tastes, was the Englishman, Protestant, and patriot.

January 14, 1956.

Erwin Stein, musician and teacher, died in London on July 19, 1958 at the age of 72.

He was born in Vienna on November 7, 1885, and educated at the Franz-Joseph Gymnasium and at Vienna University. While studying at the university he became a private pupil of Arnold Schönberg [q.v.], fortunately at the very time when Schönberg was breaking away altogether from romantic principle of tonality; later Stein was to elucidate this crisis in modern music, in an essay "New Formal Principles", which appeared in 1924 and has remained a monograph of high importance to students of contemporary techniques.

In 1910 Stein's conventional apprenticeship ended, and he began his career as *répetiteur* and conductor in various German opera houses, including Danzig and Darmstadt, and also for a period at Strasbourg. He returned to Vienna in 1919 and became closely associated with Schönberg and his circle, assisting Berg and Webern in the rehearsal and direction of concerts organized by Schönberg's *Verein für musikalische Privataufführungen.* In 1924 he joined the staff of Universal Edition in Vienna as artistic adviser, and in the same year began his editorship of the progressive musical magazine *Pult und Taktstock.* Between this time and 1938, when he left Austria, Stein was an active champion of contemporary music, as writer, teacher, lecturer, and conductor of broadcast and public concerts, and of a choral society.

When Hitler overran Austria, Stein and his family went to England, and he joined the editorial staff of Boosey and Hawkes, where he remained until his retirement. Here his championship and special knowledge of modern music brought him into touch with Benjamin Britten [Lord Britten, d. 1976], whose qualities Stein was quick to appreciate. He was responsible for the piano scores of *Albert Herring* and *Billy Budd,* and to him Britten dedicated *The Rape of Lucretia.* He also prepared new vocal scores of several operas by Mozart for an English edition. It may be mentioned here that Stein had made the piano score of Berg's unfinished opera *Lulu*, and had been responsible for reduced orchestral versions of Mahler's second symphony and Schönberg's *Gurrelieder* which have proved their value in public performance.

After his arrival in England Stein's energies were directed less towards conducting and more toward teaching and literary and editorial work, though he directed a memorable performance of *Pierrot Lunaire* in the Aeolian Hall some years ago, and his advice was constantly sought by musicians who were preparing modern works for performance. A volume of essays, chiefly on Mahler, Schönberg and Britten, was published under the title *Orpheus in New Guises,* and among others may be mentioned a series on the Vienna Opera published in *Opera* magazine. Stein had recently completed a German translation of Schönberg's *Structural Functions of Harmony,* and at the time of his death was working on a book entitled *Form and Performance,* several chapters of which were finished. His last completed task was an edition of Schönberg's letters.

It was as a sensitive and profound musician, a lucid and articulate teacher and coach, and a direct link with the mind and work shop of Schönberg that Stein was unusually valuable to London's musical life in his last years. Schönberg himself paid warm tribute to Stein's "acute and unsparing criticism" in the preface to his *Harmonielehre.*

Stein leaves a widow and their daughter, the Countess of Harewood [later Mrs. J. Thorpe].

July 22, 1958.

Cardinal Stepinac, Archbishop of Zagreb, who was imprisoned in 1946 by the Yugoslav Government and had been under close surveillance since his release in 1951, died on February 10, 1960. He was 62.

Aloizije Stepinac came of a Croat peasant family of Krašić, and was born in 1897. Having been well educated, he was an Austro-Hungarian officer in the War of 1914-18. He was taken prisoner, volunteered for the Serbian Army, and fought on the Salonika front. In 1924 he was ordained and in 1934, despite his youth, he became Bishop-Coadjutor of Zagreb, succeeding to the Archbishopric on the death of Mgr. Bauer in 1937. More universally respected than anyone in Croatia, except perhaps Dr. Maček, he was also, as an ex-volunteer, well viewed at Belgrade; though the experience of government from Belgrade intensified his Croat patriotism and western sympathies.

When the Germans set up Pavelić's state of Croatia in 1941, Mgr. Stepinac obeyed his Church's tradition of coming to terms with any Government which allows her to function. He stayed at his post, bade his flock quietly accept the situation, and publicly invoked God's guidance for the new régime. Whatever sympathy he may have had for that régime rapidly evaporated. In December 1941 he published the Croat Bishops' declaration against forced conversions of Orthodox Serbs, insisting that conversions must be voluntary and wholly withdrawn from the lay authorities' control. In 1943 he protested vigorously to the Italian Minister against Italian atrocities in the south; and earned abuse from the Croat Government by denouncing mass punishments for sabotage. Meanwhile he was constantly engaged in relieving the sufferings of Jews, Serbs, Slovenes, and any other victims of persecution, and saved many lives.

Near the end of the war, when the retreating Germans were being chased out of the country, Archbishop Stepinac, in an episcopal declaration in March 1945, condemned the communist trials of "war criminals", saying that they were being used for liquidating Catholic priests and intellectuals. He was arrested himself in May. Released the following month, he immediately called on Marshal Tito, and thereafter tried unsuccessfully to initiate discussions with the Government on future relations between the Church and the communist state.

In September 1945 he and his fellow-bishops issued a pastoral letter dwelling on the many bishops, priests, and religious killed or imprisoned; on the suppression of religious teaching and of the Catholic schools and press; on the official press's constant attacks on the clergy, to which no public reply was possible; on the confiscation of the Church's property, on which her charitable activities depended; and on other measures of persecution. The letter was not published in Yugoslavia, but was fiercely attacked in the Yugoslav Press. A pause followed, but the Archbishop was not to be brought to heel. In September 1946 he was put on trial, and was sentenced to 16 years' hard labour and five more years' loss of civil and political rights.

He was removed to Lepoglava prison, where he was confined until his conditional release in December 1951, after serving a few weeks over five years of his sentence. On his release, restricted to the life of an ordinary parish priest in his native village, he immediately challenged the régime and told foreign journalists: "I am the legitimate Archbishop, not the former archbishop [as the Government statement at the time described him]. I can fulfil my duties here or there [in gaol] or in Zagreb. I did not seek my release because I do not feel guilty. I shall never leave the country except by compulsion and will remain here until the Holy Father deems otherwise".

Then, as on other occasions—until the Government prohibited him from receiving foreign correspondents and visitors and placed a permanent police watch on the parish house, where he lived in two tiny rooms with a parish priest his only companion—he staunchly repeated the conditions for peace between the Church and State. These were recognition of religious marriage, church schools, and the freedom of the religious press.

Even in Krašić he was permitted to function only as an ordinary priest, but not as the celebrant at Mass. In the efforts to isolate him the village church itself was placed out of bounds except to actual resident members of the parish. In this lonely existence not even members of his family were permitted to visit him without official permits.

After he was named cardinal during the year following his release—a move regarded by the communist régime in Belgrade as a calculated provocation—he was offered permission to leave for Rome to receive his cardinal's hat at the hands of the Pope. But since it was intimated also that he would not be allowed to return he rejected the offer and in due course the hat was sent to him.

In December 1952 the Yugoslav Government broke off relations with the Vatican, accusing it of meddling in Yugoslav internal affairs, and closed down the papal nunciature in Belgrade. Since then one or two abortive minor gestures of a conciliatory nature have been made on the Yugoslav Government side. The conflict of Church and State has largely subsided into a passive *modus vivendi*, but the Cardinal at Krašić remained, an unyielding prisoner to the end.

February 11, 1960.

Sir Louis Sterling, the industrialist and philanthropist, died in hospital in London on June 2, 1958. He was 79.

Louis Saul Sterling was born, with no great worldly advantages, in New York on May 16, 1879. He sold newspapers on the streets of his native city as a boy and as a young man he went to Britain in a cattle boat with about £6 in his pocket.

On arrival in London he spent some of his small capital on celebration, and as a result spent the night in Vine Street police station. He recalled the incident when he was knighted by King George VI [q.v.] in 1937. Asked where he spent his first night in England, Sterling replied: "I was a guest of your grandfather, sir".

He took a job in the gramophone trade, soon to develop into a great industry, and rose to become managing director of the Columbia Gramophone Company and later of Electrical and Musical Industries, controlling H.M.V., Columbia, Marconiphone, and other companies.

A rich man, he was a princely giver and by 1956 his gifts over 30 years totalled £1,500,000. To celebrate his fiftieth birthday he divided £100,000 among the members of the staff of his company, explaining that he had intended to make provision for such a gift in his will but had decided on reflection that it would be better for the beneficiaries to have the money sooner rather than later.

On his seventy-fifth birthday he sent cheques to a total value of £200,000 to charities. Among the organizations which benefited were the British Empire Cancer Campaign, the R.A.F. Benevolent Fund, the National Playing Fields Association, the N.S.P.C.C., and various hospitals, children's homes, and theatrical charities.

In 1945 the Principal of London University announced Sterling's wish that the important collection of rare books he had formed should go to the university. In October 1956 Queen Elizabeth and the Queen Mother, Chancellor of the university, opened a special room built to house the library. It is a splendid one, for Sterling was a collector who observed the simple if not very easily imitable principle—namely, to buy the best whenever he saw it. There is not a department of English book-collecting of which his library cannot show some brilliant example. Early printing and Kelmscotts, the Romantics and the Augustans, Rowlandson and Alken, Shakespeare and the moderns, a manuscript of Mozart, Powys, or Byron: all were fish to Sterling's net.

While primarily a collection of notable books in English, a few works in other languages but by English authors are included, such as the first edition of *De Proprietatibus Rerum*, the great medieval encyclopaedia printed at Cologne in 1472.

There are important first editions of Ben Jonson, Milton, Sir Thomas Browne, Herrick, Evelyn, and Dryden, and among eighteenth-century books first editions of *Gulliver's Travels, Robinson Crusoe,* and *The Vicar of Wakefield.*

The honorary degree of D.Litt. was conferred on Sterling by London University.

He married in 1919 Cissy, daughter of Isaac Stevens.

June 3, 1958.

Lieutenant-Colonel J. Stevenson-Hamilton, to whom more than to anyone else South Africa owes the preservation of the Kruger National Park and its rich animal life, died at White River, Eastern Transvaal, on December 10, 1957. He was 90.

James Stevenson-Hamilton was born in Dublin in 1867, the son of the late Colonel James Stevenson and Eliza, daughter of James Hamilton, of Fairholm. His early years were passed in Scotland, and he was educated at Rugby and Sandhurst. He succeeded to the estates of Fairholm and Kirkton in 1888, and then assumed the name of Hamilton. In the same year he was commissioned in the 6th (Inniskilling) Dragoons, went to South Africa and served in the Zululand rebellion. His love of natural history had begun in boyhood, but it was greatly stimulated by his first sight of the African game animals, and by his friendship with Captain (afterwards Field-Marshal) Allenby, who was a keen zoologist.

After a few years his regiment was recalled to England, but Stevenson-Hamilton was strongly attracted towards Africa and returned there in 1898 as a member of Major A. St. Hill Gibbons's Cape to Cairo expedition, exploring and mapping the Congo-Zambezi watershed in that year and the following. Later he served in the South African War, obtaining the Queen's Medal with five clasps and the King's with two, and being mentioned in dispatches. In 1902 he was appointed Warden of the Transvaal Game Reserves—then just re-proclaimed—a post which he held until 1926, though during the First World War he rejoined his old regiment and served in Gallipoli, Egypt and the Sudan.

To Stevenson-Hamilton was chiefly due the success of the game reserves, their protection against the encroachment of various competing interests, and their final conversion in 1926 into the Kruger National Park, with himself still in charge. As Warden of the Kruger Park he retained control until his retirement in 1946, and it was a fitting tribute to his unrivalled position and knowledge that he should have had the privilege of showing the park to the King and Queen in 1947. Stevenson-Hamilton was a lucid writer, and published several books, the first of which, *Animal Life in Africa,* appeared in 1912. *The Low Veld,* 1929, showed the author's intimate knowledge of native life, as well as of natural history, and *South African Eden,* 1937, was a description and history of the Kruger National Park. *Wild Life in South Africa,* which appeared in 1947, was an excellent popular general account of the South African fauna.

In 1954 Chatto and Windus published *The Barotseland Journal of James Stevenson-Hamilton, 1898-99;* edited by J. P. R. Wallis, it was an honest and unpretentious diary which supplemented the records of St. Hill Gibbons's expedition of 1898-99.

A simple and modest man, he was nevertheless a hard fighter on behalf of those things which he valued.

Stevenson-Hamilton was an honorary LL.D. of Witwatersrand and Cape Town Universities. He was a corresponding member of the Zoological Society of London and received its silver medal as well as that of the Society for the Preservation of the Fauna of the Empire.

In 1930 he married Hilda, daughter of R. V. Cholmondeley, and they had a son and two daughters.

His African name was Skukuza—"He who came"—and this has now been formally inscribed on the map of Africa as the name of what was previously Sabi Bridge, the administrative centre of the Kruger Park.

December 12, 1957.

Sir Malcolm Stewart, BT., O.B.E., D.L., J.P., whose highly successful career in business may be said to have been largely due to a lively social conscience, died on February 27, 1951 at his home in Bedfordshire at the age of 78.

Percy Malcolm Stewart was the son of Sir Halley Stewart, sometime Liberal M.P. for Greenock, and was born in 1872. He was educated at the Royal High School, Edinburgh, and King's School, Rochester, and entered on his career in business at a very early age. Before he was 20 he took charge of the old-established barge building and lighterage business of James Fox and Co., Limehouse, and though many other interests soon claimed him, he retained a love of the tidal waters of the Thames for the remainder of his life, becoming in due course a foundation member of the Thames Barge Sailing Club. He was, too, an early and munificent patron of the National Maritime Museum, presenting to it a fine collection of Nelson relics.

His success in the lighterage business led to an invitation to join Stewart Brothers and Spencer, oil seed crushers, of Rochester and London, in which later he became a partner and on the sale of the firm to the British Oil and Cake Mills Limited in 1899 he joined his father in acquiring an interest in B. J. Forder and Son, brick, cement, and whiting manufacturers, and took over the management of the firm. When in 1912 Forders sold their cement, lime, and whiting assets to British Portland Cement, Stewart became a managing director of the latter firm. He had helped to form in 1906 the Inland Cement Manufacturers Alliance and was its chairman from 1910 to 1918, when he established the Cement Makers' Federation. He was the first chairman of the federation and later its president.

In 1919 he successfully worked for the formation of the National Joint Industrial Council for the cement industry and in the same year became chairman of Associated Portland Cement and British Portland Cement. Elected chairman of both companies in 1924 he inaugurated and carried through an extensive programme of reorganization, which not only benefited shareholders and employees but proved of signal service to the country during the Second World War. He had retained his interest in Forders, and when that company absorbed the London Brick Company and other brick manufacturing businesses he was elected chairman of what soon became the largest brick manufacturers in the world. In all his enterprises he acted in the conviction that fair wages must come first and that good wages and a share in profits should go hand in hand with good dividends. Not only wages, but all other conditions of the workpeople came within his purview, and the housing estate at Stewartby is a monument to his enlightened policy.

He was thus an ideal choice for the position of Commissioner for the Special Areas in England and Wales in 1934, and, having stipulated that the post must be unpaid, he took on a difficult and thankless task and spent energy and effort in abundance. His reports were models of industry and reason, and had he been given more power and more support many of the worst consequences of the depression could have been avoided. After two years of effort he resigned in order to resume his part in the industry he had done so much to build up, and his services to the country were recognized by the conferment of a baronetcy upon him in the New Year Honours of 1937. His own gifts and endowments for worthy objects were large but never indiscriminate. He presented to Peterborough a building for use as a museum and art gallery; to Mansfield House University Settlement £10,000 towards the rebuilding fund; to Ruskin College six open entrance scholarships; and he gave £35,000 to endow a cooperative farm for unemployed workers.

He was twice married, first, in 1896, to Cordelia, daughter of the late Sir Joseph Compton-Rickett. She died in 1906, having borne him a son and a daughter. He married secondly in 1907 Beatrice Maud, second daughter of the late J. B. Pratt. There were also a son and a daughter of the second marriage. The baronetcy descends on his elder son R. C. Stewart, who was born in 1903 and married Cynthia, daughter of Harold Farmiloe.

February 28, 1951.

Katharine Stewart-Murray—See **Atholl.**

Lieutenant-Colonel W. F. Stirling, D.S.O., M.C., whose wide experience of Middle Eastern affairs was of service to his country in two wars, died in Tangier at the age of 78 on February 22, 1958.

Michael Stirling, as he was called, was a regular soldier, but he was anything but orthodox. He turned aside from soldiering in India to become an Arab expert. In Arabia he was chief staff officer to Lawrence; in the Balkans he was adviser to King Zog; he plotted revolution in Liberia, tried his hand at fruit-farming in British Columbia, was a shop walker in the depression of the 1930s. His respect for official policy was uncertain, his knack of turning up at the centre of trouble uncanny. His life was active and adventurous enough without the imaginary machinations which his political enemies in the Middle East, of whom there were many, attributed to him. After an attempt to assassinate him had failed, an Arab was heard to remark: "Did they think they could kill Colonel Stirling with only six shots?"

Walter Francis Stirling was the son of Captain Francis Stirling, R.N., and was born at Portsmouth on January 31, 1880. He never knew his father, for the latter was in command of the training ship Atlanta when she left Bermuda on a trial voyage in January 1880, and was never heard of again. Educated at Kelly College and the Royal Military College Sandhurst, he was gazetted to the Royal Dublin Fusiliers in 1899 and received his first step in rank before the year was out.

After a short period with his regiment, which formed part of the Natal Field Force, he transferred to the Mounted Infantry and took part in the relief of Ladysmith. He was present at the action at Laing's Nek and served in the later operations in the Orange River Colony and in the Transvaal, for which he was mentioned in dispatches. He was awarded the D.S.O. for skill and gallantry in action at Kafferspruit in 1901. In 1906 he joined the Egyptian Army and for some six years commanded the Arab Battalion at Kassala. He thus became a fluent Arabic scholar, knowledge which was later to stand him in good stead. He retired in 1912 and became secretary of the Khedival Sporting Club.

On the outbreak of war in 1914, however, he joined the Royal Flying Corps as an observer, but finding that the 1st battalion of his old regiment was in the force allotted to the invasion of Gallipoli, he transferred to it and was appointed second-in-command. After the evacuation, in which his conduct received mention in dispatches, he was appointed G.S.O.2 Intelligence at G.H.Q., Egypt, and later held a similar appointment with the Lowland Division. Characterized by T. E. Lawrence as "Stirling the imperturbable", he was often a steadying influence on that erratic genius, especially during the early raids in the Sinai neighbourhood, and his help proved invaluable during the great advance to Damascus. His services were recognized by the award of the M.C. and a bar to his D.S.O.

His intimate knowledge of conditions in the Middle East, acquired by long residence and acute observation, was recognized by the authorities by his appointment first as acting Governor of Sinai and later as Governor of the Jaffa district. He had long since won the confidence of the Arabs and he set himself to win the confidence of the Jews in Palestine as well. He was so far successful that during his governorship his house was a recognized and genial meeting-place for both races. He remained Governor of the Jaffa district until 1923, when he went to Albania as adviser to Ahmed Bey Sogu (later King Zog I*). In this capacity he had much to do with the foundation of the force of gendarmerie.

In 1939, though verging on 60, he again volunteered for service and for a time worked in the telephone censorship, but his experience of the Levant was too valuable to be wasted and after the fall of France and the invasion of the Balkans an ugly situation arose requiring the services of the best available men. Stirling was therefore sent out by the War Office on intelligence duties and was later a most valuable member of the Spears* Mission. For a time he held the post of political officer in northern Syria and after the end of hostilities he decided to remain in the country, where he had made many friends.

He settled in Damascus, where he engaged in business and became correspondent of *The Times*. In 1949 three armed men broke into his house when he was dining, and attempted to assassinate him. His cook and night watchman died of the wounds they received, and Stirling was himself severely wounded. The crime was assumed to have a political motive, but the criminals were never traced.

Stirling then left Damascus for Egypt. He was expelled by the Egyptian Government in 1951 and had since then lived in Tangier. In 1953 he published his reminiscences in a volume aptly called *Safety Last*.

He married in 1920 Eileen Mary May, elder daughter of Lieutenant-Colonel Mackenzie-Edwards, by whom he had a daughter, Elspeth Lettys, who married Major J. A. Crankshaw, 11th Hussars.

February 24, 1958.

Richard Stokes, Labour member of Parliament for Ipswich since 1938 and a former Minister of Works and Lord Privy Seal, died on August 3, 1957 at his home in London at the age of 60. He had been injured a fortnight earlier when his car overturned. His injuries forced him to rest and caused clotting in his veins.

The Right Hon. Richard Rapier Stokes, M.C., was born on January 27, 1897, the second son of Philip Folliott Stokes, a barrister, and of Mary Fenwick Rapier. His family was Roman Catholic and he went to school at Downside, where he was prominent on cricket and football fields. In those years Downside, under the headmastership of Trafford, was for the first time introducing the prefectorial system and Stokes was selected as the first head boy under the new dispensation.

During the First World War he served in the Royal Artillery on the Western Front, winning the M.C. and bar and the French Croix de Guerre and being gazetted major at the age of 20. The inventor of the mortar was his uncle and the artillery was his natural military destination. Yet for all the gallantry of his record he returned from the front with a deep horror and hatred of war.

He then went up to Trinity College, Cambridge, where he obtained a Rugby Blue, and on going down went into the family business of Ransome and Rapier, of which he became managing director at the age of 30. When in the 1930s the National Government made its first suggestions of rearmament Stokes made to it the offer that all his firm's rearmament work should be done at cost price. This offer was rejected, and it was shortly after its rejection that Stokes joined the Labour Party.

At the general election of 1935 he contested Central Glasgow but was defeated. But in 1938 he won a notable by-election victory over [Sir] Henry Willink* at Ipswich and held the seat for his party for the rest of his life. His political opinions were always of a highly personal nature and he derived his Socialism from Henry George rather than from either Marx or Keir Hardie.

During the Second World War he was a vigorous critic of Churchill and the Government for its alleged inefficiency in the supply of tanks. When Labour came into power in 1945 he was at first considered by Attlee* too erratic and independent for political office, and throughout the first post-war Parliament he had to remain a back-bencher. While in general supporting the Government, he joined issued with them over their Palestinian policy, where he was even more pro-Arab than Ernest Bevin [q.v.], and over the acceptance of the American loan.

In 1950 the Socialists were returned again to power but with a greatly reduced majority. Feeling the need of strengthening his team and anxious perhaps to make a bid for Roman Catholic support for his party, Attlee gave Stokes office first as Minister of Works and afterwards as Lord Privy Seal and Minister of Materials. The latter posts were key offices in the Cabinet. Aneurin Bevan and Harold Wilson had resigned from the Cabinet on the ground (among others) that it was quite impossible to fulfil the projected armament programme. It was Stokes's special task to prove them wrong. As a business man, even if an unorthodox business man, he was unique as a member of a Socialist Cabinet. He entered upon his task in a spirit of good humoured efficiency and won for himself much good will and popularity, but the Government fell before he had had time to show whether he would have been successful or not. He was also during these months sent out to negotiate with the Persians about Abadan oil.

When the Conservatives returned to power in 1951 Stokes, although at first the Opposition spokesman on defence, did not attend the House very regularly or play a very prominent part there. When in 1956 he failed to secure re-election to the Labour "shadow cabinet" it was obvious that his parliamentary position was slipping. A few months before he died he joined with Sir Hartley Shawcross in criticizing further projects of nationalization and came under severe criticism both in his constituency and elsewhere in the party.

Stokes, in spite of his brief period on the Front Bench, was always, as he himself said, "a back-bencher at heart". He was essentially a hard-hitting good-humoured critic, fearing none and sparing none. He did not hesitate to tackle even Sir Winston Churchill* at the height of his power and at the height of the war. He was as completely without malice as he was without fear, and he always kept without difficulty the friendship of those from whom he most deeply differed. He was always, for instance, a popular member of White's Club, an unusual haunt for a Socialist politician. He could not feel very happy under party discipline. He enjoyed the House as long as he could criticize the Government there as an irresponsible back-bencher, and he enjoyed being a Minister. He said of himself as Minister of Works that he was "as happy as a sandboy". But he found insufferably tedious the restrained criticism of a member of the Opposition "shadow cabinet", compelled to see to it that his criticisms tallied with those of his colleagues and with a party line, and in his last years his interests more and more turned back from politics to business.

Without any ostentatious piety, Stokes was always a deeply religious man. It was said that in youth he had seriously contemplated trying his vocation in a monastery. It was to the Papal encyclicals that he turned for the inspiration of his policies, whether in politics or in industry, though his interpretation of these encyclicals was often characteristically idiosyncratic; and he would have been the first to ascribe to his religion the extraordinary generosity of his personal relations.

August 5, 1957.

William Stone, of Albany, W.1, sometimes called "The Squire of Piccadilly", died on October 25, 1958 at the age of 101.

William Stone was born at Bath on January 14, 1857, his father being a successful solicitor of that city and its town clerk. He was educated at Clifton and obtained a science scholarship to Peterhouse, Cambridge. There, in spite of his attention to his scientific studies, he seems to have found time for all the other activities enjoyed by undergraduates of the day. He considered these very important and none more so than the doings of the "Volunteers". After a course at Wellington Barracks (a memory he cherished) he was made the Captain of the Cambridge University Rifle Corps. He kept, as apparently most undergraduates did in those days, his own wine cellar and entertained lavishly in his rooms. When he came down in 1878 with first-class honours in the Natural Sciences Tripos, he also brought the remnant of his cellar, 20 dozen bottles of wine.

He next set about establishing himself in London society. To this end he joined several learned societies and also seven London clubs. He always advocated this procedure as much more worth-while for young men coming down from the university than the more frivolous application of their time and money then usual. He became a member, and on his one hundredth birthday was the senior member, of the Linnean Society, the Chemical Society, the Royal Geographical Society, and the Zoological Society. He also belonged to the Royal Institution, and these memberships brought him into contact with the leading scientists of the day, many of whom he knew well personally. He was also the senior member of the Athenaeum, the Oxford and Cambridge Club, the United Universities' Club, the Reform Club, the Garrick, Hurlingham, and Bachelors' Club.

On attaining his majority he entered into a substantial patrimony and this enabled him to travel, an occupation for which he had a great passion. In 1882 he was in Egypt and travelled up to Khartoum on a donkey, taking a fortnight for the journey. He paid many visits to India in the early days of the railways there and was successful as a big game hunter. He went to China and, since a favourite hobby was the collection of butterflies, was able to secure many rare specimens while inspecting the

Great Wall.

He ventured into politics in 1885 and contested unsuccessfully the Northern Division of Wiltshire. This enterprise greatly extended his circle of friends, but he never repeated it. In 1893 he purchased his first set of chambers in Albany—D.6—and there he received many visits from Cecil Rhodes, who interested him both romantically and financially in his projects for South Africa. It was in Albany during this period that he led the well-to-do, care-free bachelor existence of a "man-about-town".

He took a great interest in the stage and it was his boast that he had not missed a first night for 40 years. An incident which he was fond of recalling occurred in 1896. His friend Sir Alfred Welby, then commanding The Greys, was ordered to be present at the Coronation of the Tsar Nicholas II and invited Willie Stone to accompany him. His memory of those times was prodigious and the stories of his more frivolous life, in consequence, very entertaining.

He had, however, more serious pursuits, and of these Albany absorbed much of his attention. He was elected by the proprietors as a trustee in 1895 and became chairman of the trustees in 1909, a position he held till 1941. With a group of the younger proprietors he succeeded in rescuing Albany from almost certain disaster at the turn of the century. He acquired other and larger sets of chambers for his own occupation and also, as he so often insisted, to prevent any of the property being acquired by less desirable owners who might put their own profit before the interests of Albany.

He finally settled in the chambers A.1, which had once housed Sir Beerbohm Tree and Sir Squire Bancroft, to become the oldest member of yet another historical institution, enjoying his 100th birthday there, in full possession of his faculties, a charming survival from a vanished age.

October 27, 1958.

Walter E. Stoneman, M.B.E., the portrait photographer, died on May 14, 1958 at the age of 82.

Except to a few people the name of Walter Stoneman is concealed in, rather than associated with, the reference collection of photographs as the National Portrait Gallery. As may not be generally known, besides the paintings, drawings, engravings, and sculptures of great figures of the past which are normally on view, the gallery has a photographic record of "distinguished contemporaries" who may or may not be judged to be of National Portrait Gallery rank in the purgatorial interval after their death. Since willingness or financial ability to be drawn or painted is often in inverse ratio to merit, the historical value of such a record is obvious.

All the photographs in the collection were taken in the studios of J. Russell and Sons, Baker Street, and most of them were the work of Stoneman, who was chairman of the firm. It was he who suggested the scheme to the Trustees of the gallery and worked it out with James Milner, then director, and he also personally superintended the compilation of the record.

Stoneman was a man of Devon, youngest son of the late E. W. Stoneman, of Plymouth, and was born on April 6, 1876. He was educated at Plymouth College, and devoted practically the whole of his life to portrait photography and lecturing on that subject. His only recorded recreation was "studying human nature". At the time of his death he had photographed over 6,000 celebrities of all kinds and was known as the "Man's Photographer", from his reluctance to photograph women.

On this point Stoneman, who was a stoutish, chin-bearded man with a twinkle behind his spectacles, asserted that he was no misogynist, being happily married, with children. He had nothing against women personally, only he had no wish to photograph them. Beauty in woman, he said, was exceptional. Women were charming, they had grace, they might take you in with their charm, they might "get over" sex appeal, but they were not beautiful—by which he meant that their faces, as they insisted on having them photographed, lacked character.

He practised what he preached, with the exception of a few photographs of Queen Mary [q.v.] and other members of the Royal Family.

The camera he used was a massive wooden apparatus, operated by a bulb—"as old as I am", he once said.

Five monarchs had sat for him and he had taken something like nine Prime Ministers, 12 Lord Chancellors, 80 admirals, 100 generals, archbishops and bishops, authors, scientists, and every other type of famous man. Naval men, in his opinion, had the finest type of face, and generals were the easiest men to photograph, particularly if they were photographed in full uniform. "They are usually so anxious that their uniforms should photograph well that they forget to be self-conscious about their faces", he said.

Stoneman, who was made M.B.E. in 1948, was a Fellow of the Photographic Society and the Royal Geographical Society.

May 17, 1958.

Adrian Stoop, the international Rugby football player, died on November 27, 1957 at his home at Hartley Wintney, aged 74. He was not only one of the great but also one of the key players in Rugby football and his influence lasted much longer than his first-class playing career.

Adrian Dura Stoop was the son of F. C. Stoop, of Byfleet. He was educated at Rugby School and University College, Oxford. In 1908 he was called to the Bar by the Inner Temple. During the 1914-18 War he served with the 5th Battalion, The Queen's Royal Regiment, and he was awarded the M.C.

The outstanding ability of Stoop as a stand-off half-back was quickly recognized at Oxford, and he figured with distinction in the university matches of 1902, 1903, and 1904. In the last two he had for partner the soon to be famous P. Munro, of Scotland, whom Stoop was to encounter several times as an opponent in the matches for the Calcutta Cup.

Stoop at Oxford was fortunate to have as a partner a man like Munro, for about that time Cambridge produced some formidable packs, which included "Darkie" Sivright and other forwards who were no respecters of persons. At Oxford Stoop and Munro took it in turn to work the scrummage, but the division of labour at half-back had yet to be generally accepted in England. In the 1904 match, which Oxford lost, Stoop showed his quality as a beautifully balanced runner by swerving his way alone through the Cambridge defence.

It was not surprising at a time when English Rugby was seriously in the doldrums that Stoop should have been given the first of 15 caps for England in 1905. The really surprising thing was that Stoop was out of, as well as in, the national XV so often, when, as a Harlequin, he was recreating English back play and showing that what the great sides of Wales and Scotland and the All Blacks and Springboks could do England could do equally well—if they took the necessary pains. Unfortunately, Stoop was generally seen at his best among his fellow Harlequins, and there is no doubt that the broken collar-bone he received in 1907 left his fitness suspect with the English selectors.

But of course Stoop's place in the Rugby game is not to be measured by the number of honours he won on the field, though there was hardly one, if any, that he failed to get, whether playing for university, England, Harlequins or county. Stoop held an ardent belief in the essential virtues of the passing game, and he never failed to drive home, sometimes with a caustic tongue which did not please everyone, that only practice makes perfect.

There is a certain irony in recalling some of the criticism of Stoop and his Harlequins—his brother F. M. Stoop, Poulton (later to be known as Poulton-Palmer), the giant Birkett, and giant, striding Lambert among them—who were said to indulge in handball instead of football. Whether the traditionalists liked it or not, the Harlequins kept Twickenham in the news in a way no international match could quite achieve in those days shortly before the First World War. It was certainly appropriate and, as it were, a dramatic vindication of the Stoop method that he should have been largely responsible for the first try ever scored at Twickenham in an international match, in the first match played there, against Wales, in 1910.

As an administrator, Stoop was an international selector for a while, served on the Rugby Union Laws and Ground Committees, and, highest official honour, became president of the Rugby Football Union in 1932-33.

November 28, 1957.

Dr. Marie Stopes, who died on October 2, 1958 at her home at Dorking, Surrey, can fairly be said to have transformed the thoughts of her generation about the physical aspects of marriage and the role of contraception in married life. She was 77.

Immediately after the First World War she began to issue the books which made her famous and notorious. In emotional, even rhapsodic, language far removed from the scientific precision in which she had been trained, she preached the gospel of marriage as a partnership of equals, sacramentally expressed both in its physical relations and in deliberate and joyous parenthood.

Attainment of this ideal of married love required the use of contraception to remove the fear of pregnancy at the wrong time and for deliberate family planning. Her books discussed methods of contraception she favoured with uninhibited candour, though not always with medical accuracy; and she founded Britain's first birth-control clinic to give practical expression to a mission she pursued with religious fervour.

Addressed not to the learned or scientific public but to ordinary inarticulate men and women, and especially to wives and mothers, her writings at once achieved—and still retain—an enormous circulation. They helped innumerable humble folk to avoid unhappiness and ill-health. Before her advent the birth-control movement had been the preserve of a group of "Neo-Malthusian" intellectuals preoccupied chiefly by a rather academic concern about the balance between population trends and economic resources.

She transformed it into an openly discussed affair of the masses, directly and intimately concerned with the welfare of individual men and women and of their children. Her frontal attacks on old taboos, her quasi-prophetic tone, her flowery fervour aroused strong opposition from those who disagreed with her for religious reasons or felt she overstepped the bounds of good taste; and the launching of her pioneer clinics in London, Leeds, and Aberdeen was sometimes attended by stormy scenes.

Marie Carmichael Stopes was the eldest daughter of the late Henry Stopes, an anthropologist and archaeologist. Educated at St. George's, Edinburgh, and the North London Collegiate School, she went on to University College London with a chemistry scholarship. Having there gained the gold medal in junior and senior botany and her B.Sc.—she later took the D.Sc.—she went to Munich and graduated as Ph.D. In 1904 she joined the science staff of Manchester University. In 1907 she travelled to Japan, where she spent nearly two years at Tokyo University and explored the country (including some remote areas) for fossils. She returned to Manchester as a lecturer in fossil botany. She was also a fellow and sometime lecturer in palaeo-botany at University College London. During this period she wrote a number of scientific papers, as well as books on plant life and on Japan. An early marriage was, at her suit, annulled.

In 1918, retaining her maiden name, she married Humphrey Verdon-Roe, the aircraft pioneer and co-founder with his brother [Sir Alliott Verdon-Roe, [q.v.], of the firm which made the Avro biplane. In the same year she produced her two best sellers, *Married Love* and its sequel, *Wise Parenthood,* forerunners of a series of similar books which sold in hundreds of thousands. With the support of various well-known people she and her husband established "the Mothers' Clinic" in Holloway (now in Whitfield Street, St. Pancras), and used the proceeds of *Married Love* and their own private resources to keep it going and to promote other clinics through her Society for Constructive Birth Control. In 1930 a play of hers, *Our Ostriches,* forceful propaganda but without dramatic merit, was staged at the Royalty Theatre. Her husband died in 1949.

In later life, after most of the separate birth-control societies had united and achieved acceptance and respectability in the Family Planning Association, the defects of her qualities became apparent. She remained aloof, for she could not cooperate on equal terms with others. Her dogmatism in scientific matters lost her the support of most doctors sympathetic to her aims. The shortcomings of her exuberant style and literary imagination (which could not readily transcend the plane of private bodily rapture) marred the verse she occasionally published.

Her home was near Dorking, Surrey. She had two sons, one of whom survives her.

October 3, 1958.

Sir Ronald Storrs, K.C.M.G., C.B.E., who died in hospital in London on November 1, 1955 at the age of 73, was a brilliant and unusual man who in the course of a distinguished career in the Near and Middle East encountered many difficulties and registered substantial achievements.

As Military, and afterwards Civil, Governor of Jerusalem between 1917 and 1926 he did much in spite of local dissensions and disturbances, to revive the arts and to protect and improve the amenities of the Holy City. Later, as Governor and Commander-in-Chief of Cyprus, he had again another complex and trying task; but he discharged it with the imagination and understanding which were characteristic of him. In addition to being an official of long experience, who had served with Sir Eldon Gorst, Lord Kitchener, and Lord Allenby, he was a connoisseur of the arts, a witty and brilliant talker and letter-writer, with individual gifts of pungency and piquancy.

Ronald Henry Amherst Storrs was born on November 19, 1881, the eldest son of the late Very Rev. John Storrs, Dean of Rochester, by his marriage with the Hon. Lucy Cust, sister of the fifth Lord Brownlow. He was at school at Temple Grove and Charterhouse, where he was a classical scholar, and then went on to Pembroke College, Cambridge, where in 1903 he took a first class in the Classical Tripos. In the ensuing year he entered the Egyptian Civil service and was posted to the Ministry of Finance. In this and other departments he spent five years; but administration was never in his line. He preferred to throw himself into the life of the Near East and to lay the foundations of the art collection he was afterwards to lose.

It was not until 1909 that Storrs found his true place, as Oriental Secretary, under Sir Eldon Gorst, at Cairo. Although entirely English, he had a cosmopolitan outlook, to which were added a discriminating taste, a Voltairian cynicism, a lucidity of thought (which recalled Anatole France), and a zest for the good things in art, literature, music, cooking, conversation, and the company of those who were doing important things in the world of affairs and of society.

Gorst's term in Egypt was not altogether happy and was open in some respects to criticism; but Storrs, with his quick and almost feminine perception, understood what the elder man was driving at, and was to remain loyal to his memory. With Gorst's successor, Kitchener, he was even more closely *en rapport.* Both men understood the oriental mind and loved to match their wits against it, and both were art collectors. In this Storrs's taste was impeccable and his command of colloquial Arabic—he was a clever rather than a profound linguist—together with an aplomb which he could sometimes carry to excessive lengths, enabled him to defeat a Mouski dealer even on his own ground.

When Kitchener went home in 1914 Storrs remained at the Residency, and was closely concerned with the negotiations with the Sherif, afterwards King Hussein. T. E. Lawrence referred to him in *The Seven Pillars of Wisdom* and its abridgment, *Revolt in the Desert,* as "the most brilliant Englishman in the Near East".

In 1917 he was Political Officer to the Anglo-French Political Mission of the Egyptian Expeditionary Force and went to Baghdad on its behalf. He was also attached for a short time to the secretariat of the British War Cabinet. Then at the end of the year he was appointed Governor of Jerusalem, a position which he was to hold under different administrations and designations until 1926. Lawrence has, in the later portions of his book, described him as "the urbane and artful governor"; but he was something more than this. It is true that characteristically he left administration to others; but the post was new and its possibilities unfettered by precedent. Storrs, therefore, promoted musical societies, chess clubs, art exhibitions, and above all the Pro-Jerusalem Society, which, alone of the institutions of the Holy Land, created a common centre for the leaders of its varied and contending communities. His, too, was the impetus which revived the local arts and encouraged the restoration of old monuments and the construction of new buildings with the local stone.

Storrs held office at a difficult period, especially after the establishment in 1920 of a Civil Administration. In 1920 there was a clash between Arabs and Jews in Jerusalem in which blood was shed and he was attacked and criticized. Not long afterwards there were disturbances in Jaffa, and, the situation in Jerusalem continuing to be electric, he and his staff were constantly on the alert. He became, however, through the Pro-Jerusalem Society, the guardian of the city's beauties, and laboured successfully to safeguard its antiquities. The City of the Holy Places was to remain deeply in his debt.

His next post was that of Governor and Commander-in-Chief of Cyprus, where he took over under favourable auspices. Having helped to secure the cancellation of the island's share of the Turkish debt, he became for a time most popular. Pro-Hellenic intrigue was soon, however, to break out, and he became a target of attack. In 1929 obstruction became so formidable that he advised a change in the Constitution; but nothing was done. Agitation for union with Greece grew, and in the autumn of 1931 the rabble burned down Government House with all the art treasures and books Storrs had so patiently and skilfully collected. He had deserved better of the islanders. Finally ships and troops from Malta and Egypt restored order.

His dispatch on these unhappy events was published the next year as a White Paper. He attributed them to 50 years' toleration of seditious agitation, but in fact, as later events have shown, it was more deeply seated than that.

In 1932 he was appointed Governor of Northern Rhodesia, where it fell to him to organize the transfer of the capital to Lusaka. It was an uncongenial post to one of his background, and his health, which had once before been seriously affected, again became unsatisfactory. He was invalided from the service in 1934.

In 1937 he became a member of the London County Council, representing East Islington, and in the same year published his memoirs under the title *Orientations.* It was a fascinating record brilliantly told, and it achieved, in spite of its length, a remarkable success. Shortly before the outbreak of war in 1939 he toured the United States, and during his travels rendered service to the Ministry of Information and the British Council, also acting as a special correspondent for the *Sunday Times.* In his retirement from the service he became a sought-after professional lecturer and occasional broadcaster, among his subjects being Dante and T. E. Lawrence, to whom he lately paid tribute in a broadcast and in a television programme.

In 1923 he married Louisa, daughter of Rear-Admiral the Hon. Algernon Littleton, and widow of Lieutenant-Colonel H. Clowes.

November 2, 1955.

Joan P. Strachey, Principal of Newnham College, Cambridge, from 1923 to 1941, died at her home in London on December 19, 1951 at the age of 75.

Joan Pernel Strachey was one of a large and distinguished family. Her father, Lieutenant-General Sir Richard Strachey, G.C.S.I., was a well-known administrator in India; her mother was a writer; and her brother, Lytton Strachey, played an original and accomplished part in the literary history of the twentieth century. To her mother Miss Strachey owed the broad basis of her education and the first stirrings of what afterwards became the cause which lay nearest to her heart—the promotion of the higher education of women. She was brought up in a circle which had wide social, political, and literary contacts, and so acquired that tolerance and breadth of outlook which was later on so greatly to the advantage of her college.

In 1895 she went up to Cambridge and read History and Modern Languages, specializing in French. After a period of study in Paris she became in 1900 Lecturer in French at Royal Holloway College, and in 1905 Lecturer in French and Romance Languages at Newnham College, Cambridge. In 1917 she became Director of Studies in Modern and Medieval Languages. Her administrative work began in 1909 when she took charge of a house of residence for Newnham students. She became tutor in 1910 and in 1923 she was elected to the office of principal. During the years 1919-1921, when the question of admitting women to full membership of the university was under discussion, she rendered great service by her zeal and energy in organizing support and by her skill in drafting the many leaflets and statements which were sent out. When a compromise was achieved, she contributed much to its smooth working by her unfailing dignity and courtesy and by fostering in others a due appreciation of the kindness and encouragement shown by the university to women.

When she became Principal of Newnham, women began to go to Cambridge from all parts of the country and from oversea to read for the research degrees newly established by the university. She devoted much time and care to the arrangements for the admission of these candidates and to their welfare in Cambridge. From its beginning, Newnham College has had a warm interest in women's education in the Dominions and Colonies, and Miss Strachey, by her work in connexion with women's research in Cambridge, contributed to the solidarity of women throughout the Empire. She had, too, a special interest in secondary schools and in all matters concerned with the training and careers of teachers, and she was an early sponsor of the University Women's Appointments Board.

Miss Strachey's period of office was long and eventful. Every department of learning expanded under her wise encouragement. The sphere and usefulness of university women were greatly enlarged by her active interest and help. Those who lived and worked with her regarded her as unique. There was a magical quality in her delicate and imaginative sympathy which seemed to remove all barriers and at the same time to increase one's independence and self-respect. She revealed in her speeches a brilliant and penetrating wit which was the more striking because of her diffident, almost shy, delivery. The rare public lectures which she gave on French life and culture remained in the memory of her hearers as models of incisive and sympathetic comprehension. She was a worthy successor in office to Miss A. J. Clough [q.v.] and Mrs. Sidgwick, and ranks with them as one of the great pioneers in women's education.

In 1935 she carried all her energy and experience into the great task of raising money for a much-needed reconstruction of Newnham College. This was half-completed in 1938 when a new extension, Fawcett Building, was opened by Queen Mary [q.v.]. Miss Strachey's work was of inestimable benefit to the college, since not only were alterations urgently required for efficient working and reasonable living but also she was able to draw together the old members of the college in a great effort, the result of which was astonishing as an example of the successful cooperation of people of very moderate means.

December 20, 1951.

Sir Reginald Stradling, C.B., F.R.S., Dean of the Military College of Science at Shrivenham, and former Chief Scientific Adviser to the Ministry of Works, died on January 26, 1952 at the age of 60.

Reginald Edward Stradling was the son of E. J. Stradling, of Bristol, and was born in 1891. Educated at Bristol Grammar School and Bristol University, he served with the Royal Engineers during the 1914-18 war and was awarded the M.C. Later he was appointed Lecturer in Civil Engineering at Birmingham University and in 1922 he was made Head of the Civil Engineering, Architecture, and Building Department at Bradford Technical College.

In 1924 he became Director of Building Research, a post which he held for 15 years. At the outbreak of the last war Stradling was made Chief Adviser, Research and Experiments, in the Ministry of Home Security but in 1944 he went to the Ministry of Works as Chief Scientific Adviser and later did much to forward the Government's housing drive of which General Sir Frederick Pile [d. 1976] was the director.

After the war Stradling worked part-time in the Civil Defence department of the Home Office, but in 1948 the War Office appointed him Dean of the Military College of Science at Shrivenham in succession to Professor Lander.

He was made a C.B. in 1934 and knighted in 1945. In 1943 he became a Fellow of the Royal Society and was awarded the James Alfred Ewing Medal for 1942. Stradling was also awarded the America Medal for Merit for work which ultimately affected the study of explosive effects with the atomic bomb.

In 1918 he married Inda, daughter of Alfred W. Pippard, of Yeovil. There were one son and one daughter of the marriage.

January 29, 1952.

Herbert Strang—See **Ely.**

Giles Fox-Strangways—See **Ilchester.**

Dr. F. J. M. Stratton, D.S.O., O.B.E., T.D., F.R.S., who was director of the Solar Physics Observatory, Cambridge, and Professor of Astrophysics in the University of Cambridge from 1928 to 1947, died on September 2, 1960 at the age of 79. He was a leading authority on the spectra of new stars, and a prominent figure in the University of Cambridge and in international science.

Frederick John Marrian Stratton was born at Birmingham on October 16, 1881. He was educated at King Edward's Grammar School, Birmingham, and at Mason College in what subsequently became the University of Birmingham, and he then proceeded to Gonville and Caius College, Cambridge, with which he was associated for the rest of his life. He graduated Third Wrangler in the mathematical tripos of 1904, a year in which Eddington was Senior Wrangler. He was elected to an Isaac Newton Studentship in 1905, and won a Smith's Prize in 1906. In the latter year he was elected a fellow of his college.

In the 1914-18 War he commanded a signal unit in the C.U.O.T.C., rising to the rank of lieutenant-colonel. He saw much service in France, was mentioned in dispatches, and was awarded the D.S.O. and the Legion of Honour. Stratton always enjoyed soldiering, partly because it gave scope for his organizing ability, partly because it brought him into wide contact with men. In the 1939-45 War, though he was too old for active service, he was again in uniform, and went on many missions for the War Office, to Canada, the United States, New Zealand, Australia, and India.

In his earliest researches he wrote papers on planetary motions and on the latitude drift of sunspots, but his main interests soon settled on the spectra of novae. A nova outburst is the rapid rise in brightness and subsequent slow decay of a pre-existing star, accompanied by characteristic spectroscopic phenomena. The details of these spectroscopic changes and their correlation with the magnitude changes of the nova are very complicated, and Stratton became an adept at disentangling them. His familiarity with the wave-lengths of the various lines and bands was astounding.

As a result of these interests he was in 1913 appointed by the late Professor Newall as assistant director of the Solar Physics Observatory, Cambridge, and he became also university lecturer in astrophysics at Cambridge. He held these posts until 1919, when he became tutor at Caius. This temporary severance of his former connexion with the Solar Physics Observatory did not interfere with his astronomical interests. He made observations of the dying Nova Aquilae 1918, and of Nova Cygni 1920. He published his useful *Astronomical Physics* in 1925; and he contributed a lengthy and scholarly article on novae to the *Handbuch der Astrophysik* in 1928. He was Halley Lecturer at Oxford in 1927.

He was thus the natural successor to Newall when the latter retired from the chair of astrophysics in 1928, and Stratton became director of the Solar Physics Observatory and the second holder of the chair of astrophysics. Into his new duties he threw much energy. Many parts of the *Annals* of the Solar Physics Observatory appeared in rapid succession, including memoirs by Stratton himself on Nova Persei, 1901, and Nova Herculis, 1934.

He was president of the Royal Astronomical Society for the period 1933-35, and he became its foreign secretary in 1945. He was elected to the Fellowship of the Royal Society in 1947.

In addition to his personal scientific work on novae, Stratton found time to take a leading part in the organization of science both in Britain and internationally. He was general secretary of the British Association in 1930-35, general secretary of the International Astronomical Union in 1925-35, general secretary of the International Council of Scientific Unions from 1937 till 1952, and secretary of the Joint Permanent Eclipse Committee from 1923 onwards. He was also president in 1953-55 of the Society for Psychical Research. He edited the Proceedings of the I.A.U. in the three volumes devoted to the meetings at Leiden, Cambridge (Mass.), and Paris. In these various capitals he by no means contented himself with his formal duties; he radiated good fellowship, and was the personal friend of astronomers of all countries.

He was the personal friend, too, of all members of his college, past and present. He was president of his college from 1946 to 1948 and at the time of his death senior fellow. His rooms in Gonville Court, where he lived until June, were the first port of call for all Caians returning to Cambridge and there, surrounded by photographs of his friends, they could be sure of a friendly welcome and a talk about the college.

He received the Territorial Decoration in 1924, in which year he became a deputy lieutenant for the county of Cambridgeshire. He was a prominent member of the Savile Club.

In appearance he was short, and not without a certain rotundity. His nickname of "Chubby" may serve as evidence of the affectionate regard in which he was held by his colleagues in his college, in the astronomers' dining club and in science generally.

September 5, 1960.

Oscar Straus, the Austrian-born composer of *A Waltz Dream* and *The Chocolate Soldier,* died at his home in Bad Ischl, Upper Austria, on January 11, 1954 at the age of 83. Although he had no connexion with the Strauss dynasty, he struck a very similar vein of light and pleasing music.

He was born in Vienna on March 6, 1870, and began his musical career as early as 1885 as a conductor. It was about 1900 that he turned to composing light music, and during the following half-century wrote no fewer than 50 musical works, including three operas and a great number of operettas. He went to America in 1930, to France in 1939 (becoming a French citizen), and then back to America, where he became an American citizen. But he returned to die in his own land, the Austria he loved.

His music was essentially the music of Vienna—the gay, light, dainty, tuneful music of the Vienna of "the sky-blue time" (one of his light operas was entitled *Die Himmelblaue Zeit*), which is still to be heard in a thousand inn gardens on warm summer nights in the Austrian capital. The best known of his operettas was *A Waltz Dream,* which was first performed in 1917, and others included *The Brave Soldier, About Love,* and *Mariette.*

He was best known, however, for *The Chocolate Soldier,* which was successfully revived in London in the summer of 1940. It deserved its popularity both then and before. The idea was borrowed, but it had the intelligence to admit to the borrowing; its construction kept more control over the wanderings of the characters than is always the case in such pieces; and above all the music had something more than a cheerful and persistent tunefulness.

This was the truth of Straus's hold on the public. He was genuinely popular because his tunes were usually more than just catchy or gay. They had a charm and a delicacy which many of those who tried to imitate or follow him could not command. In duets, in waltzes, in choruses, Straus could always add the ingredient which others did not have to hand. Up to the very end of his life the tunes still came, and even on the day before his death he talked with his publisher of his plans to conduct first nights of a new opera in Basle and Vienna.

The greatest tragedy in Oscar Straus's life was the loss of his only son, Dr. Leo Straus, who was taken in 1943 with his wife, Myra, a writer, to the concentration camp at Theresienstadt, whence they never returned.

January 12, 1954.

Sir Arthur Street, G.C.B., who died in London on February 24, 1951 at the age of 58, was a Civil servant of outstanding zeal and ability. He had, since 1946, been deputy chairman of the National Coal Board, and was working late, as usual, on the night before he died.

He was one of the men at the head of the Government service who helped to introduce, and make reasonable for the public, that increased measure of administrative control which has marked the middle decades of this century. The nature of his work kept him out of the public eye, but those who worked with him, whether at the Ministry of Agriculture, the Air Ministry, or the National Coal Board, were always ready with praise, for they were in a position to measure his influence on the course of public policy.

Arthur William Street was born in 1892, the son of the late William Charles Street, of Cowes, Isle of Wight, and was educated at Sandown County School and King's College, London. After a distinguished career in the 1914-18 war, in which he was mentioned in dispatches and awarded the M.C., he became principal private secretary to the Minister of Agriculture. He afterwards held a similar appointment to the First Lord of the Admiralty, and then in 1922 returned to the Ministry of Agriculture as a principal. Ten years later he was principal assistant-secretary and from 1936 to 1938 Second Secretary.

His work at the Ministry of Agriculture has often been publicly acknowledged. They were years of great difficulty. The various marketing schemes, which were begun under the Labour Government of 1929 and developed by the National Government, came under his special surveillance and brought him into close touch with the farmers, who formed the highest opinion of his integrity and fairness. It was a tribute to him that he retained their confidence even when the marketing schemes did not bring all the blessings that some had expected.

In 1938 he was appointed Deputy Under-Secretary of State for Air. This appointment, at a time when the development of the country's air strength was of the first importance, underlined his high reputation in the Civil service at that time. In the following year, at the age of 47, he succeeded Sir Donald Banks as Permanent Under-Secretary of State. This onerous and exacting post—perhaps, in view of the part played in the war by the Royal Air Force and the lack of administrative tradition in the Air Ministry, it proved to be the most exacting post in the Service departments—he held for six long-drawn years of war.

His shrewdness and sagacity were of incalculable service to successive Secretaries of State, and it is no exaggeration to say that the stature of the Air Ministry in Whitehall was greatly increased under his sway. His personality was so strong and his capacity for work so phenomenal that he could be criticized for having carried the department too much on his own shoulders. If the criticism was justified it would have to be tempered by the reflection that many of the ablest of the younger Civil servants were attracted to the Air Ministry in Street's time and were given full opportunity to show their paces.

He enjoyed working during the comparative quiet of the night and his private secretaries were known to rejoice if they got to bed before 3 in the morning, and on occasions they were known to be still at work when ordinary mortals were beginning to think of breakfast.

After the defeat of Japan he was seconded to the Control Commission as permanent secretary, and in the New Year Honours List of 1946 was created G.C.B. He had already been created K.B.E. in 1938 and K.C.B. in 1941. He did not remain with the Control Commission for long, because in March 1946 his appointment was announced as deputy chairman of the National Coal Board. Yet another tremendous task of organization awaited him—and once again the high expectations of those who appointed him were fulfilled.

In 1948 he was criticized by a Labour M.P. in the House of Commons, who questioned his fitness for the post. Ebby Edwards, a colleague on the Coal Board and a former miners' leader, replied to this attack in a letter to *The Times,* declaring "most emphatically that the enormous capacity for hard work, organizing ability, intelligent foresight and tolerance displayed by the deputy chairman have been an inspiration to the other members of the National Coal Board".

This was the kind of tribute which his colleagues always paid to Street. At the Air Ministry he carried a load—especially when the complexities and controversies of civil aviation were superimposed on the department—which few other men could have borne.

At the Coal Board he made a personal contribution to the new problems of administration and, in particular, the coordination of producing units which can scarcely be over-estimated.

In appearance he was large and robust, with a manner somewhat gruff and brusque, but these hid a personality which was by nature sociable and warm. With three sons of serving age, he bore great anxieties during the war and had to endure the loss of one, a victim of the murder of R.A.F. officers in Stalag Luft III.

He leaves a widow, two sons, and a daughter.

February 26, 1951.

Johannes Strijdom—See **Strydom.**

Amid the multifarious crowd of actors, authors, directors, and producers thrown up by the film industry only a few can safely be described as significant figures sure to take a place in screen history. Such a man is **Erich von Stroheim,** who died on May 12, 1957 at his home at Maurepas, in northern France.

His career was not only distinguished but, a rarer thing in the film world, it was long and varied. Beginning as an actor, his progress on the screen chimed with a period when cold, heavy, brutal German officers were in demand, and he proved the *beau idéal* for parts like these. He then became an author, and a director of great power and insight, establishing himself with *Foolish Wives,* going on to the memorable *Greed,* and being cut off in mid-career, in 1928, with a picture half finished, by the advent of the sound-track.

After leaving Hollywood Stroheim was seen as an actor in sundry talking films, but in the early 1930s he was no longer a big name. However, in 1937 he began a fresh career in France, winning new laurels in a new arena, and 1949 saw him back in a quiet triumph at Hollywood, playing in *Sunset Boulevard* with Gloria Swanson, whose great reputation had also been made in "silent" days.

Count Erich Oswald Hans Carl Marie Stroheim von Nordenwald was born in Vienna on September 22, 1885, of good Austrian family, and educated at the Austrian Military Academy. Following a few years as an Army officer, Stroheim took a dislike to that calling, and after some time in journalism threw everything to the winds and emigrated to the United States with no profession and no capital. Like the adventurous young men who announce their readiness to "do anything", he turned his hand to a bewildering variety of jobs, being by turns dish-washer, gardener, life-saver, singer in a beer-garden, and hawker of fly-papers. But all the time he was writing articles, short stories and plays, and at last, in 1913, appeared as joint author of a play, *The Mask,* successfully produced in New York. Then came Stroheim's first real chance in life, and the beginning of his long association with the films. In 1915 he acted as technical adviser on military detail to the great D. W. Griffith in *Old Heidelberg.* Griffith quickly saw his potentialities as an actor and gave him his first small part, that of a Pharisee in *Intolerance* (1916). A year later came a part as a Prussian officer. Stroheim's "typically Teutonic" cast of countenance was an initial asset—the heavy jaw, the closely cropped bullet head, the severe, unsmiling, trap-like mouth were there; and his ability as an actor produced the piercing, incisive gaze, the leer, the scornful laugh, and the monocle worn with *panache.* The war brought abundant opportunity in these officer parts.

In 1918 Stroheim obtained the cooperation of Carl Laemmle; and a year later appeared as author, director and actor in *Blind Husbands.* With *Foolish Wives* (1921), written and directed by himself, he became an important figure in film direction and raised the firm of Universal Pictures to major status. Stroheim showed something like genius as a director, but his methods were often painful to his casts, for he would glower and bully and use icy sarcasm. Nevertheless, his belief that this technique brought out unsuspected depths in the players seemed to be justified by the event, as witness the performances of Zasu Pitts in *Greed* (1923) and of John Gilbert and Mae Murray in *The Merry Widow* (1925). These two films showed Stroheim at the peak of his silent-film fame. Both were very costly and enormously long, and both were drastically cut ("emasculated" and "butchered", Stroheim said) before exhibition.

He was selected as one of the 10 best directors of 1926; but his colossal extravagance made him more and more unpopular with the film companies as time went on. Artistically he was at his best in pieces showing with cruel humour and mordant irony the decay of an effete society. Such was *The Wedding March* (1927), a deep and weighty indictment of the Vienna he had known prior to 1914. *Queen Kelly* (1928) was his last silent film, and had Gloria Swanson as star. It was planned to enormous length, and was abandoned in the middle of the shooting because of Hollywood's sudden change-over to talking films.

In 1931 Stroheim began to work on his first sound film, *Walking Down Broadway,* but quarrelled with Fox, his backer, half-way through. His breach with Hollywood seemed complete. However he continued to act, and gave notable performances in *The Great Gabbo* and an adaptation of Pirandello's *As You Desire Me.*

There were about this time patches of semi-obscurity in which Stroheim wrote scenarios. In 1935 he produced *Paprika,* a novel of pre-war Hungary. Two years later a new and distinguished career opened out with an invitation from Raymond Bernard, the French director, to play the head of a German espionage ring in *Marthe Richard, Spy of France.*

Between 1937 and 1939 he acted in sundry French pictures, his outstanding performance being in Jean Renoir's *La Grande Illusion,* which earned him the Legion of Honour. He was very popular in France, and when the war broke out in 1939 offered his services to the French Army, but was refused on the score of age. Back in Hollywood Stroheim found himself once more in demand for German parts, this time more sinister than the last. He excelled as Rommel in *Five Graves to Cairo* (1943) and sundry other roles of similar nature.

In 1946 he was invited to return to Paris, and remained there for a considerable period, broken only by a visit to Hollywood for *Sunset Boulevard* (1950), in which both he and Gloria Swanson demonstrated that the passage of years had not blurred their quality.

Stroheim's tripartite reputation as author, director, and actor seems likely to endure. So eminent a judge as Eisenstein, visiting the United States, said: "I want to meet the three greatest men in the American cinema—Chaplin [d. 1977], Disney* and Stroheim". He was largely responsible for securing the primacy of the director, which was a necessary step in the advance of the cinema as an art. And as an actor he lived his parts with a superb skill that held audiences entranced.

Stroheim was twice married, his second wife being the French film actress, Denise Vernac.

May 14, 1957.

Isobel Strong—See **Field.**

L. A. G. Strong, the novelist and poet, died on August 17, 1958 at the age of 62.

Strong graduated to literature from schoolmastering. He remained an inspiring teacher, and indeed returned, part-time, to his first profession as instructor in drama and voice production, and as a director of the English Festival of Spoken Poetry. His students were many and devoted, and as a judge in amateur dramatics he was in demand all over Britain.

As novelist he was successful largely because of his command of macabre narrative, and the ability to contrast this with outbreaks of rustic humour. It may be, however, that he will be remembered later as a lyric poet of almost epigrammatic conciseness. This aspect of his talent has not been adequately appreciated, the style of his poetry being somewhat in eclipse. His humour, tenderness, love of nature, and finally that element of tortured striving toward a serenity which he could not find within his own personality: all these elements are revealed in poems notable for their lucid economy of structure and style. Of late years he gave much time to film script writing and radio programmes. In this last his broadcast readings of his own short stories brought him additional fame.

Leonard Alfred George Strong was born in March 1896. He was Irish by descent on his mother's side, but much of his childhood was spent in Devonshire with occasional visits to Dublin, his youth and early manhood being described in the partly autobiographical novel, *The Garden.* He was educated first at Brighton College, and from there won an open classical scholarship at Wadham College, Oxford, in 1915. His health was very uncertain at this time; he was unfit for service in the war, and for some years unable to play outdoor games, a deprivation that later had some psychological effect upon his work. In 1917 he accepted an assistant mastership in Summer Fields School, Oxford, but returned to Wadham in 1919 and graduated the following year. After taking his degree he went back to Summer Fields and remained there as a master, until his increasing reputation as a writer enabled him to devote himself solely to his literary work.

He first attracted attention as a poet with a collection of short pieces published under the title of *The Lowery Road* in 1923. His collected poems appeared under the title *The Body's Imperfections* in 1957. His first novel, *Dewer Rides* (1929), was a full-length story of the Dartmoor he had known and loved as a boy. It was written with a freedom and an occasional beauty of language, but repelled some readers by what appeared as an unnecessary brutality, and was, in fact, the writer's reaction against the ill-health of his own youth. That reaction might be traced again in a later and far more successful work, *The Brothers* (1932), in which there is also an element of cruelty, but in both cases the tendency to exaggerate a coarse, animal indifference to pain arose from a genuine expression of feeling and not from any desire to catch a sadistically minded public.

The Garden (1931) is less a novel than a series of reminiscences attributed to an imaginery hero, gifted with Strong's peculiar sensitivity. This book was written when he was first enjoying his release from the tediums and restrictions of teaching. He followed it with *The Brothers,* a story of Highland fishermen, *Sea-Wall* (1933), set chiefly in Dublin, and *Corporal Tune,* the first half of which was again pitched in the lovely scenery of Skye that so strongly appealed to him. He returned in *The Swift Shadow* (1937) to Dartmoor, the scene of his first novel.

He had known Ireland as a boy, frequently returned to it, and made it the setting of several of his novels, including some of the best. In *The Open Sky* (1939) the background to a lightly psychological story about an aspiring writer is an island off the west coast of Ireland; in *The Bay* (1941) the scene is Dublin; in *The Director* (1944) Hollywood comes to Ireland and its impact on the simple values of Irish peasant life gave Strong an occasion for some of his most perceptive characterization. His Irish sympathies also prompted him to write a useful study of James Joyce, *The Sacred River* (1950), and a life of the singer John McCormack (1949).

In his last novel, *Deliverance* (1955), as in his first, he was much occupied with the psychology of suffering. But this theme by no means obsessed him. His short stories (a collection of them, *Travellers,* earned him the James Tait Black memorial prize in 1945) were macabre, comic, fearful, ironic, or sentimental. And like the highly professional writer that he was he turned his hand to many miscellaneous tasks: a book on boxers and their fights, a discursive history of English roads, an account of Missions to Seamen, a biography of the eighteenth-century physician Dr. Thomas Dover, and a practical guide on how to write—and see yourself in print.

In 1938 Strong became a director of Methuen, Ltd., and he was a member of the Irish Academy of Letters.

He married in 1926 Dorothea Sylvia Tryce, daughter of Hubert Brinton.

August 19, 1958.

By the death of **Strube,** which occurred on March 4, 1956 at his home in London at the age of 65, a large public loses a friend whose humorous commentary on domestic and foreign politics often struck an original and gay note.

His work was clearly the product of a mind without malice and had the defects of its qualities, for malice, indeed, plays an important and sometimes a decisive part in caricature; Hogarth's "March to Finchley" from its depiction of George II's "drunken and licentious soldiery" to its dedication to the King of Prussia is full of malice, and so are Daumier's cartoons of Charles X and Louis Philippe, and Gillray's comments on the contemporary English scene. Such fierceness was foreign to Strube's nature, which is typified by his habit of addressing everyone—man or woman—as "George", and their response in bestowing that eponym on him, though in fact he had been christened Sidney soon after he was born in 1891, within the sound of Bow Bells, at Bishopsgate. His "little man", a risible figure with bowler hat, high stiff collar, umbrella and other bourgeois appendages, typified the ordinary, uncomplaining taxpayer, always being hit by the manoeuvres of politicians. Strube (the name rhymes not with "tube" but with "ruby") had a good eye for the politicians themselves, but though he often "guyed" them, his blows were those of the 8oz. practice glove in a friendly bout, and not the bare knuckles of the old London Prize Ring.

Beginning as a junior draughtsman with a furnishing firm, Strube soon tired of drawing furniture. He next went to a small advertising agency, where he drew electrical equipment and carried out lettering; but this was still uninteresting journeyman work and he pined for larger fields. He entered himself with the John Hassall School of Art in order to improve his figure work, and at last began caricaturing. Hassall liked his work and sent some of his drawings to the *Conservative and Unionist,* a periodical later published under the title *Our Flag.* It was timely. The general election of 1910 was approaching and, caricature being excellent propaganda, the editor at once bought four of Strube's drawings for publication. That success emboldened Strube to set out on the precarious path of freelance drawing, but for him the path was smooth.

He drew for the *Bystander* and the ephemeral *Evening Times* and was still a freelance when he made his first appearance in the *Daily Express.* By 1912 his drawings had become so popular that the editor of the *Daily Express* offered him an exclusive engagement, and so began his unbroken connexion with the paper as a member of the staff until his resignation through ill-health in 1948.

It was not even entirely broken by the 1914-18 War, for though Strube served in France with the Artists' Rifles, he continued to send in work from the front. So in the 36 years he served the *Daily Express* he became one of the best known and best loved contributors to the paper, and his work was syndicated all over the world. After his retirement from the *Daily Express* his irrepressible spirit found expression in weekly journalism.

Strube married in 1927 Miss Marie Allwright, then a fashion artist on the staff of the *Daily Express.* She survives him, together with a son and a daughter of the marriage.

March 5, 1956.

Ethel Strudwick, C.B.E., High Mistress of St. Paul's Girls' School from 1927 to 1948, died on August 15, 1954 at her home at East Sheen, Surrey. She was 74.

The daughter of the late John Melhuish Strudwick, she was born in London in 1880, and was educated at Queen Elizabeth's School, West Kensington. From there she took a scholarship to Bedford College, where she specialized in classical studies and graduated with honours in classics in 1900. In 1901 she was appointed classical mistress at The Laurels school for girls at Rugby, where she remained for two years. Returning to Bedford College she was appointed assistant instructor in classics there and remained on the teaching staff until 1913, being assistant lecturer for three years and for four years lecturer and head of the Latin department.

In 1913 she was appointed Headmistress of the City of London School for Girls in succession to the late Alice Blagrove, who had been the head since its foundation. During her 14 years there she proved to be as able an organizer and teacher in school as in university work and raised the standards to a high pitch of perfection. She took special care in the choice of her teaching staff, and dealt firmly with those girls who would not take their studies seriously and give proof of their progress.

Out of 46 candidates she was appointed High Mistress of St. Paul's Girls' School in 1927, in succession to Miss F. R. Gray. Besides her work in the administration of a large day school for girls, as large as any in Britain or any other country, she gave much of her time to the cause of higher education of women and served on many public boards. She was elected president of the Association of Head Mistresses in 1931 and held that office for two years. In 1934 she was made a trustee of the London Museum, and in recognition of her services to education she received the honour of O.B.E. in 1936. She was advanced to C.B.E. in 1948.

In addition to being associated with other schools and colleges for the education of women, she was a member of the Council of Westfield College from 1930 to 1950, and a member of the Senate of the University of London from 1921 to 1952. Since 1948 she has been on the Council of the Girls' Public Day School Trust. In 1949, after her retirement from St. Paul's Girls' School, she succeeded Lady Layton [q.v.] as president of the Women's Liberal Federation. A woman of boundless energy and enthusiasm, she had the capacity for getting through a great amount of work in the shortest possible time without losing her grip of essential details.

August 17, 1954.

Jan Struther—See **Placzek.**

Johannes Gerhardus Strydom, who died on August 24, 1958 at the age of 65, belonged to the generation of fanatical Afrikaans South Africans which was born too late to fight in the Anglo-Boer war but in time to be brought up in its bitter aftermath.

His childhood and youth were spent in the atmosphere of frustration and sensed inferiority that inflamed so many men who had been on the defeated side. While the British in South Africa and in Britain believed that the hatchet was being buried, that a generous settlement would lead to the setting up of a friendly bi-lingual nation, the young Strydom was brooding and biding his time. He never swerved in his personal wish to cut the link with the Empire or Commonwealth, to set up (to restore, in his view) the republican system, and to assert the uncompromising ascendancy of the Afrikaans element over the British and of the white minority over the black majority.

Doctrinaire in politics, Calvinist in religion, local in outlook (he scarcely ever left the Union), he never descended to the jealousies and pettiness of some in his camp. There was an integrity about him and a straightforwardness that made him respected and saved him from the charge, so often levelled against South African politicians, of being "slim". There was a smouldering fire in his eyes, but they looked you straight in the face. The stocky, muscular figure, the thick hair rising up from the high forehead, the grim mouth, stamped him as a man of determination. It was easy to picture him in middle age, as he confronted his opponents across the floor of the House, as the clean, hard-playing Rugby footballer that he had been in his early days.

When, after war-to-the-knife in-fighting among the rival Nationalist factions, he defeated Havenga [q.v.] in the succession to Dr. Malan [q.v.], some four years ago, he was hailed by the Transvaal as "the lion of the north". It was a triumph for Krugerism over the more cosmopolitan Cape. The Backveld hoped that he would quicken the pace, proclaim a republic, wrest the Protectorates from Britain, and put the black men where they belonged. As is often the way of fanatics when they reach office, he moved more slowly than his hotheads wished. But he moved quickly enough to show how his mind was working. Unmoved by criticisms, mildly expressed from within South Africa and heard more emphatically outside, he steered a resolute policy away from that of Botha and Smuts.

Freedom for the individual citizen as it is understood in democratic countries was for him knock-kneed liberalism. The Crown was a symbol of conquering imperialism. Any suggestion that he might be mistaken in his social and political treatment of the non-whites set those smouldering eyes on fire. There was about him the gallantry and the regardlessness of the reckoning that steeled the gladiators of old to cry "*Morituri te salutant*". He faced the lions in his path with cold courage. If *apartheid* failed, then so would the adventure of the white man in South Africa, and it would not do so, as he saw it, any quicker or any more catastrophically than it was doing farther in the north.

Strydom was born at Willowmore in the Cape Province on July 14, 1893. He was educated at French Hoek and at Stellenbosch and Pretoria universities, leaving with a B.A. and an LL.B. Then he farmed, in the south, until the boom in ostrich feathers collapsed and sent him into the Civil service. There he remained during the First World War, after which he went north to practise as an attorney in Nylstroom in the Transvaal. He became a successful cattle farmer and an acknowledged personality in the area of his adoption. The hard intransigence of the men of the northern open spaces, far from the sea and from contact with Europe, suited his temperament better than did that of his native Cape. He joined a Pretoria firm of attorneys and was admitted as Advocate in the Supreme Court. His local activities were widespread as he sunk his roots in the Transvaal, and he became president of the Waterberg Agricultural Association and chairman of various business undertakings. He took a keen interest in Afrikaans political journalism.

In 1929 he fought and won Waterberg for the Nationalists and steadily increased in political influence. In 1934 he denounced the coalition formed between Hertzog and Smuts and continued, until the outbreak of war, to fight on the extreme wing of the Afrikaans movement. When war came he was elected to the joint leadership of the Transvaal Party. Then he bided his time until, at the end of 1954, he was able to take over the leadership and to form a Ministry. Its record of legislation expressed, so far as he found it practical to do so, the political philosophy that he had always held. A weak opposition caused by doubts in the divided ranks of the United Party helped him.

But he was careful not to go too far in the direction of provoking resistance from the British elements in South Africa. The sharp warning that he gave to Natal against treating its Afrikaans citizens as "step-children" was significant of his fierce loyalty to his own people. But he hesitated, in spite of pressure from inside his own Cabinet, to proclaim a republic. He was at some pains not to antagonize the cosmopolitan business community, upon the good will of which South Africa's economic prosperity so largely depends. When he visited London in the summer of 1956, he declared that he was not drifting into isolation towards the rest of the world or, more particularly, the Commonwealth. "Well-informed business men, industrialists, bankers, and financiers", he declared, "who have invested vast sums in the industrial, mining, and economic life of our country know full well that this allegation is a complete travesty of the truth". But he made it publicly plain that he meant to have a republic as soon as he could get a sufficiently large majority of European voters in favour of such a step. Thus he was in line with each of his immediate predecessors in seeking, short of a clash, to create a South African nation with Afrikaans dominance.

Strydom was twice married. His first wife was Marda Vanne, the actress. His second wife, who survives him, with a son and a daughter, was Susannah De Klerk, the daughter of a Dutch Reformed Church *Predikant,* and sister of Senator Jan De Klerk, Minister of Labour.

He always used the old style of his name, "Strijdom". But other members of his family prefer "Strydom" and he did not mind which way it was spelt in print.

August 25, 1958.

Gen. Sir John Burnett-Stuart—See **Burnett-.**

Captain R. N. Stuart, V.C., D.S.O., R.D., R.N.R., who was awarded both the Victoria Cross and the Distinguished Service Order for his conspicuous bravery and devotion to duty while in command of "Q", or mystery, ships during the campaign against German submarines in the 1914-18 War, died at his home at Charing, Kent, on February 8, 1954 at the age of 67.

Born at Liverpool on August 26, 1886, Ronald Niel Stuart came of an old seafaring family, which for generations had given captains to the merchant service. He received his education at Shaw Street College, Liverpool, and started his sea career in 1902 in the Kirkhill, a sailing vessel. It was not long before he had a taste of adventure, for in the third year of his apprenticeship the Kirkhill was wrecked off the Falkland Islands. Later he joined the Allan Line, and when it was taken over by the Canadian Pacific Railway Company he continued in the service of the new proprietors.

During the earlier part of the 1914-18 War Stuart served in various ships of the Royal Navy, but later was fortunate enough to be selected to serve in the new "Q" ships. It was while serving in the Q-ship Pargust in June 1917 that his conduct won for him the Victoria Cross. Even among a band of heroes, as the men who manned the "Q" ships undoubtedly were, Stuart's gallantry stood out, and under Rule 13 of the Royal Warrant of January 29, 1856, he was selected by the officers and the ship's company to receive the Victoria Cross. Already Lieutenant Stuart (as Captain Stuart then was) had the D.S.O., and the further great honour of the Victoria Cross which was bestowed upon him was the first time the distinction had fallen to an Anglo-Canadian in the Imperial forces.

Captain Stuart was also the recipient of a high distinction from the United States, namely the Navy Cross. He was awarded that decoration in recognition of the heroic assistance he gave to the United States destroyer Cassin when she was torpedoed on October 15, 1917. The torpedo which struck the Cassin is understood to have been the first hit scored by the Germans against an American destroyer. When the Cassin was hit one sailor was killed, five were wounded, and the ship's stern was blown off, thus making it impossible for her to steer. Stuart, in command of the "Q" ship Tamarisk, with great difficulty, and at a great risk of having his own vessel torpedoed, got a line to the Cassin, and succeeded in towing her to port.

After the end of the war Stuart returned to more peaceful duties with the C.P.R., and in June 1934, when Captain R. G. Latta, Commodore of the C.P.R. Fleet, and Commander of the Empress of Britain, retired, he was succeeded by Captain Stuart. After nearly two years in command of the Empress of Britain, Stuart relinquished that appointment to become General Superintendent of the Canadian Pacific steamships at Montreal. He was appointed London manager of the company in 1938 and became Naval A.D.C. to the King in 1941.

He married in 1919 Evelyn, daughter of W. Wright. There were five children of the marriage, three sons and two daughters.

February 10, 1954.

Preston Sturges, one of the great originals of the American cinema, and Hollywood's leading comedy director of the 1940s, died in New York on August 6, 1959. He was 60.

He was born in Chicago on August 29, 1898, and educated in Europe and America, keeping from early days the good American's passion for Paris, where he was eventually to settle. In the First World War he served in the American Air Force, and afterwards lived for a while in New York, where he became especially interested in the theatre. During the 1920s and early 1930s he wrote a number of successful plays, mainly comedies, among them *Child of Manhattan, Recapture, Well of Romance,* and *Strictly Dishonorable.* It was the film version of this last, his greatest success to date, which brought him to Hollywood in 1931, though several of his earlier plays were subsequently made the basis of films.

During the 1930s Sturges lived and worked mainly in Hollywood, where his great facility in the writing of succinct and literate dialogue was a valuable asset. He turned his hand to many different projects, some of them rather extraordinary, such as *We Live Again,* Goldwyn's* expensive vehicle for Anna Sten, derived from Tolstoy's *Resurrection* and directed by Mamoulian, and *Imitation of Life,* a Claudette Colbert showpiece adapted from Fanny Hurst's* tearful best-seller. In 1937 he wrote his first original screenplay, a crazy comedy called *Haywire Hotel,* but more characteristic of his work were adaptations like *Port of the Seven Seas,* James Whale's American version of Pagnol's* *Marius.*

Throughout his time as scriptwriter, however, Sturges cherished the ambition to direct films, and in 1940 decided to do something about it for himself. Accordingly he wrote an original screenplay about crooked politics in an American small town, *The Great McGinty.* He then offered this to his studio free of charge (a considerable sacrifice, considering that he was a very highly paid writer), only on condition that they let him direct it himself and paid him a normal director's salary. This gamble proved irresistible and when the film came out in 1941 his own judgment was vindicated, as it was one of the year's major successes, winning him the Academy Award for the best original screenplay.

From then on he was for several years one of the most successful writer-directors in Hollywood (and incidentally started a vogue for writers-turned-directors, though none of the others achieved a comparable success). His films had certain features in common. They were all comedies, and most of them found their material in the foibles and eccentricities of ordinary American life, in small-town politics and scandals. In some ways they were the successors of Capra's political comedies of the 1930s, but less naively optimistic, more grotesque and satirical. The same people recurred in many of them—Sturges's stock company, as they came to be regarded—among them Rudy Vallee and Franklin Pangborn.

The Great McGinty was followed, in much the same style, by *Christmas in July* (1940), *Sullivan's Travels* (1942), and *Hail the Conquering Hero* (1944), all of which cast a gently satirical eye on aspects of everyday American life and institutions. A slightly different style was seen in two classic comedies of personal relationships, *The Palm Beach Story,* with Claudette Colbert, Joel McCrea, and Rudy Vallee, and *The Lady Eve.* This last, a beautifully sustained piece about a good-natured confidence trickster's pursuit of a shy and eccentric millionaire biologist (later remade by another director as *The Birds and the Bees*), was distinguished by flawless comedy performances from Henry Fonda and Barbara Stanwyck, and has a good claim to be considered Sturges's best film. *Miracle at Morgan's Creek,* a comedy about pregnancy by an unknown father, was thought tasteless, though undeniably amusing, and at the end of the war Sturges essayed a serious subject in *The Great Moment,* but levity kept breaking through and the result was not a great success.

After the war Sturges seemed to suffer a loss of direction. *The Sin of Harold Diddlebock,* an uneven come-back picture for Harold Lloyd*, was held up for several years before appearing as *Mad Wednesday; Vendetta,* which he took over from Ophüls [q.v.], was finished by two other directors; and a return to form with *Unfaithfully Yours,* a riotous fantasy about a conductor's varying plans for dealing with his wife's unfaithfulness, depending on what sort of work he is conducting at the time, was followed by a disappointing Betty Grable* comedy, *The Beautiful Blonde from Bashful Bend.*

After this Sturges left the cinema for several years, and though intriguing plans were announced from time to time, including a version of Shaw's *The Millionairess* with

Katharine Hepburn, none of them came to anything. In 1954 he settled in Paris, and continued to write and plan. His next play, *I Belong to Zozo,* was written in French, and his next film, *The Notebooks of Major Thompson,* starring Jack Buchanan [q.v.] as the perennial Englishman abroad, was made in French and English versions.

Preston Sturges was one of the few professional writers to take up film direction with complete success, and one of those rare film-creators who inevitably alter his audience's view of life, by making certain types of character and situation his own, so that if they occurred in everyday life one would immediately have the sensation of having stepped into a Sturges comedy. His invention was prodigious, and perhaps not always completely disciplined, but in his best films, like *The Lady Eve* and *Unfaithfully Yours,* he succeeded in making the form perfectly answer the content, and the result provided America with some of her most individual and diverting comedies.

August 7, 1959.

Rear-Admiral Sir Murray Sueter, C.B., who died at his home at Watlington, Oxfordshire on February 3, 1960, was one of the pioneers of naval flying and the first Director of the Air Department at the Admiralty. He was 87.

It was during his tenure of that office that the Royal Naval Air Service was organized from the naval wing of the Royal Flying Corps in 1914, and he did valuable work in developing both airships and aeroplanes. A talented and zealous officer, his enthusiasm for aircraft sometimes tended to overrun his discretion and judgment, so that he never attained the highest rank in his own service; nor, like so many of the other naval air pioneers, did he go over to the R.A.F. when it was created in 1918. Instead he turned to politics, and for 24 years he was an able M.P. for Hertford.

Murray Fraser Sueter, born in 1872, was the son of John T. Sueter, fleet paymaster, R.N. He entered the Navy as a cadet in the Britannia at Dartmouth in January 1886, and went to sea two years later as midshipman in the Swiftsure, flagship on the Pacific Station. Promoted to lieutenant in 1894, he was selected two years later to specialize in torpedoes. At the Diamond Jubilee naval review in 1897 he was lent from the course to command the destroyer Fame. The Vernon torpedo school was intimately connected with the early experiments in wireless telegraphy, and Sueter claimed to have given the first lecture on that subject in the ship.

In 1902 he joined the gunboat Hazard, which Captain Reginald Bacon commissioned as the first submarine parent ship, and assisted in the early trials of these new under-water craft. Sueter was commended by the Admiralty for saving life in a hydrogen gas explosion in submarine A1. In 1903 he was promoted to commander and appointed an assistant to the Director of Naval Ordnance. From 1906 to 1908 he commanded the cruiser Barham in the Mediterranean. He returned to the naval ordnance department and was promoted to captain in 1909.

The first naval airship, unofficially known as the Mayfly, was then under construction. Sueter, with his inventive turn of mind, took a keen and practical interest in this project, and in September 1910 was appointed to command the cruiser Hermione and to the new post of Inspecting Captain of Airships. The wreck of the Mayfly in September 1911 put a temporary stop to airship development, and in 1912 he was made director of the new Air Department at the Admiralty. The Royal Flying Corps, with naval and military wings, had just been formed, and on July 1, 1914, the naval wing became the Royal Naval Air Service.

War broke out a month later, and the R.N.A.S., under the energetic encouragement of Winston Churchill* as First Lord, expanded rapidly. Sueter, still D.A.D., was made a commodore, second class. Besides aeroplanes and seaplanes, Churchill and Lord Fisher decided to build a large number of small, non-rigid airships for submarine searching; nearly 200 of these "S.S." craft were produced, and their successful use owed much to Sueter's ingenuity. With Lieutenant-Commander Douglas Hyde-Thomson he was the joint inventor of torpedo-carrying aircraft.

In January 1915 he put forward the idea of armoured cars as an adjunct of the R.N.A.S. Before the Germans dug themselves in these cars did useful service in France and Flanders, and when of no further use there one squadron was sent to Egypt under the Duke of Westminster [q.v.] and another to Russia under Commander Oliver Locker-Lampson. More memorable was the way in which Sueter and his naval airmen pioneered the "caterpillar landship", which was developed into the tank. "I frankly admit", he wrote later, "that our work in evolving a novel weapon for trench warfare for the Army was quite outside our legitimate air work. Strictly speaking, we were misemployed"; but he was "mighty proud" of having his landship taken up, used with success in the war, and finally blossom into the Royal Tank Corps.

In September 1915 an officer of flag rank was appointed to the new post of Director of Air Services, and Sueter became Superintendent of Air Construction, in the rank of commodore first class, with charge of the material side. This post he left early in 1917 to command the R.N.A.S. units in southern Italy—"banished", he wrote afterwards, "for holding unorthodox views in advocating a separate air service". He was in Italy until 1918 and was mentioned in dispatches, but received no further naval appointment. Early in 1920 he was promoted to rear-admiral by seniority and retired. He was M.P. for Hertford from 1921 (characteristically he stood originally as an Anti-Waste candidate) until the general election of 1945.

His first and best book, *The Evolution of the Submarine, Mine, and Torpedo,* appeared in 1908, a valuable compilation and a tribute to the industry of a young officer still on naval service. He also wrote *Airmen or Noahs* (1928), which is partly autobiographical but chiefly a polemic on behalf of the claims of independent air power in preference to those of older forms of warfare.

In 1937 he produced a book on the evolution of the tank. He was thanked by three successive Postmasters-General for his valuable assistance in connexion with the development of Empire air mail services. He was appointed C.B. in 1914 and made a knight in 1934.

He married in 1903 Elinor Mary de Winton, only child of Lieutenant-General the Hon. Sir Andrew Clarke, G.C.M.G., R.E., and had two daughters. Lady Sueter died in 1948.

February 5, 1960.

Sir Lala Sukuna—Ratu Sir Joseva Lalabalayu Vanaaliali Sukuna, K.C.M.G., K.B.E.,—Paramount Chief of Fiji, who died at sea while on his way to Britain on May 29, 1958, was an outstanding representative of his people.

Of aristocratic lineage, the son of the Hon. Ratu Jione Madruiwiwi, member of the Legislative Council of the Colony, he was born in 1888 and educated at Wanganui Grammar School, New Zealand, and at Wadham College, Oxford. After taking his degree in 1921, and being called to the Bar by the Middle Temple in the same year, he was appointed to a cadetship in the Fiji Civil service.

In the course of a long career he filled with great distinction a number of important public offices, including Secretary for Fijian Affairs, Chairman of the Lands Commission, and Speaker of the Legislative Council. He was Assistant Commissioner for Fiji at the British Empire Exhibition in 1924 and represented the Fiji Government at the Coronation ceremonies in 1937 and 1953. In 1950 he attended at the United Nations as a member of the British delegation.

In the 1914-18 War he served in France with the Foreign Legion and was decorated with the French Military Medal. In the Second World War he was Colonel of the Fiji Military Forces Staff, and he led the Fijian contingent in the victory march in London in 1946. He was honorary colonel of the 2nd Battalion, Fiji Infantry, and Lieutenant-Colonel of the Fiji Defence Force.

He was a man of great personal charm as well as of outstanding ability, and he was looked up to with affection and respect not only by his own people, of whose interests he was an unwearying champion, but by all who were privileged to come into contact with him. By virtue of his innate integrity and his invariable courtesy he had the gift of getting on with men and women of all races, and he was at home equally in palace and in cottage. His happy blend of western culture and of pride in his own national heritage found expression in his custom of wearing, even with formal European dress, the kilt and sandals of his native land.

With his passing, the Fijian people have lost a great leader, and the colony as a whole has lost a wise and experienced counsellor whose influence was always exerted for the general good. Over a far wider field, many people in many places will mourn the departure of a friend.

He was made a C.B.E. in 1939 and advanced to K.B.E. in 1946 and created K.C.M.G. in 1953.

May 31, 1958.

Margaret Sullavan, one of the most delicate and charming of Hollywood actresses in the 1930s, whose death, at the age of 48, occurred on January 1, 1960, was born in Norfolk, Virginia, on May 16, 1911.

She began her career on the Broadway stage and came to the screen, already a star, in 1933, when she appeared in *Only Yesterday.* She early showed an unusual gift for comedy in such films as *The Good Fairy,* adapted from Molnar and directed by William Wyler, to whom she was married at the time, and *The Moon's Our Home,* a crazy comedy in which she played opposite Henry Fonda.

In 1938 she played one of her most famous roles in Borzage's* *Three Comrades,* based on Erich Maria Remarque's* novel of the First World War, in which she gave a superb performance as a girl in love with a shattered German veteran. This was followed by two more films directed by Borzage; *The Shining Hour,* a highly charged but rather silly emotional drama in which she starred with Joan Crawford [d. 1977], and *The Mortal Storm,* a subtle and powerful story of Hitler's rise to power, which produced another striking performance.

In contrast, Lubitsch's elegantly affectionate study of life in a Hungarian small town, *The Shop Around the Corner,* offered a graceful reminder of her comic gifts. Her last film was *No Sad Songs for Me,* in which she played a woman soon to die of an incurable disease with considerable depth and truth of feeling.

Subsequently she returned exclusively to the stage, playing leading roles in, among other plays, *Sabrina Fair, Janus* and *The Deep Blue Sea.* She was last seen on the London stage in John Van Druten's [q.v.] farce *The Voice of the Turtle.*

January 4, 1960.

Serjeant A. M. Sullivan, Q.C., who died on January 9, 1959 in Kent at the age of 87, was a well known and popular figure at the English Bar, to which he was called in 1899 after a career in Ireland, first as a journalist and later as a member of the Irish Bar. He became an Irish K.C. in 1908, and he was the last of the Serjeants-at-Law there or elsewhere.

Serjeants-at-Law formerly constituted the highest order of counsel at the English and Irish Bars. The Society of Serjeants' Inn in London was dissolved in 1877, but the title continued to be used in Ireland until the establishment of the Free State in 1922.

Alexander Martin Sullivan was the son of A. M. Sullivan, M.P. for Louth in the seventies, one of the original founders of the Home Rule League and the proprietor and editor of *The Nation* and the author of some historical, biographical, and political works.

The future Serjeant was born in 1871. He began his career as a journalist, and was a contributor to his father's paper and other journals and to various Irish periodicals. He was called to the Irish Bar in 1892. His rise was rapid and 14 years after his call he took silk. In Ireland the distinction between the common law and equity Bars was less marked than in England, so when Sullivan finally crossed the Channel after the establishment of Sinn Fein, to which (though a Nationalist) he was strongly opposed, and decided to practise at the English Bar, to which he had already been called by the Middle Temple, he found himself at home in either the King's Bench or Chancery Courts, though his advocacy was of the type more adapted to the former.

In Ireland during some of the worst periods of disturbance, especially in the west, Sullivan had displayed considerable courage in his conduct of Crown prosecutions. His life was threatened and was in real danger, but he was never deterred from the conscientious discharge of his duties, which to an adherent to the old Nationalist school in politics would never have been congenial.

From small beginnings and small fees, Sullivan soon built up a good practice both in civil and criminal work in London and on circuit. If not in the first rank he was a good advocate and an excellent cross-examiner; but the quality that perhaps most impressed his fellow practitioners was a superb memory that it was said sometimes enabled him to conduct a case without untying his brief and to cite case after case without referring to the reports.

In 1916 he defended Sir Roger Casement with conspicuous ability, and thus added greatly to his growing reputation. Three years later, in 1919, he obtained an English silk gown and in 1920 he was made a Serjeant-at-Law in Ireland. As a leader he was equally successful and his practice took him into every class of case, from a breach of promise to an appeal in the Privy Council. He appeared against Dr. Marie Stopes [q.v.] in the libel action that went up to the House of Lords.

In 1944 he was elected Treasurer of the Middle Temple, and so it fell to him to preside when the Queen first dined there as an Honorary Bencher of the Inn. He was a devout Roman Catholic, with neither rancour nor narrowness, and he combined in an unusual degree the qualities of ability, courage, humour, and charm. His sympathy and practical help in connexion with the destruction of their church will be remembered by his fellow Benchers.

In April 1949, taking an independent view of the implications of the Republic of Ireland Act, Sullivan announced that he considered himself disqualified as an alien from practising further at the English Bar, so he retired to Dublin and our courts saw him no more.

In 1952 he published his recollections under the title of *The Last Serjeant.* The background of the Casement trial is impartially sketched, and the author's adventures in remote Irish county courts and even the High Court introduces the reader into a world recalling, as a reviewer remarked, "the more fantastic work of an earlier Sullivan and his librettist collaborator".

Serjeant Sullivan married in 1900 Helen, daughter of the late Major John D. Keiley, of Brooklyn, New York. She died in 1952.

January 10, 1959.

Humphrey Sumner, one of the most distinguished historians of his generation and Warden of All Souls College, Oxford, since 1945, died in hospital at Oxford on April 25, 1951 at the age of 57.

Benedict Humphrey Sumner was born in 1893, one of the five children of Heywood Sumner and Agnes Mary Benson, a sister of Lord Charnwood and other distinguished brothers. Heywood Sumner, a figure of patriarchal dignity and the son and grandson of bishops, forsook the episcopal tradition for art. He was a disciple of William Morris and a painter, who in later life became a distinguished archaeologist. None the less, the Barchester atmosphere lingered in the Sumner household, and his mother—the foundress of the Mothers' Union—made a deep impression on the five grandchildren.

Sumner went up to Balliol, his grandfather's college, as a Brackenbury scholar from Winchester in 1912, but his career there was ended by the outbreak of war in 1914. After three gruelling years in the K.R.R.C. he was transferred to the directorate of military intelligence at the War Office in 1917. Thence he passed to the Peace Conference, and from 1920 to 1922 he served in the I.L.O. In 1919 he had been elected a Fellow of All Souls, and from Geneva he returned to Balliol to serve as Fellow and Tutor in Modern History for the next 20 years.

In this difficult period Sumner was a tower of strength in the life of the college. The effects of the war on Oxford were profound, and, to many, disquieting. The numbers of the college rose steeply; accommodation, staffing, and finance became major problems and new schools were altering the traditional balance between the humanities and the sciences. His characteristics as a tutor were of a piece with the whole man—a prodigious capacity for work, an almost over-developed conscientiousness and an immense capacity for assimilating facts. He distrusted generalization and disliked epigram. His own range was immense and if he set, both for himself and his students, an unattainable standard of detailed knowledge, yet his teaching had a wide horizon.

Sumner's personal interests ran to contemporary history, and he was closely concerned with the inception and development of Chatham House. He had already begun to learn Russian while at school and characteristically published little or nothing until he had achieved a mastery, unique in Britain, in his chosen subject. Then, in 1937, appeared *Russia and the Balkans, 1870-1880,* a work of patient learning and deeper understanding of Russian motives than then was common. He followed this up in 1944 with his *Survey of Russian History,* which was instantly recognized as the safest guide yet written to the meaning of events in contemporary Russia.

In the 1939-45 war Sumner's never robust constitution came near to breaking down under the double strain of Foreign Office work and college teaching. In 1944 he left Balliol for the less exacting post of Professor of History at Edinburgh, but only, as it proved, to return to Oxford in the course of the next year as Warden of All Souls. Succeeding Dr. Adams*, on his retirement, he threw himself into the task not only of building up the college after the war, but of ensuring its fullest cooperation with the university. In the period of reconstruction he was constantly on the alert that by its elections, its contributions to learning and scholarship, and not least by its hospitality the college should make its maximum contribution, while retaining its distinctive character as a place of liaison between public and academic life. His efforts won general confidence, founded as they were on the respect he enjoyed for his far-sighted and sober judgment; and, within the college itself, his discrimination, his consideration for each individual, and his distinguished courtesy made a deep impression. The new Fellows, who filled the ranks depleted by the suspension of elections during the war, found in the Warden a friend who took the most kindly and encouraging interest in the career on which each was embarking, whether in scholarship or in public affairs. He was particularly anxious to encourage contacts with European scholars, as could be seen from his notable speech (in French) when he entertained the Anglo-French historical conference in 1949. A countryman himself, he enjoyed visiting the college estates, where he quickly established the friendliest relations with the agricultural tenants. Careful in administration, sometimes to the point of exaggeration, he was always master of detail.

There was something almost medieval in the splendid humility with which Sumner sought to hide his light under a bushel, and it was not for nothing he was nicknamed "the Emperor". A master of silence and fundamentally reserved, he was in early years a stiff proposition as a tutor for even the most confident undergraduate, but with the years he grew steadily more easy and approachable. He had the same capacity for detail in his personal relations as in his scholarship. The influence of such an embracing personality is not easily measured, and few men of his time can have "kept up" with so wide a circle of friends. No little part of his success with the young came from an immense vitality, and if he ever felt tired in society he never showed it. He owed much to the support of the sister, unmarried like himself, who ordered the life and dispensed the hospitality of the Warden's lodgings.

With every advantage of birth and education, Sumner carried over into a more vulgar age the grace and the social accomplishments of an earlier Oxford. They made him a worthy successor to Dr. Pember [q.v.], the Warden under whom he was elected to his fellowship.

His noble profile, which suggested to the college that his commemoration in its gallery of portraits should be entrusted to a sculptor rather than a painter, was the index of a character of religious simplicity, attuned by early home discipline to "the good life". He was a man to be counted on absolutely and in his closer friendships he inspired devotion. His death will be deeply regretted in a society in which he was admired for his distinction and beloved for his friendliness.

April 26, 1951.

Millicent Duchess of Sutherland, who touched life at many points, as a great social figure, an indefatigable worker for the Red Cross and for refugees, and as an authoress, died on August 20, 1955 while on holiday at Biarritz, at the age of 87.

Lady Millicent Fanny St. Clair-Erskine was born on October 20, 1867, the eldest daughter of the fourth Earl of Rosslyn. She married the fourth Duke of Sutherland, then Marquess of Stafford, as a girl of 17, and in 1892, on the death of her father-in-law, became mistress of the great castle of Dunrobin and of Stafford (now Lancaster) House, perhaps the most magnificent of the town houses facing Buckingham Palace from the eastern fringe of the Green Park. The great house was not only the scene of much brilliant entertaining in those days but it was freely thrown open in aid of charitable causes, and artists and literary men from all over the world gathered there. Arnold Bennett was one of these and the duchess's sparkling personality may perhaps have inspired more than one of his characters.

A gifted writer herself, she submitted anonymously a play to Sir Johnstone Forbes-Robertson and only disclosed her authorship when, after he had accepted it for performance, he wanted to make some modifications. That was in 1905 and the play was *The Conqueror.*

Meanwhile, she continued to take an enthusiastic interest in such bodies as the Association of Teachers of Domestic Subjects, in workhouses, and, above all, in the Cripples' Aid Society. In all these activities she showed not merely generosity of spirit, but a capacity for hard work over long hours.

Then came the death of her husband, all too early, in 1913. Though she felt her loss deeply, she did not allow it to prostrate her and in any case the coming of war in 1914 brought for her a call to engage in work for the wounded. Three weeks after the outbreak of war she was in Namur working as a nurse. Somehow she got cut off and she and her companies crossed the frontier into Holland. As non-combatants they were not interned and quickly arrived back in England. A pamphlet *Six Weeks at the War* was written by her and published by *The Times* to raise funds for a new ambulance unit, which duly went out again and remained operating in France and Belgium until the war ended.

She had married a second time, in October 1914, Major P. D. Fitzgerald, D.S.O., but the marriage was dissolved in 1919. Later that year she married for the third time, Lieutenant-Colonel George Hawes, D.S.O., M.C., who died in 1946, when, at the urgent representations of her son, the Duke of Sutherland, she reverted to her former name, Millicent Duchess of Sutherland, by which she was best known.

She had lived in France for many years, and had done much charitable work there, including looking after many refugees from Germany. She had also published many short stories and novels, the best known of which is *That Fool of a Woman.*

August 22, 1955.

Dr. Halliday Sutherland, who, after an unusually varied medical experience and the writing of a number of works on medical or social-medical subjects, attained remarkable success as the author of *The Arches of the Years* and other volumes of personal reminiscences, died on April 19, 1960 in a London hospital. He was 77.

Halliday Gibson Sutherland was born on June 24, 1882, eldest son of Dr. J. F. Sutherland, of the Board of Control for Scotland, and was educated at Glasgow High School and Merchiston Castle School. At this time, long before he had achieved any reputation as a writer, he had given evidence of his ability, for he walked off with several essay prizes, among them the Sir Walter Scott prize, open to all Edinburgh schools. He studied at the Universities of Aberdeen, Dublin, and Edinburgh, graduated M.B. and Ch.B. in 1906 and M.D. (with honours) at Edinburgh two years later. When he had qualified and had taken a rough holiday on board a whaler he went out to Spain to practise as an assistant to an uncle. He had a high stomach for adventure, studied bull fighting under a matador, and all but lost his life attempting to put into practice the theory his preceptor had taught him.

On his return to Britain he held an appointment at the Royal Edinburgh Asylum for a short period, was resident physician at the Royal Victoria Hospital, Edinburgh, and in 1910 became Medical Superintendent of the Westmorland Sanatorium. Diseases of the chest, which were to become a life study, were now dominating his career and from 1911 to the outbreak of war in August 1914 he was a medical officer at the St. Marylebone Tuberculosis Dispensary. After the war, in which he served in an armed merchant cruiser and also in the Royal Air Force, he returned to practise his profession. He was Deputy Commissioner of Medical Services (Tuberculosis) for South-Western England and Wales from 1920 to 1925, and subsequently held a variety of posts in different parts of the country.

From 1948 to 1951 he was Medical Director of the Mass Radiography Centre, Birmingham, and a consultant under the National Health Service. He was honorary physician and member of the council of the Queen Alexandra Sanatorium Fund, a member of the Tuberculosis Association, and a past president of the Tuberculosis Society of Great Britain. He wrote several books on his speciality and in 1957 edited the forty-sixth edition of J. F. Sutherland's *First Aid to Injured and Sick.*

The Arches of the Years appeared in 1933. It was an immediate and deserved success. Sutherland's zest for living, the variousness of his experience and observation of life, his unaffectedly human sentiment, and his very real gift for anecdote and for narrative generally gave this volume of informal autobiography a very wide appeal. A best seller at home, it was promptly translated into a great many European languages.

A further volume of reminiscences, *A Time to Keep*, appeared in the following year, but here Sutherland, though he still had curious and instructive things to say in plenty, was largely engaged in gleaning the Scottish part of the field reaped in the earlier volume and in recounting his conversion to Roman Catholicism. A third selection of reminiscences, *In My Path*, appeared a couple of years later. After that there were three more books for the general reader, all of them loosely built upon a spell of travel—*Lapland Journey* (1938), *Hebridean Journey* (1939), and *Southward Journey* (1942), the last of these recording a lecture tour in Australia. *Spanish Journey* appeared in 1948 and *Irish Journey* in 1956.

Engagingly discursive in manner, all three provide a medley of recollection, anecdote, medical small-talk, folklore, history, and a great deal besides. He became a doughty Roman Catholic controversialist and, as he wrote in *A Time to Keep*, had "the honour to represent a Catholic Church in great public controversy". The matter of debate was artificial birth control: the line he took in a book on the subject made him the defendant in an action for libel decided in his favour in the House of Lords. His opponent was as doughty as he, for she was Marie Stopes [q.v.].

Sutherland married in 1920 Muriel, daughter of J. F. Fitzpatrick. They had five sons and a daughter.

April 20, 1960.

Sir James Swinburne, BT., F.R.S., a pioneer in the development of plastics, and chairman of Bakelite, Ltd., until 1948, died on March 30, 1958, just over a month since he celebrated his 100th birthday.

Born in Inverness on February 28, 1858, he was the third son of Captain T. A. Swinburne, R.N., of Eilean Shona, Inverness-shire, and as a descendant of the second baronet succeeded to the baronetcy in 1934 on the death of Sir Hubert Swinburne, the eighth baronet. He was educated at Clifton College, and received his engineering training on Tyneside from 1874 to 1881. Associated with Sir J. W. Swan in the development of the carbon incandescent electric lamp, he was sent to Antwerp at the end of the latter year to prove the working of Swan's Belgian patents, and there made one lamp which he asserted cost nearly £100.

Later, in starting lamp works in Paris, he had some amusing experiences. The payment for an engine he required had to be made in cash tipped into a leather bag brought by the man who was sent to collect it, the French at that time not understanding cheques, and after the engine had been erected there was a delay of several days in putting it to work, until he was invited to the engine room, where he found the workmen in their holiday clothes, the machine garlanded with flowers, and carafes of wine set out in which its health had to be drunk.

Subsequently he became technical manager and designer to Crompton & Co., but after 1894 he ceased to specialize in electrical engineering, settling in London as a consulting engineer. His Hedgehog transformer, so called from the rough prickly appearance given it by the projecting ends of the soft iron wires that formed its core, enjoyed a considerable vogue.

It is possibly his association with the advanced thinking of Swan, together with the interest he acquired after examining resinous materials produced by the Austrian chemist Luft, which brought Swinburne into the chemical field, and he established his laboratory in London in 1904. His independence of thought, no doubt coupled with his expert knowledge of the needs of the electrical industry for good insulating materials, directed his attention to those in-between products of chemical reactions, the sticky, resinous masses which, being neither truly crystalline nor liquid, had for long been rejected as unwanted by the conventionally minded organic chemists of that day.

He eventually established his process for the condensation of phenol and formaldehyde, but it is reported that he was anticipated by one day by Dr. Baekeland in securing patents cover. It is possibly for this reason that the part he played in the revolutionary chemical free-thinking which laid the foundation of the plastics industry has received less publicity than that attributed to Baekeland. In the subsequent development of the new products Swinburne devoted his attention to the production of materials for lacquers and impregnating compositions rather than to moulded products, and in 1910 he established a company to manufacture these in Birmingham under the very appropriate name of Damard Lacquer Ltd.

During the 1914-18 war this company concluded an agreement to use Dr. Baekeland's patents in Britain, and, after the conclusion of hostilities, combined with Mouldensite Ltd. and Redmanol Ltd. to form Bakelite Ltd. Swinburne retained his close interest with the new materials throughout the 1920s, when the scattered collection of new and old synthetics became grouped under the family name of plastics.

Swinburne was chairman of Bakelite until 1948 when he became honorary president, and he lived to see his old products and those closely allied under the general term of plastics effect a major revolution both in chemistry and engineering. His pioneer interest in plastics was further cemented on the educational side when he followed Sir Gilbert Morgan (another pioneer in phenolic plastics) in 1937-38 as the president of the Plastics Institute.

His attainments are the more remarkable when it is remembered that he had been president of the Institution of Electrical Engineers in 1902-03, and he was also a past president of the Faraday Society. He was elected a Fellow of the Royal Society in 1906.

Swinburne had a share in the work of salving the bullion from the Egypt. Soon after that vessel was sunk off Ushant in May 1922 C. P. Sandberg began to investigate the possibilities of salvage from depths much greater than had previously been possible, and engaged a Swedish salvage ship, the Fritjof, which in 1923 discovered what was believed to be the wreck. In preparation for the recovery of the bullion, to be attempted in the following year, Swinburne joined him in devising an elaborate apparatus, which they called the Eye, consisting of a submersible steel chamber to hold two men and fitted with all sorts of mechanical devices for working on the wreck. Their appliance was never used, though it was with something of the same kind, but simpler, that success was ultimately achieved.

In 1925 they contracted with a French company to retrieve the bullion with the aid of deep-diving shells of German design, but work in the following year failed to locate the ship, and not until 1930 did the Artiglio, working under an agreement between them and the Società Ricuperi-Marittimi, of Genoa, and using an observation chamber without mechanical attachments, find the wreck and prove its identity by hauling up a hydraulic crane and the captain's safe.

In 1924 he made a notable excursion from engineering into sociology with a book, *Population and the Social Problem*, the purpose of which was to urge recognition and thorough study of the "principle of population" whereby alone, he held, the social problem—the abolition of poverty—can be solved. A reviewer of the book in *The Times Literary Supplement* said of him that "he wields a sharp lance and impales on it innumerable cherished beliefs" and described his pages as bristling with "smart but dubious paradoxes which rather amuse than enlighten".

At the age of 92 he wrote a book entitled *The Mechanism of the Watch*, which was intended rather for the less informed than as a scientific treatise.

Swinburne was twice married, first in 1886 to Ellen, daughter of Dr. R. H. Wilson of Gateshead, by whom he had two sons, and second in 1898 to Lilian, daughter of Sir Godfrey Carey, of Guernsey, by whom he had two daughters.

March 31, 1958.

Major-General Sir Ernest Swinton, K.B.E., C.B., D.S.O., who died at Oxford on January 15, 1951 at the age of 82, never rose as high in the Army as his talents and imagination seemed to forecast.

Ernest Dunlop Swinton was the eldest son of B. L. Swinton, of the Madras Civil service, and was born on October 21, 1868. He went to Rugby and later to Cheltenham before passing into the Royal Military Academy. In 1888 he was gazetted into the Royal Engineers, and was appointed Assistant Instructor in Fortification at the School of Military Engineering in 1896. He remained at Chatham until after the outbreak of the South African War, but soon went out to act as adjutant to the 1st Railway Pioneer Regiment. He afterwards obtained command of this irregular unit and remained on railway work throughout the war. He received the D.S.O. in 1900.

Swinton was an observant man. The first fruits of his observation in South Africa took the form of a little work of fiction, *The Defence of Duffer's Drift,* written under the pseudonym of "Backsight-Forethought". This passed through one edition after another, and subalterns on joining their regiments were directed to read it as a tactical manual. It was followed by a series of stories purporting to depict warfare of the future. These tales, as remarkable for literary form as for their prescience, were republished in 1909 in a volume entitled *The Green Curve,* under the pseudonym of "Ole-Luk-Oie".

After serving at the War Office and having been promoted major in 1906, he went to Woolwich as chief instructor at the Royal Military Academy. In 1909 he joined the historical section of the Committee of Imperial Defence and was employed on the official history of the Russo-Japanese War. In recognition of this work he was awarded the Chesney gold medal of the Royal United Service Institution. He became assistant secretary of the Committee of Imperial Defence in October 1913. At the outbreak of war in 1914 he was appointed Deputy Director of Railway Transport.

Meanwhile Swinton had never ceased to ponder the possibilities of an armoured fighting vehicle with caterpillar tracks as the answer to the combination of barbed wire and machine-guns which made the German defence so formidable. In 1919 Mr. Justice Sargeant's commission on awards thus described Swinton's part: "This officer, acting outside the scope of his general duties, made an important contribution to the invention of the tank. This contribution included, first, the conception in October 1914 of a machine-gun destroyer of the general character of the tank; secondly, the persistent, energetic, and successful advocacy from then onwards of the value and feasibility of the employment of such an instrument of warfare; and, thirdly, the specific definition, in June 1915, of the necessary characteristics of the weapon, the conditions of its use, and the tests which it must be required to satisfy".

While production of the tank was in progress Swinton, who was promoted lieutenant-colonel in August 1915, was back in Whitehall deputizing as secretary of the Dardanelles Committee while Colonel Hankey* was in the Mediterranean. In February 1916 he wrote a memorandum on the tactical use of the tank. In March he was appointed to raise and command the "Heavy Section, Machine-Gun Corps", the first title of what became the Tank Corps. At last it seemed that his chance had come, but in November he went back to Whitehall.

When the United States entered the war, Swinton, then a brevet colonel, toured the country speaking of war aims. In August 1918 he was lent to the Ministry of Munitions for publicity work. After the armistice he continued this work as Assistant Controller-General of Publicity in the Demobilization and Resettlement Department of the Ministry of Labour. In May 1919 he retired from the Army with the honorary rank of major-general.

He afterwards went for a time to the Air Ministry as Controller of Civil Information. He had published a further collection of stories, *The Great Tab Dope,* in 1916. Other works followed, but his literary output hardly fulfilled the astonishing promise of its start. He was created a C.B. in 1917 and a K.B.E. in 1923. He was inclined to feel that his services had been inadequately recognized. It may be so, since they were very notable, but throughout the war he had not been considered eligible by G.H.Q. for any important appointment or command.

In 1925 he became Chichele Professor of Military History in the University of Oxford and Fellow of All Souls College. He was popular in All Souls common room, where his dry and shrewd humour was appreciated, and in the university generally, though he left no deep mark on its teaching.

He married in 1897 Grace Louisa, second daughter of Major Sir Edward G. Clayton, secretary to the Commissioners of Prisons, who survives him. He leaves two sons, his only daughter having been killed in a road accident during the 1939-45 war.

January 17, 1951.

Major-General Sir Frederick Sykes, G.C.S.I., G.C.I.E., G.B.E., K.C.B., C.M.G., a pioneer of wartime aviation and a former Governor of Bombay, died in a London hospital on September 30, 1954 at the age of 77.

Frederick Hugh Sykes was born on July 23, 1877, the son of Henry Sykes, of Addiscombe, Surrey. His mother was widowed when he was only two years old, and before he was 15 he went to Paris to spend two years studying, particularly French and German. At 17 he went out to Ceylon as a "creeper" on a tea estate. At 22 he volunteered for the South African War, in which he was severely wounded and was for a time a prisoner of de Wet. He obtained a commission in the 15th Hussars, but was little with that regiment, for in 1905 he was posted to the West Africa Regiment and then went to India in the Intelligence Branch.

As early as 1904 Sykes had obtained a ballooning certificate, and in 1910 at Brooklands made his first flight as a passenger in a Farman box-kite Ghnome machine of 50 h.p. He was in the list of the first hundred men to obtain the Aero Club's pilot's certificate, and was quick to see the enormous potentialities of aircraft. In 1912 he was appointed to recruit, train, and command the Military Wing of the newly established Royal Flying Corps. Night and day he worked to have the new arm ready for the impending war. When the die was cast in 1914 he had five squadrons trained and equipped, with plans for three more and a large reserve. He accompanied the first four squadrons to France, and during the retreat from Mons the B.E.F. was very greatly protected by the reconnaisances of this embryo formation. In 1915 Sykes was sent by the Admiralty to command the R.N.A.S. at the Dardanelles.

In 1916 Sykes was recalled to the War Office as Deputy Director of Organization. In the following year he went to Versailles on the British staff of the Supreme War Council. When the war was ending he was appointed chief of the Air Staff of the newly created Air Ministry, and in that capacity he was with the British delegation to the Versailles Peace Conference. In 1919 he was made Controller-General of Civil Aviation. On the expiry of his three years' term he refused an invitation from the Minister to serve for a further 12 months, on the ground that the current financial stringency was leading to undue curtailment of civil aviation.

At the general election of 1922 he entered Parliament as Conservative member for the Hallam division of Sheffield. After presiding over a government committee on the meteorological service he was appointed in 1923 chairman of the Broadcasting Committee, which laid down important principles of duly controlled monopoly. The establishment of a Broadcasting Board was recommended, and Sykes was its chairman from 1923 to 1927. Sykes resigned his seat in Parliament at the close of 1928 on appointment to succeed Sir Leslie Wilson as Governor of Bombay.

No Governor of Bombay since the establishment of Crown rule had been faced with so prolonged and intensive attempts to overthrow constituted authority, or with so devastating a drop in government revenues. Though the unpleasant duty of arranging twice for the arrest of Gandhi fell to Sykes, Congress leaders could not fail to hold him in great respect for the patience, fortitude, and breadth of view with which he faced his difficulties. The Irwin-Gandhi Pact brought a short respite to the political lawlessness, and this gave a chance for a constructive policy. Sykes seized it to make the first really determined effort in western India to introduce a scheme of village improvement which was based on the revival and modernization of the ancient *panchayat* (council of elected elders) system.

Sykes returned home at the close of 1933 to engage in many activities. In 1934 he was appointed chairman of the Miners' Welfare Committee. In his 12 years' tenure he worked persistently to secure that the conditions under which miners lived should be not less good than those of workers in other industries. In the summer of 1940 at a by-election for Central Nottingham he was again returned to Parliament and was in the House until the Labour victory at the 1945 General Election.

He was for three years from 1938 chairman of the Royal Empire Society, and thereafter vice-chairman and deputy president. He was president of the East India Association (India, Pakistan, and Burma) for five years from 1941. His philanthropy was reflected in his honorary treasurership from 1934 of the British Sailors' Society, with its world-wide beneficent activities. In the same year he was made a member of the Post Office Advisory Council. In 1938-39 he was appointed a member of the Government Licensing Board for Air Transport and he was also a director of various companies.

He married in 1920 Isabel Harrington, elder daughter of the late Bonar Law. There was a son of the marriage.

October 2, 1954.

Vernon Sylvaine died at his home at Angmering, Sussex, on November 22, 1957. He was 60.

He was an accomplished actor, had produced plays with some success and was the author of several serious pieces, but he is best remembered as a most talented exploiter of the farcical situation.

In one sense he was something of the author counterpart of the comedian who yearns to tear a passion to tatters (though the comparison is inexact), for while he wrote some dramatic pieces he made his mark with farce.

Sylvaine was born in Manchester on August 9, 1897, the son of Dr. John Conrad Scotchburn, and educated at the College of St. Francis Xavier, Mayfield, Sussex. He joined The Queen's Westminster Rifles in 1914, was commissioned in the following year, served in Belgium with The Somerset Light Infantry and was invalided out of the service in 1917.

The war behind him, he turned to the stage, studied elocution and, having appeared in Glasgow, made his first appearance on the London stage in October of the same year (1917) at the Palace Theatre as Captain Harrod in *Cash on Delivery*.

He went on to play a variety of parts, Charles Wykeham in *Charley's Aunt*, Lövborg in *Hedda Gabler*, Craig in *Craig's Wife*, Sir Colenso Ridgeon in *The Doctor's Dilemma*, and in 1928 appeared in *The Phantom Fear*, which he and Sydney Lynn had written, at His Majesty's Theatre. It was a thriller but not remarkable for its subtlety and showed few of the qualities that were seen in his piece *The Road of Poplars* (1930), a war play which was written with the feeling of one who knew both overtones and undertones of war.

Sylvaine's farcical successes made him one of the most successful theatrical authors of his time and, at the height of his career, there was hardly a break in the succession of plays from his pen at one or more London theatres—*Aren't Men Beasts?; A Spot of Bother; Worth a Million; Nap Hand; Women Aren't Angels; Madame Louise; One Wild Oat; Will Any Gentleman?;* many had long runs, became almost household names, and showed Sylvaine's ability to build up the comic situation into the wildly funny one. He was fortunate in his players (one has in mind in particular Robertson Hare and Alfred Drayton) and they in him. He exploited with great success the natural genius of Robertson Hare: in turn humorous, prim, gleeful, disastrously *déshabillé*, and the barking irascibility of Alfred Drayton. After Drayton's death Arthur Riscoe [q.v.] joined Hare, and a happy and successful partnership resulted—as witness *Will Any Gentleman?* One of Sylvaine's last big successes was *As Long as They're Happy*, in which Jack Buchanan [q.v.], who died recently, had a leading part.

November 25, 1957.

The Rev. Henry Herbert Symonds, who died at his home at Cartmel, Lancashire, on December 28, 1958 at the age of 73, had been described as "the driving force behind the National Parks and Access to the Countryside Act", and was a notable pioneer in the preservation of natural beauty. He had been in poor health for several months.

Often a most controversial figure, often under fire because of his strongly held views, at heart he was a most kindly man, completely without bitterness.

He was born in 1885 and had a brilliant career at Rugby and at Oxford, where he took a first in classical moderations and in Greats. He was an assistant master at Clifton College from 1909 to 1912 and then a senior master at Rugby, where he was in charge of the Upper Bench, the highest form on the classical side. In 1909 he was ordained. He was appointed headmaster of King's School, Chester, in 1922, and headmaster of the Liverpool Institute in 1924.

On his fiftieth birthday he retired to the Lake District and devoted the rest of his life to the preservation of its beauty and the promotion of national parks. He had known the Lake District intimately since undergraduate days and for many years had been introducing boys to the area by establishing school camps in Borrowdale and the Duddon Valley. He had been the first chairman of the Merseyside Youth Hostels Association which opened the first British youth hostels in North Wales.

He joined the newly formed Friends of the Lake District, and for the next 20 years was its guiding spirit, first as treasurer then as honorary secretary, and finally as chairman. For the same period he was a member of the Standing Committee on National Parks and later served as chairman of the North Wales (Hydro Electricity) Protection Committee formed to protest against the British Electricity Authority's designs on Snowdonia.

His principal interest, however, was in the Lake District, and thousands of walkers will remember him as the author of one of the best guides to the area, *Walking in the Lake District*, which he wrote during a Christmas holiday. Later he wrote another classic of its kind, *Afforestation in the Lake District*, which perhaps did more than anything else to save the central dale-heads from afforestation.

When the Lake District was designated as a national park Symonds was appointed to the Lake District Planning Board, but resigned after five years' active service. During many years before this he had worked tirelessly for the National Parks and Access to the Countryside Act by correspondence and in public and private meetings. In 1957 he was invited to become a member of the National Parks Commission, but six months later a serious operation left him unable to travel backwards and forwards to London.

He married first in 1911 C. Gwendolen Watson by whom he had a son and two daughters. She died in 1937 and in the following year he married Ruth B. W. Williams.

December 30, 1958.

T

Senator Robert A. Taft, who as Republican leader in the Senate in the last years of President Truman's* and the first year of President Eisenhower's* Administrations wielded great political power, died on July 31, 1953 in a New York hospital. He was 63.

Son of a Republican President and inheritor of a great name, he achieved a position of rare distinction in his party, and his allegiance to it overruled all other considerations, as his whole career, but especially the last few years of it, amply proved. He built his life round his ambition to be the second of his line to occupy the White House, but four times the honour of the Republican nomination eluded him. Immediately after his last and most bitter defeat, when his hopes had run highest, he rose to say: "I will do everything in my power to help General Eisenhower in the campaign".

To him the American way of life meant free enterprise limited only by the needs of good order, with no more restrictions on individual activity than those demanded by a communal civilization. Above all, he believed in the self-sufficiency of the United States, in its capacity to live alone and to act alone. It is only fair to say that many millions of his fellow-citizens still share his belief in a free economy at home and no commitments abroad. He opposed President Roosevelt's New Deal and President Truman's Fair Deal, thus earning a reputation for uncompromising conservatism and provoking the intense antagonism of organized labour.

Abroad, his reputation was chiefly that of an isolationist, though through the years he cautiously modified his attitude; thus, he opposed conscription, lend-lease, and President Roosevelt's plan to send destroyers to Britain. He opposed the Bretton Woods agreements, and American loans abroad. He voted against the North Atlantic Treaty Organization, but later accepted the United States' obligations under the Atlantic Pact, and though he tried originally to water down the Marshall [q.v.] Plan, he later voted for the Foreign Aid Bill.

He fully deserved his reputation for honesty and candour. Many there were, indeed, in his own party who found his candour something less than an asset. His critics maintained that in thought he belonged to the last century and was short-sighted in world affairs, and it is true that, with all his remarkable gifts for assembling and sorting facts, he had an even more striking capacity for drawing conclusions which seemed to be based on the tacit assumption that American life was at its best about 1910. His admirers, on the other hand, argued that he understood the art of government better than any man in Washington, that he was not ashamed to admit mistakes, and that he had the kind of classifying and sorting mind which particularly fitted him for the White House. Tall, bespectacled, with sparse grey hair, he dressed carelessly, spoke drily, and had a quiet humour, embellished by an engaging, almost boyish grin. In private he was a genial and witty conversationalist, but in the Senate he was, though a capable speaker, cold, aggressive, and persistent.

Robert Alphonso Taft was born in Cincinnati on September 8, 1889, the son of William Howard Taft, twenty-seventh President of the United States, by his marriage with Helen Herron. As a boy he spent some three years in the Philippine Islands, where his father was Governor. He was educated at his uncle Horace Taft's school in Connecticut, and later, during his father's Presidency, at Yale. In 1913 he went on to the Harvard Law School and, having secured top marks, was admitted in the same year to the Ohio State Bar. He then joined the Cincinnati law firm of Maxwell and Ramsay and practised in it for four years. Shortly afterwards he married Miss Martha Wheaton Bowers, daughter of Lloyd Bowers, who had been Solicitor-General in his father's Administration. She was a distinguished woman, who was destined to be of great assistance to him in his career. Her great ambition, never fulfilled, was to see her husband installed in the White House, and she bent all her efforts and all her considerable ability to this end.

In 1917 Taft sought to enlist but was rejected because of faulty vision. Soon after, however, he was appointed assistant counsel for the United States Food Administration and later counsel for the American Relief Administration in Europe. The war over, he and his younger brother Charles opened a law office in Cincinnati which eventually became, as Taft, Stettinius and Hollister, the largest and most prosperous in Ohio, its clients including many of the principal corporations in the city. Shortly after his resumption of his legal work, Taft stood for the Ohio state legislature, and was duly elected. He had been regarded as a "silk stocking" candidate unsuited to the rough and tumble of politics; but he astonished his colleagues by taking on the hardest task he could find, the overhauling of the state's antiquated tax system. By 1925 he was House Leader; in 1926 Speaker of the House; and in 1931-32 served in the Ohio Senate. Even though a new member he took—he was an effective speaker—an active role in debate, and owing to his own ability as well as his distinguished name, also became an outstanding figure in the Republican Party. In 1936, therefore, he was Ohio's "favourite son" at the Republican National Convention.

He embarked in 1938 upon an extensive campaign for the Senate at Washington in which his wife worked strenuously for him. It is told of her that in one hostile mining region which they visited she said to the miners: "My husband is not a simple man. He did not start from humble beginnings. He is a very brilliant man and trained well for his job. Isn't that what you want when you pick a man to work for you?" The appeal was not, as the result of the election showed, made in vain. In 1940 Taft was a candidate in the race for his party's nomination for the Presidency of the United States. In 1944 also he had a large following which would have supported him; but he eliminated himself as a candidate by saying: "John Bricker loyally supported my candidacy in 1940 and I intend to do the same thing for him in 1944".

The Republican national chairman appointed him in 1943 to formulate a domestic programme for consideration at the Mackinac Island party conference in September of that year. This programme he extended later in a newspaper article, explaining that in his view the issues of 1944 were predominantly domestic and national, not international. In regard to foreign policy, however, the Mackinac declaration called for "a responsible participation by the United States in a post-war cooperative organization among sovereign nations to prevent military aggression and attain permanent peace with organized justice in a free world". In 1944 he was elected chairman of the steering committee by a unanimous vote of Senate Republicans, thus becoming one of the three co-leaders of his party in the Upper House.

Although by this time he had given ground on the isolationist principles he had enunciated in and out of season before the entry of the United States into the war, the victory of 1945 did little or nothing to destroy his distrust of foreign commitments. He was one of the seven Senators who in December of that year opposed on the final vote the participation of the United States in the United Nations.

The most important result of his influence in domestic politics came in 1947 with the passage of the Taft-Hartley Act, which restricted the power of the trade unions and was particularly directed against the principle of the "closed shop". The Act was passed into law in spite of the veto of President Truman; though later Senator Taft was willing to consider modifications, he was strongly opposed to its repeal. He remained bitterly opposed to Socialism and its growth in Europe after the war did not incline him to go far to modifying his isolationism. Although he had originally voted against the ratification of the Atlantic Pact, he nevertheless declared later that Russia should be warned that an attack on western Europe would mean war with the United States.

After his defeat by General Eisenhower for the Republican nomination in 1952, Senator Taft announced that it was his last bid for the Presidency. He had been a possible choice for the nomination at every Republican Convention since 1936 but his hopes had run highest in 1952. He demonstrated his loyalty by immediately congratulating the victor, but there were reservations on both sides. After President Eisenhower was installed, Senator Taft presented him with a full list of nominations for his Cabinet. One by one Taft's nominees were passed over, but no crisis was reached until Martin Durkin, a Democrat, who had advocated the repeal of the Taft-Hartley Act, was appointed Secretary of Labour. After this incident there was for a while some doubt as to whether Taft would become majority leader in the new Senate. He was, however, elected to the office on the eve of the opening of the eighty-third Congress, and in spite of his known views loyally set himself to the task of translating the policies of President Eisenhower's Administration into legislation.

He recognized that the Republican majority had been elected on a clear policy of international cooperation, including support for the United Nations, the North Atlantic Pact, and other forms of full, and expensive, participation by the United States in the maintenance of international security. Yet, though he did not publicly impugn President Eisenhower's international outlook, he said little to indicate that he accepted cheerfully the burdens involved in world leadership. Seven years of membership of the United Nations by the United States had done little to modify his views, and even in his last two months or so, while suffering from the ailment from which he eventually died, he found means to ventilate his views. He declared, for instance, that the United States "might well forget the United Nations as far as the Korean war is concerned" and suggested a Pacific alliance headed by the United States. Later, commenting on a possible peace conference to follow the truce in Korea, he said: "I suppose we shall have a large-scale international peace conference, the kind that has not been very successful in the past. That is what we are in for, and we shall have to make the best of it".

On June 10 he announced in the Senate that his hip ailment would keep him from his duties as majority leader for the rest of the session and Senator William Knowland took over the leadership.

August 1, 1953.

The robust and genial personality of **Thomas Smith Tait,** F.R.I.B.A., who died at Aberfeldy on July 18, 1954 at the age of 72, is well indicated by the name "Tommy Tait" by which he was generally known to his colleagues.

With his combination of solidity and a surface play of emotional sensibility, he might have stood for the portrait of a typical architect as required by modern conditions, and that he should be the son of a builder was all in the picture. Experience tells that, given a sense of form, the art of architecture is more promisingly approached from a constructional foundation than from above out of a vaguely aesthetic attitude, and modern building, with its emphasis on the engineering side, gives a special point to this.

Most of Tait's earlier work was done in association with the late Sir John Burnet, R.A., upon whose death in 1938 he became senior partner in the firm of Sir John Burnet, Tait & Lorne, and there can be no doubt that the two men were in full architectural sympathy. Burnet once said that he counted himself fortunate in having begun architectural practice at a time when the demands of the client had become varied and definite. He conceived it as the business of the architect to find his artistic effect in the solution of the practical problem, whatever it might be, in all its bearings. This faith is evident in all Tait's work, and it helps to explain a building that most people regard with some disfavour—Selfridges.

What the same architects could do with different demands of the client is well shown in Adelaide House, London Bridge, which has become historical as the first—excepting

Burnet's Kodak Building, Kingsway, in which Tait was not concerned—of the big modern commercial buildings in London. The historical interest, it may be said, refers to the future rather than to the past because, though it is grandly simple and finely proportioned, Adelaide House is rather heavy and "Egyptian" in effect. It suggests an excess of material over form which Tait and other contemporary architects, like the Greeks with the post and beam principle, have learnt to avoid with the steel-frame principle of construction.

Whether by design or accident Tait's buildings were apt to run in pairs of contrasted traditional and modern. About the time of Adelaide House he was engaged with Burnet upon the King Edward VII Gallery of the British Museum, which has been described as the finest piece of pure classical architecture since St. George's Hall, Liverpool.

By the time of the new Government buildings, known as St. Andrew's House, Edinburgh, and the 1938 Empire Exhibition, Glasgow, Burnet had long ceased to take any active part in affairs, so that they may be looked upon as Tait's design throughout. Again there is a contrast, but with a change. The suggestion is that Tait's individual development was towards an architectural mean of his own to which questions of style should be merely incidental. In the case of St. Andrew's House, for which Tait was chosen as architect by a committee appointed by the Office of Works, something classical was almost imperative, both on account of the purpose of the building, to accommodate the Secretary of State's office and various Government departments for Scotland, and the character of the site, with the "Acropolis" of Calton Hill and its monuments as a background. Tait's solution was a simple, massive building with a boldly horizontal line, providing a firm base to the rocky height above and recognizing its monuments by feeling rather than by allusion. It is, perhaps, the most successful piece of "stripped classic" in the kingdom.

The Glasgow Exhibition was a different story; an occasion for high spirits in a park; and Tait seized upon it with zest under the control of the same sense of order as in St. Andrew's House and an exemplary regard for natural surroundings.

From the works named it is possible to define Tait's characteristics as an architect as a masculine common sense in meeting "the demands of the client" and in grasping the "practical problem . . . in all its bearings", to quote his old principal, Burnet, and directness with a fine sense of proportion in finding his artistic effect in the solution of the problem. No architect of his time had a clearer vision or showed a more whole-hearted acceptance of things as they are; including the circumstance that architecture becomes more and more a matter of group, or team work, and the assembling of more or less standardized building units. Both the common sense and the vision are well shown in the block of flats known as Mount Royal, near Marble Arch.

Tait, who has been described as "a dynamic little Scotsman with the vitality of a bobbing cork", was the son of John Tait, builder, and was born at Paisley in 1882. He was educated at the Paisley Technical Institute and studied art and architecture at the Glasgow School of Art and the Royal Academy Schools. As a student he won the King's Prize for Architecture and Decorative Art. Except that, like a good Scotsman, he played golf, he was completely absorbed in his profession—it is said that he would jot down notes while shaving or eating—and so far as can be remembered he never took part in any public discussion of architecture or any other subject.

Tait was married and had three sons.

July 20, 1954.

Sir Stephen Tallents, K.C.M.G., C.B., C.B.E., died in London on September 11, 1958. He was 73.

A Civil servant with imagination, completely unfettered by red tape, would be a fair description of Tallents. His trim, military figure moved briskly (with no more than a trace of limp from his first war wound) through Whitehall. But he was in it rather than of it. He was at his happiest among artists and country men who shared his enthusiasm for growing melons and cultivating a garden. This measure of detachment did not prevent him from throwing himself with zest into a miscellany of official duties—and it went with a genius for publicity or, to use his own word, "projection", in the film sense of throwing a picture upon the screen.

Stephen George Tallents was born on October 20, 1884. He was the eldest son of the late George William Tallents, barrister, and through his mother, who was the daughter of Lord Ashcombe, he was descended from Thomas Cubitt, the builder and capitalist. Tallents was educated at Harrow, under Wood, and Balliol College, Oxford, completing his academic career with a course at Grenoble.

At the age of 25 he entered the Marine Department of the Board of Trade and was instrumental in promoting measures against beri-beri, characteristically backing the men of science against the officials. Next he was transferred to help Sir William [later Lord*] Beveridge and Sir Hubert Llewellyn Smith in establishing labour or unemployment exchanges.

During the First World War Tallents, who had previously had yeomanry experience, joined the Irish Guards, served in France and was so badly wounded that it took him a year to recover. After his recovery, and under the influence of his old chiefs, he joined the Ministry of Munitions, but soon exchanged it for the Ministry of Food. This was the time of the food queues, and as principal secretary to the Ministry and member of the Food Council Tallents could claim to be the first rationer.

In 1919 Tallents was appointed chief British delegate for the relief and supply of Poland, and a year later as British Commissioner for the Baltic Provinces of Lithunania, Latvia and Estonia, with the rank of colonel. For a few days he was Governor of Riga. Before he was recalled in 1920 to make way for a more professional diplomatic representative, he had proved his resourcefulness by restoring law and order in what was then a chaotic world of conflicting interests. After his return to England Tallents became private secretary to Viscount Fitzalan, Lord-Lieutenant of Ireland, and, from 1922 until 1926, he was Imperial Secretary for Northern Ireland.

Except officially, very little is known of these earlier activities, and it was not until 1926, when Amery [q.v.] picked him out, as an exception to the prevailing orthodoxy in the ranks of Whitehall, to be Secretary of the Empire Marketing Board, that he became known to wider circles. As senior official in that transient body—much disliked and distrusted by bureacracy—he was supported by able outsiders, especially Frank Pick of the Underground and the advertising agent, William Crawford. Tallents showed himself, here, at his best, encouraging artists in poster work and playing a too little recognized part in seeing the documentary film through its teething stages. What may be called the Grierson* school owed much to his patronage.

It was in a pamphlet entitled *The Projection of England,* published in 1932 and reviewed in a turnover article in *The Times* of April 16 in that year, that Tallents first made public use of the word with which his name was especially associated. He asked for the projection upon the screen of world opinion for such a picture of England "as will create a belief in her ability to serve the world under the new order, as she has served it in the past. Deprecating "that instinct of withdrawal which has made the Government services of the world the legitimate successors of the monastic orders", he suggested the creation in the borderland lying between Government and private enterprise of a "school of national projection". Its members should be selected less on account of their existing affiliations than by reason of their diverse personal qualities, and while they must have something of the sense of responsibility, the prestige and the opportunities of Government, they must be more free to make experiments, and mistakes, than the ordinary Government cares to be.

It may be observed in passing that, whether or not through his influence, a good deal of what Tallents proposed is now covered by the activities of the British Council. It is probable, too, that the "Britain in Pictures" series of illustrated books owed something to his ideas.

When the Empire Marketing Board ceased to exist in September 1933 Tallents, who had been for some time a member of the Post Office Publicity Committee, was appointed Public Relations Officer at the General Post Office. His success there may be judged from the circumstances that in 1935 he was presented with the Cup of the Publicity Club of London, considered the highest award in the advertising world. This was the first time in the history of advertising in Britain that the cup had been presented to a Government official.

Then followed a period, begun in 1936, with the B.B.C., first as Controller (Public Relations)—this was not the happiest phase of his career for, although he found the new medium fascinating, he never got his feelings at home in the unfamiliar atmosphere of

Broadcasting House.

Tallents became Public Relations Officer of the Ministry of Town and Country Planning. On his retirement from public life he interested himself in a firm producing architectural models.

Tallents wrote several articles for *The Times*, and he was an occasional correspondent on unexpected subjects like "Plants with a History". His publications included two early collections of short stories: *The Starry Pool*, 1918, and *The Dancer*, 1922; *The Projection of England*, 1932; and *Post Office Publicity*, 1935. A volume of reminiscences, *Man and Boy*, published in 1943, gives interesting details of his childhood in Ennismore Gardens and of his war service and early activities in the diplomatic field.

He was created C.B. in 1918, C.B.E. in 1920, C.M.G. in 1929, and K.C.M.G. in 1932. There was a piquant contrast between his passion for publicity on behalf of England and the institutions he served, and his personal behaviour. At any rate to a casual acquaintance, he was an attractively shy man with pleasant and slightly apologetic manners. Perhaps the best proof of his diffidence was that in more than one chance encounter he had to introduce himself again.

In 1914 Tallents married Bridget, daughter of S. H. F. Hole, barrister of the Inner Temple and lord of the manor of Canton in Nottinghamshire. They had two sons and two daughters.

In 1943 the National Trust announced the gift from Sir Stephen and Lady Tallents of their home in Kent, St. John's Jerusalem, Sutton-at-Hone, Dartford. From the beginning of the thirtieth century to the dissolution of the Order this house, largely rebuilt in Georgian style by Hasted, the historian of Kent, was a Commandery of the Knights of St. John of Jerusalem. It was added that Sir Stephen Tallents would continue to make St. John's Jerusalem his family home as a tenant of the Trust.

September 13, 1958.

Sir Arthur Tansley, F.R.S., who died on November 25, 1955 at his home at Grantchester, Cambridge, at the age of 84, was a scientist of widely ranging interests who made an outstanding contribution to the study of ecology.

Arthur George Tansley was the son of George Tansley, one of the great figures of the Working Men's College, London. He was born in 1871, and educated at Highgate School, University College London, and Trinity College, Cambridge. Obtaining a first class in botany in Part II of the Natural Sciences Tripos in 1894, he first joined the staff at University College London, where he became assistant professor, but in 1906 he returned to Cambridge as lecturer, residing at Grantchester which remained his permanent home. Having become much interested in psychology he resigned his lectureship in 1919 in order to study under Freud at Vienna. On returning to England he continued his botanical investigations in a private capacity till in 1927 he was elected to the Sherardian professorship of botany at Oxford, from which he retired in 1937. There he infused new life into the department and gathered around him an excellent staff, all imbued with his own enthusiasm for the newer developments in botany.

Although Tansley's early interests in botany were chiefly in morphology his attention was soon diverted to ecology, in his case the study of plant communities in their widest aspects, and it is as a pioneer and leader in this field that he will be chiefly remembered. Towards the end of the nineteenth century the intensive study of natural plant communities began on the continent. A few British botanists joined the quest, and in 1904 was founded "the central committee for the survey and study of British vegetation", of which Tansley became a member and soon the acknowledged spokesman. The committee stimulated much survey work on the woodlands, moors, heaths, fens, and coastal lands of Britain, in which Tansley took a principal part.

It was Tansley who suggested that the committee should organize the first international phytogeographical excursion, which was successfully held in the British Isles during the summer of 1911, the most interesting tracts of vegetation being visited by ecologists from many countries. Apart from interruption by war these international excursions have been continued and Tansley was a prominent member of them. Largely through his instigation the British Ecological Society was founded in 1913, and he became its first president.

Throughout his career Tansley maintained his profound interest in natural vegetation and contributed much to the basic concepts of ecology, such as the classification of plant communities and their succession, and the influence of animal and human factors. It is well that in the uprising of ecology Tansley's insight and powers of analysis were at the disposal of his fellow workers. Another book which had a marked influence on the development of ecology was *Aims and Methods in the Study of Vegetation* by himself and the late T. F. Chipp, which arose out of the first Imperial Botanical Conference held in 1924.

The culmination of Tansley's scientific career came in 1939 when he published his truly monumental book *The British Isles and their Vegetation*, the result of lifelong study and unrivalled personal knowledge. In this vast work, which has a wide appeal to all interested in the countryside, he drew upon his great knowledge of climatology and geology in the elucidation of British plant communities, and numerous students repaid their debt to him in part by contributing all the information at their disposal. This book has already become a classic and will remain a stimulating guide to generations of botanists yet to come. It won for him the award of the gold medal of the Linnean Society of London.

After the conference in 1942 on nature conservation in post-war reconstruction, Tansley became chairman of a committee of the Ecological Society appointed to formulate a policy concerning the provision of nature reserves. This led to a comprehensive report on Nature Conservation and Nature Reserves, and later to a memorandum on Wild-life Conservation and ecological research from the national standpoint. His views on these matters were embodied in a beautiful little book, *Our Heritage of Wild Nature*, published in 1945.

His interest and knowledge concerning the preservation of the flora and fauna of this country were recognized by his appointment as vice-chairman of the Wild Life Conservation Special Committee of the Ministry of Town and Country Planning, and as chairman of the Nature Conservancy when that body was formed in 1949. He also took a leading part in the activities of the Council for the Promotion of Field Studies from its inception, and was its president from 1947 to 1953.

Tansley had wide intellectual interests. After his sojourn with Freud in 1919 he wrote *The New Psychology*, an excellent exposition of what was then a new school of thought, which was reprinted several times. His analytical qualities of mind were finely shown in his Herbert Spencer lecture at Oxford on *The Values of Science to Humanity* (1942). This expressed his deep convictions of liberal humanism, which also made him actively embrace the foundation of the Society for Freedom in Science. Two years ago he published *Mind and Life*, which, though vulnerable to philosophical criticism, is the testament of a biologist deeply concerned with the place of man in the scheme of nature and the heritage of the animal in the human mind.

Tansley was knighted in 1950. He was elected Fellow of the Royal Society in 1915 and an honorary fellow of Trinity College, Cambridge, in 1944, an honour which gave him particular pleasure.

He married in 1903 Edith, daughter of Samuel Chick. There were three daughters of the marriage.

November 28, 1955.

Sir William Tarn died at his home, Muirtown, Inverness, on November 7, 1957.

Born in 1869, William Woodthorpe Tarn was educated in College at Eton, as a pupil of A. C. Ainger, and was in the select for the Newcastle and a Mathematical prizeman. From Eton he went to Trinity College, Cambridge, where he became a distinguished disciple of Henry Jackson. He then read for the Bar and was called by the Inner Temple. He had already made a name as a Chancery barrister when a severe illness forced him to retire from the practice of the law. For the rest of his life, apart from a period in the 1914-18 War when he did intelligence work in London, his home was in Scotland, first near Dingwall and then at Muirtown House by Inverness.

As his health improved he devoted himself to the study of Hellenistic history. His first book, *Antigonos Gonatas*, published in 1913, displayed his power of combining political history with the interpretation of philosophic ideas, and won for him recognition in Hellenistic studies both in this country and abroad. This position he fortified by very many papers in which, on disputed points, he showed himself a forceful, while courteous, controversialist. His method of work was to collect his material during long visits to London, and then retire to the north to write with a mature judgment born of long reflection.

In 1923 an essay on the social question in the third century in *The Hellenistic Age* showed his grasp of ancient economics; five years later he published the first edition of his *Hellenistic Civilisation,* which is still the best survey of the field he had made his own. Tarn contributed chapters to four volumes of the *Cambridge Ancient History,* notably a brilliant account of Alexander the Great and a masterly chapter on Parthia. He was critical of Rome's dealings with the Greek world under the Republic, and his picture of Cleopatra, as the last of the Macedonians, was drawn with sympathy and insight.

Meanwhile his interest in ancient naval and military history had been revealed by articles on the trireme and on ancient fleets, and in particular by his Lee Knowles Lectures *Hellenistic Military and Naval Developments.* After this he spent several years on what was to be a pioneer work, *The Greeks in Bactria and India,* in which for the first time the Greek and Indian evidence was united in an original and learned synthesis. He made two striking contributions to the *Proceedings of the British Academy, Alexander the Great and the Unity of Mankind* and *Seleucid-Parthian Studies,* which exemplified the range and depth of his historical work.

During the 1939-45 War Tarn was persuaded to prepare a revision of his Alexander chapters in the *Cambridge Ancient History,* together with a companion volume of *Sources and Studies,* which preserves for scholars the wide and penetrating researches which underlay all his work on this theme. He also wrote a sketch of Greek and Roman history as a contribution to *The European Inheritance.*

His eminence as an historian was recognized by his election to the British Academy and by what he prized even more, an Honorary Fellowship of Trinity. He was an Honorary Doctor of Edinburgh and a foreign member of several academies and learned societies. He was knighted in 1952.

By the side of his historical work Tarn had lived the life of a hospitable country gentleman. He was a good shot, and had many friends among his neighbours. He was devoted to the countryside, especially of the Isle of Skye, which is the setting of a fairy story, *The Treasure of the Isle of Mist,* written for his daughter, a book widely read both in Great Britain and America. In his house at Muirtown, when he had ceased to be able to travel, he rejoiced in the occasional visits of scholars who brought him news of the world from which he was half withdrawn. He had a wide correspondence, and his learning and criticism were always at the disposal of anyone who wished to do serious work in Hellenistic history.

The study in Britain of the Ancient World has owed much to those who were able to devote themselves to scholarship without holding academical positions. Of this class, now so small, Tarn was a very eminent example. And the early phase in his career when he was at the Chancery Bar equipped him with a precision of thought and expression and a cool evaluation of evidence which was a great strength to him. But he had also a natural highminded enthusiasm, a capacity for admiration, which at times infused his writings with a warmth and colour that makes the conclusion of his account of Alexander the Great, for example, one of the great passages in English history-writing.

When, in his later years, he had to contend with ill-health he retained a notable power of work and vigour of mind, and he did not outlive his capacity for friendship and happiness, above all in the company of his daughter and grandchildren. He remained all his life the student that appears, self-revealed, in *The Treasure of the Isle of Mist.*

In 1896 he married Flora Macdonald, third daughter of John Robertson, of Orbost, Isle of Skye, and they had one daughter. His wife died in 1937.

November 8, 1957.

The well-known chessmaster **Dr. Savielly Tartakower** died in Paris on February 6, 1956, at the age of 68.

Savielly Grigorievitch Tartakower was born at Rostov-on-Don, in southern Russia, on February 9, 1887. His parents were Austro-Polish and he classed himself as Polish during the earlier part of his chess career. Leaving Russia in 1899, he matriculated at the College of Geneva in 1904 and then studied law at Vienna University, where he obtained his doctorate in 1909. From 1924 till his death he lived in Paris and he became a naturalized French citizen in the 1930s. He had a highly successful career as a tournament player, winning a large number of first prizes, notably in Vienna in 1905 and 1923, Ghent in 1926, Paris in 1929, Hastings in 1926, 1927, and 1945, Liège in 1930, and Venice in 1947. Two other fine achievements were his equal first with Nimzovitch in London, 1927, and again at Bad Niendorf in the same year. He also won matches against Spielmann, Reti, Lilienthal, and others.

Though he never quite came into the category of player who would be reckoned as a candidate for the world championship, he was recognized as a great master for most of his life; and with good reason, since when in form he was a match for the best and he included among his victims no less a player than the then world champion, Dr. Alekhine. His one weakness—an over-indulgence in imaginative complications—occasionally led to a loss, or even a succession of losses; but this was more than compensated by the large number of beautiful and original games which he constantly produced throughout his career.

A prolific writer, he exerted great influence on the theory of the game and published many books that were illuminated by his own special brand of sparkling wit. Among his more important works were: *The Hyper-modern Game, Neo-Romantic Chess, Chess Method, Breviary of Chess, Five Hundred Master Games of Modern Chess* (in collaboration with J. du Mont), and two collections of his own best games, the second of which is in the press at the moment. Dr. Tartakower was not only a master of chess but also a master of the art of conversation, in which he was equally at home in philosophy and the arts. He wrote poetry in three languages, Russian, French, and German, and was one of those versatile and many-sided men whom the University of Vienna had a habit of producing in the days of the Austro-Hungarian Empire.

February 8, 1956.

Marshal de Lattre de Tassigny—See **Lattre.**

Maurice Tate, the Sussex and England all-round cricketer, died suddenly at his home at Wadhurst, Sussex, on May 18, 1956, aged 61.

Since his retirement from first class cricket in 1937 Tate had been a publican at several Sussex inns, and for the past few years had acted as cricket coach at Tonbridge School.

Tate was born on April 29, 1895, and was the son of F. W. Tate, at one time a well-known member of the Sussex XI. Maurice showed only moderate promise as a boy, but in 1910 he was tried for the Sussex nursery and was engaged for the season. Two years later he was taken at short notice to play for Sussex against Northamptonshire. Bowling much slower in those early days, he took one wicket for 28 runs, and, going in last, scored four and six runs.

His first really successful season as a bowler was 1923, when his figures were remarkable, for he accounted for 219 wickets at a cost of 13 runs each. He was chosen to accompany the team taken out by A. E. R. Gilligan [d. 1976] to Australia in the winter of 1924-25. Though our men won only one out of the rubber of five games, our victory was the first that had come our way for more than 12 years, and was welcome on that account. Tate well justified his selection, for in the Tests he took 38 wickets, more than any bowler, English or Australian, had ever done.

This may be said to have been the high-water mark of his career, though on subsequent occasions he rendered much valuable assistance. Altogether he represented England in 20 Test matches against Australia, 10 on our grounds and 10 on theirs. Of these, seven were won, seven lost, and six drawn. He took 83 wickets at an average cost of just under 30 runs a wicket.

He made trips to Africa, India, and New Zealand, and played against the West Indies when they visited us. His first Test was against South Africa in the early summer of 1924, and was made memorable by the dismissal of our opponents for 30 runs in their first innings. The bowlers were Gilligan, the captain, and Tate himself.

His last Test was also against South Africa,

in 1935. He was recalled for the occasion, but his bowling is described as having lost much of its former fire. His batting was also successful in more than one of these important engagements. At Lord's in 1929, when South Africa had rather the best of the position, he knocked up 100 not out, a fine display of hitting, and at other times he contributed usefully to our total.

In county cricket his figures for Sussex supply remarkable evidence of his ability as an all-round player. When he was at his best, for eight consecutive seasons from 1922 to 1929 he obtained the double success of scoring 1,000 runs and taking 100 wickets. The highest score he made was in 1921 against Northamptonshire at Brighton. In partnership for the second wicket with Bowley, a leading Sussex batsman, the pair increased the score by 386 runs, Tate's share being 203.

Tate was a bowler of fast-medium pace, with a good action, He did not turn much, but came quick off the pitch. He was of the type of J. T. Hearne, always recalled by those who watched him as the ideal medium pace right-hand bowler. As a fieldsman Tate was not distinguished, but he was a safe enough catch near the wicket, he was a thorough trier from start to finish, and, when his career ended, it was well said of him that he had contributed much to the revival of our cricket after a long period of failure.

May 19, 1956.

The death in London on October 3, 1957 of **Canon Tissington Tatlow** at the age of 81 removes one who has counted far more in the Churches of Great Britain and beyond than any mere outline of his career would suggest. Indeed, at a luncheon in his honour on his eightieth birthday the Archbishop of Canterbury, who presided, testified to his far-reaching influence, and to the debt owed to him by himself and his three immediate predecessors.

Educated at St. Columbia's College and at Trinity College, Dublin, it was among students that for a major portion of his life his work lay. He was, in fact, the founder, or co-founder with Dr. Oldham, of the Student Christian Movement as it is known to-day. He was its general secretary for nearly 30 years, and became its historian. Generation after generation of students came under his spell, and he travelled widely for the Worlds Student Christian Federation, in Europe and North America. At an important stage of its life he effectively commended the movement to Anglicans of all types, and won their participation in its conferences.

But Tatlow's interests and influence were never confined to student circles. He founded the Anglican Fellowship in 1912, and as its first secretary fostered what became an important instrument of Anglican unity. But his reconciling influence extended far beyond the Church of England. His intimate understanding of all the Churches, and his host of friends in all the Churches, the rich harvest of his Student Movement days, combined with his gentle but indomitable persistence in overcoming obstacles, human and financial, equipped him for a leading part in bringing about the Edinburgh Missionary Conference of 1910, and subsequent ecumenical developments in the British Council of Churches and the World Council of Churches.

His City churches, All Hallows, Lombard Street, and later St. Edmund the King, he made acceptable centres of worship for students. Yet another foundation owes its existence and strength to Tatlow, the Institute of Christian Education at home and oversea, which he initiated in 1936 and served to the end as director.

Archbishop Davidson installed Tatlow as Honorary Canon of Canterbury in 1926, a year after the University of Edinburgh had conferred on him an honorary D.D. He was a Select Preacher at both Oxford and Cambridge.

October 5, 1957.

Dr. F. Sherwood Taylor, Director of the Science Museum, South Kensington, since 1950, died on January 5, 1956 at the age of 58.

Frank Sherwood, son of Seaton Frank and Helen Sennerth Taylor, was born in 1897. He was educated at Sherborne School, Lincoln College, Oxford, and University College London. For 12 years from 1921 he was chemistry master at various schools, including Gresham's and Repton. He was then appointed assistant lecturer in inorganic chemistry at Queen Mary College, London, where he taught until 1938. He was curator of the Museum of the History of Science at Oxford for 10 years from 1940, before his appointment as director of the Science Museum at South Kensington. There his most important work was necessarily administrative, and he was a member of numerous committees. He did much to develop the teaching side of the museum, through its lecture service, and special courses of lectures, with demonstrations, for fifth form school boys. He also showed great interest in the science library at a critical stage of its history, and under his direction the collection of early scientific books has greatly increased.

Taylor's interest in the history of science owed much to the good sense of Lincoln College. He was prevented by the First World War from taking up a classical scholarship to which he had been elected, and on his return to the university he asked, and was allowed by his college, to read science instead. The combination of classical and scientific training was the determining factor in his career. Later he was one of the first students in the Department of History and Method of Science at University College London, and there obtained his doctorate of philosophy.

His attention was drawn to the Alexandrian alchemists, for whom he had feelings as well as knowledge. He was one of the founder members of the Society for the Study of Alchemy and Early Chemistry, and published in the society's journal *Ambix* a number of translations from the Greek, as well as his own papers. He was especially successful in distinguishing between the operations used by alchemists and their meaning to those who used them.

His interest in the history of science in general was a natural outgrowth from this first love. He was an able expositor and enjoyed both lecturing and writing for audiences wider than his own immediate field of work. An example was his *The World of Science* (1936). This was neither a textbook nor a history but in his own description an attempt "to answer in simple terms the questions which the ordinary man and woman ask about living creatures, the world and the mechanical devices daily encountered by all". On the history of science he read widely and wrote carefully, and his combination of scholarship and general appeal was here his most useful asset. He was a former president of the British Society for the History of Science in which he had been interested from its beginning. In his short *Science Past and Present* (1945) he made penetrating use of the method of illustrative quotation from original sources (not always the obvious ones), and showed incidentally why his earlier *Short History of Science* had been the book that it was; he was never remote from his subject.

One other of his many books, *The Alchemists* (1952), calls for special mention. Short as it was, it distilled for his readers the results of much earlier work, and is probably the best general book on the subject. He was no believer in the universal ability of science to provide solutions for every human problem, and in his later historical books especially his views as a Roman Catholic (he had earlier been received into the Church) were represented by caveats in this sense. And he took up the subject of the relation between science and religion in such books as *The Fourfold Vision* (1945) and *Two Ways of Life* (1947). Soft-spoken and mannered, it was possible to differ from him and not quarrel. He will be remembered for himself, for his work on alchemy, and as a scholarly popular writer of science and its history.

January 7, 1956.

Sir Gordon Gordon-Taylor—See **Gordon-.**

Theodore Cooke Taylor, who died on October 19, 1952 at his home at Grassington, Yorkshire, at the age of 102, had been for many years up to the time of his death chairman of J., T. and J. Taylor, woollen manufacturers, of Batley. He was known principally as a pioneer of profit-sharing in industry. He was the leader, too, for many years in Britain of the anti-opium movement which secured the suppression of the traffic between India and China.

He was born on August 3, 1850, at the New Hall, Carlinghow, Batley, the eldest son of Joshua Taylor, by his wife Alice, a daughter of Samuel Cooke, of Liversedge, a pioneer in the West Riding carpet manufacturing industry. The Taylors had been engaged in cloth manufacture for over 100 years before he was born. His great-grandfather, Abraham Taylor, was apprenticed to the trade as long ago as 1762, and his grandfather, Thomas, bought in 1820 the factory which has ever since been, and to-day remains, the headquarters of the great concern known as J., T. and J. Taylor, Limited.

Theodore Taylor was first sent to Batley Grammar School and afterwards to Silcoates School, near Wakefield, where among his contemporaries were W. T. Stead and Sir George Newnes. On completing his education he entered the family business in 1866, which he learned in all its branches, and in 1891 became its head. In 1892 he became sole proprietor. This he did—by buying out his partners—in order to put into effect the scheme which he had long cherished for sharing the profits with the employees. He studied the experiments of Godin at Guise, and those of Leclaire in Paris, joined the Labour (now Industrial) Co-partnership Association, and made the acquaintance of other pioneers like the late Aneurin Williams, afterwards long to be his colleague in Parliament, George Thomson, Ruskin's disciple, and Sir George Livesey. From all these sources he learned something, and laid his plans. At first managers and foremen only participated in his scheme, but at the beginning of 1896 he extended its operation to include the whole of the workpeople, converting the business into a private limited company for the purpose. It was an act of the highest courage and foresight, frowned upon by many, and viewed with apprehension by others, but he persisted, worked out his ideas in detail, and made a striking appeal to the loyalty and good will of the men and women in his mills.

The scheme provided that, after paying 5 per cent. on capital, any further profit available for dividend was to be declared at a uniform rate on capital and on the year's total wages. Every employee who had been with the company during the whole of the year was to be credited with bonus at not less than the rate on his or her year's wages. From the beginning it worked without a hitch. Including two early years in which there were no profits and no dividends, dividends on capital averaged over 11 per cent., and bonuses on wages and salaries about 9 per cent. The employees, totalling more than 2,000 at three factories, own more than three-quarters of the capital, and thus receive the greater part of the profits. Since 1892 they have been paid in cash, Government securities, bonus shares, dividends on them, and allocations to the Workers' Benefit Fund, over £2,240,000, and the company is in an impregnable financial condition.

Tireless in his exposition of profit-sharing, not only upon ethical considerations, but, in his own view, as one of the surest safeguards of preserving industrial peace, he wrote much and spoke widely upon his own effort, and his scheme became the pattern for others established in many parts of the world.

He inherited Liberal principles, which he strongly maintained throughout his life, although frequently taking up an attitude upon secondary issues not in keeping with that of his party. After a good deal of local work in Yorkshire he was in 1900 elected to represent the South-East (Radcliffe-cum-Farnworth) Division of Lancashire in Parliament, and sat continuously until his retirement in 1918.

A great traveller, he had become interested in the effort of China to suppress the opium traffic, and deeply concerned at the manner in which she was being compelled against her will to accept the Indian product. With a few friends he launched and organized the anti-opium movement in Britain, and in the House in 1906 moved the famous resolution, accepted by the new Liberal Government, condemning the Indo-Chinese trade. For 11 years longer he helped to lead this cause, was its Parliamentary protagonist, and when, in April 1917, the traffic was at last ended he received at the final meeting of the Society for the Suppression of the Opium Trade an address of congratulation and thanks. Less than a year later he delivered his final speech in the House, historic because it killed one of the great controversial measures of the time—the War Charities Lotteries Bill.

Many other interests occupied his busy life. Apart from his travels abroad—he had visited every continent, and every country in the British Empire, and in his ninety-eighth year paid an extended business visit on behalf of his company to the United States and Canada—he was a loyal member and generous supporter of the Congregational Church. A keen educationist, especially an advocate of vocational and technical training, he made through his company special provision for young workers to go to the local technical colleges. Many years ago he provided the sum of £10,000 for scholarships at his old school, Silcoates. He was an omnivorous reader and his choices ranged widely over an infinite variety of subjects. Occupation of body and mind and the simple life (he was an abstainer and a non-smoker) were his recipes for longevity.

He remained almost to the end quite unbelievably active. When approaching his centenary he travelled at least twice a week from his home—the Moraine, at Grassington, in Wharfedale—to his Batley mills, where he usually spent some seven or eight hours a day at his desk. At the age of 99 he was appearing on public platforms in the north to speak about profit-sharing and actually travelled to London for this purpose.

His capacity for action and his independence of mind were well represented—and blended—in the 1950 General Election when, as a determined opponent of Socialism, he appeared, in spite of his life-long Liberal career, on the platform in support of the Conservative candidate for the Batley and Morley Division. It was an appearance the more remarkable because Taylor had been, for the better part of his life, friend and neighbour of the family of the Labour candidate, Dr. Alfred Broughton, who was elected. But he was at pains to point out that in his view principles must transcend personalities, and he remained as he always had been an unrepentant and formidable opponent of the corporate state.

He married first, in 1874, his cousin, Sara Jane, daughter of W. J. P. Ingraham, of Philadelphia, U.S.A., by whom he had a son and two daughters. She died in 1919, and a year later he married Mary Isabella, daughter of Colin A. McVean, of Kilfinichen, Isle of Mull. There was no issue of this marriage and only one daughter of his first marriage survives.

October 21, 1952.

Sir Thomas Taylor, C.B.E., Principal of the University College of the South West, Exeter, died suddenly on August 29, 1953 while on holiday in Italy.

Thomas Weston Johns Taylor was born in 1895, the son of the late T. G. Taylor, and was educated at the City of London School and Brasenose College, Oxford. He was twice wounded while serving in Gallipoli with The Essex Regiment during the 1914-18 war, and soon after his return to Oxford in 1920 he was elected a Fellow of Brasenose, where he was tutor in chemistry. An admirable and popular tutor, he became University Lecturer in Organic Chemistry in 1927, and held the post for the remainder of his time at Oxford. He was elected to a Rhodes Travelling Fellowship in 1931 and from 1936 to 1939 he was a member of the council of the Chemical Society.

Soon after the outbreak of war in 1939 he joined the chemical warfare branch of the Royal Engineers and served in the Middle East until 1942, being mentioned in dispatches. He was then appointed secretary of the British Central Scientific Office in Washington and later became director of it. In 1944 he was transferred to South-East Asia Command as head of the Operational Research Division, and remained there until the end of hostilities.

When the new University College of the West Indies was first mooted, Taylor's name was put forward, though there was some little opposition initially to appointing a scientist as the head of an institution which was to serve as a cultural centre for the whole Caribbean and to prepare students for external degrees at London University. He was, however, anything but a narrow specialist, since he had the widest interests in literature and music, and the great ease and charm of his manner quickly overbore any opposition, and in October 1946 his appointment was announced.

He began his difficult task with high courage, much ingenuity, and great tact, so that within a very short time he had won the hearts of all those West Indians who had the good of education at heart. An institution short of capital in an area with a precarious economy has to work with a great deal of improvisation. In this he was a master, so that when only a few months ago he was called home to become Principal of the University College of the South-West at Exeter, he left behind him a sturdy and growing institution in the West Indies.

His work was recognized by the conferment of a knighthood on him in July 1952.

He married in 1922 Rosamund Georgina, the younger daughter of Colonel T. E. J. Lloyd, C.B.

September 1, 1953.

The death of **Sir Godfrey Tearle,** which occurred in London on June 8, 1953, is a loss to the theatre which is not to be measured in terms only of length of service and diversity of achievement, though Tearle had indeed acted longer and acted well a greater variety of important parts than most other men of his generation.

He had above all the ability of certain actors of the older school, an ability, always rare and now perhaps almost legendary, of suggesting a greatness not be arrived at by some calculation of the intellectual score but borne in upon the senses of his audience by the mere presence and sheer authority of the man. He seemed a little larger than life. It was a surprise, when one met him, not to have to look up to him. This extra magnitude, so to speak, enabled him to invest his interpretations with an effect of inevitability beside which any critical reservations in the minds of his audience came to rank, anyhow for the moment, as quibbles. With his last Othello, at Stratford-on-Avon in 1948, there was certainly no room for quibbling, however nice. The character, meditated through the years, then seemed to have worn down to its very essentials in the actor's mind; accordingly he was able to render it in the fewest possible lines, all so rightly placed that there was plainly no need for more. He was last seen in London in *The Hanging Judge* at the Duke of York's Theatre, which he had announced beforehand would be his last appearance on the stage.

Godfrey Tearle, who was born on October 12, 1884, came of a family whose members had been actors for three generations, on both the father's and the mother's side. He was on the stage almost from babyhood, had his first speaking part in the Shakespearian touring company of his father, Osmund Tearle, when he was nine, and remained with the company until his father's death in 1901. He afterwards appeared on tour in most of the leading classical parts, from Hamlet and Romeo to Othello and Shylock, not forgetting Sir Peter Teazle. He was first seen in London when he was 22, and for more than two years played secondary Shakespearian parts with Beerbohm Tree. By the time he was 30 and entered the army in the 1914-18 war, he had appeared in important but never quite leading parts in almost every London theatre.

It was not, however, until J. B. Fagan produced *Othello* at the Court in 1921 that Godfrey Tearle, who then played the title part, appeared as a leading actor in London. He was then 37. He was afterwards seen as Mirabell in *The Way of the World* with [Dame] Edith Evans [d. 1976], as Francis Archer in *The Beaux' Stratagem,* and Hamlet in an important revival at the Haymarket in 1931.

In the next year he appeared both as Marc Antony and as Brutus, and in 1934 played Henry V. In 1936 he was the King Saul in Barrie's *Boy David.* In 1938 he went into management at the Lyric, and was the Edward Ferres of Charles Morgan's [q.v.] *The Flashing Stream.* In this play he toured the provinces and the United States, after which he confined his activities for several years to films, in which he had begun to act in 1906. Two of his most successful films were *The Thirty-Nine Steps* and *One of our Aircraft is Missing.* In 1950 he followed Sir Ralph Richardson in the chief part in *The Heiress,* at the Haymarket.

The fact that he was the first president of the British Actors Equity Association in 1932 and was vice-chairman of the London Theatre Council in 1935 gives some measure of the respect in which he was held by the other members of his profession.

He was knighted in the Birthday Honours of 1951.

June 10, 1953.

Lord Templewood died on May 7, 1959 in London. He was 79.

He was for many years an outstanding figure in British politics, worthy heir to a long family tradition of devoted public service and humanitarian endeavour, whose association with an ill-fated and notorious abortive agreement was no more than an interruption of a record of high achievement in many important spheres.

In his last public office, as Ambassador on Special Mission to Madrid during the war, he rendered signal service to the allied cause by helping in large measure to ensure Spanish neutrality and to foil Nazi machinations, notably by the part he played in the negotiations which led to the agreement for cutting off Spanish supplies of wolfram to Germany. But his positive contribution to ultimate victory had a longer history.

He rendered what were perhaps his most eminent and enduring services as Secretary of State for India. There is indeed no question of his success as an administrator. Again, as Foreign Secretary he made one of the greatest speeches ever heard at Geneva, only to ruin its efficacy and impair his own reputation by an agreement which seemed to be as much at variance with his professed policy as it was unpopular. Correct up to the verge of primness, cautious, experienced and understanding, he was nevertheless convicted by the opinion of thousands of his fellow countrymen of a grave blunder. Justice, however, demands that the consistency of principle, devotion to duty, and unfailing competence which he displayed over so many years should count heavily in the scales to his credit, while the evaluation of his arrangement with Laval may now be left to the cooler, freer judgment of historians remote from the passions of his day.

The Rt. Hon. Sir Samuel John Gurney Hoare, P.C., G.C.S.I., G.B.E., C.M.G., first and last Viscount Templewood, of Chelsea in the county of Middlesex, in the peerage of the United Kingdom, and a Baronet, was the eldest son of Sir Samuel Hoare, first Baronet of Sidestrand, Norfolk, who for 20 years had been member for Norwich. He was born on February 24, 1880, and educated at Harrow and New College, Oxford, where he took a first class in Moderations and in History.

In 1905 he became assistant private secretary to the late Alfred Lyttelton, then Colonial Secretary, and in the next year contested Ipswich. It was a bad time for Conservative candidates, and only in 1910 was he to be returned for Chelsea, to remain its member until his elevation to the peerage in 1944. In the meantime he had gained experience in the L.C.C. and in other public service. In 1909 he married Lady Maud Lygon, D.B.E., daughter of the sixth Earl of Beauchamp.

Early in the war he obtained a commission in the Norfolk Yeomanry, but a sharp illness in 1914 incapacitated him for service. He had a gift for languages and in order to fill time took lessons in Russian. When he had acquired a working knowledge of it, he obtained a position in British Military Intelligence in Russia. He was there when Rasputin was murdered, and a rumour to the effect that he was responsible for the crime was so prevalent that the British Ambassador felt bound to exculpate him at a personal interview with the Tsar.

After the war he returned to Parliament. It was already plain that his reputation would be made through sound performance rather than inspired leadership. Among the political cabals and movements of the early post-war period he picked his careful way.

In 1922, however, he spoke effectively in a dabate in which the honours recommended by the Coalition Government were strongly criticized, and wrote later in the year a letter to *The Times,* in which he argued for Conservative independence. The day before the historic meeting at the Carlton Club he asked 100 active Conservative members to his house, where they agreed that the Coalition should be ended. It was perhaps the deciding factor and helped to secure him the Air Ministry in the new administration.

Hoare, with a brief respite in 1924, was Secretary of State for Air from 1922 to 1929 (with a seat in the Cabinet from 1923). When he took office the air force of the war had been axed into comparative insignificance. He set to work to rebuild it step by step as an integral part of national defence. He realized the possibilities of civil aviation and sought to illustrate them by taking long flights which he himself treated as if they had been matters of course. In 1927, accompanied by Lady Maud Hoare, he made the first civil flight to India and on his return received a well-earned G.B.E.

Hoare entered upon his memorable tenure at the India Office with serious initial disadvantages. A considerable section of Conservatives distrusted the Round Table policy, while many leading Indian politicians, brought up in the Liberal tradition, had grave doubts of Conservative willingness to go beyond, or in some respects to implement, the Simon [q.v.] Commission proposals. The Indian delegates on their way to London included Gandhi, as the sole representative of the Congress, and in no mood to accept the dictum of the new Secretary of State in July that discussion of the question of separation of India from the Empire must be barred.

Pending the inevitable appeal to the electorate, the Federal Relations Committee could do little more than mark time; but when the National Government was confirmed in office Hoare faced his difficulties with a sure touch. Indian critics came to see that they had in the Secretary of State a man who meant serious business.

But the more convinced Hoare was made of the necessity for meeting those demands on which there was the greatest measure of agreement among the Indian delegates, the more determined grew the opposition of a considerable section of Conservative M.P.s and peers headed by Churchill* and Lord Salisbury [the 4th Marquess].

A third Round Table Conference was summoned and after its conclusion on Christmas Eve, 1932, a Burma Round Table Conference assembled and three important committees under well known Parliamentarians were sent out to India. At long last, in March 1933, the Government proposals were set out in broad outline in a White Paper providing for provincial autonomy, an All-India Federation, and responsibility with safeguards. Both Houses of Parliament set up a Joint Select Committee of 32 members to consider these proposals in consultation with a few selected Indian delegates.

There came a stage when the committee and the Indian delegates agreed that their labours would be lessened if the Secretary of State would go into the witness chair. Accompanied by the Permanent Under-Secretary and Sir Malcolm [later Lord*] Hailey, Hoare gave evidence on no fewer than 19 days—usually both morning and afternoon—and he answered some 15,000 questions on 4,500 specific points arising on the constitutional proposals outlined in the White Paper.

Soon after the publication of the J.S.C. report in November 1934 both Houses of Parliament by great majorities authorized the Government to promote legislation on the lines of the majority recommendations. The vast measure Hoare introduced early in 1935 consisted in its final form of 478 clauses and 16 schedules, covering 430 octavo pages.

The Secretary of State was between two fires—that of the Labour Opposition complaining of inadequacy and too many safeguards, and that of the Churchillians, who condemned the measure as going too far and too fast and imperilling British interests. On a few critical occasions these disparate critics found themselves in the same lobby; but such was Hoare's handling of the measure that an overwhelming Government majority was maintained.

When in June 1935, on the resignation of Ramsay MacDonald, Stanley Baldwin became Prime Minister, he expressed to Hoare a wish that he should either be the next Viceroy of India or go to the Foreign Office. The strain upon Hoare during his four years' tenure of the India Office had been far greater than that imposed on any of his predecessors in that office. The intensity of his labours had left him both physically weak and mentally tired, and he had had little time to acquaint himself, though a member of the Cabinet, with the details of foreign affairs. Nevertheless Hoare yielded to Baldwin's wish to keep him in Whitehall, and he took charge at the Foreign Office at the time when the proposed naval pact with Germany was ripe for decision.

When in the summer of 1935 he took over his new duties he said that his aim was to face facts. With a rearmed Germany openly worshipping the rule of force, and Mussolini rattling the Italian sabre and pouring troops into Africa, unpleasant facts were not far to seek. In mid-September he was at Geneva, where he made a momentous speech in which he announced his Government's intention to fulfil the obligations of the Covenant. The month was to see the failure of all diplomatic efforts to prevent a conflict, and, at the beginning of October, the Italian advance in East Africa began. He returned to Geneva. While he was there the League agreed that economic pressure should begin on November 18. He came back to London to find it rife with rumours—the General Election was in progress—that the government intended to let down the League.

In early December it was announced that he would leave London for a holiday in Switzerland and that on his way through Paris he would have discussions with Pierre Laval. On December 7 he arrived in the French capital, and the next evening the news broke that a complete agreement had been reached between them on a series of proposals which it was suggested might be sent forward to the League of Nations, to Italy, and to Abyssinia as a basis for a settlement of the dispute between the two nations. On December 9 and 10 the Cabinet met and agreed that the proposals should go forward.

Meanwhile a general outline of the plan had "leaked" in Paris and as soon as it was realized that the leakage was deliberate and substantially accurate a storm burst in Great Britain. The electors felt that the plan involved the dismemberment of Abyssinia and the reward of the aggressor at the expense of the injured party. The Ministry was faced with a threatened revolt of Government supporters in the House of Commons; Hoare returned from Switzerland to find the country aflame. He thereupon tendered his resignation to Baldwin.

On December 19 Hoare defended his policy from the back benches, and the Prime Minister admitted that he and his Government were to blame for having endorsed the Paris plan without making further inquiries. Hoare's case was that the proposals differed in degree but not in principle from those of the Committee of Five which the Emperor of Abyssinia had provisionally accepted before hostilities began, and that they were immensely less than the Italian demands.

The following June he went to the Admiralty. There he lost no time in making it clear that he regarded speed in rearmament as of vital importance. Almost at once he began placing contracts, and included two for new battleships. In the early summer of 1937 he became Home Secretary, specially interesting himself in air raid precautions, and in his early days there he was largely responsible for the development of civil defence. He effected some prison reforms—he was the great-grandnephew of Elizabeth Fry—and but for the war a new Criminal Justice Act would stand to his name.

In the following spring he was again for a brief spell Secretary of State for Air; but in May 1940 his appointment as Ambassador to Madrid on Special Mission was announced. Except perhaps for Moscow it was the most important embassy in Europe. Hoare was under the impression when he accepted the post that his mission would not extend beyond a few weeks or months. He was destined to remain in it for more than four years: it proved an excellent appointment. His paramount task was to do everything possible to keep Spain out of the war.

His endeavours took many forms, including the ceaseless supply of factual information about German reverses. He made persistent and vigorous protests against favours shown to German agents and victimization of British subjects. There was a touch of flamboyance about one such protest after the organized riots of June 1941, which had led to an attack on the British Embassy in Madrid. The Diplomatic Staff and the Service attachés—the last three in uniform—went in a body to the Minister for Foreign Affairs and demanded an official apology. It was a very effective demonstration.

In July 1944 he gave up his Chelsea seat and a peerage was conferred on him. His retirement from active politics gave him more leisure to devote to a cause very near to his heart—the reclamation of the criminal and the reform of the prison system. In February 1947 he accepted the presidency of the Howard League for Penal Reform, and a month later the chairmanship of the Magistrates Association.

In both offices he exercised an important influence on the public's attitude towards such topics as the treatment of the juvenile delinquent. His observations of the effect of the abolition of the death penalty in other European countries wrought a change in his own attitude. In 1938, when he was Home Secretary, he had not supported abolition but in later years he became increasingly convinced that there was no longer any place for capital punishment in our penal code.

At the end of the Lords debate on the second reading of the Criminal Justice Bill in 1948 he argued the case for suspension and for a separate Bill to deal with the subject—the course which was eventually taken.

In his love of sport and of the delights of the countryside he was true to a family tradition, to which his book, *The Unbroken Thread,* bears witness. He kept his trim, neat, wiry physique as well-disciplined as his mind.

As an undergraduate he had represented his university at racquets and tennis, and he was a silver medallist for skating. In such sports requiring quickness and agility he was a dexterous and stylish performer until well past middle age. For 25 years he was president of the Lawn Tennis Association.

May 9, 1959.

Lord Tennyson, whose remarkable performance as captain of the English cricket XI in the Test matches against Australia in 1921 will long be remembered, died on June 6, 1951 at Bexhill at the age of 61.

The Right Hon. Lionel Hallam Tennyson, third Baron Tennyson, of Farringford, Freshwater, Isle of Wight, in the peerage of the United Kingdom, was born on November 7, 1889, and was in the Eton eleven in 1907 and 1908. He got his place as a fast bowler, but in his second year he developed his batting and made runs instead of taking wickets. From Eton he went up to Trinity College, Cambridge, and did quite well in the Freshmen's match, but this was his only experience in university cricket, for after a year's residence he left in order to enter the Army. Nothing was heard of him for some time, but in 1913 he came out for Hampshire and batted with a success which is described by *Wisden* as one of the most striking features of the season. He was appointed vice-captain of Hampshire, and M.C.C. offered him a place in a team which they sent out to South Africa in the winter of 1913-14.

He served throughout the 1914-18 war with the Rifle Brigade, and nothing was seen of him in county cricket unitl 1919. In that and the following years he captained Hampshire, maintaining his reputation as an aggressive batsman.

In 1921 Tennyson had, as it were, greatness thrust upon him, and enjoyed an experience as unusual as it was unexpected. At this time the position of English cricket as a rival to Australia was at the lowest point it had ever reached. In the winter of 1919-20 we had dispatched to Australia a team which, for the first time in Test match history, had lost all five games of the rubber without ever looking like winning a single one of them. This was depressing enough, but when they returned our visit in 1921 the Australians, so far from giving us our revenge, seemed likely to continue their triumphs. They had brought with them two first-rate fast bowlers, Gregory* and McDonald, and against their intimidating attack our batsmen made a wretched show.

The selection committee cast about for new material, and for the second match at Lord's put into the field what was popularly supposed to be the worst eleven that had ever represented England. The last choice was Lionel Tennyson, who, when the match had gone too far to be saved, scored 74 not out, a notable display of courageous hitting. The result was that Tennyson rose from being a county player to the highest office which international cricket can offer, and was appointed captain of the English team. He took over at Leeds, where we had bad luck in losing Hobbs through illness, and Australia won the third and deciding match of the rubber. The new captain, however, going in ninth with a badly damaged hand, which caused him to bat practically one-handed, made 63 and 36. Although he received many hard knocks he treated McDonald and Gregory so severely that he reached his 50 in an hour. His driving, which when he was in form was always the best feature of his batting, was much in evidence.

It is impossible to rank Tennyson as the equal in skill of the many great players who have in their time captained England, but looking back on the action taken by the selection committee it is hard to see how they could have made a better choice, or rather one better suited to the occasion. They fixed on a hitter, who might or might not come off. He had also a cheerful spirit, which no crisis could daunt, and he was generally popular with other players. After this year of eminence, though he played no more in international cricket, Tennyson continued to captain Hampshire, and whether he himself made runs or not, his optimism encouraged the side for many more years.

Lord Tennyson, who succeeded to the barony on the death of his father in 1928, was three times married, and the title descends to the eldest son of his first marriage, the Hon. Harold Christopher Tennyson, who was born in 1919.

June 7, 1951.

Sir Eustace Tennyson-D'Eyncourt, BT., K.C.B., D.SC., LL.D., F.R.S., an eminent designer of ships and formerly Director of Naval Construction at the Admiralty, died at his home at Hailsham at the age of 82 on February 1, 1951.

The third son of the late Louis Charles Tennyson-D'Eyncourt, of Tealby, Lincoln, he was educated at Charterhouse and the Royal Naval College, Greenwich, and having served his apprenticeship at Elswick he went to Fairfield for a few years as naval architect in 1898, but returned to Elswick in 1902, also as naval architect, remaining there until appointed to the Admiralty as Director of Naval Construction and Chief Technical Adviser in 1912, which post he held for 11 years. He was also head of the Admiralty committee which produced the first tank and was vice-president of the Tank Board in 1918 and a member of the War Office Tank Committee, as well as a member of the Advisory Committee on Aeronautics during the 1914-18 war.

It was, however, in the field of ship construction that Tennyson-D'Eyncourt achieved prominence. He was responsible for the design of certain ships and boats of the Royal Navy, including the battleships Nelson and Rodney, which were characterized by certain weight-saving devices to offset the decisions of the Washington Naval Agreement of 1921; also a number of cruisers, among which were the Effingham and the Frobisher.

During the 1914-18 war he had constructed a large number of motor-boats, known as C.M.B.s, having speeds up to 40 knots. They were built on the principle of boats skimming over the water at very high speed and based on the researches of William Froude during the last century.

Tennyson-D'Eyncourt received many honours. In 1917 he was created C.B., and four years later K.C.B., and was elected F.R.S. Subsequently he received further honours, including his foreign associate membership of L'Académie de Marine. In 1931 a baronetcy was conferred upon him.

In 1898 he married Janet, widow of John Burns and elder daughter of Mathew Finlay of Langside, Glasgow. There were a son and a daughter of the marriage. The heir to the baronetcy is Eustace Gervais Tennyson-D'Eyncourt, born in 1902, who married, in 1926, Pamela, daughter of the late W. B. Gladstone. There are two sons and one daughter of the marriage.

February 2, 1951.

Julia (Mrs. Fred) Terry—See **Neilson.**

Josephine Tey—See **Mackintosh.**

Jean Tharaud, the younger of the two brothers, Jérôme [q.v.] and Jean, both members of the French Academy, whose lifelong literary partnership was in many ways among the most remarkable ever known, died unexpectedly on April 6, 1952 in hospital in Paris at the age of 74.

For more than half a century the Tharauds, inveterate travellers with an impassioned curiosity in foreign races and peoples, made a rich and distinctive contribution to French literature with their volumes of fiction, travel, and history. Theirs was indeed an astonishing feat of collaboration, in one respect at least even more notable than that of the Goncourts, since it lasted so much longer. The Tharauds were truly inseparable from one another—inseparable, that is, in literature as in life. They lived in the same house, they travelled together, they used the first person singular in their books, they signed their letters simply "J". or "J. J.", and in everything to do with the labours of literary composition it was impossible to tell when one left off and the other began.

Jean Tharaud was born on May 9, 1877, almost exactly three years after his brother, at Saint-Junien, a small town near Limoges and a shrine of pilgrimage, in that part of central France which is the scene of some of the earliest and most powerful of the Tharauds' novels.

From an early age, it would seem, Jean came under the intellectual influence of his brother, with whom, after a similar schooling at the Collège Barbe, he attended the École Normale and spent a carefree but penniless student's existence in the Latin Quarter, where they pursued the friendship and admiration for Péguy that was afterwards celebrated in the eloquent two volumes of *Notre cher Péguy* (1926). When Jérôme, in 1899, went off to Budapest as reader in the French language in the university there, Jean stayed behind. Yet their literary collaboration began in earnest in that year. It was Jérôme who, having returned to France in 1903, two years later became secretary—literary, not political—to Maurice Barrès, whose mystical nationalism was not without effect upon him, and with whom he remained until 1914. But long before then the Tharauds had made their own joint mark in literature, and it was wholly in keeping with the spirit and circumstances of their writing partnership that the names of both brothers should appear on the title-page of *Mes Années chez Barrès* (1928). Only their last publication, *La Double Confidence,* gave any hint of each brother's contribution.

The earliest of the Tharauds' books, *Le Coltineur Débile,* apparently goes back to 1899. It was with *Dingley, l'Illustre Ecrivain,* a finely ironical novel of the Boer War, for which they eventually received the Prix Goncourt, that they attracted general attention. Of the fertile and amazingly varied output of the next 40 years not even the barest catalogue can be given here. It must be sufficient to mention their novels of Jewry (for which they incurred an unmerited reputation for anti-Semitism), such as *L'Ombre de la Croix* (1917), *Un Royaume de Dieu* (1920), *Quand Israël est Roi* (1921); their North African studies, such as *Marrakech, ou les Seigneurs de l'Atlas* (1922) and *Fez, ou les Bourgeois de l'Islam* (1930); travel books of the order of *La fête arabe* (1912) and *La rose de Saron* (1927); and, among historical and biographical studies, *La Tragédie de Ravaillac* (1913) and *La vie et la mort de Déroulède* (1924). And, though it leaves speculation unanswered, there is the fascinating *Chronique des frères écrivains,* which they published in 1927.

Jérôme, the senior, was elected a member of the Academy in 1938; Jean had to wait for election until 1946.

April 10, 1952.

Jérôme Tharaud, the elder of the two brothers, both members of the French Academy, whose lifelong literary partnership was in many ways among the most remarkable ever known, died on January 28, 1953 at the age of 78. His brother, Jean [q.v.], died in April 1952.

Theirs was a remarkable collaboration. They could not be separated in life or in literature—living in the same house, travelling together, using the first person singular in their books. Their ideas and their styles were so united that it was impossible to distinguish where in a book one had left off and the other begun.

Jérôme Tharaud was born May 11, 1874, at Saint-Junien, a small town near Limoges. He was educated at the Collège Barbe and the École Normale in Paris. With his brother, who had had a similar schooling, he spent a carefree but penniless student's existence in the Latin Quarter, until, in 1899, he went off by himself to Budapest as reader in the French language at the university there. He stayed there until 1903, and two years after his return to France became a secretary to Maurice Barrès, with whom he stayed until 1914. When, in 1928, the story of these years was described in *Mes Années chez Barrès,* it was characteristic of the literary partnership that it appeared with the names of both brothers on the title-page.

The first of their joint works to attract wide attention was *Dingley, l'Illustre Ecrivain,* which was published in 1902. It was an ironical novel of the South African war and was awarded the Prix Goncourt in 1906. They quickly confirmed their reputation and the partnership was to prove so prolific and varied that to list all their books would turn a notice into a catalogue.

Their novels of Jewry, which were unjustly called anti-Semitic, included *L'Ombre de la Croix* (1917), *Un Royaume de Dieu* (1920), and *Quand Israël est Roi* (1921). Their North African studies included *Marrakech, ou les Seigneurs de l'Atlas* (1922), and *Fez, ou les Bourgeois de l'Islam* (1930). There were travel books as good as *La fête Arabe* (1912), and a romanticized autobiography, published in 1927, which did not, however, answer the speculation about the respective parts played by Jérôme and Jean in their joint work.

Both were elected members of the French Academy. When the Academy wished to honour them in 1938 there was only one seat to award. So it was given to Jérôme, as the elder. Jean had to wait until 1946.

January 30, 1953.

Jacques Thibaud, the French violinist, who was killed in an aircraft crash in the French Alps on September 1, 1953, was a few weeks short of his seventy-third birthday.

He was born at Bordeaux on September 27, 1880, and gave his first public performance there at the age of eight. He was the precociously talented child of fairy-tale or film—the child of the gods, finding inspiration in Mozart from the age of five. At the age of 13 he entered the Paris Conservatoire and studied first under Martin Marsick and afterwards under Eugène Isaye. On leaving in 1896 he won the first prize.

Thibaud was immediately engaged by the Colonne Concert Society, commenced his foreign tours in 1899, and from then on enjoyed an increasing renown in many countries. From 1930 until 1935 he formed part of a famous trio with Pablo Casals* and Alfred Cortot*. He remained in France throughout the occupation, but always refused to give concerts in Germany. His last concert was given at Biarritz on August 20, and he was on his way to undertake a concert tour of the Far East when he was killed.

It was the purity and fineness of Thibaud's tone that most struck the listener on first hearing. The tone was silvery and exquisitely polished, not without warmth or richness, nor indeed without penetrating power, but refined rather than robust. Then perhaps the elegance of his phrasing caught the attention and wooed the ear. With these qualities it was natural that he should excel in the music of his own country, and in chamber *ensemble.*

His profoundly studied and ravishingly executed interpretation of Franck's violin sonata with Alfred Cortot was justly renowned, but his readings of Fauré and Debussy were not less remarkable. The years of his collaboration with Cortot and Casals were a rare case of three great soloists who could work together as a single musician; their trio playing lives gratefully in the memory for its superb sensitiveness and masterly style, and luckily their beautiful recording of Schubert's B flat trio remains in gramophone catalogues.

When Thibaud visited England after the war his powers seemed on the wane, but he could still delight his audience on occasion with the grace and natural aristocracy of his playing. When past the age of 70 he gave a performance in the Festival Hall of a violin concerto by Mozart that was an example of style. In the slow movement, indeed, the years seemed to slip from him as he unfolded the easy cantilena of the young Mozart; the great artist found his prime again. It was a fitting farewell to a well-loved musician.

But one other English occasion is perhaps better remembered: Thibaud's first concert in London after the war, at the Royal Albert Hall, when he played Mozart's fourth concerto and Mendelssohn's concerto with the London Philharmonic Orchestra, under Basil Cameron*. The reception he received then moved him greatly.

He founded, with the French pianist, Marguerite Long, the famous international prize which bears their two names and which is competed for every two years in Paris by young pianists and violinists.

He leaves a widow and one son. A second son was killed during the 1939-45 war.

September 3, 1953.

Dylan Thomas, the Welsh poet and story writer, died in New York at the age of 39 on November 9, 1953.

Dylan Marlais Thomas was born at Swansea in 1914. He was educated at Swansea Grammar School, where his father, who died in 1952, was senior English master. He began writing early, and at the age of 12 he was able to show his parents and his friends poems which seemed to have no direct ancestry in English poetry. These poems already bore the marks of that strong individuality in pattern-making and choice of language which was to distinguish him from all his fellow-writers in maturity.

He had developed at school a passionate feeling for language which was sharpened and intensified by an acute destructive judgment. He took no reputation for granted. He approached the great masters of his art with an impudent suspicion, because, from the first, he distrusted the academic approach. Yet, when they had walked with him through the furnace of his own imagination and emerged unscathed, there was no man who loved them more. Indeed, no poet of the English language has so hoodwinked and confuted his critics. None has ever worn more brilliantly the mask of anarchy to conceal the true face of tradition. There was nothing God ever made that Dylan Thomas, the revolutionary, wanted to alter. The careful compounder of explosive imagery believed only in calm.

At the age when Rimbaud wrote his poems Dylan Thomas had left school and was working as a reporter for the *South Wales Evening Post.* His first poems, apart from those which had appeared in the school magazine, which he edited, were printed in the *Sunday Referee.* He had also at this time begun to write short stories. Then, finding newspaper work and his own writing incompatible, he left the newspaper and lived for a time in London, sharing a flat with two of his Swansea friends. Here his literary work continued, and he developed rapidly his researches into the power of language. He directed his various gifts to the concentration of verbal energy in a pattern at once musical and compact. His poems reflected the fiery, Blake-like passion of his vision, while his early stories explored the relation between immediate reality and archetypal symbols.

When in 1934 Dylan Thomas's first book, *Eighteen Poems,* was published, its impact was immediate and profound. It was at once realized by discerning readers, among whom Edith Sitwell* was one of the first, that this poet had created an idiom; that he had disturbed the roots of our language in an organic way and given it a new vitality. There was nothing stale or imitative in the book; the poems were fastidiously worked; they were poems of a man who had listened, not once but a hundred times, to the minute effects of words. It is true that still, in 1936, when this was followed by *Twenty-One Poems,* the poet had not yet found his most permanent and compelling medium of expression. Yet there was nothing topical in his work. The most mistaken of his admirers were those who loved it for its novelty. It was, even in its first phases, an ancient poetry, not rejecting antiquity for the present but seeking, with every device of language, the ancestry of the moment.

If the poetry of his first two books had been admired for the wrong reasons the poems printed in his third book, *The Map of Love,* could hardly suffer the same fate. Whereas the first book leaves an impression that the poet could extend his stanzas from the fund of invention and verbal felicities at his command, and that the same prescription could produce new poems, there is no such impression left by the poems in *The Map of Love.* Each is an experience perceived and controlled by the religious sense, and each answers its own questions. He has pared his imagery without losing any of its force; and these poems close with the statement at the end of the poem for his twenty-fourth birthday:

In the final direction of the
elementary town
I advance for as long as forever is.

The Map of Love contained also a set of stories which were clearly the work of the same hand, and these were followed two years later by the humorous stories, in quite a different vein, which Dylan Thomas collected under the title *A Portrait of the Artist as a Young Dog.* These stories, about the poet's own boyhood, written from direct experience in Swansea and the Gower peninsula, may seem to some to carry the fault of exaggerated statement, but they are as true to life as his own personality was to his friends.

It is, however, upon the poems in *Deaths and Entrances* (1946) and the few poems of the slim volume *In Country Sleep,* published in America in 1951, that his reputation as one of the greatest masters of English poetry is likely to rest. In these Dylan Thomas has not only used to perfection the idiom he himself created but has invented stanza forms which are themselves organic and which redouble the force of the entire poem. These poems form the final section of his *Collected Poems,* published in 1952.

During the war Dylan Thomas, who was always interested in the cinema, made several documentary films. His book, *The Doctor and the Devils,* published earlier in 1953, is the first instance of a film-script being printed before any film of it has been made. Among his unpublished works are several poems and a radio play, a part of which was printed in the half-yearly Italian review, *Botteghe Oscure.* The scene of this play is a Welsh village, and parts of it have been performed in New York.

In recent years Dylan Thomas had made several tours of American universities, giving readings of poetry and lectures. His reading of poetry, and particularly of his own poems (which he confessed that he did not like reading) was unrivalled; and he was almost equally accomplished in reading humorous scripts of an unparalleled adjectival richness, which were among the most popular wireless features of our time. His gift of mimicry could make each character of his stories distinct and unforgettable. He loved people. He did not write only for the few but also "for the lovers . . . Who pay no praise or wages Nor heed my craft or art".

Dylan Thomas had intended, before returning to England from this last tour, to work with Stravinsky* on the *libretto* of an opera. It is likely that by his death the world has lost a masterpiece. What it has not lost is the work of a poet who was able to live Christianity in a public way, and whose work distilled it—a poet narrow and severe with himself and wide and forgiving in his affections. Innocence is always a paradox, and Dylan Thomas presents, in retrospect, the greatest paradox of our time.

He married, in 1936, Miss Caitlin Macnamara, who survives him, together with two sons and a daughter.

November 10, 1953.

Professor F. W. Thomas, C.I.E., the doyen of British Orientalists, died at his home near Banbury, Oxfordshire, on May 6, 1956 at the age of 89.

He was a man of great learning and indefatigable industry who had great influence on the younger generation of Oriental scholars, many of whom would gladly acknowledge themselves as having been taught and trained by him. He rejoiced to have lived in a period when we are throwing off what he called a certain European provincialism, and realizing the size of the East both in space and time, and the community of experience, individual, social, and political. He was equally keen on drawing attention to Oriental art and literature. His own great part in the research which was necessary to bring the facts to light did not prevent him from giving full credit to the work of others, notably missionaries and men of the type of Sir Francis Younghusband and C. F. Andrews.

Frederick William Thomas was born on March 21, 1867, at Fazeley, in Staffordshire, the son of Frederick Thomas. His parents settled in Birmingham in 1874 and the boy was admitted to King Edward's School, where he came under the spell of its great headmaster, the Rev. A. R. Vardy, of whom Thomas always spoke with deep reverence and affection. One of the assistant masters, Mr. Donkin, had a knowledge of Sanskrit, a fact of which the boy took advantage to study that language at school, in addition to the classical curriculum. At the age of 17 he became head boy of the school and then obtained a classical scholarship at Trinity College, Cambridge, where he commenced residence in 1885.

His academic career was brilliant. He read Greek Philosophy under Henry Jackson and Archer Hind; Comparative Philology under John Peile; Latin under J. P. Postgate; Sanskrit, Pali, and other Eastern languages under R. A. Neil and Professor E. B. Cowell. In 1887 he obtained a First Class in Part I of the Classical Tripos, and in 1889 a First Class in Part II, gaining a first in pure classics, a first in philosophy, and a first with distinction in philology. In 1890 he got yet another First Class, in the Indian Languages Tripos (later, the Oriental Languages Tripos). Mention must be made, too, of his university prizes: Greek Epigram in 1887, Latin Epigram in 1888, Greek Ode in 1889, Members' Prize for Latin Essay in 1890 and again in 1891, both on Indian subjects; these were published at the time.

Yet he was no mere bookworm; he served three terms on the committee of the Union, and being blessed with a remarkably strong physique he was able to take vigorous exercise: he got his cap for lacrosse, played lawn tennis, went for long walks, ran in hare and hounds, and was a cross-country runner. In 1891 he took his first post, that of headmaster's assistant at his old school. In addition to his teaching work, Thomas took a prominent part in the general life of the school, composing a Latin school song, playing Rugby with the boys, and being chairman of the football and sports committees. In 1892 he was elected a Fellow of Trinity; he did not reside, as he retained his post at the school till 1898, but he visited Cambridge from time to time, acting as examiner both in the Classical Tripos, Part II, and in the Indian Languages Tripos. In 1898 he went to the India Office as assistant librarian, and in 1904 he succeeded C. H. Tawney as librarian, a post which he retained till 1927.

The library, by reason of its vast collections of manuscripts, and its traditions, brought him into constant communication with British and foreign Oriental scholars, and gave him a view of the whole output concerning the Middle East and the huge multilingual literary production of the Indian sphere; he was constantly engaged in research, and some of his correspondents who considered him dilatory in replying to their questions had no conception of the amount of work which he had to do before he could send them the information which they wanted. In 1908 he undertook for an exiguous salary the duty of Lecturer in Comparative Philology at University College, London, and in 1912, for no salary at all, that of Reader in Tibetan.

In the discharge of his duties as librarian at the India Office he paid many visits abroad.

He was an active member of various societies; in the Royal Asiatic he was a member of council and served in the offices of honorary secretary, vice-president, and director; on the society's behalf he conducted "Entente" Orientalist gatherings (London 1919 and Paris 1920) and he functioned at the centenary in 1923 when the Prince of Wales and the Prime Minister were present. Together with the president, Lord Chalmers, and a few others he was presented to the King at Buckingham Palace. In 1941 he was awarded the Triennial Gold Medal of the society. Of the India Society he was an early member, and he soon became a member of council. Of the Philological Society he was president from 1926 to 1929.

In 1920-21 he paid a visit of eight months to India, with instructions to see libraries; he travelled very widely and met many scholar friends; he had about a fortnight in Nepal and three weeks in Tibet, visiting numerous monasteries and inspecting their libraries; he gave public lectures at the universities of Mysore, Calcutta, and Bombay. In 1927 he became Boden Professor of Sanskrit in the University of Oxford, which carried with it a Fellowship at Balliol and the Curatorship of the Indian Institute.

The appreciation of his work by those most competent to judge of it was a source of much gratification to him. In 1937, on his seventieth birthday, he received an address signed by 99 British, Continental, and American colleagues in Oriental studies, and two years later, on his seventy-second birthday, a dinner was given in his honour by the Balliol Common Room, with Dr. Cyril Bailey [q.v.] in the chair, when there was presented to him "a volume of Eastern and Indian Studies", to which no fewer than 48 authors contributed, many of them Indians.

Between these two complimentary events he paid a second visit to India, having terminated his Professorship and Balliol Fellowship in 1937, when he was given the title Emeritus. He went to preside over the ninth All India Oriental Conference at Trivandrum, where he gave presidential and other addresses before going on to Calcutta, where he stayed over seven weeks.

In 1927 he was elected a Fellow of the British Academy (Oriental Section), and in the same year was made a C.I.E. He held degrees, ordinary or honorary, of many universities in England, on the Continent, and in India. He published a large number (well over 200) of books and papers on Indian and Orientalist subjects, the most extensive being *The Harsacarita of Bana,* which he translated in collaboration with E. B. Cowell; *Kavindravacana-samuccaya,* a Sanskrit anthology of verses; and *Tibetan Literary Texts and Documents concerning Chinese Turkestan.* These are of interest only to Indians and other Orientalists. For general readers the following may be mentioned: *The History and Prospects of British Education in India* and contributions to the *Cambridge History of India* and *The Legacy of India.* Other works of general interest include *The Making of a Sanskrit Poet.*

On his retirement he went to live in an Oxfordshire village where it might have been supposed that he would rest from his labours, physical and mental, but that was far from being the case: in his seventy-seventh year he confided to a friend that he worked in his garden and allotment for several hours a day and conducted researches at his desk till after midnight. Scholars from all over the world constantly sought his help, which he was always willing to give unstintingly, and he was, moreover, in his old age working on the preparation of a number of books for publication.

In 1948 he was elected an Honorary Fellow of the School of Oriental and African Studies in the University of London.

In 1908 he married Eleanor Grace, eldest daughter of Walter Hammond, of the Grange, Knockholt, by whom he had a son and a daughter.

May 8, 1956.

Sir Henry Thomas, for over 44 years in the service of the British Museum, and Principal Keeper of Printed Books there from 1943 to 1947, died at Birmingham on July 21, 1952 at the age of 73 after a long illness.

He entered the British Museum in October 1903 after a brilliant academic career, and a few years later joined Victor Scholderer and Dr. Arundell Esdaile on the great work then proceeding under the direction of A. W. Pollard on the British Museum's *Catalogue of Fifteenth Century Books.* His quickness of mind and natural ability, fortified by the bibliographical training he received at this time, produced in him an outstanding bibliographer—as he very soon demonstrated in the field of early Spanish literature which he took up soon after his entry into the museum.

One of his early tasks was to incorporate the extensive Cervantes collection of Henry Spencer Ashbee into the existing museum collection; this work he described in an article in the *Library* in 1908. The love of Cervantes remained with him throughout his life; he was one of the English scholars invited to take part in the important celebrations on the fourth centenary of Cervantes's birth in 1947, and one of the works which he left behind is a bibliography of English translations of Cervantes's minor works.

Thomas's reputation as a Spanish scholar quickly spread and he was invited to give the Norman MacColl Lectures at Cambridge in 1916, choosing for his subject the *Spanish and Portuguese Romances of Chivalry,* published in 1920 by the Cambridge University Press, the remarkable popular literary movement which had its origin in the Iberian Peninsula at the end of the fifteenth century and spread over western Europe. These studies were intimately connected with Thomas's work in the British Museum, and in 1921 he produced his *Short-title Catalogue of Spanish Books printed before 1601 in the British Museum,* a work which proved so successful that three years later it was followed by a corresponding catalogue of the museum's collection of fifteenth and sixteenth century French books, and in 1926 by one of Portuguese and Spanish-American books. Time has shown Thomas's wisdom in initiating this series of catalogues, and it is interesting to note that work on similar catalogues of the Italian and German books in the museum has recently been started.

A lasting friendship with Stanley Morison*, which gave great stimulus and happiness to Henry Thomas throughout his life, led to his developing still further his interest in Spanish printing. He contributed an article on the Saragossan printer Georg Coci to the *Gutenberg Jahrbuch* in 1925, and in 1926 he wrote a volume, *Spanish Sixteenth Century Printing,* for the series "Periods of Typography", edited by Morison and published by [Sir] Ernest Benn [q.v.]. He also collaborated with Morison in producing a monograph on *Andrés Brun, Calligrapher of Saragossa,* published in 1929 by the Pegasus Press. A further manifestation of his interest in printing was the exhibition of modern British and foreign printing which he arranged in the British Museum in the same year.

He published a number of reprints and facsimiles of early Spanish books in the 1930s, including an edition and a translation of Prester John's *Discovery of Abyssinia* in 1938, and in 1939 he published in the Bibliographical Society's series of "Illustrated Monographs" a remarkable collection of illustrations of early Spanish bookbindings of the eleventh to the fifteenth century, the fruits of his extensive travels in Spain and of his skill as a photographer. Thomas's travels in Spain and his friendships with the great Spanish scholars and book collectors form a separate story in themselves; they were a source of great satisfaction to him and produced such *jeux d'esprit* as his *Monster and Miracle* (privately printed at Sonning-on-Thames in 1935), which was based on his studies of the pilgrims' way across northern Spain to the shrine of St. James of Compostella.

The war put a temporary end to these visits, but his interest in the Peninsula did not flag. He amplified his catalogue of early Portuguese books in 1940, on the occasion of the tercentenary of the foundation and restoration of that country, and in 1944 he reissued his catalogue of early Spanish-American books. He also read an important paper before the Bibliographical Society on Spanish copperplate engraving and made several broadcasts in the series "La Voz de Londres". All this work was connected with Thomas's work in the British Museum, where he was appointed Deputy-Keeper in 1924, and in 1943, at the age of 65 when he would normally have retired, Keeper of the Department of Printed Books. Owing to the war and its aftermath, however, it was impossible for him to accomplish anything more for the department than the return of the books from their war-time homes. Had he become Keeper at an earlier age he would, with his great gifts, certainly have left his mark on the whole of the work of the department.

Thomas was born at Eynsham in Oxfordshire in 1878, but he was essentially a Birmingham man, and proud of it. He was educated at King Edward's School, where he became head boy, and at Mason College, later Birmingham University. He had a successful academic career in French, English and the classics and he was a brilliant linguist. He never married, and remained throughout his life devoted to his brothers and sisters.

His interests included music (he was a member of the old Oxford and Cambridge Musical Club and a singer; he also wrote on the music settings of Horace's lyric poems), walking, golf, and latterly motoring. He was a man of great spirit, and though not robust in health and in some ways inclined to be a valetudinarian, he did not in fact give way to a distressing skin trouble which marred the last years of his life in the British Museum.

His work brought him high rewards. He was knighted in 1946; he was doctor of letters of Birmingham and London and Hon. LL.D. of the former; he was a Fellow of the British Academy; Taylorian Lecturer at Oxford in 1922; corresponding or honorary member of many Spanish, Portuguese, and American academies; president of the Anglo-Spanish Society from 1931 to 1946; and of the Bibliographical Society from 1936 to 1938.

July 23, 1952.

J. P. Thomas—See **Cilcennin.**

Margaret Thomas—See **Rhondda.**

Sir William Beach Thomas, K.B.E., who died on May 12, 1957 at his home at Wheathampstead, Hertfordshire, was one of the most distinguished journalists of his generation, and was equally well known for such diverse attainments as war correspondent for the *Daily Mail* in the War of 1914-18 and as a writer on country subjects for the *Observer* and the *Spectator.*

He was a partisan of Lord Northcliffe, and was one of his most trusted lieutenants. He was one of the original regular reviewers for *The Times Literary Supplement* from the supplement's foundation in 1902. He had been a fine athlete (he was a former President of the Oxford University Athletic Club) in his youth but was opposed to the "tyranny of games".

William Beach Thomas was born in 1868, the son of the Rev. D. G. Thomas, rector of Hamerton, Huntingdonshire. He was educated at Shrewsbury, where he was in the football and cricket XIs and where his running brought him the honour of being appointed huntsman to the Royal Shrewsbury School Hunt, and at Christ Church, Oxford, where he was a scholar. For four years in succession he represented the university in the hundred yards, quarter-mile, and mile, and in 1890 and 1891 was President of the O.U.A.C. He also played cricket and football for his college. Beach Thomas started life as a schoolmaster, and was for five years at Bradfield, and later at Dulwich, but in 1897 he turned to journalism by becoming one of the writers of the "By the Way" column in the *Globe.* For some time he was on the staff of the *Saturday Review.* As a contributor to *Outlook* he worked under J. L. Garvin and it was Garvin who brought him to the *Observer,* for which he wrote a regular and never-failingly pleasing nature article (albeit in an obscure hand) for many years until April 1956.

In 1908 some 40 or 50 of Beach Thomas's essays were published under the title *From a Hertfordshire Cottage.* These showed his power of observation, which was later to make him so well known as a writer on nature or rural subjects. In 1912 he entered authoritatively into the discussion as to whether England should send a strong team to the next Olympic games at Berlin or not, and rather surprisingly, in view of his thesis that games should be played for fun, came out as opponent of the school, chiefly of Oxford rowing men, who considered that athletes who specialized and underwent rigorous professional tutorship stained their amateur status. One of Beach Thomas's arguments was that nothing was said about the cricketer, who, probably from boyhood upwards, had constant professional coaching.

During the War of 1914-18 Beach Thomas was a war correspondent in France for nearly four years, representing the *Daily Mail.* On one occasion he was sent at a moment's notice to America to find out for Northcliffe what the Americans were doing and thinking.

In the year of Northcliffe's death Beach Thomas was sent, again at a moment's notice, on one of his most important missions, a tour of the British Empire, which resulted in a series of most entertaining articles which appeared anonymously in *The Times* under the title of "The Round World". They were described as the diary of a "well-informed traveller", and had all the interest and intimacy which a journalist of the first rank can give to his writing. Three years later Beach Thomas had published his *A Traveller in News,* in which he wrote of "the Chief", Northcliffe, according to *The Times* reviewer, "as some favoured marshal might have written of Napoleon". In fact his main reason for issuing these reminiscences was because he held that Northcliffe had been misrepresented since his death. In 1928 there fell the centenary of the *Spectator,* and Beach Thomas had the honour of writing the commemorative volume—*The Story of the "Spectator".* He was created K.B.E. in 1920.

Among Beach Thomas's other works were: *The English Year, With the British on the Somme, Athletics* in the Isthmian Library, *The Happy Village, A Letter to my Dog, The Yeoman's England, Village England, The Squirrel's Granary, Hunting England, The English Landscape, The Way of a Countryman, The Poems of a Countryman, A Countryman's Creed, The Way of a Dog,* and *Hertfordshire.*

Beach Thomas married in 1900 Helen Dorothea, daughter of the late Augustus George Vernon-Harcourt, and there were two sons and one daughter of the marriage. The second son, Lieutenant-Commander Michael Beach Thomas, R.N., was killed in the late war.

May 14, 1957.

Professor A. Hamilton Thompson, C.B.E., F.B.A., F.S.A., HON. A.R.I.B.A., formerly Professor of History in the University of Leeds, died in a nursing home at Exmouth on September 4, 1952 at the age of 78.

Alexander Hamilton Thompson was the eldest son of the Rev. John Thompson, sometime vicar of St. Gabriel's, Bristol. He was born on November 7, 1873, and was educated at Clifton and St. John's College, Cambridge, where he was elected an honorary Fellow in 1938. Soon after taking his degree he joined the Cambridge local lectures syndicate and for the next 20 years or so engaged in the arduous research into English medieval records upon which his reputation chiefly rests. The firstfruits of this work were very naturally concerned with Cambridge and its colleges; the first edition of this erudite little work appeared in 1898. Two volumes on the English parish church appeared in 1911, in which Thompson's peculiarly happy appreciation of the interaction of history and architecture are abundantly evident; they were *The Ground Plan of the English Parish Church* and *The Historical Growth of the English Parish Church.*

These were followed in the course of the next year by *Military Architecture in England in the Middle Ages,* and then, with *English Monasteries* in 1913, came the first of the series of volumes which established his reputation as an outstanding authority on the medieval monastic system in England. He had published a *Students' History of English Literature* in 1903 and the quality of this little book led to his appointment as Lecturer in English at Armstrong College, Newcastle upon Tyne, in 1919. Within two years, however, he had been appointed Reader in Medieval History and Archaeology at Armstrong College and in 1922 was appointed to a similar post at Leeds. He was promoted to Professor in the same subject in 1924, and in 1927 became head of the faculty of history in the University of Leeds until 1939.

Meanwhile he continued to give to the public the results of his ever widening research, and in the years between 1914 and 1928 published his splendid volumes recording the visitations of religious houses in the vast medieval diocese of Lincoln. Three other volumes on the same subject, which brought the story up to the eve of the dissolution of the monasteries, appeared between 1940 and 1947 and together they present a picture of monastic organization, careful, scholarly and unbiased, corrective of Protestant and Catholic apologists alike.

Other works, smaller in scope and size, appeared with such copiousness that only the briefest mention of the most salient can be made here. Among them was an edition of the statutes of Durham Cathedral, a history of Welbeck Abbey before the dissolution, an excellent volume on the cathedrals of England, and an equally scholarly account of the organization of the English clergy in the later middle ages. Besides his independent work, he was for many years editor of the *Archaeological Journal* and of a number of English classics, and a contributor to the *Cambridge Medieval History,* the *Cambridge History of English Literature,* and to numerous learned periodicals. He had been a member of the Royal Commission on historical monuments and on ancient monuments since 1933 and 1935 respectively, and his sensitive appreciation of architectural quality and its historical basis was of great benefit to those bodies.

He married in 1903 Amy, daughter of Alfred Gosling. She died in 1945 and he is survived by two daughters.

September 5, 1952.

Marie-Louise Tilche, who died in October 1956 at the age of 88, was a brave friend to allied soldiers and refugees whom she protected at great personal risk during the Second World War.

French by birth, but proudly tracing her family back to a Scot who emigrated to France at the time when James II left England, she continued, although Italian by marriage, to uphold the cause of Great Britain and France, and to refuse to be intimidated in her allegiance.

After her house in Florence had been destroyed during an air raid, she withdrew with her daughter, Dudette Tilche, to a summer bungalow they had built on the slopes of Monte Senario; and there, after the armistice of 1943, braving heavy penalties, they aided and fed more than 40 fugitives from fascist and German terror—allied prisoners of war, Jews, and disbanded Italian soldiers who refused to return to military service to fight side by side with the Germans against the allied forces.

For 11 months, from the autumn of 1943 until the arrival of the allied troops in September 1944, she hid and cared for two officers of the Grenadier Guards who had escaped after being taken prisoner; although for the latter part of the time German troops occupied the house, leaving to the owners the use of only two rooms.

During those months Signora Tilche sold one thing after another to procure for the men the medicines and other needful things which her farm could not supply; and, after the British patrol had arrived and taken over the two officers, she was left with only a few lira. Although almost penniless and with a large part of her house destroyed by artillery fire, Signora Tilche and her daughter refused any reward or compensation from the Screening Commission, asking only that something should be given to their old servant, who had shared the risks.

A diploma signed by Field-Marshal Lord Alexander*, recognizing their services, was eventually awarded to them; and they were presented by the British Consul in Florence to the Duke of Gloucester* when he made a tour of the Commonwealth War cemeteries in Italy in May 1955.

October 27, 1956.

W. T. Tilden, who died at Hollywood, California, at the age of 60, in June 1953, will be regarded by many as the greatest player of lawn tennis of all time.

His claim rests not only upon his remarkable record of success in a long career but on his ability to employ almost every stroke known to the game—some of which he may be said to have invented—and to play at any speed. Furthermore, by his tall stature and generally striking appearance and his sense of the dramatic, he stamped himself at once as as great a personality as the game has seen. Indeed, one of the reasons Wimbledon moved from Worple Road to its present vast site after 1921 may be said to have been that the singles champions were Tilden and Suzanne Lenglen.

Tilden had first won the title when he beat G. L. Patterson in 1920 by his intelligent tactics in using underspin to his opponent's insecure backhand; and he was to win it for the third time as late as 1930 at the age of 37. Meanwhile, in the United States, first winning the championship in 1920 from W. M. Johnston, his previous conqueror and chief rival with whose name he will ever be associated—they were known as "Big Bill" and "Little Bill"—he then retained the title for five successive years, Johnston being four times the runner-up. During those six years he was also undefeated in fifteen Davis Cup challenge round singles. These feats have never been approached before or since. In addition he had many doubles successes with F. T. Hunter and Vincent Richards and in mixed doubles as well, although the singles game was his *métier.* And all this after overcoming the handicap of a missing finger.

After 1930, with his unequable temperament and even thirst for the bizarre, he became a controversial figure tossed to and fro between the amateur game and business interests on a growing scale; and he soon turned professional. In this he had a further long career, and in later years, when he could no longer hold his own against those far younger, such as Vines, Perry, and Budge, he was still a great attraction to spectators, many of whom remembered that it was he who did more than any other to widen the field of public interest in the game.

In recent years he fell upon adversity. But it is as the man who bestrode the centre at Wimbledon like a colossus that he will be remembered, for there is no one else for whom the description is more apt. His gaunt, long, lithe-limbed figure, with his aristocratic nose, lent atmosphere to the scene, and his very preliminaries clad in a bearskin were a thrill. Occasionally he would ask for four balls and proceed without further supply to finish the match with four "cannon-ball" services. Was it this vanity which proved his undoing in his famous match with H. Cochet in 1927 when he lost after leading by two sets to none and 5-1? At any rate as a player and a character he can deserve a word that is seldom safe to use. He was unique.

June 8, 1953.

Anne (Mrs. Josiah) Titzell—See **Parrish.**

Vesta Tilley (Lady de Frece), who died on September 16, 1952 at her London home at the age of 88, was known and loved by a great and enthusiastic public of three generations as the daintiest of male impersonators.

Vesta Tilley belonged to the great days of the London music hall, and not many living playgoers can have seen her. She was only three years younger than Dan Leno and was actually six years older than Marie Lloyd. She was already a "top of the bill" name on the halls at the age of 15, when Marie Lloyd was in the nursery; but both of them were at the height of their success in about the same period. However, nothing could be more different than the two styles of these two artists—or artistes, as the programmes of the time would have called them.

Marie Lloyd was all confidential spontaneity. She never knew quite what she was going to do when she went on to the stage. Vesta Tilley's art was a hard glitter. Every infection, every movement, was as studied and as fixed as the comic acting of Coquelin. Besides she was always impersonating, which Marie Lloyd never was, and nearly always impersonating a boy or young man, which Marie Lloyd never did. Her dapper little figure, so different from Marie Lloyd's somewhat expansive physique, was smart rather than genial. And yet her power of creating a character was such that no one who saw, for instance, her walk across the stage as the absurd little red-coated recruit with the large cigar, in her song about "the girl who loves a soldier", is ever likely to forget the picture.

She was born at Worcester on May 13, 1864, Matilda Alice, daughter of W. H. Powles (professionally known as Harry Ball), who was chairman of the St. George's Hall, Nottingham, on the stage of which she made her first public appearance at the age of four. At five she became "the pocket Sims Reeves", moustached and dressed like the great tenor and singing "The Anchor's Weighed" and others of his songs. During the next few years "the great little Tilley" (short for her first name, with "Vesta" afterwards prefixed), built up fame in the provinces as a singer in male dress. In 1878, not yet turned 14, she went to London, to triumph at two music-halls in one night, the Royal, Holborn, and Lusby's, Mile End.

Thereafter for more than 40 years she was one of the brightest stars of the variety stage. Twice she left it for pantomime: at Birmingham in 1881 and at Drury Lane in 1882. In comic opera she twice toured the provinces, and appeared also in the United States in 1894, in 1903, and in 1904, but her life's work was male impersonation in the music-halls. On her first appearance in London she had sung two songs: "The Pet of Rotten Row" and "Near the Workhouse Door" ("Poor Joe"), in which she played the part of the little urchin moved on by the big policeman.

As time went on, poor Joe, and other characters, gave way before the pet of the Row and "Algy, the Piccadilly Johnny with the little glass eye". Vesta Tilley on the stage was the most dapper little man and the dandiest "fellah turned sixteen" that could be imagined. And this "Idol of the Girls" had a way with them so free of offence that to some of her admirers the song "Following in Father's footsteps. Following the dear old Dad" seemed a shade too coarse for her, while in any other hands it might have seemed insipid.

To song after song she continued to give point and quality; but she was most adored, perhaps, when she was a sailor or a soldier. "Jolly good luck", she sang, "to the girl that loves" either of them; and during the 1914-18 war she turned her popularity directly to the benefit of her country. Her swagger and her swagger-stick—"I joined the Army yesterday, so the Army of to-day's all right!"—sent many a young man into the khaki that she wore so smartly. On a hot night in June 1920 this "London Idol" took her farewell of the variety stage; and the Coliseum was the scene of an ovation led by Ellen Terry.

On August 6, 1890, Vesta Tilley was married to Walter de Frece, controller of many theatres and music-halls in the great provincial towns, and the author and composer of many of her songs. During the 1914-18 war he did much to organize the entertainment of forces and munition workers, and for these and other public services he was knighted in 1919. From 1920 until 1931 he was a member of the House of Commons.

After her retirement from the stage Lady de Frece helped him in his career with song and speech; and she nursed him with unwearied devotion in the illness which led to his death in Monaco in January 1935. In 1934 she published a sketchy but entertaining book, *The Recollections of Vesta Tilley*. Unlike some of her fellow artists, she never returned to the stage after her retirement.

She leaves for those who saw her a memory of that farewell night at the Coliseum, when, as she sang the famous lines—

"Girls, if you'd like to love a soldier,
You can all love me . . ."

—a stentorian voice from the gallery shouted out "We do".

September 17, 1952.

Sir Henry Tizard, G.C.B., A.F.C., F.R.S., Rector of the Imperial College of Science from 1929 to 1942 and President of Magdalen College, Oxford, from 1942 to 1946, died on October 9, 1959. He was 74.

Henry Thomas Tizard was born on August 23, 1885, the son of Captain T. H. Tizard, C.B., F.R.S., R.N., who was at that time in charge of the Coastal Survey of the United Kingdom and later was Hydrographer to the Admiralty. On the mother's side Tizard's grandfather had been Chief Engineer of Malta and later of Pembroke Dockyard, so that the conspicuous way in which he combined the characteristics of the man of science with the instincts of an engineer was derived from both sides of the family. He was destined for the Navy, but a few weeks before the examination was due a blind patch in one of his eyes was discovered and a naval career had, therefore, to be abandoned.

The young Tizard was less upset than his father, and having gained an exhibition (later a scholarship) at Westminster School he went there as a boarder on the modern side in 1899. In March 1903, at the age of 17, he was awarded a demyship in mathematics and science at Magdalen College, Oxford, but, being very young for his age, he stayed on at school for another year, doing much as he liked; reading omnivorously in the library and doing special mathematics.

At Oxford he proceeded to get first-class honours in Mathematical Moderations after one year, although he always maintained he was not a real mathematician, though fairly competent and very interested. In 1905 he took seriously to chemistry with N. V. Sidgwick [q.v.] as his tutor, and obtained first-class honours in 1908. Magdalen College thereupon extended Tizard's demyship for a year and he went to Berlin to work under Nernst.

He had intended to stay for two years and take a Ph.D., but became seriously unwell there, and on Sidgwick's advice came back after his first year to work for a while at the Davy Faraday Laboratory at the Royal Institution. In spite of the short time he spent in Berlin Tizard always felt he owed a great deal to Nernst, and used to say that the average standard of work and of teaching in his laboratory was far above anything he had known at Oxford.

In the spring of 1911 Tizard was elected to a Fellowship at Oriel College, Oxford, mainly, as he used to say, because the provost at the time was an Old Westminster and refused to consider anyone else's claims.

The three years at Oriel from 1911 to 1914 were marred only by the first of what were to show themselves later as a real handicap during his life—namely, recurrent serious attacks of influenza.

In the summer of 1914 Tizard had the good luck to get a free ticket to Australia for the meeting of the British Association. Someone had dropped out at the last minute and he went at three days' notice. The best of the luck was that he made the first of the two acquaintances in the scientific world which probably influenced him more than any others, for Rutherford was on board the ss. Euripides, in which he travelled. For the first time Tizard had met someone whom he found really inspiring, and he has recorded that he registered a vow that on his return he would try to go and work with Rutherford.

That plan was prevented by the outbreak of war, but this in its turn led to the second scientific acquaintance which influenced Tizard profoundly, for it led to his association with Bertram Hopkinson, whom he regarded as the biggest man, other than Rutherford, with whom he had been on terms of intimate friendship.

Tizard did not stay long in Australia because, like so many people, he thought the war was going to be short and sharp and that he had better get back soon. On his arrival in September he went with H. G. J. Moseley to try to get a commission in the Army and, after several months, was posted to the Garrison Gunners at Portsmouth. After six months of inactivity he managed to achieve a transfer to the Central Flying School at Upavon and later took charge of the scientific work at the Aeroplane Testing Station at Martlesham Heath under Hopkinson, who was at that time Controller of Research and Experiment at the Air Board.

In 1919 Tizard returned to Oxford and to chemistry, but retained some of his engineering contacts through cooperation with Ricardo*, Pye [q.v.], and others on a large research programme on liquid fuel carried out for the Shell Oil Company. It was probably his war experience in scientific administration that led him in 1920 to accept an offer of the post of assistant secretary, under Sir Frank Heath, of the recently established Department of Scientific and Industrial Research, of which he became secretary on Heath's retirement in 1927.

Two years later he accepted the invitation to become Rector of the Imperial College of Science and Technology, and the years between that time and his resignation in 1942 were those in which the foundations were laid for the unique position he was later to be called upon to fill.

His genius for illuminating any practical problem that called for clear analysis by a well-stored scientific mind led to his being drawn into important committee work which his presence in London enabled him to combine with the headship of the Imperial College. Since 1919 he had been a member, and in 1933 became chairman, of the Aeronautical Research Committee, and he was made a development commissioner in 1934.

During the years from 1933-39 he foresaw clearly the threat of war and put his best efforts as chairman of various advisory committees into the building up of the scientific organization under the Air Ministry which successfully stood the strain of war, and, through its influence in the Battle of Britain, may have been a decisive factor in the result.

The most important stage in Tizard's work at this period was complete by 1939. Discussions under his guidance during the preparatory years had led to decisions and projects of incalculable importance to the future of the country, but during the war years, although he became an additional member of the Air Council in 1942, there were stresses and strains with leaders in the Government which meant that Tizard's influence was felt at the periphery rather than at the centre of the war machine.

The special committees over which he presided, and in which the civilian scientific members and executive officers of the Royal Air Force met on equal terms, continued. And it was in the handling of such meetings and in his power of keeping discussions fluid and easy that Tizard's genius was conspicuous. Each side felt that the chairman could speak a language which they understood, and each side therefore found it easy to contribute the results of the special experience it had to offer.

In July 1942 he was elected President of Magdalen College, Oxford. The choice of a scientist caused much comment in the university, and his career was watched with critical interest. Though he went into residence in the following September, he was much occupied for the rest of the war by government committees, but was able to give a gradually increasing amount of time to college affairs. His ability and experience in organization, his quick intelligence, and his restless energy soon proved of great value in this new environment, though they were occasionally rather disturbing. His attack upon a problem was always lively, often entertaining, but sometimes confusing; for he had so many ideas that his policy was not always consistent in every detail. He was elected to the Hebdomadal Council in 1946.

In 1946 he was pressed to take the chairmanship of the newly formed committees on defence research policy and of scientific policy. After consulting with the college about the possibility of combining the presidency with the performing of at least part of these onerous outside tasks he decided that this would not be practicable. So, to the great regret of many, he resigned.

In these last appointments in the public service he paid a large part in securing that possible applications of science in defence were considered automatically as part of a wider problem instead as—too often in the past—it being looked upon as a form of outside, even amateur, interference.

In 1950, when the burden of his commitments was extremely heavy, he asked that Sir Frederick Brundrett* should be appointed his deputy as Scientific Adviser to the Ministry of Defence, and consent was given to his request in June of that year. In March 1952 Tizard resigned as chairman of the Defence Research Policy Committee and also of the Government Scientific Advisory Policy Committee. He was president of the British Association in 1948.

He was made C.B. in 1927, K.C.B. 10 years later, and advanced to G.C.B. in 1949.

He married in 1915 Kathleen, daughter of Arthur Wilson, by whom he had three sons.

October 10, 1959.

Michael Todd, the film magnate, who died on March 22, 1958, at the age of 49, when his private aircraft crashed in mountains west of Albuquerque, New Mexico, was one of the most spectacular personalities in the American world of entertainment.

In Britain his reputation rests on his film *Around the World in 80 Days*—and on the lavish scale of his parties—but in the United States, even before the film which brought him fame and fortune, he had become one of the greatest showmen of the century, after starting from the humblest origins.

Avrom Hirsch Goldbogen, to give Todd his original name, was born on June 22, 1907, in Minneapolis, the son of a Polish Rabbi, and in his boyhood he took any job that offered while waiting for the time when he could break into the world of entertainment.

His first production was at the Chicago World's Fair in 1933, this being a Flame Dance in which a dancer would flutter close to a huge candle until her gauze wings caught fire and she would scamper off the stage apparently without clothing. His first big success in New York came in 1939, when he produced *The Hot Mikado,* in which a fifty-year-old Negro tap-dancer played the Emperor. He had four shows running at the New York World's Fair in the same year. He presented Maurice Evans in a production of *Hamlet,* and among the long runs with which he was associated were *Star and Garter* (600 performances), *Something for the Boys* (422), *Mexican Hayride* (504), and *Up in Central Park* (500). He described himself as the boy wonder who became the boy failure, and after a period of bankruptcy he turned his attention to films. With Lowell Thomas, the screen commentator, he formed a company to experiment on Cinerama, a wide screen process on which they worked secretly for 14 months, and he used to recall with pride that it was the first time in his life he had kept his mouth shut.

Todd was not satisfied with the new method of projection, because it involved the use of three cameras, three projection machines, and three separate films, which, in his view, made intimate scenes impossible. Accordingly he sold out his interests and worked on a method which would produce the effects of Cinerama with a single camera and film. The result was the Todd-Ao process, which was first used for the film of *Oklahoma!* and secondly for *Around the World in 80 Days,* the only film which Todd himself produced. The Hollywood experts assured him that he had taken on an impossible task in trying to bring Jules Verne's classic to the screen, but he was not dismayed. The task was accomplished and the picture was hailed as a milestone in the history of the screen wherever it was shown. With the generosity that was characteristic of him Todd gave the whole of the proceeds of the first performance, £15,000, to the Newspaper Press Fund.

He was married three times and leaves a widow, Miss Elizabeth Taylor, the film actress, and a baby daughter, as well as a son by a former marriage.

March 24, 1958.

George Tomlinson, Labour M.P. for Farnworth, who was successively Minister of Works and Minister of Education in the 1950 Labour Government, died, aged 62, on September 22, 1952.

When George Tomlinson was confirmed in the office of Minister of Education after the General Election of 1950 an educational commentator, in warm approval, said that he was the most popular Minister that had ever headed the Education Department. *The Times Educational Supplement* said that Tomlinson was popular because of his qualities as a man. He had sustained ardour for the business of life, whatever his assigned task; a buoyant spirit and lively sense of humour; strong sympathy with the unfortunate; and a watchful eye for the meretricious. In manner he was modest and sincere, free from pretence and vanity. Thoroughly Lancashire, he never attempted to change the accent acquired in his native county. His politics blended the evangelism of nonconformity—he was a Methodist and a lay preacher—with the evangelical socialism in a creed of zeal for the wellbeing of the bodies and souls of men.

It was not incongruous or unfitting that he, who had known little of schools, should be made Minister of Education. His qualifications were not academic but those of purpose and resolve to make effective a new and great educational instrument all ready to hand—the Education Act of 1944. The problems of the system of public education were not new to him. He had grappled with them administratively in Lancashire both as chairman of the Farnworth education committee, a "Part 3 authority", and a member of the education committee of the county. At the Ministry of Education he was confronted with administrative problems on the largest scale.

The promise of the 1944 Act awaited fulfilment and the times were not propitious, for buildings were inadequate, the ruins of war could only slowly be repaired, and teaching staffs were sadly deficient. A natural increase of the school population, the addition of a year to the compulsory period of school attendance, the necessity for rapid recruitment of additional school teachers, and the revision of secondary school examinations were all, in varying ways and degrees, exacting administrative difficulties in which the Minister's personal concern was deeply engaged. To Tomlinson, however, these were all transient problems which must not obstruct or delay the Act's great purpose of opening the door of free opportunity in the sphere of knowledge.

George Tomlinson, the son of a cotton weaver, was born at Rishton on March 21, 1890. At 12 years of age he went to the mill as a half-time worker—his father had started working when eight—and, besides his father, two brothers and two sisters had employment in the same mill. There also his mother had been employed years before, and his future wife was a workmate. He was a weaver for 25 years and then opened a small retail shop in Farnworth; but in 1935 he was among the cotton workers again as secretary of the Rishton Weavers' Association.

It was the people of the Farnworth division, which includes Rishton, who returned him to Parliament at a by-election. They had already made him their representative in the county council. He was destined for early selection for a Government post. In the all-party Government which took office under Churchill* after 10 months of war, Ernest Bevin [q.v.], at the Ministry of Labour, was given two parliamentary secretaries, one a Conservative and the other George Tomlinson, a Socialist.

Tomlinson made his mark in Parliament by able presentation of the Bill designed to resettle disabled men in industry or other suitable employment. Two important tasks were allotted to him before the end of the war. He was one of the delegates to the 1944 conference of the International Labour Organization.

The increase of his political stature was seen in the general election at the end of the war, when he was one of the party broadcasters. In the Labour Government which took office he was made head of a department and given the post of Minister of Works. The principal task then before him was, in collaboration with the Minister of Health, to provide the people with houses; but his part was the less conspicuous and less subject to criticism than that of his more flamboyant colleague. Within 18 months he was transferred, when Miss Ellen Wilkinson died, to the Ministry of Education, and the promotion gave him a seat in the Cabinet. He remained in charge of the Ministry until the defeat of the Labour Government at the elections in 1951.

September 23, 1952.

The death occurred in a London hospital on February 5, 1958 of **H. M. Tomlinson,** novelist, essayist, and travel writer, who attained his highest distinction in the long line of English authors who have commemorated the traffic of ships and the sea. He was 84.

His most celebrated book is the novel *Gallion's Reach*, in which his prose style, brooding and eloquent, is at its most evocative and felicitous. The Bible, the Elizabethan voyagers, Melville—these, perhaps, were formative influences upon a stylist much given to the grandly contemplative and elegiac.

Born at Wanstead, Essex, in 1873, Henry Major Tomlinson was the eldest of the five children of Henry and Emily Tomlinson. His father held a well-paid position in the West India Docks, but lost his entire savings in a rash stroke of speculation and died soon afterwards. The son, who on frequent visits to the docks had become familiar with ships and seamen, was taken from school and placed by an uncle in a shipping office as a clerk. He continued to spend much time at the docks—they were his university, he said afterwards—was encouraged by his mother, a well-read and talented woman, to read widely, added geology and botany to his study of the history of travel and navigation, and acquired a knowledge of languages. In 1895 he was recommended (by Sir Chalmers Mitchell, among others) as scientist to the Jackson-Harmsworth Polar Expedition, but was dissuaded from taking advantage of this by medical opinion—a thing he regretted ever afterwards.

Travel drew him more and more strongly, and opportunity eventually came in a voyage to Brazil and a journey of 1,300 miles up the Amazon and Madeira rivers by the first English steamer to make that passage. (Characteristically he heard of the matter on a visit to the docks and persuaded the owners, since they were not allowed to carry passengers, to let him ship as purser.)

Before then he had made many coastal trips on boats of all kinds and had once spent several weeks in winter with the North Sea fishing fleet. This he turned to good account some years later in an essay for the *Monthly Review*, whose editor, Ford Maddox Ford, encouraged him to go on writing. The encouragement was welcome but perhaps not strictly necessary; Tomlinson had begun to write as a child and had once astonished a headmaster with a long and meditative essay on Isaiah. He stepped firmly into serious journalism with a series of articles, critical and descriptive, in the old *Morning Leader*, joined the staff of that paper as a special writer in 1904, and remained there until it was amalgamated with the *Daily News*. From 1915 until 1917 he was an official correspondent at British G.H.Q. in France for both the *Daily News* and *The Times*. In the latter year he joined *The Nation* as literary editor and assistant to H. W. Massingham, and followed his editor when in 1923 Massingham resigned on a question of policy. Except for a very short period afterwards, Tomlinson had done with active journalism.

The Sea and the Jungle, his first book, in which he described his journey up the Amazon, had been published in 1912, and its quality was immediately apparent. This might be prose a shade too deliberate, too conspicuously studied and literary, but its evocative power and contemplative vision were undeniable. The record of later journeys, of visits to most of the Mediterranean ports, of travels in North Africa, Greece, Italy, and Spain, of voyagings in the East Indies, held a similar strength and virtue. *Old Junk* (1918) turned from travel sketches and stories to impressions of war; personal memories and musings played about *London River* (1921); impressions of war again filled *Waiting for Daylight* (1922); *Tidemarks* (1924) carried the reader to Singapore, the Malayan forest, the islands and straits of the Dutch East Indies. *Gallion's Reach* appeared in 1927, a formless novel but of compelling vividness and fine ruminative intensity, which was awarded the Femina-Vie Heureuse prize.

After that Tomlinson's work is of uneven merit. The prose of his fiction, though it retains its high seriousness, echoes a little thinly; the rolling periods begin to lack substance. At the same time a note of pessimism becomes more pronounced: from *All Our Yesterdays* (1930) onwards it gains steadily upon him. In *Mars His Idiot* (1935), an indictment of war, he takes his stand upon the supreme value of the individual personality. This indeed is the personal faith that pervades and alleviates the faintly rhetorical melancholy of his later novels and volumes of essays, sketches, and meditations.

His later books included two volumes of essays, *The Turn of the Tide* (1945) and *The Face of the Earth* (1950); two novels, *Morning Light* (1946) and *The Trumpet Shall Sound*—the latter, published in 1957, a gesture of salute to the English home front in war and, except in form, something less than fiction; and *Malay Waters* (1950), a history of the small ships of the Straits Steamship Company, whose records both in the Far East and in Liverpool were destroyed during the war. In 1953 he brought together in a single volume *A Mingled Yarn*, nearly a score of semi-autobiographical sketches, gravely eloquent and all but impersonal, written over a long period of time. In the same year, when he was 80, an admirer from a younger generation, Kenneth Hopkins, edited a volume of selections from his writings.

H. M. Tomlinson was a man of retiring and thoughtful disposition, whose reserve was deepened by the deafness from which he suffered but who kept the sincerest friendship and affection of all who were admitted to intimacy with him. He was an occasional contributor to *The Times* and also wrote for *The Times Literary Supplement*.

He married, in 1898, Miss Florence Hammond and had a son and two daughters.

February 6, 1958.

Archbishop of Toulouse—See **Saliege.**

Arturo Toscanini, who died in New York on January 16, 1957 at the age of 89, was the most renowned of living conductors, since his reputation was internationally supreme. His pre-eminence was recognized in Italy, where he was born; in America, where he worked for the greater part of his career; and in German countries, where between the wars he conducted at the Bayreuth and Salzburg Festivals. His quality as an interpreter was mainly known in Britain from gramophone records, but his visits to London in the 1930s and in 1952 confirmed and amplified the judgment that for clarity of presentation and fidelity to the composer he had no peer.

His tastes were catholic but his interpretations were always those of an Italian. Yet Siegfried Wagner made him the mainstay of the Bayreuth Festival in 1930 and 1931, and the connexion was broken only by Toscanini's refusal to appear in Germany when Jewish musicians were maltreated by the Nazi Government. That he should thus be accepted by the leading institution which stands above all others for German music is certainly a remarkable testimony to the universality of his art. It was also a characteristic fulfilment of Toscanini's career. For he had been the first to introduce Wagner's *Götterdämmerung* to Italians; he had supervised the international repertory at the Metropolitan Opera in New York from 1898 to 1915; and it is on his performances of Beethoven's symphonies that his popular fame is founded.

In Britain opportunities of hearing him in the flesh were limited to a short series of concerts in each of the years 1930, 1935, 1937-39, and a last visit in 1952, and, though we heard no opera under his direction, his performances of choral works, including Beethoven's *Mass in D* and *Choral Symphony*, Brahms's *Requiem*, and Verdi's *Requiem* were memorable. It was widely claimed for him that his readings of these and other classics revealed them in their true character as their creators conceived them, if not for the first time, certainly in a definitive manner.

The listener hearing some hitherto overlooked detail in a familiar symphony, noting some subtlety of tonal gradation or shaping of a phrase, was surprised to find that it was all marked in the score, which in point of fact the conductor never used either at rehearsal or at performances by virtue of his prodigious and, as it seems, photographic memory. Yet his interpretations were no more final than those of any other executant musician, and critics whose admiration was less idolatrous found the defects of his qualities in his reading of German music.

The Latin mind, like the Mediterranean sunshine which conditions it, views things with hard edges, clear outlines, and thorough-going logic. Toscanini's meticulous attention to detail in Beethoven's symphonies made them classical and brilliant but ultimately a little inhuman. The opening chords of the *Eroica* sounded, at any rate with the virtuoso orchestras of America, more like pistol shots than an announcement of the key of E flat, and his bourgeois German Mastersingers became a profession of Florentine nobles. This is only to say that he was true to himself, and no conductor of more single-minded integrity ever lived. This sterling honesty brought him into conflict with the Fascist Government, whose song "Giovinezza" he refused to play, as it also caused him later to break with Nazi-dominated Germany. To show with an unmistakable gesture what he thought of their intolerance he went to Palestine and

, an impressive life's
Weer more than half a
literary and poetic
espect, even admiration,
was by the enormous
al work accomplished
service of the greater
of Shaw's dramatic work
of the most voluminous,
ost ambitious tasks of its
n by a single writer; and,
of the most perfectly
fers of thought and form
into another, without loss
particular characteristics.
oup of 1938, Hitler took
na and the aged Trebitsch
e, Shaw's friendship and
ed his fate.

Orchestra,
through the
tin America
ecords which
the rest of the
while to Milan
contribute the
s towards the
ion to a financial
Festival Hall was
nnounced that he
n and direct some
This plan, however,
withstanding, he did
ll, when in September
to give two concerts
four symphonies of
exion it is worthy of
he denounced other
ing with scores he did
cks with the timpani of
hony.
so showed him sacrificing
y of the opening in favour
tely a feeling of tremendous
nt which leaves him with a
o do with the development
milder Brahms of the St.
ns and the D major symphony
re ingratiating temper, and in
n of Debussy's *La Mer* sensuous
was not neglected. But in general
intensity, the urgency, the
n of the life of a score upon which
d it was this remarkable dynamic
e preserved into extreme old age.
ncert was given at Carnegie Hall
no longer ago than in April 1954,
farewell to his orchestra and his
gner programme, at the end of
d his baton and went out not
he plaudits of his audience—a
f retirement after 68 years
ing.
redeceased him in 1951.
d two daughters of the
is married to Vladimir

first Marshal of the Royal Air
rime architect of British air
ebruary 10, 1956 at his home
d celebrated his eighty-third
before.
f the earlies
eatest—Air Fore
Seldom can a man h
ark in so short a time. In 19
own major of The Royal Sco
ed to the Royal Flying Corp
hree years later, when he w
ws of his resignation from th
post of Chief of the Air Sta
ce of opinion on a matter wh
s one of vital principle with
tate, Lord Rothermere, caus
ay to pass over the country
d acquired in so short a time
too, by the intensity of fe
fested itself in a debate in
ommons in 1918 arising out o
work in the war of 1914-18 w
be only a beginning—the earli
s of a reputation which was not
pinnacle even in his massive service
air power during his 11 years' tenure
ce of Chief of the Air Staff, when he
d the integrity and built the basic
of the great Service which was to
free world in the Battle of Britain and
predominant a share in the second
over Germany.
ions may differ about his work as
issioner of Police of the Metropolis
931 to 1935, but there are many who rate
t inferior to his service to the Air Force.
ver, his unflagging enthusiasm, his never-
g vision, and his deeply understanding
m were continually devoted to the Service
ad done so much more than anyone to
te—whether in the House of Lords, or
nd the scenes in Whitehall, or as elder
sman, guide, philosopher, and friend to a
g line of successors in the Air Ministry.
t is not easy to define the quality of real

, who died in a
New York on
as Chief of the
United States
9, and it was
he need for
nt, to build
force to
ssity of
e had
hose.
ly a
had
s of
on
d

advice in air matters. He was one of the few high officers in the air division of the Navy who had been in at the start and had worked up with the service from a time when it was a much neglected arm.

His loyalty was not altogether to his advantage in the matter of promotion, for he was twice passed over for higher commands because he was attached to the air service. It is customary in the United States Navy for an officer who is passed over three times to be retired, but in 1939 it was largely through the influence of President Roosevelt, who was personally deeply concerned in naval affairs, that he was promoted to be rear-admiral and placed in charge of the Bureau of Aeronautics.

John Henry Towers was born at Rome, in Georgia, on January 30, 1885. He was interested in applied science from his earliest days and took classes at the Georgia School of Technology, before proceeding to the United States Naval Academy at Annapolis, where he completed his studies in 1906. In 1908 he became an ensign and rose through the various ranks till he became commander in 1913. In 1911 he took up flying, one of the first men in the United States Navy to do so at a time when it was not by any means recognized as an essential part of the service and was rather looked down on. He had a flying accident in 1912 in which his left eye was injured, but it did not prevent him from continuing flying though he always had a spare pilot with him afterwards. During the 1914-18 War he was assistant director of naval air services.

In 1919 he commanded one of the first transatlantic flights, piloting one of three NC-4 aircraft attempting the crossing from Newfoundland. His machine was forced down in rough seas, but he completed the crossing by taxi-ing the craft 205 miles to the Azores. He twice represented his country as an attaché at the Embassy in London in the period between the wars, and made many friends among flying and naval men here. He was appointed Assistant Chief of the Bureau of Aeronautics at the Navy Department in 1929 and, as Captain Towers, was known as the greatest enthusiast for flying in the United States Navy. Other officers serving with him had taken up flying late in their service and had not gone in at the start as he did and learnt it from the beginning. In 1937-38 he was in command of the aircraft carrier Saratoga and then came his appointment to the chief place in the naval air service.

Not many men enjoy the fruits of their labours so quickly and so completely, for in 1942 he began to reap the benefit as a commander on active service of his earlier work as a staff officer and began to use the instrument he had so ably fashioned. Certainly the record of the United States naval air arm in the Pacific between 1942 and 1945 is a proud one, and that record is largely due to the vision and ability of Admiral Towers.

May 2, 1955.

Sir Richard Somers Travers Christmas Humphreys—See **Humphreys.**

Sir John Townsend, F.R.S., formerly Wykeham Professor of Physics in the University of Oxford, died at Oxford on February 16, 1957 at the age of 88.

John Sealy Edward Townsend was born in Galway on June 7, 1868, and educated at Trinity College, Dublin. He went to Cambridge in 1895 soon after Sir J. J. Thomson's election to the Cavendish professorship, and in time to become his second research student—Lord Rutherford, as he was later to become, being the first. The two students became great friends and Townsend, in addition to his own work, often assisted Rutherford in his experiments on the detection of electromagnetic waves. Townsend was appointed a demonstrator in the Cavendish, and was successful in winning the Clark Maxwell Studentship, becoming also a Fellow of Trinity.

He went to Oxford in 1900 to fill the newly established Wykeham Professorship of Physics with a fellowship at New College. At the time no laboratory for his own use was available and he was accommodated first in the Observatory and later in the University Museum until, in 1910, the Drapers Company built the electrical laboratory. In the 1914-18 War he volunteered for a wireless unit which was training to assist the Russian Army, and when this scheme was abandoned he undertook wireless research for the Royal Naval Air Service.

In his young days Townsend was keen on hunting, and the timetable of his routine lectures was arranged so as not to conflict with the normal hunting programme. He had all the Irishman's love of argument, possessed a stock of characteristic anecdotes, and occasionally spoke in Congregation, making speeches at once contentious and amusing, though the humour was not always intentional. In the laboratory he never had more than about half a dozen research students at a time, with the result that he took a great personal interest and even pride in them all, believing that even his geese were swans. But he had very definite scientific beliefs, and woe betide any student who tried to explain his observations by theories which ran counter to his professor's.

He took little interest in the development of physics outside his own line, and when any new theory appeared his first instinct was to attempt to prove it wrong, his point of view both in science and politics being strongly conservative. Surprisingly enough, though, it was largely due to his efforts—in the face of considerable opposition—that the Oxford Engineering School was founded. He rarely went to scientific meetings outside Oxford and this fact, together with his scientific conservatism, may explain why his work, excellent and fundamental though it was, attracted less recognition than it deserved. He became a Fellow of the Royal Society in 1903, and was knighted in 1941.

Townsend's main interest throughout his life lay in the phenomena of electrical conduction in gases, and he was one of the first to measure the charge on the electron. His pioneer work in this field led to his formulation of the theory of ionization by collision, which attributes the electrical conductivity of a gas in an electric field to the cumulative production of charged ions by the impact on the gas molecules of electrons and ions energized by the field. The first stage of ionization, by electrons only, is a process stable in time, but when the electric field is increased so that the positive ions also produce ions by collision with the molecules, the current rises without limit and a spark passes. This was the prelude to a great deal of work, which continued throughout his active life, on the movement of electrons through gases, leading among other developments to the first indication of the existence of abnormally long mean free paths. His experiments and conclusions were incorporated in his classical treatises on the subject.

He married in 1911 Mary Georgiana, daughter of Peter F. Lambert, of Castle Ellen, co. Galway, by whom he had two sons.

February 18, 1957.

Dr. Siegfried Trebitsch, who died on June 3, 1956 at Zürich, Switzerland, at the age of 86, was a gifted author in his own right, yet he reached international importance only as the winner of a vicarious, reflected fame—as George Bernard Shaw's translator into German.

Siegfried Trebitsch was born on December 21, 1869, in Vienna, and was educated there. He established himself as the author of attractive, if not very profound, society novels between 1900 and 1910, when his studies of foreign literature made him aware of Shaw's work and its importance. He got into contact with the author and became his German translator and lifelong friend, thenceforward devoting the better part of his gifts and his activity to the propagation of the master's fame. He was eminently successful, practically from the beginning; between 1911 and 1940 nine volumes of Shaw's plays appeared in Trebitsch's inspired and faithful translations, and they were played in innumerable repetitions in practically every country in which German was spoken. These translations inspired others in many other languages and were a source, not only of a huge income, but of much of Shaw's subsequent international reputation.

Trebitsch, in turn, benefited greatly from this work: Shaw manifested his friendship by translating into English in 1920 one of Trebitsch's plays, *Frau Gitta's Sühne,* and the correspondence between the two men is bound to remain an essential source of contemporary literary history and of future biographies and analyses of G.B.S., in which his adept friend will play no mean a part.

Trebitsch's own work as an author may have suffered somewhat in the shadow of his master. Yet it comprises a series of novels and of short stories which deserve mention: *Das Haus am Abhang* (1906), *Spätes Licht* (1918), *Renate Aldringen* (1924), *Mord im Nebel* (1931), *Heimkehr zum Ich* (1931), the long short stories *Weltuntergang* (1903), *Tagwandler* (1909), *Die Frau ohne Dienstag* (1919) and *Der Geheilte* (1929). There are, furthermore, some plays, several of which had a lasting success: *Gefährliche Jahre, Das Land der Treue, Ein letzter Wille, Kaiser Diocletian* (1922), &c., and a volume of sensitive verse, *Wellen und* greatness. Self-confidence without a trace of arrogance; a contemptuous yet not intolerant disregard for anything mean or petty; the capacity to shuffle aside non-essentials and put an unerring finger on the real core of a problem or the real quality of a man—a sort of instinct for the really important point: a selfless devotion to the cause of what he believed to be right; Trenchard had all these qualities, and above all a shining sincerity. Many people have disagreed with him. He was not always right—that would be too much to expect of any man. His single-minded steadfastness of purpose had its own defects. In his later years, especially, his refusal to compromise with what he believed to be unsound led him sometimes to extremes into which his warmest admirers were unable to follow him. But most of those who challenged his views lived to admit with the passage of time that he was right and they wrong. None of his critics would ever suggest that he was anything but transparently disinterested and intellectually honest: and all of them—however hotly they might disagree—regarded him with some affection.

He was the most modest of men and hated being referred to as the "Father of the Air Force". He always protested that he did not invent these ideas of air power—they became as inevitable as sunset on the day Orville Wright made his first controlled power-driven flight. That may be true. It is none the less also true that this rather inarticulate soldier was not only the first man to give expression to those principles of air power which are to-day a commonplace but also, by his single-minded energy and drive, his burning faith in his own vision, created and preserved the Service that saved England in 1940. One of his most striking characteristics was his deep humanity and understanding of the point of view of the young officer and the non-commissioned ranks—a quality enriched by his long regimental service in many countries and with a wide variety of units. There can be few officers in history who have commanded so many different types of troops.

The Right Hon. Sir Hugh Montague Trenchard, G.C.B., O.M., G.C.V.O., D.S.O., first Viscount Trenchard and Baron Trenchard, of Wolfeton, in the County of Dorset, in the Peerage of the United Kingdom, and a baronet, was born on February 3, 1873, the son of Captain Henry Montague Trenchard, The King's Own Yorkshire Light Infantry. Unable to pass the examinations for Dartmouth or Woolwich—a fact which has since brought comfort to other lesser men—he came through the back door of the Militia to The Royal Scots Fusiliers in October 1893, receiving his commission from the great-great-grandmother of our present Queen whom he regarded with such affectionate respect and pride. His early service was on the Indian Frontier, but the outbreak of the South African War gave him his first experience of action and his first acquaintance with irregular troops—Imperial Yeomanry, the Australian Bushmen Corps, and the Canadian Scouts. He was promoted to captain in February 1900, but a dangerous wound in the lung during the operations west of Pretoria laid him low for many months: but before the end he was back again, this time with the Mounted Infantry in the Transvaal, Orange River Colony, and Cape Colony, Like many other good infantry soldiers, he dearly loved a horse, and polo was a passion with him in those years before 1914.

In 1903 he was seconded with a brevet majority to the West African Frontier Force and began a new chapter of adventure which was to give him an abiding and understanding interest in the problems of Africa. For the first three years he was in Southern Nigeria where he saw much active service and played a notable part in bringing that great area under control and administration. He was awarded the D.S.O. and was twice mentioned in dispatches for his work there, and then passed to the command of the Southern Nigeria Regiment from 1908 to 1912.

Invalided home in 1912, in trouble with his old wound, he was soon besieging the War Office for another appointment oversea with mounted troops. While his applications were being considered his thoughts turned to the Royal Flying Corps—which had just taken its place in the Army list—and he determined to become a pilot. From the little grass airfield within the oval of the motor-racing track at Brooklands, where he learnt to fly, Trenchard passed to the Central Flying School at Upavon to complete his instruction; in 1912 he became an instructor and in the following September was appointed Assistant Commandant under Captain Godfrey Paine, R.N. Two years later, after the outbreak of war, he went to command the 1st Wing in France, working with the Indian Corps and IV Corps, whence after eight months he was promoted to the command of the Royal Flying Corps in the field. In the years that followed it was his duty and good fortune to build up this new service from small beginnings and to hammer out on the anvil of battle experience the new theory and practice of air warfare.

He built on foundations well and truly laid by David Henderson, and he had many able lieutenants. He had also splendid human material to work on; excellent junior commanders from the pre-War R.F.C., and a swelling stream of adventurous young spirits that soon began to flow into the squadrons from the newly formed training schools at home. None of them would deny that through those long and terrible months of Loos and the Somme, Arras and Messines, third Ypres and Cambrai, the main inspiration and driving force was Trenchard himself.

Trenchard's greatest service to the Army in that war, the priceless legacy that he bequeathed to the R.A.F. of to-day, is the policy which soon developed into an article of faith, that air mastery can be gained and maintained only by the offensive. It became the fighting doctrine of the R.A.F., as instinctive as "engage the enemy more closely" in the Royal Navy.

In January 1918, the year in which he was promoted K.C.B., he was recalled from France to be the first Chief of the newly formed Air Staff in London. Sir Douglas Haig protested strongly at his loss; and his trust in his subordinate was matched by the highest devotion on Trenchard's part. His first tour of duty as C.A.S. did not last long. In April he resigned over a difference of opinion with the Secretary of State, Lord Rothermere. Whether he was right in doing so can always be argued. But the action was typical of his refusal to compromise on a matter of principle, as also was his entire lack of self-interest in an issue which he regarded as one of right or wrong. For some time the possibility of forming an Inter-Allied force for the bombing of Germany had been under consideration, and in May the Air Council proposed to the War Cabinet the formation of an Independent Air Force to bomb Germany, with Trenchard in command responsible direct to the Air Ministry. In August it was eventually decided to form the Inter-Allied Independent Air Force with Trenchard in command answerable direct to Foch; the war ended before it had time to take shape; but the 1919 programme was of an ambitious scale and provided for large contingents of bombers from all the principal allies.

His war services were rewarded with a baronetcy, and by a grant of £10,000 by the House of Commons.

He was not destined to be long out of active employment. By April 1919 he was back as C.A.S. and began the great work of reorganization and building up the regular Air Force. The problem which faced him was to build up from the bottom a permanent Regular Service out of the ruins of our wartime air power. His policy was that the first charge on our resources should be the training of officers and men, to lay the foundations of a highly trained and efficient cadre capable of subsequent expansion should the need arise. The Cadet College at Cranwell was opened in 1920, followed by the school for apprentices at Halton, and the Staff College at Andover.

Well-equipped permanent stations began to rise, to replace the wartime hutted camps which were all there was in the way of accommodation, so that when in 1923 the expansion to the Home Defence Air Force of 52 squadrons was authorized, he had the foundations on which to build. His far-seeing wisdom in those early days was finally and triumphantly vindicated by the vast expansion to over a million men in Hitler's war. Without the invaluable cadre of Cranwell-trained officers from Halton and the other apprentice schools that followed it we could never have achieved that culmination of British air power which was such a decisive factor in the Second Great War.

Trenchard's period as Chief of the Air Staff is now a matter of history. How well and fruitfully he laboured, the story of the R.A.F. in Hitler's war bears witness. He was C.A.S. for over 10 years—abnormally long in ordinary circumstances, but the conditions of his time were not normal, and in his case it was amply justified. Many features of the R.A.F. which are commonplace to-day were innovations under Trenchard's régime, among them the short service commission, the auxiliary squadrons and university air squadrons, the introduction of airmen pilots, and the system of technical specialization by General Duties list officers. Most have stood the test of time.

One other major innovation—air control—for which he was responsible deserves special mention.

It was in Iraq that the system was first evolved and proved itself. Based on a widespread and intimate tribal intelligence network, the essence of air control was that the ultimate sanction of force was provided by a few squadrons centrally located, instead of by the large garrisons involved in the traditional method of controlling these wild and undeveloped territories. If force became necessary it was exercised, after due warning, by the bomber instead of by the old method of battle by a column of troops on the ground.

On January 1, 1930, he relinquished his appointment as Chief of the Air Staff. He had been made Colonel of his old regiment in 1916 and on transfer to the Royal Air Force had been given an honorary commission as a major-general in the Army. He was appointed Principal Air A.D.C. to King George V in 1921 and became the first Marshal of the Royal Air Force in 1927.

He became Commissioner of Police of the Metropolis in November 1931. The responsibilities of the Commissioner are always heavy, but Trenchard added to them activities of unprecedented scope and intensity in connexion with his schemes of reform and reorganization. These plans were laid before Parliament in a White Paper 18 months after his appointment and received legislative sanction in the Metropolitan Police Act of 1933. The principal feature of the Trenchard reforms were the Police College at Hendon, opened by the Duke of Windsor*, then Prince of Wales, in 1933 and closed on the outbreak of war in 1939, and the short service scheme for recruiting a substantial proportion of the police on a 10-year engagement. Among his special achievements were the forensic science laboratory at Hendon, and the many steps taken to extend and improve the application of scientific methods to police work. No commissioner ever probed so deeply into the relations of the police with the public and with criminals, or dealt more faithfully with misdoings and shortcomings. The Metropolitan Police owe him a great debt for his many contributions to their welfare—notably better housing and more facilities for recreation—and for the steps he took to rescue their provident fund from financial disaster.

When he left the police in 1935 a new vista of service opened before him. Several companies engaged in the West African trade had recently come together in the United Africa Company, within the Unilever Group. The purpose of those who formed the United Africa Company was to put the trade in West Africa on a better basis, both in the commercial sense and in the wider context of national and international relations. They were looking for a leader with the strength and prestige to secure recognition for this policy from Governments and from the public. Lord Trenchard, with his great interest in West Africa, was an ideal person. He joined the board in 1936, and accepted the chairmanship three months later, retiring from the position in 1953 after 17 years.

He married, in 1920, Katherine Isabel Salvin, second daughter of the late Edward Salvin Bowlby, of Gilston Park, Hertford, and Knoydart, Inverness-shire, and widow of Captain the Hon. James Boyle, and there were two sons of the marriage. The elder son, Hugh, born in 1921, was killed in action in North Africa in 1943, and the surviving son, Captain Thomas Trenchard, M.C., succeeds his father.

February 11, 1956.

Sir Charles Trevelyan, BT., who was President of the Board of Education in the Labour Governments of 1924 and of 1929, died on January 24, 1958 at his home in Northumberland at the age of 87.

A member of a family greatly distinguished in politics and letters, the son of Sir George Otto Trevelyan, O.M., and a brother of Dr. G. M. Trevelyan, O.M.,* Charles Trevelyan brought a strong sense of responsibility and undoubted moral courage to the political career on which he had set out immediately after leaving Cambridge. First elected to Parliament in the Liberal interest in 1899, he gave every indication of turning his intellectual abilities to good advantage there. That he achieved less in his political career than at one time seemed possible, so that he himself in the end seemed to abandon politics in some degree out of personal frustration or disappointment, may be accounted for by the defects of his qualities. There was, in Trevelyan, an impatience or contentiousness of temperament that seldom accorded well with the practical exigencies of Parliamentary discussion or Cabinet Office. It made something of a zealot of him and helped to foster those idealistic illusions about international affairs which were characteristic of a section of the Labour Party between the wars.

Having for six years held minor office as Parliamentary Secretary to the Board of Education under the three Liberal administrations immediately before 1914, he resigned in that year in order to register disapproval of the entry of Great Britain into the war. He then lent his energies to the work of the Union of Democratic Control and to the attempt to secure a negotiated peace with Germany, and in 1918 went over to the Labour cause as that was represented by the I.L.P. As President of the Board (as it then was) of Education he cherished sincere ideals, and supported them by a detailed and intimate knowledge of the educational machine. But he lacked the administrative flexibility and resource which might have enabled him to go as far as he desired in attaining the ideals set out in the Hadow reports. His resignation in March 1931 was intelligible in the circumstances, though it seemed to be made on less than wholly adequate grounds. It proved to be virtually the last act in his political career.

Charles Philips Trevelyan was born in London on October 28, 1870, the eldest son of Sir George Otto Trevelyan, second baronet of Wallington, Northumberland, by his marriage with Caroline, daughter of Robert Needham Philips, M.P. He was educated at Harrow, where Noel and Charles Roden Buxton were among his contemporaries, and at Trinity College, Cambridge, where in 1892 he was awarded a second class in the historical tripos. Almost immediately afterwards he went to Ireland as Secretary to the Lord Lieutenant, Lord Houghton (afterwards Lord Crewe). He stayed there for a year; two years later he unsuccessfully contested North Lambeth as a Liberal, then went on a grand tour of Canada, South Africa, Australia, and the Far East. In 1896 he became a member of the London School Board and during the year he served on it gained his first direct acquaintance with educational affairs. In 1899 the Elland division of the West Riding of Yorkshire returned him to Parliament in the Liberal interest and he continued to sit for it until 1918.

After two years as a Charity Commissioner, he was appointed Parliamentary Secretary to the Board of Education in 1908. He brought to his work an unmistakable personal idealism, expressed in part in a leaning towards a wholly secular system of national education. Another cause to which he notably attached himself was licensing reform.

The test of his developing political convictions came in the crisis of August 1914, when he found himself at issue with the great majority of the Liberal Party leaders in regard to British intervention. Arguing that Britain was under no treaty obligation to enter the war, and that to do so would be to fight almost entirely for Russia, he resigned his office, at the same time pleading as one of his principal reasons that "it may be we shall double our National Debt". He became an advocate of peace negotiations with Germany and was prominent in the counsels of the Union of Democratic Control, of which he was one of the founders. The Liberals of Elland asked him to resign, but he quoted Burke and refused. In 1916 he sent an open letter to President Wilson urging him to appeal to the peoples of the belligerent Powers above the heads of their Governments. These and other activities of his made him conspicuously unpopular with large sections of the public.

He joined the Labour Party in 1918 and stood for his old constituency as a Labour candidate in the "coupon" election, but was signally defeated. In the following year he drew attention to himself by the vehement terms in which he condemned the Versailles Treaty. He was elected in 1922 as Labour member for Central Newcastle (a seat which he continued to hold until his departure from active politics in 1931), and on the formation of the Labour Government in 1924 he became President of the Board of Education. Here, in his sincere but not always skilful fashion, he bent himself above all else to the practical task of achieving equality of educational opportunity. He was, perhaps, more effective in opposition than in office, proving himself an able critic of the policy of the succeeding Government in instituting cuts in the educational services. As party spokesman he urged a policy of full maintenance allowances for all children at school above the age of 14 whose parents needed them, and on his estate at Wallington, to which he succeeded on his father's death in 1928, he introduced such a scheme of allowances for his own workmen's children. Besides education, Russia—for whose achievements he expressed a fervent and uncritical admiration—was a principal source of interest and enthusiasm for him.

Back again at the Board of Education in 1929, his chief preoccupation was the raising of the school-leaving age to 15, on which indeed he set his heart. It was on the ground, first, that the House of Lords had rejected his School-leaving Age Bill, secondly, that he was very much out of sympathy with the general method and intention of Government policy, that he resigned his office and seat in the Cabinet in March 1931. Here he was following a family tradition. His father had resigned his position as a Lord of the Admiralty in 1870 as a protest against the decision of the Government of the day to provide increased grants of public money for denominational education.

Trevelyan lost his seat in the general election of 1931. The day after the election his Lord Lieutenant flag—he had been appointed his Majesty's Lieutenant for the County of Northumberland in 1930—was stolen from Wallington Hall, his beautiful Northumberland home, but was afterwards returned. Later some statuary there was tarred and feathered. In 1936 he announced his intention of bequeathing Wallington Hall, together with his large estate near Morpeth, to the nation, and in 1941 he made a gift of it, subject only to his life interest, to the National Trust.

He married in 1904 Mary Katharine, youngest daughter of Sir Hugh Bell, Bt., by whom he had two sons and four daughters. His elder son, George Lowthian Tevelyan, succeeds to the baronetcy.

January 25, 1958.

Hilda Trevelyan, the actress, died on November 10, 1959 at the age of 79.

News of her death will be received with sorrow by the generation of playgoers who recall the days before the 1914-18 War when Sir James Barrie was at the height of his powers writing parts which suited to perfection the demure young actress who appeared in so many of his most successful productions. Hilda Trevelyan always recognized the great debt she owed to Barrie but in fact the obligation was mutual. Her performance as Wendy in *Peter Pan* and as Maggie Wylie, the young Scots girl, in *What Every Woman Knows* were outstanding, and there was a fragrant naturalness in all her work.

Hilda Trevelyan (Tucker was the surname she was born with) made her first appearance on the stage at the age of nine in a production of *The Silver King* at the Princess's Theatre. She was touring in *A Gaiety Girl* before she was 14, but her first serious London engagement was at the Court in 1898, when she understudied the part of Avonia Bunn in *Trelawny of the Wells*—a part which she was later to play many times. Her association with Barrie began when she toured as Lady Babbie in *The Little Minister,* and she played the part nearly 700 times.

A tour with Sir John Hare in *Little Mary* in 1904 saw a resumption of the link with Barrie which was to continue for the rest of his life. At that time he was at work on *Peter Pan* and he selected Hilda Trevelyan to play Wendy and Nina Boucicault as Peter.

When *Alice-Sit-by-the-Fire* was produced in 1905 she made a brief appearance as a maid-of-all-work, but when it went on tour she was promoted to the leading part and she next gave an exquisite performance as the hapless terror-stricken orphan in Tree's production of *Oliver Twist.* A revival of *The Admirable Crichton* in 1908 saw her as a charming Tweeny, and then Barrie gave her probably the greatest chance of her career with the part of Maggie Wylie in *What Every Woman Knows.* The evolution from the girl who believed that she had no charm to the resourceful, courageous young wife who guided her husband's political career was delineated by author and actress alike with perfect skill.

Miss Trevelyan had one period of management with Edmund Gwenn [q.v.] at the Vaudeville, but in 1916 she scored another great success in a play by Barrie—*A Kiss for Cinderella.* A revival of *The Great Adventure* in 1924 saw her as the commonsense wife of an eccentric genius, and in another revival—*Mary Rose*—in 1926 she took over Mary Jerrold's [q.v.] part. Her last stage appearance was in 1939.

She was married to Sydney Blow, the author.

November 11, 1959.

Janet (Mrs. G. M.) Trevelyan, C.H., who will be remembered for her long and unremitting work for the children of London, died on September 7, 1956 at Newcastle upon Tyne at the age of 76.

Janet Penrose Trevelyan was born in 1879, the daughter of Mrs. Humphry Ward, the novelist, and her husband, the art critic. Matthew Arnold was her great-uncle and Arnold of Rugby her great-grandfather. In 1904 she married Dr. G. M. Trevelyan, O.M.* After marriage she lived in London, and at Berkhamsted for the education of her children. The latter part of her life was spent at Cambridge, where her husband became Regius Professor of Modern History in 1927, and was Master of Trinity from 1940 to 1951. By birth and marriage she was thus associated with a great tradition in literature and social beneficence.

The tradition no doubt influenced her choice of work, but the choice was that of an active and original mind, which shone with the light of its own qualities, not with reflected light only. Mrs. Humphry Ward was a pioneer of the movement for the promotion of play-centres for London children. Her daughter followed her in the work, and carried it on with unresting energy for more than 20 years, until it was taken over by the London County Council. The energy and ability of her advocacy and organization won hard battles for the movement; the greatest was that for saving the Foundling site.

For five years, from 1931-35, she inspired and led a campaign to keep it from the builder and for a children's playground, and it is because she and those who listened to her overthrew financial and administrative obstacles, which less brave and hopeful spirits thought insuperable, that Coram's playing fields, and not streets, are now where Coram's hospital was. For this work in particular it was, no doubt, that she was made a Companion of Honour in 1936.

Dr. Trevelyan has worked in the field of Italian history, and in the friendships with Italians which that brought her, and the opportunities which they gave for cherishing and strengthening relations between men and women of good will in England and Italy, she too found a fertile field for the activity of her clear mind and quick human sympathies, qualities congenial to Italians. One fruit of this work was the survival through evil days of the British Institute at Florence. Another was her book *A Short History of the Italian People* (1920), a work in which her keen intellectual appreciation of the glories of Italian culture, and affection for Italians skilfully woven into the complex web of their history, open a welcoming door to newcomers. Her other literary works included a life of Mrs. Humphry Ward (1923), pamphlets in support of play centres, and, in early life, a translation of Jülicher on the New Testament.

Rather more than two years ago she published a volume entitled *Two Stories.* Both stories concern children: the first is a tender and loving reminiscence of the son she lost when he was but five years old; the second is her record of the fight she fought long ago to preserve the Foundling site.

It needs, however, more than a bare record of her work to commemorate an outstanding personality, which leaves a mark on the notable world in which she lived. In her fragile frame there was a large heart quick to understand, without intrusion, and resourceful to help the troubles of others. Her mind was penetrating, particularly in its insight into the complexities of character, but wholly simple in its own integrity. So friends found in her a good pilot through the straits of life, devoted to friendship, truth, kindness, and mirth.

September 10, 1956.

R. C. Trevelyan, the poet and scholar, brother of Sir Charles Trevelyan [q.v.] and Dr. G. M. Trevelyan*, died on March 21, 1951 at his home in Surrey at the age of 78.

Though he was not a poet of original force—he made no claim to be that—Trevelyan nevertheless gave a graceful meditative charm to everything he wrote. It is, perhaps, in the verse plays whose subject is taken from Greek legend that his effect is happiest, though there are some who prefer the satirical verse of his early books. For the rest, both in manner and in choice of subject, he often recalls Bridges.

Steeped in the classics, Trevelyan communicated in his verse, whether original or renderings from the Greek or Latin, a conviction that poetry was a whole, deriving from an unbroken tradition. This is, in a sense, his "message", as the portrait Lowes Dickinson drew of him (as the young poet Coryat) in *A Modern Symposium* clearly shows, and it is also, in large part, his strength. The distinctive thing about him as poet was that he held fast to a traditional mode of poetic feeling.

At the same time he indulged in constant formal experiment. His original verse is distinguished in the first place by the rejection of rhyme; in resorting to blank verse he loved to employ novelties of metre and rhythm—he was, in his own phrase, "a confirmed metromaniac". The result was often felicitous, though at other times his experiments—for instance, in lines of 14 or 15 syllables—were inclined to be cumbrous.

Robert Calverley Trevelyan was the second son of Sir George Otto Trevelyan and was born on June 28, 1872. Educated at Harrow and at Trinity College, Cambridge, he produced his first book of poetry, *Mallow and Asphodel*, in 1898. Verse plays, dramatic poems, satirical poems, witty trifles, and translations from the Greek came with equal ease and assurance from him, and again and again Trevelyan demonstrated his skill in employing a great variety of metres. *Sisyphus* (1908), described as "an operatic table", was a lively jest; *The Bride of Dionysus* (1912) was the text of an opera composed by D. F. (afterwards Sir Donald) Tovey; *The New Parsifal* (1914), *The Foolishness of Solomon* (1915), *The Pterodamozels* (1917), and *The Death of Man* (1919) demonstrated the wide range of this poet's verse.

He continued steadily to produce books of poetry and verse plays, and in 1939 two volumes were published of his collected works. But he had by no means exhausted his impulse. His translations, moreover, occupied him almost until the end. They represent a remarkable body of work, not faultless in technical quality, but exhibiting fine taste and scholarly accomplishment. They include the *Oresteia* and *Prometheus* of Aeschylus, the *Ajax* and *Antigone* of Sophocles, the *Medea* of Euripides, renderings of Theocritus, the *De Rerum Natura* of Lucretius, and *Eclogues* and *Georgics* of Virgil, and translations from Horace, Juvenal, and others.

Trevelyan's last book of verse, published in 1947, was *From the Shiffolds*, this being the name of the house near Dorking where he had lived for many years.

He married, in 1900, Elizabeth des Amorie van der Hoeven, and there was one son of the marriage.

March 22, 1951.

Sir Frank Tribe, K.C.B., K.B.E., Comptroller and Auditor General of the Exchequer and Audit Department since 1946, collapsed while attending a ceremony at Clifton College, Bristol, on June 20, 1958 and died soon afterwards. He was 64.

His was what has been described as "one of those extraordinary jobs that could exist only in Britain". His essential function was to see that the money voted by Parliament was spent as Parliament decided it should be, and he had the power of holding Ministers and departments to account without fear or favour.

The Comptroller and Auditor General is neither a Civil servant nor a servant of the Government. Like a judge, he is appointed by the Crown, and like a judge he draws his salary from the Consolidated Fund. The post, to which Tribe came after wide experience, perhaps most of all calls for a robust common sense, and for this he was marked.

Frank Newton Tribe was born on July 15, 1893, the only son of Frank N. Tribe, of Bristol, and educated at Clifton College and Trinity College, Oxford, of which he was a foundation scholar. He was Gaisford Greek Verse Prizeman in 1914. He graduated in that year and joined the Army. For his war services he was mentioned in dispatches and made O.B.E.

Appointed to the Ministry of Labour in 1920, he was Principal Private Secretary to three Ministers of Labour in the five years from 1923 to 1928, becoming in the latter year secretary of the National Advisory Council for Juvenile Employment (England and Wales). This office he occupied until 1934, when he was chosen for the secretaryship to the Commissioner for Special Areas of England and Wales. His next appointment in 1938 was as Principal Assistant Secretary at the Treasury, where he remained until the beginning of the 1939-45 War, when he was made Deputy Secretary, Ministry of Labour and National Service (where he succeeded Humbert Wolfe), retaining the post until 1942 when he was appointed Secretary at the Ministry of Production; later in the same year he went as Permanent Secretary to the Ministry of Fuel and Power. From then to 1946 he served successively as Permanent Secretary at the Ministries of Aircraft Production and Food.

As Comptroller and Auditor General, Tribe was perhaps better known to the public than his predecessors had been. His years of office were years of mounting public expenditure, and public expenditure was very much his pigeon. Each year between Christmas and Easter, Tribe's name came prominently in the news; as one writer put it, he became "irresistibly newsworthy, simply because he signs reports that take to task Government departments whose accounts and stock records are not all that an impartial auditor would wish them to be".

He was a shrewd, likeable man with a dry sense of humour that years spent cheek by jowl with figures, forms and the bizarre nomenclature of service equipment, did not kill; indeed, they tended to develop it. He remarked on one occasion that he, the head, was the only unqualified person in a department of specialized auditors. In private he probably derived an amused satisfaction that he could be removed from office only after a vote by both Houses of Parliament. He expressed himself well and his reports were not lacking in candour; nevertheless it is doubtful if his forthrightness lost him any good will; certainly he won the respect of the politicians with whom he came in contact.

He was a member of the Joint Panel of External Auditors of the United Nations from 1950, and had been chairman since 1954. He had been External Auditor of Unesco since 1950 and since 1951 of the Food and Agricultural Organization.

Elected a member of the council of Clifton College in 1944, he had been its chairman since 1951.

He was made C.B.E. in 1930, C.B. in 1938, advanced to K.B.E. in 1941, and created K.C.B. in 1945.

June 23, 1958.

Professor E. W. Tristram, HON. D.LITT., a leading authority on medieval art, died on January 11, 1952 at the age of 69.

He was specially concerned with the discovery, preservation, and copying of medieval wall paintings throughout Britain. He did a certain amount of original painting and decorative designing, and he was for a good many years Professor of Design at the Royal College of Art, but his spiritual home, artistically speaking, was in the middle ages. Any newspaper account of the discovery of wall paintings in a village church was almost certain to contain the information that Professor Tristram had been consulted about their treatment. To quote from an article in *The Times* on October 21, 1933, by the late Dr. M. R. James, O.M., Provost of Eton, in connexion with an exhibition of copies by Tristram of English medieval wall paintings: "He is indeed, the Sherlock Holmes or the Dr. Thorndyke of the situation".

Ernest William Tristram was born at Carmarthen in 1882. He received his artistic training at the Royal College of Art under the late Professor W. R. Lethaby, an enthusiast for the middle ages, whom he was to succeed in the Chair of Design. Since 1883, when a third and enlarged edition of "A List of Buildings in Great Britain and Ireland having mural and other painted decorations", by Dr. C. F. Keyser, was published by the Victoria and Albert Museum, there had been no very systematic study or record of the subject, though a great many new paintings had been discovered, so that Tristram came with the best of preparations to a great mass of new material. He was never allowed to have an idle moment.

At Westminster Abbey he cleaned and conserved what remained of decoration on the Coronation Chair, and the newly discovered wall paintings of the Incredulity of St. Thomas and St. Christopher; and at Canterbury the early paintings in the vault of St. Gabriel's Chapel and the later legend of St. Eustace, besides cleaning and reviving the cloisters. His work at Winchester was extensive, including the paintings of the Life of Christ in the Holy Cross Chapel and those of the Miracles of the Virgin in the Lady Chapel. This last series was described by Dr. James as "a younger sister of the finer set" in Eton College Chapel.

The Eton set may well be quoted in illustration of a danger that Tristram always avoided in his work of restoration. About the middle of the nineteenth century the paintings were uncovered by the removal of panelling, and careful copies in line were made of them before the panelling was replaced. This was during the Pre-Raphaelite period, and there was a fantastic notion that the Eton paintings might be by a pupil or disciple of Fra Angelico. Obediently, and probably unconsciously, the copyist had given to his work a subtly Italianate flavour. At the memorable exhibition of British Primitives at the Royal Academy these copies were shown, together with the more objective copies made by Tristram, and it was most amusing to note the difference in "accent" between the two sets, Tristram's copies preserving the Anglo-Flemish character of the originals.

Tristram's work at Norwich was mainly in connexion with the fourteenth and fifteenth century carved bosses in the cathedral cloisters—described in an old book, according to the Dean of Norwich, as the largest and dirtiest in England. Earlier expert opinion had been that the bosses had better not be touched, lest the carved detail should crumble, but when Tristram was consulted in 1934 he decided that careful treatment would be unharmful and would add life and beauty to the cloisters, and the results of cleaning and repainting fully justified his opinion. Other notable buildings on which he worked were Exeter Cathedral, St. George's Chapel, Windsor, St. John's College, Cambridge, Oxford Cathedral, and Christchurch Priory.

There is a large collection of Tristram's copies of medieval wall paintings at the Victoria and Albert Museum. Original paintings by him are to be found in, among other buildings, York Minster and in the new church of St. Elizabeth, Eastbourne, and for the Friends of Canterbury Cathedral he designed a banner to be worked by the Royal School of Needlework.

Tristram's publications include *English Medieval Painting* (with Dr. Tancred Borenius); *The Cloister Bosses of Norwich* (with the Dean of Norwich); and his comprehensive volumes on medieval wall paintings, the last of which was published under the aegis of the Pilgrim Trust in 1951. He was a frequent contributor to *The Times* of detailed reports of preservation work in hand or completed. Concisely written, these articles are full of interesting historical information. Tristram also contributed to the *Burlington Magazine* and the publications of the Walpole Society.

He lectured on medieval art at Canterbury, Norwich, Ely, and the Royal Institute of British Architects, of which he was an honorary associate.

He married Eileen, daughter of Lieutenant-Colonel H. C. B. Dann, of the Indian Army, and had two daughters.

January 12, 1952.

Sir Arthur Trueman, K.B.E., F.R.S., who was chairman of the University Grants Committee from 1949 to 1953, and whose geological studies made an important contribution to the understanding of British coal seams and their relationships, died on January 5, 1956 at his home at Ealing. He was 61.

Arthur Elijah Trueman was the son of Elijah Trueman and Thirza Cottee and was born on April 26, 1894. He was educated at High Pavement School, Nottingham, and University College, Nottingham, graduating in 1914 with first-class honours in geology. He took his M.Sc. two years later and his doctorate of science at London in 1918. He was made assistant lecturer in geology at University College, Cardiff, in 1917, remaining there three years until he was appointed head of the geology department at University College, Swansea. When he had been there 10 years he was promoted head of the combined departments of geology and geography and appointed professor of geology. In 1933 he transferred to the Chaning Wills chair at Bristol, and in 1937 he moved to Glasgow as professor of geology. His activities at these universities were not confined to the department of which he was head, for he took a keen interest in the Workers' Educational Association and other extension work.

His early research work was mainly concerned with Jurassic rocks and fossils found in them. He also carried out much work on coal measures, the identification of coal seams and practical mining problems, including the incidence of silicosis among miners. He published two books in 1938, *The Scenery of England and Wales* and an *Introduction to Geology*.

His work as a geologist helped to bring order and sense into the complicated geology of British coalfields. By his studies of fresh-water molluscs he laid the foundations for a reinterpretation of the mutual relations of different seams and areas. This fundamental contribution was reflected in a remapping of the coalfields by the Geological Survey, of which he was chairman from 1943 to 1954. Its value to geology was recognized by the award to him in January 1955 of the Wollaston Medal of the Geological Society. But he liked as much to talk to mining engineers, and one of his favourite stories was of a robustly worded appreciation of one of these measure-identifying fossils. In 1954 he edited *The Coalfields of Great Britain,* writing himself a series of introductory chapters which set the key to the book. It was widely hailed as presenting a technical and complicated subject in a way which engineers as well as geologists could appreciate.

In 1946 Trueman was appointed deputy chairman of the University Grants Committee. He succeeded to the chairmanship on the retirement of Sir Walter Moberly* in 1949, and remained chairman until 1953. He thus served either as chairman or as deputy during the crucial years of university expansion after the war. The terms of reference of the U.G.C. had just been extended to include the duty "to assist, in consultation with the universities and other bodies concerned, the preparation and execution of such plans for the development of the universities as may from time to time be required in order to ensure that they are fully adequate to national needs". With this extension to take national needs into account, and with the growing dependence of the universities on public funds for their revenue and for almost all their capital expenditure, the maintenance of academic independence became a practical question of the first importance. That it has been maintained is in great measure due to the wise handling of its complicated task by the University Grants Committee, which is interposed between the Treasury and the universities; and as chairman of the committee Trueman impressed those with whom he came into contact by his gift for clear, cogent, yet dispassionate statement of a complex issue.

He was a member of the Elliot Commission on Higher Education in West Africa (1943-44). In 1942 he was elected a Fellow of the Royal Society; he was president of the Geological Society in 1945-47; and he was created K.B.E. in 1951.

He married, in 1920, Florence Kate Offler. They had one son.

January 7, 1956.

A. F. Tschiffely, whose ride on horseback from Buenos Aires to Washington became famous through his account of it published in 1933, died on January 5, 1954 in hospital in London at the age of 58 after a short illness.

The hero of what has often been described as the greatest feat ever accomplished by man and horse, he started from Buenos Aires in 1925 and took two and a half years on the journey with the two horses, Mancha and Gato, alternatively carrying him and his pack. In his three books describing that journey, *Southern Cross to Pole Star, Tschiffely's Ride,* and *Mancha and Gato,* he never wrote of "I" but of "we", meaning himself and the two horses, for he was careful to emphasize that the journey was undertaken to prove the worth of the native Argentine ponies and that it was their stamina and spirit that had made the spectacular journey possible.

Aimé Felix Tschiffely was born in Switzerland in 1895 and was educated in England, where for a time he taught at various preparatory schools, among them Park Hill, Lyndhurst, and The Priory, Malvern. He then went out to Buenos Aires, where he acted temporarily as headmaster of the English High School. It was after this episode that he undertook his great ride and, his first two books being immensely successful, he took up writing as a profession, gaining his material by making other, but less spectacular and exacting, journeys than that from Buenos Aires to Washington. His charming volume *Bridle Paths,* published in 1936, described a journey on horseback from Salisbury to Scotland and in 1938 he contributed two long articles to *The Times* describing a ride through Patagonia.

One of his last adventures was a tour of Spain on a motorcycle. He wrote an excellent biography of his friend, R. B. Cunninghame-Grahame, and a charming volume of reminiscences, *Bohemia Junction,* which was published in 1950. It is, however, for his famous ride that he will be best remembered, and his two horses, Mancha who died in 1947, and Gato who died in 1944, will always share his fame.

He married in 1933 Miss Violet Theodora Hume, better known under her stage name of Violet Marquesita, who was with him when he died.

January 6, 1954.

Tshekedi Khama, the former Regent of the Bamangwato Tribe in Bechuanaland, died in hospital in London on June 10, 1959 at the age of 53.

His death deprives Africa of one of the greatest of her sons. He was a man of immense drive and vigour, who also brought a quality of happy living to everything in which he engaged. Alike in Westminster and among the cattlemen of the Bamangwato, he was respected as one whose word was his bond. More than once in his life he was involved in great controversies, but he was without bitterness. For an African chief reared in primitive surroundings, he had a remarkable mastery of the British political system and scene, which served him in good stead at the time of his banishment. He was also greatly admired by other Africans in leading positions up and down the continent. He believed that white and black had to live together and his advice was always given on the side of moderation, negotiation, and faith in the future.

Tshekedi Khama was born in Serowe in 1906, the younger son of the great chief Khama of Bamangwato, the dominant tribe in Bechuanaland. Circumstances thwarted him in the full development of his talents and capacity for administration, but he had opportunity enough to show that he inherited the qualities which made his father one of the most respected and admired of Southern African chieftains in the nineteenth century.

Tshekedi was educated at the Church of Scotland College at Lovedale in the Cape. He was still a student at Fort Hare Native College when in 1926 he was summoned by the council of the Tribe to become Regent for his four-year-old nephew, Seretse, son of Khama's eldest son, Sekgoma. There was some unrest in the Tribe at the time and an attempt was actually made on Tshekedi's life.

Though only 21, Tshekedi almost immediately embarked on a course of administrative reform which secured the strong loyalty of the majority of leading members of the Tribe, but made enemies of an influential minority. Among the most important reforms he initiated were the establishment of communal granaries and a secondary school for Bamangwato children.

Tshekedi also supervised the upbringing of his nephew Seretse, and jealously watched over his interests and the interests of his Tribe, even to the successful resistance of an attempt by the Chartered Company to exploit the mineral wealth of Bechuanaland in the exercise of a concession granted to them by Khama the First.

Tshekedi's name first came into real prominence when in 1933 he ordered corporal punishment for a white man in Serowe whose misbehaviour with African women was a public scandal. Admiral E. R. G. R. Evans (later Lord Mountevans [q.v.]), then Acting High Commissioner, led a force of armed Marines from Simonstown to Serowe and, under their guns, summoned a council of the Tribe and deposed Tshekedi. There was an immediate outburst of indignant protest in Britain and Tshekedi was reinstated within a month. This incident was an example of Tshekedi's determination to uphold the privileges of the Bamangwato Tribe and Chieftainship (though in this case, as he acknowledged, he exceeded his jurisdiction), and his determination occasionally made relations between himself and local British officials difficult.

There seems to have been no basis whatever for the suspicions occasionally heard before the Seretse crisis that Tshekedi was consolidating his own position as Chief and would resist Seretse's assumption of power. He encouraged Seretse in his education and sent him to Oxford to study law. Seretse's engagement to an English girl, Ruth Williams, without consultation with the Tribe, was obviously as great a shock to Tshekedi as it was to the Tribe and to the British Government. Tshekedi called a full *Kgotla* (Council) of the Tribe and put it to them that Seretse should obtain the Tribe's consent for his marriage. They concurred and refused their consent. When Seretse returned to Bechuanaland, however, he called another *Kgotla* which consented to his marriage. A dangerous situation was obviously developing in the Tribe, for there were signs that opponents of Tshekedi and of Seretse's accession were encouraged by the dispute to reopen old tribal quarrels.

The British Government intervened by withholding recognition from Seretse as chief and banishing both him and Tshekedi from Bamangwato territory. It was the contention of the Labour Government then in power that they took these steps purely for tribal considerations. But it was widely believed that they had in mind the wider issue of the effects on liberal opinion in South Africa of the mixed marriage, and the repercussion which the alienation of such opinion might have upon the relationship of all three High Commission Territories with the South African Government. Tshekedi went to Britain and secured the support, while in opposition, of the Conservative and Liberal parties.

Once the Conservatives came into power, Lord Ismay*, the new Secretary of State for Commonwealth Relations, allowed him back into the Reserve as a private person. Tshekedi scrupulously fulfilled his part of the bargain, not to take part in tribal politics. He was allowed to take part in Protectorate politics. The final denouement came when, as a result of a reconciliation between him and his nephew, Seretse also was allowed to return. Both were at liberty to take part in politics but not to claim the chieftainship.

In recent years Tshekedi had been very active in public affairs. He was one of the three-man team which early in 1958 negotiated with mining companies in London about mineral rights in Bechuanaland. The agreement was signed last week. He pursued political as well as economic advancement and was a strong advocate of the formation of some form of legislature for the Protectorate. He was instrumental in bringing about the contemplated review of the constitution, which was announced in April.

June 11, 1959.

Gno Lean-Tuck – See **Dr. Wu.**

Hilda Tucker – See **Hilda Trevelyan.**

A long career of devotion to the improvement of the position of women in industry closes with the death on August 5, 1951, at the age of 90, of **Gertrude Tuckwell,** C.H., in hospital at Guildford, Surrey.

As a niece of that pioneer of women's trade unions Lady Dilke (the wife of the statesman) and a daughter of the Rev. William Tuckwell, the well known "Radical parson" and author of reminiscences of old Oxford, who died at the age of 90 in 1919, Gertrude Tuckwell was born into an atmosphere of progressive thought, and from the days when she was her aunt's secretary, throughout her long life, few names are more prominent than hers in all causes having for their object the improvement of the lot of women in industry.

Gertrude Mary Tuckwell was her father's second daughter and was born on July 17, 1861, when he was Master of New College School. She was educated at home, and her wide general culture can no doubt in a large measure be traced to William Tuckwell's training. In 1885 she obtained a post as elementary teacher under the London School Board, and held it until 1892, when she became Lady Dilke's secretary, and about the same time was made honorary secretary to the Women's Trade Union League. She continued to act as Lady Dilke's secretary in industrial matters, and after the latter's death in 1904 she succeeded her as president of the league. With the unremitting help of Sir Charles Dilke in Parliament, the league gained a number of notable successes, one of the most important being in its campaign against white-lead poisoning and "phossy jaw", in which Gertrude Tuckwell played a prominent part.

She had as early as 1898 urged the establishment of wages boards; in 1906 she presided over the Exhibition of Sweated Goods; and the victory was won with the passing of the Trade Boards Act, 1909. She retained the presidency of the Women's Trade Union League until its work was taken over by the General Council of the Trades Union Congress in 1921.

In her later years the campaign against maternal mortality absorbed much of her energies. She had been closely associated with the late Mary Macarthur (Mrs. Anderson), and after her death she took over the cause of the working woman during pregnancy and childbirth as her special legacy. She was a member of the Royal Commission on National Health Insurance, and was active in the national campaign against preventible maternal mortality which resulted in the formation of the Maternal Mortality Committee.

Gertrude Tuckwell's mind was perhaps not highly original, but she absorbed readily the ideas of others, and moreover she was a persuasive and indeed dramatic speaker, and had inherited from her father a clear and lucid style in writing, as *The Times* correspondence columns have borne witness across the years. She was a frequent speaker at the annual Trades Union Congress; but in her later years she became more associated with wider aspects of social work. She was president of the Women Sanitary Inspectors and Health Association and of the National Association of Probation Officers, and she was a member of the Women's Central Committee on Women's Training and Employment.

When the first women magistrates were to be appointed, Gertrude Tuckwell was made a member of the Advisory Committee to the Lord Chancellor for Women Justices of the Peace and served upon it for many years. She was also, in 1920, the first woman to be sworn a Justice of the Peace for the County of London. It need hardly be said that Gertrude Tuckwell was a member of the Labour Party, but at the same time it should be stressed that politics were to her merely ends to the promotion of social causes and never ends in themselves. She was thus never a partisan, and was regarded with respect and affection by many who, in theory at least, were politically opposed to her.

No biography of Gertrude Tuckwell would be complete without some reference to her loyalty to the memory of her uncle by marriage, Sir Charles Dilke, and to her lifelong attempts at his moral rehabilitation; to the end of her life she never doubted that he had been the victim of a miscarriage of justice. She was joint author with Stephen Gwynn of Dilke's life that was published in two volumes in 1917, and later she abridged it for the Workers' Educational Association. Her other published works include *The State and its Children, The Workers' Handbook,* and numerous articles in the monthly reviews and pamphlets on industrial matters. She was made a Companion of Honour in 1930.

In private life she was a woman of singular charm, and the striking good looks of her youth she still retained into advancing years. Her home was a pleasant meeting place for all engaged or interested in public work, and, socially gifted as she was, she enjoyed bringing persons of different classes and of political creeds together in the common object of furthering the causes she had at heart. With her death is broken a link with the early days of the organization of female labour, and the working woman of to-day owes much to the ideals to which Gertrude Tuckwell's long and well spent life had been one long devotion.

August 6, 1951.

Sir Robert Ho Tung—See **Ho.**

Frank Twyman, F.R.S., who died on March 6, 1959, was a pioneer in the application of science to industry.

He was born in Canterbury in 1876, the seventh child of a family of nine, and he maintained to the end of his life pride in his Kentish origin. From a very early age he showed two scientific attributes—keen observation and testing of statements by experiment, sometimes to the embarrassment of his teachers. He was educated at Simon Langton's School, at Finsbury Technical College under Silvanus Thompson, Perry, and Meldola, and later went as Siemens Scholar to the Central Technical College.

On leaving he worked for a time at the Fowler Waring Cables Company, testing telephone cables. He described the work as trivial but extremely tiring, and with relief he went in 1898 to Otto Hilger, who had succeeded his brother Adam Hilger in charge of the firm of that name. On the death of Otto Hilger in 1902 Twyman succeeded him as manager, although only 26 years old. In 1904 the firm was incorporated as a company, with Twyman as managing director, a post which he held until 1946. Two years later the firm was amalgamated with E. R. Watts and Son to become Hilger and Watts Ltd. He continued as a director of this company until 1952, and then became technical adviser.

In the early days he did all the testing of the optical work, and the adjustment of all the instruments. He introduced into the firm the use of proof-plates for testing optical surfaces and until 1910 designed and made complete drawings for all the instruments. He developed the testing of optical components by means of interferometers, and Twyman-Green interferometers are used wherever high quality optics are made. For example, a complete series of these interferometers was purchased by Carl Zeiss in 1929. Twyman was a master of the science of making fine optical components, and, as secrecy was anathema to him, he recorded his experience in the book *Prism and Lens Making.*

It will, however, be chiefly for his pioneer work in spectrochemical analysis that he will be remembered. Kirschhoff and Bunsen used the spectograph for the analysis of metals in 1860, and yet by 1904 this technique had not been brought into daily use. In that year Twyman designed and had made the wavelength spectrometer, which was bought by physicists and chemists for research and teaching all over the world, but it was neglected by metallurgists. This spurred him to design a fixed adjustment quartz spectograph so as to allow the ultra-violet region to be used as well as the visible, for the ultra-violet region contains most of the spectral lines important for the analysis of metals. This instrument, and a larger one more suited for the analysis of steel, were still not attractive to analysis. The situation changed dramatically when Zeiss, and Bausch and Lomb, began to make similar instruments, and persuaded professors in their respective countries to make investigations and publish papers. This was a procedure which Twyman had tried to follow in Britain, even offering the loan of instruments for the purpose. The publicity in Germany and the United States resulted in the success of Twyman's spectrographs.

Further successes followed in the infra-red and in the far ultra-violet regions of the spectrum. X-ray instruments were made for studying X-ray spectra and the structure of crystals.

In 1924 Twyman was elected a Fellow of the Royal Society. In 1926 he received the John Price Weatherill medal of the Franklin Institute of Washington, in 1927 the Duddell medal of the Physical Society, and in 1957 the gold medal of the Society of Applied Spectroscopists of the U.S.A.

He took a lively interest in current affairs, as shown, for example, by his publication of *Some New Proposals for the Amelioration of the Balance of Payments Position.* He was entertaining company, for his views were always interesting and often unorthodox. He had a prodigious memory, was quick in thought and action, but always had time for a good story. He inspired affectionate respect in those under him and will live in the memory of many.

March 10, 1959.

Admiral of the Fleet Sir Reginald Tyrwhitt, G.C.B., D.S.O., who died on May 30, 1951 after a short illness at the age of 81, was one of the outstanding commanders of the 1914-18 war, in which he had the unique distinction of holding the same command throughout.

From 1913 he had been Commodore Commanding Home Fleet Flotillas. He was thus, as Commodore, second class, the senior officer at Harwich at the outbreak of war, and he continued to command what became later known as the Harwich Force, composed of cruisers and destroyers, as Commodore, first class, from December 1914, and as acting Rear-Admiral from 1918, until six months after the close of hostilities. Harwich was the outpost nearest to enemy waters, and the command there was peculiarly suited to Tyrwhitt's bold and active temperament, for he was ever one to steer for the sound of the guns. He was a born war leader, and the officers and men of the Harwich Force would have followed him anywhere.

Tyrwhitt was the fifth son of the Rev. Richard St. John Tyrwhitt, vicar of St. Mary Magdalen, Oxford, by his second wife, Caroline, daughter of John Yorke, of Bewerley Hall, Yorkshire. Born on May 10, 1870, he entered the Navy in July 1883, and went to sea in 1885 in the Alexandra, flagship in the Mediterranean of Admiral Lord John Hay, and later of Admiral the Duke of Edinburgh. In 1888 Tyrwhitt joined the light cruiser Calypso, in the Training Squadron. He served as sub-lieutenant in the battleship Ajax, in the armoured cruiser Aurora, and in the pilot sailing tender to the training ship Impregnable at Devonport. From September 1892 to December 1895, having obtained his commission as lieutenant, he served in the light cruiser Cleopatra on the North American Station.

It was in January 1896 that Tyrwhitt obtained his first acquaintance with that arm of the

Service in which he became famous in the war, being appointed to command one of our earliest destroyers, the Hart. In 1897-99 he served as first lieutenant of the Surprise, Commander-in-Chief's yacht in the Mediterranean, and for the next three years as first lieutenant of the light cruiser Indefatigable in North American waters. Promoted to commander in 1903, he was in his old ship, the Aurora, while she was employed as a tender to the cadet training ship Britannia, and from 1904 to 1908 commanded successively the destroyer Waveney and the scouts Attentive and Skirmisher, in home waters.

He became a captain in June 1908 and was at once appointed to command the Fourth Destroyer Flotilla, with his pennant in the Topaze, and served there for two years. After a short period of study at the War College he had a spell of cruiser service as Flag-Captain to Rear-Admiral Sir Douglas Gamble in the Mediterranean, serving in the Bacchante and Good Hope. But he returned to his beloved destroyers in July 1912, being selected to command the Second Flotilla in the Home Fleet, and 18 months later he was chosen as Commodore (T) in the Fleet, with charge of all the flotillas.

On the outbreak of war he was at Harwich with his flag in the cruiser Amethyst, and the First and Third Flotillas in company—some of these were the first ships to be engaged with the enemy when they sank the German minelayer Königin Luise off the Thames Estuary on August 5, 1914. Soon after hostilities began the Commodore shifted his broad pendant from the Amethyst to the Arethusa, the first of a new type of light cruiser, and in her he revived the old glories of this famous ship name.

The Heligoland Bight action of August 28, 1914, when the British light forces destroyed the cruisers Mainz, Köln, and Ariadne, and some torpedo craft in German waters, was partly planned by Commodore Tyrwhitt in collaboration with Commodore (later Admiral of the Fleet Lord) Keyes, the two commanding respectively the destroyer and submarine flotillas employed. The Arethusa was hotly engaged, and partially disabled, but she returned safely to Sheerness. For the "great skill and gallantry" with which he delivered this attack Commodore Tyrwhitt was awarded the C.B.

In the Scarborough and Hartlepool raid of December 16, 1914, though it was too rough for the destroyers to keep the sea, the Commodore remained out with his light cruisers and narrowly missed getting into touch with the German battle-cruisers. In the seaplane raid on Cuxhaven on Christmas Day, 1914, he commanded the covering force. A month later, he was in command of the destroyers at Admiral Beatty's victory off the Dogger Bank. After 18 months' valuable service, his flagship the Arethusa was destroyed by a mine off the East Coast in February 1916, and he hoisted his broad pendant in the Cleopatra.

On May 10, 1917, he encountered a force of 11 German destroyers near the North Hinder lightship, but on his closing them and opening fire they made off, in spite of numerical superiority, and were chased under the Zeebrugge batteries. On several occasions Commodore Tyrwhitt cooperated with the vessels of the Dover Patrol in bombardments of the German positions along the Belgian coast.

He also covered attacks by aircraft such as that on July 19, 1918, upon the Zeppelin sheds at Tondern, on the Schleswig-Holstein coast. After the armistice it was to the Harwich Forces under Rear-Admiral Tyrwhitt that the "U"-boats were surrendered by the Germans.

His vessels were, except for the Dover Patrol, more frequently in contact with the enemy than any other British force in home waters, and as Lord Jellicoe says in his book, *The Crisis of the Naval War,* their duties were manifold. Tyrwhitt accepted all these demands philosophically, and the manner in which his officers and men responded to the heavy calls upon them through so many months of war was a tribute to his leadership, and the affection he inspired in them.

His war honours included the D.S.O., conferred in June 1916, and the K.C.B., in July 1917. Another honour he specially prized was the honorary degree of D.C.L. from Oxford University, and the honorary freedom of the city, where he was born, which he received in February 1919.

On hauling down his flag at Harwich, Tyrwhitt was appointed, still an acting rear-admiral, Senior Officer at Gibraltar, and in December 1919 he was promoted substantive rear-admiral. In January 1921 he returned to sea service in command of the Third Cruiser Squadron in the Mediterranean Fleet, a command which he held for two years.

On returning from the Mediterranean he was appointed Senior Officer on the Coast of Scotland and Admiral Superintendent of Rosyth Dockyard. He was promoted vice-admiral in 1925, when he relinquished the command. In 1927 he was appointed Commander-in-Chief on the China Station. Again the position was one of disturbance and difficulty, when the security of the International Settlement at Shanghai was threatened by the agitation, arising out of the Chinese civil war, for the rendition of the Treaty Ports, and for his handling of a difficult and threatening situation Tyrwhitt was awarded the G.C.B. on relinquishing command in February 1929.

In May 1930 he became for three years Commander-in-Chief at The Nore, taking over the post of First and Principal Aide-de-camp to the King in 1932. In 1934, being then senior admiral on the list—he had been promoted to that rank in 1929—he was promoted Admiral of the Fleet in the vacancy which then occurred.

In May 1936 he became one of the trustees of the National Maritime Museum, then just founded.

Admiral Tyrwhitt married, in 1903, Angela, daughter of Matthew Corbally, J.P., of Rathbeal Hall, Swords, and had one son and two daughters. The former, St. John Reginald Tyrwhitt, born in 1905, entered the Royal Navy in January 1919 as a cadet, and gained distinction for service in destroyers in the 1939-45 war.

May 31, 1951.

U

The former **Maharana of Udaipur,** the Rajputana state, **Sir Bhupal Singh,** who died on July 4, 1955 in his palace at the age of 71, was known as the "Sun of the Hindus", and the sun in splendour was emblazoned on his standard.

His Highness Maharajadhiraja Maharana Sri Sir Bhupal Singh Bahadur, G.C.S.I., G.C.I.E., was the son and successor of Maharana Sir Fateh Singh Bahadur, the head of the Sessodia Rajputs, who had personal as well as dynastic claims to veneration. With a family pedigree dating back to about A.D. 144, he was by common consent one of the noblest products of Rajput culture and chivalry, filling with dignity and charm his massive obligations.

Maharana Sir Bhupal Singh, who was born on February 22, 1884, did not inherit the magnificent figure of his father. By one of nature's surprises he was slight, frail, and partially paralysed. Though he could not ride a horse, an accomplishment which comes as by instinct to the Rajput nobility, he was a keen shot, and refused to allow his physical disabilities to hinder him from moving about the State on business and sporting expeditions. Before succeeding to the *gadi* on the death of his father on May 24, 1930, he was handicapped by an unhappy decision of the Paramount Power.

Owing to the excessive top-heaviness of the direct personal administration of Sir Fateh Singh, leading to heavy arrears in appeals—for he was his own High Court—and to lack of effective supervision of local officers, the Governor-General felt obliged to curtail his powers, though he was as loyal at heart as he was splendid in aspect. Sir Bhupal, a man of subtle brain, needed and exercised a tact and forbearance whereby he made good in an exceedingly difficult position.

Under his own rule from 1930 the State made some progress, but he scarcely had the power, even if he had the will, to modify greatly the old feudal conceptions to which his nobles tenaciously clung. The administration remained under his personal supervision, assisted by a *musahib ala* and two Ministers. Life in the medieval, far-famed capital remained much the same. The city of Udaipur which, in the words of the late Sir Walter Lawrence, "like the Taj at Agra, baffles brush and pen", is more than 2,000ft. above sea level, and in his vast, haphazard, but beautiful palace the Maharana would sit for hours in some arcaded eyrie overlooking the lake and mountains.

Here, cross-legged in Indian fashion, but in English garb and expensive English boots that never touched the ground, he received his few European guests and talked to them in fluent English.

Since the unification of the 14 Rajput States in 1949 to form the State of Rajasthan, he had been given the honorary title of "Maharajah Pramukh", and had the right to preside over the meetings of the princes of the new State, which has a population of some 12 millions.

July 5, 1955.

Maurice Utrillo, the French painter, died on November 5, 1955 at Dax in the Pyrenees, where he had gone to take the waters for his health, which had been bad for many years. He was 71.

Not inexcusably, Maurice Utrillo's bohemian reputation has distracted attention to some extent from his genius as a painter, of townscapes in particular. Unlike most of his contemporaries in Paris, he was very little touched by aesthetic theory in his passion for his craft.

The circumstances of his birth in 1883 have been so often told that no hesitation need be felt in repeating the facts. He was the child of a drunken assault upon his mother, Suzanne Valadon, a young circus performer who turned artists' model after a trapeze accident. She was employed by Puvis de Chavannes, Renoir, and Toulouse-Lautrec, under whose encouragement she developed a talent for painting that gained for her an honoured place in the modern French school. She died in 1938 at the age of 71.

Suzanne Valadon registered her son in her own name. She later married a painter named Utter, but her husband refused to give his name to the boy, and it was a Spanish journalist named Utrillo who chivalrously offered to supply a deficiency that grieved his mother. He took the boy, then aged eight, to the Mairie and brought him back as Maurice Utrillo. At first Maurice, who was devoted to his mother, refused the name, and when at the age of 19 he began to exhibit he signed his pictures Maurice Valadon. Even after persuasion he retained his mother's initial and his signature became "Maurice Utrillo V".

The life of Maurice Utrillo makes the conventional *vie de bohème* and Gauguin's self-conscious revolt from respectability seen like amateur performances. His mother's occupations as model and painter prevented her from keeping a close eye on the boy. She put him to school, but some workmen were in the habit of giving him a lift on his way home and he drank with them at wayside taverns. When his mother found this out she was terribly distressed, and in an agony of remorse at her former negligence she called in one doctor after another, took the boy away from school, and, keeping him constantly by her, taught him to paint. But he frequently escaped her vigilance and was to be found in the bars of Montmartre. She moved into the suburbs but without better success, the truth being that before he was 20 Maurice Utrillo was a confirmed dipsomaniac and was also a drug addict.

About 1919 his condition was so bad that he had to be sent to a sanatorium. He escaped by bribing an attendant and went back to Montmartre, where he engaged in a drinking bout with his boon companion Amadeo Modigliani, which ended at a police station. A few days after this bout Modigliani, who was far advanced in consumption, died. Utrillo was in and out of hospitals and sanatoria many times, and frequently in the hands of the police for disorderly conduct. In the intervals he painted, producing in fact far more than the average industrious and sober artist. Finally his mother took a house near Lyons, on the Rhône, where they lived in retirement. It was here in 1929 that a small party of artists and writers from Paris visited him to present him with the Cross of the Legion of Honour. They found him in a state of mental confusion and only able to murmur a few words of thanks.

In 1937 Utrillo brought an action for libel against the Director and Keeper of the Tate Gallery and the publishers and printers of the third edition of the catalogue of the Modern Foreign School, in which his irregular habits were described, with the erroneous information that he had died in 1934. Mr. Justice Lewis, in Chambers, refused to strike out the plea of justification and the particulars given, and Utrillo brought an appeal. It was heard before Lord Justice Greer and Lord Justice MacKinnon, who dismissed it. Except for the mistake about Utrillo's death the particulars given do not differ from those to be found in other published references to the painter, in *La Légende et la vie d'Utrillo,* by François Carco [q.v.], for example.

To turn from Utrillo's life to his work is to receive several surprises. For one thing there is not a trace in his painting of mental instability or abnormality, such as we find in the later work of Van Gogh. For another, though, as we are told, many of his pictures were made from picture-postcards, the subjects are so completely translated into terms of painting that, without information, a photographic origin would not be suspected. Intensity of vision and—until his powers declined—force of execution were his outstanding characteristics. He had an extraordinary feeling for what may be called street portraiture, for the fusion of architectural character and social atmosphere that makes a particular street different from any other street; and the same is true of his treatment of individual buildings, such as "La Maison Orange", of immense solidity, planted firmly above a green foreground under a grey-blue sky, or the graceful "Church in Autumn". Comparisons that have been made between his best work and the early work of Corot and that of Courbet are not extravagant. In some of the paintings of his so-called "white" period, between 1910 and 1914, an influence of Cubism has been suggested, but it is hardly more than an accident of subject—a cubistic character in the building. Beyond his paintings of streets and houses he does not seem to have produced much, but in 1925 he was employed by Diaghileff to design the scenery and costumes of the ballet *Barabou.*

There have been several one-man shows of works by Utrillo in London. The last was in 1951, when some of his later work was shown. In it his subjects and technique were much the same as before, but there were perceptible unexpected passages of gay and decorative colour and here and there a trace of brisk and modish stylization. He is represented in the Modern Foreign School at the Tate Gallery.

He married the artist Lucie Pauwels, who survives him.

November 7, 1955.

V

H. A. Vachell, prolific author and playwright, died at his home near Bath on January 10, 1955 at the age of 93.

He was one of the most productive and popular writers of his day. His first novel appeared when he was 33, and some 10 years later he reached what appeared to be the summit of his achievement in *The Hill.* Beyond it, however, was a high plateau of dramatic production which, after another decade, seemed to culminate in *Quinney's.* The phase continued for many years, and it was distinguished by a practised ease of accomplishment. Perhaps Vachell's most singular faculty as a writer was that of adapting a plot with equal facility to the purposes of a novel and the exigencies of the stage; it was, moreover, all the same to him whether he required to turn a novel of his into a play or a play of his into a novel.

As playwright he was no less successful than as novelist; during a good many years he offered large audiences the type of drama which, while it seldom over-strained the intellect, provided precisely the kind of entertainment they sought. He was, in fact, a skilled and honest showman of the world of which he came, and if, like the exemplary public schoolboy that in a sense he always remained, he kept within bounds which others of his day felt bound to transgress, his own public remained faithful.

Horace Annesley Vachell was born on October 30, 1861. His father, who died when he was a child, was Richard Tanfield Vachell, of Coptfold Hall, Essex; his mother was Georgina, daughter of Arthur Lyttelton Annesley, of Arley Castle, Staffordshire. He was educated at Harrow—of which he was to write one of the best known of his books and of which his memories constantly pricked him as a writer—and at Sandhurst. From Sandhurst, after a long delay during which he amused himself by painting in France and visiting the United States, he was posted to The Rifle Brigade. While in California, however, he had bought a ranch, and, tempted by the prospects which it seemed to offer, he decided to forgo a military career and to stay there.

His introduction to literary life appears to have been equally fortuitous. In 1889, while wintering in England, he wrote a short story and had it accepted by the *Pall Mall Gazette,* although others that he wrote at the time he failed to place. In the same year he married Lydie, daughter of C. H. Phillips, of San Luis Obispo, California. She bore him a son, who was killed in the 1914-18 War. To his lasting sorrow she died in 1895, after the birth of a daughter.

His first novel, *The Romance of Judge Ketchum,* which appeared in 1894, was fairly well received but sold disappointingly. He followed it with others and in collaboration with a friend tried his hand also at a "comedietta", which was produced in London; but his successes were still to come. In 1899, when affairs were going badly for him in California, he returned home determined to retrieve his fortune by his pen. In the following year he published *John Charity*, a smoothly flowing historical novel, which went well enough and helped to establish him. By 1902 he was making some £400 a year. Then, in 1904, he wrote *Brothers*, the story of a physically attractive but intellectually limited man who traded on the brains of a younger brother. This, his first real success, enabled him, among other things, to pay his debts. A year later came *The Hill*. Regarded at the time as one of the best school stories in the language, this tale of life at Harrow proved an unqualified triumph, though for his own part the author always considered that he had erred in dating it after his own time.

There were successful novels of different kinds to follow. But Vachell's mind and imagination at this remarkably fertile phase could not be contained by fiction; he was beginning to turn his eyes seriously towards the theatre. In 1907 *Her Son*, afterwards transformed into a novel, was accepted by Cyril Maude [q.v.]. It was well received in the provinces, less well received in London. But Vachell persevered and eventually had his reward with *Jelf's*, produced at Wyndham's Theatre in 1912. Of his novels round about this time, in all of which he continued to exhibit a shrewd resource in narrative and a pleasant ease in character-drawing, the one of which he himself thought best was *The Paladin*, which was duly translated to the stage as *The Case of Lady Camber*.

But it was *Quinney's*, his celebrated portrait of an idiosyncratic dealer in antique furniture, that did him most credit. Published as a novel in 1914 and produced as a play a year later, it enabled him to touch what was probably his happiest level as author and dramatist, though some felt that the astringent quality of the novel was lost in the play by the substitution of a conventional last curtain for Quinney's last words in the novel to "that maggot of a Miggot", while the later film adaptation was pure saccharine.

There followed, during the period of the 1914-18 War, a spate of dramatic productions: *Searchlights; Who is He?* adapted from a novel by Mrs. Belloc Lowndes; *Fishpingle; Humpty Dumpty; Mrs. Pomeroy's Reputation; The House of Peril*. And there were still plays to come with the return of peace.

As for the novels, Vachell assumed a closer likeness every year to the unrepentant Victorian, mourning the eclipse of a familiar order of society. From his laments for the irrecoverable past he turned to light comedy in his fiction, reserving his mood of nostalgia for volumes of reminiscence, English travel, table talk, and the like. *Phoebe's Guest House* (1939) was his fortieth novel, and by no means his last. The table talk of *Now Came Still Evening On*, published in 1946, when he was 85, showed that he could still exercise a discursive charm. *Methuselah's Diary*, and his hundredth and last book, *Quests*, showed that his gift of narrative and sense of style had not deserted him.

As a novelist Vachell was always easy to read and impossible to dislike. A natural storyteller, he had a lively turn of imagination and telling gifts of characterization and dialogue, and although, no doubt, he did not attain the highest pinnacle of achievement, yet few have upheld more consistently a standard of professional competence over so long a period.

January 11, 1955.

Maurice Valadon—See **Utrillo.**

Dr. Eduard van Beinum—See **Beinum.**

Senator Arthur Vandenberg, who died on April 18, 1951, was the outstanding figure among those American Republicans who since the war have helped in the formulation of a bipartisan foreign policy for their country.

First as an isolationist and then as an advocate of world collaboration for peace, Vandenberg was always a man of consequence in the Senate, to which he was first appointed—and later elected—in 1928, when he was 44.

But it was not until 1945 that he began the phase of his career which gave his name a meaning for many beyond his own country. In that year he was not only chosen by President Roosevelt as an American delegate to the United Nations conference at San Francisco, but he made a speech in the Senate which marked the turning point in his political development. He spoke on the eve of the Yalta conference, before anything was publicly known of the allied leaders' plans for their meeting, and he addressed himself to the problem of security against Germany and Japan after those Powers had been defeated. He proposed a bold solution. He suggested that since Russia and Great Britain did and said as they wanted in foreign policy—he was referring to recent activities in Poland and Greece—America should cease to be the silent partner in the grand alliance. America must reassert her faith in the Atlantic Charter and make clear her attitude to the future of collective security. He proposed that the allied victory over the Axis should be maintained by means of a treaty between Great Britain, France, Russia, China, and the United States, under which any sign of resurgence by Germany or Japan would be checked. At the same time he sought a just peace.

Such a forthright demand for action in the international field of the future caused concern among isolationist Republicans, who saw Vandenberg's speech as a severe blow against the party. But elsewhere—not least among that section of the Republican Party which favoured collaboration between the Powers for peace—the speech was welcomed as a significant and courageous step. It was broadcast to the outer world by the Office of War Information; and there is not much doubt that it helped President Roosevelt at Yalta in assessing the probable reactions of the American people to the terms that were agreed there.

From this time onwards Arthur Hendrik Vandenberg, the boy born of poor parents at Grand Rapids, Michigan, in 1884, could be counted as a major figure. He had succeeded in his journalistic career as editor and publisher of the *Grand Rapids Herald* from 1906 to 1928, when he went to the Senate; he had been a forceful but not destructive critic of the New Deal; now he was the advocate of a firm policy for America in international affairs at a time when official American policy had shown signs of hesitation.

Throughout 1945, at San Francisco and in the Senate, Vandenberg continued the work he had so dramatically begun. When, on June 29, he rose in the Senate to commend the United Nations Charter he had a full gathering to hear him. He warned his audience that the alternative to this projected league of the United Nations was world chaos; he saw the Charter as the one means of holding the major Powers in harmony. In meeting points put by his critics he said that the so-called special privileges of the great Powers were matched by their special responsibilities, and that the Charter, with all its limitations, was the one basis on which to launch the great venture for peace because it did in fact substantially reflect world realities. By the spring of 1946, after he had been to London for the first General Assembly of the United Nations, Vandenberg had come to declare that the United States must match Russia in bluntness and vigour; but he did not despair of agreement.

In April 1946, in the course of the Senate debate on the American loan to Britain, Vandenberg announced his support for the agreement on the grounds of intelligent American self-interest. America, he said, must assume economic as well as political leadership in world affairs. When, in the Republican mid-term electoral successes in November 1946, Vandenberg was himself re-elected, he interpreted his victory as the endorsement of the bipartisan foreign policy which he had supported. In 1947 and 1948, especially in his conduct of the debate on the European recovery programme, he displayed his ability to handle his own supporters with skill and understanding and to help to translate Marshall's [q.v.] offer to Europe, at first a cause of widespread misinterpretation, into fact.

Vandenberg had often been discussed as a likely candidate for the Republican presidential nomination, and in 1948, as was to be expected after his successes in the Senate, there were indications that he would be strongly favoured for the first place in the Republicans' fight for the presidency. But in the first ballot at the Republican convention in June he was behind Governor Dewey*, Senator Taft [q.v.], and Stassen. Though he was now outside the contest, he remained a power throughout the convention, checking by his influence any attempt by the isolationists to choose their own men for the nominations. In the Senate debate on the ratification of the Atlantic Pact in July 1949 Vandenberg again emphasized the bipartisan approach to the treaty, asking that it be ratified as rapidly and as convincingly as possible.

At the end of 1949 Vandenberg underwent a

severe pulmonary operation and he was never again able to take an active part in political affairs. In 1950, after a brief return to the Senate, he had a second operation in April. Since then he had little freedom from illness, and in March 1951 he had a further relapse. Though he was thus in 1950 unable to take his place in the diplomatic effort in Washington—at that time in a critical phase—he none the less made his influence felt. In a letter to Paul Hoffman*, then administrator of the Economic Cooperation Administration, he praised the efforts of those who were organizing aid for Europe, pointing out that though disappointments were inevitable in the fulfilment of such unprecedented programmes, the victories which they had won were there for all to see. This letter, which was a source of much encouragement to all Americans who were anxious about the future of United States help to Europe, in Britain drew from Churchill* a notable tribute in the House of Commons. The House, he said, would welcome the news (as indicated by Vandenberg's letter) that this great American statesman was recovering from his illness and that he was able once again to exert his clarifying and elevating influence on world events. The letter was, however, the close of his political career; he took no part in the dispute over foreign policy which marked the Congressional elections of 1950; and that dispute was, in fact, the evidence of his absence and of his party's loss.

Vandenberg was a tall, impressive figure, more a talker than an orator, but always a man of most effective powers in seeking support for the causes in which he believed. He had elaborate ways in public at which, it is said, he laughed in private; but there was little doubt about his earnest spirit when, at the critical and memorable moments of his later political life, he spoke for his party and for his country.

April 20, 1951.

General Hoyt S. Vandenberg, Chief of Staff of the United States Air Force from 1948 until his retirement in June 1953, died on April 2, 1954 at the age of 55.

Hoyt Sanford Vandenberg was born on January 24, 1899, and received his early education at Columbian School, whence he proceeded to West Point. There his record was far from brilliant, but after graduation he was posted to the air service, where he quickly made his mark as a pilot. He attended the Air Corps Tactical School in 1934-35, the General Staff and Command School in 1935-36, and the Army War College in 1938-39. The mere list of these courses shows that once he had got into his chosen element, the air, he was able to develop his gifts to the full and his assignment to the air war planning staff, when he left the Army War College in 1939, was due recognition of his bent. He went to England in 1942 under General James Doolittle to help in the organization of the Twelfth Air Force and accompanied that formation to North Africa.

Promoted brigadier-general in December 1942, he was appointed Chief of Staff of the North-West African Strategic Air Force, and himself flew in a great many of the sorties he had had a large hand in planning. Six months later he was recalled to Washington to fill the post of Deputy Chief of the Air Staff. While in that position he led a mission to Russia and also attended the Quebec, Cairo, and Teheran conferences.

He was Commander of the American Air Force in Europe during the period before D-day, and played a large part in planning the invasion of Normandy. In August 1944 he was appointed to command the Ninth Air Force, which gave air support to General Omar Bradley's Twelfth Army Group during the liberation of France. After the end of hostilities Vandenberg became Director of Intelligence in the War Department, and then Director of Central Intelligence, the inclusive agency established in 1946.

When in 1948 General Spaatz* retired from the post of Chief of Staff of the Air Force Vandenberg succeeded him. He worked hard to rebuild the United States Air Force, the strength of which had been allowed to decline after the end of the war. Indeed, he strove tirelessly to make his country supreme in the air and when he retired in June 1953 the United States Secretary for the Air stated that under Vandenberg's leadership the United States Air Force had become "the most powerful and effective military force ever assembled in the interests of peace". Vandenberg's latter years were clouded by the onset of the malignant disease from which he eventually died. He first entered hospital in May 1952 and underwent a serious abdominal operation. Nevertheless, in the ensuing August he was back at work, but in December 1953 he was again reported to be seriously ill and this time there was to be no recovery.

He married in 1923 Miss Gladys Rose, of Tuxedo, New York, who survives him together with a son and a daughter of the marriage.

April 3, 1954.

H. Van de Velde—See **Velde.**

John Van Druten, well known as a dramatist, stage director, and novelist on both sides of the Atlantic, died on December 19, 1957 at his home near Indio in California, where he had lived for the past 17 years. He was 56.

His circumstances at the time of his death might almost be described as retirement: retirement not indeed from work of a creative kind—his last book *The Widening Circle* was published in Britain in July 1957—but from the world as he had known it during the long period (more than a quarter of a century) of his success. Van Druten did not cut himself off from the theatre, but he came to look beyond it during his later years; and it was on such quarters of the horizon as the reading of Gerald Heard's *The Third Morality* first revealed to him that his mind dwelt with increasing interest.

His reputation, however, which was made with his plays, still rests upon these and not upon the chronicle of his spiritual adventures contained in *The Widening Circle* and in the earlier essay in autobiography, *The Way to the Present* (1938). Yet his plays, considered individually, on their own merits, cannot be said to have made a lasting impression. They show him to have had no particular delight in words, to have relied on superficial observation rather than on insight in giving an impression of truth, and to have allowed the ready wit and pleasant lucidity of his style to be frequently swamped by a genteel sentimentalism, which seemed to be an inherent part of his view of things. The merit of his plays consists in their conscientious exposition of a particular style or type of playwriting—the one that he examined faithfully and comprehensively in his book on the craft of playwriting, *Playwright at Work* (1953).

That craft, as Van Druten understood and learnt to practise it, was a matter of planning and bringing off dramatic effects. To do this in such a way as to illustrate contemporary manners and at the same time; if possible, to throw into relief some aspect of human nature in general, was to make a success of it, to justify the whole business by giving to actors and audience alike the sense of participating in something alive and worth while. In his constant and often successful endeavour to provide this experience, he developed skill in finding stage equivalents for material already popular in a different form: for Kathryn Forbes's *Mama's Bank Account* in his play *I Remember Mama* (1948), and for Christopher Isherwood's Berlin stories in *I am a Camera* (1954). These were genuinely imaginative adaptations.

John William Van Druten, the son of a Dutch father, was born in London in 1901, educated at University College School, and afterwards articled to a solicitor in the City. After being admitted a solicitor with honours in his finals in 1923 he held for three years the position of special lecturer in law at the Aberystwyth college of the University of Wales. But a play of his had already been produced by former students of R.A.D.A. in 1924, and *Young Woodley*, which established him, was staged in New York a year later and in London in 1928—at first by the 300 Club (with Frank Lawton* and with Kathleen O'Regan), and later, after the Lord Chamberlain's ban had been lifted, at the Savoy Theatre. His reputation was confirmed by such later plays as *After All,* 1931, with Dame Lilian Braithwaite; *There's Always Juliet,* 1931, with Edna Best* and Herbert Marshall*; *Behold, We Live,* 1932, with Sir Gerald du Maurier and Gertrude Lawrence [q.v.]; *The Distaff Side,* 1933, with Dame Sybil Thorndike [d. 1976]; *Old Acquaintance,* 1941, with Dame Edith Evans [d. 1976]; *The Voice of the Turtle,* 1947, with Margaret Sullavan [q.v.]; and *Bell, Book and Candle,* 1954, with Rex Harrison and Lili Palmer.

A number of his earlier plays owed much of their success to his collaborating in the staging of them with Auriol Lee as director.

In the later part of his career Van Druten, who had become an American citizen, was responsible for directing not only plays of his own but the spectacular American musical, *The King and I,* which began its long run at Drury Lane in 1953. He also published four novels.

December 21, 1957.

Lord Vansittart, Permanent Under-Secretary of State for Foreign Affairs from 1930 to 1938, died on February 14, 1957 at his home at Denham, Buckinghamshire.

Through perhaps the most critical decade in modern history he held posts of immense importance and influence. Secretaries of State may come and go, but the Permanent Head of the Foreign Office remains the repository and watchman of all that is continuous in British foreign policy, and is the leading expert adviser of the Foreign Secretary of the day. In Lord Vansittart's case these functions were entrusted to a man of conspicuous intellect and ability, strong character, great personal charm, and very definite individual views which at one time provoked much gossip in Whitehall and, later on, stirred wider controversies outside. In 1933 he never doubted that the Nazi accession to power would lead to war, for he was already convinced that Germany willed another war. As time went on and the tension created by the Nazis grew, the Permanent Head of the Foreign Office found himself increasingly at variance with the policy of the Prime Minister, Neville Chamberlain.

Winston Churchill*, in *The Gathering Storm* volume of his war memoirs, describes the situation behind the scenes: "His [Sir Robert Vansittart's] fortuitous connexion with the Hoare-Laval pact had affected his position both with the new Foreign Secretary, Mr. Eden, and in wide political circles. The Prime Minister, who leaned more and more upon his Chief Industrial Adviser, Sir Horace Wilson*, and consulted him a great deal on matters outside his province or compass, regarded Vansittart as hostile to Germany. This was indeed true, for no one more clearly realized or foresaw the growth of the German danger or was more ready to subordinate other considerations to meeting it. The Foreign Secretary felt he could work more easily with Sir Alexander Cadogan*, a Foreign Office official also of the highest character and ability. Therefore, at the end of 1937, Vansittart was apprised of his impending dismissal and on January 1, 1938, was appointed to the special post of Chief Diplomatic Adviser to His Majesty's Government. This was represented to the public as promotion and might well indeed appear to be so. In fact, however, the whole responsibility for managing the Foreign Office passed out of his hands. He kept his old traditional room but he saw the Foreign Office telegrams only after they had reached the Foreign Secretary with the Minutes of the Department upon them".

This post he retained until 1941, when he retired. He was still in office when, in the winter of 1940-41, he made some broadcasts and published them in a pamphlet entitled *Black Record.* It was a sweeping condemnation of Germany and the German people, and it provoked questions in the Commons, a debate in the Lords, and a storm of criticism outside. Objection was taken not only to the views expressed and to the harmful effect they might have in strengthening German resistance, but also to the fact that the publication constituted a breach in the tradition of the Civil Service. Events showed that *Black Record* was the beginning of a public campaign which, supported by speeches and writings, attained its full vigour after his retirement in June 1941. In and out of Parliament he reiterated his complete mistrust of the German people and ridiculed what he called the "myth" of two Germanys. His language matched the fervour of his convictions, and soon a new word had been added to the political vocabulary—"Vansittartism". He was out to tell his countrymen the truth about Germany, as he saw it, and he had no use for mincing words or "any other cookery of tough facts". Friends and admirers sometimes felt that his chief handicap as a public controversialist was his intensity.

After Germany's defeat he continued to take an active part in House of Lords debates and made some notable contributions, especially on the trend of developments in eastern Europe.

The Right Hon. Sir Robert Gilbert Vansittart, P.C., G.C.B., G.C.M.G., M.V.O., first Baron Vansittart, of Denham, in the county of Buckinghamshire, in the Peerage of the United Kingdom, was born on June 25, 1881. He was the eldest son of the late Captain Robert Arnold Vansittart. The family was descended from a merchant venturer who went to England from Danzig in 1670. He was educated at Eton, where in 1899 he won the Prince Consort's first French prize and first German prize. In 1902 he was nominated an attaché in the Diplomatic Service and sent the year after to Paris. Three years later he was promoted a Third Secretary and in 1907 he was sent to Teheran, but returned the next year to the Foreign Office and was made a Second Secretary. In 1909 he went to Cairo. From 1911 to 1913 he was again employed in London and was eventually transferred to the establishment and in 1914 promoted an assistant clerk. In 1919 he was in attendance at the Peace Conference at Paris, was given the rank of First Secretary and in the next year that of Counsellor of Embassy, being made a C.M.G.

On his return to London he became an assistant secretary, and from 1920 to 1924 was private secretary to the Secretary of State, Lord Curzon. He married in 1921 Gladys, only daughter of General Heppenheimer, of New Jersey, United States. She died, young, charming, and accomplished, in 1928. In 1928 he was appointed principal private secretary to the Prime Minister, having been made a C.B. in the previous year, and, while holding this post, was promoted to be Assistant Under-Secretary of State. Having been promoted K.C.B. in 1929, he retained the post of principal private secretary to the Prime Minister when Ramsay MacDonald succeeded Stanley Baldwin and he accompanied MacDonald on his American and Canadian tours. In 1930 he became, in succession to Sir Ronald Lindsay, Permanent Under-Secretary of State for Foreign Affairs. Promotion to G.C.M.G. followed in 1931.

In that year he married Sarita Enriqueta, daughter of Herbert Ward and widow of the Right Hon. Sir Colville Barclay. K.C.M.G. Although it was not usual for the Permanent Under-Secretary of State to go abroad he was a delegate to the Stresa Conference of 1935. Later in the same year he was in Paris with Sir Samuel Hoare [Lord Templewood, q.v.], the Secretary of State, when the ill-starred proposals for settling the Italo-Abyssinian dispute were framed. He visited Berlin in 1936 and had what was described as a general conversation with Hitler and talks with almost every other important member of the Nazi régime.

On January 1, 1938, he was appointed Chief Diplomatic Adviser to the Foreign Secretary and promoted G.C.B. It was a new office which the Government justified by the increasing pressure of foreign affairs. In 1940 he was sworn of the Privy Council, and in 1941, having retired on pension, was raised to the peerage.

In the course of his busy life he contrived to find time to write a number of poems, books, and plays. *The Singing Caravan* (1933) was perhaps his best achievement. He entered the region of Oriental romance and displayed both his dexterous gift of rhyming and his faculty for fantastic metaphor and imagery. He contributed an admirable poem upon the fall of France to *The Times* in 1940 and another in June 1944, just after D Day. In 1913 two of his comedies, *The Cap and Bells* and *People Like Ourselves,* were played in London; they were unpretentious but to their audiences amusing enough. His *Dead Heat,* produced at Malvern in 1939, pursued an entertainingly cynical theme, but not very effectively. In *Pity's Kin* he tried his hand at an historical novel, but though there was true intellectual quality behind it he attempted to put more into it than he could well express.

After his retirement he published a number of books and pamphlets, chiefly concerned with the problem of Germany, but also looking askance at Soviet Communism: *Lessons of My Life* (1943), *Bones of Contention* (1945), *Events and Shadows* (1948), *Even Now* (1949), and a volume of poems, *Green and Grey* (1944).

Lady Vansittart and one daughter by his first wife survive him.

February 15, 1957.

Daniele Varè, who spent most of his years in the Italian diplomatic service in China; who wrote with lively grace and humour of life in Peking as he himself experienced it after 1911, and as the lotos-eaters of the Corps Diplomatique knew and enjoyed it in the halcyon days before the Republic; and who was also a serious student of English history in the nineteenth century and of Anglo-Italian relations, died in February 1956 at Rome, at the age of 76.

He was born in Rome in 1880, the son of Giambatista Varè, who was a friend of Mazzini and the companion in exile of Daniele Manin and his wife Elizabeth Chalmers, a Scotswoman. In youth he studied the violin under Joachim in Berlin and for some little time hesitated between music and diplomacy in the choice of a career. He served first in the Italian Embassy in Vienna, to which he was appointed as an attaché in 1907, was recalled to the Foreign Office in Rome in 1909, and three years later went out as first secretary to the Italian Legation in Peking, where he remained until 1920.

After his return to Europe in that year he served for a period as a member of the political section of the League of Nations Secretariat, first in London and afterwards at Geneva. Then came a spell as a virtual free-lance in diplomacy, during which he worked under Mussolini at the Palazzo Chigi, until in 1927, with crisis thickening in China, he returned to Peking, a recognized expert on Chinese affairs, as Minister. It was in many ways, as he sadly acknowledged, a very different Peking from that he had known before. He remained in China until 1932. His subsequent and final appointment was as Minister in Copenhagen and Reykjavik.

A leisurely and rather cynical diplomat of the old school, Varè's reminiscences of his career, *Laughing Diplomat*, published in Britain, where it was something of a best-seller, in 1938, reveal an engaging personality of epicurean taste and whimsical humour, lightly addicted to a semi-Oriental philosophy and at all times an acute observer of the human comedy. The author is at times frankness itself about his own affairs and provides some nicely finished sketches of notable people and a great many entertaining stories (Varè was an exceptionally good *raconteur*). In his much later volume of reminiscences, *The Two Impostors* (1950), he shows a grasp of the affairs of Europe in the 1930s, only thinly disguised by his inimitable lightness of touch.

The two volumes of his history of nineteenth-century England, which appeared here in 1924, are a sound and stimulating piece of work, marked by conspicuously intelligent use of Anglo-Italian material. In a different and perhaps even more characteristic vein are *The Maker of Heavenly Trousers* and *The Gate of Happy Sparrows*, the one a delicate romance of old Peking, the other a collection of Chinese, or at least extra-territorial Chinese, stories and sketches. Varè exhibited in these books, and in one or two others of the same kind, a rare mastery of language and many felicities of style.

He married, in 1909, Elizabeth (Bettina) Maryons, *née* Stansfeld, who was of Scottish origin, and by whom he had three daughters.

February 29, 1956.

The death by his own hand of **President Vargas** of Brazil on August 24, 1954 brings to a close the remarkable career of a man who, for the past 24 years, has dominated the political scene in a country noted, in the words of one of its foreign ministers, for "the paradox of sometimes turbulent internal politics and tact and prudence in foreign relations".

For almost 19 of these 24 years Dr. Vargas occupied the Presidency. He seized it as a successful revolutionary in October 1930; used it as an instrument of authoritarian rule until he was ousted in October 1945; and was re-elected to it in October 1950, by popular vote. Brushed from power by the popular clamour for a democratic régime when the war ended, he was swept back into the Presidency after an interval of five years in which democratic liberties were established by a massive majority of votes at the free elections he had for so long denied to Brazilians. Once regarded as a thoroughgoing, if benevolent, dictator, he became President for the second time thanks to a thoroughly democratic Constitution not of his own making.

Getúlio Dornelles Vargas was born on April 19, 1883, at São Borja near the Argentine border in Rio Grande do Sul, Brazil's southernmost state. Descended from a land-owning family, Portuguese in origin, he was brought up in the free and easy life of the *gaucho* (plainsman). At 16 he entered the Army as a private and went on to train for a commission. But at 20 he turned from military life to the law, and like so many other South Americans made this a stepping-stone to politics. At 26 he became a deputy in the legislature of his native state, where several small-scale local revolutions provided him with a useful apprenticeship for his later rise to power. Not until 1923, in his fortieth year, did Dr. Vargas emerge into federal politics, to sit in the Chamber of Deputies in Rio de Janeiro as a deputy for Rio Grande do Sul. Rising rapidly in political prestige, he became Minister of Finance before returning to his own state as Governor in 1928. There he had a host of able political friends, and with their help it was an experienced and determined Vargas who returned to the federal capital in 1930 at the head of a victorious revolution.

The circumstances of this successful bid for the Presidency were rooted in the pattern of Brazilian politics. For years the two important states of São Paulo and Minas Geraes had taken it in turns to nominate candidates for the Presidency, and the victory of these alternating candidates had been taken for granted. This was a state of affairs which virtually froze southern aspirants from the state of Rio Grande do Sul out of the highest office.

Forming in the south his so-called Liberal Alliance, which promised to end political corruption and economic chaos, Dr. Vargas made for Rio de Janeiro. His *coup* was modelled on political fashions in Europe as well as South America; it was reminiscent of the first stirrings of totalitarianism in Germany and Italy. It was also favoured by Brazilian unrest engendered by the world depression, which for Brazil meant a coffee slump. And among political leaders it had the ready allegiance of idealists so diverse as Dr. Osvaldo Aranha, the country's present Minister of Finance, who championed the cause of friendship with the United States and brought Brazil into the last war, and Luiz Carlos Prestes, an orthodox communist leader who professed to speak for the "submerged masses" of under-privileged Brazilians.

Both men joined Dr. Vargas in his descent on Rio after a train journey reminiscent of Mussolini's "March on Rome". But it was not the revolution of which either the staunchly Pan American Aranha or the Marxist Prestes had dreamed. Aranha was soon "exiled" to the Brazilian Embassy in Washington, and Prestes was gaoled by Vargas for 10 years after returning from a visit to Moscow. As for Vargas himself, he gradually tightened his hold on the centres of political power where counter-revolutions might, and on three occasions did, spring up to challenge his authority. His henchmen were firmly entrenched throughout the country's 20 states when, in 1937, he formed the *Estado Novo*.

Under the *Estado Novo*, which owed much of its inspiration to Mussolini's corporate State, Congress was closed. All political parties—right, left, and centre—were suppressed. Censors and propagandists occupied the House of Deputies, where their typewriters echoed ironically. Dr. Vargas's power was at last complete, and entirely personal. Brazil, one of his War Ministers since remarked, is easier to dominate than to govern. Under the *Estado Novo* Dr. Vargas did both.

It was the end of the war, and a broken pledge, that eventually broke up the *Estado Novo*. As the war finished there was a popular cry for a democratic régime. Early in 1945 Dr. Vargas began to yield to demands for the abolition of dictatorship at home. Party politics were allowed again, press censorship was lifted and political prisoners freed. The President promised to stand aside for a successor to be chosen at free and honest elections. Five weeks before these elections were due, however, he made changes in his entourage which were taken as a sign that he was about to go back on his promise. A group of exasperated generals who had sworn to uphold the promise of free elections wrung from him his resignation. Public opinion, siding with the newly fledged political parties, was behind the Army.

For the next five years, under the constitutionally elected President Dutra*, Dr. Vargas was often out of sight but never out of mind politically. His deposition left him a free citizen with full political rights, and he won a seat in the Senate. Though he seldom sat there, he asserted his place once more in national affairs as leader of a newly formed Labour Party and lived quietly for most of the time on his ranch near São Borja. As President Dutra's term neared its end in 1950 it became clear that in the approaching presidential election, due in October of that year, Dr. Vargas would once more bid for the Presidency, this time by offering himself for election. His success at the polls made it clear that for working-class Brazilians, humble, impulsive folk who warm to personalities rather than parties, he had never really lost his appeal.

Dr. Vargas's career marks him as a consummate politician. Like many politicians in Brazil he spoke in riddles, a form of appeal which the Brazilians call *confusionismo*. It is perhaps the most important political "ism" in Brazil, one which has fogged the course of Brazilian politics and long hindered their interpretation abroad. Dr. Vargas was an adept at *confusionismo*. He was also a man of great personal courage. While he awaited the ultimatum which deposed him in 1945 he calmly discussed his dinner menu, as usual, with a manservant. And in the revolutions which threatened to unseat him before that, he personally led his troops and defended himself with a rifle in his palace in Rio. His personal courage was certainly one source of his political prowess. Another was his ability to keep his own counsel. But, although his popularity among the workers appears to have declined in recent months, he will perhaps be best remembered for what he did for them and tried to do.

August 25, 1954.

By the death of **Dr. Ralph Vaughan Williams,** O.M., which occurred at his home in London on August 26, 1958 at the age of 85, English music loses a composer of genius, which from a slow and sometimes fumbling start advanced with steadily increasing power into old age. He was a pioneer of English nationalism in music and the first composer since the Elizabethans to reflect the spirit of all things English, the permanent essence behind all manifestations of fashion and period, in an output that embraced every kind of music.

Where Elgar's service to the English musical renaissance had been to put England once more on the map of European music, Vaughan Williams's was to speak with the authentic voice of England so that its accent was unmistakable.

Continental opinion, in the persons of the critics whom the British Council invited to London in 1935, at once recognized this distinction between two near contemporaries, both composers of genius, whose musical roots were in the one case eclectic and in the other national—as men they were equally representative, though Vaughan Williams was of that rarer type that combines radical opinions with a passion for the abiding traditions of English life, like the late Lord Wedgwood—with whose family he was connected—and the late Henry Nevinson, to take instances of the same type drawn from other walks of life. Vaughan Williams's position in the revival has also to be plotted from the previous generation, *i.e.* by comparison with Parry and Stanford, who did most for the English renaissance in its early days without quite succeeding in writing as much music bearing the hall-mark of greatness as did either Elgar or Vaughan Williams. Vaughan Williams and his life-long friend, Gustav Holst, together made the clean cut from Continental, *i.e.* German-Italian, influences, that English music needed if it was to attain strong and independent growth. This aspect of his career becomes apparent in the story of his musical education.

Ralph Vaughan Williams, like Parry and Elgar, was a West countryman. He was born in the Cotswolds at Down Ampney, where his father was vicar, on October 12, 1872. The family tradition was for the law rather than the arts. His grandfather, Sir Edward Vaughan Williams, was a judge of the old Court of Common Pleas from 1847 to 1865; his great grandfather, Serjeant John Williams (1757-1810), was a profound master of the common law; and his uncle, Sir Roland Vaughan Williams, Lord Justice of Appeal from 1897 to 1914, was eminent both at the Bar and on the bench. There are Vaughan Williamses who are lawyers to-day.

But Ralph showed sufficient bent for music while still at school at Charterhouse to cause him to devote two years to study at the Royal College of Music before going up to Trinity College, Cambridge, in 1892. He took his B.Mus. while still an undergraduate in 1894. His teachers were Parry and Stanford at the R.C.M. and Charles Wood at Cambridge. The latter confessed in after years that he had no hopes of Vaughan Williams as a composer in his student days, and certainly progress towards his distinctive message was slow. He learned the organ from Alan Gray at Cambridge and from Parratt at the R.C.M., and proceeded, after a second period of study at the R.C.M. (1895-96), to an organistship at South Lambeth Church.

He was not obliged, however, to turn his whole energies to the immediate necessities of earning a living, and as he was still not satisfied with his technical equipment he took more composition lessons from Max Bruch in Berlin. He proceeded to his D.Mus. degree at Cambridge in 1901, but a year or two later the dissatisfaction which had caused him to discard his early works sent him also to work with Ravel on refining his technique. Fine points of craftsmanship have never been a feature of his work, but what he really was seeking was not so much technical facility as a basis for his style. This he found ultimately in folk-song.

Folk-song with its modal scales and pastoral atmosphere was both the major formative influence and an abiding interest in Vaughan Williams's musical life. He joined the recently founded Folk Song Society in 1904, began to collect in the field himself, made Cecil Sharp's acquaintance, and supported him in his missionary zeal. But he also went further, and as a result of his collecting experiences in Norfolk composed three *Norfolk Rhapsodies*—the orchestral rhapsody was the then accepted medium of fertilizing original work by traditional melody—and an orchestral impression, *In the Fen Country*.

This work contains no quotations of folk melody but anticipates the Pastoral Symphony of 1922, where the patience and ruminative wisdom of rural England finds its fullest expression. The inflexions of folk-song were so assimilated in his mind that they became determinants of his harmony, which has rightly been described as neo-modal.

His melodic idiom, though nourished on folk-song, became more and more personal: his folk-opera *Hugh the Drover*, written to a text by Harold Child just before the First German War, shows it in its first flush of individuality. All through his life Vaughan Williams made settings for, and arrangements of, folk-songs, and such was the affinity between the traditional and the modern musician that each enhanced the individuality of the other; his very personal idiom in some way brought out the essence of the folk-song instead of over-laying it.

Other influences that tended to make him English of the English at a time when it was the most natural thing in the world for British musicians to look abroad for models and for inspiration as well as for training, were the contact with church music already mentioned, active participation in the competitive festival movement, the editing of two volumes for the Purcell Society, and interest in the Tudor revival, which took shape during the early years of the century.

By 1912 he had formulated his nationalist creed in a striking article contributed to the *R.C.M. Magazine*, in which he asked why British composers did not "take and purify and raise to the level of great art" the forms of musical expression that surrounded them in the music-hall, the Salvation Army, Welsh hymn-singing, and other equally humble manifestations of native popular music. "Have all these nothing to say to us?" They certainly had to him, as the London Symphony testifies, but so also had the more conventional music-makings of the provincial festivals. By that time he had made his first contributions to the Three Choirs Festivals, notably the *Fantasia on a Theme of Tallis* for strings (1910), which has gone into the repertory of Continental orchestras, the "Five Mystical Songs" (1911), first of a line to be developed much further in later years, and the simple but uniquely moving *Fantasia on Christmas Carols* (1912).

Meantime the Leeds Festival of 1907 had set him on the path of choral music which is the most natural for an English composer to tread. "Toward the Unknown Region" made it clear that a new and vigorous recruit had enlisted in the forces led by Parry. The text of Walt Whitman was ethical and liberal, not religious, and he followed up this challenging cantata with a bigger work in the same vein, *A Sea Symphony*, produced at Leeds in 1910. The American rhapsodist again provided the text of a cantata in four movements dealing with that abiding call of the sea to which the Anglo-Saxon race must always attend. Whitman too provided most of the text of a cantata *Dona Nobis Pacem* which 25 years later was wrung from the composer, along with the violent symphony in F minor, during the decade of the fascist doctrine of force. *Dona Nobis Pacem* was more an occasional piece than a unified work of art in its own right, and the composer's creed of seizing upon any aspect of national life as the occasion for music prompted him to write a number of other cantatas for specific purposes and circumstances.

His setting of *Benedicite* for his own Leith Hill Festival, and his setting of the *Te Deum*, in which a morris dance tune is embedded, for the coronation of King George VI, are two instances of many. He never wrote, however, a full-scale oratorio, though *Sancta Civitas* to a text from *Revelation* comes nearest to a biblical oratorio and *Hodie* (1954) is a species of Christmas oratorio. His setting of the Mass in G minor for double unaccompanied choir was the most completely religious of his choral works, as his *Five Tudor Portraits* is the most full characteristic of his secular cantatas. The suggestion that he should set the words of the vigorous Tudor poet Skelton was made to him by Elgar, who perceived the affinity of the two outspoken Englishmen. This suite was produced at the Norwich Festival of 1936 and was not followed by any other substantial choral work until *Hodie*. One more occasional work, the *Serenade to Music* written for 16 specifically named soloists with orchestra, to celebrate Sir Henry Wood's jubilee (1938), must be mentioned, though it is not very typical Vaughan Williams and in its particular sensuousness suggests Delius, with whom he had nothing in common.

For the stage Vaughan Williams wrote, besides the two-act ballad opera *Hugh the Drover,* two one-act operas to serious texts, two full length comic operas, and two ballets. An unfinished opera on the *Pilgrim's Progress* harks back for its subject to *The Shepherds of the Delectable Mountains* of 1922, and provided some of the thematic material for the Symphony in D. The earliest incidental music for the theatre was for a Ben Jonson production at Stratford-on-Avon in 1905, but the most celebrated was for the Cambridge production in 1909 of Aristophanes's *The Wasps,* of which the overture has obtained a world-wide currency as an independent composition. The only opera that compares with those in the ordinary repertory is *Sir John in Love,* 1929, a four-act treatment of *The Merry Wives of Windsor* in which some traditional tunes, notably "Greensleeves", are incorporated as well as some settings of non-Shakespearian verse in a felicitous neo-Elizabethan style.

The Poisoned Kiss is even more an extravaganza than is constituted by the farcical antics of Sir John Falstaff, and in spite of some very lovely lyrical music, the dialogue provided by Evelyn Sharp [q.v.] was not well received by audiences who, except in the case of W. S. Gilbert, prefer humour to riotous wit. Contemporary with this comic opera (*viz.* 1926-27, though not produced till 10 years later) is the word-for-word setting of *Riders to the Sea,* which is at the opposite pole of tragic feeling and of declamatory method. The greatest and certainly the most successful of all the stage works, however, is the ballet *Job,* which was inspired not by the words of Scripture but the engravings of William Blake. Into the music is caught up the vein of mysticism which received overt expression in the short oratorio *Sancta Civitas* and many of the songs; it takes some hints from the classical and folk-dance forms in which it is composed; but its greatness lies in the way in which it combines with the other arts of drama, dancing, and design to make a perfect unity. Like other great dramatic music *Job* stands firmly on its own feet as a symphonic suite characteristic of its composer and typical of his technical modernity.

The technical freedom which constitutes modernism for him has its roots in the substitution of a modal for a major-minor framework of melody and harmony—the G Minor Mass is the *locus classicus* for this feature of Vaughan Williams's style. But the choral suite *Flos Campi* of 1925 (two years later) shows even more clearly his emancipation from all nineteenth-century procedure. It opens with an oboe solo playing a rhythmically free and unbarred melody in a sort of Dorian mode in E against a viola solo playing an equally free melody in a kind of F minor, so that clashes between flats and naturals are recurrent. For sheer dissonance, however, which is the vulgar test of modernism, the opening of the F minor symphony shows the composer's unflinching use of tonal asperity.

Flos Campi, incidentally, is the work where sheer sensuousness—in keeping with its text from the *Song of Songs*—is cultivated most assiduously in the composer's whole output until the Eighth Symphony (first performed in 1956), in which he experiments with sonority for its own sake. Elsewhere it is, though common enough in occurrence, a by-product of the thought, as in all nine symphonies, except Number Eight.

But in the last 15 years of his life it became apparent that the symphonies, nine in all, of which the last had its first performance at a philharmonic concert on April 20, 1958, form the most significant part of his output. They cover a vast range of human experience, though they do not explore the intra-subjective emotions of Beethoven's nine, and all have in some degree a specific programme. Indeed, the first three bear names—the Sea, the London, and the Pastoral. Number Four deals with the dominance of violence in European affairs that was manifest by 1935, when it came out. Number Five (1943) tells the opposite story, of inner peace, and might well have been the composer's testament. Number Six embodies the experience of war (1948), in which the finale, one of the strangest documents in the history of music, is prophetic. Number Seven is called *Sinfonia Antartica.* Number Eight is lighter and concerns itself with the musical issues of orchestral tone-colour. Number Nine resembles it in some respects but contains the only note of disillusionment and despair to be found in the whole of his published utterance.

Vaughan Williams received many honours and declined some. He avoided any official connexions that might impede the expression of his often downright and frankly unofficial opinions. He accepted an O.M. from the King in 1935, an honorary doctorate from Oxford in 1919, a life fellowship of the Worshipful Company of Musicians in 1934, and the gold badge of the English Folk Dance and Song Society in 1943.

During the war of 1914-18 he served in the R.A.M.C. as an orderly and the R.G.A. as a lieutenant.

As a practical musician he had at one time conducted the London Bach Choir, and from 1905 onwards he directed the Leith Hill Festival. He edited *The English Hymnal* and contributed to it many tunes, of which the most notable is "Sine Nomine" to "For all the Saints". Of his literary output, the chief book was *National Music,* a statement of his own artistic creed. He served upon his fair share of committees and he taught composition at the R.C.M. for 20 years. These valuable activities, which he regarded as his proper contribution to the musical life of his day and generation, never got in the way of his main business, which was to compose original music.

Complete and obvious integrity, personal modesty, a sometimes quite wicked humour, quixotic and sometimes wrongheaded chivalry, combined with a certain burliness of physique that somehow seemed to match the directness of his thought and character, made him revered by all, beloved by many, and idolized by a privileged few.

He married first in 1897 Adeline, daughter of Herbert W. Fisher, and sister of H. A. L. Fisher. She died in 1951 and he married secondly in 1953 Ursula, daughter of Major-General Sir Robert Locke and widow of Lieutenant-Colonel J. M. J. Forrester Wood, R.A.

August 27, 1958.

Professor Henry Van de Velde died in October 1957 in a Zürich clinic. He was 94. Since 1947 he had lived in Switzerland.

He was often regarded as the originator of *Art Nouveau.* Yet that convenient label for a characteristic type of decorative design adopted by a host of miscellaneous artists during the opening phase of his campaign for "liberation from the shackles of the past" is one he always deprecated for his own work, which after 1914 evinced hardly any trace of it. What is less generally realized is that he was undoubtedly the real founder of the whole Modern Movement in architecture and applied design, and gave the world the first completely untraditional examples of each—little as a superficial glance at them after the lapse of over half a century would seem to substantiate the claim.

The astonishingly wide field he covered in both, and the prestige which for long invested his name, are sufficient proof of how tenaciously he fought for his ideas and how largely they prevailed. It is no exaggeration to say that the extent to which he was emulated, or more often directly imitated, throughout Central Europe between 1898 and 1914 brought about a startling transformation in the appearance of most towns and middle-class homes in those countries. And it was on the solid foundations of the revolutionary school of arts and crafts he established in 1906 at Weimar (and in the very building he had designed for it) that Gropius* subsequently developed the Bauhaus.

Born at Antwerp on April 30, 1863, the son of a chemist, Van de Velde began his career as a painter. He studied at the Antwerp Academy of Arts and at the studio of Charles Verlat. He then went to Paris to study under Charles Duran. On his return to Belgium from Paris (where he had known Signac, Seurat, Toulouse-Lautrec, and Pissaro) he joined "Les Vingt", a group of independent artists, writers, and composers which soon reconstituted itself into "La Libre Esthétique". At the 1892 exhibition by Les Vingt, which included Kelmscott Press books and graphic work by the Art-Workers' Guild sent from England, he showed an extremely unconventional cartoon for a *pointilliste* tapestry of "angels (bereft of wings and haloes) keeping watch over a new-born child".

It was, he said, while watching his aunt, a professional embroideress, execute this design, and reading Ruskin and Morris, that he became convinced there was no social justification for his remaining "an easel painter". Although the first Continental artist to take up their crusade and to endorse their ethical repudiation of every style since Gothic, he was in no other sense a disciple of Morris or Ruskin.

His first essays, published in the review *La Société Nouvelle* (*Déblaiement d'Art* and *Aperçus en Vue d'un Synthèse* are, historically, the most important), declared that it was the manifest moral duty of the modern age to create a contemporary style, sovereignly independent of all past styles, adding as a rider, what he never ceased to reiterate throughout his life, that designers must be imbued with a high moral sense of their social mission.

The revolt against academic sterility and the slavish copying of traditional motifs, which he had begun to lead in a sort of loose association with the Liégeois cabinet-maker Serrurier-Bovy and the Brussels architects Horta and Hankar, soon shook off all remnants of English influence, and until after 1897 was entirely confined to Belgium. Well before then Van de Velde was drawing apart from the other three through the development of what became one of his basic principles: that the designer's purpose and his means of expressing it should be inseparable, ornament being the appropriate accentuation needed to inform a particular intention or function with vitality. Beginning with vignettes and decorative layouts for books, he progressively widened his scope until within a decade it included table silver and leatherware, jewelry, stained glass, ceramics, wallpapers, and textiles, besides the furniture which was his earliest title to fame and his stepping-stone to architecture. In 1899 he opened a shop in Brussels for their sale, and the following year gave his much-discussed lecture in Germany on *The Artistic Reform of Women's Clothes,* illustrated by fabrics and dresses designed by himself.

In 1894 he married Maria Sèthe, the daughter of a Belgian textile manufacturer whose German widow was one of his most ardent supporters. After the death of their first child Madame Sèthe insisted on building them a new home, at Uccle, entrusting Van de Velde with its design and that of all the furniture and household equipment. This Villa Bloemenwerf (1895) was a landmark in the evolution of modern architecture, but as the first house of radically untraditional design in Europe it aroused intense antagonism.

While it was building he received a visit from two complete strangers, Samuel Bing, the famous Parisian oriental art-dealer, accompanied by the young German art-critic Julius Meier-Graefe. Bing subsequently asked him to undertake the entire decoration and furnishing of three out of four rooms which were to stage an exhibition in Paris of what was to be called *Art Nouveau.*

That 1896 exhibition was a disastrous failure. Yet when the same three rooms, with a most peculiar rest-lounge added, were shown at the Dresden Art Exhibition the following year the whole German Press enthusiastically acclaimed them as "the genesis of the style of the future".

Through the influence of Count Harry Kessler, the enlightened connoisseur of modern art who was one of Eric Gill's earliest patrons, in 1901, Van de Velde became a court official of the Grand Duke of Saxe-Weimar charged with the duty of "raising the artistic level of design" in the manufactures and handicrafts of that then still semi-feudal Thuringian principality. By 1902 he had installed workshops at Weimar, where he taught the duchy's most promising artisans and craftsmen to execute modern designs, and in 1906 he inaugurated there the first comprehensive school of arts and crafts for training pupils concurrently in the technique and design, which was also the first to bear the since familiar designation of *Kunstgewerbeschule.* The eager demand for the new designs from the Thuringian factories at the annual Leipzig Trade Fairs reflected the outstanding success of the twin institutes he directed, and by 1908 this had given the necessary fillip for the foundation of the German *Werkbund,* of which Van de Velde was a joint-founder and one of its leading and most vigorous personalities. His curiously squat and low-pitched theatre (which had a tripartite stage) for the famous Werkbund Exhibition in Cologne of 1914 revolutionized auditorium design.

The 1914-18 War eventually compelled Van de Velde to seek refuge in Switzerland. When it was over he worked for some years in Holland. In 1925 he was appointed Directeur-Général of the Institut des Arts Décoratifs in Brussels, a post he relinquished only in 1936; he entirely reorganized the architectural school and compiled his *Formules d'une Esthétique Moderne* for the students.

The Belgian Pavilions at the Paris, 1937, and New York, 1939, international exhibitions, and the towering library block for the University of Louvain, were his last executed designs.

October 28, 1957.

Paul Cairn Vellacott, C.B.E., D.S.O., Master of Peterhouse, Cambridge, died at Cambridge on November 15, 1954 at the age of 63. He had been in poor health for some time.

The son of the late E. W. Vellacott, he was born on May 24, 1891, and was educated at Marlborough. In 1910 he went up to Cambridge with a scholarship to Peterhouse, where he read history. He obtained first-class honours in Part II of the Historical Tripos in 1913, and had it not been for the outbreak of war in August 1914 he would have taken up a history lectureship, to which he had actually been appointed, in the University of Hongkong. He enlisted as a private at the beginning of the war and was commissioned in the 7th Battalion The South Lancashire Regiment in September 1914. By 1917 he was second-in-command of his battalion, and in the same year he took over temporary command, with the rank of acting lieutenant-colonel, of the 9th Battalion The Cheshire Regiment. After Passchendaele he was appointed brigade major to a regular brigade (the 23rd) in the 8th Division.

From July 1915 he was serving with the B.E.F. in France, where he was three times mentioned in dispatches; and he received the D.S.O. in 1917 for service with his battalion in the field. In March 1918 he was wounded—his injuries seriously and permanently affected his health—and he was only picked up two days later by German stretcher-bearers. He was repatriated on New Year's Day, 1919, and from May to December in that year he was head of the Statistics Section at the Ministry of Munitions. It was possible at one moment that this would be followed by collaboration in a commercial undertaking in Africa.

In October 1919, however, he was elected a Fellow of Peterhouse, and from 1920 to 1934 he was tutor and lecturer in history there. The peculiar internal problems of that college, the post-war situation, the passage from one generation to another, and the changing character of the world at large made his tutorship important and put him in a strong position for exercising his administrative gifts. It might be said that it was really he who guided the destinies of the college as a whole throughout this period. In 1934 he became headmaster of Harrow, and once again the moment of his appointment was a strategic one; for the financial position of the school needed long and careful reconsideration and problems of large-scale reorganization had to be faced. One of these changes involved the transformation of housemasterships into salaried offices.

In 1939 he was elected Master of Peterhouse in succession to Professor Harold Temperley, his former mentor, but he remained at Harrow until the end of the year and faced the problems initially presented by the outbreak of war to a school which was at no great distance from the evacuation area.

In January 1941 he was appointed to the directorate of the Home Guard at the War Office. In 1941-42 he was touring the country as Inspector of Administration in the Home Guard. From 1942 he was in Cairo and Palestine, acting under the Foreign Secretary as head of a political warfare mission directed towards enemy-occupied countries in Europe and North Africa. It was his function to coordinate and consolidate the British effort, particularly on the Libyan front, in the Balkans, and in Italy; and, working in close relations with G.H.Q., he was responsible for propaganda and for the collection of propaganda intelligence material.

His sphere of action was about to be greatly expanded in 1944 as, under the Supreme Allied Commander, Sir Henry Maitland Wilson, he took over the whole Mediterranean theatre—a change which involved the transfer of his work from Cairo to Algiers. In the same year, however, his health made it necessary for him to resign, and he returned to Cambridge. "The work of consolidation which you achieved in Cairo", wrote the Foreign Secretary, "was a valuable contribution to the whole war effort in the Mediterranean". In 1946 he was made a C.B.E.

Vellacott was remarkable in his combination of administrative gifts (which included an unusual degree of meticulousness and patience in matters of detail, and occasionally the capacity for a swift and ruthless decision), with an extraordinary high regard for a classically austere form of scholarship, and at the same time a passion for things aesthetic. The compounding of these elements made him a distinctive figure. He was most happy when there was chaos that required to be turned into order and a considerable work of re-organization to be achieved. When this had been done he was inclined to chafe, and he recovered his deeper happiness only after he had moved to another task.

The intensity of the successive stages of his career as an administrator was attended by a considerable loss—to which a part of his personality was never reconciled—for it is only in one or two essays on the reign of James II and the period immediately afterwards that we can see him as a writer of history; though both in school and in the university he was most successful as a teacher, while in the privacy of a Cambridge "supervision" he could show to a pupil a sympathy and a kind of understanding that it would be difficult for anybody to surpass.

He married in 1929 Hilda Francesca, daughter of the late Sir Nevile Lubbock, K.C.M.G., who survives him. There were no children of the marriage.

November 16, 1954.

John Archibald Venn, C.M.G., LITT.D., President of Queens' College, Cambridge, who died in Cambridge on March 15, 1958 at the age of 74, was in many respects, and to a peculiar degree, representative of Cambridge.

Born on November 10, 1883, the son of Dr. John Venn, Senior Fellow of Caius and a conspicuous figure in the Cambridge of his day, he was nurtured in the corporate tradition of the old Cambridge, before the University became a chaos of specialized activities. After leaving Eastbourne College, John Venn went up to Trinity, where he read history and rode a motor bicycle long before the days of motor licences. He graduated in 1905, and in the next year he married Lucy, the only daughter of Sir William Ridgeway, that pugnacious Professor of Archaeology about whose name many legends still cling.

The years that followed were full of many interests, above all the study of East Anglian agriculture and birds. He was a keen tennis player and honorary secretary of the "Cock & Hen" Club. Though not a player of cricket, he came near to revolutionizing practice at the nets by inventing a bowling machine which could deliver the ball at any pace and with any required break. It bowled out the famous Australian Victor Trumper, who had doubted its efficacy, in three successive balls.

In the First World War John Venn served for two years as a captain in The Cambridgeshire Regiment; but his great abilities in the field of agricultural economics were required elsewhere, and he went, as statistician, to the Food Production Department for two years, 1917-19, and then to the Ministry of Agriculture. In 1921 he returned to Cambridge as the first holder of the Gilbey Lectureship in the History and Economics of Agriculture, though remaining for many years an advisory officer of the Ministry. Settling down to academic life, he wrote that standard work *The Foundations of Agricultural Economics,* of which he produced a second, enlarged, edition in 1933.

Wishing to share the intimate life of a small college, he incorporated at Queens' (his grandfather's college) in 1924, and was there elected a Fellow in 1927. As Junior Bursar and Director in Economics he brought to the service of his adopted college his gifts of brisk efficiency and lucid thought; and in 1930-31 he successfully discharged the duties of Senior Proctor with firmness, humour, and common sense.

He was still the Junior Fellow when the President, Dr. Fitzpatrick, died in 1931. Venn was away with his wife on a year's leave when a telegram reached him in Shanghai, telling him that his colleagues proposed to elevate him from the foot to the head of the High Table. He came back at their call, and started a new life full to the brim of ever-increasing activity.

His varied excellence as a historian, a scientist, an administrator, and a man of affairs made him an outstanding personality in the university. He was on the Council of the Senate from 1934 to 1943, a magistrate for the borough, and a member of the Town Council, 1934-39; chairman of the county's Agricultural Wages Board; and president of the Cambridge Antiquarian Society, 1933-35. Further afield, he served on many government committees at home and abroad, such as the Commission on Higher Education in the Colonies, the Hongkong University Advisory Committee, and the Commission on the sugar industry in British Guiana. For these services he was appointed C.M.G. in 1956.

As head of his college he was an active and inspiring, but never an autocratic, leader, with an immense capacity for quick work. Large schemes of college building and internal reorganization owed everything to him. A colleague, distributing adjectives one night in the Combination Room, gave the President that of "factual". Perhaps "positive" would have been better.

Venn enjoyed grappling with problems of all kinds. He went to the heart of the matter, careless whether he was right in detail. No one was less of a pedant. His vigour and assurance carried plans along while others were still considering the attendant difficulties. Always keen to raise the wages of college servants, he would characteristically suggest doing so by some method for increasing income rather than by saving on expenditure. He was certainly not as those dons whose innocence in matters of money caused Cecil Rhodes to place his academic benefactions in the hands of non-academic trustees.

He remained young. When Vice-Chancellor and nearing 60 years, he still retained the springing gait of an athlete and a boy's infectious pleasure in the ridiculous.

Among the much appreciated courtesies of John Venn and his wife was certainly their practice of treating their lovely official residence at Queens' not more as their own residence than as the common property of the college, and of keeping its doors constantly open to the Fellows, their wives, and their children.

And all the while his scanty leisure was chiefly devoted to his biographical work, *Alumni Cantabrigienses.* All who have dipped into those fascinating volumes are aware of the skill and the meticulous accuracy with which all the relevant facts about all the known Cambridge men for seven centuries have there been collected and set out. The work made John Venn an encyclopaedia of the humorous and picturesque aspects of the history of Cambridge, and provided him with an inexhaustible fund of anecdote and scandal from the past.

Venn's last year was saddened by a painful illness, but his spirit never failed. He presided at the college meeting when plans of [Sir] Basil Spence [d. 1976] for the new building on the river front were finally approved, and would explain the features of the scheme with his accustomed zest and precision.

To some, perhaps their most vivid memories of John Venn will be recollections of his after-dinner speeches in college: the neat and youthful figure in the scarlet gown, the perfect command of English, the vigorous self-confidence, the genial humour, the thought appropriate to the time and place. In him a lively sense of the past and a love of tradition were combined with an eager zest for experiment, and made him representative at once of the continuity and of the enterprise necessary to our academic and to our national life.

March 17, 1958.

Sir Alliott Verdon-Roe, O.B.E., died on January 4, 1958 in his eighty-first year.

Perhaps no man has higher claims than Alliott Verdon-Roe to be called the Father of Flying. He was not the first to fly by five years, but he was the designer who set the fashion in aeroplanes which the world was content to follow for many years. He was the first Englishman who designed his own aircraft and flew it, and, as his designs were of more value to the world than the designs of those who preceded him, he deserves the highest honour of all.

Edwin Alliott Verdon-Roe was born on April 26, 1877, at Patricroft, near Manchester. He was educated first at a boarding school at Shepperton, near Brooklands, in Surrey, and afterwards at St. Paul's School. When only 15 years old he journeyed to British Columbia to assist in getting out drawings for a flying machine. Then he went through an apprenticeship of five years at the locomotive works of the Lancashire and Yorkshire Railway at Horwich, near Manchester. During this time he won many prizes in cycle races. Following this, he passed a test as a fitter at Portsmouth

Dockyard. Then the sea called him, and he entered King's College, London, to prepare for the examination for engineer in the Royal Navy. He passed well in engineering subjects, but failed in the general knowledge paper. So he turned to the merchant service, and went to sea as a marine engineer from 1899 to 1902.

In 1903 motoring had become an important factor in life, and Roe left the sea to become a draughtsman in a motor works. Three years later he decided to devote himself to mastering the art of practical flying. He was inspired by the reports which were coming through of the success of the Wright brothers, though these were not generally credited, and he himself wrote to Wilbur Wright and was proud to receive a reply from him.

In 1907 the *Daily Mail* offered prizes for model aeroplanes to be exhibited in the Agricultural Hall and flown at the Alexandra Park. There were 200 competitors. Roe entered three models. One of his models flew the whole length of the hall, and out of doors it covered over 100 feet. The motive power was twisted elastic. For this he received £75, the highest prize awarded. The first prize was withheld, and Roe remarked afterwards that the judges were all balloon aeronauts who did not seem in full sympathy with aeroplanes. However, the prize put him in funds and also encouraged him to set to work on a full-sized aeroplane.

Roe's first real aeroplane was a biplane with an elevator out in front. The engine was a 6 h.p. J.A.P., and in September 1907, at the close of the motor racing season, he installed it in a shed at Brooklands. A prize of £2,500 had been offered to the first man to fly round the track before the end of the year, and gradually a number of pioneers assembled at Brooklands, but they were not very popular with the track authorities. Roe found his 6 h.p. engine would not lift his machine, but he had the promise of the loan of a 24 h.p. eight-cylinder Antoinette from France.

When the Antoinette engine arrived in the spring of 1908 Roe began to make progress, and on June 8, 1908, he was convinced that his machine actually lifted and flew for 75ft. at a height of 2ft. from the ground. Owing to a lack of competent witnesses the Royal Aero Club was unable to accept this officially as the first flight on British soil. The point, however, is somewhat academic. There is no doubt that shortly afterwards Roe did actually fly in this same machine, and in any case he was the first man of British blood to design his own aeroplane and fly it. He has the additional honour that before long the whole world preferred to copy his designs rather than those of America and France.

Shortly afterwards Roe was obliged to leave Brooklands, and he also had to part with his Antoinette engine. One of his brothers, Dr. S. Verdon Roe, gave him leave to use his stable in Putney, and there he built his famous triplane, and installed a 9 h.p. J.A.P. engine. This machine is now preserved in the Science Museum at South Kensington.

In September 1909 Blackpool held a great flying meeting, and Roe took his triplane there. The weather was gusty, and the 9 h.p. engine would not take the machine off the ground.

Next year another of Roe's brothers, H. V. Roe, decided to give him a helping hand. He was the head of an engineering firm in Manchester, and he put facilities for construction at his brother's disposal. The two formed the company of A. V. Roe & Company, Limited. Two triplanes were built for the 1910 Blackpool meeting, but an accidental fire destroyed both in the railway truck. By dint of furious work another machine was got ready in time, and in it Roe flew three circuits of the course, but he said it was the worst machine that he had ever made.

Towards the end of 1910 Roe designed and built a tractor biplane with a 25-h.p. engine, which was the forerunner of the famous 504 type Avro. Roe's new lay-out was revolutionary, and before long it achieved such success that well nigh the whole world became converted to the principle of the tractor biplane. This first machine of the type was afterwards fitted with floats and flown at Barrow-in-Furness, and was the first seaplane to rise off the water in England.

In 1912 came the world-famous 504 type Avro, driven in the first place by an 80-h.p. Gnôme. No other type of aircraft has rendered so many years of active usefulness. During the First World War it was first used as a bomber, and the raid on the aeroplane sheds at Friedrichshafen by Commander Briggs and two other R.N.A.S. officers was made in three Avros. When the increase in the speed of other aircraft forced the Avro out of the fighting line, it continued in use as the standard training machine of the flying services, and such, using various types of engine, it continued to be for many years after the Armistice.

Even before the supreme merits of the Avro 504 had been generally recognized Roe was producing other types. In the same year he turned out an enclosed monoplane and later an enclosed biplane, forestalling by many years the cabin type which is now in general use for civil types of aircraft. The enclosed biplane was entered for the military aircraft trials which were held on Salisbury Plain in 1912, and in it F. P. Raynham established a British duration record by flying for over seven and a half hours.

Next year the outbreak of war put an end to the financial anxieties of all British aircraft firms. Their trouble then was, not to get orders, but to comply with the demands of the Government. By 1918 Great Britain had the largest air force in the world, and practically all the pilots had been taught to fly on Avros. The country owed a debt to A. V. Roe which it first tried to repay by appointing him O.B.E. Ten years later, on June 8, 1928, the twentieth anniversary of his first flight, all the aeronautical bodies in the kingdom united in giving him a dinner. Shortly afterwards he was knighted.

About the same time a commanding interest in the management of the firm of A. V. Roe & Co., Ltd. was acquired by the firm of Armstrong-Siddeley Motors Ltd., and Sir Alliott Roe decided to sell out his share in the company which bore his name. He then bought an interest in S. E. Saunders Ltd., of Cowes, the famous firm of boat builders, which had also built a number of flying-boats. The name of this firm was then changed to Saunders-Roe Ltd., and the flying-boats which they produced were known by the name of Saro.

Verdon-Roe was always quite unspoilt by success, as he had been unabashed by early failures and criticisms. Indomitable in purpose and reckless of personal risk, he remained always the gentlest and most kindly of men, owning a host of friends and not a single enemy.

January 6, 1958.

Adela Verne, whose playing of the piano delighted audiences all over the world for more than half a century, died suddenly at her home in London on February 5, 1952.

Born at Southampton, she was the youngest member of the numerous family of the late Johann Wurm, a Bavarian musician who had settled at Southampton and became organist of St. Joseph's Church there at a salary of £20 a year. Her mother was Sophie Niggl, one of whose sisters was the mother of Eugen Pabst, the conductor, and another the mother of Sir Hubert Herkomer, R.A. The father was a dreamer, and the mother supported the family by giving piano lessons first at Southampton and then in London. Unfortunately she died soon after she had launched her elder daughters, Alice, Mary, and Mathilde, on their musical careers. Adela's musical education was thus left in the hands of her elder sister Mathilde, a pupil not only of her mother but of Clara Schumann and Franklin Taylor. Fortunately she was a splendid teacher, and until her death in 1936 conducted a very successful school of pianoforte playing in London. She was the sole teacher of her younger sister who, indeed, would learn from nobody else, and who, in order to cheat the embarrassment of family relations during a lesson, called herself Clara Jenkins and insisted upon being treated as a stranger.

As is so often the case with musicians, Adela's talent developed early and she could play many of Bach's Inventions by heart by the time she was four. At 15 she played the "Appassionata" to Paderewski, who then described her as "the little woman who plays like a man", and later sent her a fine piano, which she prized for the remainder of her life. She made her first public appearance in London in 1898, playing Tchaikovsky's Piano Concerto in B flat Minor under the baton of Sir August Manns, and at 17 began her long association with Sir Henry Wood and Queen's Hall. For many years she was a favourite with the audiences there both at the "Proms" and at the symphony concerts.

Meanwhile she made many tours of Europe and farther afield, giving concerts with such artists as Ysaye, Mischa Elman*, Clara Butt, and Tetrazzini. The famous "12 o'clock concerts" at the Aeolian Hall, organized by her sister Mathilde, owed much to her support, and the two sisters achieved a fine ensemble in works for two pianos. Both leaned towards the romantic in their style of playing and choice of programmes, in sympathy with the traditions in which they were brought up, but it was a romanticism founded upon technical mastery and the meticulous craftsmanship which was the great contribution that Mme. Schumann bequeathed to all her pupils and, through them, to later generations. Miss Verne's last recital took place at the Forum Club only a few weeks before she died.

February 6, 1952.

Sir Edmund Vestey, BT., chairman of the Union International Company and joint head of the Blue Star line, died suddenly in London on November 18, 1953 at the age of 87.

Sir Edmund Vestey's career was very similar to that of his elder brother, the first Lord Vestey, who died in 1940. They were natives of the same city, were educated at the same school, and made their large fortune in the same line of enterprise. Throughout their lives they were linked in business, each in his own way making his distinctive contribution to the success of that business—the refrigeration of food and its oversea transport—with which their names will always be associated. Sir Edmund had other interests beyond those in the Union Cold Storage Company and the Blue Star Line, but these two important concerns are the monument to the foresight, acumen, and industry of the brothers.

Edmund Hoyle Vestey, who was born on February 3, 1866, was the second son of Samuel Vestey, a Liverpool merchant. He was educated at the Liverpool Institute High School and went to America as a young man in the interests of his father's business. It was after an experience of the canning trade that he joined his brother in the foundation of the Union Cold Storage Company, which was known at first as the Union Cold Storage and Ice Company. This was started in Liverpool with a capital of £100,000. It was an immediate success, and the enterprise was extended to London where, at Blackfriars Bridge, a factory was opened. From that time forward the growth of the concern was steady and continuous. Its operations spread to many parts of the world until eventually the company's capital stood at about £12m. The first oversea factory was at Port Darwin, Northern Australia, but labour difficulties arose, and after eight years' struggle the Vesteys reluctantly transferred their activities to Argentina, and prospered in a way that placed their careers among the romances of industry.

In 1906, when they wanted to ship eggs, chickens, and other produce from China, they acquired two or three ships and converted them into refrigerated steamers. This was the beginning of the Blue Star Line, of which Sir Edmund was the joint head. But that line might never have reached its present proportions if the European steamship lines could have seen their way to guarantee the brothers regular sailings from Argentina for the transport of the output of their meat factory. Sure that the success of their venture depended on regular sailings, they decided to have their own fleet. Hence the development of the Blue Star Line, with its fine steamers operating between London and Brazil, Uruguay, and Argentina. The brothers also acquired a large number of retail shops for the sale of their chilled meat, and these proved extremely useful to them in their struggle with the American packers during the "meat war".

When war came in 1914 Sir Edmund was whole-heartedly with his brother in placing at the disposal of the Government all the vast resources of the company in cattle and cold storage accommodation at Boulogne, Havre, Dunkirk, and elsewhere, and in 1921 Sir Edmund was rewarded with a baronetcy.

His patriotism was by no means confined to the war years. In 1925 Sir Edmund announced that he and his brother had made a personal sacrifice out of their own pockets of £300,000 so that a £2,700,000 Blue Star Line contract for eight ships could go to British shipbuilders, that sum of £300,000 representing the difference between the home and the foreign contracts. In 1934 Sir Edmund joined his brother in an offer, gratefully accepted, to build, at an estimated cost of £220,000, the tower of Liverpool Cathedral in memory of their parents.

Sir Edmund's first wife, whom he married at New Jersey, United States, in 1887, was Ellen, daughter of Joseph Barker, of Formby, near Liverpool. There were five sons and two daughters. In 1926 he married secondly Ellen, daughter of the late Arthur Franklin Soward, of Sutton, Surrey. The eldest son died in 1932, leaving a son, Flight Lieutenant J. D. Vestey, R.A.F.V.R., who succeeds his grandfather in the baronetcy.

November 20, 1953.

The death of **Judge Sir Godfrey Russell Vick,** Q.C., on September 27, 1958 removes a well-known and familiar figure from the legal scene. He was 65.

He had not been in good health for some time and his friends were distressed to see the change which had come over his somewhat Pickwickian figure. If he did not achieve all that he had hoped for, he none the less had a successful career at the Bar, and his many activities showed him to be a person with a deep sense of civic duty.

Born on Christmas Eve 1892, the younger son of Richard William Vick, J.P., of West Hartlepool, Durham, he was educated at the Leys School, Cambridge, and Jesus College, Cambridge. During the First World War he was a captain in The Durham Light Infantry, and served on the General Staff of the 1st Army.

While home on leave in 1917 Vick was called to the Bar by the Inner Temple, of which he later became a Bencher. As such he was appointed Master of the Garden where, according to tradition, the Wars of the Roses started.

He built up a successful practice at the common law Bar and in criminal work, and took silk in 1935. He was a member of the North-Eastern Circuit and in 1930 was appointed Recorder of Richmond, Yorkshire, in succession to R. F. Burnand, who is now the Senior Master of the Queen's Bench Division. From 1931 to 1939 Vick was Recorder of Halifax and from 1939 to 1956 Recorder of Newcastle upon Tyne. In October of the latter year he was appointed a county court judge for the districts of Barnet, Hertford, St. Albans, Watford, and Edmonton.

In 1948 he was elected chairman of the General Council of the Bar, succeeding Gerald Slade*, K.C., who had been appointed a Judge of the High Court. In that year Vick attended the annual meeting of the Canadian Bar Association at Montreal. In 1950 he became co-president of the International Bar Association. He was knighted in the same year. He again went on duty abroad in 1952 when, as past chairman of the Bar Council, he represented the council at conferences held by the State Bar of California in Los Angeles, the American Bar Association in San Francisco, and the Canadian Bar Association in Vancouver.

Apart from his legal activities and the duties which he undertook arising therefrom, Vick also sat on a number of committees. In November 1944, he was appointed with Miss [later Dame] Myra Curtis* to consider and report on the provision of remand homes made by the London County Council and on the administration by the council of such homes. Their report was published as a White Paper in February 1945.

In 1948 Vick was the chairman of the important committee of inquiry into evasion of petrol rationing control which reported in February of that year. In October of the same year [Lord] Chuter Ede*, then Home Secretary, appointed Vick a member of the tribunal to inquire into allegations of irregularities affecting certain Ministers of the Crown and other public servants. The other members of the tribunal were the late Mr. Justice Lynskey [q.v.] (whose name is often given to the tribunal) and Gerald Upjohn, K.C. [later Lord Upjohn*].

In 1956 Vick was appointed to conduct an inquiry into allegations of ill-treatment of prisoners at Liverpool Prison.

Vick had a cheerful disposition, and was ever ready to give advice and help where needed. He was a good raconteur, and had a fund of legal stories; it was remarkable how he remembered them all and was able to produce them for the appropriate occasion. Among his recreations were hunting and golf; he captained the Bar Golfing Society in 1947. He had also played Rugby football for the Harlequins. His was a wide and sympathetic character. All human interests appealed to him and he responded to them with common sense, humour, and understanding.

He was elected Master of the Curriers' Company in 1947.

In 1920 he married Marjorie Hester, daughter of the late John Albert Compston, K.C., who with two sons and two daughters survives him.

September 29, 1958.

Professor Kenneth Hotham Vickers, Principal of University College, Southampton, from 1922 until 1946, died on September 5, 1958 at Southampton, at the age of 77.

He was the son of the Rev. Randall W. Vickers, vicar of Naburn, Yorkshire, and was educated at Oundle and Exeter College, Oxford. From 1905 to 1908 he was a lecturer in history at University College, Bristol, and for two years after that he was employed by the London County Council as organizer and lecturer in the history of London. Between 1908 and 1913 he was tutor to the London University joint committee for tutorial classes, and he was then appointed to the chair of modern history in the University of Durham. It was about this time that he published the fruits of his historical research—a biography of *Humphrey, Duke of Gloucester* (1907), *England in the Later Middle Ages* (1913), *A Short History of London* in the same year, and Vol XI of the Northumberland County History (1921).

In 1922 he was appointed principal of Hartley University College, Southampton, and from then onwards he was occupied with the administration of a growing institution. As he later recorded: "Throughout my 24 years as principal the lack of funds was a nightmare. A large part of my time and energy was spent in 'raising the wind' ". Soon after he took over, an ambitious appeal was launched to raise £500,000 to enable the university college to become the "University of Wessex". The Prime Minister, the leaders of the Liberal and Labour Parties, the Duke of Wellington, and Thomas Hardy gave the scheme their blessing. But the ultimate objective of university status was not reached until six years after Vickers's retirement, when in 1952 the University of Southampton was constituted by royal charter.

Still, large sums of money were collected, and expansion of both staff and buildings took place. A Thomas Hardy chair of English literature was founded in 1925, and the first lecturer in aeronautics appointed in the engineering department in 1936. A new library and hall were opened in 1935, and throughout his period as principal Vickers was a convinced believer in the virtues of residence for university students, to such good effect that Southampton could, and still does, manage to provide halls of residence for a higher proportion of its undergraduates than is common in university institutions.

Vickers was professor emeritus of the University of Southampton. He married in 1911 Alice Margretha, daughter of Dr. Edward Crossman. His wife died in 1948. They had one son.

September 6, 1958.

Vesta Victoria, one of the best of the women comic singers of the old music-halls, died at Swiss Cottage on April 7, 1951. She was 77.

Victoria Lawrence, daughter of Joe Lawrence, a music-hall performer, was born at Leeds on November 26, 1873, and first appeared on the stage when she was four as Baby Victoria. She was not quite 10 when, at the Cambridge Music Hall, she made her earliest London appearance. In the course of her career she performed at all the principal English music-halls and was also successful in America. She was a pleasant-faced, rather plump, fair-haired woman, with a low-pitched voice, and specialized in character songs in which she usually presented herself as the victim of some misfortune—even if it was only that "Daddy Wouldn't Buy Me a Bow-Wow", the memory of which has probably lasted longer than that of any of her other successes.

These included such numbers as "Waiting at the Church", "Now I 'ave to Call 'im Father", both of which dealt with the theme of the jilted maiden, "Poor John", "He Called Me His Own Grace Darling", and the song which she sang as an artist's model—"It's All Right in the Summer Time". She was never afraid of disguising herself in bedraggled clothes, and she delivered her songs with much energy and admirably clear diction.

Vesta Victoria retired from the music-hall stage comparatively early, about the end of the First World War, but in 1926 she made an extremely successful return to the stage, beginning at the Victoria Palace, where her revival of some of her old songs was warmly welcomed.

In 1912 she married W. G. H. Terry, whom she divorced in 1926.

April 9, 1951.

Henri Vidal, one of the most popular idols of the French screen, who died on December 10, 1959 at the age of 40, was born in Clermont-Ferrand, Puy-de-Dôme, on November 26, 1919.

After completing his schooling at Saint-Chamord he decided to try his luck in show business. He worked for some time in relative obscurity on the stage and in films, but his height, powerful physique and rugged good looks brought him before long to the notice of French film-goers, particularly the feminine members of the public, and his acting ability, though it never had any great demands made on it, proved equal to all the tasks it was set.

His first notable role was in *Fabiola,* a luxurious re-creation of ancient Rome which showed his talents to excellent effect in a number of action-sequences (he played a gladiator). While appearing in this film he met Michèle Morgan, its star, whom in 1950 he married. From then on he appeared frequently on the screen, and occasionally on the Paris stage—in such plays as *Jeunesse, Je vivrai un grand amour* and *Les Hauts de Hurlevent,* in which he made a commanding Heathcliff. His films were generally tough thrillers or comedies, and he specialized in gangster roles.

Among a large number of popular commercial films like *Quai de Grenelle, Une Manche et la Belle, Sois Belle et tais-toi,* and *Une Parisienne* (with Brigitte Bardot), a few remain memorable—Grémillon's *L'Etrange Madame X,* Guitry's [q.v.] *Napoléon* (in which he played Murat), and *Les Salauds vont en Enfer,* the first film of a member of La Nouvelle Vague, Robert Hossein—but he will probably be remembered chiefly for his appearance in René Clair's *Porte des Lilas,* in which he gave an excellent performance as the vicious and narcissistic crook whose incursion into the life of a pathetic down-and-out provides the emotional catalyst which sets the drama in motion. His last film was *Voulez-vous danser avec moi?* in which he starred with Brigitte Bardot.

December 11, 1959.

In the death of **Heitor Villa-Lobos** South America has lost an outstanding musical spokesman, Brazil its greatest musical figure, and the world its most prolific—by any standards a remarkable—composer. Villa-Lobos died on November 17, 1959, aged 72, after a cerebral haemorrhage.

He was born at Rio de Janeiro on March 5, 1887. He grew up amid Brazilian traditional music, and was encouraged by his father to learn musical instruments. Eventually he made the cello his special study, and spent several years travelling through Brazil, using his cello as a principal source of livelihood, but primarily discovering and absorbing the music of Brazil which permeated his own work.

Bach was his idol, early and late, and the inspiration of his *Bachianas brasileiras* (which numbered nine at the last count), a curious blend of Bach's style, as Villa-Lobos saw it, with the spirit of Brazilian music; Villa-Lobos once declared that he regarded Bach as a monumental folk-source valid for all countries and periods. Some of these morganatic musical children suggested neither Bach nor Brazil; but the fifth of them, written for a soprano and an orchestra of cellos, evoked an individual atmosphere and has become, perhaps, the best known of Villa-Lobos's works.

The *chorões,* Brazil's famous national music of the streets, inspired 15 works entitled *Chôros* from Villa-Lobos, scored (like the *Bachianas brasileiras*) for a variety of voices and/or instruments; thus the first *Chôros* is written for guitar, the third for a mixture of wind, brass, and male voices, the fourteenth for choir, military band, and orchestra.

A series of highly attractive and often individual piano pieces were set off by the friendship which the composer struck up in 1918 with young Artur Rubinstein. The *Prole do bêbê,* which date from this year, have become familiar through Rubinstein's recitals, as have, particularly, the *Rudepoema* and *Ciclo brasileiro;* England has also become acquainted with these, and with some of Villa-Lobos's five piano concertos, through the advocacy of Felicja Blumenthal and Ellen Ballon, who also dedicated themselves to the propagation of Villa-Lobos's music.

Often, one feels, it is not distinguished in its invention, often disparate in its resources, as might be expected of a composer whose natural genius and enthusiasm were never seriously disciplined by apprenticeship.

Besides Bach, Villa-Lobos was much influenced by his love of Wagner and Puccini, and later by Debussy. He underwent numerous ardent enthusiasms, mostly in the course of a lifelong zeal for musical education; choirs, and military and brass bands were among them. These influenced the direction that his own music took; all too often his compositions have appeared to be faulted by madcap infatuation of some temporary ideal. Yet in every one of his compositions that comes to performance (and there are so many that catalogues hesitate to list them all), an idealism and a strange individuality glow through the manifest miscalculations.

He was a pioneer, and even in his lifetime an interesting historical figure. Posterity must hesitate to judge whether he is the Bach or the Telemann of twentieth-century Brazil.

November 18, 1959.

Fred Vinson, the Chief Justice of the Supreme Court of the United States, died unexpectedly at Washington on September 8, 1953. He was 63.

As a Judge, a Congressman and an administrator, Vinson was one of the most distinguished Americans of his time. President Roosevelt used him during the war in a succession of posts of the first importance. President Truman* made him Secretary of the Treasury in 1945 and Chief Justice of the United States a year later. In each appointment he inspired confidence. Even though he was a firm Democrat and a Democratic President's nomination to the position of Chief Justice, he never inspired the same criticism or suspicion among Republicans as did some of his Democratic colleagues in the Supreme Court.

He was a Southern Democrat, having been born in Louisa, Kentucky, on January 22, 1890, the son of a lumber merchant. After graduating at Centre College, Kentucky, where he went from Kentucky Normal College, Vinson began in private law practice. In 1913 he was city attorney of Louisa and from 1921 until 1924 was commonwealth attorney for the thirty-second judicial district of Kentucky. He became a member of Congress in 1923 (his term extending until 1929) and again in 1931, this time remaining a member until he resigned in 1939 to become an associate justice of the United States Court of Appeals.

His early years in Congress were not spectacular, though he gained something of a reputation in the field of taxation and government finance, and was a strong supporter of liberal legislation. He sponsored the Goffey-Vinson Bill, regulating the bituminous coal industry, and was a keen promoter of the Walsh-Healy Act, enforcing higher standards for labour in the fulfilment of large government contracts. The Social Security Act of 1935 also had his warm support. He was the main author of the Revenue Bill of 1938, and as chairman of the internal revenue sub-committee of the Ways and Means committee of the House of Representatives he took the initiative in much other tax legislation.

Vinson, then, had made a name for himself as a loyal but not extreme, useful but not brilliant, New Dealer, when in 1939 he resigned from Congress to accept an appointment by President Roosevelt as associate justice of the United States Circuit Court of Appeals for the District of Columbia. He remained in this position until 1943, being also chief Judge of the Emergency Court of Appeal from 1942 until 1943, when Roosevelt called on him to succeed James F. Byrnes* as Director of the Office of Economic Stabilization. (Byrnes was transferred to the Office of War Mobilization). Both appointments were taken as a signal from the President that he was intent on a more vigorous prosecution of the war.

It was now that the qualities which had been recognized in Vinson as a Congressman—in particular his utter trustworthiness and his capacity for hard work—were seen to be reinforced by others of equal or even more importance in the political world. In the first place, though he was a Judge and was called "the Judge", he had learned the language of politics in his 14 years in Congress.

In the second place Vinson, though a conservative by instinct, was also acutely sensitive to political trends and popular pressures. If he was a New Dealer it was more as the result of a shrewd assessment of political realities than by passionate conviction. In Washington this gave him a start over many who were more rigidly fixed in one or other camps. In wartime it enabled him to see national needs clearly.

He became Director of Economic Stabilization at a time when the public had been brought to realize the need for price control, but there were still many interests—such as the farmers and some unions—pleading that theirs were special cases. These had powerful support in Congress, but Vinson, having determined that no section of the community should be unjustly treated or unfairly privileged, always managed to show strong grounds for any action he took and confidence in him grew rapidly.

In March 1945 Roosevelt transferred him to the post of Federal Loan Administrator, in charge of the Reconstruction Finance Corporation and its subsidiaries, but a month later Byrnes resigned from the post of Director of the Office of War Mobilization and Reconversion and Vinson was named to succeed him. On both occasions his appointments were unanimously confirmed by the Senate. There was again a unanimous confirmation when in July 1945 President Truman nominated him to succeed Henry Morgenthau* as Secretary of the Treasury.

Vinson was now in a position of supreme importance. The smooth reconversion of the United States economy was a matter of concern not only to Americans but to the rest of the world as well—and the policy of the United States Secretary of the Treasury could help or hinder that readjustment. So far as domestic policy was concerned, he was committed to "full employment", but his advocacy of it was fitted into a complete American philosophy which made it respectable and acceptable to those who might otherwise have been distrustful. For Vinson firmly believed that the enterpriser, working in a free economy, was the man best fitted to create a high level of production, a high level of national income—and, therefore, a high rate of employment. His taxation policy was based on the conviction that a United States Secretary of the Treasury should encourage the investor and the business man to expand production, and so provide the opportunity of employment.

In international financial policy Vinson's views were founded on the certainty that the world could not recover without American "investment" abroad. There could scarcely have been anyone better suited to present this case to Congress or the American public. He showed, throughout the debates on the loan to the United Kingdom in 1946, an unrivalled knack for presenting an investment in Britain's recovery not only as an "investment in peace" but also as an investment in American trade interests. If there were some who suspected this happy identification of American and British interests, many of their doubts were quietened by the awareness that both at the Bretton Woods Monetary and Financial Conference in 1944, when he was vice-chairman of the United States delegation, and during the Anglo-American financial conference in Washington, when he was chairman of the finance committee, he had shown a capacity for holding out longest which served his country well.

In June 1946 President Truman appointed Vinson Chief Justice of the Supreme Court. His nomination was widely welcomed, but it removed from the President's Cabinet one of the strongest of its members and ablest of its administrators. In his new and elevated position Vinson maintained and enhanced his reputation for integrity. In the United States, where judicial appointments are political appointments, judges are not exempt from political criticism. But no Republican could question the judicial honesty and fairness with which he faced even the most awkward issues. The two most controversial decisions taken by the Supreme Court during his term of office were the declaration, in 1952, that President Truman's seizure of the steel mills was illegal (from which Vinson dissented), and the refusal earlier in 1953 to allow Justice Douglas's stay of the Rosenbergs' execution.

Vinson was a most characteristic American. A "border-line New Dealer," accepting political realities, refusing to indulge in political dreams, he was no "egg-head". He was so firm a defender of American institutions, so unwavering an opponent of "Socialism" (with all the overtones the word carries in America), that his advocacy of liberal and New Deal policies made these more acceptable in the country and particularly in Washington. No Republican could ever fix the label of "Socialist" on so rigid an opponent of deficit-spending, so instinctive a budget-balancer. A native conservatism mingled with a native political shrewdness to make him a powerful figure in American politics.

In 1923 he married Miss Roberta Dixon, who survives him with their two sons.

September 9, 1953.

Maurice de Vlaminck, the painter, died at his home near Paris on October 11, 1958 at the age of 82.

He boasted that he had never set foot in a museum, and was given to utterances, but he was a "natural", that is, a man who *must* express himself in paint and whose vision of the external world comes from deep down inside him. "Painting", he once said, "is like cooking; it cannot be explained", it was perhaps for this reason that someone called him an anti-intellectual painter.

As his name implies, de Vlaminck was of Belgian extraction, born on April 4, 1876, in Paris, where he spent his youth, and he is generally included in the cosmopolitan "School of Paris", which dates from about the beginning of the present century. His ancestry, however, showed in his work, particularly as he grew older and, as is common, the native strain dominated over what he had acquired. His work is well known in London, where it is popular for qualities that are Flemish rather than French.

A big, athletic man, with musical and literary as well as artistic abilities, Vlaminck began life as a racing cyclist. At the age of 19 he was gaining a living by playing the violin in a café orchestra while studying painting under an academic master at Chatou. There he met André Derain [q.v.], then a student of architecture, and they became close associates.

The two young men spent their time cycling about the country, taking their sketching materials with them, and canoeing on the Seine. Both were as alert mentally as they were physically active and robust, but, though they shared a common admiration for Van Gogh, they were well contrasted. Vlaminck inherited the strong naturalistic impulses of the Netherlands, while Derain was a model of French moderation and order, so that the association between them was valuable to both.

Van Gogh was the determining influence on Vlaminck's career. Recalling his impressions of the Van Gogh exhibition at the Bernheim Gallery in 1901, he said: "That day I loved Van Gogh better than my father". This is quoted by R. H. Wilenski in *Modern French Painters,* and he adds that Matisse [q.v.], to whom Derain introduced Vlaminck at the exhibition, said in retrospect: "I saw Derain accompanied by a young giant who was voicing his enthusiasm in authoritative tones and declaring that one should paint with pure vermilion, pure Veronese green and pure cobalt; Derain, I think, was a little afraid of him—while admiring his ardours and enthusiasm". Both young men threw in their lot with the "Fauves", or "wild beasts", as the group under the leadership of Matisse of contributors to the Autumn Salon of 1905 were called in derision. It seems clear that what attracted Vlaminck to the movement was the violence of its reaction from both academism and Impressionism; a reaction quite different from the intellectual extremism which resulted in Cubism under the leadership of Picasso*.

Vlaminck made some lithographic and woodcut illustrations, but he was by temperament a painter in oil. Both his approach to art and his forcible speech are well expressed in a reported remark of his *à propos* Cubism—"Painting is a damn sight more difficult and more stupid than that", in which the operative word may be taken to be "stupid", as meaning something more instinctive than reasoned.

The work of Vlaminck consisted chiefly of landscapes, with a preference for village streets, often under snow, and still-life studies. Dramatic and agitating are the best words for the landscapes. Generally painted in stormy weather or under lowering skies, they are extremely broad and forcible in execution, with sudden transitions from dark to light. If a label must be found they partake of the general character of Expressionism, a movement of Teutonic rather than of French origin. A certain coarseness of fibre, a tendency to "hit below the belt" emotionally, is evident in them, but their power cannot be denied. Swift graduations of colour and tone give to the flower paintings of Vlaminck a peculiarly rich quality. From the nature of the case his work is best taken in small doses, and a roomful of landscapes by Vlaminck would be rather monotonously noisy. Besides painting, Vlaminck turned his attention to sculpture and ceramics, and he also wrote poetry, novels, and short comedies and scenarios for films.

Vlaminck was a downright person in everything, as an incident reported in *The Times* of February 14, 1928, will suggest. Some forged canvases signed with his name were on view. "M. de Vlaminck went to the gallery in Paris where these pictures were being exhibited, took out a penknife, and cut them to pieces".

Exhibitions of Vlaminck's work were held in London at the Independent Gallery in 1929 and at the Wildenstein Gallery in 1935, 1937, and 1939. At the last, works of his "Fauve" period, from 1905 to 1910, were compared with those of later years, the principal differences noted being a toning down of colour and the abandonment of a dark line for reinforcement.

Before and just after the Second World War the Fauve period paintings—they are comparatively few in number—would have changed hands at around £1,000, the others at perhaps £300. To-day each type sells for three or four times its previous price. In 1956 Noël Coward's* "Le Grand Quai, Le Havre" changed hands at auction for £4,800, and in June 1958 a picture of flowers on a bare table was sold in Paris for £4,085.

October 13, 1958.

Frederick Augustus Voigt, one of the most controversial writers and journalists in the field of foreign affairs in recent years and a former editor of the *Nineteenth Century and After,* died in hospital in Guildford on January 7, 1957. He was 64.

Voigt was educated at Haberdashers' Aske's School, Hampstead, and at London University. He joined the staff of the *Manchester Guardian* in 1921 and for a short time was employed in the advertisement department of that paper, but his bent was for journalism and he soon moved to the editorial side of the *Manchester Guardian* and began to write on foreign affairs, with which his name was to be associated for many years. Between 1922 and 1932 he was Berlin Correspondent, alternating with Cecil Sprigge. Later he returned to Manchester as Diplomatic Correspondent for his paper. It was Voigt's fortune or misfortune to be outspokenly anti-Nazi at a time when this attitude had not then become fashionable; and his writings in the thirties—notably his book *Unto Caesar,* in which from the standpoint of a Christian philosopher he examined with a searching scrutiny Marxism and Nazism—aroused immediate comment both favourable and unfavourable.

His regular articles in the *Nineteenth Century and After* during the late war were no less outspoken than his earlier writings, and brought him into the public eye during a hearing of an action in 1945 which he brought as editor of that periodical together with its proprietors and Constable and Company, Ltd., the publishers, against the publishers and printers of the *News Chronicle* and Cedric Belfrage for an alleged libel in that paper. The matter complained of dealt among other things with some remarks said to have been made by Lord Bracken [q.v.] (then Mr. Brendan Bracken, Minister of Information) in the House of Commons in the course of which he was reported to have referred to the *Nineteenth Century and After* as "Lord Haw Haw's favourite paper", and to have said that "Its great desire is to create the maximum amount of mischief among the United Nations". Mr. Justice Birkett* awarded the plaintiffs £1,000 damages.

Voigt was at all times an independent thinker who followed his own beliefs wherever they might lead him. Controversy he enjoyed, and the fiercer the battle the better he liked it. In his early years he had no great regard for institutional beliefs but later in life he came to terms with religion and was a regular worshipper at Anglican services. He was a brilliant talker, an outstanding linguist, and a man of great personal courage.

In addition to *Unto Caesar* Voigt wrote, in collaboration with Margaret Goldsmith, a biography of Hindenburg; *Pax Britannica; The Greek Sedition,* written after a prolonged study of Greece and the communist intrigues in that country; and (with W. A. Reichart) *Hauptmann und Shakespeare.*

January 9, 1957.

Ernst von Dohnanyi—See **Dohnanyi.**

F.-M. Gerd von Rundstedt—See **Rundstedt.**

Dr. Serge Voronoff, who was famous for his experiments in rejuvenation by grafting monkey glands into human beings, died at Lausanne on September 2, 1951 at the age of 85.

Voronoff, who was born at Voronege, Russia, on July 10, 1866, became a naturalized French citizen in 1897, and Director of the Experimental Surgery Laboratory, Collège de France. During the 1914-18 war he served as surgeon-in-chief of the Russian Hospital, treating French wounded in Paris and Bordeaux, and in 1915 was appointed head surgeon of Auxiliary Hospital 197 in Paris. Much of his military surgery was devoted to the problem of bone grafting, and "grafting" was to become the speciality by which he was best known.

While at the Collège de France he had been carrying out experiments grafting glands into sheep with a view to increasing their size and weight and to improving the growth and texture of the wool. Later he turned his attention to the grafting of monkey glands into the aged, and claimed that this process of rejuvenation restored some of their lost physical and intellectual vigour. He also grafted the thyroid from monkeys into mentally defective and backward children in an attempt to restore them to normal.

Voronoff was an enthusiast and a seeker after the truth, and his enthusiasm was undimmed by the passage of years. As a pioneer in the field of endocrine surgery, his results were empirical, for the science of biochemical control for assessing these experiments was still largely undeveloped. On the other hand he courted publicity, and it was with the public rather than his own profession that he was best known.

The implantation of monkey glands into aged men and women had very limited scientific value. On the Riviera he had a zoo of male and female monkeys for providing suitable material for grafting. Had the results been more permanent they would have been continued: the modern tendency is to replace living gland tissue by hormonal preparations.

In 1933 he was made an Officer of the Legion of Honour, and was also honoured by Spain and Italy. He was the author of many works dealing in particular with the subject of grafting.

September 3, 1951.

Bernard De Voto—See **De Voto.**

Andrei Vyshinsky, leader of the Soviet delegation to the United Nations, and the most eloquent but also the most vicious public prosecutor in Bolshevist history, died at the headquarters of the Soviet Mission in Park Avenue, New York, on November 22, 1954, at the age of 71, after a heart attack.

Although he made a name for himself as a jurist and writer on the Soviet legal system it was as the public prosecutor in the numerous Soviet purges and trials that Vyshinsky gained the greatest notoriety, at home and abroad. In the trials of Zinoviev, Kamenev, and 14 other leading revolutionaries and close collaborators of Lenin and Stalin [q.v.] as well as in the subsequent trials of Piatakov, Radek, and Sokolnikov, Vyshinsky acted as the long arm of the secret police, demanding death for all of them and denouncing them as "mad dogs" and "despicable rotten dregs of humanity". Altogether more than 5,000 Russians, including nearly all the members of Lenin's Politburo, were shot during the purges, and many of them as a result of trials which Vyshinsky conducted in the name of the Soviet authorities.

As a diplomatist, and prior to his appointment to the United Nations, Vyshinsky played an important role in organizing the Balkan States as satellites of the Soviet Union. He represented the U.S.S.R. in Romania, and also visited Bulgaria and stayed for a time in Czechoslovakia. He was chiefly responsible for the abdication of King Michael of Romania in December 1947. A fiery speaker, at times reaching great heights as an orator, he was most biting and fiery as well as offensive whenever he felt that he could intimidate an opponent.

He was of Polish origin, and in spite of his ruthlessness never lost some of the Polish charm, if he wanted to show it. He never admitted his Polish origin, except on one occasion when the Polish President visited the Kremlin and Vyshinsky saw Stalin's willingness to please the Polish guest. As main Soviet delegate to the United Nations, Vyshinsky established a reputation among others as the man who could deliver the longest speeches and at the same time the fullest of invective, of which he was a master. But he was feared by representatives of the Soviet satellite states, whom he used to insult openly if they behaved in a manner he disliked, or showed inability to act in accordance with his instructions.

Andrei Yanuarevich Vyshinsky was born in 1883 at Odessa, but passed his childhood at Baku, on the Caspian. He received his early education at Kiev. In 1902, at the age of 19, he joined the ranks of the Menshevik group in the Social Democratic Revolutionary Movement, and by 1905 he was already a leading figure in the Social Democratic militant organizations in the Caucasus, and secretary of the Baku Council of Workers' Deputies. During this period of youthful revolutionary activity, he was often arrested by the Tsarist police, and on account of his connexion with a railway strike in 1905 he was exiled for a year. On his return to revolutionary activity after his exile, both he and his wife (he appears to have married at an early age) were subjected to a violent assault in 1907 by members of an antagonistic political group.

Shortly after this event he appears to have returned to academic work at Kiev University, and graduated in jurisprudence in 1913. He was about to take up a professorship in criminal law when the Tsarist authorities intervened, and he was prevented on political grounds. After this rebuff he found employment in the literary field and in junior teaching posts. In 1915 he moved from South Russia to Moscow, where he obtained a post as an assistant advocate, and here he seems to have remained until 1919, when he volunteered for the Red Army and fought against General Denikin.

The year 1920 was a turning point in Vyshinsky's political career. Having been a Menshevik supporter for 17 years, he decided to join the ranks of the Bolshevist party and was admitted. In later life he was never accused of deviation from the Bolshevist line. Little is known of his war career but he appears to have filled an important post as a member of the Food Commissariat.

In 1921 Vyshinsky returned to Moscow, to academic life, and became a member of the teaching staff at Moscow University and later Dean of the Plekhanov Institute of National Economy. From this time on Vyshinsky began to acquire a reputation as a scholar and a jurist, and was appointed to several important academic and State posts. From 1923 to 1925 he served as Attorney-General of the Russian Socialist Federal Soviet Republic (R.S.F.S.R.) and simultaneously as Professor of Criminal Law in Moscow State University; from 1925 to 1928 he was Rector of Moscow State University; from 1928 to 1931 he was a member of the People's Commissariat for Education in the R.S.F.S.R. and vice-president of the State Scientific Council. In 1928 he became President of the Supreme Court of the U.S.S.R.

In the period 1931-33 he held the posts of Public Prosecutor of the Russian Republic and Deputy People's Commissar for Justice of the R.S.F.S.R., from 1933 to 1935 he was Deputy Public Prosecutor of the U.S.S.R., and finally, in 1935, Public Prosecutor of the U.S.S.R. From 1935 to 1939 he held the additional post of member of the Council of Educationists and headed the special State Board for Professional Education.

In the course of his work as a jurist during the period 1928-38, Vyshinsky appeared as Public Prosecutor at a number of significant state trials, among which were the so-called "Shakhtinsky" affair in 1928; the "Prompartiya" affair in 1930; the Metropolitan-Vickers trial in 1933; the investigation following the assassination of Kirov in 1934; and the State trials of various Trotskyite groups in 1936, 1937, and 1938. In the course of the Metropolitan-Vickers trial in 1933 Vyshinsky singled out *The Times* for attack, after a number of articles criticizing the conduct of the court had appeared. By this time Vyshinsky was acknowledged to be one of the most outstanding of Soviet jurists and from 1937 to 1940 he held the post of Director of the Institute of Law of the Soviet Academy of Sciences and was editor of the legal journal *Soviet State and Law*. He was elected to full membership of the Academy of Sciences of the U.S.S.R. in 1939.

In the period shortly before the outbreak of war in 1939, Vyshinsky began to acquire prestige and authority inside the organs of the Communist Party and from 1935 to 1937 he served as a member of the Central Executive Committee of the party. He was elected a deputy to the Supreme Soviet in 1937. At the eighteenth congress of the party in March, 1939, he was elected to the central committee of the Communist Party and in the same year was appointed a vice-president of the Council of People's Commissars.

The year 1940 was the beginning of what was perhaps the most significant stage in the career of Vyshinsky—namely, that of Soviet diplomatist and statesman. In this year he entered the Soviet Foreign Ministry, being at once appointed First Deputy to Molotov, who was then People's Commissar for Foreign Affairs. His new duties did not, however, signify any break with his work in the sphere of law, and indeed at this time he was also appointed to the post of president of the Juridical Commission of the Council of Ministers of the U.S.S.R. Soon after his appointment as Deputy Foreign Minister, Vyshinsky appeared with increasing regularity as one of the most important representatives of the Soviet Union at all major allied and, later, international conferences. When the Baltic States were incorporated in the U.S.S.R., he served for a time as special commissar in Latvia.

He was a prominent member of the Soviet delegation at the Yalta and Potsdam conferences; participated, as a member of the Soviet delegation, at the Moscow conferences of the Foreign Ministers in 1943 and 1945; served as Soviet representative on the Inter-Allied Mediterranean Commission at Algiers from 1943 to 1945, and as Soviet representative on the Allied Consultative Council on Italy. He was delegated by the Council of People's Commissars of the Soviet Union to participate in the discussions of the Allied Control Commission on Romania, and also represented the Soviet Foreign Ministry at the signing of the surrender of Nazi Germany.

It was particularly in the post-war period that Vyshinsky entered the international political arena as one of the leading Soviet statesmen and a champion of the Soviet Union in the "cold war". Until 1949 he appeared at almost every significant international meeting, but chiefly at the United Nations, where, with fiery and unabating vigour, he attacked the policies of the western nations and defended those of his own Government.

He led the Soviet delegation to the first session of the General Assembly of the United Nations in London in 1946, was a member of the Soviet delegation at the Paris Peace Conference and at the General Assembly in New York in the same year, and in 1947 was one of the Soviet delegates at the Moscow Conference of Foreign Ministers. In June of the same year in the United Nations Assembly Vyshinsky sharply and bitterly accused the United States of violation of the United Nations Charter by refusing to disarm and by preparing for a new war against his country.

His invective at the council table often stirred the wrath of his adversaries, and it was reported that while at a conference in Paris in 1946 he was challenged to a duel to the death by two Italian politicians, after making a derogatory remark to the effect that Italian generals possessed more prowess in running than in fighting. In the ensuing year, in America, he was threatened with a $1m. libel suit as a result of his allegations concerning the publication in that country of a book on Soviet labour camps.

Having served as deputy to Molotov since 1940, Vyshinsky was appointed to the post of Foreign Minister of the U.S.S.R. in March 1949 to release Molotov for more important work in the Politburo. In his new capacity as Soviet Foreign Minister he attended the meeting of Foreign Ministers in Paris in May of that year, and thenceforward his duties kept him for a time in Moscow, although he emerged, with his usual fiery eloquence, as the Soviet spokesman on the subject of the control of atomic energy, in the United Nations Assembly, in December 1951. At about this time his health seems to have suffered from the continual strain of political life during and since the 1939-45 War, and in 1952 he was reported to be under medical treatment. After a short rest it was announced that he was back at his post as Foreign Minister. He reverted to being deputy Foreign Minister after Stalin's death in 1953, and was appointed permanent representative of the U.S.S.R. at the United Nations.

In September 1954 he put forward a new Russian plan for disarmament by stages, to be followed by the prohibition of atomic weapons. On November 18 he announced that revisions in the proposal for international cooperation in developing atomic energy for peaceful purposes had made the proposal acceptable to the U.S.S.R., and on November 20 he informed Cabot Lodge, the United States delegate, that he intended to submit a new Soviet amendment to the plan.

Andrei Vyshinsky's achievements as a jurist tended to pass unnoticed in view of his fame as a Soviet diplomatist and statesman. These achievements are of considerable significance, and he has been referred to as "the father of the Soviet judicial system". He was a most prolific writer on Soviet law, even when engaged on exacting political and diplomatic work. Shortly after the introduction of the Stalin Constitution in 1936, which Vyshinsky had helped to formulate, he emerged as the most outstanding Soviet legal authority, to replace Pashukanis, who had been a doyen of the legal profession and writer of legal textbooks for nearly a decade.

The Pashukanis group of jurists had given their support to the idea, originally promulgated by Marx and Engels and supported by Lenin, of the "progressive withering away of the state". Vyshinsky, on the other hand, appeared with a programme for the immediate strengthening of the state as a safeguard against external enemies. Among his most important works in the field of law are: *The Judicial System in the U.S.S.R.; Course of Criminal Law; The Law of the Soviet State.* This last work was produced under his editorship in 1938 and represents the change in Soviet legal and political ideas embodied in the Stalin Constitution of 1936. It is available in English, having been translated by the American Council of Learned Societies in 1948. In 1947 Vyshinsky was awarded a First Stalin Prize of 200,000 roubles (then about £9,000) for his work on *The Theory of Legal Proof in Soviet Law.*

Vyshinsky held a number of honours and decorations in recognition of his services to the Soviet State; among these were four Orders of Lenin (one of which was specifically awarded for his services as prosecutor in the trials of the 1930s); the Order of the Red Banner; a medal for the Defence of Moscow; and another medal for "outstanding efforts in the war of 1941-45".

November 23, 1954.

W

Professor A. J. B. Wace, the archaeologist, whose name will always be associated with the Mycenae excavations, died on November 9, 1957 in Athens.

Professor Wace was 78. At the time of his death he was working on material he had excavated two years earlier at a prehistoric settlement outside the Acropolis walls at Mycenae.

Alan John Bayard Wace was born in 1879, the second son of F. C. Wace. From Shrewsbury he went up to Pembroke College, Cambridge, as a scholar and took first classes in both parts of the Classical Tripos. He was Craven Student in 1903 and Librarian of the British School at Rome two years later. After holding a fellowship at Pembroke and a lectureship in ancient history and archaeology at St. Andrews, he was appointed Director of the British School at Athens in 1914 and remained there till 1923. A year later he became deputy keeper in the Department of Textiles in the Victoria and Albert Museum, a post which he held until 1934, when he returned to Cambridge to succeed A. B. Cook [q.v.] as Laurence Professor of Classical Archaeology.

During the First World War Wace had served at the British Legation in Athens. At the outbreak of the second he was engaged in excavations in the Near East and again reported for duty at Athens. With the Greek Government he moved to Cairo, where he worked at G.H.Q. until 1943. Retiring from his Cambridge chair under the age-limit in the following year, he was appointed Professor of Classics and Archaeology in the University of Alexandria and occupied the post until 1952.

The fruit of Wace's wide experience in the Near East is seen in a number of books which bear his name such as *Prehistoric Thessaly* (written in collaboration with M. S. Thompson); *Excavations at Mycenae; Chamber Tombs at Mycenae; Mediterranean and Near Eastern Embroideries in the Collection of Mrs. F. H. Cook; Approach to Greek Sculpture;* and *Mycenae, an Archaeological History.* Wace also contributed many articles to archaeological journals.

As a teacher he would take infinite pains with his pupils and would always persevere with any who seemed to possess the right and proper feeling towards archaeological data.

His home, whether at Cambridge or at Cairo, was always open to the inquiring student and offered stores not only of learning but of kindness and good fellowship.

In 1925 he married Helen, daughter of Professor W. D. Pence, of Evanston; he leaves one daughter.

[A tribute followed this obituary on the same day and extended the scope of Professor Wace's biography.]

November 11, 1957.

George Edward Wade—See **Robey.**

A. P. Wadsworth, who retired from the post of editor of the *Manchester Guardian* only a week before, owing to ill-health, died on November 4, 1956 at the age of 65.

Wadsworth's promotion to the editorial chair when the last war seemed still far from its end was fraught with problems. International politics appeared likely to remain confused for a long time, the domestic scene uncertain, and the local interests of Lancashire hazardous. His foresight and responsibility kept his paper in the forefront of the organs of opinion in Britain both in war and in the uneasy peace that has followed it.

One of the shrewdest of his elders quickly made up his mind about Wadsworth when he joined the *Manchester Guardian.* "The best of the bunch", he said, "with a mind like a needle". Wadsworth's ascent began: special correspondent, labour correspondent, leader writer, assistant editor. Finally he became editor in 1944 in succession to W. P. Crozier. For four months before Crozier's death Wadsworth had been working under very great strain and during the winter of 1944-45 his health was often precarious, but his capacity for quick, precise work remained undiminished.

It was, and Wadsworth freely admitted it, an intimidating thought to sit in the chair occupied until 1929 by C. P. Scott. That Wadsworth succeeded in maintaining the tradition unimpaired was partly due to his own loyalty to the county in which he was born and passed all his life, but far more to the high ideals of professional integrity and historical scholarship he constantly held before himself.

Alfred Powell Wadsworth was born at Rochdale on May 26, 1891. He began his training as a journalist immediately he left school, on the staff of the *Rochdale Observer,* where he gained those valuable professional assets for a newspaperman that only experience on a local paper of standing can give—meticulous accuracy in matters of detail, the necessity for a sharp division between the reporting of news and the propagation of opinions, and the fine distinction between the service a newspaper must give to its readers and the intrusion on the private affairs of those whose activities form the raw material of its contents. Wadsworth's later career demonstrated to the full how thoroughly he had learnt these lessons from his editor, that fine journalist, W. W. Hadley [q.v.], who later edited the *Sunday Times.*

While he was working at Rochdale he had joined Professor R. H. Tawney's* famous university tutorial class, the first that was ever held, and this gave him the impulse to historical studies which were so signally to bear fruit not only in his admirable narrative of the cotton trade in Lancashire before the Industrial Revolution, but also in his balanced judgment of contemporary problems.

His historical studies centred, as was natural, on cotton, but he chose an untilled field in which to cultivate them. His history of the cotton trade in Lancashire, which was published in 1931, ended where other studies had normally begun. In collaboration with Julia de Lacy Mann (later Principal of St. Hilda's College, Oxford), he published *The Cotton Trade and Industrial Lancashire, 1600-1780.* It bridges the gap in the history of industrial development in England between the close of the Middle Ages and the rising of the tide of the Industrial Revolution. Stevenson's, Arkwright's, Hargreaves's inventions, with their consequence of the transfer of industry from the home to the factory, came towards the end of the period.

The development of the cotton industry in domestic conditions is Wadsworth's theme, and the references in the notes to his memorable narrative show the varied sources from which he drew his information. Court files, parish registers, early patents, Acts of Parliament, published and unpublished documents, which with patient research can be found by a painstaking historian, were supplemented by private correspondence and the early letter books of firms to which Wadsworth and his collaborator were given special access. Thus was the industrial history of Lancashire in the seventeenth and eighteenth centuries told in picturesque and scholarly detail. The honorary degree conferred by Manchester University upon Wadsworth in 1933 was richly merited.

When in 1917 he joined the editorial staff of the *Manchester Guardian,* a fortnight after Neville Cardus* joined it, he was already not merely an experienced journalist—his shorthand was remarkably rapid and accurate—but a journalist of high and consistent ideals.

His first big chance came in 1920 when, after the death of the paper's deputy chief reporter, George E. Leach, Wadsworth went to Ireland to help in reporting the "troubles". Then, after seeing through the press a series of reconstruction supplements, edited by the late Lord Keynes, he began his long and fruitful career as Labour Correspondent of the paper. The formation and collapse of the "Triple Alliance" were reported by him with fairness and sympathy, as also were the successive stages of unrest—the dockers' and railwaymen's strikes of 1924 and the builders' and cooperative employees' strikes of the following year—which culminated in the General Strike of 1926.

When he began to write leading articles he turned more and more to the economic aspects and so became a worthy successor in this field to E. T. Scott, who had written on economics when his father, C. P. Scott, was editor. After the former's death Wadsworth became the chief leader writer, and the balanced and humane Liberalism which had always characterized his thought was made explicit and unmistakable. This, indeed, was his strength not only as writer and editor but also as a man. Tyranny, whether from the Right or the Left, found in him an uncompromising opponent, and to the end of his life he fought the battle of the individual as against the tyranny of the mass, the tyranny of the dictator, or the more insidious threat of the protagonists of the "managerial revolution".

His fine record of 12 years as editor of the greatest of provincial newspapers in England was crowned in the summer of 1955 by the conferment upon him by Manchester University of the honorary degree of Doctor of Laws on the centenary to the day of the first appearance of the *Manchester Guardian* as a daily paper—it had previously been published since 1821 as a weekly. The centenary issue of the paper was no mean contribution to newspaper scholarship. When, a week before he died, he retired from the editorial chair he was given the unusual title (for an editor) of emeritus, and it was arranged that he would continue his connexion with the paper as a member of the board.

He married in 1922 Miss Alice Lillian Ormerod, whose wide sympathies and social gifts gave their home an unforgettable atmosphere of friendliness and good will. From her father she inherited a notable gift for music and an enthusiastic interest in social work. Her death in April 1955 was a blow from which he never completely recovered. He leaves a daughter.

November 5, 1956.

General Jonathan Wainwright, the hero of Bataan and Corregidor in 1942, died in Brooke Army Hospital, San Antonio, Texas, on September 2, 1953 at the age of 70.

The stand of Wainwright and his American and Filipino soldiers was an epic of courage and devotion to duty in the face of overwhelming odds. Throughout the stand it was Wainwright himself who was the inspiration—as he later became the symbol—of their resistance. Only rarely in military history has there been such loyalty of a commander to his men. He stayed with them when he might have escaped from the island which he had made a fortress, sending the message to Allied Headquarters: "I've been with my men from the start, and if captured will share their lot. We've been through so much together that my conscience would not let me leave before the final curtain".

Wainwright, who had been assigned to duty in the Philippines in 1940, succeeded General MacArthur* in active command in the Philippines in March 1942. The bitter defence of the Bataan peninsula had already been fought for almost three months. On April 10 it was announced that it had ended. Wainwright's men were not only heavily outnumbered, but were already worn down by successive attacks by fresh troops and exhausted by insufficient rations and by disease. President Roosevelt gave Wainwright permission to take any decision he wished in the circumstances.

Wainwright's answer was to take his men on to the island of Corregidor. The island stands in the mouth of Manila Bay—the vital harbour for which the months' long rearguard action had been fought. But by now it was obvious that the harbour could not be saved. Wainwright's action, in these circumstances, became valuable, not only because it bought time and inflicted losses on the enemy, but because it set an example of determined resistance at a psychologically vital moment.

On the rocks of Corregidor Wainwright led his men—rather the survivors of his men—with a courage which has rarely been equalled. He lived, not in the commanding general's residence, but in a battered tent outside Malinta Tunnel. In the last days of the defence he had become so deafened by shell-fire that he could hear nothing that was not shouted close to his ears. His men were devoted to him.

Wainwright went into captivity, there to endure brutality and indignity. When he returned after nearly three and a half years in a Japanese prison camp, New York and Washington gave him a hero's welcome. The President decorated him with the Congressional Medal of Honour for "intrepid" leadership, adding: "This gives me almost more pleasure than anything I have ever done".

Jonathan Mayhew Wainwright was born in Walla Walla, Washington, in 1883, the son of Major Robert P. P. Wainwright, who commanded a cavalry squadron in the battle of Santiago, Cuba, in 1898, and grandson of Commander Jonathan Mayhew Wainwright, who was killed in the United States Civil War. He graduated from the United States Military Academy at West Point in 1902, and entered the cavalry, serving for some years in the south-west, then sailing with his regiment to the Philippines.

In the 1914-18 war he saw service in the defensive sectors of Toul, Point-à-Mousson, the St. Mihiel and Meuse fronts, and was promoted to lieutenant-colonel in 1918. After the armistice he served with the U.S. Army of Occupation in Germany until 1920, and then, reverting to his peace-time rank of captain, rose through each rank until, on March 19, 1942, he was promoted lieutenant-general on assuming command in the Philippines.

September 3, 1953.

Friedrich Waismann died on November 4, 1959 in an Oxford hospital.

As University Reader, first in the philosophy of mathematics and later in the philosophy of science, Waismann was a widely respected figure among Oxford philosophers. He was particularly influential as a lecturer in the years immediately following the war, when the new methods of linguistic analysis were being formed, and the earlier, more harsh and schematic doctrines of the logical positivists were being discredited.

Waismann was born in Vienna in 1896 of partly Russian and partly Austrian parentage. He completed his education as an external student at Vienna University, supporting himself by giving tuition in mathematics. He always liked to speak of himself as largely self-educated. In 1929 he became assistant to Professor Moritz Schlick, the distinguished philosopher, who was the central figure in the Vienna Circle. This informal, and not always harmonious, group of philosophers and mathematicians was the source of much of the philosophical innovation of the last century; they were the original logical positivists.

Schlick, as friend and patron, was the strongest personal influence in Waismann's life, and Ludwig Wittgenstein [q.v.], whom he met through Schlick, was the strongest philosophical influence. In the years before the *Anschluss* Waismann wrote, and almost finished, a book which applied some of Wittgenstein's leading ideas to theory of language and to the methodology of science. This should have been his masterpiece and he took it to Cambridge to be translated when he arrived in 1937 as a lecturer in the Moral Sciences Faculty. The translation was never finished and the book was never published. Its leading ideas were later incorporated into a number of important articles in philosophical journals in England. His only published book is *Einführung in das mathematische Denken,* a short and valuable study of the foundations of mathematics.

In 1939 Waismann moved from Cambridge to Oxford. Because of his understanding of mathematics and of modern physics, combined with a fascinated interest in the forms of language, he was soon recognized as one of the most interesting philosophers in Oxford. Immediately after the war the new movement of linguistic analysis suddenly came to life, and Waismann, in lectures and published papers, elaborated his own doctrine of the necessary vagueness of language; he called it "the open texture" of language. He illustrated the subtle variety of grammatical forms with examples of English idiom carefully recorded in pocketsize notebooks. He showed why logical models could never do justice to the varying and flexible forms of any language that is adequate to varieties of experience. He naturally thought in German, and it was only by a constant effort that he expressed the refinements of his thought in English. The effect of his incursions into English slang was often bizarre and delighted his audiences.

Behind his investigations of language there was always a serious concern with metaphysics and a deeply imaginative understanding of the roots of traditional problems. His article "How I see Philosophy" in the volume *Contemporary British Philosophy* (1956) is one of the best introductions to philosophy written in English in this century.

Waismann was gentle and courteous. But he was essentially a solitary man, living an inner life of his own, imaginative and original, and always remote from practical affairs. He wrote, but did not publish, poetry and general reflections on life, tinged with his characteristic pessimism and expressing his dislike of clear cut and confident conclusions. He was the least positive of philosophers and his natural form of expression was a rhetorical question. His published work, brilliant as it is, represents only a small part of his real achievement and of the range of his thought.

November 6, 1959.

Archbishop of Wales—See **Morgan.**

Sir Robert Waley Cohen—See **Cohen.**

Dame Ethel Walker, D.B.E., A.R.A., died in a London nursing home on March 2, 1951 at the age of 89.

Comparative estimates are always risky, but it can be said with confidence that she was the most important woman artist of her time in England since Berthe Morisot. Nor was her importance of the obvious kind associated with big swaggering compositions; it came from the sheer quality of her talent as a painter.

Ethel Walker was born in Edinburgh on June 9, 1861, though she was by election a Yorkshirewoman, dividing her time in later life between her house at Robin Hood's Bay and Chelsea. As a child and young girl she was indifferent to art, her explanation being that the accurate copying of nature, which was what art meant then, did not mean anything to her. It was a chance visit in girlhood to a small private collection of Oriental works of art that aroused her. Professor Frederick Brown, the mentor of so many artists who have since become famous, under whom she studied both at the Westminster and the Slade Schools of Art, was quick to recognize her promise.

Her earlier works reflected the influence of Professor Brown and the studies pursued under his direction: mostly interiors with figures, not lacking in colour but with chief attention to values in tone; but she quickly developed the style of loose and free impressionism, with a decorative emphasis, in limited and generally light schemes of colour, which made her work easily recognizable in a mixed exhibition.

She had a full range of subjects: portraits, figure compositions, including the nude, flower paintings, landscapes, marines and mural decorations; and she also produced some excellent things in sculpture. In her mural decorations, under such titles as *The Zone of Hate* and *The Zone of Love,* there was the reflection of a theosophical bent of mind, again bearing on her affinities; and, indeed, in her wide and desultory reading she was keenly interested in the philosophical side of religion. Her portraits would sometimes leave something to seek in external likeness, as they were often casual rather than weak in construction, but they were always felt to be true to the temperament of the sitter. She painted several good portraits of men, but it was with young women that she excelled. It was perhaps in her flower and marine paintings that her taste and technical powers were most evident.

A small, active woman, Dame Ethel Walker was an extremely interesting personality. In conversation she was both witty and disconcerting. Her denunciations, delivered in a deep husky voice with her head tilted back and glancing down her nose, were unsparing, as when she described the work of a colleague as suffering from "elephantiasis of the vision". Nothing was more characteristic than her attitude to her own work. With a complete absence of self-consciousness and the enthusiasm of a person revealing some obvious truth, she would lead one up to a painting or drawing of hers and say, "Now isn't that lovely?", her contemplative enjoyment of the thing removing any suggestion of conceit.

She had the enthusiastic appreciation of her colleagues of every shade of opinion. She exhibited regularly at the New English Art Club, the Royal Academy—she was elected A.R.A. in 1940—the Royal Society of British Artists, the Society of Women Artists, and the London group, and several "one woman shows" of her work were held in London. She is represented in the Tate Gallery by ten works, including the large decorative composition "Nausicaa"; two large imaginative compositions, "The Zone of Love" and "The Zone of Hate", presented by the artist herself in 1946; a "Portrait of Miss Buchanan"; and a figure dreaming.

She was created C.B.E. in 1938 and D.B.E. in 1943.

March 3, 1951.

Sir Gilbert Walker, C.S.I., F.R.S., who effected a revolution in the forecasting of weather during the 20 years in which he was Director-General of Indian Observatories, and whose discoveries were of supreme importance for the vast population of India, died on November 4, 1958 at the age of 90.

Gilbert Thomas Walker was the son of an engineer. He was educated at St. Paul's School, where his mathematical ability quickly made itself manifest and gained for him a scholarship at Trinity College, Cambridge. There in 1889 he came out Senior Wrangler with Frank Dyson (later to be Astronomer Royal) immediately below him and Hector Munro Macdonald (later Professor of Mathematics at Aberdeen) in the same list. Two years later he was elected to a fellowship at Trinity College, to which was added in 1895 a university lectureship.

Walker's mathematical interests at Cambridge were mainly in the fields of dynamics and electromagnetism. His dynamical interests were said to have had their root in a visit to Australia, where he was fascinated by the skill with which the natives threw the boomerang. His proficiency in this subject won for him the name of "Boomerang Walker". He wrote papers on the "Motion of Elongated Projectiles", "Dynamical Tops" and "Boomerangs", which led to an invitation to write the article on "Spiel and Sport" for the *Encyclopädie der Mathematischen Wissenschaft.* In India his knowledge of the boomerang often served the delectation of his friends, but his chief dynamical interest there was the soaring flight of the great Himalayan birds, a subject on which he wrote a paper in 1923.

Walker's electrical papers began with one in 1892 on "Refulsion and Rotation produced by Alternating Electric Currents" for the Royal Society's *Philosophical Transactions.* In 1900 he won an Adams Prize with an essay on "Aberration and some other Problems connected with the Electro-magnetic Field", later published as a book. While in India he gave, in 1908, a series of lectures to the University of Calcutta which were afterwards published in a volume entitled *The Theory of Electro-magnetism.*

In 1903 Walker was appointed to succeed Sir John Eliot as Director-General of Observatories in India. His work had hitherto lain in fields not immediately connected with meteorology, but that had its advantages, for he brought a fresh mind to bear on these problems.

Walker himself encouraged his colleagues to work on subjects which seemed to have no immediate bearing on the weather but ultimately were shown to have an important connexion; for example, he set Dr. G. C. Simpson, who joined him in 1906, to work on atmospheric electricity, and allowed another worker to investigate the upper air. Walker's own first task was to collate as many facts about the Indian weather as he possibly could, and an early visitor to his office at Simla has recorded a vision of "rows and rows of pigeonholes" in which "all sorts of curious coincidences" were recorded. When Walker found two phenomena, varying in unison over a series of years he put them into one pigeonhole, and eventually into one diagram, though there was no apparent causal connexion between them. The method was frankly empirical, but it has been fully justified by its results, for Walker's "coefficients of correlation" transformed the prediction of Indian weather from augury to a science.

The whole life of India depends to a degree scarcely to be realized elsewhere on the course of the monsoon, and thanks to the work of Walker the Indian Meteorological Department was enabled to forecast in the spring what the course of the monsoon would be for months ahead.

Hitherto it had been maintained that the weather of India was the product of such relatively local factors as the quantity of snow in the Himalayas, the summer heat or winter cold in central Asia and Tibet, and storms in Persia. Walker showed that the storms which swept down from Persia had their origin in the Atlantic, and he was led to discuss the bearing on Indian weather of conditions in Mauritius, Rhodesia, South America and centres even farther afield. In 1921 a formula was found connecting the monsoon rains with the pressure at Mauritius, the pressure over South America, the rainfall at Zanzibar, and the snowfall over North-West India; the formula fitted the facts of the previous decade fairly closely.

Walker left India in 1924 and succeeded Sir Napier Shaw as professor of meteorology at the Imperial College of Science and Technology. A subject to which he gave much attention after his return to London was the formation of clouds. By direct observation and by experiments on the vortical motion of unstable layers of fluid he proved that the Helmholty wave theory would not explain, as had been hitherto thought, mackerel skies and other periodical cloud patterns. He resigned his chair at the Imperial College in 1934.

Like so many mathematicians from the days of Pythagoras, Walker was very fond of music. A love of the outdoor life, which in his youth had led him to the Alps for skating and climbing, persisted in India, and every nook and cranny of the hills round Simla were known to him. These hills were the subject of many watercolours which he showed at the Simla Art Exhibition. The breadth of his interests, the lucidity of his conversation and the sweet reasonableness of his nature made him an agreeable figure in Simla society and in London scientific circles.

Walker married in 1908 May Constance, daughter of Charles S. Carter, and they had a son and a daughter.

November 6, 1958.

David Mordeovitch Wallach—See **Litvinov.**

C. S. Walton, headmaster of University College School, London, since 1936, died suddenly on December 21, 1955 at his home near the school in Hampstead, at the age of 50.

He succeeded Guy Kendall [q.v.], who had held the position for 17 years. Walton was then just over 30 years of age. He was a brilliant classical scholar and had done well both at Rugby, where he went to school, and at Oxford. He had then spent six years as sixth-form master at Westminster, where his work had been chiefly with those who were studying for scholarships at Oxford and Cambridge. There he proved his worth as a teacher, patient and inspiring and developing in those under his tuition the same exact scholarship and good taste he himself had. On going to University College School his duties tended towards the administrative side, but he still took a share in the work of teaching, and by his enthusiasm and readiness to help soon won the affection of all members of the teaching staff and the school.

He maintained all the traditions of the school and kept its work at a high standard, while at the same time he made it his aim to instil into all boys, though they were under his care only during the day, some of the principles of loyalty, mutual trust and duty which are usually a prominent part of the training at boarding schools.

When war came in 1939 and many schools left London for other areas of the country which were thought to be safer, University College School carried on at its home. The numbers kept up and the work went on without interruption, though the staff was considerably reduced because the younger masters had gone for war service and some of the older boys left earlier than they would have done otherwise.

The transition from wartime to peacetime conditions was complicated by the bringing into force of the provisions of the Education Act of 1944, which put a still greater administrative burden on headmasters all over the country. Walton splendidly surmounted these difficulties, found time for at least some teaching, and also served on the Court of the London School of Economics.

Cecil Simpson Walton was born on February 6, 1905, the eldest son of the Rev. S. S. Walton. He was educated at Rugby and from there won a scholarship to Balliol College, Oxford. There he took a first class in Classical Moderations and a first in *Literae Humaniores* and was for a time senior student in ancient history. He was then appointed assistant master at Westminster in 1930 and remained until he was appointed to University College School.

December 23, 1955.

Arthur Sarsfield Ward—See **Rohmer.**

Fannie Ward, for whom age seemed to have no terrors, died in hospital in New York on January 27, 1952.

Public attention was for years sharply focused upon her apparent possession of the secret of eternal youth. Indeed, at an age when most women have retired to the rocking chair, she still beguiled audiences on both sides of the Atlantic by her girlish charms, and those who saw the *petite,* dark-haired, vivacious first-nighter were as much astonished by her youthful prettiness as they were by her lavish display of jewelry. Yet this single quality, remarkable as it was, was not sufficient to account for the popularity she continued to enjoy on the stage for over half a century. The stage pieces in which she chose to appear were frothy and ephemeral, yet to her work for the stage she brought a sound technique learned early, and as her experience broadened so she was able with more and more certainty to project her rich yet delicate personality across the footlights and establish a sympathetic understanding with the audience of a large theatre which was quite surprising in one so small and apparently so youthful.

Born at St. Louis, Missouri, on February 22, 1872, she was the daughter of the late John Buchanan. Brought up at local schools, she studied for the stage under John W. Norton, and when she was 18 got her first part, at the Broadway Theatre, New York, as Cupid in *Pippino.* Others of her early parts came in *Across the Potomac, The Voyage of Suzette,* and *Shenandoah.* In 1894 she made her first appearance in London, as Eva Tudor in *The Shop Girl,* at the old Gaiety, and towards the end of the next year she played Lady Cholmondeley in *Cheer! Boys, Cheer!* This first London period saw her in various other plays in like vein at the Vaudeville, Comedy, Avenue, and Savoy theatres. It continued until 1906, when she went back to America, and took the part of Rita Forrest in *A Marriage of Reason.* She returned to London to play Nance in *The Bishop's Carriage* in 1907 at the then newly built Waldorf Theatre. This part proved to be one of her more memorable performances. The run did not last long, however, and later in the year she was in Washington, taking the part of Effie Tucker in *A Fool and a Girl,* subsequently touring the American states with the same piece.

In 1908 she was in London once more, this time as Lady Kitty in *The Marriage of William Ashe.* Another resounding London success came later in the year in *Three of Us,* at the Aldwych Theatre. Thereafter she was much in demand on both sides of the Atlantic, not only in the light comedy roles of which she was the acknowledged mistress but on the variety stage and in the cinema. After a long absence from the London stage she reappeared at the Coliseum in 1927 to "demonstrate how to remain a debutante from flapper to grandmother days".

By her first marriage to the late Joseph Lewis, which was dissolved in 1913, she had a daughter, who married, first, Captain Jack Barnato. After his early death Mrs. Barnato married, in 1922, the late Lord Plunket. Both Lord and Lady Plunket were killed in an aeroplane accident in California in 1938. The loss of her only child was a severe blow and age, which she had defied so long, began at last to take its toll. She was prevented by illness from visiting England in November 1951 to attend the wedding of her grandson, the Hon. Robin Plunket. Miss Ward's second husband was John W. Dean, who had played in a number of her productions. He died in 1950.

January 28, 1952.

Francis Kingdon-Ward—See **Kingdon-.**

Sir Lancelot Barrington-Ward—See **Barrington-.**

James Wardrop, Deputy Keeper of the Library of the Victoria and Albert Museum, died suddenly in University College Hospital on July 20, 1957.

The history and criticism of the arts of illumination, calligraphy, and typography have suffered a heavy loss by his early death. He was the author of numerous monographs on the miniaturists and scribes of the middle and late Italian Renaissance. Of these periods he possessed a range and depth of knowledge unsurpassed in Britain and uncommon in Italy. He was in every way, in wit, in speech, in love of learning, in enjoyment of classic art and literature, in elegance and ceremoniousness, a living example of his own humanist ideal. One of the qualities which, beside an unusual degree of thoroughness, gave his work such high value was an individual, humanistic sensitiveness to form which marked all his faculties, intellectual and beyond.

James Wardrop was born in 1905 at Paisley, Renfrewshire, and educated at the Glasgow High School and the Glasgow School of Art. An innate interest in painting led him to the study of miniatures and thence to an appreciation of scripts. He was abroad, mainly in Italy, after leaving Glasgow and was appointed an assistant in the Library of the Victoria and Albert Museum in 1929. Although Wardrop knew that here he had found his life vocation, and resisted offers (they were hardly temptations) of more conspicuous positions outside the museum, he embraced opportunities to broaden his experience. In 1936 Dr. Thomas Jones [q.v.] attached him in a part-time capacity to the direction of the Gregynog Press. Wardrop thus gained a practical knowledge of typography as an aspect of art. In 1939 his capacities as a linguist made it inevitable that he should be called to the place known during the war as "the country".

After the war he returned to the museum and settled down to a period of specialization in Italian Studies to which he was inspired in part by Oliver Simon [q.v.], who promised (and gave) an irresistible abundance of illustration in the pages of his *Signature.* It was in the pages of this periodical that Wardrop's studies of the great Florentine miniaturists such as Pier Antonio Sallando appeared, in an English whose fastidiousness matched the elegance of Simon's choice roman print and his own decorative italic script. These studies, marked as they were by a rare depth of knowledge, range of relevance (and length of footnote), remain impeccable. The touch, too, was ever light. Those who listened to his lectures at King's College, London, will not forget the pleasure. It is hoped that the text of these, in type at the Clarendon Press, may yet appear in print.

In 1949 Wardrop visited the United States for the first time. On this occasion, and since, he lectured and made fast friends in academic circles. Wardrop's latest publication was his translation of the dialogue *De Justicia Pingenda,* written by the humanist Battista Fiera (1469-1518), which was printed recently by the Lion and Unicorn, the private press of the Royal College of Art.

July 22, 1957.

Sir Holburt Waring, BT., C.B.E., F.R.C.S., an outstanding figure in the field of surgery and medical education, and a former vice-chancellor of the University of London, died at his home, Pen-Moel, Tidenham, Gloucestershire, on February 10, 1953 at the age of 86.

Holburt Jacob Waring was born on October 3, 1866, the son of Isaac Waring, of Southport. He was educated at Owen's College, Manchester, and at the University of London, where he qualified for the Gold Medal in Surgery in 1897. From Owen's College he went to St. Bartholomew's Hospital and was successively house surgeon, surgical registrar, surgeon, and consulting surgeon. While in the medical school he was demonstrator of anatomy and teacher of operative surgery. He became interested in the University of London early in his career. He represented the Faculty of Medicine in the senate from 1911, was elected Dean of the Faculty in 1920, and acted as Vice-Chancellor from 1922 to 1924. He was also chairman of the board of Advanced Medical Studies and of the Board of Studies in Dentistry. At the Royal College of Surgeons of England he was elected a member of the council in 1913; was a member of the Court of Examiners from 1911 to 1920, and was president from 1932 to 1935. He represented the college on the General Medical Council from 1917 to 1932 and served as one of the council's treasurers. He was also a member and treasurer of the Dental Board.

When the Territorial Force was established in 1908 he accepted a commission as captain, having previously served in a similar rank in the Volunteer Medical Staff Corps. He was called up on the outbreak of war in 1914, was promoted lieutenant-colonel, and was placed in charge of the surgical division of the First London General Hospital (T.F.). He was mentioned in dispatches, was given the brevet rank of colonel, and made a C.B.E. in 1919 as a reward for his services. In 1925 he was knighted and elected president of the Medical Society of London. He also acted as president of the section of surgery at the Royal Society of Medicine. He was a governor and almoner of Christ's Hospital, a governor of the Imperial College from 1930 to 1947, a governor of the East London College, and consulting surgeon to St. Bartholomew's Hospital, the Metropolitan and Royal Dental Hospitals, and the Ministry of Pensions. He was also treasurer of the Imperial Cancer Research Fund and Hunterian Trustee of the Royal College of Surgeons.

In addition to many essays and addresses on subjects of surgical interest, he wrote a work on diseases of the liver and another on operative survey, which became a standard work.

Throughout his active professional life Waring was constantly engaged in schemes for the improvement of conditions already existing. A man of strong convictions, he sometimes pushed forward these schemes without due consideration for the opinions of his opponents. He thus alienated those whom he might have conciliated and was not always able to give effect to valuable propositions.

He was instrumental at St. Bartholomew's in getting two good pieces of work done. The surgical wards had been built in the middle of the seventeenth century and had not undergone much change. He induced the treasurer and almoners to build a new surgical block on the most modern lines. The medical school had long been proprietary, and he was instrumental in obtaining a charter making it a college and affiliating it to the University of London.

At the General Medical Council he initiated many important changes in the curriculum of medical and dental students. To study their needs he visited many of the universities and medical schools in Europe, the United States, and Canada.

Sir Holburt Waring was made a baronet in 1935. He married, in 1900, Annie Cassandra, daughter of Charles Johnston Hill. She died in 1948.

Their only son, Alfred Harold Waring, upon whom the baronetcy now devolves was born in 1902 and married in 1930 Winifred, daughter of Albert Boston, Stockton-on-Tees. There are a son and two daughters of the marriage.

February 11, 1953.

The Right Rev. Guy Warman, D.D., a prominent leader of the Evangelical movement and formerly Bishop of Manchester, died at his home at Orpington on February 12, 1953 at the age of 80.

Frederic Sumpter Guy Warman was born on November 5, 1872. He was educated at Merchant Taylors' School, from which he won a Classical Scholarship to Pembroke College, Oxford. He gained a second class in Classical Moderations in 1892, but instead of proceeding to Greats read for the Theological School, in which he gained a second in 1894. In the same year he won the Hall Houghton Junior Greek Testament prize. Ordained in 1895 to the curacy of Leyton, he was appointed in 1901 vice-principal of St. Aidan's Theological College, Birkenhead; and in 1902 he resigned that post to become vicar of Birkenhead itself. Warman remained at Birkenhead till 1908, though meanwhile he had been appointed principal of St. Aidan's in 1907. His energy and clear-headedness had so impressed his fellow-citizens that in 1907 he was elected chairman of the local Board of Guardians.

The new principal had taken his B.D. degree at Oxford in 1907; in 1911 he proceeded to D.D. In 1916 Bradford church people were very sad as they said good-bye to Theodore Woods on his appointment as Bishop of Peterborough; they felt his place could never be adequately filled, but Dr. Warman came, and their fears were dispelled. He was an outstanding success as vicar of Bradford, and his most notable achievement was his share in the formation of the Bradford diocese.

In 1919 he was appointed to the see of Truro. Once again his excellent business ability and his power as a preacher made him popular, though his Evangelical opinions were not in accord with the traditions of the diocese. He held his Evangelical opinions clearly and tenaciously, but was not in the least intolerant: he worked easily and readily with men of different views, and he strove to be fair to all parties alike. He made a first-rate joint-chairman with his neighbour the Bishop of Exeter (Lord William Gascoyne-Cecil) at the Plymouth Church Congress of 1923. In that year Dr. Warman accepted translation to the see of Chelmsford, where he had wider scope than at Truro and where he was in closer touch with the central work of the Church. He took a very large share in the work of prayer-book revision and, Evangelical though he was, supported the Revised Prayer Book of 1927, and then that of 1928, with all his considerable powers. He was also keenly interested in the training of candidates for Holy Orders and was for years chairman of the Central Advisory Council.

The resignation of Archbishop Davidson in the summer of 1928 and the consequent translation of the Archbishop of York to Canterbury involved a certain re-shuffling; and it was thought likely that Dr. Warman might be translated to York. This was not to be. Bishop William Temple, of Manchester, though nine years younger in age and two years junior in consecration, was translated to the northern Primacy and Bishop Warman succeeded him in the great see of Manchester. Here he was in a most congenial atmosphere. He had been in earlier years an examining chaplain to Bishop Knox, and at Birkenhead he had lived for 15 years on the borders of the diocese. He knew its conditions well, and he was specially adapted to appeal to a great commercial community. For his brisk and genial manner, his businesslike habits, his ability as a chairman commended him to business men, and his precise and clear preaching and speaking won their attention and respect.

Bishop Warman might easily have become a controversialist: he had gifts which tell most effectively in that technique. To his honour he resisted the temptation. He published several books: *Missions and the Minor Prophets,* 1909; *New Testament Theology,* 1910; *The English Reformation;* and *The Evangelical Movement,* 1916. But these books were written chiefly for the benefit of his pupils at St. Aidan's; they are hardly works of erudition. For though Dr. Warman knew well what scholarship was and had lectured on Hellenistic Greek in the University of Liverpool, he was too busy with practical administration to be able to afford time for research. He must have keenly appreciated the recognition of his scholarship as well as of his other outstanding qualities when he was elected an Honorary Fellow by his old college, Pembroke, in 1929.

He married in 1899 Gertrude, daughter of the late Norman Earle, of Dover. They had two sons, both of whom are in Holy Orders.

February 14, 1953.

Dr. Marjory Winsome Warren, C.B.E., who was killed in a motor car accident in France on September 5, 1960, was secretary of the International Association of Gerontology. She also held the posts of consultant physician and deputy medical director at the West Middlesex Hospital. She was 62.

She was educated at the North London Collegiate School, and after qualifying in medicine at the Royal Free Hospital and holding various resident appointments, she became assistant medical officer at the West Middlesex Hospital in 1926. When the adjacent Poor Law Infirmary was taken over by the hospital in 1935, she became responsible for reorganizing the care of several hundred aged and chronic sick patients. Dr. Warren tackled this task with characteristic energy and determination. After a few months many of the old folk who had been bedridden for years improved to such an extent that they became fit for discharge from hospital.

She then set about revolutionizing the miserable conditions under which it had been the custom to nurse old people. Infirmary wards were redecorated and re-equipped; but, in particular, Dr. Warren paid great attention to the nursing and general management of her patients. Her success in the treatment of cases suffering from cerebral thrombosis was notable. An article which she wrote for the *Lancet* about this work in 1943 attracted wide attention.

By the end of the war there was mounting interest in the medical problems of old age not in Britain alone but throughout the world. The example shown by Marjory Warren was widely followed. Doctors and nurses came in a constant stream from home and abroad to visit her wards at the West Middlesex Hospital. She herself paid numerous visits to other countries, lecturing and attending conferences on the care of the aged.

She was a founder member of the British Geriatric Society and a leading spirit in the formation of the International Association of Gerontology.

September 12, 1960.

Sir John Forbes Watson, K.C.M.G., director of the British Employers' Confederation since 1921, died at his home in London on August 25, 1952 at the age of 72.

His sudden death will come as a profound shock to all who knew him and will leave his wide circle of friends, both in Britain and overseas, with a deep sense of loss. It deprives the confederation of an outstanding leader and British industry of one of its elder statesmen. He devoted himself tirelessly to the work of the confederation, for whose direction he was responsible from shortly after its formation at the end of the 1914-18 war. It is undoubtedly due to his energy and foresight that the confederation was able to achieve the position it occupies in industrial life to-day. He set himself the highest standards in all that he did, and he was never content unless he had mastered the subject with which he was dealing down to the smallest details and, having mastered his subject, he had the capacity to express his conclusions with clarity and forthrightness. He never spared himself in his work and he inspired the same spirit in all who worked with him. Those who knew him well will cherish the memory of that example and of the kindliness which at the same time he showed in all his personal dealings.

John Ballingall Forbes Watson was born at Milnathort, Kinross-shire, on October 10, 1879, the younger son of the late John Watson. He was educated at Dollar Academy and at the universities of Edinburgh, Paris, Göttingen, and Heidelberg. He was president of the Edinburgh University Union and edited the *Student*. Having taken the degrees of M.A. and LL.B., he was called to the Scottish Bar and before the 1914-18 war was engaged in legal practice in Scotland. During the war he served in the Royal Flying Corps and the Royal Air Force from 1915 to 1919 and attained the rank of major. At the end of the war he was called to the English Bar by the Middle Temple. He served for a short time after the war as secretary of the National Light Castings Ironfounders' Federation and then took up an appointment as secretary of the newly formed National Confederation of Employers' Organizations (now the British Employers' Confederation), which had been set up in 1919 to deal at the national level on behalf of British employers with general labour questions, nationally and internationally, and of which he became director in 1921.

During the succeeding years he threw himself with great energy into his work of building up the confederation and by his determination surmounted the many difficulties with which the confederation was confronted. That work brought him in contact not only with most of the leading industrialists of the time but also with Ministers and Government Departments and the leaders of the trade union movement. He was a member of the National Joint Advisory Council and of the National Production Advisory Council on Industry from the time those councils were set up, and he also served on many other government committees.

He also played a leading part in the representation of British employers internationally. He was a member of the British employers' delegations to the annual conferences of the International Labour Organization from 1922, and led those delegations at the conferences from 1929 to 1932 and again at all the annual conferences since 1936. He was the employers' vice-president of the conference at its war-time sessions in New York and Philadelphia in 1941 and 1944 respectively, and at the post-war annual conferences in 1945 to 1947, and had been chairman of the employers' group at the conference from 1948 to 1952 inclusive. He had been a member of the governing body of the International Labour Office since 1928 and served as its employers' vice-chairman from 1941 to 1945 and again since 1948. He represented the International Labour Organization at the World Economics Conference in 1933 and at the San Francisco Conference in 1945 at which the Charter of the United Nations was drawn up. He also attended the Ottawa Conference in 1932 and was an advisory member of the British Government's delegation to the General Assembly of the United Nations and the Peace Conference in 1946. He had served on the executive committee of the International Organization of Employers since 1922 and had been chairman of that committee since 1949, having been the president of the organization in 1932-33.

He married in 1918 Alexandra Mary Georgie, only daughter of the late Canon J. N. Dalton, K.C.V.O., C.M.G., and is survived by her and by two sons and a daughter.

August 26, 1952.

Sir Malcolm Watson, who played an important part in the control of malaria and other tropical diseases in Malaya and Northern Rhodesia, died on December 28, 1955 at his home at Peaslake, Surrey, at the age of 82.

After a brilliant academic career at Glasgow and London Universities, he began the work that made his reputation at Klang, in the Federated Malay States, in 1901. Almost at once he discovered the origin of the Crescent (M.T.) malaria, and when in 1904 he extended his researches and preventive measures to the rural areas he discovered the micro-organisms which caused Quartan malaria and nephritis. He originated the method of control of malaria by species sanitation and various other naturalistic methods.

In 1914 he produced a larvicide for mosquitoes in running water. After he had returned to England to work at the Ross Institute he was approached by the Rhodesian mining companies to recommend methods of disease control in the copperbelt. The methods were so effective that within a short time the death rates of Europeans and Africans had been halved, and within 20 years the whole health picture of the area had been transformed. His interests were by no means bounded by control of these diseases, for he also patented processes for rubber tapping and for the control of dust in mines, and the prevention of silicosis and explosions in coal mines.

Born on August 24, 1873, the son of the late George Watson, Eastfield, Bridge of Allan, he was educated at Glasgow High School and University and University College London. He qualified M.B., C.M.Glas. (commended) in 1895, becoming M.D. (commended) in 1903. After holding resident posts in different hospitals in Glasgow he began anti-malarial work in towns in the Federated Malay States in 1901, and extended his work to rural areas in 1905. He also carried out anti-malarial work in India and Africa. From 1900 to 1908 he was in the Malaya Medical Service and from 1908 to 1920 Chief Medical Officer of the Estate Hospital Association. From an early stage in his career he received many prizes and distinctions. In 1914 he received a gold medal from the Rubber Growers' Association for services to the industry. He was elected an honorary LL.D. of Glasgow University in 1924, and during the next year he was elected Fellow of the Incorporated Society of Planters. In 1927 he received the Stewart prize of the British Medical Association for scientific and administrative work, and was made Sir William Jones Gold Medallist of the Asiatic Society of Bengal for contributions to science in 1928. He obtained the Mary Kingsley Medal in 1934 and in 1939 the Silver Medal of the Royal Society of Arts.

His last and most important appointment was that of Director of the Ross Institute of Tropical Hygiene of the London School of Tropical Medicine. He was a member of various committees, including the council of the British Medical Association, 1928-34, and the Malaria Advisory Board of the Federal Malay States (1911-28). Besides articles in official reports and medical journals, he was the author of *Rural Sanitation in the Tropics* (1915) and conjointly with others *Prevention of Malaria in the Federated Malay States* (2nd ed. 1921).

He was twice married; his first wife, Jean Alice, the eldest daughter of the late David Gray, of Glasgow, whom he married in 1900 and by whom he had three sons, died in 1935. His second wife was Constance Evelyn, the eldest daughter of Colonel W. L. Loring, whom he married in 1938 and by whom he had one daughter.

December 29, 1955.

G. Fiddes Watt, R.S.A., who died on November 22, 1960 in Aberdeen at the age of 87, will be best remembered as a portrait painter, and almost exclusively a painter of men. Out of the 22 portraits shown by him at the Royal Academy between 1916 and 1930 only one was the portrait of a woman—"The Artist's Mother", exhibited in 1930 and purchased for the nation out of the Chantrey Bequest Fund.

In an article which he wrote in that year Fiddes Watt explained that his reluctance to paint women was not due to misogyny but simply because: "In my experience they come to the studio full of the desire to be painted as they think they are and not as the artist sees them; consequently they conceal their true character—whether consciously or not, the result is the same—and the artist might as well expend his effort in painting a china doll". He preferred painting age to youth. Recalling that he once painted a successful portrait of Robert Louis Stevenson's nurse, affectionately known as "Cummie", he laid it down in conclusion that character is the only real beauty.

In appearance, with his solid head, heavy-lidded observant eyes and rather dour expression, dominated by a closely trimmed moustache, as in his work, Fiddes Watt was a typical Scotsman. The only son of George Watt, he was born at Aberdeen on February 15, 1873, and studied at the Royal Scottish Academy School, where he won the Chalmers' Bursary for painting, the extra painting prize and the Maclean Watters medal. In his *Scottish Painting Past and Present* Sir James L. Caw suggests that Fiddes Watt derived from Sargent through Robert Brough, but the model felt behind his work by the mere Sassenach is undoubtedly Raeburn. Not superficially attractive, though full of character, portraits by Fiddes Watt have a masculine bluntness of conception and a freedom of handling which combine to produce an effect of rugged force rather than of true solidity. Like Raeburn himself he was more remarkable for realization of character than for intellectual grasp of construction.

Fiddes Watt painted many of the celebrated men of his day, statesmen, politicians and lawyers in particular. They included Lord Haldane (for Lincoln's Inn); Lord Asquith and Lord Loreburn (both for Balliol College, Oxford); the Archbishop of York (for All Souls' College, Oxford); Lord Grey, Lord Balfour of Burleigh*, Lord Ullswater and the Duke of Atholl. It was evident that force of personality meant more to him than rank or reputation or even intellectual distinction. More articulate in words than painters generally are, he made interesting observations to this effect. He once gave it as his opinion that the men and women of the twentieth century are more obsessed with the desire to be successful than any of their forebears, and that the stamp of success could be read in their faces. Not unnaturally, this appreciation of success was reflected in his work, and his portraits seldom fail to convey the impression of men who have reached their goal.

Elected a member of the Royal Scottish Academy in 1924, Fiddes Watt was for many years a regular exhibitor at the Royal Academy, London, where he had taken up his residence.

Fiddes Watt married, in 1903, Jean, youngest daughter of William Wilcox of Park, and had three sons and one daughter.

November 23, 1960.

Major Lord Wavell was killed in action in Kenya on Christmas Eve, 1953, when his unit was attacked by 20 terrorists near the township of Theka, 30 miles from Nairobi. The second earl, aged 37, he was a notable scion of a remarkable stock.

More than a century ago one of his forebears who, like his father, the first Lord Wavell, had been in College at Winchester, served as a brilliant military free-lance in South America. While Archie John (as his father used to call him) was still at Winchester it was clear that, if he followed the family profession, his soldiering would be of no ordinary brand. It was certainly already clear that the formalities of military discipline and the conventions of military life might be expected to mean less to him than to one less gifted and less imaginative. He was able, independent, original; intrepid to the point of recklessness; and he showed already at school that love of literature and history which was to be one of the great passions of his life.

The Right Honourable Archibald John Arthur, Earl Wavell, Viscount Wavell of Cyrenaica, and Viscount Keren of Eritrea, of Winchester, in the county of Southampton, M.C., was born on May 11, 1916, the only son of the first Earl Wavell and Eugenie Marie, only daughter of the late Colonel John Owen Quirk, C.B., D.S.O. After Winchester, where he was in R. L. G. Irvine's house, he went to Sandhurst, and from there entered his father's regiment, The Black Watch. He saw his first active service in Palestine, whence he wrote back letters of extraordinary interest, describing the country and the underground movement he was helping to fight, and where he was wounded, through treating a land-mine with characteristic scepticism.

In 1940 he was in the north of Scotland training with his regiment, and the instruction he offered the Clydeside "Jocks" was typical of him, in its mixture of Shakespeare with battle practice. Nothing delighted him more than to confront those who had advised offering a less ambitious literary face with written work showing that his unbounded enthusiasm had somehow "got *Hamlet* across". In the later stages of the war he was in Burma, where he won the Military Cross, and lost a hand. Returning to England to be fitted with an artificial limb (his chief concern with which was that it should be able to control a golf club properly), he gave up most of his leave to visiting the wives and parents and sweethearts of the men serving under him—men for whom his sympathetic understanding amounted almost to genius.

It was this gift which led him to his interest in Army education, into which he flung himself at the end of the war with a devotion that threatened his orthodox military career. "We are moving into a period", he wrote, after a course he ran in India, in 1945, "where an ever-growing number of people will have something to express within their own village or borough communities. It is probably in this, far more than in an economic or political sense, that we will have a democracy in England. In education, social distinctions will soon become irrelevant". The educational courses which he devised after the war were an inspiring blend of physical and intellectual adventure. He was justly proud when one of the men he had picked out, serving under him, played a vital part in the conquest of Everest.

During the last year he had been granted prolonged leave from the Army to work on his father's papers. He attended debates in the House of Lords eagerly, and his interventions on matters of social or educational policy had an independence and vigour which, while suggesting that membership of no party would suit him, nevertheless promised great things. But his overriding ambition, when all was said, was to be Colonel of his father's regiment, and still hoping that his forays away from the beaten track had not prejudiced his chances, he rejoined them for a normal tour of service oversea a few months ago. He had been in Kenya only a few weeks when he was killed.

Between Archie John and his father there was a bond of quite unusual sympathy, whether they were partners in a foursome at St. Andrews or differing on the merits of Gerard Manley Hopkins*, a sympathy to which testimony was borne in his father's original preface to *Other Men's Flowers,* and which was emphasized again in his own preface to the memorial edition of that book. It is one of his few appearances in print, and this again shows what one day he might have done. His letters were poured out on miscellaneous oddments of paper, some of which probably bore the superscription of Viceregal Lodge or the Cabinet Office, while others appeared to have been torn from the laundry book, and there was often a colourful mixture of pen, pencil, and red chalk. T. E. Lawrence, whom his father had influenced deeply, and whom he also had known, was for him one of the prophets of the new age, one for whom, as for Archie John himself, in the splendid phrases of Sir Walter Raleigh, the world's bright glory had not blinded the eyes of the mind.

He was unmarried, and had no brothers. The title becomes extinct.

December 28, 1953.

Lord Waverley, O.M., died in St. Thomas's Hospital in London on January 4, 1958. He was 75.

Less than a month earlier—on December 8—the Order of Merit was conferred by the Queen on Lord Waverley. The insignia of the order were handed to him in St. Thomas's Hospital by Sir Michael Adeane, the Queen's private secretary.

Waverley was perhaps the finest flower of the Civil Service competitive examination system of his generation. From his entry into the Colonial Office in 1905, his career was one long series of successes in Whitehall, in Dublin, in the Governorship of Bengal, in the Chancellorship of the Exchequer in the later war years, and in the chairmanship of the Port of London Authority. No single adverse criticism can justly be recorded of his administrative capacity, or his cool judgment; by Civil Service and political colleagues he was respected and liked; and he was never known to shirk responsibility or to court either favour or publicity.

The Rt. Hon. Sir John Anderson, O.M., P.C., G.C.B., G.C.S.I., G.C.I.E., F.R.S., 1st Viscount Waverley, of Westdean in the county of Sussex in the Peerage of the United Kingdom, was the only son of D. A. P. Anderson, of

Westland House, Eskbank, Midlothian, and he was born on July 8, 1882. He was educated at George Watson's College, Edinburgh, and at Edinburgh University; he also graduated in science at the University of Leipzig. He entered the Colonial Office in 1905. His varied abilities were soon shown, and earlier than is usual in Whitehall he was appointed secretary to important committees—that on Nigerian Lands in 1909; that on West African currency in 1911. In 1912 he was one of the group of clever young Civil servants whom Lloyd George transferred to the office of the newly created National Insurance Commission to cope with the difficult administration of his famous Act. Within a short period Anderson was appointed Secretary to the Commission.

During a great part of the war of 1914-18 he was Secretary to the Ministry of Shipping. In 1919, he was made an additional Secretary of the old Local Government Board, and when in the same year that department became the Ministry of Health and absorbed the administration of the National Insurance Commission, he was made Second Secretary. Soon after, at the age of 37, he was appointed Chairman of the Board of Inland Revenue. He had been made C.B. in 1918 and was next promoted K.C.B.

In 1920, when a strong man was required to cope with the then desperate Irish situation, Anderson was made a joint Under-Secretary to the Lord Lieutenant with Sir Hamer (afterwards Lord) Greenwood as Chief Secretary. He was then sworn a member of the Irish Privy Council. In 1922, on the retirement of Sir Edward Troup, Anderson was made Permanent Under-Secretary of State at the Home Office. Older men in the office recognized very soon that they had a big man in command. He interfered but little with his subordinates so long as he was satisfied that the work was being done well. A quick worker of great industry, he was never flurried, and he got through a great deal of miscellaneous business outside the strict routine of his department. In manner he was somewhat pontifical, but he was large-minded enough to modify a proposed decision, if convinced by the criticism or advice of a colleague or subordinate.

In the spring of 1932 Anderson left one of the highest posts in the peaceful atmosphere of Whitehall to become Governor of Bengal at a most critical and even dangerous time. The call was for an administrator, rather than for following the usual practice of selecting for the three "Presidency" Governorships men of noble family or those drawn from political life. Terrorism in Bengal had been vainly fought for years and had become endemic. An attempt had recently been made on the life of the retiring Governor, the late Sir Stanley Jackson. The record of daring outrages had almost doubled in the previous two years. Financial difficulties had left the province no margin for constructive work. Economic distress—a reflex of a world-wide fall of agricultural prices—seemed to forbid all hope of industrial progress; sickness and poverty were sapping the courage of the peasantry.

Within a year of Anderson's arrival an attempt was made to wreck his train. Again, in May 1934, he narrowly escaped being shot dead at the Lebong races, Darjeeling. The latter outrage was almost the last spectacular effort of terrorism, and thereafter it scarcely showed its head. The explanation was that Anderson's firmness of action in re-establishing law and order was accompanied by definite steps to restore sanity and balance to many misguided enemies of the Raj. His efforts were more particularly directed to the welfare of the *détenus,* a great number of persons, who, usually without being actual criminals, were deemed necessarily detained, either in prison or under close surveillance.

Remedies had long been sought, though not with the realism Anderson brought to bear. He established well-equipped training camps for the *détenus* to be equipped for undertaking small industries, particularly in rural areas with state assistance. An industrial credit corporation was set up. This reclaiming work was surprisingly successful: when Anderson left Calcutta the number of *détenus* had fallen by two-thirds, and within a few months his successor, the late Lord Brabourne, was able to bring to an end the detention system. The policy was in line with Anderson's steadfastness of purpose in promoting constitutional reform. During four-fifths of his term the awkward transitional plan of diarchy was in operation, but happily it fell to him to guide the first stages of full provincial autonomy, which came into force on April 1, 1937.

It was partly to secure this guidance, but more for Anderson's strength of character and sound judgment, that leading men in Bengal pressed for the extension of his quinquennial term, and he stayed for a further six months.

On his way home by sea Anderson received a pressing invitation to be a candidate for the Scottish Universities seat in Parliament. He was elected in the following February and remained in the House of Commons until the abolition of university representation took effect with the Dissolution of 1950. He declined the chairmanship of Imperial Airways, but accepted directorates of the Midland Bank and Imperial Chemical Industries. But this association with the City was brief, for in November 1938 he was selected by Neville Chamberlain to be Lord Privy Seal and take in hand, as darkening shadows overspread Western Europe, the problems of manpower and civil defence.

Anderson had the immediate duty of considering shelter policy. He approached Mr. William (later Sir William) Paterson [q.v.], the Scottish engineer, and asked him to devise a form of shelter that could be erected in a householder's garden and could also be made in large numbers at a minimum cost. Paterson's design, with certain modifications, was accepted and soon became known as the "Anderson Shelter". It was patented to prevent its commercial exploitation and Paterson—who died in 1956—presented the patent to the nation.

When war came in September 1939 Anderson went back to the Home Office (where he had spent so many years) as Secretary of State and Minister of Home Security. The whole foundation of A.R.P., provision for widespread evacuation from large cities, the internment of aliens, and the innumerable measures and regulations in the transition from peace to "all in" war was in his strong hands. On the resignation of Neville Chamberlain on grounds of ill-health in October 1940, Churchill* made him Lord President of the Council (with charge of very secret work) and promoted him to a seat in the small War Cabinet.

Churchill's complete confidence in him was shown when in September 1943 on the death of Sir Kingsley Wood he chose Anderson for the Chancellorship of the Exchequer. His 1944 Budget was notable as being the first for 10 years which did not contain new taxation proposals, and which he grimly said was giving "the mixture as before". His Chancellorship will be chiefly remembered, however, for the introduction of the "Pay as you Earn" (P.A.Y.E.) system of income-tax collection, affecting as it did the pay packets of some 16 million workers.

During his Cabinet tenure Anderson had general responsibility for the scientific research bearing on the war, especially in respect to atomic energy, carried on by the various technical committees. When he became Chancellor a consultative council to advise him was set up under his chairmanship. It was for this service to science that in 1945 he was elected F.R.S. At the beginning of 1946 he was appointed chairman of the Port of London Authority. In May of that year, as Romanes Lecturer at Oxford, he chose the apt subject of "The Machinery of Government".

In January 1952, soon after Churchill's return to power, Anderson was raised to the peerage and took the title of Viscount Waverley, of Westdean in the county of Sussex. On February 26 the Prime Minister announced in the Commons that the new peer had been appointed chairman of the Royal Commission on the Taxation of Profits and Incomes, in replacement of Lord Cohen*, who had been made a Lord of Appeal in Ordinary, and that the terms of reference had been somewhat revised. There was a storm of protest from the Opposition benches and Hugh Gaitskell*, the ex-Chancellor, asked the Prime Minister whether he realized that in the 1945-50 Parliament Lord Waverley had shown that he held strong political views corresponding with those of the Conservative Party. Subsequently the Opposition decided to raise the issue in debate, and this led Waverley to resign. He wrote to the Prime Minister that he felt the "unjustified personal aspersions" to be the more wounding because they appeared to have the active support of wartime colleagues whom he had regarded as his personal friends. Churchill's sympathetic reply enumerated the more outstanding services of "My Dear John" to the state, expressed his confidence that he would have been a most fair-minded chairman, and added that now Waverley had become the target of organized controversy by the Opposition he could not reproach him for seeking release from fresh toils.

It was not long before Waverley's services were again in demand at national level. He was chairman of the Floods Inquiry Committee set up in March 1953 to inquire into the causes of the disastrous floods of the previous January.

A month later he was appointed chairman of a committee appointed by the Government to devise a plan for transferring responsibility for atomic energy from the Ministry of Supply to a non-departmental organization.

Since 1946 he had been chairman of the trustees of the Covent Garden Opera Trust. It was a post that he occupied with the distinction that he brought to any task, and it was said that he had seen every work in the repertoire, both opera and ballet, many times.

In June 1957 Oxford conferred her D.C.L. upon him.

He was made G.C.B. in 1923, G.C.I.E. in 1932 and G.C.S.I. in 1937.

He married in 1907 Christina, daughter of the late Andrew Mackenzie, of Edinburgh. She died in 1920, leaving a son and a daughter. He married secondly in 1941 Ava*, daughter of J. E. C. Bodley (the historian of France) and widow of Ralph Wigram, C.M.G.

January 6, 1958.

Dr. Clement Charles Julian Webb, the eminent theologian and philosopher, died on October 5, 1954 at the age of 89. He was Oriel Professor of the Philosophy of the Christian Religion, in the University of Oxford, from 1920 to 1930.

The son of the Rev. Benjamin Webb, vicar of St. Andrew's, Well Street, and Prebendary of St. Paul's, he was born in London on June 25, 1865, and was educated at Westminster and Christ Church, Oxford. He took his degree in 1888 with a first in *Lit. Hum.* and in the following year became a Fellow and Tutor in Philosophy at Magdalen. His first published work (which appeared in 1903) was an edition of the *Devotions of St. Anselm;* it was followed in 1909 by an edition of the *Policraticus* of John of Salisbury. Work as a tutor and lecturer was heavy during these years. Webb had been Senior Proctor for the year 1905-06; from 1906 to 1909 he was examining in the Final School of *Lit. Hum.;* from 1907 to 1920 he was teaching philosophy for the Non-Collegiate Students' Delegacy as well as for Magdalen. In spite of these exacting occupations, he found time to write and publish in 1911 an important volume on the philosophy of religion, based upon lectures originally delivered under the authority of the Delegates of the Common University Fund, under the title of *Problems in the Relations of God and Man.*

Webb's reputation as a thinker was immediately established. He was, in 1911, appointed Wilde Lecturer in the University in Natural and Comparative Religion, a post which he held until 1914, and published (in addition to his inaugural lecture) a valuable series of *Studies in the History of Natural Theology.* Other works followed—a discussion of *Group Theories of Religion and the Individual* (1916) and a little book called *In Time of War* published in 1918; a short *History of Philosophy* had already been contributed to the Home University Library in 1915.

During the years 1918 and 1919 Webb delivered the Gifford Lectures in the University of Aberdeen, which were published in two volumes, *God and Personality* (1918) and *Divine Personality and Human Life* (1920), of which the first contained a valuable survey of the history of the notion of "personality" as applied to God.

When these lectures appeared a graduate of Oriel College, Dr. C. F. Nolloth, offered to found and endow a professorship (to be called the Oriel Professorship) of the philosophy of the Christian religion. The University accepted the benefaction, and Dr. Nolloth, who had retained the right of first presentation, nominated Webb who, after some hesitation, accepted the offer, and in due course exchanged the Fellowship at Magdalen for a Fellowship at Oriel.

As professor he published, in addition to an inaugural lecture (*Philosophy and the Christian Religion,* 1920), a work called *A Century of Anglican Theology and other Lectures* (1923), contributions to *Contemporary British Philosophy* and *Science, Religion and Reality* (both in 1925), and a study of Kant's *Philosophy of Religion* (1926), in which he was able to make due use of the *Opus Postumum,* an *editio princeps* of which had been published in 1920 by Professor Adickes.

Academic honours were added to him: he became an Hon.LL.D. of St. Andrew's in 1921, was elected a Fellow of the British Academy in 1927, and received the honorary degrees of D. Theol. of Uppsala (1932) and D.D. of Glasgow (1938). He had been a member since 1905 of the governing body of his old school (Westminster); he served on the Archbishops' Commission on Doctrine; and he was for a number of years a valued member of the Hebdomadal Council at Oxford, as well as of the General Board of the Faculties and other boards.

In 1930 Webb retired from his Chair on reaching the age limit of 65; but in the same year he went to India and delivered the Stephanos Nirmalendu Ghosh lectures in Calcutta, and two years later he visited Uppsala as lecturer on the Olaus Petri foundation. The results were seen in his *The Contribution of Christianity to Ethics* (1932), which was translated into Arabic, and in a study of *Religious Thought in England from 1850* (1933). Meanwhile he had published in 1929 an edition of the fourth book of the *Metalogicon* of John of Salisbury, and a book bearing the title *John of Salisbury* in 1932. He later held other lecturerships which bore fruit in *Religion and Theism* (1934) and *The Historical Element in Religion* (1935). In May 1944, Webb delivered at Oxford, by invitation of his successor in the Oriel Professorship (Dr. L. W. Grensted), a public lecture on religious experience, which was printed, together with a bibliography of his published writings and a biographical foreword by Dr. Grensted, and presented to the author by a number of his friends and pupils on the occasion of his eightieth birthday in June 1945.

He married in 1905 Eleanor Theodora, daughter of the late Rev. Alexander Joseph, honorary canon of Rochester. She died in 1942.

October 7, 1954.

Maurice Webb, P.C., a former chairman of the Parliamentary Labour Party, and Minister of Food in 1950-51, died at his home in Middlesex on June 10, 1956 after a long illness. He was 51.

He had worked for years, with courage and fortitude, under the severe handicap of continued ill health and the loss of a leg. He was a brilliant political organizer, and for 10 years from 1945 a prominent member of the House of Commons, holding office in Clement Attlee's* post-war Government as Minister of Food. He will be best remembered by his many friends for his absolute honesty to his convictions, his unconcern for himself, at least in a material sense, which led him from time to time to make great sacrifices. Beyond everything else his innate kindliness and consideration for others will not be forgotten.

Maurice Webb was born on September 26, 1904, the son of George Webb, of Lancaster, a cottage weaver and tailor. He was educated at Christ Church School, Lancaster, and was in turn newspaper seller, farm worker, and milk roundsman. At 16 he was a member of the local Labour Party, and two years later he became a Methodist local preacher.

He read voraciously, and at his home, at meetings, and elsewhere he was constantly meeting, in the years after the 1914-18 War, men and women who encouraged him in his ambitions towards a political career. This began in earnest when at the age of 21 he was appointed agent for the Labour Party in the Parliamentary Division of Skipton. He was a good organizer, and could talk easily and write attractively, but he did not succeed in winning the division for his party.

He made a deep impression, however, in Lancashire and Yorkshire, and his work so convinced the national leaders of his competence that he was appointed to the staff of the Labour Party's headquarters at Transport House in 1929, mainly to organize the Labour League of Youth. This he did so successfully that within a short time he had added more than 140 new branches.

In 1935 he joined the staff of the *Daily Herald,* and soon became its political correspondent, a position he held until 1944, when he joined the staff of the *Sunday Express.* At Westminster and in Fleet Street Webb was popular and was elected, first secretary, then chairman, of the Parliamentary Lobby Journalists' organization, as well as a member of the committee of the Parliamentary Press Gallery. In those years he was combining with his newspaper work a good deal of broadcasting.

In 1945 he was returned as Labour member for Central Bradford. Almost at once he was elected vice-chairman of the Parliamentary Labour Party. He succeeded to the chairmanship in 1946, and that office he held unchallenged until, in 1950, he became Minister of Food. He was convinced of the value of bulk buying by the state, and made some hard bargains with foreign suppliers, but the change of Government in 1951 deprived him of the opportunity of justifying his ideas by the application of a long-term policy. He was sworn of the Privy Council in 1952.

He had worked assiduously, almost for the

whole time he was in Parliament, bereft of his right leg. A trifling fall at a children's party in 1944 brought on severe trouble, so that amputation was necessary in 1946 to save his life. Thereafter he was never in robust health and he was often unable, for considerable spells, to be in regular attendance in the House of Commons, or to visit his constituency. He felt acutely, in these circumstances, the loss of his only son in 1951 who, as he grew up, had greatly sustained his father in his affliction. Yet he remained as a rule his old cheery and optimistic self, encouraged and supported by his wife.

Even the knowledge that his increasing inactivity would be almost bound to debar him from office in the future, and from service such as he had rendered in the past to his party, was no deterrent to his optimistic spirit, and, in the last days, he was anxious that he should not be described as a martyr.

One of the happiest memories that he had in those trying days was the sympathy and support of members of all parties in the division which he represented in Parliament from 1945 to 1955. A major revision of the boundaries of the parliamentary divisions of Bradford in the latter year upset the balance of votes. His old constituency, Central Bradford, ceased to exist and he fought North Bradford with the sitting member as opponent. His narrow defeat by only 69 votes was the end of a clean and gallant fight.

He married in 1931 Mabel, daughter of Edgar Hughes, of Lancaster.

June 11, 1956.

Lord Webb-Johnson, the distinguished surgeon, died in London at the age of 77 on May 28, 1958.

He had the useful but somewhat rare faculty of seeing what wanted doing and getting it done. This talent he used to the great advantage of the Middlesex Hospital, where he was Surgeon, and to its medical school while he was Dean. He found the hospital structually very much in the condition in which it was built on a clay soil in 1757. A hot and dry summer caused the clay foundation to crack and there was a real danger of the hospital being scheduled as a dangerous structure.

"The Middlesex Hospital is falling down" became a useful slogan. Subscriptions were invited and several charitable persons gave large sums of money, the hospital was rebuilt on modern lines with adequate accommodation for the nursing staff, and it was opened free of debt. Queen Mary [q.v.] became interested in the work in 1921; H.R.H. Prince Francis of Teck, the Earl of Athlone [q.v.] and Prince Arthur of Connaught were successively chairmen of the hospital. Webb-Johnson was one of the moving spirits in the rebuilding, but he worked with the hearty cooperation of his colleagues. The medical school of the hospital underwent very important changes during his tenure of the office of Dean from 1919. The teachers rose to professorial rank as members of the medical faculty of the London University and were adequately paid, thanks to the liberality of generous benefactors who endowed chairs in the various branches of medical study.

In addition to his great organizing ability Webb-Johnson had a pretty wit, which always made him a good companion, for he could produce, seemingly at will, amusing topical impromptus.

The Rt. Hon. Sir Alfred Edward Webb-Johnson, G.C.V.O., C.B.E., D.S.O., Baron Webb-Johnson, of Stoke-on-Trent, in the county of Stafford, and a Baronet, was born at Stoke-on-Trent on September 4, 1880, the son of Samuel Johnson, who received his medical education in Galway and Dublin and after graduating M.D. at Queen's University settled in practice at Stoke-on-Trent, where he was Medical Officer of Health. His mother was Julia, daughter of James Webb.

Webb-Johnson had a brilliant career at the Victoria University, Manchester, where he took the M.B., C.M. with honours, winning the Tom Jones Scholarship in surgery and the Domville Surgical Prize. He became Demonstrator of Operative Surgery in the Medical Faculty of the university, Surgical Registrar at the Manchester Royal Infirmary, and Assistant Medical Officer at the Manchester Children's Hospital. Going to London, he acted as Clinical Assistant at St. Peter's Hospital and was elected Assistant Surgeon to the Middlesex Hospital in 1911, where he was promoted in due course Surgeon, Lecturer in Clinical Surgery, and finally Consulting Surgeon.

In 1919 he was made Dean of the medical school. Being already a captain R.A.M.C.(T) he was called up for service in 1914, was soon promoted major, and ended as colonel A.M.S.

For his services he received the D.S.O. in 1916; was appointed C.B.E. in 1919; and in 1936 received a knighthood. By this time he was Surgeon in Ordinary to Queen Mary, Honorary Surgeon to the Queen Alexandra Military Hospital and to the Royal Hospital Chelsea. At the Royal College of Surgeons of England he was a member of the Court of Examiners and elected to the council in 1932.

He became president in 1941, holding this position longer than any previous president, and had the task therefore of steering his college through the difficult approach stages to the Health Act and the Health Service when it came into force in 1948. His tenure of office saw him repeat for the College of Surgeons very much what he had done for the Middlesex Hospital. He successfully sought financial support for special chairs. The Bernhard Baron chair for a Research Professor was the first. Later came the two endowments for a chair of Human and Comparative Pathology and for a chair of Human and Comparative Anatomy. He attracted various related specialties to use the college for the headquarters of their professional organization. He started a wider programme of postgraduate lectures than had ever been attempted before. All this organization and administration tended to obscure what his colleagues knew—namely, that he was a first-class surgeon with a degree of judgment and a skill at operating that ranked very high. In 1945 he received a baronetcy and three years later a barony.

The mid-summer of 1949 saw the end of the longest presidency in the annals of the Royal College of Surgeons of England, for by that time Webb-Johnson had exceeded Moynihan's record by two years. It is idle to speculate why he made no endeavour to retain the surgical "woolsack" for just a little longer, since 1950 was to be an *annus mirabilis* in the history of this royal college, the 150th milestone of its corporate life.

Had he not been proud to be at the head of its affairs in 1943, the centenary of the institution of the Fellowship, an occasion celebrated, in spite of the disorderings of war, with due ceremony and by the conferment of Honorary Fellowships? Had not the centenary of the College of Surgeons in 1900 been also a historic occasion, with MacCormac as president, third only to himself in length of tenure of the presidential chair? *Dis aliter visum.*

After leaving behind him the activities of the council of the College of Surgeons, Webb-Johnson soon found fresh scope for his unabated energy; in 1950 he became president of the Royal Society of Medicine, and during his two years of office he was a driving force in a building programme there. His experience in rebuilding the Middlesex Hospital and the College of Surgeons was absolutely invaluable in this new undertaking, and by his charm of manner and his obvious business capacity he was instrumental in attracting considerable financial support for the necessary additions to the building at No. 1, Wimpole Street.

His membership of the building committee at the College of Surgeons gradually ceased, but the college remained his great love and his zeal was thenceforth directed towards an appropriate setting for what still remains of Hunter's original collection, so badly damaged by enemy action in 1941, and to the work of the Hunterian Trustees.

Not only was he an almost daily visitor to the college but the financial anxieties of the Hunterian Trustees were removed by the generous MacRae-Webb-Johnson gift from Lady Webb-Johnson, which commemorated "her own father and was also made as a tribute to the many years of devoted service given to the college by her husband".

The honorary medal of the college was presented to Webb-Johnson in 1958, and a few years later Lady Webb-Johnson was similarly honoured with this most precious of all the awards of the college, the award being made "by reason of liberal acts or distinguished labours, researches and discoveries, eminently conducive to the improvement of natural knowledge and of the healing art". Subsequently Lord and Lady Webb-Johnson were both elected to the Court of Patrons of the Royal College.

At the termination of the Second World War the great post-graduate medical centres of Europe, such as Vienna, Berlin and Paris, could no longer attract, and Webb-Johnson seized the opportunity to make London the post-graduate surgical Mecca. He inaugurated courses of teaching in the basic sciences within the college: he prevailed upon Lord Nuffield* to help generously in the creation of a residential college, which now bears the name of that great medical benefactor: all seemed set fair for the college to become a hive in surgical industry, research, and education.

The supreme satisfaction which was his, that his dream had been fulfilled, was later to be damped by the rapidly increasing costs of everything, imposing difficulties upon the council, but he was dismayed that the college should have sunk its independence by an approach to a university purse and that into the internal affairs of the college round whose dignity and sturdy independence his whole being was centred other academic organizations should insinuate themselves. Moreover, the sacrifice of the distinguished anatomist Wood Jones on the altar of an outside and perhaps critical university body distressed him greatly.

He had the vision to bring both dental surgeons and anaesthetists under the aegis of the college by founding a Faculty of Dental Surgery in 1947 and a Faculty of Anaesthetists in 1948, and he was later elected an honorary Fellow of each of these faculties, and a Webb-Johnson Commemoration Lecture was instituted to pay tribute to the man who had played the master role in the creation of the dental faculty.

He was a patron of the arts, a well-known figure at Covent Garden, a connoisseur of pictures, a lover of silver, especially that belonging to the College of Surgeons. His knowledge of London life of the past was not unworthy of the professional historian; his memory was remarkable, and while in committee he was quick in repartee and thrust, the address or oration was also delivered without a note, a practice which he always enforced on his surgical acolytes and pupils.

Throughout his career he seemed to attain success with almost mathematical certainty in all that he sought or undertook. Twice only did he fail in his objective: once, soon after the end of the 1914-18 War, his design to make Middlesex Hospital a post-graduate institution instead of an undergraduate one was defeated by the eloquence and reasoned persuasion of the late Victor Bonney and the late Dr. Harry MacCormac; secondly, his hopes that the two other Royal Colleges would come to the south side of Lincoln's Inn Fields proved vain and nugatory.

Behind the great facade of his achievements he was a man of charm and sympathy to patients: surprisingly there was a strain of emotion in him, and the tear that some thought fictitious was often very real, as was the sob that some have heard. Of him it might be truly said "he walked with kings, nor lost the common touch".

His death has robbed the surgical world of its greatest figure in this tide of time, and it will be long before another with the manifold, multifarious gifts of Webb-Johnson fills the horizon of the world of surgery.

He was made G.C.V.O. in 1954.

He married in 1911 Cecilia Flora, daughter of Douglas Gordon MacRae.

May 29, 1958.

Sir Ralph Wedgwood, BT., C.B., C.M.G., chairman of the Railway Executive Committee in 1939-41, died at his home near Dorking, Surrey, on September 5, 1956 at the age of 82.

The third son of Clement Francis Wedgwood, of Barlaston Lea and Etruria, Staffordshire, of the famous family of potters, Ralph Lewis Wedgwood was born on March 2, 1874, and was educated at Clifton and Trinity College, Cambridge. He entered the service of the North Eastern Railway under Sir George Gibb in 1896, and after three years in the dock superintendent's office at West Hartlepool became an assistant, in 1901, in the office of the general traffic manager at York. In 1902 he was transferred to Middlesbrough as district superintendent.

His next appointment was as secretary to the company in 1904, but he did not hold that position long, and in 1905 returned to the traffic department as northern divisional goods manager. In 1911 he became assistant goods manager at York and then chief goods manager, in succession to Sir Eric Geddes, who had been appointed deputy general manager, and three years later he combined with that position the control of the passenger department. Volunteering early in the 1914-18 War, he first served in the Transport Establishment in France. In 1915 he was transferred to the Ministry of Munitions, and from 1916 to 1919 he was Director of Docks under the Director-General of Transportation in France, with the rank of brigadier-general.

After the war he returned to the North Eastern Railway as deputy general manager in 1919, and in 1922 he succeeded Sir Alexander Kaye Butterworth as general manager. On the formation of the London and North Eastern Railway in 1923 by the amalgamation of the North Eastern, Great Northern, and other lines under the Railways Act of 1921, he was appointed its chief general manager, a post he retained until 1939.

He was president of the Confederation of Employers' Organizations in 1929-30, and member of the Weir [q.v.] Committee on Main Line Electrification in 1930-31, and a member of the Central Electricity Board from 1931 to 1946. From 1932 to 1951 he was a member of the Chinese Government Purchasing Commission and was chairman of the Committee of Inquiry on the Indian Railways in 1936-37. A member of King's College Delegacy since 1939, he was chairman from 1945 to 1950. A baronetcy was conferred on him in 1942.

He married in 1906 Iris Veronica, daughter of Albert H. Pawson, the author of *The Iron Age, The Livelong Day, Northumberland and Durham,* and other books. They had a son and a daughter, and the baronetcy now devolves upon the son, Major J. H. Wedgwood, who was born in 1907 and married in 1933 Diana Mildred, daughter of the late Oliver Hawkshaw. There are four sons and a daughter of the marriage.

September 6, 1956.

William Wedgwood-Benn—See **Stansgate.**

Professor Ernest Weekley, who died on May 7, 1954 at the age of 89, did much to arouse the interest of the average intelligent Englishman in the history and vicissitudes of his own language.

It has been realized of late years that popularization of knowledge is a worthy and admirable activity and Professor Weekley was a past-master in the art. Modest, even shy, in conversation, he yet displayed that keenness of wit which was manifest in his writing. His brilliant but unpedantic attitude made his books as interesting as novels and many people looked forward with pleasurable expectation to each succeeding example of "Weekley on Words". This was all the more satisfactory because he was a learned man.

Born in 1865, he served a considerable academic apprenticeship before beginning his own teaching career. He pursued his studies at the universities of Cambridge, London, Berne, Paris, and Freiburg-im-Breisgau. The part of his career that is of public interest dates from his appointment in 1896 as Professor of French in University College, Nottingham. He was to remain there for 40 years, in due course adding to his duties those of head of the modern language department.

Weekley's first writings were text-books, like the *Matriculation French Course,* excellent of their kind but not calculated to make him a wide public reputation. But in 1912 came *The Romance of Words,* a small work setting out curious and unexpected etymological facts in a manner that gave them real fascination. *The Romance of Names* and *Surnames* followed, and many people quite unconnected with academic study came to look forward with keen anticipation to each succeeding example of "Weekley on Words". Works more directly designed for the learned public appeared in the *Transactions of the Philological Society;* and Weekley made solid contributions to lexicography with his *Etymological Dictionary of Modern English* (1921) and his *Concise Etymological Dictionary* (1924). He gave help over a period of years on the etymological side of the *Oxford English Dictionary.*

Titles like *Words, Ancient and Modern* (1926), *Adjectives and Other Words* (1930), *Words and Names* (1932), and *Jack and Jill* (written in 1939, at the age of 74) followed one another at short intervals. The extent of Weekley's popularity may be gauged from the fact that even popular newspapers would give him half a column on the appearance of a new book. He was a pioneer in popular semantics. Names in particular were his speciality, and he was of the opinion that the part played by personal names in the formation of our vocabulary had been insufficiently realized and studied.

May 8, 1954.

Lord Weir, honorary president of G. & J. Weir Ltd., died on July 2, 1959 at his home at Giffnock, Renfrewshire, at the age of 82.

The Rt. Hon. Sir William Douglas Weir, P.C., G.C.B., Viscount Weir, of Eastwood in the county of Renfrew, in the Peerage of the United Kingdom, was born on May 12, 1877, the son of James Weir, inventor of the Weir feed pump. He was educated at the High School, Glasgow, and at the age of 16 was apprenticed to his father's engineering firm, G. & J. Weir, Limited, of which he was managing director when the First World War broke out. Although it had never manufactured aircraft, the firm tendered to supply complete aircraft, while other Glasgow firms were only prepared to turn out parts. So successful was it that in 1915 Weir was appointed Director of the Scottish Branch of the Ministry of Munitions, a post which gave full scope to his talent for organization.

In 1917 he became Controller of Aeronautical Supplies and a member of the Air Board, and in 1918 Director-General of Aircraft Production at the Ministry of Munitions. He was knighted in 1917. From April to December 1918, he was Secretary of State for the Royal Air Force in succession to Lord Rothermere, and President of the Air Council; in the same year his outstanding services were rewarded with a peerage and he was sworn of the Privy Council.

His attempt to provide "steel houses" with the aid of the Government subsidy was only partially successful. In vain he insisted that his houses were the cheapest of all the experimental buildings erected, and that their drawbacks were grossly misrepresented. His contention that standardized mass-production would reduce the cost and enable unemployed labour to be utilized was met by the fierce opposition of the building trade, which objected to the employment of badly trained dilutees in what it considered its own job; and more especially against the fact that, although Weir was willing enough to employ trade unionists, he was dead against collective bargaining.

In January 1928 he offered to present to the Glasgow Corporation his Cardonald factory on condition that the council proceeded with the erection of 5,000 Weir houses. This offer was rejected, and the factory was closed.

Weir was chairman of the Government committee whose recommendations resulted in the setting up of the Central Electricity Board, and in 1929-31 he presided over the committee which considered the problems of main line railway electrification.

In 1934 he was created G.C.B. and in 1935, at the joint request of Stanley Baldwin (then Prime Minister) and Neville Chamberlain, he took on advisory duties relating to air rearmament and Imperial defence, but when in 1938 Lord Swinton* resigned, Weir asked to be released from his work at the Air Ministry and at the Committee of Imperial Defence. A year later a viscountcy was conferred upon him.

In the Second World War he served as Director-General of Explosives, Ministry of Supply, from 1939 to 1941, and as chairman of the Tank Board in 1942.

He was a generous benefactor—engineering organizations in particular received large sums from him—and in 1953 gave £15,000 to the National Playing Fields Association.

He married in 1904 Alice, daughter of John MacConnachie, by whom he had two sons and a daughter. The family honours now pass to the Hon. James Kenneth Weir, C.B.E., the elder and surviving son.

July 3, 1959.

Andrew Weir—See **Inverforth.**

Sir Cecil McAlpine Weir, K.C.M.G., K.B.E., M.C., who had devoted his life for the past 50 years to the service of the state and to immense activity in the world of industry and commerce, died on October 30, 1960 at his home in London. He was 70.

Both at home and abroad he was best known as the head from 1952-55 of the United Kingdom Delegation to the High Authority of the European Coal and Steel Community, and before that he had been a prominent figure in Whitehall and in the Control Commission for Germany which, together with his other activities in Government circles, was apt to lead people to forget that he had also had a busy life in the City and as chairman and director of various companies including the British Tabulating Machine Co. Limited, whose affairs he had piloted for many years.

He was born on July 5, 1890, at Bridge of Weir, the younger son of the late Alexander Cunningham Weir, and was educated at Morrison's Academy, Crieff, in Switzerland, and in Germany. He first entered industry through the leather company of Schrader, Mitchell and Weir, of which he became one of the active partners, but his business interests in his native Scotland soon drew attention to his considerable capacity as administrator and for a period before the outbreak of the Second World War he left business to become Civil Defence Commissioner for the Western District. Early in 1940, however, more urgent and important public duties were thrust upon him and for some years he was occupying three high executive offices mainly at the same time. He was Controller-General of Factory and Storage Premises for two years, Director-General of Equipment and Stores at the Ministry of Supply (1942-46), and for six years until 1946 he was the Business Member of the Industrial and Export Council of the Board of Trade.

When in 1946 he left the Ministry of Supply he took on the post of Economic Adviser to the Control Commission for Germany followed by two years as chairman of the Dollar Exports Board. It was on completion of the latter task that he became head of the British delegation to the European Coal and Steel Community, but throughout these years he still maintained his interest in the affairs of the Glasgow leather company, with which he never severed his connexion. He had also been president of the Glasgow Chamber of Commerce, and was chairman of the Administrative Committee which organized the Empire Exhibition in Scotland in 1938.

Although it would not be proper to suggest that Weir's interests and activities were in any way circumscribed, it is true to say that because of his great sense of duty and his powers of concentration he lived very much in the atmosphere of the posts which he shouldered and discharged with such capacity and high distinction, but also with much charm and kindliness. It was said of him that he was one of the most successful representatives and administrators sent abroad by Britain in this century. It was perhaps characteristic of him that during most of his time with the High Authority he maintained a home in Luxembourg. In addition to his duties as chairman of the British Tabulating Machine Co. Ltd. he was on the boards for some time of British Enka Ltd. and the Pyrene Co. Ltd., and a part-time member of the British Transport Commission.

Weir was one of those men who, reared in private business, found satisfaction in working incredibly long hours on the jobs that offered him the widest scope. All who worked with him while he was undertaking the task of restoring the German economy after the last war will have regarded him with the highest esteem. In his autobiography, *Civilian Assignment,* published in 1953, he says that "one gets as much out of public life as one puts in. There are few spheres in which one can find so much interest, and in the real sense, enjoyment as in the arena of public affairs. It may not be very remunerative, but it provides compensations in experience and education and satisfaction which no money can buy".

His gift of organization and his capacity to see things steadily and clearly and in the minutest detail served him in good stead during the last war when, in 1941, for instance, he was in charge of the control of factory and storage premises, which commandeered and allotted space for various warlike purposes and which eventually disposed of about 20,000 buildings. Later in the war his organizing gifts released more than a quarter of a million workers for essential jobs. He was a man of unlimited energy and in Scotland was affectionately known as "wee Cecil". In the 1914-18 War he fought with The Cameronians and the Tank Brigade. He was wounded at Gallipoli, where he won the Military Cross. After the war he returned to Scotland, took an interest in politics and became Secretary of the Scottish Liberal Federation. He was knighted in 1938 for the major role he took in creating the Empire Exhibition at Glasgow.

He married in 1915 Jenny Payton Maclay, whose tragic death in an air disaster in the autumn of 1958 was a great blow to him. They had one son and one daughter.

October 31, 1960.

Dr. Chaim Weizmann, D.SC., PH.D., LL.D., the first President of Israel, died on November 9, 1952 at his home, less than three weeks before his seventy-eighth birthday.

He devoted his whole life to furthering the cause of Zionism, and no man, over so prolonged a period of time, contributed so much to the achievement of the Jewish state. In the crisis of the 1914-18 war he played a significant part in securing the Balfour Declaration, and, thereafter, as president of the World Zionist Organization, was an outstanding figure of the movement. He lived to see his vision become reality, for in May 1948 he accepted the invitation to serve as first President of the State of Israel, an honour which was confirmed when some 12 months ago he was re-elected to office, in spite of the fact that for some years previously he had been in failing health. Eminent contemporaries have paid tribute to Weizmann's statesmanship and his indomitable spirit; but if no Zionist movement had existed he would still have obtained celebrity as a scientist of the first rank.

Weizmann was born on November 27, 1874, at Motyli, near Pinsk, Poland. He had the usual religious education of a Jewish boy, then proceeded to the Gymnasium at Pinsk and later studied chemistry at the Universities of Berlin and Freiburg, of which he was respectively Ph.D. and D.Sc. He lectured for a time in chemistry at Geneva and in 1903 went to England, where he became Reader in Bio-Chemistry in the University of Manchester, which later gave him the honorary degree of LL.D. While still a student he had developed a deep interest in Zionism and early entered into Zionist politics. There he pressed for cultural work in the fields of education and colonization, in preference to political activities which then absorbed the attention of Herzl, the head of the movement. Later, after Herzl's death, he turned to a compromise, a combination of practical work in Palestine with political activity. His interest in cultural Zionism never slackened and came to the forefront in 1911, when he induced the Zionist Congress to resolve on the establishment of a Hebrew University. This resolution bore fruit when Weizmann had the happiness of laying one of the foundation-stones of such a university on Mount Scopus, near Jerusalem, in 1918, and when the university itself was inaugurated by Lord Balfour in 1925.

The great opportunity, however, came with the outbreak of the war in 1914. Weizmann was then only an ordinary member of the Greater Actions Committee, a large body that met once or twice between the biennial Zionist Congresses to consider Zionist problems. The outbreak of war broke the Zionist organization, like all other international bodies. Isolated, and without authority, he realized that the opportunity of Zionism was at hand. Introductions to Lloyd George and Viscount (then Mr. Herbert) Samuel*, members of the Cabinet, and an interview with Balfour, the most influential statesman outside the Cabinet, to whom he had once explained Zionism 10 years earlier, gave him political contacts. These were the first steps that led to the Balfour Declaration, the Mandate for Palestine, the creation of a Jewish national home, and ultimately of the state of Israel.

In the meantime the 1914-18 war was pursuing its course and the need for an unlimited supply of explosives was making itself felt. For this acetone was an essential. Acetone had previously been obtained from timber, very large quantities of which had to be used, with consequent great pressure on the transport by which the timber had to be imported. Weizmann discovered a process whereby acetone can be obtained also from maize, of which a very much smaller quantity is required than of timber, and, by his subsequent substitution of horse-chestnuts for maize, imports were entirely obviated. He had been taken to London in 1916 as director of the Admiralty laboratories. His great services to the allies in the pursuit of the war were more than once acknowledged.

At the conclusion of the 1914-18 war he declined the honours that were offered to him, being satisfied to have served his country. He had been naturalized 10 years before. Zionism and his scientific services were kept entirely apart. The Palestine policy which he always urged on the British Government he sincerely believed to be as much in British as in Jewish interests. He did not ask for it as payment, but for its intrinsic value. Already in April 1918, before the war was concluded and when only half of Palestine was in British occupation, a Zionist commission, with Weizmann at its head, was sent out from England to direct the Jewish population of the occupied territory and to act as a liaison between it and the Army. At the Peace Conference the next year he was the principal Zionist representative and gave an explanation of Zionist aims to the Council of Ten. He more than once forecast a bi-national Palestine, Jews and Arabs enjoying equal rights. This policy did not secure the undivided support of his fellow-Zionists and was undoubtedly one of the causes that deprived him temporarily of the presidency of the Zionist organization in 1931.

Weizmann was at the first opportunity, in 1920, given office as president of the Zionist organization. Henceforth, with the exception of the four years 1931 to 1935, he retained that office until 1946, adding to it in 1929 the presidency of the Jewish Agency, in which Zionists and non-Zionists at first took part. Weizmann met at times with much opposition within the organization. All schools of thought are represented there, and naturally his policy of a *modus vivendi* with the Arabs and complete confidence in and cooperation with the British Government did not always find unanimous acceptance in a body whose members are drawn from all the countries of the world. Weizmann always steered a middle course, anxious to conciliate as far as possible also non-Zionist Jewish opinion. A part of this policy was the creation of the Jewish Agency for Palestine. For five years he conducted the long-drawn-out negotiations that culminated in 1929 in the creation of the Agency. In 1934 he made a home in Palestine, and accepted the directorship of the Daniel Sieff Research Institute at Rehoboth.

The Arab outbreak of 1929 and the announcement of British policy that followed it came as severe blows to him. As a protest against the policy defined by the British Government he resigned his presidency of the organization and the agency, to resume it only after the policy had to some extent been modified by the Prime Minister. But his position was shaken, and at the next Zionist Congress, in 1937, he was not re-elected. The MacDonald White Paper of 1939 brought him still greater disappointment, as a consequence of which he gravitated noticeably towards the extreme of political Zionism. He travelled far from the teachings of Ahad Ha'Am. The creation of a political state took a definite and prominent place in his policy, and an ever-widening chasm developed between him and those who remained disciples of his former master and who held to his philosophy of cultural or spiritual Zionism.

The events in Zionist history from 1939 onwards increased his difficulties. Bitterly disappointed by them, he had to fight two continuous battles, one with a very large section of his own followers who began to attribute their disappointments to his leadership; the other with successive British Governments from whom he struggled hard to get concessions with which he might satisfy at least some of his followers. He went so far as to accept the proposal of the Royal Commission in 1937 for the partition of Palestine into Jewish and Arab independent states, although the most he could get from the Zionist Congress, and that only by a majority, was not to accept but merely not to reject his new policy. Later, partition, rejected by practically everyone, still retained the support of Weizmann, and when after the conclusion of the war in 1945 the future of Palestine became a matter of urgency, he, now in a position of greater freedom—the Zionist Congress of 1946 refused to re-elect him president and he had declined the office of honorary president—openly came forward as the principal advocate of the revived policy of partition. He owed his dismissal from office in part to this heresy.

In 1947 it became clear that he was still a force to be reckoned with, and in July he was in Jerusalem helping to present the Jewish case before the United Nations Special Committee. He expressed the belief that partition would give finality and equality, and he appealed for a quick decision. In May of the following year Weizmann, now in New York, accepted the office of President of the provisional Government of Israel, and in February 1949, under the stress of great emotion, the ageing President declared the Constituent Assembly open. In November 1949 a dinner was held in London to honour his seventy-fifth birthday. It was presided over by Lord Samuel*, and the guest of honour among a distinguished company was General Smuts, who had flown from South Africa for the occasion. In November 1951 Weizmann was re-elected President of Israel, but the office was, of necessity, merely an honorary one, for his health had given way, and the fire and enthusiasm by which he had for so long been supported were, in effect, quenched. His memoirs were published in 1949 under the title *Trial and Error.*

Dr. Weizmann married, in 1906, Dr. Vera Chatzmann, who survives him with one son. The death of their younger son, a promising young chemist, early in 1942, while on active service with the R.A.F., was a terrible blow to him.

November 10, 1952.

Ernst, Freiherr von Weizsäcker, who from 1938 to 1943, five critical years, was permanent head of the German Foreign Office, died on August 4, 1951 at Lindau, in Germany.

There has been, and probably for many years will be, an acute controversy in Britain about the part which Weizsäcker played both before and during the war in the shaping of German foreign policy. To some he appears as "the strongest influence against Ribbentrop and against war in the German Foreign Office". To others this seems altogether too naïve a view. He opposed a policy which courted war, but this was primarily because, in his own words, "We have no military recipe for defeating France and Britain . . . The war would end with our exhaustion and defeat".

Moreover, although he was anxious not to risk a war in which Germany (as he thought) would be defeated a second time, he was just as eager as Hitler to realize Germany's nationalist aims. The difference was that he hoped to attain the same objects as Hitler without provoking a war with France and Britain. "The task of German diplomacy", he wrote in 1938, "is clearly to ascertain the limits to which German policy can be pushed . . . without causing the Entente to intervene".

The publication of his memoirs, both in German and in an English translation, left the controversy where it had rested before. Those wishing to read the most favourable interpretation into his actions could naturally find much to support their case: for the whole point of the apologia was to prove how single-minded had been his struggle for peace. Those who rejected such a view could equally discover in the volume much evidence of his acquiescence—indeed complicity—in Hitler's policy.

History will probably be most interested in him as typical of the German nationalists who grew to manhood in the years before 1914, who after Versailles worked eagerly for the resurrection of German power and her expansion in Europe, who disliked Hitler and his methods but were prepared to support him as long as he seemed to be realizing their own nationalist aims, and whose influence in the shaping of German policy was always less effective than either their vanity or their need for self-justification allowed them to believe. Probably the greatest fault of Weizsäcker, as of the many others who thought and acted like him between 1933 and 1945, was his capacity for self-deception.

He was born in 1882 and spent the first part of his active life, from 1900 to 1920, in the Imperial Navy. He brought from those years the characteristic belief that the 1914-18 war was caused by a combination of German incompetence and of Sir Edward Grey's duplicity. In 1920 he entered the diplomatic service. He was for a time a member of the German delegation at Geneva, and found there only hypocrisy: "I left my Geneva post more impatient of foreign pretensions than I was when I came".

After being German Ambassador to Norway and to Switzerland he was, in June 1936, recalled to the Foreign Office as Political Director. Two years later he was appointed State Secretary, permanent head of the department. His memoirs contain many references to the searchings of his heart during these early years of the Nazi régime, but "the primary duty of the Foreign Office was to fight for peace . . . I decided to take that struggle upon myself". He remained at the Foreign Office until 1943, when he was appointed Ambassador to the Vatican.

The one clear result of his years as permanent head of the Foreign Office was that in the crucial years of 1938 and 1939 he succeeded in creating among foreign Powers the illusion that German policy was more conciliatory than in fact it was. On his actual influence on the course of German policy a final judgment must be postponed until more evidence is available. It is true that in 1938 he sought to restrain Ribbentrop, and later warned Britain of "Hitler's real intentions", in the hope that a stiffening of the British attitude would force Hitler to "draw back". But at the same time he was working for the same aims as Hitler. He sought the destruction of Czechoslovakia not by force but by a "chemical process of disruption of the Czechoslovak political structure . . . This process must, however, be a gradual one and must aim, by plebiscites and amputation of districts, at a collapse of the remaining area". The same process was to be used again later "to make the Poles more amenable".

In 1944, on the occupation of Rome by allied forces, he moved to the Vatican. He returned later to Germany, was arrested and sentenced to seven years' imprisonment by a Nuremberg military tribunal. The court afterwards set aside the charge of having waged aggressive war and reduced the sentence to five years.

In October 1950 the United States High Commissioner ordered the sentence to be commuted, and he was released.

August 7, 1951.

Joseph N. Welch, an American who crossed swords so effectively with the late Senator McCarthy [q.v.] in defending the Army against charges of communist infiltration, died at Cape Cod, at the age of 69, on October 6, 1960.

He had always been known as a "lawyer's lawyer" until, almost overnight, he became a national figure as special counsel at the Army-McCarthy hearings, which for a month or more were seen on television from coast to coast and in many ways were the beginning of the end for the power and influence of McCarthyism. Welch, who had a reputation for cross-examination, was devastating in his exchanges with McCarthy. His dry humour and satire, belied by an owlish, Dickensian appearance, often reduced the Senator to impotent rage—indeed, a new experience for the Grand Inquisitor of the American scene.

The hearings turned to a large extent on McCarthy's efforts to get exemption from Army service for his young assistant, David Schine, and, having failed in this, to secure suitably light duties for him—an aspect of the case that was denounced by the McCarthyites as a smoke-screen against their accusations that the Army was infested by communists. It was during these dramatic passages that McCarthy told General Zucker—another step to his undoing—that he was unfit to wear his uniform. But Welch remained impervious to McCarthy's heckling methods, which over-reached themselves when he made an especially nasty insinuation about a young member of Welch's firm. "Until this moment, senator", Welch remarked, "I never really gauged your cruelty or your recklessness"—a flash of anger that brought him 1,000 supporting telegrams.

It was this quiet, benevolent lawyer who perhaps more than anyone else took the measure of McCarthy and his works—this in full view of a watching nation.

After the Army hearings Welch was engaged as a narrator of mystery stories on television, and he played the part of the judge in Otto Preminger's film version of the best-selling novel, *Anatomy of Murder*—"I took it", he said, "because it looked like that was the only way I'll get to be a judge".

In recent years Welch preferred to loaf and fish—"in that order"—at a retreat near Boston where, endeared to his colleagues, he had spent most of his legal practice. He came from Indiana, the son of poor English immigrants, and always credited his mother with his success at school. He graduated from Grinnell College and in 1919 was second in his class at the Harvard Law School—having raised the tuition fees by selling maps and flagpoles, waiting on tables, and mixing cement.

October 7, 1960.

The Duchess of Wellington died on July 11, 1956 at Penns-in-the-Rocks, Withyham. She was Dorothy Violet, daughter of the late Robert Ashton, of Croughton, Cheshire, and her marriage to Lord Gerald Wellesley (now the 7th Duke of Wellington) took place in 1914. Under the name of Dorothy Wellesley she achieved a considerable poetical reputation.

W. B. Yeats in 1935, while compiling the *Oxford Book of Modern Verse,* came across her poem "Horses", and soon after wrote to her that her poems had "the noblest style I have met of late years". In 1940 a volume of his *Letters on Poetry* addressed to her was published by the Oxford University Press. Between 1938 and 1943 several of her poems appeared in *The Times.*

Dorothy Wellesley's first book, *Poems,* published in 1920, met with a rather mixed reception, and she was accused of "languishing through weary lines in quest of a dimly pagan Paradise". It was followed by *Genesis,* 1926, and by a poem-sequence, *Deserted House,* in 1931. In 1934 her collection of *Poems of Ten Years* called for some re-assessment of her standing as a poet, and critics noted the quality of rich detail for which her work was remarkable, and the inspiration she drew from the abundance and variety of created things, particularly in such poems as "Shells", "Birds", and "Moths".

Several of her poems were laments over the engulfing of fair forms of life, by a tide of commercial vulgarity. Two years later a selection of her poetry appeared, with an introduction by W. B. Yeats, which drew further attention to her talent—swift in movement and eloquently imaginative. Later volumes in verse were *Lost Planet*, 1942, *The Poets*, 1943, *Desert Wells*, 1946, and *Rhymes for Middle Years*, 1954, the last ostensibly a book of verses for children, but dedicated "to the middle-aged".

In prose she wrote, in 1935, an account of Sir George Goldie and his work in Nigeria; and in 1952 an autobiography—or something not quite that—*Far Have I Travelled*, which was described as "composed after a curious flickering fashion, so that passages of delicate perception are suddenly interrupted as if by a moment of boredom".

The Duchess of Wellington had one son, the Marquess Douro, and one daughter.

July 12, 1956.

Lady Wentworth died in hospital at Crawley, Sussex, on August 8, 1957 at the age of 84.

As a leading breeder of Arab horses and as a writer of books on breeding, Baroness Wentworth carried on the tradition of the Crabbet stud which had been built up by her father and mother. In her independence of mind, her eccentricities, her artistic pursuits, and her stormy domestic relations she reflected her ancestry—both her father, Wilfrid Scawen Blunt, the traveller and poet, and her maternal great-grandfather, Lord Byron.

Judith Anne Dorothea Blunt-Lytton, Baroness Wentworth, as sixteenth holder of the peerage, was the only daughter of Wilfrid Scawen Blunt and Lady Anne King-Noel, who as a child of the Earl of Lovelace was a granddaughter of Lord Byron, the poet. In youth she was a society beauty and her appearance made a strong impression on Burne-Jones, for some of whose last studies she sat. "She gives me the impression", he said, "of perfect beauty combined with the speed and lightness of foot of some wild creature". The second part of this tribute was not merely fanciful, for Lady Wentworth was a fine athlete. She became a champion royal tennis player, a game that is not generally regarded as suitable for women, and she built her own court at Crabbet. She was also a good squash player and went on playing the game until late in life.

In 1899 she married Neville Stephen Lytton, son of the second Earl of Lytton. The marriage took place in Cairo. The bride was given away by Lord Cromer, the Resident, who to the Queen's inquiry about the ceremony sent the laconic reply, "Marriage duly performed". She later became estranged first from her father, with whom she had differences of opinion about the management of the Crabbet estates, and afterwards from her husband, from whom she was divorced in 1923. Her mother succeeded to the Barony of Wentworth a few months before her death in 1917, when it devolved by special remainder on Judith Blunt-Lytton. The new Lady Wentworth lived for the rest of her life at Crabbet Park, in the grounds of which her father was buried.

She inherited from her parents the love of the desert and of the horse of the desert, the Arabian, and the "feeling for the desert" never left her. After her mother's death she took over the Crabbet stud which the unfortunate quarrels of her parents had allowed to reach a very low level, and gradually built it up to the dominating position which undoubtedly it holds to-day. There is hardly a stud in this country or abroad which does not owe its existence to one or other of the Crabbet stock. As a breeder she probably had few equals; she combined a voluminous knowledge of pedigree with a keen eye for a horse and with the means to breed on a big scale, and she had a certain flair or instinct which transcends scientific calculations. She was also a competent horse trainer and brought the business of preparing horses for the show ring to a fine art. The foundation of the modern Crabbet stud was undoubtedly the almost legendary Skowronek, a pure bred Arab foaled in Poland, whose sire was hanged in the market place by the revolutionaries of 1917; he was saved from a like fate by being bought for Walter Winans just before the First World War, after which Lady Wentworth acquired him. From this foundation has flowed the long line of champion Arab sires and mares which have dominated the show ring for many years in almost every country of the world.

A character as strong as Lady Wentworth's could hardly keep out of controversy; indeed, like the Biblical warhorse which she loved so much, she probably "smelled the battle from afar" and she was a doughty opponent. Just after the war she became involved in a violent controversy within the Arab Horse Society over the height and size of Arab horses in England. After much acrimony she won her point that there should be no limiting the size of Arab horses in English shows.

At Crabbet she used also to breed dogs, and her toy spaniels won innumerable championships. In later years she gave an increasing share of her time to her painting and her poetry. Among her books are two major works: *Thoroughbred Racing Stock and its Ancestors* (1938), and *The Authentic Arabian Horse and His Descendants* (1945).

She is survived by her son, the fourth Earl of Lytton, to whom the title descends, and by her two daughters.

August 10, 1957.

Lord Lyle of Westbourne—See **Lyle.**

Cardinal Archbishop of Westminster—See **Griffin.**

The Duke of Westminster died at his home in Sutherlandshire on July 19, 1953, at the age of 74.

Known to his intimate friends as "Bend Or", he was among the very fortunate in worldly standing and wealth, and though his accession to a dukedom and great estates early in life probably diverted him from any attempt to achieve distinction in politics or other of the great walks in life, it did nothing to destroy his charm of personality and his generosity of mind. He was a good and loyal friend and he earned in return the deep friendship of all those who knew him well.

Sir Hugh Richard Arthur Grosvenor, second Duke and fourth Marquess of Westminster, Earl Grosvenor, Viscount Belgrave, Baron Grosvenor, of Eaton in the County Palatine of Chester, and a baronet, G.C.V.O., D.S.O., was born on March 19, 1879, the third child and only son of Victor Alexander, Earl Grosvenor, and grandson of the first Duke of Westminster. He was styled Viscount Belgrave and, though his father died in 1884, he retained this style until his accession to the dukedom in 1899.

His early days were spent at Saighton Grange in a witty and happy family circle. He went to Eton in 1892 and left in 1897. He had no chosen career, though he had leanings towards the Army. After the outbreak of the South African war he joined Lord Roberts's staff as an A.D.C. His grandfather died on December 22, 1899. His new responsibilities in England brought him home in the middle of 1900, but his interest in South Africa did not end. A year or two later he was asked to assist in the resettlement of the annexed domains and he bought 19,000 acres in Orange River Colony. At his own expense he sent out 18 families from England, most of them from his Cheshire estates.

On his return to England in 1900 he was gazetted to the Royal Horse Guards, but soon resigned. His interest in sport was wide. He was a keen rider to hounds, he was a good shot and an enthusiastic polo player. He was an excellent car driver and in the early days he bought and drove with skill the swift Mercedes which were then holding the motor world.

At the beginning of the 1914-18 war he went to the front in an indeterminate position on Sir John French's staff, taking with him a Rolls-Royce car with a Hotchkiss machine-gun in the after compartment. With this he succeeded in waging minor war with the enemy. In November 1914 he was posted to command No. 2 Armoured Car Squadron, R.N.A.S., with the rank of temporary commander, R.N.V.R. With this squadron he went to France early in 1915 and had one or two brushes with the enemy. Later, when the idea of naval armoured cars became less popular, he took the squadron—now a military formation—to Egypt. In March 1916 he led his squadron across the desert and rescued the 60 survivors of the ship Tara, torpedoed in the Gulf of Sollum. They had been captured by the Senussi. It was a well executed operation, and for his services the Duke received the D.S.O. In the later stages of the war he was personal assistant to the Controller, Mechanical Warfare Department, Ministry of Munitions.

In the period between the wars his business acumen became clearly manifest. He was one of the first to realize that 1914 was (even more strikingly than 1939) the end of an era. The great eighteenth-century mansion, Grosvenor House, was pulled down and the site of some three acres let on a building lease in 1924. He made several gifts of land to the Westminster

City Council and the Westminster Housing Association so that work-people could be housed at reasonable rents near their work. By granting very long building leases on advantageous terms he fostered the great development of the low-lying land between Victoria and Lambeth Bridge.

His London estate suffered grievously during the 1939-45 war. Not only were many of the buildings damaged or entirely destroyed, but many that remained were no longer suitable in the changed conditions for the occupation for which, 100 and more years ago, they were originally planned. Many of the great houses in Mayfair and in the neighbourhood of Eaton Square were split up into self-contained flats and let at reasonable rents, and small, well-designed houses began to appear on vacant sites.

He also re-equipped many of his farms in Cheshire on the most modern lines, charging a maximum of 2½ per cent. advance in rent to set-off the cost of conversion, and he was busy up to the day of his death in great schemes of afforestation in Cheshire, in the Lake District, and in Scotland. His latest effort in development will eventually be of great benefit to British Columbia. Only in May he bought Annacis Island, in the Fraser River, immediately south-west of New Westminster, planning a great industrial estate, the first factories on which are to be ready for use in 1954.

He married first, in 1901, Constance Edwina, daughter of Colonel William Cornwallis-West, of Ruthin Castle, Denbigh. By her he had three children. Of these the only son, born in 1904, died in 1909. This marriage was dissolved in 1919. In November 1920 he married Violet Mary, daughter of Sir William Nelson, Bt., and formerly the wife of G. R. F. Rowley, Coldstream Guards. By her he had no issue. This marriage was dissolved in 1926. He married, thirdly, on February 20, 1930, Loelia Mary, daughter of the late Lord Sysonby. After the dissolution of this marriage in 1947 he married Anne, the only daughter of Brigadier-General E. L. Sullivan. The family honours devolve on a cousin, Mr. William Grosvenor, who is a bachelor living in retirement.

July 21, 1953.

Nicholas Jacobus De Wet—See **De Wet.**

Karl Adrien Wettach—See **Grock.**

Few men have excelled in so many different spheres of motor sport as **Kenneth Wharton,** who died of injuries received in an accident in a sports car race near Auckland, New Zealand, on January 12, 1957.

He first took part in a motor race at Donington Park in 1935, where he drove an Austin, and he later raced at Brooklands. After the war he came into prominence in trials, hill climbs, and sprints, with hybrid cars of his own construction, using an Austin Seven chassis and Ford and M.G. engines. Driving the Wharton Special, he won the R.A.C. British Trials Championship in 1948, 1949, and 1950. Then he turned to rallies, winning the Dutch Tulip Rally in 1949 and 1950, when he also won the Lisbon Rally. He won the Tulip Rally for the third time in 1952. At the same time he took up hill climbing seriously, and in 1951 he won the R.A.C. British hill climbing championship.

Breaking records at nearly every appearance, he went on to win the championship four years running, driving E.R.A. and Cooper cars. In 1953 Wharton was invited to join the B.R.M. team, and he quickly proved himself equal to the demands of handling this immensely powerful car, breaking the lap records at Goodwood and Charterhall. He took a B.R.M. to New Zealand in 1954 and finished second in the Grand Prix.

The year before he had survived a sensational crash in one of these cars at Albi, while before that he had escaped uninjured when he skidded off the road through a barbed wire fence in a sports car race at Spa. Indeed, he had many lucky escapes—another being in the Monte Carlo Rally when his Ford rolled over four times down a gorge. In 1955 Wharton joined G. A. Vandervell* as a member of the Vanwall team, but in his first race at Silverstone he crashed and the car was burnt out. He himself suffered second degree burns and a broken wrist.

Wharton was also a sports car driver of distinction, his best performance in this type of racing being as a member of the Jaguar team when the car driven by himself and P. Whitehead won the 12-hour race for sports cars at Rheims.

He will be remembered as a driver of unusual versatility, of considerable courage and skill, and of an unfailingly cheerful disposition.

Wharton was born at Smethwick in 1916 and was in business as a motor agent and engineer.

January 14, 1957.

John Wheatley, A.R.A., R.W.S., the painter and engraver, whose work is represented in the Tate Gallery and many other collections, died on November 17, 1955 at his home at Wimbledon. He was 63.

It is probable that his teaching and administrative appointments, not to speak of his own versatility, prevented Wheatley from doing full justice to talents which excited the highest hopes at the beginning of his career. As it is, his most important work was the establishment of a flourishing artistic life in South Africa. It was he who was largely responsible for the creation of the National Gallery of South Africa (formerly the South African Art Gallery, founded in 1872), of which he was the first director and chairman of trustees, and he was also for 11 years Michaelis Professor of Fine Arts in Cape Town University.

John Laviers Wheatley, who was the only son of Sir Zacariah Wheatley, mayor of Abergavenny from 1914 to 1918, was born there in 1892. He was educated at University College London, and studied art under Stanhope Forbes, Richard Sickert, and at the Slade School. During the First World War Wheatley served at first as a sergeant in the Artists Rifles, and was later appointed one of the official war artists to the Ministry of Information. From 1920 to 1925 he acted as assistant teacher at the Slade School. He was then appointed to the professorship at the University of Cape Town founded by Sir Max Michaelis, who about 10 years previously had enriched what was to become the National Gallery of South Africa with a valuable collection of old masters, mostly of the Dutch school.

In 1936 Wheatley gave up his appointments in South Africa and returned to England. That he had felt the interference of his official duties with his own development as an artist is suggested by his remarks to an interviewer at Cape Town just before his return. "I have been teaching for 16 years, and I feel that I have had enough of it. I do not intend to join any university or school of art in England, but want to settle down and do some painting for myself". Two years later, however, he became Director of the Sheffield Art Galleries in succession to Sir John Rothenstein, who had been appointed Director of the Tate Gallery. In 1947 he resigned his post at Sheffield on his appointment as director and curator of the Gallery of British Sports and Pastimes, which was founded by the late Walter Hutchinson at Derby House in London. It was not until the dispersal of that ill-starred collection was decided on after Hutchinson's death that Wheatley was without administrative duties and could give full time to his painting—and in the last five years of his life he painted much. Even so, he served, until 1952, on the Royal Fine Art Commission, and on the committees of several of the Royal Academy's winter exhibitions. At the time of his death he was chairman of the committee preparing the exhibition "English Taste in the Eighteenth Century", about to be opened at Burlington House.

As an artist Wheatley had an unusual combination of unconventionality in choice of subject and design with technical accomplishment. As was said in reviewing an exhibition of his paintings and drawings at the Wilson Gallery in 1938, he gave the impression of being incapable of working to a formula and of always obeying a particular mood of his own sensibility. From the circumstances of his life much of his work remained in the state of a brilliant suggestion, and sometimes, in defect of leisure to carry things through, he overstated his intention with an emphasis that obscured the fact that the intention really was artistic and not an attempt to catch the eye. Of Wheatley it may truly be said that, whether by choice or necessity, his private life as an artist was to some extent sacrificed to his public career.

He was a member of the New English Art Club, and most of his work before he went to South Africa appeared at its exhibitions. From 1923 onwards he exhibited regularly at the Royal Academy, mostly portraits in oil, though he also showed a good many paintings in tempera and drawings in Chinese ink.

He is represented in the Tate Gallery by

several works, including a drawing of "Mother and Child", purchased out of the Duveen Drawings Fund in 1924; by prints in the British Museum; and by paintings in the Imperial War Museum, the National Gallery of Wales, the National Gallery of South Africa, the Manchester City Art Gallery, and several other provincial galleries in England. He was elected an Associate of the Royal Academy in 1945 and a member of the Royal Society of Painters in Water Colours in 1947.

In 1912 he married Edith Grace, fourth daughter of the late James Wolfe, and had one daughter. Mrs. Wheatley is herself a painter and sculptor of great talent, and is also represented in the Tate Gallery and the British Museum.

November 19, 1955.

Sir William Cecil Dampier Whetham—See **Dampier.**

Sir Lionel Whitby, C.V.O., M.C., M.D., F.R.C.P., D.P.H., Regius Professor of Physic at Cambridge since 1945, and Master of Downing College, died in hospital in London on November 24, 1956 at the age of 61.

He was one of the most eminent bacteriologists and haematologists in Britain, who always retained a keen interest in all aspects of medicine; and he will be remembered for the distinguished services which he rendered during the 1939-45 War as consulting physician in blood-transfusion and resuscitation to the Army, and as director of the Army Blood Supply Depôt at Bristol. He took a large part in the development of blood-transfusion in the field and was responsible for the training of medical officers of the British, Dominion and Allied armies in methods which have been of inestimable value both in war and in peace.

He was also among the first in this country to make experimental studies of the sulphonamides, and in 1938 he was mainly responsible for the introduction of one of the most valuable of these drugs—sulphapyridine—in the treatment of pneumonia and allied infections.

Lionel Ernest Howard Whitby was born in 1895, the second son of Benjamin Whitby, of Yeovil, Somerset, and was educated at Bromsgrove School, whence in 1914 he won the senior open scholarship at Downing College, Cambridge. He did not go up to Cambridge until 1918, having meanwhile served in The Royal West Kent Regiment and the Machine Gun Corps in France and the Balkans. He was awarded the Military Cross and reached the rank of major, but a severe wound in 1918 caused the amputation of a leg.

After the war he completed his medical studies at the Middlesex Hospital, where he won the Freeman scholarship (1922), the Leopold Hudson prize (1922), the Hetley clinical prize (1923), and qualified as M.B., B.Ch., Cambridge in 1923. He obtained the D.P.H. in 1924, the M.D. and the M.R.C.P., London, in 1927, and was elected F.R.C.P. in 1933. In 1923 he was appointed assistant pathologist and bacteriologist to the Middlesex Hospital, and he was for some years pathologist to the Hampstead Hospital for Children and to the Hertford County Hospital.

In 1929 he was one of the team of physicians called in by Lord Dawson to attend King George V during his grave illness, and he was afterwards appointed C.V.O. He also attended Sir Winston Churchill* during his illnesses in 1943 and 1944. His appointment in 1945 as Regius Professor of Physic at Cambridge gave general satisfaction not only to the University but also to members of the medical profession, among whom his reputation stood very high.

Whitby was the author of standard books on *Medical Bacteriology* (6th edition, 1956), *The Nurse's Handbook of Hygiene* (8th edition, 1944), *The Laboratory in Surgical Practice,* jointly with Professor E. C. Dodds [later Sir Charles Dodds*] (1931), and *Disorders of the Blood,* jointly with Dr. C. J. C. Britton (7th edition, 1953). His work on chemotherapy was summarized in his Bradshaw lecture to the Royal College of Physicians in 1938. He was awarded the John Hunter triennial prize and medal by the Royal College of Surgeons in 1939 and the gold medal of the Royal Society of Medicine in 1945; in the latter year he was knighted. He was president of the B.M.A. for the year 1948, and was chairman of the education committees of both the B.M.A. and the World Medical Association. He was also president of the first world conference on medical education held in London in 1953.

On his return to Cambridge as Regius Professor, Whitby, already an honorary Fellow of Downing College, became a professorial Fellow and in 1947 was elected Master in succession to the late Sir Herbert Richmond. This new office he assumed *con amore.* Devoted to the college and all its interests, and having at his side a partner who was one of nature's hostesses, he quickly made his lodge a focus of easy and generous hospitality. At the same time he determined to organize the completion of the north side of the college. Part of the work had been accomplished during the mastership of A. C. Seward (1915-36), and it was a source of profound satisfaction to Whitby that during his own vice-chancellorship he was able to see the new building opened by the Lord Chancellor as Visitor of the College and the chapel dedicated by the late Bishop of Ely.

Meanwhile he was active as Regius Professor. It was always his hope that a clinical school would be established in Cambridge, but he knew that the achievement of this end lay in the future, and so he did not shrink from the labours of the vice-chancellorship which were imposed upon him in 1951. As chairman of innumerable committees and as principal guest at innumerable dinners, he preserved a calmness and judgment and a lightness of touch which made him *persona gratissima* at public and private functions alike. At the end of his tenure of the office he said to a friend: "Now I can get down to my proper job—the alleviation of pain".

In spite of his physical handicap Whitby was a great traveller. He would fly off gaily to conferences in remote capitals and was in great demand as a lecturer in the United States and in Australasia. When his daughter married and settled in Carolina Whitby would accept an invitation to lecture in America with added gusto.

He married in 1922 Ethel, second daughter of James Murgatroyd, of Shelf, Yorkshire. She is M.R.C.S., L.R.C.P. They had three sons and a daughter.

November 26, 1956.

Claude Grahame-White—See **Grahame-.**

L. C. White, general secretary of the Civil Service Clerical Association for the last 12 years, died in hospital in London on May 11, 1955 at the age of 57.

"Len" White was one of the two or three most brilliant trade union leaders outside the T.U.C. General Council and, indeed, a more able man than many inside it. As general secretary of one of the two largest bodies of organized Civil servants, he would have been a strong candidate for a place on the council if it had not been for communist associations which alienated some of the big votes. He said recently that he had never been a member of the Communist Party, but was a member of the Labour Party. He had a remarkable ability to deflate pomposity and expose hypocrisy, which he did with good humour but not always without offending the mighty in the movement.

He grew steadily through the years in the esteem and affection of his colleagues on the staff side of the Civil Service National Whitley Council, among whom he was respected for his sagacity, sense of humour, and negotiating ability. In 1954 they invited him to become their secretary-general and chief negotiator, and he would have taken over the post—subject to the formal approval of his own union—on July 1. He had plenty of moral courage and was never afraid to put difficult issues fairly and squarely before his members. In appearance very dark, almost swarthy, he had an encyclopaedic knowledge of civil administration and did much to raise the status of the clerical grades.

Leonard White was born on November 12, 1897. His father was a local postmaster in Cambridgeshire, and after leaving school Leonard was trained as a counter clerk. During the 1914-18 War he served with the Royal Navy and on his release went to a clerical post at the Admiralty. He soon became very active in the Admiralty branch of the C.S.C.A., being elected branch secretary, and his capabilities were noticed at the union's headquarters where he used to assist in his spare time. There also began a friendship, which was to prove a fundamental influence throughout his life, when he met W. J. Brown [q.v.], then the general secretary. Under Brown's guidance for the next few years he had an excellent introduction to everyday trade union practice, and by the time he was taken on as a full-time official he was conversant with the state of affairs in most branches of the Civil service, though the Admiralty remained his special sphere, and was expert in those problems peculiar to the Civil service, such as the marriage bar on women employees, provincial differentiation, and methods of entry.

In 1936 he was promoted to be the assistant general secretary and he was recognized as a national figure in the trade union world as a result of his work in preparation of the case for wage increases in 1936 and 1937. At this time W. J. Brown made frequent visits abroad and an increasing amount of the general secretary's responsibilities fell on White's shoulders. He began to play a prominent part on the staff side of the National Whitley Council, where the wide scope of his own union caused him to take a refreshingly broad view of most issues. With the coming of war in 1939 he was immersed in a mass of problems consequent on the opening of several new Civil service departments and the evacuation of others. The large new intake also differed in character from the permanent members and White more than once warned the authorities that while a great deal of reliance had always been placed on the tradition that Civil servants never went on strike, the same loyalty could hardly be asked of the temporary members. In 1942, after Brown's election to Parliament, White officially took over the position of general secretary.

During White's service with the union the membership grew from 20,000 in 1927 to about 150,000. By no means a negligible factor in this expansion was White's persistent support for the rights of Civil servants as citizens. He frequently came up against the Official Secrets Act in the course of his work, and during the war he disapproved of several of the inquiries made by M.I.5, which he maintained often had only the vaguest conception of what was meant by "political unreliability", into the private lives of certain Civil servants. That Ministers, because they were responsible for the policies which the Civil servants had to carry out and for which the latter often got the blame, should defend their underlings more strenuously than was customary, was one of his perennial complaints.

Yet, unlike some, White was big enough to see deficiencies in the service round which his life was centred. Thus he was prepared to accept that the Civil service was in some departments overstaffed, believing that greater use could be made of the trade unions' knowledge in reallocation of labour and in retrenchment. Addressing his own members, he would appeal to them always to act like human beings and not to consider themselves as being apart from the rest of the community. In his articles in the union journal *Red Tape* he consistently attacked any practice which was remotely suspicious of nepotism.

With the repeal of the Trades Disputes Act, White led his members back in triumph into the T.U.C. He had been president of the National Council for Civil Liberties and in 1947 presided over a conference on human rights which discussed racial and sexual discrimination and the freedom of the press. He sat on the editorial board of the *Daily Worker* and deplored the campaign led by some of his own members to remove communist influence from the C.S.C.A.'s executive, saying that there should be room for all political creeds in a democratic organization.

He played some part in the early stages of the formation of the Milk Marketing Board's Staff Association, and was for many years an adviser to the Prison Officers' Association, whose affairs he followed with the kind of zeal most men reserve for a hobby. The Civil Service Alliance's existence owes much to his efforts and from its inception he acted as secretary.

In 1946 and 1947 he paid visits to Malta and Gibraltar to assist the local Civil servants and had some success in raising the conditions of new entrants.

He leaves a widow and a son.

May 12, 1955.

Sir Thomas White, D.F.C., formerly High Commissioner for Australia in London, died suddenly at his home at South Yarra, Australia, on October 13, 1957. He was 69.

Thomas Walter White was born on April 26, 1888, at Melbourne, the son of Charles White. He was associated with flying in Australia in its early days, was the second man in that country to obtain a pilot's certificate, and was with the first oversea unit of the Australian Flying Corps in Mesopotamia in 1915.

He was awarded the D.F.C. and twice mentioned in dispatches. In November 1915 it was thought desirable that the telephone wires running north and south of Baghdad should be cut, and volunteers were called for. White and his observer, Yeats-Brown, got the job and succeeded in severing the wires but were captured by Arabs before they could get their aircraft airborne again. Thereafter, an unwilling guest of the Turks, White thought only of escape, and escape in Constantinople he finally achieved in 1918, after a progress of almost unrelieved hazard and exotic incident; the hoodwinked sentry, the café contact, the coolly cashed cheque, the dusk sortie, all were experienced by him in his efforts to get to a ship—which, when he found it, was not due to sail for 30 days. Ultimately he set sail with Captain Alan Bott, M.C., got to Odessa, and, after further trials and tribulations, reached security.

His experiences he later recounted in *Guests of the Unspeakable.*

After the war he went into business and later became managing director of C. J. White and Sons, hardware merchants and engineers. Early in life he had had ideas of entering politics and in 1929 succeeded W. A. Watt as member of the House of Representatives for Balaclava. From 1933 until 1938—when he resigned after differences with the Prime Minister, Mr. Lyons—he was Minister for Trade and Customs.

White did not again hold Cabinet rank until 1949, when he became Minister for Air and Civil Aviation, a post well suited to his talents and energy; he had founded the Australian Aero Club and had taken a leading part in the development of the flying medical services.

In 1951 he was appointed High Commissioner in London. There he was chairman of the Empire Council, the British Empire Service League, deputy president of the Royal Life-Saving Society, and a member of the executive committee of the Imperial Institute. He was a keen patron of the Australian arts, and helped form three organizations devoted to their promotion in Britain—for Australian artists, musicians, and writers.

When he opened an exhibition of Australian books at The Times Bookshop in 1955 he revealed a discriminating interest in Australian writing and particularly in present-day authorship in the Commonwealth.

White, who was made K.B.E. in 1952, married in 1920 Vera, daughter of Alfred Deakin, a former Prime Minister of Australia. There were four daughters of the marriage.

October 15, 1957.

Walter White, a fair-skinned Negro author who chose to champion his people's rights rather than pass as a white, died in New York on March 21, 1955 at the age of 61.

Though, with his fair hair, fair skin, and blue eyes he could easily have "passed" as many other technical "Negroes" have passed, whose physical appearance made them apparently a part of the ruling caste, he elected early to champion the race from which he, his father, and his mother drew a small part of their biological inheritance. The proximate cause for his decision was an incident when he was a boy of 13 in Atlanta and his father's house was attacked by a crazy white mob during the infamous riots of 1906. Crouching then, gun in hand, he realized that he was a Negro, a human being marked for persecution so that those with white skins could always feel superior. "I was glad", he wrote in his autobiography published in 1948, "I was not one of those whose story is, in the history of the world, a record of bloodshed, rapine, and pillage".

If there had been any hesitation or regret later, the manner of his father's death in Atlanta would have cured it. For his father was knocked down by a speeding doctor who rushed him to the best hospital in the city, where every effort was made to save his life. Routine inquiries revealed that this apparently white man was legally "coloured" and the desperately injured patient was consequently hastily transferred, in pouring rain, to the very inferior hospital that alone was open to Negroes. There he died, his last moments disturbed by a group of white hymn-singers who had come to speed him to another world.

At the age of 24, in 1918, the younger White joined the National Association for the Advancement of Coloured People and in 1931 became secretary. Meanwhile, he had already made a sufficient reputation as a novelist to be considered by the Guggenheim Foundation as a suitable person to be entrusted with the task of investigating the history of lynch law in the United States. The study, horrifying in its hard, cold record of man's inhumanity to man, duly appeared in 1929 and this, with his autobiography, has had a marked effect upon the opinions of thinking Americans, though as yet the effect has not been sufficiently profound for the federal anti-lynch legislation, on which he had set his heart and given his best efforts, to pass into law through Congress.

March 23, 1955.

Professor J. H. C. Whitehead, F.R.S., Waynflete Professor of Pure Mathematics in the University of Oxford and a Fellow of Magdalen College, died suddenly on May 8, 1960 at the age of 55. He was on Sabbatical leave in the United States, and during the current term had been visiting the Institute for Advanced Study at Princeton, where he died.

Henry Whitehead was one of Britain's greatest mathematicians. His contributions to topology were massive and fundamental. He also had an international reputation as a geometer and as an algebraist. In research he went from strength to strength. Profound study and ever-growing creative powers were seldom better used.

He lived in the village of Noke, where his wife Barbara ran a farm in which he took the liveliest interest. Their exuberant hospitality brought many and varied friends to Manor Farm, as it had done previously to their house in north Oxford. They shared great zest for life and enjoyed a marriage of surpassing happiness.

Whitehead was born in India in 1905. His father, Bishop of Madras and brother of the philosopher, sent him to Eton, a school for which he always had the highest regard. He went on to read mathematics at Balliol under H. W. Nicholson. After graduating he first tried financial work in the City but soon decided on a university career. In 1928 he went to Princeton for three years as a Commonwealth Fellow to study geometry under Veblen. It was there that his intellect was first challenged by the great problems of topology. After getting his Ph.D. he joined Veblen in writing a monograph on geometry which is now regarded as a classic, *The Foundations of Differential Geometry*.

On his return to Oxford as tutorial fellow at Balliol he plunged into college life with huge enjoyment. He was an inspiring teacher, a wonderful talker, and a lover of sport, especially cricket and skiing. After his marriage in 1934 he began to publish those pioneer studies which made him famous.

During the war he was elected Fellow of the Royal Society in 1944, while on Admiralty work, and after the war he succeeded Dixon as Waynflete Professor. This made him a Fellow of Magdalen, where he continued to enjoy many aspects of college life.

He inspired a lively group of research students, some of whom have now established reputations on their own. As well as his great love and knowledge of mathematics he was able to convey the deep satisfaction which it can bring. He was president of the London Mathematical Society from 1953 to 1955, and through the society and the London Mathematical Colloquium the invigorating effect of his personality was felt far beyond Oxford. Students came to him from every corner of the world.

He married in 1934 Barbara Sheila Carew Smyth, by whom he had two sons.

May 9 & 11, 1960.

J. Howard Whitehouse, the founder and for the whole of its history Warden of Bembridge School, Isle of Wight, died there at the age of 82 on September 28, 1955.

John Howard Whitehouse was born in 1873 and was educated at Mason College, Birmingham, and the Midland Institute. He began his career by organizing social schemes for Cadbury Brothers. It was evident that the writings of Ruskin influenced him greatly, for quite early in life he founded a Ruskin Society in Birmingham and on Ruskin's eightieth birthday conveyed a national address to him. His social work was almost entirely devoted to young men and boys.

Ruskin Hall, Bournville, and a boys' club in the same place were his foundations. He was successively, between 1903 and 1908, secretary of the Carnegie Dunfermline Trust and of Toynbee Hall, founder of the Secondary Schoolboys' Camp and Summer School in 1907, and of the National League of Workers with Boys. His energy was extraordinary, as may be seen from a mere list of the posts he held in the next few years. He was sub-Warden of St. George's School, Harpenden, in 1908; Warden of the Manchester University Settlement in 1909-10; a school manager in the East End of London; and he also served on Home Office committees on such subjects as the employment of children, night work for young persons, and reformatory schools.

In 1910 he added politics to his other activities, being elected as Liberal member for Mid-Lanark, and held the office of Parliamentary Private Secretary, first to the Under-Secretary of State for the Home Office and then to the Chancellor of the Exchequer (the first Earl Lloyd George) from 1913 to 1915. Since he had already had experience of relief work in the Balkans in 1912, he was chosen to be Commissioner for Belgian Refugees after the outbreak of war in 1914 and was in Antwerp until just before the city fell to the Germans.

After the war he founded Bembridge School with the intention of putting into effect his ideals on education, which he had from time to time discussed in many and various publications.

Although his admiration for Ruskin was still undimmed, Whitehouse found in Dr. Nansen an object of veneration; he wrote a *Book of Homage* to him; and in August 1931 presented part of the great down between Shanklin and Ventnor to the nation, to be called Nansen Hill, in perpetual memory of the famous explorer and humanitarian. He hoped that parties from other countries, and particularly students from Nansen's old university at Oslo, would camp there. Whitehouse was also chairman of the Fram Preservation Committee.

Though he had added Nansen to his heroes, his admiration for Ruskin continued throughout his life and in 1935 he acquired his master's old home, Brantwood, Coniston, which he presented to Oxford University in 1944. Unfortunately in 1947 the university felt compelled to return the gift to the donor for financial reasons, and Whitehouse thereupon quickly organized a new scheme, with the help of the Ruskin Society and the Friends of Brantwood, of both of which he was president, so that his scheme for using the house not only as a memorial to Ruskin but also as a centre of adult education should continue in being. Towards the end of his life he published three more books on Ruskin, *Ruskin: Renascence; Ruskin, Prophet of the Good Life;* and *Vindication of Ruskin.*

In 1954, feeling the burden of increasing years, he decided to give up the detailed administration of Bembridge, and in January 1955 G. R. Rees-Jones, a house-master at Marlborough, assumed the duties of headmaster of Bembridge; Whitehouse continued as Warden until his death.

It is an obvious criticism of such a career that he had too many irons in too many fires; but he was far too keen an idealist for anyone with knowledge to describe him as a *dilettante.* It is probably true to say that he would have been more effective if he had concentrated his enthusiasm and his energies on educational work earlier in life. Bembridge School, situated at one of the most delectable spots in the Isle of Wight, is unconventional only in the sense that it does not follow closely the English public school tradition; it is eccentric in the literal sense only. But no one who has read, for example, Whitehouse's essays *To My Boys* and the numerous other volumes on the education of boys that flowed from his pen throughout the years, could consider it in any way a "freak school". The creed he taught, at Bembridge and elsewhere, throughout his life was liberal without being partisan, international without being unpatriotic, religious without being sectarian.

September 30, 1955.

William Whiteley, C.H., who died in hospital at Durham on November 3, 1955 at the age of 73, was, outside of the House of Commons, one of the least known of all the Labour M.P.s who had sat there during the past 30 years, but for a long time, as Chief Whip of the Labour Party, he was one of the most powerful.

He was in appearance and demeanour the least likely man imaginable to have come into public life from the pits—tall, good-looking, always immaculately dressed, genial, but a man of iron will when necessary—he might have passed for a bishop in mufti. Yet until he was 30, when he became a miners' agent, he was working at a Durham colliery and there was nothing about mining life that he did not know.

William Whiteley was born on October 3, 1882, the son of Samuel and Ellen Whiteley, of Elland, and as a boy attended the Brandon Colliery School near his home, then in county

Durham. His father was a colliery check-weighman and he was reared in an atmosphere of trade union activities and Labour politics. In his young days he became a teacher in accountancy and shorthand at night schools, and some of his pupils afterwards achieved distinction in public life scarcely less than his own. Unlike some of his contemporaries, Whiteley did not enter active politics until his late twenties and he was in fact 30 or so when he joined the Labour Party and began to take part in public life in Durham. He was already active in county affairs when in 1918 he fought his first parliamentary election and was defeated. He was successful, however, four years later when he was returned for the Blaydon Division and he held the seat until the Labour *débâcle* of 1931, when he was defeated.

Whiteley was not in those days a spectacular figure at Westminster, speaking rarely, although always well and with authority; but he was recognized as a man of strong will and sterling qualities, and on the advent of Ramsay MacDonald's second administration in 1929 he became a Lord Commissioner of the Treasury, a post he held when he lost his seat. From 1931 to 1935 Whiteley knew difficult times, and was in fact only partially employed, but he won back his seat in 1935, and for five years was a useful back-bencher with an excellent record in committee work until, in May 1940, he was appointed Comptroller of the Household. In March 1942 he became joint Parliamentary Secretary to the Treasury and Chief Labour Whip, his Conservative colleague being James Stuart [Lord Stuart of Findhorn*]. This position he held until the end of the 1939-45 War and the change in administration which preceded the general election of that year.

After the Labour triumph at the polls, and the formation of Attlee's* administration, Whiteley was made Chief Government Whip and discharged his duties with a vigour and an *éclat* which won him the respect and admiration of political friends and foes alike. With his Government's huge majority he was for five years under no difficulties about possible defeat in the lobbies; but he had from time to time to handle incipient revolts, and recalcitrant, unorthodox members on the Government side, which he did with a combination of tact and admonition which invariably served its purpose. It was different, however, when in the general election of 1950 the Government returned with a working majority of only seven, and there is no doubt that his tremendous energy and his eagle eye were largely responsible for the comparatively long life of a Government so tenuously poised.

He himself worked tremendously hard night and day during the numerous crises which threatened to bring down the administration, and as a consequence the man who throughout a very long life had been almost invariably in his own words "fighting fit" developed a most troublesome attack of shingles, which kept him away from duty for some little time, although he was back again for the resumption in 1951. His consistently good health up to that time was probably attributable to his love of sport. As a youth and young man he played soccer, was in a number of Northern cricket teams, and did some rowing. In later years he liked walking, and loved watching football. However, at the end of last season he felt that his health could no longer stand the strain of work in the Whips' office and he resigned. He was too ill to attend the 1955 Labour Party Conference to receive in person the presentation that had been planned.

Whiteley never lost his interest in and contact with public affairs in Durham. For many years he was a member of the County Insurance Committee and Education Committee, and president of the Durham Mine Workers' Homes Association and of the Durham Miners' Approved Society. He was sworn of the Privy Council in 1943, and in June 1948 became a Companion of Honour.

In 1901 he married Miss Elizabeth Swordy Jackson, and there were a son and a daughter of the marriage.

November 4, 1955.

Sir Edmund Whittaker, F.R.S., the distinguished mathematician, astronomer and philosopher, died at his home at Edinburgh on March 24, 1956 at the age of 82.

Sir Edmund Whittaker was a mathematician of whom it has been said that the "astonishing quantity and quality of his work is probably unparalleled in modern mathematics". As well as his original contributions, which showed unusual versatility, he had a gift for critical and orderly exposition which made him both a great teacher and a great writer of books. He was also an historian of mathematical physics, and in this capacity showed in unusual degree an ability to reconstruct the difficulties and achievements of earlier periods, and, as if this were not enough, he contributed, especially in his later years, to the philosophy of the physical sciences. His energy and determination in fulfilling his many interests were the envy of friends and colleagues. Retirement, for Whittaker, meant leisure to work.

Among his contributions to mathematics were original work in the theories of solving dynamical problems and differential equations, and of interpolation between known values; while in recent years he contributed to the mathematics of relativity, electromagnetism, and quantum theory. As a teacher his memorial is the mathematical school at Edinburgh, which essentially was his own creation. As a writer of books his treatise on dynamics was cited by the late Sir Arthur Eddington for the modernity of its outlook. It "fairly reeked" of "action"—a key concept developed as the action-theory of dynamics before quantum theory had arrived to need it.

Independently of the wide range of his strictly mathematical writing, Whittaker had the unusual distinction of having written a classic of scientific history—*A History of the Theories of Aether and Electricity,* published in 1910—and then, more than 30 years later, of having set about its revision, expansion, and bringing up to date, to include such a quantity of new material that any lesser man would have been daunted. The first volume of the new edition was published in 1951; and, by the time that the second was being written, he had decided that a third would be needed. The special ability shown in this department of his work was his power to perceive, and present to others, the quality of the contributions which he described. As Professor McCrea has written, he showed "wherein the great pioneers were truly great".

As with Eddington, there was an element of the mystic in Whittaker's approach to the wider problems of nature, science, and philosophy. In his *Theories of the Universe and the Arguments for the Existence of God* (1946), he gave a sympathetic interpretation of Aquinas; and, from the universality of physical law, concluded that "the proof from Order is to-day more complete, more comprehensive, and more majestic than in the form in which it was presented in the thirteenth century". Not surprisingly, he was invited to be the 1951 speaker in the series of Eddington memorial lectures, and gave a distinguished interpretation in which there was perhaps as much of Whittaker as Eddington.

All the while he was a brilliant teacher, a master of his subject, with a great love of his fellow-men. His warmth and his interest in his friends and students made him the most agreeable of companions. Scholars from abroad who knew him seldom failed to visit him and enjoy his conversation, and the friendships thus founded he kept up by correspondence to all parts of the world.

Edmund Taylor was born on October 24, 1873, the son of John Whittaker, of Birkdale. He was educated at Manchester Grammar School and Trinity College, Cambridge, where he was Second Wrangler in 1895, Tyson medallist, and first Smith's prizeman. He was elected to a fellowship of his college in 1896 and was college lecturer in mathematics until 1905. The following year he was appointed Royal Astronomer of Ireland. He was already the author of various scientific works and a contributor to the publications of the Royal Society (of which he was elected a Fellow in 1905) and of the Royal Astronomical Society, when, in 1912, he was elected to succeed Professor Chrystal in the chair of mathematics in Edinburgh University. It was during his tenure of that chair (34 years, until his retirement in 1946) that his most important work was done.

He held office in a number of scientific societies, including the presidency of the Mathematical Association in 1920-21 and of the section of mathematics and physics of the British Association in 1927. And from 1939 to 1944 he was president of the Royal Society of Edinburgh. He delivered the Riddell lectures at Durham in 1941, the Donnellan lectures at Dublin in 1946, the Tarner lectures at Cambridge in 1947, and was Herbert Spencer lecturer at Oxford in 1948. He was also visiting Hitchcock Professor in the University of California in 1934. The Royal Society awarded him the Sylvester Medal in 1931 and the Copley Medal in 1954. He was a member of several foreign learned societies, and he had been elected a correspondent member of the French Academy of Sciences.

He was received into the Roman Catholic Church in 1930 and was later appointed a member of the Pontifical Academy of Sciences. In more than one of his books, including *The Beginning and End of the World* (the Riddell lectures) and *Space and Spirit*, he was concerned to re-establish a connexion between modern physical theories and natural theology.

He married, in 1901, Mary, daughter of the Rev. Thomas Boyd. There were three sons and two daughters of the marriage. The second son, Dr. J. M. Whittaker, F.R.S., was professor of mathematics in Liverpool University before becoming Vice-Chancellor of Sheffield University in 1952.

March 26, 1956.

Tom Whittaker, secretary-manager of the Arsenal Football Club since 1947, died in hospital in London on October 24, 1956. He was 59 and had been associated with the club for 37 years.

Although he had been in poor health for some months his death was quite unexpected and a great shock to all who are interested, as players, administrators, or spectators, in the Association game. During a lifetime in the game he had attained an unrivalled knowledge of all aspects of football, first as a player, then as a trainer, and finally as the manager of one of the principal clubs in the country.

Thomas James Whittaker was born at Aldershot, but while still a child went to Newcastle upon Tyne. He was apprenticed to marine engineering, but his heart was in football and in 1919, while employed by a firm of ship repairers in London, he was offered a trial by Leslie Knighton, then manager of Arsenal. He began as a centre-forward but later became a half-back of considerable promise. Unfortunately his playing days were ended by a knee injury he received while touring with the Football Association team in Australia in 1925.

Herbert Chapman, who had then taken over as manager at Highbury, persuaded him to stay with the club in the capacity of club trainer. So began the second phase of his career with Arsenal. His extraordinary skill in dealing with injuries and his rapid appreciation of modern manipulative methods led to his becoming one of the foremost therapeutists. He became trainer to many England teams, both at home and abroad, and prominent practitioners in many other sports went to him to be treated for injuries.

When war broke out in 1939 he enlisted in the R.A.F. and served in the engineering branch, rising to the rank of squadron leader. He was appointed M.B.E. for his work during the war. He returned to Highbury in 1946 as assistant manager to George Allison [q.v.], and a year later he became secretary-manager. Under his guidance Arsenal won the League Championship in 1948 and 1953 and twice reached the F.A. Cup Final. In 1950 they beat Liverpool 2-0, and two years later they returned to Wembley, losing 1-0 to Newcastle United.

Whittaker never spared himself and was ever ready to help others. Those closely connected with him often advised him to take things more easily. In April 1956 he entered hospital for a complete rest because of overwork and strain. "I am very tired", he said, "but I leave the club in good hands. I have a splendid staff to carry on the work while I am away". Although he returned to Highbury for a short while, it was clear he was far from well. He was ordered further rest and treatment, and recently he again entered hospital.

Among the tributes paid to him, perhaps that of Joe Mercer, who captained Arsenal to their post-war successes, most clearly expressed the feelings of those who knew him best. Mercer, now manager of Sheffield United, said: "I know of no one who had so many friends. He was like a father to the players. Everybody took their problems to him and he never failed them". Jack Crayston, who, as assistant manager, held the rein at Highbury in Whittaker's absence, said: "He was a great man and much more than a boss to us. In all my years with the club I never heard him say an unkind thing". To that Stanley Cullis, Wolverhampton Wanderers' manager, added: "I have never heard a harsh word said about him". Speaking on behalf of himself and the Football Association Sir Stanley Rous said: "To work with Tom was a privilege. He will remain a gracious memory".

October 25, 1956.

Geoffrey Whitworth, C.B.E., founder and for many years Director of the British Drama League, died at his home at Oxford on September 9, 1951 at the age of 68.

Geoffrey Whitworth leaves behind him two enduring theatrical memorials—the British Drama League, which in its encouragement of senior amateur actors throughout Britain "kept alive a very vital part of the country", as Bernard Shaw said on the occasion of a public tribute to Whitworth in 1934, and that National Theatre the foundation-stone of which he lived to see laid. They are two memorials to a single wide interest in the theatre which was maintained strenuously and enthusiastically for nearly 40 years.

Though the affairs of the British Drama League, which was founded in 1919, consistently went forward, those of the projected national theatre did not, and if at times the cause did not die from frustration, but continued, on the contrary, to be persistently lively, this was largely Whitworth's doing. When the Queen laid the foundation-stone on the South Bank site in July 1951, Whitworth was almost the only survivor, as he was the most pertinacious, of the few distinguished enthusiasts who by prodigies of committee work and propaganda, and in spite of public indifference kept alive the idea to which, in 1949, Parliament without a division gave its blessing and the promise of £1m. How dear Whitworth's mission was to him may be gathered from a phrase he used on his retirement from the directorship of the Drama League in 1948: it would be "a sort of minor death".

Though the League and the National Theatre might be thought engrossments enough for one man, Whitworth found time to consider other aspects of the theatre. In *The Making of a National Theatre* in 1951 and in his earlier *The Theatre of My Heart* (1930) he dealt with his main theme, but he was also the author of two plays, *Father Noah*, acted at Manchester by the Unnamed Society in 1922, and *Not Yet*, which the Repertory Players put on in London a year later.

He also wrote dramatic criticism. His other public work included the organization of the theatre sections of the Wembley Exhibition, membership of the Drama Advisory Committee of the Carnegie United Kingdom Trust, and governorship of the Stratford Memorial Theatre.

Geoffrey Whitworth, the son of William Whitworth and his wife Phyllis Mary Draper, was born in London on April 7, 1883. He was educated privately and at New College, Oxford. In 1910 he married Phyllis Bell, who survives him, together with his son and daughter.

September 11, 1951.

Pembroke Wicks, C.B.E., who died at Walton-on-Thames on February 27, 1957, had been private secretary to Lord Carson, Lord Curzon of Kedleston, and Sir Austen Chamberlain, and while Assistant Secretary to the Cabinet Office in 1918 was seconded as personal assistant to Lord Beaverbrook*.

He was born in 1882, the son of Frederick Wicks, the author, and was educated at King's College School and London University. He took first class honours in the Bar Final Examination.

He was private secretary to Lord Carson from 1911 to 1918, including the period of the Ulster campaign, and then, on Lord Milner's nomination, became an Assistant Secretary. During his term as Assistant Secretary to the Cabinet Office, he was seconded first as personal assistant to Lord Beaverbrook and then as private secretary to Sir Austen Chamberlain when the latter was a member of the War Cabinet without portfolio.

Wicks subsequently became private secretary (parliamentary) to Lord Curzon and stayed with him until his death. Wicks, whose sympathies lay with the Unionist cause, later took up the post of Principal Assistant Secretary of the Policy Secretariat of the Unionist Party in 1924, and in the following year was appointed Secretary of the Political Section of the Central Office. Wicks, though in the confidence of men of affairs at critical times in the nation's fortunes, never sought the limelight, and his unobtrusive efficiency made him a man much trusted and valued by the distinguished political figures he served.

March 1, 1957.

Former Crown Prince Wilhelm of Germany—
See **William.**

Sir Hubert Wilkins, M.C., the Polar explorer, whose death at Framingham, Massachusetts, occurred on November 30, 1958, gained distinction by his work in both the Arctic and the Antarctic. He was 70.

With the triumphs of the American nuclear-powered submarine Nautilus still fresh in the public memory, it is fitting to record that twenty-seven years ago another submarine called Nautilus, also American, but commanded by Wilkins, made the first actual cruise in the Arctic and reached a northern latitude of 82deg. 15min.

Although not the first man to use the aeroplane for exploration in the Arctic, he followed closely after Amundsen, Nobile, and Byrd [q.v.], while in the Antarctic no one before him had used aircraft, for exploration or otherwise. Wilkins was the first definitely to prove the value of the aeroplane for survey purposes and meteorological observations in Polar regions, and he had all the merits of a pioneer. By the older method of land travel he had, before he took to the air, gained, under Stefansson*, valuable experience of Arctic conditions.

At once daring and careful, his grit and determination carried him safely through many a hazardous undertaking.

George Hubert Wilkins was an Australian, born at Mount Bryan East on October 31, 1888. His father was also a South Australian—one of the first—for Wilkins senior was born in 1836, the year in which the state was founded. As a small boy George (as he called himself until his knighthood) was taken to Adelaide and was educated at the state school and the School of Mines there. But at the age of 20 he left Adelaide as a stowaway, not, as he recorded, that he had any need to be a stowaway, but he was in search of adventures and "something out of the ordinary". After four years of wandering, chiefly in Europe and America, Wilkins found himself in the Balkans during the war of 1912 and acted as official photographer to the Turkish Army. He had already formed ideas of becoming a Polar explorer and believed that in such work aeroplanes would be useful for reconnaissance. His chance to go to the Arctic came soon, and he took it.

In 1913 he joined Stefansson's Canadian Arctic expedition as second in command, and was one of the party of six which became separated from the Karluk soon after she had rounded Point Barrow; fortunately, as it proved—for the Karluk, fast in the ice, drifted to her doom. The six marooned men had to travel by dog-team and had to live "off the country"—this is, on what could be got by hunting. Wilkins remained with the expedition three years and for many weary miles—at the least 5,000—he had to trudge on foot and, though from Stefansson he learned much Arctic lore and how to take care of himself on the ice pack, he did not enjoy walking.

As he himself said "born and raised in the wide thinly populated areas of Australia, where even the poorest man's dignity demanded that he should not travel afoot, when I joined Stefansson's expedition I was unaccustomed to working and disliked walking".

He had learned to fly in 1910-12, and now he formed the idea of flying over the Arctic Ocean. His proposal to Stefansson that they should go back and get aeroplanes found, however, no favour. It was not until 1926 that Wilkins was able to take an aeroplane to the Arctic.

Returning to Europe from the Stefansson expedition, Wilkins took his part in the First World War. He joined the Australian Flying Corps and got his commission in May 1917. Though he proved an able airman he was not many months later seconded to the Military History Department as official photographer, which post he held to the end of the War. He reached the rank of captain, was twice mentioned in dispatches and was awarded the Military Cross and the bar to the Cross.

The war over, Wilkins turned again to thoughts of the Arctic and in 1919 planned a flight from Spitsbergen to Alaska. He found the money but no aircraft owner or manufacturer would let him have a machine for that purpose; they thought the idea fantastic. However the same year he was navigator in the England-Australia flight of the Blackburn-Kangaroo aeroplane, and then visited South America, Africa and other lands. In 1921 he joined Shackleton's expedition in the Quest as naturalist—he had a wide knowledge of natural history and was a skilled collector—and thus gained his first experience in Antarctic waters.

Late in 1922 Wilkins was much at the British Museum (Natural History) in connexion with the biological collection brought back by the Quest. The trustees were then looking for a leader for an expedition to tropical Australia to collect specimens of the fauna; their choice fell on Wilkins, who meanwhile had gone off to Russia. A telegram brought him post haste to London and in January 1923 he sailed for Australia. The expedition thoroughly explored, from the natural history point of view, north-eastern Australia, gaining also knowledge of the aborigines. The work of the expedition, which lasted over two years, earned high praise from the trustees.

The material obtained was of great scientific value, and rarely had an exploring expedition been managed with such economy and carried out so exactly to plan. As to economy, though the expedition lasted six months longer than had been designed, the entire cost exceeded the estimate by £10 only. This expedition in short had proved that Wilkins was a very capable leader of men and an excellent organizer.

When, in 1926, Wilkins got to Alaska with an aeroplane his intention was to fly over the unknown area of the Arctic north of Point Barrow, find out whether there was land there, and if so whether a suitable spot for a meteorological station could be found. His chief object was to study weather conditions: he also hoped to test the feasibility of air transport services in the Arctic regions.

At the request of his Detroit backers he also undertook to try to fly from Point Barrow to Spitsbergen—though he pointed out to them that that would involve covering many miles of territory already known. He had chosen as pilot Carl Ben Eielson, who made an ideal companion, and who already had some years experience of flying over Alaskan snows. Wilkins was at Point Barrow in time to see the airship Norge, in which were Amundsen and Nobile on their trans-Polar flight, pass by, in May 1926, and in that year he himself made a flight of 100 miles over the pack ice. He could, however, do little more then. The trials and disappointments he and Eielson had to endure did not extinguish Wilkins's faith though they exhausted that of his financial backers.

Perhaps they had reason, for Wilkins's summary of two years' work reads: "We begged for money, bought machines, flew them and smashed them, rebuilt them and smashed ourselves. My crooked arm and Eielson's missing finger are mute evidences of trials endured".

The most notable of those trials was in 1927 when, having started from Point Barrow, they had flown for 550 miles, there was engine trouble, and a forced landing in a blizzard had to be made on the pack ice. This was at a spot about 100 miles from "home" and Wilkins and Eielson trudged over the ice for 14 days before reaching the settlement. Indeed but for the experience Wilkins had gained with Stefansson it is doubtful if they would have won through.

With his own very limited resources Wilkins got a new machine—a Lockheed Vega—and again secured Eielson as pilot. Men and machine reached Point Barrow in the spring of 1928, and after one or two false starts the great flight began on April 16 of that year. This time Wilkins had decided to try a non-stop flight from Alaska to Spitsbergen—the first half of the way being over unknown seas, and possibly, as was hoped, over unknown lands. But no new land was seen.

Later in the flight Grant Land and Greenland were passed and the airmen turned towards Spitsbergen. Snow and clouds and the knowledge that their petrol was getting low forced them to seek a landing, and they were fortunate in coming down safely on a small level patch—they knew not exactly where. They had been 20 hours 20 minutes in the air. They found they were on a small island—named from some Arctic tragedy Dead Man Island—not far from the settlement of Green Harbour, Spitsbergen. It took them a week before they could get off: two attempts failed; at the third, Eielson piloting and Wilkins with one leg in the cockpit and the other on the ice pushing, got the machine free. With hands on the rim of the cockpit Wilkins dragged himself up and tumbled in. The machine was off and half an hour later landed at Green Harbour, where the airmen were speedily welcomed by the small colony of Norwegians and Danes living there.

From the wireless station Wilkins telegraphed to *The Times* a notable account of his memorable journey. Shortly afterwards he went to London, was knighted by the King at Buckingham Palace, and from the Royal Geographical Society received the Patron's Medal "for his many years' systematic work in Polar regions, culminating in his remarkable flight from Point Barrow to Spitsbergen".

With no more time than it took to get a new expedition together—four men in all—Wilkins again turned his attention to the Antarctic, and was the first to take an aeroplane thither. He had for pilot his old companion Eielson. In December 1928, from the base established on Deception Island, they made a flight of 1,200 miles to about latitude 72deg. South and back, and proved that Graham's Land, which had been supposed to be a peninsula jutting from the main mass of the Antarctic continent, was almost certainly two large islands separated from land farther south—which Wilkins named Hearst Land—by an ice-filled channel.

This was considered as perhaps the most important discovery in the Antarctic since Shackleton had conquered the Beardmore glacier 18 years before. A second flight yielded no big results and storing his aeroplanes at Deception Island, Wilkins returned home early in 1929.

In November of the same year he was back in the Antarctic, but Deception Island justified its name; snow conditions made it impossible of use and Wilkins put one of his aeroplanes on board the whale-catcher William Scoresby which took him south of Deception Island; several flights were made; Charcot Land was shown to be an island; and a long stretch of coast was reconnoitred. He reached longitude 101deg. in latitude 73deg.; in that area the coastline was seen to be considerably farther south than had been supposed.

Wilkins wished to make a 2,000-mile flight to the Bay of Whales, Ross Sea, where Byrd [q.v.], the United States explorer, who had flown to the South Pole, then was, but no suitable starting off point sufficiently south was found. By February 1930 Wilkins had reached Montevideo on his return journey.

These two expeditions Wilkins considered as preliminary investigations; he desired to see meteorological stations established in the Antarctic as part of a scheme for foretelling weather conditions in the southern hemisphere.

He next developed his scheme for going under the pack ice by submarine to the North Pole; he obtained the loan of a vessel, O12, which he renamed Nautilus, from the United States Navy, and he crossed the Atlantic in her in June 1931.

On the voyage Nautilus developed defects but these were made good and she reached her base at Long Year, Spitsbergen, in mid-August, and on the eighteenth of that month left for the north. This time Wilkins's luck was out for he encountered fierce storms, the submarine's diving gear was damaged and after a three-week voyage he was obliged to return to Long Year.

Nevertheless 82deg. 15min. North was attained and under the direction of Professor H. U. Sverdrup, the chief scientist on board, many important oceanographical and geophysical results were obtained. Wilkins, though disappointed, was in no wise cast down, for he was convinced of the practicability of under-ice travel. Many of his comments have a familiar ring now that a latter-day Nautilus has triumphed.

In the mid-1930s Wilkins formed plans to build a new submarine (Nautilus had been sunk—with the permission of the United States Shipping Board—outside Bergen) in England, but his plans never came to fruition. In that decade also he became more closely associated with Lincoln Ellsworth [q.v.]—who had been with him in Nautilus—and commanded the base ship Wyatt Earp during Ellsworth's later expeditions to the Antarctic.

Wilkins was a consultant to the U.S. Army Military Planning Division from 1942 to 1952, and since 1953 had been geographer to the Research and Development Command Department of Defence.

December 2, 1958.

The former German Crown Prince William died on July 20, 1951 at the age of 69.

The defeat of Germany in the 1914-18 war and the collapse of the German Empire denied to him any large opportunity for displaying his qualities of character and mind, but there is good reason for believing that if he had been given the chance he would have proved a more cautious—a more successful—wearer of the Imperial and Royal crowns than his brilliant father.

Frederick William Victor Augustus Ernest, German Crown Prince and Crown Prince of Prussia, was born at the Marble Palace in Potsdam on May 6, 1882, the eldest child of Prince William of Prussia (subsequently Emperor William II) and of Princess Augusta Victoria of Schleswig-Holstein-Sonderburg-Augustenburg. His early education was remarkable only for the predominance of English governesses and tutors (he grew up speaking English even more fluently than his father), and at the age of 14 he went to the Military Academy at Ploen. He was a student of law at Bonn from 1901 to 1903.

Tall, fair-haired, lithe and agile, he soon showed himself to be possessed of a temperament as calm as that of his father was excitable and nervous. His exuberant enjoyment of life in all its aspects and his ability to converse with all and sundry without either sacrificing his own dignity or giving the appearance of condescension ensured his popularity. He had none of the customary Prussian stiffness in social intercourse.

On June 6, 1905, shortly after his coming-of-age, the Crown Prince married Cecilia, Duchess of Mecklenburg-Schwerin. Before his marriage he had served with the First Regiment of Foot Guards at Potsdam and afterwards he passed first to the Gardes du Corps and then to the command of the famous "Death's Head" Hussars, then stationed at Danzig. He was a born cavalryman and was devoted to his regiment. In 1913 he was seconded to the General Staff in Berlin.

During the days before the 1914-18 war he occasionally clashed with his father—in the established tradition of the Hohenzollern heirs, who all started as *frondeurs*—and in his political activities was alternately the idol of the chauvinistic elements in the nation and the hope of the progressive liberals. This was not surprising, for whereas in domestic affairs he was progressive and completely free of social, racial, or other conceits, in foreign affairs he was imperialist and ambitious. Even so there is little evidence to suggest that he must share the responsibility for the war of 1914-18 and its continuation to a disastrous finish. During the years before 1914 he wielded no real political influence.

As an army leader after 1914 he proved a thoughtful, occasionally even a farseeing, strategist. He tried in vain to stop the useless and sanguinary attack of Verdun in 1916, and to press for a negotiated peace in 1917.

On November 10, 1918 he followed his father's example and fled to Holland, and lived in a small house on the dreary island of Wieringen until, in 1923, Dr. Stresemann obtained permission for him to return to Germany on condition that he abstained from politics. He lived for a considerable time on his estate of Oels, in Silesia. He continued writing his memoirs, which he had started in Holland. Although these were more independent and less biased in judgment than those of his father, it cannot be said that he made any useful contribution to the vexed question of responsibility for the 1914-18 war.

During the twenties and early thirties he was careful not to have any real association with the semi-military and avowedly monarchist organization, the Stahlhelm, and it would be an exaggeration to ascribe to him any definite hopes—much less plans—for a restoration of the monarchy. When the National Socialists came to power he accepted membership of their motor corps, but again avoided any conspicuous association with them. He was a sharp critic of "Hitler's war", in which, though technically still a German, he took no active part.

He had to flee in 1945 before the advancing Russians, and in the autumn was given accommodation in the rambling castle of a branch of the Hohenzollerns at Hechingen, in the United States zone. He latterly lived in a small villa there.

July 21, 1951.

E. G. Harcourt Williams, the actor, died in hospital in London on December 13, 1957 after a long illness. He was 77.

Harcourt Williams was in the forefront of the London theatre for nearly 60 years, during which he achieved a reputation as a producer and actor of exceptional ability. He enjoyed the friendship of many of the greatest personalities adorning the stage in that period: Ellen Terry, Sir George Alexander, Sir Herbert Tree, Arthur Bourchier, Matheson Lang, Oscar Asche, H. B. Irving, and Henry Ainley, and he played important parts in plays ranging from Shakespeare, Sheridan, and Ibsen, to Shaw, Masefield*, Drinkwater, Chesterton, and Priestley. His recollections of the theatre and his published reminiscences were rich in anecdotes of many who influenced its history and traditions.

His first appearance on the stage was as a youth of 17, and he was still impressing theatregoers long after the age of 70. During four eventful years—from 1929 to 1934—he was producer at the Old Vic, where he demonstrated his devotion to the ideals of the founders. As actor, producer, lecturer, and teacher, he was one of that goodly company that sought to establish exacting standards for the stage.

Born at Croydon on March 30, 1880, the son of John Williams, a merchant, he was educated at Beckenham Abbey and Whitgift Grammar School, Croydon. He was coached for the stage by the gifted Miss Bateman (Mrs. Crowe) and joined F. R. Benson's company in 1897. In spite of his youth he was given the part of the Duke of Bedford in *Henry V* when the play was put on at the Theatre Royal, Belfast. That he remained with the company for five years is a tribute to his industry and earnestness, and it was not until early in 1900 that he appeared on the London stage as Sir Thomas Grey in *Henry V* at the Lyceum. Two years later he toured with Kate Rorke in several plays, then with Haidee Gunn, and in 1903 with Ellen Terry.

In 1906 he went to America with H. B. Irving, and after touring for about a year, returned to Britain, where in the next few years he was associated with George Alexander, and for a second term with Irving. Though delighting in the interpretation of Shakespearian characters, he readily accepted parts in modern plays, and it was in no small measure due to his performance as the Chronicler and General Lee that *Abraham Lincoln* ran from February 1919 for a year at the Lyric, Hammersmith. He appeared in *Hamlet* with John Barrymore at the Haymarket in 1925.

When, four years later, he was appointed producer at the Old Vic, he took up the task with zest, and in the next four years put on about 50 plays, in many of which he played important roles; and he broke out of the Shakespearian repertory by including plays by Shaw and other contemporary dramatists. Throughout his long career he returned again and again to the Old Vic, and his affection for it never waned. Even when he was in greatest demand elsewhere, he would make sacrifices to appear there and, in 1944, he needed little persuasion to join a representative company from the theatre when it embarked on what proved to be a successful season at the New Theatre.

Plays he produced included *The Zeal of Thy House* by Dorothy Sayers [q.v.] (Canterbury, 1937 and Westminster, 1938) and *The Devil to Pay* (Canterbury, 1939). From 1923 he frequently took part in broadcast plays and acted in films, and in 1940 became a member of the B.B.C. Drama Repertory Company; he also appeared on television. He was the author of several interesting books, including *Four Years at the Old Vic* and *Old Vic Saga*, and also wrote a volume of short stories. He celebrated his golden jubilee as an actor in January 1948 while he was appearing in the longest run of Shaw's *You Never Can Tell* at Wyndham's Theatre.

He married in 1908 Jean Sterling Mackinlay [q.v.], a gifted *diseuse* and actress. Their son, John Sterling, is a pianist.

December 14, 1957.

Sir Herbert Williams, M.P., first baronet, died at his London home on July 25, 1954 at the age of 69. He had collapsed in the House of Commons on July 22 and was suffering from a cerebral haemorrhage.

The front bench below the gangway—on both sides of the House of Commons—is the home of the rebels and the independently minded, and of the handful of members in every Parliament whose main value to the House is their "nuisance value". There they sit—and they are among the most diligent in their attendance—fearless of Whips and enjoying every moment of the Parliamentary battle. No opportunity for an interruption or a point of order is ever allowed to pass. At times they may bore and irritate the House, but by and large they perform a valuable function: they help to keep it alert and wideawake.

Williams was, in his later years, a worthy occupier of the front bench below the gangway. His "nuisance value" was high, his independence never in doubt. He flung quips and criticism—with equal forthrightness and equal good humour—at his own and the Opposition leaders. (His affectionate baiting of Herbert Morrison [Lord Morrison of Lambeth*)] was for many years one of the innocent pleasures of the House's proceedings). But his skill as a provoker of grave and gay controversy should not be allowed to obscure the more solid achievements of a man of more than average courage and more than ordinary energy.

Herbert Geraint Williams was born at Hooton, Cheshire, on December 2, 1884, the son of a schoolmaster, and educated at Hooton Grammar School and the University of Liverpool. He entered the University as Rathbone Scholar, and besides excelling in his studies—he graduated in engineering with first-class honours in 1906—he was active in student politics. Williams followed up his engineering laboratory experience with a period of apprenticeship at the Siemens Brothers' Dynamo works at Stafford. From 1911 to 1928 he was secretary and manager of the Machine Tool Trades Association Incorporated.

During the 1914-18 War he was successively a sergeant in the special constabulary, secretary of the machine tool department of the Ministry of Munitions, and a lieutenant in the Royal Army Ordnance Corps. Afterwards, a busy, progressive, and prosperous engineering practice led him to the executive directorship of the Incorporated Association of Electric Power Companies. When, during his political career, Williams spoke on trade and industrial questions—as he often did—he spoke from a wealth of hard practical experience.

From his university days he was a keen Conservative politician. After serving for three years on the Wimbledon Borough Council he tried to enter the L.C.C., at Bow and Bromley in 1919, but without success. His early attempts to enter Parliament were also unsuccessful, and he failed in 1918 (English Universities) and in 1922 and 1923 (at Wednesbury). In 1924 he was returned to Parliament as Conservative member for Reading. From his first appearance in the House of Commons he was recognized as a quick and trenchant digester, with an unusual mastery of statistics from which he argued with cogency and adroitness.

He caught the eye of Stanley Baldwin, which was always open to catch sight of a promising young man, and in January 1928 he was appointed Parliamentary Secretary to the Board of Trade. In the following year he was defeated at the general election. Williams had, however, made an impression on the public during his five years in Parliament, and during the life of the second Labour Government he was one of its most persistent and forthright critics in the country. From then on, for many years, he was one of the Conservative Party's most effective platform speakers.

In February 1932 he was returned at a by-election in South Croydon, holding the seat until his defeat at the general election of 1945. In spite of Baldwin's prophecies and others' expectations, Williams was never again to hold office. In many ways, perhaps, he was not well fitted for it. His talents were, however, in continuous employment as a back-bench free-lance. During the 1939-45 War he was one of the most outspoken critics of Churchill's* National Government, and was a member of the Select Committee on National Expenditure from 1939 to 1944. He was returned again to Parliament, for East Croydon, in 1950, and held the seat in 1951.

Outside the House of Commons, Williams was particularly useful to his party on the propagandist and educational side, doing vigorous work for the Junior Imperial and Constitutional League, on the Grand Council of the Primrose League, and as a lecturer to many Conservative and Unionist bodies. He was chairman of the executive of the London Conservative Union from 1939 to 1948, and chairman of the Conservative Conference in 1948.

He was the author of several books on economics and politics, in which he convincingly advocated tariff reform. From 1926 to 1928 and from 1931 to 1941 he was director of the Empire Industries Association.

In 1916 he married Dorothy Frances, daughter of the late Barton Jones. She survives him, with their one daughter and one son.

July 26, 1954.

Lieutenant-Colonel James Howard Williams, O.B.E., who died on July 30, 1958 at the age of 60, was known throughout the world for his outstanding work in the training and use of elephants in Burma both in peace and war. As "Elephant Bill" he was familiar through his books to readers in many lands who took delight in his unique knowledge and experience of the largest and most useful of beasts.

He was born on November 15, 1897, and was educated at Queen's College, Taunton. He served on the Western Front in the 1914-18 War with The Devonshire Regiment. In 1920 he joined the staff of the Bombay Burma Trading Corporation. He was posted to Burma, where the corporation maintained some 2,000 elephants which were engaged mainly in timber extraction and transport. In all, some 6,000 of these sagacious animals worked in the days of

British rule in the jungles and at the ports of Burma. He had a remarkable gift of understanding the minds, actions and reactions both of elephants and of their oozies—the Burmese equivalent of the Indian mahout (driver). Without any veterinary training he knew the best treatment of sick elephants.

When the Japanese conquered Malaya the urgency of the employment of elephants in Burma for the purposes of war was recognized and acted upon. For many years up to 1895 elephants had been on the strength of the Royal Engineers in the Indian Army. It was now decided to form in Burma an Elephant Company of the Royal Indian Engineers, and Williams was appointed as adviser. The company played a highly important part not only in retarding the onslaught of the Japanese Army on Burma but also in making possible the great exodus of Indian settlers and of British wives and children, and thereafter in the expulsion of the enemy. Escape was by way of what became known as the Burma Road to the Indian sub-continent. It had been no more than a bridle track over mountainous country, through valleys, and across rivers and swamps to Imphal, in Assam. Field-Marshal Sir William Slim*, who was in command of the XIVth Army which finally expelled the invading Japanese, in his foreword to Williams's *Elephant Bill* (1950), wrote of the remarkable intelligence and dignity of the trained elephants engaged on this task, and of Williams and his assistants, "who showed jungle craft, elephant sense, dogged courage, and above all the example they set, which held the Elephant Companies together under every stress that war, terrain, and climate could inflict on them".

Williams was awarded the O.B.E. in 1945. He settled in Cornwall and, coming as he did from yeoman stock, took up farming. In connexion with filming plans he visited Ceylon twice and Siam once. He made frequent lecturing tours in Britain and on the Continent. In 1953 Williams supplemented his famous story, *Elephant Bill*, published three years earlier, by *Bandoola*, which was a detailed description and characterization of one of the elephants engaged on the Burma Road for the evacuation. In this, as in his *The Spotted Deer* (1957), Williams, as might be expected from his long years in the jungle, showed that he was not without a streak of mysticism.

He married in 1932 Susan Margaret Rowland, who shared in the anxieties and privations of British women and children who were evacuated from Burma in the early stages of the Japanese invasion. She survives him with a son and a daughter.

July 31, 1958.

Jean Sterling (Mrs. Harcourt) Williams— See **Mackinlay.**

Margaret Williams, who died on June 4, 1960, was a very successful portrait painter, numbering among her sitters several members of the Royal Family.

She became well known to the general public by her portrait group of Princess Elizabeth and Princess Margaret, which was widely reproduced in the press. This picture, painted in 1937, was approved by the Queen before being exhibited in a one-man show at the Raeburn Gallery, and it was purchased by J. W. Whitford Griffiths for presentation to a South African gallery as a Coronation gift. Subsequently she painted several more portraits of Queen Elizabeth II and portraits of the Duke of Cornwall, Princess Anne, and Queen Elizabeth the Queen Mother.

Margaret Lindsay Williams, who was the daughter of Samuel Williams, shipbroker, of Barry Dock, was born at Cardiff and educated privately and at the Cardiff Technical College. She was a brilliant student, and her artistic training could hardly have been bettered from an academic point of view. After leaving the technical college, where she won the gold medal for art, she studied first at the Pelham Street School of Painting, Kensington, under Sir Arthur S. Cope, R.A., Sir George Clausen, R.A., and J. Watson Nicholl, and then at the Royal Academy Schools. Here she carried off the gold medal and travelling scholarship, four silver medals, and the Creswick Prize for Landscape. Her artistic education was completed by travels in France, Italy, and Holland. While still a student Margaret Williams was invited by G. A. Story, R.A., Professor of Perspective at the Royal Academy, to assist him with the illustrations to his book *The Theory and Practice of Perspective*, published in 1910.

Miss Williams was loyally supported by her native city, though her reputation was by no means limited to Wales. She painted many presentation and other portraits, including larger compositions containing many figures. Among these were "The Rt. Hon. D. Lloyd George unveiling the National Statuary at Cardiff" (114 portraits); "The National Welsh War Service in Westminster Abbey, 1918" (150 portraits)—both now in the possession of the Cardiff City Council—and "The Re-opening of St. Paul's Cathedral, June 25, 1930". This, which contained portraits of the King and Queen, the Lord Mayor, the Bishop of London and other ecclesiastical dignitaries, was presented to the cathedral by Lord Riddell.

The other royal portraits by Miss Williams were those of King Edward VII, the Cardiff City memorial picture; Queen Alexandra; Queen Mary, shown at the Academy in 1938; and the Prince of Wales, which was formerly in the possession of Queen Mary.

Among the eminent people painted by Miss Williams were the late Lord Ebbisham, Master of the Stationers' Company, presented to the company by Lord Riddell; President Harding of the United States; Lord Leathers* and Sir Evelyn Wrench* (both in the possession of the English-Speaking Union); Baron Van Riemsdijk, director of the Rijks Museum, Amsterdam; Henry Ford; Dr. Thomas Ashby, director of the British School at Rome; I. M. Maisky*, Soviet Ambassador at the Court of St. James's, 1932-1943; Field Marshal Lord Slim*; the Rev. R. J. Campbell [q.v.]; and Ivor Novello [q.v.].

Portraiture occupied most of Margaret Williams's time and energy, but at least one landscape by her was seen at the Royal Academy. She also exhibited at the Royal Cambrian Academy, of which whe was a member, the Royal West of England Academy, the Royal Portrait Society, the National Museum of Wales, the Washington Art Centre, United States, and various provincial galleries in England. One-man shows of her work were held at Knoedler's Gallery, New York, and the Raeburn Gallery and the New Burlington Galleries in London. Several of her pictures were reproduced by the Fine Art Publishing Company.

Perhaps the words "professional competence" best describes the general impression made by her work. Particularly in the arrangement of her larger compositions, she evidently owed a great deal to her sound early training under Cope, and a feminine interpretation, inclining to prettiness in colour, of his workmanship will serve for her style of execution.

Though she lived for the most part in London, in St. John's Wood, Miss Williams continued to interest herself in Welsh affairs. She was a member of the South Wales Art Society, the Honourable Society of Cymmrodorion and the Gorsedd of Bards. She was also honorary corresponding secretary for Glamorgan of the English-Speaking Union.

June 6, 1960.

Dr. Ralph Vaughan Williams— See **Vaughan.**

Dr. John Thoburn Williamson, the Canadian-born diamond millionaire and owner of the Mwadui Diamond Mine in Tanganyika, died there on January 8, 1958. He was 50.

Williamson was one of the romantic figures of modern Africa. He was a man of science who by his knowledge, his persistence, and his confidence in his own scientific judgment discovered what was indeed a modern Eldorado. Although a millionaire, he never lost the simplicity of the scientist's approach to life. He was interested in mining diamonds, not in the money he got thereby. A shy man, with considerable charm of manner, he was somewhat of a recluse and lived in a small house on the mine where his bedroom table was strewn with scales and diamonds in cigarette boxes. He was a man with a strong social conscience that led him into both obstinate quixotic actions and generous practical benevolence. He made over large sums to Makerere College and was a benefactor of many other worthy causes in East Africa, particularly those aimed at improving harmony between races.

Born on February 10, 1907, in Montfort, Quebec, he was the son of a Canadian lumberman of Irish descent, and graduated in geology and mineralogy at McGill University. His first post was with the Quebec Geological Survey. When a professor from McGill was appointed as geologist to a gold mine in South Africa, Williamson, then 21, accompanied him. He became interested in diamonds when working in the Rand and formed the theory that situated somewhere in East Africa there was the original "pipe" through which, during the formation of the earth's crust, diamonds were thrown up from the subterranean cauldrons where they were formed. He was of the opinion that the "pipes" could be located by a scientific study of land formations. When he left the Rand he carried out a study of rock formation and soil composition over a great area in north-west Tanganyika, staking claims within a radius of 100 miles of Shinyanga.

His findings were encouraging and for five years he prospected. His faith was never shaken although he went down with fever and suffered from the effects of the sun in that semi-desert region. He narrowed his search to the Shinyanga area and then went north to Mwadui. It was in this district, in March 1940, that he found the first diamond to give him a clue to the location of the "pipe" six years after starting the search. It is on the site that Williamson Diamonds Ltd. now stands.

Under agreement, Tanganyika is allocated 10 per cent. of the world's annual diamond sales. As 90 per cent. of the Tanganyika supply comes from Mwadui, the Williamson Mine supplies 9 per cent. of the annual world sales. Much of the profit has been turned back into the mine itself or has been devoted to the welfare of the employees. The mine boasts a £33,000 hospital, a clubhouse for Europeans and many other amenities.

The stability of the world market was threatened when, in June 1950, Williamson stopped marketing his diamonds through the Diamond Corporation. Though the diamond market was exceptionally strong at this time, the long-term effects of any defection from the "syndicate" of a property as valuable as his would have been serious.

The dispute was based chiefly on a complaint by Williamson that the sales agreement then in force was operating in an inequitable manner so far as his enterprise was concerned. He began to talk of selling on the open market, but instead of doing this he stopped exporting altogether. Fortunately the affair was settled after two years and an agreement was reached which, as a statement at that time said, was "not only a settlement of all disputes regarding diamonds which have been produced in the past but also covers current and future production".

By this time Williamson had accumulated a considerable stock of diamonds, as was indicated by the figure of exports from Tanganyika in February 1952, the month he resumed exporting, when they totalled £224,500 compared with £11,155 the month before. After this settlement Williamson always marketed through the corporation, and production in the mine has been well maintained. Of the company's 1,200 shares it is believed that he held 894 and his brother 300. The remaining six he divided between his solicitor, Dr. I. C. Chopra, Q.C., and Chief Inspector Percy Burgess, his security officer.

Dr. I. C. Chopra was a local Indian lawyer living at Mwanza on the shores of Lake Victoria. He staked Williamson's last safari which resulted in the discovery of the diamonds, and Williamson later made him legal adviser and shareholder in the company. Dr. Chopra is now a Q.C. and member of the Tanganyika Legislative Council.

Williamson gave the world's largest pink diamond to the Queen as a wedding present. It was originally 56 carats but it was cut down to 24 to make it symmetrical. Its value is estimated at between £400,000 and £500,000. He was prevented by illness from presenting Princess Margaret with a £15,000 brooch when she visited the mine in 1956. He was to have presented the brooch to the Princess in June 1956, but again illness intervened.

In 1956 Williamson went to Canada for medical treatment and, on the advice of his doctors, completed a world cruise, returning to Tanganyika in March 1957. Secrecy surrounded his movements when he left Nairobi for London by air in June 1957, but when he returned to Nairobi later on in the month it was learnt that he had been under medical observation at a London clinic. A statement issued in July said that he was suffering from an ulcer on the tongue. He was unmarried.

January 9, 1958.

Sidonie Willy—See **Colette.**

Chester Wilmot, one of the best known war correspondents during the 1939-45 War and the author of the controversial work, *The Struggle for Europe,* was a passenger in a Comet airliner which crashed in the Mediterranean on January 10, 1954. He was 42.

Reginald William Winchester Wilmot was born on June 21, 1911, the son of the late R. W. E. Wilmot, of Melbourne, Australia. He was educated at Melbourne Grammar School and at Trinity College, University of Melbourne. In 1940, at the age of 29, he became war correspondent for the Australian Broadcasting Commission, and in the next two years was in the Middle East and New Guinea. During 1943 he edited and narrated the commentary of the documentary film *Sons of the Anzacs,* which was produced for the Commonwealth Government. In the last year of the war he was war correspondent for the B.B.C. in western Europe.

As a war correspondent he had many qualities. He was accurate and thorough. Whenever anything occurred in the area he was covering he could be relied on to be at the spot quickly—even if it meant taking personal risks. He knew and was on friendly terms with many of the most senior officers and always had the confidence of the high command. An excellent day-to-day reporter, he also had a keen interest in the wider questions of the conduct of the war.

It was this which led him—after reporting the Nuremberg trial for the B.B.C.—to start his many years' work on *The Struggle for Europe.* His decision to do this was courageous. He had made his name as one of the ablest correspondents of the war and could have had a cosy staff appointment on a newspaper for the asking. Instead he set to work on the documents of the war—living as a freelance journalist and broadcaster—and in 1952 his book was published. It was an immediate success—and not only in Britain. If he was a little provocative in his criticisms of American policy and at times gave too little weight to the political realities which he was discussing, it was yet a considerable achievement to produce an independent and documented analysis of Allied policy so soon after the war which no intelligent student can afford to ignore.

This work done, Wilmot became, in 1952, military correspondent of the *Observer.* As a military correspondent he had his faults. He was too little inclined to pursue the small matters which are the stuff of military, as of any, journalism. He preferred the big issues, the broad horizons, the large surveys. (He had never been a reporter on a daily newspaper.)

One such survey was his recent review of the development of guided missiles—a field in which he had made himself an expert and, if he had lived, might have exerted some influence. He had exceptional energy and could, at the shortest notice, master subjects that were strange to him, and make them understandable without distortion. He was the most promising of a younger generation of military correspondents who have begun to replace such established authorities as Captain [Sir Basil] Liddell Hart* and Captain Cyril Falls*.

In 1942 he married Edith French, daughter of the late Rev. W. H. Irwin, St. Peter's College, Adelaide. She survives him with their one son and two daughters.

[This obituary was followed on the same day by a tribute].

January 13, 1954.

Professor C. T. R. Wilson, C.H., F.R.S., Nobel Laureate, Emeritus Professor of Natural Philosophy in the University of Cambridge, died at his home at Carlops, Peeblesshire, on November 15, 1959. He was 90.

Charles Thomson Rees Wilson was born on February 14, 1869, at the farmhouse of Crosshouse in the Pentland Hills, near Edinburgh. But for the premature death four years later of his father, whose forebears had been farmers for generations, Wilson would certainly have become the sheep farmer for which he could readily have been mistaken, especially in his later years. He was, however, taken to Manchester, where his mother went to join her parents who had gone there from Glasgow, and young Wilson eventually entered Owens College on a biological course as preparation for a medical training.

After graduating he obtained an entrance scholarship to Sidney Sussex College, Cambridge. As he put it: "I was picked out of the Christ's College waste-paper basket, for I hadn't entered for a Sidney Scholarship but for one at Christ's". He was very fortunate in going to Sidney, and in having as tutor F. H. Neville, a kindly man with wide interests, who was quick to recognize the quality of this shy and retiring undergraduate and to encourage him to proceed to Part II in physics. For a very short time after graduating with distinction in 1892, Wilson taught in a grammar school in the Midlands, but he—and the headmaster—quickly realized that this was not his *métier,* and he was received back at the Cavendish Laboratory by J. J. Thomson, becoming Clerk Maxwell Scholar in 1895.

Wilson had spent his vacations wandering among the Scottish mountains, especially those of Arran. Throughout his long life this remained his chief joy and he came to know intimately even the most remote parts of the Scottish Highlands. When he learnt in 1894 that the authorities who operated the meteorological observatory on the summit of Ben Nevis were glad to have the help of young physicists to take the place of the permanent observers when they went on holiday, he applied and was accepted. It was here, on the summit of Ben Nevis during September 1894, that he received the impressions that led him eventually to design what Lord Rutherford described as "the most original apparatus in the whole history of physics", the cloud chamber.

The hourly observations for which he was responsible began at 5 a.m. and he described what he saw when there was a continuous sea of cloud below the summit: "The shadow of the Ben on the surface of the sea of cloud at first reached to the western horizon; its upper edge came racing eastwards as the sun rose. On the cloud surface beyond the shadow would then appear a glory, the coloured rings incomplete and rather faint and diffuse. The most striking of all were to be seen from the edge of the precipice overlooking the great corrie when the observer's shadow (The Brocken Spectre) was formed on a thin sheet of wisp of cloud only a few feet below . . . This greatly excited my interest and made me wish to imitate them in the laboratory".

On his return to Cambridge he began experiments to produce a cloud artificially by the expansion of moist air, with the aim of studying experimentally the optics of the glory. But he was immediately diverted from this by the discovery of a hitherto unknown characteristic of the process of condensation. Each droplet of the cloud formed by condensation requires a nucleus, then thought to be a particle of dust, on which to form. Wilson found that, even when all such nuclei had been removed, he could still produce some droplets, provided the expansion was sufficiently great.

The explanation of this became clear when he exposed the air in the chamber to the newly discovered X-rays. One can imagine his delight when, in 1896, he switched on the primitive X-ray tube made by the famous Everett in the Cavendish workshop and found that with a suitable expansion a dense fog was produced in the dust-free air. He thus showed conclusively that the condensation nuclei in this case were the charged atoms, soon to be known as ions.

Even in these early days he had begun to consider the possibility of making the ions visible in the positions they occupied immediately after their production and so revealing the tracks of ionizing particles like the alpha and beta rays of radio-activity. But it was only after many years of experimental work, performed with the utmost skill and the most remarkable patience, that he eventually produced in 1911 that instrument of surpassing elegance, the cloud chamber, in which the tracks of atoms or of subatomic particles appeared as thread-like trails of tiny water drops. His early cloud chamber photographs are as fine as any produced to-day and are of great historical significance, for the Wilson cloud chamber was to play a vital part in the development of nuclear physics.

Using the Wilson chamber [Professor Lord] Blackett* photographed the disintegration of nitrogen by alpha particles in 1925, and Feather the first neutron-produced disintegration in 1932. By devising the automatic control of the chamber by the rays Blackett extended the application of the Wilson method, especially in the study of cosmic rays. The evidence for mesons in cosmic rays was provided in 1937 by the cloud chamber photographs of Anderson and Neddermeyer. The bubble chamber designed to study the penetrating radiations from high energy accelerators has developed out of the cloud chamber.

The discovery in the early experiments with the cloud chamber that ions are continuously being produced in the atmosphere led Wilson into another field of research—the study of atmospheric electricity. His interest in this subject was further stimulated by an experience during a thunderstorm on the summit of the neighbour of Ben Nevis, Carn Mor Dearg when, feeling his hair stand up, he promptly scampered down off the summit just before the occurrence of a vivid flash of lightning. "This experience drew my attention very forcibly to the magnitude of the electric field of a thundercloud and to its sudden changes".

He then designed various forms of electrometer for measuring the surface density of the earth's charge and the electric field and field changes during a thunderstorm. His theory of the mechanism of the generation of electric charge in a thunderstorm derives from the systematic study of the results of these experiments; his last paper on this subject appeared in the Proceedings of the Royal Society in 1956.

The volume of Wilson's published work is not great; he would not commit any of his work to print until he had satisfied himself by all manner of tests that it was sound. While he preferred to work on his own and never collected round himself a team of research students, he had a remarkable gift for discovering and indicating new paths of research, which he left to others to explore. His scientific papers are models of lucidity, contrasting somewhat, it must be said, with his lecturing style. It was his wont to address, often in a whisper, the tiny sketches he drew on the bottom corner of the blackboard. Yet both Sir Lawrence Bragg* and Blackett have confessed to continuing to use his lecture notes on optics for their own lectures, and others have remarked on the deep insight he showed in his way of looking at a problem.

Wilson was elected a Fellow of the Royal Society and also a fellow of his college in 1900. During the next year he became university lecturer in experimental physics and in 1925 succeeded Dewar as Jacksonian Professor of Natural Philosophy. Many honours were conferred upon him by universities and scientific societies, culminating in the award of a Nobel Prize for Physics in 1927 in conjunction with [Professor] A. H. Compton*. Shortly after his retirement to Edinburgh in 1936 he was made a Companion of Honour.

He was the most lovable of men, and universally known as "C. T. R." In his college combination room he was a perpetual wonder and delight to his colleagues; he would tell stories, often against himself, in an ingenuous though somehow pawky way.

To climb with him in the mountains of Arran, which he so loved, was a revelation: here, as in his scientific work, he became a pioneer and adventurer. In his later years, indeed after he was 86, he took every opportunity of flying over the mountains to the Western Isles in flights provided for students of the class of meteorology at Edinburgh University. Modest and unassuming, he so successfully shunned the limelight that inevitably at times plays upon the great that his neighbours in the small village of Carlops (in the Pentland Hills, close to his birthplace), where he spent the last years of his life, remained for long unaware of his immense achievements. It was only when a host of distinguished scientists congregated in their village to pay homage to "C. T. R." on his ninetieth birthday that they discovered that the gentle old man whom they had welcomed back to the place of his forebears had attained international renown.

He married Jessie Fraser, the daughter of the Rev. George Hill Dick, of Glasgow, in 1908; he owed much to her never-failing devotion and counsel. They had three children, one son and two daughters.

November 16, 1959.

Mona Wilson, of Oare, Wiltshire, died on October 26, 1954 at the age of 82. She combined in a degree unusual in men and rare in women a talent for practical administration and for literature.

In administration she is best known as the first woman and one of the original National Health Insurance Commissioners appointed in 1911, under Lloyd George's National Insurance Act, for which, incidentally, she was the first woman to be paid the same rate for the job as a man. Before that she had been recognized as an expert investigator into social conditions, and after her term of office had expired her remaining years were devoted to literary pursuits, all having merit and some of even permanent value.

She was the eldest daughter of Canon J. M. Wilson, D.D., well known as a headmaster of Clifton, and afterwards Canon of Worcester. One of her half-brothers was Sir Arnold Wilson, M.P., who was killed flying in the 1914-18 War, and another is Sir Steuart Wilson. She was born in 1872 and educated at Clifton High

School, St. Leonard's School, St. Andrew's, and in 1892 went up to Newnham College, Cambridge, of which in 1932 she was made an associate.

About the time that she left Cambridge her father had recently resigned Clifton and been appointed vicar of Rochdale and archdeacon of Manchester, so in the industrial north Mona Wilson first met labour and social conditions at close quarters. She had early become acquainted with Lady Dilke and her niece Gertrude Tuckwell [q.v.], Mary Macarthur and others prominent in the fight for better conditions for working women. Her obvious ability attracting their attention, she was appointed Secretary of the Women's Trade Union League; later, she was made a member under the Trade Board Act of the chain-making and paper-box making trade boards, and she was a member of the Home Office Departmental Committee on industrial accidents.

Among investigations into social conditions in which she took part were the inquiries at West Ham and Dundee. The Dundee inquiry in 1904 was entirely under her direction and that of Miss M. L. Walker. It covered housing conditions, family incomes, employment, wages, &c., and was one of the most exhaustive ever undertaken. Thus, when the names of the Insurance Commissioners under the chairmanship of the late Sir Robert Morant were announced in November 1911 it was no surprise to those familiar with industrial matters that Mona Wilson was included as the woman member, and at the time she received the highest salary then paid to any woman in State employment. Her seven years' term of office expired in 1919, and she then retired to a pleasant house near Marlborough, and, apart from some duties she undertook as a member of the Industrial Fatigue Research Board, and work as a J.P. on the local bench, her public work was over and she was free to devote her talents to the life that had perhaps most appealed to her, though a deep sense of public duty had called her into other lines.

Her first published work was a study, in 1924, of eighteenth-century life, *These Were Muses,* nine ladies who achieved a literary reputation in their day, which was very favourably received. Her next work, published in 1927, was of greater consequence, *The Life of William Blake,* a sumptuous volume, brought out by the Nonsuch Press and one of great value to all students of the poet-painter. In 1931 followed a scholarly *Sir Philip Sidney,* a new edition of which was published in 1950, and in 1932 and 1933 *Queen Elizabeth* and *Queen Victoria.* In 1938 she returned to her favourite period with *Jane Austen and some Contemporaries,* with an introduction by her friend G. M. Young [q.v.], an interesting picture of female learning of those times. In 1950 she produced an anthology, *Johnson,* of which *The Times Literary Supplement* said it was a book for which the lover of Johnson may be grateful and one, moreover, likely to make more lovers of Johnson.

All her work bears the stamp of true scholarship, lightened by elegant humour and expressed in a graceful and lucid style. With a somewhat shy and diffident manner, Mona Wilson suggested the scholar rather than the intrepid and fearless investigator and administrator, and in her youth her ethereal beauty might well have provided a model for Sir Edward Burne-Jones.

October 30, 1954.

Major W. G. Wilson, C.M.G., who with Sir William Tritton evolved "Mother", the prototype of the Mark I tank, of which two types were used in the Somme Battles, died at Itchen Abbas on June 30, 1957.

Born on April 21, 1874, Walter Gordon Wilson was the son of George Orr Wilson, and was educated in H.M.S. Britannia and at King's College, Cambridge.

Wilson, already a well-known engineer and a member of the firm of Wilson-Pilcher, pioneers of motor car construction, was involved in the mysteries of mechanized fighting early in the war of 1914-18. As a lieutenant in the Armoured Car Squadron he had helped in the construction of these cars; and in 1915, the squadron having survived threats of disbandment, was at Burton-on-Trent supervising technical experiments on Landships. Between the summer of 1915 and early in the following year Wilson made many visits to see Tritton, of the firm of William Foster and Company, of Lincoln, in attempts to devise a land machine that would satisfy the War Office requirements.

They had just evolved the "Tritton" machine—also known as "Little Willie"—when they were told that the War Office were now thinking in terms of a machine that would be able to cross a trench 5ft. wide with a parapet 4ft. 6in. high. Wilson and Tritton thereupon began work on an entirely new type.

Finally, the "Wilson" model, afterwards named the "Centipede", later "Big Willie", and finally "Mother", was produced. This had a high degree of stability and a low centre of gravity and was in appearance the tank of common memory; it had tracks all round, an upturned nose and rhomboidal shape. The machine was given a secret trial at Hatfield in February 1916 before a distinguished company which included Lord Kitchener, Balfour, Sir William Robertson, and Lloyd George, and the results were deemed so satisfactory that an order for 100 of "Mother", the prototype of Mark I, was given later in the month.

Sir Albert Stern, secretary of the Landship Committee and later chairman of the Tank Committee, recalls in his book *Tanks, 1914-18* how at earlier trials of "Mother" trenches were dug in the grounds of Hatfield House, the Wembley proving ground not being regarded as sufficiently private, and how Balfour among others, took a ride in "Mother" but was removed feet first by his fellow Ministers before the machine tried the widest trenches.

Wilson was later granted £10,000 for his services. He was appointed C.M.G. in 1917. He was the inventor of the Wilson Self-Changing Gear Box, which has been incorporated in many cars, and was the founder and a director of Self Changing Gears Ltd., Coventry.

He married in 1904 Ethel Crommelin, daughter of S. O. Gray, and they had three sons.

July 2, 1957.

Robb Wilton, a favourite comedian of the music-halls and of broadcasting, died on May 1, 1957 in hospital in Liverpool. He was 76.

In 1898 he sacrificed a career in engineering to become an actor. His first extended engagement was with the stock company of a Liverpool theatre known as "The Old Blood Tub"—a description of the choice of plays, not of the theatre's state of repair. For three and a half years he did villains in melodrama and pantomime dames, until he sallied forth as a solo comic. Before the start of the First World War he was already popular on the music-hall stage.

A stout, well-set-up man, with a puzzled, deliberate manner, a trick of fingering his face meditatively as he spoke, and a slight northern accent, he was admirable in sketches in which he took the part of a bewildered and rather solemn official trying to combine dignity with inaction.

He was assisted by his wife, Florence Palmer, in such sketches, one of the best of them being *The Magistrate,* in which his uneasy shifts to avoid having to arrest the dramatic lady who interrupts his quiet by confessing to a murder were very funny. This sketch he played at the Royal Variety Programme at the Alhambra in 1926. In another of his sketches he was a fireman, and during the war of 1939-45 he gave an extremely amusing performance as a Home Guard who, with irresistible logic, had established his headquarters in the local public house. ("The day war broke out, my wife said to me . . .")

Though he rarely practised the art in recent years, Wilton was also a first-rate comic singer, and middle-aged music-hall frequenters remember with joy one particular song of his which consisted chiefly of dialogue sung in contrasting tones of pained surprise. As a broadcaster he made a great success of a long series of scenes relating to one "Mr. Muddlecombe, J.P."—but these could never satisfy those who knew the full richness and ripeness of Robb Wilton's act as seen upon the stage.

One of the Mr. Muddlecombe sketches provoked a protest to the B.B.C. from the Magistrates' Association. Objection was made to Wilton's portrayal of a magistrate adjudicating while under the influence of drink, and requesting an attractive female complainant to meet him in a public house after the rising of the court. The B.B.C. in reply pointed out that the broadcast was so farcical and the charges—such as racing tortoises within the 30 mile limit—so obviously fantastic, that it was not felt that it could be regarded as any reflection on magistrates' courts. Wilton expressed surprise at the protest and recalled that the best audience he ever had for a burlesque of a policeman was one composed of policemen.

Wilton's wife died in 1956.

May 2, 1957.

The death of **Arthur Wimperis,** which occurred in London on October 14, 1953, recalls the heyday of Edwardian light opera and the pointed though good-humoured satire of the "Follies".

Wit and fine craftsmanship characterized all his work and particularly his lyrics, for as a young man he had studied W. S. Gilbert to good purpose and continued throughout his career to put a high value on polish and finish in his work. His keen, quizzical face was the expression of a gently satirical mind. He was always alive to new developments in the theatre and was able for many years to write freshly and engagingly, always within the fashion of the moment, so that his writing remained popular. The span from *The Arcadians,* for which he wrote the lyrics, to the film version of *Mrs. Miniver,* for the script of which he won an "Oscar", is a long one both in time and in temperament; that each of these achievements has been so popular is the measure of Arthur Wimperis's gifts.

Arthur Harold Wimperis was born on December 3, 1874, and was educated at Dulwich. He studied to become an artist in black and white and joined the staff of the *Daily Graphic,* the pioneer of the illustrated daily newspapers, when he was 18. He had hardly begun to make much headway when the South African war broke out; he joined Paget's Horse and served with the unit in South Africa. Soon after his return to London after the end of the war he took up writing and in 1904 began his long association with the stage. In those days he was known chiefly as a lyric writer. His greatest success of the period was undoubtedly the lyrics in *The Arcadians,* though his sketches for the "Follies" were close runners up.

His name thus became widely known and his work was much in demand. He was part author of *The Girl in the Taxi* in 1912, and wrote *The Passing Show* for Herman Finck in 1914. Thereafter titles flowed thick and fast: *The Rajah's Ruby; Follow the Crowd; London, Paris and New York; The Curate's Egg* and so on. Early in the 1930s he turned to films, making such scripts as *Catherine the Great; The Private Life of Henry VIII;* the lyrics in *Sanders of the River;* above all, *Mrs. Miniver.*

While crossing the Atlantic in 1940 the ship in which he was travelling was torpedoed and he was one of the eight survivors out of 32 in his lifeboat. Only in his latest years did his touch seem to fail, for in 1951, on his return from America, he remarked that the outlook for British writers in Hollywood had deteriorated.

October 15, 1953.

H. E. Wimperis, C.B., C.B.E., formerly Director of Scientific Research to the Air Ministry, died on July 16, 1960 in Edinburgh at the age of 83.

Born on August 27, 1876, Harry Egerton Wimperis was educated at the Imperial College of Science and at Cambridge, where he was a scholar of Caius and graduated with honours in the Mechanical Sciences Tripos of 1900. A Whitworth exhibitioner in 1896 and a Whitworth scholar in 1898, he gained practical experience in the Brighton works of the London, Brighton and South Coast Railway, and the Elswick works of Armstrong Whitworth, and in 1901 joined the engineering staff of the Crown Agents for the Colonies.

As a lieutenant-commander, R.N.V.R., he was from 1915 to 1918 an experimental officer in the Royal Naval Air Service, and later he became superintendent of the Air Ministry laboratory in the Imperial College of Science. From 1925 to 1937 he was director of scientific research to the Air Ministry, and in 1934 he was responsible for the creation of the Air Ministry Committee for the Scientific Survey of Air Defence, which led to the erection of the chain of radar stations that proved their value during the Battle of Britain.

In 1937 he visited Australia to advise the Federal Government on the organization of aeronautical research, and in 1938 he became aeronautical adviser to the Council for Scientific and Industrial Research of Australia. He delivered the Wilbur Wright memorial lecture in 1932 and the Thomas Hawksley lecture of the Institution of Mechanical Engineers in 1944, and he was president of the Royal Aeronautical Society in 1936-38 and a member of the council of the British Association in 1948-54. Besides technical papers contributed mainly to the Aeronautical Research Committee, he published books on the internal-combustion engine, the application of power to road transport, air navigation and atomic energy.

He married in 1907 Grace, daughter of Sir George Parkin, and had three daughters.

July 18, 1960.

Former Dean of Windsor—See **Baillie.**

Sir Percy Winfield, Q.C., LL.D., F.B.A., the first Rouse Ball Professor of English Law in the University of Cambridge, a chair he held from 1929 to 1943, and Reader in Common Law to the Council of Legal Education from 1938 to 1949, died at Cambridge on July 7, 1953 at the age of 74.

Percy Henry Winfield was born at Stoke Ferry, Norfolk, on September 16, 1878. He was educated at the school now known as King Edward VII School, King's Lynn, and at St. John's College, Cambridge, where he was placed senior in both parts of the Law Tripos, won the Whewell Scholarship in International Law, and was elected McMahon Student of the college. Called to the Bar by the Inner Temple in 1903, he practised for a while on the South-Eastern Circuit, but eventually settled in Cambridge, where, as was not uncommon in those times, he found it necessary for several years to augment his income by undertaking a considerable burden of private coaching.

During the years 1915-19 he served as an officer in the Cambridgeshire Regiment and was wounded in action. He returned to Cambridge after the war as lecturer in law at St. John's and Trinity Colleges, and completed his researches (commenced before the war) into the history and present law of the abuse of legal procedure. These were published in 1921 and in that year he was elected to a Fellowship at St. John's College.

In 1925 his *Chief Sources of English Legal History,* based upon a course of lectures delivered at Harvard University, at once cleared the ground for research workers in legal history and proved his exceptional erudition in that wide field. He was appointed University Lecturer when the new University Statutes were introduced in 1926, and in 1929 was elected Rouse Ball Professor of English Law. Thereafter he concerned himself mainly with tort: his *Province of the Law of Tort* (1931) and *Textbook on the Law of Tort* (1938) are well known.

His academic achievements owed much both to the historical background of his learning and to an intolerance of legal theories, however elegant, which would be unworkable in practical law. His speech and writings often showed an austere liveliness and a striking turn of phrase which compelled attention. Many generations of students will remember their tasks as counsel in his problem classes: the neat diagrams and notes (additional to those previously circulated) which faced them from the blackboard before each lecture began; and the remote expression of almost gloomy detachment which lightened so readily to a friendly smile. A loyal friend and colleague, he was by nature inclined to justify rather than criticize the behaviour of his fellows.

He was keenly interested in Rugby football and it is likely that few of his academic distinctions gave him greater pleasure than did his election in 1940 to the presidency of the Rugby Football Club of the University. He was an enthusiastic tennis player and a former captain of the Cambridge County Lawn Tennis Club.

Although he was troubled by partial deafness in his later life, this did not appear to impair his appreciation of good company, nor his capacity to enjoy a social occasion. His chief interest, however, was the law, and the Squire Law Library the place where he was most likely to be found. His publications, additional to the major works already mentioned, included textbooks on contract and on international law, and he contributed numerous learned articles to legal periodicals.

In 1909 he married Helena, daughter of W. T. Scruby. There were two sons and one daughter of the marriage.

July 8, 1953.

General Sir Reginald Wingate, BT., G.C.B., G.C.V.O., G.B.E., K.C.M.G., D.S.O., who succeeded the first Lord Kitchener as Sirdar of the Egyptian Army, and was the first Governor of the Anglo-Egyptian Sudan, died on January 28,

1953 at the age of 91.

He never possessed any of the advantages normally conducive to advancement in the Army; yet from being a penniless subaltern, without ever having held any regimental command, without passing through the Staff College, without experience of the South African campaign or of any of the more important theatres of the 1914-18 war, he achieved a high reputation and filled with distinction one of the most difficult administrative posts in the service of the Crown. He did not hold an active military command from the days when he was a junior subaltern until he led his troops in pursuit of The Khalifa in 1898. He hardly served outside Egypt, but his insight, tenacity or purpose, and marvellous power of sustained office work were of more value to him than the more dashing military qualities in his chosen career.

Francis Reginald Wingate, born on June 25, 1861, was the seventh son of Andrew Wingate, of Broadfield, Renfrewshire. From St. James's School he passed into the Royal Military Academy, whence he was gazetted to the Royal Artillery in 1880. With something less than £100 as his inheritance, but possessing great courage, industry, and ambition, he arrived in India before he was 21. He immediately took up the study of eastern tongues, and passed the higher standard in Arabic, Hindustani, and other languages. He went from India to Aden, and while he was there, in 1883, the G.O.C. Aden wrote to Sir Evelyn Wood, then Sirdar in Egypt, recommending Wingate to his notice. Accordingly, he was seconded for service with the Egyptian Army, Sir Evelyn soon selecting the young gunner to be his A.D.C.

On Sir Evelyn Wood's appointment to command the Eastern District in 1886, Wingate followed him home and continued as his A.D.C.; but he found it practically impossible to live in England on his pay, and at the end of a month he asked to return to the Egyptian Army. On his arrival in Cairo he was immediately appointed Assistant Military Secretary to Major-General Grenfell, then Sirdar; but in 1887 he was transferred to the Intelligence Department, where he served for 12 years. His service in the Egyptian Intelligence was an unbroken period of patient industry. In addition to its military aspect the work had its geographical, ethnographic, and linguistic sides; and on its fruits were largely based the plans which aimed at the recovery of the Sudan from the Dervish power. In the meantime there was protracted fighting along the existing frontier. In 1889 was fought the Battle of Toski, after which Wingate received the D.S.O., and these operations dragged on until the Egyptian forces recovered Afafit and Tokar in 1891. Wingate published in the same year his monumental work *Mahdiism and the Sudan.* He also took a leading part in facilitating the escape of European captives from the Mahdi's strongholds, notably that of Father Ohrwalder, whose narrative he published in 1892 under the title *Ten Years' Captivity in the Mahdi's Camp.*

During 1894, for a few months, he had acted as Governor and Commander of the troops at Suakin. Preparations for the impending campaign of reconquest were now well forward under the direction of Colonel (afterwards Lord) Kitchener. The advance upon the Dervish stronghold at Firket began in June 1896, and throughout the subsequent operations Wingate's services were in constant request until, in September, the enemy, after being defeated at Firket and Hafir, were driven from the Dongola province.

Kitchener had now matured his plans for the next stage of the advance, and he was rejoined by his assistant in time for the latter to see the capture of Abu Hamed and the occupation of Berber. Then, in 1898, with augmented forces, Kitchener marched on Khartoum. This movement brought about the Battle of Atbara and culminated in the defeat and rout of the Dervishes at Omdurman. Wingate received the thanks of both Houses of Parliament and was created K.C.M.G. He accompanied his chief to Fashoda, where a French mission, under Major Marchand, from West Africa had anticipated the Sirdar's arrival; but the solution of that situation is now familiar history. On his return to Egypt Wingate left his intelligence work to become Adjutant-General of the Egyptian Army.

Kitchener now organized two expeditions for the pursuit of The Khalifa and his broken forces. In the first of these, which achieved little, Wingate commanded an infantry division. He was then placed in control of the operations, which proved entirely successful. Actions were fought at Abu Aadel and Om Dubreikat, where The Khalifa fell.

Later in this year, 1899, after the South African War had broken out, Kitchener was needed at the Cape and Sir Reginald Wingate was appointed Sirdar of the Egyptian Army and Governor of the Anlgo-Egyptian Sudan. The opportunity had come for him to accomplish his greatest work: the social, moral, and economic transformation of the Sudan. Slavery was abolished; industry was encouraged; justice was strictly administered; and no interference with religious beliefs was tolerated.

After the outbreak of war in 1914 he remained in the Sudan. From 1916 onwards minor operations claimed his attention, for the hostility of the ruler of Darfur was only to be quenched by military force, which eventually brought about the extension of the administration over that wide region to the confines of the French Sudan. In the same year he was placed in general control of British aid to the Sherif, with the title G.O.C. Hedjaz Operations, and it was largely due to his ability in organization that the Arab revolt against the Turks was successful.

In January 1917, when the advance into Palestine had effectually dispelled all fears of invasion, Wingate was appointed High Commissioner of Egypt, in succession to Sir A. H. McMahon, while retaining the offices of Governor-General of the Sudan and Sirdar of the Egyptian Army. It was an excellent choice, for Wingate had the respect of all classes, communities, and nationalities, and knew them well. In March 1919, Lord Allenby became High Commissioner and Sir Lee Stack, afterwards so foully murdered, was appointed Governor-General and Sirdar, in both of which posts he had acted as Wingate's deputy. In 1920 Wingate was created a baronet with the style "of Dunbar and of Port Sudan". He finally retired from the Army in 1922.

He married in 1888 Catherine Leslie, daughter of Captain J. S. Rundle, R.N. Lady Wingate, who was created D.B.E. in 1920, died in 1946. There were four children of the marriage, three sons and a daughter. The second son died in infancy and the third was killed in action in 1918. The baronetcy now devolves upon the eldest son, Colonel R. E. L. Wingate, C.I.E., O.B.E., who was born in 1889 and retired from the Indian Civil Service in 1939. He was on active service in both wars.

January 29, 1953.

Margaret Wintringham, the second woman to sit in the House of Commons, died on March 10, 1955 in a nursing home in London at the age of 76.

She was Margaret, daughter of David Longbottom, of Silsden, in the West Riding of Yorkshire. Educated at the Girls' Grammar School, Keighley, and Bedford Training College, she was headmistress of a school at Grimsby before her marriage at Ilkley Congregational Church in 1903. The early years of her marriage were passed at Grimsby, where she played an active part in the social, religious, educational, and political life of the city. When war broke out in 1914 she was made a member of the Grimsby committees for lodging and feeding Belgian refugees, and for administering the Prince of Wales's Fund for the relief of industrial distress.

After her husband had been adopted as Liberal candidate for Louth, Lincolnshire, she became a V.A.D. at the Louth Auxiliary Hospital and chairman of the Women's War Agriculture Committee at Louth. This committee had the task of replacing with women the men on the land who had been called up. After her husband's election she became president of the local Women's Liberal Association and honorary secretary of the Lindsey Federation of Women's Institutes.

Her husband's untimely death in 1921 was a great blow, but she bravely shouldered the burden of fighting the by-election which carried her triumphantly into the House of Commons as the first Liberal woman member. Her already wide experience of social work gave her an excellent background, and her work for the Women's War Agriculture Committee and for the County Agriculture Committee for Lincolnshire stood her in good stead as the representative of an almost wholly agricultural community with a Liberal tradition. Her opinions on the problems of the countryside were always listened to in the House with respectful attention. She was re-elected at the general election of 1922, but lost her seat in 1924.

Thereafter for some years she was president of the Women's National Liberal Federation, and she continued to play a prominent part in local affairs, being elected to the County Council for Parts of Lindsey in 1933. Her interest in the lot of agricultural workers she maintained unabated and, indeed, she remained until her death the same bright, helpful, and generous being whose presence so captivated the House of Commons over 30 years earlier.

March 11, 1955.

Sir Robert Witt, C.B.E., whose outstanding work for the appreciation of painting and sculpture extended over half a century, died at his home in London on March 26, 1952 at the age of 80.

Only those who have been privileged to work on committee with Robert Witt, or those who have spent their lives at the centre of the art world, can estimate how much the study of art in England owes to his initiative and taste. At this date it is hard to think of the time when there was no National Art-Collections Fund and no Witt Library; yet it needs but a little imagination to visualize the probable state of affairs if neither of these institutions had come into existence. An "amateur", in both the French and the English senses of the word, he contributed to the furtherance of art in real and solid fashion; his wholehearted love of painting and almost impeccable taste were of conspicuous service to the enlargement of British galleries; and his systematic accumulation of pictorial aids to reference earned the well-justified gratitude of scholars and connoisseurs.

Robert Clermont Witt was born in London on January 16, 1872, son of G. A. Witt, and educated at Clifton and New College, Oxford. In 1896 he served in the Matabele war; later he acted as war correspondent with Cecil Rhodes. Eventually, abandoning these adventurous courses, he settled as a solicitor in the City of London, becoming in due time senior partner in the firm of Stephenson, Harwood and Tatham. The fine arts, however, were his main interest in life, and as early as 1902 he produced a book entitled *How to Look at Pictures,* which has been many times reprinted, and which may safely be said to have the status of a minor classic in art criticism. This book alone would have been enough to give Witt a place in art history; but two other activities of his earned the appreciation and respect of all those who care for painting.

The National Art-Collections Fund was established in 1903 with about 500 members, its purpose being to raise money, by subscription, for the purchase of important works of art for British galleries. Witt was one of the prime movers in this foundation, and chairman of the fund until ill health compelled his resignation in 1945. He presided at its councils with tact and judgment, did a great deal to interest potential benefactors in its work, and saw its membership rise steeply with the passing of the years. Witt's value to the cause of art was recognized by his cooption as a trustee of the National Gallery for various periods from 1916 to 1940 (he was chairman in 1930), as trustee of the Tate Gallery from 1916 to 1931, and as chairman of the National Loan Collections Trust. He was created C.B.E. in 1918 and knighted in 1922.

The Witt Library was also started early in the present century, though it was not until after the 1914-18 war that it became a big and important aid to reference. Witt gradually accumulated great numbers of photographs of works of art, as well as reproductions from the art magazines, classifying them according to schools, with sub-classification by subject. The library (which in course of time reached a total of over half a million items) was thrown open daily to all serious students of art, and remains an important and valuable adjunct to research in the field of aesthetics. Apart from reproductions, he built up a large collection of original drawings by old and modern masters.

As a critic Witt made only modest claims for himself, but his *How to Look at Pictures* has probably been of greater utility to the average cultivated man than many more pretentious and erudite works. It set out logically and sympathetically all the elements that enter into the appreciation of a work of art. Written in a melodious, clear and graceful style, it had no *parti pris* in controversial aspects, and fulfilled extremely well its purpose of making subtle and difficult matters plain to the intelligent layman. Witt also published *One Hundred Masterpieces of Painting, The Nation and its Art Treasures,* and sundry contributions to periodicals in prose and verse.

He married, in 1899, Mary Helene, daughter of Charles Marten, and had one son.

March 27, 1952.

Dr. Ludwig Wittgenstein, who died in his sixty-second year on April 29, 1951 at Cambridge, was a philosopher with a reputation as an intellectual innovator on the highest level. His earlier and later work formed the points of origin of two schools of philosophy, both of which he himself disowned.

He came of a well-known Austrian family and was brought up in Vienna. After studying engineering at Manchester he went to Cambridge in 1912 as an "advanced student" to study under Bertrand (now Lord) Russell*. At the outbreak of war in 1914 he returned to Austria to serve with the Austrian Army until he was taken prisoner in 1918 in the Italian campaign. While thus serving he completed a manuscript, the *Tractatus Logico-Philosophicus,* which, appearing in 1921 in German in the last number of Ostwald's *Annalen der Naturphilosophie* and in English in book form in 1922, at once made for its author an international reputation.

Throughout his life Wittgenstein showed the characteristics of a religious contemplative of the hermit type. Thus he alternated between periods of great prominence in academic life and periods of extreme abnegation and retirement, and in 1922 he renounced his fortune and took a post as a schoolmaster in a mountain village near Wiener Neustadt. Here he stayed until 1928. He maintained, however, contacts with Vienna, where he went in the school holidays and where, through his acquaintance with the Professor of Philosophy, Moritz Schlick, he originated a school of philosophy—the famous Vienna Circle, later known as the logical positivists.

Quite apart from the intrinsic merit of his ideas, Wittgenstein's historical importance in this period consists in the fact that through him the work of a long series of formal logicians, culminating in Russell, became known to the inheritors of an equally long tradition of philosophy of science, culminating in Mach (Schlick's predecessor in his chair). The intellectual results of this fusion were such that, a decade later, they spread all over the philosophic world. By this time, however, Wittgenstein was reinstalled in Cambridge, having arrived there for a short visit in 1929. Trinity College elected him to a five-year research fellowship in 1930, and he also started lecturing. Apart from one paper in 1929 he published nothing in this period; but two sets of notes, dictated to groups of pupils and known respectively as *The Blue Book* and *The Brown Book,* were widely circulated, contrary to Wittgenstein's wishes. Again, it is not too much to say that he inaugurated a new "school", or perhaps rather a new method in philosophy—namely, that of which John Wisdom and Gilbert Ryle [d. 1976] are the best known exponents, and which is often referred to as "the philosophy of ordinary language". The point of view put forward in these notes diverges widely from that of the *Tractatus Logico-Philosophicus,* though it is not difficult to see how the second grew out of the first. The way had been prepared for this new philosophical departure by the emphasis placed by G. E. Moore [q.v.], who was at Cambridge, on "the language of common sense".

In 1936 Wittgenstein left Cambridge and went to Norway, where it is said that he lived in a mountain hut, and from which he returned in 1938 after the fall of Vienna. In 1939 he succeeded G. E. Moore in the Cambridge Chair of Philosophy, and was also naturalized as a British citizen. He continued lecturing for a time, but in 1943 he went to work, first as a porter in a London hospital and afterwards as a research assistant. In 1945 he returned, but found that his teaching duties prevented him from doing creative writing, and in 1947 he resigned from his chair. The second book, however, which he had sacrificed so much to complete and publish (in order, as he said, to show how very wrong the *Tractatus* was), was not destined to appear. In 1949 he became seriously ill, of a disease from which he knew there could be no great hope of recovery, and retired from active life. He formed round him a small group of philosophers who were also his friends, with whom he worked and discussed to the last.

We are still too close to Wittgenstein to form a just estimate of his work. His *Tractatus* is a logical poem, consisting as it does of the development of a gigantic metaphor, constructed round two senses of "language". It is thus an exceptionally difficult book to interpret with any reliability. His sets of notes, and his incomplete manuscript, also show, in the opinion of all who have read them, signs of indubitable genius; but Wittgenstein himself took all the steps in his power to prevent their being circulated on the ground that, if they were, they would be bound to be misunderstood. What is beyond doubt is that, like Descartes in one way, like Locke in another, he started a world-wide philosophical trend.

In so far as this can be described in one sentence, it consists in following up the idea that thinking consists in using a language. Thus thought, which it had been easy to conceive of as a private, indefinable, amorphous entity, becomes the manipulation of some symbolism; something public; something which can be "nailed down", and to which the techniques of formal logic can be applied.

May 2, 1951.

Arthur Wontner, the actor, who made his first appearance on the stage in the year of Queen Victoria's Diamond Jubilee and who continued to play leading parts till after the Second World War, died on July 10, 1960 at the age of 85.

He was 22 at the time of his first engagement, and within little more than a year—a year taken up with a season's work at Margate under Sarah Thorne and a tour with Louis Calvert—he was seen in London at the old Globe Theatre off the Strand in *The Three Musketeers.* He toured for four years under such managements as those of Mrs. Lewis Waller, Edward Compton, and Charles Sugden, and in 1903 was chosen to play Tree's part in Hall Caine's *The Eternal City* in Australia, where he stayed for the next two years. He joined Tree's company for the Shakespeare Festival at His Majesty's in 1910, supported Mrs. Patrick Campbell twice in 1911, and in 1912 was Ben-Hur in a revival of the play at Drury Lane and a member of Granville Barker's company in productions of Barker's own play *The Voysey Inheritance* and of *Twelfth Night.*

From then until the end of the First World War Wontner appeared in plays by Wilde, John Masefield* and Barrie, and was José Collins's [q.v.] leading man at Daly's during part of the long run of *The Maid of the Mountains.* For the next few years Wontner was, after Owen Nares, the most likely casting for a leading part of a romantic type on the London stage. Of the two men he had the more ascetic appearance and the more vibrant voice. Following Nares, he went into actor-management, but the play he chose, a comedy by A. A. Milne [q.v.], was perhaps too light, and the experiment did not last.

Having supported José Collins in two more musical plays, Wontner played opposite Dame Edith Evans [d. 1976] in *Tiger Cats,* and was Buckingham in Sir Lewis Casson's* production of *Henry VIII.* In the late 1920s he paid three visits to America, and in the early 1930s he appeared in London as Malvolio in Robert Atkins's* *Twelfth Night* at the New, as the Author, for whom he took Lytton Strachey as his model, in Shaw's *Village Wooing,* and in one of Leon M. Lion's cycles of plays by Galsworthy.

He toured in a thriller by [Dame] Agatha Christie [d. 1976] during the Second World War, and took part in four more plays in London in the years following it, before announcing his retirement at the end of 1955, within two months of his 81st birthday. By then he had behind him in addition to his stage work a film career of 40 years' duration, which included five appearances as Sherlock Holmes, and a number of important parts on sound-radio and television; the B.B.C.'s production of Pinero's one-act play *A Private Room* with Wontner and Mary Jerrold [q.v.] as a pair of old lovers worked out beautifully for both of them. He was grateful for such engagements, because they kept him in touch with his friends and with the profession at a time when, slender and distinguished in appearance as before, but white-haired and frail, he knew that he would not reenter a theatre by the stage-door.

He was for 11 years treasurer of British Actors' Equity Association, for more than 25 years a member of the committee of the Actors' Orphanage, and he was a trustee of the Pension Fund, established in memory of Sydney Valentine. He was married twice: first to Rosecleer Alice Kingwell, whose stage name was Rose Pendennis; secondly, after his first wife's death in 1943, to Florence Eileen Lainchbury. He had two sons and a daughter by his first marriage, one son being Hugh Wontner, M.V.O., chairman and managing director of the Savoy Hotel and director of the D'Oyly Carte Opera Company.

Alfred Cope's portrait of Arthur Wontner as Joseph Fouché in an Italian play, *Napoleon,* adapted by John Drinkwater, hangs in the Garrick Club.

July 12, 1960.

Edward Wood—See **Halifax.**

Haydn Wood, who died in London on March 11, 1959 at the age of 76, was a musician who successfully combined in one career a number of professional activities not often associated: he began as a solo violinist, took to composition, and produced serious works that gave him prestige and best-selling songs that brought him a fortune.

He was born in Yorkshire into a musical family and he used to say that he owed his Christian name to the fact that just before he was born his father went to a performance of *The Creation.* His first lessons on the violin he had from an older brother. His first appearances were in the Isle of Man as a boy prodigy. He then won an open scholarship at the Royal College of Music, where he studied under Arbos. Stanford taught him composition, which accounts for his assured technique. He played at the opening of the R.C.M. concert hall, and sufficiently impressed Joachim and Sarasate as to warrant further study abroad under César Thomson in Brussels. A world tour with Albani set the seal of success on his career as an executant.

In 1909 he married Dorothy Court, appeared with her on the musical stage, and began to write for her the popular ballads which made his name famous. Of these, "Roses of Picardy", the idea for which occurred to him on a bus in Finchley Road on his way home from the theatre, was the most famous. He jotted it down on an envelope there and then and subsequently sold thousands of copies. Other successes of this light sentimental type were "Love's Garden of Roses" and "Bird of Love Divine".

Altogether he turned out about 200 of these so-called "ballads", which had an enormous vogue among amateurs before they were killed by jazz on the one hand and serious music by radio on the other.

As a serious composer he established himself with a string quartet, which won a Cobbett prize, and a piano concerto. There were also a violin concerto, sets of orchestral variations, and pieces for small orchestra and military band.

He also wrote a number of suites which come somewhere between the ballads and the serious music and belong to the realm of entertainment music. Thus it came about that on his seventieth birthday he had a complete programme of his works performed by the B.B.C. Theatre Orchestra.

He was for a number of years on the board of the Performing Right Society as a composer-director.

March 13, 1959.

The Right Rev. Edward Sydney Woods, D.D., who had been since 1937 Bishop of Lichfield and previously Bishop Suffragan of Croydon, died at Lichfield on January 11, 1953 at the age of 75.

A man of deep, simple, and sincere piety, he was extraordinarily persuasive in the difficult art of religious broadcasting, and was thought of almost as an intimate friend by multitudes of listeners who had never seen him. In the history of the cinema his name will long be remembered in connexion with "the Croydon experiment" of 1933 and the following years, by which cinemas were allowed to open in that borough on Sundays for the showing of wholesome, cultural, and educational films.

As chairman of the executive of the Cinema Christian Council, which was later merged in the Christian Cinema and Religious Films Society, he did much to forward the interest of the Churches and of the educational world in the potentialities of the cinema in those fields. As a diocesan, Dr. Woods was a reasonable administrator, ever ready to weigh all sides of every dispute. Always approachable and always prodigal of time and effort in dealing with parochial difficulties, he was universally beloved by clergy and laity alike, and his enthusiasm for evangelism and religious education was a perpetual inspiration. He was a younger brother of the late Dr. Theodore Woods, for many years Bishop of Winchester, and compiled (in conjunction with the Very Rev. F. B. Macnutt) a memoir of him which was published in 1933.

During the recent war he paid visits to the

troops abroad and had but recently returned from Malaya.

Born at Hereford on November 1, 1877, Edward Sydney Woods was a son of the Rev. Frank Woods and Alice Octavia Fry. He was educated at Marlborough, at Trinity College, Cambridge, where he graduated in 1899, taking a second class in the Theological Tripos, and at Ridley Hall, Cambridge, whence he was ordained in 1901 as curate of Holy Trinity, Cambridge, and chaplain of the Cambridge pastorate. He was successively chaplain and lecturer at Ridley Hall from 1901 to 1903, and vice-principal from 1903 to 1907.

About this time he suffered what seemed to him at the time an almost irreparable blow. His medical adviser informed him that he had contracted tuberculosis, and that his only hope lay in another climate. It meant farewell to Cambridge and to work there in which his whole mind was absorbed. But it brought him, as chaplain first at Davos Platz (1908-13) and then at Lausanne (1913-15), wider opportunities, wider reading and contacts, and not least that deeper religious understanding which the finer spirits can derive from misfortune. With characteristic modesty, and in the third person, he has recorded something of all this in the sixth of the broadcast talks which were republished in 1942 under the title *Things I Live by.*

From 1912 to 1919 he filled the position of chaplain and commissary to the Bishop of North and Central Europe, and from 1914 to 1919 he was also a temporary Chaplain to the Forces and chaplain to the Royal Military College, Sandhurst. From 1911 to 1922 he acted as examining chaplain to the Bishop of Durham.

In restored health, Dr. Woods returned permanently to Cambridge in 1918 as vicar of his old parish of Holy Trinity, where he remained until 1927, being also a Proctor in Convocation for the diocese of Ely from 1921 to 1923 and honorary canon of Ely from 1923 to 1927, when he was appointed vicar and rural dean of Croydon and honorary canon of Canterbury.

Croydon, which was the seat of his ministry for the next ten years, and where he was to display remarkable powers of pastoral and civic leadership, is a detached portion of the diocese of Canterbury situated within greater London. It offers special opportunities and he made good use of them, especially among youth. In 1929 he was elected Proctor in Convocation for the diocese of Canterbury, and in the following year he was made Archdeacon and Bishop Suffragan of Croydon.

In 1932 the question of Sunday cinemas agitated the public mind in many areas, and the Sunday Entertainments Act of that year facilitated their opening on two conditions—namely, a day of rest for the employees and the allocation of a proportion of the profits to charity.

In brief, "The Croydon Experiment", in promoting which the Bishop gave a useful lead to other municipalities and to the public mind on this whole question, consisted in adding as a third, local condition that the pictures shown must be of a good, wholesome kind and suitable for showing on a Sunday. At the Croydon referendum of November 29, 1932, after lively polling scenes in which the Bishop took a small part, the scheme was approved by 34,617 votes to 24,386.

The Bishop subsequently was chairman for the first year of the committee which "vetted" the programmes and, thanks largely to him, the scheme worked smoothly and, on the whole, successfully. In a letter to *The Times* of October 29, 1934, reviewing the experiment, he was able to claim that they had "succeeded in eliminating films which make a special feature of crime, cruelty, and loose morality"; that some 200 undesirable films had been prevented from being shown; that practically every programme had contained some educational "shorts"; that, while the supply of "feature" films of a purely cultural type was limited, there had been no difficulty in securing plenty of clean comedy and healthy stories.

At Lichfield the Bishop's personality had a unifying effect on that scattered diocese. He was an assuager of controversies, directing the minds of all to the great tasks of religious education, including adult religious education, and above all of evangelism. In his monthly letter to his diocese for December 1940 he sounded the note which ran through all his exhortations on this latter subject.

"These are times", he wrote, "when the Ministry of the Word takes on a new significance and is charged with fresh potentialities. It is a grievous mistake at any time, and at the present time it is disastrous, for the Church's leaders and spokesmen to exalt the Ministry of the Sacraments at the expense of the Ministry of the Word. Preaching and teaching, prepared with meticulous care, based on deep thought and wide reading, and charged with the power won in the secret place of prayer is not "mere utterance", it is powerful to change the hearts of men and, indirectly but very really, to affect the course of history".

In the sphere of education he sought to end "the cleavage which too often exists between clergy and teachers"; and in the larger questions of politics he was a firm supporter of Dr. Temple's campaign to secure recognition of the fact that Christianity touches life at every point.

And no memoir of the Bishop would be complete which did not mention his infectious confidence in the triumph of right in the recent war; his earnest pleas for the early planning of post-war reconstruction; his constant "pilgrimages" through his diocese—on foot when petrol allowances failed; and his interest in old prints and water-colours.

He was appointed High Almoner by King George VI in 1946. He was the author of a number of publications including *Everyday Religion, Modern Discipleship, A Faith that Works,* and *What is this Christianity?*

He married in 1903 Clemence Rachel, daughter of Robert Barclay. She died only in October, 1952.

He is survived by three sons and three daughters of the marriage.

January 12, 1953.

The Rt. Rev. Dr. C. S. Woodward, Bishop of Bristol from 1933 to 1946 and of Gloucester from 1946 until 1953, died on April 14, 1959 at his home near Wells. If he will not rank among the prelates of his time either as a great scholar or as a leader in public thought, he will be held in affectionate remembrance by his clergy as an excellent diocesan of high character, kindly sympathy, and a wide parochial experience. Indeed, his pre-episcopal career in the Church should have provided any diocese with an almost ideal Bishop, and on the whole he fell little short of that ideal.

Clifford Salisbury Woodward, the son of the late Rev. Richard Salisbury Woodward, vicar for over 30 years of All Saints', Eastbourne, was born on August 12, 1878. He was educated at Marlborough, and afterwards at Jesus College and Wycliffe Hall, Oxford, graduating in 1901 with seconds in Classical Moderations and *Literae Humaniores.* A curacy in Bermondsey, some time as clerical secretary of the Southwark Diocese, and three years as lecturer at Wycliffe Hall and chaplain of Wadham College, were followed in 1913 by preferment to the rectory of St. Saviour's with St. Peter's, Southwark.

Woodward's evangelical training and subsequent connexion with Wycliffe Hall did not obscure his merits from prelates of quite different schools of thought. During the war he served as an Army chaplain, was slightly wounded in France, and awarded the M.C. In 1918 he was nominated by Sir Frederick Freake to the important West End living of St. Peter's, Cranley Gardens, by long tradition regarded as a stepping-stone to high ecclesiastical preferment. He interested himself in the more pressing social questions of the day, especially housing. He was not a great preacher; his force and power lay in his earnestness and deep conviction—and it should be added a beautiful voice—and it was observed that his congregations included a large proportion of young people, and especially young men.

In 1925 he was nominated by Stanley Baldwin as Canon of Westminster and rector of St. John the Evangelist, Smith Square, where he interested himself in much general social work, and he drew fairly large congregations; his sermons to young people were a popular feature with the B.B.C. In February 1933 he was appointed on the recommendation of Ramsay MacDonald to succeed Nickson as Bishop of Bristol. Woodward already had a connexion with Bristol, where his grandfather had been a prosperous merchant. His confirmation of election was unusual, perhaps unique. Sir Lewis Dibdin, the Vicar-General, was unable to officiate owing to a recent accident, so the Archbishop of Canterbury decided to confirm the election himself, which he did in Church House on May 24, 1933—believed to be the first occasion when an Archbishop had himself confirmed the election of a bishop. Woodward received the Lambeth degree of D.D.

From the first his earnest wish was to put himself on the best of terms with his clergy, and it may be said at once that he succeeded and retained their affection and regard to the end.

A more pronounced sense of humour and

a dash of worldly cynicism might perhaps have saved him from early public requests that no one would call him "My Lord" or his house "The Palace", and reminded him that titles appertain primarily to the offices rather than to the individuals holding them. In practice the first request was tacitly ignored, though it was generally conceded that the rather ordinary nineteenth century villa where the Bishop actually lived might indeed be more suitably described as a "house" than as a "palace"! But these were trivial matters and Woodward's mind was set on important ones. He had a clear conception of his duties as a bishop, and in the forefront of these he placed getting the best men he could, morally and intellectually, for the ministry, and the standard of candidates that he expected and exacted from his examining chaplains was a high one.

His views were moderate, and probably he had no very clear conception of exactly where he stood doctrinally, and that perhaps helped him to a toleration of various shades of belief and practice. His heart was really in parish work, and he used to lament that his time was so taken up with meetings and functions to the exclusion of personal contacts. His political views, which he himself called "left-centre", seldom obtruded themselves, and his obvious sincerity and sympathy with suffering and misfortune disarmed the criticism that his spoken words might sometimes evoke.

In the Second World War Bristol suffered more than most cities from air raids, and in one of them the Bishop's house was entirely destroyed while he was returning by train from London. His work had been strenuous, and his health was suffering; in 1946, on the retirement of Bishop Headlam from the See of Gloucester, he accepted the offer of translation.

Woodward was an accomplished after-dinner speaker, sometimes startling an audience who knew how genuinely kind-hearted he was, by unexpected flashes of mordant wit. His busy life left him with but little leisure for writing, and the character of his contributions to literature may be judged by their titles: *Stories Told to the Scamps, Jesus Among the Children, Christ in the Common Ways of Life, Dreams and Fables,* &c.

He married in 1905 Grace, widow of Colonel Charles Stewart of The Black Watch. She died in 1939.

There were no children.

April 15, 1959.

Frank George Woollard, M.B.E., who died in Birmingham on December 23, 1957 at the age of 74, was one of the fathers of the British motor industry.

Frank Woollard pioneered the introduction of flow production in Britain and became recognized as a world authority on automation.

He was born on September 22, 1883, and educated at the Goldsmith and the Birkbeck Colleges in London. He was trained as an apprentice in the railway workshops at Eastleigh and was then involved in the design problems of the Clarkson steam omnibus, which led him from steam locomotion to motor car design and production.

At the works of E. G. Wrigley and Co. Ltd., of Birmingham, he was responsible for designing and then putting into production under sub-contract from Lord Nuffield*, then W. R. Morris, the front and rear axles and the gearboxes for the first Morris Cowley "bull nose" motor car which went into serial production.

Later Morris appointed him to take over the engine factory of Hotchkiss et Cie at Coventry and he became director and general manager of the engines branch of Morris Motors, Ltd. It was at this factory that Frank Woollard and his associates embarked upon some remarkably far seeing ventures in production engineering. Between 1923 and 1925 they commissioned the first automatic transfer machines for the production of engineering components, and the Coventry engine factory became an outstanding example of the first large-scale attempts at continuous production in Britain. When the chief production engineer of the Ford Motor Co. of Detroit visited the plant he said that the transfer machines were 20 years ahead of time. Actually, as events have proved, Woollard was nearly 30 years ahead of British adoption of this form of automation, though the idea germinated earlier in the United States motor car industry.

In 1932 Woollard became managing director of Rudge Whitworth Ltd., and in 1936 director of the Birmingham Aluminium Casting Co., Ltd., and the Midland Motor Cylinder Co., Ltd. He associated himself strongly with professional life as an engineer and was president of the Institution of Automobile Engineers for two years from 1945, playing a leading part in the amalgamation with the Institution of Mechanical Engineers, serving on the council of that body as chairman of its automobile council. During his retirement he took a vigorous interest in education for industrial administration and contributed extensively to the teaching at the University of Birmingham and at the College of Technology, Birmingham, where he conducted a large number of executive development study groups.

In 1954 his extensive experience of production engineering management was summarized in his principal written work, *Principles of Mass and Flow Production,* which outlined the possibility of the automatic factory and stressed the importance of the human factor in such a far-reaching development. He put forward as a principle of management that "flow production must benefit everyone; consumers, workers, and owners" and showed that if this were not so waste of resources would obtain.

Large of frame and distinctive in appearance, he had a big, warm heart and endeared himself to his many professional associates, so many of whom became his firm personal friends.

His wife, who was a talented pianist, died some years ago and their daughter Joan is an outstanding sculptor and painter and has had several oils hung in the Summer Exhibitions of the Royal Academy.

December 28, 1957.

Sir Leonard Woolley, an archaeologist of international renown, died in London on February 20, 1960 at the age of 79. His career as a digger spanned a period of over 40 years; his first excavations were on the Roman wall at Corbridge in 1906 and his active work in the field was concluded in Syria in 1949. Thereafter he was fully engaged in completing the publication of his finds.

Woolley will always be remembered as one of the most successful diggers ever engaged in field archaeology. He had an extraordinary flair not only for choosing a potentially rich site but also for attacking those parts of it which concealed the most important remains. His greatest successes were obtained at Ur of the Chaldees, in southern Iraq, where he directed the excavations on behalf of the British Museum and the Museum of the University of Pennsylvania from 1922 to 1934. The climax of these expeditions was the discovery of the famous Royal Cemetery of Ur, which yielded to the spade the incomparable treasures of Sumerian civilization, many of them deposited in shafts with multiple burials, before 2500 B.C. Woolley, though employed by various institutions to conduct excavations on their behalf, remained a free-lance throughout his career and was wont to say that he was the first archaeologist who had contrived to make a living out of this profession.

The son of the Rev. George Herbert and Sarah Woolley, Charles Leonard Woolley was born on April 17, 1880, a member of a large family, and had to pay for his education through scholarships which he won for St. John's, Leatherhead, and subsequently for New College, Oxford, where he obtained an honours degree in theology. It was Warden Spooner who, with a rare discernment, told him that he must abandon his intention of becoming a schoolmaster and make archaeology his career. Much of his youth was spent in a poor parish in Bethnal Green and at an early age he acquired an interest in paintings, was a frequent visitor to the Whitechapel Art Galleries, and became familiar with the Old Masters. This taste remained with him all his life and in his retirement he collected begrimed paintings at country auctions, cleaned and repaired his acquisitions, some of which were of a high quality and found their way to important exhibitions and national art galleries. He was deft with his hands and many a delicate and fragile antiquity was salvaged in the course of his excavations by his imaginative methods, combined with an exceptional dexterity.

After graduating from Oxford he went to France and Germany in order to study modern languages, and a year later was appointed assistant to Sir Arthur Evans, then Keeper of the Ashmolean Museum, where he served a valuable apprenticeship before committing himself entirely to field archaeology. His work in the Near East began in 1907 when he excavated in Nubia in partnership with Randall MacIver, a scholar of high calibre to whose precise methods he owed much. At Karanog he dug the first big Meroitic cemetery on record; but in spite of the rich finds, which included inscribed and painted gravestones, bronze vessels of Greek workmanship, and painted pottery, he concluded that "the whole Meroitic civilization was but a backwater, remarkable as an isolated phenomenon in African history, but contributing nothing to the general stream of culture and of art". Such discoveries did not satisfy his original and creative mind, but he also dug at many other non-Egyptian sites between Korosko and Halfa, where he was all the time gaining in experience in practical problems, in the control of workmen, and in fields of discovery which ranged from the Early Dynastic down to Roman times.

A brief interlude in Italy, where he conducted a small dig in the ancient baths at Teano on a wooded hill-top in ancient Sabine territory, completed the formative stage of his training as a field archaeologist. He then made plans to dig at Leptis Magna in Tripolitania, but the outbreak of the Turco-Italian war prevented him from realizing this scheme, and it is curious to reflect that he might otherwise have spent the greater part of his archaeological career in North Africa.

Instead, in 1912 he was appointed to succeed Dr. R. Campbell-Thompson as leader of the British Museum expedition to Carchemish, where he was accompanied by a brilliant young man who was later to become famous as Lawrence of Arabia. There he made a number of spectacular discoveries in the temples and palaces of the Neo-Hittite period. A series of orthostats with carvings of north Syrian goods and rulers, many contemporary hieroglyphic inscriptions, and the layout of the town defences were considerable contributions to knowledge at the time.

While he was employed in north Syria Woolley, together with Lawrence, took the opportunity during the off season from Carchemish to make a survey in Palestine of the country stretching northwards from Akaba towards the southern end of the Dead Sea. The time available for the expedition was not much more than six weeks, in January and February 1914, but it enabled these two archaeologists to obtain a general knowledge of an area which, except for the few centuries of settled Byzantine government, had changed little since the days of Moses. The account of this work under the names of Woolley and Lawrence was published in a book entitled *The Wilderness of Zin* (1915). The discussion of the climate conditions in the past, the elucidation of the routes from Palestine to Egypt in Biblical times, and the exposition of the way in which the Byzantine Government in spite of the most unfavourable circumstances of soil and climate was able to spread over the whole district a veneer of settled civilization, were indeed a valuable contribution.

The dig at Carchemish was interrupted by the 1914-18 War, in which he served with distinction. He was blown up at sea off the coast of south Asia Minor and for the remainder of the war (1916-18) was in a Turkish prison camp, where once again his manual skill and inventiveness did much for the amenities of the place.

In 1919 he concluded the dig at Carchemish under considerable difficulties, for he found that his camp was in a no-man's-land between the French army and Kurdish irregulars; both sides consulted him at intervals. Subsequently he moved to Egypt and did fruitful work, particularly in a house quarter once occupied by ancient craftsmen on the site of Tell-el-Amarna, for the Egypt Exploration Fund.

Fortified by much experience he began his major work at Ur in 1922 and dug there systematically at intervals for 13 years. He began by concentrating on the Temenos, or sacred area within which lay the principal temples and palaces. Here he established a tremendous sequence of cities which began on water-logged soil, perhaps in the fifth millennium B.C. at what is known as the Al 'Ubaid period, and rose one over the other to form a mound some 70ft. in height, until the last occupation in the fourth century B.C. Here for the first time he exposed a complete range of town plans which revealed more fully than ever before the architectural achievements which had occurred in south Babylonia from Sumerian times onwards. It was perhaps in the revelation of Sumerian civilization that Woolley did his richest and most productive work.

The documents, which included some of the earliest literature known to mankind, were so prolific that many years will still be needed before their publication can be anything like complete. They are also of extraordinary archaeological interest because of the light they throw on all the buildings and small remains associated with them. The sculpture of these early periods, as well as the metallurgy, is of a very high order and Woolley's remarkable insight into the methods used by ancient craftsmen and builders has been one of his most valuable contributions to knowledge. His understanding of ancient methods also enabled him to follow up clues in the ground with a penetration often denied to skilled diggers.

Woolley however found so much that he was handicapped in finding time to consult other authorities and academically his work often suffered accordingly; more particularly in his chronology, which was often at variance with accepted criteria. There seems to be little doubt now that his dating of the Royal Cemetery was several centuries too early; and similarly at Carchemish there are many who cannot accept his sequence dating for the sculpture. In judging works of art, too, a Victorian outlook was not acceptable to the critics, and his book on *The Development of Sumerian Art* (1935), while invaluable in all matters touching on craftsmanship, appears to be aesthetically defective. His books on *The Sumerians* (1928) and *Abraham* (1935) were out of touch with linguistic and literary problems and thus fell short of being authoritative.

For all these defects, however, there was ample compensation in the imaginative treatment throughout his writings of whatever he found. Gifted with an unusually fluent style, an enchanting lecturer, no one has better described the sequence of his discoveries, and many of his popular books have enthralled a very wide public. *Digging up the Past* (1930) ran into many editions, and even more successful was *Ur of the Chaldees* (1930) (subsequently translated into many languages), which took the reader on a tour of the excavations and enabled him to feel at home among ancient Sumerian as well as Babylonian remains. To follow Woolley round the site at Ur and to hear him talk about the private houses was to feel oneself living among a vanished people. If his imagination sometimes outran the facts, this to him was preferable to allowing knowledge to lie dormant and inconclusive.

His industry was prodigious. While on the dig he slept little, rising with the sun and often still at work in his study or in the catalogue room until two or three o'clock in the morning. He could not have published so much had he not been exceptionally quick in composition, and he used to say that writing was an enjoyment to him. The large definitive publications of Ur came out in a steady stream from 1927 onwards and are still being produced. These volumes include *Ur Excavations,* Vol. I, "Al 'Ubaid", in collaboration with H. R. Hall (1927), mostly concerned with prehistoric and Early Dynasty remains; Vol. II, "The Royal Cemeteries" (1934) contained some 600 pages of text, illustrated by 273 plates, a *magnum opus* which no other living archaeologist could have produced in so short a space of time; Vol. V, "The Ziggurrat and its Surroundings" (1939), is a testimonial to his insight into ancient architecture, which deservedly earned him the honour of being made an honorary A.R.I.B.A.; Vol. IV, "The Early Periods" (1955), an invaluable summary of discoveries concerned with remains prior to 2000 B.C., could no longer keep pace with collateral evidence from elsewhere. Two more volumes are in MS. and still await publication. For the general reader who is not a specialist in archaeology his *Excavations at Ur, a Record of Twelve Years' Work* (1954) is a most readable summary account of these achievements. To have dug so much and left nothing unwritten is indeed a phenomenal record.

When he had completed his work at Ur he went on to dig at Al Mina, near Antioch in Syria, where he made many discoveries concerning the import and export trade between the Aegean and Syria. Even more remunerative were his discoveries at Atchana in the Hatay (1937-39 and 1946-49), where the palaces, temples, sculpture and pottery of the second millennium B.C. were of a type hitherto little known. Once again a rich find of associated documents gave us new concepts of the political history and everyday life in the small kingdoms of the time.

The scientific account of this dig was incorporated in a book entitled *Excavations at Atchana-Alalakh* (1955), full of original material and of controversial matter: his early chronology is however not generally accepted. The popular account appeared in a Pelican book entitled *A Forgotten Kingdom* (1953).

In 1938, less than a year before the outbreak of the Second World War, Woolley accepted an invitation from the Government of India to advise them about their programme of archaeological work. Here he made many vaulable recommendations on the most promising sites or areas for exploration; on the best methods and agencies for the development of exploration not only by the Government but by universities and learned societies; on the best method of training or selecting officers for exploration work. He completed this task in a remarkably short time with considerable perceptiveness. Many of his recommendations were carried out and the subsequent fruitful developments in India and also in Pakistan owed much to his advice.

From 1939-43 he served as a major in the Directorate of Public Relations and undertook the task of building up a specialized service—the monuments, fine arts, and archives branch of Civil Affairs. The object was to provide whatever protection might be possible to the ancient monuments, works of art, libraries, and collections of archives in the various areas of the war. For this work, owing to his imaginative gift for organization, he was peculiarly well fitted.

From 1943-46 he was Lieutenant-Colonel G.S. Archaeological Adviser to the Civil Affairs Directorate, and when Italy became a battlefield he was able to safeguard valuable treasures which had been removed from the Pitti, the Uffizi, and other Florentine galleries during the first days of the war. He immediately arranged with a great measure of success a systematic guarding of other captured deposits.

He was very good company, a delightful *raconteur*, and had a good understanding of his workmen in the Orient. *Dead Towns and Living Men* (1920) contains many reminiscences which well illustrate his sense of humour, ingenuity, and an unaffected *joie de vivre* which was one of the most charming facets of his character. Between him and his foreman Sheikh Hamoudi Ibn Ibrahim there was a life-long friendship. Hamoudi was foreman of all his principal expeditions from the time he went to Carchemish in 1912, and gave devoted service which Woolley would always have wished to be remembered.

Woolley married Katharine Keeling, who took an active part in his work at Ur and at Atchana; she died in 1945.

February 22, 1960.

George Grey Wornum, C.B.E., F.R.I.B.A., who died in New York on June 11, 1957, was awarded the gold medal of the Royal Institute of British Architects in 1952 after his successful replanning of Parliament Square. He was 69, and was appointed C.B.E. in the Birthday Honours list published two days after he died.

Wornum, who was connected by descent with Ralph Nicholson Wornum (1812-1877), keeper and secretary of the National Gallery, was the son of a doctor of medicine. He was born in London in 1888 and educated at Bradfield College. After studying at the Slade School he was articled to the late R. Selden Wornum, F.R.I.B.A. He also studied at the Architectural Association, where, in 1909, he won the travelling studentship and silver medal. His first professional work was a studio for H. G. Riviere, designed in 1910. From 1914 to 1918 he served with the Artists' Rifles and The Durham Light Infantry, when he was wounded and lost his right eye.

After 1919 Wornum was engaged either alone or in association with other architects in a great variety of works. They included a water garden at Hayling Island (with Louis de Soissons*) and the yacht Nyria in 1920; reconstructions and decorations at the Palais de Danse, Derby, in 1921; commercial premises in the City, and houses in various parts of the country. Two later works which received praise were the new British Girls' College, Alexandria, Egypt, in 1935, and the convalescent home of the Hearts of Oak Benefit Society at Joss Bay, near Broadstairs, in 1937.

At the time of the Coronation in 1937 Wornum was one of the three architects appointed to organize the decorations of London, Wornum being responsible for the scheme of the processional route coming within the jurisdiction of the Westminster City Council. In the same year he received another important decorative commission, being selected by the directors of the Cunard White Star Line to be decoration architect for the passenger accommodation of the Queen Elizabeth, for which he got together a team of eminent artists and craftsmen.

As designer of the premises of the Royal Institute of British Architects at Portland Place (1932), Wornum could claim to be specially honoured among his colleagues. The selection was by competition open to all members of the institute throughout the world, and no fewer than 270 sets of designs were sent in. His was one of the few to recognize a corner site, and also one of the few to observe the simplicity demanded by a setting distinguished by dignified uniformity that was nevertheless in process of change. It was criticized in its relation to context, especially the surviving work of Nash; but it is questionable if the critics recognized the extent to which Portland Place had changed and was changing. The case was well put by Sir Giles Gilbert Scott [q.v.], who said that "they had adopted the only possible solution by building with extreme simplicity; so that if others would follow, they would get another and different uniformity—that of simplicity and austerity". A more pertinent criticism is that the decorative additions to the R.I.B.A. building are not worthy of its structural design—as revealed, for instance, in the Weymouth Street elevation.

His full talents as an architect were again demonstrated in his building for the Central Cleansing and Transport Depôt of the City of Westminster, in a turning off Ebury Bridge Road, which won a bronze medal of the R.I.B.A. in 1939. It is a pity that this building is so secluded, for it is a good example of the architecture which, under the control of a sense of form, arises directly and simply out of the solution of the practical problem without self-conscious functionalism. The problem in this case was that of circulation, the building being planned primarily to facilitate the entry, operations, and exit of the refuse collection vehicles feeding the barges in Grosvenor Dock. It is upon the treatment of the walling of the road ramps and the bold use of the cantilever principle over the dock that the architectural effect of the building largely depends.

Wornum, who was president of the Architectural Association 1930-31 and a member of the R.I.B.A. council from 1935, was a sensitive, earnest man of intellectual appearance and charming manners. His characteristic limp and the monocle worn on a broad ribbon were consequences of the wounds he received in the war.

He was popular among his colleagues, and in his dealings with the young painters and sculptors recruited to assist him he was generous to a fault. In later years he became severely crippled and for reasons of health went to live first in the West Indies and then in California.

He married in 1923 Miriam Alice Gerstle, of San Francisco, a talented artist and decorator, and they had a son and two daughters.

June 14, 1957.

Frank Lloyd Wright, the most celebrated American architect of his time, and one of the outstanding architects of the world since the early years of the century, died at Phoenix, Arizona, on April 9, 1959. He was 89.

He exerted a very powerful influence on architects in America and Europe. Indeed, during the second decade of the century, when his work was beginning to be known internationally, he was perhaps more readily appreciated in Europe than in his own country where, in his early days, he met with a degree of opposition so often accorded to innovators.

His work, especially in the field of domestic building, represents the most important American contribution to modern architecture. Wright conceived building as an extension of the creative process of nature, and his work was actuated by the principles of organic growth and unity so that a building should appear as much as possible an integral part of its setting and surroundings. When speaking of the building of his own house in his autobiography he said that no house should ever be on a hill, but should be of the hill. He wanted, he said, a natural house, and he "scanned the hills of the region where the rock came cropping out in strata to suggest buildings". This indicates the essence of his domestic building.

He preached the ideas of organic architecture in his lectures and autobiography, and from these ideas formed a general philosophy of life. He was also responsible for many office buildings, a church, and the impressive Imperial Hotel in Tokyo, where trees and plants and pools of water are important elements in the composition of the exterior. When other buildings toppled and crashed during the earthquake of 1923, a year after its completion, the Imperial Hotel alone stood intact.

This was due to an extensive use of the cantilever system which enabled him to rest each concrete slab on a central support, like a tray on a waiter's fingers. The hotel was made to float like a ship on a small area of mud poised on hundreds of slender, pointed eight-foot piles with its great weight evenly distributed, a system which was followed in some of Wright's later buildings.

Frank Lloyd Wright was a native of Wisconsin. He was born on June 8, 1869 in a rural district near the town of Spring Green where his grandfather, an emigrant from Wales, settled 100 years ago.

After studying engineering at Madison, Wisconsin, for three years Wright went to Chicago in 1887 and obtained employment as a draughtsman with J. L. Silsbee. A little later he entered the office of Dankmar Adler and Louis Sullivan, the latter of whom, with his ideas of organic building, exercised a considerable influence on the young Wright. Another important early influence was the domestic architecture of Japan, with its simplicity and its integration of house and garden. Wright designed several houses while in the office of Adler and Sullivan, but in 1893 he began to work independently, and during the next 20 years he built more than 100 houses throughout the Middle West quite unlike anything that had been seen before.

They were mostly large and medium-sized houses and were all designed to integrate firmly with the earth and surrounding vegetation and were built with low pitched roofs and wide spreading eaves.

With the Husser House in Chicago, built in 1899, he developed the cruciform plan which became a distinctive feature of many houses of his middle and late periods. With this plan he often made the heating appliance the central feature of the dwelling. His method of design was generally from the interior outwards to the exterior, and the open plan, which he developed, was based on a logical sequence derived from living habits. The long horizontal masses are very pronounced in some of the large houses where the main accommodation spreads over a generous ground floor, and the merging of garden and house is often very marked, as in the Darwin Martin house at Buffalo (1904) and the Robie House in Chicago (1909).

The habit of taking suggestions from the natural setting is exemplified in the house built over a waterfall at Bear Run, Pennsylvania, in 1939, where the concrete masses of the terraces above the waterfall are formalized repetitions of the horizontal mass of rock over which the water falls—one of the most dramatic houses in the world.

Wright's early non-domestic building is of a monumental massive character and frequently included valuable technical innovations. A well-known example is the Larkin building in Buffalo (1905), which was the first in America in which such devices were used as metal bound plate glass doors and windows, all metal furniture, air conditioning, and magnesite as a building material.

Wright had married in 1890, but in 1909 he left his wife and family of six children and went to Europe. He returned in 1911 and to his ancestral valley, where his mother had bought some land on which he built a house for himself. This house he named Taliesin after a druid-bard of Wales who had sung of the glories of fine art. In 1914, while Wright was away in Chicago attending to the building of the Midway pleasure gardens, a mad negro servant killed seven of the occupants of Taliesin and set the house on fire. Little remained of the house, which he set to work to rebuild. It came as a relief after this tragedy that he should spend the next five years in Tokyo building the Imperial Hotel.

In 1925 Taliesin II was burnt down and he built a house on the same spot for the third time. Additions have been made to this house over a long period; it is one of his most characteristic works and is justly famous. After building Taliesin III matrimonial difficulties and court proceedings ruined him and lost him his practice until a number of old clients and friends gathered round and set him up in 1929. He then embarked on a third career, building even more ambitiously than before, chiefly houses in suburbs and beyond. He had visions of homes all over the country each with an acre of ground, built to fit in with natural surroundings and for comfort and enjoyment. "The future city", he said, "will be everywhere and nowhere".

Time was on his side, and when the World's Fair opened in Chicago in 1933 there was everywhere to be seen modern buildings constructed on the lines Wright had followed many years before. At his house at Taliesin and in Arizona, where he constructed the model of his idea of a modern city, many students came to study with him and a fellowship was formed devoted to his ideals in building.

Among his later works should be mentioned the Johnson building at Racine (1936-39), noteworthy for its construction and method of lighting. The office hall ceiling is supported on tall mushroom pillars which taper towards the bottom. The spaces between the mushroom discs are filled with glass tubes through which the daylight percolates. This building evoked much discussion in architectural circles, some criticizing it as theatrical and others admiring it for the infusion of poetry into building.

In 1947-48 a new research laboratory was added to the Johnson building at Racine, and Wright's design is remarkable in many ways. The laboratory is a building of 15 storeys, the floors being cantilevered like tree branches from a central core as the sole support. This core rises 154ft. high and is anchored in a foundation of concrete 54ft. into the earth. From each alternate floor hangs a glass shell composed of tubes like those in the earlier administration building. This building is of considerable structural significance because it shows the multi-storey building erected in a manner completely different from the skeleton frame and the load bearing wall, while permitting great freedom of planning.

Wright's pursuit of expressive organic forms resulted, in several of his later buildings, in the considerable use of curved forms. Noteworthy examples are his design of the Guggenheim Museum, now almost complete, and the house he built for his son David in the Arizona desert in 1952. This house is constructed of concrete blocks very much in the form of a coiled rattlesnake. The entrance is approached by a semi-circular ramp rising from the ground and the house continues the circular rhythm with the kitchen, dining and living rooms and bedrooms in sequence. It is "a plan that grows out of the earth and turns its face towards the sun".

Wright visited England in 1939 when he delivered four lectures at the Royal Institute of British Architects. These lectures were afterwards published as a book entitled *An Organic Architecture, the Architecture of Democracy.* They are a discursive exposition of his philosophy of architecture.

In 1941 he was awarded the Royal Gold Medal for architecture. In 1957, at the age of 88, Wright visited Iraq to design an opera house at Baghdad.

Wright was a powerful and picturesque personality, an assiduous propagandist with the style and appearance of a prophet. In spite of the fact that no younger architects of note have carried on his style of design, the influence of his ideas has been very great, and indeed some recent developments in modern architecture haver reached the same point that he seems to have reached by instinct many years ago.

April 10, 1959.

Richard Wright, the American Negro writer, died on November 28, 1960 in Paris, where he had been living for a number of years.

Wright was perhaps best known in Britain for his autobiographical *Black Boy,* published in 1945, a frank and moving account of his childhood and young manhood in the United States. It was to Paris he went with his wife in 1946 after he had broken with communism, an experience he recounted from a Negro viewpoint in a contribution to the collection of essays *The God That Failed.*

Born on a Mississippi plantation as the son of a Negro farm worker and a school teacher, on September 4, 1908, Wright had a hard childhood and little regular education. At 15 he took a job as a post office clerk.

He had early determined to become a writer but, in spite of publishing some verses and articles, did not have much success until in 1938 he won a $500 prize with what was to be his first book, *Uncle Tom's Children,* a collection of four longish short stories, published later in Britain, which already showed an unusual insight into the characteristics of his people. On a Guggenheim Fellowship Wright then wrote *Native Son,* a work which aroused considerable controversy in America, being based on the case of a Negro who died in the electric chair in Chicago for killing a white woman. Essentially it was an imaginative study of the inferiority psychosis of the Negro in the United States and carried a load of passionate feeling.

In 1940 Wright was awarded the Spingarn Medal, the highest award for achievement in the field of Negro interests, for his "powerful description of the effect of proscription, segregation, and denial of opportunity to the American Negro". *Native Son* was later dramatized by Orson Welles and had a London showing in 1948.

After his break with communism in 1944, and his emigration to France, Wright's writing came increasingly to reflect his travels. In 1953 he visited Ghana for several months, the result being *Black Power,* a report which not only attacked the old British colonial order but seemed dissatisfied with Dr. Nkrumah's* advancing nationalism. Earlier in 1960 another account of his travels, *Pagan Spain,* appeared in England, a book which again displayed Wright's restless critical spirit.

November 30, 1960.

Dr. Wu Lien-teh died in Penang on January 21, 1960. By his death the world of medicine has lost a heroic and almost legendary figure and the world at large one to whom it is far more indebted than it knows.

The pneumonic form of plague has a mortality rate of about 99.99 per cent. It is also the most infectious of all diseases and the most dangerous to nurse. In the winter of 1910-11 it killed some 60,000 people in Manchuria and North China. That it spread no farther and did not become another Black Death is almost wholly due to the skill and devotion of a young Malayan-born Chinese doctor, who was very fortunately put in charge and had to overcome not only the chronic inefficiency of the Manchu Empire but scientific ignorance and race prejudice on the part of European colleagues. He conquered the outbreak and a repetition of it 10 years later, threw new light upon its causes, and presided for many years over the Manchurian Plague Prevention Service.

Dr. Wu was born in 1879 at Penang. His family were Cantonese immigrants to Malaya and his father was a goldsmith whose moderate means were somewhat strained by having to support 11 children. For many years Dr. Wu was known by his Cantonese-Malayan name of Gno Lean-Tuck, and as such he appears in the British Medical Directory. His British friends and colleagues have always referred to him affectionately as "Tuck". Wu Lien-teh is the same name in Mandarin.

The boy's abilities at the local school won him a Queen's Scholarship, open to all the Straits Settlements, which enabled him to go to Cambridge. He entered Emmanuel College in 1896, was taught by Adam Sedgwick and Gowland Hopkins, obtained a first in Natural Sciences and proceeded to St. Mary's Hospital. There he defeated the future Sir Bernard Spilsbury for every hospital prize. Research, mainly in bacteriology, followed at Halle, Paris, and Johns Hopkins. He returned to Malaya as a general practitioner, but in 1908 he was invited to Tientsin as Vice-Director of the Imperial Medical College and thus entered on his Chinese career. He was only 31 when he was sent north to fight the plague.

Having beaten the two great epidemics, Dr. Wu embarked on further arduous and noble work for the League of Nations, attending conferences in every continent and becoming the world's leading expert in the opium trade. In the meantime he had reorganized and modernized Chinese medical education. His innumerable publications (many of them without collaborators) deal not only with plague but with cholera, anthrax, venereal disease, narcotics, quarantine and medical training. Two major works attained monumental status—the classical *Treatise on Pneumonic Plague* (1926) and (written jointly with K. C. Wong) the authoritative *History of Chinese Medicine* (1932). In 1959 Dr. Wu published a long and engaging, if over-modest, autobiography, *Plague-Fighter.* It ranges very widely and is full of charming stories, incise character sketches, and the reactions, kindly but not uncritical, of a tolerant Oriental to European manners, morals and religion.

In his retirement Dr. Wu lived mainly at Ipoh in his native land. He received honorary doctorates from several Far Eastern universities but, rather strangely, not from Cambridge. Nor was he an honorary Fellow of Emmanuel. And although a British subject he was never honoured by the British Crown.

Dr. Wu retained a warm affection for his English friends and, in his old age, revisited Cambridge on several occasions. His astonishingly youthful vigour, his geniality and his immensely wide interests and sympathies, made him a most welcome guest.

January 27, 1960.

Countess Nora Wydenbruck, who died in London on August 29, 1959, was a woman whose talents shone in several fields of activity. She was poet, painter, and novelist; known to the German-speaking world as a poet and translator of T. S. Eliot's* work, and to the English-speaking world as the author of a loving study of Rainer Maria Rilke, whose friend she was, and as translator and compiler of the remarkable *Memoirs of a Princess,* the reminiscences of Princess Marie von Thurn und Taxis, which were published in Britain in July 1959.

She was a serious scholar who consulted original authorities in her research, as was evident in *Placidia's Daughter,* an excellent life of Augusta Julia Grata Honoria, the unhappy fifth-century princess who could not support the bonds of late-Roman court etiquette. Of her own life Countess Wydenbruck wrote most attractively in *My Two Worlds,* which was published in 1956.

She was the daughter of Count C. A. Wydenbruck, a notable Austrian diplomatist, and was born in London in 1894 at a time when her father was Ambassador to the Court of St. James's. Educated at Copenhagen, Vienna, and Dresden, she studied art at the Women's Art School in Vienna, and at an early age exhibited in the principal cities of Austria and Germany.

Countess Wydenbruck married her compatriot, Alfons Purtscher, the brilliant painter of horses, by whom she had a son and a daughter, and shortly after the end of the First World War the Purtschers made their home in England. Like her husband, the Countess was country bred and a good horsewoman, and she had no difficulty in finding her place in a country where field sports play such a large part in social life, while her artistic abilities gained her success in London. As a painter she was chiefly interested in landscape and flowers, and some of her best work was done in Ireland, where the moist, rich greens and almost tropical exuberance of plant life suited her temperament. Romantic rather than realistic in her outlook, she inherited in her designs the spirit of Austrian baroque.

It was, however, in her woodcuts in colour of flower subjects that she found the fullest expression of her personality. In them a firm grasp of botanical character was combined with freedom in execution and decorative beauty of colour. Under the title of *Hothouse Flowers* a book of these woodcuts was published in Vienna, and similar examples were often seen in the joint exhibitions which the Purtschers held at the Bloomsbury and Claridge galleries, as also in those of the Women's International Art Club, of which she was a member.

August 31, 1959.

Sir Francis James Wylie, who died at his home on Boar's Hill on October 29, 1952, filled a place of a unique kind in the life of Oxford. As Oxford secretary to the Rhodes Trustees he represented in Oxford for over a quarter of a century an institution which, in its first years an avowed experiment, he saw become part of the settled character of the university.

The inception, in practice, of the Rhodes scholarships in Oxford was mainly his task; it fell to him in an unofficial but none the less delicate capacity to dispel early prejudices and smooth early frictions; and he retired only when the working of the scholarships, interrupted by the 1914-18 war, had been fully restored. But his death is more than the severance of these associations, for to many hundreds of Rhodes scholars now scattered over the world, who remember what he was in himself, it will seem like a personal loss.

Born in 1865, the son of the late Richard Wylie, of St. Petersburg, he had been educated at St. Edward's School, Oxford, and Glasgow University, whence he went up to Balliol. He took a first class in Classical Moderations in 1886 and a first in *Lit. Hum.* two years later. For a year he was an assistant master at his old school, and in 1891, after a short interval as a private tutor, was elected to a lectureship, tutorship and Fellowship at Brasenose. He was a well liked don, with an interest in all sides of college life and a shrewd insight into the undergraduate mind.

The Rhodes Trustees appointed him to his post in 1903 with the confidence that he would adapt himself completely to the task of settling into the university some 60 or 70 newcomers from oversea every year. The chief difficulty of the early years, and one which still recurs with every new generation, though to a decreasing extent, was to prevent the Rhodes scholars from becoming, or feeling themselves, a body apart in the university. That this danger was once and for all avoided was perhaps the greatest of Wylie's services. With the disposition of scholars among the colleges and the arrangement of their finances thereafter, the greater part of his nominal duties was done. But he knew that the relations between colleges and scholars were all-important and he did not spare his personal influence to harmonize them.

Hundreds of Rhodes scholars came and went at the house in South Parks Road and received its hospitality, and did not realize until afterwards, perhaps not until they had gone down, that they owed something to the discreet influence they met there. Nothing can be said in this regard without a reference to Lady Wylie, who was Kathleen, daughter of the late Edmond Kelly, and whom he married in 1904. She was of indefatigable help to her husband on the social side of his duties. In the recollection of Rhodes scholars of their time the two must seem to have been inseparable in the maintenance of those personal ties which many were fortunate enough to form with them. Some evidence of this regard was afforded by the subscription of a sum by former Rhodes scholars to enable Sir Francis and Lady Wylie to visit South Africa soon after his retirement.

In 1929 the office and residence of the Oxford secretary to the Rhodes Trustees were transferred to the newly completed Rhodes House. During the celebration in 1929 of the first quarter-century of the scholarships Sir Francis Wylie received convincing recognition that his services, while of necessity to be judged chiefly from the point of view of the Rhodes scholarship scheme, were appreciated as of lasting value to the university as a whole. The honour of knighthood seemed to every one well deserved.

He is survived by his widow, three sons and two daughters.

October 30, 1952.

P. Wyndham Lewis—See **Lewis.**

The Right Rev. H. E. Wynn, D.D., Bishop of Ely since 1941, died on August 12, 1956 in hospital at Cambridge at the age of 67. He had been gravely ill for more than a fortnight.

Harold Edward Wynn, son of John Wynn, Buckhurst Hill, Essex, was born on January 15, 1889. From the Mercers' School he went up to Trinity Hall, Cambridge, in 1907, and was placed in the second class of both parts of the Historical Tripos. After two years at Ely Theological College he was ordained to the chaplaincy of Jesus College, Cambridge, where he remained until the outbreak of war in 1914. As an army chaplain he had a long and varied experience, serving in France and Italy and later with the Army of the Rhine and being awarded the Croce di Guerra.

After demobilization he was appointed Vice-Principal of Westcott House, Cambridge, and in 1921 he was elected Fellow and Dean of Pembroke College. At that time Pembroke tended to look with a critical eye upon junior fellows imported from other colleges, and Wynn had need to call upon his very considerable powers of tact and persuasion. Himself a liberal Anglican, he wisely refrained from ceremonial innovation and devoted himself with disinterested simplicity to the social and spiritual welfare of undergraduates.

One change he was anxious to make, and after some years he persuaded the college to make it—the abolition of compulsory chapel. He had always regarded compulsion as militating against his influence over undergraduates and the change gave him great satisfaction. Though he never professed to be a scholar of the first rank, he was a good teacher of medieval history, and took infinite pains with his pupils.

In 1935 Pembroke suffered a disastrous series of losses among its Fellows, and in the following year Wynn was appointed Tutor. In this pivotal office he carried on, and expanded, the work that he had done as Dean. With three of its best known Fellows carried off by death within nine months, the college was faced with many difficult adjustments and Wynn, who had served as Proctor in 1927, helped greatly in re-establishing the college in its relations with the university and with the schools.

When the 1939-45 War broke out he took over the duties of Dean as well as Tutor until, in 1941, he became Bishop of Ely. Few ecclesiastics have been less troubled by ambition than Edward Wynn. In his early days he had never contemplated a bishopric or anything like it. But now that it had come to him he faced the work of a diocese in the same generous and humble spirit that he fulfilled the duties of a college don. He quickly made a point of gaining personal contact with his scattered parishes and cheered the heart of many a lonely Fenland vicar by a friendly visit. At the end of the war he put out an appeal for the needs of the diocese, and the only criticism made of it was that he did not ask for enough.

As chairman of innumerable committees he displayed remarkable patience and he found it hard to refuse an invitation to any meeting in support of what he believed to be a good cause. Similarly conscientious was his attendance from time to time at the House of Lords, at Convocation, and at the Church Assembly. He had no love of public speaking for its own sake, but if he felt it to be his duty to make a contribution to a debate he made it with sincerity. In his earlier days he was several times Select Preacher both at Oxford and Cambridge, and in 1949 made an extensive tour in the United States, where he was warmly welcomed. He also delivered a course of lectures at the Divinity School at Yale.

The fact that his elevation to a bishopric did not remove him more than 16 miles from Cambridge was a source of great satisfaction both to Wynn and to his friends. He remained a Fellow of Pembroke; Trinity Hall made him an honorary Fellow; and *ex officio* he was Visitor of Peterhouse, Jesus, and St. John's. Thus he preserved his intimacy with Cambridge life and many generations of Pembroke men in particular will not forget what they owe to him. He served university and college, Church and State with single-minded devotion. He had no desire to be a statesman-prelate; he was content to be a holy and humble man of heart.

August 13, 1956.

X

The Grand Duchess Xenia Alexandrovna, the elder sister of the last Emperor of Russia, Nicholas II, died on April 20, 1960.

She had lived in England since 1919, when she escaped from Russia with the last surviving members of the Romanoff family. She was 85.

Grand Duchess Xenia was born on April 7 (Western calendar) 1875, the daughter of Emperor Alexander III and his Danish wife Marie Federovna. From an early age she was used to tragedy and the threat of assassination. When she was only six years old her grandfather, Alexander II, the Tsar-Liberator, was killed by Nihilists while driving in his carriage through St. Petersburg.

In 1888 she was nearly the victim of a train crash when the coach in which the imperial family were travelling was derailed near Borki, and but for the exceptional strength of her father, the Emperor Alexander III, who held up the shattered roof on his broad shoulders, the whole imperial family would most probably have been crushed to death.

A happy memory of her childhood was the frequent family gatherings at Fredensborg Castle, north of Copenhagen, when her parents took their family to visit her grandfather, King Christian IX of Denmark, known as the "Grandfather of Europe" because so many of his descendants mounted thrones.

A picture painted of one of these royal gatherings by Lauritz Tuxen in 1883 shows King Christian and Queen Louise in the centre of a large group made up of the Danish, British, Russian and Greek royal families, all related to one another. The eight-year-old Grand Duchess Xenia is sitting at the children's table with Prince Charles of Denmark who became King Haakon of Norway [q.v.], Princess Maud of Wales (later his wife), Princesses Victoria and Louise of Wales, Princess Marie of Greece—all her first cousins—and Grand Duke George, her second brother. Her two other brothers, Nicholas and Michael, stand near their parents.

In July 1894 she married the strikingly handsome Grand Duke Alexander Michailovitch, a nephew of Alexander II, who later became an admiral in the Russian navy and developed the Russian air force. Her "Aunt Alix" (Queen Alexandra) went to the wedding, which was celebrated in the chapel at Peterhof. There were seven children of the marriage—six sons and one daughter, Irina, who married Prince Felix Yusupov*.

At the time of the Revolution the Grand Duchess Xenia was in Kiev with her husband, then in command of the air force, and they escaped the worst excesses of the Revolution, though for a time they were prisoners on their own estate of Ay-Todor in the Crimea. But with the advance of the German army, and later thanks to the arrival of allied naval forces in the Black Sea, the Grand Duchess and her family, including the Dowager Empress, were able to leave Russia, embarking in H.M.S. Marlborough, sent to Yalta by King George V. The Grand Duchess was his favourite cousin.

In England she settled down first in Frogmore

Cottage, in Windsor Great Park, and moved in 1936 to Wilderness House next to the Maze in Hampton Court Palace. Here she lived a very quiet and retired life, looked after by a Russian nun, Mother Martha. The Grand Duchess was a very devout woman, and a chapel was built in Wilderness House where the rites of the Greek Orthodox Church were celebrated for herself and her household.

She was patron of the Russian Benevolent Society, formerly the Russian Red Cross, and did much to help other refugees. Like her younger sister, Grand Duchess Olga [q.v.] she was a clever artist and painted many miniature water colours which she sold for charity or gave to friends. She disliked all pomp and ceremony and when people seemed astonished at her simple ways and retiring nature she would tell them: "The Russian Revolution took almost everything from me, but the Bolsheviks left me with one privilege—to be a private person". She fully used this privilege.

Her husband, the Grand Duke Alexander Michailovitch, died in 1933. The Grand Duchess Olga, born in 1882, lives in Canada.

Seton Gordon [d. 1977], who knew the Grand Duchess during the Second World War, when she was living at Craiggowan, Balmoral, has recalled her charm and distinction, great sympathy and simplicity, and complete honesty. She had been devoted to her brother, the Tsar, and on her writing desk stood a photograph of him wearing the uniform of a private soldier in the Russian Army. Her brother had marched five miles, thus dressed and fully armed, before, as Commander-in-Chief, he issued the order for the new dress.

The Grand Duchess had a great affection for King George V from the time when, as a midshipman, he visited Petrograd. The Grand Duchess had large and beautiful eyes and the King's name for her in those early days was "Owl". She was grateful to the King for having gone in person to Victoria Station to meet her on her arrival as a refugee from Russia; for in those days it was usual for the reigning sovereign to meet in person only the head of another state.

The Grand Duchess was most kindly and hospitable. She was a strong walker and used to visit regularly many of the tenants on the Balmoral estate and those of Invercauld across the River Dee. She often said that the Highland families of Upper Deeside reminded her of her friends in Russia. She retained her great love for that country and said that when she experienced the beauty of a summer sunset on Deeside her thoughts went out to that great country far to the north-east.

Latterly she had ill-health and looked frail and sad. But her charm, distinction, and great courtesy remained, for in every sense of the term she was a great lady, humble and upright, an inspiring example to all who knew her.

Seton Gordon also recalled travelling to Russia from Oxford, a year before the First World War broke out, with Prince Felix Yusupov who had just become engaged to Irina, her daughter.

April 21, 1960.

Y

Dornford Yates, as Major Cecil William Mercer was known to many readers of his novels of adventure, died on March 5, 1960 at Umtali, Southern Rhodesia, where he had made his home. He was 74.

Born on August 7, 1885, he was educated at Harrow, where he reached "The Twelve"—a special class taken by the headmaster. From Harrow he went up to Oxford, where he became president of the Oxford University Dramatic Society for the year 1906-7. He then studied law and after a year in a solicitor's office was called to the Bar. He became a pupil of Travers Humphreys, and served him as sole assistant through the whole Crippen case.

In the 1914-18 War he was commissioned in the 3rd County of London Yeomanry and later served in Egypt and Salonika, where he was afflicted with a severe form of rheumatism which gave him no respite from pain. As soon as the war ended he was accordingly advised by his doctor to spend his winters in the south of France. He chose Pau, which was his home from 1922 till 1939, when, having gained a considerable fortune from his writing, he designed and had built a house at Eaux Bonnes, 25 miles south of Pau—as described in detail in *The House That Berry Built.*

When the Germans, late in 1940, reached this region he and his wife had to escape hurriedly *via* Spain and Portugal to South Africa. There Mercer, at the age of 54, served first at the headquarters of the Imperial Forces and then with the Southern Rhodesia Force. He was soon retired sick; and as soon as the war was over returned to his beloved new house at Eaux Bonnes, only to find that during its occupation by the Germans the place had become uninhabitable. He and his wife therefore returned to Southern Rhodesia, where, at Umtali, he designed and built another house.

There he continued to write novels and finally his autobiography. This he composed in the original form of a conversation piece in two volumes, wherein four of his own characters, Berry, Daphne, Jonah, and Jill, discourse freely and amusingly with himself: (*As Berry and I Were Saying* and *B-Berry and I Look Back*). He retained to the end of his life a remarkable memory which enabled him to describe, as if they had happened the day before, his many unusual experiences.

There was something romantic and boyish in Mercer's make-up and he rejoiced to be called Victorian. Lines from two of the Harrow songs he loved so well—"Oh the great days in the distance enchanted" and "There were wonderful giants of old, you know"—seem to run like a refrain through the story of his life. He could write light-hearted farce, but most of his books are fast-moving adventure stories in which right triumphs, sometimes improbably, over wrong. His plots are packed with unexpected twists and turns. He had high ideals and preferred to observe the decencies. Only occasionally did he introduce really repulsive characters. His writing has a compulsive enthusiasm that sweeps readers, especially young readers, along; yet in fact he wrote slowly. He was a disciple of Kipling and acknowledged his debt to Anthony Hope. Well informed on many subjects, he had a scrupulous respect for accuracy when recalling historical episodes.

Having started with modest contributions to the old *Windsor Magazine* before the 1914-18 War, by the time he had finished writing more than two million of his books had been sold, and this did not include sales in the United States, where he had a large following. His first book, *The Courts of Idleness,* appeared in 1920 and was followed by a steady flow of stories at the rate of about one a year for the next 20 years. *Berry & Co.* and *Jonah and Co.*, which were published in 1921 and 1922, introduced a set of characters who enjoyed wide popularity in the years between the wars. In the thirties such novels as *Blood Royal, Storm Music,* and *She Fell Among Thieves* added to his popularity.

He was twice married, first in 1919 to Miss Bettine Edwards, of Philadelphia, by whom he had a son. The marriage was dissolved in 1933 and a year later he married Miss Elizabeth Bowie.

March 7, 1960.

As a painter, **Jack Butler Yeats,** who died in Dublin on March 28, 1957, was not in the least like anybody else. Imaginative and romantic by temperament, he had the gift of expressing directly what he felt in terms of glowing colour that sometimes only just escaped garishness. It might be said that he painted as the bird sings, without premeditation, if it were not that behind his most extravagant and reckless statements with the brush there was felt not only keen observation of character but also the discipline of drawing. Many critics held out against him for a time but most of them succumbed in the end, and when in 1942 he was given the honour of a one-man show at the National Gallery in association with Sir William Nicholson, the general feeling was that the compliment, if unexpected, was justified and that there was constructive criticism in the contrast afforded.

Yeats came of a distinguished Irish family. He was the younger son of the late John B. Yeats, R.H.A., barrister turned painter, and brother of William Butler Yeats, the poet. He was born in 1867 and educated privately in Sligo. He first attracted attention as an illustrator of books and broadsheets produced by his sisters at what was known successively as the Dun Emer and the Cuala Press at the village of Dundrum near Dublin. The general character of his work at this time, mostly in pen line with broad washes of bright colour, may be suggested by saying that he struck one as the ideal illustrator of Stevenson. He delighted "in a number of things" but more especially in the ways of the sailor ashore. He could draw the potential buccaneer to perfection, conveying in the tilt of a peaked cap all the romantic self-dramatization that is summed up in Shaw's

Captain Brassbound. An early exhibition of his work at Walker's Galleries was full of the things that excite a boy's inarticulate wonder and make him run away to sea, and it was said of Yeats that he gave you the painted equivalent of the smell of hot tin lanterns hidden under your coal.

About 1915 Yeats began to paint in oil, at first small, carefully executed landscapes, but he soon loosened his style and abandoned the use of water-colour entirely, painting freely, thickly and concentrating more and more on every day subjects near at home; incidents of Irish race meetings, impressions of the side-car in movement, and of chance encounters in bus, tram, or railway train. In these paintings there was a remarkable combination of psychological interest and visual alertness. Generally they were painted directly from the scene or else from a recent memory, and the memory was predominantly emotional.

As a rule the titles of paintings by Yeats give away nothing beyond the emotional point of departure such as "We Are Leaving You Now", "Stranger in the Circus", "Hearing the Nightingale", and "Man in the Train, Thinking"—the spectator's imagination being trusted to follow the reactions of the artist on canvas. As a member of the Royal Hibernian Academy he contributed regularly to its exhibitions, and one-man shows of his work were held periodically elsewhere in Dublin. He is represented at the Tate Gallery by "Back from the Races", a man and woman in a side-car driving madly down a suburban street, purchased out of the Clarke Fund in 1925; in the Dublin Municipal Gallery by several pictures; and at Cork and Bloemfontein, South Africa. A painting of his, "A Lift on the Long Car", was bought by the Contemporary Art Society.

For a number of yea[illegible] [illegible]eats was a contributor to *Punch* with some rather severe little drawings over the signature W. Bird.

Yeats was a writer as well as a painter, and his books have the same imaginative quality and apparently haphazard expression as his pictures. It was once said of him that as a writer he "remains the gifted amateur, and it is not unreasonable to suppose that his choice has been deliberate". *Sligo,* published in 1930, is a racy record of things remembered, detailed in observation and often recalling Dickens in the zest with which such incidents as "The Market Ordinary" are described. It was followed in 1933 by "Sailing, Sailing Swiftly", a "chronicle-story", with illustrations by the author, and later by two loosely constructed novels, *The Aramanthers,* a fantasy of daily life, published in 1936, and *The Charmed Life,* published in 1938, which consists mainly of whimsical philosophical conversations between two boon companions as they ramble at large.

He wrote also *Ah Well* (1942), *La, La Noo* (1943), *And to You Also* (1944), and *The Careless Flower* (1947). In addition to dramatizing *La, La Noo,* Yeats wrote two plays, *Harlequin's Positions,* produced in Dublin in 1939, and *In Sand,* produced in the same city in 1949.

Yeats was a lean, grey, absent-minded and rather ascetic-looking man with a musical Irish voice and charming manners.

He married Mary Cottenham White. She died in 1947.

March 29, 1957.

Dr. Walter Perceval Yetts, C.B.E., former Professor of Chinese Art and Archaeology at London University, who died on May 14, 1957 at Long Park, Chesham Bois, combined art and medicine, like his Slade school colleague the late Professor Henry Tonks.

The son of A. M. Yetts, he was born at Reading in 1878 and educated at Bradfield College, London University, and Lausanne University. He entered the Royal Navy Medical Service in 1903, and the following year he was awarded the Admiralty Gold Medal for Naval Hygiene. He retired from the service with the rank of staff surgeon in 1912, but he continued to hold medical appointments of one sort or another for a good many years. In 1913 he was acting medical officer at the British Legation, Peking.

During the war of 1914-18 he served in the R.A.M.C. as temporary major and deputy assistant Director of Medical Services, Embarkation. After serving for a year as deputy commissioner of medical services at the Ministry of Pensions he was, from 1920 to 1927, medical officer at the Ministry of Health. In 1930, thanks mainly to the generosity of Sir Percival David, a lectureship in Chinese Art and Archaeology was established at the School of Oriental Studies, University of London. This was believed to be the first lectureship of its scope not only in England but in Europe. There had been lectureships in Oriental art, but none exclusively devoted to Chinese art, and on academic and aesthetic grounds—particularly in view of the importance of English collections—systematic teaching of the subject had long been needed. Yetts was appointed to the lectureship, and two years later he became Professor of Chinese Art and Archaeology. He held the chair until 1946, when he retired with the title of Professor Emeritus.

How far Yetts's interest in Chinese art can be put down to his temporary attachment as medical officer to the British Legation at Peking in 1913 it is impossible to say, but it has been noted as an interesting coincidence that the same post had been occupied for many years by Dr. Stephen Bushell, who is famous among collectors as the pioneer of western studies in Chinese art and archaeology. However and whenever Yetts acquired his knowledge his authority was gratefully acknowledged by museum officials and students who, though well informed on the aesthetic side, did not happen to share his ability to read the Chinese literary language.

His special field was the bronzes and jades of the prehistoric period, and his most important publication was perhaps the monumental catalogue of the Eumorfopoulos Collection, to which he contributed six volumes, dealing mainly with bronzes and sculpture. His other books include *Chinese Bronzes,* published in 1925, and *Ritual Bronzes of Ancient China,* published in 1942; and he contributed articles to the *Burlington Magazine,* the *Journal of the Royal Asiatic Society,* the *Bulletin of the School of Oriental Studies, Folk Lore,* the *Geographical Review of New York* and the *International Studio.*

On the occasion of a small exhibition at the Courtauld Institute of recent archaeological finds in China, Yetts contributed to *The Times* of May 2, 1934, a learned article on Chinese Origins. Dating the site of the finds to perhaps the sixteenth century B.C., he said that they enabled some important corrections to be made, as that brush-writing was practised long before the third century B.C., to which its origin was formerly attributed, and that at the date of the site the Chinese were already expert in the *cire perdue* method of bronze casting.

Made O.B.E. in 1919 and promoted C.B.E. in 1944, he was chairman of the China Society, corresponding member of Vereeniging van Vrienden de Aziatische Kunst, The Hague, and honorary correspondent of the National Library of Peiping, Pekin.

Approaching the subject of Chinese art from the archaeological and ethnographical sides, Yetts was by no means indifferent to aesthetic qualities. His recreation was painting, and he was a member of the Society of Mural Decorators and Painters in Tempera.

May 15, 1957.

Dr. Francis Brett Young, a novelist of considerable distinction and a notably successful one, died in a Cape Town nursing home on March 28, 1954 after a long illness. He was 70.

Worcestershire formed the heart of the region he had made his own as a novelist, a region that took in the coalfields of the Black Country and the green borderlands of the Severn Valley and whose contrasts of scene and character served as a constant imaginative motive in his work. As a regional novelist, indeed, much of his quality resides in the effect of a distant romantic landscape which he carried into his minute and intimate observation of Midland life and manners. Fluent in description, in his most deeply felt passages charged with a nostalgic poetry, possessed of a fertile gift of narrative, which he employed with increasing skill and assurance, he attained a level of performance that just fell short of what might have been hoped for from him. "The successor to Galsworthy" he was called at one time, and, although the designation was not altogether apt, it implied quite justly that Brett Young achieved a certain breadth as novelist rather than depth. The temptations of popularity, it may be, stood in the way of his achieving more.

Francis Brett Young was born in 1884 at Halesowen (the "Halesby" of the novels), not far from the "North Bromwich" which was Birmingham. His father was in medical practice there (his mother also came from a Midland medical family), and Brett Young, in turn, after leaving Epsom College, proceeded to take a medical degree at Birmingham University. He began to practise in Brixham in 1907 and remained there, except for an interval spent as ship's surgeon on a voyage to Japan, until the outbreak of war in 1914.

In the following year he joined the R.A.M.C., served in the campaign in German East Africa, was invalided out of the Army, with the rank of major, in 1918, went to live in Capri, spent a holiday in South Africa, returned to Capri, and came back to England in 1929. By then Francis Brett Young was a novelist of established reputation.

His medical training and experience are clearly to be discerned in his novelist's habit of mind; Brett Young himself was always inclined to labour, possibly to excess, the discipline he owed as an observer of men and manners to his medical studies and practice. More directly, however, he continually drew upon his years of work as a general practitioner for the substance of his fiction. The fact is that his novels almost always derive in setting or circumstance from a chapter of autobiography. Medicine, Birmingham, Radnor Forest, East Africa, South Africa, most of all the familiar landscape of childhood revealed from the top of "Uffdown"—these are phases of personal experience which he directs to carefully contrived imaginative ends. No novelist, it may be argued, can work otherwise. But with Brett Young the stimulus of the immediately personal always seemed to make his imaginative ends a little less fine, more obvious and mechanical, than they promised to be.

He was, nevertheless, a remarkably accomplished story teller, whose leisurely flow of incident and observation was joined to lively romanticism of temper, and, at his best, a genuine power of lyrical evocation. His first novel, *Undergrowth* (1913), written in collaboration with a younger brother, captured the pagan quality, and with it a suggestion of supernatural horror, of a remote Welsh valley, which had been invaded by a stranger from the city; the novel showed unmistakable promise. Then, in the following year, he produced *Deep Sea,* which had Brixham for its setting and which was attractively experimental in manner; and, later, *The Dark Tower,* in which the sombre romanticism of the Welsh scene was joined to an almost Jamesian subtlety of narrative method. This was his first novel of consequence. Two years later came *The Iron Age,* the story of an infatuation for a worthless woman unfolded against a vigorously drawn industrial background.

Brett Young's war experience drew from him, besides a number of poems—he had written verse before starting out as a novelist, some of it good verse, and was always a close student of poetry—an admirably vivid impression of the East African campaign "Marching on Tanga", and a well written "shocker", *The Crescent Moon.*

With the return of peace appeared the semi-autobiographical novel, engaging in sentiment but, in the manner of its kind, somewhat formless, which he had apparently begun several years before, *The Young Physician;* and after that a series of novels exhibiting a fairly steady advance in narrative ease and craftsmanship—*The Tragic Bride* (1920), *The Black Diamond* (1921), *The Red Knight* (1921), *Pilgrim's Rest* (1922), *Woodsmoke* (1924), *Cold Harbour* (1924), *Sea Horses* (1925). Then, in 1927, he published the long, leisurely, sympathetically rendered *Portrait of Clare,* the study of an unremarkable product of Worcestershire middle-class society. It was awarded the James Tait Black memorial prize and signalized the beginning of the author's career of indubitable success.

Most of the novels which followed during the next 10 years or so were in much the same vein—copious, smooth and pleasant in texture, very English in feeling, touched here and there by a practised and often charming lyrical warmth. They include *My Brother Jonathan* (1928), *Jim Redlake* (1930), *Mr. and Mrs. Pennington* (1931), *The House Under the Water* (1932), *This Little World* (1934), and *Far Forest* (1936), all of them accomplished enough, though several were a good deal bulkier than they need or should have been. In 1937 came a soundly imagined South African novel, *They Seek a Country,* with an English hero transported for poaching, and sharing in the ardours of the great trek; and, two years later, *The City of Gold,* a graphic but too prolonged study of South African events from the founding of Kimberley to the Jameson Raid. *Mr. Lucton's Freedom* (1940) was rather innocent light entertainment, and *A Man About the House* (1942), his twenty-seventh novel, a very deft and spirited piece of story-telling, was in 1946 adapted to the stage. His last work, *In South Africa,* a descriptive piece designed for prospective visitors and settlers, appeared in 1952.

Brett Young was a person of cultivated mind and taste. He had a love of pictures and music and at one time set to music a number of poems by Robert Bridges. Besides his novels and occasional poetry he wrote short stories, a children's book, and two plays, one of them, *The Furnace,* in collaboration with William Armstrong [q.v.]. Mention must be made of his long and picturesque poem "The Island", which appeared in 1944, a "cavalcade" of English history rendered in lyric, ballad, elegy, narrative, and dialogue—a story-teller's poem rather than a poet's poem, though poetry was there. It bore the stamp of all that was English in Francis Brett Young's mind and imagination.

He married in 1908 Miss Jessie Hankinson, who survives him.

March 29, 1954.

Geoffrey Winthrop Young, D.LITT., who died at a nursing home in London on September 6, 1958 at the age of 81, was one of the greatest—if not the greatest—of the English mountaineers of this century, and the author of a book, *On High Hills,* which has become as undoubted a classic of mountaineering literature as Whymper's *Scrambles among the Alps.*

Having lost a leg in the Great War, he caused something of a sensation by re-ascending the Matterhorn in 1928. Young was also, within limits that he deliberately set himself, a gifted poet—one rather of the senses than of the mind—who sang the praises of the meadows and mountains he loved with sincerity and a genuine sense of the music of words. By profession a schoolmaster and educationist, with strong ideas on the value of a free and natural upbringing for children, he was Thomas Wall Reader in Comparative Education at London University from 1932 to 1941.

Geoffrey Winthrop Young was born on October 25, 1876, the second son of Sir George Young, third baronet, of Formosa, and Dame Alice Eacy Young, and a great-nephew of the poet Praed, from whom it is possible that he inherited some of his facility in verse. Educated at Marlborough and Trinity College, Cambridge, he soon showed his talent for poetry by winning the Chancellor's Verse Medal in 1898 and 1899, and his love of climbing by publishing the less conventional (and anonymous) "Roof-climber's Guide to Trinity"—a thorough survey of its subject, with elaborate diagrams and useful warnings as to those sections on which the proximity of senior members of the College made it advisable to be as quiet as possible. By the time he had completed his education at Jena University and Geneva, Young had become an accomplished linguist.

From 1900 to 1905 he was an assistant master at Eton, and from then until 1913 acted as a government inspector of secondary schools, but it can fairly be said that his main interest in those years centred on a few weeks each summer which he spent among the Swiss Alps. After a rigorous training in the Lake District he found little difficulty, during his first season at Belalp under the supervision of the veteran Clemenz Ruppen, in climbing such giants as the Aletschorn and Jungfrau; and he soon discovered that he was one of those in whom, above a height of 8,000ft., "the tide of life flowed with a vivacity never imagined in the plains". Of course by the time Young appeared on the scene few of the Alpine peaks remained to be climbed for the first time—but among those that still resisted, and in the invention of new methods of grappling with old antagonists, no individual climber could boast of a longer list of successes. One memorable first ascent may be recorded—that of the pinnacle "l'Isolée" of the Dames Anglaises—and other pioneer achievements were the climbing of the west ridge of the Gespaltenhorn, the south face of the Taschorn, and the Mer de Glace face of the Grepon. His leading guide on most of his later climbs was Josef Knubel, of St. Niklaus. In 1911, with Professor H. O. Jones, he ascended the Brouillard ridge of Mont Blanc and made the first complete traverse of the west ridge of the Grandes Jorasses, and the first descent of the ridge to the Col des Hirondelles.

The Great War temporarily put an end to Young's mountaineering. From October 1914 to July 1915 he was in command of the Friends' Ambulance Unit at the Front, and acted as liaison officer to the civil population in the Ypres sector for the Eighth French and Second British armies. He was awarded the Order of Leopold for "exceptional courage and resource". From 1915 to 1919 he commanded the First British Ambulance for Italy, and at the battle of Monte San Gabriele received the wounds which caused the loss of his leg.

It seemed unlikely that Young would ever go climbing again, and after the war he settled down to give young climbers the benefit of his experience, and to recapture on paper some of his adventures. The first object he fulfilled in *Mountain Craft* (1920), perhaps the most scientific treatise on climbing as it affects the minds and bodies of men. This was primarily a technical work. *On High Hills,* published in 1927, gave us the poetry and psychology of mountaineering, illustrated by a series of stories of great climbs. A reviewer in *The Times Literary Supplement* compared Young with Borrow, Hudson, or Doughty, as the possessor of that "wholly individual temperament and outlook which have so often added something memorable to English letters"—and this fascinating book would be well worth reading if only for the happy imagery which made the author speak of a climber as "crimsoning in a roast of sun heat" or "withered and brittled" by a "gurly blizzard".

Those who had settled down to mourn him as lost to active mountaineering, however, reckoned without the courage and pertinacity which Young possessed in such an exceptional degree. For several years after the war he experimented with his artificial leg on British hills, and by 1927, at the age of 51, felt sufficiently confident to return to the Alps; in the same year he climbed Monte Rosa, and in 1928 the Wellenkuppe and the Matterhorn. His own description of the latter feat was published in *The Times* of August 2, 1928. In the years that followed he reascended many of the other big peaks, the last of his exploits as a one-legged climber being the ascent, with his old guide Knubel, of the Zinal Rothorn in 1935. An account of these one-legged climbs and an analysis of the loss of balance and speed he suffered were given in *Mountains with a Difference,* which was awarded the W. H Heinemann prize in 1952.

Young's collected poems—the product of the three volumes *Wind and Hill, Freedom,* and *April and Rain*—appeared in 1936, and were well received. From 1925 until he took up his appointment at London University he had been consultant for Europe, in the humanities, to the Rockefeller Foundation.

September 8, 1958.

George Malcolm Young, C.B., who died in a nursing home near Oxford on November 18, 1959, was 77. He was born in 1882, the only son of G. F. Young, of Greenhithe.

From St. Paul's he went to Balliol as a scholar in 1900, and took a First in Classical Mods., a second in Greats and, in 1905, an All Souls fellowship. In 1908 he joined the Board of Education, in what, under the reorganization then in train at the hands of Sir Robert Morant, was to become the Universities Department. In his later life he always spoke of the stormy figure of his first official chief with a respect that amounted to reverence.

When the board's Standing Advisory Committee for University Grants—the predecessor of the University Grants Committee—was set up in 1911, Young became its first secretary. In 1917 he was appointed C.B., and was made joint secretary to the short-lived and now almost forgotten Ministry of Reconstruction. He also served in Vienna at the end of the first war, and spent some time in North Russia.

In the 1920s Young left the Civil Service to devote himself to literature. His first book, his *Gibbon,* came out in 1932, when he was in his fiftieth year. He had already, in an essay on "Victorian History" published in 1931, shown his mastery in this field, and the Oxford University Press asked him to edit two volumes of essays on *Early Victorian England.* This work came out in 1934, and at once established its authority. In the following year Young published his *Charles I and Cromwell,* a slight essay, and in 1936 there came *Victorian England: the Portrait of an Age,* an expansion of the editorial essay he had written for *Early Victorian England.* The "Portrait" was at once recognized as an outstanding piece of interpretation, and it is not too much to say that in the more than 20 years since it appeared its reputation and influence have grown steadily.

Young was now writing regularly in weekly newspapers and reviews; for a brief while after the resignation of J. L. Garvin he wrote leading articles for the *Observer,* and, in later years, he reviewed for the *Sunday Times.* He republished his essays and addresses in *Daylight and Champaign* (1937), *To-day and Yesterday* (1948), and *Last Essays* (1950).

Meanwhile he had undertaken the official biography of Earl Baldwin, and this appeared in 1952. Young was never altogether happy in the task; the materials available for his use had proved unexpectedly scanty; and his frank criticisms of Baldwin in some respects, though they were balanced by a fine recognition of his qualities, and of his great services to the country, were not everywhere accepted.

In 1947 he undertook the editorship of the Victorian volume in the series of *English Historical Documents.*

In 1937 Young was appointed a trustee of the National Portrait Gallery, in 1938 a member of the Standing Committee on Museums and Galleries, in 1947 a trustee of the British Museum, and in 1948 a member of the Historical Manuscripts Commission. The work these appointments entailed lay very close to his heart, and, until his health began to fail, he gave it a great deal of time and thought.

In his middle years Young settled in Wiltshire, and made himself an authority on the archaeology and history of his adopted county. He also interested himself in educational movements in Swindon. His re-election to an All Souls fellowship in 1947 gave him a centre at Oxford again, and he spent more and more time there, settling in his college when he gave up his Wiltshire home. Young was very much an All Souls man; the mingling of established scholars with a succession of young fellows and constant visitors from the outside world provided a society congenial both to his tastes and to his views.

The range of Young's intellectual interests reflected not only the personal discomfort he felt if he were not on terms of understanding with what he met in the world, but also his strong conviction that the maintenance of older catholic conceptions of scholarship, with what changes a changing world imposed, was important both to scholarship and to society. The break in his career was in a sense a superficial one; care for the university of knowledge, and preoccupation with the horizon of change, had been his official concerns, and they remained the dominant theme of much of his writing. The Civil servant had by no means been useless to the future historian and essayist. Young thought of scholarship, perhaps—though rather by habit than principle—as a tool for deepening and refining the common interests of the world.

He wrote always for the public, rather than for an academic audience, though for a public that he assumed to be both busy and equipped to understand. His essays had the informality, and the unexpectedness, of the best talk; his books were, in spirit, longer essays. But if, as a consequence, the shelf of his works is a short one, few writers have said so many good things on so many subjects.

As literature was, to Young, a discipline of the mind and imagination, so history was always a branch of literature. He recognized all that professional techniques had done to deepen it, but he openly feared lest, in universities, it should become too much of a profession—"historians left with no higher aim than to teach the teachers of history how to teach their successors". In an early essay, he applied—with a pardonable slight misquotation—Pope's line to historical research—"Light dies before that uncreating word". His own well-known recommendation to students of history was "to go on reading until you can hear people talking".

Personally, Young was a man of great distinction, a fascinating conversationist, drawing on the resources of an almost phenomenal memory (he would relate with unaffected vanity that he had once been dubbed a "pantomath"), generous in his acceptance of ideas and points of view not his own, and in his appreciation of people—taking as real an interest in the talk of Wiltshire countrymen and railway workers as in that of scholars and statesman.

He was an Hon. D.Litt. of Durham and of Cambridge, and an Honorary Fellow of Balliol.

November 19, 1959.

Sir Robert Arthur Young, C.B.E., M.D., F.R.C.P., F.S.A., the distinguished London physician, specialist in diseases of the chest, and medical teacher, died on August 22, 1959 in London at the age of 87.

Born on November 6, 1871, in Norfolk, the son of William Young, he was educated at the United Westminster Schools and King's College, London, and received his medical training at Middlesex Hospital, where he qualified M.B. in 1894 with first class honours in medicine, becoming M.D. (worthy of gold medal) in 1895.

In 1905 he was elected a Fellow of the Royal College of Physicians, of which he was at various times examiner, representative on the committee of the board of management of the Conjoint Board, councillor, censor, Lumleian lecturer (1929), when his subject was "A Medical Review of the Surgery of the Chest", and Harveian orator (1939). He was physician to the Middlesex Hospital, at which he was also lecturer on *materia medica* and warden of the college and hospital, to the Hospital for Consumption and Diseases of the Chest, Brompton, St. Luke's Hostel, the City of London Lying-in Hospital, the King Edward VII Sanatorium, and the Acton General Hospital.

In 1929-31 he was president of the section of medicine of the Royal Society of Medicine and in 1930 president of the Medical Society of London, of which he had been Lettsomian lecturer in 1924, when his subject was the treatment of pulmonary tuberculosis. He was vice-chairman of the council of the Chest and Heart Society, formerly the N.A.P.T. He was awarded the gold medal of the Royal Society of Medicine, which is given every third year to whoever is deemed to have done most to advance the science or art of medicine or its allied sciences.

This list of distinctions and appointments indicates the interests which Young particularly had at heart. He continued a long tradition which had associated the staffs of the Middlesex Hospital and the Brompton Hospital, and having received his training in the days before radiology, he retained a remarkable gift for diagnosis which was a constant source of amazement to his more junior colleagues. He was an exceptionally gifted teacher, and when he went back to teaching during the last war, having previously retired, he made a deep impression on the medical students of that time who had not experienced anything quite like it before.

"R. A.", as he was widely known, was the acknowledged leader of those specializing in the study of diseases of the chest. He endeared himself to younger colleagues by his unflagging interest in all their doings and his delight in their successes: they regarded him as a kind of godfather. He was a great diner out and in his later years often presided over dining clubs such as the St. Albans and the Sydenham, also on occasions at the Savage. He accelerated the progress of his branch of medicine by personal contact with many of the younger men who were doing original work, and then introducing them to one another, so that isolated individuals were drawn into a community of friends.

The Lumleian lectures of 1929 were perhaps his most fruitful contribution to progress. He laid down for the first time a clear indication from the point of view of a physician of what seemed to be the required aims and principles of chest surgery. This gave a strong impetus to young surgeons such as Tudor Edwards, J. E. H. Roberts, and [Sir] Clement Price Thomas*, who developed techniques which have been adopted by surgeons throughout the world.

R. A. was an inveterate collector, and loved to search the curiosity shops in the Fulham Road. His home was packed with Roman babies' feeding bottles, Chinese fans, glass walking-sticks, watercolour sketches, and drawers full of menu-cards signed with the names of fellow diners. His manner was courtly in a natural, unstudied fashion, and he insisted that in all dealings with patients they should be approached with gentleness and consideration.

He married Fanny Caroline Phoebe, daughter of R. M. Kennedy, I.C.S., and had one son. His wife died in 1944.

August 24, 1959.

Gladys Yule died at her home, Hanstead House, Bricket Wood, Hertfordshire, on August 24, 1957 at the age of 54.

Within a fortnight the light horse world and especially the Arabian horse breeding fraternity has suffered two heavy blows—first the death of Lady Wentworth [q.v.] in August and now Miss Yule's. They were controllers of the two biggest Arabian studs in Britain, if not in the world; Miss Yule controlled a big thoroughbred stud and famous prizewinning herds of Jersey and Aberdeen Angus cattle.

The only daughter of Sir David Yule, the East India merchant, who died in 1928, and of Lady Yule who died in 1950, Gladys Meryl Yule was born at Hanstead House, which her father bought soon after his marriage in 1900 as a permanent home for his wife, who found she could not live in the climate of Calcutta where Sir David had his business, Yule, Catto and Company.

A lifelong lover of animals, especially horses, she carried on the racing and breeding activities started by her mother, though the racing side was somewhat curtailed after Lady Yule presented Balaton Lodge, the Newmarket stables, to the Animal Health Trust for their equine research station.

However, Gladys Yule had in her stud at Bricket Wood about 140 animals, thoroughbreds, Arabians, and Anglo-Arabs; the thoroughbred stallion, Flocon, was the sire of Floss Silk, out of Life Sentence, a three-year-old filly who won five races in the 1957 season, the last one being the Hever Stakes at Lingfield the day before she died; and it gave her intense pleasure to see it win from her sickbed on a television screen.

Her main interest, however, lay in the Arabian horse. Her outstanding sire was Count Dorsaz, which won the Winston Churchill Cup for the supreme riding horse of the International Show in 1950, 1951, and 1954, and sired Count Orlando who won it in 1956 and 1957. Other well-known stallions were Blue Dominoe, General Grant, Rifaria Iridos, Grey Owl, and, recently, Orlando. She was particularly interested in the Anglo-Arab breed and she had two Anglo-Arab stallions in her stables, Connetable, imported from France, and Colonel Gainsborough.

She was a good practical rider in her youth, winning the Balmano Cup for hacks at Olympia before the war on Shecanhopit, and taking part in various riding displays at Olympia. She had, however, little use for *dressage* as such in spite of the fact that she made Bricket Wood always available to the British Horse Society for their *dressage* championships in connexion with the International Horse Show, and had two Anglo-Arabs, Casterello and M. Beaucaire, trained for *dressage* competitions. The former won the medium test at Bricket Wood in 1955 and 1957, the latter won it in 1956.

She was, of course, a member of the Arab Horse Society, its president in 1949, and on the committee of the Royal International Horse Show. In 1954 she associated herself with the Ponies of Britain Club, whose 1957 summer show was completed on the day of her death, and became its chairman, inspiration, and benefactor. In 1957 she was most deservedly awarded the British Horse Society's Medal of Honour and received it from the hands of the Duke of Edinburgh on the Tuesday evening performance of the Royal International Horse Show.

She was the most modest and unassuming of persons; her shyness and, latterly, ill-health made her seem a somewhat remote personality, but, while being a difficult person to impose upon, her kindness and generosity had no limits, but were never paraded, so that only those who have experienced it can realize its full extent.

August 26, 1957.

Abdullah ibn Yusuf Ali, C.B.E., who died in London in December 1953 at the age of 81, held a record of intellectual activity by speech and pen in varied fields scarcely equalled by any other Indian member of the I.C.S.

He was born in western India on April 4, 1872, and from Wilson College, Bombay, entered St. John's College, Cambridge. In the Indian Civil Service examination of 1894 he took the highest marks in English composition, and two years later was called to the Bar by Lincoln's Inn. In the United Provinces he served in various districts, interspersed with two short periods as acting Under-Secretary and then Deputy Secretary in the Finance Department of the Government of India. When on leave in 1905 he gave a series of six lectures at the Passmore Edwards Institute in London, and they provided the nucleus for his first considerable book, *Life and Labour in India.* The humdrum routine of district magistracy in the Sultanpur and Fatehpur collectorates was not very congenial to a man of his intellectual zest, and he welcomed the interlude provided by the task of preparing an official monograph on silk fabrics. On grounds partly of health and partly of family anxieties, he was allowed to retire from the I.C.S. in 1914 on proportionate pension.

Settling in Britain, Yusuf Ali did much useful work for the 1914-18 war effort in platform appeals for recruitment, in written propaganda in English and Urdu, as a private in the West Kent Fencibles, and as president of the Indian Students' Prisoners of War Fund. Edwin Montagu, then Secretary of State for

India, obtained his assistance for the Indian delegation at the Peace Conference. In the early years of the School of Oriental and African Studies he was Lecturer in Hindustani, Hindi, and Indian Religions, Manners and Customs.

Soon after the signature of the Treaty of Versailles, Yusuf Ali entered the service of the Nizam of Hyderabad as counsel in the *Sarf-i-Khas,* and in 1921 he was appointed Revenue Member of the Executive Council of the State. Toward the close of the next year he moved to Lucknow and took up legal practice. For three years from 1925 he was principal of the Islamia College, Lahore. In 1928 he was one of India's representatives at the ninth Assembly of the League of Nations. Next followed a round-the-world lecturing tour through the United States to Japan, China, the Philippines, Malaya, Ceylon, and India again. In 1932 he travelled through Canada from coast to coast as guest of the National Council of Education. Thence he went to India, where he presided at the All-India Muslim Educational Conference and the Sind Azad Conference. After serving as a member of the Punjab University Inquiry Committee he returned in 1935 to the principalship of the Islamia College, Lahore, and held it for a further two years.

Much of his time in Lahore was occupied by an elaborate recension in English of the Koran, with notes and commentary. He brought to this prolonged and formidable task the qualifications of an intimate knowledge of Arabic, great facility in the English tongue, and a close lifetime study of the principles and history of Islam. A second and revised edition was published in Lahore in 1940. While a great deal of the literary output of Yusuf Ali related to the history and current problems of India, his chief love was the Islamic field. He wrote that the high sounding music of the Koranic verses had haunted him like a passion from his childhood. He broke fresh ground in such studies as *Mestrovic and Serbian Sculpture* (1916) and *Social and Economic Conditions in Medieval India* (1932). Indeed no subject seemed foreign to his pen or his oratory.

He was an active supporter of the World Congress of Faiths and spoke frequently at its meetings. In advancing age he seemed to have a sense of frustration to find that so much of what he had done was vanity and vexation of spirit. In his best days he was a man of inborn courtesy and charming manners, and had warm friends in many lands.

Unhappily Yusuf Ali's last years were clouded by mental aberration. He entirely neglected his family duties and avoided financial responsibility for his nominal home. In addition to his proportionate I.C.S. pension he had private means; but he sank down to a level of apparent poverty and lack of cleanliness which brought concern to his old friends. He wandered about at the end, an unquiet spirit with no fixed abode.

He was twice married and leaves a widow of British birth together with a son of their marriage, who served in the 1939-45 War.

December 15, 1953.

Z

Mildred ("Babe") Zaharias, all-round sportswoman and breaker of many records, died peacefully in her sleep at Galveston, Texas, on September 27, 1956 at the age of 42 after a series of operations for cancer.

She was born in Texas in June 1914, the daughter of a Norwegian carpenter named Didrikson. At 15 she took time off from her work as an insurance clerk to compete in national championships at Dallas and set two records, one in the javelin throw and one in the basketball throw. She soon added successes in the long jump, pole vaulting, shot-putting, tennis, basketball, and swimming—she was a good enough swimmer to consider attempting the Channel, though she did not do so. At boxing she several times won by knockouts. She was also a capable footballer, wrestler, rifle shot, fencer, and polo player. In the 1932 Olympic Games she established Olympic and world records for the 80 metres hurdles and throwing the javelin.

In 1935 she became a golf professional and competed with success in open events. She was readmitted into the amateur ranks in 1944 and then began her greatest golfing triumphs. She won the American women's title in 1946 and a year later became the first American to win the British title. All possible amateur honours came her way and she returned in 1947 to professional golf. She became the first woman to be appointed as head professional at a leading golf club and was soon winning big money. In 1951 she won more than £5,000—an all-time record for a woman—but was taken ill the following year and had an operation for hernia.

Her husband, George Zaharias—they had married in 1938—said she was "a pretty sick girl who has been declining for some time". Not long afterwards, cancer was diagnosed and she underwent an operation in 1953. This followed her triumph in a tournament, named after her, at Beaumont, Texas. Her wonderful constitution brought her back to win more honours in 1954, including the American Women's Open for the third time. Then an operation for the removal of a spinal disc kept her out of the game in 1955. Another visit to hospital and two operations suggested that her three-year fight against cancer was being lost. In August 1956 she was again in hospital under medical supervision after two operations within three weeks.

September 28, 1956.

The Sultan of Zanzibar died in Zanzibar on October 9, 1960. He was 81.

His Highness Seyyid Khalifa-bin-Harub-bin-Thuwaini-bin-Said was born in 1879 and acceded to the throne of Zanzibar on December 9, 1911, after the abdication of Sultan Ali; he thus became the seventh descendant of the famous Seyyid Said bin Sultan of Muscat. His long reign lasted almost 49 years.

The late Sultan—affectionately known as "Bwana Said"—was beloved by his subjects and proved to be a constitutional monarch of great wisdom and breadth of mind. So he was able to move with the stormy times which included the two world wars. He was a living example of the Arab saying "With Age comes Wisdom", and his advice was at all times most valuable.

Though small in stature he had great presence and dignity. His courtesy and hospitality were, as with most Arabs of his class, renowned, and at all times he was accessible to all. He had a delightful sense of humour, which captivated all who met him, whether young or old.

Like his famous ancestor Seyyid Said of Muscat, he was a great sailor and held the Royal Navy in the highest esteem, being a friend of many of their officers, among whom were such famous names as Sir Dunbar-Nasmyth*, V.C., and Lord Fraser of North Cape.

Many constitutional changes took place during the Sultan's reign, which saw also many social and economic developments, including the building of several schools, a new road and harbour and extensive swamp reclamation work. After the last war a 10-year development programme was launched with the aid of British colonial development and welfare funds.

The Sultan's loyalty to Britain was first put to the test in 1914 and was not found wanting. In spite of the threat from German East Africa, he placed his services at the disposal of Britain and called on all Muslims in Central and East Africa to remain steadfast to the British cause. Zanzibar's aid to Britain included contributions of money and the raising of a carrier corps.

During the Second World War he and his people remained staunchly loyal to Britain. The Sultan was a keen sportsman and was renowned for his skill as a horseman. It was he who introduced polo to Zanzibar.

He attended three coronations including that of the Queen, when he was given a warm ovation from the London crowds. He was an honorary G.C.B., G.C.M.G., and G.B.E. The first of these was conferred on him at the time of Princess Margaret's visit to Zanzibar in 1956.

With his death there passes one of the last members of the old Arab aristocracy so beloved of many Englishmen.

He married a daughter of the former Sultan in 1900 and after her death in 1940 married the present Sultana, who accompanied him on his recent holiday in Britain. He is succeeded by his eldest son, Prince Seyyid Abdulla.

October 10, 1960.

Antonin Zapotocky, President of Czechoslovakia since 1953, died on November 13, 1957 in a Prague clinic. He was 72.

In the eventful days of February 1948 Zapotocky became Prime Minister of Czechoslovakia and one of the most important communist leaders in Czechoslovakia. He was President Gottwald's [q.v.] right-hand man and succeeded him as President when the latter died in March 1953. During the formative years of the Czech Communist Party he was associated with Gottwald as a mainstay of the official party line against the "deviationist" elements. For nearly a quarter of a century he had been connected with the Czechoslovak trade union movement, which he undoubtedly helped to build and strengthen, but his influence as leader of that movement was, with equal certainty, used to further the communist drive for power after the 1939-45 War. It was not as a great Marxist theorist that he fitted into the hierarchy of Eastern Europe, but rather as a man of action and of practical ability.

Antonin Zapotocky was born on December 19, 1884, at Zakolany, in the Kladno coal-mining district. His father, a tailor's assistant, was active in the socialist movement and Antonin Zapotocky therefore became acquainted with politics at a very early age. He attended school until he was 14, when he was apprenticed to a stone-mason, and in 1908 he moved to Prague to practise his trade. His youth was spent in active political work, but he also performed in a dramatic society and published a volume of his own poems.

Later he turned to novel writing, and two of his novels, *New Heroes Will Arise* and *Red Glow Over Kladno*, are much admired in Czechoslovakia. He was imprisoned as early as 1905 for taking part in a demonstration for general franchise, under the Austro-Hungarian Empire. On release he became secretary of the Social Democratic Party in Kladno. From then on until the 1914-18 War he was mixed up in numerous strikes and disturbances until he was conscribed to serve in Italy, Serbia and Romania. On his release he returned to Kladno and the Social Democratic Party.

For his part in the wave of industrial strikes in Czechoslovakia in the summer of 1920 Zapotocky was imprisoned for two and a half years. The schism in the Social Democratic Party resulted in the founding of the Czech Communist Party in 1921 by Smeral, Gottwald, and others, and on his release from prison Zapotocky joined the Communist Party to become one of its leading members and secretary of the Prague branch.

In 1925 he was elected to the Czechoslovak Parliament in which he retained his seat until the time of Munich. During this period he was very active among the trade unions in winning support for the communist case. Unlike Gottwald and others, Zapotocky failed to escape to Russia when the Germans invaded Czechoslovakia in March 1939, and was captured by the Gestapo, and after a period of imprisonment in Prague he was sent to Oranienburg concentration camp in 1940.

In April 1945 Zapotocky was released by a Red Army column and immediately returned to Prague as chairman of the Czechoslovak "Revolutionary Trade Union", which became in his hands an instrument of political pressure and figured largely in the events of February 1948. In 1946 he became a member of the National Assembly and two years later, after a series of political manoeuvres resulting in the crisis of February 1948, when Gottwald was "elected" to the Presidency to succeed Dr. Benes, Zapotocky became Prime Minister and was entrusted by Gottwald to form a new Cabinet.

Two problems faced him then and have ever since dogged him. The first was to tackle the lack of discipline within the Communist Party itself; and the second was to increase the industrial production of the country sufficiently to meet the demands Russia had constantly made on her satellites. It cannot be said that either as Prime Minister or as President he made any notable headway towards the solution of either of these problems, though during most of the time he was in a position of power in his country there was much talk of bringing the economy of Czechoslovakia within a coordinated plan.

November 14, 1957.

Georgi Zarubin, a Soviet deputy Foreign Minister, died after a serious illness in November 1958.

Zarubin, who was Soviet Ambassador in London from 1947 to 1952 and in Washington from 1952 until early in 1958, was one of a number of young Soviet diplomats who came to the attention of the western world during and after the 1939-45 War.

Georgi Nicholayevich Zarubin was born in 1900. In his youth, before the Russian Revolution, he worked as a messenger and in 1918 he joined the ranks of the Red Army, in which he served until 1924. He then began a course of study at the Moscow Textile Institute, and having successfully completed this he entered the Stalin Industrial Academy, with a view to more advanced training. Zarubin displayed energy and keenness, and in 1931 he was appointed head of the Molotov Industrial Academy—a post which he held until 1935. In this year he received a further promotion and was appointed head of the Directorate of Educational Institutions of the Peoples' Commissariat of Light Industry of the U.S.S.R., where he remained until 1938.

Zarubin's background determined his appointment in that year as assistant Commissar-General of the Soviet section of the New York World's Fair in 1938-40. He was also president of the Arts Council of the Soviet section of the fair. It was but a short step from such an appointment to the diplomatic service, and on the conclusion of the fair in 1940 he was appointed head of the Consular Bureau of the Soviet Ministry of Foreign Affairs, where he soon proved his aptitude for this work.

In 1941 he was appointed head of the Latin-American section of the Soviet Foreign Ministry, a position which he held until his appointment early in 1944 as Ambassador to Canada, where he succeeded Gusev, who had been moved to London. Zarubin held the position of Ambassador to Canada until September 1946, and although his career in Ottawa was clouded by the Canadian spy trials it was nevertheless acknowledged that he had played no part in this affair.

In September 1946 he received a further promotion and was appointed Soviet Ambassador to London, to replace Gusev, who had been recalled to Moscow. He remained in London until May 1952, when he was recalled to Moscow and subsequently appointed Soviet Ambassador in Washington to replace Panyushkin, who had been moved to Peking.

Perhaps the most fruitful act during his five and a half years in the United States was to sign a reciprocal agreement at the State Department in January 1958 providing for a wide range of cultural exchanges between the United States and Russia. An unusually strong contingent of senior State Department officers attended the Embassy reception at which Zarubin took leave of his colleagues, a mark of the personal esteem in which he was held. In February it was announced that he had been appointed a deputy Foreign Minister.

Earlier in his career, as a member of the Soviet delegation, Zarubin participated in the yearly meetings of the General Assembly of the United Nations, and also in the meetings for the drawing up of the Austrian treaty. He had been decorated by the Soviet state with the Order of the Red Banner, and the Order of the Patriotic War.

November 26, 1958.

Sir Alfred Zimmern, the authority on international law and affairs, died on November 24, 1957 at his home at Avon, Connecticut. He was 78.

He was born at Surbiton on January 26, 1879. His father, Adolf Zimmern, was of Jewish parentage, a member of one of those German-Jewish families of liberal outlook who, despairing of the prospects in their own countries after the political failures of 1848, emigrated to England and North America where they contributed appreciably to the then active political, cultural, industrial, and commercial developments. In Britain the newcomers in many cases settled in the north of England and Zimmern's ancestors made their home in Manchester. His mother was of Huguenot ancestry. Thus on both sides Zimmern was descended from immigrants who had to leave their former homes for conscience sake—political or religious. With such an ancestry Zimmern's wide international interests were not surprising, nor were the liberal tendencies by which he was inspired.

Zimmern was educated at Winchester and New College, Oxford. On graduation he remained at that college for a year as Lecturer in Ancient History, and from 1904 to 1909 as Fellow and Tutor. During a part of this period, in 1907 and 1908, he was also University secretary of the Joint Committee on Oxford and Working Class Education.

Zimmern left Oxford in 1909 in order to have more time for writing, and in 1911 published his first extended study, *The Greek Commonwealth*. In the following year he entered the Board of Education as staff inspector, and for three years devoted his thought, his knowledge, and his energies to influencing the public education policy of the country. In this first period of his career he wrote also a short book on Henry Grattan

(1902) and translated Ferrero's *Greatness and Decline of Rome* (1907).

The outbreak of war in 1914 in his case, as in those of many others, changed the whole course of his career. The first effect was the appearance of *The War and Democracy* (1914), which he edited. Later he entered the Foreign Office in the newly created Political Intelligence Department, in the meanwhile keeping in touch unofficially with the trend of events in the international field and influencing them, as one of the circle of political thinkers in which he moved, in the direction of the liberation of the subject peoples of Europe. Liberal by heredity, in touch with liberal movements on the Continent, Zimmern was fully qualified for his new role. First his independent position, later his appointment in the Foreign Office, enabled him to take advantage of many opportunities to attain the ends that he always kept in sight. And the establishment of the Institute (later Royal) of International Affairs (more familiarly known as Chatham House), of which he was one of the founders in 1920, gave him all the opportunities he needed. At the close of the 1914-18 War Zimmern was appointed to the newly created Wilson Professorship of International Politics in the University College of Wales, Aberystwyth. This office he held for only two years, resigning in 1921. In the following year he became Acting Professor of Political Science in Cornell University.

Practical participation in the development of international affairs had, however, a greater call for him than lecturing on the subject, and Zimmern was soon back in Europe. The League of Nations had not yet suffered seriously in reputation and it was as Deputy Director of its Institute of Intellectual Cooperation in Paris that he joined its forces. He held this office for four years, from 1926 to 1930. He resigned to take up the Montague Burton Professorship of International Relations in the University of Oxford. Throughout this period and for years later Zimmern was in close touch with Chatham House, of which he was recognized as one of the leading guides and inspirers. With the establishment of the Research Department at the Foreign Office, after the outbreak of war in 1939, Zimmern returned to that ministry and, after a reorganization in 1943, became Deputy Director under his long-standing colleague, Professor Arnold Toynbee*.

Zimmern retired from his chair at Oxford in 1944 and shortly after the creation of the United Nations was appointed Secretary-General of the Constituent Conference of Unesco and later First Executive Secretary, afterwards adviser, to its Preparatory Commission. In the national field he held at the same time the related office of Adviser in Information and External Relations to the Ministry of Education in London. Throughout this period he remained closely connected, in spite of his successive offices, with the work of Chatham House, at whose meetings he was always a very welcome speaker. His work as Director of the Geneva School of International Studies from 1925 to 1939 was related to this activity. In 1947, however, this phase of his career was ended. In that year he became Visiting Professor of Trinity College, Hartford, Connecticut, and in the following year, Director of the Hartford Study Centre for World Affairs.

The appearance of *The Greek Commonwealth* in 1911 was the end of the first period of literary activity, but only of the first period. Subsequent years saw the appearance of a number of other valuable works, but for the most part in his new field. *Nationality and Government* was published in 1918; *Europe in Convalescence* in 1922; *The Third British Empire* in 1926; *The Prospects of Democracy* in 1929; *The League of Nations and the Rule of Law* in its final form in 1936 (the embryo of this work appeared in 1918); *Spiritual Values and World Affairs* in 1939; and *From the British Empire to the British Commonwealth* in 1941. In 1928 he returned for a moment to his earlier interest with *Solon and Croesus, and other Greek Essays* and in the same year he produced a volume on *Learning and Leadership.* One of his last works was *The American Road to World Peace,* which appeared in 1953.

Zimmern was knighted in 1936. He was an honorary LL.D. of Aberdeen, an honorary D.Lit of Bristol and of Trinity College, Hartford, and an honorary Litt.D. of Melbourne University.

November 25, 1957.

George Zucco, the actor, died in Hollywood on May 28, 1960. He was 74.

Born at Manchester on January 11, 1886, George Zucco was in his younger days a clerk in a stockbroker's office. He made his first stage appearance in 1908 at Regina, Saskatchewan, in *What Happened to Jones,* a farce which had been popular in England 10 years before. He spent several years in Canada and the United States but returned to Britain on the outbreak of the First World War and was wounded during his military service in France. He appeared in London in 1918 in Walter Hackett's play *The Freedom of the Seas* and then decided to study at the Royal Academy of Dramatic Art. In 1920 he appeared with the New Shakespeare Company at Stratford-on-Avon and later toured in South Africa and the Far East. He was of a restless disposition and, after playing in a number of London productions, he toured Australia with Maurice Moscovitch in a repertory of plays which included *Trilby* and *The Ringer.* He was back in London, however, in January 1929 in time to give one of his most notable performances as Lieutenant Osborne in *Journey's End.*

His performance as "Uncle", the grey-haired subaltern who, being mature, sober, and with no particular aptitude for his enforced trade of war, is everything that the brilliant unbalanced young company commander is not, contributed greatly to the authenticity of the original production. Alone of the officers in the company, all of them junior to him in years, "Uncle", the professional schoolmaster, has remained entirely sane and true to himself, and Zucco showed how much patient self-discipline, how resolute a suppression of home-sickness and of a sense of his own inadequacy as a soldier, underlay this human achievement. As Zucco embodied him, this grave, shy, out of place but entirely reliable man was the point of rest which the eye of the audience returned to constantly so long as he was on the stage.

When he was engaged at the Old Vic in 1931 it was intended that Zucco should play Othello to Sir Ralph Richardson's Iago during the course of the season, but he left the company before the play went into rehearsal.

Towards the close of 1935 he appeared as Lord Beaconsfield in the American production of *Victoria Regina.* Thereafter he succumbed to the lure of Hollywood and was so successful in a long series of films that the London stage saw him no more.

May 30, 1960.

Professor Francis de Zulueta, Regius Professor of Civil Law at Oxford from 1919 to 1948 and Professor Emeritus since the latter date, died on January 16, 1958 in London. He was 79.

Francisco Maria Jose de Zulueta (to give him his full baptismal name) was born on September 12, 1878, in the Spanish Embassy in London. He was therefore by birth a Spaniard, and when he came to be of military age he drew in the ballot for military service a lot which could have conscribed him in the Spanish Army; but his father, Don Pedro de Zulueta, a member of the Spanish diplomatic service who had settled in England, was anxious that Francis should continue his studies there and made arrangements to find a substitute.

On his mother's side he was of Irish as well as Spanish extraction (she was the daughter of Sir Justin Sheil, K.C.B.), and he was a cousin of the late Marquis and of Cardinal Merry del Val. From the Oratory School at Edgbaston he was elected in 1897 to an open scholarship at New College, Oxford, where he obtained first classes in Classical Moderations, *Lit. Hum.,* and Jurisprudence, after which he was elected to a Prize Fellowship at Merton and won the Vinerian Law Scholarship in 1903. Four years later he returned to New College as a tutorial fellow with the duty of teaching for the school of jurisprudence, and from 1912 to 1917 held the post of All Souls Reader in Roman Law.

On the outbreak of the First World War he took out naturalization papers and obtained a commission in The Worcestershire Regiment before the end of 1914, seeing service later in France. During the war the Regius Chair of Civil Law fell vacant on the death of Henry Goudy, and in 1919 de Zulueta was appointed in his place. To the chair de Zulueta brought profound learning, a power of writing restrained and graceful English, and a training all the more perfect in that it had been matured under Vinogradoff, to whose instruction in methods of exact scholarship, and to whose power of taking a text or some other subject of study and squeezing the last drop out of it, he frequently acknowledged his obligation.

Like many other learned men who set themselves a high standard, he did not publish much, but the output, such as it was, justified the universal regret of his colleagues at his reluctance to increase it. What remains are chiefly pamphlets and articles in learned periodicals; his earliest work was an essay, contributed in 1909 to Vinogradoff's "Oxford Studies in Social and Legal History", on *Patronage in the Later Roman Empire.* In 1922 he published a comparatively slight, but exceedingly useful translation and commentary on Digest XLI, 1 and 2, and in 1935 a pamphlet entitled *Supplements to the Institutes of Gaius,* which brought the text up to date by the help of recently discovered fragments.

This he expanded to a text and translation of the Institutes in 1946, adding a commentary in characteristic style in 1953.

In 1945 his edition of *The Roman Law of Sale* appeared, which included appropriate parts of the French Civil Code and his valuable introduction. The range of his knowledge may be measured by his bibliographical contributions to the *Journal of Egyptian Archaeology.* His most substantial work is his edition, for the Selden Society, of the *Liber Pauperum* of Magister Vacarius, which appeared in 1927.

In 1929 he was elected a Fellow of the British Academy, and in 1938 Merton made him an honorary Fellow. As a teacher he had good success among college pupils, and during his tenure of the professorship his lectures steadily gained in popularity; but he was probably at his best when taking a small group of students in an informal class or seminar.

Tall and well proportioned, de Zulueta was a striking figure in any assembly, and especially when he led the procession of doctors at university ceremonies. As an undergraduate he was something of an athlete; he played a clever game of Association football for his college and was a useful member of the lawn tennis team. His somewhat sardonic humour, being entirely free from bitterness, was a pleasure to those who understood him, but as his temper was hot and his tongue quick, even they had to beware of the flash of his grey Irish eyes which indicated that the conversation was getting on to dangerous ground.

Such storms, however, quickly passed: no man bore less malice than he; never was there a stauncher friend nor a student more generous in sharing his knowledge with others. Finally, his most outstanding characteristic was a burning religious zeal, which guided his conduct throughout life. In his younger days he toyed with liberalism so far as to join an undergraduates' club of liberal tendencies, but such propensities were effectually checked during the modernist controversy, and in later years devotion to the Church underlay his passionate support of Franco's* cause.

He was a Fellow of All Souls from 1919 to 1948 and Sub-Warden from 1934 to 1936.

January 18, 1958.

References to Obituaries from The Times 1961-1975

Many obituaries reprinted in this volume contain references in the text to persons who died in the 1960s and 1970s. Those whose names are shown in this volume with an asterisk * were the subject of biographies in *Obituaries from The Times 1961-1970* and *Obituaries from The Times 1971-1975*, which are available from Newspaper Archive Developments Limited.

Below appear the names concerned, in each case with the year of death, the period covered by the volume concerned, and the page in that volume in which the obituary begins:—

Dean Acheson, 1971, 71-75, 6; **Dr. W. G. S. Adams**, 1966, 61-70, 6; **Dr. Konrad Adenauer**, 1967, 61-70, 6; **Max Adrian**, 1973, 71-75, 10; **F.-M. Lord Alanbrooke**, 1963, 61-70, 12; **Sir Bronson Albery**, 1971, 71-75, 12; **Lord Alexander of Hillsborough**, 1965, 61-70, 16; **F.-M. Lord Alexander of Tunis**, 1969, 61-70, 17; **Muhammad Ali**, 1970, 61-70, 19; **Florence Amery**, 1975, 71-75, 16; **Sir Donald Anderson**, 1973, 71-75, 17; **Sir Norman Angell**, 1967, 61-70, 23; **Jean Arp**, 1966, 61-70, 30; **Nancy Lady Astor**, 1964, 61-70, 32; **Lord Astor (3rd Viscount)**, 1966, 61-70, 33; **Col. Lord Astor of Hever**, 1971, 71-75, 25; **Robert Atkins**, 1972, 71-75, 29; **Lord Attlee**, 1967, 61-70, 35; **Clare Atwood**, 1962, 61-70, 40; **W. H. Auden**, 1973, 71-75, 30; **Vincent Auriol**, 1966, 61-70, 40.

Lord Balfour of Burleigh, 1967, 61-70, 46; **Tallulah Bankhead**, 1968, 61-70, 47; **Sydney F. Barnes**, 1967, 61-70, 49; **H. E. Bates**, 1974, 71-75, 36; **Clifford Bax**, 1962, 61-70, 56; **Sir Alfred Chester Beatty**, 1968, 61-70, 59; **Lord Beaverbrook**, 1964, 61-70, 60; **Joe Beckett**, 1965, 61-70, 63; **Sir Thomas Beecham**, 1961, 61-70, 63; **Queen Elisabeth of the Belgians**, 1965, 61-70, 65; **David Ben-Gurion**, 1973, 71-75, 40; **Edna Best**, 1974, 71-75, 46; **Lord Beveridge**, 1963, 61-70, 72; **Lord Birkett**, 1962, 61-70, 77; **Sir John Black**, 1965, 61-70, 78; **Lt.-Col. L. V. Stewart Blacker**, 1964, 61-70, 78; **Prof. Lord Blackett**, 1974, 71-75, 49; **Dr. T. S. R. Boase**, 1974, 71-75, 54; **Dr. Thomas Bodkin**, 1961, 61-70, 82; **Charles E. Bohlen**, 1974, 71-75, 55; **Hector Bolitho**, 1974, 71-75, 56; **James Bone**, 1962, 61-70, 85; **Georges Bonnet**, 1973, 71-75, 57; **Frank Borzage**, 1962, 61-70, 86; **Lord Boyd Orr**, 1971, 71-75, 61; **Lord Brabazon of Tara**, 1964, 61-70, 91; **James J. Braddock**, 1974, 71-75, 64; **Sir Lawrence Bragg**, 1971, 71-75, 64; **Georges Braque**, 1963, 61-70, 96; **Lord Bridges**, 1969, 61-70, 99; **Sir John Brocklebank**, 1974, 71-75, 70; **Clive Brook**, 1974, 71-75, 72; **Lord Brookeborough**, 1973, 71-75, 72; **Lord Bruce of Melbourne**, 1967, 61-70, 106; **Sir Frederick Brundrett**, 1974, 71-75, 77; **Frank Buchman**, 1961, 61-70, 110; **Sir Alfred Butt**, 1962, 61-70, 114; **James Francis Byrnes**, 1972, 71-75, 87.

Sir Alexander Cadogan, 1968, 61-70, 117; **Basil Cameron**, 1975, 71-75, 90; **Gen. Lazaro Cárdenas**, 1970, 61-70, 123; **Primo Carnera**, 1967, 61-70, 125; **Georges Carpentier**, 1975, 71-75, 92; **A. W. Carr**, 1963, 61-70, 125; **Pablo Casals**, 1973, 71-75, 94; **Sir Lewis Casson**, 1969, 61-70, 129; **Sir James Chadwick**, 1974, 71-75, 99; **Lord Chandos**, 1972, 71-75, 99; **A. P. F. Chapman**, 1961, 61-70, 130; **Prof. Sydney Chapman**, 1970, 61-70, 131; **Ruth Chatterton**, 1961, 61-70, 134; **Maurice Chevalier**, 1972, 71-75, 105; **Gen. Chiang Kai-Shek**, 1975, 71-75, 106; **John Christie**, 1962, 61-70, 137; **Randolph Churchill**, 1968, 61-70, 138; **Sir Winston Churchill**, 1965, 61-70, 139; **Lord Chuter-Ede**, 1965, 61-70, 148; **Sir Alan Cobham**, 1973, 71-75, 114; **Sir Sydney Cockerell**, 1962, 61-70, 152; **Jean Cocteau**, 1963, 61-70, 155; **Lord Cohen**, 1973, 71-75, 115; **Prof. A. H. Compton**, 1962, 61-70, 160; **Lord Constantine**, 1971, 71-75, 118; **Gary Cooper**, 1961, 61-70, 163; **Dame Gladys Cooper**, 1971, 71-75, 119; **Dr. Andrew Cordier**, 1975, 71-75, 121; **Adm. of Flt. Lord Cork and Orrery**, 1967, 61-70, 164; **Alfred Cortot**, 1962, 61-70, 164; **Sir Noël Coward**, 1973, 71-75, 124; **Edward Gordon Craig**, 1966, 61-70, 168; **Lord Crawford and Balcarres**, 1975, 71-75, 125; **Sir Herbert Creedy**, 1973, 71-75, 127; **Dame Rachel Crowdy**, 1964, 61-70, 175; **Prof. Robert Cruikshank**, 1974, 71-75, 131; **Adm. of Flt. Lord Cunningham of Hyndhope**, 1963, 61-70, 176; **Adm. of Flt. Sir John Cunningham**, 1962, 61-70, 177; **Dame Myra Curtis**, 1971, 71-75, 132.

Edouard Daladier, 1970, 61-70, 181; **Lord Dalton**, 1962, 61-70, 183; **Bernard Darwin**, 1961, 61-70, 187; **Sir Charles Darwin**, 1962, 61-70, 189; **Sir Robin Darwin**, 1974, 71-75, 137; **Clement Davies**, 1962, 61-70, 191; **Cecil Day-Lewis**, 1972, 71-75, 140; **Gen. Charles de Gaulle**, 1970, 61-70, 197; **Sir Geoffrey de Havilland**, 1965, 61-70, 206; **King Frederik IX of Denmark**, 1972, 71-75, 145; **Louis de Soissons**, 1962, 61-70, 210; **Eamon de Valera**, 1975, 71-75, 148; **Thomas E. Dewey**, 1971, 71-75, 151; **Sir William Reid Dick**, 1961, 61-70, 213; **Sir Pierson Dixon**, 1965, 61-70, 216; **Frank Dobson**, 1963, 61-70, 218; **Sir Charles Dodds**, 1973, 71-75, 154; **Marcel Duchamp**, 1968, 61-70, 227; **Georges Duhamel**, 1966, 61-70, 228; **André Dunoyer de Segonzac**, 1974, 71-75, 161; **Marshal Enrico Dutra**, 1974, 71-75, 161; **Palme Dutt**, 1974, 71-75, 161; **Julien Duvivier**, 1967, 61-70, 234.

Ebby Edwards, 1961, 61-70, 237; **Luigi Einaudi**, 1961, 61-70, 241; **Gen. Dwight Eisenhower**, 1969, 61-70, 242; **T. S. Eliot**, 1965, 61-70, 247; **Duke Ellington**, 1974, 71-75, 166; **Mischa Elman**, 1967, 61-70, 248; **Lily Elsie**, 1962, 61-70, 249; **Fritz Erler**, 1967, 61-70, 252; **St. John Ervine**, 1971, 71-75, 171; **Former Emperor Haile Selassie of Ethiopia**, 1975, 71-75, 172.

Capt. Cyril Falls, 1971, 71-75, 178; **Giuseppi (Nino) Farina**, 1966, 61-70, 260; **Geraldine Farrer**, 1967, 61-70, 261; **Edna Ferber**, 1968, 61-70, 262; **Dr. Leopold Figl**, 1965, 61-70, 264; **Prof. G. I. Finch**, 1970, 61-70, 264; **Archbishop Lord Fisher of Lambeth**, 1972, 71-75, 182; **Sir Ronald A. Fisher**, 1962, 61-70, 266; **John Ford**, 1973. 71-75, 187; **C. S. Forester**, 1966, 61-70, 274; **E. M. Forster**, 1970, 61-70, 275; **Gen. Franco**, 1975, 71-75, 190; **Pamela Frankau**, 1967, 61-70, 280; **Rudolf Friml**, 1972, 71-75, 196; **Robert Frost**, 1963, 61-70, 286; **Maj.-Gen. J. F. C. Fuller**, 1966, 61-70, 287.

Hugh Gaitskell, 1963, 61-70, 290; **Gaston Gallimard**, 1975, 71-75, 200; **Judy Garland**, 1969, 61-70, 296; **Dame Adeline Genée-Isitt**, 1970, 61-70, 299; **Duke of Gloucester**, 1974, 71-75, 204; **Samuel Goldwyn**, 1974, 71-75, 208; **Sir Victor Gollancz**, 1967, 61-70, 310; **Sir Eugene Goossens**, 1962, 61-70, 312; **Lord Gorell**, 1963, 61-70, 313; **Betty Grable**, 1973, 71-75, 210; **King Paul of Greece**, 1964, 61-70, 319; **Walter Greenwood**, 1974, 71-75, 212; **J. M. Gregory**, 1973, 71-75, 214; **John Grierson**, 1972, 71-75, 215; **James Griffiths**, 1975, 71-75; 216; **Sir James Grigg**, 1964, 61-70, 323; **Serge Grigoriev**, 1968, 61-70, 325; **Dr. Walter Gropius**, 1969, 61-70, 325; **Otto Grotewohl**, 1964, 61-70, 326; **Claude Guillebaud**, 1971, 71-75, 218; **Nubar Gulbenkian**, 1972, 71-75, 219; **Barbara Gwyer**, 1974, 71-75, 221; **Rev. R. M. Gwynn**, 1962, 61-70, 329.

George Hackenschmidt, 1968, 61-70, 330; **Grp. Capt. the Duke of Hamilton**, 1973, 71-75, 225; **Mary Agnes Hamilton**, 1962, 61-70, 339; **Dashiell Hammett**, 1961, 61-70, 341; **Walter Hammond**, 1965, 61-70, 342; **Dame Florence Hancock**, 1974, 71-75, 225; **Lord Hankey**, 1963, 61-70, 345; **Nicholas Hannen**, 1972, 71-75, 226; **Moss Hart**, 1961, 61-70, 352; **Clarence Hatry**, 1965, 61-70, 354; **Ben Hecht**, 1964, 61-70, 357; **Ernest Hemingway**, 1961, 61-70, 358; **Patsy Hendren**, 1962, 61-70, 360; **Dame Barbara Hepworth**, 1975, 71-75, 238; **Sir Alan Herbert**, 1971, 71-75, 239; **Dame Myra Hess**, 1965, 61-70, 363; **Prof. Theodor Heuss**, 1963, 61-70, 365; **Graham Hill**, 1975, 71-75, 242; **Dr. Paul Hindemith**, 1963, 61-70, 366; **Prof. Edward Hindle**, 1973, 71-75, 243; **Sir Jack Hobbs**, 1963, 61-70, 371; **Paul Hoffman**, 1974, 71-75, 246; **Herbert Hoover**, 1964, 61-70, 380; **Gerard Hopkins**, 1961, 61-70, 381; **Bobby Howes**, 1972, 71-75, 252; **Claude Hulbert**, 1964, 61-70, 389; **Sir Cecil Hurst**, 1963, 61-70, 392; **Fannie Hurst**, 1968, 61-70, 392; **Aldous Huxley**, 1963, 61-70, 395; **Sir Julian Huxley**, 1975, 71-75, 259; **Sir Harry Hylton-Foster**, 1965, 61-70, 397.

Gen. Lord Ismay of Wormington, 1965, 61-70, 403; **Lord Iveagh**, 1967, 61-70, 404.

Sir Barry Jackson, 1961, 61-70, 405; **Augustus John**, 1961, 61-70, 414; **Louis A. Johnson**, 1966, 61-70, 417; **Eric Johnston**, 1963, 61-70, 418; **Arthur Creech Jones**, 1964, 61-70, 419; **C. G. Jung**, 1961, 61-70, 425.

Lord Kemsley, 1968, 61-70, 433; **Marie Kendall**, 1964, 61-70, 434; **Nikita Khrushchev**, 1971, 71-75, 283; **Lord Killearn**, 1964, 61-70, 442; **Capt. Anthony Kimmins**, 1964, 61-70, 444; **Cmdr. Lord King-Hall**, 1966, 61-70, 445; **Prof. Hans Knappertsbusch**, 1965, 61-70, 448; **Sir Hughe Knatchbull-Hugessen**, 1971, 71-75, 289; **Dame Laura Knight**, 1970, 61-70, 449; **Dr. Zoltán Kodály**, 1967, 61-70, 451; **Victor Kravchenko**, 1966, 61-70, 453; **Shukry Kuwatly**, 1967, 61-70, 456.

Charles Laughton, 1962, 61-70, 464; **Frank Lawton**, 1969, 61-70, 467; **Lord Leathers**, 1965, 61-70, 470; **Le Corbusier**, 1965, 61-70, 470; **Vivien Leigh**, 1967, 61-70, 475; **John Llewellyn Lewis**, 1969, 61-70, 480; **Sir Basil Liddell Hart**, 1970, 61-70, 482; **Trygve Lie**, 1968, 61-70, 483; **Col. Charles Lindbergh**, 1974, 71-75, 308; **Eric Linklater**, 1974, 71-75, 309; **Walter Lippmann**, 1974, 71-75, 311; **Adm. Sir Charles Little**, 1973, 71-75, 313; **Harold Lloyd**, 1971, 71-75, 315; **Sir Robert Bruce Lockhart**, 1970, 61-70, 488; **Marie Löhr**, 1975, 71-75, 317; **Percy Lubbock**, 1965, 61-70, 495; **Sir Arnold Lunn**, 1974, 71-75, 323; **Ralph Lynn**, 1962, 61-70, 500.

Gen. of Army Douglas MacArthur, 1964, 61-70, 502; **Denis Mackail**, 1971, 71-75, 326; **Gen. Andrew McNaughton**, 1966, 61-70, 515; **Ivan M. Maisky**, 1975, 71-75, 331; **Miles Malleson**, 1969, 61-70, 519; **Dr. J. J. Mallon**, 1961, 61-70, 520; **Lord Malvern**, 1971, 71-75, 333; **F.-M. Erich von Manstein**, 1973, 71-75, 336; **Hilary Marquand**, 1972, 71-75, 340; **Herbert Marshall**, 1966, 61-70, 529; **John Masefield**, 1967, 61-70, 533; **Somerset Maugham**, 1965, 61-70, 537; **François Mauriac**, 1970, 61-70, 539; **André Maurois**, 1967, 61-70, 539; **Adolphe Menjou**, 1963, 61-70, 544; **Lord Merriman**, 1962, 61-70, 546; **Darius Milhaud**, 1974, 71-75, 352; **Lord Milner of Leeds**, 1967, 61-70, 551; **Maj.-Gen. Iskander Mirza**, 1969, 61-70, 553; **Sir Walter Moberly**, 1974, 71-75, 357; **Capt. Edward Molyneux**, 1974, 71-75, 358; **Lord Monckton**, 1965, 61-70, 555; **Marilyn Monroe**, 1962, 61-70, 556; **Henry Morgenthau**, 1967, 61-70, 560; **Stanley Morison**, 1967, 61-70, 561; **Lord Morrison of Lambeth**, 1965, 61-70, 563; **Sultan of Muscat and Oman**, 1972, 71-75, 368; **former Maharaja of Mysore (J. C. Wadiyar)**, 1974, 71-75, 368.

Adm. Sir Martin Dunbar-Nasmith, 1965, 61-70, 575; **President Gamal Abdel Nasser**, 1970, 61-70, 576; **Khwaja Nazimuddin**, 1964, 61-70, 578; **Sir John Neale**, 1975, 71-75, 370; **Jawaharlal Nehru**, 1964, 61-70, 578; **Princess Wilhelmina of the Netherlands**, 1962, 61-70, 582; **Sir Harold Nicolson**, 1968, 61-70, 587; **Flt. Adm. Chester Nimitz**, 1966, 61-70, 588; **Dr. Kwame Nkrumah**, 1972, 71-75, 379; **Duke of Norfolk**, 1975, 71-75, 380; **Lord Normanbrook**, 1967, 61-70, 590; **Lord Nuffield**, 1963, 61-70, 594; **Lt.-Gen. Sir Archibald Nye**, 1967, 61-70, 596.

Sean O'Casey, 1964, 61-70, 597; **Archbishop Gerald O'Hara**, 1963, 61-70, 599; **Adm. of Flt. Sir Henry Oliver**, 1965, 61-70, 603; **Vic Oliver**, 1964, 61-70, 604; **C. T. Onions**, 1965, 61-70, 605; **Dr. J. Robert Oppenheimer**, 1967, 61-70, 606; **Joe Orton**, 1967, 61-70, 609; **Sir Alfred Owen**, 1975, 71-75, 390.

Marcel Pagnol, 1974, 71-75, 393; **George Papandreou**, 1968, 61-70, 616; **Franz von Papen**, 1969, 61-70, 617; **Lord Parker of Waddington**, 1972, 71-75, 395; **Val Parnell**, 1972, 71-75, 397; **Lt.-Col. Frederick Peake (Peake Pasha)**, 1970, 61-70, 623; **Don Ramón Pérez de Ayala**, 1962, 61-70, 627; **Juan Perón**, 1974, 71-75, 404; **Lord Pethick-Lawrence**, 1961, 61-70, 628; **William E. W. Petter**, 1968, 61-70, 629; **Pablo Picasso**, 1973, 71-75, 408; **Lord Piercy**, 1966, 61-70, 634; **William Plomer**, 1973, 71-75, 413; **A. E. Popham**, 1970, 61-70, 640; **Ezra Pound**, 1972, 71-75, 421; **Sir Maurice Powicke**, 1963, 61-70, 644; **Lt.-Gen. Sir Henry Pownall**, 1961, 61-70, 645; **John Cowper Powys**, 1963, 61-70, 645; **Duke of Primo de Rivera**, 1964, 61-70, 648; **Princess Marina, Duchess of Kent**, 1968, 61-70, 648; **Princess Royal**, 1965, 61-70, 649.

Claude Rains, 1967, 61-70, 654; **Mátyas Rákosi**, 1971, 71-75, 430; **Lady Patricia Ramsay**, 1974, 71-75, 430; **Lord Rank**, 1972, 71-75, 433; **Arthur Ransome**, 1967, 61-70, 657; **Alan Rawsthorne**, 1971, 71-75, 434; **Sir Herbert Read**, 1968, 61-70, 662; **Eva Lady Reading**, 1973, 71-75, 435; **Erich Maria Remarque**, 1970, 61-70, 665; **Paul Reynaud**, 1966, 61-70, 668; **Wilfred Rhodes**, 1973, 71-75, 442; **Sir Harry Ricardo**, 1974, 71-75, 442; **Elmer Rice**, 1967, 61-70, 671; **Prof. Sir Albert Richardson**, 1964, 61-70, 672; **Sir Bruce Richmond**, 1964, 61-70, 672; **Sir Dennis Robertson**, 1963, 61-70, 677; **Sir Robert Robinson**, 1975, 71-75, 449; **Jules Romains**, 1972, 71-75, 451; **Lord Rosebery**, 1974, 71-75, 453; **Sir David Ross**, 1971, 71-75, 455; **Lord Russell (Bertrand Russell)**, 1970, 61-70, 691.

Louis Stephen St. Laurent, 1973, 71-75, 461; **Dr. Antonio Salazar**, 1970, 61-70, 699; **Lord Salisbury**, 1972, 71-75, 462; **Mshl. of R.A.F. Sir John Salmond**, 1968, 61-70, 701; **Lord Salter**, 1975, 71-75, 464; **Lord Samuel**, 1963, 61-70, 702; **Margaret Sanger**, 1966, 61-70, 705; **Sir Malcolm Sargent**, 1967, 61-70, 706; **Siegfried Sassoon**, 1967, 61-70, 708; **Sir Victor Sassoon**, 1961, 61-70, 709; **Lord Scarbrough**, 1969, 61-70, 711; **Dr. Hjalmar Schacht**, 1970, 61-70, 711; **Joseph Schenck**, 1961, 61-70, 713; **Robert Schuman**, 1963, 61-70, 715; **Dr. Albert Schweizer**, 1965, 61-70, 716; **Cyril Scott**, d. 1970, obit in 71-75, 474; **Sir Walford Selby**, 1965, 61-70, 719; **David Selznick**, 1965, 61-70, 720; **R. C. Sherriff**, 1975, 71-75, 482; **Brig. Adib Shishakly**, 1964, 61-70, 727; **Dmitri Shostakovich**, 1975, 71-75, 483; **Shena Lady Simon of Wythenshawe**, 1972, 71-75, 488; **Michel Simon**, 1975, 71-75, 489; **Dame Edith Sitwell**, 1964, 61-70, 732; **Sir Osbert Sitwell**, 1969, 61-70, 733; **Mr. Justice Slade**, 1962, 61-70, 735; **F.-M. Lord Slim**, 1970, 61-70, 737; **Sir Ben Smith**, 1964, 61-70, 739; **Dr. Theodore Howard Somervell**, 1975, 71-75, 498; **Gen. Carl Spaatz**, 1974, 71-75, 502; **Queen Victoria Eugénie of Spain**, 1969, 61-70, 745; **Maj.-Gen. Sir Edward Spears**, 1974, 71-75, 502; **Lieut.-Col. F. Spencer Chapman**, 1971, 71-75, 503; **Lord Spens**, 1973, 71-75, 504; **Dr. Vilhjalmur Stefansson**, 1962, 61-70, 755; **Sir Hugh Stephenson**, 1972, 71-75, 507; **G. B. Stern**, 1973, 71-75. 508; **Josef von Sternberg**, 1969, 61-70, 758; **Igor Stravinsky**, 1971, 71-75, 513; **Lord Stuart of Findhorn**, 1971, 71-75, 516; **Hussein Suhrawardy**, 1963, 61-70, 766; **Hannen Swaffer**, 1962, 61-70, 770; **King Gustav VI Adolf of Sweden**, 1973, 71-75, 518; **Queen Louise of Sweden**, 1965, 61-70, 770; **Lord Swinton**, 1972, 71-75, 519.

Prof. R. H. Tawney, 1962, 61-70, 774; **Robert Taylor**, 1969, 61-70, 776; **Ellaline Terriss (Lady Hicks)**, 1971, 71-75, 524; **Lionel Tertis**, 1975, 71-75, 524; **Dorothy Thompson**, 1961, 61-70, 783; **Sir George Thomson**, 1975, 71-75, 529; **Lord Thurso**, 1970, 61-70, 787; **Palmiro Togliatti**, 1964, 61-70, 790; **Prof. Arnold Toynbee**, 1975, 71-75, 535; **Spencer Tracy**, 1967, 61-70, 793; **Prof. G. M. Trevelyan**, 1962, 61-70, 795; **Harry S. Truman**, 1972, 71-75, 538; **Lord Twining**, 1967, 61-70, 800.

Lord Upjohn, 1971, 71-75, 545.

Tony Vandervell, 1967, 61-70, 804; **Sophocles Venizelos**, 1964, 61-70, 806; **Mshl. Klementi Voroshilov**, 1969, 61-70, 809.

Canon H. M. Waddams, 1972, 71-75, 549; **Prof. L. R. Wager**, 1965, 61-70, 811; **Anton Walbrook**, 1967, 61-70, 813; **C. C. Walker**, 1968, 61-70, 814; **Henry Agard Wallace**, 1965, 61-70, 815; **Dr. Bruno Walter**, 1962, 61-70, 816; **John Walter**, 1968, 61-70, 817; **Beatrice Warde**, 1969, 61-70, 819; **Sir Pelham Warner**, 1963, 61-70, 820; **Sir Robert Watson-Watt**, 1973, 71-75, 556; **Ava Lady Waverley**, 1974, 71-75, 556; **Naunton Wayne**, 1970, 61-70, 824; **Helene Weigel**, 1971, 71-75, 559; **Bombdr. Billy Wells**, 1967, 61-70, 828; **Sir Harold Werner**, 1973, 71-75, 562; **Gen. Weygand**, 1965, 61-70, 829; **Paul Whiteman**, 1967, 61-70, 832; **Sir Henry Willink**, 1973, 71-75, 571; **Sir Horace Wilson**, 1972, 71-75, 572; **Walter Winchell**, 1972, 71-75, 573; **Duke of Windsor**, 1972, 71-75, 574; **Sir Pelham Wodehouse**, 1975, 71-75, 581; **Sir Donald Wolfit**, 1968, 61-70, 846; **Lord Woolton**, 1964, 61-70, 852; **Sir Evelyn Wrench**, 1966, 61-70, 855; **Lord Wright**, 1964, 61-70, 855; **Diana Wynyard**, 1964, 61-70, 858.

Shigeru Yoshida, 1967, 61-70, 861; **Prince Felix Yusupov**, 1967, 61-70, 864.

GUIDE TO SUBJECTS OF THE OBITUARIES 1951-1960

The following guide to the fields of activity of persons whose obituaries have been reprinted in this volume includes nearly 300 under more than one heading—e.g., a head of State who was a soldier, a politician who was also a man of letters or historian, etc.

ROYALTY & STATECRAFT

e.g., sovereigns, other rulers, presidents, chancellors, prime ministers, and their close relatives:—

PUBLIC SERVICE & POLITICS

e.g., secretaries of state, ministers, parliamentarians, governors, diplomats, civil servants, national and local administrators, social and public workers, widows of the above:—

ARMED FORCES

e.g., defence ministers and advisers, soldiers, sailors, airmen, resistance fighters, strategists and writers on military science and history of warfare:—

EDUCATION

e.g., educationists, academics, university, college, school and departmental administrators and teachers:—

EDUCATION (continued)

ECONOMICS, TRADE & TRANSPORT

e.g., economists, traders (international, national and retail), developers and operators of transport, including shipping, aviation and railways:—

LAW

e.g., judges, barristers, solicitors, criminologists, policemen, investigators, law teachers, criminals, persons in law cases, spies and secret agents:—

PHILOSOPHY & PSYCHOLOGY

e.g., philosophers, mathematicians, psychologists:—

RELIGION

e.g., patriarchs, archbishops, bishops, other clerics, theologians, church affairs administrators, missionaries, heads of religious movements, teachers and writers:—

RELIGION (continued)

SCIENCE

e.g., physicists, chemists, zoologists, anthropologists, botanists, biochemists, anatomists, astronomers, geologists, and other scientists not mainly in medicine or industry; writers on science other than those confined to works of science fiction:—

MEDICINE

e.g., surgeons, physicians, pathologists, physiologists, anaesthetists, authorities on health, population, sex and birth control:—

INDUSTRY & ENGINEERING

e.g., manufacturers, engineers, designers, inventors, trade unionists, company directors, trade unionists, agriculturalists, oil magnates, directors of tourism, fashion designers, textile company directors:—

INDEX OF OBITUARIES AND TRIBUTES 1951-1960

EXPLANATION OF INDEX

This index has been compiled from the last edition of *The Times* each day, for the years 1951 to 1960. It contains references to all obituaries —including the 'after rules' the short death notices at the foot of the Obituary Section of the paper— and tributes, published during the period.

Where a name is printed in black type, it signifies that the full text of the Obituary is reprinted in the main section of this book, which is arranged in alphabetical order.

In each entry the first numeral(s) indicate the day of the month, the second the page, and the letter the column: for reference purposes the columns of each page are supposed to be lettered from left to right—a, b,c,d,e,f,g,h. The final numerals appearing in parenthesis indicate the year. Thus July 23, 9c (52) denotes the issue of July 23, page 9, column 3, of the year 1952.

The first date after each name refers to the date the obituary appeared in *The Times,* and each subsequent date refers to a tribute; the only exception being where the letter (t) appears, thus indicating that there was no obituary and that all references are to tributes.

A

B

Budgett, Hubert M.—Feb. 27, 6e (51)
Buhl, Hermann—July 17, 12e (57)
Buhl, Vilhelm—Dec. 20, 8e (54)
Buhla, Ernst (Dr.)—Aug. 9, 6e (51)
Buhrle, Emil G.—Nov. 30, 10d (56)
Buist, Herbert J.M. (Col.)—July 26, 12a (56)
Bukofzer, Manfred (Prof.)—Dec. 9, 13c (55); 13, 11a (55)
Bukowski, Roches J.J.—Jan. 22, 15b (60)
Bulay–Watson, Donald—Nov. 22, 8e (58)
Bulbrook, Robert—Feb. 12, 15d (60)
Bulkeley–Evans, William A. (Dr.)—May 15, 8g (52)
Bulkeley, John P.—Nov. 20, 16f (58)
Bull, Alfred—Feb. 5, 12e (59)
Bull, A.W. (Ald)—Mar. 4, 10e (55)
Bull, E. Myron—June 6, 8e (53)
Bull, Frank K—June 1, 20d (60)
Bull, John W.N. (Capt.)—Dec. 14, 13b (56)
Bull, Ludlow (Dr)—July 3, 8d (54)
Bull, Maude—(t.) Dec. 14, 8e (51)
Bullard, Quintin H. (Cdre)—July 30, 8e (53)
Bulleid, Arthur (Dr)—Jan. 11, 6d (52)
Bullen, Percy—Jan. 16, 14a (58)
Buller, Georgiana—June 23, 8d (53); 26, 8e (53); 27, 8e (53)
Buller, Henry (Adm. Sir)—Aug. 31, 12a (60)
Bullett, Gerald—Jan. 6, 14d (58); 8, 11e (58); 22, 11c (58)
Bullitt, William M.—Oct. 5, 8f (57); 9, 13d (57)
Bullock, Edward C. (Lieut.-Col.)—Dec. 10, 8g (54)
Bullock, Ernest H.—Mar. 7, 12e (57)
Bullock, Guy H.—Apr. 20, 13a (56)
Bullock, Humphry (Brig.)—(t.) Nov. 24, 15c (59)
Bullock, James—July 7, 8d (59)
Bulpitt, Walter H.—Oct. 11, 15e (57)
Bulstrode, Edward G.: see Edward (Brother)
Bulteel, John (Sir)—Feb. 20, 12b (56)
Bunbury, Henry W. (Capt.)—June 28, 13a (56)
Bune, Reginald E.—Apr. 14, 11b (56)
Bunge, Julius H.O.—Apr. 11, 10e (59)
Bunin, Ivan—Nov. 9, 11c (53)
Bunston, John S.—Oct. 18, 15b (60)
Bunting, Henry—Apr. 3, 11c (56)
Bunton, Harry M.—Sept 10, 10e (54)
Burbridge, Lilian (Lady)—Mar. 10, 10e (55)
Burchard, Ludwig—(t.) Oct. 5, 15c (60)
Burchardt, Frank A. (Dr)—Dec. 23, 8d (58)
Burden, Albert E.C.—Feb. 23, 8e (57)
Burden, Henry (Col)—Jan. 21, 10f (53)
Burdett–Coutts, Herbert S.H.—Feb. 23, 8e (57)
Burdon, Ernest (Sir)—Aug. 14, 10e (57)
Burge, Jack—Jan. 8, 10d (57)
Burger, Gerald—Feb. 22, 8e (52)
Burgess, Arthur J.W.—Apr. 18, 14a (57)
Burgess, Gelett—(t.) Oct. 24, 6f (51)
Burgess, Leslie—Aug. 11, 10d (58)
Burgess, Ralph C.—Oct. 6, 12c (55)
Burgess, W.L. (Dr.)—(t.) May 14, 8g (54)
Burgh, Alexander (6th Lord)—May 28, 17a (59)
Burgis, Edith (Lady)—Nov. 25, 13d (55)
Burian, Emil F.—(t.) Sept 3, 12d (59)
Burke, Charles D. (Rear-Adm.)—Mar. 29, 9c (52)
Burke–Gaffney (Fr)—Sept 16, 10d (58)
Burke, Gerald (Sir)—Jan. 1, 10e (55)
Burke, Kenneth—June 20, 16b (60)
Burke, Richard (Lieut. -Col. Sir)—Sept 2, 12e (60)
Burke, Roland (Sir)—Dec. 4, 18b (58)
Burke, Samuel C.—Sept 3, 8e (53)
Burke, Vincent P.—Dec. 21, 8d (53)
Burkhardt, John—Nov. 4, 6e (54)
Burkitt, Frank H.—Nov. 5, 10d (52)
Burlace, John B.—Aug. 18, 8e (54)
Burleigh, C.H.H.—Jan. 9, 12c (56); 12, 12b (56)
Burlingham, Charles C.—June 9, 14c (59)
Burman, W. J.—June 11, 11d (57)
Burmeister, Rudolf (Adm.Sir)—Dec. 29, 8e (56); Jan. 2, 11c (57)
Burn, Clive (Sir)—May 10, 13c (55); 17, 13c (55); 20, 13d (55)
Burn, Henry P—July 12, 8e (58)
Burn, John S. (Dr.)—Aug. 29, 10f (58)
Burn, Kenneth E.—July 21, 10c (56)
Burn–Murdoch, Hector (Dr)—Apr. 23, 13d (58)
Burn, Phyllis (Lady)—Jan. 21, 10e (58)
Burnaby, Hugh (Rev)—May 11, 13c (56); 16, 15d (56); 21, 10d (56)
Burnand, Rene (Dr)—May 2, 21b (60)
Burne, Alfred H. (Lieut.-Col.)—June 3, 15a (59); 8, 12e (59)
Burne, Nancy—Mar. 26, 8d (54)
Burne, Richard H.—Oct. 10, 8f (53)
Burnell, Charles E.—Apr. 6, 16f (59)
Burnett, Alexander (Maj. Sir)—May 11, 14c (59)
Burnett, Digby V. (Sir)—Nov. 5, 15f (58)
Burnett, Frances—(t.) Mar. 21, 8e (55)
Burnett, James (Maj.-Gen. Sir)—Aug. 14, 8e (53)
Burnett, Leslie (Col. Sir)—July 18, 11d (55)
Burnett of Leys, James (Sir)—(t.) Aug. 18, 8d (53)
Burnett of Leys, Sybil (Lady)—Apr. 7, 16g (60); 21, 17d (60)
Burnett, Richard G.—Mar. 21, 17e (60)
Burnett, Robert (Adm. Sir)—July 3, 9d (59)
Burnett, Roy—Feb. 17, 14b (58)
Burnett–Stuart, John (Gen. Sir)—Oct. 8, 13a (58); 13, 19e (58)
Burnett–Stuart, Nina (Lady)—July 27, 13f (60)
Burney, Arthur B. (Preb.)—Feb. 18, 10c (56)
Burney, Guy—Mar. 20, 8f (54)
Burnham, John M.—Nov. 18, 12b (57)
Burnley (Bishop of): see Prosser, Charles K.K. (Rt. Rev.)
Burnley, Frank B.—Dec. 1, 14c (55)
Burns, Edgar B. (Col.)—(t.) May 9, 18b (57)
Burns, Eric S. (Air Comm.)—Dec. 31, 9b (57)
Burns, James—June 12, 8f (54)
Burns, Jimmy—Sept 12, 14g (57)
Burns, Sybella—Dec. 13, 10g (54)
Burns, Tommy—May 12, 14e (55); 13, 13b (55)
Burnup, Cuthbert J.—(t.) Apr. 13, 15c (60)
Burr, Malcolm (Dr)—July 15, 10g (54); 16, 10f (54)
Burra, Henry C.—Jan. 9, 14e (58)
Burrage, Alfred McL.—Dec. 22, 8e (56)
Burrell, Merrick (Sir)—Dec. 23, 8d (57); Jan. 3, 11d (58)
Burrell, Percy S.—May 1, 12d (58)
Burrell, William (Sir)—Mar. 31, 10f (58); Apr. 7, 9g (58)
Burridge, Robert A.M. (Capt.)—Jan. 29, 10c (57)
Burridge, W. (Dr.)—May 19, 14b (55)
Burros, Joao de—Oct. 27, 17a (60)
Burrow, C. Severn—(t.) Aug. 3, 8e (57)
Burrow, E. (Ald.)—June 8, 10f (53)
Burrow, E.L.—(t.) May 2, 17d (55)
Burrowes, Richard B.—Oct. 5, 13c (56)
Burrows, Alfred J.—Nov. 15, 13e (57)
Burrows, Christine M.E.—Sept 11, 14d (59)
Burrows, Harold—Sept 30, 11d (55); Oct. 14, 11d (55)
Burrows, Hollis M. (Brig.)—Apr. 16, 9b (52)
Burrows, Raymond (Prof)—Oct. 25, 13d (60)
Burrows, Roland (Sir)—June 16, 8e (52)
Burrus, Maurice—Dec. 8, 15b (59)
Burstall, Francis H. (Dr)—(t.) Jan. 12, 12b (56)
Burstall, Frederick C.—Dec. 9, 13c (55)
Burston, Samuel (Maj. -Gen. Sir)—Aug. 23, 12a (60)
Burt, Beatrice (Lady)—Oct. 26, 11c (55)
Burt, H.J. Astell—(t.) June 2, 18a (60)
Burt, Joseph Barnes (Dr.)—Mar. 20, 10f (53)
Burt–White, Harold—Oct. 22, 8d (52)
Burton–Chadwick, Robert (Sir)—May 23, 8e (51)
Burton, Claud P.P.—July 15, 14b (57); 19, 14d (57)
Burton, Claude E.C.–H.—(t.) Feb. 8, 10e (55)
Burton, Geoffrey (Sir)—July 3, 8d (54); 14, 10d (54)
Burton, George (Ven)—May 5, 19a (60)
Burton, Harold J.C. (Preb.)—July 20, 11b (55)
Burton, Humphrey P.W. (Canon)—Dec. 16, 10e (57)
Burton, Llewelyn W.—(t.) Jan. 2, 9c (54)
Burton, Mark—June 10, 14a (59)
Burton, Montague (Sir)—Sept 23, 8f (52); 25, 8f (52); 30, 8e (52)
Burton, Percy C. (Lieut.-Col.)—May 22, 10e (53)
Burton, Sophia (Lady)—Nov. 28, 12d (57)
Burton, William—Oct. 14, 11a (54)
Bury, George (Sir)—July 22, 10d (58)
Bury, Henry—Mar. 29, 8g (58)
Bury, Lindsay E. (Maj.)—Feb. 1, 6e (52)
Bury, Ralph F.—Jan. 18, 8e (54)
Busbridge, Edgar G.—Oct. 18, 8e (52)
Busby, William (Canon)—Feb. 23, 8e (51)
Busch, Adolf (Dr.)—June 11, 8d (52)
Busch, Fritz (Dr.)—Sept 17, 6g (51); 26, 6e (51)
Busch, Sune—Mar. 19, 10f (53)
Buset, Max—June 29, 12e (59); 30, 12e (59)
Bush, Horace S.—June 30, 10e (54)
Bush, Horace T.—Jan. 11, 8e (58)
Bush, John (Maj.—Mar. 16, 6d (51)
Bush, Pauline de (Baroness)—Aug. 16, 8e (54); 27, 8d (54)
Bush, Percy—May 20, 13a (55)
Bushby, Elaine (Lady)—Nov. 25, 15e (59)
Bushby, Leonard C.—May 3, 15c (57)
Bushe–Fox, Joscelyn P.—Oct. 19, 11c (54)
Bushell, Christopher W. (Col.)—Feb. 7, 13a (57)
Busoni, Gerda—Sept 6, 15b (56)
Busse, John—Sept 28, 13d (56); Oct. 4, 15e (56)
Bussey, Ernest W.—(t.) July 17, 12e (58)
Bussy, Dorothy—(t.) May 13, 17c (60)
Bussy, Janie S.—(t.) May 5, 19b (60)
Bussy, Simon—June 1, 8e (54); 5, 8e (54)
Butchart, James A. (Lieut.-Col.)—May 15, 10g (53)
Butcher, Frank C.—May 27, 14d (57)
Butcher, Hubert J.E. (Canon)—Aug. 20, 12d (56)
Bute, John (5th Lord)—Aug. 16, 11d (56); 25, 11b (56)
Butler, Ann (Lady)—July 24, 10f (53); Aug. 4, 8g (53)
Butler–Bowdon, William E.I. (Lieut.-Col.)—Apr. 4, 11g (56)
Butler, C. Osburne—May 24, 9b (54)
Butler, Charles L. (Col)—Sept 26, 8e (53)
Butler, David—Mar. 12, 8e (60)
Butler, Edward H.—Feb. 21, 11c (56)
Butler, Eliza M. (Dr.)—Nov. 14, 10d (59)
Butler, George G (Dr)—Dec. 18, 10f (53)
Butler, Harold (Sir)—Mar. 28, 6d (51); Apr. 3, 6e (51); 5, 6d (51)
Butler, Harold E. (Prof.)—June 9, 8d (51); 23, 8g (51)
Butler–Henderson, Eric B.—Dec. 19, 8e (53)
Butler, Hugh A.—July 3, 8d (54)
Butler, Humphrey—(t.) Mar. 3, 10e (53)
Butler, Kathleen (Lady)—June 26, 12d (58)
Butler, Lesley J.P. (Brig-Gen)—Jan. 2, 12e (56)

C

D

Donald, David—Dec. 24, 9c (53)
Donald, Douglas—Oct. 24, 8e (53)
Donald, Henrietta (Lady)—May 9, 13b (55)
Donald, James (Sir)—Apr. 27, 8e (57)
Donald, William J.—Apr. 8, 10d (58)
Donaldson, Alexande r E. (Canon)—Sept 9, 15a (60)
Donaldson, Arthur—Oct. 1, 9b (55)
Donaldson, F. Lewis (Canon)—Oct. 8, 11a (53)
Donaldson, George—Dec. 30, 8e (52)
Donaldson, Leonard A.B. (Adm.)—June 30, 10c (56)
Donaldson, Rachel E.D.—Mar. 24, 10b (56)
Donaldson, Thorneycroft—Sept 27, 11c (55)
Donat, Robert—June 10, 13a (58)
Doncaster, Gertrude (Lady)—Feb. 25, 14b (57)
Doncaster, Robert (Sir)—July 7, 12c (55)
Done, Beatrice H.—Oct. 27, 8e (52)
Done, W.J.—Feb. 22, 11b (56)
Donegall, Violet of (Marchioness)—Oct. 14, 8e (52); 20, 8e (52)
Doneraile, Algernon (8th Lord)—Nov. 28, 12d (57)
Doneraile, Hugh (7th Lord)—Dec. 19, 10e (56)
Donker, L.A.—Feb. 6, 12a (56)
Donkin, S.B.—(t.) Nov. 28, 10e (52)
Donkin, Sydney B.—Nov. 14, 8f (52)
Donnan, Frederick G. (Prof.)—Dec. 17, 10e (56); Jan. 9, 10f (57)
Donnelly, Arthur T. (Sir)—Feb. 2, 8d (54)
Donner, Ossian—Aug. 5, 9f (57)
Donovan, Hugh—Dec. 19, 10a (59)
Donovan, William J. (Maj.-Gen.)—Feb. 9, 10f (59); 14, 10a (59)
Doorman, L.A.C.M. (Vice-Adm.)—Dec. 13, 11b (55)
Doran, George H.—Jan. 9, 12a (56)
Doran, John C.M. (Brig.)—Jan. 21, 10a (57)
Dore, Alan (Grp Capt.)—Aug. 11, 8f (53); 14, 8f (53); 17, 8e (53); 21, 8e (53)
Doria-Pamphili-landi, Gesina (Princess)—May 17, 13d (55); 17, 13d (55); 19, 14b (55)
Doria-Pamphilj, Filippo A. (Prince)—Feb. 6, 10d (58); 17, 14b (58)
Dorman, Bedford (Sir)—Sept 6, 15c (56)
Dormer, Stewart P.—Feb. 14, 8f (53)
Dorotheos (Archbishop)—July 27, 8f (57)
Dorrell, William J.—May 6, 8e (54)
Dorrell,Edmund A.—June 26, 16e (59)
Dorrien-Smith, (Lady)—(t.) Nov. 2, 6e (51)
Dorrien-Smith, Arthur A. (Maj.)—May 31, 9c (55)
Dorsey, Jimmy—June 13, 16b (57)
Dorward, Alan J. (Prof.)—Dec. 19, 10d (56)
Doubleday, Arthur (Rt Rev)—Jan. 24, 8f (51)
Doud, Elivera—Sept 30, 15a (60)
Dougherty, Denis (Card.)—June 1, 8g (51)
Doughton, Robert L.—Oct. 2, 8f (54)
Doughty, Charles (Sir)—May 3, 14b (56)
Doughty-Tichborne, Denise (Lady)—Aug. 25, 10d (59)
Douglas, Archibald (Gen.)—July 9, 10c (60)
Douglas, Archibald, P.D. (Col.)—Jan. 27, 10e (53)
Douglas, Archibald W. (Canon)—Mar. 26, 9a (55)
Douglas-Campbell, Anna—Dec. 22, 12b (60)
Douglas, C.H.—Oct. 2, 8f (54)
Douglas, Charles E. (Rev.)—Sept 28, 11b (55)
Douglas, Charles W.S.—Oct. 3, 17c (60)
Douglas, Clifford H.—Oct. 1, 9c (52)
Douglas-Downes, R. (Rev.)—Sept 12, 14g (57); 19, 14c (57)
Douglas, Findlay—Mar. 31, 10d (59)
Douglas, Francis W.—Dec. 23, 9b (53)
Douglas, Fred—Mar. 2, 10e (55)
Douglas, George P. (Dr.)—Oct. 19, 11b (54)
Douglas, George V.—Oct. 10, 15e (58)
Douglas, Harry (Maj)—Jan. 1, 10e (53)
Douglas, James—Feb. 13, 10d (58)
Douglas, John A. (Canon)—July 5, 14b (56); 12, 13a (56); 13, 14b (56); 16, 15c (56)
Douglas-Jones, Crawford (Sir)—Mar. 3, 9a (56)
Douglas, Kenneth (Sir)—Oct. 30, 8e (54)
Douglas, Langton (Capt.)—(t.) Aug. 28, 6e (51)
Douglas, Lloyd C. (Dr.)—Feb. 15, 8e (51)
Douglas, Montagu W. (Lieut.-Col.)—Feb. 26, 11f (57)
Douglas, Norman—Feb. 11, 8g (52); 13, 6e (52)
Douglas, Paul—Sept 12, 8f (59)
Douglas-Pennant, Adela—May 28, 8f (55)
Douglas-Pennant, Hilda—Feb. 13, 14d (59)
Douglas, Robert L.—Aug. 17, 6f (51)
Douglas, Robert N. (Rev.)—Feb. 28, 10e (57)
Douglas, Sholto—(t.) Mar. 13, 14g (58)
Douglas, Sholto G. (Capt.)—Feb. 10, 11b (56)
Douglas, Sholto W. (Maj.)—Apr. 15, 15b (59)
Douglas, W.D. (Dr)—(t.) Aug. 16, 10e (60)
Douglas, William (Sir)—Feb. 18, 10d (53); 20, 8e (53)
Douglas, William —May 6, 8e (54)
Douie, Charles—July 24, 10g (53)
Dounis, Dmitri—Aug. 16, 8e (54)
Douthwaite, James L.—Nov. 8, 15d (60)
Dove, Patrick G. G. (Capt.)—May 27, 14d (57)
Dovzhenko, Alexander—Nov. 28, 12g (56)
Dow, Ann (Lady)—Apr. 25, 13c (56)
Dowd, H. (Rev.)—Apr. 27, 8g (53)
Dowd, James—Mar. 17, 10a (56)
Dowdall, Harold C.—Apr. 22, 15e (55)
Dowdall, H.V.—Dec. 18, 10e (57)
Dowds, Samuel S.—Aug. 19, 11c (59)
Dowling, Alfred S. (Rev.)—Mar. 6, 8e (54)
Down, Percy—June 30, 10e (54)
Downe, Dorothy (Lady)—Mar. 28, 15d (57)
Downes, Albert J.—(t.) June 29, 12e (59)
Downes, Olin—Aug. 24, 9b (55)
Downes, Robert O.—Aug. 29, 10e (57)
Downey, Richard (Most Rev.)—June 17, 8e (53); 23, 8e (53)
Downie, B.N. (Cdr)—(t.) Jan. 15, 13d (59)
Dowsett, Ernest B.—Nov. 14, 8e (51)
Doyle, Barnard—Aug. 29, 9d (55)
Doyle, Charles J.—Mar. 26, 13d (57)
Doyle, Denis Conan—Mar. 10, 10e (55)
Doyle, E.C. (Maj.)—Oct. 8, 11d (54)
Doyle, Peadar—Aug. 6, 11c (56)
D'Oyley, Elizabeth—June 22, 14c (59)
D'Oyley, Muriel: see Crosbie, Mary
Doyne, Phillip G.—Jan. 23, 12f (59)
Drage, Geoffrey—Mar. 9, 10e (55)
Drage, Godfrey (Lieut-Col)—Oct. 24, 8e (53)
Drake, Bernard F. (Brig.-Gen.)—Oct. 27, 8d (54)
Drake-Brockman, David H. (Brig.-Gen.)—Jan. 4, 17a (60)
Drake-Brockman, Ralph A. (Rev.)—Dec. 22, 8e (52)
Drake, Elizabeth—Jan. 22, 8e (54)
Drake, Herbert L.—Feb. 28, 13b (58); Mar. 5, 13b (58)
Drake, John A. (Dr.)—Oct. 31, 8f (52)
Drake, W.H. (Col.)—Apr. 5, 13a (56)
Drakeford, Arthur S.—June 10, 9e (57)
Draper, Ruth—Dec. 31, 8e (56); Jan. 3, 12c (57); 9, 10g (57); 10, 13b (57); 16, 10d (57)
Dratvin, Mikhail I. (Lieut-Gen)—Dec. 17, 8e (53)
Drayson, Alfred P. (Col.)—June 26, 8e (53)
Dreiser, Helen—Sept 26, 12a (55)
Dresden, Sem (Dr)—July 31, 10d (57)
Drew, Charles D. (Lieut-Col)—Oct. 13, 11b (56); 29, 14b (56)
Drew, Charles E.—(t.) Sept 10, 6e (52)
Drew, Guy—(t.) Nov. 20, 16g (58)
Drew, H.D.K. (Dr)—(t.) Jan. 23, 12g (59)
Drew, J. Macalister (Dr.)—(t.) June 7, 17a (57)
Drew, James S. (Maj.-Gen. Sir)—June 28, 11a (55); July 12, 11b (55)
Drew, Ruth—Sept 21, 15d (60)
Drew, Thomas B. (Vice-Adm)—Apr. 28, 20b (60)
Drew-Wilkinson, Clennell F.M.—Apr. 13, 13c (56)
Drexel, John A.—(t.) Mar. 13, 14f (58)
Drexel, Katherine (Rev Mother)—Mar. 5, 8f (55)
Dreyer, Frederic C. (Adm.Sir)—Dec. 22, 8f (56); 25, 12e (56)
Dreyer, Holger—July 11, 13c (55)
Dreyer, John T. (Maj.-Gen.)—May 25, 15f (59)
Dreyer, Thomas F. (Dr)—July 14, 10d (54)
Dreyer, Una (Lady)—Jan. 9, 13e (59)
Dreyfus, Camille (Dr.)—Sept 29, 10f (56)
Drinkwater, Herbert—Sept 20, 13b (60)
Driscoll, Joseph—May 10, 8e (54)
Driscoll, R.A.—Feb. 15, 8f (54)
Driver, J.F.—Nov. 3, 8e (52)
Drogheda, Henry (10th Lord)—Nov. 23, 8d (57); 29, 15b (57)
Drower, Edwin M. (Sir)—Nov. 26, 6e (51)
Drummond, Eric R.B.—Apr. 15, 10e (54)
Drummond, Gertrude (Lady)—Apr. 15, 10e (54)
Drummond-Grant, Ann—Sept 12, 8g (59)
Drummond, Jack (Sir)—Aug. 6, 6d (52); 11, 8e (52); 19, 6e (52)
Drummond, John (Dr.)—(t.) Apr. 26, 8g (58)
Drummond, John R. (Ald.)—Sept 11, 8d (52)
Drummond, Maurice (Sir)—Feb. 23, 8e (57)
Drummond, Robert J. (Very Rev.)—July 23, 8d (51)
Drummond, Violet (Lady)—July 8, 11d (55)
Drury, Alfred Dru (Rev Fr)—Jan. 20, 11b (56)
Drury, Amy (Lady)—Dec. 30, 9b (53)
Drury, Edward (Cdr)—Jan. 26, 8d (51)
Drury, G. Dru (Dr)—(t.) Oct. 31, 11c (56)
Drury-Lowe, Hylda—Jan. 18, 8d (51)
Drury, Richard F. (Lieut.-Col.)—Apr. 18, 13c (56)
Drury, Thomas H. (Mgr Canon)—May 15, 13f (56)
Drury, Victor—Sept 25, 13e (57)
Dryerre, Henry (Prof.)—Feb. 7, 8d (59)
Drysdale, J.H. (Dr.)—Sept 3, 6d (51)
Drzewieski, Bernard (Dr)—Aug. 20, 8d (53)
du Bois, Guy P.—July 21, 10e (58)
Du Boulay, Freda (Lady)—Sept 4, 13d (57)
Du Cane, Ethel (Lady)—Oct. 17, 20f (60)
Du Cane, Florence—(t.) July 8, 11c (55)
Du Cros, Arthur (Sir)—Oct. 31, 12a (55); Nov. 1, 11c (55)
du Cros, Mary (Lady)—July 14, 10e (56)
du Gard, Roger M.—Aug. 25, 10d (58)
du Maurier, Muriel (Lady)—Nov. 29, 15a (57)
du Mont, Julius—Apr. 9, 14d (56); 11, 13c (56)
Du Plat (Lady)—(t.) Jan. 10, 8e (51)
Du Plat-Taylor, Francis M.G.—May 24, 9b (54)
Du Plessis, Otto (Dr)—Apr. 29, 15b (60)
Du Pont, David—Sept 5, 11c (55)
Du Pont, Lammot—July 25, 8e (52)
Du Pont, Pierre S.—Apr. 7, 11a (54)
Du Toit, M.S.—Nov. 3, 17b (60)
Du Tremblay, Pamphile R.—Oct. 8, 9a (55)
Duarte, Alfonso—Mar. 7, 13d (58)

E

F

G

H

I

J

L

Macphail, Agnes C.—Feb. 15, 8f (54)
McPherson, Alexander K.—May 27, 14d (57)
Macpherson, Arthur H.—Jan. 9, 8c (53)
McPherson, Clive (Sir)—Nov. 11, 13e (58)
McPherson, Ewan A.—Nov. 20, 9b (54)
Macpherson, Ewen A. (Brig.)—Dec. 22, 8e (52); Jan. 1, 10f (53)
Macpherson, Hector (Rev)—May 21, 10c (56)
McPherson, Hugh (Sir)—Dec. 21, 13g (60)
MacPherson, John R.—Feb. 17, 10d (55); Mar. 9, 10e (55)
MacPherson, Neil C.—Nov. 13, 13e (57); 21, 14g (57)
McPowell, Thomas (Capt.)—Jan. 10, 8d (55)
MacQueen–Pope, Walter J.—June 28, 15a (60)
Macqueen, Donald C.B.—Oct. 8, 8e (60)
Macqueen, Norman—Oct. 6, 13a (59); 9, 15c (59); Nov. 7, 18b (60); 12, 10c (60)
McQuilland, Louis J.—(t.) Oct. 13, 8f (51)
Macrae, Albert E. (Maj.–Gen.)—Jan. 11, 8e (58)
MacRae, Colin (Col. Sir)—Oct. 13, 8e (52)
MacRae, Donald M. (Dr)—Feb. 11, 10f (55)
Macrae, Ian M. (Maj–Gen)—May 17, 16a (56)
MacRae, Margaret (Lady)—June 7, 8e (54)
MacRae, Nellie E.—June 21, 13d (55)
Macrae, Russell D.—Jan. 3, 12b (57)
McRea, Charles (Sir)—June 21, 6e (51)
Macrionitus, Marius (Most Rev.—Apr. 9, 16c (59)
MacRobert, Rachel (Lady)—Sept 2, 8d (54)
Macrossan, Neal W.—Dec. 31, 9c (55)
Macself, Albert J.—Mar. 7, 8e (52)
McShee, Frederick—Oct. 5, 15d (60)
Mactaggart, John (Sir)—Apr. 9, 8e (60)
Mactaggart, John —Nov. 26, 14b (56)
MacTavish, Wilfred L.—Mar. 30, 6d (51)
M'Tighe, Robert (Very Rev.)—Apr. 15, 13d (58)
McWatters, George A. (Lieut.–Col.)—Nov. 1, 11c (55)
McWatters, Herbert C. (Col.)—Nov. 10, 11d (53)
McWeeney, A.P.—Nov. 14, 15d (58)
McWhirter, William A.—May 18, 13c (55)
MacWhite, Michael—Nov. 14, 15e (58)
McWilliams, R.F. (Mrs.)—Apr. 14, 8e (52)
Macy, George—May 22, 11d (56); 25, 13c (56); 28, 14c (56)
Madden, Cecilia C.—May 15, 15d (59)
Madden, Evelyn (Lady)—July 3, 14a (58)
Maddicks, Percy J.—Dec. 15, 14a (58)
Maddison, George—May 21, 15a (59)
Maddocks, Morris A. (Canon)—Oct. 20, 10d (53)
Madelin, Louis (Dr.)—Aug. 20, 12d (56)
Maden, Henry—Nov. 21, 17c (60)
Madibbo, Ihrahim M.—Jan. 4, 17c (60)
Madol, H.R.—Nov. 23, 13d (56); Dec. 3, 14c (56)
Madsen, Arthur W.—Apr. 10, 13d (57); 13, 11b (57)
Madsen, Thorvald (Dr.)—Apr. 16, 14a (57)
Maenan, William (Lord)—Sept 24, 6e (51); Oct. 3, 6e (51)
Maffi, Fabrizio—Feb. 24, 10e (55)
Maflin, Percy H.—May 12, 15e (58)
Magalhaes, Alfredo de—Oct. 18, 16c (57)
Magalhaes, Barbosa de (Prof. Dr)—Apr. 7, 13e (59)
Magan, Violet A.—(t.) Sept 15, 6f (51)
Magaz, Antonio de (Marques)—Oct. 14, 10e (53)
Magdalene, Francis (Sister)—(t.) Mar. 30, 6d (51)
Maggs, Ernest U.—June 6, 8f (55)
Maggs, Leonard—Aug. 25, 10d (59)
Magheramorne, Ronald T. (4th Lord)—Apr. 23, 11a (57)
Maginnis, Charles—Feb. 17, 10d (55)
Magnay, Christopher B. (Maj. Sir)—Sept 5, 14d (60)
Magnel, Gustave (Prof.)—July 7, 12c (55)
Magniac, Charles (Sir)—June 5, 8d (53)
Magnusson, Gustaf—Oct. 24, 14c (57)
Magor, Richard K.—Sept 9, 10f (57)
Magowan, John (Sir)—Apr. 7, 8d (51)
Magruder, W. Lauson—Apr. 1, 8f (52)
Magsaysay, Ramon (Pres.)—Mar. 18, 10d (57)
Maguire, Antoninus (Very Rev.)—June 19, 12e (58)
Maguire, William A. (Rev)—Sept 16, 10d (53)
Maher, Aly—Aug. 25, 10e (60)
Mahon, Audrey (Lady)—Apr. 6, 11a (57)
Mahoney, Edward J. (Very Rev.)—Jan. 9, 9b (54)
Mahony, Jeremiah V.—Apr. 6, 16f (59)
Mahony, Lewis P.—June 11, 8f (54)
Maile, John W.K.—Oct. 16, 8g (52)
Mainprise, Cecil W. (Maj.–Gen.)—Feb. 17, 8f (51)
Mainwaring, Guy R. (Brig.)—Jan. 31, 11a (56)
Mainwaring, Mary S.—(t.) Oct. 27, 11b (56)
Mairet, Ethel—Nov. 26, 10d (52)
Mais, Roger—June 22, 13b (55); 24, 13c (55)
Maitland, Arthur E. (Lieut–Col)—Nov. 19, 12e (60)
Maitland, G. Ramsay (Lieut–Col Sir)—Nov. 3, 17a (60)
Maitland, Hugh—Mar. 6, 16e (59)
Maitland–Jones, Arthur G. (Dr.)—May 27, 14d (57)
Maitland, Kathleen (Lady)—Aug. 5, 13g (59)
Maitland–Makgill–Crichton, Henry C. (Brig.)—Oct. 2, 8d (53)
Maitland, Rosalind—(t.) Oct. 28, 15a (59)
Majendie, Bernard J. (Brig–Gen)—Sept 7, 14c (59)
Majendie, V.H.B. (Maj.–Gen.)—Jan. 18, 14d (60); 20, 15d (60)
Majo, Victor J. (Gen.)—Mar. 29, 8g (58)
Major, Clare T.—Oct. 11, 8d (54)
Major, Edith H.—Mar. 19, 8d (51); 30, 6d (51)
Majoribanks, George (Rev.)—(t.) Jan. 7, 11b (55)
Majumdar, Siri Sures Chandra—Aug. 17, 8d (54)
Makary (Metropolitan)—Nov. 14, 8d (53)
Makeham, Eliot—Feb. 9, 13b (56)
Makeham, John P. (Rev.)—June 29, 10g (53)
Makepeace , Harry—Dec. 20, 8e (52)
Makins, Dorothy (Lady)—May 8, 15e (56); 11, 13c (56)
Makins, Ernest (Sir)—May 20, 14a (59); 25, 15e (59)
Malan, Daniel (Dr.)—Feb. 9, 10d (59)
Malan, L.H. (Col.)—Mar. 7, 6e (51)
Malaparte, Curzio—July 20, 8g (57)
Malcolm, Dougal (Sir)—Aug. 31, 11a (55); Sept 2, 11g (55); 6, 11d (55)
Malcolm, James A.—(t.) Aug. 14, 6e (52)
Malcolm, Neill (Sir)—Dec. 22, 8d (53); 31, 8e (53); Jan. 4, 8e (54)
Malcomson, Greer E. (Lieut–Col)—(t.) Feb. 4, 10e (55)
Malden, Richard H. (Very Rev.)—Aug. 21, 6e (51)
Male, Emile—Oct. 7, 11a (54)
Male, George P.—Dec. 14, 13b (56)
Male, Kassim—Nov. 23, 16b (59)
Malek, Guindy A.—Jan. 31, 11a (56)
Malet, Alexander W. (Lieut.–Col.)—July 23, 13a (56)
Malet, G.E.G. (Col.)—(t.) Aug. 11, 8d (52)
Maleter, Pal (Gen.)—June 18, 12d (58)
Maley, William—Apr. 3, 12d (58)
Malglaive, Pierre de—Jan. 23, 8f (53)
Malik, Teja Singh (Sir)—Feb. 5, 8e (53)
Malim, Amy G..—Dec. 20, 13e (60)
Malim, Harold C. (Cmdr.)—Aug. 22, 8f (53)
Malinin, Mikhail (Gen)—Jan. 25, 14b (60)
Malkin, George J.—Nov. 26, 13c (57)
Malkin, William H.—Oct. 15, 16b (59)
Mallabar, Herbert J.—May 26, 10b (56); June 29, 10e (56)
Malleret–Joinville, Alfred—Feb. 22, 14d (60)
Malleson, Joan (Dr)—May 16, 15d (56); 22, 11d (56)
Malleson, Rupert St. A. (Capt.)—July 14, 16g (60)
Mallik, Basanta K.—(t.) Dec. 22, 11f (58)
Mallinson, S.T.—Feb. 22, 10d (55)
Malloch, George R.—Dec. 12, 9b (53)
Mallon, Dwight S.—Apr. 9, 14e (56)
Mallory, Molla B.—Nov. 24, 15c (59)
Malmberg, Bertil.—Feb. 19, 10d (58)
Malone, E.G.S. L'Estrange (Col.)—July 6, 13b (55)
Malone, Leah L'Estrange—Sept 11, 6d (51); 18, 8e (51)
Maltby, Hugh P. (Brig)—July 1, 10e (54)
Maltby, W. Russell (Dr)—Jan. 19, 6e (51)
Maltby, William A.F. (Capt)—Jan. 7, 9c (56)
Malynowskyj, Alexander (Rt. Rev.)—Nov. 20, 13e (57)
Mamelok, Emil—May 26, 8e (54)
Man, Hubert W. (Col.)—June 29, 10f (56)
Man–Kam Lo (Sir)—Mar. 9, 12d (59)
Manchester, Ethel (Lady)—July 8, 8e (53)
Manchester, William (Sir)—May 8, 15e (56)
Mancini, Augusto (Prof.)—Sept 23, 13d (57)
Mandato, Archangelo De (Col.)—Nov. 15, 8f (52)
Mander, Charles (Sir)—Jan. 26, 8d (51)
Mandic, Ante (Dr.)—Nov. 17, 15d (59)
Meneely, John (Capt.)—Oct. 3, 12c (55)
Mangwende, Helen—(t.) June 28, 11a (55); July 6, 13c (55)
Manifold (Lady)—July 18, 13g (58)
Manifold, Courtenay C. (Maj.Gen. Sir)—June 8, 8e (57); 11, 11d (57)
Manifold, John A. (Maj.–Gen.)—Feb. 29, 14b (60)
Manipur (Maharaja of)—Dec. 12, 13a (55)
Manisty, Eldon (Rear Adm, Sir)—Aug. 29, 15f (60)
Manki Sharif (Pir of)—Jan. 30, 10d (60)
Manley–Sims, Reginald F. (Brig.–Gen.)—June 26, 6g (51)
Mann, Cathleen—Sept 10, 14d (59); Oct. 6, 13b (59)
Mann, David—July 10, 13d (56)
Mann, Dora (Dr.)—(t.) Feb. 3, 10e (53)
Mann, D.S.—June 7, 15f (56)
Mann, Edward C. (Maj)—Aug. 12, 10d (59); 26, 12a (59)
Mann, Eric W.—Feb. 16, 8e (54)
Mann, Frederick (Sir)—May 31, 8e (58)
Mann, Herbert G.—May 5, 12e (55)
Mann, John (Sir)—Mar. 7, 11b (55); 14, 10f (55)
Mann, John —Dec. 27, 10b (57)
Mann, Ludovic—Oct. 3, 12a (55)
Mann, Norman—(t.) Aug. 5, 6e (52)
Mann, Thomas—Aug. 13, 9a (55)
Mannerheim, Carl G.E. (Field-Marshal Baron)—Jan 29, 6c (51)
Manners, Charles M. (Brig.)—Nov. 15, 10d (54)
Manners, Errol (Rear–Adm Sir)—Oct. 26, 10e (53)
Manners, Zoe (Lady)—Dec. 1, 10d (53)
Mannheim, Julia (Dr.)—Dec. 19, 11b (55)
Manning, Adelaide F.O.—Sept 28, 12d (59)
Manning, Edye R. (Air Cdre)—Apr. 29, 12e (57)

O

P

Platt, Frederick (Rev Dr)—Jan. 25, 10e (55)
Platt, J. Wood—Dec. 10, 17d (59)
Platts, Walter L.—Aug. 28, 10d (58)
Play, Roger (Gen.)—Nov. 10, 8d (54)
Player, John A.—Dec. 8, 15a (59)
Player, William G.—June 30, 12e (59)
Pledge, Humphrey T.—Dec. 29, 8e (60)
Plesch, Janos O. (Dr.)—Mar. 4, 10d (57)
Plesman, Albert (Dr.)—Jan. 1, 10e (54)
Pleydell-Bouverie (Mrs.)—July 21, 10c (56)
Pleydell-Bouverie, Edwar d (Capt.)—May 7, 6e (51)
Plievier, Theodor—Mar. 15, 10e (55)
Plimmer, Robert H.A. (Prof.)—June 21, 13c (55)
Plummer, R.C.S.—June 19, 10e (53)
Plummer, Robert J.—Feb. 16, 8e (54)
Plunkett, John—Aug. 29, 15e (60)
Plymen, Frank—Mar. 11, 18e (60)
Pochon, Alfred—Feb. 28, 8e (59)
Pochon, Madeleine—Oct. 15, 9b (55)
Pocklington, Geoffrey R.—Mar. 24, 14c (58)
Pocock, Duncan R.R.—(t.) Oct. 27, 8f (51)
Pocock, Guy—Mar. 22, 10e (55)
Pocock, Ronald—(t.) Mar. 26, 6d (52)
Pocock, Roy W. (Dr)—July 6, 10e (54)
Pocock, Sydney—(t.) Nov. 1, 13b (57)
Podolskis, Vincent (Rt Rev)—May 10, 16b (60)
Podoski, Victor—Aug. 2, 10e (60)
Podrecca, Vittorio di—July 7, 8d (59)
Poducci, Raffaele (Prof.)—Sept 6, 11b (58)
Poe-Domvile, Hugo (Sir)—July 30, 8g (59)
Poe, William S. (Col.)—Mar. 21, 13c (58)
Pogany, Willy A.—Aug. 1, 9a (55)
Pohl, Robert (Dr.)—Mar. 19, 14c (56)
Point, Fernand—Mar. 7, 11c (55)
Pokora, Julien—(t.) June 22, 13f (56)
Pol, Balth van der (Dr)—Oct. 14, 15a (59); 15, 16b (59)
Polacco, Giorgio—May 3, 15a (60)
Polak, Henry S.L.—Feb. 3, 13e (59); 6, 15e (59)
Polden, E. Russell—Feb. 23, 10e (55)
Poldini, Ede—July 1, 12e (57)
Pole-Carew, Beatrice (Lady)—(t.) Mar. 18, 8d (52)
Pole, David G. (Maj.)—Dec. 1, 8e (52)
Pole, Felix (Sir)—Jan. 16, 12d (56); 20, 11c (56)
Poliakoff, Joseph—(t.) Nov. 28, 10e (59)
Poliakoff, Vladimir—June 6, 13d (56)
Polignac, Marie -Blanche de (Comtesse)—(t.) Mar. 6, 12d (58)
Politis, Ioannis—June 4, 16g (59)
Pollard, Alfred O. (Capt)—Dec. 6, 15a (60)
Pollen, John L.H. (Sir)—Mar. 16, 14c (59)
Pollinger, Heinrich—Oct. 27, 11a (53)
Pollitt, Harry—June 28, 15a (60); 30, 19c (60)
Pollock, Guy—Feb. 4, 12b (57); 8, 11c (57)
Pollock, H.B.—(t.) Oct. 31, 13d (58)
Pollock, James D.—May 17, 8e (58)
Pollock-McCall, J.B. (Brig.-Gen.)—(t.) Aug. 23, 8e (51)
Polunin, Vladimir—Mar. 18, 10d (57)
Pomeroy, Jay—June 3, 8e (55)
Poncin, Marcel—June 10, 8e (53)
Pong-Am, Clough—Feb. 16, 13f (60)
Ponsonby, George St. L.N.—May 24, 6d (51)
Ponsonby, John (Maj.-Gen. Sir)—May 27, 8e (52)
Ponto, Erich—Feb. 6, 11c (57)
Pool, Augustus F.—Oct. 1, 9b (55)
Poole, Arthur J. (Brig.-Gen.)—Mar. 12, 14c (56)
Poole, Cecil (Maj.)—Feb. 3, 11a (56)
Poole, Francis G. (Lieut-Col)—(t.) Jan. 12, 9f (51)
Pooler, Harry W. (Dr.)—Mar. 3, 10d (54)
Poore, Flora (Lady)—Jan. 30, 10e (57)
Poortenar, Jan—Oct. 21, 14b (58)
Pope, Charles G.—(t.) Feb. 11, 14b (59)
Pope, Cuthbert J. (Rear-Adm.)—Aug. 8, 10b (59)
Pope, James A.—Nov. 1, 6e (54)
Pope, Joseph—Apr. 30, 13d (57)
Pope, Mildred K. (Prof.)—Sept 19, 11a (56); 21, 13c (56)
Pope, Wilson—Sept 30, 8d (53)
Popham, Dorothy (Lady)—Mar. 16, 14c (5[illegible])
Popley, H.A. (Rev.)—July 22, 15a (60)
Poptomov, Vladimir T. (Dr.)—May 3, 8e (52)
Porras, Don Carlos—Jan. 29, 6e (51)
Portago, Alfonso de (Marquis)—May 13, 15b (57); 17, 15e (57)
Portal, Edward R.—Mar. 28, 8f (53)
Portal, Spencer (Sir)—Nov. 28, 13c (55); Dec. 6, 11c (55); 31, 9c (55)
Portarlington, Lionel (6th Lord)—July 6, 8e (59)
Porte, Marie—(t.) Mar. 15, 8e (58)
Porten, Maximilien von der (Dr.)—June 13, 10g (55)
Porteous, Roger C. (Gp. Capt.)—July 13, 8e (53); Aug. 3, 8f (53)
Porter (Mrs)—Aug. 17, 13c (59)
Porter, Bernard G.—Nov. 19, 12c (56)
Porter, Charles (Dr)—Dec. 17, 8e (52); 18, 8g (52); Jan. 9, 8d (53)
Porter, Edward—Sept 2, 12d (60)
Porter, Henry—Oct. 17, 20g (60)
Porter, Linda—May 21, 8e (54)
Porter, Samuel (Lord)—Feb. 14, 11b (56); 18, 10c (56); 22, 11c (56); 28, 11d (56)
Porter, Samuel C.—July 12, 13b (56)
Portland, Winifred of (Dowager Duchess)—July 31, 8d (54); Aug. 3, 8e (54); 5, 9d (54); 9, 8f (54)
Portman, Alan B. (Rev. Preb.)—Nov. 5, 10e (53)
Portman, Michael—Oct. 27, 15a (59)
Portugal (President of): see Carmona (Marshal)
Portugal, Amelie of (Queen)—Oct. 26, 8f (51)
Portus, Garnet V. (Prof)—June 17, 8e (54)
Portwine, John—May 23, 14e (58)
Posse, Amelie (Lady)—Mar. 7, 12d (57)
Possidonio, Alfonso T. di San (Marchese)—July 6, 13b (55)
Post, Emily—Sept 28, 18c (60)
Potocki, Alfred (Count)—(t.) Apr. 16, 13f (58)
Pott, Stanley (Sir)—Jan. 27, 8g (51)
Potter, Dorothy—(t.) Aug. 7, 8d (53)
Potter, Ernest S.—Apr. 19, 15a (56)
Potter, Frederick F.—Apr. 25, 15e (55)
Potter, Frederick W.—June 20, 8d (52)
Potter, George (Canon)—Feb. 16, 13f (60)
Potter, Harold (Prof.)—July 7, 8d (51); 20, 8d (51)
Potter, Harold B. (Capt)—Jan. 17, 11c (56)
Potter, William A. (Col.)—Mar. 12, 8f (53); 16, 10e (53)
Potter. W.T.—Feb. 16, 13g (60)
Potts, Leonard J.—Sept 3, 8e (60)
Pouishnoff, Leff N.—May 29, 17a (59)
Poulter, Arthur—Aug. 31, 10e (56)
Powdrill, Arthur H.—Dec. 8, 14c (55)
Powe, G. Hector—Mar. 11, 10e (55)
Powell, A. Maurus (Very Rev.)—(t.) Nov. 4, 16f (59)
Powell, Alfred H.—June 1, 20c (60)
Powell, Bernard—(t.) Jan. 18, 11a (57)
Powell, Claud—(t.) May 20, 14b (59); 21, 15c (59)
Powell, David H.I.—Apr. 3, 13e (57)
Powell, Edward W.M. (Brig-Gen)—July 27, 10d (54)
Powell, George B. (Vice-Adm.)—May 28, 8d (52)
Powell, H.E. (Maj.)—May 26, 8d (54)
Powell, Joseph H. (Preb.)—June 17, 10e (55)
Powell, Philip L. (Lieut.-Col.)—Jan. 5, 11c (60)
Powell, Richard A.B.—Apr. 23, 11b (57)
Power, Arthur (Adm of Flt Sir)—Jan. 29, 17a (60); Feb. 13, 8e (60)
Power, Charles M.—Mar. 8, 10e (54); 13, 8f (54)
Power, D'Arcy (Air Vice-Marsh.)—Dec. 31, 10e (58)
Power, Eileen M.W.—Oct. 6, 17a (58)
Power, Ernest—Apr. 9, 14b (57)
Power, Frederick D.—July 7, 12c (55)
Power, Ivan (Sir)—Feb. 15, 8e (54)
Power, Patia E.—Oct. 1, 16b (59)
Power, Piers D.—June 27, 16b (60); 30, 19d (60)
Power, Rhoda D. le P.—Mar. 11, 12d (57); 13, 13d (57); 16, 11a (57)
Power, Septimus—Jan. 4, 8e (51)
Power, Tyrone—Nov. 17, 15b (58); 21, 15a (58)
Power, William—June 15, 6g (51)
Powis, George (4th Lord)—Nov. 10, 8d (52)
Pownall, Assheton (Lieut. Col. Sir)—Oct. 31, 8d (53); Nov. 3, 8e (53); 6, 11b (53)
Pownall, Florence (Lady)—Dec. 16, 10g (52)
Powys, Littleton A. (Rev.)—Feb. 23, 10e (54)
Powys, Littleton C.—Sept 29, 12d (55)
Powys, Theodore F.—Nov. 28, 9c (53)
Poynter, Cherry (Lady)—May 21, 15c (59)
Poyser, Ronald (Sir)—July 2, 10e (57)
Pradera, Nicolasa—Nov. 13, 16d (58)
Praeger, Rosamond—Apr. 19, 8g (54)
Pragnell, Thomas W. (Col.)—Jan. 28, 10d (57)
Prakasam, Tanguturi—May 24, 13b (57)
Prampolini, Enrico—June 22, 13e (56)
Prandtl, Ludwig (Prof.)—Aug. 20, 8e (53)
Pratinidhi, Srimant Balasahib Pandit: see Aundh, Rajah of
Pratley, Philip L.—Aug. 4, 8d (58)
Pratt, Agnes—Aug. 13, 8e (54)
Pratt, Alfred G. (Lieut.-Col.)—Dec. 3, 9c (55)
Pratt, Douglas H. (Maj.-Gen.)—May 16, 13b (58)
Pratt, Fendall W.H. (Maj-Gen)—Apr. 28, 20a (60); May 5, 19b (60)
Pratt, Fletcher—June 12, 13c (56)
Pratt, Harry E. (Dr.)—Feb. 14, 11c (56)
Pratt, Henry S. (Sir)—May 10, 8e (54)
Pratt, Isaac H. (Ven.)—Mar. 7, 12e (57)
Pratt, John (Sir)—Oct. 29, 8f (52)
Pratt, John L.—Sept 28, 18b (60)
Pratt, William—(t.) Oct. 5, 10g (57)
Prattey, Phillip L.—Aug. 4, 8d (58)
Prattl William—(t.) Oct. 5, 10g (57)
Preece, Annie (Lady)—May 27, 13c (59)
Preece, Arthur (Sir)—Feb. 2, 8e (51); 6, 8e (51)
Premchand, Kikabhai (Sir)—Dec. 8, 10e (53)
Prendergast, Kathleen L. (Maj.)—June 4, 8e (54)
Prentice, Robert—Oct. 1, 10b (60)
Prescott, Charles (Sir)—Oct. 4, 11b (55)
Prescott, Charles W.B. (Sir)—Sept 29, 12d (55)
Prescott-Decie, Cyril (Brig-Gen)—Sept 22, 10d (53)
Prescott, Henry C. (Lieut. -Col.)—Aug. 5, 12c (60)
Prescott-Westcar, Charles H.B. (Maj.)—Aug. 14, 6d (54)
Prescott-Westcar, William (Sir)—Feb. 6, 15e (59)
Press, Edward—June 9, 14b (58)
Pressney, R.A.—Feb. 2, 8e (54)
Prestage, Edgar (Dr.)—Apr. 11, 8g (51)
Prestige, George L. (Canon)—Jan. 20, 10g (55)
Preston, Hubert—Aug. 8, 13e (60)
Preston, J.H.—(t.) Oct. 2, 8e (52)
Preston, Richard J.—Mar. 11, 10e (55)
Preston, Stanley—Jan. 20, 14b (58)

Q

R

S

T

U

V

X

Y